ENCYCLOPEDIA OF

Biography

ENCYCLOPEDIA OF
Biography

Edited by C. S. Nicholls

St. Martin's Press
New York

Acknowledgements

Cover illustration 'Dorothy Mary Crowfoot Hodgkin' by Maggi Hambling. By courtesy of the National Portrait Gallery,
London.

For permission to reproduce illustrations inside the book we are grateful to the following: Acquaella Galleries Inc;
American Embassy; Ann Ronan/Image Select; Australian Overseas Information Office; British Film Institute; Burson-
Marstellar; Californian Institute of Technology; CBS; Chanel; Danish Tourist Board; Dame Judi Dench; Dominic;
EMI; FOF/MI; Gemma Levine; Image Select; Irish Embassy; Jerry Bauer; J Wedgwood and Son; Labour Party;
Larousse; Laura Ashley plc; Library of Congress; Maxwell Davies; Mercedes-Benz/Image Select; Michael Nicholson;
NASA/Image Select; National Film Archive; Penguin Books Limited; Peter Ustinov; Philip Sauvain Picture Collection;
Phonogram; Picador; Polygram; Rank Film Distributors; Roy Skeggs; Sachem; Secker and Warburg; Sony Classical;
Sony Music; Sotheby's; St Thomas's Library; Terry Lott; The Hamling Company; Transworld/Jerry Bauer; United
Nations; United States Information Office; Vintage; Virago; WHO/Jean Mohr/Image Select.

Preface

This book contains the biographies of over 10,000 people. Many are enlivened and enriched by portraits, quotations and suggestions for further reading. Particular attention has been paid to twentieth-century lives, so that readers can find out about their contemporaries. Unlike other biographical encyclopedias, this volume also pays due attention to the lives of scientists, musicians, and artists, whose impact on our lives has often been far greater and longer lasting than the sometimes more ephemeral achievements of politicians and administrators.

ORDER OF ENTRIES
Entries are ordered alphabetically, as if there were no spaces between words. We have avoided a purely mechanical alphabetization in cases where a different order corresponds more with human logic. For example, sovereigns with the same name are grouped according to country before number, so George II of England is placed before George III of England, and not next to George II of Greece. Words beginning 'Mc' and 'Mac' are treated as if they begin 'Mac'; 'St' and 'Saint' are both treated as if they were spelt 'Saint'.

FOREIGN NAMES AND TITLES
Names of foreign sovereigns are usually shown in their English form, except where the foreign name is more familiar; thus, there is an entry for Charles V of Spain, but Juan Carlos (not John Charles). Entries for titled people are under the name by which they are best known to the general reader; thus Anthony Eden, not Lord Avon. Cross references are provided in cases where confusion is possible.

UNITS
SI (metric) units are used throughout for scientific entries. Measurements of distances, temperatures, sizes, and so on, usually include an approximate imperial equivalent.

CHINESE NAMES
Pinyin, the preferred system for transcribing Chinese names of people, is generally used: thus, there is an entry at Mao Zedong, not Mao Tse-tung; an exception is made for a few names which are more familiar in their former (Wade-Giles) form, such as Sun Yat-sen and Chiang Kai-shek. Where confusion is likely, Wade-Giles forms are given as a cross-reference.

APPENDICES
The appendices contain several useful tables listing, for example, major award winners, political leaders and other key figures. There is a full contents list on page 939.

CHRONOLOGICAL INDEX
A unique chronological index arranges all the people in this book according to the year in which they were born. This enables you, for example, to see what other playwrights were writing in Shakespeare's time, or who might have been calculating probability at the same time as Pascal.

ACKNOWLEDGEMENTS
I am most grateful to Basil Morgan, Anne Pimlott Baker, Mary Whitby, Godfrey Le May, Eric Midwinter, Alison Ambrose, Chris Murray, and Trevor Williams, who have all contributed to this book, which would have been the poorer without their scholarship and cheerfulness.

Christine Nicholls

Contributors

Alison Ambrose MA
David Armstrong PhD
Christine Avery PhD
John Ayto MA
Chris Backenist
Paul Bahn PhD, FSA
Anne Pimlott Baker MA
Mark Bindley
David Black
Malcolm Bradbury PhD, Hon D Litt, FRSL
Brendan Bradley PhD
Nigel Davis MSc
Ian D Derbyshire PhD
J Denis Derbyshire PhD
Col Michael Dewar MA
Dougal Dixon MSc
Ingrid von Essen
Sofie Fairbrass
Anna Farkas MA
Jane Farron BA
Peter Fleming PhD
Lawrence Garner BA
Derek Gjertsen BA
Wendy Grossman
Joseph Harrison PhD
Michael Hitchcock DPhil
Stuart Holroyd
Charles Kidd
Stephen Kite B Arch, RIBA
Peter Lafferty MSc

Godfrey Le May MA
Claire Lewis DPhil
Mike Lewis MBCS
Graham Ley MPhil
Carol Lister PhD, FSS
Graham Littler MSc, FSS
Tom McArthur PhD
Eric Midwinter DPhil
Basil Morgan MA
Diana Moule
David Munro PhD, FSA (Scot)
Chris Murray
Joanna O'Brien MA
Maureen O'Connor BA
Robert Paisley PhD
Paulette Pratt
Tim Pulleine
Ian Ridpath FRAS
Adrian Room MA, DipEd, FRGS
Simon Ross BA
Julian Rowe PhD
Jack Schofield MA
Emma Shackleton MA
Steve Smyth
Joe Staines BA
Callum Storrie BArch
Stephen Webster MPhil, PGCE
Mary Whitby PhD
Liz Whitelegg BSc
Trevor Williams DPhil

Managing Editor
Sara Jenkins-Jones

Consultant
Chris Murray

Project Editor
Shereen Karmali

Text Editors
Jane Anson
Avril Cridlan
Paul Davis
Ingrid von Essen
Rosemary Harris
Jane Nolan
Catherine Thompson

Production
Tony Ballsdon

Design
Roger Walker

Page Make-up
TechType

Art Editor
Terence Craven

A

Aakjaer Jeppe (1866–1930). Danish poet and novelist. Born in Jutland into a poor peasant family, he was an anticleric who became an impassioned campaigner for the rights of peasant workers. He is best remembered for his poetry, especially *Rugens sange/Song of the Rye* 1906.

Aalto (Hugo) Alvar (Henrik) (1898–1976). Finnish architect and designer. He was a pioneer of the Modern Movement in his native Finland. Initially working within the confines of the International Style, he later developed a unique architectural style, characterized by asymmetry, curved walls, and contrast of natural materials. He invented a new form of laminated bent-plywood furniture 1932 and won many design awards for household and industrial items.

Aalto's buildings include Baker House, a Hall of Residence at the Massachusetts Institute of Technology 1947–49; Technical High School, Otaniemi 1962–65; and Finlandia Hall, Helsinki 1972.

Aaltonen Wäinö (Valdemar) (1894–1966). Finnish sculptor. He was known for his monumental figures and busts portraying citizens of Finland following the country's independence 1917. The bronze monument to the athlete Paavo Nurmi (1897–1973) 1925 (Helsinki Stadium) and the bust of the composer Sibelius 1928 are examples of his work.

He was one of the early 20th-century pioneers of direct carving, favouring granite as his medium. He later developed a more sombre style of modern Classicism, well suited to his public commissions, as in the allegorical figures in the Finnish Parliament House 1930–32.

Aarestrup Carl Ludvig Emil (1800–1856). Danish poet. An aesthete with a warm admiration of female beauty and an unusual frankness in erotic description, he was little known until the posthumous publication of his poems 1863, followed by an edition of his *Samlede Digte/Collected Poems* 1877.

Born in Copenhagen, Aarestrup was a physician by profession and published only one volume of poetry, *Digte/Poems* 1838, during his lifetime.

Aaron (lived *c.* 13th century BC). In the Old Testament, the elder brother of Moses by three years and co-leader of the Hebrews in their march from Egypt to the Promised Land of Canaan. He became the associate and spokesperson of his brother in their interviews with the pharaoh. When the Hebrews despaired of Moses' return from Mount Sinai, Aaron made the Golden Calf for them to worship, yet was allowed to continue as high priest. His consecration was ratified by the budding of his rod. He married Elisheba and had four sons.

All his descendants are hereditary high priests, called the *cohanim*, or cohens, and maintain a special place in worship and ceremony in the synagogue. The lesser services are performed by Levites.

Aaron Hank (Henry Louis) (1934–). US baseball player, holder of the all-time record for home runs. In the course of his career, primarily with the Milwaukee and Atlanta Braves, he won the National League batting title twice, in 1955 and 1959. In 1957, as a member of the World Championship team, he was named the National League's most valuable player. His greatest achievement was breaking Babe Ruth's lifetime record of 714 home runs; by the time of his retirement in 1976, Aaron had hit a total of 755 home runs.

Aasen Ivar Andreas (1813–1896). Norwegian philologist, poet, and dramatist. Through a study of rural dialects, connecting them with Old Norwegian, he evolved by 1853 a native country language, which he called *Landsmål* (now known as *Nynorsk* or New Norwegian) and which he intended should replace literary Dano-Norwegian.

Landsmål was recognized 1885 alongside *Riksmål*, or *Bokmål*, which is a development of Danish (at one time the official and literary language of Norway). Aasen published a grammar 1848 and a dictionary 1850 of the 'Norwegian Popular Language'. He also wrote plays and poems in *Landsmål*.

Abbadid dynasty (lived 11th century). Muslim dynasty based in Seville, Spain, which lasted from 1023 until 1091. The dynasty was founded by Abu-el-Kasim Muhammad ibn Abbad, who led the townspeople against the Berbers when the Spanish caliphate fell. The dynasty continued under Motadid (1042–1069) and Motamid (1069–1091) when the city was taken by the Almoravids.

Abbadie Jacques (1654–1727). French ecclesiastic and writer. His works include *Traité de la vérité de la religion chrétienne* 1684 and *La Grande Conspiration d'Angleterre* 1696 (written by order of William III).

In 1688 and 1689 he accompanied Marshal Schomberg to Holland, England, and Ireland, afterwards becoming pastor of the French Church in the Savoy. In 1699 he was made dean of Killaloe by William III. He died in London.

Abbado Claudio (1933–). Italian conductor. He was principal director of the Vienna State Opera from 1986 and of the Berlin Philharmonic Orchestra from 1989. Associated early in his career with the La Scala Opera, Milan, his wide-ranging repertoire includes a significant number of 20th-century composers, among them Schoenberg, Prokofiev, Janáček, Bartók, and Stockhausen. He has also conducted the European Youth Orchestra from its inception 1977.

Abbado *Claudio Abbado was born into a musical family and at the age of eight decided to become a conductor. His phenomenal memory allows him to conduct without a musical score, though his refusal to waver from the score has led some to see his conducting as impersonal and calculated.*

Abbas or al-Abbas ibn Abd al-Muttalib (566–652). Uncle of the prophet Muhammad and founder of the Abbasid dynasty.

Abbasid dynasty Family of rulers of the Islamic empire, whose caliphs reigned in Baghdad 750–1258. They were descended from Abbas, the prophet Muhammad's uncle, and some of them, such as Harun al-Rashid and Mamun (reigned 813–33), were outstanding patrons of cultural development. Later their power dwindled, and in 1258 Baghdad was burned by the Tatars. From then until 1517 the Abbasids retained limited power as caliphs of Egypt.

Abbas I Pasha (1813–1854). Viceroy of Egypt 1848–54. He was the grandson of Mehmet Ali. He promoted the construction of the railway from Alexandria to Cairo 1851.

Abbas II Hilmi (1874–1943). Last khedive (viceroy) of Egypt, 1892–1914. Abbas II succeeded his father, Tewfik. At first he tried to overthrow British rule; he abolished and reduced taxes, and disagreed with Cromer and Kitchener before throwing in his lot with Turkey 1914. He was deposed on 19 December 1914, and the khedivate passed, with the title of sultan, to Hussein Kamil Pasha, his uncle.

Abbas I the Great (*c.* 1571–1629). Shah of Persia from 1588. He expanded Persian territory by conquest, defeating the Uzbeks near Herat 1597 and also the Turks. At his death his empire reached from the river Tigris to the Indus. He was a patron of the arts.

During his reign Abbas encouraged commerce, granted immunities and privileges to European merchants, set up a strong central administration, and gave encouragement to the building of Isfahan, which he made the capital of his kingdom. He was succeeded by his grandson, Shah Safi.

Abbas II (1632–1667). Shah of Persia 1642–67, the son of Safi I and the great-grandson of Abbas I. He received various embassies from Europe and recaptured Kandahar 1648, which had been lost by his predecessor to the Mogul emperors.

Abbas III (1732–1736). Shah of Persia, the son of Tahmasp II. His father was deposed by Quli Khan (who later became Nadir Shah Afshar) and Abbas III was crowned shah when eight months old. He was the last of the Safavid dynasty and on his death the regent, Quli Khan, succeeded him.

Abbas Mirza (1783–1833). Prince of Persia, second son of Shah Fath Ali. He commanded the Persian army in the Russian wars of 1812–13 and 1825–28. He also commanded the Persian forces in the war with Turkey, concluded by the Peace of Erzurum 1823. In 1828 he made an expedition to Khorasan to restore Persian supremacy, and died besieging Herat 1833.

Abbas Mirza was an enlightened prince and sought to reorganize his army on European lines with the help of European officers.

Abbate Niccolò dell' (*c.* 1512–1571). Italian Mannerist painter. He was active in his hometown of Modena, then in Bologna, and from the early 1550s in France where he worked with Primaticcio at Fontainebleau. He contributed significantly to the style of the Fontainebleau School with his slender, sinuous figures, and in his use of mythology prepared the way for the classical landscapes of Poussin and Claude Lorrain.

His early work in Bologna, mainly frescoes and portraits, reflects the influence of Jacopo da Pontormo.

Abbe Ernst (1840–1905). German physicist who, working with Carl Zeiss, greatly improved the design and quality of optical instruments, particularly the compound microscope. This enabled researchers to observe micro-organisms and internal cellular structures for the first time.

Abbe was born in Eisenach, Thuringia, and studied physics at Jena and Göttingen, becoming a professor at Jena 1870 and director of the observatory 1878. Zeiss supplied optical instruments to the university and repaired them. Abbe became a partner in Zeiss's firm.

Abbe worked out how to overcome spherical aberration in lenses and why, contrary to expectation, the definition of a microscope decreases with a reduction in the aperture of the objective; he found that the loss in resolving power is a diffraction effect. In 1872 he

developed the Abbe substage condenser for illuminating objects under high-power magnification.

Abbey Edwin Austin (1852–1911). US painter and illustrator who worked in both England and the USA. He was commissioned by Edward VII to paint the coronation 1902 and also decorated the Boston Public Library with a series of panels, *The Quest of the Holy Grail*. His illustrative style is at its most distinctive in delicate pen drawings for editions of Herrick, Goldsmith and Shakespeare, and in his work for *Harper's* Magazine.

Born in Philadelphia, Abbey was educated by private tutors and later studied at the Pennsylvania Academy of Fine Arts. In 1880 he moved to England. He was a member of the British Royal Academy, the US National Academy of Design, and received the French Legion of Honour.

Abbot George (1562–1633). English cleric, archbishop of Canterbury 1611–33. His works include *Exposition on the Prophet Jonah; A Brief Description of the Whole World* 1599. He was private chaplain to Thomas Sackville, Lord Buckhurst, chancellor of the University 1592, master of University College 1597, dean of Winchester 1600, and three times vice-chancellor of Oxford University 1600–05 before being promoted to the sees of Lichfield 1609, London 1610, and Canterbury 1611.

Abbott Berenice (1898–1991). US photographer. She is best known for her portrait studies of artists in the 1920s and for her comprehensive documentation of New York City in the 1930s, culminating in the publication of *Changing New York* 1939. Her straightforward style was partially influenced by the French photographer Eugène Atget, whose work she rescued from obscurity.

Abbott George (1887–1995). US playwright, theatre director, and producer. Among his many successes were *Broadway* 1926, *Three Men on a Horse* 1935, *The Boys from Syracuse* 1938, *The Pajama Game* 1954, and *Damn Yankees* 1955.

Abbott Jacob (1803–1879). US author. He entered the ministry of the Congregational Church, but is best known for his educational and religious writings. His first book, *The Young Christian* 1832, was followed by some 200 others.

Abbott and Costello Stage names of William Abbott (1895–1974) and Louis Cristillo (1906–1959) US comedy duo. They moved to films from vaudeville, and most, including *Buck Privates* 1941 and *Lost in a Harem* 1944, were showcases for their routines. They also appeared on radio and television.

Abboud Ibrahim (1900–). Sudanese general and politician. After an army coup 1958, Abboud became president of the Supreme Council of the armed forces, and subsequently premier and president. His power was severely limited after a civilian coup Oct 1964; he resigned from the presidency a month later.

Abd al-Hamid I (1725–1789). Sultan of Turkey from 1773. During his reign Turkey was occupied in a struggle with Russia and Austria. The former wrested from him control of the Crimea 1774, and the latter inflicted on him a crushing defeat at the battle of Ochakov 1788.

Abd al-Hamid II (1842–1918). Last sultan of Turkey 1876–1909. In 1908 the Young Turks under Enver Pasha forced Abdal-Hamid to restore the constitution of 1876 and in 1909 insisted on his deposition. He died in confinement. For his part in the Armenian massacres suppressing the revolt of 1894–96 he was known as the 'Great Assassin'; his actions still motivate Armenian violence against the Turks.

He succeeded on the deposition of his brother Murad V. His reign included wars with Serbia 1876, Russia 1877–78, and Greece 1897.

Abd al-Kader (*c.* 1807–1883). Algerian nationalist. Emir (Islamic chieftain) of Mascara from 1832, he led a struggle against the French until his surrender 1847.

Abd al-Karim (Abd al-Karim el-Khettabi) (1880–1963). Moroccan chief known as the 'Wolf of the Riff'. With his brother

Muhammad, he led the *Riff revolt* against the French and Spanish invaders, defeating the Spanish at Anual 1921. For five years he ruled his own Republic of the Riff, centred on Melilla. Then the Spanish sought military assistance from the French (who governed northern Morocco); a joint army of 160,000 under Marshal Pétain subdued the rebellion 1925 and Abd al-Karim surrendered 1926.

Abd Allah or Abdullah el Taaisha (1846–1899). Sudanese ruler from 1885. He succeeded the Mahdi (Islamic leader) Muhammad Ahmed, but was defeated by British forces under General Kitchener at Omdurman 1898. He was killed one year later at the battle of Umm Diwaykarat.

He controlled the Mahdists and ruled through a formal bureaucracy.

Abd al-Malik Ibn Marwan (647–705). Fifth caliph of the Umayyad dynasty, who reigned 685–705, based in Damascus. He waged military campaigns to unite Muslim groups and battled against the Greeks. He instituted a purely Arab coinage and replaced Syriac, Coptic, and Greek with Arabic as the language for his lands. His reign was turbulent but succeeded in extending and strengthening the power of the dynasty. He was also a patron of the arts.

Abd al-Mejid I (1823–1861). Sultan of Turkey from 1839. During his reign the Ottoman Empire was increasingly weakened by internal nationalist movements and the incursions of the great European powers.

He succeeded to the throne eight days after the disastrous defeat of the army of his father Mahmud II at Nezib (now Nizip) by Mehmet Ali, the rebellious viceroy of Egypt. The intervention of the European powers saved Abd al-Mejid's dynasty, and the treaty of 1841, imposed on both parties by Europe, settled the relationship of Egypt and Turkey. Abd al-Mejid instituted many reforms, and considerably improved the status of the Christians within his empire.

Well-educated, liberal-minded, and the first sultan to speak French.

Encyclopaedia Britannica on ABD AL-MEJID I
1990

Abd al-Rahman (died 732). Moorish chief. He invaded Gaul 731 at the head of the largest Muslim army that had yet menaced Europe. He was defeated by Charles Martel near Tours 732.

Abd al-Rahman I (known as al Dajil, 'the newcomer') (731–788). Emir of Córdoba 756–88. Under his leadership Moorish Spain (al-Andalus) flourished as an emirate independent of the Ummayad caliphs of Baghdad, and the foundations were laid that were to make Córdoba the cultural and intellectual capital of Europe in the 9th and 10th centuries.

A member of the Ummayad dynasty, which was ousted from power in Damascus by the Abbasids 750, Abd al-Rahman escaped and after a series of adventures reached southern Spain. He seized control of Córdoba from the Yamanites 755–56 and was successful in pacifying the warring factions of al-Andalus.

Abd-al-Rahman III (891–961). Ruler of Moorish Spain 912–61. In 929 he proclaimed himself caliph, thus formally asserting the independence from the caliphs of Baghdad which his predecessors had already enjoyed for almost two centuries. His reign witnessed the high point of Moorish cultural achievement in western Europe.

Abdul-Jabbar Kareem. Adopted name of Ferdinand Lewis Alcindor (1947–). US basketball player who played for the Milwaukee Bucks 1969–75 and the Los Angeles Lakers 1975–89. He was named basketball's most valuable player a record-breaking six times between 1971 and 1980. He played centre and, being 2 m 18 cm/7 ft 2 in tall, was noted for his 'sky hook' shot.

Born Ferdinand Lewis Alcindor in New York City, he changed his name 1971 after converting to the Muslim faith 1968. He led the basketball team of the University of California at Los Angeles

(UCLA) to the National Collegiate Athletic Association (NCAA) championship 1967–69.

Abdullah Sheik Muhammad (1905–1982). Indian politician, known as the 'Lion of Kashmir'. He headed the struggle for constitutional government against the Maharajah of Kashmir, and in 1948, following a coup, became prime minister. He agreed to the accession of the state to India, but was dismissed and imprisoned from 1953 (with brief intervals) until 1966, when he called for Kashmiri self-determination. He became chief minister of Jammu and Kashmir 1975, accepting the sovereignty of India.

Abdullah el Taaisha alternative name for ◊Abd Allah, Sudanese dervish leader.

Abdullah ibn Hussein (1882–1951). King of Jordan from 1946. He worked with the British guerrilla leader T E Lawrence in the Arab revolt of World War I. Abdullah became king of Transjordan 1946; on the incorporation of Arab Palestine (after the 1948–49 Arab–Israeli War) he renamed the country the Hashemite Kingdom of Jordan. He was assassinated.

à Beckett Gilbert Abbott (1811–1856). English humorous writer. He was the author of comic histories of England and Rome and *The Comic Blackstone* 1844 on English law. He also wrote over 50 plays and helped to dramatize some of Dickens's novels.

Abe Kōbō (1924–1993). Japanese novelist and playwright. He was a leader of the avant-garde, and his familiarity with Western literature, existentialism, surrealism, and Marxism influenced his distinctive treatment of the problems of alienation and loss of identity in postwar Japan. His books include the claustrophobic novel *Suna no onna/Woman of the Dunes* 1962 and minimalist plays such as his trilogy *Bō ni natta otoko/The Man Who Turned into a Stick* 1969.

Abel Carl Friedrich (1723–1787). German musician and composer, who played the viola da gamba. He was born at Cothen and originally played in the court band in Dresden, then moved to England 1759 and became one of the queen's chamber musicians. He joined Johann Christian Bach in giving concerts in London, where he died.

Abel Frederick Augustus (1827–1902). British scientist and inventor who developed explosives. As a chemist to the War Department, he introduced a method of making gun-cotton and was joint inventor with James Dewar of cordite. He also invented the Abel close-test instrument for determining the flash point (ignition temperature) of petroleum. Baronet 1893.

Abel John Jacob (1857–1938). US biochemist, discoverer of adrenaline. He studied the chemical composition of body tissues, and this led, in 1898, to the discovery of adrenaline, the first hormone to be identified, which Abel called epinephrine. He later became the first to isolate amino acids from blood.

Abel Niels Henrik (1802–1829). Norwegian mathematician. He demonstrated that the general quintic equation $ax^5 + bx^4 + cx^3 + dx^2 + ex + f = 0$ could not be solved algebraically. Subsequent work covered elliptic functions, integral equations, infinite series, and the binomial theorem.

Abel transformed the theory of elliptic integrals by introducing elliptic functions, and this generalization of trigonometric functions led eventually to the theory of complex multiplication, with its important implications for algebraic number theory. He also provided the first stringent proof of the binomial theorem. A number of useful concepts in modern mathematics, notably the Abelian group and the Abelian function, bear his name.

Abelard Peter, (English form of Pierre Abélard) (1079–1142). French scholastic philosopher who worked on logic and theology. His romantic liaison with his pupil Héloïse caused a medieval scandal. Details of his life are contained in the autobiographical *Historia Calamitatum Mearum/The History of My Misfortunes*.

Abelard, born at Pallet, near Nantes, became canon of Notre Dame in Paris and master of the cathedral school 1115. When his seduction of Héloïse and secret marriage to her (shortly after the birth of a son) became known, she entered a convent. He was castrated at the instigation of her uncle Canon Fulbert, and became a monk. Resuming teaching a year later, he was cited for heresy and became a hermit at Nogent, where he built the oratory of the Paraclete, and later abbot of a monastery in Brittany.

All acts are in themselves indifferent and only become good or evil according to the intention of their author.

PETER ABELARD
quoted in J P Migne (ed) *Patrologiae Latina* 178, 644a

Abell Kjeld (1901–1961). Danish dramatist. His 15 plays are chiefly concerned with moral responsibility and the need to act on ethical principles so as to avoid evil. They include *Anna Sophie Hedvig* 1939, *Dagepå en sky/Days on a Cloud* 1947, and *Skriget/The Scream* 1961.

With Kaj Munk, Abell was one of Denmark's most distinguished dramatists of the 20th century.

Abell Westcott Stile (1877–1961). British naval architect and engineer. He was the first professor of naval architecture (Liverpool University, 1910) and, as chief surveyor of shipping, Lloyd's Register (1914–28), he was largely responsible for the British government's mercantile shipbuilding programme. KBE 1920.

Abercrombie John (1726–1806). English writer on horticulture. He was employed at Kew Gardens and published *Every Man his own Gardener* 1767.

Abercrombie Lascelles (1881–1938). English poet and scholar. He published *Interludes and Poems* 1908 and several volumes of verse and verse dramas before World War I. Among Abercrombie's critical works are a study of Thomas Hardy 1912, *Principles of English Prosody* 1924, and *Poetry: Its Music and Meaning* 1932. His *Collected Poems* appeared 1930.

Abercrombie (Leslie) Patrick (1879–1957). English architect. He was a pioneer of British town planning, involved in replanning British cities, including London, after damage in World War II.

Abercrombie was born in Ashton-upon-Mersey. He was professor of civic design at Liverpool University 1915–35, and professor of town planning at London University 1935–46. He wrote *Town and Country Planning* 1933 and other books.

Abercromby Ralph (1734–1801). Scottish soldier. In 1801 he commanded an expedition to the Mediterranean, charged with the liquidation of the French forces left behind by Napoleon in Egypt. He fought a brilliant action against the French at Aboukir Bay 1801, but was mortally wounded at the battle of Alexandria a few days later. Knighted 1795.

The general who shares with Sir John Moore the credit of renewing the ancient discipline and military reputation of the British soldier.

H M Stephens on RALPH ABERCROMBY
in *Dictionary of National Biography*

Aberdare Henry Austin Bruce, 1st Baron Aberdare (1815–1895). Welsh politician. He was Liberal member of Parliament for Merthyr from 1852 and held several political appointments, including the home secretaryship 1869–73. Aberdare was made a baron 1873 and was the first chancellor of the University of Wales 1894.

Aberdeen George Hamilton Gordon, 4th Earl of Aberdeen (1784–1860). British Tory politician, prime minister 1852–55, when he resigned because of the criticism aroused by the miseries and mismanagement of the Crimean War.

Born in Edinburgh and educated at Harrow and St John's College, Cambridge, Aberdeen began his career as a diplomat; he was ambassador at Vienna 1813 and signed the Treaty of Teplitz.

His temper, naturally morose, has become licentiously peevish – (He) plagues – his colleagues with the crabbed malice of a maundering witch.

Benjamin Disraeli on GEORGE HAMILTON GORDON,
4TH EARL OF ABERDEEN
in a letter to the Press, 1853.

He was foreign secretary under Wellington 1828–30, and again under Robert Peel 1841–46. In 1852 he became prime minister in a government of Peelites and Whigs (Liberals), but resigned 1855 over the Crimean War losses. Although a Tory, he supported Catholic emancipation and followed Peel in his conversion to free trade.

He succeeded as a Scottish earl 1801, and was created an English viscount 1814.

Aberhart William (1878–1943). Canadian politician, premier of Alberta 1935–43. He tried to establish a currency system on social-credit principles, but the necessary legislation was rejected by the Supreme Court of Canada. Aberhart subsequently reverted to more orthodox financial methods.

Born in Ontario and educated at Queen's University, he was principal of the high school in Calgary, Alberta, and founder of the Calgary Prophetic Bible Institute. He organized a social credit movement, which won the provincial election 1935.

The Alberta legislature passed the necessary legislation (for his currency system), including the Bank Taxation Bill, the Credit Regulation Bill, and Press Control Bill, but all these measures were declared *ultra vires* by the Supreme Court of Canada, and their decision was upheld by the Judicial Committee of the Privy Council.

Abernethy John (1764–1831). English surgeon. During his service at St Bartholomew's Hospital, London, 1787–1827 he gained a wide reputation for his operations for the treatment of aneurysm, which extended the technique of his teacher John Hunter.

Abernethy was born in London and educated at Wolverhampton Grammar School. He was assistant surgeon at St Bartholomew's Hospital 1787–1815, and full surgeon until 1827. He published many surgical works, in which he established the principle of the constitutional origin of local disease, largely traceable in his view to disorders of the digestive system. His *Surgical and Physiological Works* was published 1830.

Abetti Giorgio (1882–1982). Italian astrophysicist who wrote a popular text on the Sun 1963. He participated in numerous expeditions to observe eclipses of the Sun, and led one such expedition to Siberia to observe the total solar eclipse of 19 June 1936.

Abetti was born in Padua and studied at the universities of Padua and Rome. He was a professor at the University of Florence 1921–57 and director of the Arcetri Observatory there 1921–52.

He wrote a handbook of astrophysics, published 1936, and a popular history of astronomy, which appeared in English 1952.

Abinger James Scarlett, 1st Baron Abinger (1769–1844). British politician and judge. He successfully carried through a bill to amend the administration of justice 1830, but opposed the Reform Bill of 1831.

He was raised to the Bench by Robert Peel 1834 as lord chief baron of the Court of Exchequer and created Baron Abinger 1835.

Abington Fanny (born Frances Barton) (1737–1815). English actress. She was engaged for Drury Lane by David Garrick, where she was the first Lady Teazle 1777 and created a number of other parts. She was also well known for Shakespearean roles, especially Beatrice in *Much Ado About Nothing*. She left Drury Lane 1782 for Covent Garden, where she remained until her retirement 1790.

Abish Walter (1931–). US writer of Austrian-Jewish origin. He moved to America 1960.

Abish uses a tight, flat-styled formalism to investigate modern history and morality in such novels as *Alphabetical Africa* 1974 and

How German Is It? 1980, an ironic guidebook that reveals the darkness and guilt behind the materialism of postwar Germany.

Abner in the Old Testament, the cousin of Saul and captain of his army. After Saul's death Abner proclaimed Ishbosheth king. To reconcile the rival claims of Ishbosheth and David he visited the latter at Hebron, where he was treacherously killed by Joab, whose youngest brother, Asahel, had been killed by Abner in battle.

About Edmond François Valentin (1828–1885). French writer. His novels include *Le Roi des montagnes* 1856, *Le Nez d'un notaire* 1862, *L'Homme à l'oreille cassée* 1862, *Le Cas de M Guérin* 1862, and *Le Roman d'un brave homme* 1880. He also contributed to journals, founded *Le XIX Siècle* 1871, and wrote *Le Progrès*, a study of social reforms.

Abrabanel Isaac Ben Jehudah, or *Abarbanel* (1437–1508). Jewish statesman. He was minister of state to King Afonso V of Portugal but was suspected of treason by John II and forced to escape. He then served Ferdinand, King of Aragon, until the expulsion of the Jews from Spain 1492.

His writings include commentaries on the Old Testament and the expected Messiah.

Abraham (lived *c.* 2300 BC). In the Old Testament, the founder of the Jewish nation. In his early life he was called Abram. God promised him heirs and land for his people in Canaan (Israel), renamed him Abraham ('father of many nations'), and tested his faith by a command (later retracted) to sacrifice his son Isaac.

Still childless at the age of 76, Abraham subsequently had a son (Ishmael) with his wife's maidservant Hagar, and then, at the age of 100, a son (Isaac) with his wife Sarah. God's promise to Abraham that his descendants would be a nation and Canaan their land was fulfilled when the descendants of Abraham's grandson Jacob were led out of Egypt by Moses.

Abraham Edward Penley (1913–). British biochemist who isolated the antibiotic cephalosporin, capable of destroying penicillin-resistant bacteria. Knighted 1980.

Abraham a Sancta Clara pseudonym of Ulrich Megerle (1644–1709). German preacher. His sermons are full of imagination and contain sound Catholic doctrine. Schiller's play *Wallensteins Lager* was inspired by his sermon 'Up, up, ye Christians!'. He joined the Augustinians, became court preacher at Vienna, went to Graz, but afterwards returned to Vienna.

Absalom in the Old Testament, the third and favourite son of King David. When defeated in a revolt against his father he fled on a mule, but caught his hair in a tree branch and was killed by Joab, one of David's officers.

Able, ambitious and handsome, he prepared the way for revolt by cunningly cultivating the goodwill of the people. After four years he raised his standard at Hebron, and had such success that David fled to Mahanaim beyond Jordan. Absalom was aided by Ahithophel, but Hushai, David's friend, joined Absalom to defeat the plan of Ahithophel who, seeing his counsel ignored, hanged himself. Absalom was routed in the Forest of Ephraim and was slain, in spite of the king's order to 'deal gently' with him.

Absalon (1128–1201). Danish statesman. He became archbishop of Lund 1178 and minister to Waldemar I and Canute VI of Denmark. He took an active part in helping with the legislation of Waldemar I, and drove the Wendish pirates from the country. Under Canute VI he helped to overthrow Bogislaw of Pomerania. He was a fine statesman and general, and a lover of art and learning, assisting Saxo Grammaticus with his great history of Denmark. He built a castle which was the nucleus of the city of Copenhagen.

Abu-al-Ala al-Maarri or Abu'l-'Ala al-Ma'arri (973–1057). Arab writer and poet. He was a notable humanist, distinguished by his hatred of injustice, hypocrisy, and superstition. His works include poems under the title *Saqt uz-Zand*, later poems the *Luzumiyyat*, and a collection of letters.

Abu Bakr or Abu-Bekr (573–634). 'Father of the virgin', name used by Abd-al-Ka'aba from about 618 when the prophet Muhammad married his daughter Ayesha. Abu Bakr was a close adviser to Muhammad in the period 622–32. On the prophet's death, he became the first caliph, adding Mesopotamia to the Muslim world and instigating expansion into Iraq and Syria.

Traditionally he is supposed to have encouraged some of those who had known Muhammad to memorize his teachings; these words were later written down to form the Koran.

Abū Hanīfah al-Nu'man (*c.* 700–780). Sunni religious leader and jurist. He was the founder of the Hanafī School, the earliest school of Islamic law, which dominates Turkey and India. He was born in Kufa, Iraq, and died in Baghdad.

Abulcasis or Albucasis or Abu'l Qasim (936–1013). Spanish physician and surgeon. His encyclopedia of medicine and surgery, *Altasrif*, greatly influenced medieval medicine. Its surgical section was the first independent work on the subject and the first to contain illustrations of surgical instruments.

Abulfeda (1273–1331). Arab historian and geographer. He was raised to royal rank 1310, becoming governor of the kingdom of Hama. His two best-known works are a universal history, which is one of the chief sources of information concerning the Saracens, and a treatise on geography.

Abul Hasan (1589–1616). Mogul painter. He worked at the court of the emperor Jahangir, specializing in portraits but also executing several delicate, closely observed animal studies. A fine example of his work is *Portrait of Jahangir Holding a Portrait of Akbar* early 17th century (Musée Guimet, Paris). Like many of the Mogul artists of the period, he was influenced by Western art, particularly in his use of colour.

Abú Nuwás Hasan ibn Háni (762–*c.* 815). Arab poet. He is celebrated for the freedom, eroticism and ironic lightness of touch he brought to traditional forms.

He was educated at Basra, spent a year in the desert among the Arabs, and later lived under the protection of the caliph Harun al-Rashid in Baghdad.

Accius Lucius, or Actius or Attius (170–*c.* 85 BC). Roman tragic poet. He wrote more than 40 tragedies on Greek themes but only two on Roman themes. About 700 lines of his work survive.

Accum Friedrich Christian (1769–1838). German chemist. He lived in England 1793–1820, where he introduced illumination by gas in his *Practical Treatise of Gaslight* 1815. His other works include 'An Essay on Chemical Reagents' 1816 and 'A Treatise on the Adulteration of Food' 1820. He worked as an assistant to Humphry Davy before establishing his own laboratory 1800 and becoming professor of chemistry in London 1802. In 1820 he was arrested for mutilating books in the library of the Royal Institution, and he returned to Germany. He was appointed professor in Berlin 1822 and died in that city.

Achad Haam pseudonym of Asher Ginzberg (1856–1927). Jewish writer, born in the Ukraine. He went to Palestine 1891 and 1893 and became convinced that Zionism needed to emphasize its cultural and spiritual nature, thus disagreeing with the political aims of many other Zionists. He founded the periodical *Ha-Shiloa* 1897, stressed the necessity for a renewal of the Hebrew spirit, and was a close adviser of the Zionist leader Chaim Weizmann.

Achaemenid dynasty family ruling the Persian Empire 550–330 BC, named after Achaemenes, ancestor of Cyrus the Great, founder of the empire. His successors include Cambyses, Darius I, Xerxes, and Darius III, who, as the last Achaemenid ruler, was killed after defeat in battle against Alexander the Great 330 BC.

Achard Franz Karl (1753–1821). German chemist who was largely responsible for developing the industrial process by which table sugar (sucrose) is extracted from sugar beet. He improved the quality of available beet and erected the first factory for the extraction of sugar in Silesia (now in Poland) 1802.

Acheampong Ignatius Kutu (born 1931). Ghanaian army officer and politician, military ruler of Ghana 1972–78. He led the coup of Jan 1972 which overthrew the president, Dr Busia, and was himself replaced by his deputy, Frederick Akuffo, in a bloodless coup 1978.

Achebe Chinua (Albert Chinualumogo) (1930–). Nigerian novelist. His themes include the social and political impact of European colonialism on African people, and the problems of newly independent African nations. Among his works are the seminal *Things Fall Apart* 1958, one of the first African novels to achieve a global reputation, and *Anthills of the Savannah* 1987.

Achebe was born in Ogidi, East Central State, and graduated in English literature 1953 from University College, Ibadan. In 1954 he was appointed talks producer for the Nigerian Broadcasting Company, and served as director of external broadcasting 1961–66. During the Nigerian Civil War, he wrote and lectured throughout the world as a spokesperson for the Biafran cause.

Suggested reading
Achebe, Chinua *Aké* (autobiography) (1983)
Achebe, Chinua *Hopes and Impediments: Selected Essays 1965–87* (1987)
Carroll, David *Chinua Achebe* (1980)
Killam, G D *The Novels of Chinua Achebe* (1969)
Wren, R *Achebe's World* (1980)

Achery Jean Luc d' (1609–1685). French Benedictine monk. His chief work is a collection of documents concerning ecclesiastical history entitled *Spicilegium* 1653–77. He collaborated with the French scholar Jean Mabillon (1632–1707) in the *Acta Sanctorum* of the Benedictines, published 1733–38.

Acheson Dean (Gooderham) (1893–1971). US politician. As undersecretary of state 1945–47 in Harry Truman's Democratic administration, he was associated with George C Marshall in preparing the Marshall Plan, and succeeded him as secretary of state 1949–52.

Acheson advocated containment of the USSR. He survived a vote calling for his resignation, but left the State Department following the election to the presidency of the Republican Dwight D Eisenhower. Acheson was highly critical of Britain's foreign-policy aims, notably of the claim to a 'special relationship' with the USA. His books include *Power and Diplomacy* 1958 and *Present at the Creation* 1969, which won the Pulitzer prize for history.

Achillas (lived 1st century BC). Minister of the young Egyptian King Ptolemy XIII. With Lucius Septimius, he murdered Pompey and supported the king against Cleopatra. Achillas led the army against Caesar, until he was put to death by Cleopatra's younger sister Arsinoë, 47 BC.

Achilles Tatius (lived 2nd century AD). Greek writer of Alexandria. His *Romance of Leucippe and Clitophon* influenced the growth of the novel in Europe.

Achillini Alessandro (1463–1512). Italian surgeon. He was one of the first to dissect the human body. He described the veins of the arm, the seven bones of the tarsus (instep), the fornix, ventricles and infundibulum of the brain, and the trochlear nerve. He also described the ducts of the submaxillary gland before Thomas Wharton to whom the discovery is traditionally ascribed, and two of the three ossicles of the ear, the malleus and incus. His chief works are *Corporis humani anatomia* 1516 and *Anatomicae annotationes* 1520.

Ackermann Rudolph (1764–1834). German photoengraver and inventor. He is best known for inventing a steering linkage for vehicles, still the basis of modern car steering. He settled in Britain and ran a print shop and drawing academy in London. He also invented a method of waterproofing paper and cloth, and introduced fine art lithographed annuals into Britain.

Ackroyd Peter (1949–). English writer. His novel *Hawksmoor* 1985 won the Whitbread award, and *T S Eliot* 1984 won the Whitbread prize for biography. Ackroyd's other books include the novel *Chatterton* 1987, and biographies *Ezra Pound and his Circle* 1980, *Dickens* 1990, and *Blake* 1995.

Acosta José de (1539–1600). Spanish Jesuit and writer. From 1571 to 1588 he lived in South America as a missionary and wrote a history of that continent, *Historia natural y moral de las Indias*, published 1590.

Acton Eliza (1799–1859). English cookery writer and poet, whose *Modern Cookery for Private Families* 1845 influenced Mrs Beeton.

Acton Harold Mario (1904–1994). Italian-born English writer and aesthete, the latter term a description he adopted at Oxford, where he was leader of the artistic set in the early 1920s. Works include *Tuscan Villas* 1973, with photographs by Alexander Zicloke, and *The Soul's Gymnasium* 1982, a collection of evocative short stories inspired by the friends he knew from other Florentine villas.

Acton lived most of his life in Villa La Pietra, a palace overlooking Florence, filled with Renaissance furniture and 15th-century Italian paintings. He was knighted 1974.

Power tends to corrupt and absolute power corrupts absolutely.

JOHN (LORD) ACTON
Letter to Mandell Creighton April 1887

Acton John Emerich Edward Dalberg, 1st Baron Acton (1834–1902). British historian and Liberal politician, leader of the liberal Catholic movement. He was a member of Parliament 1859–65, and became a friend and adviser of Prime Minister Gladstone. He was created a baron 1869.

He strenuously opposed the doctrine of papal infallibility and worked for the reunion of Christendom. Acton helped to found the *English Historical Review* 1886. His independent works include 'Lectures on Modern History' 1906, 'The History of Freedom and Historical Essays and Studies' 1907, and 'Lectures on the French Revolution' 1910. Appointed professor of modern history at Cambridge 1895, he planned and edited the *Cambridge Modern History* but did not live to complete more than the first two volumes.

Acton John Francis Edward (1736–1811). English naval officer. In 1779 he reorganized the Neapolitan navy, becoming prime minister, generalissimo, and minister of finance in Naples. In 1798 he fled with the king and queen of Naples to Palermo on account of the French invasion, but resumed his power on the king's restoration 1799. In 1806 he again fled to Sicily with the royal family. Succeeded as baronet 1791.

Acuña Cristoval de (1597–c. 1650). Spanish Jesuit missionary. He wrote an account of a journey of exploration down the Amazon river, which appeared 1641 as *Nuevo descubrimiento del gran río de las Amazonas*.

Adachi Hazato (1890–1947). Japanese general in World War II. He became commander of the Japanese 18th Army in New Guinea Nov 1942. Driven out of New Guinea by the Allied advance down the Kokoda Trail, he made a stand in Hollandia where his army was encircled by US and Australian forces. He held out until 13 Sept 1945, after the war was over, but was sentenced to life imprisonment for war crimes and died shortly afterwards.

Adair James (c. 1709–c. 1783). British trader and historian of Native North Americans. He emigrated to America 1733. He adopted the theory that the Native North Americans, among whom he lived for 40 years, came from the ten lost tribes. His *History of the American Indians* 1775, dealing with their language, habits, and character, is a valuable and interesting work.

Adalbert (c. 1000–1072). German archbishop of Hamburg-Bremen. He declined the papacy offered by Henry III and desired to found a patriarchate in the north. He exercised great power over Henry IV, whom he educated, and though the nobles accomplished his expulsion from court 1066, he was recalled 1069. He assisted in the conversion of the Wends.

Adam family of Scottish architects and designers. William Adam (1689–1748) was the leading Scottish architect of his day, and his son Robert Adam (1728–1792) is considered one of the greatest British architects of the late 18th century, responsible for transforming the prevailing Palladian fashion in architecture to a Neo-Classical style.

William Adam trained his three sons Robert, John, and James in his Edinburgh office. Robert travelled in Italy and Dalmatia, and went on to be appointed architect to King George in 1762. In his interiors, such as those at Harewood House, Luton Hoo, Syon House, and Osterley Park, he employed delicate stucco decoration with Neo-Classical motifs. He also earned a considerable reputation as a furniture designer.

We have been able to seize ... the beautiful spirit of antiquity and to transfuse it with novelty and variety.

ROBERT ADAM
Works in Architecture 1773

Robert, John, and James designed and speculatively developed the district of London between Charing Cross and the Thames, which was named the Adelphi after them (Greek for 'brothers'). The area was largely rebuilt in 1936.

Adam Adolphe Charles (1803–1856). French composer of light operas and founder of the Théâtre National, Paris, 1847. His stage works include *Le Postillion de Longjumeau/The Postillion of Longjumeau* 1836 and *Si j'étais roi/If I Were King* 1852, but he is best remembered for his ballet score for *Giselle* 1841. Some 80 of his works were staged.

Adam Juliette (born Lamber) (1836–1936). French writer. She wrote stories as well as books on political and social subjects, and founded the *Nouvelle revue* 1879. Her salon was politically influential. She was born in Verberie, Oise. Married to a lawyer, La Messine, she published 1858 under that name a volume of stories and *Idées anti-proudhoniennes sur l'amour, la femme et le mariage*. After her second marriage 1868 to Edmond Adam, prefect of police, she wrote largely under her maiden name. Her works include *Le Siège de Paris* 1873, *Le Roman de mon enfance et de ma jeunesse* 1902, *Mes Premières Armes littéraires et politiques* 1904, *Mes Sentiments et nos idées avant 1870* 1905, *Mes Illusions et nos souffrances durant le siège de Paris* 1906, *L'Angleterre en Egypte* 1922, and *L'Egypte: une leçon diplomatique* 1924.

Adam Paul Auguste Marie (1862–1920). French novelist. His work includes *Chair molle* 1885, written in the style of Emile Zola; stories of historical investigation; four romances of the Napoleonic period, including *La Force* 1899; and an autobiographical novel, *Jeunesse et amours de Manuel Hericourt* 1913. His second novel, *Soi* 1886, is a study of feminine egoism. Other works include *Robes rouges* 1891, *Le Mystère des foules* 1895, *L'Enfant d'Austerlitz* 1902, *La Ruse* 1903, and *Au Soleil de juillet* 1903. Among his later works are *Vues d'Amérique* 1906 and *Le Trust* 1910, both based on his travels in America, and *Le Lion d'Arras* 1919.

Adam de la Halle (c. 1240–c. 1290). French lyric poet, dramatist, and composer. His *Jeu de la feuillée* about 1277 is one of the earliest French comedies. His *Le Jeu de Robin et Marion*, written in Italy about 1282, is a theatrical work with dialogue and songs set to what were apparently popular tunes of the day. It is sometimes called the forerunner of comic opera.

Adamnan, St or Adomnan (c. 625–704). Irish monk. He was the author of the *Life of St Columba*. In 679 he was appointed abbot of Iona. While visiting his pupil Aldfrid, King of Northumbria, he was persuaded by the Venerable Bede to accept the Roman observance of Easter and to adopt the regulation tonsure. He endeavoured to introduce the same change of view among his own community, but failed, although some success attended similar efforts in Ireland. Feast day 23 Sept.

Adam of Bremen (died c. 1076). German historian. In 1068 he was made canon of Bremen Cathedral and principal of the cathedral school. He wrote the *Gesta Hammaburgensis Ecclesiae Pontificum* 1072–76, a history of Hamburg and of the spread of Christianity in the north.

Adamov Arthur (1908–1970). Russian-born French poet and dramatist. A Surrealist, Adamov contributed to the Theatre of the Absurd with his plays *Professeur Taranne* 1953 and *Ping Pong* 1955. His style, influenced by a Brechtian social and political awareness, is best illustrated in *Paolo Paoli* 1957 and *Le Printemps '71/Spring '71* 1961, a history of the Paris Commune of 1871.

Adams Abigail Smith (1744–1818). First lady to US president John Adams and public figure. She married lawyer John Adams of Boston 1764; one of their children, John Quincy Adams, would become the sixth US president. A strong supporter of the cause of American independence, she joined her husband on diplomatic missions to Paris and London after the Revolutionary War. As wife of the US vice president 1789–97 and later president 1797–1801, she was widely respected.

Adams Ansel Easton (1902–1984). US photographer. He is known for his printed images of dramatic landscapes and organic forms of the American West. Light and texture were important elements in his photographs. He was associated with the zone system of exposure estimation and was a founder member of the 'f/64' group which advocated precise definition.

In 1916 Adams made his first trip to the Yosemite National Park, California; the Yosemite and the High Sierras remained a major focus of his work throughout his life. Aiming to establish photography as a fine art, he founded the first museum collection of photography, at New York City's Museum of Modern Art 1937.

Although Adams first became a professional musician, he turned to professional photography in the late 1920s. His love of nature also carried over into his work as a conservationist and director of the Sierra Club from 1936.

Photography is based on my belief in the vigour and values of the world of nature.

ANSEL ADAMS
Remark made to Judy Daler 1980 at a dinner party.

Adams Charles Follen (1842–1918). US dialect poet. A dry-goods dealer in Boston, he diverted himself by writing poems in German dialect, similar to the popular ballads of Hans Breitmann. He became widely known for 'Leedle Yawcob Strauss' 1878. His collected poems were published 1910.

Adams Charles Francis (1807–1886). US political leader, journalist, diplomat, and son of John Quincy Adams. He was appointed US minister to England by Abraham Lincoln and unsuccessfully sought the 1872 Republican nomination for president.

Adams was born in Boston. After graduation from Harvard, he studied law with Daniel Webster. As a respected historian and abolitionist, he established the *Boston Whig* and accepted the vice-presidential nomination of the Free Soil party 1848. He later joined the Republican party and served in the US House of Representatives 1858–61.

Adams Franklin Pierce, popularly known as *F P A* (1881–1960). US humorist and social critic. He gained fame as a columnist for the New York *Evening Mail, Tribune, World,* and *Post*. In addition to publishing books of light verse ('The Melancholy Lute' 1936) and collections of his syndicated newspaper columns (*The Diary of Our Own Samuel Pepys* 1935), he served as a panellist on the popular radio game show *Information Please*.

Born in Chicago, Adams studied briefly at the University of Michigan, worked at a succession of odd jobs, and finally joined the *Chicago Journal* as a feature writer 1903.

Adams Gerry (Gerard) (1948–). Northern Ireland politician, president of Provisional Sinn Féin (the political wing of the Irish Republican Army) from 1978. He was elected member of Parliament for Belfast West 1983 but declined to take up his Westminster seat, stating that he did not believe in the British government; he lost his seat to a Social Democratic Labour Party candidate 1992. In Aug 1994, after initial doubts about his ability to influence the IRA, Adams announced a 'complete cessation of military operations'.

Following the IRA cease-fire 1994, the British government removed all restrictions on Adams' public appearances and freedom to travel to the UK (in force since 1988). His unwillingness to decommission IRA arms prior to full British troop withdrawal from Northern Ireland led to a delay in the start of all-party peace talks 1995.

Adams Henry Brooks (1838–1918). US historian and novelist, a grandson of President John Quincy Adams. He published the nine-volume *A History of the United States During the Administrations of Jefferson and Madison* 1889–91, a study of the evolution of democracy in the USA.

Born in Boston, he graduated 1858 from Harvard University and later taught medieval history there 1870–77. He also was editor of the *North American Review* 1870–76. His works include a study of the medieval world *Mont-Saint-Michel and Chartres* 1904, and a classic autobiography *The Education of Henry Adams* 1907, as well as the novels *Democracy, an American Novel* 1880, which reflects his disillusionment with the US political system, and *Esther* 1884, published under a pseudonym, about the conflict between religion and science.

Politics, as a practice, whatever its professions, has always been the systematic organization of hatreds.

HENRY ADAMS
The Education of Henry Adams ch 1 1906

Adams James Truslow (1878–1949). US historian. His work *The Founding of New England* 1921 was awarded the Pulitzer Prize. He

Adams, John Quincy *John Quincy Adams, 6th president of the USA. During his long second career in Congress (1831–48), 'Old Man Eloquent', as he was called, won renewed respect throughout the North as an opponent of slavery. Although never an abolitionist, Adams fought the extension of slavery in the territories.*

wrote several other books on New England, a history of *The Adams Family* 1930, and social studies.

Adams John (1735–1826). 2nd president of the USA 1797–1801, and vice president 1789–97. He was a member of the Continental Congress 1774–78 and signed the Declaration of Independence. In 1779 he went to France and negotiated the treaty of 1783 that ended the American Revolution. In 1785 he became the first US ambassador in London.

He was born in Quincy, Massachusetts, studied at Harvard and became a barrister 1758. He was ambassador to Holland 1782–85. The first vice-president of the USA, he was re-elected 1792. Adams represented the aristocratic point of view, in contrast to Thomas Jefferson, the champion of democracy. He published *A Defence of the Constitution of the United States of America* 1787.
Suggested reading
Brown, Ralph A *The Presidency of John Adams* (1975)
Peterson, Merrill D *Adams and Jefferson* (1976)
Shaw, Peter *The Character of John Adams* (1977)

Adams John Coolidge (1947–). US composer and conductor. He was director of the New Music Ensemble 1972–81, and artistic adviser to the San Francisco Symphony Orchestra from 1978. His minimalist techniques are displayed in *Electric Wake* 1968, *Heavy Metal* 1971, *Bridge of Dreams* 1982, and the operas *Nixon in China* 1988 and *The Death of Klinghoffer* 1990. He is currently creative chairman of the St Paul Chamber orchestra.

Adams John Couch (1819–1892). English astronomer who mathematically deduced the existence of the planet Neptune 1845 from the effects of its gravitational pull on the motion of Uranus, although it was not found until 1846 by J G Galle. Adams also studied the Moon's motion, the Leonid meteors, and terrestrial magnetism. Adams became a professor at Cambridge 1858 and director of the observatory 1861.

Adams John Quincy (1767–1848). 6th president of the USA 1825–29, eldest son of President John Adams. He negotiated the Treaty of Ghent to end the War of 1812 (fought with Britain) on generous terms for the USA. In 1817 he became President James Monroe's secretary of state, formulating the Monroe Doctrine 1823. As president, Adams was an advocate of strong federal government.

Think of your forefathers! Think of your posterity!

JOHN QUINCY ADAMS
Speech 22 Dec 1802

He was born in Quincy, Massachusetts, studied diplomacy in Europe and became US minister in The Hague, Berlin, St Petersburg, and London. He was elected to the US Senate in 1803. In 1824 he was elected president by the House of Representatives despite receiving fewer votes than his main rival, the Democrat Andrew Jackson, who succeeded him as president. In 1831 Adams returned to Congress, where he served until his death. After 1835 he spoke strongly against slavery.
Suggested reading
Adams, John Quincy *Memoirs* (1874–77, rep 1970)
Bemis, Samuel Flagg *John Quincy Adams* (1949–56)
Hecht, M B *John Quincy Adams: A Personal History of an Independent Man* (1972)
Richards, Leonard *The Life and Times of Congressman John Quincy Adams* (1986)

Adams Maude (1872–1953). US actress. She was the first to play Lady Babble in *The Little Minister* 1891 by the Scottish writer J M Barrie, who wrote the part for her. She became an outstanding interpreter of his heroines, and of those of the French dramatist Edmond Rostand.

Adams Neil (1958–). English judo champion. He won two junior and five senior European titles 1974–85, eight senior national titles, and two Olympic silver medals 1980, 1984. In 1981 he was world champion in the 78 kg class.

Adams, Richard *English novelist Richard Adams. His first novel Watership Down 1972, an epic story of a threatened colony of rabbits in search of a new warren, was widely read and made into a animated film 1972. He continued the animal theme in Shardik 1974, about a bear, and The Plague Dogs 1977, about laboratory animals. The Iron Wolf, a collection of short stories, appeared 1980.*

Adams Richard George (1920–). English novelist. He wrote *Watership Down* 1972, a story of rabbits who escape from a doomed warren and work together to establish a new one. As with all Adams' novels, there is an underlying social message. Later novels include *Shardik* 1974, *The Plague Dogs* 1977, *The Girl on a Swing* 1980, and *Traveller* 1988.

Many human beings say that they enjoy the winter, but what they really enjoy is feeling proof against it.
RICHARD ADAMS
Watership Down ch 50 1972

Adams Roger (1889–1971). US organic chemist, known for his painstaking analytical work to determine the composition of naturally occurring substances such as complex vegetable oils and plant alkaloids.

Adams Samuel (1722–1803). US politician, the chief instigator of the Boston Tea Party. He was a signatory to the Declaration of Independence, served in the Continental Congress, and anticipated the French emperor Napoleon in calling the British a 'nation of shopkeepers'.

Adams took the colonists' side in the disturbances caused by the Stamp Act 1765, and in 1765–74 was a member of the legislature of Massachusetts. He was lieutenant-governor of Massachusetts 1789–93 and governor until 1797. He was a second cousin of President John Adams.

Adams Walter Sydney (1876–1956). US astronomer who developed the use of spectroscopy in the study of stars and planets. He found that luminosity and the relative intensities of particular spectral lines could distinguish giant stars from dwarf stars. Spectra could also be used to study the physical properties, motions, and distances of stars.

In 1904 he assisted George Hale in the establishment of the Mount Wilson Observatory above Pasadena in California, becoming its director 1923. At Mount Wilson Adams was able to demonstrate that sunspots have a lower temperature than the rest of the solar disc. He also used Doppler displacements to study the rotation of the Sun.

Adams William (1564–1620). English sailor and shipbuilder, the only foreigner ever to become a samurai. He piloted a Dutch vessel that reached Japan 1600, and became adviser to the first Tokugawa shogun, for whom he built two warships, the first Western-style ships in Japan.

He is regarded by the Japanese as the symbolic founder of their navy.

Adamson Joy Friedericke Victoria (born Gessner) (1910–1985). German-born naturalist whose work with wildlife in Kenya, including the lioness Elsa, is described in the book *Born Free* 1960. She was murdered at her home in Kenya. She worked with her third husband, British game warden George Adamson (1906–1989), who was murdered by bandits.

Adamson Patrick (1537–1592). Scottish archbishop and writer. He came into conflict with the Presbyterian party, was sent 1583 as an ambassador to Queen Elizabeth I of England by James VI, and on his return to Scotland was charged with heresy and excommunicated 1585. He was afterwards pardoned, but again excommunicated 1588. He was the author of many theological works in Latin, both prose and verse.

Adamson became minister of Ceres, Fife, 1563. In 1566 he went to France, where he studied Calvinism, returning about 1572, when he became minister of Paisley and chaplain to the regent. He was made archbishop of St Andrews 1576.

Adamson Robert (1821–1948). Scottish photographer. He collaborated with David Octavius Hill in applying the calotype process; they produced 2,500 calotypes, both portraits and landscapes.

Adcock (Kareen) Fleur (1934–). New Zealand poet, based in England. She has developed a distinctive, unsentimental poetic voice with which she coolly explores contemporary life, love, and personal relationships. Her collections include *The Eye of the Hurricane* 1964, *High Tide in the Garden* 1971, *The Inner Harbour* 1979, and *Time Zones* 1991.

She has also edited *The Oxford Book of Contemporary New Zealand Verse* 1982 and translated medieval Latin poems under the title *The Virgin and the Nightingale* 1983. Trained as a classicist, she is a librarian by profession.

Addams Charles Samuel (1912–1988). US cartoonist, creator of the ghoulish family featured in the *New Yorker* magazine. A successful 1960s television comedy series and a feature-length film in 1991 were based on these cartoons.

Addams Jane (1860–1935). US social reformer, feminist, and pacifist. In 1889 she founded and led the social settlement of Hull House in the slums of Chicago, one of the earliest community welfare centres. She was vice president of the National American Women Suffrage Alliance 1911–14, and in 1915 led the Women's Peace Party and the first Women's Peace Congress. She shared the Nobel Peace Prize 1931.

Hull House served as a model for others throughout the USA, and provided innovative services such as day care. Addams was a US leader in attempts to reform child-labour laws and and was president of the Women's International League for Peace and Freedom 1919. Her publications include *Democracy and Social Ethics* 1902, *Newer Ideals of Peace* 1907, and *Twenty Years at Hull House* 1910.

Addington Henry, 1st Viscount Sidmouth (1757–1844). British Tory politician, prime minister 1801–04. As home secretary

I hate liberality ... Nine times out of ten it is cowardice, and the tenth time lack of principle.
HENRY ADDINGTON, 1ST VISCOUNT SIDMOUTH
quoted in John Mitford *Sayings of Lord Sidmouth*

1812–1822, he was responsible for much reprieve legislation, including the notorious Six Acts. He was created viscount 1805.

Addison Joseph (1672–1719). English writer. In 1704 he celebrated Marlborough's victory at Blenheim in a poem commissioned by the government, 'The Campaign', and subsequently held political appointments, including undersecretary of state 1706 and secretary to the Lord-Lieutenant of Ireland 1708. In 1709 he contributed to the *Tatler* magazine, begun by Richard Steele, with whom he was cofounder 1711–12 of the *Spectator*. His essays set a new standard of easy elegance in English prose.

His neoclassical blank verse tragedy *Cato* 1713 was highly respected in the 18th century, though perhaps as much for its political content as its literary merit.

In December 1715 he launched a periodical published in support of the government entitled *The Freeholder*. He was appointed secretary of state 1717 but retired from office 1718 on grounds of illness.
Suggested reading
Ketcham, M C *Transparent Designs* (1985)
Smithers, P *The Life of Joseph Addison* (1954)

From hence, let fierce contending nations know / What dire effects from civil discord flow.

JOSEPH ADDISON
Cato V iv 1713

Addison Thomas (1793–1860). British physician who first recognized the condition known as Addison's disease in 1855. He was the first to correlate a collection of symptoms with pathological changes in an endocrine gland. He is also known for his discovery of what is now called pernicious (or Addison's) anaemia. Addison also described xanthoma (flat, soft spots that appear on the skin, usually on the eyelids) and wrote about other skin diseases, tuberculosis, pneumonia, and the anatomy of the lung. He gave the first full description of appendicitis.

Ade George (1866–1944). US humorist and playwright. His *Fables in Slang* 1900 was so successful that he wrote six volumes under various titles. He also wrote novels and plays, including *The Country Chairman* 1903, *The College Widow* 1904, and *The Fair Co-ed* 1908.

Adelaide (1792–1849). Queen consort of William IV of England. Daughter of the Duke of Saxe-Meiningen, she married William, then Duke of Clarence, in 1818. No children of the marriage survived infancy.

Adeler Max. Pseudonym of Charles Heber Clark (1847–1915). US writer and journalist. Among his works, mostly humorous, are *Out of the Hurly-Burly* 1874, *Elbow-Room* 1876, *Random Shots* 1879, the novel *The Quakeress* 1905, and a collection of short stories, *By the Bend in the River* 1914.

A thick skin is a gift from God.

KONRAD ADENAUER
New York Times 30 Dec 1959

Adenauer Konrad (1876–1967). German Christian Democrat politician, chancellor of West Germany 1949–63. With the French president de Gaulle he achieved the postwar reconciliation of France and Germany and strongly supported all measures designed to strengthen the Western bloc in Europe.

Adenauer was mayor of his native city of Cologne from 1917 until his imprisonment by Hitler in 1933 for opposition to the Nazi regime. After the war he headed the Christian Democratic Union (CDU) and became chancellor, combining the office with that of foreign minister. He was re-elected chancellor 1953 and retained the post of foreign minister until 1955.

He was known as the 'Old Fox'. He supported the UK's entry into the Common Market (now the European Union).

Ader Clément (1841–1926). French aviation pioneer and inventor. He demonstrated stereophonic sound transmission by telephone at the 1881 Paris Exhibition of Electricity. His steam-driven aeroplane, the *Eole*, made the first powered takeoff in history 1890, but it could not fly. In 1897, with his *Avion III*, he failed completely, despite false claims made later.

Adjani Isabelle (1955–). French actress of Algerian-German descent. She played the title role in François Truffaut's film *L'Histoire d'Adèle H/The Story of Adèle H* 1975 and has since appeared in international productions including *Le Locataire/The Tenant*, *Nosferatu Phantom der Nacht* 1979, *Ishtar* 1987, and *La Reine Margot* 1994.

Superstars don't exist any more.

ISABELLE ADJANI
Rolling Stone 26 Aug 1976

Adler Alfred (1870–1937). Austrian psychologist who saw the 'will to power' as more influential in accounting for human behaviour than the sexual drive. A dispute over this theory led to the dissolution of his ten-year collaboration with psychiatry's founder Sigmund Freud.

The concepts of inferiority complex and overcompensation originated with Adler. In 1911 Adler, and a number of others, left the Freudian circle and founded the Individual Psychology Movement. He moved to the USA 1935.

Adler held that much neurotic behaviour is a result of feelings of inadequacy or inferiority caused by, for instance, being the youngest in a family or being a child who is trying to compete in an adult world. His works include *Organic Inferiority and Psychic Compensation* 1907, *Understanding Human Nature* 1927, and *Practice and Theory of Individual Psychology* 1927.
Suggested reading
Ansbacher, H L *Adler Revisited* (1987)
Bottome, P *Alfred Adler: A Biography* (1939)
Way, L *Alfred Adler: An Introduction to his Psychology* (1956)

Adler, Alfred   Alfred Adler was a prominent member of the circle of psychologists surrounding Sigmund Freud during the early 1900s. In 1911, after professional disagreement concerning Freud's theories, he left, and developed his psychoanalytical theory of individual psychology. (Ann Ronan/Image Select)

Adler Cyrus (1863–1940). US educator and public figure. In 1892 he was appointed curator at the Smithsonian Institution and later served as its librarian and assistant secretary. From 1908 until his death, he was president of Dropsie College and a leader of the American Jewish Committee.

His appeal for protection of the rights of religious ethnic minorities was adopted in the final text of the Treaty of Versailles after World War I.

Adler Larry (Lawrence Cecil) (1914–). US musician. He was a virtuoso performer on the harmonica. He commissioned the English composer Vaughan Williams's *Romanza in D flat* 1951.

Adler Nathan Marcus (1803–1890). German-born chief rabbi of the Jews of the British Empire. He was chief rabbi in Oldenburg 1829 and Hanover 1830, and was appointed to the chief rabbinate in London 1845, where he did much to reunite the various Jewish congregations. He published sermons and other works, including one on the Pentateuch. He was succeeded in office by his son *Hermann Adler* (1839–1911).

Adolphus John Leycester (1795–1862). English writer and lawyer. His *Letters to Richard Heber, Esq.*, published anonymously 1821, demonstrated that Walter Scott was the author of the Waverley novels; his *Letters from Spain* appeared 1858.

Adorno Theodor Ludwig Wiesengrund (1903–1969). German philosopher, social theorist, musicologist, and critic of culture. Adorno was the main contributor to *The Authoritarian Personality* 1950, a psychoanalytical and social research project stemming partly from Erich Fromm's ideas, in which the F-scale (F standing for fascism) was constructed. His early writings show the influence of the Marxist thinking of Georg Lukács and Ernst Bloch, as well as considerable interest in Sigmund Freud.

Adorno was a leading member of the Institut für Sozialforschung (Institute for Social Research) at Frankfurt, which he joined 1930. When the Nazis came to power, the institute moved with its director, Max Horkheimer, to the USA and Adorno eventually followed, acquiring US citizenship. In the 1940s he collaborated with Horkheimer on *Dialectic of Enlightenment* 1947. He returned to Germany 1949.

Adrian Edgar Douglas, 1st Baron Adrian (1889–1977). English physiologist. He received the Nobel Prize for Physiology or Medicine 1932 for his work with Charles Sherrington in the field of nerve impulses and the function of the nerve cell. Adrian was also one of the first to study the electrical activity of the brain. From 1919 he held academic posts at Cambridge. Created a baron 1955. Between 1933 and 1946 he worked on the ways in which the nervous system generates rhythmic electrical activity. He was one of the first scientists to use extensively the electroencephalogram (EEG). The last 20 years of his research life, from 1937 to 1959, were spent studying the sense of smell. Adrian's works include *The Mechanism of Nervous Action* 1932 and *The Physical Background of Perception* 1947.

Adrian IV (Nicholas Breakspear) (c. 1100–1159). Pope 1154–59, the only British pope. He secured the execution of Arnold of Brescia, crowned Frederick I Barbarossa as German emperor, refused Henry II's request that Ireland should be granted to the English crown in absolute ownership, and was at the height of a quarrel over papal supremacy with the emperor when he died.

Breakspear was born at Abbots Langley, Hertfordshire, became a monk in France, at St Rufus, near Arles, where he was elected abbot 1137 and cardinal 1146.

Adrian de Castello (c. 1460–c. 1521). Italian scholar, politician, and cleric. In 1488 he was sent by Pope Innocent VIII to England, where he held senior positions in the church. In 1517 he was accused of complicity in the plot to poison Leo X, and was stripped of all his offices 1518. He fled to Venice, and is thought to have been murdered on his return journey to Rome after the death of Leo X. Adrian was born in Tuscany. He became the agent of the English king Henry VII in Rome. In 1502 he was made bishop of Hereford, in 1503 created cardinal by Alexander VI, and in 1504 became bishop of Bath and Wells.

Ady Endre (1877–1919). Hungarian poet. Born at Ermindszent, he spent part of his youth in Paris and the influence of modern French literature can be seen in many of his earlier poems. His mature work is characterized by its violence, originality, beauty, and strength. He died in a Budapest sanatorium.

Aehrenthal Count Aloys von (1854–1912). Austro-Hungarian diplomat and politician. He was foreign minister during the Bosnian Crisis of 1908.

He studied at the universities of Prague and Bonn and entered the diplomatic service in 1877, serving as ambassador in St Petersburg 1898–1906. He became foreign minister in 1906 and directed the foreign policy of the Dual Monarchy till his death. Aehrenthal was generally identified with the peace party in Austria-Hungary.

Aelfric (c. 955–1020). Anglo-Saxon writer and abbot. He was the author of two collections of *Catholic Homilies* 990–92, sermons, and the *Lives of the Saints* 996–97, written in vernacular Old English prose.

Aelred, St also Ailred or Ethelred (1109–1167). British religious mystic and historian. His works include 'Vita et Miracula S. Edwardi Regis et Confessoris', 'De Spirituali Amicitia', and 'De Anima'. His feast day is 12 Jan. He was born in Hexham, Northumberland, and entered the household of David I of Scotland at an early age. He refused a bishopric and entered the Cistercian abbey at Rievaulx, where he became abbot 1146. On a mission to the Picts of Galloway in 1164 he persuaded the chief to become a monk.

Aeschines (389–314 BC). Athenian orator and principal rival of Demosthenes, with whom he was ambassador to Macedonia 348. His conflict with Demosthenes came to a head 330 and caused Aeschines to go into exile. He established a school of public speaking in Rhodes.

Aeschylus (c. 525–c. 456 BC). Athenian dramatist. He developed Greek tragedy by introducing the second actor, thus enabling true dialogue and dramatic action to occur independently of the chorus. Ranked with Euripides and Sophocles as one of the three great tragedians, Aeschylus composed some 90 plays between 500 and 456 BC, of which seven complete tragedies survive in his name: *Persians* 472 BC, *Seven Against Thebes* 467, *Suppliants* 463, the *Oresteia* trilogy (*Agamemnon*, *Libation-Bearers*, and *Eumenides*) 458, and *Prometheus Bound* (the last, although attributed to him, is of uncertain date and authorship).

Aeschylus was born at Eleusis in Attica and known to have fought at the battle of Marathon 490 BC. Towards the end of his life, he left Athens for Sicily. His work is characterized by spectacular tragedy, ornate language, and complex and vigorous use of choral song and dance. His *Oresteia* trilogy is the only surviving example from antiquity of three connected plays performed on the same occasion.

Aesop by tradition, a writer of Greek fables. According to the historian Herodotus, he lived in the mid-6th century BC and was a slave. The fables that are ascribed to him were collected at a later date and are anecdotal stories using animal characters to illustrate moral or satirical points.

Afonso six kings of Portugal, including:

Afonso I (1094–1185). King of Portugal from 1112. He made Portugal independent from León.

Afonso V 'el Africano' (1432–1481). King of Portugal 1438–81. His father died 1438 and, after a turbulent regency under his uncle Pedro, Afonso assumed the government 1448. He conducted a successful campaign in Morocco against the Moors 1458–71. During his reign the Portuguese explored along the west coast of Africa almost as far as the equator.

Aga Khan IV (Karim) (1936–). Spiritual head (*imam*) of the *Ismaili* Muslim sect. He succeeded his grandfather 1957.

Agassiz Jean Louis Rodolphe (1807–1873). Swiss-born US palaeontologist and geologist who developed the idea of the ice age. He established his name through his work on the classification of fossil fishes. Unlike Charles Darwin, he did not believe that individual species themselves changed, but that new species were created from time to time. In 1832 Agassiz became professor at Neuchâtel, Switzerland. Moving to the USA 1846, he joined the faculty of Harvard.

Travelling in 1836 in the Alps, Agassiz developed the novel idea that glaciers, far from being static, were in a constant state of almost imperceptible motion. Finding rocks that had been shifted or abraded, presumably by glaciers, he inferred that in earlier times much of northern Europe had been covered with ice sheets.

His book *Researches on Fossil Fish* 1833–44 described and classified over 1,700 species. *Contributions to the Natural History of the United States* 1857–62 is an exhaustive study of the American natural environment.

Agate James (Evershed) (1877–1947). English essayist and theatre critic. He wrote *Ego*, a diary in nine volumes published 1935–49.

I am not interested in what anybody else thinks. My mind is not a bed to be made and remade.

JAMES AGATE
Ego 1935–49

Agatha, St (lived 3rd century AD). Patron saint of Catania, Sicily. According to legend she was a member of the Sicilian nobility who refused the attentions of the Roman prefect. She was sentenced to be burnt alive, but when the stake was set alight an earthquake occurred. She died in prison in 251. Her feast day is 5 Feb.

Agee James Rufus (1909–1955). US journalist, screenwriter, and author. He rose to national prominence as a result of his investigation of the plight of sharecroppers in the South during the Depression. In collaboration with photographer Walker Evans, he published the photo and text essay 'Let Us Now Praise Famous Men' 1941. His screenwriting credits include *The African Queen* 1951 and *The Night of the Hunter* 1955. His novel *A Death in the Family* won a Pulitzer Prize 1958.

Born in Knoxville, Tennessee, Agee graduated from Harvard 1932 and embarked on a career as a magazine reporter and feature writer.

Agnesi Maria Gaetana (1718–1799). Italian mathematician. She produced a 1,000-page textbook, *Istituzioni analitiche ad uso della gioventù italiana/Foundations of Analysis for the Use of Italian Youth* 1748, which provided an integrated treatment of algebra, analytical geometry, and calculus. She is acknowledged as the first woman mathematician.

Agnesi was born in Milan. An infant prodigy, at the age of 11 she was familiar with French, Latin, Greek, German, Spanish, and Hebrew. In 1780 she was appointed professor of mathematics at Bologna, although she never taught there. Her name is associated with the curve $x^2y = a^2(a-y)$ which she discussed and called a *versiera*, from the Latin for 'turning'. However, *versiera* is also the colloquial word for 'witch', and in English the curve is known as the 'witch of Agnesi'.

Agnew Spiro (Theodore) (1918–1996). US vice president 1969–73, a Republican. He was governor of Maryland 1966–69, and vice president under Richard Nixon. Agnew took the lead in a campaign against the press and opponents of the Vietnam War. Although he was one of the few administration officials not to be implicated in the Watergate affair, he resigned 1973, shortly before pleading 'no contest' to a charge of income-tax evasion.

Agnon Shmuel Yosef. Pseudonym of Samuel Joseph Czaczkes (1888–1970). Israeli novelist. Born in Buczacz, Galicia (now part of W Ukraine), he made it the setting of his most celebrated work, *Tmol Shilshom/A Guest for the Night* 1945. He shared a Nobel prize 1966.

He settled in Palestine in 1909, and took the name of Agnon from his story 'Agunot' 1908. Much of his writing incorporates influences

from his childhood in Galicia, including the novel *Hakhnasat Kala/The Bridal Canopy* 1922.

Agostini Giacomo (1943–). Italian motorcyclist who won a record 122 grand prix and 15 world titles. His world titles were at 350cc and 500cc and he was five times a dual champion.

In addition he was ten times winner of the Isle of Man TT (Tourist Trophy) races; a figure bettered only by Mike Hailwood and Joey Dunlop.

Agricola Georgius. Latinized name of Georg Bauer (1494–1555). German mineralogist who pioneered mining technology. His book *De Re Metallica/On Metals* 1556, illustrated with woodcuts, became a standard text on smelting and mining.

His *The Nature of Fossils* 1546 advances one of the first comprehensive classifications of minerals. He went on to explore the origins of rocks, mountains, and volcanoes.

This is the seventh year since you started to conquer Britain in the name of imperial Rome's greatness.

GNAEUS JULIUS AGRICOLA
Address to soldiers before the battle of Mons Graupius in AD 84.
Quoted in Tacitus *Agricola* ch 33

Agricola Gnaeus Julius (AD 40–93). Roman general and politician. Born in Provence, he became consul AD 77, and then governor of Britain AD 78–85. He extended Roman rule to the Firth of Forth in Scotland and won the battle of Mons Graupius. His fleet sailed round the north of Scotland and proved Britain an island.

Agrippa Marcus Vipsanius (63–12 BC). Roman general and admiral, who was instrumental in the successful campaigns and rise to power of Augustus. He commanded the victorious fleet at the battle of Actium and married Augustus's daughter Julia.

What need is there for wine? Agrippa has sufficiently provided that men do not go thirsty by building many aqueducts.

Augustus on MARCUS VIPSANIUS AGRIPPA
commenting on a wine shortage. Quoted by Suetonius in *Augustus* ch 42.1

Agrippina the Younger (AD 15–59). Influential member of a Roman imperial family, sister of Caligula, mother of Nero, and wife of her uncle Claudius, all Roman emperors. She was suspected of poisoning Claudius, having previously persuaded him to adopt Nero as his successor over his own son, Britannicus (AD 50). She sought to rule through Nero but after five years of personal power she was poisoned on his orders.

The present-day city of Cologne (Colonia Agrippina) was named after her.

Ahab (*c.* 875–854 BC). King of Israel. His empire included the suzerainty of Moab, and Judah was his subordinate ally, but his kingdom was weakened by constant wars with Syria. By his marriage with Jezebel, princess of Sidon, Ahab introduced into Israel the worship of the Phoenician god Baal, thus provoking the hostility of Elijah and other prophets. Ahab died in battle against the Syrians at Ramoth Gilead.

Ahasuerus (Latinized Hebrew form of the Persian Khshayarsha, Greek Xerxes) name of several Persian kings in the Bible, notably the husband of Esther. Traditionally it was also the name of the Wandering Jew.

Ahmad Shah Durrani (1724–1773). Founder and first ruler of Afghanistan. Elected shah 1745, he had conquered the Punjab by 1751 and defeated the Maratha people's confederacy at Panipat, Punjab 1761.

Ahtisaari Maarti (1939–). Finnish diplomat and politician, president from 1994. Prior to being chosen as the Social Democratic

Party presidential candidate, he was under-secretary-general of the United Nations, representing it in Namibia 1989–90 and in Yugoslavia 1993. He strongly supported Finland's membership of the European Union and pledged himself to work for better relations with Russia.

Aidan, St (*c.* 600–651). Irish monk who converted Northumbria to Christianity and founded Lindisfarne monastery on Holy Island off the NE coast of England. His feast day is 31 Aug.

Aidid Muhammad Farah (1936–1996). Somali soldier and politician. A one-time colleague of the Somali president, Siad Barre, in 1990 he established an anti-Barre paramilitary organization, the United Somali Congress (USC), which eventually drove the president from office 1991. Rivalry subsequently developed within the ruling coalition and Somalia was again plunged into civil war. During 1993, United Nations peacekeeping forces (principally US Marines) targetted Aidid as the principal villain in the conflict and conducted an abortive mission to capture him. Aidid was ousted 1995. He was killed in faction fighting 1996.

Aidoo Ama Ata (1940–1996). Ghanaian dramatist and writer. *Dilemma of a Ghost* 1965, her best-known play, deals with the difficulties of reconciling a Western education and African values and traditions. She has also written novels such as *Our Sister Killjoy* 1977, and short stories.

Aiken Conrad Potter (1889–1973). US poet, novelist, and short-story writer. His *Selected Poems* 1929 won the Pulitzer Prize. His works were influenced by early psychoanalytic theory and the use of the stream-of-consciousness technique. His verse, distinguished by its musicality, includes *A Letter from Li Po and Other Poems* 1955, *A Seizure of Limericks* 1964 and *Preludes* 1966. His novels include *Great Circle* 1933, and collected short stories were published 1960.

Born in Savannah, Georgia, Aiken grew up in New England with relatives after his father, a doctor, killed his mother and then committed suicide. In his autobiography *Ushant* 1952, he confronts this traumatic experience. He graduated from Harvard University 1911 and began to write poetry. Some of Aiken's poetry is in the form of 'symphonies', works that attempt to imitate music in its ability to convey meaning on several levels at once. His poetic works include *The House of Dust* 1920, *Senlin* 1925, *Brownstone Eclogues and Other Poems* 1942, *Collected Poems* 1953, and *Sheepford Hills* 1957. His novels include *The Voyage* 1927 and *Conversation* 1940.

Rock meeting rock can know love better / Than eyes that stare or lips that touch. / All that we know in love is bitter, / And it is not much.

CONRAD AIKEN
'Annihilation'

Aiken Howard Hathaway (1900–1973). US mathematician and computer pioneer. In 1939, in conjunction with engineers from IBM, he started work on the design of an automatic calculator using standard business-machine components. In 1944 the team completed one of the first computers, the Automatic Sequence Controlled Calculator (known as the Harvard Mark I), a programmable computer controlled by punched paper tape and using punched cards. He became director of Harvard Computation Laboratory in 1946.

Ailey Alvin (1931–1989). US dancer, choreographer, and director. His Alvin Ailey City Center Dance Theater, formed 1958, was the first truly multiracial modern dance company. Its emphasis on dance as entertainment, conveyed with an infectious theatricality, brought dance to a wider audience. Ailey's highly individual choreography blends modern, jazz, and classical dance, and celebrates rural and urban black America in pieces like *Blues Suite* 1958, and the company signature piece *Revelations* 1960, which has resonances of church revivalist meetings.

Alvin Ailey's modern company offer much needed opportunities for black male and female performers: they do little to counter stereotypes of women.

Christy Adair on ALVIN AILEY
in *Woman and Dance; Sylphs and Sirens* 1992

Aimatov Chingiz (1928–). Kirghiz (central Asia) novelist. His work, drawing on oral epic tradition (the Kirghiz language had no alphabet until 1928), dramatizes the conflict between the tribal customs of the Kirghiz nomads and the Western values of the Soviet administration, as in *The White Steamship* 1970 and *The Day Lasts Longer than a Century* 1980.

Ainsworth William Harrison (1805–1882). English historical novelist. He wrote more than 40 novels and helped popularize the legends of Dick Turpin in *Rookwood* 1834 and Herne the Hunter in *Windsor Castle* 1843. His novels include *Jack Sheppard* 1939, *Old St Paul's* 1841, and *The Lancashire Witches* 1849.

Airy George Biddell (1801–1892). English astronomer. He installed a transit telescope at the Royal Observatory at Greenwich, England, and accurately measured Greenwich Mean Time by the stars as they crossed the meridian.

Airy became the seventh Astronomer Royal 1835. He began the distribution of Greenwich time signals by telegraph, and Greenwich Mean Time as measured by Airy's telescope was adopted as legal time in Britain 1880. He became professor of mathematics at Cambridge 1826 and of astronomy 1828.

As Astronomer Royal, in 1847 he had erected the alt-azimuth (an instrument he devised to calculate altitude and azimuth) for observing the Moon in every part of the sky. Airy's mathematical skills were used in establishing the border between Canada and the USA and the boundaries of the states of Oregon and Maine. His *Mathematical Tracts on Physical Astronomy* 1826 became a standard work.

Aitken Robert Grant (1864–1951). US astronomer who discovered and observed thousands of double stars. In 1891 he became professor of mathematics at the University of the Pacific. From 1895 he worked at the Lick Observatory on Mount Hamilton, California, and was its director 1930–35.

Akbar Jalal ud-Din Muhammad (1542–1605). Mogul emperor of N India from 1556, when he succeeded his father. He gradually established his rule throughout N India. He is considered the greatest of the Mogul emperors, and the firmness and wisdom of his rule won him the title 'Guardian of Mankind'; he was a patron of the arts.

Akbar was tolerant towards the majority Hindu population, suspending discriminatory taxes. He created his own eclectic royal religion (Din Illahi), reformed the land tax system and created a more centralized system of political control. He moved the Mogul court-capital temporarily from Agra to the nearby new city of Fatehpur Sikri 1569–85, and to Lahore 1585–99. *See illustration on page 14.*
Suggested reading
Gascoigne, Bamber and Christina *The Great Moghuls* (1971)
Hansen, W *The Peacock Throne: The Drama of Moghul India* (1972)
Lal, M *Akbar* (1980)
Srivastava, A L *Akbar the Great* (1962–67)

à Kempis Thomas. See ◊Thomas à Kempis, religious writer.

Akhenaton or **Ikhnaton**. King (pharaoh) of ancient Egypt of the 18th dynasty (*c.* 1353–1335 BC), who may have ruled jointly for a time with his father Amenhotep III. He developed the cult of the Sun, Aton, rather than the rival cult of Amen, and removed his capital to Akhetaton.

Akhenaton's favourite wife was Nefertiti, and two of their six daughters were married to his successors Smenkhkare and Tutankaton (later known as Tutankhamen).
Suggested reading
Aldred, Cyril *Akhenaten, Pharaoh of Egypt* (1968)
Collier, Joy *King Sun* (1970)

Akbar *The Mogul emperor Jalal ud-Din Muhammad Akbar leading the Mogul army about 1580. Akbar, who is considered the greatest of the Mogul emperors, ruled 1556–1605.*

Giles, F J *Ikhnaton: Legend and History* (1970)
Redford, D *Akhenaten* (1984)

Akhmatova Anna. Pen name of Anna Andreevna Gorenko (1889–1966). Russian poet. She was a leading member of the Acmeist movement. Among her works are the cycle *Requiem* 1963 (written in the 1930s), which deals with the Stalinist terror, and *Poem Without a Hero* 1962 (begun 1940).

In the 1920s she published several collections of poetry in the realist style of Mandelstam, but her lack of sympathy with the post-revolutionary regimes inhibited her writing, and her work was banned 1922–40 and again from 1946. From the mid-1950s her work was gradually rehabilitated in the USSR. In 1989 an Akhmatova Museum was opened in Leningrad (now St Petersburg).

Suggested reading
Driver, S *Anna Akhmatova* (1972)
Haight, Amanda *Anna Akhmatova: A Poetic Pilgrimage* (1976)
Reeder, Roberta *Akhmatova: Poet and Prophet* (1995)

In human intimacy there is a secret boundary, / Neither the experience of being in love nor passion can cross it, / Though lips be joined together in awful silence, / And the heart break asunder with love.

ANNA AKHMATOVA
'In Human Intimacy'

Akihito (1933–). Emperor of Japan from 1989, succeeding his father Hirohito (Shōwa). His reign is called the Heisei ('achievement of universal peace') era.

Unlike previous crown princes, Akihito was educated alongside commoners at the elite Gakushuin school and in 1959 he married Michiko Shoda (1934–), the daughter of a flour-company president. Their three children, the Oxford University-educated Crown Prince Hiro, Prince Aya, and Princess Nori, were raised at Akihito's home instead of being reared by tutors and chamberlains in a separate imperial dormitory.

Akins Zoe (1886–1958). US writer. She wrote poems, literary criticism, and plays, including *The Greeks Had a Word for It* 1930. She was born in Missouri.

Aksakov Sergei Timofeyevich (1791–1859). Russian writer. Born at Ufa, he became a civil servant, and under the influence of Nicolai Gogol, he wrote autobiographical novels, including *Chronicles of a Russian Family* 1856 and *Years of Childhood* 1858.

Akutagawa Ryūnosuke (1892–1927). Japanese writer of stories, plays, and poetry. Noted for stylistic virtuosity, he wrote autobiographical fiction and grim satirical fables such as 'Kappa' 1927, but his best works are stories derived from 12th- and 13th-century Japanese tales, retold in the light of modern psychology. Among the best known are 'Jigokuhen' 1918, the story of an obsessively ambitious artist, and 'Rashōmon', the basis for a film of the same name by Akira Kurosawa 1951.

Alaïa Azzedine (1940–). Tunisian-born fashion designer. He became popular during the 1980s for his soft leather, stretch fabric, and figure-hugging designs (he is nicknamed the 'King of Cling'). Alaïa began making clothes to order 1960 and launched his own label 1965. The 'body' or 'bodysuit', akin to the leotard, is credited to him.

Alain-Fournier pen name of Henri-Alban Fournier (1886–1914). French novelist. His haunting semi-autobiographical fantasy *Le Grand Meaulnes/The Lost Domain* 1913 was a cult novel of the 1920s and 1930s. His life is intimately recorded in his correspondence with his brother-in-law Jacques Rivière. He was killed in action on the Meuse in World War I.

Alanbrooke Alan Francis Brooke, 1st Viscount Alanbrooke (1883–1963). British army officer. He was Chief of Staff in World War II and largely responsible for the strategy that led to the German defeat.

Born in Ireland, Alanbrooke served in the artillery in World War I, and in World War II, as commander of the 2nd Corps 1939–40, did much to aid the extrication of the British Expeditionary Force from Dunkirk. He was commander in chief of the Home Forces 1940–41 and chief of the Imperial General Staff 1941–46. He became a field marshal 1944, was created a baron 1945 and viscount 1946.

Alarcón Pedro Antonio de (1833–1891). Spanish journalist and writer. The acclaimed *Diario/Diary* was based upon his experiences as a soldier in Morocco. His novel *El sombrero de tres picos/The Three-Cornered Hat* 1874 was the basis of Manuel de Falla's ballet of the same name.

Alarcón's other novels, including *El escandalo* 1875, *El nino de la bola/The Infant with the Globe* 1955, and *El capitan Veneno* 1881, project a romanticized picture of traditional Spanish life. He intervened in political life in defence of conservative values.

Alaric allowed his followers to plunder the wealth of Rome, but out of reverence for the apostle Peter he ordered that his great church be treated as a sanctuary.

Sozomen on ALARIC
in report of the capture of Rome in 410. *Church History* bk 9, ch 9

Alaric (c. 370–410). King of the Visigoths. In 396 he invaded Greece and retired with much booty to Illyria. In 400 and 408 he invaded Italy, and in 410 captured and sacked Rome, but died the same year on his way to invade Sicily.

Alban, St First Christian martyr in England. In 793 King Offa founded a monastery on the site of Alban's martyrdom, around which the city of St Albans grew up. His feast day is 20 June.

According to tradition, he was born at Verulamium, served in the Roman army, became a convert to Christianity after giving shelter to a priest, and, on openly professing his belief, was beheaded.

Albee Edward Franklin (1928–   ). US dramatist. His internationally performed plays are associated with the Theatre of the Absurd and include *The Zoo Story* 1960, *The American Dream* 1961, *Who's Afraid of Virginia Woolf?* 1962 (his most successful play; also filmed with Elizabeth Taylor and Richard Burton as the quarrelling, alcoholic, academic couple 1966), and *Tiny Alice* 1965. *A Delicate Balance* 1966 and *Seascape* 1975 both won Pulitzer Prizes, and *Three Tall Women* 1994 marked his return to critical acclaim.

I have a fine sense of the ridiculous, but no sense of humour.

EDWARD ALBEE
Who's Afraid of Virginia Woolf? 1962

Albéniz Isaac (1860–1909). Spanish nationalist composer and pianist. His works include numerous *zarzuelas* and operas, the orchestral suites *Española* 1886 and *Catalonia* 1899–1908 (with the assistance of Paul Dukas), and 250 piano works including the *Iberia* suite 1906–09.

Alberdi Juan Bautista (1810–1884). Argentine political theorist and diplomat. Forced into exile 1838 because of his opposition to dictator Juan Manuel de Rosas, he wrote his great work *Bases y punto de partida para la organización política de la república argentina/Bases and Starting Points for the Organization of the Argentine Republic* in Chile 1852. Its case for strong federal government formed the basis for Argentina's constitution the following year.

Alberoni Giulio (1664–1752). Spanish-Italian priest and politician, born in Piacenza, Italy. Philip V made him prime minister of Spain in 1715. In 1717 he became a cardinal. He introduced many domestic reforms, including the reorganization of the army. His invasion of Sardinia 1718 provoked the Quadruple Alliance, and in 1719 he was forced to flee to Italy.

Albers Anni (Anneliese, born Fleischmann) (1899–1994). German-born US weaver and designer, closely associated with the Bauhaus. She wrote many articles on weaving and industry, as well as two books: *Anni Albers: On designing* 1959 and *Anni Albers: On weaving* 1965. Her studies of weave structure, colour, and texture have had a continuing influence on the textile industry.

Albers wove fabrics and wall hangings for the new Bauhaus building in Dessau (designed by Walter Gropius in cooperation with staff and students) in the 1920s, and became assistant director of the weaving workshop. She was married to the Bauhaus teacher and artist Josef Albers (1888–1976).

If I had a severe illness I should give up at once ... I have no tenacity of life.

Conversation between ALBERT and Queen Victoria c. Nov 1861

Albert Prince Consort (1819–1861). Husband of British Queen Victoria from 1840. A patron of the arts, science, and industry, Albert was the second son of the Duke of Saxe Coburg-Gotha and first cousin to Queen Victoria, whose chief adviser he became. He planned the Great Exhibition of 1851; the profit was used to buy the sites in London of all the South Kensington museums and colleges and the Royal Albert Hall, built 1871. He died of typhoid. The Queen never fully recovered from his premature death, and remained in mourning for him for the rest of her life.

Albert also popularized the Christmas tree in England. He was regarded by the British people with groundless suspicion because of his German connections.

The Albert Memorial 1872, designed by Gilbert Scott, in Kensington Gardens, London, typifies Victorian decorative art.

Suggested reading
Bennet, D *King Without a Crown: Albert Prince Consort of Britain, 1819–1861* (1977)
Fulford, R *Prince Consort* (1949)
Phillips, John (ed) *Prince Albert and the Victorian Age* (1981)
Pound, Reginald *Albert: A Biography of the Prince Consort* (1973)
Richardson, Joanna *Victoria and Albert* (1977)

If I feel in good form I shall take the difficult way up. If I do not, I shall take the easy one. I shall join you in an hour.

ALBERT I
Last words before being killed in a climbing accident, 1934

Albert I (1875–1934). King of the Belgians from 1909, the younger son of Philip, Count of Flanders, and the nephew of Leopold II. In 1900 he married Duchess Elisabeth of Bavaria. In World War I he commanded the Allied army that retook the Belgian coast in 1918 and re-entered Brussels in triumph on 22 Nov.

He was killed while mountaineering in the Ardennes.

Alberti Leon Battista (1404–1472). Italian Renaissance architect and theorist. He set out the principles of Classical architecture, as well as covering their modification for Renaissance practice, in *De re aedificatoria/On Architecture*, which he started 1452 and worked on until his death (published 1485; translated as *Ten Books on Architecture* 1955).

Alberti's designs for the churches of San Sebastiano, begun 1460, and San Andrea 1470 (both in Mantua) – the only two extant buildings entirely of his design – are bold in their use of Classical language but to a certain extent anticipate Mannerism. His treatises on painting (1436) and sculpture (c. 1464) were the first to examine the theory as well as the technique of the subjects. He also wrote works on mathematics, ethics, religion, and grammar.

Suggested reading
Alberti, Leon *On Painting and Sculpture* (several editions)
Borsi, F *Leon Battista Alberti* (1977)
Gadol, J *Leon Alberti: Universal Man of the Early Renaissance* (1969)

The arts which are useful, and ... absolutely necessary to the architect are painting and mathematics.

LEON BATTISTA ALBERTI
Treatise on Architecture bk ix 1452

Albertus Magnus, St (1206–1280). German scholar of Christian theology, philosophy (especially Aristotelian), natural science, chemistry, and physics. He was known as 'doctor universalis' because of the breadth of his knowledge.

He studied at Bologna and Padua, and entered the Dominican order 1223. He taught at Cologne and lectured from 1245 at Paris University. St Thomas Aquinas was his pupil there, and followed him to Cologne 1248. He became provincial of the Dominicans in Germany 1254, and was made bishop of Ratisbon 1260. Two years later he resigned and eventually retired to his convent at Cologne. He tried to reconcile Aristotelian thought with Christian teachings.

Albinoni Tomaso (1671–1751). Italian Baroque composer. He wrote over 40 operas and numerous sonatas and *concerti à cinque* (concertos in five parts) for oboe, trumpet, bassoon, violin, organ, and strings, which helped to establish Baroque orchestral style. His work was studied and adapted by J S Bach.

The popular *Adagio*, often described as being by Albinoni, was actually composed from a fragment of original manuscript by his biographer, the Italian musicologist Remo Giazotto (1910–   ).

Alboin (lived 6th century). King of the Lombards about 561–573. At that time the Lombards were settled north of the Alps. Early in his reign he attacked the Gepidae, a Germanic tribe occupying present-day Romania, killing their king and taking his daughter Rosamund to be his wife. About 568 he crossed the Alps to invade Italy, conquering the country as far south as Rome. He was murdered at the instigation of his wife, after he forced her to drink wine from a cup made from her father's skull.

Albone Dan (1860–1906). English inventor of one of the first commercially available farm tractors, the Ivel, in 1902. It was a three-wheeled vehicle with a midmounted twin-cylinder petrol engine, and could plough an acre in 1.5 hours.

Albuquerque Afonso de (1453–1515). Viceroy and founder of the Portuguese East Indies with strongholds in Ceylon, Goa, and Malacca 1508–15. In 1515 the king of Portugal recalled him, putting Albuquerque's personal enemy Lopes Soares in his place. He died at sea on the way home when his ship *Flor del Mar* was lost between Malaysia and India.

Perhaps the first sea commander to appreciate fully the complex relation between a fleet and its bases, allowing for ... seasonal changes of wind.

J H Parry on AFONSO DE ALBUQUERQUE
The Age of Reconnaissance 1963

Alcaeus (*c.* 611–*c.* 580 BC). Greek lyric poet. Born at Mytilene in Lesvos, a contemporary of Sappho, he was a member of an aristocratic family opposed to the ruling tyrants, and spent time in exile. The surviving fragments of his poems deal with politics, drinking, and love. The Alcaic stanza is named after him.

The Alcaic metre was a favourite with Horace, and has been imitated by Tennyson in 'O Mighty-mouth'd inventor of harmonies...'.

Alcamenes (lived 5th century BC). Athenian classical sculptor, successor to Phidias. He is acclaimed for the delicacy and finish of such works as *Aphrodite of the Gardens* and *Hephaestus*.

Alcibiades (450–404 BC). Athenian politician and general. He organized a confederation of Peloponnesian states against Sparta that collapsed after the battle of Mantinea 418 BC. Although accused of profaning the Eleusinian Mysteries, he was eventually accepted as the commander of the Athenian fleet. He achieved several victories such as Cyzicus 410 BC, before his forces were defeated at Notium 406. He was murdered in Phrygia by the Persians.

I want Athens to talk about this, that it may say nothing worse about me.

ALCIBIADES
laughing response to friends, angry at his order to cut off
the tail of his prize dog, quoted in Plutarch *Life of Alcibiades* 9.

Alcmaeonidae Noble family of ancient Athens; its members included Pericles and Alcibiades.

Alcman (lived 7th century BC). Greek lyric poet. He composed choral works for Spartan festivals, especially songs to be sung by two choirs of girls. The longest surviving fragment of his work is the 'Parthenion/Maiden-song', which was discovered 1855. With Stesichorus, he was a leader of the Dorian school of choral poetry. His work is filled with colour, freshness, and delicate imagery.

Alcock John (1430–1500). English bishop. He was successively bishop of Rochester 1472, Worcester 1476, and Ely 1486. He was the founder of Jesus College, Cambridge, 1496.

Alcock John William (1892–1919). British aviator. On 14 June 1919, he and Arthur Whitten Brown (1886–1948) made the first nonstop transatlantic flight, from Newfoundland to Ireland. KBE 1919.

Alcoforado Marianna (1640–1723). Portuguese nun. The *Lettres portugaises*/*Letters of a Portuguese Nun* 1669, a series of love letters supposedly written by her to a young French nobleman (who abandoned her when their relationship became known), is no longer accepted as authentic.

I don't believe fine young ladies enjoy themselves a bit more than we do, in spite of our burnt hair, old gowns, one glove apiece and tight slippers.

LOUISA MAY ALCOTT
Little Women ch 3 1868

Alcott Louisa May (1832–1888). US author. Her children's classic *Little Women* 1869 drew on her own home circumstances, the heroine Jo being a partial self-portrait. *Good Wives* 1869 was among its sequels.

Alcott began writing to help earn money for the family. Her first book was *Flower Fables* 1848; her first success was *Hospital Sketches* 1863. The publication of *Good Wives* was followed by *Little Men* 1871. She also wrote *Eight Cousins* 1875, *Under the Lilacs* 1879, and *A Garland for Girls* 1888.

Alcuin (Flaccus Albinus Alcuinus) (735–804). English scholar. Born in York, he went to Rome 780, and in 782 took up residence at Charlemagne's court in Aachen. From 796 he was abbot of St Martin at Tours. He disseminated Anglo-Saxon scholarship, organized education and learning in the Frankish empire, gave a strong impulse to the Carolingian Renaissance, and was a prominent member of Charlemagne's academy.

The voice of the people is the voice of God.

ALCUIN
Letter to the Emperor Charlemagne AD 800

Alder Kurt (1902–1958). German organic chemist who with Otto Diels developed the diene synthesis, a fundamental process that has become known as the Diels–Alder reaction. It is used in organic chemistry to synthesize cyclic (ring) compounds, including many that can be made into plastics and others – which normally occur only in small quantities in plants and other natural sources – that are the starting materials for various drugs and dyes. Alder and Diels shared the 1950 Nobel Prize for Chemistry.

Aldhelm, St (*c.* 640–709). English prelate and scholar. He was abbot of Malmesbury from 673 and bishop of Sherborne from 705. Of his poems and treatises in Latin, some survive, notably his *Riddles* in hexameters, but his English verse has been lost. He was also known as a skilled architect.

He founded several monasteries and churches, including, according to William of Malmesbury, the church of St Lawrence at Bradford-on-Avon, Wiltshire, which alone remains of his buildings.

Patriotism is a lively sense of collective responsibility. Nationalism is a silly cock crowing on its own dunghill.

RICHARD ALDINGTON
The Colonel's Daughter 1931

Aldington Richard (1892–1962). Pen name of Edward Godfree Aldington. English poet, novelist, and critic. A leading Imagist, he published the collection *Images* 1915. He wrote biographies of the English writers D H Lawrence and T E Lawrence and his novels include *Death of a Hero* 1929 and *All Men are Enemies* 1933. He was married to the US poet Hilda Doolittle 1913–37.

Aldiss Brian Wilson (1925–). English science-fiction writer, anthologist, and critic. His novels include *Non-Stop* 1958, *The Malacia Tapestry* 1976, the 'Helliconia' trilogy, and *A Tupolev Too Far* 1993. *Trillion Year Spree* 1986 is a history of science fiction.

Whatever creativity is, it is in part a solution to a problem.

BRIAN ALDISS
Bury My Heart at W. H. Smith's, 'Apéritif' 1990

Aldred or Ealdred (died 1069). English monk. He became abbot of Tavistock about 1027, bishop of Worcester 1044, and archbishop of York 1060. He negotiated with the Holy Roman emperor Henry III for the return to England of Edmund Ironside's son 1054. He probably crowned Harold II, and certainly crowned William the Conqueror.

Aldrich Henry (1647–1710). English ecclesiastic. He wrote *A Compendium of Logic* 1691, used at Oxford for a long time; he also composed church music. He designed Peckwater Quadrangle (Christ Church College) and possibly All Saints' Church, both in Oxford.

Aldrich Robert (1918–1983). US film director and producer. He worked his theme of the individual against the institution into the framework of traditional genre material. Key films include the *noir* thriller *Kiss Me Deadly* 1955, *Attack!* 1956, *Whatever Happened to Baby Jane?* 1962, and *The Dirty Dozen* 1967.

Other films include *Ulzana's Raid* 1972, *The Killing of Sister George* 1968, and *Hustle* 1975.

Aldrich Thomas Bailey (1836–1907). US poet and editor. *The Story of a Bad Boy* 1870, which is partly autobiographical, was followed by the novels *Prudence Palfrey* 1874, *The Queen of Sheba* 1877, and *The Stillwater Tragedy* 1880. From 1881 to 1890, as editor of the *Atlantic Monthly*, he wielded a commanding influence over American letters. His collected writings were published 1907.

Aldridge Ira Frederick (1804–1867). US actor; a British citizen from 1863. He played all the major tragic Shakespearean roles, touring England and Europe. His interpretation of Othello was particularly noted.

Aldrin Edwin Eugene ('Buzz') (1930–). US astronaut who landed on the Moon with Neil Armstrong during the *Apollo 11* mission in July 1969, becoming the second person to set foot on the Moon.

He graduated from the US Military Academy, West Point, New York, and flew for the airforce in Korea and West Germany. He received a PhD for his thesis on orbital mechanics from the Massachusetts Institute of Technology 1963. During the *Gemini 12* flight with James Lovell 1966, Aldrin spent $5\frac{1}{2}$ hours in outer space without any ill effects.

He published *Return to Earth* with Wayne Warga 1975.

Aldrovandi Ulisse (1522–1605). Italian naturalist. He travelled extensively throughout Europe, researching for his great work on natural history, published 1599–1608. He established the botanic gardens at Bologna 1567, and also formed a natural history museum. He took a medical degree at Bologna 1553 and was subsequently professor of botany and natural history at that university.

Aleardi Aleardo (1812–1878). Italian poet and patriot. His poems are full of passionate hopes for the liberation of Italy. They include 'Le città italiane marinare e commercianti' 1856, 'I tre fiumi' 1857, 'Il Monte Circello' 1858, and 'Triste dramma' 1859. He was twice imprisoned by the Austrians, 1852 and 1859. After his second imprisonment he returned to Italy, and in 1864 was appointed professor of aesthetics in Florence.

Alecsandri Vasile (1821–1890). Romanian poet and dramatist. As a director 1840 of the new National Theatre in Iasi, he wrote *Chirita in Iasi* 1850 and *Chirita in provincie* 1852. Later he turned to historical drama. His collection of folk poetry, *Poesii populare* 1852, was a milestone in Romanian literature.

Aleijadinho (António Francisco Lisboa) (*c.* 1738–1814). Brazilian artist. He is generally considered to be the greatest Brazilian sculptor. Having lost the use of his hands, he sculpted with his tools strapped to them, hence his name which means 'little cripple'. He worked in a restrained and dignified Rococo style, exemplified in his finest piece *The Twelve Prophets* 1800–05, which stands outside the church of Bom Jesus de Matozinhos, Congonhas do Campo, Brazil.

Aleixandre Vicente (1898–1984). Spanish lyric poet. His verse, such as the surrealist *La destrucción o el amor*/*The Destruction of Love*

1935, had Republican sympathies, and his work was for a time banned by Franco's government. Nobel Prize for Literature 1977.

Alekhine Alexander Alexandrovich (1892–1946). Russian-born naturalized French chess master, world champion 1927–35. In 1909 he won the title of master at chess and thereafter dominated the chess world with many first prizes. He challenged the world champion José Raúl Capablanca 1927 and won the title.

Aleksandrov Pavel Sergeevich (1896–1982). Russian mathematician who was a leading expert in the field of topology and one of the founders of the theory of compact and bicompact spaces.

His passion for international cooperation led him to supervise the publication of an English–Russian dictionary of mathematical terminology 1962.

Alekseev Mikhail Vasilievich (1857–1918). Russian general. He was twice appointed Chief of Staff, under the supreme commanders in chief Nicholas II (1915) and Kerenski (1917), with a brief period inbetween as commander in chief of all Russian armies. In 1918 he organized in the Kuban region the first anti-Bolshevik volunteer army.

Alemán Mateo (1547–*c.* 1613). Spanish novelist. He was the author of the popular picaresque novel *Guzmán de Alfarache* 1599. He also published a life of St Antonio of Padua 1604 and *Ortografía castellana* 1609.

He emigrated to Mexico 1608.

Alembert Jean le Rond d' (1717–1783). French mathematician, encyclopedist, and theoretical physicist. In association with Denis

Alembert *From scandalous beginnings – he was found on a church doorstep, the illegitimate son of a courtesan – Jean le Rond d'Alembert went on to become an eminent mathematician and philosopher. He discovered the calculus of partial differences, and, in 1743, developed the principle that now bears his name, by extending the Newtonian theory of dynamics to include mobile bodies. (Ann Ronan/Image Select)*

Diderot, he helped plan the great *Encyclopédie*, for which he also wrote the 'Discours préliminaire' 1751. He framed several theorems and principles – notably *d'Alembert's principle* – in dynamics and celestial mechanics, and devised the theory of partial differential equations.

Alençon François, Duke of Alençon, later Duke of Anjou (1554–1584). Fourth son of Henry II of France and Catherine de' Medici. At one time he was considered as a suitor to Elizabeth I of England.

Alessandri Palma Arturo (1868–1950). Chilean president 1920–25 and 1932–37. Reforms proposed in his first presidential term were blocked by an opposition-controlled congress. Forced into exile, he returned to achieve a measure of economic recovery at the expense of the repression of opponents, a policy that made him a controversial figure in Chilean history.

Alexander (died 1148). English cleric. He became bishop of Lincoln 1123. In the civil war over the accession to the throne he took the side of Stephen, although he had sworn allegiance to Matilda. Suspected of disloyalty, he was arrested, imprisoned, and dispossessed of his castles.

Alexander (Conel) Hugh (O'Donel) (1909–1974). Irish chess player. He was an international master and British champion 1938 and 1956. In 1946 in a radio chess match he beat the future world champion, Mikhail Botvinnik. CBE 1955. Alexander was a mathematics teacher at Winchester College 1932–38 before joining the Foreign Office, attaining the rank of colonel in British Intelligence during World War II.

Alexander Frederick Matthias (1869–1955). Australian founder and teacher of the Alexander technique, a method of relaxing the mind and body. At one time a professional reciter, he developed throat and voice trouble, and his experiments in curing himself led him to work out the system of mental and bodily control described in his book *Use of the Self* 1931.

Alexander George. Stage name of George A Gibb Samson (1858–1918). English actor-manager. He joined Henry Irving's company at the Lyceum as a professional actor and in 1891 became manager of the St James's Theatre, where he remained until his death. He produced and played in a long list of plays, including those of Oscar Wilde and Pinero, and scored a great personal success in *The Prisoner of Zenda* and *If I Were King*. He was knighted 1911.

Alexander Harold Rupert Leofric George, 1st Earl Alexander of Tunis (1891–1969). British field marshal, a commander in World War II in France, Burma (now Myanmar), N Africa, and the Mediterranean. He was Governor-General of Canada 1946–52 and UK minister of defence 1952–54. He was appointed KCB 1942, Viscount 1946, and Earl Alexander of Tunis in 1952, and was in 1959 awarded the Order of Merit.

In World War II he was the last person to leave in the evacuation of Dunkirk. In Burma he fought a delaying action for five months against superior Japanese forces. In Aug 1942 he went to N Africa, and in 1943 became deputy to Eisenhower in charge of the Allied forces in Tunisia. After the Axis forces in N Africa surrendered, Alexander became supreme Allied commander in the Mediterranean, and in 1944, field marshal.

Alexander Samuel (1859–1938). Australian philosopher. He originated the theory of emergent evolution: that the space-time matrix evolved matter; matter evolved life; life evolved mind; and finally God emerged from mind. His books include *Space, Time and Deity* 1920. OM 1930.

He was professor at Manchester University, England, 1893–1924.

Alexander William, Earl of Stirling (*c.* 1567–1640). Scottish poet. Besides *Aurora* 1604 and *Recreations with the Muses* 1637, he wrote the four 'monarchic tragedies' *Darius* 1603, *Croesus* 1604, *The Alexandraean Tragedy* 1605, and *Julius Caesar* 1607, in the style of Seneca. As a courtier, he followed James VI to England. In 1626 he was appointed secretary of state for Scotland and in 1633 was made an earl.

Alexander eight popes, including:

Alexander III (Orlando Bandinelli) (died 1181). Pope 1159–81. His authority was opposed by Frederick I Barbarossa, but Alexander eventually compelled him to render homage 1178. He held the third Lateran Council 1179. He supported Henry II of England in his invasion of Ireland, but imposed penance on him after the murder of Thomas à Becket.

He spent the latter part of his pontificate in exile, being driven from Rome by the republic.

Alexander VI (Rodrigo Borgia) (1431–1503). Pope 1492–1503. Of Spanish origin, he bribed his way to the papacy, where he furthered the advancement of his illegitimate children, who included Cesare and Lucrezia Borgia. When Savonarola preached against his corrupt practices Alexander had him executed.

Alexander was a great patron of the arts in Italy, as were his children. He is said to have died of a poison he had prepared for his cardinals.

Alexander VII (Fabio Chigi) (1599–1667). Pope 1655–67. He succeeded Innocent X and was a patron of the arts, which he much preferred to affairs of state – he was responsible for the colonnade of St Peter's. He supported the Society of Jesus in its conflict with the Jansenists.

Alexander three tsars of Russia:

Napoleon thinks I am a fool, but he who laughs last laughs longest.

Letter from ALEXANDER I to his sister Catherine
8 Oct 1808 after meeting Napoleon at Erfurt

Alexander I (1777–1825). Tsar from 1801. Defeated by Napoleon at Austerlitz 1805, he made peace at Tilsit 1807, but economic crisis led to a break with Napoleon's Continental System and the opening of Russian ports to British trade; this led to Napoleon's ill-fated invasion of Russia 1812. After the Congress of Vienna 1815, Alexander hoped through the Holy Alliance with Austria and Prussia to establish a new Christian order in Europe. He gave a new constitution to Poland, presented to him at the Congress of Vienna.

It is better to abolish serfdom from above than to wait for it to abolish itself from below.

ALEXANDER II
Speech to the Moscow nobility March 1856

Alexander II (1818–1881). Tsar from 1855. He embarked on reforms of the army, the government, and education, and is remembered as 'the Liberator' for his emancipation of the serfs 1861, but he lacked the personnel to implement his reforms. However, the revolutionary element remained unsatisfied, and Alexander became increasingly autocratic and reactionary. He was assassinated by an anarchistic terrorist group, the Nihilists.

He had two qualities which streaked even his earliest years with light; a big heart and a vehement honesty.

E L Almedingen on ALEXANDER III
The Romanovs 1966

Alexander III (1845–1894). Tsar from 1881, when he succeeded his father, Alexander II. He pursued a reactionary policy, promoting Russification and persecuting the Jews. He married Dagmar (1847–1928), daughter of Christian IX of Denmark and sister of Queen Alexandra of Britain, 1866. In foreign affairs Alexander III strictly followed the policy of peace and non-interference; towards the end of his reign the Franco-Russian rapprochement took place.

Alexander three kings of Scotland:

Alexander I (*c.* 1078–1124). King of Scotland from 1107, known as 'the Fierce'. He ruled to the north of the rivers Forth and Clyde while his brother and successor David ruled to the south. He assisted Henry I of England in his campaign against Wales 1114, but defended the independence of the church in Scotland. Several monasteries, including the abbeys of Inchcolm and Scone, were established by him.

Alexander II (1198–1249). King of Scotland from 1214, when he succeeded his father William the Lion. Alexander supported the English barons in their struggle with King John after Magna Carta. The accession of Henry III of England allowed a rapprochement between the two countries, and the boundaries between England and Scotland were agreed by the Treaty of York 1237. Alexander consolidated the royal authority in Scotland and was a generous patron of the church.

In 1221 he married Joanna, the sister of Henry III. After her death he married Marie de Coucy 1239 with whom he had a son, Alexander III.

By the treaty of Newcastle 1244 he pledged allegiance to Henry III of England.

When Alexander our King was dead / Our Gold was changed into Lead.

ANDREW WYNTOUN on ALEXANDER II
De Orygynale Cronykil of Scotland bk vii, early 15th century

Alexander III (1241–1286). King of Scotland from 1249, son of Alexander II. In 1263, by military defeat of Norwegian forces, he extended his authority over the Western Isles, which had been dependent on Norway. The later period of his reign was devoted to administrative reforms, which limited the power of the barons and brought a period of peace and prosperity to Scotland.

He died as the result of a fall from his horse, leaving his grand-daughter Margaret, the Maid of Norway, to become queen of Scotland.

He left his kingdom independent, united, and prosperous, and his reign was viewed as a golden age ... in the long bloody conflict with England after his death.

Encyclopaedia Britannica on ALEXANDER III
1990

Alexander I Karageorgevich (1888–1934). Regent of Serbia 1912–21 and king of Yugoslavia 1921–34, as dictator from 1929. Second son of Peter I, King of Serbia, he was declared regent for his father 1912 and on his father's death became king of the state of South Slavs – Yugoslavia – that had come into being 1918.

Rivalries with neighbouring powers and among the Croats, Serbs, and Slovenes within the country led Alexander to establish a personal dictatorship. He was assassinated on a state visit to France, and Mussolini's government was later declared to have instigated the crime.

Alexander Nevski, St (1220–1263). Russian military leader, son of the grand duke of Novgorod. In 1240 he defeated the Swedes on the banks of the Neva (hence Nevski), and in 1242 defeated the Teutonic Knights on the frozen Lake Peipus.

He defended Russia equally successfully against the Lithuanians, and in 1252 was appointed grand prince of Vladimir by the Khan of the Golden Horde. Alexander Nevski spent the rest of his life endeavouring to improve the lot of the Russians and to relieve the distress caused by the Tatar invasion. He was canonized by the Russian Orthodox Church 1547.

Alexander I (1857–1893). Prince of Bulgaria (Prince Alexander of Battenberg). A nephew of Tsar Alexander II of Russia, he was, at Russia's proposal, elected first sovereign prince of Bulgaria. Once elected, however, Alexander pursued a policy which ran counter to

Russian interests and Russian pressure compelled him to step down 1886.

Alexander Obrenovich (1876–1903). King of Serbia from 1889 while still a minor, on the abdication of his father, King Milan I. He took power into his own hands 1893 and aroused great opposition by his marriage to Draga Mashin, a widow, 1900 and by his arbitrary rule. In 1903 Alexander and his queen were murdered, and Peter I Karageorgevich was placed on the throne.

Alexander I (died 326 BC). King of Epirus, Greece, about 342–330 BC. In 332 he crossed to Italy, to aid the Tarentines against the Samnites and other tribes, but was defeated and killed near Pandosia. He was the brother of Olympias, mother of Alexander the Great; he was also the son-in-law of Philip II of Macedon, whose daughter Cleopatra he married 336 and who had made him king of Epirus.

Alexander of Hales ('Doctor Irrefragabilis') (*c.* 1175–1245). English theologian. As professor of theology in Paris he taught St Bonaventure and Roger Bacon. His principal work is *Universae Theologiae Summa.*

Alexander of Hillsborough Albert Victor Alexander, Earl Alexander of Hillsborough (1885–1965). English politician. He was first lord of the Admiralty on three occasions: 1929–31, 1940, and 1945, and minister of defence 1947–50. In 1950 he was made a viscount. He was chancellor of the Duchy of Lancaster 1950–51 and Labour leader in the House of Lords 1955–64. Earl 1963.

Alexander (1893–1920). King of the Hellenes (Greece), second son of King Constantine I, on whose dethronement 1917 he ascended the throne. His government, with Eleutherios Venizelos as premier, enjoyed the confidence of the Western powers. During his reign the boundaries of Greece were much extended.

Alexander I (died 450 BC). King of Macedonia. He was obliged to submit to the Persians, and accompanied Xerxes in his invasion of Greece 480 BC. He was succeeded by Perdiccas II.

Alexander IV (commonly called Aegus) (323–310 BC). King of Macedonia. He was acknowledged as partner in the empire with his uncle Philip Arrhidaeus under a regency. Alexander and his mother were imprisoned by Cassander 316 and were put to death six years later.

After he succeeded to the empire he did everything in conjunction with his mother, so that she seemed to share power equally.

Anonymous on ALEXANDER SEVERUS
in *Life of Severus Alexander* ch 14.7

Alexander Severus (AD 208–235). Roman emperor from 222, when he succeeded his cousin Heliogabalus. He attempted to involve the Senate more closely in administration, and was the patron of the jurists Ulpian and Paulus, and the historian Dio Cassius. His campaign against the Persians 232 achieved some success, but in 235, on his way to defend Gaul against German invaders, he was killed in a mutiny.

Alexanderson Ernst Frederik Werner (1878–1957). Swedish-born US electrical and electronic pioneer. He invented the high-frequency alternator for long-range radio communication 1906 and contributed to improvements in radio antennae, railway electrification, ship propulsion, and motor control as well as the Amplidyne radionic valve. He demonstrated his system of television privately 1927 and publicly 1930, and colour television 1955.

Alexander the Great (356–323 BC). King of Macedon from 336 BC and conqueror of the large Persian empire. As commander of the vast Macedonian army he conquered Greece 336, defeated the Persian king Darius in Asia Minor 333, then moved on to Egypt, where he founded Alexandria. He defeated the Persians again in

Assyria 331, then advanced further east to reach the Indus. He conquered the Punjab before diminished troops forced his retreat.

The son of King Philip II of Macedon and Queen Olympias, Alexander was educated by the philosopher Aristotle. He first saw fighting 340, and at the battle of Chaeronea 338 contributed to the victory by a cavalry charge. At the age of 20, when his father was murdered, he assumed command of the throne and the army. He secured his northern frontier, suppressed an attempted rising in Greece by his capture of Thebes, and in 334 crossed the Dardanelles for the campaign against the vast Persian empire; at the river Granicus near the Dardanelles he won his first victory. In 333 he routed Darius at Issus, and then set out for Egypt, where he was greeted as Pharaoh. Meanwhile, Darius assembled half a million men for a final battle at Gaugamela, near Arbela on the Tigris, 331 but Alexander, with 47,000 men, drove the Persians into retreat. After the victory he stayed a month in Babylon, then marched to Susa and Persepolis and in 330 to Ecbatana (now Hamadán, Iran). Soon after, he learned that Darius was dead. In Afghanistan he founded colonies at Herat and Kandahar, and in 328 reached the plains of Sogdiana, where he married Roxana, daughter of King Oxyartes. India was his next objective, and he pressed on to the Indus. Near the river Hydaspes (now Jhelum) he fought one of his fiercest battles against the rajah Porus. At the river Hyphasis (now Beas) his depleted troops refused to go farther, and reluctantly he turned back down the Indus and along the coast. They reached Susa 324, where Alexander made Darius's daughter his second wife. He died in Babylon of a malarial fever.

Suggested reading
Fox, R L *Alexander the Great* (1970)
Fox, R L *The Search for Alexander* (1980)
Green, Peter *Alexander the Great* (1970)
Hamilton, J R *Alexander the Great* (1973)

Alexandra (1936–). Princess of the UK. Daughter of the Duke of Kent and Princess Marina, she married Angus Ogilvy (1928–), younger son of the Earl of Airlie. They have two children, James (1964–) and Marina (1966–).

Alexandra (1844–1925). Queen consort of Edward VII of England, whom she married 1863. She was the eldest daughter of Christian IX of Denmark. She bore five children, two boys and three girls. The eldest son, Albert Victor, Duke of Clarence, died 1892, and his brother reigned as George V. Alexandra was extremely popular in Britain; she had great charm, and showed a genuine interest in charitable work of all kinds. An annual Alexandra Rose Day in aid of hospitals commemorates her charitable work.

Alexandra Feodorovna (1872–1918). Last tsarina of Russia 1894–1917. She was the former Princess Alix of Hesse and granddaughter of Britain's Queen Victoria. She married Nicholas II and, from 1907, fell under the spell of Rasputin, a 'holy man' brought to the palace to try to cure her son of haemophilia. She was shot with the rest of her family by the Bolsheviks in the Russian Revolution.

Be the Emperor ... Crush them all under you ... those men who try to govern you.

Letter in English from ALEXANDRA to her husband Tsar Nicholas II 27 Dec 1916

Alexeev Vasiliy (1942–). Soviet weightlifter who broke 80 world records 1970–77, a record for any sport. He was Olympic super-heavyweight champion twice, world champion seven times, and European champion on eight occasions. At one time the most decorated man in the USSR, he was regarded as the strongest man in the world. He carried the Soviet flag at the 1980 Moscow Olympics opening ceremony, but retired shortly afterwards.

Alexeyev Mikhail (1855–1918). Russian military commander during World War I, Chief of Staff 1915–17. In 1914 he was Chief of Staff to General Ivanoff on the Southeast Front, becoming Chief of Staff to the Russian Army 1915. After the March 1917 revolution he was replaced by General Brusilov, and following the October Revolution he helped found the Volunteer Army, fighting with the counter-revolutionary 'Whites' against the Bolsheviks.

Alexi II (Alexei Mikhailovich Ridiger) (1929–). Estonian priest, patriarch of the Russian Orthodox Church from 1990. He was made bishop of Tallinn 1961, archbishop 1964, metropolitan 1968, and metropolitan of Leningrad (now St Petersburg) 1986. He is active in the World Council of Churches, and became chair of the Conference of European Churches 1987.

Alexis (Sergey Vladimirovich Simanskiy), or Aleksiy (1877–1970). Patriarch of Moscow and All Russia, head of the Russian Orthodox Church from 1945. He played a prominent part in establishing a *modus vivendi* between the Orthodox Church and the authorities, securing an extension of church work in return for loyalty to the Soviet government, but took a firm stand in the face of the renewed communist offensive against the church in the 1960s.

Alexis Mikhailovich 'the Quietest' (1629–1676). Tsar of Muscovy from 1645, second tsar of the house of Romanov, and father of Peter the Great. During his reign a code of laws was compiled which remained in force until the 19th century. A revision of prayer books by Patriarch Nikon lead to a schism in the Russian Orthodox Church. The Ukraine was reunited with Muscovy; Russian possessions in Siberia were enlarged; successful wars were waged against Poland; and there were several rebellions, including the uprising led by Stenka Razin.

Alexius five emperors of Byzantium, including:

Alexius I (Comnenus) (1048–1118). Byzantine emperor 1081–1118. The Latin (W European) Crusaders helped him repel Turkish invasions, and he devoted great skill to buttressing the threatened empire. His daughter Anna Comnena chronicled his reign.

With assistance from the Venetians, in 1085 and 1108 he repelled the Normans who were invading Albania. In 1091 he destroyed the Pechenegs who had invaded the Balkans. His appeals for Western support against Turkish invaders in Anatolia helped stimulate the 1st Crusade 1095.

Alexius III (Angelos) (died 1210). Byzantine emperor 1195–1203. He gained power by deposing and blinding his brother Isaac II, but Isaac's Venetian allies enabled him and his son Alexius IV to regain power as co-emperors.

If you leave me I shall lose my empire and the Greeks will put me to death.

ALEXIUS III
Address to the Fourth Crusaders in 1203. Quoted in Villehardouin *Conquest of Constantinople* ch 10, early 13th century

---

Alexius IV (Angelos) (1182–1204). Byzantine emperor from 1203, when, with the aid of the army of the Fourth Crusade, he deposed his uncle Alexius III. He soon lost the support of the Crusaders (by that time occupying Constantinople), and was overthrown and murdered by another Alexius, Alexius Mourtzouphlus (son-in-law of Alexius III) 1204, an act which the Crusaders used as a pretext to sack the city the same year.

Alfano Franco (1876–1954). Italian composer. He is best known for his 12 operas, including *Resurrection* 1904, *The Shade of Don Juan* performed 1914, *Sakuntala* 1922, *The Last Lord* 1930, and *Cyrano de Bergerac* 1936. He completed Puccini's unfinished work, *Turandot*.

al-Farabi Abu Nasr (*c.* 870–950). Arab philosopher of Turkish origin. He is best known as having introduced Aristotle to the Islamic world. A diligent commentator on Aristotle's works from the neo-Platonist standpoint, he applied Plato's political theories to the problems of his day. He exercised considerable influence upon

Avicenna and Averroës, and was known to the medieval schoolmen. His complete works, *Alpharabii Opera Omnia*, were published in Paris 1638.

Alfaro Eloy (1842–1912). Ecuadorian general and politician, president 1895–1901 and 1906–11. He was involved in various revolts before overthrowing President Luis Cordero 1895, backed by the military. However, despite his liberal support, he was unable to avoid political conflict or run an orderly government.

Alfieri Vittorio. Count Alfieri (1749–1803). Italian dramatist. The most successful of his 28 plays, most of them tragedies, are *Saul* 1782 and *Mirra* 1786. He is now best remembered for his *Autobiography* 1790, 1803. His works played an important role in the development of Italian nationalism.

Alfonsín Foulkes Raúl Ricardo (1927–). Argentine politician, president 1983–89, leader of the moderate Radical Union Party (UCR). As president from the country's return to civilian government, he set up an investigation of the army's human-rights violations. Economic problems caused him to seek help from the International Monetary Fund and introduce austerity measures. He stepped down 1989 several months before the end of his term to allow his successor, the Perónist Carlos Menem, to institute emergency economic measures.

Alfonso kings of Portugal; see ◊Afonso.

Alfonso thirteen kings of León, Castile, and Spain, including:

Alfonso VI 'the Brave' (1065–1109). King of León and Castile. He led organized resistance to the Moors. He was, however, defeated by the Almoravids at Zalaca 1086.

Alfonso VII (*c.* 1107–1157). King of León and Castile from 1126 who attempted to unite Spain. Although he protected the Moors, he was killed trying to check a Moorish rising.

Alfonso VIII (1155–1214). King of Castile 1158–1214. He came to power 1169, after a disputed regency. He led the Christian coalition that broke the power of the Moors.

Alfonso X 'the Wise' (1221–1284). King of Castile from 1252. His reign was politically unsuccessful but he contributed to learning: he made Castilian the official language of the country and commissioned a history of Spain and an encyclopedia, as well as several translations from Arabic concerning, among other subjects, astronomy and games.

Alfonso XI 'the Avenger' (1311–1350). King of Castile and León from 1312. He ruled cruelly, repressed a rebellion by his nobles, and defeated the last Moorish invasion 1340.

Although politically inexperienced, [he] demonstrated great natural tact and sound judgement ... and his early death ... was a great disappointment to those who looked forward to a constitutional monarchy.

Encyclopaedia Britannica on ALFONSO XII
1990

Alfonso XII (1857–1885). King of Spain from 1875, son of Isabella II. He assumed the throne after a period of republican government following his mother's flight and effective abdication 1868. His rule was peaceful. He ended the civil war started by the Carlists and drafted a constitution, both 1876.

Alfonso XIII (1886–1941). King of Spain 1886–1931. He assumed power 1906 and married Princess Ena, granddaughter of Queen Victoria of the United Kingdom, in the same year. He abdicated 1931 soon after the fall of the Primo de Rivera dictatorship 1923–30 (which he supported), and Spain became a republic. His assassination was attempted several times.

Assassination – an accident of my trade.

ALFONSO XIII
Remark after an attempt on his life May 1906

Alfred 'the Great' (*c.* 849–*c.* 901). King of Wessex from 871. He defended England against Danish invasion, founded the first English navy, and put into operation a legal code. He encouraged the translation of works from Latin (some he translated himself), and promoted the development of the Anglo-Saxon Chronicle.

Alfred was born at Wantage, Oxfordshire, the youngest son of Ethelwulf (died 858), king of the West Saxons. In 870 Alfred and his brother Ethelred fought many battles against the Danes. He gained a victory over the Danes at Ashdown 871, and succeeded Ethelred as king April 871 after a series of defeats. Five years of uneasy peace followed while the Danes were occupied in other parts of England. In 876 the Danes attacked again, and in 878 Alfred was forced to retire to the stronghold of Athelney, from where he finally emerged to win the victory of Edington, Wiltshire. By the Peace of Wedmore 878 the Danish leader Guthrum (died 890) agreed to withdraw from Wessex and from Mercia west of Watling Street. A new landing in Kent encouraged a revolt of the East Anglian Danes, which was suppressed 884–86, and after the final foreign invasion was defeated 892–96, Alfred strengthened the navy to prevent fresh incursions.

Suggested reading

Fisher, D J V *The Anglo-Saxon Age, 400–1042* (1973)
Frantzen, A *King Alfred* (1986)
Mapp, A *The Golden Dragon: Alfred the Great and his Times* (1974)
Smyth, Alfred P *King Alfred the Great* (1995)
Sturdy, David *Alfred the Great* (1995)
Woodruff, D *The Life and Times of Alfred the Great* (1974)

A king's raw materials and instruments of rule are a well-peopled land, and he must have men of prayer, men of war, and men of work.

Translation by ALFRED of Boëthius *Consolation of Philosophy* II

Alfvén Hannes Olof Gösta (1908–1995). Swedish astrophysicist who made fundamental contributions to plasma physics, particularly in the field of magnetohydrodynamics (MHD) – the study of plasmas in magnetic fields. He shared the 1970 Nobel Prize for Physics.

Alfvén was born in Norrköping, Sweden, and educated at the University of Uppsala. In 1940 he joined the Royal Institute of Technology, Stockholm, later dividing his academic career between that and the University of California, San Diego, from which he obtained a professorship in 1967. In 1972 he was among a group of Oxford scientists who appealed to governments to abandon fast-breeder nuclear reactors and concentrate efforts on nuclear fusion.

Algardi Alessandro (*c.* 1598–1654). Italian Baroque sculptor. He was active in Bologna, Rome, and at the papal court. His major works include the above life-size *Decapitation of St Paul* 1641–47 in San Paolo, Bologna, and the tomb of Pope Leo XI 1634–44 and *Pope Leo driving Attila from Rome* 1646–53, both in St Peter's, Rome.

Although Algardi's work is more restrained than that of his contemporary and rival Bernini, it is wholly Baroque in style, with figures often contorted and full of movement. He was an outstanding portrait sculptor, and it is for these busts, for example *St Philip Neri* 1640 (Sta Maria Vallicella, Rome), that he is now best remembered.

Alger Horatio (1832–1899). US writer of children's books. He wrote over 100 didactic moral tales in which the heroes rise from poverty to riches through hard work, luck, and good deeds, including the series 'Ragged Dick' from 1867 and 'Tattered Tom' from

1871. It is estimated that his books sold more than 20 million copies. In US usage a 'Horatio Alger tale' has now come to mean any rags-to-riches story, often an implausible one.

Algren Nelson Abraham (1909–1981). US novelist. His best-known novel was *The Man with the Golden Arm* 1949 (filmed 1956), a story about gambling and drug addiction, which won the first National Book Award. Other works include two travel books, the prose-poem *Chicago: City on the Make* 1951, and the novel *A Walk on the Wild Side* 1956 (filmed 1962), set in a New Orleans brothel.

Born in Detroit, Algren lived mainly in the Chicago area, the setting for most of his fiction.

Alhazen Ibn al-Haytham, (Abu Alī al-Hassan ibn al-Haytham) (*c.* 965–1038). Arabian scientist, author of the *Kitab al-Manazir/ Book of Optics*, translated into Latin as *Opticae thesaurus* (1572). For centuries it remained the most comprehensive and authoritative treatment of optics in both East and West.

Alhazen was born in Basra (now in Iraq). He made many contributions to optics, contesting the Greek view of Hero and Ptolemy that vision involves rays that emerge from the eye and are reflected by objects viewed. Alhazen postulated that light rays originate in a flame or in the Sun, strike objects, and are reflected by them into the eye.

Ali (*c.* 598–661). 4th caliph of Islam. He was born in Mecca, the son of Abu Talib, and was the cousin and close friend and supporter of the prophet Muhammad, who gave him his daughter Fatima in marriage. On Muhammad's death 632, Ali had a claim to succeed him, but this was not conceded until 656, following the murder of the third caliph, Uthman. After a brief and stormy reign, Ali was assassinated. Controversy has raged around Ali's name between the Sunni and the Shi'ites, the former denying his right to the caliphate and the latter supporting it.

His court was one of barbarous refinement, and even ... liberated Greeks looked back upon him with some respect.
    Encyclopaedia Britannica on ALI (ALI PASHA)
    1990

Ali (Ali Pasha) (1741–1822). Turkish politician, known as Arslan ('the Lion').

An Albanian, he was appointed pasha (governor) of the Janina region 1788 (now Ioánnina, Greece). He helped the Turks during the Austro-Russian War, and sided first with the French and then with the British during the Napoleonic Wars. A career of cool impudence, deliberate betrayal, and high daring ended in his being put to death by Sultan Mahmud II. His court was visited by the British poet Byron.

Ali Mehemet (1815–1871). Grand vizier (chief minister) of the Ottoman empire 1855–56, 1858–59, 1861, and 1867–71, noted for his attempts to westernize the Ottoman Empire.

After a career as ambassador to the UK, minister of foreign affairs 1846, delegate to the Congress of Vienna 1855 and of Paris 1856, he was grand vizier a total of five times. While promoting friendship with Britain and France, he defended the vizier's powers against those of the sultan.

Ali Muhammad. Adopted name of Cassius Marcellus Clay, Jr (1942–). US boxer. Olympic light-heavyweight champion 1960, he went on to become world professional heavyweight champion 1964, and was the only man to regain the title twice. He was known for his fast footwork and extrovert nature.

He had his title stripped from him 1967 for refusing to be drafted into the US Army. He regained his title 1974, lost it Feb 1978, and regained it seven months later. He had the last of his 61 professional fights 1981 against Trevor Berbick.
Suggested reading
Ali, Muhammad *The Greatest: My Own Story* (1975)

Bingham, Howard *Muhammad Ali: A Thirty-Year Journey* (1993)
Hauser, Thomas *Muhammad Ali: His Life and Times* (1991)
Mailer, Norman *The Fight* (1975)

It's just a job. Grass grows, birds fly, waves pound the sand. I beat people up.
    MUHAMMAD ALI
    New York Times 6 April 1977

Ali Mustafa (1541–1600). Historian and writer of the Ottoman Empire. Ali was responsible for much of the myth of the preceding reign of Suleiman (1520–66) as a golden age.

Ali Salim Rubayi (1934–1978). President of South Yemen 1969–78. He became a leading member of the National Liberation Front and succeeded to the presidency after a power struggle in June 1969. He was deposed and executed 1978.

Alia Ramiz (1925–). Albanian communist politician, head of state 1982–92. He gradually relaxed the isolationist policies of his predecessor Enver Hoxha and following public unrest introduced political and economic reforms, including free elections 1991, when he was elected executive president. In Sept 1994 Alia was convicted of abuse of power while in office and sentenced to eight years' imprisonment, but was released July 1995 following an appeal court ruling.

Alishan Leon (1820–1901). Armenian poet and historian. His works include *Popular Songs of the Armenians*, historical monographs, and translations of English, German, and French poetry, including Byron's *Childe Harold*. He wrote historical, geographical, and botanical works on Armenia.

Alkan pseudonym of Charles Valentin Morhange (1813–1888). French piano virtuoso and composer. His formidably difficult piano pieces were neglected until the 1970s. Works include *Grande Sonate: les quatre âges* 1848 and *12 Etudes* in every minor key 1857, of which numbers 4–7 constitute a symphony for piano solo and numbers 8–10 a concert for piano solo.

Aiken Henry Thomas (1785–1851). English sporting artist. Fox-hunting and steeplechasing were the subjects that most frequently occupied him, but the whole range of field sports was covered in his volume of 50 prints entitled *National Sports of Great Britain* 1820.

Allan David (1744–1796). Scottish history and genre painter. He studied in Glasgow and at Rome, where 1773 he won a gold medal for his *Origin of Painting* and became a member of the Academy of St Luke. He settled in Edinburgh and was known as the 'Scottish Hogarth' for his watercolours and engravings of contemporary life, his subjects, for example *The Penny Wedding* (Edinburgh), anticipating those of Wilkie.

Allan William (1782–1850). Scottish history painter. Born in Edinburgh, he spent several years in Russia and travelled widely in Europe and the Middle East, returning to Edinburgh 1814. He was elected president of the Royal Scottish Academy 1838. His paintings include scenes from Walter Scott's Waverley novels. Knighted 1842.

Allard Jean François (1785–1839). French general. He served first under Napoleon, then went to Lahore 1820 where he entered the service of Ranjit Singh. He organized the army according to the French model, and was made generalissimo of the forces.

Allbutt Thomas Clifford (1836–1925). British physician. He invented a compact medical thermometer, proved that angina is caused by narrowing of the coronary artery, and studied hydrophobia and tetanus. KCB 1907.

Allegri Gregorio (1582–1652). Italian Baroque composer. He was maestro di cappella of the Sistine Chapel, Rome, 1610–29. His output of sacred music includes Magnificats, motets, and the celebrated

You have often heard of the famous Miserere in Rome,
which is so greatly prized that the performers in the
chapel are forbidden on pain of excommunication to take
away a single part of it, or to copy it or to give it to
anyone.

Leopold Mozart on GREGORIO ALLEGRI
quoted in Anderson, *The Letters of Mozart and his Family* 1966

Miserere mei (Psalm 51) for nine voices, famously transcribed from
memory by Mozart at the age of 14.

Allen Ethan (1738–1789). US military leader who founded the
'Green Mountain Boys' 1770. At the outbreak of the American
Revolution 1775 they joined with Benedict Arnold and captured
Fort Ticonderoga, the first victory for the American side. Captured
by the British in the subsequent invasion of Canada, Allen continued
his campaign for Vermont's independence after his release in 1778.
He died before it achieved statehood in 1791.

Allen Horatio (1802–1890). US civil engineer. He made the first
railway trip in America, operating the Stourbridge Lion 1829 at
Honesdale, Pennsylvania. He was chief engineer of the South
Carolina railway and later the Erie railway, of which he was also
president. He was consulting engineer to the Panama railway and
president of the American Society of Civil Engineers.

Allen Hugh Percy (1869–1946). English professor of music. He
was conductor of the Bach Choir, London, 1901–20; professor of
music, Oxford University, from 1918; and director of the Royal
College of Music, London, until 1937. He was knighted 1920. As
professor of music at Oxford, Allen did valuable work in widening
the scope and practicality of the courses there. He was a fine choral
conductor.

Allen Viola (1869–1948). US actress. She was leading lady of
Frohman's stock company at the Empire Theatre 1891–98, and
then toured with her own company. She excelled as Viola in *Twelfth
Night* and, in later years, as Lady Macbeth.

Allen William (1532–1594). English cardinal. His Catholicism
conflicted with Elizabeth I's ecclesiastical policy and he went into
exile in Europe. He lived in Rome from 1585 and his efforts for the
reconversion of England to Catholicism became more political from
this time. He was created a cardinal 1587.

Allen founded the Catholic seminary at Douai 1568 (later transferred to Rheims) and arranged for the foundation of an English
Jesuit college in Rome 1579. The translation of the Douai Bible was
begun by Allen.

Religions change: beer and wine remain.

HERVEY ALLEN
Anthony Adverse pt 1 ch 3 1933

Allen (William) Hervey (1889–1949). US novelist, poet, and biographer. He is best known for his historical novel *Anthony Adverse*
1933 set in the Napoleonic era. He also wrote a biography of Edgar
Allen Poe, *Israfel* 1926, and several volumes of poetry.

Later novels were *Action at Aquila* 1938, *The Front and the Fort*
1943, *Bedford Village* 1945, and *The City in the Dawn* 1947.

Bisexuality immediately doubles your chances of a date
on Saturday night.

WOODY ALLEN
New York Herald Tribune 1975

Allen Woody. Adopted name of Allen Stewart Konigsberg
(1935–   ). US film writer, director, and actor. He is known for his
cynical, witty, often self-deprecating parody and offbeat humour.
His film *Annie Hall* 1977 won him three Academy Awards. From the

late 1970s, Allen mixed his output of comedies with straight dramas,
such as *Interiors* 1978 and *Another Woman* 1988, but recent works
such as *Manhattan Murder Mystery* 1994 and *Bullets over Broadway*
1994 have emphasized humour.

Suggested reading
Bjrkman, Stig *Woody Allen on Woody Allen: In Conversation with
Stig Bjrkman* (1994)
Girus, Sam *The Films of Woody Allen* (1993)
Jacobs, Diane *But We Have All The Eggs We Need: The Magic of
Woody Allen* (1982)
Lax, Eric *Woody Allen: A Biography* (1991)
Pogel, Nancy *Woody Allen* (1987)

Allenby (Edmund) Henry Hynman, 1st Viscount Allenby (1861–
1936). British field marshal. In World War I he served in France
before taking command 1917–19 of the British forces in the Middle
East.

His defeat of the Turkish forces at Megiddo in Palestine Sept 1918
was followed almost at once by the capitulation of Turkey. He was
high commissioner in Egypt 1919–35. KCB 1915, viscount 1919.

In France in 1914 he was conspicuous at Mons and in the Great
Retreat, leading a cavalry division with consummate skill and putting
up a notable resistance at Hollebeke in the Ypres battle of Oct 1914.
He was then promoted successively to corps commander and army
commander (3rd Army), and rendered valuable services at the
battle of Arras 1917.

In Egypt he took over the chief command from Sir Archibald
Murray. After considerable preparation and reorganization he captured Gaza and went on to take Beersheba and Jerusalem.

In Palestine he achieved the final overthrow of the Turkish army
in a celebrated campaign, his army sweeping forward beyond the
Jordan Valley to Damascus and Aleppo after totally crushing the
Turks in the battles of Megiddo (18 Sept–31 Oct 1918).

Allende Isabel (1942–   ). Chilean novelist. She is one of the leading exponents of magic realism. After the assassination 1973 of her
uncle, Chile's socialist president Salvador Allende, exile in
Venezuela released memories of family and country which emerged
in her first novel *La casa de los espiritus/ The House of the Spirits* 1982,
now filmed in English. Her later novels *De amor y de sombra/Of Love
and Shadows* 1984 and *Eva Luna* 1987 combine fantasy with the
'real' worlds of investigative journalism, filmmaking, and politics.
She has also published short stories and children's books.

Allende, Isabel *The niece of murdered Chilean president Salvador
Allende, Isabel Allende. Her novels combine magic realism with a frank and
penetrating account of her country's sufferings.*

Allende (Gossens) Salvador (1908–1973). Chilean left-wing politician. Elected president 1970 as the candidate of the Popular Front alliance, Allende never succeeded in keeping the electoral alliance together in government. His failure to solve the country's economic problems or to deal with political subversion allowed the army, backed by the CIA, to stage the 1973 coup which brought about the death of Allende and many of his supporters.

Allende became a Marxist activist in the 1930s and rose to prominence as a presidential candidate in 1952, 1958, and 1964. In each election he had the support of the socialist and communist movements but was defeated by the Christian Democrats and Nationalists. As president, his socialism and nationalization of US-owned copper mines led the CIA to regard him as a communist and to their involvement in the coup that replaced him by General Pinochet.

Allestree (or Allestry) Richard (1619–1681). English theologian. When the parliamentarian forces sacked the Oxford colleges during the English Civil War, he saved many Christ Church treasures. At the Restoration he was made canon of Christ Church and then professor of divinity 1663.

Alleyn Edward (1566–1626). English actor. The only actor to rival Richard Burbage, he appeared in Marlowe's plays. With his father-in-law, theatre manager Philip Henslowe, he built the Fortune Theatre 1600 and was also part owner of the Rose Theatre. He founded Dulwich College 1619. He retired to Dulwich 1604. His second wife was the daughter of the poet John Donne.

'It may only be blackmail,' said the man in the taxi hopefully.

MARGERY ALLINGHAM
The Tiger in the Smoke 1952, opening words

Allingham Margery Louise (1904–1966). English detective novelist. She created detective Albert Campion, as in *The Crime at Black Dudley* 1928. Her detective fiction displays great wit and ingenuity and includes *More Work for the Undertaker* 1948 and *The Tiger in the Smoke* 1952 (filmed 1956).

The best known of her other books is a chronicle of village life written during World War II, *The Oaken Heart* 1941.

Allingham William (1824–1889). Irish poet. His work frequently has a strong regional and nostalgic quality; in *Laurence Bloomfield in Ireland* 1864 he displays an acute agrarian realism. Other volumes of his verse include *Poems* 1850 and *Irish Songs and Poems* 1887. His *Diary*, edited 1907 by his wife, tells of his friendships with Tennyson, Leigh Hunt, and Dante Gabriel Rossetti and the influence of the Pre-Raphaelite Brotherhood.

The love of gain has never made a painter, but it has marred many.

WASHINGTON ALLSTON
Lectures on Art 1850

Allston Washington (1779–1843). US painter. He painted sea- and landscapes, and was a pioneer of the Romantic movement in the USA. His handling of light and colour earned him the title 'the American Titian'. He also painted classical, religious, and historical subjects.

His earlier work was grandiose and dramatic, *The Deluge*, 1804 (New York Metropolitan Museum), being an example. On one large picture, *Belshazzar's Feast* (in which he gave a subject to Martin), he toiled unhappily for many years after he settled in Boston, though his work there is better represented by smaller paintings of dreamy reverie such as his *Moonlit Landscape*, 1819 (Boston).

Allyson June. Stage name of Ella Geisman (1917–). US film actress with a girl-next-door image. She was popular in musicals and straight drama in the 1940s and 1950s. Her work includes *Music for Millions* 1945, *The Three Musketeers* 1948, and *The Glenn Miller Story* 1954.

Almagro Diego de (1475–1538). Spanish soldier who partnered Francisco Pizarro in the conquest of Peru. Almagro arrived in Panama 1514 with the expedition of Pedro Arias de Ávila. Almagro recruited followers and arranged shipments for the expeditions led by Pizarro 1524–28. He led an expedition of conquest to Chile 1535–36, and returned to break the siege of Cuzco, taking its governorship.

Alma-Tadema Lawrence (1836–1912). Dutch painter. He settled in England 1870. He painted romantic, idealized scenes from ancient Greek, Roman, and Egyptian life in a distinctive, detailed style. Knighted 1899.

He was determined to make Portugal the paramount power in the East and to monopolize the spice trade.

Encyclopaedia Britannica on FRANCISCO DE ALMEIDA
1990

Almeida Francisco de (c. 1450–1510). First viceroy of Portuguese India 1505–08. He consolidated rule there and sent expeditions out into the Indian Ocean and as far as Madagascar.

He was killed in a skirmish with the Hottentots (present-day Khoikhoi) at Table Bay, S Africa.

Almeida-Garrett João Baptista da Silva Leitão (1799–1854). Portuguese poet and politician. The leader of the Portuguese Romantic movement, he also took an active part in the political movements of his country. Of his plays, *Frei Luis de Sousa* 1844, built on the pattern of classical Greek tragedy, is considered the finest national drama of Portugal. His other works include an epic poem called *Dona Branca, Romanceiro*, a collection of Portuguese folk tales, and *Folhas caidas*, a volume of lyrics.

Almodóvar Pedro (1951–). Spanish film director and screenwriter. The most profitable Spanish director in both domestic and foreign markets, Almodóvar's films are often camp, frenetic melodramas, saturated in glossy colours and costumes, and peopled by characters of all shades of the sexual spectrum. His films include *Qué He Hecho Yo Para Merecer Esto?/What Have I Done to Deserve This?* 1984, *Mujeres al Borde de un Ataque de Nervios/Women on the Verge of a Nervous Breakdown* 1988, *Tacones Lejanos/High Heels* 1991, and *Kika* 1993.

His characters are firmly steeped in the post-Franco Spanish subculture of hedonism and he has sometimes been accused of excess in his portrayal of sex and violence. His other films include *Mátador* 1986 and *Atame!/Tie Me Up! Tie Me Down!* 1990.

Almohad Berber dynasty 1130–1269 founded by the Berber prophet Muhammad ibn Tumart (c. 1080–1130). The Almohads ruled much of Morocco and Spain, which they took by defeating the Almoravids; they later took the area that today forms Algeria and Tunis. Their policy of religious 'purity' involved the forced conversion and massacre of the Jewish population of Spain. The Almohads were themselves defeated by the Christian kings of Spain 1212, and in Morocco 1269.

Almoravid Berber dynasty 1056–1147 founded by the prophet Abdullah ibn Tashfin, ruling much of Morocco and Spain in the 11th–12th centuries. The Almoravids came from the Sahara and in the 11th century began laying the foundations of an empire covering the whole of Morocco and parts of Algeria; their capital was the newly founded Marrakesh. In 1086 they defeated Alfonso VI of Castile to gain much of Spain. They were later overthrown by the Almohads.

Almqvist Carl Jonas Love (1793–1866). Swedish author. His literary career began 1832 with the first of his series of romances, called *Törnrosensbok/The Book of the Thorn Rose*. His succeeding lyrics, dramas, and philosophical, aesthetic, moral, and educational works show remarkable versatility. In 1851, convicted of forgery and charged with murder, he fled to America. He returned to Europe 1865, dying in Bremen.

Alonso Alicia (born Alicia Ernestina de la Caridad dei Cobre Martinez Hoyo) (1921–). Cuban ballerina and director. Purely classical in style, her most famous role was Giselle 1959. She became prima ballerina and director of the National Ballet of Cuba 1959.

Alonso Dámaso (1898–1990). Spanish poet and critic. His best-known poetry is the volume *Hijos de la ira/Children of Wrath* 1944, but his main achievement was his reappraisal of the poetry of Góngora and St John of the Cross.

Aloysius, St (born Luigi Gonzaga) (1568–1591). Italian Jesuit. In 1585 he joined the Society of Jesus, despite parental opposition, and died while nursing plague victims. Canonized 1726, he is the patron saint of youth. Feast day 21 June.

Alp-Arslan (born Muhammad ibn Daud), 'Valiant Lion' (*c.* 1029–1072). Second sultan of the Seljuk dynasty. He came to the Persian throne 1063 and pursued a career of conquest. He reduced Armenia and Georgia, and later won a great victory over the Greek emperor, Romanus IV, whom he took prisoner but released on payment of a large ransom.

Alphege, St (954–1012). Anglo-Saxon priest, bishop of Winchester from 984, archbishop of Canterbury from 1006. When the Danes attacked Canterbury he tried to protect the city, was thrown into prison, and, refusing to deliver the treasures of his cathedral, was stoned and beheaded at Greenwich 19 April, his feast day.

Alpher Ralph Asher (1921–). US scientist who carried out the first quantitative work on nucleosynthesis and in 1948 was the first to predict the existence of primordial background radiation, which is now regarded as one of the major pieces of evidence for the validity of the Big Bang model of the universe. In 1948 Alpher and cosmologist George Gamow published the results of their work on nucleosynthesis in the early universe.

Alpini Prospero (1553–1616). Venetian botanist. He did much valuable research in Egypt. His chief works are *De medicina Aegyptiorum* 1591 and *De plantis Aegypti liber* 1592. He studied at Padua, and became professor of botany there.

Alston Richard (1948–). English choreographer. His modernist style concentrates on light, speedy, lyrical movements. Among his pieces are *Bell High* 1980, *Sacre du printemps* 1981, and *Midsummer* 1983. He was artistic director of the Rambert Dance Company 1986–92.

He prised landscape out of a merely supplementary relationship to subject matter.
CHRISTOPHER S WOOD on ALBRECHT ALTDORFER
in Albrecht Altdorfer and the Origins of Landscape 1993

Altdorfer Albrecht (*c.* 1480–1538). German painter, architect, and printmaker. He was active in Regensburg, Bavaria. He is best known for his vast panoramic battle scenes in which his use of light creates movement and drama. On a smaller scale, he also painted some of the first true landscapes.

With Albrecht Dürer and Lucas Cranach, Altdorfer is regarded as one of the leaders of the German Renaissance. He is noted for his development of landscape as a main pictorial feature, evidently being impressed by the scenery of the Austrian Alps in 1511 when he journeyed down the Danube into Austria, or perhaps by earlier journeys. As well as forests and mountains, he studied effects of light, and being city architect of Ratisbon, his architectural tastes caused him to introduce elaborate buildings into some pictures.

Alter David (1807–1881). US inventor and physicist who in 1854 put forward the idea that each element has a characteristic spectrum, and that spectroscopic analysis of a substance can therefore be used to identify the elements present.

His inventions included a successful electric clock, a model for an electric locomotive (which was not put into production), a new process for purifying bromine, an electric telegraph that spelled out words with a pointer, and a method of extracting oil from coal (which was not put into commercial practice because of the discovery of oil in Pennsylvania).

Alter Simha (1897–1992). Polish-born Israeli Hasidic rabbi. As head from 1977 of the Ger (or Gur) Hasidim, the largest Hasidic community in the world, he was also the most powerful man in Agudah, the Orthodox Religious Party of Israel, for whom all Ger Hasidim vote.

Rabbi Simha Alter escaped the Holocaust in Poland and in 1940 moved to Israel, where he went into business. In 1977 he succeeded his brother as head of the Ger Hasidim. Through the Agudah, he tried on behalf of the Hasidim to make Israel a more overtly religious society.

Altgeld John Peter (1847–1902). US political and social reformer. Born in Prussia, he was taken in infancy to the USA. During the Civil War he served in the Union army. He was a judge of the Supreme Court in Chicago 1886–91, and as governor of Illinois 1893–97 was a champion of the worker against the government-backed power of big business.

Althusser Louis (1918–1990). French philosopher and Marxist, born in Algeria, who argued that the idea that economic systems determine family and political systems is too simple. He attempted to show how the ruling class ideology of a particular era is a crucial form of class control.

Althusser divides each mode of production into four key elements – the economic, political, ideological, and theoretical – all of which interact. His structuralist analysis of capitalism sees individuals and groups as agents or bearers of the structures of social relations, rather than as independent influences on history. His works include *For Marx* 1965, *Lenin and Philosophy* 1969, and *Essays in Self-Criticism* 1976.

He dismisses mainstream sociology as bourgeois and has influenced thinkers in fields as diverse as social anthropology, literature, and history.

Althusser murdered his wife 1980 and spent the next few years in mental hospitals. His autobiography *The Future Lasts a Long Time* was published 1992.

Yeah, I have three sons working on Food for Love ... That's what sons are for. Help you run the farm.
ROBERT ALTMAN
speaking in Paris, March 1986

Altman Robert (1925–). US film director and producer. His films vary in tone from the comic to the elegiac, but are frequently ambitious in both content and form, taking a quizzical view of American life and culture and utilizing a complex and sometimes fragmentary style. His antiwar comedy *M.A.S.H* 1970 was a critical and commercial success. Subsequent films include *The Player* 1992, *Short Cuts* 1993, and *Prêt-à-Porter* 1994.

Alva Ferdinand Alvarez de Toledo, Duke of Alva (or Alba) (1508–1582). Spanish politician and general. He successfully commanded the Spanish armies of the Holy Roman emperor Charles V and his son Philip II of Spain. In 1567 he was appointed governor of the Netherlands, where he set up a reign of terror to suppress Protestantism and the revolt of the Netherlands. In 1573 he was recalled at his own request. He later led a successful expedition against Portugal 1580–81.

Alvarado Juan Bautista (1809–1882). Californian insurgent who defeated the forces of the ruling Mexican government in California in the decisive battle of San Buenaventura. From 1836 to 1838 he used the revolutionary title of 'governor', and from 1838 to 1842 was officially recognized by the Mexican government.

Alvarado Pedro de (*c.* 1485–1541). Spanish conquistador, ruler of Guatemala 1524–41. Alvarado joined Hernán Cortés' army 1519 and became his principal captain during the conquest of New Spain. Left in command at Tenochtitlán, Mexico, he provoked the Aztec rebellion that resulted in the death of Montezuma II 1520. He conquered Guatemala 1523–24 and was its governor and captain general until his death.

He also attacked Ecuador 1534 in a bid for a share of the former Inca empire, but was paid off by Francisco Pizarro.

Álvarez José (1768–1827). Spanish sculptor. He first worked with his father, a stonemason, and obtained admission into the Academy of Granada 1788. He was appointed principal sculptor to the king of Spain 1825. He also modelled portrait busts of Ferdinand VII, Rossini, and the Duchess of Alba.

There is no democracy in physics. We can't say that some second-rate guy has as much right to opinion as Fermi.

LUIS WALTER ALVAREZ
quoted in D S Greenberg *The Politics of Pure Science* 1967

Alvarez Luis Walter (1911–1988). US physicist who led the research team that discovered the ξ_0 subatomic particle 1959. He also made many other breakthroughs in fundamental physics, accelerators, and radar. He worked on the US atom bomb for two years, at Chicago and at Los Alamos, New Mexico, during World War II. Nobel prize 1968.

In 1980 Alvarez was responsible for the theory that dinosaurs disappeared because a meteorite crashed into Earth 70 million years ago, producing a dust cloud that blocked out the Sun for several years, causing dinosaurs and plants to die. The first half of the hypothesis is now widely accepted.

Alvarez de Cienfuegos Nicasio (1764–1809). Spanish playwright and poet. Of his tragedies the best known are *Zoraida* and *La Condesa de Castilla*.

Alvarez Quintero Serafin (1871–1938) and Joaquin (1873–1945). Spanish dramatists. The brothers, born near Seville, always worked together and from 1897 produced some 200 comedies, principally dealing with local life in Andalusia. Among them are *Papá Juan: Centenario* 1909 and *Los Mosquitos* 1928.

Other well known plays are *Los Galeotes* 1900, *Las Flores* 1901, *Malvaloca* 1912, and *La Calumniada* 1919. Genial and sentimental, they are not concerned with serious moral or social issues.

Alvaro Corrado (1895–1956). Italian novelist. He is best known as a writer of short stories, for example *Gente in Aspromonte* 1930 and *75 racconti* 1955, which focus on the reality as well as the myths of his home region, Calabria.

Alverstone Richard Everard Webster, Viscount Alverstone (1842–1915). British politician and lawyer. He became attorney general in the Conservative government 1885 and represented Britain in international arbitration cases. He became lord chief justice 1900.

He led as counsel for *The Times* against the Irish party before the Parnell Commission 1889; he was British representative in the Bering Sea arbitration 1893; and leading counsel in the Venezuela arbitration 1899. In May 1900 he became master of the Rolls and was created a baron, and in 1903 he was one of the three arbitrators on the Alaska Boundary question. Viscount 1913.

Alwyn William (1905–1985). English composer. Professor of composition at the Royal Academy of Music 1926–55, he wrote film music (*Desert Victory*, *The Way Ahead*) and composed symphonies and chamber music.

Alzheimer Alois (1864–1915). German neuropathologist. In 1906 he became the first to describe Alzheimer's disease, a degenerative illness affecting the nerve cells of the frontal and temporal lobes of the cerebrum of the brain, characterized by severe memory impairment. It is a major cause of presenile dementia.

Alzheimer was professor of psychiatry and neurology at Breslau University (now Wrocław, Poland) from 1912.

Amadeo Giovanni Antonio (1447–1522). Italian sculptor and architect. In collaboration with others, he decorated the Certosa at Pavia. His monument of Bartolommeo Colleoni, in the church of Sta Maria Maggiore, Bergamo, is one of the masterpieces of Renaissance sculpture. He also took part in the sculpture of the great octagonal dome of Milan Cathedral.

Amadeus I 'the White-handed' (died 1078). Ruler of Susa and Maurienne in Savoy. He governed the two states with his mother after the death of his father, the count of Maurienne. This made him master of the great pass over the Alps into Italy, by Mont Cenis, from which much of the subsequent importance of his family was derived.

Amalia Anna (1739–1807). Duchess of Saxe-Weimar-Eisenach. As widow of Duke Ernest, she reigned as regent for her son Karl August 1758–75 with prudence and skill, making the court of Weimar a literary centre of Germany. She was a friend of the writers Wieland, Goethe, and Herder.

Amanullah Khan (1892–1960). Emir (ruler) of Afghanistan 1919–29, who assumed the title of king 1926. Third son of Habibullah Khan, he seized the throne on his father's assassination and concluded a treaty with the British, but his policy of westernization led to rebellion 1928. Amanullah had to flee, abdicated 1929, and settled in Rome, Italy.

Amar Das (1495–1574). Indian religious leader, third guru (teacher) of Sikhism 1552–74. He laid emphasis on equality and opposed the caste system. He initiated the custom of the *langar* (communal meal).

Amari Michele (1806–1889). Italian historian, orientalist, and politician. His best-known work, *La Guerra del Vespro Siciliano* 1841, was prohibited and he fled to France, returning to Italy 1859 to fight under Garibaldi. He was minister of public instruction 1862–64 and professor of Arabic at Pisa and Florence until 1878.

Amaru José Gabriel Condocanqui (1742–1781). Peruvian revolutionary, known as Tupac Amaru and the 'last of the Incas'. He led a wave of Indian opposition to Spanish repression that was ruthlessly suppressed and was himself cruelly killed.

Amasis II fifth pharaoh 570–526 BC of the 26th dynasty, and Egyptian general who seized the throne from Apries. He founded Naucratis, conquered Cyprus, and maintained close relations with the Greek world.

Amaya Carmen (1913–1963). Spanish Romany dancer. She came from a family of dancers, and performed in public from the age of seven. She toured the world, and her inspired, fiery, and passionate style made her a popular performer, especially with audiences in Argentina.

Ambartsumian Viktor Amazaspovich (1908–). Soviet-Armenian astronomer who in 1955 proposed the manner in which enormous catastrophes might take place within stars and galaxies during their evolution.

Ambartsumian was born in Tiflis (now Tbilisi), Georgia, and studied at the University of Leningrad, where he later taught.

In 1946 he was appointed head of the Byurakan Observatory in Yerevan, Armenia.

The radio source in Cygnus had been associated with what appeared to be a closely connected pair of galaxies, and it was generally supposed that a galactic collision was taking place. If this were the case, such phenomena might account for many extragalactic radio sources. However, Ambartzumian presented convincing evidence in 1955 of the errors of this theory. He suggested instead that vast explosions occur within the cores of galaxies, analogous to supernovae, but on a galactic scale.

His book *Theoretical Astrophysics* 1939 was influential.

Ambler Eric (1909–). English novelist. He excels in narrating swift, suspenseful action. He used Balkan/Levant settings in the thrillers *The Mask of Dimitrios* 1939 and *Journey into Fear* 1940. His other books include *The Care of Time* 1981.

Amboise Jacques d' (1934–). US dancer. He created roles in many of George Balanchine's greatest works as a principal dancer with New York City Ballet. He also appeared in films and TV productions, including *Seven Brides for Seven Brothers* 1954.

Ambrose, St (*c.* 340–397). One of the early Christian leaders and theologians known as the Fathers of the Church. Feast day 7 Dec.

Born at Trèves, in S Gaul, the son of a Roman prefect, Ambrose became governor of N Italy. In 374 he was chosen bishop of Milan, although he was not yet a member of the church. He was then baptized and consecrated. He wrote many hymns, and devised the regulation of church music known as the *Ambrosian chant*, which is still used in Milan.

Ambrosio Vittorio (1897–1958). Italian general, initially loyal to Mussolini but later involved in his overthrow.

In World War II, Ambrosio commanded the 2nd Italian Army in Yugoslavia 1941, became Chief of Staff of the Italian Army Jan 1942, and Chief of the Italian General Staff Feb 1943. After the fall of Mussolini he made plain his opposition to the German domination of Italy following the Italian armistice with the Allies Sept 1943, and so was demoted to inspector general of the army.

Ameche Don. Stage name of Dominic Amici (1908–1993). US actor. A conventionally handsome leading man of many Hollywood films from the mid-1930s to the mid-1940s, perhaps best remembered for playing the title role in *The Story of Alexander Graham Bell* 1939. He later returned to films as a substantial character actor in *Trading Places* 1983, *Cocoon* 1985, and *Things Change* 1988.

Amenhotep four Egyptian pharaohs, including:

Amenhotep III (1391–1353 BC). King (pharaoh) of ancient Egypt who built great monuments at Thebes, including the temples at Luxor. Two portrait statues at his mortuary temple were known to the Greeks as the colossi of Memnon; one was cracked, and when the temperature changed at dawn it gave out an eerie sound, then thought supernatural. His son *Amenhotep IV* changed his name to Akhenaton.

You have sat too long here for any good you have been doing – In the name of God, go.

Speech by LEO AMERY repeating Oliver Cromwell's words, addressed to Neville Chamberlain, House of Commons 7 May 1940

Amery Leo(pold Charles Maurice Stennett) (1873–1955). English Conservative politician, First Lord of the Admiralty 1922–24, secretary for the colonies 1924–29, secretary for the dominions 1925–29, and secretary of state for India and Burma (now Myanmar) 1940–45.

Ames Adelbert (1880–1955). US scientist who studied optics and the psychology of visual perception. He concluded that much of what a person sees depends on what he or she expects to see, based (consciously or unconsciously) on previous experience.

Amici Giovanni Battista (1786–1863). Italian botanist and microscopist who in the 1820s made a series of observations clarifying the process by which pollen fertilizes the ovule in flowering plants.

Truth is not only violated by falsehood; it may be outraged by silence.

HENRI AMIEL
Journal Intime 1882–84

Amiel Henri Frédéric (1821–1881). Swiss philosopher and writer who wrote *Journal Intime* 1882–84. Born in Geneva, he became professor of philosophy at the university there.

Amies (Edwin) Hardy (1909–). English couturier. He is noted for his tailored clothes for women and menswear designs. He was formerly one of Queen Elizabeth II's dressmakers. KCVO 1989.

He began working at Lachasse 1934 where he became manager and designer, before opening his own house 1946. During World War II he contributed to the Utility scheme, creating ingenious and elegant clothes that coped with the wartime fabric restrictions. In 1950 he opened a ready-to-wear boutique and was awarded a royal warrant 1955. In 1961 he became linked with Hepworths and is now known mainly as a designer of menswear.

No other political figure in modern Africa so blatantly championed the interests of a small section of his people against the rest.

Alan Palmer on IDI AMIN (DADA)
Penguin Dictionary of Twentieth Century History 1979

Amin (Dada) Idi (1925–). Ugandan politician, president 1971–79. He led the coup that deposed Milton Obote 1971, expelled the Asian community 1972, and exercised a reign of terror over his people. He fled to Libya when insurgent Ugandan and Tanzanian troops invaded Uganda 1979.

I was never an Angry Young Man. I am angry only when I hit my thumb with a hammer.

KINGSLEY AMIS
on the labelling of authors as 'Angry Young Men', *Eton College Chronicle*

Amis Kingsley William (1922–1995). English novelist and poet. He was associated early on with the Angry Young Men group of writers. His sharply ironic works frequently debunk pretentious mediocrity; his first novel, the best-selling *Lucky Jim* 1954, is a comic portrayal of life in a provincial university. His later novels include *The Alteration* 1976, which imagines a 20th-century society dominated by the Catholic Church. He is the father of writer Martin Amis. Knighted 1990.

His other novels, written in a variety of genres, include *The Riverside Villas Murder* 1937, the spy story *The Anti-Death League* 1966, and the ghost story *The Green Man* 1969. His fascination with middle-aged sexuality is demonstrated in such novels as *Stanley and the Women* 1984 and *The Old Devils* 1986 (Booker Prize). His poetry includes *A Case of Samples: Poems 1946–56* 1956 and *Collected Poems 1944–79* 1979.

Suggested reading
Amis, Kingsley *Memoirs* (1991)
Bradford, R *Kingsley Amis* (1989)
Salwak, D *Kingsley Amis: Modern Novelist* (1992)

Amis Martin Louis (1949–). English novelist, son of Kingsley Amis. His works are characterized by their acerbic black humour

Amis, Martin English novelist Martin Amis. His darkly satirical, sometimes macabre novels depict the contemporary world as being in a period of moral decadence and decay.

and include *The Rachel Papers* 1973, a memoir of adolescence told through flashbacks, *Dead Babies* 1975, which addresses decadence and sadism, *Money* 1984, *London Fields* 1989, *Time's Arrow* 1991, and *The Information* 1995.

Ammanati Bartolommeo (1511–1592). Italian Mannerist sculptor and architect. He was influenced by Michelangelo and Andrea Sansovino. His most noted sculpture is the Fountain of Neptune in the Piazza della Signoria, Florence, 1560–75. He built the rusticated garden façade of the Palazzo Pitti, Florence, 1560 and the graceful bridge of Sta Trinità, Florence, completed 1570 (destroyed 1944 but rebuilt).

Ammanati rivalled Vasari as a Mannerist architect.

It is a much greater honour to appear ... decent and decorous, rather than ... vain and lascivious.

BARTOLOMEO AMMANATI
Letter to the Academy in Florence 22 Aug 1582,
about his dislike of nude statues.

Ammianus Marcellinus (lived 4th century). Roman soldier and historian. The surviving books of his work, dealing with contemporary affairs in the later Roman Empire, rank him as the last major Roman historian.

Ampère André Marie (1775–1836). French physicist and mathematician who made many discoveries in electromagnetism and electrodynamics. He followed up the work of Hans Oersted on the interaction between magnets and electric currents, developing a rule for determining the direction of the magnetic field associated with an

Ampère *French mathematician and physicist André Ampère, whose name is given to the basic SI unit of electric current. Although a brilliant scientist, Ampère's private life was tragic. His father was guillotined during the French Revolution in 1793, his first wife died 1804 four years after the birth of their only son, and he endured a disastrous second marriage until his death of pneumonia in 1836. (Ann Ronan/Image Select)*

The future science of government should be called 'la cybernetique'.

ANDRÉ MARIE AMPÈRE
1843

electric current. The unit of electric current, the ampere, is named after him.

Ampère's law is an equation that relates the magnetic force produced by two parallel current-carrying conductors to the product of their currents and the distance between the conductors. Today Ampère's law is usually stated in the form of calculus: the line integral of the magnetic field around an arbitrarily chosen path is proportional to the net electric current enclosed by the path. He published *Mémoire sur la théorie mathématique des phénomènes électrodynamiques uniquement déduite de l'expérience/Notes on the Mathematical Theory of Electrodynamic Phenomena Deduced Solely from Experiment* 1827.

Amsler-Laffon Jakob (born Amsler) (1823–1912). Swiss mathematical physicist who designed and manufactured precision instruments for use in engineering, including an improved tool to measure areas inside curves – the polar planimeter. It was particularly valuable to shipbuilders and railway engineers. By the time he died, his factory had produced more than 50,000 polar planimeters.

Amundsen Roald Engelbrecht Gravning (1872–1928). Norwegian explorer who in 1903–06 became the first person to navigate the Northwest Passage. Beaten to the North Pole by US explorer Robert Peary 1910, he reached the South Pole ahead of Captain Scott 1911.

In 1918, Amundsen made an unsuccessful attempt to drift across the North Pole in the airship *Maud* and in 1925 tried unsuccessfully to fly from Spitsbergen, in the Arctic Ocean north of Norway, to the Pole by aeroplane. The following year he joined the Italian explorer Umberto Nobile (1885–1978) in the airship *Norge*, which circled the North Pole twice and landed in Alaska. Amundsen was killed in a plane crash over the Arctic Ocean while searching for Nobile and his airship *Italia*.
Suggested reading
Amundsen, R *My Life as an Explorer* (1927)
Huntford, R *Scott and Amundsen* (1979)

Anami Korechika (1897–1945). Japanese general. He held several commands in China and Manchuria 1938–43, before being sent to New Guinea to take charge of operations there. He became director-general of army aviation 1944, and was appointed minister of war April 1945. He committed suicide 15 Aug 1945.

Ananda (lived 5th century BC). Favourite disciple of the Buddha. At his plea, a separate order was established for women. He played a major part in collecting the teachings of the Buddha after his death.

Anastasia (1901–1918). Russian Grand Duchess, youngest daughter of Nicholas II. During the Russian Revolution she was presumed shot with her parents by the Bolsheviks after the Revolution of 1917, but it has been alleged that Anastasia escaped.

Those who claimed her identity included Anna Anderson (1902–1984). Alleged by some detractors to be a Pole, Franziska Schanzkowski, she was rescued from a Berlin canal 1920. The German Federal Supreme Court found no proof of her claim 1970.
Suggested reading
Klier, John *The Quest for Anastasia* (1995)
Kurth, Peter *Anastasia: The Life of Anna Anderson* (1985)

Anaximander (c. 610–c. 546 BC). Greek astronomer and philosopher. He claimed that the Earth was a cylinder three times wider than it is deep, motionless at the centre of the universe, and that the celestial bodies were fire seen through holes in the hollow rims of wheels encircling the Earth. According to Anaximander, the first animals came into being from moisture and the first humans grew inside fish, emerging once fully developed.

He is thought to have been the first to determine solstices and equinoxes, by means of a sundial, and he is credited with drawing the first geographical map of the whole known world.

Anda Geza (1921–1976). Hungarian-born Swiss pianist and conductor. He excelled at Brahms, Bartók, and Mozart, whose piano concertos he conducted from the keyboard, inserting his own cadenzas. His playing was noted for its clarity and subtle nuances.

Anders Wladyslaw (1892–1970). Polish general and leader of Polish forces in exile during World War II.

On the outbreak of war 1939, he commanded a cavalry brigade during the German invasion but was captured and imprisoned by the Soviets. Released after the German invasion of the USSR June 1941, he began collecting Polish troops imprisoned in the USSR and was eventually permitted to take these men, with their families, to Palestine where he formed them into an army. The families were sent to E Africa, while the troops joined the British forces and fought at Tobruk and in the desert campaigns of 1942. They then went to Italy, where they captured Monte Cassino May 1944 and liberated Bologna April 1945.

Andersen Hans Christian (1805–1875). Danish writer of fairy tales. Well-known examples include 'The Ugly Duckling', 'The Snow Queen', 'The Little Mermaid', and 'The Emperor's New Clothes'. Their inventiveness, sensitivity, and strong sense of wonder have given these stories perennial and universal appeal; they have been translated into many languages. He also wrote adult novels and travel books.

Andersen was born the son of a shoemaker in Odense. His first children's stories were published 1835. Some are based on folklore; others are original. His other works include the novel *The Improvisatore* 1845, romances, and an autobiography *Mit Livs Eventyr* 1855 (translated 1954 as *The Tale of My Life*).

Andersen The tales of the Danish writer Hans Christian Andersen earned him international acclaim. An innovator in his method of storytelling, Andersen sometimes reveals a deep pessimism beneath the charm and childlike wonder of his stories. He also wrote novels, plays, and travel books.

Anderson, Elizabeth Garrett In 1860 Elizabeth Garrett Anderson spent a session as a medical student at the Middlesex Hospital, London, but was asked to leave when the male students objected to her presence. She was finally granted an MD by the Paris Faculty of Medicine. (Ann Ronan/Image Select)

Suggested reading
Andersen, Hans *The Fairy Tale of My Life* (autobiography) (1855, trs 1955)
Lederer, Wolfgang *The Kiss of the Snow Queen* (1986)
Spink, Reginald *The Young Hans Andersen* (1962)
Spink, Reginald *Hans Andersen and His World* (1972)
Stirling, M *The Wild Swan* (1965)

Anderson Carl David (1905–1991). US physicist who discovered the positive electron (positron) in 1932; he shared the Nobel Prize for Physics 1936. His discovery of another particle, the muon, in 1937 launched elementary-particle physics. The muon was the first elementary particle to be discovered beyond the constituents of ordinary matter (proton, neutron, and electron).

Anderson Elizabeth Garrett (1836–1917). The first English woman to qualify in medicine. Refused entry into medical school, Anderson studied privately and was licensed by the Society of Apothecaries in London 1865. She was physician to the Marylebone Dispensary for Women and Children (later renamed the Elizabeth Garrett Anderson Hospital), a London hospital now staffed by women and serving women patients.

She helped found the London School of Medicine. She was the first woman member of the British Medical Association and the first woman mayor in Britain.

Anderson Judith Francis Margaret (1898–1992). Australian stage and film actress in the USA, known particularly for her Shakespearean roles. Stage productions in which she has appeared include *Macbeth*, *Mourning Becomes Electra*, and *Medea*. Her film appearances include *Rebecca*, *Laura*, and *Cat on a Hot Tin Roof*. DBE 1960. Dame Judith was born in Adelaide and made her stage debut in 1915.

Anderson Lindsay (1932–1994). British film director. As critic and then film maker, he championed the cause of commitment to moral and social beliefs; his best-known film *If...* 1968 enunciated a message of social protest using surrealist humour and distancing effects.

His first feature film was *This Sporting Life* 1963, which ostensibly belonged to the then prevalent mode of northern realism; his later work includes *O Lucky Man* 1973. Anderson also pursued a parallel career in the theatre, directing a variety of productions, which ranged from work by ambitious modern writers such as David Storey, to popular plays, and occasional classic revivals. In 1988 he directed his only American film, *The Whales of August*, a touching portrait of two elderly sisters, played by Bette Davis and Lillian Gish.

Anderson Marian (1902–1993). US contralto, whose voice was remarkable for its range and richness. She toured Europe 1930, but in 1939 was barred from singing at Constitution Hall, Washington DC, because she was black. In 1955 she sang at the Metropolitan Opera, the first black singer to appear there. In 1958 she was appointed an alternate (deputizing) delegate to the United Nations.

Primarily a solo singer and recitalist rather than an opera singer, she won people's hearts worldwide with her beautiful, vibrant voice and her warm personality. She was one of the most important non-political figures in the civil rights movement and fight against racism in the USA.

Anderson believes that without great poetry there is no great drama.

Phyllis Hartnoll on MAXWELL ANDERSON
in Oxford Companion to the Theatre 1983

Anderson Maxwell (1888–1959). US dramatist. He is noted for *What Price Glory?* 1924, a realistic portrayal of the American soldier in action during World War I, co-written with Laurence Stallings. Most of his plays had moral and social problems as themes. He won a Pulitzer Prize for his comedic prose satire *Both Your Houses* 1933.

Anderson wrote numerous other plays, many in the form of verse tragedies, including *Elizabeth the Queen* 1930, *Winterset* 1935, and *Anne of the Thousand Days* 1948.

Anderson Philip Warren (1923–). US physicist who shared the 1977 Nobel Prize for Physics with his senior colleague John Van Vleck for his theoretical work on the behaviour of electrons in magnetic, noncrystalline solids.

In addition, Anderson has studied the relationship between super-conductivity, superfluidity, and laser action, and predicted the existence of resistance in superconductors. His studies of disordered glassy solids indicate that they could be used instead of the expensive crystalline semiconductors now used in many electronic devices, such as computer memories, electronic switches, and solar energy converters.

I found it impossible to work with security staring me in the face.

SHERWOOD ANDERSON
Remark to his publisher, on declining a weekly cheque.

Anderson Sherwood (1876–1941). US short-story writer and novelist. He is best known for his sensitive, poetic, and experimental naturalism, dealing with the desperation of small-town Midwestern life. His most highly acclaimed work is the story-cycle *Winesburg, Ohio* 1919; other works include the novel *Dark Laughter* 1925 and the collection of short stories *Death in the Woods* 1933.

A member of the Chicago Group, he was encouraged by Theodore Dreiser, Carl Sandburg, and later influenced by Gertrude Stein.

Ando Tadao (1941–). Japanese architect. His work employs vernacular materials and styles alongside Modernist techniques. His design for Azuma House in Osaka, Japan, 1975, one in a series of private houses, combines an austere, fortresslike façade with a minutely detailed interior. Materials such as timber and concrete are sensitively used, continuing the traditions of Japanese domestic architecture.

His Japanese Pavilion for Expo '92 in Seville reiterated his concern for the traditional while making a distinctly modern statement with a purely symbolic staircase of monumental proportions and massive, timber-slatted screen walls.

Andrássy Gyula, Count (1823–1890). Hungarian revolutionary and statesman who supported the Dual Monarchy of Austro-Hungary 1867 and was Hungary's first constitutional prime minister 1867–71. He became foreign minister of the Austro-Hungarian Empire 1871–79 and tried to halt Russian expansion into the Balkans.

All I am doing is putting Brancusi ... on the ground instead of in the air.

CARL ANDRÉ
Attributed remark, about his sculpture – a single row of unattached firebricks.

André Carl (1935–). US Minimalist sculptor. He is best known for his use of industrial materials. His *Equivalent VIII* 1976 (Tate Gallery, London), in which 120 bricks are stacked in two layers to form a mathematically devised rectangle, caused an outcry because it seemed to mock the traditional values of creativity and workmanship in art. André also pioneered earthworks.

André John (1751–1780). British army major in the American Revolution, with whom Benedict Arnold plotted the surrender of West Point. André was caught by Washington's army, tried, and hanged as a spy.

I am reconciled to my death, but I detest the mode. It will be but a momentary pang.

JOHN ANDRÉ
Last words before being shot as a British spy by the Americans 1780

Andrea del Sarto (Andrea d'Agnolo di Francesco) (1486–1530). Italian Renaissance painter. Active in Florence, he was one of the finest portraitists and religious painters of his time. His frescoes in Florence, such as the *Birth of the Virgin* 1514 (Sta Annunziata), rank among the greatest of the Renaissance. His style is serene and noble, characteristic of High Renaissance art.

Andrea del Sarto trained under Piero de Cosimo and others but was chiefly influenced by Masaccio and Michelangelo. He was the foremost painter in Florence after about 1510, along with Fra Bartolommeo, although he was gradually superseded by the emerging Mannerists during the 1520s. Apart from portraits, such as *A Young Man* (National Gallery, London), he painted many religious works, including the *Madonna of the Harpies* 1517 (Uffizi, Florence), an example of Classical beauty reminiscent of Raphael. His celebrated frescoes are at Sta Annunziata and the Chiostro dello Scalzo, both in Florence.

Andreas Capellanus Latin name for André le Chapelain.

André le Chapelain (Andreas Capellanus) (lived 12th century). French priest and author. He wrote *De Arte Honest Amandi/The Art of Virtuous Love*, a seminal work in courtly love literature, at the request of Marie de France, while he was chaplain at her court in Troyes, E France.

Andreotti Giulio (1919–). Italian Christian Democrat politician, a fervent European. He headed seven postwar governments: 1972–73, 1976–79 (four successive terms), and 1989–92 (two terms). In addition he was defence minister eight times, and foreign minister five times. In 1993 Andreotti was among several high-ranking politicians accused of possible involvement in Italy's corruption network, and in 1995 he was formally charged with using his influence to protect Mafia leaders.

I've nothing against it. We're born this way.
URSULA ANDRESS
answering a question on nudity at Dublin Castle Oct 1965

Andress Ursula (1936–   ). Swiss actress. She has specialized in glamour leads. Her international career started with *Dr No* 1962. Other films include *She* 1965, *Casino Royale* 1967, *Red Sun* 1971, and *Clash of the Titans* 1981.

Andrew (full name Andrew Albert Christian Edward) (1960–   ). Prince of the UK, Duke of York, second son of Queen Elizabeth II. He married Sarah Ferguson 1986; their first daughter, Princess Beatrice, was born 1988, and their second daughter, Princess Eugenie, was born 1990. The couple separated 1992 and divorced 1996. Prince Andrew is a naval helicopter pilot.

Andrew, St New Testament apostle. According to tradition, he went with John to Ephesus, preached in Scythia, and was martyred at Patras on an X-shaped cross (*St Andrew's cross*). He is the patron saint of Scotland. Feast day 30 Nov.

A native of Bethsaida, he was Simon Peter's brother. With Peter, James, and John, who worked with him as fishers at Capernaum, he formed the inner circle of Jesus' 12 disciples.

The nearer the Church the further from God.
LANCELOT ANDREWES
'Sermon on the Nativity' 1622

Andrewes Lancelot (1555–1626). Church of England bishop. He helped prepare the text of the Authorized Version of the Bible, and was known for the intellectual and literary quality of his sermons.

He was also bishop of Chichester (1605), Ely (1609), and Winchester (1618).

Andrews Dana (1909–1991). US actor. He played in several major American films of the 1940s, first attracting attention as one of the victims of a lynch mob in *The Oxbow Incident* 1943. Other films include *A Walk in the Sun* and *The Best Years of Our Lives*, both 1946. One of his last screen appearances was as the film director 'Red Riding Hood' in the screen version of Scott Fitzgerald's *The Last Tycoon* 1976.

Andrews John (1813–1885). Irish chemist who conducted a series of experiments on the behaviour of carbon dioxide under varying temperature and pressure. In 1869 he introduced the idea of a critical temperature (30.9°C in the case of carbon dioxide), beyond which no amount of pressure would liquefy a particular gas.

Andrews Julie. Stage name of Julia Elizabeth Wells (1935–   ). English-born US actress and singer. A child performer with her mother and stepfather in British music halls, she first appeared in the USA in the Broadway production *The Boy Friend* 1954. She was the original Eliza Doolittle in the Broadway production of *My Fair Lady* 1956. In 1960 she appeared in Lerner and Loewe's *Camelot* on Broadway. Her films include *Mary Poppins* 1964, *The Sound of Music* 1965, *'10'* 1979, and *Victor/Victoria* 1982.

Singing has never been particularly easy for me.
JULIE ANDREWS
Time 23 Dec 1966

Andrews Thomas (1813–1885). Irish physical chemist, best known for postulating the idea of critical temperature and pressure from his experimental work on the liquefaction of gases, which demonstrated the continuity of the liquid and gaseous states. He also studied heats of chemical combination and was the first to establish the composition of ozone, proving it to be an allotrope of oxygen.

Hydrogen, nitrogen, and air were then also liquefied by applying pressure to the gases once they had been cooled to below their critical temperatures. Andrews also worked out sets of pressure-volume isotherms at temperatures above and below the critical temperature, and brought a sense of order to what had previously been a chaotic branch of physical chemistry.

Andreyev Leonid Nicolaievich (1871–1919). Russian author. Many of his works show an obsession with death and madness, including the symbolic drama *Life of Man* 1907, the melodrama *He Who Gets Slapped* 1915, and the novels *Red Laugh* 1904 and *S.O.S.* 1919 published in Finland, where he fled after the Russian Revolution.

Andrić Ivo (1892–1975). Yugoslav novelist and nationalist. He became a diplomat, and was ambassador to Berlin 1940. *The Bridge on the Drina* 1945 is an epic history of a small Bosnian town. Nobel Prize 1961.

He was a member of the Young Bosnia organization (another member of which shot the heir to the Austrian throne 1914), and spent World War I in an internment camp because of his political views.

Andropov Yuri (1914–1984). Soviet communist politician, president of the USSR 1983–84.

As chief of the KGB 1967–82, he established a reputation for efficiently suppressing dissent.

Andropov was politically active from the 1930s. His part in quelling the Hungarian national uprising 1956, when he was Soviet ambassador, brought him into the Communist Party secretariat 1962 as a specialist on East European affairs. He became a member of the Politburo 1973 and succeeded Brezhnev as party general secretary 1982. Elected president 1983, he instituted economic reforms.

Angad (1504–1552). Indian religious leader, second guru (teacher) of Sikhism 1539–52, succeeding Nanak. He popularized the alphabet known as *Gurmukhi*, in which the Sikh scriptures are written.

Angas Australian family notable in public life in South Australia since its foundation. George Fife Angas (1789–1879), born in England, was a philanthropist and one of the founders of South Australia. He arranged for the first group of settlers to leave for Adelaide in 1836 under the South Australian Association's scheme. He himself migrated in 1851. His son, George French Angas (1822–1886), English-born artist and naturalist, visited South Australia and New Zealand 1844–46. He took part in several exploratory journeys in South Australia and published an account of his travels, *Savage Life and Scenes in Australia and New Zealand* 1847. Another son, John Howard Angas (1823–1903), preceded his father in settling in South Australia in 1843. A successful livestock breeder, he was also a politician and made numerous donations to charities and to the University of Adelaide.

Angelico Fra (Guido di Pietro) (c. 1400–1455). Italian painter. He was a monk, active in Florence, painting religious scenes. His series of frescoes at the monastery of San Marco, Florence, was begun after 1436. He also produced several altarpieces in a style characterized by a delicacy of line and colour.

Nothing is known of his training as a painter. He was no doubt involved, 1409–18, in the displacement of the brethren at Foligno and Cortona during the papal schism, but returned to the monastery at Fiesole, of which he became prior 1449. His first known work is the *Madonna dei Linaiuoli* (commissioned by the linen merchants), 1433 (Florence, San Marco Museum), and another principal undertaking was his set of frescoes for the monastery of San Marco in Florence on its architectural restoration by Michelozzo, 1436–43. From 1445 he worked in Orvieto and Rome, to which Eugene IV summoned him. An existing chapel in the Vatican was decorated by

[My own work] is the most easily understood ... good for edifying and instructing the people.
FRA ANGELICO
quoted in Landino Fiorentini excellenti in pictura et sculptura 15th century

him with scenes from the lives of St Stephen and St Lawrence, showing tendencies to a more elaborate style than that of his earlier works. This change may be attributed to his Renaissance surroundings in Rome. His art reflects a devotional character, and retains much that is Gothic rather than of the Renaissance in colour and conception. As a colourist and designer, Fra Angelico was an exquisite master, and as well as the frescoes at Florence, such works as the *Annunciation*, painted for Fiesole and now in the Prado, and *Christ Glorified* (National Gallery, London), show a resplendent beauty.

Suggested reading

Beck, James *Italian Renaissance Painting* (1981)
Guillaud, J and M *Fra Angelico* (1986)
Hartt, Frederick *Italian Renaissance Art* (1987)
Pope-Hennessy, J *Fra Angelico* (1974)

Angell (Ralph) Norman (1874–1967). British writer on politics and economics. In 1910 he acquired an international reputation with his book *The Great Illusion*, which maintained that any war must prove ruinous to the victors as well as to the vanquished. Nobel Peace Prize 1933. Knighted 1931.

[He provided] middle ground between pacifists, who thought war an absolute evil, and militarists, who thought it at best beneficial and at worst inescapable.

Frank Hardie on NORMAN ANGELL
in *Dictionary of National Biography*

Angelou Maya (born Marguerite Annie Johnson) (1928–). US writer and black activist. She became noted for her powerful autobiographical works, *I Know Why the Caged Bird Sings* 1969 and its four sequels up to *All God's Children Need Traveling Shoes* 1986. Based on her traumatic childhood, they tell of the struggles towards physical and spiritual liberation of a black woman from growing up in the South to emigrating to Ghana. She also wrote *Wouldn't Take Nothing for My Journey Now* 1993.

Suggested reading

Angelou, Maya *I Know Why the Caged Bird Sings* (1969)
Angelou, Maya *Gather Together in My Name* (1974)
Angelou, Maya *Singin' and Swingin' and Gettin' Merry Like Christmas* (1976)
Angelou, Maya *The Heart of a Woman* (1981)
Angelou, Maya *All God's Children Need Traveling Shoes* (1986)

Angelou A telling commentator on American culture, US writer Maya Angelou achieved critical and popular success with her multi-volume autobiography. A poet, singer, dancer, and stage and screen actress, she is noted for her varied and international involvement in the arts.

Africa to me ... is more than a glamorous fact. It is a historical truth. No man can know where he is going unless he knows exactly where he has been and exactly how he arrived at his present place.

MAYA ANGELOU
'Involvement in Black and White', interview in *Oregonian* 17 Feb 1951

Anger Kenneth (1929–). US avant-garde filmmaker. He was brought up in Hollywood. His films, which dispense with conventional narrative, often use homosexual iconography and a personal form of mysticism. They include *Fireworks* 1947, *Scorpio Rising* 1964, and *Lucifer Rising* 1973.

He wrote the exposé *Hollywood Babylon*, the original version of which was published in France 1959.

Lucifer is the Patron Saint of the visual arts. Colour, form ... all these are the work of Lucifer.

KENNETH ANGER
in *Independent* 18 Jan 1990

Anglesey Henry William Paget, 1st Marquess of Anglesey (1768–1854). British cavalry leader during the Napoleonic wars. He was twice Lord Lieutenant of Ireland, and succeeded his father as Earl of Uxbridge 1812. At the Battle of Waterloo he led an unsuccessful charge. Marquess 1815.

Ångström Anders Jonas (1814–1874). Swedish astrophysicist who worked in spectroscopy and solar physics. In 1861 he identified the presence of hydrogen in the Sun. His outstanding *Recherches sur le spectre solaire* 1868 presented an atlas of the solar spectrum with measurements of 1,000 spectral lines expressed in units of one-ten-millionth of a millimetre, the unit which later became the angstrom.

I have chosen to record in full my father's deeds, so that future generations may not be deprived of knowledge of them.

ANNA COMNENA
Alexiad preface

Anna Comnena (1083–after 1148). Byzantine historian, daughter of the emperor Alexius I, who was the historian of her father's reign. After a number of abortive attempts to alter the imperial succession in favour of her husband, Nicephorus Bryennius (*c*. 1062–1137), she retired to a convent to write her major work, the *Alexiad*. It describes the Byzantine view of public office, as well as the religious and intellectual life of the period.

[Her 'Alexiad'], a valuable source as a pro-Byzantine account of the early Crusades ... suffers from a defective chronology and excessive adulation of [her father].

Encyclopaedia Britannica on ANNA COMNENA
1990

Anne (1665–1714). Queen of Great Britain and Ireland 1702–14. She was the second daughter of James, Duke of York, who became James II, and Anne Hyde. She succeeded William III 1702. Events of her reign include the War of the Spanish Succession, Marlborough's victories at Blenheim, Ramillies, Oudenarde, and Malplaquet, and the union of the English and Scottish parliaments 1707. Anne was succeeded by George I.

She received a Protestant upbringing, and in 1683 married Prince George of Denmark (1653–1708). Of their many children only one survived infancy, William, Duke of Gloucester (1689–1700). For the greater part of her life Anne was a close friend of Sarah Churchill (1650–1744), wife of John Churchill (1650–1722), afterwards Duke

I know my heart to be entirely English.

of Marlborough; the Churchills' influence helped lead her to desert
her father for her brother-in-law, William of Orange, during the
Revolution of 1688, and later to engage in Jacobite intrigues. Her
replacement of the Tories by a Whig government 1703–04 was her
own act, not due to Churchillian influence.

Anne finally broke with the Marlboroughs 1710, when Mrs
Masham succeeded the duchess as her favourite, and supported the
Tory government of the same year.

Suggested reading
Curtis, G *The Life and Times of Queen Anne* (1972)
Gregg, Edward *Queen Anne* (1984)
Trevelyan, G M *England Under Queen Anne* (1930–34)

Anne (full name Anne Elizabeth Alice Louise) (1950–). Princess
of the UK, second child of Queen Elizabeth II, declared Princess
Royal 1987. She is actively involved in global charity work, especially for children. An excellent horsewoman, she won silver medals
in both individual and team events in the 1975 European
Championships, and competed in the 1976 Olympics.

In 1973 she married Capt Mark Phillips (1949–); they separated 1989 and were divorced 1992. In Dec 1992 she married
Commander Timothy Laurence. Her son Peter (1977–) was the
first direct descendant of the Queen not to bear a title. She also has a
daughter, Zara (1981–).

God does not pay at the end of every week, but He pays.

ANNE OF AUSTRIA
speaking to Cardinal Mazarin

Anne of Austria (1601–1666). Queen of France from 1615 and
regent 1643–61. Daughter of Philip III of Spain, she married Louis
XIII of France (whose chief minister, Cardinal Richelieu, worked
against her). On her husband's death she became regent for their
son, Louis XIV, until his majority.

She was much under the influence of Cardinal Mazarin, her chief
minister, to whom she was supposed to be secretly married.

*I hear no great praise, neither of her personage nor
beauty.*

John Hutton, English ambassador in the
Low Countries, on ANNE OF CLEVES 1537,
when Henry VIII was beginning to look for another
queen after Jane Seymour's death in childbirth.

Anne of Cleves (1515–1557). Fourth wife of Henry VIII of
England 1540. She was the daughter of the Duke of Cleves, and was
recommended to Henry as a wife by Thomas Cromwell, who wanted
an alliance with German Protestantism against the Holy Roman
Empire. Henry did not like her looks, had the marriage declared void
after six months, pensioned her, and had Cromwell beheaded.

Anne of Denmark (1574–1619). Queen consort of James VI of
Scotland (later James I of Great Britain 1603). She was the daughter of Frederick II of Denmark and Norway, and married James
1589. Anne was suspected of Catholic leanings and was notably
extravagant.

*An attractive blonde with gold hair, high-spirited,
frivolous and empty-headed.*

C P Hill on ANNE OF DENMARK
in *Who's Who in History* vol iii 1965

Annear Harold Desbrowe (1865–1933). Australian architect
who pioneered functional, open-plan house design, incorporating
such features as vertically sliding windows, flush doors, and built-
in furniture.

Annigoni Pietro (1910–1988). Italian portrait painter. His style
was influenced by Italian Renaissance portraiture. His sitters
included former US president John F Kennedy 1961 and Queen
Elizabeth II of Great Britain 1955 (National Portrait Gallery,
London).

Anokhin Piotre Kuzmich (1897–1974). Russian psychologist. He
worked with V M Bechterev (1857–1927), and later with Ivan
Pavlov, in examining the physiological bases of animal behaviour.

Anokhin proposed that behaviour is a system of functions, each
relating to a definite goal, and suggested that, even in simple conditioning, it is regulated by its consequences rather than reflexively
determined. His main ideas are collected in *Biology and
Neurophysiology of the Conditioned Reflex and its Role in Adaptive
Behaviour* 1974.

*Tragedy is restful and the reason is that hope, that foul,
deceitful thing, has no part in it.*

JEAN ANOUILH
Antigone 1942

Anouilh Jean (1910–1987). French dramatist. His plays, which are
often studies in the contrast between purity and cynical worldliness,
include *Antigone* 1942, *L'Invitation au château/Ring Round the Moon*
1947, *Colombe* 1950, and *Becket* 1959, about St Thomas à Becket
and Henry II.

Anquetil Jacques (1934–1988). French cyclist, the first person to
win the Tour de France five times (between 1957 and 1964), a
record later equalled by Eddie Merckx and Bernard Hinault.

Anselm, St (c. 1033–1109). Medieval priest and philosopher. As
abbot from 1078, he made the abbey of Bec in Normandy, France,
a centre of scholarship in Europe. He was appointed archbishop of
Canterbury by William II of England 1093, but was later forced into
exile. He holds an important place in the development of scholasticism.

As archbishop of Canterbury St Anselm was recalled from exile
by Henry I, with whom he bitterly disagreed on the investiture of the
clergy; a final agreement gave the king the right of temporal investiture and the clergy that of spiritual investiture.

In his *Proslogion* he developed the ontological proof of theism,
which infers God's existence from our capacity to conceive of a perfect being. His *Cur deus homo?/Why did God become Man?* treats the
subject of the atonement.

Anselm was canonized 1494.

Don't spoke! Don't spoke! If you didn't like it, you went!

ERNEST ANSERMET
to orchestra, quoted in John Culshaw, *Putting the Record Straight*, 1981

Ansermet Ernest Alexandre (1883–1969). Swiss conductor. He
worked with Diaghilev's Russian Ballet 1915–23. In 1918 he
founded the Swiss Romande Orchestra, conducting many first performances of works by Stravinsky.

*So ignorant of the world, that ... he had been round it, but
never in it.*

Horace Walpole on GEORGE ANSON
in *Memoirs*

Anson George, 1st Baron Anson (1697–1762). English admiral
who sailed around the world 1740–44. In 1740 he commanded the
squadron attacking the Spanish colonies and shipping in South

Anson *An engraving (1744) of the English admiral George Anson, who circumnavigated the world and looted £500,000 of Spanish treasure.*

America; he returned home by circumnavigating the world, with £500,000 of Spanish treasure. He carried out reforms at the Admiralty, which increased the efficiency of the British fleet and contributed to its success in the Seven Years' War (1756–63) against France. Created a baron 1748.

Antall Jozsef (1932–1993). Hungarian politician, prime minister 1990–93. He led the centre-right Hungarian Democratic Forum (MDF) to electoral victory April 1990, becoming Hungary's first post-communist prime minister. He promoted gradual, and successful, privatization and encouraged inward foreign investment.

As prime minister, heading Hungary's first democratically elected government for more than 40 years, he oversaw the establishment of a legal system to promote a market economy and attract foreign investment. Relations with Western Europe, particularly Germany and Austria, were also greatly improved. Despite being diagnosed as having lymphatic cancer 1991, Antall's deeply instilled devotion to public service persuaded him to continue with his duties until his death.

Antheil George (1900–1959). US composer and pianist. He is known for his *Ballet mécanique* 1926, scored for anvils, aeroplane propellers, electric bells, car horns, and pianos.

Anthony John (1938–). US fashion designer. Running his own business from 1971, he is noted for cardigans, trousers, and evening dresses in satin and sheer wool. He designs for the top end of ready-to-wear fashion, using only natural fabrics. He also designs a menswear collection.

Anthony Susan B(rownell) (1820–1906). US pioneering campaigner for women's rights who also worked for the antislavery and

temperance movements. Her causes included equality of pay for women teachers, married women's property rights, and women's suffrage. In 1869, with Elizabeth Cady Stanton, she founded the National Woman Suffrage Association. Her profile appears on the 1979 US dollar coin.

She edited and published a radical women's newspaper, *The Revolution* 1868–70, and co-edited with Elizabeth Cady Stanton the *History of Woman Suffrage* 1881–86. She organized the International Council of Women and founded the International Woman Suffrage Alliance in Berlin 1904.

Anthony of Padua, St (1195–1231). Portuguese Franciscan preacher who opposed the relaxations introduced into the order. Born in Lisbon, the son of a nobleman, he became an Augustinian monk, but in 1220 joined the Franciscans. Like St Francis, he is said to have preached to animals. He died in Padua, Italy, and was canonized 1232. He is popularly designated the patron saint of lost property. Feast day 13 June.

After joining the Franciscans, he sailed to Morocco, hoping to preach to the Saracens and be martyred. Illness forced him to return to Europe. In 1221 he attended the General Chapter in Assisi and thereafter taught theology at Bologna, Montepellier, Toulouse, and Puy-en-Valence, gaining a great reputation as a preacher.

Anthony, St or Anthony of Thebes (c. 251–356). Egyptian founder of Christian monasticism. At the age of 20, he renounced all his possessions and began a hermetic life of study and prayer, later seeking further solitude in a cave in the desert.

In 305 Anthony founded the first cenobitic order, a community of Christians following a rule of life under a superior. Late in his life he went to Alexandria and preached against Arianism. He lived to over 100, and a good deal is known about his life since a biography (by St Athanasius) has survived. Anthony's temptations in the desert were a popular subject in art; he is also often depicted with a pig and a bell.

All the Greeks should be free.

ANTIGONUS
Proclamation of 314 BC. Quoted in Diodorus *Library of History* bk 19, ch 61

Antigonus (382–301 BC). A general of Alexander the Great after whose death 323 BC Antigonus made himself master of Asia Minor. He was defeated and killed by Seleucus I at the battle of Ipsus.

Antiochus IV Epiphanes (lived 1st century AD). King of Commagene, son of Antiochus III. He was made king 38 by Caligula, who deposed him immediately. He was restored 41 by Claudius, and reigned as an ally of Rome against Parthia. He was deposed on suspicion of treason 72.

I am Antiochus the great king, the legitimate king, the king of the world, king of Babylon, king of all countries.

ANTIOCHUS
Royal proclamation at Babylon. Quoted in J B Pritchard *Ancient Near Eastern Texts Relating to the New Testament* p 317 1950

Antiochus thirteen kings of Syria of the Seleucid dynasty, including:

Antiochus I (c. 324–c. 261 BC). King of Syria from 281 BC, son of Seleucus I, one of the generals of Alexander the Great. He earned the title of Antiochus Soter, or Saviour, by his defeat of the Gauls in Galatia 276.

Antiochus II (c. 286–c. 246 BC). King of Syria 261–246 BC, son of Antiochus I. He was known as Antiochus Theos, 'the Divine'. During his reign the eastern provinces broke away from Graeco-Macedonian rule and set up native princes. He made peace with Egypt by marrying the daughter of Ptolemy Philadelphus, but was a tyrant among his own people.

The true Republic: men, their rights and nothing more; women, their rights and nothing less.

SUSAN ANTHONY
Motto of her newspaper *Revolution*

*ntiochus asked the Romans not to meddle in the affairs of
Asia as he had not interfered in Italian affairs.*

Polybius on ANTIOCHUS (III) THE GREAT
about his negotiations with Roman ambassadors 196 BC. bk 18, ch 51

Antiochus (III) the Great (*c.* 241–187 BC). King of Syria from
223 BC, nephew of Antiochus II. He secured a loose control over
Armenia and Parthia 209, overcame Bactria, received the homage of
the Indian king of the Kabul valley, and returned by way of the
Persian Gulf 204. He took possession of Palestine, entering
Jerusalem 198. He crossed into NW Greece, but was decisively
defeated by the Romans at Thermopylae 191 and at Magnesia 190.
The Peace of Apamea 188 BC confined Seleucid rule to Asia.

Antiochus IV (*c.* 215–164 BC). King of Syria from 175 BC, known
as Antiochus Epiphanes, 'the Illustrious', son of Antiochus III. He
occupied Jerusalem about 170, seizing much of the Temple treasure,
and instituted worship of the Greek type in the Temple in an attempt
to eradicate Judaism. This produced the revolt of the Hebrews under
the Maccabees; Antiochus died before he could suppress it.

*When we have restored our kingdom, we will confer on
you, the Jewish people, and the Temple such great
honours that your glory will be manifest the world over.*

ANTIOCHUS VII
quoted in The Bible, 1 Maccabbees 15.9

Antiochus VII (*c.* 159–129 BC). King of Syria from 138 BC. The
last strong ruler of the Seleucid dynasty, he took Jerusalem 134,
reducing the Maccabees to subjection. He was defeated and killed in
battle against the Parthians.

Antiochus XIII (lived 1st century BC). King of Syria 69–65 BC,
the last of the Seleucid dynasty. During his reign Syria was made a
Roman province by Pompey the Great.

Antoine André (1858–1943). French theatre director. Founder of
the *Théâtre Libre* 1887, he introduced to France the work of international dramatists such as Ibsen (*Ghosts*, performed there 1890) and
Strindberg (*Miss Julie*, 1893). He resigned from the company 1894,
but returned to directing 1896–1916.

Antonello da Messina (*c.* 1430–1479). Italian painter. He was
a pioneer in his country of the technique of oil painting developed by
Flemish artists; he probably acquired his knowledge of it in Naples.
Flemish influence is reflected in his brushwork, his use of light, and
sometimes in his imagery, although his sense of structure is entirely
Italian. Surviving works include bust-length portraits and sombre
religious paintings.

He visited Venice in the 1470s where his work inspired, among
other Venetian painters, the young Giovanni Bellini. His paintings
include *St Jerome in His Study* about 1460 (National Gallery,
London) and *A Young Man* 1478 (Staatliche Museum, Berlin).

Antonescu Ion (1882–1946). Romanian general and politician.
He headed a pro-German government during World War II which
enforced the Nazis' anti-Semitic policies and was executed for war
crimes 1946.

Antonescu became prime minister 1940 and seized power, forcing King Carol to abdicate and installing Carol's son Michael as
monarch. He allied Romania with Germany against the Soviet
Union. King Michael had him arrested Aug 1944; he was tried 1945
and shot 1946.

*One of the very few people whose advice in matters of
strategy Hitler was prepared to listen to.*

James Joll on ION ANTONESCU
in *Europe Since 1870* 2nd ed 1976

Antoniadi Eugène Marie (1870–1944). Turkish-born French
astronomer who demolished the theory of canals on Mars. Antoniadi
was born in Constantinople (now Istanbul). He began to make astronomical observations 1888, and in 1893 went to France to utilize
better telescopes, first at the observatory at Juvisy-sur-Orge and then
at Meudon. Detecting an apparent spot on the surface of Mars, he
soon realized that it was merely an optical effect caused by the diffraction of light by the Earth's atmosphere. There was at that time
widespread belief that there was an intricate pattern of canals on the
surface of Mars suggestive of advanced technology, as proposed
1877 by Italian astronomer Giovanni Schiaparelli. Antoniadi suggested that the canals were also an optical illusion, produced by the
eye's linking of many tiny surface details into an apparently meaningful pattern.

Antoniadi's later work included research into the behaviour and
properties of Mercury (published in *La planète Mercure/The Planet
Mercury* 1934). He then turned to a study of the history of astronomy and, in particular, the work of the ancient Greek and Egyptian
astronomers.

*Foolish wife, now that we have gained an empire we have
lost even what we had before.*

The reaction of ANTONINUS PIUS to his wife's
happiness at his accession. Quoted in *Life of Antoninus* ch 4.8

Antoninus Pius (Titus Aurelius Fulvus) (AD 86–161). Roman
emperor who had been adopted 138 as Hadrian's heir, and succeeded him later that year. He enjoyed a prosperous reign, during
which the Antonine Wall was built. His daughter Faustina the
Younger married his successor Marcus Aurelius.

Antonio Stage name of Antonio Ruiz Soler (1922–1996). Spanish
dancer, choreographer, and director. He toured the world with his
partner, Rosario. He established a National Ballet Company 1953,
choreographing in a blend of classical ballet and Spanish dance, but
is remembered primarily for his mesmerizing personality and dazzling technique as a soloist in pure Spanish dance.

Antonioni Michelangelo (1912–   ). Italian film director. He is
known for his subtle presentations of neuroses and personal relationships among the leisured classes. His elliptical approach to
narrative is best seen in *L'Avventura* 1960.

Antonioni Italian film director Michelangelo Antonioni. He established
himself in the 1950s and 1960s as a director of slow character studies of
rootless people, particularly with L'Avventura *1960 and* La Notte *1961.* Blow-
Up *1966 and* Zabriskie Point *1970 aimed to catch the flavour of the 1960s in
Britain and the USA.*

Beginning his career making documentaries, Antonioni directed his first feature film, *Cronaca di un Amore/Story of a Love Affair* 1950. His other films include *Blow-Up* 1966, *Zabriskie Point* 1970, and *The Passenger* 1975.

Suggested reading

Cameron, I and Wood, R *Antonioni* (1969)

Leprohon, Pierre *The Italian Cinema* (1972)

Aosta Duke Amadeo (1898–1942). Italian general, cousin of King Emmanuel of Italy. During World War II, he was a general of the Italian Air Force and Viceroy of Abyssinia (now Ethiopia).

He led an Italian army in an invasion of British Somaliland Aug 1940, but a British counterattack drove him back into Ethiopia where he took up a position at Amba Alagi and was forced to surrender. He was taken prisoner and sent to a camp in Kenya where he died 1942.

Aouita Said (1960–). Moroccan runner. Outstanding at middle and long distances, he won the 1984 Olympic and 1987 World Championship 5,000-metres title, and has set many world records.

In 1985 he held world records at both 1,500 and 5,000 metres, the first person for 30 years to hold both. He has since broken the 2 miles, 3,000 metres, and 2,000 metres world records.

Aoun Michel (1935–). Lebanese soldier and Maronite Christian politician, president 1988–90. As commander of the Lebanese army, he was made president without Muslim support, his appointment precipitating a civil war between Christians and Muslims. His unwillingness to accept a 1989 Arab League-sponsored peace agreement increased his isolation until the following year when he surrendered to military pressure. He left the country 1991 and was pardoned by the new government the same year.

Apelles (lived 4th century BC). Greek painter, court artist of Alexander the Great. He studied in the studio of Pamphilos at Sicyon, near Corinth, one of the centres of Greek painting, and was later employed by Philip of Macedon and Alexander, whose portrait Apelles alone was allowed to paint. No trace of his work remains and its nature can only be estimated by his reputation in the ancient world.

Realism and an ability to convey three-dimensional effect are suggested by anecdote; thus in his *Alexander wielding a Thunderbolt* the hand, according to Pliny, seemed to come out of the picture.

When painting Alexander wielding the thunderbolt, Apelles did not reproduce his complexion but made it too swarthy.

Plutarch on APELLES
Life of Alexander ch 4.3

Apollinaire Guillaume. Pen name of Guillaume Apollinaire de Kostrowitsky (1880–1918). French poet of aristocratic Polish descent. He was a leader of the avant-garde in Parisian literary and artistic circles. His novel *Le Poète assassiné/The Poet Assassinated* 1916, followed by the experimental poems *Alcools/Alcohols* 1913 and *Calligrammes/Word Pictures* 1918, show him as a representative of the Cubist and Futurist movements.

Alcools juxtaposes short lyrics, Symbolist elegies, and the 'conversation poems' and urban ironies of poetic modernism. Traditional rhetoric and discontinuity of form and tone are also displayed in *Calligrammes*, which contains love poems, war poems, manifesto poems, and ideograms.

Apollinaire's other writings include the fiction works *L'Enchanteur pourrissant* 1909 and *L'Hérésiarque et Cie* 1910; art criticism (*Les Peintres cubistes/The Cubist Painters* 1913); and erotic novels. Much of his work was published posthumously, comprising 15 volumes of poems and letters, 1920–69 (*La Femme assise* to *Lettres à Lou*).

Apollinarius of Laodicea (*c.* 310–*c.* 390). Bishop of Laodicea in Phrygia (Asia Minor). His views on the nature of Christ were condemned by the Council of Constantine 381, but he nonetheless laid the foundations for the later Nestorian controversy. Rather than seeing the nature of Jesus as a human and divine soul somehow joined in the person of Christ, he saw Christ as having a divine mind only, and not a human one.

Apollonius of Perga (*c.* 245–*c.* 190 BC). Greek mathematician, called 'the Great Geometer'. In his work *Conica/The Conics* he showed that a plane intersecting a cone will generate an ellipse, a parabola, or a hyperbola, depending on the angle of intersection. In astronomy, he used a system of circles called epicycles and deferents to explain the motion of the planets; this system, as refined by Ptolemy, was used until the Renaissance.

Apollonius proved that all sections can be obtained in any cone according to different relations of the plane to the cone.

Geminus on APOLLONIUS OF PERGA,
quoted in Eutocius' commentary on *Conics*

Apollonius of Rhodes or Apollonius Rhodius (lived 3rd century BC). Greek poet. He was the author of the epic *Argonautica*, which tells the story of Jason and the Argonauts and their quest for the Golden Fleece. A pupil of Callimachus, he was for a time head of the library at Alexandria.

Apollonius was innovative in making Medea's love for Jason an integral part of his story. It is likely that Virgil was influenced by this when he wrote about Dido's love for Aeneas.

Although he was born at Alexandria or Naucratis, he was called 'the Rhodian' because he lived much of his life in retirement at Rhodes. He had a feud with Callimachus over the merits of long epic narrative as against Callimachus's short, highly polished poems.

The soul is an immortal thing, not yours to own but Providence's. When the body wastes, like a swift horse that breaks its bonds, the soul leaps nimbly out and mingles with the air.

APOLLONIUS OF TYANA
quoted in Philostratus *Life of Apollonius* bk 8, ch 31

Apollonius of Tyana (lived 1st century AD). Greek ascetic philosopher of the neo-Pythagorean school. He travelled in Babylonia and India, where he acquired a wide knowledge of oriental religions and philosophies, and taught at Ephesus. He was said to have had miraculous powers but claimed only that he could see the future.

Painting is always a fight with yourself and the material.

KAREL APPEL
quoted in Colin Naylor (ed) *Contemporary Artists* 1989

Appel Karel Christian (1921–). Dutch painter and sculptor. He founded the Expressionist group Cobra 1948. His style employed vivid colours and vigorous brushwork, with often childlike imagery.

Appert Nicolas François (*c.* 1750–1841). French pioneer of food preservation by canning. He devised a system of sealing food in glass bottles and subjecting it to heat, described in his book *L'Art de conserver les substances animales et végétales/The Art of Preserving all Kinds of Animal and Vegetable Substances for Several Years* 1810. In 1822 he changed to using cylindrical tin-plated steel cans. In addition to his work on food preservation, Appert was responsible for the invention of the bouillon cube and he devised a method of extracting gelatin from bones without using acid.

Appia Adolphe (1862–1928). Swiss stage designer and theorist. A proponent of symbolic design, he advocated reducing the importance of the actor as well as developing the atmospheric use of theatrical lighting. His theories were expressed in *Die Musik und die Inszenierung/Music and Staging* 1899.

An admirer of Wagner, Appia rebelled against the prevailing illusionistic naturalism of the theatre of his time and advocated settings that would be 'atmospheric' rather than representational. He was the first to understand the artistic possibilities of electric stage lighting and to work out a complete theory of stage design based on it. Although he designed few productions himself, his ideas have had a great influence on modern stage practice.

Appleton Edward Victor (1892–1965). British physicist who worked at Cambridge under Ernest Rutherford from 1920. He proved the existence of the Kennelly–Heaviside layer (now called the E layer) in the atmosphere, and the Appleton layer beyond it (now the F layer), and was involved in the initial work on the atom bomb. Nobel Prize 1947, KCB 1941, GBE 1946.

Apuleius Lucius (lived 2nd century AD). Roman lawyer, philosopher, and writer. He was the author of *The Golden Ass*, or *Metamorphoses*, a prose fantasy.

Born at Madaura in North Africa, he was educated at Carthage and Athens. He travelled extensively in the East in order to become an initiate of religious mysteries, and then practised for some time as an advocate in Rome. Returning to Africa he married a rich widow, Aemilia Pudentilla, whose family charged him with having won her by magic. His defence survives: *Apologia* or *De Magia*. He was acquitted and devoted the remainder of his life to philosophy and literature. His main work, *The Golden Ass*, is the only complete Latin novel to survive.

Aquaviva Claudius (Claudio) (1543–1615). Italian monk, fifth general of the Roman Catholic monastic order of Jesuits. He entered the order in 1567 and became its head in 1581. Under his rule they greatly increased in numbers, and the revolt of the Spanish Jesuits was put down. He published a treatise on education.

All I have written seems to me like so much straw ... compared with what has been revealed to me.
ST THOMAS AQUINAS
quoted in F C Copleston *Aquinas* 1955

Aquinas St Thomas (1225–1274). Italian philosopher and theologian, the greatest figure of the school of scholasticism. He was a Dominican monk, known as the 'Angelic Doctor'. In 1879 his works were recognized as the basis of Catholic theology. His *Summa contra Gentiles/Against the Errors of the Infidels* 1259–64 argues that reason and faith are compatible. He assimilated the philosophy of Aristotle into Christian doctrine. He was canonized 1323.

His unfinished *Summa Theologica*, begun 1265, deals with the nature of God, morality, and the work of Jesus.

His works embodied the world view taught in universities until the mid-17th century, and include scientific ideas derived from Aristotle. The philosophy of Aquinas is known as *Thomism*.
Suggested reading
Copleston, F *Aquinas* (1955)
Foster, K (ed) *The Life of Saint Thomas Aquinas* (1959)
Kenny, Anthony *Aquinas* (1980)
McInerny, Ralph *Saint Thomas Aquinas* (1977)

Aquino (Maria) Corazon (born Cojuangco) (1933–). President of the Philippines 1986–92. She was instrumental in the nonviolent overthrow of President Ferdinand Marcos 1986. As president, she sought to rule in a conciliatory manner, but encountered opposition from left (communist guerrillas) and right (army coup attempts), and her land reforms were seen as inadequate.

The USA provided strong support as well and was instrumental in turning back a 1989 coup attempt. She did not contest the 1992 presidential elections, which were won by her defence secretary Fidel Ramos.

Arafat Yassir (born Mohammed Abed Ar'ouf Arafat) (1929–). Palestinian nationalist politician, cofounder of al-Fatah 1957 and president of the Palestine Liberation Organization (PLO) from 1969. His support for Saddam Hussein after Iraq's invasion of

Arafat *As leader of the Palestinian Liberation Organization, Yassir Arafat has been the focus of controversy since 1969. He has campaigned to win international recognition of the rights of Palestinians to self-determination and of the PLO as their sole political representative. In 1993 he and Israeli prime minister Yitzhak Rabin signed an accord allowing limited Palestinian autonomy.*

Kuwait 1990 weakened his international standing, but he was subsequently influential in the Middle East peace talks and in 1993 reached a historic peace accord of mutual recognition with Israel, under which the Gaza Strip and Jericho were transferred to PLO control. He returned to the former occupied territories 1994 as head of an embryonic Palestinian state, and in 1995 reached agreement on further Israeli troop withdrawals from areas in the West Bank. He took the unprecedented step Oct 1995 of inviting the terrorist organization Hamas to talks on Palestinian self-rule. He was elected president, with almost 90% of the popular vote, of the self-governing Palestinian National Council 1996.

He was awarded the 1994 Nobel Prize for Peace jointly with the then Israeli president Yitzhak Rabin and foreign minister Shimon Peres.
Suggested reading
Hart, Alan *Arafat* (1994)
Mishal, S *The PLO Under Arafat* (1986)
Wallach, John and Janet *Arafat: In The Eyes of the Beholder* (1991)

The PLO recognizes the right of the State of Israel to exist in peace and security.
YASSIR ARAFAT
on signing peace agreement with Israel, Sept 1993

Arago Dominique François Jean (1786–1853). French physicist and astronomer who made major contributions to the early study of electromagnetism. In 1820 he found that iron enclosed in a wire coil could be magnetized by the passage of an electric current. In 1824, he was the first to observe the ability of a floating copper disc to deflect a magnetic needle, the phenomenon of magnetic rotation.

From 1815, Arago worked with French physicist Augustin Fresnel on the polarization of light and was able to elucidate the fundamental laws governing it. Together they established the wave theory of light. His studies in astronomy included investigations of the solar corona and chromosphere, measurements of the diameters of the planets, and a theory that light interference is responsible for the twinkling of stars.

Aragon Louis (1897–1982). French poet and novelist. Beginning as a Dadaist, he became one of the leaders of Surrealism, published volumes of verse, and in 1930 joined the Communist Party. Taken prisoner in World War II, he escaped to join the Resistance; his experiences are reflected in the poetry of *Le Crève-coeur* 1942 and *Les Yeux d'Elsa* 1944.

His novels include the Surrealist *Le Paysan de Paris* 1926, describing the decay of the European bourgeoisie, and later social-realistic novels, including *Les Communistes* 1949–51, *La Semaine sainte* 1958, *La Mise à mort* 1965, and *Blanche, ou l'oubli* 1967.

With André Breton, he cofounded the review *Littérature* 1919; he also edited *Ce Soir* 1935–39 and *Les Lettres françaises* 1944–72, and was active in making Russian literature known in France. He was married to the novelist and critic Elsa Triolet 1896–1970.

His peculiar distinction is to have lighted upon a truth of the greatest moment ... the affinity of the Celtic to the other European languages.

Richard Garnett on EUGENE ARAM
in *Dictionary of National Biography*

Aram Eugene (1704–1759). English murderer, the subject of works by the English novelist Edward Bulwer-Lytton, the English poet Thomas Hood, and others. He was a schoolmaster in Knaresborough, Yorkshire, and achieved some distinction as a philologist. In 1745 he was tried and acquitted on a charge concerned with the disappearance of a local shoemaker. Later a skeleton was discovered in a cave at Knaresborough. He was tried at York, convicted and hanged.

Arany János (1817–1882). Hungarian writer. His comic epic *The Lost Constitution* 1846 was followed 1847 by *Toldi*, a product of the popular nationalist school. In 1864 his epic masterpiece *The Death of King Buda* appeared. During his last years Arany produced the rest of the *Toldi* trilogy, and his most personal lyrics.

Aratus of Sicyon (271–213 BC). Greek soldier and politician. He was instrumental in the growth of the Achaean League, the political and military confederation of Greek cities, and prevented its disintegration under pressure from Macedon and Sparta in 224 BC.

Aratus was born at Sicyon. His father was put to death by the tyrant Abantidas 266, and he was brought up at Argos. At the age of 20 he freed Sicyon and brought that city into the Achaean League, whose general he became 245.

Arbenz Guzmán Jácobo (1913–1971). Guatemalan social democratic politician and president from 1951 until his overthrow 1954 by rebels operating with the help of the CIA.

Guzmán brought in policies to redistribute land, much of which was owned by overseas companies, to landless peasants; he also encouraged labour organization. His last years were spent in exile in Mexico, Uruguay, and Cuba.

Roscoe always said, I'll make it, darling, and you spend it.

FATTY (ROSCOE) ARBUCKLE
quoted by his wife, Minta Dufee.

Arbuckle Fatty (Roscoe Conkling) (1887–1933). US silent-film comedian; also a writer and director. His successful career in such films as *The Butcher Boy* 1917 and *The Hayseed* 1919 ended 1921 after a sex-party scandal in which a starlet died.

Arbus Diane (1923–1971). US photographer. Although she practised as a fashion photographer for 20 years, Arbus is best known for her later work which examined the fringes of American society: the misfits, the eccentrics, and the bizarre. Her work has been attacked as cruel and voyeuristic, but it is essentially sympathetic in its unflinching curiosity. *A Box of Ten Photographs*, a limited edition of her work, was published 1970.

Arbuthnot John (1667–1735). Scottish writer and physician. He attended Prince George and then Queen Anne 1705–14. He was a friend of Alexander Pope, Thomas Gray, and Jonathan Swift and was the chief author of the satiric *Memoirs of Martinus Scriblerus* 1741. He created the English national character of John Bull, a prosperous farmer, in his 'History of John Bull' 1712, pamphlets advocating peace with France.

Born at Arbuthnott, Kincardineshire, he studied at Aberdeen, Oxford, and St Andrews universities, where he obtained the first recorded MD degree 1696.

He also wrote 'A Treatise concerning the Altercation or Scolding of the Ancients' and 'The Art of Political Lying', the style of which is modelled on Swift, but without his ferocity.

Law is a bottomless pit.

JOHN ARBUTHNOT
The History of John Bull 1712

Arch Joseph (1826–1919). English Radical member of Parliament and trade unionist, founder of the National Agricultural Union (the first of its kind) 1872.

Archer Frederick (1857–1886). English jockey. He rode 2,748 winners in 8,084 races 1870–86, including 21 classic winners.

He won the Derby five times, Oaks four times, St Leger six times, the Two Thousand Guineas four times, and the One Thousand Guineas twice. He rode 246 winners in the 1885 season, a record that stood until 1933. Archer shot himself in a fit of depression.

War and Peace maddens me because I didn't write it myself, and worse, I couldn't.

JEFFREY ARCHER
'The Spell of Words' in Brian Redhead and
Kenneth McLeish *The Anti-Booklist* 1981

Archer Jeffrey Howard, Baron Archer of Weston-super-Mare (1940–). English writer and politician. A Conservative member of Parliament 1969–74, he lost a fortune in a disastrous investment, but recouped it as a best-selling novelist and dramatist. His books, which often concern the rise of insignificant characters to high political office or great business success, include *Not a Penny More, Not a Penny Less* 1975 and *First Among Equals* 1984. Created a baron 1992.

In 1985 he became deputy chair of the Conservative Party but resigned Nov 1986 after a scandal involving an alleged payment to a prostitute.

Archer John Lee (1791–1852). Irish-born architect and engineer in Australia. His many Regency buildings in Tasmania did much to establish the island's English character and include the Anglesea Barracks 1828, the Customs House, Hobart, 1835, and St Luke's church, Campbell Town, 1836.

Archer Thomas (1668–1743). English architect. He is noted for his interpretations of Italian Baroque, which he studied at first hand during a continental Grand Tour 1691–95. He was active 1703–15, after which he took up the post of Controller of Customs at Newcastle. Notable among his designs are the north front of Chatsworth House 1704–05, the church of St John, Smith Square, London, 1714–28, and the cathedral of St Philip, Birmingham, 1710–15.

Archibald Jules François (1815–1919). Australian journalist. He was one of the founders of the *Bulletin*, and was its editor from 1902 to 1904. His will provided for the Archibald Prize and for the Archibald Memorial which stands in Hyde Park, Sydney, in commemoration of the joint action of Australian and French troops during World War I.

Archimedes (*c.* 287–212 BC). Greek mathematician who made major discoveries in geometry, hydrostatics, and mechanics. He formulated a law of fluid displacement (Archimedes' principle), and is credited with the invention of the Archimedes screw, a cylindrical device for raising water.

Archimedes was born in Syracuse, Sicily. He designed engines of war for the defence of Syracuse, and was killed when the Romans seized the town. It is alleged that Archimedes' principle was discovered when he stepped into the public bath and saw the water overflow. He was so delighted that he rushed home naked, crying 'Eureka! Eureka!' ('I have found it! I have found it!'). He used his discovery to prove that the goldsmith of Hieron II, King of Syracuse, had adulterated a gold crown with silver.

Suggested reading
Dijksterhuis, E J *Archimedes* (1956)
Farrington, Benjamin *Greek Science* (1953)

Archipenko Alexander (1887–1964). Ukrainian-born abstract sculptor. He lived in France from 1908 and in the USA from 1923. He pioneered Cubist works, experimenting with sculptures in which 'negative form' (holes, voids, and spaces) is as significant as solid form. He also made polychrome reliefs, and later experimented with clear plastic and sculptures incorporating lights.

By experimenting with new materials and by making space, light, and colour important, Archipenko greatly influenced the development of 20th-century sculpture.

Arcimboldo Giuseppe (*c.* 1530–1593). Italian painter and designer. He is known for his fantastical portraits, human in form but composed of fruit, plant, and animal details. He also designed tapestries and was a successful portrait painter at the court of Rudolf II in Prague. The Surrealists helped to revive interest in his symbolic portraits, which were considered in bad taste at the time of their conception.

Arden Elizabeth. Adopted name of Florence Nightingale Graham (1884–1966). Canadian-born US beauty expert and mass merchandiser. Born in Woodbridge, Ontario, she moved to New York 1908. Possessing an extraordinary business sense, she opened a beauty salon 1910 and expanded the firm in 1914 under the corporate name of 'Elizabeth Arden', a name she soon adopted herself. She developed and merchandised a line of cosmetic products and also utilized new techniques of mass advertising to introduce her products to the public. She later opened a chain of beauty salons and spas throughout the USA.

Arden John (1930–). English dramatist. His early plays *Serjeant Musgrave's Dance* 1959 and *The Workhouse Donkey* 1963 contain trenchant social criticism and show the influence of Brecht. Subsequent works, often written in collaboration with his wife, Margaretta D'Arcy, express increasing concern with the political situation in Northern Ireland and dissatisfaction with the professional and subsidized theatre world.

Arden was born at Barnsley and educated at King's College, Cambridge, and Edinburgh College of Art, where he qualified as an architect. He first came to attention with a prize-winning radio play, *The Life of Man* 1956. This was followed by *The Waters of Babylon* 1957 and *Live Like Pigs* 1958, both produced at the Royal Court Theatre. *Serjeant Musgrave's Dance* is generally regarded as his finest work; it deals with the realities of war and the tragically unsuccessful attempt by a group of deserters to act effectively against those guilty of encouraging war.

Later plays include *The Happy Haven* 1960 (written with Margaretta d'Arcy), *Armstrong's Last Goodnight* 1964, adventurously extending the techniques and political concerns of *Serjeant Musgrave's Dance*, and *Left-handed Liberty* 1965. *The Island of the Mighty* provoked considerable controversy when performed by the Royal Shakespeare Company 1973.

Ardizzone Edward (1900–1979). British illustrator, author, and teacher. A prolific artist, he illustrated over 180 books, and as an official war artist during World War II he completed some 520 works 1940–45. He was author of the 'Tim' series of children's books, the first of which was *Little Tim and the Brave Sea Captain* 1936.

Under conditions of tyranny it is far easier to act than to think.

HANNAH ARENDT
quoted by W H Auden *A Certain World* 1970

Arendt Hannah (1906–1975). German-born US political philosopher. Her concerns included totalitarianism, the nature of evil, and the erosion of public participation in the political process. Her works include *Eichmann in Jerusalem* 1963 and *On Violence* 1972.

In *The Origins of Modern Totalitarianism* 1951, she pointed out the similarities between Nazism and Soviet communism, and in her report of the trial of a leading Nazi war criminal, *Eichmann in Jerusalem*, she coined the phrase 'the banality of evil' to describe how bureaucratic efficiency can facilitate the acceptance of the most terrible deeds.

Suggested reading
Ettinger, Elzbieta *Hannah Arendt/Martin Heidegger* (1995)
Kateb, George *Hannah Arendt: Politics, Conscience, Evil* (1984)
May, Derwent *Hannah Arendt* (1986)
Villa, Dana *Arendt and Heidegger* (1995)
Young-Bruehl, Elisabeth *Hannah Arendt: For Love of the World* (1982)

Aretino Pietro (1492–1556). Italian writer. He earned his living, both in Rome and Venice, by publishing satirical pamphlets while under the protection of a highly placed family. His 'Letters' 1537–57 are a unique record of the cultural and political events of his time, and illustrate his vivacious, exuberant character. He also wrote poems and comedies.

Aretino, born in Arezzo, began as a protégé of Pope Leo X, but left Rome after the publication of his lewd verses. He settled in Venice, and quickly became known as the 'Scourge of Princes' with his vicious satires on powerful contemporaries; he was also well paid for not taking up his pen.

Arevalo Bermejo Juan José (1904–1990). Guatemalan president 1945–51, elected to head a civilian government after a popular revolt ended a 14-year period of military rule. However, many of his liberal reforms were later undone by subsequent military rulers.

Argand Jean-Robert (1768–1822). Swiss mathematician who 1806 invented a method of geometrically representing complex numbers and their operations – the *Argand diagram*. Argand's book *Essai sur une manière de représenter les quantités imaginaires dans les constructions géométriques* 1806 was published anonymously and it was not until 1813 that he became known as the author.

Argelander Friedrich Wilhelm August (1799–1875). Prussian astronomer who made a catalogue of 324,198 stars in the northern hemisphere, the *Bonner Durchmusterung/Bonn Survey* 1859–62. This catalogued the position and brightness of nearly 324,000 stars, and although it was the last major catalogue to be produced without the aid of photography, its value is such that it was reprinted as recently as 1950. His *Uranometrica nova* 1843 introduced the 'estimation by steps' method for determining stellar magnitudes with the naked eye.

Argentina La. Stage name of Antonia Merce (1890–1936). Argentine Spanish dancer, choreographer, and director. She took her artistic name from the land of her birth. Through the brilliance of her personality and sparkling technique, she became one of the most famous exponents of Spanish dance. She was also known for the sensitive technique of her castanet playing.

Argyll line of Scottish peers who trace their descent to the Campbells of Lochow. The earldom dates from 1457.

It was created by James I, who conferred the title on Lord Campbell (died 1493), from whom the greatness of the family dates. The 2nd Earl was killed at Flodden, the 3rd Earl died 1530, whilst the 4th Earl was the first of the great Scottish nobility to become Protestant. Successors include:

Argyll Archibald Campbell, 5th Earl of Argyll (1530–1573). Adherent of the Scottish presbyterian John Knox. A supporter of Mary Queen of Scots from 1561, he commanded her forces after her escape from Lochleven Castle 1568. Following her defeat at Langside, he revised his position, made peace with the regent, James Stuart, Earl of Murray, and became Lord High Chancellor of Scotland 1572. Succeeded to earldom 1558.

Argyris Chris (1923–). US psychologist who specialized in the personal development of individuals within organizations and the defence mechanisms managers employ to resist change. He developed the 'goal congruence theory' 1964, which stated that organizational design should ensure that the individual's needs for personal development are matched with the organization's needs for productivity.

Argyris was professor at Yale, moving to Harvard 1971. He has also worked as a consultant to industry, notably for IBM, Shell, and Du Pont, as well as for government departments in the USA and Europe.

Arias Sanchez Oscar (1940–). Costa Rican politician, president 1986–90, secretary general of the left-wing National Liberation Party (PLN) from 1979. He advocated a neutralist policy and in 1987 was the leading promoter of the Central American Peace Plan. He lost the presidency to Rafael Angel Calderón 1990. He was awarded the Nobel Prize for Peace 1987.

Arion (lived 7th century BC). Greek writer, reputedly the first to introduce choral works known as dithyrambs. He returned to the court of Periander of Corinth after visiting Italy and Sicily.

Legend records that he was saved from drowning by a dolphin, which was charmed by his song.

Ariosto Ludovico (1474–1533). Italian poet. He wrote Latin poems and comedies on Classical lines. His major work is the poem *Orlando furioso* 1516, published 1532, an epic treatment of the Roland story, the perfect poetic expression of the Italian Renaissance.

He was frequently engaged in ambassadorial missions and diplomacy for the Duke of Ferrara, whose service he entered 1518. In 1521 he became governor of Garfagnana, a province in the Apennines, where he was mostly occupied in suppressing bandits and enforcing order. After three years he retired to Ferrara to work on the final revision of *Orlando furioso*.

Ariosto's great work perfects and enriches the half satiric, fantastic, yet restrained manner which Boiardo had employed. It is remarkable the zest which he was able to sustain on such a huge scale. He also completed four comedies, seven satires in the style of Horace, some Latin poems, a prose dialogue on the subject of hygiene, *Rime* (sonnets and other poems), and *Cinque canti*, five cantos withheld from *Orlando furioso*.

Aristagoras (died 497 BC). Tyrant of the ancient Greek city of Miletus in SW Asia Minor. He incited a revolt of the Ionian Greeks against the Persians 499 BC, involving Athens in the conflict, which led to the Persian Wars of 499–449 BC and the end of Persian dominance in the ancient world.

He was the brother-in-law of Histiaeus, for whom he acted as regent during the latter's absence at the Persian court. Having failed in an attack upon Naxos, and thereby fallen into disfavour with the Persians, Aristagoras raised the whole of Ionia in revolt.

The moon receives its light from the sun.

ARISTARCHUS OF SAMOS
Magnitudes and Distances of the Sun and Moon 1

Aristarchus of Samos (*c.* 320–*c.* 250 BC). Greek astronomer. The first to argue that the Earth moves around the Sun, he was ridiculed for his beliefs. He was also the first astronomer to estimate (quite inaccurately) the sizes of the Sun and Moon and their distances from the Earth.

Aristide Jean-Bertrand (1953–). President of Haiti Dec 1990–Oct 1991 and from Oct 1994. A left-wing Catholic priest opposed to the right-wing regime of the Duvalier family, he campaigned for the National Front for Change and Democracy, representing a loose coalition of peasants, trade unionists, and clerics, and won 70% of the vote. He was deposed by the military Sept 1991 and took refuge in the United States. In Sept 1994, under an agreement brokered by former US president Jimmy Carter, the military stepped down and allowed Aristide to return. He later relinquished his priesthood to concentrate on the presidency.

Aristides (*c.* 530–468 BC). Athenian politician. He was one of the ten Athenian generals at the battle of Marathon 490 BC and was elected chief archon, or magistrate. Later he came into conflict with the democratic leader Themistocles, and was exiled about 483 BC. He returned to fight against the Persians at Salamis 480 BC and in the following year commanded the Athenians at Plataea. As commander of the Athenian fleet he established the alliance of Ionian states known as the Delian League.

I don't even know the man, but I am fed up of hearing him called the Just.

Comment of an illiterate man whom ARISTIDES had just assisted in voting for his exile, quoted in Plutarch *Life of Aristides* 7:6

Aristippus (*c.* 435–356 BC). Greek philosopher, founder of the Cyrenaic or hedonist school. A pupil of Socrates, he developed the doctrine that pleasure is the highest good in life. He lived at the court of Dionysius of Syracuse and then with Laïs, a courtesan, in Corinth.

His doctrines were taught after his death by his daughter Arete, and later by her son, Aristippus the Younger.

Our poet says that he deserves a rich reward at your hands for having stopped you being too easily deceived by the words of foreigners, taking pleasure in flattery, being citizens of Emptyhead.

ARISTOPHANES
Autobiographical comment put into mouths of the chorus in *Acharnians* lines 633–5

Aristophanes (*c.* 448–380 BC). Greek comedy dramatist. Of his 11 extant plays (of a total of over 40), the early comedies are remarkable for the violent satire with which he ridiculed the democratic war leaders. He also satirized contemporary issues such as the new learning of Socrates in *The Clouds* 423 BC and the obsession with war, with the sex-strike of women in *Lysistrata* 411 BC. The chorus plays a prominent role, frequently giving the play its title, as in *The Wasps* 422, *The Birds* 414, and *The Frogs* 405.

The first evil he attacked was the Peloponnesian War, to which he ascribed the influence of such demagogues as Cleon at Athens; other objects of his indignation include the excessive love of litigation at Athens (*The Wasps*). His other surviving plays are: *The Acharnians* 425, *The Knights* 424, *The Peace* 421, *Thesmophoriazusae* 410, *Ecclesiazusae* 393, and *Plutus* 388. Aristophanes was a master of the Attic dialect. His dramatic greatness lies in his wit and humanitarian feeling, which insists that, in spite of their aberrations, humans are essentially wholesome creatures.

Aristophanes was probably born in Athens. His father had property in Aegina, and may originally have come from there; hence the doubt as to whether Aristophanes was a genuine Athenian citizen and Cleon's attempt to deprive him of his civic rights. He had three sons, but nothing else is known of his private life.

Aristotle (384–322 BC). Greek philosopher who advocated reason and moderation. He maintained that sense experience is our only source of knowledge, and that by reasoning we can discover the essences of things, that is, their distinguishing qualities. In his works on ethics and politics, he suggested that human happiness consists in living in conformity with nature. He derived his political theory from the recognition that mutual aid is natural to humankind, and refused to set up any one constitution as universally ideal. Of Aristotle's works some 22 treatises survive, dealing with logic, metaphysics, physics, astronomy, meteorology, biology, psychology, ethics, politics, and literary criticism.

Aristotle was born in Stagira in Thrace and studied in Athens, where he became a distinguished member of the Academy founded by Plato. He then opened a school at Assos. At this time he regarded himself as a Platonist, but his subsequent thought led him further from the traditions that had formed his early background and he was later critical of Plato. In about 344 he moved to Mytilene in Lesvos, and devoted the next two years to the study of natural history. Meanwhile, during his residence at Assos, he had married Pythias, niece and adopted daughter of Hermeias, ruler of Atarneus.

In 342 he accepted an invitation from Philip II of Macedon to go to Pella as tutor to Philip's son Alexander the Great. In 335 he opened a school in the Lyceum (grove sacred to Apollo) in Athens. It became known as the 'peripatetic school' because he walked up and down as he talked, and his works are a collection of his lecture notes. When Alexander died 323, Aristotle was forced to flee to Chalcis, where he died.

Among his many contributions to political thought were the first systematic attempts to distinguish between different forms of government, ideas about the role of law in the state, and the conception of a science of politics.

In the *Poetics*, Aristotle defines tragic drama as an imitation (mimesis) of the actions of human beings, with character subordinated to plot. The audience is affected by pity and fear, but experiences a purgation (catharsis) of these emotions through watching the play. The second book of the *Poetics*, on comedy, is lost. The three books of the *Rhetoric* form the earliest analytical discussion of the techniques of persuasion, and the last presents a theory of the emotions to which a speaker must appeal.

In the Middle Ages, Aristotle's philosophy first became the foundation of Islamic philosophy, and was then incorporated into Christian theology; medieval scholars tended to accept his vast output without question. Aristotle held that all matter consisted of a single 'prime matter', which was always determined by some form. The simplest kinds of matter were the four elements – earth, water, air, and fire – which in varying proportions constituted all things. According to Aristotle's laws of motion, bodies moved upwards or downwards in straight lines. Earth and water fell, air and fire rose. To explain the motion of the heavenly spheres, Aristotle introduced a fifth element, ether, whose natural movement was circular.

His works were lost to Europe after the decline of Rome, but they were reintroduced in the Middle Ages by Arab and Jewish scholars and became the basis of medieval scholasticism.

Suggested reading
Ackrill, J L *Aristotle the Philosopher* (1981)
Allan, D J *The Philosophy of Aristotle* (1970)
Barnes, Jonathan *Aristotle* (1982)
Grene, Marjorie *A Portrait of Aristotle* (1963)
Ferguson, John *Aristotle* (1972)
Lear, Jonathan *Aristotle* (1988)

Arius (*c.* 256–336). Egyptian priest whose ideas gave rise to Arianism, a Christian belief that denied the complete divinity of Jesus.

Arius was born in Libya and became a priest in Alexandria 311. In 318 he was excommunicated and fled to Palestine, but his theology spread to such an extent that the Roman emperor Constantine called a council at Nicaea 325 to resolve the question. Arius and his adherents were condemned and banished.

The heresy of Arius, in a less well developed form, had long been current in Antioch, where he had received his education. He denied that the Son was consubstantial with the Father, though affirming that he was begotten before time, and that by him the Father created all things. Arius's aim was to prevent the idea of there being two Gods; and to avoid this he described the Son as a created Being, though far surpassing all others.

When Arius was excommunicated, many of the bishops favoured him, and the chief of his supporters was Eusebius, Bishop of Nicomedia, who had been his fellow student at Antioch. Arius was a skilled propagandist, and in his *Thalia* he explained his doctrines in verse set to music. The controversy soon reached Rome, and Constantine, not realizing the importance of the dogma in debate, at first made efforts for a compromise. When this failed, he called the first ecumenical council at Nicaea 325.

Athanasius, then deacon of Alexandria, was the chief exponent of the orthodox view, which insisted that the Son was 'of the same substance' (*homoousios*) with the Father, and the battle raged around this word. Arius was condemned and banished to Illyria, while the orthodox (Nicene) creed was promulgated. The continued support of Eusebius of Nicomedia achieved the recall of Arius 330, and he secured the ear of the emperor. Constantine, finding it impossible to compel Athanasius, now Bishop of Alexandria, to reinstate the heretic, banished him to Gaul 335. At last, in 336, Alexander, Bishop of Constantinople, was persuaded to consent reluctantly to admit Arius to communion, but before this was done Arius was taken suddenly ill and died.

Arianism became practically extinct in the empire before the end of the 4th century. For about 200 years longer it lingered among the Goths and other Teutonic tribes who had received Christianity from Arian missionaries, the chief of whom was Ulfilas.

Arjan Indian religious leader, fifth guru (teacher) of Sikhism 1581–1606. He built the Golden Temple in Amritsar and compiled the *Adi Granth*, the first volume of Sikh scriptures. He died in Muslim custody.

Arkwright Richard (1732–1792). English inventor and manufacturing pioneer who developed a machine for spinning cotton (he called it a 'spinning frame') 1768. He set up a water-powered spinning factory 1771 and installed steam power in a Nottingham factory 1790. Knighted 1786.

In 1773 Arkwright produced the first cloth made entirely from cotton; previously, the warp had been of linen and only the weft was cotton. A special Act of Parliament was passed 1774 to exempt Arkwright's fabric from the double duty imposed on cottons by an act of 1736. By 1782 Arkwright employed 5,000 workers.

It is a sorry business to inquire into what men think,
when we are every day ... confronted with what they do.

MICHAEL ARLEN
'The Three Cornered Moon'

Arlen Michael. Adopted name of Dikran Kuyumjian (1895–1956). Bulgarian writer of Armenian descent. He became a naturalized British subject 1922. His best-selling novel, *The Green Hat* 1924, reflected the stylishly irresponsible spirit of the 1920s.

His other books include *Ghost Stories* 1927, *Lily Christine* 1928, and *Hell! said the Duchess* 1934.

The London Venture 1920 was his first book, and two years later his *Piracy* was favourably received. Among his other novels and collections of stories are *These Charming People* 1923, *May Fair* 1925, *Young Men in Love* 1929, *Babes in the World* 1930, *Men Dislike Women* 1931, and *Flying Dutchman* 1939. He also wrote four plays, including a dramatization of *The Green Hat*. He died in New York.

Armani Giorgio (1935–   ). Italian fashion designer. He launched his first menswear collection 1974 and the following year started designing women's clothing. His work is known for understated styles, and fine fabrics. He pioneered the 'unstructured jacket' and his designs are marketed under different labels, from exclusive models to the less expensive diffusion range.

Arminius Latin form of Hermann (17 BC–AD 19). German chieftain of the Cherusci tribe. An ex-soldier of the Roman army, he annihilated a Roman force led by Quintilius Varus in the Teutoburger Forest area AD 9, and saved Germany from becoming a Roman province. He was later treacherously killed by some of his kinsmen.

Arminius is regarded as a German national hero and a monument to his memory was unveiled near Detmold 1875.

If you prefer your country, parents and traditions to foreign domination, follow Arminius to glory and freedom.

Tacitus on ARMINIUS
in *Annals* bk 1, ch 59

Arminius Jacobus. Latinized name of Jakob Harmensen (1560–1609). Dutch Protestant priest who founded Arminianism, a school of Christian theology opposed to John Calvin's doctrine of predestination. His views were developed by Simon Episcopius (1583–1643). Arminianism is the basis of Wesleyan Methodism.

Arminius was born in S Holland, ordained in Amsterdam 1588, and from 1603 was professor of theology at Leyden. He asserted that forgiveness and eternal life are bestowed on all who repent of their sins and sincerely believe in Jesus Christ. He was drawn into many controversies, and his followers were expelled from the church and persecuted.

Armstrong Edwin Howard (1890–1954). US radio engineer who developed a system known as superheterodyne tuning for reception over a very wide spectrum of radio frequencies and frequency modulation (FM) radio transmission for static-free reception.

Armstrong became a professor at Columbia University. He was involved in much litigation over patents and eventually killed himself.

Armstrong Gillian May (1950–). Australian writer and director of films and documentaries. Her first feature film *My Brilliant Career* 1980 established her concern with the theme of female role models. Her subsequent Australian films include *High Tide* 1987, and *Last Days of Chez Nous* 1992, while in the US she has made *Mrs Soffel* 1984, and a popular adaptation of Louisa M Alcott's *Little Women* 1995.

Armstrong Henry, 'Homicide Hank' (born Henry Jackson) (1912–1988). US boxer. He was the only man to hold world titles at three different weights simultaneously. Between May and Nov 1938 he held the feather-, welter-, and lightweight titles. He retired 1945 and became a Baptist minister.

Making money ain't nothing exciting to me. You might be able to buy a little better booze than the wino on the corner. But you get sick just like the next cat and when you die you're just as graveyard dead.

LOUIS ARMSTRONG
quoted in *Observer* 5 July 1970

Armstrong Louis ('Satchmo') (1901–1971). US jazz cornet and trumpet player and singer. His Chicago recordings in the 1920s with the Hot Five and Hot Seven brought him recognition for his warm and pure trumpet tone, his skill at improvisation, and his quirky, gravelly voice. From the 1930s he also appeared in films.

Armstrong was born in New Orleans. In 1923 he joined the Creole Jazz Band led by the cornet player Joe 'King' Oliver in Chicago, but soon broke away and fronted various bands of his own. In 1947 he formed the Louis Armstrong All-Stars. He firmly established the pre-eminence of the virtuoso jazz soloist. He is also credited with the invention of scat singing.

Suggested reading
Armstrong, Louis *Satchmo: My Life in New Orleans* (1954)
Colliet, James Lincoln *Louis Armstrong: An American Genius* (1983)
Jones, M and Chilton, J *Louis* (1971)
Pinfold, M *Louis Armstrong: His Life and Times* (1987)

Armstrong Neil Alden (1930–). US astronaut. In 1969, he became the first person to set foot on the Moon, and said, 'That's one small step for a man, one giant leap for mankind.' The Moon landing was part of the Apollo project.

Born in Ohio, Armstrong gained his pilot's licence at 16, studied aeronautics at Purdue University, and served as a naval pilot in Korea 1949–52 before joining NASA as a test pilot. He joined the US National Aerospace Program 1962, and commanded *Gemini 8* March 1966, linking with an unmanned *Agena* rocket. With Edwin 'Buzz' Aldrin and Michael Collins in *Apollo 11* on 16 July 1969, he lifted off from Cape Kennedy to land, four days later, on the Moon.

They collected soil samples, explored, and set up scientific instruments during $21\frac{1}{2}$ hours on the lunar surface.

Armstrong Robert Temple. Baron Armstrong of Ilminster (1927–). British civil servant, cabinet secretary in Margaret Thatcher's government. He achieved notoriety as a key witness in the *Spycatcher* trial in Australia 1987. Defending the British Government's attempts to prevent Peter Wright's book alleging 'dirty tricks' from being published, he admitted to having sometimes been 'economical with the truth'.

In 1970 he became Prime Minister Edward Heath's principal private secretary; Thatcher later made him cabinet secretary and head of the home civil service. He retired 1988 and was made a life peer.

Armstrong William George. Baron Armstrong of Cragside (1810–1900). English engineer. He developed hydraulic equipment and a revolutionary method of making gun barrels 1855, by building a breech-loading artillery piece with a steel and wrought-iron barrel (previous guns were muzzle-loaded and had cast-bronze barrels). By 1880 the 150-mm/16-in Armstrong gun was the standard for all British ordnance. In 1850 Armstrong invented the hydraulic pressure accumulator. It consisted of a large cylinder containing a piston that could be loaded to any desired pressure, the water being pumped in below it by a steam engine or other prime mover. This device made possible the installation of hydraulic power in almost any situation, and it was particularly used for the manipulation of heavy naval guns. Created a baron 1887.

Arnauld (1560–1619). French advocate of Jansenism. Strongly critical of the Jesuits, he produced not only Jansenist pamphlets, but works on logic, grammar, and geometry. Many of his 20 children were associated with the abbey of Port Royal, which became the centre of Jansenism. His youngest child was *Antoine*, 'the great Arnauld'.

For years Arnauld had to live in hiding, and the last 16 years of his life were spent in Brussels.

Arne Thomas Augustine (1710–1778). English composer of incidental music for theatre who introduced opera in the Italian manner to the London stage with works such as *Artaxerxes* 1762, revised 1777. He is remembered for the songs 'Where the bee sucks' from *The Tempest* 1746, 'Blow, blow thou winter wind' from *As You Like It* 1740, and 'Rule Britannia!' from the masque *Alfred* 1740.

Arne produced his first opera, *Rosamond*, 1733. He wrote music for Henry Fielding's *Tom Thumb*, William Congreve's *Judgement of Paris*, and John Milton's *Comus*. In 1744 he was appointed composer to the Drury Lane theatre, and in 1745 composer to the Vauxhall Gardens. In 1746 he supplied music for the masque *Neptune and Amphitrite* and the songs in *The Tempest*. He composed two oratorios, *Abel* and *Judith*. In 1760 he became composer to Covent Garden theatre, where his popular dramatic pastoral *Thomas and Sally* was produced. He was buried at St Paul's, Covent Garden.

Arne's dramatic works are very numerous. He also wrote some church music, cantatas, odes, overtures, concertos, sonatas, and songs. His son Michael (c. 1740–1786) was also a composer, mainly for the stage.

Arne had kept bad company: he had written for vulgar singers and hearers too long to be able to comport himself properly at the opera-house, in the first circle of taste and fashion.

Charles Burney on THOMAS ARNE
in *A General History of Music*, 1776

Arnim Jurgen von (1889–1971). German general in World War II. He commanded a division during the invasion of the USSR 1941 and then a corps. Late in 1942 he was appointed to command the 5th Panzer Army in Africa, and in March 1943 became commander Army Group Afrika and commander in chief of German Forces in Tunisia. With his supply lines cut, he was unable to stem the Allied advance and surrendered 12 May 1942. He remained a prisoner until the end of the war.

Arnim Ludwig Achim von (1781–1831). German Romantic poet and novelist. Born in Berlin, he wrote short stories, a romance (*Gräfin Dolores*/*Countess Dolores* 1810), and plays, but left the historical novel *Die Kronenwächter* 1817 unfinished. With Clemens Brentano he collected the German folk songs in *Des Knaben Wunderhorn*/*The Boy's Magic Horn* 1805–08, several of which were set to music by Mahler.

Arnold Benedict (1741–1801). US soldier and military strategist who, during the American Revolution, won the turning-point battle at Saratoga 1777 for the Americans. He is chiefly remembered as a traitor to the American side, having plotted to betray the strategic post at West Point to the British. Since the plot failed, he was paid only a fraction of the money promised him.

Somewhere there waiteth in this world of ours / For one lone soul another lonely soul, / Each choosing each through all the weary hours, / And meeting strangely at one sudden goal.

EDWIN ARNOLD
'Somewhere There Waiteth'

Arnold Edwin (1832–1904). English scholar and poet. He wrote *The Light of Asia* 1879, a rendering of the life and teaching of the Buddha in blank verse. *The Light of the World* 1891 retells the life of Jesus. CSI 1877, KCIE 1888.

Arnold was born in Gravesend and educated at King's School, Rochester; King's College, London; and University College, Oxford, where he gained the Newdigate prize for a poem on Belshazzar's feast 1852. He went to India as a schoolmaster and later became a journalist, joining the staff of the *Daily Telegraph*, of which he was ultimately editor. He was largely responsible for sending Henry Morton Stanley to the Congo.

Arnold Henry ('Hap') (1886–1950). US general and aviator; he was largely responsible for preparing the US aviation industry for the war and the training programme which allowed the air corps to expand. A firm believer in the ability of bombing to win wars, he favoured attacking specific targets rather than bombing whole areas.

In 1936 he became assistant chief of the US Army Air Corps and in 1938 Chief of the Air Staff. He then served on the US Joint Chiefs of Staff Committee and the Allied Combined Chiefs of Staff Committee. He was promoted to general of the army 1944, and when the US Army Air Corps was disbanded upon the formation of the US Air Force 1947, he became the first five star commanding general of the Air Force.

Arnold Malcolm Henry (1921–). English composer. His work is tonal and includes a large amount of orchestral, chamber, ballet, and vocal music. His overtures *Beckus the Dandipratt* 1948, *A Sussex Overture* 1951, and *Tam O'Shanter* 1955 are well known. His operas include *The Dancing Master* 1951, and he has written music for more than 80 films, including *The Bridge on the River Kwai* 1957, for which he won an Academy Award.

Arnold was born in Northampton and studied at the Royal College of Music in London. He began his career as a trumpeter, becoming principal trumpet in the London Philharmonic Orchestra. He soon became known for his witty, high-spirited, and well-designed compositions.

Culture, the acquainting ourselves with the best that has been known and said in the world, and thus with the history of the human spirit.

MATTHEW ARNOLD
Literature and Dogma preface to 1873 ed

Arnold Matthew (1822–1888). English poet and critic. His poem 'Dover Beach' 1867 was widely regarded as one of the most eloquent expressions of the spiritual anxieties of Victorian England. The critical essays collected in *Culture and Anarchy* 1869 were highly influential.

Arnold's poems, characterized by their elegiac mood and pastoral themes, include 'The Forsaken Merman' 1849, 'Sohrab and Rustum' 1853, 'Thyrsis' 1867 (commemorating his friend Arthur Hugh Clough), and 'The Scholar-Gipsy' 1853. His *Essays in Criticism* were published 1865 and 1888, and *Literature and Dogma*, on biblical interpretation, 1872. In *Culture and Anarchy* he attacked the smugness and philistinism of the Victorian middle classes, and argued for a new culture based on the pursuit of artistic and intellectual values.
Suggested reading
Anderson, W D *Arnold and the Classical Tradition* (1965)
Bush, Douglas *Matthew Arnold* (1971)
Holloway, John *The Victorian Sage* (1953)
Honan, P *Matthew Arnold: A Life* (1981)
Trilling, Lionel *Matthew Arnold* (1949)

The same heart beats in every human breast.

MATTHEW ARNOLD
'The Buried Life'

Arnold Thomas (1795–1842). English schoolmaster, father of the poet and critic Matthew Arnold. He was headmaster of Rugby School 1828–42. His regime has been graphically described in Thomas Hughes's *Tom Brown's Schooldays* 1857. He emphasized training of character, and had a profound influence on public school education.

My object will be, if possible, to form Christian men, for Christian boys I can scarcely hope to make.

THOMAS ARNOLD
Letter, on appointment to headmastership of Rugby 1828

Arnold of Brescia (1100–1155). Italian Augustinian monk who attacked the holding of property by the Catholic Church; he was hanged and burned, and his ashes thrown into the river Tiber.

Born in Brescia of noble parents, Arnold was educated in Paris and may possibly have studied under Abelard. On his return to Italy he became a canon regular, and was noted for his extreme asceticism. Accused by St Bernard of Clairvaux of being a follower of Abelard, he shared Abelard's condemnation 1140 and took refuge in Zürich.

Returning to Rome 1145, Arnold joined the republican movement and became its most prominent leader; he made continual attacks upon the clergy, vehemently denying their right to hold property. He was excommunicated 1148 by Pope Eugenius III. On the accession to the papacy of Adrian IV (Nicholas Breakspear) 1154, Arnold was forced to flee into Campagna. He was seized by the emperor Frederick Barbarossa and brought back to Rome 1155 where he was condemned and put to death.

Aron Raymond (1905–1983). French sociologist and political commentator. Never afraid to follow an independent view, however unfashionable, he stressed the importance of the political element in social change. He saw industrial societies as characterized by pluralism and by a diversity of values and he was highly critical of Marxism.

Aron was professor of sociology at the University of Paris 1955–68 (resigning during the 1968 riots) and was a highly influential commentator on politics through his articles in the newspaper *Le Figaro*.

Arp Halton Christian (1927–). US astronomer who has worked particularly on the identification of galaxies. He published *Atlas of Peculiar Galaxies* 1965. He also carried out the first photometric work on the Magellanic Clouds – the nearest extragalactic system.

During his research on globular clusters, globular-cluster variable stars, novae, Cepheid variables, extragalactic nebulae, and so on, Arp has attempted to relate the listings of galaxies to radio sources; the optical identification of these sources can now be done fairly accurately. He is working with other astronomers on the question whether the red shifts in the spectrum of quasars are due to the general expansion of the universe.

Arp Hans, or Jean (1887–1966). French abstract painter and sculptor. He was one of the founders of the Dada movement 1916, and was later associated with the Surrealists. Using chance and automatism, Arp developed an abstract sculpture whose sensuous form suggests organic shapes. In his early experimental works, such as collages, he collaborated with his wife Sophie Taeuber-Arp (1889–1943).

Arrau Claudio (1903–1991). Chilean-born US pianist. A concert performer from the age of five, he specialized in 19th-century music and was known for his magisterial interpretations of Chopin, Beethoven, and Brahms.

Arrhenius Svante August (1859–1927). Swedish scientist, the founder of physical chemistry. For his study of electrolysis, he received the Nobel Prize for Chemistry 1903. In 1905 he predicted global warming as a result of carbon dioxide emission from burning fossil fuels.

Arrhenius explained that in an electrolyte the dissolved substance is dissociated into electrically charged ions. The electrolyte conducts electricity because the ions migrate through the solution.

Arrhenius Svante August Arrhenius's doctoral thesis was almost rejected by the University of Uppsala, because of his innovative and novel ideas. He was fortunate enough to be highly regarded by several prominent chemists, such as Ostwald and van't Hoff, and was able to continue his pioneering work in Europe on a travelling scholarship.In 1887, by consolidating and extending his doctoral thesis, Arrhenius published his theory of electrolytic dissociation, which is still largely accepted today. In 1903, he was awarded the Nobel Prize for Chemistry. (Ann Ronan/Image Select)

Arrian (lived 2nd century AD). Greek historian. His *Anabasis/ Expedition* is the chief literary source of information on the campaigns of Alexander the Great, drawn with care from much earlier material. Arrian was a governor and commander under Roman emperor Hadrian.

Arrow Kenneth Joseph (1921–). US economist. With Gerard Debreu, he developed mathematical models of the conditions necessary for economic equilibrium, where demand and supply are equal. Nobel Prize for Economics 1972. His works include *Social Choice and Individual Values* 1951 and *Essays in the Theory of Risk-bearing* 1971.

Arsacid dynasty rulers of ancient Parthia *c.* 250 BC–AD 226, who took their titles from their founder Arsaces. At its peak the dynasty controlled a territory from E India to W Mesopotamia, with a summer capital at Ecbatana and a winter palace at Ctesiphon. Claiming descent from the Persian Achaemenids, but adopting Hellenistic Greek methods of administration, they successfully challenged Roman expansion, defeating the Roman general Crassus at the battle of Carrhae 53 BC. The Arsacid dynasty came to an end with the overthrow of Parthia by Ardashir AD 226; it was succeeded by the Sassanian Empire.

No one has ever written, painted, sculpted, modelled, built, or invented except literally to get out of hell.

ANTONIN ARTAUD
Van Gogh, the Man Suicided by Society 1959

Artaud Antonin (1896–1948). French actor, theatre director, and theorist. Although his play *Les Cenci/The Cenci* 1935 was a failure, his passionate manifestos in *Theatre of Cruelty*, advocating the release of feelings usually repressed in the unconscious, have been an important influence on modern dramatists and directors, such as Brook and Grotowski.

Arthur (lived 6th century AD). Legendary British king and hero in stories of Camelot and the quest for the Holy Grail. Arthur is said to have been born in Tintagel, Cornwall, and buried in Glastonbury, Somerset. He may have been a Romano-Celtic leader against pagan Saxon invaders.

The legends of Arthur and the knights of the Round Table were developed in the 12th century by Geoffrey of Monmouth, Chrétien de Troyes, and the Norman writer Wace. Later writers on the theme include the anonymous author of *Sir Gawayne and the Greene Knight* 1346, Thomas Malory, Tennyson, T H White, and Mark Twain.

Suggested reading
Jenkins, Elizabeth *The Mystery of King Arthur* (1975)
Barber, Richard *King Arthur in Legend and History* (1973)
Lacy, N L *The Arthurian Handbook* (1988)
Morris, John *The Age of Arthur: A History of the British Isles from 350 to 650* (1973)

Arthurian scholarship of our own day is patchy: some of it muscular and austere, much of it mushy and credulous.

Richard Fletcher on ARTHUR
in *Who's Who in Roman Britain and Anglo-Saxon England* 1989

Arthur Chester Alan (1830–1886). 21st president of the USA 1881–85, a Republican. In 1880 he was chosen as James Garfield's vice president, and was his successor when Garfield was assassinated the following year.

He was born in Vermont, the son of a Baptist minister, and became a lawyer and Republican political appointee in New York.

Suggested reading
Cardinale, E J *Chester A Arthur* (1989)
Doenecke, J D *The Presidencies of James A Garfield and Chester A Arthur* (1981)
Reeves, Thomas *President Chester A Arthur* (1975)

Arthur Duke of Brittany (1187–1203). Grandson of Henry II of England and nephew of King John, who is supposed to have had him murdered, 13 April 1203, as a rival for the crown.

Arthur George (1784–1854). Scottish-born colonial administrator in Australia. He was lieutenant governor of Tasmania 1823–37, during which period the Port Arthur convict settlement was established, the Van Diemen's Land Company was formed, the Black War occurred, and the expeditions of Batman and Fawkner set out, which led to the settlement at Port Phillip. Although his rule brought increased prosperity to the colony, Arthur's despotic methods alienated both local residents and the local and Sydney press.

Arthur Prince of Wales (1486–1502). Eldest son of Henry VII of England. He married Catherine of Aragon 1501, when he was 16 and she was 15, but died the next year.

Artigas José Gervasio (1764–1850). Uruguayan independence campaigner. Artigas became governor of Montevideo 1815 but soon fell out with the Buenos Aires regime because it lacked commitment to his province's liberation. Although he was forced into exile 1820, his federalist plans laid the foundations of an independent Uruguay 1828.

Artin Emil (1898–1962). Austrian mathematician who made important contributions to the development of class field theory and the theory of hypercomplex numbers. He was one of the creators of modern algebra. In 1944 his discovery of rings with minimum conditions for right ideals – now known as Artin rings – was a fertile addition to the theory of associative ring algebras. *Class Field Theory* 1961 is a summation of his life's work.

Arundel Thomas Howard, 2nd Earl of Arundel (1586–1646). English politician and patron of the arts. Succeeded to earldom 1595.

The Arundel Marbles, part of his collection of Italian sculptures, were given to Oxford University in 1667 by his grandson. Succeeded to earldom 1595.

Arup Ove (1895–1988). Danish engineer. He founded the British-based architectural practice, Arup Associates, a firm noted for the considered and elegant manner in which modern materials, especially concrete, are employed in its designs. Set up 1963, the practice represented Arup's ideal of interdisciplinary cooperation. Examples of its work are at Somerville College, Oxford, 1958–62, and Corpus Christi, Cambridge, 1961–64.

During the 1930s Arup worked with Berthold Lubetkin and the Tecton group on a number of projects, including the Penguin Pool, London Zoo, 1934–35, which used reinforced concrete in a sculptural fashion (later developed in Arup's own designs).

He that will write well in any tongue must follow the counsel of Aristotle: to speak as the common people do, to think as wise men do.

ROGER ASCHAM
Toxophilus 1545

Ascham Roger (c. 1515–1568). English scholar and royal tutor, author of *The Scholemaster* 1570 on the art of education.

After writing a treatise on archery, King Henry VIII's favourite sport, Ascham was appointed tutor to Princess Elizabeth in 1548. He retained favour under Edward VI and Queen Mary (despite his Protestant views), and returned to Elizabeth's service as her secretary after she became queen.

Asche (John Stanger Heiss) Oscar (1871–1957). Australian actor, producer, and writer who worked in the UK. The play *Chu-Chin-Chow*, which he wrote and produced, ran for five years, 1916–21, on the London stage.

Asche was born at Geelong, Victoria, and his first stage appearance was in London in 1893. He had three successful Australian tours, 1909–10, 1912–13, and 1922. He also appeared in several films.

Ascher Zika (Zigmund) George (1910–1992) and Lida (1910–1983). Czechoslovakian fabric designers. They were known for producing scarves with designs by modern artists, including Braque, Picasso, and Matisse, and for designing neon-coloured shaggy mohairs, cheesecloth, lacy fabrics, and dress- and coat-weighted chenilles that were popular from the late 1950s to the early 1970s. Their fabrics were used by leading couturiers including Christian Dior, Elsa Schiaparelli, and Mary Quant.

Ashbee Charles Robert (1863–1942). English designer, architect, and writer. He was one of the major figures of the Arts and Crafts movement. He founded a Guild and School of Handicraft in the East End of London 1888, but later modified his views, accepting the importance of machinery and design for industry.

I'm famous for being famous.

JOHN ASHBERY
Interview in *PN Review* No 46 1985

Ashbery John Lawrence (1927–). US poet and art critic. His collections of poetry – including *Self-Portrait in a Convex Mirror* 1975, which won a Pulitzer Prize – are distinguished by their exuberant artifice and strong visual and musical elements. His most experimental work, *Europe* (in *The Tennis Court Oath* 1962), uses montage and collage methods derived from Cubist painting. Other volumes include *Some Trees* 1956, *Houseboat Days* 1977, *As We Know* 1979, *A Wave* 1984, and *And the Stars Were Shining* 1994.

Ashcroft Peggy (1907–1991). English actress. Her Shakespearean roles included Desdemona in *Othello* (with Paul Robeson) and Juliet in *Romeo and Juliet* 1935 (with Laurence Olivier and John Gielgud), and she appeared in the British TV play *Caught on a Train* 1980 (BAFTA award), the series *The Jewel in the Crown* 1984, and the film *A Passage to India* 1985. DBE 1956.

She was born in Croydon, Surrey, where a theatre is named after her.

Ashdown Paddy (Jeremy John Durham) (1941–). English politician, leader of the merged Social and Liberal Democrats from 1988. He served in the Royal Marines as a commando, leading a Special Boat Section in Borneo, and was a member of the Diplomatic Service 1971–76. He became a Liberal member of Parliament 1983. His constituency is Yeovil, Somerset.

Ashe Arthur Robert (1943–1993). US tennis player and coach. He won the US national men's singles title at Forest Hills and the first US Open 1968. Known for his exceptionally strong serve, Ashe turned professional 1969. He won the Australian men's title 1970 and Wimbledon 1975. Cardiac problems ended his playing career 1979, but he continued his involvement with the sport as captain of the US Davis Cup team. In 1992 he launched a fund-raising campaign to combat AIDS, which he had contracted from a blood transfusion.

Ashford Daisy (Margaret Mary Julia) (1881–1972). English author. She is known for *The Young Visiters* 1919, a novel of unconscious humour written when she was nine.

My life will be sour grapes and ashes without you.

DAISY ASHFORD
The Young Visiters ch 8 1919

Ashikaga in Japanese history, the family who held the office of shogun 1338–1573, a period of civil wars. Nō drama evolved under the patronage of Ashikaga shoguns. Relations with China improved intermittently and there was trade with Korea. The last (15th) Ashikaga shogun was ousted by Oda Nobunaga at the start of the Momoyama period. The Ashikaga belonged to the Minamoto clan.

Ashkenazy *The pianist and conductor Vladimir Ashkenazy. He began his career as a pianist, taking lessons from the age of six. A champion of Russian composers including Rachmaninov and Prokofiev, his wide-ranging gifts of intellect, expression and technique are evident in the varying demands of the music.*

Ashkenazy Vladimir (1937–). Russian-born pianist and conductor. He was music director of the Royal Philharmonic, London, from 1987 and of the Berlin Radio Symphony Orchestra from 1989. He excels in Rachmaninov, Prokofiev, and Liszt.

After studying in Moscow, he toured the USA 1958. In 1962 he was joint winner of the Tchaikovsky Competition with John Ogdon. He settled in England 1963 and moved to Iceland 1968.

Ashley *Welsh designer Laura Ashley who became successful marketing floral-print fabrics and clothes that created a romantic vision of pre-industrial rural life. In the 1980s her chain of shops expanded to include all aspects of interior decoration.*

Ashley Laura (born Mountney) (1925–1985). Welsh designer. She established and gave her name to a Neo-Victorian country style in clothes and furnishings manufactured by her company from 1953. She founded a highly successful international chain of shops.

Ashmole Elias (1617–1692). English antiquary, whose collection forms the basis of the Ashmolean Museum, Oxford, England.

He wrote books on alchemy and on antiquarian subjects, and amassed a fine library and a collection of curiosities, both of which he presented to Oxford University 1682. His collection was housed in the 'Old Ashmolean' (built 1679–83); the present Ashmolean Museum was erected 1897.

> *[He was] critically skilled in ancient coins, Chemistry, heraldry, mathematics, and what not.*
>
> Thomas Fuller on ELIAS ASHMOLE
> *Worthies of England* 1662

Ashrawi Hanan (1946–). Palestinian political leader. She was chief spokesperson of the Palestinian Liberation Organization delegation at the Madrid peace conference 1991, but refused to join Yassir Arafat's Palestine National Authority. In 1994 she launched the Palestinian Independent Commission for Citizen's Rights to defend the rights of citizens in the Palestinian self-rule areas of Gaza and Jericho.

Born in Ramallah, in the British mandate for Palestine (now the West Bank), she opposed the Israeli occupation of the West Bank and Gaza. She became professor of English literature at Bir Zeit University in the West Bank 1981.

Ashton Frederick William Mallandaine (1904–1988). English choreographer and dancer. He was director of the Royal Ballet, London, 1963–70. He studied with Marie Rambert before joining the Sadler's Wells (now Royal) Ballet 1935 as chief choreographer. His choreography is marked by a soft, pliant, classical lyricism. His many works and long association with Margot Fonteyn, for whom he created her most famous roles, contributed to the worldwide reputation of British ballet and to the popularity of ballet in the mid-20th century. Knighted 1962.

His major works include *Façade* 1931 and *Les Rendezvous* 1933 for Rambert; *Symphonic Variations* 1946, *Cinderella* 1948, *Ondine* 1958, *La Fille mal gardée* 1960, *Marguerite and Armand* – for Margot Fonteyn and Rudolf Nureyev – 1963, and *A Month in the Country* 1976.

Ashton Julian Rossi (1851–1942). Australian landscape painter and art teacher. In 1895 he established in Sydney an influential art school, now the Julian Ashton Art School. His work includes a number of watercolours such as *The Milkmaid* 1888 (Art Gallery of New South Wales, Sydney), painted in part in the open air, which captures accurately the hues of crisp winter sunlight. Among his students were Thea Proctor, William Dobell, and Sydney Long.

Asimov Isaac (1920–1992). Russian-born US author and editor of science fiction and nonfiction. He published more than 400 books, including his science-fiction novels *I, Robot* 1950 and the *Foundation* trilogy 1951–53, continued in *Foundation's Edge* 1983. His two-volume work *The Intelligent Man's Guide to Science* 1960 gained critical acclaim.

> *If my doctor told me I only had six months to live, I wouldn't brood. I'd type a little faster.*
>
> ISAAC ASIMOV
> *Life* 1981

Askin Robert William (1907–1981). Australian Liberal politician, premier of New South Wales 1965–75. When he led his party to electoral victory in 1965 he ended 24 years of Labor government in New South Wales. He was noted for political shrewdness and conservative policies, strongly opposing the Whitlam Labor federal government and curbing public demonstrations against the Vietnam War. His reputation has been tarnished by allegations that he allowed corruption to flourish during his term of office.

Asoka (lived *c.* 273–228 BC). Mauryan emperor of India *c.* 268–232 BC, the greatest of the Mauryan rulers. He inherited an empire covering most of north and south-central India which, at its height, had a population of at least 30 million, with its capital at Pataliputra. A devout Buddhist, he renounced militarism and concentrated on establishing an efficient administration with a large standing army and a secret police.

He issued edicts carved on pillars and rocks throughout his dominions, promoting wise government and the cultivation of moral virtues according to Buddhist teachings. Many still survive, and are among the oldest deciphered texts in India.

Those who praise themselves and criticize their neighbours are merely self-seekers, who wish to excel but only harm themselves.

ASOKA
Proclamation at Kandahar

Aspasia (lived *c.* 440 BC). Greek courtesan, the mistress of the Athenian politician Pericles. As a 'foreigner' from Miletus, she could not be recognized as his wife, but their son was later legitimized.

The philosopher Socrates visited her salon, a meeting place for the celebrities of Athens. Her free thinking led to a charge of impiety, from which Pericles had to defend her.

Asimov *Science fiction author Isaac Asimov. Asimov published more than 400 books and gained much of his recognition through his adeptness at presenting science to the general public. He won the Hugo award for his* Foundation *trilogy published 1951–53.* (Image Select)

What great art this woman had to manage as she pleased the foremost men of state and to afford philosophers occasion to discuss her in exalted terms.

Plutarch on ASPASIA
Life of Pericles ch 24.1

Asplund (Erik) Gunnar (1885–1940). Swedish architect. His early work, for example at the Stockholm South Cemetery 1914, was in the Neo-Classical tradition. Later buildings, such as the Stockholm City Library 1924–27 and the extension of the Gothenburg City Hall 1934–37, developed a refined Modernist-Classical style, culminating in the Stockholm South Cemetery Crematorium 1935–40.

His fusion of Classicism and Modernism holds great appeal for many Post-Modern architects and designers.

He recrafted a former gravel pit into a resonant dialogue between building and site.

Randall J Van Vynckt (ed) on GUNNAR ASPLUND
in *International Dictionary of Architects and Architecture* 1993

Asquith Herbert Henry, 1st Earl of Oxford and Asquith (1852–1928). British Liberal politician, prime minister 1908–16. As chancellor of the Exchequer he introduced old-age pensions 1908. He limited the powers of the House of Lords and attempted to give Ireland Home Rule.

Asquith was born in Yorkshire. Elected a member of Parliament 1886, he was home secretary in Gladstone's 1892–95 government. He was chancellor of the Exchequer 1905–08 and succeeded Campbell-Bannerman as prime minister. Forcing through the radical budget of his chancellor Lloyd George led him into two elections 1910, which resulted in the Parliament Act 1911, limiting the right of the Lords to veto legislation. His endeavours to pass the Home Rule for Ireland Bill led to the Curragh 'Mutiny' and incipient civil war. Unity was re-established by the outbreak of World War I 1914, and a coalition government was formed May 1915. However, his attitude of 'wait and see' was not adapted to all-out war, and in Dec 1916 he was replaced by Lloyd George. In 1918 the Liberal election defeat led to the eclipse of the party. Created an earl 1925.
Suggested reading
Jenkins, Roy *Asquith* (1964)
Koss, Stephen *Asquith* (1976)
Levine, Naomi *Asquith* (1991)

Youth would be an ideal state if it came a little later in life.

HERBERT ASQUITH
Observer 15 Apr 1923

Assad Hafez al (1930–). Syrian Ba'athist politician, president from 1971. He became prime minister after a bloodless military coup 1970, and the following year was the first president to be elected by popular vote. Having suppressed dissent, he was re-elected 1978, 1985, and 1991. He is a Shia (Alawite) Muslim.

He has ruthlessly suppressed domestic opposition, and was Iran's only major Arab ally in its war against Iraq. He steadfastly pursued military parity with Israel, and made himself a key player in any settlement of the Lebanese civil war or Middle East conflict generally. His support for United Nations action against Iraq following its invasion of Kuwait 1990 raised his international standing. In 1995, following intense US diplomatic pressure, he was close to reaching a mutual peace agreement with Israel.

Astaire Fred. Adopted name of Frederick Austerlitz (1899–1987). US dancer, actor, singer, and choreographer. He starred in numerous films, including *Top Hat* 1935, *Easter Parade* 1948, and *Funny Face* 1957, many containing inventive sequences which he designed and choreographed himself. He made ten classic films with the most

Astaire *US dancer, singer, and film star Fred Astaire with his dancing partner Ginger Rogers in* Flying Down to Rio *1933, the first of the ten films they made together. The sophisticated and intimate style of dancing, its grace and technical excellence, and the integration of plot and music in the Rogers–Astaire films revolutionized the musical comedy. Astaire's later co-stars included Judy Garland, Leslie Caron, and Audrey Hepburn.*

Astley Thea (1925–   ). Australian novelist and short-story writer. Her published works include *Girl with a Monkey* 1958, *A Descant for Gossips* 1960 (dramatized for ABC television in 1983) and a collection of short-stories, *Hunting the Wild Pineapple* 1979. She has won the Miles Franklin Award on three occasions.

Aston Francis William (1877–1945). English physicist who developed the mass spectrometer, which separates isotopes by projecting their ions (charged atoms) through a magnetic field. Aston first examined neon gas and found that it consists of two isotopes. Over the next few years he examined the isotopic composition of more than 50 elements, and published *Isotopes* 1922. For his contribution to analytic chemistry and the study of atomic theory he was awarded the 1922 Nobel Prize for Chemistry.

Selfish, narrow-minded, quite blandly antisocial, he went after whatever he sought and took it by fair means or foul.

> Kenneth W Porter on JOHN JACOB ASTOR
> in *John Jacob Astor* 1931

Astor prominent US and British family. John Jacob Astor (1763–1848) was a US millionaire. His great-grandson Waldorf Astor, 2nd Viscount Astor (1879–1952), was a British politician, and served as Conservative member of Parliament for Plymouth 1910–19, when he succeeded to the peerage. His US-born wife Nancy Witcher Langhorne (1879–1964), Lady Astor, was the first woman member of Parliament to take a seat in the House of Commons 1919, when she succeeded her husband for the constituency of Plymouth.

William Backhouse Astor (1792–1875) was known as the 'landlord of New York'. John Jacob Astor's grandson William Waldorf Astor (1848–1919), a US diplomat and writer, became naturalized British 1899. In 1917 he was made 1st Viscount Astor.

Astor John Jacob (1763–1848). German-born US merchant who founded the monopolistic American Fur Company 1808. His subsidiary enterprise, the Pacific Fur Company, was created 1811 following the US government's Louisiana Purchase 1803 facilitating trade with the West. He founded Astoria, now in Oregon, as his trading post at the mouth of the Columbia River. His estate endowed the Astor library, now a part of The New York Public Library.

Astor Mary. Stage name of Lucille Langhanke (1906–1987). US film actress. Renowned for her poise, her many films included *Don Juan* 1926, *Dodsworth* 1936, and *The Maltese Falcon* 1941. Her memoirs *My Story* 1959 were remarkable for their frankness.

Asturias Miguel Ángel (1899–1974). Guatemalan author and diplomat. He published poetry, Guatemalan legends, and novels, such as *El señor presidente/The President* 1946, *Men of Corn* 1949, and *Strong Wind* 1950, attacking Latin-American dictatorships and 'Yankee imperialism'. Nobel prize 1967.

Atahualpa (*c.* 1502–1533). Last emperor of the Incas of Peru. He was taken prisoner 1532 when the Spaniards arrived and agreed to pay a substantial ransom, but he was accused of plotting against the conquistador Pizarro and was sentenced to be burned. On his consenting to Christian baptism, the sentence was commuted to strangulation.

popular of his dancing partners, Ginger Rogers. He later played straight dramatic roles in such films as *On the Beach* 1959. He was the greatest popular dancer of his time. As a singer, he used first-rate material (some of which he wrote himself) and interpreted it intelligently; songs he recorded include 'Isn't This a Lovely Day?' 1935, 'I'm Building Up to an Awful Letdown' 1936, and 'A Fine Romance' 1937.

Suggested reading
Adler, Bill *Fred Astaire* (1987)
Giles, Sarah *Fred Astaire* (1988)
Thomas, B *Astaire: The Man, the Dancer* (1984)

I have no desire to prove anything by dancing ... I just dance.

> FRED ASTAIRE
> attributed remark

I don't act for public opinion. I act for the nation and for my own satisfaction.

> KEMAL ATATÜRK
> quoted in Lord Kinross *Atatürk* 1964

Atatürk Mustafa Kemal, (Turkish 'Father of the Turks') Name assumed 1934 by Mustafa Kemal (1881–1938). Turkish politician and general, first president of Turkey from 1923. After World War I he established a provisional rebel government and in 1921–22 the

Turkish armies under his leadership expelled the Greeks who were occupying Turkey. He was the founder of the modern republic, which he ruled as virtual dictator, with a policy of consistent and radical westernization.

Suggested reading
Kazoncigil, Ali and Özbudun, Ergun *Atatürk: Father of a Modern State* (1981)
Kinross, J P D *Atatürk: The Rebirth of a Nation* (1964)
Renda, Gunsel and Kortpeter, C M (eds) *The Transformation of Turkish Culture: The Atatürk Legacy* (1986)
Zürcher, Erik J *Turkey: A Modern History* (1993)

Atget Eugène (1857–1927). French photographer. He took up photography at the age of 40, and for 30 years documented urban Paris in some 10,000 images. His photographs were sometimes used by painters and he was admired by the Surrealists. After his death his work was rescued and promoted by the photographer Berenice Abbott.

Athanasius, St (298–373). Bishop of Alexandria, Egypt, supporter of the doctrines of the Trinity and Incarnation. He was a disciple of St Anthony the hermit, and an opponent of Arianism in the great Arian controversy. Following the official condemnation of Arianism at the Council of Nicaea 325, Athanasius was appointed bishop of Alexandria 328. The Athanasian creed was not actually written by him, although it reflects his views.

Banished 335 by Emperor Constantine because of his intransigence towards the defeated Arians, Athanasius was recalled in 346 but suffered three more banishments before his final reinstatement about 366.

Athelstan (*c.* 895–939). King of the Mercians and West Saxons. Son of Edward the Elder and grandson of Alfred the Great, he was crowned king 925 at Kingston upon Thames. He subdued parts of Cornwall and Wales, and defeated the Welsh, Scots, and Danes at Brunanburh 937.

Atherton Michael Andrew (1968–). Lancashire and England cricketer, who first played for Lancashire when a Cambridge University student 1987. He captained Cambridge University 1988–89, made his Test debut 1989, and took over as England captain 1993.

Atkinson Harry Albert (1831–1892). New Zealand politician, born in England, prime minister 1876–77, 1883–84, 1887–91. In his second term of office he abolished the provinces and in his third handled the financial depression by measures then regarded as socialistic – for example, reduction of civil service salaries, abolition of land tax, and introduction of income tax.

Atkinson Richard (1920–1994). British archaeologist who carried out important investigations at the major prehistoric monuments of Stonehenge and Silbury Hill, Wiltshire, England; his work set new standards for excavation.

Atkinson's career began in 1944 when he joined the staff of the Ashmolean Museum in Oxford. His first book, *Field Archaeology* 1946 was the first textbook of fieldwork and excavation to be published in the UK, and greatly influenced succeeding archaeologists. After several years of lecturing in prehistoric archaeology at Edinburgh University, he became in 1958 professor of archaeology at Cardiff, where he remained until retiring in 1983.

Atkinson Robert D'escourt (1898–1982). Welsh astronomer and inventor. His research was in the field of atomic synthesis, stellar energy, and positional astronomy.

His contributions were fundamental to our basic understanding of how stars like the Sun work and how they evolve. He was also involved in instrument design.

Attalid dynasty (282–133 BC). Greek rulers of the ancient Greek city of Pergamum in NW Asia Minor. The Attalids pursued an active cultural policy, with the aim of making Pergamum a successor to Athens in architecture and the arts.

Attalus I (ruled 241–197 BC) decisively defeated the invading Galatians (before 230 BC), and defeated Antiochus Hierax of Syria in three battles 229–228. He allied himself with Rome against Philip V of Macedon. His son Eumenes II (ruled 197–159 BC) drew Rome into conflict with Antiochus III. He was succeeded first by his brother Attalus II (ruled 159–138 BC), and then by his son Attalus III (ruled 138–133 BC), who bequeathed Pergamum to the Romans in his will.

Anyone who spends any time watching animals has to conclude that the overriding purpose of an individual's existence is to pass on some part of it to the next generation.

DAVID ATTENBOROUGH
The Trials of Life 1990

Attenborough David Frederick (1926–). English traveller and zoologist who has made numerous wildlife films for television. He was the writer and presenter of the television series *Life on Earth* 1979, *The Living Planet* 1983, *The Trials of Life* 1990, and *The Private Life of Plants* 1995. He was director of programmes for BBC Television 1969–72 and a member of its board of management. Knighted 1985. He is the brother of the actor and director Richard Attenborough.

Attenborough Richard, Baron Attenborough (1923–). English director, actor, and producer. He made his screen acting debut in *In Which We Serve* 1942, and later appeared in such films as *Brighton Rock* 1947 and *10 Rillington Place* 1970. He co-produced the socially-conscious *The Angry Silence* 1960, and directed *Oh! What a Lovely War* 1969. He subsequently concentrated on directing, including the epic biographies of *Gandhi* (which won eight Academy Awards) 1982, *Cry Freedom* 1987, and *Chaplin* 1992. He is the brother of naturalist David Attenborough. He was knighted 1976 and created a baron 1993.

[He was] familiar with all the artifices which make falsehood look like truth and ignorance like knowledge.

T B Macaulay on FRANCIS ATTERBURY
Life of Atterbury 1866

Atterbury Francis (1662–1732). English bishop and Jacobite politician. In 1687 he was appointed a royal chaplain by William III. Under Queen Anne he received rapid promotion, becoming bishop of Rochester 1713. His Jacobite sympathies prevented his further rise, and in 1722 he was sent to the Tower of London and subsequently banished. He was a friend of the writers Alexander Pope and Jonathan Swift.

Is not slavery to Attila better than wealth among the Romans?

Onegesius on ATTILA,
quoted by Byzantine historian Priscus (fragment 11.2; Blockley)

Attila (*c.* 406–453). King of the Huns in an area from the Alps to the Caspian Sea from 434, known to later Christian history as the 'Scourge of God'. He twice attacked the Eastern Roman Empire to increase the quantity of tribute paid to him, 441–443 and 447–449, and then attacked the Western Roman Empire 450–452.

Attila first ruled jointly with his brother Bleda, whom he murdered in 444. In 450 Honoria, the sister of the western emperor Valentinian III, appealed to him to rescue her from an arranged marriage, and Attila used her appeal to attack the West. He was forced back from Orléans by Aetius and Theodoric, king of the Visigoths, and defeated by them on the Catalaunian Fields in 451. In 452 he led the Huns into Italy, and was induced to withdraw by Pope Leo I.

Suggested reading
Howarth, Patrick *Attila, King of the Huns* (1994)
Thompson, E A *A History of Attila and the Huns* (1948)

I should be a sad subject for any publicity expert. I have none of the qualities which create publicity.

CLEMENT ATTLEE
quoted in Harold Nicolson *Diary* 14 Jan 1949

Attlee Clement Richard, 1st Earl Attlee (1883–1967). British Labour politician. In the coalition government during World War II he was Lord Privy Seal 1940–42, dominions secretary 1942–43, and Lord President of the Council 1943–45, as well as deputy prime minister from 1942. As prime minister 1945–51 he introduced a sweeping programme of nationalization and a whole new system of social services.

Attlee was educated at Oxford and practised as a barrister 1906–09. Social work in London's East End and cooperation in poor-law reform led him to become a socialist; he joined the Fabian Society and the Independent Labour Party 1908. He became lecturer in social science at the London School of Economics 1913. After service in World War I he was mayor of Stepney, E London, 1919–20; Labour member of Parliament for Limehouse 1922–50 and for W Walthamstow 1950–55. In the first and second Labour governments he was undersecretary for war 1924 and chancellor of the Duchy of Lancaster and postmaster general 1929–31. In 1935 he became leader of the opposition. In July 1945 he became prime minister after a Labour landslide in the general election. The government was returned to power with a much reduced majority 1950 and was defeated 1951. He was created an earl 1955 on his retirement as leader of the opposition.

Attwell Mabel Lucie (1879–1964). English artist. She illustrated many books for children, including her own stories and verse.

Atwood Margaret Eleanor (1939–). Canadian novelist, short-story writer, and poet. Her novels, which often treat feminist themes with wit and irony, include *The Edible Woman* 1969, *Life Before Man* 1979, *Bodily Harm* 1981, *The Handmaid's Tale* 1986, *Cat's Eye* 1989, and *The Robber Bride* 1993. Collections of poetry include *Power Politics* 1971, *You are Happy* 1974, and *Interlunar* 1984.
Suggested reading
Davidson, Arnold and Cathy *The Art of Margaret Atwood* (1981)
Grace, S E *Violent Duality: A Study of Margaret Atwood* (1980)
Ingersoll, E E (ed) *Atwood: Conversations* (1990)
Rigney, B H *Margaret Atwood* (1987)

Auber Daniel François Esprit (1782–1871). French operatic composer. He studied under the Italian composer and teacher Luigi Cherubini and wrote about 50 operas, including *La Muette de Portici/The Mute Girl of Portici* 1828 and the comic opera *Fra Diavolo* 1830.

How these curiosities would be quite forgot, did not such idle fellows as I am put them down.

JOHN AUBREY
Brief Lives 'Venetia Digby' 1898

Aubrey John (1626–1697). English biographer and antiquary. His *Lives*, begun 1667, contains gossip, anecdotes, and valuable insights into the celebrities of his time. It was published as *Brief Lives* 1898 in two volumes (edited by A Clark). *Miscellanies* 1696, a work on folklore and ghost stories, was the only work to be published during his lifetime.

Aubrey was born in Wiltshire. He studied law but became dependent on patrons, including the antiquary Ashmole and the philosopher Hobbes. A one-volume edition of three of his works *Miscellanies, Remaines of Gentilisme and Judaisme*, and *Observations* appeared 1972 under the title *Three Prose Works* (edited by J Buchanan-Brown). Aubrey was the first to claim Stonehenge as a Druid temple.

Auchinleck Claude John Eyre (1884–1981). British commander in World War II. He won the First Battle of El Alamein 1942 in N Egypt. In 1943 he became commander in chief in India and founded the modern Indian and Pakistani armies. In 1946 he was promoted to field marshal; he retired 1947.

Auchinleck, nicknamed 'the Auk', succeeded Wavell as commander in chief Middle East July 1941, and in the summer of 1942 was forced back to the Egyptian frontier by the German field marshal Rommel, but his victory at the First Battle of El Alamein is regarded by some as more important to the outcome of World War II than the Second Battle. From India he gave background support to the Burma campaign. GCIE 1940, GCB 1945.

Auckland George Eden, 1st Earl of Auckland (1784–1849). British Tory politician after whom Auckland, New Zealand, is named. He became a member of Parliament 1810, and 1835–41 was governor general of India. He was created earl 1893.

A conscientious mediocrity, without experience of war or of Indian affairs.

E L Woodward on GEORGE EDEN, 1ST EARL OF AUCKLAND
in *The Age of Reform 1815–1870* 1938

Auden W(ystan) H(ugh) (1907–1973). English-born US poet. He wrote some of his most original poetry, such as *Look, Stranger!* 1936, in the 1930s when he led the influential left-wing literary group that included Louis MacNeice, Stephen Spender, and Cecil Day Lewis. He moved to the USA 1939, became a US citizen 1946, and adopted a more conservative and Christian viewpoint, for example in *The Age of Anxiety* 1947.

Born in York, Auden was associate professor of English literature at the University of Michigan from 1939, and professor of poetry at Oxford 1956–61. He also wrote verse dramas with Christopher Isherwood, such as *The Dog Beneath the Skin* and *The Ascent of F6* 1951, and opera librettos, notably for Stravinsky's *The Rake's Progress* 1951.
Suggested reading
Callan, E *Auden: A Carnival of Intellect* (1983)
Carpenter, H *Auden: A Biography* (1981)
Gingerich, M E *Auden: A Reference Guide* (1978)
Mendelson, E *Early Auden* (1981)
Rodway, A *Preface to Auden* (1984)
Rowse, A L *The Poet Auden* (1988)
Spender, S (ed) *W H Auden: A Tribute* (1975)

Audubon John James (1785–1851). US naturalist and artist. Before Audubon most painters of birds used stylized techniques; stuffed birds were often used as subjects. Audubon painted from life and his compositions were startling, his detail minute. In 1827, after extensive travels and observations of birds, he published the first part of his *Birds of North America*, with a remarkable series of colour plates. He illustrated *Viviparous Quadrupeds of North America* 1845–48, compiling the text 1846–54 with his sons and John Bachman (1790–1874).

The National Audubon Society (founded 1886) has branches throughout the USA and Canada for the study and protection of birds.

Auer Carl. Austrian chemist and engineer; see Baron von ◊Welsbach.

This heavy paint ... is ... laid onto the picture like pâté.

FRANK AUERBACH
quoted in Colin Naylor (ed) *Contemporary Artists* 1989

Auerbach Frank Helmuth (1931–). German-born British painter. He is best known for his portraits and views of London; his style is characterized by thick, heavily worked paint.

Auger Arleen (1939–1993). US soprano. She made her Vienna State Opera debut 1967 as the Queen of the Night in Mozart's *The Magic Flute*. In 1986 she sang at the wedding of Prince Andrew and

Sarah Ferguson in Westminster Abbey, to a worldwide television audience of 500 million. Millions heard her again Dec 1991 in the television broadcast of Mozart's *Requiem* live from Vienna in commemoration of the bicentenary of the composer's death.

Augier (Guillaume Victor) Émile (1820–1889). French dramatist. Reacting against Romanticism, in collaboration with Jules Sandeau he wrote *Le Gendre de M Poirier* 1854, a realistic delineation of bourgeois society.

Augustin Eugène (1791–1861). French dramatist. He was the originator and exponent of 'well-made' plays, which achieved success but were subsequently forgotten. He wrote *Une Nuit de la Garde Nationale* 1815.

Give me chastity and continency, but do not give it yet.
ST AUGUSTINE OF HIPPO
Confessions

Augustine of Hippo, St (Aurelius Augustinus) (354–430). One of the early Christian leaders and writers known as the Fathers of the Church. He was converted to Christianity by Ambrose in Milan and became bishop of Hippo (modern Annaba, Algeria) 396. Among Augustine's many writings are his *Confessions*, a spiritual autobiography, and *De Civitate Dei/The City of God*, vindicating the Christian church and divine providence in 22 books.

Augustine's written output was vast, with 113 books and treatises, over 200 letters, and more than 500 sermons surviving. Many of Augustine's books resulted from his participation in three great theological controversies: he refuted Manichaeism; attacked (and did much to eliminate) the exclusive N African Donatist sect at the conference of Carthage 411; and devoted the last 20 years of his life to refute Pelagius, maintaining the doctrine of original sin and the necessity of divine grace.

Suggested reading
Battenhouse, Roy (ed) *A Companion to the Study of St Augustine* (1955)
Brown, Peter *Augustine of Hippo* (1967)
Chadwick, Henry *Augustine* (1986)
Smith, W T *Augustine: His Life and Thought* (1980)

Augustine, St (died 605). first archbishop of Canterbury, England. He was sent from Rome to convert England to Christianity by Pope Gregory I. He landed at Ebbsfleet in Kent 597 and soon after baptized Ethelbert, King of Kent, along with many of his subjects. He was consecrated bishop of the English at Arles in the same year, and appointed archbishop 601, establishing his see at Canterbury. Feast day 26 May.

Augustine was originally prior of the Benedictine monastery of St Andrew, Rome. In 603 he attempted unsuccessfully to unite the Roman and native Celtic churches at a conference on the Severn. He founded Christ Church, Canterbury, in 603, and the abbey of Saints Peter and Paul, now the site of Saint Augustine's Missionary College.

He so improved the city that he justly boasted that he found it brick and left it marble.
Suetonius on AUGUSTUS
in *Life of Augustus*

Augustus (63 BC–AD 14). Title of Octavian (Gaius Julius Caesar Octavianus), first of the Roman emperors. The son of a senator who married a niece of Julius Caesar, he became Caesar's adopted son and principal heir. Following Caesar's murder, he joined forces with Mark Antony and Lepidus in the Second Triumvirate. Following Mark Antony's liaison with the Egyptian queen Cleopatra, Augustus defeated her troops at Actium 31 BC. As emperor (from 27 BC) he reformed the government of the empire, the army, and Rome's public services and was a patron of the arts. The period of his rule is known as the Augustan Age.

Aung San (1916–1947). Burmese (Myanmar) politician. He was a founder and leader of the Anti-Fascist People's Freedom League, which led Burma's fight for independence from Great Britain. During World War II he collaborated first with Japan and then with the UK. In 1947 he became head of Burma's provisional government but was assassinated the same year by political opponents. His daughter Suu Kyi (1945–) spearheaded a nonviolent prodemocracy movement in Myanmar from 1988.

Imprisoned for his nationalist activities while a student in Rangoon, Aung escaped to Japan 1940. He returned to lead the Burma Independence Army, which assisted the Japanese invasion 1942, and became defence minister in the puppet government set up. Before long, however, he secretly contacted the Resistance movement, and from March 1945 openly cooperated with the British in the expulsion of the Japanese. Burma became independent 1948, after his death.

Aung San Suu Kyi Burmese (Myanmar) politician; see ◊Suu Kyi.

Strange that I came with nothing into the world and now go away with this stupendous caravan of sin; wherever I look I see only God.
AURANGZEB
words spoken shortly before his death, 1707.

Aurangzeb or Aurungzebe (1618–1707). Mogul emperor of N India from 1658. Third son of Shah Jahan, he made himself master

Audubon *US biologist and artist John James Audubon. Audubon published artworks depicting the wildlife of North America in the early nineteenth century. Most of his paintings are of birds.* (Image Select)

of the court by a palace revolution. His reign was the most brilliant period of the Mogul dynasty, but his despotic tendencies and Muslim fanaticism aroused much opposition. His latter years were spent in war with the princes of Rajputana and the Marathas and Sikhs. His drive south into the Deccan overextended Mogul resources.

Such was the death of Aurelian, a prince who was necessary rather than good.

ANONYMOUS on AURELIAN
in *Life of Aurelian* ch 37.1

Aurelian (Lucius Domitius Aurelianus) (*c.* 215–275 AD). Roman emperor from 270. A successful soldier, he was chosen emperor by his troops on the death of Claudius II. He defeated the Goths and Vandals, defeated and captured Zenobia of Palmyra, and was planning a campaign against Parthia when he was murdered. The Aurelian Wall, a fortification surrounding Rome, was built by Aurelian 271. It was made of concrete, and substantial ruins exist.

The Aurelian Way ran from Rome through Pisa and Genoa to Antipolis (Antibes) in Gaul.

Aurelius Marcus. Roman emperor; see ◊Marcus Aurelius Antoninus.

Aurenche Jean (1904–1992). French screenwriter. He was especially noted for adaptations of major literary works, including Stendhal's *The Red and the Black/Le Rouge et le Noir* 1954, Zola's *L'Assommoir* as *Gervaise* 1956, and Dostoevsky's *The Gambler/Le Joueur* 1958. A prolific writer, Aurenche contributed to some 50 films, among them some of the finest French cinema has produced.

Auric Georges (1899–1983). French composer. His works include a comic opera, several ballets, and incidental music to films including Jean Cocteau's *Orphée/Orpheus* 1950. He was one of the musical group called Les Six who were influenced by Erik Satie.

Auriol Vincent (1884–1966). French Socialist politician. He was president of the two Constituent Assemblies of 1946 and first president of the Fourth Republic 1947–54.

Aurobindo Ghose known as Shri Aurobindo (1872–1950). Indian religious writer and leader, founder of Aurobindo Ashram (a centre for religious study) at Pondicherry, S India. He wrote extensively on Hindu theology and philosophy, proposing a system called integral yoga to bring together body and soul, individual and community. Through his widespread influence on the Hindu intelligentsia he strengthened the modern Hindu movement in the 1930s and 1940s. After his death his followers developed the city of Auroville at his ashram.

It is a truth universally acknowledged, that a single man in possession of a good fortune, must be in want of a wife.

JANE AUSTEN
Pride and Prejudice ch 1 1813

Austen Jane (1775–1817). English novelist. She described her raw material as 'three or four families in a Country Village'. *Sense and Sensibility* was published 1811, *Pride and Prejudice* 1813, *Mansfield Park* 1814, *Emma* 1816, *Northanger Abbey* and *Persuasion* 1818, all anonymously. She observed speech and manners with wit and precision, revealing her characters' absurdities in relation to high standards of integrity and appropriateness.

She was born at Steventon, Hampshire, where her father was rector, and began writing early; the burlesque *Love and Freindship* (sic), published 1922, was written 1790. In 1801 the family moved to Bath and after the death of her father in 1805, to Southampton, finally settling in Chawton, Hampshire, with her brother Edward. Between 1795 and 1798 she worked on three novels. The first to be published (like its successors, anonymously) was *Sense and*

Let other pens dwell on guilt and misery.

JANE AUSTEN
Mansfield Park ch 48 1814

Sensibility (drafted in letter form 1797–98). *Pride and Prejudice* (written 1796–97) followed, but *Northanger Abbey*, a skit on the contemporary Gothic novel (written 1798, sold to a London publisher 1803, and bought back 1816), did not appear until 1818. The fragmentary *Watsons* and *Lady Susan*, written about 1803–05, remained unfinished. The small success of her published works, however, stimulated Jane Austen to write in rapid succession *Mansfield Park, Emma, Persuasion*, and the final fragment *Sanditon*, written 1817. She died in Winchester, and is buried in the cathedral.

Suggested reading
Cecil, David *A Portrait of Jane Austen* (1978)
Halperin, John *The Life of Jane Austen* (1984)
Hodge, Aiken *The Double Life of Jane Austen* (1972)
Honan, P *Jane Austen: Her Life* (1988)
Pilgrim, C *Dear Jane* (1971)
Tanner, Tony *Jane Austen* (1986)

Auster Paul (1947–). US novelist. Making experimental use of detective story techniques, he has explored modern urban identity in his acclaimed *New York Trilogy: City of Glass* 1985, *Ghosts* 1986, and *The Locked Room* 1986. Later works in different genres include *In the Country of Last Things* 1987, *Moon Palace* 1989, *The Music of Chance* 1991, and *Mr Vertigo* 1994.

I dare not alter these things, they come to me from above.

ALFRED AUSTIN
Remark rejecting the accusation of writing ungrammatical verse

---

Austin Alfred (1835–1913). English poet. He published the satirical poem *The Season* 1861, which was followed by plays and volumes of poetry little read today. He was poet laureate 1896–1913.

Austin Herbert, 1st Baron Austin (1866–1941). English industrialist who began manufacturing cars 1905 in Northfield, Birmingham, notably the Austin Seven 1921. KBE 1917, baron 1936.

Austin John (1790–1859). English jurist. His analysis of the chaotic state of the English legal system led him to define law as the enforceable command of a sovereign authority, thus distinguishing it from other kinds of rules and from morality. His work had a strong impact on jurisprudential thought, though many of his ideas were derived from his friend Jeremy Bentham. He was professor of jurisprudence at the University of London 1826–35.

Austin J(ohn) L(angshaw) (1911–1960). British philosopher, a pioneer in the investigation of the way words are used in everyday speech. His later work was influential on the philosophy of language.

According to Austin's theory of speech acts, there are three kinds: *locutions*, or the uttering of meaningful sentences; *illocutions*, or what one does in saying things, such as stating, promising, urging; and *perlocutions*, or what one does by saying things, such as persuading, frightening, embarrassing.

His lectures *Sense and Sensibilia* and *How to do Things with Words* were published posthumously in 1962.

Austin Stephen Fuller (1793–1836). American pioneer and political leader. A settler in Texas 1821, he was a supporter of the colony's autonomy and was imprisoned 1833–35 for his opposition to Mexican rule. Released during the Texas revolution, he campaigned for US support. After the end of the war 1836, he was appointed secretary of state of the independent Republic of Texas but died shortly afterwards.

Born in Austinville, Virginia, USA, Austin grew up in Missouri and followed his father to Texas 1821 where he accepted Mexican citizenship and political privileges in spite of his support of the colony's independence. The state capital of Austin was named in his honour.

We profit little by books we do not enjoy.
JOHN LUBBOCK, 1ST BARON AVEBURY
in Pleasures of Life ch 5 1887

Avebury John Lubbock, 1st Baron Avebury (1834–1913). British banker. A Liberal (from 1886 Liberal Unionist) member of Parliament 1870–1900, he was responsible for the Bank Holidays Act 1871 introducing statutory public holidays.

Avedon Richard (1923–   ). US photographer. A fashion photographer with *Harper's Bazaar* magazine in New York from the mid-1940s, he moved to *Vogue* 1965. He later became the highest-paid fashion and advertising photographer in the world. He became associated with the *New Yorker* 1993. Using large-format cameras, his work consists of intensely realistic images, chiefly portraits.

Born in New York City, Avedon was already pursuing an interest in photography by the age of 10. After studying photography in the US merchant marine and at the New School for Social Research, he turned professional. His primary subject, aside from fashion, was portraits. Many of his dramatic portraits were assembled in such books as *Observations* 1959 (text by Truman Capote) and *Nothing Personal* 1974 (text by James Baldwin).

Daylight is something I rarely see ... something I must give up ... like childhood.
RICHARD AVEDON
quoted in Cecil Beaton and Gail Buckland The Magic Image 1975

Avercamp Hendrick (1585–1634). Dutch landscape painter. He specialized in winter scenes enlivened by colourful, carefully arranged groups of people, skating or talking together. *Winter Scene* about 1609 (National Gallery, London) is typical.

Averroës (Ibn Rushd in Arabic) (1126–1198). Arabian philosopher who argued for the eternity of matter and against the immortality of the individual soul. His philosophical writings, including commentaries on Aristotle and on Plato's *Republic*, became known to the West through Latin translations. He influenced Christian and Jewish writers into the Renaissance, and reconciled Islamic and Greek thought in asserting that philosophic truth comes through reason. St Thomas Aquinas opposed this position.

Averroës was born in Córdoba, Spain, trained in medicine, and became physician to the caliph as well as judge of Seville and Córdoba. He was accused of heresy by the Islamic authorities and banished 1195. Later he was recalled, and died in Marrakesh, N Africa.

'Averroism' was taught at Paris and elsewhere in the 13th century by the 'Averroists', who defended a distinction between philosophical truth and revealed religion.

Philosophy is the friend and milk-sister of the Law.
AVERROËS
The Decisive Treatise

Avery Milton (1893–1965). US painter. His early work was inspired by Matisse, portraying subjects in thin, flat, richly coloured strokes. His later work, although still figurative, shows the influence of Mark Rothko and other experimental US artists. Born in Altmar, New York, Avery received little formal training.

Avery Oswald Theodore (1877–1955). Canadian-born US bacteriologist whose work on transformation in bacteria established 1944 that DNA (deoxyribonucleic acid) is responsible for the transmission of heritable characteristics. He also proved that polysaccharides play an important part in immunity.

Avery Tex (Frederick Bean) (1907–1980). US cartoon-film director. He used violent, sometimes surreal humour. At Warner Bros he helped develop Bugs Bunny and Daffy Duck, before moving to MGM 1942 where he created, among others, Droopy the dog and Screwball Squirrel.

Avianus (lived *c.* AD 400). Roman fable writer. Written in elegiac couplets, his fables number 42 in total.

Avicenna (Ibn Sina in Arabic) (979–1037). Arabian philosopher and physician. He was the most renowned philosopher of medieval Islam. His *Canon Medicinae* was a standard work for many centuries. His philosophical writings were influenced by al-Farabi, Aristotle, and the neo-Platonists, and in turn influenced the scholastics of the 13th century.

Avicenna was born near Bokhara, and died in Hamadan, where he had been vizier. His concept of God as the being in which essence and existence are identical gained wide currency, influencing Moses Maimonides and Thomas Aquinas.

A horse is simply a horse.
AVICENNA
quoted in Gordon Leff Medieval Thought: St Augustine to Ockham 1959

Avogadro Amedeo, Conte di Quaregna (1776–1856). Italian physicist, one of the founders of physical chemistry, who proposed *Avogadro's hypothesis* on gases 1811. His work enabled scientists to calculate *Avogadro's number*, and still has relevance for atomic studies.

Avogadro made it clear that the gas particles need not be individual atoms but might consist of molecules, the term he introduced to describe combinations of atoms. No previous scientists had made this fundamental distinction between the atoms of a substance and its molecules.

Using his hypothesis Avogadro provided the theoretical explanation of Gay-Lussac's law of combining volumes. It had already been observed that the electrolysis of water (to form hydrogen and oxygen) produces twice as much hydrogen (by volume) as oxygen. He reasoned that each molecule of water must contain hydrogen and oxygen atoms in the proportion of 2 to 1. Also, because the

Avery, Oswald Bacteriologist Oswald Theodore Avery. Oswald purified a molecule from heat-killed pathogenic smooth *pneumococci* bacteria extracts that could transform nonpathogenic mutant rough *pneumococci* into the smooth form in vitro. This molecule was deoxyribonucleic acid, DNA. (Image Select)

oxygen gas collected weighs eight times as much as the hydrogen, oxygen atoms must be 16 times as heavy as hydrogen atoms.

Axelrod Julius (1912–). US neuropharmacologist who shared the 1970 Nobel Prize for Physiology or Medicine with the biophysicists Bernard Katz (1911–) and Ulf von Euler (1905–1983) for his work on neurotransmitters (the chemical messengers of the brain).

Axelrod wanted to know why the messengers, once transmitted, should stop operating. Through his studies he found a number of specific enzymes that rapidly degraded the neurotransmitters.

Axthelm Walther von (1893–1961). German Luftwaffe general in World War II. He was appointed inspector general of anti-aircraft artillery 1942, with considerable responsibility for the air defences of Germany. In 1944 he was in overall command of the V-1 'flying bomb' campaign against Britain.

You must come to our house next time. Absolute peace. Neither of us ever says a word to each other. That's the secret of a successful union.

ALAN AYCKBOURN
Absent Friends 1974

Ayckbourn Alan (1939–). English playwright, and artistic director of the Stephen Joseph Theatre, Scarborough from 1970. His prolific output, characterized by comic dialogue and teasing experiments in dramatic structure, includes *Relatively Speaking* 1967, *Absurd Person Singular* 1972, a trilogy *The Norman Conquests* 1974, *Intimate Exchanges* 1982, *A Woman in Mind* 1986, and *Haunting Julia* 1994. He has recently written a number of plays for children, including *Invisible Friends* 1989 and *This Is Where We Came In* 1990.

Ayer A(lfred) J(ules) (1910–1989). English philosopher. He wrote *Language, Truth and Logic* 1936, an exposition of the theory of 'logical positivism', presenting a criterion by which meaningful statements (essentially truths of logic, as well as statements derived from experience) could be distinguished from meaningless metaphysical utterances (for example, claims that there is a God or that the world external to our own minds is illusory). Knighted 1970.

He was professor of logic at Oxford 1959–78. Later works include *Probability and Evidence* 1972 and *Philosophy in the Twentieth Century* 1982.

Suggested reading
Ayer, A J *Part of My Life* (1977)
Ayer, A J *More of My Life* (1984)
Magee, Bryan *Men of Ideas* (1978)

No morality can be founded on authority, even if the authority were divine.

A J AYER
Essay on Humanism

Ayesha (611–678). Third and favourite wife of the prophet Muhammad, who married her when she was nine. Her father, Abu Bakr, became caliph on Muhammad's death 632. She bitterly opposed the later succession to the caliphate of Ali, who had once accused her of infidelity.

Ayrton Michael (1921–1975). English painter, sculptor, illustrator, and writer. From 1961, he concentrated on the Daedalus myth, producing bronzes of Icarus and a fictional autobiography of Daedalus, *The Maze Maker* 1967.

He built a maze with 2 m/6 ft walls, 1,000 m/3,300 ft long, at Arkville, New York State, USA.

The image I seek is a paraphrase of the human body.

MICHAEL AYRTON
on 'The suicide of Icarus' *Catalogue of the Matthieson gallery exhibition* Oct 1961

Ayrton, William English electrical engineer and inventor William Edward Ayrton. As well as establishing the world's first laboratory devoted to the teaching of applied electricity, he co-invented the ammeter and the world's first electric tricycle. (Ann Ronan/Image Select)

Ayrton William Edward (1847–1908). English physicist and electrical engineer who invented many of the prototypes of modern electrical measuring instruments. He also created the world's first laboratory for teaching applied electricity, in Tokyo, Japan, 1873.

In 1881 Ayrton and his colleague John Perry (1850–1920) invented the surface-contact system for electric railways, and they brought out the first electric tricycle 1882. There followed a series of portable electrical measuring instruments, including the ammeter (so named by its inventors), an electric power meter, various forms of improved voltmeters, and an instrument used for measuring self and mutual induction. In this, great use was made of an ingeniously devised flat spiral spring which yields a relatively large rotation for a small axial elongation.

I loved thee once, I'll love no more, / Thine be the grief, as is the blame; / Thou art not what thou wast before, / What reason I should be the same?

ROBERT AYTOUN
'To an Inconstant Mistress'

Aytoun Robert, or Ayton (1570–1638). Scottish poet. He was employed and knighted by James I and was noted for his love poems. Aytoun is the reputed author of the lines on which Robert Burns based 'Auld Lang Syne'. Knighted 1612.

The earth is all the home I have, / The heavens my wide roof-tree.

WILLIAM AYTOUN
'The Wandering Jew'

Aytoun W(illiam) E(dmonstoune) (1813–1865). Scottish poet. He is chiefly remembered for his *Lays of the Scottish Cavaliers* 1848 and *Bon Gaultier Ballads* 1855, which he wrote in collaboration with the Scottish nationalist Theodore Martin (1816–1909).

Ayub Khan Muhammad (1907–1974). Pakistani soldier and president 1958–69. He served in the Burma Campaign 1942–45, and was commander in chief of the Pakistan army 1951. In 1958 Ayub Khan assumed power after a bloodless army coup. He won the presidential elections 1960 and 1965, and established a stable economy and achieved limited land reforms. His militaristic form of government was unpopular, particularly with the Bengalis. He resigned 1969 after widespread opposition and civil disorder, notably in Kashmir.

Azaña Manuel (1880–1940). Spanish politician and first prime minister 1931–33 of the second Spanish republic. He was last president of the republic during the Civil War 1936–39, before the establishment of a dictatorship under Franco.

Azikiwe Nnamdi (1904–   ). Nigerian politician and president of Nigeria 1963–66. A leading nationalist in the 1940s, he advocated self-government for Nigeria. He was prime minister of Eastern Nigeria 1954–59 and on independence became governor general of the Federation of Nigeria 1960–63. During the civil war triggered by the secession of Biafra 1967–70 he initially backed his own ethnic group, the Ibo, but switched his support to the federal government 1969.

Leader of the Nigeria People's Party from 1978 until political parties were banned 1984, he retired from politics 1986.

Azikiwe was born in Zungeru, Niger State, and educated in the USA. He worked as a newspaper editor in the Gold Coast from 1934, returning to Nigeria 1937 to start the *West African Pilot* in Lagos, where he built up a chain of newspapers. In 1946 he was a founder of the National Council of Nigeria and the Cameroons and acted as its president 1946–60. He was accused of using government funds to save the African Continental Bank in which he held shares 1956, and was censured by a tribunal. His books, mainly on African nationalism, include *Renascent Africa* 1937, *The African in Ancient and Medieval History* 1938, *Political Blueprint of Nigeria* 1943, and *Military Revolution in Nigeria* 1972.

Azorín pen name of José Martínez Ruiz (1873–1967). Spanish writer. His works include volumes of critical essays and short stories, plays and novels, such as the autobiographical *La voluntad/The Choice* 1902, describing the spiritual pessimism of his generation, and *Antonio Azorín* 1903. He adopted the name of the hero of the latter as his pen name.

B

Baade (Wilhelm Heinrich) Walter (1893–1960). German-born US astronomer who made observations that doubled the distance, scale, and age of the universe. He discovered that stars are in two distinct populations according to their age, known as Population I and Population II. Population I stars, bluish, are young and formed from the dusty material of the spiral arms – hydrogen, helium, and heavier elements; Population II stars, reddish, are old, were created near the nucleus and contain fewer heavy elements. Later, he found that Cepheid variable stars of Population I are brighter than had been supposed and that distances calculated from them were wrong.

Baader Andreas (1943–1977). German radical left-wing political activist. With Ulrike Meinhof (1934–1976) and Gudrun Ensslin (1940–1977) he formed the *Rote Armee Fraktion*/Red Army Faction (RAF), also known as the Baader-Meinhof gang, urban guerrillas who aimed to bring down the West German state through acts of violence and political assassination. Sentenced to life imprisonment 1977, he and Ensslin both died in prison, allegedly by suicide.

Baader was born in Munich. He studied under the Palestinian revolutionary group al-Fatah in Jordan, before returning to Germany to join the 1960s student protest movement. He was imprisoned 1968 for setting fire to shops in Frankfurt, but escaped 1970. His death followed the failure of the RAF to secure the release of the three leaders by holding a Lufthansa plane hostage at Mogadishu, Somalia.

Baader Benedict Franz (1765–1841). German theologian and philosopher. His writings, though mystical and often obscure, led some to consider him the greatest Catholic thinker of modern times. He opposed the claims of ecclesiastical authority in the field of speculation, which led to a papal decree 1838 preventing lay persons from lecturing on the philosophy of religion.

Baader was born in Munich. He studied medicine at Ingolstadt and Vienna and spent some years in England (1791–96), where his attention first turned to philosophy. In 1826 he was appointed professor of philosophy and theology at Munich. His works were published in 16 volumes at Leipzig 1851–60.

Bab (Arabic 'gate'). Adopted name of Mirza Ali Mohammad (1819–1850). Persian religious leader, born in Shiraz, founder of Babism, an offshoot of Islam. In 1844 he proclaimed that he was a gateway to the Hidden Imam, a new messenger of Allah who was to come. He gained a large following whose activities caused the Persian authorities to fear a rebellion, and who were therefore persecuted. The Bab was executed for heresy.

Babangida Ibrahim (1941–). Nigerian politician and soldier, president 1985–93. He became head of the Nigerian army 1983 and in 1985 led a coup against President Buhari, assuming the presidency himself. From 1992 he promised a return to civilian rule but resigned 1993, his commitment to democracy increasingly in doubt.

Babbage Charles (1792–1871). English mathematician who devised a precursor of the computer. He designed an analytical engine, a general-purpose mechanical computing device for performing different calculations according to a program input on punched cards (an idea borrowed from the Jacquard loom). This device was never built, but it embodied many of the principles on which digital computers are based.

Babbage was a founder member of the Royal Astronomical Society, the British Association, the Cambridge Philosophical Society, and the Statistical Society of London. He was elected Fellow of the Royal Society 1816. His book *On the Economy of Machinery and Manufactures* 1832 is an analysis of industrial production systems and their economics. Babbage also assisted in establishing the British postal system and compiled the first reliable actuarial tables. Altogether he wrote about 100 books.

Suggested reading
Babbage, Charles *Passages from the Life of a Philosopher* (autobiography) (1864, rep 1969)
Halacy, D *Charles Babbage* (1970)
Hyman, A *Charles Babbage* (1982)
Moseley, M *Irascible Genius* (1964)

Babbitt Milton (1916–). US composer and theorist. He pioneered the application of information theory to music in the 1950s, introducing set theory to series manipulations and the term 'pitch class' to define every octave identity of a note name. His works include four string quartets, works for orchestra, *Philomel* for soprano and electronic tape 1963–64, and *Ensembles for Synthesizer* 1967, both composed using the 1960 RCA Princeton-Columbia Mark II Synthesizer, which he helped to design.

Babcock George Herman (1832–1893). US co-inventor of the first polychromatic printing press. He devised the Babcock–Wilcox steam boiler 1867 with his partner, Stephen Wilcox.

This boiler was able to withstand very high pressures and ensured a high standard of protection against explosions. It was first manufactured in Providence and then in New York, where the firm of Babcock and Wilcox was incorporated 1881.

Babcock Harold Delos (1882–1968). US astronomer and physicist. He measured the Sun's general magnetic field 1948 and studied the relationship between sunspots and local magnetic fields. He also did important work in spectroscopy. He produced a revised table of wavelengths for the solar spectrum, published 1928 and including 22,000 spectral lines (extended 1947 and 1948).

Babel Isaak Emmanuilovich (1894–1941). Russian writer. Born in Odessa, he was an ardent supporter of the Revolution and fought with Budyenny's cavalry in the Polish campaign of 1921–22, an experience which inspired *Red Cavalry* 1926. His other works include *Stories from Odessa* 1924, which portrays the life of the Odessa Jews.

Babeuf François-Noël (1760–1797). French revolutionary journalist, a pioneer of practical socialism. In 1794 he founded a newspaper in Paris, later known as the *Tribune of the People*, in which he demanded the equality of all people. He was guillotined for conspiring against the ruling Directory during the French Revolution.

The whole of the developments and operations of analysis are now capable of being executed by machinery...As soon as an Analytical Engine exists, it will necessarily guide the future course of science.

CHARLES BABBAGE
Passages from the Life of a Philosopher 1864

The murder of the Queen has been represented to me as a deed lawful and meritorious. I die a firm Catholic.

ANTHONY BABINGTON
Last words before execution 1586 for attempting to assassinate Queen Elizabeth I.

Babington Anthony (1561–1586). English traitor who hatched a plot to assassinate Elizabeth I and replace her with Mary Queen of Scots; its discovery led to Mary's execution and his own.

I shall adorn each of Aesop's fables with the flower of my own Muse and present a poetical honeycomb, dripping with sweetness.

BABRIUS
Fables preface

Babrius (lived 3rd century AD). Roman writer of fables, written in Greek. He probably lived in Syria, where his stories first gained popularity. In 1842 a manuscript of his fables was discovered in a convent on Mount Athos, Greece. There were 123 fables, arranged alphabetically, but stopping at the letter O.

Babur (Arabic 'lion') (Zahir ud-Din Muhammad) (1483–1530). First Great Mogul of India from 1526. He was the great-grandson of the Mogul conqueror Tamerlane and, at the age of 11, succeeded his father, Omar Sheik Mirza, as ruler of Ferghana (Turkestan). In 1526 he defeated the emperor of Delhi at Panipat in the Punjab, captured Delhi and Agra (the site of the Taj Mahal), and established a dynasty that lasted until 1858.

Baby Doc nickname of Jean-Claude ◊Duvalier, president of Haiti 1971–86.

Bacall Lauren. Stage name of Betty Joan Perske (1924–). US actress. She became an overnight star when cast by Howard Hawks opposite Humphrey Bogart in *To Have and Have Not* 1944. She and Bogart married 1945 and starred together in *The Big Sleep* 1946. She returned to Hollywood after an eight-year absence with *Murder on the Orient Express* 1974 and two years later appeared in *The Shootist* 1976, subsequently playing occasional cameo roles.

She also appeared in *The Cobweb* 1955 and *Harper* 1966.

Bach is the father, we are the children.

Joseph Haydn on CARL PHILIP EMMANUEL BACH
Bodley Head History of Music, 1974

Bach Carl Philip Emmanuel (1714–1788). German composer. He was the third son of J S Bach. He introduced a new 'homophonic' style, light and easy to follow, which influenced Mozart, Haydn, and Beethoven.

In the service of Frederick the Great 1740–67, he left to become master of church music at Hamburg 1768. He wrote over 200 pieces for keyboard instruments, and published a guide to playing the piano. Through his music and concert performances he helped to establish a leading solo role for the piano in Western music.

Bach Johann Christian (1735–1782). German composer. The eleventh son of J S Bach, he became celebrated in Italy as a composer of operas. In 1762 he was invited to London, where he became music master to the royal family. He remained in England until his death, enjoying great popularity both as a composer and a performer.

For the glory of the most high God alone / And for my neighbour to learn from.

JOHANN SEBASTIAN BACH
epigraph to *The Little Organ Book*, 1717

Bach Johann Sebastian (1685–1750). German composer. A master of counterpoint, his music epitomizes the Baroque polyphonic style. His orchestral music includes the six *Brandenburg Concertos* 1721, other concertos for keyboard instrument and violin, four orchestral suites, sonatas for various instruments, six violin partitas, and six unaccompanied cello suites. Bach's keyboard music, for clavier and organ, his fugues, and his choral music are of equal importance. He also wrote chamber music and songs.

Born at Eisenach, Bach came from a distinguished musical family. At 15 he became a chorister at Lüneburg, and at 19 he was organist at Arnstadt. His appointments included positions at the courts of

Bach, J S *J S Bach (1685–1750) represented in his later years in a painting by Gemäide von Elias Gottlieb Haussmann (1746). The seminal figure of the Baroque period, Bach's greatest legacy was his extensive oeuvre of sacred and keyboard works; as a composer for the organ he is unrivalled.* (Image Select)

Weimar and Anhalt-Köthen, and from 1723 until his death he was musical director at St Thomas' choir school in Leipzig.

He married twice and had over 20 children (although several died in infancy). His second wife, Anna Magdalena Wülkens, was a soprano; she also worked for him when his sight failed in later years.

Bach's sacred music includes 200 church cantatas; the Christmas and Easter oratorios 1734 and 1736; the two great Passions, of St John and St Matthew, first performed 1723 and 1729, and the Mass in B minor 1749. His keyboard music includes a collection of 48 preludes and fugues known as *Das wohltemperierte Clavier/The Well-Tempered Clavier* 1742, the *Goldberg Variations* 1742, and the *Italian Concerto* 1735. Of his organ music the finest examples are the chorale preludes. Two works written in his later years illustrate the principles and potential of his polyphonic art – *Das Musikalische Opfer/The Musical Offering* 1747 and *Die Kunst der Fuge/The Art of Fugue*, published posthumously 1751.

Suggested reading
Boyd, M *Bach* (1983)
David, H and Mendel, A (eds) *The Bach Reader* (1966)
Dowley, T *Bach His Life and Times* (1985)
Mellers, W *Bach and the Dance of God* (1980)
Neumann, W *Bach and his World* (1970)

Bach almost persuades me to be a Christian.

Roger Fry on JOHANN SEBASTIAN BACH
quoted in Virginia Woolf *Roger Fry* 1940

Bach Wilhelm Friedemann (1710–1784). German composer. He was also an organist, improviser, and master of counterpoint. He was the eldest son of J S Bach.

Bachelard Gaston (1884–1962). French philosopher and scientist who argued for a creative interplay between reason and experience. He attacked both Cartesian and positivist positions, insisting that science was derived neither from first principles nor directly from experience.

Even a minor event in the life of a child is an event of that child's world and thus a world event.

GASTON BACHELARD
Fragments of a Poetics of Fire ch 1

Bacon Francis (1909–1992). Irish painter. Self-taught, he practised abstract art, then developed a stark Expressionist style characterized by distorted, blurred figures enclosed in loosely defined space. One of his best-known works is *Study after Velázquez's Portrait of Pope Innocent X* 1953 (Museum of Modern Art, New York).

Bacon moved to London 1925, began to paint about 1930, and held his first show in London 1949. He destroyed much of his early work. *Three Studies for Figures at the Base of a Crucifixion* about 1944 (Tate Gallery, London) is an early example of his mature style, which is often seen as a powerful expression of the existential anxiety and nihilism of 20th-century life.

Suggested reading
Ades, D and Farge, A *Francis Bacon* (1985)
Archimbaud, M *Francis Bacon: In Conversation* (1993)
Russell, J *Francis Bacon* (1971)
Sylvester, D *Interviews with Francis Bacon 1962–1979* (1980)

It's an attempt to bring the figurative thing up onto the nervous system more violently and more poignantly.

FRANCIS BACON
in David Sylvester *The Brutality of Fact: Interviews with Francis Bacon* 1975

Bacon Francis, 1st Baron Verulam and Viscount St Albans (1561–1626). English politician, philosopher, and essayist. He became Lord Chancellor 1618, and the same year confessed to bribe-taking, was fined £40,000 (which was later remitted by the king), and spent four days in the Tower of London. His works include *Essays* 1597, characterized by pith and brevity; *The Advancement of Learning* 1605, a seminal work discussing scientific method; *Novum organum* 1620, in which he redefined the task of natural science, seeing it as a means of empirical discovery and a method of increasing human power over nature; and *The New Atlantis* 1626, describing a utopian state in which scientific knowledge is systematically sought and exploited.

Bacon was born in London, studied law at Cambridge from 1573, was part of the embassy in France until 1579, and became a member of Parliament 1584. He was the nephew of Queen Elizabeth's adviser Lord Burghley, but turned against him when he failed to provide Bacon with patronage. He helped secure the execution of the earl of Essex as a traitor 1601, after formerly being his follower. Bacon was accused of ingratitude, but he defended himself in *Apology* 1604.

Satirist Alexander Pope called Bacon 'the wisest, brightest, and meanest of mankind'. Knighted on the accession of James I 1603, he became Baron Verulam 1618 and Viscount St Albans 1621. His writings helped to inspire the founding of the Royal Society. The *Baconian Theory*, originated by James Willmot 1785, suggesting that

I have taken all knowledge to be my province.

FRANCIS BACON
Letter to Lord Burleigh 1592

Bacon, Francis *After a bribery scandal that left his political career in ruins, Francis Bacon devoted the rest of his life to the advancement of science. His own scientific work was generally behind the times, but it was his ideas and philosophies, particularly his insistence of the importance of experiment over deduction, that made him such an influential figure.* (Image Select)

the works of Shakespeare were written by Bacon, is not taken seriously by scholars.

Suggested reading
Anderson, F H *Francis Bacon: His Career and his Thought* (1962)
Farrington, B *Francis Bacon: Philosopher of Planned Science* (1963)
Quinton, A *Francis Bacon* (1980)
Weinberger, J *Science, Faith and Politics: Francis Bacon and the Utopian Roots of the Modern Age* (1985)
Whitney, C *Francis Bacon and Modernity* (1986)

Bacon Nathaniel (1647–1676). American colonial leader and wealthy plantation owner. An advocate of social reform in Virginia and an opponent of Governor William Berkeley, he gained wide public support and was proclaimed 'General of Virginia'. In 1676 he organized Bacon's Rebellion, forcing Berkeley to flee from the capital at Jamestown. Bacon's sudden death ended the uprising but Berkeley was removed from power for his brutal treatment of the rebels.

Bacon Roger (c. 1214–1294). English philosopher and scientist. He was interested in alchemy, the biological and physical sciences, and magic. Many discoveries have been credited to him, including the magnifying lens. He foresaw the extensive use of gunpowder and mechanical cars, boats, and planes.

In 1266, at the invitation of his friend Pope Clement IV, he began his *Opus majus/Great Work*, a compendium of all branches of knowledge. In 1268 he sent this with his *Opus minus/Lesser Work* and other writings to the pope. In 1277 Bacon was condemned and imprisoned by the Christian church for 'certain novelties' (heresy) and not released until 1292.

Bacon wrote in Latin and his works include *On Mirrors, Metaphysical,* and *On the Multiplication of Species.* He followed the maxim 'Cease to be ruled by dogmas and authorities; look at the world!'

Bacon was born in Somerset and educated at Oxford and Paris. He became a Franciscan monk and lectured in Paris about 1241–47, then at Oxford University. He described a hypothetical diving apparatus and some of the properties of gunpowder. He promoted the use of latitude and longitude in mapmaking, and suggested the changes necessary to improve the Western calendar that were carried out by Pope Gregory XIII in 1582.

Mathematics is the door and the key to the sciences.
ROGER BACON
Opus Majus pt 4 *Distinctia Prima* ch 1, 1267 transl Robert Belle Burke 1928

Baden-Powell Agnes (1854–1945). Sister of Robert Baden-Powell, she helped him found the Girl Guides.

Baden-Powell Olave St Clair (1889–1977). Wife of Robert Baden-Powell from 1912, she was the first and only World Chief Guide 1918–1977.

Baden-Powell Robert Stephenson Smyth, 1st Baron Baden-Powell (1857–1941). British general, founder of the Scout Association. He fought in defence of Mafeking (now Mafikeng) during the Second South African War. After 1907 he devoted his time to developing the Scout movement, which rapidly spread throughout the world.

Born in London, he was educated at Charterhouse. After failing to gain a place at Oxford University he joined the Indian Army, being commissioned in the Hussars in 1876; he became its youngest colonel by the age of 40. His defence of Mafikeng brought him worldwide fame.

Baden-Powell began the Scout movement in 1907 with a camp for 20 boys on Brownsea Island, Poole Harbour, Dorset. He published *Scouting for Boys* 1908 and about thirty other books. He was World Chief Scout from 1920. Knighted 1909, created baron 1929.

Suggested reading
Jeal, Tim *Baden-Powell* (1989)
Kiernan, R H *Baden-Powell* (1939)
Wade, E K *The Chief: The Life Story of Robert Baden-Powell* (1975)

A Scout smiles and whistles under all circumstances.
ROBERT BADEN-POWELL
Scouting for Boys 1908

Bader Douglas Robert Steuart (1910–1982). British fighter pilot. He lost both legs in a flying accident 1931, but had a distinguished flying career in World War II. He was credited with 22 planes shot down before himself being shot down and captured Aug 1941. He was twice decorated for his war service and was knighted 1976 for his work with disabled people.

Badoglio Pietro (1871–1956). Italian soldier and Fascist politician. He served as a general in World War I and subsequently in the campaigns against the peoples of Tripoli and Cyrenaica. In 1935 he became commander in chief in Ethiopia, adopting ruthless measures to break patriot resistance. He was created viceroy of Ethiopia and duke of Addis Ababa in 1936. He resigned during the disastrous campaign into Greece 1940 and succeeded Mussolini as prime minister of Italy from July 1943 to June 1944, negotiating the armistice with the Allies.

Badura-Skoda Paul (1927–). Austrian pianist. He has recorded on both the fortepiano and the modern piano, particularly the work of Mozart, and his interpretations are noted for their attention to authenticity.

Baedeker Karl (1801–1859). German editor and publisher of foreign travel guides; the first was for Coblenz 1829. These are now published from Hamburg (before World War II from Leipzig).

Oxford is ... more attractive than Cambridge to the ordinary visitor; ... the traveller is therefore recommended to visit Cambridge first, or to omit it altogether if he cannot visit both.
KARL BAEDEKER
Baedeker's Great Britain 'From London to Oxford' 1887

Baekeland Leo Hendrik (1863–1944). Belgian-born US chemist. He invented Bakelite, the first commercial plastic, made from formaldehyde and phenol. He also made a photographic paper, Velox, which could be developed in artificial light. In 1909 he founded the General Bakelite Corporation, later to become part of the Union Carbide and Carbon Company.

Baer Karl Ernst von (1792–1876). Estonian embryologist who discovered the mammalian ovum 1827. He made a significant contribution to the systematic study of the development of animals, and showed that an embryo develops from simple to complex, from a homogeneous to a heterogeneous stage.

Baer conceived that the goal of early development is the formation of three layers in the vertebrate embryo – the ectoderm, endoderm, and mesoderm – out of which all later organs are formed. He also suggested that the younger the embryos of various species are, the stronger is the resemblance between them.

In his observations of the embryo, von Baer discovered the extraembryonic membranes – the chorion, amnion, and allantois – and described their functions. He also identified for the first time the notochord and revealed the neural folds.

Baer *Using a colleague's pet dog as a subject for dissection, von Baer was the first embryologist to show that mammalian reproduction involved the fusion of a female ovum with male sperm, instead of, as previously thought, a mingling of mutual seminal fluids. He also showed that during embryonic development, general characteristics appeared before species-dependent ones: this concept eventually became known as the 'biogenetic law'. (Ann Ronan/Image Select)*

Baeyer Johann Friedrich Wilhelm Adolf von (1835–1917). German organic chemist who synthesized the dye indigo 1880. He discovered barbituric acid 1863, later to become the parent substance of a major class of hypnotic drugs. In 1888 he carried out the first synthesis of a terpene. Nobel Prize for Chemistry 1905.

His work with ring compounds and the highly unstable polyacetylenes led him to consider the effects of carbon–carbon bond angles on the stability of organic compounds. He concluded that the more a bond is deformed away from the ideal tetrahedral angle, the more unstable it is; this is known as Baeyer's strain theory. It explains why rings with five or six atoms are much more common, and stable, than those with fewer or more atoms.

Baez Joan (1941–). US folk singer and pacifist activist. Her pure soprano in the early 1960s popularized traditional English and American folk songs such as 'Silver Dagger' and 'We Shall Overcome' (an anthem of the civil-rights movement). She helped Bob Dylan at the start of his career and has recorded many of his songs. She founded the Institute for the Study of Non-Violence in Carmel, California, 1965.

I've never had a humble opinion. If you've got an opinion, why be humble about it?

JOAN BAEZ
Attributed remark

Baffin William (1584–1622). English explorer and navigator. In 1616 he and Robert Bylot explored Baffin Bay, NE Canada, and reached latitude 77° 45′ N, which for 236 years remained the 'furthest north'.

In 1612, Baffin was chief pilot of an expedition in search of the Northwest Passage, and in 1613–14 commanded a whaling fleet near Spitsbergen, Norway. He piloted the *Discovery* on an expedition to Hudson Bay led by Bylot in 1615. After 1617, Baffin worked for the East India Company and made surveys of the Red Sea and Persian Gulf. In 1622 he was killed in an Anglo-Persian attack on Hormuz.

Bagehot Walter (1826–1877). British writer and economist. His *English Constitution* 1867, a classic analysis of the British political system, is still a standard work.

Bagehot was editor of the *Economist* magazine 1860–77. His *Physics and Politics* 1872 was one of the first books to apply the theory of evolution to politics.

Bagnold Enid Algerine (1889–1981). English author. Her novel *National Velvet* 1935, about horse racing, was also successful as a film (1944) starring Elizabeth Taylor. She wrote the play *The Chalk Garden* 1954.

Bagritsky Eduard. Pen name of Eduard Dzyubin (1895–1934). Russian poet. One of the Constructivist group, he published the heroic poem *Lay About Opanas* 1926, and collections of verse called *The Victors* 1932 and *The Last Night* 1932.

A poet, musician, and calligrapher, more an aesthete than a political leader ... for most of his reign he was a client of the British without authority.

Encyclopaedia Britannica on BAHADUR SHAH II
1990

Bahadur Shah II (1775–1862). Last of the Mogul emperors of India. He reigned, though in name only, as king of Delhi 1837–57, when he was hailed by the mutineers of the Indian Mutiny as an independent emperor at Delhi. After the rebellion he was exiled to Burma (now Myanmar) with his family.

Baha'u'llah title of Mirza Hosein Ali (1817–1892). Persian founder of the Baha'i religion. Baha'u'llah, 'God's Glory', proclaimed himself as the prophet the Bab had foretold.

Bainbridge, Beryl *The English novelist and journalist Beryl Bainbridge. Her novels, full of comic and sometimes macabre incidents, are wry and compassionate depictions of the pains and complexities of domestic life.*

Bailey David (1938–). English fashion photographer. His work for *Vogue* magazine in the 1960s and his black-and-white portraits of fashionable celebrities did much to define the image of 'swinging London'. He has published several books, including *Box of Pin-ups* 1965 and *Goodbye Baby and Amen* 1969.

If I have to explain my pictures in words, it means that my images have not worked.

DAVID BAILEY
Attributed remark.

Bailey Donald Coleman (1901–1985). English engineer, inventor in World War II of the portable Bailey bridge, made of interlocking, interchangeable, adjustable, and easily transportable units. Knighted 1946.

Baillie Isobel (1895–1983). British soprano. Celebrated for her work in oratorio, she was professor of singing at Cornell University in New York 1960–61. DBE 1978.

Bailly Jean Sylvain (1736–1793). French astronomer who wrote about the satellites of Jupiter and the history of astronomy. Early in the French Revolution he was president of the national assembly and mayor of Paris, but resigned in 1791; he was guillotined during the Reign of Terror.

It is time for me to enjoy another pinch of snuff. Tomorrow my hands will be bound, so as to make it impossible.

JEAN SYLVAIN BAILLY
Remark made on the evening before his execution,
quoted in H Hoffmeister *Anekdotenschatz*

Baily Francis (1774–1844). British astronomer who described in 1836 the light effect called Baily's beads, observable during a total eclipse of the Sun. Baily began to publish his astronomical observations 1811. He was the author of an accurate revised star catalogue in which he plotted the positions of nearly 3,000 stars. He also measured the Earth's elliptical shape.

Bainbridge Beryl (1934–). English novelist, originally an actress. Her writing has dramatic economy and pace. Acutely observed, peppered with ironic black humour, and often dealing with the tragedy and comedy of human self-delusion, her works include *The Dressmaker* 1973, *The Bottle Factory Outing* 1974, *Injury Time* 1977, *An Awfully Big Adventure* 1990, and *The Birthday Boys* 1991.

Among her other works are *Young Adolf* 1978, *The Winter Garden* 1980, and the collected short stories in *Mum and Mr Armitage* 1985.

> *There are so many ways of dying it's astonishing any of us choose old age.*
>
> BERYL BAINBRIDGE
> *Young Adolf* ch 12 1978

Bainbridge Kenneth Tompkins (1904–). US physicist who was director of the first atomic-bomb test at Alamogordo, New Mexico, 1945. He also made important innovations in the mass spectrometer.

The mass spectrometer invented by English physicist Francis Aston focused ion beams of varying velocity but not varying direction. In 1936 Bainbridge developed a machine in which ion beams that are nonuniform in both direction and velocity can be brought to a focus.

Baird John Logie (1888–1946). Scottish electrical engineer who pioneered television. In 1925 he gave the first public demonstration of television and in 1926 pioneered fibre optics, radar (in advance of Robert Watson-Watt), and 'noctovision', a system for seeing at night by using infrared rays.

Born at Helensburgh, Scotland, Baird studied electrical engineering in Glasgow at what is now the University of Strathclyde, at the

Baker, Benjamin British civil engineer Benjamin Baker 1896. Baker worked in the latter half of the nineteenth century and is famous for designing the Forth Rail Bridge. (Image Select)

Baird John Logie Baird. In April 1927 in New York, a year after the first public demonstration of an early television set, Bell Telephone made a historic black and white broadcast on a screen just two inches high and three inches wide: the programme consisted of a brief speech by the Secretary of Commerce, Herbert Hoover, followed by a vaudeville comic. In 1928, Baird demonstrated the first colour transmission in London with a programme devoted to a man repeatedly sticking his tongue out. (Image Select)

same time serving several practical apprenticeships. He was working on television possibly as early as 1912, and he took out his first provisional patent 1923. He also developed video recording on both wax records and magnetic steel discs (1926–27), colour TV (1925–28), 3-D colour TV (1925–46), and transatlantic TV (1928). In 1936 his mechanically scanned 240-line system competed with EMI-Marconi's 405-line, but the latter was preferred for the BBC service from 1937, partly because it used electronic scanning and partly because it handled live indoor scenes with smaller, more manoeuvrable cameras. In 1944 he developed facsimile television, the forerunner of Ceefax, and demonstrated the world's first all-electronic colour and 3-D colour receiver (500 lines).

> *Well, if you knows of a better 'ole, go to it.*
>
> BRUCE BAIRNSFATHER
> *Fragments from France* 1

Bairnsfather (Charles) Bruce (1888–1959). British artist, celebrated for his 'Old Bill' cartoons of World War I. In World War II he was official cartoonist to the US Army in Europe 1942–44.

Baker Alan (1939–). English mathematician whose chief work has been devoted to the study of transcendental numbers (numbers that cannot be expressed as roots or as the solution of an algebraic equation with rational coefficients).

Baker was born in London and studied mathematics there and at Cambridge. He remained at Cambridge, except for many visiting professorships abroad, becoming professor 1974.

Baker Benjamin (1840–1907). English engineer who designed, with English engineer John Fowler (1817–1898), London's first underground railway (the Metropolitan and District) 1869; the Forth Rail Bridge, Scotland, 1890; and the original Aswan Dam on the river Nile, Egypt. KCMG 1890.

Baker was born near Frome, Somerset, and at 16 was apprenticed at Neath Abbey ironworks. In 1862 he joined the staff of John

Baker, Janet *Following her 1957 operatic debut in Smetana's* The Secret *at Glyndebourne, mezzo-soprano Janet Baker enjoyed an extensive operatic career. Especially admired for her stylish performance of early Italian opera and the works of Benjamin Britten, she also excelled as an interpreter of Bach, Schubert, and Mahler.*

Fowler, becoming his partner 1875. In the construction of the Central Line of the London Underground, Baker incorporated an ingenious energy-conservation measure: he dipped the line between stations to reduce the need both for braking to a halt and for the increase in power required to accelerate away.

The Forth Bridge was built just after the collapse of the Tay Bridge 1879, and made Baker's name internationally. It is a cantilever structure of mild steel, which had just become available through the new Siemens open-hearth process. The two main spans are each of 521 m/1,710 ft.

Baker Chet (Chesney) (1929–1988). US jazz trumpeter. His good looks, occasional vocal performances, and romantic interpretations of ballads helped make him a cult figure. He became known with the Gerry Mulligan Quartet 1952 and formed his own quartet 1953. Recordings include 'My Funny Valentine' and 'The Thrill Is Gone'.

Baker Howard Henry (1925–1994). US Republican politician. He was senator from Tennessee 1967–85, Senate minority leader 1977–81, and majority leader 1981–85. As White House chief of staff 1987–88, he helped the administration deal with the revelation of the Irangate scandal (the illegal sale of arms to Iran by members of the US government in order to fund the rebels in Nicaragua).

After serving in the US Navy during World War II, Baker joined the family law firm in Knoxville, Tennessee. He was a member of the Senate select committee to investigate the Watergate scandal 1973, which brought down President Nixon. After poor results in the New Hampshire primary, he withdrew from the contest for the Republican nomination for president 1980.

Baker James Addison III (1930–   ). US Republican politician. Under President Reagan, he was White House chief of staff 1981–85 and Treasury secretary 1985–88. After managing George Bush's successful presidential campaign, Baker was appointed secretary of state 1989 and played a prominent role in the 1990–91 Gulf crisis and the subsequent search for a lasting Middle East peace settlement. In 1992 he left the State Department to become White House chief of staff and to oversee Bush's unsuccessful re-election campaign.

He was criticized for the unscrupulousness of the 1988 Bush campaign.

Baker Janet Abbott (1933–   ). English mezzo-soprano noted for the emotional strength and richness of her interpretations of lieder (musical settings for poems), oratorio, and opera from Purcell to Britten, including a notable Dido in Purcell's *Dido and Aeneas*. She retired from the stage 1981. DBE 1976.

Performances include Dido in both *Dido and Aeneas* and *The Trojans*, and Marguerite in *Faust*; also *The Dream of Gerontius* and *The Song of the Earth*.

Singing lieder is like putting a piece of music under a microscope.

JANET BAKER
Opera News July 1977

Baker Kenneth Wilfrid (1934–   ). British Conservative politician, home secretary 1990–92. He was environment secretary 1985–86, education secretary 1986–89, and chair of the Conservative Party 1989–90, retaining his cabinet seat, before becoming home secretary in John Major's government. Since his dismissal in 1992, he has become a strong government critic.

Baker Nicholson (1957–   ). US novelist. His first novel, *The Mezzanine* 1988, was followed by *Room Temperature* 1990, *Vox* 1992, and *The Fermata* 1994. Often pornographic, his novels are notable for their attention to detail and lack of plot.

Baker was born in Rochester, New York, and worked as a Wall Street oil analyst and stockbroker before turning to writing. In 1991 he published *U and I: A True Story*, an autobiographical work about his fixation on the writer John Updike.

Baker Samuel White (1821–1893). English explorer, in 1864 the first European to sight Lake Albert Nyanza (now Lake Mobutu Sese Seko) in central Africa, and discover that the river Nile flowed through it.

He founded an agricultural colony in Ceylon (now Sri Lanka), built a railway across the Dobruja, and in 1861 set out to discover the source of the Nile. His wife, Florence von Sass, accompanied him. From 1869 to 1873 he was governor general of the Nile equatorial regions. Knighted 1866.

Bakewell Robert (1725–1795). British pioneer improver of farm livestock. From his home in Leicestershire, England, he developed the Dishley or New Leicester breed of sheep and worked on raising the beef-producing qualities of Longhorn cattle. Known as 'breeding in and in', his technique was adopted widely.

Bakewell's Longhorns found less favour because they were outshone by the rapidly emerging Shorthorns, but his New Leicesters proved popular as crosses to improve other native breeds of sheep.

Bakhtiar Shahpur (1914–1991). Iranian politician, the last prime minister under the Shah, in 1979. He was a supporter of the political leader Muhammad Mossadeq in the 1950s, and was active in the National Front opposition to the Shah from 1960. He lived in exile after the 1979 Islamic revolution, until his assassination by Islamic zealots at his home in a Paris suburb.

Bakhuyzen Ludolf (1631–1708). Dutch marine painter and etcher, the pupil of van Everdingen at Amsterdam, where his life was mainly spent. He worked for Peter the Great, and in his own day was as highly esteemed for 'storms' (*Boats in a Storm* in the Dulwich Gallery, London, and *Stormy Sea* in the Rijksmuseum, Amsterdam being examples) as Willem van de Velde for 'calms'. He is well represented in the National Gallery, London.

Bakke Allan (1940–). US student who, in 1978, gave his name to a test case claiming 'reverse discrimination' when appealing against his exclusion from medical school, since less well-qualified blacks were to be admitted as part of a special programme for ethnic minorities. He won his case against quotas before the Supreme Court, although other affirmative action for minority groups was still endorsed.

Bakst Leon. Assumed name of Leon Rosenberg (1866–1924). Russian painter and theatrical designer. He combined intense colours and fantastic images adapted from Oriental and folk art with an Art Nouveau tendency toward graceful surface pattern. His designs for Diaghilev's touring *Ballets Russes* made a deep impression in Paris 1909–14.

Does it follow that I reject all authority? Perish the thought. In the matter of boots, I defer to the authority of the bootmaker.

MIKHAIL BAKUNIN
God and the State 1882

Bakunin Mikhail (1814–1876). Russian anarchist, active in Europe. In 1848 he was expelled from France as a revolutionary agitator. In Switzerland in the 1860s he became recognized as the leader of the anarchist movement. In 1869 he joined the First International (a coordinating socialist body) but, after stormy conflicts with Karl Marx, was expelled 1872. He wrote books and pamphlets, including *God and the State*.

Balakirev Mily Alexeyevich (1837–1910). Russian composer. He wrote orchestral works including the fantasy *Islamey* 1869/1902, piano music, songs, and a symphonic poem *Tamara*, all imbued with the Russian national character and spirit. He was leader of the group known as 'The Five' and taught its members, Mussorgsky, Cui, Rimsky-Korsakov, and Borodin.

Balakirev was born at Nizhni-Novgorod. At St Petersburg he worked with Mikhail Glinka, established the Free School of Music 1862, which stressed the national element, and was director of the Imperial Chapel 1883–95.

In time he will be a second Glinka.

Mikhail Glinka on MILY ALEXEYEVICH BALAKIREV
quoted in *Edward Garden* 'Balakirev' 1967

Balanchine George (born Georgi Melitonivich Balanchivadze) (1904–1983). Russian-born US choreographer. After leaving the USSR 1924, he worked with Diaghilev in France. Moving to the USA 1933, he became a major influence on dance, starting the New York City Ballet 1948. He was the most influential 20th-century choreographer of ballet in the USA. He developed an 'American Neo-Classic' dance style and made the New York City Ballet one of the world's great companies. His ballets are usually plotless and are performed in practice clothes to modern music. He also choreographed dances for five Hollywood films.

His many works include *Apollon Musagète* 1928 and *The Prodigal Son* 1929 for Diaghilev; *Serenade* 1934; several works with music by Stravinsky, such as *Agon* 1957 and *Duo Concertante* 1972; and Broadway musicals, such as *On Your Toes* 1936 and *The Boys from Syracuse* 1938.
Suggested reading
Balanchine, George and Mason F *Balanchine's Book of Ballet* (1985)
Balanchine, George *Choreography by Balanchine: A Catalogue of Works* (1984)
Caras, Steven *Balanchine* (1985)
Kirstein, L *Portrait of Mr Balanchine* (1984)

Balbo Italo, Count (1896–1940). Italian aviator and politician. He was one of the main figures in Mussolini's 'March on Rome' but later quarrelled with him over the alliance with Germany.

A well-known aviator, famed for his long-distance flights to demonstrate Italian aviation, he served as minister of aviation in the

1930s. His popularity irked Mussolini, and he was despatched as governor to Libya 1936. This did not stop him voicing his objections to Mussolini's growing friendship with Hitler and he tried to persuade Mussolini to stay out of the war. Shortly after Italy's entry into the war, Balbo was flying back to Libya from Italy when his aircraft was shot down over Tobruk by Italian anti-aircraft guns and he was killed.

Decisive, unscrupulous, no respecter of persons ... first of the great conquistadors of the American mainland.

J H Parry on VASCO NÚÑEZ DE BALBOA
in *The Age of Reconnaissance* 1963

Balboa Vasco Núñez de (1475–1519). Spanish conquistador. He founded a settlement at Darien (now Panama) 1511 and crossed the Isthmus in search of gold, reaching the Pacific Ocean (which he called the South Sea) on 25 Sept 1513, after a 25-day expedition. He was made admiral of the Pacific and governor of Panama but was removed by Spanish court intrigue, imprisoned, and executed.

He was the first European to see the eastern side of the Pacific Ocean.

Balchin Nigel Marlin (1908–1970). English author. During World War II he was engaged on scientific work for the army and wrote *The Small Back Room* 1943, a novel dealing with the psychology of the 'back room boys' of wartime research.

Who are the people who've been wrong every single time all through the war? The experienced soldiers.

NIGEL BALCHIN
The Small Back Room ch 3 1943

Balcon Michael Elias (1896–1977). English film producer. He was responsible for the influential Ealing comedies of the 1940s and early 1950s, such as *Kind Hearts and Coronets* 1949, *Whisky Galore!* 1949, and *The Lavender Hill Mob* 1951. Knighted 1948.

Baldung Grien Hans (1484/85–1545). German Renaissance painter, engraver, and designer. He was based in Strasbourg. A prolific artist, he designed tapestries and stained glass, produced many graphic works, and painted religious subjects, portraits, and allegories, notably his several versions of *Death and the Maiden*. His principal religious paintings were his altarpiece for the cathedral at Freiburg, *The Adoration of the Kings* (Berlin) and *Crucifixion* (Basel), showing an ornate invention.

To be a Negro in this country and to be relatively conscious is to be in a rage almost all the time.

JAMES BALDWIN
Time Aug 1965

Baldwin James Arthur (1924–1987). US writer and civil-rights activist. He portrayed with vivid intensity the suffering and despair of black Americans in contemporary society. After his first novel, *Go Tell It On The Mountain* 1953, set in Harlem, and *Giovanni's Room* 1956, about a homosexual relationship in Paris, his writing became more politically indignant with *Another Country* 1962 and *The Fire Next Time* 1963, a collection of essays.

Other works include his play *The Amen Corner* 1955, the autobiographical essays *Notes of a Native Son* 1955, and the novel *Just Above My Head* 1979.
Suggested reading
Macebush, S *James Baldwin* (1973)
O'Daniel, T B *James Baldwin: A Critical Evaluation* (1977)
Pratt, L H *James Baldwin* (1978)
Sylvander, C W *James Baldwin* (1981)

Baldwin Stanley, 1st Earl Baldwin of Bewdley (1867–1947). British Conservative politician, prime minister 1923–24, 1924–29,

The gift of rhetoric has been responsible for more bloodshed on this earth than all the guns and explosives that were ever invented.

STANLEY BALDWIN
quoted in *Observer* 16 March 1924

and 1935–37; he weathered the general strike 1926, secured complete adult suffrage 1928, and handled the abdication crisis of Edward VIII 1936, but failed to prepare Britain for World War II.

Born in Bewdley, Worcestershire, the son of an iron and steel magnate, in 1908 he was elected Unionist member of Parliament for Bewdley, and in 1916 he became parliamentary private secretary to Bonar Law. He was financial secretary to the Treasury 1917–21, and then appointed to the presidency of the Board of Trade. In 1919 he gave the Treasury £50,000 of War Loan for cancellation, representing about 20% of his fortune. He was a leader in the disruption of the Lloyd George coalition 1922, and, as chancellor under Bonar Law, achieved a settlement of war debts with the USA.

Baldwin believed that it was rarely possible to solve problems. The forces which created them might be diverted or weakened, and this perpetual struggle was an 'Endless Adventure'.

Keith Middlemas and John Barnes on STANLEY BALDWIN
in *Baldwin* 1969

As prime minister 1923–24 and again 1924–29, Baldwin passed the Trades Disputes Act of 1927 after the general strike, granted widows' and orphans' pensions, and complete adult suffrage 1928. He joined the national government of Ramsay MacDonald 1931 as Lord President of the Council. He handled the abdication crisis during his third premiership 1935–37, but was later much criticized for

Balfour, Arthur *Arthur Balfour, British statesman, formulator of the Balfour Declaration. An intellectual – he delivered the Gifford Lectures on Theism and Humanism 1915 – he was sometimes considered too detached to excel in politics.*

his failures to resist popular desire for an accommodation with the dictators Hitler and Mussolini, and to rearm more effectively. Created earl 1937.

Suggested reading
Ball, Stuart *Baldwin and the Conservative Party: The Crisis 1929–1931* (1988)
Middlemas, Keith and Barnes, John *Baldwin: A Biography* (1969)
Montgomery Hyde, H *Baldwin: The Unexpected Prime Minister* (1973)
Young, Kenneth *Baldwin* (1976)

Baldwin five kings of the Latin kingdom of Jerusalem, including:

Baldwin I (1058–1118). King of Jerusalem from 1100. A French nobleman, he joined his brother Godfrey de Bouillon on the First Crusade 1096 and established the kingdom of Jerusalem 1100. It was destroyed by Islamic conquest 1187.

Baldwin III (1129–1162). King of the Latin kingdom of Jerusalem from 1144, succeeding his father, Fulk of Anjou. Baldwin III ruled Jerusalem during the ill-fated Second Crusade.

Baldwin IV the Leper (1160–1185). King of the Latin kingdom of Jerusalem from 1173.

Balenciaga Cristóbal (1895–1972). Spanish couturier. His influential innovations in women's clothing included drop shoulder lines, nipped-in waists, and rounded hips, followed by three-quarter length sleeves and the pillbox hat. During the 1950s–1960s he moved away from fitted outfits to show loose designs such as a dress known as the 'sack', cut full around the body and gathered or tapered into a narrow hem-band just below the knees, in 1956 and loose full jackets in the 1960s. He retired 1968.

Balewa alternative title of Nigerian politician ◊Tafawa Balewa.

Balfe Michael William (1808–1870). Irish composer and singer. He was a violinist and baritone at Drury Lane, London, when only 16. In 1825 he went to Italy, where he sang in Palermo and at La Scala, and in 1846 he was appointed conductor at Her Majesty's Theatre, London. His operas include *The Bohemian Girl* 1843.

Balfour Arthur James, 1st Earl of Balfour (1848–1930). British Conservative politician, prime minister 1902–05 and foreign secretary 1916–19. He was involved in peace negotiations after World War I, signing the Treaty of Versailles.

Son of a Scottish landowner, Balfour was elected a Conservative member of Parliament 1874. In Lord Salisbury's ministry he was secretary for Ireland 1887, and for his ruthless vigour was called 'Bloody Balfour' by Irish nationalists. In 1891 and again in 1895 he became First Lord of the Treasury and leader of the Commons, and in 1902 he succeeded Salisbury as prime minister. His cabinet was divided over Joseph Chamberlain's tariff-reform proposals, and in the 1905 elections he suffered a crushing defeat.

Balfour retired from the party leadership 1911. In 1915 he joined the Asquith coalition as First Lord of the Admiralty. As foreign secretary 1916–19 he issued the Balfour Declaration 1917 in favour of a national home in Palestine for the Jews. He was Lord President of the Council 1919–22 and 1925–29. Created earl 1922. He also wrote books on philosophy.

Suggested reading
Egremont, Max *Balfour: A Life of Arthur James Balfour* (1980)
Mackay, Ruddock *Balfour: Intellectual Statesman* (1985)
Ramsden, John *The Age of Balfour and Baldwin* (1978)
Young, Kenneth *Arthur James Balfour* (1963)

I never forgive but I always forget.

ARTHUR JAMES BALFOUR
quoted by Robert Blake *Conservative Party* ch 7 1970

Balfour Eve (1898–1990). English agriculturalist and pioneer of modern organic farming. She established the Haughley Experiment, a farm research project at New Bells Farm near Haughley, Suffolk, to demonstrate that a more sustainable agricultural alternative existed. The experiment ran for almost 30 years, comparing organic and chemical farming systems. The wide-ranging support it attracted led to the formation of the Soil Association 1946.

Baliol John de (or Balliol) (*c.* 1249–1315). King of Scotland 1292–96. As an heir to the Scottish throne on the death of Margaret, the Maid of Norway, his cause was supported by the English king, Edward I, against 12 other claimants. Having paid homage to Edward, Baliol was proclaimed king but soon rebelled and gave up the kingdom when English forces attacked Scotland.

Ball Albert (1896–1917). British fighter pilot and air ace. He was awarded the MC, DSO and Bar, and, posthumously, the Victoria Cross. At the time of his death May 1917 he had attained the rank of captain and was credited with over 40 enemy aircraft shot down.

Ball John (died *c.* 1381). English priest, one of the leaders of the Peasants' Revolt 1381, known as 'the mad priest of Kent'. A follower of John Wycliffe and a believer in social equality, he was imprisoned for disagreeing with the archbishop of Canterbury. During the revolt he was released from prison, and when in Blackheath, London, incited people against the ruling classes by preaching from the text 'When Adam delved and Eve span, who was then the gentleman?' When the revolt collapsed he escaped but was captured near Coventry and executed.

Ball Lucille Desirée (1911–1989). US comedy actress. She began her film career as a bit player 1933, and appeared in dozens of movies over the next few years, including *Room Service* 1938 (with the Marx Brothers) and *Fancy Pants* 1950 (with Bob Hope). From 1951 to 1957 she starred with her husband, Cuban bandleader Desi Arnaz, in the television sitcom *I Love Lucy*, the first US television show filmed before an audience. It was followed by *The Lucy Show* 1962–68 and *Here's Lucy* 1968–74.

Her TV success limited her film output after 1950; her later films include *Mame* 1974. The television series are still transmitted in many countries.

Balla Giacomo (1871–1958). Italian painter. A leading member of the Futurist group, his work is concerned with themes of time and movement. Influenced by photographic techniques, he developed a style using multiple images and blurred outlines. His *Dog on a Leash* 1912 (Fine Arts Academy, Buffalo) is one of the best-known Futurist works.

Balladur Edouard (1929–). French Conservative politician, prime minister 1993–95. During his first year of 'co-habitation' with socialist president, François Mitterrand, he demonstrated the sureness of his political touch, retaining popular support despite active opposition to some of his more right-wing policies. He unsuccessfully contested the presidency 1995. He is a supporter of the European Union and of maintaining close relations between France and Germany.

Ballance John (1839–1893). New Zealand Liberal politician, born in Northern Ireland; prime minister 1891–93. He emigrated to New Zealand, founded and edited the *Wanganui Herald*, and held many cabinet posts. He passed social legislation and opposed federation with Australia.

Ballantyne R(obert) M(ichael) (1825–1894). Scottish writer of children's books. Childhood visits to Canada and six years as a trapper for the Hudson's Bay Company provided material for his adventure stories, which include *The Young Fur Traders* 1856, *Coral Island* 1857, and *Martin Rattler* 1858.

Ballard J(ames) G(raham) (1930–). English novelist. His works include science fiction on the theme of catastrophe and collapse of the urban landscape, such as *The Drowned World* 1962, *Crash!* 1973, and *High-Rise* 1975; the partly autobiographical *Empire of the Sun* 1984, dealing with his internment in China during World War II; and the autobiographical novel *The Kindness of Women* 1991. His fundamentally moral vision is expressed with an untrammelled imagination and pessimistic irony.

Later, as he sat on his balcony eating the dog, Dr Robert Laing reflected on the unusual events.

J G BALLARD
High-Rise opening words 1975

Ballesteros Seve(riano) (1957–). Spanish golfer who came to prominence 1976 and has won several leading tournaments in the USA, including the Masters Tournament 1980 and 1983. He has also won the British Open three times: in 1979, 1984, and 1988.

Born in Pedrena, N Spain, he is one of four golf-playing brothers. He has won more than 60 tournaments worldwide.

Balmaceda José Manuel (1840–1891). Chilean president 1886–91. He inaugurated a vast reform programme including education, railways, communications, and public utilities, and invested revenue from Chile's nitrate fields in public works. The volatility of this key market led him to denounce foreign interests in Chile.

Balmer Johann Jakob (1825–1898). Swiss physicist and mathematician who developed a formula in 1884 that gave the wavelengths of the light emitted by the hydrogen atom (the hydrogen spectrum). This simple formula played a central role in the development of spectral and atomic theory.

Balthus (Balthazar Klossowski de Rola) (1908–). Polish-born French painter. He is famed for his enigmatic paintings of interiors featuring languid, pubescent girls, both clothed and nude, for example *Nude with Cat* about 1954 (National Gallery of Victoria, Melbourne). The studied, intense realism with which his self-absorbed figures are depicted lends his pictures a dreamlike quality.

Although initially associated with the Surrealists, his early paintings of street scenes, in which figures appear rigid and entranced, more closely ally him to magic realism, as in *The Street* 1933 (Museum of Modern Art, New York).

It is easier to be a lover than a husband, for the same reason that it is more difficult to show a ready wit all day long than to produce an occasional bon mot.

HONORÉ DE BALZAC
Attributed remark

Balzac Honoré de (1799–1850). French writer. He was one of the major novelists of the 19th century. His first success was *Les Chouans/The Chouans*, inspired by Walter Scott. This was the beginning of the long series of novels *La Comédie humaine/The Human Comedy* which includes *Eugénie Grandet* 1833, *Le Père Goriot* 1834, and *Cousine Bette* 1846. He also wrote the Rabelaisian *Contes drolatiques/Ribald Tales* 1833.

Born in Tours, Balzac studied law and worked as a notary's clerk in Paris before turning to literature. His first attempts included tragedies such as *Cromwell* and novels published under a pseudonym with no great success. A venture in printing and publishing 1825–28 involved him in a lifelong web of debt. His patroness, Madame de Berny, figures in *Le Lys dans la vallée/The Lily in the Valley* 1836. Balzac intended his major work *La Comédie humaine/The Human Comedy* to comprise 143 volumes, depicting every aspect of society in 19th-century France, of which he completed 80. Titles and characters include *Cousin Pons* 1847; and the doctor of *Le Médicin de la campagne/The Country Doctor* 1833, the great businessman of *La Maison de Nucingen/The House of Nucingen* 1838, and the cleric of *Le Curé de village/The Village Parson* 1839. Balzac corresponded constantly with the Polish countess Evelina Hanska after meeting her 1833, and they married four months before his death in Paris. He was buried in Père Lachaise cemetery.

Suggested reading
Brooks, Peter *The Melodramatic Imagination* (1976)
Maurois, André *Prometheus: The Life of Balzac* (1965)
McCormick, D F *Honoré de Balzac* (1979)
Pritchett, V S *Balzac* (1973)
Robb, Graham *Balzac* (1994)

Bancks James Charles (1889–1952). Australian cartoonist. He created the comic strip *Ginger Meggs*, which first appeared in the Sydney *Sun* 1921 and was later syndicated nationally and internationally.

The world is growing weary of that most costly of all luxuries, hereditary kings.

GEORGE BANCROFT
letter, London, March 1848

Bancroft George (1800–1891). US diplomat and historian. A Democrat, he was secretary of the navy 1845 when he established the US Naval Academy at Annapolis, Maryland, and as acting secretary of war (May 1846) was instrumental in bringing about the occupation of California and the Mexican War. He wrote a *History of the United States* 1834–76.

I wish I could bring Stonehenge to Nyasaland to show there was a time when Britain had a savage culture.

HASTINGS BANDA
Observer 10 March 1963

Banda Hastings Kamuzu (1905–). Malawi politician, president 1966–94. He led his country's independence movement and was prime minister of Nyasaland (the former name of Malawi) from 1963. He became Malawi's first president 1966 and was named president for life 1971; his rule was authoritarian. Having bowed to opposition pressure and opened the way for a pluralist system, Banda stood in the first free presidential elections for 30 years 1994, but was defeated by Bakili Muluzi. In Jan 1996 he and his former aide, John Tembo, were acquitted of the murders of three senior politicians and a lawyer in 1983.

Banda studied in the USA, and was a doctor in Britain until 1953.

She carried on her husband's policies of socialism, neutrality in international relations, and ... active encouragement of the Buddhist religion and ... Sinhalese language and culture.

Encyclopaedia Britannica on SIRIMAVO BANDARANAIKE
1990

Bandaranaike Sirimavo, (born Ratwatte) (1916–). Sri Lankan politician who succeeded her husband Solomon Bandaranaike to become the world's first female prime minister, 1960–65 and 1970–77, but was expelled from parliament 1980 for abuse of her powers while in office.

Bandaranaike Solomon West Ridgeway Dias (1899–1959). Sri Lankan nationalist politician. In 1952 he founded the Sri Lanka Freedom party and in 1956 became prime minister, pledged to a socialist programme and a neutral foreign policy. He failed to satisfy extremists and was assassinated by a Buddhist monk.

Oxford ... revealed to me my life's mission and ... was the dearer to me because she had taught me to love my country better.

SOLOMON BANDARANAIKE
on Magdalen Bridge on his last afternoon at Oxford University,
contrasting the mellowness of the scene with the
disease and poverty of his own country.

Bankhead Tallulah (1903–1968). US actress. She was renowned for her wit and flamboyant lifestyle. Her stage appearances included *Dark Victory* 1934, Lillian Hellman's *The Little Foxes* 1939, and Thornton Wilder's *The Skin of Our Teeth* 1942. Her films include Alfred Hitchcock's *Lifeboat* 1943.

I'm as pure as the driven slush.

TALLULAH BANKHEAD
Saturday Evening Post 12 April 1947

Banks Jeff (1943–). English textile, fashion, and interior designer. He helped establish the Warehouse Utility chain 1974 and combines imaginative designs with inexpensive materials to provide stylish and affordable garments for the younger market. Today he is the familiar presenter of the popular TV programme *The Clothes Show*, which has encouraged broader interest in fashion among the British public.

Banks Joseph (1743–1820). British naturalist and explorer. The *Banksia* genus of shrubs is named after him. Created a baronet 1781.

Banks was born in London and educated at Oxford. Inheriting a fortune, he made his first voyage 1766, to Labrador and Newfoundland. In 1768 Banks obtained the position of naturalist on an expedition to the southern hemisphere in the *Endeavour*, commanded by Capt James Cook. The expedition explored the coasts of New Zealand and Australia. Banks's plant-collecting activities at the first landing place in Australia (near present-day Sydney) gave rise to the name of the area – Botany Bay. He also studied the Australian fauna.

Returning to England 1771, he brought back a vast number of plant specimens, more than 800 of which were previously unknown. As a result of the friendship between Banks and George III, the Royal Botanic Gardens at Kew – of which Banks was the honorary director – became a focus of botanical research.

In 1772 Banks went on his last expedition, to Iceland, where he studied geysers. He was instrumental in establishing the first colony at Botany Bay in 1788.

Banneker Benjamin (1731–1806). American astronomer, surveyor, and mathematician who published almanacs 1792–97. He took part in the survey that prepared the establishment of the US capital, Washington DC.

Bannister Roger Gilbert (1929–). English track and field athlete, the first person to run a mile in under four minutes. He achieved this feat at Oxford, England, on 6 May 1954, in a time of 3 min 59.4 sec.

Studying at Oxford to be a doctor at the time, Bannister broke the four-minute barrier on one more occasion: at the 1954 Commonwealth Games in Vancouver, Canada, when he was involved with John Landy (1930–) from Australia, in the 'Mile of the Century', so called because it was a clash between the only two people to have broken the four-minute barrier for the mile at that time. Knighted 1975.

Banting Frederick Grant (1891–1941). Canadian physician who discovered a technique for isolating the hormone insulin 1921 when he and his colleague Charles Best tied off the ducts of the pancreas to determine the function of the cells known as the islets of Langerhans. This made possible the treatment of diabetes. Banting and John J R Macleod (1876–1935), his mentor, shared the 1923 Nobel Prize for Physiology or Medicine, and Banting divided his prize with Best. KBE 1934.
Suggested reading
Bliss, Michael *The Discovery of Insulin* (1982)
Harris, Seale *Banting's Miracle* (1946)
Levine, Israel *The Discoverer of Insulin* (1959)
Rowland, John *The Insulin Man* (1966)

Bantock Granville Ransome (1868–1946). English composer and conductor; professor of music at the University of Birmingham 1908–34. His works include the oratorio *Omar Khayyám* 1906–09, *Hebridean Symphony* 1915, and *Pagan Symphony* 1928.

Banu Musa (Arabic 'sons of Musa') Three brothers, Muhammad (died 873), Ahmad, and al-Hasan, who lived in Baghdad. They compiled an important mathematical work on the measurement of plane and spherical figures, and one of the earliest works on mechanical engineering, *Kitab al-Hiyal/The Book of Ingenious Devices*.

Bara Theda. Stage name of Theodosia Goodman (1890–1955). US silent-film actress. She became known as 'the vamp', and the first movie sex symbol, after appearing in *A Fool There Was* 1915, based on a poem by Rudyard Kipling, 'The Vampire'.

She was born in Cincinnati, Ohio. As the most popular star of the Fox studios, Bara made more than 40 films during her relatively brief film career that extended from 1915 to 1920. After unsuccessfully attempting a career on the Broadway stage, she retired from show business and lived the rest of her life in relative obscurity.

The reason good women like me and flock to my pictures is that there is a little bit of vampire instinct in every woman.

THEDA BARA
Attributed remark

Barabbas in the New Testament, a condemned robber released by Pilate at Passover instead of Jesus to appease a mob.

Baraka (Imamu) Amiri. Adopted name of LeRoi Jones (1934–   ). US poet, dramatist, and militant black activist. One of the major black voices of his generation, he promoted black poetry and theatre, as well as producing volumes of poetry, novels, plays, and cultural analyses including *Blues People* 1963, a study of jazz. He began his literary career with personal and romantic poetry as in *Preface to a Twenty Volume Suicide Note* 1961, before turning to the theatre as a revolutionary force for black separatism in such plays as *Dutchman* and *The Slave* both 1964.

In 1965 he converted to Islam, changing his name, as part of his campaign for African-American consciousness. His ideological focus shifted in the 1970s, attacking capitalism as much as racism.

Banting With his assistant Charles Best, Frederick Banting developed the first practical method for the commercial preparation of insulin. Insulin is a pancreatic hormone which reduces glucose levels in blood, and is effective in the treatment of diabetes. For his discovery, Banting was awarded the 1923 Nobel Prize for Physiology or Medicine. (Ann Ronan/Image Select)

Bara US silent-film actress Theda Bara who created and popularized the image of the 1920s 'vamp'. Her sensational success in more than 40 silent films was aided by massive publicity campaigns.

His *Selected Plays and Prose* and *Selected Poetry* were both published 1979 and *The Autobiography of LeRoi Jones* appeared 1984.

Barba Eugenio (1936–   ). Italian-born theatre director and theorist. A former assistant to Jerzy Grotowski, he founded Odin Teatret in 1964 in Oslo, later moving with the company to Holstebro in Denmark, where he established an International School for Theatre Anthropology 1979 for research into trans-cultural performance. He has organized conventions for the Third Theatre, a loose grouping of alternative companies across several continents, and with Odin has promoted the idea of 'barter', where visiting companies exchange performances with their hosts. Productions with Odin range from *Kaspariana* 1967 to *Kaosmos* 1993.

Barbarossa nickname 'red beard' given to the Holy Roman emperor Frederick I, and also to two brothers, Horuk and Khair-ed-Din, who were Barbary pirates. Horuk was killed by the Spaniards 1518; Khair-ed-Din took Tunis 1534 and died in Constantinople 1546.

Give me the man who will surrender the whole world for a moss or a caterpillar, and impracticable visions for a simple human delight.

W N P BARBELLION
Enjoying Life and Other Literary Remains, 'Crying for the Moon' 1919

Barbellion W N P. Pen name of Bruce Frederick Cummings (1889–1919). English diarist. His *The Journal of a Disappointed Man* 1919 is an account of his struggle with the illness multiple sclerosis.

Barber Samuel (1910–1981). US composer. He worked in a Neo-Classical, astringent style. Compositions include *Adagio for Strings* 1936 and the opera *Vanessa* 1958, which won one of his two Pulitzer prizes. Another Barber opera, *Antony and Cleopatra* 1966, was commissioned for the opening of the new Metropolitan Opera House at the Lincoln Center, New York City. Barber's music is lyrical and fastidiously worked. His later works include *The Lovers* 1971.

Suggested reading
Broder, Nathan *Samuel Barber* (1954)
Heyman, Barbara B *Samuel Barber: The Composer and His Music*
(1992)

Barbey Daniel E(dward) (1889–1969). US rear admiral. Commissioned into the US Navy 1912, Barbey had a varied career, divided between sea service and administrative posts, and designed the DUKW amphibious truck 1941.

He was a captain in the war plans section of the bureau of navigation 1937–40 and 1941 established the amphibious warfare section of the US Navy Department. Promoted to rear admiral 1942, in 1943 he was given command of VII Amphibious Force of the 7th Fleet and took responsibility for all amphibious operations in the SW Pacific Area. In late 1945 he became commander of 7th Fleet before retiring 1951.

Barbie Klaus (1913–1991). German Nazi, a member of the SS from 1936. During World War II he was involved in the deportation of Jews from the occupied Netherlands 1940–42 and in tracking down Jews and Resistance workers in France 1942–45. He was arrested 1983 and convicted of crimes against humanity in France 1987.

Three farts and a raspberry, orchestrated.
JOHN BARBIROLLI
on 'modern music', quoted in Michael Kennedy,
Barbirolli, Conductor Laureate, 1971

Barbirolli John (Giovanni Battista) (1899–1970). English conductor. He was noted for his interpretation of Vaughan Williams and Sibelius symphonies. Trained as a cellist, he succeeded Toscanini as conductor of the New York Philharmonic Orchestra 1937–43 and was conductor of the Hallé Orchestra, Manchester, England, 1943–70. Knighted 1949.

Barbour John (*c.* 1320–1395). Scottish poet. His epic 13,000-line poem, *The Bruce* 1375–78, chronicles the war of Scottish independence and includes a vivid account of Robert Bruce's victory over the English at Bannockburn 1314. It is among the earliest known works of Scottish poetry.

A! fredome is a noble thing!
JOHN BARBOUR
The Bruce I, 1, 225 1375

Barbour Philip Pendleton (1783–1841). US jurist and political leader. He served as Speaker of the House in the US House of Representatives 1821–23. A strong supporter of states' rights, he was appointed federal district judge by President Jackson 1830. He served on the US Supreme Court 1836–41, consistently ruling in favour of the prerogative of the states over federal authority.

Bardeen John (1908–1991). US physicist who won a Nobel Prize 1956, with Walter Brattain and William Shockley, for the development of the transistor 1948. In 1972 he became the first double winner of a Nobel Prize in the same subject (with Leon Cooper and Robert Schrieffer (1931–)) for his work on superconductivity. The theory developed in 1957 by Bardeen, Schrieffer, and Cooper states that superconductivity arises when electrons travelling through a metal interact with the vibrating atoms of the metal.

It is better to be unfaithful than faithful without wanting to be.
BRIGITTE BARDOT
quoted in *Observer* 18 Feb 1968

Bardot Brigitte (born Camille Javal) (1934–). French film actress. A celebrated sex symbol of the 1960s, she did much to popularize French cinema internationally. Her films include *Et Dieu créa la femme*/*And God Created Woman* 1950, *Viva Maria* 1965, and

Shalako 1968. She has subsequently devoted herself to animal welfare.

Barenboim Daniel (1942–). Israeli pianist and conductor. Pianist/conductor with the English Chamber Orchestra from 1964, he became conductor of the New York Philharmonic Orchestra 1970, musical director of the Orchestre de Paris 1975, and director of the Chicago Symphony Orchestra 1991. As a pianist he specialized in the German classic and romantic repertoire; as a conductor he has extended into 19th- and 20th-century French music, including Boulez. He was married to the cellist Jacqueline Du Pré.

Today, conducting is a question of ego: a lot of people believe they are actually playing the music.
DANIEL BARENBOIM
quoted in Robert Jacobson, *Reverberations*, 1975

Barents Willem (*c.* 1550–1597). Dutch explorer and navigator. He made three expeditions to seek the Northeast Passage; he died on the last voyage. The Barents Sea, part of the Arctic Ocean N of Norway, is named after him.

Barham Richard Harris (1788–1845). English writer and clergyman. He was the author of verse tales of the supernatural, and *The Ingoldsby Legends*, published under his pen name Thomas Ingoldsby.

He cursed him in sleeping, that every night / He should dream of the devil, and wake in a fright.
RICHARD HARRIS BARHAM
Ingoldsby Legends 'Jackdaw of Rheims' 1837

Baring-Gould Sabine (1834–1924). English author. He was rector of Lew Trenchard in N Devon from 1881. A prolific writer, his work includes novels and books of travel, mythology, and folklore; he also wrote the words of the hymn 'Onward, Christian Soldiers'.

Onward, Christian soldiers, / Marching as to war.
SABINE BARING-GOULD
Hymn, 1864

Barker Clive (1952–). English writer. His *Books of Blood* 1984–85 are in the sensationalist tradition of horror fiction.

When the guns begin to rattle / And the men to die / Does the Goddess of the Battle / Smile or sigh?
GEORGE BARKER
'Battle Hymn of the New Republic'

Barker George Granville (1913–1991). English poet. He is known for his vivid imagery, as in *Calamiterror* 1937, *The True Confessions of George Barker* 1950, *Collected Poems* 1930–50, and the posthumously published *Street Ballads* 1992.

Barker Herbert Atkinson (1869–1950). British manipulative surgeon, whose work established the popular standing of orthopaedics (the study and treatment of disorders of the spine and joints), but who was never recognized by the world of orthodox medicine. Knighted 1922.

The working class criminals in my plays are victims of phoney individualism.
HOWARD BARKER
The Bloomsbury Theatre Guide 1988

Barker Howard (1946–). English playwright whose plays examine the human spirit when it is subjected to dictatorship, whether mental or physical. Among his works are *Victory* 1982; *The Castle* 1985; *The Last Supper, The Possibilities,* and *The Bite of the Night,* all 1988; *Seven Lears* 1989; *Hated Nightfall* 1993; and *Wounds to the Face* 1994. In 1988 he formed The Wrestling School, a theatre company dedicated to the performance of his own work.

Barkla Charles Glover (1877–1944). English physicist who studied the phenomenon of X-ray scattering. He found that X-ray emissions are a form of transverse electromagnetic radiation, like visible light, and monochromatic. Barkla named the two types of characteristic emissions the K-series (for the more penetrating emissions) and the L-series (for the less penetrating emissions). He later predicted that an M-series and a J-series of emissions with different penetrances might exist, and an M-series was subsequently discovered. Nobel Prize for Physics 1917.

Barlach Ernst (1870–1938). German Expressionist sculptor, painter, and poet. Influenced by Russian folk art and by medieval wood sculpture, his simple blocklike figure carvings were intended to express human spiritual longings. His work was condemned as Degenerate Art by the Nazi regime and much of it destroyed. The war memorial in Güstrow Cathedral is one of his finest surviving works.

Barlow Joel (1754–1812). US poet and diplomat. A member of the literary circle the 'Connecticut Wits', he published an epic entitled *The Vision of Columbus* 1787, but is particularly remembered for 'Hasty Pudding' 1796, a celebration of an American dessert. As US consul in Algiers 1795–97, he gained the release of American hostages taken by the Barbary pirates operating against US and European shipping. On a diplomatic mission to France 1811, he died while accompanying Napoleon in his retreat from Russia 1812.

Barnabas, St (lived 1st century AD). In the New Testament, a 'fellow labourer' with St Paul; he went with St Mark on a missionary journey to Cyprus, his birthplace. Feast day 11 June.

Barnard Christiaan Neethling (1922–   ). South African surgeon who performed the first human heart transplant 1967 at Groote Schuur Hospital in Cape Town. The 54-year-old patient lived for 18 days.

Barnard also discovered that intestinal artresia – a congenital deformity in the form of a hole in the small intestine – is the result of an insufficient supply of blood to the fetus during pregnancy. It was a fatal defect before he developed the corrective surgery.

Barnard Edward Emerson (1857–1923). US observational astronomer who discovered the fifth satellite of Jupiter 1892 and Barnard's star 1916. He was the first to realize that the apparent voids in the Milky Way are in fact dark nebulae of dust and gas.

Barnardo Thomas John (1845–1905). British philanthropist, who was known as Dr Barnardo, although not medically qualified. He opened the first of a series of homes for destitute children 1867 in Stepney, E London.

Barnes Djuna Chappell (1892–1982). US writer. Her most celebrated novel was *Nightwood* 1936, a dark and idiosyncratic study of decadence. She lived in Paris from the 1920s and her work was much influenced by European Surrealism. She was also the author of short stories, plays, poems, essays, and portraits.

Barnes Ernest William (1874–1953). British cleric. A lecturer in mathematics at Cambridge 1902–15, he was an ardent advocate of the influence of scientific thought on religion. In 1924 he became bishop of Birmingham; he published *The Rise of Christianity* 1947.

Barnes Thomas (1785–1841). British journalist, forthright and influential editor of *The Times* of London from 1817, during whose editorship it became known as 'the Thunderer'.

Barnes William (1800–1886). English poet and cleric. He published volumes of poems in the Dorset dialect. His poetry was admired for its charm, linguistic interest, and metrical innovation by English poets Thomas Hardy, Alfred Lord Tennyson, and Gerard Manley Hopkins. Among his works are *Poems of Rural Life in the*

Dorset Dialect 1844, *Hwomely Rhymes* 1859, and *Poems of Rural Life in Common English* 1868.

The son of farmers, Barnes went to Cambridge University at the age of 36, becoming a schoolteacher and then a cleric.

How were the receipts today in Madison Square Garden?

PHINEAS T BARNUM
Last words

Barnum P(hineas) T(aylor) (1810–1891). US showman. In 1871 he established the 'Greatest Show on Earth', which included the midget 'Tom Thumb', a circus, a menagerie, and an exhibition of 'freaks', conveyed in 100 railway carriages. In 1881, it merged with its chief competitor and has continued to this day as the Ringling Brothers and Barnum and Bailey Circus.

His American Museum in New York (1843–68) contained a theatre alongside numerous curiosities. He coined the phrase 'there's a sucker born every minute'. In 1850, in an attempt to change his image to that of an art promoter, Barnum managed the hugely successful US concert tour of Swedish soprano Jenny Lind, whom he dubbed 'The Swedish Nightingale'.

Suggested reading
Barnum, P T *Struggles and Triumphs* (autobiography) (1927, rep 1986)
Harris, N *Humbug: The Art of P T Barnum* (1973)
Tompert, Ann *The Greatest Show on Earth* (1987)

Barocci Federico, or Baroccio (c. 1535–1612). Italian artist. Based in Urbino, he painted religious themes in a highly coloured, sensitive style that falls between Renaissance and Baroque. Many of his pictures such as his *Holy Family* about 1570 show the influence of Raphael (also from Urbino) and Correggio.

He decorated the palace of the Cardinal della Rovere with frescoes, and at the invitation of Pope Pius IV assisted in the decoration of the Belvedere.

Baroja Pio (1872–1956). Spanish novelist of Basque extraction. His works include a trilogy dealing with the Madrid underworld, *La lucha por la vida/The Struggle for Life* 1904–05, and the multivolume *Memorias de un hombre de acción/Memoirs of a Man of Action* 1913–28.

Barr Murray Llewellyn (1908–   ). Canadian anatomist and geneticist who carried out research into defects of the human reproductive system, and simplified diagnostic tests for chromosomal defects. From his investigations, the sex chromatin (called the Barr body) is now known to be one of the two X-chromosomes in the cells of females; it is more condensed than the other chromosomes and is genetically inactive.

Barragán Luis (1902–1988). Mexican architect. He is known for his use of rough wooden beams, cobbles, lava, and adobe, which he combines in striking and colourful compositions. Mexican vernacular architecture provided the inspiration for much of his work, although Le Corbusier's influence is also evident in his early designs.

The construction and enjoyment of a garden accustoms people to beauty,

LUIS BARRAGÁN
quoted in Muriel Emanuel (ed) *Contemporary Architects* 1994

Barras Paul François Jean Nicolas, Count (1755–1829). French revolutionary. He was elected to the National Convention 1792 and helped to overthrow Robespierre 1794. In 1795 he became a member of the ruling Directory. In 1796 he brought about the marriage of his former mistress, Joséphine de Beauharnais, with Napoleon and assumed dictatorial powers. After Napoleon's coup d'état 19 Nov 1799, Barras fell into disgrace.

Barrault Jean-Louis (1910–1994). French actor and stage director. He appeared in such films as *La Symphonie fantastique* 1942 and

La Ronde 1950, and is perhaps best known for his role as the mime, Baptiste, in Marcel Carné's classic of the cinema *Les Enfants du Paradis* 1945.

He was producer and director to the Comédie Française 1940–46, and set up the Compagnie Renaud-Barrault 1946 with his wife Madeleine Renaud, the company's leading actress. He became director of the Théâtre de France (formerly Odéon) from 1958, and presented a wide repertory, including a production of Eugène Ionesco's *Rhinocéros*, playing the lead himself. He was dismissed 1968 because of statements made during the student unrest of that year, but continued to stage shows and spectacles in Paris and around the world.

Barre Raymond (1924–). French politician, member of the centre-right Union pour la Démocratie Française; prime minister 1976–81, when he also held the Finance Ministry portfolio and gained a reputation as a tough and determined budget-cutter. He built up a strong political base in the Lyon region during the early 1980s. Once considered a candidate for the presidency, in 1988 he effectively ruled himself out of contention.

How do I love thee? Let me count the ways.

ELIZABETH BARRETT BROWNING
Sonnets from the Portuguese XLIII 1846

Barrett Browning Elizabeth (1806–1861). English poet. As a child she fell from her pony and injured her spine and was subsequently treated by her father as a confirmed invalid. Freed from her father's oppressive influence, her health improved. She wrote strong verse about social injustice and oppression in Victorian England. In 1844 she published *Poems* (including 'The Cry of the Children'), which led to her friendship with and secret marriage to Robert Browning 1846. The *Sonnets from the Portuguese* published 1847 were written during their courtship. Later works include *Casa Guidi Windows* 1851 and the poetic novel *Aurora Leigh* 1857. She was a learned, fiery, and metrically experimental poet.

Suggested reading
Forster, M *Elizabeth Barrett Browning* (1988)
Leighton, A *Elizabeth Barrett Browning* (1986)
Radley, V *Elizabeth Barrett Browning* (1972)

Barrie J(ames) M(atthew) (1860–1937). Scottish dramatist and novelist. His work includes *The Admirable Crichton* 1902 and the children's fantasy *Peter Pan* 1904.

After early studies of Scottish rural life in plays such as *A Window in Thrums* 1889, his reputation as a dramatist was established with *The Professor's Love Story* 1894 and *The Little Minister* 1897. Later plays include *Quality Street* 1901 and *What Every Woman Knows* 1908. Created a baronet 1913.

Suggested reading
Asquith, Cynthia *Portrait of Barrie* (1954)
Birkin, Andrew *J M Barrie and the Lost Boys* (1979)
Dunbar, Janet *J M Barrie: The Man Behind the Image* (1970)

Barrios de Chamorro Violeta. President of Nicaragua from 1990; see ◊Chamorro.

Barrow Clyde. US criminal; see ◊Bonnie and Clyde.

Barrow Isaac (1630–1677). British mathematician, theologian, and classicist. His *Lectiones geometricae* 1670 contains the essence of the theory of calculus, which was later expanded by Isaac Newton and Gottfried Leibniz.

His sermons and treatises, especially the splendid *Treatise on the Pope's Supremacy* (1680), have gained a permanent place in ecclesiastical literature.

He was pliable and accommodating with the commissions and committees ... careful not to say too much.

Randall J Van Vynckt (ed) on CHARLES BARRY
in *International Dictionary of Architects and Architecture* 1993

Barry Charles (1795–1860). English architect. He designed the Neo-Gothic Houses of Parliament at Westminster, London, 1840–60, in collaboration with Augustus Pugin. His early designs for the Travellers Club, 1829–31, and for the Reform Club, 1837, both in London, were in Renaissance style. Knighted 1852.

Barry Comtesse du; see ◊du Barry, mistress of Louis XV of France.

Barry Marion S (1936–). US Democrat politician, mayor of Washington DC 1978–90 and from 1995. He was active in the civil-rights movement from 1960 as cofounder and chair until 1967 of the Student Nonviolent Coordinating Committee (SNCC).

As a student at the University of Tennessee, Barry became involved in the campaign for civil rights and organized the first lunch-counter sit-ins in Nashville, Tennessee, 1960. He met Martin Luther King that year and helped to establish the SNCC, based in Atlanta, Georgia, which advocated direct action through protests, sit-ins, and boycotts. In 1967 Barry set up the Youth Pride programme to help poor, unemployed blacks in Washington DC. He was elected to the Washington city council 1974, elected mayor 1978, and re-elected 1982 and 1986. Convicted of cocaine possession 1990, he was imprisoned for six months. Emerging a born-again Christian, he revived his political career and was re-elected mayor Nov 1994.

Barrymore US family of actors, the children of British-born Maurice Barrymore and Georgie Drew, both stage personalities. Lionel Barrymore (1878–1954) first appeared on the stage with his grandmother, Mrs John Drew, 1893. He played numerous film roles from 1909, including *A Free Soul* 1931 and *Grand Hotel* 1932, but was perhaps best known for his annual radio portrayal of Scrooge in Dickens' *A Christmas Carol*.

Love ... the delightful interval between meeting a beautiful girl and discovering that she looks like a haddock.

JOHN BARRYMORE
Attributed remark

John Barrymore (1882–1942), a flamboyant actor who often appeared on stage and screen with his brother and sister. In his early years he was a Shakespearean actor. From 1923 he acted almost entirely in films, including *Dinner at Eight* 1933, and became a screen idol, nicknamed 'the Profile'.

Ethel Barrymore (1879–1959) played with the British actor Henry Irving in London 1898 and opened the Ethel Barrymore Theater in New York 1928; she also appeared in many films from 1914, including *None but the Lonely Heart* 1944.

Barstow Stan (1928–). English novelist. His realist novels describe northern working-class life and include *A Kind of Loving* 1960 (filmed 1962), a first-person, present tense narrative of a young man forced to marry his pregnant girlfriend.

His other novels include *A Raging Calm* 1968, *B Movie* 1987, and *Next of Kin* 1991.

Bart Lionel (1930–). English composer. He wrote both the words and music for many musicals including *Fings Ain't Wot They Us'd T'Be* 1959 and *Oliver!* 1960.

Barth Heinrich (1821–1865). German geographer and explorer who in explorations of N Africa between 1844 and 1855 established the exact course of the river Niger.

He studied the coast of N Africa from Tunis to Egypt 1844–45, travelled in the Middle East 1845–47, crossed the Sahara from Tripoli 1850, and then spent five years exploring the country between Lake Chad and Cameroon which he described in the five-volume *Travels and Discoveries in Central Africa* 1857–58.

Barth John Simmons (1930–). US novelist and short-story writer. He was influential in the 'academic' experimental movement of the 1960s. His works, typically encyclopedic in scale, are usually interwoven fictions based on language games, his principal concerns being the nature of narrative and the relationship of language to reality. His novels include *The Sot-Weed Factor* 1960, *Giles Goat-Boy*

1966, *Letters* 1979, *Sabbatical: A Romance* 1982, and *The Last Voyage of Somebody the Sailor* 1991.

Barth Karl (1886–1968). Swiss Protestant theologian. A socialist in his political views, he attacked the Nazis. His *Church Dogmatics* 1932–62 makes the resurrection of Jesus the focal point of Christianity.

Barth is generally considered the greatest Christian theologian of the 20th century. His *Theology of Crisis* rejected liberal theology and stressed scripture and the infinite gulf that separates God from humanity, which can be overcome only by the grace of God.

Suggested reading
Bromiley, G W *An Introduction to the Theology of Karl Barth* (1981)
Busch, Eberhard *Karl Barth: His Life from Letters and
    Autobiographical Texts* (1976)
Hartwell, H *The Theology of Karl Barth* (1964)
Torrance, T F *Karl Barth* (1966)

Barthelme Donald (1931–1989). US writer. His innovative short stories, often first published in the *New Yorker* magazine, display a minimalist economy and a playful sense of the absurd and irrational, as in the collection *Sixty Stories* 1981. He also wrote the novellas *Snow White* 1967, *The Dead Father* 1975, *Paradise* 1986, and *The King* 1991. Barthelme's works have been seen as model texts for literary criticism based on Deconstruction.

Barthes Roland (1915–1980). French critic and theorist of semiology, the science of signs and symbols. One of the French 'new critics' and an exponent of structuralism, he attacked traditional literary criticism in his first collection of essays, *Le Degré zéro de l'ecriture/Writing Degree Zero* 1953.

Barthes's main aim was to expose the bourgeois values and ideology he saw as implicit in the seemingly 'natural' and innocent language of French literature. For Barthes, a text was not a depiction of the world or the expression of an author's personality, but a system of signs in which meanings are generated solely by the interplay of these signs. Among his works are *Mythologies* 1957, *Sur Racine/On Racine* 1963, and *Roland Barthes sur Roland Barthes* 1975.

Suggested reading
Barthes, Roland *Roland Barthes by Roland Barthes* (an essay in
    autobiography) (1977)
Calvet, Louis-Jean *Roland Barthes: A Biography* (trs 1994)
Cullers, Jonathan *Roland Barthes* (1983)
Moriarty, Michael *Roland Barthes* (1991)
Thody, P *Roland Barthes: A Conservative Estimate* (1984)

Bartholdi Frédéric Auguste (1834–1904). French sculptor. He designed the Statue of Liberty overlooking New York harbour, 1884–86.

Bartholomew, St in the New Testament, one of the apostles. Some legends relate that after the Crucifixion he took Christianity to India; others that he was a missionary in Anatolia and Armenia, where he suffered martyrdom by being flayed alive. Feast day 24 Aug.

Bartlett Frederic Charles (1886–1969). English psychologist. He put forward the view of sensory and memory processes as the expression of a dynamic integration of an organism's past experience with its current situation and needs. The results of his extensive researches, centred on perception, recognition, and recall processes, are collected in his book *Remembering: A Study of Experimental and Social Psychology* 1932. Knighted 1948.

Bartlett Neil (1932–). British-born chemist who in 1962 prepared the first compound of one of the inert gases, which were previously thought to be incapable of reacting with anything. He took an appointment at the University of British Columbia, Canada, 1958, became professor of chemistry at Princeton, USA, 1966, and

A genuine peasant melody of our land is a musical example of perfected art.
BÉLA BARTÓK
quoted in Joseph Machlis *Introduction to Contemporary Music* 1963

at the University of California, Berkeley, 1969.

Bartók Béla (1881–1945). Hungarian composer. His works combine folk elements with mathematical concepts of tonal and rhythmic proportion. His large output includes six string quartets, a *Divertimento* for string orchestra 1939, concertos for piano, violin, and viola, the *Concerto for Orchestra* 1942–45, a one-act opera *Duke Bluebeard's Castle* 1918, and graded teaching pieces for piano.

Suggested reading
Antokoletz E *The Music of Béla Bartók* (1985)
Griffiths, P *Bartók* (1984)
Stevens, H *The Life and Music of Béla Bartók* (1967)

Bartolommeo Fra, also called Baccio della Porta (*c.* 1472–1517). Italian religious painter of the High Renaissance. He was active in Florence. He introduced Venetian artists to the Florentine High Renaissance style during a visit to Venice 1508, and took back with him to Florence a Venetian sense of colour. *The Mystical Marriage of St Catherine* 1511 (Louvre, Paris) is one of his finest works. He worked with Albertinelli after 1508 and visited Rome 1514, when he was impressed by Michelangelo and Leonardo, his *Deposition*, 1516 (Pitti Palace), showing Leonardo's influence. Among the works in which he collaborated with Albertinelli are the fresco of the *Last Judgment*, 1498 (Santa Maria Nuova), *Madonna and Saints* (Pitti) and *Assumption* (Berlin). Some of his best work is at Lucca, including the *Madonna della Misericordia* of 1515.

Barton Clara (1821–1912). US health worker, founder of the American Red Cross 1881 and its president until 1904. A volunteer nurse, she tended the casualties of the American Civil War 1861–65 and in 1864 General Benjamin Butler named her superintendent of nurses for his forces. *See illustration on p. 72.*

Bartók The composer Béla Bartók (1881–1945). As one of the first ethnomusicologists he drew upon the music of his native Hungary for inspiration; his knowledge of Bach is also evident in his own often complex contrapuntal procedures. Bartók's music, often very dissonant, is nevertheless highly individual. (Image Select)

Barton, Clara *An American Florence Nightingale, Clara Barton attended soldiers during the American Civil War and later the Franco-Prussian War, before setting up the American Red Cross 1881.*

Barton Derek Harold Richard (1918–). English organic chemist who investigated the stereochemistry of natural compounds. He showed that their biological activity often depends on the shapes of their molecules and the positions and orientations of key functional groups. He shared the 1969 Nobel Prize for Chemistry.

Barton Edmund (1849–1920). Australian politician. He was leader of the federation movement from 1896 and first prime minister of Australia 1901–03. GCMG 1902.

He tempered natural dignity with charm of manner; and ... his mastery of both constitutional and common law was universally recognised.

H E Egerton on EDMUND BARTON
in *Dictionary of National Biography*

Barton John (1928–). English theatre director. He was associate director of the Royal Shakespeare Company from 1960. He directed and devised numerous productions for the company, including *The Hollow Crown* 1961, *The Wars of the Roses* 1963, Shakespeare's history plays 1964, and *The Greeks* 1980. Television work includes the series of workshops *Playing Shakespeare* 1982.

Baruch Bernard Mannes (1870–1965). US financier. He was a friend of the British prime minister, Winston Churchill, and a self-appointed, unpaid adviser to US presidents Wilson, F D Roosevelt, and Truman. He strongly advocated international control of nuclear energy.

To me old age is always fifteen years older than I am.

BERNARD BARUCH
Newsweek 29 Aug 1955

Baryshnikov Mikhail Nikolayevich (1948–). Latvian-born dancer, now based in the USA. He joined the Kirov Ballet 1967 and, after defecting from the Soviet Union 1974, joined the American Ballet Theater (ABT) as principal dancer, partnering Gelsey Kirkland. He left to join the New York City Ballet 1978–80, but rejoined ABT as director 1980–90. From 1990 he has danced for various companies including his own modern dance company, White Oak Project. His physical prowess and amazing aerial feats have combined with an impish sense of humour and dash to make him one of the most accessible of dancers.

Barzun Jacques Martin (1907–). French-born US historian and educator whose speciality was 19th-century European intellectual life. His book *The Modern Researcher* 1970 is recognized as a classic study of historical method. Among his many historical works is *Romanticism and the Modern Ego* 1943.

If it were possible to talk to the unborn, one could never explain to them how it feels to be alive, for life is washed in the speechless real.

JACQUES BARZUN
The House of Intellect ch 6 1959

Basawan (1556–1605). Mogul painter. He was one of the finest artists of the period.

He contributed paintings to many of the albums of miniatures that were a feature of the Mogul courts, in particular the *Akbar-nama*. His works are renowned for their subtle characterization and also show a novel use of perspective and composition, suggesting that he may have been influenced by Western art.

Bashkirtseff Marie (1860–1884). Russian diarist and painter. Her journals, written in French, were cited by Simone de Beauvoir as the archetypal example of 'self-centred female narcissism', but also revealed the discovery by the female of her independent existence. She died of tuberculosis at 24.

If I had been born a man, I would have conquered Europe. As I was born a woman, I exhausted my energy in tirades against fate, and in eccentricities.

MARIE BASHKIRTSEFF
Journal June 1884

Bashō pen name of Matsuo Munefusa (1644–1694). Japanese poet. He was a master of the haiku, a 17-syllable poetic form with lines of 5, 7, and 5 syllables, which he infused with subtle allusiveness. His *Oku-no-hosomichi/The Narrow Road to the Deep North* 1694, an account of a visit to northern and western Honshū, consists of haiku interspersed with prose passages.

Basie Count (William) (1904–1984). US jazz band leader and pianist. He developed the big-band sound and a simplified, swinging style of music. He led impressive groups of musicians in a career spanning more than 50 years. Basie's compositions include 'One O'Clock Jump' and 'Jumpin'' at the Woodside'.

His solo piano technique was influenced by the style of Fats Waller. Some consider his the definitive dance band.

Basil II (*c.* 958–1025). Byzantine emperor from 976. His achievement as emperor was to contain, and later decisively defeat, the Bulgarians, earning for himself the title 'Bulgar-Slayer' after a victory 1014. After the battle he blinded almost all 15,000 of the defeated, leaving only a few men with one eye to lead their fellows home. The Byzantine empire had reached its largest extent at the time of his death.

Basil, St (c. 330–379). Cappadocian monk, known as 'the Great', founder of the Basilian monks. Elected bishop of Caesarea 370, Basil opposed the heresy of Arianism. He wrote many theological works and composed the *Liturgy of St Basil*, in use in the Eastern Orthodox Church. Feast day 2 Jan.

Baskerville John (1706–1775). English printer and typographer. He experimented in casting types from 1750 onwards. The Baskerville typeface is named after him. He manufactured fine printing paper and inks, and in 1756 published a quarto edition of the Classical poet Virgil, which was followed by 54 highly crafted books.

Basov Nikolai Gennadievich (1922–). Soviet physicist who, with his compatriot Aleksandr Prokhorov, developed the microwave amplifier called a maser. They were both awarded the Nobel Prize for Physics 1964, which they shared with Charles Townes of the USA.

Bass George (1763–c. 1808). English naval surgeon who with Matthew Flinders explored the coast of New South Wales and the strait that bears his name between Tasmania and Australia 1795–99.

Bastos Augusto Roa (1917–). Paraguayan writer. He wrote short stories and novels, including *Son of Man* 1960 about the Chaco War between Bolivia and Paraguay, in which he fought.

Bateman H(enry) M(ayo) (1887–1970). Australian cartoonist who lived in England. His cartoons were based on themes of social embarrassment and confusion, in such series as *The Man who...* (as in *The Guardsman who Dropped his Rifle*).

Of course you start with dreams of being a star, you want recognition, public recognition. And why not? You're doing public work.

ALAN BATES
Sunday Times 3 Oct 1971

Bates Alan (1934–). English actor. He has proved himself a versatile male lead in over 60 plays and films. His films include *Zorba the Greek* 1965, *Far from the Madding Crowd* 1967, *Women in Love* 1970, *The Go-Between* 1971, *The Shout* 1978, and *Duet for One* 1986.

Bates Daisy May (1863–1951). Australian social worker, anthropologist, and journalist, born in Ireland. She went to Australia 1884 and is noted for her work with Aborigines which began in 1901 with a study of the language, kinship, and rites of the Aborigines of the Broome district of NW Western Australia. In later years she lived in isolated camps, and the newspaper articles she wrote describing the deprivation of the Aborigines prompted government medical assistance.

Bates H(erbert) E(rnest) (1905–1974). English author. Of his many novels and short stories, *The Jacaranda Tree* 1949 and *The Darling Buds of May* 1958 demonstrate the fineness of his natural observation and compassionate portrayal of character. *Fair Stood the Wind for France* 1959 was based on his experience as a squadron leader in World War II.

The five chronicles of the Larkin family, began with *The Darling Buds of May* and *Fair Stood the Wind for France*, included *When the Green Woods Laugh* 1960, and were filmed as a television series in the 1990s.

Bates H(enry) W(alter) (1825–1892). English naturalist and explorer, who spent 11 years collecting animals and plants in South America and identified 8,000 new species of insects. He made a special study of camouflage in animals, and his observation of insect imitation of species that are unpleasant to predators is known as 'Batesian mimicry'. In *The Naturalist on the River Amazon* 1863, Bates described both his explorations and his scientific findings.

Bateson Gregory (1904–1980). English-born US anthropologist and cyberneticist. His interests were wide-ranging – from the study of ritual in a New Guinea people to the exploration of communication methods in schizophrenics and dolphins – but all his work shows an interest in how systems operate and a willingness to break down the boundaries between intellectual disciplines. His publications include *Steps to an Ecology of Mind* 1973 and *Mind and Nature* 1978.

Bateson William (1861–1926). English geneticist who was one of the founders of the science of genetics (a term he introduced), and a leading proponent of Austrian biologist Gregor Mendel's work on heredity. Bateson also made contributions to embryology and he carried out breeding experiments, described in *Mendel's Principles of Heredity* 1908. He showed that certain traits are consistently inherited together; this phenomenon (called linkage) is now known to result from genes being situated close together on the same chromosome.

Báthory Stephen (1533–1586). King of Poland, elected by a diet convened 1575 and crowned 1576. Báthory succeeded in driving the Russian troops of Ivan the Terrible out of his country. His military successes brought potential conflicts with Sweden, but he died before these developed.

Batista Fulgencio (1901–1973). Cuban dictator 1933–44, when he stood down, and again 1952–59, after seizing power in a coup. His authoritarian methods enabled him to jail his opponents and amass a large personal fortune. He was overthrown by rebel forces led by Fidel Castro 1959.

Batoni Pompeo Girolamo (1708–1787). Italian painter. Based in Rome, he was celebrated for his detailed portraits of princes and British visitors on the Grand Tour. Most of his portraits are painted with a Roman antiquity in the background.

Batten Jean (1909–1982). New Zealand aviator who made the first return solo flight by a woman Australia–Britain 1935, and established speed records.

Bates, H W *During a two-year insect hunting expedition to the Amazon, H W Bates collected over 14,000 specimens, including almost 8,000 that were new to science. On his return, he published a paper describing the phenomenon of insect mimicry, now known as Batesian mimicry. His theory proposes that edible species of insects may gradually evolve markings which are very similar to poisonous species in an attempt to deceive predators. (Ann Ronan/Image Select)*

Battenberg title (conferred 1851) of German noble family; its members included Louis, Prince of Battenberg, and Louis Alexander, Prince of Battenberg, the father of Louis Mountbatten, who anglicized his name to Mountbatten 1917 due to anti-German feeling in Britain during World War I.

Battenberg (Mountbatten) Prince Louis Alexander, Marquess of Milford Haven (1854–1921). British admiral. A member of a British family of German extraction, Battenberg joined the Royal Navy and became an admiral. In 1914 he was First Sea Lord but was forced to retire due to anti-German public feeling as a result of World War I. He was created Marquess of Milford Haven 1917 and in the same year changed the family name to Mountbatten.

There are as many kinds of beauty as there are habitual ways of seeking happiness.

CHARLES BAUDELAIRE
Curiosités Esthétiques, 'Salon of 1846' 2 1946 ed

Baudelaire Charles Pierre (1821–1867). French poet. His immensely influential work combined rhythmical and musical perfection with a morbid romanticism and eroticism, finding beauty in decadence and evil. His first and best-known book of verse was *Les Fleurs du mal/Flowers of Evil* 1857. He was one of the main figures in the development of Symbolism.
Suggested reading
Fairlie, A *Baudelaire* (1960)
Pichois, Claude *Baudelaire* (1987)
Richardson, Joanna *Baudelaire* (1994)
Starkie, Enid *Baudelaire* (1957)
Turnell, Martin *Baudelaire: A Study of His Poetry* (1953)

It takes twenty years ... of peace to make a man; it takes only twenty seconds of war to destroy him.

BAUDOUIN
Address to a joint session of the US Congress 12 May 1959

Baudouin (1930–1993). King of the Belgians 1951–93. In 1950 his father, Leopold III, abdicated and Baudouin was known until his succession 1951 as *Le Prince Royal*. During his reign he succeeded in holding together a country divided by religion and language, while presiding over the dismemberment of Belgium's imperial past. In 1960 he married Fabiola de Mora y Aragón (1928–), member of a Spanish noble family. They were unable to have any children, and he was succeeded by his brother, Alberto, 1993.

Terror is as much a part of the concept of truth as runniness is of the concept of jam ... We wouldn't like truth if it wasn't sticky, if, from time to time, it didn't ooze blood.

JEAN BAUDRILLARD
Cool Memories ch 5 1987

Baudrillard Jean (1929–). French cultural theorist. Originally influenced by Marxism and structuralism in works such as *The System of Objects* 1968, Baudrillard evolved a critique of consumer society and of an information-world dominated by the reproduction of images, producing a state which he called 'hyper-reality'. His theories are expressed in a wide range of writings, including *In the Shadow of the Silent Majorities* 1978 and *Simulacra and Simulations* 1981.

Bauer Ferdinand Lukas (1760–1826). Austrian painter. As the botanical artist on Matthew Flinders' second voyage to Australia 1801 he made more than 1,500 painstakingly detailed drawings of Australian plants and animals. He is commemorated in the name of the Australian plant species *Bauera*.

Baum L(yman) Frank (1856–1919). US writer. He was the author of the children's fantasy *The Wonderful Wizard of Oz* 1900 and its 13 sequels.

The series was continued by another author after his death. The film *The Wizard of Oz* 1939 with Judy Garland became a US classic.

'The road to the City of Emeralds is paved with yellow brick,' said the Witch, 'so you cannot miss it.'

L FRANK BAUM
The Wonderful Wizard of Oz 1900

Bausch Pina (1940–). German avant-garde dance choreographer, director from 1974 of the Wuppertal Tanztheater (dance theatre). Her works incorporate dialogue, elements of psychoanalysis, comedy, and drama, and have been performed on floors covered with churned earth (*Le Sacre du printemps* 1975), water (*Arien* 1979), and rose petals (*Nelken* 1982). Her dramatic form of dance has all the emotional involvement of theatre without recourse to narrative structures. She has been a major influence in breaking the stranglehold of American post-modernism on European dance.

Bausch's work is inspiring in a number of ways. Frequently activities within performance are simultaneous so that as the audience you create your own performance by choosing where and when you look at actions on the stage.

Christy Adair on PINA BAUSCH
in *Woman and Dance; Sylphs and Sirens* 1992

Bawa Geoffrey (1919–). Sri Lankan architect. His buildings are a contemporary interpretation of vernacular traditions, and include houses, hotels, and gardens. More recently he has designed public buildings such as the new parliamentary complex, near Colombo, 1982, and Ruhuana University, Matara, 1984.

It is rational to give presence to both function and form, to admit beauty and pleasure.

GEOFFREY BAWA
quoted in Muriel Emanuel (ed) *Contemporary Architects* 1994

Bax Arnold Edward Trevor (1883–1953). English composer. His works, often based on Celtic legends, include seven symphonies and *The Garden of Fand* 1913–16 and *Tintagel* 1917–19 (both tone poems).

He was Master of the King's Musick 1942–53. Knighted 1937.

One should try everything once, except incest and folk-dancing.

ARNOLD BAX
Farewell, my Youth, 1943

Baxter George (1804–1867). English engraver and printmaker; inventor 1834 of a special process for printing in oil colours, which he applied successfully in book illustrations.

Baxter Richard (1615–1691). English cleric. During the English Civil War he was a chaplain in the Parliamentary army, and after the Restoration became a royal chaplain. Baxter was driven out of the church by the Act of Uniformity of 1662, which he saw as an unacceptable administrative and spiritual imposition. In 1685 he was imprisoned for nearly 18 months for alleged sedition.

Bayard Pierre du Terrail, Chevalier de (1473–1524). French soldier. He served under Charles VIII, Louis XII, and Francis I, and was killed in action at the crossing of the Sesia in Italy. His heroic exploits in battle and in tournaments, and his chivalry and magnanimity, won him the accolade of 'knight without fear and without reproach'.

Bayes Thomas (1702–1761). English mathematician whose investigations into probability led to what is now known as Bayes' theorem. Bayes' theorem relates the probability of particular events taking place to the probability that events conditional upon them have occurred.

Bayle Pierre (1647–1706). French critic and philosopher. In *Dictionnaire historique et critique/Historical and Critical Dictionary* 1696, he wrote learned and highly sceptical articles attacking almost all the contemporary religious, philosophical, moral, scientific, and historical views. Bayle was professor of philosophy at Sedan and Rotterdam. He was suspended from his post at Rotterdam under suspicion of religious scepticism 1693.

Baylis Lilian Mary (1874–1937). English theatre manager. After a period in South Africa, she returned to London 1895, and managed the Old Vic Theatre from 1912, starting a complete series of productions of Shakespeare's plays. She was responsible for re-opening Sadler's Wells Theatre, London, 1931. From 1934 Sadler's Wells specialized in productions of opera and ballet: the resultant companies eventually became the Royal Ballet and the English National Opera.

Bayliss William Maddock (1860–1924). English physiologist who discovered the digestive hormone secretin, the first hormone to be found, with Ernest Starling 1902. During World War I, Bayliss introduced the use of saline (salt water) injections to help the injured recover from shock. Knighted 1922. Bayliss's *Principles of General Physiology* 1915 became a standard work.

Bazaine Achille François (1811–1888). Marshal of France. From being a private soldier 1831 he rose to command the French troops in Mexico 1862–67 and was made a marshal 1864. In the Franco-Prussian War Bazaine allowed himself to be taken in the fortress of Metz, surrendering 27 Oct 1870 with nearly 180,000 men. For this he was court-martialled 1873 and imprisoned; he escaped to Spain 1874.

Bazalgette Joseph William (1819–1890). British civil engineer who, as chief engineer to the London Board of Works, designed London's sewer system, a total of 155 km/83 mi of sewers, covering an area of 256 sq km/100 sq mi. It was completed 1865.

He also designed the Victoria Embankment 1864–70, which was built over the river Thames and combined a main sewer, a water frontage, an underground railway, and a road. Knighted 1874.

I was a useless little vegetable. I made everybody very angry at me because I wasn't able to work, to get off my butt. Coke every day.

Brian Wilson of the THE BEACH BOYS quoted in David Felton *Rolling Stone Encyclopedia of Rock, Pop and Soul* 1989

Beach Boys, the US pop group formed 1961. They began as exponents of vocal-harmony surf music with Chuck Berry guitar riffs (their hits include 'Surfin' USA' 1963 and 'Help Me, Rhonda' 1965), but the compositions, arrangements, and production by Brian Wilson (1942–) became highly complex under the influence of psychedelic rock, as in 'Good Vibrations' 1966. Wilson spent most of the next 20 years in retirement but returned with a solo album 1988.

Beaconsfield title taken by Benjamin ◊Disraeli, prime minister of Britain 1868 and 1874–80.

Beadle George Wells (1903–1989). US biologist. In 1958 he shared a Nobel prize with Edward L Tatum and Joshua Lederberg for his work in biochemical genetics, forming the 'one-gene-one-enzyme' hypothesis (a single gene code for a single kind of enzyme).

Beale Dorothea (1831–1906). British pioneer in women's education whose work helped to raise the standard of women's education and the status of women teachers.

She was headmistress of the Ladies' College in Cheltenham from 1858, and founder of St Hilda's Hall (later College), Oxford, 1892.

The world is not a mere bog in which men and women trample themselves in the mire and die.

CHARLES BEARD
quoted in Will Durant *Meaning of Life* 43 1933

Beard Charles Austin (1874–1948). US historian and a leader of the Progressive movement, active in promoting political and social reform. As a chief exponent of critical economic history, he published *An Economic Interpretation of the Constitution of the United States* 1913 and *The Economic Origins of Jeffersonian Democracy* 1915. With his wife, Mary, he wrote *A Basic History of the United States* 1944, long a standard textbook in the USA.

Beardsley Aubrey Vincent (1872–1898). English illustrator and leading member of the Aesthetic Movement. His meticulously executed black-and-white drawings show the influence of Japanese prints and French Rococo, and also display the sinuous line and decorative mannerisms of Art Nouveau. His work was often charged with being grotesque and decadent.

He became known through *The Yellow Book* magazine, for which he was the art editor, and through his drawings for Oscar Wilde's *Salome* 1893.

Beatles, the English pop group 1960–70. The members, all born in Liverpool, were John Lennon (1940–1980, rhythm guitar, vocals), Paul McCartney (1942– , bass, vocals), George Harrison (1943– , lead guitar, vocals), and Ringo Starr (formerly Richard Starkey, 1940– , drums). Using songs written largely by Lennon and McCartney, the Beatles dominated rock music and pop culture in the 1960s.

The Beatles gained early experience in Liverpool and Hamburg, West Germany. They had a top-30 hit with their first record, 'Love Me Do' 1962, followed by 'Please Please Me' which reached number two. Every subsequent single and album released until 1967 reached number one in the UK charts.

At the peak of Beatlemania they starred in two films, *A Hard Day's Night* 1964 and *Help!* 1965, and provided songs for the animated film *Yellow Submarine* 1968. Their ballad 'Yesterday' 1965 was covered by 1,186 different performers in the first ten years. The album *Sgt Pepper's Lonely Hearts Club Band* 1967, recorded on two four-track machines, anticipated subsequent technological developments.

I had two careers – photography and set designing. They overflowed constantly.

CECIL BEATON
Attributed remark.

Beaton Cecil Walter Hardy (1904–1980). English photographer. His elegant and sophisticated fashion pictures and society portraits often employed exotic props and settings. He adopted a more simple style for his wartime photographs of bomb-damaged London. He also worked as a stage and film designer, notably for the musicals *Gigi* 1959 and *My Fair Lady* 1965. Knighted 1972.

Beaton David (1494–1546). Scottish nationalist cardinal and politician, adviser to James V. Under Mary Queen of Scots, he was opposed to the alliance with England and persecuted reformers such

His greatest gift was the power he had of gaining ascendancy over the minds of others.

Margaret MacArthur on DAVID BEATON
in *Dictionary of National Biography*

as George Wishart, who was condemned to the stake; he was killed by Wishart's friends.

Beatrix (Wilhelmina Armgard) (1938–). Queen of the Netherlands. The eldest daughter of Queen Juliana, she succeeded to the throne on her mother's abdication 1980. In 1966 she married West German diplomat Claus von Amsberg (1926–), who was created Prince of the Netherlands. Her heir is Prince Willem Alexander (1967–).

Beattie John Hugh Marshall (1915–1990). British anthropologist whose work on cross-cultural analysis influenced researchers in other fields, particularly philosophy. His book *Other Cultures: Aims, Methods and Achievements in Social Anthropology* 1964 has been translated into many languages.

There's something wrong with our bloody ships today, Chatfield.

DAVID BEATTY
Remark during the Battle of Jutland 1916

Beatty David, 1st Earl Beatty (1871–1936). British admiral in World War I. He commanded the cruiser squadron 1912–16 and bore the brunt of the Battle of Jutland 1916. In 1916 he became commander of the fleet, and in 1918 received the surrender of the German fleet. Created an earl 1919.

You love somebody once, you love them forever – only maybe not as much as the next person.

WARREN BEATTY
Photoplay 1979

Beatty Warren. Stage name of Warren Beaty (1937–). US actor, director, and producer. He attracted attention as a young man in such films as *Splendour in the Grass* 1961, then produced and starred as gangster Clyde Barrow in the hugely successful *Bonnie and Clyde* 1967. Later, he directed *Reds* 1981, *Dick Tracy* 1990, and co-produced *Bugsy* 1992, in which he played the gangster Bugsy Siegel. He is the brother of actress Shirley MacLaine.

Beauclerk family name of the dukes of St Albans, descended from King Charles II by his mistress Nell Gwyn.

Beaufort Francis (1774–1857). British admiral, hydrographer to the Royal Navy from 1829; the Beaufort scale and the Beaufort Sea in the Arctic Ocean are named after him. KCB 1848.

At once the greatest ecclesiastic and the most grasping usurer of his day.

A V Dicey on HENRY BEAUFORT
in *The Privy Council* 1860

Beaufort Henry (1375–1447). English priest, bishop of Lincoln from 1398, of Winchester from 1405. As chancellor of England, he supported his half-brother Henry IV and made enormous personal loans to Henry V to finance war against France. As a guardian of Henry VI from 1421, he was in effective control of the country until 1426. In the same year he was created a cardinal. In 1431 he crowned Henry VI as king of France in Paris.

Beaufort Margaret. Countess of Richmond and Derby (1443–1509). English noblewoman. She married Edmund Tudor, Earl of Richmond 1455. Their son, Henry VII, claimed the English throne through his mother's descent from John of Gaunt.

Her third husband, Thomas Stanley, defected from the Yorkists to the Lancastrians, aiding Henry's victory at the Battle of Bosworth 1485.

Beaufoy Merlin Henry (1803–1873). Australian documentary photographer. He recorded everyday life in small pioneer settlements in Victoria 1868–70 and from 1870 travelled around the goldfields and mining camps of Hill End, Gulgong, and Sofala in New South Wales photographing the inhabitants at work, at school, and in front of their shanties and shops.

Beauharnais Alexandre, Vicomte de (1760–1794). French liberal aristocrat and general who served in the American Revolution and became a member of the National Convention in the early days of the French Revolution. He was the first husband of Josephine (consort of Napoleon I). Their daughter Hortense (1783–1837) married Louis, a younger brother of Napoleon, and their son became Napoleon III. Beauharnais was guillotined during the Terror for his alleged lack of zeal for the revolutionary cause and his lack of success as Commander of the Republican Army of the North.

Today if something is not worth saying, people sing it.

PIERRE-AUGUSTIN CARON DE BEAUMARCHAIS
Le Barbier de Séville 1775

Beaumarchais Pierre Augustin Caron de (1732–1799). French dramatist. His great comedies, *Le Barbier de Seville/The Barber of Seville* 1775 and *Le Mariage de Figaro/The Marriage of Figaro* (1778, but prohibited until 1784), form the basis of operas by Rossini and Mozart, with their blend of social criticism and sharp humour.

Louis XVI entrusted Beaumarchais with secret missions, notably for the profitable shipment of arms to the American colonies during the War of Independence. Accused of treason 1792, he fled to Holland and England, but in 1799 he returned to Paris.

Those have most power to hurt us that we love.

FRANCIS BEAUMONT
Maid's Tragedy V:vi 1611

Beaumont Francis (1584–1616). English dramatist and poet. From about 1608 he collaborated with John Fletcher. Their joint plays include the tragicomedies *Philaster* 1610 and *A King and No King* c. 1611, and *The Maid's Tragedy* c. 1611, *The Woman Hater* c. 1606 and *The Knight of the Burning Pestle* c. 1607, which is a satire on the audience, are ascribed to Beaumont alone.

Beaumont William (1785–1853). US surgeon who conducted pioneering experiments on the digestive system. In 1822 he saved the life of a Canadian trapper wounded in the side by a gun blast; the wound only partially healed, and through an opening in the stomach wall, Beaumont was able to observe the workings of the stomach. His *Experiments and Observations on the Gastric Juice and the Physiology of Digestion* was published 1833.

Beauregard Pierre Gustave Toutant (1818–1893). US military leader and Confederate general whose opening fire on Fort Sumter, South Carolina, started the American Civil War 1861. His military successes were clouded by his conflicts with Confederate president Jefferson Davis.

One is not born a woman. One becomes one.

SIMONE DE BEAUVOIR
The Second Sex 1953

Beauvoir Simone de (1908–1986). French socialist, feminist, and writer who played a large role in French intellectual life from the 1940s to the 1980s. Her book *Le Deuxième sexe/The Second Sex* 1949, one of the first major feminist texts, is an encyclopedic study of the role of women in society, drawing on literature, myth and history.

In it, she argues that the subservient position of women is the result of their systematic repression by a male-dominated society that denies their independence, identity and sexuality. She also published novels, including *Les Mandarins/The Mandarins* 1954, and many autobiographical volumes. She was a lifelong companion of the philosopher Jean-Paul Sartre.

Suggested reading
Asher, Carol *Simone de Beauvoir: A Life of Freedom* (1981)
Bair, Deirdre *Simone de Beauvoir* (1990)
Beauvoir, Simone de *Memoirs of a Dutiful Daughter* (autobiography vol 1) (trs 1959)
Beauvoir, Simone de *The Prime of Life* (autobiography vol 2) (trs 1962)
Beauvoir, Simone de *The Force of Circumstances* (autobiography vol 3) (trs 1964)
Beauvoir, Simone de *All Said and Done* (autobiography vol 4) (trs 1972)
Evans, M *Simone de Beauvoir: A Feminist Mandarin* (1985)
Whitmarsh, A *Simone de Beauvoir and the Limits of Commitment* (1981)

The Daily Express declares that Great Britain will not be involved in a European war this year or next year either.

MAX AITKEN, 1ST BARON BEAVERBROOK
Daily Express 19 Sept 1938

Beaverbrook (William) Max(well) Aitken, 1st Baron Beaverbrook (1879–1964). British financier, newspaper proprietor, and politician, born in Canada. He bought a majority interest in the *Daily Express* 1919, founded the *Sunday Express* 1921, and bought the London *Evening Standard* 1929. He served in Lloyd George's World War I cabinet and Churchill's World War II cabinet.

Beauregard Remembered as the Confederate general who fired on Fort Sumter and so opened the American Civil War, Pierre Beauregard had a distinguished career, fighting at Bull Run, Shiloh, and Charleston.

Between the wars he used his newspapers, in particular the *Daily Express*, to campaign for empire and free trade and against Prime Minister Baldwin. He was created a baron 1917.

Suggested reading
Chisholm, Anne and Davie, Michael *Beaverbrook: A Life* (1992)
Driberg, T *Beaverbrook* (1956)
Gourlay, Logan (ed) *The Beaverbrook I Knew* (1994)
Taylor, A J P *Beaverbrook* (1972)

Bebel (Ferdinand) August (1840–1913). German socialist. In 1869, with Wilhelm Liebknecht, he was a founding member of the Verband deutsche Arbeitervereine (League of German Workers' Clubs), and became its leading speaker in the Reichstag. Also known as the Eisenach Party, it was based in Saxony and SW Germany before being incorporated into the SPD (Sozialdemokratische Partei Deutschlands/German Social Democratic Party) 1875.

Beccaria Cesare, Marchese di Beccaria (1738–1794). Italian philanthropist, born in Milan. He opposed capital punishment and torture, advocated education as a crime preventive, influenced English philosopher Jeremy Bentham, and coined the phrase 'the greatest happiness of the greatest number', the tenet of utilitarianism.

Bechet Sidney Joseph (1897–1959). US jazz musician. He played clarinet and was the first to forge an individual style on soprano saxophone. Bechet was based in Paris in the late 1920s and the 1950s, where he was recognized by classical musicians as a serious artist.

Bechstein (Friedrich Wilhelm) Carl (1826–1900). German piano maker. He founded his own firm 1856, after having worked as an employee of several other companies. It expanded rapidly, taking advantage of new technological developments, some of which were invented by Steinway. The company was bankrupt 1993, but was saved by the intervention of the German government. Bechstein pianos are noted for their smooth but not particularly brilliant tone.

Beckenbauer Franz (1945–). German footballer who captained West Germany to the 1972 European Championship and the 1974 World Cup, and was twice European Footballer of the Year. After retiring as a player, he became West Germany's team manager, taking them to the runners-up spot in the 1986 World Cup and victory in the 1990 World Cup. He is the only person both to captain and manage a winning World Cup team.

Becker Boris (1967–). German tennis player. In 1985, at the age of 17, he became the youngest winner of a singles title at Wimbledon. He has won the title three times and helped West Germany to win the Davis Cup 1988 and 1989. He also won the US Open 1989 and the Grand Prix Masters/ATP Tour World Championship 1992.

Becker Lydia Ernestine (1827–1890). English botanist and campaigner for women's rights. She established the Manchester Ladies' Literary Society 1865 as a forum for women to study scientific subjects. In 1867 she co-founded and became secretary of the National Society for Women's Suffrage. In 1870 she founded a monthly newsletter, the *Women's Suffrage Journal*.

The boldness of this man wore out his victims and others in England; they fell upon him and killed him (I say it with sorrow).

Henry II on ST THOMAS À BECKET
in letter to Pope Alexander III

Becket St Thomas à (1118–1170). English priest and politician. He was chancellor to Henry II 1155–62, when he was appointed archbishop of Canterbury. The interests of the church soon conflicted with those of the crown and Becket was assassinated; he was canonized 1172.

A friend of Henry II, Becket was a loyal chancellor, but on becoming archbishop of Canterbury transferred his allegiance to the church. In 1164 he opposed Henry's attempt to regulate the relations between church and state, and had to flee the country; he

Becket *The murder of Thomas à Becket, archbishop of Canterbury, depicted by the artist and chronicler Matthew Paris. After his death, Becket's tomb at Canterbury became one of the most important English pilgrimage sites of the middle ages.*

returned 1170, but the reconciliation soon broke down. Encouraged by a hasty outburst from the king, four knights murdered Becket before the altar of Canterbury cathedral. He was declared a saint, and his shrine became the busiest centre of pilgrimage in England until the Reformation.

Suggested reading
Barlow, Frank *Thomas Becket* (1986)
Jones, T M *The Becket Controversy* (1970)
Knowles, David *Thomas Becket* (1971)
Winston, Richard *Becket* (1967)

Beckett Samuel Barclay (1906–1989). Irish novelist and dramatist. He wrote in both French and English. His play *En attendant Godot* – first performed in Paris 1952, and then in his own translation as *Waiting for Godot* 1955 in London, and New York 1956 – is possibly the best-known example of Theatre of the Absurd, in which life is taken to be meaningless. This genre is taken to further extremes in *Fin de Partie/Endgame* 1957 and *Happy Days* 1961. Nobel Prize for Literature 1969.

Originally a novelist and strongly influenced by James Joyce, Beckett also wrote successfully for radio in plays such as *All That Fall* 1957 and *Embers* 1959.

Vladimir: 'That passed the time.' Estragon: 'It would have passed in any case.' Vladimir: 'Yes, but not so rapidly.'

SAMUEL BECKETT
Waiting for Godot 1953

Beckford William Thomas (1760–1844). English author and eccentric. Forced out of England by scandals about his private life, he published *Vathek* 1787 in Paris, a fantastic Arabian Nights tale, and on returning to England 1796 rebuilt his home, Fonthill Abbey in Wiltshire, as a Gothic fantasy.

He did not think ... that it was necessary to make a hell of this world to enjoy paradise in the next.

WILLIAM BECKFORD
Vathek 1786

Beckmann Max (1884–1950). German Expressionist painter and graphic artist. He was influenced both by medieval art and by the *Neue Sachlichkeit* movement and after World War I his art concentrated on themes of cruelty in human society, as in *Night* 1918–19 (Kunstsammlung Nardrheim-Westfalen, Düsseldorf).

Becquerel (Antoine) Henri (1852–1908). French physicist who discovered penetrating radiation coming from uranium salts, the first

indication of radioactivity, and shared a Nobel Prize with Marie and Pierre Curie 1903. Becquerel subsequently investigated the radioactivity of radium, and showed in 1900 that it consists of a stream of electrons. In the same year, Becquerel also obtained evidence that radioactivity causes the transformation of one element into another.

If there were dreams to sell, / What would you buy? / Some cost a passing bell; / Some a light sigh.

THOMAS LOVELL BEDDOES
'Dream-Pedlary'

Beddoes Thomas Lovell (1803–1849). English poet and dramatist. His play *Death's Jest Book* was begun 1825, but it was not published until 1850, much revised.

Bede (*c.* 673–735). English theologian and historian, known as *the Venerable Bede*, active in Durham and Northumbria. He wrote many scientific, theological, and historical works. His *Historia Ecclesiastica Gentis Anglorum/Ecclesiastical History of the English People* 731 is a seminal source for early English history.

Born at Monkwearmouth, Durham, he entered the local monastery at the age of seven, later transferring to Jarrow, where he became a priest in about 703. He devoted his life to writing and teaching; among his pupils was Egbert, archbishop of York.

He alone attempts to paint for us and explain the spectacle of Anglo-Saxon England in its first phase.

Winston Churchill on BEDE
in *History of the English-Speaking People* i, 1956

Bedell Smith Walter (1895–1961). US general; Eisenhower's staff officer for much of World War II. Among his many achievements was the negotiation of the Italian surrender 1943 and the surrender of German forces in NW Europe 1945.

A staff officer who had risen from the ranks, in 1941 he became secretary to the Joint Chiefs of Staff and US secretary of the Anglo-American Combined Chiefs of Staff. He became Chief of Staff to

Becquerel *In 1896, Henri Becquerel discovered radioactivity while investigating the X-ray emission of fluorescent uranium salts using photographic plates. His accidental discovery marked the beginning of the nuclear age and in 1903 he was awarded the Nobel Prize for Physics – an award he shared with Marie and Pierre Curie. (Ann Ronan/Image Select)*

General Eisenhower Sept 1942 and remained in this post until the end of the war.

Bedford John Robert Russell, 13th Duke of Bedford (1917–). English peer. Succeeding to the title 1953, he restored the family seat Woburn Abbey, Bedfordshire, now a tourist attraction.

Beebe Charles (1877–1962). US naturalist, explorer, and writer. His interest in deep-sea exploration led to a collaboration with the engineer Otis Barton and the development of a spherical diving vessel, the bathysphere. On 24 Aug 1934 the two men made a record-breaking dive to 923 m/3,028 ft. Beebe was curator of birds for the New York Zoological Society 1899–1952. He wrote the comprehensive *Monograph of the Pheasants* 1918–22, and his expeditions are described in a series of memoirs.

The English may not like music, but they absolutely love the noise it makes.

THOMAS BEECHAM
New York Herald Tribune 1961

Beecham Thomas (1879–1961). English conductor and impresario. He established the Royal Philharmonic Orchestra 1946 and fostered the works of composers such as Delius, Sibelius, and Richard Strauss. Knighted and succeeded to baronetcy 1916.

There are two golden rules for an orchestra: start together and finish together. The public doesn't give a damn what goes on in between.

THOMAS BEECHAM
in *Beecham Stories*, 1978

Beecher Harriet. Unmarried name of Harriet Beecher Stowe, author of *Uncle Tom's Cabin*.

Beecher Henry Ward (1813–1887). US Congregational minister and militant opponent of slavery, son of the pulpit orator Lyman Beecher and brother of the writer Harriet Beecher Stowe. He travelled to Britain and did much to turn sentiment against the South.

Beecher Lyman (1775–1863). US Congregational and Presbyterian minister, one of the most popular pulpit orators of his time. He was the father of Harriet Beecher Stowe and Henry Ward Beecher.

As pastor from 1847 of Plymouth church, Brooklyn, New York, he was a leader in the movement for the abolition of slavery.

Beeching Richard, Baron Beeching (1913–1985). British scientist and administrator. He was chair of the British Railways Board 1963–65, producing the controversial *Beeching Report* 1963, which advocated concentrating resources on intercity passenger traffic and freight, at the cost of closing many rural and branch lines. Created a baron 1965.

The dullard's envy of brilliant men is always assuaged by the suspicion that they will come to a bad end.

MAX BEERBOHM
Zuleika Dobson 1911

Beerbohm (Henry) Max(imilian) (1872–1956). English caricaturist and author. A perfectionist in style, he contributed to *The Yellow Book* 1894; wrote a novel of Oxford undergraduate life, *Zuleika Dobson* 1911; and published volumes of caricature, including *Rossetti and His Circle* 1922. He succeeded George Bernard Shaw as critic to the *Saturday Review* 1898. Knighted 1939.

Beethoven Ludwig van (1770–1827). German composer and pianist. His mastery of musical expression in every genre made him the dominant influence on 19th-century music. Beethoven's repertoire includes concert overtures; the opera *Fidelio* 1805, revised 1814; five piano concertos and two for violin (one unfinished); 32 piano sonatas, including the *Moonlight* 1801 and *Appassionata* 1804–05; 17 string quartets; the Mass in D (*Missa solemnis*) 1824; and nine symphonies, as well as many youthful works. He usually played his own piano pieces and conducted his orchestral works until he was hampered by deafness 1801; nevertheless he continued to compose.

Prince, what you are, you are by the accident of your birth; what I am, I am of myself.

LUDWIG VAN BEETHOVEN
in a letter to Prince Lichnowsky, 1806

Born in Bonn, the son and grandson of musicians, Beethoven became deputy organist at the court of the Elector of Cologne at Bonn before he was 12; later he studied under Haydn and possibly Mozart, whose influence dominated his early work. From 1809, he received a small allowance from aristocratic patrons.

Beethoven's career spanned the transition from Classicism to Romanticism. Of his symphonies the best-known are the Third (*Eroica*) 1803–04, originally intended to be dedicated to Napoleon with whom Beethoven became disillusioned, the Fifth 1807–08, the Sixth (*Pastoral*) 1803–08, and Ninth (*Choral*) 1815–24, which includes the passage from Schiller's 'Ode to Joy' chosen as the national anthem of Europe.

Suggested reading

Arnold, D and Fortune, N (eds) *Beethoven Reader* (1971)
Crabbe, J *Beethoven's Empire of the Mind* (1987)
Kendall, A *The Life of Beethoven* (1978)
Kerman, J and Tyson, A *The New Grove Beethoven* (1983)
Matthews, D *Beethoven* (1985)
Solomon, M *Beethoven* (1977)

Beethoven *Ludwig van Beethoven (1770-1827) as drawn in a period sketch by Johann Peter Lyser. The composer is depicted rambling in the street, oblivious to the outside world. Most of his contemporaries tolerated his dishevelled appearance and unsophisticated manners, believing them to be symptoms of his genius. (Image Select)*

Beeton Mrs (Isabella Mary Mayson) (1836–1865). British writer on cookery and domestic management. She produced *Beeton's Household Management* 1859, the first comprehensive work on domestic science.

Begin Menachem (1913–1992). Israeli politician. He was leader of the extremist Irgun Zvai Leumi organization in Palestine from 1942 and prime minister of Israel 1977–83, as head of the right-wing Likud party. In 1978 Begin shared a Nobel Peace Prize with President Sadat of Egypt for work on the Camp David Agreements for a Middle East peace settlement.

Begin was born in Brest-Litovsk, Russia (now Brest, in Belarus), studied law in Warsaw, and fled to the USSR 1939. As leader of the Irgun group, he was responsible in 1946 for a bomb attack at the King David Hotel, Jerusalem, which killed over 100 people.

Other people have a nationality. The Irish and the Jews have a psychosis.

BRENDAN BEHAN
Richard's Cork Leg I 1973

Behan Brendan Francis (1923–1964). Irish dramatist. His early experience of prison and knowledge of the workings of the IRA (recounted in his autobiography *Borstal Boy* 1958) provided him with two recurrent themes in his plays. *The Quare Fellow* 1954 was followed by the tragicomedy *The Hostage* 1958, first written in Gaelic.

Love ceases to be a pleasure, when it ceases to be a secret.

APHRA BEHN
The Lover's Watch 'Four o'clock' 1686

Behn Aphra (1640–1689). English novelist and playwright, the first woman in England to earn her living as a writer. Her writings were criticized for their explicitness; they frequently present events from a woman's point of view. Her novel *Oroonoko* 1688 is an attack on slavery.

Between 1670 and 1687 fifteen of her plays were produced, including *The Rover*, which attacked forced and mercenary marriages. She was employed as a government spy in Holland 1666.
Suggested reading
Duffy, Maureen *The Passionate Shepherdess: Aphra Behn 1640–89* (1977)
Fraser, Antonia *The Weaker Vessel* (1984)
Goreau, Angeline *Reconstructing Aphra* (1980)
Link, Frederick *Aphra Behn* (1968)

Architecture comprises two ideas: the mastery of the practical, and the art of the beautiful.

PETER BEHRENS
Architectural Press 1981

Behrens Peter (1868–1940). German architect. He pioneered the adaptation of architecture to industry and designed the AEG turbine factory in Berlin 1909, a landmark in industrial architecture. He taught Le Corbusier, Walter Gropius, and Mies van der Rohe.

Behring Emil von (1854–1917). German physician who discovered that the body produces antitoxins, substances able to counteract poisons released by bacteria. Using this knowledge, he developed new treatments for such diseases as diphtheria, tuberculosis, and tetanus. He won the first Nobel Prize for Physiology or Medicine, in 1901.

Beiderbecke Bix (Leon Bismarck) (1903–1931). US jazz cornetist, composer, and pianist. A romantic soloist with the bands of King Oliver, Louis Armstrong, and Paul Whiteman, Beiderbecke was the first acknowledged white jazz innovator. He was influenced by the classical composers Debussy, Ravel, and Stravinsky.

His reputation grew after his early death with the publication of Dorothy Baker's novel *Young Man with a Horn* 1938, based on his life.

Contemporaries said his notes sounded like they had been struck, as with a mallet on a bell.

BIX BEIDERBECKE
described by Donald Clarke (ed) *The Penguin Encyclopedia of Popular Music* 1989

Beijerinck Martinus Willem (1851–1931). Dutch bacteriologist who in 1898 published his finding that an agent smaller than bacteria could cause diseases, an agent that he called a virus.

Béjart Maurice. Adopted name of Maurice Jean Berger (1927–). French choreographer and ballet director. Believing dance to be 'total theatre', he has staged huge, spectacular productions, for example *Romeo and Juliet* 1966. As director of his Ballet of the 20th Century 1960, based in Brussels until 1987, Béjart's productions included *The Firebird* 1970 (where the ballerina's role is taken by a male leader of a band of partisans) and *Kabuki* 1986, which features the suicide of 47 samurai in the finale. Other ballets include *Bolero* 1961 and *Notre Faust* 1975.

The last refuge in our world where a man can discover the exact measure of his own soul.

MAURICE BÉJART
Of the stage, in *Ballet and Modern Dance*, 'Dynamic Tradition'

Békésy Georg von (1899–1972). Hungarian-born US scientist who resolved a long-standing controversy on how the inner ear functions. For his discovery concerning the mechanism of stimulation within the cochlea, he received the 1961 Nobel Prize for Physiology or Medicine.

Békésy Scientist Georg von Békésy. Békésy worked in telecommunications holding both academic and industrial positions. He won the 1961 Nobel Prize for Physiology or Medicine after discovering how the inner ear works. Fascinated by the senses, he also investigated the mechanisms underlying sight and touch. (Image Select)

Belasco David (1859–1931). US dramatist and producer. His works include *Madame Butterfly* 1900 and *The Girl of the Golden West* 1905, both of which Puccini used as libretti for operas.

Many of his plays were written in collaboration with others, including J A Herne. As a producer, Belasco was known more for his technical innovations than for the quality of the plays he chose. His name was a big draw for theatre audiences, and he made stars out of many unknown performers.

Belaúnde Terry Fernando (1913–). President of Peru 1963–68 and 1980–85. He championed land reform and the construction of roads to open up the Amazon valley. He fled to the USA 1968 after being deposed by a military junta. After his return, his second term in office was marked by rampant inflation, enormous foreign debts, terrorism, mass killings, and human-rights violations by the armed forces.

Bel Geddes Norman (1893–1958). US industrial designer. He was a key member of the small group of US pioneers who helped to establish the profession of industrial design in the interwar years. Throughout his career he was motivated by a desire to create a utopian, futuristic environment.

Belgrano Manuel (1770–1820). Argentine revolutionary. He was a member of the military group that led the 1810 revolt against Spain. Later, he commanded the revolutionary army until he was replaced by José de San Martín 1814.

Belisarius brought two kings captive to Constantinople, and unexpectedly made the possessions of Geiseric and Theoderic Roman spoil.

Procopius on BELISARIUS
Wars 7.14

Belisarius (*c.* 505–565). Roman general under Emperor Justinian I. He won major victories over the Persians in 530 and the Vandals in 533 when he sacked Carthage. Later he invaded Sicily and fought a series of campaigns against the Goths in Italy.

As a young man he was a member of Justinian's bodyguard before becoming commander of the eastern army. Although he was not always favoured by the Emperor, it was largely his military skill which preserved the Byzantine Empire from being overthrown.

Bell Alexander Graham (1847–1922). Scottish-born US scientist and inventor, the first person ever to transmit speech from one point to another by electrical means. This invention – the telephone – was made 1876. Later Bell experimented with a type of phonograph and, in aeronautics, invented the tricycle undercarriage.

Bell also invented a photophone, which used selenium crystals to apply the telephone principle to transmitting words in a beam of light. He thus achieved the first wireless transmission of speech.

Born in Edinburgh, Bell was educated at the universities of Edinburgh and London and studied under his father, who developed a method for teaching the deaf to speak. In 1870 the family moved to Canada and Bell went to the US, where he opened a school 1872 for teachers of the deaf in Boston. In 1873 he began teaching vocal physiology at Boston University. He became a US citizen 1882. Bell also worked on converting seawater to drinking water and on air conditioning and sheep breeding.

Suggested reading
Bruce, R V *Alexander Graham Bell and the Conquest of Solitude* (1973)
Eber, Dorothy *Genius at Work: Images of Alexander Graham Bell* (1982)

Bell Charles (1774–1842). Scottish anatomist and surgeon who carried out pioneering research on the human nervous system. He gave his name to Bell's palsy, an extracranial paralysis of the facial nerve, and to the long thoracic nerve of Bell, which supplies a muscle in the chest wall. His findings first appeared 1811; his main written work was *The Nervous System of the Human Body* 1830. Knighted 1829.

Bell Daniel (1919–). US sociologist. He was editor of the report *Toward the Year 2000* 1968, which reflects his interest in contemporary history and social forecasting. In *The End of Ideology* 1960, he tried to show how the West, as a result of welfare state and mixed economy, had come to the 'end of the ideological age'. *The Coming of Post-Industrial Society* underlined his view of the importance of scientific and technical knowledge in social and political life and predicted greater power for scientific elites.

Bell Francis Henry Dillon (1851–1936). New Zealand politician, prime minister 1925. He was attorney-general 1918–26 and minister for external affairs 1923–26, being best known in the international sphere as New Zealand delegate to League of Nations conferences and to the Imperial Conference 1928. KCMG 1915.

Bell John (1928–1990). British physicist who in 1964 devised a test to verify a point in quantum theory: whether two particles that were once connected are always afterwards interconnected even if they become widely separated. As well as investigating fundamental problems in theoretical physics, Bell contributed to the design of particle accelerators. Bell worked for 30 years at CERN, the European research laboratory near Geneva, Switzerland.

Bell John Anthony (1940–). Australian actor and theatrical director. In 1970 he became the founding artistic director of the Nimrod Theatre, Sydney, where he developed a distinctive style, particularly with his productions of Shakespeare.

Bell Patrick (1799–1869). Scottish inventor of a reaping machine, developed around 1828. It was pushed by two horses and used a rotating cylinder of horizontal bars to bend the standing corn on to a reciprocating cutter that was driven off the machine's wheels (in much the same way as on a combine harvester).

Bell, Alexander Graham *Scottish-born US scientist Alexander Graham Bell, who invented the telephone in 1876. Bell had always been fascinated with the mechanics of speech – he spent his early twenties teaching deaf-mutes – and, in 1880, with money he made from his inventions, established the Volta Laboratory in Washington for research into deafness. (Ann Ronan/Image Select)*

In the years to 1832 at least 20 machines were produced, and later, since Bell did not take out a patent, the design was widely copied and improved on, until mechanical harvesting became the norm.

Bellamy Edward (1850–1898). US author and social critic. His utopian novel *Looking Backward: 2000–1887* 1888, was a huge best-seller and inspired wide public support for his political programme of state socialism. He published a second utopian novel, *Equality* 1897.

Bellarmine Roberto Francesco Romolo (1542–1621). Italian Roman Catholic theologian and cardinal. He taught at the Jesuit College in Rome and became archbishop of Capua 1602. His *Disputationes de controversiis fidei christianae* 1581–93 was a major defence of Catholicism in the 16th century. He was canonized 1930.

Bell Burnell (Susan) Jocelyn (1943–). British astronomer. In 1967 she discovered the first pulsar (rapidly flashing star) with Antony Hewish and colleagues at Cambridge University, England.

Belli Giuseppe Giocchomo (1791–1863). Italian poet. He wrote more than 2,000 sonnets in the Roman dialect which provide a brilliantly observed satiric account of early 19th-century papal Rome.

Bellingshausen Fabian Gottlieb von (1778–1852). Russian Antarctic explorer, the first to sight and circumnavigate the Antarctic continent 1819–21, although he did not realize what it was.

Carve in your head by letters of brass: An Opera must draw tears, cause horror, bring death, by means of song.

VINCENCO BELLINI
in a letter, 1834

Bellini Venetian family of artists, founders of the Venetian School in the 15th and early 16th centuries. Jacopo (*c.* 1400–1470/71), the father-in-law of Andrea Mantegna, worked at Venice, Padua, Verona and Ferrara. Gentile (*c.* 1429–1507) was probably the elder son of Jacopo and was trained by him. Gentile's great ability in portraiture is shown by the *Man with a Pair of Dividers* (National Gallery, London), though the superb *St Dominic*, long attributed to him, is now assigned to Giovanni. He painted a series of history pictures for the Doge's Palace 1474, which were later destroyed, but extant compositions are his paintings of Venetian ceremonies and pageants, in which he gives a fascinating view of the city, his *Procession in the Piazza San Marco* (Accademia, Venice) being famous. Although now overshadowed by his brother, he was no less famous in his own day. Giovanni (*c.* 1430–1516) contributed more than any painter of his time to the creation of the great Venetian School. He worked to an advanced age on paintings for public buildings and churches in Venice and other cities, including numerous versions of the Madonna and Child. Altarpieces for San Pietro Martire, Murano, the church of the Frari and the church of San Zaccaria are notable, as also is a late mythological composition, *The Feast of the Gods*, 1514 (Washington), in which Titian may have had a hand.

Suggested reading
Goffen, Rona *Giovanni Bellini* (1989)
Robertson, Giles *Giovanni Bellini* (1968)
Steer, John *Venetian Painting* (1970)
Wilde, Johannes *Venetian Art from Bellini to Titian* (1974)
Wind, Edgar *Bellini's Feast of the Gods* (1948)

Bellini Mario (1935–). Italian architect and industrial designer. He was one of the figures who helped establish Italy as a leading nation in industrial design from the 1960s. He is known for his elegant pieces of office machinery for the Olivetti company (from 1962) and his sophisticated furniture designs for Cassina (from 1964).

Bellini Vincenzo (1801–1835). Italian composer of operas. He collaborated with the tenor Giovanni Battista Rubini (1794–1854) to develop a new simplicity of melodic expression in romantic evocations of classic themes, as in *La Sonnambula/The Sleepwalker* and *Norma*, both 1831. In *I Puritani/The Puritans* 1835, his last work, he discovered a new boldness and vigour of orchestral effect.

Bello Andrés (1781–1865). Venezuelan poet and polymath. Regarded as the intellectual father of Latin America, a friend and teacher of the patriot Simón Bolívar, he translated the Romantics Byron and Hugo but defended Neo-Classicism in literature. He celebrated the flora of tropical America in the widely read Virgilian stanzas *Silvas a la agricultura de la zona tórrida/Agriculture in the Tropics* 1826, part of an unfinished epic *América*. In the service of the new republic of Chile he was an enormously influential educational and legal reformer; he also published an important grammar of the Spanish language 1847 which is still in use.

When I am dead, I hope it may be said: / 'His sins were scarlet, but his books were read.'

HILAIRE BELLOC
'On His Books'

Belloc (Joseph) Hilaire (René Pierre) (1870–1953). English author. He is remembered primarily for his nonsense verse for children *The Bad Child's Book of Beasts* 1896 and *Cautionary Tales* 1907. Belloc also wrote travel and religious books (he was a devout Catholic). With G K Chesterton, he advocated a return to the late medieval guild system of commercial association in place of capitalism or socialism.

Bellot Joseph René (1826–1853). French Arctic explorer who reached the strait now named after him 1852, and lost his life while searching for English explorer John Franklin.

Bellow Saul (1915–). Canadian-born US novelist. From his first novel, *Dangling Man* 1944, Bellow has typically set his naturalistic narratives in Chicago and made his central character an anxious, Jewish-American intellectual. In *The Adventures of Augie March* 1953 and *Henderson the Rain King* 1959, he created confident and comic picaresque heroes, before *Herzog* 1964, which pitches a comic but distressed scholar into a world of darkening humanism. Later works, developing Bellow's depiction of an age of urban disorder and indifference, include the near-apocalyptic *Mr Sammler's Planet* 1970, *Humboldt's Gift* 1975, *The Dean's December* 1982, *More Die of Heartbreak* 1987, and the novella *A Theft* 1989. His finely styled works and skilled characterizations won him the Nobel Prize for Literature 1976. Other works include *Him with His Foot in His Mouth* 1984 and *Something to Remember Me By* 1992.

Suggested reading
Fuchs, D *Saul Bellow: Vision and Revision* (1983)
Goldman, L H *Saul Bellow's Moral Vision* (1983)
Wilson, J *On Bellow's Planet* (1985)

Bellows George Wesley (1882–1925). US painter. He is associated with the Ashcan School, and known for his vigorous portrayals of the drama of street life and sport. His most famous works, such as *Stag at Sharkey's* 1909, depict the violence and excitement of illegal boxing matches.

Women over thirty are at their best, but men over thirty are too old to recognize it.

JEAN-PAUL BELMONDO
Attributed remark

Belmondo Jean-Paul (1933–). French film actor who became a star in Jean-Luc Godard's *A bout de souffle/Breathless* 1959. He is best known for his racy personality in French vehicles. His other films include *Cartouche* 1962, *That Man from Rio* 1964, *The Brain* 1968, *Borsalino* 1970, and *Stavisky* 1974.

Belmont August (1816–1890). German-born US financier, who became the Rothschilds' exclusive representative in the USA when he established a private bank in New York 1837. Belmont was a leading member of New York City society's most exclusive clique (the '400') and was instrumental in financing the costs of the Mexican War (1846–48).

Beloff Max, Baron Beloff (1913–). British historian. From 1974 to 1979 he was principal of the University College at Buckingham, the UK's first independent institution at university level. Created a baron 1981.

Belshazzar in the Old Testament, the last king of Babylon, son of Nebuchadnezzar. During a feast (known as *Belshazzar's Feast*) he saw a message, interpreted by Daniel as prophesying the fall of Babylon and death of Belshazzar. All of this is said to have happened on the same night that the city was invaded by the Medes and Persians (539 BC).

Beltrami Eugenio (1835–1899). Italian mathematician who pioneered modern non-Euclidean geometry. His work ranged over almost the whole field of pure and applied mathematics, but especially theories of surfaces and space of constant curvature. He demonstrated the usefulness of employing differential parameters in surface theory, thereby beginning the use of invariant methods in differential geometry. After 1872 Beltrami switched his attention to questions of applied mathematics, especially problems in elasticity and electromagnetism.

Ben Ali Zine el Abidine (1936–). Tunisian politician, president from 1987. After training in France and the USA, he returned to Tunisia and became director-general of national security. He was made minister of the interior and then prime minister under the ageing president for life, Habib Bourguiba, whom he deposed 1987 in a

bloodless coup with the aid of ministerial colleagues. He ended the personality cult established by Bourguiba and moved toward a pluralist political system. He was re-elected 1994, with 99% of the popular vote.

Ben Barka Mehdi (1920–1965). Moroccan politician. He became president of the National Consultative Assembly 1956 on the country's independence from France. He was assassinated by Moroccan agents with the aid of the French secret service because of his alleged involvement in an attempt on King Hassan's life and for supporting Algeria in Algerian-Moroccan border disputes.

His assassination followed his alleged involvement in an attempt on King Hassan's life and for supporting Algeria in Algerian-Moroccan border disputes.

Ben Bella Mohammed Ahmed (1916–). Algerian politician. He was leader of the National Liberation Front (FLN) from 1952, the first prime minister of independent Algeria 1962–63, and its first president 1963–65. In 1965 Ben Bella was overthrown by Col Houari Boumédienne and detained until 1979. In 1985 he founded a new party, Mouvement pour la Démocratie en Algérie, and returned to Algeria 1990 after nine years in exile.

In no one instance where he commanded was any success over the enemy obtained.

J K Laughton on JOHN BENBOW
in *Dictionary of National Biography*

Benbow John (1653–1702). English admiral, hero of several battles with France. He ran away to sea as a boy, and from 1689 served in the navy. He fought at the battles of Beachy Head 1690 and La Hogue 1692, and died of wounds received in a fight with the French off Jamaica.

My only solution for the problem of habitual accidents and, so far, nobody has asked me for my solution, is to stay in bed all day. Even then, there is always the chance that you will fall out.

ROBERT BENCHLEY
Chips off the old Benchley, 'Safety Second' 1949

Benchley Robert Charles (1889–1945). US humorist, actor, and drama critic. His books include *Of All Things* 1921 and *Benchley Beside Himself* 1943. His film skit *How to Sleep* illustrates his ability to extract humour from everyday life.

Born in Massachusetts, he was associated with the writer Dorothy Parker, *The New Yorker* magazine, and the circle of wits at the Algonquin Round Table in New York. He was a master of gentle satire, left New York City for Hollywood, and wrote and appeared in several 1930s and 1940s films.

The Treason of the Intellectuals.

JULIEN BENDA
Book title 1927

Benda Julien (1867–1956). French writer and philosopher. He was an outspoken opponent of the philosophy of Henri Bergson, and in 1927 published a manifesto on the necessity of devotion to the absolute truth, which he felt his contemporaries had betrayed, *La Trahison des clercs/The Treason of the Intellectuals*.

Benedict fifteen popes, including:

Benedict XV (Giacomo della Chiesa) (1854–1922). Pope from 1914. During World War I he endeavoured to bring about a peace settlement, and it was during his papacy that British, French, and Dutch official relations were renewed with the Vatican.

Bellow The works of US novelist Saul Bellow combine cultural sophistication with the wisdom of the streets. Mainly set in Chicago and New York, they present characterizations of modern urban life and contain a sense of moral and social alarm. His many literary awards include the National Book Award 1965 and 1971, the Pulitzer Prize 1976, and the Nobel Prize 1976.

Benedict, St (*c.* 480–*c.* 547). Founder of Christian monasticism in the West and of the Benedictine order. He founded the monastery of Monte Cassino and others in Italy. His feast day is 11 July.

Nothing harsh, nothing burdensome.

ST BENEDICT
Rule of St Benedict

Beneš Eduard (1884–1948). Czechoslovak politician. He worked with Tomáš Masaryk towards Czechoslovak nationalism from 1918 and was foreign minister and representative at the League of Nations. He was president of the republic from 1935 until forced to resign by the Germans; he headed a government in exile in London during World War II. He returned home as president 1945 but resigned again after the Communist coup 1948.

To make peace in Europe possible … the pre-war generation must die and take [their] pre-war mentality into the grave.

EDUARD BENEŠ
Interview Dec 1929

Benét Stephen Vincent (1898–1943). US poet, novelist, and short-story writer. He won a Pulitzer Prize 1929 for his narrative poem of the Civil War, *John Brown's Body* 1928. One of his short stories, 'The Devil and Daniel Webster', became a classic and was made into a play, an opera, and a film *All That Money Can Buy*. He published more than 17 volumes of verse and prose.

Bury my heart at Wounded Knee.

STEPHEN VINCENT BENÉT
Yale Review vol 17 1927 , 'American Names'

Ben-Gurion David. Adopted name of David Gruen (1886–1973). Israeli statesman and socialist politician, one of the founders of the state of Israel, the country's first prime minister 1948–53, and again 1955–63.

He was born in Poland and went to Palestine 1906 to farm. He was a leader of the Zionist movement, and as defence minister he presided over the development of Israel's armed forces into one of the strongest armies in the Middle East.

Ours is a country built more on people than on territory. The Jews will come from everywhere: from France, from Russia, from America, from Yemen … Their faith is their passport.

DAVID BEN-GURION
Recalled by Shimon Peres *New York Times* 5 Oct 1986

Benjamin Arthur (1893–1960). Australian pianist and composer. He taught composition at the Royal College of Music in London from 1925, where Benjamin Britten was one of his pupils. His works include *Jamaican Rumba*, inspired by a visit to the West Indies 1937.

Benjamin George William John (1960–   ). English composer, conductor, and pianist. A pupil of Messiaen, his colourful and sonorous works include *Ringed by the Flat Horizon* 1980, *At First Light* 1982, *Antara* 1987, and *Cascade* 1990.

Benjamin Judah Philip (1811–1884). US Confederate official. Holding office in the US Senate 1852–61, he was a proponent of secession of the South and resigned from office at the outbreak of the American Civil War. As one of the leaders of the Confederacy, he served as attorney general, secretary of war, and secretary of state.

Benjamin Walter (1892–1940). German Marxist essayist, one of the most important cultural critics of the 20th century. He wrote on literature, film, art, and society. Some of his essays were collected in *Einbahnstrasse/One-Way Street* 1928 and *Illuminationen/Illuminations* 1961.

Benjamin's works are a complex and unlikely blend of Marxism and Jewish mysticism. Rejecting more orthodox Marxist aesthetic theory, he was a staunch supporter of Modernism, and wrote important essays on the writers Franz Kafka, Bertolt Brecht, and Charles Baudelaire, and on the relationship between technology, the arts, and society.

Like ultraviolet rays memory shows to each man in the book of life a script that invisibly and prophetically glosses the text.

WALTER BENJAMIN
One-Way Street, 'Madame Ariane – Second Courtyard on the Left' 1928

Benn Gottfried (1886–1956). German lyric poet. Experience as a military physician during World War I encouraged a cynically pessimistic emphasis on human degeneracy and physical decay in his early collections such as *Morgue* and *Fleisch/Flesh*, both 1917. His autobiography *Doppelleben/Double Life* 1950 describes a gradual

Benjamin, Judah Philip US lawyer and politician Judah Philip Benjamin was Confederate secretary of state during the American Civil War. Escaping to England at the end of the war, he became a lawyer and wrote a classic legal work, The Sale of Personal Property 1868.

mellowing into pragmatism. *Primal Vision*, an English translation of selected verse and prose, was published 1961.

Benn Tony (Anthony Neil Wedgwood) (1925–   ). British Labour politician, formerly the leading figure on the party's left wing. He was minister of technology 1966–70 and of industry 1974–75, but his campaign against entry to the European Community (now the European Union) led to his transfer to the Department of Energy 1975–79. A skilled parliamentary orator, he unsuccessfully contested the Labour Party leadership 1988.

Son of the 1st Viscount Stansgate, a Labour peer, Benn was MP for Bristol SE 1950–60, succeeded his father 1960, but never used his title, and in 1963 was the first person to disclaim a title under the Peerage Act. He was again MP for Bristol SE 1963–83. In 1981 he challenged Denis Healey for the deputy leadership of the party and was so narrowly defeated that he established himself as the acknowledged leader of the left. His diaries cover in enormous detail the events of the period. In 1984 he became MP for Chesterfield.

A faith is something you die for, a doctrine is something you kill for. There is all the difference in the world.

TONY BENN
BBC TV 11 April 1989

Bennelong (*c.* 1764–1813). Australian Aborigine captured 1789 by Governor Phillip with the aim of exposing him to the benefits of European civilization and installed with his family in a hut in Sydney at what is now Bennelong Point. He was taken to England by Phillip 1792–95 but on his return was unable to fit back into Aboriginal society and eventually was killed in a fight with other Aborigines.

Bennet Donald (1910–1968). Australian air vice-marshal, commander of the Royal Air Force Pathfinder Force in World War II from Aug 1942.

In the early part of the war, he controlled the 'transatlantic ferry' system of flying aircraft from the USA to Britain. He then rejoined the RAF, commanded a bomber squadron, and was shot down over Norway 1941 while attacking the *Tirpitz*. He led his crew back to the UK via Sweden.

Bennett Agnes Elizabeth Lloyd (1872–1960). Australian medical practitioner in New Zealand. She was the first woman science graduate from the University of Sydney 1894. During World War II she became the first woman commissioned officer in the British Army.

Bennett Alan (1934–   ). English dramatist, screenwriter, and actor. His works (often set in his native north of England) treat subjects such as class, senility, illness, and death with macabre comedy. They include *Talking Heads* 1988, a series of monologues for television, and the play *The Madness of George III* 1991, made into the film *The Madness of King George* 1995.

Bennett began his career writing and acting in *Beyond the Fringe*, a satirical revue in the 1960s. Other works include the TV film *An Englishman Abroad* 1982, the cinema film *A Private Function* 1984, and plays such as *Forty Years On* 1968, *Getting On* 1971, and *Kafka's Dick* 1986. He also wrote the screenplay for *Prick Up Your Ears* 1987, based on the relationship between the dramatist Joe Orton and his lover Kenneth Halliwell. A selection of prose writings was published as *Writing Home* 1994.

Life is rather like a tin of sardines – we're all of us looking for the key.

ALAN BENNETT and others
Beyond the Fringe 1963

Bennett (Enoch) Arnold (1867–1931). English novelist. His major books are set in the industrial Five Towns of the Midlands and are concerned with the manner in which the environment dictates the pattern of his characters' lives. His many novels include *Anna of the Five Towns* 1904, *The Old Wives' Tale* 1908, and the trilogy *Clayhanger, Hilda Lessways*, and *These Twain* 1910–16.

Suggested reading
Bennett, Arnold *The Journals of Arnold Bennett 1896–1928* (1932–33)
Bennett, Arnold (ed J Hepburn) *Sketches for Autobiography* (1979)
Broomfield, O R *Arnold Bennett* (1984)
Drabble, Margaret *Arnold Bennett* (1974)
Lucas, John *Arnold Bennett: A Study in his Fiction* (1974)

Ye can call it influenza if ye like ... There was no influenza in my young days. We called a cold a cold.

ARNOLD BENNETT
The Card ch 8 1911

Bennett Richard Rodney (1936–   ). English composer of jazz, film music, symphonies, and operas. His film scores for *Far from the Madding Crowd* 1967, *Nicholas and Alexandra* 1971, and *Murder on the Orient Express* 1974 all received Oscar nominations. His operas include *The Mines of Sulphur* 1963 and *Victory* 1970.

Benny Jack. Stage name of Benjamin Kubelsky (1894–1974). US comedian notable for his perfect timing and lugubrious manner. Over the years, Benny appeared on the stage, in films, and on radio and television. His radio programme, *The Jack Benny Show* from 1932, made him a national institution. Featuring his wife Mary Livingston, singer Dennis Day, announcer Don Wilson, and valet Eddie 'Rochester' Anderson, it was produced for television in the 1950s. His film appearances, mostly in the 1930s and 1940s, included *To Be or Not to Be* 1942. He also played in *Charley's Aunt* 1941, *It's In the Bag* 1945, and *A Guide for the Married Man* 1967.

Born in Chicago, he began a musical career in local theatre orchestras (playing the violin) and joined a vaudeville troupe. During the 1920s, he turned to comedy, taking the stage name 'Jack Benny' and developing his familiar miserly, yet harmless character.

I'm thinking.

JACK BENNY
Part of Benny's comedy routine, in reply to a highwayman's
question 'Your money or your life! Come on, come on, hurry up!'

Benson E(dward) F(rederic) (1867–1940). English writer. He specialized in novels gently satirizing the foibles of upper-middle-class society, and wrote a series of books featuring the formidable female antagonists Mapp and Lucia, including *Queen Lucia* 1920. He was the son of Edward White Benson, archbishop of Canterbury 1883–96.

Benson Edward White (1829–1896). English cleric, first headmaster of Wellington College 1859–68, and, as archbishop of Canterbury from 1883, responsible for the 'Lincoln Judgment' on questions of ritual 1887.

The greatest happiness of the greatest number is the foundation of morals and legislation.

JEREMY BENTHAM
Works x.142 1842

Bentham Jeremy (1748–1832). English philosopher, legal and social reformer, and founder of utilitarianism. The essence of his moral philosophy is found in the pronouncement of his *Principles of Morals and Legislation* (written 1780, published 1789): that the object of all legislation should be 'the greatest happiness for the greatest number'.

Bentham declared that the 'utility' of any law is to be measured by the extent to which it promotes the pleasure, good, and happiness of the people concerned. In 1776 he published *Fragments on Government*. He made suggestions for the reform of the poor law 1798, which formed the basis of the reforms enacted 1834, and in his *Catechism of Parliamentary Reform* 1817 he proposed annual elections, the secret ballot, and universal male suffrage. He was also a pioneer of prison reform.

Bentham English Utilitarian philosopher Jeremy Bentham. His failure to appreciate quality and poetry was criticized by John Stuart Mill, among others, but his radical social reformism greatly influenced subsequent practice.

In economics he was an apostle of *laissez-faire*, and in his *Defence of Usury* 1787 and *Manual of Political Economy* 1798 he contended that his principle of 'utility' was best served by allowing every man (sic) to pursue his own interests unhindered by restrictive legislation. He was made a citizen of the French Republic 1792.

Suggested reading
Harrison, Ross *Bentham* (1983)
Letwin, S R *The Pursuit of Certainty* (1965)
Mack, Mary P *Jeremy Bentham 1748–1792* (1962)

Bentinck Lord (William) George (Frederic Cavendish) (1802–1848). English nobleman and politician, son of the 4th Duke of Portland. He was a leading opponent of the repeal of the Corn Laws 1848 but after the repeal helped defeat Peel's government. He was best known as a racehorse owner.

He infused into oriental despotism the spirit of British freedom ... (and) never forgot that the end of government is the happiness of the governed.

T B Macaulay on LORD WILLIAM HENRY CAVENDISH BENTINCK, inscription on the statue of Bentinck in Calcutta.

Bentinck Lord William Henry Cavendish (1774–1839). British colonial administrator, first governor general of India 1828–35. He acted against the ancient Indian rituals of thuggee and suttee, and established English as the medium of instruction. He was the son of the 3rd Duke of Portland.

Bentley Edmund Clerihew (1875–1956). English author. He invented the four-line humorous verse form known as the *clerihew*, used in *Biography for Beginners* 1905 and in *Baseless Biography* 1939. He was also the author of the classic detective story *Trent's Last Case* 1913.

The Art of Biography / Is different from Geography. / Geography is about Maps, / But Biography is about Chaps.

EDMUND CLERIHEW BENTLEY
Biography for Beginners, introduction 1905

Bentley John Francis (1839–1902). English architect. He designed Westminster Cathedral, London, 1895–1903. It is outwardly Byzantine but inwardly shaped by shadowy vaults of bare brickwork.

The campanile is the tallest church tower in London.

He had a genius for taking infinite pains with detail.

Cardinal Herbert Vaughan on JOHN FRANCIS BENTLEY
in letter to Lady Herbert of Lea

Bentley Richard (1662–1742). English classical scholar whose textual criticism includes *Dissertation upon the Epistles of Phalaris* 1699. He was Master of Trinity College, Cambridge University, from 1700.

Benton Thomas Hart (1782–1858). US political leader. He was elected to the US Senate 1820, where he served for the next 30 years. He distinguished himself as an outspoken opponent of the Bank of the United States and the extension of slavery as well as a strong supporter of westward expansion.

Moving to St Louis 1815, he opened a law practice and published the *Missouri Enquirer* 1818–20.

Bentsen Lloyd Millard (1921–). US Democrat politician. Elected to the House of Representatives 1948, he served three terms. He was a senator for Texas 1971–93, chairing the Senate Finance Committee 1986–92. He was chosen by Michael Dukakis as the

Bentinck Lord George Bentinck, English Tory politician, supporter of emancipation. A keen sportsman, he reformed abuses in horse racing and field sports. He was greatly admired by Disraeli.

Benz *Karl Benz's 'Motorenveloziped' drove on the streets of Mannheim for the first time in 1886 and is generally regarded as one of the world's first vehicles to be successfully propelled by an internal combustion engine.* (Mercedes–Benz/Image Select)

vice-presidential nominee in the 1988 election. Bentsen was secretary to the Treasury 1993–94.

Benz Karl Friedrich (1844–1929). German automobile engineer who produced the world's first petrol-driven motor vehicle. He built his first model engine 1878 and the petrol-driven car 1885.

Benz made his first four-wheeled prototype in 1891 and by 1895, he was building a range of four-wheeled vehicles that were light, strong, inexpensive, and simple to operate. These automobiles ran at speeds of about 24 kph/15 mph. In 1926, the thriving company merged with the German firm of Daimler to form Daimler-Benz.

Ben Zvi Izhak (1884–1963). Israeli politician, president 1952–63. He was born in Poltava, Russia, and became active in the Zionist movement in Ukraine. In 1907 he went to Palestine but was deported 1915 with Ben-Gurion. They served in the Jewish Legion under Field Marshal Allenby, who commanded the British forces in the Middle East.

Béranger Pierre Jean de (1780–1857). French poet. He wrote light satirical lyrics dealing with love, wine, popular philosophy, and politics.

Berchtold Leopold Anton Johann Sigismond Joseph Korsinus Ferdinand, Count von (1863–1942). Foreign minister of Austria–Hungary 1912–15 and a crucial figure in the events that led to World War I, because his indecisive stance caused tension with Serbia.

Berdyaev Nikolai Alexandrovich (1874–1948). Russian philosopher who often challenged official Soviet viewpoints after the Revolution of 1917. Although appointed professor of philosophy in 1919 at Moscow University, he was exiled 1922 for defending Orthodox Christian religion. His books include *The Meaning of History* 1923 and *The Destiny of Man* 1935.

Bérégovoy Pierre Eugène (1925–1993). French socialist politician, prime minister 1992–93. A close ally of François Mitterrand,

he was named Chief of Staff 1981 after managing the successful presidential campaign. He was social affairs minister 1982–84 and finance minister 1984–86 and 1988–92. He resigned as premier following the Socialists' defeat in the March 1993 general election, and shortly afterwards committed suicide.

Berengaria of Navarre (1165–c. 1230). Queen of England. The only English queen never to set foot in England, she was the daughter of King Sancho VI of Navarre. She married Richard I of England in Cyprus 1191, and accompanied him on his crusade to the Holy Land.

Berenson Bernard (originally Bernhard) (1865–1959). Lithuanian-born US art historian and connoisseur. He was once revered as a leading scholar of Italian Renaissance art. He became wealthy through his advisory work for art galleries and for such collectors as Joseph Duveen (1869–1939), although many of his attributions of anonymous Italian paintings were later questioned. His books include *The Drawings of the Florentine Painters* 1903.

When I compose I always feel I am like Beethoven; only afterwards do I become aware that at best I am only Bizet.

ALBAN BERG
in Theodor W Adorno *Alban Berg* 1968

Berg Alban (1885–1935). Austrian composer. He studied under Arnold Schoenberg and developed a personal twelve-tone idiom of great emotional and stylistic versatility. His relatively small output includes two operas: *Wozzeck* 1920, a grim story of working-class life,

Berg *The composer Alban Berg (1885–1935). Regarded as the most 'human' of the Second Viennese School composers, Berg adapted the normally strict 12-note procedures to suit his own needs. In the* Lyric Suite *and other works he enciphered his initials and showed an obsession with numbers.*

and the unfinished *Lulu* 1929–35; and chamber music incorporating coded references to friends and family.

His music is emotionally expressive, and sometimes anguished, but it can also be lyrical, as in the *Violin Concerto* 1935.

Suggested reading
Carner, Mosco *Alban Berg: The Man and his Work* (1975)
Jarman, Douglas *Alban Berg: Wozzeck* (1989)
Monson, Karen *Alban Berg* (1979)
Reich, W *The Life and Work of Alban Berg* (1965)

Berg Paul (1926–). US molecular biologist. In 1972, using gene-splicing techniques developed by others, Berg spliced and combined into a single hybrid the DNA from an animal tumour virus (SV40) and the DNA from a bacterial virus. For his work on recombinant DNA, he shared the 1980 Nobel Prize for Chemistry.

Berger Hans (1873–1941). German psychiatrist and philosopher of science. He first described the human electroencephalogram (EEG) 1929. The differential patterns of cortical electrical activity he observed in alert and relaxed subjects led him to attempt the application of EEG to the study of psychophysical relationships and of conscious processes in general. He saw EEG as a key to the mind–body problem, a problem with which he was preoccupied for much of his life.

Berger John Peter (1926–). English left-wing art critic and writer. In his best-known book, *Ways of Seeing* 1972, he valued art for social rather than aesthetic reasons. He also attacked museums for preserving what is by nature ephemeral. His novels include *A Painter of Our Time* 1958 and *G* 1972 (Booker Prize).

Berger, John *English art critic and novelist John Berger. Starting from a Marxist position, and indebted in particular to Walter Benjamin, Berger has sought to analyze art in terms of its social and political significance.*

In later works this concern with the multiple layers of meaning of an image led him to examine photography, as in Another Way of Telling 1982. His later fiction, such as Pig Earth which depicts the lives of French peasants, looks at the nature of authentic social life.

All weddings are similar but every marriage is different. Death comes to everyone but one mourns alone.

JOHN BERGER
White Bird, 'Storyteller' 1985

Berger Thomas Louis (1924–). US writer. His parodic novels include the picaresque sequence *Crazy in Berlin* 1958, *Reinhart in Love* 1961, *Vital Parts* 1970, and *Reinhart's Women* 1981. Berger also parodied the Western in *Little Big Man* 1964 (filmed 1970), and the detective genre in *Who is Teddy Villanova?* 1977.

Bergius Friedrich Karl Rudolph (1884–1949). German research chemist who invented processes for converting coal into oil and wood into sugar. Yielding nearly 1 tonne of petrol from 4.5 tonnes of coal, the process became important to Germany during World War II as an alternative source of supply of petrol and aviation fuel. He shared a Nobel prize 1931 with Carl Bosch for his part in inventing and developing high-pressure industrial methods.

Directing is more fun with women ... everything is.

INGMAR BERGMAN
Film Yearbook 1990

Bergman (Ernst) Ingmar (1918–). Swedish stage producer (from the 1930s) and film director (from the 1940s). He is regarded by many as one of the great masters of modern cinema. His work deals with complex moral, psychological, and metaphysical problems and is often strongly pessimistic. His films include *Wild Strawberries* 1957, *The Seventh Seal* 1957, *Persona* 1966, *Autumn Sonata* 1978 and *Fanny and Alexander* 1982.

Suggested reading
Bergman, Ingmar *The Magic Lantern* (1987)
Cowie, P *Ingmar Bergman* (1982)
Donner, Jorn *The Personal Vision of Ingmar Bergman* (1964)
Marker, L L and Frederick, J *Ingmar Bergman* (1982)

Keep it simple. Make a blank face and the music and the story will fill it in.

INGRID BERGMAN
Advice on film-acting

Bergman Ingrid (1915–1982). Swedish-born actress. She went to the USA 1939 to appear in David Selznick's *Intermezzo* 1939 and later appeared in *Casablanca* 1942, *For Whom the Bell Tolls* 1943, and *Gaslight* 1944, for which she won an Academy Award. She projected a combination of radiance, refined beauty, and fortitude.

Her last film, *Autumn Sonata* 1978, was made by Ingmar Bergman. She also did stage plays and received an Emmy for the television film *A Woman Called Golda* 1982, portraying the Israeli prime minister.

Bergson Henri Louis (1859–1941). French philosopher who believed that time, change, and development were the essence of reality. He thought that time was a continuous process in which one period merged imperceptibly into the next. In *Creative Evolution* 1907 he attempted to prove that all evolution and progress are due to the working of the *élan vital*, or life force. Nobel Prize for Literature 1928.

The essential function of the universe, which is a machine for making gods.

HENRI BERGSON
Les deux sources de la morale et de la religion 1932

Beria Lavrenti Pavlovich (1899–1953). Soviet politician who in 1938 became minister of the interior and head of the Soviet police force that imprisoned, liquidated, and transported millions of Soviet citizens. On Stalin's death 1953, he attempted to seize power but was foiled and shot after a secret trial. Apologists for Stalin have blamed Beria for the atrocities committed by Soviet police during Stalin's dictatorship.

Bering Vitus Jonassen (1681–1741). Danish explorer, the first European to sight Alaska. He died on Bering Island in the Bering Sea, both named after him, as is the Bering Strait, which separates Asia (Russia) from North America (Alaska).

Berio Luciano (1925–). Italian composer. His work combines serial techniques with commedia dell'arte and antiphonal practices, as in *Alleluiah II* 1958 for five instrumental groups. His prolific output includes nine *Sequenzas/Sequences* 1957–75 for various solo instruments or voice, *Sinfonia* 1969 for voices and orchestra, *Formazioni/Formations* 1987 for orchestra, and the opera *Un re in ascolto/A King Listens* 1984.

Beriosova Svetlana (1932–). British ballerina. Born in Lithuania and brought up partly in the USA, she danced with the Royal Ballet from 1952. Her style had a lyrical dignity and she excelled in *The Lady and the Fool, Ondine,* and *Giselle.*

Berkeley Busby. Stage name of William Berkeley Enos (1895–1976). US choreographer and film director. He used ingenious and extravagant sets and teams of female dancers to create song and dance sequences that formed large-scale kaleidoscopic patterns when filmed from above, as in *Gold Diggers of 1933* and *Footlight Parade* 1933.

I do know that I, who am a spirit or thinking substance, exist as certainly as I know my ideas exist.

GEORGE BERKELEY
Three Dialogues between Hylas and Philonous 1713

Berkeley George (1685–1753). Irish philosopher and cleric who believed that nothing exists apart from perception, and that the all-seeing mind of God makes possible the continued apparent existence of things. For Berkeley, everyday objects are collections of

Bergman Swedish film actress Ingrid Bergman. She established herself as a Hollywood star with films such as Casablanca 1942, starring with Humphrey Bogart, also shown here, and the two Hitchcock films Spellbound 1945 and Notorious 1946. In 1948 her romance with Italian director Roberto Rossellini took her to Italy but she returned to Hollywood 1956. Her last film was Autumn Sonata 1978, directed by Ingmar Bergman (no relation).

ideas or sensations, hence the dictum *esse est percipi* ('to exist is to be perceived'). He became bishop of Cloyne 1734.

With John Locke and David Hume he is considered to be one of the British empiricists, but his philosophy – that nothing exists except in the mind – is also described as subjective idealism.
Suggested reading
Luce, A A *Life of Berkeley* (1949)
Ritchie, A D *George Berkeley: A Reappraisal* (1967)
Urmson, J *Berkeley* (1987)
Warnock, G J *Berkeley* (1953)

Berkeley Lennox Randal Francis (1903–1989). English composer. His works for the voice include *The Hill of the Graces* 1975, verses from Spenser's *Faerie Queene* set for eight-part unaccompanied chorus; and his operas *Nelson* 1953 and *Ruth* 1956. Knighted 1974.

Berkeley William (1606–1677). British colonial administrator in North America, governor of the colony of Virginia 1641–77. Siding with the Royalists during the English Civil War, he was removed from the governorship by Oliver Cromwell 1652. He was reappointed 1660 by Charles II after the Restoration of the monarchy. However, growing opposition to him in the colony culminated in Bacon's Rebellion 1676 and in 1677 Berkeley was removed from office for his brutal repression of that uprising.

Born in Bruton, England, Berkeley was educated at Oxford University. When first appointed as governor of Virginia, he proved himself to be an able administrator, but was drawn into English politics and neglected the affairs of his colony. Knighted 1639.

Berkoff Steven (1937–). English dramatist and actor. His abrasive and satirical plays include *East* 1975, *Greek* 1979, and *West* 1983. Berkoff's production of Oscar Wilde's *Salome* was staged 1991. His *Collected Plays* (2 vols) were published 1994.

He formed the London Theatre Group 1968 as a vehicle for his own productions, which have included his adaptations of Kafka's *Metamorphosis* 1969 and *The Trial* 1970, and Poe's *The Fall of the House of Usher* 1974. In his acting career, he has often been cast as a villainous 'heavy' as in *Beverly Hills Cop* 1984 and *The Krays* 1990. He published his exploration of a leading role in *I Am Hamlet* 1989.

An architect should concentrate on the effect of volumes and mass.

HENDRIK BERLAGE
quoted in Randall J Van Vynckt (ed) *International Dictionary of Architects and Architecture* 1993

Berlage Hendrik Petrus (1856–1934). Dutch architect. He is known principally for his design for the Amsterdam Stock Exchange 1897–1903. His individualist style marked a move away from 19th-century historicism towards Dutch Expressionism.

There's no business like show business.

IRVING BERLIN
Song title

Berlin Irving. Adopted name of Israel Baline (1888–1989). Russian-born US songwriter. His songs include hits such as 'Alexander's Ragtime Band' 1911, 'Always' 1925, 'God Bless America' 1917 (published 1939), and 'White Christmas' 1942, and the musicals *Top Hat* 1935, *Annie Get Your Gun* 1946, and *Call Me Madam* 1950. He also provided songs for films like *Blue Skies* 1946 and *Easter Parade* 1948.

Berlin grew up in New York and had his first song published 1907. He began providing songs for vaudeville and revues and went on to own a theatre, the Music Box, where he appeared in his own revues 1921 and 1923. Generally writing both lyrics and music, he was instrumental in the development of the popular song, taking it from jazz and ragtime to swing and romantic ballads.

The son of a poor Jewish cantor, Berlin learned music by ear. Many of his songs are 'standards', the most popular and enduring of all time.

Berlin Isaiah (1909–). Latvian-born British philosopher and historian of ideas. Berlin emigrated to England with his family 1920, and was professor of social and political theory at Oxford 1957–67. In *The Hedgehog and the Fox*, he wrote about Leo Tolstoy's theory of irresistible historical forces; and in *Historical Inevitability* 1954 and *Four Essays on Liberty* 1969, he attacked all forms of historical determinism. His other works include *Karl Marx* 1939 and *Vico and Herder* 1976. Knighted 1957.

Liberty is liberty, not equality or fairness or justice or human happiness or a quiet conscience.

ISAIAH BERLIN
Two Concepts of Liberty 1959

Berlinguer Enrico (1922–1984). Italian Communist who freed the party from Soviet influence. Secretary general of the Italian Communist Party, by 1976 he was near to the premiership, but the murder of Aldo Moro, the prime minister, by Red Brigade guerrillas, prompted a move toward support for the socialists.

A hard worker if not a brilliant speaker, and a realistic rather than a flamboyant man.

Encyclopaedia Britannica on ENRICO BERLINGUER
1990

Berlioz (Louis) Hector (1803–1869). French Romantic composer. He is noted as the founder of modern orchestration. Much of his music was inspired by drama and literature and has a theatrical quality. He wrote symphonic works, such as *Symphonie fantastique* 1830–31 and *Roméo et Juliette* 1839; dramatic cantatas including *La Damnation de Faust* 1846 and *L'Enfance du Christ* 1854; sacred music; and three operas: *Benvenuto Cellini* 1838, *Les Troyens* 1856–58, and *Béatrice et Bénédict* 1862.
Suggested reading
Barzun, J *Berlioz and his Century* (1982)
Berlioz, Hector *Memoirs* (tr 1969)
Caitus, David *Berlioz: The Making of an Artist* (1989)
Holoman, D K *Berlioz* (1989)
Primmer, B *The Berlioz Style* (1973)

Time is a great teacher, but unfortunately it kills all its pupils.

HECTOR BERLIOZ
Almanach des lettres françaises

Berlusconi Silvio (1936–). Italian businessman and right-of-centre politician, prime minister March–Dec 1994. After building up an extremely profitable business empire, Fininvest, he turned his Milan-based pressure group, Forza Italia, into a political party to fight the March 1994 general election and, with the federalist Northern League and right-wing National Alliance, won a clear parliamentary majority. He resigned, following allegations of corruption in his business dealings, and in 1996 stood trial on charges of company bribery and tax evasion.

Bernadette, St of Lourdes (originally Marie Bernard Soubirous) (1844–1879). French saint, born in Lourdes in the French Pyrenees. In Feb 1858 she had a vision of the Virgin Mary in a grotto, and it became a centre of pilgrimage. Many sick people who were dipped in the water of a spring there were said to have been cured. Canonized 1933. Her feast day is 16 April.

The grotto of Massabielle was opened to the public by command of Napoleon III, and a church built on the rock above became a shrine. At the age of 20 Bernadette became a nun at Nevers, and nursed the wounded of the Franco-Prussian War.

Bernadotte Folke, Count (1895–1948). Swedish diplomat and president of the Swedish Red Cross. In 1945 he conveyed Nazi

Berlioz *The composer Hector Berlioz (1803-1869). At a time in France when literature was considered the greatest art form, Berlioz achieved more than any other composer in placing music on a par with it. He prepared the way for the later Romantics in France and abroad, including Liszt (who settled in Paris) and Wagner.* (Image Select)

commander Himmler's offer of capitulation to the British and US governments, and in 1948 was United Nations mediator in Palestine, where he was assassinated by Israeli Stern Gang guerrillas. He was a nephew of Gustaf VI of Sweden.

Bernadotte Jean-Baptiste Jules (1763–1844). Marshal in Napoleon's army who in 1818 became ◊Charles XIV of Sweden. Hence, Bernadotte is the family name of the present royal house of Sweden.

The first sign of corruption in a society that is still alive is that the end justifies the means.

GEORGES BERNANOS
The Last Essays of Georges Bernanos, 'Why Freedom?'

Bernanos Georges (1888–1948). French author. He achieved fame 1926 with *Sous le Soleil de Satan/The Star of Satan*. His strongly Catholic viewpoint is also expressed in his *Journal d'un curé de campagne/The Diary of a Country Priest* 1936.

Bernard Claude (1813–1878). French physiologist and founder of experimental medicine. Bernard first demonstrated that digestion is not restricted to the stomach, but takes place throughout the small intestine. He discovered the digestive input of the pancreas, several functions of the liver, and the vasomotor nerves which dilate and contract the blood vessels and thus regulate body temperature. This led him to the concept of the *milieu intérieur* ('internal environment') whose stability is essential to good health. He summed up his work in *The Introduction to the Study of Experimental Medicine* 1865.

Bernard of Clairvaux, St (1090–1153). Christian founder in 1115 of Clairvaux monastery in Champagne, France. He reinvigorated the Cistercian order, preached in support of the Second Crusade in 1146, and had the scholastic philosopher Abelard condemned for heresy. He is often depicted with a beehive. Canonized 1174. His feast day is 20 Aug.

Bernard of Menthon, St or Bernard of Montjoux (923–1008). Christian priest, founder of the hospices for travellers on the Alpine passes that bear his name. The large, heavily built St Bernard dogs, formerly employed to find travellers lost in the snow, were also named after him. He is the patron saint of mountaineers. Canonized 1115. His feast day is 28 May.

Bernays Paul Isaak (1888–1977). British-born Swiss mathematician whose theory of sets and classes is now widely believed to be the most useful arrangement, and a major contribution to the modern development of logic. A set is a multitude forming a real mathematical object, whereas a class is a predicate to be regarded only with respect to its extension.

Bernhard Leopold Prince of the Netherlands (1911–). Formerly Prince Bernhard of Lippe-Biesterfeld, he married Princess Juliana in 1937. When Germany invaded the Netherlands in 1940, he escaped to England and became liaison officer for the Dutch and British forces, playing a part in the organization of the Dutch Resistance.

In 1976 he was widely censured for his involvement in the purchase of Lockheed aircraft by the Netherlands.

Bernhardt Sarah. Stage name of Henriette Rosine Bernard (1844–1923). French actress. She dominated the stage in her day, frequently performing at the Comédie-Française in Paris. She excelled in tragic roles, including Cordelia in Shakespeare's *King Lear*, the title role in Racine's *Phèdre*, and the male roles of Hamlet and of Napoleon's son in Edmond Rostand's *L'Aiglon*.

He painted the scenes, cut the statues, composed the music, wrote the comedy ... built the theatre.

John Evelyn on GIANLORENZO BERNINI
in *John Evelyn's Diaries* 1644

Bernini Gianlorenzo (Giovanni Lorenzo) (1598–1680). Italian sculptor, architect, and painter. He was a leading figure in the development of the Baroque style. His work in Rome includes the colonnaded piazza in front of St Peter's Basilica 1656, fountains (as in the Piazza Navona), and papal monuments. His sculpture includes *The Ecstasy of St Theresa* 1645–52 (Sta Maria della Vittoria, Rome) and numerous portrait busts.

Bernini's sculptural style is full of movement and drama, captured in billowing drapery and facial expressions. His subjects are religious and mythological. A fine example is the marble *Apollo and Daphne* for Cardinal Borghese 1622–25 (Borghese Palace, Rome), with the figures shown in full flight. Inside St Peter's, he created several marble monuments and the elaborate canopy over the high altar. His many fine portrait busts include one of Louis XIV of France.
Suggested reading
Borsi, F *Bernini* (1985)
Hibbard, H *Bernini* (1965)
Lavin, Irving (ed) *Gianlorenzo Bernini: New Aspects of his Life and Art* (1985)
Wallace, Robert *The World of Bernini* (1970)

Bernard , Claude French Physiologist Claude Bernard discovered the role of the small intestine and pancreas in the digestive process. He later served in the French Senate. (Image Select)

Bernoulli Daniel (1700–1782). Swiss mathematical physicist who made important contributions to trigonometry and differential equations. In hydrodynamics he proposed Bernoulli's principle, an early formulation of the idea of conservation of energy. He demonstrated how the differential calculus could be used in problems of probability. He did pioneering work in trigonometrical series and the computation of trigonometrical functions. Bernoulli also showed the shape of the curve known as the lemniscate.

Bernoulli was born in Groningen in the Netherlands, the son of mathematician Johann Bernoulli. Having studied philosophy, logic, and medicine in Basel, Switzerland, he became professor of mathematics at the St Petersburg Academy, Russia, 1725–32, and professor of anatomy and botany at the University of Basel from 1733.

Bernoulli Jakob (1654–1705). Swiss mathematician who with his brother Johann pioneered German mathematician Gottfried Leibniz's calculus. Jakob used calculus to study the forms of many curves arising in practical situations, and studied mathematical probability (*Ars conjectandi* 1713); Bernoulli numbers are named after him.

Jakob Bernoulli's papers on transcendental curves (1696) and isoperimetry (1700, 1701) contain the first principles of the calculus of variations. It is probable that these papers owed something to collaboration with Johann. His other great achievement was his treatise on probability, *Ars Conjectandi*, which contained both the Bernoulli numbers (a series of complex fractions) and the Bernoulli theorem.

Jakob Bernoulli was born in Basel. On a trip to England 1676 he met Irish physicist Robert Boyle and other leading scientists, and decided to devote himself to science. He became particularly interested in comets (which he explained by an erroneous theory 1681) and in 1682 began to lecture in mechanics and natural philosophy at

Bernoulli *Johann Bernoulli was an early pioneer of differential calculus, working particularly on the nature and mathematical properties of curves.* (Ann Ronan/Image Select)

the University of Basel. During the next few years he came to know the work of Leibniz and began a correspondence with him. In 1687 he was made professor of mathematics at Basel.

Bernoulli Johann (1667–1748). Swiss mathematician who with his brother Jakob Bernoulli pioneered German mathematician Gottfried Leibniz's calculus. He was the father of Daniel Bernoulli.

Johann also contributed to many areas of applied mathematics, including the problem of a particle moving in a gravitational field. He found the equation of the catenary 1690 and developed exponential calculus 1691.

Bernoulli was born in Basel and studied medicine, but became professor of mathematics at Groningen, the Netherlands, 1694–1705, and then at Basel. Both Johann and Jakob wrote papers on a wide variety of mathematical and physical subjects, and it is often difficult to separate their work, although they never published together.

Bernstein Basil Bernard (1924–). British sociologist of education. He observed that the language of working-class children, who were often socially disadvantaged, was considerably more restricted than that of middle-class children. This led him to study how social origins affect the ability to communicate with others. He reported his research in several academic articles; many are published in *Class, Codes and Control. Vol 1: Theoretical Studies in the Sociology of Language* 1971.

He held that Socialism is the final result of the liberalism inherent in human aspiration, not the mere product of a revolt against the capitalist middle-class.

Encyclopaedia Britannica on EDUARD BERNSTEIN
1990

Bernstein Eduard (1850–1932). German socialist thinker, journalist, and politician. He was elected to the Reichstag 1902. He was a proponent of reformist rather than revolutionary socialism, whereby a socialist society could be achieved within an existing parliamentary structure merely by workers' parties obtaining a majority.

Bernstein Jeremy (1929–). US mathematical physicist who has written many articles and books on various topics of pure and applied science for the nonspecialist reader. He has also sought to give a mathematical analysis and description of the behaviour of elementary particles.

In 1962 Bernstein joined the staff of the urbane magazine the *New Yorker*. His lengthy articles for that magazine include 'The analytical engine: computers, past, present and future'. He published a general survey of the historical progress of scientific knowledge, *Ascent*, 1965, and a biography of Albert Einstein 1973.

Bernstein Leonard (1918–1990). US composer, conductor, and pianist. He was one of the most energetic and versatile of US musicians in the 20th century. His works, which established a vogue for realistic, contemporary themes, include symphonies such as *The Age of Anxiety* 1949, ballets such as *Fancy Free* 1944, and scores for musicals, including *Wonderful Town* 1953, *West Side Story* 1957, and *Mass* 1971 in memory of President J F Kennedy.

From 1958 to 1970 he was musical director of the New York Philharmonic. Among his other works are the symphony *Jeremiah* 1944, the ballet *Facsimile* 1946, and the musicals *Candide* 1956 and the *Chichester Psalms* 1965.

Suggested reading
Bernstein, Leonard *The Infinite Variety of Music* (1966)
Briggs, John *Leonard Bernstein: The Man, His Work and His World* (1961)
Gradenwitz, Peter *Leonard Bernstein* (1987)
Peyser, J *Bernstein: A Biography* (1987)
Secrest, Meryle *Leonard Bernstein: A Life* (1995)

Bernstein, Leonard *US composer, conductor, and pianist Leonard Bernstein juxtaposed a romantic intensity with jazz and Latin American elements in his large instrumental and choral works. He wrote in widely different styles, from* West Side Story *1957, a musical based on the* Romeo and Juliet *theme, to the* Chichester Psalms *1965.*

Bernstein Sidney Lewis (1899–1993). English entrepreneur and film producer. As founder of Granada Television, chair of the Granada group 1934–79, and president of the group until his death, he was a dominant influence on commercial television in the UK.

During World War II, Bernstein was films adviser to the Ministry of Information, while his chain of 30 cinemas flourished. After the war, he spent five years in Hollywood, where he produced three films directed by Alfred Hitchcock: *Rope* 1948, *Under Capricorn* 1949, and *I Confess* 1953. In 1954, when the passage of the Television Act opened the way for commercial broadcasting, Bernstein applied for a licence, despite being a long-time believer in public-service broadcasting. After struggles in the early years, the television company became hugely successful, and Granada diversified into TV-set rentals, motorway service centres, and publishing. Bernstein remained active on the board of the company until he was 80.

Berri Nabih (1939–   ). Lebanese politician and soldier, leader of Amal ('Hope'), the Syrian-backed Shi'ite nationalist movement. He became minister of justice in the government of President Gemayel 1984. In 1988 Amal was disbanded after defeat by the Iranian-backed Hezbollah ('Children of God') during the Lebanese civil wars, and Berri joined the cabinet of Selim Hoss 1989. In Dec 1990 Berri was made minister of state in the newly formed Karami cabinet, and in 1992 retained the same post in the cabinet of Rashid al-Sohl. He subsequently became president of the national assembly.

Berrigan Daniel (1921–   ) and Philip (1924–   ). US Roman Catholic priests. The brothers, opponents of the Vietnam War, broke into the draft-records offices at Catonsville, Maryland, to burn the files with napalm. They were sentenced in 1968 to three and six years' imprisonment respectively, but went underground. Subsequently Philip Berrigan was tried with others in 1972 for allegedly conspiring to kidnap President Nixon's adviser Henry Kissinger and blow up government offices in Washington DC; he was then sentenced to two years' imprisonment.

Berry family name of Viscount ◊Camrose, Viscount ◊Kemsley, and Baron ◊Hartwell.

Berry Chuck (Charles Edward Anderson) (1926–   ). US rock-and-roll singer, songwriter, and guitarist. His characteristic guitar riffs became staples of rock music, and his humorous storytelling lyrics were also emulated. He had a string of hits in the 1950s and 1960s, such as 'Maybellene' 1955, 'Roll Over Beethoven' 1956, 'Rock 'n' Roll Music' 1957, 'Sweet Little Sixteen' 1958, and 'Johnny B Goode' 1958.

The statue, tolerant through years of weather, / Spares the unity Sunday throng its look.

JOHN BERRYMAN
'The Statue'

Berryman John (1914–1972). US poet. His emotionally intense, witty, and personal works often deal with sexual torments and are informed by a sense of suffering. After collections of short poems and sonnets, he wrote *Homage to Mistress Broadstreet* 1956, a romantic narrative featuring the first American poet, Anne Dudley (born 1612), and then introduced his guilt-ridden, anti-heroic alter-ego, Henry, in *77 Dream Songs* 1964 (Pulitzer Prize) and *His Toy, His Dream, His Rest* 1968.

Berthelot Pierre Eugène Marcellin (1827–1907). French chemist and politician who carried out research into dyes and explosives, proving that hydrocarbons and other organic compounds can be synthesized from inorganic materials. His work during the 1850s was summed up in his book *Chimie organique fondée sur la synthèse* 1860. He published *Mécanique chimique* 1878 and *Thermochimie* 1897.

Berthelot was born in Paris, where he studied and became professor of organic chemistry. In 1870–71, during the siege of Paris in the Franco-Prussian War, he was consulted about the defence of the capital and supervised the manufacture of guns and explosives. Thereafter he took an increasing part in politics, becoming a senator

1881, minister for public instruction 1886, and foreign minister 1895–96.

Berthollet Claude Louis, Count (1748–1822). French chemist who carried out research into dyes and bleaches (introducing the use of chlorine as a bleach) and determined the composition of ammonia. Modern chemical nomenclature is based on a system worked out by Berthollet and Antoine Lavoisier. He was appointed inspector of dye-works and director of the Gobelins tapestry factory 1784. He taught chemistry to Napoleon and went with him to Egypt 1798. In 1804 he became a senator but ten years later voted for the deposition of Napoleon.

Berthoud Ferdinand (1727–1807). Swiss clockmaker and maker of scientific instruments. He improved the work of John Harrison, devoting 30 years to the perfection of the marine chronometer, giving it practically its modern form.

I adore TV ... like everyone else. But I watch very little. There's so very little worth watching.

BERNARDO BERTOLUCCI
Film Yearbook 1989

Bertolucci Bernardo (1940–   ). Italian film director. His work combines political and historical perspectives with an elegant and lyrical visual appeal. His films include *The Spider's Stratagem* 1970, *Last Tango in Paris* 1972, *1900* 1976, *The Last Emperor* 1987 (for which he received an Academy Award), *The Sheltering Sky* 1990, and *Little Buddha* 1992. He is regarded as one of the most talented of the younger generation of Italian film directors. Among his other films are *The Conformist* 1970.

Bertrand de Born (c. 1140–c. 1215). Provençal troubadour. He was viscount of Hautefort in Périgord, accompanied Richard the Lionheart to Palestine, and died a monk.

He was brought up to uphold a sinking cause, and to utilize in adversity every latent resource.

Charles Louis de Secondat, Baron de la Brède Montesquieu
on JAMES FITZJAMES, 1ST DUKE OF BERWICK
in éloge prefixed to Berwick's memoirs 1777

Berwick James Fitzjames, 1st Duke of Berwick (1670–1734). French marshal, illegitimate son of the Duke of York (afterwards James II of England) and Arabella Churchill (1648–1730), sister of the great Duke of Marlborough, his enemy in battle. He was made Duke of Berwick in 1687. After the revolution of 1688 he served under his father in Ireland, joined the French army, fought against William III and Marlborough, and in 1707 defeated the English at Almansa in Spain. He was killed at the siege of Philippsburg.

Berzelius Jöns Jakob (1779–1848). Swedish chemist who accurately determined more than 2,000 relative atomic and molecular masses. He devised (1813–14) the system of chemical symbols and formulae now in use and proposed oxygen as a reference standard for atomic masses. His discoveries include the elements cerium (1804), selenium (1817), and thorium (1828); he was the first to prepare silicon in its amorphous form and to isolate zirconium. The words 'isomerism', 'allotropy', and 'protein' were coined by him.

Berzelius noted that some reactions appeared to work faster in the presence of another substance which itself did not appear to change, and postulated that such a substance contained a catalytic force. Platinum, for example, was capable of speeding up reactions between gases. Although he appreciated the nature of catalysis, he was unable to give any real explanation of the mechanism. In 1807 he was appointed professor of medicine and pharmacy at what in 1810 became the Karolinska Institute.

Besant Annie (born Wood) (1847–1933). English socialist and feminist activist. She was associated with the radical atheist Charles

Bradlaugh and the socialist Fabian Society. In 1889 she became a disciple of Madame Blavatsky. She thereafter preached theosophy, went to India, and became president of the Indian National Congress in 1917. Her *Theosophy and the New Psychology* was published 1904.

She was the sister-in-law of Walter Besant.

Besant Walter (1836–1901). English writer. He wrote novels in partnership with James Rice (1844–1882), and produced an attack on the social evils of the East End of London, *All Sorts and Conditions of Men* 1882, and an unfinished *Survey of London* 1902–12. He was the brother-in-law of Annie Besant. Knighted 1895.

Beseler Hans von (1850–1921). German general. In World War I he commanded the force attacking Antwerp, which he captured Oct 1915, before going to the Eastern Front to command the siege artillery. He was subsequently appointed governor of Warsaw and then governor-general of Poland.

Bessel Friedrich Wilhelm (1784–1846). German astronomer and mathematician, the first person to find the approximate distance to a star by direct methods when he measured the parallax (annual displacement) of the star 61 Cygni in 1838. In mathematics, he introduced the series of functions now known as Bessel functions.

Bessel was born in Minden, NW Germany. As an amateur, he wrote a paper on Halley's comet 1804 which got him a post as an assistant at Lilienthal Observatory. After only four years the Prussian government commissioned Bessel to construct the first large German observatory at Königsberg; this was completed 1813 and Bessel spent his life as its director.

Bessemer *While trying to devise a method for manufacturing stronger rifle barrels for use in the Crimean War, Henry Bessemer discovered a process in which molten pig-iron could be turned directly into steel. This process used a special furnace, a Bessemer converter, and was much cheaper than previous methods.* (Ann Ronan/Image Select)

Bessemer Henry (1813–1898). British engineer and inventor who developed a method of converting molten pig iron into steel (the Bessemer process) 1856. By modifying the standard process, he found a way to produce steel without an intermediate wrought-iron stage, reducing its cost dramatically. However, to obtain high-quality steel, phosphorus-free ore was required. In 1860 Bessemer erected his own steel works in Sheffield, importing phosphorus-free iron ore from Sweden. Knighted 1879.

Bessmertnykh Aleksandr (1934–). Soviet politician, foreign minister Jan–Aug 1991. He began as a diplomat and worked mostly in the USA, at the United Nations headquarters in New York and the Soviet embassy in Washington DC. He succeeded Edvard Shevardnadze as foreign minister in Jan 1991, but was dismissed in August of the same year for exhibiting 'passivity' during the abortive anti-Gorbachev coup attempt.

Best Charles H(erbert) (1899–1978). Canadian physiologist, one of the team of Canadian scientists including Frederick Banting whose research resulted in 1922 in the discovery of insulin as a treatment for diabetes.

Best also discovered the vitamin choline and the enzyme histaminase, and introduced the use of the anticoagulant heparin. A Banting–Best Department of Medical Research was founded in Toronto, and Best was its director 1941–67.

Best George (1946–). Irish footballer. He won two League championship medals and was a member of the Manchester United side that won the European Cup in 1968.

Born in Belfast, he joined Manchester United as a youth and made his debut at 17; seven months later he made his international debut for Northern Ireland. Trouble with managers, fellow players, and the media led to his early retirement.

Betancourt Rómulo (1908–1981). Venezuelan president 1959–64 whose rule was plagued by guerrilla violence and economic and political division. He expanded welfare programmes, increased expenditure on education, encouraged foreign investment, and tried to diversify the Venezuelan economy to decrease its dependence on oil exports.

Bethe Hans Albrecht (1906–). German-born US physicist who in 1938 worked out the details of how nuclear mechanisms power stars. He also worked on the first atom bomb but later became a peace campaigner. He left Germany 1933, moving first to England and in 1935 to the USA, where he became professor of theoretical physics at Cornell University; his research was interrupted by World War II and by his appointment as head of the theoretical division of the Los Alamos atom-bomb project. Nobel prize 1967.

'World power or downfall' will be our rallying cry.
THEOBALD VON BETHMANN-HOLLWEG
quoted by Friedrich von Bernhardi *Germany and the Next War* ch 3 1914

Bethmann Hollweg Theobald Theodor Friedrich Alfred von (1856–1921). German politician, imperial chancellor 1909–17, largely responsible for engineering popular support for World War I in Germany, but his power was overthrown by a military dictatorship under Ludendorff and Hindenburg.

One cannot assess in terms of cash or exports and imports an imponderable thing like the turn of a lane or an inn or a church tower or a familiar skyline.
JOHN BETJEMAN
Observer 1969

Betjeman John (1906–1984). English poet and essayist. He was the originator of a peculiarly English light verse, nostalgic, and delighting in Victorian and Edwardian architecture. His *Collected Poems* appeared 1968 and a verse autobiography, *Summoned by Bells*, 1960. Knighted 1969. He became poet laureate 1972.

Suggested reading
Betjeman, John *Summoned By Bells* (autobiography in verse) (1960)
Delaney, Frank *Betjeman Country* (1984)
Hillier, Bevis *Young Betjeman* (1988)
Press, John *John Betjeman* (1975)

Poetry is the shortest way of saying things.

JOHN BETJEMAN
quoted in postscript to Michael Harrison and Christopher
Stuart-Clark (ed) *New Dragon Book of Verse* 1977

Bettelheim Bruno (1903–1990). Austrian-born US child psychologist. At the University of Chicago he founded a treatment centre for emotionally disturbed children based on the principle of a supportive home environment. Among his books are *Love Is Not Enough* 1950 and *The Uses of Enchantment: The Meaning and Importance of Fairy Tales* 1976.

Imprisoned in the Dachau and Buchenwald concentration camps 1933–35, he emigrated to the USA in 1939. His other books include *Truants from Life* 1954, *Children of the Dream* 1962, and *A Good Enough Parent* 1987. He took his own life.

Suggested reading
Sutton, Nina *Bruno Bettelheim: The Other Side of Madness* (1996)

Betterton Thomas (*c.* 1635–1710). English actor. A member of the Duke of York's company after the Restoration, he was greatly admired in many Shakespearean parts, including Hamlet and Othello.

Betti Enrico (1823–1892). Italian mathematician who was the first to provide a thorough exposition and development of the theory of equations formulated by French mathematician Evariste Galois. This greatly advanced the transition from classical to abstract algebra. In 1878 he gave the law of reciprocity in elasticity theory which became known as Betti's theorem. Along the way, conducting research into 'analysis situs' in hyperspace in 1871, he also did valuable work on numbers characterizing the connection of a variety, these later becoming known as Betti numbers.

Betti was born near Pistoia, Tuscany, and studied physical and mathematical sciences at Pisa, where he was professor from 1856. Betti had fought against Austria during the first wars of Italian independence and in 1862 he became a member of the new Italian parliament. He entered the government as undersecretary of state for education 1874 and served in the senate after 1884.

Betti Ugo (1892–1953). Italian dramatist. Some of his most important plays, such as *Frana allo scalo nord/Landslide at the North Station* 1936, concern the legal process (Betti was a judge for many years) and focus on the themes of justice and moral responsibility. Of his many other plays, often austere, even pessimistic, the best known include *La padrone/The Mistress* 1927, *Delitto all'isola delle capre/Crime on Goat Island* 1948 and *La Regina e gli insorte/The Queen and the Rebels* 1949.

Betty William Henry West (1791–1874). English boy actor. He was called the 'Young Roscius' after the greatest comic actor of ancient Rome. He was famous, particularly in Shakespearean roles, from the age of 11 to 17.

Beuys Joseph (1921–1986). German sculptor and performance artist. He was one of the leaders of the European avant-garde during the 1970s and 1980s. An exponent of Arte Povera, he made use of so-called 'worthless', unusual materials such as felt and fat. His best-known performance was *How to Explain Pictures to a Dead Hare* 1965. He was also an influential exponent of video art, for example, *Felt TV* 1968.

Beuys saw the artist as a shaman and art as an agent of social and spiritual change.

Freedom is the by-product of economic surplus.

ANEURIN BEVAN
quoted in Michael Foot *Aneurin Bevan* vol 1, ch 3 1962

Bevin *British Labour politician Ernest Bevin while minister of labour 1942. During World War II, all able-bodied men between the ages of 18 and 51 were eligible for national service under a scheme devised by Bevin. Some 30,000 men under the age of 25, known as 'Bevin boys', were sent to work in the mines.* (Image Select)

Bevan Aneurin ('Nye') (1897–1960). British Labour politician. Son of a Welsh miner, and himself a miner at 13, he became member of Parliament for Ebbw Vale 1929–60. As minister of health 1945–51, he inaugurated the National Health Service (NHS); he was minister of labour Jan–April 1951, when he resigned (with Harold Wilson) on the introduction of NHS charges and led a Bevanite faction against the government. In 1956 he became chief Labour spokesperson on foreign affairs, and deputy leader of the Labour party 1959. He was an outstanding speaker.

Suggested reading
Foot, Michael *Aneurin Bevan, 1897–1945* (1962)
Foot, Michael *Aneurin Bevan, 1945–1960* (1973)
Krug, Mark *Aneurin Bevan, Cautious Rebel* (1961)
Lee, Jenny *My Life with Nye* (1960)

Bevan Brian (1924–1991). Australian-born rugby league player. Bevan's total of 796 tries for Warrington, Blackpool Borough, and representative sides is an unequalled record. Lean and almost scrawny in appearance, he was known for speed, swerve, and a characteristic sidestep which enabled him to score many of his tries untouched.

Scratch a pessimist, and you find often a defender of privilege.

WILLIAM BEVERIDGE
Observer 17 Dec 1943

Beveridge William Henry, 1st Baron Beveridge (1879–1963). British economist. A civil servant, he acted as Lloyd George's lieutenant in the social legislation of the Liberal government before World War I. The *Beveridge Report* 1942 formed the basis of the welfare state in Britain. KCB 1919, baron 1946.

My [foreign] policy is to be able to take a ticket at Victoria Station and go anywhere I damn well please.

ERNEST BEVIN
Spectator April 1951

Bevin Ernest (1881–1951). British Labour politician. Chief creator of the Transport and General Workers' Union, he was its general secretary from 1921 to 1940, when he entered the war cabinet as minister of labour and national service. He organized the 'Bevin boys', chosen by ballot to work in the coal mines as war service, and was foreign secretary in the Labour government 1945–51.

Bewick Thomas (1753–1828). English wood engraver. He excelled in animal subjects and some of his finest works appear in his illustrated *A General History of Quadrupeds* 1790 and *A History of British Birds* 1797–1804.

Beza Théodore (properly De Bèsze) (1519–1605). French church reformer. He settled in Geneva, Switzerland, where he worked with the Protestant leader John Calvin and succeeded him as head of the reformed church there 1564. He wrote in defence of the burning of Spanish theologian Michael Servetus (1554) and translated the New Testament into Latin.

Bhabha Homi Jehangir (1909–1966). Indian theoretical physicist who made several important explanations of the behaviour of sub-atomic particles. In 1935, Bhabha became the first person to determine the cross-section (and thus the probability) of electrons scattering positrons. This phenomenon is now known as Bhabha scattering. He was also responsible for the development of research and teaching of advanced physics in India, and for the establishment and direction of the nuclear-power programme in India. The Tata Institute of Fundamental Research was established in Bombay 1945 with Bhabha as director.

Bhaktivedanta Prabhupada (1896–1977). Indian religious writer and teacher; founder of the International Society for Krishna Consciousness. He produced numerous scholarly translations and commentaries from Vedic devotional texts. By teaching devotion to Krishna as the universal religion, he did much to assist the spread of Hinduism in the West. He initiated over 5,000 disciples and established over 100 Hare Krishna communities outside India.

Bhindranwale Sant Jarnail Singh (1947–1984). Indian Sikh fundamentalist leader who campaigned for the creation of a separate state of Khalistan during the early 1980s, precipitating a bloody Hindu–Sikh conflict in the Punjab. Having taken refuge in the Golden Temple complex in Amritsar and built up an arms cache for guerrilla activities, Bhindranwale, along with around 500 followers, died at the hands of Indian security forces who stormed the temple in 'Operation Blue Star' June 1984.

Bhumibol Adulyadej (1927–   ). King of Thailand from 1946. Born in the USA and educated in Bangkok and Switzerland, he succeeded to the throne on the assassination of his brother. In 1973 he was active, with popular support, in overthrowing the military government of Marshal Thanom Kittikachorn and thus ended a sequence of army-dominated regimes in power from 1932.

Bhutto Benazir (1953–   ). Pakistani politician, leader of the Pakistan People's Party (PPP) from 1984 (in exile until 1986), prime minister of Pakistan 1988–90 (when the opposition manoeuvred her from office and charged her with corruption) and again from 1993. In her first year in office she struck an uneasy balance with the military establishment, improved Pakistan's relations with India, and led her country back into the Commonwealth 1989.

He had a flair for populist leadership, linking an ability to play upon the passions of the crowd with skill in tailoring political platforms to fit ... contradictory demands.

Neville Maxwell on ZULFIKAR ALI BHUTTO
Dictionary of National Biography

Bhutto Zulfikar Ali (1928–1979). Pakistani politician, president 1971–73; prime minister from 1973 until the 1977 military coup led by General Zia ul-Haq. In 1978 Bhutto was sentenced to death for conspiring to murder a political opponent and was hanged the following year. He was the father of Benazir Bhutto.

Biber Heinrich Ignaz Franz von (1644–1704). Bohemian composer, virtuoso violinist, and kapellmeister at the archbishop of Salzburg's court. He composed a wide variety of music including 16 *Mystery Sonatas* about 1676 for violin; church music; the opera *Chi la dura la vince* 1687; and various pieces, for example the *Nightwatchman Serenade*.

Bichat Marie François Xavier (1771–1802). French physician and founder of histology, the study of tissues. He studied the organs of the body, their structure, and the ways in which they are affected by disease.

This led to his discovery and naming of 'tissue', a basic biological and medical concept; he identified 21 types. He argued that disease does not affect the whole organ but only certain of its constituent tissues.

Bickford William (1774–1834). English inventor of the miner's safety fuse 1831. He made a major contribution to safety and productivity in mines and quarries.

Freedom is when one hears the bell at 7 o'clock in the morning and knows it is the milkman and not the Gestapo.

GEORGES BIDAULT
quoted in *Observer* 23 April 1950

Bidault Georges Augustin (1899–1983). French politician, prime minister 1946, 1949–50. He was a leader of the French Resistance during World War II and foreign minister and president in de Gaulle's provisional government. He left the Gaullists over Algerian independence, and in 1962 he became head of the Organisation de l'Armée Secrète (OAS), formed 1961 by French settlers devoted to perpetuating their own rule in Algeria. He was charged with treason 1963 and left the country, but was allowed to return 1968.

Biddle Nicholas (1786–1844). US financier and public figure. Born in Philadelphia, Biddle was admitted to the Pennsylvania bar 1809 and elected to the state legislature 1814. An expert in international commerce, he was appointed a director of the Bank of the United States by President James Monroe 1819 and became president of the bank 1822. An extreme fiscal conservative, Biddle became the focus of Andrew Jackson's campaigns against the power of the bank in 1828 and 1832. After the withdrawal of the bank's federal charter 1836, he remained its president under a state charter.

Bienville Jean Baptiste Le Moyne, Sieur de (1680–1768). French colonial administrator, governor of the North American colony of Louisiana 1706–13, 1717–23, and 1733–43. During his first term he founded the settlement at Mobile in Alabama and in his second term established the Louisiana colonial capital at New Orleans. During his final term Bienville was drawn into a costly and ultimately unsuccessful war with the Indians of the lower Mississippi Valley.

Admiration: our polite recognition of another's resemblance to ourselves.

AMBROSE BIERCE
Cynic's Word Book 1906

Bierce Ambrose Gwinett (1842–c. 1914). US author. After service in the American Civil War, he established his reputation as a master of the short story, his themes being war and the supernatural, as in *Tales of Soldiers and Civilians* 1891 and *Can Such Things Be?* 1893. He also wrote *The Devil's Dictionary* 1911 (first published as *The Cynic's Word Book* 1906), a collection of ironic definitions showing his sardonic humour. He disappeared in Mexico 1913.

He was writer-editor of the *San Francisco Newsletter*, publisher of short stories by Mark Twain and Bret Harte, and the satirical columnist known as 'The Prattler' 1887–1906.

Quoting: the act of repeating erroneously the words of another.

AMBROSE BIERCE
Devil's Dictionary 1911

Bierstadt Albert (1830–1902). German-born US landscape painter. His spectacular panoramas of the American wilderness fell out of favour after his death until interest in the Hudson River School was rekindled in the late 20th century. A classic work is *Thunderstorm in the Rocky Mountains* 1859 (Museum of Fine Arts, Boston). His *Discovery of the Hudson* hangs in the Capitol in Washington DC.

Biffen (William) John (1930–). British Conservative politician. In 1971 he was elected to Parliament for a Shropshire seat. Despite being to the left of Margaret Thatcher, he held key positions in government from 1979, including leader of the House of Commons from 1982, but was dropped after the general election of 1987. He subsequently became a greatly respected backbencher.

Bigelow Erastus Brigham (1814–1879). US inventor and industrialist who devised power looms for weaving various patterned fabrics and carpets, such as Wilton and Brussels carpets. Carpets could now be made of virtually any colour, to virtually any pattern. His power loom was developed between 1845 and 1851. Together with his other looms, this made the company so successful that the town of Clinton, Massachusetts, grew up around the plant. Bigelow helped found the Massachusetts Institute of Technology 1861.

Bihzad Kamal al-Din (c. 1450–1536). Persian painter of miniatures. He is known as the 'Persian Raphael'. Although only a few works are firmly attributed to him, he is widely regarded as the finest painter of the Persian miniature. His work shows a novel subtlety in composition and use of colour, as well as enhanced realism.

The power of a movement lies in the fact that it can indeed change the habits of people. This change is not the result of force but of dedication, of moral persuasion.

STEVE BIKO
Interview, July 1976

Biko Steve (Stephen) (1946–1977). South African civil-rights leader. An active opponent of apartheid, he was arrested in Sept 1977; he died in detention six days later. Following his death in the custody of South African police, he became a symbol of the anti-apartheid movement.

He founded the South African Students Organization (SASO) in 1968 and was cofounder in 1972 of the Black People's Convention, also called the Black Consciousness movement, a radical association of South African students that aimed to develop black pride. His death in the hands of the police caused much controversy.

Bildt Carl (1949–). Swedish politician, prime minister 1991–94. Leader of the Moderate Party (MS) from 1986, he pledged an end to the 'age of collectivism' and in 1991 formed a right-of-centre coalition after decades of social democratic politics. A year later, after battling unsuccessfully with Sweden's worst economic crisis since the 1920s, he persuaded his former political opponents to join him in a fight for economic recovery, heading what was, in effect, a government of national unity. In 1995 he succeeded David Owen as European Union negotiator in the former Yugoslavia.

Bildt was elected to the Riksdag (parliament) 1979. He became leader of the Moderate Party (MS) 1986 and when the ruling Social Democratic Labour Party lost its parliamentary majority after the 1991 general election, he formed with other right-of-centre parties what became known as the 'bourgeois coalition'. He won widespread support for Swedish membership of the European Community (now the European Union) before he and his party were defeated in the 1994 elections.

Billy the Kid nickname of William H Bonney (1859–1881). US outlaw, a leader in the 1878 Lincoln County cattle war in New Mexico, who allegedly killed his first victim at 12 and was reputed to have killed 21 men by age 22, when he died.

Born in Brooklyn, New York, Bonney moved west with his family to Kansas and then New Mexico. He was sentenced to death for murdering a sheriff, but escaped (killing two guards), and was finally shot by Sheriff Pat Garrett while trying to avoid recapture.

Binet Alfred (1857–1911). French psychologist who introduced the first intelligence tests 1905. They were standardized so that the last of a set of graded tests the child could successfully complete gave the level described as 'mental age'. If the test was passed by most children over 12, for instance, but failed by those younger, it was said to show a mental age of 12. Binet published these in collaboration with Théodore Simon.

Binet was born in Nice and studied neurology and psychology in Paris, becoming director of the physiological psychology laboratory at the Sorbonne 1895.

Bingham George Caleb (1811–1879). American painter of pioneer life. Taken by his parents to the edge of settlement in Missouri, he drew as a boy, had some training at the Pennsylvania Academy of Fine Arts, and after a period of travel returned to Missouri to paint vivid pictures of trappers and traders, raftsmen and steamboat crews. *The Fur Traders descending the Missouri* (New York Metropolitan Museum) is typical.

Bingham Hiram (1875–1956). US explorer and politician who from 1907 visited Latin America, discovering Machu Picchu, Vitcos, and other Inca settlements in Peru. He later entered politics, becoming a senator.

They shall grow not old, as we that are left grow old: / Age shall not weary them, nor the years condemn. / At the going down of the sun and in the morning / We will remember them.

LAURENCE BINYON
'Poems For the Fallen'

Binyon (Robert) Laurence (1869–1943). English poet. His verse volumes include *Lyric Poems* 1894 and *London Visions*, but he is best remembered for his ode 'For the Fallen' 1914, set to music by English composer Edward Elgar. His art criticism includes *Japanese Art* 1909.

Biot Jean Baptiste (1774–1862). French physicist who studied the polarization of light. In 1804 he made a balloon ascent to a height of 5 km/3 mi, in an early investigation of the Earth's atmosphere.

Birch James Frederick Noel (1865–1939). British general. Commissioned into the Royal Artillery 1885, he served in Ashanti and South Africa. During World War I he acted as artillery adviser to the commander in chief in France and was promoted to lieutenant-general. KCMG 1918.

He became director-general of the Territorial Army 1921 and later master general of the Ordnance.

Birch John M (1918–1945). US Baptist missionary, commissioned by the US Air Force to carry out intelligence work behind the Chinese lines where he was killed by the communists; the US extreme right-wing John Birch Society 1958 is named after him.

Bird Isabella Lucy (1831–1904). British traveller and writer who wrote extensively of her journeys in the USA, Persia, Tibet, Kurdistan, China, Japan, and Korea. Her published works include *The Englishwoman in America* 1856, *A Lady's Life in the Rocky Mountains* 1874, *Unbeaten Tracks in Japan* 1880, *Among the Tibetans* 1894, and *Pictures from China* 1900. Her last great journey was made 1901 when she travelled over 1,600 km/1,000 mi in Morocco.

Birdseye Clarence (1886–1956). US inventor who pioneered food refrigeration processes. While working as a fur trader in Labrador 1912–16 he was struck by the ease with which food could be preserved in an Arctic climate. Back in the USA he found that the same effect could be obtained by rapidly freezing prepared food between two refrigerated metal plates. To market his products he founded the General Sea Foods Company 1924, which he sold to General Foods 1929.

Birendra Bir Bikram Shah Dev (1945–). King of Nepal from 1972, when he succeeded his father Mahendra; he was formally crowned 1975. King Birendra oversaw Nepal's return to multiparty politics and introduced a new constitution 1990.

Birinus, St (died *c.* 650). English saint and first bishop of Dorchester, Oxon, who in 635 converted and baptized the Saxon king Cynegils.

The world continues to offer glittering prizes to those who have stout hearts and sharp swords.

F E SMITH, 1ST EARL OF BIRKENHEAD
Rectorial address at Glasgow University 7 Nov 1923

Birkenhead F(rederick) E(dwin) Smith, 1st Earl of Birkenhead (1872–1930). British Conservative politician. A flamboyant character, known as 'FE', he joined with Edward Carson in organizing armed resistance in Ulster to Irish Home Rule. He was Lord Chancellor 1919–22 and a much criticized secretary for India 1924–28. Viscount 1919, earl 1922.

Birkhoff George David (1884–1944). US mathematician who made fundamental contributions to the study of dynamical systems such as the Solar System. He formulated the 'weak form' of the ergodic theorem. Birkhoff developed a system of differential equations which is still inspiring research. His work on difference equations was notable for the prominence he gave to the use of

matrix algebra. From 1912 he taught at Harvard, and was made professor 1919.

Biró Lazlo (1900–1985). Hungarian-born Argentine who invented a ballpoint pen 1944. His name became generic for ballpoint pens in the UK.

Birtwistle Harrison (1934–). English avant-garde composer. He has specialized in chamber music – for example, his chamber opera *Punch and Judy* 1967 and *Down by the Greenwood Side* 1969.

Birtwistle's early music was influenced by US composer Igor Stravinsky and by the medieval and Renaissance masters, and for many years he worked alongside Peter Maxwell Davies. Orchestral works include *The Triumph of Time* 1972 and *Silbury Air* 1977; he has also written operas including *The Mask of Orpheus* 1986 (with electronic music by Barry Anderson (1935–1987)) and *Gawain* 1991, a reworking of the medieval English poem 'Sir Gawain and the Green Knight'. His tape composition *Chronometer* 1972 (assisted by Peter Zinovieff (1934–)) is based on clock sounds. Knighted 1988.

Bishop Isabella. Married name of the travel writer Isabella ◊Bird.

Bishop Ronald Eric (1903–1989). British aircraft designer. He joined the de Havilland Aircraft Company 1931 as an apprentice, and designed the Mosquito bomber, the Vampire fighter, and the Comet jet airliner.

Bishop William Avery (1894–1956). Canadian air ace. He shot down over 70 enemy aircraft in World War I, and was awarded the Victoria Cross 1917.

Politics is not an exact science.

OTTO, PRINCE VON BISMARCK
Speech in Prussian Chamber 18 Dec 1863

Bismarck Otto Eduard Leopold, Prince von (1815–1898). German politician, prime minister of Prussia 1862–90 and chancellor of the German Empire 1871–90. He pursued an aggressively expansionist policy, waging wars against Denmark 1863–64, Austria 1866, and France 1870–71, which brought about the unification of Germany. He became prince 1871.

Bismarck was ambitious to establish Prussia's leadership within Germany and eliminate the influence of Austria. He secured Austria's support for his successful war against Denmark and then, in 1866, went to war against Austria and its allies (the Seven Weeks' War), his victory forcing Austria out of the German Bund and unifying the N German states into the North German Confederation under his own chancellorship 1867. He then defeated France, under Napoleon III, in the Franco-Prussian War 1870–71, proclaimed the German Empire 1871, and annexed Alsace-Lorraine. He tried to secure his work by the Triple Alliance 1881 with Austria and Italy but ran into difficulties at home with the Roman Catholic church and the socialist movement and was forced to resign by Wilhelm II 18 March 1890.

Suggested reading
Crankshaw, E *Bismarck* (1982)
Rose, J E *Bismarck* (1987)
Taylor, A J P *Bismarck: The Man and the Statesman* (1955)

As a musician I tell you that if you were to suppress adultery, fanaticism, crime, evil, the supernatural, there would no longer be the means for writing one note.

GEORGES BIZET
in a letter to Edmond Galabert, October 1866

Bismarck *The imperialist 'Iron Chancellor' Prince Otto von Bismarck, from a photograph published* c. 1880. *Bismarck's expansionist policies and autocratic rule secured Prussia's dominance in his new German Empire.* (Image Select)

Bizet Georges (Alexandre César Léopold) (1838–1875). French composer of operas. Among his works are *Les Pêcheurs de perles/The Pearl Fishers* 1863 and *La Jolie Fille de Perth/The Fair Maid of Perth* 1866. He also wrote the concert overture *Patrie* and incidental music to Alphonse Daudet's play *L'Arlésienne*. His operatic

Bizet *The composer Georges Bizet (1838–1875) as portrayed in a chromolithograph published in London 1912. Often criticized for being cynical and complacent in his private life, his letters reveal a caring man, especially with regard to his mentally unstable wife and mother-in-law.* (Image Select)

masterpiece *Carmen* was produced a few months before his death 1875.

Bjelke-Petersen Joh(annes) (1911–). Australian right-wing politician, leader of the Queensland National Party (QNP) and premier of Queensland 1968–87. His Queensland state chauvinism and extremely conservative policies, such as lack of support for Aboriginal land rights or for conservation issues, and attacks on the trade-union movement, made him a controversial figure outside as well as within Queensland, and he was accused more than once of electoral gerrymandering. Honorary KCMG 1982.

Bjerknes Vilhelm Firman Koren (1862–1951). Norwegian scientist whose theory of polar fronts formed the basis of all modern weather forecasting and meteorological studies. He also developed hydrodynamic models of the oceans and the atmosphere and showed how weather prediction could be carried out on a statistical basis, dependent on the use of mathematical models. He coined the word 'front' to denote the boundary between such air masses.

Björk Stage name of Björk Gudmundsdóttir (1966–). Icelandic pop singer and songwriter with a highly distinctive soprano vocal style. She became known internationally as lead singer with Sykurmolar/the Sugarcubes (1986–92) and released solo albums *Debut* 1993 and *Post* 1995. In her solo work Björk abandoned the guitar-pop of the Sugarcubes in favour of jazz, house, techno, and world-music influences.

Björnson Björnstjerne Martinius (1832–1910). Norwegian novelist, playwright, poet, and journalist. His plays include *The Newly Married Couple* 1865 and *Beyond Human Power* 1883, dealing with politics and sexual morality. Among his novels is *In God's Way* 1889. Nobel Prize for Literature 1903.

Black Conrad Moffat (1940–). Canadian newspaper publisher. Between 1985 and 1990 he gained control of the right-wing *Daily Telegraph*, *Sunday Telegraph*, and *Spectator* weekly magazine in the UK, and he owns a number of Canadian newspapers.

Black Davidson (1884–1934). Canadian anatomist. In 1927, when professor of anatomy at the Union Medical College, Peking (Beijing), he unearthed the remains of Peking man, an example of one of our human ancestors.

Black Hugo LaFayette (1886–1971). US jurist. He was elected to the US Senate 1926 and despite his earlier association with the Ku Klux Klan, distinguished himself as a progressive populist. He was appointed to the US Supreme Court by F D Roosevelt 1937, resigning shortly before his death. Among his decisions concerning personal and civil rights were those rendered in *Board of Education* v. *Barnette* 1943, *Korematsu* v. *US* 1944, and *Gideon* v. *Wainwright* 1963.

Black James Whyte (1924–). British physiologist, director of therapeutic research at Wellcome Laboratories (near London) from 1978. He was active in the development of beta-blockers (which reduce the rate of heartbeat) and anti-ulcer drugs. He shared the Nobel Prize for Physiology or Medicine 1988 with US scientists George Hitchings (1905–) and Gertrude Elion (1918–). Knighted 1981.

Black Joseph (1728–1799). Scottish physicist and chemist who in 1754 discovered carbon dioxide (which he called 'fixed air'). By his investigations in 1761 of latent heat and specific heat, he laid the foundation for the work of his pupil James Watt.

In 1756 Black described how carbonates become more alkaline when they lose carbon dioxide, whereas the taking-up of carbon dioxide reconverts them. He discovered that carbon dioxide behaves like an acid, is produced by fermentation, respiration, and the combustion of carbon, and guessed that it is present in the atmosphere. He also discovered the bicarbonates (hydrogen carbonates).

Black Max (1909–). Azeri-born US philosopher and mathematician. Investigating the question, 'What is mathematics?', he divided the answers into three schools: the logical, the formalist, and the intuitional. This approach has had most influence in the theory of sets of points. Black's works include *The Nature of Mathematics* 1950 and *Problems of Analysis* 1954.

Black, born in Baku, studied philosophy at Cambridge and London universities. Moving to the USA 1940, he worked from 1946 at Cornell, where he was professor of philosophy 1954–77.

Blackburn James (1803–1854). English-born Australian engineer and architect, transported to Tasmania in 1833 for forgery and granted a free pardon in 1841. Among the churches he designed in Tasmania are the gothic revival Holy Trinity, Hobart, 1840–47, and the Norman style St Mark's, Pontville, 1839. He also surveyed and designed the Yan Yean water-supply works in Victoria 1850–51.

Black Elk (1863–1950). American Indian religious leader, born into the Oglala Lakota people. He tried to find ways of reconciling indigenous traditions with Christianity and the new reality of white dominance. Although he continued his calling as a shaman, he converted to Christianity 1886.

At the age of 17, Black Elk had a vision of the Lakota people rising up and freeing their lands from the white settlers. In order to understand more about this invading culture, he joined Buffalo Bill's Wild West Show and toured the USA and Europe. When he returned home, he witnessed the disaster of the Ghost Dance movement, which swept through American Indian communities in the late 19th century and taught that they would be made invincible and throw out the white settlers. The movement was crushed at Wounded Knee 1890. This seems to have led Black Elk to question his call and he converted to Catholicism 1904.

Blacket Edmund Thomas (1817–1883). English-born architect in Australia known for his churches in Sydney, which include St Philip's, Church Hill 1848 and St Mark's, Darling Point 1848. He also completed St Andrew's Cathedral 1847. In 1854 he began work on the University of Sydney, especially noted for its Great Hall. He was born in Surrey, and arrived in Australia with his wife Sarah in 1842.

Blackett Patrick Maynard Stuart, Baron Blackett (1897–1974). British physicist. He was awarded a Nobel prize 1948 for work in cosmic radiation and his perfection of the cloud chamber, an apparatus for tracking ionized particles, with which he confirmed the existence of positrons. Created baron 1969.

Black Hawk or Black Sparrow Hawk (Sauk name Makataimeshekiakiak) (1767–1838). North American Sauk Indian leader. A principal opponent of the cession of Indian lands to the US government, he sided with the British during the Anglo-American War 1812–14 and joined his people in their removal to Iowa at the end of the war. In 1832 he led a large contingent back to Illinois to resettle the Sauk homeland. Defeated by Illinois militia in the bloody 'Black Hawk War', he was captured and permanently exiled to Iowa.

Blacking John Anthony Randall (1928–1990). British anthropologist and ethnomusicologist who researched the relationship between music and body movement, and the patterns of social and musical organization. His most widely read book is *How Musical is Man?* 1973.

He worked in South Africa in the 1950s and 1960s, but left because of his opposition to apartheid. From 1970 he was professor of social anthropology at Queen's University, Belfast, where he established a centre for ethnomusicology.

Blackman Charles Raymond (1928–). Australian artist. He is noted for his figure paintings of children. His work is characterized by simple shapes, often no more than silhouettes, that are boldly coloured and large scale, as in *Suite of Paintings* 1960 (Art Gallery of South Australia, Adelaide).

Blackmore R(ichard) D(oddridge) (1825–1900). English novelist. He was the author of *Lorna Doone* 1869, a romance set on Exmoor, SW England, in the late 17th century.

Black Prince nickname of ◊Edward, Prince of Wales, eldest son of Edward III of England.

Mankind will not be reasoned out of the feelings of humanity.

WILLIAM BLACKSTONE
Commentaries 1765–70

Blackstone William (1723–1780). English jurist who wrote to defend the common law of England as a natural and coherent system, and published his *Commentaries on the Laws of England* 1765–70. A barrister from 1746, he became the first professor of English Law at Oxford 1758, and a justice of the Court of Common Pleas 1770. Knighted 1770.

Blackwell Elizabeth (1821–1910). English-born US physician, the first woman to qualify in medicine in the USA 1849, and the first woman to be recognized as a qualified physician in the UK 1869. She was professor of gynaecology at the London School of Medicine for Women 1875–1907.

Her example inspired Elizabeth Garrett Anderson and many other aspiring female doctors.

Blaine James Gillespie (1830–1893). US politician and diplomat. Elected to the US House of Representatives 1862, he became Speaker 1868. Unsuccessful in the Republican presidential nominations 1876 and 1880, he served briefly as President Garfield's secretary of state. Gaining the Republican presidential nomination 1884, he was defeated by Grover Cleveland. During the Harrison administration 1889–93, Blaine again served as secretary of state.

Blair Tony (Anthony Charles Lynton) (1953–). British politician, leader of the Labour Party from 1994. A centrist in the manner of his predecessor John Smith, he became Labour's youngest leader by a large majority in the first fully democratic elections to the post July 1994. In 1995, after a hard-fought campaign, he won approval of a new Labour Party charter, intended to distance the party from its traditional socialist base and promote 'social market' values.

Blair practised as a lawyer before entering the House of Commons 1983 as member for the Durham constituency of Sedgfield. He was elected to Labour's shadow cabinet 1988 and given the energy portfolio; he shadowed employment from 1991 and home affairs from 1992. Like John Smith, he did not ally himself with any particular faction and, in drawing a distinction between 'academic and ethical socialism', succeeded in winning over most sections of his party, apart from the extreme left. During 1995, Blair established an opinion poll lead of more than 20% for Labour over the Conservatives.

Blake George (1922–). British double agent who worked for MI6 and also for the USSR. Blake was unmasked by a Polish defector 1960 and imprisoned, but escaped to the Eastern bloc 1966. He is said to have betrayed at least 42 British agents to the Soviet side.

Blake Quentin Saxby (1932–). English book illustrator. His animated pen-and-ink drawings are instantly recognizable. A prolific illustrator of children's books written by others, he has also written and illustrated his own books, including *The Marzipan Pig* 1986.

How typically were his qualities those which Englishmen like to claim as their own.

ROBERT BLAKE
described by Roger Beadon in *Robert Blake* 1935

Blake Robert (1599–1657). British admiral of the Parliamentary forces during the English Civil War. Appointed 'general-at-sea' 1649, he destroyed Prince Rupert's privateering fleet off Cartagena, Spain, in the following year. In 1652 he won several engagements against the Dutch navy. In 1654 he bombarded Tunis, the stronghold of the Barbary corsairs, and in 1657 captured the Spanish treasure fleet in Santa Cruz.

He represented his native Bridgwater, Somerset, in the Short Parliament of 1640, and distinguished himself in defending Bristol 1643 and Taunton 1644–45 in the Civil War. In the naval war with the Netherlands (1652–54) he was eventually defeated by Tromp off Dungeness, but had his revenge 1653 when he defeated the Dutch admiral off Portsmouth and the northern Foreland.

To see a World in a Grain of Sand, / And a Heaven in a Wild Flower, Hold Infinity in the palm of your hand, / And Eternity in an hour.

WILLIAM BLAKE
Auguries of Innocence 1914 ed

Blake William (1757–1827). English poet, artist, engraver, and visionary. He was one of the most important figures of English Romanticism. His lyrics, as in *Songs of Innocence* 1789 and *Songs of Experience* 1794, express spiritual wisdom in radiant imagery and symbolism and are often written with a childlike simplicity. In prophetic books like *The Marriage of Heaven and Hell* 1790, *America* 1793, and *Milton* 1804, he created a vast personal mythology. He illustrated his own works with hand-coloured engravings. His figures are usually elongated and heavily muscled. Blake's poem 'Jerusalem' 1820 was set to music by Charles Parry.

Suggested reading
Bloom, H *Blake's Apocalypse* (1963)
Blunt, A *The Art of William Blake* (1959)
Bronowski, J *William Blake and the Age of Revolution* (1944)
Crehan, S *Blake in Context* (1984)
Frye, N *Fearful Symmetry: A Study of William Blake* (1947)
Lindsay, J *William Blake* (1978)
Raine, K *Blake* (1970)

Blakemore Colin Brian (1944–). English physiologist who has made advanced studies of how the brain works. In his book *Mechanics* *of the Mind* 1977 he explains the mechanics of sensation, sleep, memory, and thought, and discusses a number of philosophical questions.

Blakey Art(hur). Muslim name Abdullah ibn Buhaina (1919–1990). US jazz drummer and bandleader. His dynamic, innovative style made him one of the jazz greats. He contributed to the development of bebop in the 1940s and subsequently to hard bop, and formed the Jazz Messengers in the mid-1950s, continuing to lead the band for most of his life and discovering many talented musicians.

The rabbit that runs away is the rabbit that gets shot.

THOMAS BLAMEY
Address to his troops

Blamey Thomas Albert (1884–1951). Australian field marshal. Born in New South Wales, he served at Gallipoli, Turkey, and on the Western Front in World War I. After his recall to Australia in 1942 and appointment as commander in chief, Allied Land Forces, he commanded operations on the Kokoda Trail and the recapture of Papua. Knighted 1935.

Blanc (Jean Joseph Charles) Louis (1811–1882). French socialist and journalist. In 1839 he founded the *Revue du progrès*, in which he published his *Organisation du travail*, advocating the establishment of cooperative workshops and other socialist schemes. He was a member of the provisional government of 1848 and from its fall lived in the UK until 1871.

Blanchard Jean Pierre François (1753–1809). French balloonist who made the first hot air balloon flight across the English Channel with John Jeffries 1785. He made the first balloon flight in the USA 1793.

Blanche of Castile (1188–1252). Queen of France, wife of Louis VIII of France, and regent for her son Louis IX (St Louis of France) from the death of her husband 1226 until Louis IX's majority 1234, and again from 1247 while he was on a Crusade.

She quelled a series of revolts by the barons and in 1229 negotiated the Treaty of Paris, by which Toulouse came under control of the monarchy.

Blanchflower Danny (Robert Dennis) (1926–1994). British football player, captain of Tottenham Hotspur 1959–64, during which time it became the first club since Victorian times to win both the Championship and FA Cup in one season (1960–61). He also captained Northern Ireland in the 1958 World Cup finals, when the team reached the quarterfinals, and was Footballer of the Year 1958 and 1961. His play was characterized by its inventiveness and subtlety.

He retired 1964 and went on to manage Northern Ireland 1976–79 and, briefly, Chelsea 1978–79.

Blanco Serge (1958–). French rugby union player, renowned for his pace, skill, and ingenuity on the field. Blanco played a world-record 93 internationals before his retirement in 1991, scoring 38 tries of which 34 were from full back – another world record. He was instrumental in France's Grand Slam wins of 1981 and 1987.

Blanqui (Louis) Auguste (1805–1881). French revolutionary politician. He formulated the theory of the 'dictatorship of the proletariat', used by Karl Marx, and spent a total of 33 years in prison for insurrection. Although in prison, he was elected president of the Commune of Paris 1871. His followers, the Blanquists, joined with the Marxists 1881.

He became a martyr figure for the French workers' movement.

Blashford-Snell John (1936–). British explorer and soldier. His expeditions have included the first descent and exploration of the Blue Nile 1968; the journey N to S from Alaska to Cape Horn, crossing the Darien Gap between Panama and Colombia for the first time 1971–72; and the first complete navigation of the Zaïre River, Africa 1974–75.

From 1963 he organized adventure training at Sandhurst military academy. He was director of Operation Drake 1977–81 and Operation Raleigh 1978–82. His books include *A Taste for Adventure* 1978.

Blasis Carlo (1795–1878). Italian ballet teacher of French extraction. He was successful as a dancer in Paris and in Milan, where he established a dancing school 1837. His celebrated treatise on the art of dancing, *Traité élémentaire, théoretique et pratique de l'art de la danse/Treatise on the Dance* 1820, forms the basis of classical dance training.

Blaskowitz Johann Albrecht (1883–1948). German general in World War II. He was military governor of Poland 1939–40, but was removed after complaining about the excesses of the SS in dealing with Jews in the territory. He subsequently served on the Eastern Front and in France following the Allied invasion of Europe. He was captured and arraigned for trial at Nuremberg 1945 but committed suicide in prison.

Blau Peter Michael (1918–). US sociologist. In his studies of organizations, particularly bureaucracies, he has shown how a system of reciprocation and obligation can create social bonding and how less formal controls can increase involvement in decision-making. His writings include *The Dynamics of Bureaucracy* 1952 and *On the Nature of Organizations* 1974.

Blavatsky Helena Petrovna (born Hahn) (1831–1891). Russian spiritualist and mystic, cofounder of the Theosophical Society 1875, which has its headquarters near Madras, India. In Tibet she underwent spiritual training and later became a Buddhist. Her books include *Isis Unveiled* 1877 and *The Secret Doctrine* 1888. She was declared a fraud by the London Society for Psychical Research 1885.
Suggested reading
Ryan, Charles J *H P Blavatsky and the Theosophical Movement* (1937)
Symonds, John *Madame Blavatsky* (1959)
Williams, G M *Priestess of the Occult* (1946)

Bleasdale Alan (1946–). English dramatist. He gained a national reputation with the series of television dramas, *The Boys From the Blackstuff* 1982, which portrayed the pressures and tensions of unemployment on a group of men. It was followed by *GBH* 1991, a psychological study of the leader of a city council in northern England. His stage plays include *Having a Ball* 1981 and *On the Ledge* 1993.

A Liverpudlian, he wrote several early plays including *Down the Dock Road* 1976 for the Everyman Theatre in Liverpool, where he was artistic director from 1977. His early *Scully* stories about an adolescent boy were adapted for television 1984.

Blériot Louis (1872–1936). French aviator who, in a 24-horse-power monoplane of his own construction, made the first flight across the English Channel on 25 July 1909.

Love-matches are made by people who are content, for a month of honey, to condemn themselves to a life of vinegar.

MARGUERITE BLESSINGTON
Commonplace Book

Blessington Marguerite Gardiner, Countess of Blessington (1789–1849). Irish writer. A doyenne of literary society, she published *Conversations with Lord Byron* 1834, travel sketches, and novels.

Bread-fruit Bligh

Nickname acquired when WILLIAM BLIGH was sailing-master in the *Resolution* on Captain Cook's second voyage round the world 1772–74 on which the breadfruit was discovered at Otaheite.

Bligh William (1754–1817). English sailor who accompanied Captain James Cook on his second voyage around the world 1772–74, and in 1787 commanded HMS *Bounty* on an expedition to the Pacific.

On the return voyage the crew mutinied 1789, and Bligh was cast adrift in a boat with 18 men. He was appointed governor of New South Wales 1805, where his discipline again provoked a mutiny 1808 (the Rum Rebellion). He returned to Britain, and was made an admiral 1811.

Bliss Arthur Edward Drummond (1891–1975). English composer and conductor. He became Master of the Queen's Musick 1953. Among his works are *A Colour Symphony* 1922; music for the ballets *Checkmate* 1937, *Miracle in the Gorbals* 1944, and *Adam Zero* 1946; an opera *The Olympians* 1949; and dramatic film music, including *Things to Come* 1935. He conducted the first performance of US composer Igor Stravinsky's *Ragtime* for 11 instruments 1918. Knighted 1950, KCVO 1969.

Blitzstein Marc (1905–1964). US composer. Born in Philadelphia, he was a child prodigy as a pianist at the age of six. He served with the US Army 8th Air Force 1942–45, for which he wrote *The Airborne* 1946, a choral symphony. His operas include *The Cradle Will Rock* 1937.

Blixen Karen Christentze, Baroness Blixen (born Dinesen) (1885–1962). Danish writer. She wrote mainly in English and is best known for her short stories, Gothic fantasies with a haunting, often mythic quality, published in such collections as *Seven Gothic Tales* 1934 and *Winter's Tales* 1942 under the pen name Isak Dinesen. Her autobiography *Out of Africa* 1937 (filmed 1985) is based on her experience of running a coffee plantation in Kenya.
Suggested reading
Lasser, F and Svendsen, C *The Life and Destiny of Karen Blixen* (1970)
Thurman, Judith *Isak Dinesen: The Life of Karen Blixen* (1982)

Bloch Ernest (1880–1959). Swiss-born US composer. Among his works are the lyrical drama *Macbeth* 1910, *Schelomo* for cello and orchestra 1916, five string quartets, and *Suite Hébraïque* for viola and orchestra 1953. He often used themes based on Jewish liturgical music and folk song.
Born in Geneva, Switzerland, he went to the US 1916 and became founder-director of the Cleveland Institute of Music 1920–25.

Bloch Felix (1905–1983). Swiss-born US physicist who invented the analytical technique of nuclear magnetic resonance (NMR) spectroscopy 1946. For this work he shared the Nobel Prize for Physics 1952 with US physicist Edward Purcell (1912–). He was born in Zürich and was professor of physics at Stanford University, USA, 1934–71.

Bloch Konrad Emil (1912–). German-born US chemist whose research concerned cholesterol. Making use of the radioisotope carbon-14 (the radioactive form of carbon), Bloch was able to follow the complex steps by which the body chemically transforms acetic acid into cholesterol. In 1954 he became a professor at Harvard. He shared the 1964 Nobel Prize for Physiology or Medicine with his collaborator in Germany, Feodor Lynen.

Bloch Marc (1886–1944). French historian, leading member of the Annales school. Most of his research was into medieval European history. He held that economic structures and systems of belief were just as important to the study of history as legal norms and institutional practices, and pioneered the use of comparative history.
Bloch was professor of economic history at the Sorbonne from 1936. Forced out of teaching during World War II, he joined the Resistance 1943 but was captured and shot by German soldiers 1944.
Bloch explored the relationship between freedom and servitude in his thesis *Kings and Serfs* 1920 and *Feudal Society* 1939–40.

Blok Alexander Alexandrovich (1880–1921). Russian poet. As a follower of the French Symbolist movement, he used words for their symbolic rather than actual meaning. He backed the 1917 Revolution, as in his poems *The Twelve* 1918 and *The Scythians* 1918, the latter appealing to the West to join in the revolution.

Blomberg Werner Eduard Fritz von (1878–1946). German field marshal. After a sound but unremarkable career in World War I, Blomberg became minister of war Jan 1933 and commander in chief of German armed forces May 1935. Hitler forced him to resign shortly after he was appointed field marshal 1936. He was interrogated about war crimes by the Nuremberg tribunal, but died during the trial.

Blomdahl Karl-Birger (1916–1968). Swedish composer. He wrote ballets and symphonies in Expressionist style. His opera *Aniara* 1959 incorporates electronic music and is set in a spaceship fleeing Earth after nuclear war.

Blondin Charles. Assumed name of Jean François Gravelet (1824–1897). French tightrope walker who walked across a rope suspended above Niagara Falls, USA. He first crossed the falls 1859 at a height of 49 m/160 ft, and later repeated the feat blindfold and then pushing a wheelbarrow.

Here lies the man who boldly hath run through / More villainies than ever England knew; / And ne're to any friend he had was true.

THOMAS BLOOD
Epitaph ending 'An Elegie on Colonel Blood' 1680, reprinted in *Roxburghe Ballads* vol vi

Blood Thomas (1618–1680). Irish adventurer, known as Colonel Blood, who attempted to steal the crown jewels from the Tower of London, England, 1671.

Bloom Claire (originally Clair Blume) (1931–). English actress. Her career has stretched over four decades. She began her film career in Chaplin's *Limelight* 1952 and continued with such films as *Richard III* 1956 and *The Brothers Karamazov* 1958. Her more recent films have included supporting roles in *Sammy and Rosie Get Laid* 1987 and Woody Allen's *Crimes and Misdemeanours* 1990.
Her television appearances include *Brideshead Revisited* 1980.

The costume of woman … should conduce at once to her health, comfort, and usefulness … while it should not fail also to conduce to her personal adornment, it should make that end of secondary importance.

AMELIA JENKS BLOOMER
Letter June 1857

Bloomer Amelia (born Jenks) (1818–1894). US campaigner for women's rights. In 1849, when unwieldy crinolines were the fashion, she introduced a knee-length skirt combined with loose trousers gathered at the ankles, which became known as bloomers (also called 'rational dress'). She published the magazine *The Lily* 1849–54, which campaigned for women's rights and dress reform, and lectured with Susan B Anthony in New York, USA.

Bloomfield Leonard (1887–1949). US linguist who carried out extensive field research, notably on Tagalog (Filipino), spoken in the Philippines, and on the languages of North American Indians. His widely influential *Languages* 1933 is a rigorous analysis of the theory and methodology of linguistic research.

Blount Charles, Earl of Devonshire, 8th Baron Mountjoy (1563–1606). English soldier, a friend of the 2nd Earl of Essex. Blount accompanied him and Raleigh on their unsuccessful expedition to the Azores 1597. He became Lord Deputy of Ireland 1601 and quelled the revolt led by the Irish chief Hugh O'Neill, 2nd Earl of Tyrone, when the Irish failed in their attempt to reach a Spanish force that had arrived at Kinsale 1601. He subdued most of Ireland and was created earl 1603. Knighted 1586.

Blow John (1648–1708). English composer. He taught English composer Henry Purcell and wrote church music, for example the anthem 'I Was Glad When They Said Unto Me' 1697. His masque *Venus and Adonis* 1685 is sometimes called the first English opera.

Bloy Léon-Marie (1846–1917). French author. He achieved a considerable reputation with his literary lampoons in the 1880s.

What a place to plunder!

GEBHART VON BLUCHER
on viewing London from St Paul's 1814

Blücher Gebhard Leberecht von (1742–1819). Prussian general and field marshal, popularly known as 'Marshal Forward'. He took an active part in the patriotic movement, and in the War of German Liberation defeated the French as commander in chief at Leipzig 1813, crossed the Rhine to Paris 1814, and was made prince of Wahlstadt (Silesia).

In 1815 he was defeated by Napoleon at Ligny but came to the aid of British commander Wellington at Waterloo.

Blum Léon (1872–1950). French politician. He was converted to socialism by the Dreyfus affair 1899 and in 1936 became the first socialist prime minister of France. He was again premier for a few weeks 1938. Imprisoned under the Vichy government 1942 as a danger to French security, he was released by the Allies 1945. He again became premier for a few weeks 1946.

Blumentritt Gunther (1892–1967). German general. A general staff officer, he was chief of operations for Field Marshal von Rundstedt throughout the Polish and French campaigns 1939–40, and planned French counter–invasion defences 1942. He commanded several units in his own right 1944–45 then surrendered to the British May 1945.

Cricket to us, like you, was more than play, / It was a worship in the summer sun.

EDMUND BLUNDEN
'Pride of the Village'

Blunden Edmund Charles (1896–1974). English poet. He served in World War I and published the prose work *Undertones of War* 1928. His poetry is mainly about rural life. Among his scholarly contributions was the discovery and publication of some poems by the 19th-century poet John Clare.

His career [shows] the fatal conjunction ... of his own outstanding gifts and his desire to be at once part of the establishment and against it.

Michael Kitson on ANTHONY BLUNT
Dictionary of National Biography

Blunt Anthony Frederick (1907–1983). British art historian and double agent. As a Cambridge lecturer, he recruited for the Soviet secret service and, as a member of the British Secret Service 1940–45, passed information to the USSR. In 1951 he assisted the defection to the USSR of the British agents Guy Burgess and Donald Maclean (1913-1983). He was the author of many respected works on French and Italian art. Unmasked 1964, he was given immunity after his confession.

He was director of the Courtauld Institute of Art 1947–74 and Surveyor of the Queen's Pictures 1945–72. KCVO 1956. He was stripped of his knighthood 1979 when the affair became public.

Blunt Wilfrid Scawen (1840–1922). English poet. He married Lady Anne Noel, Byron's grand-daughter, and travelled with her in the Middle East, becoming a supporter of Arab nationalism. He also supported Irish Home Rule (he was imprisoned 1887–88), and wrote anti-imperialist books, poetry, and diaries.

Bly Robert Elwood (1926–). US writer. His book *Iron John: A Book About Men* 1990, in which he argued that men needed to rediscover the warrior side of their natures, started the 'men's movement'. His *Light Around the Body* 1967 won the National Book Award for poetry.

Bly championed new American poetry through his literary magazine the *Fifties*, publishing his first collection of poetry, *Silence in the Snowy Fields* 1962. He helped to organize American Writers Against the Vietnam War 1966, denouncing the war in his own poetry. Collections include *The Spirit Boy and Insatiable Soul* 1994. He translated the poems of Pablo Neruda from Spanish and the novel *Hunger* by Knut Hamsun from Norwegian. Becoming interested in matriarchal religions, Bly conducted seminars on the Great Mother, a pre-Christian deity, in the 1960s and 1970s. In *Iron John* he argued that men had moved away from the traditional male values as a result of the feminist movement, and needed to distance themselves from their mothers and learn from older men. This was seen as a backlash against the feminist movement.

Blyth Chay (Charles) (1940–). British sailing adventurer who rowed across the Atlantic with John Ridgeway 1966 and sailed solo around the world in a westerly direction during 1970–71. He sailed around the world with a crew in the opposite direction 1973–74, and in 1977 he made a record-breaking transatlantic crossing from Cape Verde to Antigua.

Blyton Enid Mary (1897–1968). English writer of children's books. She created the character Noddy and the adventures of the 'Famous Five' and 'Secret Seven'.

She dealt with 17 different publishers, and on average wrote some 15 new books per year; she was able to complete a 50,000-word Famous Five adventure in a week. She has been criticized by educationalists for social, racial, and sexual stereotyping.

Sales of Enid Blyton books now number more than 8 million copies a year, with translations into 27 languages. Noddy alone sold over 100 million copies 1949–95.

In 1996 Trocadero plc, the entertainment company, purchased the remaining 43 years of copyright to all Blyton's books – more than 600 titles – for £13 million.

Boadicea alternative spelling of British queen ◊Boudicca.

Boas Franz (1858–1942). German-born US anthropologist. He stressed the need to study 'four fields' – ethnology, linguistics, physical anthropology, and archaeology – before generalizations might be made about any one culture or comparisons about any number of cultures. In 1896 he was appointed professor at Columbia University, where he trained the first generation of US anthropologists, such as Alfred Kroeber and Margaret Mead. From 1901 to 1905 he was also curator of the American Museum of Natural History in New York City.

Boas spent much of his later career battling against unscientific theories of racial inequality.

Boateng Paul Yaw (1951–). British Labour politician and broadcaster. Elected member of Parliament for Brent South 1987, he was appointed to Labour's Treasury team 1989, the first black appointee to a front-bench post. He served on numerous committees on crime and race relations.

Boberg Ferdinand (1860–1945). Swedish architect. The most important exponent of early 20th-century architecture in Sweden, he designed mainly large-scale civic buildings in the style of US architects Henry Richardson and Louis Sullivan. Typical of his work is a contrast between large, plain areas and highly intricate Art Nouveau elements. His plan for a Nobel Festival Hall was rejected following criticisms by his chief rival Ragnar Östberg.

He who has once been happy is for aye / Out of Destruction's reach.

WILFRED BLUNT
Esther ch 1 1892

Boccaccio Giovanni (1313–1375). Italian writer and poet. He is chiefly known for the collection of tales called the *Decameron* 1348–53. Equally at home with tragic and comic narrative, he laid the foundations for the Humanism of the Renaissance and raised vernacular literature to the status enjoyed by the ancient classics.

Son of a Florentine merchant, he lived in Naples 1328–41, where he fell in love with the unfaithful 'Fiammetta' who inspired his early poetry. Before returning to Florence 1341 he had written the prose romance *Filostrato* and the verse narrative *Teseide* (used by Chaucer in his *Troilus and Criseyde* and 'The Knight's Tale'). He was much influenced by Petrarch, whom he met 1350.

Suggested reading
Bergin, Thomas *Boccaccio* (1981)
Chubb, Thomas C *The Life of Boccaccio* (1930, rep 1979)
Dombroski, Robert S (ed) *Critical Perspectives on the Decameron* (1976)

Boccherini (Ridolfo) Luigi (1743–1805). Italian composer and cellist. He studied in Rome, made his mark in Paris 1768, and was court composer in Prussia and Spain. Boccherini composed some 350 instrumental works, an opera, and oratorios.

Boccioni Umberto (1882–1916). Italian painter, sculptor, and theorist. One of the founders of Futurism, he pioneered a semi-abstract style that sought to depict movement and speed, as in his sculpture *Unique Forms of Continuity in Space* 1913 (Tate Gallery, London).

Bock Fedor von (1880–1945). German field marshal of World War II. He commanded an army group during the German invasions of Poland 1939, Belgium and the Netherlands 1940, and the USSR 1941. After the failure to take Moscow and the Soviet counteroffensive, he was removed from his post, but early 1942 was given command of Army Group South in the Caucasus. He was dismissed July 1942 after a dispute over strategy with Hitler.

Böcklin Arnold (1827–1901). Swiss Symbolist painter. His mainly imaginary landscapes have a dreamlike atmosphere, as in his best-known work *Island of the Dead* 1880 (Metropolitan Museum of Art, New York).

He was strongly attracted to Italy and lived for years in Rome. Many of his paintings are peopled with mythical beings, such as nymphs and naiads.

Bode Johann Elert (1747–1826). German astronomer and mathematician who contributed greatly to the popularization of astronomy. He published the first atlas of all stars visible to the naked eye, *Uranographia* 1801, and devised Bode's law. This predicted the existence of a planet between Mars and Jupiter, which led to the discovery of the asteroids. Bode was director of the Berlin observatory 1786–1825.

Bodhidharma (lived 6th century AD). Indian Buddhist and teacher. He entered China from S India about 520 and was the founder of the Ch'an school. Ch'an focuses on contemplation leading to intuitive meditation, a direct pointing to and stilling of the human mind. In the 20th century, the Japanese variation, Zen, has attracted many followers in the West.

Bodichon Barbara (born Leigh-Smith) (1827–1891). English feminist and campaigner for women's education and suffrage. She wrote *Women and Work* 1857, and was a founder of the magazine *The Englishwoman's Journal* 1858.

Born into a radical family that believed in female equality, she attended Bedford College, London. She was a founder of the college for women that became Girton College, Cambridge.

Bodin Jean (1530–1596). French political philosopher whose six-volume *De la République* 1576 is considered the first work on political economy.

Bodin was a lawyer in Paris. He published 1574 a tract explaining that prevalent high prices were due to the influx of precious metals from the New World. His theory of an ideal government emphasized obedience to a sovereign ruler.

Th' hast made us all thine Heirs: whatever we / Hereafter write, 'tis thy Posterity.

Henry Vaughan on THOMAS BODLEY
in *On Sir Thomas Bodley's Library*

Bodley Thomas (1545–1613). English scholar and diplomat, after whom the Bodleian Library in Oxford is named. After retiring from Queen Elizabeth I's service 1597, he restored the university's library, which was opened as the Bodleian Library 1602. The library had originally been founded in the 15th century by Humphrey, Duke of Gloucester (1391–1447). Knighted 1604.

Bodoni Giambattista (1740–1813). Italian printer. He managed the printing press of the duke of Parma and produced high-quality editions of the classics. He designed several typefaces, including one bearing his name, which is in use today.

Boehm Theobald (1794–1881). German flautist and composer. He invented the Boehm system of improvements to the flute 1832. Using metalworking skills, he applied a series of levers and keypads to the instrument which improved performance and enabled the pitch holes to be drilled at optimum acoustical positions instead of, as formerly, to suit the player's fingers. His system was later applied to other woodwind instruments.

Boehme Jakob (1575–1624). German mystic who had many followers in Germany, Holland, and England. He claimed divine revelation of the unity of everything and nothing, and found in God's eternal nature a principle to reconcile good and evil. He was the author of the treatise *Aurora* 1612.

Boelke Oskar (1889–1916). One of the foremost German fighter pilots of World War I. By 1916 he had more enemy aircraft to his credit than any other German flier and received the *Order pour le Merite*.

At the time of his death Oct 1916, he was credited with 40 victories.

Boerhaave Hermann (1668–1738). Dutch physician and chemist who made Leiden a European centre of medical knowledge. He re-established the technique of clinical teaching, taking his students to the bedsides of his patients. Boerhaave described the structure and function of the sweat glands, and was the first to realize that smallpox is spread by contact. His *Elementia chemiae* 1732 presented a clear and precise approach to the chemistry of the day.

It is the nature of human affairs to be fraught with anxiety.

BOETHIUS
The Consolation of Philosophy II. iv

Boethius Anicius Manlius Severinus (AD 480–524). Roman philosopher. He wrote treatises on music and mathematics and *De Consolatione Philosophiae/The Consolation of Philosophy*, a dialogue in prose. It was translated into European languages during the Middle Ages.

Boethius wrote *De Consolatione Philosophiae* while imprisoned on suspicion of treason by Emperor Theodoric the Great. In it, a lady, Philosophy, responds to Boethius' account of his misfortunes with stoic, Platonic, and Christian advice. English translations were written by by Alfred the Great, Geoffrey Chaucer, and Elizabeth I. Boethius also translated Aristotle's works on logic and wrote treatises on Christian philosophy.

Bofill Ricardo (1939–). Spanish architect. He has been active largely in France since the late 1970s. In 1965 he set up the Taller de Arquitectura practice in his native Barcelona, in which an economist and a poet worked alongside architects. He established his reputation with low-cost designs for social housing, notably Walden 7, near

Barcelona, 1970–75, a geometrically complex scheme incorporating a disused cement works in a towering, picturesque composition. An increasingly grandiose form of Classicism characterizes his later work in France.

Bogarde Dirk. Stage name of Derek Niven van den Bogaerde (1921–   ). English actor. He appeared in comedies and adventure films such as *Doctor in the House* 1954 and *Campbell's Kingdom* 1957, before acquiring international recognition for complex roles in Joseph Losey's *The Servant* 1963 and *Accident* 1967, and Luchino Visconti's *Death in Venice* 1971. His other films include *A Bridge Too Far* 1977. Knighted 1992.

He has also written autobiographical books and novels including *A Postillion Struck by Lightning* 1977, *Backcloth* 1986, *A Particular Friendship* 1989, and *A Short Walk from Harrods* 1993.

> *There's something wrong with actors. We've always been a suspect breed. Socially, I find myself more admissible now in England because I've written books.*
>
> DIRK BOGARDE
> *Ritz* April 1983

Bogart Humphrey De Forest (1899–1957). US film actor. He achieved fame as the gangster in *The Petrified Forest* 1936. He became an international cult figure as the tough, romantic 'loner' in such films as *The Maltese Falcon* 1941 and *Casablanca* 1942, a status resurrected in the 1960s and still celebrated today. He won an Academy Award for his role in *The African Queen* 1952.

He co-starred in *To Have and Have Not* 1944 and *The Big Sleep* 1946 with Lauren Bacall, who became his fourth wife.

Suggested reading
Barbour, A D *Humphrey Bogart* (1973)
Eyles, Allen *Humphrey Bogart* (1990)
Goodman, Ezra *Bogey: The Good Bad Guy* (1965)
McCarthy, C *Bogey: The Films of Humphrey Bogart* (1965)

Bogart US actor Humphrey Bogart with Lauren Bacall in To Have and Have Not *1944. Playing gangster roles in the 1930s, Bogart had by the 1940s developed the role of the tough, laconic loner that made him a cult figure. He and Bacall married 1945 and went on to make several more films together, notably* The Big Sleep *1946 and* Key Largo *1948. His other co-stars included Ingrid Bergman and Katherine Hepburn.*

Bogarde English actor Dirk Bogarde began his film career with a series of solid but unexciting roles in thrillers and comedies. He later took on more complex roles – as in The Servant *1963 – portraying subtlety and ambiguity with great finesse.*

Bogdanovich Peter (1939–   ). US film director, screenwriter, and producer. He was formerly a critic. *The Last Picture Show* 1971, a nostalgic look at a small Texas town in the 1950s, was followed by two films that attempted to capture the style of old Hollywood, *What's Up Doc?* 1972 and *Paper Moon* 1973. Both made money but neither was a critical success. In 1990 he made *Texasville*, an unsuccessful follow-up to *The Last Picture Show*.

> *I've always been a self-confessed opportunist.*
>
> PETER BOGDANOVICH
> *Film Illustrated* April 1972

Bohan Marc (1926–   ). French fashion designer who joined the Dior firm 1958, replacing Yves Saint-Laurent, to design couture and ready-to-wear ranges. He was designer to the British couture house Hartnell 1991–92. He is noted for refined, romantic clothes, soft prints, and flattering colours.

Bohlen Chip (Charles) (1904–1974). US diplomat. Educated at Harvard, he entered the foreign service 1929. Interpreter and adviser to presidents Franklin Roosevelt at Tehran and Yalta, and Harry S Truman at Potsdam, he served as ambassador to the USSR 1953–57.

Bohm David Joseph (1917–1992). US-born British physicist who specialized in quantum mechanics but also worked on plasmas, metals, and liquid helium. In 1959 he and his student Yakir Aharanov discovered the Aharanov–Bohm effect, showing that the motions of charged particles can be affected by magnetic fields even if they never enter the regions to which those fields are confined. He settled permanently in London 1961, where he was professor of theoretical physics at Birkbeck College until 1983.

Böhm Karl (1894–1981). Austrian conductor. He is known for his stately interpretations of Beethoven, and of Mozart and Strauss operas.

Bohr Aage Niels (1922–). Danish physicist who produced a new model of the nucleus of the atom 1952, known as the collective model. For this work, he shared the 1975 Nobel Prize for Physics. He was the son of Niels Bohr.

An expert is a man who has made all the mistakes which can be made in a very narrow field.

NIELS BOHR
quoted in Mackay *The Harvest of a Quiet Eye*

Bohr Niels Henrik David (1885–1962). Danish physicist. His theoretical work produced a new model of atomic structure, now called the Bohr model, and helped establish the validity of quantum theory. He also explained the process of nuclear fission. Nobel Prize for Physics 1922.

Bohr's first model of the atom was developed working with Ernest Rutherford at Manchester, UK. He was director of the Institute of Theoretical Physics in Copenhagen from 1920. During World War II he took part in work on the atomic bomb in the USA. In 1952 he helped to set up CERN, the European nuclear research organization in Geneva. He proposed the doctrine of complementarity: that a fundamental particle is neither a wave nor a particle, because these are complementary modes of description.

Bohr, Niels *Danish physicist Niels Bohr, who recieved the Nobel Prize for Physics 1922 for his theory of the structure of the atom. Bohr escaped from German-occupied Denmark in a fishing boat during World War II and assisted in the development of the atom bomb in the United States. After the war he returned to Denmark and campaigned publicly against the spread of nuclear weapons.* (Ann Ronan/Image Select)

When Denmark was invaded by Nazi Germany, Bohr took an active part in the resistance movement. In 1943, he escaped to Sweden and on to the USA. After working on the atomic bomb, he became a passionate advocate for the control of nuclear weapons.

Suggested reading
Moore, Ruth E *Niels Bohr: The Man and the Scientist* (1967)
Rozental, S (ed) *Niels Bohr: His Life and Work* (1967)

Boiardo Matteo Maria, Count of Scandiano (1434–1494). Italian poet. He is famed for his *Orlando innamorato/Roland in Love* 1487, a chivalrous epic glorifying military honour, patriotism, and religion. Ariosto's *Orlando furioso* 1516 was conceived as a sequel to this work.

Boileau Despréaux Nicolas (1636–1711). French poet and critic. After a series of contemporary satires, his 'Epîtres/Epistles' 1669–77 led to his joint appointment with Racine as royal historiographer 1677. Later works include *L'Art poétique/The Art of Poetry* 1674 and the mock-heroic *Le Lutrin/The Lectern* 1674–83.

Bok Bart (Jan) (1906–1983). Dutch-born US astrophysicist who discovered small, circular dark spots in nebulae (now Bok's globules). Bok suggested that the globules were clouds of gas in the process of condensation and that stars might be in the early stages of formation there. His work broadened our understanding of the formation of stars.

Bok, born in Hoorn, was educated at Leiden and Groningen in the Netherlands and in the USA at Harvard, where he remained and became professor 1947. In 1957 he went to Australia as head of the department of astronomy at the Australian National University as well as director of the Mount Stromlo Observatory near Canberra. He ended his career as professor at the University of Arizona 1966–74.

His regime became renowned not so much for its brutality ... but for extravagance and folly on a scale unsurpassed in modern Africa.

Michael Meredith on JEAN-BÉDEL BOKASSA
in *The First Dance of Freedom: Black Africa in the Postwar Era* 1984

Bokassa Jean-Bédel (1921–1996). President of the Central African Republic 1966–79 and later self-proclaimed emperor 1977–79. Commander in chief from 1963, in Dec 1965 he led the military coup that gave him the presidency. On 4 Dec 1976 he proclaimed the Central African Empire and one year later crowned himself as emperor for life.

His regime was characterized by arbitrary state violence and cruelty. Overthrown in 1979, Bokassa was in exile until 1986. Upon his return he was sentenced to death, but this was commuted to life imprisonment 1988.

Boksenberg Alexander (1936–). English astronomer and physicist who devised a light-detecting system that can be attached to telescopes, vastly improving their optical powers. His image photon-counting system (IPCS) revolutionized observational astronomy, enabling Boksenberg and others to study distant quasars. Boksenberg studied at London University. He became professor of physics 1978 and director of the Royal Greenwich Observatory 1981.

Bol Ferdinand (*c.* 1616–1680). Dutch painter, a pupil (before 1640) of Rembrandt in Amsterdam, and probably the most prolific of his followers in portraiture, his works sometimes being confused with those of his master. In his later style he tended towards a Baroque elegance, and painted a number of civic group portraits, of which the Rijksmuseum has several examples.

Boldrewood Rolf. Pen name of Thomas Alexander Browne (1826–1915). Australian writer. Born in London, he was taken to Australia as a child 1830. He became a pioneer squatter, and a police magistrate in the goldfields. He wrote 17 novels, mostly rather stilted and 'literary' romances, but is remembered mainly for *Robbery*

Under Arms 1888 and *A Squatter's Life* 1890, which give graphic accounts of life in the outback.

Anne Boleyn was not a catalyst in the English Reformation; she was an element in the equation.

E W IVES on ANNE BOLEYN
in *Anne Boleyn* 1986

Boleyn Anne (*c.* 1501–1536). Queen of England 1533–36. Henry VIII broke with the pope in order to divorce his first wife and marry Anne. She was married to him 1533 and gave birth to the future Queen Elizabeth I in the same year. Accused of adultery and incest with her half-brother (a charge invented by Thomas Cromwell), she was beheaded.
Suggested reading
Chapman, Hester *Anne Boleyn c 1504–36* (1974)
Fraser, Antonia *The Six Wives of Henry VIII* (1992)
Lofts, Norah *Anne Boleyn* (1979)
Warnicke, Retha M *The Rise and Fall of Anne Boleyn* (1989)

Bolger Jim (James Brendan) (1935–   ). New Zealand politician, prime minister from 1990. A successful sheep and cattle farmer, Bolger was elected to Parliament 1972. He held a variety of cabinet posts under Robert Muldoon's leadership 1977–84 and was an effective, if uncharismatic, leader of the opposition from March 1986, taking the National Party to electoral victory Oct 1990. His subsequent failure to honour election pledges, leading to cuts in welfare provision, led to a sharp fall in his popularity. He retained power in the 1993 general election with a majority of one.

Bolingbroke title of Henry of Bolingbroke, ◊Henry IV of England.

Nations, like men, have their infancy.

HENRY ST JOHN, VISCOUNT BOLINGBROKE
Letters on the Study of History 1752

Bolingbroke Henry St John, 1st Viscount Bolingbroke (1678–1751). British Tory politician and political philosopher. His books, such as *Idea of a Patriot King* 1738 and *The Dissertation upon Parties* 1735, laid the foundations for 19th-century Toryism.
   Secretary of war 1704–08, he became foreign secretary in Robert Harley's ministry 1710, and in 1713 negotiated the Treaty of Utrecht. His plans to restore the 'Old Pretender' James Francis Edward Stuart were ruined by Queen Anne's death only five days after he had secured the dismissal of Harley 1714. He fled abroad, returning 1723, when he worked to overthrow Robert Walpole. Viscount 1712.

Plain truth will influence half a score men at most ... while mystery will lead millions by the nose.

HENRY ST JOHN, VISCOUNT BOLINGBROKE
letter 28 July 1721

Bolívar Simón (1783–1830). South American nationalist, leader of revolutionary armies, known as the Liberator. He fought the Spanish colonial forces in several uprisings and eventually liberated his native Venezuela 1821, Colombia and Ecuador 1822, Peru 1824, and Bolivia (a new state named after him, formerly Upper Peru) 1825.
Suggested reading
Bushnell, David *The Liberator: Simón Bolívar* (1970)
Fitzgerald, G E *The Political Thought of Bolívar* (1971)
Madariaga, Salvador de *Bolívar* (1951)
Masur, G *Simón Bolívar* (1969)
Wepman, Dennis *Bolívar* (1985)

Bolkiah Hassanal (1946–   ). Sultan of Brunei from 1967, following the abdication of his father, Omar Ali Saifuddin (1916–1986).

As absolute ruler, Bolkiah also assumed the posts of prime minister and defence minister on independence 1984.
   As head of an oil- and gas-rich microstate, the sultan is reputedly the world's richest individual, with an estimated total wealth of $22 billion, which includes the Dorchester and Beverly Hills hotels in London and Los Angeles and, at a cost of $40 million, the world's largest palace. He was educated at a British military academy.

Böll Heinrich Theodor (1917–1985). German novelist. A radical Catholic and anti-Nazi, he attacked Germany's political past and the materialism of its contemporary society. His many publications include poems, short stories, and novels which satirized West German society, for example *Billard um Halbzehn/Billiards at Half-Past Nine* 1959 and *Gruppenbild mit Dame/Group Portrait with Lady* 1971. He won the Nobel Prize for Literature 1972.
Suggested reading
Böll, Heinrich *What's to Become of the Boy?* (autobiography) (trs 1984)
Macpherson, E *A Student's Guide to Böll* (1972)
Reid, James A *Heinrich Böll: A German for His Time* (1988)

Bolo Paul (Pasha) (died 1918). French traitor and confidence trickster. In Feb 1915 he gained the confidence of the Khedive of Egypt and got his backing for a scheme to get money from Germany to promote a campaign for peace in France. It was later discovered that before his arrest in Sept 1917 he had received some £300,000 from German sources. He was tried and executed for obtaining money from an enemy in order to create a pacifist movement in France.

Brecht is the writer I would most wish to resemble.

ROBERT BOLT
The Bloomsbury Theatre Guide 1988

Bolt Robert Oxton (1924–1995). English dramatist and screenwriter. He is known for his historical plays, such as *A Man for All Seasons* 1960 (filmed 1966), and for his screenplays, including *Lawrence of Arabia* 1962, *Dr Zhivago* 1965 (both Academy Awards), *Ryan's Daughter* 1970, and *The Bounty* 1984.

Boltzmann Ludwig Eduard (1844–1906). Austrian physicist who studied the kinetic theory of gases, which explains the properties of gases by reference to the motion of their constituent atoms and molecules. He established the branch of physics now known as statistical mechanics.
   He derived a formula, the Boltzmann distribution, which gives the number of atoms or molecules with a given energy at a specific temperature. The constant in the formula is called the *Boltzmann constant.*

Bolyai (Farkas) Wolfgang (1775–1856). Hungarian mathematician, father of János Bolyai; their work on geometry is closely interlinked.

Bolyai János (1802–1860). Hungarian mathematician, one of the founders of non-Euclidean geometry. By about 1820, Bolyai had become convinced that a proof of Euclid's postulate about parallel lines was impossible; he began instead to construct a geometry which did not depend upon Euclid's axiom. This was a theory of absolute space in which several lines pass through the point P without intersecting the line L. He developed his formula relating the angle of parallelism of two lines with a term characterizing the line. In his new theory Euclidean space was simply a limiting case of the new space, and Bolyai introduced his formula to express what later became known as the space constant. He was the son of Wolfgang Bolyai.

Bolzano Bernardus Placidus Johann Nepomuk (1781–1848). Czech philosopher and mathematician who formulated a theory of real functions and introduced the nondifferentiable Bolzano function. He was also able to prove the existence and define the properties of infinite sets. Bolzano formulated a proof of the binomial theorem and, in one of his few works published in his lifetime (1817), attempted to lay down a rigorous foundation of analysis. One of the most interesting parts of the book was his definition of continuous functions. During the 1830s Bolzano concentrated on the study of real numbers.

My object is the construction of pure form.

DAVID BOMBERG
quoted in *Catalogue of the Bomberg exhibition* 1914

Bomberg David Garshen (1890–1957). English painter. He applied forms inspired by Cubism and Vorticism to figurative subjects in such early works as *The Mud Bath* 1914 (Tate Gallery, London). Moving away from semi-abstraction in the mid-1920s, his work became more representational and Expressionist.

Bomberg was apprenticed to a lithographer, then studied at the Slade School in London 1911–13, and was a founder member of the London Group. He gained recognition only towards the end of his life.

Bonaparte Corsican family of Italian origin that gave rise to the Napoleonic dynasty: see ◊Napoleon I, ◊Napoleon II, and ◊Napoleon III. Others were the brothers and sister of Napoleon I:

Joseph (1768–1844) whom Napoleon made king of Naples 1806 and Spain 1808;

Lucien (1775–1840) whose handling of the Council of Five Hundred on 10 Nov 1799 ensured Napoleon's future;

Louis (1778–1846) the father of Napoleon III, who was made king of Holland 1806–10; also called (from 1810) Comte de Saint Leu;

Caroline (1782–1839) who married Joachim Murat 1800; full name Maria Annunciata Caroline;

Jerome (1784–1860) made king of Westphalia 1807.

Bonar Law British Conservative politician; see ◊Law, Andrew Bonar.

Bonaventura, St (Giovanni di Fidanza) (1221–1274). Italian Roman Catholic theologian. He entered the Franciscan order 1243, became professor of theology in Paris, and in 1256 general of his order. In 1273 he was created cardinal and bishop of Albano. Canonized 1482. Feast day 15 July.

Bond Alan (1938–). English-born Australian entrepreneur. He was chair of the Bond Corporation 1969–90 during the years when its aggressive takeover strategy gave the company interests in brewing, the media, mining, and retailing. In 1983 Bond led a syndicate that sponsored the winning yacht in the America's Cup race. The collapse of the Bond empire 1990 left thousands of investors impoverished and shook both Australian and international business confidence. In Jan 1995 he was arrested and charged with fraud and misconduct relating to corporate deals in the 1980s. He was voted out of bankruptcy by his creditors Feb 1995.

We have only one thing to keep us sane, pity; and the man without pity is mad.

EDWARD BOND
Lear 1972

Bond Edward (1934–). English dramatist. His early work aroused controversy because of the savagery of some of his imagery, for example, the brutal stoning of a baby by bored youths in *Saved* 1965. Other works include *Early Morning* 1968, *Lear* 1972, a reworking of Shakespeare's play; *Bingo* 1973, an account of Shakespeare's last days; and *The War Plays* 1985, and *Tuesday* 1993.

Early Morning was the last play to be banned in the UK by the Lord Chamberlain.

Bond George Phillips (1825–1865). US astronomer who developed astronomical photography and in 1850 took the first photograph of a star (Vega). His research was carried out at the Harvard Observatory together with his father, William Cranch Bond. Bond also made numerous studies of comets. He discovered 11 new comets and made calculations on the factors affecting their orbits.

Bond was born in Dorchester, Massachusetts, and educated at Harvard, remaining there at the observatory under his father and succeeding him as director when he died 1859.

Bond William Cranch (1789–1859). US astronomer who established the Harvard College Observatory as a centre of astronomical research. Much of his work was done in collaboration with his son George Phillips Bond. He also designed chronometers. William and George Bond discovered Hyperion (the eighth satellite of Saturn) 1848 and the Crêpe Ring (a faint ring inside two bright rings) around Saturn 1850. Their observation that stars could be seen through the Crêpe Ring led to their conclusion that the rings of Saturn are not solid.

The two Bonds also collaborated on the development of photographic techniques for astronomy. They took superior photographs of the Moon, and the first photographs of stars.

Bondarchuk Sergei Feodorovich (1920–1994). Soviet actor and film director. In 1967 he directed one of the most lavish film productions ever undertaken, an eight-hour long version of Leo Tolstoy's novel *War and Peace*, in which he also played the central role. Made as a self-conscious bid for Soviet cultural prestige, the undertaking was bankrolled by the government to an estimated equivalent of $100 million. But it is debatable whether the film, which deployed 20,000 extras in its recreation of the Battle of Borodino, matched its physical scale in narrative command.

Bondfield Margaret Grace (1873–1953). British socialist who became a trade-union organizer to improve working conditions for women. She was a Labour member of Parliament 1923–24 and 1926–31, and was the first woman to enter the cabinet – as minister of labour 1929–31.

[Science doesn't deal with facts; indeed] fact is an emotion-loaded word for which there is little place in scientific debate. Science is above all a cooperative enterprise.

HERMANN BONDI
in *Nature* 1977

Bondi Hermann (1919–). Austrian-born British cosmologist. In 1948 he joined with Fred Hoyle and Thomas Gold in developing the steady-state theory of cosmology 1948, which suggested that matter is continuously created in the universe. Bondi also described the likely characteristics and physical properties of gravitational waves, and demonstrated that such waves are compatible with and are indeed a necessary consequence of the general theory of relativity. Bondi's academic career after the war was spent mostly at Cambridge and King's College, London. KCB 1973.

Bonestell Chesley (1888–1986). US artist who specialized in such realistic-looking astronomical illustrations that many believe they were instrumental in persuading the US government that space exploration was possible. *The Conquest of Space* 1949, written by German-born rocket scientist Willy Ley (1906–1969), was the first popular astronomy book to carry Bonestell's illustrations, many in colour.

Tories are not always wrong, but they are always wrong at the right moment.

VIOLET BONHAM-CARTER
Observer 26 April 1964

Bonham-Carter (Helen) Violet, Baroness Asquith of Yarnbury (1887–1969). British president of the Liberal party 1945–47. DBE 1953, Baroness 1964.

Bonheur Rosa (Marie Rosalie) (1822–1899). French painter. She is best known for her realistic animal painting, including *Horse Fair* 1853 (Metropolitan Museum of Art, New York).

She exhibited at the Paris Salon every year from 1841 and received international awards. In 1894 she became the first woman Officer of the Légion d'Honneur.

Bonhoeffer Dietrich (1906–1945). German Lutheran theologian and opponent of Nazism. Involved in a plot against Hitler, he was executed by the Nazis in Flossenburg concentration camp. His *Letters and Papers from Prison* 1953 became the textbook of modern radical theology, advocating the idea of a 'religionless' Christianity.

Boniface name of nine popes, including:

Boniface VIII (Benedict Caetani) (*c.* 1235–1303). Pope from 1294. He clashed unsuccessfully with Philip IV of France over his taxation of the clergy, and also with Henry III of England.

Boniface exempted the clergy from taxation by the secular government in a bull (edict) 1296, but was forced to give way when the clergy were excluded from certain lay privileges. His bull of 1302 *Unam sanctam*, asserting the complete temporal and spiritual power of the papacy, was equally ineffective.

Boniface, St (680–754). English Benedictine monk, known as the 'Apostle of Germany'; originally named Wynfrith. After a missionary journey to Frisia 716, he was given the task of bringing Christianity to Germany 718 by Pope Gregory II, and was appointed archbishop of Mainz 746. He returned to Frisia 754 and was martyred near Dockum. His feast day is 5 June.

Bonington Chris(tian) John Storey (1934–). British mountaineer. He took part in the first ascent of Annapurna II 1960, Nuptse 1961, and the first British ascent of the north face of the Eiger 1962, climbed the central Tower of Paine in Patagonia 1963, and was the leader of an Everest expedition 1975 and again 1985, reaching the summit. Publications include the autobiographical *I Chose to Climb* 1966. Knighted 1996.

Bonington Richard Parkes (1801–1828). English painter. He lived in France from 1817. He is noted for his fresh, atmospheric seascapes and landscapes in oil and watercolour, mainly viewed from a high perspective; he also painted historic genre works. He was much admired by Delacroix.

Bonnard Pierre (1867–1947). French painter, designer, and graphic artist. Influenced by Gauguin and Japanese prints, he specialized in intimate domestic scenes and landscapes, his paintings shimmering with colour and light. With other members of *les Nabis*, he explored the decorative arts (posters, stained glass, furniture), but is most widely known for his series of nudes, for example, *Nude in the Bath* 1938 (Petit Palais, Paris).

Bonner Yelena (1923–). Soviet human-rights campaigner. Disillusioned by the Soviet invasion of Czechoslovakia 1968, she resigned from the Communist Party after marrying her second husband, Andrei Sakharov, 1971, and became active in the dissident movement.

Bonney Charles (1813–1897). Australian politician and overlander, born in England. He is claimed to be Australia's first overlander, having taken 10,000 sheep south from the Murray River to the Goulburn River in 1837 and the next year helping to overland the first stock to Adelaide. He was later an administrator and member of the House of Assembly in South Australia.

Bonney William H. US outlaw known by the name of ◊Billy the Kid.

Bonnie and Clyde Bonnie Parker (1911–1934) and Clyde Barrow (1909–1934). Infamous US criminals who carried out a series of small-scale robberies in Texas, Oklahoma, New Mexico, and Missouri between Aug 1932 and May 1934. They were eventually betrayed and then killed in a police ambush.

Much of their fame emanated from encounters with the police and their coverage by the press. Their story was filmed as *Bonnie and Clyde* 1967 by the US director Arthur Penn.

Bonnie Prince Charlie Scottish name for ◊Charles Edward Stuart, pretender to the throne.

Boole George (1815–1864). English mathematician whose work *The Mathematical Analysis of Logic* 1847 established the basis of modern mathematical logic, and whose Boolean algebra can be used in designing computers.

Boole's system is essentially two-valued. By subdividing objects into separate classes, each with a given property, his algebra makes it possible to treat different classes according to the presence or absence of the same property. Hence it involves just two numbers, 0 and 1 – the binary system used in the computer.

Boone Daniel (1734–1820). US pioneer who explored the Wilderness Road (East Virginia–Kentucky) 1775 and paved the way for the first westward migration of settlers. Boone was born in Pennsylvania and spent most of his youth in North Carolina. During the American Revolution, he led militias against Indians allied with the British. He was captured by a Shawnee war party and so impressed the chief that he was adopted by the tribe. He left the Indians and continued to explore westward.

Boorman John (1933–). English film director. He started out in television, and has directed successful films both in Hollywood (*Point Blank* 1967, *Deliverance* 1972) and in Britain (*Excalibur* 1981, *Hope and Glory* 1987).

He is the author of a telling book on film finance, *Money into Light* 1985.

Boot Jesse, 1st Baron Trent (1850–1931). British entrepreneur and founder of the Boots pharmacy chain. In 1863 Boot took over his father's small Nottingham shop trading in medicinal herbs. Recognizing that the future lay with patent medicines, he concentrated on selling cheaply, advertising widely, and offering a wide range of medicines. In 1892, Boot also began to manufacture drugs. He had 126 shops by 1900 and more than 1,000 by his death. Knighted 1909, baronet 1917, baron 1929.

Booth Charles (1840–1916). English sociologist, author of the study *Life and Labour of the People in London* 1891–1903, and pioneer of an old-age pension scheme.

Boole George Boole was the founder of the modern science of symbolic logic and the first mathematician to consider logic algebraically. Boolean algebra, applied to binary addition and subtraction, is important today in the design and construction of circuits and computers. (Ann Ronan/Image Select)

Booth Edwin Thomas (1833–1893). US actor. He was one of America's most acclaimed Shakespearean performers, famous for his portrayal of Hamlet. As lead actor, theatre manager, and producer, he successfully brought to the New York stage numerous Shakespearean tragedies. His career suffered in the wake of the public disgrace of his brother, John Wilkes Booth, who assassinated President Lincoln 1865.

Booth Hubert Cecil (1871–1955). English mechanical and civil engineer who invented the vacuum cleaner 1901. In his machine, one end of a tube was connected to an air pump, while the other, with nozzle attached, was pushed over the surface being cleaned. The cleaner incorporated an air filter.

Tell mother – tell mother – I died for my country.

JOHN WILKES BOOTH
Remark after having assassinated President Lincoln 1865

Booth John Wilkes (1838–1865). US actor and fanatical Confederate sympathizer who assassinated President Abraham Lincoln 14 April 1865; he escaped with a broken leg and was later shot in a barn in Virginia when he refused to surrender.
Suggested reading
Clarke, A B *The Unlocked Book: A Memoir of John Wilkes Booth* (by his sister) (1938)
Samples, Gordon *Lust for Fame* (1982)

Booth William (1829–1912). British founder of the Salvation Army 1878, and its first 'general'.

Booth, William *Portrait of English evangelist William Booth by Hubert Herkomer. Booth founded the Salvation Army and became its first 'general', modelling its operations on those of the British army. His movement grew rapidly, and its work soon extended to the USA, Australia, India, and elsewhere, and Booth's standing was such that he was invited to the coronation of Edward VII 1901.*

Booth was born in Nottingham. He experienced religious conversion at the age of 15. In 1865 he founded the Christian Mission in Whitechapel, E London, which became the Salvation Army 1878. 'In Darkest England, and the Way Out' 1890 contained proposals for the physical and spiritual redemption of the many down-and-outs. His wife Catherine (1829–1890, born Mumford), whom he married 1855, became a public preacher about 1860, initiating the ministry of women. Their eldest son, William Bramwell Booth (1856–1929), became chief of staff of the Salvation Army 1880 and was general from 1912 until his deposition 1929. Evangeline Cora Booth (1865–1950), seventh child of General William Booth, was a prominent Salvation Army officer, and 1934–39 was general. She became a US citizen. Catherine Bramwell Booth (1884–1987), a granddaughter of William Booth, was a commissioner in the Salvation Army.
Suggested reading
Barnes, Cyril *William Booth and His Army of Peace* (1965)
Collier, R *The General Next to God* (1965)
Sandall, Robert *The History of the Salvation Army* (1947–73)

Compassion ... the urge to diminish the sum of human suffering ... brings the most abiding personal happiness.

BOB BOOTHBY
quoted in Robert Rhodes James *Bob Boothby – A Portrait* 1991

Boothby Bob (Robert) John Graham, Baron Boothby (1900–1986). Scottish politician. He became a Unionist member of Parliament 1924 and was parliamentary private secretary to Churchill 1926–29. He advocated Britain's entry into the European Community (now the European Union), and was a powerful speaker. KBE 1958, baron 1958.

Boothroyd Betty (1929–). British Labour politician, speaker of the House of Commons from 1992. She was elected MP for West Bromwich in the West Midlands 1973 and was a member of the European Parliament 1975–77. The first woman to hold the office of speaker, she has controlled Parliamentary proceedings with a mixture of firmness and good humour.

Borah William Edgar (1865–1940). US Republican politician. Born in Illinois, he was a senator for Idaho from 1906. An arch-isolationist, he was chiefly responsible for the USA's repudiation of the League of Nations following World War I.

Borchert Wolfgang (1921–1947). German playwright and prose writer. Borchert was sent home wounded during World War II while serving on the Russian front, where he had been sent for making anti-Nazi comments. *Draussen vor der Tür/The Outsider* 1947 is a surreal play about the chaotic conditions that a German soldier finds when he returns to Germany after walking home from the Russian front.

Borden Robert Laird (1854–1937). Canadian Conservative politician, prime minister 1911–20. Throughout World War I he represented Canada at meetings of the Imperial War Cabinet, and he was the chief Canadian delegate at the Paris Peace Conference 1919. He played an important role in transforming Canada from a colony to a nation, notably by insisting on separate membership of the League of Nations 1919.

Borden was born in Grand Pré, Nova Scotia. He practised law in Halifax, and was a member of the House of Commons 1896–1921, representing Halifax for most of that time. After his retirement from politics he published two volumes of lectures: *Canadian Constitutional Studies* 1922 and *Canada in the Commonwealth* 1929. His *Memoirs* were published posthumously 1938. GCMG 1914.

Border Allan Robert (1955–). Australian cricketer, left-handed batsman, and captain of Australia 1985–94. He retired from international cricket in 1994 as holder of world records for most test runs (11,174), most test matches as captain (93), most appearances in test matches (156), most consecutive appearances in test matches (153), most catches in test matches by an outfielder (156) and most appearances in one-day internationals (263). Border plays for Queensland after starting his career with NSW and has played in England for Gloucestershire and Essex.

Bordet Jules Jean Baptiste Vincent (1870–1961). Belgian bacteriologist and immunologist who researched the role of blood serum in the human immune response. He was the first to isolate 1906 the whooping-cough bacillus.

Borel Emile Félix Edouard Justin (1871–1956). French mathematician who rationalized the theory of functions of real variables. In the 1890s Borel did his most important work: on probability, the infinitesimal calculus, divergent series, and, most influential of all, the theory of measure. He provided a proof of Charles Emile Picard's theorem 1896.

Borelli Giovanni Alfonso (1608–1679). Italian scientist who explored the links between physics and medicine and showed how mechanical principles could be applied to animal physiology. This approach, known as iatrophysics, has proved basic to understanding how the mammalian body works.

Borg Björn Rune (1956–). Swedish tennis player who won the men's singles title at Wimbledon five times 1976–80, a record since the abolition of the challenge system 1922. He also won six French Open singles titles 1974–75 and 1978–81 inclusive. In 1990 Borg announced plans to return to professional tennis, but he enjoyed little competitive success.

Borge Victor. Stage name of Börg Rosenbaum (1909–). Danish-born US pianist and comedian. His Broadway show *Comedy in Music*, which ran for 849 performances 1953–56, was the longest-running one-person show in US theatrical history, and he continued to perform it all over the world until the 1980s. One of his acts involved indicating punctuation marks by different sounds.

Borge was born in Copenhagen, the son of a Russian Jewish violinist, and had a successful career as an entertainer before leaving for the USA 1940, the year Denmark was occupied by Nazi Germany. By 1945 he had his own *Victor Borge Show* on NBC radio. In the 1970s he was guest conductor for several major orchestras, including the Royal Concertgebouw of Amsterdam. He published an autobiography, *My Favourite Intermissions* 1971.

Writing is nothing more than a guided dream.
JORGE LUIS BORGES
Dr Brodie's Report 1972

Borges Jorge Luis (1899–1986). Argentine poet and short-story writer. He was an exponent of magic realism. In 1961 he became director of the National Library, Buenos Aires, and was professor of English literature at the university there. He is known for his fantastic and paradoxical work *Ficciones/Fictions* 1944.

Borges explored metaphysical themes in early works such as *Ficciones* and *El Aleph/The Aleph, and other Stories* 1949. In a later collection of tales *El informe de Brodie/Dr Brodie's Report* 1972 he adopted a more realistic style, reminiscent of the work of the young Rudyard Kipling, of whom he was a great admirer. *El libro de arena/The Book of Sand* 1975 marked a return to more fantastic themes.

Borgia Cesare (*c.* 1475–1507). Italian general, illegitimate son of Pope Alexander VI. Made a cardinal at 17 by his father, he resigned to become captain-general of the papacy, campaigning successfully against the city republics of Italy. Ruthless and treacherous in war, he was an able ruler (the model for Machiavelli's *The Prince*), but his power crumbled on the death of his father. He was a patron of artists, including Leonardo da Vinci.
Suggested reading
Bradford, S *Cesare Borgia: His Life and Times* (1976)
Hansen, W P and Haney, J (eds) *Cesare Borgia* (1986)
Johnson, Marion *The Borgias* (1981)
Mallett, Michael *The Borgias: The Rise and Fall of a Renaissance Dynasty* (1969)

My husbands have been very unlucky.
LUCREZIA BORGIA
on the murder of her second husband.
Quoted in R Erlanger *Lucrezia Borgia* 1979

Borgia Lucrezia (1480–1519). Duchess of Ferrara from 1501. She was the illegitimate daughter of Pope Alexander VI and sister of Cesare Borgia. She was married at 12 and again at 13 to further her father's ambitions, both marriages being annulled by him. At 18 she was married again, but her husband was murdered in 1500 on the order of her brother, with whom (as well as with her father) she was said to have committed incest. Her final marriage was to the Duke of Este, the son and heir of the Duke of Ferrara. She made the court a centre of culture and was a patron of authors and artists such as Ariosto and Titian.
Suggested reading
Johnson, Marion *The Borgias* (1981)
Erlanger, R *Lucrezia Borgia* (1979)
Fusero, Clemente *The Borgias* (trs 1972)
Mallett, Michael *The Borgias: The Rise and Fall of a Renaissance Dynasty* (1969)

I approach the end of my life with pleasure, knowing that in a few hours ... I shall be released.
LUCREZIA BORGIA
Last words to her father Pope Alexander VI 1519.

Borglum (John) Gutzon (de la Mothe) (1867–1941). US sculptor. He created a six-ton marble head of Abraham Lincoln in Washington, DC, and the series of giant heads of presidents Washington, Jefferson, Lincoln, and Theodore Roosevelt, carved on Mount Rushmore, South Dakota (begun 1930).

Intelligent, astute and devious: to safeguard his person and throne he gave an impression of boredom with politics, delighting in the mechanics of clocks and railway engines.
Alan Palmer on BORIS III
Penguin Dictionary of Twentieth Century History 1979

Boris III (1894–1943). Tsar of Bulgaria from 1918, when he succeeded his father, Ferdinand I. From 1934 he was virtual dictator until his sudden and mysterious death following a visit to Hitler. His son Simeon II was tsar until deposed 1946.

Boris Godunov (1552–1605). See ◊Godunov, Boris, tsar of Russia from 1598.

Bor-Komorowski Tadeusz (1895–1956). Polish general and resistance leader during the German occupation of Poland in World War II. He went underground after the Polish defeat 1939 and organized resistance groups, taking the cover-name 'Bor' and eventually becoming commander in chief of the Polish Home Army. He was captured by the Germans after the Warsaw Rising 1944 and imprisoned in Colditz.

Borlaug Norman Ernest (1914–). US microbiologist and agronomist. He developed high-yielding varieties of wheat and other grain crops to be grown in Third World countries, and was the first to use the term 'Green Revolution'. Nobel Prize for Peace 1970.

Bormann Martin (1900–1945). German Nazi leader. He took part in the abortive Munich beer-hall putsch (uprising) 1923 and rose to high positions in the Nazi (National Socialist) Party, becoming deputy party leader May 1941 following the flight of Rudolf Hess to Britain.

In 1943 Hitler made him his personal secretary, a position in which he controlled access to Hitler, preventing bad news from reaching him and exercised enormous influence over Hitler's decisions. Bormann was believed to have escaped the fall of Berlin May

1945 and was tried in his absence and sentenced to death at the Nuremberg trials 1945–46, but a skeleton uncovered by a mechanical excavator in Berlin 1972 was officially recognized as his by forensic experts 1973.

I am now convinced that theoretical physics is actual philosophy.

MAX BORN
My Life and My Views 1968

Born Max (1882–1970). German-born British physicist who received a Nobel prize 1954 for fundamental work on the quantum theory, especially his 1926 discovery that the wave function of an electron is linked to the probability that the electron is to be found at any point.

In 1924 Born coined the term 'quantum mechanics'. Born made Göttingen a leading centre for theoretical physics and together with his students and collaborators – notably Werner Heisenberg – he devised 1925 a system called matrix mechanics that accounted mathematically for the position and momentum of the electron in the atom. He also devised a technique, called the Born approximation method, for computing the behaviour of subatomic particles, which is of great use in high-energy physics.

Music is a pastime, a relaxation from more serious occupations.

ALEXANDER BORODIN
in a letter to Krylov 1867

Borodin Alexander Porfiryevich (1833–1887). Russian composer. Born in St Petersburg, the illegitimate son of a Russian prince, he became by profession an expert in medical chemistry, but in his spare time devoted himself to writing music. His principal work is the opera *Prince Igor*, left unfinished; it was completed by Rimsky-Korsakov and Glazunov and includes the Polovtsian Dances. His other works include symphonies, songs, and chamber music, using traditional Russian themes.

Borodina Olga (1963–   ). Russian mezzo-soprano. She has been a member of the Kirov Opera at St Petersburg from 1987, singing

Borodina *Russian mezzo-soprano Olga Borodina. Although her coloratura is widely admired in the Russian repertory, she is also successful in such roles as Carmen (at St Petersburg and elsewhere), Rosina and Angelina in* La Cenerentola, *which she sang for the first time on stage at Covent Garden in 1994.*

there and on tour to Europe and the USA. She made her Paris Opéra, Covent Garden, and New York Metropolitan Opera House debuts in 1992. She is also admired as a concert artist.

Boross Peter (1928–   ). Hungarian politician, prime minister 1993–94. Brought into Joszef Antall's government as a nonpolitical technocrat, he became deputy chairman of the ruling Hungarian Democratic Forum 1991 and acting prime minister during Antall's recurring bouts of illness. When Antall died Dec 1993, Boross succeeded him, but lost office to Gyula Horn, of the ex-communist Hungarian Socialist Party, in the July 1994 elections.

Borromeo St Carlo (1538–1584). Italian Roman Catholic saint and cardinal. He was instrumental in bringing the Council of Trent (1562–63) to a successful conclusion, and in drawing up the catechism that contained its findings. Feast day 4 Nov. He was canonized 1610.

It has the springiness of a sheet of metal which has been slightly curved under pressure.

FRANCESCO BORROMINI on Baroque fascination with movement, quoted in Anthony Blunt *Borromini* 1979

Borromini Francesco, originally Francesco Castelli (1599–1667). Swiss-born Italian Baroque architect. He was one of the two most important architects (with Bernini, his main rival) in 17th-century Rome. Whereas Bernini designed in a florid, expansive style, his pupil Borromini developed a highly idiosyncratic and austere use of the Classical language of architecture. His genius may be seen in the cathedrals of San Carlo alle Quatro Fontane 1637–41, San Ivo della Sapienza 1643–60, and the Oratory of St Philip Neri 1638–50.

My favourite, I might say, my only study, is man.

GEORGE BORROW
The Bible in Spain ch 5 1843

Borrow George Henry (1803–1881). English author and traveller. He travelled on foot through Europe and the East. His books, incorporating his knowledge of languages and Romany lore, include *Zincali* 1840, *The Bible in Spain* 1843, *Lavengro* 1851, *The Romany Rye* 1857, and *Wild Wales* 1862.

His concern for the interest, and unwearied attention to the health, of all under his command, softened the necessary exactions of duty and the rigours of discipline.

Inscription on EDWARD BOSCAWEN's monument in the parish church of St Michael Penkivel, Cornwall.

Boscawen Edward (1711–1761). English admiral who served against the French in the mid-18th-century wars, including the War of Austrian Succession and the Seven Years' War. He led expeditions to the East Indies 1748–50 and served as lord of the Admiralty from 1751, vice admiral from 1755, and admiral from 1758. To his men he was known as 'Old Dreadnought'.

Bosch Carl (1874–1940). German metallurgist and chemist. He developed the Haber process from a small-scale technique for the production of ammonia into an industrial high-pressure process that made use of water gas as a source of hydrogen. He shared the Nobel Prize for Chemistry 1931 with Friedrich Bergius. From 1925 Bosch was chair of the vast industrial conglomerate IG Farbenindustrie AG after its formation from the merger of BASF with other German industrial concerns.

Bosch Hieronymus (Jerome) (*c.* 1460–1516). Early Dutch painter. His fantastic visions of weird and hellish creatures, as shown in *The Garden of Earthly Delights c.* 1505–10 (Prado, Madrid), show astonishing imagination and a complex imagery. His religious subjects focused not on the holy figures but on the mass of ordinary witnesses, placing the religious event in a contemporary Dutch context and creating cruel caricatures of human sinfulness.

Bosch is named after his birthplace, 's-Hertogenbosch, in North Brabant, the Netherlands. His work, which influenced Brueghel the Elder and foreshadowed Surrealism, was probably inspired by a local religious brotherhood. However, he was an orthodox Catholic and a prosperous painter, not a heretic, as was once believed. After his death, his work was collected by Philip II of Spain.

Suggested reading
Bosing, Walter *Hieronymus Bosch: Between Heaven and Hell* (trs 1973)
Combe, Jacques *Hieronimus Bosch* (1946)
Gibson, Walter *Hieronymous Bosch* (1985)
Harris, L *The Secret Heresy of Hieronymus Bosch* (1995)

It seems as though you just / saw all infernal spectres fly close around your ears.

Lampsonius on HIERONYMUS BOSCH
quoted in Karel van Mander *The Lives of the Illustrious Netherlandish and German Painters* 1603–04

Bosch (Gavino) Juan (1909–). President of the Dominican Republic 1963. His left-wing Partido Revolucionario Dominicano won a landslide victory in the 1962 elections. In office, he attempted agrarian reform and labour legislation. He was opposed by the USA, and overthrown by the army. His achievement was to establish a democratic political party after three decades of dictatorship.

Boscovich Ruggero Giuseppe (1711–1787). Croatian-born Italian scientist. An early supporter of Newton, he developed a theory, popular in the 19th century, of the atom as a single point with surrounding fields of repulsive and attractive forces.

Bose Jagadis Chunder (1858–1937). Indian physicist and plant physiologist. He was professor of physical science at Calcutta 1885–1915, and studied the growth and minute movements of plants and their reaction to electrical stimuli. He founded the Bose Research Institute, Calcutta. Knighted 1917.

Bose Satyendra Nath (1894–1974). Indian physicist who formulated the Bose–Einstein law of quantum theory with Einstein. He was professor of physics at the University of Calcutta 1945–58. The boson particle is named after him.

Bose Subhas Chandra (1897–1945). Indian nationalist politician, president of the Indian Congress Party. During World War II, he recruited Indian prisoners of war to fight the British in his Indian National Army (INA).

He left India 1941 to go to Germany in an attempt to recruit prisoners of war to the INA. A similar drive in Japan 1943 gained only a small number of recruits and the INA was ineffectual as a fighting force, most of its members defecting to the British as soon as the opportunity occurred. Bose was killed while flying to Japan for a further recruiting drive 1945.

Bossuet Jacques Bénigne (1627–1704). French Roman Catholic priest and theologian. Appointed to the Chapel Royal, Paris 1662, he became known for his funeral orations.

Bossuet was tutor to the young dauphin (crown prince). He became involved in a controversy between Louis XIV and the pope and did his best to effect a compromise. He wrote an 'Exposition de la foi catholique' 1670 and 'Histoire des variations des églises protestantes' 1688.

Boswell James (1740–1795). Scottish biographer and diarist. He was a member of Samuel Johnson's London Literary Club and the two men travelled to Scotland together 1773, as recorded in Boswell's *Journal of the Tour to the Hebrides* 1785. His *Life of Samuel Johnson* was published 1791. Boswell's ability to record Johnson's pithy conversation verbatim makes this a classic of English biography.

Establishing a place in his intimate circle, he became a member of the Literary Club 1773. On his succession to his father's estate 1782, he made further attempts to enter Parliament, was called to the English Bar 1786, and was recorder of Carlisle 1788–90. In 1789 he settled in London.

Suggested reading
Brady, Frank *Boswell: The Later Years, 1769–1795* (1984)
Craik, Roger *James Boswell, 1740–1795: The Scottish Perspective* (1994)
Finlayson, Iain *The Moth and the Candle* (1984)
Hutchinson, Roger *All the Sweets of Life: A Life of James Boswell* (1995)
Pottle, Frederick *James Boswell: The Earlier Years, 1740–69* (1984)

Botero Fernando (1932–). Colombian painter. He studied in Spain and Italy, developing a naive style influenced by South American peasant art, in which, with ironic humour, he depicted fat, doll-like figures, often as parodies of conventional sensuality.

His was the largest, most beautiful, sweetest soul of all my land and days.

Remark by J C Smuts on LOUIS BOTHA
at Botha's graveside 1919

Botha Louis (1862–1919). South African soldier and politician, a commander in the Second South African War (Boer War). In 1907 Botha became premier of the Transvaal and in 1910 of the first Union South African government. On the outbreak of World War I 1914 he rallied South Africa to the Commonwealth, suppressed a Boer revolt, and conquered German South West Africa.

After all, Moses had a mixed marriage.

P W BOTHA
Speech 4 Sept 1980

Botha P(ieter) W(illem) (1916–). South African politician, prime minister from 1978–89. Botha initiated a modification of apartheid, which later slowed in the face of Afrikaner (Boer) opposition. In 1984 he became the first executive state president. In 1989 he unwillingly resigned both party leadership and presidency after suffering a stroke, and was succeeded by F W de Klerk.

Botham Ian Terence (1955–). English cricketer whose Test record places him among the world's greatest all-rounders. He has played county cricket for Somerset, Worcestershire, and Durham, as well as playing in Australia. He played for England 1977–89 and returned to the England side 1991.

Botham made his Somerset debut 1974 and first played for England against Australia at Trent Bridge 1977; he took five wickets for 74 runs in Australia's first innings. In 1987 he moved from Somerset to Worcestershire and helped them to win the Refuge Assurance League in his first season.

Botham also played Football League soccer for Scunthorpe United 1979–84. He raised money for leukaemia research with much-publicized walks from John o'Groats to Land's End in the UK, and Hannibal-style across the Alps.

Bothe Walther Wilhelm Georg (1891–1957). German physicist who showed 1929 that the cosmic rays bombarding the Earth are composed not of photons but of more massive particles. Nobel Prize for Physics 1954.

Bothwell James Hepburn, 4th Earl of Bothwell and Duke of Orkney and Shetland (*c.* 1536–1578). Scottish nobleman, third husband of Mary Queen of Scots, 1567–70, alleged to have arranged the explosion that killed Darnley, her previous husband, 1567.

Tried and acquitted a few weeks after the assassination, he abducted Mary and married her on 15 May. A revolt ensued, and Bothwell was forced to flee. In 1570 Mary obtained a divorce, and

Bothwell was confined in a castle in the Netherlands where he died insane. Succeeded as earl 1556. Duke 1567.

[He had a] natural predilection for lawless violence ... cool, resolute determination characterized his every step.

J G Alger on JAMES HEPBURN, 4TH EARL OF BOTHWELL
in Dictionary of National Biography

Botta Mario (1943–   ). Swiss architect. Most of his work is in Ticino (the Italian canton of Switzerland). A key figure of the Ticino school, his work shows a strong regionalist interpretation of modern architecture, close attention to topography, and a very formal geometry. These aspects are expressed in a striking series of single-family houses, including Riva San Vitale 1972–73 and Ligometto 1975–76.

Between architecture and environment a real exchange takes place, which is reciprocal and continuous.

MARIO BOTTA
quoted in Muriel Emanuel (ed) Contemporary Architects 1994

Botticelli Sandro (born Alessandro Filipepi) (1445–1510). Florentine painter. He depicted religious and mythological subjects. He was patronized by the ruling Medici family and was deeply influenced by their Neo-Platonic circle. It was for the Medicis that he painted *Primavera* 1478 and *The Birth of Venus c.* 1482–84. From the 1490s he was influenced by the religious fanatic Savonarola, and developed a harshly expressive and emotional style, as seen in his *Mystic Nativity* 1500.

His work for the Medicis was designed to cater to the educated classical tastes of the day. As well as his sentimental and beautiful young Madonnas, he produced a series of inventive compositions, including *tondi* (circular paintings) and illustrations for Dante's *Divine Comedy*. He broke with the Medicis after their execution of Savonarola.

A change is perceptible in his work from about 1490, a religious disquiet almost certainly produced or intensified by the influence of the religious reformer Savonarola. He seems to have consigned a number of his pagan subjects to the reformer's bonfire, and the triumph of religious enthusiasm over the sensuousness of the Renaissance can subsequently be traced in his work. He made his series of illustrations for Dante's *Inferno* between 1492 and 1497, *The Calumny of Apelles* 1495, being his last secular masterpiece. The year 1498, in which Savonarola was put to death, saw the production of his passionate *Pietà*, and in the great *Nativity* of 1500 he returned to the medieval spirit and conception. His last works express melancholy and suffering with dramatic intensity, as in the *Crucifixion* and the four scenes from the life of St Zenobius.

In composition and detail he shows an unrivalled poetic invention. The delicacy of his art (which imitators at various periods have vainly tried to recapture) is accompanied by a dynamic linear energy and dramatic power.

Suggested reading
Ettlinger, L D and H *Botticelli* (1977)
Horne, H *Botticelli: Painter of Florence* (1980)
Lightbrown, R *Sandro Botticelli* (1978)
Santi, B *Botticelli* (1981)

Botticelli, a most excellent painter ... His works have a virile air ... and perfect proportion.

BOTTICELLI
15th century document without signature or
date quoted in H P Horne Botticelli 1908

Bottomley Virginia Hilda Brunette Maxwell (1948–   ). British Conservative politician, National Heritage secretary from 1995. She was health secretary 1992–95, during which period she oversaw a radical restructuring of, and cutbacks in, the National Health Service in the name of increased efficiency and competitiveness.

Before entering Parliament she was a magistrate and psychiatric social worker. She became a member of Parliament for Surrey Southwest 1984. As an MP she became parliamentary private secretary to Chris Patten, then to Geoffrey Howe, and was made a junior environment minister 1988. Her husband, Peter Bottomley (1944–   ), is Conservative MP for Eltham.

Boucher François (1703–1770). French Rococo painter. Court painter to Louis XV from 1765, he was much patronized for his light-hearted, decorative scenes which often convey a playful eroticism, as in *Diana Bathing* 1742 (Louvre, Paris).

Stemming from Watteau, and perhaps owing something to his Italian contemporary Tiepolo, his art is the triumph of the Rococo style in France, his frivolous mythologies and artificial pastorals being skilfully planned in relation to the Louis Quinze interior and expressing the spirit of the age in terms of decoration. Criticized by Diderot and others since for a lack of seriousness, he was capable of figure painting (like that of Louis XV's mistress, Louise O'Murphy) of a quality that aroused the admiration of Renoir. Fragonard was among his many pupils.

Boucher de Crèvecoeur de Perthes Jacques (1788–1868). French geologist whose discovery of palaeolithic hand axes 1837 challenged the accepted view of human history dating only from 4004 BC, as proclaimed by the calculations of Bishop James Ussher.

Boucicault Dion(ysus) Larner (1822–1890). Irish dramatist and actor. His first success was with the social comedy *London Assurance* 1841, and during his long career he wrote or adapted about 200 plays, many of them melodramas, including *The Corsican Brothers* 1852 and *Louis XI* 1855. He moved to the USA 1872 where *The Poor of New York* 1857, *The Octoroon* 1859, and *The Colleen Bawn* 1860 had been produced.

Boudicca (died AD 61). Queen of the Iceni (native Britons), often referred to by the Latin form Boadicea. Her husband, King Prasutagus, had been a tributary of the Romans, but on his death AD 60 the territory of the Iceni was violently annexed. Boudicca was scourged and her daughters raped. Boudicca raised the whole of SE England in revolt, and before the main Roman armies could return from campaigning in Wales she burned Londinium (London), Verulamium (St Albans), and Camulodunum (Colchester). Later the Romans under governor Suetonius Paulinus defeated the British between London and Chester; they were virtually annihilated and Boudicca poisoned herself.
Suggested reading
Dudley, D R and Webster, G *The Rebellion of Boudicca* (1962)
Webster, G *Boudicca: The British Revolt Against Rome* (1978)

The sun drenched beaches and the ... skies ... the joy of painting them in the sea breezes.

EUGÈNE BOUDIN
Letter to M Martin 14 June 1869

Boudin (Louis) Eugène (1824–1898). French artist. A forerunner of the Impressionists, he is known for his luminous seaside scenes painted in the open air, such as *Harbour of Trouville* (National Gallery, London).

Bougainville Louis Antoine de (1729–1811). French navigator. After service with the French in Canada during the Seven Years' War, he made the first French circumnavigation of the world 1766–69 and the first systematic observations of longitude.

Several Pacific islands are named after him, as is the climbing plant bougainvillea.

Bouguereau Adolphe William (1825–1905). French academic painter. His subjects were historical and mythological. He was respected in his day, though not by the Impressionists for whom he was the embodiment of insipid middle-class taste.

Boulanger Georges Ernest Jean Marie (1837–1891). French general. He became minister of war 1886, and his anti-German speeches nearly provoked war with Germany 1887. In 1889 he was suspected of aspiring to dictatorship by a coup d'état. Accused of treason, he fled into exile and committed suicide on the grave of his mistress.

Boulanger Lili (Juliette Marie Olga) (1893–1918). French composer. She was the younger sister of Nadia Boulanger. At the age of 19, she won the Prix de Rome with the cantata *Faust et Hélène* for voices and orchestra.

Boulanger Nadia Juliette (1887–1979). French music teacher and conductor. A pupil of Fauré, and admirer of Stravinsky, she included among her composition pupils at the American Conservatory in Fontainebleau, France, (from 1921) Aaron Copland, Roy Harris, Walter Piston, and Philip Glass.

She was the first woman to conduct the Royal Philharmonic, London, 1937, and the Boston Symphony, the New York Philharmonic, and the Philadelphia Orchestra 1938.

Boulestin Marcel (1878–1943). French cookery writer and restaurateur. He spread the principles of simple but high-quality French cooking in Britain in the first half of the 20th century, with a succession of popular books such as *What Shall We Have Today?* 1931.

Boulez Pierre (1925–). French composer and conductor. He is the founder and director of IRCAM, a music research studio in Paris opened 1977. His music, strictly serial and expressionistic in style, includes the cantatas *Le Visage Nuptial* 1946–52 and *Le Marteau Sans Maître* 1955, both to texts by René Char; *Pli Selon Pli* 1962 for soprano and orchestra; and *Répons* 1981 for soloists, orchestra, tapes, and computer-generated sounds.

Symmetry, regularity and variety. All three combine to produce harmony and proportion.

ETIENNE-LOUIS BOULLÉE
Architecture. Essai sur l'Art 1790 published 1953

Boullée Etienne-Louis (1728–1799). French Neo-Classical architect. Although he built very little, he was a major influence on the architecture of his day, and his austere, visionary works have influenced late 20th-century architects such as the Italian Aldo Rossi. Boullée's abstract, geometric style is exemplified in his design for a spherical monument to the scientist Isaac Newton, 150 m/500 ft high.

Boult Adrian Cedric (1889–1983). English conductor. He conducted the BBC Symphony Orchestra 1930–50 and the London Philharmonic 1950–57. He promoted the work of Holst and Vaughan Williams, and was a celebrated interpreter of Elgar. Knighted 1937.

Boulting John Edward (1913–1985) and Roy (1913–) English director–producer team that was successful in the years following World War II. Their films include *Brighton Rock* 1947, *Lucky Jim* 1957, and *I'm All Right Jack* 1959. They were twins.

I sell here, Sir, what all the world desire to have – POWER.

MATTHEW BOULTON
to James Boswell, of his engineering works 1776

Boulton Matthew (1728–1809). English factory owner who helped to finance James Watt's development of the steam engine.

Boulton had an engineering works near Birmingham. He went into partnership with Watt 1775 to develop engines to power factory machines that had previously been driven by water. Boulton's machines for the Royal Mint continued in efficient operation until 1882.

Boulez *Composer and conductor Pierre Boulez. Working first as a mathematician and then as a composer, Boulez has been at the leading edge of musical developments since World War II. His uncompromising brand of modernism has ignored current populist trends. Since the 1970s he has also been influential as a conductor of 20th-century music.*

Boumédienne Houari. Adopted name of Mohammed Boukharouba (1925–1978). Algerian politician who brought the nationalist leader Ben Bella to power by a revolt 1962 and superseded him as president in 1965 by a further coup.

Bourbon Charles, 8th Duke of (1490–1527). Constable of France, honoured for his courage at the Battle of Marignano 1515. Later he served the Holy Roman Emperor Charles V, and helped to drive the French from Italy. In 1526 he was made duke of Milan, and in 1527 allowed his troops to sack Rome. He was killed by a shot the artist Cellini claimed to have fired.

Bourbon dynasty French royal house (succeeding that of Valois), beginning with Henry IV and ending with Louis XVI, with a brief revival under Louis XVIII, Charles X, and Louis Philippe. The Bourbons also ruled Spain almost uninterruptedly from Philip V to Alfonso XIII and were restored in 1975 (Juan Carlos); at one point they also ruled Naples and several Italian duchies. The Grand Duke of Luxembourg is also a Bourbon by male descent.

Bourdon Eugène (1808–1884). French engineer and instrument-maker who 1849 invented the pressure gauge that bears his name. The Bourdon gauge contains a C-shaped tube, closed at one end. When the pressure inside the tube increases, the tube uncurls slightly, causing a small movement at its closed end. A system of levers and gears magnifies this movement and turns a pointer, which indicates the pressure on a circular scale.

Bourgeois Léon Victor Auguste (1851–1925). French politician. Entering politics as a Radical, he was prime minister in 1895, and later served in many cabinets. One of the pioneer advocates of the League of Nations, he was awarded the Nobel Peace Prize 1920.

Bourguiba Habib ben Ali (1903–). Tunisian politician, first president of Tunisia 1957–87. He became prime minister 1956, president (for life from 1974) and prime minister of the Tunisian republic 1957; he was overthrown in a bloodless coup 1987.

Bourguiba was the youngest of seven children and was educated at the University of Paris. He became a journalist and leader of the nationalist Néo-Destour party. Due to his nationalist aspirations, he was imprisoned by the French protectorate of Tunisia 1934–36, 1938–43, and 1952–55. Although he was an autocrat, his rule as president was both moderate and progressive.

Bourke-White Margaret (1906–1971). US photographer. As an editor of *Fortune* magazine 1929–33, she travelled extensively in the USSR, publishing several collections of photographs. Later, with husband Erskine Caldwell, she also published photo collections of American and European subjects. She began working for *Life* magazine 1936, covered combat in World War II, and documented India's struggle for independence.

Bournonville August (1805–1879). Danish dancer and choreographer. In 1830 he was appointed director of the Royal Danish Ballet, the company for which he both danced and created his ballets. His works, unlike that of the then prevalent Romantic era, are ebullient, warmly good-humoured, and give equal importance to both male and female dancers. His style is marked by swift, fluid footwork accompanied by patterns of arcing leaps. His works, of which only a dozen survive, include a version of *La Sylphide* 1836 and *Napoli* 1842.

Boutros-Ghali Boutros (1922–). Egyptian diplomat and politician, deputy prime minister 1991–92, secretary general of the United Nations (UN) from 1992. He worked towards peace in the Middle East in the foreign ministry posts he held 1977–91. Since taking office at the UN he has encountered a succession of challenges regarding the organization's role in conflict areas such as Bosnia-Herzegovina, Somalia, Haiti, and Rwanda, with which he has dealt with varying success.

Bouts Dirk (Dierick) (*c.* 1420–1475). Early Dutch painter. Born in Haarlem, he settled in Louvain, painting portraits and religious scenes influenced by Rogier van der Weyden and Petrus Christus. *The Last Supper* 1464–68 (St Pierre, Louvain) is one of his finest works.

Boveri Theodor Heinrich (1862–1915). German biologist who showed that it is not a specific number but a specific assortment of chromosomes that is responsible for normal development, indicating that individual chromosomes possess different qualities. In 1914, he theorized that tumours may become malignant as the result of abnormal chromosome numbers, and was the first to view the tumour as a cell problem.

Bovet Daniel (1907–1992). Swiss physiologist. He pioneered research into antihistamine drugs used in the treatment of nettle rash and hay fever, and was awarded the Nobel Prize for Physiology or Medicine 1957 for his production of a synthetic form of curare, used as a muscle relaxant in anaesthesia.

Bow Clara (1905–1965). US film actress. She was known as a 'Jazz Baby' and the 'It Girl' after her portrayal of a glamorous flapper in the silent film *It* 1927.

She made a smooth transition to sound with *The Wild Party* 1929. Other films include *Down to the Sea in Ships* 1925; *The Plastic Age*, *Kid Boots*, *Mantrap*, and *Dancing Mothers*, all 1926; *Rough House Rosie* 1927; *Red Hair* and *Three Weekends*, both 1928; and *The Saturday Night Kid* 1929. She made her last film *Hoopla* 1933 and retired to her husband's ranch in Nevada.

Bowden Frank Philip (1903–1968). Australian physicist and chemist who worked mainly in Britain. He studied friction, lubricants, and surface erosion. For example, he realized that the thin layer of water between a ski or an ice skate and the snow or ice is produced not by pressure due to the weight on them but by friction-induced heat caused by irregularities in the sliding surfaces. His war research covered a broad range of areas of military significance: machine and tool lubricants, flame-throwing fuels, the accurate measurement of shell velocities for gun calibration, and the casting of aircraft bearings.

Bowditch Nathaniel (1773–1838). US astronomer. He wrote *The New American Practical Navigator* 1802, having discovered many inaccuracies in the standard navigation guide of the day. *Celestial Mechanics* 1829–39 was his translation of the first four volumes of French astronomer Pierre Laplace's *Traité de mécanique céleste* 1799–1825.

Bowdler Thomas (1754–1825). English editor. His prudishly expurgated versions of Shakespeare and other authors gave rise to the verb bowdlerize.

Bowdoin James (1726–1790). American public official. A supporter of American independence, he was elected to the Massachusetts General Court 1753, chosen as a member of the Governor's Council 1757, and served on the Massachusetts Executive Council 1775–76. He was president of the state constitutional convention 1779–80 and governor 1785–87.

Bowen Elizabeth Dorothea Cole (1899–1973). Irish novelist. She published her first volume of short stories, *Encounters*, 1923. Her novels include *The Death of the Heart* 1938, *The Heat of the Day* 1949, and *The Little Girls* 1964.

Bowen Ira Sprague (1898–1973). US astrophysicist who studied the spectra of planetary nebulae. He showed that strong green lines in such spectra are due to ionized oxygen and nitrogen under extreme conditions not found on Earth. He was director of the Mount Wilson and Palomar Observatories 1946–64.

Bowen Norman Levi (1887–1956). Canadian geologist whose work helped found modern petrology. He demonstrated the principles governing the formation of magma by partial melting, and the fractional crystallization of magma.

The idea was to concoct surrealist or minimalist stage pieces to accompany rock-and-roll songs.

DAVID BOWIE
on his performance *New York Times* 2 Aug 1987

Bowie David. Stage name of David Robert Jones (1947–). English pop singer, songwriter, and actor. His career has been a series of image changes. His hits include 'Jean Genie' 1973, 'Rebel, Rebel' 1974, 'Golden Years' 1975, and 'Underground' 1986. He has acted in plays and films, including Nicolas Roeg's *The Man Who Fell to Earth* 1976.

Bowie's first hit was 'Space Oddity' 1969. He became a glam-rock star with the album *The Rise and Fall of Ziggy Stardust and the Spiders from Mars* 1972 but shed the Ziggy persona the next year. Much of his best work has been created in collaboration, such as the 1975 hit 'Fame' written with John Lennon, the 1985 duet with Mick Jagger on 'Dancing in the Street', songwriting with Iggy Pop, and production. Bowie's albums include *Aladdin Sane* 1973, *Station to Station* 1976, *Low* 1977, *Heroes* 1977, *Lodger* 1979, *Let's Dance* 1983, and *Black Tie/White Noise* 1993. In 1989 he formed the hard-rock band Tin Machine.

Bowie Jim (James) (1796–1836). US frontiersman and folk hero. A colonel in the Texan forces during the Mexican War, he is said to have invented the single-edge, guarded hunting and throwing knife known as a Bowie knife. He was killed in the battle of the Alamo.

Bowlby (Edward) John (Mostyn) (1907–1990). English psychologist and author of *Child Care and the Growth of Love* 1953, in which he argued that a home environment for children is preferable to an institution, and stressed the bond between mother and child. He was consultant in mental health for the World Health Organization 1972–90.

Bowles Paul Frederick (1910–). US writer and composer. Born in New York City, he studied music composition with Aaron Copland and Virgil Thomson, writing scores for ballets, films, and an opera, *The Wind Remains* 1943, as well as incidental music for plays. He settled in Morocco, the setting of his novels *The Sheltering*

Sky 1949 (filmed 1990) and *Let It Come Down* 1952, which chillingly depict the existential breakdown of Westerners unable to survive self-exposure in an alien culture. Other works include *A Thousand Days for Mokhtar* 1989 and *Too Far from Home* 1994. His autobiography, *Without Stopping*, was published 1972.

Bowles settled permanently in Tangier with his wife, the writer Jane Bowles (1917–1973), after World War II and became greatly influenced by Moroccan storytelling – he later turned to transcribing and translating tales by Mohammed Mrabet and others.

Small, with blonde hair and an olive complexion, she was saved from prettiness by the intensity of her gaze.

PAUL BOWLES
The Sheltering Sky, bk 1, ll 1949

Boyce William (1710–1779). English composer and organist. He was one of the most respected English composers of his time. He wrote church music, symphonies, and chamber music, but is best known for his song 'Heart of Oak' 1759. Much of his music exhibits a fresh liveliness, particularly his many dance movements.

Boycott Charles Cunningham (1832–1897). English land agent in County Mayo, Ireland, who strongly opposed the demands for agrarian reform by the Irish Land League 1879–81, with the result that the peasants refused to work for him; hence the word boycott.

Boycott Geoffrey (1940–). English cricketer born in Yorkshire, England's most prolific run-maker with 8,114 runs in Test cricket until overtaken by David Gower in 1992. He was banned as a Test player in 1982 for taking part in matches against South Africa.

Bowie, David A pop star with a frequently changing image, David Bowie is particularly associated with the glam-rock period of the 1970s. While producing albums in a variety of musical styles, he has also appeared on Broadway in The Elephant Man 1980 and in a number of films, including The Man Who Fell to Earth 1976, from which this still is taken.

He played in 108 Test matches and in 1981 overtook Gary Sobers' world record total of Test runs. Twice, in 1971 and 1979, his average was over 100 runs in an English season. He was released by Yorkshire after a dispute in 1986.

Boyd Arthur Merric Bloomfield (1920–). Australian painter, sculptor, and potter. His work is broadly Expressionist, and often deals with social themes. He established his international reputation with an exhibition held in London 1960. His paintings include *Wimmera Landscape* 1950 and *The Blind Nebuchadnezzar with a Lion* 1967; he is also known for the ceramic sculpture at the Melbourne Olympic Swimming Pool, 1955.
Suggested reading
Framz, Phillip *Arthur Boyd* (1967)

Boyd Orr John Boyd, 1st Baron Boyd Orr (1880–1971). British nutritionist and health campaigner. He was awarded the Nobel Prize for Peace in 1949 in recognition of his work towards alleviating world hunger. Knighted 1939, baron 1945.

Boyer Charles (1899–1978). French film actor. He made his name in Hollywood in the 1930s as the 'great lover' in such films as *The Garden of Allah* 1936 and *Conquest/Maria Walewska* 1937, in which he played Napoleon. Later films include *Love Affair* 1939 and *Gaslight* 1942. He continued as a leading man into the 1950s.

Boyle Charles, 4th Earl of Orrery (1676–1731). Irish soldier and diplomat. The orrery, a mechanical model of the Solar System in which the planets move at the correct relative velocities, is named after him. Succeeded to earldom 1703.

Boyle Robert (1627–1691). Irish chemist and physicist who published the seminal *The Sceptical Chymist* 1661. He formulated Boyle's law 1662 which states that the volume of a given mass of gas at a constant temperature is inversely proportional to its pressure. He was a pioneer in the use of experiment and scientific method.

Boyle questioned the alchemical basis of the chemical theory of his day and taught that the proper object of chemistry was to determine the compositions of substances. The term 'analysis' was coined by Boyle and many of the reactions still used in qualitative work were known to him. He introduced certain plant extracts, notably litmus, for the indication of acids and bases. He was also the first chemist to collect a sample of gas.

Boys Charles Vernon (1855–1944). English inventor and physicist who designed several scientific instruments, including a very sensitive torsion balance used 1895 to determine Isaac Newton's gravitational constant and the mean density of the Earth. Boys' other work included the invention of a 'radio-micrometer' 1890 to measure the heat radiated by the planets in the Solar System. He also developed a special camera to record fast-moving objects such as bullets and lightning flashes, and devised a calorimeter which became the standard instrument used to measure the calorific value of fuel gas in Britain. In addition, he performed a series of experiments on soap bubbles, which increased knowledge of surface tension and of the properties of thin films. Knighted 1935.

Bo Zhu Yi or Po Chü-i (772–846). Chinese poet. President from 841 of the imperial war department, he criticized government policy and wrote poems dealing with the social problems of his age. He is said to have checked his work with an old peasant woman for clarity of expression.

Bracegirdle Anne (*c.* 1663–1748). English actress. She was the mistress of William Congreve, and possibly his wife; she played Millamant in his *The Way of the World*.

Bracton Henry de (died 1268). English judge, writer on English law, and chancellor of Exeter cathedral from 1264. The account of the laws and customs of the English attributed to Henry de Bracton, *De Legibus et consuetudinibus Anglie/The Laws and Customs of England*, the first of its kind, was not in fact written by him.

Bradbury Malcolm Stanley (1932–). English novelist and critic. His writings include comic and satiric portrayals of academic life. He became professor of American studies at the University of East

Anglia 1970, and his major work is *The History Man* 1975, set in a provincial English university. Other works include *Rates of Exchange* 1983 and *Dr Criminale* 1992.

Marriage is the most advanced form of warfare in the modern world.

MALCOLM BRADBURY
The History Man 1975

Bradbury Ray(mond Douglas) (1920–). US author. He is best known as a writer of science fiction, a genre he helped make 'respectable' to a wider readership. His work shows nostalgia for small-town Midwestern life, and includes *The Martian Chronicles* 1950, *Fahrenheit 451* 1953, *R is for Rocket, S is for Space* 1962, *Something Wicked This Way Comes* 1962, and *Yestermorrow* 1991. Some of his short stories are collected in *The Stories of Ray Bradbury* 1980. He also has written several volumes of poetry, television and motion-picture screenplays, radio dramas, and children's stories.

Bradfield John Job Crew (1867–1943). Australian civil engineer best known for his work as supervising engineer on the Sydney Harbour Bridge and its approaches. The Bradfield Plan, a water conservation scheme devised by him but never carried out, involved damming the Burdekin and other northern Queensland rivers on the coastal side of the Great Dividing Range and transporting the water to dry inland areas by tunnel.

Bradford William (1590–1657). British colonial administrator in America, the first governor of Plymouth colony, Massachusetts, 1621–57. As one of the Pilgrim Fathers, he sailed for America aboard the *Mayflower* 1620 and was among the signatories of the Mayflower Compact, the first written constitution in the New World. His memoirs, *History of Plimoth Plantation*, are an important source for the colony's early history.

The member for India.

CHARLES BRADLAUGH's nickname as an MP because of his deep interest in the social and political condition of the Indian natives.

Bradlaugh Charles (1833–1891). British freethinker and radical politician. In 1880 he was elected Liberal member of Parliament for Northampton, but was not allowed to take his seat until 1886 because, as an atheist, he (unsuccessfully) claimed the right to affirm instead of taking the oath. He was associated with the feminist Annie Besant.

He served in the army, was a lawyer's clerk, became well known as a speaker and journalist under the name of Iconoclast, and from 1860 ran the *National Reformer*. He advocated the freedom of the press, contraception, and other social reforms.

Bradley A(ndrew) C(ecil) (1851–1935). English literary critic and scholar. His study of the plays *Hamlet*, *King Lear*, *Othello*, and *Macbeth* in *Shakespearean Tragedy* 1904 looked at the plays in terms of their major characters. His *Oxford Lectures on Poetry* 1909 were delivered while he was professor of poetry at Oxford 1901–06.

Bradley Francis Herbert (1846–1924). British philosopher who argued for absolute idealism – the theory, influenced by German philosopher G W F Hegel, that there is only one ultimately real thing, the Absolute, which is spiritual in nature. In ethics he attacked the utilitarianism of J S Mill. Bradley's works include *Ethical Studies* 1876, *Principles of Logic* 1883, *Appearance and Reality* 1893, and *Truth and Reality* 1914.

Bradley James (1693–1762). English astronomer who in 1728 discovered the aberration of starlight. From the amount of aberration in star positions, he was able to calculate the speed of light. As Astronomer Royal from 1742 he sought to modernize the observatory in Greenwich, and embarked on an extensive programme of stellar observation. In 1748, he announced the discovery of nutation (variation in the Earth's axial tilt).

Brady The most prolific US photographer of the 19th century, Mathew Brady left an invaluable record of the period. He is known in particular for his portraits of famous men and women (including 18 presidents), and his many images of the American Civil War.

Bradley Omar Nelson (1893–1981). US general in World War II. In 1943 he commanded the 2nd US Corps in their victories in Tunisia and Sicily, leading to the surrender of 250,000 Axis troops, and in 1944 led the US troops in the invasion of France. His command, as the 12th Army Group, grew to 1.3 million troops, the largest US force ever assembled.

He was Chief of Staff of the US Army 1948–49 and chair of the joint Chiefs of Staff 1949–53. He was appointed general of the army 1950.

In war there is no second prize for the runner up.

OMAR BRADLEY
Military Review, Sept 1951

Bradley Scott (1914–). US composer of animation film music. Working for the US film-production company Metro-Goldwyn-Mayer (MGM), with Carl Stalling he developed the click-track which enables a composer to write a music track to any desired tempo for a given length of film. He also introduced classical music to *Tom and Jerry* cartoons, arranging Liszt's *Hungarian Rhapsody No 2* for *Cat Concerto* 1947, and in *The Cat that Hated People* using a twelve-tone row on piccolo to represent Jerry and the same row in reverse played by oboe to represent Tom.

Bradman Don(ald) George (1908–). Australian Test cricketer with the highest average in Test history. From 52 Test matches he averaged 99.94 runs per innings. He only needed four runs from his final Test innings to average 100 but was dismissed second ball. Knighted 1949.

Bradman was born in Bowral, New South Wales, came to prominence at an early age, and made his Test debut in 1928. He played for Australia for 20 years and was captain 1936–48.

He twice scored triple centuries against England and in 1930 scored 452 not out for New South Wales against Queensland, the highest first-class innings until 1959. In 1989 a Bradman Museum was opened in his home town.

Suggested reading
Bradman, Donald *Farewell to Cricket* (autobiography) (1950)
Docker, E *Bradman and the Bodyline Series* (1978)
Page, Michael *Bradman: The Illustrated History* (1983)
Pollard, J *Bradman Years: Australian Cricket 1918–48* (1988)

The game of cricket existed long before I was born. It will be played centuries after my demise. During my career I was privileged to give the public my interpretation of its character in the same way that a pianist might interpret the works of Beethoven.

DON BRADMAN
Farewell to Cricket 1950

Bradshaw George (1801–1853). British publisher who brought out the first railway timetable in 1839. Thereafter *Bradshaw's Railway Companion* appeared at regular intervals.

He was apprenticed to an engraver on leaving school, and set up his own printing and engraving business in the 1820s, beginning in 1827 with an engraved map of Lancashire.

Brady Mathew B (*c.* 1823–1896). US photographer. Famed for his skill in photographic portraiture, he published *The Gallery of Illustrious Americans* 1850. With the outbreak of the US Civil War 1861, Brady and his staff became the foremost photographers of battle scenes and military life. Although his war photos were widely reproduced, Brady later suffered a series of financial reverses and died in poverty.

Braganza Royal house of Portugal whose members reigned 1640–1910; another branch were emperors of Brazil 1822–89.

Bragg William Henry (1862–1942). English physicist. In 1915 he shared with his son Lawrence Bragg the Nobel Prize for Physics for their research work on X-rays and crystals. KBE 1920.

The Braggs' work gave a method of determining the positions of atoms in the lattices making up the crystals, and for accurate determination of X-ray wavelengths. This led to an understanding of the ways in which atoms combine with each other and revolutionized mineralogy and later molecular biology, in which X-ray diffraction was crucial to the elucidation of the structure of DNA.

Bragg (William) Lawrence (1890–1971). Australian-born British physicist. In 1915 he shared with his father William Bragg the Nobel Prize for Physics for their research work on X-rays and crystals. Knighted 1941.

Brahe Tycho (1546–1601). Danish astronomer whose accurate observations of the planets enabled German astronomer and mathematician Johannes Kepler to prove that planets orbit the Sun in ellipses. Brahe's discovery and report of the 1572 supernova brought him recognition, and his observations of the comet of 1577 proved that it moved in an orbit among the planets, thus disproving the Greek view that comets were in the Earth's atmosphere. He prepared tables of the motion of the Sun and determined the length of a year to within less than a second, necessitating the calendar reform of 1582.

It is a verbosity which outfaces its commonplaceness by dint of sheer magnitude.

George Bernard Shaw on the music of JOHANNES BRAHMS
The Star, 1892

Bragg, Lawrence *Lawrence Bragg was still at university when, in 1912, he discovered the famous law, describing the condition for X-ray diffraction in crystals, which now bears his name. In 1915, at the age of 25, he became the youngest person ever to be awarded the Nobel Prize for Physics – an award he shared with his father, William. (Ann Ronan/Image Select)*

Brahms Johannes (1833–1897). German composer, pianist, and conductor. Considered one of the greatest composers of symphonic music and of songs, his works include four symphonies, lieder (songs), concertos for piano and for violin, chamber music, sonatas, and the choral *Ein Deutsches Requiem/A German Requiem* 1868. He performed and conducted his own works.

He had suddenly remembered I was a girl, to take whom seriously, was beneath a man's dignity, and the quality of the work, which had I been an obscure male he would have upheld against anyone, simply passed from his mind.

Ethel Smyth on JOHANNES BRAHMS
in *Impressions That Remained*, 1919

In 1853 the violinist Joachim introduced him to Liszt and Schumann, who encouraged his work. From 1868 Brahms made his home in Vienna. Although his music belongs to a reflective strain of Romanticism, similar to Wordsworth in poetry, Brahms saw himself as continuing the classical tradition from the point to which Beethoven had brought it. To his contemporaries, he was a strict formalist, in opposition to the romantic sensuality of Wagner. His influence on Mahler and Schoenberg was profound.

Suggested reading
Geiringer, K *Brahms: His Life and Work* (1981)
Holmes, P *Brahms: His Life and Times* (1984)
James, B *Brahms: A Critical Study* (1972)
Musgrave, M *The Music of Brahms* (1985)

Brain Dennis (1921–1957). English horn player. The greatest virtuoso of his day, he inspired composers including Britten and

Brahms *The composer Brahms (1833–1897), as pictured in 1860. During this early period he fell in love with Clara Schumann, who, along with her husband Robert, gave him the encouragement and support needed to help launch his career. He became the greatest Romantic composer still to adhere to traditional formal models.* (Image Select)

Hindemith to write pieces for him, such as Britten's *Serenade* 1943 for tenor, horn, and strings.

Braine John Gerard (1922–1986). English novelist. His novel *Room at the Top* 1957 created the character of Joe Lampton, one of the first of the northern working-class antiheroes. His other novels include *The Vodi* 1959 and *Life at the Top* 1962.

Braithwaite Eustace Adolphe (1912–). Guyanese author. His experiences as a teacher in London prompted *To Sir With Love* 1959. His *Reluctant Neighbours* 1972 deals with black–white relations.

Braithwaite Richard Bevan (1900–1990). British philosopher, physicist, and mathematician. Although mainly a philosopher of science, he also tried to give an empiricist account of religious belief as a belief in morally uplifting stories and to put moral choice on a rational basis by applying the mathematical theory of games to situations of moral conflict.

He was professor of moral philosophy at Cambridge 1953–67.

Bramah Ernest. Pen name of Ernest Brammah Smith (1868–1942). English short-story writer. He created the characters Kai Lung and Max Carrados, a blind detective.

Bramah Joseph. Adopted name of Joe Brammer (1748–1814). British inventor of a flushing water closet 1778, an 'unpickable' lock 1784, and the hydraulic press 1795. The press made use of Pascal's principle (that pressure in fluid contained in a vessel is evenly distributed) and employed water as the hydraulic fluid; it enabled the 19th-century bridge builders to lift massive girders.

He revived the good architecture which had been buried from the days of the Ancients.

SEBASTIANO SERLIO on DONATO BRAMANTE
in *Books on Architecture* 1537

Bramante Donato (1444–1514). Italian Renaissance architect and artist. Inspired by Classical designs and by the work of Leonardo da Vinci, he was employed by Pope Julius II in rebuilding part of the Vatican and St Peter's in Rome. The circular Tempietto of San Pietro in Montorio, Rome (commissioned 1502; built about 1510), is possibly his most important completed work. Though small in size, this circular collonaded building possesses much of the grandeur of ancient Roman buildings.

I don't go around saying, 'Hello, did you know I'm the new Olivier?'

KENNETH BRANAGH
Newsweek 9 Oct 1989

Branagh Kenneth Charles (1960–). Northern Irish actor, director, and producer. Branagh brought his immense energy to his adaptation of Shakespeare's *Henry V* 1989 to the screen. His other directorial and acting credits include the films *Dead Again* 1991, *Peter's Friends* 1992, *Much Ado About Nothing* 1993, and *Mary Shelley's Frankenstein* 1994. He is married to actress Emma Thompson with whom he frequently co-stars.

He cofounded, with David Parfitt, the Renaissance Theatre Company 1987–1994, and was a notable Hamlet 1988 and 1992, and Touchstone 1988.

Brancusi Constantin (1876–1957). Romanian sculptor. He is a seminal figure in 20th-century art.

Active in Paris from 1904, he was a pioneer of abstract sculpture, developing increasingly simplified representations of natural, or organic, forms, for example the *Sleeping Muse* 1910 (Musée National d'Art Moderne, Paris), a sculpted head that gradually comes to resemble an egg. By the 1930s he had achieved monumental simplicity with structures of simple repeated forms, for example, *Endless Column* and other works commissioned for Tirgu Jiu public park, Romania.

Brand Dollar (Adolf Johannes). Former name of South African jazz musician Abdullah ◊Ibrahim.

Brand Max. Pen name of Frederick Faust (1892–1944). US novelist and poet. Brand was one of the earliest mass-market writers, author of over 500 novels. The majority of these were Westerns, the first of which was *The Untamed* 1918. His most famous Western novel was *Destry Rides Again* 1930, which was made into a film 1939. He was the creator of Dr Kildare, later a popular television series.

Brandeis Louis Dembitz (1856–1941). US jurist. As a crusader for progressive causes, he helped draft social-welfare and labour legislation. In 1916, with his appointment to the US Supreme Court by President Wilson, he became the first Jewish justice and maintained his support of individual rights in his opposition to the 1917 Espionage Act and in his dissenting opinion in the first wiretap case, *Olmstead* v *US* 1928.

Born in Louisville, Kentucky, Brandeis was educated at Harvard and was admitted to the bar 1877. Brandeis University in Waltham, Massachusetts, is named in his honour.

An actor is a guy who, if you aren't talking about him, isn't listening.

MARLON BRANDO
Observer Jan 1956

Brando Marlon (1924–). US actor. His powerful presence, mumbling speech, and use of Method acting earned him a place as a distinctive actor. He won best-actor Academy Awards for *On the Waterfront* 1954 and *The Godfather* 1972.

I coulda been a contender. I coulda had class and been somebody.

MARLON BRANDO
in the film *On the Waterfront* 1954

He made his Broadway debut in *I Remember Mama* 1944, and achieved fame in *A Streetcar Named Desire* 1947. His films include *The Men* 1950, *A Streetcar Named Desire* 1951, *Julius Caesar* 1953, *The Wild One* 1954, *Mutiny on the Bounty* 1962, *Last Tango in Paris* 1973, *Apocalypse Now* 1979, *The Freshman* 1990, and *Don Juan De Marco* 1995.

Brandt Bill (Hermann Wilhelm) (1904–1983). English photographer. During the 1930s he made a series of social records contrasting the lives of the rich and the poor, some of which were presented in his book *The English at Home* 1936. During World War II he documented conditions in London in the Blitz. The strong contrasts in his black-and-white prints often produced a gloomy and threatening atmosphere. His outstanding creative work was his treatment of the nude, published in *Perspective of Nudes* and *Shadows of Light*, both 1966.

> *Only rarely are we able to free ourselves from the burden of our thoughts and emotions and ... see.*
>
> BILL BRANDT
> quoted in Colin Naylor (ed) *Contemporary Photographers* 1988

Brandt Willy. Adopted name of Karl Herbert Frahm (1913–1992). German socialist politician, federal chancellor (premier) of West Germany 1969–74. He played a key role in the remoulding of the Social Democratic Party (SPD) as a moderate socialist force (leader 1964–87). As mayor of West Berlin 1957–66, Brandt became internationally known during the Berlin Wall crisis 1961. He was awarded the Nobel Peace Prize 1971.

In the 'grand coalition' 1966–69, Brandt served as foreign minister and introduced Ostpolitik, a policy of reconciliation between East and West Europe, which was continued when he became federal chancellor 1969 and culminated in the 1972 signing of the Basic Treaty with East Germany. He chaired the Brandt Commission on Third World problems 1977–83 and was a member of the European Parliament 1979–83.

> *Recognized as the outstanding pragmatic social democrat on the Continent.*
>
> Alan Palmer on WILLY BRANDT
> in *Penguin Dictionary of Twentieth Century History* 1979

Brangwyn Frank (François Guillaume) (1867–1956). British artist. He initially worked for William Morris as a textile designer, and subsequently produced furniture, pottery, carpets, schemes for interior decoration and architectural designs, as well as book illustrations, lithographs, and etchings. Knighted 1941.

Branly Edouard Eugène Désiré (1844–1940). French physicist and inventor who in 1890 demonstrated the possibility of detecting radio waves; the apparatus he devised (the coherer) was soon used in the invention of wireless telegraphy and radio.

> *Borrow fivers off everyone you meet.*
>
> RICHARD BRANSON's answer on being asked
> what is the quickest way to become a millionaire

Branson Richard (1950–). British entrepreneur whose Virgin company developed quickly, diversifying from retailing records to the airline business.

He was born in Surrey, England, and the 1968 launch of *Student* magazine proved to be the first of his many successful business ventures.

> *Art is meant to disturb, science reassures.*
>
> GEORGES BRAQUE
> *Pensées sur l'Art*

Braque Georges (1882–1963). French painter. With Picasso, he founded the Cubist movement around 1907–10. His early work was influenced by Fauvism in its use of pure, bright colour, but from 1907 he developed a geometric style and during the next few years he and Picasso worked very closely developing Cubism. It was during this period that he began to experiment with collage and invented the technique of gluing paper, wood, and other materials to canvas. His later work was more decorative but more restrained in its use of colour.

> *I invent nothing, I imagine everything.*
>
> BRASSAÏ
> Remark made 1982 and quoted in Colin
> Naylor (ed) *Contemporary Photographers* 1988

Brassaï adopted name of Gyula Halasz (1899–1984). French photographer of Hungarian origin. He chronicled, mainly by flash, the nightlife of Paris: the prostitutes, street cleaners, and criminals. These pictures were published as *Paris by Night* 1933. Later he turned to more abstract work.

> *The chip frier was ... put there ... for the purpose of improving the composition.*
>
> JOHN BRATBY
> describing his painting *Still Life with Chip Frier 1954* Aug 1956

Bratby John (1928–1992). English painter. He was one of the leading exponents of the 'kitchen sink' school of the 1950s whose work concentrated on working-class domestic life.

Brathwaite Edward Kamau (1930–). West Indian historian and poet. Using calypso and work songs as well as more literary verse forms, he has explored the ways in which the West Indian legacy of slavery has been transcended by the traditions of ritual, music, and dance originating in West Africa, particularly in *Masks* 1968. Other works include *Mother Poem* 1977, *Sun Poem* 1982, and *The Folk Culture of the Slaves of Jamaica* 1970.

Brattain Walter Houser (1902–1987). US physicist. In 1956 he was awarded a Nobel prize jointly with William Shockley and John Bardeen for their work on the development of the transistor, which replaced the comparatively costly and clumsy vacuum tube in electronics.

He was born in Amoy, China, the son of a teacher. From 1929 to 1967 he was on the staff of Bell Telephone Laboratories.

> *The Führer spoke of Brauchitsch only in terms of contempt. A vain, cowardly wretch who could not even appraise the situation, much less master it.*
>
> Goebbels on Hitler's assessment of WALTHER VON BRAUCHITSCH
> in his diary, quoted in Alan Bullock *Hitler* 1962 ed

Brauchitsch (Heinrich Alfred) Walther von (1881–1948). German field marshal. A staff officer in World War I, he became commander in chief of the army and a member of Hitler's secret cabinet council 1938. He resigned after a heart attack and his failure to repel Marshal Zhukov's counterattack outside Moscow 1941. He was captured 1945, but died before he could be tried in the Nuremberg trials.

Braudel (Paul Achille) Fernand (1902–1985). French historian. While in a German prisoner-of-war camp during World War II he wrote *La Mediterranée et le monde mediterranéen à l'époque de Philippe II/ The Mediterranean and the Mediterranean World in the Age of Philip II* 1949, a work which revolutionized the writing of history by taking a global view of long-term trends.

Braudel taught in Algeria and Brazil before returning to France in 1938. He became a professor at the Collège de France 1949–72 and a leading member of the Annales school, editing the journal *Annales d'histoire économique et sociale*. During this period, he published extensively and championed the ideas of using the social sciences and problem-based research as a means of historical enquiry.

Braun Emma Lucy (1889–1971). US botanist, an early pioneer in recognizing the importance of plant ecology and conservation. Her book *Deciduous Forests of Eastern North America* 1950 describes the evolution of forest communities and their survival during periods of glaciation.

She made no pretensions to intellectual gifts or to any understanding of politics. Her interests in life were sport ... animals, the cinema, sex and clothes.

Alan Bullock on EVA BRAUN
in *Hitler* 1962 ed

Braun Eva (1912–1945). German mistress of Adolf Hitler. Secretary to Hitler's photographer and personal friend, Heinrich Hoffmann, she became Hitler's mistress in the 1930s and married him in the air-raid shelter of the Chancellery in Berlin on 29 April 1945. The next day they committed suicide together.

Braun Karl Ferdinand (1850–1918). German physicist who made improvements to Guglielmo Marconi's system of wireless telegraphy; they shared the 1909 Nobel Prize for Physics. Braun also discovered crystal rectifiers (used in early radios), and invented the oscilloscope 1895. Braun's oscilloscope was an adaptation of the cathode-ray tube. A laboratory instrument to study high-frequency alternating currents, it was the forerunner of television and radar display tubes.

Braun Wernher von (1912–1977). German scientist responsible for Germany's rocket development programme in World War II. He was technical director of the army rocket research centre at Peenemunde and designed a number of rockets including the V2. He was taken to the USA with his research team 1945 and became a prominent figure in the NASA space programme.

Brautigan Richard Gary (1935–1984). US novelist. He lived in San Francisco, the setting for many of his playfully inventive and humorous short fictions, often written as deadpan parodies. He became a cult figure in the late 1960s with such works as *A Confederate General from Big Sur* 1964, his best-seller *Trout Fishing in America* 1967, and *In Watermelon Sugar* 1968. His last novels, before committing suicide, were *The Tokyo–Montana Express* 1980 and *So The Wind Won't Blow It All Away* 1982.

Bravo Manuel Alvarez (1902–). Mexican photographer. He was self-taught but received advice from the US photographer Edward Weston. His dark and brooding images convey an essentially tragic vision of his native land.

Breakspear Nicholas. Original name of ◊Adrian IV, the only English pope.

Bream Julian Alexander (1933–). English guitar and lute virtuoso. He has revived much Elizabethan lute music and encouraged composition by contemporaries for both instruments. Benjamin Britten and Hans Henze have written for him.

Breasted James Henry (1865–1935). US Orientalist. Well known as the author of textbooks and popular works on the history of the ancient Near East, Breasted founded the University of Chicago Oriental Institute, funded by John D Rockefeller, as a centre of American archaeological research. He published *A History of Egypt* 1905, and directed the Chicago expedition to Egypt and Sudan 1905–07.

Brecht Bertolt (Eugen Berthold Friedrich) (1898–1956). German dramatist and poet, one of the most influential figures in 20th-century theatre. A committed Marxist, he sought to develop an 'epic theatre' which aimed to destroy the 'suspension of disbelief' usual in the theatre and so encourage audiences to develop an active and critical attitude to a play's subject. He adapted John Gay's *The Beggar's*

Opera as *Die Dreigroschenoper/The Threepenny Opera* 1928, set to music by Kurt Weill. Later plays include *Mutter Courage/Mother Courage* 1941, set during the Thirty Years' War, and *Der kaukasische Kreidekreis/The Caucasian Chalk Circle* 1949. He established the Berliner Ensemble theatre group in East Germany 1949, and in the same year published *A Short Organum for the Theatre*, a concise expression of his theatrical philosophy.

As an anti-Nazi, he left Germany 1933 for Scandinavia and the USA; he became an Austrian citizen after World War II. His other works include *Galileo* 1938, *Der gute Mensch von Setzuan/The Good Woman of Setzuan* 1943, and *Der aufhaltsame Aufstieg des Arturo Ui/The Preventable Rise of Arturo Ui* 1958.

Food comes first, then morals.

BERTOLT BRECHT
Dreigroschenoper/Threepenny Opera 1928

Bredig Georg (1868–1944). German physical chemist who devised a method of preparing colloidal solutions 1898. He studied the catalytic action of colloidal platinum and the 'poisoning' of catalysts by impurities.

Breker Arno (1900–1991). German Neo-Classical sculptor who created several pieces on commission for the Nazi regime. After World War II much of his work was destroyed.

Brel Jacques (1929–1978). Belgian singer and songwriter. He was active in France from 1953, where his fatalistic ballads made him a star. Of his more than 400 songs, many have been recorded in translation by singers as diverse as Frank Sinatra and David Bowie. 'Ne me quitte pas/If You Go Away' 1964 is one of his best-known songs.

Brel worked in the *chansonnier* (singer-songwriter) tradition, often with orchestral arrangements. He also appeared in films. Other Brel songs are 'Marieke' 1964, 'Les Moribonds/Seasons in the Sun', 'La Colombe', 'Jackie', and 'Amsterdam'. The album *Brel* 1977 was his last work.

Brendel Alfred (1931–). Austrian pianist. He is known for his fastidious and searching interpretations of Beethoven, Schubert, and Liszt. He is the author of *Musical Thoughts and Afterthoughts* 1976 and *Music Sounded Out* 1990. Honorary KBE 1989.

Brennan Christopher John (1870–1932). Australian Symbolist poet. He was influenced by Baudelaire and Mallarmé. Although one of Australia's greatest poets, he is virtually unknown outside his native country. His complex, idiosyncratic verse includes *Poems* 1914 and *A Chant of Doom and Other Verses* 1918.
Suggested reading
Clark, Axel *Christopher John Brennan* (1980)

Brennan Walter (1894–1974). US actor. He is often seen in Westerns as the hero's sidekick, although he was a versatile performer. His work includes *The Westerner* 1940, *Bad Day at Black Rock* 1955, and *Rio Bravo* 1959.

Brennan William J(oseph), Jr (1906–). US jurist and associate justice of the US Supreme Court 1956–90. He wrote many important Supreme Court majority decisions that assured the freedoms set forth in the First Amendment and established the rights of minority groups. He is especially noted for writing the majority opinion in *Baker v Carr* 1962, in which state voting reapportionment ensured 'one person, one vote', and in *US v Eichman* 1990, which ruled that the law banning desecration of the flag was a violation of the right to free speech as provided for in the First Amendment.

Born in Newark, New Jersey, Brennan graduated from the University of Pennsylvania and Harvard Law School. A New Jersey superior court 1949–52 and supreme court 1952–56 judge, he was appointed to the US Supreme Court by President Eisenhower. Considered a moderate liberal, his vote was usually cast with the majority during the years of the Court under Chief Justice Earl Warren, but he became a key liberal influence when the court majority, under chief justices Burger and Rehnquist, shifted to the

Brendel The pianist Alfred Brendel. Although an eccentric, who wears sticking plaster on his finger tips while performing, Brendel's interpretations of the Classical repertoire are unsurpassed for their well-balanced phrasing and dignity. His recording of the Liszt sonata is also highly regarded.

conservative side in the 1980s. He retired from the Court 1990, citing health reasons.

Brenner Sidney (1927–). South African biochemist, one of the pioneers of genetic engineering. Brenner discovered messenger RNA (a link between DNA and the ribosomes in which proteins are synthesized) 1960.

Brenner became engaged in one of the most elaborate efforts in anatomy ever attempted: investigating the nervous system of nematode worms and comparing the nervous systems of different mutant forms of the animal. About 100 genes are involved in constructing the nervous system of a nematode and most of the mutations that occur affect the overall design of a section of the nervous system.

Progress in science depends on new techniques, new discoveries and new ideas, probably in that order.

SIDNEY BRENNER
in *Nature* May 1980

Brentano Clemens (1778–1842). German Romantic writer. He published a seminal collection of folk tales and songs with Ludwig von Arnim (*Des Knaben Wunderhorn/The Boy's Magic Horn*) 1805–08, and popularized the legend of the Lorelei (a rock in the river Rhine). He also wrote mystic religious verse, as in *Romanzen von Rosenkranz* 1852.

Brentano Franz (1838–1916). German-Austrian philosopher and psychologist. In *Psychology from the Empirical Standpoint* 1874 he developed the theory that mental phenomena can be identified as those that have 'intentionality'; that is, have an object within themselves. For example, fear is always fear of something and joy or sorrow are always about something.

Brenton Howard (1942–). English dramatist. His political theatre, deliberately provocative, includes *The Churchill Play* 1974 and *The Romans in Britain* 1980.

Bloody Poetry 1984 is an examination of the poet Shelley, and he co-wrote *Pravda* 1985 with David Hare and *Moscow Gold* 1990 with activist/writer Tariq Ali.

His is an uncomfortable talent, with a particular capacity for anatomising the unhealthy state of Britain today.

Trevor and Carole Woddis Griffiths on HOWARD BRENTON
in *The Bloomsbury Theatre Guide* 1988

Breton André (1896–1966). French writer and poet. He was among the leaders of the Dada art movement and was also a founder of Surrealism, publishing *Le Manifeste de surréalisme/Surrealist Manifesto* 1924.

Les Champs magnétiques/Magnetic Fields 1921, written with fellow Dadaist Philippe Soupault, was an experiment in automatic writing. Breton soon turned to Surrealism. Influenced by communism and the theories of psychoanalyst Sigmund Freud, he believed that on both a personal and a political level Surrealist techniques could shatter the inhibiting order and propriety of the conscious mind (bourgeois society) and release deep reserves of creative energy.

Other works include *Najda* 1928, the story of his love affair with a medium.

It is living and ceasing to live that are imaginary solutions. Existence is elsewhere.

ANDRÉ BRETON
Surrealist Manifesto 1924

Brenner South African born biochemist Sidney Brenner. Brenner discovered messenger RNA and the ribosomes which function to synthesize proteins encoded by DNA. He succeeded Max Perutz as director of the Laboratory for Molecular Biology in Cambridge in 1980, a post he held until 1986. He then became professor of genetic medicine at Cambridge University. (Image Select)

Breuer Josef (1842–1925). Viennese physician, one of the pioneers of psychoanalysis. He applied it successfully to cases of hysteria, and collaborated with Freud on *Studien über Hysterie/Studies in Hysteria* 1895.

The taste of space on your tongue;/ The fragrance of dimensions;/ The juice of stone.

MARCEL BREUER
quoted in Muriel Emanuel (ed) *Contemporary Architects* 1994

Breuer Marcel Lajos (1902–1981). Hungarian-born architect and designer. He studied and taught at the Bauhaus school in Germany. His tubular steel chair 1925 was the first of its kind. He moved to England, then to the USA, where he was in partnership with Walter Gropius 1937–40. His buildings show an affinity with natural materials, as exemplified in the Bijenkorf, Rotterdam, the Netherlands (with Elzas) 1953.

Breuil Henri Édouard Prosper (1877–1961). French prehistorian who was enormously influential in the world of archaeology throughout the first half of this century, particularly the study of the Palaeolithic (Old Stone Age), and who specialized in the tracing of prehistoric rock art, especially Palaeolithic cave art, which he interpreted in terms of hunting and fertility magic.

Brewster David (1781–1868). Scottish physicist who made discoveries about the diffraction and polarization of light, and invented the kaleidoscope 1816. Knighted 1831.

Brezhnev Leonid Ilyich (1906–1982). Soviet leader. A protégé of Stalin and Khrushchev, he came to power (after he and Kosygin forced Khrushchev to resign) as general secretary of the Soviet Communist Party (CPSU) 1964–82 and was president 1977–82. Domestically he was conservative; abroad the USSR was established as a military and political superpower during the Brezhnev era, extending its influence in Africa and Asia.

Brewster *Although trained as a priest, David Brewster was never ordained and spent most of his scientific career investigating the polarization of light. In 1815 he discovered the optical law, which now bears his name, that relates the angle of maximum polarization for light reflecting off a surface to the refractive index of the reflecting material. (Ann Ronan/Image Select)*

Suggested reading
Kelley, D R (ed) *Soviet Politics in the Brezhnev Era* (1980)
McCauley, M (ed) *The Soviet Union Under Brezhnev* (1983)
Navazelskis, Ina *Leonid Brezhnev* (1988)

Good-humoured and patient, he was very much a 'consensus' leader, content to blunt the differences between opposing factions, even when that meant adopting no clear policy line.

Geoffrey Hosking on LEONID BREZHNEV
in *A History of the Soviet Union* 1985

Brian known as Brian Boru ('Brian of the Tribute') (926–1014). High king of Ireland from 976, who took Munster, Leinster, and Connacht to become ruler of all Ireland. He defeated the Norse at Clontarf, thus ending Norse control of Dublin, although he was himself killed. He was the last high king with jurisdiction over most of Scotland. His exploits were celebrated in several chronicles.

Brian (William) Havergal (1876–1972). English composer. He wrote 32 symphonies in visionary Romantic style, including the *Gothic* 1919–27 for large choral and orchestral forces.

A country grows in history ... when it turns to justice and to right for the conservation of its interests.

ARISTIDE BRIAND
Speech welcoming Germany to the
League of Nations, Geneva 10 Sept 1926

Briand Aristide (1862–1932). French radical socialist politician. He was prime minister 1909–11, 1913, 1915–17, 1921–22, 1925–26 and 1929, and foreign minister 1925–32. In 1925 he concluded the Pact of Locarno (settling Germany's western frontier) and in 1928 the Kellogg–Briand pact renouncing war; in 1930 he outlined a scheme for a United States of Europe.

Brickhill Paul Chester Jerome (1916–1991). Australian writer. His *The Great Escape* 1951 was based on his own experience as a prisoner of war during World War II. It was filmed 1963. He also wrote *The Dambusters* 1951 and *Reach for the Sky* 1954.

Bridge Frank (1879–1941). English composer. His works include the orchestral suite *The Sea* 1912, and *Oration* 1930 for cello and orchestra. He taught English composer Benjamin Britten.

Bridges Harry (1901–1990). Australian-born US labour leader. In 1931 he formed a trade union of clockworkers and in 1934, after police opened fire on a picket line and killed two strikers, he organized a successful general strike. He was head of the International Longshoremen's and Warehousemen's Union for many years.

I love all beauteous things, / I seek and adore them; / God hath no better praise, / And man in his hasty days / Is honoured for them.

ROBERT BRIDGES
'I Love All Beauteous Things'

Bridges Robert Seymour (1844–1930). English poet. Poet laureate 1913–30, he wrote *The Testament of Beauty* 1929, a long philosophical poem. In 1918 he edited and published posthumously the poems of Gerard Manley Hopkins.

Bridget, St (453–523). A patron saint of Ireland, also known as St Brigit or St Bride. She founded a church and monastery at Kildare, and is said to have been the daughter of a prince of Ulster. Feast day 1 Feb.

Bridgewater Francis Egerton, 3rd Duke of Bridgewater (1736–1803). Pioneer of British inland navigation. With James Brindley as his engineer, he constructed 1762–72 the Bridgewater canal from

interest in astronomy and navigation. For that reason Briggs's logarithms were 10^9 times 'larger' than those in modern tables.

Brighouse Harold (1882–1958). English dramatist. He was born and bred in Lancashire and in his most famous play, *Hobson's Choice* 1916, he dealt with a Salford bootmaker's courtship, using the local idiom.

England is the mother of Parliaments.

JOHN BRIGHT
Speech in House of Commons 1865

Bright John (1811–1889). British Liberal politician, a campaigner for free trade, peace, and social reform. A Quaker millowner, he was among the founders of the Anti-Corn Law League in 1839, and was largely instrumental in securing the passage of the Reform Bill of 1867.

After entering Parliament in 1843 Bright led the struggle there for free trade, together with Richard Cobden, which achieved success in 1846. His *laissez-faire* principles also made him a prominent opponent of factory reform. His influence was constantly exerted on behalf of peace, as when he opposed the Crimean War, Palmerston's aggressive policy in China, Disraeli's anti-Russian policy, and the bombardment of Alexandria. During the American Civil War he was outspoken in support of the North. He sat in Gladstone's cabinets as president of the Board of Trade 1868–70 and chancellor of the Duchy of Lancaster 1873–74 and 1880–82, but broke with him over the Irish Home Rule Bill. Bright owed much of his influence to his skill as a speaker.

Bright Richard (1789–1858). British physician who described many conditions and linked oedema (fluid accumulation) to kidney disease. Bright's disease, an acute inflammation of the kidneys, is named after him.

Brillat-Savarin Jean Anthelme (1755–1826). French gastronome, author of *La Physiologie du Goût/The Physiology of Taste* 1825, a compilation of observations on food and drink regarded as the first great classic of gastronomic literature. Most of his professional life was spent as a politician.

Brindley James (1716–1772). British canal builder, the first to employ tunnels and aqueducts extensively, in order to reduce the

Bright, John John Bright, British Victorian politician and humanitarian campaigner against the Corn Laws and the Crimean War. A stirring orator, he said of the Crimean War: 'The angel of death has been abroad throughout the land; you may almost hear the beating of his wings'.

Worsley to Manchester and on to the Mersey, a distance of 67.5 km/42 mi. Initially built to carry coal, the canal crosses the Irwell valley on an aqueduct. Succeeded as duke 1748.

Bridgman Percy Williams (1882–1961). US physicist. His research into machinery producing high pressure led in 1955 to the creation of synthetic diamonds by General Electric. He was awarded the Nobel Prize for Physics 1946. His technique for synthesizing diamonds was used to synthesize many more minerals and a new school of geology developed, based on experimental work at high pressure and temperature. Born in Cambridge, Massachusetts, he was educated at Harvard, where he spent his entire academic career.

Bridie James. Pen name of Osborne Henry Mavor (1888–1951). Scottish dramatist and professor of medicine. He was a founder of the Glasgow Citizens' Theatre. His plays include the comedies *Tobias and the Angel* 1930 and *The Anatomist* 1931.

Brieux Eugène (1858–1932). French dramatist. He was an exponent of the naturalistic problem play attacking social evils. His most powerful plays are *Les Trois Filles de M Dupont* 1897; *Les Avariés/Damaged Goods* 1901, long banned for its outspoken treatment of syphilis; and *Maternité* 1903.

Briggs Barry (1934–). New Zealand motorcyclist who won four individual world speedway titles 1957–66 and took part in a record 87 world championship races.

Briggs Henry (1561–1630). English mathematician, with John Napier one of the founders of calculation by logarithms. Briggs's tables remain the basis of those used to this day. The logarithms of Briggs (and Napier) were logarithms of sines, a reflection of their

Brindley *A portrait of the engineer James Brindley. In the left-hand corner of the picture is the Barton Aqueduct, which carries the Bridgewater Canal over the river Irwell at a height of 12 m/40 ft. Brindley's ingenious design established him as the leading canal builder in England. (Ann Ronan/Image Select)*

Britten *The composer Benjamin Britten pictured with his lifelong companion, the tenor Peter Pears. An essentially vocal composer, Britten left his mark on all such genres, especially opera: he is sometimes considered the greatest composer for the stage in the 20th century.* (Image Select)

number of locks on a direct-route canal. His 580 km/360 mi of canals included the Bridgewater (Manchester–Liverpool) and Grand Union (Manchester–Potteries) canals.

Brinell Johan August (1849–1925). Swedish engineer who devised the Brinell hardness test, for measuring the hardness of substances, in 1900. It is based on the idea that a material's response to a load placed on one small point is related to its ability to deform permanently. Brinell also carried out investigations into the abrasion resistance of selected materials.

The founder of Australian science.

John Herschel on THOMAS BRISBANE
awarding him the gold medal of the Astronomical Society 8 Feb 1828

Brisbane Thomas Makdougall (1773–1860). Scottish soldier, colonial administrator, and astronomer. After serving in the Napoleonic Wars under Wellington, he was governor of New South Wales 1821–25. Brisbane in Queensland is named after him. He catalogued over 7,000 stars. KCB 1814, baronet 1836.

Brissot Jacques Pierre (1754–1793). French revolutionary leader, born in Chartres. He became a member of the legislative assembly and the National Convention, but his party of moderate republicans, the Girondins, or Brissotins, fell foul of Robespierre, and Brissot was guillotined.

Bristow Eric (1957–). English darts player nicknamed 'the Crafty Cockney'. He has won all the game's major titles, including the world professional title a record five times between 1980 and 1986.

Britannicus Tiberius Claudius Caesar (c. AD 41–55). Roman prince, son of the Emperor Claudius and Messalina; so-called from his father's conquest of Britain. He was poisoned by Nero.

He is said to have been intelligent, but the reputation was never tested and may have been due to sympathy for his perils.

Tacitus on BRITANNICUS
in *Annals* bk 12, ch 26

Brittain Vera Mary (1893–1970). English socialist writer. She was a nurse to the troops overseas 1915–19, as told in her *Testament of Youth* 1933; *Testament of Friendship* 1950 commemorated English novelist Winifred Holtby. She married political scientist Sir George Catlin (1896–1979); their daughter is Shirley Williams, member of the Social and Liberal Democratic Party (SLDP).

Brittan Leon (1939–). British Conservative politician and lawyer. Chief secretary to the Treasury 1981–83, home secretary 1983–85, secretary for trade and industry 1985–86 (resigned over his part in the Westland affair), and senior European commissioner from 1988. Appointed commissioner for external trade from 1993, he was at the forefront of the negotiating team that concluded the Uruguay round of GATT trade talks, leading to greater trade liberalization. Knighted 1989.

There are many dangers which hedge around the unfortunate composer: pressure groups which demand true proletarian music; snobs who demand the latest avant-garde tricks; critics who are already trying to document today for tomorrow, to be the first to find the correct pigeonhole definition.

BENJAMIN BRITTEN
On receiving the first Aspen Award 1964

Britten (Edward) Benjamin, Baron Britten (1913–1976). English composer. He often wrote for the individual voice; for example, the role in the opera *Peter Grimes* 1945, based on verses by George Crabbe, was created for his life companion Peter Pears. Among his many works are the *Young Person's Guide to the Orchestra* 1946; the chamber opera *The Rape of Lucretia* 1946; *Billy Budd* 1951; *A Midsummer Night's Dream* 1960; and *Death in Venice* 1973. Created baron 1976.

Suggested reading
Evans, Peter *The Music of Benjamin Britten* (1979)
Kennedy, M *Britten* (1981)
Palmer, C (ed) *The Britten Companion* (1984)
White, E W *Benjamin Britten: His Life and Operas* (1970)

Broad Charles Dunbar (1887–1971). British philosopher who appreciated the importance of science and psychology. His books include *Perception, Physics and Reality* 1914 and *Lectures on Psychic Research* 1962, discussing scientific evidence for survival after death.

Broad was born in London; he was educated at Cambridge, and was professor of moral philosophy at the university 1933–53.

Broch Hermann (1886–1951). Austrian novelist. He used experimental techniques in *Die Schlafwandler/The Sleepwalkers* 1932, *Der Tod des Vergil/The Death of Virgil* 1945, and *Die Schuldlosen/The Guiltless*, a novel in 11 stories. He moved to the USA 1938 after being persecuted by the Nazis.

The real history of consciousness starts with one's first lie.

JOSEPH BRODSKY
Less Than One, title essay 1981

Brodsky Joseph Alexandrovich (1940–1996). Russian poet. He emigrated to the USA 1972. His work, often dealing with themes of exile, is admired for its wit and economy of language, particularly in its use of understatement. Many of his poems, written in Russian, have been translated into English (*A Part of Speech* 1980). More recently he has also written in English. He was awarded the Nobel Prize for Literature in 1987 and became US poet laureate 1991.

No poem is ever written for its story line's sake, just as no life is lived for the sake of an obituary.

JOSEPH BRODSKY
'Keening Muse'

Broglie (Louis César Victor) Maurice, 6th Duc de (1875–1960). French physicist. He worked on X-rays and gamma rays, and helped to establish the Einsteinian description of light in terms of photons. He was the brother of Louis de Broglie.

Maurice, after a short naval career, equipped an extensive private laboratory at the family home, where he was assisted by his brother Louis. Maurice pioneered the study of X-ray spectra.

Broglie Louis Victor Pierre Raymond, 7th Duc de (1892–1987). French theoretical physicist. He established that all subatomic particles can be described either by particle equations or by wave equations, thus laying the foundations of wave mechanics. He was awarded the 1929 Nobel Prize for Physics. Succeeded as Duke 1960.

De Broglie's discovery of wave–particle duality enabled physicists to view Einstein's conviction that matter and energy are interconvertible as being fundamental to the structure of matter. The study of matter waves led not only to a much deeper understanding of the

Brodsky The protégé of the great Russian poet Anna Akhmatova during the 1950s, Joseph Brodsky was arrested by the Soviet authorities 1964 as a 'parasite'. After years of internal exile, he emigrated to the USA, where he wrote both in Russian and English. His book of essays Less than One appeared 1985.

nature of the atom but also to explanations of chemical bonds and the practical application of electron waves in electron microscopes.

Two seemingly incompatible conceptions can each represent an aspect of the truth .... They may serve in turn to represent the facts without ever entering into direct conflict.

LOUIS DE BROGLIE
Dialectical 326

Bromfield Louis Brucker (1896–1956). US novelist. Among his books are *The Strange Case of Miss Annie Spragg* 1928, *The Rains Came* 1937, and *Mrs Parkington* 1943, dealing with the golden age of New York society.

That is the essence of science: ask an impertinent question, and you are on the way to a pertinent answer.

JACOB BRONOWSKI
Ascent of Man, BBC television series 1971–2

Bronowski Jacob (1908–1974). Polish-born British scientist, broadcaster, and writer, who enthusiastically popularized scientific knowledge in several books and in the 13-part BBC television documentary *The Ascent of Man*, issued as a book 1973.

His book *The Common Sense of Science* 1951 displayed the history and workings of science around three central notions: cause, chance, and order. *Science and Human Values* 1958 collected newspaper articles written for the *New York Times* about nuclear science and the morality of nuclear weapons. *The Western Intellectual Tradition* 1960 is an illuminating survey of the growth of political, philosophical, and scientific knowledge from the Renaissance to the 19th century, written with Bruce Mazlish. Bronowski also wrote about literature; for example, *William Blake and the Age of Revolution* 1965.

Acting is the easiest thing I've ever done. I guess that's why I'm sticking with it.

CHARLES BRONSON
Leslie Halliwell *Filmgoer's Companion* 1965

Bronson Charles. Stage name of Charles Buchinsky (1922–). US film actor. He began in a variety of supporting roles from 1952, graduating to larger roles in such films as *The Magnificent Seven* 1960. He worked in Europe in films such as *C'era una Volta il West*/*Once Upon a Time in the West* 1968 and returned to the USA taking starring roles, often as a hard-bitten loner, such as the vigilante in *Death Wish* 1974 and its sequels.

He often appeared with his second wife, actress Jill Ireland until her death 1990.

Brønsted Johannes Nicolaus (1879–1947). Danish physical chemist whose work in solution chemistry, particularly electrolytes, resulted in a new theory of acids and bases. In 1923, Brønsted defined an acid as a proton donor and a base as a proton acceptor. The definition applies to all solvents, not just water. It also explains the different behaviour of pure acids and acids in solution. In Brønsted's scheme, every acid is related to a conjugate base, and every base to a conjugate acid.

Because the road is rough and long, / Shall we despise the skylark's song?

ANNE BRONTË
'Views of Life'

Brontë three English novelists, daughters of a Yorkshire parson. Charlotte (1816–1855), notably with *Jane Eyre* 1847 and *Villette* 1853, reshaped autobiographical material into vivid narrative. Emily

(1818–1848) in *Wuthering Heights* 1847 expressed the intensity and nature mysticism which also pervades her poetry (*Poems* 1846). The more modest talent of Anne (1820–1849) produced *Agnes Grey* 1847 and *The Tenant of Wildfell Hall* 1848.

No coward soul is mine.

EMILY BRONTË
'Last Lines'

The Brontës were brought up by an aunt at Haworth rectory (now a museum) in Yorkshire. In 1846 the sisters published a volume of poems under the pen names Currer (Charlotte), Ellis (Emily) and Acton (Anne) Bell. In 1847 (using the same names), they published the novels *Jane Eyre*, *Wuthering Heights*, and *Agnes Grey*, Anne's much weaker work. During 1848–49 Emily, Anne, and their brother Patrick Branwell all died of tuberculosis, aided in Branwell's case by alcohol and opium addiction; he is remembered for his portrait of the sisters.

Reader, I married him.

CHARLOTTE BRONTË
Jane Eyre 1847

Charlotte married her father's curate, A B Nicholls, 1854, and died during pregnancy.

Suggested reading
Barker, Juliet *The Brontës* (1994)
Bentley, Phyllis *The Brontës and their World* (1979)
Fraser, Rebecca *The Brontës* (1988)
Myer, V G *Charlotte Brontë: Truculent Spirit* (1987)
Gérin, Winifred *The Brontës* (1974)
Peters, Margot *Unquiet Soul* (1987)
Wilks, Brian *The Brontës* (1975)

If all else perished, and he remained, I should still continue to be; and if all else remained and he were annihilated, the universe would change to a mighty stranger.

EMILY BRONTË
Wuthering Heights ch 9 1848

Bronzino Agnolo (1503–1572). Italian Mannerist painter. Active in Florence, he was court painter to Cosimo I, Duke of Tuscany. He is known for his cool, elegant portraits – *Lucrezia Panciatichi c.* 1540 (Uffizi, Florence) is typical – and for the allegory *Venus, Cupid, Folly and Time* about 1545 (National Gallery, London). His religious works were held in lesser esteem.

Brook Peter Stephen Paul (1925–). English theatre director. He is renowned for his innovative productions. His work with the Royal Shakespeare Company (joined 1962) included a production of Shakespeare's *A Midsummer Night's Dream* 1970, set in a white gymnasium and combining elements of circus and commedia dell'arte. In the same year he founded an independent initiative, Le Centre International de Créations Théâtrales/The International Centre for Theatre Research in Paris. Brook's later productions aim to combine elements from different cultures and include *The Conference of the Birds* 1973, based on a Persian story, and *The Mahabarata* 1985–88, a cycle of three plays based on the Hindu epic.

His films include *Lord of the Flies* 1962 and *Meetings with Remarkable Men* 1979. He is the author of the influential study of contemporary theatre, *The Empty Space* 1968, and of the essays and observations published in *The Shifting Point* 1988.

I find it easier to govern thirty thousand Malays and Dayaks than to manage a dozen of your majesty's subjects.

JAMES BROOKE
Said to Queen Victoria on a visit to Windsor in 1847.

Brooke James (1803–1868). British administrator who became rajah of Sarawak, on Borneo, 1841. In 1838 he headed a private expedition to Borneo, where he helped to suppress a revolt, for which the sultan gave him the title. Brooke became known as the 'the white rajah'. KCB 1848.

Brooke Peter Leonard (1934–). British Conservative politician, a member of Parliament from 1977. Appointed chair of the Conservative Party by Margaret Thatcher 1987, he was Northern Ireland secretary 1989–92, and National Heritage secretary 1992–94.

As Northern Ireland secretary, he aroused criticism (and praise) for observing that at some future time negotiations with the IRA might take place. In 1991 his efforts to institute all-party, and all-Ireland, talks on reconciliation proved abortive but he continued to be held in high regard on both sides of the border.

If I should die, think only this of me ... That there's some corner of a foreign field / That is forever England.

RUPERT BROOKE
'The Soldier'

Brooke Rupert Chawner (1887–1915). English poet. He stands as a symbol of the World War I 'lost generation'. His five war sonnets, the best known of which is 'The Patriot', were published posthumously. Other notable works include 'Grantchester' and 'The Great Lover'.

Born in Rugby, where he was educated, Brooke travelled abroad after a nervous breakdown 1911, but in 1913 won a fellowship at King's College, Cambridge. Later that year he toured America (*Letters from America* 1916), New Zealand, and the South Seas, and in 1914 became an officer in the Royal Naval Division. After fighting at Antwerp, he sailed for the Dardanelles, but died of blood-poisoning on the Greek island of Skyros, where he is buried.

Suggested reading
Delany, P *The Neo-Pagans* (1987)
Hassall, Christopher *Rupert Brooke: A Biography* (1964)
Hastings, M *The Handsomest Young Man In England: Rupert Brooke* (1967)
Lehmann, John *The Strange Case of Rupert Brooke* (1981)

A lazy man of limited ability and considerable charm, he ... much preferred country pursuits ... to the work of government.

P J Buckland on VISCOUNT BROOKEBOROUGH
in *Dictionary of National Biography*

Brookeborough Basil Stanlake Brooke, 1st Viscount Brookeborough (1888–1973). Unionist politician of Northern Ireland. He entered Parliament in 1929, held ministerial posts 1933–45, and was prime minister of Northern Ireland 1943–63. He was a staunch advocate of strong links with Britain. Viscount 1952.

There are moments when you feel free, moments when you have energy, moments when you have hope, but you can't rely on any of these things to see you through. Circumstances do that.

ANITA BROOKNER
John Haffenden (ed) *Novelists in Interview* 1985

Brookner Anita (1928–). English novelist. Her books include *Hotel du Lac* 1984 (Booker Prize), *A Misalliance* 1986, *Latecomers* 1988, *A Closed Eye* 1991, and *Family Romance* 1993. Her skill is in the subtle portrayal of hopelessness and lack of vitality in her female characters. She also lectures in art history.

Brooks Louise (1906–1985). US actress. She was known for her dark, enigmatic beauty and for her roles in silent films such as *A Girl*

Brooks *Louise Brooks as Lulu in* Pandora's Box *1929. Brooks began her professional career at 15 as a dancer. Eventually her appearances in* George White's Scandals *and in the Ziegfeld Follies led to a Hollywood contract.*

in Every Port 1928 and *Die Büchse der Pandora/Pandora's Box* and *Das Tagebuch einer Verlorenen/The Diary of a Lost Girl*, both 1929 and both directed by G W Pabst. At 25 she had appeared in 17 films. She retired from the screen 1938.

That's it baby, when you got it, flaunt it.
MEL BROOKS
The Producers

Brooks Mel. Stage name of Melvin Kaminsky (1926–). US film director and comedian. He is known for madcap and slapstick verbal humour. He became well known with his record album *The 2,000-Year-Old Man* 1960. His films include *The Producers* 1968, *Blazing Saddles* 1974, *Young Frankenstein* 1975, *History of the World Part I* 1981, and *To Be or Not to Be* 1983.

His wife not only edited his works but edited him.
VAN WYCK BROOKS
Ordeal of Mark Twain ch 5 1934

Brooks Van Wyck (1886–1963). US literary critic and biographer. His five-volume *Makers and Finders: A History of the Writer in America, 1800–1915* 1936–52 was an influential series of critical works on US literature. The first volume *The Flowering of New England* 1936 won a Pulitzer Prize.

An earlier work, *America's Coming-of-Age* 1915, concerned the Puritan heritage and its effects on American literature. His other works include studies of Mark Twain, Henry James, and Ralph Waldo Emerson.

Broome David (1940–). British show jumper. He won the 1970 world title on a horse named Beethoven. His sister Liz Edgar is also a top-class show jumper.

Brosnan Pierce (1953–). Irish actor who became the fifth to play the role of secret agent James Bond in *Goldeneye* 1995. As a young actor he struggled to make his mark despite extensive London stage experience. Brosnan first found success in a string of elegantly mounted television roles, especially in the thriller series *Remington*

Steele. He was first offered the role of James Bond in 1986, but turned it down due to television commitments.

Education makes a people easy to lead but difficult to drive; easy to govern, but impossible to enslave.
HENRY, 1ST BARON BROUGHAM
Speech in House of Commons 29 Jan 1828

Brougham Henry Peter, 1st Baron Brougham and Vaux (1778–1868). British Whig politician and lawyer. From 1811 he was chief adviser to the Princess of Wales (afterwards Queen Caroline), and in 1820 he defeated the attempt of George IV to divorce her. He was Lord Chancellor 1830–34, supporting the Reform Bill.

Born in Edinburgh, he was a founder of the *Edinburgh Review* 1802. He sat in Parliament 1810–12 and from 1816, and supported the causes of public education and law reform. He was one of the founders of University College, London, 1828. When the Whigs returned to power 1830, Brougham accepted the chancellorship and a peerage a few weeks later. His allegedly dictatorial and eccentric ways led to his exclusion from office when the Whigs next assumed power 1835. After 1837 he was active in the House of Lords.

Brouwer Adriaen (1605–1638). Flemish painter of genre who worked both in Flanders and Holland, and was equally esteemed by Flemish and Dutch masters, both Rembrandt and Rubens possessing examples of his work. Typical of his tavern scenes are *A Quarrel between Two Peasants* (Dresden) and *Spanish Soldiers playing Dice* (Munich).

Brouwer Luitzen Egbertus Jan (1881–1966). Dutch mathematician. He worked on the nature and foundation of mathematics, and was the founder of the intuitionist school of mathematics, or intuitionism. He held that the foundation of mathematics is a fundamental intuition of temporal sequence – the counting of moments of time – and that numbers and mathematical entities are constructible from this intuition.

Brougham *Scottish-born English politician, lawyer, and reformer, Henry Brougham was often considered arrogant and eccentric. He campaigned vigorously for Benthamite legal reforms and co-founded London University. The carriage specially built for him became the prototype of the 'brougham'.*

Brown Capability (Lancelot) (1715–1783). English landscape gardener. He acquired his nickname because of his continual enthusiasm for the 'capabilities' of natural landscapes.

He advised on gardens of stately homes, including Blenheim, Oxfordshire; Stowe, Buckinghamshire; and Petworth, W Sussex, sometimes also contributing to the architectural designs.

Parks ... lakes ... trees ... walks ... a grand house like punctuation marks in a literary masterpiece.

Randall J Van Vynckt (ed) on CAPABILITY BROWN
in *International Dictionary of Architects* 1993

Brown Charles Brockden (1771–1810). US novelist and magazine editor. He introduced the American Indian into fiction and is called the 'father of the American novel'. Inspired by the writings of William Godwin and Mrs Radcliffe, his *Wieland* 1798, *Ormond* 1799, *Edgar Huntly* 1799, and *Arthur Mervyn* (two volumes 1799, 1800) imported the Gothic and fantastic traditions into US fiction.

Brown Earle (1926–). US composer. He pioneered graph notation and mobile form during the 1950s, as in *Available Forms II* 1958 for ensemble and two conductors. He was an associate of John Cage.

Brown Ernest William (1866–1938). English mathematician who studied the effect of gravity on the motions of the planets and smaller members of the Solar System. He published extremely accurate tables of the Moon's movements.

Brown Ford Madox (1821–1893). English painter. He was associated with the Pre-Raphaelite Brotherhood. His pictures, which include *The Last of England* 1855 (City Art Gallery, Birmingham) and *Work* 1852–65 (City Art Gallery, Manchester), are character-

Brown , John *Believing he was an instrument in the hands of God, the US abolitionist John Brown took direct action to liberate the slaves of the southern states. He organized the 'underground railway', a secret network that may have helped as many as 100,000 slaves to escape from southern states, and in 1859, believing he could lead an armed insurrection, he seized a government arsenal.*

ized by their abundance of realistic detail and their use of symbolism. His later subject pictures, romantically historico-literary, are not always harmonious in design and colour, but as a colourist he excels in some small landscapes.

I know by experience that from originality to eccentricity there is but one step.

FORD MADOX BROWN
Letter to Davis 4 Jan 1859

Brown George Alfred. Baron George-Brown (1914–1985). British Labour politician. He entered Parliament in 1945, was briefly minister of works 1951, and contested the leadership of the party on the death of Gaitskell, but was defeated by Harold Wilson.

He was secretary for economic affairs 1964–66 and foreign secretary 1966–68. He was created a life peer 1970.

If my own life proves anything, it proves that people still respond to convictions passionately held.

GEORGE BROWN
In My Way 1971

Brown James (1928–). US rhythm-and-blues and soul singer. He was a pioneer of funk. Staccato horn arrangements and shouted vocals characterize his hits, which include 'Please, Please, Please' 1956, 'Papa's Got a Brand New Bag' 1965, and 'Say It Loud, I'm Black and I'm Proud' 1968. In that year his TV appearance appealing for calm succeeded in restraining race riots in US cities.

I was a juvenile delinquent ... I tell kids it's not the end of things if they go to jail and to go on.

JAMES BROWN
talking to Dinah Shore, Nov 1971, NBC-TV

Brown (James) Gordon (1951–). British Labour politician. He entered Parliament in 1983, rising quickly to the opposition front bench, with a reputation as an outstanding debater. He took over from John Smith as shadow chancellor 1992. After Smith's death May 1994, he generously declined to challenge his close ally, Tony Blair, for the leadership, retaining his post as shadow chancellor.

Brown John (1800–1859). US slavery abolitionist. With 18 men, on the night of 16 Oct 1859, he seized the government arsenal at Harper's Ferry in W Virginia, apparently intending to distribute weapons to runaway slaves who would then defend a mountain stronghold, which Brown hoped would become a republic of former slaves. On 18 Oct the arsenal was stormed by US Marines under Col Robert E Lee. Brown was tried and hanged on 2 Dec, becoming a martyr and the hero of the popular song 'John Brown's Body' *c.* 1860.

Suggested reading
Boyer, R O *The Legend of John Brown* (1973)
Keller, Allan *Thunder at Harper's Ferry* (1958)
Oates, Stephen *To Purge this Land of Blood: A Biography of John Brown* (1984)
Scott, John A *John Brown at Harper's Ferry* (1987)

Brown John (1826–1883). Scottish servant and confidant of Queen Victoria from 1858.

Brown Robert (1773–1858). Scottish botanist who in 1827 discovered Brownian motion. The concept of Brownian motion arose from his observation that very fine pollen grains suspended in water move about in a continuously agitated manner. He was able to establish that inorganic materials such as carbon and various metals are equally subject to it, but he could not find the cause of the movement (now explained by kinetic theory). As a botanist, his more lasting work was in the field of plant morphology. He was the first to establish the real basis for the distinction between gymnosperms (pines) and angiosperms (flowering plants).

Brown Trisha (1936–). US dancer and choreographer. One of the leading Post-Modernist choreographers, she founded the improvisational Grand Union 1970–76. During the 1960s and early 1970s, Brown devised a series of 'equipment pieces' that utilized harnesses to enable the dancers to perform movements, cantilevered out from the wall. Her works include *Roof Piece* 1973 (where 15 dancers, scattered over the Manhattan rooftops, were watched by an audience on an adjacent rooftop), *Accumulation* 1971, and *Glacial Decoy* 1979.

Her current style is more fluid and supple, in contrast to her earlier, deliberately angular movements. These works include *Son of Gone Fishin'* 1981, *Set and Reset* 1983, and *Lateral Pass* 1985.

Browne Hablot Knight (1815–1882). Real name of English illustrator ◊Phiz.

Browne Robert (1550–1633). English Puritan leader, founder of the Brownists. He founded communities in Norwich, East Anglia, and in the Netherlands which developed into present-day Congregationalism.

Browne, born in Stamford, Lincolnshire, preached in Norwich and then retired to Middelburg in the Netherlands, but returned after making his peace with the church and became head of Stamford Grammar School. In a work published in 1582 Browne advocated Congregationalist doctrine; he was imprisoned several times in 1581–82 for attacking Episcopalianism (church government by bishops). From 1591 he was a rector in Northamptonshire.

We all labour against our own cure; for death is the cure of all diseases.

THOMAS BROWNE
Religio medici 1642

Browne Thomas (1605–1682). English author and physician. Born in London, he travelled widely in Europe before settling in Norwich 1637. His works display a richness of style as in *Religio medici/The Religion of a Doctor* 1643, a justification of his profession; *Vulgar Errors* 1646, an examination of popular legend and superstition; *Urn Burial* and *The Garden of Cyrus* 1658; and *Christian Morals*, published posthumously 1717. Knighted 1671.

Oh, to be in England / Now that April's there.

ROBERT BROWNING
'Home Thoughts from Abroad'

Browning Robert (1812–1889). English poet. His work is characterized by the use of dramatic monologue and an interest in obscure literary and historical figures. It includes the play *Pippa Passes* 1841 and the poems 'The Pied Piper of Hamelin' 1842, 'My Last Duchess' 1842, 'Home Thoughts from Abroad' 1845, and 'Rabbi Ben Ezra' 1864.

Browning, born in Camberwell, London, wrote his first poem 'Pauline' 1833 under the influence of Shelley; it was followed by 'Paracelsus' 1835 and 'Sordello' 1840. From 1837 he achieved moderate success with his play *Strafford* and several other works. In the pamphlet series of *Bells and Pomegranates* 1841–46, which contained *Pippa Passes*, *Dramatic Lyrics* 1842, and *Dramatic Romances* 1845, he included the dramas *King Victor and King Charles*, *Return of the Druses*, and *Colombe's Birthday*. In 1846 he met Elizabeth Barrett; they married the same year and went to Italy. There he wrote *Christmas Eve and Easter Day* 1850 and *Men and Women* 1855, the latter containing some of his finest love poems and dramatic monologues, which were followed by *Dramatis Personae* 1864 and *The Ring and the Book* 1868–69, based on an Italian murder story. After his wife's death 1861 Browning settled in England and enjoyed an established reputation, although his later works, such as *Red-Cotton Night-Cap Country* 1873, *Dramatic Idylls* 1879–80, and *Asolando* 1889, prompted opposition by their rugged obscurity of style.

Suggested reading
Eriksen, L *Robert Browning* (1984)
Irvine, W and Honan, P *The Book, the Ring, and the Poet: A Biography of Robert Browning* (1974)
King, R *The Bow and the Lyre: The Art of Robert Browning* (1957)
Pearsall, R *Robert Browning* (1974)
Ryals, C de L *The Life of Robert Browning* (1993)

Brubeck Dave (David Warren) (1920–). US jazz pianist and composer. He was the leader of the Dave Brubeck Quartet (formed 1951). A student of composers Darius Milhaud and Arnold Schoenberg, Brubeck combines improvisation with classical discipline. Included in his large body of compositions is the internationally popular *Take Five*.

Bruce one of the chief Scottish noble houses. Robert (I) the Bruce and his son, David II, were both kings of Scotland descended from Robert de Bruis (died 1094), a Norman knight who arrived in England with William the Conqueror 1066.

Bruce Christopher (1945–). English choreographer and dancer. He became artistic director of the Rambert Dance Company 1992. Bruce often mixes modern and classical idioms with overtly political and social themes, as in *Ghost Dances* 1981, which treats the theme of political oppression. His other pieces include *Cruel Garden* 1977 and *The Dream is Over* 1987, a tribute to John Lennon.

As a dancer, Bruce's famous roles have been *Pierrot lunaire* 1967 (for Ballet Rambert), the Faun in *L'Après-midi d'un faune*, and *Petrushka* 1988 (for London Festival Ballet).

Bruce James (1730–1794). Scottish explorer, the first European to reach the source of the Blue Nile 1770, and to follow the river downstream to Cairo 1773. He was British consul at Algiers 1763–65.

Bruce Lenny. Born Leonard Alfred Schneider (1925–1966). US comedian, whose rapid-fire delivery, scatological language, and fearless tackling of taboo subjects, such as race relations and liberal hypocrisy, religion, and sexuality, were ground-breaking in the field of stand-up comedy. His constant iconoclasm and irreverence caused offence to the authorities and he was imprisoned for obscenity 1961. Convicted of drugs possession 1963, he died of an overdose 1966. He wrote a series of autobiographical articles 1963–66 for *Playboy* magazine, eventually published as *How To Talk Dirty and Influence People* 1972.

Bruce Robert. King of Scotland; see ◊Robert (I) the Bruce.

Bruce Robert de, 5th Lord of Annandale (1210–1295). Scottish noble, one of the unsuccessful claimants to the throne at the death of Alexander II 1290. His grandson was Robert the Bruce.

Bruce Stanley Melbourne, 1st Viscount Bruce of Melbourne (1883–1967). Australian National Party politician, prime minister 1923–29.

He was elected to parliament in 1918. As prime minister he introduced a number of social welfare measures. Viscount 1947.

Bruch Max (1838–1920). German composer. He was professor at the Berlin Academy 1891. He wrote three operas, including *Hermione* 1872. Among the most celebrated of his works are the *Kol Nidrei* 1881 for cello and orchestra, violin concertos, and many choral pieces.

When God finally calls me and asks 'What have you done with the talent I gave you, my lad?', I will present to him the score of my Te Deum *and I hope he will judge me mercifully.*

ANTON BRUCKNER
quoted in Sutton, *Introduction to the* Te Deum 1993

Bruckner (Josef) Anton (1824–1896). Austrian Romantic composer. He was cathedral organist at Linz 1856–68, and professor at the Vienna Conservatoire from 1868.

His works include many choral pieces and 11 symphonies, the last unfinished. His compositions were influenced by Wagner and Beethoven.

Suggested reading
Simpson, Robert *The Essence of Bruckner* (1968)
Watson, D *Bruckner* (1975)
Wolff, W *Anton Bruckner* (1942)

Brueghel or *Bruegel*. Family of Flemish painters. Pieter Brueghel the Elder (c. 1525–1569) was one of the greatest artists of his time. His pictures of peasant life helped to establish genre painting, and he also popularized works illustrating proverbs, such as *The Blind leading the Blind* 1568 (Museo di Capodimonte, Naples). A contemporary taste for the macabre can be seen in *The Triumph of Death* 1562 (Prado, Madrid), which clearly shows the influence of Hieronymus Bosch. One of his best-known works is *Hunters in the Snow* 1565 (Kunsthistorisches Museum, Vienna).

The elder Pieter was nicknamed 'Peasant' Brueghel. Two of his sons were also painters. Pieter Brueghel the Younger (1564–1638), called 'Hell' Brueghel, specialized in religious subjects, and another son, Jan Brueghel (1568–1625), called 'Velvet' Brueghel, painted flowers, landscapes, and seascapes.

Suggested reading
Gibson, W *Bruegel* (1977)
Grossmann, F *Bruegel, the Paintings* (1966)
Osten, G Von der and Vey, H *Painting and Sculpture in Germany and the Netherlands, 1500–1600* (1969)

Brulé Étienne (c. 1592–1632). French adventurer and explorer. He travelled with Champlain to the New World in 1608 and settled in Quebec, where he lived with the Algonquin Indians. He explored the Great Lakes and travelled as far south as Chesapeake Bay. Returning north, he was killed by Huron Indians.

Who's your fat friend?

BEAU BRUMMELL
Referring to the Prince Regent, in R H Gronow *Reminiscences* 1964 ed

---

Brummell Beau (George Bryan) (1778–1840). British dandy and leader of fashion. He introduced long trousers as conventional day and evening wear for men. A friend of the Prince of Wales, the future George IV, he later quarrelled with him. Gambling losses drove him in 1816 to exile in France, where he died in an asylum.

I always like to have the morning well-aired before I get up.

BEAU BRUMMELL
in Charles Macfarlane *Reminiscences of a Literary Life* 27 1917

Brundtland Gro Harlem (1939–   ). Norwegian Labour politician. Environment minister 1974–76, she briefly took over as prime minister 1981, a post to which she was re-elected 1986, 1990, and 1993. In 1992 she resigned as leader of the Norwegian Labour Party (a post she had held since 1981) but continued as prime minister. Retaining her seat count in the 1993 general election, she led a minority Labour government committed to European Union membership, but failed to secure backing for the membership application in a 1994 national referendum.

She chaired the World Commission on Environment and Development which produced the Brundtland Report, published as *Our Common Future* 1987.

Brunel Isambard Kingdom (1806–1859). British engineer and inventor. In 1833 he became engineer to the Great Western Railway, which adopted the 2.1-m/7-ft gauge on his advice. He built the Clifton Suspension Bridge over the river Avon at Bristol and the Saltash Bridge over the river Tamar near Plymouth. His shipbuilding designs include the *Great Western* 1837, the first steamship to cross the Atlantic regularly; the *Great Britain* 1843, the first large iron ship to have a screw propeller; and the *Great Eastern* 1858, which laid the first transatlantic telegraph cable and was to remain the largest ship in service until the end of the 19th century.

Suggested reading
Nobel, C B *The Brunels: Father and Son* (1938)
Pudney, J *Brunel and his World* (1974)
Rolt, L T C *Isambard Kingdom Brunel* (1957)
Vaughan, Adrian *Isambard Kingdom Brunel* (1991)

Brunel Marc Isambard (1769–1849). French-born British engineer and inventor, father of Isambard Kingdom Brunel. He constructed the tunnel under the river Thames in London from Wapping to Rotherhithe 1825–43. Knighted 1841.

Brunel fled to the USA 1793 to escape the French Revolution. He became chief engineer in New York. In 1799 he moved to England to mass-produce pulley blocks, which were needed by the navy. Brunel demonstrated that with specially designed machine tools 10 men could do the work of 100, more quickly, more cheaply, and yield a better product. Cheating partners and fire damage to his factory caused the business to fail and he was imprisoned for debt 1821. He spent the latter part of his life working on the Rotherhithe tunnel.

I wonder, if even the ancients ever raised a vault as daunting as this will be.

FILIPPO BRUNELLESCHI
in Vasari *Lives of the Artists* 1568 (on vaulting in a church)

Brunelleschi Filippo (1377–1446). Italian Renaissance architect. The first and one of the greatest of the Renaissance architects, he pioneered the scientific use of perspective. He was responsible for the construction of the dome of Florence Cathedral (completed 1436), a feat deemed impossible by many of his contemporaries.

His use of simple geometries and a modified Classical language lend his buildings a feeling of tranquillity, to which many other early Renaissance architects aspired. His other works include the Ospedale degli Innocenti 1419 and the Pazzi Chapel 1429, both in Florence.

The last resolute opponent of Nazism in the Weimar Republic.

Alan Palmer on HEINRICH BRÜNING
in *Penguin Dictionary of Twentieth Century History* 1979

Brüning Heinrich (1885–1970). German politician. Elected to the Reichstag (parliament) 1924, he led the Catholic Centre Party from 1929 and was federal chancellor 1930–32 when political and economic crisis forced his resignation.

Boxing is just show business with blood.

FRANK BRUNO
Guardian 19 Nov 1991

Bruno Frank (1961–   ). English heavyweight boxer who won the World Boxing Association (WBA) world title after defeating Oliver McCall 1995. He had previously made 3 unsuccessful attempts to win a world title, against Tim Witherspoon 1986 (WBA title), Mike Tyson 1989 (undisputed world title), and Lennox Lewis 1993 (World Boxing Council (WBC) title).

Bruno was born in London and had an ambition from an early age to become world heavyweight champion. He won the Amateur Boxing Association (ABA) championship 1980, and in 1982 fought his first professional fight, defeating Lupe Guerra by a knockout in the first round. In 1985 he won the European heavyweight championship against Anders Eklund. After his second world title defeat in 1989 Bruno retired, but returned to boxing in 1992.

Bruno Giordano (born Filippo Bruno) (1548–1600). Italian philosopher. He entered the Dominican order of monks 1563, but his sceptical attitude to Catholic doctrines forced him to flee Italy 1577. He was arrested by the Inquisition 1593 in Venice and burned at the stake for his adoption of Copernican astronomy and his heretical religious views.

After visiting Geneva and Paris, he lived in England 1583–85, where he wrote some of his finest works. Drawing both on contemporary science (in particular the theories of Copernicus) and on magic and esoteric wisdom, he developed a radical form of pantheism in which all things are aspects of a single, infinite reality animated by God as the 'world soul'. His views had a profound influence on the philosophers Benedict Spinoza and Gottfried Leibniz.

Bruno, St (*c.* 1030–1101). German founder of the monastic Catholic Carthusian order. He was born in Cologne, became a priest, and controlled the cathedral school of Rheims 1057–76. Withdrawing to the mountains near Grenoble after an ecclesiastical controversy, he founded the monastery at Chartreuse in 1084. Canonized 1514. Feast day 6 Oct.

Brusilov Aleksei Alekseevich (1853–1926). Russian general, military leader in World War I who achieved major successes against the Austro-Hungarian forces in 1916. Later he was commander of the Red Army 1920, which drove the Poles to within a few miles of Warsaw before being repulsed by them.

He was responsible for the Brusilov offensive of June 1916 which relieved pressure on the Western and Italian Fronts by drawing German units east to cover the losses sustained by Austro-Hungarian forces. The attack so decimated the Austo-Hungarians that they were never able to play an equal role in the Central Powers' alliance again. However, it cost the Russians nearly one million casualties which further exacerbated the dissatisfaction which was to lead to revolution the following year.

Brut Trojan in medieval British legend, chronicle, and romance who was the great-grandson of Aeneas and who founded Britain, to which he gave his name.

Bruton John (1947–). Irish politician, leader of Fine Gael (United Ireland Party) from 1990 and prime minister from 1994. The collapse of Albert Reynolds' Fianna Fáil–Labour government Nov 1994 thrust Bruton, as a leader of a new coalition with Labour, into the prime ministerial vacancy. He pledged himself to the continuation of the Anglo-Irish peace process as pursued by his predecessor; in 1995 he pressed for greater urgency in negotiations for a permanent peace agreement.

A Dublin-trained lawyer and working farmer, Bruton entered parliament 1969 and, as party spokesman, made steady progress through the departments of agriculture, industry and commerce, and education. He served in the government of Garret FitzGerald 1982–87 before succeeding him as party leader.

---

*On the Ides of March I gave my own life to my country,
and thereafter for her have lived another life of liberty
and glory.*

BRUTUS
quoted in Plutarch *Life of Brutus* ch 40.6

Brutus Marcus Junius (*c.* 85–42 BC). Roman senator and general, a supporter of Pompey (against Caesar) in the civil war. Pardoned by Caesar and raised to high office by him, he nevertheless plotted Caesar's assassination to restore the purity of the Republic. Brutus committed suicide when he was defeated (with Cassius) by Mark Antony, Caesar's lieutenant, at Philippi 42 BC.

---

*You shall not press down upon the brow of labour this
crown of thorns, you shall not crucify mankind upon a
cross of gold.*

WILLIAM BRYAN
Speech at the National Democratic Convention, Chicago 1896

Bryan William Jennings (1860–1925). US politician who campaigned unsuccessfully for the presidency three times: as the Populist and Democratic nominee 1896, as an anti-imperialist Democrat 1900, and as a Democratic tariff reformer 1908. He served as President Wilson's secretary of state 1913–15. In the early 1920s he was a leading fundamentalist and opponent of Clarence Darrow in the Scopes monkey trial. He died shortly after from the strain.

---

*Believing history to be a branch of literature he placed
himself boldly in the tradition of Macaulay and
Trevelyan.*

Robert Blake on ARTHUR BRYANT
in *Dictionary of National Biography*

Bryant Arthur Wynne Morgan (1899–1985). British historian who produced studies of Restoration figures such as Pepys and Charles II, and a series covering the Napoleonic Wars including *The Age of Elegance* 1950. Knighted 1954.

Bryant David John (1931–). English flat-green (lawn) bowls player. He has won every honour the game has offered, including four outdoor world titles (three singles and one triples) 1966–88 and three indoor titles 1979–81.

Bryant William Cullen (1794–1878). US poet and literary figure. His most famous poem, 'Thanatopsis', was published 1817. He was co-owner and co-editor of the *New York Evening Post* 1829–78 and was involved in Democratic party politics. However, his resolute opposition to slavery converted him to Republicanism at the inception of the party 1856.

Bryant, William *US poet, critic, and journalist William Bryant. As co-editor of the* New York Evening Post *for almost 50 years, he argued for the abolition of slavery. His literary works include translations of Homer's* Iliad *and* Odyssey.

Bryce James, 1st Viscount Bryce (1838–1922). British Liberal politician, professor of civil law at Oxford University 1870–93. He entered Parliament 1880, holding office under Gladstone and Rosebery. He was author of *The American Commonwealth* 1888, ambassador to Washington 1907–13, and improved US–Canadian relations. Viscount 1914.

Law will never be strong or respected unless it has the sentiment of the people behind it.

JAMES BRYCE
The American Commonwealth vol 1, 352 1888

Brynner Yul. Stage name of Taidje Khan (1915–1985). Actor, in the USA from 1940, who had a distinctive stage presence and made a shaven head his trademark. He played the king in *The King and I* both on stage 1951 and on film 1956 (Academy Award), and was the leader of *The Magnificent Seven* 1960.

Although his origins were deliberately shrouded in mystery he is believed to have been born in Sakhalin, an island east of Siberia and north of Japan. He later acknowledged a gypsy background. He made his film debut in a B picture *Port of New York* 1949. His other films include *Taras Bulba* 1962, and *Westworld* 1973.

People don't know my real self, and they're not about to find out.

YUL BRYNNER
quoted in Leslie Halliwell *Filmgoer's Companion* 1965

Bryusov Valery Yakovlevich (1873–1924). Russian Symbolist poet, novelist, and critic. He wrote *The Fiery Angel* 1908.

Brzezinski Zbigniew (1928–). US Democrat politician, born in Poland; he taught at Harvard University, USA, and became a US citizen 1949. He was national security adviser to President Carter 1977–81 and chief architect of Carter's human-rights policy.

Buber Martin (1878–1965). Austrian-born Israeli philosopher, a Zionist and advocate of the reappraisal of ancient Jewish thought in contemporary terms. His book *I and Thou* 1923 posited a direct dialogue between the individual and God; it had great impact on Christian and Jewish theology.

Buber was born in Vienna. When forced by the Nazis to abandon a professorship in comparative religion at Frankfurt, he went to Jerusalem and taught social philosophy at the Hebrew University 1937–51.

Suggested reading
Diamond, Malcolm *Buber: Jewish Existentialist* (1960)
Friedman, Maurice *Martin Buber's Life and Work* (1987)
Hodes, Aubrey *Martin Buber: An Intimate Portrait* (1971)
Schlipp, P and Friedman, M *The Philosophy of Martin Buber* (1967)
Smith, R G *Martin Buber* (1967)

Bubka Sergey Nazarovich (1963–). Russian pole vaulter who achieved the world's first six-metre vault in 1985. World champion in 1983, he was unbeaten in a major event from 1981 to 1990. From 1984 he has broken the world record on 32 occasions.

Bucer Martin (1491–1551). German Protestant reformer, professor of divinity at Cambridge University from 1549, who tried to reconcile the views of his fellow Protestants Martin Luther and Ulrich Zwingli with the significance of the eucharist.

To live for a time close to great minds is the best kind of education.

JOHN BUCHAN
Memory Hold-the-Door 1940

Buchan John, 1st Baron Tweedsmuir (1875–1940). Scottish politician and author. Called to the Bar 1901, he was Conservative member of Parliament for the Scottish universities 1927–35, and

governor general of Canada 1934–40. His adventure stories, today criticized for their anti-semitism, include *The Thirty-Nine Steps* 1915, *Greenmantle* 1916, and *The Three Hostages* 1924. Baron 1935.

Buchanan George (1506–1582). Scottish humanist. He wrote *Rerum Scoticarum Historia/A History of Scotland* 1582, which was biased against Mary Queen of Scots.

Forced to flee to France 1539 owing to his satirical verses on the Franciscans, Buchanan returned to Scotland about 1562 as tutor to Mary Queen of Scots. He became principal of St Leonard's College, St Andrews, 1566.

Good-looking, long-legged, nasal of voice and debonair in appearance.

Leslie Halliwell on JACK BUCHANAN
in *The Filmgoer's Companion* 1965

Buchanan Jack (Walter John) (1890–1957). Scottish musical-comedy actor. His songs such as 'Good-Night Vienna' epitomized the period between World Wars I and II.

Buchanan James (1791–1868). 15th president of the USA 1857–61, a Democrat. He was a member of the US House of Representatives 1821–31 and was US minister to Russia 1832–34 when he was elected to the Senate.

Adhering to a policy of compromise on the issue of slavery, he left his Senate seat to serve as US secretary of state during the Mexican War (1846–48). Nominated by the Democrats and elected president 1856, he could do little to avert the secession of the South over the issue of slavery, precipitating the outbreak of the Civil War 1861.

Suggested reading
Hoyt, Edwin *James Buchanan* (1966)
Klein, Philip *President James Buchanan: A Biography* (1962)
Smith, Elbert *The Presidency of James Buchanan* (1975)

Buchanan, James The 15th president of the United States of America, James Buchanan, a Democrat, 1857–1861.

Buchanan Pat(rick) Joseph (1938–   ). US right-wing Republican activist, a TV and radio commentator.

He was special assistant and speechwriter to President Richard Nixon, and was President Ronald Reagan's White House director of communications 1985–87. In 1993 Buchanan became chair of his own broadcasting company. A candidate for the Republican nomination for president 1992, he ran again 1996.

Buchanan was born in Washington DC. He was a journalist on the *St Louis Globe-Democrat* 1962–65 before taking a job in Nixon's law firm. When Nixon became president 1969, it was Buchanan who prepared his daily briefing. Buchanan attacked the television networks, which he believed were under the control of antigovernment liberals and were too influential. Appointed special consultant to the president 1972, he stayed on under Gerald Ford, and from 1975 to 1978 wrote a syndicated political column. In the book *Conservative Voters, Liberal Victories* 1975 he attacked the media for undermining public support for the Vietnam War. From 1978 to 1982 he introduced the commentary programme *Confrontation* on NBC radio. He was moderator of the TV show *Capital Gang* 1988–92 and editor of the newsletter *PJB – From the Right* 1990–91.

Buchman Frank Nathan Daniel (1878–1961). US Christian evangelist. In 1938 he launched in London the anticommunist campaign, the Moral Re-Armament movement.

Buchner Eduard (1860–1917). German chemist who researched the process of fermentation. In 1897 he observed that fermentation could be produced mechanically, by cell-free extracts. Buchner argued that it was not the whole yeast cell that produced fermentation, but only the presence of the enzyme he named zymase. Nobel Prize for Chemistry 1907.

Büchner Georg (1813–1837). German dramatist. His characters were often individuals pitted against the forces of society. Büchner's plays include *Danton's Death* 1835, which chronicles the power struggle between Danton and Robespierre during the French Revolution; and *Woyzeck* 1836, unfinished at his death, which depicts the despair of a common soldier, crushed by his social superiors. Büchner's third play is the comedy *Leonce and Lena* 1836.

His plays remained unperformed until well after his death, but have been repeatedly produced in the 20th century.

It is better to be first with an ugly woman than the hundredth with a beauty.

PEARL S BUCK
The Good Earth ch 1 1931

Buck Pearl S(ydenstricker) (1892–1973). US novelist. Daughter of missionaries to China, she spent much of her life there and wrote novels about Chinese life, such as *East Wind–West Wind* 1930 and *The Good Earth* 1931, for which she received a Pulitzer Prize 1932. She received the Nobel Prize for Literature 1938.

Buckingham George Villiers, 1st Duke of Buckingham (1592–1628). English courtier, adviser to James I and later Charles I. After Charles's accession, Buckingham attempted to form a Protestant coalition in Europe, which led to war with France, but he failed to relieve the Protestants (Huguenots) besieged in La Rochelle 1627. This added to his unpopularity with Parliament, and he was assassinated. Earl 1617, duke 1623.

Stiff in Opinions, always in the wrong; / Was Everything by starts and Nothing long.

John Dryden on GEORGE VILLIERS, 2ND DUKE OF BUCKINGHAM
Absalom and Achitophel 1681

Buckingham George Villiers, 2nd Duke of Buckingham (1628–1687). English politician, a member of the Cabal under Charles II. A dissolute son of the first duke, he was brought up with the royal children. His play *The Rehearsal* satirized the style of the poet Dryden, who portrayed him as Zimri in *Absalom and Achitophel*. Succeeded to dukedom 1628.

His ascent was so quick, that it seemed rather a flight than a growth.

Edward Hyde, Earl of Clarendon on
GEORGE VILLIERS, 2ND DUKE OF BUCKINGHAM
History of the Rebellion 1702–04

Buckland William (1784–1856). English geologist and palaeontologist, a principal pioneer of British geology. He contributed to the descriptive and historical stratigraphy of the British Isles, inferring from the vertical succession of the strata a stage-by-stage temporal development of the Earth's crust. He was also a cleric and in 1845 became dean of Westminster.

Buckler Ernest Redmond (1908–1984). Canadian novelist. From a Novia Scotia farming background, he has published verse and distinguished short stories, including *The Rebellion of Young David and Other Stories* 1975. He is best known for his first novel, *The Mountain and the Valley* 1952, which traces the secret growth of artistic vision in a country boy.

Buckley William (1780–1856). Australian convict who escaped from Port Phillip and lived 1803–35 among the Aborigines before giving himself up, hence 'Buckley's chance' meaning an 'outside chance'.

Buckley William F(rank) (1925–   ). US conservative political writer, novelist, and founder-editor of the *National Review* 1955. In such books as *Up from Liberalism* 1959, and in a weekly television debate *Firing Line*, he represented the 'intellectual' right-wing, antiliberal stance in US political thought.

Budaeus Latin form of the name of Guillaume Budé (1467–1540). French scholar. He persuaded Francis I to found the Collège de France, and also the library that formed the nucleus of the French national library, the Bibliothèque Nationale.

Buddha 'enlightened one'. Title of Prince Gautama Siddhārtha (*c.* 563–483 BC). Religious leader, founder of Buddhism, born at Lumbini in Nepal. At the age of 29 he left his wife and son and a life of luxury, to escape from the material burdens of existence. After six years of austerity he realized that asceticism, like overindulgence, was futile, and chose the middle way of meditation. He became enlightened under a bo, or bodhi, tree near Buddh Gaya in Bihar, India. He began teaching at Varanasi, and founded the Sangha, or order of monks. He spent the rest of his life travelling around N India, and died at Kusinagara in Uttar Pradesh.

The Buddha's teaching consisted of the Four Noble Truths: the fact of frustration or suffering; that suffering has a cause; that it can be ended; and that it can be ended by following the Noble Eightfold Path – right views, right intention, right speech, right action, right livelihood, right effort, right mindfulness, and right concentration – eventually arriving at nirvana, the extinction of all craving for things of the senses and release from the cycle of rebirth.

Suggested reading
Auboyer, J *Buddha* (1983)
Carrithers, Michael *The Buddha* (1983)
Thomas, E J *The Life of Buddha as Legend and History* (1952)
Foucher, A C A *The Life of the Buddha* (1963)

Budenny Semyon Mikhailovich (1883–1973). Soviet general. A sergeant-major in the Tsar's army, Budenny joined the Bolsheviks 1917 and rose rapidly, commanding a cavalry army by 1920 and being made Marshal of the Soviet Union 1935. One of Stalin's 'Old Guard', he survived the Great Purge of Red Army Officers 1936–38 and after the German invasion of the USSR 1941 became commander in chief in the Ukraine and Bessarabia.

A man of limited military talent, Budenny was outmanoeuvred by the Germans and lost Kiev along with half his army. He survived this defeat although he took no further active part in the war. He was made a Hero of the Soviet Union and inspector of recruiting, becoming commander of cavalry forces 1943.

Budge (John) Donald (1915–   ). US tennis player. He was the first to perform the Grand Slam when he won the Wimbledon, French, US, and Australian championships all in 1938.

He won 14 Grand Slam events, including the Wimbledon singles twice.

Buffet Bernard (1928–   ). French figurative painter. He created distinctive, thin, spiky forms with bold, dark outlines. He was a precocious talent in the late 1940s.

Genius is only a great aptitude for patience.
> GEORGES-LOUIS LECLERC BUFFON
> Attributed remark

Buffon Georges Louis Leclerc, Comte de (1707–1788). French naturalist and author of the 18th century's most significant work of natural history, the 44-volume *Histoire naturelle génerale et particulière* 1749–67. In *The Epochs of Nature*, one of the volumes, he questioned biblical chronology for the first time, and raised the Earth's age from the traditional figure of 6,000 years to the seemingly colossal estimate of 75,000 years. Became count 1773.

Bujones Fernando (1955–   ). US ballet dancer. He joined the American Ballet Theater 1972. A virtuoso performer, he has danced leading roles both in the major classics and in contemporary ballets, including *Swan Lake*, *La Bayadère*, and *Fancy Free*.

We might have a two-party system, but one of the two parties would be in office and the other in prison.
> NIKOLAI IVANOVICH BUKHARIN
> Attributed remark

Bukharin Nikolai Ivanovich (1888–1938). Soviet politician and theorist. A moderate, he was the chief Bolshevik thinker after Lenin. Executed on Stalin's orders for treason 1938, he was posthumously rehabilitated 1988.

He wrote the main defence of war communism in his *Economics of the Transition Period* 1920. He drafted the Soviet constitution of 1936 but in 1938 was imprisoned and tried for treason in one of Stalin's 'show trials'. He pleaded guilty to treason, but defended his moderate policies and denied criminal charges. Nevertheless, he was executed, as were all other former members of Lenin's Politburo except Trotsky, who was murdered, and Stalin himself.

Bukowski Charles Henry (1920–1994). German-born US writer and poet. He was a prolific author of poems, stories, and novels in which he creates the persona of himself as an ugly lover and angry drunk, an outsider trapped in a gutter world of comic pathos and glimpsed beauty. His works include *Post Office* 1971, *Ham on Rye* 1982, and a collection of short stories under the title of *Erections, Ejaculations, Exhibitions and General Tales of Ordinary Madness* 1971.

Bukowski's works were typically printed by small presses or underground magazines. A film version of some of his stories appeared 1982 under the title *Tales of Ordinary Madness*, and his 1979 screenplay *Barfly* was filmed 1987. His verse, a revolt against academic or intellectual tradition, is widely popular and has a genuine appeal beyond its immoderate subject matter.

Bulatović Moidrag (1930–1991). Serbian writer. Self-educated and first noted as a lyric poet drawing on his country's oral tradition, he later disclosed a gift for original, courageous, and grimly satiric narrative. He has published short stories and popular novels of which *Crveni petao leti prema nebu/The Red Cockerel* 1959 and *Heroj na magarcu/Hero on a Donkey* 1964 are the best known.

Bulfinch Charles (1763–1844). US architect. He became one of New England's leading architects after his design for the

Massachusetts State House was accepted 1787. His designs include the Hollis Street Church, Harvard's University Hall, the Massachusetts General Hospital, and the Connecticut State House. In 1817 he was appointed architect of the US Capitol by President Monroe.

Some say he developed a national style that was simple, frugal and dignified.
> Randall J Van Vynckt (ed) on CHARLES BULFINCH
> in *International Dictionary of Architects* 1993

Bulgakov Mikhail Afanasyevich (1891–1940). Russian novelist and playwright. His novel *The White Guard* 1924, dramatized as *The Days of the Turbins* 1926, deals with the Revolution and the civil war. His satiric approach made him unpopular with the Stalin regime, and he was unpublished from the 1930s. *The Master and Margarita*, a fantasy about the devil in Moscow, was not published until 1967.

Bulganin Nikolai Aleksandrovich (1895–1975). Soviet politician and military leader. His career began in 1918 when he joined the Cheka, the Soviet secret police. He helped to organize Moscow's defence in World War II, became a marshal of the USSR 1947, and was minister of defence 1947–49 and 1953–55. On the fall of Malenkov he became prime minister (chair of Council of Ministers) 1955–58 until ousted by Khrushchev.

Bull John. Imaginary figure personifying England.

Bull John (*c.* 1562–1628). English composer, organist, and virginalist. Most of his output is for keyboard, and includes 'God Save the King'. He also wrote sacred vocal music.

Bull Olaf Jacob Martin Luther (1883–1933). Norwegian lyric poet. He often celebrated his birthplace Christiania (now Oslo) in his poetry. He was the son of humorist and fiction writer Jacob Breda Bull (1853–1930).

Bullard Edward Crisp (1907–1980). English geophysicist who, with US geologist Maurice Ewing, is generally considered to have founded the discipline of marine geophysics. He pioneered the application of the seismic method to study the sea floor. He also studied continental drift before the theory became generally accepted. Knighted 1953.

He saved Natal.
> Inscription on the equestrian statue of
> REDVERS BULLER in Exeter, erected 1905.

Buller Redvers Henry (1839–1908). British commander against the Boers in the South African War 1899–1902. He was defeated at Colenso and Spion Kop, but relieved Ladysmith; he was superseded by British field marshal Lord Roberts. KCMG 1882.

We desire to throw no one into the shade (in East Asia), but we also demand our own place in the sun.
> BERNHARD, PRINCE VON BÜLOW
> Speech in the Reichstag 6 Dec 1897

Bülow Bernhard Heinrich Martin Karl, Prince von (1849–1929). German diplomat and politician. He was chancellor of the German Empire 1900–09 under Kaiser Wilhelm II and, holding that self-interest was the only rule for any state, adopted attitudes to France and Russia that unintentionally reinforced the trend towards opposing European power groups: the Triple Entente (Britain, France, Russia) and the Triple Alliance (Germany, Austria–Hungary, Italy). He resigned after losing the confidence of Emperor William II and the Reichstag.

Bülow Hans Guido, Freiherr von (1830–1894). German conductor and pianist. He studied with Wagner and Liszt and in 1857 married Cosima, daughter of Liszt. From 1864 he served Ludwig II of

Bavaria, conducting first performances of Wagner's *Tristan und Isolde* and *Die Meistersinger*. His wife left him and married Wagner 1870.

Bülow Karl Wilhelm Paul von (1846–1921). German field marshal. In World War I, he commanded the German 2nd Army in the invasion of Belgium, before advancing into France. He was heavily defeated in the Battle of the Marne Sept 1914 and was transferred to a defensive post on the Northern Command. He retired 1916 due to ill health.

Bultmann Rudolf Karl (1884–1976). German Lutheran theologian and New Testament scholar. He was a professor at Marburg University 1921–51, and during the Third Reich played a leading role in the Confessing Church, a Protestant anti-Nazi movement. A pioneer of form criticism (the analysis of biblical texts in terms of their literary form), he made the controversial claim that the gospels are largely composed of 'myths', which have to be reinterpreted in existentialist terms if they are to be relevant to contemporary needs.

Born in Oldenburg, Lower Saxony, the son of a Lutheran pastor, Bultmann taught at Breslau and Giessen before becoming professor of New Testament studies at Marburg. In his two central works, *History of the Synoptic Gospels* 1921, and *Jesus* 1926, he argues that the gospels are not a reliable guide to life or even to the teachings of Jesus, being not 'biographies', but collections of various 1st-century Christian texts brought together by the evangelists. Many of these texts, he claims, embody mythic forms of thought and expression of the period, which are irrelevant or misleading in a scientific age and hence need to be reinterpreted, or 'demythologized', if their essential meaning – Christ's call to the spiritual life – is to be recognized. For this reinterpretation, Bultmann draws heavily on the existentialist approach of the German philosopher Martin Heidegger (a colleague at Marburg during the late 1920s), and in effect reaffirms the Lutheran principle of 'justification by faith'.

His other major works include *Kerygma and Myth* 1948, *Theology of the New Testament* 1948–53, and *Essays Philosophical and Theological* 1955.

Bulwer-Lytton Edward George Earle Lytton, 1st Baron Lytton (1803– 1873). See ◊Lytton.

Bunche Ralph Johnson (1904–1971). US diplomat. Grandson of a slave, he was principal director of the UN Department of Trusteeship 1947–54, and UN undersecretary acting as mediator in Palestine 1948–49 and as special representative in the Congo 1960. He taught at Harvard and Howard universities and was involved in the planning of the United Nations. In 1950 he was awarded the Nobel Prize for Peace, the first awarded to a black man.

Bundelas Rajput clan prominent in the 14th century, which gave its name to the Bundelkhand region in N central India. The clan had replaced the Chandelā in the 11th century and continued to resist the attacks of other Indian rulers until coming under British control after 1812.

Bunin Ivan Alexeyevich (1870–1953). Russian writer. He was the author of *The Village* 1910, a novel which tells of the passing of peasant life; and the short story collection *The Gentleman from San Francisco* 1916 (about the death of a millionaire on Capri), for which he received a Nobel prize 1933. He was also a poet and translated Byron into Russian.

Bunsen Robert Wilhelm (1811–1899). German chemist credited with the invention of the Bunsen burner. The Bunsen burner, used in laboratories, consists of a vertical metal tube through which a fine jet of gas is directed. Air is drawn in through holes near the base of the tube and the mixture is ignited and burns at the tube's upper opening. His name is also given to the carbon–zinc electric cell, which he invented 1841 for use in arc lamps. In 1860 he discovered two new elements, caesium and rubidium.

Buildings ... They are the language I use, not the written word.

GORDON BUNSHAFT
quoted in Muriel Emanuel (ed) *Contemporary Architects* 1994

Bunshaft Gordon (1909–1990). US architect. While working for the architectural practice Skidmore, Owings & Merrill, he produced the first Modernist building to be completely enclosed in curtain walling (walls which hang from a rigid steel frame), the Lever Building 1952 in New York. He also designed the Heinz Company's UK headquarters 1965 at Hayes Park, London.

Buntline Ned. Adopted name of US author Edward Zane Carroll ◊Judson.

Our memory is our coherence, our reason, our feeling, even our action. Without it, we are nothing.

LUIS BUÑUEL
My Last Sigh ch 1 1984

Buñuel Luis (1900–1983). Spanish Surrealist film director. He collaborated with Salvador Dali on *Un chien andalou* 1928 and *L'Age d'or/The Golden Age* 1930, and established his solo career with *Los olvidados/The Young and the Damned* 1950. His works are often anticlerical, with black humour and erotic imagery. Later films include *Le Charme discret de la bourgeoisie/The Discreet Charm of the Bourgeoisie* 1972 and *Cet obscur objet du désir/That Obscure Object of Desire* 1977.
Suggested reading
Buache, F *The Cinema of Luis Buñuel* (1973)
Edwards, G *The Discreet Art and Life of Luis Buñuel* (1983)
Sandro, P *Diversions of Pleasure* (1987)

Bunyan John (1628–1688). English author. A Baptist, he was imprisoned in Bedford 1660–72 for unlicensed preaching and wrote *Grace Abounding* 1666, which describes his early spiritual life. During a second jail sentence 1675 he started to write *The Pilgrim's Progress*, the first part of which was published 1678. The fervour and imagination of this allegorical story of Christian's spiritual quest has ensured its continued popularity.

Bunsen *Robert Wilhelm Bunsen, German chemist and physicist. As well as the Bunsen burner, he invented a grease-spot photometer (a means of comparing the intensities of two light sources), an electric cell and, with Gustav Kirchhoff, the method of spectrum analysis which facilitated the discovery of new elements.*

Suggested reading
Forrest, J T and Greaves, R L *John Bunyan: A Reference Guide* (1982)
Furlong, M *Puritan's Progress: A Study of John Bunyan* (1975)
Sadler, L V *John Bunyan* (1979)
Sharrock, R *John Bunyan* (1954)

Who would true valour see, / Let him come hither; / One here will constant be, / Come wind, come weather. / There's no discouragement / Shall make him once relent / His first avow'd intent / To be a pilgrim.

JOHN BUNYAN
Pilgrim's Progress 1678

Burali Forti Cesare (1861–1931). Italian mathematician who worked in the field of vector analysis, especially on the linear transformations of vectors. He also framed the Burali Forti paradox 1897, which contradicted the notion that mathematics (or at least its foundations) could be adequately expressed in purely logical terms.

Burbage Richard (*c.* 1567–1619). English actor. He is thought to have been Shakespeare's original Hamlet, Othello, and Lear. He also appeared in first productions of works by Ben Jonson, Thomas Kyd, and John Webster. His father James Burbage (*c.* 1530–1597) built the first English playhouse, known as 'the Theatre'; his brother Cuthbert Burbage (*c.* 1566–1636) built the original Globe Theatre 1599 in London.

Burbidge (Eleanor) Margaret (born Peachey) (1922–   ). British astrophysicist who, with her husband Geoffrey Burbidge, discovered processes by which elements are formed in the nuclei of stars. Together they published *Quasi-Stellar Objects* 1967, based on her research. Later, they suggested that quasars and galaxies are linked in some way. In addition to the work done jointly with her husband, Margaret Burbidge measured the red shifts of several objects suspected of being quasars, and in the process she found that some quasars do not give off any radio radiation.

Burckhardt Jacob Christoph (1818–1897). Swiss art historian, one of the founders of cultural history as a discipline. His *The Civilization of the Renaissance in Italy* 1860, intended as part of a study of world cultural history, profoundly influenced thought on the Renaissance. Burckhardt was professor of history at Basel 1858–93. He also wrote on Greek cultural history.

Burckhardt Johann Ludwig (1784–1817). Swiss explorer sponsored 1806 by the African Association in England to explore Africa. He discovered the ancient city of Petra 1812 and in 1814, disguised as a Muslim pilgrim, became the first Christian to visit Mecca, as described in his *Travels in Arabia* 1829.

Bürger Gottfried August (1747–1794). German Romantic poet, remembered for his ballad 'Lenore' 1773.

Burger Warren Earl (1907–1995). US jurist, chief justice of the US Supreme Court 1969–86. Appointed to the court by President Richard Nixon because of his conservative views, Burger showed himself to be pragmatic and liberal on some social issues, including abortion and desegregation. It was Burger's ruling against presidential executive privilege 1974, at the height of the Watergate scandal, which forced the release of damning tapes and documents that were to prompt the resignation of Nixon. He stepped down as chief justice 1986 to concentrate on his work as chairman of the commission organizing the bicentennial celebrations of the US constitution. The succeeding 'Rehnquist Court', infused by New Right justices appointed by the Republican presidents Reagan and Bush, was significantly more conservative.

Burges William (1827–1881). English Gothic Revival architect and designer. His style is characterized by sumptuous interiors with carving, painting, and gilding. His chief works are Cork Cathedral 1862–76, and additions to and the remodelling of Cardiff Castle 1868–85 and Castle Coch near Cardiff 1875–91.

The poetry of a building lies in its decoration.

WILLIAM BURGES
quoted in J Mordaunt Crook *William Burges and the High Victorian Dream* 1981

Burgess Anthony. Pen name of John Anthony Burgess Wilson (1917–1993). English novelist, critic, and composer. A prolific and versatile writer, Burgess wrote some 60 books as well as screenplays, television scripts, and reviews. His work includes *A Clockwork Orange* 1962, a despairing depiction of high technology and violence set in a future London terrorized by teenage gangs, and the panoramic *Earthly Powers* 1980. The former was made into a notorious film by Stanley Kubrick 1971. *Earthly Powers*, a vast survey of the 20th century narrated by a fictional world-famous novelist, was short-listed for the Booker Prize. Equally ambitious was *The Kingdom of the Wicked* 1985, a spectacular retelling of the Acts of the Apostles. Burgess also wrote many works of literary criticism, particularly on James Joyce, as well as several on language and on music and composing. His memoirs, *Little Wilson and Big God* 1987 and *You've Had Your Time* 1990, are as exciting as his fiction and in many respects an extension of it.

Suggested reading
Aggler, Geoffrey *Anthony Burgess* (1986)
Burgess, Anthony *Little Wilson and Big God* (autobiography) (1987)
Cole, Samuel *Anthony Burgess* (1981)
Mathews, Richard *The Clockwork Universe of Anthony Burgess* (1978)

A work of fiction should be, for its author, a journey into the unknown, and the prose should convey the difficulties of the journey.

ANTHONY BURGESS
Homage to Qwert Yuiop 1987

Burgess Guy Francis de Moncy (1911–1963). British spy, a diplomat recruited by the USSR as an agent. He was linked with Kim Philby, Donald Maclean (1913–1983), and Anthony Blunt.

Burgh Hubert de (died 1243). English justiciar and regent of England. He began his career in the administration of Richard I, and was promoted to the justiciarship by King John; he remained in that position under Henry III from 1216 until his dismissal. He was a supporter of King John against the barons, and ended French intervention in England by his defeat of the French fleet in the Strait of Dover 1217. He reorganized royal administration and the Common Law.

The first of our statesmen to convert the emotion of nationality into a principle of political action.

Shirley on HUBERT DE BURGH
in *Introduction to Royal Letters of Henry VIII* Rolls Series

---

Burghley William Cecil, 1st Baron Burghley (1520–1598). English politician, chief adviser to Elizabeth I as secretary of state from 1558 and Lord High Treasurer from 1572. He was largely responsible for the religious settlement of 1559, and took a leading role in the events preceding the execution of Mary Queen of Scots 1587. Knighted 1551, baron 1572.

One of Edward VI's secretaries, he lost office under Queen Mary, but on Queen Elizabeth's succession became one of her most trusted ministers. He carefully avoided a premature breach with Spain in the difficult period leading up to the attack by the Spanish Armada 1588, and did a great deal towards abolishing monopolies and opening up trade.

Burgoyne John (1722–1792). British general and dramatist. He served in the American Revolution and surrendered 1777 to the colonists at Saratoga, New York State, in one of the pivotal battles of the war. He wrote comedies, among them *The Maid of the Oaks* 1775 and *The Heiress* 1786. He figures in George Bernard Shaw's play *The Devil's Disciple* 1896.

Burke Arleigh Albert (1901–1996). US rear admiral. During World War II, he earned the nickname '31-knot Burke' from his aggressive patrolling policy in the South Pacific. His squadron covered the US landings at Bougainville 1944 and fought over 20 separate engagements with Japanese naval forces. He later became Chief of Staff to Carrier Task Force 58, and was appointed to head the research and development department in the Naval Bureau of Ordnance 1945.

A state without the means of some change is without the means of its conservation.
EDMUND BURKE
Reflections on the Revolution in France 1790

Burke Edmund (1729–1797). British Whig politician and political theorist, born in Dublin, Ireland. In Parliament from 1765, he opposed the government's attempts to coerce the American colonists, for example in *Thoughts on the Present Discontents* 1770, and supported the emancipation of Ireland, but denounced the French Revolution, for example in *Reflections on the Revolution in France* 1790.

Burke wrote *A Philosophical Inquiry into the Origin of our Ideas on the Sublime and Beautiful* 1756, on aesthetics. He was paymaster of the forces in Rockingham's government 1782 and in the Fox–North coalition 1783, and after the collapse of the latter spent the rest of his career in opposition. He attacked Warren Hastings's misgovernment in India and promoted his impeachment. Burke defended his inconsistency in supporting the American but not the French Revolution in his *Appeal from the New to the Old Whigs* 1791 and *Letter to a Noble Lord* 1796, and attacked the suggestion of peace with France in *Letters on a Regicide Peace* 1795–97. He retired 1794. He was a skilled orator and is regarded by British Conservatives as the greatest of their political theorists.

Burke John (1787–1848). First publisher, in 1826, of *Burke's Peerage*.

Burke Martha Jane (born Cannary) (*c.* 1852–1903). Real name of US heroine ◊Calamity Jane.

Burke Robert O'Hara (1821–1861). Irish-born Australian explorer who made the first south-north crossing of Australia (from Victoria to the Gulf of Carpentaria), with William Wills (1834–1861). Both died on the return journey, and only one of their party survived.

Burke William (1792–1829). Irish murderer. He and his partner William Hare, living in Edinburgh, sold the body of an old man who had died from natural causes in their lodging house. After that, they increased their supplies by murdering at least 15 people. Burke was hanged on the evidence of Hare. Hare is said to have died a beggar in London in the 1860s.

Burkitt Denis Parsons (1911–1993). British surgeon who first described the childhood tumour named after him, Burkitt's lymphoma. He also pioneered the trend towards high-fibre diets.

Burle Marx Roberto (1909–   ). Brazilian landscape architect. His work exploits the vivid colours of tropical plants to create spacious painterly landscapes of rhythmic abstract form. Exemplary are the Garden-Yacht Club, Pampulha, 1943, and Del-Este Park, Caracas, 1956. The setting for the new capital of Brasilia, designed by Lucio Costa (1902–   ), owes much to his designs.

Burlington Richard Boyle, 3rd Earl of Burlington (1695–1753). Anglo-Irish architectural patron and architect. He was one of the premier exponents of the Palladian style in Britain. His buildings are characterized by absolute adherence to the Classical rules. Succeeded to earldom 1704.

Chiswick House in London, built by Burlington 1725–29, is based on Palladio's Villa Rotonda, Italy. His major protégé was William Kent.

The problem was not that he looked to the past but he did so unimaginatively.
Rowan Moore on RICHARD BOYLE, 3RD EARL OF BURLINGTON
Daily Telegraph 1 Feb 1995

Burnaby Frederick Gustavus (1842–1885). English soldier, traveller, and founder of the weekly critical journal *Vanity Fair*. He travelled to Spain, Sudan, and Russian Asia during his leave from the Horse Guards. His books include *A Ride to Khiva* 1876 and *On Horseback through Asia Minor* 1877. Burnaby joined the British Nile expedition to relieve General Gordon, under siege in Khartoum, Sudan, and was killed in action at the battle of Abu Klea.

I mean by a picture a beautiful romantic dream.
EDWARD BURNE-JONES
quoted in introduction to catalogue by John Christian *Burne-Jones* 1975

Burne-Jones Edward Coley (1833–1898). English painter. In 1856 he was apprenticed to the Pre-Raphaelite painter and poet Dante Gabriel Rossetti, who remained a dominant influence. His paintings, inspired by legend and myth, were characterized by elongated forms and subdued tones, as in *King Cophetua and the Beggar Maid* 1880–84 (Tate Gallery, London). He also designed tapestries and stained glass in association with William Morris. His work influenced both Symbolism and Art Nouveau. Created baronet 1894. The best collection of his work is in the Birmingham City Art Gallery.

Burnell (Susan) Jocelyn Bell. British astronomer. See ◊Bell Burnell.

Burnes Alexander (1805–1841). Scottish soldier, linguist, diplomat, and traveller in Central Asia. Following journeys to Rajputana and Lahore he led an expedition across the Hindu Kush to Bokhara described in his *Travels into Bokhara* 1834. In 1836–37 he led a diplomatic mission to the Afghan leader Dost Mohammed, described in his book *Kabul* 1842. He was killed in Kabul during a rising that sparked off the first Afghan War. Knighted 1839.

The law of England is the greatest grievance of the nation, very expensive and dilatory.
GILBERT BURNET
History of His Own Times 1723–34

Burnet Gilbert (1643–1715). English historian and bishop, author of *History of His Own Times* 1723–34. His Whig views having brought him into disfavour, he retired to the Netherlands on the accession of James II and became the confidential adviser of William of Orange, with whom he sailed to England 1688. He was appointed bishop of Salisbury 1689.

Burnet (Frank) Macfarlane (1899–1985). Australian physician, an authority on immunology and viral diseases such as influenza, poliomyelitis, and cholera. From 1927 he was associated with the Walter and Eliza Hall Institute for Medical Research in Melbourne, becoming its director 1944. He shared the 1960 Nobel Prize for Physiology or Medicine with immunologist Peter Medawar for his work on skin grafting. Knighted in 1951.

The idea of man as a dominant animal of the earth whose whole behaviour tends to be dominated by his own desire for dominance gripped me. It seemed to explain almost everything.
MACFARLANE BURNET
Dominant Manual 1970

Burnett Frances Eliza Hodgson (1849–1924). English writer. She emigrated with her family to the USA 1865. Her novels for children include the sentimental rags-to-riches tale *Little Lord Fauntleroy* 1886 and the less cloying *The Secret Garden* 1911, which has its values anchored in nature mysticism.

Travelling is the ruin of all happiness! There's no looking at a building here after seeing Italy.

FANNY BURNEY
Cecilia 1782

Burney Fanny (Frances) (1752–1840). English novelist and diarist. She achieved success with *Evelina*, a novel published anonymously 1778, became a member of Dr Johnson's circle, received a post at court from Queen Charlotte, and in 1793 married the French émigré General d'Arblay (died 1818). She published three further novels, *Cecilia* 1782, *Camilla* 1796, and *The Wanderer* 1814; her diaries and letters appeared 1842. She was the daughter of musician Dr Charles Burney (1726–1814).
Suggested reading
Burney, Fanny *Diaries* (many editions available)
Simons, J *Fanny Burney* (1987)
Wallace, T G *A Busy Day* (1984)

Burnham James (1905–1987). US philosopher who argued in *The Managerial Revolution* 1941 that world control is passing from politicians and capitalists to the new class of business executives, the managers.

Burnham (Linden) Forbes (Sampson) (1923–1985). Guyanese Marxist-Leninist politician. He was prime minister 1964–80, leading the country to independence 1966 and declaring it the world's first cooperative republic 1970. He was executive president 1980–85. Resistance to the US landing in Grenada 1983 was said to be due to his forewarning the Grenadans of the attack.

Burnside , Ambrose US Union general Ambrose Everett Burnside. He resigned his position as commander of the Army of the Potomac after the loss of the battle of Fredericksburg 1862, during which the Union army lost over 10,000 men. He later took Knoxville 1863, but resigned after the defeat at Petersburg 1864, when Union troops failed to break Robert E Lee's hold on the city.

Burns John Elliot (1858–1943). British labour leader, sentenced to six weeks' imprisonment for his part in the Trafalgar Square demonstration on 'Bloody Sunday' 13 Nov 1887, and leader of the strike in 1889 securing the 'dockers' tanner' (wage of 6d per hour). An Independent Labour member of Parliament 1892–1918, he was the first working-class person to be a member of the cabinet, as president of the Local Government Board 1906–14.

The Mississippi ... is muddy water ... the St Lawrence ... is crystal water. But the Thames is liquid history.

JOHN BURNS
Attributed remark

Burns John Horne (1916–1953). US novelist. He is known for his acclaimed novel *The Gallery* 1946, a passionate, episodic story set in Naples and North Africa and based on his service in the US army during World War II. He wrote two other novels while an expatriate in Italy, where he died.

The best laid schemes o' mice an' men / Gang aft a-gley.

ROBERT BURNS
'To a Mouse'

Burns Robert (1759–1796). Scottish poet. He used the Scots dialect at a time when it was not considered suitably 'elevated' for literature. Burns' first volume, *Poems, Chiefly in the Scottish Dialect*, appeared 1786. In addition to his poetry, Burns wrote or adapted many songs, including 'Auld Lang Syne'.

Burns' fame rests equally on his poems (such as 'Holy Willie's Prayer', 'Tam o' Shanter', 'The Jolly Beggars', and 'To a Mouse') and his songs – sometimes wholly original, sometimes adaptations – of which he contributed some 300 to Johnson's *Scots Musical Museum* 1787–1803 and Thomson's *Scottish Airs with Poetry* 1793–1811.

Born at Alloway near Ayr, he became joint tenant with his brother of his late father's farm at Mossgiel in 1784, but it was unsuccessful. Following the publication of his first volume of poems in 1786 he farmed at Ellisland, near Dumfries.

He became district excise officer on the failure of his farm in 1791. Burns Night is celebrated on 25 January.
Suggested reading
Hecht, H *Robert Burns: The Man and his Work* (1985)
Lindsay, M *Robert Burns: The Man, His Work, The Legend* (1954)
Low, D *Robert Burns* (1986)
Mackay, J *Burns* (1992)
McIntyre, Ian *Dirt and Deity: A Life of Robert Burns* (1995)

Burns Terence (1944–   ). British economist. A monetarist, he was director of the London Business School for Economic Forecasting 1976–79, and chief economic adviser to the Thatcher government 1980–91. Knighted 1983.

Burnside Ambrose Everett (1824–1881). US military leader and politician. He was appointed brigadier general in the Union army soon after the outbreak of the Civil War 1861. Named as George McClellan's successor as commander of the Army of the Potomac, Burnside served briefly in that position before being transferred to the West. He was governor of Rhode Island 1866–69 and US Senator 1874–81. His distinctive side whiskers and moustache framing a clean-shaven chin became popularly known as 'burnsides', of which 'sideburns' is a modification.

Burnside William (1852–1927). English mathematician who made advances in automorphic functions, group theory, and the theory of probability. In 1897 he published the first book on group theory to appear in English; the revised edition 1911 is considered a standard work. A nearly completed manuscript on probability theory was published after his death.

Burr Aaron (1756–1836). US politician, Republican vice president 1800–04, in which year he killed his political rival Alexander

Hamilton in a duel. In 1807 Burr was tried and acquitted of treason charges, which implicated him variously in a scheme to conquer Mexico, or part of Florida, or to rule over a seceded Louisiana.

Burr was born in Newark, New Jersey, of an eminent Puritan family. He was on George Washington's staff during the American Revolution but was critical of the general and was distrusted in turn. He tied with Thomas Jefferson in the presidential election of 1800, but Alexander Hamilton, Burr's longtime adversary, influenced the House of Representatives to vote Jefferson in, Burr becoming vice president. After killing Hamilton, Burr fled to South Carolina, but returned briefly to Washington to complete his term of office. He spent some years in Europe, seeking British and French aid in overthrowing Jefferson, but re-entered the USA 1812 under an assumed name. He died in poverty at the age of 80.

Burr Raymond (1917–1993). Canadian actor. He graduated from playing assorted Hollywood villains to the heroes Perry Mason and Ironside in the long-running television series of the same names. He played the murderer in Alfred Hitchcock's *Rear Window* 1954.

Burra Edward John (1905–1976). English painter. He was devoted to themes of city life, its bustle, humour, and grimy squalor. *The Snack Bar* 1930 (Tate Gallery, London) and his watercolour scenes of Harlem, New York, 1933–34, are characteristic. Postwar works include religious paintings and landscapes.

Burroughs Edgar Rice (1875–1950). US novelist. He wrote *Tarzan of the Apes* 1914, the story of an aristocratic child lost in the jungle and reared by apes, and followed it with over 20 more books about the Tarzan character. He also wrote a series of novels about life on Mars.

After one look at this planet any visitor from outer space would say 'I WANT TO SEE THE MANAGER.'
WILLIAM BURROUGHS
The Adding Machine, 'Women: A Biological Mistake?' 1985

Burroughs William S(eward) (1914–). US writer. One of the most culturally influential postwar writers, his work is noted for its experimental methods, black humour, explicit homo-eroticism, and apocalyptic vision. In 1944 he met Allen Ginsberg and Jack Kerouac, all three becoming leading members of the Beat Generation. His first novel, *Junkie* 1953, documented his heroin addiction and expatriation to Mexico, where in 1951, he accidentally killed his common-law wife. He settled in Tangier 1954 and wrote his celebrated anti-novel *Naked Lunch* 1959. In Paris, he developed collage-based techniques of writing, resulting in his 'cut-up' science-fiction trilogy, *The Soft Machine* 1961, *The Ticket That Exploded* 1962, and *Nova Express* 1964.

Later, more conventionally written novels, include *Cities of the Red Night* 1981, *Place of Dead Roads* 1984, and *The Western Lands* 1987. His *Selected Letters 1945–59* was published 1993.

Burroughs William Seward (1855–1898). US industrialist who invented the first hand-operated adding machine to give printed results.

Burt Cyril Lodowic (1883–1971). British psychologist. A specialist in children's mental development, he argued in *The Young Delinquent* 1925 the importance of social and environmental factors in delinquency. After his death it was claimed that he had falsified experimental results in an attempt to prove his theory that intelligence is largely inherited. Knighted 1946.

Burton Richard. Stage name of Richard Walter Jenkins (1925–1984). Welsh stage and screen actor. He had a rich, dramatic voice but his career was dogged by personal problems and an often poor choice of roles. Films in which he appeared with his wife, Elizabeth Taylor, include *Cleopatra* 1962 and *Who's Afraid of Virginia Woolf?* 1966. Among his later films are *Equus* 1977 and *Nineteen Eighty-Four* 1984.

Other films include *Beckett* 1964 and *The Spy Who Came in from the Cold* 1966. His rendition of Dylan Thomas' *Under Milk Wood* for radio was another of his career highspots. He also won acclaim for his stage performances in both Shakespearean and contemporary dramas throughout his film career.

This diamond has so many carats, it's almost a turnip.
RICHARD BURTON
on his gift to Elizabeth Taylor, quoted in *Observer* 5 March 1972

Burton Richard Francis (1821–1890). British explorer and translator (he knew 35 oriental languages). He travelled mainly in the Middle East and NE Africa, often disguised as a Muslim; made two attempts to find the source of the Nile, 1855 and 1857–58 (on the second, with John Speke, he reached Lake Tanganyika); and wrote many travel books. He translated oriental erotica and the *Arabian Nights* 1885–88. KCMG 1885.

After military service in India, Burton explored the Arabian peninsula and Somaliland. In 1853 he visited Mecca and Medina disguised as an Afghan pilgrim; he was then commissioned by the Foreign Office to explore the sources of the Nile. Later travels took him to North and South America. His translations include the *Kama Sutra of Vatsyayana* 1883 and *The Perfumed Garden* 1886.

One religion is as true as another.
ROBERT BURTON
Anatomy of Melancholy 1621

Burton Robert (1577–1640). English philosopher who wrote an analysis of depression, *Anatomy of Melancholy* 1621, a compendium of information on the medical and religious opinions of the time, much used by later authors.

Burton was born in Leicester. He studied at Oxford, and remained there for the rest of his life as a fellow of Christ Church.

Burton Tim (1960–). US film director. Black humour and a visual sensibility inspired by comic strips characterize such films as the comedy ghost story *Beetlejuice* 1988 and *Batman* 1989. Before

Burroughs, William S US novelist William S. Burroughs, a leading figure of the Beat Generation, became notorious for his graphic depictions of the often sordid and sometimes violent world of drug addiction. His frank and innovative novels are regarded by some as dreary exercises in narcissism, and by others as strikingly original satires on the spiritual and emotional emptiness of contemporary life.

making the sequel *Batman Returns* 1992, he directed *Edward Scissorhands* 1990, a suburban fable that gave full rein to Burton's penchant for gothic fantasy.

Before he directed his first full-length feature film, *Pee Wee's Big Adventure* 1985, Burton worked as an animator with Disney and made several short experimental films.

Busby Matt(hew) (1909–1994). Scottish football player and manager, synonymous with the success of Manchester United both on and off the field. He was best known as manager of Manchester United 1945–1969. His 'Busby Babes' won the championship 1952, 1956, and 1957, before eight members were killed in an air crash in Munich 1958. Busby's reassembled team reached the 1958 FA Cup final, and won the FA Cup 1963. Championship wins 1965 and 1967 ensured a further onslaught on European Cup competition, and the team went on to win the European Cup 1968, the first English side to do so. Knighted 1968.

Matt Busby is a symbol of everything that is best in our national game.

British prime minister Harold Wilson on MATT BUSBY 1978

Busby Richard (1606–1695). English headmaster of Westminster school from 1640, renowned for his use of flogging. Among his pupils were Dryden, Locke, Atterbury, and Prior.

Bush Alan Dudley (1900–). English composer. A student of the composer John Ireland, he later adopted a didactic simplicity in his compositions in line with his Marxist beliefs. He has written a large number of works for orchestra, voice, and chamber groups. His operas include *Wat Tyler* 1952 and *Men of Blackmoor* 1956.

Read my lips – no new taxes.

GEORGE BUSH
Promise made during 1988 US presidential campaign

Bush George Herbert Walker (1924–). 41st president of the USA 1989–93, a Republican. He was director of the Central Intelligence Agency (CIA) 1976–81 and US vice president 1981– 89. As president, his response to the Soviet leader Gorbachev's diplomatic initiatives was initially criticized as inadequate, but his sending of US troops to depose his former ally, General Noriega of Panama, proved a popular move at home. Success in the 1991 Gulf War against Iraq further raised his standing. Despite this success, the signing of the long-awaited Strategic Arms Reduction Treaty (START I) July 1991, and Bush's unprecedented unilateral reduction in US nuclear weapons two months later, his popularity at home began to wane as criticism of his handling of domestic affairs mounted.

Domestic economic problems 1991–92 were followed by his defeat in the 1992 presidential elections by Democrat Bill Clinton. After his defeat at the polls Nov 1992 and prior to handing over to his successor Bill Clinton 20 Jan 1993, Bush initiated 'Operation Restore Hope' in Somalia, in which US Marines were drafted in as part of a multinational effort to deliver aid to famine-striken areas, and signed the START II treaty with Russia, which bound both countries to cut long-range nuclear weapons by two thirds by the year 2003. He also supported the more controversial bombing of strategic targets in Iraq after alleged infringements of the UN-imposed 'no-fly zone'.

Suggested reading
Campbell, Colin (ed) *The Bush Presidency* (1991)
Green, F *George Bush* (1989)
Sufrin, M *George Bush* (1989)

Bush Vannevar (1890–1974). US electrical engineer and scientist who in the 1920s and 1930s developed several mechanical and mechanical-electrical analogue computers which were highly effective in the solution of differential equations. The standard electricity meter is based on one of his designs. From 1932 he held senior positions at MIT. During World War I he worked on a magnetic device for detecting submarines. During World War II, as scientific adviser to President F D Roosevelt, Bush was one of the initiators of the atomic-bomb project. After the war he took part in the setting-up and running of the Office of Scientific Research and Development and its successor, the Research and Development Board.

In matters concerning art my feelings are those of an autocrat.

FERRUCCIO BUSONI
in a letter to Heinrich Burkard 1923

Busoni Ferruccio Dante Benvenuto (1866–1924). Italian pianist, composer, and music critic. Much of his music was for the piano, but he also composed several operas including *Doktor Faust*, completed by Philipp Jarnach after his death. An apostle of Futurism, he encouraged the French composer Edgard Varèse.

Buss Frances Mary (1827–1894). British pioneer in education for women. She first taught in a school run by her mother, and at 18 she founded her own school for girls in London. Her work helped to raise the status of women teachers and the academic standard of women's education in the UK.

Her first school became the North London Collegiate School in 1850. She founded the Camden School for Girls in 1871. She is often associated with Dorothea Beale, a fellow pioneer.

Bustamante (William) Alexander (born Clarke) (1884–1977). Jamaican politician. As leader of the Labour Party, he was the first prime minister of independent Jamaica 1962–67. Knighted 1955.

Butcher Rosemary (1947–). English choreographer and dancer. She is a leading exponent of avant-garde dance. Her minimalist pieces display a quiet assurance and fluidity and are often performed in unorthodox settings, such as on beaches and in art galleries. They include *Flying Lines* 1985 and *Touch the Earth* 1986.

Bute John Stuart, 3rd Earl of Bute (1713–1792). British Tory politician, prime minister 1762–63. On the accession of George III in 1760, he became the chief instrument in the king's policy for breaking the power of the Whigs and establishing the personal rule of the monarch through Parliament.

Bute succeeded his father as earl 1723, and in 1737 was elected a representative peer for Scotland. His position as the king's favourite

Bush *The US president 1989–93, George Bush. His failure to pull the economy out of recession was the main factor in his landslide defeat 1992.*

and supplanter of the popular prime minister Pitt the Elder made him hated in the country. He resigned 1763 after the Seven Years' War.

Proud, aristocratical, pompous, imposing, with a great deal of superficial knowledge, and a very false taste in everything.

William Petty Fitzmaurice, 2nd Earl of Shelburne on
JOHN STUART, 3RD EARL OF BUTE
quoted in Alan Lloyd *The Wickedest Age* 1971

Butenandt Adolf Friedrich Johann (1903–1995). German biochemist who isolated the first sex hormones (oestrone, androsterone, and progesterone), and determined their structure. He shared the 1939 Nobel Prize for Chemistry with Leopold Ruzicka (1887–1976).

Buthelezi Chief Mangosuthu Gatsha (1928–). South African Zulu leader and politician, president of the Zulu-based Inkatha Freedom Party (IFP), which he founded as a paramilitary organization for attaining a nonracial democratic society in 1975. Buthelezi's threatened boycott of South Africa's first multiracial elections led to a dramatic escalation in politically motivated violence, but he eventually agreed to register his party and in May 1994 was appointed home affairs minister in the country's first post-apartheid government.

Buthelezi, great-grandson of King Cetewayo, became chief minister of KwaZulu, then a black homeland in the Republic of South Africa, 1970. Opposed to KwaZulu becoming a Black National State, he argued instead for a confederation of black areas, with eventual majority rule over all South Africa under a one-party socialist system. He was accused of complicity in the factional violence between Inkatha and African National Congress supporters that racked the townships during the early 1990s.

Butler Joseph (1692–1752). English priest and theologian who became dean of St Paul's in 1740 and bishop of Durham in 1750; his *Analogy of Religion* 1736 argued that it is no more rational to accept deism (arguing for God as the first cause) than revealed religion (not arrived at by reasoning).

Butler Josephine Elizabeth (born Gray) (1828–1906). English social reformer. She promoted women's education and the Married Women's Property Act, and campaigned against the Contagious Diseases Acts of 1862–70, which made women in garrison towns suspected of prostitution liable to compulsory examination for venereal disease. Refusal to undergo examination meant imprisonment. As a result of her campaigns, the acts were repealed in 1883.

Butler Reg(inald) Cotterell (1913–1981). English sculptor. He taught architecture 1937–39 and was then a blacksmith for many years before becoming known for cast and forged iron works, both abstract and figurative. In 1953 he won an international competition for a monument to *The Unknown Political Prisoner* (a model is in the Tate Gallery, London).

My own career ... exemplifies the advantages of the long haul ... the steady influence one may exert by being at all times on the inside.

RICHARD AUSTEN ('RAB') BUTLER
quoted in Roy Jenkins *Gallery of 20th Century Portraits* 1988

Butler Richard Austen ('Rab'), Baron Butler of Saffron Walden (1902–1982). British Conservative politician. As minister of education 1941–45, he was responsible for the 1944 Education Act; he was chancellor of the Exchequer 1951–55, Lord Privy Seal 1955–59, and foreign minister 1963–64. As a candidate for the prime ministership, he was defeated by Harold Macmillan in 1957 (under whom he was home secretary 1957–62), and by Alec Douglas Home in 1963. Baron 1965.

Butler Samuel (1612–1680). English satirist. His poem *Hudibras*, published in three parts 1663, 1664, and 1678, became immediately popular for its biting satire against the Puritans.

Love is a boy, by poets styled / then spare the rod and spoil the child.

SAMUEL BUTLER
Hudibras pt 2 1663

Butler Samuel (1835–1902). English author. He made his name 1872 with a satiric attack on contemporary utopianism, *Erewhon* (*nowhere* reversed), but is now remembered for his autobiographical *The Way of All Flesh* written 1872–85 and published 1903.

The Fair Haven 1873 examined the miraculous element in Christianity. *Life and Habit* 1877 and other works were devoted to a criticism of the theory of natural selection. In *The Authoress of the Odyssey* 1897 he maintained that Homer's *Odyssey* was the work of a woman.
Suggested reading
Cole, G D *Samuel Butler* (1961)
Harris, J F *Samuel Butler, Author of Erewhon: The Man and His Work* (1973)

Life is like playing a violin solo in public and learning the instrument as one goes on.

SAMUEL BUTLER
Speech at the Somerville Club 27 Feb 1895

Butlin Billy (William Heygate Edmund Colborne) (1899–1980). British holiday-camp entrepreneur. Born in South Africa, he went in early life to Canada, but later entered the fairground business in the UK. He originated a chain of camps (the first was at Skegness 1936) that provided accommodation, meals, and amusements at an inclusive price. Knighted 1964.

Butor Michel Marie François (1926–). French writer. He was one of the *nouveau roman* novelists who made radical changes in the traditional form. His works include *Passage de Milan/Passage from Milan* 1954, *Dégrès/Degrees* 1960, *L'Emploi du temps/Passing Time* 1963, and *Improvisations sur Michel Butor* 1993. *Mobile* 1962 is a volume of essays.

The brick diapers are distributed with taste, if not with discretion.

John Summerson on WILLIAM BUTTERFIELD
in *Heavenly Mansion* 1949 (on Keble College, Oxford)

Butterfield William (1814–1900). English Gothic Revival architect. His work is characterized by vigorous, aggressive forms and multicoloured striped and patterned brickwork. His schools, parsonages, and cottages developed an appealing functional secular style that anticipated Philip Webb and other Arts and Crafts architects.

Typical buildings by Butterfield are the church of All Saints, Margaret Street, London, 1849–59, and Keble College and chapel, Oxford, 1867–83. At Baldersby, Yorkshire, UK, he designed a whole village of church, rectory, almshouse, school, and cottages 1855–57.

Buxtehude Diderik (1637–1707). Danish composer. In 1668 he was appointed organist at the Marienkirche, Lübeck, Germany, where his fame attracted J S Bach and Handel. He is remembered for his organ works and cantatas, written for his evening concerts or *Abendmusiken*; he also wrote numerous trio sonatas for two violins, viola da gamba, and harpsichord.

Byatt A(ntonia) S(usan) (1936–). English novelist and critic. Her fifth novel, *Possession*, won the 1990 Booker Prize. *The Virgin in the Garden* 1978 is a confident, zestfully handled account of a varied group of characters putting on a school play during Coronation year, 1953. It has a sequel, *Still Life* 1985.

in Turkey and France, where, after a victory at Vimy Ridge, he took command of the Third Army.

From 20 Nov to 7 Dec 1917 he led the successful tank attack on Cambrai. He was governor general of Canada 1921–26, and was made a field marshal 1932. KCMG 1915, baron 1919, viscount 1928.

Byrd Richard Evelyn (1888–1957). US aviator and explorer. The first to fly over the North Pole (1926), he also flew over the South Pole (1929) and led five overland expeditions in Antarctica. At the request of President Franklin Roosevelt, he took command of the US Antarctic Service. Byrd maintained that new techniques could be used as supplements to traditional methods, rather than as replacements for them. In holding this view, he disagreed with Norwegian explorer Roald Amundsen.

Byrd William (1543–1623). English composer. His sacred and secular choral music, including over 200 motets and masses for three, four, and five voices, exemplifies the English polyphonic style.

Probably born in Lincoln, he became organist at the cathedral there 1563. He shared with Thomas Tallis the honorary post of organist in Queen Elizabeth's Chapel Royal, and in 1575 he and Tallis were granted a monopoly in the printing and selling of music.

Byron (Augusta) Ada, Countess of Lovelace (1815–1852). English mathematician, a pioneer in writing programs for Charles Babbage's analytical engine. In 1983 a new, high-level computer language, Ada, was named after her. She was the daughter of the poet Lord Byron.

I love not man the less, but Nature more.

LORD BYRON
Childe Harold IV. 178 1817

Byron George Gordon, 6th Baron Byron (1788–1824). English poet. He became the symbol of Romanticism and political liberalism throughout Europe in the 19th century. His reputation was established with the first two cantos of *Childe Harold* 1812. Later works include *The Prisoner of Chillon* 1816, *Beppo* 1818, *Mazeppa* 1819, and, most notably, the satirical *Don Juan* 1819–24. He left England 1816, spending most of his later life in Italy.

Born in London and educated at Harrow and Cambridge, Byron published his first volume *Hours of Idleness* 1807 and attacked its harsh critics in *English Bards and Scotch Reviewers* 1809. Overnight fame came with the first two cantos of *Childe Harold*, romantically describing his tours in Portugal, Spain, and the Balkans (third canto 1816, fourth 1818). In 1815 he married mathematician Anne Milbanke (1792–1860), with whom he had a daughter, Augusta Ada Byron, separating from her a year later amid much scandal. He then went to Europe, where he became friendly with Percy and Mary Shelley. He engaged in Italian revolutionary politics and sailed for Greece 1823 to further the Greek struggle for independence, but died of fever at Missolonghi. He is remembered for his lyrics, his colloquially easy 'Letters', and as the 'patron saint' of Romantic liberalism. Succeeded as baron 1798.

Suggested reading
Coote, S *Byron: The Making of a Myth* (1988)
Knight, G W *Lord Byron* (1952)
Marchand, L *Byron: A Portrait* (1970)
Quennell, P *Byron* (1967)
Quennell, P *Byron: A Portrait in his Own Words* (1989)
Raphael, F *Byron* (1982)

Byron Robert (1905–1941). English writer on travel and architecture, including *The Byzantine Achievement* 1929 and *The Road to Oxiana* 1937, an account of a journey from Iran to Afghanistan 1933–34.

(I consider myself) a victim destroyed to divert the indignation and resentment of an injured and deluded people.

Dudley Pope *At Twelve Mr Byng Was Shot* 1987
on JOHN BYNG's court-martial and death sentence

Byatt *English novelist and critic A S Byatt is one of the prominent literary figures writing in England today. Among her scholarly works is the first book-length study of Iris Murdoch,* Degrees of Freedom *1965.*

She was born in Sheffield and educated at a Quaker boarding school (with her sister, novelist Margaret Drabble) and at Newnham College, Cambridge.

Autobiographies tell more lies than all but the most self-indulgent fiction.

A S BYATT
'The Day that E M Forster Died' in *Sugar* 1987

Bykau Vasil (Russian Vasily Bykov) (1924–). Belorussian writer. In novels such as *The Ordeal* 1970 and *The Mark of Doom* 1982 Bykau seeks to crystallize a specifically Belorussian sense of identity by exploring the severe wartime ordeals of small groups of ordinary people under German occupation.

He left nothing to fortune that could be accomplished by foresight and application.

Thomas Corbett on GEORGE BYNG
in *An Account of the Expedition of the British Fleet to Sicily in the Years 1718, 1719 and 1720 under the command of Sir George Byng, Bart* 1739

Byng George, 1st Viscount Torrington (1663–1733). British admiral. He captured Gibraltar 1704, commanded the fleet that prevented an invasion of England by the 'Old Pretender' James Francis Edward Stuart 1708, and destroyed the Spanish fleet at Messina 1718. John Byng was his fourth son. Knighted 1704, created viscount 1721.

Byng John (1704–1757). British admiral. Byng failed in the attempt to relieve Fort St Philip when in 1756 the island of Minorca was invaded by France. He was court-martialled and shot. The French writer Voltaire ironically commented that it was done 'to encourage the others'.

Byng Julian Hedworth George, 1st Viscount Byng of Vimy (1862–1935). British general in World War I, commanding troops

C

Caballé Montserrat (1933–). Spanish operatic soprano. Specializing in the operas of Bellini, Donizetti, and Verdi, she became famous overnight after a concert performance of Donizetti's *Lucrezia Borgia* at Carnegie Hall, New York 1965. Her secure technique and excellent breathing control enable her to sing a very wide repertory.

Caballero Fernan. Pseudonym of Cecilia Francisca Josefa Bohl von Faber (1796–1877). Spanish novelist, born at Morges, Switzerland. Her first novel, *La gaviota* 1849, created the type of the Andalusian village romances in Spain. She published many other works, including *Cuentos y poesias populares Andaluces* 1859, the earliest collection of Spanish folk tales and songs.

Cabot Sebastian (1474–1557). Italian navigator and cartographer, the second son of Giovanni Caboto. He explored the Brazilian coast and the Rio de la Plata for the Holy Roman Emperor Charles V 1526–30.

Cabot was also employed by Henry VIII, Edward VI, and Ferdinand of Spain. He planned a voyage to China by way of the North-East Passage, the sea route along the N Eurasian coast, encouraged the formation of the Company of Merchant Adventurers of London 1551, and in 1553 and 1556 directed the company's expeditions to Russia, where he opened British trade.

Caboto Giovanni, or John Cabot (*c.* 1450–*c.* 1498). Italian navigator. Commissioned, with his three sons, by Henry VII of England to discover unknown lands, he arrived at Cape Breton Island on 24 June 1497, thus becoming the first European to reach the North American mainland (he thought he was in NE Asia). In 1498 he sailed again, touching Greenland, and probably died on the voyage.

Cabral Pedro Alvarez (1460–1526). Portuguese explorer who made Brazil a Portuguese possession in 1500 and negotiated the first commercial treaty between Portugal and India.

Cabral set sail from Lisbon for the East Indies in March 1500, and accidentally reached Brazil by taking a course too far west. He claimed the country for Portugal 25 April, since Spain had not followed up Vicente Pinzón's (*c.* 1460–1523) landing there earlier in the year. Continuing around Africa, he lost seven of his fleet of 13 ships (the explorer Bartolomeu Diaz was one of those drowned), and landed in Mozambique. Proceeding to India, he negotiated the first Indo-Portuguese treaties for trade, and returned to Lisbon July 1501.

Cabrini Frances, or Francesca Xavier ('Mother Cabrini') (1850–1917). First Roman Catholic US citizen to become a saint. Born in Lombardy, Italy, she founded the Missionary Sisters of the Sacred Heart, and established many schools and hospitals in the care of her nuns. She was canonized 1946. Feast day 22 Dec.

Cacoyannis Michael (1922–). Greek film and stage director and writer. He directed *Zorba the Greek* 1965; other films include *Stella* 1955, *Electra* 1961, *The Trojan Women* 1971, and *Up, Down and Sideways* 1992.

Cade Jack (died 1450). English rebel. He was a prosperous landowner, but led a revolt 1450 in Kent against the high taxes and court corruption of Henry VI and demanded the recall from Ireland of Richard, Duke of York. The rebels defeated the royal forces at Sevenoaks and occupied London. After being promised reforms and pardon they dispersed, but Cade was hunted down and killed.

Cadell Francis (1822–1879). Australian navigator, shipowner and merchant, born in Scotland. He was a pioneer in the navigation of the Murray River in the 1850s.

Cadorna Luigi, Count (1850–1928). Italian soldier. He was appointed commander in chief of Italian forces on Italy's entry into World War I 1915. He held this post until after the Battle of Caporetto Nov 1917, when he was relieved by General Diaz. He represented Italy in the military council at Versailles and was retired Sept 1919.

Cadwalader (died *c.* 633). Welsh hero. The son of Cadwallon, king of Gwynedd, N Wales, he defeated and killed Eadwine of Northumbria in 633. About a year later he was killed in battle.

Cadwallon (lived 6th century). King of Gwynedd, N Wales, father of Cadwalader.

Caecus Appius Claudius (lived 4th–3rd century BC). Roman politician, the most famous member of the Appii Claudii, one of the great patrician families of the republic. As censor in 312 BC and consul 307 and 296 BC, he was responsible for reforms giving more privileges to the plebeians.

He also constructed Rome's first aqueduct, the Aqua Appia, and built the Via Appia road (312 BC), connecting Rome with Capua, and hence the main line between Rome and Greece.

Light was first / Through the Lord's word / Named day: / Beauteous, bright creation.

CAEDMON
'Creation. The First Day'.

Caedmon (lived 7th century). Earliest known English poet. According to the Northumbrian historian Bede, when Caedmon was a cowherd at the Christian monastery of Whitby, he was commanded to sing by a stranger in a dream, and on waking produced a hymn on the Creation. The poem is preserved in some manuscripts. Caedmon became a monk and may have composed other religious poems.

Caesar powerful family of ancient Rome, which included Gaius Julius Caesar, whose grand-nephew and adopted son Augustus assumed the name of Caesar and passed it on to his adopted son Tiberius. From then on, it was used by the successive emperors, becoming a title of the Roman rulers. The titles 'tsar' in Russia and 'kaiser' in Germany were both derived from the name Caesar.

I came, I saw, I conquered.

JULIUS CAESAR
on his campaign in Pontus, quoted in Suetonius
Lives of the Caesars, 'Divus Julius'

Caesar (Gaius) Julius (100–44 BC). Roman statesman and general. A patrician, Caesar allied himself with the popular party, and when elected to the office of aedile (magistrate) 65, nearly ruined himself with lavish amusements for the Roman populace. Although a free thinker, he was elected chief pontiff 63 and appointed governor of Spain 61. He formed with Pompey and Crassus the First Triumvirate 60 BC. He conquered Gaul 58–50 and invaded Britain 55 and 54. A revolt by the Gauls under Vercingetorix 52 was crushed 51. His governorship of Gaul ended 49, and after the death of Crassus, Pompey became his rival. He fought against Pompey 49–48, defeating him at Pharsalus. He followed Pompey to Egypt, where Pompey was murdered. Caesar stayed some months in Egypt, where Cleopatra, queen of Egypt, gave birth to his son, Caesarion. Caesar executed a lightning campaign 47 against King Pharnaces II (ruled 63–47 BC) in Asia Minor, which he summarized: *Veni vidi vici* 'I came, I saw, I conquered'. He was awarded a ten-year dictatorship 46, and with his final victory over the sons of Pompey at Munda in Spain 45, he was awarded the dictatorship for life 44. On 15 March 44, he was stabbed to death by conspirators (led by Brutus and Cassius) at the foot of Pompey's statue in the Senate house. His commentaries on the campaigns and the civil war survive.

Suggested reading
Bradford, E *Julius Caesar: The Pursuit of Power* (1984)
Gelzer, M *Julius Caesar: Politician and Statesman* (1968)
Grant, Michael *Julius Caesar* (1975)
Meier, Christian *Caesar* (trs 1995)
Weinstock, S *Divus Julius* (1971)
Yavetz, Z *Julius Caesar and his Public Image* (1983)

Caetano Marcello José des Neves Alves (1906–1980). Portuguese right-wing politician. Professor of administrative law at Lisbon from 1940, he succeeded the dictator Salazar as prime minister from 1968 until his exile after the military coup of 1974. He was granted political asylum in Brazil.

Try as we might to make a silence, we cannot.

JOHN CAGE
Silence, 1961

Cage John (1912–1992). US composer. His interest in Indian classical music led him to the view that the purpose of music was to change the way people listen. From 1948 he experimented with instruments, graphics, and methods of random selection in an effort to generate a music of pure incident. For example, he used 24 radios, tuned to random stations, in *Imaginary Landscape No 4* 1951. His ideas profoundly influenced late 20th-century aesthetics.

Cage studied briefly with Arnold Schoenberg, also with Henry Cowell, and joined others in reacting against the European music tradition in favour of a freer idiom open to non-Western attitudes. Working in films during the 1930s, Cage assembled and toured a percussion orchestra incorporating ethnic instruments and noise-makers, for which *Double Music* 1941 was composed (with Lou Harrison). He invented the prepared piano to tour as accompanist with the dancer Merce Cunningham, a lifelong collaborator. In a later work, *4 Minutes and 33 Seconds* 1952, the pianist sits at the piano reading a score for that length of time but does not play.

Cage's essays and writings were collected in, for example, *Silence* 1961 and *For the Birds* 1981.

Cagliostro Alessandro di, Count Cagliostro. Assumed name of Giuseppe Balsamo (1743–1795). Italian adventurer, swindler, and specialist in the occult, born in Palermo. In Paris in 1785 he was involved in the affair of the diamond necklace – obtained by a band of swindlers supposedly on behalf of Marie Antoinette, dismantled and sold – and was imprisoned in the Bastille. Later arrested by the Inquisition in Rome, he died in the fortress of San Leone.

Once a song-and-dance man, always a song-and-dance man. Those few words tell as much about me professionally as there is to tell.

JAMES CAGNEY
Time obituary 1 Apr 1986

Cagney James (1899–1986). US actor. His physical dynamism and staccato vocal delivery made him one of the first stars of talking pictures. Often associated with gangster roles (for example, *The Public Enemy* 1931), he was an actor of great versatility, playing Bottom in *A Midsummer Night's Dream* 1935 and singing and dancing in *Yankee Doodle Dandy* 1942. He starred in *Mr Roberts* 1955, and *One Two Three* was his last film before retirement; but in 1981 he came back for *Ragtime*.

Cahn Sammy. Adopted name of Samuel Cohen (1913–1993). US song lyricist whose career took him from Tin Pan Alley to Hollywood and Broadway. For over 20 years he provided Frank Sinatra with material, including 'Come Fly With Me' 1958 and 'My Kind of Town' 1964. His chief collaborators were composers Jule Styne (1905–) and Jimmy van Heusen (1913–1990). He wrote 'Three Coins in the Fountain' 1954 with Styne and 'The Tender Trap' 1955 with van Heusen, both for Sinatra. Cahn's favourite among his own songs was 'Call Me Irresponsible' 1963, which he described, with characteristic immodesty, as 'the epitome of matching words to music'.

Love and marriage, love and marriage, / Go together like a horse and carriage, / This I tell ya, brother, / Ya can't have one without the other.

SAMMY CAHN
'Love and Marriage'

Cailletet Louis Paul (1832–1913). French physicist and inventor who in 1877–78 was the first to liquefy oxygen, hydrogen, nitrogen, and air. He did it by cooling them below their critical temperatures, first compressing the gas, then cooling it, then allowing it to expand to cool it still further. Cailletet's other achievements included the installation of a 300-m/985-ft high manometer on the Eiffel Tower; an investigation of air resistance on falling bodies; a study of a liquid-oxygen breathing apparatus for high-altitude ascents; and the construction of numerous devices, including automatic cameras, an altimeter, and air-sample collectors for sounding-balloon studies of the upper atmosphere.

Cain James M(allahan) (1892–1977). US novelist. He wrote a series of popular novels in the taut, economical idiom of 'hard-boiled' fiction, derived in the main from Ernest Hemingway. Written with compelling power, his major novels – *The Postman Always Rings Twice* 1934, *Mildred Pierce* 1941, and *Double Indemnity* 1943 – were made into key works of *film noir* during the 1940s.

Caine Michael. Stage name of Maurice Joseph Micklewhite (1933–). English actor. He is an accomplished performer with an enduring Cockney streak. His films include *Alfie* 1966, *Sleuth* 1972, *The Man Who Would Be King* 1975, *Educating Rita* 1983, *Hannah and Her Sisters* 1986, and many others.

Cairns Hugh John Forster (1922–). English virologist whose research has focused on cancer and influenza. In 1959 he succeeded in carrying out genetic mapping of an animal virus for the first time. He worked at the Viruses Research Institute, Entebbe, Uganda, 1951–63 and was director of the Cold Spring Harbor Laboratory of Quantitative Biology in New York 1963–68. He then took professorships at the State University of New York and with the American Cancer Society. From 1973 to 1981 he was in charge of the Mill Hill laboratories of the Imperial Cancer Research Fund, London. In 1982 he moved to the Harvard School of Public Health, Boston, USA.

Cairns Jim (James Ford) (1914–). Australian Labor politician, regarded as the leader of Labor's left wing in the 1960s and early 1970s when he was heavily involved in the movement against the Vietnam War and conscription. He was treasurer in the Whitlam government 1974–75 but was dismissed for his role in the 'loans affair' which centred on unorthodox loan negotiations by the minister for minerals and energy, Rex Connor.

Caitanya (1486–1533). Principal leader in Bengal of the bhakti movement which revitalized medieval Hinduism. He inspired a mass movement of devotion for Krishna, especially through *sankirtan*, public singing of the name of God accompanied by dancing and musical instruments. (The modern Hare Krishna movement is descended from Caitanya.)

Cajori Florian (1859–1930). Swiss-born US historian of mathematics. His books dealt with the history of both elementary and advanced mathematics, as well as the teaching of mathematics. His two-volume *History of Mathematical Notations* 1928–29 is a standard reference text. He also wrote biographies of eminent mathematicians.

Calamity Jane nickname of Martha Jane Burke (born Cannary) (*c.* 1852–1903). US heroine of Deadwood, South Dakota. She worked as a teamster, transporting supplies to the mining camps, adopted male dress and, as an excellent shot, promised 'calamity' to any aggressor. Many fictional accounts of the Wild West featured her exploits.

Calas Jean (1698–1762). French Protestant, executed in 1762 for allegedly murdering his son to prevent his conversion to Catholicism. His widow escaped to Switzerland and, aided by the writer Voltaire, succeeded in getting the trial reviewed, proving Calas' innocence.

Calatrava Santiago (1951–). Spanish architect and engineer. He is noted for his highly expressive and elegant structural solutions. Of these, the Mérida Bridge, Spain (begun 1988), spans the river Guadiana with a 195 m/640 ft arch; the dramatic TGV railway station, Lyon (begun 1989), has a wing roof resembling a bird taking flight; and the East London River Crossing Bridge 1990, 630 m/ 2,067 ft in length, has a central arch spanning 450 m/1,477 ft contained within its internal structure. More recently, he designed two spectacular suspension bridges in Seville 1992.

Caldecott Randolph (1846–1886). English artist and illustrator. He illustrated books for children, including *John Gilpin* 1848, and became an illustrator for *Punch* during the 1870s.

The Caldecott medal, given annually by the American Library Association to the artist of the year's best illustrated book, is named for him.

Calder Alexander Stirling (1898–1976). US abstract sculptor. He invented mobiles, suspended shapes that move in the lightest current of air. In the 1920s he began making wire sculptures and stabiles (static mobiles), coloured abstract shapes attached by lines of wire. Huge versions adorn the Lincoln Center in New York City and UNESCO in Paris.

Even in dreams good works are not wasted.

PEDRO CALDERÓN DE LA BARCA
La Vida es Sueño 1636

Calderón de la Barca Pedro (1600–1681). Spanish dramatist and poet. After the death of Lope de Vega 1635, he was considered to be the leading Spanish dramatist. Most celebrated of the 118 plays is the philosophical *La vida es sueño/Life is a Dream* 1635.

Calderón was born in Madrid and 1613–19 studied law at Salamanca. In 1620 and 1622 he was successful in poetry contests in Madrid; while still writing dramas, he served in the army in Milan and the Netherlands (1625–35). By 1636 his first volume of plays was published and he had been made master of the revels at the court of Philip IV, receiving a knighthood in 1637. In 1640 he assisted in the suppression of the Catalan rebellion. After the death of his mistress he became a Franciscan 1650, was ordained 1651, and appointed as a prebendary of Toledo in 1653. As honorary chaplain to the king 1663, he produced outdoor religious plays for the festival of the Holy Eucharist. He died in poverty.

His works include the tragedies *El pintor de su deshonra/The Painter of His Own Dishonour* 1645, *El alcalde de Zalamea/The Mayor of Zalamea* 1640, and *El médico de su honra/The Surgeon of His Honour* 1635; the historical *El príncipe constante/The Constant Prince* 1629; and the dashing intrigue *La dama duende/The Phantom Lady* 1629.

Caldwell Erskine Preston (1903–1987). US novelist. He achieved great popular success with *Tobacco Road* 1932 and *God's Little Acre* 1933. These were vivid, bawdy depictions of poverty-stricken Southern sharecroppers in the Depression, which bordered on sensationalist melodrama. His literary autobiography, *Call It Experience*, was published 1951.

Born in White Oak, Georgia, Caldwell travelled with his father, a minister, and worked among poor whites in the South as a cotton picker. He was married to photojournalist Margaret Bourke-White, who collaborated with him on three books, notably *You Have Seen Their Faces* 1937, about the rural South. His other works include *Trouble in July* 1940 and *Georgia Boy* 1943.

Caley George (1770–1829). English botanist and explorer in Australia whose many excursions resulted in a detailed knowledge of the country surrounding the settlement of Sydney.

Calhoun John C(aldwell) (1782–1850). US politician; vice president 1825–29 under John Quincy Adams and 1829–33 under Andrew Jackson. Throughout his vice-presidency, he was a defender of strong states' rights against an overpowerful federal government and of the institution of slavery. He served in the US Senate 1842–43 and 1845–50, where he continued to espouse the right of states to legislate on slavery. As President Tyler's secretary of state 1844–45, he was responsible for effecting the annexation of Texas.

Would that the Roman people had but one neck!

CALIGULA
Suetonius *Life of Caligula*

Caligula (Gaius Caesar) (AD 12–41). Roman emperor, son of Germanicus and successor to Tiberius AD 37. Caligula was a cruel tyrant and was assassinated by an officer of his guard. He is believed to have been mentally unstable. He was nicknamed after the soldier's boot he wore (*caliga*) when with the army as a young man.

A lie can be half-way round the world before the truth has got its boots on.

JAMES CALLAGHAN
Speech 1 Nov 1976

Callaghan (Leonard) James, Baron Callaghan of Cardiff (1912–). British Labour politician. As chancellor of the Exchequer 1964–67, he introduced corporation and capital-gains taxes, and resigned following devaluation. He was home secretary 1967–70 and prime minister 1976–79 in a period of increasing economic stress.

As foreign secretary 1974, Callaghan renegotiated Britain's membership of the European Community (now the European Union). In 1976 he succeeded Harold Wilson as prime minister and in 1977 entered into a pact with the Liberals to maintain his government in office. Strikes in the so-called 'winter of discontent' 1978–79 led to the government losing a vote of no confidence in the Commons, forcing him to call an election, and his party was defeated at the polls May 1979.

This made Callaghan the first prime minister since Ramsay MacDonald 1924 to be forced into an election by the will of the Commons. In 1980 he resigned the party leadership under left-wing pressure, and in 1985 announced that he would not stand for Parliament in the next election. Created baron and KG 1987.

See illustration on page 148.
Suggested reading
Callaghan, James *Time and Chance* (memoirs) (1987)
Donoughue, B *Prime Minister: The Conduct of Policy under Harold Wilson and James Callaghan* (1987)

Callaghan Morley Edward (1903–1990). Canadian novelist and short-story writer. His realistic novels include *Such Is My Beloved* 1934, *More Joy in Heaven* 1937, and *Close to the Sun Again* 1977.

Deeply influenced both by the Depression and the teaching of the Catholic modernist Jacques Maritain, he characteristically writes about social misfits and outcasts and the possibilities of personal salvation through the power of love. His other works include *They Shall Inherit the Earth* 1935, *The Loved and the Lost* 1951, *Stories* 1959, and *A Passion in Rome* 1961.

Suggested reading
Callaghan, Morley *That Summer in Paris* (memoirs) (1963)
Conron, Brandon *Morley Callaghan* (1966)
Hoar, Victor *Morley Callaghan* (1969)

Callaghan, James *British Labour politician James Callaghan, prime minister 1976–79. His premiership, which began when Harold Wilson unexpectedly resigned, was marked by currency crises and the collapse of any kind of working relationship between government and trades unions. His government was forced into a general election when it lost a vote of no confidence in the Commons.*

Callas Maria. Adopted name of Maria Cecilia Sophia Anna Kalogeropoulos (1923–1977). US lyric soprano. She was born in New York of Greek parents. With a voice of fine range and a gift for dramatic expression, she excelled in operas including *Norma, La Sonnambula, Madame Butterfly, Aïda, Tosca,* and *Medea.*

She debuted in Verona, Italy, 1947 and at New York's Metropolitan Opera 1956. Although her technique was not considered perfect, she helped to popularize classical coloratura roles through her expressiveness and charisma.

Suggested reading
Ardoin, J and Fitzgerald, G *Callas* (1974)
Kesting, Jürgen *Maria Callas* (trs 1992)
Stancioff, N *Maria* (1987)
Stassinopoulos, Arianna *Maria: Beyond the Callas Legend* (1980)

She shone all too brief a while in the world of opera, like a vivid flame attracting the attention of the whole world, and she had a strange magic that was all her own.

Tito Gobbi on MARIA CALLAS
in *My Life*, 1980

Callendar Hugh Longbourne (1863–1930). English physicist and engineer who carried out fundamental investigations into the behaviour of steam. One of the results was the compilation of reliable steam tables that enabled engineers to design advanced steam machinery. He was professor of physics at the Royal Holloway College, Egham, Surrey, 1888–93, at McGill College, Montreal, 1893–98, at University College, London, 1898–1901, and at the Royal College of Science, London, from 1901.

Life in the brightest lights of nature ... nothing harrowing, nothing problematic ... nothing blurred.

Nikolaus Pevsner on CALLICRATES
in *An Outline of European Architecture* 1943 (on the Parthenon).

Callicrates (lived 5th century BC). Athenian architect. With Ictinus, he designed the Parthenon 447–438 on the Acropolis.

Callimachus (*c.* 310–*c.* 240 BC). Greek poet and critic. He is known for his epigrams. Born in Cyrene, he taught in Alexandria, Egypt, where he is reputed to have been head of the great library.

Callot Jacques (1592/93–1635). French engraver and painter. He was influenced by Mannerism. His series of etchings *Great Miseries of War* 1633, prompted by his own experience of the Thirty Years' War, are arrestingly composed and full of horrific detail. He is regarded as one of the greatest etchers, and his enormous output includes over 1,400 prints and 1,500 drawings. His love of the grotesque was later to influence Goya.

Calloway Cab(ell) (1907–1994). US band leader, singer, and actor. An extrovert performer, he became a big star as leader of the house band at the Cotton Club in New York 1931. He was a pioneer of scat singing with his catch phrase 'Hi-de-ho', used in his theme song 'Minnie the Moocher' 1931. His biggest hit songs were 'Jumping Jive' 1939 and 'Blues in the Night' 1942.

Calmette (Léon Charles) Albert (1863–1933). French bacteriologist. A student of Pasteur, he developed, with Camille Guérin, the BCG vaccine against tuberculosis 1921.

Calne Roy Yorke (1930–). British surgeon who developed the technique of organ transplants in human patients and pioneered kidney-transplant surgery in the UK. He became professor of surgery at Cambridge University 1965. Knighted 1986.

Calvert George, 1st Baron Baltimore (1579–1632). English politician who founded the North American colony of Maryland 1632. As a supporter of colonization, he was granted land in Newfoundland 1628 but, finding the climate too harsh, obtained a royal charter for the more temperate Maryland 1632. Knighted 1617, baron 1625.

Calvin John (also known as Cauvin or Chauvin) (1509–1564). French-born Swiss Protestant church reformer and theologian. He was a leader of the Reformation in Geneva and set up a strict religious community there. His theological system is known as Calvinism, and his church government as Presbyterianism. Calvin wrote (in Latin) *Institutes of the Christian Religion* 1536 and commentaries on the New Testament and much of the Old Testament.

Calvin, born in Noyon, Picardie, studied theology and then law, and about 1533 became prominent in Paris as an evangelical preacher. In 1534 he was obliged to leave Paris and retired to Basel, where he studied Hebrew. In 1536 he accepted an invitation to go to Geneva, Switzerland, and assist in the Reformation, but was expelled 1538 because of public resentment against the numerous and too drastic changes he introduced. He returned to Geneva 1541 and, in the face of strong opposition, established a rigorous theocracy (government by priests). In 1553 he had the Spanish theologian Servetus burned for heresy. He supported the Huguenots in their struggle in France and the English Protestants persecuted by Queen Mary I.

Suggested reading
Bouwsma, W J *Calvin* (1987)
McGrath, Alister E *A Life of John Calvin* (1990)
Parker, T H L *John Calvin* (1976)
Stauffer, R *The Humanness of John Calvin* (1971)

Calvin Melvin (1911–). US chemist who, using radioactive carbon-14 as a tracer, determined the biochemical processes of photosynthesis, in which green plants use chlorophyll to convert carbon dioxide and water into sugar and oxygen. Nobel prize 1961. From 1937 he was on the staff of the University of California, becoming professor 1947.

Calvino Italo (1923–1985). Italian novelist. Inspired by folk tales, his novels have a fairy-tale quality. *If on a Winter's Night a Traveller* 1979 is a pastiche of ten literary modes, parodying the *nouveau roman* and other contemporary trends. He was an avowed opponent of Fascism, as he shows in his writings, which contain both allegory and fantasy.

Born in Cuba to Italian parents, he grew up in Italy. *The Path to the Nest of Spiders* 1947 is based on his experiences in the Italian Resistance, which he joined 1943. He was a member of the Italian Communist Party in the 1950s. His other novels include *Invisible Cities* 1972 and *The Castle of Crossed Destinies* 1973.

Calwell Arthur Augustus (1896–1973). Australian Labor politician. He entered the federal parliament 1940 and became minister for immigration 1945, in which position he initiated a programme that was based for the first time on large-scale non-British immigration from Europe. He was leader of the Labor Party and leader of the opposition 1960–67, surviving an assassination attempt in 1966.

She was excellent technically, a virtuoso.

Christy Adair on MARIE-ANNE DE CUPIS DE CAMARGO
in *Woman and Dance; Sylphs and Sirens* 1992
concerning her debut at the Paris Opera 1726

Camargo Marie-Anne de Cupis de (1710–1770). French ballerina. She became a ballet star in Paris 1726 and was the first ballerina to attain the 'batterie' (movements involving beating the legs together) previously danced only by men. She shortened her skirt to expose her ankles and her brilliant footwork, thereby gaining more freedom of movement.

Calvin, John *The Protestant theologian and reformer John Calvin. Calvin was born in France, and trained in theology and law before becoming a preacher in Paris. He then went to Geneva, Switzerland, where he became a prominent figure in the Reformation.*

I. CALVIN

Cambon (Pierre) Paul (1843–1924). French diplomat who was ambassador to London during the years leading to the outbreak of World War I, and a major figure in the creation of the Anglo-French entente during 1903–04.

Although the judges could discover no law that allowed a brother to marry a sister, there was undoubtedly a law that the King of Persia could do what he pleased.

HERODOTUS on CAMBYSES
in *History* bk 3, ch 31

Cambyses (lived 6th century BC). King of Persia 529–522 BC. Succeeding his father Cyrus, he assassinated his brother Smerdis and conquered Egypt in 525 BC. There he outraged many of the local religious customs and was said to have become insane. He died in Syria.

Camden William (1551–1623). English antiquary. He published his topographical survey *Britannia* 1586, and was headmaster of Westminster School from 1593. The *Camden Society* (1838) commemorates his work.

Cameron Alastair Graham Walter (1925–   ). Canadian-born US astrophysicist responsible for theories regarding the formation of the unstable element technetium within the core of red giant stars and of the disappearance of Earth's original atmosphere. He emigrated to the USA 1959 and held successive posts at the California Institute of Technology; the Goddard Institute for Space Studies, New York; and Yeshiva University, New York. In 1973 he became professor of astronomy at Harvard.

Cameron Charles (c. 1743–1812). Scottish architect. His work was classical in spirit and very scholarly. He trained under Isaac Ware (1717–1766) in the Palladian tradition before being summoned to Russia by Catherine the Great 1779. He decorated the palace complex at Tsarskoe Selo (now Pushkin), laid out the park of the royal villa at Pavlovsk (rebuilding it with two temples, an aviary, and a colonnade), and planned the city of Sofia. After a period in England 1796–1800, he returned to Russia as chief architect of the Admiralty, and from 1803 executed many buildings, including the Naval Hospital and barracks at Kronstadt 1805. His work was largely destroyed in World War II.

Whilst all that we love best in classic art / is stamped forever on the immortal face.

JULIA MARGARET CAMERON
Poem 'On a Portrait' Sept 1875

Cameron Julia Margaret (born Pattle) (1815–1879). British photographer. She made lively and dramatic portraits of the Victorian intelligentsia, often posed as historical or literary figures. Her sitters included her friends the English astronomer John Herschel, the poet Alfred Lord Tennyson, whose *Idylls of the King* she illustrated 1872, and Charles Darwin. She used a large camera, five-minute exposures, and wet plates.

Suggested reading
Gernsheim, Helmut *Julia Margaret Cameron* (1973)
Hill, Brian *Julia Margaret Cameron: A Victorian Family Portrait* (1973)
Weaver, Mike *Julia Margaret Cameron* (1984)

Cameron Simon (1799–1889). US political leader. He served two partial terms in the US Senate 1845–49 and 1857–60. A supporter of Abraham Lincoln at the 1860 Republican nominating convention, he was appointed secretary of war at the outbreak of the American Civil War 1861. A dismal failure in that position, Cameron was named minister to Russia 1862. After the end of the war 1865 he returned to the Senate 1867–77.

Camillus Marcus Furius (lived 4th century BC). Roman general and statesman, five times dictator. Following early successes against the Etruscans, he rallied the Romans after the Gallic invasion 387 BC. Camillus was an important leader of the patrician cause in the political crises that followed, and was later victorious in campaigns against the Aequi.

Camoëns or Camões, Luís Vaz de (1524–1580). Portuguese poet and soldier. He went on various military expeditions, and was shipwrecked 1558. His poem *Os Lusiades/The Lusiads* 1572 tells the story of the explorer Vasco da Gama and incorporates much Portuguese history; it has become the country's national epic. His posthumously published lyric poetry is also now valued.

Having wounded an equerry of the king 1552, he was banished to India. He received a small pension, but died in poverty of plague.

Camp Walter Chauncey (1859–1925). US football coach who was responsible for instituting some of the most basic rules of the game of American football, including team size, field dimensions, and the four-down system. He also initiated the tradition of selecting an annual all-American football team.

Born in New Britain, Connecticut, USA, Camp was educated at Yale University. In 1888, after a brief business career, he returned to Yale as athletic director, football coach, and member of the Intercollegiate Football Rules Committee.

Campbell Colen (1676–1729). Scottish architect. He was one of the principal figures in British Palladian architecture. His widely influential book *Vitruvius Britannicus* was published 1712. Among his best-known works are Burlington House, London, 1718–19 and Merewith Castle, Kent, 1722–25.

Campbell Colin, 1st Baron Clyde (1792–1863). British field marshal. He commanded the Highland Brigade at Balaclava in the Crimean War and, as commander in chief during the Indian Mutiny, raised the siege of Lucknow and captured Cawnpore. KCB 1849, baron 1858.

Campbell Donald Malcolm (1921–1967). British car and speedboat enthusiast, son of Malcolm Campbell, who simultaneously held the land-speed and water-speed records. In 1964 he set the world water-speed record of 444.57 kph/276.3 mph on Lake Dumbleyung, Australia, with the turbojet hydroplane *Bluebird*, and achieved the land-speed record of 648.7 kph/403.1 mph at Lake Eyre salt flats, Australia. He was killed in an attempt to raise his water-speed record on Coniston Water, England.

Campbell Gordon (1886–1953). British admiral in World War I. He commanded Q-ships, armed vessels that masqueraded as merchant ships to decoy German U-boats to destruction.

Campbell Kim (1947–). Canadian Progressive Conservative politician, prime minister (briefly) 1993. She was the country's first woman prime minister. She held the posts of minister for state affairs

Campbell, Donald Land and water-speed champion Donald Campbell, pictured with the car *Bluebird. He held the water speed record in a boat of the same name, but was tragically killed during an attempt to break his own speed record.* (Image Select)

and northern development 1989–90, attorney general 1990–92, and defence 1992. Four months after taking over as prime minister, she lost the Oct 1993 election to the Liberal Party's candidate, Jean Chretien, and in Dec resigned as leader of the Progressive Conservative Party.

Don't mess with me, I got tanks.

KIM CAMPBELL
Remark while defence minister

Campbell Malcolm (1885–1948). British racing driver who once held both land- and water-speed records. He set the land-speed record nine times, pushing it up to 484.8 kph/301.1 mph at Bonneville Flats, Utah, USA, in 1935, and broke the water-speed record three times, the best being 228.2 kph/141.74 mph on Coniston Water, England, in 1939. His car and boat were both called *Bluebird*. Knighted 1931.

His son Donald Campbell emulated his feats.

The deep, deep peace of the double-bed after the hurly-burly of the chaise-longue.

MRS PATRICK CAMPBELL
on her recent marriage. Quoted in A Woollcott *While Rome Burns* 1989

Campbell Mrs Patrick (born Beatrice Stella Tanner) (1865–1940). English actress. Her roles included Paula in Pinero's *The Second Mrs Tanqueray* 1893 and Eliza in *Pygmalion*, written for her by G B Shaw, with whom she had an amusing correspondence.

Campbell Robert (1769–1846). Australian pioneer settler and merchant, born in Scotland. In 1819 he co-founded Australia's first savings bank. He was one of the first settlers in the Canberra area, his property Duntroon remaining in his family until 1910 when it was acquired by the federal government for a military college.

Translations (like wives) are seldom strictly faithful if they are in the least attractive.

ROY CAMPBELL
Quoted in *Poetry Review* June-July 1949

Campbell Roy (born Ignatius Royston Dunnachie Campbell) (1901–1957). South African poet. He wrote *The Flaming Terrapin* 1924. His poetry displays technical virtuosity, narrative verve, and brilliant metaphor, sometimes applied to satiric ends as in his attack on English literary coteries *The Georgiad* 1931. Among his most successful works are translations from Baudelaire, Lorca, and St John of the Cross.

Born in Durban, he became a professional jouster and bullfighter in Spain and Provence, France. He fought for Franco in the Spanish Civil War and was with the Commonwealth forces in World War II. He recorded his flamboyant life in *Light in a Dark House* 1951.

O leave this barren spot to me! / Spare, woodman, spare the beechen tree.

THOMAS CAMPBELL
'The Beech-Tree's Petition'

Campbell Thomas (1777–1844). Scottish poet. After the successful publication of his *Pleasures of Hope* 1799, he travelled in Europe, and there wrote his war poems 'Hohenlinden' and 'Ye Mariners of England'.

Campbell William Wallace (1862–1938). US astronomer and mathematician who published a catalogue of nearly 3,000 radial velocities of stars 1928. His spectroscopic observations of Nova Auriga 1892 enabled him to describe the changes in its spectral pattern with time. From 1891 he worked at the newly established Lick

Observatory, California, becoming director of the observatory 1901–30. There he was responsible for much of the spectroscopic work undertaken and was an active participant in and organizer of seven eclipse expeditions to many parts of the world.

I am a great believer in bed, in constantly keeping horizontal – the heart and everything else go slower, and the whole system is refreshed.
HENRY CAMPBELL-BANNERMAN
Letter to Mrs Whiteley 11 Sept 1906

Campbell-Bannerman Henry (born Henry Campbell) (1836–1908). British Liberal politician, prime minister 1905–08. It was during his term of office that the South African colonies achieved self-government, and the Trades Disputes Act 1906 was passed.

Campbell-Bannerman, born in Glasgow, was chief secretary for Ireland 1884–85, war minister 1886 and again 1892–95, and leader of the Liberals in the House of Commons from 1899. In 1905 he became prime minister and led the Liberals to an overwhelming electoral victory 1906. He began the conflict between Commons and Lords that led to the Parliament Act of 1911. He resigned 1908. GCB 1895.
Suggested reading
Hirst, F W *In the Golden Days* (1947)
Wilson, John *CB: A Life of Campbell-Bannerman* (1973)

Campese David (1962–). Australian rugby union player, one of the outstanding entertainers of the game. He holds the world record for the most tries scored in international rugby and is the most-capped Australian international (91 by 15 July 1995). He was a key element in Australia's 1991 World Cup victory.

Campese was a member of the 1984 Australia team, which won all four internationals in Britain. He plays for Randwick (New South Wales) and Milan (Italy).

Campi family of Italian painters practising in Cremona, N Italy, in the 16th century, the best-known member being *Giulio Campi* (*c.* 1502–1572).

Campin Robert, also known as the Master of Flémalle (*c.* 1378–1444). Dutch painter of the early Renaissance. Active in Tournai from 1406, he was one of the first northern masters to use oil. Several altarpieces are attributed to him. Rogier van der Weyden was his pupil.

His outstanding work is the *Mérode Altarpiece* about 1425 (Metropolitan Museum of Art, New York), which shows a characteristic blend of naturalism and elaborate symbolism, together with a new subtlety in modelling and a grasp of pictorial space.

Campion Edmund (1540–1581). English Jesuit and Roman Catholic martyr. He became a Jesuit in Rome 1573 and in 1580 was sent to England as a missionary. He took orders as a deacon in the English church, but fled to Douai, France, where he recanted Protestantism 1571. He was betrayed as a spy 1581, imprisoned in the Tower of London, and hanged, drawn, and quartered as a traitor. Canonized 1970.

Campion Jane (1954–). New Zealand film director and screenwriter. She made her feature debut with *Sweetie* 1989, a dark tale of family dysfunction, then went on to make *An Angel at My Table* 1990, based on the autobiography of writer Janet Frame, originally shown as a television miniseries. Her international status was confirmed by the success of *The Piano* 1993, co-winner of the Cannes Film Festival Palme d'Or. She also earned an Academy Award for her screenplay.

Campion Thomas (1567–1620). English poet and musician. He was the author of the critical *Art of English Poesie* 1602 and four *Bookes of Ayres*, for which he composed both words and music.

An intellectual is someone whose mind watches itself.
ALBERT CAMUS
Notebooks 1963

Camus Albert (1913–1960). Algerian-born French writer. His works, such as the novels *L'Etranger/The Outsider* 1942 and *La Peste/The Plague* 1948, owe much to existentialism in their emphasis on the absurdity and arbitrariness of life. Nobel Prize for Literature 1957.

Other works include *Le Mythe de Sisyphe/The Myth of Sisyphus* 1943 and *L'Homme révolté/The Rebel* 1951. Camus' criticism of communism in the latter book led to a protracted quarrel with the philosopher Jean-Paul Sartre.

Camus was born in Algeria, then a French colony. He went on to become a journalist in France, and was active in the Resistance during World War II.
Suggested reading
Cruickshank, John *Albert Camus and the Literature of Revolt* (1960)
Lottman, Herbert R *Albert Camus* (1979)
O'Brien, Conor Cruise *Camus* (1970)

Canaletto Antonio (born Giovanni Antonio Canal) (1697–1768). Italian painter. He is celebrated for his paintings of views (*vedute*) of Venice (his native city) and of London and the river Thames 1746–56. Encouraged to visit England, he worked mainly in London and its environs, with brief intervals in Venice, finally returning to his native city 1756.

Much of his work is very detailed and precise, with a warm light and a sparkling of tiny highlights on the green waters of canals and rivers. *The Upper Reaches of the Grand Canal* about 1738 (National Gallery, London) is typical.
Suggested reading
Links, J G *Canaletto* (1982)
Levey, Michael *Canaletto Paintings in the Royal Collection* (1964)
Potterton, H *Pageant and Panorama: The Elegant World of Canaletto* (1978)

Canaris Wilhelm Franz (1887–1945). German admiral and intelligence expert. A U-boat commander during World War I, he remained in the navy after the war and became an intelligence specialist. He ran the Abwehr, the German armed forces Intelligence Service, from 1935 until his arrest after the July Plot against Hitler 1944.

There has never been any evidence that Canaris was involved in the plot against Hitler and it is probable that he was 'framed' by SS head Heinrich Himmler so that the SS could take over the Abwehr. He was executed in Flossenberg concentration camp 9 April 1945.

Candela (Outeriño) Félix (1910–). Spanish-born architect-engineer. His most outstanding work was carried out in Mexico, where he emigrated 1939; since 1970 he has lived in the USA. He has pioneered, and excelled in the artistic presentation of thin concrete shell roofs, creating beautiful forms based on the geometry of the hyperbolic paraboloid. His Cosmic Ray Building, University City, Mexico, 1952, has a hyperbolic paraboloid roof 15 mm/0.63 in thick to allow cosmic rays to penetrate.

In his Church of the Immaculate Virgin, Mexico City, 1953, parabolic vaults create a Gothic feeling of space.

Candella Rajput dynasty. See ◊Chandelā.

When you write down your life, every page should contain something no one has ever heard about.
ELIAS CANETTI
The Secret Heart of the Clock: Notes, Aphorisms, Fragments 1973

Canetti Elias (1905–1994). Bulgarian-born writer. He was exiled from Austria as a Jew 1937 and settled in England 1939. His books, written in German, include *Die Blendung/Auto da Fé* 1935. Nobel Prize for Literature 1981.

He was concerned with crowd behaviour and the psychology of power, and wrote the anthropological study *Masse und Macht/Crowds and Power* 1960. His three volumes of memoirs are *Die gerettete Zunge: Geschichte einer Jugend/The Tongue Set Free:*

Remembrance of a Childhood 1977, in which he writes of his earliest years; *Die Fackel im Ohr: Lebensgeschichte 1921–31/The Torch in My Ear* 1980, set mainly in Vienna and covering the period when Canetti came under the spell of satirist Karl Kraus; and *Das Augenspeil/The Play of the Eyes* 1985, which covers the years 1931–37, and is rich in satirical insights into the artistic Viennese society of the time.

Canning Charles John, 1st Earl Canning (1812–1862). British administrator, first viceroy of India from 1858. As governor general of India from 1856, he suppressed the Indian Mutiny with a fair but firm hand which earned him the nickname 'Clemency Canning'. He was the son of George Canning. Succeeded as viscount 1837, earl 1859.

In our Indian empire [peace] depends upon a greater variety of chances and a more precarious tenure than in any other quarter of the globe.

CHARLES, LST EARL CANNING
Speech by Canning at a banquet given by the court of directors of the East India Company in his honour before his departure to be governor-general of India, 1856.

Canning George (1770–1827). British Tory politician, foreign secretary 1807–10 and 1822–27, and prime minister 1827 in coalition with the Whigs. He was largely responsible, during the Napoleonic Wars, for the seizure of the Danish fleet and British intervention in the Spanish peninsula.

Canning entered Parliament 1793. His verse, satires, and parodies for the *Anti-Jacobin* 1797–98 led to his advancement by Pitt the Younger. His disapproval of the Walcheren expedition 1809 involved him in a duel with the war minister, Castlereagh, and led

Canning , George *George Canning, British Tory politician and prime minister for four months during 1827. He resigned as foreign secretary 1809 after blaming his colleague Viscount Castlereagh, secretary of war, for two British defeats. The two men fought a duel on Wimbledon Common to settle the matter, during which Canning was wounded in the thigh.*

to Canning's resignation as foreign secretary. He was president of the Board of Control 1816–20. On Castlereagh's death 1822, he again became foreign secretary, supported the national movements in Greece and South America, and was made prime minister 1827. When Wellington, Peel, and other Tories refused to serve under him, he formed a coalition with the Whigs. He died in office.

Save me, oh, save me from the candid friend.

GEORGE CANNING
New Morality 1826

Canning Stratford, 1st Viscount Stratford de Redcliffe (1786–1880). British nobleman and diplomat. He negotiated the treaty of Bucharest between Russia and Turkey 1812 and helped establish a federal government in Switzerland 1815. He was minister to the United States 1820–23 and ambassador in Constantinople 1825–28, 1831, and 1842–58. GCB 1828, viscount 1852.

Cannizzaro Stanislao (1826–1910). Italian chemist who revived interest in the work of Avogadro that had, in 1811, revealed the difference between atoms and molecules, and so established atomic and molecular weights as the basis of chemical calculations.

Cannizzaro also worked in aromatic organic chemistry. In 1853 he discovered reactions (named after him) that make benzyl alcohol and benzoic acid from benzaldehyde.

In 1848 he fought in the Sicilian Revolution, and was condemned to death, but in 1849 escaped to Marseille and went on to Paris. He was a professor at the Technical Institute of Alessandria, Piedmont, 1851–55. This was followed by professorships at Genoa, Palermo, and Rome. He became a senator 1871 and eventually vice president.

Cannon Annie Jump (1863–1941). US astronomer who carried out revolutionary work on the classification of stars by examining their spectra. Her system, still used today, has spectra arranged according to temperature into categories labelled O, B, A, F, G, K, M, R, N, and S. O-type stars are the hottest, with surface temperatures of over 25,000 K.

Studying photographs, Cannon discovered 300 new variable stars. In 1901 she published a catalogue of the spectra of more than 1,000 stars, using her new classification system. She went on to classify the spectra of over 300,000 stars. Most of this work was published in a ten-volume set which was completed 1924. She spent her career at the Harvard College Observatory, as assistant 1896–1911, curator of astronomical photographs 1911–38, and astronomer and curator 1938–40.

Cano Alonso (1601–1667). Spanish sculptor, painter, and architect. He was an exponent of the Baroque style in Spain. He was active in Seville, Madrid, and Granada and designed the façade of Granada Cathedral 1667. He also created monumental carved screens, such as the reredos (altar screen) in Lebrija, near Seville, and graceful free-standing polychrome carved figures.

From 1637 he was employed by Philip IV to restore the royal collection at the Prado Museum in Madrid. Many of his religious paintings show the influence of the Venetian masters.

Cano Juan Sebastian del (*c.* 1476–1526). Spanish voyager. It is claimed that he was the first sea captain to sail around the world. He sailed with Magellan 1519 and, after the latter's death in the Philippines, brought the *Victoria* safely home to Spain.

Canova Antonio, Marquese d'Ischia (1757–1822). Italian Neo-Classical sculptor. He was based in Rome from 1781. He received commissions from popes, kings, and emperors for his highly finished marble portrait busts and groups of figures. He made several portraits of Napoleon.

Canova was born near Treviso. His reclining marble *Pauline Borghese as Venus* 1805–07 (Borghese Gallery, Rome) is a fine example of his cool, polished Classicism. He executed the tombs of popes Clement XIII, Pius VII, and Clement XIV. His marble sculptures include *Cupid and Psyche* 1793 (Louvre, Paris) and *The Three Graces* (the Victoria and Albert Museum, London).

Cánovas del Castillo Antonio (1828–1897). Spanish politician and chief architect of the political system known as the *turno politico* through which his own Conservative party, and that of the Liberals under Práxedes Sagasta, alternated in power. Elections were rigged to ensure the appropriate majorities. Cánovas was assassinated 1897 by anarchists.

Cantinflas (1911–1993). Mexican comedian. He briefly achieved international fame when he played Passepartout, quizzical valet to the globetrotting Phineas Fogg in the lavish screen version of Jules Verne's *Around the World in 80 Days* 1956.

Cantona Eric (1966–). French footballer who played in three English Championship teams 1992–94. In France he played for Auxerre, Martigues, Marseilles, Bordeaux, Montpellier, and Nimes, and won medals for the French League Championship 1990 and the French Cup 1989–1990. He joined Leeds United during their Championship season 1991–92, and in Nov 1992 moved to Manchester United, whom he helped win the Premier League 1992–93 and the League and FA Cup double 1993–94. He was PFA Player of the Year 1994. An incident at Crystal Palace in 1995, when he attacked a spectator, resulted in an eight-month suspension and a court sentence of community service.

Cantor Georg Ferdinand Ludwig Philipp (1845–1918). German mathematician who followed his work on number theory and trigonometry by considering the foundations of mathematics. He defined real numbers and produced a treatment of irrational numbers using a series of transfinite numbers. Cantor's set theory has been used in the development of topology and real function theory. From 1869 he was on the staff at Halle University, as professor from 1879.

Sea, I command thee that thou touch not my feet!

William Camden *Remains Concerning Britain* 1605, describing the famous incident when CANUTE failed to stay the waves.

Canute (*c.* 995–1035). King of England from 1016, Denmark from 1018, and Norway from 1028. Having invaded England 1013 with his father, Sweyn, king of Denmark, he was acclaimed king on his father's death 1014 by his Viking army. Canute defeated Edmund (II) Ironside at Assandun, Essex, 1016, and became king of all England on Edmund's death. He succeeded his brother Harold as king of Denmark 1018, compelled King Malcolm to pay homage by invading Scotland about 1027, and conquered Norway 1028. He was succeeded by his illegitimate son Harold I.

The legend of Canute disenchanting his flattering courtiers by showing that the sea would not retreat at his command was first told by Henry of Huntingdon 1130.

Canute VI or Cnut VI (1163–1202). King of Denmark from 1182, son and successor of Waldemar Knudsson. With his brother and successor, Waldemar II, he resisted Frederick I's northward expansion, and established Denmark as the dominant power in the Baltic.

Cao Cao or Ts'ao Ts'ao (155–220). Chinese general who reunified and pacified N China after the collapse of the Han dynasty. Cao's exploits are recorded in *The Romance of the Three Kingdoms*, China's oldest extant novel, and in other works, in which he appears as a heroic figure. His son Cao Bei (or Ts'ao P'ei) founded the Wei state, one of the Three Kingdoms.

Cao Chan or Ts'ao Chan (1719–1763). Chinese novelist. His tragicomic love story *Hung Lou Meng/The Dream of the Red Chamber*, published 1792, involves the downfall of a Manchu family and is semi-autobiographical.

Capa Robert. Adopted name of André Friedmann (1913–1954). US photographer, born in Hungary. He specialized in war photography. He covered the Spanish Civil War as a freelance and World War II for *Life* and *Collier's* magazines. His pictures emphasize the human tragedy of war. He was a founder member of the Magnum photographic agency. He died while on an assignment in Vietnam.

Čapek Karel (1890–1938). Czech writer. His works often deal with social injustice in an imaginative, satirical way. *R.U.R.* 1921 is a play in which robots (a term he coined) rebel against their controllers; the novel *War with the Newts* 1936 is a science-fiction classic.

Capet Hugh (938–996). King of France from 987, when he claimed the throne on the death of Louis V. He founded the Capetian dynasty, of which various branches continued to reign until the French Revolution, for example, Valois and Bourbon.

I've been accused of every death except the casualty list of the World War.

AL CAPONE
Newspaper interview.

Capone Al(phonse), ('Scarface') (1899–1947). US gangster. During the Prohibition period, he built a formidable criminal organization in Chicago. He was brutal in his pursuit of dominance, killing seven members of a rival gang in the St Valentine's Day massacre. He was imprisoned 1931–39 for income-tax evasion, the only charge that could be sustained against him.

Capote Truman. Pen name of Truman Streckfus Persons (1924–1984). US novelist, journalist, and playwright. After achieving early success as a writer of sparkling prose in the stories of *Other Voices, Other Rooms* 1948 and the novel *Breakfast at Tiffany's* 1958, Capote's career flagged until the sensational 'nonfiction novel' *In Cold Blood* 1965 made him a celebrity.

Later works included *Music for Chameleons* 1980 and the posthumously published *Answered Prayers* 1986, an unfinished novel of scandalous socialite gossip.

I made mistakes in drama. I thought drama was when actors cried. But drama is when the audience cries.

FRANK CAPRA
Cinéma No 12, *Antenne 2* (French TV) Feb 1983

Capra Frank (1897–1991). Italian-born US film director. His satirical comedies, which often have the common man pitted against corrupt institutions, were hugely successful in the Depression years of the 1930s. He won Academy Awards for the fairy-tale comedy romance *It Happened One Night* 1934, *Mr Deeds Goes to Town* 1936, and *You Can't Take It with You* 1938. Among his other classic films are *Mr Smith Goes to Washington* 1939, and *It's a Wonderful Life* 1946.

Capra began as a gagman for silent comedies, then directed several films with Harry Langdon (1884–1944). His later films included *A Hole in the Head* 1959 and *A Pocketful of Miracles* 1961.

Suggested reading
Capra, Frank *The Name Above the Title* (1971)
Carney, R *American Vision: The Films of Frank Capra* (1986)
Griffith, R *Frank Capra* (1979)
Willis, D *The Films of Frank Capra* (1974)

Caprivi (Georg) Leo, Graf von (1831–1899). German soldier and politician. While chief of the admiralty (1883–88) he reorganized the German navy. He became imperial chancellor 1890–94 succeeding Bismarck and renewed the Triple Alliance but wavered between European allies and Russia. Although he strengthened the army, he alienated the conservatives.

If you wish you may; don't you know that you are emperor and make the laws.

Response of CARACALLA's mother to his proposition of an incestuous relationship. Anon *Life of Antoninus Caracalla* ch 10.3

Caracalla (Marcus Aurelius Antoninus) (AD *c.* 186–217). Roman emperor. He succeeded his father Septimius Severus AD 211 and, with the support of the army, he murdered his brother Geta 212 to become sole ruler of the empire. During his reign in 212, Roman citizenship was given to all subjects of the empire.

He built on a grandiose scale, and campaigned in Germany and against the Parthians. He was nicknamed after the Celtic cloak (*caracalla*) that he wore. He was assassinated.

Preserve my life, and I shall be, to late posterity, a monument of Roman clemency.

Plea by CARACTACUS to Emperor Claudius, granted by the Emperor, quoted in Tacitus *Annals* bks 36–7

Caractacus (died *c.* 54). British chieftain who headed resistance to the Romans in SE England AD 43–51, but was defeated on the Welsh border. Shown in Claudius's triumphal procession, he was released in tribute to his courage and died in Rome.

Caradon Baron. Title of Hugh ◊Foot, British Labour politician.

Carathéodory Constantin (1873–1950). German mathematician who made significant advances to the calculus of variations and to function theory. His work also covered theory of measure and applied mathematics. He held professorships at various universities in Germany and, 1920–24, in Greece; from 1924 he was at the University of Munich.

Caravaggio Michelangelo Merisi da (1573–1610). Italian early Baroque painter. He was active in Rome 1592–1606, then in Naples, and finally in Malta. He created a forceful style, using contrasts of light and shade, dramatic foreshortening, and a meticulous attention to detail. His life was as dramatic as his art (he had to leave Rome after killing a man in a brawl).

The son of a mason in the village of Caravaggio near Milan, he had some early training in Milan, but was painting in Rome before he was 20, quickly developing that famous 'naturalism' which was in strong contrast to the prevailing Mannerism of Zuccaro and the Cavaliere d'Arpino. Instead of ideal figures, he painted the types he saw and knew, delighting in plebeian traits of character, contemporary dress and carefully delineated still life. Early examples are the *Bacchus* (Uffizi), the *Fortune Teller* (Louvre) and the *Fruit Basket* (Ambrosiana, Milan). The innovation that gave him fame and made him the centre of controversy was not only that he applied this realistic method to religious painting, but also intensified its effect by combining it with a depth and drama of light and shade that he may have adapted from Tintoretto. It appears in his first commission for the Contarelli Chapel of St Luigi dei Francesi, *St Matthew and the Angel*, the *Vocation of St Matthew* and *Martyrdom of the Apostle*. These and other works in Rome, painted 1600–07, including the *Madonna of the Serpent* (Borghese Gallery), the *Death of the Virgin* (Louvre) and the *Madonna del Rosario* (Vienna), were either refused by his patrons or were the subject of fierce argument.

Suggested reading
Berenson, Bernard *Caravaggio: His Incongruity and His Fame* (1953)
Friedlaender, Walter *Caravaggio Studies* (1955)
Hibbard, Howard *Caravaggio* (1983)
Moir, Albert *Caravaggio* (1982)

Carboni Raffaello (1820–1875). Italian writer, poet, and goldminer in Australia. He fled from Italy because of his involvement in the Young Italy movement and arrived in Australia in 1852. With Lalor, he was a leader of the Ballarat Reform League. After the Eureka rebellion, he was acquitted, wrote his version of events in *The Eureka Stockade* 1855 and returned to Italy.

Cardano Girolamo (1501–1576). Italian physician, mathematician, philosopher, astrologer, and gambler. He is remembered for his theory of chance, his use of algebra, and many medical publications, notably the first clinical description of typhus fever.

Born in Pavia, he became professor of medicine there 1543, and wrote two works on physics and natural science, *De subtilitate rerum* 1551 and *De varietate rerum* 1557.

Cárdenas Lázaro (1895–1970). Mexican centre-left politician and general, president 1934–40. A civil servant in early life, Cárdenas took part in the revolutionary campaigns 1915–29 that followed the fall of President Díaz (1830–1915). As president of the republic, he attempted to achieve the goals of the revolution by building schools, distributing land to the peasants, and developing transport and industry. He was minister of defence 1943–45.

Cardiff Jack (1914–). English director of photography. He is considered one of cinema's finest colour-camera operators for his work on such films as *A Matter of Life and Death* 1946, *The Red Shoes* 1948, and *The African Queen* 1951. He won an Academy Award for *Black Narcissus* 1947. He later directed several films including *Sons and Lovers* 1960.

Cardin Pierre (1922–). French pioneering fashion designer. He was the first to launch menswear (1960) and designer ready-to-wear collections (1963) and has given his name to a perfume. Cardin has franchised his name for labelling many different acessories and household products. He was particularly influential in the 1960s, creating his 'Space Age Collection' of catsuits, tight leather trousers, jumpsuits with bat wings, and close-fitting helmet-style caps 1964, followed 1966 by shift dresses with ring collars from which the fabric was suspended.

Cardozo Benjamin Nathan (1870–1938). US jurist and Supreme Court justice. He was appointed to the US Supreme Court by President Hoover 1932. During the F D Roosevelt administration, he upheld the constitutionality of New Deal programmes to counter the depression of 1929 conveyed in such famous cases as *Ashwander v Tennessee Valley Authority* 1936.

Cardozo William Warrick (1905–1962). US physician and paediatrician who made pioneering investigations into sickle-cell anaemia. He concluded in 1937 that the disease was inherited following Mendelian law and almost always occurred in black people or people of African descent; not all persons with sickle cells were necessarily anaemic and not all patients died of the disease.

In 1937 he started private practice in Washington DC, and was appointed part-time instructor in paediatrics at Howard University College of Medicine and Freedmen's Hospital, later being promoted to associate professor.

Far better in one's work to forget than to seek to solve the vast riddles of the universe.

GIOSUÈ CARDUCCI
'Idillio Maremmano'

Carducci Giosuè (1835–1907). Italian poet. Born in Tuscany, he was appointed professor of Italian literature at Bologna 1860, and won distinction through his lecturing, critical work, and poetry. His revolutionary *Inno a Satana/Hymn to Satan* 1865 was followed by several other volumes of verse, in which his nationalist sympathies are apparent. Nobel prize 1906.

The country was served more brilliantly by other men of his generation, but by none more faithfully ... more strenuously, or with more lasting fruit.

George (Murray) Smith on EDWARD, 1ST VISCOUNT CARDWELL
in *Dictionary of National Biography*

Cardwell Edward, 1st Viscount Cardwell (1813–1886). British Liberal politician. He entered Parliament as a supporter of the Conservative prime minister Peel 1842, and was secretary for war under Gladstone 1868–74, when he carried out many reforms, including the abolition of the purchase of military commissions and promotions. Viscount 1874.

Carême Antonin (Marie Antoine) (1784–1833). French chef who is regarded as the founder of classic French *haute cuisine*. At various times he was chief cook to the Prince Regent in England and Tsar Alexander I in Russia.

Then fly betimes for only they / Conquer love, that run away.

THOMAS CAREW
'Conquest by Flight'

Carew Thomas (*c*. 1595–*c*. 1640). English poet. Often associated with the 'Cavalier poets', he was a courtier and gentleman of the privy chamber to Charles I, for whom he wrote the spectacular masque *Coelum Britannicum* 1634. *Poems* 1640 reveal his ability to weave metaphysical wit, eroticism, and a jewelled lyricism in his work.

His first important work was an elegy written on the death of the metaphysical poet John Donne, which was published 1633 in the first edition of Donne's poetry.

Carey George Leonard (1935–). 103rd archbishop of Canterbury from 1991. A product of a liberal evangelical background, he was appointed bishop of Bath and Wells 1987.

His support of the ordination of women priests brought disagreement during his first meeting with Pope John Paul II in 1992.

Carey Henry (*c*. 1690–1743). English poet and musician. He is remembered for the song 'Sally in Our Alley'. 'God Save the King' (both words and music) has also been attributed to him.

Carey Peter Philip (1943–). Australian novelist. His works include *Bliss* 1981, *Illywhacker* (Australian slang for 'con man') 1985, and *Oscar and Lucinda* 1988, which won the Booker Prize. *The Tax Inspector* 1991 is set in modern-day Sydney, and depicts an eccentric Greek family under investigation for tax fraud.
Suggested reading
Lamb, Karen *Peter Carey: The Genesis of Fame* (1992)

Carissimi Giacomo (1605–1674). Italian composer. He wrote sacred and secular cantatas and motets. As maestro di capella at Sant' Apollinaire, Rome, 1630–74, he pioneered the use of expressive solo aria as a commentary on the Latin biblical text. He wrote five oratorios, including *Jephtha* 1650.

Carl XVI Gustaf (1946–). King of Sweden from 1973. He succeeded his grandfather Gustaf VI, his father having been killed in an air crash 1947. Under the new Swedish constitution, which became effective on his grandfather's death, the monarchy was stripped of all power at his accession.

Carling Will(iam) David Charles (1965–). English rugby union player. He made his full England debut in Jan 1988, and was appointed England captain when only 22 years old. He captained England to Grand Slam Championships 1991, 1992, and 1995, the World Cup final 1991, and the World Cup semi-final 1995. He was sacked as captain 1995 after remarks made in a television interview, but was quickly reinstated by popular demand. He holds the world record for international appearances as captain.

Carlos I (1863–1908). King of Portugal, of the Braganza-Coburg line, from 1889 until he was assassinated in Lisbon with his elder son Luis. He was succeeded by his younger son Manuel.

With his outsize head and frail body, his constant stammer and frequent illnesses ... he was an irascible paranoiac and a sadistic voyeur.

E N Williams on DON CARLOS
in *Penguin Dictionary of English and European History 1485–1789* 1980

Carlos Don (1545–1568). Spanish prince. Son of Philip II, he was recognized as heir to the thrones of Castile and Aragon but became mentally unstable and had to be placed under restraint following a plot to assassinate his father. His story was the subject of plays by Friedrich von Schiller, Vittorio Alfieri, Thomas Otway, and others.

Carlos four kings of Spain; see ◊Charles.

Carlson Chester Floyd (1906–1968). US scientist who invented xerography. A research worker with Bell Telephone, he lost his job 1930 during the Depression and set to work on his own to develop an efficient copying machine. By 1938 he had invented the Xerox photocopier.

Carlsson Ingvar Gösta (1934–). Swedish socialist politician. Leader of the Social Democratic Labour Party (SDAP) from 1986, he was deputy prime minister 1982–86, and prime minister 1986–91 and 1994–96.

After studying in Sweden and the USA, Carlsson became president of the Swedish Social Democratic Youth League 1961. He was elected to the Riksdag (parliament) 1964 and served in the governments of Olof Palme, 1969–75 and 1982–86, becoming deputy prime minister 1982. On Palme's untimely assassination Feb 1986, Carlsson replaced him as SAP leader and prime minister. He lost his majority Sept 1991 and resigned, but was returned Sept 1994 at the head of a minority SDAP government. In 1995 he announced his intention to resign March 1996, citing personal reasons.

Carlucci Frank Charles (1930–). US politician. A former diplomat and deputy director of the Central Intelligence Agency (CIA), he was national security adviser 1986–87 and defence secretary 1987–89 under President Reagan, supporting Soviet–US arms reduction.

Educated at Princeton and Harvard, Carlucci, after fighting in the Korean War, was a career diplomat during the later 1950s and 1960s. He returned to the USA 1969 to work under presidents Nixon, Ford, and Carter, his posts including US ambassador to Portugal and deputy director of the CIA. An apolitical Atlanticist, Carlucci found himself out of step with the hawks (pro-war advisers) in the Reagan administration, and left to work in industry after barely a year as deputy secretary of defence. In Dec 1986, after the Irangate scandal, he replaced John Poindexter as national security adviser.

Carlyle Thomas (1795–1881). Scottish essayist and social historian. His works include *Sartor Resartus* 1833–34, describing his loss of Christian belief; *The French Revolution* 1837; the pamphlet *Chartism* 1839, attacking the doctrine of *laissez-faire*, *Past and Present* 1843, the notable *Letters and Speeches of Cromwell* 1845, and the miniature life of his friend John Sterling 1851. His prose style was idiosyncratic, encompassing grand, thunderous rhetoric and deliberate obscurity.
Suggested reading
Collis, J S *The Carlyles* (1971)
Holloway, J *The Victorian Sage* (1953)
Holme, T *The Carlyles at Home* (1965)
Kaplan, F *Thomas Carlyle: A Biography* (1983)
Le Quesne, A L *Carlyle* (1983)

Carmichael Hoagy (Hoagland Howard) (1899–1981). US composer, pianist, singer, and actor. His songs include 'Stardust' 1927, 'Rockin' Chair' 1930, 'Lazy River' 1931, and 'In the Cool, Cool, Cool of the Evening' 1951 (Academy Award).

While studying law at Indiana University, he began to compose, and he came to perform with such jazz greats as Bix Beiderbecke. Later he worked in Hollywood, where he also appeared in films, including *To Have and Have Not* 1944.

Carmichael Stokely. Former name of Kwame Touré (1941–). Trinidad-born US civil-rights activist. He coined the term Black Power. As leader of the Black Panthers 1967–69, he demanded black liberation rather than integration, and called for armed revolution. He then moved to Guinea, changed his name, and worked for the Pan-African movement.

Although born in Port-of-Spain, Trinidad, Carmichael was educated in the USA. He took part in civil-rights demonstrations from 1961 and joined the Student Nonviolent Coordinating Committee (SNCC) 1964, organizing volunteers to teach southern blacks to read and to help them to register for the vote. He was president 1966–67 of SNCC when it became the radical wing of the civil-rights movement after the murder of Malcolm X. He left the Black Panthers 1969 when they decided to cooperate with white radicals.

Carnap Rudolf (1891–1970). German philosopher, in the USA from 1935. He was a member of the Vienna Circle and an exponent of logical positivism, the theory that the only meaningful propositions are those that can be verified empirically. He tried to show that metaphysics arose from a confusion between talk about the world and talk about language. He was professor of philosophy at the University of California 1954–62. His books include *The Logical Syntax of Language* 1934 and *Meaning and Necessity* 1956.

Carné Marcel (1909–1996). French director. He is known for the romantic fatalism of such films as *Drôle de Drame* 1936, *Hôtel du Nord* 1938, *Le Quai des brumes/Port of Shadows* 1938, and *Le Jour se lève/Daybreak* 1939. His masterpiece, *Les Enfants du paradis/The Children of Paradise* 1943–45, was made with his longtime collaborator, poet and screenwriter Jacques Prévert (1900–1977).

Carnegie family name of the earls of Northesk and Southesk and of the duke of Fife, who is descended from Queen Victoria.

Carnegie Andrew (1835–1919). US industrialist and philanthropist, born in Scotland, who developed the Pittsburgh iron and steel industries, making the USA the world's leading producer. He endowed public libraries, education, and various research trusts.

Carnegie invested successfully in railways, land, and oil. From 1873 he engaged in steelmaking, adopting new techniques. Having built up a vast empire, he disposed of it to the US Steel Trust 1901. After his death the Carnegie trusts continued his philanthropic activities. *Carnegie Hall* in New York, opened 1891 as the Music Hall, was renamed 1898 because of his large contribution to its construction.

How to Win Friends and Influence People.

DALE CARNEGIE
Book title 1937

Carnegie Dale (1888–1955). US author and teacher. He wrote the best-selling self-help book *How to Win Friends and Influence People* 1937. His courses in public speaking, which drew huge audiences, first won him fame, and he was asked to publish them as a book. His other books include *Little Known Facts About Well Known People* 1934 and *How to Stop Worrying and Start Living* 1948.

Carnot Lazare Nicolas Marguerite (1753–1823). French general and politician. A member of the National Convention in the French Revolution, he organized the armies of the republic. He was war minister 1800–01 and minister of the interior 1815 under Napoleon. His work on fortification, *De la Défense de places fortes* 1810, became a military textbook. Minister of the interior during the hundred days, he was proscribed at the restoration of the monarchy and retired to Germany.

Carnot joined the army as an engineer, and his transformation of French military technique in the revolutionary period earned him the title of 'Organizer of Victory'. After the coup d'état of 1797 he went abroad, but returned 1799 when Napoleon seized power. In 1814, as governor of Antwerp, he put up a brilliant defence.

Carnot (Marie François) Sadi (1837–1894). French president from 1887, grandson of Lazare Carnot. He successfully countered the Boulangist anti-German movement and in 1892 the scandals arising out of French financial activities in Panama. He was assassinated by an Italian anarchist in Lyon.

Carnot (Nicolas Leonard) Sadi (1796–1832). French scientist and military engineer who founded the science of thermodynamics. His pioneering work was *Reflexions sur la puissance motrice du feu/On the Motive Power of Fire*, which considered the changes that would take place in an idealized, frictionless steam engine. At the time he wrote *Reflexions*, Carnot believed that heat was a form of fluid. But notes discovered 1878 indicate that he later arrived at the idea that heat is essentially work, or rather work that has changed its form. He had calculated a conversion constant for heat and work and showed he

believed that the total quantity of work in the universe is constant – the first law of thermodynamics.

You cannot explain abstract art in ten minutes.

ANTHONY CARO
quoted in Colin Naylor (ed) *Contemporary Artists* 1989

Caro Anthony Alfred (1924–   ). English sculptor. He has made brightly coloured abstract sculpture from prefabricated metal parts, such as I-beams, angles, and mesh. An example is *Early One Morning* 1962 (Tate Gallery, London). Knighted 1987.

Carol two kings of Romania:

His long reign brought notable military and economic development along Western lines but signally failed to confront the basic problems of an overwhelmingly rural nation.

Encyclopaedia Britannica on CAROL I
1990

Carol I (1839–1914). First king of Romania 1881–1914. A prince of the house of Hohenzollern-Sigmaringen, he was invited to become prince of Romania, then part of the Ottoman Empire, 1866. In 1877, in alliance with Russia, he declared war on Turkey, and the Congress of Berlin 1878 recognized Romanian independence.

He promoted economic development and industrial reforms but failed to address rural problems. This led to a peasant rebellion 1907 which he brutally crushed. At the beginning of World War I, King Carol declared Romania's neutrality but his successor (his nephew King Ferdinand I) declared for the Allies.

Carol II (1893–1953). King of Romania 1930–40. Son of King Ferdinand, he married Princess Helen of Greece and they had a son, Michael. In 1925 he renounced the succession because of his affair with Elena Lupescu and went into exile in Paris. Michael succeeded to the throne 1927, but in 1930 Carol returned to Romania and was proclaimed king.

In 1938 he introduced a new constitution under which he practically became an absolute ruler. He was forced to abdicate by the pro-Nazi Iron Guard Sept 1940, went to Mexico, and married his mistress 1947.

Though she dissimulated she remained obstinately and grandly herself.

Peter Quennell on CAROLINE OF ANSPACH
in *Caroline of England* 1939

Caroline of Anspach (1683–1737). Queen of George II of Great Britain and Ireland. The daughter of the Margrave of Brandenburg-Anspach, she married George, Electoral Prince of Hanover, 1705, and followed him to England 1714 when his father became King George I.

She was the patron of many leading writers and politicians such as Alexander Pope, John Gay, and the Earl of Chesterfield. She supported Robert Walpole and kept him in power and acted as regent during her husband's four absences.

The Queen, and may all your wives be like her.

Said by Henry Paget, 1st Marquess of Anglesey, when pressed by a mob of her sympathizers to cheer George IV's queen, CAROLINE OF BRUNSWICK, at the time of her trial, 1820

Caroline of Brunswick (1768–1821). Queen of George IV of Great Britain, who unsuccessfully attempted to divorce her on his accession to the throne 1820.

Second daughter of Karl Wilhelm, Duke of Brunswick, and Augusta, sister of George III, she married her first cousin, the Prince of Wales, 1795, but after the birth of Princess Charlotte Augusta a separation was arranged. When her husband ascended the throne 1820 she was offered an annuity of £50,000 provided she agreed to renounce the title of queen and to continue to live abroad. She returned forthwith to London, where she assumed royal state. In July 1820 the government brought in a bill to dissolve the marriage, but Lord Brougham's brilliant defence led to the bill's abandonment. On 19 July 1821 Caroline was prevented by royal order from entering Westminster Abbey for the coronation. Her funeral was the occasion of popular riots.

Most Gracious Queen, we thee implore / To go away and sin no more, / But if that effort be too great, / To go away at any rate.

Lord Colchester on CAROLINE OF BRUNSWICK
Diary 15 Nov 1826 (Anon)

Carolingian dynasty Frankish dynasty descending from Pepin the Short (died 768) and named after his son Charlemagne; its last ruler was Louis V of France (reigned 966–87), who was followed by Hugh Capet, first ruler of the Capetian dynasty.

Carothers Wallace Hume (1896–1937). US chemist who carried out research into polymerization. He discovered that some polymers were fibre-forming, and in 1931 he produced nylon and neoprene, one of the first synthetic rubbers. In 1928 he became head of organic chemistry research at the Du Pont research laboratory in Wilmington, Delaware. He committed suicide.

Carpaccio Vittore (1450/60–1525/26). Italian painter. He is famous for scenes of his native Venice, for example, the series *The Legend of St Ursula* 1490–98 (Accademia, Venice). His paintings are a graceful blend of fantasy and closely observed details from everyday life.

His real name was Scarpazza, and he probably came from a family established in the Venetian islands. He is said to have been a pupil of Lorenzo Bastiani, but was evidently influenced by Gentile Bellini, with whom he vied in depicting the aspect and ceremony of Venice. He was much employed by the *scuole* or confraternities of Venice and his charm and narrative gift are beautifully displayed in his cycles of the *Life of St Ursula*, 1490–95, painted for the Scuola di Sant' Orsola and now in the Accademia, Venice, and the *Life of St George* and other saints for the Scuola di San Giorgio degli Schiavoni, 1502–07. *The Miracle of the Cross at Rialto* (Accademia) is remarkable for its typically Venetian background and, as a form of genre picture (though perhaps a fragment of a larger work), also famous is the so-called *Courtesans* (Correr Museum, Venice).

Carpeaux Jean-Baptiste (1827–1875). French sculptor. His lively naturalistic subjects include *La Danse* 1865–69 for the Opéra, Paris (now in the Louvre, Paris) and the *Neapolitan Fisherboy* 1858 (Louvre, Paris).

The Romantic charm of his work belies his admiration for Michelangelo. He studied in Italy 1856–62 and won the Prix de Rome scholarship 1854.

Carpenter Alfred Francis (1881–1955). British naval captain. Carpenter entered the Royal Navy 1907 and was promoted to commander 1915. He commanded HMS *Vindictive* in the attack on Zeebrugge April 1918, for which he received the Victoria Cross. He was then promoted to captain and appointed to the Naval Intelligence Department.

Carpenter Edward (1844–1929). English socialist and writer who campaigned for such causes as sexual reform, women's rights, and vegetarianism. He lived openly as a homosexual and made a plea for sexual toleration in *Love's Coming of Age* 1896. His books include *The Simplification of Life* 1884, *Civilization: Its Cause and Cure* 1889, and the long poem *Towards Democracy* 1883–1902.

Carpenter John Howard (1948–). US director of horror and science-fiction films. He is notable for such films as *Dark Star* 1974 and *Assault on Precinct 13* 1976.

His subsequent films include the low-budget thriller *Halloween* 1978, *The Fog* 1979, *The Thing* 1982, *Christine* 1983 (adapted from a Stephen King story about a vindictive car), *Starman* 1984, *They Live* 1988, and *Memoirs of an Invisible Man* 1992. He composes his own film scores, which have often added to the atmosphere of menace that often haunts his movies.

Carpini Johannes de Plano (c. 1182–c. 1252). Italian Franciscan friar and traveller. Sent by Pope Innocent IV on a mission to the Great Khan, he visited Mongolia 1245–47 and wrote a history of the Mongols in Latin.

Carr Emma Perry (1880–1972). US chemist who in the USA pioneered techniques to synthesize and analyse the structure of complex organic molecules using absorption spectroscopy. She also did research into unsaturated hydrocarbons and far ultraviolet vacuum spectroscopy. From 1910 she was on the staff of Mount Holyoke, as professor of chemistry 1913–46.

Carrà Carlo (1881–1966). Italian painter. He was one of the original members of the Futurist group. His best-known work of the period is *The Funeral of the Anarchist Galli* 1911 (Museum of Modern Art, New York). In 1917 he broke away to form the Metaphysical Painting movement with Giorgio de Chirico, and subsequently developed a fresco-like style based on the works of early Renaissance painters such as Masaccio.

Carracci three related Italian painters who represent an important phase of late-Renaissance art, Lodovico Carracci and his cousins (who were brothers) Agostino and Annibale. Lodovico (1555–1619), pupil of Prospero Fontana and in the school of Passignano at Florence, was an artist of scholarly inclination who made an extensive study of Renaissance masters, especially of Correggio and Titian. Agostino (1557–1602), painter and engraver, also studied under Fontana and in Parma and Venice. Annibale (1560–1609) was the most original artist of the three. He studied Correggio's work and was an excellent draughtsman (drawing from life being one of Carraccis' tenets).

Carradine John Richmond Reed (1906–1988). US film character actor. He appeared in many major Hollywood films, such as *Stagecoach* 1939 and *The Grapes of Wrath* 1940, but was later often seen in horror B-movies, including *House of Frankenstein* 1944.

Carrel Alexis (1873–1944). US surgeon born in France, whose experiments paved the way for organ transplantation. Working at the Rockefeller Institute, New York City, he devised a way of joining blood vessels end to end (anastomosing). This was a key move in the development of transplant surgery, as was his work on keeping organs viable outside the body, for which he was awarded the Nobel Prize for Physiology or Medicine 1912.

Carreras José Maria (1947–). Spanish operatic tenor. His comprehensive repertoire includes Handel's Samson and his recordings include *West Side Story* 1984 under Leonard Bernstein. His vocal presence, charmingly insinuating rather than forceful, is favoured for Italian and French romantic roles.

In 1987 he was seriously ill with leukaemia, but resumed his career 1988. Together with Placido Domingo and Luciano Pavarotti, he achieved worldwide fame in a recording of operatic hits released to coincide with the World Cup soccer series in Rome 1990. *See illustration on page 158.*

Carrington Dora (1893–1932). English painter, a member of the Bloomsbury Group. She developed a style which, in its emphasis on design and bold colours, is typical of English Post-Impressionism of the period from World War I to the 1930s. Among her best known works are an elegant portrait of her close friend, the writer Lytton Strachey (1918, private collection), and the landscape *The Mill House at Tidmarsh* (1918, private collection).

Carrington studied at the Slade School of Fine Art, London 1910–14 – then one of the most avant-garde art schools in England

Carreras *Spanish lyric tenor José Carreras made his mark playing opposite Montserrat Caballé. Favoured for romantic roles including Flavio in Bellini's* Norma *and Ismaele in Verdi's* Nabucco, *he brings a distinctive intimacy to opera.*

– where she came into contact with artists such as Mark Gertler, who had a marked impact on her development, Paul Nash, and Stanley Spencer. In 1915 she met Lytton Strachey, with whom she lived for the rest of her life, even after her marriage to Ralph Partridge 1921. Her style, broadly similar to that of her Bloomsbury friends Duncan Grant and Vanessa Bell, was well suited to the decorative arts, and her work includes sign boards, painted tiles and furniture, and designs for book covers; for several years she worked for Roger Fry's Omega Workshop. She killed herself in 1932 shortly after Strachey died of cancer. A critically acclaimed film of her life, *Carrington*, appeared 1995.

Suggested reading
Garnett, David (ed) *Carrington: Letters and Extracts from Her Diary* (1980)
Gerzina, Gretchen *Carrington: A Life of Dora Carrington* (1989)
Hill, Jane *The Art of Dora Carrington* (1994)

Carrington Peter Alexander Rupert, 6th Baron Carrington (1919–   ). British Conservative politician. He was defence secretary 1970–74, and led the opposition in the House of Lords 1964–70 and 1974–79. While foreign secretary 1979–82, he negotiated independence for Zimbabwe, but resigned after failing to anticipate the Falklands crisis. He was secretary general of NATO 1984–88. He chaired European Community-sponsored peace talks on Yugoslavia 1991. KCMG 1958; succeeded as baron 1938.

Carrington Richard Christopher (1826–1875). English astronomer who by studying sunspots established the Sun's axis and rotation. He was the first to record the observation of a solar flare, in 1859. He became an astronomical observer at Durham University. In 1853 he set up his own observatory at Redhill, Surrey; in 1865 he moved to Churt, near Farnham, Surrey, where he built another observatory.

Carroll Charles (1737–1832). American public official who, as a member of the Continental Congress, was one of the signatories of the Declaration of Independence 1776. He was one of Maryland's first US senators 1789–92.

Carroll James (1858–1927). New Zealand Maori politician and advocate of Maori rights. He was minister for Maori affairs 1899–

1912 and acting prime minister in 1909 and 1911. His main work was in arbitrating between the Maori and the government over land settlements, adopting a policy of *taihoa* (marking time or delaying) rather than forcing the Maori to accept European ways.

'You are old, Father William,' the young man said, / 'And your hair has become very white; / And yet you incessantly stand on your head / – Do you think, at your age, it is right?'

LEWIS CARROLL
Alice's Adventures in Wonderland ch 5 1865

Carroll Lewis. Pen name of Charles Lutwidge Dodgson (1832–1898). English author of the children's classics *Alice's Adventures in Wonderland* 1865 and its sequel *Through the Looking-Glass* 1872. Among later works was the mock-heroic narrative poem *The Hunting of the Snark* 1876. He was fascinated by the limits and paradoxes of language and thought, the exploration of which leads to the apparent nonsense of Alice's adventures. He also published mathematical works.

Dodgson was a mathematics lecturer at Oxford 1855–81. There he first told the fantasy stories to Alice Liddell and her sisters, daughters of the dean of Christ Church. Dodgson was a prolific letter writer and one of the pioneers of portrait photography. He was also responsible, in his publication of mathematical games and problems requiring the use of logic, for a general upsurge of interest in such pastimes. He is said to be, after Shakespeare, the most quoted writer in the English language.

Suggested reading
Cohen, M *Lewis Carroll: A Biography* (1995)
Elwyn Jones, Jo and Gladstone, J Francis *The Red King's Dream, or Lewis Carroll in Wonderland* (1995)
Pudney, John *Lewis Carroll and His World* (1976)
Williams, Sidney and Green, Roger *The Lewis Carroll Handbook* (1962)
Wood, James *The Snark was a Boojum: A Life of Lewis Carroll* (1966)

My only great qualification for being put in charge of the Navy is that I am very much at sea.

EDWARD, BARON CARSON
addressing senior Admiralty staff on formation of the Coalition
Government 1916, quoted in H Montgomery Hyde *Carson* ch 7 1974

Carson Edward Henry, Baron Carson (1854–1935). Irish politician and lawyer who played a decisive part in the trial of the writer Oscar Wilde. In the years before World War I he led the movement in Ulster to resist Irish Home Rule by force of arms if need be. Knighted 1896, baron 1921.

Carson was a highly respected barrister both in England and Ireland. He acted as counsel for the Marquess of Queensbury in the trial that ruined Wilde's career. On the outbreak of war he campaigned in Ulster in support of the government, and took office under both Asquith and Lloyd George (attorney general 1915, First Lord of the Admiralty 1916, member of the war cabinet 1917–18). He was a Lord of Appeal in Ordinary 1921–29.

Carson Kit (Christopher) (1809–1868). US frontier settler, guide, and Indian agent, who later fought for the federal side in the Civil War. Carson City, Nevada, was named after him.

Carson Rachel Louise (1907–1964). US biologist, writer, and conservationist. Her first book, *The Sea Around Us* 1951, was a best seller and won several literary awards. It was followed by *The Edge of the Sea* 1955, an ecological exploration of the seashore. Her book *Silent Spring* 1962, attacking the indiscriminate use of pesticides, inspired the creation of the modern environmental movement.

Carson Willie (William Fisher Hunter) (1942–   ). Scottish jockey who has ridden four Epsom Derby winners as well as the winners of most major races worldwide.

The top flat-race jockey on five occasions, he has ridden over 3,000 winners in Britain. For many years he rode for the royal trainer, Major Dick Hern. Since 1962 to the start of the 1994 season he has ridden 16 classic winners and 3,541 winners.

Comedy is tragedy that happens to other people.

ANGELA CARTER
Wise Children ch 4 1991

Carter Angela (1940–1992). English writer of the magic realist school. Her works are marked by elements of Gothic fantasy, a fascination with the erotic and the violent, tempered by a complex lyricism and a comic touch. Her novels include *The Magic Toyshop* 1967 (filmed 1987) and *Nights at the Circus* 1984. She co-wrote the script for the film *The Company of Wolves* 1984, based on one of her stories. Her last novel was *Wise Children* 1991.

Carter Elliott Cook (1908–). US composer. He created intricately structured works in Schoenbergian serial idiom, incorporating 'metrical modulation', an adaptation of standard notation allowing different instruments or groups to remain synchronized while playing at changing speeds. This practice was first employed in his *String Quartet No 1* 1950–51, and to dense effect in *Double Concerto* 1961 for harpsichord and piano. In his eighth decade, his music has shown a new tautness and vitality, as in *Three Occasions for Orchestra* 1986–89.

Carter Herbert James (1858–1940). Australian entomologist, born in England. He migrated to Australia in 1881 and worked as a school teacher. He became interested in entomology, particularly beetles, and was an avid collector and classifier, describing over 1,000 new species. He was joint editor of the first *Australian Encyclopaedia* 1925–27, supervising the science articles. His published work includes 65 papers and the book *Gulliver in the Bush* 1933, recording his field experiences in Australia.

We should live our lives as though Christ were coming this afternoon.

JIMMY CARTER
Speech to Bible class in Plains, Georgia March 1976

Carter Jimmy (James Earl) (1924–). 39th president of the USA 1977–81, a Democrat. Born in Plains, Georgia, Carter served in the navy as a physicist until 1953, when he took over the family peanut business. He first entered politics 1962 when he made a successful bid for the Georgia State Senate, and in 1970 was elected governor. In 1976, after a long and hard-fought campaign, he won the Democratic presidential nomination and went on to secure a narrow victory over Gerald Ford, becoming the first Southern president since the American Civil War. Features of his presidency were the return of the Panama Canal Zone to Panama, the introduction of an amnesty program for deserters and draft dodgers of the Vietnam War, the Camp David Agreements for peace in the Middle East, and the Iranian seizure of US embassy hostages. He was defeated by Ronald Reagan 1980. During the 1990s he emerged as a leading mediator and peace negotiator, securing President Aristide's safe return to Haiti Oct 1994.
Suggested reading
Carter, Jimmy *Keeping Faith: Memoirs of a President* (1982)
Hargrove, Erwin *Jimmy Carter as President* (1988)
Meyer, P *James Earl Carter* (1978)
Miller, W L *Yankee from Georgia* (1978)

Cartier George Etienne (1814–1873). French-Canadian politician. He fought against the British in the rebellion 1837, was elected to the Canadian parliament 1848, and was joint prime minister with John A Macdonald 1858–62. He brought Quebec into the Canadian federation 1867. Baronet 1868.
Suggested reading
Boyd, John *Georges Étienne Cartier* (1914, rep 1971)
Young, Brian *Georges Étienne Cartier* (1981)

Cartier Jacques (1491–1557). French navigator who, while seeking a north-west passage to China, was the first European to sail up the St Lawrence River 1534. He named the site of Montréal.

You have to approach your prey carefully and strike at the right time.

HENRI CARTIER-BRESSON
Interview *Le Monde* 5 Sept 1974

Cartier-Bresson Henri (1908–). French photographer. He is considered one of the greatest photographic artists. His documentary work was shot in black and white, using a small-format Leica camera. His work is remarkable for its tightly structured composition and his ability to capture the decisive moment. He was a founder member of the Magnum photographic agency.

At fifty you have the choice of keeping your face or your figure, and it's much better to keep your face.

BARBARA CARTLAND
Daily Mail 10 July 1981

Cartland (Mary) Barbara (Hamilton) (1904–). English romantic novelist. She published her first book, *Jigsaw* 1921 and since then has produced a prolific stream of stories of chastely romantic love, usually in idealized or exotic settings, for a mainly female audience (such as *Love Climbs In* 1978 and *Moments of Love* 1981). DBE 1991.

Cartwright Edmund (1743–1823). British inventor. He patented the power loom 1785, built a weaving mill 1787, and patented a wool-combing machine 1789.
He became rector of Goadby Marwood, Leicestershire, 1779 and was prebendary of Lincoln from 1786. He set up a factory in Doncaster, Yorkshire, for weaving and spinning, went bankrupt 1793, but was awarded £10,000 by the government 1809.

Caruso was dragging out his arias. 'Chi son? Chi son? (Who am I?)' he sang slowly. 'Sei un imbecile! (You're a fool!)', retorted Puccini, to general delight.

Henry Russell on ENRICO CARUSO
The Passing Show, 1926

Caruso Enrico (1873–1921). Italian operatic tenor. His voice was dark, with full-bodied tone and remarkable dynamic range. In 1902 he starred, with Nellie Melba, in Puccini's *La Bohème/Bohemian Life*. He was among the first opera singers to achieve lasting fame through gramophone recordings. *See illustration on page 160.*

Carvel Robert (1919–1990). British journalist. He was political editor of the *Evening Standard* for 25 years, retiring 1985.
His columns did much to inform and entertain the ordinary reader who looked for a lighter, but still serious window on politics. He was widely respected in political and journalistic circles.

Carver George Washington (1860–1943). US agricultural chemist. Born a slave in Missouri, he was kidnapped and raised by his former owner, Moses Carver. He devoted his life to improving the economy of the US South and the condition of blacks. He advocated the diversification of crops, promoted peanut production, and was a pioneer in the field of plastics.

Carver Raymond (1938–1988). US short-story writer and poet. His writing deals mainly with blue-collar middle America, depicting failed, empty lives in a spare prose. His major works include *Will You Please Be Quiet, Please* 1976, *What We Talk About When We Talk About Love* 1981, *Cathedral* 1983, and *In a Marine Light* 1988, a collection of poetry.

Cary (Arthur) Joyce (Lunel) (1888–1957). English novelist. He used his experiences gained in Nigeria in the Colonial Service

Caruso The Italian operatic tenor Enrico Caruso. Caruso was born in Naples, and made his first stage appearance there at 21. Roles which he made his own include Canio in Leoncavallo's I Pagliacci/The Strolling Players *and the Duke in Verdi's* Rigoletto. (Image Select)

(which he entered 1918) as a backdrop to such novels as *Mister Johnson* 1939. Other books include *The Horse's Mouth* 1944, part of a trilogy about the life of an artist, Gulley Jimson.

The will is never free – it is always attached to an object, a purpose. It is simply the engine in the car – it can't steer.

JOYCE CARY
Interview in Malcolm Cowley (ed) *Writers at Work*, First Series 1959

Casals Pablo (Pau) (1876–1973). Catalan cellist, composer, and conductor. He was largely self-taught. As a cellist, he was celebrated for his interpretations of J S Bach's unaccompanied suites. He wrote instrumental and choral works, including the Christmas oratorio *The Manger*.

He was an outspoken critic of fascism who openly defied Franco, and a tireless crusader for peace.

Casals was born in Tarragona. His pioneer recordings of Schubert and Beethoven trios 1905, with violinist Jacques Thibaut and pianist

---

To make divine things human, and human things divine; such is Bach, the greatest and purest moment in music of all times.

PABLO CASALS
Speech at Prades Bach Festival 1950

Alfred Corot, launched his international career and established the popularity of the cello as a solo instrument, notably the solo suites of J S Bach recorded 1916. In 1919 he founded the Barcelona orchestra, which he conducted until leaving Spain 1939 to live in Prades in the French Pyrenees, where he founded an annual music festival. In 1956 he moved to Puerto Rico, where he launched the Casals Festival 1957, and toured extensively in the USA.

Casanova de Seingalt Giovanni Giacomo (1725–1798). Italian adventurer, spy, violinist, librarian, and, according to his *Memoirs,* one of the world's great lovers. From 1774 he was a spy in the Venetian police service. In 1782 a libel got him into trouble, and after more wanderings he was in 1785 appointed librarian to Count Waldstein at his castle of Dûx in Bohemia. Here Casanova wrote his *Memoirs* (published 1826–38, although the complete text did not appear until 1960–61).
Suggested reading
Casanova, Giovanni *Story of My Life* (1826–38, trs 1967–69)
Childs, J R *Casanova* (1987)
Master, John *Casanova* (1969)

It is a cruel thing to die with all men misunderstanding.

ROGER CASEMENT
From his last letter to his sister before being hanged as a spy, 1916.

Casement Roger David (1864–1916). Irish nationalist. While in the British consular service, he exposed the ruthless exploitation of the people of the Belgian Congo and Peru, for which he was knighted 1911 (degraded 1916).

In 1914 Casement went to Germany and attempted to induce Irish prisoners of war to form an Irish brigade to take part in a republican

Casals The career of Pablo Casals spanned 75 years. He played a leading role in raising the status of the cello as a solo instrument, his performances acclaimed for their warmth and beauty. He was passionately committed to the political freedom of Spain and Catalonia, and spent many years in exile during the Franco era.

Casement *Sir Roger Casement appearing at Bow Street magistrates'
court charged with High Treason. A former British diplomat, Casement was
an ardent supporter of Irish Home Rule; he was captured when he was
dropped off the Irish coast by a German submarine at the start of the Easter
Rising April 1916.*

insurrection. He returned to Ireland in a submarine 1916 (actually to
postpone, not start, the Easter Rising), was arrested, tried for treason,
and hanged.

Casey Richard Gardiner, Baron Casey (1890–1976). Australian
diplomat, Liberal politician, and governor-general 1965–69. In 1924
he was involved in the formulation of the Statute of Westminster
and, after a time in the House of Representatives, in 1940 was
appointed minister plenipotentiary in Washington, US, beginning
Australia's formal diplomatic representation overseas. He was a
member of the British war cabinet in World War II and governor of
Bengal, India, 1944–46. Re-elected to federal parliament 1949, he
was minister for external affairs 1951–60, working to build up
Australia's relations with Asia and to foster the American alliance.
Unable to work harmoniously with prime minister Menzies, he
retired in 1960 and was granted a life peerage.

Cash Johnny (1932–   ). US country singer, songwriter, and
guitarist. His early hits, recorded for Sun Records in Memphis,
Tennessee, include the million-selling 'I Walk the Line' 1956. Many
of his songs have become classics.

Cash's gruff delivery and storytelling ability distinguish his work.
He is widely respected beyond the country-music field for his concern for the underprivileged, expressed in albums like *Bitter Tears*
1964 about American Indians and *Live At Folsom Prison* 1968. He is
known as the 'Man in Black' because of his penchant for dressing
entirely in black.

Cash Pat (1965–   ). Australian tennis player. An attacking player
with a powerful serve, he set up Australia's victory in the 1986 Davis
Cup in an epic match against Mikael Pernfors of Sweden. In the
same year he was a semi-finalist at Wimbledon and in 1987 he won
the Wimbledon men's singles title, defeating Ivan Lendl. His career
has been marred by injuries.

Caslavska Vera (1942–   ). Czechoslovak gymnast, the first of
the great present-day stylists. She won a record 21 world, Olympic,
and European gold medals 1959–68; she also won eight silver and
three bronze medals.

Cass Lewis (1782–1866). US political leader and diplomat. He
was appointed secretary of war 1831 by President Jackson, and

served as US minister to France 1836–42. He was the unsuccessful
Democratic presidential candidate in 1848, returning to the Senate
1849–57. In the Buchanan administration 1856–60, he served as
secretary of state 1857–60.

Cassab Judy (1920–   ). Austrian-born painter in Australia. She is
best known as a portrait artist. Her *Portrait of Margo Lewers* (Art
Gallery of New South Wales), which won the Archibald Prize in
1967, combines broad abstract forms with the demands of portraiture to project a likeness of the subject. She first won the Archibald
Prize in 1960.

Cassatt Mary (1845–1926). US Impressionist painter and printmaker. She settled in Paris 1868. Her popular, colourful pictures of
mothers and children show the influence of Japanese prints, for
example *The Bath* 1892 (Art Institute, Chicago). She excelled in
etching and pastel.

Cassatt's work, always respected in France, has gained recognition in the USA in recent years; the largest collection is owned by the
Philadelphia Art Museum.

Cassavetes John (1929–1989). US director and actor. His independent experimental films include *Shadows* 1960 and *The Killing of
a Chinese Bookie* 1980. His acting credits include *The Dirty Dozen*
1967 and *Rosemary's Baby* 1968.

Cassegrain (*c.* 1650–1700). French inventor of the system of
mirrors within many modern reflecting telescopes and sometimes used in large refraction telescopes.

Nothing is known for certain about Cassegrain's life – not even his
first name. Believed to have been a professor at the College of
Chartres, he is variously credited with having been an astronomer, a
physician, and a sculptor at the court of Louis XIV.

Cassini Giovanni Domenico (1625–1712). Italian-born French
astronomer who discovered four moons of Saturn and the gap in the
rings of Saturn now called the Cassini division.

Cassini was born near Nice (then in Italy). Having assisted two
astronomers at an observatory near Bologna, Cassini was made professor of astronomy at the University of Bologna at the age of 25. In
1669 he departed for France at the invitation of King Louis XIV, to
construct and run the Paris Observatory. When he went blind 1710,
his son *Jacques Cassini* (1677–1756) succeeded him.

Cassirer Ernst (1874–1945). German philosopher of the neo-
Kantian school. Immanuel Kant had taught that human experience
was conditioned by the categories or forms of thought to which all
human experience was limited. Cassirer held that, in addition to
Kant's list of categories, there are also forms of thought conditioning
mythical, historical, and practical thinking. These forms of thought
could be discovered by the study of language.

Cassirer was born in Breslau. With the rise of Nazism in Germany,
he fled to the USA 1932. He became a professor at Yale 1941.

His main work is the three-volume *Die Philosophie der
Symbolischen Formen*/*Philosophy of Symbolic Forms* 1923–29.

Brutus called Cassius the last of the Romans.

Plutarch on CASSIUS
in *Brutus* ch 44.1

Cassius (Gaius Cassius Longinus) (died 42 BC). Roman soldier,
one of the conspirators who killed Julius Caesar 44 BC. He fought
with Pompey against Caesar, and was pardoned after the battle of
Pharsalus 48, but became a leader in the conspiracy of 44. After
Caesar's death he joined Brutus, and committed suicide after their
defeat at Philippi 42.

Cassivelaunus chieftain of the British tribe, the Catuvellauni,
who led the British resistance to the Romans under Caesar 54 BC.

Casson Hugh Maxwell (1910–   ). English architect. He was professor at the Royal College of Art 1953–75, and president of the
Royal Academy 1976–84. He was director of architecture for the

Festival of Britain on the South Bank in London 1948–51, in which pavilions designed by young architects helped to popularize the Modern Movement. His books include *Victorian Architecture* 1948. Knighted 1952.

Castagno Andrea del (assumed name of Andrea di Bartolo de Bargilla) (*c.* 1421–1457). Italian Renaissance painter. He was active in Florence. In his frescoes in Sta Apollonia, Florence, he adapted the pictorial space to the architectural framework and followed Masaccio's lead in his use of perspective. His work is sculptural and strongly expressive, anticipating the Florentine late 15th-century style, as in his *David, c.* 1450–57 (National Gallery, Washington DC).

Castello Branco Camillo Ferreira Botelho, Visconde de Corrêa Botelho (1825–1890). Portuguese novelist. Born illegitimately and then orphaned, he led a dramatic life. His work fluctuates between mysticism and bohemianism, and includes *Amor de perdição/Love of Perdition* 1862, written during his imprisonment for adultery, and *Novelas do Minho* 1875, stories of the rural north. Other works include *Onde está a felicidade?/Where is Happiness?* 1856 and *A brazileira de Prazins/The Brazilian Girl from Prazins* 1882. He was made a viscount 1885, and committed suicide when overtaken by blindness.

Castelnau (Noel) Marie-Joseph (Edouard) Vicomte de Curieres de (1851–1944). French general. In World War I he directed the Champagne offensive in the autumn of 1915 and was responsible for the defence of Verdun. He took command of the Eastern Army Group 1918, directing the campaign into Lorraine, and was preparing to besiege Metz and march on the Rhine when the Armistice was signed. He was elected to the Chamber of Deputies 1919.

Castiglione Achille (1918–). Italian industrial designer. He worked with his brothers Livio (1911–1979) and Pier Giacomo (1913–1968) until they died. A key member of the generation of Italian designers who trained as architects before 1939 and became consultant designers for industry after 1945, his work represents modern Italian design at its most innovative and dramatic.

Castiglione Baldassare. Count, (1478–1529). Italian author and diplomat. He described the perfect Renaissance gentleman in *Il Cortegiano/The Courtier* 1528. He became count 1511.

Castilla Ramón (1797–1867). President of Peru 1841–51 and 1855–62. He dominated Peruvian politics for over two decades, bringing political stability. Income from guano exports was used to reduce the national debt and improve transport and educational facilities. He abolished black slavery and the head tax on Indians.

She was immensely self-centred, and she could be maddeningly obsessive, vain and coy. But she did not dissimulate.

Roy Jenkins on BARBARA CASTLE
in *Gallery of 20th Century Portraits* 1988

Castle Barbara Anne, Baroness Castle (born Betts) (1911–). British Labour politician, a cabinet minister in the Labour governments of the 1960s and 1970s. She led the Labour group in the European Parliament 1979–89. Baroness 1990.

Castle was minister of overseas development 1964–65, transport 1965–68, employment 1968–70 (when her White Paper *In Place of Strife*, on trade-union reform, was abandoned because it suggested state intervention in industrial relations), and social services 1974–76, when she was dropped from the cabinet by Prime Minister James Callaghan. She criticized him in her *Diaries* 1980.

Castle Roy (1932–1994). British entertainer. Noted for his versatility, he combined the talents of comic, singer, dancer, and musician; he was a particularly enthusiastic trumpeter. He presented the long-running TV series, *Record Breakers*, based on entries in the *The Guinness Book of Records*, and held two records himself; for tap dancing and wing walking. In his last years he was an active campaigner for cancer research.

Castlemaine Countess of (born Barbara Villiers) (1641–1709). Mistress of Charles II of England 1660–70 and mother of his son, the Duke of Grafton (1663–1690).

She was the wife from 1659 of Roger Palmer (1634–1705), created Earl of Castlemaine 1661. In 1670 she was created Duchess of Cleveland. Among her descendants through the Duke of Grafton is Diana, Princess of Wales.

Curse of our nation.

John Evelyn on COUNTESS OF CASTLEMAINE
in *Diary* 1 Mar 1671

Castlereagh Robert Stewart, Viscount Castlereagh (1769–1822). British Tory politician. As chief secretary for Ireland 1797–1801, he suppressed the rebellion of 1798 and helped the younger Pitt secure the union of England, Scotland, and Ireland 1801. As foreign secretary 1812–22, he coordinated European opposition to Napoleon and represented Britain at the Congress of Vienna 1814–15.

Castlereagh sat in the Irish House of Commons from 1790. When his father, an Ulster landowner, was made an earl 1796, he took the courtesy title of Viscount Castlereagh. In Parliament he was secretary for war and the colonies 1805–06 and 1807–09, when he had to resign after a duel with foreign secretary George Canning. Castlereagh was foreign secretary from 1812, when he devoted himself to the overthrow of Napoleon and subsequently to the Congress of Vienna and the congress system. Abroad, his policy favoured the development of material liberalism, but at home he repressed the Reform movement, and popular opinion held him responsible for the Peterloo massacre of peaceful demonstrators 1819. In 1821 he succeeded his father as Marquess of Londonderry.

Castro Cipriano (1858–1924). Venezuelan dictator 1899–1908, known as 'the Lion of the Andes'. When he refused to pay off foreign debts 1902, British, German, and Italian ships blockaded the country. He presided over a corrupt government. There were frequent rebellions during his rule, and opponents of his regime were exiled or murdered.

A revolution is not a bed of roses. A revolution is a struggle to the death between the future and the past.

FIDEL CASTRO
Speech given on the second anniversary
of the revolution, Havana Jan 1961

Castro (Ruz) Fidel (1927–). Cuban communist politician, prime minister 1959–76 and president from 1976. He led two unsuccessful coups against the right-wing Batista regime and led the revolution that overthrew the dictator 1959. He raised the standard of living for most Cubans but dealt harshly with dissenters. From 1990, deprived of the support of the USSR and experiencing the long-term effects of a US trade embargo, Castro faced increasing pressure for reform; in Sept 1995 he moved towards greater economic flexibility by permitting foreign ownership in major areas of commerce and industry.

Suggested reading
Bourne, Peter *Fidel* (1986)
Martin, Lionel *The Early Fidel* (1978)
Oppenheimer, A *Castro's Final Hour* (1992)
Szulc, Tad *Fidel: A Critical Portrait* (1986)

Catesby Robert (1573–1605). English conspirator and leader of the Gunpowder Plot 1605. He took part in the uprising of the 2nd Earl of Essex 1601 and was an accomplice in the plot of 1603 to capture James I and force religious concessions from him. He was killed resisting arrest following the failure of the Gunpowder Plot to blow up parliament.

Cather Willa Sibert (1873–1947). US novelist and short-story writer. Her novels frequently explore life in the pioneer West, both in her own time and in past eras; for example, *O Pioneers!* 1913 *My Antonia* 1918, and *A Lost Lady* 1923. *Death Comes for the Archbishop* 1927 is a celebration of the spiritual pioneering of the Catholic Church in New Mexico. She also wrote poetry and essays on fiction.

I like trees because they seem more resigned to the way they have to live than other things do.

WILLA CATHER
O Pioneers! 1913

Catherine two empresses of Russia:

Catherine I (1684–1727). Empress of Russia from 1725. A Lithuanian peasant, born Martha Skavronsky, she married a Swedish dragoon and eventually became the mistress of Peter the Great. In 1703 she was rechristened Katarina Alexeievna. The tsar divorced his wife 1711 and married Catherine 1712. She accompanied him on his campaigns, and showed tact and shrewdness. In 1724 she was proclaimed empress, and after Peter's death 1725 she ruled capably with the help of her ministers. She allied Russia with Austria and Spain in an anti-English bloc.

Coarse and corpulent, licentious and illiterate ... [she inaugurated] a period of declining autocracy and crumbling centralization.

E N Williams on CATHERINE I
in *Penguin Dictionary of English and European History 1485–1789* 1980

Castro, Fidel The Cuban revolutionary leader Fidel Castro. After his overthrow of the right-wing Batista regime 1959, Castro maintained his leadership of Cuba despite the enmity of his powerful neighbour, the USA. Since 1990 events in E Europe and the former USSR have left Castro increasingly isolated.

Catherine (II) the Great (1729–1796). Empress of Russia from 1762, and daughter of the German prince of Anhalt-Zerbst. In 1745, she married the Russian grand duke Peter. Catherine was able to dominate him; six months after he became Tsar Peter III in 1762, he was murdered in a coup and Catherine ruled alone. During her reign Russia extended its boundaries to include territory from wars with the Turks 1768–74, 1787–92, and from the partitions of Poland 1772, 1793, and 1795, as well as establishing hegemony over the Black Sea.

Catherine's private life was notorious throughout Europe, but except for Grigory Potemkin she did not permit her lovers to influence her policy.

She admired and aided the French Encyclopédistes, including d'Alembert, and corresponded with the radical writer Voltaire.

Suggested reading
Alexander, J T *Catherine the Great: Life and Legend* (1989)
Cronin, V *Catherine, Empress of All the Russias* (1990)
Troyat, H *Catherine the Great* (1977)

I shall be an autocrat: that's my trade. And the good Lord will forgive me: that's his.

CATHERINE THE GREAT
Attributed remark

Catherine de' Medici (1519–1589). French queen consort of Henry II, whom she married 1533; daughter of Lorenzo de' Medici, Duke of Urbino; and mother of Francis II, Charles IX, and Henry III. At first outshone by Henry's mistress Diane de Poitiers (1490–1566), she became regent 1560–63 for Charles IX and remained in power until his death 1574.

During the religious wars of 1562–69, she first supported the Protestant Huguenots against the Roman Catholic *Guises* to ensure her own position as ruler; she later opposed them, and has been traditionally implicated in the Massacre of St Bartholomew 1572.

She was never afraid of hard work, but usually had her eye on short-term political gains rather than on long-term statesmanship.

E N Williams on CATHERINE DE' MEDICI
in *Penguin Dictionary of English and European History 1485–1789* 1980

Catherine of Alexandria, St (lived early 4th century). Christian martyr. According to legend she disputed with 50 scholars, refusing to give up her faith and marry Emperor Maxentius. Her emblem is a wheel, on which her persecutors tried to kill her (the wheel broke and she was beheaded). Feast day 25 Nov; removed from church calendar 1969.

Catherine of Aragon (1485–1536). First queen of Henry VIII of England, 1509–33, and mother of Mary I. Catherine had married Henry's elder brother Prince Arthur 1501 and on his death 1502 was betrothed to Henry, marrying him on his accession. She failed to produce a male heir and Henry divorced her without papal approval, thus creating the basis for the English Reformation.

Of their six children, only Mary lived. Wanting a male heir, Henry sought an annulment 1526 when Catherine was too old to bear children. When the pope demanded that the case be referred to him, Henry married Anne Boleyn, afterward receiving the desired decree of nullity from Cranmer, the archbishop of Canterbury, in 1533. The Reformation in England followed, and Catherine went into retirement until her death.

A little woman, no breeder.

Anthony à Wood on CATHERINE OF BRAGANZA
in *Life and Times* 20 May 1662

Catherine of Braganza (1638–1705). Queen of Charles II of England 1662–85. Her childlessness and Catholic faith were unpopular, but Charles resisted pressure for divorce. She returned to Lisbon 1692 after his death.

The daughter of John IV of Portugal (1604–1656), she brought the Portuguese possessions of Bombay and Tangier as her dowry and introduced tea drinking and citrus fruits to England.

Catherine of Genoa, St (born Caterina Fieschi) (1447–1510). Italian mystic who devoted herself to the sick and to meditation. Feast day 15 Sept. Canonized 1737.

Catherine of Siena (born Caterina Benicasa) (1347–1380). Italian mystic, born in Siena. She persuaded Pope Gregory XI to return to Rome from Avignon 1376. In 1375 she is said to have received on her body the stigmata, the impression of Jesus' wounds. Her *Dialogue* is a classic mystical work. Feast day 29 April. Canonized 1461.

Catherine of Valois (1401–1437). Queen of Henry V of England, whom she married 1420; the mother of Henry VI. After the death of Henry V, she secretly married Owen Tudor (*c.* 1400–1461) about 1425, and their son Edmund Tudor was the father of Henry VII.

Catherwood Frederick (1799–1854). English topographical artist and archaeological illustrator who accompanied John Lloyd Stephens in his exploration of Central America 1839–40 and the Yucatán 1841–42. His engravings, published 1844, were the first accurate representation of Maya civilization in the West.

Catholic Monarchs, the the two monarchs ◊Ferdinand V of Castile and ◊Isabella I, so-called because they catholicized Spain after 700 years of Moorish rule.

I have adopted a course of action which offers hopes of saving what remains of my honour.

Letter from CATILINE to a senatorial friend. Quoted in Sallust *Catilinarian Conspiracy* ch 35

Catiline (Lucius Sergius Catilina) (*c.* 108–62 BC). Roman politician. Twice failing to be elected to the consulship in 64/63 BC, he planned a military coup, but Cicero exposed his conspiracy. He died at the head of the insurgents.

Catlin George (1796–1872). US painter and explorer. From the 1830s he made a series of visits to the Great Plains, painting landscapes and scenes of American Indian life. His style is factual, with close attention to detail.

Catlin produced an exhibition of over 500 paintings with which he toured America and Europe. Many of his pictures are in the Smithsonian Institution, Washington, DC.

Cato Marcus Porcius. Known as 'the Censor' (234–149 BC). Roman politician. Having significantly developed Roman rule in Spain, Cato was appointed censor 184 BC. He acted severely, taxing luxuries and heavily revising the senatorial and equestrian lists. He was violently opposed to Greek influence on Roman culture and his suspicion of the re-emergence of Carthaginian power led him to remark: 'Carthage must be destroyed.'

Cato Marcus Porcius of Utica, (Cato the Younger) (95–46 BC). Roman politician, great-grandson of Cato 'the Censor'. His staunch republican views led him to support Pompey in the civil war, but failed to hold Sicily for him. He withdrew (48 BC) to Utica in Africa, where he committed suicide after learning of Caesar's victory at the battle of Thapsus.

His suicide made him a hero to those with republican sympathies, a martyrdom aided by a virulent attack by Caesar in his pamphlet *Anticato*.

What a woman says to her ardent lover should be written in wind and running water.

CATULLUS
Odes no 70

Catullus Gaius Valerius (*c.* 84–54 BC). Roman lyric poet. He wrote in a variety of metres and forms, from short narratives and hymns to epigrams. He was born in Verona, N Italy. He moved with ease through the literary and political society of late republican Rome. His love affair with the woman he called Lesbia provided the inspiration for many of his poems.

Cauchy Augustin Louis, Baron de (1789–1857). French mathematician who employed rigorous methods of analysis. His prolific output included work on complex functions, determinants, and probability, and on the convergence of infinite series. In calculus, he refined the concepts of the limit and the definite integral.

Cauchy has the credit for 16 fundamental concepts and theorems in mathematics and mathematical physics, more than any other mathematician.

Cauchy was born in Paris, studied engineering there and worked for a time in construction, then became a professor at the Ecole Polytechnique 1816 and later at the Collège de France. In 1830 Charles X was overthrown, and, refusing to take the new oath of allegiance, Cauchy went into exile. He became professor of mathematical physics at the University of Turin, and from 1833 he was tutor to Charles X's son in Prague, returning to Paris 1838 to resume his professorship at the Ecole Polytechnique. In 1843 he published a defence of academic freedom of thought, which was instrumental in the abolition of the oath of allegiance soon after the fall of Louis Philippe 1848. From 1848 to 1852 Cauchy was a professor at the Sorbonne.

Causley Charles Stanley (1917–). English poet. He published his first volume *Hands to Dance* 1951. Later volumes include *Johnny Alleluia* 1961, *Underneath the Water* 1968, *Figgie Hobbin* 1970, and *Secret Destinations* 1989. His work is rooted in the life and folklore of his native Cornwall and makes use of ballad material and religious themes.

Cauthen Steve (1960–). US jockey. He rode Affirmed to the US Triple Crown 1978 at the age of 18 and won 487 races 1977. He twice won the English Derby, on Slip Anchor 1985 and on Reference Point 1987, and was UK champion jockey 1984, 1985, and 1987.

Cavaco Silva Anibal (1939–). Portuguese politician, finance minister 1980–81, and prime minister and Social Democratic Party (PSD) leader 1985–95. Under his leadership Portugal joined the European Community 1985 and the Western European Union 1988.

Body, remember not only how much you were loved, / not only the beds you lay on, / but also those desires glowing openly / in eyes that looked at you, / trembling for you in voices.

CONSTANTINOS CAVAFY
'Body, Remember'

Cavafy Constantinos. Pen name of Konstantínos Pétrou Kaváfis (1863–1933). Greek poet. An Alexandrian, he shed light on Greek history, recreating the classical period with zest. He published only one book of poetry and remained almost unknown until translations of his works appeared 1952.

Cavalcanti Guido (*c.* 1255–1300). Italian poet. A Florentine and friend of Dante, he was a leading exponent of the *dolce stil nuovo* (sweet new style).

He is remembered for 'Donna mi prega/A Lady Asks Me', a philosophical poem about love, and for his sonnets and *ballate* or ballads. English translators include D G Rossetti and Ezra Pound.

Cavalli (Pietro) Francesco (1602–1676). Italian composer. He was organist at St Mark's, Venice, and the first to make opera a popular entertainment with such works as *Equisto* 1643 and *Xerxes* 1654, later performed in honour of Louis XIV's wedding in Paris. Twenty-seven of his operas survive.

Cave Edward (1691–1754). British printer and founder, under the pseudonym Sylvanus Urban, of *The Gentleman's Magazine* 1731–1914, the first periodical to be called a magazine. Samuel Johnson was a contributor 1738–44.

I realize that patriotism is not enough. I must have no hatred or bitterness towards any one.

EDITH CAVELL
Last words 12 Oct 1915, quoted in *The Times* 23 Oct 1915

Cavell Edith Louisa (1865–1915). English matron of a Red Cross hospital in Brussels, Belgium, in World War I, who helped Allied soldiers escape to the Dutch frontier. She was court-martialled by the Germans and condemned to death.

Cavendish family name of dukes of Devonshire; the family seat is at Chatsworth, Derbyshire, England.

Cavendish Lord Frederick Charles (1836–1882). British administrator, second son of the 7th Duke of Devonshire. He was appointed chief secretary to the lord lieutenant of Ireland in 1882. On the evening of his arrival in Dublin he was murdered in Phoenix Park with Thomas Burke, the permanent Irish undersecretary, by members of the Irish Invincibles, a group of Irish Fenian extremists founded 1881.

Cavendish Henry (1731–1810). English physicist and chemist. He discovered hydrogen (which he called 'inflammable air') 1766, and determined the compositions of water and of nitric acid. The Cavendish experiment 1798 enabled him to discover the mass and density of the Earth. He spent the rest of his life in seclusion in London. Most of his work, especially his experiments with electricity, was unknown for 100 years or more. He believed electricity to be an elastic fluid.

Suggested reading
Berry, A J *Henry Cavendish: His Life and Scientific Work* (1960)

Cavendish Spencer. See ◊Hartington, Spencer Compton Cavendish, British politician.

Cavendish Thomas (1560–1592). English navigator, and commander of the third circumnavigation of the world. He sailed in July 1586, touched Brazil, sailed down the coast to Patagonia, passed through the Straits of Magellan, and returned to Britain via the Philippines, the Cape of Good Hope, and St Helena, reaching Plymouth after two years and 50 days.

Cavendish-Bentinck family name of the dukes of Portland.

Rome must be the capital of Italy because without Rome Italy cannot be constituted.

COUNT CAVOUR
Speech in Turin 25 March 1861

Cavour Camillo Benso di, Count (1810–1861). Italian nationalist politician, a leading figure in the Italian *Risorgimento*. As prime minister of Piedmont 1852–59 and 1860–61, he enlisted the support of Britain and France for the concept of a united Italy, achieved 1861; after expelling the Austrians 1859, he assisted Garibaldi in liberating southern Italy 1860.

Cawley Evonne Fay (born Goolagong) (1951–). Australian tennis player who won the Wimbledon singles title in 1971 and 1980. She has won every Australian mainland state title as well as the Australian singles title 1974–76.

Caxton William (*c.* 1422–1491). The first English printer. He learned the art of printing in Cologne, Germany, 1471 and set up a press in Belgium where he produced the first book printed in English, his own version of a French romance, *Recuyell of the Historyes of Troye* 1474. Returning to England 1476, he established himself in London, where he produced the first book printed in England, *Dictes or Sayengis of the Philosophres* 1477. The books from

Cavell *English nurse Edith Cavell who ran a Red Cross hospital in Belgium during World War I which treated Allied and German wounded. She was executed by the Germans Oct 1915 for helping Allied soldiers to escape to Holland. She became a national hero in Britain and a statue was erected in her honour in St Martin's Place, London. (Image Select)*

Caxton's press in Westminster included editions of the poets Chaucer, John Gower, and John Lydgate (*c.* 1370–1449). He translated many texts from French and Latin and revised some English ones, such as Malory's *Morte d'Arthur*. Altogether he printed about 100 books.

Suggested reading
Blake, N *Caxton and his Age* (1977)
Blumenthal, J *The Art of the Printed Book, 1435–1955* (1973)
Hindley, Geoffrey *England in the Age of Caxton* (1979)
Painter, George *William Caxton: A Biography* (1977)

Cayley Arthur (1821–1895). English mathematician who developed matrix algebra, used by Werner Heisenberg in his elucidation of quantum mechanics. He also developed the study of *n*-dimensional geometry, introducing the concept of the 'absolute', and formulated the theory of algebraic invariants. In 1863 he became professor of pure mathematics at Cambridge.

Cayley George (1773–1857). English aviation pioneer, inventor of the first piloted glider 1853, and the caterpillar tractor. The 1853 glider was a triplane, in which his reluctant coach driver travelled 275 m/900 ft across a small valley – the first recorded flight by a person in an aircraft. Although delighted with the result, Cayley realized that control of flight could not be achieved until a lightweight engine was developed to give the thrust and lift required. Succeeded as 6th baronet 1792.

Cayley Neville William (1886–1950). Australian ornithological artist who specialized in Australian birds. His best-selling book *What Bird is That?* first appeared in 1931 and gives colour illustrations and descriptions of all Australian birds.

Cazneaux Harold (1878–1953). Australian photographer known for his portraits and landscapes. His work has been acquired by the National and New South Wales art galleries.

Ceaușescu Nicolae (1918–1989). Romanian politician, leader of the Romanian Communist Party (RCP), in power 1965–89. He pursued a policy line independent of and critical of the USSR. He appointed family members, including his wife Elena Ceaușescu, to senior state and party posts, and governed in an increasingly repressive manner, zealously implementing schemes that impoverished the nation. The Ceaușescus were overthrown in a bloody revolutionary coup Dec 1989 and executed.

Cecchetti Enrico (1850–1928). Italian ballet master. He evolved a system of teaching that greatly improved the technical standards of the dance. His system has been preserved by the Cecchetti Society (founded 1922 and incorporated into the Imperial Society of Teachers of Dancing 1924) and is still widely used. He taught Anna Pavlova.

As a dancer he created the roles of Bluebird and Carabosse in *Sleeping Beauty* 1887. He taught at the Imperial Russian Ballet school 1890–1902 and was the instructor for Diaghilev's Ballets Russes 1910–18. He founded a school in London 1918–25, and then became director of the La Scala ballet school in Milan 1925–28.

Cecil Henry Richard Amherst (1943–). Scottish-born racehorse trainer with stables at Warren Place, Newmarket. He was the first trainer to win over £1 million in a season (1985). He trained Slip Anchor and Reference Point to win the Epsom Derby.

Cecil Robert, 1st Earl of Salisbury (1563–1612). Secretary of state to Elizabeth I of England, succeeding his father, Lord Burghley; he was afterwards chief minister to James I (James VI of Scotland) whose accession to the English throne he secured. He discovered the Gunpowder Plot, the conspiracy to blow up the King and Parliament 1605. James I created him Earl of Salisbury 1605. Knighted 1591, baron 1603, viscount 1604.

Cecilia, St (lived 2nd or 3rd century AD). Christian patron saint of music. She was martyred in Rome in the 2nd or 3rd century, and is said to have sung hymns while undergoing torture. Feast day 22 Nov.

Cela Camilo José (1916–). Spanish novelist. Among his novels, characterized by their violence and brutal realism, are *La familia de Pascual Duarte/The Family of Pascal Duarte* 1942, and *La colmena/The Hive* 1951. Nobel Prize for Literature 1989.

Almost every desire a poor man has is a punishable offence.
LOUIS-FERDINAND CÉLINE
Journey to the End of the Night 176 1932

Céline Louis Ferdinand. Pen name of Louis Destouches (1894–1961). French novelist. His writings aroused controversy over their cynicism and misanthropy. His best-known work is *Voyage au bout de la nuit/Journey to the End of the Night* 1932.

Cellini Benvenuto (1500–1571). Italian sculptor and goldsmith. He worked in the Mannerist style and wrote an arrogant but entertaining and informative autobiography (begun 1558). Among his works are a graceful bronze *Perseus* 1545–54 (Loggia dei Lanzi, Florence) and a celebrated gold salt cellar made for Francis I of France 1540–43 (Kunsthistorisches Museum, Vienna), topped by nude reclining figures.

The difference between a painting and a sculpture is the difference between a shadow and the thing that casts it.
BENVENUTO CELLINI
Letter to Benedetto Varchi 1547

Suggested reading
Cellini, Benvenuto *Autobiography* (trs 1956)
Pope-Hennessy, J *Cellini* (1985)

Celsius Anders (1701–1744). Swedish astronomer, physicist, and mathematician who introduced the Celsius scale of temperature. His other scientifc works include a paper on accurately determining the shape and size of the Earth, some of the first attempts to gauge the magnitude of the stars in the constellation Aries, and a study of falling water level of the Baltic Sea.

Celsius was born in Uppsala, where he succeeded his father as professor of astronomy 1730. He travelled extensively in Europe, visiting astronomers and observatories in particular. In Uppsala he built Sweden's first observatory.

Cennini Cennino (*c.* 1370–*c.* 1440). Italian painter and writer. He is remembered for his practical manual on painting *Il libro dell'arte/The Craftsman's Handbook*, about 1390, a source of fascinating insights into early Italian Renaissance workshop techniques, especially tempera painting. None of his paintings survive.

When the glowing of passion's over, and pinching winter comes, will amorous sighs supply the want of fire, or kind looks and kisses keep off hunger?
SUSANNAH CENTLIVRE
Artifice 1761

Centlivre Susannah (born Freeman) (*c.* 1667–*c.* 1723). English dramatist and actress. Her first play was a tragedy, *The Perjured Husband* 1700. Success as a dramatist came with the comedy *The Gamester* 1705, which was followed by *The Busie Body* 1709 and *A Bold Stroke for a Wife* 1718. As an actress, she specialized in male roles, as in *The Beau's Duel* 1702.

Cerf Bennett Alfred (1898–1971). US editor and publisher. In 1925 he co-purchased the rights to the Modern Library series, and subsequently founded Random House 1927. The company grew to be one of the world's largest publishing houses.

Love and War are the same thing, and stratagems and policy are as allowable in the one as in the other.
MIGUEL DE CERVANTES
Don Quixote pt 2 bk 3 1605

Cervantes (Saavedra), Miguel de (1547–1616). Spanish novelist, playwright, and poet. His masterpiece *Don Quixote* (in full *El ingenioso hidalgo Don Quixote de la Mancha*) was published 1605. In 1613, his *Novelas ejemplares/Exemplary Novels* appeared, followed by *Viaje del Parnaso/The Voyage to Parnassus* 1614. A spurious second part of *Don Quixote* prompted Cervantes to bring out his own second part 1615, often considered superior to the first in construction and characterization.

Born at Alcalá de Henares, he entered the army in Italy, and was wounded in the battle of Lepanto 1571. While on his way back to Spain 1575, he was captured by Barbary pirates and taken to Algiers, where he became a slave until ransomed 1580.

Returning to Spain, he wrote several plays, and in 1585 his pastoral romance *Galatea* was printed. He was employed in Seville 1587 provisioning the Armada. While working as a tax collector, he was imprisoned more than once for deficiencies in his accounts. He sank into poverty, and little is known of him until 1605 when he published *Don Quixote*. The novel was an immediate success and was soon translated into English and French.

Suggested reading
Byron, W *Cervantes: A Biography* (1978)
Caravaggio, J *Cervantes* (1990)
Predmore, R L *Cervantes* (1973)
Russell, P *Cervantes* (1985)

Cesalpino Andrea (1519–1603). Italian botanist who showed that plants could be and should be classified by their anatomy and structure. In *De plantis* 1583, Cesalpino offered the first remotely modern classification of plants. Before this plants were classed by their location – for example marsh plants, moorland plants, and even foreign plants.

César adopted name of César Baldaccini (1921–). French sculptor. He created imaginary insects and animals using iron and scrap metal and, in the 1960s, crushed car bodies. From the late 1960s he experimented with works in plastic and polyurethane.

Cesaro Ernesto (1859–1906). Italian mathematician who made important contributions to intrinsic geometry. He first defined Cesaro's curves 1896. He was professor of higher algebra at the University of Palermo 1886–91, and then professor of mathematical analysis at Naples.

Cetewayo or Cetshwayo (*c.* 1826–1884). King of Zululand, South Africa, 1873–83, whose rule was threatened by British annexation of the Transvaal 1877. Although he defeated the British at Isandhlwana 1879, he was later that year defeated by them at Ulundi. Restored to his throne 1883, he was then expelled by his subjects.

Treat nature by the cylinder, the sphere, the cone, everything in proper perspective.

Letter from PAUL CÉZANNE to Emile Bernard 15 April 1904

Cézanne Paul (1839–1906). French Post-Impressionist painter. He was a leading figure in the development of modern art. He broke away from the Impressionists' concern with the ever-changing effects of light to develop a style that tried to capture the structure of natural forms, whether in landscapes, still lifes, or portraits. *Cardplayers* about 1890–95 (Louvre, Paris) is typical of his work.

He was educated at the Collège Bourbon of Aix (where he became the friend of Zola) and was intended for the law, but persuaded his parents to allow him to study art in Paris. He had, however, no regular training, failing in the entrance examination of the École des Beaux-Arts, and his early work had an undisciplined and Romantic enthusiasm for Delacroix, Daumier, and Courbet, sensational subject matter (*L'Orgie*, *L'Enlèvement*) being rendered with violent and dark colour, heavily plastered on the canvas. His real apprenticeship began in the 1870s when his friendship with Camille Pissarro brought him within the orbit of Impressionism. A further result of Impressionist influence was to wean him from Romantic ideas and to confront him simply with the study of nature, *La Maison du Pendu*, which he contributed to the first Impressionist exhibition of 1874, marking a transitional stage in his art.

He found Paris unsympathetic, and his later life, the most creative phase, was spent largely in seclusion at Aix.
Suggested reading
Geist, S *Interpreting Cézanne* (1988)
Rewald, J *Paul Cézanne* (1986)
Schapiro, M *Cézanne* (1988)
Venturi, L *Cézanne* (1978)

Chabrier (Alexis) Emmanuel (1841–1894). French composer. He wrote *España* 1883, an orchestral rhapsody, and the light opera *Le Roi malgré lui*/*The Reluctant King* 1887. His colourful orchestration inspired Debussy and Ravel.

Chabrol Claude (1930–). French film director. Originally a critic, he was one of the New Wave directors. His works of murder and suspense, which owe much to Hitchcock, include *Les Cousins*/*The Cousins* 1959, *Les Biches*/*The Girlfriends* 1968, *Le Boucher*/*The Butcher* 1970, *Cop au Vin* 1984, and *L'Enfer*.

Chadli Benjedid (1929–). Algerian socialist politician, president 1979–92. An army colonel, he supported Boumédienne in the overthrow of Ben Bella 1965, and succeeded Boumédienne 1979, pursuing more moderate policies. Chadli resigned Jan 1992 following a victory for Islamic fundamentalists in the first round of assembly elections.

Chadwick Edwin (1800–1890). English social reformer, author of the Poor Law Report 1834. He played a prominent part in the campaign that resulted in the Public Health Act 1848. He was commissioner of the first Board of Health 1848–54. Knighted 1889.

A self-educated protégé of the philosopher Jeremy Bentham and advocate of utilitarianism, Chadwick used his influence to implement measures to eradicate cholera, improve sanitation in urban areas, and clear slums in British cities.

Chadwick James (1891–1974). English physicist. In 1932 he discovered the particle in the nucleus of an atom that became known as the neutron because it has no electric charge. Nobel Prize for Physics 1935. Knighted 1945.

Chadwick established the equivalence of atomic number and atomic charge. During World War II, he was closely involved with the atomic bomb, and from 1943 he led the British team working on the Manhattan Project in the USA.

Chadwick Lynn (1914–). English abstract sculptor. She is known for her 1940s mobiles (influenced by Alexander Calder) and for welded ironwork from the 1950s, typically spiky, pyramidal 'creatures'.

Chagall Marc (1887–1985). Russian-born French painter and designer. Much of his highly coloured, fantastic imagery was inspired by the village life of his boyhood and by Jewish and Russian folk traditions. He designed stained glass, mosaics (for Israel's Knesset in the 1960s), the ceiling of the Paris Opera House 1964, tapestries, and stage sets. He was an original figure, often seen as a precursor of Surrealism, as in *I and the Village* 1911 (Museum of Modern Art, New York).

Chagall lived mainly in France from 1922. Examples of his stained glass can be found in a chapel in Vence, the south of France, 1950s, and a synagogue near Jerusalem 1961. He also produced illustrated books.
Suggested reading
Cassou, J *Chagall* (1965)
Chagall, M *My Life* (1960)
Meyer, F *Marc Chagall* (1963)
Verdet, A *Chagall's World* (1984)

Chaillu Paul Belloni du (1835–1903). French-born US explorer. In 1855 he began a four-year journey of exploration in West Africa, covering 8,000 miles on foot. His *Explorations and Adventures in Equatorial Africa* 1861 describes his discovery of gorillas in Gabon.

He brought back 2,000 stuffed birds and 1,000 stuffed animals from his 1855–59 African expedition.

Chain Ernst Boris (1906–1979). German-born British biochemist. After the discovery of penicillin by Alexander Fleming, Chain worked to isolate and purify it. For this work, he shared the 1945 Nobel Prize for Medicine with Fleming and Howard Florey. Chain also discovered penicillinase, an enzyme that destroys penicillin. Knighted 1969.

Born and educated in Berlin, Chain fled to Britain from the Nazis 1933. He worked at Cambridge University 1933–35, and then with Florey at Oxford. In 1949 Chain was invited to the Istituto Superiore di Sanità in Rome; he stayed there as professor until 1961, when he returned to the UK as professor of biochemistry at Imperial College, London.

Chaka alternative spelling of ◊Shaka, Zulu chief.

Chaliapin Fyodor Ivanovich (1873–1938). Russian bass singer, born in Kazan (Tatar Republic). He achieved fame in the West through his charismatic recordings, notably as Boris in Mussorgsky's opera *Boris Godunov*. He specialized in Russian, French, and Italian roles.
Suggested reading
Borovsky, Victor *Chaliapin* (1988)
Chaliapin, Fyodor *Chaliapin: An Autobiography as Told to Maxim Gorky* (1967)

Challis James (1803–1882). English astronomer who failed to take the advice of John Couch Adams on where to search for the planet Neptune, leaving its discovery to French and German astronomers.

Challis was born in Braintree, Essex, and educated at Cambridge. An Anglican cleric, he was rector at Papworth Everard, Cambridgeshire, 1830–52, as well as professor of astronomy and director of the observatory at Cambridge from 1836.

Chalmers Thomas (1780–1847). Scottish theologian. At the Disruption of the Church of Scotland 1843, Chalmers withdrew from the church along with a large number of other priests, and became principal of the Free Church college, thus founding the Free Church of Scotland.

As minister of Tron Church, Glasgow, from 1815, Chalmers gained a reputation for eloquence and made proposals for social reform. In 1823 he became professor of moral philosophy at St Andrews, and in 1828 of theology at Edinburgh.

Peace with honour. I believe it is peace for our time.
NEVILLE CHAMBERLAIN
Speech from 10 Downing Street 30 Sept 1938

Chamberlain (Arthur) Neville (1869–1940). British Conservative politician, son of Joseph Chamberlain. He was prime minister 1937–40; his policy of appeasement toward the fascist dictators Mussolini and Hitler (with whom he concluded the Munich Agreement 1938) failed to prevent the outbreak of World War II. He resigned 1940 following the defeat of the British forces in Norway.

Younger son of Joseph Chamberlain and half-brother of Austen Chamberlain, he was born in Birmingham, of which he was lord mayor 1915. He was minister of health 1923 and 1924–29 and worked at slum clearance. In 1931 he was chancellor of the Exchequer in the national government, and in 1937 succeeded Baldwin as prime minister. Trying to close the old Anglo-Irish feud, he agreed to return to Eire those ports that had been occupied by the navy.

He also attempted to appease the demands of the European dictators, particularly Mussolini. In 1938 he went to Munich and negotiated with Hitler the settlement of the Czechoslovak question. He was ecstatically received on his return, and claimed that the Munich Agreement brought 'peace in our time'. Within a year, however, Britain was at war with Germany.

Suggested reading
Charmley, John *Chamberlain and the Lost Peace* (1989)
Dilks, David *Neville Chamberlain, 1869–1929* (1985)
Fuchser, L W *Neville Chamberlain and Appeasement* (1982)
Mackintosh, John P *British Prime Ministers in the Twentieth Century* (1977)
Rock, William *Neville Chamberlain* (1969)

Chamberlain Joseph (1836–1914). British politician, reformist mayor of and member of Parliament for Birmingham; in 1886, he resigned from the cabinet over Gladstone's policy of home rule for Ireland, and led the revolt of the Liberal-Unionists.

By 1874 Chamberlain had made a sufficient fortune in the Birmingham screw-manufacturing business to devote himself entirely to politics. He adopted radical views, and took an active part in local affairs. Three times mayor of Birmingham, he carried through many schemes of municipal development. In 1876 he was elected to Parliament and joined the republican group led by Charles Dilke, the extreme left wing of the Liberal Party. In 1880 he entered Gladstone's cabinet as president of the Board of Trade. The climax of his radical period was reached with the unauthorized programme, advocating, among other things, free education, graduated taxation, and smallholdings of 'three acres and a cow'.

As colonial secretary in Salisbury's Conservative government, Chamberlain was responsible for relations with the Boer republics up to the outbreak of war 1899. In 1903 he resigned to campaign for imperial preference or tariff reform as a means of consolidating the empire. From 1906 he was incapacitated by a stroke. Chamberlain was one of the most colourful figures of British politics, and his monocle and orchid made him a favourite subject for political cartoonists.

The day of small nations has long passed away. The day of Empires has come.
JOSEPH CHAMBERLAIN
Speech in Birmingham 12 May 1904

Chamberlain (Joseph) Austen (1863–1937). British Conservative politician, elder son of Joseph Chamberlain.

He was elected to Parliament 1892 as a Liberal-Unionist, and after holding several minor posts was chancellor of the Exchequer 1903–06. During World War I he was secretary of state for India 1915–17 and member of the war cabinet 1918. He was chancellor of the Exchequer 1919–21 and Lord Privy Seal 1921–22, but failed to secure the leadership of the party 1922, as many Conservatives resented the part he had taken in the Irish settlement of 1921. He was foreign secretary in the Baldwin government 1924–29, and negotiated and signed the Locarno Pact 1925 (for which he won the Nobel Peace Prize) to fix the boundaries of Germany, and the Kellogg–Briand pact 1928 to ban war and provide for peaceful settlement of disputes. Knighted 1925.

Chamberlain Owen (1920–). US physicist whose graduate studies were interrupted by work on the Manhattan Project at Los Alamos. After World War II, working with Italian physicist Emilio Segrè, he discovered the existence of the antiproton. Both scientists were awarded the Nobel Prize for Physics 1959.

Chamberlain Wilt(on) Norman (1936–). US basketball player who set a record by averaging 50.4 points a game during the 1962 season, and was the only man to score 100 points in a game.

He was known as 'Wilt the Stilt' because of his height of 2.16 m/ 7 ft 1 in. He retired 1973.

Chamberlin Thomas Chrowder (1843–1928). US geophysicist who asserted that the Earth was far older than then believed. He developed the planetesimal hypothesis for the origin of the Earth and other planetary bodies – that they had been formed gradually by accretion of particles. Partly self-taught in science, he joined the Wisconsin Geological Survey 1873, and rose to become its chief geologist, publishing *Geology of Wisconsin* 1877–83. He went on to work for the US Geological Survey before becoming professor at Chicago 1892–1918.

Even men of inferior rank now aspire to taste in the fine arts.
WILLIAM CHAMBERS
Treatise on Civil Architecture 1769

Chambers William (1726–1796). Swedish-born English architect. Although he worked in the Neo-Palladian style, he was also a popularizer of Chinese influence (for example, the pagoda in Kew Gardens, London, 1762). His best-known work in the Neo-Palladian style is Somerset House, London, 1776–86.

Chamisso Adelbert von. Pen name of Louis Charles Adélaïde Chamisso de Boncourt (1781–1838). German writer. He is known for the story *Peter Schlemihl*, about a man who sold his shadow. Chamisso was born into a French family who left France because of the French Revolution; subsequently he went as a botanist on Otto von Kotzebue's trip around the world 1815–18, recounted in *Reise um de Welt* 1821. His verse includes the cycle of lyrics *Frauenliebe und Frauenleben* 1831, set to music by Schumann.

Chamorro Violeta Barrios de (c. 1939–). President of Nicaragua from 1990. With strong US support, she was elected to be the candidate for the National Opposition Union (UNO) 1989, winning the presidency from David Ortega Saavedra Feb 1990 and thus ending the period of Sandinista rule.

Chamorro's political career began 1978 with the assassination by the right-wing dictatorship of her husband, Pedro Joaquín Chamorro. Violeta became candidate for UNO, a 14-party coalition,

Sept 1989. In the 1990 elections, UNO won 51 of the 92 seats in the National Assembly. The Sandinista Liberation Front (FSLN), however, remained the largest party, and together with reactionary elements within Chamorro's own coalition, obstructed the implementation of her policies. Her early presidency was marked by rising unemployment, strikes, and continuing skirmishes between Contra rebels and Sandinista militants in the mountains (despite official disbanding of the Contras June 1990). A peace accord was reached with the rebels 1994.

Champaigne Philippe de (1602–1674). French artist. He was the leading portrait painter of the court of Louis XIII. Of Flemish origin, he went to Paris 1621 and gained the patronage of Cardinal Richelieu. His style is elegant, cool, and restrained. *Ex Voto* 1662 (Louvre, Paris) is his best-known work. He devoted himself to religious painting after 1659, decorating several Paris churches. His nephew, Jean Baptiste de Champaigne (1631–81), was also a painter and his collaborator.

Champlain Samuel de (1567–1635). French pioneer, soldier, and explorer in Canada. Having served in the army of Henry IV and on an expedition to the West Indies, he began his exploration of Canada 1603. In a third expedition 1608 he founded and named Quebec, and was appointed lieutenant governor of French Canada 1612.

Champollion Jean François, le Jeune (1790–1832). French Egyptologist who in 1822 deciphered Egyptian hieroglyphics with the aid of the Rosetta Stone.

Chandelā or Candella. Rajput dynasty that ruled the Bundelkhand region of central India from the 9th to the 11th century. The Chandelās fought against Muslim invaders, until they were replaced by the Bundelās. The Chandelā capital was Khajurāho.

Chamberlin US geophysicist Thomas Chamberlin is best known for his work on the geology of the Solar System and the development of the planetesimal hypothesis. This states that, during their early formation, planetary bodies attract material through gravitational contraction, and not, as previously thought, that they cool steadily from a large molten mass. (Image Select)

Chanel The French couturier Coco Chanel in 1937. The predominant influence on dress design for almost 60 years, she created simple, comfortable clothes that were a dramatically successful reaction to previous fashions in women's wear.

Chandler Happy (Albert Benjamin) (1898–1991). US politician and sports administrator. He was governor of Kentucky 1934–39 and 1955–59. After his first term as governor he resigned to enter the US Senate. In 1945 Chandler was appointed baseball commissioner but resigned 1951, mainly because of personality conflicts with several team owners.

When I split an infinitive, God damn it, I split it so it will stay split.

RAYMOND CHANDLER
Letter to Edward Weeks 18 Jan 1947

Chandler Raymond Thornton (1888–1959). US novelist. He turned the pulp detective mystery form into a successful genre of literature and created the quintessential private eye in the tough but chivalric loner, Philip Marlowe. Marlowe is the narrator of such books as *The Big Sleep* 1939 (filmed 1946), *Farewell My Lovely* 1940 (filmed 1944), *The Lady in the Lake* 1943 (filmed 1947), and *The Long Goodbye* 1954 (filmed 1975). He also wrote numerous screenplays, notably *Double Indemnity* 1944, *Blue Dahlia* 1946, and *Strangers on a Train* 1951.

Chandragupta Maurya ruler of N India *c.* 325–*c.* 297 BC, founder of the Mauryan dynasty. He overthrew the Nanda dynasty 325 and then conquered the Punjab 322 after the death of Alexander the Great, expanding his empire west to Persia. He is credited with having united most of India.

Chandrasekhar Subrahmanyan (1910–1995). Indian-born US astrophysicist who made pioneering studies of the structure and evolution of stars. The Chandrasekhar limit is the maximum mass of a white dwarf before it turns into a neutron star. Nobel Prize for Physics 1983.

Chandrasekhar has also investigated the transfer of energy in stellar atmospheres by radiation and convection, and the polarization of light emitted from particular stars.

Chanel Coco (Gabrielle) (1883–1971). French fashion designer. She was renowned as a trendsetter and her designs have been copied worldwide. She created the 'little black dress', the informal cardigan suit, costume jewellery, and perfumes.
Suggested reading
Baillén, Claude *Chanel Solitaire* (trs 1974)
Charles-Roux, Edmonde *Chanel and Her World* (1981)
Madsen, Axel *Chanel* (1990)

Chaney US film actor Lon Chaney in the silent film The Hunchback of Notre Dame 1923. Starring in over 150 films, he became famous for his portrayal of deformed and grotesque villains.

Chaney Lon (Alonso) (1883–1930). US star of silent films. He often played grotesque or monstrous roles such as *The Phantom of the Opera* 1925. A master of make-up, he was nicknamed 'the Man of a Thousand Faces'. He sometimes used extremely painful devices for added effect, as in the title role in *The Hunchback of Notre Dame* 1923, when he carried over 30 kg/70 lb of costume in the form of a heavy hump and harness.

Chaney Lon, Jr (Creighton) (1907–1973). US actor. The son of Lon Chaney, he gave an acclaimed performance as Lennie in *Of Mice and Men* 1940. He went on to star in many 1940s horror films, including the title role in *The Wolf Man* 1941. His other work includes *My Favorite Brunette* 1947 and *The Haunted Palace* 1963.

Chang Ch'ien (lived 2nd century BC). Chinese explorer who pioneered the Silk Road.

Channing William Ellery (1780–1842). US minister and theologian. He became a leader of the Unitarian movement 1819, opposing the strict Calvinism of the New England Congregationalist churches. He was an instrumental figure in the establishment of the American Unitarian Association. In his later years, Channing campaigned to end the institution of slavery.

Chantrey Francis Legatt (1781–1841). English sculptor. He is known for portrait busts and monuments. His unaffected studies of children were much loved in his day, notably *Sleeping Children* 1817 (Lichfield Cathedral). Knighted 1835.

The Chantrey Bequest provides for the Royal Academy of Arts to buy works of art for the nation, which are housed in the Tate Gallery, London.

Chaplin Charlie (Charles Spencer) (1889–1977). English film actor and director. He made his reputation as a tramp with a smudge moustache, bowler hat, and twirling cane in silent comedies from the mid-1910s, including *The Rink* 1916, *The Kid* 1920, and *The Gold Rush* 1925. His work combines buffoonery with pathos, as in *The Great Dictator* 1940 and *Limelight* 1952. He was one of cinema's most popular and greatest stars. KBE 1975.

Chaplin was born in south London and first appeared on the music hall stage at the age of five. He joined Mack Sennett's Keystone Company in Los Angeles 1913. Along with Mary Pickford, Douglas Fairbanks, and D W Griffith, Chaplin formed United Artists 1919 as an independent company to distribute their films. His other films include *City Lights* 1931, *Modern Times* 1936, and *Monsieur Verdoux* 1947. *Limelight* 1952 was awarded an Oscar for Chaplin's musical theme. When accused of communist sympathies during the McCarthy witchhunt, he left the USA 1952 and moved to Switzerland. He received special Oscars 1928 and 1972.

Until sound films became common, he was the best known and most popular film star of his day. He was married four times, his third wife being actress Paulette Goddard, and his fourth, Oona, was the daughter of the dramatist Eugene O'Neill.

Suggested reading

Chaplin, Charlie *My Autobiography* (1964, published as *My Early Years* 1982)

Huff, Theodore *Charlie Chaplin* (1952)

Lahue, K C *World of Laughter: The Motion Picture Comedy Short, 1910–1930* (1966)

McCabe, John *Charlie Chaplin* (1978)

Manvell, Roger *Chaplin* (1973)

Robinson, David *Chaplin: His Life and Art* (1984)

Chapman Frederick Spencer (1907–1971). British explorer, mountaineer, and writer who explored Greenland, the Himalayas, and Malaysia. He accompanied Gino Watkins on the British Arctic Air Routes Expedition 1930–31, recalled in *Northern Lights* 1932, and in 1935 he joined a climbing expedition to the Himalayas. For two years he participated in a government mission to Tibet described in *Lhasa, the Holy City* 1938, before setting out to climb the 7,315-m/24,000-ft peak Chomollari.

Chapman George (c. 1559–1634). English poet and dramatist. His translations of the Greek epics of Homer (completed 1616) were celebrated; his plays include the comedy *Eastward Ho!* (with Jonson and Marston) 1605 and the tragedy *Bussy d'Amboise* 1607.

Chapman John ('Johnny Appleseed') (1774–1845). US pioneer and folk hero, credited with establishing orchards throughout the Midwest by planting seeds as he travelled. Famous as the subject of local legends and folk tales, Chapman was described as a religious visionary with boundless generosity.

Born in Leominster, Massachusetts, Chapman roamed westward from Pennsylvania in the years after 1800, planting apple seeds in

Chaplin English film actor and director Charlie Chaplin in The Kid 1920. He made a successful transition from silent films to those with soundtrack, such as Limelight 1952. (Image Select)

Ohio and Indiana. However, few specific details about his later life can be verified.

Chappell Greg(ory) Stephen (1948–). Australian cricketer, born in Adelaide. He replaced his brother Ian as test captain in 1975, leading Australia in a record 48 tests of which 21 were won, 13 lost and 14 drawn. When he retired in 1984 he was Australia's highest scoring batsman with 7,110 runs. He scored a century in his first and last tests.

Chappell Ian Michael (1943–). Australian cricketer, born in Adelaide. An aggressive batsman, he was test captain 1971–75 and captain in world series cricket 1977–78 during which time he led his team to 15 wins, 10 draws and 5 losses.

Charcot Jean-Martin (1825–1893). French neurologist who studied hysteria, sclerosis, locomotor ataxia, and senile diseases. Among his pupils was the founder of psychiatry, Sigmund Freud.

One of the most influential neurologists of his day, Charcot exhibited hysterical women at weekly public lectures, which became fashionable events. He was also fascinated by the relations between hysteria and hypnotic phenomena.

Charcot was born and educated in Paris and worked at the Salpétrière hospital there. He was convinced that all psychiatric conditions followed natural laws, and studied the way certain mental illnesses correlate with physical changes in the brain. He published the results in a series of memoirs.

Chardin Jean Baptiste Siméon (1699–1779). French painter. He took as his subjects naturalistic still lifes and quiet domestic scenes that recall the Dutch tradition. His work is a complete contrast to that of his contemporaries, the Rococo painters. He developed his own technique, using successive layers of paint to achieve depth of tone, and is generally considered one of the finest exponents of genre painting. He is a 'modern' among 17th-century French painters in the largeness of design and the study of light which gave both to his figures (for example *La Pourvoyeuse*, Louvre) and to the vessels and foodstuffs of the bourgeois table a dignity and interest of their own.

Chardonnet (Louis-Marie) Hilaire Bernigaud, Comte de (1839–1924). French chemist who developed artificial silk 1883, the first artificial fibre. He also worked on cellulose nitrate.

He trained first as a civil engineer in Paris, and then went to work under Louis Pasteur, who was studying diseases in silkworms. This inspired Chardonnet to seek an artificial replacement for silk. He opened a factory in Besançon 1889 and another in Hungary 1904. Chardonnet's starting point was mulberry leaves, the food of silkworms; he turned them into a cellulose pulp with nitric and sulphuric acids and stretched it into fibres. The original fibre was highly flammable, but by 1889 he had eliminated this and developed rayon.

Chareau Pierre (1883–1950). French designer. He is best known for his Maison de Verre, Paris, 1928–31. This predated and influenced development of the 1970s High Tech approach to design in its innovative use of industrial materials, such as studded rubber flooring and glass bricks.

Charlemagne (Charles I the Great) (742–814). King of the Franks from 768 and Holy Roman emperor from 800. By inheritance (his father was Pepin the Short) and extensive campaigns of conquest, he united most of W Europe by 804, when after 30 years of war the Saxons came under his control. He reformed the legal, judicial, and military systems; established schools; and promoted Christianity, commerce, agriculture, arts, and literature. In his capital, Aachen, scholars gathered from all over Europe.

Pepin had been mayor of the palace in Merovingian Neustria until he was crowned king by Pope Stephen II (died 757) in 754, and his sons Carl (Charlemagne) and Carloman were crowned as joint heirs. When Pepin died 768, Charlemagne inherited the N Frankish kingdom, and when Carloman died 771, he also took possession of his domains.

He was engaged in his first Saxon campaign when the Pope's call for help against the Lombards reached him; he crossed the Alps, captured Pavia, and took the title of king of the Lombards. The

pacification and christianizing of the Saxon peoples occupied the greater part of Charlemagne's reign. From 792 N Saxony was subdued, and in 804 the whole region came under his rule.

In 777 the emir of Zaragoza asked for Charlemagne's help against the emir of Córdoba. Charlemagne crossed the Pyrenees 778 and reached the Ebro but had to turn back from Zaragoza. The rearguard action of Roncesvalles, in which Roland, warden of the Breton March, and other Frankish nobles were ambushed and killed by Basques, was later glorified in the *Chanson de Roland*. In 801 the district between the Pyrenees and the Llobregat was organized as the Spanish March. The independent duchy of Bavaria was incorporated in the kingdom 788, and the Avar people were subdued 791–96 and accepted Christianity. Charlemagne's last campaign was against a Danish attack on his northern frontier 810.

The supremacy of the Frankish king in Europe found outward expression in the bestowal of the imperial title: in Rome, during Mass on Christmas Day 800, Pope Leo III crowned Charlemagne emperor. He enjoyed diplomatic relations with Byzantium, Baghdad, Mercia, Northumbria, and other regions. Jury courts were introduced, the laws of the Franks revised, and other peoples' laws written down. A new coinage was introduced, weights and measures were reformed, and communications were improved. Charlemagne also took a lively interest in theology, organized the church in his dominions, and furthered missionary enterprises and monastic reform.

The Carolingian Renaissance of learning began when he persuaded the Northumbrian scholar Alcuin to enter his service 781. Charlemagne gathered a kind of academy around him. Although he never learned to read, he collected the old heroic sagas, began a Frankish grammar, and promoted religious instruction in the vernacular. He died 28 Jan 814 in Aachen, where he was buried.

Soon a cycle of heroic legends and romances developed around him, including epics by Ariosto, Boiardo, and Tasso.

Suggested reading
Bullough, D A *The Age of Charlemagne* (1965)
Chamberlin, R *The Emperor Charlemagne* (1986)
Heer, F *The World of Charlemagne* (1975)
Lamb, H *Charlemagne: The Legend and the Man* (1954)

Charles Jacques Alexandre César (1746–1823). French physicist who studied gases and made the first ascent in a hydrogen-filled balloon 1783. His work on the expansion of gases led to the formulation of Charles's law.

Hearing of the hot-air balloons of the Montgolfier brothers, Charles and his brothers began experimenting with hydrogen balloons and made their ascent only ten days after the Montgolfiers' first flight. In later flights Charles ascended to an altitude of 3,000 m/ 10,000 ft.

Charles (Mary) Eugenia (1919–). Dominican politician, prime minister 1980–95; cofounder and first leader of the centrist Dominica Freedom Party (DFP). Two years after Dominica's independence the DFP won the 1980 general election and Charles became the Caribbean's first female prime minister. In 1993 she resigned the leadership of the DFP, but remained as prime minister until the 1995 elections, which were won by the opposition United Workers' Party (UNP).

Charles Ray (born Ray Charles Robinson) (1930–). US singer, songwriter, and pianist. His first hits were 'I've Got a Woman' 1955, 'What'd I Say' 1959, and 'Georgia on My Mind' 1960. He has recorded gospel, blues, rock, soul, country, and rhythm and blues.

Charles two kings of Great Britain and Ireland:

Charles I (1600–1649). King of Great Britain and Ireland from 1625, son of James I of England (James VI of Scotland).

Charles was born at Dunfermline, and became heir to the throne on the death of his brother Henry 1612. He married Henrietta Maria, daughter of Henry IV of France. When he succeeded his father, friction with Parliament began at once. The parliaments of 1625 and 1626 were dissolved, and that of 1628 refused supplies until Charles had accepted the Petition of Right. In 1629 it attacked Charles's illegal taxation and support of the Arminians in the church, whereupon he dissolved Parliament and imprisoned its leaders.

For 11 years he ruled without a parliament, the Eleven Years' Tyranny, raising money by expedients, such as ship money, that alienated the nation, while the Star Chamber suppressed opposition by persecuting the Puritans. When Charles attempted 1637 to force a prayer book on the English model on Presbyterian Scotland he found himself confronted with a nation in arms. The Short Parliament, which met April 1640, refused to grant money until grievances were redressed, and was speedily dissolved. The Scots then advanced into England and forced their own terms on Charles. The Long Parliament met 3 Nov 1640 and declared extraparliamentary taxation illegal, abolished the Star Chamber and other prerogative courts, and voted that Parliament could not be dissolved without its own consent. Laud and other ministers were imprisoned, and Strafford condemned to death. After the failure of his attempt to arrest the parliamentary leaders 4 Jan 1642, Charles, confident that he had substantial support among those who felt that Parliament was becoming too radical and zealous, withdrew from London, and on 22 Aug declared war on Parliament by raising his standard at Nottingham.

Charles's defeat at Naseby June 1645 ended all hopes of victory; in May 1646 he surrendered at Newark to the Scots, who handed him over to Parliament Jan 1647. In June the army seized him and carried him off to Hampton Court. While the army leaders strove to find a settlement, Charles secretly intrigued for a Scottish invasion. In Nov he escaped, but was recaptured and held at Carisbrooke Castle; a Scottish invasion followed 1648, and was shattered by Cromwell at Preston. In Jan 1649 the House of Commons set up a high court of justice, which tried Charles and condemned him to death. He was beheaded 30 Jan before the Banqueting House in Whitehall.

Suggested reading
Ashley, Maurice *Charles I and Cromwell* (1988)
Carlton, Charles *Charles I: The Personal Monarch* (1983)
Gregg, P *King Charles I* (1984)
Hibbert, Christopher *Charles I* (1968)
Hill, Christopher *The Century of Revolution, 1603–1714* (1961)
Wedgwood, C V *The King's Peace, 1637–1641* (1955)
Wedgwood, C V *The King's War, 1641–1647* (1958)
Wedgwood, C V *A Coffin for King Charles* (1964)

Let not poor Nelly starve.

CHARLES II
quoted in Gilbert Burnet, *History of His Own Times* 1723–34

Charles II (1630–1685). King of Great Britain and Ireland from 1660.

Charles was born in St James's Palace, London; during the Civil War he lived with his father at Oxford 1642–45, and after the victory of Cromwell's Parliamentary forces withdrew to France. Accepting the Covenanters' offer to make him king, he landed in Scotland 1650, and was crowned at Scone 1 Jan 1651. An attempt to invade England was ended 3 Sept by Cromwell's victory at Worcester. Charles escaped, and for nine years he wandered through France, Germany, Flanders, Spain, and Holland until the opening of negotiations by George Monk (1608–1670) 1660.

In April Charles issued the Declaration of Breda, promising a general amnesty and freedom of conscience. Parliament accepted the Declaration and he was proclaimed king 8 May 1660, landed at Dover on 26 May, and entered London three days later. Charles wanted to make himself absolute, and favoured Catholicism for his subjects as most consistent with absolute monarchy. The disasters of the Dutch war furnished an excuse for banishing Clarendon 1667,

---

Here lies a great and mighty king / Whose promise none relies on; / He never said a foolish thing, / Nor ever did a wise one.

John, Earl of Rochester on CHARLES II
'The King's Epitaph'

---

and he was replaced by the Cabal of Clifford and Arlington, both secret Catholics, and Buckingham, Ashley (Lord Shaftesbury), and Lauderdale, who had links with the Dissenters.

In 1670 Charles signed the Secret Treaty of Dover, the full details of which were known only to Clifford and Arlington, whereby he promised Louis XIV of France he would declare himself a Catholic, re-establish Catholicism in England, and support Louis's projected war against the Dutch; in return Louis was to finance Charles and in the event of resistance to supply him with troops. War with the Netherlands followed 1672, and at the same time Charles issued the Declaration of Indulgence, suspending all penal laws against Catholics and Dissenters. In 1673, Parliament forced Charles to withdraw the Indulgence and accept a Test Act excluding all Catholics from office, and in 1674 to end the Dutch war. The Test Act broke up the Cabal, while Shaftesbury, who had learned the truth about the treaty, assumed the leadership of the opposition. Danby, the new chief minister, built up a court party in the Commons by bribery, while subsidies from Louis relieved Charles from dependence on Parliament. In 1678 Titus Oates's announcement of a 'popish plot' released a general panic, which Shaftesbury exploited to introduce his Exclusion Bill, excluding James, Duke of York, from the succession as a Catholic; instead he hoped to substitute Charles's illegitimate son Monmouth.

In 1681 Parliament was summoned at Oxford, which had been the Royalist headquarters during the Civil War. The Whigs attended armed, but when Shaftesbury rejected a last compromise, Charles dissolved Parliament and the Whigs fled in terror. Charles now ruled without a parliament, financed by Louis XIV. When the Whigs plotted a revolt, their leaders were executed, while Shaftesbury and Monmouth fled to the Netherlands.

Charles was a patron of the arts and science. His mistresses included Lady Castlemaine, Nell Gwyn, Lady Portsmouth, and Lucy Walter.

Suggested reading
Ashley, Maurice *Charles II* (1973)
Fraser, Antonia *King Charles II* (1979)
Hill, Christopher *The Century of Revolution, 1603–1714* (1961)
Miller, John *Charles II* (1991)
Ogg, David *England in the Reign of Charles II* (1962)

Charles (full name Charles Philip Arthur George) (1948–). Prince of the UK, heir to the British throne, and Prince of Wales since 1958 (invested 1969). He is the first-born child of Queen Elizabeth II and the Duke of Edinburgh. He studied at Trinity College, Cambridge, 1967–70, before serving in the Royal Air Force and Royal Navy. He is the first royal heir since 1659 to have an English wife, Lady Diana Spencer, daughter of the 8th Earl Spencer. They have two sons and heirs, William (1982–) and Henry (1984–). Amid much publicity, Charles and Diana separated 1992 and divorced 1996.

Prince Charles's concern for social and environmental issues has led to many self-help projects for the young and underprivileged, and he is a leading critic of unsympathetic features of contemporary architecture.

Conservation must come before recreation.

PRINCE CHARLES
Times 5 July 1989

Charles ten kings of France:

Charles I King of France, better known as the Holy Roman emperor ◊Charlemagne.

Charles (II) the Bald King of France, see ◊Charles II, Holy Roman emperor.

Charles (III) the Simple (879–929). King of France 893–922, son of Louis the Stammerer. He was crowned at Reims. In 911 he ceded what later became the duchy of Normandy to the Norman chief Rollo.

Charles (IV) the Fair (1294–1328). King of France from 1322, when he succeeded Philip V as the last of the direct Capetian line.

Charles (V) the Wise (1337–1380). King of France from 1364. He was regent during the captivity of his father, John II, in England 1356–60, and became king on John's death. He reconquered nearly all France from England 1369–80.

Charles (VI) the Mad or the Well-Beloved (1368–1422). King of France from 1380, succeeding his father Charles V; he was under the regency of his uncles until 1388. He became mentally unstable 1392, and civil war broke out between the dukes of Orléans and Burgundy. Henry V of England invaded France 1415, conquering Normandy, and in 1420 forced Charles to sign the Treaty of Troyes, recognizing Henry as his successor.

Charles VII (1403–1461). King of France from 1429. Son of Charles VI, he was excluded from the succession by the Treaty of Troyes, but recognized by the south of France. In 1429 Joan of Arc raised the siege of Orléans and had him crowned at Reims. He organized France's first standing army and by 1453 had expelled the English from all of France except Calais.

Charles VIII (1470–1498). King of France from 1483, when he succeeded his father, Louis XI. In 1494 he unsuccessfully tried to claim the Neapolitan crown, and when he entered Naples 1495 was forced to withdraw by a coalition of Milan, Venice, Spain, and the Holy Roman Empire. He defeated them at Fornovo, but lost Naples. He died while preparing a second expedition.

Charles IX (1550–1574). King of France from 1560. Second son of Henry II and Catherine de' Medici, he succeeded his brother Francis II at the age of ten but remained under the domination of his mother's regency for ten years while France was torn by religious wars. In 1570 he fell under the influence of the Huguenot leader Gaspard de Coligny (1517–1572); alarmed by this, Catherine instigated his order for the Massacre of St Bartholomew, which led to a new religious war.

Charles X (1757–1836). King of France from 1824. Grandson of Louis XV and brother of Louis XVI and Louis XVIII, he was known as the Comte d'Artois before his accession. He fled to England at the beginning of the French Revolution, and when he came to the throne on the death of Louis XVIII, he attempted to reverse the achievements of the Revolution. A revolt ensued 1830, and he again fled to England.

Charles seven rulers of the Holy Roman Empire:

Charles I Holy Roman emperor, better known as ◊Charlemagne.

Charles (II) the Bald (823–877). Holy Roman emperor from 875 and (as Charles II) king of France from 843. Younger son of Louis I (the Pious), he warred against his eldest brother, Emperor Lothair I. The Treaty of Verdun 843 made him king of the West Frankish Kingdom (now France and the Spanish Marches).

Charles (III) the Fat (839–888). Holy Roman emperor 881–87; he became king of the West Franks 885, thus uniting for the last time the whole of Charlemagne's dominions, but was deposed.

Charles IV (1316–1378). Holy Roman emperor from 1355 and king of Bohemia from 1346. Son of John of Luxembourg, king of Bohemia, he was elected king of Germany 1346 and ruled all Germany from 1347. He was the founder of the first German university in Prague 1348.

I came, I saw, God conquered.

CHARLES V
after defeating the Protestant princes at
the Battle of Muhlberg, 23 April 1547

Charles V (1500–1558). Holy Roman emperor 1519–56. Son of Philip of Burgundy and Joanna of Castile, he inherited vast possessions, which led to rivalry from Francis I of France, whose alliance with the Ottoman Empire brought Vienna under siege 1529 and 1532. Charles was also in conflict with the Protestants in Germany

until the Treaty of Passau 1552, which allowed the Lutherans religious liberty.

Charles was born in Ghent and received the Netherlands from his father 1506; Spain, Naples, Sicily, Sardinia, and the Spanish dominions in N Africa and the Americas on the death of his maternal grandfather, Ferdinand V of Castile (1452–1516); and from his paternal grandfather, Maximilian I, the Habsburg dominions 1519, when he was elected emperor. He was crowned in Aachen 1520. From 1517 the empire was split by the rise of Lutheranism, Charles making unsuccessful attempts to reach a settlement at Augsburg 1530, and being forced by the Treaty of Passau to yield most of the Protestant demands. Worn out, he abdicated in favour of his son Philip II in the Netherlands 1555 and Spain 1556. He yielded the imperial crown to his brother Ferdinand I, and retired to the monastery of Yuste, Spain.

Suggested reading
Brandi, Karl *The Emperor Charles V* (trs 1938)
Koenigsberger, H G *The Hapsburgs and Europe 1516–1660* (1971)

He put his trust in military and diplomatic adventures in scattered parts of Europe instead of building sound institutions at home.

E N Williams on CHARLES VI
in *Penguin Dictionary of English and European History 1485–1789* 1980

Charles VI (1685–1740). Holy Roman emperor from 1711, father of Maria Theresa, whose succession to his Austrian dominions he tried to ensure, and himself claimant to the Spanish throne 1700, thus causing the War of the Spanish Succession.

Charles VII (1697–1745). Holy Roman emperor from 1742, opponent of Maria Theresa's claim to the Austrian dominions of Charles VI.

Charles (Karl Franz Josef) (1887–1922). Emperor of Austria and king of Hungary from 1916, the last of the Habsburg emperors. He succeeded his great-uncle Franz Josef 1916 but was forced to withdraw to Switzerland 1918, although he refused to abdicate. In 1921 he attempted unsuccessfully to regain the crown of Hungary and was deported to Madeira, where he died.

Charles (Spanish Carlos) four kings of Spain:

Charles I (1500–1558). See ◊Charles V, Holy Roman emperor.

Charles II (1661–1700). King of Spain from 1665. The second son of Philip IV, he was the last of the Spanish Habsburg kings. Mentally disabled from birth, he bequeathed his dominions to Philip of Anjou, grandson of Louis XIV, which led to the War of the Spanish Succession.

He chose his ministers with sound judgment, and he was as reluctant to change them as he was his timetable or his clothes.

E N Williams on CHARLES III
in *Penguin Dictionary of English and European History 1485–1789* 1980

Charles III (1716–1788). King of Spain from 1759. Son of Philip V, he became duke of Parma 1732 and conquered Naples and Sicily 1734. On the death of his half-brother Ferdinand VI (1713–1759), he became king of Spain, handing over Naples and Sicily to his son Ferdinand (1751–1825). At home, he reformed state finances, strengthened the armed forces, and expelled the Jesuits. During his reign, Spain was involved in the Seven Years' War with France against England. This led to the loss of Florida 1763, which was only regained when Spain and France supported the colonists during the American Revolution.

Charles IV (1748–1819). King of Spain from 1788, when he succeeded his father, Charles III; he left the government in the hands of his wife and her lover, the minister Manuel de Godoy (1767–1851).

In 1808 Charles was induced to abdicate by Napoleon's machinations in favour of his son Ferdinand VII (1784–1833), who was subsequently deposed by Napoleon's brother Joseph. Charles was awarded a pension by Napoleon and died in Rome.

Charles (Swedish Carl) fifteen kings of Sweden (the first six were local chieftains), including:

Charles VII King of Sweden from about 1161. He helped to establish Christianity in Sweden.

Charles VIII (1408–1470). King of Sweden from 1448. He was elected regent of Sweden 1438, when Sweden broke away from Denmark and Norway. He stepped down 1441 when Christopher III of Bavaria (1418–1448) was elected king, but after his death became king. He was twice expelled by the Danes and twice restored.

Charles IX (1550–1611). King of Sweden from 1604, the youngest son of Gustavus Vasa. In 1568 he and his brother John led the rebellion against Eric XIV (1533–1577); John became king as John III and attempted to catholicize Sweden, and Charles led the opposition. John's son Sigismund, king of Poland and a Catholic, succeeded to the Swedish throne 1592, and Charles led the Protestants. He was made regent 1595 and deposed Sigismund 1599. Charles was elected king of Sweden 1604 and was involved in unsuccessful wars with Russia, Poland, and Denmark. He was the father of Gustavus Adolphus.

Charles X (1622–1660). King of Sweden from 1654, when he succeeded his cousin Christina. He waged war with Poland and Denmark and in 1657 invaded Denmark by leading his army over the frozen sea.

Charles XI (1655–1697). King of Sweden from 1660, when he succeeded his father Charles X. His mother acted as regent until 1672 when Charles took over the government. He was a remarkable general and reformed the administration.

Charles XII (1682–1718). King of Sweden from 1697, when he succeeded his father, Charles XI. From 1700 he was involved in wars with Denmark, Poland, and Russia.

He won a succession of victories until, in 1709 while invading Russia, he was defeated at Poltava in the Ukraine, and forced to take refuge in Turkey until 1714. He was killed while besieging Fredrikshall, Norway, although it was not known whether he was murdered by his own side or by the enemy.

Charles XIII (1748–1818). King of Sweden from 1809, when he was elected; he became the first king of Sweden and Norway 1814.

Charles XIV (Jean Baptiste Jules Bernadotte) (1763–1844). King of Sweden and Norway from 1818. A former marshal in the French army, in 1810 he was elected crown prince of Sweden under the name of Charles John (Carl Johan). Loyal to his adopted country, he brought Sweden into the alliance against Napoleon 1813, as a reward for which Sweden received Norway. He was the founder of the present dynasty.

A Republican by principle and devotion, I will, until my death, oppose all Royalists.

Charles XIV of Sweden (JEAN-BAPTISTE BERNADOTTE)
in letter to the French Directory Sept 1797

Charles XV (1826–1872). King of Sweden and Norway from 1859, when he succeeded his father Oscar I. A popular and liberal monarch, his main achievement was the reform of the constitution.

Charles Albert (1798–1849). King of Sardinia from 1831. He showed liberal sympathies in early life, and after his accession introduced some reforms. On the outbreak of the 1848 revolution he granted a constitution and declared war on Austria. His troops were defeated at Custozza and Novara. In 1849 he abdicated in favour of his son Victor Emmanuel and retired to a monastery, where he died.

Charles Augustus (1757–1828). Grand Duke of Saxe-Weimar in Germany. He succeeded his father in infancy, fought against the

French in 1792–94 and 1806, and was the patron and friend of the writer Goethe.

Charles Edward Stuart the Young Pretender or Bonnie Prince Charlie (1720–1788). British prince, grandson of James II and son of James, the Old Pretender. In the Jacobite rebellion 1745 Charles won the support of the Scottish Highlanders; his army invaded England to claim the throne but was beaten back by the duke of Cumberland and routed at Culloden 1746. Charles went into exile.

He was born in Rome, and created Prince of Wales at birth. In July 1745 he sailed for Scotland, and landed in Inverness-shire with seven companions. On 19 Aug he raised his father's standard, and within a week had rallied an army of 2,000 Highlanders. He entered Edinburgh almost without resistance, won an easy victory at Prestonpans, invaded England, and by 4 Dec had reached Derby, where his officers insisted on a retreat. The army returned to Scotland and won a victory at Falkirk, but was forced to retire to the Highlands before Cumberland's advance.

The wretched today be happy tomorrow. All great men would be the better to feel a little of what I do.

CHARLES EDWARD STUART
after defeat at Culloden 1746, quoted in James
Hogg *The Jacobite Relics of Scotland* 1819

On 16 April at Culloden Charles's army was routed by Cumberland, and he fled. For five months he wandered through the Highlands with a price of £30,000 on his head, before escaping to France. He visited England secretly in 1750, and may have made other visits. In later life he degenerated into a friendless drunkard. He settled in Italy 1766.

Suggested reading
Daiches, David *Charles Edward Stuart* (1973)
Forster, Margaret *The Rash Adventurer* (1973)
Kybett, Susan *Bonnie Prince Charlie* (1988)
Maclean, Fitzroy *Bonnie Prince Charlie* (1988)
Prebble, John *Culloden* (1961)

Charles Martel (*c.* 688–741). Frankish ruler (Mayor of the Palace) of the E Frankish kingdom from 717 and the whole kingdom from 731. His victory against the Moors at Moussais-la-Bataille near Tours 732 earned him his nickname of Martel, 'the Hammer', because he halted the Islamic advance by the Moors into Europe.

An illegitimate son of Pepin of Heristal (Pepin II, Mayor of the Palace *c.* 640–714), he was a grandfather of Charlemagne.

Charles the Bold Duke of Burgundy (1433–1477). Son of Philip the Good, he inherited Burgundy and the Low Countries from him 1465. He waged wars attempting to free the duchy from dependence on France and restore it as a kingdom. He was killed in battle.

Charles' ambition was to create a kingdom stretching from the mouth of the Rhine to the mouth of the Rhône. He formed the League of the Public Weal against Louis XI of France, invaded France 1471, and conquered the country as far as Rouen. The Holy Roman emperor, the Swiss, and Lorraine united against him; he captured Nancy, but was defeated at Granson and again at Morat 1476. Nancy was lost, and he was killed while attempting to recapture it. His possessions in the Netherlands passed to the Habsburgs by the marriage of his daughter Mary to Maximilian I of Austria.

Charlotte Augusta Princess (1796–1817). Only child of George IV and Caroline of Brunswick, and heir to the British throne. In 1816 she married Prince Leopold of Saxe-Coburg (later Leopold I of the Belgians), but died in childbirth 18 months later.

I do think that the bloom of her ugliness is going off.

Colonel Disbrowe, CHARLOTTE SOPHIA's
chamberlain, to J W Croker, quoted in John Timbs
A Century of Anecdote 1760–1860 1864

Charlotte Sophia (1744–1818). British queen consort. The daughter of the German duke of Mecklenburg-Strelitz, she married

George III of Great Britain and Ireland 1761, and they had nine sons and six daughters.

Charlton Andrew ('Boy') (1907–1975). Australian swimmer, born in Sydney. He broke the world record for 440 yards at the age of 16 and won the gold medal in the 1,500 metres freestyle at the 1924 Olympics.

Charlton Bobby (Robert) (1937–). English footballer, younger brother of Jack Charlton, who scored a record 49 goals in 106 appearances. An elegant midfield player who specialized in fierce long-range shots, he spent most of his playing career with Manchester United and played in the England team that won the World Cup 1966.

On retiring Charlton had an unsuccessful spell as manager of Preston North End. He later became a director of Manchester United. He was knighted 1994.

Charlton Eddie (Edward) (1929–). Australian snooker player. Born in Merewether, New South Wales, he became a professional snooker player in 1960 and won the World Open Snooker Championship 1968 and the World Professional title 1972.

Charlton Jack (John) (1935–). English footballer, older brother of Bobby and nephew of Jackie Milburn. He spent all his playing career with Leeds United and played more than 750 games for them. He appeared in the England team that won the World Cup 1966.

After retiring, Charlton managed Middlesbrough to the 2nd division title. Appointed manager of the Republic of Ireland national squad in 1986, he took the team to the 1988 European Championship finals, after which he was made an 'honorary Irishman'. He led Ireland to the World Cup finals for the first time 1990 and again 1994.

Charnley John (1911–1982). English orthopaedic surgeon who applied engineering principles to the practice of orthopaedics. He worked on degenerative hip disease and developed a new technique, the total hip replacement, or arthroplasty. He also successfully pioneered arthrodeses (fusing joint surfaces) for the knee and hip. Knighted 1977.

He worked at Manchester Royal Infirmary from 1947 until the mid-1960s, and then became director of the Centre of Hip Surgery at Wrightington Hospital, Lancashire, turning it into the primary unit for hip replacement in the world.

Charpentier Gustave (1860–1956). French composer. He wrote an opera about Paris working-class life, *Louise* 1900. He was a pupil of Massenet.

Charpentier Marc-Antoine (c. 1645–1704). French composer. He wrote incidental music in Italian style to plays by Molière, including *Le Malade imaginaire/The Hypochondriac* 1673. Later in life, as official composer to the Sainte Chapelle, Paris, he composed sacred music in French style and the opera *Médée* 1693.

Charrière Isabelle Agnès Elizabeth van Zuylen de (1740–1805). Dutch writer who wrote in French. She settled in Colombier, Switzerland, 1761. Her works include plays, tracts, and novels, among them *Caliste* 1786. She had many early feminist ideas.

Charteris Leslie Charles Bowyer Yin (1907–1993). British novelist, who became a US citizen 1946. Charteris, the son of a Chinese surgeon and an Englishwoman, was born Leslie Charles Bowyer Yin in Singapore. His varied career in many exotic occupations gave authentic background to some 40 novels about Simon Templar, the 'Saint', a gentleman adventurer on the wrong side of the law. The novels have been adapted for films, radio, and television. The first was *Enter The Saint* 1930.

Chase James Hadley. Pen name of René Raymond (1906–1985). English author. He wrote the hard-boiled thriller *No Orchids for Miss Blandish* 1939 and other popular novels.

Chase Mary Agnes (born Meara) (1869–1963). US botanist and suffragist who made outstanding contributions to the study of grasses. During the course of several research expeditions she

Chase , Salmon Portland *Salmon Portland Chase who in President Lincoln's administration became secretary to the Treasury and then chief justice of the Supreme Court. A committed abolitionist, he often defended escaped slaves.*

collected many plants previously unknown to science, and her work provided much important information about naturally occurring cereals and other food crops. From 1903 she worked in Washington DC for the US Department of Agriculture Bureau of Plant Industry and Exploration, and became the principal scientist for agrostology (study of grasses). Chase's publications include the authoritative *Manual of the Grasses of the United States* 1950.

Chase Salmon Portland (1808–1873). US public official and chief justice of the USA. He held a US Senate seat 1849–55 and 1860; helped found the Republican Party 1854–56; was elected governor of Ohio 1855; became Abraham Lincoln's secretary of the treasury 1861; and was appointed chief justice of the US Supreme Court 1864. He presided over the impeachment trial of President A Johnson 1868.

Chase William C (1895–1986). US general. He served with the US cavalry in World War I. In World War II, he served mainly in the Far East and Sept 1945 led the 1st Cavalry Division, the first US military force to enter Tokyo. After the war he became Chief of Staff 3rd Army, then went to Taiwan as military adviser to Chiang Kai-shek until his retirement 1956.

From 1943, he commanded 1 Cavalry Brigade which recaptured the Admiralty Islands March 1944. He later took part in the invasion of the Philippines and led the first US troops into Manila 3 Feb 1945. He then took command of 38 Infantry Division and cleared the Japanese out of Bataan and supervised the airborne assault on Corregidor.

Chateaubriand François Auguste René, Vicomte de (1768–1848). French writer, a founder of Romanticism. He was in exile from the French Revolution 1794–1800, and wrote *Atala* 1801 (based on his encounters with North American Indians), *Le Génie du*

Christianisme/The Genius of Christianity 1802 – a defence of the Christian faith in terms of its social, cultural, and spiritual benefits – and the autobiographical *René* 1805. Vicomte 1815.

The original writer is not he who refrains from imitating others, but he who can be imitated by none.

FRANÇOIS RENÉ CHATEAUBRIAND
Le Génie du Christianisme 1802

He visited the USA 1791 and, on his return to France, fought for the royalist side, which was defeated at Thionville 1792. He lived in exile in England until 1800. When he returned to France, he held diplomatic appointments under Louis XVIII, becoming ambassador to Britain 1822. He later wrote *Mémoires d'outre-tombe/Memoirs from Beyond the Tomb* 1848–50.

Châtelet (Gabrielle) Emilie de Breteuil, Marquise du (1706–1749). French scientific writer and translator into French of Isaac Newton's *Principia*.

Her marriage to the Marquis du Châtelet 1725 gave her the leisure to study physics and mathematics. She met controversial French writer Voltaire 1733, and settled with him at her husband's estate at Cirey, in the Duchy of Lorraine. Her study of Newton, with whom she collaborated on various scientific works, influenced Voltaire's work. She independently produced the first (and only) French translation of Newton's *Principia* (published posthumously in 1759).

Chatterji Bankim Chandra (1838–1894). Indian novelist. Born in Bengal, where he established his reputation with his first book, *Durges-Nandini* 1864, he became a favourite of the nationalists. His book *Ananda Math* 1882 contains the Indian national song

'Bande-Mataram'.

What is love? 'tis nature's treasure, / 'Tis the storehouse of her joys; / 'Tis the highest heaven of pleasure, / 'Tis a bliss which never cloys.

THOMAS CHATTERTON
'Revenge I. ii'

Chatterton Thomas (1752–1770). English poet. His medieval-style poems and brief life were to inspire English Romanticism. Born in Bristol, he studied ancient documents he found in the Church of St Mary Redcliffe and composed poems he ascribed to a 15th-century monk, 'Thomas Rowley', which were accepted as genuine. He sent examples to Horace Walpole who was advised that they were forgeries. He then began contributing to periodicals in many styles, including Junius. He committed suicide in London, after becoming destitute.

Wandering re-establishes the original harmony which once existed between man and the universe.

BRUCE CHATWIN
The Songlines ch 30 1987

Chatwin (Charles) Bruce (1940–1989). English writer. His works include *The Songlines* 1987, written after living with Australian Aborigines; the novel *Utz* 1988, about a manic porcelain collector in Prague; and travel pieces and journalism collected in *What Am I Doing Here* 1989.

The lyf so short, the craft so long to lerne, / Thassay so hard, so sharp the conquering.

GEOFFREY CHAUCER
The Parlement of Foules – translation of an aphorism of Hippocrates *c.* 1380

Chaucer *Posthumous portrait of English poet Geoffrey Chaucer by an unknown artist, National Portrait Gallery, London. Chaucer's work has been admired from his own time to the present day. It confirmed the domination of southern English as the language of literature throughout England.*

Chaucer Geoffrey (*c.* 1340–1400). English poet. *The Canterbury Tales*, a collection of stories told by a group of pilgrims on their way to Canterbury, reveals his knowledge of human nature and his stylistic variety, from urbane and ironic to simple and bawdy. Early allegorical poems, including *The Book of the Duchess*, were influenced by French poems like the *Roman de la Rose*. His *Troilus and Criseyde* is a substantial narrative poem about the tragic betrayal of an idealized courtly love.

Chaucer was born in London. Taken prisoner in the French wars, he had to be ransomed by Edward III 1360. He married Philippa Roet 1366, becoming in later life the brother-in-law of John of Gaunt. He achieved various appointments and was sent on missions to Italy (where he may have met Boccaccio and Petrarch), France, and Flanders. His early work showed formal French influence, as in his adaptation of the French allegorical poem on courtly love, *The Romaunt of the Rose*; more mature works reflected the influence of Italian realism, as in his long narrative poem *Troilus and Criseyde*, adapted from Boccaccio. In *The Canterbury Tales* he showed his own genius for metre and characterization. He was the most influential English poet of the Middle Ages.

Suggested reading
Bowden, M A *A Reader's Guide to Chaucer* (1964)
Brewer, D *Chaucer and his World* (1978)
Gardner, J *The Life and Times of Chaucer* (1977)
Howard, D R *Chaucer: His Life, His Works, His World* (1987)
North, J D *Chaucer's Universe* (1988)
Pearsall, D *The Life of Geoffrey Chaucer* (1992)
Rowland, B (ed) *Companion to Chaucer Studies* (1979)

Chaudhuri Nirad Chandra (1897–). Indian writer and broadcaster. He attracted attention with his *Autobiography of an Unknown Indian* 1950 which illuminates the clash of British and Indian civilizations. A first visit to England, previously known to him only through its literature, produced the quirky *A Passage to England* 1959. Later works include *The Continent of Circe* 1965, an erudite critique of Indian culture, and *Thy Hand Great Anarch* 1987, critical of the impact of British culture on India.

Chávez Carlos Antonio de Padua (1899–1978). Mexican composer and pianist. His music incorporates national and pre-Columbian folk elements, for example *Chapultepec: Republican Overture* 1935. He composed a number of ballets, seven symphonies, and concertos for both violin and piano.

He was founder-director of the Mexico Symphony Orchestra 1928–48.

Chavez Cesar Estrada (1927–1993). US labour organizer who founded the National Farm Workers Association 1962 and, with the support of the AFL-CIO and other major unions, embarked on a successful campaign to unionize California grape workers. He led boycotts of citrus fruits, lettuce, and grapes in the early 1970s, but disagreement and exploitation of migrant farm labourers continued despite his successes.

Chavis Benjamin Franklin (1948–). US civil-rights campaigner. As executive director of the National Association for the Advancement of Colored People from 1993, he succeeded in putting the NAACP more in touch with the concerns of the black community, recruiting 160,000 new members, although he was criticized by conservative blacks for his friendly relations with Louis Farrakhan of the Nation of Islam.

Chavis was a direct descendant of John Chavis (1763–1838), a former slave who graduated from Princeton University. He was sentenced to 34 years in prison 1972 as leader of the Wilmington Ten, convicted of conspiracy and arson. While in prison he gained a master of divinity degree and taught a seminar on black church studies at Duke University, North Carolina. The convictions were overturned 1980. He became executive director of the Commission for Racial Justice and commissioned a study, *Toxic Wastes and Race in the United States* 1987, which showed that a large number of hazardous-waste dumps were in black neighbourhoods.

Chayefsky Paddy (Sidney) (1923–1981). US screenwriter and dramatist of great passion and insight. He established his reputation with naturalistic television plays, at least two of which were adapted for cinema: *Marty* 1955 (for which he won an Oscar for the film screenplay) and *Bachelor Party* 1957. He also won Oscars for the bitterly satirical *The Hospital* 1971 and *Network* 1976.

His stage plays include *The Tenth Man* 1959 and *Gideon* 1961. He wrote the screenplay for Ken Russell's *Altered States* 1980, which was very loosely based on Chayefsky's novel of the same name.

Cheever John (1912–1982). US writer. His stories and novels focus on the ironies of upper-middle-class life in suburban America. His short stories were frequently published in the *New Yorker* magazine. His first novel was *The Wapshot Chronicle* 1957, for which he won the National Book Award. Others include *Falconer* 1977. His *Stories of John Cheever* 1978 won the Pulitzer Prize.

Cheever was born in Quincy, Massachusetts. His collections of short stories include *The Way Some People Live* 1943, *The Housebreaker of Shady Hill* 1958, and *The Brigadier and the Golf Widow* 1964. Among his novels are *Bullet Park* 1969 and *Oh What a Paradise It Seems* 1982.

A woman can become a man's friend only in the following stages – first an acquaintance, next a mistress, and only then a friend.

ANTON CHEKHOV
Uncle Vanya 1897

Chekhov Anton Pavlovich (1860–1904). Russian dramatist and writer of short stories. His plays concentrate on the creation of atmosphere and delineation of internal development, rather than external action. His first play, *Ivanov* 1887, was a failure, as was *The*

Seagull 1896 until revived by Stanislavsky 1898 at the Moscow Art Theatre, for which Chekhov went on to write his finest plays: *Uncle Vanya* 1897, *The Three Sisters* 1901, and *The Cherry Orchard* 1904.

Chekhov was born in Taganrog, S Russia. He qualified as a doctor 1884, but devoted himself to writing short stories rather than practising medicine. The collection *Particoloured Stories* 1886 consolidated his reputation and gave him leisure to develop his style, as seen in *My Life* 1895, *The Lady with the Dog* 1898, and *In the Ravine* 1900.

Suggested reading
Hingley, Ronald *A New Life of Anton Chekhov* (1976)
Lantz, K *Anton Chekhov: A Reference Guide* (1985)
Pritchett, V S *Chekhov: A Spirit Set Free* (1988)
Troyat, Henri *Chekhov* (1986)
Valency, M J *The Breaking String: The Plays of Anton Chekhov* (1966)

Cheng-Ho Chinese admiral and emperor; see ◊Zheng He.

Chénier André Marie de (1762–1794). French poet. His lyrical poetry was later to inspire the Romantic movement, but he was known in his own time for his uncompromising support of the constitutional royalists after the Revolution. In 1793 he went into hiding, but finally he was arrested and, on 25 July 1794, guillotined. While in prison he wrote *Jeune Captive/Captive Girl* and the political *Iambes*, published after his death.

Chen Kaige (1954–). Chinese film director, one of the 'Fifth Generation' of Chinese directors (those graduating from the Beijing Film Academy in the early 1980s) in the aftermath of the Cultural Revolution. His films are notable for their visual impact as well as their re-examination of Chinese culture and history. They include *Huang Tudi/Yellow Earth* 1984, *Da Yuebing/The Big Parade* 1986, the semi-autobiographical *Haizi Wang/King of the Children* 1988, and the co-winner of the Cannes Palme d'Or *Bawang Bie Ji/Farewell My Concubine* 1993.

Chen acted in a cameo role in Bertolucci's *The Last Emperor* 1987.

Chennault Claire Lee (1890–1958). US pilot. He became famous during World War II as the leader of the 'Flying Tigers', a volunteer force of 200 US pilots and engineers fighting alongside Chinese Nationalist forces.

Originally a pilot in the US Army Air Corps, Chennault was retired on medical grounds 1937 and then became an adviser and trainer on aviation for the Chinese Nationalist forces. He returned to duty with the US Army Air Force 1942 when the Flying Tigers were absorbed with the regular US air forces. An offensive against the Japanese 1943 was met with a strong counterattack which destroyed much of his force both in the air and on the ground. He resigned July 1945 after his advice on the future reorganization of the Chinese air force was rejected.

Chen Yun adopted name of Liao Chenyun (1905–1995). Chinese communist politician, economics expert, and second-ranking 'party elder' at the time of his death. A veteran of the Long March of 1934–35, he was a member of the Chinese Communist Party (CCP) Politburo for a record 53 years (1934–87). He favoured a planned economy in which market forces would be allowed to operate in a controlled manner, 'like a bird in a cage'. Formerly an ally of China's paramount leader Deng Xiaoping, Chen became a conservative opponent in his later years, voicing concern at the destabilizing effects of Deng's 'uncaged' market socialism.

Cherenkov Pavel Alexeevich (1904–1990). Soviet physicist. In 1934 he discovered Cherenkov radiation; this occurs as a bluish light when charged atomic particles pass through water or other media at a speed in excess of that of light. He shared a Nobel prize 1958 with his colleagues Ilya Frank and Igor Tamm for work resulting in a cosmic-ray counter.

Cherenkov discovered that this effect was independent of any medium and depended for its production on the passage of high velocity electrons.

Chéret Jules (1836–1932). French lithographer and poster artist.

His early posters, such as those in the 1860s for the Circus Rancy, pioneered the medium.

Later works show the influence of the Impressionists and Toulouse-Lautrec.

Chernenko Konstantin Ustinovich (1911–1985). Soviet politician, leader of the Soviet Communist Party (CPSU) and president 1984–85. He was a protégé of Brezhnev and from 1978 a member of the Politburo.

Chernenko, born in central Siberia, joined the Komsomol (Communist Youth League) 1929 and the CPSU 1931. The future CPSU leader Brezhnev brought him to Moscow to work in the central apparatus 1956 and later sought to establish Chernenko as his successor, but he was passed over in favour of the KGB chief Andropov. When Andropov died Feb 1984 Chernenko was selected as the CPSU's stopgap leader by cautious party colleagues and was also elected president. From July 1984 he gradually retired from public life because of failing health.

Chernomyrdin Viktor Stepanovich (1938–). Russian politician, prime minister from 1992. A former manager in the state gas industry and communist party *apparatchik* (full-time senior official), he became prime minister Dec 1992 after Russia's ex-communist-dominated parliament had ousted the market reformer, Yegor Gaidar. In Nov 1995 he assumed temporary control over foreign and security policy after President Yeltsin suffered a heart attack.

Although lacking charisma, Chernomyrdin emerged as a respected and pragmatic reformer who, enjoying strong establishment support, brought a measure of stability to the country. He formed the Russia is Our Home party May 1995 and was viewed as a leading challenger for the Russian presidency 1996. His negotiated settlement of a hostage crisis in S Russia June 1995, although controversial, won him popular support, leading to a temporary cease-fire in the civil war in Chechnya and peace talks between the two sides.

Cherubini Luigi Carlo Zanobi Salvadore Maria (1760–1842). Italian composer. His first opera *Quinto Fabio* 1779 was produced at Alessandria. Following his appointment as court composer to King George III of England 1784–88, he settled in Paris where he produced a number of dramatic works including *Médée* 1797, *Les Deux Journées* 1800, and the ballet *Anacréon* 1803. After 1809 he devoted himself largely to church music.

Cherwell Frederick Alexander Lindemann, 1st Viscount Cherwell (1886–1957). British physicist. He served as director of the Clarendon Laboratory, Oxford, 1919–56, and oversaw its transformation into a major research institute.

Lindemann was born in Baden-Baden, Germany, and studied at Berlin, leaving on the outbreak of World War I 1914 to become director of the Royal Air Force Physical Laboratory, where he was concerned with aircraft stability. From 1919 he was professor of experimental philosophy at Oxford. He was also a member of the government as paymaster-general 1942–45 and 1951–53, helping to direct scientific research during World War II and to create the Atomic Energy Authority afterwards. Baron 1941, viscount 1956.

Cheshire (Geoffrey) Leonard (1917–1992). British pilot. Commissioned into the Royal Air Force on the outbreak of World War II, he won the Victoria Cross, Distinguished Service Order (with 2 bars), and Distinguished Flying Cross. In 1945 he was an official observer at the dropping of the atom bomb on Nagasaki. A devout Roman Catholic, he founded the first Cheshire Foundation Home for the Incurably Sick 1948. In 1959 he married Susan Ryder (1923–) who established a foundation for the sick and disabled of all ages and became a life peeress 1978. Baron 1991.

Advice is seldom welcome; and those who want it the most always like it the least.

EARL OF CHESTERFIELD
Letter to his son 29 Jan 1748

Chesterfield Philip Dormer Stanhope, 4th Earl of Chesterfield (1694–1773). English politician and writer. He was the author of *Letters to his Son* 1774, which gave voluminous instruction on aristocratic manners and morals. A member of the literary circle of Swift, Pope, and Bolingbroke, he incurred the wrath of Dr Samuel Johnson by failing to carry out an offer of patronage.

He was ambassador to Holland 1728–32 and 1744. In Ireland, he established schools, helped to reconcile Protestants and Catholics, and encouraged manufacturing. An opponent of Walpole, he was a Whig member of Parliament 1715–26, Lord Lieutenant of Ireland 1745–46, and secretary of state 1746–48. Succeeded to earldom 1726.

Chesterton G(ilbert) K(eith) (1874–1936). English novelist, essayist, and poet. He wrote numerous short stories featuring a Catholic priest, Father Brown, who solves crimes by drawing on his knowledge of human nature. Other novels include the fantastic *The Napoleon of Notting Hill* 1904 and *The Man Who Was Thursday* 1908, a deeply emotional allegory about the problem of evil.

Born in London, he studied art but quickly turned to journalism. Like Hilaire Belloc, he was initially a socialist sympathizer.

Suggested reading
Baker, Dudley *G K Chesterton* (1973)
Coren, Michael *Gilbert: The Man Who was G K Chesterton* (1989)
Dale, A S *The Art of G K Chesterton* (1985)
Ffinch, Michael *G K Chesterton* (1989)
Sullivan, J (ed) *G K Chesterton: A Centenary Appraisal* (1974)

Chetwode Philip Walhouse, 1st Baron Chetwode (1869–1950). British soldier. Chetwode entered the 19th Hussars 1889, and served in Burma and South Africa. He commanded the 5th cavalry brigade in action against the Germans before Mons 1914. In 1916 he went to Egypt to assume command of the desert mounted column of the Egyptian expeditionary force, which he led in the early campaigns in Palestine.

Allenby based his plans during the conquest of Palestine largely on Chetwode's experience and advice. He was promoted to lieutenant-general 1919. Succeeded as baronet 1905, became baron 1945.

Chesterton English journalist, novelist, and broadcaster G K Chesterton.

Chevalier Maurice (1888–1972). French singer and actor. He began as dancing partner to the revue artiste Mistinguett at the Folies-Bergère, and made numerous films including *Innocents of Paris* 1929 (which revived his song 'Louise'), *The Merry Widow* 1934, and *Gigi* 1958.

Many a man has fallen in love with a girl in a light so dim he would not have chosen a suit by it.

MAURICE CHEVALIER
Attributed remark 1955

Chevreul Michel-Eugène (1786–1889). French chemist who studied the composition of fats and identified a number of fatty acids, including 'margaric acid', which became the basis of margarine. He also studied sugars and dyes. From 1824 he was director of dyeing at the Gobelins tapestry factory. He became professor of chemistry at the Museum of Natural History, and its director 1864.

At the Gobelins dyeworks he made various chemical discoveries, and his interest in the creation of the illusion of continuous colour gradation by using massed small monochromatic dots (as in an embroidery or tapestry) later influenced the Pointillist and Impressionist painters.

Cheyne John (1777–1836). Scottish physician who, with William Stokes, gave his name to Cheyne–Stokes breathing, or periodic respiration.

Cheyne was born in Leith and apprenticed to his physician father at the age of 13. In 1809 he settled in Dublin. He took the first professorial chair in medicine at the Royal College of Surgeons of Ireland 1813. In 1818 Cheyne described the periodic respiration that occurs in patients with intracranial disease or cardiac disease. His paper described the breathing that would cease entirely for a quarter of a minute or more, then would become perceptible and increase by degrees to quick, heaving breaths which gradually subside again.

Chiang Ching alternative transliteration of ◊Jiang Qing, Chinese actress, third wife of Mao Zedong.

Chiang Ching-kuo (1910–1988). Taiwanese politician, son of Chiang Kai-shek, prime minister 1971–78, president 1978–88.

We shall not talk lightly about sacrifice until we are driven to the last extremity which makes sacrifice inevitable.

CHIANG KAI-SHEK
Speech to Fifth Congress of the Guomindang

Chiang Kai-shek (Jiang Jie Shi in Pingin) (1887–1975). Chinese nationalist Guomindang (Kuomintang) general and politician, president of China 1928–31 and 1943–49, and of Taiwan from 1949, where he set up a US-supported right-wing government on his expulsion from the mainland by the communist forces.

Chiang took part in the revolution of 1911 that overthrew the Qing dynasty of the Manchus, and on the death of the Guomindang leader Sun Yat-sen was made commander in chief of the nationalist armies in S China 1925. Collaboration with the communists, broken 1927, was resumed after the Xian Incident 1936 when China needed to pool military strength in the struggle against the Japanese invaders of World War II. After the Japanese surrender 1945, civil war between the nationalists and communists erupted, and in Dec 1949 Chiang and his followers took refuge on the island of Taiwan, maintaining a large army in the hope of reclaiming the mainland. His authoritarian regime enjoyed US support until his death. His son Chiang Ching-kuo then became president.
Suggested reading
Crozier, B and Chou, E *The Man Who Lost China* (1976)
Miller, M *Chiang Kai-shek* (1988)
Morwood, W *Duel for the Middle Kingdom: The Struggle Between Chiang Kai-Shek and Mao Tse-Tung for Control of China* (1979)

Chichester Francis Charles (1901–1972). English sailor and navigator. In 1931 he made the first east–west crossing of the Tasman Sea in *Gipsy Moth*, and in 1966–67 circumnavigated the world in his yacht *Gipsy Moth IV*. KBE 1967.

A typical Australian Labor amalgam of radical, socialist and conservative.

L F Crisp on BEN CHIFLEY
in *Dictionary of National Biography*

Chifley Ben (Joseph Benedict) (1885–1951). Australian Labor prime minister 1945–49. He united the party in fulfilling a welfare and nationalization programme (although he failed in an attempt to nationalize the banks 1947) and initiated an immigration programme and the Snowy Mountains hydroelectric project.

Chifley was minister of postwar reconstruction 1942–45 under John Curtin, when he succeeded him as prime minister. He crushed a coal miners' strike 1949 by using troops as mine labour. He was leader of the Opposition from 1949 until his death.
Suggested reading
Crisp, L F *Ben Chifley* (1961)

Chikamatsu Monzaemon (born Sugimori Nobumori) (1653–1725). Japanese dramatist. He wrote over 150 plays for the puppet and kabuki theatres in Osaka. His plays for puppets were usually either domestic tragedies such as *The Love Suicides at Sonezaki* 1703, or heroic historical dramas like *The Battles of Coxinga* 1715. The plays are written in prose.

Child Charles Manning (1869–1954). US zoologist who developed a theory of how the various cells and tissues in organisms are organized – by a gradation in the rate of physiological processes leading to relationships of dominance and subordination. Although not now thought to be correct, it was an important early contribution to the problem of functional organization within living organisms. He spent his academic career at the University of Chicago, becoming professor 1916.

Child Lydia Maria Francis (1802–1880). US writer, social critic, and feminist, author of the popular women's guides *The Frugal Housewife* 1829 and *The Mother's Book* 1831. With her husband, David Child, she worked for the abolition of slavery, advocating educational support for black Americans. The Childs edited the weekly *National Anti-Slavery Standard* 1840–44.

Child, born in Medford, Massachusetts, received little formal education but read widely and published several historical novels about life in colonial New England.

Tall, ungainly, and ugly, eccentric in dress and often abrupt in manner, the generous, kindly, rather naive person hidden behind … was known to few.

Stuart Piggott on V GORDON CHILDE
in *Dictionary of National Biography*

Childe V(ere) Gordon (1892–1957). Australian archaeologist who was an authority on early European and Middle Eastern societies. He pioneered current methods of analytical archaeology. His books include *The Dawn of European Civilization* 1925 and *What Happened in History* 1942.

He was professor of prehistoric archaeology at Edinburgh University 1927–46, and director of the London Institute of Archaeology 1946–57. He excavated the prehistoric village of Skara Brae in the Orkneys, and defined civilization for archaeological reconstruction. Childe was born in Sydney. He committed suicide by stepping off a cliff.

Childers (Robert) Erskine (1870–1922). British civil servant and, from 1921, Irish Sinn Féin politician, author of the spy novel *The Riddle of the Sands* 1903.

Before turning to Irish politics, Childers was a clerk in the House of Commons in London. In 1921 he was elected to the Irish Parliament as a supporter of the Sinn Féin leader de Valera, and took up arms against the Irish Free State 1922. Shortly afterwards he was captured, court-martialled, and shot by the Irish Free State government of William T Cosgrave.

Come closer, boys, it will be easier for you.

ERSKINE CHILDERS
Words to his firing squad taking up position across the prison yard, quoted in Burke Wilkinson *The Zeal of the Convert* 1976

Chiluba Frederick (1943–). Zambian politician and trade unionist, president from 1991. In 1993 he was forced to declare a state of emergency, following the discovery of documents suggesting an impending coup. He later carried out a major reorganization of his cabinet but failed to silence his critics.

Chin dynasty hereditary rulers of N China 1122–1234; see ◊Jin dynasty.

Chippendale Thomas (1718–1779). English furniture designer. He set up his workshop in St Martin's Lane, London, 1753. His book *The Gentleman and Cabinet Maker's Director* 1754, was a significant contribution to furniture design. Although many of his most characteristic designs are Rococo, he also employed Louis XVI, Chinese, Gothic, and Neo-Classical styles. He worked mainly in mahogany.

Chirac Jacques René (1932–). French conservative politician, prime minister 1974–76 and 1986–88, and president from 1995. He established the neo-Gaullist Rassemblement pour la République (RPR) 1976, and became mayor of Paris 1977. His decision to resume French nuclear-testing in the Pacific region 1995 was widely condemned.

Chirac held ministerial posts during the Pompidou presidency and gained the nickname 'the Bulldozer'. In 1974 he became prime minister to President Giscard d'Estaing, but the relationship was uneasy. Chirac contested the 1981 presidential election and

Chladni *By combining music with experimental physics, Ernst Chladni helped establish the science of acoustics. His most famous acoustic experiment used geometrically shaped metal or glass plates covered with a fine layer of sand. When the plates were struck, or even played with a bow, the sand moved to form patterns known as 'Chladni figures'.* (Ann Ronan/Image Select)

emerged as the National Assembly leader for the parties of the right during the socialist administration of 1981–86.

Following the rightist coalition's victory 1986, Chirac was appointed prime minister by President Mitterrand in a 'cohabitation' experiment. The term was marked by economic decline, nationality reforms, and student unrest. Student demonstrations in autumn 1986 forced him to scrap plans for educational reform. He stood in the May 1988 presidential elections and was defeated by Mitterrand, who replaced him with the moderate socialist Michel Rocard. He was elected president 1995 with a comfortable majority over his socialist rival Lionel Jospin, but soon lost popular support as a result of confusion in his economic programme and the decision to resume the Pacific nuclear tests.

Chirico Giorgio de (1888–1978). Greek-born Italian painter. His style presaged Surrealism in its use of enigmatic imagery and dreamlike settings, for example, *Nostalgia of the Infinite* 1911 (Museum of Modern Art, New York).

In 1917, with Carlo Carrà, he founded the school of Metaphysical Painting, which aimed to convey a sense of mystery and hallucination. This was achieved by distorted perspective, dramatic lighting, and the use of dummies and statues in place of human figures. In the 1930s he repudiated the modern movement in art, and began reworking the styles of the old masters.

Chisholm Caroline (born Jones) (1808–1877). English welfare worker and philanthropist in Australia. She arrived in New South Wales 1838 and began aiding immigrant women, setting up a home for unemployed girls. Her policy of finding employment for girls in rural areas helped in alleviating unemployment in Sydney and the rural labour shortage. She returned to England in 1846 and in 1850 her Family Colonization Loan Scheme was established.

Chisholm Jesse (*c.* 1806–*c.* 1868). US pioneer who gained a reputation as a resourceful guide, trader, and military scout during the early 19th century. He established one of the main paths of the yearly Texas cattle drive, known among cowboys as the 'Chisholm Trail'. Ranging over the south part of the Great Plains, he customarily followed a route from the Mexican border to Kansas, ending at the market town of Abilene.

Chisholm Shirley Anita St Hill (1924–). US Democrat politician. The first black woman elected to the US Congress, in 1964, she served until 1983.

Although born in Brooklyn, New York city, the child of an immigrant from British Guiana (now Guyana), she spent her childhood in Barbados. A specialist in early-childhood education, she worked at the Mount Calvary Child Care Center 1946–52, before running her own nursery school. She later became director to the city of New York on day-care facilities. In Congress she campaigned successfully for the extension of employment protection to domestic workers, and assaulted sexism and racism. Her autobiography *Unbought and Unbossed* was published 1970. From 1983 she has been a member of the faculty at Mount Holyoke College in Massachusetts.

Chissano Joaquim (1939–). Mozambique nationalist politician, president from 1986; foreign minister 1975–86. In Oct 1992 Chissano signed a peace accord with the leader of the rebel Mozambique National Resistance (MNR) party, bringing to an end 16 years of civil war, and in 1994 won the first free presidential elections.

He was secretary to Samora Machel, who led the National Front for the Liberation of Mozambique (Frelimo) during the campaign for independence in the early 1960s. When Mozambique achieved internal self-government 1974, Chissano was appointed prime minister. After independence he served under Machel as foreign minister and on his death succeeded him as president.

Chladni Ernst Florens Friedrich (1756–1827). German physicist, a pioneer in the field of acoustics. He developed an experimental technique whereby sand is vibrated on a metal plate and settles into regular and symmetric patterns (Chladni's figures), indicating the nodes of the vibration's wave pattern.

Chodowiecki Daniel Nikolaus (1726–1801). German painter and engraver. He is known for his intimate pictures of German middle-class life. His works include engravings of scenes from the Seven Years' War and the life of Christ, and the portrait *The Parting of Jean Calas from his Family* 1767 (Berlin-Dahlem Museum).

Choiseul Etienne François, Duc de Choiseul (1719–1785). French politician. Originally a protégé of Madame de Pompadour, the mistress of Louis XV, he became minister for foreign affairs 1758, and held this and other offices until 1770. He banished the Jesuits, and was a supporter of the Enlightenment philosophers Diderot and Voltaire. Duke 1758.

Chola dynasty S Indian family of rulers that flourished in the 9th–13th centuries. Based on the banks of the Cauvery River, the Cholas overthrew their Pallava and Pandya neighbours and established themselves as the major pan-regional force. The two greatest Chola kings were Rajaraja I (reigned 985–1014) who invaded Northern Cyprus and his son Rajendra Cholavarma (reigned 1014–1044).

During their reigns, Chola military expeditions were sent to the Ganges valley and the Malay archipelago, and magnificent temples were built at Tanjore. The dynasty lasted until *c.* 1279, but lost much of its territory in W and central India during the 12th century. In addition to making themselves into a maritime power, the Cholas built a system of local government and supported commerce and the arts.

If we don't believe in freedom of expression for people we despise, we don't believe in it at all.

NOAM CHOMSKY
on BBC TV 'The Late Show' 25 Nov 1992

Chomsky (Avram) Noam (1928–). US professor of linguistics and political commentator. He proposed a theory of transformational generative grammar, which attracted widespread interest because of the claims it made about the relationship between language and the mind and the universality of an underlying language structure. He has been a leading critic of the imperialist tendencies of the US government.

Chomsky distinguished between knowledge and behaviour and maintained that the focus of scientific enquiry should be on knowledge. In order to define and describe linguistic knowledge, he posited a set of abstract principles of grammar that appear to be universal and may have a biological basis.

Choong Eddy (Ewe Beng) (1930–). Malaysian badminton player. Only 157 cm/5 ft 2 in tall, he was a dynamic player and won most major honours during his career 1950–57, including All-England singles title four times 1953–57.

Choonhavan Chatichai (1922–). Thai conservative politician, prime minister of Thailand 1988–91. He promoted a peace settlement in neighbouring Cambodia as part of a vision of transforming Indochina into a thriving open-trade zone. Despite economic success, he was ousted in a bloodless military coup 1991.

A field marshal's son, Choonhavan fought in World War II and the Korean War, rising to major-general. After a career as a diplomat and entrepreneur, he moved into politics and became leader of the conservative Chat Thai party and, in 1988, prime minister. He was overthrown Feb 1991 and was allowed, the following month, to leave the country for Switzerland.

I'm a revolutionary, money means nothing to me.

FRÉDÉRIC CHOPIN
quoted in Arthur Hedley *Chopin* 1947

Chopin Frédéric François (1810–1849). Polish composer and pianist. He made his debut as a pianist at the age of eight. As a performer, Chopin revolutionized the technique of pianoforte-playing, turning the hands outward and favouring a light, responsive touch. His compositions for piano, which include two concertos and other works with orchestra, are characterized by great volatility of mood, and rhythmic fluidity.

From 1831 he lived in Paris, where he became known in the fashionable salons, although he rarely performed in public. In 1836 the composer Liszt introduced him to Madame Dudevant (George Sand), with whom he had a close relationship 1838–46. During this time she nursed him in Majorca for tuberculosis, while he composed intensively and for a time regained his health. His music was used as the basis of the ballet *Les Sylphides* by Fokine 1909 and orchestrated by Alexander Gretchaninov (1864–1956), a pupil of Rimsky-Korsakov.

Suggested reading
Attwood, W G *Fryderyk Chopin* (1987)
Hedley, A *Chopin* (1947)
Marek, G R and Gordon-Smith, M *Chopin* (1978)
Orga, A *Chopin: His Life and Times* (1976)

Chopin Kate (born Katherine O'Flaherty) (1851–1904). US novelist and short-story writer. Her novel *The Awakening* 1899, the story of a married New Orleans woman's awakening to her sexuality, caused a sensation of hostile criticism, which effectively ended her career. It is now regarded as a classic of feminist sensibility.

Following the death of her father, she was brought up by her mother, grandmother, and great-grandmother in St Louis, Missouri, USA. An avid reader, Chopin first began to write to support her six children following the death of her husband and then her mother. She was the author of poignant tales of Creole and Cajun life in *Bayou Folk* 1894.

Chou En-lai alternative transliteration of ◊Zhou Enlai.

Chrétien (Joseph Jacques) Jean (1934–). French-Canadian politician, prime minister from 1993. He won the leadership of the

Chopin The composer Frédéric Chopin (1810–1849) as depicted on a cigarette card of 1912. He died of lung disease (tuberculosis) at an early age, but he nevertheless left behind a large quantity of quintessentially romantic music, written mostly for piano solo. (Image Select)

Liberal Party 1990 and defeated Kim Campbell in the Oct 1993 election. He has been a vigorous advocate of national unity and, although himself a Quebecois, has consistently opposed the province's separatist ambitions.

He held ministerial posts in the cabinets of Lester Pearson and Pierre Trudeau. After unsuccessfully contesting the Liberal Party leadership 1984, he resigned his parliamentary seat, returning 1990 to win the leadership on his second attempt.

Chrétien de Troyes (died c. 1183). French poet. His epics, which introduced the concept of the Holy Grail, include *Lancelot, ou le chevalier de la charrette*; *Perceval, ou le conte du Graal*, written for Philip, Count of Flanders; *Erec*; *Yvain, ou le chevalier au Lion*; and other Arthurian romances.

Christ (Greek *khristos* 'anointed one') the Messiah as prophesied in the Hebrew Bible, or Old Testament. See ◊Jesus.

Christian Fletcher (c. 1764–c. 1794). English seaman who led the mutiny on HMS *Bounty* 1789. He and eight others settled on Pitcairn Island where their descendants live today.

Christian ten kings of Denmark and Norway, including:

Christian I (1426–1481). King of Denmark from 1448, and founder of the Oldenburg dynasty. In 1450 he established the union of Denmark and Norway that lasted until 1814. He was King of Sweden 1457–64 and 1465–67.

Christian III (1503–1559). King of Denmark and Norway from 1534. During his reign the Reformation was introduced.

A bluff, red-faced, hard-drinking hedonist, who could command the fleet in battle as well as plan new cities.
E N Williams on CHRISTIAN IV
in *Penguin Dictionary of English and European History 1485–1789* 1980

Christie, Julie *English film actress Julie Christie. In such films as* Billy Liar *1963 and* Darling *1965 she came to epitomize the liberated woman of the 'Swinging Sixties'. In 1965 she won an Academy Award for her role in David Lean's* Dr Zhivago.

Christian IV (1577–1648). King of Denmark and Norway from 1588. He sided with the Protestants in the Thirty Years' War (1618–48), and founded Christiania (now Oslo, capital of Norway). He was succeeded by Frederick II 1648.

Christian VIII (1786–1848). King of Denmark 1839–48. He was unpopular because of his opposition to reform. His attempt to encourage the Danish language and culture in Schleswig and Holstein led to an insurrection there shortly after his death. He was succeeded by Frederick VII.

Christian IX (1818–1906). King of Denmark from 1863. His daughter Alexandra married Edward VII of the UK and another, Dagmar, married Tsar Alexander III of Russia; his second son, George, became king of Greece. In 1864 he lost the duchies of Schleswig and Holstein after a war with Austria and Prussia.

Christian X (1870–1947). King of Denmark and Iceland from 1912, when he succeeded his father Frederick VIII. He married Alexandrine, Duchess of Mecklenburg-Schwerin, and was popular for his democratic attitude. During World War II he was held prisoner by the Germans in Copenhagen. He was succeeded by Frederick IX.

An archaeologist is the best husband any woman can have: the older she gets, the more interested he is in her.
AGATHA CHRISTIE
Attributed remark 1954

Christie Agatha Mary Clarissa (born Miller) (1890–1976). English detective novelist. She created the characters Hercule Poirot and Miss Jane Marple. She wrote more than 70 novels, including *The Murder of Roger Ackroyd* 1926 and *Ten Little Indians* 1939. A number of her books have been filmed, for example *Murder on the Orient Express* 1975. Her play *The Mousetrap*, which opened in London 1952, is the longest continuously running show in the world. DBE 1971.

She was born in Torquay, married Col Archibald Christie 1914, and served during World War I as a nurse. Her first crime novel, *The Mysterious Affair at Styles* 1920, introduced Hercule Poirot. She often broke 'purist' rules, as in *The Murder of Roger Ackroyd* in which the narrator is the murderer. She caused a nationwide sensation 1926 by disappearing for ten days, possibly because of amnesia, when her husband fell in love with another woman. After a divorce 1928, in 1930 she married the archaeologist Max Mallowan (1904–1978).

Suggested reading
Barnard, R *A Talent to Deceive: An Appreciation of Agatha Christie* (1980)
Christie, Agatha *An Autobiography* (1977)
Morgan, Janet *Agatha Christie* (1986)
Osborne, Charles *The Life and Times of Agatha Christie* (1982)

Christie Julie Frances (1940–). English film actress. She became a star following her award-winning performance in *Darling* 1965. She also appeared in *Dr Zhivago* 1965; *The Go-Between* and *McCabe and Mrs Miller*, both 1971; *Don't Look Now* 1973; *Heat and Dust* 1982; and *Power* 1986.

Christie Linford (1960–). Jamaican-born English sprinter who, with his win in the 1993 World Championships, became the first track athlete ever to hold World, Olympic, European, and Commonwealth titles simultaneously.

He has won more medals in major events than any other athlete in British athletics history. His time of 9.87 seconds was, in 1993, the second-fastest time ever recorded for a 100-metre sprinting event.

Christina (1626–1689). Queen of Sweden 1632–54. Succeeding her father Gustavus Adolphus at the age of six, she assumed power 1644, but disagreed with the former regent Oxenstjerna. Refusing to marry, she eventually nominated her cousin Charles Gustavus (Charles X) as her successor. As a secret convert to Roman

Catholicism, which was then illegal in Sweden, she had to abdicate 1654, and went to live in Rome, twice returning to Sweden unsuccessfully to claim the throne.

Christine de Pisan (1364–*c.* 1430). French poet and historian. Her works include love lyrics, philosophical poems, a poem in praise of Joan of Arc, a history of Charles V, and various defences of women, including *La Cité des dames/The City of Ladies* 1405.

Christo adopted name of Christo Javacheff (1935–   ). US sculptor. Born in Bulgaria, he was active in Paris in the 1950s and in New York from 1964. He is known for his 'packages': structures, such as bridges and buildings, and even areas of coastline, temporarily wrapped in synthetic fabric tied down with rope.

The *Running Fence* 1976 installed across several miles of open country in California was a typically ephemeral work. In 1991 he mounted a simultaneous project, *The Umbrellas*, in which a series of enormous umbrellas were erected across valleys in both the USA and Japan.

In his *Wrapped Reichstag* June–July 1995, the German former government building was temporarily wrapped in 93,000 sq m/1 million sq ft of silver fabric secured by 15,500 m/49,000 ft of blue rope. The project had won government approval Feb 1994 after a 20-year campaign by the artist.

Christoff Boris (1919–1993). Bulgarian bass singer. His extraordinary stage presence and his distinctive, powerfully projected voice, with its astonishing range of colour and nuance, made him one of this century's greatest interpreters of Verdi and of Russian operas. He was known for roles such as Mussorgsky's Boris Godunov, Philip II in Verdi's *Don Carlos*, Ivan the Terrible in Rimsky-Korsakov's *The Maid of Pskov*, and the title role in *Mefistofele/Mephistopheles* by the Italian composer Arrigo Boito (1842–1918). His greater range is revealed in recordings of the complete songs of Mussorgsky.

Christoffel Elwin Bruno (1829–1900). German mathematician who made a fundamental contribution to the differential geometry of surfaces, carried out some of the first investigations that later resulted in the theory of shock waves, and introduced what are now known as the Christoffel symbols into the theory of invariants. His first professorship was at the Polytechnicum in Zürich, Switzerland, 1862–69; the second at Berlin; and from 1872 he was at the University of Strasbourg.

Christophe Henri (1767–1820). West Indian slave, one of the leaders of the revolt against the French 1791, who was proclaimed king of Haiti 1811. His government distributed plantations to military leaders. He shot himself when his troops deserted him because of his alleged cruelty.

Christopher, St patron saint of travellers. His feast day, 25 July, was dropped from the Roman Catholic liturgical calendar 1969.

Traditionally he was a martyr in Syria in the 3rd century, and legend describes his carrying the child Jesus over the stream; despite his great strength, he found the burden increasingly heavy, and was told that the child was Jesus Christ bearing the sins of all the world.

Christopher Warren (1925–   ). US Democrat politician, secretary of state from 1993. Trained as a lawyer, he was deputy attorney general under Jimmy Carter 1977–81 and led negotiations for the release of US hostages in Iran. In 1992 he masterminded the selection of Clinton's cabinet team, in Sept 1993 he secured the signing of a historic Israeli–PLO accord in Washington, and in Nov 1995 he brokered a peace agreement for Bosnia-Herzegovina. He is regarded as a skilled negotiator, unrestricted by strong political bias.

Chrysler Walter Percy (1875–1940). US industrialist. After World War I, he became president of the independent Maxwell Motor Company and went on to found the Chrysler Corporation 1925. By 1928 he had acquired Dodge and Plymouth, making Chrysler Corporation one of the largest US motor-vehicle manufacturers.

Chrysler was born in Wamego, Kansas. He worked first as a railway machinist, rising through the ranks to become manager of the

American Locomotive Company in Pittsburgh 1912. Shifting to the car industry, he was hired by General Motors and was appointed president of the Buick division 1916.

Chuang Tzu (*c.* 370–300 BC). Chinese philosopher, the second most important writer in the Taoist tradition, following Lao Zi. He was renowned for his wit, storytelling, and discourses on the inadequacy of words to describe anything of meaning. Stories about him were collected into a book called the *Chuang Tzu*, which became one of the most influential books in the rise of philosophical Taoism.

Chuikov Vasily Ivanovich (1900–1982). Soviet general. He joined the Red Army 1918, fighting against the Poles and in the Civil War. He then served as an adviser to Chinese nationalist leader Chiang Kai-shek 1926–37. He served with distinction in World War II, making his name at the siege of Stalingrad and taking his 8th Guards Army through to Berlin. He held several command positions following the war, finally becoming commander in chief Soviet Land Forces 1960.

Chukovsky Kornei Ivanovich (1882–1969). Russian critic and poet. The leading authority on the 19th-century Russian poet Nekrasov, he was also an expert on the Russian language, as in, for example, *Alive as Life* 1963. He was also beloved as 'Grandpa' Kornei Chukovsky for his nonsense poems, which owe much to English nursery rhymes and nonsense verse.

Chulalongkorn or *Rama V* (1853–1910). King of Siam (modern Thailand) from 1868. He studied Western administrative practices and launched an ambitious modernization programme after reaching his majority in 1873. He protected Siam from colonization by astutely playing off French and British interests.

Chulalongkorn was partly educated by English tutors and travelled to Europe 1897. His wide-ranging reforms, introduced after reaching his majority in 1873, included the abolition of slavery, centralization of administration to check the power of local chiefs, and reorganization of court and educational systems.

Chun Doo-hwan (1931–   ). South Korean military ruler who seized power 1979, president 1981–88 as head of the newly formed Democratic Justice Party.

Chun, trained in Korea and the USA, served as an army commander from 1967 and was in charge of military intelligence 1979 when President Park was assassinated by the chief of the Korean Central Intelligence Agency (KCIA). General Chun took charge of the KCIA and, in a coup, assumed control of the army and the South Korean government. In 1981 Chun was appointed president, and oversaw a period of rapid economic growth, governing in an authoritarian manner. In 1988 he retired to a Buddhist retreat.

Church Alonzo (1903–   ). US mathematician who in 1936 published the first precise definition of a calculable function, and so contributed enormously to the systematic development of the theory of algorithms. Church was educated at Princeton and remained there for 40 years, becoming professor of mathematics and philosophy. In 1967 he moved to the University of California in Los Angeles.

Church Frederick Edwin (1826–1900). US painter. He was a student of Thomas Cole and follower of the Hudson River School's tradition of grand landscape. During the 1850s he visited South America and the Arctic and became known for his meticulous and dramatic depictions of exotic landscapes. He is known for his portrayal of light, as in *Heart of the Andes* 1855 and *Niagara Falls* 1857.

Churchill Caryl (1938–   ). English dramatist. Her plays include the innovative and feminist *Cloud Nine* 1979 and *Top Girls* 1982, a study of the hazards encountered by 'career' women throughout history; *Serious Money* 1987, which satirized the world of London's brash young financial brokers; and *Mad Forest* 1990, set in Romania during the overthrow of the Ceausescu regime. Her most recent works include a translation of Seneca's *Thyestes*, and *The Skriker*, both 1994.

Churchill Charles (1731–1764). English satirical poet. At one time a priest in the Church of England, he wrote coarse personal satires dealing with political issues. His poems include *The Rosciad* 1761, a satire on the London stage; *The Prophecy of Famine* 1763, the first of his political satires; and *Epistle to Hogarth* 1763, which he wrote after a quarrel with the English artist, William Hogarth.

A joke's a very serious thing.

CHARLES CHURCHILL
The Ghost bk 4 1764

Churchill Lord Randolph Henry Spencer (1849–1895). British Conservative politician, chancellor of the Exchequer and leader of the House of Commons 1886; father of Winston Churchill.

Born at Blenheim Palace, son of the 7th duke of Marlborough, he entered Parliament 1874. In 1880 he formed a Conservative group known as the Fourth Party with Drummond Wolff (1830–1908), J E Gorst, and Arthur Balfour, and in 1885 his policy of Tory democracy was widely accepted by the party. In 1886 he became chancellor of the Exchequer, but resigned within six months because he did not agree with the demands made on the Treasury by the War Office and the Admiralty. In 1874 he married Jennie Jerome (1854–1921), daughter of a wealthy New Yorker.

The duty of an Opposition is to oppose.

RANDOLPH CHURCHILL
quoted in W S Churchill *Life of Lord Randolph Churchill* vol 1 ch 5 1906

Churchill Winston Leonard Spencer (1874–1965). British Conservative politician, prime minister 1940–45 and 1951–55. In Parliament from 1900, as a Liberal until 1923, he held a number of ministerial offices, including First Lord of the Admiralty 1911–15 and chancellor of the Exchequer 1924–29. Absent from the cabinet in the 1930s, he returned Sept 1939 to lead a coalition government 1940–45, negotiating with Allied leaders in World War II to achieve the unconditional surrender of Germany 1945; he led a Conservative government 1951–55. He received the Nobel Prize for Literature 1953. Knight of the Garter 1953.

He was born at Blenheim Palace, the elder son of Lord Randolph Churchill. During the Boer War he was a war correspondent and made a dramatic escape from imprisonment in Pretoria. In 1900 he was elected Conservative member of Parliament for Oldham, but he disagreed with Chamberlain's tariff-reform policy and joined the Liberals. Asquith made him president of the Board of Trade 1908, where he introduced legislation for the establishment of labour exchanges. He became home secretary 1910. In 1911 Asquith appointed him First Lord of the Admiralty. In 1915–16 he served in the trenches in France, but then resumed his parliamentary duties and was minister of munitions under Lloyd George 1917, when he was concerned with the development of the tank. After the armistice he was secretary for war 1918–21 and then as colonial secretary played a leading part in the establishment of the Irish Free State. During the postwar years he was active in support of the Whites (anti-Bolsheviks) in Russia.

It was a nation and race dwelling all around the globe that had the lion's heart. I had the luck to be called upon to give the roar.

WINSTON CHURCHILL
Speech on his eightieth birthday 30 Nov 1954

In 1922–24 Churchill was out of Parliament. He left the Liberals 1923, and was returned for Epping as a Conservative 1924. Baldwin made him chancellor of the Exchequer, and he brought about Britain's return to the gold standard and was prominent in the defeat of the General Strike 1926. In 1929–39 he was out of office as he disagreed with the Conservatives on India, rearmament, and Chamberlain's policy of appeasement.

On the first day of World War II he went back to his old post at the Admiralty. In May 1940 he was called to the premiership as head of an all-party administration and made a much quoted 'blood, tears, toil, and sweat' speech to the House of Commons. He had a close relationship with US president Roosevelt, and in Aug 1941 concluded the Atlantic Charter with him. He travelled to Washington, Casablanca, Cairo, Moscow, and Tehran, meeting the other leaders of the Allied war effort. He met Stalin and Roosevelt in the Crimea Feb 1945 and agreed on the final plans for victory. On 8 May he announced the unconditional surrender of Germany.

The coalition was dissolved 23 May 1945, and Churchill formed a caretaker government drawn mainly from the Conservatives. Defeated in the general election July, he became leader of the opposition until the election Oct 1951, in which he again became prime minister. In April 1955 he resigned. His home from 1922, Chartwell in Kent, is a museum. His books include a six-volume history of World War II (1948–54) and a four-volume *History of the English-Speaking Peoples* (1956–58).

Suggested reading
Brendan, P *Churchill: A Brief Life* (1987)
Churchill, Winston *My Early Life* (1930)
Gilbert, M *Churchill: A Life* (1991)
Manchester, W *The Last Lion: Visions of Glory* (1983)
Manchester, W *The Caged Lion* (1988)
Taylor, A J P and others *Churchill Revisited: A Critical Assessment* (1969)

Chu Ta (Pa Ta Shan Jen) (*c.* 1625–*c.* 1705). Chinese painter. A member of the Ming imperial family, he became a Buddhist priest and led a solitary life. He painted many landscapes but is better known for his often whimsical portrayals of birds, animals, and plants. His style is remarkable for its simplicity and spontaneity, a bird or leaf being depicted with just a few bold strokes.

Ciano Galeazzo, Count (1903–1944). Italian Fascist politician. Son-in-law of the dictator Mussolini, he was foreign minister and member of the Fascist Supreme Council 1936–43. He voted against Mussolini at the meeting of the Grand Council July 1943 that overthrew the dictator, but was later tried for treason and shot by the Fascists.

What times, what customs!

CICERO
In Catilinam I. 1

Cicero Marcus Tullius (106–43 BC). Roman orator, writer, and politician. His speeches and philosophical and rhetorical works are models of Latin prose, and his letters provide a picture of contemporary Roman life. As consul 63 BC he exposed the Roman politician Catiline's conspiracy in four major orations.

Born in Arpinium, Cicero became an advocate in Rome, spent three years in Greece studying oratory, and after the dictator Sulla's death distinguished himself in Rome with the prosecution of the corrupt Roman governor, Verres. When the First Triumvirate was formed 59 BC, Cicero was briefly exiled and devoted himself to literature. He sided with Pompey during the civil war (49–48) but was pardoned by Julius Caesar and returned to Rome. After Caesar's assassination 44 BC he supported Octavian (the future emperor Augustus) and violently attacked Antony in speeches known as the *Philippics*. On the reconciliation of Antony and Octavian, he was executed by Antony's agents.

Suggested reading
Dorey, T A *Cicero* (1965)
Mitchell, T N *Cicero* (1979)
Powell, J G F (ed) *Cicero the Philosopher* (1995)
Rawson, Elizabeth *Cicero: A Portrait* (1983)
Stockton, D *Cicero: A Political Biography* (1971)

O fortunate Rome, to have been born in my consulship.

CICERO
On his Consulship fr. 7

Cid, El (Rodrigo Díaz de Bivar) (*c.* 1043–1099). Spanish soldier, nicknamed El Cid ('the lord') by the Moors. Born in Castile of a noble family, he fought against the king of Navarre and won his nickname el Campeador ('the Champion') by killing the Navarrese champion in single combat. Essentially a mercenary, fighting both with and against the Moors, he died while defending Valencia against them, and in subsequent romances became Spain's national hero.

Much of El Cid's present-day reputation is the result of the exploitation of the legendary character as a model Christian military hero by the Nationalists during the Civil War, with Franco presented as a modern equivalent in his reconquest of Spain.

Cierva Juan de la (1895–1936). Spanish engineer. In trying to produce an aircraft that would not stall and could fly slowly, he invented the autogiro 1923, the forerunner of the helicopter but differing from it in having unpowered rotors that revolve freely.

Cierva was born in Murcia and studied engineering in Madrid. He was twice elected to the Cortes (parliament), in 1919 and 1922. In 1925 he founded the Cierva Autogyro Company in the UK. Test-flying his own aircraft, he was killed in a crash in Croydon, S London.

Ciller Tansu (1946–). Turkish politician, prime minister from 1993. A forthright exponent of free-market economic policies, she won the leadership of the centre-right True Path Party and the premiership on the election of Suleyman Demirel as president. Her support for a military, as opposed to a diplomatic, approach to Kurdish insurgency provoked international criticism; in 1995 relations with her coalition partners deteriorated, and a general election was called for Dec.

Trained as an economist, Ciller became economic adviser to Prime Minister Demirel 1990. She joined the government 1991 and, on assuming the premiership May 1993, embarked on an extensive economic-reform programme, combining privatization with austerity measures.

Cimabue Giovanni, (Cenni di Peppi) (*c.* 1240–1302). Italian painter. Active in Florence, he is traditionally styled the 'father of Italian painting'. His paintings retain the golden background of Byzantine art but the figures have a new naturalism. Among the works attributed to him are *Maestà* about 1280 (Uffizi, Florence), a huge Gothic image of the Virgin, with a novel softness and solidity that points forwards to Giotto.

Very little is known of his life, though he worked in Rome, where he may have received his training, also at Pisa and Florence. He is buried in the cathedral at Florence. The brief reference by his contemporary Dante indicates that he was famous in his own time and believed himself without equal, but was eclipsed in fame by Giotto. Vasari's account of him lacks historical confirmation, and a number of works attributed to him, such as the Rucellai altarpiece of Santa Maria Novella, Florence, are now assigned to Duccio or his school. His only certainly authentic work is the figure of St John in the absidal mosaic of Pisa Cathedral. Frescoes in the Upper Church of St Francis, Assisi (much deteriorated), are credibly attributed to him, and also the versions of the *Maestà* (Madonna and Child with Angels) now in the Uffizi and Louvre, Byzantine in conception but showing a far from conventional vigour of line and humanity of expression. His *Crucifix* in Sta Croce, Florence, was damaged by the flood of 1966.

Cimarosa Domenico (1749–1801). Italian composer. His witty operas include *Il Matrimonio segreto/The Secret Marriage* 1792. He also wrote orchestral and keyboard music.

Cimino Michael (1943–). US film director. His reputation was made by *The Deer Hunter* 1978, a moral epic set against the Vietnam War (five Academy Awards). A later film, the Western *Heaven's Gate* 1980, lost its backers, United Artists, some $40 million, and subsequently became a byword for commercial disaster in the industry.

He also made *The Year of the Dragon* 1986, and *Desperate Hours* 1990.

Cimon (*c.* 512–449 BC). Athenian general, son of Miltiades. He helped Aristides in the formation of the Delian League (478–77 BC) against Persia and campaigned repeatedly in the Aegean, defeating the Persians decisively at the battle of Eurymedon *c.* 467 BC. He induced Athens to aid the suppression of the helots in Sparta 462 BC, the failure of which led to his ostracism 461–457 BC. He returned to lead an expedition against Cyprus in 449 BC, where he died.

Cincinnatus Lucius Quinctius (born *c.* 519 BC). Roman general. Appointed dictator 458 BC, he defeated the Aequi (an Italian people) in a brief campaign, then resumed life as a yeoman farmer. He became a legend for his republican idealism.

Claes Willy (1938–). Belgian politician, secretary-general of the North Atlantic Treaty Organization (NATO) 1994–95. With a proven reputation as a consensus-builder, he was a clear favourite for the post, but subsequent allegations about his involvement (while Belgian foreign minister) in illegal dealings with Agusta, the Italian aircraft manufacturer, eventually forced his resignation Nov 1995.

Prior to becoming secretary-general, he was Belgium's foreign affairs minister and deputy prime minister. A Flemish-speaking socialist, he had risen to high political office via the trade union movement.

Clair René. Adopted name of René-Lucien Chomette (1898–1981). French filmmaker. He was originally a poet, novelist, and journalist. His early comedy *Sous les Toits de Paris/Under the Roofs of Paris* 1930 made great use of the new innovation of sound. His other films include *Entr'acte* 1924, *Le Million* 1931, *A nous la Liberté* 1931, *Le Silence est d'Or* 1947, and *Porte des Lilas* 1957.

Clampitt Amy (1920–1994). US poet. Her first major collection of poems, *The Kingfisher* 1983, influenced by the poetry of Gerard Manley Hopkins, contained descriptions of the New England coast.

Working for a publisher in New York from the 1940s, she did not begin to write poetry until the 1960s, and she published her first work, *Multitudes, Multitudes* 1974, at her own expense. From then on her poems were regularly published in such magazines as the *New Yorker*. Later volumes of poetry included *What the Light was Like* 1985, *Archaic Figure* 1987, *Westward* 1990, and *A Silence Opens* 1994.

Clapperton Hugh (1788–1827). English explorer who crossed the Sahara from Tripoli with Dixon Denham (1785–1828) and reached Lake Chad, of whose existence they had been unaware, 1823. With his servant Richard Lander (1804–1834), he attempted to reach the river Niger, but died at Sokoto. Lander eventually reached the mouth of the Niger 1830.

Clapton Eric (1945–). English blues and rock guitarist, singer, and songwriter. Originally a blues purist, then one of the pioneers of heavy rock with Cream 1966–68, he returned to the blues after making the landmark album *Layla and Other Assorted Love Songs* 1970 by Derek and the Dominos. Solo albums include *Journeyman* 1989 and the acoustic *Unplugged* 1992, for which he received six Grammy awards 1993.

Clapton, born in Surrey, was a member of the Yardbirds 1963–65 but left when the group turned from rhythm and blues to experimental rock. During his year with John Mayall's Bluesbreakers 1965–66, 'Clapton is God' graffiti began to appear on British walls. After the groundbreaking rock of Cream, he formed the short-lived supergroup Blind Faith 1969. He sought a lower profile 1970–72, playing with US duo Delaney and Bonnie, and adopted a more laid-back style with his solo album *461 Ocean Boulevard* 1974. Other albums include *Money and Cigarettes* 1983 and *August* 1986.

Clare John (1793–1864). English poet. His work includes *Poems Descriptive of Rural Life and Scenery* 1820, *The Village Minstrel* 1821, and *The Shepherd's Calendar* 1827. The dignified simplicity and truth of his descriptions of both landscape and emotions have been rediscovered and appreciated in the 20th century.

Born at Helpstone, near Peterborough, the son of a farm labourer, Clare spent most of his life in poverty. He was given an annuity from the Duke of Exeter and other patrons, but had to turn to work on the land. He spent his last 20 years in Northampton asylum. His early life is described in his autobiography, first published 1931.

He could not die when trees were green, / For he loved the time too well.

JOHN CLARE
'The Dying Child'

Clare, St (c. 1194–1253). Christian saint. Born in Assisi, Italy, at 18 she became a follower of St Francis, who founded for her the convent of San Damiano. Here she gathered the first members of the Order of Poor Clares. In 1958 she was proclaimed the patron saint of television by Pius XII, since in 1252 she saw from her convent sickbed the Christmas services being held in the Basilica of St Francis in Assisi. Feast day 12 Aug. Canonized 1255.

It is his combination of marvellous style and personal insight, experience and need for self-justification that makes his history so readable, so important and so untrustworthy to posterity.

Ronald Hutton on EDWARD HYDE, EARL OF CLARENDON
in *Blackwell's Dictionary of Historians* 1988

Clarendon Edward Hyde, 1st Earl of Clarendon (1609–1674). English politician and historian, chief adviser to Charles II 1651–67. A member of Parliament 1640, he joined the Royalist side 1641. The Clarendon Code 1661–65, a series of acts passed by the government, was directed at Nonconformists (or Dissenters) and was designed to secure the supremacy of the Church of England.

In the Short and Long Parliaments Clarendon attacked Charles I's unconstitutional actions and supported the impeachment of Charles's minister Strafford. In 1641 he broke with the revolutionary party and became one of the royal advisers. When civil war began he followed Charles to Oxford, and was knighted and made chancellor of the Exchequer. On the king's defeat 1646 he followed Prince Charles to Jersey, where he began his *History of the Rebellion*, published 1702–04, which provides memorable portraits of his contemporaries. In 1651 he became chief adviser to the exiled Charles II. At the Restoration he was created Earl of Clarendon, while his influence was further increased by the marriage of his daughter Anne to James, Duke of York. His moderation earned the hatred of the extremists, however, and he lost Charles's support by openly expressing disapproval of the king's private life. After the disasters of the Dutch war 1667, he went into exile. Knighted 1643, baron 1660.

Clarendon George William Frederick Villiers, 4th Earl of Clarendon (1800–1870). British Liberal diplomat, lord lieutenant of Ireland 1847–52, foreign secretary 1853–58, 1865–66, and 1868–70. Succeeded to earldom 1838.

He was posted to Ireland at the time of the potato famine. His diplomatic skill was shown at the Congress of Paris 1856 and in the settlement of the dispute between Britain and the USA over the *Alabama* cruiser.

Clark (Charles) Manning (Hope) (1915–). Australian historian. He was first professor of Australian history at the Australian National University 1949–75. His writings, television appearances, outspoken political stance opposing, for example, the Vietnam War and his comments on Australian culture have made him a public figure. His six-volume *A History of Australia* 1962–87 has attracted both intense admiration and criticism.

Clark (Harold) Gene (1941–1991). US rock and folk singer, songwriter, and guitarist, a founder member 1964–66 of the influential rock group the Byrds; he was a member of the New Christy Minstrels (a folk group) 1963–64, and later of Dillard & Clark, a bluegrass duo; he also recorded solo.

Clark George Rogers (1752–1818). American military leader and explorer. He was made commander of the Virginia frontier militia at the outbreak of the American Revolution 1775. During 1778–79 he led an attack on the Indian allies of the British to the W of the Ohio River and founded a settlement at the site of Louisville, Kentucky.

Born near Charlottesville, Virginia, Clark spent his early adult years surveying and exploring Kentucky. After the war he remained in the Northwest Territory as Indian commissioner, leading an attack on the Wabash 1786. After leaving office, he accepted commissions from the French and Spanish colonial authorities.

Clark Jim (James) (1936–1968). Scottish-born motor-racing driver who was twice world champion 1963 and 1965. He spent all his Formula One career with Lotus.

His partnership with Lotus boss Colin Chapman (1928–1982) was one of the closest in the sport. He won 25 Formula One Grand Prix races, a record at the time, before losing his life at Hockenheim, West Germany during a Formula Two race 1968.

Clark Joe (Charles Joseph) (1939–). Canadian Progressive Conservative politician who became party leader 1976, and May 1979 defeated Pierre Trudeau at the polls to become the youngest prime minister in Canada's history. Following the rejection of his government's budget, he was defeated in a second election Feb 1980. He became secretary of state for external affairs (foreign minister) 1984 in the Mulroney government.

Clark Kenneth Mackenzie, Baron Clark (1903–1983). English art historian. He was director of the National Gallery, London, 1934–45. His books include *Leonardo da Vinci* 1939, *Landscape into Art* 1949, and *The Nude* 1956, which he considered his best book.

He popularized the history of art through his television series *Civilization*, broadcast in the UK 1969, and also published a book in the same year. KCB 1938, baron 1969.

Clark Mark Wayne (1896–1984). US general in World War II. In 1942 he became Chief of Staff for ground forces, and deputy to General Eisenhower. He led a successful secret mission by submarine to get information in North Africa to prepare for the Allied invasion, and commanded the 5th Army in the invasion of Italy. He remained in this command until the end of the war when he took charge of the US occupation forces in Austria.

Clark, born in New York, fought in France in World War I and between the wars held various military appointments in the USA. He was commander in chief of the United Nations forces in the Korean War 1952–53.

Clark Michael (1962–). Scottish avant-garde dancer. His barebottomed costumes and outlandish stage props have earned him as much celebrity as his innovative dance technique. A graduate of the Royal Ballet school, he formed his own company, the Michael Clark Dance Company, in the mid-1980s and became a leading figure in the British avant-garde dance scene. In 1991 he played Caliban in Peter Greenaway's film *Prospero's Books*. He premiered his *Mmm... Modern Masterpiece* 1992.

Clark Wilfrid Edward Le Gros (1895–1971). English anatomist and surgeon whose research made a major contribution to the understanding of the structural anatomy of the brain. By emphasizing the importance of relating structure to function, he had a profound influence on the teaching of anatomy. He became professor of anatomy first at St Bartholomew's Hospital, London, then at St Thomas's, and 1934–62 at Oxford, where he created a new department of anatomy. Knighted 1955.

Clarke Arthur C(harles) (1917–). English science-fiction and nonfiction writer who originated the plan for a system of communications satellites in geostationary orbit 1945. His works include the short story 'The Sentinel' 1951 (filmed 1968 by Stanley Kubrick as *2001: A Space Odyssey*), *Childhood's End* 1953, *2010: Odyssey Two* 1982, and *The Hammer of God* 1993.

Clarke was born in Minehead, Somerset, served in the Royal Air Force during World War II, and then studied at King's College, London. He became chair of the British Interplanetary Society 1946, the year his first story was published. In 1956 he moved to Sri Lanka. His popular-science books generally concern space exploration; his fiction is marked by an optimistic belief in the potential of science and technology.

Clarke Jeremiah (c. 1669–1707). English composer. Organist at St Paul's, he composed 'The Prince of Denmark's March', a harpsichord piece that was arranged by Henry Wood as a 'Trumpet Voluntary' and wrongly attributed to Purcell.

Clarke Kenneth Harry (1940–). British Conservative politician. A cabinet minister from 1985, he held the posts of education secretary 1990–92 and home secretary 1992–93. He succeeded Norman Lamont as chancellor of the Exchequer May 1993, bringing to the office a more open and combative approach.

Clarke was politically active as a law student at Cambridge. He was elected to Parliament for Rushcliff, Nottinghamshire, 1970. From 1965–66, Clarke was secretary for the Birmingham Bow Group. He became a minister of state 1982, paymaster general 1985, with special responsibility for employment, and chancellor of the Duchy of Lancaster 1987. In 1988 he was made minister of health, in 1990 education secretary, in 1992 home secretary, and chancellor in 1993.

Clarke Marcus Andrew Hislop (1846–1881). Australian writer. Born in London, he went to Australia when he was 18 and worked as a journalist in Victoria. He wrote *For the Term of his Natural Life* 1874, a novel dealing with life in the early Australian prison settlements.

Clarke Ron(ald) William (1937–). Australian middle- and long-distance runner. He broke 17 world records, ranging from 2 miles to the one-hour run.

The first man to break 13 minutes for the 3 miles 1966, he was also the first to better 28 minutes for the 10,000 metres. Despite his record-breaking achievements, he never won a gold medal at a major championship.

Clarkson Thomas (1760–1846). British philanthropist. From 1785 he devoted himself to a campaign against slavery. He was one of the founders of the Anti-Slavery Society 1823 and was largely responsible for the abolition of slavery in British colonies 1833.

Claude Georges (1870–1960). French industrial chemist, responsible for inventing neon signs. He discovered 1896 that acetylene, normally explosive, could be safely transported when dissolved in acetone. He later demonstrated that neon gas could be used to provide a bright red light in tubes. These were displayed publicly for the first time at the Paris Motor Show 1910. As an old man, Claude spent the period 1945–49 in prison as a collaborator.

Claudel Paul Louis Charles Marie (1868–1955). French poet and dramatist. A fervent Catholic, he was influenced by the Symbolists and achieved an effect of mystic allegory in such plays as *L'Annonce faite à Marie*/*Tidings Brought to Mary* 1912 and *Le Soulier de satin*/*The Satin Slipper* 1929, set in 16th-century Spain. His verse includes *Cinq Grandes Odes*/*Five Great Odes* 1910.

Claude Lorrain (Claude Gelée) (1600–1682). French landscape painter. He was active in Rome from 1627. His distinctive, luminous, Classical style had a great impact on late 17th- and 18th-century taste. In his paintings, insignificant figures (mostly mythological or historical) are typically lost in great expanses of poetic scenery, as in *The Enchanted Castle* 1664 (National Gallery, London).

Left an orphan as a child, he is thought to have lived for a while with his brother, a woodcarver, at Freiburg, and is said to have worked in his early days as a pastry cook. Travelling merchants, possibly relatives, took the boy to Italy, where he found humble employment in artists' studios. He may have studied under an obscure view-painter, Gottfried Waals, at Naples, and at Rome was servant-assistant to Agostino Tassi, the landscape painter and former pupil of Paul Bril. He made one journey back to his native country 1625, but at the age of 27 settled in Rome, where he spent the rest of his life, painting works which were highly esteemed and in great demand among patrons resident in Rome, and visiting connoisseurs, French and English. His pictorial record of his compositions, the *Liber Veritatis* (engraved by Earlom in 1777), seems to have been as much a reference list of works that had gone abroad as a list of authentic pictures that could expose forgery.

Claudet Antoine François Jean (1797–1867). French-born pioneer of photography. Working in London, he made daguerreotype portraiture commercially viable when he discovered that chlorine and iodine vapour increased the sensitivity of the plate and greatly reduced exposure time. His other innovations include the earliest light meter and the introduction of painted backgrounds into studio portraits.

Claudian (Claudius Claudianus) (c. 370–404). Last of the great Latin poets of the Roman Empire. He was probably born in Alexandria, Egypt. He wrote official panegyrics, epigrams, and the mythological epic *The Rape of Proserpine*.

Claudius (Tiberius Claudius Drusus Nero Germanicus) (10 BC– AD 54). Nephew of Tiberius, made Roman emperor by his troops AD 41, after the murder of his nephew Caligula. Claudius was a scholar, historian, and able administrator. During his reign the Roman empire was considerably extended, and in 43 he took part in the invasion of Britain.

His rule was marked by the increased political power enjoyed by his private secretaries who exercised ministerial functions. Claudius was dominated by his third wife, Messalina, whom he ultimately had executed, and is thought to have been poisoned by his fourth wife, Agrippina the Younger.

Clausewitz Carl Philipp Gottlieb von (1780–1831). Prussian officer whose book *Vom Kriege*/*On War* 1833 exerted a powerful influence on military strategists well into the 20th century. Although he advocated the total destruction of an enemy's forces as one of the strategic targets of warfare, his most important idea was to see war as an extension of political policy and not as an end in itself.

Clausius Rudolf Julius Emanuel (1822–1888). German physicist, one of the founders of the science of thermodynamics. In 1850 he enunciated its second law: heat cannot pass from a colder to a hotter body. He became professor of physics at Zürich 1855, returning to Germany 1867 for similar posts first at Würtzburg and then at Bonn.

According to Clausius, there are two types of entropy: the conversion of heat into work, and the transfer of heat from high to low temperature. He concluded that entropy must inevitably increase in the universe.

Clavell James du Maresq (1924–1994). British writer, scriptwriter, film director, and producer. His best-selling novels include *King Rat* 1962, *Taipan* 1966, *Shogun* 1975, *Noble House* 1981, *Whirlwind* 1986, *Gai-Jin* 1993. His highly successful work as a scriptwriter included the cult sci-fi film *The Fly* 1958, the prisoner-of-war drama *The Great Escape* 1966, and *To Sir With Love* 1966, which he wrote, directed, and produced. In 1941 he was captured by the Japanese in Java and, at the age of 18, was shipped to Changi jail in Singapore, where he remained until the end of the war.

In 1953 he moved to Hollywood where he embarked on his career as a scriptwriter and, later, producer and director. By the time his film, *The Last Valley* 1969, a meditation on men at war starring Michael Caine, appeared, Clavell was already established as a best-selling novelist.

Claverhouse John Graham, Viscount Dundee (c. 1649–1689). Scottish soldier. Appointed by Charles II to suppress the Covenanters from 1677, he was routed at Drumclog 1679, but three weeks later won the battle of Bothwell Bridge, by which the rebellion was crushed. Until 1688 he was engaged in continued persecution and became known as 'Bloody Clavers', regarded by the Scottish people as a figure of evil. His army then joined the first Jacobite rebellion and defeated the loyalist forces in the pass of Killiecrankie, where he was mortally wounded. Viscount 1688.

Clay Cassius Marcellus, Jr. Original name of boxer Muhammad ◊Ali.

Clay Frederic (1838–1889). English composer. Clay wrote light operas and the cantata *Lalla Rookh* 1877, based on a poem by Thomas Moore.

I had rather be right than be President.

HENRY CLAY
Remark to Senator Preston of South Carolina 1839

Clay Henry (1777–1852). US politician. He stood unsuccessfully three times for the presidency: as a Democratic Republican 1824, as a National Republican 1832, and as a Whig 1844. He supported the war of 1812 against Britain, and tried to hold the Union together on the slavery issue by the Missouri Compromise of 1820 and again in the compromise of 1850. He was secretary of state 1825–29 and devised an 'American system' for the national economy.

A powerful orator, he was a strong leader of the House of Representatives. He fought a duel over the accusation that he had struck a corrupt deal with John Quincy Adams to ensure the latter would be named president by the House in 1824.

Clay Lucius DuBignon (1897–1978). US commander in chief of the US occupation forces in Germany 1947–49. He broke the Soviet blockade of Berlin 1948 after 327 days, with an airlift – a term he brought into general use – which involved bringing all supplies into West Berlin by air.

Clayton Jack (1921–1995). English film director, originally a producer. His first feature, *Room at the Top* 1958, heralded a new maturity in British cinema, not only for the frankness of its sex scenes, but also for the harshly drawn realism of its setting in the north of England. Other works include *The Innocents* 1961, *The Great Gatsby* 1974, and *The Lonely Passion of Judith Hearne* 1987.

Cleaver (Leroy) Eldridge (1935–   ). US political activist. He joined the Black Panthers 1967, becoming minister of information, and stood for US president 1968. After a fight with the police, he fled to Cuba 1968 and Algeria 1969. His political autobiography *Soul on Ice* was published 1968.

While in prison 1957–66, Cleaver became a Black Muslim minister. Later he became a born-again Christian in France, and toured the USA as an evangelist. His *Post-Prison Writings and Speeches* were published 1969.

This parrot is no more. It's ceased to be. It has expired. The parrot has gone to meet its maker. This is a late parrot ... If you hadn't nailed it to the perch, it would be pushin' up the daisies.

JOHN CLEESE
'Monty Python's Flying Circus' 1969

Cleese John Harwood (1939–   ). English actor and comedian. He has written for and appeared in both television programmes and films. On British television, he is particularly associated with the comedy series *Monty Python's Flying Circus* and *Fawlty Towers*. His films include *Monty Python and the Holy Grail* 1974, *The Life of Brian* 1979, and *A Fish Called Wanda* 1988.

He also wrote for and appeared in the satirical television programmes *That Was The Week That Was* and *The Frost Report*.

Cleisthenes (*c.* 570–*c.* 508 BC). Athenian statesman, the founder of Athenian democracy. He was exiled with his family, the Alcmaeonidae, and intrigued and campaigned against the Athenian tyrants, the Pisistratids. After their removal in 510 BC he developed a popular faction in favour of democracy, which was established by his reforms over the next decade.

Truth! stark naked truth is the word.

JOHN CLELAND
Memoirs of a Woman of Pleasure, also known as *Fanny Hill* 1750

Cleland John (1709–1789). English author. He is best known for his bawdy novel *Fanny Hill, the Memoirs of a Woman of Pleasure* 1748–49 which he wrote to free himself from his creditors. The book was considered immoral.

Cleland was called before the Privy Council, but was granted a pension to prevent further misdemeanours.

It is easier to make war than to make peace.

GEORGES CLEMENCEAU
Speech at Verdun 20 July 1919

Clemenceau *French prime minister Georges Clemenceau. An outspoken radical, his appointment of Marshal Foch secured the victory of the Allies in World War I.*

Clemenceau Georges (1841–1929). French politician and journalist (prominent in the defence of Alfred Dreyfus). He was prime minister 1906–09 and 1917–20. After World War I he presided over the peace conference in Paris that drew up the Treaty of Versailles, but failed to secure for France the Rhine as a frontier.

Clemenceau was mayor of Montmartre, Paris, in the war of 1870, and 1871 was elected a member of the National Assembly at Bordeaux. He was elected a deputy 1876 after the formation of the Third Republic. An extreme radical, he soon earned the nickname of 'the Tiger' on account of his ferocious attacks on politicians whom he disliked. He lost his seat 1893 and spent the next ten years in journalism. In 1902 he was elected senator for the Var, and was soon one of the most powerful politicians in France. When he became prime minister for the second time 1917, he made the decisive appointment of Marshal Foch as supreme commander.

Suggested reading
Dallas, Gregor *At the Heart of a Tiger: Clemenceau and His World* (1993)
Gottfried, Ted *Georges Clemenceau* (1987)
Watson, D R *Clemenceau: A Political Biography* (1976)

Clemens Samuel Langhorne. Real name of the US writer Mark ◊Twain.

Clement VII (1478–1534). Pope 1523–34. He refused to allow the divorce of Henry VIII of England and Catherine of Aragon. Illegitimate son of a brother of Lorenzo de' Medici, the ruler of

Florence, he commissioned monuments for the Medici chapel in Florence from the Renaissance artist Michelangelo.

For lust is not easily restrained, when it has no fear.

CLEMENT OF ALEXANDRIA
Exhortation to the Greeks ch iv 43

Clement of Alexandria (c. AD 150–c. 215). Greek theologian who applied Greek philosophical ideas to Christian doctrine, believing that Greek philosophy was a divine gift to humanity. He was one of the early Christian writers whose writings are considered authoritative by the church, known as fathers of the church. His works include *The Exhortation to the Greeks* and *Miscellanies*.

Clement of Rome, St (lived late 1st century AD). One of the early Christian leaders and writers known as the fathers of the church. According to tradition he was the third or fourth bishop of Rome, and a disciple of St Peter. He was pope AD 88–97 or 92–101. He wrote a letter addressed to the church at Corinth (First Epistle of Clement), and many other writings have been attributed to him.

Clemente Francesco (1952–). Italian painter. He was at the forefront of Neo-Expressionism in the 1970s. His use of hand-drawn imagery, rendered in an expressive, naive, and colourful style, was a reaction to the high-tech approach of Photorealism. The erotic, gesturing figures that characterize his work are frequently mutilated and often images of himself, as in *Midnight Sun No VI* 1982 (private collection).

Roman art and Indian mystical and folkloric references have provided the inspiration for much of his work.

Clemente Roberto Walker (1934–1972). Puerto Rican-born US baseball player who played for the Pittsburgh Pirates 1955–72. He had a career batting average of .317, was the 11th player in history to reach 3,000 hits, and was an outstanding right fielder.

Clemente was born in Carolina, Puerto Rico. He led the league in hitting four times, hit 240 career home runs, and was the National League's Most Valuable Player 1966. He died in a plane crash while flying to aid Nicaraguan earthquake victims. He was elected to the Baseball Hall of Fame 1973.

Clementi Muzio (1752–1832). Italian pianist and composer. He settled in London 1782 as a teacher and then as proprietor of a successful piano and music business. He was the founder of the present-day technique of piano playing, and his series of studies, *Gradus ad Parnassum* 1817, is still in use.

Clements John Selby (1910–1988). English actor and director. His productions included revivals of Restoration comedies and the plays of George Bernard Shaw. Knighted 1968.

Cleon stripped the assembly of its decorum, setting the fashion of yelling when he harangued the people, of throwing back his robe, slapping his thigh and running about while speaking.

Plutarch on CLEON
in *Life of Nicias* ch 8.3

Cleon (died 422 BC). Athenian politician and general in the Peloponnesian War. He became 'leader of the people' (demagogue) after the death of Pericles to whom he was opposed. He was an aggressive imperialist and advocated a vigorous war policy against the Spartans. He was killed by the Spartans at Amphipolis 422 BC.

Cleopatra (c. 68–30 BC). Queen of Egypt 51–48 and 47–30 BC. When the Roman general Julius Caesar arrived in Egypt, he restored her to the throne from which she had been ousted. Cleopatra and Caesar became lovers and she went with him to Rome. After Caesar's assassination 44 BC she returned to Alexandria and resumed her position as queen of Egypt. In 41 BC she was joined there by Mark Antony, one of Rome's rulers. In 31 BC Rome declared war on Egypt and scored a decisive victory in the naval Battle of Actium off the W coast of Greece. Cleopatra fled with her 60 ships to Egypt; Antony abandoned the struggle and followed her. Both he and Cleopatra committed suicide.

Cleopatra was Macedonian, and the last ruler of the Macedonian dynasty, which ruled Egypt from 323 until annexation by Rome 31. She succeeded her father Ptolemy XII jointly with her brother Ptolemy XIII, and they ruled together from 51 to 49 BC, when she was expelled by him.

Her reinstatement in 48 BC by Caesar caused a war between Caesar and Ptolemy XIII, who was defeated and killed. The younger brother, Ptolemy XIV, was elevated to the throne and married to her, in the tradition of the pharaohs, although she actually lived with Caesar and they had a son, Ptolemy XV, known as Caesarion (he was later killed by Octavian).

Yet she, seeking to die a nobler death, showed for the dagger's point no woman's fear.

Horace on CLEOPATRA
in *Odes* 1 37: 21

After Caesar's death, Cleopatra and Mark Antony had three sons, and he divorced in 32 BC his wife Octavia, the sister of Octavian, who then induced the Roman senate to declare war on Egypt. Shakespeare's play *Antony and Cleopatra* recounts that Cleopatra killed herself with an asp (poisonous snake) after Antony's suicide.

Film versions of her life were made 1934 and 1963.
Suggested reading
Grant, Michael *Cleopatra* (1972)
Hughes-Hallett, Lucy *Cleopatra* (1990)
Lindsay, Jack *Cleopatra* (1971)
Volkmann, H *Cleopatra* (trs 1958)

Clerides Glafkos John (1919–). Greek Cypriot lawyer and politician, president of Cyprus from 1993. Leader of the right-of-centre Democratic Rally, he unsuccessfully contested the presidency 1978, 1983, and 1988, and then won it by a narrow majority 1993 at the age of 73. His personal ties with the Turkish leader, Rauf Denktas, raised expectations that he might be more successful than his predecessors in resolving his country's divisions.

Cleve Per Teodor (1840–1905). Swedish chemist and geologist who discovered the elements holmium and hulium 1879. He also demonstrated that the substance didymium, previously supposed to be an element, was in fact two elements, now known as neodymium and praseodymium.

Towards the end of his life he developed a method for identifying the age of glacial and postglacial deposits from the diatom fossils found in them.

Cleveland (Stephen) Grover (1837–1908). 22nd and 24th president of the USA, 1885–89 and 1893–97; the first Democratic president elected after the Civil War, and the only president to hold office for two nonconsecutive terms. He attempted to check corruption in public life, and in 1895 initiated arbitration proceedings that eventually settled a territorial dispute with Britain concerning the Venezuelan boundary.

An unswerving conservative, Cleveland refused to involve the government in economic affairs. Within a year of his taking office for the second time, 4 million were unemployed and the USA was virtually bankrupt. *See illustration on page 190.*
Suggested reading
Tugwell, R G *Grover Cleveland* (1968)
Merrill, H S *President Grover Cleveland* (1957)
Welch, R E, Jr *The Presidencies of Grover Cleveland* (1988)

Cliff Clarice (1899–1972). English pottery designer. Her Bizarre ware, characterized by brightly coloured floral and geometric decoration on often geometrically shaped china, became increasingly popular in the 1930s and increasingly collectable in the 1970s and 1980s.

Cleveland *The 22nd and 24th president of the United States, Grover Cleveland, a Democrat. Cleveland is the only president to have served for two non-consecutive terms of office.*

Born in the Potteries, she started as a factory apprentice at the age of 13, trained at evening classes and worked for many years at the Wilkinson factory. In 1963 she became art director of the factory, which was part of the Royal Staffordshire Pottery in Burslem.

Clifford William Kingdon (1845–1879). English mathematician and scientific philosopher who developed the theory of biquaternions and made advances in non-Euclidean geometry. Clifford parallels and Clifford surfaces are named after him.

Clifford was born in Exeter, Devon, and educated at Cambridge, where he spent his academic career until 1871, when he was appointed professor of applied mathematics at University College, London. From 1876 he lived in the Mediterranean region.

Clift (Edward) Montgomery (1920–1966). US film and theatre actor. A star of the late 1940s and 1950s in films such as *Red River* 1948, *A Place in the Sun* 1951, and *From Here to Eternity* 1953, he was disfigured in a car accident in 1957 but continued to make films. He played the title role in *Freud* 1962.

There is nothing wrong with America that cannot be cured by what is right with America.

BILL CLINTON
Inaugural speech as US president, 1993

Clinton Bill (William Jefferson) (1946–). 42nd president of the USA from 1993, a Democrat. He served as governor of Arkansas 1979–81 and 1983–93, establishing a liberal and progressive reputation. As president, he sought to implement a New Democrat programme, combining social reform with economic conservatism as a means of bringing the country out of recession. He was initially successful in introducing legislation to reduce the federal deficit and cut crime, but the loss of both houses of Congress to the Republicans in the 1994 midterm elections presented a serious obstacle to further social reform.

Born in the railway town of Hope, Arkansas, Clinton graduated from Georgetown University 1968, won a Rhodes scholarship to Oxford University 1968–70, and graduated from Yale University Law School 1973. He was elected attorney general for Arkansas 1975. With running mate Al Gore, he won the 1992 presidential campaign by focusing on domestic issues and the ailing economy. He became the first Democrat in the White House for 13 years.

During his first year in office Clinton secured passage of an ambitious deficit-reduction plan, combining spending cuts with tax increases targeted against the rich, and won Congressional approval of the controversial North American Free Trade Agreement (NAFTA) and wide-ranging anticrime bills. His alleged involvement in irregular financial dealings in the 1980s (the Whitewater affair) thereafter clouded his presidency and in the autumn of 1994 his much-championed health-care reform proposals were blocked by Congress. A subsequent diplomatic success in Haiti and the return of its democratically elected president Aristide failed to prevent a devastating defeat for his party in the Nov 1994 midterm elections.

In June 1995 Clinton issued the first veto of his presidency in an attempt to block proposed cuts in public-spending programmes that had earlier been approved by Congress. The Israeli–PLO accord on the West Bank, the Bosnia-Herzegovina peace agreements in the former Yugoslavia, and the Northern Ireland cease-fire have been significant foreign policy successes for the Clinton administration.

Clinton De Witt (1769–1828). American political leader. After serving in the US Senate 1802–03, he was elected mayor of New York City 1803–15 and governor of New York from 1817. A strong promoter of the Erie Canal, he was instrumental in the initiation of that project, completed 1825.

Born in Little Britain, New York, Clinton was educated at Columbia University, studied law, and became the personal assistant of his uncle George Clinton, governor of New York. He served in the state legislature 1797–1802 serving simultaneously as lieutenant governor.

Clinton Hillary Diane Rodham (1947–). US lawyer and First Lady. In 1993 President Clinton appointed her to head his task force on the reform of the national health-care system, but her proposal of health insurance for all US citizens was blocked by Congress in 1994. In 1994 the Justice Department appointed a special prosecutor to

Clinton, Bill *Bill Clinton who defeated George Bush in the US presidential election of November 1992 to become the first Democratic president for 12 years. He had been governor of Arkansas since 1983.*

COBDEN

investigate the Whitewater affair relating to alleged irregularities in property deals made by the Clintons in Arkansas.

Hillary Rodham was born in Chicago. She graduated from Yale law school 1973 and married Bill Clinton 1975. She was one of the team of lawyers appointed to work on the impeachment of President Richard Nixon 1974. The Clintons moved to Arkansas 1976, and she joined the Rose law firm. As head of the Arkansas Education Standards Committee from 1983, she succeeded in getting the state to pass a law 1985 allowing the dismissal of teachers for incompetence.

Clive Robert, 1st Baron Clive (1725–1774). British soldier and administrator who established British rule in India by victories over French troops at Arcot 1751 and over the nawab of Bengal at Plassey 1757. He was governor of Bengal 1757–60 and 1765–66. Baron (Irish peerage) 1762. On his return to Britain in 1766, his wealth led to allegations that he had abused his power. Although acquitted, he committed suicide.
Suggested reading
Edwardes, M *Plassey: The Founding of an Empire* (1970)
Lawford, J *Clive* (1976)
Stephens, L *Robert Clive and Imperialism* (1981)
Turnbull, P *Clive of India* (1976)

I never wanted to be a man. I feel sorry for them.
GLENN CLOSE
quoted in *Film Yearbook* 1990

Close Glenn (1947–). US actress. She received Academy Award nominations for her roles as the embittered 'other woman' in *Fatal Attraction* 1987 and as the scheming antiheroine of *Dangerous Liaisons* 1988. She played Gertrude in Franco Zeffirelli's film of *Hamlet* 1990 and appeared as an opera star in *Meeting Venus* 1991.

Her first film was *The World According to Garp* 1982; other screen appearances include *The Big Chill* 1983 and *Jagged Edge* 1985. More recently, she has had roles on Broadway in Tom Stoppard's *The Real Thing* and Michael Frayn's *Benefactors*.

Clouet French portrait painters and draughtsmen of the 16th century, father and son. The father, Jean (or Janet) (*c.* 1485–1541), is assumed to have been of Flemish origin. He became painter and *valet de chambre* to Francis I 1516. His son, François (*c.* 1520–1572), succeeded his father in Francis I's service 1541 and worked also under Henry II, Francis II, and Charles IX.

Clough Arthur Hugh (1819–1861). English poet. Many of his lyrics are marked by a melancholy scepticism that reflects his struggle with his religious doubt.

'How sad a thing to live among strangers with none of my relatives to help me'. He said this not out of grief but cunning, hoping to find some more living relatives to kill.
St Gregory of Tours on CLOVIS
in *Histories* bk 2 ch 43

Clovis (465–511). Merovingian king of the Franks from 481. He succeeded his father Childeric as king of the Salian (northern) Franks; defeated the Gallo-Romans (Romanized Gauls) near Soissons 486, ending their rule in France; and defeated the Alemanni, a confederation of Germanic tribes, near Cologne 496. He embraced Christianity and subsequently proved a powerful defender of orthodoxy against the Arian Visigoths, whom he defeated at Poitiers 507. He made Paris his capital.

Clunies-Ross family that established a benevolently paternal rule in the Cocos Islands. John Clunies-Ross, a Scottish seaman, settled on Home Island in 1827. The family's rule ended in 1978 with the purchase of the Cocos by the Australian government.

Clurman Harold Edgar (1901–1980). US theatre director and critic. He helped found the independent Group Theatre in 1931

(other members were Lee Strasberg and Elia Kazan), and directed plays by Clifford Odets (*Awake and Sing* 1935) and William Saroyan. He wrote theatre criticism for the *New Republic* 1948–52 and the *Nation* from 1953.

Cnut alternative spelling of ◊Canute.

Coates Eric (1886–1957). English composer. He is remembered for the orchestral suites *London* 1933, including the 'Knightsbridge' march; 'By the Sleepy Lagoon' 1939; 'The Dam Busters March' 1942; and the songs 'Bird Songs at Eventide' and 'The Green Hills of Somerset'.

Coates Joseph Gordon (1878–1943). New Zealand Reform Party politician, prime minister 1925–28. During his term highways and hydro-electric power were developed and race relations improved.

It will be evolution rather than revolution.
NIGEL COATES
on his appointment as professor of architecture at the
Royal College of Art *Architects Journal* 4 May 1995

Coates Nigel (1949–). English architect. While teaching at the Architectural Association in London in the early 1980s, Coates and a group of students founded NATO (Narrative Architecture Today) and produced an influential series of manifestos and drawings on the theme of the imaginative regeneration of derelict areas of London.

Drawing parallels with the ideas of the Situationists in the 1960s and of punk in the 1970s, Coates promoted an eclectic and narrative form of architecture that went against the contemporary grain.

Cobain Kurt (1967–1994). US rock singer, songwriter, and guitarist, founder member of Nirvana. The group popularized grunge rock with the breakthrough of their second album, *Nevermind* 1991. Their biggest hit was 'Smells Like Teen Spirit' 1991. Cobain's suicide 1994 shocked fans worldwide.

Cobb Ty(rus) Raymond, nicknamed 'the Georgia Peach' (1886–1961). US baseball player, one of the greatest batters and base runners of all time. He played for Detroit and Philadelphia 1905–28, and won the American League batting average championship 12 times. He holds the record for runs scored (2,254) and lifetime batting average (.367). He had 4,191 hits in his career – a record that stood for almost 60 years.

From a very early age, I had imbibed the opinion, that it was every man's duty to do all that lay in his power to leave his country as good as he had found it.
WILLIAM COBBETT
Political Register 22 Dec 1832

Cobbett William (1763–1835). English Radical politician and journalist, who published the weekly *Political Register* 1802–35. He spent much time in North America. His crusading essays on the conditions of the rural poor were collected as 'Rural Rides' 1830.

Born in Surrey, the self-taught son of a farmer, Cobbett enlisted in the army 1784 and served in Canada. He subsequently lived in the USA as a teacher of English, and became a vigorous pamphleteer, at this time supporting the Tories. In 1800 he returned to England. With increasing knowledge of the sufferings of the farm labourers, he became a Radical and leader of the working-class movement.

He was imprisoned 1809–11 for criticizing the flogging of British troops by German mercenaries. He visited the USA again 1817–19. He became a strong advocate of parliamentary reform, and represented Oldham in the Reformed Parliament after 1832.

Cobden Richard (1804–1865). British Liberal politician and economist, co-founder with John Bright of the Anti-Corn Law League 1839. A member of Parliament from 1841, he opposed class and religious privileges and believed in disarmament and free trade.

Cobden *The British Liberal politician Richard Cobden, a portrait by L Dickinson. Cobden's early struggles as a cloth merchant shaped his thinking on free trade and the increase of British commerce.*

A typical early Victorian radical, he believed in the abolition of privileges, a minimum of government interference, and the securing of international peace through free trade and by disarmament and arbitration. He opposed trade unionism and most of the factory legislation of his time, because he regarded them as opposed to liberty of contract. His opposition to the Crimean War made him unpopular. He was largely responsible for the commercial treaty with France in 1860.

Born in Sussex, the son of a farmer, Cobden had become a calico manufacturer in Manchester.

Cobden-Sanderson Thomas James (1840–1922). English bookbinder and painter. Influenced by the English designer William Morris and the Pre-Raphaelite painter Burne-Jones, he opened his own workshop in Maiden Lane, London, 1884; he founded the Doves Press 1900–16.

Coburn Alvin Langdon (1882–1966). American-born photographer who settled in Britain. He produced several books of atmospheric photogravures, including *New York* 1910 and a portrait album *Men of Mark* 1913. His work tended towards abstraction and in 1917 he exhibited with the Vorticists (an English avant-garde group of artists) a number of fragmented, abstract images which he called 'Vortographs'.

Coburn James (1928–). US film actor. He was popular in the 1960s and 1970s. Rough-hewn and tall, he was ideal for starring roles in action films such as *The Magnificent Seven* 1960, *Pat Garrett and Billy the Kid* 1973, and *Cross of Iron* 1977.

Cochise (*c.* 1812–1874). American Apache Indian leader who campaigned relentlessly against white settlement of his territory.

Unjustly arrested by US authorities 1850, he escaped from custody and took American hostages, whom he later executed. A Chiricahua Apache, Cochise joined forces with the Mimbrēno Apache and successfully fought off a large force of California settlers 1862. Finally apprehended by General George Crook 1871, Cochise made peace with the US government the following year.

Cochise was born in Arizona. He gained a large number of followers in his long and bitter dispute with the US government and conducted repeated raids on American posts.

Cochran C(harles) B(lake) (1872–1951). English impresario. He promoted entertainment ranging from wrestling and roller-skating to Diaghilev's Ballets Russes. Knighted 1948.

Cochran Eddie (1938–1960). US rock-and-roll singer, songwriter, and guitarist. He created classic rock songs like 'Summertime Blues' 1958 and 'C'mon Everybody' 1959 as well as slower romantic numbers ('Dark, Lonely Street' 1958, 'Three Steps to Heaven' 1960).

Cochran was born in Oklahoma but began his career in Los Angeles as a session musician. His first record was 'Skinny Jim' 1956, and he appeared in the 1956 film *The Girl Can't Help It* singing 'Twenty Flight Rock'. He was killed in a car crash while touring the UK with fellow rocker Gene Vincent (1935–1971).

Cockcroft John Douglas (1897–1967). British physicist. In 1932 he and Irish physicist Ernest Walton succeeded in splitting the nucleus of an atom for the first time. For this they were jointly awarded a Nobel prize 1951. Knighted 1948.

The voltage multiplier built by Cockcroft and Walton to accelerate protons was the first particle accelerator. They used it to bombard lithium, artificially transforming it into helium. The production of the helium nuclei was confirmed by observing their tracks in a cloud chamber. They then worked on the artificial disintegration of other elements, such as boron.

Having been in charge of the construction of the first nuclear-power station in Canada during World War II, he returned to the UK to be director of Harwell Atomic Energy Research Establishment 1946–58, and in 1959 became first Master of Churchill College, Cambridge.

Something imposing, grand, massive and high is wanted in our buildings at present.

CHARLES COCKERELL
Diary 1822

Cockerell Charles Robert (1788–1863). English architect. He built mainly in a Neo-Classical style derived from antiquity and from the work of Christopher Wren. His buildings include the Cambridge University Library (now the Cambridge Law Library) 1837–42 and the Ashmolean Museum and Taylorian Institute in Oxford 1841–45.

Cockerell Christopher Sydney (1910–). English engineer who invented the hovercraft in the 1950s. Cockerell tested various ways of maintaining the air cushion. In 1957 he came up with the idea of a flexible skirt, which gave rise to much derision because nobody could believe that a piece of fabric could be made to support a large vessel. Knighted 1969.

Cockerell was born and educated at Cambridge. Employed by the Marconi Company 1935–50, he made a major contribution to aircraft radio navigation and communications. During this period he filed 36 patents. In the 1970s he began to interest himself in the generation of energy by wave power.

Cockerill William (1759–1832). English engineer who is generally regarded as the founder of the European textile-machinery industry. He was mainly active in Russia and Belgium.

Cockerill was born in Lancashire. His working career began with the building of spinning jennies and flying shuttles. In 1794 he went to St Petersburg, Russia, and enjoyed the patronage of Catherine II. Her successor, however, imprisoned Cockerill for failing to complete a contract within the given time. Eventually he escaped via Sweden to Belgium 1799, where he established himself as a manufacturer of textile machinery, first in Verviers and from 1807 in nearby Liège. There, together with his three sons William, Charles, and John, he made rotary carding machines, spinning frames, and looms for the French woollen industry.

Cocteau Jean (1889–1963). French poet, dramatist, and film director. A leading figure in European Modernism, he worked with Picasso, Diaghilev, and Stravinsky. He produced many volumes of poetry, ballets such as *Le Boeuf sur le toit/The Ox on the Roof* 1920, plays, for example, *Orphée/Orpheus* 1926, and a mature novel of bourgeois French life, *Les Enfants terribles/Children of the Game* 1929, which he made into a film 1950.

Cody Samuel Franklin (1862–1913). US-born British aviation pioneer. He made his first powered flight on 16 Oct 1908 at Farnborough, England, in a machine of his own design. He was killed in a flying accident.

Born in Texas, USA, he took British nationality in 1909. He spent his early days with a cowboy stage and circus act, and made kites capable of lifting people.

Cody William Frederick ('Buffalo Bill') (1846–1917). US scout and performer. From 1883 he toured the USA and Europe with a Wild West show which featured the recreation of Indian attacks and, for a time, the cast included Chief Sitting Bull as well as Annie Oakley. His nickname derives from a time when he had a contract to supply buffalo carcasses to railway labourers (over 4,000 in 18 months).

He was a heavy drinker and a trusting investor; he died in poverty after seeing his exploits recounted and exaggerated in novels of the West.

Coe Sebastian Newbold (1956–   ). English middle-distance runner, Olympic 1,500-metres champion 1980 and 1984. He became Britain's most prolific world-record breaker with eight outdoor world records and three indoor world records 1979–81.

After his retirement from running in 1990 he pursued a political career with the Conservative party, and in 1992 was elected member of Parliament for Falmouth and Camborne in Cornwall.

Coen Joel (1954–   ) and Ethan (1957–   ). US filmmakers. With Joel directing, Ethan producing, and both collaborating on their screenplays, they made a succession of stylish, offbeat movies beginning with *Blood Simple* 1984. Other films include *Raising Arizona* 1987, *Miller's Crossing* 1990, *Barton Fink* 1991, and *The Hudsucker Proxy* 1994. Their films are often marked by self-conscious reference to the conventions of bygone Hollywood genres – *Blood Simple* to film noir, *Raising Arizona* and *The Hudsucker Proxy* to 1930s comedy, *Miller's Crossing* to the gangster film.

Coetzee J(ohn) M(ichael) (1940–   ). South African author. His novel *In the Heart of the Country* 1975 dealt with the rape of a white woman by a black man. In 1983 he won Britain's Booker Prize for *The Life and Times of Michael K*.

Other works include *Waiting for the Barbarians* 1982, *Foe* 1987, and *The Master of Petersburg* 1994.

Cohan George M(ichael) (1878–1942). US composer. His Broadway hit musical *Little Johnny Jones* 1904 included his songs 'Give My Regards to Broadway' and 'Yankee Doodle Boy'. 'You're a Grand Old Flag' 1906 further associated him with popular patriotism, as did his World War I song 'Over There' 1917.

Born to a theatrical family in Providence, Rhode Island, USA, Cohan spent his youth touring, writing songs, and appearing in musical comedies. A film version of his life, *Yankee Doodle Dandy*, appeared 1942.

Cohan Robert Paul (1925–   ). US choreographer. He was founding artistic director of the London Contemporary Dance Theatre (LCDT) 1969–89 and artistic adviser from 1992. A student of Martha Graham and co-director of her company 1966–69, his choreography is a development of her style. Blending elements of American jazz dance and Graham's modern dance, Cohan's work is marked by a thematic vagueness and a willingness to utilize modern

technology as in *Video-Life* 1987. His works include *Cell* 1969, a study on the loss of individuality; *Waterless Method of Swimming Instruction* 1974; and the television ballet *A Mass for Man* 1985.

Coke Edward (1552–1634). Lord Chief Justice of England 1613–17. He was a defender of common law against royal prerogative; against Charles I he drew up the Petition of Right 1628, which defines and protects Parliament's liberties.

Coke became a barrister 1578, and in 1592 speaker of the House of Commons and solicitor-general. As attorney-general from 1594, he conducted the prosecution of Elizabeth I's former favourites Essex and Raleigh, and of the Gunpowder Plot conspirators. In 1606 he became Chief Justice of the Common Pleas, and began his struggle, as champion of the common law, against James I's attempts to exalt the royal prerogative. An attempt to silence him by promoting him to the dignity of Lord Chief Justice proved unsuccessful, and from 1620 he led the parliamentary opposition and the attack on Charles I's adviser Buckingham. Coke's *Institutes* are a legal classic, and he ranks as the supreme common lawyer.

Coke Thomas William, 1st Earl of Leicester (1754–1842). English pioneer and promoter of the improvements associated with the Agricultural Revolution. His innovations included regular manuring of the soil, the cultivation of fodder crops in association with corn, and the drilling of wheat and turnips.

He also developed a fine flock of Southdown sheep at Holkham, Norfolk, which were superior to the native Norfolks, and encouraged his farm tenants to do likewise. These ideas attracted attention at the annual sheep shearings, an early form of agricultural show, which Coke held on his home farm from 1776. By the end of the century these had become major events, with many visitors coming to see and discuss new stock, crops, and equipment. Earl 1837.

Colbert Claudette. Stage name of Lily Claudette Chauchoin (1903–   ). French-born film actress. She lived in Hollywood from childhood. She was ideally cast in sophisticated, romantic roles, but had a natural instinct for comedy and appeared in several of Hollywood's finest, including *It Happened One Night* 1934 and *The Palm Beach Story* 1942.

Colbert Jean-Baptiste (1619–1683). French politician, chief minister to Louis XIV, and controller-general (finance minister) from 1665. He reformed the Treasury, promoted French industry and commerce by protectionist measures, and tried to make France a naval power equal to England or the Netherlands, while favouring a peaceful foreign policy.

Colbert, born in Reims, entered the service of Cardinal Mazarin and succeeded him as chief minister to Louis XIV. In 1661 he set to work to reform the Treasury. The national debt was largely repaid, and the system of tax collection was drastically reformed. Industry was brought under state control, shipbuilding was encouraged by bounties, companies were established to trade with India and America, and colonies were founded in Louisiana, Guiana, and Madagascar. In his later years Colbert was supplanted in Louis's favour by the war minister Louvois (1641–1691), who supported a policy of conquests.

Cole Thomas (1801–1848). US painter. He founded the Hudson River School of landscape artists. Apart from panoramic views such as *The Oxbow* 1836 (Metropolitan Museum of Art, New York), he painted a dramatic historical series, *The Course of Empire* 1836 (New York Historical Society), influenced by the European artists Claude Lorrain, J M W Turner, and John Martin.

He was able to travel to England and Italy, 1829–32, and returned with larger Romantic ambitions, producing a series of landscape allegories (*The Voyage of Life*, *The Course of Empire*) and nostalgic Italian compositions. He wrote 'An Essay on American Scenery' 1835.

Coleman Ornette (1930–   ). US alto saxophonist and jazz composer. In the late 1950s he rejected the established structural principles of jazz for free avant-garde improvisation. He has worked with small and large groups, ethnic musicians of different traditions, and symphony orchestras. His albums include *The Shape of Jazz to Come* 1959, *Chappaqua Suite* 1965, and *Skies of America* 1972.

Colenso John William (1814–1883). British cleric, Anglican bishop of Natal, South Africa, from 1853. He was the first to write down the Zulu language. He championed the Zulu way of life (including polygamy) in relation to Christianity, and applied Christian morality to race relations in South Africa.

He incurred furious attack from traditionalists by his *Pentateuch and Book of Joshua Critically Examined* 1862. Deposed 1863 by the bishop of Cape Town, he was reinstated on appeal to the Privy Council.

Coleridge Samuel Taylor (1772–1834). English poet. He was one of the founders of the Romantic movement. A friend of the poets Robert Southey and William Wordsworth, he collaborated with the latter on *Lyrical Ballads* 1798. His poems include 'The Rime of the Ancient Mariner', 'Christabel', and 'Kubla Khan'; critical works include *Biographia Literaria* 1817.

A brilliant talker and lecturer, Coleridge was expected to produce some great work of philosophy or criticism. His *Biographia Literaria*, much of it based on German ideas, is full of insight but its formlessness and the limited extent of his poetic output represents a partial failure of promise. Coleridge became addicted to opium and from 1816 lived in Highgate, London, under medical care.

Suggested reading
Bate, W J *Coleridge* (1968)
Doughty, O *Perturbed Spirit* (1981)
Holmes, R *Coleridge: Early Visions* (1989)
Lefebure, M *Samuel Taylor Coleridge: A Bondage to Opium* (1974)

Coleridge Sara (1802–1852). English woman of letters. She edited the work of her father Samuel Taylor Coleridge. She was also a writer and translator.

Coleridge-Taylor Samuel (1875–1912). English composer who wrote the cantata *Hiawatha's Wedding Feast* 1898, a setting in three parts of Longfellow's poem. The son of a West African doctor and an Englishwoman, he was a student and champion of traditional black music.

Coleridge-Taylor *The English composer Samuel Coleridge-Taylor. Coleridge-Taylor was born in London and educated at the Royal College of Music. He is known for his cantata* Hiawatha's Wedding Feast, *a musical arrangement of Longfellow's poem* The Song of Hiawatha. *(Image Select)*

Colet John (c. 1467–1519). English humanist, influenced by the Italian reformer Savonarola and the Dutch scholar Erasmus. He reacted against the scholastic tradition in his interpretation of the Bible, and founded modern biblical exegesis. In 1505 he became dean of St Paul's Cathedral, London.

The day after that wedding night I found that a distance of a thousand miles, abyss and discovery and irremediable metamorphosis, separated me from the day before.

COLETTE
'Wedding Night'

Colette (Sidonie-Gabrielle) (1873–1954). French writer. At 20 she married Henri Gauthier-Villars, a journalist known as 'Willy', under whose name and direction her four 'Claudine' novels, based on her own early life, were written. Divorced 1906, she worked as a striptease and mime artist for a while, but continued to write. Works from this later period include *Chéri* 1920, *La Fin de Chéri/The End of Chéri* 1926, and *Gigi* 1944.

Suggested reading
Colette *Earthly Paradise* (autobiographical writings ed by Robert Phelps) (1966)
Crosland, M *Colette* (1985)
Dormann, G *Colette: A Passion for Life* (1985)
Jouve, N W *Colette* (1987)
Mitchell, Yvonne *Colette: A Taste for Life* (1975)
Richardson, Joanna *Colette* (1983)

Colfax Schuyler (1823–1885). US political leader. He was elected to the US House of Representatives 1854 and served as Speaker of the House 1863–69. A radical Republican, Colfax was elected vice president for President Grant's first term 1869–73. He was not renominated because of charges of corruption and financial improprieties.

Born in New York, USA, Colfax moved with his family to Indiana 1836 and, although having the benefit of little formal education, worked in a succession of jobs, including county auditor, newspaper reporter, and legal assistant before becoming active in Indiana state politics.

Coligny Gaspard de (c. 1519–1572). French admiral and soldier, and prominent Huguenot. About 1557 he joined the Protestant party, helping to lead the Huguenot forces during the Wars of Religion. After the Treaty of St Germain 1570, he became a favourite of the young king Charles IX, but was killed on the first night of the Massacre of St Bartholomew.

Colles Abraham (1773–1843). Irish surgeon who in 1814 observed and described a common fracture of the wrist, now named after him. Colles was born in County Kilkenny and educated at Dublin and Edinburgh. He set up in practice in Dublin 1797 and began to teach anatomy and surgery. At the age of 29 he became president of the Royal College of Surgeons, where he was a professor 1804–36.

Context was his delight; he was not be be frighted from his purpose or his prey.

Samuel Johnson on JEREMY COLLIER
in *Lives of the Poets* 1779

Collier Jeremy (1650–1726). British Anglican cleric, a Nonjuror, who was outlawed 1696 for granting absolution on the scaffold to two men who had tried to assassinate William III. His *Short View of the Immorality and Profaneness of the English Stage* 1698 was aimed at the dramatists William Congreve and John Vanbrugh.

Collier Lesley Faye (1947–). English ballerina. She became a principal dancer of the Royal Ballet 1972. She created roles in Kenneth MacMillan's *Anastasia* 1971 and *Four Seasons* 1975, Hans van Manen's *Four Schumann Pieces* 1975, Frederick Ashton's *Rhapsody* 1980, and Glen Tetley's *Dance of Albiar* both 1980.

Let us do something today which the world may talk of hereafter.

LORD COLLINGWOOD
before the Battle of Trafalgar 21 Oct 1805, quoted in G L Newnham
Collingwood (ed) *Correspondence and Memoir of Lord Collingwood*

Collingwood Cuthbert, 1st Baron Collingwood (1750–1810). British admiral who served with Horatio Nelson in the West Indies against France and blockaded French ports 1803–05; after Nelson's death he took command at the Battle of Trafalgar. Baron 1805.

Collingwood Robin George (1889–1943). English philosopher who believed that any philosophical theory or position could be properly understood only within its own historical context and not from the point of view of the present. His aesthetic theory, outlined in *Principles of Art* 1938, bases art on expression and imagination.

Collingwood was professor of philosophy at Oxford, and also an authority on the history and archaeology of Roman Britain.

Collins Albert (1932–1993). US blues guitarist, singer, and songwriter. His distinctive guitar sound was based on open D-minor tuning; calling it 'cold blues', he gave his albums titles such as *Frosty* 1962, *Frostbite* 1980, and *Cold Snap* 1986. The albums *Don't Lose Your Cool* 1983 and *Showdown!* 1985 both won awards.

Collins David (1756–1810). British administrator in Australia, first lieutenant governor of Van Diemen's Land (Tasmania) 1804–10. He arrived in New South Wales with the First Fleet as judge-advocate of the new settlement and gave a first-hand account of the early days of the colony in the first volume of *An Account of the English Colony in New South Wales* 1798.

Collins J(ames) Lawton (1882–1963). US general. He first came to prominence on Guadalcanal 1942 leading the US 25th Infantry Division, which relieved the US Marines and completed the capture of the island. He then went to Europe and took part in the D-Day landings 6 June 1944 and the subsequent Allied drive through Europe.

Collins Joan Henrietta (1933–). English film and television actress. Her role as Alexis Carrington in the TV series *Dynasty* 1981–89 brought her international fame.

Collins was born in London and made her West End stage debut 1946 and her film debut 1952 in *Lady Godiva Rides Again*. She appeared in undemanding roles in a series of mediocre films for the Rank Organization 1952–55, and in Hollywood for 20th-Century-Fox 1955–62, including the role of Beth Throgmorton in *The Virgin Queen* 1955. From the late 1960s she gained a glamorous and slightly disreputable reputation on and off screen, especially after *The Stud* 1979. Her autobiography *Past Imperfect* was published 1978. She has written some 'sex-and-shopping' novels, and won a legal case brought by Random House 1996, when the publishing firm accused her of supplying it with a novel which would have required much editing, rather than a completed novel. She is the sister of the novelist Jackie Collins.

Collins Michael (1890–1922). Irish nationalist. He was a Sinn Féin leader, a founder and director of intelligence of the Irish Republican Army 1919, minister for finance in the provisional government of the Irish Free State 1922, commander of the Free State forces in the civil war, and for ten days head of state before being killed by Irishmen opposed to the partition treaty with Britain.

Born in County Cork, Collins became an active member of the Irish Republican Brotherhood, and in 1916 fought in the Easter Rising. In 1918 he was elected a Sinn Féin member to the Dáil, and became a minister in the Republican Provisional government. In 1921 he and Arthur Griffith (1872–1922) were mainly responsible for the treaty that established the Irish Free State. During the ensuing civil war, Collins took command and crushed the opposition in Dublin and the large towns within a few weeks. When Griffith died on 12 Aug Collins became head of the state and the army, but he was ambushed near Cork by fellow Irishmen on 22 Aug and killed.

Suggested reading
O'Connor, Frank *Big Fellow* (1937)
Ryan, Desmond *Michael Collins* (1985)

Collins Phil(lip) David Charles (1951–). English pop singer, drummer, and actor. A member of the group Genesis from 1970, he has also pursued a successful middle-of-the-road solo career since 1981, with hits (often new versions of old songs) including 'In the Air Tonight' 1981 and 'Groovy Kind of Love' 1988. He starred as the train robber Buster Edwards in the film *Buster* 1988.

How sleep the brave, who sink to rest, / By all their country's wishes blest!

WILLIAM COLLINS
'Ode Written in the Year 1746'

Collins William (1721–1759). English poet. His *Persian Eclogues* 1742 were followed in 1746 by his series *Odes*, including the poem 'To Evening'.

I have always held the old-fashioned opinion that the primary object of a work of fiction should be to tell a story.

WILKIE COLLINS
Preface to *The Woman in White* 1860

Collins (William) Wilkie (1824–1889). English author of mystery and suspense novels. He wrote *The Woman in White* 1860 (with its fat villain Count Fosco), often called the first English detective novel, and *The Moonstone* 1868 (with Sergeant Cuff, one of the first detectives in English literature).

Collodi Carlo. Pen name of Carlo Lorenzini (1826–1890). Italian journalist and writer. In 1881–83 he wrote *Le avventure di Pinocchio/The Adventures of Pinocchio*, a children's story of a wooden puppet that became a human boy.

Collor de Mello Fernando (1949–). Brazilian politician, president 1990–92. He founded the centre-right National Reconstruction Party 1989. As its candidate, he won that year's presidential election by promising to root out government corruption and entrenched privileges. However, rumours of his own past wrongdoings led to his constitutional removal from office by a vote of impeachment in Congress Sept 1992. He resigned in Dec at the start of his trial and was subsequently banned from public office for eight years.

He is as ingratiating when he talks as when he is silent.

New York Times on RONALD COLMAN
1929

Colman Ronald Charles (1891–1958). English film actor. In Hollywood from 1920, he played suave and dashing roles in *Beau Geste* 1924, *The Prisoner of Zenda* 1937, *Lost Horizon* 1937, and *A Double Life* 1947, for which he received an Academy Award.

Colombo Joe Cesare (1930–1971). Italian industrial designer. He was a member of the postwar generation of designers who created a sophisticated, sculptural style for banal industrial goods. He is best known for his plastic chairs designed for Kartell, notable among them his 'Chair 4860' 1965 which brought a new respectability to the material.

Colombo moved from a background in fine art into design 1955. Based in Milan, he designed many other furniture pieces and domestic appliances with the same rigorous style, among them his 'Poker' card table 1968 and his air conditioner for Candy 1970, for a wide range of manufacturers. He was placed among the most innovative designers of his generation.

Colombo Matteo Realdo (c. 1516–1559). Italian anatomist who discovered pulmonary circulation, the process of blood circulating from the heart to the lungs and back.

This showed that Galen's teachings were wrong, and was of help to William Harvey in his work on the heart and circulation. Colombo was a pupil of Andreas Vesalius and became his successor at the University of Padua.

Colonna Vittoria (c. 1492–1547). Italian poet. Many of her Petrarchan sonnets idealize her husband, who was killed at the battle of Pavia 1525. She was a friend of Michelangelo, who addressed sonnets to her.

Colt Samuel (1814–1862). US gunsmith who invented the revolver 1835 that bears his name. With its rotating breech which turned, locked, and unlocked by cocking the hammer, the Colt was superior to other revolving pistols, and it revolutionized military tactics.

Colt built a large factory in Hartford, Connecticut, 1854. During the Crimean War 1853–56 he also manufactured arms in Pimlico, London. By 1855 he had the largest private armoury in the world. When the American Civil War broke out 1861, he supplied thousands of guns to the US government.

Coltrane John William (1926–1967). US jazz saxophonist. He first came to prominence 1955 with the Miles Davis quintet, later playing with Thelonious Monk 1957. He was a powerful and individual artist, whose performances featured much experimentation. His 1960s quartet was highly regarded for its innovations in melody

Colt US inventor Samuel Colt shown holding a Colt revolver. In a time when firearms were notoriously unreliable, Colt's designs were revolutionary and were quickly adopted by many fighting forces. His first revolver, the 'Colt Patterson', fired five shots and was used extensively by Texas Rangers in the Mexican–American War. He also supplied weaponry to both the Unionist North in the American Civil War and the British in Crimea. (Ann Ronan/Image Select)

and harmony.

Like Charlie Parker, Coltrane marked a watershed in jazz and has been deified by his fans. The free-jazz movement of the 1960s owed much to his extended exploratory solos, for example on 'Giant Steps' 1959, the year he traded tenor saxophone for soprano. A highly original musician, he has been much imitated, but the deeply emotional tone of his playing, for example on 'A Love Supreme' 1964, is impossible to copy.

May I never leave this world / Until my ill-luck is gone; / Till I have cows and sheep, / And the lad that I love for my own.

PADRAIC COLUM
'The Poor Girl's Meditation'

Colum Padraic (1881–1972). Irish poet and dramatist. He was associated with the foundation of the Abbey Theatre, Dublin, where his plays *Land* 1905 and *Thomas Muskerry* 1910 were performed. His *Collected Poems* 1932 show his gift for lyrical expression.

Even if Columba was a holy miracle worker, can he be placed above St Peter to whom our Lord said, 'You are Peter and upon this rock I will build my Church'?

St Wilfrid on ST COLUMBA
quoted in Bede *Ecclesiastical History* bk 3, ch 25

Columba, St (Latin form of Colum-cille, 'Colum of the cell') (521–597). Irish Christian abbot, missionary to Scotland. He was born in County Donegal of royal descent, and founded monasteries and churches in Ireland. In 563 he sailed with 12 companions to Iona, and built a monastery there that was to play a leading part in the conversion of Britain. Feast day 9 June.

From his base on Iona St Columba made missionary journeys to the mainland. Legend has it that he drove a monster from the river Ness, and he crowned Aidan, an Irish king of Argyll.

Columban, St (543–615). Irish Christian abbot. He was born in Leinster, studied at Bangor, and about 585 went to the Vosges, France, with 12 other monks and founded the monastery of Luxeuil. Later, he preached in Switzerland, then went to Italy, where he built the abbey of Bobbio in the Apennines. Feast day 23 Nov.

Columbus thought he was a flop, probably, when they sent him back in chains. Which didn't prove there was no America.

Saul Bellow on CHRISTOPHER COLUMBUS
in *The Adventures of Augie March* 1953

Columbus Christopher (Spanish Cristóbal Colón) (1451–1506). Italian navigator and explorer who made four voyages to the New World: 1492 to San Salvador Island, Cuba, and Haiti; 1493–96 to Guadaloupe, Montserrat, Antigua, Puerto Rico, and Jamaica; 1498 to Trinidad and the mainland of South America; 1502–04 to Honduras and Nicaragua.

Believing that Asia could be reached by sailing westwards, he eventually won the support of King Ferdinand and Queen Isabella of Spain and set off on his first voyage from Palos 3 Aug 1492 with three small ships, the *Niña*, the *Pinta*, and his flagship the *Santa Maria*. Land was sighted 12 Oct, probably Watling Island (now San Salvador Island), and within a few weeks he reached Cuba and Haiti, returning to Spain March 1493.

Born in Genoa, Columbus went to sea at an early age, and settled in Portugal 1478. After his third voyage 1498, he became involved in quarrels among the colonists sent to Haiti, and in 1500 the governor sent him back to Spain in chains. Released and compensated by the king, he made his last voyage 1502–04, during which he hoped to find a strait leading to India. He died in poverty in Valladolid and is buried in Seville cathedral. In 1968 the site of the wreck of the *Santa Maria*, sunk off Hispaniola 25 Dec 1492, was located.

Columbus Day (12 Oct), a public holiday, is named after him.

Suggested reading

Axtell, James *Beyond 1492* (1992)

Canzotto, G *Christopher Columbus: The Dream and the Obsession* (1986)

Cohen, J M *The Four Voyages of Christopher Columbus* (1969)

Collis, John *Christopher Columbus* (1977)

Fernández-Armesto, F *Columbus* (1991)

Fernández-Armesto, F *Columbus on Himself* (1992)

Philips, C R *The Worlds of Christopher Columbus* (1992)

Ryan, C *Columbus in Poetry, History and Art* (1976)

Taviani, E *Christopher Columbus: The Grand Design* (1985)

Colville Alex (1920–). Canadian painter. A prominent Realist artist, his style has affinities with that of Andrew Wyeth. His somewhat melancholic paintings depict smooth, broad-bodied nudes and figures of working men as remote from the Canadian landscape they inhabit. He is also an accomplished animal painter, for example *Hound in Field* 1958 (National Gallery of Canada, Ottawa).

Comaneci Nadia (1961–). Romanian gymnast. She won three gold medals at the 1976 Olympics at the age of 14, and was the first gymnast to record a perfect score of 10 in international competition. Upon retirement she became a coach of the Romanian team, but defected to Canada 1989.

Comines Philippe de (*c.* 1445–1511). French diplomat in the service of Charles the Bold, Louis XI, and Charles VIII; author of *Mémoires* 1489–98.

Comme des Garçons trade name of Rei Kawakubo (1942–). Japanese fashion designer. Her asymmetrical, seemingly shapeless designs combine Eastern and Western ideas of clothing. They are often sombre in colour and sometimes torn and crumpled. She became a freelance designer 1966, after working in a Japanese textile company, and formed Comme des Garçons 1969. In the early 1980s her avant-garde designs received acclaim in Paris and were widely influential. She continued to question conventions in 1993, producing outfits turned inside out, with unpicked seams and slashed hems, as well as jackets and coats with three sleeves.

His great simplicity and cowardice made him the slave of his companions.

Dio Cassius on LUCIUS AELIUS AURELIUS COMMODUS
in *History* bk 73, ch 1

Commodus Lucius Aelius Aurelius (AD 161–192). Roman emperor from 177 (jointly with his father), sole emperor from 180, son of Marcus Aurelius Antoninus. He was a tyrant, spending lavishly on gladiatorial combats, confiscating the property of the wealthy, persecuting the Senate, and renaming Rome 'Colonia Commodiana'. There were many attempts against his life, and he was finally strangled at the instigation of his mistress and advisers, who had discovered themselves on the emperor's death list.

Compton Arthur Holly (1892–1962). US physicist who in 1923 found that X-rays scattered by such light elements as carbon increased their wavelengths. He concluded from this unexpected result that the X-rays were displaying both wavelike and particlelike properties, since named the Compton effect. He shared a Nobel prize 1927 with Scottish physicist Charles Wilson. Compton was also a principal contributor to the development of the atomic bomb. His academic career in the USA was spent at Washington University, St Louis, 1920–23 and 1945–61, and at the University of Chicago 1923–45.

As regards plots I find real life no help at all. Real life seems to have no plots.

IVY COMPTON-BURNETT
quoted in R Lehmann et al *Orion I* 1945

Compton-Burnett Ivy (1884–1969). English novelist. She used dialogue to show reactions of small groups of characters dominated by the tyranny of family relationships. Her novels, set at the turn of the century, include *Pastors and Masters* 1925, *More Women Than Men* 1933, and *Mother and Son* 1955. DBE 1967.

Men are not allowed to think freely about chemistry and biology, why should they be allowed to think freely about political philosophy?

AUGUSTE COMTE
Positive Philosophy 1830–42

Comte (Isidore) Auguste (Marie François Xavier) (1798–1857). French philosopher regarded as the founder of sociology, a term he coined 1830. He sought to establish sociology as an intellectual discipline, using a scientific approach ('positivism') as the basis of a new science of social order and social development.

In his six-volume *Cours de philosophie positive* 1830–42, Comte argued that human thought and social development evolve through three stages: the theological, the metaphysical, and the positive or scientific. Although he originally sought to proclaim society's evolution to a new golden age of science, industry, and rational morality, his radical ideas were increasingly tempered by the political and social upheavals of his time. His influence continued in Europe and the USA until the early 20th century.

From 1816–18 he taught mathematics. He divided human knowledge into a hierarchy, with sociology at the top of the academic pyramid. Positivism offered a method of logical analysis and provided an ethical and moral basis for predicting and evaluating social progress.

Conchobar in Celtic mythology, king of Ulster whose intended bride, Deirdre, eloped with Noísi. She died of sorrow when Conchobar killed her husband and his brothers.

Condé Louis de Bourbon, Prince of Condé (1530–1569). Prominent French Huguenot leader, founder of the house of Condé and uncle of Henry IV of France. He fought in the wars between Henry II and the Holy Roman emperor Charles V, including the defence of Metz.

Condé Louis II (1621–1686). Prince of Condé, called the Great Condé. French commander who won brilliant victories during the Thirty Years' War at Rocroi 1643 and Lens 1648, but rebelled 1651 and entered the Spanish service. Pardoned 1660, he commanded Louis XIV's armies against the Spanish and the Dutch.

Conder Charles Edward (1868–1909). Australian artist. He painted in watercolour and oil. In 1888 Conder joined Tom Roberts in Melbourne forming the Australian Impressionist group which became known as the Heidelberg School.

Although his early work, such as *The Departure of the SS Orient – Circular Quay* 1888 (Art Gallery of New South Wales, Sydney), is distinctly Impressionist in style, he later became known for his delicate watercolours painted on silk and for series of lithograph prints, such as *Carnival* 1905 (executed following his return to Europe 1890).

Condillac Étienne Bonnot de (1715–1780). French philosopher. He mainly followed English philosopher John Locke, but his *Traité de sensations* 1754 claims that all mental activity stems from the transformation of sensations. He was a collaborator on the French *Encyclopédie*.

Condillac was born in Grenoble of noble parentage. He entered the church and was appointed tutor to Louis XV's grandson, the duke of Parma.

Condorcet Marie Jean Antoine Nicolas de Caritat, Marquis de (1743–1794). French philosopher, mathematician, and politician, associated with the *Encyclopédistes*. In *Esquisse d'un tableau des progrès de l'esprit humain/Historical Survey of the Progress of Human Understanding* 1795, he traced human development from barbarity to the brink of perfection. As a mathematician he made important contributions to the theory of probability.

Although a keen supporter of the French Revolution, Condorcet opposed the execution of Louis XVI, and was imprisoned and poisoned himself. The *Esquisse* was written in prison. He also wrote in support of pacifism, sexual equality, and social services.

Confucius (Latinized form of Kong Zi or K'ung Fu Tzu, 'Kong the master') (551–479 BC). Chinese sage whose name is given to the ethical system of Confucianism. He placed emphasis on moral order and observance of the established patriarchal family and social relationships of authority, obedience, and mutual respect. His emphasis on tradition and ethics attracted a growing number of pupils during his lifetime. *The Analects of Confucius*, a compilation of his teachings, was published after his death.

Confucius was born in Lu, in what is now the province of Shangdong, and his early years were spent in poverty. Married at 19, he worked as a minor official, then as a teacher. In 517 there was an uprising in Lu, and Confucius spent the next year or two in the adjoining state of Ch'i. As a teacher he was able to place many of his pupils in government posts but a powerful position eluded him. Only in his fifties was he given an office, but he soon resigned because of the lack of power it conveyed. Then for 14 years he wandered from state to state looking for a ruler who could give him a post where he could put into practice his ideas for relieving suffering among the poor. At the age of 67 he returned to Lu and devoted himself to teaching. At his death five years later he was buried with great pomp, and his grave outside Qufu has remained a centre of pilgrimage. Within 300 years of his death, his teaching was adopted by the Chinese state.

Suggested reading
Creel, H G *Confucius: The Man and His Myth* (1949)
Dawson, Raymond *Confucius* (1981)
Fingarette, Herbert *Confucius: The Secular as Sacred* (1972)

Musick has charms to sooth a savage breast.

WILLIAM CONGREVE
The Mourning Bride I i 1697

Congreve William (1670–1729). English dramatist and poet. His first success was the comedy *The Old Bachelor* 1693, followed by *The Double Dealer* 1694, *Love for Love* 1695, the tragedy *The Mourning Bride* 1697, and *The Way of the World* 1700. His plays, which satirize the social affectations of the time, are characterized by elegant wit and wordplay, and complex plots.

Coningham Arthur (1895–1948). British air marshal. After service with the New Zealand Army in World War I, he joined the Royal Flying Corps 1916 then transferred to the Royal Air Force on its formation. In World War II, he developed the techniques of air support for ground forces while commanding the Desert Air Force in N Africa. KCB 1942.

Conkling Roscoe (1829–1888). US political leader, one of the founders of the Republican Party 1854. He served in the US House of Representatives 1859–63 and 1865–67, and in the US Senate 1867–81. A radical Republican, Conkling was an active prosecutor in President A Johnson's impeachment trial.

Born in Albany, New York, USA, Conkling was admitted to the bar 1850 and soon appointed district attorney. As an opponent of President Garfield, Conkling declined an appointment to the US Supreme Court 1882 and returned to private law practice.

Tho' cowards flinch and traitors sneer, / We'll keep the red flag flying here.

Traditionally sung at close of annual conference of the
Labour Party, from JAMES CONNELL's 'The Red Flag'

Connell James (1850–1929). Irish socialist who wrote the British Labour Party anthem 'The Red Flag' during the 1889 London strike.

Connery Sean Thomas (1930–). Scottish film actor. He was the first interpreter of James Bond in several films based on the novels of Ian Fleming. His films include *Dr No* 1962, *From Russia with Love* 1963, *Marnie* 1964, *Goldfinger* 1964, *Diamonds Are Forever* 1971, *A Bridge Too Far* 1977, *The Name of the Rose* 1986, *The Untouchables* 1987 (Academy Award), and *Rising Sun* 1993.

There is no more sombre enemy of good art than the pram in the hall.

CYRIL CONNOLLY
Enemies of Promise ch 14 1938

Connolly Cyril Vernon (1903–1974). English critic and author. As founder and editor of the literary magazine *Horizon* 1930–50, he had considerable critical influence. His works include *The Rock Pool* 1935, a novel of artists on the Riviera, and *The Unquiet Grave* 1944, a series of reflections published under the pseudonym of Palinurus.

Connolly Maureen Catherine (1934–1969). US lawn-tennis player, nicknamed 'Little Mo' because she was just 157 cm/5 ft 2 in tall. In 1953 she became the first woman to complete the Grand Slam by winning all four major tournaments.

All her singles titles (won at nine major championships) and her Grand Slam titles were won between 1951 and 1954. She also represented the USA in the Wightman Cup. Her career ended 1954 after a riding accident.

Connors Jimmy (James Scott) (1952–). US tennis player who won the Wimbledon title 1974 and 1982, and subsequently won ten Grand Slam events. He was one of the first players to popularize the two-handed backhand.

Conrad Franz Xaver Josef, Count Conrad von Hötzendorf (1852–1925). Austrian general, field marshal from 1916.

Appointed Chief of Staff 1906, he was largely responsible for modernizing and reorganizing the Austro-Hungarian army. Believing in an aggressive policy towards Italy and Serbia, he supported the diplomatic moves which set the war in motion. He was a good organizer and strategist but his performance in the field was poor and his successes were largely due to German support.

Any work that aspires, however humbly, to the condition of art should carry its justification in every line.

JOSEPH CONRAD
The Nigger of the Narcissus, author's note 1897

Conrad Joseph. Pen name of Jozef Teodor Konrad Nalecz Korzeniowski (1857–1924). English novelist, born in the Ukraine of Polish parents. He joined the French merchant navy at the age of 17 and first learned English at 21. His greatest works include the novels *Lord Jim* 1900, *Nostromo* 1904, *The Secret Agent* 1907, and *Under Western Eyes* 1911, the short novel *Heart of Darkness* 1902 and the short story 'The Shadow Line' 1917. These combine a vivid sensuous evocation of various lands and seas with a rigorous, humane scrutiny of moral dilemmas, pitfalls, and desperation.

Conrad is regarded as one of the greatest of modern novelists. His prose style, varying from eloquently sensuous to bare and astringent, keeps the reader in constant touch with a mature, truth-seeking, creative mind.

Suggested reading
Baines, J *Joseph Conrad: A Critical Biography* (1960)
Batchelor, J *The Life of Joseph Conrad* (1994)
Karl, F R *Joseph Conrad: The Three Lives* (1979)
Page, N *A Conrad Companion* (1986)
Sherry, N *Conrad* (1972)
Watts, C *A Preface to Conrad* (1982)

Conrad five German kings:

Conrad I (died 918). King of the Germans from 911, when he succeeded Louis the Child, the last of the German Carolingians. During his reign the realm was harassed by Magyar invaders.

Conrad II (*c.* 990–1039). King of the Germans from 1024, Holy Roman emperor from 1027. He ceded the Sleswick (Schleswig) borderland, S of the Jutland peninsula, to King Canute, but extended his rule into Lombardy and Burgundy.

Conrad III (1093–1152). King of Germany and Holy Roman emperor from 1138, the first king of the Hohenstaufen dynasty. Throughout his reign there was a fierce struggle between his followers, the Ghibellines, and the Guelphs, the followers of Henry the Proud, duke of Saxony and Bavaria (1108–1139), and later of his son Henry the Lion (1129–1195).

Conrad IV (1228–1254). Elected king of the Germans 1237. Son of the Holy Roman emperor Frederick II, he had to defend his right of succession against Henry Raspe of Thuringia (died 1247) and William of Holland (1227–56).

Conrad V (Conradin) (1252–1268). Son of Conrad IV, recognized as king of the Germans, Sicily, and Jerusalem by German supporters of the Hohenstaufens 1254. He led Ghibelline forces against Charles of Anjou at the battle of Tagliacozzo, N Italy 1266, and was captured and executed.

Conran Jasper Alexander Thirlby (1959–). English fashion designer. He is known for using quality fabrics to create comfortable garments. He launched his first collection 1978 and has rarely altered the simple, successful style he then adopted. He has also designed costumes for the stage. He is the son of Terence Conran.

Conran Terence Orby (1931–). English designer and retailer of furnishings, fashion, and household goods. He was founder of the Storehouse group of companies, including Habitat and Conran Design, with retail outlets in the UK, the USA, and elsewhere. He has been influential in popularizing French country style in the UK.

In 1964 he started the Habitat company, then developed Mothercare. Knighted 1983. The Storehouse group gained control of British Home Stores 1986.

The sky is the source of light in nature and governs everything.
JOHN CONSTABLE
Letter to Archdeacon Fisher 23 Oct 1821

Constable John (1776–1837). English artist. He was one of the greatest landscape painters of the 19th century. He painted scenes of his native Suffolk, including *The Haywain* 1821 (National Gallery, London), as well as castles, cathedrals, landscapes, and coastal scenes in other parts of Britain. Constable inherited the Dutch tradition of sombre Realism, in particular the style of Jacob Ruisdael. He aimed to capture the momentary changes of the weather as well as to create monumental images of British scenery, as in *The White Horse* 1819 (Frick Collection, New York) and *Salisbury Cathedral from the Bishop's Grounds* 1827 (Victoria and Albert Museum, London).

Constable's paintings are remarkable for their atmospheric effects and were admired by many French painters including Eugène Delacroix. Notable are *The Leaping Horse* 1825 (Royal Academy of Arts, London), *The Cornfield* 1826 (National Gallery, London), and *Dedham Vale* 1828 (National Gallery of Scotland, Edinburgh). His many oil sketches are often considered among his best work.
Suggested reading
Barrell, J *The Darker Side of the Landscape: The Rural Poor in English Painting, 1730–1840* (1980)
Cormack, M *Constable* (1986)
Reynolds, G *Constable, the Natural Painter* (1965)
Rosenthal, M *Constable: The Painter and his Landscape* (1986)

Constant de Rebecque (Henri) Benjamin (1767–1830). French writer and politician. An advocate of the Revolution, he opposed Napoleon and in 1803 went into exile. Returning to Paris after the fall of Napoleon in 1814 he proposed a constitutional monarchy. He published the autobiographical novel *Adolphe* 1816, which reflects his affair with Madame de Staël, and later wrote the monumental study *De la Religion* 1825–31.

Constantine II (1940–). King of the Hellenes (Greece). In 1964 he succeeded his father Paul I, went into exile 1967, and was formally deposed 1973.

He married Princess Anne-Marie of Denmark in 1964.

The privileges which have been granted in consideration of religion must benefit only the catholic church.
CONSTANTINE THE GREAT
Law of AD 326 *Theodosian Code* bk 16 ch 5.1

Constantine the Great (c. AD 285–337). First Christian emperor of Rome and founder of Constantinople. He defeated Maxentius, joint emperor of Rome AD 312, and in 313 formally recognized Christianity. As sole emperor of the west of the empire, he defeated Licinius, emperor of the east, to become ruler of the Roman world 324. He presided over the church's first council at Nicaea 325. Constantine moved his capital to Byzantium on the Bosporus 330, renaming it Constantinople (now Istanbul).
Suggested reading
Burckhardt, J *The Age of Constantine the Great* (trs 1983)
MacMullen, R *Constantine* (1969)
Saughter, F G *Constantine* (1972)
Smith, J H *Constantine* (1971)

A filmset is just a never ending hell.
TOM CONTI
Remark at Cannes 15 May 1983

Conti Tom (1942–). Scottish stage and film actor. Specializing in character roles, his films include *The Duellists* 1977, *Merry Christmas Mr Lawrence* 1982, *Reuben, Reuben* 1983, *Beyond Therapy* 1987, and *Shirley Valentine* 1989.

Cooder Ry(land) Peter (1947–). US guitarist, singer, and composer. His explorations of various forms of American music (Tex-Mex, jazz, Hawaiian, and so on) and bottleneck slide playing have gained him much session work and a cult following. His records include *Into the Purple Valley* 1972, *Borderline* 1980, and *Get Rhythm* 1987; he has written music for many films, including *Paris, Texas* 1984.

Was this country settled by an Industrus people they would very soon be suppl'd not only with the necessarys but many of the luxuries of life.
JAMES COOK
Of New Zealand, *Journal* March 1770

Cook James (1728–1779). British naval explorer. After surveying the St Lawrence River in North America 1759, he made three voyages: 1768–71 to Tahiti, New Zealand, and Australia; 1772–75 to the South Pacific; and 1776–79 to the South and North Pacific, attempting to find the Northwest Passage and charting the Siberian coast. He was killed in Hawaii.

In 1768 Cook was given command of an expedition to the South Pacific to witness Venus eclipsing the Sun. He sailed in the *Endeavour* with Joseph Banks and other scientists, reaching Tahiti in April 1769. He then sailed around New Zealand and made a detailed survey of the east coast of Australia, naming New South Wales and Botany Bay. He returned to England 12 June 1771.

Now a commander, Cook set out 1772 with the *Resolution* and *Adventure* to search for the southern continent. The location of Easter Island was determined, and the Marquesas and Tonga

Cook, James *The British naval explorer James Cook. Cook sailed to Tahiti in the* Endeavour *1768 to observe the transit of Venus across the Sun. This done, he travelled on to explore New Zealand and Australia, returning to England 1771. He made two further exploratory voyages, and was killed in Hawaii 1779.* (Image Select)

Islands plotted. He also went to New Caledonia and Norfolk Island. Cook returned 25 July 1775, having sailed 100,000 km/60,000 mi in three years.

On 25 June 1776, he began his third and last voyage with the *Resolution* and *Discovery*. On the way to New Zealand, he visited several of the Cook or Hervey Islands and revisited the Hawaiian or Sandwich Islands. The ships sighted the North American coast at latitude 45° N and sailed north hoping to discover the Northwest Passage. He made a continuous survey as far as the Bering Strait, where the way was blocked by ice. Cook then surveyed the opposite coast of the strait (Siberia), and returned to Hawaii early 1779, where he was killed in a scuffle with islanders.

Suggested reading
Beaglehole, J *The Life of Captain James Cook* (1974)
Hough, Richard *Captain James Cook* (1994)
Moorhead, Alan *The Fatal Impact* (1966)
Withey, L *Voyages of Discovery: Captain Cook and the Exploration of the Pacific* (1989)

Cook Peter Edward (1937–1995). English satirist and entertainer. With his partner Dudley Moore, he appeared in the revue *Beyond the Fringe* 1959–64. He opened London's first satirical nightclub, the Establishment, 1960, and backed the satirical magazine *Private Eye*. Cook's distinctive humour, best exemplified in the 'Pete and Dud' routines with Moore, was as little restrained by any concern for political correctness as by good taste, and frequently tended towards a kind of verbal surrealism. His films include *The Wrong Box* 1966, *Bedazzled* 1968, *The Bed Sitting Room* 1969, a parody of *The Hound of the Baskervilles* 1977, and *Supergirl* 1984.

Cook Robin (Robert Finlayson) (1946–). English Labour politician. A member of the moderate-left Tribune Group, he entered Parliament 1974 and became a leading member of Labour's shadow cabinet, specializing in health matters. When John Smith assumed the party leadership July 1992, Cook

remained in the shadow cabinet as spokesman for trade and industry. He became shadow foreign secretary under Smith's successor, Tony Blair, Oct 1994.

Cook Thomas (1808–1892). Pioneer British travel agent and founder of Thomas Cook & Son. He organized his first tour, to Switzerland, in 1863. He introduced traveller's cheques (then called 'circular notes') in the early 1870s.

The path to his prose led through the bile duct.
ALISTAIR COOKE
'Letter from America' 29 June 1969

Cooke (Alfred) Alistair (1908–). British-born US journalist. He was *Guardian* correspondent in the USA 1948–72, and broadcasts a weekly *Letter from America* on BBC radio.

Cooke Sam (1931–1964). US soul singer and songwriter. He began his career as a gospel singer and turned to pop music 1956. His hits include 'You Send Me' 1957 and 'Wonderful World' 1960 (re-released 1986). His smooth tenor voice gilded some indifferent material, but his own song 'A Change Is Gonna Come' 1965 is a moving civil-rights anthem.

Coolidge (John) Calvin (1872–1933). 30th president of the USA 1923–29, a Republican. As governor of Massachusetts 1919, he was responsible for crushing a Boston police strike. As Warren Harding's vice president 1921–23, he succeeded to the presidency on Harding's death (2 Aug 1923). He won the 1924 presidential election, and his period of office was marked by economic growth.

Coolidge declined to run for re-election in 1928, supporting his secretary of the interior, Herbert Hoover, who won the presidency.
Suggested reading
Coolidge, Calvin *The Autobiography of Calvin Coolidge* (1929, rep 1972)
McCoy, Donald R *Calvin Coolidge: The Quiet President* (1967)
White, William *Puritan in Babylon: The Story of Calvin Coolidge* (1938, rep 1973)

Coolidge Julian Lowell (1873–1954). US geometrician who wrote many mathematical textbooks, in which he not only reported his results but also described the historical background, together with contemporary developments. From 1900 he taught at Harvard, where he became professor 1918 and remained until 1940.

Coombs Herbert Cole ('Nugget') (1906–). Australian economist. He was appointed governor of the Commonwealth Bank in

Cooke, Alistair *Journalist and broadcaster Alistair Cooke (on left). He is well known for his* Letter from America, *first broadcast by the BBC 1946 – the longest-running solo radio feature program. A sympathetic and versatile commentator on US current affairs and popular culture, Cooke has also written numerous books.*

Coolidge, Calvin *The US president Calvin Coolidge. Coolidge was born in Vermont, the son of a farmer and storekeeper. He became the 30th president of the USA 1923.* (Image Select)

1949, and when the central and trading functions of the bank were separated in 1959, Coombs became governor of the Reserve Bank and chair of its board. He was also personal adviser to seven Australian prime ministers, from Curtin to Whitlam, chancellor of the Australian National University from 1968 to 1976, and was active in the area of Aboriginal welfare and land rights.

Cooney Ray(mond) George Alfred (1932–). English actor, director, and dramatist. He is known for his farces *Two into One* 1981 and *Run for Your Wife* 1983.

Cooper Gary (born Frank James Cooper) (1901–1961). US film actor. He epitomized the lean, true-hearted American, slow of speech but capable of outdoing the 'bad guys'. His films include *Lives of a Bengal Lancer* 1935, *Mr Deeds Goes to Town* 1936, *Sergeant York* 1940 (Academy Award), and *High Noon* 1952 (Academy Award).

In 1960 he received a special Academy Award for his lifetime contribution to cinema.

Cooper Henry (1934–). English heavyweight boxer, the only man to win three Lonsdale Belts outright, 1961, 1965, and 1970. He held the British heavyweight title 1959–71 and lost it to Joe Bugner. He fought for the world heavyweight title but lost in the sixth round to Muhammad Ali 1966.

Cooper James Fenimore (1789–1851). US writer. He wrote some 50 novels, becoming popular with *The Spy* 1821. His volumes of *Leatherstocking Tales* focused on the frontier hero Leatherstocking and the American Indians before and after the American Revolution; they included *The Last of the Mohicans* 1826. Still popular as adventures, his novels have been reappraised for their treatment of social and moral issues in the settling of the American frontier.

Suggested reading
Dekker, George *James Fenimore Cooper, the Novelist* (1967)
Franklin, W *The New World of James Fenimore Cooper* (1982)
Motley, W *The American Abraham: James Fenimore Cooper and the Frontier Patriarch* (1988)
Ringe, Donald *James Fenimore Cooper* (1962)

Cooper Leon Niels (1930–). US physicist who in 1955 began work on the phenomenon of superconductivity. He proposed that

at low temperatures electrons would be bound in pairs (since known as Cooper pairs) and in this state electrical resistance to their flow through solids would disappear. He shared the 1972 Nobel Prize for Physics with John Bardeen and J Robert Schrieffer (1931–). His work with John Bardeen was carried out at the University of Illinois. In 1958 Cooper moved to Brown University, Rhode Island, and in 1978 became director of the Centre for Neural Science at Brown.

The painting is so extraordinary as I do never expect to see the like again.

Samuel Pepys on SAMUEL COOPER
Diary March 1688

Cooper Samuel (1609–1672). English portrait miniaturist. His subjects included Milton, members of Charles II's court, the diarist Samuel Pepys' wife, and Oliver Cromwell.

He departed from the tradition of Hilliard and Oliver in giving the miniature some of the quality of the large oil portrait, being known as a 'van Dyck in little'. His contemporaries greatly admired him, and to Aubrey he was 'the prince of limners'. His brother Alexander (fl. 1630–60) was also a miniature painter who worked at Amsterdam and at the court of Queen Christina of Sweden.

Cooper Susie. Married name Susan Vera Barker (1902–1995). English pottery designer. Her style has varied from colourful Art Deco to softer, pastel decoration on more classical shapes. She started her own company 1929, which later became part of the Wedgwood factory, where she was senior designer from 1966.

Cooper Whina Josephine (1895–1994). New Zealand campaigner for Maori rights, and particularly claims to traditionally-held land. Despite traditional prejudice about the role women should play, by the strength of her intellect and personality she became the leading voice of the Maori people and the best-known advocate of racial harmony in her country. DBE 1980.

Cooper, Gary US film actor Gary Cooper in the Western classic High Noon 1952. With an image as the unwilling hero, laconic and somewhat awkward, Cooper was a leading Hollywood star for many years. Other films include The Virginian 1929 and For Whom the Bell Tolls 1943.

Coote Eyre (1726–1783). Irish general in British India. His victory 1760 at Wandiwash, followed by the capture of Pondicherry, ended French hopes of supremacy. He returned to India as commander in chief 1779, and several times defeated Hyder Ali, sultan of Mysore. Knighted 1771.

Not an agreeable man, he … quarrelled with everybody … but he was also ready to die in his saddle and his spirit did much to save British India.
Geoffrey Treasure on EYRE COOTE
in *Who's Who in Early Hanoverian Britain* 1991

Coover Robert Lowell (1932–). US novelist. He writes stylized, satirical fantasies using American myths to reinterpret history such as *The Origin of the Brunists* 1965, an investigation of mystical sects. Later novels include *Gerald's Party* 1986, a fantastic, babbling text that parodies the murder mystery, and *Pinocchio in Venice* 1991, a scatological reworking of the classic fable.

He also wrote *The Public Burning* 1977, which dramatizes Vice President Nixon meeting Uncle Sam shortly before the execution of the Rosenberg spies.

Copeau Jacques (1879–1949). French theatre director. He advocated a simplification of stage setting. He founded a company at the Vieux-Columbier Theatre 1913, where he directed plays by Molière and Shakespeare, notably *The Winter's Tale* 1921. In 1924 he established a school for young performers in Burgundy. He was a director of the Comédie Française 1936–41.

Coper Hans (1920–1981). German potter. He was originally an engineer. His work resembles Cycladic Greek pots in its monumental quality.

Coperario John. Assumed name of John Cooper (*c.* 1570–1626). English composer of songs with lute or viol accompaniment. His works include several masques, such as *The Masque of Flowers* 1614, and sets of fantasies for organ and solo viol.

Finally we shall place the Sun himself at the centre of the Universe.
NICOLAUS COPERNICUS
De revolutionibus orbium coelestium 1543

Copernicus Nicolaus (1473–1543). Polish astronomer who believed that the Sun, not the Earth, is at the centre of the Solar System, thus defying the Christian church doctrine of the time. For 30 years he worked on the hypothesis that the rotation and the orbital motion of the Earth were responsible for the apparent movement of the heavenly bodies. His great work *De revolutionibus orbium coelestium/On the Revolutions of the Heavenly Spheres* was not published until the year of his death.

Copernicus relegated the Earth from being the centre of the universe to being merely a planet (the centre only of its own gravity and the orbit of its solitary Moon). This forced a fundamental revision of the anthropocentric view of the universe and came as an enormous psychological shock to European culture. Copernicus's model could not be proved right, because it contained several fundamental flaws, but it was the important first step to the more accurate picture built up by later astronomers.

Copernicus was born in Toruń on the Vistula. He studied mathematics, astronomy, classics, law, and medicine at Kraków and various universities in Italy. On his return to Poland 1506 he became physician to his uncle, the bishop of Varmia, who had also got him the post of canon at Frombork, enabling him to intersperse astronomical work with the duties of various civil offices.

Music that is born complex is not inherently better or worse than music that is born simple.
AARON COPLAND
quoted in Robert Jacobson *Reverberations* 1975

Copland Aaron (1900–1990). US composer. His early works, such as his piano concerto 1926, were in the jazz idiom but he gradually developed a gentler style with a regional flavour drawn from American folk music. Among his works are the ballets *Billy the Kid* 1939, *Rodeo* 1942, and *Appalachian Spring* 1944 (based on a poem by Hart Crane), and *Inscape for Orchestra* 1967.

Born in New York, Copland studied in France with Nadia Boulanger, and taught from 1940 at the Berkshire Music Center, now the Tanglewood Music Center, near Lenox, Massachusetts. He took avant-garde European styles and gave them a distinctive American accent. His eight film scores, including *The Heiress* 1949, set new standards for Hollywood.

Suggested reading
Butterworth, Neil *The Music of Aaron Copland* (1986)
Copland, Aaron *What to Listen for in Music* (1957)
Copland, Aaron *The New Music, 1900–1960* (1968)
Dobrin, A *Aaron Copland: His Life and Times* (1967)

Copland Douglas Berry (1894–1971). New Zealand-born Australian economist and diplomat. He was financial adviser to the Australian government from the 1930s to the end of World War II. He spent two years as Australian minister to China (1946–48) and was the first vice-chancellor of the Australian National University. KBE 1950.

Copley John Singleton (1738–1815). US painter. He was the leading portraitist of the colonial period, but from 1775 lived mainly in London where he painted lively historical scenes such as *The Death of Major Pierson* 1783 (Tate Gallery, London).

Some of his historical paintings are unusual in that they portray dramatic events of his time, such as *Brook Watson and the Shark* 1778 (National Gallery, Washington, DC).

In some ways this is Death of a Salesman *Italian style with my family.*
FRANCIS FORD COPPOLA
describing *Godfather III*, MTV 19 June 1991

Coppola Francis Ford (1939–). US film director and screenwriter of wide-ranging ambition. He directed *The Godfather* 1972, which became one of the biggest moneymaking films of all time, and its sequels *The Godfather Part II* 1974, which won seven Academy Awards, and *The Godfather Part III* 1990. His other films include *Apocalypse Now* 1979, *One from the Heart* 1982, *Rumblefish* 1983, *The Outsiders* 1983, and *Bram Stoker's Dracula* 1992.

After working on horror B-films, his first successes were *Finian's Rainbow* 1968 and *Patton* 1969, for which his screenplay won an

Copland, Aaron US composer Aaron Copland. The many styles and forms in which he has worked have brought him wide recognition, including a Pulitzer Prize for music 1945, and an Academy Award for his film score for *The Heiresss* 1949.

Academy Award. Among his other films are *The Conversation* 1972, *The Cotton Club* 1984, *Tucker: The Man and His Dream* 1988, and *Gardens of Stone* 1987.

Coralli Jean (born Jean Coralli Peracini) (1779–1854). French dancer and choreographer. He made his debut as a dancer 1802. He choreographed *Le Diable boîteux* 1836 for the Austrian ballerina Fanny Elssler (1810–1884), *Giselle* 1841, and *La Péri* 1843 for the Italian ballerina Carlotta Grisi (1819–1899).

Coram Thomas (1668–1751). English philanthropist who established the Foundling Hospital for orphaned and abandoned children in Holborn, London, 1741. The site, now Coram Fields, is still a children's foundation.

Corbett James John ('Gentleman Jim') (1866–1933). US boxer who gained the heavyweight title in his 1892 New Orleans fight with reigning champion John L Sullivan. It was the first title bout to be fought with gloves and according to the Marquess of Queensberry rules. Corbett held the title until his defeat 1897 by Robert Fitzsimmons.

Corbière Tristan (born Edouard Joachim Corbière) (1845–1875). French poet. His volume of poems *Les Amours jaunes/Yellow Loves* 1873 went unrecognized until Paul Verlaine called attention to it 1884. Many of his poems, such as *La Rhapsodie foraine/Wandering Rhapsody*, deal with life in his native Brittany.

Corbusier, Le French architect; see ◊Le Corbusier.

I have done my task, let others do theirs.
CHARLOTTE CORDAY
Remark on being interrogated for the murder of Marat July 1793

Corday Charlotte. Full name Marie-Anne Charlotte Corday d'Armont (1768–1793). French Girondin (right-wing republican during the French Revolution). After the overthrow of the Girondins by the extreme left-wing Jacobins May 1793, she stabbed to death the Jacobin leader, Jean Paul Marat, with a bread knife as he sat in his bath in July of the same year. She was guillotined.

Corelli Arcangelo (1653–1713). Italian composer and violinist. He was one of the first virtuoso exponents of the Baroque violin and his music, marked by graceful melody, includes a set of *concerti grossi* and five sets of chamber sonatas.

Born near Milan, he studied in Bologna and in about 1685 settled in Rome, under the patronage of Cardinal Pietro Ottoboni, where he published his first violin sonatas.

Corelli Marie. Pseudonym of Mary Mackay (1855–1924). English romantic novelist. Trained for a musical career, she turned instead to writing (she was said to be Queen Victoria's favourite novelist) and published *The Romance of Two Worlds* 1886. Her works were later ridiculed for their pretentious style.

Cori Carl Ferdinand (1896–1984) and Gerty (Theresa, born Radnitz) (1896–1957) US biochemists born in Austro-Hungary who, together with Argentine physiologist Bernardo Houssay (1887–1971), received a Nobel prize 1947 for their discovery of how glycogen (animal starch) – a derivative of glucose – is broken down and resynthesized in the body, for use as a store and source of energy.

Both were born in Prague and married while studying at the medical school there. They emigrated to the USA 1922, and in 1931 Carl Cori was appointed professor of biochemistry at Washington University School of Medicine in St Louis, Missouri. Gerty Cori also worked there, becoming professor 1947. Carl Cori remained at St Louis until 1967, when he moved to Harvard Medical School.

Corinna (lived 6th century BC). Greek lyric poet. From Tanagra in Boeotia, she may have been a contemporary of Pindar. Only fragments of her poetry survive.

Coriolis Gaspard Gustave de (1792–1843). French physicist who in 1835 discovered the Coriolis effect, which governs the movements of winds in the atmosphere and currents in the ocean. Coriolis was also the first to derive formulas expressing kinetic energy and mechanical work.

Coriolis was born in Paris and studied there, graduating in highway engineering. He was professor of mechanics at the Ecole Centrale des Arts et Manufactures 1829–36 and then at the Ecole des Ponts et Chaussées. In 1838 he became director of studies at the Ecole Polytechnique.

Corliss George Henry (1817–1888). US engineer and inventor of many improvements to steam engines, particularly the Corliss valve for controlling the flow of steam to and through cylinders.

He took out the first of his many patents in 1849, for the Corliss valve. In 1856 he founded the Corliss Engine Company in Providence, Rhode Island. This company designed and built the largest steam engine then in existence to power all the exhibits in the Machinery Hall at the 1876 Philadelphia Centennial Exposition.

Corman Roger William (1926–). US film director and producer. His low-budget, highly profitable films are mainly in the youth and science-fiction genres. One of the most consistently commercial filmmakers working outside the Hollywood studio system, Corman has over 200 films to his credit since 1954. Among his directed work was a series of Edgar Allan Poe adaptations, beginning with *The House of Usher* 1960.

Corman also fostered some of the leading names in cinema such as Francis Ford Coppola, Martin Scorsese, and Jack Nicholson, who benefited from Corman's independent company New World Pictures, and later Concorde/New Horizons.

When there is no peril in the fight, there is no glory in the triumph.
PIERRE CORNEILLE
Le Cid 1636

Corneille Pierre (1606–1684). French dramatist. His tragedies, such as *Horace* 1640, *Cinna* 1641, and *Oedipe* 1659, glorify the strength of will governed by reason, and established the French classical dramatic tradition. His first comedy, *Mélite*, was performed 1629, followed by others that gained him a brief period of favour with Cardinal Richelieu. His early masterpiece, *Le Cid* 1636, was attacked by the Academicians, although it received public acclaim, and was produced in the same year as *L'Illusion comique/The Comic Illusion*.

Although Corneille enjoyed public popularity, periodic disfavour with Richelieu marred his career, and it was not until 1639 that Corneille (again in favour) produced plays such as *Polyeucte* 1643, *Le Menteur* 1643, and *Rodogune* 1645, leading to his election to the Académie 1647. His later plays were approved by Louis XIV.

Cornell Joseph (1903–1972). US assemblage artist. Cornell's art consisted of collecting ephemera in junkshops, which then gained power by their juxtaposition in a box or display-case (termed 'magic peep holes'), expressing the 'endlessly mysterious processes of the mind'. He described the process of collecting materials 'metaphysics of ephemera'. Although he never left his native New York, and never even moved house, his best works convey a sense of unexpected beauty ('intangible visitations').

Cornell Katherine (1898–1974). German-born US actress. Her first major success came with an appearance on Broadway in *Nice People* 1921. This debut was followed by a long string of New York stage successes, several of which were directed by her husband, Guthrie McClintic. From 1930 she began to produce her own plays; the most famous of them, *The Barretts of Wimpole Street* 1931, was later taken on tour and produced for television 1956.

Cornforth John Warcup (1917–). Australian chemist. Using radioisotopes as markers, he found out how cholesterol is manufactured in the living cell and how enzymes synthesize chemicals that are mirror images of each other (optical isomers).

He shared a Nobel prize 1975 with Swiss chemist Vladimir Prelog. Knighted 1977.

Cornforth was born in Sydney and educated there and at Oxford University. He settled in the UK 1941, and worked for the British Medical Research Council 1946–62, when he became director of the Milstead Laboratory of Chemical Enzymology, Shell Research Ltd. He remained there until 1975, when he accepted a professorship at the University of Sussex.

Cornwallis Charles, 1st Marquis and 2nd Earl (1738–1805). British general in the American Revolution until 1781, when his defeat at Yorktown led to final surrender and ended the war. He then served twice as governor general of India and once as viceroy of Ireland. Earl 1762, marquis 1792.

Coronado Francisco Vásquez de (c. 1510–1554). Spanish explorer who sailed to the New World 1535 in search of gold. In 1540 he set out with several hundred men from the Gulf of California on an exploration of what are today the Southern states. Although he failed to discover any gold, his expedition came across the impressive Grand Canyon of the Colorado and introduced the use of the horse to the indigenous Indians.

To enter fully into one of my landscapes, one must have the patience to allow the mists to clear ...
JEAN-BAPTISTE COROT
Remark made to T Silvestre 1856

Corot Jean-Baptiste Camille (1796–1875). French painter. He created a distinctive landscape style using a soft focus and a low-key palette of browns, ochres, and greens. His early work, including Italian scenes of the 1820s, influenced the Barbizon School of painters. Like them, Corot worked outdoors, but he also continued a conventional academic tradition with his romanticized paintings of women.

It is reasonable to suppose that he was impressed by Constable in the Salon of 1824; going to Rome the following year he showed in his first Italian landscapes a response to effects of sun and cloud that seems, as in the *Claudian Aqueduct* (National Gallery), related to the work of the English master. Their breadth and directness of style marked a new conception of landscape in French art. His first Salon picture, 1827, was the *Vue prise à Narni* (National Gallery of Canada), and he returned to France 1828, painting some of his best pictures in the following six years, and working in Paris and Normandy, at Fontainebleau, Ville d'Avray and elsewhere, the light of Italy giving place to harmonies of silvery grey. His stay at Fontainebleau places him in close relation to the Barbizon School.

I remained speechless on seeing such a mighty work.
Annibale Carracci
in letter to his cousin Lodovico, 18 April 1580
on seeing CORREGGIO's frescoes in Parma

Correggio assumed name of Antonio Allegri (c. 1494–1534). Italian painter of the High Renaissance. His style followed the Classical grandeur of Leonardo da Vinci and Titian, but anticipated the Baroque in its emphasis on movement, softer forms, and contrasts of light and shade.

Based in Parma, he painted splendid illusionistic visions in the cathedral there, including the remarkable *Assumption of the Virgin* 1526–30. His religious paintings, for example, the night scene *Adoration of the Shepherds* about 1527–30 (Gemäldegalerie, Dresden), and mythological scenes, such as *Jupiter and Io* about 1532 (Wallace Collection, London), were much admired in the 18th century.

As an oil painter of both religious and mythological subjects he perfected a rich technique, and famous examples are the *Nativity* (Dresden), *Ecce Homo* and *Mercury instructing Cupid* (National Gallery), the *Marriage of St Catherine* and *Jupiter and Antiope* (Louvre), *Jupiter and Io* (Vienna) and *Danae* (Rome). In the pagan subjects especially there appears a sensuous charm and softness of modelling, another aspect of the genius which provided a model for the artists of the Counter-Reformation.

Cort Henry (1740–1800). English iron manufacturer. For the manufacture of wrought iron, he invented the puddling process and developed the rolling mill (shaping the iron into bars), both of which were significant in the Industrial Revolution.

Cort's work meant that Britain no longer had to rely on imported iron and could become self-sufficient. His method of manufacture combined previously separate actions into one process, removing the impurities of pig iron and producing high-class metal relatively cheaply and quickly.

Cortázar Julio (1914–1984). Argentine writer. His novels include *The Winners* 1960, *Hopscotch* 1963, and *Sixty-two: A Model Kit* 1968. One of his several volumes of short stories includes *Blow-up*, adapted for a film by the Italian director Michelangelo Antonioni.

Cortés Hernán Ferdinand (1485–1547). Spanish conquistador. He conquered the Aztec empire 1519–21, and secured Mexico for Spain.

Cortés went to the West Indies as a young man and in 1518 was given command of an expedition to Mexico. Landing with only 600 men, he was at first received as a god by the Aztec emperor Montezuma II but was expelled from Tenochtitlán (Mexico City) when he was found not to be 'divine'. With the aid of Indian allies he recaptured the city 1521, and overthrew the Aztec empire. His conquests eventually included most of Mexico and N Central America.

Suggested reading
Cortés, Hernán *Letters from Mexico* (trs 1986)
Johnson, W W *Cortés: Conquering the New World* (1987)
Madariaga, S de *Hernán Cortés: Conqueror of Mexico* (1979)
Prescott, W H *Conquest of Mexico* (1843; several recent editions)

Cortona Pietro da. Italian Baroque painter; see ◊Pietro da Cortona.

Corvo Baron (1860–1913). Assumed name of English writer Frederick ◊Rolfe.

Cosby Bill (William Henry) (1937–). US comedian and actor. His portrayal of the dashing, handsome secret agent in the television series *I Spy* 1965–68 revolutionized the way in which blacks were presented on screen. His sardonic humour, based on wry observations of domestic life and parenthood, found its widest audience in *The Cosby Show* 1984–92.

He won three Emmy awards for the *I Spy* series and *The Cosby Show* consistently topped the national ratings and provided new role models for young African Americans. It also made him one of the richest performers in show business. Among his other TV series was *Fat Albert and the Cosby Kids* 1972–84.

He hosted the game show *You Bet Your Life* from 1992.

Cosgrave Liam (1920–). Irish Fine Gael politician, prime minister of the Republic of Ireland 1973–77. As party leader 1965–77, he headed a Fine Gael–Labour coalition government from 1973. Relations between the Irish and UK governments improved under his premiership.

He never grew out of the idea of government by repression.
Owen Dudley Edwards on WILLIAM THOMAS COSGRAVE
in *Eamon de Valera* 1987

Cosgrave William Thomas (1880–1965). Irish politician. He took part in the Easter Rising 1916 and sat in the Sinn Féin cabinet of 1919–21. Head of the Free State government 1922–33, he founded and led the Fine Gael opposition 1933–44. His eldest son is Liam Cosgrave.

Costas Bob (Robert Quinlan) (1952–). US sports broadcaster. Working for NBC from 1980, he was host of *NFL Live*, the NBC Sunday coverage of professional football, 1984–93, and from 1988 host of *Later with Bob Costas*, an interview show broadcast four times a week. He was the chief NBC broadcaster at the Olympic Games in Barcelona, Spain, 1992.

He covered baseball for NBC's *Game of the Week* 1983–89, and from 1991 was host of *NBA Showtime*, covering professional basketball. Winner of three Emmy awards, he also won four National Sportscaster of the Year awards from 1985 onwards.

I don't want to go cruising in Hollywood or hang out at all the star parties. I'm not interested in any of that … I'm just interested in playing.

ELVIS COSTELLO
quoted in Irwin Stambler *The Encyclopedia of Pop, Rock and Soul* 1989

Costello Elvis. Stage name of Declan Patrick McManus (1954–). English rock singer, songwriter, and guitarist. He emerged as part of the New Wave. His intricate yet impassioned lyrics have made him one of Britain's foremost songwriters, and he dominated the UK rock scene into the early 1980s. His hits range from the political rocker 'Oliver's Army' 1979 to the country weepy 'Good Year for the Roses' 1981 and the punning pop of 'Everyday I Write the Book' 1983.

The great stylistic range of his work was evident from his 1977 debut 'My Aim Is True' and was further extended 1993 when he collaborated with the classical Brodsky Quartet on the song cycle 'The Juliet Letters'. From his second album (*This Year's Model* 1978) to 'Goodbye Cruel World' 1984 he worked exclusively with his backing group, the Attractions; the group also appeared on *Blood and Chocolate* 1986. Other musicians were used on, for example, *King of America* 1986 and *Mighty Like a Rose* 1991.

Coster Laurens Janszoon (*c.* 1370–1440). Dutch printer. According to some sources, he invented movable type, but after his death an apprentice ran off to Mainz with the blocks and, taking Johann Gutenberg into his confidence, began a printing business with him.

If you say what you mean in this town you're an outlaw.

KEVIN COSTNER
on Hollywood *Time* 26 June 1989

Costner Kevin (1955–). US film actor. He emerged as a star in the late 1980s, with his role as law-enforcer Elliot Ness in *The Untouchables* 1987. Increasingly identified with the embodiment of idealism and high principle, Costner went on to direct and star in *Dances with Wolves* 1990, a Western sympathetic to the native American Indians, which won several Academy Awards. Subsequent films include *Robin Hood – Prince of Thieves* 1991, *JFK* 1991, *The Bodyguard* 1992, *A Perfect World* 1993, and *Waterworld* 1995.

Cosway Richard (1742–1821). English artist. Elected to the Royal Academy 1771, he was an accomplished miniaturist and painted members of the Prince Regent's court.

He led the 18th-century revival of the miniature, showing an exceptional lightness of touch and becoming very successful through the favour of the Prince of Wales, who greatly admired his portrait of Mrs Fitzherbert (Wallace Collection, London). He lived a life of lavish splendour with his wife Maria Cecilia Louisa, also a miniature painter, who lived abroad after his death and published a volume of his designs, Florence, 1826.

It's … a sorry drudgery … when a man fags from door to door merely for the pound sterling.

JOHN SELL COTMAN
on teaching art, in letter to Dawson Turner 17 Dec 1811

Cotman John Sell (1782–1842). English landscape painter. With John Crome, he was a founder of the Norwich School. His early watercolours were bold designs in simple flat washes of colour, for example *Greta Bridge, Yorkshire* about 1805 (British Museum, London).

He studied in London, was one of Dr Monro's protégés, and exhibited at the Royal Academy, 1800–06, early watercolours made in Yorkshire, such as *Greta Bridge* being among the classics of the art. He returned to Norwich 1807, worked there and at Yarmouth as drawing master, and with Crome was a leader of the 'Norwich School'. His appointment as drawing master at King's College, London 1834 lightened a constant burden of financial difficulties.

In the simplification of design to broad, expressively silhouetted areas, he was highly original and unlike any of his contemporaries. Time spent on drawing antiquities for his patron in Norfolk, Dawson Turner, was largely wasted, and his later work is unequal, but it included oil-paintings in his own distinct manner as well as some masterly drawings. Of his two painter sons, Joseph John (1814–78) and Miles Edmund (1810–58), the latter is the more distinguished for his river and sea views.

Cotten Joseph (1905–1994). US actor. Intelligent and low-keyed, he was brought into films by director Orson Welles. Cotten gave outstanding performances in *Citizen Kane* 1941, *The Magnificent Ambersons* 1942, and *The Third Man* 1949. Perhaps his most memorable role was that of a sardonic serial killer in Alfred Hitchcock's *Shadow of a Doubt* 1943.

Cotten was not conventionally handsome, but his air of rugged intelligence and his distinctively husky voice lent him a strong screen presence, although his days as a top-rank star proved relatively brief.

Cotton John (1585–1652). English-born American religious leader. In England, his extreme Puritan views led to charges of heterodoxy being filed against him 1633. In the same year, he immigrated to the Massachusetts Bay Colony, where he was named teacher of Boston's First Congregational Church. A powerful force in the colony, he published widely circulated sermons and theological works.

Cotton was born in Derby and educated at Cambridge University. He was named vicar in Boston, Lincolnshire, 1612 before the persecution of Puritans under Charles I forced him to leave the country.

His rich collection of Saxon charters proved the foundation of the scholarly study of pre-Norman English history.

Sidney Lee on ROBERT BRUCE COTTON
in *Dictionary of National Biography*

Cotton Robert Bruce (1571–1631). English antiquary. At his home in Westminster he built up a fine collection of manuscripts and coins, many of which had come from the despoiled monasteries. His son Thomas Cotton (1594–1662) added to the library. The collection is now in the British Museum, London. Created baronet 1611.

Cotton William (1786–1866). English inventor, financier, and philanthropist who in 1864 invented a knitting machine for the production of hosiery. This machine had a straight-bar frame which automatically made fully fashioned stockings knitted flat and sewn up the back. In 1821 Cotton was elected a director of the Bank of England, and was its governor 1843–46. He invented an automatic weighing machine for sovereigns.

Coué Emile (1857–1926). French psychological healer, the pioneer of autosuggestion. He coined the slogan 'Every day, in every way, I am getting better and better'. Couéism reached the height of its popularity in the 1920s.

Coulomb Charles Augustin de (1736–1806). French scientist, inventor of the torsion balance for measuring the force of electric and magnetic attraction. The coulomb was named after him. In the fields of structural engineering and friction, Coulomb greatly influenced and helped to develop engineering in the 19th century.

Coulomb's law of 1787 states that the force between two electric charges is proportional to the product of the charges and inversely proportional to the square of the distance between them. He was posted to Martinique to undertake construction work 1764–72.

From 1781 he was in Paris, resigning from the army during the French Revolution.

Coulson Charles Alfred (1910–1974). English theoretical chemist who developed a molecular orbital theory and the concept of partial valency. He developed many mathematical techniques for solving chemical and physical problems.

Coulson was born in Dudley, Yorkshire, and studied at Cambridge. He became professor of theoretical physics at King's College, London, 1947, professor of mathematics at Oxford 1952, and later Oxford's first professor of theoretical chemistry. He was chair of the charity Oxfam 1965–71. He wrote three best-selling books: *Waves* 1941, *Electricity* 1948, and *Valence* 1952.

Couperin François le Grand (1668–1733). French composer. He is the best-known member of a musical family which included his uncle Louis Couperin (1626–1661), composer for organ and harpsichord. A favoured composer of Louis XIV, Couperin composed numerous chamber concertos and harpsichord suites, and published a standard keyboard tutor *L'Art de toucher le clavecin/The Art of Playing the Harpsichord* 1716 in which he laid down guidelines for fingering, phrasing, and ornamentation.

Courant Richard (1888–1972). German-born US mathematician who wrote several textbooks that became standard reference works, and founded three highly influential mathematical institutes, one at Göttingen and two in New York.

During World War I, he interested the military authorities in a device for sending electromagnetic radiation through the earth to carry messages. He was professor at Göttingen until the rise of the Nazis, and emigrated to the USA 1934, joining the teaching staff at New York University. He was director of the Institute of Mathematical Sciences of New York University 1953–58, and a new institute opened 1965 as the Courant Institute of Mathematical Sciences.

I deny that art can be taught.
GUSTAVE COURBET
Letter to prospective students 1861

Courbet Gustave (1819–1877). French artist. He was a portrait, genre, and landscape painter. Reacting against academic trends, both Classicist and Romantic, he became a major exponent of Realism, depicting contemporary life with an unflattering frankness. His *Burial at Ornans* 1850 (Musée d'Orsay, Paris), showing ordinary working people gathered around a village grave, shocked the public and the critics with its 'vulgarity'.

His powerful genius found expression in portraiture, figure composition, landscape (the gorges and forests of his native Franche-Comté, and superb paintings of the Normandy coast, *The Wave* being famous in several versions), sensuous paintings of the nude, animal studies, and still life.

Suggested reading
Clark, T J *Image of the People: Gustave Courbet and the 1848 Revolution* (1978)
Lindsay, Jack *Gustave Courbet: His Life and Art* (1974)
Nochlin, Linda *Gustave Courbet: A Study in Style and Society* (1976)

Courrèges André (1923–). French fashion designer. He is credited with inventing the miniskirt 1964. His 'space-age' designs – square-shaped short skirts and trousers – were copied worldwide in the 1960s.

Courrèges worked for Cristóbal Balenciaga 1950–61, and founded his own label 1961. From 1966 he produced both couture and ready-to-wear lines of well-tailored designs, often in pastel shades.

Court Margaret (born Smith) (1942–). Australian tennis player. The most prolific winner in the women's game, she won a record 64 Grand Slam titles, including 25 at singles.

Court was the first from her country to win the ladies title at Wimbledon 1963, and the second woman after Maureen Connolly to complete the Grand Slam 1970.

Courtauld Samuel (1793–1881). British industrialist who developed the production of viscose rayon and other synthetic fibres from 1904. He founded the firm of Courtaulds 1816 in Bocking, Essex, and at first specialized in silk and crepe manufacture.

His great-nephew Samuel Courtauld (1876–1947) was chair of the firm from 1921, and in 1931 gave his house and art collection to the University of London as the Courtauld Institute.

The institute is based in Somerset House, London.

Courtneidge Cicely Esmeralda (1893–1980). English comic actress and singer. She appeared both on stage and in films. She married comedian Jack Hulbert (1892–1978), with whom she formed a successful variety partnership. DBE 1972.

Cousin Victor (1792–1867). French philosopher who helped to introduce German philosophical ideas into France. In 1840 he was minister of public instruction and reorganized the system of elementary education.

Cousteau Jacques Yves (1910–). French oceanographer who pioneered the invention of the aqualung 1943 and techniques in underwater filming. In 1951 he began the first of many research voyages in the ship *Calypso*. His film and television documentaries and books established him as a household name.

He joined the navy and worked for naval intelligence during the Nazi occupation. From 1936 he experimented with diving techniques. The compressed air cylinder had been invented 1933 but restricted the diver to very short periods of time beneath the surface. Testing new breathing equipment, Cousteau was several times nearly killed.

Coutts Thomas (1735–1822). British banker. He established with his brother the firm of Coutts & Co (one of London's oldest banking houses, founded 1692 in the Strand), becoming sole head on the latter's death 1778. Since the reign of George III an account has been maintained there by every succeeding sovereign.

Other customers have included the politicians the Earl of Chatham, William Pitt, Charles Fox, and the Duke of Wellington, and the biographer, James Boswell.

Coverdale Miles (1488–1568). English Protestant priest whose translation of the Bible 1535 was the first to be printed in English. His translation of the psalms is that retained in the Book of Common Prayer.

Coverdale, born in Yorkshire, became a Catholic priest, but turned to Protestantism and 1528 went to the continent to avoid persecution. In 1539 he edited the Great Bible which was ordered to be placed in churches. After some years in Germany, he returned to England 1548, and in 1551 was made bishop of Exeter. During the reign of Mary I he left the country.

Coveri Enrico (1952–1990). Italian fashion designer. He set up his own business 1979. A bold designer of young, fun-loving clothes, he was best known for knitted tops and trousers in strong colours, and for incorporating comic characters and Pop art into his designs.

Coveri was born in Florence and studied at the Accademia delle Belle Arti. He started working freelance for several companies, creating knitwear and sportswear under the Touche label, in 1973, and five years later moved to Paris to work at the Espace Cardin. By the time of his death, his own business had achieved a turnover of £100 million.

Cowan Edith Dircksey (1861–1932). Australian social worker and politician. She became the first woman in Australia to be elected a member of parliament, when elected to the Western Australian Legislative Assembly 1921.

Coward Noël Peirce (1899–1973). English dramatist, actor, revue-writer, director, and composer. He epitomized the witty and sophisticated man of the theatre. From his first success with *The*

Mad dogs and Englishmen / Go out in the midday sun.
NOËL COWARD
'Mad Dogs and Englishmen'

Young Idea 1923, he wrote and appeared in plays and comedies on both sides of the Atlantic such as *Hay Fever* 1925, *Private Lives* 1930 with Gertrude Lawrence, *Design for Living* 1933, *Blithe Spirit* 1941, and *A Song at Twilight* 1966. His revues and musicals included *On With the Dance* 1925 and *Bitter Sweet* 1929. Knighted 1970.

Coward also wrote for and acted in films, including the patriotic *In Which We Serve* 1942 and the sentimental *Brief Encounter* 1945. After World War II he became a nightclub and cabaret entertainer, performing songs like 'Mad Dogs and Englishmen'.

Suggested reading
Castle, Charles *Noël* (1972)
Coward, Noël *Future Indefinite* (autobiography) (1954)
Gray, Frances *Noel Coward* (1987)
Hoare, Noel *Noel Coward* (1995)
Kiernan, R F *Noel Coward* (1986)
Lesley, Cole *The Life of Noel Coward* (1976)
Morley, Sheridan *A Talent to Amuse* (1969)
Morley, Sheridan *Noel Coward Autobiography* (1986)

Cowell Henry Dixon (1897–1965). US composer and theorist. His pioneering *New Musical Resources* 1930 sought to establish a rationale for modern music. He worked with Percy Grainger 1941 and alongside John Cage. Although remembered as a discoverer of piano effects such as strumming the strings in *Aeolian Harp* 1923, and for introducing clusters, using a ruler on the keys in *The Banshee* 1925, he was also an astute observer and writer of new music developments.

Cowell also wrote chamber and orchestral music and was active as a critic and publisher of 20th-century music.

God the first garden made, and the first city Cain.
ABRAHAM COWLEY
'The Garden'

Cowley Abraham (1618–1667). English poet. He introduced the Pindaric ode (based on the work of the Greek poet Pindar) to English poetry, and published metaphysical verse with elaborate imagery, as well as essays. His best-known collection is *The Mistress* 1647.

Cowling Thomas George (1906–1990). English applied mathematician and physicist who contributed significantly to modern research into stellar energy, with special reference to the Sun. He was professor of mathematics at University College, Bangor, 1945–48, and at Leeds University 1948–70.

Variety's the very spice of life, / That gives it all its flavour.
WILLIAM COWPER
The Task bk 2 1783

Cowper William (1731–1800). English poet. He trained as a lawyer, but suffered a mental breakdown 1763 and entered an asylum, where he underwent an evangelical conversion. He later wrote hymns (including 'God Moves in a Mysterious Way'). His verse includes the six books of *The Task* 1785.

He who devotes his time to the completion of a perfect outline has more than half finished his piece.
DAVID COX
Treatise on Landscape Painting and its Effect on Watercolours 1814

Cox David (1783–1859). English artist. He studied under John Varley and made a living as a drawing master. His watercolour landscapes, many of scenes in N Wales, show attractive cloud effects, and are characterized by broad colour washes on rough, tinted paper. In later years he painted much in North Wales and his inn sign for the Royal Oak, Bettws-y-Coed, is famous. He is noted for watercolours in which broken touches and atmospheric effect give a distant anticipation of Impressionism. He took to oils late in life, adapting his watercolour technique. *A Windy Day* (Tate Gallery) well shows his special gift. His treatises on painting are the more conventional recipes of the drawing master.

Cox Jacob Dolson (1828–1900). Canadian-born US educator and public figure. After service in the US Congress 1876–79, Cox was president of the University of Cincinnati 1885–89. He was elected governor of Ohio 1866 and served as secretary of the interior 1869–70 under President Grant.

Coysevox Antoine (1640–1720). French Baroque sculptor at the court of Louis XIV. He was employed at the palace of Versailles, contributing a stucco relief of a triumphant Louis XIV to the Salon de la Guerre.

He also produced portrait busts, for example a terracotta of the artist Le Brun 1676 (Wallace Collection, London), and more sombre monuments, such as the *Tomb of Cardinal Mazarin* 1689–93 (Louvre, Paris).

Cozens John Robert (1752–1797). English landscape painter, a watercolourist. His Romantic views of Europe, painted on tours in the 1770s and 1780s, influenced both Thomas Girtin and Turner. He was the son of the painter Alexander Cozens (*c.* 1717–1786).

The ring so worn, as you behold, / So thin, so pale, is yet of gold: / The passion such it was to prove; / Worn with life's cares, love yet was love.
GEORGE CRABBE
'His Late Wife's Wedding-Ring'

Crabbe George (1754–1832). English poet. Originally a doctor, he became a cleric 1781, and wrote grimly realistic verse on the poor of his own time: *The Village* 1783, *The Parish Register* 1807, *The Borough* 1810 (which includes the story used in Benjamin Britten's opera *Peter Grimes*), and *Tales of the Hall* 1819.

Crabtree William (1905–1991). English architect. He designed the Peter Jones department store in Sloane Square, London,

Cowper *English poet William Cowper. Despite being plagued by melancholia, he wrote the long poem* The Task, *the amusing narrative* John Gilpin, *and such hymns as* 'God moves in a mysterious way'. *His letters to friends are graceful and personal models of letter-writing.*

1935–39, regarded as one of the finest Modern Movement buildings in England. The building was technically innovative in its early application of the curtain wall, which flows in a gentle curve from the King's Road into the square.

Craig (Edward Henry) Gordon (1872–1966). English director and stage designer. His innovations and theories on stage design and lighting effects, expounded in *On the Art of the Theatre* 1911, had a profound influence on stage production in Europe and the USA. He was the son of actress Ellen Terry.

A man of undaunted courage, high character, sound judgement, and devotion to duty ... his powers of leadership were conspicuous.

John M Andrews on JAMES CRAIG, 1ST VISCOUNT CRAIGAVON
in *Dictionary of National Biography*

Craig James, 1st Viscount Craigavon (1871–1940). Ulster Unionist politician, the first prime minister of Northern Ireland 1921–40. Craig became a member of Parliament 1906, and was a highly effective organizer of Unionist resistance to Home Rule. As prime minister he carried out systematic discrimination against the Catholic minority, abolishing proportional representation 1929 and redrawing constituency boundaries to ensure Protestant majorities. Baronet 1918, viscount 1927.

Oh, my son's my son till he gets him a wife, / But my daughter's my daughter all her life.

MRS CRAIK
'Young and Old'

Craik Dinah Maria (born Mulock; popularly known as Mrs Craik) (1826–1887). English novelist. She was the author of *John Halifax, Gentleman* 1857, the story of the social betterment of a poor orphan through his own efforts.

Craik Kenneth John William (1914–1945). Scottish psychologist. Initially involved in the study of vision, Craik became increasingly interested in the nature of cognition, believing that the brain has mechanisms similar in principle to devices used, for example, in calculating machines and anti-aircraft predictors. In several aspects of his work he anticipated later ideas in cybernetics and artificial intelligence and, were it not for his early death, would have made important contributions to these fields.

Craik's views were presented in *The Nature of Explanation* 1943 and developed in a posthumously published collection of essays, notes, and papers titled *The Nature of Psychology* 1966.

Cramer Gabriel (1704–1752). Swiss mathematician who introduced Cramer's rule 1750, a method for the solution of linear equations which revived interest in the use of determinants; Cramer's paradox; and the concept of utility in mathematics.

Cramer was born and educated in Geneva, where from the age of 20 he was professor of mathematics at the Académie de la Rive. In 1750 he was made professor of philosophy. Cramer travelled in Europe and met leading mathematicians.

Cramer Johann Baptist (1771–1858). German-born composer, pianist, and teacher. He lived mostly in London and composed in a conservative style for his day, trying to emulate the music of Mozart. He is most famous for his 84 studies for piano 1804 and 1810, which are still used today. As a pianist he was admired for his technical command and legato touch. He was one of a group of composers known as the London Pianoforte School.

Cranach Lucas the Elder, originally Lucas Müller (1472–1553). German painter, etcher, and woodcut artist. He was a leading figure in the German Renaissance. He painted many full-length nudes and precise and polished portraits, such as *Martin Luther* 1521 (Uffizi, Florence).

Born at Kronach in Bavaria, he settled at Wittenberg 1504 to work for the elector of Saxony. He is associated with the artists Albrecht Dürer and Albrecht Altdorfer and was a close friend of the Christian reformer Martin Luther, whose portrait he painted several times. *The Flight into Egypt* 1504 (Staatliche Museum, Berlin) is typical. His religious paintings feature splendid landscapes. His second son, Lucas Cranach the Younger (1515–1586), had a similar style and succeeded his father as director of the Cranach workshop.

Stars scribble on our eyes the frosty sagas. / The gleaming cantos of unvanquished space.

HART CRANE
'Cape Hatteras' in *The Bridge* 1930

Crane (Harold) Hart (1899–1932). US poet. His long mystical poem *The Bridge* 1930 uses the Brooklyn Bridge as a symbolic key to the harmonizing myth of modern America, seeking to link humanity's present with its past in an epic continuum. His work, which was influenced by T S Eliot, is notable for its exotic diction and dramatic rhetoric.

He committed suicide by jumping overboard from a steamer bringing him back to the USA after a visit to Mexico.

Crane Stephen (1871–1900). US writer. He introduced grim realism into the US novel. His book *The Red Badge of Courage* 1895 deals vividly with the US Civil War in a prose of impressionist, visionary naturalism.

Born in Newark, New Jersey, he moved to the tenements of New York City to work as a journalist. There he wrote his naturalistic fables of urban misery, the self-published *Maggie: A Girl of the Streets: A Story of New York* 1893, which was rejected by many editors because of its shocking subject matter. He was a war correspondent in Mexico, Greece, and Cuba, the latter assignment inspiring one of his most acclaimed stories, 'The Open Boat' 1897, an account of a shipwreck that dramatizes man's exposure to indifferent nature. He also published two volumes of poetry: *The Black Riders* 1895 and *War is Kind* 1899.

Suggested reading
Benfey, Christopher *The Double Life of Stephen Crane: A Biography* (1992)
Berryman, John *Stephen Crane* (1950)
Colvert, J B *Stephen Crane* (1984)
Knapp, B L *Stephen Crane* (1987)

End-papers must be delicately suggestive of the character and contents of the book.

WALTER CRANE
Decorative Illustration of Books 1986

Crane Walter (1845–1915). English artist, designer, and book illustrator. He was influenced by William Morris and became an active socialist in the 1880s.

While apprenticed to W J Linton (1812–1898), a wood engraver, he came under the influence of the Pre-Raphaelites. His book illustrations, both for children's and for adult books, included an edition of Spenser's *Faerie Queene* 1894–96.

Cranko John Cyril (1927–1973). South African-born British choreographer. He was a pivotal figure in the ballet boom of the 1960s. He joined Sadler's Wells, London, 1946 as a dancer, becoming resident choreographer 1950. In 1961 he became director of the Stuttgart Ballet, where he achieved the 'Stuttgart Ballet Miracle', turning it into a world-class company with a vital and exhilarating repertory. He excelled in the creation of full-length narrative ballets, such as *Romeo and Juliet* 1958 and *Onegin* 1965. He is also known for his one-act ballets, peopled with comic characters, as in *Pineapple Poll* 1951 and *Jeu de cartes* 1965.

Cranmer Thomas (1489–1556). English cleric, archbishop of Canterbury from 1533. A Protestant convert, he helped to shape the defeated by the Parthians at the battle of Carrhae, captured, and put to death.

I like playing bitches. There's a lot of bitch in every woman ... a lot in every man.

JOAN CRAWFORD
in *Variety* April 1973

Crawford Joan. Stage name of Lucille Le Sueur (1908–1977). US film actress. She became a star with her performance as a flapper (liberated young woman) in *Our Dancing Daughters* 1928. Later she appeared as a sultry, often suffering, mature woman. Her films include *Mildred Pierce* 1945 (for which she won an Academy Award), *Sudden Fear* 1952, and *Whatever Happened to Baby Jane?* 1962.

Beginning her career as a chorus girl 1924, Crawford made her first film appearance 1925. In the 1930s she played in many Clark Gable films, and in *Grand Hotel* 1932. *Whatever Happened to Baby Jane?* was her last 'great' film, before cameo appearances and *Trog* 1970.

Crawford Michael. Stage name of Michael Patrick Dumble-Smith (1942–). English actor and singer. He played the title role in Andrew Lloyd Webber's musical *The Phantom of the Opera*, which opened in London 1986 and New York 1988.

His early television, film, and stage appearances were mainly in comedy, including the TV series *Not so Much a Programme, More a Way of Life* 1964 and *Some Mothers Do 'ave 'em* 1973–78, the film *A Funny Thing Happened on the Way to the Forum* 1966, and the play *No Sex, Please – We're British* 1971. His musical theatre performances included *Barnum* 1981, in which he played the part of the circus impresario P T Barnum. He toured the USA in *The Music of Andrew Lloyd Webber*, a revue.

Going from Greats to Geography was like leaving the parlour for the basement; one lost caste but one did see life.

O G S CRAWFORD
describing his change of course at Oxford University
from the study of Latin and Greek philosophy and history.

Crawford Osbert Guy Stanhope (1886–1957). British archaeologist, who introduced aerial survey as a means of finding and interpreting remains, an idea conceived during World War I.

Craxi Bettino (Benedetto) (1934–). Italian socialist politician, leader of the Italian Socialist Party (PSI) 1976–93, prime minister 1983–87. In 1993 he was one of many politicians suspected of involvement in Italy's corruption network; in 1994 he was sentenced in absentia to eight and a half years in prison for accepting bribes, and in 1995 he received a further four-year sentence for corruption.

Craxi, born in Milan, became a member of the Chamber of Deputies 1968 and general secretary of the PSI 1976. In 1983 he became Italy's first socialist prime minister, successfully leading a broad coalition until 1987. In Feb 1993 he was forced to resign the PSI leadership in the face of mounting allegations of corruption, but was later absolved from prosecution on several charges. He was in Tunisia, and claimed to be too ill to return to Italy, when he was tried and sentenced for accepting bribes July 1994.

Crazy Horse Sioux name Ta-Sunko-Witko (1849–1877). Sioux Indian chief, one of the Indian leaders at the massacre of Little Bighorn. He was killed when captured.
Suggested reading
Ambrose, S E *Crazy Horse and Custer: Parallel Lives of Two American Warriors* (1988)
Brown, V *Crazy Horse, Hoka Hey: It is a Good Time to Die!* (1987)
Kadlecek, Edward and Mabell *To Kill an Eagle: Indian Views of the Killing of Crazy Horse* (1981)

Cranmer *Thomas Cranmer, the archbishop of Canterbury who declared the marriage between Henry VIII and Catherine of Aragon null and void. He played a large part in the creation of the liturgy of the Church of England and drew up the Thirty-nine Articles of faith, to which Anglican clergy are still required to subscribe.*

doctrines of the Church of England under Edward VI. He was responsible for the issue of the Prayer Books of 1549 and 1552, and supported the succession of Lady Jane Grey 1553.

Condemned for heresy under the Catholic Mary Tudor, he at first recanted, but when his life was not spared, resumed his position and was burned at the stake, first holding to the fire the hand which had signed his recantation.

Cranmer suggested 1529 that the question of Henry VIII's marriage to Catherine of Aragon should be referred to the universities of Europe rather than to the pope, and in 1533 he declared it null and void.

I would be married but I'd have no wife, / I would be married to a single life.

RICHARD CRASHAW
'On Marriage'

Crashaw Richard (*c.* 1613–1649). English religious poet of the metaphysical school. He published a book of Latin sacred epigrams 1634, then went to Paris, where he joined the Roman Catholic Church; his collection of poems *Steps to the Temple* appeared 1646.

Such is old age; but no weapon will fall from these hands.

MARCUS LICINIUS CRASSUS
Comment after dropping the sacrifice.
Quoted in Plutarch *Life of Crassus* ch 19.6

Crassus Marcus Licinius (*c.* 115–53 BC). Roman general who crushed the Spartacus uprising 71 BC and became consul 70. In 60 BC he joined with Caesar and Pompey in the First Triumvirate and obtained a command in the east 55 BC. Eager to gain his own reputation for military glory, he invaded Parthia (Mesopotamia), but was

Creed Frederick George (1871–1957). Canadian inventor who developed the teleprinter. He perfected the Creed telegraphy system (teleprinter), first used in Fleet Street, the headquarters of the British press, 1912 and subsequently, usually under the name Telex, in offices throughout the world.

He conveys vividly the absurdity of a situation, but he is incurious about the underlying processes which shape it.
William Thomas on THOMAS CREEVEY
in *Dictionary of National Biography Missing Persons* 1993

Creevey Thomas (1768–1838). British Whig politician and diarist whose lively letters and journals give information on early 19th-century society and politics. He was a member of Parliament and opposed the slave trade.

Crerar Henry Duncan Graham (1888–1965). Canadian general. Appointed Chief of the Canadian General Staff 1940, he was sent to Britain to organize the training of Canadian troops as they arrived. He resigned 1941 and took a drop in rank to command the 1st Canadian Corps which he led in the invasion of Sicily 1944. He commanded 1st Canadian Army in the D-Day invasion of France. His force was later involved in clearing the Scheldt Estuary and 1945 broke the Siegfried Line and entered Germany.

Crick *English molecular biologist Francis Crick. Crick shared the Nobel Prize for Physiology or Medicine with James Watson and Maurice Wilkins 1962, after discovering the molecular structure of the genetic material DNA, at the Cavendish Laboratory in Cambridge. He later turned his attention to investigating the nature of human consciousness.* (Image Select)

Crespo Joaquín (1845–1898). Venezuelan president 1884–86, 1892–98. A puppet of Antonia Guzman Blanco during his first term in office, Crespo seized power 1892 and is noted for his involvement in a boundary dispute with Great Britain over Guiana, where gold had been discovered.

Cresson Edith (born Campion) (1934–). French politician and founder member of the Socialist Party, prime minister 1991–92. Cresson held successive ministerial portfolios in François Mitterrand's government 1981–86 and 1988–90. Her government was troubled by a struggling economy, a series of strikes, and unrest in many of the country's poor suburban areas, which eventually forced her resignation.

A long-time supporter of François Mitterrand, and an outspoken defender of French trade rights, she became minister of agriculture 1981, minister of tourism 1983, minister of trade 1984, and minister of European affairs 1988, resigning from the last-named post 1990 on the grounds that France was 'in danger of being undermined by a lack of industrial mobilization'. She replaced Michel Rocard as prime minister May 1991. Increasingly unpopular with the public, Cresson was replaced as prime minister April 1992 by Pierre Bérégovoy, the former finance minister.

His memory was such that anything that he once heard or read he could repeat without an error.
J M Rigg on JAMES CRICHTON
in *Dictionary of National Biography*

Crichton James (1560–1582). Scottish scholar, known as 'the Admirable Crichton' because of his extraordinary gifts as a poet, scholar, and linguist. He was also an athlete and fencer. According to one account he was killed at Mantua in a street brawl by his pupil, a son of the Duke of Mantua, who resented Crichton's popularity.

Crichton Michael (1942–). US novelist, screenwriter, and director. Educated at Harvard Medical School, he combined his medical experience with science fiction themes to produce a series of highly popular novels, his first success being *The Andromeda Strain* 1969. This, and many of his later novels, have been filmed, including *Westworld* 1974, a fantasy science fiction film which he wrote and directed. Subsequent novels include *Congo* 1980, *Jurassic Park* 1992, and *Disclosure* 1994.

If you want to understand function, study structure.
FRANCIS CRICK
What Mad Pursuit p 150 1988

Crick Francis Harry Compton (1916–). English molecular biologist. From 1949 he researched the molecular structure of DNA, and the means whereby characteristics are transmitted from one generation to another. For this work he was awarded a Nobel prize (with Maurice Wilkins and James Watson) 1962.

Using Wilkins's and others' discoveries, Crick and Watson postulated that DNA consists of a double helix consisting of two parallel chains of alternate sugar and phosphate groups linked by pairs of organic bases. They built molecular models which also explained how genetic information could be coded – in the sequence of organic bases. Crick and Watson published their work on the proposed structure of DNA in 1953. Their model is now generally accepted as correct.

Crippen Hawley Harvey (1861–1910). US murderer who killed his wife, variety artist Belle Elmore, in 1910. He buried her remains in the cellar of his London home and tried to escape to the USA with his mistress Ethel le Neve (dressed as a boy). He was arrested on board ship following a radio message, the first criminal captured 'by radio', and was hanged.

Cripps (Richard) Stafford (1889–1952). British Labour politician, expelled from the Labour Party 1939–45 for supporting a 'Popular

Front' against Chamberlain's appeasement policy. He was ambassador to Moscow 1940–42, minister of aircraft production 1942–45, and chancellor of the Exchequer 1947–50. Knighted 1930.

Inducements of a material kind can never replace the spiritual urge ... from our sense of devotion to a cause which transcends our own personal interests.
STAFFORD CRIPPS
Address in a Birmingham church 11 May 1947

Crispi Francesco (1819–1901). Italian prime minister 1887–91 and 1893–96. He advocated the Triple Alliance of Italy with Germany and Austria, but was deposed 1896.

He made Italy run in the hope that she would learn to walk.
Norman Stone
quoting A J P Taylor on FRANCESCO CRISPI,
in *Europe Transformed 1878–1919* 1985

Cristofori Bartolommeo di Francesco (1665–1731). Italian harpsichordmaker, inventor of the piano. In 1709 he constructed a *gravicembalo col piano e forte* (harpsichord with softness and loudness), consisting of a harpsichord frame with a new action mechanism: hammers hitting the strings instead of plucking them, allowing for the first time a gradation of soft to loud.

Critias (*c.* 460–403 BC). Athenian politician and orator. He was one of the Thirty Tyrants installed as rulers of Athens by the Spartans at the end of the Peloponnesian War 404 BC. He was killed while at war against the Athenian general Thrasybulus (died 388 BC).

A pupil of Socrates, he was introduced by Plato in one of his dialogues 'Critias'.

Crivelli Carlo (*c.* 1435–*c.* 1495). Italian painter in the early Renaissance style. He was active in Venice and painted extremely detailed, decorated religious works, sometimes festooned with garlands of fruit. His figurative style is strongly Italian, reflecting the influence of Mantegna and Tura. His *Annunciation* 1486 (National Gallery, London) is his best-known work.

Croce Benedetto (1866–1952). Italian philosopher, historian, and literary critic; an opponent of fascism. His *Filosofia dello spirito/Philosophy of the Spirit* 1902–17 was a landmark in idealism. Like the German philosopher G W F Hegel, he held that ideas do not represent reality but *are* reality; but unlike Hegel, he rejected every kind of transcendence.

Crockett Davy (David) (1786–1836). US folk hero, born in Tennessee, a Democratic Congressman 1827–31 and 1833–35. A series of books, of which he may have been part-author, made him into a mythical hero of the frontier, but their Whig associations cost him his office. He clashed with Andrew Jackson, claiming Jackson had betrayed his frontier constituency, and left for Texas in bitterness. He died in the battle of the Alamo during the War of Texan Independence.

Suggested reading
Burke, J W *Crockett: The Man Behind the Myth* (1984)
Crockett, David *A Narrative of the Life of David Crockett* (autobiography) (1834, rep 1977)
Shackford, James *David Crockett: The Man and the Legend* (1986)

Crockford William (1775–1844). British gambler, founder in 1827 of Crockford's Club in St James's Street, which became the fashionable place for London society to gamble.

Both oracles foretold that if Croesus attacked the Persians he would destroy a great empire.
Herodotus on CROESUS
in *History* bk 1 ch 53

Croesus (died *c.* 546 BC). Last king of Lydia *c.* 560–546 BC, famed for his wealth. Dominant over the Greek cities of the Asia Minor coast, he was defeated and captured by Cyrus the Great and Lydia was absorbed into the Persian empire.

Croker Richard (1841–1922). US politician, 'boss' of Tammany Hall, the Democratic Party political machine in New York 1886–1902.

Crome John (1768–1821). English landscape painter. He was a founder of the Norwich School with John Sell Cotman 1803. His masterpieces include the *Boy keeping Sheep* (Victoria and Albert Museum); *Mousehold Heath* ('painted for air and space') and *The Poringland Oak* (National Gallery); and *The Slate Quarries* and *Moonlight on the Yare* (Tate Gallery): all products of his later life. As 'Old Crome' he is distinguished from his son, *John Bernay Crome* (1794–1842), who also worked at Norwich as painter and art master and specialized in effects of moonlight.

The son of a journeyman weaver and in youth a doctor's errand-boy and then apprentice to a coach painter, he was largely self-taught but studied with profit Dutch and other paintings in a local collection. He seems to have learned mainly from Hobbema, Gainsborough, Morland, and as regards luminous effect, from Richard Wilson. Earning a living as a drawing master at Norwich, he founded with others the Norwich Society of Artists 1803, thus becoming the main strength of the remarkable provincial phenomenon the 'Norwich School'. Cotman inspired him to produce some watercolours and he also made a number of etchings, but his main work is in oil-paintings, broadly treated and with true grandeur of design.

'All right,' she said calmly, 'I'll thcream then. I'll thcream, an' thcream, an' thcream till I'm sick'
RICHMAL CROMPTON
Just William 1922

Crompton Richmal. Pen name of Richmal Crompton Lamburn (1890–1969). English writer. She is remembered for her stories about the mischievous schoolboy William, the first of which was *Just William* 1922.

Crompton Rookes Evelyn Bell (1845–1940). English engineer who pioneered the dynamo, electric lighting, and road transport. He also contributed to the development of industry standards, both electrical and mechanical, and was involved in the founding of the National Physical Laboratory and what is now the British Standards Institution.

Crompton Samuel (1753–1827). British inventor at the time of the Industrial Revolution. He invented the 'spinning mule' 1779, combining the ideas of Richard Arkwright and James Hargreaves. This spun a fine, continuous yarn and revolutionized the production of high-quality cotton textiles.

Cromwell Oliver (1599–1658). English general and politician, Puritan leader of the Parliamentary side in the Civil War. He raised cavalry forces (later called Ironsides) which aided the victories at Edgehill 1642 and Marston Moor 1644, and organized the New Model Army, which he led (with General Fairfax) to victory at Naseby 1645. He declared Britain a republic ('the Commonwealth') 1649, following the execution of Charles I. As Lord Protector (ruler) from 1653, Cromwell established religious toleration and raised Britain's prestige in Europe on the basis of an alliance with France against Spain.

Cromwell was born at Huntingdon, NW of Cambridge, son of a small landowner. He entered Parliament 1629 and became active in events leading to the Civil War. Failing to secure a constitutional settlement with Charles I 1646–48, he defeated the 1648 Scottish invasion at Preston. A special commission, of which Cromwell was a member, tried the king and condemned him to death, and a republic, known as 'the Commonwealth', was set up.

The Levellers demanded radical reforms, but he executed their leaders 1649. He used terror to crush Irish clan resistance 1649–50, and defeated the Scots (who had acknowledged Charles II) at

Dunbar 1650 and Worcester 1651. In 1653, having forcibly expelled the corrupt 'Rump' Parliament, he summoned a convention ('Barebone's Parliament'), soon dissolved as too radical, and under a constitution (Instrument of Government) drawn up by the army leaders, became Protector (king in all but name). The parliament of 1654–55 was dissolved as uncooperative, and after a period of military dictatorship, his last parliament offered him the crown; he refused because he feared the army's republicanism.

Suggested reading

Ashley, M *Charles I and Oliver Cromwell* (1988)
Coward, Barry *Oliver Cromwell* (1991)
Fraser, A *Cromwell Our Chief of Men* (1973)
Gregg, P *Oliver Cromwell* (1988)
Hill, C *God's Englishman* (1970)
Kennelly, B *Cromwell* (1988)
Woolrych, Austin *Commonwealth and Protectorate* (1982)

Crookes *A cartoon published in* Vanity Fair *in 1903 of English chemist William Crookes, shown holding the discharge tube which carries his name. The Crookes tube was used to investigate the passage of cathode rays through rarified gases in a vacuum. Crooke's experimental work using high-voltage discharge tubes was one of the key steps towards the discovery of X-rays and the electron. (Ann Ronan/Image Select)*

I will not have a drop of blood spilt for the preservation of my greatness, which is a burden to me.

RICHARD CROMWELL
quoted in Grant Uden (ed) *Anecdotes from History* 123 1968

Cromwell Richard (1626–1712). Son of Oliver Cromwell, he succeeded his father as Lord Protector but resigned May 1659, having been forced to abdicate by the army. He lived in exile after the Restoration until 1680, when he returned.

An iron-fisted bureaucrat who crammed into his brief reign the kind of process which in England, we like to maintain, is carried out insensibly, over centuries.

H R Trevor-Roper on THOMAS CROMWELL
in *Historical Essays* 1957

Cromwell Thomas, Earl of Essex (*c.* 1485–1540). English politician who drafted the legislation that made the Church of England independent of Rome. Originally in Lord Chancellor Wolsey's service, he became secretary to Henry VIII 1534 and the real director of government policy; he was executed for treason. Created baron 1536.

Cromwell had Henry divorced from Catherine of Aragon by a series of acts that proclaimed him head of the church. From 1536 to 1540 Cromwell suppressed the monasteries, ruthlessly crushed all opposition, and favoured Protestantism, which denied the divine right of the pope. His mistake in arranging Henry's marriage to Anne of Cleves (to cement an alliance with the German Protestant princes against France and the Holy Roman Empire) led to his being accused of treason and beheaded.

Suggested reading

Beckinsale, B W *Thomas Cromwell* (1978)
Dickens, A G *Thomas Cromwell and the English Reformation* (1959)
Elton, G R *The Tudor Revolution in Government* (1953)

Cronenberg David (1943–). Canadian filmmaker of horror and science-fiction films. His works include *The Fly* 1986, a remake of a 1950s film, and *Dead Ringers* 1988, about twin psychotic gynaecologists.

His first film, *Shivers* 1974, concerns the invasion of human bodies by parasites. In 1991 he made a film of the novelist William Burroughs's *Naked Lunch*.

Cronin James Watson (1931–). US physicist who shared the 1980 Nobel Prize for Physics with Val Fitch for their work in particle physics. They showed for the first time that left–right asymmetry is not always preserved when some particles are changed in state from matter to antimatter. He was at Princeton 1958–71, as professor from 1965, and became professor at the University of Chicago 1971.

Cronje Piet Arnoldus (1835–1911). Boer commander who fought the British in both South African Wars (1881 and 1899–1902). He was defeated and surrendered his 4,000-strong force to Field Marshal Roberts at Paardeberg, Feb 1900.

Cronkite Walter Leland (1916–). US broadcast journalist who was anchorperson of the national evening news programme for CBS, a US television network, from 1962 to 1981.

Crookes William (1832–1919). English scientist whose many chemical and physical discoveries include the metallic element thallium 1861, the radiometer 1875, and the Crookes high-vacuum tube used in X-ray techniques. Knighted 1897.

The radiometer consists of a four-bladed paddle wheel mounted horizontally on a pinpoint bearing inside an evacuated glass globe. Each vane of the wheel is black on one side (making it a good absorber of heat) and silvered on the other side (making it a good reflector). When the radiometer is put in strong sunlight, the paddle wheel spins round.

Crosby Bing (Harry Lillis) (1904–1977). US film actor and singer. He achieved world success with his distinctive style of crooning in such songs as 'Pennies from Heaven' 1936 (featured in a film of the same name) and 'White Christmas' 1942. He won an acting Oscar for 'Going My Way' 1944, and made a series of 'road' film comedies with Dorothy Lamour and Bob Hope, the last being *Road to Hong Kong* 1962.

He was an average guy who could carry a tune.

BING CROSBY's own chosen epitaph.

Crossley Paul Christopher Richard (1944–). English pianist. He became joint artistic director of the London Sinfonietta 1988. A specialist in the works of such composers as Ravel, Messiaen, and Michael Tippett, he studied with Messiaen and French pianist Yvonne Loriod (1924–).

Whitehall envelops me.

RICHARD CROSSMAN
Diary entry after his first week in Cabinet 22 Oct 1964

Crossman Richard Howard Stafford (1907–1974). British Labour politician. He was minister of housing and local government 1964–66 and of health and social security 1968–70. His posthumous *Crossman Papers* 1975 revealed confidential cabinet discussions.

Do what thou wilt shall be the whole of the Law.

ALEISTER CROWLEY
Book of the Law 1909

Crowley Aleister (Edward Alexander) (1875–1947). British occultist, a member of the theosophical Order of the Golden Dawn; he claimed to practise black magic, and his books include the novel *Diary of a Drug Fiend* 1923. He designed a tarot pack that bears his name.

Known as the Great Beast, he was vehemently anti-Christian. He advocated drug taking and sexual magic as means to deeper levels of consciousness; his beliefs are set out in *Magick in Theory and Practice* 1929.

Crowley John (1942–). US writer of science fiction and fantasy. His work notably includes *Little, Big* 1980 and *Aegypt* 1987, which contain esoteric knowledge and theoretical puzzles.

Cruden Alexander (1701–1770). Scottish compiler of a biblical *Concordance* 1737.

Cruft Charles (1852–1938). British dog expert. He organized his first dog show 1886, and from that year annual shows bearing his name were held in Islington, London. In 1948 the show's venue moved to Olympia and in 1979 to Earl's Court.

Cruikshank George (1792–1878). English painter and illustrator. He is remembered for his political cartoons and illustrations for Charles Dickens' *Oliver Twist* and Daniel Defoe's *Robinson Crusoe*.

Following his father, he began with political and social caricatures in the Gillray and Rowlandson style, but evolved a grotesque and humorous manner of his own in sketches of Victorian London life and in book illustration. Notable productions are his etchings, 1823–26, for Grimms' fairy-tales and the spirited melodrama of those for Harrison Ainsworth's *Old St Paul's*. His brother Robert (1789–1856) was also a caricaturist and a miniature painter. They collaborated 1821 in illustrating the late-Georgian humours of Pierce Egan's *Life in London*.

Cruise Tom. Adopted name of Thomas Cruise Mapother IV (1962–). US film actor, one of Hollywood's biggest box-office attractions of the late 1980s and 1990s. His clean-cut good looks earned him a succession of teen roles in the early 1980s but he proved his dramatic metal against Paul Newman in *The Color of Money* 1986. He went on to star in such films as *Top Gun* 1986, *Rain Man* 1988, *Born on the Fourth of July* 1989, and *Days of Thunder* 1990. His other films include *Far and Away* 1992 with his wife Nicole Kidman, *Cocktail* 1988, *A Few Good Men* 1993, and *Interview with the Vampire* 1994.

Crumb George Henry (1929–). US composer of imagist works. He employed unusual graphics and imaginative sonorities, such as the musical saw in *Ancient Voices of Children* 1970, settings of poems by the Spanish poet Lorca.

Cruwell Ludwig (1892–1953). German general. Cruwell served in World War I and remained in the postwar *Reichsheer*. He was promoted to major-general Dec 1939 and by 1940 commanded a Panzer division. He became commander of the Afrika Korps 1941 but he was shot down and captured while making an air reconnaissance May 1942.

Cruyff Johan (1947–). Dutch footballer, an outstanding European player in the 1970s. He was capped 48 times by his country, scoring 33 goals. He spent most of his career playing with Ajax and Barcelona and was named European Footballer of the Year three times. As coach, he took both clubs to domestic and European honours.

Cruyff was a slightly built player with razor-sharp reactions, excellent control, speed, acceleration, and the ability to change direction instantly.

Cruz, Juana Inés de la Sor (born Juana Inés de Asbaje y Ramirez) (1651–1695). Mexican poet and dramatist. A nun from the age of 17, she was both poet and writer, defending her secular writings in her eloquent *Respuesta a Sor Filotea/Response to Sister Philotea* 1691, which also argues for women's rights to education. Her poems, baroque in style, include sonnets and lyrics; her plays, in the style of Calderón de la Barca, include *El Divino Narciso* 1690.

Cubitt Thomas (1788–1855). English builder and property developer. One of the earliest speculators, Cubitt, together with his brother Lewis Cubitt (1799–1883), rebuilt much of Belgravia, London, an area of Brighton, and the east front of Buckingham Palace.

Cudworth Ralph (1617–1688). English philosopher and leading member of the Cambridge Platonists. He opposed the materialism of Thomas Hobbes, and tried to combine the science of his day with the Platonic tradition in metaphysics and theology. Holding that mechanical and atomic principles do not suffice to explain nature, he posited the existence of a Plastic Nature, or Platonic world soul, to relate the material and spiritual orders.

Cudworth was born in Aller, Somerset. He spent most of his life at Cambridge University, where he became Master of Clare Hall and then Master of Christ's College. He was professor of Hebrew 1645–88. His works include *The True Intellectual System of the Universe* 1678 and the posthumously published *A Treatise Concerning Eternal and Immutable Morality* 1731.

Cugnot Nicolas-Joseph (1725–1804). French engineer who produced the first high-pressure steam engine and, in 1769, the first self-propelled road vehicle. Although it proved the viability of steam-powered traction, the problems of water supply and pressure maintenance severely handicapped the vehicle.

While serving in the army, Cugnot was asked to design a steam-operated gun carriage. After several years, he produced a three-wheeled, high-pressure carriage capable of carrying 1,800 litres/400 gallons of water and four passengers at a speed of 5 kph/3 mph. Although he worked further on the carriage, the political upheavals of the French revolutionary era obstructed progress and his invention was ignored.

Cui César Antonovich (1835–1918). Russian composer and writer, of French parentage. An army engineer by profession, he became a member of 'The Five' group of composers and an enthusiastic proponent of Russian nationalist music in the press. Despite this, his own musical tastes tended towards the France of Auber and

Meyerbeer in operas *Angelo* 1876 based on Victor Hugo and *Le Flibustier/The Buccaneer* 1889 based on a play by Jean Richepin.

I was too shaken to make the announcement. No one else could do it either. Audrey said simply: 'I'll do it'. Taking a hand microphone, she said simply: 'The President of the United States is dead. Shall we have two minutes silence to pray or do whatever you think is appropriate.'

GEORGE CUKOR
recounting how Audrey Hepburn helped him
announce Kennedy's death *Daily Mail* 1964

Cukor George Dewey (1899–1983). US film director. He is known for sophisticated dramas and light comedies. He moved to the cinema from the theatre and was praised for his skilled handling of such stars as Greta Garbo (in *Camille* 1937) and Katharine Hepburn (in *The Philadelphia Story* 1940). He won an Academy Award for the direction of *My Fair Lady* 1964.
Suggested reading
Bernardoni, J *George Cukor* (1985)
Phillips, Gene *George Cukor* (1982)

Culshaw John Royds (1924–1980). British record producer who developed recording techniques. Managing classical recordings for the Decca record company in the 1950s and 1960s, he introduced echo chambers and the speeding and slowing of tapes to achieve effects not possible in live performance. He produced the first complete recordings of Wagner's *Ring* cycle.

Cumberland Ernest Augustus, Duke of Cumberland (1771–1851). King of Hanover from 1837, the fifth son of George III of Britain. A high Tory and an opponent of all reforms, he attempted to suppress the constitution but met with open resistance that had to be put down by force. Duke 1799.

All the good that we have done has been a little blood-letting, which has only weakened the madness, but not at all cured.

WILLIAM AUGUSTUS, DUKE OF CUMBERLAND
Letter 29 June 1746, after crushing the Jacobite rebellion in Scotland.

Cumberland William Augustus, Duke of Cumberland (1721–1765). British general who ended the Jacobite rising in Scotland with the Battle of Culloden 1746; his brutal repression of the Highlanders earned him the nickname of 'Butcher'. KCB 1725, duke 1726.

Third son of George II, he was created Duke of Cumberland 1726. He fought in the War of the Austrian Succession at Dettingen 1743 and Fontenoy 1745. In the Seven Years' War he surrendered with his army at Kloster-Zeven 1757.

Listen: there's a hell of a good universe next door: let's go.

E E CUMMINGS
'Pity this busy monster, manunkind'

cummings e(dward) e(stlin) (1894–1962). US poet. His work is marked by idiosyncratic punctuation and typography (for example, his own name is always written in lower case), and a subtle, lyric celebration of life. Before his first collection *Tulips and Chimneys* 1923, cummings published an avant-garde novel, *The Enormous Room* 1922, based on his internment in a French concentration camp during World War I.

His typographical experiments were antecedents of the concrete and sound poetry of the 1960s.
Suggested reading
Friedman, N *e e cummings: The Growth of a Writer* (1964)
Kennedy, R S *Dreams in the Mirror: A Biography of e e cummings* (1980)
Kidder, R M *e e cummings: An Introduction to his Poetry* (1979)

Cunha Euclydes Rodrigues Pimenta da (1866–1909). Brazilian writer. His novel *Os Sertões/Rebellion in the Backlands* 1902 describes the Brazilian *sertão* (backlands), and how a small group of rebels resisted government troops.

Cunningham Alan Gordon (1887–1983). British general of World War II. Although he led the British offensive against the Italians in Ethiopia 1940–41 with great success, Cunningham failed to show his usual drive during Operation Crusader when he was commander of the British 8th Army. He was relieved of his post by Field Marshal Auchinleck and spent the rest of the war in administrative posts before becoming the last High Commissioner in Palestine. Knighted 1941.

Cunningham Allan (1791–1839). English botanist and explorer in Australia whose explorations 1823–29 opened up stock routes to the NW of the E coast and located the valuable pastures of the Darling Downs. Several Australian trees are named after him, as well as Cunningham's Gap, a pass through the Great Dividing Range, Queensland.

Cunningham Andrew Browne, 1st Viscount Cunningham of Hyndhope (1883–1963). British admiral in World War II, commander in chief in the Mediterranean 1939–42, maintaining British control; as commander in chief of the Allied Naval Forces in the Mediterranean Feb–Oct 1943 he received the surrender of the Italian fleet. He then became First Sea Lord and Chief of Naval Staff until 1946. KCB 1939, baron 1945, viscount 1946.

Cunningham Imogen (1883–1976). US photographer. Her early photographs were romantic but she gradually rejected pictorialism, producing clear and detailed plant studies 1922–29. With Ansel Adams and Edward Weston, she was a founder member of the 'f/64' group which advocated precise definition. From the mid-1930s she concentrated on portraiture.

Cunningham John (1917–). British air ace of World War II. He was among the first pilots to be given airborne radar for night fighting. His successes with this led to his nickname 'Cats-Eyes Cunningham', a public relations stunt to conceal the fact that radar was in use.

Cunningham was a test pilot for the De Havilland Aircraft company prior to the war; he was commissioned into the RAF and rose to the rank of Group Captain.

Cunningham John Henry Dacres (1885–1962). British admiral in World War II. He was commander in chief in the Mediterranean 1943–46, First Sea Lord 1946–48, and became admiral of the fleet in 1948. KCB 1941.

In 1940 he assisted in the evacuation of Norway and, as Fourth Sea Lord in charge of supplies and transport 1941–43, prepared the way for the N African invasion in 1942.

Cunningham Merce (1919–). US choreographer and dancer. He is recognized as the father of post-modernist, or experimental, dance. He liberated dance from its relationship with music, allowing it to obey its own dynamics.

Along with his friend and collaborator, composer John Cage, he introduced chance into the creative process, such as tossing coins to determine options. Influenced by Martha Graham, with whose company he was soloist 1939–45, he formed his own avant-garde dance company and school in New York 1953. His works include *The Seasons* 1947, *Antic Meet* 1958, *Squaregame* 1976, and *Arcade* 1985.

Cunningham worked closely with composers, such as Cage, and artists, such as Robert Rauschenberg, when staging his works; among them *Septet* 1953, *Suite for Five* 1956, *Crises* 1960, *Winterbranch* 1964, *Scramble* 1967, *Signals* 1970, and *Sounddance* 1974.

Cunninghame-Graham Robert Bontine (1852–1936). Scottish writer, politician, and adventurer. He was the author of essays and short stories such as 'Success' 1902, 'Faith' 1909, 'Hope' 1910, and 'Charity' 1912. He wrote many travel books based on his experiences as a rancher in Texas and Argentina 1869–83, and as a traveller in Spain and Morocco 1893–98. He became the first president of the Scottish Labour Party in 1888 and the first president of the Scottish National Party in 1928.

Cuno Wilhelm Carl Josef (1876–1933). German industrialist and politician who was briefly chancellor of the Weimar Republic 1923.

Cunobelin King of the Catuvellauni; see ◊Cymbeline.

Cuomo Mario Matthew (1932–   ). US Democrat politician. He was governor of New York State 1983–95. One of his party's foremost thinkers, he was for many years seen as a future president. His key concern was that rich and poor America should unite.

Cuomo was born in New York and became a lawyer. Following the publication of *Forest Hills Diary: The Crisis of Low Income Housing* 1974, an account of his assessment of a proposed public housing project in a middle-class community, he became secretary of state of the State of New York, acting as the governor's negotiator in statewide crises. In 1994 he wrote *The New York Idea: An Experiment in Democracy.*

It would be impossible, it would be against the scientific spirit .... Physicists should always publish their researches completely. If our discovery has a commercial future that is a circumstance from which we should not profit. If radium is to be used in the treatment of disease, it is impossible for us to take advantage of that.

MARIE CURIE
quoted in Eve Curie *Marie Curie* transl V Sheean 1938

Curie Marie (born Manya Skłodowska) (1867–1934). Polish scientist. In 1898 she and her husband Pierre Curie discovered two new, radioactive elements in pitchblende ores: polonium and radium. They isolated the pure elements 1902. Both scientists refused to take out a patent on their discovery and were jointly awarded the Nobel Prize for Physics 1903, with Henri Becquerel. Marie Curie wrote a *Treatise on Radioactivity* 1910, and was awarded the Nobel Prize for Chemistry 1911.

From 1896 the Curies worked together on radioactivity, building on the results of Wilhelm Röntgen (who had discovered X-rays) and Becquerel (who had discovered that similar rays are emitted by uranium salts). They took no precautions against radioactivity and Marie Curie died of radiation poisoning. Her notebooks, even today, are too contaminated to handle.

Suggested reading
Giroud, F *Marie Curie: A Life* (trs 1986)
Quinn, Susan *Marie Curie: A Life* (1995)
Reid, Robert *Marie Curie* (1974)

Curie Pierre (1859–1906). French scientist who shared the Nobel Prize for Physics 1903 with his wife Marie Curie and Henri Becquerel. From 1896 the Curies had worked together on radioactivity, discovering two radioactive elements.

Pierre Curie was born in Paris and educated at the Sorbonne, becoming an assistant there 1878. He discovered the piezoelectric effect and, after being appointed head of the laboratory of the Ecole de Physique et Chimie, went on to study magnetism and formulate Curie's law, which states that magnetic susceptibility is inversely proportional to absolute temperature. In 1895 he discovered the Curie point, the critical temperature at which a paramagnetic substance becomes ferromagnetic. In 1904 he became professor of physics at the Sorbonne.

Curley James Michael (1874–1958). US Democratic politician. He was a member of the US House of Representatives 1912–14, several times mayor of Boston between 1914 and 1934, when he was elected governor. He lost a bid for the US Senate 1936 and did not hold political office again until elected to the House 1942. His fourth and last mayoral term began 1946, during which time he spent six months in federal prison on a mail-fraud conviction. The flamboyant Curley's political career inspired Edwin O'Connor's *The Last Hurrah* 1956.

Curie Marie and Pierre Curie with their eldest daughter Irène 1904. All three members of the family won Nobel prizes – Marie and Pierre won the Nobel Prize for Physics for their work on radioactivity in 1903, Marie won the Nobel Prize for Chemistry for the discovery of polonium and radium in 1911, and Irène Joliet-Curie won the Nobel Prize for Chemistry in 1935 for her work on preparing the first artificial isotope. (Ann Ronan/Image Select)

Curnonsky pseudonym of Maurice Edmond Sailland (1872–1956). French gastronome and cookery writer, who was a pioneer in the cataloguing of French regional cuisine.

Curnow Allen (1911–   ). New Zealand poet, dramatist, anthologist, and critic. Associated with the important Phoenix group in the 1930s, as a poet and critic he has influentially explored the possibilities of cultural identity in New Zealand, stressing both the isolation of the poet (particularly in *Island and Time* 1941) and the need for poets and the people to speak the same language. Language itself is the focus of more recent work such as *Trees, Effigies, Moving Objects* 1972 and *An Incorrigible Music* 1979. A selection of his plays was published 1972 and *Collected Poems, 1933–1973* appeared 1974.

Currie Arthur William (1875–1933). Canadian soldier, the first Canadian officer to become a general. His success at commanding a Canadian brigade in the Second Battle of Ypres 1915 led to his promotion to general and from 1917 he was commander of the Canadian Corps for the rest of World War I. KCMG 1917.

He forced the Quéant Switch line and captured Cambrai 1918. In 1920 he became principal of McGill University, Montreal.

Curry John Anthony (1949–1994). English ice skater, British champion 1970 and 1972–75, and European, Olympic, and world champion 1976. He excelled in the free interpretation of music on ice, and moved the emphasis of the sport from the athletic to the artistic.

Curtin John (1885–1945). Australian Labor politician, prime minister and minister of defence 1941–45. He was elected leader of the Labor Party 1935. As prime minister, he organized the mobilization of Australia's resources to meet the danger of Japanese invasion during World War II. He died in office before the end of the war.

He proved a capable and inspirational leader in World War II, mobilizing Australia's resources to meet the threat of Japanese invasion. He clashed with Churchill over the latter's view that Australia was dispensable, withdrawing Australian troops from the Middle East 1942 to help defend against the Japanese threat. At the same time, he reassessed the need for US support and invited General Douglas MacArthur to establish his headquarters in Australia.

A man of great sincerity and force of character ... his leadership of Australia in the most critical years of her history won the respect of all parties.

K C Wheare on JOHN CURTIN
in *Dictionary of National Biography*

Curtis Heber Doust (1872–1942). US astronomer who deduced that spiral nebulae were galaxies that produced a cloud of debris which accumulated in the plane of the galaxy. At the age of 22, he became professor of Latin at Napa College, California. Access to the small observatory there changed his career, and in 1897 he became professor of mathematics and astronomy at the University of the Pacific. He subsequently worked at a number of US observatories and 1906–09 in Chile, but most of his research was done at the Lick Observatory, Mount Hamilton, California, between 1898 and 1920.

We've no control over our conception, only over our creation.

TONY CURTIS
on filmmaking, Cannes May 1982

Curtis Tony. Stage name of Bernard Schwartz (1925–). Versatile US film actor. His best work was characterized by a nervous energy, as the press agent in *Sweet Smell of Success* 1957 and the drag-disguised musician on the run from the Mob in *Some Like It Hot* 1959.

He also starred in *The Vikings* 1958 and *The Boston Strangler* 1968.

Curtiss Glenn Hammond (1878–1930). US aeronautical inventor, pioneer aviator, and aircraft designer. In 1908 he made the first public flights in the USA, including the one-mile flight. He belonged to Alexander Graham Bell's Aerial Experiment Association 1907–09 and established the first flying school 1909. In 1910 Curtiss staged his sensational flight down the Hudson River from Albany to New York City.

In 1916 he founded the Curtiss Aeroplane and Motor Corp, based on his invention of ailerons, which he designed for the first seaplanes 1911. He designed and constructed many planes for the Allied nations during World War I. After the end of the war 1918 he continued to improve plane and motor designs.

Curtiz Michael. Adopted name of Mihaly Kertész (1888–1962). Hungarian-born film director. He worked in Austria, Germany, and France before moving to the USA 1926, where he made several films with Errol Flynn (*Captain Blood* 1935). He directed *Mildred Pierce* 1945, which revitalized Joan Crawford's career, and *Casablanca* 1942 (Academy Award).

His wide range of films include *The Private Lives of Elizabeth and Essex* 1939, *The Adventures of Robin Hood* 1938, *Yankee Doodle Dandy* 1942, and *White Christmas* 1954.

Curwen John (1816–1880). English cleric and educator. In about 1840 he established the tonic sol-fa system of music notation (originated in the 11th century by Guido d'Arezzo) in which the notes of the diatonic major scale are named by syllables (doh, ray, me, fah, soh, lah, te) to simplify singing by sight.

Curzon Clifford (1907–1982). English pianist. He made his reputation as a pianist specializing in 18th-century composers, though he also played 19th- and 20th-century works in his early years. He was known as perhaps the greatest Mozartian of his day. Knighted 1977.

Curzon George Nathaniel, 1st Marquess Curzon of Kedleston (1859–1925). British Conservative politician, viceroy of India

Cushing , Peter *Gaunt and intense, Peter Cushing specialized in horror film roles, though he also played a range of character parts such as Sherlock Holmes. He is seen here in* The Hound of the Baskervilles *1959.*

1899–1905. As viceroy he partitioned Bengal, created the North West Frontier province, and introduced political and social reforms. He resigned over a dispute with Lord Kitchener. During World War I, he was a member of the cabinet 1916–19. As foreign secretary 1919–24, he set up a British protectorate over Persia. Baron (Irish peerage) 1898, earl 1911, marquess 1921.

Suggested reading
Dilks, David *Curzon of India* (1969)
Gilmour, David *Curzon* (1994)
Rose, Kenneth *Superior Person* (1969)

The British Empire is under Providence the greatest instrument for good that the world has seen.

GEORGE CURZON
Dedication of his book *Problems of the Far East* 1894

Curzon Robert, 14th Baron Zouche (1810–1873). English diplomat and traveller, author of *Monasteries in the Levant* 1849. Succeeded to barony 1870.

Cusack Cyril James (1910–1993). Irish actor. He joined the Abbey Theatre, Dublin, 1932 and appeared in many of its productions. In Paris he won an award for his solo performance in Beckett's *Krapp's Last Tape*. In the UK he played many roles as a member of the Royal Shakespeare Company and the National Theatre Company.

He also played a number of small parts in films, including *The Spy Who Came in from the Cold* 1965, Zeffirelli's *The Taming of the Shrew* 1968, *The Day of the Jackal* 1973 and *My Left Foot* 1989. However, the theatre was his first love, and he is remembered for the parts he played in Irish drama, particularly as the naive and charming Christy Mahon in Synge's *The Playboy of the Western World* and the impertinent young Covey in Sean O'Casey's *The Plough and the Stars*.

Cushing Harvey Williams (1869–1939). US neurologist who pioneered neurosurgery. He developed a range of techniques for the surgical treatment of brain tumours, and also studied the link between the pituitary gland and conditions such as dwarfism. He first described the chronic wasting disease now known as Cushing's syndrome.

From 1912 to 1932 he was professor of surgery at the Harvard Medical School; in 1933 he became professor of neurology at Yale.

Teeth are a vitally important part of an actor's equipment. I have over thirty toothbrushes at home, and always keep a good supply at the studio.

PETER CUSHING
Publicity release for *Scream and Scream again* 1969

Cushing Peter (1913–1994). English actor. Elegant and often sinister, he specialized in horror roles in films made at Hammer studios 1957–73, including *Dracula* 1958, *The Mummy* 1959, and *Frankenstein Must Be Destroyed* 1969. Other films include *Doctor Who and the Daleks* 1966, *Star Wars* 1977, and *Top Secret* 1984.

Custer George Armstrong (1839–1876). US Civil War general, who became the Union's youngest brigadier general 1863 as a result of a brilliant war record. Some historians accuse Custer of a reckless desire to advance his career. He was made a major general 1865, but following the end of the Civil War, his rank was reduced to captain. He campaigned against the Sioux from 1874, and was killed with a detachment of his troops by the forces of Sioux chief Sitting Bull in the Battle of Little Bighorn, Montana, also called Custer's last stand, 25 June 1876.

Suggested reading
Ambrose, S E *Crazy Horse and Custer: Parallel Lives of Two American Warriors* (1988)
Connell, E *Sun of the Morning Star* (1984)
Custer, George Armstrong *My Life on the Plains* (1874, rep 1986)
Goble, P and D *Custer's Last Battle* (1970)
Utley, R *Cavalier in Buckskin* (1988)

God's grace made clear the glory of the saint. For when his monks dug up his body after eleven years, they found it all whole as if he were still alive, and the joints of the limbs, supple, more like one sleeping than dead.

Bede on ST CUTHBERT
Church History bk 4, ch 30

Cuthbert, St (died 687). Christian saint. A shepherd in Northumbria, England, he entered the monastery of Melrose, Scotland, after receiving a vision. He travelled widely as a missionary and because of his alleged miracles was known as the 'wonderworker of Britain'.

He became prior of Lindisfarne 664, and retired 676 to Farne Island. In 684 he became bishop of Hexham and later of Lindisfarne. Feast day 20 March.

Cuvier Georges Léopold Chrétien Frédéric Dagobert., Baron (1769–1832). French comparative anatomist, the founder of palaeontology. In 1799 he showed that some species have become extinct by reconstructing extinct giant animals that he believed were destroyed in a series of giant deluges. These ideas are expressed in *Recherches sur les ossiments fossiles de quadrupèdes/Researches on the Fossil Bones of Quadrupeds* 1812 and *Discours sur les révolutions de la surface du globe* 1825.

In 1798 Cuvier produced *Tableau élémentaire de l'histoire naturelle des animaux*, in which his scheme of classification is outlined. He was the first to relate the structure of fossil animals to that of their living relatives. His great work *Le Règne animal/The Animal Kingdom* 1817 is a systematic survey.

Cuyp Aelbert (1620–1691). Dutch painter. His subjects were countryside scenes, seascapes, and portraits. His idyllically peaceful landscapes are bathed in a golden light, reflecting the influence of

Custer *US general George A Custer (centre) during a Black Hills expedition 1874. Custer was now engaged on the campaign against the Sioux Indians that would lead to his famous 'last stand' at the Battle of Little Big Horn 1876.*

Claude Lorrain, for example, *A Herdsman with Cows by a River* about 1650 (National Gallery, London). His father, Jacob Gerritsz Cuyp (1594–1652), was also a landscape and portrait painter.

His coins far surpass those of previous British kings, both in excellence of workmanship and in the artistic character of their design.

T F Tout on CYMBELINE
'Cunobelinus'

Cymbeline or Cunobelin (lived 1st century AD). King of the Catuvellauni AD 5–40, who fought unsuccessfully against the Roman invasion of Britain. His capital was at Colchester.

Cynewulf (lived early 8th century). Anglo-Saxon poet. He is thought to have been a Northumbrian monk and is the undoubted author of 'Juliana' and part of the 'Christ' in the Exeter Book (a collection of poems now in Exeter Cathedral, England), and of the 'Fates of the Apostles' and 'Elene' in the Vercelli Book (a collection of Old English manuscripts housed in Vercelli, Italy), in all of which he inserted his name by using runic acrostics.

Cyprian, St (c. 210–258). Christian martyr, one of the earliest Christian writers, and bishop of Carthage about 249. He wrote a treatise on the unity of the church. Feast day 16 Sept.

Cyrano de Bergerac Savinien (1619–1655). French writer. He joined a corps of guards at 19 and performed heroic feats which brought him fame. He is the hero of a classic play by Edmond Rostand, in which his excessively long nose is used as a counterpoint to his chivalrous character.

Cyril and Methodius, Sts two brothers, both Christian saints: Cyril 826–869 and Methodius 815–885. Born in Thessalonica, they were sent as missionaries to what is today Moravia. They invented a Slavonic alphabet, and translated the Bible and the liturgy from Greek to Slavonic. The language (known as Old Church Slavonic) remained in use in churches and for literature among Bulgars, Serbs, and

Russians up to the 17th century. The cyrillic alphabet is named after Cyril and may also have been invented by him. Feast day 14 Feb.

Cyril of Alexandria, St (376–444). Bishop of Alexandria from 412, persecutor of Jews and other non-Christians, and suspected of ordering the murder of Hypatia (*c.* 370–*c.* 415), a philosopher whose influence was increasing at the expense of his. He was violently opposed to Nestorianism.

I have never feared men who have a special place in the city where they swear oaths and cheat each other.

CYRUS THE GREAT
on Greek commercial practices, quoted in Herodotus *History* bk 1, ch 153

Cyrus the Great (died 529 BC). Founder of the Persian Empire. As king of Persia, he was originally subject to the Medes, whose empire he overthrew 550 BC. He captured Croesus 546 BC, and conquered Lydia, adding Babylonia (including Syria and Palestine) to his empire 539 BC, allowing exiled Jews to return to Jersualem. He died fighting in Afghanistan.

Czartoryski Adam Jerzy (1770–1861). Polish statesman and general. The most famous member of the Czartoryski family, he campaigned for the restoration of an independent Polish state. In 1830 he headed the Polish November Insurrection, but on its suppression by Russia the following year, he went into exile in Paris.

Having lost his family estate in the 1795 partition of Poland, he became a friend and adviser of the future Tsar Alexander, went to Russia and was appointed Russian minister of foreign affairs 1804–1806. As Polish spokesman at the Congress of Vienna 1815, he negotiated the creation of a kingdom of Poland with Alexander as king. He retired from public life in 1816. He was chosen to lead the provisional Polish government in the 1830 revolution, and was subsequently elected president of the national government in 1831. While in Paris, he was acknowledged as the Polish king in exile.

Czerny Carl (1791–1857). Austrian composer and pianist. He wrote an enormous quantity of religious and concert music, but is chiefly remembered for his books of graded studies and technical exercises used in piano teaching, including the *Complete Theoretical and Practical Pianoforte School* 1839 which is still in widespread use.

D

Dadd Richard (1817–1886). English painter. In 1843 he murdered his father and was committed to an asylum, but continued to paint minutely detailed pictures of fantasies and fairy tales, such as *The Fairy Feller's Master Stroke* 1855–64 (Tate Gallery, London).

Dafydd ap Gwilym (*c.* 1340–*c.* 1400). Welsh poet. His work is notable for its complex but graceful style, its concern with nature and love rather than with heroic martial deeds, and for its references to Classical and Italian poetry.

Daglish Eric Fitch (1892–1966). English artist and author. He wrote a number of natural history books, and illustrated both these and classics by Izaak Walton, Henry Thoreau, Gilbert White, and W H Hudson with exquisite wood engravings.

Daguerre Louis Jacques Mandé (1787–1851). French pioneer of photography. Together with Joseph Niépce, he is credited with the invention of photography (though others were reaching the same point simultaneously). In 1838 he invented the daguerreotype, a single image process superseded ten years later by Fox Talbot's negative/positive process.

Dahl Johann Christian Clausen (1788–1857). Norwegian landscape painter in the Romantic style. He trained in Copenhagen but was active chiefly in Dresden from 1818. The first great painter of the Norwegian landscape, his style recalls that of the Dutch artist Jacob van Ruisdael.

Dahl Roald (1916–1990). British writer of Norwegian ancestry. He is celebrated for short stories with a twist, for example, *Tales of the Unexpected* 1979, and for children's books, including *Charlie and the Chocolate Factory* 1964. He also wrote the screenplay for the James Bond film *You Only Live Twice* 1967.

His autobiography *Going Solo* 1986 recounted his experiences as a fighter pilot in the RAF.

Grown-ups should keep well away from Dahl's stories for children unless there's a youngster handy to help them with the shocking bits.

Chris Powling on ROALD DAHL
in *Roald Dahl* ch 1 1993

Dahrendorf Ralf Gustav, Baron Dahrendorf (1929–). German-born British sociologist whose works include *Life Chances* 1980, which sees the aim of society as the improvement of the range of opportunities open to the individual. He was director of the London School of Economics 1974–84. KBE 1982, baron 1993.

Daimler Gottlieb Wilhelm (1834–1900). German engineer who pioneered the car and the internal-combustion engine together with Wilhelm Maybach. In 1885 he produced a motor bicycle and in 1889 his first four-wheeled motor vehicle. He combined the vaporization of fuel with the high-speed four-stroke petrol engine.

Daimler's work on the internal-combustion engine began in earnest in 1872 when he teamed up with Nikolaus Otto at a gas-engine works; Maybach was the chief designer. Daimler built his first petrol engines 1883. The Daimler Motoren Gesellschaft was founded 1890, and Daimler engines were also manufactured under licence; a Daimler-powered car won the first international car race: Paris to Rouen 1894.

Daladier Edouard (1884–1970). French Radical politician. As prime minister April 1938–March 1940, he signed the Munich Agreement 1938 (by which the Sudeten districts of Czechoslovakia were ceded to Germany) and declared war on Germany 1939. He resigned 1940 because of his unpopularity for failing to assist Finland against Russia. He was arrested on the fall of France 1940 and was a prisoner in Germany 1943–45. Following the end of World War II he was re-elected to the Chamber of Deputies 1946–58.

It is a phoney war.

EDOUARD DALADIER
Speech in Chamber of Deputies Paris 22 Dec 1939

Dalai Lama (Tibetan 'oceanic guru') 14th incarnation. Title of Tenzin Gyatso (1935–). Tibetan Buddhist monk, political ruler of Tibet from 1940 until 1959, when he went into exile in protest against Chinese annexation and oppression. He has continued to campaign for self-government; Nobel Peace Prize 1989. Tibetan Buddhists believe that each Dalai Lama is a reincarnation of his predecessor and also of Avalokiteśvara.
Suggested reading
Avedon, J *In Exile from the Land of Snows* (1984)
Dalai Lama *Freedom in Exile* (1990)
Goodman, M H *The Last Dalai Lama* (1986)

Dalcroze Emile Jaques. See ◊Jaques-Dalcroze.

Dale Henry Hallett (1875–1968). British physiologist who in 1936 shared the Nobel Prize for Physiology or Medicine with Otto Loewi for proving that chemical substances are involved in the transmission of nerve impulses. He was director of the Wellcome Physiological Research Laboratories 1906–14; worked at the Medical Research Council 1914–28, and was director of the National Institute for Medical Research 1928–42. Knighted 1932.

d'Alembert French mathematician. See ◊Alembert.

Dalén Nils Gustav (1869–1937). Swedish industrial engineer who invented the light-controlled valve. This allowed lighthouses to operate automatically and won him the 1912 Nobel Prize for Physics.

Daley Richard Joseph (1902–1976). US politician and controversial mayor of Chicago 1955–76. He built a formidable political machine and ensured a Democratic presidential victory 1960 when J F Kennedy was elected. He hosted the turbulent national Democratic convention 1968.

Born in Chicago, Daley became involved in local Democratic politics at an early age. He attended law school at DePaul University, gaining admission to the bar 1933. He served in the Illinois legislature 1936–46. He was Cook County clerk 1935–55 before being elected mayor of Chicago, remaining in office until his death.

Dalgarno George (*c.* 1626–1687). Scottish schoolteacher and the inventor of the first sign-language alphabet 1680.

Dalglish Kenny (Kenneth Mathieson) (1951–). Scottish footballer and football manager. He was the first man to play 200 League games in both England and Scotland, and to score 100 goals in each country.

He played for Celtic 1967–77, who won four Scottish League Championships, four Scottish Cups and one Scottish League Cup. He moved to Liverpool and won 12 major medals in the next eight years; five League Championships, four League Cups, and three European Cups. He made a record 102 international appearances for Scotland and equalled Denis Law's record of 30 goals. He was

Footballer of the Year 1979 and 1983, and Players' Player of the Year 1983. He was player-manager of Liverpool when they won the Cup and League double 1985–86; as manager he added two more League titles 1987–88, 1989–90, and another FA Cup win 1989. He became manager of Blackburn Rovers 1991, taking them into the Premier League and on to the Championship 1994–95. He is one of only three managers to win the English Championship with two clubs.

To him India owes railways and telegraphs, the reform of the postal system, and the development of irrigation and roadmaking.

A J Arbuthnot on JAMES DALHOUSIE
in *Dictionary of National Biography*

Dalhousie James Andrew Broun Ramsay, 1st Marquess and 10th Earl of Dalhousie (1812–1860). British administrator, governor general of India 1848–56. In the second Sikh War he annexed the Punjab 1849, and, following the second Burmese War, Lower Burma 1853. He reformed the Indian army and civil service and furthered social and economic progress. Succeeded to earldom 1838, marquis 1849.

Surrealism is destructive, but it destroys only what it considers to be shackles limiting our vision.

SALVADOR DALI
Declaration

Dali Salvador Felippe Jacinto (1904–1989). Spanish painter and designer. In 1929 he joined the Surrealists and became notorious for his flamboyant eccentricity. Influenced by the psychoanalytic theories of Sigmund Freud, he developed a repertoire of striking, hallucinatory images – distorted human figures, limp pocket watches, and burning giraffes – in superbly executed works, which he termed 'hand-painted dream photographs'. *The Persistence of Memory* 1931 (Museum of Modern Art, New York) is typical. By the late 1930s he had developed a more conventional style – this, and his apparent Fascist sympathies, led to his expulsion from the Surrealist movement 1938. It was in this more traditional though still highly inventive and idiosyncratic style that he painted such celebrated religious works as *The Crucifixion* 1951 (Glasgow Art School). He also painted portraits of his wife Gala.

Dali, born near Barcelona, initially came under the influence of the Italian Futurists. He is credited as co-creator of Luis Buñuel's Surrealist film *Un Chien andalou* 1928, but his role is thought to have been subordinate; he abandoned filmmaking after collaborating on the script for Buñuel's *L'Age d'or*/*The Golden Age* 1930. He also designed ballet costumes, scenery, jewellery, and furniture. The books *The Secret Life of Salvador Dali* 1942 and *Diary of a Genius* 1966 are autobiographical. He was buried beneath a crystal dome in the museum of his work at Figueras on the Costa Brava, Spain.

Suggested reading
Ades, D *Dali and Surrealism* (1982)
Dali, S *The Secret Life of Salvador Dali* (1942)
Dali, S *Confessions of a Genius* (1965)
Dali, S *Dali by Dali* (1970)
Gerard, M *Salvador Dali* (1970)
Secrest, M *Salvador Dali, the Surrealist Jester* (1986)

Dallapiccola Luigi (1904–1975). Italian composer. Initially a Neo-Classicist, he adopted a lyrical twelve-tone style after 1945. His works include the operas *Il prigioniero*/*The Prisoner* 1949 and *Ulisse*/*Ulysses* 1968, as well as many vocal and instrumental compositions.

Dalton (Edward) Hugh (John Neale), Baron Dalton (1887–1962). British Labour politician and economist. Chancellor of the Exchequer from 1945, he oversaw nationalization of the Bank of England, but resigned 1947 after making a disclosure to a lobby correspondent before a budget speech. Baron 1960.

He was suspicious of the upper class, contemptuous of the middle class, and nervously patronizing of the working class.

Roy Jenkins on HUGH DALTON
in *Gallery of 20th Century Portraits* 1988

Dalton John (1766–1844). English chemist who proposed the theory of atoms, which he considered to be the smallest parts of matter. He produced the first list of relative atomic masses in *Absorption of Gases* 1805 and put forward the law of partial pressures of gases (Dalton's law).
Suggested reading
Cardwell, D (ed) *John Dalton and the Progress of Science* (1968)
Thackrey, A *John Dalton: Critical Assessments of His Life and Science* (1973)

Daly (John) Augustin (1838–1899). US theatre manager. He began as a drama critic and dramatist before building his own theatre in New York 1879 and another, Daly's, in Leicester Square, London, 1893.

Dalziel family of British wood engravers. George (1815–1902), Edward (1817–1905), John (1822–1860), and Thomas Bolton (1823–1906) were all sons of Alexander Dalziel of Wooler, Northumberland. George went to London in 1835 and was joined by his brothers. They produced illustrations for classic works of literature and for magazines.

Dam Carl Peter Henrik (1895–1976). Danish biochemist who discovered vitamin K. For his success in this field he shared the 1943 Nobel Prize for Physiology or Medicine with US biochemist Edward Doisy (1893–1986).

Damien, Father name adopted by Belgian missionary Joseph de ◊Veuster.

Damocles (lived 4th century BC). In Classical legend, a courtier of the elder Dionysius, ruler of Syracuse, Sicily. When Damocles made too much of his sovereign's good fortune, Dionysius invited him to a feast where he symbolically hung a sword over Damocles' head to demonstrate the precariousness of the happiness of kings.

Dampier William (1651–1715). English explorer and hydrographic surveyor who circumnavigated the world three times.

He was born in Somerset, and went to sea in 1668. He led a life of buccaneering adventure, circumnavigated the globe, and published his *New Voyage Round the World* in 1697. In 1699 he was sent by the government on a voyage to Australia and New Guinea, and again circled the world. He accomplished a third circumnavigation 1703–07, and on his final voyage 1708–11 rescued Alexander Selkirk (on whose life Daniel Defoe's *Robinson Crusoe* is based) from Juan Fernandez in the S Pacific.

When a dog bites a man that is not news, but when a man bites a dog that is news.

CHARLES DANA
'What is News?' in *New York Sun* 1882

Dana Charles Anderson (1819–1897). US journalist who covered the European revolutions of 1848 and earned a reputation as one of America's most able foreign correspondents. During the US Civil War he served as assistant secretary of war 1863–65 and in 1868 purchased the *New York Sun*, with which he pioneered the daily tabloid format.

Dana was manager of Brook Farm, an experimental community in West Roxbury, Massachusetts, 1841–47. He was later managing editor of the *New York Tribune* under Horace Greeley.

Dana Richard Henry, Jr (1815–1882). US author and lawyer. He went to sea and worked for his passage around Cape Horn to California and back, then wrote an account of the journey *Two Years before the Mast* 1840. He also published *The Seaman's Friend* 1841, a guide to maritime law.

He rejoiced more in the votes of ninety-nine silent legislators than the conversion of one notable opponent.

David Ogg on THOMAS DANBY
in *England in the Reign of Charles II* 1934

Danby Thomas Osborne, 1st Earl of Danby (1631–1712). British Tory politician. He entered Parliament 1665, acted as Charles II's chief minister 1673–78 and was created earl of Danby 1674, but was imprisoned in the Tower of London 1678–84. In 1688 he signed the invitation to William of Orange to take the throne. Succeeded to baronetcy 1647. Danby was again chief minister 1690–95, and in 1694 was created duke of Leeds.

Dance Charles (1946–). English film and television actor. He became known when he played the sympathetic Guy Perron in *The Jewel in the Crown* 1984. He has also appeared in *Plenty* 1986, *Good Morning Babylon*, *The Golden Child* both 1987, and *White Mischief* 1988.

Dance George, the Younger (1741–1825). English architect. He is best remembered for his unorthodox designs for Newgate Prison 1770–80, London (demolished 1902).

An exponent of the Neo-Classical tradition, absorbed on a visit to Italy as a young man, he retained a highly individual and innovative style. He was to exert a lasting influence on his pupil, John Soane. Indeed, his design for All-Hallows Church, London Wall, 1765–67, can be seen as a precursor of Soane's refined Classicism. His father George Dance, the Elder (1700–1768) was the architect of the Mansion House 1739–42, London.

Dancer John Benjamin (1812–1887). British optician and instrumentmaker who pioneered microphotography. By 1840 he had developed a method of taking photographs of microscopic objects, using silver plates. The photographic image was capable of magnification up to 20 times before clarity was lost. By 1859 he was showing microscope slides which carried portraits or whole pages of books.

Dandolo Venetian family that produced four doges (rulers), of whom the most outstanding, Enrico (*c.* 1120–1205), became doge in 1193. He greatly increased the dominions of the Venetian republic and accompanied the crusading army that took Constantinople in 1203.

Daniel (lived 6th century BC). Jewish folk hero and prophet at the court of Nebuchadnezzar; also the name of a book of the Old Testament, probably compiled in the 2nd century BC. It includes stories about Daniel and his companions Shadrach, Meshach, and Abednego, set during the Babylonian captivity of the Jews.

One of the best-known stories is that of Daniel in the den of lions, where he was thrown for refusing to compromise his beliefs, and was preserved by divine intervention. The book also contains a prophetic section dealing with the rise and fall of a number of empires.

Daniel Glyn Edmund (1914–1986). British archaeologist. Prominent in the development of the subject, he was Disney professor of archaeology, Cambridge, 1974–81. His books include *Megaliths in History* 1973 and *A Short History of Archaeology* 1981.

Daniel Samuel (1562–1619). English poet. He was the author of the sonnet collection *Delia* 1592. From 1603 he was master of the revels at court, for which he wrote masques.

Daniell John Frederic (1790–1845). British chemist and meteorologist who invented a primary electrical cell 1836. The Daniell cell consists of a central zinc cathode dipping into a porous pot containing zinc sulphate solution. The porous pot is, in turn, immersed in a solution of copper sulphate contained in a copper can, which acts as the cell's anode. The use of a porous barrier prevents polarization (the covering of the anode with small bubbles of hydrogen gas) and allows the cell to generate a continuous current of electricity.

The Daniell cell was the first reliable source of direct-current electricity. He was the first professor of chemistry at King's College, London, 1831–45.

Daniels Sarah (1957–). British dramatist. Her plays explore contemporary feminist issues, and include *Ripen Our Darkness* 1981, *Masterpieces* 1983, *Byrthrite* 1987, *Neaptide* 1984, *Beside Herself* 1990, and *Head-Rot Holiday* 1992, concerning women condemned to mental institutions.

Daninos Pierre (1913–). French author. Originally a journalist, he was liaison agent with the British Army at Dunkirk 1940, and created in *Les Carnets du Major Thompson/The Notebooks of Major Thompson* 1954, a humorous Englishman who caught the French imagination.

Dankl Victor (1854–1941). Austrian general; commander in chief of Austrian troops in N Italy in World War I.

Dankl joined the Austro-Hungarian cavalry 1874 and became a general of the Austrian cavalry 1912. In 1914 he took command of the 1st Austrian Army which invaded SE Poland Aug 1914 and was heavily defeated by the Russians in the battles of Rava Russka Sept 1914. After operations against Ivangorod July–Aug 1915, he was transferred to the Italian front.

Dankworth John Philip William (1927–). English jazz musician, composer, and bandleader. He was a leading figure in the development of British jazz from about 1950. His film scores include *Saturday Night and Sunday Morning* 1960 and *The Servant* 1963.

D'Annunzio Gabriele (1863–1938). Italian poet, novelist, and playwright. Marking a departure from 19th-century Italian literary traditions, his use of language and style of writing earned him much criticism in his own time. His novels, often combining elements of corruption, snobbery, and scandal, include *L'innocente* 1891 and *Il triomfo della morte/The Triumph of Death* 1894.

His first volume of poetry, *Primo vere/In Early Spring* 1879, was followed by further collections of verse, short stories, novels, and plays (he wrote the play *La Gioconda* for the actress Eleonora Duse 1898). During World War I, he was active in turning public opinion to the side of the Allies 1915. He joined the air service and flew many bombing missions, losing an eye as a result of an accident. After the war, he led an expedition of volunteers 1919 to capture Fiume, which he held until 1921. He became a national hero, and was created Prince of Montenevoso 1924. Influenced by Nietzsche's writings, he later became an ardent exponent of Fascism.

All hope abandon, ye who enter here.

DANTE ALIGHIERI
Divine Comedy, 'Inferno' III 1307–21

Dante Alighieri (1265–1321). Italian poet. His masterpiece *La divina commedia/The Divine Comedy* 1307–21 is an epic account in three parts of his journey through Hell, Purgatory, and Paradise, during which he is guided part of the way by the poet Virgil; on a metaphorical level, the journey is also one of Dante's own spiritual development. Other works include the philosophical prose treatise *Convivio/The Banquet* 1306–08, the first major work of its kind to be written in Italian rather than Latin; *Monarchia/On World Government* 1310–13, expounding his political theories; *De vulgari eloquentia/Concerning the Vulgar Tongue* 1304–06, an original Latin work on Italian, its dialects, and kindred languages; and *Canzoniere/Lyrics*, containing his scattered lyrics.

Dante was born in Florence, where in 1274 he first met and fell in love with Beatrice Portinari (described in *La vita nuova/New Life* 1283–92). His love for her survived her marriage to another and her death 1290 at the age of 24. He married Gemma Donati 1291.

In 1289 Dante fought in the battle of Campaldino, won by Florence against Arezzo, and from 1295 took an active part in Florentine politics. In 1300 he was one of the six Priors of the Republic, favouring the moderate 'White' Guelph party rather than the extreme papal 'Black' Ghibelline faction; when the Ghibellines seized power 1302, he was convicted in his absence of misapplication of public money and sentenced first to a fine and then to death. He escaped from Florence and spent the remainder of his life in exile, in central and N Italy.

Suggested reading

Caesar, Michael *Dante* (1989)
Chubb, T C *Dante and His World* (1966)
Grandgent, C *Companion to the Divine Comedy* (1975)
Holmes, G *Dante* (1980)
Mazzotta, G *Dante: Poet of the Desert* (1987)

To conquer them we must dare, and dare again, and dare for ever; and thus will France be saved.

GEORGES DANTON
Speech to rally support against foreign invaders
in French Legislative Committee 2 Sept 1792

Danton Georges Jacques (1759–1794). French revolutionary. Originally a lawyer, during the early years of the Revolution he was one of the most influential people in Paris. He organized the uprising 10 Aug 1792 that overthrew Louis XVI and the monarchy, roused the country to expel the Prussian invaders, and in April 1793 formed the revolutionary tribunal and the Committee of Public Safety, of which he was the leader until July of that year.

Thereafter he lost power to the Jacobins, and, when he attempted to recover it, was arrested and guillotined.

Dantzig George Bernard (1914–   ). US mathematician, an expert in linear computer programming and operations research. His work is fundamental to many university courses in business studies, industrial engineering, and managerial sciences. Dantzig has been involved in all the main areas of mathematical programming. He was a research mathematician with the Rand Corporation at Santa Monica, California, 1952–60, and then became a professor at the University of California at Berkeley, moving 1966 to Stanford University, Palo Alto, California.

Da Ponte Lorenzo (born Conegliano Emmanuele) (1749–1838). Italian librettist. He is renowned for his collaboration with Mozart in *The Marriage of Figaro* 1786, *Don Giovanni* 1787, and *Così fan tutte* 1790. His adaptations of contemporary plays are deepened by a rich life experience and understanding of human nature.

Born in Ceneda (now Vittorio Veneto), he studied to take holy orders, proving a skilful versifier in both Italian and Latin. Appointed as a professor in literature at Treviso Seminary 1773, his radical views and immoral behaviour led to his banishment from Venice 1779. Travelling to Vienna, he was appointed as librettist to the New Italian Theatre 1781 on the recommendation of Salieri. His first major success was in adapting Beaumarchais' comedy for Mozart's *The Marriage of Figaro*. *Don Giovanni* and *Così fan tutte* followed, together with libretti for other composers. In 1805 he emigrated to the USA, eventually becoming a teacher of Italian language and literature.

d'Arblay, Madame married name of English writer Fanny ◊Burney.

Darboux (Jean) Gaston (1842–1917). French mathematician who contributed immensely to the differential geometry of his time, and to the theory of surfaces. In defining the Riemann integral 1879, he derived the Darboux sums and used the Darboux integrals.

Darboux was born in Nîmes and educated at the Ecole Normale Supérieure and at the Sorbonne in Paris, where he became a professor 1873 and assistant to mathematician Joseph Liouville.

Darby Abraham (1677–1717). English iron manufacturer who developed a process for smelting iron ore using coke instead of the more expensive charcoal 1709.

He employed the cheaper iron to cast strong thin pots for domestic use, and after his death it was used for the huge cylinders required by the new steam pumping-engines. In 1779 his grandson Abraham Darby (1750–1791) constructed the world's first iron bridge, over the river Severn at Coalbrookdale, Shropshire.

Dare Virginia (born 1587). First English child born in America. She was the granddaughter of John White, the governor of Roanoke colony (now in North Carolina). White returned to England soon after her birth, leaving Dare in Roanoke with the rest of her settler family. English communication with Roanoke was cut off for nearly four years during the war with Spain 1585–88. In 1591 the crew of an English ship found the colony deserted.

The enigmatic inscription 'Croatan' carved in a tree led to speculation that the settlers, fearful of hostile Indians, had perhaps taken refuge with the friendly Croatan.

Darío Rubén. Pen name of Félix Rubén García Sarmiento (1867–1916). Nicaraguan poet. His first major work *Azul/Azure* 1888, a collection of prose and verse influenced by French Symbolism, created a sensation. He went on to establish modernismo, the Spanish-American modernist literary movement, distinguished by an idiosyncratic and deliberately frivolous style that broke away from the prevailing Spanish provincialism and adapted French poetic models. His vitality and eclecticism influenced every poet writing in Spanish after him, both in the New World and in Spain.

I was not wicked, nor a liar, nor tyrannical; I walked according to right and justice.

DARIUS
Royal proclamation at Behistun in Iran

Darius (I) the Great (c. 558–486 BC). King of Persia 521–486 BC. A member of a younger branch of the Achaemenid dynasty, he won the throne from the usurper Gaumata (died 522 BC) and reorganized the government. In 512 BC he marched against the Scythians, a people north of the Black Sea, and subjugated Thrace and Macedonia.

An expedition in 492 BC under his general Mardonius to crush a rebellion in Greece failed, and the army sent into Attica 490 BC was defeated at the battle of Marathon. Darius had an account of his reign inscribed on the mountain at Behistun, Persia.

Darlan Jean Louis Xavier François (1881–1942). French admiral and politician. He entered the navy 1899, and was appointed admiral and commander in chief 1939. He commanded the French navy 1939–40, took part in the evacuation of Dunkirk, and entered the Pétain cabinet as naval minister. In 1941 he was appointed vice premier, and adopted a strongly pro-German stance in the hope of obtaining better conditions for the French people, with little success. When Pétain was replaced by Laval 1942, he was dropped from the cabinet and sent to N Africa, where he was assassinated by a French monarchist 24 Dec.

Applications for locks of hair came in until Grace was in danger of baldness.

Dictionary of National Biography on GRACE DARLING

Darling Grace Horsley (1815–1842). British heroine. She was the daughter of a lighthouse keeper on the Farne Islands, off Northumberland. On 7 Sept 1838 the *Forfarshire* was wrecked, and Grace Darling and her father rowed through a storm to the wreck, saving nine lives. She was awarded a medal for her bravery.

Darnand Joseph (1897–1945). French admiral and right-wing politician. During World War II, he set up the *Milice Française* security police, which collaborated with the German army and Gestapo. After the liberation of France he fled to Germany, but was captured and executed by the French.

Darnley Henry Stewart (or Stuart), Lord Darnley (1545–1567). British aristocrat, second husband of Mary Queen of Scots from

1565, and father of James I of England (James VI of Scotland).

On the advice of her secretary, David Rizzio, Mary refused Darnley the crown matrimonial; in revenge, Darnley led a band of nobles who murdered Rizzio in Mary's presence. Darnley was assassinated 1567. Knighted and became Earl of Ross and Duke of Albany 1565.

[Although] handsome and notably athletic ... his intelligence was of the meanest and he was vain, arrogant, irritable and vicious.

C R N Routh on LORD DARNLEY
in *Who's Who in Tudor England*

He was born in England, the son of the 4th Earl of Lennox (1516–1571) and Lady Margaret Douglas (1515–1578), through whom he inherited a claim to the English throne. Mary was his first cousin. Mary and Darnley were reconciled after the murder of Rizzio 1566, but soon Darnley alienated all parties and a plot to kill him was formed by Bothwell. Mary's part in it remains a subject of controversy.

Suggested reading
Bingham, Caroline *Darnley: A Life of Henry Stuart, Lord Darnley, Consort of Mary Queen of Scots* (1995)

Darrell George (born Frederick Price) (1841–1921). Australian actor, dramatist, and theatrical manager, born in England. He wrote more than fifty plays on Australian themes and is best known for *The Sunny South* 1883, which was produced in London in 1884 and 1898, and in 1914 was made into a film.

Darrow Clarence Seward (1857–1938). US lawyer, born in Ohio, a champion of liberal causes and defender of the underdog. He defended many trade-union leaders, including Eugene Debs 1894. He was counsel for the defence in the Nathan Leopold and Richard Loeb murder trial in Chicago 1924, and in the Scopes monkey trial. Darrow matched wits in the latter trial with prosecution attorney William Jennings Bryan. He was an opponent of capital punishment.

Suggested reading
Darrow, Clarence *The Story of My Life* (1932)
Weinberg, A and L *Clarence Darrow* (1987)

Dart Raymond Arthur (1893–1988). Australian-born South African palaeontologist and anthropologist who in 1924 discovered the first fossil remains of the australopithecines, early hominids, near Taungs in Botswana. He was professor of anatomy at the University of Witwatersrand, Johannesburg, South Africa, 1922–58.

Dart (Robert) Thurston (1921–1971). English harpsichordist and musicologist. His pioneer reinterpretations of Baroque classics such as Bach's *Brandenburg Concertos* helped to launch the trend towards authenticity in early music.

Darwin Charles Robert (1809–1882). English scientist who developed the modern theory of evolution and proposed, with Alfred Russel Wallace, the principle of natural selection. After research in South America and the Galápagos Islands as naturalist on HMS *Beagle* 1831–36, Darwin published *On the Origin of Species by Means of Natural Selection or the Preservation of Favoured Races in the Struggle for Life* 1859. This explained the evolutionary process through the principles of natural and sexual selection. It aroused bitter controversy because it disagreed with the literal interpretation of the Book of Genesis in the Bible.

The theory of natural selection concerned the variation existing between members of a sexually reproducing population. According to Darwin, those members with variations better fitted to the environment would be more likely to survive and breed, subsequently passing on these favourable characteristics to their offspring.

On the Origin of Species also refuted earlier evolutionary theories, such as those of French naturalist J B de Lamarck. Darwin himself played little part in the debates, but his *Descent of Man* 1871 added fuel to the theological discussion, in which English scientist T H Huxley

and German zoologist Ernst Haeckel took leading parts.

Darwin also made important discoveries in many other areas, including the fertilization mechanisms of plants, the classification of barnacles, and the formation of coral reefs.

Suggested reading
Bowlby, John *Charles Darwin: A Biography* (1990)
Brent, Peter *Charles Darwin: A Man of Enlarged Curiosity* (1981)
Browne, Janet *Charles Darwin: Voyaging* (1995)
Chancellor, John *Charles Darwin* (1973)
Clark, R W *The Survival of Charles Darwin* (1985)
de Beer, Gavin *Charles Darwin: A Scientific Biography* (1963)
George, Wilma *Darwin* (1982)

Darwin Erasmus (1731–1802). British poet, physician, and naturalist; he was the grandfather of Charles Darwin. He wrote *The Botanic Garden* 1792, which included a versification of the Linnaean system entitled *The Loves of the Plants*, and *Zoonomia* 1794–96, which anticipated aspects of evolutionary theory, but tended to French naturalist J B de Lamarck's interpretation.

Dassin Jules (1911–). US-born international film director. After directing the violent prison film *Brute Force* 1947 and the thriller *Naked City* 1948, he left the US in the wake of the anti-Communist witch-hunts. The French-made gangster film *Rififi* 1954 was an international success, as was *Never on Sunday* 1960, filmed in Greece, in which Dassin starred opposite Melina Mercouri, his wife from 1966.

He later returned to the USA to film *Up Tight* 1968.

Daudet Alphonse (1840–1897). French novelist. He wrote about his native Provence in *Lettres de mon moulin/Letters from My Mill* 1866, and created the character Tartarin, a hero epitomizing southern temperament, in *Tartarin de Tarascon* 1872 and two sequels.

Other works include the play *L'Arlésienne/The Woman from Arles* 1872, for which Bizet composed the music; and *Souvenirs d'un homme de lettres/Recollections of a Literary Man* 1889.

Daudet (Alphonse Marie) Léon (1867–1942). French writer and journalist. He founded the militant right-wing royalist periodical *Action Française* 1899 after the Dreyfus case. During World War II he was a collaborator with the Germans. He was the son of Alphonse Daudet.

Darwin, Charles *Charles Darwin, the founder of modern evolutionary theory, photographed by Elliott G Fry on the verandah of his home, Down House, Kent, c. 1880. (Image Select)*

Daumier Honoré Victorin (1808–1879). French artist. His sharply dramatic and satirical cartoons dissected Parisian society. He produced over 4,000 lithographs and, mainly after 1860, powerful, sardonic oil paintings that were little appreciated in his lifetime.

Daumier drew for *La Caricature*, *Charivari*, and other periodicals. He created several fictitious stereotypes of contemporary figures and was once imprisoned for an attack on King Louis Philippe. His paintings show a fluent technique and a mainly monochrome palette. He also produced sculptures of his caricatures, such as the bronze statuette of *Ratapoil* about 1850 (Louvre, Paris).

For I must go where lazy Peace / Will hide her drowsy head; / And, for the sport of kings increase / The number of the dead.

WILLIAM DAVENANT
'The Soldier Going to the Field'

Davenant William (1606–1668). English poet and dramatist, poet laureate from 1638. His *Siege of Rhodes* 1656 is sometimes considered the first English opera. His plays include *The Wits* and *Love and Honour*, both 1634. Knighted 1643.

David (*c.* 1060–*c.* 970 BC). Second king of Israel. According to the Old Testament he played the harp for King Saul to banish Saul's melancholy; he later slew the Philistine giant Goliath with a sling and stone. After Saul's death David was anointed king at Hebron, took Jerusalem, and made it his capital.

David was celebrated as a secular poet and probably wrote some of the psalms attributed to him. He was the youngest son of Jesse of Bethlehem. While still a shepherd boy he was anointed by Samuel, a judge who ruled Israel before Saul. Saul's son Jonathan became David's friend, but Saul, jealous of David's prowess, schemed to murder him. David married Michal, Saul's daughter, but after further attempts on his life went into exile until Saul and Jonathan fell in battle with the Philistines at Gilboa. Once David was king, Absalom, his favourite son, led a rebellion but was defeated and killed.

David sent Uriah (a soldier in his army) to his death in the front line of battle in order that he might marry his widow, Bathsheba. Their son Solomon became the third king.

In both Jewish and Christian belief, the messiah would be a descendant of David; Christians hold this prophecy to have been fulfilled by Jesus.

David Elizabeth (1914–1992). British cookery writer. Her *Mediterranean Food* 1950 and *French Country Cooking* 1951 helped to spark an interest in foreign cuisine in Britain, and also inspired a growing school of informed, highly literate writing on food and wine.

David Félicien César (1810–1876). French composer. His symphonic fantasy *The Desert* 1844 was inspired by travels in Palestine. He was one of the first Western composers to introduce oriental scales and melodies into his music.

David Gerard (*c.* 1450–*c.* 1523). Netherlandish painter. He was active chiefly in Bruges from about 1484. His style follows that of Rogier van der Weyden, but he was also influenced by the taste in Antwerp for Italianate ornament. *The Marriage at Cana* about 1503 (Louvre, Paris) is an example of his work. Famous paintings are the panels ordered by the magistrates of Bruges for the Hall of Justice depicting the arrest and punishment of the corrupt judge, Sisamnes (Bruges, Musée Communal), and the *Baptism of Christ*, also at Bruges. Some miniatures are attributed to him.

I want to give meaning to that deep great and religious feeling inspired by love for one's country.

JACQUES-LOUIS DAVID
quoted in *Journal de Délécluze* 1824

David Jacques-Louis (1748–1825). French Neo-Classical painter. He was an active supporter of, and unofficial painter to, the republic

during the French Revolution, and was imprisoned 1794–95. In his *Death of Marat* 1793 (Musées Royaux, Brussels), he turned political murder into Classical tragedy. Later he devoted himself to the newly created Empire in paintings such as the vast, pompous *Coronation of Napoleon* 1805–07 (Louvre, Paris). After Napoleon's fall, David was banished by the Bourbons and settled in Brussels. Among his finest works are *The Rape of Sabine Women* 1799 (Louvre, Paris) and *Mme Récamier* 1800 (Louvre, Paris).

Suggested reading
Brookner, Anita *J-L David: A Personal Interpretation* (1974)
Friedlaender, W *From David to Delacroix* (1968)
Lindsay, J *Death of the Hero* (1960)
Roberts, Warren *Jacques-Louis David, Revolutionary Artist* (1989)

David two kings of Scotland:

David I (1084–1153). King of Scotland from 1124. The youngest son of Malcolm III Canmore and St Margaret, he was brought up in the English court of Henry I, and in 1113 married Matilda, widow of the 1st earl of Northampton.

He invaded England 1138 in support of Queen Matilda, but was defeated at Northallerton in the Battle of the Standard, and again 1141.

At no period of its history has Scotland ever stood as high in the scale of nations.

Hume Brown on DAVID I
in *History of Scotland* vol i 1899

David II (1324–1371). King of Scotland from 1329, son of Robert (I) the Bruce. David was married at the age of four to Joanna, daughter of Edward II of England. In 1346 David invaded England, was captured at the battle of Neville's Cross, and imprisoned for 11 years.

After the defeat of the Scots by Edward III at Halidon Hill 1333, the young David and Joanna were sent to France for safety. They returned 1341. On Joanna's death 1362 David married Margaret Logie, but divorced her 1370.

Inconsistent, passionate and headstrong ... at bottom weak ... in the end yielding to the persistent policy and will of the English King [Edward III].

A J G Mackay on DAVID II
in *Dictionary of National Biography*

David, St or Dewi (lived 5th–6th century). Patron saint of Wales, Christian abbot and bishop. According to legend he was the son of a prince of Dyfed and uncle of King Arthur; he was responsible for the adoption of the leek as the national emblem of Wales, but his own emblem is a dove. Feast day 1 March.

Tradition has it that David made a pilgrimage to Jerusalem, where he was consecrated bishop. He founded 12 monasteries in Wales, including one at Menevia (now St Davids), which he made his bishop's seat; he presided over a synod at Brefi and condemned the ideas of the British theologian Pelagius.

In anguish we uplift / A new unhallowed song: / The race is to the swift, / The battle to the strong.

JOHN DAVIDSON
'War Song'

Davidson John (1857–1909). Scottish poet. His modern, realistic idiom, as in 'Thirty Bob a Week', influenced T S Eliot.

Davies Henry Walford (1869–1941). English composer and broadcaster. His compositions include the cantata *Everyman* 1904, the 'Solemn Melody' 1908 for organ and strings, chamber music, and part songs.

From 1934 he was Master of the King's Musick, and he contributed to the musical education of Britain through regular radio talks. Knighted 1922.

Davies Jonathan (1962–). Welsh rugby league player. He was capped 27 times between 1985 and 1988 for the Wales rugby union team. In 1988 he changed codes, joining Widnes for a fee of £225,000, and became a member of the Great Britain XIII.

Davies Laura (1963–). English golfer, and member of Europe's Solheim Cup team 1990, 1992, and 1994. Winner of many major tournaments, including the Ladies British Open 1986, the US Women's Open 1987, and the McDonald's LPGA 1993, she was top of the LPGA Money List 1994. She was a member of the Curtis Cup team 1984, and turned professional 1985, when she became Rookie of the Year.

Davies Peter Maxwell (1934–). English composer and conductor. His music combines medieval and serial codes of practice with a heightened Expressionism as in his opera *Taverner* 1962–68. Other works include the opera *The Lighthouse* 1980. He was appointed conductor of the BBC Scottish Symphony Orchestra 1985. Knighted 1987.

Davies Siobhan (Susan) (1950–). English choreographer and dancer. She was a founding member of the London Contemporary Dance Theatre (LCDT) 1967 and became its resident choreographer 1983–87. She is the founder and director of Siobhan Davies and Dancers 1981. Her Siobhan Davies Company was premiered during the 10th Dance Umbrella festival 1988. Her works, such as *Bridge the Distance* (for LCDT) 1985, display a quiet, cool intensity.

Other works include *Celebration* 1978 and *Embarque* 1988 (both for the Rambert Dance Company).

Davies Terence (1945–). British film director. He forged his reputation on the strength of films dealing impressionistically with his own family background and early life in Liverpool. The two-part *Distant Voices/Still Lives* 1988 won the Cannes critics' award and was succeeded by *The Long Day Closes* 1992. He subsequently made a non-autobiographical film in the US, *The Neon Bible* 1995.

What is this life if, full of care, / We have no time to stand and stare?

W H DAVIES
'Leisure'

Davies W(illiam) H(enry) (1871–1940). Welsh poet. He went to the USA where he lived the life of a vagrant and lost his right foot stealing a ride under a freight car. His first volume of poems was *Soul's Destroyer* 1906. He published his *Autobiography of a Super-Tramp* 1908.

The world does so well without me that I am moved to wish that I could do equally well without the world.

ROBERTSON DAVIES
The Papers of Samuel Marchbanks ch 38 1986

Davies (William) Robertson (1913–1996). Canadian novelist. He published the first novel of his Deptford trilogy *Fifth Business* 1970, a panoramic work blending philosophy, humour, the occult, and ordinary life. Other works include *A Mixture of Frailties* 1958, *The Rebel Angels* 1981, *What's Bred in the Bone* 1986, *The Lyre of Orpheus* 1988, and *Murther and Walking Spirits* 1991.
Suggested reading
Monk, Patricia *The Smaller Infinity* (1982)

Davin Dan(iel) Marcus (1913–1990). New Zealand novelist and short-story writer. He was based in Oxford after 1945. His Irish Catholic upbringing and his wartime experience with the New Zealand Division provided the background for his acclaimed early novels *Cliffs of Fall* 1945 and *For the Rest of Our Lives* 1947.

Davies, Peter Maxwell *The composer Peter Maxwell Davies is probably the foremost British composer of our time. His early avant garde works have given way more recently to an accessible means of expression admired by both critics and the general public. He is active in support of the arts in the face of funding cuts.*

His social and psychological concerns are reflected in *Selected Stories* 1981, in critical studies, and in an autobiography *Closing Times* 1975.

da Vinci Italian Renaissance artist. See ◊Leonardo da Vinci.

Davis Angela Yvonne (1944–). US left-wing activist for black rights, prominent in the student movement of the 1960s. In 1970 she went into hiding after being accused of supplying guns used in the murder of a judge who had been seized as a hostage in an attempt to secure the release of three black convicts. She was captured, tried, and acquitted. At the University of California she studied under Herbert Marcuse, and was assistant professor of philosophy at UCLA 1969–70. In 1980 she was the Communist vice-presidential candidate.

I will never be below the title.

BETTE DAVIS
Playboy July 1982

Davis Bette, assumed name of Ruth Elizabeth Davis (1908–1989). US actress. She entered films 1930, and established a reputation as a forceful dramatic actress with *Of Human Bondage* 1934. Later films included *Dangerous* 1935 and *Jezebel* 1938, both winning her Academy Awards; *All About Eve* 1950; and *Whatever Happened to Baby Jane?* 1962. She continued to make films throughout the 1980s such as *The Whales of August* 1987, in which she co-starred with Lillian Gish.

Her screen trademarks were a clipped, precise diction and a flamboyant use of cigarettes. Her appeal to female audiences came from her portrayal of wilful, fiercely independent women who survived despite the adversities thrown at them.

Davis Colin Rex (1927–). English conductor. He was musical director at Sadler's Wells 1961–65, chief conductor of the BBC Symphony Orchestra 1967–71, musical director of the Royal Opera, Covent Garden, 1971–86, and chief conductor of the Bavarian Radio Symphony Orchestra from 1986. He is particularly associated with the music of Berlioz, Mozart, and Tippett. Knighted 1980.

Davis Jefferson (1808–1889). US politician, president of the short-lived Confederate States of America 1861–65. He was a leader of the Southern Democrats in the US Senate from 1857, and a defender of 'humane' slavery; in 1860 he issued a declaration in favour of secession from the USA. During the Civil War he assumed strong political leadership, but often disagreed with military policy. He was imprisoned for two years after the war, one of the few cases of judicial retribution against Confederate leaders.

Born in Kentucky, he graduated from West Point military academy and served in the US army before becoming a cotton planter in Mississippi. He sat in the US Senate 1847–51, was secretary of war 1853–57, and returned to the Senate 1857. His fiery temper and self-righteousness hindered efforts to achieve broad unity among the Southern states. His call for conscription in the South raised protests that he was a military dictator, violating the very ideals of freedom for which the Confederacy was fighting.

Davis Joe (Joseph) (1901–1978). British billiards and snooker player. He was world snooker champion a record 15 times 1927–46 and responsible for much of the popularity of the game. His brother Fred (1913–) was also a billiards and snooker world champion.

Davis John (c. 1550–1605). English navigator and explorer. He sailed in search of the Northwest Passage through the Canadian Arctic to the Pacific Ocean 1585, and in 1587 sailed to Baffin Bay through the straits named after him. He was the first European to see the Falkland Islands 1592.

Davis Judy (1956–). Australian stage and film actress. Her films include *My Brilliant Career* 1979 and *Passage to India* 1984, for which she was nominated for an Academy Award. She was born in Perth and after graduating from NIDA in 1977 began her stage career in Adelaide.

Davis Miles Dewey, Jr (1926–1991). US jazz trumpeter, composer, and bandleader. He was one of the most influential and innovative figures in jazz. He pioneered bebop with Charlie Parker 1945, cool jazz in the 1950s, and jazz-rock fusion from the late 1960s. His albums include *Birth of the Cool* 1957 (recorded 1949 and 1950), *Sketches of Spain* 1959, *Bitches Brew* 1970, and *Tutu* 1985.

Davis, born in Illinois, joined Charlie Parker's group 1946–48. In 1948 he began an association with composer and arranger Gil Evans (1912–1988) that was to last throughout his career. His quintet in 1955 featured the saxophone player John Coltrane, who recorded with Davis until 1961; for example, *Kind of Blue* 1959. In 1968 Davis introduced electric instruments, later adding electronic devices to his trumpet and more percussion to his band. He went on to use disco backings, record pop songs, and collaborate with rock musicians, remaining changeable to the end.

I was brought up in the business that said there was room for everybody, for all tastes ... That's why they called it variety.

SAMMY DAVIS, JR
quoted in Donald Clarke (ed) *The Penguin Encyclopedia of Popular Music* 1989

Davis Sammy, Jr (1925–1990). US entertainer. His starring role in the Broadway show *Mr Wonderful* 1956, his television work, and his roles in films with Frank Sinatra's 'rat pack' – among them, *Ocean's Eleven* 1960 and *Robin and the Seven Hoods* 1964 – made him a celebrity. He also appeared in the film version of the opera *Porgy and Bess* 1959. He published two memoirs, *Yes I Can* 1965 and *Why Me?* 1989.

Born in New York City, Davis appeared on stage at the age of four and became a member of the Will Mastin Trio 1932. Recognized as one of the best tap dancers in the country, Davis served as an army entertainer during World War II and became a nightclub headliner in the 1950s.

Davis Steve (1957–). English snooker player who has won every major honour in the game since turning professional 1978. He has been world champion six times.

Davis won his first major title 1980 when he won the Coral UK Championship. He has also won world titles at Pairs and with the England team. His earnings regularly top £1 million through on- and off-the-table prize money and endorsements.

Davis Stuart (1894–1964). US abstract painter. Much of his work shows the influence of both jazz tempos and Cubism in its use of hard-edged geometric shapes in primary colours and collage. In the 1920s he produced paintings of commercial packaging, such as *Lucky Strike* 1921 (Museum of Modern Art, New York), that foreshadowed Pop art.

His early abstracts reflect the impact of Cubism, and he was deeply influenced by the Armory Show in New York 1913. He often used numbers or letters as the focus for his compositions.

Davis William Morris (1850–1934). US physical geographer who analysed landforms. In the 1890s he developed the organizing concept of a regular cycle of erosion, a theory that dominated geomorphology and physical geography for half a century. Davis was born in Philadelphia and studied science at Harvard, where he taught 1877–1912.

Davison Emily Wilding (1872–1913). English militant suffragette who died after throwing herself under the king's horse at the Derby at Epsom (she was trampled by the horse). She joined the Women's Social and Political Union in 1906 and served several prison sentences for militant action such as stone throwing, setting fire to pillar boxes, and bombing Lloyd George's country house.

Her coffin was carried through London draped in the colours of the suffragette movement, purple, white, and green. It was escorted by 2,000 uniformed suffragettes. She was a teacher with degrees from Oxford and London universities.

Davisson Clinton Joseph (1881–1958). US physicist who in 1927 made the first experimental observation of the wave nature of electrons. George Thomson carried through the same research independently, and in 1937 they shared the Nobel Prize for Physics. He worked for the Western Electric Company (later Bell Telephone) in New York 1917–46.

Although he never wavered ... from the ultimate idea of an independent Ireland, he abandoned ... those methods of secret conspiracy and armed rebellion ... generally associated with the separatist ideal.

F S Skeffington on MICHAEL DAVITT
in *Dictionary of National Biography*

Davitt Michael (1846–1906). Irish nationalist. He joined the Fenians (forerunners of the Irish Republican Army) 1865, and was imprisoned for treason 1870–77. After his release, he and the politician Charles Parnell founded the Land League 1879. Davitt was jailed several times for land-reform agitation. He was a member of Parliament 1895–99, advocating the reconciliation of extreme and constitutional nationalism.

Davy Humphry (1778–1829). English chemist. He discovered, by electrolysis, the metallic elements sodium and potassium in 1807, and calcium, boron, magnesium, strontium, and barium in 1808. In addition, he established that chlorine is an element and proposed that hydrogen is present in all acids. He invented the safety lamp for use in mines where methane was present, enabling miners to work in previously unsafe conditions. Knighted 1812, baronet 1818.

Davy's experiments on electrolysis of aqueous solutions from 1800 led him to suggest its large-scale use in the alkali industry. He theorized that the mechanism of electrolysis could be explained in terms of species that have opposite electric charges, which could be arranged on a scale of relative affinities – the foundation of the modern electrochemical series. His study of the alkali metals provided proof of French chemist Antoine Lavoisier's idea that all alkalis contain oxygen.

Suggested reading
Hartley, Harold *Humphry Davy* (1966)
Treneer, Anne *The Mercurial Chemist: A Life of Sir Humphry Davy* (1963)

Dawe (Donald) Bruce (1930–). Australian poet. His most successful poems are distinguished by wittily inventive deployment of everyday language and imagery, addressing serious subjects with unsentimental yet gentle dignity. Collections include *No Fixed Address* 1962, *Condolences of the Season* 1971, and *Just a Dugong at Twilight* 1975. His collected poems were published as *Sometimes Gladness* 1978.

Dawes Charles Gates (1865–1951). US Republican politician. In 1923 he was appointed by the Allied Reparations Commission president of the committee that produced the Dawes Plan, a $200 million loan that enabled Germany to pay enormous war debts after World War I. It reduced tensions temporarily in Europe but was superseded by the Young Plan (which reduced the total reparations bill) 1929. Dawes was made US vice president (under Calvin Coolidge) 1924, received the Nobel Peace Prize 1925, and was ambassador to Britain 1929–32.

We are survival machines – robot vehicles blindly programmed to preserve the selfish molecules known as genes. This is a truth which still fills me with astonishment.

RICHARD DAWKINS
The Selfish Gene preface1976

Dawkins (Clinton) Richard (1941–). British zoologist whose book *The Selfish Gene* 1976 popularized the theories of sociobiology (social behaviour in humans and animals in the context of evolution). In *The Blind Watchmaker* 1986 he explained the modern theory of evolution.

Dawkins was born in Nairobi, Kenya, and educated at Oxford, where from 1975 he held academic posts.

In *The Selfish Gene* he argued that genes – not individuals, populations, or species – are the driving force of evolution. He suggested an analogous system of cultural transmission in human societies, and proposed the term 'mimeme', abbreviated to 'meme', as the unit of such a scheme. He considered the idea of God to be a meme with a high survival value. His contentions were further developed in *The Extended Phenotype* 1982, primarily an academic work.

Dawson Les (1934–1993). British comedian. After a long apprenticeship in working men's clubs and similar venues, he gained popularity on television, especially as host of the quiz show *Blankety Blank*.

In mining a vein of determinedly glum humour, full of derogatory references to wives and mothers-in-law, Dawson was a natural successor to bygone exponents of northern working-class comedy. However, his best routines possessed qualities of verbal elaboration and near-surreal fantasy.

Dawson Peter (1882–1961). Australian bass-baritone. He is remembered for his elegant recordings of marching songs and ballads from World War I.

Day Clarence Shepard, Jr (1874–1935). US cartoonist and author. His autobiographical memoir *Life with Father* 1935 became a national bestseller, a long-running Broadway play from 1939, and a popular feature film 1947. Day's sequels to that work, *Life with Mother* 1937 and *Father and I* 1940, were published after his death.

Born in New York and educated at Yale, Day joined his father's Wall Street firm soon after graduation. Poor health forced his retirement from business at an early age, and he devoted himself to freelance cartooning and humour writing for a number of New York-based magazines.

Day Doris. Stage name of Doris von Kappelhoff (1924–). US film actress and singing star of the 1950s and early 1960s.

She appeared in musicals and, often with Rock Hudson, coy sex comedies. Her films include *Tea for Two* 1950, *Calamity Jane* 1953, *Love Me or Leave Me* 1955, and Alfred Hitchcock's *The Man Who Knew Too Much* 1956. With *Pillow Talk* 1959, *Lover Come Back* 1962, and other 1960s light sex comedies, she played a self-confident but coy woman who caused some of the biggest male stars to capitulate.

I never retired. I just did something else.

DORIS DAY
Time 29 July 1985

Day Robin (1923–). British broadcasting journalist. A barrister, he pioneered the probing political interview, notably when he questioned Harold Macmillan on the composition of his cabinet in 1958. Knighted 1981.

Dayan Moshe (1915–1981). Israeli general and politician. As minister of defence 1967 and 1969–74, he was largely responsible for the victory over neighbouring Arab states in the 1967 Six-Day War, but he was criticized for Israel's alleged unpreparedness in the 1973 October War and resigned along with Prime Minister Golda Meir.

Foreign minister from 1977, Dayan resigned 1979 in protest over the refusal of the Begin government to negotiate with the Palestinians.

Dayananda Sarasvati (born Mula Sankara) (1824–1883). Hindu religious reformer. In about 1875 he founded the Arya Samaj, a society named after the Aryans, who were believed to have originated the Vedic hymns. By returning to the original hymns of the Vedas, he tried to simplify and purify Hinduism.

Now the peak of summer's past, the sky is overcast / And the love we swore would last for an age seems deceit.

CECIL DAY-LEWIS
'Hornpipe'

Day-Lewis Cecil (1904–1972). Irish poet, British poet laureate 1968–72. With W H Auden and Stephen Spender, he was one of the influential left-wing poets of the 1930s. He also wrote detective novels under the pseudonym Nicholas Blake.

Born at Ballintubber, Ireland, he was educated at Oxford and then taught at Cheltenham College 1930–35. His work, which includes *From Feathers to Iron* 1931 and *Overtures to Death* 1938, is marked by accomplished lyrics and sustained narrative power. Professor of poetry at Oxford 1951–56, he published critical works and translations from Latin of Virgil's *Georgics* and the *Aeneid*.

In 1968 he succeeded John Masefield as poet laureate. His autobiography, *The Buried Day* 1960, was followed by a biography written by his eldest son, Sean, 1980.

Day-Lewis Daniel (1958–). English actor, noted for his chameleon-like versatility. He first came to prominence in *My Beautiful Laundrette* and *A Room With a View* both 1985. He won an Academy Award for his performance as Christy Brown, the painter suffering from cerebral palsy, in *My Left Foot* 1989. His other films include *The Last of the Mohicans* 1992, *The Age of Innocence*, and *In the Name of the Father* both 1993, in which he played Gerry Conlon, one of the wrongly convicted Guildford Four.

Dazai Osamu. Pen name of Shuji Tsushima (1909–1948). Japanese novelist. The title of his novel *The Setting Sun* 1947 became identified in Japan with the dead of World War II.

His ideals were ... sane and moderate, but his anxiety to secure rapid results led him ... to seek coalitions which were not very effective.

A B Keith on ALFRED DEAKIN
in *Dictionary of National Biography*

Deakin Alfred (1856–1919). Australian politician, prime minister 1903–04, 1905–08, and 1909–10. In his second administration, he enacted legislation on defence and pensions.

Dean Basil Herbert (1888–1978). English founder and director-general of Entertainments National Service Association (ENSA) 1939, which provided entertainment for the Allied forces in World War II.

Dean Dizzy (Jay Hanna) (1911–1974). US baseball player. He joined the St Louis Cardinals 1930 and made his major-league pitching debut 1932. Winning 30 games and leading the Cardinals to a World Series win, he was voted the National League's most valuable player 1934. Following an injury in the 1937 All-Star Game, his pitching suffered. He was traded to the Chicago Cubs, for whom he pitched until his retirement 1941.

Born in Lucas, Arkansas, Dean worked as a farmhand until he was old enough to join the army, where his pitching skills were recognized. The offbeat brashness and good-natured arrogance that won him the nickname 'Dizzy' are as legendary as his explosive fast-ball pitch. Dean was elected to the Baseball Hall of Fame 1953.

Death is the only thing left to respect. Everything else can be questioned. But death is truth.

JAMES DEAN
quoted in *Photoplay* Sept 1985

Dean James Byron (1931–1955). US actor. Killed in a car accident soon after the public showing of his first film, *East of Eden* 1955, he posthumously became a cult hero with *Rebel Without a Cause* 1955 and *Giant* 1956.

His image has endured as the classic icon of teenage rebellion throughout the decades since his death.

Suggested reading
Dalton, David and Cayen, Ron *James Dean: American Icon* (1984)
Howlett, John *James Dean* (1984)

Dean, James *American film star and cult hero James Dean, who personified the restless American youth of the 1950s. In just over a year, with only three films to his name, Dean became a screen icon. His posthumous growth in popularity reached legendary proportions, rivaling that of Rudolf Valentino.*

Deane Silas (1737–1789). American public leader and diplomat. He served in the Continental Congress 1774–76 and was dispatched to Paris to gain support from the French government during the American Revolution (1775–83), recruiting French soldier Marie Lafayette, amongst others, for the Continental army. Falsely accused of financial improprieties, Deane was discharged from his post; he was exonerated posthumously by Congress 1842.

de Beer Gavin Rylands (1899–1972). English zoologist who made important contributions to embryology and evolution. He disproved the germ-layer theory and developed the concept of paedomorphism (the retention of juvenile characteristics of ancestors in mature adults). Knighted 1954.

In 1945 he became professor of embryology at University College, London, then was director of the British Museum (Natural History) 1950–60.

Debeney Marie-Eugene (1864–1943). French general in World War I. He defended Amiens March–April 1918, captured Montdidier, and then advanced to the river Somme Aug 1918. He was appointed commandant of St Cyr military academy June 1919.

After education at St Cyr, he entered the army as a lieutenant of Chasseurs 1886. In 1914 he was sub-Chief of Staff of the 1st French Army. He subsequently commanded the 33rd and 32nd Corps and the 7th Army 1916, and was appointed to command the 1st Army Dec 1917.

de Bono Edward Francis Charles Publius (1933–). Maltese-born British medical doctor and psychologist whose concept of lateral thinking, first expounded in *The Use of Lateral Thinking* 1967, involves thinking round a problem rather than tackling it head on.

Deborah Old Testament prophet and judge (leader). She helped lead an Israelite army against the Canaanite general Sisera, who was killed trying to flee; her song of triumph at his death is regarded as an excellent example of early Hebrew poetry.

We are never completely contemporaneous with our present. History advances in disguise.

RÉGIS DEBRAY
Revolution in the Revolution? ch 1 1967

Debray Régis (1941–). French Marxist theorist. He was associated with Che Guevara in the revolutionary movement in Latin America in the 1960s. In 1967 he was sentenced to 30 years' imprisonment in Bolivia but was released after three years. His writings on Latin American politics include *Strategy for Revolution* 1970. He became a specialist adviser to President Mitterrand of France on Latin American affairs.

Debreu Gerard (1921–). French-born US economist. He developed mathematical economic models with Kenneth Arrow, analysing the conditions for economic equilibrium, where demand and supply are equal. He further developed such models in his chief work, *Theory of Value* 1959, which integrates the theory of location of firms, the theory of capital, and the theory of behaviour under uncertainty into general economic equilibrium theory. He was awarded the Nobel Prize for Economics 1983 for his work on general equilibrium theory.

de Broglie Maurice and Louis. French physicists; see ◊Broglie.

I said then, I say now, that while there is a lower class, I am in it; while there is a criminal element, I am of it; while there is a soul in prison, I am not free.

EUGENE V DEBS
Speech at his trial 14 Sept 1918

Debs Eugene V(ictor) (1855–1926). US labour leader and socialist who organized the Social Democratic Party 1897. He was the founder and first president of the American Railway Union 1893, and was imprisoned for six months in 1894 for defying a federal injunction to end the Pullman strike in Chicago. He was socialist candidate for the presidency in every election from 1900 to 1920, except that of 1916.

Debs was born in Terre Haute, Indiana. He opposed US intervention in World War I and was imprisoned 1918–21 for allegedly advocating resistance to conscription, but was pardoned by President Harding 1921. In 1920 he polled nearly 1 million votes, the highest socialist vote ever in US presidential elections, despite having to conduct the campaign from a federal penitentiary in Atlanta, Georgia. His powerful oratory and his evocation of homespun American ideals were the source of his appeal rather than any doctrinaire adherence to socialist theory.

Debussy (Achille-) Claude (1862–1918). French composer. He broke with German Romanticism and introduced new qualities of melody and harmony based on the whole-tone scale, evoking oriental music. His work includes *Prélude à l'après-midi d'un faune/Prelude to the Afternoon of a Faun* 1894, illustrating a poem by Mallarmé, and the opera *Pelléas et Mélisande* 1902.

Among his other works are numerous piano pieces, songs, orchestral pieces such as *La Mer* 1903–05, and the ballet *Jeux* 1910–13. Debussy also published witty and humorous critical writing about the music of his day, featuring the fictional character Monsieur Croche 'antidilettante' (professional debunker), a figure based on Erik Satie.

Suggested reading
Dawes, Frank *Debussy Piano Music* (1969)
Howat, R *Debussy in Proportion* (1984)

de Bono *Psychologist and author Edward de Bono. He developed the concept of 'lateral thinking' as a creative way of approaching problems. His approach to problem solving became influential in education and business.*

Debussy *The composer Claude Debussy (1862–1918) pictured with his first wife, Rosalie Texier. During the years they spent together (1899–1904)* Pelléas et Mélisande *was produced and Debussy consolidated his reputation as the leading impressionist composer. Following their separation his technique evolved in works such as* La Mer *and* Images. (Image Select)

Lesure, F and Nichols, R (eds) *Debussy: Letters* (1987)
Lockspeiser, E *Debussy* (1980)
Nichols, Roger *Debussy Remembered* (1992)
Wenk, A *Claude Debussy and Twentieth Century Music* (1983)

Debye Peter. Anglicized name of Petrus Josephus Wilhelmus Debije (1884–1966). Dutch-born US physicist. A pioneer of X-ray powder crystallography, he also worked on polar molecules, dipole moments, molecular structure, and polymers. The Debye–Hückel theory, developed with German chemist Erich Hückel, concerns the ordering of ions in solution. He held a series of professorships in Switzerland and Germany, starting at Zürich 1910. In 1934 he went to the Max Planck Institute, Berlin. Nobel Prize for Chemistry 1936. He was lecturing at Cornell University in the USA in 1940 when Germany invaded the Netherlands, so he remained at Cornell as professor 1940–52.

De Carlo Giancarlo (1919–). Italian architect. His series of buildings in the Renaissance hill town of Urbino (begun 1952) are notable in their sensitivity towards context and urban continuity. The Faculty of Education, Urbino, 1968–76, respects the fabric of the town while opening out towards the Umbrian countryside with a glazed cascade of lecture theatres.

De Carlo worked under the patronship of Carlo Bo, rector of Urbino University, and in 1959 helped to found Team 10, following the collapse of CIAM. His other works include the student residences, Urbino, 1962–66 and 1973–83, and the Mazzorbo housing scheme, Venice, 1979–85.

Our country, right or wrong.

STEPHEN DECATUR
quoted in A S Mackenzie *Life of Decatur* ch 14 1846

Decatur Stephen (1779–1820). US naval hero who, during the war with Tripoli 1801–05, succeeded in burning the *Philadelphia*, which the enemy had captured. During the War of 1812 with Britain, he surrendered only after a desperate resistance 1814. In 1815, he was active against Algerian pirates. Decatur coined the phrase 'our country, right or wrong'. He was killed in a duel.

Decius Gaius Messius Quintus Traianus (*c.* 201–251). Roman emperor from 249. He fought a number of campaigns against the Goths but was finally beaten and killed by them near Abrittus. He ruthlessly persecuted the Christians.

Dedekind (Julius Wilhelm) Richard (1831–1916). German mathematician who made contributions to number theory. In 1872 he introduced the Dedekind cut (which divides a line of infinite length representing all real numbers) to define irrational numbers in terms of pairs of sequences of rational numbers. He was professor at the Technische Hochschule in Brunswick 1862–94.

Dee John (1527–1608). English alchemist, astrologer, and mathematician who claimed to have transmuted metals into gold, although he died in poverty. He long enjoyed the favour of Elizabeth I, and was employed as a secret diplomatic agent.

de Falla Manuel. Spanish composer; see ◊Falla, Manuel de.

de Filippo Eduardo (1900–1984). Italian actor and dramatist. He founded his own company in Naples 1932, which was strongly influenced by the commedia dell'arte, and for which he wrote many plays. These include his finest comedies, *Filumena Marturano* 1946, *Napoli milionaria!* 1945, *Questi fantasmi!/These Ghosts!* 1946, *Grande magia/Grand Magic* 1951, and *Saturday, Sunday, Monday* 1959.

Defoe Daniel (1660–1731). English writer. His *Robinson Crusoe* 1719, though purporting to be a factual account of shipwreck and solitary survival, was influential in the development of the novel. The fictional *Moll Flanders* 1722 and the partly factual *A Journal of the Plague Year* 1724 are still read for their concrete realism. A prolific journalist and pamphleteer, he was imprisoned 1702–04 for the ironic *The Shortest Way with Dissenters* 1702.

Born in Cripplegate, London, Defoe was educated for the Nonconformist ministry, but became a hosier. He took part in Monmouth's rebellion, and joined William of Orange 1688. He was bankrupted three times as a result of various business ventures, once for the then enormous amount of £17,000. After his business had failed, he held a civil-service post 1695–99. He wrote numerous pamphlets, and first achieved fame with the satire *The True-Born Englishman* 1701, followed in 1702 by the ironic *The Shortest Way with Dissenters*, for which he was fined, imprisoned, and pilloried. In Newgate he wrote his *Hymn to the Pillory* and started a paper, *The Review* 1704–13. Released 1704, he travelled in Scotland 1706–07, working to promote the Union, and published *A History of the Union* 1709. During the next ten years he was almost constantly employed as a political controversialist and pamphleteer. His version of the contemporary short story 'True Relation of the Apparition of one Mrs Veal' 1706 had revealed a gift for realistic narrative, and *Robinson Crusoe*, based on the story of Alexander Selkirk, appeared 1719. It was followed, among others, by the pirate story *Captain Singleton* 1720, and the picaresque *Colonel Jack* 1722 and *Roxana* 1724. Since Defoe's death, an increasing number of works have been attributed to him, bringing the total from 128 in 1790 to 561 in 1960.

Suggested reading
Backschneider, P R *Daniel Defoe* (1989)
Bastian, Frank *Defoe's Early Life* (1981)
Moore, J R *Daniel Defoe, Citizen of the Modern World* (1958)
Richetti, J *Daniel Defoe* (1987)

De Forest Lee (1873–1961). US physicist and inventor who in 1906 invented the triode valve, which contributed to the development of radio, radar, and television. Ambrose Fleming invented the diode valve 1904. De Forest saw that if a third electrode were added, the triode valve would serve as an amplifier as well as a rectifier, and radio communications would become a practical possibility.

Everybody has talent at twenty-five. The difficult thing is to have it at fifty.

EDGAR DEGAS
quoted in R H Ives Gammell *The Shop-Talk of Edgar Degas* 1961

Degas (Hilaire Germain) Edgar (1834–1917). French Impressionist painter and sculptor. He devoted himself to lively, informal studies (often using pastels) of ballet, horse racing, and young women working. From the 1890s he turned increasingly to sculpture, modelling figures in wax in a fluent, naturalistic style.

Degas studied under a pupil of Ingres and worked in Italy in the 1850s, painting Classical themes. In 1861 he met Manet, and

exhibited regularly with the Impressionists 1874–86. His characteristic style soon emerged, showing the influence of Japanese prints and photography in inventive compositions and unusual viewpoints, as in *Woman with Chrysanthemums* 1865 (Metropolitan Museum of Art, New York). An example of his sculpture is *The Little Dancer* 1881 (Tate Gallery, London). From middle age onwards he tended to concentrate increasingly on the study of women, adding to his dancers, in the 1880s, remarkable pastels and drawings of the 'femme au tub'. Failing sight turned him to sculpture, which he called a 'blind man's art', and his small bronzes of dancers or horses are of great beauty. Somewhat isolated, Degas had no direct following in France, though through his English pupil, Sickert, he may be said to have benefited English art.

Suggested reading
Gordon, R and Forge, A *Degas* (1988)
Lipton, E *Looking into Degas: Uneasy Images of Women and Modern Life* (1986)
Reff, T *Degas: The Artist's Mind* (1976)
Rich, D *Degas* (1954)

A man of great integrity and considerable stamina, gentle and conciliatory in his approach, he combined shrewdness with an extraordinary firmness of purpose.

Walter Laqueur on ALCIDE DE GASPERI
in *Europe Since Hitler* 1970

De Gasperi Alcide (1881–1954). Italian politician. A founder of the Christian Democrat Party, he was prime minister 1945–53 and worked for European unification.

de Gaulle Charles André Joseph Marie (1890–1970). French general and first president of the Fifth Republic 1958–69. He organized the Free French troops fighting the Nazis 1940–44, was head of the provisional French government 1944–46, and leader of his own Gaullist party. In 1958 the national assembly asked him to form a government during France's economic recovery and to solve the crisis in Algeria. He became president at the end of 1958, having changed the constitution to provide for a presidential system, and served until 1969.

Diplomats are useful only in fair weather. As soon as it rains they drown in every drop.

CHARLES DE GAULLE
Newsweek 1 Oct 1962

Born in Lille, he graduated from Saint-Cyr 1911 and was severely wounded and captured by the Germans 1916. In June 1940 he refused to accept the new prime minister Pétain's truce with the Germans and 18 June made his historic broadcast calling on the French to continue the war against Germany. He based himself in England as leader of the Free French troops fighting the Germans 1940–44. In 1944 he entered Paris in triumph and was briefly head of the provisional government before resigning over the new constitution of the Fourth Republic 1946. In 1947 he founded the Rassemblement du Peuple Français, a nonparty constitutional reform movement, then withdrew from politics 1953. When national bankruptcy and civil war in Algeria loomed 1958, de Gaulle was called to form a government. As prime minister he promulgated a constitution subordinating the legislature to the presidency and took office as president Dec 1958. Economic recovery followed, as well as Algerian independence after a bloody war. A nationalist, he opposed 'Anglo-Saxon' influence in Europe.

Re-elected president 1965, he pursued a foreign policy that opposed British entry to the EEC, withdrew French forces from NATO 1966, and pursued the development of a French nuclear deterrent. He violently quelled student demonstrations May 1968 when they were joined by workers. The Gaullist party, reorganized as Union des Democrats pour la Cinquième République, won an overwhelming majority in the elections of the same year. In 1969 he resigned after the defeat of the government in a referendum on constitutional reform. He retired to the village of Colombey-les-Deux-Eglises in NE France.

Suggested reading
Banfield, Susan *De Gaulle* (1985)
Crozier, Brian *De Gaulle: The Warrior* (1973)
Crozier, Brian *De Gaulle: The Statesman* (1974)
Ledwige, B *De Gaulle* (1982)
Shennan, Andrew *De Gaulle* (1993)

Degoutte Jean Marie Joseph (1866–1938). French general in World War I. In June 1918 he commanded the 6th Army at the Battle of Chateau-Thierry and at the second Battle of the Marne, and played an important part in the liberation of Belgium.

Degoutte entered the French army as a volunteer, and was commissioned into the 4th Zouaves 1890. After extensive service in the French colonies during 1914, he became Chief of Staff of the 4th Army Corps. Promoted to brigadier-general March 1916, he commanded the Moroccan Division and became general of division March 1918. He became commander in chief of the Allied Armies of Occupation in Germany 1920.

Dehaene Jean-Luc (1940–). Belgian politician, prime minister from 1992. He successfully negotiated constitutional changes to make Belgium a federal state. His centre-left coalition was re-elected 1995.

Born in Montpellier, France, and educated at the university of Namur, he entered politics by joining the trade-union wing of the Flemish Christian Socialists (CVP). He was a government adviser 1972–81, establishing a reputation as a skilful mediator. In this role in 1988 he negotiated the formation of a five-party coalition, led by Wilfried Martens, and became his deputy. When the coalition collapsed 1992 he constructed another three-party government which he led.

Dehaene came to the notice of a wider public 1994 when he was proposed by Germany and France as the successor to European Commission president, Jacques Delors. Seeing Dehaene as a 'federalist', UK prime minister John Major vetoed his appointment, in contrast to the other 11 European Union heads of government.

De Havilland Geoffrey (1882–1965). British aircraft designer who designed and whose company produced the Moth biplane, the Mosquito fighter-bomber of World War II, and in 1949 the Comet, the world's first jet-driven airliner to enter commercial service. Knighted 1944.

After designing a fighter and a bomber for use in World War I, he founded the De Havilland Aircraft Company 1920. This was eventually absorbed into the Hawker Siddeley conglomerate.

De Havilland Olivia Mary (1916–). US actress. She was a star in Hollywood from the age of 19, when she appeared in *A Midsummer Night's Dream* 1935. She later successfully played challenging dramatic roles in *Gone with the Wind* 1939, *To Each His Own* (Academy Award) and *Dark Mirror* 1946, and *The Snake Pit* 1948. She won her second Academy Award for *The Heiress* 1949, and played in *Lady in a Cage* and *Hush, Hush, Sweet Charlotte*, both 1964.

She is the sister of actress Joan Fontaine.

Dehn Max Wilhelm (1878–1952). German-born US mathematician who in 1907 provided one of the first systematic studies of topology. His work was mainly concerned with the geometric properties of polyhedra.

After World War I Dehn became professor of mathematics at Frankfurt University, but lost his position 1935 because of the Nazi anti-Semitism laws. He emigrated 1940 to the USA, and worked from 1945 at the Black Mountain College in North Carolina.

Divorce is a system whereby two people make a mistake and one of them goes on paying for it.

LEN DEIGHTON
quoted in A Alvarez *Life after Marriage* 1982

Deighton Len (Leonard Cyril) (1929–). English author of spy fiction. His novels include *The Ipcress File* 1963 and the trilogy *Berlin Game, Mexico Set,* and *London Match* 1983–85, featuring the spy Bernard Samson. Samson was also the main character in Deighton's trilogy *Spy Hook* 1988, *Spy Line* 1989, and *Spy Sinker* 1990.

Charlotte Street runs north from Oxford Street and there are few who will blame it.

LEN DEIGHTON
Funeral in Berlin ch 13 1964

Dekker Thomas (*c.* 1572–*c.* 1632). English dramatist and pamphleteer. He wrote mainly in collaboration with others. His play *The Shoemaker's Holiday* 1600 was followed by collaborations with Thomas Middleton, John Webster, Philip Massinger, and others. His pamphlets include *The Gull's Hornbook* 1609, a lively satire on the fashions of the day.

Dekker's plays include *The Honest Whore* 1604–05 and *The Roaring Girl* 1611 (both with Middleton), *Famous History of Sir Thomas Wyat* 1607 (with Webster), *Virgin Martyr* 1622 (with Massinger), and *The Witch of Edmonton* 1621 (with John Ford and William Rowley).

Golden slumbers kiss your eyes, / Smiles awake you when you rise.

THOMAS DEKKER
Patient Grissill IV. ii 1603

de Klerk F(rederik) W(illem) (1936–). South African National Party politician, president 1989–94. Projecting himself as a pragmatic conservative who sought gradual reform of the apartheid system, he won the Sept 1989 elections for his party, but with a reduced majority. In Feb 1990 he ended the ban on the African National Congress (ANC) opposition movement and released its effective leader, Nelson Mandela, and by June 1991 he had repealed all racially discriminating laws. After a landslide victory for Mandela

De Havilland US film actress Olivia De Havilland won critical and public acclaim for the role of Melanie in Gone with the Wind *1939. In a celebrated court case against Warner Bros, De Havilland won her fight for better roles and in the process broke the power of the studio over its stars. From that point, players' contracts were limited to a seven-year period.*

and the ANC in the first universal suffrage elections April 1994, de Klerk became second executive deputy president.

He was awarded the Nobel Peace Prize jointly with Mandela 1993.

Trained as a lawyer, he entered the South African parliament 1972. He served in the cabinets of B J Vorster and P W Botha 1978–89, replacing P W Botha as party leader Feb 1989 and as state president Aug 1989. He entered into negotiations with the ANC Dec 1991 and in March 1992 a nationwide, whites-only referendum gave him a clear mandate to proceed with plans for major constitutional reform to end white minority rule. In Feb 1993 he and Mandela agreed to the formation of a government of national unity after multiracial elections 1994.

As soon as an artist fills a certain area on the canvas or circumscribes it, he becomes historical. He acts from or upon other artists.

WILLEM DE KOONING
'A Desperate View', paper delivered to friends 18 Feb 1949

---

de Kooning Willem (1904–   ). Dutch-born US painter. He emigrated to the USA 1926 and worked as a commercial artist. After World War II he became, together with Jackson Pollock, one of the leaders of the Abstract Expressionist movement, although he retained figural images, painted with quick, violent brushstrokes. His *Women* series, exhibited 1953, was criticized for its grotesque depictions of women.

De Kooning joined the faculty of the Yale Art School and became a member of the National Institute of Arts 1960. He received the Presidential Medal of Freedom 1964. His paintings were commissioned for numerous Work Projects Administration (WPA) projects, and he won praise for his mural in the Hall of Pharmacy at the 1939 New York World's Fair.
Suggested reading
Gaugh, H *Willem de Kooning* (1983)
Hess, T B *Willem de Kooning* (1969)
Rosenberg, H *De Kooning* (1974)
Sylvester, D and others *Willem de Kooning Paintings* (1994)
Waldman, D *Willem de Kooning* (1988)

De la Beche Henry Thomas (born Beach) (1796–1855). English geologist who secured the founding of the Geological Survey 1835, a government-sponsored geological study of Britain, region by region. His main work is *The Geological Observer* 1851.

The colour of the red slippers goes into one's eyes like a glass of wine down one's throat.

Paul Cézanne
commenting on *Women of Algiers* 1834 by EUGÈNE DELACROIX

Delacroix (Ferdinand Victor) Eugène (1798–1863). French Romantic painter. His prolific output included religious and historical subjects and portraits of friends, among them the musicians Paganini and Chopin. Antagonistic to the French academic tradition, he evolved a highly coloured, fluid style, as in *The Death of Sardanapalus* 1829 (Louvre, Paris).

The *Massacre at Chios* 1824 (Louvre, Paris) shows Greeks enslaved by wild Turkish horsemen, a contemporary atrocity (his use of a contemporary theme recalls Géricault's example). His style was influenced by the English landscape painter Constable. Delacroix also produced illustrations for works by Shakespeare, Dante, and Byron. His *Journal* is a fascinating record of his times.
Suggested reading
Friedlaender, W *From David to Delacroix* (1968)
Johnson, L *Delacroix* (1963)
Lindsay, J *Death of the Hero* (1960)
Pool, P *Delacroix* (1969)
Trapp, F *Delacroix and the Romantic Image* (1988)

Delafield E M. Pen name of Edmée Elizabeth Monica Dashwood, born de la Pasture (1890–1943). English writer. She is remembered for her amusing *Diary of a Provincial Lady* 1931, skilfully exploiting the foibles of middle-class life.

Delalande Michel-Richard (1657–1726). French organist and composer for the court of Louis XIV. His works include grand motets and numerous orchestral suites.

Look thy last on all things lovely, / Every hour.

WALTER DE LA MARE
'Fare Well'

---

de la Mare Walter John (1873–1956). English poet. He is known for his verse for children, such as *Songs of Childhood* 1902, and the novels *The Three Royal Monkeys* 1910 for children and, for adults, *The Memoirs of a Midget* 1921. He excelled at creating a sense of eeriness and supernatural mystery.

His first book, *Songs of Childhood*, appeared under the pseudonym Walter Ramal. Later works include poetry for adults (*The Listeners* 1912 and *Collected Poems* 1942), anthologies (*Come Hither* 1923 and *Behold this Dreamer* 1939), and short stories.

Delane John Thadeus (1817–1879). British journalist. As editor of *The Times* 1841–77, he gave the newspaper international standing. He pioneered the first newspaper war reports.

de la Renta Oscar (1932–   ). US fashion designer. He launched his luxury ready-to-wear label 1965, later diversifying into perfumes, swimwear, and jewellery. In 1993 he began designing the couture collections for the couture house Balmain. He is noted for the use of opulent fabrics in evening clothes.

de la Roche Mazo (1885–1961). Canadian novelist. Experience of life in an area of southern Ontario characterized by large estates centred on big houses gave her the idea for the immensely popular 15-novel saga of the Whiteoaks of Jalna 1927–60, characterized by primitive passions seen against a background of nature and animal life and given unity by the brooding presence of the Anglo-Irish matriarch Adeline Whiteoak and her descendants.
Suggested reading
de la Roche, Mazo *Ringing the Changes* (autobiography) (1957)
Hambleton, Ronald *Mazo de la Roche of Jalna* (1966)
Hendrick, George *Mazo de la Roche* (1970)

Delaroche (Hippolyte) Paul (1797–1856). French historical artist. His melodramatic, often sentimental, historical paintings achieved great contemporary popularity; an example is *Lady Jane Grey* 1833 (National Gallery, London).

de la Rue Warren (1815–1889). British astronomer and instrumentmaker who pioneered celestial photography. Besides inventing the first photoheliographic telescope, he took the first photograph of a solar eclipse 1860 and used it to prove that the prominences observed during an eclipse are of solar rather than lunar origin. De la Rue was born in Guernsey and joined his father in the printing business. He was one of the first printers to adopt electrotyping and in 1851 he invented the first envelope-making machine. He also invented the silver chloride battery.

Delaunay Robert (1885–1941). French painter. He was a pioneer of abstract art. With his wife Sonia Delaunay-Terk, he developed a style known as Orphism, an early variation of Cubism, focusing on the effects of pure colour contrasts.

Working from the colour theories of the French chemist Michel Chevreul, Delaunay and his wife explored the simultaneous effects of light on disc-like planes of radiant, contrasting colour, their aim being to produce a visual equivalent to music. Delaunay painted several series 1912, notably *Circular Forms* (almost purely abstract) and *Simultaneous Windows* (inspired by Parisian cityscapes). His art was described as 'Orphist' (essentially musical) by Guillaume Apollinaire. He carried out a huge decorative scheme (ten large reliefs in colour and a vast *Rhythm*) for the Palace of Air and Railway

Pavilion of the Paris Exposition of 1937, and with other artists, including his wife, Sonia Delaunay-Terk, decorated the sculpture hall at the Salon des Tuileries 1938.

Delaunay-Terk Sonia (1885–1979). French painter and textile designer. Born in Russia, she was active in Paris from 1905. With her husband Robert Delaunay, she was a pioneer of abstract art.

De Laurentiis Dino (1919–). Italian film producer. His early films, including Fellini's *La strada/The Street* 1954, brought more acclaim than later epics such as *Waterloo* 1970. He then produced a series of undistinguished Hollywood films: *Death Wish* 1974, *King Kong* (remake) 1976, and *Dune* 1984.

de la Warr Thomas West, 3rd or 12th Baron de la Warr (1577–1618). US colonial administrator, known as Delaware. Appointed governor of Virginia 1609, he arrived 1610 just in time to prevent the desertion of the Jamestown colonists, and by 1611 had revitalized the settlement. He fell ill, returned to England, and died during his return voyage to the colony 1618. Succeeded to barony 24 March 1601–02.

Both the river and state are named after him.

Delbruck Max (1906–1981). German-born US biologist who pioneered techniques in molecular biology, studying genetic changes occurring when viruses invade bacteria. He was awarded the Nobel Prize for Physiology or Medicine 1969, which he shared with Salvador Luria and Alfred Hershey (1908–).

Delcassé Théophile (1852–1923). French politician. He became foreign minister 1898, but had to resign 1905 because of German hostility; he held that post again 1914–15. To a large extent he was responsible for the Entente Cordiale 1904 with Britain.

de Lesseps Ferdinand, Vicomte. French engineer; see ◊Lesseps, Ferdinand, Vicomte de Lesseps.

Delibes (Clément Philibert) Léo (1836–1891). French composer. His lightweight, perfectly judged works include the ballets *Coppélia* 1870 and *Sylvia* 1876, and the opera *Lakmé* 1883.

Delilah in the Old Testament, the Philistine mistress of Samson. Following instructions from the lords of the Philistines she sought to find the source of Samson's great strength. When Samson eventually revealed that his physical power lay in the length of his hair, she shaved his head while he slept and then delivered him into the hands of the Philistines.

DeLillo Don (1936–). US novelist. His dark and highly complex novels examine images of American culture, power, conspiracy, and obsession. They include: the news media as a network of controls in *Americana* 1971; sport as a cult in *End Zone* 1972; mathematics and myth in *Ratner's Star* 1976; the Kennedy assassination in *Libra* 1988; and celebrity, terrorism, and disaster in *Mao II* 1991.

What should have been evident at first hearing was the remotely alien sound of it, a note in English music stranger than any heard for over two hundred years.

Thomas Beecham on FREDERICK DELIUS
in *A Mingled Chime* 1944

Delius Frederick Theodore Albert (1862–1934). English composer. His haunting, richly harmonious works include the opera *A Village Romeo and Juliet* 1901; the choral pieces *Appalachia* 1903, *Sea Drift* 1904, *A Mass of Life* 1905; orchestral works such as *In a Summer Garden* 1908 and *A Song of the High Hills* 1911; chamber music; and songs.

Born in Bradford, he tried orange-growing in Florida, before studying music in Leipzig 1888, where he met the Norwegian composer Grieg. From 1890 Delius lived mainly in France and in 1903 married the artist Jelka Rosen. Although blind and paralysed for the last ten years of his life, he continued to compose.

Suggested reading
Beecham, Sir Thomas *Frederick Delius* (1959)
Carley, L *Delius: A Life in Letters* (1984)

Fenby, Eric *Delius as I Knew Him* (1936)
Jefferson, A *Delius* (1972)
Redwood, C (ed) *A Delius Companion* (1976)

Dell Ethel M(ary) (1881–1939). British writer of romantic fiction. Her commercially successful novels usually included a hero who was ugly: *Way of an Eagle* 1912, *The Keeper of the Door* 1915, and *Storm Drift* 1930.

della Robbia Italian family of artists; see ◊Robbia, della.

Deller Alfred (1912–1979). English singer. He revived the countertenor voice and repertoire of 16th- to 18th-century music and founded the Deller Consort 1950.

Del Mar Norman Rene (1919–1994). English conductor, composer, and horn player. He founded the Chelsea Symphony Orchestra 1944, and was a guest conductor with leading orchestras. He conducted an enormously wide range of music, but was especially known for his Mahler, Elgar, and other late romantics, above all Strauss, and was noted for his clear interpretations of complex scores. He also composed two symphonies, a string quartet, and a number of horn pieces.

He wrote three volumes on Richard Strauss 1960–72, as well as *Orchestral Variations* 1981 and *Companion to the Orchestra* 1987.

Delon Alain (1935–). French film actor. He graduated from youthful charmer to character roles, appearing in *Purple Noon* 1960, *Rocco e i suoi fratelli/Rocco and His Brothers* 1960, *Il gattopardo/The Leopard* 1963, *Texas Across the River* 1966, *Scorpio* 1972, and *Swann in Love* 1983.

Delorme Philibert (c. 1512–1570). French Renaissance architect. He is remembered principally as author of two important architectural treatises 'Nouvelles Intentions' 1561 and 'Architecture' 1567. His building work includes the tomb of Francis I in St Denis, begun 1547, and extensions to the château of Chenonceaux 1557, including the first storey of the picturesque covered bridge. Little else remains intact.

Delors Jacques Lucien Jean (1925–). French socialist politician, finance minister 1981–84. As president of the European Commission 1984–94, he oversaw significant budgetary reform and the move towards a free European Community (now European Union) market, with increased powers residing in Brussels.

Delors worked as social-affairs adviser to Prime Minister Jacques Chaban-Delmas 1969–72 before joining the Socialist Party 1973. He served as minister of economy and finance (and, later, budget) in the administration of President Mitterrand 1981–84, overseeing an austerity programme ('rigueur') from June 1982. Having been passed over for the post of prime minister, Delors left to become president of the European Commission. Although criticized by some as being too federalist in outlook, he generally enjoyed a high-profile, successful presidency, including overseeing final ratification and implementation of the Maastricht Treaty on European union and negotiating the Uruguay round of General Agreement on Tariffs and Trade (GATT), concluded 1993.

Delsarte (François) Alexandre (Nicolas Chéri) (1811–1871). French music teacher and theoretician. Teaching at the Paris Conservatoire, he devised a system of body movements designed to develop coordination, grace, and expressiveness, which greatly inspired the pioneers of modern dance, such as Emile Jaques-Dalcroze and Ted Shawn.

He divided the movements of the human body into three categories: eccentric, concentric, and normal; and the expressions into three zones: head, torso, and limbs.

del Sarto Andrea. Italian Renaissance painter; see ◊Andrea del Sarto.

Delvaux Paul (1897–1994). Belgian Surrealist painter. He is renowned for his unearthly canvases portraying female nudes in settings of ruined, classical architecture. He was initially influenced by Dali, de Chirico, and Magritte, but later developed his own unique style, reflecting a preoccupation with time, eroticism, and death. His nudes are typically somnambulant and frequently accompanied by stilled locomotives, skeletons, half-moons, and mirrors, as in *Sleeping Venus* 1944. Occasionally an elegantly clothed woman or man appears among Delvaux's nudes, but his characters rarely interact. Any erotic message is held in suspense.

Demachy Robert (1859–1936). French photographer. By a complex manipulation of the printing process, using oils and gums, he produced hazy and impressionistic images, largely of young women in landscape or 'backstage' settings. He wrote several books about his printing techniques.

de Maizière Lothar (1940–   ). German politician, leader 1989–90 of the conservative Christian Democratic Union (CDU) in East Germany. He became premier after East Germany's first democratic election April 1990 and negotiated the country's reunion with West Germany. In Dec 1990 he resigned from Chancellor Kohl's cabinet and as deputy leader of the CDU, following allegations that he had been an informer to the Stasi (East German secret police). In Sept 1991, he resigned from the legislature, effectively leaving active politics.

His departure followed criticisms that he had not done enough to promote reform in the East. Shortly after his resignation, the press published allegations that, for at least a year, the western CDU had been actively working to discredit de Maizière. Known as the 'CDU affair', the scandal threatened to embroil Chancellor Kohl.

Demetrius Donskoi (or Dmitry of the Don) (1350–1389). Grand prince of Moscow from 1363. In 1380 he achieved the first Russian victory over the Tatars on the plain of Kulikovo, next to the river Don (hence his nickname).

DeMille Agnes George (1909–1993). US dancer and choreographer. She introduced popular dance idioms into ballet with such works as *Rodeo* 1942. One of the most significant contributors to the American Ballet Theater with dramatic ballets like *Fall River Legend* 1948, based on the Lizzie Borden murder case, she also led the change on Broadway to new-style musicals with her choreography of *Oklahoma!* 1943, *Carousel* 1945, and others.

DeMille studied ballet with Marie Rambert in the UK, dancing in ballets and musicals in Europe before making her debut as a choreographer in the USA. She was the daughter of William C DeMille, the playwright, and the niece of film director Cecil B DeMille.

I make pictures for people not critics.

CECIL B DE MILLE
Attributed remark

DeMille Cecil B(lount) (1881–1959). US film director and producer. He entered films 1913 with Jesse L Lasky (with whom he later established Paramount Pictures), and was one of the founders of Hollywood. He specialized in lavish biblical epics, such as *The Sign of the Cross* 1932 and *The Ten Commandments* 1923; remade 1956. He also made the 1952 Academy-Award-winning *The Greatest Show on Earth*.

Demirel Süleyman (1924–   ). Turkish politician, president from 1993. Leader from 1964 of the Justice Party, he was prime minister 1965–71, 1975–77, and 1979–80. He has favoured links with the West, full membership of the European Union, and foreign investment in Turkish industry.

De Mita Luigi Ciriaco (1928–   ). Italian conservative politician, leader of the Christian Democratic Party (DC) from 1982, prime minister 1988–90. He entered the chamber of deputies 1963 and held a number of ministerial posts in the 1970s before becoming DC secretary general. In 1993 he resigned as head of a commission on parliamentary reform, and was subsequently under investigation for extortion in connection with misuse of government aid.

Demme Jonathan (1944–   ). US film director and screenwriter. One of the most intelligent filmmakers working in Hollywood's

mainstream, Demme's films often deal with contemporary American values, sometimes with a satiric tone. His films include *Melvin and Howard* 1980, *Swimming to Cambodia* 1987, *Married to the Mob* 1988, *The Silence of the Lambs* 1991 (Academy Award), and *Philadelphia* 1994, the first Hollywood mainstream picture to deal with the subject of AIDS.

In reality we know nothing, for truth is in the depths.

DEMOCRITUS
quoted in Diogenes Laertius *Lives of the Philosophers* bk 9, ch 72

Democritus (c. 460–c. 370 BC). Greek philosopher and speculative scientist who made a significant contribution to metaphysics with his atomic theory of the universe: all things originate from a vortex of tiny, indivisible particles, which he called atoms, and differ according to the shape and arrangement of their atoms.

Democritus' discussion of the constant motion of atoms to explain the origins of the universe was the most scientific theory proposed in his time. His concepts come to us through Aristotle's work in this area.

Great fleas have little fleas upon their backs to bite 'em, / And little fleas have lesser fleas, and so ad infinitum.

AUGUSTUS DE MORGAN
Budget of Paradoxes 1915

De Morgan Augustus (1806–1871). British mathematician who initiated and developed a theory of relations in logic. He devised a symbolism that could express such notions as the contradictory, the converse, and the transitivity of a relation, as well as the union of two relations. He was the first professor of mathematics at University College, London, 1828–58.

de Morgan William Frend (1839–1917). English pottery designer. He set up his own factory 1888 in Fulham, London, producing tiles and pottery painted with flora and fauna in a style typical of the Arts and Crafts movement.

Inspired by William Morris and Edward Burne-Jones, he started designing tiles and glass for Morris' Merton Abbey factory. His work was influenced by Persian and Italian styles – he spent many months in Italy in later years – and he also developed lustre techniques (a way of covering pottery with an iridescent metallic surface).

A man is his own easiest dupe, for what he wishes to be true he generally believes to be true.

DEMOSTHENES
Third Olynthiac 19

Demosthenes (c. 384–322 BC). Athenian politician, famed for his oratory. From 351 BC he led the party that advocated resistance to the growing power of Philip of Macedon, and in his *Philippics*, a series of speeches, incited the Athenians to war. This policy resulted in the defeat of Chaeronea 338, and the establishment of Macedonian supremacy. After the death of Alexander he organized a revolt; when it failed, he took poison to avoid capture by the Macedonians.

You can today choose whether you must fight there or Philip of Macedon must fight here.

DEMOSTHENES
Orations 1.25

Dempsey Jack (William Harrison) (1895–1983). US heavyweight boxing champion, nicknamed 'the Manassa Mauler'. He beat Jess Willard 1919 to win the title and held it until 1926, when he lost it to Gene Tunney. He engaged in the 'Battle of the Long Count' with Tunney 1927.

Suggested reading
Roberts, Randy *The Manassa Mauler* (1979)
Smith, T *Kid Blackie: The Colorado Days of Jack Dempsey* (1987)

Dempsey Miles Christopher (1896–1969). British general. He commanded an infantry brigade in France 1939–40, then took command of an armoured division June 1941. In 1942 he was in command of XIII Corps in both Sicily and Italy. He returned to Britain 1944 and took command of the British 2nd Army for the D-day invasion, leading them through NW Europe to the final surrender. He then became commander in chief of Allied Forces in SE Asia, a post he held until the end of the war. KCB 1944.

Dench Judi (Judith Olivia) (1934–   ). English actress. She made her professional debut as Ophelia in *Hamlet* 1957 with the Old Vic Company. Her Shakespearean roles include Viola in *Twelfth Night* 1969, Lady Macbeth 1976, and Cleopatra 1987. Her films include *Wetherby* 1985, *A Room with a View* 1986, and *A Handful of Dust* 1988. DBE 1988.

She is also a versatile comedy actress and has directed *Much Ado about Nothing* 1988 and John Osborne's *Look Back in Anger* 1989 for the Renaissance Theatre Company.

I don't see any reason for marriage when there is divorce.

CATHERINE DENEUVE
in *LA Times* 13 Apr 1975

Deneuve Catherine (born Dorléac) (1943–   ). French actress. She was acclaimed for her performance in Roman Polanski's film *Repulsion* 1965. She also appeared in *Les Parapluies de Cherbourg/Umbrellas of Cherbourg* 1964 (with her sister Françoise Dorléac (1942–1967)), *Belle de jour* 1967, *Hustle* 1975, *Le Dernier Métro/The Last Metro* 1980, *The Hunger* 1983, and *Indochine* 1993.

Deng Xiaoping or Teng Hsiao-ping (1904–1997). Chinese political leader. Deng, born in Sichuan province into a middle-class landlord family, joined the Chinese Communist Party (CCP) as a student in Paris, where he adopted the name Xiaoping ('Little Peace') 1925, and studied in Moscow 1926. After the Long March, he served as a political commissar to the People's Liberation Army during the civil war of 1937–49. He entered the CCP Politburo 1955 and headed the secretariat during the early 1960s, working closely with President Liu Shaoqi. During the Cultural Revolution Deng was dismissed as a 'capitalist roader' and sent to work in a tractor factory in Nanchang for 're-education'.

Deng was rehabilitated by his patron Zhou Enlai 1973 and served as acting prime minister after Zhou's heart attack 1974. On Zhou's death Jan 1976 he was forced into hiding but returned to office as vice premier July 1977. By Dec 1978, although nominally a CCP vice chair, state vice premier, and Chief of Staff to the PLA, Deng was the controlling force in China. His policy of 'socialism with Chinese characteristics', misinterpreted in the West as a drift to capitalism, had success in rural areas. He helped to oust Hua Guofeng in favour of his protégés Hu Yaobang (later in turn ousted) and Zhao Ziyang.

His reputation, both at home and in the West, was tarnished by his sanctioning of the army's massacre of more than 2,000 prodemocracy demonstrators in Tiananmen Square, Beijing, in June 1989. When Deng officially retired from his party and army posts, he claimed to have renounced political involvement, but in 1992 publicly announced his support for market-oriented economic reforms. A subsequent purge of military leaders was later claimed to have been carried out at Deng's instigation.

Denikin Anton Ivanovich (1872–1947). Russian general. He distinguished himself in the Russo-Japanese War 1904–05 and World War I. After the outbreak of the Bolshevik Revolution 1917 he organized a volunteer army of 60,000 Whites (loyalists) but was routed 1919 and escaped to France. He wrote a history of the Revolution and the Civil War.

Dench *One of Britain's leading and most versatile classical actresses, Judi Dench won high critical acclaim for her performances in Shakespeare, Brecht, and Chekhov. A versatile performer, with a soft, distinctive voice and a gift for comedy, she has also appeared on television and in films, such as* A Room with a View *1987.*

There's nothing more offensive to me than watching an actor act with their ego.

ROBERT DE NIRO
in *Newsweek* 16 May 1977

De Niro Robert (1943–   ). US actor of great magnetism and physical presence. He won Academy Awards for his performances in *The Godfather Part II* 1974 and *Raging Bull* 1980, for which role he put on weight in the interests of authenticity as the boxer gone to seed, Jake LaMotta. His other films include *Mean Streets* 1973, *Taxi Driver* 1976, *The Deer Hunter* 1978, *The Untouchables* 1987, *Midnight Run* 1988, and *Cape Fear* 1991. He showed his versatility in *The King of Comedy* 1982 and other Martin Scorsese films. He directed *A Bronx Tale* 1993. *See illustration on page 236.*

Denis Maurice (1870–1943). French painter, illustrator, and art theorist. He is chiefly important as a founder-member and spokesman for *les Nabis*. His friendship with Paul Gauguin and admiration for Italian Renaissance art are reflected in his flat, decorative paintings of figures and landscapes, for example *The Muses or Sacred Wood* 1893 (Musée National d'Art Moderne, Paris).

Denis was the author of several influential articles and books on art theory, including *Théories, 1890–1910*, republished 1920. He also illustrated numerous books and executed large murals on religious themes, notably that in Sainte-Marguerite du Vésinet 1901–03.

Denis, St first bishop of Paris and one of the patron saints of France, who was martyred by the Romans. Feast day 9 Oct.

St Denis is often confused with Dionysius the Areopagite, as well as with the original martyr of the 1st century AD. According to legend, he was sent as a missionary to Gaul in 250, and was beheaded several years later at what is today Montmartre in Paris, during the reign of Emperor Valerian. He is often represented as carrying his head in his hands.

De Niro *US film actor Robert de Niro, seen here in the film A Bronx Tale 1993. Although he is a versatile actor, his most successful roles have been as psychotics. He has won critical acclaim for his striving for authenticity.*

Denktas Rauf R (1924–   ). Turkish-Cypriot nationalist politician. In 1975 the Turkish Federated State of Cyprus (TFSC) was formed in the northern third of the island, with Denktas as its head, and in 1983 he became president of the breakaway Turkish Republic of Northern Cyprus (TRNC). He was re-elected 1995.

Denktas held law-officer posts under the British crown before independence in 1960. Relations between the Greek and Turkish communities progressively deteriorated, leading to the formation of the TFSC. In 1983 the TRNC, with Denktas as its president, was formally constituted, but recognized internationally only by Turkey.

The accession of the independent politician Georgios Vassilou to the Cyprus presidency offered hopes of reconciliation, but meetings between him and Denktas during 1989, under UN auspices, failed to produce an agreement. The talks resumed 1992 but failed to reach a successful conclusion.

Denning Alfred Thompson, Baron Denning (1899–   ). British judge, Master of the Rolls 1962–82. In 1963 he conducted the inquiry into the Profumo scandal. A vigorous and highly innovative civil lawyer, he was controversial in his defence of the rights of the individual against the state, the unions, and big business. Knighted 1944, baron 1957.

Violence is extremely beautiful.
BRIAN DE PALMA
in Film Yearbook 1985

De Palma Brian Russell (1940–   ). US film director, especially of thrillers. His technical mastery and enthusiasm for spilling blood are shown in films such as *Sisters* 1973, *Carrie* 1976, and *The Untouchables* 1987. His *Bonfire of the Vanities* 1990 was a critical and commercial failure.

At 20 you have many desires that hide the truth, but beyond 40 there are only real and fragile truths – your abilities and your failings.
GÉRARD DEPARDIEU
in Observer March 1991

Depardieu Gérard (1948–   ). French actor. He is renowned for his imposing physique and screen presence. His films include *Deux Hommes dans la ville* 1973, *Le Camion* 1977, *Mon Oncle d'Amérique* 1980, *The Moon in the Gutter* 1983, *Jean de Florette* 1985, *Cyrano de Bergerac* 1990, and *Le Colonel Chabert* 1994. His English-speaking films include the US romantic comedy *Green Card* 1990, *1492 – Conquest of Paradise* 1992, and *My Father the Hero* 1994.

De Quincey Thomas (1785–1859). English author. His works include *Confessions of an English Opium-Eater* 1821 and the essays 'On the Knocking at the Gate in Macbeth' 1823 and 'On Murder Considered as One of the Fine Arts' 1827. He was a friend of the poets Wordsworth and Coleridge.

Born in Manchester, De Quincey ran away from school there to wander and study in Wales. He then went to London, where he lived in extreme poverty but with the constant companionship of the young orphan Ann, of whom he writes in the *Confessions*. In 1803 he was reconciled to his guardians and was sent to university at Oxford, where his opium habit began. In 1809 he settled with the Wordsworths and Coleridge in the Lake District. He moved to Edinburgh 1828, where he eventually died. De Quincey's work had a powerful influence on Charles Baudelaire and Edgar Allan Poe among others.

I curse painting every day, it gives me so much trouble!
ANDRÉ DERAIN
Letter to Vlaminck 1917

Derain André (1880–1954). French painter. He experimented with the strong, almost primary colours associated with Fauvism but

Depardieu *French film actor Gérard Depardieu. A compelling screen presence, versatile acting ability, and burly yet sympathetic looks made him a leading figure in French cinema in the 1980s. With Jean de Florette 1985, Cyrano de Bergerac 1990, and Green Card 1991 he became widely known to international audiences.*

later developed a more sombre landscape and figurative style. *Pool of London* 1906 (Tate Gallery, London) is a typical work. He also produced costumes and scenery for Diaghilev's Ballets Russes.

The duty of an Opposition (is) very simple – to oppose everything, and propose nothing.

EDWARD STANLEY, 14TH EARL OF DERBY
Speech in House of Commons 4 June 1841

Derby Edward George Geoffrey Smith Stanley, 14th Earl of Derby (1799–1869). British politician, prime minister 1852, 1858–59, and 1866–68.

Originally a Whig, he became secretary for the colonies 1830, and introduced the bill for the abolition of slavery. He joined the Tories 1834, and the split in the Tory Party over Robert Peel's free-trade policy gave Derby the leadership for 20 years. Succeeded to earldom 1851.

D. is a very weak-minded fellow I am afraid, and, like the feather pillow, bears the marks of the last person who has sat on him!

Douglas Haig on EDWARD STANLEY, 17TH EARL OF DERBY
in letter to Lady Haig 14 Jan 1918

Derby Edward George Villiers Stanley, 17th Earl of Derby (1865–1948). British Conservative politician, member of Parliament from 1892. He was secretary of war 1916–18 and 1922–24, and ambassador to France 1918–20. KCVO 1905, succeeded to earldom 1908.

De Robeck John Michael (1862–1928). British admiral in World War I. He commanded British naval forces at Gallipoli, directing operations off the coast until the evacuation 1916. In 1919 he became commander in chief in the Mediterranean and high commissioner at Constantinople. Knighted 1916, he was made a full admiral 1920.

De Roburt Hammer (1923–1992). President of Nauru 1968–76, 1978–83, and 1987–89. During the country's occupation 1942–45, he was deported to Japan. He became head chief of Nauru 1956 and was elected the country's first president 1968. He secured only a narrow majority in the 1987 elections and in 1989 was ousted on a no-confidence motion.

Derrida Jacques (1930–   ). French philosopher who introduced the deconstruction theory into literary criticism. His approach involves looking at how a text is put together in order to reveal its hidden meanings and the assumptions of the author. Derrida's main publications are *De la Grammatologie/Of Grammatology* 1967 and *La Voix et le phénomène/Speech and Writing* 1967.

Derrida was born in Algeria. He taught in Paris at the Sorbonne 1960–64 and subsequently at the Ecole Normale Supérieure. His analysis of language draws on the German philosophers Friedrich Nietzsche, Edmund Husserl, and Martin Heidegger, and the Swiss linguist Ferdinand de Saussure. Although obscurely presented, his conclusions have some similarity to those of Anglo-American linguistic philosophers.

Desai Morarji Ranchhodji (1896–1995). Indian politician. An early follower of Mahatma Gandhi, he was independent India's first non-Congress Party prime minister 1977–79, as leader of the Janata party, after toppling Indira Gandhi. Party infighting led to his resignation of both the premiership and the party leadership.

Born in Gujarat, W India, Desai's early career was as a civil servant working for the British Raj. Strongly influenced by Mahatma Gandhi, Desai resigned from the civil service 1930 and committed his life to the Indian freedom movement. Although jailed for his participation in the Civil Disobedience Campaign, he was elected to the Bombay legislature 1935 and became the state's chief minister 1951. A disciplined teetotaller, vegetarian and, from the age of 32, celibate, he imposed prohibition in the state.

Jawaharlal Nehru brought Desai into the federal administration of independent India 1956 and appointed him finance minister 1958. However, his relations with Nehru's daughter Indira Gandhi, who became prime minister in 1966, were strained; Desai, who had previously derided her as a 'mere schoolgirl' and, being politically more conservative, resigned in 1969 in opposition to plans to nationalize India's banks. His departure caused a serious split in the ruling Congress Party; Desai went on to form the Janata Party, which gained power after the state of emergency 1975–77 imposed by Indira Gandhi when she was found guilty of electoral malpractice.

At the age of 81, Desai became the world's oldest prime minister and, as a true Gandhian, sought to encourage the revival of cottage industries, and delayed the manufacture of India's nuclear bomb. However, the fractious Janata coalition stayed together for only two years. Desai's frank, difficult, obdurate, and eccentric personality contributed to his demise as premier July 1979, when he retired from politics. He remained in remarkable health and ascribed his longevity to his ascetic regimen and, in particular, the health-giving powers of his remarkable twice daily ritual of drinking his own urine, which he described as 'the water of life'.

De Savary Peter John (1944–   ). British entrepreneur. He acquired Land's End, Cornwall, England, 1987 and built a theme park there. He revived Falmouth dock and the port of Hayle in N Cornwall.

A yachting enthusiast, he sponsored the Blue Arrow America's Cup challenge team.

Descartes René (1596–1650). French philosopher and mathematician. He believed that commonly accepted knowledge was doubtful because of the subjective nature of the senses, and attempted to rebuild human knowledge using as his foundation *cogito ergo sum* ('I think, therefore I am'). He also believed that the entire material universe could be explained in terms of mathematical physics, and founded coordinate geometry as a way of defining and manipulating geometrical shapes by means of algebraic expressions. Cartesian coordinates, the means by which points are represented in

Descartes *French philosopher and mathematician René Descartes, who reformulated scientific thinking in the 17th century with his attempts to describe the whole of knowledge using mathematics. He devised the Cartesian system of coordinate geometry, which allows points to be described numerically on a set of perpendicular axes.* (Ann Ronan/Image Select)

this system, are named after him. Descartes also established the science of optics, and helped to shape contemporary theories of astronomy and animal behaviour.

Descartes identified the 'thinking thing' (*res cogitans*) or mind with the human soul or consciousness; the body, though somehow interacting with the soul, was a physical machine, secondary to, and in principle separable from, the soul. He held that everything has a cause; nothing can result from nothing. He believed that, although all matter is in motion, matter does not move of its own accord; the initial impulse comes from God. He also postulated two quite distinct substances: spatial substance, or matter, and thinking substance, or mind. This is called 'Cartesian dualism', and it preserved him from serious controversy with the church.

Suggested reading
Balz, A G *Descartes and the Modern Mind* (1952)
Gauk, Roger *Descartes: An Intellectual Biography* (1995)
Grene, Marjorie *Descartes* (1985)
Sorell, T *Descartes* (1987)
Vrooman, J R *Rene Descartes: A Biography* (1970)

Deschamps Eustache (*c.* 1346–*c.* 1406). French poet. He was the author of more than 1,000 ballades, and the *Miroir de mariage/The Mirror of Marriage*, an attack on women.

Moral indignation is in most cases 2% moral, 48% indignation and 50% envy.

VITTORIO DE SICA
quoted in *Observer* 17 Dec 1961

De Sica Vittorio (1901–1974). Italian film director and actor. His *Bicycle Thieves* 1949 is a landmark of Italian neorealism. Later films included *Umberto D* 1955, *Two Women* 1960, and *The Garden of the Finzi-Continis* 1971. His considerable acting credits include *The Earrings of Madame de...* 1953 and *The Millionaires* 1960.

He won four Academy Awards for best foreign film with *Shoeshine* 1946; *Bicycle Thieves*; *Yesterday, Today and Tomorrow* 1964; and *The Garden of the Finzi-Continis*.

De Sica Italian film director and actor Vittorio de Sica. After World War II, he emerged as one of the leading Italian neorealist directors with Shoeshine 1946, Bicycle Thieves 1948, and Miracle in Milan 1950. *He continued to make films until the early 1970s.*

Deslandres Henri Alexandre (1853–1948). French physicist and astronomer. His work in spectroscopy led to his construction of the spectroheliograph for his solar studies. In 1902 he predicted that the Sun would be found to be a source of radio waves, and 40 years later this was confirmed. In 1897 he moved to the observatory at Meudon, where he became director 1907. The Paris and Meudon Observatories were combined in 1926. Deslandres retired 1929.

Desmarest Nicolas (1725–1815). French naturalist who became a champion of volcanist geology, countering the widely held belief that all rocks were sedimentary. He wrote extensively for the *Encyclopédie*.

Desmarest, born near Troyes, moved to Paris and occupied minor government offices. Gradually he staked out for himself a scientific career, publishing charts of the English Channel and making geological tours.

Studying the large basalt deposits of central France, Desmarest traced their origin to ancient volcanic activity in the Auvergne region. In 1768 he produced a detailed study of the geology and eruptive history of the volcanoes responsible. However, he did not believe that all rocks had igneous origin, and emphasized the critical role of water in the shaping of the Earth's history.

Desmoulins (Lucie Simplice) Camille (Benoist) (1760–1794). French revolutionary who summoned the mob to arms on 12 July 1789, so precipitating the revolt that culminated in the storming of the Bastille. A prominent left-wing Jacobin, he was elected to the National Convention 1792. His *Histoire des Brissotins* was largely responsible for the overthrow of the right-wing Girondins, but shortly after he was sent to the guillotine as too moderate.

Désormes Charles Bernard (1777–1862). French physicist and chemist who determined the ratio of the specific heats of gases 1819. He did this and almost all his scientific work in collaboration with his son-in-law Nicolas Clément (1779–1841).

Désormes was born in Dijon, Côte d'Or. He was a student at the Ecole Polytechnique in Paris from 1794, when it opened, and subsequently worked there as a demonstrator. Désormes met Clément at the Ecole Polytechnique 1801, beginning a scientific collaboration that lasted until 1824. He left the Ecole 1804 to establish an alum refinery at Berberie, Oise, with Clément and Joseph Montgolfier, who had earlier pioneered balloon flight. Desormes was elected counsellor for Oise 1830 and in 1848 to the national assembly, in which he sat with the Republicans.

de Soto Hernando (*c.* 1496–1542). Spanish explorer who sailed with d'Avila (*c.* 1400–1531) to Darien, Central America, 1519, explored the Yucatán Peninsula 1528, and travelled with Francisco Pizarro in Peru 1530–35. In 1538 he was made governor of Cuba and Florida. In his expedition of 1539, he explored Florida, Georgia, and the Mississippi River.

Emperor Charles V appointed de Soto governor of Florida in 1537. His expeditions may have penetrated Missouri and Louisiana. Upon his death on May 21, 1542, his companions buried his body in a river to preserve the local Indians' belief that de Soto had descended from heaven.

Desprez Josquin. Franco-Flemish composer; see ◊Josquin Desprez.

Dessalines Jean Jacques (*c.* 1758–1806). Emperor of Haiti 1804–06. Born in Guinea, he was taken to Haiti as a slave, where in 1802 he succeeded Toussaint L'Ouverture as leader of the black revolt against the French. After defeating the French, he proclaimed Haiti's independence and made himself emperor. He was killed when trying to suppress an uprising provoked by his cruelty.

Dessau Paul (1894–1979). German composer. His work includes incidental music to Bertolt Brecht's theatre pieces; an opera, *Der Verurteilung des Lukullus/The Trial of Lucullus* 1949, also to a libretto by Brecht; and numerous choral works and songs.

He studied in Berlin, becoming a theatre conductor until moving to Paris 1933, where he studied Schoenberg's serial method with

René Leibowitz. He collaborated with Brecht from 1942, when they met as political exiles in the USA, returning with him to East Berlin 1948.

de Tocqueville Alexis. French politician; see ◊Tocqueville, Alexis de.

Dev Kapil (1959–). Indian cricketer who is one of the world's outstanding all-rounders. At the age of 20 he became the youngest player to complete the 'double' of 1,000 runs and 100 wickets in test cricket. In 1992 he followed Richard Hadlee as the second bowler to reach 400 wickets.

de Valera Eamon (1882–1975). Irish nationalist politician, prime minister of the Irish Free State/Eire/Republic of Ireland 1932–48, 1951–54, and 1957–59, and president 1959–73. Repeatedly imprisoned, he participated in the Easter Rising 1916 and was leader of the nationalist Sinn Féin party 1917–26, when he formed the republican Fianna Fáil party; he directed negotiations with Britain 1921 but refused to accept the partition of Ireland until 1937.

De Valera was born in New York, the son of a Spanish father and an Irish mother, and sent to Ireland as a child, where he became a teacher of mathematics. He was sentenced to death for his part in the Easter Rising, but the sentence was commuted, and he was released under an amnesty 1917. In the same year he was elected member of Parliament for E Clare, and president of Sinn Féin. He was rearrested May 1918, but escaped to the USA 1919. He returned to Ireland 1920 and directed the struggle against the British government from a hiding place in Dublin. He authorized the negotiations of 1921, but refused to accept the ensuing treaty which divided Ireland into the Free State and the North.

Civil war followed. De Valera was arrested by the Free State government 1923, and spent a year in prison. In 1926 he formed a new party, Fianna Fáil, which secured a majority in 1932. De Valera became prime minister and foreign minister of the Free State, and at once abolished the oath of allegiance and suspended payment of the annuities due under the Land Purchase Acts. In 1938 he negotiated an agreement with Britain, under which all outstanding points were settled. Throughout World War II he maintained a strict neutrality, rejecting an offer by Winston Churchill 1940 to recognize the principle of a united Ireland in return for Eire's entry into the war. He resigned after his defeat at the 1948 elections but was again prime minister in the 1950s, and then president of the republic.

Suggested reading
Coogan, Tim Pat *De Valera: Long Fellow, Long Shadow* (1995)
Edwards, O D *Eamon de Valera* (1988)
Fitzgibbon, C and Morrison, G *The Life and Times of Eamon de Valera* (1974)
O'Carroll, John and Murphy, John (eds) *De Valera and His Times* (1986)

Whenever I wanted to know what the Irish people wanted I had only to examine my own heart.
EAMON DE VALERA
Speech in the Dail 6 Jan 1922

de Valois Ninette. Stage name of Edris Stannus (1898–). Irish choreographer, dancer, and teacher. In setting up the Vic-Wells Ballet 1931 (later the Royal Ballet and Royal Ballet School) she was, along with choreographer Frederick Ashton, one of the architects of British ballet. Among her works are *Job* 1931 and *Checkmate* 1937.

She worked with Sergei Diaghilev in Paris (1923–25) before opening a dance academy in London 1926. DBE 1951.

De Vaucouleurs Gerard Henri (1918–). French-born US astronomer who carried out important research into extragalactic nebulae. In 1956 he suggested that there is a pattern in the location of nebulae, clusters of stars formerly thought to be randomly scattered. He worked in Australia 1951–57 and then moved to the USA. In 1965 he became professor of astronomy at the University of Texas, Austin.

Deventer Jacob Louis (1874–1922). South African soldier. Originally a farmer, he became second-in-command to General Smuts in the Boer invasion of Cape Colony. When a Boer rebellion broke out in South Africa 1914, he prevented the rebels capturing Upington. He was commander in chief East Africa May 1917 until the colony was captured. He was knighted 1917 and made honorary lieutenant-general 1919.

Devine George Alexander Cassady (1910–1966). English actor and theatre director. A director of the Young Vic training school from 1946, he was appointed artistic director of the English Stage Company at the Royal Court Theatre, London, 1956, which became the home of the new wave of British dramatists, including John Osborne, Arnold Wesker, and John Arden.

Devlin Patrick Arthur, Baron Devlin (1905–1992). British judge, a distinguished jurist and commentator on the English legal system. He was justice of the High Court in the Queen's Bench Division 1948–60, Lord Justice of Appeal 1960–61, and Lord of Appeal in Ordinary 1961–64. Knighted 1948, baron 1961.

Devonshire William Cavendish, 7th Duke of Devonshire (1808–1891). British aristocrat whose development of Eastbourne, Sussex, England, was an early example of town planning. 2nd earl 1834, succeeded to dukedom 1858.

Devonshire, 8th Duke of See ◊Hartington, Spencer Compton Cavendish, British politician.

De Vries Hugo Marie (1848–1935). Dutch botanist who conducted important research on osmosis in plant cells and was a pioneer in the study of plant evolution. His work led to the rediscovery of Austrian biologist Gregor Mendel's laws and the discovery of spontaneously occurring mutations. He spent most of his academic career at the University of Amsterdam, and was professor of botany there 1881–1918.

Dewar James (1842–1923). Scottish chemist and physicist who invented the vacuum flask (Thermos) 1872 during his research into the properties of matter at extremely low temperatures. He became professor of chemistry at Cambridge 1875, as well as at the Royal Institute in London 1877.

Working on the liquefaction of gases, Dewar found, in 1891, that both liquid oxygen and ozone are magnetic. In 1895 he became the first to produce liquid hydrogen, and in 1899 succeeded in solidifying hydrogen at a temperature of −259°C/−434°F. He also invented the explosive cordite 1889. Knighted 1904.

de Wet Christiaan Rudolf (1854–1922). Boer general and politician. He served in the South African Wars 1880 and 1899. When World War I began, he headed a pro-German rising of 12,000 Afrikaners but was defeated, convicted of treason, and imprisoned. He was sentenced to six years' imprisonment for his part in the uprising, but was released 1915.

Dewey George (1837–1917). US naval officer. Dewey saw action on the Mississippi River and in the blockade of Southern ports during the American Civil War 1861–65. He was appointed chief of the Bureau of Equipment 1889 and of the Board of Inspection and Survey 1895.

As commodore, Dewey was dispatched to the Pacific 1896. He destroyed the Spanish fleet in Manila harbour at the outbreak of the Spanish-American War 1898. Dewey was promoted to the rank of admiral of the navy (the highest naval rank ever awarded) 1899. He retired from active service 1900.

Dewey John (1859–1952). US philosopher who believed that the exigencies of a democratic and industrial society demanded new educational techniques. He expounded his ideas in numerous writings, including *School and Society* 1899, and founded a progressive school in Chicago. A pragmatist thinker, influenced by William James, Dewey maintained that there is only the reality of experience and made 'inquiry' the essence of logic.

Dewey was born in Vermont and from 1904 was professor of philosophy at Columbia University, New York.

His other writings include *Experimental Logic* 1916, *Reconstruction in Philosophy* 1920, *Quest for Certainty* 1929, and *Problems of Men* 1946.

Suggested reading
Archambault, R (ed) *Dewey on Education: Appraisals* (1966)
Bernstein, R J *John Dewey* (1966)
Bullert, G *The Politics of John Dewey* (1983)
Dykhuizen, G *The Life and Mind of John Dewey* (1973)
Hook, S (ed) *John Dewey: An Intellectual Portrait* (1971)
Wirth, A G *John Dewey as Educator* (1989)

Dewey Melvil (1851–1931). US librarian. In 1876, he devised the Dewey decimal system of classification for accessing, storing, and retrieving books, widely used in libraries. The system uses the numbers 000 to 999 to designate the major fields of knowledge, then breaks these down into more specific subjects by the use of decimals.

Dewey founded the American Library Association 1876 and the first school of library science, at Columbia University, 1887.

Dewey Thomas Edmund (1902–1971). US public official. He was Manhattan district attorney 1937–38 and served as governor of New York 1942–54. Dewey was twice the Republican presidential candidate, losing to F D Roosevelt 1944 and to Truman 1948, the latter race being one of the greatest electoral upsets in US history.

Born in Owosso, Michigan, USA, Dewey received a law degree from Columbia University 1925. He was appointed chief assistant to the US attorney in the Southern District of New York 1931. He gained a reputation as a crime fighter while serving as special investigator of organized crime 1935–37.

de Wint Peter (1784–1849). Landscape painter of Dutch-American descent born in Staffordshire, USA where his father, a doctor (born in New York), had his practice. He was apprenticed to the engraver John Raphael Smith, but was directed towards watercolour by the advice of John Varley and the example of Girtin, whose work he admired in Dr Monro's collection. From 1806 watercolour was his chief means of expression, and the country round Lincoln (the home of his wife) his main theme, his best work being executed with broad washes summarizing natural forms.

Diabelli Anton (1781–1858). Austrian publisher and composer. He was the original publisher of Beethoven, Haydn, and Schubert. He is most famous today for appearing in the title of Beethoven's *Diabelli Variations* 1823, which formed part of a contribution by 50 composers, each of whom was asked to compose a piece based on a waltz theme written by Diabelli himself.

Diaghilev Sergei Pavlovich (1872–1929). Russian ballet impresario. In 1909 he founded the Ballets Russes/Russian Ballet (headquarters in Monaco), which he directed for 20 years. Through this company he brought Russian ballet to the West, encouraging a dazzling array of dancers, choreographers, composers, and artists, such as Anna Pavlova, Vaslav Nijinsky, Bronislava Nijinksa, Mikhail Fokine, Léonide Massine, George Balanchine, Igor Stravinsky, Sergey Prokofiev, Pablo Picasso, and Henri Matisse.

Suggested reading
Buckle, Richard *Diaghilev* (1979)
Kochno, Boris *Diaghilev and the Ballet Russe* (1970)
Percival, J *The World of Diaghilev* (1971)
Spencer, C and Dyer, P *The World of Serge Diaghilev* (1974)

Diana Princess of Wales (born Diana Frances Spencer) (1961–   ). daughter of the 8th Earl Spencer, Diana married Prince Charles in St Paul's Cathedral, London 1981, the first English bride of a royal heir since 1659. She is descended from the only sovereigns from whom Prince Charles is not descended, Charles II and James II. She had two sons, William and Henry, before her separation from Charles 1992.

Charles and Diana's decision to separate was announced by Prime Minister John Major Dec 1992, when he stated that they had no plans to divorce, and that their constitutional positions were not affected. The Church of England issued a statement saying that the separation would not prevent Charles from leading the church. However, Diana admitted in a television interview Nov 1995 that she had had an affair following her separation from Prince Charles, and that she had suffered from bulimia and practised self-mutilation. The couple divorced 1996.

Diaz Armando (1861–1928). Italian general in World War I. After the Battle of Caporetto Nov 1917 he replaced Cadorna as Italian commander in chief and held the Austro-Hungarian advance on the line of the Piave. He comprehensively defeated the Austrians along their whole line Oct–Nov 1918.

Educated in the military academy of Turin, he joined the army 1881 and saw active service in Abyssinia 1896. In 1915 he was a junior major-general and commanded the 23rd Corps in the battles of the Carso 1916. After the war, he became inspector-general of the Italian Army 1919.

Diaz Bartolomeu (*c.* 1450–1500). Portuguese explorer, the first European to reach the Cape of Good Hope 1488, and to establish a route around Africa. He drowned during an expedition with Pedro Cabral.

Poor Mexico, so far from God, and so close to the United States!

PORFIRIO DÍAZ
Attributed remark

Díaz (José de la Cruz) Porfirio (1830–1915). Dictator of Mexico 1877–80 and 1884–1911. After losing the 1876 election, he overthrew the government and seized power. He was supported by conservative landowners and foreign capitalists, who invested in railways and mines. He centralized the state at the expense of the peasants and Indians, and dismantled all local and regional leadership. He faced mounting and revolutionary opposition in his final years and was forced into exile 1911.

Díaz del Castillo Bernal (*c.* 1492–*c.* 1581). Spanish soldier and chronicler. He arrived in the New World 1514 with conquistador Pedro Arias de Ávila (*c.* 1440–1531) and took part in the exploration of the Gulf coast of Mexico 1517 and 1518. He served as a common soldier under Pedro de Alvarado during the conquest of Mexico, and is known for his account, *Historia verdadera de la conquista de la Nueva España/True Account of the History of New Spain*.

Diaz de Solís Juan (*c.* 1471–*c.* 1516). Spanish explorer in South America who reached the estuary of the Río de la Plata, and was killed and reputedly eaten by cannibals.

Dick Philip K(endred) (1928–1982). US science-fiction writer. His works often deal with religion and the subjectivity of reality. His protagonists are often alienated individuals struggling to retain their integrity in a technologically dominated world. His novels include *The Man in the High Castle* 1962, *Simulcra* 1964, and *Do Androids Dream of Electric Sheep?* 1968 (filmed as *Blade Runner* 1982).

Dicke Robert Henry (1916–   ). US physicist who in 1964 proposed a version of the Big Bang theory known as the 'hot Big Bang': he suggested that the present expansion of the universe had been preceded by a collapse in which high temperatures had been generated. From 1946 he was on the staff at Princeton, becoming professor 1957.

Annual income twenty pounds, annual expenditure nineteen nineteen six, result happiness. Annual income twenty pounds, annual expenditure twenty pounds ought and six, result misery.

CHARLES DICKENS
Mr Micawber in *David Copperfield* ch 12 1849

Dickens Charles John Huffam (1812–1870). English novelist. He is enduringly popular for his memorable characters and his portrayal of the social evils of Victorian England. In 1836 he published the first number of the *Pickwick Papers*, followed by *Oliver Twist* 1838, the

Dickens: major works

title	date	well-known characters
The Pickwick Papers	1836	Mr Pickwick, Sam Weller, Mr Snodgrass, Mr Jingle, Mr and Mrs Bardell
Oliver Twist	1838	Oliver Twist, Fagin, Mr Bumble, The Artful Dodger
Nicholas Nickleby	1839	Nicholas Nickleby, Wackford Squeers, Madame Mantalini, Smike, Vincent Crummles
The Old Curiosity Shop	1841	Little Nell, Dick Swiveller, Daniel Quilp
Barnaby Rudge	1841	Simon Tappertit (Sim), Miss Miggs, Gashford
A Christmas Carol	1843	Ebenezer Scrooge, Bob Cratchit, Marley's Ghost, Tiny Tim
Martin Chuzzlewit	1843	Martin Chuzzlewit (Junior), Mr Pecksniff, Mrs Gamp, Tom Pinch
Dombey and Son	1848	Dombey, Paul and Florence Dombey, Edith Granger, James Carker, Major Bagstock
David Copperfield	1849	David Copperfield, Mr Micawber, Mr Dick, Uriah Heep, Little Em'ly, Betsey Trotwood
Bleak House	1853	John Jarndyce, Esther Summerson, Harold Skimpole, Lady Dedlock, Mrs Jellyby
Hard Times	1854	Gradgrind, Tom and Louisa Gradgrind, Josiah Bounderby, Bitzer, Cissy Jupe
Little Dorrit	1857	Amy Dorrit, Flora Finching, Mr Merille
A Tale of Two Cities	1859	Dr Manette, Charles Darnay, Sydney Carton, Jerry Cruncher, Madame Defarge
Great Expectations	1861	Pip, Estella, Miss Havisham, Joe Gargery, Wemmick, Magwitch
Our Mutual Friend	1865	Noddy Boffin, Silas Wegg, Mr Podsnap, Betty Higden, Bradley Headstone, Reginald Wilfer
The Mystery of Edwin Drood (unfinished)	1870	Rosa Bud, John Jasper

first of his 'reforming' novels; *Nicholas Nickleby* 1839; *Barnaby Rudge* 1841; *The Old Curiosity Shop* 1841; and *David Copperfield* 1849. Among his later books are *A Tale of Two Cities* 1859 and *Great Expectations* 1861.

Born in Portsea, Hampshire, the son of a clerk, Dickens received little formal education, although a short period spent working in a blacking factory in S London, while his father was imprisoned for debt in the Marshalsea prison during 1824, was followed by three years in a private school. In 1827 he became a lawyer's clerk, and then after four years a reporter for the *Morning Chronicle*, to which he contributed the *Sketches by Boz*. In 1836 he married Catherine Hogarth, three days after the publication of the first number of the *Pickwick Papers*. Originally intended merely as an accompaniment to a series of sporting illustrations, the adventures of Pickwick outgrew their setting and established Dickens' reputation. In 1842 he visited the USA, where his attack on the pirating of English books by American publishers chilled his welcome; his experiences are reflected in *American Notes* and *Martin Chuzzlewit* 1843. In 1843 he published the first of his Christmas books, *A Christmas Carol*, followed 1844 by *The Chimes*, written in Genoa during his first long sojourn abroad, and in 1845 by the even more successful *Cricket on the Hearth*. A venture as editor of the Liberal *Daily News* 1846 was short-lived, and *Dombey and Son* 1848 was largely written abroad. *David Copperfield*, his most popular novel, appeared 1849 and contains many autobiographical incidents and characters. Returning to

journalism, Dickens inaugurated the weekly magazine *Household Words* 1850, reorganizing it 1859 as *All the Year Round*; many of his later stories were published serially in these periodicals. In 1857 Dickens met the actress Ellen Ternan and in 1858 agreed with his wife on a separation; his sister-in-law remained with him to care for his children. In 1858 he began giving public readings from his novels, which proved such a success that he was invited to make a second US tour 1867. Among his later novels are *Bleak House* 1853, *Hard Times* 1854, *Little Dorrit* 1857, and *Our Mutual Friend* 1865. *Edwin Drood*, a mystery story influenced by the style of his friend Wilkie Collins, was left incomplete on his death.

Suggested reading
Ackroyd, P *Dickens* (1990)
Collins, P *Charles Dickens* (1987)
Hardwick, M and M *The Charles Dickens Encyclopedia* (1973)
Hobsbaum, P *A Reader's Guide to Charles Dickens* (1973)
Kaplan, F *Dickens: A Biography* (1988)
Page, N *A Dickens Companion* (1987)
Wilson, A *The World of Charles Dickens* (1970)

Dickens Monica Enid (1915–1992). English writer. Her first books were humorous accounts of her experiences in various jobs, beginning as a cook (*One Pair of Hands* 1939); she went on to become a novelist. Her first novel, *Mariana*, was published 1940. In the early years of World War II she worked as a hospital nurse and then later as a fitter in a factory producing aircraft spare parts. Her experiences again provided material for her next books, *One Pair of Feet* 1942, *The Fancy* 1943, and *Thursday Afternoons* 1945, the latter two attracting much praise. She was a great-granddaughter of Charles Dickens.

A close friend of the Samaritans' founder, Chad Varah, she founded the Samaritans in the USA.

Dickey James Lafayette (1923–1997). US poet, critic, and novelist. His fiction deals mainly with guilt arising from acts of individual or collective cruelty and the struggle for survival. His powerful best seller *Deliverance* 1970 (filmed 1972) is a menacing thriller about four men canoeing down a dangerous river. His poetry, initially conservative, turned to more open forms as in *The Central Motion: Poems 1968–1978* 1979. His non-fiction *To the White Sea* was published 1994.

Parting is all we know of heaven, / And all we need of hell.

EMILY DICKINSON
'Parting'

Dickinson Emily Elizabeth (1830–1886). US poet. She wrote most of her poetry between 1850 and the late 1860s and was particularly prolific during the Civil War years. She experimented with poetic rhythms, rhymes, and forms, as well as language and syntax. Her work is characterized by a wit and boldness that seem to contrast sharply with the reclusive life she led in Amherst, Massachusetts. Very few of her many short, mystical poems were published during her lifetime, and her work became well known only in the 20th century. The first collection of her poetry, *Poems by Emily Dickinson*, was published 1890.

Born in Amherst, she lived in near seclusion there after 1862. Dickinson also carried on lengthy correspondences with a number of friends and acquaintances, and many of her letters are extraordinary artistic achievements in themselves.

Suggested reading
Ferlazzo, P J *Emily Dickinson* (1976)
Knapp, B L *Emily Dickinson* (1986)
Luce, W *The Belle of Amherst* (1978)
Sewall, R B *The Life of Emily Dickinson* (1974)
Wolff, C G *Emily Dickinson* (1986)

Dick-Read Grantly (1890–1959). British gynaecologist. In private practice in London 1923–48, he developed the concept of natural childbirth: that by the elimination of fear and tension, labour pain could be minimized and anaesthetics, which can be hazardous to both mother and child, rendered unnecessary.

Dicksee Cedric Bernard (1888–1981). British engineer who was a pioneer in developing the compression-ignition (diesel) engine into a suitable unit for road transport. This became standard in commercial vehicles.

He worked in the USA 1919–26 for the Westinghouse Electric and Manufacturing Company, then joined the manufacturing subsidiary of the London General Omnibus Company (LGOC) 1928. During World War II he worked on combustion-chamber design for the De Havilland series of jet engines.

Dickson Leonard Eugene (1874–1954). US mathematician who gave the first extensive exposition of the theory of fields. In *History of the Theory of Numbers* 1919–23, now a standard work, he investigated abundant numbers, perfect numbers, and Pierre de Fermat's last theorem.

Dickson was born in Independence, Iowa, and studied at the universities of Texas and Chicago, spending nearly all his academic career at the latter and becoming professor 1910.

Diddley Bo. Stage name of Ellas Bates McDaniel (1928–). US rhythm-and-blues guitarist, singer, and songwriter. His distinctive syncopated beat ('Shave and a haircut, two bits') became a rock staple; it can be heard in many of his classic songs, including 'Bo Diddley' 1955, 'Who Do You Love?' 1955, and 'Mona' 1956.

Bo Diddley, born in Mississippi, recorded for the Chess label in Chicago 1955–74. Muddy Waters had a hit with his song 'Mannish Boy' (also known as 'I'm a Man') 1955. Relying more on distortion than technique, Bo Diddley's guitar style has influenced generations of garage bands, and his lyrics are often humorous.

It is said that desire is a product of the will, but the converse is in fact true: will is a product of desire.

DENIS DIDEROT
Elements of Physiology, 'Will, Freedom' 1964 ed

Diderot Denis (1713–1784). French philosopher. He is closely associated with the Enlightenment, the European intellectual movement for social and scientific progress, and was editor of the enormously influential *Encyclopédie* 1751–80.

An expanded and politicized version of the English encyclopedia 1728 of Ephraim Chambers (c. 1680–1740), this work exerted an enormous influence on contemporary social thinking with its materialism and anticlericalism. Its compilers were known as Encyclopédistes.

Diderot's materialism, most articulately expressed in *D'Alembert's Dream*, published after Diderot's death, sees the natural world as nothing more than matter and motion.

His account of the origin and development of life is purely mechanical.

Suggested reading
Crocker, L G *Diderot, the Embattled Philosopher* (1966)
France, Peter *Diderot* (1983)
Mason, John *The Irresistible Diderot* (1982)

That is one last thing to remember: writers are always selling somebody out.

JOAN DIDION
Slouching towards Bethlehem preface 1968

Didion Joan (1934–). US author and journalist. She is known for her terse yet eloquent views of modern American society, especially California, where she grew up. Her sharp, culturally evocative writing includes the novel *A Book of Common Prayer* 1970 and the essays of *The White Album* 1979.

Her other works include the essays *Slouching toward Bethlehem* 1968 and the novels *Run River* 1963, *Play It As It Lays* 1970, and *Democracy* 1984, which depict the cultural disintegration of modern life.

She reported on current events in *Salvador* 1983 and the state of affairs in the city in *Miami* 1987.

Diebenkorn Richard (1922–1993). US painter. A leading member of the second generation of Abstract Expressionists, he gained worldwide renown for his *Ocean Park* series of mainly abstract canvases 1967–88. His earliest work was representational and full of light, showing the influence of the older American artist, Edward Hopper.

In 1955 he turned to figurative art, painting still-lifes and landscapes, until 1967 when he moved to Santa Monica, Los Angeles. It was here he returned to abstraction and began the *Ocean Park* paintings, named after a district of Santa Monica. He represented the USA at the Venice Biennale 1978 but his work remained largely unseen in Europe until a retrospective exhibition held first at the Whitechapel Gallery in London 1991, and then in galleries in Germany and Spain.

He brought the fresh wind of the prairies into the Conservative Party, long dominated by the urban tycoons, and made it the party of reform.

H Lintott on JOHN DIEFENBAKER
in *Dictionary of National Biography*

Diefenbaker John George (1895–1979). Canadian Progressive Conservative politician, prime minister 1957–63; he was defeated after criticism of the proposed manufacture of nuclear weapons in Canada.

Diefenbaker was born in Ontario, and moved to Saskatchewan. A brilliant defence counsel, he became known as the 'prairie lawyer'. He became leader of his party 1956 and prime minister 1957. In 1958 he achieved the greatest landslide in Canadian history. A 'radical' Tory, he was also a strong supporter of Commonwealth unity. He resigned the party leadership 1967, repudiating a 'two nations' policy for Canada. He was known as 'the Chief'.

Diels Otto Paul Hermann (1876–1954). German chemist. In 1950 he and his former assistant, Kurt Alder, were jointly awarded the Nobel Prize for Chemistry for their research into the synthesis of organic chemical compounds.

In 1927 Diels dehydrogenated cholesterol to produce 'Diels hydrocarbon' ($C_{18}H_{16}$), an aromatic hydrocarbon closely related to the skeletal structure of all steroids, of which cholesterol is one. In 1935 he synthesized it. This work proved to be a turning point in the understanding of the chemistry of cholesterol and other steroids. He was director of the Chemical Institute at the Christian Albrecht University in Kiel 1916–48.

Diemen Anthony van (1593–1645). Dutch admiral. In 1636 he was appointed governor general of Dutch settlements in the E Indies, and wrested Ceylon and Malacca from the Portuguese. In 1636 and 1642 he supervised expeditions to Australia, on the second of which the navigator Abel Tasman discovered land not charted by Europeans and named it *Van Diemen's Land*, now Tasmania.

Diesel Rudolf Christian Karl (1858–1913). German engineer who patented the diesel engine. He began his career as a refrigerator engineer and, like many engineers of the period, sought to develop a better power source than the conventional steam engine. Able to operate with greater efficiency and economy, the diesel engine soon found a ready market.

Born in Paris, Diesel moved to Germany after the outbreak of the Franco-Prussian War 1870, and studied at Munich Polytechnic.

His ideas for an engine where the combustion would be carried out within the cylinder were first published 1893, one year after he had taken out his first patent. In his first engine, Diesel is thought to have used coal dust as a fuel, but he later discarded this along with several other types in favour of a form of refined mineral oil. A very high pressure must be used to compress the air before fuel injection, and he was nearly killed when a cylinder head blew off one of his prototype engines. In 1899, he founded his own manufacturing company in Augsburg.

Dietrich *German film actress and singer Marlene Dietrich in the classic film* The Blue Angel *1930. She created a mesmerizing and sexually alluring persona as a husky-voiced femme fatale through her collaboration with director Josef von Sternberg in films such as this and* Shanghai Express *1932. She later developed this image as a singer and entertainer.*

Dietl Eduard (1890–1944). German general. Dietl joined the Nazi Party 1920 and by 1939 was a major-general commanding 3rd Mountain Division which he led in Poland and Norway 1939–40. During the invasion of the USSR 1941 he commanded a mountain corps in an unsuccessful attempt to seize Murmansk. He was appointed commander of all German forces in Lapland 1942 but died in an air crash in the summer of 1944.

Dietrich Marlene (born Maria Magdalene Dietrich von Losch) (1901–1992). German-born US actress and singer. She appeared with Emil Jannings in both the German and American versions of the film *Der Blaue Engel/The Blue Angel* 1930, directed by Josef von Sternberg. She stayed in Hollywood, becoming a US citizen 1937. Her husky, sultry singing voice added to her appeal. Her other films include *Blonde Venus* 1932, *Destry Rides Again* 1939, and *Just a Gigolo* 1978.

Her last screen role was a brief appearance in *Just a Gigolo* 1978. She was the subject of Maximilian Schell's documentary *Marlene* 1983.

Dietrich Sepp (1892–1976). German SS officer. He founded the *Liebstandarte SS Adolf Hitler*, Hitler's personal bodyguard, 1928 and led it during World War II when it operated as a combat unit of the Waffen SS. He was convicted of war crimes 1945, notably the murder of US prisoners at Malmédy, and served 10 years of a 25-year sentence. He received a further 18-month sentence from a German court 1957 for his part in suppressing the SA (Sturmabteilung) in the 'Night of the Long Knives' 1934.

Dilke Charles Wentworth (1843–1911). British Liberal politician, member of Parliament 1868–86 and 1892–1911. A Radical, he supported a minimum wage and legalization of trade unions. Succeeded to baronetcy 1869.

Dill John Greer (1881–1944). British field marshal in World War II. A former commandant of the Staff College and Director of Operations, he commanded British I Corps in France 1939. He returned to the UK April 1940 to become Vice-Chief of the Imperial General Staff, succeeding General Ironside as Chief of Staff May 1940. He was replaced by General Alanbrooke Dec 1941 and went to the USA as head of the British Military Mission. KCB 1937.

Dillinger John Herbert (1903–1934). US bank robber and murderer. In 1923 he was convicted of armed robbery and spent the next ten years in state prison. Released in 1933, he led a gang on a robbery spree throughout the Midwest, staging daring raids on police stations to obtain guns. Named 'Public Enemy Number One' by the Federal Bureau of Investigation (FBI), Dillinger led the authorities on a long chase. He was finally betrayed by his mistress, the mysterious 'Lady in Red', and was killed by FBI agents in Chicago as he left a cinema.

Dilthey Wilhelm (1833–1911). German philosopher, a major figure in the interpretive tradition of hermeneutics. He argued that the 'human sciences' (*Geisteswissenschaften*) could not employ the same methods as the natural sciences but must use the procedure of 'understanding' (*Verstehen*) to grasp the inner life of an alien culture or past historical period. Thus Dilthey extended the significance of hermeneutics far beyond the interpretation of texts to the whole of human history and culture.

DiMaggio Joe (Joseph Paul) (1914–   ). US baseball player with the New York Yankees 1936–51. In 1941 he set a record by getting hits in 56 consecutive games. He was an outstanding fielder, played centre field, hit 361 home runs, and had a career average of 325. DiMaggio was married to the actress Marilyn Monroe. He was elected to the Baseball Hall of Fame 1955.

Suggested reading
De Gregorio, G *Joe DiMaggio* (1981)
Moore, J G *Joe DiMaggio* (1987)

Dimbleby Richard Frederick (1913–1965). British broadcaster. He joined the BBC in 1936 and became the foremost commentator on royal and state events and current affairs on radio and television. He is commemorated by the Dimbleby Lectures.

Dilke *English politician Charles Dilke's progress to high office in Gladstone's government was reversed when he was cited as co-respondent in a divorce case. He subsequently organized members of the early Labour Party and wrote brilliantly on the subject of politics.*

Dimitrov Georgi Mikhailovich (1882–1949). Bulgarian communist, prime minister from 1946. He was elected a deputy in 1913 and from 1919 was a member of the executive of the Comintern, an international communist organization. In 1933 he was arrested in Berlin and tried with others in Leipzig for allegedly setting fire to the parliament building. Acquitted, he went to the USSR, where he became general secretary of the Comintern until its dissolution 1943.

Dine Jim (James) (1935–   ). US Pop artist. He experimented with combinations of paintings and objects, such as a bathroom sink attached to a canvas. Dine was a pioneer of happenings in the 1960s and of environment art.

Dinesen Isak. Pen name of Danish writer Karen ◊Blixen, born Karen Christentze Dinesen.

Dingaan (1795–c. 1843). Zulu chief who obtained the throne in 1828 by murdering his predecessor, Shaka, and became notorious for his cruelty. In warfare with the Boer immigrants into Natal he was defeated on 16 Dec 1838 – 'Dingaan's Day'. He escaped to Swaziland, where he was deposed by his brother Mpande and subsequently assassinated.

Ding Ling assumed name of Chiang Wei-Chih (1904–1986). Chinese novelist. Her works include *Wei Hu* 1930 and *The Sun Shines over the Sanggan River* 1951.

She was imprisoned by the Guomindang (Chiang Kai-shek's nationalists) in the 1930s, wrongly labelled as rightist and expelled from the Communist Party 1957, imprisoned in the 1960s and intellectually ostracized for not keeping to Maoist literary rules; she was rehabilitated 1979. Her husband was the writer Hu Yapin, executed by Chiang Kai-shek's police 1931.

Dini Lamberto (1932–   ). Italian politician, prime minister from 1995. Director general of the Bank of Italy from 1979, he was brought into government, as treasury minister, by Premier Silvio Berlusconi 1994. On the latter's resignation, Dini was asked to form a non-political 'technocrat' government of 20 members. He declared three priorities: improving public finances, regulating political parties' access to the media, and reforming electoral procedures.

In the months following his appointment, Dini made real progress in achieving his objectives, but in Nov 1995 faced a no-confidence motion from Berlusconi's party, Forza Italia, over his economic policy.

Dinkins David (1927–   ). Mayor of New York City 1990–93, a Democrat. He won a reputation as a moderate and consensual community politician and was Manhattan borough president before succeeding Edward I Koch to become New York's first black mayor. He lost his re-election bid 1993.

Dio Cassius (c. AD 150–c. 235). Roman historian. He wrote, in Greek, a Roman history in 80 books (of which 26 survive), covering the period from the founding of the city to AD 229, including the only surviving account of the invasion of Britain by Claudius 43 BC.

It is wrong to desert the ancient religion for some new one, for it is the height of criminality to revise doctrine that was established by the ancients.

DIOCLETIAN
Order to the governor of Egypt, quoted in
M Hyamson (ed) *Collation of Roman and Mosaic Law* 1913

Diocletian (Gaius Aurelius Valerius Diocletianus) (AD 245–313). Roman emperor 284–305, when he abdicated in favour of Galerius. He reorganized and subdivided the empire, with two joint and two subordinate emperors, and in 303 initiated severe persecution of Christians.

Diogenes (c. 412–c. 323 BC). Ascetic Greek philosopher of the Cynic school. He believed in freedom and self-sufficiency for the individual, and that the virtuous life was the simple life; he did not

believe in social mores. His writings do not survive.

Stand out of my sun a little.

DIOGENES
Response to Alexander the Great when he asked him
if he wanted anything, quoted in Plutarch *Life of Alexander*

He was born in Sinope, Asia Minor, on the Black Sea, captured by pirates, and sold as a slave to a Corinthian named Xeniades, who appointed Diogenes tutor to his two sons. He spent the rest of his life in Corinth. He is said to have carried a lamp during the daytime, looking for one honest man. The story of his having lived in a barrel arose when Seneca said that was where a man so crabbed ought to have lived.

Diogenes Laertius (lived 3rd century AD). Greek writer. He was the author of an important compilation of anecdotes and quotations from the ancient Greek philosophers. It is the sole source of information we have about many of the philosophers it covers.

Dionysius two tyrants of the ancient Greek city of Syracuse in Sicily. Dionysius the Elder (c. 430–367 BC) seized power 405 BC. His first two wars with Carthage further extended the power of Syracuse, but in a third (383–378 BC) he was defeated. He was a patron of Plato. He was succeeded by his son, Dionysius the Younger, who was driven out of Syracuse by Dion 356; he was tyrant again 353, but in 343 returned to Corinth.

Dionysius of Halicarnassus (lived 1st century BC). Greek critic and historian, who settled in Rome 30 BC and wrote 20 books on the early history of Rome, ten of which are extant. He also wrote on rhetoric (prose style).

Diophantus (lived AD 250). Greek mathematician in Alexandria whose *Arithmetica* is one of the first known works on problem solving by algebra, in which both words and symbols are used.

His main mathematical study was in the solution of what are now known as 'indeterminate' or 'Diophantine' equations – equations that do not contain enough facts to give a specific answer but enough to reduce the answer to a definite type. These equations have led to the formulation of the theory of numbers, regarded as the purest branch of present-day mathematics.

My dream is to save [women] from nature.

CHRISTIAN DIOR
quoted in *Collier's* 1955

Dior Christian (1905–1957). French couturier. He established his own Paris salon 1947 and made an impact with the 'New Look' – long, cinch-waisted, and full-skirted – after wartime austerity.

He worked with Robert Piquet as design assistant 1938 and for Lucien Lelong 1941–46. His first collection 1947 was an instant success and he continued to be popular during the 1950s when he created elegant and sophisticated looks with slim skirts and large box-shaped jackets. His last collection 1957 was based on a waistless shift-style dress with the skirt narrowing towards the hem.

Diouf Abdou (1935–   ). Senegalese left-wing politician, president from 1980. He became prime minister 1970 under President Leopold Senghor and, on his retirement, succeeded him, being re-elected 1983, 1988, and 1993. His presidency has been characterized by authoritarianism.

Diouf was born in Louga in NW Senegal, studied at Paris University, and was a civil servant before entering politics. He was chair of the Organization of African Unity 1985–86. He leads the Senegalese Socialist Party.

Di Pietro Antonio (1950–   ). Italian judge, head of the *mani puliti* (clean hands) series of anti-corruption investigations which began 1992. His investigations into allegations of corruption in Milan's local government proved instrumental in discrediting, and eventually bringing down, Italy's old political order, and opened the door for Silvio Berlusconi's right-wing alliance to win the 1994 general election. In Dec 1994 Di Pietro resigned, claiming his work had been increasingly hampered by government interference.

A theory with mathematical beauty is more likely to be correct than an ugly one that fits some experimental data. God is a mathematician of a very high order, and He used very advanced mathematics in constructing the universe.

PAUL DIRAC
Scientific American May 1963

Dirac Paul Adrien Maurice (1902–1984). British physicist who worked out a version of quantum mechanics consistent with special relativity. The existence of antiparticles, such as the positron (positive electron), was one of its predictions. He shared the Nobel Prize for Physics 1933 with Austrian physicist Erwin Schrödinger.

Dirac was born and educated in Bristol and from 1923 at Cambridge, where he was professor of mathematics 1932–69. From 1971 he was professor of physics at Florida State University.

Dirichlet (Peter Gustav) Lejeune (1805–1859). German mathematician whose work in applying analytical techniques to mathematical theory resulted in the fundamental development of the theory of numbers. He was also a physicist interested in dynamics. He became professor at the University of Berlin at the age of 23, and at Göttingen 1855. In 1837 he presented his first paper on analytic number theory, proving Dirichlet's theorem: in every arithmetical sequence a, $a + d$, $a + 2d$, and so on, where a and d are relatively prime (that is, have no common divisors other than 1), there is an infinite number of prime numbers.

Disch Thomas M(ichael) (1940–   ). US writer and poet. He is the author of such science-fiction novels as *Camp Concentration* 1968 and *334* 1972.

Disney Walt(er Elias) (1901–1966). US filmmaker and animator, a pioneer of family entertainment. He established his own studio in Hollywood 1923, and his first Mickey Mouse cartoons (*Plane Crazy*, which was silent, and *Steamboat Willie*, which had sound) appeared 1928.

In addition to short cartoons, the studio later made feature-length animated films, including *Snow White and the Seven Dwarfs* 1938, *Pinocchio* 1940, and *Dumbo* 1941. Disney's cartoon figures, for example Donald Duck, also appeared in comic books worldwide. In 1955, Disney opened the first theme park, Disneyland, in California.

Using the new medium of sound film, Disney developed the 'Silly Symphony', a type of cartoon based on the close association of music with visual images. He produced these in colour from 1932, culminating in the feature-length *Fantasia* 1940. The Disney studio also made nature-study films such as *The Living Desert* 1953, which have been criticized for their fictionalization of nature: wild animals were placed in unnatural situations to create 'drama'. Feature films with human casts were made from 1946, such as *The Swiss Family Robinson* 1960 and *Mary Poppins* 1964. Disney also produced the first television series in colour 1961.

At the end of 1995 Disney emerged as the leader in home-video sales, with an annual growth of 10%. The two biggest sellers were *Lion King* 1995 and the re-released *Snow White*. 1995 sales in the USA were above $2 billion for the first time.

Suggested reading
Eliot, Marc *Walt Disney* (1993)
Finch, Christopher *The Art of Walt Disney* (1973)
Schickel, Richard *The Disney Version* (1968)
Thomas, Bob *Walt Disney: An American Original* (1976)

Disraeli Benjamin, 1st Earl of Beaconsfield (1804–1881). British Conservative politician and novelist. Elected to Parliament 1837, he was chancellor of the Exchequer under Lord Derby 1852, 1858–59, and 1866–68, and prime minister 1868 and 1874–80. His imperialist policies brought India directly under the crown, and he was

Disraeli Cartoon from Punch *1872 depicting Disraeli (front) and Gladstone as two opposing lions making speeches in Lancashire*

personally responsible for purchasing control of the Suez Canal. The central Conservative Party organization is his creation. His popular, political novels reflect an interest in social reform and include *Coningsby* 1844 and *Sybil* 1845.

Increased means and increased leisure are the two civilizers of man.

BENJAMIN DISRAELI
Speech in Manchester 3 April 1872

After a period in a solicitor's office, Disraeli wrote the novels *Vivian Grey* 1826, *Contarini Fleming* 1832, and others, and the pamphlet *Vindication of the English Constitution* 1835. Entering Parliament in 1837 after four unsuccessful attempts, he was laughed at as a dandy, but when his maiden speech was shouted down, he said: 'The time will come when you will hear me.' Excluded from Peel's government of 1841–46, Disraeli formed his Young England group to keep a critical eye on Peel's Conservatism. Its ideas were expounded in the novel trilogy *Coningsby*, *Sybil*, and *Tancred* 1847.

When Peel decided in 1846 to repeal the Corn Laws, Disraeli opposed the measure in a series of witty and effective speeches; Peel's government fell soon after, and Disraeli gradually came to be recognized as the leader of the Conservative Party in the Commons. During the next 20 years the Conservatives formed short-lived minority governments in 1852, 1858–59, and 1866–68, with Lord Derby as prime minister and Disraeli as chancellor of the Exchequer and leader of the Commons. In 1852 Disraeli first proposed discrimination in income tax between earned and unearned income, but without success. The 1858–59 government legalized the admission of Jews to Parliament, and transferred the government of India from the East India Company to the crown. In 1866 the Conservatives took office after defeating a Liberal Reform Bill, and then attempted to secure the credit of widening the franchise by the Reform Bill of 1867. On Lord Derby's retirement in 1868 Disraeli became prime minister, but a few months later was defeated by Gladstone in a general election. During the six years of opposition that followed he published another novel, *Lothair* 1870, and established Conservative Central Office, the prototype of modern party organizations.

In 1874 Disraeli took office for the second time, with a majority of 100. Some useful reform measures were carried, such as the Artisans' Dwelling Act, which empowered local authorities to undertake slum clearance, but the outstanding feature of the government's policy was its imperialism. It was Disraeli's personal initiative that purchased from the Khedive of Egypt a controlling interest in the Suez Canal, conferred on the Queen the title of Empress of India, and sent the Prince of Wales on the first royal tour of that country. Disraeli accepted an earldom 1876. The Bulgarian revolt of 1876 and the subsequent Russo-Turkish War of 1877–78 provoked one of many political duels between Disraeli and Gladstone, the Liberal leader, and was concluded by the Congress of Berlin 1878, where Disraeli was the principal British delegate and brought home 'peace with honour' and Cyprus. The government was defeated in 1880, and a year later Disraeli died.

Suggested reading
Blake, R *Disraeli* (1966)
Bradford, S *Disraeli* (1982)
Davis, R W *Disraeli* (1976)
Hibbert, C *Disraeli and his World* (1978)
Pearson, H *Dizzy* (1951)
Ridley, Jane *The Young Disraeli* (1995)
Salter, Richard (ed) *Peel, Gladstone and Disraeli* (1991)
Weintraub, Stanley *Disraeli: A Biography* (1993)

What does Ben know of dukes?
ISAAC D'ISRAELI
on his son Benjamin's publication of *The Young Duke* 1830

D'Israeli Isaac (1766–1848). English scholar. He was the father of Benjamin Disraeli and author of *Curiosities of Literature* 1791–93 and 1823.

Dix Dorothea Lynde (1802–1887). US educator and medical reformer. From 1841 she devoted herself to a campaign for the rights of the mentally ill, helping to improve conditions and treatment in public institutions for the insane in the USA, Canada, and Japan. During the American Civil War 1861–65, she served as superintendent of nurses.

Born in Hampden, Maine, and raised in Boston, Dix began her career as a teacher at a girls' school in Worcester, Massachusetts, and opened her own school in Boston 1821. Forced by ill health to retire in 1835, she travelled in Europe and published several books.

So many persons think divorce a panacea for every ill, who find out, when they try it, that the remedy is worse than the disease.
DOROTHEA DIX
quoted in E Gilmer *Dorothy Dix, Her Book* ch 13 1926

Dix Otto (1891–1969). German painter. He was a major exponent of the harsh Realism current in Germany in the 1920s and closely associated with the *Neue Sachlichkeit* group. He is known chiefly for his unsettling 1920s paintings of prostitutes and sex murders and for his powerful series of works depicting the hell of trench warfare, for example *Flanders: After Henri Barbusse 'Le Feu'* 1934–36 (Nationalgalerie, Berlin).

Dix was a considerable portraitist, as exemplified in *Dr Heinrich Stadelmann* 1920 (Art Gallery of Ontario, Toronto), and he also painted allegorical works in a style reminiscent of 16th-century Flemish and Italian masters. He trained at the art academies of Dresden and Dusseldorf, and his early work shows the influence of Kokoschka and Italian Futurism. In 1933 he was dismissed from his teaching post at the Dresden Art Academy by the Nazis, and branded a decadent. His experiences as a serving soldier in World War I and as a prisoner-of-war 1945–46 instilled in him a profound horror of armed conflict.

Djilas Milovan (1911–1995). Yugoslav dissident and political writer. Djilas was born in Montenegro and was a partisan during World War II. He joined the illegal CPY after studying philosophy and law in Belgrade and was imprisoned 1933–36 for protesting against the Yugoslav monarchy. He entered the CPY's controlling Politburo in 1940, during World War II, when he became a ruthless military leader of Tito's anti-Nazi partisan guerrillas.

In postwar Yugoslavia, Djilas held key positions, but as a romantic communist of principle he became disillusioned and critical of Soviet-style communism, where ends justified means and where a party elite had emerged as a privileged social stratum. This was the subject of his first book, *The New Class*, which was smuggled to the West and published in 1957. These criticisms led to his censure 1954 and resignation from the CPY, and his imprisonment 1956.

Released from prison 1961, he was jailed within a year after castigating the former Soviet leader Josef Stalin as 'the greatest criminal in history' in *Conversations with Stalin* 1962, which recounted Djilas's own meetings with Stalin during 1944–45. Released in 1966, though still subject to surveillance, he wrote further works on communism and Yugoslav recent history, most notably *Memoir of a Revolutionary* 1973, which chronicles his own career.

Officially rehabilitated in 1989, Djilas predicted that Mikhail Gorbachev's glasnost (political openness) and perestroika (economic restructuring) reforms would lead to the collapse of Soviet communism and a dangerous resurgence of nationalism. He became reviled in his final years in what had become an increasingly nationalistic Yugoslavia for his humanistic criticisms of Serb aggression in Croatia and Bosnia.

Dobell William (1899–1970). Australian portraitist and genre painter, born in New South Wales. He studied art in the UK and the Netherlands 1929–39. His portrait of *Joshua Smith* 1943 (Sir Edward Hayward, Adelaide, Australia) provoked a court case (Dobell was accused of caricaturing his subject). Knighted 1966.
Suggested reading
Adams, Brian *Portrait of an Artist* (1983)
Penton, B *The Art of William Dobell* (1946)

Döblin Alfred (1878–1957). German novelist. His *Berlin-Alexanderplatz* 1929 owes much to James Joyce in its minutely detailed depiction of the inner lives of a city's inhabitants, and is considered by many to be the finest 20th-century German novel. Other works include *November 1918: Eine deutsche Revolution/A German Revolution* 1939–50 (published in four parts) about the formation of the Weimar Republic.

Born in Stettin (modern Szczecin, Poland) to a Yiddish-speaking family, he grew up in Berlin where he practised as a doctor until 1933 when his books were banned and he was exiled; he moved first to France and from 1941 lived in the USA.

Dobrynin Anatoliy Fedorovich (1919–). Soviet diplomat, ambassador to the USA 1962–86, emerging during the 1970s as a warm supporter of détente.

Dobrynin joined the Soviet diplomatic service in 1941. He served as counsellor at the Soviet embassy in Washington DC 1952–55, assistant to the minister for foreign affairs 1955–57, undersecretary at the United Nations 1957–59, and head of the USSR's American department 1959–61, before being appointed Soviet ambassador to Washington in 1962. He remained at this post for 25 years. Brought back to Moscow by the new Soviet leader Mikhail Gorbachev, he was appointed to the Communist Party's Secretariat as head of the International Department, before retiring in 1988.

Dobzhansky Theodosius, originally Feodosy Grigorevich Dobrzhansky (1900–1975). Ukrainian-born US geneticist who established evolutionary genetics as an independent discipline. He showed that genetic variability between individuals of the same species is very high and that this diversity is vital to the process of evolution.

His book *Genetics and the Origin of Species* 1937 was the first significant synthesis of Darwinian evolutionary theory and Mendelian genetics. Dobzhansky also proved that there is a period when speciation is only partly complete and during which several races coexist.

After teaching at Kiev and Leningrad universities, he went to the USA 1927. He was at the California Institute of Technology 1929–40. He became professor of zoology at Columbia University, New York City, 1940; worked at the Rockefeller Institute (later the Rockefeller University) 1962–71; then he moved to the University of California at Davis.

His book *Mankind Evolving* 1962 had great influence among anthropologists. He wrote on the philosophical aspects of evolution in *The Biological Basis of Human Freedom* 1956 and *The Biology of Ultimate Concern* 1967.

It's like driving a car at night. You never see further than your headlights, but you can make the whole trip that way.

E L DOCTOROW
on his writing technique, interviewed in George
Plimpton (ed) *Writers at Work* Eighth Series 1988

Doctorow E(dgar) L(awrence) (1931–). US novelist. He achieved critical and commercial success with his third novel, *The Book of Daniel* 1971, the story of the Rosenberg spy case told by their fictional son, which established Doctorow as an imaginative and experimental revisionist of American history. It was followed by his best-seller, *Ragtime* 1975, which dramatized the Jazz Age.

His other novels include *Loon Lake* 1980, a montage narrative set in 1936; *World's Fair* 1985, about Jewish boyhood in 1930s New York; *Billy Bathgate* 1989, the story of a child apprenticed to the gangster Dutch Schultz; and *The Waterworks* 1994, a detective story set in New York.

Dodds (Edward) Charles (1899–1973). English biochemist who was largely responsible for the discovery of stilboestrol, a powerful synthetic hormone used in treating prostate conditions and also for fattening cattle. He was Courtauld professor of biochemistry at London University 1927–65. Knighted 1954, baronet 1964.

Dodds Johnny (John M) (1892–1940). US jazz clarinetist. He is generally ranked among the top New Orleans jazz clarinetists. He played with Louis Armstrong, Jelly Roll Morton, and the New Orleans Wanderers, as well as his own trio and orchestra, and was acclaimed for his warmth of tone and improvisation.

Dodgson Charles Lutwidge. Real name of writer Lewis ◊Carroll.

He proclaimed he was leading a revolution but made few changes other than to award soldiers a pay increase.

Martin Meredith on SAMUEL DOE
in *The First Dance of Freedom: Black Africa in the Postwar Era* 1984

Doe Samuel Kanyon (1950–1990). Liberian politician and soldier, head of state 1980–90. He seized power in a coup. In 1981 he made himself general and army commander in chief. In 1985 he narrowly elected president, as leader of the newly formed National Democratic Party of Liberia. Having successfully put down an uprising April 1990, Doe was deposed and killed by rebel forces Sept 1990. His human-rights record was poor.

Dōgen (1200–1253). Japanese Buddhist monk, pupil of Eisai; founder of the Sōtō school of Zen. He did not reject study, but stressed the importance of *zazen*, seated meditation, for its own sake.

Dōgen trained as a monk with the Tendai school of Buddhism, then studied in China 1223–27. In 1246 he established the Eihei temple as headquarters for the Sōtō school.

His teachings are outlined in *Shōbōgenzō/The Eye Treasury of the Right Dharma* 1231–53.

Dohnányi Ernst (Ernö) von (1877–1960). Hungarian pianist, conductor, composer, and teacher. His compositions include *Variations on a Nursery Song* 1914 and *Second Symphony for Orchestra* 1948.

Born in Bratislava, he studied in Budapest, then established his name as a concert pianist in the UK and the USA. He became conductor of the Budapest Philharmonic 1919, musical director of Hungarian Broadcasting 1931, and director of the Budapest conservatory 1934. Rumoured to have been friendly with the Nazis during the 1930s and 1940s, he left Hungary 1948 and subsequently settled in the USA.

Doi Takako (1929–). Japanese socialist politician, leader of the Social Democratic Party of Japan (SDJP), formerly the Japan Socialist Party (JSP), 1986–1991. The country's first female major party leader, she was largely responsible for the SDJP's revival in the late 1980s. Her resignation followed the party's crushing defeat in local elections April 1991.

Doisneau Robert (1912–1994). French photographer. He is known for his sensitive and often witty depictions of ordinary people and everyday situations within the environs of Paris. His most famous image, *Baiser de l'Hôtel de Ville/The Kiss at the Hôtel de Ville*, was produced for *Life* magazine 1950. His work endeared him to millions who would normally profess little interest in art or photography.

Some 40 books of his photographs have been published, including a few for children, and there have been many exhibitions; his 80th birthday retrospective at the Oxford Museum of Modern Art was one of the most memorable.

Doisy Edward Adelbert (1893–1986). US biochemist. In 1939 he succeeded in synthesizing vitamin K, a compound earlier discovered by Carl Dam, with whom he shared the 1943 Nobel Prize for Physiology or Medicine.

Dolci Carlo (1616–1686). Italian painter of the late Baroque period. He was active in Florence, creating intensely emotional versions of religious subjects such as *The Martyrdom of St Andrew* 1646 (Pitti, Florence).

Dolci was the foremost painter in Florence of his day and continued to be much admired in the 18th century. He was also a portraitist, and was sent to Austria 1675 to paint the Medici wife of the emperor Leopold I.

Dole Bob (Robert Joseph) (1923–). US Republican politician, leader of his party in the Senate from 1985. He first became a senator from Kansas 1969, and was chair of the Senate Finance Committee 1981, responsible for getting President Reagan's tax bills through Congress. Dole was a candidate for the Republican presidential nomination 1980, 1988, and 1996.

Dole was born in Kansas. He was badly wounded in Italy while serving in the US army during World War II. He was elected to the House of Representatives 1960 and served four terms. As Gerald Ford's running mate during the 1976 presidential campaign, he got the reputation of being a ruthless manipulator. During the Irangate scandal (revelation of the illegal sale of arms to Iran by members of the US government in order to fund the rebels in Nicaragua)1986–87, he was spokesperson for the Republican Party.

Dolin Anton. Stage name of (Sydney Francis) Patrick (Chippendall Healey) Kay (1904–1983). English dancer and choreographer. He was the first British male dancer to win an international reputation. As a dancer, his reputation rested on his commanding presence, theatricality, and gymnastic ability. His most famous partnership was with Alicia Markova. After studying under Nijinsky, he was a leading member of Diaghilev's company 1924–29. He formed the Markova–Dolin Ballet Company with Markova 1935–38, and was a guest soloist with the American Ballet Theater 1940–46. Knighted 1981.

He created roles in Nijinska's *Le Train bleu* 1924 and Balanchine's *The Prodigal Son* 1929 while with the Ballets Russes; and Satan in de Valois' *Job* 1931.

Doll (William) Richard (Shaboe) (1912–). British physician who, working with Professor Bradford Hill (1897–), provided the first statistical proof of the link between smoking and lung cancer in 1950. In a later study of the smoking habits of doctors, they were

Dollfuss *Austrian chancellor Engelbert Dollfuss. He was murdered by Austrian Nazis during an unsuccessful 'coup' attempt on the Chancellery, and was succeeded by Kurt von Schuschnigg.* (Image Select)

From 1927, he directed research at the Laboratories for Experimental Pathology and Bacteriology of I G Farbenindustrie, Düsseldorf, a dyemaking company. But he also remained on the staff of Münster University, as professor from 1928.

Domenichino Assumed name of Domenico Zampieri (1581–1641). Italian Baroque painter and architect. He was active in Bologna, Naples, and Rome. He began as an assistant to the Carracci family of painters and continued the early Baroque style in, for example, frescoes 1624–28 in the choir of S Andrea della Valle, Rome. He is considered a pioneer of landscape painting in the Baroque period.

Good examples of his landscape are in the National Gallery, London, and Constable regarded his *Landscape with a Fortified Building* (formerly at Bridgewater House and now in a private collection) as 'of the highest order'.

Domenico Veneziano (*c.* 1400–1461). Italian painter. He was active in Florence. His few surviving frescoes and altarpieces show a remarkably subtle use of colour and light (which recurs in the work of Piero della Francesca, who worked with him).

He worked in Sta Egidio, Florence, on frescoes now lost. Remaining works include the *Carnesecchi Madonna and Two Saints* (National Gallery, London) and the *St Lucy Altarpiece*, now divided between Florence (Uffizi), Berlin (Staatliche Museen), Cambridge (Fitzwilliam), and Washington, DC (National Gallery).

Domingo Placido (1941–). Spanish lyric tenor. He specializes in Italian and French 19th-century operatic roles to which he brings a finely-tuned dramatic temperament. As a youth in Mexico, he sang baritone roles in zarzuela (musical theatre), moving up to tenor as a member of the Israel National Opera 1961–64. Since his New York debut 1965 he has established a world reputation as a sympathetic leading tenor, and has made many films including the 1988 version of Puccini's *Tosca* set in Rome, and the 1990 Zeffirelli production of Leoncavallo's *I Pagliacci/The Strolling Players*. He also sang with José Carreras and Luciano Pavarotti in a recording of operatic hits released to coincide with the World Cup soccer series in Rome 1990, and again in the USA 1994. A member of a musical family, he emigrated to Mexico in 1950. In 1986 he starred in the film version of *Otello*. He sung his first Parsifal at the New York Met, 1991.

able to show that stopping smoking immediately reduces the risk of cancer. Knighted 1971.

Dollfus Audouin Charles (1924–). French physicist and astronomer whose preferred method of research is to use polarization of light. He was the first to detect a faint atmosphere round the planet Mercury, in 1950, and established that the Moon does not have one. In pursuit of his detailed investigations into Mars, Dollfus made the first French ascent in a stratospheric balloon.

Dollfus was born and educated in Paris. In 1946 he became an astronomer at the Meudon Observatory there.

Hoping to establish the mineral composition of the Martian deserts, Dollfus checked the polarization of light by several hundreds of different terrestrial minerals to try to find one for which the light matched that polarized by the bright Martian desert areas. He found only one, and that was pulverized limonite.

In 1966 Dollfus discovered Janus, the innermost moon of Saturn, at a time when the rings – to which it is very close – were seen from Earth edgeways on and were practically invisible.

I have only desired peace. We have never attacked anybody. We have always fought to defend ourselves. May God forgive them.

ENGELBERT DOLLFUSS
Last words at his assassination 1934

Dollfuss Engelbert (1892–1934). Austrian Christian Socialist politician. He was appointed chancellor in 1932, and in 1933 suppressed parliament and ruled by decree. In Feb 1934 he crushed a protest by the socialist workers by force, and in May Austria was declared a 'corporative' state. The Nazis attempted a coup d'état on 25 July; the Chancellery was seized and Dollfuss murdered.

Dolmetsch (Eugène) Arnold (1858–1940). Swiss-born English musician and instrumentmaker. Together with his family, including his son Carl (1911–), he revived interest in the practical performance of solo and consort music for lute, recorders, and viols, and established the Baroque soprano (descant) recorder as an inexpensive musical instrument for schools.

He worked in Boston, USA, and Paris, France, as a restorer and maker of early musical instruments before establishing his workshop in Haslemere, England, 1917.

Domagk Gerhard Johannes Paul (1895–1964). German pathologist, discoverer of antibacterial sulphonamide drugs. He found in 1932 that a coal-tar dye called Prontosil red contains chemicals with powerful antibacterial properties. Sulphanilamide became the first of the sulphonamide drugs, used – before antibiotics were discovered – to treat a wide range of conditions, including pneumonia and septic wounds. Nobel prize 1939.

Domingo *Placido Domingo is regarded as the greatest lyric-dramatic tenor of our time. His supreme musicianship and versatility is matched by his dramatic conviction. Possessing an exceptionally wide repertory, Domingo has nevertheless been identified especially as Verdi's Otello.*

Dominic, St (*c.* 1170–1221). Founder of the Roman Catholic Dominican order of preaching friars. Feast day 7 Aug. Canonized 1234.

Born in Old Castile, Dominic was sent by Pope Innocent III in 1205 to preach to the heretic Albigensian sect in Provence. In 1208 the Pope instigated the Albigensian crusade to suppress the heretics by force, and this was supported by Dominic. In 1215 the Dominican order was given premises in Toulouse; during the following years Dominic established friaries in Bologna and elsewhere in Italy, and by the time of his death the order was established all over W Europe.

When I get an idea for a song, I sit down at the piano and sing into the tape.

FATS DOMINO
quoted in Irwin Stambler *The Encyclopedia of Pop, Rock and Soul* 1989

Domino Fats (Antoine) (1928–). US rock-and-roll pianist, singer, and songwriter. He was an exponent of the New Orleans style. His hits include 'Ain't That a Shame' 1955 and 'Blueberry Hill' 1956.

The fate of princes is most unhappy, since when they discover a conspiracy no-one believes them until they have been killed.

Suetonius on DOMITIAN
Domitian ch 21

Domitian (Titus Flavius Domitianus) (AD 51–96). Roman emperor from AD 81. He finalized the conquest of Britain , strengthened the Rhine–Danube frontier, and suppressed immorality as well as freedom of thought in philosophy and religion. His reign of terror led to his assassination.

Donald Ian (1910–1987). English obstetrician who introduced ultrasound (very high-frequency sound wave) scanning. He pioneered its use in obstetrics as a means of scanning the growing fetus without exposure to the danger of X-rays. Donald's experience of using radar in World War II suggested to him the use of ultrasound for medical purposes.

Donald III Bane ('fair') (*c.* 1039–*c.* 1100). King of Scotland. He came to the throne 1093 after seizing it on the death of his brother Malcolm III. He was dethroned 1094 by Malcolm's brother, Duncan II. He regained power 1094 but was defeated and captured 1097 by another brother, Edgar, who had him blinded and imprisoned until his death.

As Donalbain, he appears in Shakespeare's play *Macbeth* 1605.

Donaldson Stephen (1947–). US fantasy writer, author of two Thomas Covenant trilogies 1978–83.

Donat (Friederich) Robert (1905–1958). English actor of Anglo-Polish parentage. He started out in the theatre and made one film in Hollywood (*The Count of Monte Cristo* 1934). His other films include Alfred Hitchcock's *The Thirty-Nine Steps* 1935, *Goodbye, Mr Chips* 1939 for which he won an Academy Award, and *The Winslow Boy* 1948.

Donatello (Donato di Niccolo) (*c.* 1386–1466). Italian sculptor of the early Renaissance. He was instrumental in reviving the Classical style, as in his graceful bronze statue of the youthful *David* about 1433 (Bargello, Florence) and his equestrian statue of the general *Gattamelata* 1447–50 (Piazza del Santo, Padua). The course of Florentine art in the 15th century was strongly influenced by his work.

Donatello introduced true perspective in his relief sculptures, such as the panel of *St George Slaying the Dragon* about 1415–17 (Or San Michele, Florence). He absorbed Classical influences during a stay in Rome 1430–32, and *David* is said to be the first life-size, free-

standing nude since antiquity. In his later work, such as his wood-carving of the aged *Mary Magdalene* about 1456 (Baptistry, Florence), he sought dramatic expression through a distorted, emaciated figural style.

Suggested reading
Avery, Charles *Donatello: An Introduction* (1994)
Bennett, B and Wilkins, D *Donatello* (1985)
Hartt, Frederick *Donatello* (1972)
Janson, H *The Sculpture of Donatello* (1957)
Pope-Hennessy, J *Italian Renaissance Sculpture* (1958)
Sachs, H *Donatello* (1981)
Seymour, Charles, Jr *Sculpture in Italy 1400–1500* (1966)

Donati Giovanni Battista (1826–1873). Italian astronomer who discovered six comets. He made important contributions to the early development of stellar spectroscopy and applied spectroscopic methods to the understanding of the nature of comets. He also studied cosmic meteorology.

Donati was born and educated in Pisa. From 1852 he worked at the observatory in Florence, becoming its director 1864.

During the 1850s Donati was an enthusiastic comet-seeker, and the most dramatic of his discoveries was named after him. Donati's comet, first sighted 1858, had, in addition to its major tail, two narrow extra tails.

Donellan Declan (1953–). Theatre director, born in Manchester of an Irish family. He was cofounder of the Cheek by Jowl theatre company 1981, and associate director of the National Theatre from 1989. His irreverent and audacious productions include many classics, such as Racine's *Andromaque* 1985, Corneille's *Le Cid* 1987, and Ibsen's *Peer Gynt* 1990.

Donen Stanley (1924–). US film director. Formerly a dancer, he co-directed two of Gene Kelly's best musicals, *On the Town* 1949 and *Singin' in the Rain* 1952. His other films include *Seven Brides for Seven Brothers* 1954, *Charade* 1963, *Two for the Road* 1968, and *Blame It on Rio* 1984.

Dönitz Karl (1891–1980). German admiral, originator of the wolf-pack submarine technique, which sank 15 million tonnes of Allied shipping in World War II. He succeeded Hitler 1945, capitulated, and was imprisoned 1946–56.

He was in charge of Germany's U-boat force 1939–43 and his 'wolf-packs' sank 15 million tonnes of Allied shipping during the course of the war. He succeeded Raeder as commander in chief of the Navy Jan 1943 and devoted himself to trying to overcome Allied naval superiority. Hitler trusted him when he had lost faith in his Army and Luftwaffe commanders, and so Dönitz was appointed to succeed him May 1945. His sole deed as leader of the Reich was to negotiate its surrender. He was arrested 23 May, tried at Nuremberg and was sentenced to 10 years' imprisonment.

While his magical tunes bring joy to the world, while everyone sings them and trills them, he himself sits, a terrible picture of insanity, in a lunatic asylum near Paris.

Heinrich Heine on DONIZETTI
in *Letters on the French Stage* 1837

Donizetti (Domenico) Gaetano (Maria) (1797–1848). Italian composer. He created more than 60 operas, including *Lucrezia Borgia* 1833, *Lucia di Lammermoor* 1835, *La Fille du régiment* 1840, *La Favorite* 1840, and *Don Pasquale* 1843. They show the influence of Rossini and Bellini, and are characterized by a flow of expressive melodies. *See illustration on page 250.*

Donkin Bryan (1768–1855). English engineer who made several innovations in papermaking and printing; he invented the forerunner of the rotary press. He also contributed to food preservation by taking the bottling process introduced by Nicolas Appert and modifying it to use metal cans instead of glass bottles.

Donne was brought up in the Roman Catholic faith and matriculated early at Oxford to avoid taking the oath of supremacy. Before becoming a law student 1592 he travelled in Europe. During his four years at the law courts he was notorious for his wit and reckless living. In 1596 he sailed as a volunteer in an expedition against Spain with the Earl of Essex and Walter Raleigh, and on his return became private secretary to Sir Thomas Egerton, Keeper of the Seal. This appointment was ended by his secret marriage to Ann More (died 1617), niece of Egerton's wife, and they endured many years of poverty. The more passionate and tender of his love poems were probably written to her. From 1621 to his death Donne was dean of St Paul's. His sermons rank him with the century's greatest orators, and his fervent poems of love and hate, violent, tender, or abusive, give him a unique position among English poets. His verse was not published in collected form until after his death, and was long out of favour, but he is now recognized as one of the greatest English poets.

Suggested reading
Bald, R C *John Donne: A Life* (1970)
Carey, J *John Donne: Life, Mind and Art* (1980)
Roston, M *The Soul of Wit* (1974)
Warnke, F J *John Donne* (1987)

Love built on beauty, soon as beauty, dies.

JOHN DONNE
Elegies, 'The Anagram' 1965 ed

Donoghue Steve (Stephen) (1884–1945). British jockey. Between 1915 and 1925 he won the Epsom Derby six times, equalling the record of Jem Robinson (since beaten by Lester Piggott). Donoghue is the only jockey to have won the race in three successive years.

Donovan William Joseph (1883–1959). US military leader and public official. Donovan served as US district attorney 1922–24 and as

Donizetti *The composer Gaetano Donizetti (1797—1848). Following the death of Bellini in 1835, Donizetti was the unrivalled leader of Italian opera until Verdi emerged in the 1840s. Donizetti's comedies have endured especially well, thanks largely to their melodic spontaneity and charm. (Image Select)*

Donne *The poet John Donne. Donne is now recognized as one of the greatest English poets for his poems of love and faith, but during his life he suffered for his Catholic faith, which he later renounced for the Church of England, and for his secret marriage to Ann More, as a result of which he lost his job and suffered many years of poverty. (Image Select)*

In printing, Donkin tackled the problem of increasing the speed of presses. The original flat-bed press, with its back-and-forth movement, was too slow. Donkin arranged four (flat) formes of type around a spindle – a rudimentary rotary press. He introduced a composition of glue and treacle for the inking rollers, an innovation which was still widely used long after his press had been superseded.

Donleavy J(ames) P(atrick) (1926–   ). US-born Irish writer. His picaresque novel *The Ginger Man* (published in France 1955), regarded as a comic masterpiece, was banned in Britain and the USA until the 1960s. Set in Dublin in the 1940s, it is the story of an expatriate American.

Donleavy was born in New York, the son of Irish immigrants. He studied at Trinity College, Dublin, and became an Irish citizen 1967. Later novels include *A Singular Man* 1963, *The Destinies of Darcy Dancer, Gentleman* 1977, *Leila: Further in the Life and Destinies of Darcy Dancer, Gentleman* 1983, and *Are You Listening Rabbi Löw* 1987. His novels, which are about eccentrics, have a fierce comic energy. *The History of the Ginger Man* 1994 is part autobiography, part literary history.

Donne John (1572–1631). English metaphysical poet. His work consists of love poems, religious poems, verse satires, and sermons, most of which were first published after his death. His religious poems show the same passion and ingenuity as his love poetry. A Roman Catholic in his youth, he converted to the Church of England and finally became dean of St Paul's Cathedral, where he is buried.

assistant to the US attorney general 1925–29. He was national security adviser to Presidents Hoover and F D Roosevelt and founded the Office of Strategic Services (OSS) 1942. As OSS director 1942–45, Donovan coordinated US intelligence during World War II.

Dooley Thomas Anthony (1927–1961). US medical missionary. He founded Medico, an international welfare organization, 1957, after tending refugees in Vietnam who were streaming south after the partition of the country 1954. As well as Medico, he established medical clinics in Cambodia, Laos, and Vietnam.

Doolittle Hilda. Pen name *HD* (1886–1961). US poet. She went to Europe 1911, and was associated with Ezra Pound and the English writer Richard Aldington (to whom she was married 1913–37) in founding the Imagist school of poetry, advocating simplicity, precision, and brevity. Her work includes the *Sea Garden* 1916 and *Helen in Egypt* 1961, as well as *End to Torment* 1958, a memoir of Ezra Pound.

Doolittle James Harold (1896–1993). US aviation pioneer who took part in the development of new aircraft designs and more efficient aircraft fuel. During World War II he saw active service and in 1942 led a daring bombing raid over Tokyo. He later participated in the invasion of North Africa and the intensive bombing of Germany.

Born in Alameda, California, USA, Doolittle attended the University of California and served as an army flying instructor during World War I. Later, in the Army Air Corps, he became an aviation specialist, earning an engineering degree from the Massachusetts Institute of Technology (MIT).

Doone English family of freebooters who, according to legend, lived on Exmoor, Devon, until they were exterminated in the 17th century. They feature in R D Blackmore's novel *Lorna Doone* 1869.

Doppler Christian Johann (1803–1853). Austrian physicist who in 1842 described the Doppler effect and derived the observed frequency mathematically in Doppler's principle. In 1835 he went to Prague to teach mathematics; in 1850 he became director of the new Physical Institute at the Royal Imperial University of Vienna.

The Doppler effect is the change in observed frequency, or wavelength, of waves due to relative motion between the wave source and the observer; for example, the perceived pitch change of a siren as it approaches and then recedes.

Dorati Antál (1906–1988). US conductor, born in Hungary. He toured with ballet companies 1933–45 and went on to conduct orchestras in the USA and Europe in a career spanning more than half a century. Dorati gave many first performances of Bartók's music and recorded all Haydn's symphonies with the Philharmonia Hungarica.

Doré (Paul) Gustave (1832–1883). French artist. Chiefly known as a prolific illustrator, he was also active as a painter, etcher, and sculptor. He produced closely worked engravings of scenes from, for example, Rabelais, Dante, Cervantes, the Bible, Milton, and Edgar Allan Poe.

Doré was born in Strasbourg. His views of Victorian London 1869–71, concentrating on desperate poverty and overcrowding in the swollen city, were admired by van Gogh.

Dornier Claude (1884–1969). German pioneer aircraft designer who invented the seaplane and during World War II designed the Do-17 'flying pencil' bomber, the mainstay of the Luftwaffe during the air raids on Britain 1940–41.

Born in Bavaria, he founded the Dornier Metallbau works at Friedrichshafen, Lake Constance, in 1922.

d'Orsay Alfred Guillaume Gabriel, Count d'Orsay (1801–1857). French dandy. For 20 years he resided with the Irish writer Lady Blessington in London at Gore House, where he became known as an arbiter of taste.

Dorset 1st Earl of Dorset. Title of English poet Thomas ♦Sackville.

Dorsey Tommy (Thomas) (1905–1956) and Jimmy (James) (1904–1957). US bandleaders, musicians, and composers during the swing era. They worked together in the Dorsey Brothers Orchestra 1934–35 and 1953–56, but led separate bands in the intervening period. The Jimmy Dorsey band was primarily a dance band; the Tommy Dorsey band was more jazz-oriented and featured the singer Frank Sinatra 1940–42. Both Dorsey bands featured in a number of films in the 1940s, and the brothers appeared together in *The Fabulous Dorseys* 1947.

Dos Passos John Roderigo (1896–1970). US author. He made his reputation with the war novels *One Man's Initiation* 1919 and *Three Soldiers* 1921. His major work is the trilogy *U.S.A.* 1930–36. An epic, panoramic view of US life through three decades, and inspired by a communist and anarchist historical approach, it used such innovative structural devices as the 'Newsreel', a collage of documentary information, and the 'Camera Eye', the novelist's own stream-of-consciousness.

His other works include *Manhattan Transfer* 1925, an expressionist montage novel of the modern city. Born in Chicago, Dos Passos was a member of the post-World War I 'lost generation', and his writing was shaped by his radical sympathies. He also wrote a second, less ambitious trilogy, *District of Columbia* 1939–49. Other works include *One Man's Initiation – 1917* 1919 and *Midcentury* 1961.

Dos Santos José Eduardo (1942–). Angolan left-wing politician, president from 1979, a member of the People's Movement for the Liberation of Angola (MPLA). By 1989, he had negotiated the withdrawal of South African and Cuban forces, and in 1991 a peace agreement to end the civil war. In 1992 his victory in multiparty elections was disputed by UNITA rebel leader Jonas Savimbi, and fighting resumed, escalating into full-scale civil war 1993. Representatives of the two leaders signed a peace agreement 1994.

Dostoevsky Fyodor Mihailovich (1821–1881). Russian novelist. Remarkable for their profound psychological insight, Dostoevsky's novels have greatly influenced Russian writers, and since the beginning of the 20th century have been increasingly influential abroad. In 1849 he was sentenced to four years' hard labour in Siberia, followed by army service, for printing socialist propaganda. *The House of the Dead* 1861 recalls his prison experiences, followed by his major works *Crime and Punishment* 1866, *The Idiot* 1868–69, and *The Brothers Karamazov* 1879–80.

Born in Moscow, the son of a physician, Dostoevsky was for a short time an army officer. His first novel, *Poor Folk*, appeared 1846. In 1849, during a period of intense tsarist censorship, he was arrested as a member of a free-thinking literary circle and sentenced to death. After a last-minute reprieve he was sent to the penal settlement at Omsk for four years, where the terrible conditions increased his epileptic tendency. Finally pardoned in 1859, he published the humorous *Village of Stepanchikovo*, *The House of the Dead*, and *The Insulted and the Injured* 1862. Meanwhile he had launched two unsuccessful liberal periodicals, in the second of which his *Letters from the Underworld* 1864 appeared. Compelled to work by pressure of debt, he quickly produced *Crime and Punishment* 1866 and *The Gambler* 1867, before fleeing the country to escape from his creditors. He then wrote *The Idiot* (in which the hero is an epileptic like himself), *The Eternal Husband* 1870, and *The Possessed* 1871–72. Returning to Russia 1871, he again entered journalism and issued the personal miscellany *Journal of an Author*, in which he discussed contemporary problems. In 1875 he published *A Raw Youth*, but the great work of his last years is *The Brothers Karamazov*.

Suggested reading
Chapple, Richard *A Dostoevsky Dictionary* (1983)
Frank, Joseph *Dostoevsky: The Seeds of Revolt, 1821–1849* (1977)
Frank, Joseph *Dostoevsky: The Years of Ordeal, 1850–1859* (1984)
Frank, Joseph *Dostoevsky: The Stir of Liberation, 1860–1865* (1986)
Grossman, L *Dostoevsky* (1974)
Gunn, Judith *Dostoevsky: Dreamer and Prophet* (1990)
Hingley, Ronald *Dostoevsky: His Life and Work* (1978)

Dou Gerrit (Gerard) (1613–1675). Dutch genre painter. A pupil of Rembrandt, he is known for small domestic interiors, minutely observed. His teacher's influence can be clearly seen in *Tobit* 1632–33 (National Gallery, London).

Doub was born in Leiden, where he founded a painters' guild with Jan Steen. His many pupils included Gabriel Metsu.

Doubleday Abner (1819–1893). American Civil War military leader and reputed inventor of baseball. He served as major general in the Shenandoah Valley campaign and at the Battles of Bull Run and Antietam 1862, and Gettysburg 1863. He retired from active service 1873. In an investigation into the origins of baseball 1907, testimony was given that Doubleday invented the game 1839 in Cooperstown, New York, a claim refuted by sports historians ever since.

Born in Ballston Spa, New York, Doubleday graduated from West Point military academy 1842 and saw action in the Mexican War 1846–48 and was present at Fort Sumter 1861 at the outbreak of the Civil War.

Strange and horrible as a pit, in an inhuman deadness of nature, is this site of the Nabateans' metropolis.

CHARLES DOUGHTY
Travels in Arabia Deserta vol 1 ch 2 'Monuments of Petra' 1888

Doughty Charles Montagu (1843–1926). English travel writer, author of *Travels in Arabia Deserta* 1888, written after two years in the Middle East searching for Biblical relics. He was a role model for English soldier T E Lawrence ('Lawrence of Arabia').

I am the Love that dare not speak its name.

ALFRED DOUGLAS
'Two Loves'

Douglas Alfred Bruce (1870–1945). English poet. He became closely associated in London with the Irish writer Oscar Wilde. Their relationship led to Wilde's conviction for homosexual activity, imprisonment, and early death, through the enmity of Douglas' father, the 9th Marquess of Queensberry. Douglas wrote the self-justifactory *Oscar Wilde and Myself* 1914 and *Oscar Wilde, A Summing-Up* 1940.

Douglas Clifford Hugh, known as Major Douglas (1879–1952). English social reformer, founder of the economic theory of social credit, which held that interest should be abolished and credit should become a state monopoly. During a depression, the state should provide purchasing power by subsidizing manufacture and paying dividends to individuals; as long as there was spare capacity in the economy, this credit would not cause inflation.

And all small fowlys singis on the spray: / Welcum the lord of lycht and lamp of day.

GAVIN DOUGLAS
Eneados bk 12, prologue 1.251 1415

Douglas Gavin, (or Gawain) (*c.* 1475–1522). Scottish poet. His translation into Scots of Virgil's *Aeneid* 1515 was the first translation from the classics into a vernacular of the British Isles.

Actors have a universal language, like athletes and musicians. They're good ambassadors for their countries ... they transcend political lines.

KIRK DOUGLAS
Photoplay Sept 1978

Douglas Kirk. Stage name of Issur Danielovitch Demsky (1916–). US film actor. Usually cast as a dynamic though often ill-fated hero, as in *Spartacus* 1960, he was a major star of the 1950s and 1960s in such films as *Ace in the Hole* 1951, *The Bad and the Beautiful* 1953, *Lust for Life* 1956, *The Vikings* 1958, *Seven Days in May* 1964, and *The War Wagon* 1967. He often produced his own films. He is the father of actor Michael Douglas.

Douglas Michael Kirk (1944–). US film actor and producer. His acting range includes both romantic and heroic leads in films such as *Romancing the Stone* 1984 and *Jewel of the Nile* 1985, both of which he produced. He won an Academy Award for his portrayal of a ruthless businessman in *Wall Street* 1987. Among his other films are *Fatal Attraction* 1987, *Basic Instinct* 1991, and *Falling Down* 1993.

Douglas first achieved recognition in the television series *The Streets of San Francisco* 1972–76. He is the son of actor Kirk Douglas.

The one thing that men and women have in common – they both like the company of men.

MICHAEL DOUGLAS
Playboy Nov 1980

Douglas (George) Norman (1868–1952). Scottish diplomat and travel writer. His travel books include *Siren Land* 1911 and *Old Calabria* 1915, dealing with Italy; his novel *South Wind* 1917 is set in his adopted island of Capri.

Douglas Stephen Arnold (1813–1861). US politician. He served in the US House of Representatives 1843–47 and as US senator for Illinois 1847–61. An active Democrat, he urged a compromise on slavery, and debated Abraham Lincoln during the 1858 Senate race, winning that election. After losing the 1860 presidential race to Lincoln, Douglas pledged his loyal support to the latter's administration 1861–65.

Born in Brandon, Vermont, Douglas moved west, settling in Illinois, where he studied law and was admitted to the bar 1834. He served in the Illinois state legislature 1836 and as a judge of the state supreme court 1841. He acquired the nickname 'Little Giant' for his support of westward expansion.

Douglas-Hamilton family name of dukes of Hamilton, seated at Lennoxlove, East Lothian, Scotland.

There are two problems in my life. The political ones are insoluble and the economic ones are incomprehensible.

ALEC DOUGLAS-HOME
Speech Jan 1964

Douglas-Home Alec (Alexander Frederick), Baron Home of the Hirsel (1903–1995). British Conservative politician. He was foreign secretary 1960–63, and succeeded Harold Macmillan as prime minister 1963. He renounced his peerage (as 14th Earl of Home) and re-entered the Commons after successfully contesting a by-election, but failed to win the 1964 general election, and resigned as party leader 1965. Knighted 1962. He was again foreign secretary 1970–74, when he received a life peerage. The playwright William Douglas-Home was his brother.
Suggested reading
Douglas-Home, Sir Alex *The Way the Wind Blows* (autobiography) (1976)
Young, Kenneth *Sir Alec Douglas-Home* (1970)

Every morning I read the obits in The Times. *If I'm not there, I carry on.*

WILLIAM DOUGLAS-HOME
quoted in *Observer* 16 Aug 1987

Douglas-Home William (1912–1992). Scottish dramatist. He is noted for his comedies, which include *The Chiltern Hundreds* 1947, *The Secretary Bird* 1968, *Lloyd George Knew My Father* 1972, and *The Kingfisher* 1977. He was the younger brother of the politician Alec Douglas-Home.

As a captain in the Royal Armoured Corps during World War II, he disobeyed orders by refusing to take part in the bombardment of Le Havre because the citizens had not been evacuated. This led to a court martial and a year in prison, an experience upon which his first real success, *Now Barabbas* 1945, was based.

Douglas of Kirtleside William Sholto Douglas, 1st Baron Douglas of Kirtleside (1893–1969). British air marshal. During World War II he was air officer commander in chief of Fighter Command 1940–42, Middle East Command 1943–44, and Coastal Command 1944–45. KCB 1941, baron 1948.

Douglass Frederick. Born Frederick Augustus Washington Bailey (1817–1895). US antislavery campaigner active during the American Civil War 1861–65. He issued a call to blacks to take up arms against the South and helped organize two black regiments. After the Civil War, he held several US government posts, including minister to Haiti 1889–91. He published appeals for full civil rights for blacks and also campaigned for women's suffrage.

Born a slave in Maryland, Douglass escaped 1838 and fled to Britain to avoid re-enslavement. He returned to the USA after he had secured sufficient funds to purchase his freedom. He campaigned relentlessly against slavery, especially through his speeches and his newspaper the *North Star*. His autobiographical *Narrative of the Life of Frederick Douglass* 1845 aroused support for the abolition of slavery.

Suggested reading
Bontemps, Arna *Free at Last: The Life of Frederick Douglass* (1971)
Douglass, Frederick *Narrative of the Life of Frederick Douglass* (1845, rep as *Life and Times of Frederick Douglass* 1962)
Martin, W E, Jr *The Mind of Frederick Douglass* (1986)
Ruuth, Marianne *Frederick Douglass: Patriot and Activist* (1991)

Doulton Henry (1820–1897). English ceramicist. He developed special wares for the chemical, electrical, and building industries, and established the world's first stoneware-drainpipe factory 1846. From 1870 he created art pottery and domestic tablewares in Lambeth, S London, and Burslem, near Stoke-on-Trent. Knighted 1887.

Ah, a road accident ... a road accident.

Words spoken by PAUL DOUMER at his assassination, 1932. He never knew a bullet not a car had hit him, and his aides refused to reveal the truth.

Doumer Paul (1857–1932). French politician. He was elected president of the Chamber 1905, president of the Senate 1927, and president of the republic 1931. He was assassinated by Gorgulov, a White Russian emigre.

Doumergue Gaston (1863–1937). French prime minister Dec 1913–June 1914 (during the time leading up to World War I); president 1924–31; and premier again Feb–Nov 1934 at the head of a 'national union' government.

Dowding Hugh Caswall Tremenheere, 1st Baron Dowding (1882–1970). British air chief marshal. He was chief of Fighter Command at the outbreak of World War II in 1939, a post he held through the Battle of Britain 10 July–12 Oct 1940.

His refusal to commit more fighters to France in 1940, when he could see that the campaign was doomed, proved to be a vital factor in the later Battle of Britain, but his uncompromising attitude upset Churchill and other political leaders and he was replaced in Fighter Command Nov 1940. He retired 1942. KCB 1933, baron 1943.

Dowell Anthony James (1943–). English Classical ballet dancer. He is known for his refined, polished style. He was principal dancer with the Royal Ballet 1966–86, and director from 1986.

Dowell joined the Royal Ballet 1961. The choreographer Frederick Ashton chose him to create the role of Oberon in *The Dream* 1964 opposite Antoinette Sibley, the start of an outstanding partnership. His other noted performances include those in Anthony Tudor's *Shadowplay* 1967, Ashton's *Monotones* 1965, and van Manen's *Four Schumann Pieces* 1975.

Always Dowland, always sad.

JOHN DOWLAND
Title of pavan

Douglass *An escaped slave, Frederick Douglass (born Frederick Augustus Washington Bailey) played a major role in fighting for the abolition of slavery in the southern states of the USA. His volumes of autobiography gave a vivid and moving account of slavery, and countered the argument that slaves were born intellectually inferior.*

Dowland John (c. 1563–c. 1626). English composer of lute songs. He introduced daring expressive refinements of harmony and ornamentation to English Renaissance style in the service of an elevated aesthetic of melancholy, as in the masterly *Lachrymae* 1605.

They are not long, the weeping and the laughter, / Love and desire and hate; / I think they have no portion in us after / We pass the gate.

ERNEST DOWSON
'Vitae Summa Brevis'

Dowson Ernest Christopher (1867–1900). English poet. He was one of the 'decadent' poets of the 1890s. He wrote the lyric with the refrain 'I have been faithful to thee, Cynara! in my fashion'.

Doxiadis Constantinos Apostolos (1913–1975). Greek architect and town planner. He designed Islamabad, the capital of Pakistan.

How often have I said to you that when you have eliminated the impossible, whatever remains, however improbable, must be the truth?

ARTHUR CONAN DOYLE
The Sign of Four 1890

Doyle Arthur Conan (1859–1930). Scottish writer. He created the detective Sherlock Holmes and his assistant Dr Watson, who first appeared in *A Study in Scarlet* 1887 and featured in a number of subsequent stories, including *The Hound of the Baskervilles* 1902. Conan Doyle also wrote historical romances (*Micah Clarke* 1889 and *The White Company* 1891) and the scientific romance *The Lost World* 1912.

Born in Edinburgh, he qualified as a doctor, and during the second South African War (or Boer War) was senior physician of a field hospital. His Sherlock Holmes character featured in several books, including *The Sign of Four* 1889 and *The Valley of Fear* 1915, as well as in volumes of short stories, first published in the *Strand Magazine*. In his later years Conan Doyle became a spiritualist. Knighted 1902.

Suggested reading
Cox, D R *Arthur Conan Doyle* (1985)
Dudley-Edwards, Owen *The Quest for Sherlock Holmes: A Biographical Study of Arthur Conan Doyle* (1988)
Pearson, Hesketh *Conan Doyle: His Life and His Art* (1961)
Symons, Julian *Conan Doyle: Portrait of an Artist* (1987)

Doyle Richard (1824–1883). English caricaturist and book illustrator. In 1849 he designed the original cover for the humorous magazine *Punch*.

D'Oyly Carte Richard (1844–1901). English producer of the Gilbert and Sullivan operas. They were performed at the Savoy Theatre, London, which he built. The D'Oyly Carte Opera Company, founded 1876, was disbanded 1982 following the ending of its monopoly on the Gilbert and Sullivan operas. The present company, founded 1988, moved to the Alexandra Theatre, Birmingham, 1991.

What fools middle-class girls are to expect other people to respect the same gods and E M Forster.
MARGARET DRABBLE
A Summer Birdcage ch 11 1962

Drabble Margaret (1939–   ). English writer. Her novels include *The Millstone* 1965, *The Middle Ground* 1980, *The Radiant Way* 1987, *A Natural Curiosity* 1989, and *The Gates of Ivory* 1991. She portrays contemporary life with toughness and sensitivity, often through the eyes of intelligent modern women. She edited the 1985 edition of the *Oxford Companion to English Literature*.

With the exception of those on murder, Solon repealed the laws of Draco because they were too severe.
PLUTARCH on DRACO
in *Life of Solon* ch 17.1

Draco (lived 7th century BC). Athenian politician, the first to codify the laws of the Athenian city-state. These were notorious for their severity; hence *draconian*, meaning particularly harsh.

Dragonetti Domenico (1763–1846). Italian-born virtuoso double bass player and composer. He established the instrument's solo credentials in tours of Britain and Europe, performing a repertoire including a transcription for bass of Beethoven's *Cello Sonata in D* 1811. His own compositions include eight concertos and numerous string quartets.

There must be a beginning of any great matter, but the continuing ... until it be thoroughly finished yields the true glory.
FRANCIS DRAKE
Despatch to Sir Francis Walsingham 17 May 1587

Drake Francis (c. 1540–1596). English buccaneer and explorer. Having enriched himself as a pirate against Spanish interests in the Caribbean 1567–72, he was sponsored by Elizabeth I for an expedition to the Pacific, sailing round the world 1577–80 in the *Golden Hind*, robbing Spanish ships as he went. This was the second circumnavigation of the globe (the first was by the Portuguese explorer Ferdinand Magellan). Drake also helped to defeat the Spanish Armada 1588 as a vice admiral in the *Revenge*.

Drake was born in Devon and apprenticed to the master of a coasting vessel, who left him the ship at his death. He accompanied

his relative, the navigator John Hawkins, 1567 and 1572 to plunder the Caribbean, and returned to England 1573 with considerable booty. After serving in Ireland as a volunteer, he suggested to Queen Elizabeth I an expedition to the Pacific, and Dec 1577 he sailed in the *Pelican* with four other ships and 166 men towards South America. In Aug 1578 the fleet passed through the Straits of Magellan and was then blown south to Cape Horn. The ships became separated and returned to England, all but the *Pelican*, now renamed the *Golden Hind*. Drake sailed north along the coast of Chile and Peru, robbing Spanish ships as far north as California, and then, in 1579, headed southwest across the Pacific. He rounded the South African Cape June 1580, and reached England Sept 1580. Thus the second voyage around the world, and the first made by an English person, was completed in a little under three years. When the Spanish ambassador demanded Drake's punishment, the Queen knighted him on the deck of the *Golden Hind* at Deptford, London.

In 1581 Drake was made mayor of Plymouth, in which capacity he brought fresh water into the city by constructing leats from Dartmoor. In 1584–85 he represented the town of Bosinney in Parliament. In a raid on Cadiz 1587 he burned 10,000 tons of shipping, 'singed the King of Spain's beard', and delayed the invasion of England by the Spanish Armada for a year. He was stationed off the French island of Ushant 1588 to intercept the Armada, but was driven back to England by unfavourable winds. During the fight in the Channel he served as a vice admiral in the *Revenge*. Drake sailed on his last expedition to the West Indies with Hawkins 1595, capturing Nombre de Dios on the north coast of Panama but failing to seize Panama City. In Jan 1596 he died of dysentery off the town of Puerto Bello (now Portobello), Panama.

Suggested reading
Andrews, K R *Drake's Voyages* (1967)
Sugden, John *Drake* (1990)
Williams, N *Francis Drake* (1973)
Williamson, J A *Sir Francis Drake* (1966)
Wilson, D *The World Encompassed: Francis Drake and his Great Voyage* (1987)

Draper Henry (1837–1882). US astronomer who used a spectrograph of his own devising to obtain high-quality spectra of celestial objects. His work is commemorated by the *Henry Draper Catalogue* of stellar spectral types.

Draper was born in Virginia and studied medicine at the University of the City of New York. Travelling in Europe, he became interested in telescope-making and photography. In 1860, he was appointed professor of natural science at the University of the City of New York.

Drayton Michael (1563–1631). English poet. His volume of poems *The Harmony of the Church* 1591 was destroyed by order of the archbishop of Canterbury. His greatest poetical work was the topographical survey of England, *Poly-Olbion* 1612–22, in 30 books.

Drees Willem (1886–1988). Dutch socialist politician, prime minister 1948–58. Chair of the Socialist Democratic Workers' Party from 1911 until the German invasion of 1940, he returned to politics in 1947, after being active in the resistance movement. In 1947, as the responsible minister, he introduced a state pension scheme.

Dreiser Theodore Herman Albert (1871–1945). US writer. His works include the naturalist novels *Sister Carrie* 1900 and *An American Tragedy* 1925, based on the real-life crime of a young man, who in his drive to 'make good', drowns a shop assistant he has made pregnant. It was filmed as *A Place in the Sun* 1951.

Born in Terre Haute, Indiana, Dreiser was a journalist 1889–90 in Chicago and was editor of several magazines. His other novels include *The Financier* 1912, *The Titan* 1914, and *The Genius* 1915. *An American Tragedy* finally won him great popularity after years of publishing works that had been largely ignored. His other works range from autobiographical pieces to poems and short stories. Although his work is criticized for being technically unpolished, it is praised for its powerful realism and sincerity. In the 1930s he devoted much of his energy to the radical reform movement.

Suggested reading
Lingeman, Richard *Theodore Dreiser* (1986–90)
Matthiessen, F O *Theodore Dreiser* (1951)
Moers, Ellen *Two Dreisers: The Man and the Novelist* (1969)
Shapiro, Charles *Theodore Dreiser: Our Bitter Patriot* (1964)

Drew Charles Richard (1904–1950). US surgeon who demonstrated that plasma had a longer life than whole blood and therefore could be better used for transfusion.

Drew was born in Washington DC and studied at Amherst College and McGill University Medical School. He became professor of surgery at Howard University Medical School 1942.

In 1939, he established a blood bank and was in charge of collecting blood for the British army at the beginning of World War II. In 1941, he became director of the American Red Cross Blood Bank in New York, which collected blood for the US armed forces. Drew resigned, however, when the Red Cross decided to segregate blood according to the race of the donor.

Dreyer Carl Theodor (1889–1968). Danish film director. His wide range of films includes the austere silent classic *La Passion de Jeanne d'Arc/The Passion of Joan of Arc* 1928 and the Expressionist horror film *Vampyr* 1932, after the failure of which Dreyer made no full-length films until *Vredens Dag/Day of Wrath* 1943. His two late masterpieces are *Ordet/The Word* 1955 and *Gertrud* 1964.

Dreyer John Louis Emil (1852–1926). Danish astronomer, in Ireland from 1874. He compiled three catalogues which together described more than 13,000 nebulae and star clusters; these achieved international recognition as standard reference material. He also wrote a biography of Danish astronomer Tycho Brahe 1890.

Dreyer was born and educated in Copenhagen. In 1874 he was appointed assistant at Lord Rosse's Observatory at Birr Castle in Parsonstown, Ireland. Four years later he took up a similar post at Dunsink Observatory at the University of Dublin, and he was director of the Armagh Observatory 1882–1916.

The Dreyfus case ... provided an example of the way in which French public opinion could genuinely make itself felt so as to expose injustice and to right wrongs.

James Joll on ALFRED DREYFUS
in *Europe Since 1870* 2nd ed 1976

Dreyfus Alfred (1859–1935). French army officer, victim of miscarriage of justice, anti-Semitism, and cover-up. Employed in the War Ministry, in 1894 he was accused of betraying military secrets to Germany, court-martialled, and sent to the penal colony on Devil's Island, French Guiana. When his innocence was discovered 1896 the military establishment tried to conceal it, and the implications of the Dreyfus affair were passionately discussed in the press until he was exonerated in 1906.

Dreyfus was born in Mulhouse, E France, of a Jewish family. He had been a prisoner in the French Guiana penal colony for two years when it emerged that the real criminal was a Major Esterhazy; the high command nevertheless attempted to suppress the facts and used forged documents to strengthen their case. After a violent controversy, in which the future prime minister Georges Clemenceau and the novelist Emile Zola championed Dreyfus, he was brought back for a retrial 1899, found guilty with extenuating circumstances, and received a pardon. In 1906 the court of appeal declared him innocent, and he was reinstated in his military rank.

Suggested reading
Bredin, Jean-Denis *The Affair: The Case of Alfred Dreyfus* (trs 1986)
Burns, Michael *Dreyfus: A Family Affair 1789–1945* (1992)
Chapman, Guy *The Dreyfus Trials* (1972)
Kleenblatt, Norman L (ed) *The Dreyfus Affair* (1987)

Dreyfuss Henry (1904–1972). US industrial designer. He was a major pioneer of design in the interwar years. He moved through stage and store design before setting up an independent office 1929 from which he collaborated with a number of manufacturers.

Notable designs include his black bakelite telephone 'Bell 33' 1933 for Bell Telephone and the streamlined train 'Twentieth Century Limited' 1941 for the New York Central Railroad.

After World War II he worked on a system of anthropometrics (the study of the size and proportions of the human body), disseminated through his two influential books *Designing for People* 1955 and *The Measure of Man* 1960.

Driesch Hans Adolf Eduard (1867–1941). German embryologist and philosopher who was one of the last advocates of vitalism, the theory that life is directed by a vital principle and cannot be explained solely in terms of chemical and physical processes. He made several important discoveries in embryology. He was professor of philosophy at Heidelberg 1911–20, moving to Cologne and Leipzig before being forced to retire 1935 by the Nazi regime.

Those book-learned fools who miss the world.

JOHN DRINKWATER
'From Generation to Generation'

Drinkwater John (1882–1937). English poet and dramatist. He was a prolific writer of lyrical and reflective verse, and also many historical plays, including *Abraham Lincoln* 1918.

Drucker Peter Ferdinand (1909–   ). Austrian-born US management expert who set out the theory of 'management by objectives' (MBO), now a field of management theory in its own right, in his classic *The Practices of Management* 1954. He is also responsible for the idea of privatization, although he referred to it as 'reprivatization'.

Drucker's five basic objectives for management – setting objectives, organization, motivation and communication, laying down performance targets, and personnel development – are still applicable today.

Only the echoes which he made relent / Ring from their marble caves repent, repent.

WILLIAM DRUMMOND
'For the Baptist'

Drummond William (1585–1649). Scottish poet, also known as Drummond of Hawthornden. He was one of the first Scottish poets to use southern English, and his *Poems* 1614 also show the strong influence of continental models.

Drummond de Andrade Carlos (1902–1987). Brazilian writer. He is generally considered the greatest modern Brazilian poet, and was a prominent member of the Modernist school. His verse, often seemingly casual, continually confounds the reader's expectations of the 'poetical'.

Dryden John (1631–1700). English poet and dramatist. He is noted for his satirical verse and for his use of the heroic couplet. His poetry includes the verse satire *Absalom and Achitophel* 1681, *Annus Mirabilis* 1667, and 'St Cecilia's Day' 1687. Plays include the heroic drama *The Conquest of Granada* 1670–71, the comedy *Marriage à la Mode* 1672, and *All for Love* 1678, a reworking of Shakespeare's *Antony and Cleopatra*.

On occasion, Dryden trimmed his politics and his religion to the prevailing wind, and, as a Roman Catholic convert under James II, lost the post of poet laureate (to which he had been appointed 1668) at the Revolution of 1688. Critical works include *Essay on Dramatic Poesy* 1668. Later ventures to support himself include a translation of Virgil 1697.

Suggested reading
Davidson, D *Dryden* (1968)
Myers, W *Dryden* (1973)
Winn, J A *Dryden and his World* (1987)
Wykes, D *Preface to Dryden* (1977)

Drysdale (George) Russell (1912–1981). Australian artist. In 1944 he produced a series of wash drawings for the *Sydney Morning*

Herald recording the effects of a severe drought in W New South Wales. The bleakness of life in the Australian outback is a recurring theme in his work, which typically depicts the dried-out, scorched landscape with gaunt figures reflecting fortitude in desolation and poverty. Children appear frequently, as in *The Gatekeeper's Wife* 1965 (National Library, Canberra).

He is also known for his paintings of the old gold-mining towns of Hill End and Sofala in New South Wales. Knighted 1969.
Suggested reading
Dutton, Geoffrey *Drysdale* (1981)
Hughes, Robert *The Art of Australia* (1970)

Duarte José Napoleon (1925–1990). El Salvadorean politician, president 1980–82 and 1984–88. He was mayor of San Salvador 1964–70, and was elected president 1972, but was exiled by the army 1982. On becoming president again 1984, he sought a negotiated settlement with the left-wing guerrillas 1986, but resigned on health grounds.

Dubail Augustin Yvon Edmond (1851–1934). French soldier. After service in the Franco-Prussian War and as Chief of Staff in Algeria, by the outbreak of World War I he was Chief of Staff of the French Army and a member of the military council. He successfully defended Nancy, and then held the German attack on the Heights of the Meuse. He was appointed military governor of Paris April 1916 and remained in that post for the rest of the war.

You are going to hurt me! Oh, please, do not hurt me!
COMTESSE DU BARRY
Last words before being guillotined 1793.

---

du Barry Marie Jeanne, Comtesse (born Bécu) (1743–1793). Mistress of Louis XV of France from 1768. At his death 1774 she was banished to a convent, and during the Revolution fled to London. Returning to Paris 1793, she was guillotined.

Socialism with a Human Face.

Motto on the Prague Spring attributed to ALEXANDER DUBČEK

Dubček Alexander (1921–1992). Czechoslovak politician, chair of the federal assembly 1989–92. He was a member of the Slovak resistance movement during World War II, and became first secretary of the Communist Party 1967–69. He launched a liberalization campaign (called the Prague Spring) that was opposed by the USSR and led to the Soviet invasion of Czechoslovakia 1968. He was arrested by Soviet troops and expelled from the party 1970. In 1989 he gave speeches at prodemocracy rallies, and after the fall of the hardline regime, he was elected speaker of the National Assembly in Prague, a position to which he was re-elected 1990. He was fatally injured in a car crash Sept 1992.

Du Bellay Joaquim (c. 1522–1560). French poet and prose writer. He published the great manifesto of the new school of French poetry, the Pléiade: *Défense et illustration de la langue française* 1549. He also wrote sonnets inspired by Petrarch and his meditations on the vanished glories of Rome, *Antiquités de Rome* 1558, influenced English writers such as Edmund Spenser who translated some of his work.

Dubois Marie Eugène François Thomas (1858–1940). Dutch palaeontologist who in Indonesia 1891 discovered the remains of an early species of human, *Homo erectus*, known as Java man.

In 1887 he joined the Army Medical Service and was posted to Java – then a Dutch possession – where he was commissioned by the Dutch government to search for fossils. He returned to Europe 1895 and became a professor at Amsterdam 1899.

Du Bois W(illiam) E(dward) B(urghardt) (1868–1963). US educator and social critic. Du Bois was one of the early leaders of the National Association for the Advancement of Colored People (NAACP) and the editor of its journal *Crisis* 1909–32. As a staunch advocate of black American rights, he came into conflict with Booker T Washington, opposing the latter's policy of compromise on the issue of slavery. Du Bois was born in Great Barrington, Massachusetts. He earned a PhD from Harvard 1895 and was appointed to the faculty of Atlanta University. In 1962 he established his home in Accra, Ghana.

Du Bois-Reymond Emil Heinrich (1818–1896). German physiologist who showed the existence of electrical currents in nerves, correctly arguing that it would be possible to transmit nerve impulses chemically. His experimental techniques proved the basis for almost all future work in electrophysiology. Du Bois-Reymond was born and educated in Berlin, and became professor of physiology there 1858.

Dubos René Jules (1901–1982). French-US microbiologist who studied soil microorganisms and became interested in their antibacterial properties.

The antibacterials he discovered had limited therapeutic use since they were toxic. However, he opened up a new field of research that eventually led to the discovery of such major drugs as penicillin and streptomycin.

Dubuffet Jean Philippe Arthur (1901–1985). French artist. He originated *Art Brut*, 'raw or brutal art', in the 1940s. Inspired by graffiti and children's drawings, he used such varied materials as plaster, steel wool, and straw in his paintings and sculptures to produce highly textured surfaces.

Art Brut emerged 1945 with an exhibition of Dubuffet's own work and of paintings by psychiatric patients and naive, or untrained, artists. His own paintings and sculptural works have a similar quality, primitive and expressive.

It is the meeting of a beauty steeped in sentiment, like the impassioned beauty of a woman.

E Cecchi on DUCCIO DI BUONINSEGNA
in *The Sienese painters of the Trecento*
translated 1931 (comment on his madonnas)

Duccio di Buoninsegna (c. 1255–c. 1319). Italian painter. A major figure in the Sienese school, his influence on the development of painting was profound. His greatest work is his altarpiece for Siena Cathedral, the *Maestà* 1308–11 (Cathedral Museum, Siena). The figure of the Virgin is essentially Byzantine in style, with much gold detail, but depicted with warmth and tenderness. His skill in narrative is displayed on the back of the main panel of the *Maestà* in scenes from the Passion of Christ.

Duce (Italian 'leader') title bestowed on the fascist dictator Benito ◊Mussolini by his followers and later adopted as his official title.

Duchamp Marcel (1887–1968). French-born US artist. He achieved notoriety with his *Nude Descending a Staircase No 2* 1912 (Philadelphia Museum of Art), influenced by Cubism and Futurism. An active exponent of Dada, he invented ready-mades, everyday items (for example, a bicycle wheel mounted on a kitchen stool) which he displayed as works of art.

A major early work that focuses on mechanical objects endowed with mysterious significance is *La Mariée mise à nu par ses célibataires, même/The Bride Stripped Bare by Her Bachelors, Even* 1915–23 (Philadelphia Museum of Art). Duchamp continued to experiment with collage, mechanical imagery, and sculptural assemblages throughout his career. He lived mostly in New York and became a US citizen 1954.
Suggested reading
Bailly, J-C *Duchamp* (1986)
d'Harnoncourt, Anne and McShine, Kynaston *Marcel Duchamp* (1973)
Kuenzli, Rudolf and Maumann, Francis (eds) *Marcel Duchamp: Artist of the Century* (1989)

Moure, G *Marcel Duchamp* (1988)
Tomkins, Calvin *The World of Marcel Duchamp* (1966)

Dudintsev Vladimir Dmitriyevich (1918–). Soviet novelist. He wrote the remarkably frank *Not by Bread Alone* 1956, a depiction of Soviet bureaucracy and inefficiency.

Dudley Lord Guildford (died 1554). English nobleman, fourth son of the Duke of Northumberland. He was married by his father to Lady Jane Grey 1553, against her wishes, in an attempt to prevent the succession of Mary I to the throne. The plot failed, and he and his wife were executed.

Dufay Guillaume (*c.* 1400–1474). Flemish composer. He wrote secular songs and sacred music, including 84 songs and eight masses. His work marks a transition from the style of the Middle Ages to the expressive melodies and rich harmonies of the Renaissance.

Du Fu another name for the Chinese poet ◊Tu Fu.

Pictures have broken away from their frames to continue on dresses and on walls.
RAOUL DUFY
Les Tissus Imprimés Amour de l'Art No 1 1920

Dufy Raoul (1877–1953). French painter and designer. Inspired by Fauvism he developed a fluent, brightly coloured style in watercolour and oils, painting scenes of gaiety and leisure, such as horse racing, yachting, and life on the beach. He also designed tapestries, textiles, and ceramics.

Duguit Léon (1859–1928). French jurist. He attacked abstract notions of sovereignty and the state, believing that the law exists to promote social solidarity; that is, the interaction and interdependence of groups of people. When it fails to do so, it should be rejected. He was professor of constitution law at the University of Bordeaux.

Duiker Johannes (1890–1935). Dutch architect of the 1920s and 1930s avant-garde period. A member of the De Stijl group, his works demonstrate great structural vigour. They include the Zonnestraal Sanatorium, Hilversum, 1926–28, co-designed with Bernard Bijvoet (1889–), and the Open Air School 1929–30 and Handelsblad-Cineac News Cinema 1934, both in Amsterdam.

Dukakis Michael Stanley (1933–). US Democrat politician, governor of Massachusetts 1974–78 and 1982–90, presiding over a high-tech economic boom, the 'Massachusetts miracle'.

Dukakis was born in Boston, Massachusetts, the son of Greek immigrants. After studying law at Harvard and serving in Korea (1955–57), he concentrated on a political career in his home state. Elected as a Democrat to the Massachusetts legislature 1962, he became state governor 1974. After an unsuccessful first term, marred by his unwillingness to compromise, he was defeated 1978. He returned as governor 1982, committed to working in a more consensual manner, was re-elected 1986, and captured the Democratic Party's presidential nomination 1988. After a poor campaign, Dukakis was defeated by the incumbent vice president George Bush. His standing in Massachusetts dropped and he announced that he would not seek a new term.

Dukas Paul Abraham (1865–1935). French composer and teacher. His scrupulous orchestration and chromatically enriched harmonies were admired by Debussy. His small output includes the opera *Ariane et Barbe-Bleue/Ariane and Bluebeard* 1907, the ballet *La Péri/The Peri* 1912, and the animated orchestral scherzo *L'Apprenti sorcier/The Sorcerer's Apprentice* 1897.

He was professor of composition at the Paris Conservatoire.

Dulles Allen Welsh (1893–1969). US lawyer, director of the Central Intelligence Agency (CIA) 1953–61. He helped found the CIA 1950. He was embroiled in the Bay of Pigs, Cuba, controversial invasion attempt, among others, which forced his resignation. He was the brother of John Foster Dulles.

Dulles John Foster (1888–1959). US politician. Senior US adviser at the founding of the United Nations, he was largely responsible for drafting the Japanese peace treaty of 1951. As secretary of state 1952–59, he was the architect of US Cold War foreign policy, secured US intervention in South Vietnam after the expulsion of the French 1954, and was critical of Britain during the Suez Crisis 1956.

Dulong Pierre Louis (1785–1838). French chemist and physicist. In 1819 he discovered, together with physicist Alexis Petit, the law that now bears their names. Dulong and Petit's law states that, for many elements solid at room temperature, the product of relative atomic mass and specific heat capacity is approximately constant. He also discovered the explosive nitrogen trichloride 1811. He was professor of chemistry at Paris 1820–30, and then director of studies at the Ecole Polytechnique. He collaborated with Petit 1815–20, and continued on his own to work on specific heat capacities, publishing his findings in 1829.

Dumas Alexandre (1802–1870). French author, known as Dumas *père* (the father). He is remembered for his historical romances, the reworked output of a 'fiction-factory' of collaborators. They include *Les Trois Mousquetaires/The Three Musketeers* 1844 and its sequels. His play *Henri III et sa cour/Henry III and His Court* 1829 established French romantic historical drama.

Dumas *fils* was his son.
Suggested reading
Bell, Craig *Alexandre Dumas* (1950)
Hemmings, F W *Alexandre Dumas* (1980)
Maurois, André *The Titans: A Three-Generation Biography of the Dumas* (trs 1957)
Ross, Michael *Alexandre Dumas* (1980)
Stowe, R W *Alexandre Dumas Père* (1976)

Dumas Alexandre (1824–1895). French author, known as Dumas *fils* (the son of Dumas *père*). He is remembered for the play *La Dame aux camélias/The Lady of the Camellias* 1852, based on his own novel, and the source of Verdi's opera *La Traviata*.

Dumas Jean Baptiste André (1800–1884). French chemist who made contributions to organic analysis and synthesis, and to the determination of atomic weights (relative atomic masses) through the measurement of vapour densities. In 1822 he went to Paris, where he became professor of chemistry first at the Lyceum and 1835 at the Ecole Polytechnique. After the political upheavals of 1848 Dumas abandoned much of his scientific work for politics, and held ministerial posts under Napoleon III.

Studying blood, Dumas showed that urea is present in the blood of animals from which the kidneys have been removed, proving that one of the functions of the kidneys is to remove urea from the blood, not to produce it.

In 1826, Dumas began working on atomic theory, and concluded that 'all elastic fluids observed under the same conditions, the molecules are placed at equal distances' – that is, they are present in equal numbers.

Last night I dreamt I went to Manderley again.
DAPHNE DU MAURIER
Rebecca opening words 1938

Du Maurier Daphne (1907–1989). English novelist. Her romantic fiction includes *Jamaica Inn* 1936, *Rebecca* 1938, and *My Cousin Rachel* 1951, and is set in Cornwall. Her work, though lacking in depth and original insights, is made compelling by her fine story-telling gift. *Jamaica Inn, Rebecca*, and her short story *The Birds* were made into films by the English director Alfred Hitchcock. DBE 1969.

She was the granddaughter of British cartoonist and novelist George Du Maurier. She married Sir Frederick ('Boy') Browning, who planned the Arnhem operation in 1944.
Suggested reading
Cook, Judith *Daphne: A Portrait of Daphne Du Maurier* (1991)
Du Maurier, Daphne *Growing Pains: The Shaping of a Writer* (autobiography) (1977)
Forster, Margaret *Daphne Du Maurier* (1993)

Du Maurier George Louis Palmella Busson (1834–1896). French-born British author and illustrator. He is remembered for the novel *Trilby* 1894, the story of a natural singer able to perform only under the hypnosis of Svengali, her tutor.

Dumont d'Urville Jules Sébastien César (1790–1842). French explorer in Australasia and the Pacific. In 1838–40 he sailed round Cape Horn on a voyage to study terrestial magnetism and reached Adélie Land in Antarctica.

The courtiers who surround Louis XVIII have forgotten nothing and learnt nothing.

Said by CHARLES DUMOURIEZ at the time of the
Declaration of Verona Sept 1795, later used by Napoleon
in his Declaration to the French on his return from Elba.

Dumouriez Charles François du Périer (1739–1823). French general during the Revolution. In 1792 he was appointed foreign minister, supported the declaration of war against Austria, and after the fall of the monarchy was given command of the army defending Paris. After intriguing with the royalists he had to flee for his life, and from 1804 he lived in England.

Dunant Jean Henri (1828–1910). Swiss philanthropist, originator of the international relief agency the Red Cross. At the Battle of Solferino 1859 he helped tend the wounded, and in *Un Souvenir de Solferino* 1862 he proposed the establishment of an international body for the aid of the wounded – an idea that was realized in the Geneva Convention 1864. He shared the 1901 Nobel Peace Prize.

To be in love with your director – that way lies madness. You lose your judgement sometimes in a love affair.

FAYE DUNAWAY
quoted in *Film Yearbook* 1989

Dunaway (Dorothy) Faye (1941–). US film actress. Her first starring role was in *Bonnie and Clyde* 1967. Her subsequent films, including *Network* 1976 (for which she won an Academy Award) and *Mommie Dearest* 1981, received a varying critical reception. She also starred in Polanski's *Chinatown* 1974 and *The Handmaid's Tale* 1990.

Fear of death throws me into confusion.

WILLIAM DUNBAR
Lament for the Makaris 1511

Dunbar William (*c.* 1460–*c.* 1520). Scottish poet at the court of James IV. His poems include a political allegory, 'The Thrissil and the Rois' 1503, and the lament with the refrain 'Timor mortis conturbat me/Fear of death disturbs me' about 1508.

Duncan Isadora, originally Angela (1878–1927). US dancer. A pioneer of modern dance, she adopted an emotionally expressive free form, dancing barefoot and wearing a loose tunic, inspired by the ideal of Hellenic beauty. She danced solos accompanied to music by Beethoven and other great composers, believing that the music should fit the grandeur of the dance.

Having made her base in Paris 1908, she toured extensively, often returning to Russia after her initial success there 1904.

She died in an accident when her long scarf caught in the wheel of the sportscar in which she was travelling. She was as notorious for her private life as for her work, which was considered scandalous at

---

To her the idea that lust could be evoked in the audience by her body was unthinkable.

D Jowitt on ISADORA DUNCAN
in *Time and Dancing Image* 1988

---

the time. Her frequent alliances with artists and industrialists, her marriage to the Russian poet Sergei Esenin, and the tragedy of her two children who were drowned in a freak car accident, were documented in her autobiography *My Life* 1927.

Suggested reading
Blair, Fredrika *Isadora: Portrait of the Artist as a Woman* (1987)
Duncan, Isadora *My Life* (1927, rep 1955)
Seroff, Victor *The Real Isadora* (1971)
Steegmuller, F *Your Isadora* (1974)
Terry, W *Isadora Duncan* (1984)

Duncan Robert Edward (1919–1988). US poet. A key figure in the San Francisco Renaissance of the 1950s (other poets include Kenneth Rexroth (1905–1982), Gary Snyder, and Philip Lamantia (1927–), he was also, after meeting the poet Charles Olson, an important member of the Black Mountain poets. His first major collection, *The Opening of the Field* 1960, was influenced by Walt Whitman, Ezra Pound, William Carlos Williams, and Olson. His politically radical and formally open-ended sequence 'Passages' appeared in *Roots and Branches* 1964, *Bending the Bow* 1968, and *Ground Work: Before the War* 1984.

Duncan-Sandys Duncan (Edwin) British politician; see ◊Sandys, Duncan Edwin.

I know not any advice which he ever gave, for the government of India, that was not either very obvious or wrong.

J S Mill on HENRY DUNDAS
in *History of British India* vol iv 1858

Dundas Henry, 1st Viscount Melville (1742–1811). Scottish Conservative politician. In 1791 he became home secretary and, with revolution raging in France, carried through the prosecution of the English and Scottish radicals. After holding other high cabinet posts, he was impeached 1806 for corruption and, although acquitted on the main charge, held no further office.

An MP from 1774, he became Lord Advocate 1775. He was the leading political figure in Scotland for over 15 years, and was responsible for many reform acts passed by Parliament, especially those concerning Scotland. He transferred his allegiance from Lord North to Pitt 1783, and became one of Pitt's closest supporters. Viscount 1802.

But we cannot appear where people such as ourselves cannot sit next to people such as you.

KATHERINE DUNHAM
addressing a Kentucky audience, where blacks were only
allowed in the balcony, in R Beckford *Kathrine Dunham* 1979

Dunham Katherine (1909–). US dancer and choreographer. She was noted for a free, strongly emotional method, and employed her extensive knowledge of anthropology as a basis for her dance techniques and choreography. Her interests lay in the fusion of modern and Afro-Caribbean dance. In 1940 Dunham established an all-black dance company, which toured extensively. She also choreographed for and appeared in Hollywood films.

Dunlop John Boyd (1840–1921). Scottish inventor who founded the rubber company that bears his name. In 1888, to help his child win a tricycle race, he bound an inflated rubber hose to the wheels. The same year he developed commercially practical pneumatic tyres, first patented by Robert William Thomson (1822–1873) 1845 for bicycles and cars.

Thomson's invention had gone practically unnoticed, whereas Dunlop's arrived at a crucial time in the development of transport, and with the rubber industry well established. He founded his own company for the mass production of tyres. In 1896, after trading for only about five years, Dunlop sold both his patent and his business for £3 million.

Dunne Finley Peter (1867–1936). US humorist and social critic. His fictional character 'Mr Dooley', the Irish saloonkeeper and sage, gained a national readership. Written in dialect, Mr Dooley's humorous yet pointed reflections on US politics and society appeared 1892–1915. From 1900 the 'Mr Dooley columns' appeared in such national magazines as *Collier's* and *Metropolitan*.

Born in Chicago, Dunne wrote humour pieces for local newspapers before becoming editor-in-chief of the *Chicago Journal* 1897.

Dunne Irene (1904–1990). US actress. From 1930 to 1952, she appeared in a wide variety of films, including musicals and comedies, but was perhaps most closely associated with the genre of romantic melodrama, for example, *Back Street* 1932.

She brought a poised vitality and an instinctive sense of timing to 'screwball' comedies like *The Awful Truth* 1937 and to such musicals as *Roberta* 1935. Complementing these qualities was a sense of gravity, which came to the fore when she played the self-sacrificing heroines of such films as *Magnificent Obsession* 1935.

After Dunne retired from acting, she was for many years active in support of the Republican Party.

Duns Scotus John (*c*. 1265–*c*. 1308). Scottish monk, a leading figure in the theological and philosophical system of medieval scholasticism. The church rejected his ideas, and the word dunce is derived from Dunses, a term of ridicule applied to his followers.

Dunsany Edward John Moreton Drax Plunkett, 18th Baron of Dunsany (1878–1957). Irish writer. He was the author of the 'Jorkens' stories, beginning with *The Travel Tales of Mr Joseph Jorkens*, which employed the convention of a narrator (Jorkens) sitting in a club or bar. He also wrote short ironic heroic fantasies, collected in *The Gods of Pegana* 1905 and other books. His first play, *The Glittering Gate*, was performed at the Abbey Theatre, Dublin, 1909. Succeeded to barony 1890.

In the medieval controversy over universals he advocated nominalism, maintaining that classes of things have no independent reality. He belonged to the Franciscan order, and was known as Doctor Subtilis.

On many points he turned against the orthodoxy of Thomas Aquinas; for example, he rejected the idea of a necessary world, favouring a concept of God as absolute freedom capable of spontaneous activity.

Dunstable John (*c*. 1385–1453). English composer of songs and anthems. He is considered one of the founders of Renaissance harmony.

Dunstan, St (924–988). English priest and politician, archbishop of Canterbury from 960. He was abbot of Glastonbury from 945, and made it a centre of learning. Feast day 19 May.

Dunsterville Lionel Charles (1865–1946). British general. He joined the infantry 1884 then transferred to the Indian Army with whom he served on the Northwest Frontier, in Waziristan, and in China. After various posts in India, he went to Mesopotamia 1918 and commanded the expedition to Baku. He was promoted to major-general 1918.

He was a schoolmate of Rudyard Kipling, who used him as the model for 'Stalky', the hero of his book *Stalky & Co*.

Duparc (Marie Eugène) Henri Fouques (1848–1933). French composer. He studied under César Franck. His songs, though only 15 in number, are memorable for their lyric sensibility.

Dupleix Joseph-François (1697–1763). Governor general of the French East India Company 1741–54. He wanted to establish an extensive French empire in India and, through skilful diplomacy with local Indian rulers, briefly achieved French domination within the Carnatic (SE India), capturing Madras 1746 and defending Pondicherry against the English 1748. His wider aims were frustrated by British general Robert Clive, and Dupleix was recalled to France 1754.

Du Pré Jacqueline Mary (1945–1987). English cellist. She was celebrated for her proficient technique and powerful interpretations of the classical cello repertory, particularly of Elgar. She had an international concert career while still in her teens and made many recordings.

She married the Israeli pianist and conductor Daniel Barenboim 1967 and worked with him in concerts, as a duo, and in a conductor-soloist relationship until her playing career was ended by multiple sclerosis. Although confined to a wheelchair for the last 14 years of her life, she continued to work as a teacher and to campaign on behalf of other sufferers of the disease.

Durand Asher Brown (1796–1886). US painter and engraver. His paintings express communion with nature, as in *Kindred Spirits* 1849, a tribute to Thomas Cole, William Cullen Bryant, and the Catskill Mountains. The founding of the Hudson River School of landscape art is ascribed to Cole and Durand.

Born in Jefferson Village, New Jersey, Durand began as an engraver of portraits, landscapes, and banknotes but, influenced by Cole, turned to painting. Having studied in Europe 1840–41, he returned as a master of landscapes. Durand was president of the National Academy of Design 1840–61.

Duras Marguerite. Assumed name of Marguerite Donnadieu (1914–1996). French author. Her work includes short stories ('Des Journées entières dans les arbres' 1954, stage adaptation *Days in the Trees* 1965), plays (*La Musica* 1967), and film scripts (*Hiroshima mon amour* 1960). She also wrote novels including *Le Vice-Consul* 1966, evoking an existentialist world from the setting of Calcutta, *L'Amant* 1984 (Prix Goncourt), which deals with a love affair between a young French woman and a Chinese man, and *Emily L.* 1989. *La Vie materielle* 1987 appeared in England as *Practicalities* 1990. Her autobiographical novel, *La Douleur* 1986, is set in Paris in 1945.

If a man devotes himself to art, much evil is avoided that happens otherwise if one is idle.

ALBRECHT DÜRER
Outline of a General Treatise on Painting

Dürer Albrecht (1471–1528). German artist. He was the leading figure of the northern Renaissance. He was born in Nuremberg and travelled widely in Europe. Highly skilled in drawing and a keen student of nature, he perfected the technique of woodcut and engraving, producing woodcut series such as the *Apocalypse* 1498 and copperplate engravings such as *The Knight, Death, and the Devil* 1513 and *Melancholia* 1514. His paintings include altarpieces and meticulously observed portraits, including many self-portraits.

He was apprenticed first to his father, a goldsmith, then 1486 to Michael Wolgemut (1434–1519), a painter, woodcut artist, and master of a large workshop in Nuremberg. At the age of 13 he drew a portrait of himself from the mirror, the first known self-portrait in the history of European art. From 1490 he travelled widely, studying Netherlandish and Italian art, then visited Colmar, Basel, and Strasbourg and returned to Nuremberg 1495. Other notable journeys were to Venice 1505–07, where he met the painter Giovanni Bellini, and to Antwerp 1520, where he was made court painter to Charles V of Spain and the Netherlands (recorded in detail in his diary).
Suggested reading
Anzelewsky, F *Dürer: His Art and Life* (1983)
Panofsky, E *The Life and Art of Albrecht Dürer* (1955)
Strieder, P *Dürer: Paintings, Prints, Drawings* (1982)

The English race ... predominate [in Lower Canada] ... by their superior knowledge, energy, enterprise and wealth.

JOHN LAMBTON, 1ST EARL OF DURHAM
Durham Report 1839

Durham John George Lambton, 1st Earl of Durham (1792–1840). British politician. Appointed Lord Privy Seal 1830, he drew up the first Reform Bill 1832, and as governor general of Canada briefly in 1837 he drafted the Durham Report which resulted in the union of Upper and Lower Canada. Baron 1828, earl 1833.

Durkheim Emile (1858–1917). French sociologist, one of the founders of modern sociology, who also influenced social anthropology. He worked to establish sociology as a respectable and scientific discipline, capable of diagnosing social ills and recommending possible cures.

He was the first lecturer in social science at Bordeaux University 1887–1902, professor of education at the Sorbonne from 1902 and the first professor of sociology there 1913. He examined the bases of social order and the effects of industrialization on traditional social and moral order.

His four key works are *De la division du travail social/ The Division of Labour in Society* 1893, comparing social order in small-scale societies with that in industrial ones; *Les Régles de la méthode/ The Rules of Sociological Method* 1895, outlining his own brand of functionalism and proclaiming positivism as the way forward for sociology as a science; *Suicide* 1897, showing social causes of this apparently individual act; and *Les Formes élémentaires de la vie religieuse/ The Elementary Forms of Religion* 1912, a study of the beliefs of Australian Aborigines, showing the place of religion in social solidarity.

Suggested reading
Lukes, S *Emile Durkheim* (1973)
Parkin, Frank *Durkheim* (1992)
Thompson, K *Emile Durkheim* (1982)

Durrell Gerald Malcolm (1925–1995). English naturalist, writer, and zoo curator. He became director of Jersey Zoological Park 1958, and wrote 37 books, including the humorous memoir *My Family and Other Animals* 1956. He was the brother of the writer Lawrence Durrell.

Born in Jamshedpur, India, Durrell spent part of his childhood in Corfu, where he set up his own childhood zoo of scorpions, lizards, and eagle owls.

Durrell Lawrence George (1912–1990). English novelist and poet. Born in India, he joined the foreign service and lived mainly in the E Mediterranean, the setting of his novels, including the Alexandria Quartet: *Justine, Balthazar, Mountolive*, and *Clea* 1957–60; he also wrote travel books. His heady prose and bizarre characters reflect his exotic sources of inspiration. He was the brother of the naturalist Gerald Durrell.

The content of physics is the concern of physicists, its effect the concern of all men.

FRIEDRICH DÜRRENMATT
The Physicists 1962

Dürrenmatt Friedrich (1921–1990). Swiss dramatist. He wrote grotesque and ironical tragicomedies, for example *The Visit* 1956 and *The Physicists* 1962. His fascination with the absurd and with black humour can also be seen in his novels, such as *Das Versprechen/ The Pledge* 1958.

Our disintegrating world is a subject for comedy rather than tragedy.

FRIEDRICH DÜRRENMATT
Theme of his essay *Threatreprobleme* 1955

Duse Eleonora (1858–1924). Italian actress. She was the mistress of the poet Gabriele D'Annunzio from 1897, as recorded in his novel *Il fuoco/ The Flame of Life.*

Dussek Jan Ladislav (1760–1812). Bohemian (Czech) composer and pianist. A virtuoso pianist, his compositions, which include 28 piano sonatas and 15 piano concertos, often display technically challenging passages, by the standard of his day. Composing more fully textured (and often more harmonically adventurous) music than most of his contemporaries, Dussek foreshadowed many of the musical developments of the 19th century. He was one of a group of composers known as the London Pianoforte School.

Dutilleux Henri (1916–). French composer. He wrote instrumental music in elegant Neo-Romantic style. His works include *Métaboles* 1962–65 for orchestra and *Ainsi la nuit/ Thus the Night* 1975–76 for string quartet.

Du Toit Alexander Logie (1878–1948). South African geologist whose work was to form one of the foundations for the synthesis of continental drift theory and plate tectonics that created the geological revolution of the 1960s.

The theory of continental drift put forward by German geophysicist Alfred Wegener inspired Du Toit's book *A Geological Comparison of South America and South Africa* 1927, in which he suggested that they had probably once been joined. In *Our Wandering Continents* 1937, he maintained that the southern continents had, in earlier times, formed the supercontinent of Gondwanaland, which was distinct from the northern supercontinent of Laurasia.

Here lies Du Vall: Reader, if male thou art, / Look to thy purse, if female, to thy heart.

Epitaph on CLAUDE DUVAL's tomb in Covent Garden church

Duval Claude (1643–1670). English criminal. He was born in Normandy and turned highwayman after coming to England at the Restoration.

He was known for his gallantry. Duval was hanged at Tyburn, London.

Duvalier François (1907–1971). Right-wing president of Haiti 1957–71. Known as Papa Doc, he ruled as a dictator, organizing the Tontons Macoutes ('bogeymen') as a private security force to intimidate and assassinate opponents of his regime. He rigged the 1961 elections to have his term of office extended until 1967, and in 1964 declared himself president for life. He was excommunicated by the Vatican for harassing the church, and was succeeded on his death by his son Jean-Claude Duvalier.

Duvalier Jean-Claude (1951–). Right-wing president of Haiti 1971–86. Known as Baby Doc, he succeeded his father François Duvalier, becoming, at the age of 19, the youngest president in the world. He continued to receive support from the USA but was pressured into moderating some elements of his father's regime, yet still tolerated no opposition. In 1986, with Haiti's economy stagnating and with increasing civil disorder, Duvalier fled to France, taking much of the Haitian treasury with him.

Duve Christian René de (1917–). British-born Belgian biochemist who discovered two organelles, the lysosome and the peroxisome. For this contribution to cell biology he shared the 1974 Nobel Prize for Physiology or Medicine.

De Duve was born in Thames Ditton, Surrey, and educated at the University of Louvain, Belgium. He then held positions at the Nobel Institute, Stockholm, Sweden, and Washington University, St Louis, USA, before returning to Belgium 1947. From 1951 he was professor of biochemistry at Louvain, and from 1962 also at the Rockefeller Institute, New York.

Duvivier Julien Henri Nicolas (1896–1967). French film director. His work includes *La Belle Equipe* 1936, *Un Carnet de bal* 1937, *La Fin du jour* 1938, as well as several Hollywood films including *Tales of Manhattan* 1942.

Duwez Pol (1907–). US scientist, born in Belgium, who in 1959 developed metallic glasses (alloys rapidly cooled from the melt, which combine properties of glass and metal) with his team at the California Institute of Technology.

Dvořák Antonín Leopold (1841–1904). Czech composer. International recognition came with two sets of *Slavonic Dances*

1878 and 1886. He was director of the National Conservatory, New York, 1892–95. Works such as his *New World Symphony* 1893 reflect his interest in American folk themes, including black and native American. He wrote nine symphonies; tone poems; operas, including *Rusalka* 1900; large-scale choral works; the *Carnival* 1891–92 and other overtures; violin and cello concertos; chamber music; piano pieces; and songs. His Romantic music extends the Classical tradition of Beethoven and Brahms and displays the influence of Czech folk music.

Why on earth didn't I know that one could write a violincello concerto like this? If I had only known, I would have written one long ago.

Johannes Brahms on DVOŘÁK
quoted in Alec Robertson, *Dvořák* 1964

Suggested reading
Butterworth, Neil *Dvořák: His Life and Times* (1980)
Clapham, John *Antonín Dvořák* (1966)
Hughes, Gervase *Dvořák: His Life and Work* (1967)
Schonzeler, H H *Dvořák* (1984)
Young, Percy *Dvořák* (1970)

Dworkin Andrea (1946–). US feminist writer. Arguing that pornography is a form of sexual discrimination, she has worked with the lawyer Catharine MacKinnon (1946–) to draft legislation outlawing pornography. They published *Pornography and Civil Rights: A New Day for Women's Equality* 1988.

Woman Hating 1974 is a history of the ways in which women have been subjugated by men, such as by foot-binding in China and witch-hunting. She edited the anthology *Take Back the Night: Women on Pornography* 1982. In *Right Wing Women* 1983 she discussed the reasons why women join the Republican Party. Her novels include the semi-autobiographical *Mercy* 1990.

Dworkin Ronald (1931–). US jurist. A leading exponent of liberalism, he has consistently challenged the positivist notion of law – that a legal system is the sum of its rules – by stressing the importance of moral principles or rights in assessing particular cases. His publications include *Taking Rights Seriously* 1977 and *Life's Dominion* 1993, a discussion of euthanasia and abortion in which he argues against the belief in fetal rights and in favour of the right to terminate a pregnancy when necessary.

He is professor of jurisprudence at Oxford University and professor of law at New York University.

Van Dyck ... turned the crudest model into an aristocratic image.

Erik Larsen on ANTHONY VAN DYCK
in *The Paintings of Anthony Van Dyck* 1988

Dyck Anthony van (1599–1641). Flemish painter. Born in Antwerp, van Dyck was an assistant to Rubens 1618–20, then briefly worked in England at the court of James I, and moved to Italy 1622. In 1626 he returned to Antwerp, where he continued to paint religious works and portraits. From 1632 he lived in England and produced numerous portraits of royalty and aristocrats, such as *Charles I on Horseback* about 1638 (National Gallery, London). Knighted 1632.

Suggested reading
Brown, Christopher *Van Dyck* (1982)
Piper, David *Van Dyck* (1968)
Strong, Roy *Van Dyck* (1972)
Waterhouse, Ellis *Painting in Britain 1530–1790* (1978)

Dylan Bob. Adopted name of Robert Allen Zimmerman (1941–). US singer and songwriter. His lyrics provided catchphrases for a generation and influenced innumerable songwriters. He began in the folk-music tradition. His early songs, as on his albums *The Freewheelin' Bob Dylan* 1963 and *The Times They Are A-Changin'* 1964, were associated with the US civil-rights move-

Dvořák *The composer Antonín Dvořák (1841–1904) in a portrait with his wife. Dvořák successfully blends the two most important factors influencing music in the 19th century: Romanticism, as expressed formally by composers such as Brahms, and Nationalism, as embodied in the growing prominence of regional folk song. (Image Select)*

ment and antiwar protest. From 1965 he worked in an individualistic rock style, as on the albums *Highway 61 Revisited* 1965 and *Blonde on Blonde* 1966.

Dylan's early songs range from the simple, preachy 'Blowin' in the Wind' 1962 to brooding indictments of social injustice like 'The Ballad of Hollis Brown' 1963. When he first used an electric rock band 1965, he was criticized by purists, but the albums that immediately followed are often cited as his best work, with songs of spite ('Like a Rolling Stone') and surrealistic imagery ('Visions of Johanna') delivered in his characteristic nasal whine. The film *Don't Look Back* 1967 documents the 1965 British tour. Of Dylan's 1970s albums, *Blood on the Tracks* 1975 was the strongest.

Slow Train Coming 1979 was his first album as a born-again Christian, a phase that lasted several years and alienated all but the die-hard fans. *Oh, Mercy* 1989 was seen as a partial return to form, but *Under the Red Sky* 1990 did not bear this out. However, *The Bootleg Years* 1991, a collection of 58 previously unreleased items from past years, reasserted his standing. In 1992 he released *Good As I Been to You*, which consisted of traditional tunes and was his first completely solo acoustic album since *Another Side of Bob Dylan* 1964.

How many roads must a man walk down / Before you can call him a man? ... / The answer, my friend, is blowin' in the wind, / The answer is blowin' in the wind.

BOB DYLAN
'Blowin' in the Wind' 1962

Suggested reading
Dylan, Bob *Bob Dylan, Self-Portrait* (1970)
Rinzler, Alan *Bob Dylan* (1978)
Shelton, Robert *No Direction Home* (1986)
Shepard, Sam *Rolling Thunder Logbook* (1977)
Spitz, Bob *Dylan* (1988)

Dyson Frank Watson (1868–1939). English astronomer especially interested in stellar motion and time determination. He initiated the public broadcasting of time signals by the British Broadcasting Corporation over the radio 1924.

Dyson was born in Ashby-de-la-Zouch, Leicestershire, and studied at Cambridge. He was Astronomer Royal for Scotland 1906–10 and for England 1910–33. Dyson was one of a number of astronomers who confirmed the observations of Jacobus Kapteyn on the proper motions of stars, which indicated that the stars in our Galaxy seemed to be moving in two great streams. These results were later realized to be the first evidence for the rotation of our Galaxy. Dyson organized several expeditions to study total eclipses of the Sun. Other areas to which he made important contributions include the study of the Sun's corona and of stellar parallaxes. Knighted 1915.

E

Eagleburger Lawrence S(idney) (1930–). US Republican government official. He spent his career in the foreign service and the State Department and briefly acted as secretary of state in 1992, having been deputy from 1989.

Eagleburger entered the foreign service 1957. He became assistant to the national security adviser Henry Kissinger 1968 and an executive assistant to Kissinger when the latter became secretary of state 1973. Having been ambassador to Yugoslavia 1977–81, Eagleburger became assistant secretary for European affairs in the State Department 1981, and undersecretary for political affairs 1982–84. He supported President Reagan's funding of the Contra rebels fighting to overthrow the government of Nicaragua. From 1984 to 1989 he worked for Kissinger Associates.

Eagling Wayne John (1950–). Canadian dancer. He joined the Royal Ballet in London 1969, becoming a soloist 1972 and a principal dancer 1975. He appeared in *Gloria* 1980 and other productions. In Sept 1991 he became artistic director of the Dutch National Ballet.

Eaker Ira Clarence (1898–1971). US air force general of World War II. He commanded the US 8th Air Force Bomber Command, based in the UK from the end of 1942, and drew up plans for the Allied Combined Bomber Offensive, prioritizing targets for both the USAAF and RAF. He commanded the air support for Operation Dragoon, the landings in S France 1944, and then moved his force over to French airfields to give support to the Allied armies.

A strong believer in precision daylight bombing, he was initially over-optimistic about the ability of his bomber force to penetrate Germany in daylight and was forced to modify his tactics in the face of the German defences.

Eakins Thomas (1844–1916). US painter. A trained observer of human anatomy and a devotee of photography, Eakins attempted to achieve a powerful visual Realism. His most memorable subjects are medical and sporting scenes, characterized by strong contrasts between light and shade, as in *The Gross Clinic* 1875 (Jefferson Medical College, Philadelphia), a group portrait of a surgeon, his assistants, and students.

Born in Philadelphia, Eakins attended the Pennsylvania Academy of the Fine Arts and the Ecole des Beaux-Arts in Paris, later becoming an instructor at the Pennsylvania Academy. He studied with the French academic painter Jean-Léon Gérôme (1824–1904) in Paris in the 1860s and on a European tour drew inspiration from Rembrandt, Velázquez, and Ribera. He was dismissed from his post at the Pennsylvania Academy for removing the loincloth from a nude model. In his later years he painted distinguished portraits. His most memorable subjects were medical and sporting scenes. Among his larger-than-life-size sculptures commissioned for public monuments are the war memorials in Trenton, New Jersey, and Brooklyn, New York.

Suggested reading
Goodrick, L *Thomas Eakins* (1961)
Hendricks, G *The Life and Works of Thomas Eakins* (1974)
Porter, F *Thomas Eakins* (1959)
Schendler, S *Eakins* (1967)

Eames Charles (1907–1978) and Ray (born Kaiser) (1916–1988). US designers. A husband-and-wife team, they worked together in California 1941–78. They created some of the most highly acclaimed furniture designs of the 20th century: a moulded plywood chair 1945–46; the Lounge Chair, a black leather-upholstered chair 1956; and a fibreglass armchair 1950–53.

Eanes António dos Santos Ramalho (1935–). Portuguese politician. He helped plan the 1974 coup that ended the Caetano regime, and as army Chief of Staff put down a left-wing revolt Nov 1975. He was president 1976–86.

Failure must be but a challenge to others.

AMELIA EARHART
Last Flight 1937

Earhart Amelia (1898–1937). US aviation pioneer and author. Born in Atchison, Kansas, Earhart worked as an army nurse and social worker, before discovering that her true calling lay in aviation. In 1928 she became the first woman to fly across the Atlantic as a passenger and in 1932 completed a solo transatlantic flight. During a flight over the Pacific 1937, her plane disappeared without trace, although clues found 1989 on Nikumaroro island, SE of Kiribati's main island group, suggest that she and her copilot might have survived a crash only to die of thirst.

Suggested reading
Brennan, T C and Rosenblum, R *Witness to the Execution: The Odyssey of Amelia Earhart* (1989)
Devine, Thomas and Daley, Richard *Eyewitness: The Amelia Earhart Incident* (1987)
Lovell, Mary S *The Sound of Wings: The Biography of Amelia Earhart* (1989)
Rich, Doris *Amelia Earhart* (1989)

Early Jubal Anderson (1816–1894). American Confederate military leader. Although long a supporter of the Union, he joined the Confederate army at the outbreak of the American Civil War 1861. After the Battle of Bull Run 1862 he was made general in the Army of Northern Virginia, leading campaigns in the Shenandoah Valley 1862 and threatening Washington DC 1864.

Born in Franklin County, Virginia, Early graduated from West Point military academy 1837. After studying law, he was admitted to the bar 1840 and later served in the Virginia legislature. After a brief period of exile following the end of the Civil War, he resumed his Virginia law practice.

Earp Wyatt Berry Stapp (1848–1929). US frontier law officer. With his brothers Virgil and Morgan, Doc Holliday, and the legendary Bat Masterson he was involved in the famous gunfight at the OK Corral in Tombstone, Arizona, on 26 Oct 1881. Famous as a scout and buffalo hunter, he also gained a reputation as a gambler and brawler. After leaving Tombstone 1882, he travelled before settling in Los Angeles.

Born in Monmouth, Illinois, USA, Earp moved with his family to Iowa, finally settling in California 1864. He moved to Wichita, Kansas, 1874, where he was occasionally employed by the US marshal and was appointed assistant marshal in Dodge City, Kansas 1876. *See illustration on page 264.*

My work is done. Why wait?

GEORGE EASTMAN
Suicide note

Eastman George (1854–1932). US entrepreneur and inventor who founded the Eastman Kodak photographic company 1892. He patented flexible film 1884, invented the Kodak box camera 1888, and introduced daylight-loading film 1892. By 1900 his company was selling a pocket camera for as little as one dollar.

Earp *Wyatt Earp (second from left, front row) was one of several 19th-century law officers of the American West who were turned into folk heroes by journalists and then filmmakers. Earp was best known for the gunfight at the OK Corral in Tombstone, Arizona.*

The films first worked with chemicals fixed to a paper base 1884 and later on celluloid 1889. In 1928 he perfected a film process for color photography and development, an important service offered on fine papers. He was known for his contributions to education and music.

Eastwood Alice (1859–1953). US botanist who provided critical specimens for professional botanists as well as advising travellers on methods of plant collecting and arousing popular support for saving native species.

Eastwood studied plants in the Colorado Mountains while working as a schoolteacher. In 1892, she went to the California Academy of Sciences, San Francisco, where she became curator of the herbarium and founded and ran the California Botanical Club. After the San Francisco earthquake of 1906, she spent years rebuilding the collections, involving field trips to the coastal ranges and the Sierra Nevada and visits to botanical gardens around the world. Between 1912 and her retirement 1949, over 340,000 specimens were added to the herbarium.

Eastwood's early fieldwork led to the publication of *A Handbook of the Trees of California* 1905.

Eastwood Clint(on) (1930–). US film actor and director. As the 'Man with No Name' in *A Fistful of Dollars* 1964 and *The Good, the Bad, and the Ugly* 1966, he started the vogue for 'spaghetti westerns' (made in Italy or Spain). Later westerns which he both starred in and directed include *High Plains Drifter* 1973, *The Outlaw Josey Wales* 1976, and *Unforgiven* 1992 (two Academy Awards). Other films include *In The Line of Fire* 1993 and *The Bridges of Madison County* 1995.

Eastwood starred in the TV series *Rawhide* and in the 'Dirty Harry' series of films, and directed *Bird* 1988. He was elected mayor of Carmel, California, 1986.

Eastwood Eric (1910–1981). British electronics engineer who made major contributions to the development of radar for both military and civilian purposes.

Eastwood studied at Manchester University and Cambridge before entering the Signals branch of the Royal Air Force during World War II, and becoming involved with the solution of technical problems concerning radar. He worked at the Marconi Research

Laboratory 1948–62 and ended his career as director of research for General Electric.

At Marconi, Eastwood concentrated on telecommunications, radar, and applied physics. With the aid of the Marconi experimental station at Bushy Hill, Essex, he applied radar methods to the study of various meteorological phenomena (such as the aurorae) and carried out extensive investigations into the flight behaviour of birds and migration; his book *Radar Ornithology* was published 1967.

History teaches us that men and nations behave wisely once they have exhausted other alternatives.

ABBA EBAN
Speech 16 Dec 1970

Eban Abba (born Aubrey Solomon) (1915–). South-African-born Israeli diplomat and politician, ambassador in Washington 1950–59 and foreign minister 1966–74.

Eban was born in Cape Town, South Africa, and educated in England; he taught at Cambridge University before serving at Allied HQ during World War II. He subsequently settled in Israel.

Ebbinghaus Hermann (1850–1909). German experimental psychologist. Influenced by Gustav Fechner's *Elements of Psychophysics* 1860, he applied quantitative principles to the study of higher mental processes, in particular to human memory.

Ebbinghaus invented nonsensical syllables, consonant-vowel-consonant letter groups that he believed (wrongly) had no meaning and would therefore all be equally difficult to memorize. Using himself as subject, he used this material to investigate learning and forgetting, publishing the results in his *Memory* 1885. It was the first research to attempt, experimentally, to isolate the principal factors that generate learning curves. Although of great influence, Ebbinghaus's methods were later extensively criticized, notably by Frederic Charles Bartlett.

Eccles John Carew (1903–). Australian physiologist who shared (with Alan Hodgkin and Andrew Huxley) the 1963 Nobel Prize for Physiology or Medicine for work on conduction in the central nervous system. In some of his later works, he argued that the mind has an existence independent of the brain.

Echegaray José (1832–1916). Spanish dramatist. His social dramas include *O locura o santidad/Madman or Saint* 1877, and *El gran Galeoto/The World and his Wife* 1881. Nobel prize 1904.

Eckert John Presper (1919–1995). US electronics engineer and mathematician. During World War II he worked on radar ranging systems and then turned to the design of calculating devices, building the Electronic Numerical Integrator and Calculator (ENIAC) with Mauchly. The Eckert–Mauchly Computer Corporation, formed 1947, was incorporated in Remington Rand 1950 and subsequently came under the control of the Sperry Rand Corporation. The ENIAC weighed many tonnes and lacked a memory, but could store a limited amount of information and perform mathematical functions. It was used for calculating ballistic firing tables and for meteorological and research problems.

ENIAC was superseded by BINAC, also designed in part by Eckert, and in the early 1950s, Eckert's group began to produce computers for the commercial market with the construction of the UNIVAC 1. Its chief advance was the capacity to store programs.

Eckhart Johannes, called Meister Eckhart (c. 1260–c. 1327). German theologian and leader of a popular mystical movement. In 1326 he was accused of heresy, and in 1329 a number of his doctrines were condemned by the pope as heretical. His theology stressed the absolute transcendence of God, and the internal spiritual development through which union with the divine could be attained.

Eckhart was born near Gotha. He became a Dominican friar, and was provincial of the order for Saxony 1304–11. He taught theology in Paris, Strasbourg, and Cologne.

Eckstine Billy (William Clarence, originally Eckstein) (1913–1993). US jazz singer, bandleader, and trumpeter whose mid-1940s orchestra included bebop greats Dizzy Gillespie and Charlie Parker, and singer Sarah Vaughan. He had several top-ten hits, including 'I Apologize' 1950 and 'Passing Strangers' 1957 (a duet with Vaughan).

With his deep baritone vibrato and liking for ballads, he began as a night-club singer and was always equally at home with pop and jazz. As vocalist 1939–43 in the orchestra led by pianist Earl Hines, Eckstine learned to play trumpet and trombone, and had his first hit in 1940 with 'Jelly, Jelly'. The big band he led 1944–47 became legendary for the number of outstanding jazz musicians it employed (the teenage Miles Davis and the drummer Art Blakey among them) and for its bebop innovation, but was not a commercial success. Returning for a solo career, he became the most popular vocalist in the USA, with hits like 'Blue Moon' 1948 and 'Caravan' 1949. In the late 1950s he disappeared from the charts and returned to night clubs.

Eco Umberto (1932–). Italian writer, semiologist, and literary critic. His works include *The Role of the Reader* 1979, the 'philosophical thriller' *The Name of the Rose* 1983, and *Foucault's Pendulum* 1988.

Edberg Stefan (1966–). Swedish tennis player. He won the junior Grand Slam 1983 and his first Grand Slam title, the Australian Open, 1985, repeated 1987. Other Grand Slam singles titles include Wimbledon 1988, 1990 and the US Open 1991 and 1992.

At Wimbledon in 1987 he became the first male player in 40 years to win a match without conceding a game.

Eddery Pat(rick) James John (1952–). Irish-born flat-racing jockey who has won the jockey's championship eight times, including four in succession.

He has won all the major races, including the Epsom Derby twice. He won the Prix de L'Arc de Triomphe four times, including three in succession 1985–87.

Eddington Arthur Stanley (1882–1944). British astrophysicist who studied the motions, equilibrium, luminosity, and atomic structure of the stars. In 1913, Eddington went to Cambridge as professor, and was director of the university's observatory from 1914. In 1919 his observation of stars during a solar eclipse confirmed Albert Einstein's prediction that light is bent when passing near the Sun, in accordance with the general theory of relativity. In *The Expanding Universe* 1933 Eddington expressed the theory that in the spherical universe the outer galaxies or spiral nebulae are receding from one another.

Eddington discovered the fundamental role of radiation pressure in the maintenance of stellar equilibrium, explained the method by which the energy of a star moves from its interior to its exterior, and in 1924 showed that the luminosity of a star depends almost exclusively on its mass – a discovery that caused a complete revision of contemporary ideas on stellar evolution.

Suggested reading
Douglas, A V *Arthur Stanley Eddington* (1956)
Kilmister, C W *Sir Arthur Eddington* (1966)

Eddison Eric Rucker (1882–1945). British author of heroic fantasies, notably *The Worm Ouroboros* 1922.

Eddy Mary Baker (1821–1910). US founder of the Christian Science movement. Her pamphlet *Science of Man* 1869 was followed by *Science and Health with Key to the Scriptures* 1875, which systematically set forth the basis of Christian Science.

Her faith in divine healing was confirmed by her recovery from injuries caused by a fall, and she based a religious sect on this belief.

She was born in New Hampshire and brought up as a Congregationalist. She founded the Christian Science Association 1876. In 1879 the Church of Christ, Scientist, was established, and although living in retirement after 1892, she continued to direct the activities of the movement until her death.

Suggested reading
Beasley, N *The Cross and the Crown: The History of Christian Science* (1953)
Peel, Robert *Mary Baker Eddy: The Years of Discovery* (1966)
Peel, Robert *Mary Baker Eddy: The Years of Trial* (1971)
Peel, Robert *Mary Baker Eddy: The Years of Authority* (1977)

Edelman Gerald Maurice (1929–). US biochemist who worked out the sequence of 1,330 amino acids that makes up human immunoglobulin, a task completed 1969. For this work he shared the Nobel Prize for Physiology or Medicine 1972 with Rodney Porter.

Eden (Robert) Anthony, 1st Earl of Avon (1897–1977). British Conservative politician, foreign secretary 1935–38, 1940–45, and 1951–55; prime minister 1955–57, when he resigned after the failure of the Anglo-French military intervention in the Suez Crisis. KG 1954, earl 1961.

Upset by his prime minister's rejection of a peace plan secretly proposed by Roosevelt Jan 1938, Eden resigned as foreign secretary Feb 1938 in protest against Chamberlain's decision to open conversations with the Fascist dictator Mussolini. He was foreign secretary again in the wartime coalition, formed Dec 1940, and in the Conservative government, elected 1951. With the Soviets, he negotiated an interim peace in Vietnam 1954. In April 1955 he succeeded Churchill as prime minister. His use of force in the Suez Crisis led to his resignation Jan 1957, but he continued to maintain that his action was justified.

Suggested reading
Carlton, David *Anthony Eden: A Biography* (1981)
Eden, Anthony *The Eden Memoirs* (1960–65)
Rhodes James, Robert *Anthony Eden* (1986)

Edgar known as the Atheling ('of royal blood') (*c.* 1050–*c.* 1130). English prince, born in Hungary. Grandson of Edmund Ironside, he was supplanted as heir to Edward the Confessor by William the Conqueror. He led two rebellions against William 1068 and 1069, but made peace 1074.

Edgar David (1940–). English dramatist. After early work as a journalist, Edgar turned to documentary and political theatre. *Destiny*, about the extreme right wing in Britain, was produced by the Royal Shakespeare Company 1976. Other plays include *The Jail Diary of Albie Sachs* 1978; his adaptation from Dickens for the RSC, *The Life and Adventures of Nicholas Nickleby* 1980; *The Shape of the Table* 1990, on the collapse of the Eastern bloc in Europe; and *Pentecost* 1994.

It is a sign of his competence as a ruler that his reign is singularly devoid of recorded incident.

F A Stenton on EDGAR THE PEACEFUL
in *Anglo-Saxon England* 1943

Edgar the Peaceful (944–975). King of all England from 959. He was the younger son of Edmund I, and strove successfully to unite English and Danes as fellow subjects.

Some people talk of morality, and some of religion, but give me a little snug property.

MARIA EDGEWORTH
The Absentee 1812

Edgeworth Maria (1767–1849). Irish novelist. Her first novel, *Castle Rackrent* 1800, dealt with Anglo-Irish country society and was followed by the similar *The Absentee* 1812 and *Ormond* 1817. As a writer of socially concerned and historical novels, she influenced Walter Scott. She was a fervent proponent of women's education and has been re-evaluated by 20th-century feminists.

Edinburgh, Duke of title of Prince ◊Philip of the UK.

Edinger Tilly (Johanna Gabrielle Ottilie) (1897–1967). German-born US palaeontologist whose work in vertebrate palaeontology laid the foundations for the study of palaeoneurology. She demonstrated that the evolution of the brain could be studied directly from fossil cranial casts.

Edinger was born in Frankfurt and studied there and at Heidelberg and Munich. With the Nazis's rise to power, she was forced to leave Germany. After a year in the UK, she went to Cambridge, Massachusetts, in 1940, to take up a job at the Museum of Comparative Zoology at Harvard. Her research shed new light on the evolution of the brain and showed that the progression of brain structure does not proceed at a constant rate in a given family but varies over time; also that the enlarged forebrain evolved several times independently among advanced groups of mammals and there was no single evolutionary scale. Edinger's main works are *Die fossilen Gehirne/Fossil Brains* 1929 and *The Evolution of the Horse Brain* 1948.

Genius is one per cent inspiration and ninety-nine per cent perspiration.

THOMAS EDISON
Life ch 24

Edison Thomas Alva (1847–1931). US scientist and inventor, with over 1,000 patents. In Menlo Park, New Jersey, 1876–87, he produced his most important inventions, including the electric light bulb 1879. He constructed a system of electric power distribution for consumers, the telephone transmitter, and the phonograph.

Edison's first invention was an automatic repeater for telegraphic messages. Later came the carbon transmitter (used as a microphone in the production of the Bell telephone), the electric filament lamp, a new type of storage battery, and the kinetoscopic camera, an early cine camera. He also anticipated the Fleming thermionic valve. He supported direct current (DC) transmission, but alternating current (AC) was eventually found to be more efficient and economical.

Edison *US scientist and inventor Thomas Edison at work in his laboratory on electric filament lamps. In 1889 he formed the Edison Light Company, which later became the General Electric Company.* (Image Select)

Edison was born in Milan, Ohio, and self-educated. As a 19-year-old telegraph operator, he took out his first patent, for an electric vote recorder. With the proceeds of an improved stock ticker (a machine that printed stock-market prices on continuous paper tape), he opened an industrial research laboratory in Newark, New Jersey, 1869, later moving to Menlo Park and then to West Orange. In 1889 he formed the Edison Light Company, which became the General Electric Company.

Suggested reading
Connot, R *Thomas A Edison* (1987)
Edison, Thomas (ed D Runes) *Diary and Sundry Observations* (1949)
Josephson, M *Edison: A Biography* (1959)
Millard, A *Edison and the Business of Invention* (1990)
Wachhorst, W *Thomas Alva Edison: An American Myth* (1981)

Edlén Bengt (1906–). Swedish astrophysicist who resolved the identification of certain lines in spectra of the solar corona that had misled scientists for the previous 70 years. Edlén was born in Östergötland and educated at Uppsala University, where he was on the staff 1928–44. He was professor of physics at Lund University 1944–73.

During the eclipse of 1869, astronomers recorded unexpected spectral lines in the Sun's corona that they ascribed to the presence of a new element which they called 'coronium'. Similar lines were later discovered to originate nearer the Earth; these were attributed to 'geocoronium'. In the early 1940s, Edlén showed that, if iron atoms are deprived of many of their electrons, they can produce spectral lines like those of 'coronium'. Similarly ionized atoms of nickel, calcium, and argon produced even more lines. It was determined that such high stages of ionization would require temperatures of about 1,000,000°C/1,800,000°F and when, in the 1950s, it was verified that such high temperatures did exist in the solar corona, it became accepted that 'coronium' did not exist. The lines thought to be caused by 'geocoronium' were found to be produced by atomic nitrogen emitting radiation in the Earth's upper atmosphere.

He had a reputation of the kind which made a king formidable in disaster.

F M Stenton on EDMUND (II) IRONSIDE
in *Anglo-Saxon England* 2nd ed 1947

Edmund (II) Ironside (*c.* 989–1016). King of England 1016, the son of Ethelred the Unready. He led the resistance to Canute's invasion 1015, and on Ethelred's death 1016 was chosen king by the citizens of London, whereas the Witan (the king's council) elected Canute. In the struggle for the throne, Edmund was defeated by Canute at Assandun (Ashington), Essex, and they divided the kingdom between them; when Edmund died the same year, Canute ruled the whole kingdom.

The early development of his cult suggests very strongly that a basis of fact underlay the legends of his martyrdom.

F M Stenton on ST EDMUND
Anglo-Saxon England 2nd ed 1947

Edmund, St (*c.* 840–870). King of East Anglia from 855. In 870 he was defeated and captured by the Danes at Hoxne, Suffolk, and martyred on refusing to renounce Christianity. He was canonized and his shrine at Bury St Edmunds became a place of pilgrimage.

Edric the Forester or Edric the Wild (lived mid-11th century). English chieftain on the Welsh border who revolted against William the Conqueror 1067, around what is today Herefordshire, burning Shrewsbury. He was subsequently reconciled with William, and fought with him against the Scots 1072. Later writings describe him as a legendary figure.

Edson J(ohn) T(homas) (1928–   ). English writer of Western novels. His books, numbering 129 by 1990 and with 25 million copies sold, have such titles as *The Fastest Gun in Texas* and feature a recurring hero, Rapido Clint.

Edward (full name Edward Antony Richard Louis) (1964–   ). Prince of the UK, third son of Queen Elizabeth II. He is seventh in line to the throne after Charles, Charles's two sons, Andrew, and Andrew's two daughters.

The flower of chivalry of all the world.

> Froissart on EDWARD
> in Michael Hicks *Who's Who in Late Medieval England* 1991

Edward (called the Black Prince) (1330–1376). Prince of Wales, eldest son of Edward III of England. The epithet (probably post-humous) may refer to his black armour. During the Hundred Years' War he fought at the Battle of Crécy 1346 and captured the French king at Poitiers 1356. He ruled Aquitaine 1360–71; during the revolt that eventually ousted him, he caused the massacre of Limoges 1370.

In 1367 he invaded Castile and restored to the throne the deposed king, Pedro the Cruel (1334–69).

Suggested reading
Barber, R *Edward Prince of Wales and Aquitaine* (1978)
Emerson, B *The Black Prince* (1976)

Edward eight kings of England or Great Britain:

The English Justinian.

> David Hume on EDWARD I
> in *History of England* 1761

Edward I (1239–1307). King of England from 1272, son of Henry III. Edward led the royal forces against Simon de Montfort in the Barons' War 1264–67, and was on a crusade when he succeeded to the throne. He established English rule over all Wales 1282–84, and secured recognition of his overlordship from the Scottish king, although the Scots (under Wallace and Bruce) fiercely resisted actual conquest. In his reign Parliament took its approximate modern form with the Model Parliament 1295. He was succeeded by his son Edward II.

Suggested reading
Harvey, J H *The Plantagenets* (1970)
Powicke, F *King Henry III and the Lord Edward* (1947)
Prestwich, M *Edward I* (1988)
Tout, T F *Edward the First* (1920)

The first king after the Norman Conquest who was not a man of business.

> William Stubbs on EDWARD II
> quoted in T F Tout *The Captivity and Death of Edward of Carnarvon* 1920

Edward II (1284–1327). King of England from 1307, son of Edward I. Born at Caernarvon Castle, he was created the first Prince of Wales 1301. His invasion of Scotland 1314 to suppress revolt resulted in defeat at Bannockburn. He was deposed 1327 by his wife Isabella (1292–1358), daughter of Philip IV of France, and her lover Roger de Mortimer, and murdered in Berkeley Castle, Gloucestershire. He was succeeded by his son Edward III.

Incompetent and frivolous, and entirely under the influence of his favourites, Edward I struggled throughout his reign with discontented barons.

Suggested reading
Bingham, C *The Life and Times of Edward II* (1973)
Fryde, Natalie *The Tyranny and Fall of Edward II, 1321–1326* (1979)
Harvey, J H *The Plantagenets* (1970)
Johnstone, Hilda *Edward of Carnarvon, 1284–1307* (1947)

Edward III (1312–1377). King of England from 1327, son of Edward II. He assumed the government 1330 from his mother, through whom in 1337 he laid claim to the French throne and thus began the Hundred Years' War. He was succeeded by his grandson Richard II.

Evil be to him who evil thinks.

> EDWARD III
> Alleged remark at the falling of the Countess of Salisbury's garter,
> presumably when the Order of the Garter was founded 1344

Edward began his reign by attempting to force his rule on Scotland, winning a victory at Halidon Hill 1333. During the first stage of the Hundred Years' War, English victories included the Battle of Crécy 1346 and the capture of Calais 1347. In 1360 Edward surrendered his claim to the French throne, but the war resumed 1369. During his last years his son John of Gaunt acted as head of government.

Suggested reading
Johnson, P *The Life and Times of Edward III* (1973)
Packe, Michael *Edward III: Seaman* (1984)
Vale, J *Edward III and Chivalry* (1983)

His achievements ... did not stem from consistent pursuit of coherent policy, but were rather piecemeal reactions to particular crises and circumstances.

> Michael Hicks on EDWARD IV
> in *Who's Who in Late Medieval England* 1991

Edward IV (1442–1483). King of England 1461–70 and from 1471. He was the son of Richard, Duke of York, and succeeded Henry VI in the Wars of the Roses, temporarily losing the throne to Henry when Edward fell out with his adviser Warwick, but regaining it at the Battle of Barnet 1471. He was succeeded by his son Edward V.

Edward was known as Earl of March until his accession. After his father's death he occupied London 1461, and was proclaimed king in place of Henry VI by a council of peers. His position was secured by the defeat of the Lancastrians at Towton 1461 and by the capture of Henry. He quarrelled, however, with Warwick, his strongest supporter, who in 1470–71 temporarily restored Henry, until Edward recovered the throne by his victories at Barnet and Tewkesbury.

Edward V (1470–1483). King of England 1483. Son of Edward IV, he was deposed three months after his accession in favour of his uncle (Richard III), and is traditionally believed to have been murdered (with his brother) in the Tower of London on Richard's orders.

Forced into the mould of a saviour and a genius, while being treated as a catspaw, he died in the process: probably because of it.

> H W Chapman on EDWARD VI
> in *The Last Tudor King* 1958

Edward VI (1537–1553). King of England from 1547, son of Henry VIII and Jane Seymour. The government was entrusted to his uncle the Duke of Somerset (who fell from power 1549), and then to the Earl of Warwick, later created Duke of Northumberland. He was succeeded by his sister, Mary I.

Jane Seymour was Henry VIII's third wife, and Edward was his only son. Edward became a staunch Protestant and during his reign the Reformation progressed. He died from tuberculosis.

Suggested reading
Chapman, H W *The Last Tudor King* (1958)
Jordan, W K *Edward VI* (1968–70)

Edward VII (1841–1910). King of Great Britain and Ireland from 1901. As Prince of Wales he was a prominent social figure, but his mother Queen Victoria considered him too frivolous to take part in political life. In 1860 he made the first tour of Canada and the USA ever undertaken by a British prince.

You can tell when you have crossed the frontier into Germany because of the badness of the coffee.

EDWARD VII
quoted in Lord Haldane *Autobiography* 1929

Edward was born at Buckingham Palace, the eldest son of Queen Victoria and Prince Albert. After his father's death 1861 he undertook many public duties, took a close interest in politics, and was on friendly terms with the party leaders. In 1863 he married Princess Alexandra of Denmark, and they had six children. He toured India 1875–76. He succeeded to the throne 1901 and was crowned 1902.

Although he overrated his political influence, he contributed to the Entente Cordiale 1904 with France and the Anglo-Russian agreement 1907.

Suggested reading
Hibbert, Christopher *The Royal Victorians* (1976)
Magnus, P *Edward VII* (1967)
Middlemas, K *The Life and Times of Edward VII* (1972)
Roby, Kinley *The King, the Press and the People* (1975)
St Aubyn, G *Edward VII, Prince and King* (1979)

The thing that impresses me most about America is the way parents obey their children.

EDWARD VIII
quoted in *Look* 5 Mar 1957

Edward VIII (1894–1972). King of Great Britain and Northern Ireland Jan–Dec 1936, when he renounced the throne to marry Wallis Warfield Simpson. He was created Duke of Windsor and was governor of the Bahamas 1940–45, subsequently settling in France.

Eldest son of George V, he received the title of Prince of Wales 1910 and succeeded to the throne 20 Jan 1936. In Nov 1936 a constitutional crisis arose when Edward wished to marry Mrs Simpson; it was felt that, as a divorcee, she would be unacceptable as queen. On 11 Dec Edward abdicated and left for France, where the couple were married 1937. He was succeeded by his brother, George VI.

Edward was extremely popular as prince of Wales, and he made fashion statements that changed the way men dressed throughout the 20th century in the Western world – soft collars, tweed sport jackets, cuffed trousers, low shoes, the Windsor knotted tie, and V-necked sweaters freed men from the starched look that characterized the turn of the century.

Suggested reading
Bloch, Michael *The Reign and Abdication of Edward VIII* (1990)
Donaldson, Frances *Edward VIII* (1974)
Duke of Windsor *A King's Story* (1951)
Sitwell, Osbert *Tar Week: An Essay on Abdication* (1984)
Warwick, C *Abdication* (1986)
Ziegler, Philip *Edward VIII: The Official Biography* (1990)

I have found it impossible to discharge my duties as King as I would wish to do without the help and support of the woman I love.

EDWARD VIII
Abdication speech, broadcast on radio 11 Dec 1936

Edward the Confessor (*c.* 1003–1066). King of England from 1042, the son of Ethelred II. He lived in Normandy until shortly before his accession. During his reign power was held by Earl Godwin and his son Harold, while the king devoted himself to religion, including the rebuilding of Westminster Abbey (consecrated 1065), where he is buried. His childlessness led ultimately to the Norman Conquest 1066. He was canonized 1161.

Suggested reading
Barlow, F *Edward the Confessor* (1970)
Fisher, D J V *The Anglo-Saxon Age, 400-1042* (1973)

His virtues would have adorned the cloister, his failings ill became a throne.

William Hunt on EDWARD THE CONFESSOR
in *Dictionary of National Biography*

Edward the Elder (*c.* 870–924). King of the West Saxons. He succeeded his father Alfred the Great 899. He reconquered SE England and the Midlands from the Danes, uniting Wessex and Mercia with the help of his sister, Athelflad.

By the time Edward died, his kingdom was the most powerful in the British Isles. He was succeeded by his son Athelstan.

The ablest strategist ever produced by the Anglo-Saxons.

Richard Fletcher on EDWARD THE ELDER
in *Who's Who in Roman Britain and Anglo-Saxon England* 1989

Edward the Martyr (*c.* 963–978). King of England from 975. Son of King Edgar, he was murdered at Corfe Castle, Dorset, probably at his stepmother Aelfthryth's instigation (she wished to secure the crown for her son, Ethelred). He was canonized 1001.

An unnattractive personality, given to outbursts of rage which struck terror into his household.

Richard Fletcher on EDWARD THE MARTYR
in *Who's Who in Roman Britain and Anglo-Saxon England* 1989

Edwards Blake. Adopted name of William Blake McEdwards (1922–). US film director and writer. He was formerly an actor. Specializing in comedies, he directed the series of *Pink Panther* films 1963–78, starring Peter Sellers. His other work includes *Breakfast at Tiffany's* 1961 and *Blind Date* 1986.

Edwards Gareth Owen (1947–). Welsh rugby union player. He was appointed captain of his country when only 20 years old.

He appeared in seven championship winning teams, five Triple Crown winning teams, and two Grand Slam winning teams. In 53 internationals he scored a Welsh record equalling 20 tries. He toured with the British Lions three times.

Edwards George Robert (1908–). British civil and military aircraft designer, associated with the Viking, Viscount, Valiant V-bomber, VC-10, and Concorde. Knighted 1957.

The bodies of those that made such a noise and tumult when alive, when dead, lie as quietly among the graves of their neighbours as any others.

JONATHAN EDWARDS
'Procrastination'

Edwards Jonathan (1703–1758). US theologian who took a Calvinist view of predestination and initiated a religious revival, the 'Great Awakening'. His *The Freedom of the Will* 1754 (defending determinism) received renewed attention in the 20th century.

Edwards Robert Geoffrey (1925–). British physiologist who with Patrick Steptoe devised a technique for fertilizing a human egg outside the body and transferring the fertilized embryo to the uterus of a woman. A child born following the use of this technique is popularly known as a 'test-tube baby'. Edwards's research has added to knowledge of the development of the human egg and young embryo.

Edwards was educated at the universities of Wales and Edinburgh. He has held academic positions in Scotland and California, and was at the National Institute of Medical Research,

London, 1958–62. In 1963 he moved to the Department of Physiology at Cambridge.

In the 1950s Edwards successfully replanted mouse embryos into the uterus of a mouse and he wondered if the same process could be applied to humans. In 1965 he first attempted the *in vitro* fertilization of human eggs, not succeeding until 1967. Steptoe had just invented a new technique, laparoscopy, to view the internal organs. Edwards and Steptoe met 1968 and arranged to collaborate.

Steptoe treated volunteer patients with a fertility drug to stimulate maturation of the eggs in the ovary, while Edwards devised a simple piece of apparatus to be used with the laparoscope for collecting mature eggs from human ovaries. He then prepared them for fertilization. In 1971, once they were sure that the fertilized eggs were developing normally, Edwards and Steptoe were ready to introduce an eight-celled embryo into the uterus of a volunteer patient, but their attempts were unsuccessful until 1977, when they abandoned the use of the fertility drug.

Under King Edwin's jurisdiction ... a woman could carry her newborn babe across the island from sea to sea without any fear or harm.

Bede on EDWIN
in *Ecclesiastical History of the English People*

Edwin (*c.* 585–633). King of Northumbria from 617. He captured and fortified Edinburgh, which was named after him, and was killed in battle with Penda of Mercia 632.

He had for the first time united all the English race under one overlordship, and ... his work was never wholly undone.

William Hunt on EGBERT
in *Dictionary of National Biography*

Egbert (died 839). King of the West Saxons from 802, the son of Ealhmund, an under-king of Kent. By 829 he had united England for the first time under one king.

Egerton family name of dukes of Sutherland, seated at Mertoun, Roxburghshire, Scotland.

Eggen Olin Jenck (1919–). US astronomer whose work has included studies of high-velocity stars, red giants (using narrow- and broadband photometry), and subluminous stars.

Born in Orfordville, Wisconsin, Eggen graduated from Wisconsin University. He has spent much of his working life in senior appointments all round the world; he was director of Mount Stromlo and Siding Spring observatories, Australia, 1966–77, when he moved to the Observatory Interamericano de Cerro Tololo, Chile.

During the mid-1970s, Eggen completed a study – based on ultraviolet photometry and every available apparent motion – of all red giants brighter than apparent magnitude 5. As a result he was able to classify these stars, categorizing them as very young discs, young discs, and old discs. A few remained unclassifiable (haloes). He also systematically investigated the efficiency of the method of stellar parallax using visual binaries originally suggested by William Herschel in 1781, and reviewed the original correspondence of English astronomers John Flamsteed and Edmond Halley.

Eggleston William (1937–). US photographer. His banal scenes of life in the deep south are transformed by his use of the dye transfer technique into intense, superreal images of richly saturated colour. In 1984 he documented Graceland, Elvis Presley's home.

Egmont Lamoral, Graaf von (1522–1568). Flemish nobleman, born in Hainault. As a servant of the Spanish crown, he defeated the French first at St Quentin 1557 and then at Gravelines 1558, and became stadholder (chief magistrate) of Flanders and Artois. From 1561 he opposed Philip II's religious policy in the Netherlands of persecuting Protestants, but in 1567 the duke of Alva was sent to

crush the resistance, and Egmont was beheaded. Succeeded as count 1541.

Egoyan Atom (1960–). Canadian filmmaker. *Family Viewing* 1987 won many prizes, and *Exotica* 1994 won the International Critics' Prize at the Cannes Film Festival. His films explore isolation and obsession.

Egoyan was born in Cairo, Egypt, to Armenian refugees who emigrated to British Columbia when he was three years old. His first feature film was *Next of Kin* 1984. Other films include *Speaking Parts* 1989, *The Adjuster* 1991, and *Calendar* 1992, which is set in Armenia.

Ehrenburg Ilya Grigorievich (1891–1967). Soviet writer, born in Kiev, Ukraine. His controversial work *The Thaw* 1954 depicted artistic circles in the USSR and contributed to the growing literary freedom of the 1950s.

Ehrenfels (Maria) Christian (Julius Leopold Karl) von (1859–1933). Austrian philosopher and psychologist. In his paper *Über Gestalt Qualitäten/On Gestalt Qualities* 1891, he introduced the notion of gestalt to explain observations of wholeness and object-constancy in perception.

For example, a circle is still seen as a circle even after its size or colour has changed. A whole that retains its specific character when changes occur that affect all its parts he termed a *Gestalt* and its special property a *Gestalt quality*. His ideas were important in the early history of Gestalt psychology.

Ehrlich Paul (1854–1915). German bacteriologist and immunologist who produced the first cure for syphilis. He developed the arsenic compounds, in particular Salvarsan, that were used in the treatment of syphilis before the discovery of antibiotics. He shared the 1908 Nobel Prize for Physiology or Medicine with Ilya Mechnikov for his work on immunity.

Ehrlich founded chemotherapy – the use of a chemical substance to destroy disease organisms in the body. He was also one of the earliest workers on immunology, and through his studies on blood samples the discipline of haematology was recognized. In 1884 he became a professor in Berlin, but spent 1886–88 in Egypt, curing himself of tuberculosis contracted in the course of research. He set up a small private laboratory in Berlin 1889, in addition to his academic posts.

Eichelberger Robert L(awrence) (1886–1961). US general. He was commandant of West Point Military Academy when the USA entered the war and was sent to take command of US I Corps in the Pacific. He fought in New Guinea, defeating the Japanese at Buna Jan 1943, and then took command of the US 8th Army for the assault on the Philippines 1945.

Eichendorff Joseph Freiherr von (1788–1857). German Romantic poet and novelist. His work was set to music by Schumann, Mendelssohn, and Wolf. He held various judicial posts.

Eichhorn Hermann von (1848–1918). German field marshal. As a general on the Eastern Front in World War I he captured Kovno (now Kaunas) Aug 1915 and Vilna the following month, resulting in his promotion to field marshal. He was military commander of the Ukraine 1918, acting as virtual dictator. His oppressive regime made him unpopular with the local population and he was murdered by Ukrainian activists in Kiev Oct 1918.

Eichmann (Karl) Adolf (1906–1962). Austrian Nazi. As an SS official during Hitler's regime (1933–1945), he was responsible for atrocities against Jews and others, including the implementation of genocide. He managed to escape at the fall of Germany 1945, but was discovered in Argentina 1960, abducted by Israeli agents, tried in Israel 1961 for war crimes, and executed.

He was in charge of the Gestapo department controlling the Jewish population of all German-occupied territory. He organized the mass deportation of Jews from Germany and Bohemia to concentration camps in Poland 1941. He was given the task of organizing the Final Solution to the 'Jewish problem' at the Wannsee

Eichmann *The Austrian Nazi Adolf Eichmann. Eichmann, who was a Nazi official responsible for the deportation and killing of Jews in World War II, escaped at the end of the war, but was found, tried, and executed as a war criminal in the 1960s.* (Image Select)

Conference 1942 and set up extermination camps, specifying the design of the gas chambers and crematoria.

Eiffel (Alexandre) Gustave (1832–1923). French engineer who constructed the *Eiffel Tower* for the 1889 Paris Exhibition. The tower, made of iron, is 320 m/1,050 ft high and stands in the Champ de Mars, Paris. Sightseers may ride to the top for a view.

Eiffel set up his own business in Paris 1867 and quickly established his reputation with the construction of a series of ambitious railway bridges, of which the span across the Douro at Oporto, Portugal, was the longest at 160 m/525 ft. In 1881 he provided the iron skeleton for the Statue of Liberty. Originally, the Eiffel Tower was intended to be dismantled at the conclusion of the exhibition, but it was preserved as a radio transmitting station. For some time it was by far the highest artificial structure in the world.

Why should we disguise the industrial nature of iron, even in the city?

GUSTAVE EIFFEL
quoted in Randall J Van Vynckt (ed)
International Dictionary of Architects 1993

Eigen Manfred (1927–). German chemist who worked on extremely rapid chemical reactions (those taking less than 1 millisecond). From 1954 he developed a technique by which very short bursts of energy could be applied to solutions, disrupting their equilibrium and enabling him to investigate momentary reactions, such as the formation and dissociation of water. Nobel prize 1967. From 1953 he worked at the Max Planck Institute for Physical Chemistry in Göttingen, eventually becoming its director.

A theory has only the alternative of being right or wrong. A model has a third possibility: it may be right, but irrelevant.

MANFRED EIGEN
quoted in Jagdish Mehra (ed) *The Physicist's Conception of Nature* p 618 1973

Eijkman Christiaan (1858–1930). Dutch bacteriologist. He pioneered the recognition of vitamins as essential to health and identified vitamin B_1 deficiency as the cause of the disease beriberi. He shared the 1929 Nobel Prize for Physiology or Medicine with Frederick Gowland Hopkins.

Eilenberg Samuel (1913–). Polish-born US mathematician whose research in the field of algebraic topology led to considerable development in the theory of cohomology.

Eilenberg was born and educated in Warsaw. In the 1930s he emigrated to the USA. He was professor of mathematics at the University of Indiana 1946–49, and ended his career at Columbia University, New York.

Einem Rothmaier Karl von (1853–1934). German general. He was promoted to lieutenant-general and became Prussian minister of war 1903. He took command of an army corps 1910 and held various staff positions during World War I. He was given command of the 3rd German Army July 1918 and mounted the unsuccessful attack on the French near Reims.

Nationalism is an infantile sickness. It is the measles of the human race.

ALBERT EINSTEIN
quoted in H Dukas and B Hoffman *Albert Einstein, the Human Side* 1979

Einstein Albert (1879–1955). German-born US physicist who formulated the theories of relativity, and worked on radiation physics and thermodynamics. In 1905 he published the special

Einstein *German physicist Albert Enstein. He is best known for his theories of relativity which shed new light on the concepts of matter, space, and time.* (Image Select)

theory of relativity, and in 1915 issued his general theory of relativity. He received the Nobel Prize for Physics 1921. His last conception of the basic laws governing the universe was outlined in his unified field theory, made public 1953.

The theories of relativity revolutionized our understanding of matter, space, and time. Einstein also established that light may have a particle nature and deduced 1905 the photoelectric law that governs the production of electricity from light-sensitive metals. He investigated Brownian movement, also 1905, and was able to explain it so that it not only confirmed the existence of atoms but could be used to determine their dimensions. He also proposed the equivalence of mass and energy, which enabled physicists to deepen their understanding of the nature of the atom, and explained radioactivity and other nuclear processes.

Einstein was born in Ulm, Württemberg, and lived in Munich and Italy before settling in Switzerland. Disapproving of German militarism, he became a Swiss citizen and was appointed an inspector of patents in Berne. In his spare time, he took his PhD at Zürich. In 1909 he became a lecturer in theoretical physics at the university. After holding a similar post at Prague 1911, he returned to teach at Zürich 1912. In 1913 he took up a specially created post as director of the Kaiser Wilhelm Institute for Physics, Berlin. Confirmation of the general theory of relativity by the solar eclipse of 1919 made Einstein world famous. Deprived of his position at Berlin by the Nazis, he emigrated to the USA 1933 and became professor of mathematics and a permanent member of the Institute for Advanced Study at Princeton, New Jersey.

In 1939, Einstein drew the attention of the president of the USA to the possibility that Germany might be developing the atomic bomb. This prompted US efforts to produce the bomb, though Einstein did not take part in them. After World War II he was actively involved in the movement to abolish nuclear weapons. In 1952, the state of Israel paid him the highest honour it could by offering him the presidency, which he declined.

Suggested reading
Bernstein, Jeremy *Einstein* (1973)
Hoffmann, Banesh *Albert Einstein: Creator and Rebel* (1973)
Michelmore, Peter *Einstein: Profile of the Man* (1963)
Pais, Abraham *'Subtle is the Lord': The Life and Science of Albert Einstein* (1982)

Einthoven Willem (1860–1927). Dutch physiologist and inventor of the electrocardiogram. He demonstrated that certain disorders of the heart alter its electrical activity in characteristic ways. He was awarded the 1924 Nobel Prize for Physiology or Medicine.

Eisai or Yōsai (1141–1215). Japanese Buddhist monk who introduced Zen from China to Japan and founded the Rinzai school. He popularized the use of tea in Japan.

Eisai trained as a Tendai monk and visited China twice, receiving the Rinzai transmission on his second visit 1189–91. He also brought back tea seeds, but was not the first to do so. On his return, he founded in Kyushu the first Rinzai temple, and later the Kennin temple in Kyoto 1202.

His works include *Kōzen gokokuron/Propagation of Zen for the Protection of the Nation* 1198 and *Kissa yōjōki/Drink Tea and Prolong Life* 1214.

Eisenhart Luther Pfahler (1876–1965). US theoretical geometrist who formulated a unifying principle to the theory of the deformation of surfaces. In the 1920s he attempted to develop his own geometry theory from that of German mathematician Georg Riemann. His life's work in mathematical research was spent at Princeton University 1900–45.

Eisenhower Dwight David ('Ike') (1890–1969). 34th president of the USA 1953–60, a Republican. A general in World War II, he commanded the Allied forces in Italy 1943, then the Allied invasion of Europe, and from Oct 1944 all the Allied armies in the West. As president he promoted business interests at home and conducted the Cold War abroad. His vice president was Richard Nixon.

Eisenhower was born in Texas. A graduate of West Point military

Eisenhower *US soldier and politician Dwight D Eisenhower. After commanding Allied forces in Europe during World War II, he became the 34th president of the USA 1953.*

academy in 1915, he served in a variety of staff and command posts before World War II. He became commander in chief of the US and British forces for the invasion of North Africa Nov 1942; commanded the Allied invasion of Sicily July 1943; and announced the surrender of Italy 8 Sept 1943. In Dec he became commander of the Allied Expeditionary Force for the invasion of Europe and was promoted to General of the Army Dec 1944. After the war he served as commander of the US Occupation Forces in Germany, then returned to the USA to become Chief of Staff. He served as president of Columbia University and chair of the joint Chiefs of Staff between 1949 and 1950. He resigned from the army 1952 to campaign for the presidency; he was elected, and re-elected by a wide margin in 1956. A popular politician, Eisenhower held office during a period of domestic and international tension, with the growing civil-rights movement at home and the Cold War dominating international politics, although the USA was experiencing an era of postwar prosperity and growth.

Every gun that is made, every warship launched, every rocket fired signifies, in the final sense, a theft from those who hunger and are not fed, those who are cold and are not clothed.

DWIGHT EISENHOWER
Speech in Washington 16 Apr 1953

Suggested reading
Ambrose, Stephen E *Eisenhower* (1983)
Brendon, Piers *Ike* (1987)
Eisenhower, David *Eisenhower: At War, 1943–1945* (1986)
Kreig, J P *Dwight D Eisenhower: Soldier, President, Statesman* (1987)
Miller, M *Ike the Soldier* (1987)
Sixsmith, E K G *Eisenhower as Military Commander* (1973)

Eisenman Peter (1932–   ). US architect. He came to prominence as a member of the New York Five group, along with Richard Meier and Michael Graves. His work draws on mathematics and philosophy, especially Deconstructionism. Early experiments in complexity, such as House X 1978, led to increasingly scrambled designs, for example, Fin d'Ou T Hou S 1983.

A more recent commission, the Wexner Centre for the Visual Arts, Ohio, 1985–90, has enabled him to explore his interest in grids and the concept of 'non-building' in a large public project.

Eisenstein Sergei Mikhailovich (1898–1948). Latvian-born Soviet film director. He pioneered film theory and introduced the use of montage (the juxtaposition of shots to create a particular effect) as a means of propaganda, as in *The Battleship Potemkin* 1925.

The Soviet dictator Stalin banned the second (and last) part of Eisenstein's projected three-film epic *Ivan the Terrible* 1944–46. His other films include *Strike* 1925, *October* 1928, *Que Viva Mexico!* 1931–32, and *Alexander Nevsky* 1938.

Suggested reading
Barna, Yon *Eisenstein* (1973)
Eisenstein, Sergei *Film Form: Essays in Film Theory* (1949)
Eisenstein, Sergei *The Film Sense* (1942)
Eisenstein, Sergei *Immoral Memories: An Autobiography* (1983)
Eisenstein, Sergei *Collected Works, vol iv* memoirs (1942)
Leyda, J *Kino: A History of the Russian and Soviet Film* (1960)
Swallow, Norman *Eisenstein: A Documentary Portrait* (1976)

Eisner Thomas (1929–). German-born US entomologist and conservation activist. He is an authority on the role of chemicals in insect behaviour. A campaigner for the preservation of biodiversity, in order to prevent the extinction of species and the loss of potentially useful chemicals he advocates 'chemical prospecting', whereby drug companies buy the rights to extract chemically rich organic matter from forests, leaving the forests themselves intact.

Thomas was born in Berlin but moved to New York with his family in 1947. His early entomological work concentrated on the bombardier beetle. He became professor of biology at Cornell University, New York, 1976, and director of the Cornell Institute for Research in Chemical Ecology. Concerned at the environmental implications of the population explosion, he is a member of Zero Population Growth.

El Cid Spanish soldier. See ◊Cid, El.

Eldem Sedad Hakki (1908–). Turkish architect. His work is inspired by the spatial harmony and regular rhythms of the traditional Turkish house. These qualities are reinterpreted in modern forms with great sensitivity to context, as in the Social Security Agency Complex, Zeyrek, Istanbul, 1962–64 and the Ataturk Library, Istanbul, 1973.

Elder Mark Philip (1947–). English conductor. He was music director of the English National Opera (ENO) 1979–92 and of the Rochester Philharmonic Orchestra, USA, 1989.

Elder worked at Glyndebourne from 1970, conducted with the Australian Opera from 1972, and joined the ENO 1974. As principal conductor of the ENO, he specializes in 19th- and 20th-century repertoire.

Elders (Minnie) Joycelyn (born Jones) (1933–). US physician, surgeon general (head of the public health service) 1993–94. She was director of the Arkansas Department of Health 1987–93 and a member of Hillary Clinton's health-care task force 1993.

She was born in Schaal, Arkansas, graduated from the University of Arkansas Medical School 1960, and became a paediatric endocrinologist, working on children's growth patterns and hormone-related illnesses. At the Arkansas Department of Health she promoted sex education, contraception, and abortion rights. As surgeon general she called for higher taxes on alcohol and tobacco and, being the second woman and first black American to be appointed to the post, was under heavy scrutiny by the media, resigning Dec 1994.

Eldon John Scott, 1st Earl of Eldon (1751–1838). English politician, born in Newcastle. He became a member of Parliament 1782, solicitor-general 1788, attorney-general 1793, and Lord Chancellor 1801–05 and 1807–27. During his term the rules of the Lord Chancellor's court governing the use of the injunction and precedent in equity finally became fixed. Knighted 1788, baron 1799, earl 1821.

If I were to begin life again, d-n my eyes, but I would begin as an agitator.

JOHN SCOTT, 1ST EARL OF ELDON
quoted in Walter Bagehot *Biographical Studies: Lord Brougham* 1881

Eleanor of Aquitaine (*c.* 1122–1204). Queen of France 1137–51 as wife of Louis VII, and of England from 1154 as wife of Henry II. Henry imprisoned her 1174–89 for supporting their sons, the future Richard I and King John, in revolt against him.

She was the daughter of William X, Duke of Aquitaine, and was married 1137–52 to Louis VII of France, but the marriage was annulled. The same year she married Henry of Anjou, who became king of England 1154.

Suggested reading
Meade, Marion *Eleanor of Aquitaine: A Biography* (1977)
Pernoud, R *Eleanor of Aquitaine* (1967)
Seward, D *Eleanor of Aquitaine* (1986)

Eleanor of Castile (*c.* 1245–1290). Queen of Edward I of England, the daughter of Ferdinand III of Castile. She married Prince Edward 1254, and accompanied him on his crusade 1270. She died at Harby, Nottinghamshire, and Edward erected stone crosses in towns where her body rested on the funeral journey to London. Several Eleanor crosses are still standing, for example, at Northampton.

Elgar Edward William (1857–1934). English composer whose *Enigma Variations* 1899 brought him lasting fame. Although his celebrated oratorio *The Dream of Gerontius* 1900 (based on the written

Elgar *The composer Edward Elgar (1857–1934). His works, the greatest expressions of a romantic English composer, range from the dignified and publicly oriented* Pomp and Circumstance *marches and the First Symphony to the intimate and emotive* Dream of Gerontius *and the Cello Concerto.* (Image Select)

work by theologian John Henry Newman) was initially unpopular in Britain, it was well received at Düsseldorf 1902, leading to a surge of interest in his earlier works, including the *Pomp and Circumstance Marches* 1901.

Among his later works, which tend to be more introspective than the earlier ones, are oratorios, two symphonies, a violin concerto, chamber music, songs, and the symphonic poem *Falstaff* 1913, culminating in the poignant cello concerto of 1919. After this piece, Elgar published no further music of significance. He concentrated on transcriptions and made some early gramophone recordings of his own work. KCVO 1928, baronet 1931.

Suggested reading
De-la-Noy, Michael *Elgar the Man* (1983)
Kennedy, M *Portrait of Elgar* (1968)
McVeagh, D *Edward Elgar* (1955)
Moore, J N *Edward Elgar: A Creative Life* (1989)
Parrott, I *Elgar* (1971)

Eli in the Old Testament, a priest and childhood teacher of the first prophet, Samuel.

Eliade Mircea (1907–1986). Romanian philosopher and anthropologist of religion. He was a leading figure in the phenomenology of religion, bringing anthropological insights and data to bear on the phenomena of religion. His influence has been extensive and his studies of previously marginalized religious groups, such as the shamans, led to a re-evaluation of many aspects of religious practice and history.

Eliade was born in Bucharest and studied there and at the University of Calcutta, India. He moved to Paris, France, 1945, and worked in the USA from 1956 as professor at Chicago. His most significant books include *From Primitives to Zen: A Thematic Sourcebook of the History of Religion* and *Patterns in Comparative Religion* 1958. He was editor in chief of a 16-volume *Encyclopedia of Religion* published 1987.

Elijah (lived c. mid-9th century BC). In the Old Testament, a Hebrew prophet during the reigns of the Israelite kings Ahab and Ahaziah. He came from Gilead. He defeated the prophets of Baal, and was said to have been carried up to heaven in a fiery chariot in a whirlwind. In Jewish belief, Elijah will return to Earth to herald the coming of the Messiah.

Eliot Charles William (1834–1926). US educator credited with establishing the standards of modern American higher education. He was appointed professor at the Massachusetts Institute of Technology (MIT) 1865 and was named president of Harvard University 1869. Under Eliot's administration, the college and its graduate and professional schools were reorganized and the curriculum and admission requirements standardized. He retired 1909.

Eliot George. Pen name of Mary Ann Evans (1819–1880). English novelist. Her works include the pastoral *Adam Bede* 1859; *The Mill on the Floss* 1860, with its autobiographical elements; *Silas Marner* 1861, containing elements of the folktale; and *Daniel Deronda* 1876. *Middlemarch*, published serially 1871–72, is considered her greatest novel for its confident handling of numerous characters and central social and moral issues. Her work is pervaded by a penetrating and compassionate intelligence.

Born at Chilvers Coton, Warwickshire, George Eliot had a strict evangelical upbringing. In 1841 she was converted to free thought. As assistant editor of the *Westminster Review* under John Chapman 1851–53, she made the acquaintance of Thomas Carlyle, Harriet Martineau, Herbert Spencer, and the philosopher and critic George Henry Lewes (1817–1878). Lewes was married but separated from his wife, and from 1854 he and Eliot lived together in a relationship that she regarded as a true marriage and that continued until his death. In 1880 she married John Cross (1840–1924).

Suggested reading
Ashton, R *George Eliot* (1983)
Dodd, V A *George Eliot: An Intellectual Life* (1989)
Ermarth, E D *George Eliot* (1985)
Haight, G S *George Eliot: A Biography* (1968)

Taylor, I *George Eliot, Woman of Contradictions* (1989)
Uglow, J *George Eliot* (1987)

The greatest orator of his time ... sensitive, emotional, impetuous ... he was a bad tactician [and] temperamentally averse to compromise.

C P Hill on JOHN ELIOT
in *Who's Who in History* vol 3 1965

Eliot John (1592–1632). English politician, born in Cornwall. He became a member of Parliament 1614, and with the Earl of Buckingham's patronage was made a vice-admiral 1619. In 1626 he was imprisoned in the Tower of London for demanding Buckingham's impeachment. In 1628 he was a formidable supporter of the petition of right opposing Charles I, and with other parliamentary leaders was again imprisoned in the Tower of London 1629, where he died. Knighted 1618.

I will show you fear in a handful of dust.

T S ELIOT
The Waste Land 1922

Eliot T(homas) S(tearns) (1888–1965). US-born British poet, playwright, and critic. He lived in London from 1915. His first volume of poetry, *Prufrock and Other Observations* 1917, introduced new verse forms and rhythms; subsequent major poems were *The Waste Land* 1922 and 'The Hollow Men' 1925. For children he published *Old Possum's Book of Practical Cats* 1939. His plays include *Murder in the*

Eliot, T S Poet, critic, and dramatist T S Eliot, one of the major figures of 20th-century literature. Born in the USA, Eliot embraced British nationality, culture, and religious traditions. His early and most influential poems, Prufrock *1917* and The Waste Land *1922*, portrayed the disillusionment engendered by World War I in a radically modernist style.

Cathedral 1935 and *The Cocktail Party* 1949. His critical works include *The Sacred Wood* 1920. Nobel Prize for Literature 1948.

Eliot was born in St Louis, Missouri, and was educated at Harvard, in France at the Sorbonne, and in the UK at Oxford. He settled in London 1915 and became a British subject 1927. He was for a time a bank clerk, later lecturing and entering publishing at Faber & Faber. As editor of the highly influential *Criterion* literary magazine 1922–39, he was responsible for a critical re-evaluation of metaphysical poetry and Jacobean drama, and wrote perceptively about such European poets as Dante, Charles Baudelaire, and Jules Laforgue.

Prufrock and Other Observations expressed the disillusionment of the generation affected by World War I and caused a sensation with its experimental form and rhythms. His reputation was established by the desolate modernity of *The Waste Land*. 'The Hollow Men' continued on the same note, but 'Ash Wednesday' 1930 revealed the change in religious attitude that had led him to join the Church of England 1927. Among his other works are *Four Quartets* 1943, a religious sequence in which he seeks the eternal reality, and the poetic dramas *Murder in the Cathedral* (about Thomas à Becket); *The Cocktail Party*; *The Confidential Clerk* 1953; and *The Elder Statesman* 1958. His collection *Old Possum's Book of Practical Cats* was used for the popular English composer Andrew Lloyd Webber's musical *Cats* 1981.

Eliot's critical works, which include *The Use of Poetry and the Use of Criticism* 1933, *The Idea of a Christian Society* 1940, and *Notes toward the Definition of Culture* 1948, are conservative in tone, emphasizing the traditional values of ritual and community. He coined two important literary critical terms: dissociation of sensibility and objective correlative.

Suggested reading
Ackroyd, P *T S Eliot: A Life* (1984)
Frye, N *T S Eliot* (1981)
Gardner, H *The Art of T S Eliot* (1949)
Gordon, L *Eliot's Early Years* (1977)
Gordon, L *Eliot's New Life* (1988)
Spender, S *Eliot* (1975)
Williamson, G *A Reader's Guide to T S Eliot* (1966)

Elisha (lived mid-9th century BC). In the Old Testament, a Hebrew prophet, successor to Elijah.

Elizabeth in the New Testament, mother of John the Baptist. She was a cousin of Jesus' mother Mary, who came to see her shortly after the Annunciation; on this visit (called the Visitation), Mary sang the hymn of praise later to be known as the 'Magnificat'.

I'm glad we've been bombed. It makes me feel I can look the East End in the face.

ELIZABETH, THE QUEEN MOTHER
Remark to a policeman 13 Sept 1940 following German bombing of Buckingham Palace

---

Elizabeth the Queen Mother (1900–). Wife of King George VI of England. She was born Lady Elizabeth Angela Marguerite Bowes-Lyon, and on 26 April 1923 she married Albert, Duke of York, who became King George VI in 1936. Their children are Queen Elizabeth II and Princess Margaret.

She is the youngest daughter of the 14th Earl of Strathmore and Kinghorne (died 1944), through whom she is descended from Robert Bruce, king of Scotland. When her husband became King George VI she became Queen Consort, and was crowned with him 1937. She adopted the title Queen Elizabeth, the Queen Mother after his death.

Elizabeth two queens of England or the UK:

Elizabeth I (1533–1603). Queen of England 1558–1603, the daughter of Henry VIII and Anne Boleyn. Through her Religious Settlement of 1559 she enforced the Protestant religion by law. She had Mary Queen of Scots executed 1587. Her conflict with Roman

Catholic Spain led to the defeat of the Spanish Armada 1588. The Elizabethan age was expansionist in commerce and geographical exploration, and arts and literature flourished. The rulers of many European states made unsuccessful bids to marry Elizabeth, and she used these bids to strengthen her power. She was succeeded by James I.

This judgement I have of you, that you will not be corrupted with any manner of gift and that you will ... give me that counsel that you think best.

ELIZABETH I
to Lord Burghley 1558

Elizabeth was born at Greenwich, London, 7 Sept 1533. She was well educated in several languages. During her Roman Catholic half-sister Mary's reign, Elizabeth's Protestant sympathies brought her under suspicion, and she lived in seclusion at Hatfield, Hertfordshire, until on Mary's death she became queen. Her first task was to bring about a broad religious settlement.

My favour is not so lockt up for you, that others shall not partake thereof ... I will have here but one Mistress, and no Master.

ELIZABETH I
addressing Robert Dudley, Earl of Leicester,
quoted in Robert Naunton *Fragmenta Regalia* 1641

Many unsuccessful attempts were made by Parliament to persuade Elizabeth to marry or settle the succession. She found courtship a useful political weapon, and she maintained friendships with, among others, the courtiers Leicester, Sir Walter Raleigh, and Essex. She was known as the Virgin Queen.

The arrival in England 1568 of Mary Queen of Scots and her imprisonment by Elizabeth caused a political crisis, and a rebellion of the feudal nobility of the north followed 1569. Friction between English and Spanish sailors hastened the breach with Spain. When the Dutch rebelled against Spanish tyranny Elizabeth secretly encouraged them; Philip II retaliated by aiding Catholic conspiracies against her. This undeclared war continued for many years, until the landing of an English army in the Netherlands 1585 and Mary's execution 1587, brought it into the open. Philip's Armada (the fleet sent to invade England 1588) met with total disaster.

The war with Spain continued with varying fortunes to the end of the reign, while events at home foreshadowed the conflicts of the 17th century. Among the Puritans discontent was developing with Elizabeth's religious settlement, and several were imprisoned or executed. Parliament showed a new independence, and in 1601 forced Elizabeth to retreat on the question of the crown granting manufacturing and trading monopolies. Yet her prestige remained unabated, as was shown by the failure of Essex's rebellion 1601.

Suggested reading
Bassnett, S *Elizabeth the First: A Feminist Perspective* (1988)
Haigh, C *Elizabeth the First* (1988)
Johnson, P *Elizabeth: A Study in Power and Intellect* (1974)
Marshall, Rosalind K *Elizabeth I* (1991)
Perry, Maria *The Word of a Prince: A Life of Elizabeth I from Contemporary Documents* (1990)
Ridley, Jasper *Elizabeth I* (1988)
Rowse, A L *The England of Elizabeth* (1950)
Williams, Neville *The Life and Times of Elizabeth I* (1972)

My whole life ... shall be devoted to your service and the service of our great Imperial family to which we all belong.

ELIZABETH II
Broadcast speech (as Princess Elizabeth) to the Commonwealth
from Cape Town 21 April 1947 quoted in *The Times* 22 April 1947

Elizabeth II (Elizabeth Alexandra Mary) (1926–). Queen of Great Britain and Northern Ireland from 1952, the elder daughter of George VI. She married her third cousin, Philip, the Duke of Edinburgh, 1947. They have four children: Charles, Anne, Andrew, and Edward.

Princess Elizabeth was born in London 21 April 1926; she was educated privately, and assumed official duties at 16.

During World War II she served in the Auxiliary Territorial Service, and by an amendment to the Regency Act she became a state counsellor on her 18th birthday. On the death of George VI in 1952 she succeeded to the throne while in Kenya with her husband and was crowned on 2 June 1953.

With an estimated wealth of £5 billion (1994), the Queen is one of the richest woman in Britain. In April 1993 she voluntarily began paying full rates of income tax and capital gains on her private income, which chiefly consists of the proceeds of a share portfolio and is estimated to be worth around £45 million.

Suggested reading
Lacey, Robert *Majesty* (1977)
Longford, Elizabeth *The Queen* (1984)

Elizabeth (1709–1762). Empress of Russia from 1741, daughter of Peter the Great. She carried through a palace revolution and supplanted her cousin, the infant Ivan VI (1730–1764), on the throne. She continued the policy of westernization begun by Peter and allied herself with Austria against Prussia.

Elkington George Richards (1801–1865). English inventor who pioneered the use of electroplating for finishing metal objects.

Elkington was born in Birmingham and in 1818 he became an apprentice in the local small-arms factory; in due course he became its proprietor. With his cousin Henry Elkington (1810–1852), he explored the alternatives to traditional methods of plating from about 1832. The process of plating base metals with silver and gold by electrodeposition was announced in a patent taken out by the Elkington cousins in 1840. In 1841 they established a workshop for electroplating in Birmingham, and successfully patented their ideas in France. George Elkington also established large copper-smelting works in South Wales, providing houses for his workers and schools for their children.

Ellet Charles (1810–1862). US civil engineer who designed the first wire-cable suspension bridge in the USA, in 1842. He also designed the world's first long-span wire-cable suspension bridge, crossing the Ohio River at Wheeling, West Virginia.

Ellet was born in Pennsylvania and began his career as a surveyor and assistant engineer on the Chesapeake and Ohio Canal 1828. In 1831–32 he was in Europe, enrolled at the Ecole Polytechnique in Paris and studied the various engineering works taking place in France, Germany, and Britain.

For his first wire-cable suspension bridge, over the Schuylkill River at Fairmount, Pennsylvania, Ellet introduced a technique he had learned in France of binding small wires together to make the cables.

The central span of the suspension bridge over the Ohio River was at 308 m/1,010 ft the longest ever built when completed 1849. The bridge failed under wind forces in 1854; however, Ellet's towers remained standing and the bridge was rebuilt.

Ellington Duke (Edward Kennedy) (1899–1974). US pianist. He had an outstanding career as a composer and arranger of jazz. He wrote numerous pieces for his own jazz orchestra, accentuating the strengths of individual virtuoso instrumentalists, and became one of the leading figures in jazz over a 55-year period. Some of his most popular compositions include 'Mood Indigo', 'Sophisticated Lady', 'Solitude', and 'Black and Tan Fantasy'. He was one of the founders of big-band jazz.

Suggested reading
Collier, James *Duke Ellington* (1987)
Dance, Stanley *The World of Duke Ellington* (1971)
Ellington, Duke *Music is My Mistress* (memoirs) (1973)
Jewell, Derek *Duke: A Portrait of Duke Ellington* (1977)

Elliott Denholm Mitchell (1922–1992). English film, stage, and television actor. In his early career he was known especially for playing youthful parts and stiff-upper-lip Englishmen, and later for his portrayal of somewhat degenerate upper-class characters. In his first film for Hollywood he was a cynical prisoner in *King Rat* 1965. He followed this a year later with the part of the villainous back-street abortionist in *Alfie*.

His first film part was that of the minor civil servant in *Dear Mr Prohack* 1949; then followed leading roles in *The Cruel Sea* 1953 and *The Heart of the Matter* 1953, and several minor roles until 1964 when his con man aristocrat in *Nothing but the Best*, instructing Alan Bates on how to get into high society, marked a turning point for him. He played many villains in films after this. He is also remembered as the conceited butler in *Trading Places* 1983, the Fleet Street hack in *Defence of the Realm* 1985, and as Mr Emerson in *A Room with a View* 1986. He appeared in many TV plays and series, including *Bleak House* 1987. He received the BAFTA award for best TV actor 1981 and for best supporting film actor 1984, 1985, and 1986.

Ellis Bret Easton (1964–). US novelist. He is the author of *Less Than Zero* 1985, a rites-of-passage novel dealing with the alienation of affluent youth; *The Rules of Attraction* 1987, about sex on a college campus; and the controversial *American Psycho* 1991, about a Wall Street psychopath, which vividly depicts the urban violence of contemporary American life.

The sun, the moon and the stars would have disappeared long ago ... had they happened to be within the reach of predatory human hands.

HAVELOCK ELLIS
The Dance of Life ch 7 1923

Ellis (Henry) Havelock (1859–1939). English psychologist and writer of many works on the psychology of sex, including *Studies in the Psychology of Sex* (seven volumes) 1898–1928.

He trained as a physician, and was also a literary critic and essayist.

I am an invisible man. I am invisible, understand, because people refuse to see me.

RALPH ELLISON
Invisible Man 1952

Ellison Ralph Waldo (1914–1994). US novelist. His *Invisible Man* 1952 portrays with humour and energy the plight of a black man whom postwar American society cannot acknowledge. It is regarded as one of the most impressive novels published in the USA in the 1950s. He also wrote essays collected in *Shadow and Act* 1964.

Ellison saw black people not as separate or marginalized but right in the centre of US national life. He identified 'being invisible' as a complex condition, applying to himself 'simply because people refuse to see me', but emphasizing that part of the problem was that the invisible man was also invisible to himself. Ellison was an instructor in Russian and American Literature at Bard College, Annadale-on-Hudson 1958–61 and held visiting professorships at Chicago 1961, Rutgers 1962–64, and Yale University 1966. He was Albert Schweitzer Professor of Humanities at New York University 1970–79.

Ellsworth Oliver (1745–1807). US jurist and chief justice of the US Supreme Court 1796–1800. As a Connecticut delegate to the Constitutional Convention 1777, he was instrumental in effecting the 'Connecticut Compromise,' which balanced large and small state interests. He was selected as US senator from Connecticut in 1787. Appointed chief justice by President Washington, his opinions shaped admiralty law and treaty law.

Born in Windsor, Connecticut, he attended Yale College and graduated from Princeton University 1766. After establishing himself as a lawyer he served concurrently in a number of political posts in Connecticut. He became a judge of the new state court of appeals in 1785, moving to the new state superior court as a judge in the same year.

Elsasser Walter Maurice (1904–1991). German-born US geophysicist who pioneered analysis of the Earth's former magnetic fields, frozen in rocks. Born in Mannheim and educated at Göttingen, Elsasser left in 1933 following Hitler's rise to power, and spent three years in Paris working on the theory of atomic nuclei. After settling in 1936 in the USA and joining the staff of the California Institute of Technology, he specialized in geophysics. Elsasser became a professor at the University of Pennsylvania 1947; in 1962 he was made professor of geophysics at Princeton.

His magnetical researches in the 1940s yielded the dynamo model of the Earth's magnetic field. The field is explained in terms of the activity of electric currents flowing in the Earth's fluid metallic outer core. The theory premises that these currents are magnified through mechanical motions, rather as currents are sustained in power-station generators.

Elsheimer Adam (1578–1610). German painter and etcher. He was active in Rome from 1600. His small paintings, nearly all on copper, depict landscapes darkened by storm or night, with figures picked out by beams of light, as in *The Rest on the Flight into Egypt* 1609 (Alte Pinakothek, Munich).

He is noted for the effective contrast between different sources of light in the same picture, for example the firelight, torchlight and moonlight in his *Rest on the Flight into Egypt*, which may well have inspired Rembrandt's *Flight into Egypt* (Dublin). Effects of this kind delighted and influenced Rubens, who bought works by him. He also made a study of the country round Rome, and his sketches in the Campagna foreshadow the 'classical' landscape with ruins that Claude was to perfect.

Elton Charles Sutherland (1900–1991). British ecologist, a pioneer of the study of animal and plant forms in their natural environments, and of animal behaviour as part of the complex pattern of life. He defined the concept of food chains and was an early conservationist, instrumental in establishing the Nature Conservancy Council 1949, and much concerned with the impact of introduced species on natural systems.

Elton carried out a 20-year research project of interrelationships of animals in meadows, woods, and water near Oxford. He originated the concept of the 'pyramid of numbers' as a method of representing the structure of an ecosystem in terms of feeding relationships. His books include *Animal Ecology and Evolution* 1930 and *The Pattern of Animal Communities* 1966.

Elton Geoffrey Rudolph (1921–1994). Czechoslovakian-born British historian. During World War II he worked in intelligence before teaching at Cambridge University from 1949 and becoming Regius Professor of History in 1983. His reputation was made through his study of the Tudor monarchs of England and the 'Tudor revolution' in government in the 1530s. He has since written a series of books on this and related subjects, the best known being *England under the Tudors* and *The Practice of History*.

Eluard Paul. Pen name of Eugène Grindel (1895–1952). French poet. He expressed the suffering of poverty in his verse, and was a leader of the Surrealists. He fought in World War I, which inspired his *Poèmes pour la paix/Poems for Peace* 1918, and was a member of the Resistance in World War II. His books include *Poésie et vérité/Poetry and Truth* 1942 and *Au Rendezvous allemand/To the German Rendezvous* 1944.

Ely Richard Theodore (1854–1943). US economist and an early advocate of government economic intervention, central planning, and the organization of the labour force. He was appointed professor of political economy at Johns Hopkins University 1881 and in 1885 founded the American Economic Association. In 1892 he became chair of the department of economics at the University of Wisconsin before joining the faculty of Northwestern University 1925.

Elyot Thomas (c. 1490–1546). English diplomat and scholar. In 1531 he published *The Governour*, the first treatise on education in English. Knighted 1530.

Abstinence is whereby a man refraineth from anything which he may lawfully take.

THOMAS ELYOT
Thomas Elyot *The Governour* pt iii ch 16 1531

Elytis Odysseus. Pen name of Odysseus Alepoudelis (1911–1996). Greek poet. His verse celebrates the importance of the people's attempts to shape an individual existence in freedom. His major work *To Axion Esti/Worthy It Is* 1959 is a lyric cycle, parts of which have been set to music by Theodorakis. Nobel Prize for Literature 1979.

Elzevir Louis (c. 1540–1617). Founder of the Dutch printing house Elzevir in the 17th century. Among the firm's publications were editions of Latin, Greek, and Hebrew works, as well as French and Italian classics.

Born at Louvain, Elzevir was obliged to leave Belgium 1580 because of his Protestant and political views. He settled at Leyden as a bookseller and printer.

Emanuel David (1952–) and Elizabeth (1953–). British fashion designers who opened their own salon 1977. They specialized in off-the-shoulder, ornate and opulent evening wear. In 1981 Lady Diana Spencer, now Princess of Wales, commissioned the Emanuels to design her wedding dress. In 1990 Elizabeth Emanuel established her own label in London, continuing to design outfits for singers, actresses, and members of the British royal family.

Eméleus Harry Julius (1903–). English chemist who made wide-ranging investigations in inorganic chemistry, studying particularly nonmetallic elements and their compounds. He worked on chemical kinetics and studied the hydrides of silicon and the halogen fluorides. He was professor of inorganic chemistry at Cambridge 1945–70. Eméleus summarized much of his work in *The Chemistry of Fluorine and its Compounds* 1969.

Emerson Peter Henry (1856–1936). English landscape photographer. His aim was to produce uncontrived naturalistic images of the countryside. He believed in differential focusing, the idea that only part of the picture should be sharply focused. His first book, *Life and Landscape on the Norfolk Broads*, was produced in collaboration with the painter T F Goodall 1886. His theories were set out in *Naturalistic Photography* 1889 but a year later he recanted and largely gave up photography.

The louder he talked of his honour, the faster we counted our spoons.

RALPH EMERSON
Conduct of Life, 'Worship' 1870

Emerson Ralph Waldo (1803–1882). US philosopher, essayist, and poet. He settled in Concord, Massachusetts, which he made a centre of transcendentalism, and wrote *Nature* 1836, which states the movement's main principles emphasizing the value of self-reliance and the godlike nature of human souls. His two volumes of *Essays* (1841, 1844) made his reputation: 'Self-Reliance' and 'Compensation' in the earlier volume are among the best known.

Born in Boston, Massachusetts, and educated at Harvard, Emerson became a Unitarian minister. In 1832 he resigned and travelled to Europe, meeting the British writers Thomas Carlyle, Samuel Coleridge, and William Wordsworth. On his return to Massachusetts in 1833 he settled in Concord. He made a second visit to England 1847 and incorporated his impressions in *English Traits* 1856. Much of his verse was published in the literary magazine *The Dial*. His poems include 'The Rhodora', 'Threnody', and 'Brahma'. His later works include *Representative Men* 1850 and *The Conduct of Life* 1870.

Suggested reading
Allen, G W *Waldo Emerson* (1981)
Porte, J *Emerson* (1982)

Wagenknecht, E C *Ralph Waldo Emerson* (1974)
Yannelle, D *Ralph Waldo Emerson* (1982)

Emery (Walter) Bryan (1903–1971). British archaeologist, who in 1929–34 in Nubia, N Africa, excavated the barrows at Ballana and Qustol, rich royal tombs of the mysterious X-group people (3rd to 6th centuries AD). He also surveyed the whole region 1963–64 before it was flooded as a result of the building of the Aswan High Dam.

Emin Pasha Mehmed. Adopted name of Eduard Schnitzer (1840–1892). German explorer, physician, and linguist. Appointed by British general Charles Gordon chief medical officer and then governor of the Equatorial province of S Sudan, he carried out extensive research in anthropology, botany, zoology, and meteorology.

Schnitzer practised medicine in Albania. In 1876 he joined the Egyptian Service, where he was known as Emin Pasha. Isolated by his remote location in Sudan and cut off from the outside world by Arab slave traders, he was 'rescued' by an expedition led by H M Stanley in 1889. He travelled with Stanley as far as Zanzibar but returned to continue his work near Lake Victoria. Three years later he was killed while leading an expedition to the W coast of Africa.

Let my character and motives rest in obscurity and peace, till other times and other men can do them justice.
ROBERT EMMET
Speech on his conviction for treason Sept 1803

Emmet Robert (1778–1803). Irish nationalist leader. In 1803 he led an unsuccessful revolt in Dublin against British rule and was captured, tried, and hanged. His youth and courage made him an Irish hero.

Empedocles (*c.* 493–433 BC). Greek philosopher and scientist who proposed that the universe is composed of four elements – fire, air, earth, and water – which through the action of love and discord are eternally constructed, destroyed, and constructed anew. He lived in Acragas (Agrigentum), Sicily, and according to tradition, he committed suicide by throwing himself into the crater of Mount Etna.

Empson William (1906–1984). English poet and critic. He was professor of English literature at Tokyo and Beijing (Peking), and from 1953 to 1971 at Sheffield University. His critical work examined the potential variety of meaning in poetry, as in *Seven Types of Ambiguity* 1930 and *The Structure of Complex Words* 1951. His *Collected Poems* were published 1955. Knighted 1979.

Encke Johann Franz (1791–1865). German astronomer whose work on star charts during the 1840s contributed to the discovery of the planet Neptune in 1846. He also worked out the path of the comet that bears his name. He was a professor at the Academy of Sciences in Berlin and director of the Berlin Observatory 1825–65. The new star charts took nearly 20 years to draw up, compiled from both old and new observations. They were completed 1859 but were soon improved upon by those of Friedrich Argelander.

Ender Kornelia (1958–   ). German swimmer. She won a record-tying four gold medals at the 1976 Olympics at freestyle, butterfly, and relay; a total of eight Olympic medals 1972–76; and a record ten world championship medals 1973 and 1975.

Enders John Franklin (1897–1985). US virologist. With Thomas Weller (1915–   ) and Frederick Robbins (1916–   ), he developed a technique for culturing virus material in sufficient quantity for experimental work. This led to the creation of effective vaccines against polio and measles. The three were awarded the Nobel Prize for Physiology or Medicine 1954.

Enders was born in West Hartford, Connecticut. He interrupted his studies at Yale to become a flying instructor during World War I and then took up a business career but left it to study English at Harvard, before changing to medicine. He remained at Harvard Medical School, becoming professor 1962.

Viruses cannot be grown, as bacteria can, in nutrient substances, and so a method had been developed for growing them in a living chick embryo. In 1948, Enders and his colleagues prepared a medium of homogenized chick embryo and blood and, adding penicillin to suppress bacteria, managed to grow a mumps virus in it. Previously the polio virus could be grown only in living nerve tissue from primates. But using their method, Enders managed to grow the virus successfully on tissue scraps obtained from stillborn human embryos, and then on other tissue. The general application of this technique meant that viruses could be more readily isolated and identified.

Endo Shusako Paul (1923–1996). Japanese novelist. A convert to Catholic Christianity, he studied modern French religious writing in Lyons 1950. This encouraged his fictional explorations of cultural conflict and moral and spiritual perplexity in sympathetically treated unheroic lives, disclosing a 'mudswamp' of moral inertia in contemporary Japanese life. Among his best-known works, much-translated, are the historical novel *Chinmoky/Silence* 1967 and *Kuchibue o fuku toki/When I Whistle* 1979.

Engel (Johann) Carl (Ludwig) (1778–1840). German architect. From 1815 he worked in Finland. His great Neo-Classical achievement is the Senate Square in Helsinki, which is defined by his Senate House 1818–22 and University Building 1828–32, and crowned by the domed Lutheran cathedral 1830–40.

Engels Friedrich (1820–1895). German social and political philosopher, a friend of, and collaborator with, Karl Marx on *The Communist Manifesto* 1848 and other key works. His later interpretations of Marxism, and his own philosophical and historical studies such as *Origins of the Family, Private Property, and the State* 1884 (which linked patriarchy with the development of private property), developed such concepts as historical materialism. His use of positivism and Darwinian ideas gave Marxism a scientific and deterministic flavour which was to influence Soviet thinking.

In 1842 Engels's father sent him to work in the cotton factory owned by his family in Manchester, England, where he became involved with Chartism. In 1844 his lifelong friendship with Karl Marx began, and together they worked out the materialist interpretation of history and in 1847–48 wrote the *Communist Manifesto*. Returning to Germany during the 1848–49 revolution, Engels worked with Marx on the *Neue Rheinische Zeitung/New Rhineland Newspaper* and fought on the barricades in Baden. After the defeat of the revolution he returned to Manchester, and for the rest of his life largely supported the Marx family.

Engels's first book was *The Condition of the Working Classes in England* 1845. He summed up the lessons of 1848 in *The Peasants' War in Germany* 1850 and *Revolution and Counter-Revolution in Germany* 1851. After Marx's death Engels was largely responsible for the wider dissemination of his ideas; he edited the second and third volumes of Marx's *Das Kapital* 1885 and 1894. Although Engels himself regarded his ideas as identical with those of Marx, discrepancies between their works are the basis of many Marxist debates.

Suggested reading
Carver, Terrell *Engels* (1981)
Henderson, W O *The Life of Friedrich Engels* (1976)
Mayer, Gustav *Friedrich Engels* (1936, rep 1969)
McLellan, David *Engels* (1977)

Engleheart George (1752–1839). English miniature painter. Born in Kew, London, he studied under Joshua Reynolds and in over 40 years painted nearly 5,000 miniatures, including copies of many of Reynolds's portraits.

Ennius Quintus (*c.* 239–169 BC). Early Roman poet. He wrote tragedies based on the Greek pattern. His epic poem *Annales* deals with Roman history.

Enright D(enis) J(oseph) (1920–   ). English poet. His poetry is wide-ranging, often dealing with cultural differences, and is passionate about inequality. Its unpretentious tone is ironic and unsentimental. Collections include *Old Men and Comets* 1993.

For over 20 years Enright taught at universities abroad, mostly in the East (where many of his poems are set), until his return to the UK in the 1970s. Between 1955 and 1965 he wrote four novels about British academics abroad. His criticism has appeared mainly in book reviews and essays, collected in *Man is an Onion* 1972. He made his debut as a poet in 1953 and published a *Collected Poems* 1981. He has edited several anthologies, such as *The Oxford Book of Death* 1983.

Ensor James Sidney, Baron Ensor (1860–1949). Belgian painter and printmaker. In a bold style employing vivid colours, he created a surreal and macabre world inhabited by masked figures and skeletons. Such works as his famous *Entry of Christ into Brussels* 1888 (Musée Royale des Beaux-Arts, Brussels) anticipated Expressionism. Baron 1929.

Enver Pasha (1881–1922). Turkish politician and soldier. He led the military revolt 1908 that resulted in the Young Turks' revolution. He was killed fighting the Bolsheviks in Turkestan.

He entered the army 1898, became active in the 'Young Turk' movement 1905, and following the 1908 revolution was appointed military attaché to Berlin. He returned to Salonika 1909 when the Turkish counter-revolution began and assisted in the overthrow of Abdul Hamid. He was active in organizing the Arabs of Tripoli in the Tripoli War against Italy 1911, and in the Second Balkan War he recaptured Adrianople from the Bulgarians 1913. By that time he had been appointed minister of war, with the rank of Pasha and married a princess.

His pro-German influence was a major factor in the Turkish decision to align with Germany against the Allies in World War I, although his attempts at military command during the war were invariably failures. After the Turkish surrender he fled to the Caucasus, from where he urged resistance to the terms of the Peace Treaty. Having no success in returning to power in Turkey, he joined a group of anti-Bolsheviks in Uzbekistan and was killed leading them in a skirmish.

Eötvös Roland, Baron von (1848–1919). Hungarian scientist who investigated problems of gravitation. He constructed the double-armed torsion balance for determining variations of gravity.

If we are victorious, it is time to die.

EPAMINONDAS
Dying words quoted in Diodorus Siculus *Bibliotheca Historiae* bk 15, ch 87

Epaminondas (*c.* 420–362 BC). Theban general and politician who won a decisive victory over the Spartans at Leuctra 371. He brought independence to Messenia and Arcadia, and consolidated Theban supremacy before dying from wounds received at the battle of Mantinea 362 BC.

Ephron Nora (1941–). US writer. Her semi-autobiographical novel *Heartburn* 1983 was adapted for film 1986. Her screenplays include *Silkwood* 1983, based on the life of Karen Silkwood (1946–1974) who exposed the hazardous conditions at a plutonium plant; *When Harry Met Sally* 1989; and *Sleepless in Seattle* 1993.

Ephron was born in New York and worked for the *New York Post* 1963–68. Collections of her articles include *Wallflower at the Orgy* 1970, *Crazy Salad: Some Things about Women* 1975, and *Scribble, Scribble: Notes on the Media* 1978. She has also written short stories.

Epicharmus (*c.* 530–*c.* 440 BC). Greek comic writer from Sicily, reputedly one of the founders of comedy. He was also regarded as a philosopher because of a philosophical poem, probably by somebody else, written under his name.

Epictetus (c. AD 55–135). Greek Stoic philosopher who encouraged people to refrain from self-interest and to promote the common good of humanity. He believed that people were in the hands of an all-wise providence and that they should endeavour to do their duty in the position to which they were called.

Born at Hierapolis in Phrygia, he lived for many years in Rome as

a slave but eventually secured his freedom. He was banished by the emperor Domitian from Rome in AD 89.

Epicurus (341–270 BC). Greek philosopher, founder of Epicureanism, who held that all things are made up of atoms. His theory of knowledge stresses the role of sense perception, and in his ethics the most desired condition is a serene detachment based on the avoidance of anxiety and physical pain.

Epicurus taught at Athens from 306 BC, and was influential in both Greek and Roman thinking. For example, his atomic theory was adopted by the Roman Epicurean Lucretius.

Epstein Jacob (1880–1959). US-born British sculptor. Initially influenced by Rodin, he turned to primitive forms after Brancusi and is chiefly known for his controversial muscular nude figures such as *Genesis* 1931 (Whitworth Art Gallery, Manchester). He was better appreciated as a portraitist (bust of Einstein, 1933), and in later years executed several monumental figures, notably the expressive bronze of *St Michael and the Devil* 1959 (Coventry Cathedral).

In 1904 he moved to England, where most of his major work was done. An early example showing the strong influence of ancient sculptural styles is the angel over the tomb of Oscar Wilde 1912 (Père Lachaise cemetery, Paris), while *Rock Drill* 1913–14 (Tate Gallery, London) is Modernist and semi-abstract. These and his nude figures outraged public sensibilities. KBE 1954.

Equiano Olaudah (*c.* 1745–1797). African antislavery campaigner and writer. He travelled widely as a free man. His autobiography, *The Interesting Narrative of the Life of Olaudah Equiano, or Gustavus Vassa, the African* 1789, is one of the earliest significant works by an African written in English.

Equiano was born near the river Niger in what is now Nigeria, captured at the age of ten and sold to slavers, who transported him to the West Indies. He learned English and bought his freedom at the age of 21. He subsequently sailed to the Mediterranean and the Arctic, before being appointed commissary of stores for freed slaves returning to Sierra Leone. He was an active campaigner against slavery.

Erasistratus (*c.* 304–*c.* 250 BC). Greek physician and anatomist regarded as the founder of physiology. He came close to discovering the true function of several important systems of the body, which were not fully understood until nearly 1,000 years later.

Erasistratus was born on the Aegean island of Ceos (now Khios). He learned his skills in Athens and became court physician to Seleucus I, who governed western Asia. He then moved on to Alexandria, where he taught.

Erasistratus dissected and examined the human brain, noting the convolutions of the outer surface, and observed that the organ is divided into larger and smaller portions (the cerebrum and cerebellum). He compared the human brain with those of other animals and made the correct hypothesis that the surface area/volume complexity is directly related to the intelligence of the animal.

Erasmus Desiderius (*c.* 1466–1536). Dutch scholar and leading humanist of the Renaissance era, who taught and studied all over Europe and was a prolific writer. His pioneer translation of the Greek New Testament (with parallel Latin text) 1516 exposed the Vulgate as a second-hand document. Although opposed to dogmatism and abuse of church power, he remained impartial during Martin Luther's conflict with the pope.

Erasmus was born in Rotterdam, and as a youth he was a monk in an Augustinian monastery near Gouda. After becoming a priest, he went to study in Paris 1495. He paid the first of a number of visits to England 1499, where he met the physician Thomas Linacre, the politician Thomas More, and the Bible interpreter John Colet, and

---

Let a king recall that to improve his realm is better than to increase his territory.

DESIDERIUS ERASMUS
Querella Pacis July 1517

for a time was professor of divinity and Greek at Cambridge University. He also edited the writings of St Jerome and the early Christian authorities, and published *Encomium Moriae/The Praise of Folly* 1511 (a satire on church and society that quickly became an international bestseller) and *Colloquia* (dialogues on contemporary subjects) 1519. In 1521 he went to Basel, Switzerland, where he edited the writings of the early Christian leaders.

Suggested reading

Bainton, R H *Erasmus* (1969)
Huizinga, Johan *Erasmus and the Age of the Reformation* (trs 1952)
Jardine, Lisa *Erasmus, Man of Letters* (1993)
McConica, James *Erasmus* (1991)
Sowards, J K *Desiderius Erasmus* (1975)

The earth has a circumference of 31,000 miles.

ERATOSTHENES
On the Measurement of the Earth

Eratosthenes (*c.* 276–*c.* 194 BC). Greek geographer and mathematician whose map of the ancient world was the first to contain lines of latitude and longitude, and who calculated the Earth's circumference with an error of about 10%. His mathematical achievements include a method for duplicating the cube, and for finding prime numbers (Eratosthenes' sieve).

No work of Eratosthenes survives complete. The most important that remains is on geography – a word that he virtually coined as the title of his three-volume study of the Earth (as much as he knew of it) and its measurement. Eratosthenes divided the Earth into five zones: two frigid zones around each pole; two temperate zones; and a torrid zone comprising the two areas from the equator to each tropic. In *Chronography* and *Olympic Victors*, many of the dates he

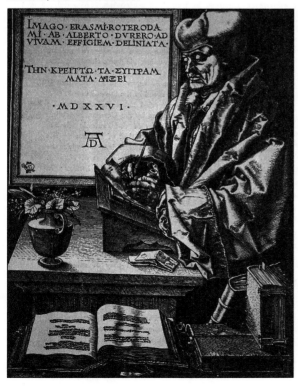

Erasmus *The Dutch Renaissance humanist and scholar Desiderius Erasmus. The illegitimate son of Rogerius Gerardus, Erasmus adopted his new name, which means 'beloved'.*

set for events (for example, the fall of Troy) have been accepted by later historians. He also wrote many books on literary criticism in a series entitled *On the Old Comedy*.

A compromise is the art of dividing a cake in such a way that everyone believes that he has got the biggest piece.

LUDWIG ERHARD
quoted in *Observer* 28 Dec 1958

Erhard Ludwig (1897–1977). West German Christian Democrat politician, chancellor of the Federal Republic 1963–66. The 'economic miracle' of West Germany's recovery after World War II is largely attributed to Erhard's policy of social free enterprise which he initiated during his period as federal economics minister (1949–63).

Ericsson John (1803–1889). Swedish-born US engineer who took out a patent to produce screw-propeller-powered paddle-wheel ships 1836. He built a number of such ships, including the *Monitor*, which was successfully deployed during the American Civil War.

In 1829 he built the *Novelty*, a steam locomotive which competed unsuccessfully against George Stephenson's *Rocket*. Ericsson turned to building ships fitted with steam engines and screw propellers, and moved to the USA 1839. In 1849, he built the *Princeton*, the first metal-hulled, screw-propelled warship and the first to have its engines below the waterline for added protection.

Ericsson Leif (lived *c.* 970). Norse explorer, son of Eric the Red, who sailed west from Greenland to find a country first sighted by Norsemen 986. He visited Baffin Island then sailed along the Labrador coast to Newfoundland, which was named 'Vinland' (Wine Land), because he discovered grape vines growing there.

The story was confirmed 1961 when a Norwegian expedition, led by Helge Ingstad, discovered the remains of a Viking settlement (dated *c.* 1000) near the fishing village of L'Anse-aux-Meadows at the northern tip of Newfoundland.

Eric the Red (*c.* 950–1010). Allegedly the first European to find Greenland. According to a 13th-century saga, he was the son of a Norwegian chieftain, and was banished from Iceland about 982 for murder. He then sailed westward and discovered a land that he called Greenland.

Erigena Johannes Scotus (*c.* 815–*c.* 877). Medieval philosopher. He was probably Irish and, according to tradition, travelled in Greece and Italy. The French king Charles (II) the Bald invited him to France (before 847), where he became head of the court school. He is said to have visited Oxford, to have taught at Malmesbury, and to have been stabbed to death by his pupils. In his philosophy, he defied church orthodoxy in his writings on cosmology and predestination, and tried to combine Christianity with neo-Platonism.

Erikson Erik Homburger (1902–1994). German-born US psychoanalytic theorist who contributed to the understanding of human mental development. He coined the phrase *identity crisis*, and proposed that the ego is not fixed at birth or during childhood, but continues to be moulded throughout life by experience and environment. He established his reputation with the book *Childhood and Society* 1950.

Other works include his so-called psychobiographies of German religious reformer Martin Luther and Indian nationalist Mahatma Gandhi. Among his more significant papers was 'Ego Development and Historical Chance', which argued that an individual could be affected at the deepest levels by the progress of history and society. His last book, *Vital Involvement in Old Age*, written with his wife, was published 1986.

Erim Kenan Tevfig (1929–1990). Turkish-born US historian and archaeologist. From 1961 he began to excavate the city of Aphrodisias in Turkey while teaching at New York University. In his efforts to conserve and protect the site, the excavation took 30 years to complete.

Erlang Agner Krarup (1878–1929). Danish mathematician who applied the theory of probabilities to problems connected with telephone traffic, such as congestion and waiting time. The erlang is now the unit of telephone-traffic flow. From 1908 he was leader of the laboratory of the Copenhagen Telephone Company.

Ernst Max (1891–1976). German Surrealist artist. He worked in France 1922–38 and in the USA from 1941. He was an active Dadaist, experimenting with collage, photomontage, and surreal images, and helped found the Surrealist movement 1924.

Ernst first exhibited in Berlin 1916. He produced a 'collage novel', *La Femme cent têtes* 1929, worked on films with Salvador Dali and Luis Buñuel, and designed sets and costumes for Sergei Diaghilev's Ballets Russes.

His pictures range from precise Surrealist images to highly textured, imaginary landscapes, employing *frottage* (rubbing colour or graphite on to paper laid over a textured surface).

Suggested reading
Ernst, Max *Beyond Painting* (1948)
Legge, E *Max Ernst* (1989)
Russell, John *Max Ernst: Life and Work* (1967)

Ershad Hussain Muhammad (1930–). Military ruler of Bangladesh 1982–90. He became chief of staff of the Bangladeshi army 1979 and assumed power in a military coup 1982. As president from 1983, Ershad introduced a successful rural-oriented economic programme. He was re-elected 1986 and lifted martial law, but faced continuing political opposition, which forced him to resign Dec 1990.

In 1991 he was formally charged with the illegal possession of arms, convicted, and sentenced to ten years' imprisonment. He received a further sentence of three years' imprisonment Feb 1992 after being convicted of corruption.

Erskine Ralph (1914–). English-born architect. He settled in Sweden 1939. He specialized in community architecture before it was named as such. A deep social consciousness and a concern to mould building form in response to climate determine his architecture. His Byker Estate in Newcastle-upon-Tyne 1969–80, where a sheltering wall of dwellings embraces the development, involved a lengthy process of consultation with the residents.

A later project is the 'Ark', an office building in Hammersmith, London, 1989–91. Its shiplike form shelters the internal activities from an adjoining motorway.

The job of buildings is to improve human relations;
architecture must ease them, not make them worse.
RALPH ERSKINE
The Times 16 Sept 1992

Erskine Thomas, 1st Baron Erskine (1750–1823). British barrister and lord chancellor. He was called to the Bar in 1778 and defended a number of parliamentary reformers on charges of sedition. When the Whig Party returned to power 1806 he became lord chancellor and a baron. Among his speeches were those in defence of Lord George Gordon, Thomas Paine, and Queen Caroline.

The tongue of Cicero and the soul of Hampden.
Lord John Russell on THOMAS ERSKINE
in *Dictionary of National Biography*

Erté adopted name of Romain de Tirtoff (1892–1990). Russian designer and illustrator. He was active in France and the USA. An exponent of Art Deco, he designed sets and costumes for opera, theatre, and ballet, and his drawings were highly stylized and expressive, featuring elegant, curvilinear women.

Erté (the name was derived from the French pronunciation of his initials) went to Paris 1911 to work as a theatre and ballet set designer. From 1916 to 1926 he produced covers for the US fashion magazine *Harper's Bazaar*, and went to Hollywood 1925 to work as a designer on several films. He continued to design sets and costumes in Europe and the USA for many decades. His illustrations were influenced by 16th-century Persian and Indian miniatures.

Esaki Leo (born Esaki Reiona) (1925–). Japanese physicist who in 1957 noticed that electrons could sometimes 'tunnel' through the barrier formed at the junctions of certain semiconductors. The effect is now widely used in the electronics industry. For this early discovery Esaki shared the 1973 Nobel Prize for Physics with British physicist Brian Josephson and Norwegian-born US physicist Ivar Giaever (1929–).

Esaki, born in Osaka, graduated from the University of Tokyo and worked for electronics manufacturer Sony 1956–60. He then joined IBM's research centre in Yorktown Heights, New York, but returned to Japan 1992 as president of the University of Tsukuba.

Esarhaddon (died 669 BC). King of Assyria from 680 BC, when he succeeded his father Sennacherib. He conquered Egypt 674–671 BC.

Esau in the Old Testament, the son of Isaac and Rebekah, and the hirsute elder twin brother of Jacob. Jacob tricked the blind Isaac into giving him the blessing intended for Esau by putting on goatskins for Isaac to feel. Earlier Esau had sold his birthright to Jacob for a 'mess of red pottage'. Esau was the ancestor of the Edomites.

Escher M(aurits) C(ornelis) (1898–1972). Dutch graphic artist. His prints are often based on mathematical concepts and contain paradoxes and illusions. The lithograph *Ascending and Descending* 1960, with interlocking staircases creating a perspective puzzle, is a typical work.

Escobar Pablo Gaviria (1949–1993). Colombian drug dealer, racketeer, and politician. From humble beginnings he became the leader of an international drugs cartel based on the city of Medellín. His activities, which included political assassinations and terrorism, brought international condemnation.

As head of the Medellín cartel, Escobar transformed the law-abiding city of Medellín into the narcotics capital of South America. His political ambitions in the 1980s led to the assassination of opponents as well as indiscriminate acts of terrorism. After escaping from 'voluntary imprisonment' he was killed by police while resisting arrest.

Esenin or Yesenin, Sergey Aleksandrovich (1895–1925). Soviet poet, born in Konstantinovo (renamed Esenino in his honour). He went to Petrograd 1915, attached himself to the Symbolists, welcomed the Russian Revolution, revived peasant traditions and folklore, and initiated the Imaginist group of poets 1919. A selection of his poetry was translated in *Confessions of a Hooligan* 1973. He was married briefly to US dancer Isadora Duncan 1922–23.

Eskola Pentti Eelis (1883–1964). Finnish geologist who was one of the first to apply physicochemical postulates on a far-reaching basis to the study of metamorphism, thereby laying the foundations of most subsequent studies in metamorphic petrology. In the early 1920s he worked in Norway and in Washington DC, USA. He was professor at Helsinki 1924–53.

Throughout his life Eskola was fascinated by the study of metamorphic rocks, taking early interest in the Precambrian rocks of England. Building largely on Scandinavian studies, he was concerned to define the changing pressure and temperature conditions under which metamorphic rocks were formed. His approach enabled comparison of rocks of widely differing compositions in respect of the pressure and temperature under which they had originated.

Espronceda José de (1808–1842). Spanish poet. Originally one of the Queen's guards, he lost his commission because of his political activities, and was involved in the Republican uprisings of 1835 and 1836. His lyric poetry and lifestyle both owed much to Lord Byron.

Esquivel Adolfo (1932–). Argentinian sculptor and architect. As leader of the Servicio de Paz y Justicia (Peace and Justice Service), a Catholic–Protestant human-rights organization, he was awarded the 1980 Nobel Peace Prize.

Reasons are not like garments, the worse for wearing.
ROBERT DEVEREUX 2ND EARL OF ESSEX
to Lord Willoughby 1598 or 1599

Essex Robert Devereux, 2nd Earl of Essex (1566–1601). English soldier and politician. He became a favourite with Queen Elizabeth I from 1587, but was executed because of his policies in Ireland. Succeeded to earldom 1576.

Essex fought in the Netherlands 1585–86 and distinguished himself at the Battle of Zutphen. In 1596 he jointly commanded a force that seized and sacked Cádiz. In 1599 he became Lieutenant of Ireland and led an army against Irish rebels under the Earl of Tyrone in Ulster, but was unsuccessful, made an unauthorized truce with Tyrone, and returned without permission to England. He was forbidden to return to court, and when he marched into the City of London at the head of a body of supporters, he was promptly arrested, tried for treason, and beheaded on Tower Green.

Suggested reading
Lacey, Robert *Robert, Earl of Essex: An Elizabethan Icarus* (1971)
Strachey, Lytton *Elizabeth and Essex* (1928, rep 1986)

Essex Robert Devereux, 3rd Earl of Essex (1591–1646). English soldier. Eldest son of the 2nd earl, he commanded the Parliamentary army at the inconclusive English Civil War battle of Edgehill 1642. Following a disastrous campaign in Cornwall, he resigned his command 1645. Succeeded to earldom 1604.

Esson (Thomas) Louis (Buvelot) (1878–1943). Australian dramatist and freelance writer born in Edinburgh, Scotland. His plays were distinctively Australian in setting and include *Dead Timber* 1911, *The Bride of Gospel Place* 1911, and *The Drovers* 1920. In 1921, with his wife, Dr Hilda Bull, he helped set up the Pioneer Players Movement, a company dedicated to performing Australian plays.

Esteve-Coll Elizabeth Anne Loosemore (1938–). British museum administrator. Keeper of the National Art Library at the Victoria and Albert Museum 1985–88, she was director of the museum itself 1988–95. Her reorganization of the museum staff 1989, when she split the administrative and research roles, led to widespread criticism and the resignation of several senior curators.

Esther in the Old Testament, the wife of the Persian king Ahasuerus (Xerxes I), who prevented the extermination of her people by the king's vizier Haman. Their deliverance is celebrated in the Jewish festival of Purim. Her story is told in the Old Testament Book of Esther.

The laws of Ethelbert ... written in English ... are of unique interest as by far the earliest body of law expressed in any Germanic language.

F M Stenton on ETHELBERT
in Anglo-Saxon England 2nd ed 1947

Ethelbert (*c.* 552–616). King of Kent 560–616. He was defeated by the West Saxons 568 but later became ruler of England S of the river Humber. Ethelbert received the Christian missionary Augustine 597 and later converted to become the first Christian ruler of Anglo-Saxon England. He issued the first written code of laws known in England.

He married a French princess, Bertha.

... called the Unready because he was never ready when the Danes were.

R J Sellar and W C Yeatman on ETHELRED (II) THE UNREADY
in 1066 And All That 1930

Ethelred (II) the Unready (968–1016). King of England from 978. He tried to buy off the Danish raiders by paying Danegeld. In 1002, he ordered the massacre of the Danish settlers, provoking an invasion by Sweyn I of Denmark. War with Sweyn and Sweyn's son, Canute, occupied the rest of Ethelred's reign. He was nicknamed the 'Unready' because of his apparent lack of foresight.

The son of King Edgar, Ethelred became king after the murder of his half-brother, Edward the Martyr.

Etherege George (*c.* 1635–1691). English Restoration dramatist. His play *Love in a Tub* 1664 was the first attempt at the comedy of manners (a genre further developed by Congreve and Sheridan). Later plays include *She Would If She Could* 1668 and *The Man of Mode, or Sir Fopling Flutter* 1676. Knighted by 1680.

Etty William (1787–1849). English painter. He specialized in nudes, as well as mythological or historical subjects such as *Telemachus Rescuing Antiope* 1811. In his work Etty aimed to paint great moral truths and regarded his numerous nude paintings as a dedication to 'God's most glorious work'. Many of his paintings are in the York City Art Gallery, England.

There is no royal road to geometry.

EUCLID
to Ptolemy I in Proclus Commentary on Euclid Prologue

Euclid (*c.* 330–*c.* 260 BC). Greek mathematician who wrote the *Stoicheia/Elements* in 13 books, of which nine deal with plane and solid geometry and four with number theory. His great achievement lay in the systematic arrangement of previous discoveries, based on axioms, definitions, and theorems.

Euclid's works, and the style in which they were presented, formed the basis for all mathematical thought and expression for the next 2,000 years. He used two main styles of presentation: the synthetic (in which one proceeds from the known to the unknown via logical steps) and the analytical (in which one posits the unknown and works towards it from the known, again via logical steps).

Eudoxus was the first to increase the number of the so called general theorems.

Proclus on EUDOXUS
in Commentary on Euclid's Elements

Eudoxus of Cnidus (*c.* 400–*c.* 347 BC). Greek mathematician and astronomer. He devised the first system to account for the motions of celestial bodies, believing them to be carried around the Earth on sets of spheres. Work attributed to Eudoxus includes methods to calculate the area of a circle and to derive the volume of a pyramid or a cone.

Probably Eudoxus regarded the celestial spheres as a mathematical device for ease of computation rather than as physically real, but the idea was taken up by Aristotle and became entrenched in astronomical thought until the time of Tycho Brahe.

In mathematics Eudoxus' early success was in the removal of many of the limitations imposed by Pythagoras on the theory of proportion. Eudoxus also established a test for the equality of two ratios.

The model of planetary motion was published in a book called *On Rates*. Further astronomical observations were included in two other works, *The Mirror* and *Phaenomena*, providing the basis of the constellation system still in use today. In a series of geographical books with the overall title of *A Tour of the Earth*, Eudoxus described the political, historical, and religious customs of the countries of the E Mediterranean.

Eugène Prince of Savoy (full name François Eugène de Savoie Carignan) (1663–1736). Austrian general who had many victories against the Turkish invaders (whom he expelled from Hungary 1697 in the Battle of Zenta) and against France in the War of the Spanish Succession (battles of Blenheim, Oudenaarde, and Malplaquet).

The son of Prince Eugène Maurice of Savoy-Carignano, he was born in Paris. When Louis XIV refused him a commission he entered the Austrian army, and served against the Turks at the defence of Vienna 1683, and against the French on the Rhine and in Italy ten years later. In the War of the Spanish Succession 1701–14 he shared with the British commander Marlborough in his great victories against the French and won many successes as an independent commander in Italy. He again defeated the Turks 1716–18, and fought a last campaign against the French 1734–35.

Suggested reading
Henderson, Nicholas *Prince Eugene of Savoy* (1965)
McKay, Derek *Prince Eugene of Savoy* (1977)

Eugénie Marie Ignace Augustine de Montijo (1826–1920). Empress of France, daughter of the Spanish count of Montijo. In 1853 she married Louis Napoleon, who had become emperor as Napoleon III.

She encouraged court extravagance and Napoleon III's intervention in Mexico, and urged him to fight the Prussians. After his surrender to the Germans at Sedan, NE France, 1870 she fled to England.

Euler Leonhard (1707–1783). Swiss mathematician. He developed the theory of differential equations and the calculus of variations, and worked in astronomy and optics. He also enlarged mathematical notation.

Euler developed spherical trigonometry and demonstrated the significance of the coefficients of trigonometric expansions; Euler's number (e, as it is now called) has various useful theoretical properties and is used in the summation of particular series.

He became professor of physics at the University of St Petersburg 1730. In 1741 he was invited to Berlin by Frederick the Great, where he spent 25 years before returning to Russia.

Euler carried out research into the motion and positions of the Moon, and the gravitational relationships between the Moon, the Sun, and the Earth. His resulting work on tidal fluctuations took him into the realm of fluid mechanics.

Euphronius (*c.* 520–470 BC). Greek vase painter of the Attic School, one of those who introduced the red-figured style, a new form of figure drawing, more advanced in anatomy and foreshortening. Many of his works survive. The bowl showing Herakles and Antaeos wrestling (Louvre) signed by him is a notable example.

Eupolis (*c.* 445–*c.* 411 BC). Greek comic dramatist. He was a contemporary and rival of Aristophanes, with whom he helped create the Old Comedy form. Only fragments of his plays survive.

Euripides (*c.* 485–*c.* 406 BC). Athenian tragic dramatist. He is ranked with Aeschylus and Sophocles as one of the three great tragedians. He wrote about 90 plays, of which 18 and some long fragments survive. These include *Alcestis* 438 BC, *Medea* 431, *Hippolytus* 428, the satyr-drama *Cyclops* about 424–423, *Electra* 417, *Trojan Women* 415, *Iphigenia in Tauris* 413, *Iphigenia in Aulis* about 414–412, and *The Bacchae* about 405 (the last two were produced shortly after his death).

Never say that marriage has more of joy than pain.

EURIPIDES
Alcestis 238

Euripides' questioning of contemporary mores and shrewd psychological analyses made him unpopular, even notorious, during his lifetime, and he was cruelly mocked by the contemporary comic playwright Aristophanes, but he had more influence on the development of later drama than either Aeschylus or Sophocles. Drawing on the sophists, he transformed tragedy with unheroic themes, sympathetic and disturbing portrayals of women's anger, and plots of incident and reunion. Towards the end of his life he left Athens for Macedon.

Eusebio adopted name of Eusebio Ferreira da Silva (1942–). Portuguese footballer, born in Lourenço Marques (now Maputo). He made his international debut 1961 and played for his country 77 times. He spent most of his league career with Benfica, but also played in the USA. He was European Footballer of the Year 1965.

Eusebius (*c.* 260–340). Bishop of Caesarea (modern Qisarya, Israel); author of a history of the Christian church to 324.

Eustachio Bartolommeo (1520–1574). Italian anatomist, the discoverer of the Eustachian tube, leading from the middle ear to the pharynx, and of the Eustachian valve in the right auricle of the heart.

Eutyches (*c.* 384–*c.* 456). Christian theologian. An archimandrite (monastic head) in Constantinople, he held that Jesus had only one nature, the human nature being subsumed in the divine (a belief which became known as Monophysitism). He was exiled after his ideas were condemned as heretical by the Council of Chalcedon 451.

Evans Alice Catherine (1881–1975). US microbiologist whose research into the bacterial contamination of milk led to the recognition of the danger of unpasteurized milk. As a result of her research the incidence of brucellosis was greatly reduced when the dairy industry accepted that all milk should be pasteurized. In 1918 she moved to the Hygienic Laboratories of the United States Public Health Service to research into epidemic meningitis and influenza as well as milk flora.

Evans Arthur John (1851–1941). English archaeologist. His excavation of Knossos on Crete resulted in the discovery of pre-Phoenician Minoan script and proved the existence of the legendary Minoan civilization. Knighted 1911.

Suggested reading
Brown, Ann *Arthur Evans and the Palace of Minos* (1983)
Evans, Joan *Time and Chance* (1943)
Harden, D D *Sir Arthur Evans* (1983)

When a woman behaves like a man, why doesn't she behave like a nice man?

EDITH EVANS
Observer 30 Sept 1956

Evans Edith Mary (1888–1976). English character actress. She performed on the London stage and on Broadway. Her many imposing performances include the Nurse in *Romeo and Juliet* (first performed 1926); her film roles include Lady Bracknell in Wilde's comedy *The Importance of Being Earnest* 1952. Among her other films are *Tom Jones* 1963 and *Crooks and Coronets* 1969. DBE 1946.

Evans Edward Ratcliffe (1881–1957). British naval commander. Evans was second-in-command of the ill-fated Antarctic Expedition of 1909 and led the expedition safely home after the death of Capt Scott 1913. During World War I, he commanded HMS *Broke* in the Dover Patrol.

Evans Geraint Llewellyn (1922–1992). Welsh operatic baritone. In a career spanning 36 years, he sang more than 70 roles. He is best remembered for his singing of the title role in Verdi's *Falstaff*, which he sang and acted at Glyndebourne, Covent Garden, and elsewhere. The warmth of his voice, the clarity of his diction and his engaging stage presence endeared him to opera house audiences, television viewers, and music enthusiasts all over the world.

He made his Glyndebourne debut in 1950 as Guglielmo, one of the lovers in Mozart's *Così Fan Tutte*. Other Mozart roles followed, including Papageno in *The Magic Flute* and Leporello in *Don Giovanni*. Other roles he famously interpreted include Schaunard, the Bohemian musician in Puccini's *La Bohème*, with which he made his Vienna State Opera debut; Beckmesser in Wagner's *Die Meistersinger*, the first of many roles he sang for San Francisco; and Dulcamara, the quack seller of love potions in Donizetti's *L'Elisir d'Amore*, the role in which he made his farewell appearance at Covent Garden 1984. To coincide with this occasion he published his memoirs, *A Knight at the Opera*; he had been knighted in 1969.

Evans Oliver (1755–1819). US engineer who developed high-pressure steam engines and various machines powered by them. He also pioneered production-line techniques in manufacturing.

Evans moved to Philadelphia, where he spent more than ten years unsuccessfully trying to develop a steam carriage. He then turned to stationary steam engines, and built about 50, as well as the *Orukter Amphibole*, a steam dredger he constructed 1804. It had power-driven rollers as well as a paddle so that it could be moved on land under its own power.

Evans Walker (1903–1975). US photographer. He is best known for his documentary photographs of people in the rural American South during the Great Depression. Many of his photographs appeared in James Agee's book *Let Us Now Praise Famous Men* 1941.

Evans-Pritchard Edward Evan (1902–1973). English social anthropologist. His studies, in the 1920s and 1930s, of the Azande and the Nuer peoples of the S Sudan were attempts to understand both how a tribal society was organized and the way in which its people thought. Evans-Pritchard was professor at Oxford 1946–70. He regarded social anthropology as more of an art, like history, than a science. His works include *Witchcraft, Oracles and Magic among the Azande* 1937, marked by the elegance and clarity of his prose style. Knighted 1971.

Evelyn John (1620–1706). English diarist and author. He was a friend of Samuel Pepys, and like him remained in London during the Plague and the Great Fire of London. His fascinating diary, covering the years 1641–1706, and first published 1818, is an important source of information about 17th-century England. He also wrote some 30 books on a wide variety of subjects, including horticulture and the cultivation of trees, history, religion, and the arts. He was one of the founders of the Royal Society.

Born at Wotton House, near Dorking, Surrey, Evelyn was educated at Southover Free School and went, in 1637, to Balliol College, Oxford, but left without a degree. He had earlier been admitted as a law student, and in 1640 took up residence in the Temple, though he did not practise as a barrister. He was interested in horticulture and improved the grounds of his father's estate at Wotton.
Suggested reading
Bowle, John *John Evelyn and His World* (1981)
Hiscock, W G *John Evelyn and His Family Circle* (1955)

Everett Edward (1794–1865). US religious leader, educator, and public figure. He served in the US House of Representatives 1825–35, as governor of Massachusetts 1835–39, and as US minister to England 1841–45. He was president of Harvard University 1846–49. His four-month role as President Fillmore's secretary of state 1852–53 was followed by a short tenure in the US Senate 1853–54. After retiring from public office, he spent the rest of his life as a private citizen speaking out against slavery and in favour of the preservation of the Union.

Everett Kenny. Professional name of Maurice Cole (1944–1995). British television and radio broadcaster, renowned for his zany and surreal style as a disc jockey and comic. His professional progress was hampered by his tendency to make gaffes.

Everett was diagnosed as having AIDS in 1993 and, in an effort to remove the taboo from the subject, made a public announcement of the fact, characteristically making a joke about it.

Evershed John (1864–1956). English astronomer who made solar observations. In 1909, he discovered the radial movements of gases in sunspots (the Evershed effect). He also gave his name to a spectroheliograph, the Evershed spectroscope.

Evert Chris(tine) Marie (1954–). US tennis player. She won her first Wimbledon title 1974, and has since won 21 Grand Slam titles. She became the first woman tennis player to win $1 million in prize money. She has an outstanding two-handed backhand and is a great exponent of baseline technique. Evert retired from competitive tennis 1989.

From 1974 to 1989 she never failed to reach the quarter-finals at Wimbledon. She married British Davis Cup player John Lloyd 1979 but subsequently divorced him.

Ewing (William) Maurice (1906–1974). US geologist whose studies of the ocean floor provided crucial data for the plate-tectonics revolution in geology in the 1960s. He demonstrated that midocean ridges, with deep central canyons, are common to all oceans. He developed his geological interests by working for oil companies. In 1944 he joined the Lamont–Doherty Geological Observatory, New York. From 1947 he was professor of geology at Columbia University, while also holding a position at the Woods Hole Oceanographic Institute.

Exekias (*c.* 550–525 BC). Athenian potter and leading vase painter of the Attic School in the archaic black-figured style. He is known from 11 signed works. A notable example is an amphora from Vulci, Etruria (Vatican), depicting Kastor and Polydeukes and signed by the painter.

Eyck Aldo van (1918–). Dutch architect. He has a strong commitment to social architecture. His works include an orphans' home, the Children's Home 1957–60, and a refuge for single mothers, Mothers' House 1978 (both in Amsterdam).

Eyck Jan van (*c.* 1390–1441). Early Netherlandish painter, brother of Hubert van Eyck, and traditionally regarded as his collaborator in the Ghent masterpiece *The Adoration of the Lamb*. A succession of signed and dated masterpieces shows his profound ability in portraiture, his magical sense of detail, and an appreciation of perspective that goes beyond the efforts of Italian contemporaries. They include the *Madonna of the Chancellor Rolin*, *c.* 1425–26 (Louvre), the *Portrait of Timotheus*, 1432, the *Man with a Turban*, 1433, and the matchless *Marriage of Giovanni Arnolfini and Giovanna Cenami*, 1434, of the National Gallery, the *Madonna of Canon van der Paele*, 1434 (Bruges), the *Madonna of the Fountain*, 1439 (Antwerp), and the *Portrait of the Artist's Wife*, 1439 (Bruges).

One of the great European masters, he is, unlike his brother, a clearly defined historical figure, the products of whose single genius are distinct and unquestioned. He worked as a miniaturist for the Duke of Bavaria, 1422–25, and 1425 entered the service of Philip the Good, Duke of Burgundy, as court painter and 'valet de chambre', on his behalf visiting Spain and Portugal. He settled at Bruges *c.* 1430, still working for the duke, but employed also by the wealthy burgesses of Bruges and the visitors to this international seat of trade.

He (and, it may be, his brother) improved on the already existing technique of oil painting, perhaps by the use of a clarified medium and varnish, though the brilliance of colour and perfection of enamel-like surface attained by Jan must be attributed also to his superbly skilled and methodical handling of paint.

He may be said to have founded a school in the broadest sense, not by an immediate following of pupils and assistants, but in establishing the essential character that art in the southern Netherlands retained until the 16th century.
Suggested reading
Baldiss, L *Jan van Eyck* (1952)
Dhanens, E *Van Eyck* (1990)
Hughes, R and Faggin, G *The Complete Paintings of the van Eycks* (1970)

Eyde Samuel (1866–1940). Norwegian industrial chemist who helped to develop a commercial process for the manufacture of nitric acid that made use of comparatively cheap hydroelectricity. He obtained the hydroelectric rights on some waterfalls in Norway and became director of an electrochemical company 1904, founding a hydroelectric company 1905. He was a member of the Norwegian parliament.

In 1901, while studying the problem of the fixation of nitrogen (the conversion of atmospheric nitrogen into chemically useful compounds), he met his compatriot Christian Birkeland (1867–1917). Together they developed the Birkeland–Eyde process for the economic combination of nitrogen and oxygen (from air) in an electric arc to produce nitrogen oxides and, eventually, nitric oxide.

Eyre Edward John (1815–1901). English explorer who wrote *Expeditions into Central Australia* 1845. He was governor of Jamaica 1864–65. *Lake Eyre* in South Australia is named after him.

Eyre Richard Charles Hastings (1943–). English stage and film director. He succeeded Peter Hall as artistic director of the National Theatre, London 1988. His stage productions include *Guys and Dolls* 1982, *Bartholomew Fair* 1988, *Richard III* 1990, which he set in

1930s Britain; and *Night of the Iguana* 1992. His films include *The Ploughman's Lunch* 1983, *Laughterhouse* (US *Singleton's Pluck*) 1984, and *Tumbledown* 1988 for television.

He has announced his intention to step down as artistic director 1997.

Eysenck Hans Jürgen (1916–). British psychologist. His work concentrates on personality theory and testing by developing behaviour therapy. He is an outspoken critic of psychoanalysis as a therapeutic method. His theory that intelligence is almost entirely inherited and can be only slightly modified by education aroused controversy.

Eysenck was born in Berlin, but left his native Germany for the UK when the Nazis came to power in the 1930s. He studied at London University, where he became professor of psychology 1955.

Suggested reading
Eysenck H *Uses and Abuses of Psychology* (1951)
Eysenck H *Race, Intelligence and Education* (1971)
Eysenck H *The Measurement of Intelligence* (1973)
Gibson, H B *Hans Eysenck* (1981)

Ezekiel (lived *c.* 600 BC). In the Old Testament, a Hebrew prophet. Carried into captivity in Babylon by Nebuchadnezzar 597, he preached that Jerusalem's fall was due to the sins of Israel. The book of Ezekiel begins with a description of a vision of supernatural beings.

Ezra in the Old Testament, a Hebrew scribe who was allowed by Artaxerxes, king of Persia (probably Artaxerxes I, 464–423 BC), to lead his people back to Jerusalem from Babylon 458 BC. He reestablished the Mosaic law (laid down by Moses) and forbade intermarriage.

F

Faber Frederick William (1814–1863). British hymn writer. At first a minister of the Church of England, he became a Roman Catholic priest in 1845, and superior of the Oratory of St Philip Neri (Brompton Oratory, London) in 1849. He wrote 'Hark, Hark, My Soul'.

Fabergé Peter Carl (born Karl Gustavovich) (1846–1920). Russian goldsmith and jeweller. Among his masterpieces was a series of jewelled Easter eggs, the first of which was commissioned by Alexander III for the tsarina 1884.

His workshops in St Petersburg and Moscow were celebrated for the exquisite delicacy of their products, especially the use of gold in various shades. Fabergé died in exile in Switzerland.

Fabius Laurent (1946–). French politician, leader of the Socialist Party (PS) 1992–93. As prime minister 1984–86, he introduced a liberal, free-market economic programme, but his career was damaged by the 1985 Greenpeace sabotage scandal.

Fabius became economic adviser to PS leader François Mitterrand 1976, entered the National Assembly 1978, and was a member of the socialist government from 1981. In 1984, at a time of economic crisis, he was appointed prime minister. He resigned after his party's electoral defeat March 1986, but remained influential as speaker of the National Assembly and as its president from 1988. In Jan 1992 he was elected PS first secretary (leader), replacing Pierre Mauroy. He was ousted as leader April 1993, after the Socialists lost more than 200 seats in the March general election.

Fabius Maximus (Quintus Fabius Maximus Verrucosus) (c. 260–203 BC). Roman general, known as *Cunctator* or 'Delayer' because of his cautious tactics against Hannibal 217–214 BC, when he continually harassed Hannibal's armies but never risked a set battle.

History celebrates the battlefields whereon we meet our death, but scorns to speak of the ploughed fields whereby we live. It knows the names of the kings' bastards, but cannot tell us the origin of wheat.

HENRI FABRE
Souvenirs entomologiques 1879–1907

Fabre Jean Henri Casimir (1823–1915). French entomologist whose studies of wasps, bees, and other insects, particularly their anatomy and behaviour, have become classics. In 1852 he became professor of physics and chemistry at the lycée in Avignon. He held this post for 20 years, eventually resigning because the authorities would not allow girls to attend his science classes. He then abandoned his teaching career and embarked on a serious study of entomology. In addition to numerous entomological papers, Fabre wrote the ten-volume *Souvenirs entomologiques* 1879–1907. Based almost entirely on observations Fabre made in his small plot, this work is a model of meticulous attention to detail.

Fabricius Geronimo. Latinized name of Girolamo Fabrizio (1537–1619). Italian anatomist and embryologist. He made a detailed study of the veins and discovered the valves that direct the blood flow towards the heart. He also studied the development of chick embryos.

Fabricius also investigated the mechanics of respiration, the action of muscles, the anatomy of the larynx (about which he was the first to give a full description) and the eye (he was the first to correctly describe the location of the lens and the first to demonstrate that the pupil changes size).

Fabricius was born in Aquapendente, near Orvieto, and studied at Padua, where he was taught by anatomist Gabriel Fallopius. In 1565 he succeeded Fallopius as professor and remained at Padua for the rest of his career. Fabricius built up an international reputation that attracted students from many countries, including William Harvey.

Fabritius Carel (1622–1654). Dutch painter. He was a pupil of Rembrandt. His own style, lighter and with more precise detail than his master's, is evident for example in *The Goldfinch* 1654 (Mauritshuis, The Hague). He painted religious scenes and portraits.

He settled at Delft, and was killed in the Delft explosion of 1654, a number of his works (which are now rare) perishing with him. Those which survive show an original genius and an unusual capacity for experiment, as in his *View of Delft* (National Gallery). Other remarkable paintings are his *Self-Portrait* (National Gallery) and the famous *The Goldfinch* (The Hague, Mauritshuis), painted in the year of his death. He may well have inspired Vermeer. His brother, Barent Fabritius (1624–73), was also a pupil of Rembrandt, a painter of religious subjects and portraits, but of less note.

Fabry (Marie Paul Auguste) Charles (1867–1945). French physicist who specialized in optics, devising methods for the accurate measurement of interference effects. He took part in inventing a device known as the Fabry–Pérot interferometer. In 1913, Fabry demonstrated that ozone is plentiful in the upper atmosphere and is responsible for filtering out ultraviolet radiation from the Sun.

Fabry was born in Marseille and studied in Paris at the Ecole Polytechnique and the Sorbonne. He became professor at the University of Marseille 1904. The Ministry of Inventions recalled him to Paris in 1914 to investigate interference phenomena in light and sound waves, and in 1921 Fabry became professor of physics at the Sorbonne.

Fadden Artie (Arthur William) (1895–1973). Australian politician, leader of the Country Party 1941–58 and prime minister Aug–Oct 1941. KCMG 1951.

Fadiman Clifton Paul (1904–). US editor and media personality. Following his appointment as book reviewer for the *New Yorker* 1933, Fadiman became moderator of the national radio program *Information Please* 1938–48. In 1944 he was appointed to the editorial board of the Book of the Month Club. From the 1950s, he published literary anthologies and continued to be a popular radio and television personality.

Born in Brooklyn, New York, USA, and educated at Columbia University, Fadiman began his career as a teacher at the New York Ethical Culture School. He became an editor for the US book publishing concern Simon and Schuster 1927.

Fahd (Ibn Abdul Aziz) (1923–). King of Saudi Arabia from 1982, when he succeeded his half-brother Khalid. As head of government, he has been active in trying to bring about a solution to the Middle East conflicts.

Fahrenheit Gabriel Daniel (1686–1736). Polish-born Dutch physicist who invented the first accurate thermometer 1724 and devised the Fahrenheit temperature scale. Using his thermometer, Fahrenheit was able to determine the boiling points of liquids and found that they vary with atmospheric pressure.

Fahrenheit was born in Danzig (Gdańsk). He learned the manufacture of scientific instruments in Amsterdam from 1701, and spent ten years travelling round Europe, meeting scientists. In 1717 he set himself up as an instrumentmaker in Amsterdam, and remained in the Netherlands for the rest of his life.

Fahrenheit's first thermometers contained a column of alcohol which expanded and contracted directly, as originally devised by Danish astronomer Ole Römer in 1701. Fahrenheit substituted mercury for alcohol because its rate of expansion, although less than that of alcohol, is more constant. Furthermore, mercury could be used over a much wider temperature range than alcohol.

Fairbairn William (1789–1874). Scottish engineer who designed a riveting machine that revolutionized the making of boilers for steam engines. He also worked on many bridges, including the wrought iron box-girder construction used first on the railway bridge across the Menai Straits in North Wales.

In Manchester, Fairbairn set up as a manufacturer of cotton-mill machinery. In 1824 he erected two watermills in Zürich. From 1830, he concentrated on shipbuilding, first in Manchester (where he built ships in sections) and then, from 1835, on the river Thames, where his Millwall Iron Works employed some 2,000 people. Baronet 1869.

Fairbanks Douglas, Sr. Stage name of Douglas Elton Ulman (1883–1939). US actor. He played acrobatic swashbuckling heroes in silent films such as *The Mark of Zorro* 1920, *The Three Musketeers* 1921, *Robin Hood* 1922, *The Thief of Bagdad* 1924, and *Don Quixote* 1925. He was married to film star Mary Pickford ('America's Sweetheart') 1920–35. In 1919 he founded United Artists with Charlie Chaplin and D W Griffith.

Fairbanks Douglas Elton, Jr (1909–). US actor. He initially appeared in the same type of swashbuckling film roles as his father, Douglas Fairbanks; for example, in *Catherine the Great* 1934 and *The Prisoner of Zenda* 1937. Later he produced TV films and acted in a variety of productions.

Fairburn Arthur Rex Dugard (1904–1957). New Zealand poet and publicist. His sharply critical engagement with New Zealand life, art, and letters, stimulated by absence in England in the early 1930s, issued in a stream of pamphlets, satiric verse, and colourfully imaginative poetic works. His numerous publications include *Strange Rendezvous* 1952 and *Three Poems: Dominion, The Voyage, To a Friend in the Wilderness* 1952 and the satirical volumes *The Rakehelly Man* 1946 and *The Disadvantages of Being Dead* (published posthumously 1958).

His name in armes through Europe rings / Filling each mouth with envy, or with praise, / And all her jealous monarchs with amaze.

John Milton on THOMAS FAIRFAX
in 'On the Lord General Fairfax at the siege of Colchester'

Fairfax Thomas, 3rd Baron Fairfax (1612–1671). English general, commander in chief of the Parliamentary army in the English Civil War. With Oliver Cromwell he formed the New Model Army and defeated Charles I at Naseby. He opposed the king's execution, resigned in protest 1650 against the invasion of Scotland, and participated in the restoration of Charles II after Cromwell's death. Knighted 1640, succeeded to barony 1648.

Fairweather Ian (1891–1974). Australian artist. He travelled extensively in Asia before settling in Australia and the influence of contact with Chinese, Indonesian, and Australian Aboriginal cultures is evident in works such as *Monastery* 1960 (Australian National Gallery, Canberra). His paintings are abstract in style, and use the natural colours of the earth.

Faisal I (1885–1933). King of Iraq 1921–33. An Arab nationalist leader during World War I, he was instrumental in liberating the Middle East from Ottoman control and was declared king of Syria in 1918 but deposed by the French in 1920. The British then installed him as king in Iraq, where he continued to foster pan-Arabism.

Faisal ibn Abd al-Aziz (1905–1975). King of Saudi Arabia from 1964. He was the younger brother of King Saud, on whose accession 1953 he was declared crown prince. He was prime minister 1953–60

and 1962–75. In 1964 he emerged victorious from a lengthy conflict with his brother and adopted a policy of steady modernization of his country. He was assassinated by his nephew.

Fajans Kasimir (1887–1975). Polish-born US chemist who did pioneering work on radioactivity and isotopes. He also formulated rules that help to explain valence and chemical bonding. He worked in Germany 1911–35, becoming director of the Munich Institute of Physical Chemistry. In 1936, he emigrated to the USA and served as a professor at the University of Michigan, Ann Arbor.

Falcón Juan Crisóstomo (1820–1870). Venezuelan marshal and president 1863–68. Falcón's rule saw the beginnings of economic recovery after the chaos of the Federal Wars 1858–63. He travelled around the country putting down uprisings, while his ministers in Caracas built roads, restored the nation's finances, and established foreign trade links. He fell from power because he was unable to tackle splits in the ruling Liberal party.

Falconet Etienne-Maurice (1716–1791). French sculptor. His works range from Baroque to gentle Rococo in style. He directed sculptural modelling at the Sèvres porcelain factory 1757–66. His bronze equestrian statue *Peter the Great* in St Petersburg was commissioned 1766 by Catherine II.

Faldo Nick (Nicholas Alexander) (1957–). English golfer who was the first Briton in 54 years to win three British Open titles, and the only person after Jack Nicklaus to win two successive US Masters titles (1989 and 1990). He is one of only six golfers to win the Masters and British Open in the same year.

Since turning professional in 1976 he has won more than 25 tournaments worldwide, with career earnings in excess of £3 million.

Falkender Marcia Matilda Williams, Baroness Falkender (1932–). British political secretary to Labour prime minister Harold Wilson from 1956. She was influential in the 'kitchen cabinet' of the 1964–70 government, as described in her book *Inside No 10* 1972.

Falkenhausen Alexander (1878–1966). German general; military governor of Belgium and N France 1940–44. He maintained strict control of his area though he deliberately ignored many Gestapo directives and did his best to make life tolerable for the population. He was implicated by others in the July Plot against Hitler, and was recalled to Berlin and interrogated, but no evidence was found against him. At the end of the war he was arrested by the Allies and was sentenced to 12 years imprisonment by a Belgian court 1951.

Falkenhayn Erich Georg Anton Sebastian von (1861–1922). German soldier. Falkenhayn served on the expedition to China 1900

Faldo The English golfer Nick Faldo, 1993. Faldo has won more than 25 tournaments since turning professional 1976. (Image Select)

and became minister of war 1913. On the outbreak of World War I he became Chief of the General Staff and remained in this post until he was removed by the Kaiser Aug 1916 after the failure of the German attacks on Verdun. He was sent to the Eastern Front where he succeeded in subduing Romania before handing over his command to General von Mackensen 1917. He then took up an unsuccessful command in support of the Turks against the British in the Middle East and was recalled March 1918.

Considered by many to be the German Army's finest strategist, Falkenhayn was less successful as a field commander.

When it is not necessary to change, it is necessary not to change.

LUCIUS CARY, 2ND VISCOUNT FALKLAND
Speech concerning Episcopacy in House of Commons
22 Nov 1641 quoted in *A Discourse of Infallibility* 1660

Falkland Lucius Cary, 2nd Viscount Falkland (*c.* 1610–1643). English soldier and politician. He was elected to the Long Parliament 1640 and tried hard to secure a compromise peace between Royalists and Parliamentarians. He was killed at the Battle of Newbury in the Civil War. Viscount 1633.

The excellence of natural Andalusian melody is revealed by the fact that it is the only music continuously and abundantly used by foreign composers.

MANUEL DE FALLA
Cante Jondo 1922

Falla Manuel de (full name Manuel Maria de Falla y Matheu) (1876–1946). Spanish composer. His opera *La vida breve/Brief Life* 1905 (performed 1913) was followed by the ballets *El amor brujo/Love the Magician* 1915 and *El sombrero de tres picos/The Three-Cornered Hat* 1919, and his most ambitious concert work, *Noches en los jardines de España/Nights in the Gardens of Spain* 1916.

Born in Cádiz, he lived in France, where he was influenced by the Impressionist composers Debussy and Ravel. In 1939 he moved to Argentina. The folk idiom of southern Spain is an integral part of his compositions. He also wrote songs and pieces for piano and guitar.

Fallopius Gabriel. Latinized name of Gabriele Falloppio (1523–1562). Italian anatomist who discovered the Fallopian tubes, which he described as 'trumpets of the uterus', and named the *vagina*. As well as the reproductive system, he studied the anatomy of the brain and eyes, and gave the first accurate description of the inner ear.

Fallopius, born in Modena, studied at Padua under Andreas Vesalius, becoming professor of anatomy at Pisa 1548 and Padua 1551. He was the teacher of Geronimo Fabricius.

Faludi Susan (1959–). US journalist. In *Backlash: The Undeclared War Against American Women* 1991, she argued that in the 1980s there had been a backlash against the advances made by women, instilling the idea that feminism had led women to expect to be able to have a career and a family, and their new roles had made them miserable.

Faludi was born in New York and began her career as a journalist 1981. She won the Pulitzer Prize 1991 for 'The Reckoning', an investigation into the human costs of the 1986 buyout of Safeway Stores, which appeared in the *Wall Street Journal* 1990.

Fangio Juan Manuel (1911–1995). Argentine racing-car driver who won the drivers' world championship a record five times 1951–57. For most of his career he drove a blue and yellow Maserati.

Fang Lizhi (1936–). Chinese political dissident and astrophysicist. He advocated human rights and Western-style pluralism and encouraged his students to campaign for democracy. In 1989, after the Tiananmen Square massacre, he sought refuge in the US embassy in Beijing and, over a year later, received official permission to leave China.

Fanon Frantz Omar (1925–1961). French political writer. His experiences in Algeria during the war for liberation in the 1950s led to the writing of *Les Damnés de la terre/The Wretched of the Earth* 1964, which calls for violent revolution by the peasants of the Third World.

Suggested reading
Caute, David *Fanon* (1970)
Gendzier, Irene *Frantz Fanon: A Critical Study* (1973)
Onwuanibe, R C *A Critique of Revolutionary Humanism: Frantz Fanon* (1983)

Fantin-Latour (Ignace) Henri (Jean Théodore) (1836–1904). French painter. He excelled in delicate still lifes, flower paintings, and portraits. *Homage à Delacroix* 1864 (Musée d'Orsay, Paris) is a portrait group featuring several poets, authors, and painters, including Charles Baudelaire and James McNeill Whistler.

At Whistler's suggestion he visited England and perhaps was influenced by the meticulous detail of the Pre-Raphaelites, though the sincerely executed still lifes and flower-pieces by which he is best known err if anything towards photographic realism. He produced also some allegorical fancies, often carried out in lithography, but it is by virtue of his still life that he has stood the test of time.

Faraday Michael (1791–1867). English chemist and physicist. He became a laboratory assistant to Humphry Davy at the Royal Institution 1813, and in 1833 succeeded him as professor of chemistry. Faraday delivered highly popular lectures at the Royal Institution 1825–62. In 1821 he began experimenting with electromagnetism, and ten years later discovered the induction of electric currents and made the first dynamo. He subsequently found that a magnetic field will rotate the plane of polarization of light. Faraday produced the basic laws of electrolysis 1834.

In 1821 he devised an apparatus that demonstrated the conversion of electrical energy into motive force, for which he is usually credited with the invention of the electric motor. Faraday's work in chemistry included the isolation of benzene from gas oils 1835. He demonstrated the use of platinum as a catalyst and showed the importance in chemical reactions of surfaces and inhibitors.

Suggested reading
Gooding, David and James, Frank (eds) *Faraday Rediscovered* (1986)
Williams, Leslie *Michael Faraday: A Biography* (1965)

Faraday *An artist's impression of Michael Faraday giving one of his famous lectures at the Royal Institution in the presence of Prince Albert and the Prince of Wales. The first of these immensely popular lectures took place in 1825 and they continued until 1862, long after the end of Faraday's own experimental career.* (Ann Ronan/Image Select)

Fargo William George (1818–1881). US pioneer of long-distance transport. In 1844 he established with Henry Wells (1805–1878) and Daniel Dunning the first express company to carry freight west of Buffalo. Its success led to his appointment 1850 as secretary of the newly established American Express Company, of which he was president 1868–81. He also established *Wells, Fargo & Company* 1851, carrying goods express between New York and San Francisco via Panama.

Farman Henry (1874–1958). Anglo-French aviation pioneer. He designed a biplane 1907–08 and in 1909 flew a record distance of 160 km/100 mi. With his brother Maurice Farman (1878–1964), he founded an aircraft works at Billancourt, Brittany, supplying the army in France and other countries. The UK also made use of Farman's inventions, for example, air-screw reduction gears, in World War II.

Farmer Frances (1913–1970). US actress. She starred in such films as *Come and Get It* 1936, *The Toast of New York* 1937, and *Son of Fury* 1942, before her career was ended by alcoholism and mental illness.

Farnaby Giles (1563–1640). English composer. He wrote madrigals, psalms for the *Whole Booke of Psalms* 1621, edited by Thomas Ravenscroft (1582–1633), and music for virginals (an early keyboard instrument), over 50 pieces being represented in the 17th-century manuscript collection the *Fitzwilliam Virginal Book*.

Farnese Italian family, originating in upper Lazio, who held the duchy of Parma 1545–1731. Among the family's most notable members were Alessandro Farnese (1468–1549), who became Pope Paul III in 1534 and granted his duchy to his illegitimate son Pier Luigi (1503–1547); and Elizabeth (1692–1766), niece of the last Farnese duke, who married Philip V of Spain and was a force in European politics of the time.

The whole world is in revolt. Soon there will be only five Kings left – the King of England, the King of Spades, the King of Clubs, the King of Hearts and the King of Diamonds.

FAROUK
Remark at a conference in Cairo 1948

Farouk (1920–1965). King of Egypt 1936–52. He succeeded his father Fuad I. In 1952 a coup headed by General Muhammed Neguib and Colonel Gamal Nasser compelled him to abdicate, and his son Fuad II was temporarily proclaimed in his place.

Hanging and marriage, you know, go by Destiny.

GEORGE FARQUHAR
Recruiting Officer III. ii 1706

Farquhar George (*c.* 1677–1707). Irish dramatist. His plays *The Recruiting Officer* 1706 and *The Beaux' Stratagem* 1707 are in the tradition of the Restoration comedy of manners, although less robust.

Farragut David Glasgow (1801–1870). US admiral, born near Knoxville, Tennessee. During the US Civil War he took New Orleans 1862, after destroying the Confederate fleet, and in 1864 effectively put an end to blockade-running at Mobile. The ranks of vice admiral (1864) and admiral (1866) were created for him by Congress.

Farrakhan Louis (born Louis Eugene Walcott) (1933–). African-American religious and political figure, leader of the Nation of Islam. Farrakhan preaches strict adherence to Muslim values and black separatism. His outspoken views against Jews, homosexuals, and whites have caused outrage. In 1995 he organized a march of some 400,000 black men in Washington.

In 1986 Farrakhan was banned from entering the UK for his anti-Semitic views. In one speech he referred to Judaism as a 'gutter religion'.

Born in the Bronx in New York, Farrakhan studied to be a teacher and worked as a singer before he was recruited to the Black Muslims by Malcolm X. When the group was dissolved in 1985 he remained faithful to its original principles, forming a splinter group using its original name, the Nation of Islam. A powerful leader and impressive speaker, he has increased the group's membership to over 15,000.

Farrell J(ames) G(ordon) (1935–1979). English historical novelist. His work includes *Troubles* 1970, set in Ireland, and *The Siege of Krishnapur* 1973.

Farrell James T(homas) (1904–1979). US novelist and short-story writer. His naturalistic documentary of the Depression, the *Studs Lonigan* trilogy 1932–35 comprising *Young Lonigan*, *The Young Manhood of Studs Lonigan*, and *Judgment Day*, describes the development of a young Catholic man in Chicago after World War I, and was written from his own experience. *The Face of Time* 1953 is one of his finest works.

Farrell Terry (Terence) (1938–). English architect. He works in a Post-Modern idiom, largely for corporate clients seeking an alternative to the rigours of Modernist or High Tech office blocks. His Embankment Place scheme 1991 sits theatrically on top of Charing Cross station in Westminster, London, and has been likened to a giant jukebox. Alban Gate in the City of London 1992 is a continuation of the language but is more towerlike in form.

Farrell's style is robust and eclectic, and he is not afraid to make jokes in architecture, such as the gaily painted giant egg cups that adorn the parapet of his TV AM building in Camden, London, 1981–82. Other works include studios for Limehouse Productions, Henley Royal Regatta HQ, and the Craft Council Galleries.

Farrelly Bernard ('Midget') (1944–). Australian surfer. In 1963 he became the first non-Hawaiian to win the Makaha International event in Hawaii, then the unofficial world championship. The next year he won the first official world championship at Manly Beach, Sydney, and was runner-up in the 1968 world championships.

Farr-Jones Nick (Nicholas) (1962–). Australian rugby union player. He is Australia's most capped scrum half and has captained his country on more than 30 occasions. He was captain of Australia's 1991 World Cup winning team, and plays for Sydney University and New South Wales.

If I seem to be running, it's because I'm pursued.

MIA FARROW
quoted in *Leslie Halliwell's Filmgoer's Companion* 1965

Farrow Mia Villiers (1945–). US film and television actress. Popular since the late 1960s, she was associated with the director Woody Allen, both on and off screen, 1982–92. She starred in his films *Zelig* 1983, *Hannah and Her Sisters* 1986, and *Crimes and Misdemeanors* 1990, as well as in Roman Polanski's *Rosemary's Baby* 1968. In 1992 she split acrimoniously from Allen.

Fassbinder Rainer Werner (1946–1982). West German film director. He began as a fringe actor and founded his own 'anti-theatre' before moving into films. His works are mainly stylized indictments of contemporary German society. He made more than 40 films, including *Die bitteren Tränen der Petra von Kant/The Bitter Tears of Petra von Kant* 1972, *Angst essen Seele auf/Fear Eats the Soul* 1974, and *Die Ehe von Maria Braun/The Marriage of Maria Braun* 1979.

Fassett Kaffe (1940–). US knitwear and textile designer. He has been based in the UK from 1964. He co-owns a knitwear company and his textiles appear in important art collections around the world. Fassett took up knitting when encountering Shetland yarns on a trip to Scotland, and now designs and produces for Missoni, Bill Gibb, and others.

Fathy Hassan (1900–1989). Egyptian architect. In his work at the village of New Gournia in Upper Egypt 1945–48, he demonstrated the value of indigenous building technology and natural materials in solving contemporary housing problems. This, together with his book *The Architecture of the Poor* 1973, influenced the growth of community architecture enabling people to work directly with architects in building their homes.

Fatimid dynasty of Muslim Shi'ite caliphs founded 909 by Obaidallah, who claimed to be a descendant of Fatima (the prophet Muhammad's daughter) and her husband Ali, in N Africa. In 969 the Fatimids conquered Egypt, and the dynasty continued until overthrown by Saladin 1171.

A politician to his fingertips, he was essentially a political manager, a doer rather than a talker.

Lord Windlesham on BRIAN FAULKNER
Dictionary of National Biography

Faulkner (Arthur) Brian (Deane), Baron Faulkner of Downpatrick (1921–1977). Northern Ireland Unionist politician. He was the last prime minister of Northern Ireland 1971–72 before the Stormont Parliament was suspended. Baron 1977.

I believe man will not merely endure, he will prevail. He is immortal, not because he, alone among creatures, has an inexhaustible voice but because he has a soul, a spirit capable of compassion and sacrifice and endurance.

WILLIAM FAULKNER
Nobel prize speech 1950

Faulkner William Cuthbert (1897–1962). US novelist. His works are noted for their difficult narrative styles and epic mapping of a quasi-imaginary Southern region, Yoknapatawpha County. His third and most celebrated novel, *The Sound and the Fury* 1929, deals with the decline of a Southern family, told in four voices, beginning with an especially complex stream-of-consciousness narrative. He was recognized as one of America's greatest writers only after World War II, and was awarded the Nobel Prize for Literature 1949.

Faulkner served in World War I and his first novel, *Soldier's Pay* 1929, is about a war veteran. After the war he returned to Oxford, Mississippi, on which he was to model the town of Jefferson in the county of Yoknapatawpha, the setting of his major novels. Later works using highly complex structures include *As I Lay Dying* 1930, *Light in August* 1932, and *Absalom, Absalom!* 1936. These were followed by his less experimental trilogy, *The Hamlet* 1940, *The Town* 1957, and *The Mansion* 1959, covering the rise of the materialistic Snopes family. Other works include *The Unvanquished* 1938, stories of the Civil War, and *The Wild Palms* 1939.

Suggested reading
Blotner, J *Faulkner: A Biography* (1972)
Brooks, C *William Faulkner: The Yoknapatawpha County* (1964)
Friedman, A W *William Faulkner* (1985)
McHaney, T *William Faulkner: A Reference Guide* (1976)

For me ... music exists to elevate us as far as possible above everyday existence.

GABRIEL FAURÉ
letter to his son, Philippe, 1908

Fauré Gabriel Urbain (1845–1924). French composer. He wrote songs, chamber music, and a choral *Requiem* 1888. He was a pupil of Saint-Saëns, became professor of composition at the Paris Conservatoire 1896, and was director 1905–20.

Fawcett Millicent (born Garrett) (1847–1929). English suffragette, younger sister of Elizabeth Garrett Anderson. A nonmilitant, she rejected the violent acts of some of her contemporaries in the suffrage movement. She joined the first Women's Suffrage Committee 1867 and became president of the Women's Unionist Association 1889.

She was also active in property reform and campaigned for the right of married women to own their own property. Her publications include *Political Economy for Beginners* 1870, *Women's Suffrage* 1912, and *Women's Victory and After*. DBE 1925.

Fawcett Percy Harrison (1867–1925). British explorer. After several expeditions to delineate frontiers in South America during the rubber boom, he set off in 1925, with his eldest son John and a friend, into the Mato Grosso to find the legendary 'lost cities' of the ancient Indians, the 'cradle of Brazilian civilization'. They were never seen again.

A desperate disease requires a dangerous remedy.

GUY FAWKES
6 Nov 1605

Fawkes Guy (1570–1606). English conspirator in the Gunpowder Plot to blow up King James I and the members of both Houses of Parliament. Fawkes, a Roman Catholic convert, was arrested in the cellar underneath the House 4 Nov 1605, tortured, and executed. The event is still commemorated in Britain and elsewhere every 5 Nov with bonfires, fireworks, and the burning of the 'guy', an effigy.

Suggested reading
Edwards, F *Guy Fawkes* (1962)
Garnett, Henry *Portrait of Guy Fawkes* (1962)
Parkinson, Northcote *Gunpowder, Treason and Plot* (1977)

Fayol Henri (1841–1925). French pioneer of management theory. He is generally regarded as the first to question the nature of management and put forward a theory designed to be applicable in all managerial contexts.

Fayol attempted to postulate his theory in such a way that the business procedures he had studied and developed as managing director of a mining and metallurgical combine in France could be applied to any organization, regardless of size or nature. He stipulated that managerial activity should involve five major elements: forecasting and planning; organizing; commanding; coordinating; and controlling. His ideas remained influential for much of the 20th century.

Fayolle Marie Emile (1852–1928). French general. He replaced General Castelnau as commander of French armies in the Somme 1916. In 1917 he took command of the Army of the Centre, fighting the battles of the Aisne, and became commander in chief of French forces in Italy Oct 1917. He returned to France 1918 and after the Armistice commanded the French Army of Occupation in Germany.

Febvre Lucien (1878–1956). French historian who in 1929 founded, with his colleague Marc Bloch, the highly influential journal *Annales d'histoire économique et sociale*. His pupil Fernand Braudel became the leading exponent of the Annales school, of which Febvre and Bloch were the pioneers. This new kind of history emphasized economic and social change, studying human affairs and the impersonal forces that really influenced people rather than narrating the deeds of the famous or dealing with only dramatic events.

Drawing on research in social psychology and human geography, and influenced by the anthropologist and philosopher Lucien Lévy-Bruhl, Febvre developed the idea of 'collective mentalities' that went beyond individual thinkers, their beliefs and values and that differed from age to age. For example, in his classic *Le Problème de l'incroyance au XVIème siècle: La Religion de Rabelais/The Problem of Unbelief in the 16th Century: The Religion of Rabelais* 1942, he argues that the writer Rabelais and his contemporaries could not have been atheists because the mentality required for disbelief did not exist at the time.

For much of his career Febvre was a professor at Strasbourg University and then president of the VIth section of the Ecole Practique des Hautes Etudes in Paris, now the Ecole des Hautes

Etudes en Sciences Sociales. In the latter post he was succeeded by Braudel.

Fechner Gustav Theodor (1801–1887). German psychologist. He became professor of physics at Leipzig in 1834, but in 1839 turned to the study of psychophysics (the relationship between physiology and psychology). He devised *Fechner's law*, a method for the exact measurement of sensation.

Federman Raymond (1928–). US writer. His playful postmodernist texts draw on his French-Jewish boyhood, his family's death in Auschwitz, and his postwar emigration to America. He coined the term 'surfiction' to describe a form of writing, including that of his own, Steve Katz (1935–), Gilbert Sorrentino (1929–), and Ronald Sukenick, which lays bare narrative conventions, resists interpretation, and engages with historical reality. His works include *Double or Nothing* 1971, *The Voice in the Closet* 1979, and *The Twofold Vibration* 1982.

Feijó Diogo Antônio (1784–1843). Brazilian politician, regent of Brazil 1835–37. The illegitimate son of a priest, Feijó trained for the priesthood and was a teacher before his election to the Portuguese Cortes (parliament) 1821. A dedicated liberal and opponent of the slave trade, he was appointed minister of justice after the abdication of Pedro II 1831. A hostile parliament allowed him to accomplish little as regent.

Feininger Lyonel Charles Adrian (1871–1956). US abstract artist, an early Cubist. He worked at the Bauhaus school of design and architecture in Germany 1919–33, and later helped to found the Bauhaus in Chicago. Inspired by Cubism and *der Blaue Reiter*, he developed a style based on translucent geometric planes arranged in subtle harmonic patterns.

Feininger was born in New York, the son of German immigrants. While in Germany, he formed the *Blaue Vier* (Blue Four) 1924 with the painters Alexei von Jawlensky, Wassily Kandinsky, and Paul Klee. He returned to the USA after the rise of the Nazis.

Feinstein Dianne (born Goldman) (1933–). US Democrat politician. She was mayor of San Francisco 1978–88, the first woman in the post, and became senator from California 1993.

She was born in San Francisco. An expert on criminal justice, she was appointed to the California Women's Board of Terms and Paroles 1962, elected to the Board of Supervisors 1969, and was president 1970–72 and 1974–76. In Dec 1978, following the assassination of Mayor George Moscone (1949–1978), she was elected to

finish Moscone's term as mayor to the end of 1979, and then re-elected mayor. She achieved a reputation as a hands-on governor, with no detail too small for her attention.

She was defeated by Senator Pete Wilson (1933–) in the election for governor of California 1991, and elected to the Senate 1992 to fill the vacancy left by him. She was re-elected 1994.

Feldman Morton (1926–1987). US composer. An associate of John Cage and Earle Brown in the 1950s, he devised an indeterminate notation based on high, middle, and low instrumental registers and time cells of fixed duration for his *Projection* series for various ensembles 1950–51, later exploiting the freedoms of classical notation in a succession of reflective studies in vertical tone mixtures including *Madame Press Died Last Week at 90* 1970.

Feller Bob (Robert William Andrew) (1918–). US baseball pitcher. He made his major-league debut 1936 and went on to a brilliant pitching career that lasted for the next 20 years. He led the American League six times by winning 20 or more games in a season; he pitched 3 no-hitters and 12 one-hitters and posted 266 career wins. Feller was famed for his powerful fastball and pinpoint control.

Born in Van Meter, Iowa, USA, Feller was signed by the Cleveland Indians organization while he was still in high school. He was elected to the Baseball Hall of Fame 1962.

Feller William (1906–1970). Yugoslavian-born US mathematician largely responsible for making the theory of probability accessible to students of subjects other than mathematics through his textbook on the subject. In the theory of limits, he formulated the law of the iterated logarithm. His work is set out in *Introduction to Probability Theory and its Applications* 1950–66.

Feller was born and educated in Zagreb and also studied in Germany at Göttingen. He worked at the University of Stockholm 1933–39. On the outbreak of World War II, he emigrated to the USA. He was professor of mathematics at Cornell University, New York, 1945–50, and at Princeton from 1950.

Fellini Federico (1920–1993). Italian film director and screenwriter. His work has been a major influence on modern cinema. His films combine dream and fantasy sequences with satire and autobiographical detail. They include *I vitelloni/The Young and the Passionate* 1953, *La strada/The Street* 1954 (Academy Award), *Le notti di Cabiria/Nights of Cabiria* 1956 (Academy Award), *La dolce vita* 1960, *Otto e mezzo/8½* 1963 (Academy Award), *Satyricon* 1969, *Roma/Fellini's Rome* 1972, *Amarcord* 1974 (Academy Award), *La città delle donne/City of Women* 1980, and *Ginger e Fred/Ginger and Fred* 1986. He was presented with a Special Academy Award for his life's work 1993.

Distinctively 'Felliniesque', his work is intensely personal and vividly original. Peopled with circus, carnival, and music-hall characters and the high society of Rome, his films created iconic images such as that of actress Anita Ekberg in the Trevi Fountain, Rome, in *La dolce vita*.

Fellini was one of the most celebrated creators the Italian cinema has produced, and achieved near-legendary status in his home country. His significance as a film director gained him 'superstar' status in the 1960s, and was instrumental in establishing the artistic authenticity of filmmaking. His two most famous films, *La dolce vita* and *Otto e mezzo* are daring in both form and content and rank among the classics of world cinema.

Suggested reading
Baxter, John *Fellini* (1993)
Burke, F *Federico Fellini* (1984)
Fava, C and Vigano, A *The Films of Federico Fellini* (1985)
Fellini, Federico *Fellini on Fellini* (1976)
Leprohon, Pierre *The Italian Cinema* (1972)

Fellows Charles (1799–1860). English archaeologist. A wealthy amateur, he discovered several ancient sites of the region of Lycia, Turkey, including in 1838 the ruins of Xanthos, and successfully negotiated with the Turkish government for the purchase of sculptural remains from the site for the British Museum. On his return he

Fellini Italian film director Federico Fellini. One of the most original filmmakers in the history of cinema, Fellini moved from the comparative realism and astringent satire of Nights of Cabiria *1956 and* La dolce vita *1960 to the Baroque fantasy and autobiography of* 8½ *1963 and* The Ship Sails On *1983.*

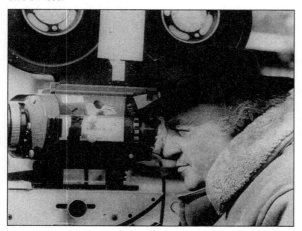

was given a knighthood (1845), and a room in the British Museum was named in his honour.

Fender (Clarence) Leo (1909–1991). US guitarmaker. He created the solid-body electric guitar, the Fender Broadcaster 1948 (renamed the Telecaster 1950), and the first electric bass guitar, the Fender Precision, 1951. The Fender Stratocaster guitar dates from 1954. In 1965 he sold the Fender name to CBS, which continues to make the instruments.

Fender began making amplifiers and Hawaiian-style guitars 1945, and built solid-body guitars for several country musicians. Although the guitarist and producer Les Paul was also working independently on a solid-body electric guitar, Fender was the first to get his model on the market. The design was totally new, with a one-piece neck bolted on to a wooden body, and could easily be mass-produced. Its clear trebly sound was particularly suited to country music; rock guitarists have generally preferred its successor, the futuristically streamlined Stratocaster, whose three pickups made possible various electronic modifications of tone and volume.

Fenech Jeff (Jeffrey) (1964–). Australian boxer. He turned professional in 1984 and the next year won the IBF world bantamweight title, defeating Japan's Satoshi Shingaki. He subsequently captured the WBC junior featherweight title 1987, defeating Samart Payakarum of Thailand, and the WBC featherweight title 1988, defeating Victor Callejas of Puerto Rico. He has since successfully defended that title three times.

Fénelon François de Salignac de la Mothe (1651–1715). French writer and ecclesiastic. He entered the priesthood 1675 and in 1689 was appointed tutor to the duke of Burgundy, grandson of Louis XIV. For him he wrote his *Fables* and *Dialogues des morts/Dialogues of the Dead* 1690, *Télémaque/Telemachus* 1699, and *Plans de gouvernement/Plans of Government*.

Télémaque, with its picture of an ideal commonwealth, had the effect of a political manifesto, and Louis banished Fénelon to Cambrai, where he had been consecrated archbishop 1695. Fénelon's mystical *Maximes des saints/Sayings of the Saints* 1697 had also led to condemnation by Pope Innocent XII and a quarrel with the Jansenists, who believed that only those chosen by God beforehand received salvation.

Fenoglio Beppe (1922–1963). Italian novelist. His work is set mainly during World War II and depicts the Italian resistance fighters of his native region near Alba, N Italy; novels include *Il Partigiano Johnny* (unfinished) 1968 and *I ventrito' giorni della citta' di Alba* 1952.

Fenton Roger (1819–1869). English photographer. He is best known for his comprehensive documentation of the Crimean War 1855. He was a founder member of the Photographic Society (later the Royal Photographic Society) in London 1853 but completely gave up photography 1860.

Being an old maid is like death by drowning, a really delightful sensation after you cease to struggle.

EDNA FERBER
quoted in R E Drennan *Wit's End* 1973

Ferber Edna (1887–1968). US novelist and dramatist. Her novel *Show Boat* 1926 was adapted as an operetta 1927 by Jerome Kern and Oscar Hammerstein II, and her plays, in which she collaborated with George S Kaufmann, include *The Royal Family* 1927, about the Barrymore theatrical family, *Dinner at Eight* 1932, and *Stage Door* 1936. Her novels include *The Girls* 1921, *So Big* 1924 (Pulitzer Prize), *Cimarron* 1930, *Giant* 1952 (filmed 1956), about Texas, and *Ice Palace* 1959, about Alaska.

Ferdinand II King of Aragon from 1479, also known as ◊Ferdinand V of Castile.

Ferdinand (1861–1948). King of Bulgaria 1908–18. Son of Prince Augustus of Saxe-Coburg-Gotha, he was elected prince of Bulgaria 1887 and, in 1908, proclaimed Bulgaria's independence from Turkey and assumed the title of tsar. In 1915 he entered World War I as Germany's ally, and in 1918 abdicated.

Fox of the Balkans.

Nickname given to FERDINAND for his sly
political behaviour and political astuteness.

Ferdinand five kings of Castile:

Ferdinand (I) the Great (*c.* 1016–1065). King of Castile from 1035. He began the reconquest of Spain from the Moors and united all NW Spain under his and his brothers' rule.

For over seven hundred years the Crown of Spain has not been as great or as resplendent it is now, both in the west and the east, and all, after God, by my work and labour.

FERDINAND V
quoted in John Lotherington *Years of Renewal* 1988

Ferdinand V (1452–1516). King of Castile from 1474, *Ferdinand II* of Aragon from 1479, and *Ferdinand III* of Naples from 1504; first king of all Spain. In 1469 he married his cousin Isabella I, who succeeded to the throne of Castile 1474; they were known as *the Catholic Monarchs* because after 700 years of rule by the Moors, they catholicized Spain. When Ferdinand inherited the throne of Aragon 1479, the two great Spanish kingdoms were brought under a single government for the first time. They introduced the Inquisition 1480; expelled the Jews, forced the final surrender of the Moors at Granada, and financed Columbus' expedition to the Americas, 1492.

Fenton English photographer Roger Fenton, whose coverage of the Crimean war made him the first photographer ever to document a war. He took over 350 pictures, travelling in a specially converted 'photographic van' that served as a mobile dark room. His stark pictures did much to publicize the inadequacies of the British campaign.

Ferdinand conquered Naples 1500–03 and Navarre 1512, completing the unification of Spain and making it one of the chief powers in Europe.

Suggested reading

Fernández-Armesto, Felipe *Ferdinand and Isabella* (1975)

Mariéjol, J H *The Spain of Ferdinand and Isabella* (trs 1961)

Ferdinand three Holy Roman emperors:

Let justice be done, though the world perish.

FERDINAND I
Motto (attributed) quoted in Johannes Manlius
Locorum Communium Collectanea II 290 1565

Ferdinand I (1503–1564). Holy Roman emperor who succeeded his brother Charles V 1558; king of Bohemia and Hungary from 1526, king of the Germans from 1531. He reformed the German monetary system and reorganized the judicial Aulic council (*Reichshofrat*). He was the son of Philip the Handsome and grandson of Maximilian I.

Genial and ascetic by turns ... privately amiable and kind-hearted while pursuing his joint aims of absolutism and orthodoxy with unflinching ruthlessness, if insufficient realism.

E N Williams on FERDINAND II
in *Penguin Dictionary of English and European History 1485–1789* 1980

Ferdinand II (1578–1637). Holy Roman emperor from 1619, when he succeeded his uncle Matthias; king of Bohemia from 1617 and of Hungary from 1618. A zealous Catholic, he provoked the Bohemian revolt that led to the Thirty Years' War. He was a grandson of Ferdinand I.

Sad, shy and taciturn ... he was too artistic and scholarly to be a heroic crusader for church and Empire.

E N Williams on FERDINAND III
in *Penguin Dictionary of English and European History 1485–1789* 1980

Ferdinand III (1608–1657). Holy Roman emperor from 1637 when he succeeded his father Ferdinand II; king of Hungary from 1625. Although anxious to conclude the Thirty Years' War, he did not give religious liberty to Protestants.

Ferdinand five kings of Naples, including:

Ferdinand I (1423–1494). King of Naples 1458–94, known as Ferrante. He was the son of Alphonso V of Aragon (1396–1458) and his illegitimacy brought him into conflict with the papacy many times during his reign. His authoritarian rule provoked several baronial revolts, including major ones in 1462 and 1485. He promoted learning and trade, but his hold on his territories was weak. He fought a series of campaigns against the French and Turks to retain his dominions, but the French invaded soon after his death.

Ferdinand III King of Naples from 1504, also known as ◊Ferdinand V of Castile.

Ferdinand (1865–1927). King of Romania from 1914, when he succeeded his uncle Charles I. In 1916 he declared war on Austria. After the Allied victory in World War I, Ferdinand acquired Transylvania and Bukovina from Austria-Hungary, and Bessarabia from Russia. In 1922 he became king of this Greater Romania. His reign saw agrarian reform and the introduction of universal suffrage.

Ferguson Harry George (1884–1960). Northern Irish engineer who pioneered the development of the tractor, joining forces with Henry Ford 1938 to manufacture it in the USA. He also experimented in automobile and aircraft development.

Ferguson was born near Belfast. In 1902 he joined his brother in a car- and cycle-repair business. He built his own aeroplane and flew it 1909, becoming one of the first Britons to do so. He started to import tractors, then, from 1936, designed his own. In 1946, with British government backing, the Ferguson tractor, made by the Standard Motor Company in Coventry, was launched. In the USA Ferguson and Ford fought a massive antitrust suit, largely over a similar machine produced by Ford. Ferguson set up his own US plant 1948, but sold it to Massey-Harris 1953.

For the first Ferguson tractor, he designed a plough that would not rear up and crush the driver when encountering an obstacle. But it was his system of draught control, patented 1925, that revolutionized farming methods by improving the effective traction so that expensive, heavy machines were no longer necessary.

Ferguson Margaret Clay (1863–1951). US botanist who made important contributions as a teacher and administrator. Studying plant genetics, she worked particularly on the genus *Petunia*. She taught at Wellesley 1893–1938, becoming professor 1906. Ferguson's department became a major centre for botanical education.

Her early work focused on the life history and reproductive physiology of a species of North American pine. Turning to *Petunia*, she analysed the inheritance of features such as petal colour, flower pattern, and pollen colour, and built up a large database of genetic information.

To divide a cube into two other cubes, a fourth power or in general any power whatever into two powers of the same denomination above the second is impossible, and I have assuredly found an admirable proof of this, but the margin is too narrow to contain it.

PIERRE DE FERMAT
[written in the margin of his copy of Diophantus *Arithmetica*]
Translated from Latin in *Source Book of Mathematics* 1929

Fermat Pierre de (1601–1665). French mathematician who, with Blaise Pascal, founded the theory of probability and the modern theory of numbers. Fermat also made contributions to analytical geometry. In 1657, Fermat published a series of problems as challenges to other mathematicians, in the form of theorems to be proved.

Fermat's last theorem states that equations of the form $x^n + y^n = z^n$ where x, y, z, and n are all integers have no solutions if $n > 2$. Fermat scribbled the theorem in the margin of a mathematics textbook and noted that he could have shown it to be true had he enough space in which to write the proof. The theorem remained unproven for 300 years (and therefore, strictly speaking, constituted a conjecture rather than a theorem). In 1993, Andrew Wiles of Princeton University, USA, announced a proof; this turned out to be premature, but he put forward a revised proof 1994 which was accepted.

Fermi Enrico (1901–1954). Italian-born US physicist who proved the existence of new radioactive elements produced by bombardment with neutrons, and discovered nuclear reactions produced by low-energy neutrons. He took part in the Manhattan Project to construct an atom bomb. His theoretical work included study of the weak nuclear force, one of the fundamental forces of nature. Nobel prize 1938.

Fermi's experimental work on beta-decay in radioactive materials provided further evidence for the existence of the neutrino, as predicted by Austrian physicist Wolfgang Pauli. At the University of Chicago, Fermi built the first nuclear reactor 1942. This was the basis for studies leading to the atomic bomb and nuclear energy.

He was professor of theoretical physics at Rome 1926–38, when the rise of Fascism in Italy caused him to emigrate to the USA. He was professor at Columbia University, New York, 1939–42, and from 1946 at the University of Chicago. With British physicist Paul Dirac, Fermi studied the quantum statistics of fermion particles, which are named after him.

Suggested reading
Fermi, Laura *Atoms in the Family: My Life with Enrico Fermi* (1954)
Segrè, Emilio *Enrico Fermi, Physicist* (1970)

*After Don Quixote, [The Good Soldier Svejk] is the other
fictitious figure who has succeeded in representing ... a
whole nation.*

PATRICK LEIGH FERMOR
Time of Gifts 'Prague under Snow' 1977

Fermor Patrick (Michael) Leigh (1915–). English travel writer
who joined the Irish Guards in 1939 after four years' travel in central
Europe and the Balkans. His books include *The Traveller's Tree*
1950, *A Time to Keep Silence* 1953, *Mani* 1958, *Roumeli* 1966, *A
Time of Gifts* 1977, and *Between the Woods and the Water* 1986.

Fernández Juan (*c.* 1536–*c.* 1604). Spanish explorer and navigator. As a pilot on the Pacific coast of South America 1563, he
reached the islands off the coast of Chile that now bear his name.
Alexander Selkirk was later marooned on one of these islands, and
his life story formed the basis of Daniel Defoe's *Robinson Crusoe*.

Fernandez de Quirós Pedro (1565–1614). Spanish navigator,
one of the first Europeans to search for the great southern continent
that Ferdinand Magellan believed lay to the south of the Magellan
Strait. Despite a series of disastrous expeditions, he took part in the
discovery of the Marquesas Islands and the main island of Espíritu
Santo in the New Hebrides.

Fernel Jean François (1497–1558). French physician who introduced the terms 'physiology' and 'pathology' into medicine.

Ferneyhough Brian John Peter (1943–). English composer.
His uncompromising, detailed compositions include *Carceri*

Fermi *Italian-born US physicist Enrico Fermi pictured around 1942. Fermi
won the Nobel Prize for Physics 1938 following his work with radioactive
material which led to considerable insights into the structure of the nucleus.*
(Image Select)

d'invenzione, a cycle of seven works inspired by the engravings of
Piranesi, *Time and Motion Studies* 1974–77, and string quartets.

Ferragamo Salvatore (1898–1960). Italian shoe designer. He created elegant and sophisticated shoes and was known for his
innovative designs. He experimented with cork, lace, needlework,
raffia, and snail shells, among other materials, and is credited with
creating the wedge heel 1938, followed by the platform shoe, and the
'invisible' shoe 1947 which consisted of clear nylon uppers and a
suede heel. During his lifetime he created over 20,000 shoes and reg-
istered 350 patents.

Born near Naples, Ferragamo emigrated to the USA, aged 16,
where he made shoes for American film companies and actresses
such as Gloria Swanson and Dolores del Río. When he returned to
Italy 1927 he founded a workshop in Florence.

Ferranti Sebastian Ziani de (1864–1930). British electrical engineer who established the principle of a national grid and an
electricity-generating system based on alternating current (AC)
(successfully arguing against Thomas Edison's proposal). He
brought electricity to much of central London. In 1881 he made and
sold his first alternator. Ferranti also designed, constructed, and
experimented with many other electrical and mechanical devices,
including high-tension cables, circuit breakers, transformers, turbines, and spinning machines.

He was chief engineer with the London Electric Supply Company
1887–92, and worked on the design of a large power station at
Deptford. He set up a company in Oldham, Lancashire, 1896, to
design and build all kinds of electrical equipment, most of which was
designed by Ferranti himself, and to develop high-voltage systems
for long-distance transmission. He was also involved with heat
engines of various kinds.

Ferrar Nicolas (1592–1637). English mystic and founder in 1625
of the Anglican monastic community at Little Gidding,
Cambridgeshire, in 1625, which devoted itself to work and prayer. It
was broken up by the Puritans in 1647.

Ferrari Enzo (1898–1988). Italian founder of the Ferrari car-
manufacturing company, which specializes in Grand Prix racing
cars and high-quality sports cars. He was a racing driver for Alfa
Romeo in the 1920s, went on to become one of their designers, and
took over their racing division 1929. In 1947 the first 'true' Ferrari
was seen. The Ferrari car won more world championship Grand
Prix than any other car until very recently, when the McLaren
Formula One team equalled their record.

Ferraro Geraldine Anne (1935–). US Democrat politician, vice-
presidential candidate in the 1984 election. Ferraro, a lawyer, was
elected to Congress in 1981 and was selected in 1984 by Walter
Mondale to be the USA's first female vice-presidential candidate from
one of the major parties. The Democrats were defeated by the incumbent president Reagan, and Ferraro, damaged by investigations of her
husband's business affairs, retired temporarily from politics.

Ferré Gianfranco (1944–). Italian couturier, whose style is
strongly influenced by his training as an architect. His clothes are
marked by simple shapes and clearly defined lines punctuated by
such flourishes as oversized bows and theatrical sashes, rendered in
the most luxurious fabrics. His first collection under his own name
was shown 1979 and scored an immediate success. In 1989 he was
offered the artistic directorship of the house of Christian Dior,
arguably the crowning post in the world of international fashion.

Ferrier Kathleen Mary (1912–1953). English contralto. She
brought warmth and depth of conviction to English oratorio roles
during wartime and subsequently to opera and lieder (songs),
including Gluck's *Orfeo ed Euridice*, Mahler's *Das Lied von der
Erde/The Song of the Earth*, and the role of Lucretia in Benjamin
Britten's *The Rape of Lucretia* 1946.

Ferrier Susan Edmonstone (1782–1854). Scottish novelist. Her
anonymously published books include *Marriage* 1818, *Inheritance*
1824, and *Destiny* 1831, all of which give a lively picture of Scottish
manners and society.

Ferry Jules François Camille (1832–1893). French republican politician, mayor of Paris during the siege of 1870–71. As a member of the republican governments of 1879–85 (prime minister 1880–81 and 1883–85), he was responsible for the 1882 law making primary education free, compulsory, and secular. He directed French colonial expansion in Tunisia 1881 and Indochina (the acquisition of Tonkin in 1885).

Fessenden Reginald Aubrey (1866–1932). Canadian physicist who worked in the USA. He patented the modulation of radio waves (transmission of a signal using a carrier wave), an essential technique for voice transmission. At the time of his death, he held 500 patents. Early radio communications relied on telegraphy by using bursts of single-frequency signals in Morse code. In 1900 Fessenden devised a method of making audio-frequency speech (or music) signals modulate the amplitude of a transmitted radio-frequency carrier wave – the basis of AM radio broadcasting. Fessenden's other major invention was the heterodyne effect. In this, the received radio wave is combined with a wave of frequency slightly different to that of the carrier wave. The resulting intermediate frequency wave is easier to amplify before being demodulated to generate the original sound wave.

Fessenden became professor of electrical engineering at Purdue University, Lafayette, and then at the Western University of Pennsylvania (now the University of Pittsburgh). It was there that Fessenden began major work on the problems of radio communication.

Feynman US physicist Richard Feynman, noted for the major theoretical advances he made in quantum electrodynamics. Feynman began working on the Manhattan Project while at Princeton University and then worked in Los Alamos 1943–46, on the development of the first atomic bomb.

Feuerbach Ludwig Andreas (1804–1872). German philosopher who argued that religion is the elevation of human qualities into an object of worship. His main work is *Das Wesen des Christentums/The Essence of Christianity* 1841. He influenced political theorist Karl Marx.

Feuerbach was born in Landshut, Bavaria. He studied philosophy under G W F Hegel in Berlin, but abandoned Hegel's idealism for a form of materialism. He also studied theology and science. *Das Wesen des Christentums* was translated into English by novelist George Eliot 1854.

Feydeau Georges Léon Jules Marie (1862–1921). French comic dramatist. He is the author of over 60 farces and light comedies, which have been repeatedly revived in France at the Comédie Française and abroad. These include *La Dame de chez Maxim/The Girl from Maxim's* 1899, *Une Puce à l'oreille/A Flea in her Ear* 1907, *Feu la mère de Madame/My Late Mother-in-Law*, and *Occupe-toi d'Amélie/Look after Lulu*, both 1908.

Variety of opinion is necessary for objective knowledge.
PAUL K FEYERABEND
Against Method 1975

Feyerabend Paul K (1924–1994). Austrian-born US philosopher of science, who rejected the attempt by certain philosophers (such as Karl Popper) to find a methodology applicable to all scientific research. His works include *Against Method* 1975.

Feyerabend argues that successive theories that apparently concern the same subject (for instance the motion of the planets) cannot in principle be subjected to any comparison that would aim at finding the truer explanation. According to this notion of incommensurability, there is no neutral or objective standpoint, and therefore no rational and objective way in which one particular theory can be chosen over another. Instead, scientific progress is claimed to be the result of a range of sociological factors working to promote politically convenient notions of how nature operates. In the best-selling *Against Method*, he applied an anarchic approach to the study of knowledge and espoused practices, such as the Haitian cult of voodoo, that flew in the face of conventional scientific wisdom.

One does not, by knowing all the physical laws as we know them today, immediately obtain an understanding of anything much.
RICHARD P FEYNMAN
The Character of Physical Law 1992

Feynman Richard P(hillips) (1918–1988). US physicist whose work laid the foundations of quantum electrodynamics. For his work on the theory of radiation he shared the Nobel Prize for Physics 1965 with Julian Schwinger and Sin-Itiro Tomonaga (1906–1979). He also contributed to many aspects of particle physics, including quark theory and the nature of the weak nuclear force.

For his work on quantum electrodynamics, he developed a simple and elegant system of *Feynman diagrams* to represent interactions between particles and how they moved from one space-time point to another. He had rules for calculating the probability associated with each diagram. His other major discoveries are the theory of superfluidity (frictionless flow) in liquid helium, developed in the early 1950s; his work on the weak interaction (with US physicist Murray Gell-Mann) and the strong force; and his prediction that the proton and neutron are not elementary particles. Both particles are now known to be composed of quarks. Feynman was professor of theoretical physics at Caltech (California Institute of Technology) from 1950 until his death.

As a member of the committee investigating the *Challenger* space-shuttle disaster 1986, he demonstrated the faults in rubber seals on the shuttle's booster rocket.

The Feynman Lectures on Physics 1963 became a standard work. He also published two volumes of autobiography: *Surely You're*

Joking, Mr Feynman! 1985 and *What Do You Care What Other People Think?* 1988.
Suggested reading
Feynman, Richard *Surely You're Joking, Mr Feynman!* (memoirs) (1985)
Gleick, James *The Life and Science of Richard Feynman* (1992)

Fibonacci Leonardo, also known as Leonardo of Pisa (*c.* 1170–*c.* 1250). Italian mathematician. He published *Liber abaci/The Book of the Calculator* in Pisa 1202, which was instrumental in the introduction of Arabic notation into Europe. From 1960, interest increased in Fibonacci numbers, in their simplest form a sequence in which each number is the sum of its two predecessors (1, 1, 2, 3, 5, 8, 13, ...). They have unusual characteristics with possible applications in botany, psychology, and astronomy (for example, a more exact correspondence than is given by Bode's law to the distances between the planets and the Sun).

In 1220, Fibonacci published *Practica geometriae*, in which he used algebraic methods to solve many arithmetical and geometrical problems.

Fichte Johann Gottlieb (1762–1814). German philosopher who developed a comprehensive form of subjective idealism, expounded in *The Science of Knowledge* 1794. He was an admirer of Immanuel Kant.

In 1792, Fichte published *Critique of Religious Revelation*, a critical study of Kant's doctrine of the 'thing-in-itself'. For Fichte, the absolute ego posits both the external world (the non-ego) and finite self. Morality consists in the striving of this finite self to rejoin the absolute. In 1799 he was accused of atheism, and was forced to resign his post as professor of philosophy at Jena. He moved to Berlin, where he devoted himself to public affairs and delivered lectures, including *Reden an die deutsche Nation/Addresses to the German People* 1807–08, which influenced contemporary liberal nationalism.

Ficino Marsilio (1433–1499). Italian philosopher. He created an influential synthesis of Platonism and medieval theology. He assigned to the human soul the central place in the hierarchy of the universe, and he believed that the soul ascended towards God through contemplation. His doctrine of platonic love became one of the most popular concepts of later Renaissance literature.

Ficino founded a Platonic Academy in Florence 1462. He was ordained a priest 1473 and retired 1494. He translated both Plato and Plotinus, the founder of neo-Platonism, into Latin. His main work is *Theologica Platonica de immortalitate animae/Platonic Theology Concerning the Immortality of the Soul* 1482.

Fiedler Arthur (1894–1979). US orchestra conductor. Concerned to promote appreciation of music among the public, he founded the Boston Sinfonietta chamber-music group 1924. He reached an even wider audience with the Esplanade concerts along the Charles River from 1929.

Fiedler's greatest fame was as founder and conductor of the Boston Pops Orchestra 1930, dedicated to popularizing light classical music through live and televised concert appearances.

Born in Boston and trained at the Academy of Music in Berlin, Fiedler joined the Boston Symphony Orchestra 1916.

Field George Brooks (1929–). US theoretical astrophysicist whose main research has been into the nature and composition of intergalactic matter and the properties of residual radiation in space. He became professor at the University of California at Berkeley 1965 and at Harvard University 1972; from 1973 he was also director of the Center of Astrophysics at the Harvard College Observatory and the Smithsonian Astrophysical Observatory.

One of Field's major areas of research has been to investigate why a cluster of galaxies remains a cluster rather than dispersing. They are thought to be stabilized gravitationally by intergalactic matter, mainly hydrogen and helium. By studying part of the spectrum of the radio source Cygnus A, Field found in 1958 some evidence of atomic hydrogen distributed intergalactically.

Field has also carried out research into the lines in the spectra of stars.

Field John (1782–1837). Irish-born composer and pianist. Often regarded as one of a group of composers known as the London Pianoforte School, all of his works include the piano, reaching their peak artistically with his nocturnes, a genre he named and devised. These anticipate Chopin's nocturnes by 20 years, especially regarding their forward-looking textures and passage work.

As an apprentice to Muzio Clementi, he travelled throughout Europe demonstrating instruments for the firm of piano makers established by his master. He settled in St Petersburg 1803, where he composed most of his mature music.

Field Sally (1946–). US film and television actress. She won an Academy Award for *Norma Rae* 1979 and again for *Places in the Heart* 1984. Her other films include *Hooper* 1978, *Absence of Malice* 1981, and *Murphy's Romance* 1985.

His designs were strictly honourable, as the phrase is; that is, to rob a lady of her fortune by way of marriage.

HENRY FIELDING
Tom Jones bk 11 ch 4 1749

Fielding Henry (1707–1754). English novelist. His greatest work, *The History of Tom Jones, a Foundling* 1749 (which he described as 'a comic epic in prose'), realized for the first time in English the novel's potential for memorable characterization, coherent plotting, and perceptive analysis. In youth a prolific dramatist, he began writing novels with *An Apology for the Life of Mrs Shamela Andrews* 1741, a merciless parody of Samuel Richardson's *Pamela*.

He was appointed Justice of the Peace for Middlesex and Westminster 1748. In failing health, he went to recuperate in Lisbon 1754, writing on the way *A Journal of a Voyage to Lisbon*.
Suggested reading
Battestin, M and R B *Henry Fielding: A Life* (1989)
Dircks, R J *Henry Fielding* (1983)
Macallister, H *Fielding* (1967)
Rogers, P *Henry Fielding: A Biography* (1979)
Varey, S *Henry Fielding* (1986)

Fields Gracie. Stage name of Grace Stansfield (1898–1979). English comedian and singer. Much loved by the public, her humorously sentimental films include *Sally in Our Alley* 1931 and *Sing as We Go* 1934.

I was in love with a beautiful blonde once, dear. She drove me to drink. That's the one thing I'm indebted to her for.

W C FIELDS
quoted in R J Anobile *Flask of Fields* 1973

Fields W C. Stage name of William Claude Dukenfield (1880–1946). US actor and screenwriter. His distinctive speech and professed attitudes such as hatred of children and dogs gained him enormous popularity in such films as *David Copperfield* 1935, *My Little Chickadee* (co-written with Mae West) and *The Bank Dick* both 1940, and *Never Give a Sucker an Even Break* 1941.

Originally a vaudeville performer, he incorporated his former stage routines, such as juggling and pool playing, into his films. He was also a popular radio performer.
Suggested reading
Deschner, D *The Films of W C Fields* (1966)
Everson, W K *The Art of W C Fields* (1967)
Fields, Ronald *W C Fields: A Life in Film* (1984)

Fiennes Ranulph Twisleton-Wykeham (1944–). British explorer who made the first surface journey around the world's polar circumference between 1979 and 1982. Earlier expeditions include explorations of the White Nile 1969, Jostedalsbre Glacier, Norway, 1970, and the Headless Valley, Canada, 1971. Accounts of his adventures include *A Talent for Trouble* 1970, *Hell on Ice* 1979, and the autobiographical *Living Dangerously* 1987. Succeeded to baronetcy 1944.

Filchner Wilhelm (1877–1957). German explorer who travelled extensively in Central Asia, but is remembered for his expedition into the Weddell Sea of Antarctica 1911, where his ship became icebound for a whole winter. He landed a party and built a hut on the floating ice shelf, which eventually broke up and floated northwards. Filchner also conducted cartographic surveys and magnetic observations in Tibet 1926–28 and made a magnetic survey of Nepal 1939–40.

Filene Edward Albert (1860–1937). US store owner who introduced innovative retailing methods. One of his most imaginative merchandising ideas was the 'bargain basement', where prices were dramatically lowered on certain goods. Incorporating his father's dry-goods store in Boston as William Filene's Sons 1891, Filene was committed to employee profit-sharing and for that reason was removed by his partners 1928.

Fillmore Millard (1800–1874). 13th president of the USA 1850–53, a Whig. Born into a poor farming family in New Cayuga County, New York State, he was Zachary Taylor's vice-president from 1849, and succeeded him on Taylor's death, 9 July 1850. Fillmore supported a compromise on slavery 1850 to reconcile North and South. This compromise pleased neither side, and it contained a harsh fugitive slave act requiring escaped slaves to be returned to their owners. He threatened to enforce this act with troops, if necessary, earning the wrath of the abolitionists. Fillmore failed to be nominated for another term.
Suggested reading
Grayson, Benson L *The Unknown President: The Administration of President Millard Fillmore* (1981)
Rayback, Robert *Millard Fillmore: Biography of a President* (1959)

Hollywood must have been terrific once.

PETER FINCH
Evening Standard Sept 1972

Finch Peter William Mitchell (1916–1977). Australian-born English cinema actor. He began his career in Australia before moving to London 1949 to start on an international career in films such as *A Town Like Alice* 1956, *The Trials of Oscar Wilde* 1960, *Sunday, Bloody Sunday* 1971, and *Network* 1976, for which he won an Academy Award.

Finney Albert (1936–). English stage and film actor. He created the title roles in Keith Waterhouse's stage play *Billy Liar* 1960 and John Osborne's *Luther* 1961, and was associate artistic director of the Royal Court Theatre 1972–75. Later roles for the National Theatre include Tamburlaine in Marlowe's tragedy 1976 and *Macbeth* 1978. His films include *Saturday Night and Sunday Morning* 1960, *Tom Jones* 1963, *Murder on the Orient Express* 1974, and *The Dresser* 1984.

Finney Tom (Thomas) (1922–). English footballer, known as the 'Preston Plumber'. He played for England 76 times, and in every forward position. He was celebrated for his ball control and goal-scoring skills, and was the first person to win the Footballer of the Year award twice.

Finn Mac Cumhaill or Finn McCool. Legendary Irish hero, identified with a general who organized an Irish regular army in the 3rd century. The Scottish writer James Macpherson featured him (as Fingal) and his followers in the verse of his popular epics 1762–63, which were supposedly written by a 3rd-century bard called Ossian.

Finsen Niels Ryberg (1860–1904). Danish physician, the first to use ultraviolet light treatment for skin diseases. Nobel Prize for Physiology or Medicine 1903.

Fiorucci Elio (1935–). Italian fashion designer and retailer. He established the Fiorucci label in the 1960s, but became best known in the 1970s for bright, casual clothing including slimfit jeans, sold internationally through Fiorucci boutiques.

Firbank (Arthur Annesley) Ronald (1886–1926). English novelist. His work, set in the Edwardian decadent period, has a malicious

humour and includes *Caprice* 1916, *Valmouth* 1918, and the posthumous *Concerning the Eccentricities of Cardinal Pirelli* 1926.

Firdausi Abdul Qasim Mansur (*c.* 935–*c.* 1020). Persian poet. His epic *Shahnama/The Book of Kings* relates the history of Persia in 60,000 verses.

Firestone Harvey Samuel (1868–1938). US industrialist who established a tyre-manufacturing firm, the Firestone Tire and Rubber Co., in Akron, Ohio, in 1900. He pioneered the principle of the detachable rim and, from 1906, was the major supplier of tyres to the Ford Motor Co.

Born in Columbiana, Ohio, Firestone was educated at local schools. He entered the family buggy business and quickly recognized the advantages of rubber for wheel rims, originally founding a retail tyre outlet in Chicago 1896. A strong opponent of organized labour, he long resisted the unionization of his work force.

Firestone Shulamith (1945–). Canadian feminist writer and editor. Her book *The Dialectic of Sex: the Case for Feminist Revolution* 1970, which analysed the limited future of feminism under Marxist and Freudian theories, exerted considerable influence on feminist thought. She was one of the early organizers of the women's liberation movement in the USA. Her other works include *Notes from the Second Year* 1970.

Firth John Rupert (1890–1960). English linguist. Influenced by the anthropologist Bronislaw Malinowski, he made semantics central to his approach to linguistics and developed the latter's theory of the 'context of the situation'. Whatever anyone said must be understood in the entire context of the utterance, including such nonlinguistic factors as the status and personal history of the speakers and the social character of the situation.

Firth described typical contexts of situation and 'typical repetitive events in the social process'; for example, the occurrence of ready-made, socially prescribed utterances such as 'How do you do?' He also studied phonological features of speech such as stress, intonation, and nasalization, which he emphasized, varied considerably in different languages.

In 1944 he was appointed professor of general linguistics at London University, the first such post in Britain. Firth wrote two books, *Speech* 1930 and *The Tongues of Men* 1937. His most important academic articles are found in *Papers in Linguistics 1934–51* 1957 and *Selected Papers of J R Firth* 1968.

Fischer Bobby (Robert James) (1943–). US World Chess Champion 1972–5, 1992. In 1958, after proving himself in international competition, he became the youngest grand master in history. He was the author of *Games of Chess* 1959, and was also celebrated for his unorthodox psychological tactics. By 1956 he had won the US junior chess title and, within two years, had also won the US Chess Federation championship for adults. Afer winning the world title from Boris Spassky in Reykjavik, Iceland, 1972 he retired without defending his title. He emerged from retirement Sept 1992 to play Spassky, completing his victory after a nine-week contest Nov 1992.
Suggested reading
Brady, Frank *Profile of a Prodigy: The Life and Games of Bobby Fischer* (1973)
Steiner, George *Fields of Force: Fischer and Spassky at Reykjavik* (1974)

Fischer Emil Hermann (1852–1919). German chemist who produced synthetic sugars and, from these, various enzymes. His descriptions of the chemistry of the carbohydrates and peptides laid the foundations for the science of biochemistry. Nobel prize 1902.

About 1882, Fischer began working on a group of compounds that included uric acid and caffeine. He realized that they were all related to a hitherto unknown substance, which he called purine. Over the next few years he synthesized about 130 related compounds, one of which was the first synthetic nucleotide. These studies led to the synthesis of powerful hypnotic drugs derived from barbituric acids (barbiturates). Fischer held professorships at Erlangen 1882–85, Würzburg 1885–92, and Berlin from 1892.

Fischer Ernst Otto (1918–). German inorganic chemist who showed that transition metals can bond chemically to carbon. He and English chemist Geoffrey Wilkinson shared the 1973 Nobel Prize for Chemistry for their work on organometallic compounds, which they carried out independently.

Fischer was born in Munich and educated at the Munich Technical University. He remained there, becoming professor 1959.

Investigating a synthetic compound called ferrocene, both Fischer and Wilkinson separately came to the conclusion that each molecule of ferrocene consists of a single iron atom sandwiched between two five-sided carbon rings – an organometallic compound. A combination of chemical and physical studies, finally confirmed by X-ray analysis, showed the compound's structure.

With this work came the general realization that transition metals can bond chemically to carbon, and other ring systems were then studied. All the elements of the first transition series have now been incorporated into molecules of this kind and all except that of manganese have the ferrocene-type structure. Only ferrocene, however, is stable in air, the others being sensitive to oxidation.

Fischer Hans (1881–1945). German chemist awarded a Nobel prize 1930 for his work on haemoglobin, the oxygen-carrying, red colouring matter in blood.

Fischer was born in Höchst-am-Main, near Frankfurt, and studied at Marburg and Munich. He went to Austria as professor at Innsbruck 1915–18 and Vienna 1918–21, returning to Germany as professor at the Munich Technische Hochschule.

In 1921 Fischer began investigating haemoglobin, concentrating on haem, the iron-containing non-protein part of the molecule. By 1929 he had elucidated the complete structure and synthesized haem. Chlorophyll, he found in the 1930s, has a similar structure. He then turned to the bile pigments, particularly bilirubin (the pigment responsible for the colour of the skin of patients suffering from jaundice), and by 1944 had achieved a complete synthesis of bilirubin. In 1945 Fischer's laboratories were destroyed in an Allied bombing raid and in a fit of despair he committed suicide.

Fischer Hermann Otto Laurenz (1888–1960). German organic chemist who carried out research into the synthetic and structural chemistry of carbohydrates, glycerides, and inositols.

Fischer was born in Würzburg, Bavaria, the son of chemist Emil Fischer, and studied in the UK at Cambridge and in Germany at Berlin and Jena. In 1912, he returned to the Chemical Institute of Berlin University to continue research with his father, interrupted two years later by the outbreak of World War I. With the rise of Nazi leader Adolf Hitler, the Fischers left Berlin in 1932 and went to Basel, Switzerland. In 1937 Hermann moved to the Banting Institute in Toronto, Canada, where he stayed until moving, in 1948, to the University of California at Berkeley.

Between 1920 and 1932 Fischer worked out the exact structure of quinic acid and investigated the difficult chemistry of the trioses glyceraldehyde and dihydroxyacetone and the related two-, three-, and four-carbon compounds.

Fischer also worked on glyceraldehydes, extending it from 1937 to glycerides (esters of glycerol, i.e. propan-1,2,3-triol) and demonstrated the action of lipase enzymes on these biologically important substances.

Fischer-Dieskau Dietrich (1925–). German baritone singer. His intelligently focused and subtly understated interpretations of opera and lieder (songs) introduced a new depth and intimacy to a wide-ranging repertoire extending in opera from Gluck to Berg's Wozzeck, Henze, and Britten, and from Bach arias to lieder (songs) of Schubert, Wolf, and Schoenberg. Since 1973 he has also conducted.

Fischl Eric (1948–). US Realist painter. The most prominent artist of his generation, he is known for his narrative, frequently disturbing paintings of suburban Americans at play. His figures are shown on the beach or indoors, often engaged in such intimate activities as dressing or making love. His straightforward handling of sexual themes has been considered shocking, as in *Bad Boy* 1981 (Saatchi Collection, London).

Fischl's work has affinities with that of Edward Hopper and of Balthus, but unlike the latter's his voyeurism is detached and unerotic. Instead he seeks to reveal the emptiness of instantly gratified, materialistic lives.

Fish Hamilton (1808–1893). US public figure and diplomat. He held office in the US Senate 1851–57, by which time he had become a member of the Republican Party. As secretary of state under President Grant 1869–77, his office was marked by moderation in his pursuit of US claims against the UK in the *Alabama* case and in averting war with Spain over Cuba.

Fish was born in New York, USA, and educated at Columbia University; he was admitted to the bar 1830. Active in Whig politics, he served as governor of New York 1849–50.

Three of his qualities need particular emphasis ... personal modesty ... exact knowledge of his own limitations; ... and ... strong devotion to the Empire as a whole.

A W Jose on ANDREW FISHER
in *Dictionary of National Biography*

Fisher Andrew (1862–1928). Australian Labor politician. Born in Scotland, he went to Australia 1885, and entered the Australian parliament in 1901.

He was prime minister 1908–09, 1910–13, and 1914–15, and Australian high commissioner to the UK 1916–21.

Fisher Geoffrey Francis, Baron Fisher of Lambeth (1887–1972). English priest, archbishop of Canterbury 1945–61. He was the first holder of this office to visit the pope since the 14th century. GCVO 1953, baron 1961.

Fisher Irving (1867–1947). US economist. He developed the quantity theory of money from the quantity equation, which he formulated as MV = PT, M being the quantity of money in circulation (the money supply), V the velocity of circulation of money around the economy, P the average price level, and T the number of transactions (equivalent to output). This equation is sometimes known as the Fisher equation. The quantity theory assumes that V and T are relatively constant, and therefore suggests that an increase in the money supply causes inflation.

Fisher John Arbuthnot, 1st Baron Fisher (1841–1920). British admiral, First Sea Lord 1904–10, when he carried out many radical reforms and innovations, including the introduction of the dreadnought battleship.

He served in the Crimean War 1855 and the China War 1859–60. He held various commands before becoming First Sea Lord, and returned to the post 1914, but resigned the following year, disagreeing with Winston Churchill over sending more ships to the Dardanelles, Turkey, in World War I. KCB 1894, baron 1909.

Fisher John, St (*c.* 1469–1535). English cleric, created bishop of Rochester 1504. He was an enthusiastic supporter of the revival in the study of Greek, and a friend of the humanists Thomas More and Desiderius Erasmus. In 1535 he was tried on a charge of denying the royal supremacy of Henry VIII and beheaded. Canonized 1935.

Fisher Ronald Aylmer (1890–1962). English statistician and geneticist. He modernized Charles Darwin's theory of evolution, thus securing the key biological concept of genetic change by natural selection. Fisher developed several new statistical techniques and, applying his methods to genetics, published *The Genetical Theory of Natural Selection* 1930.

This classic work established that the discoveries of the geneticist Gregor Mendel could be shown to support Darwin's theory of evolution.

In 1919 he was appointed head of Rothamstead Experimental Station, where he made a statistical analysis of a backlog of experimental data that had built up over more than 60 years. At Rothamstead, Fisher also bred poultry, mice, snails, and other creatures, and in his papers on genetics contributed to the contemporary understanding of genetic dominance. As a result, in 1933 he was appointed professor of eugenics at University College, London. He was professor of genetics at Cambridge 1943–57. In statistics, Fisher evolved the rules for decisionmaking that are now used almost automatically, and many other methods that have since been extended to virtually every academic field in which statistical analysis can be applied.

Fitch John (1743–1798). US inventor and early experimenter with steam engines and steamships. In 1786 he designed the first steamboat to serve the Delaware River. His venture failed, so Robert Fulton is erroneously credited with the invention of the steamship.

Fitch Val Logsdon (1923–). US physicist who shared the 1980 Nobel prize for Physics with James Cronin for their joint work in particle physics, studying the surprising way certain mesons change from matter to antimatter. He became professor at Princeton University 1960.

The discovery for which Fitch and Cronin received the 1980 Nobel prize was first published in 1964. They had set up an experiment with the proton accelerator at the Brookhaven Laboratory in New York to study the properties of K^0 mesons. K^0 is a mixture of two 'basic states' which have a long and a short lifetime and are therefore called K^0_L and K^0_S respectively. These two basic states can also mix together to form not K^0 but an antimatter particle (anti-K^0), and K^0 can oscillate from particle to antiparticle through either of its basic states. Fitch and Cronin found that decays of K^0_L mesons sometimes violate the known rules, and so are different from all other known particle interactions.

Fitzalan-Howard family name of dukes of Norfolk; seated at Arundel Castle, Sussex, England.

Fitzgerald family name of the dukes of Leinster.

Fitzgerald Edward (1809–1883). English poet and translator. His poetic version of the *Rubaiyat of Omar Khayyám* 1859, with its resonant and melancholy tone, is generally considered more an original creation than a true translation.

Ah, fill the Cup: what boots it to repeat/How time is slipping underneath our feet.

EDWARD FITZGERALD
The Rubaiyat of Omar Khayyam 1859

Fitzgerald Ella (1918–1996). US jazz singer. She is recognized as one of the finest, most lyrical voices in jazz, both in solo work and with big bands. She is celebrated for her smooth interpretations of George and Ira Gershwin and Cole Porter songs.

Fitzgerald's first hit was 'A-Tisket, A-Tasket' 1938. She excelled at scat singing and was widely imitated in the 1950s and 1960s. She is among the best-selling recording artists in the history of jazz. Her albums include *Ella Fitzgerald Sings the Rodgers and Hart Songbook, Duke Ellington Songbook,* and other single-composer sets in the 1950s, and *Ella and Louis* 1956 with trumpeter Louis Armstrong.

Her scat-singing is without equal; clear, accurate; flexible voice combined with warm vocal colour and sympathetic phrasing.

ELLA FITZGERALD
described in Donald Clarke (ed) *The Penguin Encyclopedia of Popular Music* 1989

Fitzgerald F(rancis) Scott (Key) (1896–1940). US novelist and short-story writer. His early autobiographical novel *This Side of Paradise* 1920 made him known in the postwar society of the East Coast, and *The Great Gatsby* 1925 epitomizes the Jazz Age.

Fitzgerald was born in Minnesota. His first book, *This Side of Paradise*, reflected his experiences at Princeton University. In *The*

In a real dark night of the soul it is always three o'clock in the morning, day after day.

F SCOTT FITZGERALD
The Crack-Up 1945

Great Gatsby 1925 the narrator resembles his author, and Gatsby, the self-made millionaire, is lost in the soulless society he enters. Fitzgerald's wife Zelda Sayre (1900–1948), a schizophrenic, entered an asylum 1930, after which he declined into alcoholism. Her descent into mental illness forms the subject of *Tender is the Night* 1934. His other works include numerous short stories and the novels *The Beautiful and the Damned* 1922 and *The Last Tycoon*, which was unfinished at his death.

Suggested reading
Bruccoli, J *Some Sort of Epic Grandeur* (1981)
Chambers, J B *The Novels of F Scott Fitzgerald* (1989)
Mellow, James *Invented Lives: The Marriage of F Scott Fitzgerald and Zelda Fitzgerald* (1984)
Mitford, N *Zelda Fitzgerald* (1970)

Happiness ... is only the first hour after the alleviation of some especially intense misery.

F SCOTT FITZGERALD
The Beautiful and Damned 1922

FitzGerald Garret Michael (1926–). Irish politician. As *Taoiseach* (prime minister) 1981–82 and again 1982–86, he was noted for his attempts to solve the Northern Ireland dispute, ultimately by participating in the Anglo-Irish agreement 1985. He tried to remove some of the overtly Catholic features of the constitution to make the Republic more attractive to Northern Protestants. He retired as leader of the Fine Gael Party 1987.

FitzGerald George Francis (1851–1901). Irish physicist known for his work on electromagnetics. In 1892 he explained the anomalous results of the Michelson–Morley experiment 1887 by supposing that bodies moving through the ether contracted as their velocity increased, an effect since known as the Fitzgerald–Lorentz contraction.

Fitzgerald was born in Dublin and studied there at Trinity College, where he was professor of natural and experimental philosophy from 1888.

FitzGerald R(obert) D(avid) (1902–). Australian poet noted for the complex intellectual themes of his work. His collections include *To Meet the Sun* 1929, *Moonlight Acre* 1938, *Heemskerck Shoals* 1949, *Between Two Tides* 1952, and *This Night's Orbit* 1953.

Fitzherbert Maria Anne (born Smythe) (1756–1837). Wife of the Prince of Wales, later George IV. She became Mrs Fitzherbert by her second marriage 1778 and, after her husband's death 1781, entered London society. She secretly married the Prince of Wales 1785 and finally parted from him 1803.

Fitzroy family name of dukes of Grafton; descended from King Charles II by his mistress Barbara Villiers; seated at Euston Hall, Norfolk, England.

Fitzroy Robert (1805–1865). British vice admiral and meteorologist. In 1828 he succeeded to the command of HMS *Beagle*, then engaged on a survey of the Patagonian coast of South America, and in 1831 was accompanied by naturalist Charles Darwin on a five-year survey. Fitzroy was governor of New Zealand 1843–45. In 1855 the Admiralty founded the Meteorological Office, which issued weather forecasts and charts, under his charge.

Fitzsimmons Robert Prometheus (1863–1917). English prizefighter best known for his US fights. He won the middleweight title in New Orleans 1891. Although he weighed only 73 kg/160 lb, he also competed as a heavyweight and in 1897 won the title from James J ('Gentleman Jim') Corbett in Carson City, Nevada. He lost that title to James J Jeffries in New York 1899.

Fitzsimmons was born in England and raised in New Zealand. He began boxing at an early age and continued to fight professionally until 1914.

Fixx James (1932–1984). US popularizer of jogging for cardiovascular fitness with his book *The Complete Book of Running* 1978. He died of a heart attack while jogging.

Fizeau Armand Hippolyte Louis (1819–1896). French physicist who in 1849 was the first to measure the speed of light on the Earth's surface. He also found that light travels faster in air than in water, which confirmed the wave theory of light, and that the motion of a star affects the position of the lines in its spectrum.

Fizeau, born in Paris, studied at the College de France and with François Arago at the Paris Observatory. Many of his discoveries were made in collaboration with Léon Foucault 1839–47.

Fizeau began to research into the new science of photography in 1839, and with Foucault developed daguerreotype photography for astronomical observations by taking the first detailed pictures of the Sun's surface 1845. They also found, in 1847, that heat rays from the Sun undergo interference and that radiant heat therefore behaves as a wave motion.

Flagg James Montgomery (1877–1960). US illustrator. His World War I recruiting poster 'I want You', features a haggard image of Uncle Sam modelled on Flagg himself.

Flagler Henry Morrison (1830–1913). US entrepreneur. He founded a salt factory in Saginaw, Michigan, 1862, but when that failed moved to Cleveland and entered the oil-refining business with John D Rockefeller 1867. Flagler served as a director of Standard Oil 1870–1911 and invested in the Florida tourist industry. He established the Florida East Coast Railroad 1886 and built a string of luxury hotels.

Flagstad Kirsten Malfrid (1895–1962). Norwegian soprano. Her Bayreuth debut 1933 established her as a Wagnerian leading soprano of majestic presence, notably as Fricka in *Das Rheingold/The Rhinegold* and Brünnhilde in *Götterdämmerung/Twilight of the Gods*. In 1950 she gave the premiere of Richard Strauss' *Four Last Songs* 1948.

Flaherty Robert Joseph (1884–1951). US film director. He was one of the pioneers of documentary filmmaking. He exerted great influence through his pioneer documentary of Inuit life, *Nanook of the North* 1922, a critical and commercial success. Later films include *Moana* 1926, a South Seas documentary; *Man of Aran* 1934, *Elephant Boy* 1936, and the Standard Oil-sponsored *Louisiana Story* 1948. Critics subsequently raised questions about the truthfulness of his documentary method.

Dig out the standards if you are too weak to pull them out.

GAIUS FLAMINIUS
His order to his troops to remove legionary
standards from the ground before a disastrous march.
Quoted in Livy *From the Foundation of the City* bk 22, ch 3

Flaminius Gaius (died 217 BC). Roman consul and general. He constructed the Flaminian Way northward from Rome to Rimini 220 BC, and was killed at the battle of Lake Trasimene fighting Hannibal.

Flamsteed John (1646–1719). English astronomer who began systematic observations of the positions of the stars, Moon, and planets at the Royal Observatory he founded at Greenwich, London, 1676. His observations were published in *Historia Coelestis Britannica* 1725.

As the first Astronomer Royal of England, Flamsteed determined the latitude of Greenwich, the slant of the ecliptic, and the position of the equinox. He also worked out an ingenious method of observing the absolute right ascension – a coordinate of the position of a heavenly body – which removed all errors of parallax, refraction, and

Flagg *This World War I recruitment poster is the most familiar work by US illustrator James Flagg. It features Uncle Sam, a personification of the US government.*

latitude. Having obtained the positions of 40 reference stars, he then went back and computed positions for the rest of the 3,000 stars in his catalogue.

Flanagan Bud. Stage name of Chaim Reeven Weintrop (Robert Winthrop) (1896–1968). English comedian. He was the leader of the 'Crazy Gang' 1931–1962. He played in variety theatre all over the world and, with his partner Chesney Allen, popularized such songs as 'Underneath the Arches'.

Of all the icy blasts that blow on love, a request for money is the most chilling and havoc-wreaking.

GUSTAVE FLAUBERT
Madame Bovary ch 8 1857

Flaubert Gustave (1821–1880). French writer. One of the major novelists of the 19th century, he was the author of *Madame Bovary* 1857, *Salammbô* 1862, *L'Education sentimentale/Sentimental Education* 1869, and *La Tentation de Saint Antoine/The Temptation of St Anthony* 1874. Flaubert also wrote the short stories *Trois Contes/Three Tales* 1877. His dedication to art resulted in a meticulous prose style, realistic detail, and psychological depth, which is often revealed through interior monologue.
Suggested reading
Bart, Benjamin *Flaubert* (1967)
Lottman, Herbert *Flaubert* (1989)

Starkie, Enid *Flaubert: The Making of the Master* (1967)
Starkie, Enid *Flaubert: The Master* (1971)

Flavin Dan (1933–   ). US sculptor and environmental artist. He specializes in the use of light technology. His simple installations using standard coloured or white neon tubes alter the viewer's perceptions of the surrounding space. The tactics are reductive, yet the results are often sublimely decorative, as in the coloured-neon arrangement *Untitled (to Agrati)* 1964 (Saatchi Collection, London).

Flavin began as a Minimalist, exhibiting his 'light boxes' in the 1960s; he later evolved to constructing elegant clusters of neon tubes.

Flaxman John (1755–1826). English Neo-Classical sculptor and illustrator. From 1775 he worked for the Wedgwood pottery as a designer. His public works include the monuments of Nelson 1808–10 in St Paul's Cathedral, London, and of Robert Burns and Kemble in Westminster Abbey.

Flaxman was born in York and studied at the Royal Academy in London. From 1787 to 1794 he was in Rome directing the Wedgwood studio there. Apart from designs for Wedgwood ware, he modelled friezes on classical subjects and produced relief portraits. In 1810 he became the first professor of sculpture at the Royal Academy.

We take the Golden Road to Samarkand.

JAMES ELROY FLECKER
Hassan V ii 1922

Flecker (Herman) James Elroy (1884–1915). English poet. During a career in the consular service, he wrote several volumes of verse, including *The Bridge of Fire* 1907, *The Golden Journey to Samarkand* 1913, and *The Old Ships* 1915.

Fleischer Max (1889–1972). Austrian-born US cartoonist. With his younger brother, Dave (1894–1972), as director, Fleischer animated and produced cartoon films from 1917. His first major series was *Out of the Inkwell* 1918 starring Koko the Clown. He created the long-running characters Betty Boop and Popeye. His feature films include *Gulliver's Travels* 1939 and *Superman* 1941.

Fleming (John) Ambrose (1849–1945). English electrical physicist and engineer who invented the thermionic valve 1904 and devised Fleming's rules. Fleming's rules are memory aids used to recall the relative directions of the magnetic field, current, and motion in an electric generator or motor, using one's fingers. The three directions are represented by the thu*m*b (for *m*otion), *f*orefinger (*f*ield), and se*c*ond finger (*c*urrent), all held at right angles to each other. The right hand is used for generators and the left for motors.

Fleming was born in Lancaster, Lancashire, and educated at University College and South Kensington, London, and at Cambridge, where he worked in the Cavendish Laboratory and studied under Scottish physicist James Clerk Maxwell. In 1882–83, Fleming was professor at Nottingham, and from 1885 at University College, London. He was a consultant at various times to the Edison, Swan, and Ferranti electric-lighting companies and the Marconi Wireless Telegraph Company, for which he designed many parts of their early radio apparatus. Knighted 1929.

Fleming Alexander (1881–1955). Scottish bacteriologist who discovered the first antibiotic drug, penicillin, in 1928. In 1922 he had discovered lysozyme, an antibacterial enzyme present in saliva, nasal secretions, and tears. While studying this, he found an unusual mould growing on a neglected culture dish, which he isolated and grew into a pure culture; this led to his discovery of penicillin. It came into use in 1941. In 1945 he won the Nobel Prize for Physiology or Medicine with Howard W Florey and Ernst B Chain, whose research had brought widespread realization of the value of penicillin.

Fleming was born in Lochfield, Ayrshire, and studied medicine at St Mary's Hospital, London, where he remained in the bacteriology department for his entire career, becoming professor 1928. Knighted 1944.

Suggested reading
MacFarlane, Gwyn *Alexander Fleming* (1985)
Maurois, André *The Life of Sir Alexander Fleming* (trs 1959)
Rowland, John *The Penicillin Man* (1957)

Most marriages don't add two people together. They subtract one from the other.

IAN FLEMING
Diamonds are Forever 1956

Fleming Ian Lancaster (1908–1964). English author. His suspense novels feature the ruthless, laconic James Bond, British Secret Service agent 007. The first novel in the series was *Casino Royale* 1953. Most of the novels were made into successful films.

During World War II he worked for British Intelligence where he had the opportunity to give full rein to his vivid imagination in disseminating false information and rumours.

Fleming (Robert) Peter (1907–1971). British journalist and travel writer, remembered for his journeys up the Amazon and across the Gobi Desert recounted in *Brazilian Adventure* 1933 and *News from Tartary* 1941.

Fleming Williamina Paton Stevens (1857–1911). Scottish-born US astronomer, assistant to Edward Pickering, with whom she compiled the first general catalogue classifying stellar spectra.

Fleming was born in Dundee and emigrated to the USA 1878. From 1879 she was employed by Pickering, director of the Harvard College Observatory, initially as a 'computer' and copy editor. In 1898 she was appointed curator of astronomical photographs.

Photographs were taken of the spectra obtained using prisms placed in front of the objectives of telescopes. In the course of her analysis of these spectra, Fleming discovered 59 nebulae, more than 300 variable stars, and 10 novae.

The spectra of the stars observed in this manner could be classified into categories. Fleming designed the system adopted in the 1890 *Draper Catalogues*, in which 10,351 stellar spectra were listed in 17 categories ('A' to 'Q'). This system was to be superseded by the work of Annie Jump Cannon at the same observatory.

Fletcher Andrew of Saltoun (1655–1716). Scottish patriot, the most outspoken critic of the Union of Scotland with England of 1707. He advocated an independent Scotland, and a republic or limited monarchy, and proposed 'limitations' to the treaty, such as annual Parliaments. After the Treaty of Union he retired to private life.

Fletcher Frank Jack (1885–1973). US admiral. He commanded the US naval forces in the Battle of the Coral Sea 1942 but had to withdraw from the Battle of the Midway after his flagship, USS *Yorktown*, was damaged. He was hostile to naval aircraft providing cover for the ground operations on Guadalcanal, but was overruled by Admiral Nimitz. He was then transferred to command of the Northern Pacific Fleet and remained there until the end of the war; he retired 1946.

Fletcher Horace (1849–1919). Writer and lecturer on nutrition. In 1895 a life-insurance company refused to accept him as a risk because he was 23 kg/50 lb overweight and was frequently ill. He attributed his recovery to a change in eating habits, popularized as Fletcherism: eat only when hungry; eat whatever appeals; chew each mouthful until it swallows itself; eat only when relaxed. He made no money from his zealous instruction.

Of all the paths lead to a woman's love / Pity's the straightest.

JOHN FLETCHER
Knight of Malta I 1619

Fletcher John (1579–1625). English dramatist. He is remarkable for his range, which included tragicomedy and pastoral dramas, in addition to comedy and tragedy. He collaborated with Beaumont, producing, most notably, *Philaster* 1609 and *The Maid's Tragedy* 1610–11. He is alleged to have collaborated with Shakespeare on *The Two Noble Kinsmen* and *Henry VIII* 1612.

Among plays credited to Fletcher alone are the pastoral drama *The Faithful Shepherdess* 1610, the tragedy *Bonduca* c. 1611–14, and the comedy *The Wild Goose Chase* 1621.

Flett John (1963–1991). English fashion designer. He achieved international recognition while still training at St Martin's School of Art, London. In the late 1980s his collections were bought by top fashion houses. In 1989 he moved to Paris to join Claude Montana, and from there went to Enrico Coveri's Italian house.

Flinders Matthew (1774–1814). English navigator who explored the Australian coasts 1795–99 and 1801–03. Named after him are *Flinders Island*, NE of Tasmania, Australia; the *Flinders Range* in S Australia; and *Flinders River* in Queensland, Australia.

Flint William Russell (1880–1969). Scottish artist. He is known for his watercolours of mildly erotic nudes. He was president of the Royal Society of Painters in Water-Colour 1936–56. Knighted 1947.

Flores Juan José (1801–1864). Ecuadorian general, president 1830–35 and 1839–45. Born in Venezuela, he joined Simón Bolívar's patriot army in his teens, and soon became one of its most trusted generals. Flores convoked the assembly declaring Ecuador's independence 1830 and was elected its first constitutional president the same year. During his two terms in office Ecuador was an oasis of stability in Spanish America.

Flores refused to step down at the end of his second period of office 1843 and was deposed and fled the country 1845. An attempt to invade Ecuador from Peru 1852 failed, but he was later recalled as a military commander and ended Ecuador's civil war 1860.

Florey Howard Walter, Baron Florey (1898–1968). Australian pathologist whose research into lysozyme, an antibacterial enzyme discovered by Alexander Fleming, led him to study penicillin (another of Fleming's discoveries), which he and Ernst Chain isolated and prepared for widespread use. With Fleming, they were awarded the Nobel Prize for Physiology or Medicine 1945.

Florey was born in Adelaide and educated there and at Oxford University, England. He was professor of pathology at Sheffield 1932–35 and at Oxford from 1935. Knighted 1944, baron 1965.

Florio Giovanni (c. 1553–1625). English translator, born in London, the son of Italian refugees. He translated Michel Montaigne's essays in 1603.

Flory Paul John (1910–1985). US polymer chemist who was awarded the 1974 Nobel Prize for Chemistry for his investigations of synthetic and natural macromolecules. With Wallace Carothers, he developed nylon, the first synthetic polyamide, and the synthetic rubber neoprene.

He worked successively for Du Pont (with Carothers), Esso, and the Goodyear Tire and Rubber Company. He was professor of chemistry at Cornell University 1948–56 and at Stanford University from 1961. Flory pioneered research substances made up of giant molecules, such as rubbers, plastics, fibres, films, and proteins. In addition to developing polymerization techniques, he discovered ways of analysing polymers. Many of these substances are able to increase the lengths of their component molecular chains and Flory found that one extending molecule can stop growing and pass on its growing ability to another molecule.

Flotow Friedrich Adolf Ferdinand, Freiherr von (1812–1883). German composer. He wrote 18 operas, including *Martha* 1847.

Fludd Robert (1574–1637). British physician and alchemist who attempted to present a comprehensive account of the universe based on Hermetic principles.

Flynn Errol (born Leslie Thomson Flynn) (1909–1959). Australian-born US film actor. He is renowned for his portrayal of swashbuckling heroes in such films as *Captain Blood* 1935, *Robin*

Hood 1938, *The Charge of the Light Brigade* 1938, *The Private Lives of Elizabeth and Essex* 1939, *The Sea Hawk* 1940, and *The Master of Ballantrae* 1953. In *The Sun Also Rises* 1957 he portrayed a middle-aged Hemingway roué, and in *Too Much Too Soon* 1958 he portrayed actor John Barrymore. Flynn wrote an autobiography, *My Wicked, Wicked Ways* 1959. He became a US citizen 1942.

Flynn John (1880–1951). Australian missionary. Inspired by the use of aircraft to transport the wounded of World War I, he instituted in 1928 the *flying doctor* service in Australia, which can be summoned to the outback by radios in individual homesteads.

Fo Dario (1926–   ). Italian dramatist. His plays are predominantly political satires combining black humour with slapstick. They include *Morte accidentale di un anarchico/Accidental Death of an Anarchist* 1970, and *Non si paga non si paga/Can't Pay? Won't Pay!* 1975/1981. He has also written a one-man show, *Mistero buffo* 1969, based on the medieval mystery plays; and a handbook on the skills of the comic performer, *Tricks of the Trade* 1991.

My centre is giving way, my right is in retreat; situation excellent. I am attacking.

FERDINAND FOCH
Attributed remark quoted in G G Aston
The Biography of the Late Marshall Foch 1929

Foch Ferdinand (1851–1929). Marshal of France during World War I. He was largely responsible for the Allied victory at the first battle of the Marne Sept 1914, and commanded on the NW front Oct 1914–Sept 1916. He was appointed commander in chief of the Allied armies in the spring of 1918, and launched the Allied counter-offensive in July that brought about the negotiation of an armistice to end the war.

Following his success at the Marne, he was made assistant commander of the French Forces of the North, taking full command Jan 1915. He commanded the French right wing during the battle of the Somme 1916 and later that year was side-lined into various administrative and consultative posts. His retirement was more due to

Flynn, Errol Australian-born Hollywood film actor Errol Flynn in The Adventures of Robin Hood *1938. Flynn played the swashbuckling hero in many films such as* Captain Blood *1935 and* The Private Lives of Elizabeth and Essex *1939. His personal life attracted as much interest as the roles he played, and during the 1940s various scandals led to a decline in his career.*

Foch Ferdinand Foch, French Marshal in World War I. He initiated the Allied counter-offensive in July 1918 which led to negotiations for an armistice to end the war. (Image Select)

political infighting than his age and he was recalled by Pétain to serve as Chief of the General Staff 1917 to co-ordinate Allied support for Italy following the defeat at Caporetto. He went on to co-ordinate Anglo-French forces in France, and became the Allied commander in chief April 1918. He was elected Marshal of France 6 Aug.

Focillon Henri (1881–1943). French art historian. He taught both in Europe and the USA. He was an authority on the Middle Ages, discussed in, for example, *Art d'Occident/Art of the West* 1938. His writings explore two themes in particular: the role of technique in artistic creation and the extent to which art reflects the world-view of a period. In *Vie des formes/The Life of Forms in Art* 1934, he analyses the evolution of style in terms of three interrelated stages: the experimental, the classical, and the baroque.

Fokine and Pavlova clashed with the authorities when they led a group in support of revolutionary activities against the Tsar.

Christy Adair on MIKHAIL FOKINE
in *Woman and Dance; Sylphs and Sirens* 1992

Fokine Mikhail (1880–1942). Russian choreographer and dancer. He was chief choreographer to the *Ballets Russes* 1909–14, and with Diaghilev revitalized and reformed the art of ballet, promoting the idea of artistic unity among dramatic, musical, and stylistic elements.

Fokine was born in St Petersburg. His creations for Diaghilev include some of the most famous works in the ballet repertory, such as *Les Sylphides* 1909, *Schéhérazade* and *The Firebird*, both 1910, and *Le Spectre de la rose* and *Petrushka*, both 1911. He also created *The Dying Swan* for Anna Pavlova 1907. As a dancer, he was first soloist with the Maryinsky Theatre (later the Kirov) 1904.

Foley Thomas S(tephen) (1929–). US Democrat politician. He was speaker of the House of Representatives 1989–94.

Foley was born in Spokane, Washington. A member of the House of Representatives from 1965, he was chair of the Democratic Study Group from 1974 and chair of the Congressional Agriculture Committee 1974–80. He became majority whip 1980 and majority leader 1986. He was a reform-minded liberal who did not upset his opponents. He was the first incumbent speaker to be defeated in an election since 1960.

Fonck René (1896–1953). French fighter ace of World War I. He shot down his first German aircraft 6 Aug 1916 and on 9 May 1918, over Montdidier, he shot down six German aircraft in one dogfight. By the end of the war he had claimed 75 enemy aircraft and was the highest-scoring French ace. He was awarded the British MC and DCM, as well as many French honours.

I'm Goddam ashamed of it.

HENRY FONDA
on his five marriages, quoted in *Film Yearbook* 1983

Fonda Henry Jaynes (1905–1982). US actor. His engaging style made him ideal in the role of the American pioneer and honourable man. His many films include *The Grapes of Wrath* 1940, *My Darling Clementine* 1946, *12 Angry Men* 1957, and *On Golden Pond* 1981, for which he won the Academy Award for best actor. He was the father of actress Jane Fonda and actor and director Peter Fonda (1939–).

I'm perfect; the areas that I need help on are not negotiable. They have to do with gravity.

JANE FONDA
People 12 Nov 1990

Fonda Jane Seymour (1937–). US actress. Her varied film roles include *Cat Ballou* 1965, *Barefoot in the Park* 1967, *Barbarella* 1968, *They Shoot Horses, Don't They?* 1969, *Julia*, 1977, *The China Syndrome* 1979, *On Golden Pond* 1981 (in which she appeared with her father, Henry Fonda), and *Old Gringo* 1989. She won Academy Awards for *Klute* 1971 and *Coming Home* 1978.

She is active in left-wing politics and in promoting physical fitness.

Fontaine Joan. Stage name of Joan De Beauvoir De Havilland (1917–). US film actress of cool, delicate beauty. She achieved stardom in two Alfred Hitchcock films *Rebecca* 1940 with Laurence Olivier, and *Suspicion* 1941 (Academy Award) with Cary Grant. Fontaine continued to play both sympathetic and scheming roles until the 1960s, appearing to notable effect in *Letter from an Unknown Woman* 1948 and *Beyond a Reasonable Doubt* 1956. She is the sister of the actress Olivia De Havilland.

Fontana Domenico (1543–1607). Italian architect, born in Melide, Canton Tizino. He was appointed architect to Pope Sixtus V and undertook various important commissions in Rome, notably the Lateran Palace 1586–88 and the Vatican library 1587–90. He also assisted in the completion of the dome of St Peter's 1588–90. After 1592 he settled in Naples, where he designed the Royal Palace 1600–02.

Fontana Lucio (1899–1968). Italian painter and sculptor. He developed a unique abstract style, presenting bare canvases with straight parallel slashes. His *White Manifesto* 1946 argued for the blending of scientific ideas with new art forms.

Fontana Niccolò (*c.* 1499–1557). Italian mathematician and physicist known as ◊Tartaglia.

Fontane Theodor (1819–1898). German novelist. His best work, such as the historical novel *Vor den Sturm/Before the Storm* 1878, a critical but sympathetic account of Prussian aristocratic life, and *Effi Briest* 1898, is marked by superb characterization and a concern with the position of women.

He was born in Brandenburg, the vividly rendered setting of his novels. He worked as a journalist and wrote stirring popular ballads and topographical books before turning to realist fiction.

Fontanne Lynn (1887–1983). US actress. She was one-half of the husband-and-wife acting partnership known as the 'Lunts' with her husband Alfred Lunt.

Fonteyn Margot. Stage name of Peggy (Margaret) Hookham (1919–1991). English ballet dancer. She made her debut with the Vic-Wells Ballet in *Nutcracker* 1934 and first appeared as Giselle 1937, eventually becoming prima ballerina of the Royal Ballet, London. Renowned for her perfect physique, clear line, musicality, and interpretive powers, she created many roles in Frederick Ashton's ballets and formed a legendary partnership with Rudolf Nureyev. She did not retire from dancing until 1979.

Fonteyn's first major role was in Ashton's *Le Baiser de la fée* 1935; other Ashton ballets include *Symphonic Variations* 1946, *Ondine* 1958 (filmed 1959), and *Marguerite and Armand* 1963 (filmed 1972). She also appeared in Macmillan's *Romeo and Juliet* 1965 (filmed 1966) with Nureyev. DBE 1956.
Suggested reading
Money, K *The Art of Fonteyn* (1965)
Money, K *Fonteyn: The Making of a Legend* (1973)

Racial and colour prejudice were to him not so much detestable as incomprehensible.

Lord Elwyn-Jones on DINGLE FOOT
in *Dictionary of National Biography*

Foot Dingle Mackintosh (1905–1978). British lawyer and Labour politician, solicitor-general 1964–67. He was the brother of Michael Foot. Knighted 1964.

Foot Hugh Mackintosh, Baron Caradon (1907–1990). British Labour politician. As governor of Cyprus 1957–60, he guided the independence negotiations, and he represented the UK at the United Nations 1964–70. He was the son of Isaac Foot and brother of Michael Foot. KCMG 1951, baron 1964.

Men of power have no time to read; yet men who do not read are unfit for power.

ISAAC FOOT
Debts of Honour

Foot Isaac (1880–1960). British Liberal politician. A staunch Nonconformist, he was minister of mines 1931–32. He was the father of Dingle, Hugh, and Michael Foot.

Foot Michael Mackintosh (1913–). British Labour politician and writer. A leader of the left-wing Tribune Group, he was secretary of state for employment 1974–76, Lord President of the Council and leader of the House 1976–79, and succeeded James Callaghan as Labour Party leader 1980–83.
Suggested reading
Hoggart, Simon and Leigh, David *Michael Foot: A Portrait* (1981)

Forbes Bryan John Clarke (1926–). English film producer, director, and screenwriter. After acting in such films as *An Inspector Calls* 1954, he made his directorial debut with *Whistle Down the Wind* 1961; among his other films are *The L-Shaped Room* 1962, *The Wrong Box* 1966, and *The Raging Moon* 1971.

Forbes Edward (1815–1854). British naturalist who studied molluscs and made significant contributions to oceanography. In palaeobotany, he divided British plants into five groups, and proposed that Britain had once been joined to the continent by a land bridge.

Forbes was born on the Isle of Man and studied at Edinburgh. He became palaeontologist to the Geological Society of London, then professor of natural history at Edinburgh and from 1851 at the Royal School of Mines in London.

Forbes discounted the contemporary conviction that marine life subsisted only close to the sea surface, spectacularly dredging a starfish from a depth of 400 m/1,300 ft in the Mediterranean. His *The Natural History of European Seas* 1859 was a pioneering oceanographical text. It developed his favourite idea of 'centres of creation'; that is, the notion that species had come into being at one particularly favoured location. Though not an evolutionist, Forbes' ideas could be commandeered for evolutionary purposes.

Ford Ford Madox. Adopted name of Ford Hermann Hueffer (1873–1939). English author. He wrote more than 82 books, the best known of which is the novel *The Good Soldier* 1915. He founded and edited the *English Review* 1909, to which Thomas Hardy, D H Lawrence, and Joseph Conrad contributed. He excelled at a comic mixture of invention and reportage. He also founded *The Transatlantic Review* 1924. He was a grandson of the painter Ford Madox Brown.

Ford Gerald R(udolph) (1913–). 38th president of the USA 1974–77, a Republican. He was elected to the House of Representatives 1949, was nominated to the vice-presidency by Richard Nixon 1973 following the resignation of Spiro Agnew, and became president 1974, when Nixon was forced to resign following the Watergate scandal. He granted Nixon a full pardon Sept 1974. Ford's visit to Vladivostok 1974 resulted in agreement with the USSR on strategic arms limitation. He was defeated by Carter in the 1976 election by a narrow margin.
Suggested reading
Fitzgerald, Carol (ed) *Gerald R Ford* (1988)
Ford, Gerald *A Time to Heal* (memoirs) (1979)
Osborne, John *The White House Watch: The Ford Years* (1977)

Ford Glenn (Gwyllym Samuel Newton) (1916–). Canadian-born US actor. He was active in Hollywood from the 1940s to the 1960s. Usually cast as the tough but good-natured hero, he was equally at home in Westerns, thrillers, and comedies. His films include *Gilda* 1946, *The Big Heat* 1953, and *Dear Heart* 1965.

Ford *US film actor Harrison Ford. He made his reputation in a series of popular adventure movies, including* Star Wars *1977 and* Raiders of the Lost Ark *1981. He has also appeared in more serious films, such as* Witness *1985,* Presumed Innocent *1990, and* The Fugitive *1993.*

Ford, John *US film director John Ford. One of the USA's greatest directors and a pioneer of the Western, he made such classics as* Stagecoach *1939 (with John Wayne) and* Young Mr Lincoln *1939,* The Grapes of Wrath *1940, and* My Darling Clementine *1946 (all with Henry Fonda).*

Ford Harrison (1942–   ). US film actor. He became internationally known as Han Solo in George Lucas' *Star Wars* 1977, playing the role in the rest of the trilogy, and created the lead role in Steven Spielberg's series of *Indiana Jones* films 1981–89. Other films include *Blade Runner* 1982, *The Mosquito Coast* 1987, *Presumed Innocent* 1990, and *The Fugitive* 1993. *See illustration on page 303.*

People can have the Model T in any colour – so long as it's black.

HENRY FORD
quoted in J A Nevins *Ford, the Times, the Man, the Company* 1954

Ford Henry (1863–1947). US automobile manufacturer. He built his first car 1896 and founded the Ford Motor Company 1903. His Model T (1908–27) was the first car to be constructed solely by assembly-line methods and to be mass-marketed; 15 million of these

Ford, Henry *US automotive engineer Henry Ford, shown in his first car. Ford's early cars were named alphabetically, albeit in a rather erratic fashion. His first eight models were the A, B, C, F, K, N, R and S before he finally produced, in 1908, his first mass produced car, the Model T. When, after nineteen years, he ceased production of the Model T, he succeeded it not with the Model U, but another Model A. (Image Select)*

FIRST · CAR

cars were sold. Ford's innovative policies, such as a $5 daily minimum wage and a five-day working week, revolutionized employment practices, but he opposed the introduction of trade unions. In 1928 he launched the Model A, a stepped-up version of the Model T.

Ford was politically active and a pacifist; he opposed US intervention in both world wars and promoted his own anti-Semitic views. In 1936 he founded, with his son Edsel Ford (1893–1943), the philanthropic Ford Foundation; he retired in 1945 from the Ford Motor Company, then valued at over $1 billion.

Suggested reading
Herndon, B *Ford* (1969)
Lacey, R *Ford: The Man and the Machine* (1986)
Nye, D *Henry Ford: Ignorant Idealist* (1979)
Rae, J B *Henry Ford* (1969)

Love is the tyrant of the heart; it darkens / Reason, confounds discretion; deaf to counsel, / It runs a headlong course to desperate madness.

JOHN FORD
Lover's Melancholy III iii 1629

Ford John (*c.* 1586–*c.* 1640). English poet and dramatist. His play *'Tis Pity She's a Whore* (performed about 1626, printed 1633) is a study of incest between brother and sister. His other plays include *The Lover's Melancholy* 1629, *The Broken Heart* 1633, *Love's Sacrifice* 1633, and *The Chronicle History of Perkin Warbeck* 1634. Dwelling on themes of pathos and frustration, they reflect the transition from a general to an aristocratic audience for drama.

Tempt not the stars, young man, thou canst not play / With the severity of fate.

JOHN FORD
The Broken Heart I iii 1633

Ford John. Adopted name of Sean Aloysius O'Feeney (1895–1973). US film director. Active from the silent film era, he was one of the key creators of the 'Western', directing *The Iron Horse* 1924; *Stagecoach* 1939 became his masterpiece. He won Academy Awards for *The Informer* 1935, *The Grapes of Wrath* 1940, *How Green Was My Valley* 1941, and *The Quiet Man* 1952. Other films include *They Were Expendable* 1945, *Rio Grande* 1950, *Mr Roberts* 1955, *The Last Hurrah* 1958, and *The Man Who Shot Liberty Valance* 1962.

Suggested reading
Baxter, John *The Cinema of John Ford* (1971)
Bogdanovich, Peter *John Ford* (1978)
Gallagher, T *John Ford: The Man and his Works* (1988)
Stowell, Peter *John Ford* (1986)

Forde Francis Michael (1890–1983). Australian Labor politician, prime minister for six days 1945. He was deputy prime minister and minister for the army under John Curtin from 1941 and on Curtin's death was sworn in as caretaker prime minister 6–13 July. He was defeated by Ben Chifley in the subsequent leadership contest and in 1946 was appointed high commissioner to Canada.

Foreman George (1948–   ). US heavyweight boxer who was the undisputed world heavyweight champion 1973–74. In Nov 1994, at the age of 45, Foreman became the oldest boxer ever to win a championship when he knocked out Michael Moorer to win the International Boxing Federation and World Boxing Association heavyweight title belts. Foreman had retired from boxing 1977, but returned to the sport 1987.

Forester C(ecil) S(cott) (1899–1966). English novelist. He wrote a series of historical novels set in the Napoleonic era that, beginning with *The Happy Return* 1937, cover the career – from midshipman to admiral – of Horatio Hornblower. He also wrote *Payment Deferred* 1926, a subtle crime novel, and *The African Queen* 1938, later filmed with Humphrey Bogart.

Never, never never, would England forgive the man who allowed Nelson's coffin to sink ... in Thames mud.

C S FORESTER
Hornblower and the Atropos IV 1953

Forman Milos (1932–). Czech-born film director noted for his film *One Flew Over the Cuckoo's Nest* 1975, which won the five top Academy Awards. His other films include *Ragtime* 1981 and the lavishly designed *Amadeus* 1984 (Academy Award). Such films as *The Fireman's Ball* 1967 established Forman as one of the major talents of the 'new wave' cinema, which emerged from the temporary liberalization of Czechoslovakia in the 1960s. After the 1968 Soviet invasion, Forman escaped to the United States.

The Czechs voted for the jungle, while the Slovaks voted for the zoo. It is clear that a compromise is impossible.

MILOS FORMAN
Remark on the division of Czechoslovakia 1992

Formby George (1904–1961). English comedian. He established a stage and screen reputation as an apparently simple Lancashire working lad, and sang such songs as 'Mr Wu' and 'Cleaning Windows', accompanying himself on the ukulele. His father was a music-hall star of the same name.

I'm leaning on a lamp-post at the corner of the street / In case a certain little lady comes by.

GEORGE FORMBY
'Leaning on a Lamp-post'

Forrest John, 1st Baron Forrest of Bunbury (1847–1918). Australian explorer and politician. He crossed Western Australia W–E 1870, when he went along the southern coast route, and in 1874, when he crossed much further north, exploring the Musgrave Ranges. He was born in Western Australia, and was its first premier 1890–1901. Knighted 1891, baron 1918.
Suggested reading
Crowley, F K *Forrest* (1971)
Rawson, Geoffrey *Desert Journeys* (1948)

Forrest Nathan Bedford (1821–1877). US Confederate military leader and founder of the Ku Klux Klan 1866, a secret and sinister society dedicated to white supremacy. At the outbreak of the American Civil War 1861, Forrest escaped from Union troops before the fall of Fort Donelson in Tennessee 1862. After the Battle of Shiloh 1862, he was promoted to the rank of brigadier general.

Born in Chapel Hill, Tennessee, Forrest had little formal schooling but accumulated enough wealth through slave dealing to buy land in Mississippi and establish a cotton plantation. He founded the Klan while working as a civilian railroad executive after the end of the Civil War.

Forrestal James Vincent (1892–1949). US Democratic politician. As under secretary from 1940 and secretary of the navy from 1944, he organized its war effort, accompanying the US landings on the Japanese island Iwo Jima. He was the first secretary of the Department of Defense 1947–49, a post created to unify the three armed forces at the end of World War II.

Forssmann Werner (1904–1979). German heart surgeon. In 1929 he originated, by experiment on himself, the technique of cardiac catheterization (passing a thin tube from an arm artery up into the heart for diagnostic purposes). He shared the 1956 Nobel Prize for Physiology or Medicine.

Forster E(dward) M(organ) (1879–1970). English novelist. He was concerned with the interplay of personality and the conflict between convention and instinct. His novels include *A Room with a View* 1908, *Howards End* 1910, and *A Passage to India* 1924. He also

wrote short stories, for example 'The Eternal Omnibus' 1914; criticism, including *Aspects of the Novel* 1927; and essays, including 'Abinger Harvest' 1936.

Personal relations are the important thing for ever and ever, and not this outer life of telegrams and anger.

E M FORSTER
Howards End ch 19 1910

Forster published his first novel, *Where Angels Fear to Tread*, 1905. He enhances the superficial situations of his plots with unexpected insights in *The Longest Journey* 1907, *A Room with a View*, and *Howards End*. His many years spent in India and as secretary to the Maharajah of Dewas 1921 provided him with the material for *A Passage to India*, which explores the relationship between the English and the Indians. *Maurice*, published 1971, has a homosexual theme.
Suggested reading
Arlott, J *Aspects of Forster* (1969)
Furbank, P *E M Forster: A Life* (1978)
McDowell, F *E M Forster* (1965)
Tambling, J *E M Forster* (1995)
Trilling, L *E M Forster* (1943)

Forster Margaret (1938–). English novelist and biographer. Her *Georgy Girl* 1965 (filmed 1966) encapsulated the mood of 1960s London; later novels include *Have the Men Had Enough?* 1989 on the tragedy of Alzheimer's disease. The subjects of her biographies, mostly writers, include the poet Elizabeth Barrett Browning 1988.

Forster's first novel, *Dame's Delight* 1964, set in Oxford, exposed the nostalgic aura surrounding Oxbridge. She has written lives of Prince Charles Edward Stuart (the Young Pretender) 1973 and the novelists William Makepeace Thackeray 1978 and Daphne du Maurier 1993.

Forster William Edward (1818–1886). British Liberal reformer. In Gladstone's government 1868–74 he was vice president of the council, and secured the passing of the Education Act 1870 and the Ballot Act 1872. He was chief secretary for Ireland 1880–82.

Forsyth Andrew Russell (1858–1942). Scottish mathematician whose *Theory of Functions* 1893 introduced the main strands of European mathematical study to British mathematicians. Bringing together the work of all the various schools in a single volume, the book completely changed the nature of mathematical thinking.

Forsyth was born in Glasgow and studied at Cambridge. He was professor at Liverpool College 1882–84, but spent most of his career at Cambridge. From 1913 to 1923 he was professor at Imperial College, London.

He formulated a theorem that generalized a large number of identities between double theta functions; because this work was also carried out independently yet simultaneously by Henry Smith (1826–1883), the theorem is now called the *Smith–Forsyth theorem*. Forsyth also studied languages, enabling him to translate the works of others and to introduce their ideas to the UK. His *Theory of Functions* stimulated such rapid developments in mathematics that Forsyth was soon left behind.

Forsyth Bill (1947–). Scottish film director and screenwriter. Forsyth established a reputation with a series of comedies, set in Scotland, including *Gregory's Girl* 1980 and *Local Hero* 1983, which combined whimsy and dry humour. His first feature film was *That Sinking Feeling* 1979. Other films include *Comfort and Joy* 1984 and *Housekeeping* 1987.

It is cold at six-forty in the morning ... when a man is about to be executed by a firing squad.

FREDERICK FORSYTH
Day of the Jackal, opening words 1970

Forsyth Frederick (1938–). English thriller writer. His books include *The Day of the Jackal* 1970, *The Dogs of War* 1974, *The*

Fourth Protocol 1984, and *The Negotiator* 1990. He was a Reuters correspondent and BBC radio and television reporter before making his name with *The Day of the Jackal*, dealing with an attempted assassination of president de Gaulle of France. Later novels were *The Odessa File* 1972 and *The Devil's Alternative* 1979.

Fortin Jean Nicolas (1750–1831). French physicist and instrumentmaker who invented a portable mercury barometer in 1800. Any barometer in which the mercury level can be adjusted to zero is now known as a Fortin barometer. The barometer Fortin designed incorporated a mercury-filled leather bag, a glass cylinder, and an ivory pointer for marking the mercury level. Fortin did not invent these features but he was the first to use them together in a sensitive portable barometer.

Fortin was born in Ile de France and worked in Paris at the Bureau de Longitudes, and later for the Paris Observatory, constructing instruments for astronomical studies and surveying. He also made clocks, and precision equipment for many scientists, including a balance for French chemist Antoine Lavoisier which could measure masses as little as 70 mg/0.0025 oz. In 1799 he adjusted the weight standard, the platinum kilogram, which was stored in the French National Archives.

Foscolo Ugo (1778–1827). Italian author. An intensely patriotic Venetian, he fought with the French against the invading Austrians. Disillusionment with Napoleon inspired his very popular novel *Ultime lettere di Jacopo Ortis/Last Letters of Jacopo Ortis* 1802. His blank-verse patriotic poem 'Dei sepolchri'/'Of the Sepulchres' 1807 made his name and was followed by the tragedies *Aiace/Ajax* 1811 and *Ricciarda* 1812. His last years were spent in exile in England as a literary journalist and Italian teacher.

Foss (born Fuchs) Lukas (1922–). US composer and conductor. His stylistically varied works, including the cantata *The Prairie* 1942 and *Time Cycle* for soprano and orchestra 1960, express an ironic view of tradition.

Born in Germany, he studied in Europe before settling in the USA 1937. A student of Hindemith, he composed vocal music in Neo-Classical style; in the mid-1950s he began increasingly to employ improvisation. Foss has also written chamber and orchestral music in which the players reproduce tape-recorded effects.

Directors are never in short supply of girlfriends.

BOB FOSSE
quoted in *Film Yearbook* 1985

Fosse Bob (Robert Louis) (1927–1987). US film director. He entered films as a dancer and choreographer from Broadway, making his directorial debut with *Sweet Charity* 1968. He received an Academy Award for his second film as director, *Cabaret* 1972. Other films include *All That Jazz* 1979.

Fossey Dian (1938–1985). US zoologist. Almost completely untrained, Fossey was sent by Louis Leakey into the African wild. From 1975, she studied mountain gorillas in Rwanda and discovered that they committed infanticide and that females were transferred to nearby established groups. Living in close proximity to them, she discovered that they led peaceful family lives. She was murdered by poachers whose snares she had cut.

Foster Greg (1958–). US hurdler. He has won three consecutive World Championship gold medals (1983, 1987, 1991), the only athlete to achieve this feat.

When you know your text, that's when you can improvise.

JODIE FOSTER
quoted in *Photoplay* Oct 1984

Foster Jodie. Stage name of Alicia Christian Foster (1962–). US film actress and director. She began acting as a child in a great variety

of roles. She starred in *Taxi Driver* and *Bugsy Malone* both 1976, when only 14. Subsequent films include *The Accused* 1988 and *The Silence of the Lambs* 1991 (she won Academy Awards for both), *Sommersby* 1993, and *Nell* 1994. She made her directorial debut with *Little Man Tate* 1991.

Foster Norman Robert (1935–). English architect of the High Tech school. His buildings include the Willis Faber & Dumas insurance offices, Ipswich 1975, the Sainsbury Centre for the Visual Arts, Norwich 1977, the headquarters of the Hong Kong and Shanghai Bank, Hong Kong 1986, and Stansted Airport, Essex, 1991.

He has won numerous international awards for his industrial architecture and design, including RIBA awards for the Stansted project and the Sackler Galleries extension at the Royal Academy of Art, London, 1992, which is a sensitive, yet overtly modern, addition to an existing historic building. Knighted 1990.

Foster Stephen Collins (1826–1864). US songwriter. He wrote sentimental popular songs including 'My Old Kentucky Home' 1853 and 'Beautiful Dreamer' 1864, and rhythmic minstrel songs such as 'Oh! Susanna' 1848 and 'Camptown Races' 1850.

Foucault Jean Bernard Léon (1819–1868). French physicist who used a pendulum to demonstrate the rotation of the Earth on its axis, and invented the gyroscope 1852. In 1862 he made the first accurate determination of the velocity of light.

Foucault investigated heat and light, discovered eddy currents induced in a copper disc moving in a magnetic field, invented a polarizer, and made improvements in the electric arc. In 1860, he invented high-quality regulators for driving machinery at a constant speed; these were used in telescope motors and factory engines. Foucault was born and educated in Paris and became a physicist at the Paris Observatory 1855.

Freedom of conscience entails more dangers than authority and despotism.

MICHEL FOUCAULT
Madness and Civilization ch 7 1961

Foucault Michel Paul (1926–1984). French philosopher who argued that human knowledge and subjectivity are dependent upon specific institutions and practices, and that they change through history. In particular, he was concerned to subvert conventional assumptions about 'social deviants' – the mentally ill, the sick, and the criminal – who, he believed, are oppressed by the approved knowledge of the period in which they live.

Foucault rejected phenomenology and existentialism, and his historicization of the self challenges the ideas of Marxism. He was deeply influenced by the German philosopher Friedrich Nietzsche, and developed an analysis of the operation of power in society using Nietzschean concepts. His publications include *Histoire de la folie/Madness and Civilization* 1961 and *Les Mots et les choses/The Order of Things* 1966.

Suggested reading
Dreyfus, Hubert and Rabinow, Paul *Foucault* (1982)
Eribon, Didier *Michel Foucault* (trs 1991)
Michel, R *Foucault* (1985)
Miller, James *The Passion of Michel Foucault* (1993)
Sheridan, A *The Will to Truth* (1980)
Williams, K *Pauperism to Poverty* (1980)

It is worse than a crime; it is a blunder.

JOSEPH FOUCHÉ
referring to the political murder of the Duc d'Enghien by Napoleon
21 March 1804 (attributed also to Doulay de la Meurthe and Talleyrand)

Fouché Joseph, Duke of Otranto (1759–1820). French politician. He was elected to the National Convention (the post-Revolutionary legislature), and organized the conspiracy that overthrew the Jacobin leader Robespierre. Napoleon employed him as police minister.

Fouquet or Foucquet, Jean (*c.* 1420–*c.* 1481). French painter. He became court painter to Charles VIII 1448 and to Louis XI 1475. His *Melun Diptych* about 1450 (Musées Royaux, Antwerp, and Staatliche Museen, Berlin) shows Italian Renaissance influence.

He possibly trained in Paris, and was an accomplished master when he visited Italy, *c.* 1445, having already painted his famous portrait of Charles VII (Louvre). His art was admired in Rome, where he painted the portrait of Pope Eugene IV and evidently studied Italian Renaissance art with profit. He produced exquisite miniatures, notably those for a Book of Hours for his patron, Etienne Chevalier, Charles VII's treasurer (Chantilly, Musée Condé), a Boccaccio (Munich) and historical compilations, Jewish and French (Bibliothèque Nationale); but on a larger scale he showed a grandeur and firmness of design (with something of the quality of Gothic sculpture) as well as appreciation of human character, which are magnificently displayed in the *Deposition, c.* 1466, of the Church of Nouans.

Fouquet Nicolas (1615–1680). French politician, a rival to Louis XIV's minister J-B Colbert. Fouquet became *procureur général* of the Paris parlement 1650 and superintendent of finance 1651, responsible for raising funds for the long war against Spain, a post he held until arrested and imprisoned for embezzlement (at the instigation of Colbert, who succeeded him).

Fourier (François Marie) Charles (1772–1837). French socialist. In *Le Nouveau monde industriel/The New Industrial World* 1829–30, he advocated that society should be organized in self-sufficient cooperative units of about 1,500 people, and marriage should be abandoned.
Suggested reading
Riasanovsky, Nicholas *The Teachings of Charles Fourier* (1969)
Zeldin, David *The Educational Ideas of Charles Fourier* (1969)

Fourier Jean Baptiste Joseph (1768–1830). French applied mathematician whose formulation of heat flow 1807 contains the proposal that, with certain constraints, any mathematical function can be represented by trigonometrical series. This principle forms the basis of *Fourier analysis*, used today in many different fields of physics. His idea, not immediately well received, gained currency and is embodied in his *Théorie analytique de la chaleur/The Analytical Theory of Heat* 1822.

Light, sound, and other wavelike forms of energy can be studied using Fourier's method, a developed version of which is now called harmonic analysis.
Suggested reading
Grattan-Guinness, I *Joseph Fourier* (1972)
Herivel, John *Joseph Fourier: The Man and the Physics* (1975)

Fourneyron Benoit (1802–1867). French engineer who invented the first practical water turbine 1827. Fourneyron's water turbine was an outward-flow turbine. Water passed into guide passages in the movable outer wheel. When the water impinged on these wheel vanes, its direction was changed and it escaped round the periphery of the wheel. But the outward-flow turbine was unstable and speed regulation was difficult. Fourneyron patented an improved design which incorporated a three-turbine installation 1832. In 1855 he produced an improved version. He went on to build more than 1,000 hydraulic turbines of various forms and for use in different parts of the world, including Niagara Falls, USA.

Fowler Gerald (1935–1993). British politician and academic. A Labour MP 1966–79, he campaigned for equal access for all to higher education.

The loss of his parliamentary seat 1970 allowed him to experience as an academic the Open University and the new polytechnics – two of the innovations in which he had been involved politically. Later, as rector of the Polytechnic of North London 1982–92, and as a combative chairman of the Committee of Directors of Polytechnics, he was involved in the transfer of the polytechnics from local government control and their elevation to university status 1992.

Fowler Henry Watson (1858–1933) and Francis George (1870–1918) English brothers who were scholars and authors of a number of English dictionaries. *Modern English Usage* 1926, the work of Henry Fowler, has become a classic reference work for matters of style and disputed usage.

Fowler (Peter) Norman (1938–). British Conservative politician, chair of the party 1992–94. He was a junior minister in the Heath government, transport secretary in the first Thatcher administration 1979, social services secretary 1981, and employment secretary 1987–89. Knighted 1990.

Fowler William Alfred (1911–1995). US astrophysicist. In 1983 he and Subrahmanyan Chandrasekhar were awarded the Nobel Prize for Physics for their work on the life cycle of stars and the origin of chemical elements.

He attended the California Institute of Technology, gained a PhD, and became a research fellow there 1936. He spent his entire career at Caltech, rising from assistant professor to professor and, in 1970, instructor professor.

Fowler concentrated on research into the abundance of helium in the universe. The helium abundance was first defined as the result of the 'hot Big Bang' theory proposed by US physicist Ralph Alpher, Hans Bethe, and George Gamow 1948. In its original form, the Big Bang theory accounted only for the creation of the lightest elements, hydrogen and helium. In their classic paper 1957, Fowler, Hoyle, and the Burbages described how, in a star like the Sun, two hydrogen nuclei, or protons, combine to create the next heavier element, helium, thus generating energy. Over time, more and heavier elements are produced until, after millions of years, the star finally explodes into a supernova, scattering its material across the Universe.

We all write poems; it is simply that poets are the ones that write in words.

JOHN FOWLES
The French Lieutenant's Woman ch 19 1969

Fowles John Robert (1926–). English writer. His novels, often concerned with illusion and reality and with the creative process, include *The Collector* 1963, *The Magus* 1965, *The French Lieutenant's Woman* 1969 (filmed 1981), *Daniel Martin* 1977, *Mantissa* 1982, and *A Maggot* 1985.

Fox Charles James (1749–1806). English Whig politician, son of the 1st Baron Holland. He entered Parliament 1769 as a supporter of the court, but went over to the opposition 1774. As secretary of state 1782, leader of the opposition to Pitt, and foreign secretary 1806, he welcomed the French Revolution and brought about the abolition of the slave trade.

In 1782 he became secretary of state in Rockingham's government, but resigned when Shelburne succeeded Rockingham. He allied with North 1783 to overthrow Shelburne, and formed a coalition ministry with himself as secretary of state. When the Lords threw out Fox's bill to reform the government of India, George III dismissed the ministry, and in their place installed Pitt. Fox now became leader of the opposition, although co-operating with Pitt in the impeachment of Warren Hastings, the governor-general of India.

The 'Old Whigs' deserted to the government 1792 over the French Revolution, leaving Fox and a small group of 'New Whigs' to oppose Pitt's war of intervention and his persecution of the reformers. On Pitt's death 1806 a ministry was formed with Fox as foreign secretary, which at Fox's insistence abolished the slave trade. He opened peace negotiations with France, but died before their completion.
Suggested reading
Ayling, Stanley *Fox: The Life of Charles James Fox* (1991)
Derry, John *Charles James Fox* (1972)

Fox George (1624–1691). English founder of the Society of Friends. After developing his belief in a mystical 'inner light', he became a travelling preacher 1647, and in 1650 was imprisoned for blasphemy at Derby, where the name Quakers was first applied derogatorily to him and his followers, supposedly because he enjoined Judge Bennet to 'quake at the word of the Lord'.

Fox was born in Leicestershire. He suffered further imprisonments, made a missionary journey to America in 1671–72, and wrote many evangelical and meditative works, including a *Journal*, published 1694.

Suggested reading
Barbour, H *Quakers in Puritan England* (1964)
Wildes, H E *The Voice of the Lord* (1965)
Yolen, J *Friend: The Story of George Fox and the Quakers* (1972)

Fox James (1939–). English film actor. He is usually cast in upper-class, refined roles but was celebrated for his portrayal of a psychotic gangster in Nicolas Roeg's *Performance* 1970, which was followed by an eight-year break from acting. Fox appeared in *The Servant* 1963 and *Isadora* 1968. He returned to acting in *No Longer Alone* 1978 and other films include *Runners* 1984, *A Passage to India* 1984, and *The Russia House* 1990.

Fox Margaret (1833–1893). Canadian-born US spiritual medium. With her sister Katherine, she became famous for her psychic ability. The girls gave public demonstrations of their powers, sparking widespread public interest in spiritualism as a modern religious movement. In 1888 Margaret publicly confessed that her 'psychic powers' were a hoax.

Suggested reading
Braude, Ann *Radical Spirits: Spiritualism and Women's Rights in 19th Century America* (1989)

Foxe John (1516–1587). English Protestant propagandist. He became a canon of Salisbury 1563. His *Book of Martyrs* 1563 (originally titled *Actes and Monuments*) luridly described persecutions under Queen Mary, reinforcing popular hatred of Roman Catholicism.

Fracastoro Girolamo (c. 1478–1553). Italian physician known for two medical books. *Syphilis sive morbus gallicus/Syphilis or the French disease* 1530 was written in verse. It was one of the earliest texts on syphilis, a disease Fracastoro named. In *De contagione/On contagion* 1546, he wrote, far ahead of his time, about 'seeds of contagion'. He was born and worked mainly in Verona.

Fra Diavolo nickname of Michele Pezza (c. 1771–1806). Italian brigand. A renegade monk, he led a gang in the mountains of Calabria, S Italy, for many years, and was eventually executed in Naples.

Fraenkel Abraham Adolf (1891–1965). German-born Israeli mathematician who wrote many textbooks on set theory. He also investigated the axiomatic foundations of mathematical theories.

He was professor at Marburg 1922–28. In 1929 he emigrated to Israel and taught until 1959 at the Hebrew University of Jerusalem. Fraenkel's works include *Einleitung in die Mengenlehre* 1919, *Abstract Set Theory* 1953, and *Foundations of Set Theory* 1958.

Fraenkel-Conrat Heinz Ludwig (1910–). German-born US biochemist who showed that the infectivity of bacteriophages (viruses that infect bacteria) is a property of their inner nucleic acid component, not the outer protein case.

Fraenkel-Conrat was born and educated in Breslau (now Wrocław, Poland). With the Nazis' rise to power, he left Germany for the UK and the University of Edinburgh, after which he went to the USA. He became professor at the University of California 1958.

In 1955, Fraenkel-Conrat developed a technique for separating the outer protein coat from the inner nucleic acid core of bacteriophages without seriously damaging either portion. He also succeeded in reassembling the components and showed that these reformed bacteriophages are still capable of infecting bacteria. This work raised fundamental questions about the molecular basis of life. He then showed that the protein component of bacteriophages is inert and that the nucleic acid component alone has the capacity to infect bacteria. Thus, it seemed the fundamental properties of life resulted from the activity of nucleic acids.

Fragonard Jean-Honoré (1732–1806). French painter. He was the leading exponent of the Rococo style (along with his master

Boucher). His light-hearted subjects, often erotic, include *The Swing* c. 1766 (Wallace Collection, London). Mme de Pompadour was one of his patrons.

He was the son of a mercer, and studied art (for six months) with Chardin and then with Boucher. Winning the Prix de Rome 1752, he spent three years in Paris under Carle van Loo before travelling to Italy, where he stayed, 1756–61, being much impressed by the art of Tiepolo. A successful and immensely productive career was virtually ended by the Revolution. During the last 15 years of his life, divided between Grasse and Paris, though befriended by David, he ceased to paint, as if in the revolutionary epoch his art had become an anachronism.

His 500 paintings and thousands of drawings reveal a personality far transcending that of Boucher, and his vein of fantasy had its anticipation, as in his *Fontaine d'Amour*, of the spirit of Romanticism. His son, Alexandre Evariste (1780–1850), a decorative painter, and his sister-in-law, Marguerite Gérard, were his pupils.

Frame Janet Paterson (1924–). New Zealand novelist. After being wrongly diagnosed as schizophrenic, she reflected her experiences 1945–54 in the novel *Faces in the Water* 1961 and the autobiographical *An Angel at My Table* 1984 (filmed 1990).

Suggested reading
Frame, Janet *An Autobiography* (1989)

Frampton George James (1860–1928). English sculptor. His work includes the statue of *Peter Pan* 1911 in Kensington Gardens and the Edith Cavell memorial near St Martin-in-the-Fields, London, 1920.

France Anatole. Pen name of Jacques Anatole François Thibault (1844–1924). French writer. He is renowned for the wit, urbanity, and style of his works. His earliest novel was *Le Crime de Sylvestre Bonnard/The Crime of Sylvester Bonnard* 1881; later books include the autobiographical series beginning with *Le Livre de mon ami/My Friend's Book* 1885, the satiric *L'Île des pingouins/Penguin Island* 1908, and *Les Dieux ont soif/The Gods Are Athirst* 1912. Nobel Prize for Literature 1921.

France was born in Paris. He published a critical study of Alfred de Vigny 1868, which was followed by several volumes of poetry and short stories. He was elected to the French Academy 1896. His other books include *Thaïs* 1890 and *Crainquebille* 1905. He was a socialist and supporter of Dreyfus.

Francesca Piero della. See ◊Piero della Francesca, Italian painter.

Franchet d'Esperey Louis Félix Marie François (1856–1942). French soldier. In World War I, he fought in the first Battle of the Marne Sept 1914, then held the Aisne bridgeheads. He was placed in command of the Armies of Eastern France April 1916, and of the Armies of the North Jan 1917. He was appointed supreme commander of the Allied armies in the East June 1918, accepting the surrender of Bulgaria Sept 1918. He commanded the Allied forces in Turkey until 1920 and was created Marshal of France 1921.

Francia José Gaspar Rodríguez de (1766–1840). Paraguayan dictator 1814–40, known as *El Supremo*. A lawyer, he emerged as a strongman after independence was achieved 1811, and was designated dictator by congress 1814. Hostile to the Argentine regime, he sealed off the country and followed an isolationist policy.

Francis James Bicheno (1815–1892). English-born US hydraulics engineer who was active in the industrial development of New England. He made significant contributions to the understanding of fluid flow and to the development of the Francis-type water turbine.

In 1833 he went to the USA and worked for a locks and canals company, rising to chief engineer 1837. He advised on a number of dam projects, was a member of the Massachusetts state legislature, and was president of the Stonybrook Railroad for 20 years.

Francis devised a complete system of water supply for fire protection and had it working in the Lowell district for many years before anything similar was in operation anywhere else. He designed and built hydraulic lifts for the guard gates of the Pawtucket Canal and reconstructed the Pawtucket Dam 1875–76. His book *The Lowell*

Hydraulic Experiments 1855 gives the *Francis formula* for the flow of fluids over weirs.

Francis Sam (1923–1994). US painter and printmaker. A leading second-generation Abstract Expressionist, his buoyant paintings fuse American and European abstract styles. He is known for his large, splashed and splattered, floating forms, executed in a high-keyed palette against a white ground, for example *Middle Blue No.5* 1960.

Initially influenced by the gestural approaches of Clyfford Still and Mark Rothko, he developed his own more structured manner in Paris 1950–57 where, under the influence of French Tachisme, he produced largely monochromatic canvases covered with patches of translucent colour and runnels of pigment, as in *Blue-Black* 1952. His Blue-and-White and Edge series – all-white canvases with coloured edges – followed in the 1960s.

Francis I Emperor of Austria from 1804, also known as ◊Francis II, Holy Roman emperor.

Francis or *François*. Two kings of France:

Out of all I had, only honour remains, and my life, which is safe.

FRANCIS I
Letter to his mother after losing the Battle of Pavia 1525

Francis I (1494–1547). King of France from 1515. He succeeded his cousin Louis XII, and from 1519 European politics turned on the rivalry between him and the Holy Roman emperor Charles V, which led to war 1521–29, 1536–38, and 1542–44. In 1525 Francis was defeated and captured at Pavia and released only after signing a humiliating treaty. At home, he developed absolute monarchy.
Suggested reading
Hackett, Francis *Francis I* (1935, rep 1968)
Knecht, R J *Renaissance Warrior and Patron: The Reign of Francis I* (1994)
Seward, Desmond *Prince of the Renaissance* (1973)

In times of necessity all privileges cease, and not only privileges, but common laws as well, for necessity has no law.

FRANCIS I
quoted by R J Knecht *French Renaissance Monarchy: Francis I & Henry II* 1984

Francis II (1544–1560). King of France from 1559 when he succeeded his father, Henri II. He married Mary Queen of Scots 1558. He was completely under the influence of his mother, Catherine de' Medici.

Francis or *Franz*. Two Holy Roman emperors:

Francis I (1708–1765). Holy Roman emperor from 1745, who married Maria Theresa of Austria 1736.

Francis II (1768–1835). Holy Roman emperor 1792–1806. He became Francis I, Emperor of Austria 1804, and abandoned the title of Holy Roman emperor 1806. During his reign Austria was five times involved in war with France, 1792–97, 1798–1801, 1805, 1809, and 1813–14. He succeeded his father, Leopold II.

Francis Ferdinand Archduke of Austria, also known as ◊Franz Ferdinand.

Francis Joseph Emperor of Austria-Hungary, also known as ◊Franz Joseph.

Francis of Assisi, St (born Giovanni Bernadone) (1182–1226). Italian founder of the Roman Catholic Franciscan order of friars 1209 and, with St Clare, of the Poor Clares 1212. In 1224 he is said to have undergone a mystical experience during which he received the *stigmata* (five wounds of Jesus). Many stories are told of his ability to charm wild animals, and he is the patron saint of ecologists. His feast day is 4 Oct. Canonized 1228.

The son of a wealthy merchant, Francis changed his life after two dreams he had during an illness following spells of military service when he was in his early twenties. He resolved to follow literally the behests of the New Testament and live a life of poverty and service while preaching a simple form of the Christian gospel. In 1219 he went to Egypt to convert the sultan, and lived for a month in his camp. Returning to Italy, he resigned his leadership of the friars.
Suggested reading
Chesterton, G K *Saint Francis of Assisi* (1924, rep 1957)
Cunningham, Lawrence *Saint Francis of Assisi* (1976)
Moorman, J R H *Sources for the Life of Saint Francis of Assisi* (1967)

Make friends with the angels, who though invisible are always with you.

ST FRANCIS OF SALES
Introduction to the Devout Life pt 2 ch 16 1609

Francis of Sales, St (1567–1622). French bishop and theologian. He became bishop of Geneva 1602, and in 1610 founded the order of the Visitation, an order of nuns. He is the patron saint of journalists and other writers. His feast day is 24 Jan. Canonized 1655.

Francis of Sales was born in Savoy. His *Introduction à la vie dévote/Introduction to the Devout Life* 1609 was written to reconcile the Christian life with living in the real world.

The Choral is not a choral and the Fugue is not a fugue.

Camille Saint-Saëns
on CÉSAR AUGUSTE FRANCK's Prelude, Choral and Fugue, quoted in Norman Demuth *Vincent d'Indy* 1951

Franck César Auguste (1822–1890). Belgian composer. His music, mainly religious and Romantic in style, includes the *Symphony in D Minor* 1866–68, *Symphonic Variations* 1885 for piano and orchestra, the *Violin Sonata* 1886, the oratorio *Les Béatitudes/The Beatitudes* 1879, and many organ pieces.

Franck James (1882–1964). German-born US physicist. He shared a Nobel prize 1925 with his co-worker Gustav Hertz (1887–1975) for their experiments of 1914 on the energy transferred by colliding electrons to mercury atoms, showing that the transfer was governed by the rules of quantum theory.

In 1920 he became professor of experimental physics at Göttingen, but emigrated to the USA 1933 after publicly protesting against the Nazis' racial policies. He was a professor at the University of Chicago 1938–49. He participated in the wartime atomic-bomb project at Los Alamos but organized the 'Franck petition' 1945, which argued that the bomb should not be used against Japanese cities. After World War II he turned his research to photosynthesis.

Franco Francisco (Paulino Hermenegildo Teódulo Bahamonde) (1892–1975). Spanish dictator from 1939. As a general, he led the insurgent Nationalists to victory in the Spanish Civil War 1936–39, supported by Fascist Italy and Nazi Germany, and established a dictatorship. In 1942 Franco reinstated a Cortes (Spanish parliament), which in 1947 passed an act by which he became head of state for life.

Franco was born in Galicia, NW Spain. He entered the army 1910, served in Morocco 1920–26, and was appointed Chief of Staff 1935, but demoted to governor of the Canary Islands 1936. Dismissed from this post by the Popular Front (Republican) government, he plotted an uprising with German and Italian assistance, and on the outbreak of the Civil War organized the invasion of Spain by N African troops and foreign legionaries. After the death of General Sanjurjo, he took command of the Nationalists, proclaiming himself *Caudillo* (leader) of Spain. The defeat of the Republic with the surrender of Madrid 1939 brought all Spain under his government. On the outbreak of World War II, in spite of Spain's official attitude of 'strictest neutrality', his pro-Axis sympathies led him to send aid, later withdrawn, to the German side.

At home, he curbed the growing power of the Falange Española (the fascist party), and in later years slightly liberalized his regime. In 1969 he nominated Juan Carlos as his successor and future king of Spain. He relinquished the premiership 1973, but remained head of state until his death.

Suggested reading
Crozier, Brian *Franco: A Biographical History* (1967)
Ellwood, Sheelagh *Franco* (1994)
Gallo, Max *Spain Under Franco: A History* (trs 1974)
Hills, George *Franco: The Man and His Nation* (1967)
Preston, Paul *Franco: A Biography* (1993)
Trythall, J W D *Il Caudillo: A Political Biography of Franco* (1970)

Franco Itamar (1931–). Brazilian politician, president 1992–94. Replacing President Fernando Collor after his removal on charges of corruption, Franco came to the office with a clean record. He promised reform with stability but during his first months in office attracted widespread criticism, both from friends (for his working methods and lack of clear policies) and opponents (for his rapid privatization programme). He was defeated by Fernando Henrique Cardoso in the Oct 1994 presidential election.

Although vice president 1990–92, he had a largely low-profile political career until his elevation to head of state.

François French form of ◊Francis, two kings of France.

Francome John (1952–). British jockey. He holds the record for the most National Hunt winners (over hurdles or fences). Between 1970 and 1985 he rode 1,138 winners from 5,061 mounts – the second person (after Stan Mellor) to ride 1,000 winners. He took up training after retiring from riding.

Frank Anne (Anneliese Marie) (1929–1945). German diarist. She fled to the Netherlands with her family 1933 to escape Nazi anti-Semitism (the Holocaust). During the German occupation of Amsterdam, they and two other families remained in a sealed-off room, protected by Dutch sympathizers 1942–44, when betrayal resulted in their deportation and Anne's death in Belsen concentration camp. Her diary of her time in hiding was published 1947.

Previously suppressed portions of her diary were published 1989. The house in which the family took refuge is preserved as a museum. Her diary has sold 20 million copies in more than 50 languages and has been made into a play and a film publicizing the fate of millions.

Suggested reading
Frank, Anne *The Diary of Anne Frank* (trs 1953)
Gies, Miep *Anne Frank Remembered* (1987)
Schnabel, Ernst *Anne Frank: A Portrait in Courage* (1958)

Frank Hans (1900–1946). German bureaucrat and governor of Poland in World War II. Originally a lawyer and a member of the Nazi Party from its early years, he became Reichs Commissioner for Justice 1933. After the German invasion of Poland 1939 he was appointed governor-general of the *Generalgouvernement*, that part of Poland not incorporated into the Reich.

He ran a brutal and repressive regime aimed at total subjugation of the Poles and the extraction of every possible economic advantage from the territory using slave labour and Jewish extermination. As the Soviet Army approached Aug 1944 he resigned his post and fled. He was captured after the defeat of Germany, tried at Nuremberg, and hanged 16 Oct 1946.

Frank Ilya Mikhailovich (1908–1990). Russian physicist known for his work on radiation. In 1934 Pavel Cherenkov had noted a peculiar blue radiation sometimes emitted as electrons passed through water. It was left to Frank and his colleague at Moscow University, Igor Tamm (1895–1971), to realize that this form of radiation was produced by charged particles travelling faster through the medium than the speed of light in the same medium. Frank shared the 1958 Nobel Prize for Physics with Cherenkov and Tamm.

Frank Karl Hermann (1898–1946). Czech Nazi politician. Originally a leader of the Sudeten German Nazi Party, he became secretary of state for Bohemia and Moravia after their annexation by Germany 1939. Among other atrocities, he was responsible for the destruction of Lidice and the murder of its inhabitants June 1942 as a reprisal for the assassination of Heydrich. He was captured at the end of the war, tried, and publicly hanged near Prague May 1946.

Frank Robert (1924–). US photographer. He is best known for his informal and unromanticized pictures of American life. These were published, with a foreword by the US novelist Jack Kerouac, as *The Americans* 1959. Since then he has concentrated mainly on film-making.

Frankel Benjamin (1906–1973). English composer and teacher. He studied the piano in Germany and continued his studies in London while playing jazz violin in nightclubs. His output includes chamber music and numerous film scores, notably *The Man in the White Suit* 1951 and *A Kid for Two Farthings* 1955.

Frankenthaler Helen (1928–). US Abstract Expressionist painter. She invented the colour-staining technique whereby the unprimed, absorbent canvas is stained or soaked with thinned-out paint, creating deep, soft veils of translucent colour.

Frankfurter Felix (1882–1965). Austrian-born US jurist and Supreme Court justice. As a supporter of liberal causes, Frankfurter was one of the founders of the American Civil Liberties Union 1920. Appointed to the US Supreme Court 1939 by F D Roosevelt, he opposed the use of the judicial veto to advance political ends.

Frankl Peter (1935–). Hungarian-born British pianist. Both a solo and chamber-music pianist, Frankl's wide repertory ranges from Mozart to Bartók. He is noted for both his technique and sensitivity of expression.

Franklin (Stella Marian Sarah) Miles (1879–1954). Australian novelist. Her first novel, *My Brilliant Career* 1901, autobiographical and feminist, drew on her experiences of rural Australian life. *My Career Goes Bung*, written as a sequel, was not published until 1946. Novels she wrote under the name 'Brent of Bin Bin' include *Up the Country* 1928, *Ten Creeks Run* 1931, and the family saga *All That Swagger* 1936.

Franklin Aretha (1942–). US soul singer. Her gospel background infuses her four-octave voice with a passionate conviction and authority. Her hits include 'Respect' 1967, 'Chain of Fools' 1968, and the albums *Lady Soul* 1968, *Amazing Grace* 1972, and *Who's Zoomin' Who?* 1985.

But in this world nothing can be said to be certain, except death and taxes.

BENJAMIN FRANKLIN
Letter to Jean Baptiste Le Roy 13 Nov 1789

Franklin Benjamin (1706–1790). US scientist, statesman, writer, printer, and publisher. He proved that lightning is a form of electricity, distinguished between positive and negative electricity, and invented the lightning conductor. He was the first US ambassador to France 1776–85, and negotiated peace with Britain 1783. As a delegate to the Continental Congress from Pennsylvania 1785–88, he helped to draft the Declaration of Independence and the US Constitution.

A printer, Franklin wrote and published the popular *Poor Richard's Almanac* 1733–58, as well as engaging in scientific experiment and making useful inventions, including bifocal spectacles. A member of the Pennsylvania Assembly 1751–64, he was sent to Britain to lobby Parliament about tax grievances and achieved the repeal of the Stamp Act; on his return to the USA he was prominent in the deliberations leading up to independence. As ambassador in Paris he enlisted French help for the American Revolution. After independence he became president of Pennsylvania and worked hard to abolish slavery.

Franklin, Benjamin *US statesman and scientist Benjamin Franklin, who helped draft the Declaration of Independence and performed some of the early investigations into the nature of electricity. Franklin was also a manic inventor. He gave the world bifocals, the lightning rod, extendible grippers for taking items off high shelves, and the Franklin stove. (Ann Ronan/Image Select)*

Franklin was born in Boston and self-educated. He became one of the most widely travelled of the leaders of the American colonies, bringing an internationalist perspective to the Constitutional Convention. He organized an effective postal system; taught himself Spanish, French, Italian, and Latin; and mapped the Gulf Stream. By flying a kite in a thunderstorm, he was able to charge up a condenser and produce sparks. He recognized the aurora borealis as an electrical phenomenon, and speculated on the existence of the ionosphere.

His autobiography first appeared 1781 (in complete form, 1868).

Suggested reading
Clark, R W *Benjamin Franklin: A Biography* (1983)
Doren, Carl van *Benjamin Franklin* (1938)
Franklin, Benjamin *Autobiography of Benjamin Franklin* (1771 and many other editions)
Ketcham, R L *Benjamin Franklin* (1965)

Franklin John (1786–1847). English naval explorer who took part in expeditions to Australia, the Arctic, and N Canada, and in 1845 commanded an expedition to look for the Northwest Passage from the Atlantic to the Pacific, during which he and his crew perished. The 1845 expedition had virtually found the Passage when it became trapped in the ice. No trace of the team was discovered until 1859. In 1984, two of its members, buried on King Edward Island, were found to be perfectly preserved in the frozen ground of their graves. Knighted 1829.

Franklin Rosalind Elsie (1920–1958). English biophysicist whose research on X-ray diffraction of DNA crystals helped Francis Crick and James D Watson to deduce the chemical structure of DNA.

Sophie, don't die, live for the children.
FRANZ FERDINAND
Last words to his wife, on his assassination at Sarajevo1914.

Franz Ferdinand or *Francis Ferdinand* (1863–1914). Archduke of Austria. He became heir to his uncle, Emperor Franz Joseph, in 1884 but while visiting Sarajevo 28 June 1914, he and his wife were assassinated by a Serbian nationalist. Austria used the episode to make unreasonable demands on Serbia that ultimately precipitated World War I.

You see in me the last monarch of the old school.
FRANZ JOSEPH
in conversation with Theodore Roosevelt 1910

Franz Joseph or *Francis Joseph* (1830–1916). Emperor of Austria-Hungary from 1848, when his uncle, Ferdinand I, abdicated. After the suppression of the 1848 revolution, Franz Joseph tried to establish an absolute monarchy but had to grant Austria a parliamentary constitution 1861 and Hungary equality with Austria 1867. He was defeated in the Italian War 1859 and the Prussian War 1866. In 1914 he made the assassination of his heir and nephew Franz Ferdinand the excuse for attacking Serbia, thus precipitating World War I.

Suggested reading
Clark, C W *Franz Joseph and Bismarck* (1934, rep 1968)
Crankshaw, Edward *The Fall of the House of Habsburg* (1963)
Marek, G B *The Eagles Die* (1974)

Fraser Antonia (1932–). English author. She has published authoritative biographies, including *Mary Queen of Scots* 1969; historical works, such as *The Weaker Vessel* 1984; and a series of detective novels featuring investigator Jemima Shore. She is married to the dramatist Harold Pinter, and is the daughter of Lord Longford.

Fraser Bruce Austin, 1st Baron Fraser of North Cape (1888–1981). British admiral. As commander in chief of the Home Fleet in World War II, he directed the search for and subsequent sinking of the *Scharnhorst* Dec 1943. He became commander in chief of the Eastern Fleet in the Indian Ocean Aug 1944 and Nov 1944 took command of the Pacific Fleet. He was the British representative at the signing of the Japanese surrender in Tokyo Bay 2 Sept 1945. After the war he became First Sea Lord and Chief of the Naval Staff 1948–51. KBE 1941, baron 1946.

Fraser Dawn (1937–). Australian swimmer. The only person to win the same swimming event at three consecutive Olympic Games: 100 metres freestyle in 1956, 1960, and 1964. The holder of 27 world records, she was the first woman to break the one-minute barrier for the 100 metres.

Fraser (John) Malcolm (1930–). Australian Liberal politician, prime minister 1975–83; nicknamed 'the Prefect' because of a supposed disregard of subordinates.

Fraser was educated at Oxford University, and later became a millionaire sheep farmer. In March 1975 he replaced Snedden as Liberal Party leader. In Nov, following the Whitlam government's economic difficulties, he blocked finance bills in the Senate, became prime minister of a caretaker government, and in the consequent general election won a large majority. He lost to Hawke in the 1983 election.

As a speaker he was powerful in agitation, in opposition, or in debate; on a purely formal occasion he plumbed the gulfs.
J C Beaglehole on PETER FRASER
in *Dictionary of National Biography*

Fraser Peter (1884–1950). New Zealand Labour politician, born in Scotland. He held various cabinet posts 1935–40, and was prime minister 1940–49 during which time he co-ordinated the New Zealand war effort. After 1945 he concentrated on problems of social legislation and in 1949 promoted controversial legislation to bring in military conscription.

Suggested reading
Thorn, James *Peter Fraser* (1952)

Fraser Simon (1776–1862). Canadian explorer and surveyor for the Hudson Bay Company who crossed the Rockies and travelled most of the way down the river that bears his name 1805–07.
Suggested reading
Fraser, Simon *The Letters and Journals of Simon Fraser* (ed W K Lamb) (1960)

Fraunhofer Joseph von (1787–1826). German physicist who did important work in optics. The dark lines in the solar spectrum (*Fraunhofer lines*), which reveal the chemical composition of the Sun's atmosphere, were accurately mapped by him.

Fraunhofer determined the dispersion powers and refractive indices of different kinds of optical glass. In the process, he developed the spectroscope, and in 1821 he became the first to use a diffraction grating to produce a spectrum from white light.

Fraunhofer was born in Bavaria and started work in his father's glazing workshop at the age of ten. In 1806 he entered the optical shop of the Munich Philosophical Instrument Company, which produced scientific instruments, and by 1811 he had become a director. From 1823 he was director of the Physics Museum of the Bavarian Academy of Sciences.

Fraze Ermal Cleon (1913–1989). US inventor of the ring-pull on drink cans, after having had to resort to a car bumper to open a can while picnicking.

The awe and dread with which the untutored savage contemplates his mother-in-law are amongst the most familiar facts of anthropology.

J G FRAZER
Golden Bough vol I 1890

Frazer James George (1854–1941). Scottish anthropologist, author of *The Golden Bough* 1890, a pioneer study of the origins of religion and sociology on a comparative basis. It exerted considerable influence on writers such as T S Eliot and D H Lawrence, but by the standards of modern anthropology, many of its methods and findings are unsound. Knighted 1914.
Suggested reading
Downie, Robert *Frazer and the Golden Bough* (1970)
Frazer, James G *The Golden Bough* (1890)
Frazer, James G *Folk-lore in the Old Testament* (1918)

Frears Stephen Arthur (1941–   ). English film director. His keen visual sensibility and an ability to tell a good story have made him one of the leading British directors of the 1980s and 1990s. He made such films as *My Beautiful Laundrette* 1985 and *Sammy and Rosie Get Laid* 1987, both dealing with the effects of racism and inequalities in British society. His biography of playwright Joe Orton, *Prick Up Your Ears* 1986, was followed by a move to Hollywood with an adaptation of *Dangerous Liaisons* 1988, and the thriller *The Grifters* 1988. His other films include the comedy thriller *Gumshoe* 1971 and *Accidental Hero* 1992.

Frederick V ('the Winter King') (1596–1632). Elector palatine of the Rhine 1610–23 and king of Bohemia 1619–20 (for one winter, hence the name), having been chosen by the Protestant Bohemians as ruler after the deposition of Catholic emperor Ferdinand II. His selection was the cause of the Thirty Years' War. Frederick was defeated at the Battle of the White Mountain, near Prague, in Nov 1620, by the army of the Catholic League and fled to Holland.

He was the son-in-law of James I of England.

Frederick nine kings of Denmark, including:

Frederick IX (1899–1972). King of Denmark from 1947. He was succeeded by his daughter who became Queen Margrethe II.

Frederick two Holy Roman emperors:

Frederick (I) Barbarossa ('red-beard') (*c.* 1123–1190). Holy Roman emperor from 1152. Originally duke of Swabia, he was elected emperor 1152, and was engaged in a struggle with Pope

Alexander III 1159–77, which ended in his submission; the Lombard cities, headed by Milan, took advantage of this to establish their independence of imperial control. Frederick joined the Third Crusade, and was drowned while crossing a river in Anatolia.
Suggested reading
Munz, Peter *Frederick Barbarossa* (1970)
Pacaut, M *Frederick Barbarossa* (1970)

Deeply religious, but physically and mentally unimpressive ... [he] concentrated on ostentation.

E N Williams on FREDERICK I
in *Penguin Dictionary of English and European History 1485–1789* 1980

Frederick II (1194–1250). Holy Roman emperor from 1212, called 'the Wonder of the World'. He led a crusade 1228–29 that recovered Jerusalem by treaty, without fighting. He quarrelled with the pope, who excommunicated him three times, and a feud began that lasted with intervals until the end of his reign. Frederick, who was a religious sceptic, is often considered the most cultured man of his age. He was the son of Henry VI.
Suggested reading
Abulafia, David *Frederick II: A Medieval Emperor* (1988)
Van Cleve, Thomas *Emperor Frederick II of Hohenstaufen* (1972)

Frederick three kings of Prussia:

Frederick I (1657–1713). King of Prussia from 1701. He became elector of Brandenburg 1688.

Frederick (II) the Great (1712–1786). King of Prussia from 1740, when he succeeded his father Frederick William I. In that year he started the War of the Austrian Succession by his attack on Austria. In the peace of 1745 he secured Silesia. The struggle was renewed in the Seven Years' War 1756–63. He acquired West Prussia in the first partition of Poland 1772 and left Prussia as Germany's foremost state. He was an efficient and just ruler in the spirit of the Enlightenment and a patron of the arts.

In his domestic policy he encouraged industry and agriculture, reformed the judicial system, fostered education, and established religious toleration. He corresponded with the French writer Voltaire, and was a talented musician.

He received a harsh military education from his father, and in 1730 was threatened with death for attempting to run away. In the Seven Years' War, in spite of assistance from Britain, Frederick had a hard task holding his own against the Austrians and their Russian allies; the skill with which he did so proved him to be one of the great soldiers of history.
Suggested reading
Horn, D B *Frederick the Great and the Rise of Prussia* (1964)
Mitford, Nancy *Frederick the Great* (1970)
Simon, Edith *The Making of Frederick the Great* (1963)

Frederick III (1831–1888). King of Prussia and emperor of Germany 1888. The son of Wilhelm I, he married the eldest daughter (Victoria) of Queen Victoria of the UK 1858 and, as a liberal, frequently opposed Chancellor Bismarck. He died three months after his accession.

His achievement was to give Brandenburg-Prussia, not merely external security, but also a positive international role.

E N Williams on FREDERICK WILLIAM
in *Penguin Dictionary of English and European History 1485–1789* 1980

Frederick William (1620–1688). Elector of Brandenburg from 1640, 'the Great Elector'. By successful wars against Sweden and Poland, he prepared the way for Prussian power in the 18th century.

Frederick William (1882–1951). Last crown prince of Germany, eldest son of Wilhelm II. During World War I he commanded a group of armies on the western front. In 1918, he retired into private life.

Frederick William four kings of Prussia:

Frederick William I (1688–1740). King of Prussia from 1713, who developed Prussia's military might and commerce.

Frederick William II (1744–1797). King of Prussia from 1786. He was a nephew of Frederick II but had little of his relative's military skill. He was unsuccessful in waging war on the French 1792–95 and lost all Prussia west of the Rhine.

Frederick William III (1770–1840). King of Prussia from 1797. He was defeated by Napoleon 1806, but contributed to his final overthrow 1813–15 and profited by being allotted territory at the Congress of Vienna.

Henceforth Prussia merges into Germany.

FREDERICK WILLIAM IV
Proclamation in response to nationalistic
revolutionary pressure, Berlin 21 March 1848

Frederick William IV (1795–1861). King of Prussia from 1840. He upheld the principle of the divine right of kings, but was forced to grant a constitution 1850 after the Prussian revolution 1848. He suffered two strokes 1857 and became mentally debilitated. His brother William (later emperor) took over his duties.

Fredholm Erik Ivar (1866–1927). Swedish mathematician and mathematical physicist who founded the modern theory of integral equations. His work provided the foundations for much of the research later carried out by German mathematician David Hilbert. He became professor at Stockholm University 1906.

Freeman (Lawrence) Bud (1906–1991). US jazz saxophonist. He took part in developing the Chicago style in the 1920s. His playing was soft and elegant, and he worked and recorded with a number of bands, as well as cofounding the World's Greatest Jazz Band in the 1970s. As a member of Benny Goodman's orchestra 1936–39 he was given insufficient freedom to improvise; he left to form his own Summa cum Laude 1939–40, and then to work with a variety of line-ups. In the 1960s he recorded again with McPartland. He was based in London 1974–84.

Frege (Friedrich Ludwig) Gottlob (1848–1925). German philosopher, the founder of modern mathematical logic. He created symbols for concepts like 'or' and 'if...then', which are now in standard use in mathematics. His *Die Grundlagen der Arithmetik/The Foundations of Arithmetic* 1884 influenced Bertrand Russell and Ludwig Wittgenstein. Frege's chief work is *Begriffsschrift/Conceptual Notation* 1879.

Frege was born in Wismar on the Baltic coast and studied at Jena and Göttingen; he became professor at Jena 1879.

Frei Eduardo (1911–1982). Chilean president 1964–70. Elected as the only effective anti-Marxist candidate, he pursued a moderate programme of 'Chileanization' of US-owned copper interests. His regime was plagued by inflation and labour unrest, but saw considerable economic development.

He split with the Conservatives 1938 to help found the Falanga Nacional, an anti-fascist Social Christian party, which joined forces with the Social Christian Conservatives 1957. He was a shrewd opposition leader, arguing for reform within a democratic framework.

Frémont John Charles (1813–1890). US explorer and politician who travelled extensively throughout the western USA. He surveyed much of the territory between the Mississippi River and the coast of California with the aim of establishing an overland route E–W across the continent. In 1842 he crossed the Rocky Mountains, climbing a peak that is named after him.

In 1850 he was elected a senator of the newly created state of California and six years later he stood as Republican candidate for the US presidency. Between 1878 and 1883 he was governor of Arizona.

French Daniel Chester (1850–1931). US sculptor. He produced mainly public monuments. His most famous works include *The Minute Man* 1875 in Concord, Massachusetts, *John Harvard* 1884 at Harvard College, *Alma Mater* at Columbia University, and the imposing seated *Abraham Lincoln* 1922 in the Lincoln Memorial, Washington DC.

French John Denton Pinkstone, 1st Earl of Ypres (1852–1925). British field marshal. In the second South African War 1899–1902, he relieved Kimberley and took Bloemfontein; in World War I he was commander in chief of the British Expeditionary Force in France 1914–15; he resigned after being criticized as indecisive and became commander in chief of home forces. KCB 1900, viscount 1916, earl 1922.

French Marilyn (1929–). US feminist writer. Her first novel, *The Women's Room* 1977, the story of a generation of 1950s housewives who transform themselves into independent women in the 1970s, sold 4 million copies, and was made into a television film 1980. In *The War against Women* 1992 she discusses the harm done to women for the sake of religion and cultural customs, such as female infanticide in China.

Her other novels include *Her Mother's Daughter* 1987, which takes the lives of four generations of women in a Polish-American family, and *Our Father* 1994. As well as a book on James Joyce's *Ulysses* 1976, she has written *Beyond Power: On Women, Men, and Morals* 1985, which explores theories of power and control and the morality that continues to glorify war.

Freneau Philip Morin (1752–1832). US poet. His *A Political Litany* 1775 was a mock prayer for deliverance from British tyranny. His other works include *The British Prison-Ship* 1781, about his experiences as a British prisoner. He was a professional journalist, the first in the USA.

Frere John (1740–1807). English antiquary, a pioneering discoverer of Old Stone Age (Palaeolithic) tools in association with large extinct animals at Hoxne, Suffolk, in 1797. He suggested (long before Charles Darwin) that they predated the conventional biblical timescale. Frere was high sheriff of Suffolk and member of Parliament for Norwich.

Frescobaldi Girolamo (1583–1643). Italian composer and virtuoso keyboard player. He was organist at St Peter's, Rome, 1608–28. His fame rests on numerous keyboard toccatas, fugues, ricercares, and capriccios in which he advanced keyboard technique and exploited ingenious and daring modulations of key.

If you cannot saw with a file or file with a saw, then you will be no good as an experimentalist.

AUGUSTIN JEAN FRESNEL
quoted in *Hutchinson Dictionary of Scientific Biography*

Fresnel Augustin Jean (1788–1827). French physicist who refined the theory of polarized light. Fresnel realized in 1821 that light waves do not vibrate like sound waves longitudinally, in the direction of their motion, but transversely, at right angles to the direction of the propagated wave.

Fresnel first had to confirm the wave theory of light. He demonstrated mathematically that the dimensions of light and dark bands produced by diffraction could be related to the wavelength of the light producing them if light consisted of waves. To explain double refraction, he then arrived at the theory of transverse waves. Fresnel was born in Broglie, Normandy, and studied in Paris, becoming a civil engineer for the government.

Freud Anna (1895–1982). Austrian-born founder of child psychoanalysis in the UK. Her work was influenced by the theories of her father, Sigmund Freud. She held that understanding the stages of psychological development was essential to the treatment of children,

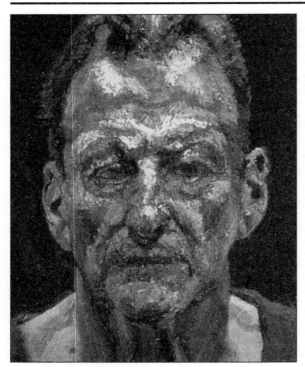

Freud, Lucian *A self-portrait (1990–91) by the English painter Lucian Freud. One of the outstanding figurative artists of his day, Freud combines acute observation with disquieting intensity, emphasizing the physicality of his subjects, which include nudes, still lifes, interiors, and street scenes.*

and that this knowledge could only be obtained through observation of the child.

Anna Freud and her father left Nazi-controlled Vienna in 1938 and settled in London. There she began working in a Hampstead nursery. In 1947 she founded the Hampstead Child Therapy Course and Clinic, which specialized in the treatment of children and the training of child therapists.

Suggested reading

Coles, R and Piers, M *The Wages of Neglect* (1969)
Coles, R *Anna Freud* (1992)
Dyer, Raymond *Her Father's Daughter* (1983)
Young-Bruehl, Elizabeth *Anna Freud* (1989)

Freud Clement Raphael (1924–). British journalist, television personality, and until 1987 Liberal member of Parliament; a grandson of Sigmund Freud. Knighted 1987.

Freud Lucian (1922–). German-born British painter. He is one of the greatest contemporary figurative artists. He combines meticulous accuracy with a disquieting intensity, emphasizing the physicality of his subjects, whether nudes, still lifes, or interiors. His *Portrait of Francis Bacon* 1952 (Tate Gallery, London) is one of his best-known works. He is a grandson of Sigmund Freud.

Freud Sigmund (1856–1939). Austrian physician who pioneered the study of the unconscious mind. He developed the methods of free association and interpretation of dreams that are basic techniques of psychoanalysis. The influence of unconscious forces on people's thoughts and actions was Freud's discovery, as was his controversial theory of the repression of infantile sexuality as the root of neuroses in the adult. His books include *Die Traumdeutung/The Interpretation of Dreams* 1900, *Jenseits des Lustprinzips/Beyond the Pleasure Principle* 1920, *Das Ich und das Es/The Ego and the Id* 1923, and *Das Unbehagen in der Kultur/Civilization and its Discontents*

1930. His influence has permeated the world to such an extent that it may be discerned today in almost every branch of thought.

From 1886 to 1938 Freud had a private practice in Vienna, and his theories and writings drew largely on case studies of his own patients, who were mainly upper-middle-class, middle-aged women. The word 'psychoanalysis' was, like much of its terminology, coined by Freud, and many terms have passed into popular usage, not without distortion. His theories have changed the way people think about human nature and brought about a more open approach to sexual matters. Antisocial behaviour is now understood to result in many cases from unconscious forces, and these new concepts have led to wider expression of the human condition in art and literature. Nevertheless, Freud's theories have caused disagreement among psychologists and psychiatrists, and his methods of psychoanalysis cannot be applied in every case.

Freud was born in Freiburg, Moravia (now Příbor in the Czech Republic). After first intending to study law, he studied medicine in Vienna from 1873, working under Ernst Wilhelm von Brücke. During this time Freud was a member of the research team that discovered the local anaesthetic effects of cocaine. In 1884 he became assistant physician at the General Hospital of Vienna, and was appointed lecturer in neurology 1885.

In the same year Freud began to study hypnosis as a treatment for hysteria under French physiologist Jean Charcot at the Saltpêtrière hospital, Paris. He was influenced by Charcot's belief that hysteria is of psychical origin and that ideas can produce physical changes, and in 1886 he returned to Vienna with this first inspiration that led to psychoanalysis.

Freud was also influenced by Viennese physician Josef Breuer's research into hysteria, and in 1893 he and Breuer published *Studien über Hysterie/Studies on Hysteria*, outlining the theory that hysterical cases can successfully be treated while under hypnosis by freeing the idea at the root of the condition from the unconscious mind.

Freud, Sigmund *Austrian physician Sigmund Freud. Freud initially investigated the relationship between the unconscious mind and the psychological health of an individual. He was a pioneer of psychoanalysis and an early investigator of human consciousness.* (Image Select)

In about 1895 Freud abandoned hypnosis for the technique of free association, which led to an interest in the interpretation of dreams. From this point he progressed rapidly with his studies and consequent discoveries in psychoanalysis, and published successively *Die Traumdeutung/The Interpretation of Dreams* 1900, *Zur Psychopathologie des Alltagslebens/The Psychopathology of Everyday Life* 1904, and *Drei Abhandlungen zur Sexualtheorie/Three Treatises on the Sexual Theory* 1905. *Die Traumdeutung* put forward the important idea that the recollected parts of dreams are symbols of the activities of the unconscious mind during sleep when the will is ineffective and conscious self-control is suspended. Freud drew a comparison between the symbolism of dreams and of mythology and religion, stating that religion was infantile (God as the father image) and neurotic (projection of repressed wishes).

The revolutionary nature of his theories aroused great hostility, since to assert that nearly all cases of neurosis are due to the repression of sexual desires shocked the public idea of morality at the time. Informed observers, however, found much to interest them in the consequent doctrine that a disturbance in a child's sexual growth explains many cases of emotional disturbance, and that under proper direction sexual impulses may be 'sublimated' into forces which can inspire great achievements.

In 1903 he founded the Vienna Psychoanalytical Circle, and by 1906 branches were established in several other countries. By 1908 his influence had spread further, and the first International Psychoanalytical Congress was held at Salzburg, Austria. In 1909 the International Psychoanalytical Association was formed. Following the Nazi occupation of Vienna, Freud sought refuge in London 1938 and died there the following year.

Suggested reading
Bettelheim, Bruno *Freud and Man's Soul* (1993)
Eysenck, Hans *Decline and Fall of the Freudian Empire* (1985)
Gay, Peter *Freud: A Life for Our Times* (1988)
Jones, Ernest *The Life and Works of Sigmund Freud* (1961)
Klein, Paul *Psychology and Freudian Theory* (1984)
McGrath, W J *Freud's Discovery of Psychoanalysis* (1986)
Sulloway, Frank *Freud, Biologist of the Mind* (1979)

Freundlich Herbert Max Finlay (1880–1941). German physical chemist who worked on the nature of colloids, particularly sols and gels. He introduced the term 'thixotropy' to describe the behaviour of gels.

Freundlich was born in Berlin and studied at Munich and Leipzig. In 1911 he became professor at the Technische Hochschule in Brunswick. He worked at the Kaiser Wilhelm Institut in Berlin 1914–33. When Adolf Hitler came to power, Freundlich emigrated first to Britain and then, in 1938, to the USA, where he became professor of colloid chemistry at the University of Minnesota.

Freundlich's research was mainly devoted to all aspects of colloid science. He investigated colloid optics, the scattering of light by dispersed particles of various shapes. He studied the electrical properties of colloids, since electrostatic charges are largely responsible for holding colloidal dispersions in place. He investigated mechanical properties such as viscosity and elasticity, and studied the behaviour of certain systems under other types of mechanical force. One application of this work has been the development of nondrip paints.

Freyberg Bernard Cyril, 1st Baron Freyberg (1889–1963). New Zealand soldier and administrator born in England. He fought in World War I, winning the Victoria Cross and three DSOs, and during World War II he commanded the New Zealand expeditionary force. He was governor general of New Zealand 1946–52. KCB 1942, baron 1951.

During World War II he commanded the New Zealand 2nd Division in the N African desert, then went to Greece, was evacuated

---

The salamander of the British Empire.

Winston Churchill on BERNARD FREYBERG
at Tripoli 1943, after its capture from Rommel.

---

to Crete and commanded the troops there during the German airborne attack. Returning to Libya he took the New Zealanders through to the final victory in Tunisia, from where they went to Italy as part of the 8th Army. He was corps commander at Cassino and has often, wrongly, been identified as 'the man who ordered the bombing of the monastery'. After the war he was governor-general of New Zealand 1946–52. He commanded Allied forces in Crete 1941.

Freysinnet (Marie) Eugène (Léon) (1879–1962). French engineer. He revealed the full structural potential of reinforced concrete with his technically innovative designs, and later pioneered the use of prestressed concrete. His huge airship hangars in reinforced concrete at Orly 1916–24 (destroyed 1944) were purely functional structures and yet the elegance of their slender, arched forms, rising dramatically out of the ground, made them architectural landmarks. From the 1920s, his experiments in prestressing concrete allowed for the use of ever more slender shapes, as employed in his scheme for rebuilding Le Havre harbour 1946–52.

Frick Wilhelm (1877–1946). German Nazi politician and governor of part of Czechoslovakia in World War II. As minister of the interior 1933–43 he was responsible for many of the laws and decrees which kept the Nazi party firmly in control of Germany. He became Reichs Protector for Bohemia and Moravia 1943, although his secretary Frank actually wielded most of the power. Arrested after the war, he was tried at Nuremberg and hanged Oct 1946.

Friedan Betty (born Elizabeth Goldstein) (1921–   ). US liberal feminist. Her book *The Feminine Mystique* 1963 started the contemporary women's movement in the USA and the UK. She was a founder of the National Organization for Women (NOW) 1966 (and its president 1966–70), the National Women's Political Caucus 1971, and the First Women's Bank 1973. Friedan also helped to organize the Women's Strike for Equality 1970 and called the First International Feminist Congress 1973.

Friedeburg Hans von (1895–1945). German admiral. Otherwise obscure, he signed the document which surrendered all German forces in N Europe and ended World War II 7 May 1945.

A relatively unknown German naval staff officer, Friedeburg succeeded Dönitz as commander in chief of the German Navy April 1945 and so was sent to negotiate surrender with Field Marshal Montgomery 3 May 1945.

Friedel Charles (1832–1899). French organic chemist and mineralogist who with US chemist James Mason Crafts (1839–1917) discovered the Friedel–Crafts reaction, which is useful in organic synthesis. Throughout his career, Friedel successfully combined his interests in chemistry and minerals.

Friedel was born in Strasbourg and studied at the Sorbonne in Paris. He qualified in both chemistry and mineralogy and in 1856 was made curator of the collection of minerals at the Ecole des Mines. In 1871 he became an instructor at the Ecole Normale and from 1876 was professor of mineralogy at the Sorbonne.

Friedman Aleksandr Aleksandrovich (1888–1925). Russian mathematician and cosmologist, who made fundamental contributions to the development of theories regarding the expansion of the universe.

Friedman was born and educated in St Petersburg, where he joined the mathematics faculty. From 1918 to 1920 he was professor of theoretical mechanics at Perm University, but he returned to St Petersburg in 1920 to conduct research at the Academy of Sciences.

Friedman's early research was in the fields of geomagnetism, hydromechanics. and, above all, theoretical meteorology. His work of the greatest relevance to astronomy was his independent and original approach to the solution of Albert Einstein's field equation in the general theory of relativity. Einstein had produced a static solution, which indicated a closed universe. Friedman derived several solutions, all of which suggested that space and time were isotropic (uniform at all points and in every direction), but that the mean density and radius of the universe varied with time – indicating an either expanding or contracting universe.

Friedman Maurice (1903–1991). US physician who in the 1930s developed the 'rabbit test' to determine if a woman was pregnant. Following injection of a woman's urine into a female rabbit, changes would occur in the animal's ovaries if the woman was pregnant. However, such changes could only be detected on dissection of the rabbit.

Friedman Milton (1912–). US economist, a pioneer of monetarism. He argued that a country's economy, and hence inflation, can be controlled through its money supply, although most governments lack the 'political will' to cut government spending and thereby increase unemployment. Nobel Prize for Economics 1976.

Friedman believed that inflation is 'always and everywhere a monetary phenomenon'. If the rate of growth of the money supply is limited to the rate of growth of output in the economy (through monetary policy such as changes in interest rates), it should be impossible for increases in costs, such as wages or imports, to be translated into a rise in prices in the economy as a whole.

His advocacy of the use of monetary policy, and his rejection of Keynesian economics, stemmed from his belief in the self-regulating nature of market forces, and the idea that there is a 'natural rate of unemployment'. He argued that this was determined by 'structural and institutional forces in the labour market', such as unemployment benefits and trade unions, and could not be reduced in the long term by increases in government spending.

Friedman was professor of economics at Chicago University 1948–79. His published works include *A Theory of the Consumption Function* 1957, *Capitalism and Freedom* 1962, *A Monetary History of the United States 1867–1960* 1963, *A Theoretical Framework for Monetary Analysis* 1971, and *Free to Choose* 1980.

Friedrich German form of Frederick.

Friedrich Caspar David (1774–1840). German Romantic landscape painter. He was active mainly in Dresden. He imbued his subjects – mountain scenes and moonlit seas – with poetic melancholy and was later admired by Symbolist painters. *The Cross in the Mountains* 1808 (Gemäldegalerie, Dresden) and *Moonrise over the Sea* 1822 (Nationalgalerie, Berlin) are among his best-known works.
Suggested reading
Borsch-Supon, H *Caspar David Friedrich* (1974)
Cardinal, M *The German Romantics in Context* (1975)
Etlinger, L *Caspar David Friedrich* (1967)

Friel Brian (1929–). Northern Irish dramatist. His work often deals with the social and historical pressures that contribute to the Irish political situation. His first success was with *Philadelphia, Here I Come!* 1964, which dealt with the theme of exile.

In 1980 he founded the Field Day Theatre Company, which produced *Translations* 1981, a study of British cultural colonialism in 19th-century Ireland. Other plays include *The Freedom of the City* 1973, about victims of the Ulster conflict, *Faith Healer* 1980, *Making History* 1988, *Dancing at Lughnasa* 1990, and *Molly Sweeney* 1994.

Friese-Greene William (1855–1921). English photographer, inventor, and early experimenter in cinematography.

Friese-Greene was born in Bristol. In about 1875 he opened a portrait photography studio in Bath, moving to London 1885. Asked to produce slides for a magic lantern (forerunner of the slide projector), he became interested in moving pictures, and in 1889 patented a camera that could take ten photographs per second on a roll of sensitized paper. Using his own apparatus, he was able to project a jerky picture of people and horse-drawn vehicles moving past Hyde Park Corner – probably the first time a film of an actual event had been projected on a screen. In 1890, he substituted celluloid film for the paper in the camera, and in the next few years he patented other inventions: a three-colour camera, moving pictures using a two-colour process, and machinery for rapid photographic processing and printing.

Although Friese-Greene's patent of 1890 was upheld in the USA in 1910, the first functional cine camera is generally credited to French physiologist Etienne-Jules Marey (1830–1904) in 1888.

Frink Elisabeth (1930–1993). English sculptor. She created rugged, naturalistic bronzes, mainly based on human and animal forms, for example the *Alcock Brown Memorial* for Manchester airport 1962, *In Memoriam* (heads), and *Running Man* 1980.

From 1967 to 1973 she lived in France and expressed her horror of the Algerian War and other troubles in North Africa in a series of 'goggle heads' resembling torturers in sunglasses or the messengers of death in motor-cycle goggles in Jean Cocteau's film *Orphée*. In her later years, influenced by the *Riace* bronzes, the Classical Greek figures found in the sea off the coast of southern Italy, her male figures became more aggressive. Her use of startling colour effects was inspired by the Aboriginal art she had seen on a visit to Australia.

Frink's other public commissions include the *Dorset Martyrs* in Dorchester and the *Shepherd with Three Lambs* in Paternoster Square, London. She also undertook a few commissions for churches, the last being a bronze *Christ* for Liverpool Cathedral, unveiled only weeks before her death.

Frisch Karl von (1886–1982). Austrian zoologist, founder with Konrad Lorenz of ethology, the study of animal behaviour. He specialized in bees, discovering how they communicate the location of sources of nectar by movements called 'dances'. He was awarded the Nobel Prize for Physiology or Medicine 1973 together with Lorenz and Nikolaas Tinbergen.

Frisch Max Rudolf (1911–1991). Swiss dramatist. Inspired by Brecht, his early plays such as *Als der Krieg zu Ende war/When the War Is Over* 1949 are more romantic in tone than his later symbolic dramas, such as *Andorra* 1962, dealing with questions of identity. He wrote *Biedermann und die Brandstifter/The Fire Raisers* 1958.

Frisch Otto Robert (1904–1979). Austrian-born British physicist who first described the fission of uranium nuclei under neutron bombardment, coining the term 'fission' to describe the splitting of a nucleus.

Frisch was born and educated in Vienna. Doing research at Hamburg, he fled from Nazi Germany in 1933, initially to the UK and in 1934 to the Institute of Theoretical Physics in Copenhagen. The German occupation of Denmark at the beginning of World War II forced Frisch to return to Britain. He then worked 1943–45 on the atom bomb at Los Alamos, New Mexico, USA. He was professor of natural philosophy at Cambridge University 1947–71.

Frisch worked on methods of separating the rare uranium-235 isotope that would undergo fission. He also calculated details such as the critical mass needed to produce a chain reaction and make an atomic bomb, and urged the British government to undertake nuclear research. At the first test explosion of the atomic bomb, Frisch conducted experiments from a distance of 40 km/25 mi.

He was the nephew of physicist Lise Meitner.

Frisch Ragnar Anton Kittil (1895–1973). Norwegian economist, pioneer of econometrics (the application of mathematical and statistical methods in economics). He shared the first Nobel Prize for Economics in 1969 with Jan Tinbergen.

Frith William Powell (1819–1909). English painter. His canvases depict large contemporary scenes featuring numerous figures and incidental detail. *Ramsgate Sands* 1854 (Royal Collection, London), bought by Queen Victoria, is a fine example, as is *Derby Day* 1856–58 (Tate Gallery, London).

Fritsch Werner von (1880–1939). German general. He served with distinction in World War I and by 1934 was a general. Contemptuous of politics, he was nonetheless appointed commander in chief of the Army 1934, but his opposition to the introduction of Nazi ideology in the military soon upset Hitler and he was forced into retirement 1938 by a false charge of homosexuality.

His departure removed the only obstacle to Hitler's reorganization of the Army High Command. He remained an honorary colonel of his old artillery regiment and accompanied them in the invasion of Poland 1939, where he was killed by a sniper outside Warsaw.

Frobenius Ferdinand Georg (1849–1917). German mathematician who formulated the concept of the abstract group – the first abstract structure of 'new' mathematics. His research into the theory of groups and complex number systems would prove useful to the development of quantum mechanics. He also made contributions to the theory of elliptic functions and to the solution of differential equations.

Frobenius was born in Berlin and studied at Göttingen. He was professor at the Eidgenossische Polytechnikum in Zürich, Switzerland, 1875–92, and at Berlin for the rest of his career.

Frobisher Martin (c. 1535–1594). English navigator. He made his first voyage to Guinea, West Africa, 1554. In 1576 he set out in search of the Northwest Passage, and visited Labrador, and Frobisher Bay, Baffin Island. Second and third expeditions sailed 1577 and 1578.

He was vice admiral in Drake's West Indian expedition 1585. In 1588, he was knighted for helping to defeat the Armada. He was mortally wounded 1594 fighting against the Spanish off the coast of France.

Suggested reading
Bert, George *The Three Voyages of Martin Frobisher* (1938)
Kenyon, W A *Tokens of Possession: The Northern Voyages of Martin Frobisher* (1975)

Fröding Gustaf (1860–1911). Swedish lyric poet. Inspired by the European Romantics, radical in politics, engaged in the revolt against Naturalism, he charted new possibilities for Swedish verse by uniting colloquial language with musical form. His themes are often melancholy and despairing, reflecting his history of mental instability. His collections include *Guitarr och dragharmonika/Guitar and Concertina* 1891 and *Stänk och flikar/Splashes and Rags* 1896.

Froebel Friedrich Wilhelm August (1782–1852). German educationist. He evolved a new system of education using instructive play, described in *Education of Man* 1826 and other works. In 1836 he founded the first kindergarten (German 'garden for children') in Blankenburg, Germany. He was influenced by the Swiss Johann Pestalozzi.

Suggested reading
Lilley, Irene *Friedrich Froebel: A Selection from his Writings* (1967)

Fröhlich Herbert (1905–1991). German-born British physicist who helped lay the foundations for modern theoretical physics in the UK. He revolutionized solid-state theory by importing into it the methods of quantum field theory – the application of quantum theory to particle interactions.

In particular, he proposed a theory to explain superconductivity using the methods of quantum field theory. He made important advances in the understanding of low-temperature superconductivity. His work also led him to the idea that quantum methods might elucidate some aspects of biological systems, such as the electrical properties of cell membranes.

Fröhlich studied in Munich under Arnold Sommerfeld, one of Germany's foremost theoretical physicists. When the Nazis engineered Fröhlich's dismissal from his teaching post 1933, he went to Bristol. From 1948 he was professor of theoretical physics at Liverpool University.

Froissart Jean (1338–1401). French historian, secretary to Queen Philippa, wife of Edward III of England. He travelled in Scotland and Brittany, went with Edward the Black Prince to Aquitaine, and in 1368 was in Milan at the same time as the writers Chaucer and Petrarch. He recorded in his *Chronicles* events of 1326–1400, often at first hand. Later he entered the church; he died, a canon, at Chimay.

Fromm Erich (1900–1980). German psychoanalyst who moved to the USA 1933 to escape the Nazis. He believed that human beings experience a separation from nature and from other people which gives them the freedom to decide on the course their lives should take. This gives their lives meaning but also causes anxiety.

Fromm was influenced by Karl Marx and existentialism as much as by psychoanalysis. He stressed the role of culture in the formation of personality, a view that distinguished him from traditional psychoanalysts. He also described the authoritarian personality (the servile, obedient type of person who wants to accept authority), particularly to explain the success of Nazism.

Fromm's basic ideas are set out in *The Fear of Freedom* 1941 and *The Sane Society* 1955. He urged people to give up the materialistic way of life for one based on meaningful love in *The Art of Loving* 1956 and *To Have or to Be* 1976.

Suggested reading
Funk, Rainer *Erich Fromm: The Courage to be Human* (1982)
Hausdorff, Don *Erich Fromm* (1972)
Schaar, John *Escape from Authority: The Perspectives of Erich Fromm* (1961)

Man is the only animal for whom his own existence is a problem which he has to solve.

ERICH FROMM
Man for Himself ch 3 1949

Fromm Friedrich (1888–1945). German general. An officer of the German general staff, he was responsible for all home army units, the administration of the general staff, and maintaining a supply of trained replacements for front-line units. Although he did his job well, he became involved in the July Plot through Count von Stauffenberg, who was on his staff. When the plot failed, Fromm attempted to cover up his involvement and display his loyalty by having his fellow conspirators rounded up, court-martialled, and shot. This did him no good; he was arrested by the Gestapo and hanged 19 March 1945.

Frontenac Louis de Buade, Comte de Frontenac et Palluau (1622–1698). French colonial governor. He began his military career 1635, and was appointed governor of the French possessions in North America 1672. Although efficient, he quarrelled with the local bishop and his followers and was recalled 1682. After the Iroquois, supported by the English, won several military victories, Frontenac was reinstated 1689. He defended Quebec against the English 1690 and defeated the Iroquois 1696.

Frost John (1784–1877). English Chartist, transported to Tasmania, Australia, 1840 as a political prisoner. On his return to England he publicized the horrors of convict life.

Frost 'Johnnie' Dutton (1912–1993). British military officer, commander of the 2nd Parachute Battalion, who held the bridge at Arnhem.

Frost carved his name in the annals of Anglo-American military history by reaching and holding the bridge at Arnhem until his ammunition ran out Sept 1944, although surrounded by SS Panzers. His name was later illuminated by Cornelius Ryan's book and Richard Attenborough's film *A Bridge Too Far*, in which he was portrayed by Anthony Hopkins. Frost's epic fight at Arnhem was the climax of his wartime service with the 2nd Parachute Battalion. He was a founder member of '2 Para' and his indomitable leadership as adjutant, company commander, and commanding officer, established its fighting traditions.

Frost Robert Lee (1874–1963). US poet. His accessible, colloquial blank verse, often flavoured with New England speech patterns, is written with an individual voice and penetrating vision. His poems include 'Mending Wall' ('Something there is that does not love a wall'), 'The Road Not Taken', and 'Stopping by Woods on a Snowy Evening' and are collected in *A Boy's Will* 1913, *North of Boston* 1914, *New Hampshire* 1924 (Pulitzer Prize), *Collected Poems* 1930 (Pulitzer Prize), *A Further Range* 1936 (Pulitzer Prize), and *A Witness Tree* 1942 (Pulitzer Prize).

I would have written of me on my stone: / I had a lover's quarrel with the world.

ROBERT FROST
'Lesson for Today'

Fry, Elizabeth *English Quaker and social reformer Elizabeth Fry reading to women prisoners in Newgate Prison. She first visited the prison 1813 and was so shocked by conditions that she devoted herself to prison reform.* (Image Select)

Suggested reading
Burnshaw, S *Robert Frost Himself* (1986)
Poirer, W R *Robert Frost: The Work of Knowing* (1977)
Pritchard, W H *Frost: A Literary Life Reconsidered* (1984)
Thompson, L and Winnick, R H *Robert Frost: A Biography* (1982)

The woods are lovely, dark and deep. / But I have promises to keep, / And miles to go before I sleep.
ROBERT FROST
'Stopping by Woods on a Snowy Evening'

Froude James Anthony (1818–1894). English historian whose *History of England from the Fall of Wolsey to the Defeat of the Spanish Armada* in 12 volumes 1856–70 was a classic Victorian work. He was influenced by the Oxford Movement in the Church of England, in which his brother, *Richard Hurrell Froude* (1803–1836), collaborated with Cardinal Newman.

Truth only smells sweet forever, and illusions, however innocent, are deadly as the canker-worm.
J A FROUDE
Short Studies on Great Subjects ' Calvinism' 1867–82

Froude William (1810–1879). English engineer and hydrodynamicist who first formulated reliable laws for the resistance that water offers to ships and for predicting their stability. *Froude's law of comparison* stated that the wave-making resistance of similar-shaped models varies as the cube of their dimensions if their speeds are as the square root of their dimensions. He also invented the hydraulic dynameter (1877) for measuring the output of high-power engines. These achievements were fundamental to marine development.

Comedy is an escape, not from truth but from despair; a narrow escape into faith.
CHRISTOPHER FRY
Time 20 Nov 1950

Fry Christopher Harris (1907–). English dramatist. He was a leader of the revival of verse drama after World War II with *The Lady's Not for Burning* 1948, *Venus Observed* 1950, and *A Sleep of Prisoners* 1951.

He has also written screenplays and made successful translations of Anouilh and Giraudoux.

Fry (Edwin) Maxwell (1899–1987). English architect. He was a pioneer of the Modern Movement in Britain. Representative is his Sun House, Hampstead, London, 1935, with its horizontally banded windows and white stucco finish. Fry worked in partnership with Walter Gropius 1934–36, and with Denys Lasdun (among others) 1951–58. He was Le Corbusier's senior architect at Chandigarh, India, 1951–54.

The pathos of her voice was almost miraculous, and melted alike the hardest criminals and the most impervious men of the world.
W G Blaikie on ELIZABETH FRY
in *Dictionary of National Biography*

Fry Elizabeth (born Gurney) (1780–1845). English Quaker philanthropist. She formed an association for the improvement of conditions for female prisoners 1817, and worked with her brother, *Joseph Gurney* (1788–1847), on an 1819 report on prison reform.
Suggested reading
Kent, John *Elizabeth Fry* (1962)
Rose, June *Elizabeth Fry* (1980)

Fry Roger Eliot (1866–1934). English artist and art critic. He was a champion of Post-Impressionism and an admirer of the French painter Cézanne. He was a member of the Bloomsbury Group and founded the Omega Workshops to improve design and to encourage young artists. His critical essays, which were influential in the 1920s and 1930s, are contained in *Vision and Design* 1920.

Frye (Herman) Northrop (1912–). Canadian literary critic. He is concerned especially with the role and practice of criticism and the relationship between literature and society. His *Anatomy of Criticism* 1957 was very influential.
Suggested reading
Cook, David *Northrop Frye* (1986)
Denham, Robert *Northrop Frye and the Critical Method* (1978)

Fuad two kings of Egypt:

Fuad I (1868–1936). King of Egypt from 1922. Son of the Khedive Ismail, he succeeded his elder brother Hussein Kiamil as sultan of Egypt 1917; when Egypt was declared independent 1922 he assumed the title of king.

Fuad II (1952–). King of Egypt 1952–53, between the abdication of his father Farouk and the establishment of the republic. He was a grandson of Fuad I.

Fuchida Mitsuo (1902–1976). Japanese naval pilot who led the attack on Pearl Harbor 7 Dec 1941. He co-ordinated the various elements of the operation and personally led the first wave of the attack. He remained active in naval aviation operations throughout the war.

Fuchs (Emil Julius) Klaus (1911–1988). German spy who worked on atom-bomb research in the USA in World War II, and subsequently in the UK. He was imprisoned 1950–59 for passing information to the USSR and resettled in eastern Germany.

Fuchs Immanuel Lazarus (1833–1902). German mathematician whose work on Georg Riemann's method for the solution of differential equations led to a study of the theory of functions that was later crucial to Henri Poincaré in his investigation of function theory.
Fuchs was born in Moschin (now in Poland), and studied at Berlin, where he became professor 1866. After holding posts at Göttingen and Heidelberg, he returned to Berlin 1882.

Fuchs Vivian Ernest (1908–). British explorer and geologist. Before World War II, he accompanied several Cambridge University expeditions to E Africa. From 1947 he worked in the Falkland Islands as director of the Scientific Bureau. In 1957–58, he led the overland Commonwealth Trans-Antarctic Expedition. He published his autobiography *A Time to Speak* in 1991. Knighted 1958.

Fuentes Carlos (1928–). Mexican novelist, lawyer, and diplomat. His first novel *La región más transparente/Where the Air Is Clear* 1958 encompasses the history of the country from the Aztecs to the present day.

More than other Mexican novelists, he presents the frustrated social philosophy of the failed Mexican revolution. He received international attention for *The Death of Artemio Cruz* 1962, *Terra nostra* 1975, and *El gringo veijo/The Old Gringo* 1985. *The Campaign* 1991 is set during the revolutionary wars leading to independence in Latin America.

Suggested reading
Brady, Robert and Rossman, Charles (eds) *Carlos Fuentes: A Critical View* (1982)
Faris, Wendy *Carlos Fuentes* (1983)
Guzmán, Daniel *Carlos Fuentes* (1972)

Fugard Athol Harold Lanigan (1932–). South African dramatist, director, and actor. His plays often deal with the effects of apartheid. His first successful play was *The Blood Knot* 1961, which was produced in London and New York. This was followed by *Hello and Goodbye* 1965 and *Boesman and Lena* 1969. Other plays include *Statements After an Arrest under the Immorality Act* 1973, *A Lesson from Aloes* 1980, *Master Harold and the Boys* 1982, *A Place with the Pigs* 1987, *My Children! My Africa!* 1989, and *The Township Plays* 1993. His film roles include General Smuts in *Gandhi* 1982.

Führer (German 'leader') or *Fuehrer*. Title adopted by Adolf ◊Hitler as leader of the Nazi Party.

Fujimori Alberto (1939–). Peruvian politician, president from 1990. As leader of the newly formed Cambio 90 (Change 90) he campaigned on a reformist ticket and defeated his more experienced Democratic Front opponent. Lacking an assembly majority and faced with increasing opposition to his policies, he imposed military rule early 1992. In 1993 a plebiscite narrowly approved his constitutional reform proposals, allowing him to seek, and achieve, re-election 1995. In Aug 1994 Fujimori dismissed his wife as first lady, claiming that she was 'disloyal' and opposed him politically. She denied the charges and challenged his leadership.

Fujiwara in Japanese history, the ruling clan 858–1185. During that period (the latter part of the Heian), the office of emperor became merely ceremonial, with power exercised by chancellors and regents, who were all Fujiwara and whose daughters in every generation married into the imperial family. There was a Fujiwara in Japanese government as recently as during World War II.

The name Fujiwara dates from 669; the family claimed divine descent. The son of the first Fujiwara became a minister and the grandfather of an emperor, and as this pattern repeated itself for centuries, the clan accumulated wealth and power through the control of government appointments. In 1868, when the last shogun had been ousted, it was a Fujiwara that the Meiji emperor appointed to the highest government post.

Fulbright (James) William (1905–1995). US Democratic politician. A US senator 1945–75, he was responsible for the *Fulbright Act* 1946, which provided grants for thousands of Americans to study abroad and for overseas students to study in the USA. Fulbright chaired the Senate Foreign Relations Committee 1959–74, and was a strong internationalist and supporter of the United Nations.

Born in Sumner, Missouri, Fulbright studied at Oxford University on a Rhodes scholarship, and at the George Washington University law school. He served in the US House of Representatives 1942–45 before becoming a senator. He anticipated the creation of the UN, calling for US membership in an international peacekeeping body. He was an advocate of military and economic aid to Western nations but a powerful critic of US involvement in the Vietnam War.

In 1954 Fulbright stood out publicly against the notorious campaign against left-wingers that was being orchestrated by Senator Joseph McCarthy, and during the 1960s and 1970s Fulbright

advocated a more liberal US foreign policy. He led the congressional opposition to the use of presidential power to launch armed interventions overseas – notably the Bay of Pigs invasion of Cuba in 1961, the intervention in the Dominican Republic in 1965, and the escalation of the war in Vietnam – and chaired many influential televised hearings on the Vietnam War.

Fuller John Frederick Charles (1878–1966). British major general and military theorist who propounded the concept of armoured warfare which, when interpreted by the Germans, became *blitzkrieg* in 1940.

Fuller Melville Weston (1833–1910). US jurist and chief justice of the US Supreme Court 1888–1910. Fuller endorsed court options that limited state and federal strengths to regulate private business. He sided with the majority of the Court in *Pollack* v *Farmers Loan and Trust Co* 1895, which held invalid a flat-rate US income tax, leading to passage of the 16th Amendment to the Constitution in 1913, authorizing an income tax.

Fuller Peter (1947–1990). English art critic. From the mid-1970s, he attacked the complacency of the art establishment and emphasized tradition over fashion. From 1988 these views, and an increased interest in the spiritual power of art, were voiced in his own magazine *Modern Painters*.

> *Now there is one outstandingly important fact regarding Spaceship Earth, and that is that no instruction book came with it.*
>
> BUCKMINSTER FULLER
> *Operating Manual for Spaceship Earth* 1969

Fuller (Richard) Buckminster (1895–1983). US architect, engineer, and social philosopher. He embarked on an unorthodox career in an attempt to maximize energy resources through improved technology. In 1947 he invented the lightweight geodesic dome, a hemispherical space-frame of triangular components linked by rods, independent of buttress or vault and capable of covering large-span areas. Within 30 years over 50,000 had been built.

He also invented a Dymaxion (a combination of the words 'dynamics' and 'maximum') house 1928 and car 1933 that were inexpensive and utilized his concept of using the least amount of energy output to gain maximum interior space and efficiency, respectively. Among his books are *Ideas and Integrities* 1963, *Utopia or Oblivion* 1969, and *Critical Path* 1981.

Suggested reading
Fuller, R Buckminster *Operating Manual for Spaceship Earth* (1969)
Fuller, R Buckminster *Earth Inc* (1973)
Hatch, A *Buckminster Fuller* (1974)
Mellor, James (ed) *The Buckminster Fuller Reader* (1970)
Pawley, M *Buckminster Fuller* (1990)

> *A book that is shut is but a block.*
>
> ROY FULLER
> 'Middle of a War'

Fuller Roy Broadbent (1912–1991). English poet and novelist. His collections of poetry include *Poems* 1939, *Epitaphs and Occasions* 1951, *Brutus's Orchard* 1957, *Collected Poems* 1962, and *The Reign of Sparrows* 1980. Novels include *My Child, My Sister* 1965 and *The Carnal Island* 1970.

> *As horrible thoughts / Loud fluttering aircraft slope above his head / At dusk.*
>
> ROY FULLER
> *Gnomologia* no 23 1969

Fuller (Sarah) Margaret (1810–1850). US author and reformer. She was the editor of *The Dial*, the Transcendentalist magazine

1839–44, and noted for her public 'conversations' for the edification of the women of Boston during the same period. She became the literary critic for the *New York Tribune* 1844. Later, while on assignment in Italy, she joined Giuseppe Mazzini's doomed nationalist revolt 1848. Fuller was lost at sea while returning to the USA 1850.

Suggested reading
Blanchard, Paula *Margaret Fuller* (1978)
Fuller, Margaret *Memoirs of Margaret Fuller* (ed by Emerson 1852, rep 1972)
Myerson, Joel *Margaret Fuller* (1977–78)
Wade, Mason *Margaret Fuller: Whetstone of Genius* (1940)

Fuller Solomon Carter (1872–1953). US physician, neurologist, psychiatrist, and pathologist. He worked on degenerative brain diseases including Alzheimer's disease, which he attributed to causes other than arteriosclerosis; this was supported by medical researchers in 1953. He practised medicine in Boston and at his home in Framingham and taught pathology, neurology, and psychology at Boston University until he retired as professor emeritus 1937.

Fuller Thomas (1608–1661). English writer. He was chaplain to the Royalist army during the Civil War and, at the Restoration, became the king's chaplain. He wrote a *History of the Holy War* 1639, *Good Thoughts in Bad Times* 1645, its sequel *Good Thoughts in Worse Times* 1647, and the biographical *Worthies of England* 1662.

Anger is one of the sinews of the soul.

THOMAS FULLER
The Holy State and the Profane State bk 3 'Of Anger' 1642

Fulton Robert (1765–1815). US engineer and inventor who designed the first successful steamships. He produced a submarine, the *Nautilus*, for Napoleon's government in France 1801, and experimented with steam navigation on the Seine, then returned to the USA. The first steam vessel of note, known as the *Clermont*, appeared on the river Hudson 1807, sailing between New York and Albany. The first steam warship was the USS *Fulton*, of 38 tonnes, built 1815.

Funj Islamic dynasty that ruled the Sudan from 1505 to the 1820s, when the territory was taken over by the Turkish government of Egypt. During the 16th and 17th centuries the Funj extended their territories westwards and in the 18th century fought a series of wars against Ethiopia. From the late 1600s there were severe internal conflicts, with the warrior aristocracy challenging and eventually supplanting the ruling family.

Funk Casimir (1884–1967). Polish-born US biochemist who pioneered research into vitamins. He was the first to isolate niacin (nicotinic acid, one of the vitamins of the B complex).

Funk proposed that certain diseases are caused by dietary deficiencies. In 1911 he demonstrated that rice extracts cure beriberi in pigeons. As the extract contains an amine, he mistakenly concluded that he had discovered a class of 'vital amines', a phrase soon reduced to 'vitamins'.

Funk, born in Warsaw, studied in Berne, Switzerland, and worked at research institutes in Europe before emigrating to the USA 1915. He returned to Warsaw 1923 but, because of the country's uncertain political situation, went in 1927 to Paris, where he founded a research institution, the Casa Biochemica. With the German invasion of France at the outbreak of World War II in 1939, Funk

returned to the USA. In 1940, he became president of the Funk Foundation for Medical Research.

Furness Frank Heyling (1839–1912). US architect. His eclectic yet highly original work has had considerable influence on the development of his country's architecture. His best-known building is the Pennsylvania Academy of Fine Arts, Philadelphia, 1871–76, which reflects the influence of Viollet-le-Duc while anticipating Post-Modernism, in particular the work of Michael Graves, in its dramatic manipulation of space and idiosyncratic decoration.

Furphy Joseph (1843–1912). Australian writer and poet. His most successful novel, *Such is Life* 1903, is an anecdotal account of life in the Australian Riverina district in the 1880s. Two other works, *Rigby's Romance* 1921 and *The Buln Buln and the Brolga* 1948, were created from sections deleted from the overlong original manuscript of *Such is Life*.

Furtwängler (Gustav Heinrich Ernst Martin) Wilhelm (1886–1954). German conductor. He was leader of the Berlin Philharmonic Orchestra 1924–54. His interpretations of Wagner, Bruckner, and Beethoven were valued expressions of monumental national grandeur, but he also gave first performances of Bartók, Schoenberg's *Variations for Orchestra* 1928, and Hindemith's opera *Mathis der Maler/Mathis the Painter* 1934, a work implicitly critical of the Nazi regime. He ascended rapidly from theatre to opera orchestras in Mannheim 1915–20 and Vienna 1919–24, then to major appointments in Leipzig and Vienna.

Fuseli (John) Henry (born Johann Heinrich Füssli) (1741–1825). Swiss-born British Romantic artist. He painted macabre and dreamlike images, such as *The Nightmare* 1781 (Institute of Arts, Detroit), which come close in feelings of horror and the unnatural to the English Gothic novels of his day. His subjects include scenes from Milton and Shakespeare.

The son of a Swiss portrait painter, he emigrated to England 1764, and was encouraged by Reynolds to become a painter and study in Italy. The period spent there, 1770–78, made him a devotee of Michelangelo, though his own work depends for its interest on so different an element as the Romantic love of horror and fantasy. *The Nightmare* made him immediately famous, and the contributions to Boydell's 'Shakespeare Gallery' that followed gave further scope to his imagination. The sensation produced by the subject, rather than beauty of paint, was his main concern. Paintings and drawings of elongated female figures with exaggerated head-dresses in which there is a strain of erotic fancy form another aspect of his work. Witty, learned and an able writer, he appears in his later years, when Keeper of the Royal Academy, as an eccentric figure. He was the friend of Blake. He was also a perceptive critic, and translated Winckelmann's highly influential *Reflections on the Painting and Sculpture of the Greeks*.

Fux Johann Joseph (1660–1741). Austrian composer and theorist. His rules of counterpoint, compiled in his *Gradus ad Parnassum,* are still used as a teaching formula by many music schools. He wrote a considerable quantity of sacred music, including 50 masses and 10 oratorios.

Fyfe David Maxwell, 1st Earl of Kilmuir. Scottish lawyer and Conservative politician; see ◊Kilmuir.

Fyffe Will (1885–1947). Scottish music-hall comedian. He is remembered for his vivid character sketches and for his song 'I Belong to Glasgow'.

Gable (William) Clark (1901–1960). US actor. A star for more than 30 years in 90 films, he played romantic roles such as Rhett Butler in *Gone with the Wind* 1939. His other films include *The Painted Desert* 1931 (his first), *It Happened One Night* 1934 (Academy Award), *Mutiny on the Bounty* 1935, and *The Misfits* 1961. He was nicknamed the 'King of Hollywood'.
Suggested reading
Samuels, Charles *The King* (1962)
Tornabene, Lye *Long Live the King* (1977)

Gabo Naum. Adopted name of Naum Neemia Pevsner (1890–1977). US abstract sculptor, born in Russia. One of the leading exponents of Constructivism, he left the USSR for Germany 1922 and taught at the Bauhaus in Berlin, a key centre of design. He lived in Paris and England in the 1930s, then settled in the USA 1946. He was one of the first artists to make kinetic sculpture and often used transparent coloured plastics. Many of his drawings and sculptures are in the Tate Gallery, London.

> *Till now man has been up against Nature, from now on he will be up against his own nature.*
>
> DENNIS GABOR
> *Inventing the Future* 1963

Gabor Dennis (1900–1979). Hungarian-born British physicist. In 1947 he invented the holographic method of three-dimensional photography. He was awarded a Nobel prize 1971.

Born in Budapest, Gabor studied at the Budapest Technical University and then at the Technishe Hochschule in Berlin. He worked in Germany until he fled to Britain in 1933 to escape the Nazis. He was professor of applied electron physics at the Imperial College of Science and Technology, London, 1958–67.

Gabrieli Giovanni (*c.* 1555–1612). Italian composer. He succeeded his uncle Andrea Gabrieli (*c.* 1533–1585) as organist of St Mark's, Venice. His sacred and secular works include numerous madrigals, motets, and the antiphonal *Sacrae Symphoniae* 1597, sacred canzonas and sonatas for brass choirs, strings, and organ, in spatial counterpoint.

Gadamer Hans-Georg (1900–). German hermeneutic philosopher. In *Truth and Method* 1960, he argued that 'understanding' is fundamental to human existence, and that all understanding takes place within a tradition. The relation between text and interpreter can be viewed as a dialogue, in which the interpreter must remain open to the truth of the text.

Gaddafi Alternative form of ◊Khaddhafi, Libyan leader.

Gaddi Italian family of artists. Gaddo (*c.* 1260–1332) was a painter and mosaic worker, a friend of Cimabue, whose influence has been perceived in the *Coronation of the Virgin with Saints and Angels*, a mosaic in the cathedral at Florence attributed to Gaddo. Other works attributed to him are the mosaics in Santa Maria Maggiore and those of the choir of the old St Peter's, Rome. His son, Taddeo (*c.* 1300–1366) was a pupil of Giotto and is considered one of his most important followers. His paintings include the frescoes *Virgin and Child between Four Prophets* and other scenes from the life of the Virgin in the Baroncelli Chapel in Santa Croce at Florence, 1332, as well as works at Pisa, Pistoia and in various galleries. The son of Taddeo, Agnolo (active 1369–1396), perhaps trained by his father, was placed on the latter's death in the care of Jacopo del Casentino and Giovanni da Milano. He worked in the Vatican 1369, probably with his brother Giovanni. Frescoes in Santa Croce depicting the

Gable US film actor Clark Gable in The Misfits *1960. Rugged good looks and an impudent grin helped to made him one of Hollywood's leading stars. His talent for comedy was proved in* It Happened One Night *1934 while his lead role in* Gone With the Wind *1939 was a melodramatic one. His last appearance (and also that of Marilyn Monroe) was in the elegiac* The Misfits.

legend of the Cross, and in the cathedral of Prato, 1392–95, representing the legends of the Virgin and the Sacred Girdle, are attributed to him. He died while working on an altarpiece for San Miniato. He employed a number of assistants, and Cennino Cennini was among his pupils, embodying the methods of the followers of Giotto in his famous treatise.

Gaddis William (1922–). US novelist. He is a distinctive and satirical stylist of non-psychological work, often written on a vast, perplexing scale. His first novel, *The Recognitions* 1955, explores the idea of forgery in social and sexual relations and in art. It was followed by the encyclopedic *JR* 1975, written entirely in dialogue, which deals with money and power, *Carpenter's Gothic* 1985, and *A Frolic of His Own* 1994. *See illustration on page 322.*

Gadsden James (1788–1858). US military leader and diplomat. In 1823 he was appointed by President Monroe to supervise the forced resettlement of the North American Seminole Indians to S Florida and participated in the ensuing Seminole Wars. He was appointed US minister to Mexico 1853 and negotiated the Gadsden Purchase, acquiring for the USA from Mexico what is now New Mexico and Arizona.

Gadsden was born in Charleston, South Carolina, USA, and educated at Yale University. He served in the Anglo-American War of 1812 as well as in the Seminole Wars. After several years as a railroad executive, he was named US minister to Mexico and agreed the sale of Mexican territory south of the Gila River, to be used as a route to California. The Gadsden Purchase was approved by the Senate 1854.

Gaetano Mosca (1858–1941). Italian jurist, politician, and political scientist. His best-known work *Elementi di scienza politica* 1896

Gaddis *US novelist William Gaddis. His three highly innovative novels to date, written at long intervals, consist of gargantuan tours de force of verbal playfulness and black humour, in which he sees the contemporary world as essentially bleak and loveless.*

(translated as *The Ruling Class* 1939) set out his theory of the political elite. In all societies, the majority is ruled by a minority in the upper stratum of society and, in the endless struggle for power, the membership of the elite political class is determined by natural selection. Although his theory of the elite appears to justify fascism, Mosca spurned both Mussolini and Hitler.

He was elected a deputy in the Italian parliament 1908 and became a life senator 1919. He was a professor at the University of Rome from 1923 and taught both there and at the universities of Palermo and Turin.

Gagarin Yuri Alexeyevich (1934–1968). Soviet cosmonaut who in 1961 became the first human in space aboard the spacecraft *Vostok 1*. Gagarin was born in the Smolensk region. He became a pilot 1957, and on 12 April 1961 completed one orbit of the Earth, taking 108 minutes from launch to landing. He died in a plane crash while training for the *Soyuz 3* mission.

Gaillard Slim (Bulee) (1916–1991). US jazz singer, songwriter, actor, and musician. A light, humorous performer, he claimed to have invented his own language, Vout (nonsense syllables as in scat singing). His first hit was 'Flat Foot Floogie' 1938.

Gainsborough Thomas (1727–1788). English landscape and portrait painter. In 1760 he settled in Bath and painted society portraits. In 1774 he went to London and became one of the original members of the Royal Academy. He was one of the first British artists to follow the Dutch example in painting realistic landscapes rather than imaginative Italianate scenery.

Born in Sudbury, Suffolk, Gainsborough began to paint while still at school. In London he learned etching and painting, but remained largely self taught. His method of painting – what Reynolds called 'those odd scratches and marks... this chaos which by a kind of magic at a certain distance assumes form' – is full of temperament and life.

His *Blue Boy* (San Marino, California) is a homage to van Dyck. The landscapes he painted for his own pleasure took on an imaginary look; rhythmic in movement, the *Harvest Wagon* (Birmingham) already has this Utopian character. A foundation member of the Royal Academy and elected to its Council 1774, Gainsborough moved in

We are all going to heaven, and Vandyke is of the company.

THOMAS GAINSBOROUGH
Last words

that year to Schomberg House in London, becoming the principal rival of Sir Joshua Reynolds in portraiture. The portrait of his wife (Courtauld Institute, London) and *The Morning Walk* (National Gallery, London) show his sense of character, and the great elegance of style he had developed. In landscape, influenced by Rubens rather than, as in his youth, by Ruisdael, he produced, for example, the massing and play of light of *The Market Cart* of 1786 (National Gallery). Hundreds of drawings, often in a mixture of media, show his continued pursuit of landscape for its own sake. A constant tendency to experiment produced the remarkable 'fancy pictures' or imaginative compositions of his late years, the *Diana and Actaeon* (Royal Collection), unfinished when he died, being an example.

Suggested reading
Leonard, J *The World of Gainsborough* (1969)
Lindsay, J *Gainsborough: His Life and Work* (1985)
Rothschild, M *The Life and Work of Thomas Gainsborough* (1983)
Waterhouse, E *Gainsborough* (1958)

Gair Vincent Clair (1902–1980). Australian Labor, later Democratic Labor Party, politician. He was premier of Queensland 1952–57 when he was expelled from the Australian Labor Party as a consequence of the split in the party. Gair continued as premier and formed the Queensland Labor Party but lost the election later the same year to the Country-Liberal Party coalition. In 1962 the Queensland Labor Party became a state branch of the Democratic Labor Party (DLP) and Gair entered federal parliament as a Queensland senator and leader of the DLP. He was appointed ambassador to Ireland in 1974 in an unsuccessful move by the Labor government to gain an extra Senate seat and was recalled by the new Fraser government in 1976.

I became a Socialist because I hated poverty and squalor.

HUGH GAITSKELL
Labour Party Conference 1955

Gaitskell Hugh Todd Naylor (1906–1963). British Labour politician. In 1950 he became minister of economic affairs, and then chancellor of the Exchequer until Oct 1951. In 1955 he defeated Aneurin Bevan for the succession to Attlee as party leader, and tried to reconcile internal differences on nationalization and disarmament. He was re-elected leader in 1960.

Suggested reading
McDermott, G *Leader Lost: A Biography of Hugh Gaitskell* (1971)
Rodgers, W T (ed) *Hugh Gaitskell* (1964)
Williams, P M *Hugh Gaitskell* (1979)

Gajdusek D(aniel) Carleton (1923–). US virologist and paediatrician who won the Nobel prize 1976 for his work on identifying and describing slow virus infections in humans. This was based on his studies of kuru, a disease of neural degeneration found in people in New Guinea.

The affected people practised a form of ritual cannibalism, in which the women and children consumed the brains of the dead. Analyses of brain tissue failed to reveal any signs of infective organisms, but when Gajdusek injected extracts from the brains of kuru victims into the brains of chimpanzees, the animals began to display signs of the disease after about a year. This led Gajdusek to propose that kuru was caused by a virus that has a very long incubation period. Further work by his team showed that Creutzfeldt–Jakob disease is similarly caused by slow viruses. Since then such a mechanism has been proposed for many illnesses, including AIDS and multiple sclerosis. From 1958 he has worked at the National Institute of Neurology and Communicative Disorders and Stroke in Bethesda, Maryland.

Galbraith John Kenneth (1908–). Canadian-born US economist who criticized the neoclassical view that in the economy market forces were in a state approximating perfect competition. He suggested that the 'affluent society' develops an economic imbalance, devoting too many resources to the production of consumer goods and not enough to public services and infrastructure.

Galbraith was critical of the view put forward by the advocates of monetarism that state spending was unable to reduce unemployment. His commitment to the development of the public sector was in sympathy with Keynesian economics. In his book *The Affluent Society* 1958, he documents the tendency of free-market capitalism to create private splendour and public squalor.

Politics is not the art of the possible. It consists in choosing between the disastrous and the unpalatable.

J K GALBRAITH
Letter to President Kennedy 2 March 1962

Galbraith became a US citizen 1937. He was a professor of economics at Harvard 1949–75, worked for the Office of Price Administration during World War II, and served as ambassador to India 1961–63. He was an adviser to President Kennedy and the Democratic presidential candidates Adlai Stevenson, Eugene McCarthy, and George McGovern, and believed strongly in a governmental role in economic planning.

His works include *American Capitalism* 1952, *The New Industrial State* 1967, *Economics and the Public Purpose* 1973, and *The Culture of Containment* 1992. He has also written novels.

Suggested reading
Galbraith, J K *A Life in Our Time* (1981)
Gambs, John *John Kenneth Galbraith* (1975)
Munro, C L *Galbraithian Vision: The Cultural Criticism of John Kenneth Galbraith* (1977)

Gale George Stafford (1927–1990). British journalist and broadcaster. He worked for the *Manchester Guardian, Daily Mirror, Daily Express*, and, towards the end of his life, *Daily Mail*. His sometimes raw, iconoclastic views earned him a formidable reputation as a political journalist.

Gale Humphrey Middleton (1890–1971). British general. After serving in World War I, he remained in the Army and at the outbreak of World War II went to France with the British Expeditionary Force 1939. He then served in a variety of administrative posts, mainly under General Eisenhower, before returning to the UK 1944 to take over the administration of Operation Overlord, the D-Day landings in Normandy. He then returned to his post as Eisenhower's right-hand man until the end of the war in Europe. KBE 1943.

Gale Richard Nelson (1896–1982). British general. In World War II, he raised and trained the 1st Parachute Brigade and during the D-Day landings led the small force which dropped ahead of the main invasion to capture the Orne bridges flanking the British beachhead. After the war he commanded the British Army of the Rhine and later became Chief of the General Staff.

He served with the British and Indian armies prior to 1939 and was among the first to volunteer for parachute training 1940. KBE 1950.

Galen (*c.* 129–*c.* 200). Greek physician and anatomist whose ideas dominated Western medicine for almost 1,500 years. Central to his thinking were the theories of humours and the threefold circulation of the blood. The humours were four kinds of fluid of which the human body was supposed to consist: phlegm, blood, choler or yellow bile, and melancholy or black bile. Physical and mental characteristics were explained by different proportions of humours in individuals. He remained the highest medical authority until Andreas Vesalius and William Harvey exposed the fundamental errors of his system.

Galen postulated a circulation system in which the liver produced the natural spirit, the heart the vital spirit, and the brain the animal spirit. He also wrote about philosophy and believed that Nature expressed a divine purpose, a belief that became increasingly popular with the rise of Christianity (Galen himself was not a Christian). This helped to account for the enormous influence of his ideas.

Galen was born in Pergamum in Asia Minor and studied medicine there and at Smyrna (now Izmir), Corinth in Greece, and Alexandria in Egypt, after which he returned home to become chief physician to the gladiators at Pergamum. In 161 he went to Rome, where he became a society physician and attended the Roman emperor Marcus Aurelius Antoninus. Although Galen made relatively few discoveries and relied heavily on the teachings of Hippocrates, he wrote a large number of books, more than 100 of which are known.

Galileo properly Galileo Galilei (1564–1642). Italian mathematician, astronomer, and physicist. He developed the astronomical telescope and was the first to see sunspots, the four main satellites of Jupiter, and the appearance of Venus going through phases, thus proving it was orbiting the Sun. In mechanics, Galileo discovered that freely falling bodies, heavy or light, have the same, constant acceleration and that a body moving on a perfectly smooth horizontal surface would neither speed up nor slow down.

Galileo's work founded the modern scientific method of deducing laws to explain the results of observation and experiment (although the story of his dropping cannonballs from the Leaning Tower of Pisa is questionable). His observations were an unwelcome refutation of the ideas of Aristotle taught at the (church-run) universities, largely because they made plausible for the first time the heliocentric (Sun-centred) theory of Polish astronomer Nicolaus Copernicus. Galileo's persuasive *Dialogo sopra i due massimi sistemi del mondo/Dialogues on the Two Chief Systems of the World* 1632 was banned by the church authorities in Rome and he was made to recant by the Inquisition.

Galileo was born and educated in Pisa, and in 1589 became professor of mathematics at the university there; in 1592 he became a professor at Padua, and in 1610 was appointed chief mathematician to the Grand Duke of Tuscany. When tried for heresy in 1633, and forced to abjure his belief that the Earth moves around the Sun, Galileo is reputed to have muttered: '*Eppur si muove*' ('Yet it does move'). He was put under house arrest for his last years.

Galileo discovered in 1583 that each oscillation of a pendulum takes the same amount of time despite the difference in amplitude. He invented the thermometer and a hydrostatic balance, and discovered that the path of a projectile is a parabola.

Galileo published *De motu/On Motion* 1590. Having made his own telescopes, he published his first findings in *Sidereus nuncius/The Starry Messenger* 1610; the book was a sensation throughout Europe. He summed up his life's work in *Discorsi e dimostrazioni matematiche intorno a due nove scienze/Discourses and Mathematical Discoveries Concerning Two New Sciences*. The manuscript of this book was smuggled out of Italy and published in Holland 1638.

Suggested reading
Allan-Olney, M *The Private Life of Galileo* (1970)
Drake, Stillman *Galileo at Work: His Scientific Biography* (1978)
Geymonat, L *Galileo Galilei: A Biography* (trs 1965)

Galinski Heinz (1912–1992). German Jewish community leader. A survivor of the Auschwitz and Buchenwald death camps, he helped to re-establish a strong Jewish community in postwar Germany, and was chairman of the Central Council of German Jews 1988–92.

Gall (*c.* 1840–1894). American Sioux Indian leader. He became a noted warrior of the Hunkpapa Sioux and a protégé of Chief Sitting Bull. Gall accompanied Sitting Bull to Montana 1876 and led the encirclement and annihilation of Custer's force at Little Bighorn.

Born along the Moreau river in the Dakota Territory, Gall participated in raids against the US Army along the Bozeman Trail and opposed the Treaty of Fort Laramie 1868, which established the reservation system in the N plains. After Custer's last stand 1876, he escaped to Canada with Sitting Bull and later settled on a reservation, becoming an Indian judge.

Gall Franz Joseph (1758–1828). Austrian anatomist, instigator of the discredited theory of phrenology.

Galland Adolf (1912–1996). German air ace of World War II. He served in the Spanish Civil War 1936–39 and then the Polish and French campaigns 1939 and the Battle of Britain 1940. By June 1941 he had claimed 70 enemy aircraft and was the first German pilot to be awarded the Swords to the Knight's Cross.

He was promoted to general in charge of fighter operations on all European fronts Nov 1941 but found that the administrative role was not his forte, particularly as he was faced with increasing Allied air strength, bureaucratic interference, and internal political wrangling. He was relieved of his post late 1944 and at Hitler's personal request trained and led a jet fighter squadron. He raised his score to 104 enemy aircraft before injuries put an end to his flying career.

Gallant Mavis (born Young) (1922–). Canadian short-story writer and novelist, based in Paris. A regular contributor to the *New Yorker* magazine, she has published novels and collections of short fiction, notably *The Pegnitz Junction* 1973, dealing with German life alienated from its immediate past after 1945, *From the Fifteenth District* 1979, set in various European countries, and *Across the Bridge* 1994.

Her work, which is distinguished by adroitly shifting points of view, perhaps influenced by cinema technique, often deals with the themes of cultural isolation and displacement.

Gallatin (Abraham Alphonse) Albert (1761–1849). Swiss-born US political leader and diplomat. He served in the US House of Representatives 1795–1801 and was secretary of the treasury 1801–13 during the administrations of Jefferson and Madison. He negotiated the treaty ending the Anglo-American War of 1812–14 and served as US minister to France 1815–22 and to England 1826–27.

Gallatin served in the Pennsylvania state legislature 1790–94. A critic of the Federalists, he helped establish the fiscal power of the US House of Representatives. After the end of his political career, he devoted himself to banking and American Indian ethnology.

Gallé Emile (1846–1904). French Art Nouveau glassmaker. He produced glass in sinuous forms or rounded, solid-looking shapes almost as heavy as stone, typically decorated with flowers or leaves in colour on colour.

After training in Europe, he worked at his father's glass factory and eventually took it over. He was a founder of the Ecole de Nancy, a group of French Art Nouveau artists who drew inspiration from his 1890s work and adopted his style of decoration and techniques.

Galle Johann Gottfried (1812–1910). German astronomer who located the planet Neptune 1846, close to the position predicted by French mathematician Urbain Leverrier.

Galle was born in Saxony, Prussia, and educated at Berlin. He worked at the Berlin Observatory until 1851, when he became professor of astronomy and director of the Breslau Observatory (now in Wroclaw, Poland).

Gallegos Rómulo (1884–1969). Venezuelan politician and writer. He was Venezuela's first democratically elected president 1948 before being overthrown by a military coup the same year. He was also a professor of philosophy and literature. His novels include *La trepadora/The Climber* 1925 and *Doña Bárbara* 1929.

Galliano John (1960–). English fashion designer. His elegant and innovative designs are often inspired by historical motifs (for example, 'Dickensian' clothing), the elements of which he redesigns to create progressive collections. He became known before graduating from St Martin's School of Art 1984 for his technical expertise and imaginative flair. In 1990 he designed the costumes for a production of Ashley Page's ballet *Corrulao*, performed by the Ballet Rambert. In the same year he began showing his collections in Paris.

Gallico Paul William (1897–1976). US author. Originally a sports columnist, he began writing fiction 1936. His many books include *The Snow Goose* 1941.

Gallieni Joseph Simon (1849–1916). French general, nicknamed 'The Saviour of Paris' from his plans for the defence of the city as military governor in World War I. He brought the city's fortifications to a state of readiness and rendered considerable assistance to the French 6th Army operating outside Paris. His rallying of all the Parisian taxicabs to take reinforcements to the front became a legend.

As governor of Madagascar 1896–1905, he organized the island as a French colony. He became minister of war Oct 1915 but

resigned due to ill-health and died 27 May 1916. He was posthumously awarded the distinction of Marshal of France 1921.

Gallo Robert Charles (1937–). US scientist credited with identifying the virus responsible for AIDS. Gallo discovered the virus, now known as human immunodeficiency virus (HIV), in 1984; the French scientist Luc Montagnier (1932–) of the Pasteur Institute, Paris, discovered the virus, independently, in 1983. The sample in which Gallo discovered the virus was supplied by Montagnier, and it has been alleged that this may have been contaminated by specimens of the virus isolated by Montagnier a few months earlier.

Gallup George Horace (1901–1984). US journalist and statistician, who founded in 1935 the American Institute of Public Opinion and devised the Gallup Poll, in which public opinion is sampled by questioning a number of representative individuals.

Gallwitz Max Karl Wilhelm von (1852–1937). German general. Gallwitz was attached to the general staff 1883–85 and was appointed inspector general of field artillery 1911. In World War I, he served with Hindenburg on the Eastern Front and Mackensen in the conquest of Serbia. He then moved to the Western Front where he fought at the Somme and was defeated at Verdun. Temporarily relieved of his command late 1917, he was reinstated to command an army group on the Western Front 1918.

Although never famous, Gallwitz was a highly competent tactician and, apart from his defeat at Verdun, rarely put a foot wrong on the battlefield.

Galois Evariste (1811–1832). French mathematician who originated the theory of groups and greatly extended the understanding of the conditions in which an algebraic equation is solvable.

In 1830, Galois joined the revolutionary movement. In the next year he was twice arrested, and was imprisoned for nine months for taking part in a republican demonstration. Shortly after his release he was killed in a duel. The night before, he had hurriedly written out his discoveries on group theory. His only published work was a paper on number theory 1830. What has come to be known as the *Galois theorem* demonstrated the insolubility of higher-than-fourth-degree equations by radicals. *Galois theory* involved groups formed from the arrangements of the roots of equations and their subgroups, which he fitted into each other rather like Chinese boxes.

I am probably the most happily married man in England. ... I know ... the value and beauty of a perfect union.

JOHN GALSWORTHY
quoted in H V Marrot *Life and Letters of John Galsworthy* 1935

Galsworthy John (1867–1933). English novelist and dramatist. His work examines the social issues of the Victorian period. He wrote *The Forsyte Saga* 1922 and its sequel *A Modern Comedy* 1929. His other novels include *The Country House* 1907 and *Fraternity* 1909; plays include *The Silver Box* 1906. Nobel prize 1932.

Galsworthy first achieved recognition with *The Man of Property* 1906, the first instalment of the *Forsyte* series, which includes *In Chancery* and *To Let*. Soames Forsyte, the central character, is the embodiment of Victorian values and feeling for property, and the wife whom he also 'owns' – Irene – was based on Galsworthy's wife. Later additions to the series are *A Modern Comedy* 1929, which contained *The White Monkey*, *The Silver Spoon*, and *Swan Song*, and the short stories *On Forsyte Change* 1930.

Yet still the blood is strong, the heart is Highland / And we in dreams behold the Hebrides!

JOHN GALT
'Canadian Boat Song' in *Blackwoods Edinburgh Magazine* Sept 1829

Galt John (1779–1839). Scottish novelist. He was the author of *Annals of the Parish* 1821, in which he portrays the life of a Lowlands village, using the local dialect. Born in Ayrshire, he moved to

London 1804 and lived in Canada 1826–29. He founded the Canadian town of Guelph, and Galt, on the Grand River, Ontario, was named after him.

Galtieri Leopoldo Fortunato (1926–). Argentine general, president 1981–82. A leading member from 1979 of the ruling right-wing military junta and commander of the army, Galtieri became president in 1981. Under his leadership the junta ordered the seizure 1982 of the Falkland Islands (Malvinas), a British colony in the SW Atlantic claimed by Argentina. After the surrender of his forces he resigned as army commander and was replaced as president. He and his fellow junta members were tried for abuse of human rights and court-martialled for their conduct of the war; he was sentenced to 12 years in prison in 1986.

Galton Francis (1822–1911). English scientist, inventor, and explorer who studied the inheritance of physical and mental attributes with the aim of improving the human species. He was the first to use twins to try to assess the influence of environment on development, and is considered the founder of eugenics (a term he coined).

Galton believed that genius was inherited, and was principally to be found in the British; he also attempted to compile a map of human physical beauty in Britain. He invented the 'silent' dog whistle, the weather map, a teletype printer, and forensic fingerprinting, and discovered the existence of anticyclones. Knighted 1909.

Galvani Luigi (1737–1798). Italian physiologist who discovered galvanic, or voltaic, electricity in 1762, when investigating the contractions produced in the muscles of dead frogs by contact with pairs of different metals. His work led quickly to Alessandro Volta's invention of the electrical cell, and later to an understanding of how nerves control muscles.

Galvani was born and educated in Bologna, where he taught anatomy. He was professor 1775–97, when he resigned rather than swear allegiance to Napoleon as head of the new Cisalpine Republic.

In 1786 Galvani noticed that touching a frog with a metal instrument during a thunderstorm made the frog twitch. He concluded that electricity was causing the contraction and postulated (incorrectly) that it came from the animal's muscle and nerve tissues. He summarized his findings in 1791 in a paper called 'De viribus electricitatis in motu musculari commentarius/Commentary on the Effect of Electricity on Muscular Motion', which gained general acceptance. But by 1800, Volta had proved that Galvani had been wrong and that the source of the electricity in his experiments had been two different metals and the animal's body fluids. Nevertheless, for many years current electricity was called Galvanic electricity.

Galway James (1939–). Irish flautist. He played with the London Symphony Orchestra 1966, Royal Philharmonic Orchestra 1967–69, and was principal flautist with the Berlin Philharmonic Orchestra 1969–75 before taking up a solo career.

Gama Vasco da (c. 1469–1524). Portuguese navigator who commanded an expedition in 1497 to discover the route to India around the Cape of Good Hope in modern South Africa. On Christmas Day 1497 he reached land, which he named Natal. He then crossed the Indian Ocean, arriving at Calicut May 1498, and returning to Portugal Sept 1499.

Da Gama was born at Sines, and chosen by Portuguese King Manoel I for his 1497 expedition. In 1502 he founded a Portuguese colony at Mozambique. In the same year he attacked and plundered Calicut in revenge for the murder of some Portuguese sailors. After 20 years of retirement, he was dispatched to India again as Portuguese viceroy in 1524, but died two months after his arrival in Goa.

Suggested reading
Correa, G (ed) *The Three Voyages of Vasco da Gama* (1869, rep 1964)
Hart, H H *Sea Route to the West Indies* (1950)
Ravenstein, E (ed) *A Journal of the First Voyage of Vasco da Gama* (1898, rep 1963)

Gamarra Augustín (1786–1841). Peruvian president 1829–33 and from 1839. His first period of rule saw chaos, and he went into exile, but was re-elected president 1839. He died during an attempted invasion of Bolivia.

Gamarra had emerged along with Andrés Santa Cruz (1792–1865) and José de La Mar (1776–1830) after the Battle of Ayacucho 1824, the last great contest in the struggle for independence in South America.

Let us never speak of it to the foreigner but see to it that he understands we think of it always.

LÉON MICHEL GAMBETTA
Speech at St Quentin Sept 1871 on the loss of Alsace-Lorraine to Germany

---

Gambetta Léon Michel (1838–1882). French politician, organizer of resistance during the Franco-Prussian War, and founder in 1871 of the Third Republic. In 1881–82 he was prime minister for a few weeks.

Game Philip Woolcott (1876–1961). English soldier and administrator, governor of New South Wales, Australia, 1930–35. In a crisis caused by the default of Labor premier J T Lang on paying state revenue to the Commonwealth during the Depression, he took the unprecedented step of dismissing the premier and his cabinet in May 1932. After his return to England he was commissioner of the London Metropolitan Police. KCB 1924.

Gamelin Maurice Gustave (1872–1958). French commander in chief of the Allied armies in France at the outset of World War II 1939. Replaced by Maxime Weygand after the German breakthrough at Sedan 1940, he was tried by the Vichy government as a scapegoat before the Riom 'war guilt' court 1942. He refused to defend himself and was detained in Germany until released by the Allies 1945.

Gamow George (Georgi Antonovich) (1904–1968). Russian-born US cosmologist, nuclear physicist, and popularizer of science. His work in astrophysics included a study of the structure and evolution of stars and the creation of the elements. He explained how the

Gambetta Léon Gambetta, French politician who took a leading role in proclaiming the Third Republic after the fall of Napoleon III in 1870.

collision of nuclei in the solar interior could produce the nuclear reactions that power the Sun. With the 'hot Big Bang' theory, he indicated the origin of the universe.

Gamow predicted that the electromagnetic radiation left over from the universe's formation should, after having cooled down during the subsequent expansion of the universe, manifest itself as a microwave cosmic background radiation. He also made an important contribution to the understanding of protein synthesis.

Gamow was born in Odessa (now in Ukraine), and studied at Leningrad (St Petersburg) and Göttingen, Germany. He then worked at the Institute of Theoretical Physics in Copenhagen, Denmark, and at the Cavendish Laboratory, Cambridge, England. From 1931 to 1933 he was at the Academy of Science in Leningrad, and then defected to the USA, becoming professor at George Washington University in Washington DC 1934–56 and then at the University of Colorado. In the late 1940s, he worked on the hydrogen bomb at Los Alamos, New Mexico.

Gamsakhurdia Zviad (1939–1993). Georgian politician, president 1990–92. He was a fervent nationalist and an active anti-communist. After nationalist success in parliamentary elections when Georgia achieved independence 1991, he was elected head of state by a huge margin. His increasingly dictatorial style of government and his attitude to non-ethnic Georgians led to his forced removal and flight to neighbouring Armenia 1992. He returned to W Georgia 1993 to lead a rebellion against Edvard Shevardnadze's presidency, but Shevardnadze, with Russian help, destroyed his ill-equipped supporters, and the deposed president was later reported dead, although uncertainty remained as to whether he had committed suicide or been killed by Russian troops.

Born in Tbilisi, the son of the Georgian novelist Konstantin Gamsakhurdia, he was a highly literate scholar who became a university lecturer in American studies, translated Shakespeare into Georgian, and spoke Russian, German, and French.

Gance Abel (1889–1981). French film director. His films were grandiose melodramas. *Napoléon* 1927 was one of the most ambitious silent epic films. It features colour tinting and triple-screen sequences, as well as multiple-exposure shots, and purported to suggest that Napoleon was the fulfilment of the French Revolution. He took film technologically and aesthetically further than any of his contemporaries.

Politics is the art of acquiring, holding and wielding power.

INDIRA GANDHI
quoted in *Observer* 4 May 1975

Gandhi Indira Priyadarshani (born Nehru) (1917–1984). Indian politician, prime minister of India 1966–77 and 1980–84, and leader of the Congress Party 1966–77 and subsequently of the Congress (I) Party. She was assassinated 1984 by members of her Sikh bodyguard, resentful of her use of troops to clear malcontents from the Sikh temple at Amritsar.

Her father, Jawaharlal Nehru, was India's first prime minister. She married Feroze Gandhi in 1942 (died 1960, not related to Mahatma Gandhi) and had two sons, Sanjay Gandhi (1946–1980), who died in an aeroplane crash, and Rajiv Gandhi, who was assassinated 21 May 1991. In 1975 the validity of her re-election to parliament was questioned, and she declared a state of emergency. During this time Sanjay Gandhi implemented a social and economic programme (including an unpopular family-planning policy) which led to his mother's defeat 1977.

Suggested reading
Ali, Tariq *Nehru and the Gandhis* (1985)
Carras, M *Indira Gandhi* (1979)
Moraes, D *Indira Gandhi* (1980)

Gandhi Mahatma (Sanskrit 'Great Soul'). Honorific name of Mohandas Karamchand Gandhi (1869–1948). Indian nationalist leader. A pacifist, he led the struggle for Indian independence from

the UK by advocating nonviolent noncooperation (*satyagraha*, defence of and by truth) from 1915. He was imprisoned several times by the British authorities and was influential in the nationalist Congress Party and in the independence negotiations 1947. He was assassinated by a Hindu nationalist in the violence that followed the partition of British India into India and Pakistan.

Gandhi was born in Porbandar and studied law in London, later practising as a barrister. He settled in South Africa where until 1914 he led the Indian community in opposition to racial discrimination. Returning to India, he emerged as leader of the Indian National Congress. He organized hunger strikes and events of civil disobedience, and campaigned for social reform, including religious tolerance and an end to discrimination against the so-called untouchable caste.

Suggested reading
Brown, J M *Gandhi: Prisoner of Hope* (1990)
Gandhi, Mahatma *Autobiography* (1948)
Mehta, V *Mahatma Gandhi and his Apostles* (1977)
Payne, R *The Life and Death of Mahatma Gandhi* (1969)
Richards, G *The Philosophy of Gandhi: A Study of his Ideas* (1982)

Gandhi Rajiv (1944–1991). Indian politician, prime minister from 1984 (following his mother Indira Gandhi's assassination) to Nov 1989. As prime minister, he faced growing discontent with his party's elitism and lack of concern for social issues. He was assassinated by a bomb at an election rally.

Elder son of Indira Gandhi and grandson of Nehru, Rajiv Gandhi was born into the Kashmiri Brahmin family that had governed India for all but four years since 1947. He initially displayed little interest in politics and became a pilot with Indian Airlines. But after the death in a plane crash of his brother *Sanjay* (1946–1980), he was elected to his brother's Amethi parliamentary seat 1981. In the Dec 1984 parliamentary elections he won a record majority. His reputation was tarnished by a scandal concerning alleged kickbacks to senior officials from an arms deal with the Swedish munitions firm Bofors and, following his party's defeat in the general election of Nov 1989, Gandhi was forced to resign as premier. He was killed in the middle of the 1991 election campaign at a rally near Madras, while attempting to regain office.

What, when drunk, one sees in other women, one sees in Garbo sober.

Kenneth Tynan on GRETA GARBO
in *Curtains* 1961

Garbo Greta. Stage name of Greta Lovisa Gustafsson (1905–1990). Swedish-born US film actress. She went to the USA 1925, and her captivating beauty and leading role in *Flesh and the Devil* 1927 made her one of Hollywood's greatest stars. Her later films include *Mata Hari* 1931, *Grand Hotel* 1932, *Queen Christina* 1933, *Anna Karenina* 1935, *Camille* 1936, and *Ninotchka* 1939. Her ethereal qualities and romantic mystery on the screen intermingled with her seclusion in private life. She retired 1941.

Suggested reading
Conway, Michael *The Films of Greta Garbo* (1968)
Corliss, Richard *Greta Garbo* (1974)
Payne, R *The Great Garbo* (1976)
Sands, Frederick and Broman, Sven *Divine Garbo* (1979)
Walker, Alexander *Garbo* (1980)

Garbus Martin (1930–   ). US lawyer specializing in civil-liberty cases. His clients have included Soviet dissident Andrei Sacharov, Nelson Mandela, and Vaclav Havel, for whom he drafted the section on civil liberties in the Czech constitution.

Garbus was born into a poor immigrant family in New York. He has been a law professor at Yale and Colombia, has represented the comedian Lenny Bruce, has been the advocate of Timothy Leary, Viking Penguin in the Salman Rushdie case, and black people in Mississippi wanting to exercise their right to vote. His books include *Ready for the Defence* 1987 and *Traitors and Heroes*.

García Lorca Federico, Spanish poet. See ◊Lorca, Federico García.

García Márquez Gabriel Gabo (1928–). Colombian novelist. His sweeping novel *Cien años de soledad/One Hundred Years of Solitude* 1967 (which tells the story of a family over a period of six generations) is an example of magic realism, a technique used to heighten the intensity of realistic portrayal of social and political issues by introducing grotesque or fanciful material. Nobel Prize for Literature 1982.

His other books include *El amor en los tiempos del cólera/Love in the Time of Cholera* 1985 and *The General in His Labyrinth* 1991, which describes the last four months of Simón Bolívar's life.

Suggested reading
McMurray, G H *Gabriel García Márquez* (1977)
Wood, Michael *Gabriel García Márquez* (1990)

She discovered with great delight that one does not love one's children just because they are one's children, but because of the friendship formed while raising them.

GABRIEL GARCÍA MÁRQUEZ
Love in the Time of Cholera 207 1985

García Perez Alan (1949–). Peruvian politician, leader of the moderate, left-wing America Popular Revolutionary Alliance (APRA) party; president 1985–90. He inherited an ailing economy and was forced to trim his socialist programme, losing to political novice Alberto Fujimori in the 1990 presidential elections.

He was born in Lima and educated in Peru, Guatemala, Spain, and France. He became APRA's secretary general 1982. In 1985 he succeeded Fernando Belaúnde Terry as president, becoming the first civilian president democratically elected.

Garbo *Swedish film actress Greta Garbo in* Queen Christina *1933. Garbo went to Hollywood in the mid-1920s and created a legend as the mysterious and often tragic heroine in historical dramas such as* Queen Christina *and* Anna Karenina *1935, though she also appeared in comedies such as* Ninotchka *1939. Her sudden retirement 1941, after which she lived as a recluse, added to her aura of mystery.*

García Márquez *The power of the Colombian writer Gabriel García Márquez's novels and short stories lies in their innocence, their epic range, and their calm acceptance of the fantastic. Most of his works are set in the imaginary town of Macondo, which closely resembles the N Colombian town of his birth.*

Garcilaso de la Vega (1503–1536). Spanish poet. A soldier, he was a member of Charles V's expedition in 1535 to Tunis; he was killed in battle at Nice. His verse, some of the greatest of the Spanish Renaissance, includes sonnets, songs, and elegies, often on the model of Petrarch.

Garcilaso de la Vega (*c.* 1539–*c.* 1616). Spanish writer, called 'el Inca'. Son of a Spanish conquistador and an Inca princess, he wrote an account of the conquest of Florida and *Comentarios reales de los Incas* on the history of Peru.

Gardiner Gerald Austin, Baron Gardiner (1900–1990). British lawyer. As Lord Chancellor in the 1964–70 Labour governments, Gardiner introduced the office of ombudsman to Britain, and played a major role in the movement for abolition of capital punishment for murder (which became law in 1965). Baron 1963.

Gardiner John Eliot (1943–). English conductor. He first made his mark establishing the Monteverdi Choir 1966, which he continues to conduct. He is an authority on 17th- and 18th-century music, and an exponent of the authenticity movement. He has also recorded modern music.

Gardiner Stephen (*c.* 1493–1555). English priest and politician. After being secretary to Cardinal Wolsey, he became bishop of Winchester in 1531. An opponent of Protestantism, he was imprisoned under Edward VI, and as Lord Chancellor 1553–55 under Queen Mary he tried to restore Roman Catholicism.

Gardner Ava (born Lucy Johnson) (1922–1990). US film actress. She was a sensuous star in such films as *The Killers* 1946, *Pandora and the Flying Dutchman* 1951, and *The Barefoot Contessa* 1954, a tragically slanted Cinderella tale of a Romany girl who becomes an international celebrity. Her later roles include that of Lillie Langtry in *The Life and Times of Judge Roy Bean* 1972. She remained active in films until the 1980s, when she retired to London.

Although no one believes me, I have always been a country girl, and still have a country girl's values.

AVA GARDNER
quoted in Leslie Halliwell *Filmgoer's Companion* 1965

Gardner Erle Stanley (1889–1970). US author of best-selling crime fiction. He created the character of the lawyer-detective Perry Mason, who was later featured in film and on television. Originally a lawyer, Gardner gave up his practice with the success of the first Perry Mason stories.

Gardner Helen Louise (1908–1986). English scholar and critic. She edited the poetry and prose of Donne and other metaphysical poets and the *New Oxford Book of English Verse* 1972. She was Merton Professor of English Literature at Oxford 1966–75. She wrote a study of T S Eliot's *Four Quartets* published 1978. DBE 1967.

I don't think any words are brutal and disgusting in themselves.

HELEN GARDNER quoted in
C H Rolph (ed) *Trial of Lady Chatterley*
(testimony in Regina v Penguin Books Limited)

Gardner Isabella Stewart (1840–1924). US art collector. She founded the Isabella Stewart Gardner Museum in Boston, USA. As an art collector, she specialized in the works of the Renaissance and of the Dutch masters. Her private art gallery in Boston was opened as a public museum 1903.

Born in New York and educated in Paris, France, she married prominent Boston manufacturer John Gardner 1860. She was participant in the intellectual life of the city but as a tireless world traveller, socialite, and local celebrity, she scandalized Bostonians with her lavish parties and public appearances. She was a patron of the Boston Symphony Orchestra (founded 1881).

Gardner Julia Anna (1882–1960). US geologist and palaeontologist whose work was important for petroleum geologists establishing standard stratigraphic sections for Tertiary rocks in the southern Caribbean.

She worked for the US Geological Survey 1911–54. During World War II, she joined the Military Geologic Unit where she helped to locate Japanese beaches from which incendiary bombs were being launched, by identifying shells in the sand ballast of the balloons.

Her work on the Cenozoic stratigraphic palaeontology of the Coastal Plain, Texas, and the Rio Grande Embayment in northeast Mexico led to the publication of *Correlation of the Cenozoic Formations of the Atlantic and Gulf Coastal Plain and the Caribbean Region* 1943 (with two co-authors).

Gardner Wayne Michael (1959–   ). Australian motorcycle racer. He gained international recognition in 1984 when he won the British 500 cc and the British Masters titles. In 1987, riding with Honda, he won the World Road Racing Championship (500 cc), 20 points ahead of his nearest rival.

Garfield James A(bram) (1831–1881). 20th president of the USA 1881, a Republican. A compromise candidate for the presidency, he held office for only four months before being assassinated in a Washington DC railway station by a disappointed office-seeker. His short tenure was marked primarily by struggles within the Republican party over influence and cabinet posts.

He was born in a log cabin in Ohio, and served in the Civil War with the Union forces.

Suggested reading
Leech, Margaret and Brown, Harry *The Garfield Orbit: The Life of President James A Garfield* (1978)
Peskin, Allan *Garfield* (1978)
Taylor, John M *Garfield of Ohio* (1970)

Garibaldi Giuseppe (1807–1882). Italian soldier who played a central role in the unification of Italy by conquering Sicily and Naples 1860. From 1834 a member of the nationalist Mazzini's Young Italy society, he was forced into exile until 1848 and again 1849–54. He fought against Austria 1848–49, 1859, and 1866, and led two unsuccessful expeditions to liberate Rome from papal rule in 1862 and 1867.

Born in Nice, he became a sailor and then joined the nationalist movement *Risorgimento*. Condemned to death for treason, he escaped to South America where he became a mercenary. He returned to Italy during the 1848 revolution, served with the Sardinian army against the Austrians, and commanded the army of the Roman republic in its defence of the city against the French. He subsequently lived in exile until 1854, when he settled on the island of Caprera.

In 1860, at the head of his 1,000 redshirts, he won Sicily and Naples for the new kingdom of Italy. He served in the Austrian War of 1866 and fought for France in the Franco-Prussian War 1870–71.

Suggested reading
Hibbert, Christopher *Garibaldi and His Enemies* (1965)
Parris, John *The Lion of Caprera* (1962)
Ridley, J *Garibaldi* (1976)

Garland Judy. Stage name of Frances Gumm (1922–1969). US singer and actress. Her performances are marked by a compelling

Garfield James Garfield, the 20th president of the USA, 1881. After graduating from Williams College, Garfield became a teacher, a lawyer, and a general in the US Civil War. During the war he was elected to Congress, and sat in the House of Representatives 1863–80, as Republican leader during the last four years.

Garibaldi Italian hero of the Risorgimento, Giuseppe Garibaldi. His enthusiastic leadership and colourful exploits fired the hearts of Italians. He never wavered from his single purpose, the unification of Italy under Italian rule, and he perhaps did more than any other person to bring it about. (Image Select)

intensity. Her films include *The Wizard of Oz* 1939 (which featured the tune that was to become her theme song, 'Over the Rainbow'), *Babes in Arms* 1939, *Strike Up the Band* 1940, *Meet Me in St Louis* 1944, *Easter Parade* 1948, *A Star is Born* 1954, and *Judgment at Nuremberg* 1961.

She began her acting career 1935 in the Andy Hardy series. She was the mother of actress and singer Liza Minnelli.

You see that girl? She used to be a hunchback. You see what I've made her into?

JUDY GARLAND
quoted by Louis B Mayer in Leslie Halliwell *Filmgoer's Companion* 1965

Garner Helen (1942–   ). Australian novelist, journalist, and short-story writer. Her early experience as a secondary-school teacher has helped her to engage realistically with the inner-city life of Melbourne. She won the National Book Council's Award for her novel *Monkey Grip* 1977 (filmed 1981). Her other books include *Honour and Other People's Children* 1980 and *The Children's Bach* 1984.

Garner John Nance (1868–1967). US political leader and vice president of the USA 1933–41. He served in the US House of Representatives 1903–33. A Democratic leader in the House, he was chosen as Speaker 1931. Garner later served as vice president during Franklin Roosevelt's first two terms. Opposing Roosevelt's re-election in 1940, he retired from public life.

Garner was born in Red River County, Texas, and briefly attended Vanderbilt University. After privately studying law in

Clarksville, Texas, he was admitted to the bar 1890. He was appointed county judge 1895 before embarking on a career in Democratic party politics and serving in the state legislature 1898–1902.

Garrett Almeida (1799–1854). Portuguese poet, novelist, and dramatist. As a liberal, in 1823 he was forced into 14 years of exile. His works, which he saw as a single-handed attempt to create a national literature, include the prose *Viagens na Minha Terra/Travels in My Homeland* 1843–46 and the tragedy *Frei Luis de Sousa* 1843.

A fellow-feeling makes one wond'rous kind.

DAVID GARRICK
'An Occasional Prologue on Quitting the Theatre' 10 June 1776

Garrick David (1717–1779). English actor and theatre manager. From 1747 he became joint licensee of the Drury Lane Theatre with his own company, and instituted a number of significant theatrical conventions including concealed stage lighting and banishing spectators from the stage. He played Shakespearean characters such as Richard III, King Lear, Hamlet, and Benedick, and collaborated with George Colman (1732–1794) in writing the play *The Clandestine Marriage* 1766. He retired from the stage 1766, but continued as a manager.

He was a pupil of Samuel Johnson.

There was not one of his scene-shifters who could not have spoken 'To be or not to be' better than he did, yet he was the only actor I ever saw who I would call a master both in comedy and tragedy.

Samuel Johnson on DAVID GARRICK
to Mrs Siddons, quoted by Boswell 1797

Garrison William Lloyd (1805–1879). US editor and reformer who was an uncompromising opponent of slavery. He founded the

Garrick Portrait of the English actor David Garrick by William Hogarth.

Garrison *Through his journal* The Liberator, *which he edited for over 30 years, US reformer William Lloyd Garrison denounced slavery, capital punishment, and war (though he supported the North in the American Civil War), and argued in favour of women's rights.*

abolitionist journal *The Liberator* 1831 and became a leader of the American Anti-Slavery Society. Although initially opposed to violence, he supported the Union cause in the Civil War. After the Emancipation Proclamation, he disbanded the Anti-Slavery Society and devoted his energies to prohibition, feminism, and Indian rights.

Garrod Archibald Edward (1857–1936). English physician who first recognized a class of metabolic diseases, while studying the rare disease alcaptonuria, in which the patient's urine turns black on contact with air. He calculated that the cause was a failure of the body's metabolism to break down certain amino acids into harmless substances like water and carbon dioxide. KCMG 1918.

Garros Roland (1888–1918). French fighter pilot in World War I. He held several aviation records 1911–12 and made his name with a 800 km/500 mi flight across the Mediterranean from St Raphael to Bizerta. He had some success as a fighter pilot but crash-landed in enemy territory April 1915 and was taken prisoner. He escaped Feb 1918 and returned to France, rejoined the air service and scored several more victories before being shot down and killed 5 Oct 1918.

Garros was the first pilot to fire machine guns through the propeller blades, giving him a considerable advantage over his enemies. He had sheets of steel attached to the propeller blades so that bullets would be deflected if they hit, but a sufficient number passed between the blades to be effective.

Garshin Vsevolod Mikhailovich (1855–1888). Russian short-story writer. He served in the Russo-Turkish War and was invalided home 1878. His stories, fewer than 20, include allegories, fairy tales, and war stories, among them 'The Red Flower' 1883 and 'Four Days' 1877, set during the war.

Garvey Marcus Moziah (1887–1940). Jamaican political thinker and activist, an early advocate of black nationalism. He led a Back to Africa movement for black Americans to establish a black-governed country in Africa. The Jamaican cult of Rastafarianism is based largely on his ideas.

Garvey founded the UNIA (Universal Negro Improvement Association) in 1914, and moved to the USA in 1916, where he established branches in New York and other northern cities. Aiming to achieve human rights and dignity for black people through black pride and economic self-sufficiency, he was considered one of the first militant black nationalists.

Gascoigne Paul ('Gazza') (1967–). English footballer who played for Tottenham Hotspur 1988–91, Lazio, Italy 1992–95, and then joined Glasgow Rangers. At the 1990 World Cup semifinal against West Germany, he committed a foul for which he was booked (cautioned by the referee), meaning that he would be unable to play in the final, should England win. His tearful response drew public sympathy, and he was subsequently lionized by the British press.

A little credulity helps one on through life very smoothly.
ELIZABETH GASKELL
Cranford ch 11 1853

Gaskell Mrs (Elizabeth Cleghorn, born Stevenson) (1810–1865). English novelist. Her most popular book, *Cranford* 1853, is the study of a small, close-knit circle in a small town, modelled on Knutsford, Cheshire. Her other books, which often deal with social concerns, include *Mary Barton* 1848, *North and South* 1855, *Sylvia's Lovers* 1863–64, and the unfinished *Wives and Daughters* 1866. Also of note is her frank and sympathetic biography of her friend Charlotte Brontë 1857.

Suggested reading
Brodetsky, T *Elizabeth Gaskell* (1987)
Easson, A *Elizabeth Gaskell* (1979)
Gerin, Winifred *Elizabeth Gaskell: A Biography* (1976)
Stoneman, P *Elizabeth Gaskell* (1987)

Gass William Howard (1924–). US experimental writer and theoretician. His novels, which parody genres and use typography and layout variations to emphasize the physical reality of the book, include *Omensetter's Luck* 1966 and *Willie Master's Lonesome Wife* 1968. Other works include the short-story collection *In the Heart of the Heart of the Country* 1968, two volumes of criticism, *Fiction and the Figures of Life* 1970 and *The World Within the Word* 1978, and the novel *The Tunnel* 1994.

Gassendi Pierre (1592–1655). French physicist and philosopher who played a crucial role in the revival of atomism (the theory that the world is made of small, indivisible particles), and the rejection of Aristotelianism so characteristic of the period. He was a propagandist and critic of other views rather than an original thinker.

Gates Henry Louis (1950–). US academic and social activist. A scholar of African-American studies, he has republished such forgotten works as *Our Nig* by Harriet E Wilson 1859, the earliest known novel by a black American. He published *The Signifying Monkey: A Theory of African-American Literary Criticism* 1988.

Gates was born in Keyser, West Virginia. He was the first black American to get a PhD from Cambridge University, England, for a thesis on attitudes to black American and African culture in the 18th century. He received the MacArthur Foundation 'genius' award for his work on literary theory 1981. In 1991 he was made professor of humanities and chair of the department of Afro-American studies at Harvard University. He wants to increase the number of black-studies courses in colleges in the USA in order to raise public awareness of the cultural achievements of black Americans. Other publications include *Colored People: A Memoir* 1994.

Gates Horatio (c. 1727–1806). British-born American military leader. George Washington appointed him brigadier general in the Continental army 1775 at the outbreak of the American Revolution. In command of the Northern Department, Gates won a tide-turning victory at the Battle of Saratoga 1777 after several American losses and retreats.

Born in England, Gates joined the British army, serving in Nova Scotia, Canada, and seeing action in the French and Indian War 1755–60. After returning to England, he emigrated to America

1772. Falling out of favour with Washington, he was dispatched to the South, where his defeat at the Battle of Camden in 1780 effectively ended his military career.

Gates William Henry ('Bill'), III (1955–). US businessman and computer scientist. He co-founded Microsoft Corporation 1975 and was responsible for supplying MS-DOS, the operating system that IBM chose to use in the IBM PC.

When the IBM deal was struck, Microsoft did not actually have an operating system, but Gates bought one from another company, renamed it MS-DOS, and modified it to suit IBM's new computer. Microsoft also retained the right to sell MS-DOS to other computer manufacturers, and because the IBM PC was not only successful but easily copied by other manufacturers, MS-DOS found its way onto the vast majority of PCs. The revenue from MS-DOS allowed Microsoft to expand into other areas of software, guided by Gates.

Gatling Richard Jordan (1818–1903). US inventor of a rapid-fire gun. Patented in 1862, the Gatling gun had ten barrels arranged as a cylinder rotated by a hand crank. Cartridges from an overhead hopper or drum dropped into the breech mechanism, which loaded, fired, and extracted them at a rate of 320 rounds per minute.

The Gatling gun was used in the US Civil War, in the Indian Wars that followed the settling of the American West, and in the Franco-Prussian War of 1870. By 1882 rates of fire of up to 1,200 rounds per minute were achieved, but the weapon was soon superseded by Hiram Maxim's machine gun in 1889.

Gatling was born in North Carolina; from 1870 his main factory was in Hartford, Connecticut. He manufactured other machines of his invention: for sowing, for breaking hemp, a steam plough, and a marine steam ram.

Gatting Michael William (1957–). Middlesex and England cricketer. He joined Middlesex in 1975 and captained the county from 1983. He was a member of seven championship-winning teams 1976, 1977, 1980, 1982, 1985, 1990, and 1993, and captain of the Sunday League champions 1992. He first played for England 1977 and captained England 1986–88.

Gaudí Antonio (1852–1926). Spanish architect. He is distinguished for his flamboyant Art Nouveau style. Gaudí worked mainly in Barcelona, designing both domestic and industrial buildings. He introduced colour, unusual materials, and audacious technical innovations. His spectacular Church of the Holy Family, Barcelona, begun 1883, is still under construction.

His design for Casa Milà, a block of flats in Barcelona (begun 1905), is wildly imaginative, with an undulating façade, vertically thrusting wrought-iron balconies, and a series of sculpted shapes that protrude from the roof. The central feature of his Parque Güell in Barcelona is a snakelike seat faced with a mosaic of broken tiles and cutlery.

Gaudier-Brzeska Henri (born Henri Gaudier) (1891–1915). French sculptor. He was active in London from 1911. He is regarded as one of the outstanding sculptors of his generation. He studied art in Bristol, Nuremberg, and Munich, and became a member of the English Vorticist movement, which sought to reflect the energy of the industrial age through an angular, semi-abstract style. From 1913 his sculptures showed the influence of Brancusi, Jacob Epstein, and primitive art. He was killed in action during World War I.

Suggested reading
Cole, Roger *Gaudier-Brzeska: Artist and Myth* (1995)
Ede, H S *Savage Messiah* (1972)

Art is either plagiarism or revolution.
PAUL GAUGUIN
quoted in J Huneker *Pathos of Distance* 128

Gauguin (Eugène Henri) Paul (1848–1903). French Post-Impressionist painter. Going beyond the Impressionists' notion of reality, he sought a more direct experience of life in the rich colours of the South Sea islands and the magical rites of its people. His work, often heavily symbolic and decorative, is characterized by his sensuous use of pure colours. Among his paintings is *Le Christe jaune* 1889 (Albright-Knox Art Gallery, Buffalo, New York State).

Born in Paris, Gauguin spent his childhood in Peru. After a few years as a stockbroker, he took up full-time painting 1883 and became a regular contributor to the Impressionists' last four group exhibitions 1880–86. From 1886–91 he spent much of his time in the village of Pont Aven in Brittany, where he concentrated on his new style, Synthetism, based on the use of powerful, expressive colours and boldly outlined areas of flat tone. Influenced by Symbolism, he chose subjects reflecting his interest in the beliefs of other cultures. He made brief visits to Martinique and Panama 1887–88, and 1888 spent two troubled months with van Gogh in Arles. He lived in Tahiti 1891–93 and 1895–1901, and from 1901 in the Marquesas Islands, where he died. It was in Tahiti that he painted one of his best-known works, *Where Do We Come From? What Are We? Where Are We Going?*, 1897 (Museum of Fine Art, Boston). Gauguin has touched the modern imagination as an escapist from a sophisticated civilization, but the new life he gave to colour was his great legacy to modern painting. In letters, journals and the poetical fragment of autobiography *Noa-Noa* he vividly recorded impressions in writing.

Suggested reading
Andersen, Wayne *Gauguin's Paradise Lost* (1971)
Boudaille, Georges *Gauguin* (1964)
Chassé, C *The Nabis and Their Period* (1969)
Thomson, B *Gauguin* (1987)

Gaulle Charles de. French politician, see Charles ◊de Gaulle.

Gaultier Jean-Paul (1952–). French fashion designer. After working for Pierre Cardin, he launched his first collection 1978, designing clothes that went against fashion trends, inspired by London's street style. Humorous and showy, his clothes are among the most influential in the French ready-to-wear market. He designed the costumes for Peter Greenaway's film *The Cook, the Thief, His Wife and Her Lover* 1989 and the singer Madonna's outfits for her world tour 1990.

He is also a popular media figure amongst the young through his Gaultier Junior Collection, and being a presenter of the *Eurotrash* TV programme.

Gauquelin Michel (1928–1991). French neo-astrologist. Gauquelin trained as a psychologist and statistician, but became widely known for neo-astrology, or the scientific measurement of the correlations between the exact position of certain planets at birth and individual fame. His work attracted strong criticism as well as much interest. His book *Neo-Astrology: a Copernican Revolution* was published posthumously 1991.

Gauquelin studied the relationship between planet and personality, discovering that athletes were more likely to be born with Mars in the crucial positions, actors with Jupiter, and scientists and doctors with Saturn. Gauquelin studied thousands of eminent people to obtain his data, using thousands of non-eminent people as a control group.

Gauss Carl Friedrich (1777–1855). German mathematician who worked on the theory of numbers, non-Euclidean geometry, and the mathematical development of electric and magnetic theory. A method of neutralizing a magnetic field, used to protect ships from magnetic mines, is called 'degaussing'. In statistics, the normal distribution curve, which he studied, is sometimes known as the Gaussian distribution.

Between 1800 and 1810 Gauss concentrated on astronomy. He developed a quick method for calculating an asteroid's orbit from only three observations and published this work – a classic in astronomy – 1809.

Gauss was born in Brunswick and studied there at the Collegium Carolinum, and at Göttingen and Helmstedt. By 1799 he had already made nearly all his fundamental mathematical discoveries. He spent most of his career at Göttingen, becoming professor of mathematics and director of the observatory.

Gauss *German mathematician, astronomer and physicist Karl Friedrich Gauss was born in 1777 in Brunswick to poor parents. His prodigious talent for mathematics was noticed at the age of fourteen by the Duke of Brunswick, who subsequently financed the remainder of his academic schooling. Gauss went on to make discoveries in virtually every field of physics and mathematics, many of which were not discovered until after his death.* (Image Select)

Suggested reading
Buhler, W K *Gauss: A Biographical Study* (1981)
Hall, T *Carl Friedrich Gauss: A Biography* (1970)

Gautama family name of the historical ◊Buddha.

Gautier Théophile (1811–1872). French Romantic poet. His later works emphasized the perfection of form and the polished beauty of language and imagery (for example, *Emaux et camées/Enamels and Cameos* 1852). He was also a novelist (*Mlle de Maupin* 1835) and later turned to journalism.

Gavaskar Sunil Manohar (1949–). Indian cricketer. Between 1971 and 1987 he scored a record 10,122 test runs in a record 125 matches (including 106 consecutive tests) until overtaken by Allan Border in 1993.

Gaviria (Trujillo) Cesar (1947–). Colombian Liberal Party politician, president 1990–94; he was finance minister 1986–87 and minister of government 1987–89. He supported the extradition of drug traffickers wanted in the USA and sought more US aid in return for stepping up the drug war.

An economist, Gaviria began his career in local government at the age of 22 and became mayor of his home town Pereira at 27. He went on to the house of representatives and became a deputy minister at 31. As acting president in 1988, while President Virgilio Barco was out of the country, Gaviria negotiated the freedom of a kidnapped presidential candidate. In 1989 he left the government to manage the campaign of another presidential candidate, who was assassinated later the same year.

Gay John (1685–1732). English poet and dramatist. He wrote *Trivia* 1716, a verse picture of 18th-century London. His *The Beggar's Opera* 1728, a 'Newgate pastoral' using traditional songs and telling of the love of Polly for highwayman Captain Macheath, was an extraordinarily popular success. Its satiric political touches led to the banning of *Polly*, a sequel. He was a friend of the writers Alexander Pope and John Arbuthnot.

Gaye Marvin (1939–1984). US pop singer and songwriter. His hits, including 'Stubborn Kinda Fellow' 1962, 'I Heard It Through the Grapevine' 1968, and 'What's Goin' On' 1971, exemplified the Detroit Motown sound.

Gay-Lussac Joseph Louis (1778–1850). French physicist and chemist who investigated the physical properties of gases, and discovered new methods of producing sulphuric and oxalic acids. In 1802 he discovered the approximate rule for the expansion of gases now known as Charles's law.

He became assistant to chemist Claude Berthollet 1801, made balloon ascents to study the weather in 1804, and accompanied Alexander von Humboldt on an expedition 1805–06 to measure terrestrial magnetism. In 1809 Gay-Lussac became professor of chemistry at the Ecole and professor of physics at the Sorbonne. He held various government appointments, including that of superintendent of a gunpowder factory (1818) and chief assayer to the Mint (1829). He was a member of the chamber of deputies for a short time in the 1830s.

With Humboldt he accurately determined the proportions of hydrogen and oxygen in water, showing the volume ratio to be 2:1; they also established the existence of explosive limits in mixtures of the two gases. In 1808 he formulated *Gay-Lussac's law* of combining volumes, which states that gases combine in simple proportions by volume and that the volumes of the products are related to the original volumes.

Geber Latinized form of Jabir ibn Hayyan (*c.* 721–*c.* 776). Arabian alchemist. His influence lasted for more than 600 years, and in the late 1300s his name was adopted by a Spanish alchemist whose writings spread the knowledge and practice of alchemy throughout Europe.

The Spanish alchemist Geber probably discovered nitric and sulphuric acids, and he propounded a theory that all metals are composed of various mixtures of mercury and sulphur.

Geddes Patrick (1854–1932). Scottish town planner. He established the importance of surveys, research work, and properly planned 'diagnoses before treatment'. His major work is *City Development* 1904. His protégé was Lewis Mumford. Knighted 1932.

Geertgen tot Sint Jans (*c.* 1460–*c.* 1490). Dutch painter. His name means 'Little Gerard of (the Order of) St John', but little is known about him. Of the few works firmly attributed to him, two best exhibit his characteristic charm and delicacy: *The Nativity* (National Gallery, London), a night scene lit solely by the radiance of the infant Jesus, and *St John in the Wilderness* (Staatliche Museum, Berlin), which shows a subtle mastery of landscape (both dated around the 1480s).

Geertz Clifford James (1926–). US cultural anthropologist. He has consistently argued for a more open and interdisciplinary approach to his subject. He views the structures of society less like an 'elaborate machine' and more like a 'serious game'. He maintains that the task of the anthropologist is to interpret the signs and symbols of society in the same way that a critic interprets a text.

He has been professor of social sciences at Princetown University, USA, since 1970 and his publications include *The Interpretation of Cultures* 1973.

Gehlen Reinhard (1902–1979). German World War II general and intelligence specialist. He became responsible for all intelligence relating to the Eastern Front 1942 and at the end of the war secured all the archives and files of his department and surrendered to US forces. He then set up his own intelligence agency working with the Western powers and specializing in Soviet intelligence.

Gehrig Lou (Henry Louis) (1903–1941). US baseball player. Nicknamed 'the Iron Horse' for his incomparable stamina and strength, he was signed by the New York Yankees 1923. Voted the American League's most valuable player 1927, 1931, 1934, and 1936, he achieved a remarkable lifetime 493 home runs, a .340 lifetime batting average, and a record 2,130 consecutive games played.

Born in New York, USA, Gehrig attended Columbia University. He stayed with the Yankees for 17 years as their first baseman and most consistent hitter. Diagnosed with a degenerative muscle disease (now known as 'Lou Gehrig's disease'), he retired from baseball 1939. A film biography, *Pride of the Yankees*, appeared 1942. He was elected to the Baseball Hall of Fame 1939.

Gehry Frank Owen (1929–   ). US architect, based in Los Angeles. His architecture approaches abstract art in its use of collage and montage techniques. His own experimental house in Santa Monica 1977, Edgemar Shopping Center and Museum, Santa Monica, 1988, and the Vitra Furniture Museum, Weil am Rhein, Switzerland, 1989 – his first building in Europe – demonstrate his vitality.

Geiger Hans Wilhelm (1882–1945). German physicist who produced the Geiger counter. He spent the period 1906–12 in Manchester, England, working with Ernest Rutherford on radioactivity. In 1908 they designed an instrument to detect and count alpha particles, positively charged ionizing particles produced by radioactive decay.

In 1928 Geiger and Walther Müller produced a more sensitive version of the counter, which could detect all kinds of ionizing radiation.

Geiger was born in Neustadt, Rheinland-Pfalz, and studied at Munich and Erlangen. On his return from Manchester 1912, Geiger became head of the Radioactivity Laboratories at the Physikalische Technische Reichsanstalt in Berlin, where he established a successful research group. He subsequently held other academic posts in Germany; from 1936 he was at the Technical University, Berlin.

Geingob Hage Gottfried (1941–   ). Namibian politician, prime minister from 1990. Geingob was appointed founding director of the United Nations Institute for Namibia in Lusaka, 1975. He became the first prime minister of an independent Namibia March 1990.

He played a major role in the South West Africa's People's Organization (SWAPO), acting as a petitioner to the United Nations 1964–71, to obtain international recognition for SWAPO.

Our whole thing is geared towards playing rock'n'roll and making it the exciting thing it was when I used to go to dances.

BOB GELDOF
quoted by Irwin Stambler *The Encyclopedia of Rock, Pop and Soul* 1989

Geldof Bob (1954–   ). Irish rock singer. He was the leader of the group the Boomtown Rats 1975–86. In the mid-1980s he instigated the charity Band Aid, which raised about £60 million for famine relief, primarily for Ethiopia.

In partnership with musician Midge Ure (1953–   ), Geldof gathered together many pop celebrities of the day to record Geldof's song 'Do They Know It's Christmas?' 1984, donating all proceeds to charity (it sold 7 million copies). He followed it up with two simultaneous celebrity concerts 1985 under the name Live Aid, one in London and one in Philadelphia, which were broadcast live worldwide. Honorary knighthood 1986.

Gell-Mann Murray (1929–   ). US theoretical physicist. Gell-Mann proposed in 1953 a new quantum number called the strangeness number, together with the law of conservation of strangeness, which states that the total strangeness must be conserved on both sides of an equation describing a strong or an electromagnetic interaction but *not* a weak interaction. This led to his theory of associated production 1955 concerning the creation of strange particles. Gell-Mann used these rules to group mesons, nucleons (neutrons and protons), and hyperons, and was thereby able to form successful predictions. In 1964 he formulated the theory of the quark as one of the fundamental constituents of matter. In 1969 he was awarded a Nobel prize for his work on elementary particles and their interaction.

Gell-Mann proposed in 1962 a classification system for elementary particles called the *eightfold way*. It postulated the existence of supermultiplets, or groups of eight particles which have the same spin value but different values for charge, isotopic spin, mass, and strangeness. The model also predicted the existence of supermultiplets of different sizes.

Gell-Mann was born in New York and studied at Yale and the Massachusetts Institute of Technology. He became professor at the California Institute of Technology 1956.

Gelon (*c.* 540–478 BC). Tyrant of Syracuse. Gelon took power in Gela, then capital of Sicily 491, and then transferred the capital to Syracuse. He refused to help the mainland Greeks against Xerxes 480 BC, but later the same year defeated the Carthaginians under Hamilcar Barca at Himera, on the north coast of Sicily, leaving Syracuse as the leading city in the western Greek world.

Gemayel Amin (1942–   ). Lebanese politician, a Maronite Christian; president 1982–88.

He succeeded his brother, president-elect *Bechir Gemayel* (1947–1982), on his assassination on 14 Sept 1982. The Lebanese parliament was unable to agree on a successor when his term expired, so separate governments were formed under rival Christian and Muslim leaders.

Geminiani Francesco (1687–1762). Italian violinist and composer. His treatise *The Art of Playing the Violin* 1740 was the first violin tutor ever published. His music was influenced by Corelli and is typically brilliant in fast movements and expressive in slow movements. He lived in London, Paris, and Dublin.

Genée Adeline. Stage name of Anina Margarete Kirstina Petra Jensen (1878–1970). Danish-born British dancer. She was president of the Royal Academy of Dancing 1920–54. Her most famous role was Swanilda in *Coppélia*, which she danced with infectious vivacity and charm. DBE 1950.

Geldof Irish rock musician and philanthropist Bob Geldof, celebrated for his fund-raising activities and his bluntly outspoken manner. Geldof worked as a pop journalist in Canada before becoming a professional musician. He was awarded a KBE 1986 and a variety of international honours for his role in pop charity events.

Born in Aarhus, she settled in England 1897. Her work was commemorated by the *Adeline Genée Theatre* 1967–89, East Grinstead, Sussex.

Genet Jean (1910–1986). French dramatist, novelist, and poet. His turbulent life and early years spent in prison are reflected in his drama, characterized by ritual, role-play, and illusion, in which his characters come to act out their bizarre and violent fantasies. His plays include *Les Bonnes/The Maids* 1947, *Le Balcon/The Balcony* 1957, and two plays dealing with the Algerian situation: *Les Nègres/The Blacks* 1959 and *Les Paravents/The Screens* 1961. His best-known novels include *Notre Dame des fleurs/Our Lady of the Flowers* 1944 and *Miracle de la rose/Miracle of the Rose* 1946.

Genghis Khan (*c.* 1167–1227). Mongol conqueror, ruler of all Mongol peoples from 1206. He began the conquest of N China 1213, overran the empire of the shah of Khiva 1219–25, and invaded N India, while his lieutenants advanced as far as the Crimea. When he died, his empire ranged from the Yellow Sea to the Black Sea; it continued to expand after his death to extend from Hungary to Korea. Genghis Khan controlled probably a larger area than any other individual in history. He was not only a great military leader, but the creator of a stable political system.

The ruins of his capital Karakorum are SW of Ulaanbaatar in Mongolia; his alleged remains are preserved at Ejin Horo, Inner Mongolia.

Temujin, as he was originally called, was the son of a chieftain. After a long struggle he established his supremacy over all the Mongols, when he assumed the title of Chingis or 'perfect warrior'.

Suggested reading
Brent, P *Genghis Khan* (1976)
Lister, R *Genghis Khan* (1969)
Martin, H *The Rise of Chingis Khan and His Conquest of North China* (1950)

Genji alternative name for ◊Minamoto, an ancient Japanese clan. Prince Genji, 'the shining prince', is the hero of one of Japan's best-known literary works, *Genji Monogatari/The Tale of Genji*, whose author is known as Murasaki.

Genscher Hans-Dietrich (1927–). German politician, chair of the West German Free Democratic Party (FDP) 1974–85, foreign minister 1974–92. A skilled and pragmatic tactician, Genscher became the reunified Germany's most popular politician.

Born in Halle, East Germany, Genscher settled in West Germany 1952. He served as interior minister 1969–74 and then as foreign minister, committed to Ostpolitik and European cooperation. As FDP leader, Genscher masterminded the party's switch of allegiance from the Social Democratic Party to the Christian Democratic Union, which resulted in the downfall of the Helmut Schmidt government 1982.

Gentile da Fabriano (born Niccolo di Giovanni di Massio) (*c.* 1370–*c.* 1427). Italian painter of frescoes and altarpieces. He was one of the most important exponents of the International Gothic style. Gentile was active in Venice, Florence, Siena, Orvieto, and Rome and collaborated with the artists Pisanello and Jacopo Bellini.

He worked in Venice, 1408–14, on frescoes for the Doge's Palace and was the master of Jacopo Bellini. His most famous work is *The Adoration of the Magi*, painted for the church of Santa Trinità in Florence (Uffizi), which in gay colour and richness of detail and ornament is a masterpiece of what is known as the 'International Gothic' style. Other notable works are the altarpiece of the Quaratesi family, 1425, of which the centre panel, Madonna and Child, is in the English Royal Collection and the wings and panels in the Uffizi and Vatican galleries; and a *Madonna with Saints* (Berlin). His last work was a series of frescoes (since destroyed) for San Giovanni in Laterano, Rome. These were finished by Pisanello, who was influenced by Gentile's Gothic manner.

Gentile Giovanni (1875–1944). Italian philosopher and politician, whose writings formed the basis of the Italian fascist state under Mussolini. As minister of education from 1924, he reformed both the school and university systems. He edited the *Encyclopedia Italiana* and wrote the entry in it for 'fascism'. He was assassinated by partisans.

Gentile's doctrine of 'actualism' was seized by the Fascists, to justify their authoritarian policies.

Gentileschi Artemisia (*c.* 1593–*c.* 1652). Italian painter. She trained under Agostino Tassi (*c.* 1580–1644) and her father Orazio Gentileschi, though her work is more melodramatic than his. Active in England (1638–39), Florence, and Rome, she settled in Naples from about 1630, working in a heavily Caravaggesque style. She focused on macabre and grisly subjects popular during her day, most notably *Judith Decapitating Holofernes c.* 1620.

Gentileschi Orazio (*c.* 1563–*c.* 1639). Italian painter. He was a follower and friend of Caravaggio, whose influence can be seen in the dramatic treatment of light and shade in his most noted picture, *The Annunciation* 1623. From 1626 he lived in London, painting for King Charles I. His daughter was the painter Artemisia Gentileschi.

Gentili Alberico (1552–1608). Italian jurist. He practised law in Italy but having adopted Protestantism was compelled to flee to England, where he lectured on Roman law in Oxford. His publications, such as *De Jure Belli libri tres/On the Law of War, Book Three* 1598, made him the first true international law writer and scholar.

Geoffrey of Monmouth (*c.* 1100–1154). Welsh writer and chronicler. While a canon at Oxford, he wrote *Historia Regum Britanniae/History of the Kings of Britain c.* 1139, which included accounts of the semi-legendary kings Lear, Cymbeline, and Arthur, and *Vita Merlini*, a life of the legendary wizard. He was bishop-elect of St Asaph, N Wales, 1151 and ordained a priest 1152.

Capital is a result of labor, and is used by labor to assist it in further production. Labor is the active and initial force, and labor is therefore the employer of capital.

HENRY GEORGE
Progress and Poverty bk 3 ch 1 1879

George Henry (1839–1897). US economist. His *Progress and Poverty* 1879 suggested a 'single tax' on land, to replace all other taxes on earnings and savings. He hoped such a land tax would abolish poverty, by ending speculation on land values. George's ideas have never been implemented thoroughly, although they have influenced taxation policy in many countries.

George Stefan (1868–1933). German poet. His early poetry was inspired by French Symbolism, but his concept of himself as regenerating the German spirit first appears in *Des Teppich des Lebens/The Tapestry of Life* 1899, and later in *Der siebente Ring/The Seventh Ring* 1907.

Das neue Reich/The New Empire 1928 shows his realization that World War I had not had the right purifying effect on German culture. He rejected Nazi overtures and emigrated to Switzerland 1933.

George six kings of Great Britain:

I hate all Boets and Bainters.

GEORGE I
quoted in Campbell *Lives of the Chief Justices* ch 30 1849

George I (1660–1727). King of Great Britain and Ireland from 1714. He was the son of the first elector of Hanover, Ernest Augustus (1629–1698), and his wife Sophia, and a great-grandson of James I. He succeeded to the electorate 1698, and became king on the death of Queen Anne. He attached himself to the Whigs, and spent most of his reign in Hanover, never having learned English.

He was heir through his father to the hereditary lay bishopric of Osnabrück and the duchy of Calenberg, which was one part of the Hanoverian possessions of the house of Brunswick. He acquired the other part by his marriage to *Sophia Dorothea of Zell* (1666–1726) in 1682. They were divorced 1694, and she remained in seclusion until her death. George's children were George II and *Sophia Dorothea* (1687–1757), who married Frederick William (later king of Prussia) 1706 and was the mother of Frederick the Great.

Suggested reading
Hatton, R *George I: Elector and King* (1978)
Marlow, Joyce *The Life and Times of George I* (1973)
Plumb, J H *The First Four Georges, 1714–1830* (1956)
Redman, A *The House of Hanover* (1960)
Williams, Basil *The Whig Supremacy, 1714–60* (1962)

George II (1683–1760). King of Great Britain and Ireland from 1727, when he succeeded his father, George I. His victory at Dettingen 1743, in the War of the Austrian Succession, was the last battle commanded by a British king. He married Caroline of Anspach 1705. He was succeeded by his grandson George III.

Suggested reading
Plumb, J H *The First Four Georges, 1714–1830* (1956)
Redman, A *The House of Hanover* (1960)
Williams, Basil *The Whig Supremacy, 1714–60* (1962)

I desire what is good; therefore, everyone who does not agree with me is a traitor.

GEORGE III
quoted in John Fortescue (ed) *The Correspondence of George III* 1927–28

George III (1738–1820). King of Great Britain and Ireland from 1760, when he succeeded his grandfather George II. His rule was marked by intransigence resulting in the loss of the American colonies, for which he shared the blame with his chief minister Lord North, and the emancipation of Catholics in England. Possibly suffering from porphyria, he had repeated attacks of insanity, permanent from 1811. He was succeeded by his son George IV.

He married Princess Charlotte Sophia of Mecklenburg-Strelitz 1761.

Suggested reading
Brooke, John *George III* (1972)
Clarke, J *The Life and Times of George III* (1972)
Plumb, J H *The First Four Georges, 1714–1830* (1956)
Redman, A *The House of Hanover* (1960)
Watson, J S *The Reign of George III, 1760–1815* (1960)

A more contemptible, cowardly, selfish, unfeeling dog does not exist than this King.

Charles Greville on GEORGE IV
in *The Greville Memoirs* 1874

George IV (1762–1830). King of Great Britain and Ireland from 1820, when he succeeded his father George III, for whom he had been regent during the king's period of insanity 1811–20. In 1785 he secretly married a Catholic widow, Maria Fitzherbert, but in 1795 also married Princess Caroline of Brunswick, in return for payment of his debts. He was a patron of the arts. His prestige was undermined by his treatment of Caroline (they separated 1796), his dissipation, and his extravagance. He was succeeded by his brother, the duke of Clarence, who became William IV.

Suggested reading
Hibbert, Christopher *George IV, Prince of Wales, 1762–1811* (1973)
Hibbert, Christopher *George IV, Regent and King, 1811–1830* (1973)
Palmer, Alan *The Life and Times of George IV* (1972)
Plumb, J H *The First Four Georges, 1714–1830* (1956)
Redman, A *The House of Hanover* (1960)

George V (1865–1936). King of Great Britain from 1910, when he succeeded his father Edward VII. He was the second son, and became heir 1892 on the death of his elder brother Albert, Duke of Clarence. In 1893, he married Princess Victoria Mary of Teck (Queen Mary), formerly engaged to his brother. During World

War I he made several visits to the front. In 1917, he abandoned all German titles for himself and his family. The name of the royal house was changed from Saxe-Coburg-Gotha (popularly known as Brunswick or Hanover) to Windsor.

His mother was Princess Alexandra of Denmark, sister of Empress Marie of Russia.

Suggested reading
Judd, D *The Life and Times of George V* (1973)
Nicolson, Harold *George V* (1952)
Rose, Kenneth *King George V* (1984)
Sinclair, David *Two Georges: The Making of the Modern Monarchy* (1988)

I can't understand it. I'm really quite an ordinary sort of chap.

GEORGE V
Attributed remark at Jubilee celebrations 1935

George VI (1895–1952). King of Great Britain from 1936, when he succeeded after the abdication of his brother Edward VIII, who had succeeded their father George V. Created Duke of York 1920, he married in 1923 Lady Elizabeth Bowes-Lyon (1900–   ), and their children are Elizabeth II and Princess Margaret. During World War II, he visited the Normandy and Italian battlefields.

Suggested reading
Donaldson, Frances *King George VI and Queen Elizabeth* (1977)
Sinclair, David *Two Georges: The Making of the Modern Monarchy* (1988)
Wheeler-Bennett, J *King George VI* (1958)

George two kings of Greece:

George I (1845–1913). King of Greece 1863–1913. The son of Christian IX of Denmark, he was nominated to the Greek throne and, in spite of early unpopularity, became a highly successful constitutional monarch. He was assassinated by a Greek, Schinas, at Salonika.

George II (1890–1947). King of Greece 1922–23 and 1935–47. He became king on the expulsion of his father Constantine I 1922 but was himself overthrown 1923. Restored by the military 1935, he set up a dictatorship under Joannis Metaxas, and went into exile during the German occupation 1941–45.

George, St patron saint of England. The story of St George rescuing a woman by slaying a dragon, evidently derived from the Perseus legend, first appears in the 6th century. The cult of St George was introduced into W Europe by the Crusaders. His feast day is 23 April.

He is said to have been martyred at Lydda in Palestine 303, probably under the Roman emperor Diocletian, but the other elements of his legend are of doubtful historical accuracy.

His association with England probably began when his story became popular among medieval Crusaders. He is the patron of the Order of the Garter, founded about 1348, and the feast of St George was given official status 1415.

Gerald of Wales English name of ◊Giraldus Cambrensis, medieval Welsh bishop and historian.

Gerhard Roberto (1896–1970). Spanish-born British composer. He studied with Enrique Granados and Arnold Schoenberg and settled in England 1939, where he composed twelve-tone works in Spanish style. He composed the *Symphony No 1* 1952–55, followed by three more symphonies and chamber music incorporating advanced techniques. His opera *The Duenna* 1947 received its British premiere 1992 (it was premiered in Wiesbaden, Germany, 1957).

Gerhardie William Alexander (born Gerhardi) (1895–1977). English novelist, born in Russia. His novels include *Futility: A Novel on Russian Themes* 1922 and *The Polyglots* 1925, both of which draw on his Russian upbringing.

She even sighed offensively ... as if she meant to charge me with the necessity of doing so.

WILLIAM GERHARDIE
Futility pt 3 ch 3 1922

Géricault (Jean Louis André) Théodore (1791–1824). French Romantic painter and graphic artist. *The Raft of the Medusa* 1819 (Louvre, Paris) was notorious in its day for exposing a relatively recent scandal in which shipwrecked sailors had been cut adrift and left to drown. His other works include *The Derby at Epsom* 1821 (Louvre, Paris) and pictures of cavalry. He also painted portraits, including remarkable studies of the insane, such as *A Kleptomaniac* 1822–23 (Musée des Beaux Arts, Ghent).

He studied first under the painter of hunting and racing scenes, Carle Vernet, 1808–10, then under the classicist Guérin, 1810–11, though it was Baron Gros who really inspired him to the dash and spirit of his early pictures of Napoleonic cavalry officers. After an unhappy love-affair he left Paris for Italy, 1816–17, where he conceived ambitious projects of painting in the grand style of Michelangelo and Raphael, making studies for a large canvas suggested by the Barberi horse race. On his return he painted his most famous picture, *The Raft of the Medusa*, a painting in which the classic nude of David, realism of subject and a Romantic force of feeling were characteristically blended: it made a strong impression on the young Delacroix, who incidentally posed for one of the figures. The visit to England which followed, 1820–22, marked a change of direction. The sporting print and English genre picture alike attracted him, *The Derby at Epsom* (Louvre) being a striking result, while he made several lithographs of London life and character and in addition an equestrian portrait of the Prince Regent (Wallace Collection). In 1822–23, back in Paris, he executed a series of portraits, clinical in their veracity, of insane patients in the Salpetrière hospital.

Germain Sophie (1776–1831). French mathematician, born in Paris. Although she was not allowed to study at the newly opened Ecole Polytechnique, she corresponded with the mathematicians Joseph Lagrange and Karl Gauss. She is remembered for work she carried out in studying Fermat's principle.

German Edward (born Edward German Jones) (1862–1936). English composer. He is remembered for his operettas *Merrie England* 1902 and *Tom Jones* 1907, and he wrote many other instrumental, orchestral, and vocal works. Knighted 1928.

Germanicus Caesar (15 BC–AD 19). Roman general. He was the adopted son of the emperor Tiberius and married the emperor Augustus' granddaughter Agrippina. Although he refused the suggestion of his troops that he claim the throne on the death of Augustus, his military victories in Germany made Tiberius jealous. Sent to the Middle East, he died near Antioch, possibly murdered at the instigation of Tiberius. He was the father of Caligula and Agrippina, mother of Nero.

Geronimo (Spanish name for *Goyahkla*) (1829–1909). Chief of the Chiricahua Apache Indians and war leader. From 1875 to 1885, he fought US federal troops, as well as settlers encroaching on tribal reservations in the Southwest, especially in SE Arizona and New Mexico.

After surrendering to General George Crook March 1886, and agreeing to go to Florida where their families were being held, Geronimo and his followers escaped. Captured again Aug 1886, they were taken to Florida, then to Alabama. The climate proved unhealthy, and they were taken to Fort Sill, Oklahoma, where Geronimo became a farmer. He dictated *Geronimo's Story of His Life* 1906.

Suggested reading
Adams, A *Geronimo: A Biography* (1971)
Debo, A *Geronimo: The Man, His Time, His Place* (1976)

Gerrald Joseph (1763–1796). English social reformer, born in the West Indies. He was one of the Scottish Martyrs sentenced to transportation to Australia in 1794.

Gershwin George (born Jacob Gershwin) (1898–1937). US composer. He wrote concert works including the tone poems *Rhapsody in Blue* 1924 and *An American in Paris* 1928, and popular musicals and songs, many with lyrics by his brother *Ira Gershwin* (1896–1983), including 'I Got Rhythm', ''S Wonderful', and 'Embraceable You'. His opera *Porgy and Bess* 1935 incorporated jazz rhythms and popular song styles in an operatic format.

He was born in Brooklyn, New York. Although his scores to musicals made him famous, his 'serious' work earned him much critical acclaim. *Of Thee I Sing* 1931, a collaboration between the Gershwin brothers, was the first musical to win a Pulitzer prize.

Suggested reading
Goldberg, Isaac and Garson, Edith *George Gershwin: A Study in American Music* (1958)
Jablonski, Edward *Gershwin* (1987)
Kendall, Alan *Gershwin* (1987)
Rosenberg, D *Fascinating Rhythm: The Collaboration of George and Ira Gershwin* (1992)
Schwartz, C *Gershwin: His Life and Music* (1973)

I don't think there has been such an inspired melodist on this earth since Tchaikovsky ... but if you want to speak of a composer, that's another matter.

Leonard Bernstein on GEORGE GERSHWIN
in *Atlantic Monthly*, 1955

Gerson Jean le Charlier de (1363–1429). French theologian. He was leader of the concilliar movement, which argued for the supremacy of church councils over popes, and denounced John Huss at the Council of Constance 1415. His theological works greatly influenced 15th-century thought.

He was chancellor of Notre Dame cathedral in Paris and of the University of Paris from 1405.

Gertler Mark (1891–1939). English painter. He was a pacifist and a noncombatant during World War I, and his best-known work, *Merry-Go-Round* 1916 (Tate Gallery, London), is often seen as an expressive symbol of anti-militarism. He suffered from depression and committed suicide.

Gesell Arnold Lucius (1880–1961). US psychologist and educator. He founded the Yale Clinic of Child Development, which he directed 1911–48. Among the first to study the stages of normal development, he worked as a consultant to the Gesell Institute of Child Development, New Haven, Connecticut, which was founded 1950 to promote his educational ideas.

Gesner Konrad von (1516–1565). Swiss naturalist who produced an encyclopedia of the animal world, the *Historia animalium* 1551–58. He began a similar project on plants that was incomplete at the time of his death. He is considered the founder of zoology.

Gesualdo Carlo, Prince of Venosa (c. 1561–1613). Italian composer and lutenist. His compositions, which comprise sacred and secular vocal music, and some instrumental pieces, are noted for their complex (modern-sounding) harmonic structure, most unlike the work of his contemporaries. His highly chromatic madrigals (in six books 1594–1611), set to emotional, passionate texts, have been admired in the 20th century by Stravinsky, among others.

In 1590 he had his wife and her lover murdered; he married Leonora d'Este of Ferrara 1593, and lived at the court in Ferrara to 1596.

Getty J(ean) Paul (1892–1976). US oil billionaire, president of the Getty Oil Company from 1947, and founder of the Getty Museum (housing the world's highest-funded art collections) in Malibu, California.

Getty *Tycoon and oil billionaire J Paul Getty devoted much of his personal fortune to art collecting. Getty acquired and controlled more than 100 companies and became one of the richest men in the world; in 1968 his personal wealth was estimated at over $1 billion.*

In 1985 his son John Paul Getty Jr (1932–) established an endowment fund of £50 million for the National Gallery, London.

If you can actually count your money, then you are not really a rich man.

J PAUL GETTY
quoted in *Observer* 3 Nov 1957

Getz Stan(ley) (born Gayetzby) (1927–1991). US saxophonist. He was one of the foremost tenor-sax players of his generation. In the 1950s he was a leading exponent of the cool jazz school, as on the album *West Coast Jazz* 1955. In the 1960s he turned to the Latin American bossa nova sound, which gave him a hit single, 'The Girl from Ipanema' 1964. Later he experimented with jazz-rock fusion.

Getz became a professional musician at 15, working with the big-band leaders of the era: Tommy Dorsey, Stan Kenton, Benny Goodman, and Woody Herman. Technically brilliant but never showy, he was influenced by Lester Young, and became a cult hero in the cool-jazz movement with its tendency towards subtlety and restraint. In the early 1960s *Jazz Samba*, *Big Band Bossa Nova*, and other albums brought jazz to a wider public.

Geulincx Arnold (*c.* 1625–1669). Belgian philosopher. He formed the theory of occasionalism, according to which God synchronizes body and mind, like two clocks that act together but have no influence on each other. Occasionalism was his solution to the mind–body problem.

Geulincx was professor at Louvain 1646–58. To avoid persecution, he often used the pseudonym of Philaretus. His main works are *Quaestiones Quodlibeticae/Miscellaneous Questions* 1653 and *Metaphysica Vera/True Metaphysics* 1691.

Ghazzali, al- (1058–1111). Muslim philosopher and Sufi (Muslim mystic). He was responsible for easing the conflict between the Sufi and the Ulema, a body of Muslim religious and legal scholars. Initially, he believed that God's existence could be proved by reason, but later he became a wandering Sufi, seeking God through mystical experience; his book *The Alchemy of Happiness* was written on his travels.

Gheorgiu-Dej Gheorge (1901–1965). Romanian communist politician. A member of the Romanian Communist Party from 1930, he played a leading part in establishing a communist regime 1945. He was prime minister 1952–55 and state president 1961–65. Although retaining the support of Moscow, he adopted an increasingly independent line during his final years.

Ghiberti Lorenzo (1378–1455). Italian sculptor and goldsmith. In 1402 he won the commission for a pair of gilded bronze doors for Florence's Baptistry. He produced a second pair (1425–52), the *Gates of Paradise*, one of the masterpieces of the early Italian Renaissance. They show a sophisticated use of composition and perspective, and the influence of Classical models. He also wrote *Commentarii/Commentaries* about 1450, a mixture of art history, manual, and autobiography.

Ghirlandaio Domenico, (adopted name of Domenico di Tommaso Bigordi) (*c.* 1449–1494). Italian fresco painter. He was the head of a large and prosperous workshop in Florence. His fresco cycle 1486–90 in Sta Maria Novella, Florence, includes portraits of many Florentines and much contemporary domestic detail. He also worked in Pisa, Rome, and San Gimignano, and painted many portraits.

He was styled Il Ghirlandaio or Grillandaio (garland-maker) after his father Tommaso, who was a goldsmith, and is notable not only as the master of Michelangelo, but as one of the greatest Italian masters of fresco and a principal representative of the narrative art of the late 15th century. He studied under Baldovinetti and his style was influenced by Castagno, Masaccio and Verrocchio. His first major work was the *Life of St Fina* in the Cappella Fina, 1475, and his frescoes in Florence include those for the Sassetti Chapel in Santa Trinità, 1485, and for the choir of Santa Maria Novella (the *Life of St Francis*, 1485, and the scenes from the life of St John the Baptist and the Virgin, his masterpiece, 1486–90). A prolific painter with a flourishing studio, Ghirlandaio produced not only frescoes and mosaics but many religious subjects on panel and portraits. Of the two frescoes he contributed to the Sistine Chapel to the order of Sixtus IV, 1481, the *Calling of St Andrew and St Peter* remains. His altarpiece from Santa Maria Novella is at Munich.

Ghirlandaio was assisted by his brothers, Davide (1452–1525) and Benedetto (1458–1497). Davide helped in the mosaic of the *Annunciation* over the north portal of Florence Cathedral and executed others at Orvieto, Florence and Siena. The son of Domenico, Ridolfo (1483–1561), was also a painter and was a friend of Raphael. He too had a busy studio and was employed by the Signoria of Florence and the Medici. There are paintings by him in galleries at Berlin, Paris (Louvre) and Florence (Uffizi and Pitti).

Ghormley Robert Lee (1883–1953). US admiral. He became US Commander South Pacific 1942 and was ordered to organize the capture of Tulagi and Guadalcanal. He complained there was not enough time for adequate preparation and although he was proved right his attitude made him enemies. He was responsible for the decision which made Admiral Fletcher withdraw his ships from Guadalcanal, leaving the ground operations exposed, which contributed to US losses in the Battle of Savo Island. He was replaced by Admiral Halsey Oct 1942 and sent to a staff post in Washington, holding no further active command.

Giacconi Riccardo (1931–). Italian-born US physicist, the head of a team whose work has been fundamental in the development of X-ray astronomy. In 1970 they launched a satellite devoted entirely to X-ray astronomy.

Giacconi was born in Genoa and obtained his doctorate from Milan. He emigrated to the USA 1956. In 1959 he joined American Science and Engineering, Inc., rising to executive vice president 1969. In 1973 he was made professor of astronomy at Harvard University. Later he became director of the European Southern Observatory.

In 1962, a rocket sent up by Giacconi and his group to observe secondary spectral emission from the Moon detected strong X-rays from a source evidently located outside the Solar System. X-ray research has since led to the discovery of many types of stellar and interstellar material. Giacconi's team have developed a telescope capable of producing X-ray images.

Giacconi has also worked with a Cherenkov detector, by means of which it is possible to observe the existence and velocity of high-speed particles.

Giacometti Alberto (1901–1966). Swiss sculptor and painter. He trained in Italy and Paris. In the 1930s, in his Surrealist period, he began to develop his characteristic spindly constructions. His mature style of emaciated, rough-textured, single figures in bronze, based on wire frames, emerged in the 1940s. *Man Pointing* 1947 is one of many examples in the Tate Gallery, London.

Suggested reading
Hohl, R *Alberto Giacometti* (trs 1972)
Juliet, Charles *Giacometti* (1986)
Lord, James *Giacometti: A Biography* (1985)
Sylvester, D *Looking at Giacometti* (1995)

Giambologna (Giovanni da Bologna or Jean de Boulogne) (1529–1608). Flemish-born sculptor. He was active mainly in Florence and Bologna. In 1583 he completed his public commission for the Loggia dei Lanzi in Florence, *The Rape of the Sabine Women*, a dynamic group of muscular, contorted figures and a prime example of Mannerist sculpture. He also produced the *Neptune Fountain* 1563–67 in Bologna and the equestrian statues of the Medici grand dukes Cosimo and Ferdinando.

Giap Vo Nguyen (1910–   ). Vietnamese military leader and communist politician. When Ho Chi Minh formed the Vietminh 1941 in China, Giap organized the army that returned to Indochina 1944 to fight the Japanese and liberated Hanoi 19 Aug 1945. As commander in chief of a guerrilla force of 60,000, he led the struggle against the French colonial forces, conclusively defeating them at Dien Bien Phu 7 May 1954. With the growth of US influence in South Vietnam, Giap sent North Vietnamese troops to help the Vietcong (the National Liberation Front), and he took direct control of communist military operations in South Vietnam 1967, launching the Tet Offensive Feb 1968. He was responsible for the defeat of the US army 1973.

Born in Quangbiln Province, then part of the French protectorate of Indochina, Giap joined the Communist Party 1930. With a doctorate in law from the University of Hanoi 1938, he fled to China when the party was banned 1939, and became military aide to Ho Chi Minh. When Vietnam was partitioned 1954, he became commander in chief of the North Vietnam army. His training manual on guerrilla warfare (1960) was published in English as *People's War, People's Army* 1962. He was minister of national defence and deputy prime minister of Vietnam 1976–80.

Gibberd Frederick Ernest (1908–1984). English architect and town planner. He was a pioneer of the Modern Movement in England. His works include the new towns of Harlow, England, and Santa Teresa, Venezuela; the Catholic Cathedral, Liverpool 1960; and the Central London Mosque, Regent's Park 1969. Knighted 1967.

Gibbon Edward (1737–1794). English historian. He wrote one major work, arranged in three parts, *The History of the Decline and Fall of the Roman Empire* 1776–88, a continuous narrative from the 2nd century AD to the fall of Constantinople 1453. He began work on it while in Rome 1764. Although immediately successful, he was

It was at Rome, on the 15th of October, 1764, as I sat musing amidst the ruins of the Capitol, while the barefooted friars were singing vespers in the Temple of Jupiter, that the idea of writing the decline and fall of the city first started to my mind.

EDWARD GIBBON
Memoirs of My Life 1966 ed

compelled to reply to attacks on his account of the early development of Christianity by a *Vindication* 1779. His *Autobiography*, pieced together from fragments, appeared 1796.

From 1783 Gibbon lived in Lausanne, Switzerland, but he returned to England and died in London.

Suggested reading
Beer, Gavin de *Gibbon and His World* (1968)
Braddock, Patricia *Young Edward Gibbon, Man of Letters* (1982)
Burrow, J W *Gibbon* (1985)
Gibbon, Edward *Memoirs of My Life* (1827, ed Betty Radice 1984)
Porter, Roy *Gibbon: Making History* (1988)

Gibbon John Heysham (1903–1974). US surgeon who invented the heart–lung machine in 1953. It has become indispensable in heart surgery, maintaining the circulation while the heart is temporarily inactivated.

Gibbon Lewis Grassic. Pen name of James Leslie Mitchell (1901–1935). Scottish novelist. He was the author of the trilogy *A Scots Quair: Sunset Song, Cloud Howe*, and *Grey Granite* 1932–34, set in the Mearns, south of Aberdeen, where he was born and brought up. Under his real name he wrote *Stained Radiance* 1930 and *Spartacus* 1933.

Gibbons Grinling (1648–1720). Dutch woodcarver who settled in England c. 1667. He produced carved wooden panels (largely of birds, flowers, and fruit) for St Paul's Cathedral, London, and for many large English country houses including Petworth House, Sussex, and Hampton Court, Surrey. He was carpenter to English monarchs from Charles II to George I. Features of his style include acanthus whorls in oak, and trophies of musical instruments in oak and limewood.

It is proportion that beautifies everything, this whole universe consists of it, and music is measured by it.

ORLANDO GIBBONS
The First Set of Madrigals and Motets 1612

Gibbons Orlando (1583–1625). English composer. He wrote sacred anthems, instrumental fantasias, and madrigals including *The Silver Swan* for five voices 1612. From a family of musicians, he became organist at Westminster Abbey, London, 1623.

Gibbons Stella Dorothea (1902–1989). English journalist. She is remembered for her *Cold Comfort Farm* 1932, a classic satire on the regional novel, in particular the works of Mary Webb.

When you were very small ... you had seen something nasty in the woodshed.

STELLA GIBBONS
Cold Comfort Farm ch 10 1932

Gibbs James (1682–1754). Scottish Neo-Classical architect. He studied under the late-Baroque architect Carlo Fontana (1638–1714) in Rome and was a close friend and follower of Christopher Wren. His buildings include St Mary-le-Strand, London, 1714–17, St Martin-in-the-Fields, London, 1722–26, and the circular Radcliffe Camera, Oxford, 1737–49, which shows the influence of Italian Mannerism.

Gibbs Josiah Willard (1839–1903). US theoretical physicist and chemist who developed a mathematical approach to thermodynamics and established vector methods in physics. He devised the phase rule and formulated the Gibbs adsorption isotherm. Gibbs showed how many thermodynamic laws could be interpreted in terms of the results of the movements of enormous numbers of bodies such as molecules. His ensemble method equated the behaviour of a large number of systems at once to that of a single system over a period of time.

Gibbs was born in New Haven, Connecticut, and studied at Yale and 1866–69 in Europe. From 1871 he was professor of mathematical physics at Yale.

Gibran Kahlil (1883–1931). Lebanese-American essayist, artist, and mystic poet. Brought to Boston 1895, he studied in Beirut and Paris before settling in New York 1912. A Maronite Christian influenced by the Bible, William Blake, and Nietzsche, he wrote in both Arabic and English, exploring the themes of love, nature, longing for homeland, and romantic rebellion, including, controversially, the rebellion of women against arranged marriages. He is best known in the West for *The Prophet* 1923.

Everyone has experienced that truth: that love, like a running brook, is disregarded, taken for granted; but when the brook freezes over, then people begin to remember how it was when it ran, and they want it to run again.

KAHLIL GIBRAN
Beloved Prophet 1972

Gibson Althea (1927–). US tennis player, the first black American woman to compete at the US Championships at Forest Hills 1950 and at Wimbledon 1951. In 1957 she took both the women's singles and doubles titles at Wimbledon and the singles at Forest Hills. In 1958 she successfully defended all three titles.

Born in Silver, South Carolina, USA, and raised in New York, Gibson was hindered in her tennis career by racial discrimination and segregation. In 1943 she won the New York State Negro girls' singles title, and in 1948 the national Negro women's title. She later played professional golf.

Gibson Charles Dana (1867–1944). US illustrator. He portrayed an idealized type of American young woman, known as the 'Gibson Girl'.

Gibson Guy Penrose (1918–1944). British bomber pilot of World War II. He became famous as leader of the 'dambuster raids' 16–17 May 1942; he formed 617 squadron specifically to bomb the Ruhr Dams, and as wing commander led the raid personally, dropping the first bomb on the Mohne Dam. He was awarded the Victoria Cross for his leadership in this action.

Gibson joined the RAF 1936 and by 1939 was an operational bomber pilot. Following the dambuster raid, he was relieved of operational duties and accompanied Churchill to Canada and the USA late 1944. On returning to Britain he obtained permission for 'one more operation', flying a De Havilland Mosquito on a raid on targets in Bavaria. On the return flight his plane crashed in Holland and he was killed.

Gibson James Jerome (1904–1979). US psychologist who did influential and highly original work on visual perception. An outspoken critic of the German physiologist Hermann Helmholtz's notion that perception involves unconscious inferences from sense data and learning-based associations, he proposed that perceptual information is gained directly from the environment, without the need for intermediate processing.

Educated at Princeton, Gibson went on to teach at Smith College, Massachusetts, 1928–49, where he was influenced by Kurt Koffka (1886–1941), and at Cornell University 1949–72.

In his experimental work, Gibson dispensed with the use of two-dimensional, static images and instead explored the perception of motion in freely moving subjects under natural conditions, publishing his results in *The Perception of the Visual World* 1950. He went on to develop what he called an ecological theory of perception in *Senses Considered as Perceptual Systems* 1966.

Gibson Mel (1956–). Australian actor. He became an international star following lead roles in *Mad Max* 1979 and *Mad Max II*

I'll work anywhere, anytime, any price.

MEL GIBSON
quoted in *Photoplay* 1983

1982 which was released in the USA as *Road Warrior*. His other films include *The Year of Living Dangerously* 1982, *Mutiny on the Bounty* 1984 as Fletcher Christian, and the *Lethal Weapon* series, in which Danny Glover co-starred. He directed *Man Without a Face* 1993.

Gibson Mike (Cameron Michael Henderson) (1942–). Irish rugby player. He made a world record 81 international appearances between the years 1964 and 1979; 69 for Ireland and 12 for the British Lions on a record five tours. Of his 69 Ireland caps, 40 were played as centre, 25 at outside-half, and 4 on the wing.

Gibson William (1948–). US writer. His debut novel *Neuromancer* 1984 established the 'cyberpunk' genre of computer-talk fantasy adventure and won both the Hugo and Nebula awards for science fiction. Gibson is credited with inventing the concept of virtual reality in *Neuromancer*. It was followed by *Count Zero* 1986 and *Mona Lisa Overdrive* 1988. Other works include *The Difference Engine* 1990, co-written with Bruce Sterling (1954–), about Babbage's original 19th-century computer.

Sadness is almost never anything but a form of fatigue.

ANDRÉ GIDE
Journal 1889–1949

Gide André Paul Guillaume (1869–1951). French novelist, playwright, and critic. His work is largely autobiographical and concerned with the conflict between desire and conventional morality. It includes *L'Immoraliste/The Immoralist* 1902, *La Porte étroite/Strait Is the Gate* 1909, *Les Caves du Vatican/The Vatican Cellars* 1914, and *Les Faux-monnayeurs/The Counterfeiters* 1926. He was a cofounder of the influential literary periodical *Nouvelle Revue française* and kept an almost lifelong *Journal*. Nobel Prize for Literature 1947.

Suggested reading
Bettinson, Christopher *Gide: A Study* (1977)
Cordel, Thomas *André Gide* (1975)
Fowlie, Wallace *André Gide: His Life and Art* (1969)
Gide, André *If it Die...* (autobiography) (trs 1935, rep 1957)
Painter, George *André Gide: A Critical Biography* (1968)

An elderly fallen angel travelling incognito.

Peter Quennell on ANDRÉ GIDE
in *Sign of the Fish* ch 2 1960

Gideon in the Old Testament, one of the Judges of Israel, who led a small band of Israelite warriors which succeeded in routing an invading Midianite army of overwhelming number in a surprise night attack.

When you're my age, you just never risk being ill – because then everyone says: Oh, he's done for.

JOHN GIELGUD
on being 84, in *Sunday Express Magazine* 17 July 1988

Gielgud (Arthur) John (1904–). English actor and director. He is renowned as one of the greatest Shakespearean actors of his time. He made his debut at the Old Vic 1921, and his numerous stage appearances ranged from roles in works by Chekhov and Sheridan to those of Alan Bennett, Harold Pinter, and David Storey. Gielgud's films include *Becket* 1964, *Oh! What a Lovely War* 1969, *Providence* 1977, *Chariots of Fire* 1980, and *Prospero's Books* 1991. He won an Academy Award for his role as a butler in *Arthur* 1981. Knighted 1953.

Gierek Edward (1913–). Polish communist politician. He entered the Politburo of the ruling Polish United Workers' Party (PUWP) in 1956 and was party leader 1970–80. His industrialization programme plunged the country heavily into debt and sparked a series of Solidarity-led strikes.

Gierek, a miner's son, lived in France and Belgium for much of the period between 1923 and 1948, becoming a member of the Belgian Resistance. He served as party boss in Silesia during the 1960s. After replacing Gomulka as PUWP leader in Dec 1970, he embarked on an ambitious programme of industrialization. A wave of strikes in Warsaw and Gdańsk, spearheaded by the Solidarity free trade-union movement, forced Gierek to resign in Sept 1980.

Giffard Henri (1825–1882). French inventor of the first passenger-carrying powered and steerable airship, called a dirigible, built 1852. On 24 Sept 1852 he took off from the Hippodrome in Paris and flew to Elancourt, near Trappes. The hydrogen-filled airship was 43 m/144 ft long, had a 2,200-W/3-hp steam engine that drove a three-bladed propeller, and was steered using a saillike rudder. It flew at an average speed of 5 kph/3 mph. Giffard went on to build another airship 1855, and a series of large balloons. This was funded by money from other inventions, such as an injector to feed water into a steam-engine boiler to prevent it running out of steam when not in motion.

Gigli Beniamino (1890–1957). Italian lyric tenor. His radiant tone and affectionate characterizations brought a natural realism to roles in Puccini, Gounod, and Massenet.

Gigli Romeo (1950–). Italian fashion designer. He founded his own label 1984 and achieved acclaim for his sombre colours, long languid dresses, and exaggerated shaped garments. He also designs for the label Callaghan and in 1993 launched a collection of carpets.

Gilbert Alfred (1854–1934). English sculptor. He was influenced by Art Nouveau. His statue *Eros* 1887–93 in Piccadilly Circus, London, was erected as a memorial to the 7th Earl of Shaftesbury. Knighted 1932.

Gilbert Cass (1859–1934). US architect. He was a major developer of the skyscraper. He designed the Woolworth Building, New York, 1913, the highest building in America (265 m/868 ft) when built and famous for its use of Gothic decorative detail. He was also architect of the US Supreme Court building in Washington DC, the Minnesota state capitol in St Paul, and the US Customs House in New York City.

We are as near to heaven by sea as by land!
HUMPHREY GILBERT
in Hakluyt's Collection of Early Voyages 1809

Gilbert Humphrey (c. 1539–1583). English soldier and navigator who claimed Newfoundland (landing at St John's) for Elizabeth I in 1583. He died when his ship sank on the return voyage. Knighted 1570.

Gilbert Walter (1932–). US molecular biologist who studied genetic control, seeking the mechanisms that switch genes on and off. By 1966 he had established the existence of the lac repressor, a molecule that suppresses lactose production. Further work on the sequencing of DNA nucleotides won him a share of the 1980 Nobel Prize for Chemistry, with Frederick Sanger and Paul Berg.

Gilbert was born in Boston, Massachusetts, and educated as a physicist at Harvard and at Cambridge, England. In 1960 he changed to biology, becoming professor of biophysics at Harvard 1964, then professor of molecular biology 1969.

Gilbert William (1540–1603). English scientist who studied magnetism and static electricity, deducing that the Earth's magnetic field behaves as if a bar magnet joined the North and South poles. His book on magnets, published 1600, is the first printed scientific book based wholly on experimentation and observation.

Gilbert was the first English scientist to accept Nicolas Copernicus' idea that the Earth rotates on its axis and revolves around the Sun. He also believed that the stars are at different distances from the Earth and might be orbited by habitable planets, but erroneously thought that the planets were held in their orbits by magnetic forces.

Gilbert was born in Colchester, Essex, and educated at Cambridge. In about 1573, he settled in London, where he established a medical practice. He was appointed physician to Queen Elizabeth I 1600 and later briefly to James I.

Gilbert discovered many important facts about magnetism, such as the laws of attraction and repulsion and magnetic dip. He also investigated static electricity and differentiated between magnetic attraction and electric attraction (as he called the ability of an electrostatically charged body to attract light objects). This is described in his book *De magnete, magneticisque corporibus, et de magno magnete tellure/Concerning Magnetism, Magnetic Bodies, and the Great Magnet Earth* 1600.

The idiot who praises, with enthusiastic tone, / All centuries but this, and every country but his own.
W S GILBERT
The Mikado 1885

Gilbert W(illiam) S(chwenk) (1836–1911). English humorist and dramatist. He collaborated with composer Arthur Sullivan, providing the libretti for their series of light comic operas from 1871 performed by the D'Oyly Carte Opera Company; they include *HMS Pinafore* 1878, *The Pirates of Penzance* 1879, and *The Mikado* 1885. Knighted 1907.

Born in London, he became a lawyer 1863, but in 1869 published a collection of his humorous verse and drawings, *Bab Ballads*, which was followed by a second volume 1873.

Suggested reading
Ayre, Leslie *The Gilbert and Sullivan Companion* (1972)
Brahms, Caryl *Gilbert and Sullivan* (1975)
Eden, D *Gilbert and Sullivan* (1986)
Hibbert, Christopher *Gilbert and Sullivan and Their Victorian World* (1976)

Gilbert and George Gilbert Proesch (1943–) and George Passmore (1942–). English painters and performance artists. They became known in the 1960s for their presentations of themselves as works of art, or 'living sculptures'. They also produce large emblematic photoworks. Their use of both erotic and ambiguous political material has made them controversial. They received the Turner Award 1986.

Gilchrist Ellen (1935–). US short-story writer and novelist. She is noted for sharp and stylish social tragicomedy. Her collections include *In the Land of Dreamy Dreams* 1981, *Victory Over Japan* 1985, *Light Can Be Both Wave and Particle* 1990, and *Star Carbon* 1994. Her novels include *Net of Jewels* 1992.

Gilchrist Percy Carlyle (1851–1935). British metallurgist who devised a method of producing low-phosphorus steel from high-phosphorus ores, such as those commonly occurring in the UK. This meant that steel became cheaply available to British industry.

Gilchrist was born in Lyme Regis, Dorset, and studied at the Royal School of Mines. He developed the steelmaking process 1875–77, together with his cousin Sidney Gilchrist Thomas. The product became known at first as 'Thomas steel'. Pig iron was melted in a convector similar to that used in the Bessemer process and subjected to prolonged blowing. The oxygen in the blast of air oxidized carbon and other impurities, and the addition of lime at this stage caused the oxides to separate out as a slag on the surface of the molten metal. Continued blowing then brought about oxidation of the phosphorus.

Giles Carl Ronald (1916–1995). British cartoonist for the *Daily Express* and *Sunday Express* from 1943, noted for his creation of a family with a formidable 'Grandma'.

Giles (William) Ernest (Powell) (1835–1897). English-born explorer in Australia whose double crossing over the unknown desert country of the western half of Australia provided valuable information about the centre of the continent. In 1875 he crossed east–west, from Port Augusta to Perth, and in 1876 went from Geraldton west–east across the Gibson Desert.

Gill (Arthur) Eric (Rowton) (1882–1940). English sculptor, engraver, and writer. He designed the typefaces Perpetua 1925 and Gill Sans (without serifs) 1927, and created monumental stone sculptures with clean, simplified outlines, such as *Prospero and Ariel* 1929–31 (on Broadcasting House, London).

He studied lettering at the Central School of Art in London under Edward Johnston (1872–1944), and began his career carving inscriptions for tombstones. Gill was a leader in the revival of interest in the craft of lettering and book design. His views on art combine Catholicism, socialism, and the Arts and Crafts tradition.

Gill David (1843–1914). Scottish astronomer who pioneered the use of photography to catalogue stars. He also made much use of a heliometer, determining the solar parallax and measuring the distances of 20 of the brighter and nearer southern stars. KCB 1900.

Gill was born in Aberdeen and studied there at Marischal College; he then went to Switzerland to learn clockmaking. In 1872, he became director of Lord Lindsay's private observatory at Dun Echt, near Aberdeen. He was astronomer at the observatory at the Cape of Good Hope, South Africa, 1879–1906.

With Lord Lindsay, Gill went on an expedition to Mauritius 1872–78 in order to measure the distance of the Sun and other related constants, particularly during the 1874 transit of Venus. In 1882 Gill realized it should be possible to chart and measure star positions by photography. He initiated a vast project, with the help of other observatories, to produce the *Cape Durchmusterung*, which gives the positions and brightness of more than 450,000 southern stars. Gill also served on the council for the *International Astrographic Chart and Catalogue*, which was to give precise positions for all stars to the 11th magnitude. It was not completed until 1961, although all the photographs had been taken by 1900.

Gillespie Dizzy (John Birks) (1917–1993). US jazz trumpeter. With Charlie Parker, he was the chief creator and exponent of the bebop style (*Groovin' High* is a CD re-issue of their seminal 78-rpm recordings). Gillespie influenced many modern jazz trumpeters, including Miles Davis.

Gillespie was born in South Carolina. He moved to Philadelphia and then, in 1937, to New York, where he made his first recordings as a soloist. He was a member of popular bandleader Cab Calloway's orchestra 1939–41, with shorter spells in other bands, and formed his own quartet 1942. The following year he made his first recording with Parker. Although associated mainly with small combos, Gillespie formed his first big band 1945 and toured with a big band in the late 1980s, as well as in the intervening decades; a big band can be heard on *Dizzy Gillespie at Newport* 1957.

Gillette King Camp (1855–1932). US inventor of the Gillette safety razor.

Gillray James (1757–1815). English caricaturist. His 1,500 cartoons, 1779–1811, satirized the French, George III, politicians, and social follies of his day. After being a letter-engraver and actor, he was encouraged to become a caricaturist by the works of Hogarth, and he was celebrated for his coloured etchings, fiercely satirical and topical, and directed against both the English court and France. They compose an unconventional history of the late Georgian and Napoleonic period. He became insane in later life.

Gilman Charlotte Anna (born Perkins) (1860–1935). US feminist socialist poet, novelist, and historian, author of *Women and Economics* 1898, proposing the ending of the division between 'men's work' and 'women's work' by abolishing housework.

From 1909 to 1916 she wrote and published a magazine called *The Forerunner*, in which her feminist Utopian novel *Herland* 1915 was serialized.

The people people have for friends / Your common sense appall, / But the people people marry / Are the queerest folk of all.

CHARLOTTE PERKINS GILMAN
'Queer People'

Gilman Henry (1893–1986). US organic chemist who made a comprehensive study of methods of high-yield synthesis, quantitative and qualitative analysis, and uses of organometallic compounds, particularly Grignard reagents.

Gilman was born in Boston, Massachusetts, and studied at Harvard. He was professor at Iowa State University 1923–47.

Gilman investigated the organic chemistry of 26 different metals, from aluminium, arsenic, and barium to thallium, uranium, and zinc, and discovered several new types of compounds. He was the first to study organocuprates, now known as *Gilman reagents*, and his early work with organomagnesium compounds (Grignard reagents) would later play an important part in the preparation of polythene.

Gilmore Mary Jean (1865–1962). Australian poet, author, journalist, and worker for social justice and political reform. She is best known for her many volumes of poetry which are noted for their radical themes and their nationalism. They include *The Passionate Heart* 1918, a response to World War I expressing dismay at the waste and futility of war; *The Wild Swan* 1930, showing deep concern at the destruction of Aboriginal culture and the despoilation of the landscape by white civilization; *Battlefields* 1939, the title referring to her own campaigns and containing her most radical verse; and her final volume *Fourteen Men* 1954.

Gilpin William (1724–1804). English artist. He is remembered for his essays on the 'picturesque', which set out precise rules for the production of this effect.

Gilson Etienne Henry (1884–1978). French philosopher. He studied medieval philosophy, through which he became deeply influenced by Thomas Aquinas, and contributed to the philosophy of neo-Thomism. His works include *L'Esprit de la philosophie médiéval/The Spirit of Medieval Philosophy* 1932.

Gilson was born in Paris. He taught there at the Sorbonne from 1921 and later at the Collège de France. From 1945 he spent much time at the University of Toronto, Canada.

Gimbutas Marija (1921–1994). Lithuanian-born US-based archaeologist whose feminist theories challenged traditional views of society in prehistoric Europe. She proposed that Stone Age Europe was a peaceful and harmonious place, where men and women were equals and worshipped life-giving goddesses, in particular the great Mother Goddess; the invading Indo-Europeans brought a male-dominated society and warlike gods.

Gimbutas' radical ideas are treated with considerable scepticism by most scholars in the field, but they have been adopted with enthusiasm by many feminists. Works include *The Language of the Goddess* 1989 and *The Civilization of the Goddess* 1991.

Gimbutas first established her reputation with solid works such as *The Prehistory of Eastern Europe* 1956 and the enormous *Bronze Age Cultures of Central and Eastern Europe* 1965. Appointed a professor at the University of California at Los Angeles, she organized and directed Neolithic excavations in Yugoslavia, Greece, and Italy, and developed her theories about the *Gods and Goddesses of Old Europe* 1974, theories which culminated in her last two works, on the supposed Mother Goddess cult.

Ginastera Alberto Evaristo (1916–1983). Argentinian composer. His early works, including his *Pampeana No. 3* 1954, are mostly in a nationalistic style, but after 1958 he turned to modern techniques of serialism, aleatory rhythms, and the use of microtones. He is best known for his operas *Don Rodrigo* 1964, *Bomarzo* 1967, and *Beatrix Cenci* 1971.

Gingrich Newt(on Leroy) (1943–). US Republican politician, speaker (leader) of the House of Representatives from 1995. A radical-right 'Reaganite', he was the driving force behind his party's sensational victory in the 1994 congressional elections, when it gained a House majority for the first time since 1954. On taking office, he sought to implement a ten-point conservative, populist manifesto, 'Contract with America', designed to reduce federal powers, balance the budget, tackle crime, and limit congressional terms.

The stepson of a peripatetic army officer, Gingrich was a professor of military history before entering Congress as House representative for Georgia 1979. He established himself as a powerful and partisan speaker, and became House minority whip for the Republicans 1989. He set about attacking the leadership of the incumbent Democrats with charges of sleaze and corruption and, following their defeat in the 1994 mid-term elections, was elected speaker. He fulfilled his party's pledge to put all measures in its manifesto to a House floor vote within the first 100 days of the new Congress.

Ginner (Isaac) Charles (1878–1952). English painter. His street scenes and landscapes were strongly influenced by Post-Impressionism. He settled in London 1910, and was one of the London Group.

Ginsberg (Irwin) Allen (1926–). US poet and political activist. His reputation as a visionary, overtly political poet was established by *Howl* 1956, which expressed and shaped the spirit of the Beat Generation and criticized the materialism of contemporary US society. His poetry draws heavily on Oriental philosophies and utilizes mantric breath meditations.

Ginsberg travelled widely – to Cuba, India, and Czechoslovakia in the 1960s, and China and Nicaragua in the 1980s – spreading his Zen-socialist politics of radical but passive dissent. His other major poem, *Kaddish* 1961, deals with the breakdown and death of his schizophrenic mother. His *Collected Poems 1947–1980* was published 1985.

Ginsburg Ruth Joan Bader (1933–). US judge. Appointed Supreme Court justice by President Clinton 1993, she is only the second woman to serve on the court. Ginsburg made her reputation

Ginsberg, Allen US poet Allen Ginsberg, one of the outspoken leaders of the Beat Generation. His spontaneous, loosely structured verse draws heavily on personal experience and freely expresses his outrage at the spiritual emptiness of modern life. His imagery is stark and sometimes shocking.

as a civil liberties lawyer in the 1960s and 1970s, particularly with the six cases on gender equality she argued before the Supreme Court 1973–76. She won five, establishing a legal framework for women's rights.

Ginzburg Vitalii Lazarevich (1916–). Russian astrophysicist whose use of quantum theory in a study of Cherenkov radiation contributed to the development of nuclear physics. He was one of the first to believe that cosmic background radiation comes from beyond our own Galaxy.

Ginzburg was born and educated in Moscow and spent his career there at the Physics Institute of the Academy of Sciences.

Ginzburg also formulated the theory of a molecule containing particles with varying degrees of motion, for which he devised the first relativistically invariant wave equation. After 1950, he concentrated on problems in thermonuclear reactions. His work on cosmic rays led him to a hypothesis about their origin and to the conclusion that they can be accelerated in a supernova.

A hard-working and ascetic, almost puritanical, legal bureaucrat.

Norman Stone on GIOVANNI GIOLITTI
in *Europe Transformed 1878–1919* 1985

Giolitti Giovanni (1842–1928). Italian liberal politician, born in Mondovi. He was prime minister 1892–93, 1903–05, 1906–09, 1911–14, and 1920–21. He opposed Italian intervention in World War I and pursued a policy of broad coalitions, which proved ineffective in controlling Fascism after 1921.

Giono Jean (1895–1970). French novelist. His books are chiefly set in Provence. *Que ma Joie demeure/Joy of Man's Desiring* 1935 is an attack on life in towns and a plea for a return to country life.

In 1956 he published a defence of Gaston Dominici, who allegedly murdered an English family on holiday, maintaining that the old farmer exemplified the misunderstandings between town and country people.

Giordano Luca (c.1634–1705). Italian Baroque painter. He was active in Florence in the 1680s. In 1692 he was summoned to Spain by Charles II and painted ceilings in the Escorial palace for the next ten years.

In Florence, Giordano painted a ceiling in the Palazzo Medici-Riccardi 1682–83. He also produced altarpieces and frescoes for churches. His work shows a variety of influences, including Paolo Veronese, and tends to be livelier than that of earlier Baroque painters.

Giorgione da Castelfranco (Giorgio Barbarelli) (c. 1475–1510). Italian Renaissance painter. He was active in Venice, and was probably trained by Giovanni Bellini. His work greatly influenced Titian and other Venetian painters. His subjects are imbued with a sense of mystery and treated with a soft technique, reminiscent of Leonardo da Vinci's later works, as in *The Tempest* 1504 (Accademia, Venice). He created the Renaissance poetic landscape, with rich colours and a sense of intimacy; an example is the *Sleeping Venus*, about 1510 (Gemäldegalerie, Dresden), a work which may have been completed by Titian. Giorgione died of the plague 1510.

In 1500, at the age of 23, he was chosen to paint portraits of the Doge Agostino Barberigo and the *condottiere* Consalvo Ferrante. He decorated the façades of several Venetian palaces, working with Titian on that of the Fondaco dei Tedeschi, when it was rebuilt 1504. He is described by Vasari as a person of social charm, a musician and a romantic lover. Vasari speaks of Sebastiano del Piombo and Titian as his 'disciples'.

Four pictures are generally accepted as certainly his: the Castelfranco altarpiece, the *Three Philosophers* (Vienna), the *Portrait of a Lady* (Vienna) and *The Tempest* (or *Storm*) (Venice, Accademia). To these are added with probability the *Judith* (Leningrad), *Portrait of a Young Man* (Berlin), *Venus* (Dresden), *Madonna with Saints* (Prado), *Christ and the Adulteress* (Glasgow), the *Judgment of Solomon* (Kingston Lacy), the *Concert Champêtre* (Louvre) and *Concert* (Florence, Pitti).

Suggested reading
Baldass, Ludwig *Giorgione* (1965)
Freeberg, S J *Painting in Italy 1500–1600* (1975)
Pignatti, T *Giorgione* (1971)
Wind, Edgar *Giorgione's Tempesta* (1969)
Zampetti, Pietro *The Complete Paintings of Giorgione* (1970)

Giotto di Bondone (*c.* 1267–1337). Italian painter and architect. His influence on the development of painting in Europe was profound. He broke away from the conventions of International Gothic and introduced a naturalistic style, painting saints as real people, life-like and expressive; an enhanced sense of volume and space also characterizes his work. He painted cycles of frescoes in churches at Assisi, Florence, and Padua.

Giotto was born in Vespignano, north of Florence. The interior of the Arena Chapel, Padua, was covered by him in a fresco cycle (completed by 1306) illustrating the life of Mary and the life of Jesus. Giotto's figures occupy a definite pictorial space, and there is an unusual emotional intensity and dignity in the presentation of the story. In one of the frescoes he made the Star of Bethlehem appear as a comet; Halley's comet had appeared 1303, just two years before.

From 1334 he was official architect to the city of Florence and from 1335 overseer of works at the cathedral; he designed the campanile, which was completed after his death by Andrea Pisano.

Suggested reading
Barasch, M *Giotto and the Language of Gesture* (1987)
Baxandall, Michael *Giotto and the Orators* (1971)
Cole, B *Giotto and Florentine Painting, 1200–1375* (1976)
Eimerl, S *The World of Giotto* (1967)
Martindale, A *The Complete Paintings of Giotto* (1969)
White, J *Art and Architecture in Italy, 1250–1400* (1966)

The sun has set; no night has followed.

GIRALDUS CAMBRENSIS
referring (1189) to the succession of Richard I
to the English throne on the death of Henry II.

Giraldus Cambrensis (Welsh *Gerallt Gymro*) (*c.* 1146–*c.* 1220). Welsh historian, born in Pembrokeshire. He was elected bishop of St Davids in 1198. He wrote a history of the conquest of Ireland by Henry II, and *Itinerarium Cambriae/Journey through Wales* 1191.

Girardon François (1628–1715). French academic sculptor. His *Apollo Tended by Nymphs*, commissioned 1666, is one of several marble groups sculpted for the gardens of Louis XIV's palace at Versailles.

Giraud Henri Honoré (1879–1949). French general. He put up stiff resistance to the German invasion of France but was captured and imprisoned by the Germans 1940–42, when he escaped to Algiers. He succeeded Admiral Darlan as local commander of the Free French in Algiers Dec 1942. He became co-president, with de Gaulle, of the National Committee for Liberation May 1943 and was made commander in chief of the French Army, liberating Corsica Sept 1943. However, de Gaulle's political manoeuvring led to him resigning his co-presidency Oct 1943 and his command in N Africa April 1944.

Faithful women are all alike, they think only of their fidelity, never of their husbands.

JEAN GIRAUDOUX
Amphitryon 38 1929

Giraudoux (Hippolyte) Jean (1882–1944). French playwright and novelist. He wrote the plays *Amphitryon 38* 1929 and *La Folle de Chaillot/The Madwoman of Chaillot* 1945. His novels include *Suzanne et la Pacifique/Suzanne and the Pacific* 1921, *Eglantine* 1927,

and *Les Aventures de Jérôme Bardini* 1930. His other plays include *La Guerre de Troie n'aura pas lieu/Tiger at the Gates* 1935.

Girtin Thomas (1775–1802). English painter of watercolour landscapes. His work is characterized by broad washes of strong colour and bold compositions, for example *The White House at Chelsea* 1800 (Tate Gallery, London). He was a friend of J M W Turner.

To views of the English countryside, such as *View on the Wharfe*, he added, 1801–02, some excellent views of Paris (subsequently made into soft-ground etchings), and on his return from his Parisian visit worked on a panorama of London (the *Eidometropolis*). Six sketches for this work are preserved in the British Museum. Though he died of tuberculosis at the age of 27, he made an important contribution to the development of English watercolour painting.

Giscard d'Estaing Valéry (1926–). French conservative politician, president 1974–81. He was finance minister to de Gaulle 1962–66 and Pompidou 1969–74. As leader of the Union pour la Démocratie Française, which he formed in 1978, Giscard sought to project himself as leader of a 'new centre'.

Giscard was active in the wartime Resistance. After a distinguished academic career, he worked in the Ministry of Finance and entered the National Assembly for Puy de Dôme in 1956 as an Independent Republican. After Pompidou's death he was narrowly elected president in 1974, in difficult economic circumstances; he was defeated by the socialist Mitterrand in 1981. He returned to the National Assembly in 1984. In 1989 he resigned from the National Assembly to play a leading role in the European Parliament.

Lionel Barrymore first played my grandfather, later my father, and finally, he played my husband. If he'd lived, I'm sure I'd have played his mother. That's the way it is in Hollywood. The men get younger and the women get older.

LILLIAN GISH
quoted in *Film Yearbook* 1984

Gish Lillian Diana. Stage name of Lillian de Guiche (1899–1993). US film and stage actress. She worked with the director D W Griffith, playing virtuous heroines in *Way Down East* and *Orphans of the Storm* both 1920. Deceptively fragile, she made a notable Hester in Victor Sjöström's *The Scarlet Letter* 1926 (based on the novel by Nathaniel Hawthorne). Her career continued well into the 1980s with films such as *The Whales of August* 1987.

Gish appeared in over 100 films. Her pure style was far removed from the gesticulation often thought of as silent film acting. She was renowned for the lengths to which she was prepared to go in pursuit of physical conviction; she deprived herself of food and water for several days to make her death scene in *La Boheme* 1924 look authentic. She was the sister of the actress *Dorothy Gish* (1898–1968).

Gissing George Robert (1857–1903). English writer. His work deals with social issues. Among his books are *New Grub Street* 1891, about a writer whose marriage breaks up, and the autobiographical *Private Papers of Henry Ryecroft* 1903.

He was born in Yorkshire, and taught for many years in London and the USA. His first novel, *Workers in the Dawn*, appeared 1880. Between 1885 and 1895 he wrote 14 novels including *The Odd Woman* which is about early feminists, and *The Nether World* about the London poor.

Giugiaro Giorgio (1938–). Italian industrial designer. He established himself internationally as an independent automotive designer with his Volkswagen Golf car 1973, the popular successor to the Beetle. He went on to create other memorable automotive designs as well as a large number of diverse products, including cameras for Nikon in the late 1970s. His design for a pasta shape 1983, dubbed 'Marielle', confirmed his role as a universal 'form-giver'.

Giulini Carlo Maria (1914–). Italian conductor. He was joint musical director of the Los Angeles Philharmonic Orchestra

1978–84. As principal conductor at La Scala, Milan, 1953–55 he worked with Maria Callas, Zeffirelli, and Visconti. He is noted for interpretations of Verdi, Bach, Mozart, and Beethoven, blending Italian lyricism with the austere monumentality of the German tradition.

At Milan Radio 1946–51 he revived rare operas by Scarlatti, Malapiero, and Bartók; his 1951 radio production of Haydn's opera *Il mondo della luna/The World on the Moon* 1777 attracted Toscanini who recommended his appointment at La Scala.

Giulio Romano (born Giulio Pippi) (*c.* 1499–1546). Italian painter and architect. An assistant to Raphael, he developed a Mannerist style, creating effects of exaggerated movement and using rich colours, for example the frescoes in the Palazzo del Tè, Mantua, begun 1526.

Givenchy Hubert James Marcel Taffin de (1927–). French fashion designer. His simple, reasonably priced mix-and-match blouses, skirts, and slacks earned him instant acclaim when he opened his couture house in Paris 1952. He was noted for his embroidered and printed fabrics and his imaginative use of accessories.

At 17 Givenchy was apprenticed to Parisian designer Jacques Fath and spent eight years working for other designers, including Elsa Schiaparelli. In the 1960s he designed both screen and personal wardrobes for Audrey Hepburn, creating for her the princess dress of the 1961 film *Breakfast at Tiffany's*.

Glackens William James (1870–1938). US painter. He was a member of the Ashcan School and one of 'the Eight', a group of Realists who exhibited at New York's Macbeth Gallery 1908. Glackens' painting eventually evolved into a Realism that was strongly influenced by Impressionism. He painted subjects from everyday urban life, as well as those from fashionable society.

Born in Philadelphia, he studied at the Pennsylvania Academy of Fine Arts under Robert Henri.

Gladstone William Ewart (1809–1898). British Liberal politician, repeatedly prime minister. He entered Parliament as a Tory in 1833 and held ministerial office, but left the party 1846 and after 1859 identified himself with the Liberals. He was chancellor of the Exchequer 1852–55 and 1859–66, and prime minister 1868–74, 1880–85, 1886, and 1892–94. He introduced elementary education 1870 and vote by secret ballot 1872 and many reforms in Ireland, although he failed in his efforts to get a Home Rule Bill passed.

Gladstone was born in Liverpool, the son of a rich merchant. In Peel's government he was president of the Board of Trade 1843–45, and colonial secretary 1845–46. He left the Tory Party with the Peelite group in 1846. He was chancellor of the Exchequer in Aberdeen's government 1852–55 and in the Liberal governments of Palmerston and Russell 1859–66. In his first term as·prime minister he carried through a series of reforms, including the disestablishment of the Church of Ireland, the Irish Land Act, and the abolition of the purchase of army commissions and of religious tests in the universities.

Gladstone strongly resisted Disraeli's imperialist and pro-Turkish policy during the latter's government of 1874–80, not least because of Turkish pogroms against subject Christians, and by his Midlothian campaign of 1879 helped to overthrow Disraeli. Gladstone's second government carried the second Irish Land Act and the Reform Act 1884 but was confronted with problems in Ireland, Egypt, and South Africa, and lost prestige through its failure to relieve General Gordon. Returning to office in 1886, Gladstone introduced his first Home Rule Bill, which was defeated by the secession of the Liberal Unionists, and he thereupon resigned. After six years' opposition he formed his last government; his second Home Rule Bill was rejected by the Lords, and in 1894 he resigned. He led a final crusade against the massacre of Armenian Christians in 1896.

Suggested reading
Adelman, Paul *Gladstone, Disraeli and Later Victorian Politics* (1970)
Checkland, S G *The Gladstones: A Family Biography* (1971)
Feuchtwanger, E J *Gladstone* (1975)

Jenkins, Roy *Gladstone* (1995)
Magnus, P *Gladstone* (1954)
Marlow, J *Mr and Mrs Gladstone: An Intimate Biography* (1977)
Matthew, H C G *Gladstone 1809–1874* (1986)
Matthew, H C G *Gladstone 1875–1898* (1995)
Morley, John *Life of Gladstone* (3 vols 1903)
Shannon, Richard *Gladstone I: 1809–1865* (1982)
Salter, Richard (ed) *Peel, Gladstone and Disraeli* (1991)
Shannon, Richard *Gladstone 1809–1865* (1982)
Winstanley, Michael *Gladstone and the Liberal Party* (1990)

Glanville Ranalf (died 1190). English justiciar from 1180 and legal writer. His *Treatise on the Laws and Customs of England* 1188 was written to instruct practising lawyers and judges and is now a historical source on medieval common law.

Glaser Donald Arthur (1926–). US physicist who invented the bubble chamber for detecting high-energy elementary particles in 1952, for which he received the Nobel Prize for Physics 1960. Glaser's first bubble chamber consisted of a vessel only a few centimetres across, containing superheated liquid ether under pressure. When the pressure was released suddenly, particles traversing the chamber left tracks consisting of streams of small bubbles formed when the ether boiled locally; the tracks were photographed using a high-speed camera. In later, larger bubble chambers, liquid hydrogen was substituted for ether.

In 1957 he became professor at the University of Michigan, moving 1959 to the University of California. In the early 1960s he turned from physics to molecular biology.

Glasgow Ellen Anderson Gholson (1873–1945). US novelist. Her books, set mainly in her native Virginia, often deal with the survival of tough heroines in a world of adversity and include *Barren Ground* 1925, *The Sheltered Life* 1932, *Vein of Iron* 1935, and *In This Our Life* 1941 (Pulitzer Prize).

Suggested reading
Auchincloss, Louis *Ellen Glasgow* (1964)
Glasgow, Ellen *The Woman Within* (autobiography) (1954)
Wagner, Linda *Ellen Glasgow: Beyond Convention* (1982)

Glashow Sheldon Lee· (1932–). US particle physicist. In 1964 he proposed the existence of a fourth, 'charmed' quark, and later argued that quarks must be coloured. Insights gained from these theoretical studies enabled Glashow to consider ways in which the weak nuclear force and the electromagnetic force (two of the fundamental forces of nature) could be unified as a single force now called the electroweak force. For this work he shared the Nobel Prize for Physics 1979 with Abdus Salam and Steven Weinberg. He worked at the Niels Bohr Institute in Copenhagen before becoming professor at Harvard 1967.

Glass Philip (1937–). US composer. As a student of Nadia Boulanger, he was strongly influenced by Indian music; his work is characterized by repeated rhythmic figures that are continually expanded and modified. His compositions include the operas *Einstein on the Beach* 1976, *Akhnaten* 1984, *The Making of the Representative for Planet 8* 1988, and the *'Low' Symphony* 1992 on themes from David Bowie's *Low* album.

Glasse Hannah (1708–1770). British cookery writer whose *The Art of Cookery made Plain and Easy* 1747 is regarded as the first classic recipe book in Britain.

Glauber Johann Rudolf (1604–1670). German chemist who about 1625 discovered the salt known variously as *Glauber's salt* and *'sal mirabile'* (sodium sulphate). He made his living selling patent medicines and used the salt to treat almost any complaint. Glauber investigated and developed processes that could have industrial application. He prepared nitric acid by substituting saltpetre (potassium nitrate) for salt in the reaction with sulphuric acid. He made many metal chlorides and nitrates from the mineral acids, and produced organic liquids containing such solvents as acetone (dimethylketone) and benzene – although he did not identify them – by reacting and distilling natural substances such as wood, wine, and vegetable oils. The chemical techniques involved are described in his book *Opera omnia chymica* 1651–61. He outlined his views on a possible utopian future for Germany in *Teutschlands-Wohlfahrt/ Germany's Prosperity*.

Glauber was born in Karlstadt, Franconia, and was self-educated. After many years of travelling in Europe, he settled in Amsterdam 1655 and built a chemical laboratory there.

Glazunov Alexander Konstantinovich (1865–1936). Russian composer. He achieved fame with his first symphony, which was written when he was only 17. He absorbed a range of influences, from his teacher Rimsky-Korsakov's orchestrational skill to Tchaikovsky's lyricism. His own style fits between that of the Russian national school of The Five and that of the Western European 'cosmopolitan' composers. He made a significant impact as a teacher on the following generation of composers, including Prokofiev and Shostakovich.

Gleizes Albert (1881–1953). French Cubist painter and theorist. He is chiefly remembered for his pioneering book *De Cubisme* 1912, written with Jean Metzinger (1883–1956). Influenced initially by Picasso and Braque and later by Robert Delaunay, Gleizes painted in an exuberant manner, filling the entire canvas with tilting, interpenetrating planes, as in *Harvest Threshing* 1912 (Solomon R Guggenheim Museum, New York).

He helped found the *Section d'Or* in Paris 1912–14, an exhibition society for disseminating the work of Cubist painters, and was greatly inspired by his visits to the USA in 1915 and 1917–18, producing *On Brooklyn Bridge* 1917 (Solomon R Guggenheim Museum, New York).

Glendower Owen (Welsh Owain Glyndwr) (*c.* 1359–*c.* 1416). Welsh nationalist leader of a successful revolt against the English in N Wales, who defeated Henry IV in three campaigns 1400–02, although Wales was reconquered 1405–13. Glendower disappeared 1416 after some years of guerrilla warfare.

Glass *Philip Glass revolutionized opera in the 1980s. His music appealed to a younger, wider audience, and was performed both in opera houses and at pop concerts.*

Suggested reading
Davies, R R *The Revolt of Owain Glyndwr* (1995)

Glenn John Herschel (1921–). US astronaut and politician. On 20 Feb 1962, he became the first American to orbit the Earth, doing so three times in the Mercury spacecraft *Friendship 7*, in a flight lasting 4 hr 55 min. After retiring from NASA, he was elected to the US Senate as a Democrat from Ohio 1974; re-elected 1980 and 1986. He unsuccessfully sought the Democratic presidential nomination 1984.

As a senator, he advocated nuclear-arms-production limitations and increased aid to education and job-skills programmes.

Glinka Mikhail Ivanovich (1804–1857). Russian composer. He broke away from the prevailing Italian influence and turned to Russian folk music as the inspiration for his opera *A Life for the Tsar* (originally *Ivan Susanin*) 1836. His later works include the opera *Ruslan and Lyudmila* 1842 and the instrumental fantasia *Kamarinskaya* 1848.

Gloucester Richard Alexander Walter George, Duke of Gloucester (1944–). Prince of the UK. Grandson of George V, he succeeded his father to the dukedom when his elder brother Prince William (1941–1972) was killed in an air crash. In 1972 he married Birgitte van Deurs (1946–), daughter of a Danish lawyer. His heir is his son Alexander, Earl of Ulster (1974–).

Glover Denis (1912–1980). New Zealand poet. A member of the influential Phoenix group in the 1930s, he was first noted for impudently satirical works such as *Six Easy Ways of Dodging Debt Collectors* 1936 and *The Arraignment of Paris* 1937, lampooning some women poets. His unobtrusively well-crafted poems democratically shunned pretension and evinced sympathy with ordinary lives, the world of the pilot or engineer in *The Wind and the Sand* 1945 or of the unsuccessful gold prospector in his popular sequence *Arawata Bill* 1952.

Glover John (1767–1849). Australian pioneer landscape painter. Born in England, he emigrated to Australia at the age of 64 and settled in Tasmania, where in three years he produced 68 paintings, 'descriptive of the scenery and customs of Van Diemen's Land'. His *Australian Landscape with Cattle* (National Library, Canberra) sensitively depicts sprawling gum trees and grey-green ranges, while also bringing to the Australian bush the feeling of 'a Gentleman's Park in England'.

Glubb John Bagot (known as Glubb Pasha) (1897–1986). British military commander.

Glubb was a member of the Royal Engineers in World War I, and in 1920 volunteered for service in Iraq. On Iraqi independence 1930, he went to Transjordan as second in command of the Arab Legion (the Jordanian army), taking over as commander from 1939. Under his leadership the Legion grew in number from 1,000 to 9,000, becoming the most powerful Arab military force. The Legion distinguished itself during World War II. Glubb was dismissed by King Hussein 1956. Knighted 1956.

There is no musical rule that I have not willingly sacrificed to dramatic effect.

GLUCK
Preface to *Alceste* 1767

Gluck Christoph Willibald von (1714–1787). German composer. He settled in Vienna as kapellmeister to Maria Theresa 1754. In 1762 his *Orfeo ed Euridice/Orpheus and Eurydice* revolutionized the 18th-century conception of opera by giving free scope to dramatic effect. *Orfeo* was followed by *Alceste/Alcestis* 1767 and *Paride ed Elena/Paris and Helen* 1770.

Born in Erasbach, Bavaria, he studied music at Prague, Vienna, and Milan, and went to London 1745 to compose operas for the Haymarket but returned to Vienna 1746 where he was knighted by the pope.

In 1762 his *Iphigénie en Aulide/Iphigenia in Aulis* 1774, produced in Paris, brought to a head the fierce debate over the future of opera in

Glyn *British author Elinor Glyn. Her novels were immensely popular in the 1920s and 1930s, despite their dubious literary value, largely because of their risqué themes. She popularized the use of the term 'It' to describe sex appeal. (Image Select)*

which Gluck's French style had the support of Marie Antoinette while his Italian rival Nicolò Piccinni (1728–1800) had the support of Madame Du Barry. With *Armide* 1777 and *Iphigénie en Tauride/Iphigenia in Tauris* 1779 Gluck won a complete victory over Piccinni.

Suggested reading
Einstein, Alfred *Gluck* (trs 1936, rep 1973)
Howard, Patricia *Gluck and the Birth of Modern Opera* (1963)

Glyn Elinor (born Sutherland) (1864–1943). British writer. Her novel of an exotic love affair, *Three Weeks* 1907, scandalized Edwardian society.

I don't particularly like your voice, but when you sing I forget to play.

Orchestral player on TITO GOBBI
in Gobbi *My Life* 1979

Gobbi Tito (1913–1984). Italian baritone singer. His vibrant bel canto was allied to a resourceful talent for verismo characterization in Italian opera, notably Verdi and Puccini, and as Figaro in *Le Nozze di Figaro/The Marriage of Figaro*.

Gobind Singh (1666–1708). Indian religious leader, the tenth and last guru (teacher) of Sikhism, 1675–1708, and founder of the Sikh brotherhood known as the Khalsa. On his death, the Sikh holy book, the *Guru Granth Sahib*, replaced the line of human gurus as the teacher and guide of the Sikh community.

During a period of Sikh persecution, Gobind Singh asked those who were willing to die for their faith to join him. The first five willing to risk their lives were named the *panj pyares* 'faithful ones' by him and proclaimed the first members of the Khalsa. He also introduced the names Singh (lion) for male Sikhs, and Kaur (princess) for female Sikhs.

Godard Jean-Luc (1930–   ). French film director. He was one of the leaders of New Wave cinema. His works are often characterized by experimental editing techniques and an unconventional dramatic form. His films include *A bout de souffle/Breathless* 1959, *Vivre sa Vie/It's My Life* 1962, *Weekend* 1968, *Sauve qui peut (la vie)/Slow Motion* 1980, and *Je vous salue, Marie/Hail Mary* 1985. His other films include *Pierrot le fou* 1965.

Goddard Paulette. Stage name of Marion Levy (1911–1990). US film actress. She starred with comedian Charlie Chaplin (to whom she was married 1936–42) in *Modern Times* 1936 and *The Great Dictator* 1940, and her other films include the British-made version of Oscar Wilde's play *An Ideal Husband* 1948.

Goddard Robert Hutchings (1882–1945). US rocket pioneer. His first liquid-fuelled rocket was launched at Auburn, Massachusetts, in 1926. By 1935 his rockets had gyroscopic control and carried cameras to record instrument readings. Two years later a Goddard rocket gained the world altitude record with an ascent of 3 km/1.9 mi.

Goddard developed the principle of combining liquid fuels in a rocket motor, the technique used subsequently in every practical space vehicle. He was the first to prove by actual test that a rocket will work in a vacuum and he was the first to fire a rocket faster than the speed of sound.

Gödel Kurt (1906–1978). Austrian-born US mathematician and philosopher. He proved that a mathematical system always contains statements that can be neither proved nor disproved within the system; in other words, as a science, mathematics can never be totally

Godard *French film director Jean-Luc Godard. One of the leaders of the French New Wave of cinema directors of the 1950s and 1960s, he made his reputation with* A Bout de souffle/Breathless *1959 and* Pierrot le fou *1965. His films became increasingly experimental as he sought to create a cinema that was concerned both with itself as a self-conscious medium and also with the undermining of capitalism.*

consistent and totally complete. He worked on relativity, constructing a mathematical model of the universe that made travel back through time theoretically possible.

Gödel was born in Brünn, Moravia (now Brno in the Czech Republic) and educated at the University of Vienna, where he worked until 1938. When Austria was annexed by Nazi Germany, he emigrated to the USA. He settled at Princeton, where he was appointed professor 1953.

In 1930, Gödel showed that a particular logical system (predicate calculus of the first order) was such that every valid formula could be proved within the system; in other words, the system was what mathematicians call complete. He then investigated a much larger logical system – that constructed by English philosophers Bertrand Russell and Alfred Whitehead as the logical basis of mathematics. The resultant paper, 'On formally undecidable propositions of *Principia Mathematica* and related systems' 1931, is the one in which Gödel dashed the hopes of philosophers and mathematicians alike.

Godfrey de Bouillon (c. 1060–1100). French crusader, second son of Count Eustace II of Boulogne. He and his brothers, Baldwin I and Eustace, led 40,000 Germans in the First Crusade 1096. When Jerusalem was taken 1099, he was elected its ruler, but refused the title of king. After his death, Baldwin was elected king.

Tennyson's handling [of the legend] ... is one of the many indications that the nineteenth century is in some ways more remote from us than the eleventh.

> Richard Fletcher on GODGIFU or Lady GODIVA
> *Who's Who in Roman Britain and Anglo-Saxon England* 1989

Godiva or Godgifu, Lady (c. 1040–1080). Wife of Leofric, Earl of Mercia (died 1057). Legend has it that her husband promised to reduce the heavy taxes on the people of Coventry if she rode naked through the streets at noon. The grateful citizens remained indoors as she did so, but 'Peeping Tom' bored a hole in his shutters and was struck blind.

Godkin Edwin Lawrence (1831–1902). Irish-born US editor and writer on political affairs who founded the liberal weekly magazine *The Nation* 1865.

There will not be a poor man in my Tsardom! ... Even to my last shirt I will share with all.

> BORIS GODUNOV
> at his coronation Moscow 1 Sept 1598

Godunov Boris Fyodorovich (1552–1605). Tsar of Russia from 1598, elected after the death of Fyodor I, son of Ivan the Terrible. He was assassinated by a pretender to the throne who professed to be Dmitri, a brother of Fyodor and the rightful heir. The legend that has grown up around this forms the basis of Pushkin's play *Boris Godunov* 1831 and Mussorgsky's opera of the same name 1874.

An apocryphal story of Boris killing the true Dmitri in order to gain the throne was fostered by Russian historians anxious to discredit Boris because he was not descended from the main ruling families. Godunov's rule was marked by a strengthening of the Russian church. It was also the beginning of the Time of Troubles, a period of instability.

Godwin Earl of Wessex from 1020. He secured the succession to the throne in 1042 of Edward the Confessor, to whom he married his daughter Edith, and whose chief minister he became. King Harold II was his son.

Godwin Edward William (1833–1886). English architect. His reputation was established by his competition-winning Gothic Revival design for Northampton Town Hall 1861. However, his style was at its most original in his domestic buildings. His White House in Tite Street, Chelsea, London, 1877–79, designed for the painter James Whistler (now demolished), suggested Japanese influence with its varied façade and startlingly simple interior of bare, plain-coloured walls.

This jostling, upstart clan [Godwin and his six sons] ... the Kennedys of the eleventh century.

> Richard Fletcher on GODWIN, EARL OF WESSEX
> in *Who's Who in Roman Britain and Anglo-Saxon England* 1989

Godwin William (1756–1836). English philosopher, novelist, and father of the writer Mary Shelley. His *Enquiry concerning Political Justice* 1793 advocated an anarchic society based on a faith in people's essential rationality. At first a Nonconformist minister, he later became an atheist. His first wife was Mary Wollstonecraft.

Godwin was born in Wisbech, East Anglia, and studied at the Dissenting Academy, Hoxton, London. He became an active campaigner for civil liberties and eventually a publisher of children's books. *Enquiry concerning Political Justice, and its Influence on General Virtue and Happiness* was written as part of the debate about the French Revolution.

His philosophical outlook was deterministic, yet he believed that people should increase their awareness of moral choices. Morality was defined by reference to the greatest general good, and he argued that selfish actions bring less pleasure than benevolent ones. His adventure thriller *Caleb Williams* 1794 promoted his views. *The Enquirer* 1797 contains essays on education and economics. Other works include the novels *St Leon* 1799, *Fleetwood* 1805, and *Mandeville* 1817, biographies of Mary Wollstonecraft 1798 and Geoffrey Chaucer 1803, a number of political pamphlets, and *The History of the Commonwealth* 1824–28.

Goebbels (Paul) Joseph (1897–1945). German Nazi leader. As minister of propaganda from 1933, he brought all cultural and

Goebbels *Josef Goebbels, German Nazi minister of propaganda under Hitler. Exempted from military service through a foot deformity, he attended eight universities before drifting into the Nazi party. There his ambition and ruthlessness and his skill in public relations made him second in power only to Hitler himself.*

Goering *Nazi leader Hermann Goering. Creator of the Luftwaffe and founder of concentration camps and the Gestapo, Goering was found guilty of war crimes at the Nuremberg trials but committed suicide rather than face execution.* (Image Select)

educational activities under Nazi control and built up sympathetic movements abroad to carry on the 'war of nerves' against Hitler's intended victims. On the capture of Berlin by the Allies, he poisoned himself.

He was born in the Rhineland, became a journalist, joined the Nazi party 1924 when it was still in its early days, and was given control of its propaganda 1929. He was totally committed to Nazism and as minister of propaganda his organizational abilities and oratory were major factors in disseminating the party line throughout Germany and abroad. He was appointed special plenipotentiary for total war Aug 1944 and was granted powers to draft any able-bodied person in the Reich into war work. In the final days of Berlin he moved into the Führerbunker, poisoned his six children, and then ordered an SS officer to shoot him and his wife.

We can manage without butter but not, for example, without guns. If we are attacked we can only defend ourselves with guns not with butter.

JOSEPH GOEBBELS
Speech in Berlin 17 Jan 1936

His swift reaction to the 1944 July Plot was instrumental in preventing the anti-Nazi conspirators gaining any advantage. He fomented the myth of the last-ditch 'National Redoubt' and the 'Werewolf' resistance organization which gave many Allied leaders sleepless nights and led to complex military tactical dispositions to deal with threats which never actually existed.

Goehr (Peter) Alexander (1932–). German-born English composer. He was professor of music at Cambridge from 1976. A lyrical but often hard-edged serialist, he nevertheless usually remained within the forms of the symphony and traditional chamber works, and more recently turned to tonal and even Neo-Baroque models. Works include the opera *Arden muss sterben/Arden Must Die* 1966, the music theatre piece *Naboth's Vineyard* 1968, and *Metamorphosis/Dance* 1974.

Goeppert-Mayer Maria (born Goeppert) (1906–1972). German-born US physicist who studied the structure of the atomic nucleus. Her explanation of the stability of particular atoms 1948 envisaged atomic nuclei as shell-like layers of protons and neutrons, with the most stable atoms having completely filled outermost shells. She shared the 1963 Nobel Prize for Physics with Eugene Wigner and Hans Jensen.

Goeppert was born in Kattowitz, Upper Silesia (now Katowice in Poland) and studied at Göttingen. Emigrating to the USA 1930, she was professor at Chicago 1946–60 and at the University of California from 1960.

In 1945, Goeppert-Mayer developed a 'little bang' theory of cosmic origin with US physicist Edward Teller to explain element and isotope abundances in the universe. This led her to study the stability of nuclei. In 1948, she published evidence of the special stability of the following numbers of protons and neutrons: 2, 8, 20, 50, 82 and 126. These are commonly called magic numbers. She and Jensen independently proposed a shell model, and in 1955 they wrote a book together, *Elementary Theory of Nuclear Shell Structure.*

When I hear the word culture I reach for my pistol

HERMANN GOERING
Attributed *c.* 1935

Goering Hermann Wilhelm (1893–1946). Nazi leader, German field marshal from 1938. He was part of Hitler's inner circle, and with Hitler's rise to power was appointed commissioner for aviation from 1933 and built up the Luftwaffe (airforce). He built a vast economic empire in occupied Europe, but later lost favour and was expelled from the party in 1945. Tried at Nuremberg for war crimes, he poisoned himself before he could be executed.

Goering was born in Bavaria. He was a renowned fighter pilot in World War I, and joined the Nazi party in 1922. He was elected to the Reichstag in 1928 and became its president in 1932. He was appointed minister of the interior for Prussia 1933. This position gave him full control of the police and security forces; he organized the Gestapo and had the first concentration camps built then handed control to the SS to enable him to concentrate on developing the Luftwaffe. He supervised the four-year economic plan to ready the country for war 1935–39. The Luftwaffe's failure to break the British air defences was a serious blow to his reputation from which he never really recovered and he retired to his country estate 1942.

Goes Hugo van der, Flemish painter. He was chiefly active in Ghent. His *Portinari Altarpiece* about 1475 (Uffizi, Florence) is a huge oil painting of the Nativity, full of symbolism and naturalistic detail, while his *Death of the Virgin*, about 1480 (Musée Communale des Beaux Arts, Bruges), is remarkable for the varied expressions on the faces of the apostles.

One of the greatest 15th-century masters, he began with small panels warmly coloured and detailed in the van Eyck fashion, but from about 1474 he worked on a larger scale, using cool and translucent colour and often expressing great emotional intensity. His most famous work is the *Portinari Altarpiece*, executed for the agent of the Medici at Bruges, Tommaso Portinari. It made a great impression on the Florentines, being closely studied by Ghirlandaio, while its author was favourably mentioned by Vasari. Other works are the *Adoration of the Magi* (Berlin), *Death of the Virgin* (Bruges) and *Monk meditating* (New York, Metropolitan Museum). He became a monk in the Roode-Clooster, Brussels, 1475 but continued to paint, though suffering intermittently in the last years of his life from fits of severe depression.

Goethe Johann Wolfgang von (1749–1832). German poet, novelist, dramatist, and scholar. He is generally considered the founder of modern German literature, and was the leader of the Romantic *Sturm und Drang* movement. His works include the autobiographical *Die Leiden des Jungen Werthers/The Sorrows of the Young Werther* 1774 and the poetic play *Faust* 1808 and 1832, his masterpiece.

Among his interests were geology, the occult, physics, philosophy, biology, comparative anatomy, and optics. His many works – in poetry, drama, fiction, and science – made him known throughout Europe. Between 1775 and 1785 he served as prime minister at the court of Weimar. A visit to Italy 1786–88 inspired the classical dramas *Iphigenie auf Tauris/Iphigenia in Tauris* 1787 and *Torquato Tasso* 1790. Other works include the *Wilhelm Meister* novels 1795–1829, the short novel *Die Wahlverwandschaften/Elective Affinities* 1809, and *Farbenlehre/Treatise on Colour* 1810.

Suggested reading
Boyle, N *Goethe: Faust, Part 1* (1987)
Diekmann, L *Johann Wolfgang Goethe* (1974)

Goethe, J W *Poetry and Truth* (autobiography, several translations) (1811–1814)
Gray, R *Goethe: A Critical Introduction* (1967)
Reed, T *Goethe* (1984)

Goff Bruce Alonzo (1904–1982). US architect. His work is frequently described as 'organic' in form. Initially influenced by Frank Lloyd Wright, he later developed a highly individual approach, characterized by unlikely combinations of materials and styles. His most striking project is the Bavinger House, Oklahoma, 1949, composed of a spiralling wall of stone with a steel mast at its centre; 'living bowls' and a staircase are suspended from the mast.

Although poetic in the expression of free-flowing space, the quality of his executed designs has been criticized.

Goffman Erving (1922–1982). Canadian social scientist. He studied the ways people try to create, present, and defend a self-image within the social structures surrounding, controlling, and defining human interaction. He analysed the ways people behave in public places, for example. His works include *The Presentation of Self in Everyday Life* 1956, *Gender Advertisements* 1979, and *Forms of Talk* 1981.

Gogarty Oliver St John (1878–1957). Irish writer. A successful Dublin physician, he was a member of the literary circle which included Yeats, George Moore, and Joyce, and figures in *Ulysses* as Buck Mulligan. A wit and a poet, he wrote several books, including the autobiographical *As I was going down Sackville Street* 1937. He took an active interest in Irish politics, being a senator of the Irish Free State 1922–36.

Gogh Vincent Willem van (1853–1890). Dutch Post-Impressionist painter. He tried various careers, including preaching, and began painting in the 1880s, his early works often being sombre depictions of peasant life, such as *The Potato Eaters* 1885 (Van Gogh Museum, Amsterdam). Influenced by both the Impressionists and Japanese prints, he developed a freer style characterized by intense colour and expressive brushwork, as seen in his *Sunflowers* series 1888. Both the number and the splendour of his pictures produced during a short and unhappy life remain astonishing, and his influence on modern art in the conception of colour and individual expression has been immense.

He was the son of a Dutch pastor. He did not take to art seriously until he was 27, having by that time failed in various projected careers, in the firm of Goupil & Co, art dealers at The Hague and in London and Paris, as an usher in schools at Ramsgate and Isleworth, and as lay preacher among the miners of the Borinage. The first stage of his career as artist may be dated 1880–86 in Holland and Belgium. Supported by an allowance from his brother Theo, he took drawing lessons in Brussels, was with his uncle Anton Mauve for a while at The Hague, and for a year in the Academy at Antwerp. *The Potato-Eaters* of 1885 was the remarkable product of this period. There follows the Paris period, 1886–88, in which he was much influenced by Japanese prints, by Impressionism and the division of colour as practised by Seurat and Signac. His famous *Boots* was a last effort in his early dark, proletarian style; his new sense of colour and design found wonderful expression at Arles 1888, to which period belong such famous pictures as his views of Arles, *The Drawbridge, Orchard in Blossom, Boats at Saintes-Maries, The Chair and Pipe, The Night Café, The Zouave Officer* and his several *Sunflowers*. Following the mental crisis of 1888, when after a quarrel with Gauguin he mutilated his ear, his genius struggled with the depression of mental illness and hospital surroundings. The year 1889 at St-Rémy produced his free copies after the works of various artists and his paintings of cypress trees; 1890 at Auvers-sur-Oise (with Dr Gachet), the last agitated paintings of cornfields before he shot himself. His letters to his brother Theo are an illuminating commentary on his work and ideas.

His numerous works (over 800 paintings and 700 drawings) include still lifes, portraits (also many self-portraits), and landscapes, including *The Starry Night* 1889 (Museum of Modern Art, New York) and *Crows over Wheatfield* 1890 (Van Gogh Museum, Amsterdam). The Arles paintings vividly testify to his intense

Gogh *A self-portrait of Vincent van Gogh, titled* Portrait of the Artist. (Image Select)

emotional involvement in his art; among them is *The Night Café* 1888 (Yale University Art Gallery, New Haven) of which he wrote 'I have tried to express with red and green the terrible passions of human nature'.

Suggested reading
Hammacher, A M and R *Van Gogh* (trs 1982)
McQuillan, Melissa *Van Gogh* (1989)
Pollock, Griselda and Orton, F *Vincent van Gogh: Artist of His Time* (1978)
Schapiro, Meyer *Van Gogh* (1950)
van Gogh, Vincent *Letters of Vincent van Gogh* (trs 1958)

Gogol Nicolai Vasilyevich (1809–1852). Russian writer. His first success was a collection of stories, *Evenings on a Farm near Dikanka* 1831–32, followed by *Mirgorod* 1835. Later works include *Arabesques* 1835, the comedy play *The Inspector General* 1836, and the picaresque novel *Dead Souls* 1842, which satirizes Russian provincial society.

Gogol was born near Poltava. He tried several careers before entering the St Petersburg civil service. From 1835 he travelled in Europe, and it was in Rome that he completed the earlier part of *Dead Souls* 1842. Other works include the short stories 'The Overcoat' and 'The Nose'.

Suggested reading
Nabokov, Vladimir *Nikolai Gogol* (1961)
Peace, Richard *The Enigma of Gogol* (1981)
Troyat, Henri *Gogol: The Biography of a Divided Soul* (trs 1974)

Goh Chok Tong (1941–). Singapore politician, prime minister from 1990. A trained economist, Goh became a member of Parliament for the ruling People's Action Party 1976. Rising steadily through the party ranks, he was appointed deputy prime minister 1985, and subsequently chosen by the cabinet as Lee Kuan Yew's successor, first as prime minister and from 1992 also as party leader.

Gokhale Gopal Krishna (1866–1915). Indian political adviser and friend of Mahatma Gandhi, leader of the Moderate group in the Indian National Congress before World War I.

Gold Thomas (1920–). Austrian-born US astronomer and physicist who in 1948 formulated, with Fred Hoyle and Hermann Bondi, the steady-state theory regarding the creation of the universe.

Gold was born in Vienna and studied at Cambridge. In 1956 he emigrated to the USA and became professor of astronomy at Harvard 1958 and at Cornell University from 1959. Gold has served as an adviser to NASA.

The steady-state theory assumes an expanding universe in which the density of matter remains constant because, as galaxies recede from one another, new matter is continually created (at an undetectably slow rate). The implications that follow are that galaxies are not all of the same age, and that the rate of recession is uniform. With the discovery in the 1960s of cosmic background radiation, the steady-state hypothesis was abandoned by most cosmologists in favour of the Big Bang model.

Goldberg Leo (1913–1981). US astrophysicist who carried out research into the composition of stellar atmospheres and the dynamics of the loss of mass from cool stars. His main subject of research was the Sun.

Goldberg was born in Brooklyn, New York, and studied at Harvard, where, after 23 years at the University of Michigan, he was professor 1960–73 and director of Harvard College Observatory 1966–71. From 1971 to 1977 he was director of the Kitt Peak National Observatory in Arizona.

At Harvard, Goldberg and his colleagues designed an instrument that could function either as a spectrograph or as a spectrohelio-graph (a device to photograph the Sun using monochromatic light). This formed part of the equipment of *Orbital Solar Observatory IV*, launched 1967. He has also carried out research on the temperature variations and chemical composition of the Sun and of its atmosphere, in which he succeeded in detecting carbon monoxide.

Goldberg Rube (Reuben Lucius) (1883–1970). US cartoonist whose most famous and widely read of his strips featured ridiculously complicated inventions. He produced several popular comic strips that were nationally syndicated from 1915. Goldberg also devoted time to political cartooning, winning a Pulitzer Prize 1948.

Goldberg Whoopi. Stage name of Caryn Johnson (1949–). US actress and comedienne. Having made her film debut in Spielberg's *The Color Purple* 1985, she starred in a number of lightweight comedies such as *Jumpin' Jack Flash* 1986 and *Fatal Beauty* 1987, but featured most successfully as the reluctant medium in *Ghost* 1990. Her *Sister Act* 1992, was one of the highest grossing films of that year, and led to *Sister Act 2* 1993.

She initially made her name as a stand-up comedienne during the early 1980s. Her other films include *The Telephone* 1988, *The Long Walk Home* 1990, and *Made in America* 1993.

Ralph wept for the end of innocence, the darkness of man's heart, and the fall through the air of the true, wise friend called Piggy.

WILLIAM GOLDING
Lord of the Flies penultimate paragraph 1954

Golding William Gerald (1911–1993). English novelist. His work is often principally concerned with the fundamental corruption and evil inherent in human nature. His first book, *Lord of the Flies* 1954, concerns the degeneration into savagery of a group of English schoolboys marooned on a Pacific island. *Pincher Martin* 1956 is a study of greed and self-delusion. Later novels include *The Spire* 1964 and *Darkness Visible* 1979. He was awarded the Nobel Prize for Literature 1983, and knighted 1988.

The Sea Trilogy, *Rites of Passage* 1980 (Booker Prize), *Close Quarters* 1987, and *Fire Down Below* 1989, tells the story of a voyage to Australia through the eyes of a callow young aristocrat. *Lord of the Flies*, although initially turned down by no less than 15 publishers, sold over 2 million copies in ten years. Translated into several languages, it became a cult book, especially in the USA, and remains a

prescribed text for many English literature courses. The film version, by Peter Brook 1962, was also highly successful.

Golding's novels were never about trivial or ephemeral matters. They dealt with universal themes and anxieties: evil, greed, guilt, primal instincts, and unknown forces.

Suggested reading
Carey, J (ed) *William Golding: The Man and his Books* (1986)
Crompton, D *A View from the Spire: William Golding's Later Novels* (1985)
Tiger, V *William Golding: The Dark Fields of Discovery* (1974)

The history of progress is written in the blood of men and women who have dared to espouse an unpopular cause, as, for instance, the black man's right to his body, or woman's right to her soul.

EMMA GOLDMAN
'What I Believe' *New York World* 1908

Goldman Emma (1869–1940). US political organizer, feminist and co-editor of the anarchist monthly *Mother Earth* 1906–17. In 1908 her citizenship was revoked and in 1919 she was deported to Russia. Breaking with the Bolsheviks 1921, she spent the rest of her life in exile. Her writings include *My Disillusionment in Russia* 1923 and *Living My Life* 1931.

Born in Lithuania and raised in Russia, Goldman emigrated to the USA 1885 and worked in a clothing factory in Rochester, New York. There she became attracted to radical socialism and moved to New York City 1889, where she became part of the anarchist movement. In 1893 she was jailed for inciting unemployed workers to riot; she was again imprisoned for opposing military conscription during World War I.

Suggested reading
Drinnon, Richard *Rebel in Paradise: A Biography of Emma Goldman* (1961)
Goldman, Emma *Living My Life* (autobiography) (1931)
Shulman, Alex *To the Barricades: The Anarchist Life of Emma Goldman* (1971)

Goldoni Carlo (1707–1793). Italian dramatist. He wrote popular comedies for the Sant'Angelo theatre, which drew on the traditions of the commedia dell'arte, *Il servitore di due padroni/The Servant of Two Masters* 1743, *Il bugiardo/The Liar* 1750, and *La locandiera/Mine Hostess* 1753. In 1761 he moved to Paris, where he directed the Italian theatre and wrote more plays, including *L'Eventail/The Fan* 1763.

Goldring Winifred (1888–1971). US palaeontologist whose research focused on Devonian fossils. She worked 1914–54 at the New York State Museum. In 1939 she was made state palaeontologist. Goldring began her work in palaeobotany 1916. During the late 1920s and the 1930s, as well as geologically mapping the Coxsackie and Berne quadrangles of New York, she developed and maintained the State Museum's public programme in palaeontology. Her works include *The Devonian Crinoids of the State of New York* 1923 and *Handbook of Paleontology for Beginners and Amateurs* 1929–31. She did much to popularize geology.

Goldschmidt Victor Moritz (1888–1947). Swiss-born Norwegian chemist who did fundamental work in geochemistry, particularly on the distribution of elements in the Earth's crust. He considered the colossal chemical processes of geological time to be interpretable in terms of the laws of chemical equilibrium.

Goldschmidt was born in Zürich but moved to Norway as a child and studied at the University of Christiania (now Oslo). He was professor and director of the Mineralogical Institute 1914–29, when he moved to Göttingen, Germany. The rise of Nazism forced him to return to Norway 1935, but during World War II he had to flee again, first to Sweden and then to Britain, where he worked at Aberdeen and Rothamsted (on soil science). He returned to Norway after the end of the war.

Goldsmith James Michael (1933–   ). Franco-British entrepreneur, one of the UK's wealthiest people. Early in his career he built up a grocery empire, Cavenham Foods; he went on to become the owner of several industrial, commercial (he was cofounder of Mothercare), and financial enterprises. His magazine *Now!*, launched 1979, closed two years later. Knighted 1976.

He became a director of the *Daily Telegraph* 1990 and began his own political party 1996.

Goldsmith Jerry (Jerrald) (1930–   ). US composer of film music. He originally worked in radio and television. His prolific output includes *Planet of the Apes* 1968, *The Wind and the Lion* 1975, *The Omen* 1976 (Academy Award), and *Gremlins* 1984.

And still they gaz'd, and still the wonder grew, / That one small head could carry all he knew.

OLIVER GOLDSMITH
'The Deserted Village' 1770

Goldsmith Oliver (1728–1774). Irish writer. His works include the novel *The Vicar of Wakefield* 1766; the poem 'The Deserted Village' 1770; and the play *She Stoops to Conquer* 1773. In 1761 Goldsmith met Samuel Johnson, and became a member of his 'club'. *The Vicar of Wakefield* was sold (according to Johnson's account) to save him from imprisonment for debt.

Goldsmith was the son of a cleric. He was educated at Trinity College, Dublin, and Edinburgh, where he studied medicine 1752. After travelling extensively in Europe, he returned to England and became a hack writer, producing many works, including *History of England* 1764 and *Animated Nature* 1774. One of his early works was *The Citizen of the World* 1762, a series of letters by an imaginary Chinese traveller. In 1764 he published the poem 'The Traveller', and followed it with collected essays 1765.

Goldstein Eugen (1850–1930). German physicist who investigated electrical discharges through gases at low pressures. Goldstein was born at Gleiwitz, Upper Silesia (now Gliwice, Poland), and studied at Breslau and Berlin. He worked at the Berlin Observatory 1878–90, and was eventually appointed head of the Astrophysical Section of Potsdam Observatory.

In 1876 Goldstein demonstrated that cathode rays can cast shadows and that the rays are emitted perpendicular to the cathode surface. He then showed how cathode rays could be deflected by magnetic fields. In an experiment 1886, he perforated the anode and observed glowing yellow streamers emanating from the perforations. He termed them *Kanalstrahlen* or canal rays. Goldstein later investigated the wavelengths of light emitted by metals and oxides when canal rays impinge on them, and observed that alkali metals show bright spectral lines.

In his last paper, published 1928, he observed that a trace of ammonia was present after the discharge in a tube containing nitrogen and hydrogen. Much later investigations were begun to see if biologically important molecules, and hence life, could have originated in this way.

Goldstein Vida (1869–1949). Australian feminist and suffragette. In 1903 she stood as an independent female candidate for the Australian senate, becoming the first woman in the British Empire to stand for election to a national parliament. Although unsuccessful, she polled more than 51,000 votes. She later campaigned in Victoria for women's suffrage, which was granted in 1908, and during World War I formed the pacifist Women's Peace Army.

Goldwater Barry Morris (1909–   ). US Republican politician; presidential candidate in the 1964 election, when he was overwhelmingly defeated by Lyndon Johnson. As a US senator for Arizona 1953–86, he voiced the views of his party's right-wing faction. Many of Goldwater's conservative ideas were later adopted by the Republican right, especially the Reagan administration.

Goldwyn Samuel. Adopted name of Schmuel Gelbfisz (Samuel Goldfish) (1882–1974). US film producer. Born in Poland, he emigrated to the USA 1896. He founded the Goldwyn Pictures Corporation 1917, which eventually merged into Metro-Goldwyn-Mayer (MGM) 1924, although he was not part of the deal. He remained an independent producer for many years, making classics such as *Wuthering Heights* 1939, *The Little Foxes* 1941, *The Best Years of Our Lives* 1946, and *Guys and Dolls* 1955. He was famed for his illogical aphorisms known as 'goldwynisms', for example, 'Include me out'.

Golgi Camillo (1843–1926). Italian cell biologist who produced the first detailed knowledge of the fine structure of the nervous system. He shared the 1906 Nobel Prize for Physiology or Medicine with Santiago Ramón y Cajal, who followed up Golgi's work.

Golgi's use of silver salts in staining cells proved so effective in showing up the components and fine processes of nerve cells that even the synapses – tiny gaps between the cells – were visible. The *Golgi apparatus*, a series of flattened membranous cavities found in the cytoplasm of cells, was first described by him 1898.

Golgi was born near Brescia and studied at Pavia, where he spent most of his academic career, becoming professor 1876. He was elected to the senate 1900.

From his examinations of different parts of the brain, Golgi put forward the theory that there are two types of nerve cells, sensory and motor cells, and that axons are concerned with the transmission of nerve impulses. He discovered tension receptors in the tendons – now called the organs of Golgi. Between 1885 and 1893 Golgi investigated malaria. This was known to be caused by the protozoon *Plasmodium*, and Golgi showed how the fever attacks coincide with the release into the bloodstream of a new generation of the parasites. He also established a method of treatment.

Goliath in the Old Testament, a champion of the Philistines, who was said to have been slain by a stone from a sling by the young David in single combat in front of their opposing armies.

Gollancz Victor (1893–1967). British left-wing writer and publisher, founder in 1936 of the Left Book Club. His own firm published plays by R C Sherriff and novels by Daphne Du Maurier, Elizabeth Bowen, and Dorothy L Sayers, among others. Knighted 1965.

Goltz Wilhelm Leopold Colmar, Freiherr von der (1843–1916). German soldier. Goltz served on Prince Frederick's staff during the Franco-Prussian war 1870–71 and then with the general staff in Berlin. He was attached to the Turkish Army 1883 and reorganized

Goldwyn US film producer Sam Goldwyn became one of the most powerful figures in Hollywood during its golden age. Many stars, including Rudolf Valentino, Ronald Colman, Gary Cooper, Danny Kaye, and David Niven, began their screen careers in Goldwyn's studios.

it along German lines. In World War I he accompanied the German Army into Belgium to become governor-general, first of Brussels and then of Belgium. He returned to Turkey 1915 and commanded a Turkish army during the Gallipoli campaign. He directed Turkish operations in the Middle East until his death from fever 19 April 1916.

Gombrich Ernst Hans Joseph (1909–). Austrian-born British art historian. His work on art history and theory is noted for its depth of analysis and the connections it makes with other fields, such as psychology. His best-known work is *The Story of Art* 1950, written for a popular audience.

He came to Britain 1936 to work at the University of London Warburg Institute, where he was director 1959–76. Knighted 1972.

Gombrowicz Witold (1904–1969). Polish dramatist and novelist. His technique of grotesque and fantastic allegory was expressed in *Iowna, Princess of Burgundy* 1957, *Marriage* 1963, and *Operetta* 1969. He was an exile from 1939.

Gomez Diego (1440–1482). Portuguese navigator who discovered the coast of Liberia during a voyage sponsored by Henry the Navigator 1458–60.

Gómez Juan Vicente (1864–1935). Venezuelan dictator 1908–35. The discovery of oil during his rule attracted US, British, and Dutch oil interests and made Venezuela one of the wealthiest countries in Latin America. Gómez amassed a considerable personal fortune and used his well-equipped army to dominate the civilian population.

Gompers Samuel (1850–1924). US labour leader. His early career in the Cigarmakers' Union led him to found and lead the American Federation of Labor 1886. Gompers advocated nonpolitical activity within the existing capitalist system to secure improved wages and working conditions for members.

Gomuʹka Wʹadysʹaw (1905–1982). Polish communist politician, party leader 1943–48 and 1956–70. He introduced moderate reforms, including private farming and tolerance for Roman Catholicism.

Gomuʹka, born in Krosno in SE Poland, was involved in underground resistance to the Germans during World War II, taking part in the defence of Warsaw. Leader of the Communist Party in Poland from 1943, he was ousted by the Moscow-backed Boʹeslaw Bierut (1892–1956) in 1948, but was restored to the leadership in 1956, following riots in Poznań. Gomuʹka was forced to resign in Dec 1970 after sudden food-price rises induced a new wave of strikes and riots.

His programme was 'national communism', which meant combining patriotism (... including restrained anti-Russianism) with the search for a 'separate road to socialism'.

Walter Laqueur on WŁADYSŁAW GOMUŁKA
in *Europe Since Hitler* 1970

Goncharov Ivan Alexandrovitch (1812–1891). Russian novelist. His first novel, *A Common Story* 1847, was followed 1858 by his humorous masterpiece *Oblomov*, which satirized the indolent Russian landed gentry. From 1852 to 1855 he was secretary on the ship *Pallada*, which was sent to Japan by the tsar to open it to trade. His wry description of the world cruise was published as *The Frigate 'Pallada'* 1858.

Man is a mind betrayed, not served, by his organs.

EDMOND AND JULES DE GONCOURT
The Goncourt Journals 30 July 1861

Goncourt, de Edmond (1822–1896) and Jules (1830–1870) French writers. The brothers collaborated in producing a compendium, *L'Art du XVIIIème siècle/18th-Century Art* 1859–75,

historical studies, and a *Journal* published 1887–96 that depicts French literary life of their day. Edmond de Goncourt founded the Académie Goncourt, opened 1903, which awards an annual prize, the Prix Goncourt, to the author of the best French novel of the year. Equivalent to the Commonwealth Booker Prize in prestige, it has a monetary value of only 50 francs.

A book is never a masterpiece: it becomes one. Genius is the talent of a dead man.

EDMOND AND CHARLES DE GONCOURT
The Goncourt Journals 23 July 1864

González Julio (1876–1942). Spanish sculptor and painter. He is notable for establishing the use of wrought and welded iron as an expressive sculptural medium. Influenced by the Cubism of his close friend Picasso, and also by Russian Constructivism and Surrealism, his early sculptures are open, linear designs using rods and bands of iron; for example, *Woman with a Mirror* about 1936–37 (IVAM, Centre Julio González, Valencia). From the mid-1930s, he produced moulded, fragmented torsos from sheet iron and naturalistic, commemorative sculptures of Spanish peasant women in revolt, for example *Montserrat* 1936–37 (Stedelijk Museum, Amsterdam), that many consider to be his finest work.

Trained in metalwork by his father in Barcelona, he moved to Paris 1900 where he met and was influenced by Picasso. He worked first as a painter and jewellery-maker, and from 1928 taught Picasso welding techniques, a collaboration that was to change the direction of his work. Contemporary sculptors influenced by González include David Smith and Anthony Caro.

González Márquez Felipe (1942–). Spanish socialist politician, leader of the Socialist Workers' Party (PSOE), prime minister from 1982. His party was re-elected 1989 and 1993, but his popularity suffered as a result of economic upheaval and revelations of corruption within his administration. During 1995 he was himself briefly under investigation for alleged involvement with anti-terrorist death squads in the 1980s.

After studying law in Spain and Belgium, in 1966 he opened the first labour-law office in his home city of Seville. In 1964 he had joined the PSOE, and he rose rapidly to the position of leader. In 1982 the PSOE won a sweeping electoral victory and González became prime minister. Under his administration left-wing members of the PSOE, disenchanted with González's policies, formed a new party called Social Democracy 1990. After his party's failure to retain an absolute majority in the 1989 parliamentary elections, González formed a coalition with Catalan and Basque nationalist parties, promising increased devolution to the country's regions.

The PSOE suffered, during the early 1990s, from a series of corruption scandals, and in 1995 González was accused of having been personally involved in the setting up of the Anti-terrorist Liberation Group, a paramilitary group which had been responsible for the deaths of scores of Basque separatists in the 1980s. A preliminary probe into the allegations was abandoned as a result of insufficient evidence, but the scandal cost him the support of his Catalan coalition partner.

Gooch Graham Alan (1953–). English cricketer who plays for Essex, England's leading run-scorer in test cricket since he overtook David Gower's record at The Oval in 1993. He made his first-class debut 1973, and his England debut 1975. Banned for three years for captaining an unofficial England side to South Africa 1982, he went on to captain England on 34 occasions. He scored a world record match total of 456 runs against India 1990. In 1993 he joined the select band of cricketers to reach the milestone of 100 centuries.

He became the fourth person to average 100 runs per innings in an English season and has appeared in more than 80 test matches.

Goodall Reginald (1901–1990). English conductor, known for his slow, expansive interpretations of Wagner. He conducted without a baton, and never took curtain calls. Knighted 1985.

Goodman Arnold Abraham, Baron Goodman (1913–1995). English lawyer and political adviser. Once described as the most powerful man in Britain, he was adviser to three prime ministers: Harold Wilson, Edward Heath, and John Major. He has the unique distinction of having been made a peer by a Labour prime minister and a Companion of Honour by a Conservative one. Baron 1965.

A lifelong bachelor who thought women intellectually inferior, he said that he could accomplish so much in a day (he was chair of the Arts Council, master of an Oxford college, chair of the *Observer* newspaper, director of two national opera houses, cofounder of the National Theatre, government negotiator in dealings with Rhodesia (as it was), chair of the Newspaper Publishers' Association, and of the Housing Association, and lawyer to trade unions and popular media stars) because he had no domestic distractions.

Goodman Benny (Benjamin David) (1909–1986). US clarinetist. He was nicknamed the 'King of Swing' for the new jazz idiom he introduced with arranger Fletcher Henderson (1897–1952). In 1934 he founded his own 12-piece band, which combined the expressive improvisatory style of black jazz with disciplined precision ensemble playing. He is associated with such numbers as 'Blue Skies' and 'Let's Dance'.

He introduced jazz to New York's Carnegie Hall 1938. In the same year he embarked on a parallel classical career, recording the Mozart *Clarinet Quintet* with the Budapest String Quartet, and commissioning new works from Bartók (*Contrasts* 1938), Copland, Hindemith, and others. He also recorded jazz with a sextet 1939–41 that included the guitarist Charlie Christian (1916–1942). When swing lost popularity in the 1950s, Goodman took a series of smaller groups on world tours, culminating in a US-government-sponsored visit to Moscow 1962.

Goodman Nelson (1906–). US philosopher who tried to dispel the confusions of everyday language by the use of formal logic. His alleged 'new riddle of induction' (Goodman's paradox) posits the lack of justification for the way in which we prefer one of the many conceivable characteristics of a set of things we have observed to other, less obvious ones when we generalize about the set as a whole. In aesthetics, he attacked the idea that art represents reality by resembling it. He taught at Harvard for most of his career, before becoming a professor at the University of Pennsylvania. His most important work is *The Structure of Appearance* 1951.

Goodman Paul (1911–1972). US writer and social critic whose many works (novels, plays, essays) express his anarchist, anti-authoritarian ideas. He studied young offenders in *Growing up Absurd* 1960.

Goodyear Charles (1800–1860). US inventor who developed rubber coating 1837 and vulcanized rubber 1839, a method of curing raw rubber to make it strong and elastic.

Goodyear was born in New Haven, Connecticut, and entered his father's hardware business. He began to investigate rubber in the 1830s and obtained US patents for his process 1844, but both Britain and France refused his applications because of legal technicalities. His attempts to set up companies in both countries failed, and for a while he was imprisoned for debt in Paris. When he returned to the USA, many of his patents had been pirated by associates, and he died in poverty.

Goodyear discovered the vulcanization process by accident. One day he was mixing rubber with sulphur and various other ingredients when he dropped some on top of a hot stove. The next morning the stove had cooled and the rubber had vulcanized.

Gorbachev Mikhail Sergeyevich (1931–). Soviet president, in power 1985–91. He was a member of the Politburo from 1980. As general secretary of the Communist Party (CPSU) 1985–91 and president of the Supreme Soviet 1988–91, he introduced liberal reforms at home (*perestroika* and *glasnost*), proposed the introduction of multiparty democracy, and attempted to halt the arms race abroad. He became head of state 1989. Nobel Peace Prize 1990.

Gorbachev, born in the N Caucasus, studied law at Moscow University and joined the CPSU 1952. In 1955–62 he worked for the

Goodyear *American Charles Goodyear who invented the vulcanization process for rubber. During this process rubber is heated to a high temperature in the presence of sulphur in order to increase its elasticity and strength. Goodyear went on to invent many applications for rubber including the motor-vehicle tyre.* (Image Select)

Komsomol (Communist Youth League) before being appointed regional agriculture secretary. As Stavropol party leader from 1970 he impressed Andropov, and was brought into the CPSU secretariat 1978.

Gorbachev was promoted into the Politburo and in 1983, when Andropov was general secretary, took broader charge of the Soviet economy. During the Chernenko administration 1984–85, he was chair of the Foreign Affairs Commission. On Chernenko's death 1985 he was appointed party leader. He initiated wide-ranging reforms and broad economic restructuring, and introduced campaigns against alcoholism, corruption, and inefficiency. In the 1988 presidential election by members of the Soviet parliament, he was the sole candidate.

The market came with the dawn of civilization and is not the invention of capitalism. If the market leads to the improvement of people's daily lives, then there is no contradiction with socialism.

MIKHAIL GORBACHEV
rebutting the complaints of his conservative rivals that he was
attempting to restore capitalism in the Soviet Union, June 1990

In March 1990 he was elected to a five-year term as executive president with greater powers. At home his plans for economic reform failed to avert a food crisis in the winter of 1990–91 and his desire to preserve a single, centrally controlled USSR met with resistance from Soviet republics seeking more independence. Early in 1991, Gorbachev shifted to the right in order to placate the conservative wing of the party and appointed some of the hardliners to positions of power. In late spring, he produced a plan for a new union treaty to satisfy the demands of reformers. This plan alarmed the hardliners, who, in late summer, temporarily removed him from

Gorbachev *Mikhail Gorbachev, president of the USSR 1985–91. He led the USSR into political pluralism but was criticized for remaining too close to the party that had brought him to power and for failing to make the food-distribution system work.*

office. He was saved from this attempted coup mainly by the efforts of Boris Yeltsin and the ineptness of the plotters.

Soon after his reinstatement, Gorbachev was obliged to relinquish his leadership of the party, renounce communism as a state doctrine, suspend all activities of the Communist Party (including its most powerful organs, the Politburo and the Secretariat), and surrender many of his central powers to the states. He continued to press for an agreement on his proposed union treaty in the hope of preventing a disintegration of the Soviet Union, but was unable to maintain control and on 25 Dec 1991 resigned as president, effectively yielding power to Boris Yeltsin. In the 1996 elections he polled only 0.5% of the vote.

Suggested reading
Aslund, Anders *Gorbachev's Struggle for Reform* (1989)
Brown, Archie *The Gorbachev Factor* (1996)
Lewin, Moshe *The Gorbachev Phenomenon* (1988)
Medvedev, Zhores *Gorbachev* (1986)
Sheehy, Gail *Gorbachev: The Making of the Man Who Shook the World* (1991)

Censorship ... is a brand on the imagination that affects the individual who has suffered it, forever.

NADINE GORDIMER
Address to Writer's day conference, London,
June 1990: 'Censorship and its Aftermath'

Gordimer Nadine (1923–). South African novelist, an opponent of apartheid and censorship. Her finest writing is characterized by beautiful evocations of the rural Transvaal, effective renderings of sexuality, and interacting characters from different racial backgrounds. Her first novel, *The Lying Days*, appeared 1953, her other works include *The Conservationist* 1974, the volume of short stories *A Soldier's Embrace* 1980, *July's People* 1981, and *Why Haven't You Written?* 1992. Nobel Prize for Literature 1991.

Gordon Adam Lindsay (1833–1870). Australian poet known particularly for vigorous narrative verse, such as 'The Sick Stockrider' (1870), which extols horses, riders, and life in outback Australia. He committed suicide the day after his verse collection *Bush Ballards and Galloping Rhymes* 1870, was published. He is the only Australian to have a memorial in Poets' Corner, Westminster Abbey, London.

Better a ball in the brain than to flicker out unheeded.

CHARLES GORDON
Diary Nov 1884

Gordon Charles George (1833–1885). British general sent to Khartoum in the Sudan 1884 to rescue English garrisons that were under attack by the Mahdi, Muhammad Ahmed; he was himself besieged for ten months by the Mahdi's army. A relief expedition arrived 28 Jan 1885 to find that Khartoum had been captured and Gordon killed two days before.

Gordon served in the Crimean War and in China 1864, where he earned his nickname 'Chinese' Gordon in ending the Taiping Rebellion. In 1874 he was employed by the Khedive of Egypt to open the country and 1877–80 was British governor of the Sudan.

Suggested reading
Garrett, R *General Gordon* (1974)
Tames, R *General Gordon* (1983)
Walker, J *Gordon of Khartoum* (1988)

A somewhat feckless critic of institutions and personalities in the eighteenth century 'establishment' ... [after 1780] his future could only lie in the milder paths of eccentricity.

Geoffrey Treasure on LORD GEORGE GORDON
in *Who's Who in Early Hanoverian England* 1991

Gordon Lord George (1751–1793). British organizer of the so-called *Gordon Riots* of 1778, a protest against removal of penalties

Gordon, Charles *British army general Charles Gordon was governor of the Sudan 1877–80, and attempted to suppress the slave trade there. In 1860 he took part in the expedition that captured Beijing and was personally responsible for the burning of the Summer Palace.*

imposed on Roman Catholics in the Catholic Relief Act of 1778; he was acquitted on a treason charge. Gordon and the 'No Popery' riots figure in Charles Dickens's novel *Barnaby Rudge*.

Gordon Richard. Pen name of Gordon Ostlere (1921–). British author. He produced a series of light-hearted novels on the career of a young doctor, beginning with *Doctor in the House* 1952, many of which were filmed.

I began to suffer an attack of terror celibans or bachelor's panic.

RICHARD GORDON
Doctor at Sea

Gordon-Lennox family name of dukes of Richmond; seated at Goodwood, Sussex; descended from King Charles II by his mistress Louise de Keroualle.

Gore Al(bert) (1948–). US politician, vice president from 1993. A Democrat, he became a member of the House of Representatives 1977–79, and was elected senator for Tennessee 1985–92. He is on the conservative wing of the party, but holds liberal views on such matters as women's rights, environmental issues, and abortion.

Born into a wealthy patrician family in Tennessee, where his father was senator, Gore was a journalist, a property developer, and a farmer before going into politics. He is known to have strong views on arms control, military, and foreign policy.

Górecki Henryk Mikolaj (1933–). Polish composer. His study with Messiaen and exposure to avant-garde influences after 1956 led him to abandon a politically correct Neo-Classical style and seek out new sonorities. He later adopted a slow-moving tonal idiom appealing to revived religious tradition, often on tragic themes from Polish history, as in *Old Polish Music* for orchestra 1969, and his *Symphony No 3* 1976, which propelled him to fame in the West 1992.

Goria Giovanni (1943–1994). Italian Christian Democrat (DC) politician, prime minister 1987–88. He entered the chamber of deputies 1976 and held a number of posts, including treasury minister, until he was asked to form a coalition government 1987. He resigned as finance minister 1993 to fight allegations of corruption.

Göring Hermann. German spelling of ◊Goering, Nazi leader.

Gorky Arshile. Adopted name of Vosdanig Manoüg Adoian (1904–1948). Armenian-born US painter. He painted in several Modernist styles before developing a semi-abstract surreal style, using organic shapes and vigorous brushwork. His works, such as *The Liver Is the Cock's Comb* 1944 (Albright-Knox Art Gallery, Buffalo), are noted for their sense of fantasy.

Among Gorky's major influences were Picasso, Kandinsky, Miró, and Cézanne, and he in turn influenced the emerging Abstract Expressionists. He lived in the USA from 1920.

When a woman gets married it is like jumping into a hole in the ice in the middle of winter; you do it once and you remember it the rest of your days.

MAXIM GORKY
Lower Depths 1912

Gorky Maxim. Pen name of Alexei Maximovich Peshkov (1868–1936). Russian writer. Born in Nizhni-Novgorod (named Gorky 1932–90 in his honour), he was exiled 1906–13 for his revolutionary principles. His works, which include the play *The Lower Depths* 1902 and the memoir *My Childhood* 1913–14, combine realism with optimistic faith in the potential of the industrial proletariat.

Suggested reading
Borras, F *Maxim Gorky the Writer: An Interpretation* (1967)

Hare, Richard *Maxim Gorky: Romantic Realist and Conservative Revolutionary* (1962)
Levin, Dan *Stormy Petrel: The Life and Work of Maxim Gorky* (1965)
Wolf, Bertram *The Bridge and the Abyss* (1967)

Gorshkov Sergei Georgievich (1910–1988). Soviet admiral, commander in chief of the navy 1956–85.

That [he] was less successful than might have been expected from his energy and ability was probably [because] he could not attach himself wholeheartedly to any political party.

MYRA CURTISS ON J E GORST
in *Dictionary of National Biography*

Gorst J(ohn) E(ldon) (1835–1916). English Conservative Party administrator. A supporter of Disraeli, Gorst was largely responsible for extending the Victorian Conservative Party electoral base to include middle- and working-class support. Appointed Conservative Party agent in 1870, he established Conservative Central Office, and became secretary of the National Union in 1871. He was solicitor-general 1885–86. Knighted 1885.

Gort John Standish Surtees Prendergast Vereker, 1st Viscount Gort (1886–1946). British general who in World War II commanded the British Expeditionary Force 1939–40, conducting a fighting retreat from Dunkirk, France. Although he had no experience of major command, he handled the BEF with great skill in the face of the German onslaught and French collapse, taking the vital decision 23 May 1940 to withdraw the British Army via Dunkirk before it was entirely destroyed. 6th viscount (Irish peerage) 1902, viscount (UK) 1945.

Gorton John Grey (1911–). Australian Liberal politician. He was minister for education and science 1966–68, and prime minister 1968–71. GCMG 1977.

We have stood alone in that which is called isolation – our splendid isolation.

GEORGE, 1ST VISCOUNT GOSCHEN
Speech at Lewes 26 Feb 1896

Goschen George Joachim, 1st Viscount Goschen (1831–1907). British Liberal politician. He held several cabinet posts under Gladstone 1868–74, but broke with him in 1886 over Irish Home Rule. In Salisbury's Unionist government of 1886–92 he was chancellor of the Exchequer, and 1895–1900 was First Lord of the Admiralty. Viscount 1900.

Gossaert Jan. Flemish painter, known as ◊Mabuse.

Gosse Edmund William (1849–1928). English writer and critic. His strict Victorian upbringing is reflected in his masterly autobiographical work *Father and Son* (published anonymously 1907). His father was a member of the Plymouth Brethren, a Christian fundamentalist sect that rejected the evolutionary ideas of Darwin. As a literary critic and biographer, he was responsible for introducing the Norwegian dramatist Ibsen to England. Knighted 1925.

Gosset William Sealy (1876–1937). British industrial research scientist whose work on statistical analysis of the normal distribution opened the door to developments in the analysis of variance. Gosset spent his career with the Guinness brewery firm, first in Dublin, Ireland, and from 1935 in London.

Gottschalk Louis Moreau (1829–1869). US composer and pianist. His adoption of Creole and American folk music, Latin American rhythms and dance forms, and striking coloristic effects won the admiration of Berlioz, Liszt, Offenbach, and others. His compositions include *Souvenir d'Andalousie/Souvenir of Andalusia*

1851 for piano and orchestra and numerous piano pieces, among which are *La Gallina: danse cubaine/La Gallina: Cuban Dance c.* 1868 and *Le Banjo – esquisse américaine/Banjo – American Sketch* 1854–55.

Gough Hubert de la Poer (1870–1963). British general. As commander of the Fifth Army 1916–18, he led it through the battles of the Somme 1916 and Ypres 1917, where he was criticized for the high rate of casualties. He was initially blamed for the German breakthrough on the Somme 1918, but his force was later admitted to have been too small for the length of the front. KBE 1926.

Goujon Jean (*c.* 1510–*c.* 1565). French Renaissance sculptor. His Mannerist style, developed under the influence of Primaticcio and Cellini at Fontainebleau, is tempered with a graceful Classicism. Characteristic of his work are the slender nymphs in bas relief on his *Fountain of the Innocents* 1549 (Louvre, Paris).

Gould Bryan Charles (1939–   ). British Labour politician, a member of the shadow cabinet 1986–92. He was an unsuccessful candidate in the 1992 Labour Party leadership election and resigned from the shadow cabinet in Sept. In 1994 he announced his retirement from active politics, and returned to an academic career in his native New Zealand.

Gould Elliott. Stage name of Elliot Goldstein (1938–   ). US film actor. A successful child actor, his film debut *The Night They Raided Minsky's* 1968 led rapidly to starring roles in such films as *M.A.S.H.* 1970, *The Long Goodbye* 1972, and *Capricorn One* 1978.

My only enemy is me.

ELLIOTT GOULD
Photoplay April 1979

Gould Glenn Herbert (1932–1982). Canadian pianist. He was launched to fame with his first recording of Bach's *Goldberg Variations*, and built his reputation as one of the greatest interpreters of Bach. His eccentricities, especially his unusual choice of tempo, ultimately led to his giving up live performance in favour of making recordings.
Suggested reading
Cott, John *Conversations with Glenn Gould* (1984)
Page, Tim (ed) *The Glenn Gould Reader* (1984)
Sachs, H *Virtuoso* (1982)

Gould Jay (Jason) (1836–1892). US financier, born in New York. He is said to have caused the financial panic on 'Black Friday', 24 Sept 1869, through his efforts to corner the gold market.
    Gould was one of the 'robber barons' who built the transportation and communications structures of the USA while accumulating great wealth. His first major success came when he was made an associate of the Erie Railroad by Cornelius Vanderbilt. Following financial and political scandals, Gould was forced to relinquish control of the Erie Railroad, but he used the large fortune he had amassed to acquire control of western railroads, including the Union Pacific. He also controlled the Western Union Telegraph Company and elevated railways in New York City.

Gould John (1804–1881). English zoologist who with his wife Elizabeth (1804–1841), a natural-history artist, published a successful series of illustrated bird books. They visited Australia 1838–40 and afterwards produced *The Birds of Australia*, issued in 36 parts from 1840. *Mammals of Australia* followed 1845–63, and *Handbook to the Birds of Australia* 1865.

Gould Stephen Jay (1941–   ). US palaeontologist and writer. In 1972 he proposed the theory of punctuated equilibrium, suggesting that the evolution of species did not occur at a steady rate but could suddenly accelerate, with rapid change occurring over a few hundred thousand years. His books include *Ever Since Darwin* 1977, *The Panda's Thumb* 1980, *The Flamingo's Smile* 1985, and *Wonderful Life* 1990. He became professor of geology at Harvard 1973 and was

later also given posts in the departments of zoology and the history of science.

Musical ideas sprang to my mind like a flight of butterflies, and all I had to do was to stretch out my hand to catch them.

CHARLES GOUNOD
quoted in James Harding *Gounod* 1973

Gounod Charles François (1818–1893). French composer and organist. His operas, notably *Faust* 1859 and *Roméo et Juliette* 1867, and church music, including *Messe solennelle/Solemn Mass* 1849, combine graceful melody and elegant harmonization. His *Méditation sur le prélude de Bach/Meditation on Bach's 'Prelude'* 1889 for soprano and instruments, based on Prelude No 1 of Bach's *Well-Tempered Clavier*, achieved popularity as 'Gounod's *Ave Maria*'.

Aesthetic emotion puts man in a state favourable to the reception of erotic emotion. Art is the accomplice of love. Take love away and there is no longer art.

RÉMY DE GOURMONT
Decadence

Gourmont Rémy de (1858–1915). French critic and novelist. A prolific essayist, he influentially disseminated the aesthetic doctrines of French Symbolism, committed to the relativity of truth and the necessarily aesthetic basis of all literary judgement. His rather cerebral novels include *Sixtine: Roman de la vie cérébrale/Very Woman* 1890.

Govorov Leonid (1897–1955). Soviet marshal. Appointed to command the 5th Soviet Army in front of Moscow Nov 1941, he played a major part in the Soviet defence and counteroffensive. He then took over the Leningrad front, at the time besieged by the Germans, conducting an active defence and opening up a supply route across Lake Ladoga. He eventually broke the siege Jan 1944 and pursued the retreating German forces all the way into E Prussia.

Gow Ian Reginald Edward (1937–1990). British Conservative politician. After qualifying as a solicitor, he was elected member of Parliament for Eastbourne 1974. He became parliamentary private secretary to Margaret Thatcher, 1979, and her close ally. He secured steady promotion but resigned his post as minister of state 1985 in protest at the signing of the Anglo-Irish Agreement. A strong critic of terrorist acts, he was killed by an Irish Republican Army car bomb.

Gower David Ivon (1957–   ). English left-handed cricketer who played for Leicestershire 1975–89 and for Hampshire 1990–93. He was England's record run scorer in test cricket from 1992, when he surpassed Geoffrey Boycott's record, until 1993, when his total was overtaken by Graham Gooch. He retired in 1993.

It hath and schal ben evermor / That love is maister wher he wile.

JOHN GOWER
Confessio Amantis, prologue 1390

Gower John (*c.* 1330–1408). English poet. He is remembered for his tales of love *Confessio Amantis* 1390, written in English, and other poems in French and Latin. He was a friend and contemporary of Geoffrey Chaucer.

Gowon Yakubu (1934–   ). Nigerian politician, head of state 1966–75. Educated at Sandhurst military college in the UK, he became Chief of Staff, and in the military coup of 1966 seized power. After the Biafran civil war 1967–70, he reunited the country with his policy of 'no victor, no vanquished'. In 1975 he was overthrown by a military coup.

Goya Francisco José de Goya y Lucientes (1746–1828). Spanish painter and engraver. He painted portraits of four successive kings of Spain; his series of etchings include the famous *Caprichos* 1797–98 and *The Disasters of War* 1810–14, both depicting the horrors of the French invasion of Spain. Among his later works are the 'Black Paintings' (Prado, Madrid), with such horrific images as *Saturn Devouring One of His Sons* about 1822.

Goya was born in Aragon and was for a time a bullfighter, the subject of some of his etchings. After studying in Italy, he returned to Spain and was employed on a number of paintings for the royal tapestry factory as well as numerous portraits. In 1789 he was appointed court painter to Charles IV. The eroticism of his *Naked Maja* and *Clothed Maja* about 1800–05 (Prado, Madrid) caused such outrage that he was questioned by the Inquisition. *The Shootings of May 3rd 1808* 1814 (Prado, Madrid), painted for Ferdinand VII, is passionate in its condemnation of the inhumanity of war. Technically, Goya attained brilliant effects by thin painting over a red earth ground. Much influenced by Rembrandt ('Rembrandt, Velasquez and Nature' were, he said, his guides), he turned in later years to a dusky near-monochrome. His skill, however, seemed to increase with age, and the *Milkmaid of Bordeaux*, one of his last paintings, shows him using colour with great freedom.

Suggested reading
Chabrun, J F *Goya* (1965)
Gassier, P and Wilson, J *Goya* (1971)
Licht, F *Goya: The Origins of the Modern Temper in Art* (1979)
Malraux, A *Saturn: An Essay on Goya* (1957)
Symmons, S *Goya: In Pursuit of Patronage* (1988)

Goyen Jan Josephszoon van (1596–1656). Dutch landscape painter. He was active in Leiden, Haarlem, and from 1631 in The Hague. A pioneer of the Realist style of landscape with Ruisdael, he sketched from nature and studied clouds and light effects.

He worked with Esaias van de Velde at Haarlem, after some study with other masters, and settled at The Hague. His art was creative in the development of Dutch landscape painting, gradually replacing the incidental interest of boats, figures and buildings in his river scenes with a larger concern with space, light and atmosphere conceived in what was virtually a warm monochrome. Rembrandt derived some inspiration from him.

Gozzoli Benozzo (c. 1421–1497). Florentine painter. He was a late exponent of the International Gothic style. He is known for his fresco *The Procession of the Magi* 1459–61 in the chapel of the Palazzo Medici-Riccardi, Florence, where the walls are crowded with figures, many of them portraits of the Medici family.

Graaf Regnier de (1641–1673). Dutch physician and anatomist who discovered the ovarian follicles, which were later named Graafian follicles. He named the ovaries and gave exact descriptions of the testicles. He was also the first to isolate and collect the secretions of the pancreas and gall bladder.

There are two reasons why I'm in show-business, and I'm standing on both of them.

BETTY GRABLE
on her career

Grable Betty (Elizabeth Ruth) (1916–1973). US actress, singer, and dancer. She starred in *Moon over Miami* 1941, *I Wake Up Screaming* 1941, and *How to Marry a Millionaire* 1953. As a publicity stunt, her legs were insured for a million dollars. Her popularity peaked during World War II when US soldiers voted her their number-one pin-up girl.

Gaius Gracchus said that he had himself thrown daggers into the forum with which the citizens might stab each other.

Cicero on GRACCHUS
in *On Laws* bk 3 ch 9

Gracchus Tiberius Sempronius (c. 163–133 BC) and Gaius Sempronius (c. 153–121 BC) in ancient Rome, two brothers who worked for agrarian reform. As tribune (magistrate) 133 BC, Tiberius tried to redistribute land away from the large slave-labour farms in order to benefit the poor as well as increase the number of those eligible for military service by providing them with the minimum property requirement. He was murdered by a mob of senators. Gaius, tribune 123–122 BC, revived his brother's legislation, and introduced other reforms, but was outlawed by the Senate and killed in a riot.

The wild beasts that roam Italy have each their lair, but the men who fight and die for Italy enjoy the common air but nothing else.

TIBERIUS SEMPRONIUS GRACCHUS
Justification for land reform. Quoted in Plutarch
Life of Tiberius Gracchus ch 9.4

Grace W(illiam) G(ilbert) (1848–1915). English cricketer. By profession a doctor, he became the best batsman in England. He began playing first-class cricket at the age of 16, scored 152 runs in his first test match, and scored the first triple century 1876. Throughout his career, which lasted nearly 45 years, he scored more than 54,000 runs.

He scored 2,739 runs in 1871, the first time any batsman had scored 2,000 runs in a season. An all-rounder, he took nearly 3,000 first-class wickets. Grace played in 22 test matches.

Graf Steffi (1969–). German lawn-tennis player who brought Martina Navratilova's long reign as the world's number-one female player to an end. Graf reached the semi-final of the US Open 1985 at the age of 16, and won five consecutive Grand Slam singles titles 1988–89. In 1994 she became the first defending Wimbledon ladies' singles champion to lose her title in the first round.

Shy and serious, but difficult and ill-at-ease in public, he was a useful debater and efficient administrator ... with liberal views ... but not suitable for high office.

E N Williams on AUGUSTUS HENRY
FITZROY, 3RD DUKE OF GRAFTON
in *Penguin Dictionary of English and European History 1485–1789* 1980

Grafton Augustus Henry Fitzroy, 3rd Duke of Grafton (1735–1811). British politician. Grandson of the first duke, who was the son of Charles II and Barbara Villiers (1641–1709), Duchess of Cleveland. He became First Lord of the Treasury in 1766 and an unsuccessful acting prime minister 1767–70. Succeeded to dukedom 1757.

Graham family name of dukes of Montrose.

Graham Billy (William Franklin) (1918–). US Protestant evangelist, known for the dramatic staging and charismatic eloquence of his preaching. Graham has preached to millions during worldwide crusades and on television, bringing many thousands to conversion to, or renewal of, Christian faith.

No artist is ahead of his time, he is his time; it is just that others are behind the times.

MARTHA GRAHAM
Observer Magazine 8 July 1979

Graham Martha (1894–1991). US dancer, choreographer, teacher, and director. The greatest exponent of modern dance in the USA, she developed a distinctive vocabulary of movement, the *Graham Technique*, now taught worldwide. Her pioneering technique, designed to express inner emotion and intention through dance forms, represented the first real alternative to classical ballet.

Graham founded her own dance school 1927 and started a company with students from the school 1929. She created over 170 works, including *Appalachian Spring* 1944 (score by Aaron Copland), *Clytemnestra* 1958, the first full-length modern dance work, and *Lucifer* 1975. She danced in most of the pieces she choreographed until her retirement from performance in the 1960s. Graham had a major influence on such choreographers in the contemporary dance movement as Robert Cohan, Glen Tetley, Merce Cunningham, Norman Morrice, Paul Taylor, and Robert North.

Suggested reading
Graham, Martha *The Notebooks of Martha Graham* (1973)
de Mille, Agnes *Martha: The Life and the Works of Martha Graham* (1991)
Leatherman, L *Martha Graham* (1966)
Stodelle, E *Deep Song* (1984)

Graham Thomas (1805–1869). Scottish chemist who laid the foundations of physical chemistry (the branch of chemistry concerned with changes in energy during a chemical transformation) by his work on the diffusion of gases and liquids. *Graham's law* 1829 states that the diffusion rate of a gas is inversely proportional to the square root of its density.

His work on colloids (which have larger particles than true solutions) was equally fundamental; he discovered the principle of dialysis, that colloids can be separated from solutions containing smaller molecules by the differing rates at which they pass through a semipermeable membrane. The human kidney uses the same principle to extract nitrogenous waste.

Graham was born in Glasgow and studied at Glasgow and Edinburgh. In 1830, Graham became professor at Anderson's College, Glasgow, moving to University College, London, 1837–54. In 1855, he was appointed Master of the Royal Mint.

The clever men at Oxford / Know all that there is to be knowed. / But they none of them know one half as much / As intelligent Mr Toad!

KENNETH GRAHAME
Wind in the Willows ch 10 1908

Grahame Kenneth (1859–1932). Scottish author. The early volumes of sketches of childhood, *The Golden Age* 1895 and *Dream Days* 1898, were followed by his masterpiece *The Wind in the Willows* 1908, an animal fantasy created for his young son, which was dramatized by A A Milne as *Toad of Toad Hall* 1929.

Grainger Percy Aldridge (1882–1961). Australian-born experimental composer and pianist. He is remembered for piano transcriptions, songs, and short instrumental pieces drawing on folk idioms, including *Country Gardens* 1925, and for his settings of folk songs, such as *Molly on the Shore* 1921.

He studied in Frankfurt, moved to London, then settled in the USA 1914. Grainger shared his friend Ferruccio Busoni's vision of a free music, devising a synthesizer and composing machine far ahead of its time.

Suggested reading
Bird, John *Percy Grainger* (1976)
Slattery, Thomas *Percy Grainger* (1974)

Salvation Army Booth objected to the devil having all the good tunes. I object to jazz and vaudeville having all the best instruments!

PERCY GRAINGER
preface to *Spoon River* 1930

Gramsci Antonio (1891–1937). Italian Marxist who attempted to unify social theory and political practice. He helped to found the Italian Communist Party 1921 and was elected to parliament 1924, but was imprisoned by the Fascist leader Mussolini from 1926; his *Quaderni di carcere/Prison Notebooks* were published posthumously 1947.

A thinker of some originality who sought to harmonize historical materialism with the specifically Italian tradition of metaphysical philosophy.

Alan Palmer on ANTONIO GRAMSCI
in *Penguin Dictionary of Twentieth Century History* 1979

Gramsci believed that politics and ideology were independent of the economic base, that no ruling class could dominate by economic factors alone, and that the working class could achieve liberation by political and intellectual struggle. His concept of *hegemony* argued that real class control in capitalist societies is ideological and cultural rather than physical, and that only the working class 'educated' by radical intellectuals could see through and overthrow such bourgeois propaganda.

His humane and gradualist approach to Marxism, specifically his emphasis on the need to overthrow bourgeois ideology, influenced European Marxists in their attempt to distance themselves from orthodox determinist Soviet communism.

Suggested reading
Clark, M N *Antonio Gramsci and the Revolution that Failed* (1977)
Davidson, A *Antonio Gramsci: Towards an Intellectual Biography* (1977)
Joll, James *Antonio Gramsci* (1977)
Sassoon, S *Gramsci's Politics* (1980)

Granados Enrique (1867–1916). Spanish composer and pianist. His piano-work *Goyescas* 1911, inspired by the art of the artist Goya, was converted to an opera 1916.

Swinging inn-signs recall the name of a brave and spectacular general.

Geoffrey Treasure on JOHN MANNERS, MARQUESS OF GRANBY
in *Who's Who in Early Hanoverian Britain* 1991

Granby John Manners, Marquess of Granby (1721–1770). British soldier. His head appears on many inn-signs in England as a result of his popularity as a commander of the British forces fighting in Europe in the Seven Years' War.

He wanted Italy to become more Machiavellian, more isolated, less anglophile, and militarily so strong that she would tip the scales in Europe when the great day of war came.

Denis Mack Smith on DINO, COUNT GRANDI
Mussolini 1981

Grandi Dino, Count (1895–1988). Italian politician who challenged Mussolini for leadership of the Italian Fascist Party in 1921 and was subsequently largely responsible for Mussolini's downfall in July 1943.

Grandi, a leading figure in the Fascist Party during the 1920s, was Italian foreign minister 1929–32 and ambassador to the UK 1932–39. After Mussolini's deposure and rescue Grandi fled from Italy and lived for four years in Lisbon.

Grandi Guido (1671–1742). Italian mathematician who worked on the definition of curves. He devised the curves now known as the 'versiera', the 'rose', and the 'cliela', and his theory of curves also comprehended the means of finding the equations of curves of known form. He was mainly responsible, in addition, for introducing calculus into Italy 1703.

Grandi was born in Cremona. He became professor of philosophy at Pisa in 1700 and of mathematics 1714.

Grange Kenneth Henry (1929–). English industrial designer. He was among the first British designers to work as a consultant to industry and, from the late 1950s, has created a vast number of lasting designs for a range of manufacturers both at home and abroad.

Notable examples include the Kodak 'Brownie 44A' camera 1959 and the 'Chef' food mixer for Kenwood 1964. They demonstrate a simple elegance and pragmatism. He has been a member of the London-based Pentagram group of graphic and industrial designers since 1972.

Grange Red (Harold Edward). Nickname 'the Galloping Ghost' (1903–1991). US American football player. He joined the Chicago Bears professional football team 1925, becoming one of the first superstars of the newly founded National Football League. In both the 1923 and 1924 seasons he was chosen All-American halfback and won his nickname for his extraordinary open-field running ability.

I've never done a film I'm proud of.

STEWART GRANGER
Attributed remark

Granger (James Lablache) Stewart (1913–1993). English film actor. After several leading roles in British romantic melodramas during World War II (such as *The Man in Grey* 1940) he moved to Hollywood 1950 and subsequently appeared in such films as *Scaramouche* 1952, *The Prisoner of Zenda* 1952, *Beau Brummel* 1954, and *Moonfleet* 1955. Some of Granger's performances tended to inflexibility, and hardly any of his films made after 1960 rose above the level of potboilers. By 1978 he was reduced to a minor supporting role in *The Wild Geese*. He returned to the theatre 1990, appearing in a revival of *The Circle* on Broadway in New York, and on an English tour.

I often wonder how I'm going to die. You don't want to embarrass friends.

CARY GRANT
Variety 6 Dec 1983

Grant Cary. Stage name of Archibald Alexander Leach (1904–1986). British-born actor, a US citizen from 1942. His witty, debonair personality made him a screen favourite for more than three decades. He was directed by Alfred Hitchcock in *Suspicion* 1941, *Notorious* 1946, *To Catch a Thief* 1955, and *North by Northwest* 1959. He received a 1970 Academy Award for general excellence. His other films include *She Done Him Wrong* 1933, *Bringing Up Baby* 1937, and *The Philadelphia Story* 1940.

Grant Duncan James Corrowr (1885–1978). Scottish painter and designer. He was a member of the Bloomsbury Group and a pioneer of Post-Impressionism in the UK. He lived with the painter Vanessa Bell (1879–1961) from about 1914 and worked with her on decorative projects, such as those at the Omega Workshops. Later works, such as *Snow Scene* 1921, show great fluency and a subtle use of colour.

Grant Hugh (1962–). British actor, who broke through to widespread popular success with his embodiment of languid romantic charm in the film *Four Weddings and a Funeral* 1994. His performance won a best actor award from the British Academy of Film and Television Arts. He made his screen debut in *Privileged* 1982. Other film roles include *Impromptu* 1990, in which he played Frederick Chopin, *An Awfully Big Adventure* 1994, *The Englishman Who Went Up a Hill But Came Down a Mountain* 1995, and *Nine Months* 1995. In private life he has had a widely publicized relationship with the actress and model Elizabeth Hurley (1965–), though his charming image suffered a blow in 1995 following a liaison with a Hollywood prostitute.

Grant James Augustus (1827–1892). Scottish soldier and explorer who served in India and Abyssinia and, with Captain John Speke, explored the sources of the Nile 1860–63. Accounts of his travels include *A Walk across Africa* 1864 and *Botany of the Speke and Grant Expedition*.

Grant, Ulysses *General Ulysses S Grant at City Point, near Hopewell, Virginia, June 1864. Respected as a war hero, Grant was nominated as the Republican Party's presidential candidate in 1868. He was elected and served two terms, marred by poor administration, financial scandals, and official corruption.*

I know no method to secure the repeal of bad or obnoxious laws so effective as their stringent execution.

ULYSSES S GRANT
Inaugural Address 4 March 1869

Grant Ulysses S(impson) (born Hiram Ulysses Grant) (1822–1885). US Civil War general in chief for the Union and 18th president of the USA 1869–77. As a Republican president, he carried through a liberal Reconstruction policy in the South. He failed to suppress extensive political corruption within his own party and cabinet, which tarnished the reputation of his second term.

Grant was the son of an Ohio farmer. He had an unsuccessful career in the army 1839–54 and in business. On the outbreak of the Civil War he received a commission on the Mississippi front. He took command there in 1862, and by his capture of Vicksburg in 1863 brought the whole Mississippi front under Northern control. In 1864 he was made commander in chief. He slowly wore down the

Confederate general Lee's resistance, and in 1865 received his surrender at Appomattox. He was elected president 1868 and re-elected 1872. As president, he reformed the civil service and ratified the Treaty of Washington with the UK 1871.

Suggested reading
Barber, James G *U S Grant: The Man and the Image* (1986)
Goldhurst, Richard *Many are the Hearts: The Agony and the Triumph of Ulysses S Grant* (1975)
Grant, Ulysses S *Personal Memoirs of Ulysses S Grant* (1885–86, rep 1962)
McFeeley, William S *Grant: A Biography* (1981)

Granvelle Antoine Perrenot de (1517–1586). French diplomat and prelate, adviser to Holy Roman emperor Charles V and Philip II of Spain. As president of the Netherlands' Council of State 1559–64, he introduced the Inquisition to the Netherlands, where he provoked such hostility that Philip II was obliged to recall him.

He was born in Besançon, eastern France, which was then part of the Holy Roman Empire. He was a diplomat in the service of Charles V, became bishop of Arras 1543, and imperial chancellor 1550. In 1554 he helped with the negotiations for the marriage of the future Philip II and Mary I of England. After Charles V's abdication 1555 he served Philip II of Spain, negotiating a number of important treaties and acting as prime minister to the regent in the Low Countries 1559–64. He was created cardinal 1561. His career after his recall from the Netherlands was less important. He returned from retirement to be viceroy of Naples 1571–75, then president of the supreme council of Italy 1579–84 and later of Castile.

Granville-Barker Harley Granville (1877–1946). English theatre director and author. He was director and manager with J E Vedrenne at the Royal Court Theatre, London, 1904–18, producing plays by Shaw, Yeats, Ibsen, Galsworthy, and Masefield. His works include the plays *Waste* 1907, *The Voysey Inheritance* 1905, and *The Madras House* 1910. His series of *Prefaces to Shakespeare* 1927–47 influenced the staging of Shakespeare for many years.

Grappelli Stephane (1908–). French jazz violinist. He played in the Quintette du Hot Club de France 1934–39, in partnership with the guitarist Django Reinhardt. Romantic improvisation is a hallmark of his style.

Grappelli spent World War II in the UK and returned several times to record there, including a number of jazz albums with the classical violinist Yehudi Menuhin in the 1970s. Of his other collaborations, an LP with the mandolinist David Grisman (1945–) reached the US pop chart 1981. He continues to give live performances.

Grass Günter Wilhelm (1927–). German writer. The grotesque humour and socialist feeling of his novels *Die Blechtrommel/The Tin Drum* 1959 and *Der Butt/The Flounder* 1977 are also characteristic of many of his poems.

Born in Danzig (now Gdańsk), he studied at the art academies of Düsseldorf and Berlin, worked as a writer and sculptor (first in Paris and later in Berlin), and in 1958 won the coveted 'Group 47' prize.

Suggested reading
Hayman, R *Günter Grass* (1985)
Lawson, R *Günter Grass* (1984)
Miles, K *Günter Grass* (1975)

Grassmann Hermann Günther (1809–1877). German mathematician and linguist who discovered a new calculus. It was one of the earliest mathematical attempts to investigate n-dimensional space, where n is greater than 3. He also studied ancient languages and comparative linguistics.

Grassmann developed his method of calculus, which he called the theory of extension, from 1840. He published it 1844, but his vocabulary was so obscure that the book had virtually no impact at all until after his death. He used the method to reformulate Ampère's law and investigate the subject of algebraic curves, but again the work was ignored.

Grassmann learned and examined many ancient languages, such as Persian, Sanskrit, and Lithuanian. From his investigations he derived a theory of speech. He published a glossary to the Rig-Veda (Hindu sacred writings) 1873–75.

Grattan Henry (1746–1820). Irish politician. He entered the Irish parliament in 1775, led the patriot opposition, and obtained free trade and legislative independence for Ireland 1782. He failed to prevent the Act of Union of Ireland and England in 1805, sat in the British Parliament from that year, and pressed for Catholic emancipation.

To all Irishmen he gave the wing-beat of his words and the example of his integrity.

R J McHugh on HENRY GRATTAN
in *Henry Grattan* 1936

Graves Michael (1934–). US architect. His work, in the Post-Modernist idiom, is distinctive for the refined, elegant manner in which it blends classical and vernacular elements. Originally a member of the New York Five group, with Peter Eisenman and Richard Meier, Graves went on to develop a highly idiosyncratic, colourful style, as represented in the Public Services building, Portland, Oregon, 1980–82, and Humana Tower, Louisville, Kentucky, 1986.

Graves Robert Ranke (1895–1985). English poet and author. He was severely wounded on the Somme in World War I, and his frank autobiography *Goodbye to All That* 1929 is one of the outstanding war books. Other works include the poems *Over the Brazier* 1916; two historical novels of imperial Rome, *I Claudius* and *Claudius the God*, both 1934; and books on myth – for example, *The White Goddess* 1948.

Suggested reading
Graves, Robert *Goodbye to All That* (early autobiography) (1929)
Graves, Richard P *Robert Graves: The Assault Heroic* (1986)
Graves, Richard P *Robert Graves: The Years with Laura* (1990)
Graves, Richard P *Robert Graves and the White Goddess* (1995)
Seymour, Miranda *Robert Graves: Life on the Edge* (1995)
Seymour-Smith, Martin *Robert Graves: His Life* (1995)

Gray Asa (1810–1888). US botanist and taxonomist who became America's leading expert in the field. His major publications include *Elements of Botany* 1836 and the definitive *Flora of North America* 1838, 1843. He based his revision of the Linnaean system of plant classification on fruit form rather than gross morphology. A friend and supporter of Charles Darwin, he was one of the founders of the American National Academy of Sciences. His *Manual of Botany* 1850 remains the standard reference work on flora east of the Rockies.

Gray Henry (c. 1827–1861). British anatomist who compiled a book on his subject, published 1858 with illustrations by his colleague H Vandyke Carter. What is now known as *Gray's Anatomy* was based on his own dissections. Unlike other contemporary works on the subject, it was organized in terms of systems, rather than areas of the body. Such sections as neuroanatomy have been greatly enlarged in later editions but the section that deals with, for example, the skeletal system is almost identical to Gray's original work. It remains a standard text for students and surgeons alike.

Gray studied at St George's Hospital, London, where he became demonstrator of anatomy and curator of the St George's Museum.

Gray (Kathleen) Eileen (Moray) (1879–1976). Irish-born architect and furniture designer. Her Art Deco furniture explored the use of tubular metal, glass, and new materials such as aluminium.

After training as a painter at the Slade School of Art, London, she worked for a Japanese lacquer painter in Paris. She set up her own workshop and gradually concentrated on the design of furniture, woven textiles, and interiors.

Gray Thomas (1716–1771). English poet. His 'Elegy Written in a Country Churchyard' 1751 is one of the most quoted poems in English. Other poems include 'Ode on a Distant Prospect of Eton College', 'The Progress of Poesy', and 'The Bard'; these poems are now seen as the precursors of Romanticism.

A close friend of Horace Walpole at Eton, Gray made a continental tour with him 1739–41, an account of which is given in his vivid letters. His first poem 'Ode on a Distant Prospect of Eton College' was published 1747 and again 1748 with 'Ode on the Spring' in Robert Dodsley's (1703–1764) *A Collection of Poems By Several Hands*.

The curfew tolls the knell of parting day, / The lowing herd winds slowly o'er the lea, / The ploughman homeward plods his weary way, / And leaves the world to darkness and to me.

THOMAS GRAY
'Elegy Written in a Country Churchyard' 1 1751

Graziani Rodolfo, Marquess (1882–1955). Italian general. He was commander in chief of Italian forces in North Africa during World War II and had some initial success in an advance into Egypt but was comprehensively defeated by British forces 1940, and subsequently replaced. Later, as defence minister in the new Mussolini government, he failed to reorganize a republican Fascist army, was captured by the Allies 1945, tried by an Italian military court, and finally released 1950. He remained active in neo-fascist politics until his death.

Graziano Rocky (Thomas Rocco Barbella) (1922–1990). US middleweight boxing champion who fought in the 1940s and 1950s. Although he was not noted for his boxing skills or finesse, his colourful, brawling style made him popular. He compiled a record of 67 wins, 10 losses and 6 draws between 1942 and 1952. Three of his bouts, with Tony Zale 1946, 1947, and 1948, were considered classics.

Greco Juliette (1927–   ). French singer. She was part of the avant-garde Left Bank café culture of Paris after World War II, singing songs with lyrics by Jacques Prévert (1900–1977) and music by Joseph Kosma (1905–1969), such as 'Les Feuilles mortes' 1947. She appeared in many films, including Jean Cocteau's *Orphée* 1949 and Jean Renoir's *Eléna et les Hommes* 1955. In the 1960s she sang songs by Serge Gainsbourg and Jacques Brel.

Following the arrest of her mother, a member of the French Resistance in the Dordogne, she went to Paris 1943, and became hostess of the all-night basement bistro, Le Tabou, on the rue Dauphine, 1946. In the 1940s Greco was regarded as the 'muse of existentialism'. Her circle included the writers and philosophers Albert Camus, Jean-Paul Sartre, Simone de Beauvoir, and Maurice Merleau-Ponty. She began to tour all over the world in the 1950s, and appeared in several films directed by Darryl F Zanuck, such as *The Sun Also Rises* 1957. Her autobiography *Jujube* was published 1982.

Greco, El (Doménikos Theotokopoulos) (1541–1614). Painter called 'the Greek' because he was born in Crete. He studied in Italy, worked in Rome from about 1570, and by 1577 had settled in Toledo, Spain. He painted elegant portraits and intensely emotional religious scenes with increasingly distorted figures and flickering light; for example, *The Burial of Count Orgaz* 1586 (church of San Tomé, Toledo).

His passionate insistence on rhythm and movement and vehement desire for intensity of expression were conveyed by the elongation and distortion of figures, and unusual and disturbing colour schemes with calculated discords of crimson, lemon yellow, green and blue, and livid flesh tones. Perspective and normal effects of lighting were disregarded, and the significance of the young El Greco's remarks to Giulio Clovio, that the daylight blinded him to the inner light, is apparent. In a modern and 'expressionist' fashion he was projecting a vision conceived in the mind and emotions. The characteristic El Greco can be seen in the *Martyrdom of St Maurice*, 1581–84 (Madrid, Escorial). The huge *The Burial of Count Orgaz* combined austere Spanish dignity with rapturous sublimity. Later compositions include the *Agony in the Garden* (National Gallery, London and

other versions) and the soaring vertical ascent of the *Pentecost, Resurrection* and *Adoration of the Shepherds* (Prado).

The later period of his life produced portraits superbly characterized (and refuting the supposition that El Greco's elongations in other works were due to some defect of eyesight). *Cardinal Niño de Guevara* (New York, Metropolitan Museum) is one of his great portraits, and a remarkable collection is in the Prado. His famous and single pure landscape, *View of Toledo* (Metropolitan Museum), typically selects the intense and abnormal atmosphere of storm. It may be noted that El Greco, as in his *Boy blowing on Coals* (Naples), was the first of those painters who exploited the mysterious and rich effects of shadow produced by artificial light.

Go West, young man, and grow up with the country.

HORACE GREELEY
Hints toward Reform 1850

Greeley Horace (1811–1872). US editor, publisher, and politician. He founded the *New York Tribune* 1841 and, as a strong supporter of the Whig party, advocated many reform causes in his newspaper – among them, feminism and abolitionism. He was an advocate of American westward expansion, and is remembered for his advice 'Go west, young man'. One of the founders of the Republican party 1854, Greeley was the unsuccessful presidential candidate of the breakaway Liberal Republicans 1872.

Green George (1793–1841). English mathematician who coined the term 'potential', now a central concept in electricity, and introduced Green's theorem, which is still applied in the solution of partial differential equations; for instance, in the study of relativity.

Green was born in Nottingham and studied mathematics by himself until at the age of 40 he became a student at Cambridge, and later a member of the staff.

Green's groundbreaking paper was published 1828 and in it he demonstrated the importance of 'potential function' (also known as the Green function) in both magnetism and electricity, and showed how the Green theorem enabled volume integrals to be reduced to surface integrals. It stimulated great interest, and was to influence such scientists as James Clerk Maxwell and Lord Kelvin.

Green went on to produce other important papers on fluids (1832, 1833), attraction (1833), waves in fluids (1837), sound (1837), and light (1837).

Green Henry. Pen name of Henry Vincent Yorke (1905–1973). English novelist. His works (for example *Loving* 1945, and *Nothing* 1950) are characterized by an experimental colloquial prose style and extensive use of dialogue.

Green Lucinda Jane (born Prior-Palmer) (1953–   ). British three-day eventer. She has won the Badminton Horse Trials a record six times 1973–84 and was world individual champion 1982.

Green Thomas Hill (1836–1882). English philosopher. He attempted to show the limitations of Herbert Spencer and John Stuart Mill, and advocated the study of the German philosophers Immanuel Kant and G W F Hegel. He was professor of moral philosophy at Oxford from 1878. His chief works are *Prolegomena to Ethics* 1883 and *Principles of Political Obligation* 1895.

Greenaway Kate (Catherine) (1846–1901). English illustrator. She is known for her drawings of children. In 1877 she first exhibited at the Royal Academy, London, and began her collaboration with the colour-printer Edmund Evans, with whom she produced a number of children's books, including *Mother Goose*.
Suggested reading
Ernst, Edward (ed) *The Kate Greenaway Treasury* (1967)
Thomson, Susan *Kate Greenaway* (1977)

Greenaway Peter (1942–   ). English film director. His films are highly stylized and cerebral, richly visual, and often controversial. His feeling for perspective and lighting reveal his early training as a painter. His films, such as *A Zed & Two Noughts* 1985, are hallmarked by puzzle motifs and numerical games. Greenaway's other films include *The Draughtsman's Contract* 1983, *Belly of an Architect* 1986, *Drowning by Numbers* 1988, the controversially violent *The Cook, the Thief, his Wife and her Lover* 1989, *Prospero's Books* 1991, and *The Baby of Macon* 1993.

> *God ... created a number of possibilities in case some of his prototypes failed – that is the meaning of evolution.*
>
> GRAHAM GREENE
> *Travels With My Aunt* pt 2, ch 7 1981

Greene (Henry) Graham (1904–1991). English writer. His novels of guilt, despair, and penitence are set in a world of urban seediness or political corruption in many parts of the world. They include *Brighton Rock* 1938, *The Power and the Glory* 1940, *The Heart of the Matter* 1948, *The Third Man* 1949, *The Honorary Consul* 1973, and *Monsignor Quixote* 1982.

Greene was born in Berkhamsted. In World War II he served in the Foreign Office. He converted to Catholicism 1926.

Suggested reading
Greene, Graham *A Sort of Life* (autobiography) (1972)
Lodge, David *Graham Greene* (1966)
O'Prey, Paul *A Reader's Guide to Graham Greene* (1988)
Sharrock, R *Saints, Sinners and Comedians: The Novels of Graham Greene* (1984)
Shelden, Michael *Graham Greene: The Man Within* (1994)
Sherry, Norman *The Life of Graham Greene:1904–1939* (1989)

Greene Nathanael (1742–1786). American military leader. During the American Revolution 1775–83 he was commander of the Rhode Island regiments and later brigadier general in the Continental army, seeing action at the Battle of Long Island 1776 and Washington's New Jersey campaigns 1777. He commanded the successful American offensive in the South that ended the war.

Greene was born in Warwick, Rhode Island. Although a member of a Quaker family, he showed an exceptional interest in military affairs.

Greer *The Australian feminist Germaine Greer came to prominence in the 1970s with her polemical study* The Female Eunuch, *which argues that women have to determine their own social and sexual identities. Some feminists criticized her later works, such as* Sex and Identity *1984, in which she argued that sexual liberation was often to women's detriment. Greer has also written on Shakespeare and on the nature of ageing.*

Greenspan Alan (1926–). US economist who succeeded Paul Volcker as chair of the Federal Reserve System 1987 and successfully pumped liquidity into the market to avert a sudden 'free fall' into recession after the Wall Street share crash of Oct 1987. He served as economics adviser and member of a variety of 'task forces' under the Republican presidents Nixon, Ford, and Reagan.

Greenstein Jesse Leonard (1909–). US astronomer who took part in the discovery of the interstellar magnetic field and the discovery and interpretation of quasars. His early work involved the spectroscopic investigation of stellar atmospheres; later work included a study of the structure and composition of white dwarf stars.

Greenstein was born in New York and studied at Harvard. In 1948, he joined the California Institute of Technology and also the staff of the Mount Wilson and Palomar Observatories. He became professor of astrophysics 1971. During the 1970s he guided both the US space agency NASA and the National Academy of Sciences in their policies.

Greenstreet Sydney (1879–1954). English character actor. He made an impressive film debut in *The Maltese Falcon* 1941 and became one of the cinema's best-known villains. His other films include *Casablanca* 1942 and *The Mask of Dimitrios* 1944.

Greenway Francis Howard (1777–1837). English-born architect in Australia, who arrived in New South Wales as a convict in 1814 and was granted a ticket-of-leave in 1815 by Governor Macquarie and a free pardon in 1819. His elegantly proportioned Georgian buildings were designed to suit the Australian climate and landscape and used attractive local building materials. Examples of his work include the Hyde Park convict barracks, 1817, now a museum, St Mark's, Windsor 1817, and the St James's, Sydney 1819.

Greenwood Walter (1903–1974). English novelist of the Depression. His own lack of a job gave authenticity to *Love on the Dole* 1933, later dramatized and filmed.

> *Human beings have an inalienable right to invent themselves; when that right is pre-empted it is called brain-washing.*
>
> GERMAINE GREER
> *The Times* 1 Feb 1986

Greer Germaine (1939–). Australian academic and feminist, author of *The Female Eunuch* 1970. The book is a polemical study of how patriarchy – through the nuclear family and capitalism – subordinates women by forcing them to conform to feminine stereotypes that effectively 'castrate' them.

With its publication, Greer became identified as a leading figure of the women's movement. However, the book has been criticized by other feminists for placing too much emphasis on sexual liberation as the way forward. In *Sex and Destiny: The Politics of Human Fertility* 1984, a critique of the politics of fertility and contraception, Greer seemed to reverse this position. Other works include *The Obstacle Race* 1979, a study of women and painting; and *The Change* 1991, a positive view of the menopause.

Suggested reading
Greer, Germaine *Daddy, We Hardly Knew You* (autobiography) (1989)

Gregg Norman McAlister (1892–1966). Australian ophthalmic surgeon who discovered 1941 that German measles in a pregnant woman could cause physical defects in her child. Knighted 1953.

Gregory Augustus Charles (1819–1905). English-born explorer and surveyor in Australia who in 1855–56 led an expedition of scientific exploration which crossed from Victoria River, on the NW coast of Australia, to Rockhampton on the NE coast, and located valuable pastures. In 1858 his expedition in search of Leichhardt found traces of the lost explorer but failed to clear up the mystery of his disappearance. KCMG 1903.

Gregory Isabella Augusta, Lady (born Persse) (1852–1932). Irish dramatist. She was associated with W B Yeats in creating the Abbey Theatre, Dublin, 1904. Her plays include the comedy *Spreading the News* 1904 and the tragedy *Gaol Gate* 1906. Her journals 1916–30 were published 1946.

Gregory name of 16 popes, including:

Gregory (I) the Great (St Gregory) (*c*. 540–604). Pope from 590 who asserted Rome's supremacy and exercised almost imperial powers. In 596 he sent St Augustine to England. He introduced the choral *Gregorian chant* into the liturgy. Feast day 12 March.
Suggested reading
Dudden, F H *Gregory the Great* (1905, rep 1967)

Gregory VII (monastic name *Hildebrand*) (*c*. 1023–1085). Chief minister to several popes before his election to the papacy 1073. In 1077 he forced the Holy Roman emperor Henry IV to wait in the snow at Canossa for four days, dressed as a penitent, before receiving pardon. He was driven from Rome and died in exile. His feast day is 25 May. Canonized 1606.

He claimed power to depose kings, denied lay rights to make clerical appointments, and attempted to suppress simony (the buying and selling of church preferments) and to enforce clerical celibacy, making enemies of both rulers and the church.
Suggested reading
Blumenthal, U-R *The Investiture Controversy* (trs 1988)
MacDonald, Allan *Hildebrand: A Life of Gregory the Seventh* (1932, rep 1977)
Williams, S *Gregory VII: Church Reformer or World Monarch?* (1967)

Gregory XIII (1502–1585). Pope from 1572 who introduced the reformed *Gregorian calendar*, still in use, in which a century year is not a leap year unless it is divisible by 400.

Gregory of Tours, St (*c*. 538–594). French Christian bishop of Tours from 573, author of a *History of the Franks*. His feast day is 17 Nov.

The fighting man shall from the sun / Take warmth, and life from the glowing earth.
> JULIAN GRENFELL
> 'Into Battle' 1915

Grenfell Julian Henry Francis (1888–1915). British poet, killed in World War I. His poem 'Into Battle' was first published in *The Times* 1915.

Grenville George (1712–1770). British Whig politician, prime minister, and chancellor of the Exchequer, whose introduction of the Stamp Act 1765 to raise revenue from the colonies was one of the causes of the American Revolution. His government was also responsible for prosecuting the radical John Wilkes. Grenville took other measures to reduce the military and civil costs in North America, including the Sugar Act and the Quartering Act. His inept management of the Regency Act 1765 damaged his relationship with George III.

He was the raven of the House of Commons, always croaking defeat in the midst of triumphs, and bankruptcy with an overflowing exchequer.
> T B Macaulay on GEORGE GRENVILLE
> in *Essays*, 'Chatham' 1866

Grenville Richard (*c*. 1541–1591). English naval commander and adventurer who died heroically aboard his ship *The Revenge* when attacked by Spanish warships. Grenville fought in Hungary and Ireland 1566–69, and was knighted about 1577. In 1585 he commanded the expedition that founded Virginia, USA, for his cousin Walter Raleigh. From 1586 to 1588 he organized the defence of England against the Spanish Armada.

In 1591 Grenville was second in command of a fleet under Lord Thomas Howard that sailed to seize Spanish treasure ships returning from South America, when his ship became isolated from the rest of the fleet off the Azores and was attacked by Spanish warships. After many hours of hand-to-hand combat, *The Revenge* succumbed; Grenville was captured and fatally wounded. He became a symbol of English nationalism and was commemorated in the poem 'The Revenge' 1880 by Alfred Tennyson.

It is perfect blindness not to see that in the establishment of the French Republic (1793) is included the overthrow of all the other governments of Europe.
> WILLIAM WYNDHAM, BARON GRENVILLE
> quoting the words of St Just in a letter to his elder brother
> 17 Sept 1794 after the outbreak of war with France

Grenville William Wyndham, 1st Baron Grenville (1759–1834). British Whig politician. Grenville, son of George Grenville, entered the House of Commons 1782, held the secretaryship for Ireland, was home secretary 1791–94 and foreign secretary 1794–1801. He resigned along with Prime Minister Pitt the Younger 1801 over George III's refusal to assent to Catholic emancipation. He refused office in Pitt's government of 1804 because of the exclusion of Charles James Fox. He headed the 'All the Talents' coalition of 1806–07 that abolished the slave trade. Baron 1790.

Gresham Thomas (*c*. 1519–1579). English merchant financier who founded and paid for the Royal Exchange and propounded Gresham's law: 'bad money tends to drive out good money from circulation'. Knighted 1559.

Gresham Thomas Gresham, financial adviser and agent to Elizabeth I and founder of the Royal Exchange, revenues from which funded the establishment of Gresham College.

Gretzky Wayne (1961–   ). Canadian ice-hockey player, probably the best in the history of the National Hockey League (NHL). Gretzky played with the Edmonton Oilers 1979–88 and with the Los Angeles Kings from 1988. He took just 11 years to break the NHL scoring record of 1,850 goals (accumulated by Gordie Howe over 26 years) and won the Hart Memorial Trophy as the NHL's most valuable player of the season a record nine times (1980–87, 1989). By the start of the 1990–91 season he had scored 1,979 goals.

Greuze Jean Baptiste (1725–1805). French painter. His sentimental narrative works include *The Bible Reading* 1755 (Louvre, Paris). Many of his works were reproduced in engravings.

Greville Charles Cavendish Fulke (1794–1865). English diarist. He was Clerk of the Council in Ordinary 1821–59, an office which brought him into close contact with all the personalities of the court and of both political parties. They provided him with much of the material for his *Memoirs* 1817–60.

O wearisome condition of humanity! / Born under one law, to another bound; / Vainly begot, and yet forbidden vanity; / Created sick, commanded to be sound.
FULKE GREVILLE
The Tragedy of Mustapha V iv 1633

Greville Fulke, 1st Baron Brooke (1554–1628). English poet and courtier. He was the friend and biographer of Philip Sidney. Greville's works, none of them published during his lifetime, include *Caelica*, a sequence of poems in different metres; *The Tragedy of Mustapha* and *The Tragedy of Alaham*, tragedies modelled on the Roman Seneca; and the *Life of Sir Philip Sidney* 1652. He has been commended for his plain style and tough political thought. Knighted 1603, baron 1621.

Grey Beryl (1927–   ). English dancer. Prima ballerina with the Sadler's Wells Company 1942–57, she then danced internationally, and was artistic director of the London Festival Ballet 1968–79. Her roles included the Black Queen in *Checkmate* and Odette-Odile in *Swan Lake*. DBE 1988.

The only way with newspaper attacks is, as the Irish say, 'to keep never minding'.
CHARLES, 2ND EARL GREY
in conversation during his final months as prime minister, summer 1834

Grey Charles, 2nd Earl Grey (1764–1845). British Whig politician. He entered Parliament 1786, and in 1806 became First Lord of the Admiralty, and foreign secretary soon afterwards. As prime minister 1830–34, he carried the Great Reform Bill that reshaped the parliamentary representative system 1832 and the act abolishing slavery throughout the British Empire 1833. Succeeded to earldom 1807.

The lamps are going out all over Europe; we shall not see them lit again in our lifetime.
EDWARD GREY
On the impending war 3 Aug 1914 Twenty-Five Years 1925

Grey Edward, 1st Viscount Grey of Fallodon (1862–1933). British Liberal politician, nephew of Charles Grey. As foreign secretary 1905–16 he negotiated an entente with Russia 1907, and backed France against Germany in the Agadir Incident of 1911.

Grey George (1812–1898). British colonial administrator in Australia and New Zealand, born in Portugal. After several unsuccessful exploratory expeditions in Western Australia, he was appointed governor of South Australia 1840. Autocratic in attitude, he managed to bring the colony out of bankruptcy by 1844. He was lieutenant governor of New Zealand 1845–53, governor of Cape

Colony, S Africa, 1854–61, and governor of New Zealand 1861–68. He then entered the New Zealand parliament and was premier 1877–79. KCB 1848.

His opinions were a curious compound of democratic idealism akin to Jefferson's, and a species of pacific imperialism.
W P Reeves on GEORGE GREY
in Dictionary of National Biography

Grey Henry George, 3rd Earl Grey (1802–1894). British politician, son of Charles Grey. He served under his father as undersecretary for the colonies 1830–33, resigning because the cabinet would not back the immediate emancipation of slaves; he was secretary of war 1835–39 and colonial secretary 1846–52.

He was unique among politicians of the period in maintaining that the colonies should be governed for their own benefit, not that of Britain, and in his policy of granting self-government wherever possible. Yet he advocated convict transportation and was opposed to Gladstone's Home Rule policy. He was known as Viscount Howick from 1806 until 1845, when he succeeded to the earldom.

Not merely worthless, but pernicious ... enlarging the range of our responsibilities, while yielding no additional resources for properly sustaining them.
HENRY, 3RD EARL GREY
quoted in K N Bell and W P Morrell Select Documents on British Colonial
Policy 1830–1860 1928. On acquisitions of African land, Nov 1846.

Grey Lady Jane (1537–1554). Queen of England for nine days, 10–19 July 1553, the great-granddaughter of Henry VII. She was married 1553 to Lord Guildford Dudley (died 1554), son of the Duke of Northumberland. Edward VI was persuaded by Northumberland to set aside the claims to the throne of his sisters Mary and Elizabeth. When Edward died on 6 July 1553, Jane reluctantly accepted the crown and was proclaimed queen four days later. Mary, although a Roman Catholic, had the support of the populace, and the Lord Mayor of London announced that she was queen 19 July. But Grey was executed on Tower Green to make way for Mary I.

Suggested reading
Chapman, H W *Lady Jane Grey* (1962)
Malvern, G *The World of Lady Jane Grey* (1964)

One of the greatest benefits ... God gave me, is, that he sent me so sharp and severe parents, and so gentle a schoolmaster.
LADY JANE GREY
to the humanist Roger Ascham on the eve of his departure for
Germany 1550. Her parents were the Duke of Suffolk and
Lady Frances Brandon: her schoolmaster was John Aylmer
later Bishop of London, quoted in The Schoolmaster 1570

Grey (Pearl) Zane (1872–1939). US author of Westerns. He wrote more than 80 books, including *Riders of the Purple Sage* 1912, and was primarily responsible for the creation of the Western as a literary genre.

Grieg Edvard Hagerup (1843–1907). Norwegian nationalist composer. Much of his music is small-scale, particularly his songs, dances, sonatas, and piano works, strongly identifying with

I am sure my music has a taste of codfish in it.
EDVARD GRIEG
Speech 1903

Grieg *The composer Edvard Grieg, whose output consists largely of keyboard and vocal works of a characteristic Norwegian flavour, reflecting the fact that he was a fine pianist and that his wife Nina was a singer (he considered her the greatest interpreter of his songs).* (Image Select)

Norwegian folk music. Among his orchestral works are the *Piano Concerto in A Minor* 1869 and the incidental music for Ibsen's *Peer Gynt* 1876, commissioned by Ibsen and the Norwegian government.

Grieg studied at the Leipzig Conservatoire and in Copenhagen. He was a director of the Christiania (Oslo) Philharmonic Society 1866 and played a part in the formation of the Norwegian Academy of Music.

Suggested reading
Horton, J *Grieg* (1974)
Benestad, Finn and Schjelderup-Ebbe, Dag *Grieg* (tr 1988)
Schlotel, B *Grieg* (1986)

Grierson John (1898–1972). Scottish film producer, director, and theoretician. He was a sociologist who pioneered the documentary film in Britain, describing it as 'the creative treatment of actuality'. He directed *Drifters* 1929 and produced 1930–35 *Industrial Britain*, *Song of Ceylon*, and *Night Mail*. During World War II he created the National Film Board of Canada. Some of his writings were gathered in *Grierson on Documentary* 1946.

Griffin Walter Burley (1876–1937). US-born architect in Australia best known as the designer of the original plan, later modified, for the city of Canberra. He later settled in Australia and other works include Newman College 1917 and the Capitol Theatre 1924 in Melbourne, and the development of the Sydney harbourside suburb of Castlecrag using an organic style of architecture to blend with natural bushland.

Griffith D(avid) W(ark) (1875–1948). US film director. He was an influential figure in the development of cinema as an art. He made hundreds of 'one-reelers' 1908–13, in which he pioneered the techniques of masking, fade-out, flashback, crosscut, close-up, and long shot. After much experimentation with photography and new techniques he directed *The Birth of a Nation* 1915, about the aftermath of the Civil War, later criticized as degrading to blacks. His other films include the epic *Intolerance* 1916, *Broken Blossoms* 1919, *Way Down East* 1920, *Orphans of the Storm* 1921, and *The Struggle* 1931. He was a cofounder of United Artists 1919. He made two unsuccessful sound films and subsequently lived forgotten in Hollywood until his death.

Suggested reading
Henderson, Robert *D W Griffith: His Life and Work* (1972)
O'Dell *Griffith and the Rise of Hollywood* (1970)
Schickel, Richard *D W Griffith: An American Life* (1984)

Griffith Melanie (1957–). US film actress. Bubbly and vivacious, with a talent for projecting 'kookiness', she showed a gift for light comedy as the secretary with ambitions in *Working Girl* 1988, for which she received an Academy Award nomination. She initially attracted notice as the perverse anti-heroine of *Something Wild* 1986. Other films include *Pacific Heights* 1990 and *Born Yesterday* 1993.

Griffith-Joyner (Delorez) Florence (born Griffith) (1959–). US track athlete who won three gold medals at the 1988 Seoul Olympics, the 100 and 200 metres and the sprint relay. Her time in the 200 metres was a world record 21.34 seconds.

Grignard (François Auguste) Victor (1871–1935). French chemist. In 1900 he discovered a series of organic compounds, the *Grignard reagents*, that found applications as some of the most versatile reagents in organic synthesis. Members of the class contain a hydrocarbon radical, magnesium, and a halogen such as chlorine. Grignard reagents added to formaldehyde (methanal) produce a primary alcohol; with any other aldehyde they form secondary alcohols, and added to ketones give rise to tertiary alcohols. They will also add to a carboxylic acid to produce first a ketone and ultimately a tertiary alcohol. He shared the Nobel Prize for Chemistry 1912.

He became professor at Nancy 1910. During World War I he headed a department at the Sorbonne concerned with the development of chemical warfare. From 1919 he was professor at Lyon.

Grillparzer Franz (1791–1872). Austrian poet and dramatist. His plays include the tragedy *Die Ahnfrau/The Ancestress* 1817, the classical *Sappho* 1818, and the trilogy *Das goldene Vliess/The Golden Fleece* 1821.

Born in Vienna, Grillparzer worked for the Austrian government service 1813–56. His historical tragedies *König Ottokars Glück und Ende/King Ottocar, His Rise and Fall* 1825 and *Ein treuer Diener seines Herrn/A True Servant of His Master* 1826 both involved him with the censor. There followed his two greatest dramas, *Des Meeres und der Liebe Wellen/The Waves of Sea and Love* 1831, returning to the Hellenic world, and *Der Traum, ein Leben/A Dream Is Life* 1834. He wrote a bitter cycle of poems *Tristia ex Ponto* 1835 after an unhappy love affair.

Grimaldi Francesco Maria (1618–1663). Italian physicist who discovered the diffraction of light. In physiology, he observed muscle action and was the first to note that minute sounds are produced by muscles during contraction.

Grimaldi was born in Bologna and was professor of mathematics at the Jesuit College there from 1648. He also helped with astronomical observations.

Grimaldi let a beam of sunlight enter a darkened room through a small circular aperture and observed that, when the beam passed through a second aperture onto a screen, the spot of light was slightly larger than the second aperture and had coloured fringes. Grimaldi concluded that the light rays had diverged slightly, becoming bent outwards, or diffracted. On placing a narrow obstruction in the light beam, he noticed bright bands at each side of its shadow on the screen. This phenomenon can be explained readily only if light is regarded as travelling in waves – contrary to the then accepted corpuscular theory of light.

A description of the experiments was published in *Physicomathesis de lumine, coloribus, et iride/Physicomathematical Thesis of Light, Colours and the Rainbow* 1665.

Grimaldi Joseph (1779–1837). English clown. Born in London, he was the son of an Italian actor. He appeared on the stage at two years

With him the days of genuine pantomime drollery are held to have expired.

Dictionary of National Biography on JOSEPH GRIMALDI

old. He gave his name 'Joey' to all later clowns, and excelled as 'Mother Goose' performed at Covent Garden 1806.

Grimm brothers Jakob Ludwig Karl (1785–1863) and Wilhelm (1786–1859), philologists and collectors of German fairy tales such as 'Hansel and Gretel' and 'Rumpelstiltskin'. Joint compilers of an exhaustive dictionary of German, they saw the study of language and the collecting of folk tales as strands in a single enterprise.

Encouraged by a spirit of Romantic nationalism, the brothers collected stories from friends, relatives, and villagers. *Kinder und Hausmärchen/Nursery and Household Tales* were published as successive volumes 1812, 1815, and 1822. Jakob was professor of philology at Göttingen and formulator of Grimm's law. His *Deutsche Grammatick/German Grammar* 1819 was the first historical treatment of the Germanic languages.

Suggested reading
Ellis, J *One Fairy Story Too Many* (1983)
Peppard, Murray *Paths Through the Forest: A Biography of the Brothers Grimm* (1971)
Zipes, Jack *The Brothers Grimm* (1989)

Grimmelshausen Hans Jakob Christofel von (1625–1676). German picaresque novelist. *Der Abenteuerliche Simplicissimus/The Adventurous Simplicissimus* 1669 reflects his experiences in the Thirty Years' War.

Grimond Jo(seph), Baron Grimond (1913–1993). British Liberal politician. As leader of the Liberal Party 1956–67, he aimed at making it 'a new radical party to take the place of the Socialist Party as an alternative to Conservatism'. An old-style Whig and a man of culture and personal charm, he had a considerable influence on postwar British politics, although he never held a major public position. During his term of office, the number of Liberal seats in Parliament doubled.

Born in St Andrews, he studied law, but after wartime service began a political career. It was his ill luck to become leader of the Liberal Party at a time when the Labour Party, in its ascendancy, was, with the Conservatives, squeezing the Liberals almost out of existence. The party may well have ceased to survive without his inspiration. However, when he passed it to Jeremy Thorpe 1967 it was in much better shape. After Thorpe's resignation 1976, Grimond became leader again for three months before handing over to David Steel.

He married Laura Bonham Carter, of the great Liberal dynasty, who was also politically active, and they had four children. He represented the remote Orkney and Shetland constituency for 33 years until entering the House of Lords 1983.

Grimshaw Nicholas Thomas (1939–). English architect. His work has developed along distinctly High Tech lines, diverging sharply from that of his former partner, Terry Farrell. His *Financial Times* printing works, London 1988, is an uncompromising industrial building, exposing machinery to view through a glass outer wall. The British Pavilion for Expo '92 in Seville, created in similar vein, addressed problems of climatic control, incorporating a huge wall of water in its façade and sail-like mechanisms on the roof.

Gris Juan. Adopted name of José Victoriano Gonzalez (1887–1927). Spanish painter, one of the earliest Cubists. He developed a distinctive geometrical style, often strongly coloured. He experimented with paper collage and made designs for Diaghilev's Ballets Russes 1922–23.

He went to Paris 1906, meeting Picasso, whose disciple he became, and began to paint about 1910. First trained as an engineer, he had a precise and scientific outlook and delighted in variations of geometric form effectively combined with an imitative rendering of substance, for example the grain of wood and the use of *papiers collés* – pieces of wallpaper, etc. 'With a mind as precise as mine', he said, 'I can never smudge a blue or bend a straight line.' In addition to oil-paintings he produced some etchings and lithographs as book illustrations.

Grisham John (1955–). US writer. His courtroom thrillers *A Time to Kill* 1987, *The Firm* 1991, *The Pelican Brief* 1992, *The Client*

1993, *The Chamber* 1994, and *The Rain Maker* 1995 were all best sellers.

Grisham was born in Arkansas, the son of a migrant construction worker who moved around the southern USA. He worked as a tax lawyer in Mississippi, and sat as a Democrat in the Mississippi state legislature 1983–90. *The Firm* was made into a film 1993, directed by Sydney Pollack (1934–).

Grivas George (Georgios Theodoros) (1898–1974). Greek Cypriot general who from 1955 led the underground group EOKA's attempts to secure the union (Greek *enosis*) of Cyprus with Greece.

Gromyko Andrei Andreyevich (1909–1989). President of the USSR 1985–88. As ambassador to the USA from 1943, he took part in the Tehran, Yalta, and Potsdam conferences; as United Nations representative 1946–49, he exercised the Soviet veto 26 times. He was foreign minister 1957–85. It was Gromyko who formally nominated Mikhail Gorbachev as Communist Party leader 1985.

Gropius Walter Adolf (1883–1969). German architect, in the USA from 1937. He was an early exponent of the International Style, defined by glass curtain walls, cubic blocks, and unsupported corners. A founder-director of the Bauhaus school in Weimar 1919–28, he advocated teamwork in design and artistic standards in industrial production. He was responsible for the new Bauhaus premises in Dessau 1925–26. The model factory and office building at the 1914 Cologne Werkbund exhibition, designed with Adolph Meyer, was an early example of the International Style.

From 1937 he was professor of architecture at Harvard. His other works include the Fagus Works (a shoe factory in Prussia) 1911 and the Harvard Graduate Centre 1949–50.

Suggested reading
Busignani, Alberto *Gropius* (1973)
Fitch, James *Walter Gropius* (1960)
Franciscono, M *Walter Gropius and the Creation of the Bauhaus in Weimar* (1971)

Grose Francis (1758–1814). English army officer and colonial administrator in Australia. He arrived in 1792 with the New South Wales Corps which he had raised and of which he was the first commander. He was also lieutenant governor and, after Phillip's departure, was acting governor until 1794, during which time the officers of the NSW Corps established their hold over trading and farming in the colony.

Gross Michael (1964–). German swimmer who won gold medals at the 1984 and 1988 Olympics. He has also won gold medals at the World and European Championships. Gross won a record six gold medals at the 1985 European Championships. He is known as 'the albatross' because of his exceptional arm span.

Grosseteste Robert (c. 1169–1253). English scholar and bishop. His prolific writings include scientific works as well as translations of Aristotle and commentaries on the Bible. He was a forerunner of the empirical school, being one of the earliest to suggest testing ancient Greek theories by practical experiment. He was bishop of Lincoln from 1235 to his death, attempting to reform morals and clerical discipline, and engaging in controversy with Innocent IV over the pope's finances.

Grosseteste was born in Suffolk and studied at Oxford and perhaps Paris, later becoming chancellor of Oxford University.

I left the room with silent dignity, but caught my foot in the mat.

GEORGE AND WEEDON GROSSMITH
The Diary of a Nobody ch 12 1894

Grossmith George (1847–1912). English actor and singer. Turning from journalism to the stage, in 1877 he began a long association with the Gilbert and Sullivan operas, in which he created a number of parts. He collaborated with his brother *Weedon Grossmith* (1854–1919) on the comic novel *Diary of a Nobody* 1894.

Grosvenor family name of dukes of Westminster; seated at Eaton Hall, Cheshire, England.

Grosvenor Gilbert Hovey (1875–1966). US publisher, named editor of *National Geographic Magazine* 1899. Its financial status was shaky, but Grosvenor soon transformed it to a mass circulation periodical through the use of colour photography from 1910. He also changed the parent body, the National Geographic Society, from a small scientific body to a national institution. As president of the Society 1920–54 and chair of its directors 1954–66, Grosvenor sponsored scientific expeditions all over the world.

Grosz George (1893–1959). German Expressionist painter and graphic artist. He was a founder of the Berlin Dada group 1918. Grosz excelled in savage satirical drawings criticizing the government and the military establishment. After numerous prosecutions he fled his native Berlin 1932 and went to the USA where he became a naturalized American 1938.

Suggested reading

Eberle, M *World War I and the Weimar Artists: Dix, Grosz, Beckmann, Schlemmer* (1985)

Grosz, G *A Little Yes and a Big No: The Autobiography of George Grosz* (1946)

Hess, Hans *George Grosz* (1974)

Whitfield *Grosz* (1981)

Grosz Károly (1930–1996). Hungarian Communist politician, prime minister 1987–88. As leader of the ruling Hungarian Socialist Workers' Party (HSWP) 1988–89, he sought to establish a flexible system of 'socialist pluralism'.

Grosz, a steelworker's son, was a printer and then a newspaper editor before moving to Budapest to serve as first deputy head and then head of the HSWP agitprop (agitation and propaganda) department 1968–79. He was Budapest party chief 1984–87 and briefly prime minister before succeeding János Kádár as HSWP leader May 1988. In Oct 1989 the HSWP reconstituted itself as the Hungarian Socialist Party and Grosz was replaced as party leader by the social democrat Rezso Nyers.

Grotefend Georg Friedrich (1775–1853). German scholar. Although a student of the classical rather than the oriental languages, he nevertheless solved the riddle of the wedgelike cuneiform script as used in ancient Persia: decipherment of Babylonian cuneiform followed from his work.

Grotius Hugo, or *Huig de Groot* (1583–1645). Dutch jurist and politician. His book *De Jure Belli et Pacis/On the Law of War and Peace* 1625 is the foundation of international law. Grotius held that the rules governing human and international relations are founded on human nature, which is rational and social. These rules constitute a natural law binding on citizens, rulers, and God.

Grotius was born in Delft and educated at the University of London. He became a lawyer, and later received political appointments. In 1618 he was arrested as a republican and sentenced to imprisonment for life. His wife contrived his escape 1620, and he settled in France, where he composed *De Jure Belli*. He was Swedish ambassador in Paris 1634–45.

Grotowski Jerzy (1933–). Polish theatre director. His ascetic theoery of performance in *Towards a Poor Theatre* 1968 has had a great influence on experimental theatre in the USA and Europe. His most famous productions were *Akropolis* 1962, *The Constant Prince* 1965, and *Apocalypsis cum Figuris* 1969, which he toured widely.

He directed in Opole (from 1959) and then in Wroclaw (from 1965); his company, originally the Theatre of the Thirteen Rows, was renamed the Laboratory Theatre 1962.

Grounds Roy Burman (1905–1981). Australian architect. He was a pioneer of modern architecture in Australia with projects such as Clendon, a block of bachelor units. Other works include Wrest Point Casino, Hobart, the Victorian Arts Centre, Melbourne and the Australian Academy of Science headquarters, Canberra. Knighted 1969.

Grove Frederick Philip (1879–1948). Canadian novelist and essayist. His experiences as an itinerant farm hand and schoolteacher on the prairies gave substance to his evocative sketches 'Over Prairie Trails' 1922 and his realist tragedies *Settlers of the Marsh* 1925 and *Fruits of the Earth* 1933, exploring the emotional and spiritual costs of pioneer life, material success, and family conflict in rural Manitoba.

Born in Prussia, he wrote poems, plays, and novels in German and worked as a translator before debt drove him to Canada.

Grove George (1820–1900). English scholar. He edited the original *Dictionary of Music and Musicians* 1889, which in its expanded and revised form is still one of the standard music reference sources. He was also the first director of the Royal College of Music. Knighted 1882.

Groves Charles Barnard (1915–). English conductor. Known both as a choral and symphonic conductor, he is an outstanding interpreter of British music, especially the works of Delius. Knighted 1973.

Groves Leslie (1896–1970). US general and engineer. Groves had spent most of his career on civil engineering projects and so was appointed 1942 to supervise the engineering of the Manhattan Project, the codename for the US atomic bomb. He was responsible for the erection of factories, towns, power stations, and the acquisition of all the raw materials necessary to complete the project. He

Groves, Charles *The conductor Charles Groves. In addition to his secure foundation in the symphonic repertory, Groves could have been considered Beecham's spiritual heir in terms of his affinity for the choral works of Delius, such as* A Mass of Life *and* Sea Drift.

employed over 125,000 people and had an annual budget in excess of $500 million.

Grumiaux Arthur, Baron (1921–1986). Belgian violinist. He was admired for his purity of tone and controlled intensity. He excelled in the 18th-century repertory, and is famous for his recordings of the unaccompanied Bach violin sonatas, and the Mozart and Beethoven violin/piano sonatas with Romanian pianist Clara Haskil (1895–1960). In addition he played the 20th-century concertos of Bartók, Berg, and Stravinsky. Baron 1973.

Grünewald Matthias, or Mathis Gothardt-Neithardt (c. 1475–1528). German painter. He was active in Mainz, Frankfurt, and Halle. He was court painter, architect, and engineer to the archbishop of Mainz 1508–14. His few surviving paintings show an intense involvement with religious subjects. His Isenheim altarpiece, 1515 (Unterlinden Museum, Colmar, France), with its tortured figure of Jesus, recalls medieval traditions.

To his contemporaries he was 'Matthis of Aschaffenburg'. He was trained in Alsace in the style of Martin Schongauer (though unlike the latter he produced no engravings), and is first mentioned, 1501, in the archives of Seligenstadt. 1508–1514 he was painter to the Archbishop of Mainz at Aschaffenburg, and after 1514 to the Elector of Mainz, Albrecht von Brandenburg. His master work is the altarpiece for Isenheim in Alsace. His later years were occupied by a series of paintings ordered by the Elector of Mainz for the cathedral of Halle (where Grünewald also had the function of hydraulic engineer). Apart from the Isenheim altarpiece, his remaining work is fragmentary: the *Christ Mocked* (Munich); a Crucifixion (Basel); parts of altarpieces at Stuppach, Freiburg-Breisgau, Karlsruhe and Aschaffenburg; a fine late work (part of the Halle commission) is the *Meeting of St Erasmus and St Maurice* (Munich). Unlike his contemporary, Dürer, he was untouched by the spirit of the Renaissance, yet he seems in his own way to open up to art prospects hitherto unknown in the intensity of tragedy and pathos he achieves.

Guardi Francesco (1712–1793). Italian painter. He produced souvenir views of his native Venice that were commercially less successful than Canaletto's but are now considered more atmospheric, with subtler use of reflected light.

A figure of *Hope*, 1747 (Sarasota, Ringling Museum), and five large canvases (based on illustrations by Piazzetta to Tasso), discovered in Ireland 1959 and identified as his, show his decorative skill in Rococo figure painting, in which, however, he does not challenge comparison with his brother-in-law, Tiepolo. His views of Venice and the islands of the lagoon are his main product. His output was large and he seems to have been assisted by his son *Giacomo* (1764–1835), who produced *gouache* views in a style of his own. Guardi painted not only famous buildings and splendid occasions like Canaletto but insular byways and architectural caprices with ruins, with a sparkling touch and a sense of atmosphere that might be called Impressionist.

Guare John (1938–). US dramatist. He wrote the screenplay of Louis Malle's *Atlantic City* 1980. His stage plays include *House of Blue Leaves* 1971 and *Six Degrees of Separation* 1990.

Guareschi Giovanni (1909–1968). Italian author. His short stories feature the friendly feud between parish priest Don Camillo and the communist village mayor.

Guarini Giovanni (1624–1683). Italian architect. His intricate carved Baroque designs were produced without formal architectural training. Guarini was a secular priest of the Theatine Order, and many of his buildings are religious; for example, the Chapel of the Holy Shroud, Turin, 1667–90. His greatest secular work is the undulating Palazzo Carignano, Turin, 1679.

Guarneri family of stringed-instrument makers of Cremona, Italy. Giuseppe 'del Gesù' Guarneri (1698–1744) produced the finest models.

Guderian Heinz Wilhelm (1888–1954). German general in World War II. He created the Panzer (German 'armour') divisions that formed the ground spearhead of Hitler's *Blitzkrieg* attack strategy, achieving a significant breakthrough at Sedan in Ardennes, France 1940, and leading the advance to Moscow 1941. His initial advance on Moscow was rapid but winter and determined Soviet resistance led him to make a partial withdrawal and Hitler dismissed him from his post. He was reinstated as inspector general of armoured troops 1943 and became Chief of Staff after the July plot against Hitler 1944, but was dismissed by Hitler March 1945.

The man who showed what the German Panzer divisions could do when used with imagination.

Alan Bullock on HEINZ WILHELM GUDERIAN
in *Hitler* 1962

Guercino, Il (Giovanni Francesco Barbieri) (1591–1666). Italian Baroque painter. He was active chiefly in Rome. In his ceiling painting of *Aurora* 1621–23 (Villa Ludovisi, Rome), the chariot-borne figure of Dawn rides across the heavens; the architectural framework is imitated in the painting, giving the illusion that the ceiling opens into the sky. His work in Rome, 1621–22, when he was employed by Pope Gregory XV, included his *Petronilla*, which was placed in the Capitol, and his ceiling decoration *Aurora* for the Villa Ludovisi, which rivals Guido Reni's famous version of the same subject. He worked at Cento 1623–42, then removed to Bologna, where, following Reni, he produced many vapid religious paintings which show a decline from his early work. He was a prolific and able draughtsman and his drawings were highly prized in 18th-century England, many fine examples being among the 600 in the Royal Collection at Windsor Castle.

Guericke Otto von (1602–1686). German physicist and politician who invented the air pump and demonstrated the pressure of the atmosphere. He also constructed the first machine for generating static electricity.

Guericke constructed an air pump in an attempt to produce a vacuum, to test French mathematician René Descartes's idea that space was matter. In 1647 Guericke imploded a copper sphere from which he pumped the air via an outlet at the bottom. But when he built a stronger vessel, he succeeded in evacuating it without causing it to collapse. He also demonstrated that a candle is extinguished as the air is removed, and gradually the theory that a vacuum cannot exist was discarded.

While experimenting with a globe of sulphur constructed to simulate the magnetic properties of the Earth, Guericke discovered that it produced static electricity when rubbed; he went on to develop a primitive machine for the production of static electricity. He also demonstrated the magnetization of iron by hammering in a north–south direction.

Another first with which he is credited is the observation of coloured shadows.

Guérin Camille (1872–1961). French bacteriologist who, with Albert Calmette, developed the BCG vaccine for tuberculosis 1921.

A dedicated professional politician who, although lacking in personal charm ... had the powers of exposition to spread Marx's ideas and the organizing ability to found a major socialist party.

James Joll on JULES GUESDES
in *Europe Since 1870* 2nd ed 1976

Guesdes Jules. Adopted name of Mathieu Basile (1845–1922). French socialist leader from the 1880s who espoused Marxism and revolutionary change. His movement, the Partie Ouvrier Français (French Workers' Party), was eventually incorporated in the foundation of the SFIO (Section Française de l'International Ouvrière/French Section of International Labour) 1905.

Guest Edgar Albert (1881–1959). US journalist and poet. From 1900 he wrote 'Breakfast Table Chat' for the *Detroit Free Press*. The column combined light verse and folksy wisdom and was later nationally syndicated. Guest's best-selling collections of verse include *A Heap o' Livin'* 1916 and *Harbor Lights of Home* 1928.

Guettard Jean-Etienne (1715–1786). French naturalist who pioneered geological mapping. He also studied botany and medicine, as well as the origin of various types of rock.

Guettard was born in Etampes, Ile-de-France, and became keeper of the natural-history collection of the Duc d'Orléans. In 1746 he presented his first mineralogical map of France to the Académie des Sciences; and in 1766, he and chemist Antoine Lavoisier were commissioned to prepare a geological survey of France, though only a fraction was ever completed.

Guevara Che (Ernesto) (1928–1967). Latin American revolutionary. He was born in Argentina and trained there as a doctor, but left his homeland 1953 because of his opposition to the right-wing president Perón. In effecting the Cuban revolution of 1959, he was second only to Castro and Castro's brother Raúl. In 1965 he went to the Congo to fight against white mercenaries, and then to Bolivia, where he was killed in an unsuccessful attempt to lead a peasant rising. He was an orthodox Marxist and renowned for his guerrilla techniques.

Suggested reading
Ebon, Martin *Che: The Making of a Legend* (1969)
Harris, Richard *Death of a Revolutionary* (1970)
Sauvage, Leo *Che Guevara: The Failure of a Revolutionary* (1974)
Sinclair, A *Che Guevara* (1970)

Guido Reni. Italian painter, see ◊Reni.

Guillaume Charles Edouard (1861–1938). Swiss physicist who studied measurement and alloy development. He discovered a nickel-steel alloy, Invar, which showed negligible expansion with rising temperatures. He was awarded the Nobel Prize for Physics 1920.

As the son of a clockmaker, Guillaume came to appreciate early in life the value of precision in measurement. He spent most of his life at the International Bureau of Weights and Measures in Sèvres, France, which established the standards for the metre, litre, and kilogram.

Guillemin Roger Charles Louis (1924–). French-born US endocrinologist. He has isolated and identified various hormones, for which he received the 1977 Nobel Prize for Physiology or Medicine, together with his co-worker Andrew Schally (1926–) and US physicist Rosalyn Yalow. Guillemin also discovered endorphins.

He moved to the USA 1953 and did most of his work at Baylor College of Medicine, Houston, Texas, becoming professor 1963. In 1970 he joined the Salk Institute in La Jolla, California.

Guillemin found that the brain controls the pituitary gland by means of hormones produced by central neurons – the neurosecretory cells of the hypothalamus. He worked with Lithuanian refugee Schally 1957–62, and later their investigations were parallel. Between 1968 and 1973 they isolated and synthesized three hypothalamic hormones which regulate the secretion of the anterior pituitary gland.

Guimard Hector Germain (1867–1942). French architect. He was a leading exponent of the Art Nouveau style in France. His flamboyant designs of glazed canopies for a number of Paris Métro station exteriors are one of Art Nouveau's most enduring images. In another of his projects, the Castel Béranger apartment block, Paris, 1894–98, he emphasized the importance of detail by designing each apartment to a different plan. Within the building, the Art Nouveau style is apparent on everything from stonework to door handles.

Guinness Alec (1914–). English actor of stage and screen. His films include *Great Expectations* 1946, *Kind Hearts and Coronets* 1949 (in which he played eight parts), *The Bridge on the River Kwai* 1957 (Academy Award), and *Star Wars* 1977.

Guinness joined the Old Vic 1936. A subtle character actor, he played the enigmatic spymaster in TV adaptations of John Le

Carré's *Tinker, Tailor, Soldier, Spy* 1979 and *Smiley's People* 1981. Knighted 1959.

Güiraldes Ricardo (1886–1927). Argentine novelist and poet. Contact with French avant-garde writing in Paris in 1910 influenced the controversially innovative poetry and prose of his collection *El cencerro de cristal/The Crystal Bell* 1915. Deep feeling for his native land characterizes his stories *Cuentos de muerte y de sangre/Tales of Death and Blood* 1915 and his novel *Don Segundo Sombra* 1926, a poetic idealization of Argentinian *gaucho* (nomadic cattleman) life, his best-known work.

Guise Francis, 2nd Duke of Guise (1519–1563). French soldier and politician. He led the French victory over Germany at Metz 1552 and captured Calais from the English 1558. Along with his brother Charles (1527–1574), he was powerful in the government of France during the reign of Francis II. He was assassinated attempting to crush the Huguenots.

Guise Henri, 3rd Duke of Guise (1550–1588). French noble who persecuted the Huguenots and was partly responsible for the Massacre of St Bartholomew 1572. He was assassinated.

The spirit of revolution ... of insurrection is a spirit radically opposed to liberty.

FRANÇOIS GUIZOT
Speech in Paris 29 Dec 1830

Guizot François Pierre Guillaume (1787–1874). French politician and historian, professor of modern history at the Sorbonne, Paris 1812–30. He wrote histories of French and European culture and became prime minister 1847. His resistance to all reforms led to the revolution of 1848.

Gullit Ruud (1962–). Dutch international footballer who was captain when the Netherlands captured the European Championship 1988. After playing in the Netherlands with Haarlem, Feyenoord, and PSV Eindhoven, he transferred to AC Milan 1987.

Gulpilil David (1953–). Australian actor and Aboriginal dancer. His film appearances include *Walkabout* 1971, *The Last Wave* 1977, *Crocodile Dundee* 1986, and *Until the End of the World* 1991. Gulpilil has worked internationally as a dancer and is also a traditional storyteller.

Gummer John Selwyn (1939–). British Conservative politician, secretary of state for the environment from 1993. He was minister of state for employment 1983–84, paymaster general 1984–85, minister for agriculture 1985–89, secretary of state for agriculture 1989–93, and chair of the party 1983–85. A prominent lay member of the Church of England, he left in 1994, after its decision to permit the ordination of women priests, and became a Roman Catholic.

Gunnell Sally (1966–). British hurdler. She won the 1986 Commonwealth 100-metre hurdles gold medal before moving on to 400-metre hurdles. In 1994 she became the first woman athlete to complete the athletics Grand Slam, winning gold medals over 400-metre hurdles at the 1992 Olympics, 1993 World Championships (breaking the world record), 1990 and 1994 Commonwealth Games, and 1994 European Championships.

Gunter Edmund (1581–1626). English mathematician who became professor of astronomy at Gresham College, London 1619. He is reputed to have invented a number of surveying instruments as well as the trigonometrical terms 'cosine' and 'cotangent'.

Gupta dynasty Indian hereditary rulers that reunified and ruled over much of northern and central India 320–550. The dynasty's stronghold lay in the Magadha region of the middle Ganges valley, with the capital Pataliputra. Gupta influence was extended through military conquest E, W, and S by Chandragupta I, Chandragupta II, and Samudragupta. Hun raids in the NW from the 6th century undermined the Guptas' decentralized administrative structure.

The dynasty grew out of the array of states left from the disintegration of the Kushan empire (about 200). Its conquest brought about varying degrees of independence and created a prosperous society in which Sanskrit grew out of its religious sphere to become the official language, at least in N India. At the empire's height, the Hindu and Buddhist religions, commerce, and the arts flourished in what is seen as a golden or classical age of Indian civilization.

A man may be born, but in order to be born he must first die, and in order to die he must first awake.

GEORGE GURDJIEFF
quoted in P D Ouspensky, *Search of the Miraculous* ch 11 1987

Gurdjieff George Ivanovitch (1877–1949). Russian occultist and mystic who influenced the modern human-potential movement. His famous text is *Meetings with Remarkable Men* (English translation 1963). The mystic Ouspensky was a disciple who expanded his ideas.

After years of wandering in central Asia, in 1912 Gurdjieff founded in Moscow the Institute for the Harmonious Development of Man, based on a system of raising consciousness (involving learning, group movement, manual labour, dance, and a minimum of sleep) known as the Fourth Way. After the 1917 Revolution he established similar schools in parts of Europe.

Suggested reading
Moore, James *Gurdjieff: The Anatomy of a Myth* (1991)

Gurdon John Bertrand (1933–). English molecular biologist who has studied nuclear transplantation and the effects of known protein fractions on gene activity. In 1972 he joined the Laboratory of Molecular Biology at Cambridge.

Transplanting nuclei and nuclear constituents, such as DNA, into enucleated eggs, mainly frog's eggs, Gurdon showed how the genetic activity changes in the recipient eggs. He concluded that the changes in gene activity induced by nuclear transplantation are indistinguishable from those that occur in normal early development. He also demonstrated how nuclear transplantation and microinjection techniques can be used to elucidate the intracellular movements of proteins.

Gustavus or Gustaf. Six kings of Sweden, including:

Gutenberg *German printer Johann Gutenberg, who invented moveable type, shown at work in his printing shop. Gutenberg produced the first major work to come off a printing press, the so-called 'Gutenberg Bible', of which there are 47 surviving copies.* (Ann Ronan/Image Select)

Gustavus I or Gustaf I. King of Sweden, better known as ◊Gustavus Vasa.

Gustavus II or Gustaf II. King of Sweden, better known as ◊Gustavus Adolphus.

Gustavus V or Gustaf V (1858–1950). King of Sweden from 1907, when he succeeded his father Oscar II. He married Princess Victoria, daughter of the Grand Duke of Baden 1881, thus uniting the reigning Bernadotte dynasty with the former royal house of Vasa.

Gustavus VI or Gustaf VI (1882–1973). King of Sweden from 1950, when he succeeded his father Gustavus V. He was an archaeologist and expert on Chinese art. He was succeeded by his grandson Carl XVI Gustavus.

His first wife was Princess Margaret of Connacht (1882–1920), and in 1923 he married Lady Louise Mountbatten (1889–1965), sister of the Earl of Mountbatten of Burma.

I have taken the water from them; I would take the air if I could.

GUSTAVUS ADOLPHUS
to Louis de Geer who had tried to persuade him to lift the blockade of Gdansk during the Swedo-Polish conflict 1627

Gustavus Adolphus (Gustavus II or Gustaf II) (1594–1632). King of Sweden from 1611, when he succeeded his father Charles IX. He waged successful wars with Denmark, Russia, and Poland, and in the Thirty Years' War became a champion of the Protestant cause. Landing in Germany 1630, he defeated the German general Wallenstein at Lützen, SW of Leipzig 6 Nov 1632, but was killed in the battle. He was known as the 'Lion of the North'.

Suggested reading
Dupuy, Trevor *The Military Life of Gustavus Adolphus* (1969)
Roberts, Michael *Gustavus Adolphus and the Rise of Sweden* (1973)

Gustavus Vasa (Gustavus I or Gustaf I) (1496–1560). King of Sweden from 1523, when he was elected after leading the Swedish revolt against Danish rule. He united and pacified the country and established Lutheranism as the state religion.

Guston Philip (1913–1980). Canadian-born US painter. Initially inspired by the Mexican muralists, he developed a fluid, abstract style in the 1950s. He later returned to a harsh, dynamic figuration, satirizing contemporary life with cartoonlike drawings in livid pinks, greys, white, and black, as in *Painting, Smoking, Eating* 1973 (Stedelijk Museum, Amsterdam).

Largely self-taught, Guston began his career executing murals for the Federal Arts Project 1935–42. The Impressionist style of abstraction he adopted in the 1950s placed him squarely within the New York School of Abstract Expressionism.

Suggested reading
Ashton, Dore *Yes, But … :A Critical Study of Philip Guston* (1976)

Gutenberg Johann Gensfleisch (*c.* 1398–1468). German printer, the inventor of printing from movable metal type, based on the Chinese wood-block-type method (although Laurens Janszoon Coster has a rival claim).

Gutenberg began work on the process in the 1440s and in 1450 set up a printing business in Mainz. By 1456 he had produced the first printed Bible (known as the Gutenberg Bible). It is not known what other books he printed.

He punched and engraved a steel character (letter shape) into a piece of copper to form a mould which he filled with molten metal. The letters were in the Gothic style and of equal height. By 1500, more than 180 European towns had working presses of this kind.

Gutenberg was born in Mainz and set up a printing firm in Strasbourg in the late 1430s, where he may have invented movable type. This business folded, as did the subsequent one in Mainz with Johann Fust (*c.* 1400–1466) as a backer: Fust seized the press for nonpayment of the loan. Gutenberg is believed to have gone on to set up a third press and print the Mazarin and Bamberg bibles. In 1462, Mainz was involved in a local feud, and in the upheaval

Gutenberg was expelled from the city for five years before being reinstated, offered a pension, and given tax exemption.

Suggested reading
Ing, Janet *Johann Gutenberg and His Bible* (1988)
Scholderer, Victor *Johann Gutenberg: The Inventor of Printing* (1963)

Guthrie Edwin R(ay) (1886–1959). US behaviourist who attempted to develop a learning theory in which the role of reinforcement (reward or punishment) in a stimulus-response connection is secondary. Contiguity between the stimulus and the response was the crucial factor. Reinforcement merely brought the learning trial or incident to an end, preventing further responses that might become bonded to the stimulus.

Guthrie (William) Tyrone (1900–1971). English theatre director. He was notable for his innovative approach. Administrator of the Old Vic and Sadler's Wells theatres 1939–45, he helped found the Ontario (Stratford) Shakespeare Festival 1953 and the Minneapolis theatre now named after him. He pioneered the modern concept of open-stage productions for medieval and Renaissance plays. Knighted 1961.

Guthrie Woody (Woodrow Wilson) (1912–1967). US folk singer and songwriter. His left-wing protest songs, 'dustbowl ballads', and 'talking blues' influenced, among others, Bob Dylan; they include 'Deportees', 'Hard Travelin'', and 'This Land Is Your Land'.

His son *Arlo Guthrie* (1947–   ), also a folk singer, is best known for the Vietnam-draft epic 'Alice's Restaurant' 1967.

Guttuso Renato (1912–1987). Italian painter. He was a leading exponent of Social Realism during and after World War II and a committed anti-Fascist. While other artists explored abstraction in the 1950s, Guttuso adhered to his forceful Realist style. Social and political comment remained an essential part of his work, as in *Occupation of Uncultivated Land in Sicily* 1949–50 (Gemaldgalerie Neue Meister, Dresden).

His varied subject matter includes street scenes, land and seascapes, still lifes, interiors, nudes, and large allegories of contemporary life based on well-known works by old and modern masters.

Guys Constantin (1805–1892). Dutch-born French illustrator. He is remembered for his witty drawings of Paris life during the Second Empire. He was with the English poet Byron at Missolonghi, Greece, and made sketches of the Crimean War for the *Illustrated London News*. Baudelaire praised his 'modernity'.

London was his headquarters until the 1860s, but afterwards he worked in Paris. He depicted bourgeois society and the *demi-monde*, military occasions, horses and carriages, and women of various degree, in pen and wash drawings and watercolours of remarkable character. Baudelaire's magnificient study of his art, *Le Peintre de la Vie Moderne* justly called attention to his distinctive work.

Guzmán Blanco Antonio (1829–1899). Venezuelan dictator and military leader (*caudillo*), who seized power 1870 and remained absolute ruler until 1889. He modernized Caracas to become the political capital; committed resources to education, communications, and agriculture; and encouraged foreign trade.

Gwyn Nell (Eleanor), (or Gwynn) (1650–1687). English comedy actress from 1665. She was formerly an orange-seller at Drury Lane Theatre, London. The poet Dryden wrote parts for her, and from 1669 she was the mistress of Charles II.

Suggested reading
Bevan, Bryan *Nell Gwynn* (1969)
MacGregor-Hastie, Roy *Nell Gwyn* (1987)

Gyokudō Uragami (1745–1820). Japanese painter. He is known for the vibrant quality of his brushwork. He painted mainly landscapes, executed in a Chinese style but with a sense of the personal and intimate typical of Japanese art.

Gysi Gregor (1948–   ). German politician, elected leader of the Communist Party Dec 1989 following the resignation of Egon Krenz. He continued to lead the party after it was renamed the Party of Democratic Socialism (PDS) and oversaw its electoral success Oct 1994, when the PDS captured 30 Bundestag seats.

A lawyer, Gysi acted as defence counsel for dissidents during the 1970s.

H

Haakon seven kings of Norway, including:

Haakon (I) the Good (*c.* 915–961). King of Norway from about 935. The son of Harald Hárfagri ('Finehair') (*c.* 850–930), king of Norway, he was raised in England. He seized the Norwegian throne and tried unsuccessfully to introduce Christianity there. His capital was at Trondheim.

Haakon IV (1204–1263). King of Norway from 1217, the son of Haakon III. Under his rule, Norway flourished both militarily and culturally; he took control of the Faroe Islands, Greenland 1261, and Iceland 1262–64. His court was famed throughout N Europe.

Haakon VII (1872–1957). King of Norway from 1905. Born Prince Charles, the second son of Frederick VIII of Denmark, he was elected king of Norway on separation from Sweden, and in 1906 he took the name Haakon. In World War II he carried on the resistance from Britain during the Nazi occupation of his country. He returned 1945.

For more than forty years I have selected my collaborators on the basis of their intelligence and their character and I am not willing for the rest of my life to change this method which I have found so good.

FRITZ HABER
Letter of Resignation 30 April 1933 [Haber was
unwilling to follow the Nazi requirements for racial purity.]

Haber Fritz (1868–1934). German chemist whose conversion of atmospheric nitrogen to ammonia opened the way for the synthetic fertilizer industry. His study of the combustion of hydrocarbons led to the commercial 'cracking' or fractional distillation of natural oil (petroleum) into its components (for example, diesel, petrol, and paraffin). In electrochemistry, he was the first to demonstrate that oxidation and reduction take place at the electrodes; from this he developed a general electrochemical theory.

At the outbreak of World War I in 1914, Haber was asked to devise a method of producing nitric acid for making high explosives. Later he became one of the principals in the German chemical-warfare effort, devising weapons and gas masks, which led to protests against his Nobel prize 1918.

He was professor at Karlsruhe 1906–11, and then was made director of the newly established Kaiser Wilhelm Institute for Physical Chemistry in Berlin. When Adolf Hitler rose to power in 1933, Haber sought exile in Britain, where he worked at the Cavendish Laboratory, Cambridge.

Habermas Jürgen (1929–). German social theorist, a member of the Frankfurt school. His central concern is how a meaningful engagement in politics and society is possible in a society dominated by science and the technology and bureaucracy based on it.

In *Theorie und Praxis/Theory and Practice* 1963 and *Erkenntnis und Interesse/Knowledge and Human Interest* 1968, he argues that reason, which had long been a weapon of intellectual and political freedom, has been appropriated by science. Far from being a disinterested pursuit of knowledge, it is an instrument for achieving a range of unquestioned social and political ends. In *Theory of Communicative Action* 1981 he describes how a 'communicative rationality' can be developed, reclaiming lost ground and allowing rational political commitment.

Habsburg or *Hapsburg*. European royal family, former imperial house of Austria–Hungary. A Habsburg, Rudolf I, became king of Germany 1273 and began the family's control of Austria and Styria. They acquired a series of lands and titles, including that of Holy Roman emperor which they held 1273–91, 1298–1308, 1438–1740, and 1745–1806. The Habsburgs reached the zenith of their power under the emperor Charles V (1519–1556) who divided his lands, creating an Austrian Habsburg line (which ruled until 1918) and a Spanish line (which ruled to 1700).

The name comes from the family castle in Aargau, Switzerland.

Suggested reading
Crankshaw, Edward *The Hapsburgs* (1971)
Kann, R A *A History of the Habsburg Empire, 1526–1918* (1974)
Tapié, V L *The Rise and Fall of the Hapsburg Monarchy* (1971)

Hackman Gene (1931–). US actor. He became a star as 'Popeye' Doyle in *The French Connection* 1971 and continued to play a variety of often combative roles in such films as *The Conversation* 1974, *The French Connection II* 1975, *Mississippi Burning* 1988, *Unforgiven* 1992, and *The Quick and the Dead* 1995.

Actors who are in it for any length of time either evolve into directors or drunks.

GENE HACKMAN
quoted in *Film Yearbook* 1985

Hadamard Jacques Salomon (1865–1963). French mathematician who originated functional analysis, one of the most fertile branches of modern mathematics. He also made contributions to number theory and formulated the concept of a correctly posed problem.

Hadamard was born in Versailles and studied at the Ecole Normale Supérieure in Paris. He was professor of mathematics at the Collège de France in Paris 1909–37. During the German occupation of France in World War II, he went into exile, returning 1945.

Hadamard's early work was on analytic functions; that is, functions that can be developed as power series that converge. He began to study the Riemann zeta function and in 1896 solved the problem of determining the number of prime numbers less than a given number x. Hadamard was able to demonstrate that this number was asymptotically equal to $x/\log x$, which was the most important single result ever obtained in number theory.

Hadfield Robert Abbott (1858–1940). British industrial chemist and metallurgist who invented stainless steel and developed various other ferrous alloys. In making ordinary mild steel, pig iron is oxidized, to lower the carbon content. Hadfield carried out many experiments in which he mixed other metals to the steel. He found, for example, that a small amount of manganese gave a tough, wear-resistant steel suitable for such applications as railway track and grinding machinery. By adding nickel and chromium he produced corrosion-resistant stainless steels. Knighted 1908, baronet 1917.

Hadid Zahia (1950–). British architect, born in Baghdad. An exponent of Deconstructionism, she has been influential through her drawings rather than buildings. Her unbuilt competition-winning entry for Hong Kong's Peak Club 1983 established her reputation, and in 1993 she completed her first major building, a fire station for the Vitra Furniture Factory at Weil-am-Rhein, Germany.

Hadlee Richard John (1951–). New Zealand cricketer who broke Ian Botham's world record of 373 test wickets and improved the total to 431, a figure then beaten by Kapil Dev 1994. He played for Canterbury (NZ) and Nottinghamshire (England). In 1990 he retired from test cricket after being the first to take the field in a test match after being knighted that year for services to cricket.

Hadlee played first-class cricket in Australia for Tasmania. His father Walter Arnold Hadlee also played Test cricket for New Zealand, as did his brother Dayle Robert Hadlee.

If you have no time to answer, then do not be a king.

Comment by an old woman after HADRIAN said he was too busy to attend to her request. Quoted in Dio Cassius *History* bk 59, ch 6

Hadrian (Publius Aelius Hadrianus) (AD 76–138). Roman emperor from 117. He was adopted by his relative, the emperor Trajan, whom he succeeded. He abandoned Trajan's conquests in Mesopotamia and adopted a defensive policy aimed at fixing the boundaries of the empire, which included the building of Hadrian's Wall in Britain. He travelled more widely than any other emperor, and consolidated both the army and Roman administration.

A very capable ruler, Hadrian introduced administrative, financial, and legal reforms, while his magnificent buildings, often the result of his travels, are found throughout the empire. Some of his largest building projects were at Rome (including the Pantheon, his own mausoleum, and his villa at Tivoli) and Athens, where his new town and appointment as archon of Athens 112 reveals his fondness for Greek culture. He was also a cultivated poet and patron of the arts.

Hadrian was born at Italica (modern Santiponce, near Seville, Spain), where his family, originally from Atria in Picenum, had resided for nearly 200 years. On his father's death (85 or 86) he was placed under the guardianship of Marcus Ulpius Traianus (later to become the emperor Trajan), and of Caelius Attianus, a future praetorian prefect. Hadrian spent the next six years at Rome, but at the age of 15 returned to Spain and joined the army. Summoned by Trajan to Rome in 93, he held various minor civil posts, then went as tribune of the Second Legion at Aquincum in Lower Pannonia, where he remained until his return to Rome with Trajan in 99. In the following year the empress Plotina arranged a marriage between him and Trajan's great-niece, Vibia Sabina. Hadrian's public career from this date until his accession was as follows: quaestor, 101; tribune of the plebeians, 105; praetor, 106; distinguished himself in both Dacian campaigns, 101–02 and 105–06; legatus praetorius of Lower Pannonia, 107; legatus in the Parthian campaign, 113–17. In this last year Trajan fell ill and set out for home, leaving Hadrian as commander of the army and governor of Syria. Hadrian was at Antioch when he learned of his adoption by Trajan and two days later of the emperor's death. His succession was confirmed by the army and the Senate.

At the time of Hadrian's succession, the empire was threatened on all sides. Hadrian abandoned Assyria, Mesopotamia, and Armenia, which his predecessor had annexed. He pacified the Lower Danube, and then in 118 hurried to Rome to remove the unfavourable impression created by the execution of four consulars alleged to have conspired against him. The first of his two great tours of the empire (121–25) included Gaul, Germany, Britain, Spain, Mauretania, Greece, and Sicily. Among its principal events were the beginning of Hadrian's Wall in 122 and the emperor's initiation into the Eleusinian Mysteries 125.

The second major tour (128–34) took in Athens (where he completed and dedicated the buildings begun during his first visit), Asia Minor, Syria, Palestine (where he ordered the rebuilding of Jerusalem), Arabia, and Egypt. On his way back to Europe in 133 he was recalled to deal with the Jewish revolt which had broken out in the previous year, possibly in reaction to Hadrian's decision to build a temple to Jupiter Capitolinus on the site of the Jewish temple of Jerusalem, and ban circumcision. In 134 he entrusted the command to Julius Severus, returned to Rome and passed the remainder of his life between the capital and his villa at Tibur. He died at Baiae, and was succeeded by his adopted son Antoninus Pius.

Man creates God in his own image.

ERNST HAECKEL
Generelle Morphologie vol I p 174 1866

Haeckel Ernst Heinrich Philipp August (1834–1919). German zoologist and philosopher. His theory of 'recapitulation', expressed as 'ontogeny repeats phylogeny' (or that embryonic stages represent past stages in the organism's evolution), has been superseded, but it stimulated research in embryology.

Haeckel was born in Potsdam, Prussia, and studied at Würtzburg and Berlin. He was professor at Jena 1865–1909.

Hâfiz Shams al-Din Muhammad (*c.* 1326–*c.* 1390). Persian lyric poet. He was born in Shiraz and taught in a Dervish college there. His *Diwan*, a collection of short odes, extols the pleasures of life and satirizes his fellow Dervishes.

Hagen Walter Charles (1892–1969). US golfer, a flamboyant character. He won 11 major championships 1914–29. An exponent of the match-play game, he won the US PGA Championship five times, four in succession.

Hagenbeck Carl (1844–1913). German zoo proprietor. In 1907 he founded Hagenbeck's Zoo, near his native Hamburg. He was a pioneer in the display of animals against a natural setting, rather than in restrictive cages.

Haggai minor Old Testament prophet (lived *c.* 520 BC) who promoted the rebuilding of the Temple in Jerusalem.

I cannot help thinking that simple things are always the most impressive, and books are easier to understand when they are written in plain language.

H RIDER HAGGARD
Preface to *King Solomon's Mines* 1885

Haggard H(enry) Rider (1856–1925). English novelist. He used his experience in the South African colonial service in his romantic adventure tales, including *King Solomon's Mines* 1885 and *She* 1887. Knighted 1912.

Haggard Merle (1937–). US country singer, songwriter, and musician (guitar and fiddle). His songs deal with working-class tribulations and extol patriotism. He had hits with, among others, 'I Am a Lonesome Fugitive' 1966, 'Sing Me Back Home' 1967, 'Mama Tried' 1968, and 'Okie from Muskogee' 1969.

Hagler Marvin (1954–). US boxer who was the undisputed world middleweight champion from 1980 to 1987. He won 13 of his 15 World Title fights, losing only to Sugar Ray Leonard. Subsequently, he became a movie actor.

Hahn Kurt Matthias Robert Martin (1886–1974). German educationist. He was the founder of Salem School in Germany. After his expulsion by the Nazi dictator Hitler, he founded Gordonstoun School in Scotland and was its head teacher 1934–53. He cofounded the Atlantic College project 1960, and was associated with the Outward Bound Trust and the Duke of Edinburgh Award scheme.

Hahn Otto (1879–1968). German physical chemist who discovered nuclear fission. In 1938 with Fritz Strassmann (1902–1980), he discovered that uranium nuclei split when bombarded with neutrons. Hahn did not participate in the resultant development of the atom bomb. Nobel Prize for Chemistry 1944.

Hahn was born in Frankfurt-am-Main and studied at Marburg. From 1904 to 1906 he worked in London with William Ramsay, who introduced Hahn to radiochemistry, and at McGill University in Montréal, Canada, with Ernest Rutherford. Returning to Germany, Hahn was joined at Berlin in 1907 by Meitner, beginning a long collaboration. Hahn was director of the Kaiser Wilhelm Institute for Chemistry in Berlin 1928–44, and then president of the Max Planck Institute in Göttingen.

Haidar Ali ruler of Mysore, India, from 1761; see ◊Hyder Ali.

Haig Alexander Meigs (1924–). US general and Republican politician. He became President Nixon's White House Chief of Staff at the height of the Watergate scandal, was NATO commander 1974–79, and secretary of state to President Reagan 1981–82.

Haitink *The conductor Bernard Haitink divides his time between orchestral and operatic work. In both fields he has been praised for his 'no-nonsense' approach, which seeks to reproduce the composer's intentions without introducing indulgent affectations.*

Haig Douglas, 1st Earl Haig (1861–1928). British army officer, commander in chief in World War I. His Somme offensive in France in the summer of 1916 made considerable advances only at enormous cost to human life, and his Passchendaele offensive in Belgium from July to Nov 1917 achieved little at a similar loss. He was created field marshal 1917 and, after retiring, became first president of the British Legion 1921. KCVO 1909, earl 1919.

A national hero at the time of his funeral, Haig's reputation began to fall after Lloyd George's memoirs depicted him as treating soldiers' lives with disdain, while remaining far from battle himself.

Haile Selassie Ras (Prince) Tafari ('the Lion of Judah') (1892–1975). Emperor of Ethiopia 1930–74. He pleaded unsuccessfully to the League of Nations against the Italian conquest of his country 1935–36, and was then deposed and fled to the UK. He went to Egypt 1940 and raised an army which he led into Ethiopia Jan 1941 alongside British forces and was restored to the throne 5 May. He was deposed by a military coup 1974 and died in captivity the following year. Followers of the Rastafarian religion believe that he was the Messiah, the incarnation of God (Jah).

Suggested reading
Haile Selassie I *The Autobiography of Haile Selassie I* (trs 1976)
Kapuscinski, Ryszard *The Emperor* (trs 1983)
Schwab, Peter *Haile Selassie* (1979)

Hailsham Quintin McGarel Hogg, Baron Hailsham of St Marylebone (1907–). British lawyer and Conservative politician.

Having succeeded as 2nd Viscount Hailsham 1950, he renounced the title 1963 to re-enter the House of Commons, and was then able to contest the Conservative Party leadership elections, but took a life peerage 1970 on his appointment as Lord Chancellor 1970–74. He was Lord Chancellor again 1979–87.

Hailwood Mike (Stanley Michael Bailey) (1940–1981). English motorcyclist. Between 1961 and 1967 he won nine world titles and a record 14 titles at the Isle of Man TT races between 1961 and 1979.

Haitink Bernard (1929–). Dutch conductor. He has been associated with the Concertgebouw Orchestra, Amsterdam, from 1958, and the London Philharmonic Orchestra from 1967; musical director at Glyndebourne 1977–87 and at the Royal Opera House, Covent Garden, London, from 1987. A noted interpreter of Mahler and Shostakovitch, he also conducted Mozart's music for the film *Amadeus*, after the play by Peter Schaffer.

Hakluyt Richard (*c.* 1552–1616). English geographer whose chief work is *The Principal Navigations, Voyages and Discoveries of the English Nation* 1598–1600. He was assisted by Sir Walter Raleigh. He lectured on cartography at Oxford, became geographical adviser to the East India Company, and was an original member of the Virginia Company.

The Hakluyt Society, established 1846, published later accounts of exploration.

Halas George Stanley (1895–1983). US athlete and sports promoter. He was founder of the Chicago Bears of the National Football League and was an active player until 1929. He acted as coach until retirement 1967, introducing the T-formation and giving special emphasis to the passing offence.

Born in Chicago, and educated at the University of Illinois, Halas was an exceptional athlete and in 1919 briefly played professional baseball for the New York Yankees. From 1921 he devoted himself to professional football. He became a charter member of the Football Hall of Fame 1963.

I have no doubt that in reality the future will be vastly more surprising than anything I can imagine. Now my own suspicion is that the universe is not only queerer than we suppose, but queerer than we can suppose.

J B S HALDANE
Possible Worlds and Other Papers p 286 1927

Haldane J(ohn) B(urdon) S(anderson) (1892–1964). British physiologist, geneticist, and author of popular science books. In 1936 he showed the genetic link between haemophilia and colour blindness.

In 1933 he became professor of genetics at University College, London. He emigrated to India 1957 in protest at the Anglo-French invasion of Suez and was appointed director of the Genetics and Biometry Laboratory in Orissa. He became a naturalized Indian citizen in 1961. In 1924 Haldane produced the first proof that enzymes obey the laws of thermodynamics. Haldane investigated how carbon dioxide in the bloodstream of human beings enables the muscles to regulate breathing under different conditions. During World War II, in 1942, Haldane, who often used his own body in biochemical experiments, spent two days in a submarine to test an air-purifying system.

Haldane was convinced that natural selection and not mutation is the driving force behind evolution. In 1932, he estimated for the first time the rate of mutation of the human gene and worked out the effect of recurrent harmful mutations on a population. He is supposed to have remarked: 'I'd lay down my life for two brothers or eight cousins.'

Haldane John Scott (1860–1936). Scottish physiologist whose studies of the exchange of gases during respiration led to an interest in the health hazards of coal mining and deep-sea diving. His aim was to bridge the gap between theoretical and applied science.

He was director of the Mining Research Laboratory (first in Doncaster, then in Birmingham) 1913–28. He also lectured at various universities in the UK, the USA, and Ireland.

In 1905, Haldane published his idea that breathing is controlled by the effect of the concentration of carbon dioxide in arterial blood on the respiratory centre of the brain. In 1907, he announced a technique of decompression by stages which allows a deep-sea diver to rise to the surface safely; it is still used today.

He also researched the reaction of the kidneys to the water content of the blood, and the physiology of sweating.

Haldane Richard Burdon, 1st Viscount Haldane (1856–1928). British Liberal politician. As secretary for war 1905–12, he sponsored the army reforms that established an expeditionary force, backed by a territorial army and under the unified control of an imperial general staff. He was Lord Chancellor 1912–15 and in the Labour government of 1924. His writings on German philosophy led to accusations of his having pro-German sympathies. Viscount 1911.

Once the toothpaste is out of the tube, it is awfully hard to get it back in.

H R HALDEMAN
Comment on the Watergate affair 1973

Haldeman H(arry) R(obbins) (1926–1993). US businessman and presidential aide. He was Chief of Staff to Richard Nixon 1969–1974. Immensely protective and loyal towards his president, Haldeman was crucially involved in the Watergate cover-up and, after being convicted of obstructing justice and lying, served 18 months in a federal prison.

Halder Franz (1884–1971). German general. As Chief of Staff from Sept 1938, he was responsible for much of the planning for the invasion of the USSR 1941, though it seems he did not dare draw attention to possible problems. He was arrested in the aftermath of the July Plot against Hitler 1944 and imprisoned in Dachau concentration camp. Liberated by US troops 1945, he gave evidence for the prosecution at the Nuremberg trials of Nazi war criminals.

Hale George Ellery (1868–1938). US astronomer who made pioneer studies of the Sun and founded three major observatories. In 1889 he invented the spectroheliograph, a device for photographing the Sun at particular wavelengths. In 1917 he established on Mount Wilson, California, a 2.5-m/100-in reflector, the world's largest telescope until superseded 1948 by the 5-m/200-in reflector on Mount Palomar, which Hale had planned just before he died. In 1897 he founded the Yerkes Observatory in Wisconsin, with the largest refractor, 102 cm/40 in, ever built at that time.

In 1892 he became professor at Chicago, moving to Mount Wilson as director 1904–23. He was elected to the governing body of Throop Polytechnic Institute in Pasadena, and through his influence this developed into the California Institute of Technology.

Hale Nathan (1755–1776). US nationalist hanged by the British as a spy in the American Revolution. Reputedly his final words were 'I only regret that I have but one life to lose for my country'.

Hale Sarah Josepha Buell (1788–1879). US poet. She was the author of 'Mary had a Little Lamb' 1830.

Hales Stephen (1677–1761). English scientist who studied the role of water and air in the maintenance of life. He gave accurate accounts of water movement in plants. He demonstrated that plants absorb air, and that some part of that air is involved in their nutrition. His work laid emphasis on measurement and experimentation.

Hales's work on air revealed to him the dangers of breathing 'spent' air in enclosed places, and he invented a ventilator which improved survival rates when introduced on naval, merchant, and slave ships, in hospitals, and in prisons.

A cleric, he was curate at Teddington, Middlesex, from 1709. His experiments on plants took place mainly between 1719 and 1725.

Hales's findings were published in his book *Vegetable Staticks* 1727, enlarged 1733 and retitled *Statical Essays, Containing Haemastaticks, etc.*

Halévy Ludovic (1834–1908). French novelist and librettist. He collaborated with Hector Crémieux in the libretto for Offenbach's *Orpheus in the Underworld*; and with Henri Meilhac on librettos for Offenbach's *La Belle Hélène* and *La Vie parisienne*, as well as for Bizet's *Carmen*.

Haley Bill (1927–1981). US pioneer of rock and roll. He was originally a western-swing musician. His songs 'Rock Around the Clock' 1954 (recorded with his group the Comets and featured in the 1955 film *Blackboard Jungle*) and 'Shake, Rattle and Roll' 1955 were big hits of the early rock-and-roll era.

Halifax Charles Montagu, 1st Earl of Halifax (1661–1715). British financier. Appointed commissioner of the Treasury 1692, he raised money for the French war by instituting the national debt and in 1694 carried out William Paterson's plan for a national bank (the Bank of England) and became chancellor of the Exchequer.

In 1695 he reformed the currency and issued the first 'Exchequer Bills', and in 1696 inaugurated the Consolidated Fund, used to pay interest on foreign loans. He was created a baron 1700, and at the accession of George I became again first Lord of the Treasury and was made an earl 1714.

Halifax Edward Frederick Lindley Wood, 1st Earl of Halifax (2nd creation) (1881–1959). British Conservative politician, viceroy of India 1926–31. As foreign secretary 1938–40 he was associated with Chamberlain's 'appeasement' policy. He received an earldom 1944 for services to the Allied cause while ambassador to the USA 1941–46. Baron 1925, succeeded as viscount 1934.

Men are not hanged for stealing horses, but that horses may not be stolen.

GEORGE SAVILE, 1ST MARQUIS OF HALIFAX
Political, Moral and Miscellaneous Thoughts and Reflections 'Of Punishment' *c.* 1690

Halifax George Savile, 1st Marquess of Halifax (1633–1695). English politician. He entered Parliament 1660, and was raised to the peerage by Charles II, by whom he was also later dismissed. He strove to steer a middle course between extremists, and became known as 'the Trimmer'. He played a prominent part in the revolution of 1688. Baronet 1644, viscount 1668, marquess 1682.

Hall Asaph (1829–1907). US astronomer who discovered the two Martian satellites, Deimos and Phobos, 1877. He determined the orbits of satellites of other planets and of double stars, the rotation of Saturn, and the mass of Mars.

Hall became assistant astronomer at the US Naval Observatory in Washington DC 1862, and within a year of his arrival he was made professor.

In 1875 Hall was given responsibility for a 66-cm/26-in telescope, the largest refractor in the world at the time. He noticed a white spot on Saturn which he used as a marker to ascertain the planet's rotational period. In 1884, he showed that the position of the elliptical orbit of Saturn's moon, Hyperion, was retrograding by about 20° per year. Hall also investigated stellar parallaxes and the position of the stars in the Pleiades cluster.

Hall Charles Martin (1863–1914). US chemist who developed a process for the commercial production of aluminium 1886. A similar process was independently but simultaneously developed in France by Paul Héroult. He invented the aluminium process at 22 and, after initial difficulties, formed the Pittsburgh Reduction Company (later to become the Aluminum Company of America) and became a multimillionaire. He found that when aluminium was mixed with cryolite (sodium aluminium fluoride), its melting point was lowered and electrolysis became commercially viable. It had previously been as costly as gold, but by 1914 its price was 40 cents a kilogram.

Hall James (1761–1832). Scottish geologist, one of the founders of experimental geology. He provided evidence in support of the theories of Scottish naturalist James Hutton regarding the formation of the Earth's crust. Succeeded to baronetcy 1776.

Hall was born in Berwickshire (Borders region) and spent much of the 1780s travelling in Europe. He undertook extensive geological observations in the Alps and studying Mount Etna in Sicily. He was also won over to the new chemistry of Antoine Lavoisier.

Hall set out to prove his friend Hutton's 'Plutonist' geological theories (the view that heat rather than water was the chief rock-building agent and shaper of the Earth's crust). By means of furnace experiments, he showed with fair success that Hutton had been correct to maintain that igneous rocks would generate crystalline structures if cooled very slowly. Hall also demonstrated that there was a degree of interconvertibility between basaltine and granitic rocks; and that, even though subjected to immense heat, limestone would not decompose if sustained under suitable pressure.

Hall Ken (1901–1994). Australian film and TV director and producer, a pioneer of feature film production in Australia, with 19 credits to his name between 1932 and 1946. While the films he made for Cinesound were often artless, they represented Australia's chief demonstration of an indigenous production base until the 'new wave' of the 1970s.

Under Hall's leadership Cinesound became in its modest way an impressive production power. From 1932 he directed a succession of films for the company – homespun comedies such as *Dad and Dave Come to Town* 1936, which introduced Peter Finch to the screen, and rural dramas like *Orphan of the Wilderness* 1936. His last feature was *Smithy* 1946. Hall was also the moving spirit behind the Cinesound newsreel. In 1956, he took on the running of Australia's first television station, Channel Nine.

Hall (Marguerite Antonia) Radclyffe (1880–1943). English novelist. *The Well of Loneliness* 1928 brought her notoriety because of its lesbian theme. Its review in the *Sunday Express* newspaper stated: 'I had rather give a healthy boy or girl a phial of prussic acid than this novel'. Her other works include the novel *Adam's Bread* 1926 and four volumes of poetry.

Halley English astronomer and mathematician Edmond Halley, who carried out important work on the motion and positions of planetary and celestial bodies, and is chiefly known for the identification of the comet that now bears his name. Halley's comet approaches the Earth every 76 years and is depicted in the Bayeaux tapestry. (Ann Ronan/Image Select)

Hall Peter Reginald Frederick (1930–). English theatre, opera, and film director. He was director of the Royal Shakespeare Theatre in Stratford-upon-Avon 1960–68 and developed the Royal Shakespeare Company 1968–73 until appointed director of the National Theatre 1973–88, succeeding Laurence Olivier. He founded the Peter Hall Company 1988.

Hall's stage productions include Beckett's *Waiting for Godot* 1955, *The Wars of the Roses* 1963, Pinter's *The Homecoming* stage 1967 and film 1973, *The Oresteia* 1981, and *Orpheus Descending* 1988. He has directed operas at Covent Garden, Bayreuth, and New York, and in 1984 was appointed artistic director of opera at Glyndebourne, with productions of *Carmen* 1985 and *Albert Herring* 1985–86. Knighted 1977.

Hall Philip (1904–1982). English mathematician who specialized in the study of group theory.

Hall was born in London and studied at Cambridge, where he spent his whole career. He was professor of pure mathematics 1953–67.

In 1928 Hall began a study of prime power groups. From this work he developed his 1933 theory of regular groups. An investigation of the conditions under which finite groups are soluble led him in 1937 to postulate a general structure theory for finite soluble groups. In 1954, he published an examination of finitely generated soluble groups in which he demonstrated that they could be divided into two classes of unequal size. At the end of the 1950s Hall turned to the subject of simple groups, and later also examined non-strictly-simple groups.

Hall (William) Reginald (1870–1943). British admiral. In Oct 1914 as director of Naval Intelligence he founded 'Room 40', the naval cryptanalysis office which successfully broke German naval codes and was responsible for decoding the Zimmerman Telegram. KCMG 1918.

Hall joined the Royal Navy 1883, was promoted to commander 1898, inspecting captain of mechanical training 1906–07, and assistant controller to the Navy 1911–13. Knighted 1918, he resigned 1919 and became the Conservative Member of Parliament for West Derby, Liverpool.

Hallam Henry (1777–1859). British historian. He was called to the Bar, but a private fortune enabled him to devote himself to historical study from 1812 and his *Constitutional History of England* 1827 established his reputation.

Hallé Charles (Carl) (1819–1895). German conductor and pianist. Settling in England 1848, he established and led Manchester's Hallé Orchestra 1858, until his death. As a pianist, he was the first to play all 32 Beethoven piano sonatas in London (also in Manchester and Paris).

Haller Albrecht von (1708–1777). Swiss physician and scientist, founder of neurology. He studied the muscles and nerves, and concluded that nerves provide the stimulus that triggers muscle contraction. He also showed that it is the nerves, not muscle or skin, that receive sensation. He was professor at Göttingen, Germany, 1736–53.

Haller published *De respiratione experimenta anatomica/ Experiments in the Anatomy of Respiration* 1747 and *Elementa physiologiae corporis humani/ The Physiological Elements of the Human Body* 1757–66.

Halley Edmond (1656–1742). English astronomer who not only identified 1705 the comet that was later to be known by his name, but also compiled a star catalogue, detected the proper motion of stars, using historical records, and began a line of research that – after his death – resulted in a reasonably accurate calculation of the astronomical unit.

Halley calculated that the cometary sightings reported in 1456, 1531, 1607, and 1682 all represented reappearances of the same comet. He reasoned that the comet would follow a parabolic path and announced 1705 that it would reappear 1758. When it did, public acclaim for the astronomer was such that his name was irrevocably attached to it. He became professor of geometry at Oxford 1703.

Halley was also a pioneer geophysicist and meteorologist and worked in many other fields, including mathematics. He became the second Astronomer Royal 1720. He was a friend of Isaac Newton, whose *Principia* he financed.

Suggested reading
Baldwin, Louis *Edmond Halley and His Comet* (1985)
Lancaster-Brown, Peter *Halley and His Comet* (1985)
Ronan, Colin *Edmond Halley: Genius in Eclipse* (1969)

Hals Frans (*c.* 1581–1666). Flemish-born painter of lively portraits. His work includes the *Laughing Cavalier* 1624 (Wallace Collection, London), and large groups of military companies, governors of charities, and others (many examples in the Frans Hals Museum, Haarlem, the Netherlands). In the 1620s he experimented with genre scenes.

He developed a broad and fluent method of painting, disciplined by great economy of colour, with which he inimitably rendered liveliness of expression, as in his *Laughing Cavalier*. His work comprises the group portraiture of the Military Guilds, composed with remarkable skill to provide variety of interest while paying equal attention to each person represented; individual commissioned portraits; and the studies of Bohemian types which appealed to him (*La Bohémienne* – Louvre, *Hille Bobbe* – Berlin). Late works in which he was most penetrating and nearest to Rembrandt were the groups of 1664 depicting the regents, male and female, of the Old Peoples' Almshouse.

Halsey William Frederick (1882–1959). US admiral. A highly skilled naval air tactician, his handling of carrier fleets in World War II played a significant role in the eventual defeat of Japan. He was appointed commander of US Task Force 16 in the Pacific 1942 and almost immediately launched the Doolittle raid on Tokyo. He took part in operations throughout the Far East, including Santa Cruz, Guadalcanal, Bougainville, and the Battle of Leyte Gulf. He was promoted to fleet admiral 1945 and retired 1947.

Halston trade name of Roy Halston Frowick (1932–1990). US fashion designer. He showed his first collection 1969 and created a vogue for easy-to-wear clothes that emphasized the body but left it free to move. In 1973 he diversified into loungewear, luggage, and cosmetics.

Hamaguchi Osachi, also known as Hamaguchi Yūko (1870–1931). Japanese politician, prime minister 1929–30. His policies created social unrest and alienated military interests. His acceptance of the terms of the London Naval Agreement 1930 was also unpopular. Shot by an assassin Nov 1930, he died of his wounds nine months later.

Hamed Nassem ('Prince') (1974–). English boxer. Winner of the European bantamweight title 1994, and the WBC International super-bantamweight championship.

The general to whom the prize for daring and genius must be given is Hamilcar, surnamed Barca.

Polybius on HAMILCAR BARCA
History bk 1 ch 64

Hamilcar Barca (*c.* 270–228 BC). Carthaginian general, father of Hannibal. From 247 to 241 BC in the First Punic War he harassed the Romans in Sicily and Italy and then led an expedition to Spain, where he died in battle.

Hamilton family name of the dukes of Abercorn; seated at Barons Court, County Tyrone. The 3rd duke was the great-grandfather of Diana, Princess of Wales.

Hamilton Alexander (1757–1804). US politician who influenced the adoption of a constitution with a strong central government and was the first secretary of the Treasury 1789–95. He led the Federalist Party, and incurred the bitter hatred of Aaron Burr when he voted against Burr and in favour of Thomas Jefferson for the presidency 1801. Challenged to a duel by Burr, Hamilton was wounded and died the next day.

Hamilton, born in the West Indies, served during the American Revolution as captain and was George Washington's secretary and aide-de-camp 1777–81. After the war he practised as a lawyer. He was a member of the Constitutional Convention of 1787, and in the *Federalist* influenced public opinion in favour of the ratification of the Constitution. He was a strong advocate of the wealthy urban sector of American life and encouraged renewed ties with Britain, remaining distrustful of revolutionary France. As the first secretary of the treasury, he proved an able controller of the national finances.

Hamilton Alice (1869–1970). US physician, social reformer, and antiwar campaigner who pioneered the study of industrial diseases and industrial toxicology.

As a member of the Illinois Commission on Occupational Diseases, she supervised in 1910 a survey of industrial poisons. She and her staff identified many hazardous procedures and consequent state legislature introduced safety measures in the workplace and medical examinations for workers at risk. The following year Hamilton was appointed special investigator for the US Bureau of Labor and rapidly became the leading authority on lead poisoning in particular and industrial diseases in general. She lectured at Harvard from 1919, almost 30 years before Harvard accepted women as medical students.

During and after World War I she attended International Congresses of Women and was a pacifist until 1940, when she urged US participation in World War II. During the 1940s and 1950s she spoke out on such subjects as contraception, civil liberties, and workers' rights. In the 1960s she was still considered worthy of attention by the Federal Bureau of Investigation when she protested against US military actions in Vietnam.

Hamilton's *Industrial Poisons in the United States* established her reputation worldwide. She also wrote the classic textbook *Industrial Toxicology* 1934 and an autobiography, *Exploring the Dangerous Trades*, 1943.

Brave Emma! ... Good Emma! ... If there were more Emmas, there would be more Nelsons.

Robert Southey on EMMA, LADY HAMILTON
in Life of Nelson 1813

Hamilton Emma, Lady (born Amy Lyon) (*c.* 1761–1815). English courtesan. In 1782 she became the mistress of Charles Greville and in 1786 of his uncle Sir William Hamilton (1730–1803), the British envoy to the court of Naples, who married her 1791. After Admiral Nelson's return from the Nile 1798 during the Napoleonic Wars, she became his mistress and their daughter, Horatia, was born 1801.

Suggested reading
Fraser, Flora *Beloved Emma* (1986)
Lofts, Nora *Emma Hamilton* (1978)

Hamilton Iain Ellis (1922–). Scottish composer. His intensely emotional and harmonically rich works include striking viola and cello sonatas; the ballet *Clerk Saunders* 1951; the operas *Pharsalia* 1968 and *The Royal Hunt of the Sun* 1967–69, which renounced melody for inventive chordal formations; and symphonies.

Hamilton Ian Standish Monteith (1853–1947). Scottish general. He was Chief of Staff and deputy to Lord Kitchener, commander in chief in the second South African War. In 1915 he directed the land operations in Gallipoli, Turkey, but was replaced Oct 1915. KCB 1900.

Hammarskjöld *As secretary general 1953–61, Dag Hammarskjöld greatly increased the power and prestige of the UN, having the courage and determination to play a leading role in such major conflicts as the Korean War, the Suez Crisis, and the war in the Congo. His book of reflections, Markings, was published 1964.*

Hamilton James, 3rd Marquis and 1st Duke of Hamilton (1606–1649). Scottish adviser to Charles I. He led an army against the Covenanters (supporters of the National Covenant 1638 to establish Presbyterianism) 1639 and subsequently took part in the negotiations between Charles and the Scots. In the second English Civil War he led the Scottish invasion of England, but was captured at Preston and executed. Marquis 1625, duke 1643.

Slow and unimaginative as a general as he was inept and vacillating as a politician.

C P Hill on JAMES HAMILTON
in *Who's Who in History* vol iii 1965

Hamilton Richard (1922–). English artist. He was a pioneer of Pop art. His collage *Just What Is It That Makes Today's Homes So Different, So Appealing?* 1956 (Kunsthalle, Tübingen, Germany) is often cited as the first Pop art work: its 1950s interior, inhabited by the bodybuilder Charles Atlas and a pin-up, is typically humorous, concerned with popular culture and contemporary kitsch.

His series *Swingeing London 67* 1967 comments on the prosecution for drugs of his art dealer Robert Fraser and the singer Mick Jagger.

Hamilton William (1730–1803). British diplomat, envoy to the court of Naples 1764–1800, whose collection of Greek vases was bought by the British Museum. Knighted 1772.

Hamilton William D(onald) (1936–). British biologist. By developing the concept of inclusive fitness, he was able to solve the theoretical problem of explaining altruism in animal behaviour in terms of neo-Darwinism.

Hamilton William Rowan (1805–1865). Irish mathematician whose formulation of Isaac Newton's dynamics proved adaptable to quantum theory, and whose 'quarternion' theory was a forerunner of the branch of mathematics known as vector analysis. Knighted 1835.

Hamilton was born in Dublin and educated there at Trinity College. In 1827, while still an undergraduate, he was appointed professor of astronomy and royal astronomer of Ireland.

Hamlin Hannibal (1809–1891). US political leader and vice-president 1861–65. Originally a Democrat, he served in the US House of

Representatives 1843–47 and the US Senate 1848–61. Opposed to slavery, he joined the Republican Party 1856. He served as vice-president in Lincoln's first term. Returning to the Senate as a radical Republican 1868–80, he later served as US minister to Spain 1881–82.

Born in Paris Hill, Maine, USA, Hamlin worked at a succession of jobs before studying law and being admitted to the bar 1833. He served in the state legislature 1836–41 and was briefly governor of Maine 1857.

Hammarskjöld Dag Hjalmar Agne Carl (1905–1961). Swedish secretary general of the United Nations 1953–61. He opposed Britain over the Suez Crisis 1956. His attempts to solve the problem of the Congo (now Zaire), where he was killed in a plane crash, were criticized by the USSR. He was awarded the Nobel Prize for Peace 1961.
Suggested reading
Hammarskjöld, Dag *Markings* (trs 1964)
Urquhart, Brian *Hammarskjöld* (1972)

Hammer Stage name of Stanley Kirk Burrell (until 1991 *MC Hammer*) (1963–). US rap vocalist and songwriter. His pop-oriented rap style and exuberant dancing gave him a wide appeal, especially in the video-based market, and his second LP, *Please Hammer Don't Hurt 'Em* 1990, sold 13 million copies in one year.

Hammer Armand (1898–1990). US entrepreneur, one of the most remarkable business figures of the 20th century. A pioneer in trading with the USSR from 1921, he later acted as a political mediator. He was chair of the US oil company Occidental Petroleum until his death, and was also an expert on art.

Hammer visited the USSR 1921 and acquired the first private concession awarded by the Soviet government, an asbestos mine. He built up fortunes in several business areas, including the import-export business. He was renowned for his dynamism, his championing of East–West relations, and his many philanthropic and cultural activities.

Hammershøi Vilhelm (1864–1916). Danish painter. He is known for his evocative domestic interiors rendered with monumental simplicity in a muted palette of greys, greens, and soft blacks. His quiet, Neo-Classical rooms often feature a young woman, alone and with her back turned, as in *Interior with a Seated Woman* 1908 (Aarhus Kunstmuseum, Aarhus). His work, exemplifying the inner strength and mysticism of the Nordic spirit, occupies a central place in Scandinavian art.

Some enchanted evening, / You may see a stranger, / You may see a stranger, / Across a crowded room.

OSCAR HAMMERSTEIN
'Some Enchanted Evening'

Hammerstein Oscar, II (1895–1960). US lyricist and librettist. He collaborated with Richard Rodgers over a period of 16 years on some of the best-known American musicals, including *Oklahoma!* 1943 (Pulitzer Prize), *Carousel* 1945, *South Pacific* 1949 (Pulitzer Prize), *The King and I* 1951, and *The Sound of Music* 1959.

He was a grandson of opera impresario Oscar Hammerstein. He earned his first successes with *Rose Marie* 1924, music by Rudolf Friml (1879–1972); *Desert Song* 1926, music by Sigmund Romberg (1887–1951); and *Show Boat* 1927, music by Jerome Kern. *Show Boat* represented a major step forward in integration of plot and character. After a period of moderate success in film music, he joined Rodgers and began a 16-year collaboration.
Suggested reading
Fordin, H *Getting to Know Him* (1977)
Green, Stanley *The Rodgers and Hammerstein Story* (1963)

Hammett (Samuel) Dashiell (1894–1961). US crime novelist. He introduced the 'hard-boiled' detective character into fiction and attracted a host of imitators, with works including *The Maltese Falcon* 1930 (filmed 1941), *The Glass Key* 1931 (filmed 1942), and his most successful novel, the light-hearted *The Thin Man* 1932 (filmed

1934). His Marxist politics were best expressed in *Red Harvest* 1929, which depicts the corruption of capitalism in 'Poisonville'.

Hammett was a former Pinkerton detective agent. In 1951 he was imprisoned for contempt of court for refusing to testify during the McCarthy era of anticommunist witch hunts. He lived with the dramatist Lillian Hellman for the latter half of his life.

Suggested reading
Layman, Richard *Shadow Man: The Life of Dashiell Hammett* (1981)
Nolan, William *Hammett: A Life on the Edge* (1983)
Wolfe, Peter *Beams Falling* (1979)

Hammick Dalziel Llewellyn (1887–1966). English chemist whose major contributions were in the fields of theoretical and synthetic organic chemistry. He devised a rule to predict the order of substitution in benzene derivatives.

Hammick was born in London and studied at Oxford and Munich, Germany. In 1921, he returned to Oxford as a lecturer.

Hammond Joan Hood (1912–1996). Australian soprano. She made her debut in *The Messiah* 1938 and in opera the following year. Her principal repertoire is Wagner and Italian opera to Puccini. DBE 1974.

Hammurabi (died *c.* 1750 BC). King of Babylon from *c.* 1792 BC. He united his country and took it to the height of its power. He authorized a legal code, of which a copy was found in 1902.

Hamnett Katharine (1948–). English fashion designer. She is particularly popular in the UK and Italy. Her oversized T-shirts promoting peace and environmental campaigns attracted attention 1983–84. She produces well-cut designs for men and women, predominantly in natural fabrics. In 1989 she began showing her collections in Paris, and in 1993 launched hand-knitwear and leather collections.

He had a head to contrive, a tongue to persuade, and a hand to execute, any mischief.

Edward Hyde, Earl of Clarendon on JOHN HAMPDEN
in *History of the Rebellion* 1702–04

Hampden John (1594–1643). English politician. His refusal in 1636 to pay ship money, a compulsory tax levied to support the navy, made him a national figure. In the Short and Long Parliaments he proved himself a skilful debater and parliamentary strategist.

King Charles's attempt to arrest him and four other leading MPs made the Civil War inevitable. He raised his own regiment on the outbreak of hostilities, and on 18 June 1643 was mortally wounded at the skirmish of Chalgrove Field in Oxfordshire.

Hampton Lionel (1909–). US jazz musician. He was a top bandleader of the 1940s and 1950s. Originally a drummer, Hampton introduced the vibraphone, an electronically vibrated percussion instrument, to jazz music. With the Benny Goodman band from 1936, he fronted his own big band 1941–65 and subsequently led small groups.

Hampton Wade (1818–1902). US politician and Confederate military leader. During the American Civil War 1861–65, he was appointed brigadier general in the cavalry 1862 and commander of the entire Confederate cavalry corps 1864. After the end of the war 1865 he returned to South Carolina, serving as governor 1876–79 and US senator 1879–91.

Born in Charleston, South Carolina, Hampton was educated at Carolina College and later administered his family's plantation. At the outbreak of the Civil War, he raised and led a regiment of Confederate volunteers.

Hamsun Knut Pedersen (1859–1952). Norwegian novelist. His first novel *Sult*/*Hunger* 1890 was largely autobiographical. Other works include *Pan* 1894 and *Markens Grode*/*The Growth of the Soil* 1917, which won him a Nobel prize 1920. His hatred of capitalism made him sympathize with Nazism, and he was fined in 1946 for collaboration.

Suggested reading
Ferguson, Robert *Enigma: The Life of Knut Hamsun* (1987)
Hamsun, Knut *On Overgrown Paths* (memoirs) (1949, trs 1967)

Hanbury-Brown Robert (1916–). British radio astronomer who participated in the early development of radio-astronomy techniques and later in designing a radio interferometer that permits considerably greater resolution in the results provided by radio telescopes.

After World War II he joined the staff at the Jodrell Bank Observatory in Cheshire. In 1960 he was made professor at Victoria University, Manchester, moving in 1962 to the University of Sydney, Australia.

Hanbury-Brown became one of the first astronomers to construct a radio map of the sky. In 1949 he detected radio waves emanating from the Andromeda nebula at a distance of 2.2 million light years. To improve resolution, Hanbury-Brown and his colleagues devised the radio interferometer, and as a result Cygnus A became the first radio source traced to a definite optical identification, even though it had a magnitude (brightness) of only 17.9.

Hanbury-Tenison (Airling) Robin (1936–). Irish adventurer, explorer, and writer who made the first land crossing of South America at its widest point 1958. He explored the southern Sahara intermittently during 1962–66, and in South America sailed in a small boat from the Orinoco River to Buenos Aires 1964–65. After expeditions to Ecuador, Brazil, and Venezuela, he rode across France 1984 and along the Great Wall of China 1986. In 1969 he became chair of Survival International, an organization campaigning for the rights of threatened tribal peoples.

Hancock John (1737–1793). US politician and a leader of the American Revolution. As president of the Continental Congress 1775–77, he was the first to sign the Declaration of Independence 1776. Because he signed it in a large, bold hand (in popular belief, so that it would be big enough for George III to see), his name became a colloquial term for a signature in the USA. He coveted command of the Continental Army, deeply resenting the selection of George Washington. He was governor of Massachusetts 1780–85 and 1787–93.

Hancock Thomas (1786–1865). English inventor who developed various processes used in the rubber industry, such as the 'masticator', a machine which kneaded raw rubber to produce a solid block.

In 1820 he opened a factory in London for making rubber products. Between 1820 and 1847 he took out 17 patents connected with working rubber, and set up a research laboratory. He also collaborated with Charles Macintosh of Glasgow, inventor of a waterproof cloth. Like Charles Goodyear in the USA, Hancock wanted to solve the problems of rubber's tackiness and inconsistency at different temperatures. After experimenting with sulphur additives and learning of Goodyear's work, Hancock adopted the heat process of vulcanization. In 1857 he published *Personal Narrative of the Origin and Progress of the Caoutchouc or India Rubber Manufacture in England*.

Hancock Tony (Anthony John) (1924–1968). English lugubrious radio and television comedian. *Hancock's Half Hour* from 1954 showed him famously at odds with everyday life. He also appeared in films, including *The Rebel* 1960 and *The Wrong Box* 1966.

Hand Learned Billings (1872–1961). US jurist. He became federal district judge under President Taft 1909 and was appointed to the Second Circuit Court of Appeals by President Coolidge 1924. He served as chief judge of that court 1939–51, handing down opinions in landmark copyright, antitrust, and the constitutional First Amendment cases.

Born in Albany, New York, USA, and educated at Harvard University, Hand received his law degree 1896. Although never appointed to the US Supreme Court, Hand was considered a leading jurist of his day. A collection of his essays, *The Spirit of Liberty*, was published 1952.

Handel Georg Friedrich, (originally Händel) (1685–1759). German composer, a British subject from 1726. His first opera,

Handel *The composer George Friedrich Handel (1685-1759), German by birth and later naturalized British, was almost an exact contemporary of J S Bach. Although both composers wrote many vocal works, Handel wrote for the theatre as well as for the church; his compositions also admit a greater range of influences. (Image Select)*

Almira, was performed in Hamburg 1705. In 1710 he was appointed Kapellmeister to the elector of Hanover (the future George I of England). In 1712 he settled in England, where he established his popularity with such works as the *Water Music* 1717 (written for George I). His great choral works include the *Messiah* 1742 and the later oratorios *Samson* 1743, *Belshazzar* 1745, *Judas Maccabaeus* 1747, and *Jephtha* 1752.

Born in Halle, he abandoned the study of law 1703 to become a violinist at Keiser's Opera House in Hamburg. Visits to Italy (1706–10) inspired a number of operas and oratorios, and in 1711 his opera *Rinaldo* was performed in London. *Saul* and *Israel in Egypt* (both 1739) were unsuccessful, but his masterpiece the *Messiah* was acclaimed on its first performance in Dublin 1742. Other works include the pastoral *Acis and Galatea* 1718 and a set of variations for harpsichord that were later nicknamed 'The Harmonious Blacksmith'. In 1751 he became totally blind.

Suggested reading

Burrows, Donald *Handel* (1994)
Dean, Winton *The New Grove Handel* (1983)
Hogwood, Christopher *Handel* (1988)
Keats, J *Handel: The Man and his Music* (1985)
Landon, H C *Handel and his World* (1984)

My Lord, I should be sorry if I only entertained them; I wished to make them better.

HANDEL
to Lord Kinnol, after a performance of
The Messiah, quoted in Young *Handel* 1947

Handke Peter (1942–   ). Austrian novelist and playwright. His first play *Insulting the Audience* 1966 was an example of 'anti-theatre writing'. His novels include *Die Hornissen/The Hornets* 1966 and *Die Angst des Tormanns beim Elfmeter/The Goalie's Anxiety at the Penalty Kick* 1970. He wrote and directed the film *Linkshandige Frau/The Left-handed Woman* 1977.

Handley Tommy (Thomas Reginald) (1892–1949). English radio comedian. His popular programme *ITMA (It's That Man Again)* ran from 1939 until his death.

Handley Page Frederick (1885–1962). English aeronautical engineer who designed the first large bomber 1915. In 1908 he set up as an aeronautical engineer and a year later, with a capital of £10,000, he established the first private British company of this kind, in Barking, Essex. The outbreak of World War I led to his design of the first two-engined bomber, enlarged before the end of the war into a four-engined bomber with a fully laden weight of 13 tonnes.

Handley Page then turned to civil aviation, but found this not to be viable without government subsidies, and these were only to be had when the Handley Page airline merged with Imperial Airways, the forerunner of BOAC (now part of British Airways). In 1930, Handley Page produced the first 40-seat airliner, the Hercules, a four-engined plane. During World War II Handley Page produced the Halifax, of which 7,000 were constructed. Work on the bomber continued after the end of the war, resulting in a four-engined jet of unusual design, the Victor, which made its first flight 1952. Knighted 1942.

Han dynasty Chinese ruling family 206 BC–AD 220 established by Liu Bang (256–195 BC) after he overthrew the Qin dynasty, and named after the Han River. There was territorial expansion to the W, SW, and N, including the conquest of Korea by emperor Wudi (Wu-ti, ruled 141–87 BC) and the suppression of the Xiongnu invaders. Under the Han, a Confucianist-educated civil service was established and Buddhism introduced.

Divided into the eras of the Western Han 206 BC–AD 8 and the Eastern Han AD 25–220, it was a time of internal peace, except AD 8–25. The building of new canals allowed long-distance trading, while the arts and technologies (including the invention of paper) flourished. The dynasty collapsed under the weight of court intrigues, rebellions, and renewed threat from the Xiongnu, and was replaced by the Three Kingdoms.

Handsome Lake or Ganioda Yo (1735–1815). American Indian religious leader, belonging to the Seneca people, who preached a combination of Christianity and indigenous traditions. Handsome Lake became a typical victim of the arrival of white settlers. He collapsed from drink and depression 1800, and was thought to be dead. During the funeral procession, he awoke and believed he had been resurrected to be a preacher. For the next 15 years he received messages from God which stressed a combination of Christianity – as put forward by the Shakers, in particular – and American Indian traditions.

Hani Chris (Martin Thembisile) (1942–1993). South African communist and anti-apartheid activist, leader of Umkhonto we Sizwe (the military wing of the African National Congress) from 1987 and secretary general of the South African Communist Party (SACP) from 1991. One of the most popular black South African leaders, particularly among the radical young, he was seen as a potential successor to Nelson Mandela. He was assassinated by a white right-wing extremist.

Hani joined Umkhonto we Sizwe 1962, but fled the country later the same year after being sentenced to prison under the Suppression of Communism Act. While in exile he fought against white rule in Rhodesia (now Zimbabwe) and subsequently ran an Umkhonto network in Lesotho, where he survived two assassination attempts. In 1987 he was made Chief of Staff of Umkhonto. His death April 1993 came as a serious blow to the ANC, for whom he provided a vital and influential link with black militant groups.

Hankel Hermann (1839–1873). German mathematician and mathematical historian who made significant contributions to the study of complex and hypercomplex numbers and the theory of functions. Much of his work was also in developing that of others. He lectured at Leipzig and Tübingen.

Hankel's *Theorie der complexen Zahlensysteme* 1867 dealt with the real, complex, and hypercomplex number systems, and demonstrated that no hypercomplex number system can satisfy all the laws of ordinary arithmetic.

In *Untersuchungen über die unendlich oft oscillerenden und unstetigen Functionen*, he presented a method for constructing functions with singularities at every rational point. He also explicitly stated that functions do not possess general properties; this work was an important advance towards modern integration theory.

Hanks Tom (1956–   ). US actor. His amiable features and mainstream appeal, often seen to best advantage in romantic comedies such as *Sleepless in Seattle* 1993, made his casting as the AIDS-afflicted lawyer in *Philadelphia* 1993 (Academy Award) all the more controversial. His other notable roles include the drunken baseball coach in *A League of their Own* 1992, and the title role in *Forrest Gump* 1994 (Academy Award).

He featured in a number of lightweight comedy dramas during the 1980s, most notably in *Splash* 1984, and *Big* 1988, in which he played a boy transformed into a grown man. His other films include *Dragnet* 1987 and *Turner and Hooch* 1989.

Hanley Ellery (1965–   ). English rugby league player, a regular member of the Great Britain team since 1984 and the inspiration behind Wigan's domination of the sport in the 1980s. He joined Leeds 1991.

Hanley started his career in 1981 with Bradford Northern before his transfer to Wigan 1985 for a then world record £85,000. He has since won all the top honours of the game in Britain as well as earning a reputation in Australia, the world's top rugby league nation.

Hanna Mark (1837–1904). US politician. A Republican, he supported James Garfield in his presidential campaign 1880. He served in the US Senate 1896–1900 and, as chair of the Republican National Committee, engineered McKinley's victories in 1896 and 1900, becoming his closest adviser.

Born in New Lisbon, Ohio, USA, Hanna attended Case Western Reserve College before joining his father in business. He later became one of Cleveland's civic leaders, founding the Union National Bank and buying the *Cleveland Herald*.

Destiny, both personal and public, has since boyhood taught me all a soldier should know, and I think I have learned my lesson well.

HANNIBAL
Comment to Scipio before his defeat at Zama in 202.
Quoted in Livy *From the Foundation of the City* bk 30 ch 37

Hannibal (247–*c.* 182 BC). Carthaginian general from 221 BC, son of Hamilcar Barca. His siege of Saguntum (now Sagunto, near Valencia) precipitated the Second Punic War with Rome. Following a campaign in Italy (after crossing the Alps in 218), Hannibal was the victor at Trasimene in 217 and Cannae in 216, but he failed to take Rome. In 203 he returned to Carthage to meet a Roman invasion but was defeated at Zama in 202 and exiled in 196 at Rome's insistence.

Suggested reading
Bradford, Ernie *Hannibal* (1981)
De Beer, Gavin *Hannibal: Challenging Rome's Supremacy* (1969)
Jacobs, W J *Hannibal: An African Hero* (1973)

Hanover German royal dynasty that ruled Great Britain and Ireland 1714–1901. Under the Act of Settlement 1701, the succession passed on the ruling family of Hanover, Germany, on the death of Queen Anne. On the death of Queen Victoria, the crown passed to Edward VII of the house of Saxe-Coburg.

Hansom Joseph Aloysius (1803–1882). English architect and inventor. His works include the Birmingham town hall 1831, but he is remembered as the designer of the *hansom cab* 1834, a two-wheel carriage with a seat for the driver on the outside.

Hanway Jonas (1712–1786). British traveller in Russia and Persia, and advocate of prison reform. He is believed to have been the first Englishman to carry an umbrella.

Hapsburg English form of ◊Habsburg, former imperial house of Austria–Hungary.

Haq Fazlul (1873–1962). Leader of the Bengali Muslim peasantry. He was a member of the Viceroy's Defence Council, established 1941, and was Bengal's first Indian prime minister 1937–43.

Harald (III) Hardrada or Harald the Ruthless (Norwegian Harald Hardråde) (1015–1066). King of Norway 1045–66, ruling jointly with Magnus I 1045–47. He engaged in an unsuccessful attempt to conquer Denmark 1045–62; extended Norwegian rule in Orkney, Shetland, and the Hebrides; and tried to conquer England together with Tostig, Earl of Northumbria. They were defeated by King Harold of England at Stamford Bridge and both died in battle.

A good old-fashioned parliamentary bruiser.

Augustine Birrell on WILLIAM HARCOURT
in *Things Past Redress* 1937

Harcourt William George Granville Venables Vernon (1827–1904). British Liberal politician. Under Gladstone he was home secretary 1880–85 and chancellor of the Exchequer 1886 and 1892–95. He is remembered for his remark 1892: 'We are all Socialists now.' Knighted 1873.

Harden Arthur (1865–1940). English biochemist who investigated the mechanism of sugar fermentation and the role of enzymes in this process. For this work he shared the 1929 Nobel Prize for Chemistry. Knighted 1936.

He worked at the British Institute of Preventative Medicine (later called the Jenner Institute) 1897–1912, when he became professor at the University of London.

Hardenberg Karl August Fürst von (1750–1822). Prussian politician, foreign minister to King Frederick William III of Prussia during the Napoleonic Wars; he later became chancellor. His military and civic reforms were restrained by the reactionary tendencies of the king.

Hardicanute (*c.* 1019–1042). King of Denmark from 1028, and of England from 1040; son of Canute. In England he was considered a harsh ruler.

I understand what Christ suffered in Gethsemane as well as any man living.

KEIR HARDIE
speaking to friends after hostility in Aberdare 6 Aug 1914

Hardie (James) Keir (1856–1915). Scottish socialist, member of Parliament 1892–95 and 1900–15. He worked in the mines as a boy and in 1886 became secretary of the Scottish Miners' Federation. In 1888 he was the first Labour candidate to stand for Parliament; he entered Parliament independently as a Labour member 1892 and was a chief founder of the Independent Labour Party 1893.

Hardie was born in Lanarkshire but represented the parliamentary constituencies of West Ham, London 1892–95 and Merthyr Tydfil, Wales, from 1900. A pacifist, he strongly opposed the Boer War, and his idealism in his work for socialism and the unemployed made him a popular hero. *See illustration on page 382.*

Suggested reading
McLean, Ian *Keir Hardie* (1975)
Morgan, K O *Keir Hardie: Radical and Socialist* (1975)
Reid, F *Keir Hardie* (1978)

Hardie *Kier Hardie addressing an antiwar rally in London 1914. Hardie played an important part in the establishment of the early Labour Party, and was an ardent pacifist who campaigned against Britain's involvement in World War I. (Image Select)*

Harding John (Allan Francis), 1st Baron Harding of Petherton (1896–1989). British field marshal. During World War II he was Chief of Staff in Egypt 1940 and Italy 1944. As governor of Cyprus 1955–57, during the period of political agitation prior to independence 1960, he was responsible for the deportation of Makarios III from Cyprus 1955. KCB 1944, baron 1958.

Harding Warren G(amaliel) (1865–1923). 29th president of the USA 1921–23, a Republican. He opposed US membership of the League of Nations. There was corruption among members of his cabinet (the Teapot Dome Scandal), with the secretary of the interior later convicted for taking bribes.

Harding was born in Ohio, and entered the US Senate 1914. As president he concluded the peace treaties of 1921 with Germany, Austria, and Hungary, and in the same year called the Washington

Harding, Warren *The Republican Warren G Harding, the 29th president of the United States of America 1921–23. Elected on a 'back to normalcy' platform after World War I, his administration soon collapsed amid widespread corruption.*

Naval Conference to resolve conflicting British, Japanese, and US ambitions in the Pacific. He died in office shortly after undeniable evidence of corruption in his administration began to surface.

Suggested reading
Harding, Warren *From Printer to President* (1922)
Mee, Charles *The Ohio Gang* (1981)
Russell, Francis *The Shadow of Blooming Grove* (1968)
Sinclair, Andrew *The Available Man: The Life Behind the Masks of Warren Gamaliel Harding* (1965)
Wade, L R *Warren G Harding* (1989)

America's present need is not heroics, but healing; not nostrums but normalcy; not revolution, but restoration.
WARREN G HARDING
Speech at Boston 14 May 1920

Hardouin-Mansart Jules (1646–1708). French architect to Louis XIV from 1675. He designed the lavish Baroque extensions to the palace of Versailles (from 1678) and the Grand Trianon. Other works include the Invalides Chapel (1680–91), the Place de Vendôme (from 1698), and the Place des Victoires, all in Paris.

Hardy Alister Clavering (1896–1985). English marine biologist who developed methods for ascertaining the numbers and types of minute sea organisms.

In 1924 he joined an expedition to the Antarctic, and on his return in 1928 he was appointed professor at Hull University, where he founded the Department of Oceanography. Clavering was professor of zoology and comparative anatomy at Oxford 1946–65 and master of the Unitarian College, Manchester College, Oxford, 1958–65.

Hardy made his special study of plankton on the 1924 *Discovery* expedition. The aim of quantitative plankton studies is to estimate the numbers or weights of organisms beneath a unit area of sea surface or in a unit volume of water. He developed the Hardy plankton continuous recorder – a net that can be used behind faster-moving vessels, at a depth of 10 m/33 ft, giving a larger area in which accurate recordings can be made. Surveys using this device now annually cover many thousands of kilometres in the Atlantic, North Sea, and Icelandic waters, for the benefit of fisheries.

He also attempted to apply scientific methods to religious phenomena, conducting a number of research projects into religious experience. He concluded that such experiences were common and classified them into types. Although he held back from claiming that his results proved that religious experience was genuine and therefore that God existed, his work has been cited as evidence for the existence of God by some and of the inappropriateness of scientific methodology in religion by others.

Hardy Frank (Francis) (1917–). Australian radical political writer. He is best known for the novel *Power Without Glory* 1950, a semi-fictional account of the life of Melbourne millionaire sports promoter and financier John Wren and for which Hardy faced court proceedings for libel. His other works include *The Yarns of Billy Borker* 1965, a collection of tall tales, *The Outcasts of Foolgarah* 1971, and *But the Dead Are Many* 1975.

Hardy Godfrey Harold (1877–1947). English mathematician whose research was at a very advanced level in the fields of pure mathematics known as analysis and number theory. His *Course in Pure Mathematics* 1908 revolutionized the teaching of mathematics at senior school and university levels. Hardy was born in Cranleigh, Surrey, and studied at Cambridge.

Hardy Oliver (born Norvell Hardy) (1892–1957). US film comedian, member of the duo ◊Laurel and Hardy.

Hardy Thomas (1840–1928). English novelist and poet. His novels, set in rural 'Wessex' (his native West Country), portray intense human relationships played out in a harshly indifferent natural world. They include *Far From the Madding Crowd* 1874, *The Return of the Native* 1878, *The Mayor of Casterbridge* 1886, *The Woodlanders* 1887, *Tess of the d'Urbervilles* 1891, and *Jude the Obscure* 1895. His poetry

Hardy: major works

title	date	well-known characters
Under the Greenwood Tree	1872	Joseph Bowman, Fancy Day, Dick Dewy, Reuben Dewy, William Dewy, Arthur Maybold, Farmer Fred Shiner
Far From the Madding Crowd	1874	William Boldwood, Bathsheba Everdene, Gabriel Oak, Joseph Poorgrass, Fanny Robin, Lyddy Smallbury, Sergeant Francis Troy
The Return of the Native	1878	Christian Cantle, Grandfer Cantle, Diggory Venn, Eustacia Vye, Clym Yeobright, Mrs Yeobright, Thomasin Yeobright, Damon Wildeve
The Trumpet Major	1880	Festus Derriman, Anne Garland, Mrs Garland, Bob Loveday, John Loveday
The Mayor of Casterbridge	1886	Suke Damson, Donald Farfrae, Elizabeth Jane Henchard, Mrs Henchard, Michael Henchard, Richard Newson, Lucetta Templeman/Le Sueur
The Woodlanders	1887	Felice Charmond, Robert Creedle, Edred Fitzpiers, Grace Melbury, Marty South, Giles Winterbourne
Tess of the d'Urbervilles	1891	Mercy Chant, Angel Clare, Rev James Clare, Dairyman Crick, Car Darch, Izz Huett, Marian, Retty Priddle, Alec d'Urberville, Tess Durbeyfield, John and Joan Durbeyfield
Jude the Obscure	1895	Sue Bridehead, Arabella Donn, Jude Fawley, Little Father Time, Richard Phillotson

includes the *Wessex Poems* 1898, the blank-verse epic of the Napoleonic Wars *The Dynasts* 1904–08, and several volumes of lyrics.

Hardy was born in Dorset and trained as an architect. His first success was *Far From the Madding Crowd*. *Tess of the d'Urbervilles*, subtitled 'A Pure Woman', outraged public opinion by portraying as its heroine a woman who had been seduced. The even greater outcry that followed *Jude the Obscure* 1895 reinforced Hardy's decision to confine himself to verse.

Suggested reading
Gittings, R *Young Thomas Hardy* (1975)
Gittings, R *The Older Hardy* (1978)
Goode, J *Thomas Hardy* (1988)
Millgate, M *Thomas Hardy: His Career as a Novelist* (1971)
Millgate, M *Thomas Hardy: A Biography* (1982)
Page, N *Thomas Hardy* (1980)
Pinion, F *A Hardy Companion: A Guide to the Works of Thomas Hardy* (1968)

Ah! Stirring times we live in – stirring times.

THOMAS HARDY
Far From the Madding Crowd 1874

Hardy Thomas Masterman (1769–1839). British sailor. At Trafalgar he was Nelson's flag captain in the *Victory*, attending him during his dying moments. He became First Sea Lord 1830. KCB 1815.

Hare David (1947–). British dramatist and screenwriter, who co-founded the theatre company Joint Stock 1974. His plays satirize the decadence of post-war Britain, and include *Slag* 1970, *Teeth 'n' Smiles* 1975, *Fanshen* 1975 on revolutionary Chinese communism, *Plenty* 1978, and *Pravda* 1985 (with Howard Brenton) on Fleet Street journalism. A recent trilogy of plays looks critically at three aspects of the establishment in Britain: *Racing Demon* 1990 at the Church of England, *Murmuring Judges* 1991 at the legal system, and *The Absence of War* 1994. His screenplays include *Wetherby* and *Plenty* both 1985, *Paris by Night* 1988, and *The Absence of War* 1994. He has also published an autobiography *Writing Left-Handed* 1991.

[He had] a highly charged political consciousness.

Trevor and Carole Woddis Griffiths on DAVID HARE
in *The Bloomsbury Theatre Guide* 1988

Harewood George Henry Hubert Lascelles, 7th Earl of Harewood (1923–). Artistic director of the Edinburgh Festival 1961–65, director of the English National Opera 1972–85, and a governor of the BBC 1985–87. Earl 1947.

Hargobind (1595–1644). Indian religious leader, sixth guru (teacher) of Sikhism 1606–44. He encouraged Sikhs to develop military skills in response to growing persecution. At the festival of Diwali, Sikhs celebrate his release from prison.

Hargraves Edward Hammond (1816–1891). Australian prospector, born in England. In 1851 he found gold in the Blue Mountains of New South Wales, thus beginning the first Australian gold rush.

Hargreaves James (*c.* 1720–1778). English inventor who co-invented a carding machine for combing wool 1760. About 1764 he invented his 'spinning jenny' (patented 1770), which enabled a number of threads to be spun simultaneously by one person.

When he began to sell the machines, spinners with the old-fashioned wheel became alarmed by the possibility of cheaper competition and in 1768 a mob from Blackburn gutted Hargreaves's house and destroyed his equipment. Hargreaves moved to Nottingham, where he formed a partnership and built a small cotton mill in which the jenny was used.

The spinning jenny multiplied eightfold the output of the spinner and could be worked easily by children. It did not entirely supersede the spinning wheel in cotton manufacturing (and was itself overtaken by Samuel Crompton's mule). But for woollen textiles the jenny could be used to make both the warp and the weft.

Harington Charles (1872–1940). British general. Harington served on the staff during the South African War 1899–1902, and in World War I became chief of the General Staff, British Forces Italy 1917. In 1918 he was appointed deputy chief of the Imperial General Staff, War Office.

Harington joined the King's Regiment 1892, served on the staff during the South African War, as an instructor at the Royal Military College, and then on intelligence duties at the War Office. In 1911–13 he was brigade major at Aldershot, and in the early part of the war was a brigadier-general on the staff of and then Chief of Staff to General Plumer. When Plumer went to Italy 1917, Harington accompanied him and became chief of the General Staff, British Forces Italy. He was promoted to lieutenant-general in command of the army of the Black Sea 1920. KCB 1919.

Treason doth never prosper: what's the reason? / For if it prosper, none dare call it treason.

JOHN HARINGTON
'Of Treason'

Harington John (1561–1612). English writer and translator. He translated Ariosto's *Orlando furioso* and was the author of *The Metamorphosis of Ajax*, a ribald history of the privy ('jakes'). Elizabeth I of England referred to him as 'that saucy poet, my godson', and banished him from court on several occasions but also installed the water closet he invented. Knighted 1599.

Har Krishen (1656–1664). Indian religious leader, eighth guru (teacher) of Sikhism 1661–64, who died at the age of eight.

Harlan John Marshall (1833–1911). US politician and jurist, associate justice of the US Supreme Court 1877–1911. Harlan supported the Union during the American Civil War 1861–65, serving as colonel in the 10th Kentucky Volunteer Infantry and elected

Kentucky attorney general 1863. He was defeated as Republican candidate for governor of Kentucky 1871 and 1875.

Before embarking on his political career, Harlan practised law in Kentucky. He was appointed associate justice by President Hayes after service on a federal reconstruction commission in Louisiana 1877 and held the office until his death.

He was really a dull puzzleheaded man.

T B Macaulay on ROBERT HARLEY
in *History of England* 1839

Harley Robert, 1st Earl of Oxford (1661–1724). British Tory politician, chief minister to Queen Anne 1711–14, when he negotiated the Treaty of Utrecht 1713. Accused of treason as a Jacobite after the accession of George I, he was imprisoned 1714–17. Earl 1711.

Harlow Jean. Stage name of Harlean Carpentier (1911–1937). US film actress. She was the original 'platinum blonde' and the wise-cracking sex symbol of the 1930s. Her films include *Hell's Angels* 1930, *Red Dust* 1932, *Platinum Blonde* 1932, *Dinner at Eight* 1933, *China Seas* 1935, and *Saratoga* 1937, during the filming of which she died (her part was completed by a double).

Harmon Millard F (1888–1945). US general and aviator. In 1942 he was placed in command of US forces in the South Pacific and was responsible for the campaigns in the Solomon Islands and Guadalcanal. He was appointed to command US Air Forces Pacific Ocean July 1944 with the primary task of organizing the bombing campaign against Japan. He died 1945 when his aircraft disappeared over the sea.

Harnoncourt Nikolaus (1929–). German conductor, cellist, and musicologist. A leading figure in the authenticity movement, he established the Vienna Consensus Musicus 1953, an ensemble playing early music on period instruments. He has conducted notable recordings of Monteverdi's operas and Bach's choral and orchestral

Harlow *After joining Metro-Goldwyn-Meyer 1932, Jean Harlow quickly developed into a superstar. She was cast opposite such stars as Clark Gable and Spencer Tracy, and her early image as a coarse, flashy sexpot was transformed into that of a subtle actress with a flair for comedy.*

music. Since 1969 his wife, violinist Alice Harnoncourt (1930–), has led the Consensus Musicus.

Harold two kings of England:

Harold I (*c.* 1016–1040). King of England from 1035. The illegitimate son of Canute, known as 'Harefoot', he claimed the throne 1035 when the legitimate heir Hardicanute was in Denmark. He was elected king 1037.

We march straight on; we march to victory.

HAROLD II
Attributed remark before the Battle of Hastings

Harold II (*c.* 1020–1066). King of England from Jan 1066. He succeeded his father Earl Godwin 1053 as earl of Wessex. In 1063 William of Normandy (William the Conqueror) tricked him into swearing to support his claim to the English throne, and when the Witan (a council of high-ranking religious and secular men) elected Harold to succeed Edward the Confessor, William prepared to invade. Meanwhile, Harold's treacherous brother Tostig (died 1066) joined the king of Norway, Harald Hardrada (1015–1066), in invading Northumbria. Harold routed and killed them at Stamford Bridge 25 Sept. Three days later William landed at Pevensey, Sussex, and Harold was killed at the Battle of Hastings 14 Oct 1066.
Suggested reading
Swanton, M *Three Lives of the Last Englishman* (1984)

Har Rai (1630–1661). Indian religious leader, seventh guru (teacher) of Sikhism 1644–61.

Harriman (William) Averell (1891–1986). US diplomat, administrator of lend-lease in World War II, Democratic secretary of commerce in Truman's administration 1946–48, negotiator of the Nuclear Test Ban Treaty with the USSR 1963, and governor of New York 1955–58.

Harris Arthur Travers (1892–1984). British marshal of the Royal Air Force in World War II. Known as 'Bomber Harris', he was commander in chief of Bomber Command 1942–45.

He was an autocratic and single-minded leader, and was criticized for his policy of civilian-bombing of selected cities in Germany; he authorized the fire-bombing raids on Dresden, in which more than 100,000 died. He never lost his conviction that area bombing could, by itself, bring the war to an end, and stretched his theories to the utmost with the devastating raids on Hamburg, Berlin, and Dresden. He also showed a flair for dramatic actions, such as the celebrated 'thousand bomber raid' on Cologne May 1942. Although his policies were endorsed by the War Cabinet, Harris was the only senior British commander not to receive a peerage after the war, and no medal was ever struck for the men of Bomber Command. KCB 1942.

Harris Emmylou (1947–). US country-and-western singer and songwriter. Her pure soprano voice gives a sensitive treatment to material ranging from old hymns to country rock. She enjoyed crossover success right from her solo debut, *Pieces of the Sky* 1975; others include *Luxury Liner* 1977 and *White Shoes* 1983.

She teamed up 1972 with Gram Parsons (1946–1973), a former member of the Byrds rock group, and after his death went on performing his songs as well as her own, drawing also on a wide range of traditions and contemporary songwriters. *Blue Kentucky Girl* 1979 won a Grammy award for the best country vocal performance by a woman. She was inducted into Grand Ole Opry 1992, the highest honour in country music.

Harris was born in Birmingham, Alabama, and began singing folk songs in the late 1960s. In 1974 she formed the Hot Band as a backup group, which she dissolved 1991 to form the Nash Ramblers, giving up electric instruments for acoustic ones. Notable Hot Band guitarists included James Burton (1939–) and Albert Lee (1943–).

Harris Frank. Pen name of James Thomas Harris (1856–1931). Irish journalist, later in the USA, who wrote colourful biographies of

Oscar Wilde and George Bernard Shaw, and an autobiography, *My Life and Loves* 1926, originally banned in the UK and the USA for its sexual content.

Tar-baby ain't sayin' nuthin', en Brer Fox, he lay low.

JOEL CHANDLER HARRIS
Uncle Remus, Legends of the Old Plantation ch 2 1880

Harris Joel Chandler (1848–1908). US author. He wrote tales narrated by the former slave 'Uncle Remus', based on black folklore and involving the characters Brer Rabbit, Brer Fox, Brer Wolf, and Brer Bear.

Suggested reading
Bickley, R B, Jr *Joel Chandler Harris* (1978)
Cousins, P M *Joel Chandler Harris: A Biography* (1968)

Harris Louis (1921–). US pollster. He joined the Roper opinion polling organization 1947 and became a partner in that firm 1954. Developing his own research techniques, he founded Louis Harris and Associates 1956. Hired by the 1960 Kennedy presidential campaign, Harris gained a national reputation and later served as a consultant to the CBS television network and as a political columnist.

Born in New Haven, Connecticut, he was educated at the University of North Carolina. After World War II, Harris gained his first experience in testing public opinion in his work for the American Veterans' Committee.

Harris Paul Percy (1868–1947). US lawyer who founded the first Rotary Club in Chicago 1905; the International Association followed 1912.

Harris Richard St Johns (1933–). Irish film actor. He is known for playing dominating characters in such films as *This Sporting Life* 1963. His other films include *Camelot* 1967, *A Man Called Horse* 1970, *Robin and Marian* 1976, *Tarzan the Ape Man* 1981, *The Field* 1990, and *Unforgiven* 1992.

Harris Roy (Leroy Ellsworth) (1898–1979). US composer. His works, which make use of American folk tunes, include the *Symphony No 10* 1965 (known as 'Abraham Lincoln') and the orchestral *When Johnny Comes Marching Home* 1935.

Harris William Wadé (c. 1865–1929). Liberian Christian evangelist. Using healing and dramatic symbolism, he converted over 120,000 people in the Ivory Coast to Christianity in the space of a few years. He was expelled from the Ivory Coast by the French authorities 1915 and died in poverty in Liberia. His followers founded a number of the independent churches which still flourish today.

Harrison Benjamin (1833–1901). 23rd president of the USA 1889–93, a Republican. He called the first Pan-American Conference, which led to the establishment of the Pan American Union, to improve inter-American cooperation, and develop commercial ties. In 1948 this became the Organization of American States.

Suggested reading
Harrison, Benjamin *Autobiographic Memoirs* (1911)
Rothman, H *Benjamin Harrison* (1989)
Sievers, Harry *Benjamin Harrison* (1952–68)

Harrison John (1693–1776). English horologist and instrument-maker who made the first chronometers that were accurate enough to allow the precise determination of longitude at sea, and so permit reliable (and safe) navigation over long distances.

In 1714, the British government's Board of Longitude announced a prize of up to £20,000 for anyone who could make an instrument to determine longitude at sea to an accuracy of 30 minutes (half a degree). Between 1735 and 1760, Harrison submitted four instruments for the award. When his fourth marine chronometer was tested at sea, it kept accurate time to within 5 seconds over the duration of two voyages to the West Indies, equivalent to just over one minute of longitude. Harrison was eventually awarded the prize money. A unique feature that contributed to the chronometer's

accuracy was a device that enabled it to be rewound without temporarily stopping the mechanism. This was subsequently incorporated into other chronometers.

Harrison Rex (Reginald Carey) (1908–1990). English film and theatre actor. He appeared in over 40 films and numerous plays, often portraying sophisticated and somewhat eccentric characters, such as the waspish Professor Higgins in *My Fair Lady* 1964 (Academy Award), the musical version of *Pygmalion*. His other films include *Blithe Spirit* 1945, *The Ghost and Mrs Muir* 1947, and *Dr Doolittle* 1967. Knighted 1989.

Harrison Tony (1937–). English poet, translator, and dramatist. He caused controversy with his poem *V* 1987, dealing with the desecration of his parents' grave by Liverpool football supporters, and the play *The Blasphemers' Banquet* 1989, which attacked (in the name of Molière, Voltaire, Byron, and Omar Khayyam) the death sentence on Salman Rushdie. He has also translated and adapted Molière. *Black Daisies for the Bride* (poems) appeared 1993.

Harrison William Henry (1773–1841). 9th president of the US 1841. Elected 1840 as a Whig, he died one month after taking office. His political career was based largely on his reputation as an Indian fighter, and his campaign was constructed to give the impression that he was a man of the people with simple tastes and that the New Yorker, Martin Van Buren, his opponent, was a 'foppish' sophisticate.

Born in Charles City County, Virginia, he joined the army 1791 at the age of 18. He resigned from the army 1798 and served as secretary of the Northwest Territory 1798–1800 and governor of the Indiana Territory 1801–12, where he drove off a minor Indian attack at Tippecanoe Creek, which was reported as a rout. Recalled to the army during the War of 1812, Harrison led his troops in the recapture of Detroit and was victorious at the Battle of the Thames River in Ontario, Canada. He served in the US House of Representatives 1816–19 and the Senate 1825–28. Benjamin Harrison was his grandson.

Suggested reading
Gunderson, Robert G *The Log Cabin Campaign* (1957)
Hoffnagle, W M *Road to Fame* (1959)
Huston, James *Counterpoint: Tecumseh vs William Henry Harrison* (1987)

Harrisson Tom (Thomas Harnett) (1911–1976). British anthropologist who set up Mass Observation with Charles Madge 1937, the earliest of the organizations for the analysis of public opinions and attitudes. After working among the people of Borneo, Harrisson decided to apply the same study techniques among Bolton cotton-mill operators.

Harsha-Vardhana (c. 590–c. 647). Supreme ruler (*sakala-Uttarapathanatha*) of N India from 606. Through a succession of military victories, he established a large pan-regional empire in N and central India, extending to Kashmir in the NW. It was connected by loose feudalistic tributary ties.

Originally chief of the Pushyabhutis, based in Thanesar near Delhi, he united his throne through a marriage alliance with the Maukharis, whose headquarters at Kanauj, in the upper Ganges valley, became his capital. A devout Buddhist, he was an enlightened and cultured ruler.

Hart Gary (born Gary Hartpence) (1936–). US Democrat politician, senator for Colorado from 1974. In 1980 he contested the Democratic nomination for the presidency, and stepped down from his Senate seat 1986 to run, again unsuccessfully, in the 1988 presidential campaign.

Hart H(erbert) L(ionel) A(dolphus) (1907–1993). English jurist and philosopher. In *The Concept of Law* 1961, he argued that rules of obligation are felt to be necessary for society to function and that they are maintained through social pressure. A legal system is a union of primary rules (those which govern behaviour) and secondary rules (those which identify and modify primary rules). He was professor of jurisprudence at Oxford University 1952–68.

Hart Judith Constance Mary, Baroness Hart (1924–1991). British Labour politician and sociologist. She was minister of overseas development 1967–70 and 77–79, and minister of state 1974–75. DBE 1979, baroness 1988.

Hart Moss (1904–1961). US dramatist. He collaborated with such major figures as Irving Berlin, Cole Porter, Kurt Weill, and Ira Gershwin. Among Hart's most famous works are *The Man Who Came to Dinner* 1939 and the films *Gentlemen's Agreement* 1947 and *A Star is Born* 1954. His autobiography, *Act One*, appeared 1959.

Harte (Francis) Bret (born Francis Brett Harte) (1836–1902). US writer. He became a goldminer at 18 before founding the *Overland Monthly* 1868 in which he wrote short stories of the pioneer West, for example 'The Luck of Roaring Camp', and poems such as 'The Heathen Chinee'. From 1885 he settled in England after five years as US consul in Glasgow.

Hartington Spencer Compton Cavendish, Marquess of Hartington and 8th Duke of Devonshire (1833–1908). British politician, first leader of the Liberal Unionists 1886–1903. As war minister he opposed devolution for Ireland in cabinet and later led the revolt of the Liberal Unionists that defeated Gladstone's Irish Home Rule bill 1886. Hartington refused the premiership three times, 1880, 1886, and 1887, and led the opposition to the Irish Home Rule bill in the House of Lords 1893. Marquess 1858, duke 1891.

Hartley L(eslie) P(oles) (1895–1972). English novelist, noted for his exploration of the sinister. His books include the trilogy *The Shrimp and the Anemone* 1944, *The Sixth Heaven* 1946, and *Eustace and Hilda* 1947, on the intertwined lives of a brother and sister. Later works include *The Boat* 1949, *The Go-Between* 1953 (also a film), and *The Hireling* 1957.

Hartley Marsden (1877–1943). US avant-garde painter. His works range from abstract, brightly coloured representations of German soldiers and German military symbols, such as *Portrait of a*

German Officer 1914 (Metropolitan Museum of Art, New York), to New England landscapes, such as *Log Jam, Penobscot Bay* 1940–41 (Detroit Institute of Art).

Born in Lewiston, Maine, USA, he travelled in Europe to study art. He exhibited 1913 with the *Blaue Reiter* group and returned to the USA to exhibit with the Armory Show 1913. Typical of his later 'primitive' style is the painting *Fisherman's Last Supper* portraying the influence of the early German Expressionists.

Hartnell Norman Bishop (1901–1979). English fashion designer. He was known for his ornate evening gowns and tailored suits and coats. He worked for the designer Lucille 1923 before founding his own studio. Appointed dressmaker to the British royal family 1938, he created Queen Elizabeth II's wedding dress, when she was Princess Elizabeth, 1947, and her coronation gown 1953. The Hartnell fashion house closed 1992. KCVO 1977.

Hartnett Laurence John (1898–1986). Australian engineer and company director, born in England. He was the creator of the Holden car, the first mass-produced all-Australian car. Knighted 1967.

Harunobu Suzuki (1725–1770). Japanese artist; see Harunobu ◊Suzuki.

Harvey Ethel Browne (1885–1965). US embryologist and cell biologist who discovered the mechanisms of cell division, using sea-urchin eggs as her experimental model. From 1931 she was an independent research worker attached to the biology department of Princeton. She was a frequent visitor to the Stazione Zoologica in Naples.

Harvey's work concentrated on the role in cell fertilization and development of non-nuclear cell components in the cytoplasm. She undertook morphological studies and physiological experiments to examine the factors that affect the process of cell division and was able to stimulate division in fragments of sea-urchin eggs that contained no nucleus. This was an important contribution to unravelling the connections between different cellular structures in controlling cell division and development.

Harvey Jonathan Dean (1939–). English composer. His use of avant-garde and computer synthesis techniques is allied to a tradition of visionary Romanticism in works such as *Inner Light II* 1977 for voices, instruments, and tape music and *Mortuos plango, vivos voco*/*I Mourn the Dead, I Call the Living* 1980.

Harvey Laurence. Adopted name of Lauruska Mischa Skikne (1929–1973). British film actor of Lithuanian descent. He worked both in England (*Room at the Top* 1958) and in Hollywood (*The Alamo* 1960, *The Manchurian Candidate* 1962).

Harvey William (1578–1657). English physician who discovered the circulation of blood. In 1628 he published his book *De motu cordis*/*On the Motion of the Heart and the Blood in Animals*. He also explored the development of chick and deer embryos. Harvey's discovery marked the beginning of the end of medicine as taught by Greek physician Galen, which had been accepted for 1,400 years.

Harvey was born in Folkestone, Kent, and studied at Cambridge and at Padua, Italy, under Geronimo Fabricius. He worked at St Bartholomew's Hospital, London, and served as a professor there 1615–43. From 1618, he was court physician to James I and later to Charles I. Examining the heart and blood vessels of mammals, Harvey deduced that the blood in the veins must flow only towards the heart. He also calculated the amount of blood that left the heart at each beat, and realized that the same blood must be circulating continuously around the body. He reasoned that it passes from the right side of the heart to the left through the lungs (pulmonary circulation).

Suggested reading
Keynes, G L *The Life of William Harvey* (1966)
Pagel, W *New Light on William Harvey* (1975)

Hasan (625–670). Eldest grandson of the prophet Muhammad. He was the son of Ali bin Abu Talib and Muhammad's daughter Fatima. He was caliph for six months in 611 AD before resigning. It is through Hasan and his brother Husayn that the descendants of the prophet trace their lineage.

Harvey, William English physician William Harvey, who discovered the circulation of blood after viewing it experimentally in animals. Harvey also showed that the heart acted as a pump and that blood flowed through the body via the lungs along arteries, and back to the heart along veins. His observations met with initial hostility but were generally accepted by the time of his death in 1657. (Ann Ronan/Image Select)

Hašek Jaroslav (1883–1923). Czech writer. His masterpiece is an anti-authoritarian comic satire on military life under Austro-Hungarian rule, *The Good Soldier Svejk* 1921–23. During World War I he deserted to Russia, and eventually joined the Bolsheviks.

Hassam (Frederick) Childe (1859–1935). US Impressionist painter and printmaker. He studied in Paris 1886–89 and later became one of the members of 'the Ten', a group of American Impressionists who exhibited together until World War I. His *Flag Day* 1919 (County Museum, Los Angeles) is typical.

Morocco is like a tree nourished by roots deep in the soil of Africa which breathes through foliage rustling to the winds of Europe.

HASSAN II
The Challenge 1979

Hassan II (1929–). King of Morocco from 1961 and a moderating influence in the Middle East in recent years. Following riots in Casablanca 1965, he established a royal dictatorship, but returned to constitutional government, with a civilian prime minister leading a government of national unity 1984. From 1976 he undertook the occupation of the part of Western Sahara ceded by Spain.

Hastings Andrew Gavin (1962–). Scottish rugby union player. He first played for Scotland in 1986, and was a member of Scotland's Grand Slam team 1990, British Lions in Australia 1989, and New Zealand 1993. He scored 44 points in a World Cup game against the Ivory Coast 1995; he retired 1995 after 61 internationals.

Hastings Warren (1732–1818). British colonial administrator. A protégé of Lord Clive, who established British rule in India, Hastings carried out major reforms, and became governor-general of Bengal 1774. Impeached for corruption on his return to England 1785, he was acquitted 1795.
Suggested reading
Edwardes, M *Warren Hastings: King of the Nabobs* (1976)
Feiling, Keith *Warren Hastings* (1954)
Moon, Penderel *Warren Hastings and British India* (1947)

Hathaway Anne (1556–1623). Englishwoman, daughter of a yeoman farmer, who married William Shakespeare 1582. She was born at Shottery, near Stratford, where her cottage can still be seen.

Hatshepsut (c. 1473–c. 1458 BC). Queen (pharaoh) of ancient Egypt during the 18th dynasty. She was the daughter of Thothmes I, and the wife and half-sister of Thothmes II. Throughout his reign real power lay with Hatshepsut, and she continued to rule after his death, as regent for her nephew Thothmes III.

Her reign was a peaceful and prosperous time. Hatshepsut reigned as a man, and is shown dressed as a pharaoh, with a beard. When she died or was forced to abdicate, Thothmes III defaced her monuments. The ruins of her temple at Deir el-Bahri survive.

Hattersley Roy Sydney George (1932–). British Labour politician and author. On the right wing of the Labour Party, he was prices secretary 1976–79, and deputy leader of the party 1983–92. In 1994 he announced his retirement from active politics, and later expressed disagreement with some policies of the new party leadership.

Hatton Derek (1948–). British left-wing politician, former deputy leader of Liverpool Council. A leading member of the Militant Tendency, Hatton was removed from office and expelled from the Labour Party 1987. He revealed in his autobiography 1988 how Militant acted as a subversive party-within-a-party. Subsequently he embarked on a career in advertising and public relations.

Haughey Charles James (1925–). Irish Fianna Fáil politician of Ulster descent. Dismissed 1970 from Jack Lynch's cabinet for alleged complicity in IRA gun-running, he was afterward acquitted. He was prime minister 1979–81, March–Nov 1982, and 1986–92, when he was replaced by Albert Reynolds.

Suggested reading
Dwyer, T R *Charlie: The Political Biography of Charles J Haughey* (1987)
Joyce, Joe and Murtagh, Peter *The Boss: Charles J Haughey in Government* (1983)

Hauptmann Gerhart Johann Robert (1862–1946). German dramatist. A strong proponent of an uncompromising naturalism in the theatre, Hauptmann's work has been widely produced. *Die Weber/The Weavers* 1892, his finest play, is an account of a revolt of Silesian weavers in 1844. His other plays include *Vor Sonnenaufgang/Before Dawn* 1889, the comedy *Der Biberpelz/The Beaver Coat* 1893, and a tragicomedy of the Berlin underworld *Die Ratten/The Rats* 1910.

Hausdorff Felix (1868–1942). German mathematician and philosopher who developed the branch of mathematics known as topology, in which he formulated the theory of point sets. He investigated general closure spaces, and formulated Hausdorff's maximal principle in general set theory. His major work is *Grundzuge der Mengenlehre/Basic Features of Set Theory* 1914.

In 1902 he was appointed professor at Leipzig, later moving to Bonn. During World War II he committed suicide rather than be sent to a concentration camp.

Haussmann Georges Eugène, Baron (1809–1891). French administrator. He replanned medieval Paris 1853–70 to achieve the current city plan, with long wide boulevards and parks. The cost of his scheme and his authoritarianism caused opposition, and he was made to resign from his post.

Haüy René-Just (1743–1822). French mineralogist, the founder of modern crystallography. He regarded crystals as geometrically structured assemblages of units (integrant molecules), and developed a classification system on this basis. His two major works are *Traité de minéralogie/Treatise of Mineralogy* 1801 and *Treatise of Crystallography* 1822.

He trained as a priest, then became professor of mineralogy in Paris 1802. During the Revolutionary era, he was protected from anticlerical attacks by Napoleon's patronage.

Havel Václav (1936–). Czech dramatist and politician, president of Czechoslovakia 1989–92 and of the Czech Republic from 1993. His plays include *The Garden Party* 1963 and *Largo Desolato* 1985, about a dissident intellectual. Havel became widely known as a human-rights activist. He was imprisoned 1979–83 and again 1989 for support of Charter 77, a human-rights manifesto. As president of Czechoslovakia he sought to preserve a united republic, but resigned in recognition of the breakup of the federation 1992. In 1993 he became president of the newly independent Czech Republic.
Suggested reading
Havel, Vaclav *Letters to Olga* (trs 1988)
Simmons, Michael *The Reluctant President: A Political Life of Vaclav Havel* (1991)

Havers Robert Michael Oldfield, Baron Havers (1923–1992). British lawyer, Lord Chancellor 1987–88. After a successful legal career he became Conservative member of Parliament for Wimbledon 1970 and was solicitor general under Edward Heath and attorney general under Margaret Thatcher. He was made a life peer 1987 and served briefly, and unhappily, as Lord Chancellor before retiring 1988. Knighted 1972, baron 1987.

Hawke Bob (Robert James Lee) (1929–). Australian Labor politician, prime minister 1983–91, on the right wing of the party. He was president of the Australian Council of Trade Unions 1970–80. He announced his retirement from politics 1992.
Suggested reading
D'Alpuget, Blanche *Bob Hawke* (1982)
Hurst, John *Bob Hawke* (1979)

Hawkes (Charles Francis) Christopher (1905–1992). British archaeologist, professor of European archaeology in the University of Oxford. A pioneer in the study of the prehistoric periods of Britain and Europe, Hawkes helped to found international prehistory as a discipline in Britain in the late 1920s and early 1930s. Later, his interest in the application of scientific techniques to archaeological material led in 1955 to the creation of the Research Laboratory for Archaeology and the History of Art at Oxford.

Hawkes John Clendennin Burne Jr (1925–). US novelist. His writing is characterized by a Gothic, macabre violence, nightmarish landscapes, and oblique plotting. His novels include *The Cannibal* 1949, dealing with the horror of authoritarian power in Nazi Germany; *The Lime Twig* 1961, a thriller set in postwar London; and *Second Skin* 1964, a first-person recollection set on a tropical island.

His later novels became more accessible and include *Travesty* 1976, a suicide note in the form of a monologue; *The Passion Artist* 1979, narrating a widower's fantastic experiences in a European city; *Whistlejacket* 1988, which combines photography, anatomy, painting, and fox-hunting into a metaphysical thriller, and *Hawkes Scrapbook* 1991.

How can the complexity of the universe and all its trivial details be determined by a simple set of equations? Alternatively, can one really believe that God chose all the trivial details, like who should be on the cover of Cosmospolitan?

STEPHEN HAWKING
Black Holes and Baby Universes 1993

Hawking Stephen William (1942–). English physicist whose work in general relativity – particularly gravitational field theory – led to a search for a quantum theory of gravity to explain black holes and the Big Bang, singularities that classical relativity theory does not adequately explain.

Hawking's objective of producing an overall synthesis of quantum mechanics and relativity theory began around the time of the publication of his seminal book *The Large Scale Stucture of Space-Time*, written with G F R Ellis, 1973. His most remarkable result, published in 1974, was that black holes could in fact emit particles in the form of thermal radiation – the so-called Hawking radiation.

Hawking was born in Oxford, studied at Oxford and Cambridge, and became Lucasian Professor of Mathematics at Cambridge 1979. Hawking's most fruitful work was with black holes, stars that have undergone total gravitational collapse and whose gravity is so great that nothing, not even light, can escape from them. Since 1974, he has studied the behaviour of matter in the immediate vicinity of a black hole, concluding that black holes do, contrary to expectation, emit radiation. He has proposed a physical explanation for this 'Hawking radiation' which relies on the quantum-mechanical concept of 'virtual particles' – these exist as particle–antiparticle pairs and are supposed to fill 'empty' space. Hawking suggested that, when such a particle is created near a black hole, one half of the pair might disappear into the black hole, leaving the other half, which could escape to infinity. This would be seen by a distant observer as thermal radiation.

Confined to a wheelchair because of a rare and progressive neuromotor disease, Hawking remains mentally active. His book *A Brief History of Time* 1988 gives a popular account of cosmology and became an international bestseller.
Suggested reading
Bowe, Frank *Comeback* (1981)
White, Michael *Stephen Hawking: a Life in Science* (1992)

Hawkins Coleman Randolph (1904–1969). US virtuoso tenor saxophonist. He was, until 1934, a soloist in the swing band led by Fletcher Henderson (1898–1952), and was an influential figure in bringing the jazz saxophone to prominence as a solo instrument.

Hawkins Jack (1910–1973). English film actor. He was often cast in military roles. His films include *The Cruel Sea* 1953, *Bridge on the River Kwai* 1957, *The League of Gentlemen* 1959, *Zulu* 1963, and *Waterloo* 1970. After an operation for throat cancer that removed his vocal chords 1966 his voice had to be dubbed.

Hawkins John (1532–1595). English navigator, born in Plymouth. Treasurer to the navy 1573–89, he was knighted for his services as a commander against the Spanish Armada 1588.

Serve God daily, love one another, preserve your victuals, beware of fire and keep good fellowship [i.e. ships close together].

JOHN HAWKINS
Hawkins's orders to his ships on his second slaving voyage 1564, quoted in C R N Routh *Who's Who in Tudor England*

Hawkins Richard (c. 1560–1622). English navigator, son of John Hawkins. He held a command against the Spanish Armada 1588, was captured in an expedition against Spanish possessions 1593–94 and released 1602. Knighted 1603.

Hawks Howard Winchester (1896–1977). US director, screenwriter, and producer of a wide range of classic films in virtually every American genre. Swift-moving and immensely accomplished, his films include the gangster movie *Scarface* 1932, screwball comedy *Bringing Up Baby* 1938, the *film noir The Big Sleep* 1946, and *Gentlemen Prefer Blondes* 1953.
Suggested reading
Branson, C *Howard Hawks* (1987)
Poague, L *Howard Hawks* (1982)
Willis, D *The Films of Howard Hawks* (1975)

Hawksmoor Nicholas (1661–1736). English architect. He was assistant to Christopher Wren in designing various London churches and St Paul's Cathedral and joint architect with John Vanbrugh of Castle Howard and Blenheim Palace. His genius is displayed in a quirky and uncompromising style incorporating elements from both Gothic and Classical sources.

The original west towers of Westminster Abbey, long attributed to Wren, were designed by Hawksmoor 1734–36, and were completed after his death 1745. After 1712 Hawksmoor completed six of the 50 new churches planned for London under the provisions made by the Fifty New Churches Act 1711.

Haworth (Walter) Norman (1883–1950). English organic chemist who was the first to synthesize a vitamin (ascorbic acid, vitamin C) 1933, for which he shared a Nobel prize 1937. He made significant advances in determining the structures of many carbohydrates, particularly sugars. He was professor at Birmingham 1925–48. Haworth's book *The Constitution of the Sugars* 1929 became a standard work. Knighted 1947.

Hawthorne Nathaniel (1804–1864). US writer. He was the author of American literature's first great classic novel, *The Scarlet Letter* 1850. Set in 17th-century Puritan Boston, it tells the powerful allegorical story of a 'fallen woman' and her daughter who are judged guilty according to men's, not nature's laws. He wrote three other novels, including *The House of the Seven Gables* 1851, and many short stories, a form he was instrumental in developing, including *Tanglewood Tales* 1853, classic Greek legends retold for children.

Born in Salem, Massachusetts, Hawthorne graduated from Bowdoin College and worked as a customs official. He was the US consul 1853–57 in Liverpool, England, and then lived in Italy until 1860. Hawthorne's fiction is marked by its haunting symbolism and its exploration of guilt, sin, and other complex moral and psychological issues. It had a profound effect on writers of his own time, notably his friend Herman Melville, and continues to influence writers.
Suggested reading
Dauber, K *Rediscovering Hawthorne* (1977)
Martin, T *Nathaniel Hawthorne* (1983)
Mellow, J R *Nathaniel Hawthorne and his Times* (1980)
Turner, A *Nathaniel Hawthorne: An Introduction and Interpretation* (1961)
Turner, A *Nathaniel Hawthorne: A Biography* (1980)

Hay Will(iam Thomson) (1888–1949). English comedy actor. Originally a music-hall comedian, he made many films in the 1930s, in which he was usually cast as an incompetent in a position of authority, including *Good Morning Boys* 1937, *Oh Mr Porter* 1938, *Ask a Policeman* 1939, and *My Learned Friend* 1944.

A good comedy scene is very near pathos. The character I play is really a pathetic character.

WILL HAY
quoted in Leslie Halliwell *Filmgoer's Companion* 1965

Hayashi Chushiro (1920–). Japanese physicist whose research in 1950 exposed a fallacy in the 'hot Big Bang' theory proposed two years earlier by Ralph Alpher and others. Hayashi has published many papers on the origin of the chemical elements in stellar evolution and on the composition of primordial matter in an expanding universe.

Hayashi pointed out that in the Big Bang earlier than the first two seconds, the temperature would have been greater than 10^{10}K, which is above the threshold for the making of electron–positron pairs. This radically altered the timescale proposed in the 'hot Big Bang' theory. He also showed that the abundance of neutrons at the heart of the Big Bang did not depend on the material density but on the temperature and the properties of the weak interreactions. Provided the density is great enough for the reaction between neutrons and protons to combine at a rate faster than the expansion rate, a fixed concentration of neutrons will be incorporated into helium nuclei, however great the material density is – producing a plateau in the relationship between helium abundance and material density. Hayashi was born and educated in Kyoto, where he became professor of physics 1957.

Hayden Bill (William George) (1933–). Australian Labor politician. He was leader of the Australian Labor Party and of the opposition 1977–83, and minister of foreign affairs 1983. He became governor-general 1989.

As minister for social security 1972–75 and treasurer 1975, he introduced much welfare legislation including the universal health insurance scheme Medibank. He spoke openly in support of euthanasia and marriage and adoption rights for homosexuals 1995.

Hayden Sterling. Stage name of John Hamilton (1916–1986). US film actor. He played leading Hollywood roles in the 1940s and early 1950s. Although later seen in some impressive character roles, his career as a whole failed to do justice to his talent. His work includes *The Asphalt Jungle* 1950, *Johnny Guitar* 1954, *Dr Strangelove* 1964, and *The Godfather* 1972.

Haydn (Franz) Joseph (1732–1809). Austrian composer. A teacher of Mozart and Beethoven, he was a major exponent of the classical sonata form in his numerous chamber and orchestral works (he wrote more than 100 symphonies). He also composed choral music, including the oratorios *The Creation* 1798 and *The Seasons* 1801. He was the first great master of the string quartet.

Born in Lower Austria, he was Kapellmeister 1761–90 to Prince Esterházy. His work also includes operas, church music, and songs, and the 'Emperor's Hymn', adopted as the Austrian, and later the German, national anthem.

Suggested reading
Butterworth, N *Haydn* (1978)
Hughes, R *Haydn* (1978)
Larsen, J P *The New Grove Haydn* (1983)
Rosen, C *The Classical Style* (1972)

Haydon Benjamin Robert (1786–1846). English painter. His attempts at the 'grand style' include many gigantic canvases such as *Christ's Entry into Jerusalem* 1820 (Philadelphia, USA), but he is better known for his genre pictures such as *The Mock Election* and *Chairing the Member*. He also painted portraits of Wordsworth and Keats. He published *Autobiography and Memoirs* 1853, a lively account of the contemporary art scene and his own tragicomic life.

Hayek Friedrich August von (1899–1992). Austrian economist who taught at the London School of Economics 1931–50. His *The*

Road to Serfdom 1944 was a critical study of socialist trends in Britain. He won the 1974 Nobel Prize for Economics with Gunnar Myrdal.

Hayek was born in Vienna. He was professor of social and moral science at the University of Chicago 1950–62.

Hayes Helen (1900–1993). US film and theatre actress. Her long theatre career included the title role in *Victoria Regina* 1938–39. She appeared in several silent films and won an Academy Award for her first performance in a talkie, *The Sin of Madelon Claudet* 1931. However, she did not care for the atmosphere of Hollywood, and during the years of her Broadway eminence made only a few sorties into the cinema, of which the best remembered is probably the role of the dowager Empress in *Anastasia* 1956. She gained wider fame for her appearance as the stowaway passenger in the film *Airport* 1970 (Academy Award).

Hayes Rutherford Birchard (1822–1893). 19th president of the USA 1877–81, a Republican. Born in Ohio, he was a major general on the Union side in the Civil War. During his presidency federal troops were withdrawn from the Southern states (after the Reconstruction) and the Civil Service reformed. He was noted for his honesty, and his integrity was viewed by many as a way to overcome the aura of corruption that had surrounded the Grant administration. Under Hayes, the political role of federal employees was curtailed.

Suggested reading
Davidson, Kenneth E *The Presidency of Rutherford B Hayes* (1972)
Fitzgerald, C B (ed) *Rutherford B Hayes* (1989)
Hoogenboom, Ari *The Presidency of Rutherford B Hayes* (1988)

Haywood William Dudley (1869–1928). US labour leader. One of the founders of the Industrial Workers of the World (IWW, 'Wobblies') 1905, Haywood was arrested for conspiracy to murder

Haydn *The composer Joseph Haydn (1732-1809) in an engraving of c. 1792 by Luigi Schiavotti. One of the great composers who defined the universal style of Viennese Classical music, Haydn spent most of his creative life, however, in isolation at the estate of the Esterházy family in Hungary. (Image Select)*

Hayworth *With her flame-red hair which became her trademark, US actress Rita Hayworth brought to her varied roles an erotic and alluring screen image. Frequently associated with tempestuous femme fatale roles, she was also the dancing star of 1940s musicals. She was seen to best advantage in the title role of the film* Gilda *1946.*

an anti-union politician. His acquittal in 1907 made him a labour hero. Arrested again for sedition during World War I, he spent his later years in exile in the Soviet Union.

Born in Salt Lake City, Utah, USA, Haywood worked in the mines, joining the Western Federation of Miners (WFM) 1896. By 1899 he had become a national leader of the WFM and, in his tireless tours of the country, won the nickname 'Big Bill'.

I never really thought of myself as a sex-symbol – more an actress who could dance.

RITA HAYWORTH
Leslie Halliwell *Filmgoer's Companion* 1965

Hayworth Rita. Stage name of Margarita Carmen Cansino (1918–1987). US dancer and film actress. She gave vivacious performances in 1940s musicals and played erotic roles in *Gilda* 1946 and *Affair in Trinidad* 1952. She was known as Hollywood's 'goddess' during the height of her career. She was married to Orson Welles 1943–48 and appeared in his film *The Lady from Shanghai* 1948. She gave assured performances in *Pal Joey* 1957 and *Separate Tables* 1958.

Her later appearances were intermittent and she retired in 1972, a victim of Alzheimer's disease.

It is well that there is no one without a fault; for he would not have a friend in the world.

WILLIAM HAZLITT
Characteristics: In the Manner of Rochefoucault's Maxims no. 66 1823

Hazlitt William (1778–1830). English essayist and critic. His work is characterized by invective, scathing irony, and a gift for epigram. His critical essays include 'Characters of Shakespeare's Plays' 1817–18, 'Lectures on the English Poets' 1818–19, 'English Comic Writers' 1819, and 'Dramatic Literature of the Age of Elizabeth' 1820. Other works are *Table Talk* 1821–22, *The Spirit of the Age* 1825, and *Liber Amoris* 1823.

Head Bessie Emery (1937–1986). South African writer. She lived in exile in Botswana. Her work is concerned with questions of private and national identity, incorporating an unidealized sense of social and communal history. Her novels include *When Rain Clouds Gather* 1969, *Maru* 1971, and *A Question of Power* 1973.

Head Edith (1900–1981). US costume designer for Hollywood films. She won eight Academy Awards for her designs, in such films as *The Heiress* 1949, *All About Eve* 1950, and *The Sting* 1973.

Heal Ambrose (1872–1959). English cabinetmaker. He took over the Heal's shop from his father and developed it into a large London store. He initially designed furniture in the Arts and Crafts style, often in oak, but in the 1930s he started using materials such as tubular steel.

Heal was a founder member of the Design and Industries Association, which aimed to improve the quality of mass-produced items. Knighted 1933.

Healey Denis Winston, Baron Healey (1917–). British Labour politician. While minister of defence 1964–70 he was in charge of the reduction of British forces east of Suez. He was chancellor of the Exchequer 1974–79. In 1976 he contested the party leadership, losing to James Callaghan, and again in 1980, losing to Michael Foot, to whom he was deputy leader 1980–83. In 1987 he resigned from the shadow cabinet. Baron 1992.
Suggested reading
Healey, Denis *The Time of My Life* (memoirs) (1989)
Reed, B and Williams, G *Denis Healey and the Politics of Power* (1971)

We are voluptuaries of the morning after.

SEAMUS HEANEY
'Holding Course'

Heaney Seamus Justin (1939–). Irish poet. He has written powerful verse about the political situation in Northern Ireland. Collections include *North* 1975, *Field Work* 1979, *Station Island* 1984, and *Joy or Night* 1993. He was the elected professor of poetry at Oxford University 1989–94. In 1995 he was awarded the Nobel Prize for Literature.
Suggested reading
Curtis, Tony (ed) *The Art of Seamus Heaney* (1982)
Heaney, Seamus *Preoccupations: Selected Prose, 1968–1978* (1980)
Morrison, Blake *Seamus Heaney* (1982)
Parker, Michael *Seamus Heaney: The Making of the Poet* (1994)

Hearn (Patrick) Lafcadio (Tessima Carlos) (1850–1904). Greek-born US writer and translator. He lived in Japan from 1890 and became a Japanese citizen. His many books on Japanese life and customs introduced the country to many Western readers, for example, *Glimpses of Unfamiliar Japan* 1893 and *In Ghostly Japan* 1904.

A journalist, Hearn was sent to Japan to write an article for a US magazine and never left. His sympathetic understanding of the country and its culture made him accepted and appreciated by the Japanese, and his writings are still widely read. From 1896 he taught English literature at Tokyo University.

Hearns Thomas (1958–). US boxer who in 1988 became the first man to win world titles at five different weight classes in five separate fights.

Hearst Patty (Patricia Campbell) (1955–). US socialite. A granddaughter of the newspaper tycoon William Randolph Hearst, she was kidnapped 1974 by an urban guerrilla group, the Symbionese Liberation Army. She joined her captors in a bank robbery, was sought, tried, convicted, and imprisoned 1976–79. She has since married and become active in charities and fundraising.

Hearst William Randolph (1863–1951). US newspaper publisher, celebrated for his introduction of banner headlines, lavish illustration, and the sensationalist approach known as 'yellow journalism'. A campaigner in numerous controversies, and a strong isolationist, he was said to be the model for Citizen Kane in the 1941 film of that name by Orson Welles.

Heartfield John (born Helmut Hertzfelde) (1891–1968). German painter and graphic artist. He was one of the greatest exponents of photomontage. Influenced by the aims and techniques of both Dada and the *Neue Sachlichkeit* group, he developed a highly original style, employing incongruous images of contemporary German life to satirize capitalism and Nazism.

Heath Edward Richard George (1916–). British Conservative politician, party leader 1965–75. As prime minister 1970–74 he took the UK into the European Community but was brought down by economic and industrial relations crises at home. He was replaced as party leader by Margaret Thatcher 1975, and became increasingly critical of her policies and her opposition to the UK's full participation in the EC. During John Major's administration, he continued his attacks on 'Eurosceptics' within the party. In 1990 he undertook a mission to Iraq in an attempt to secure the release of British hostages. He returned 1993 to negotiate the release of three Britons held prisoner by Iraq.

Heath entered Parliament 1950, was minister of Labour 1959–60, and as Lord Privy Seal 1960–63 conducted abortive negotiations for Common Market membership. He succeeded Alec Douglas Home as Conservative leader 1965, the first elected leader of his party. Defeated in the general election 1966, he achieved a surprise victory 1970, but his confrontation with the striking miners as part of his campaign to control inflation led to Conservative defeats in the general elections of Feb 1974 and Oct 1974. KG 1992.
Suggested reading
Campbell, John *Edward Heath:A Biography* (1994)
Laing, Margaret *Edward Heath* (1973)
Roth, Andrew *Heath and the Heathmen* (1972)

Heath Thomas Little (1861–1940). English mathematical historian who specialized in ancient Greece. His *History of Greek Mathematics* 1921 is regarded as the standard work on the subject in the English language. KCB 1909.

Heath was born in Lincolnshire, studied at Cambridge and joined the civil service. He rose through the ranks in the Treasury Office; in 1913 he was appointed joint permanent secretary to the Treasury and auditor of the Civil List, and he was comptroller general and secretary to the Commissioners for the Reduction of the National Debt 1919–26.

Heathcoat John (1783–1861). English inventor of lacemaking machinery 1807. Throughout his life, he took out patents for further inventions in textile manufacture. In 1832 he patented a steam plough to assist with agricultural improvements in Ireland.

Heathcoat was born near Derby, apprenticed in the hosiery trade, and became a master mechanic about 1803. His lace factory in Loughborough was destroyed by Luddites 1816, and Heathcoat moved to Tiverton, Devon. In 1832 he was elected to represent Tiverton in the new reformed Parliament and remained MP for the borough until 1859.

Heaviside Oliver (1850–1925). English physicist. In 1902 he predicted the existence of an ionized layer of air in the upper atmosphere, which was known as the Kennelly–Heaviside layer but is now called the E layer of the ionosphere. Deflection from it makes possible the transmission of radio signals around the world which would otherwise be lost in outer space. His studies of electricity published in *Electrical Papers* 1892 had considerable impact on long-distance telephony, and he added the concepts of inductance, capacitance, and impedance to electrical science.

Heaviside was born in London. Because of severe hearing difficulties, he was mainly self-taught and was unemployed most of his life.

Hecataeus (lived 6th–5th century BC). Greek historian and geographer from Miletus. An intellectual successor to the early Ionian philosophers, Hecataeus wrote what was probably the first historical work of a genealogical kind. He was a major influence on the historian Herodotus.

I discovered early in my movie work that a movie is never any better than the stupidest man connected with it.

BEN HECHT
A Child of the Century bk 5, 'Illustrations by Doré (Gustave)' 1954

Hecht Ben (1893–1964). US dramatist, screenwriter and film director. He was formerly a journalist. His play *The Front Page* 1928 was adapted several times for the cinema by other writers. His own screenplays included *Twentieth Century* 1934, *Gunga Din* and *Wuthering Heights* both 1939, *Spellbound* 1945, and *Actors and Sin* 1952. His directorial credits include *Crime without Passion* 1934. His autobiography, *A Child of the Century*, was published 1954.

Born in New York City and raised in Racine, Wisconsin, Hecht began his writing career as a reporter for the *Chicago Journal* and as a foreign correspondent for the *Chicago Daily News*. Also interested in fiction writing, he published his first novel, *Erik Dorn*, 1921. A collection of his newspaper feature stories, *1001 Nights in Chicago*, appeared 1922.

Heckel Erich (1883–1970). German painter, lithographer, and illustrator. Trained as an architect, he turned to painting 1905, founding the German Expressionist group *Die Brücke* 1905 with fellow students Ernst Ludwig Kirchner and Karl Schmidt-Rottluff. *Two Men at a Table* 1912 (Kunsthaus, Hamburg) exemplifies his severe, angular, heavily contoured style. His most expressive tool was the coloured woodcut.

Heckel was also a prolific painter in oil, watercolour, and tempera, working in a diagrammatic, fluid style, as in *Women by a Lake* 1913 (Wilhelm-Lehmbruck Museum, Duisburg). His subject matter ranges from starved figures, interiors, and landscapes to primitive nudes in bucolic settings.

Hedin Sven Anders (1865–1952). Swedish archaeologist, geographer, and explorer in central Asia and China. Between 1891 and 1908 he explored routes across the Himalayas and produced the first maps of Tibet. During 1928–33 he travelled with a Sino-Swedish expedition which crossed the Gobi Desert. His publications include *My Life as Explorer* 1925 and *Across the Gobi Desert* 1928.

Heffer Eric Samuel (1922–1991). English Labour politician, member of Parliament for Walton, Liverpool 1964–91. He held a ministerial post 1974–75, joined Michael Foot's shadow cabinet 1981, and was regularly elected to Labour's National Executive Committee, but found it difficult to follow the majority view.

Hefner Hugh Marston (1926–). US publisher, founder of *Playboy* magazine 1953. With its centrefolds of nude women, and columns of opinion, fashion, and advice on sex, *Playboy* helped reshape the social attitudes of the postwar generation. Its success declined in the 1980s owing to the rise of competing men's magazines and feminist protest.

Hegel Georg Wilhelm Friedrich (1770–1831). German philosopher who conceived of mind and nature as two abstractions of one indivisible whole, Spirit. His system, which is a type of idealism, traces the emergence of Spirit in the logical study of concepts and the process of world history.

For Hegel, concepts unfold, and in unfolding they generate the reality that is described by them. To understand reality is to understand our concepts, and vice versa. The development of a concept involves three stages, which he calls *dialectic*. The dialectic moves from the thesis, or indeterminate concept (for example, a thing in space), to the antithesis, or determinate concept (for example, an animal), and then to the synthesis (for example, a cat), which is the resolution of what Hegel thinks is the contradiction between the indeterminate and determinate concepts. As logic, Hegel's dialectic is worthless. As an account of how intellectual and social development occurs, it is shrewd. Hegel's works include *The Phenomenology of Spirit* 1807, *Encyclopaedia of the Philosophical Sciences* 1817, and *Philosophy of Right* 1821. Hegel was professor of philosophy at Heidelberg 1817–18 and at Berlin 1818–31.

Suggested reading
Findlay, J N *Hegel: A Re-examination* (1958)
Kaufman, Walter *Hegel: Reinterpretation, Texts, and Commentary* (1965)
Rosen, Stanley *Hegel* (1974)
Singer, Peter *Hegel* (1983)
Taylor, Charles *Hegel* (1975)

Heidegger Martin (1889–1976). German philosopher, often classed as an existentialist. He believed that Western philosophy had 'forgotten' the fundamental question of the 'meaning of Being', and his work concerns the investigation of what he thought were the different types of being appropriate to people and to things in general. Heidegger was born in Baden and taught mainly at Freiburg. His sympathy with the Nazis damaged his reputation. His works include *Sein und Zeit/Being and Time* 1927.

I occasionally play works by contemporary composers and for two reasons. First, to discourage the composer from writing any more, and secondly to remind myself how much I appreciate Beethoven.

JASCHA HEIFETZ
Life 1961

Heifetz Jascha (1901–1987). Russian-born US violinist. He was one of the great virtuosos of the 20th century. He first performed at the age of five, and before he was 17 had played in most European capitals, and in the USA, where he settled 1917. He popularized a clear, unemotional delivery suited to radio and recordings.

He appeared in several Hollywood movies, played in a trio with Artur Rubenstein and Grigor Piatigorsky, and after returning from the concert stage taught several violinists including Eugene Fodor.

Heike alternative name for ◊Taira, an ancient Japanese clan.

Heine (Christian Johann) Heinrich (1797–1856). German Romantic poet and journalist. He wrote *Reisebilder* 1826–31, blending travel writing and satire, and *Buch der Lieder/Book of Songs* 1827. From 1831 he lived mainly in Paris, working as a correspondent for German newspapers and publishing *Neue Gedichte/New Poems* 1844. He excelled in both the Romantic lyric and satire. Schubert and Schumann set many of his lyrics to music.

In 1835 he headed a list of writers forbidden to publish in Germany. He contracted a spinal disease 1845 that confined him to his bed from 1848 until his death.

Heine Heinrich Eduard (1812–1881). German mathematician who completed the formulation of the notion of uniform continuity. He subsequently provided a proof of the classic theorem on uniform continuity of continuous functions, which has since become known as *Heine's theorem*.

Heine was born in Berlin and studied there and at Göttingen. In 1848, he was appointed professor at Halle University and remained there for the rest of his life. His *Handbuch der Kugelfunctionen* 1861 became the standard work on spherical functions for the next 50 years.

Suggested reading
Butler, E M *Heinrich Heine: A Biography* (1956)
Prawer, S S *Heine the Tragic Satirist* (1961)
Prawer, S S *Heine's Jewish Comedy* (1983)
Sammons, Jeffrey *Heinrich Heine: A Modern Biography* (1979)

Heinkel Ernst Heinrich (1888–1958). German aircraft designer who pioneered jet aircraft. He founded his firm 1922 and built the first jet aircraft 1939. During World War II his company was Germany's biggest producer of warplanes, mostly propeller-driven.

Notable Heinkel aircraft of World War II include the He 111, originally designed as a civilian airliner but adapted almost immediately as a medium bomber. It was used extensively in air raids over England 1940, but was found to be vulnerable to attack and so was redeployed as a night bomber and mine-layer.

Heinlein Robert A(nson) (1907–). US science-fiction writer. Associated with the pulp magazines of the 1940s, he wrote the militaristic novel *Starship Troopers* 1959 and the utopian cult novel *Stranger in a Strange Land* 1961. His work helped to increase the legitimacy of science fiction as a literary genre.

Heinz Henry John (1844–1919). US industrialist. Heinz, born in Pittsburgh, entered his family's brick business but became interested in the possibilities of wholesale food marketing, founding a firm for that purpose 1876. The firm, renamed the H J Heinz Co 1888, specialized in the manufacture of prepared foods and condiments. Heinz popularized the use of ketchup and made famous his company's slogan '57 Varieties'.

As president, Heinz oversaw every phase of production, from farming to advertising. Unlike some of his competitors, he was a strong supporter of the 1906 US Pure Food and Drug Act.

An expert is someone who knows some of the worst mistakes that can be made in his subject and how to avoid them.

WERNER HEISENBERG
The Part and the Whole

Heisenberg Werner Karl (1901–1976). German physicist who developed quantum theory and formulated the uncertainty principle, which concerns matter, radiation, and their reactions, and places absolute limits on the achievable accuracy of measurement. He was awarded a Nobel prize 1932 for work he carried out when only 24.

During World War II Heisenberg worked for the Nazis on nuclear fission, but his team were many months behind the Allied atom-bomb project. After the war he worked on superconductivity.

In 1923 he became assistant to Max Born at Göttingen, then worked with Danish physicist Niels Bohr in Copenhagen 1924–26. Heisenberg became professor at Leipzig 1927 at the age of only 26, and stayed until 1941. He was director of the Max Planck Institute for Physics 1942–70.

Hekmatyar Gulbuddin (1949–). Afghani Islamic fundamentalist guerrilla leader, prime minister of Afghanistan 1993–94. Strongly anticommunist, he resisted the takeover of Kabul by moderate mujaheddin forces April 1992 and refused to join the interim administration, continuing to bombard the city until being driven out. A year later he became prime minister under a peace agreement, but his forces renewed attacks on Kabul during 1994 and he was subsequently dismissed from the premiership.

Helena, St (*c.* 248–*c.* 328). Roman empress, mother of Constantine the Great, and a convert to Christianity. According to legend, she discovered the true cross of Jesus in Jerusalem. Her feast day is 18 Aug.

Some men are born mediocre, some men achieve mediocrity, and some men have mediocrity thrust upon them. With Major Major it had been all three.

JOSEPH HELLER
Catch-22 1961

Heller Joseph (1923–). US novelist. He drew on his experiences in the US air force in World War II to write his best-selling *Catch-22*

Heller US novelist Joseph Heller, best known for his anti-war novel Catch 22 *1961. His later novels, often as bleakly pessimistic as* Catch 22, *include* God Knows *1984, a lively retelling of the Old Testament story of King David, for which he was awarded the French Prix Medici Etranger 1985.*

1961, satirizing war, the conspiracy of bureaucratic control, and the absurdism of history. A film based on the book appeared 1970.

His other works include the novels *Something Happened* 1974, *Good As Gold* 1979, and *Closing Time* 1994; and the plays *We Bombed in New Haven* 1968 and *Clevinger's Trial* 1974.

Hellman Lillian Florence (1907–1984). US dramatist. Her work is concerned with contemporary political and social issues. *The Children's Hour* 1934 on accusations of lesbianism, *The Little Foxes* 1939 on industrialists, and *Toys in the Attic* 1960 are all examples of a social critique cast in the form of the 'well-made play'. In the 1950s she was summoned to appear before the House Committee on Un-American Activities.

She lived 31 years with the writer Dashiell Hammett, and in her will set up a fund to promote Marxist doctrine. Since her death there has been dispute over the accuracy of her memoirs, for example *Pentimento* 1973.

Helmholtz Hermann Ludwig Ferdinand von (1821–1894). German physiologist, physicist, and inventor of the ophthalmoscope for examining the inside of the eye. He was the first to explain how the cochlea of the inner ear works, and the first to measure the speed of nerve impulses. In physics he formulated the law of conservation of energy, and worked in thermodynamics.

Helmholtz's scientific work in many fields was intended to prove that living things possess no innate vital force, and that their life processes are driven by the same forces and obey the same principles as nonliving systems. He arrived at the principle of conservation of energy 1847, observing that the energy of life processes is derived entirely from oxidation of food, and that animal heat and muscle action are generated by chemical changes in the muscles.

He first became professor at Bonn 1855 and ended his career as director of the Physico-Technical Institute of Berlin from 1887.

Helmont Jean Baptiste van (1579–1644). Belgian doctor who was the first to realize that there are gases other than air, and claimed to have coined the word 'gas' (from Greek *cháos*). Helmont identified four gases: carbon dioxide, carbon monoxide, nitrous oxide, and methane. He was the first to take the melting point of ice and the boiling point of water as standards for temperature and the first to use the term 'saturation' to signify the combination of an acid and a base. In medicine, Helmont used remedies that specifically considered the type of disease, the organ affected and the causative agent. He demonstrated acid as the digestive agent in the stomach. His works were collectively published posthumously as *Ortus medicinae* 1648.

Helms Richard McGarrah (1913–). US director of the Central Intelligence Agency (CIA) 1966–73, when he was dismissed by President Nixon. In 1977 he was convicted of lying before a congressional committee because his oath as chief of intelligence compelled him to keep secrets from the public. He was originally with the Office of Strategic Services, before it developed into the CIA 1947.

Héloïse (1101–1164). Abbess of Paraclete in Champagne, France, correspondent and lover of Abelard. She became deeply interested in intellectual study in her youth and was impressed by the brilliance of Abelard, her teacher, whom she secretly married.

After her affair with Abelard, and the birth of a son, Astrolabe, she became a nun 1129, and with Abelard's assistance, founded a nunnery at Paraclete. Her letters show her strong and pious character and her devotion to Abelard.

Helmholtz Hermann von Helmholtz spent six years as an army surgeon before being released from military service 1848 to embark on a scientific career. Helmholtz was a remarkable scientist, publishing pioneering work in both physics and physiology. He is best known for the principle of the conservation of energy and his discoveries in the physiology of vision. (Image Select)

Suggested reading
Pernoud, Regine *Heloise and Abelard* (trs 1973)
Robertson, D W, Jr *Abelard and Heloise* (1972)
Worthington, Marjorie *The Immortal Lovers* (1960)

Helpmann Robert Murray (1909–1986). Australian dancer, choreographer, and actor. The leading male dancer with the Sadler's Wells Ballet, London 1933–50, he partnered Margot Fonteyn in the 1940s. Knighted 1968.

His forte was characterization rather than virtuosity, best displayed in his memorable role as the comic Ugly Sister in Frederick Ashton's *Cinderella*, for which he used his gift for mime and other theatrical effects. His other comic roles include Doctor Coppelius in *Coppélia* and the bridegroom in Ashton's *A Wedding Bouquet*, but he was equally at home in dramatic roles, such as the Red King in de Valois' *Checkmate*. His film appearances include *The Red Shoes* 1948, *The Tales of Hoffman* 1951, *Chitty Chitty Bang Bang* 1968, and the title role in Nureyev's *Don Quixote* 1973.

Helvetius Claude Adrien (1715–1771). French philosopher. In *De l'Esprit* 1758 he argued, following David Hume, that self-interest, however disguised, is the mainspring of all human action and that, since conceptions of good and evil vary according to period and locality, there is no absolute good or evil. He also believed that intellectual differences are only a matter of education.

Helvetius's principle of artificial identity of interests (those manipulated by governments) influenced the utilitarian philosopher Jeremy Bentham. *De l'Esprit* was denounced and burned by the public hangman.

Hemingway Ernest Miller (1899–1961). US writer. War, bullfighting, and fishing are used symbolically in his work to represent honour, dignity, and primitivism – prominent themes in his short stories and novels, which include *A Farewell to Arms* 1929, *For Whom the Bell Tolls* 1941, and *The Old Man and the Sea* 1952 (Pulitzer Prize). His deceptively simple writing styles attracted many imitators. He received the Nobel Prize for Literature 1954.

He was born in Oak Park, Illinois, and in his youth developed a passion for hunting and adventure. He became a journalist and was wounded while serving on a volunteer ambulance crew in Italy in World War I. His style was influenced by Gertrude Stein, who also introduced him to bullfighting, a theme in his first novel, *Fiesta (The Sun Also Rises)* 1927, and the memoir *Death in the Afternoon* 1932. *A Farewell to Arms* deals with wartime experiences on the Italian front, and *For Whom the Bell Tolls* has a Spanish Civil War setting. He served as war correspondent both in that conflict and in Europe during World War II. After a full life, physical weakness, age, and depression contributed to his suicide.

Suggested reading
Baker, Carlos *Ernest Hemingway: A Life Story* (1969)
Lynn, Kenneth *Hemingway* (1987)
Meyers, J (ed) *Hemingway: The Critical Heritage* (1982)
Meyers, J *Hemingway* (1986)

The most essential gift for a good writer is a built-in, shock-proof shit detector. This is the writer's radar and all great writers have had it.

ERNEST HEMINGWAY
Paris Review Spring 1958

Hench Philip Showalter (1896–1965). US physician who introduced cortisone treatment for rheumatoid arthritis, for which he shared the 1950 Nobel Prize for Physiology or Medicine with Edward Kendall and Tadeus Reichstein.

Hench noticed that arthritic patients improved greatly during pregnancy or an attack of jaundice and concluded that a hormone secreted in increased quantity during both these conditions caused the improvement. This turned out to be cortisol, a steroid converted to cortisone in the liver.

Henderson Arthur (1863–1935). British Labour politician, foreign secretary 1929–31, when he accorded the Soviet government full recognition. He was awarded the Nobel Peace Prize 1934.

Hendrix Jimi (James Marshall) (1942–1970). US rock guitarist, songwriter, and singer. He was legendary for his virtuoso experimental technique and flamboyance. *Are You Experienced?* 1967 was his first album. His performance at the 1969 Woodstock festival included a memorable version of *The Star-Spangled Banner* and is recorded in the film *Woodstock* 1970. He greatly expanded the vocabulary of the electric guitar and influenced both rock and jazz musicians.

Hendrix moved to the UK 1966 and formed a trio, the Jimi Hendrix Experience, which produced hit singles with their first recorded songs ('Hey Joe' and 'Purple Haze', both 1967), and attracted notice in the USA when Hendrix burned his guitar at the 1967 Monterey Pop Festival. The group disbanded early 1969 after three albums; Hendrix continued to record and occasionally perform until his death the following year.

Suggested reading
Hopkins, J *Hit and Run* (1983)

Hendry Stephen (1970–). Scottish snooker player. He replaced Steve Davis as the top-ranking player during the 1989–90 season as well as becoming the youngest ever world champion.

Hendry was the youngest winner of a professional tournament when he claimed the 1986 Scottish professional title. He won his first ranking event in the 1987 Rothmans Grand Prix.

For a time, the land was ruled by squabbling gangs of Nordic nonentities, among whom the names of Hengist and Horsa ring a dim sort of bell.

Nicolas Bentley on HENGIST
in *Golden Sovereigns* 1970

Hengist (died c. 488). Legendary leader, with his brother Horsa, of the Jutes, who originated in Jutland and settled in Kent about 450, the first Anglo-Saxon settlers in Britain.

Heng Samrin (1934–). Cambodian politician. A Khmer Rouge commander 1976–78, he became disillusioned with its brutal tactics. He led an unsuccessful coup against Pol Pot 1978 and established the Kampuchean People's Revolutionary Party (KPRP) in Vietnam, before returning 1979 to head the new Vietnamese-backed government. He was replaced as prime minister by the reformist Hun Sen 1985.

Henie Sonja (1912–1969). Norwegian skater. Champion of her country at 11, she won ten world championships and three Olympic titles. She turned professional 1936 and went on to make numerous films in Hollywood.

Henlein Konrad (1898–1945). Sudeten-German leader of the Sudeten Nazi Party in Czechoslovakia, and closely allied with Hitler's Nazis. He was partly responsible for the destabilization of the Czechoslovak state 1938, which led to the Munich Agreement and secession of the Sudetenland to Germany.

Henri Robert. Adopted name of Robert Henry Cozad (1865–1929). US painter. He was a leading figure in the transition between 19th-century conventions and Modern art in America, and a principal member of the Ashcan School.

Suggested reading
Homer, W I *Robert Henri and his Circle* (1969)
Hoopes, D F *Robert Henri, 1865–1929* (1976)
Perlman, B B *Robert Henri: His Life and Art* (1984)

Queens of England are never drowned.

Said by HENRIETTA MARIA during a storm at sea Feb 1642

Henrietta Maria (1609–1669). Queen of England 1625–49. The daughter of Henry IV of France, she married Charles I of England 1625. By encouraging him to aid Roman Catholics and make himself an absolute ruler, she became highly unpopular and was exiled 1644–60. She returned to England at the Restoration but retired to France 1665.

Henry (Charles Albert David), known as Harry (1984–). Prince of the UK; second child of the Prince and Princess of Wales.

Henry Alice (1857–1943). Australian journalist and women's suffragette. Her first articles appeared in 1884, and over the following two decades she covered a variety of social causes, including women's hospitals and care of the disabled. She was a pioneer of women's trade-union movements in Australia and later settled in the USA, where she became a powerful speaker and key figure in the National Women's Trade Union League of America.

Henry Joseph (1797–1878). US physicist, inventor of the electromagnetic motor 1829 and of a telegraphic apparatus. He also discovered the principle of electromagnetic induction, roughly at the same time as Michael Faraday, and the phenomenon of self-induction. The unit of inductance, the *henry*, is named after him.

Born in Albany, New York, Henry studied at Albany Academy, where he became professor 1826, moving 1832 to New Jersey College (later Princeton). He was the Smithsonian Institution's first director, from 1846.

Turn up the lights; I don't want to go home in the dark.

O HENRY
Last words

Henry, O pen name of William Sydney Porter (1862–1910). US short-story writer. His collections include *Cabbages and Kings* 1904 and *The Four Million* 1906. His stories are written in a colloquial style and employ skilled construction with surprise endings.

I know not what course others may take; but as for me, give me liberty, or give me death!

PATRICK HENRY
Speech in the Virginia Convention 23 Mar 1775

Henry Patrick (1736–1799). US politician who in 1775 supported the arming of the Virginia militia against the British by a speech ending, 'Give me liberty or give me death!' He was governor of Virginia 1776–79 and 1784–86.

Henry assisted in the creation of the Continental Congress, of which he was a member. He opposed ratification of the US Constitution on the grounds that it jeopardized states' rights. His influence, however, helped to ensure the passage of ten amendments to it, constituting the Bill of Rights.

Henry William (1774–1836). English chemist and physician. In 1803 he formulated *Henry's law*, which states that when a gas is dissolved in a liquid at a given temperature, the mass that dissolves is in direct proportion to the pressure of the gas. In poor health after a childhood accident, he worked mainly for his father, an industrial chemist. A series of chemistry lectures which he gave 1798–99 were later published as *Elements of Experimental Chemistry* and became a highly successful textbook.

Henry eight kings of England:

The king praises no one whom he has not resolved to ruin.

Bishop Block on HENRY I
quoted in Henry of Huntingdon *History of England*

Henry I (1068–1135). King of England from 1100. Youngest son of William the Conqueror, he succeeded his brother William II. He won the support of the Saxons by granting them a charter and marrying a Saxon princess. An able administrator, he established a professional bureaucracy and a system of travelling judges. He was succeeded by Stephen.
Suggested reading
Barlow, F *The Feudal Kingdom of England, 1042–1216* (1962)

Will no one revenge me of the injuries I have sustained from one turbulent priest?

HENRY II
referring to Thomas à Becket, archbishop of Canterbury;
four of Henry's household knights took these words literally
and killed Becket in Canterbury Cathedral. Oral tradition quoted
in G Lyttleton *History of the Life of King Henry the Second* 1769 IV 353

Henry II (1133–1189). King of England from 1154, when he succeeded Stephen. He was the son of Matilda and Geoffrey of Anjou (1113–1151). He curbed the power of the barons, but his attempt to bring the church courts under control had to be abandoned after the murder of Thomas à Becket. During his reign the English conquest of Ireland began. He was succeeded by his son Richard I.

He was lord of Scotland, Ireland, and Wales, and count of Anjou, Brittany, Poitou, Normandy, Maine, Gascony, and Aquitaine. He was married to Eleanor of Aquitaine.
Suggested reading
Harvey, J H *The Plantagenets* (1970)
Warren, W *Henry II* (1973)

I fear thunder and lightning exceedingly but ... I fear thee more than all the thunder and lightning in the world.

HENRY III
to Simon de Montfort, July 1258, quoted in Matthew Paris
Chronica Majora H R Luard (ed) Rolls Series 1872–1883 vol v

Henry III (1207–1272). King of England from 1216, when he succeeded John, but he did not rule until 1227. His financial commitments to the papacy and his foreign favourites led to de Montfort's revolt 1264. Henry was defeated at Lewes, Sussex, and imprisoned. He was restored to the throne after the royalist victory at Evesham 1265. He was succeeded by his son Edward I.

The royal powers were exercised by a regency until 1232 and by two French nobles, Peter des Roches and Peter des Rivaux, until the barons forced their expulsion 1234, marking the start of Henry's personal rule. While he was in prison, de Montfort ruled in his name. On his release Henry was weak and senile and his eldest son, Edward, took charge of the government.
Suggested reading
Hallam, E (ed) *The Four Gothic Kings* (1987)
Harvey, J H *The Plantagenets* (1970)
Powicke, F *King Henry III and the Lord Edward* (1947)

He provided not firm leadership but well-meaning incompetence ... ultimately he became a cipher, a mere symbol of allegiance.

Michael Hicks on HENRY IV (BOLINGBROKE)
in *Who's Who in Later Medieval England* 1991

Henry IV (Bolingbroke) (1367–1413). King of England from 1399, the son of John of Gaunt. In 1398 he was banished by Richard II for political activity but returned 1399 to head a revolt and be accepted as king by Parliament. He was succeeded by his son Henry V.

He had difficulty in keeping the support of Parliament and the clergy, and had to deal with baronial unrest and Glendower's rising in Wales. In order to win support he had to conciliate the church by a law for the burning of heretics, and to make many concessions to Parliament.

Suggested reading
Bevan, Bryan *Henry IV* (1994)
Kirby, J L *Henry IV of England* (1970)
Jacob, E F *The Fifteenth Century, 1399–1485* (1961)

Henry V (1387–1422). King of England from 1413, son of Henry IV. Invading Normandy 1415 (during the Hundred Years' War), he captured Harfleur and defeated the French at Agincourt. He invaded again 1417–19, capturing Rouen. His military victory forced the French into the Treaty of Troyes 1420, which gave Henry control of the French government. He married Catherine of Valois 1420 and gained recognition as heir to the French throne by his father-in-law Charles VI, but died before him. He was succeeded by his son Henry VI.

Suggested reading
Earl, P *The Life and Times of Henry V* (1972)
Harriss, G L (ed) *Henry V: The Practice of Kingship* (1985)
Jacob, E F *Henry V and the Invasion of France* (1947)
Labarge, M W *Henry V: The Cautious Conqueror* (1976)
Pugh, T B *Henry V and the Southampton Plot* (1988)
Seward, D *Henry V* (1988)

I shall play such a ball game with the French in their own courtyards, that they will in the end ... win grief instead of the game.

HENRY V
to ambassadors returning from France
with an insulting gift of tennis balls 1414

Henry VI (1421–1471). King of England from 1422, son of Henry V. He assumed royal power 1442 and sided with the party opposed to the continuation of the Hundred Years' War with France. After his marriage 1445, he was dominated by his wife, Margaret of Anjou. The unpopularity of the government, especially after the loss of the English conquests in France, encouraged Richard, Duke of York, to claim the throne, and though York was killed 1460, his son Edward IV proclaimed himself king 1461. Henry was captured 1465, temporarily restored 1470, but again imprisoned 1471 and then murdered.

Suggested reading
Jacob, E F *The Fifteenth Century, 1399–1485* (1961)
Lander, J R *Crown and Nobility, 1450–1509* (1976)

Henry VII (1457–1509). King of England from 1485, son of Edmund Tudor, Earl of Richmond (*c.* 1430–1456), and a descendant of John of Gaunt.

He spent his early life in Brittany until 1485, when he landed in Britain to lead the rebellion against Richard III which ended with Richard's defeat and death at Bosworth. By his marriage to Elizabeth of York 1486, he united the houses of York and Lancaster. Yorkist revolts continued until 1497, but Henry restored order after the Wars of the Roses by the Star Chamber and achieved independence from Parliament by amassing a private fortune through confiscations. He was succeeded by his son Henry VIII.

Suggested reading
Alexander, Michael van Cleave *The First of the Tudors: A Study of Henry VII and his Reign* (1981)
Chrimes, S *Henry VII* (1972)
Elton, G R *England Under the Tudors* (1955)
Griffiths, Ralph A and Thomas, Roger S *The Making of the Tudor Dynasty* (1985)
Plowden, Alison *The House of Tudor* (1976)
Williams, Neville *The Life and Times of Henry VII* (1973)

Henry VIII (1491–1547). King of England from 1509, when he succeeded his father Henry VII and married Catherine of Aragon, the widow of his brother.

During the period 1513–29 Henry pursued an active foreign policy, largely under the guidance of his Lord Chancellor, Cardinal Wolsey, who shared Henry's desire to make England stronger. Wolsey was replaced by Thomas More 1529 for failing to persuade the pope to grant Henry a divorce. After 1532 Henry broke with papal authority, proclaimed himself head of the church in England, dissolved the monasteries, and divorced Catherine. His subsequent wives were Anne Boleyn, Jane Seymour, Anne of Cleves, Catherine Howard, and Catherine Parr.

He was succeeded by his son Edward VI.

My Lord, if it were not to satisfy the world, and my Realm, I would not do that I must do this day for none earthly thing.

HENRY VIII
Remark to Thomas Cromwell, on the day
of his wedding to Anne of Cleves, 5 Jan 1540

Henry divorced Catherine of Aragon 1533 because she was too old to give him an heir, and married Anne Boleyn, who was beheaded 1536, ostensibly for adultery. Henry's third wife, Jane Seymour, died 1537. He married Anne of Cleves 1540 in pursuance of Thomas Cromwell's policy of allying with the German Protestants, but rapidly abandoned this policy, divorced Anne, and beheaded Cromwell. His fifth wife, Catherine Howard, was beheaded 1542, and the following year he married Catherine Parr, who survived him. Henry never completely lost his popularity, but wars with France and Scotland towards the end of his reign sapped the economy, and in religion he not only executed Roman Catholics, including Thomas More, for refusing to acknowledge his supremacy in the church, but also Protestants who maintained his changes had not gone far enough.

Suggested reading
Bruce, Marie Louise *The Making of Henry VIII* (1977)
Fraser, Antonia *The Six Wives of Henry VIII* (1992)
Loaders, David *The Politics of Marriage: Henry VIII and his Queens* (1994)
Ridley, Jasper *Henry VIII* (1985)
Scarisbrick, J J *Henry VIII* (1968)
Simons, E N *Henry VIII: The First Tudor King* (1968)
Starkey, David *The Reign of Henry VIII* (1986)
Williams, Neville *Henry VIII and his Court* (1971)

Henry four kings of France, including:

Henry I (*c.* 1008–1060). King of France from 1031. He spent much of his reign in conflict with William the Conqueror, then duke of Normandy.

Henry II (1519–1559). King of France from 1547. He captured the fortresses of Metz and Verdun from the Holy Roman emperor Charles V and Calais from the English. He was killed in a tournament.

In 1526 he was sent with his brother to Spain as a hostage, being returned when there was peace 1530. He married Catherine de' Medici 1533, and from then on was dominated by her, Diane de Poitiers, and Duke Montmorency. Three of his sons, Francis II, Charles IX, and Henry III, became kings of France.

He was intelligent and artistic, but unstable and extravagant, oscillating between bouts of Counter-Reformation religiosity and orgies of wasteful indulgence with his male harem, his 'mignons'.

E N Williams on HENRY III
in *Penguin Dictionary of English and European History 1485–1789* 1980

Henry III (1551–1589). King of France from 1574. He fought both the Huguenots (headed by his successor, Henry of Navarre) and the Catholic League (headed by the third Duke of Guise). Guise expelled Henry from Paris 1588 but was assassinated. Henry allied with the Huguenots under Henry of Navarre to besiege the city, but was assassinated by a monk.

Henry IV (1553–1610). King of France from 1589. Son of Antoine de Bourbon and Jeanne, Queen of Navarre, he was brought up as a Protestant and from 1576 led the Huguenots. On his accession he settled the religious question by adopting Catholicism while tolerating Protestantism. He restored peace and strong government to France and brought back prosperity by measures for the promotion of industry and agriculture and the improvement of communications. He was assassinated by a Catholic extremist.

Henry seven Holy Roman emperors, including:

Henry (I) the Fowler (c. 876–936). King of Germany from 919, and duke of Saxony from 912. He secured the frontiers of Saxony, ruled in harmony with its nobles, and extended German influence over the Danes, the Hungarians, and the Slavonic tribes. He was about to claim the imperial crown when he died.

Henry (II) the Saint (973–1024). King of Germany from 1002, Holy Roman emperor from 1014, when he recognized Benedict VIII as pope. He was canonized 1146.

Henry (III) the Black (1017–1056). King of Germany from 1028, Holy Roman emperor from 1039 (crowned 1046). He raised the empire to the height of its power, and extended its authority over Poland, Bohemia, and Hungary.

Henry IV (1050–1106). Holy Roman emperor from 1056, who was involved from 1075 in a struggle with the papacy. Excommunicated twice (1076 and 1080), Henry deposed Gregory VII and set up the antipope Clement III by whom he was crowned Holy Roman emperor 1084.

Henry V (1086–1125). Holy Roman emperor from 1106. He continued the struggle with the church until the settlement of the investiture contest 1122.

Henry VI (1165–1197). Holy Roman emperor from 1190. As part of his plan for making the empire universal, he captured and imprisoned Richard I of England and compelled him to do homage.

Henry VII (c. 1269–1313). Holy Roman emperor from 1308. He attempted unsuccessfully to revive the imperial supremacy in Italy.

Henry Frederick Prince of Wales (1594–1612). Eldest son of James I of England and Anne of Denmark; a keen patron of Italian art.

Henry of Blois (died 1171). Brother of King Stephen of England, he was bishop of Winchester from 1129, and Pope Innocent II's legate to England from 1139. While remaining loyal to Henry II, he tried to effect a compromise between Becket and the king. He was a generous benefactor to Winchester and Cluny, and he built Westminster Abbey.

Henry the Lion (1129–1195). Duke of Bavaria 1156–80, duke of Saxony 1142–80, and duke of Lüneburg 1180–85. He was granted the Duchy of Bavaria by the Emperor Frederick Barbarossa. He founded Lübeck and Munich. In 1162 he married Matilda, daughter of Henry II of England. His refusal in 1176 to accompany Frederick Barbarossa to Italy led in 1180 to his being deprived of the duchies of Bavaria and Saxony. Henry led several military expeditions to conquer territory in the East.

Henry the Navigator (1394–1460). Portuguese prince, the fourth son of John I. He set up a school for navigators 1419 and under his patronage Portuguese sailors explored and colonized Madeira, the Cape Verde Islands, and the Azores; they sailed down the African coast almost to Sierra Leone.
Suggested reading
Sanceau, Elaine *Henry the Navigator* (1946)
Ure, John *Prince Henry the Navigator* (1977)

Henryson Robert (c. 1430–c. 1505). Scottish poet. His works include versions of Aesop and the *Testament of Cresseid*, a work once attributed to Chaucer, which continues Chaucer's story of *Troilus and Criseyde* by depicting the betrayal and wretched afterlife of Troilus.

Henslowe Philip. (died 1616). English theatre manager. He owned the Fortune, Hope, and Rose Theatres in London. He wrote a diary, in which he kept his accounts of transactions for his theatres, and of loans and payments to actors and dramatists. The diary provides invaluable material evidence for the study of the English theatre in the age of Shakespeare.

Henson Jim (James Maury) (1936–1990). US puppeteer who created the television Muppet characters, including Kermit the Frog, Miss Piggy, and Fozzie Bear. The Muppets became popular on the children's educational TV series *Sesame Street*, which first appeared in 1969 and soon became regular viewing in over 80 countries. In 1976 Henson created *The Muppet Show*, which ran for five years and became one of the world's most widely seen TV programmes, reaching 235 million viewers in 100 countries. Three Muppet movies followed.

Henty Edward (1810–1878). Australian grazier, born in England. A member of a pioneering family whose members settled in Tasmania and Victoria between 1829 and 1837, Edward was the first person to settle permanently in what is now Victoria 1834. He established a large grazing estate and was a member of the Victorian Legislative Assembly 1856–61.

Henty G(eorge) A(lfred) (1832–1902). English war correspondent and author. He wrote numerous historical novels for children, including *With the Allies to Peking* 1904.

I have taken the decision that in my work I will embody all the difficulties and all the problems of contemporary bourgeois music, and that I will, however, try to transform these into something usable, into something that the masses can understand.

HANS WERNER HENZE
Music and Politics 1982

Henze Hans Werner (1926–   ). German composer. His immense and stylistically restless output is marked by a keen literary sensibility and seductive use of orchestral coloration, as in the opera *Elegy for Young Lovers* 1959–61 and the cantata *Being Beauteous* 1963. Among recent works are the opera *Das Verratene Meer/The Sea Betrayed* 1992.

Following the student unrest of 1968 he suddenly renounced the wealthy musical establishment in favour of a militantly socialist stance in works such as the abrasive *El Cimarrón* 1969–70 and *Voices* 1973, austere settings of 22 revolutionary texts in often magical sonorities. In 1953 he moved to Italy where his music became more expansive, as in the opera *The Bassarids* 1966.

When the chips are down, Audrey is there.

George Cukor on AUDREY HEPBURN

Hepburn Audrey (born Edda van Heemstra Hepburn-Rushton) (1929–1993). British actress of Anglo-Dutch descent. She often played innocent, childlike characters. Slender and doe-eyed, she set a different style from the more ample women stars of the 1950s. After playing minor parts in British films in the early 1950s, she became a Hollywood star in *Roman Holiday* 1951, for which she won an Academy Award, and later starred in such films as *Funny Face* 1957, *My Fair Lady* 1964, and *Wait Until Dark* 1968. Among her later films were *Robin and Marian* 1976.

Afraid of death? Not at all. Be a great relief. Then I wouldn't have to talk to you.

KATHARINE HEPBURN
Directed at her interviewer from *People* 5 Nov 1990

Hepburn Katharine (1909–   ). US actress. She made feisty self-assurance her trademark. She appeared in such films as *Morning Glory* 1933 (Academy Award), *Little Women* 1933, *Bringing Up*

Hepburn, Katherine *The face of US actress Katherine Hepburn dominates a film poster for* Morning Glory *1933. Her long career has included many stage appearances and films such as* The African Queen *and* On Golden Pond. *(Image Select)*

Baby 1938, *The Philadelphia Story* 1940, *Woman of the Year* 1942 (her first film with her frequent partner Spencer Tracy), *The African Queen* 1951, *Pat and Mike* 1952, *Guess Who's Coming to Dinner* 1967 (Academy Award), *Lion in Winter* 1968 (Academy Award), and *On Golden Pond* 1981 (Academy Award). She also had a distinguished stage career.

Suggested reading
Anderson, C *Young Kate* (1988)
Carey, Gary *Katharine Hepburn: A Hollywood Yankee* (1984)
Edwards, Anne *A Remarkable Woman* (1985)
Leamington, Barbara *Katharine Hepburn* (1995)

Hepplewhite George (died 1786). English furnituremaker. His name is associated with Neo-Classicism. His reputation rests upon his book of designs *The Cabinetmaker and Upholsterer's Guide*, published posthumously 1788, which contains over 300 designs, characterized by simple elegance and utility. No piece of furniture has been identified as being made by him.

Hepworth (Jocelyn) Barbara (1903–1975). English sculptor. She developed a distinctive abstract style, creating hollowed forms of stone or wood with spaces bridged by wires or strings; many later works are in bronze.

She worked in concrete, bronze, wood, and aluminium, but her preferred medium was stone. She married first the sculptor John Skeaping and later the painter Ben Nicholson. Under Nicholson's influence she became more interested in abstract form. In 1939 she moved to St Ives, Cornwall (where her studio is now a museum). DBE 1965.

To do the same thing over and over again is not only boredom: it is to be controlled by rather than to control what you do.
HERACLITUS
Herakleitos and Diogenes pt 1, 89

Heraclitus (*c.* 544–*c.* 483 BC). Greek philosopher who believed that the cosmos is in a ceaseless state of flux and motion, fire being the fundamental material that accounts for all change and motion in the world. Nothing in the world ever stays the same; hence the dictum, 'one cannot step in the same river twice'. Wisdom came from understanding this eternal dynamic, which unified the diversity of nature, as he wrote in *On Nature*. Heraclitus was born in Ephesus.

Heraclius (*c.* 575–641). Byzantine emperor from 610. His reign marked a turning point in the empire's fortunes. Of Armenian descent, he recaptured Armenia 622, and other provinces 622–28 from the Persians, but lost them to the Muslims 629–41.

Is this how you have governed the empire?
HERACLIUS
Question to his predecessor, before having him
executed. Quoted in Nicephorus Short History ch 4

Heraklides of Pontus (388–315 BC). Greek philosopher and astronomer who may have been the first to realize that the Earth turns on its axis, from west to east, once every 24 hours. He also thought that the observed motions of Mercury and Venus suggested that they orbited the Sun rather than the Earth.

Born in Heraklea, near the Black Sea, Heraklides migrated to Athens and studied at the Academy of Plato. He is said also to have attended the schools of the Pythagorean philosophers, and would thus have come into contact with Aristotle. All his writings are lost, so his astronomical theories are known only at second hand.

In proposing the doctrine of a rotating Earth (not to be accepted for another 1,800 years), Heraklides contradicted the accepted model of the universe put forward by Aristotle. Heraklides thought that the immense spheres in which the stars and planets were assumed to be fixed could not rotate so fast. He did not completely adopt the heliocentric view of the universe stated later by Aristarchus, but proposed instead that the Sun moved in a circular orbit (in its sphere) and that Mercury and Venus moved on epicycles around the Sun as centre.

Herapath John (1790–1868). English mathematician. His work on the behaviour of gases, though seriously flawed, was acknowledged by the physicist James Joule in his own more successful investigations.

Herbert A(lan) P(atrick) (1890–1971). English politician and writer. He was an Independent member of Parliament for Oxford University 1935–50, author of several novels, including *The Water Gipsies* 1930, and a contributor to the humorous magazine *Punch*.

He was called to the bar 1918, but never practised. His first novel, *The Secret Battle* 1919, dealing with an officer's breakdown on the western front during World War I, was reissued just before World War II and led to an improvement in court-martial procedure. Herbert joined *Punch* 1924, and his series of articles satirizing legal anomalies was published as *Misleading Cases* 1927. The novel *Holy Deadlock* 1934 exposed the limitations of English divorce law, and Herbert brought in as a private member's bill the Matrimonial Causes Bill, which became law 1937. Among his other campaigns was a successful attack on the proposal to subject books to purchase tax. His musical revues included *Bless the Bridge* 1950. He published *A. P. H.; His Life and Times* 1970. Knighted 1945.

Herbert (Alfred Francis) Xavier (1901–1984). Australian novelist and short-story writer. He is best known for *Poor Fellow My Country* 1975, winner of the Miles Franklin Award, and at 850,000 words the longest novel ever published in Australia. His other works include *Capricornia* 1938, *Soldier's Women* 1959, set in Sydney during World War II, his autobiography *Disturbing Element* 1961, and a collection of short stories 'Larger than Life' 1963. The treatment of Australian Aborigines by white Australians, his own attachment to the land, and the search for personal and national identity are recurring themes in his work.

Herbert Edward, 1st Baron Herbert of Cherbury (1583–1648). English philosopher. His virtual rejection of revelation and his advocacy of rational religion founded English deism. His main work is *De veritate* 1624. He was the brother of the poet George Herbert. KB 1603, Irish baron 1624, UK baron 1629.

Herbert Frank Patrick (1920–1986). US science-fiction writer. He was the author of the *Dune* series from 1965 (filmed by David Lynch 1984), large-scale adventure stories containing serious ideas about ecology and religion.

Herbert George (1593–1633). English poet. His volume of religious poems, *The Temple*, appeared 1633, shortly before his death. His intense though quiet poems embody his religious struggles ('The Temper', 'The Collar') or poignantly contrast mortality and eternal truth ('Vertue', 'Life') in a deceptively simple language.

He became orator to Cambridge University 1619, and a prebendary in Huntingdonshire 1625. After ordination in 1630 he became vicar of Bemerton, Wiltshire, and died of consumption.

Herbert Sidney, 1st Baron Herbert of Lea (1810–1861). British politician. He was secretary for war in Aberdeen's Liberal-Peelite coalition of 1852–55, and during the Crimean War was responsible for sending Florence Nightingale to the front. Baron 1860.

I wish ... one of the thousand who ... justly celebrate Miss Nightingale would say a single word for the man ... who devised ... her going [to the Dardanelles] ... Sidney Herbert.

W E Gladstone on SIDNEY HERBERT
in letter to R M Milnes (later Lord Houghton) 15 Oct 1855

Herbert Victor (1859–1924). Irish-born US conductor and composer. In 1893 he became conductor of the 22nd Regiment Band, also composing light operettas for the New York stage. He was conductor of the Pittsburgh Philharmonic 1898–1904, returning to New York to help found the American Society of Composers, Authors, and Publishers (ASCAP) 1914.

Herbert Wally (Walter William) (1934–). British surveyor and explorer. His first surface crossing by dog sledge of the Arctic Ocean 1968–69, from Alaska to Spitsbergen via the North Pole, was the longest sustained sledging journey (6,000 km/3,800 mi) in polar exploration.

Herbert Zbigniew (1924–). Polish poet and essayist. His poetry, avant-garde, ironic, and formally accomplished, achieves classical precision and control amidst and against the observed chaos of Poland's human suffering. He published few poems in the communist-inspired epoch of Socialist Realism 1949–54 but his collection *Struna swiatla/Chord of Light* 1956 was soon followed by *Hermes, pies i gwiazda/Hermes, a Dog and a Star* 1957 and *Studium przedmiotu/A Study of the Object* 1961. He has also written plays for broadcasting and essays on art and history.

Herbig George Howard (1920–). US astronomer who specialized in spectroscopic research into irregular variable stars, notably those of the T Tauri group. He also worked on binary stars. In 1944, he became a member of the staff at the Lick Observatory, California, rising to professor 1966.

Herblock pen name of Herbert Lawrence Block (1909–). US cartoonist who gained a national reputation during the 1950s with his syndicated cartoons. He won Pulitzer Prizes 1942 and 1952 and published several collections of his work. He played a leading role in the public campaign against the communist witch-hunting tactics of Senator Joseph McCarthy.

Born in Chicago, USA, Herblock joined the staff of the *Chicago Daily News* 1929 as an editorial cartoonist. After serving in the army during World War II, he joined the staff of the *Washington Post* 1946.

Herbrand Jacques (1908–1931). French mathematical prodigy who originated some innovatory concepts in the field of mathematical logic. He formulated the Herbrand theorem, which established a link between quantification theory and sentential logic. This has since found many applications in such fields as decision and reduction problems. Herbrand was also fascinated by modern algebra and wrote a number of papers on class-field theory.

Herder Johann Gottfried von (1744–1803). German poet, critic, and philosopher. Herder's critical writings indicated his intuitive rather than reasoning trend of thought. He collected folk songs of all nations 1778, and in the *Ideen zur Philosophie der Geschichte der Menschheit/Outlines of a Philosophy of the History of Man* 1784–91 he outlined the stages of human cultural development.

Herder was born in East Prussia and studied at Königsberg, where he was influenced by the philosopher Immanuel Kant. Herder became pastor in Riga, Latvia. He met the writer J W Goethe in 1770, and in 1776 was called to Weimar (where Goethe was prime minister) as court preacher. Herder gave considerable impetus to the *Sturm und Drang* (storm and stress) Romantic movement in German literature.

(His) genius for amphibious guerrilla warfare ... the last and noblest of a series of regional revolts undertaken too late.

G M Trevelyan on HEREWARD THE WAKE
in *History of England* 1926

Hereward the Wake (lived 11th century). English leader of a revolt against the Normans 1070. His stronghold in the Isle of Ely was captured by William the Conqueror 1071. Hereward escaped, but his fate is unknown.

Hergé pen name of Georges Remi (1907–1983). Belgian artist, creator of the boy reporter Tintin, who first appeared in strip-cartoon form as *Tintin in the Land of the Soviets* 1929–30.

Herling-Grudziński Gustaw (1919–). Polish novelist and essayist. An anti-Nazi journalist in 1939, he was deported to a Russian labour camp during the war, an experience reflected in the juxtaposed horror and beauty of his distinguished autobiographical novel *Inny świat/A World Apart* 1953. He later fought with the Allies and eventually settled in Italy. Some of his stories, humane but detached, with medieval settings, were collected and translated as *The Island* 1967. His work was officially suppressed in Poland until 1988.

Herman Woody (Woodrow Charles) (1913–1987). US jazz bandleader and clarinetist. A child prodigy, he was leader of his own orchestra at 23, and after 1945 formed his Thundering Herd band. Soloists in this or later versions of the band included Lester Young and Stan Getz.

Hermite Charles (1822–1901). French mathematician who was a principal contributor to the development of the theory of algebraic forms, the arithmetical theory of quadratic forms, and the theories of elliptic and Abelian functions. Much of his work was highly innovative, especially his solution of the quintic equation through elliptic modular functions, and his proof of the transcendence of e. He became professor at the Ecole Normale 1869, moving to the Sorbonne 1870.

I who was called immortal by you am now under sentence of death.

HEROD AGRIPPA
quoted in Josephus *Jewish Antiquities* bk 19.347

Herod Agrippa I (10 BC–AD 44). Ruler of Palestine from AD 41. His real name was Marcus Julius Agrippa, erroneously called 'Herod' in the Bible. Grandson of Herod the Great, he was made tetrarch (governor) of Palestine by the Roman emperor Caligula and king by Emperor Claudius AD 41. He put the apostle James to death and imprisoned the apostle Peter. His son was Herod Agrippa II.

Herod Agrippa II (c. 40–c. 93 AD). King of Chalcis (now S Lebanon), son of Herod Agrippa I. He was appointed by the Roman emperor Claudius about AD 50, and in AD 60 tried the apostle Paul. He helped the Roman commander Titus (subsequently emperor) take and sack Jerusalem AD 70, then went to Rome, where he died.

Antipas was skilful in calumniating those who were innocent and inciting the king to seek information about plots against his life.

Josephus on HEROD ANTIPAS
in *Jewish Antiquities* bk 16.246

Herod Antipas (21 BC–AD 39). Tetrarch (governor) of the Roman province of Galilee, N Palestine, 4 BC–AD 39, son of Herod the Great. He divorced his wife to marry his niece Herodias, and was responsible for the death of John the Baptist. Jesus was brought before him on Pontius Pilate's discovery that he was a Galilean and hence of Herod's jurisdiction, but Herod returned him without giving any verdict. In AD 38 Herod Antipas went to Rome to try to persuade Emperor Caligula to give him the title of king, but was instead banished.

Remains of one of his royal palaces were excavated at Masada 1963–64. There were important finds of ancient texts, mosaic floors, decorated walls of the royal palace, and reservoirs.

You can find out from my past actions how I behave towards my benefactors.
HEROD THE GREAT
quoted in Josephus *Jewish Antiquities* bk 15.193

Herod the Great (74–4 BC). King of the Roman province of Judaea, S Palestine, from 40 BC.

With the aid of Mark Antony, he established his government in Jerusalem 37 BC. He rebuilt the Temple in Jerusalem, but his Hellenizing tendencies made him suspect to orthodox Jewry. His last years were a reign of terror, and in the New Testament Matthew alleges that he ordered the slaughter of all the infants in Bethlehem to ensure the death of Jesus, whom he foresaw as a rival. He was the father of Herod Antipas.

Herodotus made his prose style resemble the finest poetry by its persuasiveness, its charm and its utterly delightful effect.
Dionysius of Halicarnassus on HERODOTUS
in *Essay on Thucydides* ch 23

Herodotus (c. 484–c. 424 BC). Greek historian. After four years in Athens, he travelled widely in Egypt, Asia, and the Black Sea region of E Europe, before settling at Thurii in S Italy 443 BC. He wrote a nine-book history of the Greek-Persian struggle that culminated in the defeat of the Persian invasion attempts 490 and 480 BC. Herodotus was the first historian to apply critical evaluation to his material, while also recording divergent opinions.
Suggested reading
Fornara, C W *Herodotus* (1971)
Myres, J L *Herodotus: Father of History* (1953)
Waters, K H *Herodotus the Historian* (1985)

We must first discuss the nature of the vacuum; some writers deny its existence, but through experiments we will provide a true account.
HERO OF ALEXANDRIA
Pneumatics bk1 ch 1

Hero of Alexandria (lived AD 62). Greek mathematician and engineer, the greatest experimentalist of antiquity. Among his many inventions was an automatic fountain and a kind of stationary steam engine. His books have survived mainly in Arabic.

Hero was also a teacher and in Alexandria founded a technical school with one section devoted entirely to research.

He regarded air as a substance that could be compressed and expanded, and explained the phenomenon of suction and associated apparatus, such as the pipette. His assumption that air is composed of minute particles was 1,500 years ahead of its time.

In mechanics, he devised a system of gear wheels which could lift a mass of 1,000 kg/2,200 lb by means of a mere 5 kg/11 lb. His work *Mechanics* contains the parallelogram of velocity and the laws of levers, and his construction of a variable ratio via a friction disc has been used to build a motor vehicle with a semi-automatic transmission.

Hero's book *Metrica* explains the measurement of geometrical figures. *Pneumatica* describes numerous mechanical devices operated by gas, water, steam, or atmospheric pressure, and siphons, pumps, and working automata in the likeness of animals or birds.

Herophilus of Chalcedon (c. 330–c. 260 BC). Greek physician, active in Alexandria. His handbooks on anatomy make pioneering use of dissection, which, according to several ancient sources, he carried out on live criminals condemned to death.

A doctor is a man who can distinguish the possible from the impossible.
HEROPHILUS OF CHALCEDON
quoted in John Stobaeus *Florilegium* bk 4 ch 38

Héroult Paul Louis Toussaint (1863–1914). French metallurgist who developed the electrolytic manufacturing process for aluminium, simultaneously with US chemist Charles Hall. Like Hall in the USA, Héroult used direct-current electrolysis to extract aluminium from compounds, dissolving aluminium oxide in a variety of molten fluorides to find the best combination of material, and finding cryolite (sodium aluminium flouride) the most promising. Héroult's process differed from Hall's in that the former used one large, central graphite electrode in the graphite cell holding the molten material. Héroult also invented the electric arc furnace for the production of steels.

Herr Michael (1940–). US writer. *Dispatches* 1977, his book of Vietnam reportage, became an international best seller, praised for its bold and savage depiction of war. Co-author of several screenplays, including *Apocalypse Now* 1979 and *Full Metal Jacket* 1987, he also wrote *Walter Winchell* 1990, a hybrid screenplay/novel vividly dramatizing the life of the famous 1940s gossip columnist.

Herrera, de Spanish painters, father and son. Francisco the Elder (El Viejo, 1576–1656) was a painter of frescoes and history pictures, etcher and medallist. He worked in a coarse and forcible style of which some trace may be discovered in the early 'kitchen pictures' of Velázquez, whose first master he was. He was a man of such difficult temper, however, that neither his children nor his pupils would stay with him. His enemies accused him of coining false money and he took refuge in the Jesuits' College at Seville, where he painted the *St Hermengild in Glory* which won him the pardon of Philip IV.

Francisco the Younger (El Mozo, 1622–1685) was the second son and the pupil of his father, but fled to Rome to escape his cruelty. He became celebrated for his pictures of still life, flowers, fruit, and fish. He also painted frescoes and, in later life, portraits. He became sub-director of the academy at Seville under Murillo 1660. His painting of St Francis is in Seville Cathedral, and his *Assumption of the Virgin* in the Atocha church in Madrid won him appointment as painter to the king.

Herrick Robert (1591–1674). English poet and cleric. He published *Hesperides* 1648, a collection of sacred and pastoral poetry admired for its lyric quality, including 'Gather ye rosebuds' and 'Cherry ripe'.
Suggested reading
Hageman, Elizabeth *Robert Herrick: A Reference Guide* (1983)
Musgrove, S *The Universe of Robert Herrick* (1950)
Scott, George *Robert Herrick* (1974)

When it's a question of peace one must talk to the Devil himself.
EDOUARD HERRIOT
Observer 21 Sept 1953

Herriot Edouard (1872–1957). French Radical socialist politician. An opponent of Poincaré, who as prime minister carried out the French occupation of the Ruhr, Germany, he was briefly prime minister 1924–25, 1926, and 1932. As president of the chamber of deputies 1940, he opposed the policies of the right-wing Vichy government and was arrested and later taken to Germany; he was released 1945 by the Soviets.

Herriot James. Pen name of James Alfred Wight (1916–1995). English writer. A practising veterinary surgeon in Yorkshire from

1939, he wrote of his experiences in a series of humorous books which described the life of a young vet working in a Yorkshire village in the late 1930s. His first three books were published as a compilation under the title *All Creatures Great and Small* 1972. In 1974 a film version of *All Creatures Great and Small* was made, and by the 1980s his books had been translated into every major language, including Japanese, and a long-running television series was being sold worldwide.

I have long held the notion that if a vet can't catch his patient there's not much to worry about.

JAMES HERRIOT
Vet in Harness 1974

Herrmann Bernard (1911–1975). US film composer. His long career began with *Citizen Kane* 1940 and included collaborations with Alfred Hitchcock (*North by Northwest* 1959 and *Psycho* 1960) and François Truffaut (*Fahrenheit 451* 1966). He wrote his best scores for thriller and mystery movies, and was a major influence in the establishment of a distinctively American musical imagery.

He joined CBS (Columbia Broadcasting System) 1933 as a composer and conductor of music for drama and documentary programmes and worked with Orson Welles on a number of radio projects before making his film debut. An eclectic stylist, he made his own orchestrations and sought out many new and exotic instruments for special effects and authentic colour.

Herron Ron(ald James) (1930–1994). English architect and founder member of Archigram, a radical architectural group of the 1960s. He designed Walking City, a proposed city on wheels with full environmental controls, inspired by space exploration. Walking City became a seminal icon of technology and mobility.

Herschel Caroline Lucretia (1750–1848). German-born English astronomer, sister of William Herschel, and from 1772 his assistant in England. She discovered eight comets and worked on her brother's catalogue of star clusters and nebulae.

Herschel was born in Hanover. She received no formal education. In 1787, she was granted an annual salary by George III. On her brother's death 1822, she returned to Hanover but continued to work on his catalogue.

Herschel John Frederick William (1792–1871). English scientist, astronomer, and photographer who discovered thousands of close double stars, clusters, and nebulae. He coined the terms 'photography', 'negative', and 'positive', discovered sodium thiosulphite as a fixer of silver halides, and invented the cyanotype process; his inventions also include astronomical instruments. Baronet 1838.

His works include *Outlines of Astronomy* 1849, which became a standard textbook; *General Catalogue of Nebulae and Clusters*, still the standard reference catalogue; and *General Catalogue of 10,300 Multiple and Double Stars*, published posthumously.

Suggested reading
Lubbock, Constance *The Herschel Chronicle* (1933)
Schweber, S and Cohen, I B (eds) *Aspects of the Life and Thought of Sir John Herschel* (1981)

Herschel (Frederick) William (1738–1822). German-born English astronomer. He was a skilled telescope maker, and pioneered the study of binary stars and nebulae. He discovered the planet Uranus 1781 and infrared solar rays 1801. The discovery of Uranus brought him fame and, in 1782, the post of private astronomer to George III. He catalogued over 800 double stars, and found over 2,500 nebulae, catalogued by his sister Caroline Herschel; this work was continued by his son John Herschel. By studying the distribution of stars, William established the basic form of our Galaxy, the Milky Way. Knighted 1816.

Suggested reading
Crawford, Deborah *The King's Astronomer* (1968)
Hoskin, M *Herschel and the Construction of the Heavens* (1963)
Sidgwick, J B *William Herschel, Explorer of the Heavens* (1963)
Warner, B and N *Maclear and Herschel* (1984)

Hertling Georg Friedrich, Count von (1843–1919). German politician who was appointed imperial chancellor Nov 1917. He maintained a degree of support in the Reichstag (parliament) but was powerless to control the military leadership under Ludendorff.

Hertz Heinrich Rudolf (1857–1894). German physicist who studied electromagnetic waves, showing that their behaviour resembles that of light and heat waves.

Hertz confirmed James Clerk Maxwell's theory of electromagnetic waves. In 1888, he realized that electric waves could be produced and would travel through air, and he confirmed this experimentally. He went on to determine the velocity of these waves (which were later called radio waves) and, on showing that it was the same as that of light, devised experiments to show that the waves could be reflected, refracted, and diffracted. He was professor at Karlsruhe 1885–89 and at Bonn from 1889.

Hertzberger Herman (1932–). Dutch architect. His work is in the tradition of Brutalism but with the added element of user-friendliness. In similar style to Aldo van Eyck, his designs create a spatial framework that invites the user to occupy and complete the building. Notable examples of his work are the Central Beheer office building, Apeldoorn, 1970–72, and the Music Centre, Utrecht, 1976–78.

Hertzog James Barry Munnik (1866–1942). South African politician, prime minister 1924–39, founder of the Nationalist Party 1913 (the United South African National Party from 1933). He opposed South Africa's entry into both world wars.

Hertzog was born in Cape Colony of Boer descent. In 1914 he opposed South African participation in World War I. After the 1924 elections Hertzog became prime minister, and in 1933 the Nationalist Party and General Smuts's South African Party were

Herschel, William *German-born English astronomer William Herschel, who discovered the planet Uranus in 1781. Herschel named the planet, which was the first to be discovered telescopically, Georgium Sidus (George's Star) in honour of King George III, who appointed him his private astronomer a year later. (Ann Ronan/Image Select)*

merged as the United South African National Party. In Sept 1939 his motion against participation in World War II was rejected, and he resigned.

Hertzsprung Ejnar (1873–1967). Danish astronomer and physicist who introduced the concept of the absolute magnitude (brightness) of a star, and described the relationship between the absolute magnitude and the temperature of a star, formulating his results in the form of a diagram that has become a standard reference. In 1919 he became professor of astronomy at Leiden, the Netherlands. He retired 1945 and returned to Denmark, but did not cease his astronomical research until well into the 1960s.

Herzberg Gerhard (1904–). German-born Canadian physicist who used spectroscopy to determine the electronic structure and geometry of molecules, especially free radicals (atoms or groups of atoms that possess a free, unbonded electron). Nobel Prize for Chemistry 1971.

In 1935, with the rise to power of Adolf Hitler, he fled to Canada, where he became professor of physics at the University of Saskatchewan, Saskatoon, and director of the Division of Pure Physics for the National Research Council in Ottawa 1949–69. He spent 1945–49 at the Yerkes Observatory in Wisconsin, USA.

Don't forget that your people need young, healthy strength and that you are the heir to the name Herzl.

THEODOR HERZL
Last words (to his son) 1904

Herzl Theodor (1860–1904). Austrian founder of the Zionist movement. The Dreyfus case convinced him that the only solution to the problem of anti-Semitism was the resettlement of the Jews in a state of their own. His book *Jewish State* 1896 launched political Zionism, and he became the first president of the World Zionist Organization 1897.

He was born in Budapest and became a successful playwright and journalist, mainly in Vienna.

Suggested reading
Bein, A *Theodor Herzl* (1957)
Gurko, M *Theodor Herzl* (1988)
Pawel, Ernst *The Labyrinth of Exile* (1989)
Stewart, D *Theodor Herzl* (1972)

Herzog Bertram (1929–). German-born computer scientist, one of the pioneers in the use of computer graphics in engineering design.

Herzog was born in Offenburg, near Strasbourg, but emigrated to the USA and studied at the Case Institute of Technology. He has alternated academic posts with working in industry. In 1965 he became professor of industrial engineering at the University of Michigan. Two years later he became professor of electrical engineering and computer science at the University of Colorado.

In 1963, Herzog joined the Ford Motor Company as engineering methods manager, where he extensively applied computers to tasks involved in planning and design. Herzog remained as a consultant to Ford after his return to academic life.

Herzog Werner. Adopted name of Werner Stipetic (1942–). German film director. He often takes his camera to exotic and impractical locations. His original and visually splendid films include *Aguirre der Zorn Gottes/Aguirre Wrath of God* 1972, *Nosferatu Phantom der Nacht/Nosferatu Phantom of the Night* 1979, and *Fitzcarraldo* 1982.

Heseltine Michael Ray Dibdin (1933–). English Conservative politician, deputy prime minister from 1995. A member of Parliament from 1966 (for Henley from 1974), he was secretary of state for the environment 1990–92 and for trade and industry 1992–95. He was appointed deputy prime minister in the cabinet reshuffle that followed the July 1995 snap leadership election, which was called, but only narrowly won, by Prime Minister John Major.

Heseltine was minister of the environment 1979–83, when he succeeded John Nott. As minister of defence from 1983, he resigned Jan 1986 over the Westland affair and was then seen as a major rival to Margaret Thatcher. In Nov 1990, Heseltine's challenge to Thatcher's leadership of the Conservative Party brought about her resignation.

Suggested reading
Critchley, Julian *Heseltine* (1987)

Heseltine Philip (Arnold). Real name of the English composer Peter ◊Warlock.

Between us and virtue the immortal gods placed sweat: long and steep is the path that leads to her.

HESIOD OF ASCRA
Works and Days 289–90

Hesiod (lived 8th century BC). Greek poet. He is supposed to have lived a little later than Homer, and, according to his own account, to have been born in Boeotia. He is the author of *Works and Days*, a moralizing and didactic poem of rural life, and *Theogony*, an account of the origin of the world and of the gods. Both poems include the myth of Pandora.

Hess Germain Henri (1802–1850). Swiss-born Russian chemist, a pioneer in the field of thermochemistry. The law of constant heat summation is named after him.

Hess was born in Geneva, but his family emigrated to Russia. Hess studied at the University of Dorpat (now Tartu, Estonia), and in Stockholm, Sweden, under chemist Jöns Berzelius. Returning to Russia, he took part in a geological expedition to the Urals before setting up a medical practice in Irkutsk. In 1830 he settled in St Petersburg, where he held various academic appointments, becoming professor at the Technological Institute.

Hess's law was published 1840 and states that the heat change in a given chemical reaction depends only on the initial and final states of the system and is independent of the path followed, provided that heat is the only form of energy to enter or leave the system. Every chemical change is either endothermic (absorbing heat) or exothermic (evolving heat). Hess's law is in fact an application of the law of conservation of energy, but this was not formulated until 1842. In 1842 Hess proposed his second law, the law of thermoneutrality, which states that in exchange reactions of neutral salts in aqueous solution, no heat effect is observed.

Hess Harry Hammond (1906–1969). US geologist who in 1962 proposed the notion of seafloor spreading. This played a key part in the acceptance of plate tectonics as an explanation of how the Earth's crust is formed and moves.

Hess was born in New York and studied at Yale and Princeton, where he eventually became professor. From 1931, he carried out geophysical research into the oceans, continuing during World War II while in the navy. Later he was one of the main advocates of the Mohole project, whose aim was to drill down through the Earth's crust to gain access to the upper mantle.

Building on the recognition that certain parts of the ocean floor were anomalously young, and the discovery of the global distribution of mid-ocean ridges and central rift valleys, Hess suggested that convection within the Earth was continually creating new ocean floor, rising at mid-ocean ridges and then flowing horizontally to form new oceanic crust. It would follow that the further from the mid-ocean ridge, the older would be the crust – an expectation confirmed by research 1963.

Hess (Julia) Myra (1890–1965). British pianist. She is remembered for her morale-boosting National Gallery concerts in World War II, her transcription of the Bach chorale 'Jesu, Joy of Man's Desiring', and her interpretations of Beethoven. DBE 1941.

Hess Victor Francis (1883–1964). Austrian physicist who emigrated to the USA shortly after sharing a Nobel prize in 1936 for the discovery of cosmic radiation.

From 1906 to 1920 he worked in Vienna, studying radioactivity and atmospheric ionization. He was professor at Graz 1920–31 and at Innsbruck 1931–38, founding a cosmic-ray observatory on the nearby Hafelekar mountain. After the Nazi annexation of Austria, he emigrated to the USA, becoming professor at Fordham University, New York.

Hess made ten balloon ascents in 1911–12 to collect data about atmospheric ionization. Ascending to altitudes of more than 5,000 m/16,000 ft, he established that the intensity of ionization decreased to a minimum at about 1,000 m/3,000 ft, then increased steadily. By making ascents at night – and one during a nearly total solar eclipse – he proved that the ionization was not caused by the Sun. He concluded that radiation enters the atmosphere from outer space.

Another improvement we made ... was that we built our gas-chambers to accommodate two thousand people at one time.

RUDOLF HESS
Affidavit quoted in Alan Bullock *Hitler* ch 12 1952

Hess (Walter Richard) Rudolf (1894–1987). German Nazi leader. Imprisoned with Hitler 1924–25, he became his private secretary, taking down *Mein Kampf* from his dictation. In 1933 he was appointed deputy *Führer* to Hitler, a post he held until replaced by Goering Sept 1939. On 10 May 1941 he landed by air in the UK with his own compromise peace proposals and was held a prisoner of war until 1945, when he was tried at Nuremberg as a war criminal and sentenced to life imprisonment. He died in Spandau prison, Berlin.

He was effectively in charge of the Nazi party organization until his flight 1941. For the last years of his life he was the only prisoner left in Spandau.

Suggested reading
Douglas-Hamilton, James *Motive for a Mission* (1971)
Padfield, Peter *Hess: Fight for the Führer* (1991)
Schwarzwaller, Wulf *Rudolf Hess: The Last Nazi* (1988)

Hesse Hermann (1877–1962). German writer, a Swiss citizen from 1923. A conscientious objector in World War I and a pacifist opponent of Hitler, he published short stories, poetry, and novels, including *Peter Camenzind* 1904, *Siddhartha* 1922, and *Steppenwolf* 1927. Later works, such as *Das Glasperlenspiel/The Glass Bead Game* 1943, show the influence of Indian mysticism and Jungian psychoanalysis. Nobel Prize for Literature 1946.

Suggested reading
Field, G *Hermann Hesse* (1970)
Freeman, R *Hermann Hesse: Pilgrim in Crisis – A Biography* (1979)

Heston Charlton. Stage name of John Charles Carter (1924–). US film actor. He often starred in biblical and historical epics, for example, as Moses in *The Ten Commandments* 1956, and in the title role in *Ben Hur* 1959 (Academy Award). His other film appearances include *Major Dundee* 1965 and *Earthquake* 1974.

I have played three presidents, three saints and two geniuses. If that doesn't create an ego problem, nothing does.

CHARLTON HESTON
quoted in Leslie Halliwell *Filmgoer's Companion* 1965

Hevelius Johannes. Latinized form of Jan Hewel or Hewelcke (1611–1687). German astronomer who in 1647 published the first comparatively detailed map of the Moon in his *Selenographia*. He also discovered four comets and suggested that these bodies orbited in parabolic paths about the Sun.

Hevelius was born in Danzig (now Gdańsk). He worked as a brewing merchant and was a city councillor, but spent his evenings on the roof of his house, where he had an observatory installed 1641. This was destroyed by fire in 1679, with some of his notes. His wife Elizabeth assisted him in his work and, after his death, she edited and published his *Prodromus astronomiae* 1690.

Between 1642 and 1645, Hevelius deduced a fairly accurate value for the period of the solar rotation and gave the first description of the bright areas in the neighbourhood of sunspots. The name he gave to them, *faculae*, is still used.

Although Hevelius used telescopes for details on the Moon and planets, he refused to apply them to his measuring apparatus, and his observations of the positions of stars were made with the naked eye, not always accurately. His *Uranographia* 1690 contains a catalogue of more than 1,500 stars and a celestial atlas with 54 plates.

Hevesy Georg Karl von (1885–1966). Hungarian-born Swedish chemist, discoverer of the element hafnium. He was the first to use a radioactive isotope to follow the steps of a biological process, for which he won the Nobel Prize for Chemistry 1943.

He worked in Copenhagen at the Institute of Physics under Niels Bohr 1920–26 and 1934–43. During the German occupation of Denmark in World War II, Hevesy escaped to Sweden and became professor at Stockholm.

Hewett Dorothy Coade (1923–). Australian dramatist, poet and, writer. Her work is characterized by humorous and bawdy treatment of confessional and romantic themes. She is best known for her plays, including *The Chapel Perilous* 1972 and *The Man from Muckinupin* 1979. Her collections of poetry include *Rapunzel in Suburbia* 1975 and *Journeys* 1982.

Hewish Antony (1924–). English radio astronomer who was awarded, with Martin Ryle, the Nobel Prize for Physics 1974 for his work on pulsars, rapidly rotating neutron stars that emit pulses of energy.

The discovery by Jocelyn Bell Burnell of a regularly fluctuating signal, which turned out to be the first pulsar, began a period of intensive research. Hewish discovered another three straight away, and more than 170 pulsars have been found since 1967. Hewish has patented a system of space navigation using three pulsars as reference points, which would provide coordinates in outer space accurate up to a few hundred kilometres. He worked at the Cavendish Laboratory, and became professor at Cambridge 1972.

Hewitt Henry Kent (1887–1972). US admiral. An expert in amphibious operations, he commanded the landings at Casablanca 1942, after which he took charge of the US 8th Fleet in N African waters. He commanded the task force which landed US troops in Sicily and Italy 1943, and in 1944 commanded the US landings in S France.

Hey James Stanley (1909–). English physicist whose work in radar led to pioneering research in radioastronomy. He discovered that large sunspots were powerful ultra-shortwave radio transmitters, and pinpointed a radio source in the Milky Way. From 1940 to 1952 he was on the staff of an Army Operational Research Group. He then became a research scientist at the Royal Radar Establishment.

Cold, clever and ambitious, he was sceptical about everything except the obsessive pursuit of power.

Alan Bullock on REINHARD HEYDRICH
in *Hitler and Stalin* 1991

Heydrich Reinhard Tristan Eugen (1904–1942). German Nazi, head of the *Sicherheitsdienst* (SD), the party's security service, and Heinrich Himmler's deputy. He was instrumental in organizing the final solution, the policy of genocide used against Jews and others. 'Protector' of Bohemia and Moravia from 1941, he was ambushed and killed the following year by three members of the Czechoslovak forces in Britain, who had landed by parachute. Reprisals followed, including several hundred executions and the massacre in Lidice.

Heydrich is believed to have had Jewish ancestry, although this was not widely known at the time and seems, if anything, only to have made him a more fanatical Nazi. He was responsible for the fake attack on a German radio station at Gleiwicz 1939 which provided the pretext for the German invasion of Poland, and went on to organize the Einsatzgruppen 1941.

Heyerdahl Thor (1914–   ). Norwegian ethnologist. He sailed on the ancient-Peruvian-style raft *Kon-Tiki* from Peru to the Tuamotu Archipelago along the Humboldt Current 1947, and in 1969–70 used ancient-Egyptian-style papyrus-reed boats to cross the Atlantic. His experimental approach to historical reconstruction is not regarded as having made any important scientific contribution.

His expeditions were intended to establish that ancient civilizations could have travelled the oceans in similar fashion, but his theories are largely discounted by anthropologists, who rely on linguistic, sociological, and archaeological information. His voyages are described in *Kon-Tiki* and *The Ra Expeditions*. He also crossed the Persian Gulf 1977, written about in *The Tigris Expedition*.

Heyrovský Jaroslav (1890–1967). Czech chemist who was awarded the 1959 Nobel prize for his invention and development of polarography, an electrochemical technique of chemical analysis. Heyrovský's technique depends on detecting the discharge of ions during electrolysis of aqueous solutions. From 1920 he was on the staff of the Institute of Analytical Chemistry in Prague; in 1950 he became director of the newly founded Polarographic Institute of the Czechoslovak Academy of Sciences.

Seven cities warr'd for Homer, being dead, who, living, had no roof to shroud his head.

THOMAS HEYWOOD
The Hierarchy of the Blessed Angels 1635

Heywood Thomas (*c*. 1570–*c*. 1650). English actor and dramatist. He wrote or adapted over 220 plays, including the domestic tragedy *A Woman Kilde with Kindnesse* 1602–03. He also wrote an *Apology for Actors* 1612, in answer to attacks on the morality of the theatre.

Hezekiah in the Old Testament, king of Judah from 719 BC. Against the advice of the prophet Isaiah he rebelled against Assyrian suzerainty in alliance with Egypt, but was defeated by Sennacherib and had to pay out large amounts in indemnities. He carried out religious reforms.

Hiawatha 16th-century North American Indian teacher and Onondaga chieftain. He is said to have welded the Five Nations (later joined by a sixth) of the Iroquois into the league of the Long House, as the confederacy was known in what is now upper New York State. Hiawatha is the hero of H W Longfellow's epic poem *The Song of Hiawatha*.

Hibberd Jack (John Charles) (1940–   ). Australian dramatist. He is best known for *Dimboola* 1974, a warm-hearted send-up of a country wedding, which came to popular notice in a production directed by David Williamson and is now the most performed of all Australian plays. His other works include *A Stretch of the Imagination* 1973 and *One of Nature's Gentlemen* 1976.

Hick Graeme Ashley (1966–   ). Rhodesian-born cricketer who became Zimbabwe's youngest professional cricketer at the age of 17. A prolific batsman, he joined Worcestershire, England, in 1984. He achieved the highest score in England in the 20th century in 1988 against Somerset with 405 not out. He made his test debut for England in 1991 after a seven-year qualification period.

Hickey William (1749–1830). Irish writer. His entertaining *Memoirs* were first published 1913–25. Educated at Westminster School, he was intended to follow his father as an attorney in England but dissipation led to his being sent first to the East Indies and then to Jamaica, before he finally made good at the Indian Bar.

Hickok 'Wild Bill' (born James Butler Hickok) (1837–1876). US pioneer and law enforcer, a legendary figure in the West. In the Civil War he was a sharpshooter and scout for the Union army. He then served as marshal in Kansas, killing as many as 27 people. He was a prodigious gambler and was fatally shot from behind while playing poker in Deadwood, South Dakota.

He established his reputation as a gunfighter when he killed a fellow scout, turned traitor.

Suggested reading
Rosa, Joseph *They Called Him Wild Bill: The Life and Adventures of James Butler Hickok* (1964)

Hicks John Richard (1904–1989). English economist. He developed a theoretical framework for Keynesian analysis (known as IS–LM analysis) with an expenditure sector incorporating investment and savings (IS, investment–savings) and a monetary sector incorporating the demand for and supply of money (LM, liquidity–money). The extent to which an increase in the money supply affects expenditure depends on the sensitivity of expenditure to changes in interest rates.

He also developed, in his work *Theory of Wages* 1963, a model of industrial disputes which relates the length of strikes to the expected net costs of the strike to unions and management. Knighted 1964, Nobel Prize for Economics 1972.

Hidalgo y Costilla Miguel (1753–1811). Catholic priest, known as 'the Father of Mexican Independence'. He led a violent social protest 1810 against Spanish rule in which his forces swelled to 100,000. During the unrest the Indian population threatened Creoles as well as Spaniards, provoking a counter-revolution by the forces of law and order. Hidalgo attempted to form a separatist government but failed, losing the key battle of Calderón 1811. He was captured and shot by Creole-Spanish forces.

Hideyoshi Japanese warlord; see ◊Toyotomi Hideyoshi.

Higgins George Vincent (1939–   ). US novelist. He has written many detective and underworld novels, often set in Boston, including *The Friends of Eddie Coyle* 1972, *The Impostors* 1986, and *Trust* 1989.

Higgins Jack. Pseudonym of English novelist Harry ◊Patterson.

Highsmith Patricia (1921–1995). US crime novelist. Her first book, *Strangers on a Train* 1950, was filmed by Alfred Hitchcock. She excels in tension and psychological exploration of character. She wrote a series dealing with the amoral Tom Ripley, including *The Talented Mr Ripley* 1957, *Ripley Under Ground* 1971, *Ripley's Game* 1974, and *Ripley Under Water* 1991.

Hikmet Nazim (1902–1963). Turkish poet. Acclaimed since his death as a revolutionary hero, he was educated at Moscow University and was imprisoned in Turkey for his activities as a communist propagandist. His much-translated poems, which were banned in Turkey during his lifetime, include *Memleketimden insan manzaralari/Portraits of People from My Land* and *Seyh Bedreddin destani/The Epic of Shayk Bedreddin* 1936, about a religious revolutionary in 15th-century Anatolia.

Hilbert David (1862–1943). German mathematician, philosopher, and physicist whose work was fundamental to 20th-century mathematics. He founded the formalist school with *Grundlagen der Geometrie/Foundations of Geometry* 1899, which was based on his idea of postulates.

Hilbert attempted to put mathematics on a logical foundation through defining it in terms of a number of basic principles, which Kurt Gödel later showed to be impossible. In 1900 Hilbert proposed a set of 23 problems for future mathematicians to solve, and gave 20 axioms to provide a logical basis for Euclidean geometry. He was professor at Königsberg 1892–95 and at Göttingen 1895–1930.

Hildebrand Benedictine monk who became Pope ◊Gregory VII.

Hildebrandt Johann Lucas von (1668–1745). Italian-born Austrian architect. He trained under Carlo Fontana (1638–1714), the leading Baroque architect in late 17th-century Rome, and was successor to Viennese court architect Johann Fischer von Erlach (1656–1723). His Baroque masterpiece is the Belvedere, Vienna, 1693–1724, which comprises the Upper and Lower Palaces, divided by magnificent gardens.

Hildegard of Bingen (1098–1179). German abbess, writer, and composer. Her encyclopedia of natural history, *Liber simplicis medicinae* 1150–60, giving both Latin and German names for the species described as well as their medicinal uses, is the earliest surviving scientific book by a woman.

Hildegard was abbess of the Benedictine convent of St Disibode, near the Rhine, from 1136.

She wrote a mystical treatise, *Liber Scivias* 1141, and collected her lyric poetry in the 1150s into one volume, providing each individual text with music. The poetry is vivid, reflecting the visions she experienced throughout her life. The melodic structure of her music is based on a small number of patterns (similar to motifs), which are repeated in different modes.

Suggested reading

Beer, Frances *Women and Mystical Experience in the Middle Ages* (1992)

Flanagan, Sabina *Hildegard of Bingen: A Visionary Life* (1989)

Hill Archibald Vivian (1886–1977). English physiologist who studied muscle action and especially the amount of heat produced during muscle activity. For this work he shared the 1922 Nobel Prize for Physiology or Medicine.

He was professor at Manchester 1920–23 and at the Royal Society 1923–51. He also served as scientific adviser to India 1943–44 and was a member of the War Cabinet Scientific Advisory Committee during World War II.

Hill Austin Bradford (1897–1991). English epidemiologist and statistician. He pioneered rigorous statistical study of patterns of disease and, together with William Richard Doll, was the first to demonstrate the connection between cigarette smoking and lung cancer. Knighted 1961.

Hill took a degree in economics, and in 1923 began working for the Medical Research Council as a statistician. In 1933 he moved to the London School of Hygiene and Tropical Medicine, where he later became professor of medical statistics. His work on smoking and lung cancer, which involved collecting data on the smoking habits and health of over 30,000 British doctors for several years, in the precomputer age, is considered to be among the great medical achievements of the century.

Hill Benny (born Alfred Hawthorne) (1925–1992). English comedian. His television shows, which first appeared in 1952, combined the bawdy humour of the seaside postcard with the manic slapstick of the silent cinema, a format which he perfected but never really changed.

Hill was born in Southampton. His early career included work as a milkman and a period in the army during World War II, where he also appeared as a forces entertainer. As well as writing all the scripts and music for his shows, he often played all the characters himself. Regarded as too risqué early in his career, he was later condemned for being sexist, but many critics nevertheless saw him as the last of the great visual comics.

Hill (Norman) Graham (1929–1975). English motor-racing driver. He won the Dutch Grand Prix 1962, progressing to the world driver's title 1962 and 1968. In 1972 he became the first Formula One World Champion to win the Le Mans Grand Prix d'Endurance (Le Mans 24-Hour Race). He was also the only driver to win the Formula One World Championship, Le Mans 24-Hour Race, and the Indianapolis 500 Race in his career as a driver.

Hill started his Formula One career with Lotus 1958, went to BRM 1960–66, returned to Lotus 1967–69, moved to Brabham 1970–72, and formed his own team, Embassy Shadow, 1973–75. He was killed in an air crash. His son Damon won his first Grand Prix 1993, making them the first father and son to both win a Grand Prix.

Hill Joe (born Joel Emmanuel Hägglund) (*c.* 1872–1915). Swedish-born US labour organizer. A member of the Industrial Workers of the World (IWW, 'Wobblies'), he was convicted of murder on circumstantial evidence in Salt Lake City, Utah, 1914. Despite calls by President Wilson and the Swedish government for a retrial, Hill was executed 1915, becoming a martyr for the labour movement.

Hill Octavia (1838–1912). English campaigner for housing reform and public open spaces. She cofounded the National Trust 1894.

Hill Robert (1899–1991). British biochemist who showed that during photosynthesis, oxygen is produced, and that this derived oxygen comes from water. This process is now known as the Hill reaction. He also demonstrated the evolution of oxygen in human blood cells by the conversion of haemoglobin to oxyhaemoglobin.

Hill was educated at Cambridge and remained researching there until 1938. From 1943 to 1966 he was a member of the scientific staff of the Agricultural Research Council.

Hill Rowland (1795–1879). British Post Office official who invented adhesive stamps and prompted the introduction of the penny prepaid post in 1840 (previously the addressee paid, according to distance, on receipt). KCB 1860.

Hill and Adamson David Octavius Hill (1802–1870) and Robert R Adamson (1821–1848). Scottish photographers who worked together 1843–48. They made extensive use of the calotype process in their portraits of leading members of the Free Church of Scotland and their views of Edinburgh and the Scottish fishing village of Newhaven. They produced some 2,500 calotypes. Their work was rediscovered around 1900.

Hillary Edmund Percival (1919–). New Zealand mountaineer. He was in the reconnaissance party to Everest in 1951. In 1953, with Nepalese Sherpa mountaineer Tenzing Norgay, he reached the summit of Mount Everest, the first to climb the world's highest peak. As a member of the Commonwealth Transantarctic Expedition 1957–58, he was the first person since Scott to reach the South Pole overland, on 3 Jan 1958. On the way to the South Pole he laid depots for Vivian Fuchs's completion of the crossing of the continent. KCB 1953.

Suggested reading

Hillary, Edmund *High Adventure* (1955)

Hillary, Edmund *Nothing Venture, Nothing Win* (autobiography) (1975)

Hillel (born *c.* 60 BC). Hebrew scholar, lawyer, and teacher; member of the Pharisaic movement. His work was accepted by later rabbinic Judaism and is noted for its tolerance.

Hiller Wendy (1912–). English actress. Her many roles include Catherine Sloper in *The Heiress* 1947 and Eliza in the film version of Shaw's *Pygmalion* 1938. Her other films include *The Elephant Man* 1980. DBE 1975.

Hilliard Nicholas (*c.* 1547–1619). English miniaturist and goldsmith. He was court artist to Elizabeth I and James I. His sitters included the explorers Francis Drake and Walter Raleigh.

Hilliard was born in Exeter. After 1600 he was gradually superseded by his pupil Isaac Oliver, and in 1617 imprisoned for debt. His son Lawrence was also a miniaturist.

A fine collection of his brilliant, highly detailed portraits, set in gold cases, including *An Unknown Young Man Amid Roses* about 1590, is in the Victoria and Albert Museum, London. Between 1597 and 1603 he wrote a treatise on miniature painting called *The Arte of Limning*.

Suggested reading

Edmond, M *Hilliard and Oliver* (1984)

Reynolds, G *Nicholas Hilliard and Isaac Oliver* (1971)

Strong, R *Nicholas Hilliard* (1975)

Hilton Conrad Nicholson (1887–1979). US entrepreneur, founder of the Hilton Hotel Corporation 1946. During the 1930s he steadily expanded his chain of luxury hotels and resorts and reorganized it as the Hilton Hotel Corporation 1946. He based the firm's marketing appeal on its recognizable name and high-quality standardized service.

Born in San Antonio, New Mexico, USA, Hilton attended the New Mexico School of Mines and joined his father in various business ventures after graduation 1909. Originally successful in banking, he entered the hotel business after World War I, retiring 1966. His autobiography, *Be My Guest*, was published 1957.

Hilton James (1900–1954). English novelist. He settled in Hollywood as one of its most successful scriptwriters, for example, *Mrs Miniver*. His books include *Lost Horizon* 1933, envisaging Shangri-la, a remote district of Tibet where time stands still; *Goodbye, Mr Chips* 1934, a portrait of an old schoolmaster; and *Random Harvest* 1941.

> *Nothing really wrong with him – only anno domini, but that's the most fatal complaint of all, in the end.*
>
> JAMES HILTON
> *Goodbye, Mr Chips* 1934

Hilton Walter (*c.* 1340–1396). English mystic. He wrote *The Ladder of Perfection*, a treatise on asceticism and contemplation. It was widely circulated in manuscript and was one of the first books printed 1494 by Wynkyn de Worde (died *c.* 1534). It prescribes for the restoration of God's image in the soul by enduring the 'dark night' of detachment from worldly things. Hilton spent most of his life as an Augustinian canon.

Himes Chester Bomar (1909–1984). US novelist. After serving seven years in prison for armed robbery, he published his first novel *If He Hollers Let Him Go* 1945, a powerful depiction of racist victimization set in a Californian shipyard. He later wrote in the crime thriller genre, most notably in *The Real Cool Killers* 1958, *Rage in Harlem* 1965, and *Cotton Comes to Harlem* 1965. He also published two volumes of autobiography, *The Quality of Hurt* 1972 and *My Life of Absurdity* 1976.

> *We shall never be rough and heartless when it is not necessary.*
>
> HEINRICH HIMMLER
> Speech 4 Oct 1943

Himmler Heinrich (1900–1945). German Nazi leader, head of the SS elite corps from 1929, the police and the Gestapo secret police from 1936, and supervisor of the extermination of the Jews in E Europe. During World War II he replaced Goering as Hitler's second-in-command. He was captured May 1945 and committed suicide.

Hindenburg *German soldier and statesman Paul von Hindenburg (centre). As president of the German Republic he reluctantly appointed Adolf Hitler (left) as chancellor, on the recommendations of his advisers. Hermann Goering (right) was made president (speaker) of the Reichstag under Hindenburg. (Image Select)*

Born in Munich, he joined the Nazi Party in 1925 and became chief of the Bavarian police 1933. His accumulation of offices meant he had command of all German police forces by 1936, which made him one of the most powerful people in Germany. He was appointed minister of the interior 1943 in an attempt to stamp out defeatism and following the July Plot 1944 became commander in chief of the home forces. In April 1945 he made a proposal to the Allies that Germany should surrender to the USA and Britain but not to the USSR, which was rejected.

Hinault Bernard (1954–   ). French cyclist, one of three men to have won the Tour de France five times (1978–85); the others being Jacques Anquetil and Eddie Merckx.

> *We are no longer the prisoners of the key.*
>
> PAUL HINDEMITH
> *The Craft of Musical Composition* 1937

Hindemith Paul (1895–1963). German composer and teacher. His operas *Cardillac* 1926, revised 1952, and *Mathis der Maler/ Mathis the Painter* 1933–35, are theatrically astute and politically aware; as a teacher in Berlin 1927–33 he encouraged the development of a functional modern repertoire ('Gebrauchsmusik'/'utility music') for home and school.

In 1939 he emigrated to the USA, where he taught at Yale University and was influential in promoting a measured Neo-Classical idiom of self-evident contrapuntal mastery but matter-of-fact tone, exemplified in *Ludus Tonalis* for piano 1942 and the *Symphonic Metamorphoses on Themes of Carl Maria von Weber* 1944. In later life he revised many of his earlier compositions to conform with a personal theory of tonality.

Suggested reading
Hindemith, Paul *A Composer's World* (memoirs) (1952)
Kemp, I *Hindemith* (1970)
Skelton, Geoffrey *Paul Hindemith: The Man Behind the Music* (1975)

Hindenburg Paul Ludwig Hans Anton von Beneckendorf und Hindenburg (1847–1934). German field marshal and right-wing politician. During World War I he was supreme commander and, with Ludendorff, practically directed Germany's policy until the end of the war. He was president of Germany 1925–33.

Born in Posen of a Prussian Junker (aristocratic landowner) family, he was commissioned 1866, served in the Austro-Prussian and Franco-German wars, and retired 1911. Given the command in East Prussia Aug 1914, he received the credit for the defeat of the Russians at Tannenberg and was promoted to supreme commander and field marshal. Re-elected president 1932, he was compelled to invite Hitler to assume the chancellorship Jan 1933.

> *The German army was stabbed in the back.*
>
> PAUL VON HINDENBURG
> quoting an English general in a statement read to
> a Reichstag Committee of Inquiry 18 Nov 1919

Hindmarsh John (*c.* 1785–1860). English naval officer and colonial administrator in Australia, first governor of South Australia 1836–38. His attempts to move the settlement to the coast caused conflict with William Light and the South Australian Colonization Commissioners' representative J Fisher (1790–1875), and led to his replacement.

Hine Lewis Wickes (1874–1940). US sociologist and photographer. His dramatic photographs of child labour conditions in US factories at the beginning of the 20th century led to changes in state and local labour laws.

Trained as a sociologist at the University of Chicago and New York University, Hine documented social conditions by photographing the immigrants coming into the US at New York's Ellis Island 1904–08, as well as their tenement homes and the places and sweatshops in which they worked. His publication of those photos 1908 is considered the first 'photo story'. The National Child Labor Committee hired him to travel extensively in the US, photographing child labor conditions 1911–16. In later years, Hine photographed various government projects and construction of the Empire State Building, published 1930 in his *Men at Work*.

Hines Duncan (1880–1959). US travel author and publisher. He published restaurant and hotel reviews such as *Adventures in Good Eating* 1936 and *Lodging for a Night* 1939. A pioneer travel critic, Hines helped raise the standard of travel accommodation in the USA.

He was born in Bowling Green, Kentucky, USA. His guides were based on notes compiled during his work as a travelling salesman.

Hinkler Herbert John Louis (1892–1933). Australian pilot who in 1928 made the first solo flight from England to Australia. He was killed while making another attempt to fly to Australia.

Hinshelwood Cyril Norman (1897–1967). English chemist who shared the 1956 Nobel prize for his work on chemical chain reactions. He also studied the chemistry of bacterial growth. Knighted 1948.

Hinshelwood was born in London and studied at Oxford, where he became professor 1937. During World War I he worked in the Department of Explosives at the Royal Ordnance Factory in Queensferry, Scotland.

Studying gas reactions and the decomposition of solid substances in the presence and absence of catalysts, Hinshelwood went on to demonstrate that many reactions can be explained in terms of a series – a chain – of interdependent stages. At high temperatures the chain reactions of some elements accelerate the process to explosion point. He provided experimental evidence for the role of activated molecules in initiating the chain reaction. In his bacterial-growth experiments, too, he considered that all the various chemical reactions that occurred were interconnected and mutually dependent, the product of one reaction becoming the reactant for the next.

Hinton William Augustus (1883–1959). US bacteriologist and pathologist who worked on syphilis, in particular the development of the Hinton test.

In 1915 he was made chief of the Wasserman Laboratory, and from 1918 he was an instructor at the Harvard Medical School. In 1949, he became the first black professor in the university's history.

Hinton developed a blood-serum test for syphilis which reduced the number of false positive diagnoses of the disease; in 1934, the US Public Health Service showed the Hinton test for syphilis to be the best. He wrote many scientific papers and his book *Syphilis and its Treatment* 1926 was the first medical textbook by a black American to be published. Hinton was also the discoverer of the Davies–Hinton tests of blood and spinal fluid.

Hipparchus (*c.* 555–514 BC). Son of Pisistratus (*c.* 605–527 BC), he was associated with his elder brother Hippias who was tyrant of Athens. His affection being spurned by Harmodius, he insulted his sister, and was assassinated 514 BC by Harmodius and Aristogiton. This pair came to be known as the Tyrannicides, and were celebrated in a sculptural monument in the agora of Athens. The historian Thucydides challenged the contemporary popular notion that the pair had acted out of a hatred of tyranny.

Hipparchus (*c.* 190–*c.* 120 BC). Greek astronomer and mathematician who invented trigonometry and calculated the lengths of the solar year and the lunar month. He discovered the precession of the equinoxes, made a catalogue of 850 fixed stars, and advanced Eratosthenes' method of determining the situation of places on the Earth's surface by lines of latitude and longitude.

The difference in the length of the year can be accurately observed from the records on the bronze sphere in the Square Stoa at Alexandria.

HIPPARCHUS
On the Length of the Year

Hipparchus was born in Nicaea, Bithynia (now in Turkey), and lived on the island of Rhodes and in Alexandria, Egypt.

In 134 BC Hipparchus noticed a new star in the constellation Scorpio, a discovery which inspired him to put together a star catalogue – the first of its kind. He entered his observations of stellar positions using a system of celestial latitude and longitude, and taking the precaution wherever possible to state the alignments of other stars as a check on present position. He classified the stars by magnitude (brightness). His finished work, completed in 129 BC, was used by Edmond Halley some 1,800 years later.

Hipper Franz von (1863–1932). German vice-admiral. A rear-admiral at the start of World War I, he commanded the cruiser squadron which bombarded the Hartlepools 1914. He later commanded cruisers in the battles of the Dogger Bank and Jutland 1916, after which he was awarded the *Pour le Merite* by the Kaiser. He was promoted to commander in chief of the High Seas Fleet 1918.

Life is short, the Art long, opportunity fleeting, experience treacherous, judgment difficult.

HIPPOCRATES
Aphorisms I.1

Hippocrates (*c.* 460–*c.* 377 BC). Greek physician, often called the founder of medicine. Important Hippocratic ideas include cleanliness (for patients and physicians), moderation in eating and drinking, letting nature take its course, and living where the air is good. He believed that health was the result of the 'humours' of the body being in balance; imbalance caused disease. These ideas were later adopted by Galen.

He was born and practised on the island of Kos, where he founded a medical school. He travelled throughout Greece and Asia Minor, and died in Larisa, Thessaly. He is known to have discovered aspirin in willow bark. The *Corpus Hippocraticum/Hippocratic Collection*, a group of some 70 works, is attributed to him but was probably not written by him, although the works outline his approach to medicine. They include *Aphorisms* and the Hippocratic Oath, which embodies the essence of medical ethics.

Hippodamus (lived 5th century BC). Greek architect and town planner from Miletus. He was responsible for laying out the Athenian port of Piraeus. His reputation rests on the 'Hippodamian' design of criss-crossed streets. He also laid out the city of Rhodes.

Hirohito (regnal era name Shōwa) (1901–1989). Emperor of Japan from 1926, when he succeeded his father Taishō (Yoshihito). After the defeat of Japan in World War II 1945, he was made a figurehead monarch by the US-backed 1946 constitution. He is believed to have played a reluctant role in General Tōjō's prewar expansion plans. He was succeeded by his son Akihito.

As the war turned against Japan from June 1942, Tōjō involved him more in national life, calling upon the people to make sacrifices in his name. He belatedly began to exert more influence over his government as defeat became imminent in 1945, but was too late to act before the atomic bombs were dropped on Hiroshima and Nagasaki. His speech on Japanese radio 15 Aug 1945 announcing the previous day's surrender was the first time a Japanese emperor had directly addressed his people. The Shōwa emperor ruled Japan following World War II, during and after the US occupation, with dignity. He was a scholar of botany and zoology and the author of books on marine biology.

Hiroshige Andō (1797–1858). Japanese artist. He was one of the leading exponents of ukiyo-e prints, an art form whose flat, decorative style and choice of everyday subjects greatly influenced the development of Western art. His landscape prints, often employing snow or rain to create atmosphere, include *53 Stations on the Tokaido Highway* 1833. Whistler and van Gogh were among Western painters influenced by him.

Hitchcock *Suspense, melodrama, and fleeting personal appearances are the hallmarks of Alfred Hitchcock's films. A meticulous director, a supreme technician and visual artist, Hitchcock contributed significantly to the growth of cinema as an art form.*

Hiroshige was born in Edo (now Tokyo), and his last series, *100 Famous Views of Edo* 1856–58, was incomplete at his death. He is thought to have made over 5,000 different prints.

Hirst Damien (1965–   ). English artist. He won the Turner Prize 1995 with *Mother and Child Divided*, a bisected cow and calf presented in a glass case. His installation works include *Away from the Flock* 1994, a sheep pickled in formaldehyde and displayed in glass.

The main focus of his work has been an exploration of mortality, notably in his Natural History series in which dead animals are presented as reminders of death, evoking the fragility of life. Some of these works have provoked demonstrations by animal lovers.

Hiss Alger (1904–1996). US diplomat and liberal Democrat, a former State Department official, imprisoned 1950 for perjury when he denied having been a Soviet spy. There are doubts about the justice of Hiss's conviction.

Hiss, president of the Carnegie Endowment for International Peace and one of President Roosevelt's advisers at the 1945 Yalta Conference, was accused 1948 by a former Soviet agent, Whittaker Chambers (1901–1961), of having passed information to the USSR during the period 1926–37. He was convicted of perjury for swearing before the House Un-American Activities Committee that he had not spied for the USSR (under the statute of limitations he could not be tried for the original crime). Richard Nixon was a prominent member of the committee, which inspired the subsequent anticommunist witch-hunts of Senator Joseph McCarthy. The official Soviet commission on KGB archives reported in 1992 that Hiss had never been a spy.

Hitchcock Alfred Joseph (1899–1980). English film director, a US citizen from 1955. A master of the suspense thriller, he was noted for his meticulously drawn storyboards that determined his camera angles and for his cameo 'walk-ons' in his own films. His *Blackmail* 1929 was the first successful British talking film; *The Thirty-Nine Steps* 1935 and *The Lady Vanishes* 1939 are British suspense classics. He went to Hollywood 1940, and his work there included *Rebecca* 1940, *Notorious* 1946, *Strangers on a Train* 1951,

Rear Window 1954, *Vertigo* 1958, *Psycho* 1960, and *The Birds* 1963. His last film was the comedy thriller *Family Plot* 1976.

He also hosted two US television mystery series, *Alfred Hitchcock Presents* 1955–62 and *The Alfred Hitchcock Hour* 1963–65. KBE 1980.
Suggested reading
Deutelbaum, M and Poague, L (eds) *A Hitchcock Reader* (1986)
LaValley, Albert (ed) *Focus on Hitchcock* (1972)
Rohmer, Eric and Chabrol, Claude *Hitchcock* (1979)
Rothman, W *Hitchcock* (1982)
Spoto, D *The Dark Side of Genius* (1983)
Sterritt, David *The Films of Alfred Hitchcock* (1993)

Television has brought back murder into the home – where it belongs.

ALFRED HITCHCOCK
in the *Observer* 19 Dec 1965

Hitchens Ivon (1893–1979). English painter. His semi-abstract landscapes were painted initially in natural tones, later in more vibrant colours. He also painted murals, for example *Day's Rest, Day's Work* 1963 (Sussex University).

From the 1940s Hitchens lived in a forest near Midhurst in Sussex, which provided the setting for many of his paintings.

Hitchings George Herbert (1905–   ). US pharmacologist who shared the Nobel Prize for Physiology or Medicine 1988 with his co-worker Gertrude Elion (1918–   ). His work was on anticancer agents, and immunosuppressive drugs and antibiotics that were of vital importance in the growing surgical field of transplantation. In the 1970s, Hitchings and Elion's research produced an antiviral compound, acyclovir, active against the herpes virus, which preceded the development by Burroughs Wellcome of AZT, the anti-AIDS compound.

In 1942 he joined the biochemical research laboratory of Burroughs Wellcome, where he was joined two years later by Elion. Hitchings rose to vice president of the company 1967.

Hitler Adolf (1889–1945). German Nazi dictator, born in Austria. He was *Führer* (leader) of the Nazi Party from 1921 and wrote *Mein Kampf/My Struggle* 1925–27. As chancellor of Germany from 1933 and head of state from 1934, he created a dictatorship by playing party and state institutions against each other and continually creating new offices and appointments. His position was not seriously challenged until the failed July Plot 1944 to assassinate him. In foreign affairs, he reoccupied the Rhineland and formed an alliance with the Italian Fascist Benito Mussolini 1936, annexed Austria 1938, and occupied the Sudetenland under the Munich Agreement. The rest of Czechoslovakia was annexed March 1939. The Ribbentrop–Molotov pact was followed in Sept by the invasion of Poland and the declaration of war by Britain and France.

Hitler was born in Braunau-am-Inn, and spent his early years in poverty in Vienna and Munich. After serving as a volunteer in the German army during World War I, he was employed as a spy by the military authorities in Munich and in 1919 joined, in this capacity, the German Workers' Party. By 1921 he had assumed its leadership, renamed it the National Socialist German Workers' Party (Nazi Party for short), and provided it with a programme that mixed nationalism with anti-Semitism. Having led an unsuccessful uprising in Munich 1923, he served nine months in prison during which he wrote his political testament, *Mein Kampf*.

The party did not achieve national importance until the elections of 1930; by 1932, although Field Marshal Hindenburg defeated Hitler in the presidential elections, it formed the largest group in the Reichstag (parliament). As the result of an intrigue directed by Chancellor Franz von Papen, Hitler became chancellor in a Nazi–Nationalist coalition 30 Jan 1933. The opposition was rapidly suppressed, the Nationalists removed from the government, and the Nazis declared the only legal party. In 1934 Hitler succeeded Hindenburg as head of state. Meanwhile, the drive to war began;

Hitler *Führer of the Nazi dictatorship in Germany, Adolf Hitler. Whilst serving his prison sentence after the abortive Munich Putsch, Hitler wrote* Mein Kampf *outlining his expansionist politics and his anti-Semitic and anti-Communist beliefs.*

Ruisdael, with whose work Hobbema's has several points of similarity, though he did not possess Ruisdael's range. He was the outstanding interpreter of the Dutch rural picturesque in the second half of the 17th century, painting woods, water mills, winding tracks, streams and cottages with delightful sympathy. There is much that is obscure about his career and the chronology of his work. He obtained a post in the excise at 30, and it has been assumed that he then gave up painting, with the superb exception of his masterpiece, *The Avenue, Middelharnis.*

The nine paintings in the National Gallery, London, reflect the admiration which English connoisseurs had for his work in the 18th and 19th centuries, while his influence on English landscape is exemplified in Crome's reputed dying words: 'Hobbema, Hobbema, how I have loved you.'

> *No arts; no letters; no society; and which is worst of all, continual fear and danger of violent death; and the life of man, solitary, poor, nasty, brutish, and short.*
>
> THOMAS HOBBES
> *Leviathan* pt 1 ch 13 1651

Hobbes Thomas (1588–1679). English political philosopher and the first thinker since Aristotle to attempt to develop a comprehensive theory of nature, including human behaviour. In *Leviathan* 1651, he advocates absolutist government as the only means of ensuring order and security; he saw this as deriving from the social contract.

Hobbes analysed everything, including human behaviour, in terms of matter and motion. He is now best remembered for his political philosophy, in which he defended absolute sovereignty as the only way to prevent life from being 'nasty, brutish, and short', as he alleged it was in a state of nature. He based this absolute sovereignty on a social contract among individuals, but the sovereign has duties only to God.

Suggested reading
Dietz, M (ed) *Thomas Hobbes and Political Theory* (1990)
Goldsmith, M *Hobbes's Science of Politics* (1966)
Peters, Richard *Hobbes* (1956)
Rowse, A L *Four Caroline Portraits* (1993)
Sorrell, T *Hobbes* (1986)

Hobbs Jack (John Berry) (1882–1963). English cricketer who represented his country 61 times. In all first-class cricket he scored a world record 61,237 runs, including a record 197 centuries in a career that lasted nearly 30 years. Knighted 1953.

Hobson John Atkinson (1858–1940). British economist and publicist who was a staunch opponent of the Boer War 1899–1902. He condemned it as a conflict orchestrated by and fought for the preservation of finance capitalism at the expense of the British working class. In his *Imperialism: A Study* 1902, he argued that imperial expansion was driven by a search for new markets and opportunities for investment overseas. Resultant underconsumption of finance capital in the domestic arena stifled the development of social welfare policies which would benefit the impoverished classes.

Hochhuth Rolf (1931–). Swiss dramatist. His controversial play *Soldaten/Soldiers* 1968 implied that the British politician Churchill was involved in a plot to assassinate the Polish general Sikorski. *Der Stellvertieter/The Representative* 1963 dealt with the Nazi holocaust of the Jews.

Ho Chi Minh adopted name of Nguyen Tat Thanh (1890–1969). North Vietnamese communist politician, premier and president 1954–69. Having trained in Moscow shortly after the Russian Revolution, he headed the communist Vietminh from 1941 and fought against the French during the Indochina War 1946–54, becoming president and prime minister of the republic at the armistice. Aided by the communist bloc, he did much to develop industrial potential. He relinquished the premiership 1955, but continued as president. In the years before his death, Ho successfully led

Germany left the League of Nations, conscription was reintroduced, and in 1936 the Rhineland was reoccupied.

Hitler and Mussolini, who were already both involved in Spain, formed an alliance (the Axis) 1936, joined by Japan 1940. Hitler conducted the war in a ruthless but idiosyncratic way, took and ruled most of the neighbouring countries with repressive occupation forces, and had millions of Slavs, Jews, Romanies, homosexuals, and political enemies killed in concentration camps and massacres. He narrowly escaped death 20 July 1944 from a bomb explosion at a staff meeting, prepared by high-ranking officers. On 29 April 1945, when Berlin was largely in Soviet hands, he married his mistress Eva Braun in his bunker under the chancellery building and on the following day committed suicide with her.

Suggested reading
Bullock, Alan *Hitler: A Study in Tyranny* (1952)
Davidson, Eugene *The Making of Adolf Hitler* (1978)
Hamilton, Richard *Who Voted for Hitler?* (1982)
Payne, Robert *The Life and Death of Adolf Hitler* (1973)
Trevor-Roper, Hugh *The Last Days of Hitler* (1947)

Hoagland Mahlon Bush (1921–). US biochemist who was the first to isolate transfer RNA (tRNA), a nucleic acid that plays an essential part in intracellular protein synthesis.

He studied at Harvard University Medical School, and worked there 1953–67. In 1967, he was appointed professor at Dartmouth Medical School and scientific director of the Worcester Foundation for Experimental Biology in Shrewsbury, Massachusetts.

Hoban James C (1762–1831). Irish-born architect. He emigrated to the USA where he designed the White House, Washington, DC; he also worked on the Capitol and other public buildings.

Hobbema Meindert Lubbertzsoon (1638–1709). Dutch landscape painter. He is thought to have been the pupil of Jacob van

Hodgkin, Dorothy *British crystallographer Dorothy Hodgkin, who determined the structure of penicillin and vitamin B$_{12}$ using crystallographic methods. Hodgkin became the third woman to win a Nobel prize 1964 (for chemistry) and was admitted to the Order of Merit 1965 – the first female since Florence Nightingale.* (Image Select)

his country's fight against US-aided South Vietnam in the Vietnam War 1954–75.

Hockney David (1937–). English painter, printmaker, and designer, resident in California. He exhibited at the Young Contemporaries Show of 1961 and contributed to the Pop art movement. He developed an individual figurative style, as in his portrait *Mr and Mrs Clark and Percy* 1971 (Tate Gallery, London) and has experimented prolifically with technique. His views of swimming pools reflect a preoccupation with surface pattern and effects of light. He has also produced drawings, etchings (*Six Fairy Tales from the Brothers Grimm* 1970), photo collages, and sets for opera at La Scala, Milan, and the Metropolitan Opera House, New York.

If we are to change our world view, images have to change. The artist now has a very important job to do. He's not just a little peripheral figure entertaining rich people, he's really needed.

DAVID HOCKNEY
Hockney on Photography, 'New York: September 1986' 1988

Hockney, born in Yorkshire, studied at Bradford School of Art and the Royal College of Art, London. He was the subject of Jack Hazan's semi-documentary film *A Bigger Splash* 1974.

Suggested reading
Hockney, D *David Hockney by David Hockney* (1976)
Joyce, P *Hockney on Photography* (1988)
Livingstone, M *David Hockney* (1981)
Webb, P *Portrait of David Hockney* (1988)

Hodges Courtney (1887–1966). US general; one of the most competent, if not so well-known, US commanders of the war. He

organized the US landings on Omaha and Utah beaches on D-Day and succeeded Bradley in command of 1st Army Aug 1944. By Oct he had led the army through Luxembourg and Belgium, broken through the Siegfried Line, and captured Aachen. He held and eventually repulsed the main thrust of the German attack in the Battle of the Bulge and went on to cross the Rhine and link up with the 9th Army in encircling the Ruhr pocket.

Hodgkin Alan Lloyd (1914–). British physiologist engaged in research with Andrew Huxley on the mechanism of conduction in peripheral nerves 1945–60. He devised techniques for measuring electric currents flowing across a cell membrane. In 1963 they shared the Nobel prize. KBE 1972.

Hodgkin was born in Banbury, Oxfordshire, and educated at Cambridge, where he spent most of his career and became professor 1952.

Hodgkin and Huxley managed for the first time to record electrical changes across the cell membrane, and Hodgkin then built on these findings working with Bernhard Katz, another cell physiologist. They proposed that during the resting phase a nerve membrane allows only potassium ions to diffuse into the cell, but when the cell is excited it allows sodium ions (which are positively charged) to enter and potassium ions to move out. The extrusion of sodium is probably dependent on the metabolic energy supplied either directly or indirectly in the form of ATP (adenosine triphosphate). The amount of sodium flowing in equals that of the potassium flowing out.

Hodgkin Dorothy Mary Crowfoot (1910–1994). English biochemist who analysed the structure of penicillin, insulin, and vitamin B$_{12}$. Hodgkin was the first to use a computer to analyse the molecular structure of complex chemicals, and this enabled her to produce three-dimensional models. Nobel Prize for Chemistry 1964.

Hodgkin studied the structures of calciferol (vitamin D$_2$), lumisterol, and cholesterol iodide, the first complex organic molecule to be determined completely by the pioneering technique of X-ray crystallography, a physical analysis technique devised by Lawrence Bragg (1890–1971), and at the time used only to confirm formulas predicted by organic chemical techniques. She also used this technique to determine the structure of penicillin, insulin, and vitamin B$_{12}$.

Hodgkin Thomas (1798–1866). English physician who first recognized Hodgkin's disease. He pioneered the use of the stethoscope in the UK. He was also the first person to stress the importance of postmortem examinations. Hodgkin was born in London and studied at Guy's Hospital, London, and at Edinburgh, and lectured at Guy's 1827–37. He was active in the Aborigines Protection Society, and died in Jaffa (now in Israel) while on a mercy mission. His paper describing Hodgkin's disease was published 1832.

Hodgkinson Eaton (1789–1861). English civil engineer who introduced scientific methods of measuring the strength of materials. From a theoretical analysis, he devised experiments to determine the strongest iron beam, which resulted in the discovery of what is known as 'Hodgkinson's beam'. Hodgkinson helped civil engineer Robert Stephenson in the construction of the Menai and Conway tubular bridges by fixing the best forms and dimensions of tubes.

Hodgkinson was born in Anderton, Cheshire, and became a pawnbroker. He presented a number of scientific papers to the Literary and Philosophical Society in Manchester, and in 1847–49 was a member of a Royal Commission to inquire into the application of iron to railway structures. Also in 1847 he was appointed professor of the mechanical principles of engineering at University College, London.

Hodler Ferdinand (1853–1918). Swiss painter. His dramatic Art Nouveau paintings of allegorical, historical, and mythological subjects include large murals with dreamy Symbolist female figures, such as *Day* about 1900 (Kunsthaus, Zürich). His work prefigured Expressionism.

He studied art at Geneva with Barthélémy Menn and by copying old masters. He competed successfully for the decoration of the national museum at Zürich. Beginning as a portrait and landscape painter he turned to historical themes and finally evolved a decorative and symbolic style, as in his *Towards the Infinite*, which made a great impression in his lifetime and caused him to be regarded as the most distinguished of the purely Swiss school.

Hodza Milan (1878–1944). Czechoslovak politician, prime minister 1936–38. He and President Beneš were forced to agree to the secession of the Sudeten areas of Czechoslovakia to Germany before resigning 22 Sept 1938.

Hoe Richard March (1812–1886). US inventor of the rotary printing press 1846, which revolutionized newspaper printing. He also improved on the cylinder press for use in lithographic and letterpress work, and introduced the web press in the USA, making it efficient enough to supersede the rotary press in the 1880s.

Hoe was born in New York and worked in his father's firm manufacturing printing presses. His inventions led to expansion in New York, Boston, and the UK; between 1865 and 1870, a large manufacturing branch was built up in London, employing 600 people. Concerned for the welfare of his employees, he ran free evening classes for apprentices.

Hoess Rudolf Franz (1900–1947). German commandant of Auschwitz concentration camp 1940–43. Under his control, more than 2.5 million people were exterminated. Arrested by Allied military police in 1946, he was handed over to the Polish authorities, who tried and executed him in 1947.

Hoess was adjutant of Sachsenhausen concentration camp 1939 until his appointment to the newly-built camp at Auschwitz early 1940. It was originally run simply as a forced labour camp, but when he received orders to convert it into an extermination camp he installed four gas chambers and crematoria. Hoess found that gassing by carbon monoxide, the recommended method, was inefficient and introduced the cyanide gas Zyklon B, which improved his execution rate to 6,000 people per day. In late 1943 he was appointed chief inspector of concentration camps and worked hard to improve the 'efficiency' of the other extermination centres. Arrested and arraigned at Nuremberg, he appeared to be more upset about being thought inefficient than being thought callous. He was handed over to a Polish court, sentenced to death, and hanged at Auschwitz.

An ego is just imagination. And if a man doesn't have imagination he'll be working for someone else for the rest of his life.

JIMMY HOFFA
in *Esquire*

Hoffa Jimmy (James Riddle) (1913–c. 1975). US labour leader, president of the International Brotherhood of Teamsters (transport workers) from 1957. He was jailed 1967–71 for attempted bribery of a federal court jury after he was charged with corruption. He was released by President Nixon with the stipulation that he did not engage in union activities, but was evidently attempting to reassert influence when he disappeared. He is generally believed to have been murdered.

Suggested reading
Hoffa, James R *The Trials of Jimmy Hoffa* (autobiography) (1970)
Sheridan, Walter *The Fall and Rise of Jimmy Hoffa* (1972)

Hoffman Abbie (Abbot) (1936–1989). US left-wing political activist, founder of the Yippies (Youth International Party), a political offshoot of the hippies. He was a member of the Chicago Seven, a radical group tried for attempting to disrupt the 1968 Democratic Convention.

Hoffman was arrested 52 times and was a fugitive from justice 1973–80. He specialized in imaginative political gestures to gain media attention, for example throwing dollar bills to the floor of the New York Stock Exchange 1967. His books include *Revolution for the Hell of It* 1969. He campaigned against the Vietnam War and, later, for the environment. He committed suicide.

Hoffman Dustin (1937–   ). US actor. He became popular in the 1960s with his unconventional looks, short stature, and versatility. He won Academy Awards for his performances in *Kramer vs Kramer*

1979 and *Rain Man* 1988. His other films include *The Graduate* 1967, *Midnight Cowboy* 1969, *Little Big Man* 1970, *All the President's Men* 1976, *Tootsie* 1982, *Hook* 1991, and *Outbreak* 1995. He appeared on Broadway in the 1984 revival of *Death of a Salesman*, which was also filmed for television 1985.

Hoffmann Amadeus (born Ernst Theodor Wilhelm Hoffmann) (1776–1822). German composer and writer. He composed the opera *Undine* 1816, but is chiefly remembered as an author and librettist of fairy stories, including 'Nussknacker/Nutcracker' 1816. His stories inspired Offenbach's *Tales of Hoffmann*.

Hoffmann Josef (1870–1956). Austrian architect. Influenced by Art Nouveau, he was one of the founders of the Wiener Werkstätte/Vienna Workshops (a modern design cooperative of early 20th-century Vienna), and a pupil of Otto Wagner. One of his best-known works is the Purkersdorf Sanatorium 1903–05.

Hofmann August Wilhelm von (1818–1892). German chemist who studied the extraction and exploitation of coal-tar derivatives, mainly for dyes. He was professor at the Royal College of Chemistry in London 1845–65 and at Berlin from 1865.

In 1858 Hofmann obtained the dye known as fuchsine or magenta by the reaction of carbon tetrachloride (tetrachloromethane) with aniline (phenylamine). Later he isolated from it a compound which he called rosaniline and used this as a starting point for other aniline dyes, including aniline blue (triphenyl rosaniline). With alkyl iodides (iodoalkanes) he obtained a series of violet dyes, which he patented 1863. These became known as 'Hofmann's violets' and were a considerable commercial and financial success.

The term 'valence' is a contraction of his notion of 'quantivalence' and he devised much of the terminology of the paraffins (alkanes)

Hoffman, Dustin US film actor Dustin Hoffman in Rain Man *1988. A versatile performer, he is noted for his meticulous characterizations, often of vulnerable and unheroic men. His films include* The Graduate *1967 and* Midnight Cowboy *1969. In 1989 he appeared on the London stage as Shylock in Peter Hall's production of* The Merchant of Venice.

and their derivatives that was accepted at the 1892 Geneva Conference on nomenclature.

In 1881 he devised a process for the production of pure primary amines from amides.

Hofmann Hans (1880–1966). German-born painter. He was active in Paris and Munich 1915–32, when he moved to the USA. In addition to bold brushwork (he experimented with dribbling and dripping painting techniques in the 1940s), he used strong expressive colours. In the 1960s he moved towards a hard-edged abstract style.

He opened two art schools, in New York City and Provincetown, Massachusetts, and was influential among New York artists in the 1930s and 1940s. His teaching had a great impact on the Abstract Expressionists.

Hofmann Josef Casimir (1876–1957). Polish-born US pianist and composer. One of the great pianists of the Romantic repertory, his interpretation of Chopin and Liszt was considered to be his strongpoint. He influenced many young pianists as director of the Curtis Institute 1925–38.

Hofmeister Wilhelm Friedrich Benedikt (1824–1877). German botanist. He studied plant development and determined how a plant embryo, lying within a seed, is itself formed out of a single fertilized egg (ovule).

Hofmeister also discovered that mosses and ferns display an alternation of generations, in which the plant has two forms, spore-forming and gamete-forming.

Hofstadter Robert (1915–1990). US nuclear physicist who made pioneering studies of nuclear structure and the elementary nuclear constituents, the proton and the neutron. He established that the proton and neutron were not pointlike, but had a definite volume and shape. He shared the 1961 Nobel Prize for Physics.

Hofstadter demonstrated that the nucleus is composed of a high-energy core and a surrounding area of decreasing density.

He helped to construct a new high-energy accelerator at Stanford University, California, with which he showed that the proton and the neutron have complex structures and cannot be considered elementary particles.

From 1950 he was at Stanford, where his early work involved bouncing, or scattering, electrons from complex nuclei, such as gold. This produced accurate pictures of the charge distribution within nuclei. Gradually, smaller nuclei were studied by Hofstadter and his team, using electrons of increasing energy. By 1960, accurate data had been obtained for the proton and neutron, revealing the spatial distribution of charge and magnetization within these particles.

Hogan Ben (William Benjamin) (1912–). US golfer who won the Masters, the US Open, and the British Open in the same year, 1953, after a courageous recovery from a near-fatal car accident. He was a member of four Ryder Cup teams, playing captain in 1947 and 1949.

Hogan Paul (1940–). Australian TV comic, film actor, and producer. The box-office hit *Crocodile Dundee* (considered the most profitable film in Australian history) 1986 and *Crocodile Dundee II* 1988 (of which he was also co-writer and producer) brought him international fame.

Hogarth William (1697–1764). English painter and engraver. He produced portraits and moralizing genre scenes, such as the series of prints *A Rake's Progress* 1735. His portraits are remarkably direct and full of character, for example *Heads of Six of Hogarth's Servants* about 1750–55 (Tate Gallery, London).

Hogarth was born in London and apprenticed to an engraver. He published *A Harlot's Progress*, a series of six engravings, 1732. Other series followed, including *Marriage à la Mode* 1745, *Industry and Idleness* 1749, and *The Four Stages of Cruelty* 1751. In his book *The Analysis of Beauty* 1753 he attacked uncritical appreciation of the arts and proposed a double curved line as a key to visual beauty.

Suggested reading
Antal, Frederick *Hogarth and His Place in European Art* (1962)

Bindman, David *Hogarth* (1981)
Jarrett, Derek *The Ingenious Mr Hogarth* (1976)
Lindsay, J *Hogarth* (1979)
Paulson, R *Hogarth* (1971)

Hogben Lancelot Thomas (1895–1975). English zoologist and geneticist who wrote the best-selling *Mathematics for the Million* 1933. He applied mathematical principles to genetics and was concerned with the way statistical methods were used in the biological and behavioural sciences.

He held various academic posts in the UK, Canada, and South Africa, becoming professor of social biology at London University 1930. During World War II he was put in charge of the medical statistics records for the British army. After the war he became professor of medical statistics at the University of Birmingham, where he remained until he retired 1961.

Will you no come back again?

JAMES HOGG
'Will You No Come Back Again'

Hogg James (1770–1835). Scottish novelist and poet. He was known as the 'Ettrick Shepherd', being born in Ettrick Forest, Selkirkshire. He worked as a shepherd at Yarrow 1790–99. Until the age of 30 he was illiterate. His novel *Confessions of a Justified Sinner* 1824 is a masterly portrayal of personified evil.

Hogg Quintin. British politician; see Lord ◊Hailsham.

Hohenlohe-Schillingsfürst Prince Chlodwig Karl Victor von (1819–1901). German imperial chancellor from Oct 1894 until his replacement by Prince von Bülow Oct 1900.

Hohenstaufen German family of princes, several members of which were Holy Roman emperors 1138–1208 and 1214–54. They were the first German emperors to make use of associations with Roman law and tradition to aggrandize their office, and included Conrad III; Frederick I (Barbarossa), the first to use the title Holy Roman emperor (previously the title Roman emperor was used); Henry VI; and Frederick II.

The last of the line, Conradin, was executed 1268 with the approval of Pope Clement IV while attempting to gain his Sicilian inheritance. They were supported by the Ghibellines, who took their name from the family's castle of Waiblingen.

Hohenzollern German family, originating in Württemberg, the main branch of which held the titles of elector of Brandenburg from 1415, king of Prussia from 1701, and German emperor from 1871. The last emperor, Wilhelm II, was dethroned 1918 after the disastrous course of World War I. Another branch of the family were kings of Romania 1881–1947.

Hohfeld Wesley N(ewcomb) (1879–1918). US jurist. In his posthumously published *Fundamental Legal Conceptions as Applied to Judicial Reasoning* 1919 he criticized the imprecision of much legal terminology and formulated a system of jural relationships.

Hōjō family family that were regents (*shikken*) and effective rulers of Japan 1203–1333, during most of the Kamakura (Minamoto) shogunate. Among its members were Hōjō Yasutoki (regent 1224–42), Hōjō Tokiyori (regent 1245–56), and Hōjō Shigetoki (1198–1261), a high official whose writings on politics were influential.

The Hōjō were also among the last to hold out against the unification of Japan in the 16th century under Toyotomi Hideyoshi. Their castle of Odawara blocked his access to the Kantō area of central Honshu until 1590 when their ally Tokugawa Ieyasu, to whom they were related by marriage, sided with Hideyoshi and the castle capitulated after a siege.

Hokusai Katsushika (1760–1849). Japanese artist. He was the leading printmaker of his time and a major exponent of ukiyo-e. He published *36 Views of Mount Fuji* about 1823–29, and produced outstanding pictures of almost every kind of subject – birds, flowers, courtesans, and scenes from legend and everyday life. *Under the Wave at Kanagawa* (British Museum, London) is typical.

Hokusai was born in Edo (now Tokyo) and studied wood engraving and book illustration. He was interested in Western painting and perspective and introduced landscape as a woodblock-print genre. His *Manga*, a book crammed with inventive sketches, was published in 13 volumes from 1814.

Holbein Hans, the Elder (*c.* 1464–1524). German painter mainly of religious works, belonging to the school of van der Weyden and Memlinc in his early paintings but showing Renaissance influence in such a work as the *Basilica of St Paul*, 1502 (Augsburg). His principal painting is the altarpiece *St Sebastian*, 1515–17 (Munich). Financial failure ended his career as artist at Augsburg and ill success then seems to have pursued him at Isenheim and elsewhere. He had a strong sense of character in portrait drawings (as in the sketchbooks preserved at Berlin), which reappears in his great son, Hans Holbein the Younger.

Holbein Hans, the Younger (1497–1543). German painter and woodcut artist. The son and pupil of Hans Holbein the Elder, he was born in Augsburg. In 1515 he went to Basel, where he became friendly with the scholar and humanist Erasmus and illustrated his *Praise of Folly*; he painted three portraits of Erasmus 1523. He travelled widely in Europe and while in England as painter to Henry VIII he created a remarkable evocation of the English court in a series of graphic, perceptive portraits, the best-known being those of Henry VIII and of Thomas More. During his time at the English court, he also painted miniature portraits, inspiring Nicholas Hilliard. One of the finest graphic artists of his age, he executed a woodcut series *Dance of Death* about 1525, and designed title pages for Luther's New Testament and More's *Utopia*.

From 1532 London was his headquarters. He painted the German merchants of the steelyard, for example Jörg Gyze (Berlin), the famous portrait of *The (French) Ambassadors* (National Gallery, London) 1533, remarkable in technical skill and curious detail, though not his greatest triumph, and became court painter to Henry VIII 1536. The dynastic group for the Privy Chamber at Whitehall, including Henry VII, Henry VIII, Jane Seymour and Elizabeth of York, was destroyed by fire 1698, but in other works Holbein has left an imperishable record of the Tudors. Of his numerous portrayals of Henry VIII an authentic example is in the Thyssen Collection. He was compelled to paint elaborate details of court dress, but his later work is remarkable for an exquisite refinement of line and essential simplicity of design, as in the portrait he was sent to make at Brussels of the Duchess of Milan 1537 (National Gallery), and that of Anne of Cleves 1539 (Louvre). His other work in England included ornamental design (for example the drawing for the *Jane Seymour Cup* – Bodleian Library) and miniatures, beautiful examples of which are in the Victoria and Albert Museum. Holbein, though he may have inspired the miniaturist Hilliard in some degree, stands alone in the history of the English School and may be called a great internationalist of portraiture.

Suggested reading
Ganz, P *The Paintings of Hans Holbein* (1956)
Rowlands, John *The Paintings of Hans Holbein the Younger* (1985)
Strong, Roy *Holbein and Henry VIII* (1967)

Holborne Anthony (1584–1602). English composer. He was in the service of Queen Elizabeth I. His collection *The Cittharn Schoole* 1597 contains pieces for cittern and bass viol. A further collection, *Pavans, Galliards, Almains and Other Short Aeirs*, was published 1599.

Holbrooke Richard (1941–). US diplomat. He was appointed head of the US negotiating team in the Balkans July 1994 and within seven months had persuaded Bosnian Muslim and Croat leaders to sign an accord, leading to the creation of a Bosnian Muslim-Croat federation. He went on to negotiate an overall peace agreement Sept 1995.

Holbrooke served as an aide to Henry Cabot Lodge in Vietnam and returned to the state department in President Carter's administration, becoming assistant secretary at the age of 35. On Reagan's election, he left government to take up a financial career in Wall Street but returned to public service under President Bill Clinton, first as ambassador to Germany and then, from 1994, as assistant secretary of state for European and Canadian affairs. Disillusioned with the failure of the US administration to provide leadership in tackling the United Nations crisis in Bosnia-Herzegovina, Holbrooke was on the point of leaving his post when Clinton intervened personally, appointing him US special envoy in the former Yugoslavia.

Holden Charles Henry (1875–1960). English Modernist architect. He is known for his massive, austere, stone-faced buildings such as the headquarters of London Transport, over St James's station, London, 1927–29, and the Senate House, University of London, 1932. Following World War II, he was responsible, with William Holford, for the town-planning report for the City of London 1946–47. Early works of note include the King Edward VII Sanatorium at Midhurst, West Sussex 1903–06.

Holden Edith (1871–1920). English artist and naturalist. Daughter of a Birmingham manufacturer, she made most of her observations near her native city, and her journal, illustrated with her own watercolours, was published 1977 as *The Country Diary of an Edwardian Lady*.

Holden William. Stage name of William Franklin Beedle (1918–1981). US film actor. He was a star in the late 1940s and 1950s. He played a wide variety of leading roles in such films as *Sunset Boulevard* 1950, *Stalag 17* 1953, *Bridge on the River Kwai* 1957, *The Wild Bunch* 1969, and *Network* 1976.

Hölderlin (Johann Christian) Friedrich (1770–1843). German lyric poet. His poetry attempted to reconcile Christianity and the religious spirit of ancient Greece and to naturalize the forms of Greek verse in German. His work includes *Hyperion* 1797–99, an epistolary novel, translations of Sophocles 1804, and visionary poems such as the elegy 'Menons Klagen um Diotima/Menon's Lament for Diotima' and the brilliantly apocalyptic 'Patmos', written just before the onset of madness 1806.
Suggested reading
Peacock, Reginald *Hölderlin* (1973)
Shelton, R C *The Young Hölderlin* (1973)
Unger, Richard *Friedrich Hölderlin* (1984)

Holford William Graham, Baron Holford (1907–1975). British architect, born in South Africa. A leading architect/planner of his generation, he was responsible for much postwar redevelopment, including the plan for the City of London (with Charles Holden) and the precinct for St Paul's Cathedral, London, 1955–56. Knighted 1953, baron 1965.

Mom and Pop were just a couple of kids when they got married. He was eighteen, she was sixteen, and I was three.

BILLIE HOLIDAY
Lady Sings the Blues 1958

Holiday Billie. Stage name of Eleanora Gough McKay (1915–1959). US jazz singer, also known as 'Lady Day'. She made her debut in Harlem clubs and became known for her emotionally charged delivery and idiosyncratic phrasing; she brought a blues feel to performances with swing bands. Songs she made her own include 'Stormy Weather', 'Strange Fruit', and 'I Cover the Waterfront'.
Suggested reading
Clarke, Donald *Wishing on the Moon: The Life and Times of Billie Holiday* (1994)
Holiday, Billie *Lady Sings the Blues* (autobiography) (1956)
White, John *Billie Holiday: Her Life and Times* (1987)

Holinshed Raphael (*c.* 1520–*c.* 1580). English historian who published two volumes of the *Chronicles of England, Scotland and Ireland* 1578, on which Shakespeare based his history plays.

Times change, and we change with them.

RAPHAEL HOLINSHED
Chronicles of England Fo 996 1578

Holkeri Harri Hermanni (1937–). Finnish politician, prime minister 1987–91. Joining the centrist National Coalition Party (KOK) at an early age, he eventually became its national secretary.

Holland Henry Richard Vassall Fox, 3rd Baron Holland (1773–1840). British Whig politician. He was Lord Privy Seal 1806–07. His home, at Holland House, London, was for many years the centre of Whig political and literary society. Baron 1796.

Nephew of Fox, and friend of Grey, / Enough my need of fame / If those who deigned to observe me say / I injured neither name.

HENRY FOX, 3RD BARON HOLLAND
Lines found in Holland's handwriting on
his dressing-table after his death 1840.

Holland John Philip (1840–1914). Irish engineer who developed some of the first submarines. He began work in Ireland in the late 1860s and emigrated to the USA 1873. His first successful boat was launched 1881 and, after several failures, he built the *Holland* 1893, which was bought by the US Navy two years later.

Holland Sidney George (1893–1961). New Zealand politician, leader of the National Party 1940–57 and prime minister 1949–57. He removed wartime controls, abolished the upper house of parliament, the Legislative Council, suppressed the dock workers' strike of 1951 and participated in conferences on the Suez Crisis 1956. Knighted 1957.

An effective spokesman for uncomplicated ideas, dear to the 'average man'.

F L W Wood on SIDNEY GEORGE HOLLAND
in *Dictionary of National Biography*

Hollar Wenceslaus (1607–1677). Bohemian engraver. He was active in England from 1637, the first landscape engraver to work in England. He recorded views of London before the Great Fire of 1666. Born in Prague, he was appointed drawing master to the Prince of Wales. He made numerous plates of various other cities which he visited.

Hollerith Herman (1860–1929). US inventor of a mechanical tabulating machine, the first device for data processing. Hollerith's tabulator was widely publicized after being successfully used in the 1890 census. The firm he established, the Tabulating Machine Company, was later one of the founding companies of IBM.

Working on the 1880 US census, he saw the need for an automated recording process for data, and had the idea of punching holes in cards or rolls of paper. By 1889 he had developed machines for recording, counting, and collating census data. The system was used 1891 for censuses in several countries, and was soon adapted to the needs of government departments and businesses that handled large quantities of data.

Holley Robert William (1922–). US biochemist who established the existence of transfer RNA (tRNA) and its function. For this work he shared the 1968 Nobel Prize for Physiology or Medicine. He was on the staff at Cornell from 1948, becoming professor 1962. In 1966 he moved to the Salk Institute for Biological Studies in San Diego, California.

At Cornell he obtained evidence for the role of tRNAs as acceptors of activated amino acids. In 1958, he succeeded in isolating the alanine-, tyrosine- and valene-specific tRNAs from baker's yeast, and eventually Holley and his colleagues succeeded in solving the entire nucleotide sequence of this RNA.

Holliger Heinz (1939–). Swiss oboist and composer. He has created avant-garde works in lyric expressionist style, including *Siebengesang/Sevensong* 1967 for amplified oboe, voices, and orchestra. He has given first performances of Berio, Krenek, Henze, and Stockhausen.

He was ... well adapted to [a career in the security service]: ... a hard and conscientious worker, level-headed, fair-minded, and always calm.

Dick White on ROGER HOLLIS
in *Dictionary of National Biography*

Hollis Roger Henry (1905–1973). British civil servant, head of the secret intelligence service MI5 1956–65. He was alleged to have been a double agent together with Kim Philby, but this was denied by the KGB 1991. Knighted 1960.

Holloway Thomas (1800–1883). English manufacturer and philanthropist who made a fortune from patent medicines. He founded Royal Holloway College, London, opened 1886, as a college for women 'because they are the greatest sufferers'. The building cost him some £800,000.

They kicked us out the front door, so we went in the back door.

BUDDY HOLLY
quoted in Irwin Stambler *The Encyclopedia of Rock, Pop and Soul* 1989

Holly Buddy. Stage name of Charles Hardin Holley (1936–1959). US rock-and-roll singer, guitarist, and songwriter. He had a distinctive, hiccuping vocal style and was an early experimenter with recording techniques. Many of his hits with his band, the Crickets, such as 'That'll Be the Day' 1957, 'Peggy Sue' 1957, and 'Maybe Baby' 1958, have become classics. He died in a plane crash.
Suggested reading
Goldrosen, J and Beecher, J *Remembering Buddy Holly* (1987)
Laing, Dave *Buddy Holly* (1971)

Holmes Arthur (1890–1965). English geologist who helped develop interest in the theory of continental drift. He also pioneered the use of radioactive decay methods for rock dating, giving the first reliable estimate of the age of the Earth.

He was appointed in 1924 head of the Geology Department at Durham, moving in 1943 to Edinburgh University.

In 1928, Holmes proposed that convection currents within the Earth's mantle, driven by radioactive heat, might furnish the mechanism for the continental drift theory broached a few years earlier by German geophysicist Alfred Wegener. In Holmes's view, new rocks were forming throughout the ocean ridges. Little attention was given to these ideas until the 1950s. His books include *The Age of the Earth* 1913, *Petrographic Methods and Calculations* 1921, and *Principles of Physical Geology* 1944.

Holmes Oliver Wendell (1809–1894). US writer and physician. In 1857 he founded *The Atlantic Monthly* with J R Lowell, in which were published the essays and verse collected 1858 as *The Autocrat of the Breakfast-Table*, a record of the imaginary conversation of boarding-house guests. This was followed by *The Professor at the Breakfast-Table* 1860 and other 'Breakfast-Table' collections, and the novel *Elsie Venner* 1861. 'The Chambered Nautilus' is among his best-known poems.
Suggested reading
Small, Miriam *Oliver Wendell Holmes* (1962)
Tilton, Eleanor *Amiable Autocrat: A Biography of Oliver Wendell Holmes* (1947)

Holmes Oliver Wendell (1841–1935). US jurist and Supreme Court justice 1902–32, noted for the elegance of his written opinions. He was appointed to the US Supreme Court by President T Roosevelt, and during his office handed down landmark decisions in a number of antitrust, constitutional First Amendment, and labour law cases. He retired from the Court 1932.

Holmes was born in Boston, Massachusetts, the son of the writer and physician of the same name. He was educated at Harvard University. After service in the American Civil War 1861–65, he studied law and was admitted to the bar 1867. Holmes established a private practice in Boston and gained a reputation as an author and lecturer on legal subjects. He was appointed to the Massachusetts Supreme Court 1882.

Suggested reading

Burton, David *Oliver Wendell Holmes, Jr* (1980)
Howe, M D *Justice Oliver Wendell Holmes* (1957–63)
Monagan, J S *Grand Panjandrum* (1988)
White, G Edward *Justice Oliver Wendell Holmes: Law and the Inner Self* (1994)

Holmes à Court (Michael) Robert (Hamilton) (1937–1990). Australian entrepreneur. At the peak of his financial strength, before the stock-market crash 1987, he was the richest individual in Australia.

Holmes à Court owned 30% of Broken Hill Proprietary, Australia's biggest company; 10% of Texaco; and had substantial media, transport, and property interests. His personal fortune of about A$1.3 billion/£555 million halved in a matter of weeks after the stock-market crash. Having sold his master company, the Bell Group, to Alan Bond in 1988, he retired to being a private investor.

Holst Gustav(us Theodore von) (1874–1934). English composer of distant Swedish descent. He wrote operas, including *Sávitri* 1908 and *At the Boar's Head* 1924; ballets; choral works, including *Hymns from the Rig Veda* 1908–12 and *The Hymn of Jesus* 1917; orchestral suites, including *The Planets* 1914–16; and songs. He was a lifelong friend of Ralph Vaughan Williams, with whom he shared an enthusiasm for English folk music. His musical style, although tonal and drawing on folk song, tends to be severe. He was the father of Imogen Holst (1907–), musicologist and his biographer.

Holmes, Oliver Wendell *Oliver Wendell Holmes, US scientist and man of letters. His reflections in* The Autocrat of the Breakfast Table *and its sequels, many first published in* The Atlantic Monthly *are learned, witty, and humane.*

Suggested reading

Holst, Imogen *Gustav Holst: A Biography* (1938)
Rubbra, Edmund *Gustav Holst* (1947)
Short, Michael *Gustav Holst: the Man and his Music* (1990)

Holstein Friedrich August von (1839–1909). German diplomat and foreign-affairs expert. He refused the post of foreign minister, but played a key role in German diplomacy from the 1880s until his death.

Holt Harold Edward (1908–1967). Australian Liberal politician, prime minister 1966–67. His brief prime ministership was dominated by the Vietnam War, to which he committed increased Australian troops.

Holt was born in Sydney. He was minister of labour 1940–41 and 1949–58, and federal treasurer 1958–66, when he succeeded Menzies as prime minister. He was also minister for immigration 1949–56, during which time he made the first modifications to the White Australia Policy, relaxing some restrictions on Asian immigration. He was drowned in a swimming accident.

> *God give me work while I may live and life till my work is done.*
>
> WINIFRED HOLTBY
> Inscription on her grave.

Holtby Winifred (1898–1935). English novelist, poet, and journalist. She was an ardent advocate of women's freedom and racial equality, and wrote the novel *South Riding* 1936, set in her native Yorkshire. Her other works include an analysis of women's position in contemporary society, *Women and a Changing Civilization* 1934.

Holub Miroslav (1923–). Czech poet. A doctor specializing in immunology, amidst the discouragements of communist rule he courageously testified to humanistic values in terse and allusive poems. His collections include *Kam tece krev/Where the Blood Flows* 1963, *Udalosti/Events* 1971, and *Naopal/On the Contrary* 1982. *Notes of a Clay Pigeon*, a volume of poems in English translation, appeared 1977.

Holyoake Keith Jacka (1904–1983). New Zealand National Party politician, prime minister 1957 (for two months) and 1960–72, during which time he was also foreign minister. He favoured a property-owning democracy. He was governor-general 1977–80. GCMG 1970.

Home Alec Douglas-. British conservative politician. See ◊Douglas-Home.

Homer according to ancient tradition, the author of the Greek narrative epics, the *Iliad* and the *Odyssey* (both derived from oral tradition). Little is known about the man, but modern research suggests that both poems should be assigned to the 8th century BC, with the *Odyssey* the later of the two.

The epics, dealing with military values, social hierarchy, and the emotions and objectives of a heroic class of warriors, supported or opposed by the gods, had an immediate and profound effect on Greek society and culture and were a strong influence on the Roman poet Virgil in the composition of his *Aeneid*. The predominant dialect in the poems indicates that Homer may have come from an Ionian Greek settlement, such as Smyrna or Chios, as was traditionally believed.

Suggested reading

Camps, W A *An Introduction to Homer* (1980)
Kirk, G S *Homer and the Epic* (1965)
Vivante, P *Homer* (1985)
Wace, A J B and Stubbings, F H (eds) *A Companion to Homer* (1962)

Homer Winslow (1836–1910). US painter and lithographer. He is known for his vivid seascapes, in both oil and watercolour, which date from the 1880s and 1890s. Born in Boston, Homer made his reputation as a Realist painter with *Prisoners from the Front* 1866

(Metropolitan Museum of Art, New York), recording the miseries of the American Civil War. After a visit to Paris he turned to lighter subjects, such as studies of country life, which reflect early Impressionist influence.

Suggested reading
Beam, P *Winslow Homer* (1975)
Cooper, H *Winslow Homer's Watercolors* (1987)
Judge, M *Winslow Homer* (1986)
Wilmerding, J *Winslow Homer* (1972)

Homma Masaharu (1888–1946). Japanese general. Homma spent most of his military career in intelligence duties and had little experience of field command. He unwisely boasted he could complete the invasion of the Philippine Islands 1941 within 45 days. MacArthur withdrew into the Bataan Peninsula, prolonging the defence considerably, and Homma was reprimanded and replaced in all but name by General Yamashita. Homma was recalled to Japan and held administrative posts for the rest of the war. He was arrested by US troops Sept 1945, tried for his part in the 'Bataan Death March', and executed in Manila 1946.

Hon'ami Kōetsu (1558–1637). Japanese designer, calligrapher, and potter. As the central figure of a community dedicated to reviving the traditional arts and crafts of Kyoto, Kōetsu influenced all aspects of Japanese design. Famed for his calligraphy and ceramics for tea ceremonies, he also produced lacquer pieces, one of the finest of which is the *Boat Bridge Writing Box* early 17th century (National Museum, Tokyo).

Hondecoeter Melchior d' (1636–1695). Dutch artist. He painted large pictures of birds, both domestic fowl and exotic species, in grandiose settings. He was the pupil of his father, Gisbert Hondecoeter, and his maternal uncle Jan Weenix. He worked at The Hague, 1659–63, and then at Amsterdam. His most famous picture is *The Floating Feather* (Rijksmuseum).

Hone William (1780–1842). British journalist and publisher. In 1817, he was unsuccessfully prosecuted for his *Political Litany*, in which he expounded the journalist's right to free expression.

Honecker Erich (1912–1994). German communist politician, in power in East Germany 1973–89, elected chair of the council of state (head of state) 1976. He governed in an outwardly austere and efficient manner and, while favouring East–West détente, was a loyal ally of the USSR. In 1989, following a wave of prodemocracy demonstrations, he was replaced as leader of the Socialist Unity Party (SED) and head of state by Egon Krenz, and expelled from the Communist Party.

He directed the party's youth movement in East Germany after World War II, was elected to the East German parliament (Volkskammer) 1949, and became a member of the SED Politburo 1958. He was responsible for security, and instigated the building of the Berlin Wall 1961 and the infamous *Schiessbefehl* (shoot-to-kill order) against would-be escapees. During the 1960s he served as a secretary of the National Defence Council before being appointed first secretary of the SED 1971. After Walter Ulbricht's death 1973, Honecker became leader of East Germany. He permitted only limited economic reform and cultural liberalization during the 1970s and 1980s, but did foster closer relations with West Germany.

Mikhail Gorbachev's *glasnost* and *perestroika* initiatives in the Soviet Union, combined with the loss of Moscow's backing, resulted in large-scale civil disturbances 1989, and Honecker was replaced by his protégé Egon Krenz. Three weeks after his overthrow as Communist Party leader, the Berlin Wall was opened and the process of German reunification began. Within a year the two Germanies were reunited. He was placed under house arrest 1990 and charged with high treason, misuse of office, and corruption. In 1991 he was transferred from a Soviet military hospital to Moscow, but the German government demanded his return to face manslaughter charges in connection with the killing of those illegally crossing the Berlin Wall 1961–89. He returned to Germany 1992, but the courts ruled that he was too ill to stand trial (he had been terminally ill with liver cancer from mid-1989) and he was allowed to go into exile in Chile 1993. Unrepentant to his death, he was described by *Die Zeit* as 'the last German communist'.

Honegger Arthur (1892–1955). Swiss composer. He was one of the group of composers known as *Les Six*. His work was varied in form, for example, the opera *Antigone* 1927, the ballet *Skating Rink* 1922, the oratorio *Le Roi David/King David* 1921, programme music (*Pacific 231* 1923), and the *Symphonie liturgique/Liturgical Symphony* 1946. He also composed incidental music for Abel Gance's silent movie classics *La Roue/The Wheel* 1923 and *Napoléon* 1927.

Hōnen (1133–1212). Japanese Buddhist monk who founded the Pure Land school of Buddhism. Hōnen trained as a priest of the Tendai school before deciding in 1175 that calling on the name of the Buddha was sufficient to gain the believer entry to the Western Paradise after death. He travelled the country, teaching people the invocation *Namu Amida Butsu*. The popularity of his simple formula, with no ethics attached, attracted resentment from the established schools of Buddhism, and Hōnen was exiled to the island of Shikoku 1207–11.

His works are *Senjaku shū/Collection of Passages* 1198 and *Ichimai kishōmon/One-Page Testament* 1212.

Honthorst Gerrit van (1590–1656). Dutch painter. He used extremes of light and shade, influenced by Caravaggio, and painted biblical, mythological, and genre pictures. Around 1610–12 he was in Rome, studying Caravaggio. Later he visited England, painting *Charles I* 1628 (National Portrait Gallery, London), and later became court painter in The Hague.

Hooch Pieter de (1629–1684). Dutch painter. He was active in Delft and, later, Amsterdam. The harmonious domestic interiors and courtyards of his Delft period were influenced by Vermeer.

He is something more than a genre painter, for though his courtyards and interiors with their domestic figures and visitors give fascinating glimpses of everyday life, the beauty of these compositions primarily depends on the sense of space, the effect of light and exquisitely calculated arrangement, as for example in the *Courtyard of a Dutch House* (National Gallery, London) and the *Boy bringing Pomegranates* (Wallace Collection, London). An unfortunate change came over his work after 1657 and his move to Amsterdam, when his efforts to depict fashionable society in luxurious surroundings retained little trace of his earlier quality. At his best he comes near to Vermeer.

Hood Raymond Mathewson (1881–1934). US architect. He designed several New York skyscrapers of the 1920s and 1930s, and was a member of the team responsible for the Rockefeller Center, New York, 1929. Two of his skyscrapers, the *Daily News* building 1930 and the McGraw-Hill building, 1931, with its distinctive green-tile cladding, are seminal works of the Art Deco style. With S Gordon Jeeves he built the National Radiator building in London 1928, faced with black tiles and coloured Egyptian-style decoration.

Hood Samuel, 1st Viscount Hood (1724–1816). British admiral. A masterly tactician, he defeated the French at Dominica in the West Indies 1783, and in the Revolutionary Wars captured Toulon and Corsica. Baronet 1779, viscount 1796.

I remember, I remember, / The house where I was born.

THOMAS HOOD
'I Remember'

Hood Thomas (1799–1845). English poet and humorist. Born in London, he entered journalism, and edited periodicals, for example, *Hood's Monthly Magazine* 1844. Although remembered primarily for his comic verse, for example, 'Miss Kilmansegg', he also wrote serious poems such as 'Song of the Shirt' 1843, a protest against poorly paid labour, and 'Bridge of Sighs' 1843, about the suicide of a prostitute.

Hook Sidney (1902–1989). US philosopher. He is noted for his interpretations of John Dewey and Karl Marx. He held that our ideas are not true or false propositions but guides to action and experiment, and that Marx held that knowledge was primarily an activity, too. Accordingly, he saw philosophy as an empirical discipline, similar to the social sciences. He attacked Martin Heidegger's notion of being. Born in New York, he taught at New York University 1927–69. His works include *From Hegel to Marx* 1936 and *The Quest for Being* 1961.

Hooke Robert (1635–1703). English scientist and inventor, originator of Hooke's law, and considered the foremost mechanic of his time. Hooke's law, formulated 1676, states that the tension in a lightly stretched spring is proportional to its extension from its natural length. His inventions included a telegraph system, the spirit level, marine barometer, and sea gauge. He coined the term 'cell' in biology.

He studied elasticity, furthered the sciences of mechanics and microscopy, invented the hairspring regulator in timepieces, perfected the air pump, and helped improve such scientific instruments as microscopes, telescopes, and barometers. His work on gravitation and in optics contributed to the achievements of his contemporary Isaac Newton.

Hooke was born in Freshwater on the Isle of Wight and educated at Oxford, where he became assistant to Irish physicist Robert Boyle. Moving to London 1663, he became curator of the newly established Royal Society, which entailed demonstrating new experiments at weekly meetings. He was also professor of geometry at Gresham College, London, from 1665.

Hooker John Lee (1917–). US blues guitarist, singer, and songwriter. He was one of the foremost blues musicians. His first record, 'Boogie Chillen' 1948, was a blues hit and his percussive guitar style made him popular with rock audiences from the 1950s. His albums include *Urban Blues* 1968 and *Boom Boom* 1992 (also the title of his 1962 song).

Hooker Joseph Dalton (1817–1911). English botanist who travelled to the Antarctic and India, and made many botanical discoveries. His works include *Flora Antarctica* 1844–47, *Genera plantarum* 1862–83, and *Flora of British India* 1875–97.

In 1865 he succeeded his father, William Jackson Hooker (1785–1865), as director of the Royal Botanic Gardens, Kew, London. Knighted 1877.

He joined an expedition to locate the magnetic South Pole 1839–43, in the course of which he visited the Falkland Islands, Tasmania, and New Zealand. From 1847 to 1850 he undertook a botanical exploration of NE India and the Himalayas, and sent back to England many previously unknown species of rhododendron. From 1855 he worked at Kew; under his directorship, the *Index Kewensis* was founded 1883; this is a list of all scientific plant names, accompanied by descriptions.

Hooker Richard (*c.* 1554–1600). English theologian, author of *The Laws of Ecclesiastical Polity* 1594, a defence of the episcopalian system of the Church of England.

Hooker Stanley George (1907–1984). English engineer responsible for the development of aircraft engines such as the Proteus turboprop 1957, Orpheus turbojet 1958, Pegasus vectored-thrust turbofan, Olympus turbojet, and RB-211 turbofan. Knighted 1974.

He spent his career at Rolls-Royce (from 1938) and the Bristol Aeroplane Company, which merged with Rolls-Royce 1966.

Hooker Thomas (1586–1647). British colonial religious leader in America. A Puritan, he opposed the religious leadership of Cambridge colony, and led a group of his followers westward to the Connecticut Valley, founding Hartford 1636. He became the *de facto* leader of the colony and in 1639 helped to formulate Connecticut's first constitution, the Fundamental Orders.

Born in England and educated as a minister at Cambridge, Hooker served at parishes in England before fleeing to Holland in 1630 because of his Puritan beliefs. In 1633 he emigrated to the Massachusetts Bay Colony, settling in Cambridge.

Hooper John (*c.* 1495–1555). English Protestant reformer and martyr. He adopted the views of the Swiss Protestant Ulrich Zwingli and was appointed bishop of Gloucester 1550. He was burned to death for heresy.

When there is a lack of honour in government, the morals of the whole people are poisoned.

HERBERT HOOVER
in *New York Times* 9 Aug 1964

Hoover Herbert Clark (1874–1964). 31st president of the USA 1929–33, a Republican. He was secretary of commerce 1921–28. Hoover lost public confidence after the stock-market crash of 1929, when he opposed direct government aid for the unemployed in the Depression that followed.

As a mining engineer, Hoover travelled widely before World War I. After the war he organized relief work in occupied Europe; a talented administrator, he was subsequently associated with numerous international relief organizations, and became food administrator for the USA 1917–19. He defeated the Democratic candidate for the presidency, Al Smith (1873–1944), by a wide margin. The shantytowns, or Hoovervilles, of the homeless that sprang up around large cities after the stock-market crash were evidence of his failure to cope with the effects of the Depression and prevent the decline of the economy. He was severely criticized for his adamant opposition to federal relief for the unemployed, even after the funds of states, cities, and charities were exhausted. In 1933 he was succeeded by F D Roosevelt.

Hoover was called upon to administer the European Food Program 1947, and in the late 1950s he headed two Hoover commissions that recommended reforms in government structure and operations.

Suggested reading
Burner, D *Herbert Hoover: A Public Life* (1979)
Nash, G H *The Life of Herbert Hoover* (1983–88)
Smith, R *An Uncommon Man* (1984)
Warren, H G *Hoover and the Great Depression* (1959)
Wilson, Joan H *Herbert Hoover: Forgotten Progressive* (1975)

Hoover, Herbert US Republican politician Herbert Hoover, whose term as president coincided with the financial collapse of 1929 and the ensuing Depression. Hoover, who believed in ultimate recovery through private enterprise, was criticized for the ineffectiveness of the measures he initiated.

Hoover J(ohn) Edgar (1895–1972). US director of the Federal Bureau of Investigation (FBI) from 1924. He built up a powerful network for the detection of organized crime. His drive against alleged communist activities after World War II, and his opposition to the Kennedy administration and others brought much criticism over abuse of power.

He served under eight presidents, none of whom would dismiss him, since he kept files on them and their associates. Hoover waged a personal campaign of harassment against leaders of the civil rights movement, notably Dr Martin Luther King, Jr.

Suggested reading
Gentry, Curt *J Edgar Hoover: The Man and His Secrets* (1991)
Nash, J R *Citizen Hoover* (1972)
Theoharis, A G and Cox, J S *The Boss* (1988)

Hoover William Henry (1849–1932). US manufacturer who developed the vacuum cleaner. 'Hoover' soon became a generic name for vacuum cleaner.

When Hoover's business as a leather manufacturer for carriages and wagons was threatened by the advent of the automobile, he concentrated on developing a primitive existing cleaner into an effective tool for domestic use.

Hope A(lec) D(erwent) (1907–). Australian poet and critic noted for his skilfully crafted verse rich in biblical and literary allusions. His published collections include *The Wandering Islands* 1955, *Collected Poems 1930–1965* 1966, *A Late Picking* 1975, and *Antechinus* 1981. He has also published several collections of essays.

'Boys will be boys ' / 'And even that ... wouldn't matter if we could only prevent girls from being girls.'

ANTHONY HOPE
Dolly Dialogues 1894

Hope Anthony. Pen name of Anthony Hope Hawkins (1863–1933). English novelist. His romance *The Prisoner of Zenda* 1894, and its sequel *Rupert of Hentzau* 1898, introduced the imaginary Balkan state of Ruritania. Knighted 1918.

The girls call me Pilgrim because every time I dance with one I make a little progress.

BOB HOPE
Ghost Breakers 1940

Hope Bob. Stage name of Leslie Townes Hope (1903–). British-born US comedian. He is best remembered for seven films he made with Bing Crosby and Dorothy Lamour between 1940 and 1953, whose titles all began *The Road to* (*Singapore, Zanzibar, Morocco, Utopia, Rio, Bali,* and *Hong Kong*). Other films include *The Cat and the Canary* 1939 and *The Facts of Life* 1960.

He was taken to the USA 1907, and became a Broadway and radio star in the 1930s. He has received several special Academy Awards.

Suggested reading
Hope, Bob *Have Tux, Will Travel* (autobiography) (1954)
Trescott, P *Bob Hope* (1988)

Hope John Adrian Louis, 7th Earl of Hopetoun, 1st Marquess Linlithgow (1860–1908). British administrator in Australia, born in Scotland. He was governor of Victoria 1889–95 and first governor-general of Australia 1901–03. Earl 1873, marquess 1902.

Hopkins Anthony Philip (1937–). Welsh actor. Among his stage appearances are *Equus, Macbeth, Pravda,* and the title role in *King Lear*. His films include *The Lion in Winter* 1968, *A Bridge Too Far* 1977, *The Elephant Man* 1980, *84 Charing Cross Road* 1986, *The Silence of the Lambs* (Academy Award) 1991, *Howards End* 1992, and *Shadowlands* and *The Remains of the Day*, both 1993. Knighted 1995.

Hopkins Frederick Gowland (1861–1947). English biochemist whose research into diets revealed the necessity of certain trace sub-

stances, now known as vitamins, for the maintenance of health. Hopkins shared the 1929 Nobel Prize for Physiology or Medicine with Christiaan Eijkman, who had arrived at similar conclusions. In 1914 he was appointed professor of biochemistry at Cambridge. Knighted 1925.

Hopkins also established that there are certain amino acids that the body cannot produce itself. Another discovery he took part in was that contracting muscle accumulates lactic acid. Experimenting on rats fed on artificial milk, Hopkins noticed in 1906 that animals cannot survive on a diet containing only proteins, fats, and carbohydrates. When a small quantity of cow's milk was added, the rats grew. He concluded that the milk must contain accessory food factors in trace amounts, but he failed to isolate these.

Glory be to God for dappled things – / For skies of couple-colour as a brinded cow.

GERARD MANLEY HOPKINS
'Pied Beauty'

Hopkins Gerard Manley (1844–1889). English poet and Jesuit priest. His work, which is marked by its originality of diction and rhythm, and includes 'The Wreck of the Deutschland' and 'The Windhover', was published posthumously 1918 by Robert Bridges. His poetry is profoundly religious and records his struggle to gain faith and peace, but also shows freshness of feeling and delight in nature. His employment of 'sprung rhythm' (combination of traditional regularity of stresses with varying numbers of syllables in each line) greatly influenced later 20th-century poetry.

Hopkins was born at Stratford, Essex. He converted to Roman Catholicism 1866 and in 1868 began training as a Jesuit. He was ordained 1877 and taught Greek and Latin at University College, Dublin, 1884–89.

Suggested reading
Bergonzi, Bernard *Gerard Manley Hopkins* (1977)
Gardner, W H *Gerard Manley Hopkins* (1944–49)
Kitchen, Paddy *Gerard Manley Hopkins* (1978)
Mackenzie, N H *A Reader's Guide to Gerard Manley Hopkins* (1981)
Martin, R B *Gerard Manley Hopkins: A Very Private Life* (1991)
White, Norman *Hopkins: A Literary Biography* (1992)

Hopkins Harry Lloyd (1890–1946). US government official. Originally a social worker, in 1935 he became head of the WPA (Works Progress Administration), which was concerned with Depression relief work. After a period as secretary of commerce 1938–40, he was appointed supervisor of the lend-lease programme 1941, and undertook missions to Britain and the USSR during World War II.

Hopkins Mark (1802–1887). US educator and religious leader, president of Williams College 1836–72 and of the American Board of Commissioners for Foreign Missions 1857–87. He was also known as a popular lecturer and author on religious subjects.

Born in Stockbridge, Massachusetts, Hopkins was educated at Williams College and received an MD degree from Berkshire College 1829. In 1830 he was appointed professor of philosophy at Williams College and president 1836–72. Increasingly involved in religious affairs, Hopkins was ordained a Congregationalist minister 1836.

Höpner Erich (1886–1944). German general, skilled in armoured warfare. Höpner was involved in a plot to arrest Hitler if he ordered an attack on Czechoslovakia 1938, but it came to nothing when the Munich Agreement allowed him to take the country without military force. Höpner was dismissed from his command of a Panzer group by Hitler and discharged from the Army in disgrace after he was forced to withdraw from an attack on Moscow by a Soviet counter-attack. He then became involved with anti-Nazi groups and was designated to become commander in chief of the Home Army after the July Plot 1944. The plot failed and, along with thousands of others, Höpner was arrested and executed 8 Aug 1944.

Hopper Dennis (1936–   ). US film actor and director. He caused a sensation with the anti-establishment *Easy Rider* 1969, but his *The Last Movie* 1971 was poorly received by the critics. He made a comeback in the 1980s directing such films as *Colors* 1988. His work as an actor includes *Rebel Without a Cause* 1955, *The American Friend/Der amerikanische Freund* 1977, *Apocalypse Now* 1979, *Blue Velvet* 1986, and *Speed* 1994.

I sure learned a lot from the guy – and it sure got me into trouble.

Dennis Hopper
speaking of his friendship with JAMES DEAN, at Cannes 26 May 1976

Hopper Edward (1882–1967). US painter and etcher. He was one of the foremost American Realists, and never followed avant-garde trends. His views of life in New England and New York in the 1930s and 1940s, painted in rich, dark colours, convey a brooding sense of emptiness and solitude, as in *Nighthawks* 1942 (Art Institute, Chicago). Hopper's teacher Robert Henri, associated with the Ashcan School, was a formative influence.

Hopper Grace (1906–1992). US computer pioneer who created the first compiler and helped invent the computer language COBOL. She also coined the term 'debug'.

Hopper was educated at Vassar and Yale. She volunteered for duty in World War II with the Naval Ordinance Computation Project. This was the beginning of a long association with the Navy (she was appointed rear admiral 1983). After the war, Hopper joined a firm that eventually would become the Univac division of Sperry-Rand, to manufacture a commercial computer.

In 1945 she was ordered to Harvard University to assist Howard Aiken in building a computer. One day a breakdown of the machine was found to be due to a moth that had flown into the computer. Aiken came into the laboratory as Hopper was dealing with the insect. 'Why aren't you making numbers, Hopper?' he asked. Hopper replied: 'I am debugging the machine!'

Hopper's main contribution was to create the first computer language, together with the compiler needed to translate the instructions into a form that the computer could work with. In 1959, she was invited to join a Pentagon team attempting to create and standardize a single computer language for commercial use. This led to the development of COBOL, still one of the most widely used languages.

Hopper Hedda (1890–1966). US actress and celebrity reporter. From 1915 she appeared in many silent films and after a brief retirement was hired as a radio gossip reporter in 1936. From 1938 Hopper wrote a syndicated newspaper column about the private lives of the Hollywood stars. She carried on a widely publicized feud with rival columnist Louella Parsons.

Born Elda Furry in Hollidaysburg, Pennsylvania, she left home as a teenager to begin a theatrical career. First appearing on the Broadway stage in 1909, she adopted her professional name after marrying actor DeWolf Hopper.

Hoppner John (1758–1810). English portrait painter, born in England of German parentage. He studied at the Royal Academy Schools, and became portrait painter to the Prince of Wales (later George IV) 1789. He was a follower of Joshua Reynolds and in popularity a rival to Thomas Lawrence, though in quality and technique by no means of the same rank. Among his paintings are portraits of the royal princesses, William Pitt, and Admiral Nelson. His *Mrs Williams* (Tate Gallery) shows him at his best.

Horace (full name Quintus Horatius Flaccus) (65–8 BC). Roman lyric poet and satirist. He became a leading poet under the patronage

---

It is a sweet and becoming thing to die for one's country.

HORACE
Odes III. 2

---

of Emperor Augustus. His works include *Satires* 35–30 BC; the four books of *Odes*, about 25–24 BC; *Epistles*, a series of verse letters; and an influential critical work, *Ars poetica*. They are distinguished by their style, wit, discretion, and patriotism.

Born at Venusia, S Italy, the son of a freedman, Horace fought under Brutus at Philippi, lost his estate, and was reduced to poverty. In about 38 Virgil introduced him to Maecenas, who gave him a farm in the Sabine hills and recommended him to the patronage of Augustus.

Suggested reading
Fraenkel, E *Horace* (1957)
Monagan, John *Horace: Priest of the Poor* (1985)
Shackleton-Bailey, D R *Profile of Horace* (1982)

Hordern Michael Murray (1911–1995). English character actor. He has appeared in stage roles such as Shakespeare's Lear and Prospero, and in plays by Tom Stoppard and Harold Pinter. His films include *The Man Who Never Was* 1956, *The Spy Who Came in From the Cold* 1965, *The Bed Sitting Room* 1969, and *Joseph Andrews* 1976. Knighted 1983.

[He has] very exceptional qualities of courage, imagination, and drive ... he has done more for the army than anyone since Haldane.

Neville Chamberlain on LESLIE HORE-BELISHA
in *Dictionary of National Biography*

Hore-Belisha (Isaac) Leslie, 1st Baron Hore-Belisha (1893–1957). British politician. A National Liberal, he was minister of transport 1934–37, introducing Belisha beacons to mark pedestrian crossings. As war minister from 1937, until removed by Chamberlain 1940 on grounds of temperament, he introduced peacetime conscription 1939. Baron 1954.

Horkheimer Max (1895–1973). German social theorist. He rejected empiricism and positivism and believed technology posed a threat to culture and civilization because the physical sciences upon which it is based ignored human values.

Horkheimer was director of the Institut für Sozialforschung (Institute for Social Research) in Frankfurt from 1930. When the Nazis came to power, he moved with the institute to Columbia University, New York, and later to California. He returned to Frankfurt 1949 and became rector of the university there 1951.

In his seminal papers of the 1930s, collected under the title *Kritische Theorie/Critical Theory: Selected Essays* 1968, he argues that only a radical transformation in social theory and practice will cure modern civilization of its sickness. The analysis of society is partly a function of social life – its concepts, as well as what it studies, are products of social and economic processes – but it is also autonomous. 'Critical theory' has to discover and describe the social origins of knowledge in order to emancipate human beings.

He collaborated with, among others, Theodor W Adorno on *Dialectic of Enlightenment* 1947, and also with Herbert Marcuse.

Horn Gyula (1932–   ). Hungarian economist and politician, president of the Hungarian Socialist Party (HSP) from 1990 and prime minister from 1994. Under his leadership the ex-communist HSP enjoyed a resurgence, capturing an absolute majority in the July 1994 assembly elections. Despite opposition to the ongoing economic restructuring programme, Horn, as a trained economist, recognized the need to press on with reforms and formed a coalition with the centrist Free Democrats.

Horn worked in the international department of the Hungarian Socialist Workers' Party (HSWP) 1969–85 and, during the period of one-party communist rule, was under-secretary and then minister for foreign affairs 1985–90. In anticipation of the introduction of multiparty politics, the HSWP transformed itself into the HSP 1990, and the pragmatic Horn was chosen as its new president. He is the author of several books on East–West relations.

Horowitz Vladimir Horowitz enjoyed world acclaim as a virtuoso pianist, particularly with his interpretations of the Romantic repertoire. As a boy he expected to become a composer, but to earn a living he became a pianist. Apart from some bravura transcriptions, none of his own compositions have yet been made public.

Horn Philip de Montmorency, Count of (c. 1518–1568). Flemish politician. He held high offices under the Holy Roman emperor Charles V and his son Philip II. From 1563 he was one of the leaders of the opposition to the rule of Cardinal Granvella (1517–1586) and to the introduction of the Inquisition. In 1567 he was arrested, together with the Resistance leader Egmont, and both were beheaded in Brussels.

Horne Henry Sinclair, Baron Horne of Stirkoke (1861–1929). British general, the only artillery officer to command a field army in World War I. He was responsible for many of the technical and tactical improvements in artillery, including the perfection of the creeping barrage.

Commissioned into the Royal Artillery 1880, he served in the South African War and became lieutenant-colonel 1905. He was inspector of artillery 1912–14, and on the outbreak of war went to France commanding an artillery brigade. He went to the Middle East to report on the defences of Egypt and the Suez Canal, then returned to France and commanded 15th Corps in the battle of the Somme. He took command of the 1st British Army from 1916 until the war ended. KCB 1916, baron 1919.

Horniman Annie Elizabeth Fredericka (1860–1937). English pioneer of repertory theatre. She subsidized the Abbey Theatre, Dublin (built 1904), and founded the Manchester company at the Gaiety Theatre 1908.

Hornsby Rajah (Rogers) (1896–1963). US baseball player. He won the National League batting title in six consecutive seasons 1920–25. His .424 batting average 1924 is the highest achieved in the National League and he was voted the National League's most valuable player 1925. His lifetime batting average of .358 is the second highest in history.

Born in Winters, Texas, USA, Hornsby was signed by the St Louis Cardinals and broke into the major leagues 1915. In 1925 he was named the Cardinals' player-manager and, in the same year, he became the first player to win baseball's Triple Crown twice. Traded to the New York Giants 1927 he served variously as player/player-manager for the Boston Braves 1928, the Chicago Cubs 1929–32, the Cardinals 1933, and the St Louis Browns 1933–37.

Hornung E(rnest) W(illiam) (1866–1921). English novelist. Prompted by Conan Doyle, he created A J Raffles, the gentleman-burglar, and his assistant Bunny Manders, in *The Amateur Cracksman* 1899.

Horowitz Vladimir (1904–1989). Russian-born US pianist. He made his US debut 1928 with the New York Philharmonic Orchestra. A leading interpreter of Liszt, Schumann, and Rachmaninov, he toured worldwide until the early 1950s, when he retired to devote more time to recording. His rare concert appearances 1965–86 displayed undiminished brilliance.

Horowitz married Arturo Toscanini's daughter, Wanda, 1933. In 1986 he made a pilgrimage to his homeland, giving a brilliant performance at the Moscow Conservatory of Music.

The British Army always fights uphill, in the rain, at the junction of two maps.

Remark by Sir Brian Horrocks

Horrocks Brian Gwynne (1895–1985). British general. He served in World War I, and in World War II under Montgomery at Alamein and with the British Liberation Army in Europe. KBE 1945.

When Montgomery went to Africa he sent for Horrocks 1942. Horrocks repaid his confidence at Alam Halfa, holding off German and Italian attacks without sustaining heavy casualties. He was given command of the British 1st Army with which he took Tunis 7 May 1943 but was wounded and returned to England. He returned to command XXX Corps at Normandy, again under Montgomery, and retained this position until the end of the war.

Horsa Anglo-Saxon leader, brother of ◊Hengist.

Horsley John Callcott (1817–1903). English artist. A skilled painter of domestic scenes, he was also responsible for frescoes in the Houses of Parliament and is credited with designing the first Christmas card.

Horszowski Mieczyslaw (1892–1993). Polish-born US pianist. His concert career of over 90 years is by far the longest ever. He was a fine interpreter of Bach, Beethoven, Schubert, and Chopin, and a champion of new music, particularly that of his compatriot, Karol Szymanowski.

A noted chamber music player, he formed duos and trios with the Catalan cellist, conductor and composer Pablo Casals, the Russian-born violinist Alexander Schneider, and the Hungarian-born violinist Joseph Szigeti. He frequently took part in festivals, including the Prades Festival in southwest France, organized by Casals, the Marlboro Festival in Vermont, USA and, in later years, the Aldeburgh Festival in the UK. Among his most famous students are Eugene Istomin, Peter Serkin, Murray Perahia, and Andras Schiff.

Horta Victor, Baron Horta (1861–1947). Belgian Art Nouveau architect. He was responsible for a series of apartment buildings in Brussels, the first of which, Hôtel Tassel 1892, is striking in its use of sinuous forms and decorative ironwork in the interior, particularly the staircase. His sumptuous Hôtel Solvay 1895–1900 and Maison du Peuple 1896–99 are more complete, interior and exterior being unified in a stylistic whole.

Horthy Nicholas Horthy de Nagybánya (1868–1957). Hungarian politician and admiral. Leader of the counter-revolutionary White government, he became regent 1920 on the overthrow of the communist Bela Kun regime by Romanian and Czechoslovak intervention. He represented the conservative and military class, and retained power until World War II, trying (although allied to Hitler) to retain independence of action. In 1944 he tried to negotiate a surrender to the USSR but Hungary was taken over by the Nazis and he was deported to Germany. He was released from German captivity the same year by the Western Allies and allowed to go to Portugal, where he died.

Horthy's relations with Germany were somewhat ambivalent. He ordered Hungarian forces to invade Yugoslavia Aug 1941 in support of Hitler's aims in the region and the following month formally declared an anti-Soviet alliance with Germany. However, he refused to send more troops to the Eastern Front May 1943 and went further in 1944, demanding the return of Hungarian troops from Germany and an end to the use of Hungary as a supply base and attempting to halt the deportation of Hungarian Jews. He backed down on all these points when Hitler threatened to occupy Hungary and from then on began trying to remove Hungary from the war.

Horton Max Kennedy (1883–1951). British admiral and submarine specialist in World War II. In 1942 he became commander in chief on the Western Approaches, responsible for convoys crossing the Atlantic. He rapidly made his mark, adopting a variety of measures and tactics to neutralize the U-boat threat and eventually gained the upper hand. He remained in this post until the war ended.

He commanded the Reserve Fleet 1937–39 and on the outbreak of war was given command of the Northern Patrol and became flag officer for submarines Jan 1940. KCB 1939.

Hosea (lived 8th century BC). Prophet in the Old Testament. His prophecy draws parallels between his own marriage and the relationship between God and Israel.

Hosking Eric John (1909–1990). English wildlife photographer. He is known for his documentation of British birds, especially owls. Beginning at the age of eight and still photographing in Africa at 80, he covered all aspects of birdlife and illustrated a large number of books, published between 1940 and 1990.

All you want is a bacon sandwich and there they are.

BOB HOSKINS
on being persistently asked questions during his directorial
début, quoted in *Screen International* 13 May 1988

Hoskins Bob (Robert William) (1942–   ). English character actor. He progressed to fame from a series of supporting roles. Films include *The Long Good Friday* 1980, *The Cotton Club* 1984, *Mona Lisa* 1985, *A Prayer for the Dying* 1987, and *Who Framed Roger Rabbit?* 1988.

Hoth Hermann (1895–1971). German general. A cavalry officer in World War I, he remained in the army after the war, specializing in tank warfare. In World War II, he commanded the 3rd Panzer Army in the invasion of the USSR 1941, getting within 19 km/12 mi of Moscow before being repulsed. He was given command of 4th Panzer Army in the advance toward Stalingrad but was again beaten back. He had no more success at the Battle of Kursk 1943, and after the fall of Kiev he was relieved by Hitler and retired.

Hotham Charles (1806–1855). English naval officer and colonial administrator in Australia. He was lieutenant governor of Victoria 1854 and governor 1855 during which time he greatly curtailed public expenditure and enforced the gold-licensing laws which were one of the causes of the Eureka Stockade.

Hotteterre Jacques-Martin (1674–1763). French flautist, bassoonist, and instrument-maker. He came from a family of woodwind instrument-makers and composers responsible for developing the orchestral Baroque flute and bassoon from folk antecedents. A respected performer and teacher, he wrote a tutor for the transverse flute and composed trio sonatas and suites for flute and bassoon.

Houdini Harry. Stage name of Erich Weiss (1874–1926). US escapologist and conjurer. He was renowned for his escapes from ropes and handcuffs, from trunks under water, from straitjackets and prison cells.

Born in Budapest, he was the son of a rabbi. He wrote books and articles on magic and was deeply interested in spiritualism, and campaigned against fraudulent mindreaders and mediums.

Suggested reading
Brandon, Ruth *The Life and Many Deaths of Harry Houdini* (1993)
Fitzsimons, Raymund *Death and the Magician: The Mystery of Houdini* (1980)
Hennig, Doug and Reynolds, Charles *Houdini* (1977)

Houdon Jean-Antoine (1741–1828). French sculptor. A portraitist, he made characterful studies of Voltaire and a Neo-Classical statue of George Washington, commissioned 1785. His other subjects included the philosophers Diderot and Rousseau, the composer Gluck, the emperor Napoleon, and the American politician Benjamin Franklin. Houdon also produced popular mythological figures, such as *Diana* and *Minerva*.

Hounsfield Godfrey Newbold (1919–   ). English engineer, a pioneer of tomography, the application of computer techniques to X-raying the human body. He shared the Nobel Prize for Physiology or Medicine 1979. Knighted 1981.

He joined British electronics company EMI (now Thorn EMI) 1951 as a researcher in medical technology.

The EMI scanner he invented 1972, a computerized transverse axial tomography system for X-ray examination, enables the whole body to be screened at one time. The X-ray crystal detectors, more sensitive than film, are rotated round the body and can distinguish between, for example, tumours and healthy tissue.

Houphouët-Boigny Félix (1905–1993). Ivory Coast right-wing politician, president 1960–93. He held posts in French ministries, and became president of the Republic of the Ivory Coast on independence 1960, maintaining close links with France, which helped to boost an already thriving economy and encourage political stability. Pro-Western and opposed to communist intervention in Africa,

Hoskins *The English actor Bob Hoskins in* Who Framed Roger Rabbit? *1988, a film that integrated animation and live action. It won an Academy Award for its visual effects.* (Image Select)

Houphouët-Boigny was strongly criticized for maintaining diplomatic relations with South Africa. He was re-elected for a seventh term 1990 in multiparty elections, amid allegations of ballot rigging and political pressure.

He was Africa's longest-serving head of state, having begun his political career as a left-wing nationalist under French colonial rule, and became the first president of the independent Ivory Coast, with closer links with France than any other African state. Under his guidance his country became one of the most stable and prosperous states in the continent, and he became known in Paris as 'the grand old man of Africa'. After 30 years of one-man, one-party rule, he conceded 1990 to demands for free elections, which he and his party won with ease.

House Edward Mandell (1858–1938). US politician and diplomat. He was instrumental in obtaining the presidential nomination for Woodrow Wilson 1912 and later served as Wilson's closest adviser. During World War I 1914–1918, House served as US liaison with Great Britain and was an important behind-the-scenes participant in the 1919 Versailles Peace Conference.

Born in Houston, Texas, USA, House attended Cornell University and, after working for many years on his family's holdings, became active in state Democratic politics. As personal adviser to a succession of Texas governors 1892–1904, he was awarded the honorary title of colonel.

The police admitted afterwards that if I had continued to live my normal life ... they would not have been able to protect me.

GEOFFREY HOUSEHOLD
Watcher in the Shadows ch 1 1960

Household Geoffrey Edward West (1900–1988). English espionage and adventure novelist. His *Rogue Male* 1939 concerned an Englishman's attempt to kill Hitler, and the enemy hunt for him after his failure. Household served with British intelligence in World War II.

Houseman John. Adopted name of Jacques Haussman (1902–1988). US theatre, film, and television producer and character actor. He co-founded the Mercury Theater with Orson Welles, and collaborated with such directors as Max Ophuls, Vincente Minnelli, and Nicholas Ray. He won an Academy Award for his acting debut in *The Paper Chase* 1973, and recreated his role in the subsequent TV series. Among the films he produced are *The Bad and the Beautiful* 1952 and *Lust for Life* 1956.

Loveliest of trees, the cherry now / Is hung with bloom along the bough, / And stands about the woodland ride / Wearing white for Eastertide.

A E HOUSMAN
A Shropshire Lad 2 1892

Housman A(lfred) E(dward) (1859–1936). English poet and classical scholar. His *A Shropshire Lad* 1896, a series of deceptively simple, nostalgic, balladlike poems, was popular during World War I. This was followed by *Last Poems* 1922 and *More Poems* 1936. In 1892 he became professor of Latin at University College, London; he held a similar post at Cambridge from 1911.
Suggested reading
Graves, Richard Perceval *A E Housman: The Scholar-Poet* (1979)
Housman, Laurence *My Brother: A E Housman* (1936, rep 1969)
Page, Norman *A E Housman: a Critical Biography* (1983)
Scott-Kilvert *A E Housman* (1955)

Houston Sam (Samuel) (1793–1863). US general who won independence for Texas from Mexico 1836 and was president of the Republic of Texas 1836–45. Houston, Texas, is named after him. Houston was governor of the state of Tennessee and later US senator

for and governor of the state of Texas. He took Indian citizenship when he married a Cherokee.
Suggested reading
Hopewell, Clifford *Sam Houston: Man of Destiny* (1987)
James, M *The Raven: A Biography of Sam Houston* (1929, rep 1977)

Houston Whitney (1963–). US soul ballad singer. She has had a string of consecutive number-one hits in the USA and Britain. They include 'Saving All My Love for You' 1985, 'I Wanna Dance With Somebody (Who Loves Me)' 1987, 'Where Do Broken Hearts Go' 1988, and 'I Will Always Love You' 1992. She made her acting debut in the film *The Bodyguard* 1992.

Hovell William Hilton (1786–1875). English-born explorer in Australia who, with Hamilton Hume, travelled overland from Gunning, SW of Sydney, to Port Phillip in 1824.

Hovell was born in Yarmouth, England. A mistake in his calculations on the expedition to Port Phillip led him to believe they had reached Westernport and that the hinterland was suitable for agriculture. Based on these reports a party, accompanied by Hovell, sailed south, but attempts to settle were abandoned when the error was realized.

Howard Alan Mackenzie (1937–). English actor. His appearances with the Royal Shakespeare Company include the title roles in *Henry V*, *Henry VI*, *Coriolanus*, and *Richard III*.

I die a Queen, but I would rather die the wife of Culpeper.

CATHERINE HOWARD
Last words at her execution 1542

Howard Catherine (c. 1520–1542). Queen consort of Henry VIII of England from 1540. In 1541 the archbishop of Canterbury, Thomas Cranmer, accused her of being unchaste before marriage to Henry and she was beheaded 1542 after Cranmer made further charges of adultery.

Howard Charles, 2nd Baron Howard of Effingham and 1st Earl of Nottingham (1536–1624). English admiral, a cousin of Queen Elizabeth I. He commanded the fleet against the Spanish Armada while Lord High Admiral 1585–1618. He co-operated with the Earl of Essex in the attack on Cadiz 1596. Baron 1573, earl 1596.

Howard Constance (1919–). English embroiderer. She helped to revive creative craftwork after World War II. Her work included framed pictures with fabrics outlined in bold black threads, wall hangings, and geometric studies in strong colour.

Howard Ebenezer (1850–1928). English town planner. He pioneered the ideal of the garden city through his book *Tomorrow* 1898 (republished as *Garden Cities of Tomorrow* 1902). In these, every house was to have its own plot of land; land usage was to be arranged zonally with civic amenities at the centre and factories on the edge of the city; and the whole city was to be surrounded by a 'green belt'. Knighted 1927.

Howard John (1726–1790). English philanthropist whose work to improve prison conditions is continued today by the Howard League for Penal Reform.

On his appointment as high sheriff for Bedfordshire 1773, he undertook a tour of English prisons which led to two acts of Parliament 1774, making jailers salaried officers and setting standards of cleanliness. After touring Europe 1775, he published *State of the Prisons in England and Wales, with an account of some Foreign Prisons* 1777. He died of typhus fever while visiting Russian military hospitals at Kherson in the Crimea.

Howard Leslie. Stage name of Leslie Howard Stainer (1893–1943). English actor. His films include *The Scarlet Pimpernel* 1935, *The Petrified Forest* 1936, *Pygmalion* 1938, and *Gone with the Wind* 1939. He was killed during a secret wartime mission when the plane he was travelling in was shot down by the Germans, allegedly because Winston Churchill was thought to be aboard.

He had a passion for England and the English ideal that was almost Shakespearean.

C A Lejeune on LESLIE HOWARD
in Leslie Halliwell *Filmgoer's Companion* 1965

Howard Michael (1941–). British Conservative politician, home secretary from 1993. On the right of the Conservative Party, he championed the restoration of law and order as a key electoral issue, but encountered stiff opposition to his proposals for changes to the criminal-justice system and for increased police powers, as embodied in the 1994 Criminal Justice and Public Order Bill. A new crime bill, focusing on tougher sentencing, was announced by Howard at the 1995 Conservative Party conference, and immediately condemned by the Lord Chief Justice.

After a successful legal career, Howard entered the House of Commons 1983 and, under Margaret Thatcher, made rapid ministerial progress through the departments of Trade and Industry, Environment, and Employment, until being appointed home secretary by John Major 1993. His populist approach to law and order won him the plaudits of grass-roots party members, but he was forced to retreat on a number of key points, including that of police restructuring, in the face of criticism from senior Conservative figures as well as members of the judiciary.

Howard Trevor Wallace (1913–1988). English actor. His films include *Brief Encounter* 1945, *Sons and Lovers* 1960, *Mutiny on the Bounty* 1962, *Ryan's Daughter* 1970, and *Conduct Unbecoming* 1975.

Howe Elias (1819–1867). US inventor, in 1846, of a sewing machine using two threads, thus producing a lock stitch.

Howard, Leslie *English actor Leslie Howard, whose qualities of restraint and reserve won him the role of Ashley Wilkes in* Gone with the Wind *1939. He accepted this part reluctantly and returned to England to make patriotic films such as* Pimpernel Smith *1941. He was shot down by the Germans in World War II on a mission between Lisbon and London.*

Howe was born in Spencer, Massachusetts, and trained as a machinist. He began work on the design of a sewing machine in about 1843, and in 1846 he was granted a US patent for a practical machine. He was the first to patent a lock-stitch mechanism, and his machine had two other important features: a curved needle with the eye (for the thread) at the point, and an under-thread shuttle (this had been invented by a Walter Hunt in 1834, probably unbeknown to Howe).

Howe went to the UK and sold the invention for £250 to a corset manufacturer named William Thomas of Cheapside, London.

Thomas secured the British patent in his own name, and although Howe worked with Thomas until 1849, his career in London was unsuccessful. Returning in poverty to the USA, he found that various people – among them Isaac Singer – were making machines similar to his own. Howe redeemed his patent, which he had pawned, and sued for infringement. The courts eventually found in his favour and Howe became a millionaire on his royalties. In his last years he manufactured the machine in Bridgeport, Connecticut.

Howe (Richard Edward) Geoffrey, Baron Howe of Aberavon (1926–). British Conservative politician, member of Parliament for Surrey East. Under Edward Heath he was solicitor general 1970–72 and minister for trade 1972–74; as chancellor of the Exchequer 1979–83 under Margaret Thatcher, he put into practice the monetarist policy which reduced inflation at the cost of a rise in unemployment. In 1983 he became foreign secretary, and in 1989 deputy prime minister and leader of the House of Commons. On 1 Nov 1990 he resigned in protest at Thatcher's continued opposition to Britain's greater integration in Europe. Knighted 1970, baron 1992.

Many of the ideas proposed by Howe in the early 1960s were subsequently taken up by the Thatcher government.
Suggested reading
Hillman, J and Clarke, P *Geoffrey Howe: A Quiet Revolutionary* (1988)

Howe George (1769–1821). The first editor and printer in Australia. He issued the first book printed in Australia, *New South Wales General Standing Orders* 1802, and the first newspaper, the *Sydney Gazette and New South Wales Advertiser*. His son, Robert Howe (1795–1829), also a printer and publisher, produced the first periodical in Australia, the *Australian Magazine* 1821, and also the first hymn book in Australia, *An Abridgement of the Wesleyan Hymns* 1821.

Howe Gordie (Gordon) (1926–). Canadian ice-hockey player who played for the Detroit Red Wings (National Hockey League) 1946–71 and then the New England Whalers (World Hockey Association). In the NHL, he scored more goals (801), assists (1,049), and points (1,850) than any other player in ice-hockey history until beaten by Wayne Gretsky. Howe played professional hockey until he was over 50.

Howe James Wong. Adopted name of Wong Tung Jim (1899–1976). Chinese-born director of film photography. He lived in the USA from childhood. One of Hollywood's best cinematographers, he is credited with introducing the use of hand-held cameras. His work ranges from *The Alaskan* 1924 to *Funny Lady* 1975 and notably includes *Sweet Smell of Success* 1957.

Howe Julia Ward (1819–1910). US feminist and antislavery campaigner who wrote the 'Battle Hymn of the Republic' 1862, sung to the tune of 'John Brown's Body'. She wrote a biography 1883 of Margaret Fuller, a prominent literary figure and a member of Ralph Waldo Emerson's Transcendentalists.

Mine eyes have seen the glory of the coming of the Lord: / He is trampling out the vintage where the grapes of wrath are stored.

JULIA WARD HOWE
'Battle Hymn of the American Republic'

Howe Richard, 1st Earl Howe (1726–1799). British admiral. He co-operated with his brother William against the colonists during the American Revolution and in the French Revolutionary Wars commanded the Channel fleets 1792–96. Viscount 1758, earl 1788.

Howe William, 5th Viscount Howe (1729–1814). British general. During the American Revolution he won the Battle of Bunker Hill 1775, and as commander in chief in America 1776–78 captured New York and defeated Washington at Brandywine and Germantown. He resigned in protest at lack of home government support. KB 1775, Irish viscount 1799.

Howells Herbert Norman (1892–1983). English composer, organist, and teacher. His works are filled with an 'English' quality, as with those of Elgar and Vaughan Williams. Often elegiac in expression, as in some of the *Six Pieces for Organ* 1940, much of his music after the mid-1930s reflects his mourning over the death of his son. He wrote choral and chamber music, as well as solo works, both sacred and secular.

Howells William Dean (1837–1920). US novelist and editor. The 'dean' of US letters in the post-Civil War era, and editor of *The Atlantic Monthly*, he championed the realist movement in fiction and encouraged many younger authors. He wrote 35 novels, 35 plays, and many books of poetry, essays, and commentary.

His novels, filled with vivid social detail, include *A Modern Instance* 1882 and *The Rise of Silas Lapham* 1885, about the social fall and moral rise of a New England paint manufacturer, a central fable of the 'Gilded Age'.

Suggested reading

Cady, Edwin *The Road to Realism: The Early Years, 1837–1885, of William Dean Howells* (1956)
Cady, Edwin *The Realist at War: The Mature Years, 1885–1920, of William Dean Howells* (1958)
Eble, Kenneth *William Dean Howells* (1982)
Lynn, Kenneth S *William Dean Howells: An American Life* (1971)

Howerd Frankie (Francis Alex Howard) (1922–1992). English comedian and actor. He was best known for his role as the Roman slave Lurcio in the television series *Up Pompeii*. The trademark of his rambling monologues was suggestive innuendo followed by aggrieved disapproval when audiences laughed.

Howerd was born in York and moved to Eltham in Kent at an early age. After failing to get into RADA, he joined the Royal Artillery during World War II and performed as a forces entertainer. From there he went into radio, and throughout the 1950s he appeared as a stand-up comedian, in revue, films, pantomime, and occasionally in straight theatre. An appearance in *A Funny Thing Happened on the Way to the Forum* 1963 provided him with the inspiration for *Up Pompeii*.

Howlin' Wolf stage name of Chester Arthur Burnett (1910–1976). US blues singer, songwriter, harmonica player, and guitarist. His music was characterized by a harsh, compelling vocal style. His most influential recordings, made in Chicago, feature the electric guitarist Hubert Sumlin (1931–) and include 'Smokestack Lightnin'' 1956, 'Little Red Rooster' 1961, and 'Killin'' Floor' 1965.

Hoxha Enver (1908–1985). Albanian Communist politician, the country's leader from 1954. He founded the Albanian Communist Party 1941, and headed the liberation movement 1939–44. He was prime minister 1944–54, combining with foreign affairs 1946–53, and from 1954 was first secretary of the Albanian Party of Labour. In policy he was a Stalinist and independent of both Chinese and Soviet communism.

Hoyle Fred(erick) (1915–). English astronomer, cosmologist, and writer. In 1948 he joined with Hermann Bondi and Thomas Gold in developing the steady-state theory of the universe. In 1957,

---

Space isn't remote at all. It's only an hour's drive away if your car could go straight upwards.

FRED HOYLE
Observer Sept 1979

---

with William Fowler, he showed that chemical elements heavier than hydrogen and helium may be built up by nuclear reactions inside stars.

According to Hoyle's theory on gravitation, matter is not evenly distributed throughout space, but forms self-gravitating systems. These may range in diameter from a few kilometres to a million light years. Formed from clouds of hydrogen gas, they vary greatly in density.

Hoyle has suggested that life originated in bacteria and viruses contained in the gas clouds of space and was then delivered to the Earth by passing comets. His first science-fiction novel was *The Black Cloud* 1957; he has also written many popular science books. Knighted 1972.

Hoyle was born in Bingley, Yorkshire, and studied at Cambridge. His academic career was spent at Cambridge and 1956–66 at Mount Palomar Observatory, California. On his return he became director of the Cambridge Institute of Theoretical Astronomy.

Hrabal Bohumil (1914–1997). Czechoslovak writer. He began writing after 1962. His novels depict ordinary people caught up in events they do not control or comprehend, including *Ostre sledované vlaky/Closely Observed Trains* 1965 (filmed 1967).

Hsia dynasty (*c*. 2200–*c*. 1500 BC). China's first legendary ruling family see ◊Xia dynasty.

Hsuan Tung name adopted by Henry ◊P'u-i on becoming emperor of China 1908.

Hsun Tzu (300–230 BC). Chinese philosopher, a sceptical rationalist. He argued that human nature is essentially evil and needs to be constrained into moral behaviour by laws and punishments.

Hua Guofeng or Hua Kuofeng (1920–). Chinese politician, leader of the Chinese Communist Party (CCP) 1976–81, premier 1976–80. He dominated Chinese politics 1976–77, seeking economic modernization without major structural reform. From 1978 he was gradually eclipsed by Deng Xiaoping. Hua was ousted from the Politburo Sept 1982 but remained a member of the CCP Central Committee.

Hua, born in Shanxi into a peasant family, fought under Zhu De, the Red Army leader, during the liberation war 1937–49. He entered the CCP Central Committee 1969 and the Politburo 1973. An orthodox, loyal Maoist, Hua was selected to succeed Zhou Enlai as prime minister Jan 1976 and became party leader on Mao Zedong's death Sept 1976. He was replaced as prime minister by Zhao Ziyang Sept 1980 and as CCP chair by Hu Yaobang June 1981.

Huáscar (*c*. 1495–1532). King of the Incas. He shared the throne with his half-brother Atahualpa from 1525, but the latter overthrew and murdered him during the Spanish conquest.

Hubbard L(afayette) Ron(ald) (1911–1986). US science-fiction and fantasy writer, founder in 1954 of Scientology.

Despite his later claims to be a war hero, he was in fact relieved of his command in the navy for incompetence.

His first story was published in the pulp magazine *Astounding Science Fiction* 1938. His novels have been described as melodramatic and paranoid space operas. They include *Return to Tomorrow* 1954 and *Fear* 1957.

Hubble Edwin Powell (1889–1953). US astronomer who discovered the existence of other galaxies outside our own, and classified them according to their shape. His theory that the universe is expanding is now generally accepted.

Hubble discovered Cepheid variable stars in the Andromeda galaxy 1923, proving it to lie far beyond our own Galaxy. In 1925 he introduced the classification of galaxies as spirals, barred spirals, and ellipticals. In 1929 he announced Hubble's law, which states that the galaxies are moving apart at a rate that increases with their distance.

Hubble was born in Marshfield, Missouri, and studied at Chicago and in the UK at Oxford. He briefly practised law before returning to Chicago to join Yerkes Observatory 1914. From 1919 he worked at Mount Wilson, near Pasadena, California.

His data on the speed at which galaxies were receding (based on their red shifts) were used to determine the portion of the universe that we can ever come to know, the radius of which is called the *Hubble radius*. Beyond this limit, any matter will be travelling at the speed of light, so communication with it will never be possible. The ratio of the velocity of galactic recession to distance has been named the *Hubble constant*.

Hubel David Hunter (1926–). US neurophysiologist who worked with Torsten Wiesel (1924–) on the physiology of vision and the way in which the higher centres of the brain process visual information. They shared the 1981 Nobel Prize for Physiology or Medicine. From 1959 he worked at Harvard, becoming professor 1965.

At Harvard he met Wiesel, and they began experiments implanting electrodes into the brain of anaesthetized cats, correlating the anatomical structure of the visual cortex of the brain with the physiological responses to different types of visual stimulation. They built up a complex picture of how the brain analysed visual information by an increasingly sophisticated system of detection by the nerve cells.

Later study of the development of the visual system in young animals suggested that eye defects should be treated and corrected immediately, and the then routine ophthalmological practice of leaving a defect to correct itself was abandoned.

Huc Evariste Régis, Abbé (1813–1860). French missionary in China. In 1845 he travelled to the border of Tibet, where he stopped for eight months to study the Tibetan language and Buddhist literature before moving on to the city of Lhasa.

Hückel Erich Armand Arthur Joseph (1896–1980). German physical chemist who, with Peter Debye, developed in 1923 the modern theory that accounts for the electrochemical behaviour of strong electrolytes in solution. Hückel also made discoveries relating to the structures of benzene and similar compounds that exhibit aromaticity.

He worked with Debye at Göttingen and the Eidgenössische Technische Hochschule, Zürich, and held various academic posts, becoming professor of theoretical physics at the University of Marburg 1937.

Hudson Henry (*c.* 1565–1611). English explorer. Under the auspices of the Muscovy Company 1607–08, he made two unsuccessful attempts to find the Northeast Passage to China. In Sept 1609, commissioned by the Dutch East India Company, he reached New York Bay and sailed 240 km/150 mi up the river that now bears his name, establishing Dutch claims to the area. In 1610, he sailed from London in the *Discovery* and entered what is now the Hudson Strait. After an icebound winter, he was turned adrift by a mutinous crew in what is now Hudson Bay.

Hudson had heard reports of two possible channels to the Pacific Ocean across North America. One of these had been described by English soldier and colonist John Smith. Since Hudson's search for the Northeast Passage proved unsuccessful, he chose to pursue Smith's suggestion.
Suggested reading
O'Connell, Richard *Hudson's Fourth Voyage* (1978)
Vail, P *The Magnificent Adventures of Henry Hudson* (1965)

Hudson Rock. Stage name of Roy Scherer Jr (1925–1985). US film actor. He was a star from the mid-1950s to the mid-1960s, and appeared in several melodramas directed by Douglas Sirk and in three comedies co-starring Doris Day (including *Pillow Talk* 1959). He went on to have a successful TV career in the 1970s.

I can't play a loser: I don't look like one.
ROCK HUDSON
quoted in Leslie Halliwell *Filmgoer's Companion* 1965

Hudson W(illiam) H(enry) (1841–1922). British author, born of US parents in Argentina. He was inspired by recollections of early days in Argentina to write the romances *The Purple Land* 1885 and *Green Mansions* 1904, and his autobiographical *Far Away and Long Ago* 1918. He wrote several books on birds, and on the English countryside, for example, *Nature in Down-Land* 1900 and *A Shepherd's Life* 1910.

Huggins William (1824–1910). English astronomer and pioneer of astrophysics. He revolutionized astronomy by using spectroscopy to determine the chemical make-up of stars and by using photography in stellar spectroscopy.

Huggins was born in London, where he ran the family drapery business until 1854. He then built a private observatory at Tulse Hill, London, and devoted himself entirely to science.

In 1860, with his friend W A Miller (a professor of chemistry), Huggins designed a spectroscope and attached it to the telescope. By observing the spectral lines of stars, he established that the universe was made up of well-known elements. At that time, some nebulae had been observed to be faint clusters of stars, but others could not be resolved without more powerful telescopes. Huggins realized that if they were composed of stars, they would give a characteristic stellar spectrum. However, when he turned to the unresolved nebulae in the constellation of Draco in 1864, only a single bright line was observed. Seeing this, he understood the nature of unresolved nebulae: they were clouds of luminous gas and not clusters of stars. KCB 1897.

Hughes Charles Evans (1862–1948). US jurist and public official, appointed to the US Supreme Court by President Taft 1910. He resigned 1916 to accept the Republican nomination for president, losing narrowly to the incumbent Wilson. He served as secretary of state 1921–25 under President Harding. As Supreme Court chief justice 1930–41, he presided over the constitutional tests of President F D Roosevelt's New Deal legislation.

Hughes, born in Glens Falls, New York, received his law degree from Columbia University 1884. After joining the Columbia law

Hudson, Rock US film actor Rock Hudson whose good looks made him one of Hollywood's leading stars. A former truck driver, Hudson had no acting experience when he was given his first chance in films, and later had to undergo intensive coaching and grooming. His death from AIDS 1985 shocked film-goers around the world.

faculty 1891–93, he directed a state investigation of public utilities 1905 and served two terms as New York governor 1906–10. He retired from the US Supreme Court 1941.

Suggested reading
Hughes, Charles Evans (edited by Danelski and Tulchin) *The Autobiographical Notes of Charles Evans Hughes* (1973)
Pusey, Merlo *Charles Evans Hughes of the Supreme Court* (1951)

Hughes David (1831–1900). British-born US inventor who patented an early form of telex in 1855, a type-printing instrument for use with the telegraph. In 1857 he took the instrument to Europe, where it became widely used.

Hughes Howard Robard (1905–1976). US tycoon. Inheriting wealth from his father, who had patented a successful oil-drilling bit, he created a legendary financial empire. A skilled pilot, he manufactured and designed aircraft. He formed a film company in Hollywood and made the classic film *Hell's Angels* 1930, about aviators of World War I; later successes included *Scarface* 1932 and *The Outlaw* 1944. From his middle years he was a recluse.

He founded the Hughes Aircraft Company and broke the air speed record in a craft of his own design in 1935, reaching a speed of 352 mph/566 kph.

Suggested reading
Bartlett, D and Steele, J B *Empire* (1981)
Drosnin, M *Citizen Hughes* (1985)
Higham, Charles *Howard Hughes: The Secret Life* (1993)

Hughes (James Mercer) Langston (1902–1967). US poet and novelist. Known as 'the poet laureate of Harlem', he became one of the foremost black American literary figures, writing such collections of poems as *The Weary Blues* 1926. In addition to his poetry he wrote a series of novels, short stories, and essays. His autobiography *The Big Sea* appeared 1940.

Born in Joplin, Missouri, USA, and raised in Cleveland, Ohio, Hughes had a poem published while still in high school. After briefly attending Columbia University, he travelled widely and continued to write. He published *The Weary Blues* shortly after graduating from Lincoln University.

Suggested reading
Barksdale, R *Langston Hughes* (1977)
Berry, Faith *Langston Hughes* (1983)
Hughes, Langston *The Big Sea* (autobiography) (1940)
Rampersad, Arnold *The Life of Langston Hughes* (1986–88)

Hughes Richard Arthur Warren (1900–1976). English writer. His study of childhood, *A High Wind in Jamaica*, was published 1929, and the trilogy *The Human Predicament* 1961–73.

It took the whole of Creation / To produce my foot, my each feather: / Now I hold Creation in my foot.

TED HUGHES
'Hawk Roosting'

Hughes Ted (Edward James) (1930–   ). English poet, poet laureate from 1984. His work includes *The Hawk in the Rain* 1957, *Lupercal* 1960, *Wodwo* 1967, *River* 1983, and *Rain-Charm for the Duchy* 1992, and is characterized by its harsh portrayal of the crueller aspects of nature. In 1956 he married the poet Sylvia Plath.

Suggested reading
Gifford, T and Roberts, N *Ted Hughes* (1986)
Sagar, K *The Art of Ted Hughes* (1978)

Hughes Thomas (1822–1896). English writer. He was the author of the children's book *Tom Brown's School Days* 1857, a story of Rugby School under Thomas Arnold. It had a sequel, *Tom Brown at Oxford* 1861.

Life isn't all beer and skittles.

THOMAS HUGHES
Tom Brown's Schooldays pt 1, ch 2 1857

Hughes William Morris (1862–1952). Australian politician, prime minister 1915–23; originally Labor, he headed a national cabinet. After resigning as prime minister 1923, he held many other cabinet posts 1934–41.

Born in London, he emigrated to Australia 1884. He represented Australia in the peace conference after World War I at Versailles.

Without the Empire we should be tossed like a cork in the cross current of world politics. It is ... our sword and shield.

WILLIAM HUGHES
Speech to Australian Historical Society Melbourne 1926

Hugo Victor Marie (1802–1885). French poet, novelist, and dramatist. The *Odes et poésies diverses* appeared 1822, and his verse play *Hernani* 1830 established him as the leader of French Romanticism. More volumes of verse followed between his series of dramatic novels, which included *Notre-Dame de Paris* 1831, later filmed as *The Hunchback of Notre Dame* 1924, 1939, and *Les Misérables* 1862, adapted as a musical 1980.

Born at Besançon, Hugo was the son of one of Napoleon's generals. Originally a monarchist, his support of republican ideals in the 1840s led to his banishment 1851 for opposing Louis Napoleon's coup d'état. He lived in exile in Guernsey until the fall of the empire 1870, later becoming a senator under the Third Republic. He died a national hero and is buried in the Panthéon, Paris.

Suggested reading
Edwards, Samuel *Victor Hugo: A Tumultuous Life* (1971)
Maurois, André *Victor Hugo* (trs 1954)
Richardson, Joanna *Victor Hugo* (1976)

Huizinga Johan (1872–1945). Dutch historian and, in his time, a leading intellectual and popular writer. He is probably best known for *The Waning of the Middle Ages* 1919, an account of cultural decline in 14th- and 15th-century Burgundy.

Huizinga preferred broad themes and his writings ranged widely from classical Indian drama and Oriental cultural history to Western history from the 12th century to the present day. His eclecticism is brilliantly displayed in *Homo Ludens* 1938, a classic study of culture as play. His *Dutch Civilization in the Seventeenth Century* 1933 is an important contribution to Dutch history, as is his biography of Erasmus (*Erasmus* 1924), whose heir many consider him to be.

He taught Indian literature at the University of Amsterdam before being appointed professor of history at Groningen 1905. From 1915 he was professor of general history at London University and became rector of Leyden University 1933.

Hull Cordell (1871–1955). US Democratic politician. As F D Roosevelt's secretary of state 1933–44, he opposed German and Japanese aggression. He was identified with the Good Neighbour policy of non-intervention in Latin America. In his last months of office he paved the way for a system of collective security, for which he was called 'father' of the United Nations. He was awarded the Nobel Peace Prize 1945.

He was born in Tennessee. He was a member of Congress 1907–33. After Dec 1941 foreign policy was handled more directly by Roosevelt, but Hull was active in reaching agreements with Vichy France, though these were largely cancelled by the rising influence of de Gaulle.

Hulme Keri (1947–   ). New Zealand poet and novelist. She won the Commonwealth Booker Prize with her first novel *The Bone People* 1985. This centres on an autistic child and those close to him. Acutely responsive to maritime landscape, it lyrically incorporates the more mystical aspects of Maori experience. Other works include the novella *Lost Possessions* 1985, *The Windeater/Te Kaihau* 1986, a collection of short stories, and *Strands* 1990, a book of poetry.

Hulme T(homas) E(rnest) (1883–1917). British philosopher, critic, and poet, killed on active service in World War I. His

Speculations 1924 influenced T S Eliot and his few poems inspired the Imagist movement.

And round about were the wistful stars / With white faces like town children.

T E HULME
'Autumn'

Humason Milton Lasell (1891–1972). US astronomer who carried out a spectroscopic study of distant galaxies, determining their velocities from their red shift.

From 1954 he was astronomer at the Mount Wilson and Palomar Observatories. At Mount Wilson Observatory Humason took part in an extensive study of the properties of galaxies, initiated by Edwin Hubble 1928. The work consisted of making a series of systematic spectroscopic observations to test and extend the relationship that Hubble had found between the red shifts and the apparent magnitudes of galaxies. But because of the low surface brightness of galaxies there were severe technical difficulties. Humason developed the technique and made most of the exposures and plate measurements. The velocities of 620 galaxies were measured, and the results, published 1956, still represent the majority of known values of radial velocities for normal galaxies.

Humayun also known as Nasir ud-Din Muhammad (1508–1556). Second Mogul emperor of N India 1530–40 and 1554–56. The son of Babur, he inherited an unsettled empire and faced constant challenges from his three brothers. Following defeat by the Afghan Sher Shad Suri (died 1545), he fled into exile in Persia 1540. Returning to India, he reoccupied Delhi and Agra 1555 but died within a year. He was succeeded by his son Akbar.

Humbert Anglicized form of ◊Umberto, two kings of Italy.

Humboldt (Friedrich Wilhelm Heinrich) Alexander, Baron von (1769–1859). German geophysicist, botanist, geologist, and writer who, with French botanist Aimé Bonpland (1773–1858), explored the regions of the Orinoco and Amazon rivers in South America 1800–04, and gathered 60,000 plant specimens. He was a founder of ecology.

Humboldt aimed to erect a new science, a 'physics of the globe', analysing the deep physical interconnectedness of all terrestrial phenomena. He believed that geological phenomena were to be understood in terms of basic physical causes (for example, terrestrial magnetism or rotation).

One of the first popularizers of science, he gave a series of lectures later published as *Kosmos/Cosmos* 1845–62, an account of the relations between physical environment and flora and fauna.

In meteorology, he introduced isobars and isotherms on weather maps, made a general study of global temperature and pressure, and instituted a worldwide programme for compiling magnetic and weather observations. His studies of American volcanoes demonstrated they corresponded to underlying geological faults; on that basis he deduced that volcanic action had been pivotal in geological history and that many rocks were igneous in origin. In 1804, he discovered that the Earth's magnetic field decreased from the poles to the equator.

Suggested reading
Botting, Douglas *Humboldt and the Cosmos* (1973)
De Terra, Helmut *The Life and Times of Alexander Humboldt* (1955)
Kellner, Charlotte *Alexander von Humboldt* (1963)

Humboldt (Karl) Wilhelm Baron von Humboldt (1767–1835). German philologist whose stress on the identity of thought and language influenced Noam Chomsky. He was the brother of Friedrich Humboldt.

Hume (Andrew) Hamilton (1797–1873). Australian explorer. In 1824, with William Hovell, he led an expedition from Sydney to the Murray River and Port Phillip. The Melbourne–Sydney *Hume Highway* is named after him.

Hume David (1711–1776). Scottish philosopher whose *Treatise of Human Nature* 1739–40 is a central text of British empiricism. Examining meticulously our modes of thinking, he concluded that they are more habitual than rational. Consequently, he not only held that speculative metaphysics was impossible, but also arrived at generally sceptical positions about reason, causation, necessity, identity, and the self.

Hume became secretary to the British embassy in Paris 1763. His *History of Great Britain* 1754–62 was popular within his own lifetime but *A Treatise of Human Nature* was indifferently received. However, the German philosopher Immanuel Kant claimed that Hume's scepticism woke him from his 'dogmatic slumbers'. Among Hume's other publications is the *Enquiry concerning the Principles of Morals* 1751.

Hume's law in moral philosophy states that it is never possible to deduce evaluative conclusions from factual premises; this has come to be known as the 'is/ought problem'.

Suggested reading
Ayer, A J *Hume* (1980)
Basson, A H *David Hume* (1958)
Flew, Anthony *David Hume* (1986)
Mossner, E C *The Life of David Hume* (1971)

Hume Fergus (1859–1932). British writer. Educated in New Zealand, he returned to England in 1888; his *Mystery of a Hansom Cab* 1887 was one of the first detective stories.

Hume (George) Basil (1923–   ). English Roman Catholic cardinal from 1976. A Benedictine monk, he was abbot of Ampleforth in Yorkshire 1963–76, and in 1976 became archbishop of Westminster, the first monk to hold the office.

Humboldt, Alexander German geologist, naturalist and explorer Alexander von Humboldt shown during his pioneering expedition across South America. Humboldt, often described as the founder of ecology, gathered a massive collection of geological, botanical and zoological specimens, and, on his return to Europe in 1804, aimed to create a new science – a 'physics of the globe' – based on his observations. (Ann Ronan/Image Select)

Hume John (1937–). Northern Ireland Catholic politician, leader of the Social Democratic Labour Party (SDLP) from 1979. Hume was a founder member of the Credit Union Party, which later became the SDLP. In 1993 he held talks with Sinn Féin leader, Gerry Adams, on the possibility of securing peace in Northern Ireland. This prompted a joint Anglo-Irish peace initiative, which in turn led to a general cease-fire 1994–96.

It was chiefly through his efforts that 'retrenchment' was added to the words 'peace and reform' as the [radical] party watchword.

W A J Archbold on JOSEPH HUME
in *Dictionary of National Biography*

Hume Joseph (1777–1855). British Radical politician. Born in Montrose, Scotland, he went to India as an army surgeon 1797, made a fortune, and on his return bought a seat in Parliament. In 1818 he secured election as a Philosophic Radical and supported many progressive measures.

Hume-Rothery William (1899–1968). British metallurgist who studied the constitution of alloys. He established that the microstructure of an alloy depends on the different sizes of the component atoms, the valency electron concentration, and electrochemical differences. He was appointed to the first chair of metallurgy at Oxford 1958.

With atoms of widely different sizes, at least two types of crystal lattice may form, one rich in one metal and one rich in the other. The presence of two types of structure can increase the strength of an alloy. This is why some brasses are much stronger than their component metals zinc and copper.

If the two elements differ considerably in electronegativity, a definite chemical compound is formed. Thus steel, an 'alloy' of iron and carbon, contains various iron carbides. Hume-Rothery and his team constructed the equilibrium diagrams for a great number of alloy systems.

Hummel Johann Nepomuk (1778–1837). Austrian composer and pianist. Following in the steps of Mozart (his teacher), his melodies are graceful if somewhat overly symmetrical and 'square'. He was known as a conservative in his lifetime, clinging to a decaying tradition in the face of growing Romanticism. In addition to his keyboard works, which include seven concertos, he wrote choral and chamber works and operas.

Humperdinck Engelbert (1854–1921). German composer. He studied in Cologne and Munich and assisted Richard Wagner in the preparation of *Parsifal* 1879 at Bayreuth. He wrote the musical fairy operas *Hänsel und Gretel* 1893, and *Königskinder/King's Children* 1910.

Humphrey Doris (1895–1958). US choreographer, dancer, and teacher. She was one of the pioneers of modern dance. Her movement technique was based on the shifting imbalance of weight, either falling towards or recovering from two absolute positions – the upright or horizontal. Her works include *The Shakers* 1930, *With My Red Fires* 1936, and *Day on Earth* 1947. Her book *The Art of Making Dances* 1959 is still a highly regarded study on choreography.

A graduate of the Denishawn School of Dancing and Related Arts, Humphrey taught at Bennington College, Vermont, USA, from 1934 and at the Juilliard from 1952. As a teacher and theorist, she was responsible for codifying the radical ideas of the 1920s and 1930s into a usable vocabulary of movement and has influenced two generations of modern dance exponents.

Humphrey Hubert Horatio (1911–1978). US political leader, vice president 1965–69. He was elected to the US Senate 1948,

Freedom is the most contagious virus known to man.

HUBERT HUMPHREY
Speech, New York City, 29 Oct 1964

serving for three terms, distinguishing himself as an eloquent and effective promoter of key legislation. He was an unsuccessful presidential candidate 1960. Serving as vice president under L B Johnson, he made another unsuccessful run for the presidency 1968. He was re-elected to the Senate in 1970 and 1976.

Humphrey was born in Wallace, South Dakota, USA, and trained as a pharmacist. Settling in Minnesota, he became active in Democratic party politics and was elected mayor of Minneapolis 1945. He strongly supported the 1964 Civil Rights Act.

Those extraordinary euphemisms for vomiting – parking the tiger, yodelling on the lawn, the technicolour yawn, the liquid laugh.

BARRY HUMPHRIES
From Fringe to Flying Circus

Humphries (John) Barry (1934–). Australian actor and author. He is best known for his satirical one-person shows and especially for the creation of the character of Mrs (later Dame) Edna Everage. His comic strip 'The Adventures of Barry Mackenzie', published in the British weekly *Private Eye* 1963–74, was the basis for two films, *The Adventures of Barry Mackenzie* 1972 and *Barry Mackenzie Holds His Own* 1974, in which Humphries also acted.
Suggested reading
Humphries, Barry *More Please: Barry Humphries: An Autobiography* (1992)

Hun Sen (1950–). Cambodian political leader, prime minister 1985–93, deputy prime minister from 1993. Originally a member of the Khmer Rouge army, he defected in 1977 to join Vietnam-based anti-Khmer Cambodian forces. His leadership was characterized by the promotion of economic liberalization and a thawing in relations with exiled non-Khmer opposition forces as a prelude to a compromise political settlement. After the defeat of his Cambodian People's Party (CCP) in the 1993 elections, Hun Sen agreed to participate in a power-sharing arrangement as second premier.

Hunt Geoffrey Brian (1948–). Australian squash player. He won four Australian Amateur Championships, eight Australian Open Championships, eight British Open titles and was the winner of the first World Open Championship 1976, winning again 1977, 1979, 1980.

Hunt (James Henry) Leigh (1784–1859). English poet and essayist. The appearance in his Liberal newspaper *The Examiner* of an unfavourable article that he had written about the Prince Regent caused him to be convicted for libel and imprisoned 1813. He was a friend and later an enemy of Byron, and also knew Keats and Shelley.

His verse is little appreciated today, but he influenced the Romantics, and his book on London *The Town* 1848 and his *Autobiography* 1850 survive. The character of Harold Skimpole in Dickens' *Bleak House* was allegedly based on him.

Hunt James Simon Wallis (1947–1993). English motor-racing driver who won his first Formula One race at the 1975 Dutch Grand Prix. He went on to win the 1976 world driver's title. Hunt started his Formula One career with Hesketh 1973 and moved to Maclaren 1976–79, finishing in 1979 with Wolf. He later took up commentating for the BBC's Grand Prix coverage until his sudden death of a heart attack June 1993.

Hunt John Horbury (1838–1904). Canadian-born architect in Australia. His buildings make skilful use of the natural qualities of timber and brickwork and are powerful and direct in character. Examples include Tudor House, Moss Vale, New South Wales 1891 and the Convent of the Sacred Heart, Rose Bay, Sydney 1897–1900, the chapel of which featured the first use of a groined stone-vaulted roof in Australia.

Hunt (Henry Cecil) John, Baron Hunt (1910–). British mountaineer, leader of the successful Everest expedition 1953 (with Edmund Hillary and Norgay Tenzing). Knighted 1953, baron 1966.

Hunt William Holman (1827–1910). English painter. He was one of the founders of the Pre-Raphaelite Brotherhood 1848. Obsessed with realistic detail, he travelled from 1854 onwards to Syria and Palestine to paint biblical subjects. His works include *The Awakening Conscience* 1853 (Tate Gallery, London) and *The Light of the World* 1854 (Keble College, Oxford).

> *Our purpose had not only a newness in its outer form, but also took up in more extended aspiration the principle exemplifying that 'Art is Love'.*
>
> WILLIAM HOLMAN HUNT
> *Pre-Raphaelitism and the Pre-Raphaelite Brotherhood* 1905

Hunter Holly (1958–). US actress. She has often been cast in roles that contrast her diminutive frame with a larger-than-life, passionate, personality. She first came to prominence with *Broadcast News* and *Raising Arizona*, both 1987. Her hallmark Southern accent was jettisoned in the virtuoso performance she gave as a mute woman in *The Piano* 1993 (Academy Award).

Her other films include *Always* and *Miss Firecracker* both 1989.

Hunter John (1728–1793). Scottish surgeon, pathologist, and comparative anatomist who insisted on rigorous scientific method. He was the first to understand the nature of digestion.

Hunter was born in Lanarkshire and trained in London under his elder brother William Hunter (1718–1783), anatomist and obstetrician, who became professor of anatomy in the Royal Academy 1768 and president of the Medical Society 1781. His collection of specimens and preparations is now in the Hunterian Museum of Glasgow University; John Hunter's is housed in the Royal College of Surgeons, London.

He experimented extensively on animals, and kept a number of animal specimens in his garden for dissection. He also dissected human bodies obtained from 'resurrectionists', who raided graveyards at night to sell newly buried corpses to surgeons. During the late 1760s he took up a senior surgical post at St George's Hospital, London, and was appointed physician to George III. Serving on the army surgical staff during the Seven Years' War, he gained the knowledge for a treatise on gunshot wounds.

Hunter made studies of lymph and blood circulation, the sense of smell, the structure of teeth and bone, and various diseases. Experimenting with the transplantation of tissues, he fixed a human tooth into a cock's comb. He often carried out experiments on himself, and eventually died of syphilis with which he had injected himself in an attempt to prove it to be a type of gonorrhoea.

Hunter John (1738–1821). British naval officer and colonial administrator, born in Scotland. He was second captain of the First Fleet to Australia, in command of HMS *Sirius*. He did much survey work in the new colony and in 1788–89 sailed to the Cape Colony to obtain supplies, making a pioneer circumnavigation of the world in Antarctic latitudes. He returned to England but was appointed governor of New South Wales 1794. He ruled the colony 1795–1800 but was unable to control the New South Wales Corps which, during the acting governorship of Francis Grose, had gained control of trade, the courts, land management, and convict labour. When he was recalled he had contributed much to Australian exploration and to the knowledge of Australian zoology and botany.

Huntziger Charles (1880–1941). French general. After a distinguished career in World War I, Huntziger was in command of the French 2nd Army 1940 when the Germans invaded. He deployed his troops to prevent an outflanking attack on the Maginot Line, but his left flank was weak and was pierced by the German advance on Sedan. Huntziger then inexplicably pulled his force back to protect the Maginot Line and was trapped in a fort at Verdun until the French collapse, when he emerged to lead the French delegation which signed the armistice with Germany 22 June.

Hunyadi János Corvinus (*c.* 1387–1456). Hungarian politician and general. Born in Transylvania, reputedly the son of the emperor

Sigismund, he won battles against the Turks from the 1440s. In 1456 he defeated them at Belgrade, but died shortly afterwards of the plague.

Huppert Isabelle Anne (1953–). French actress. She has an international reputation for her versatility, displayed in such films as *La Dentellière/The Lacemaker* 1977, *Violette Nozière* 1978, *Heaven's Gate* 1980, and *Madame Bovary* 1990.

Hurd Douglas (Richard) (1930–). English Conservative politician, home secretary 1985–89 and foreign secretary 1989–95. He was appointed foreign secretary 1989 in the reshuffle that followed Nigel Lawson's resignation as chancellor of the Exchequer and retained his post in Prime Minister John Major's new cabinet formed after the 1992 general election. He was replaced as foreign secretary in the reshuffle that followed Major's re-election as party leader July 1995, having earlier announced his intention to retire.

Hurd entered the House of Commons 1974, representing Witney in Oxfordshire from 1983. He was made a junior minister by Margaret Thatcher, and the sudden resignation of Leon Brittan projected him into the home secretary's post early in 1986. In Nov 1990 he was an unsuccessful candidate in the Tory leadership contest following Margaret Thatcher's unexpected resignation.

Hurd was in the diplomatic service 1952–66, serving in Beijing and at the United Nations in New York and Rome. He then joined the Conservative research department and became a secretary to the party leader Edward Heath. As a hobby, he writes thrillers.

Hurley James Francis (1885–1962). Australian photographer and film maker, best known for Antarctic work done on expeditions with Douglas Mawson and Ernest Shackleton and for documentaries made in Papua New Guinea. He was an official photographer in both world wars.

Hurok Sol(omon) (1888–1974). Russian-born US theatrical producer. From 1914 he produced musical and theatrical events and over the years arranged US appearances for the most prominent figures in European music and dance. His autobiographical *Impresario* and *S Hurok Presents* appeared 1946 and 1953 respectively.

Hurok emigrated to the USA 1906. As a lifelong devotee of music, he originally organized concerts for New York unions and social groups.

Hurston Zora Neale (1901–1960). US writer. She was associated with the Harlem Renaissance. She collected traditional Afro-American folk tales in *Mules and Men* 1935 and *Tell My Horse* 1938. Among her many other works are the novel *Their Eyes Were Watching God* 1937 and her autobiography *Dust Tracks on a Road* 1942.

Although her conservative philosophy of her later years alienated many of her contemporaries, she was a key figure for following generations of black women writers, including Alice Walker, who edited a collection of her writings, *I Love Myself When I Am Laughing* 1979.

Suggested reading

Hemenway, R E *Hurston: A Literary Biography* (1977)

Hurston, Zora Neale *Dust Tracks on the Road* (autobiography) (1942)

Newson, A S *Zora Neale Hurston* (1987)

> *You learn as much from the hand that you lead across the street, as it learns from you. Do you know what I mean?*
>
> WILLIAM HURT
> quoted in *Film Yearbook* 1985

Hurt William (1950–). US actor. His films include *Altered States* 1980, *The Big Chill* 1983, *Kiss of the Spider Woman* 1985 (Academy Award), *Broadcast News* 1987, and *The Accidental Tourist* 1988.

Husák Gustáv (1913–1991). Leader of the Communist Party of Czechoslovakia (CCP) 1969–87 and president 1975–89. After the 1968 Prague Spring of liberalization, his task was to restore control, purge the CCP, and oversee the implementation of a new, federalist constitution. He was deposed in the popular uprising of Nov–Dec 1989 and expelled from the Communist Party Feb 1990.

Husák, a lawyer, was active in the Resistance movement during World War II, and afterwards in the Slovak Communist Party (SCP), and was imprisoned on political grounds 1951–60. Rehabilitated, he was appointed first secretary of the SCP 1968 and CCP leader 1969–87. As titular state president he pursued a policy of cautious reform. He stepped down as party leader 1987, and was replaced as state president by Václav Havel Dec 1989 following the 'gentle revolution'.

Husayn (627–680). Second grandson of the prophet Muhammad. He was the son of Ali bin Abu Talib and Muhammad's daughter Fatima. He was murdered at Karbala (modern Iraq), and his death is commemorated every year by Shia Muslims. It is through Husayn and his brother Hasan that Muhammad's descendants trace their lineage.

He is a very good bridge for rats to run over.

Arthur Wellesley, 1st Duke of Wellington on WILLIAM HUSKISSON
when making Huskisson a cabinet minister.
in Lord Holland's Diary 8 Mar 1828.

Huskisson William (1770–1830). British Conservative politician, financier, and advocate of free trade. He served as secretary to the Treasury 1807–09 and colonial agent for Ceylon (now Sri Lanka). He was active in the Corn Law debates and supported their relaxation in 1821. He was the first person to be killed by a train when he was hit at the opening of the Liverpool and Manchester Railway.

O holy simplicity!

JOHN HUSS
Attributed remark at the stake, on an old
peasant who was bringing wood to throw on the pile

Huss John (Czech Jan) (*c.* 1373–1415). Bohemian Christian church reformer, rector of Prague University from 1402, who was excommunicated for attacks on ecclesiastical abuses. He was summoned before the Council of Constance 1414, defended the English reformer John Wycliffe, rejected the pope's authority, and was burned at the stake. His followers were called Hussites.

Suggested reading
Spinka, Matthew *John Huss: A Biography* (1968)

Hussein Saddam (1937–). Iraqi politician, in power from 1968, president from 1979. He presided over the Iran-Iraq war 1980–88, and harshly repressed Kurdish rebels in N Iraq. He annexed Kuwait 1990 but was driven out by a US-dominated coalition army Feb 1991. Defeat in the Gulf War led to unrest, and both the Kurds in the north and Shi'ites in the south rebelled. His savage repression of both revolts led to charges of genocide and the United Nations (UN) established 'safe havens' in the north and 'no-fly zones' in the south. Infringement of the latter led to US air strikes Jan 1993. In 1995, to counter evidence of rifts among his closest supporters, he called a presidential election, in which he was elected (unopposed) with 99.6% of the vote.

Hussein joined the Arab Ba'ath Socialist Party as a young man and soon became involved in revolutionary activities. In 1959 he was sentenced to death and took refuge in Egypt, but a coup in 1963 made his return possible, although in the following year he was imprisoned for plotting to overthrow the regime he had helped to install. After his release he took a leading part in the 1968 revolution, removing the civilian government and establishing a Revolutionary Command Council (RCC). At first discreetly, and then more openly, Hussein strengthened his position and in 1979 became RCC chair and state president, progressively eliminating real or imagined opposition factions as he gained increasing dictatorial control.

In 1977 Saddam Hussein al-Tikriti abolished the use of surnames in Iraq to conceal the fact that a large number of people in the government and ruling party all came from his home village of Tikrit

and therefore bore the same surname. Ruthless in the pursuit of his objectives, he fought a bitter war against Iran 1980–88, with US economic aid, and opposed Kurdish rebels seeking independence, using chemical weapons against civilian populations. The 1990 Kuwait annexation followed a long-running border dispute and was prompted by the need for more oil resources after the expensive war against Iran. Saddam, who had enjoyed US support for being the enemy of Iran and had used poison gas against his own people in Kurdistan without any falling-off in trade with the West, suddenly found himself almost universally condemned.

He is neither a strategist, nor is he schooled in the operational art, nor is he a tactician, nor is he a general, nor is he a soldier. Other than that, he is a great military man.

H Norman Schwarzkopf on SADDAM HUSSEIN
March 1991

Iraq's defeat in the ensuing Gulf War undermined Saddam's position as the country's leader; when the Kurds rebelled again after the end of the war, he sent the remainder of his army to crush them, bringing international charges of genocide against him and causing hundreds of thousands of Kurds to flee their homes in N Iraq. His continued indiscriminate bombardment of Shi'ites in S Iraq led the UN to impose a 'no-fly zone' in the area Aug 1992. Another potential confrontation with the West was averted 1994.

Suggested reading
Bullock, John and Morris, Harvey *Saddam's War* (1991)
Henderson, Simon *Instant Empire: Saddam Hussein's Ambition for Iraq* (1991)
Karsh, E and Rantsi, I *Saddam Hussein* (1991)

Hussein ibn Ali (*c.* 1854–1931). Leader of the Arab revolt 1916–18 against the Turks. He proclaimed himself king of the Hejaz 1916, accepted the caliphate 1924, but was unable to retain it due to internal fighting. He was deposed 1924 by Ibn Saud.

Hussein ibn Talal (1935–). King of Jordan from 1952. By 1967 he had lost all his kingdom west of the river Jordan in the Arab-Israeli Wars, and in 1970 he suppressed the Palestine Liberation Organization, which was acting as a guerrilla force against his rule on the remaining East Bank territories. Subsequently, he became a moderating force in Middle Eastern politics, and in 1994 signed a peace agreement with Israel, ending a 46-year-old 'state of war' between the two countries.

Great-grandson of Hussein ibn Ali, he became king following the mental incapacitation of his father, Talal. After Iraq's annexation of Kuwait 1990 he attempted to mediate between the opposing sides, at the risk of damaging his relations with both sides. In 1993 he publicly distanced himself from Iraqi leader Saddam Hussein.

Husserl Edmund Gustav Albrecht (1859–1938). German philosopher, regarded as the founder of phenomenology, the study of mental states as consciously experienced. His early phenomenology resembles linguistic philosophy because he examined the meaning and our understanding of words. He hoped phenomenology would become the science of all sciences. He influenced Martin Heidegger and affected sociology through the work of Alfred Schütz (1899–1959). Husserl's main works are *Logical Investigations* 1900, *Phenomenological Philosophy* 1913, and *The Crisis of the European Sciences* 1936.

Hussey Obed (1792–1860). US inventor who developed one of the first successful reaping machines 1833 and various other agricultural machinery.

Hussey was born in Maine. His reaping machine used the principle of a reciprocating knife cutting against stationary guards or figures. The cutter was attached to a crank activated by gearing, connected to one of the wheels. The contraption was pulled by horses walking alongside the standing grain. During the harvest of 1834, he demonstrated the reaper to farmers and began to sell the machines.

In 1851 he went to Britain and demonstrated the reaper at Hull and Barnardscastle. He was invited to show it to Prince Albert, who bought two (at £21 each). An earlier rival design of reaper had been developed by Cyrus McCormick in 1831, although Hussey's was patented first.

Hussey also invented a steam plough, a machine for making hooks and eyes, a grinding mill for maize and a horse-powered husking machine, a sugar-cane crusher, and an ice-making machine.

Concentrate on the story, leave the details to others ... and sit whenever you can.

JOHN HUSTON
speaking at Cap d'Antibes 23 May 1979

Huston John Marcellus (1906–1987). US film director, screenwriter, and actor. An impulsive and individualistic film maker, he often dealt with the themes of greed, treachery in human relationships, and the loner. His works as a director include *The Maltese Falcon* 1941 (his debut), *The Treasure of the Sierra Madre* 1948 (in which his father Walter Huston starred and for which both won Academy Awards), *The African Queen* 1951, and his last, *The Dead* 1987. His other films include *Key Largo* 1948, *Moby Dick* 1956, *The Misfits* 1961, *Fat City* 1972, and *Prizzi's Honor* 1984. He was the father of actress Anjelica Huston.
Suggested reading
Grobel, Lawrence *The Hustons* (1989)
Huston, John *An Open Book* (1980)
Kaminsky, Stuart *John Huston* (1978)

Threatened with boredom, I'll run like a hare.

JOHN HUSTON
in *Time Out* 18 April 1980

Huston Walter (1884–1950). Canadian-born US actor. His career alternated between stage acting and appearances in feature films. He received critical acclaim for his Broadway performance in *Desire Under the Elms* 1924. In 1948 he won the Academy Award for the best supporting actor for his role in *The Treasure of the Sierra Madre*.

Huston who was born in Toronto, Canada, trained and worked as an engineer before choosing a theatrical career. He was the father of director John Huston who wrote and directed *The Treasure of the Sierra Madre*.

Hutchinson Anne Marbury (1591–1643). American colonial religious leader. In 1634, she and her family followed John Cotton from England to Massachusetts Bay Colony. Preaching a unique theology which emphasized the role of faith, she gained a wide following. The colony's leaders, including Cotton, felt threatened by Hutchinson and in 1637 she was banished and excommunicated. Settling in Long Island, she and her family were killed by Indians.
Suggested reading
Battis, E J *Saints and Sectaries* (1962)
Bremer, F J *Anne Hutchinson* (1981)
Rimmer, R H *The Resurrection of Anne Hutchinson* (1986)

Hutier Oskar von (1857–1934). German general. During the capture of Riga Sept 1917, he developed the tactic of using small armed parties of well-trained infantry to infiltrate the enemy positions, outflank and turn them, and thus force gaps for larger parties to follow up; this was assisted by well-planned artillery support devised by his artillery commander Col Bruchmuller.

Hutton Barbara (1912–1979). US heiress, granddaughter of retail magnate F W Woolworth, notorious in her day as the original 'poor little rich girl'. Her seven husbands included the actor Cary Grant.

Hutton Edward Thomas Henry (1848–1923). English army officer who was military commander in New South Wales, Australia, 1893–97. He led a brigade of Australian, New Zealand, Canadian, and British troops during the Boer War and returned to Australia after federation to form a single army out of the state forces and organize land defence 1902–04.

Hutton James (1726–1797). Scottish geologist, known as the 'founder of geology', who formulated the concept of uniformitarianism. In 1785 he developed a theory of the igneous origin of many rocks.

His *Theory of the Earth* 1788 proposed that the Earth was incalculably old. Uniformitarianism suggests that past events could be explained in terms of processes that work today. For example, the kind of river current that produces a certain settling pattern in a bed of sand today must have been operating many millions of years ago, if that same pattern is visible in ancient sandstones.
Suggested reading
Bailey, E B *James Hutton* (1967)
Playfair, John *Illustrations of the Huttonian Theory of the Earth* (1802, rep 1956)

Hutton Len (Leonard) (1916–1990). English cricketer, born in Pudsey, West Yorkshire. He captained England in 23 test matches 1952–56 and was England's first professional captain. In 1938 at the Oval he scored 364 against Australia, a world record test score until beaten by Gary Sobers 1958. He was knighted for services to the game 1956.

Huxley Aldous Leonard (1894–1963). English writer of novels, essays, and verse. From the disillusionment and satirical eloquence of *Crome Yellow* 1921, *Antic Hay* 1923, and *Point Counter Point* 1928, Huxley developed towards the Utopianism exemplified by *Island* 1962. The science fiction novel *Brave New World* 1932 shows human beings mass-produced in laboratories and rendered incapable of freedom by indoctrination and drugs. He was the grandson of Thomas Henry Huxley and brother of Julian Huxley.

Huxley, Aldous *The English writer Aldous Huxley. His 1932 novel* Brave New World *is a fable about individual freedom in a scientific age. It describes a future state in which humans are hatched in incubators and controlled by drugs.* (Image Select)

That men do not learn very much from the lessons of history is the most important of all the lessons that history has to teach.

ALDOUS HUXLEY
Collected Essays, 'Case of Voluntary Ignorance' 1960

Huxley's later devotion to mysticism led to his experiments with the hallucinogenic drug mescalin, recorded in *The Doors of Perception* 1954. He also wrote the novel *Eyeless in Gaza* 1936, and two historical studies, *Grey Eminence* 1941 and *The Devils of Loudun* 1952.

Suggested reading
Bedford, Sybille *Aldous Huxley: A Biography* (1985)
Nance, G A *Aldous Huxley* (1989)
Woodcock, George *Dawn and the Darkest Hour: A Study of Aldous Huxley* (1972)
Wyatt, Donald *Aldous Huxley* (1985)

Man's greatest strength lies in his capacity for irrelevance. In the midst of pestilences, wars and famines, he builds cathedrals.

ALDOUS HUXLEY
Antic Hay ch 13 1923

Huxley Andrew Fielding (1917–). English physiologist, awarded the Nobel prize 1963 with Alan Hodgkin for work on nerve impulses, discovering how ionic mechanisms are used in nerves to transmit impulses. Knighted 1974.

Huxley was born in London, the grandson of scientist T H Huxley. He was educated at Cambridge and did military research during World War II. After the war, he returned to Cambridge. In 1960 he became professor at University College, London.

In 1945 at Cambridge, Hodgkin and Huxley began to measure the electrochemical behaviour of nerve membranes. They experimented on axons of the giant squid – each axon is about 0.7 mm/0.03 in in diameter. They inserted a glass capillary tube filled with sea water into the axon to test the composition of the ions in and surrounding the cell, which also had a microelectrode inserted into it. Stimulating the axon with a pair of outside electrodes, they showed that the inside of the cell was at first negative (the resting potential) and the outside positive, and that during the conduction of the nerve impulse the membrane potential reversed.

Huxley Hugh Esmor (1924–). English physiologist who, using the electron microscope and thin slicing techniques, established the detailed structural basis of muscle contraction.

Huxley was born in Birkenhead, Cheshire, and studied at Cambridge. He returned to Cambridge as a lecturer 1961.

Muscle fibres contain a large number of longitudinally arranged myofibrils, which, Huxley demonstrated, are composed of thick and thin filaments of the proteins myosin and actin. He showed how the filaments are attached to one another in a woven pattern, and suggested that muscle contraction is brought about by sliding movements of two sets of filaments.

He discovered that the myosin filaments are able to aggregate under suitable conditions to form 'artificial' filaments of varying lengths. He proposed that the 'tails' of the myosin molecules become attached to each other to form a filament with the heads projecting from the body of the filament, and that this plays an important part in the sliding effect.

By coincidence, Andrew Huxley (no relation), working separately, came to the same conclusions at about the same time in the 1950s, although they disagree on the exact details.

Huxley Julian Sorell (1887–1975). English biologist, first director general of UNESCO, and a founder of the World Wildlife Fund (now the World Wide Fund for Nature). He wrote popular science books, including *Essays of a Biologist* 1923. Knighted 1958.

Huxley Thomas Henry (1825–1895). English scientist and humanist. Following the publication of Charles Darwin's *On the Origin of Species* 1859, he became known as 'Darwin's bulldog', and for many years was a prominent champion of evolution. In 1869, he coined the word 'agnostic' to express his own religious attitude, and is considered the founder of scientific humanism.

From 1846 to 1850 Huxley was the assistant ship's surgeon on HMS *Rattlesnake* on its voyage around the South Seas. The observations he made on the voyage, especially of invertebrates, were published and made his name in the UK.

In 1854 he became professor of natural history at the Royal School of Mines. His grandsons include Aldous, Andrew, and Julian Huxley. Huxley found the system of classification introduced by French anatomist Georges Cuvier to be inadequate for the sea creatures he studied on his voyage. He reclassified the animal kingdom into Annuloida, Annulosa, Infusoria, Coelenterata, Mollusca, Molluscoida, Protozoa, and Vertebrata, and started a fundamental revision of the Mollusca. He also produced a new system of classification of birds, based mainly on the palate and other bony structures, which is the foundation of the modern system. His scientific works include *Man's Place in Nature* 1863; later books, such as *Lay Sermons* 1870, *Science and Culture* 1881, and *Evolution and Ethics* 1893, were expositions of scientific humanism.

Suggested reading
Ashforth, Albert *Thomas Henry Huxley* (1969)
Bibby, Cyril *Scientist Extraordinary: The Life and Scientific Work of T H Huxley* (1972)
Irvine, W *Darwin, Huxley and Evolution* (1961)

Logical consequences are the scarecrows of fools and the beacons of wise men.

THOMAS HENRY HUXLEY
Science and Culture, 'On the Hypothesis that Animals are Automata' 1882

Hu Yaobang (1915–1989). Chinese politician, Communist Party (CCP) chair 1981–87. A protégé of the communist leader Deng Xiaoping, Hu presided over a radical overhaul of the party structure and personnel 1982–86. His death ignited the prodemocracy movement, which was eventually crushed in Tiananmen Square in June 1989.

Hu, born into a peasant family in Hunan province, was a political commissar during the 1934–35 Long March. In 1941 he served under Deng and later worked under him in provincial and central government. Hu was purged as a 'capitalist roader' during the 1966–69 Cultural Revolution and sent into the countryside for 're-education'. He was rehabilitated 1975 but disgraced again when Deng fell from prominence 1976. In Dec 1978, with Deng established in power, Hu was inducted into the CCP Politburo and became head of the revived secretariat 1980 and CCP chair 1981. He attempted to quicken reaction against Mao. He was dismissed Jan 1987 for his relaxed handling of a wave of student unrest Dec 1986.

Huygens Christiaan (1629–1695). Dutch mathematical physicist and astronomer who proposed the wave theory of light. He developed the pendulum clock 1657, discovered polarization, and observed Saturn's rings. He made important advances in pure mathematics, applied mathematics, and mechanics, which he virtually founded. Huygens's study of probability, including game theory, originated the modern concept of the expectation of a variable.

Huygens was born in The Hague and studied at Leiden and Breda. He spent his life in research, based 1666–81 at the Bibliothèque Royale, Paris.

Huysmans J(oris) K(arl). Adopted name of Charles Marie Georges Huysmans (1848–1907). French novelist of Dutch ancestry. His novel *Marthe* 1876, the story of a courtesan, was followed by other novels, all of which feature solitary protagonists. His best-known work is *A rebours/Against Nature* 1884, a novel of self-absorbed aestheticism that symbolized the 'decadent' movement. He ended his life in a religious order.

Born in Paris, he worked 30 years as a civil servant, and also wrote art criticism.

Hyakutake Haruyoshi (1888–1947). Japanese general in World War II. He failed to evict US troops from Guadalcanal 1942, barely managing to escape with 10,000 of his troops. The US landings at Rendova June 1943 took him by surprise and he failed to defeat the Americans on Bougainville. In April 1945 he was removed from his command and employed in an administrative post for the remainder of the war.

Hyatt John Wesley (1837–1920). US inventor who in 1869 invented celluloid, the first artificial plastic, intended as a substitute for ivory. It became popular for making a wide range of products, from shirt collars and combs to toys and babies' rattles, and is still used in the manufacture of table-tennis balls.

Hyatt was born in Starkey, New York, and worked in Illinois as a printer. In the early 1860s, the New York company of Phelan and Collender offered a prize of $10,000 for a satisfactory substitute for ivory for making billiard balls. Using pyroxylin, a partly nitrated cellulose, Hyatt developed celluloid (the US trade name: it was called Xylonite in Britain). Although celluloid did come to be used for billiard balls, Hyatt was never awarded the prize money. He continued to patent his inventions – more than 200 of them, including roller bearings and a multiple-stitch sewing machine.

Celluloid consisted of a mouldable mixture of nitrated cellulose and camphor. Its chief disadvantage was its flammability. Celluloid was also used as a substrate for photographic film and as the filling in sandwich-type safety glass for car windscreens. It has been largely superseded by other synthetic materials.

Hyde Douglas (1860–1949). Irish scholar and politician. Founder president of the Gaelic League 1893–1915 (aiming to promote a

His habit of flattery and picturesque speech sometimes suggested the stage Irishman of fiction.

Denis Gwynn on DOUGLAS HYDE
in *Dictionary of National Biography*

cultural, rather than political, nationalism), he was president of Eire 1938–45. He was the first person to write a book in modern Irish and to collect Irish folklore, as well as being the author of the first literary history of Ireland. His works include *Love Songs of Connacht* 1894.

Hyder Ali or Haidar Ali (*c.* 1722–1782). Indian general, sultan of Mysore in SW India from 1759. In command of the army in Mysore from 1749, he became the ruler of the state 1761, and rivalled British power in the area until his triple defeat by Sir Eyre Coote 1781 during the Anglo-French wars. He was the father of Tipu Sultan.

Hyde-White Wilfred (1903–1991). English actor. He is best known for character roles in British and occasionally US films, especially the role of Colonel Pickering in the screen version of *My Fair Lady* 1964. He tended to be cast as an eccentric or a pillar of the establishment, and sometimes as a mixture of the two.

Hyman Libbie Henrietta (1888–1969). US zoologist whose six-volume *The Invertebrates* 1940–68 provided an encyclopedic account of most phyla of invertebrates.

Hyman was born in Des Moines, Iowa, and studied at the University of Chicago, where she remained as a research assistant until 1930. She then travelled to several European laboratories, working for a period at the Stazione Zoologica, Naples, Italy, before returning to New York City to begin to write a comprehensive reference book on the invertebrates, for which she was given office and laboratory space, but no salary, by the American Museum of Natural History.

Initially she worked on flatworms, but soon extended her investigations to a wide spread of invertebrates, especially their taxonomy (classification) and anatomy.

Hypatia (*c.* 370–*c.* 415). Greek philosopher, born in Alexandria. She studied Neo-Platonism in Athens, and succeeded her father Theon as professor of philosophy at Alexandria. She was probably murdered by Christian fanatics.

Ibáñez Vicente Blasco (1867–1928). Spanish novelist and politician. His novels include *La barraca/The Cabin* 1898, the most successful of his regional works; *Sangre y arena/Blood and Sand* 1908, the story of a famous bullfighter; and *Los cuatro jinetes del Apocalipsis/The Four Horsemen of the Apocalypse* 1916, a product of the effects of World War I. He was actively involved in revolutionary politics.

It is better to die on your feet than to live on your knees.
DOLORES IBARRURI
Speech in Paris 3 Sept 1936

Ibarruri Dolores, known as 'La Pasionaria' ('the passion flower') (1895–1989). Spanish Basque politician, journalist, and orator; she was first elected to the Cortes in 1936. She helped to establish the Popular Front government and was a Loyalist leader in the Civil War. When Franco came to power in 1939 she left Spain for the USSR, where she was active in the Communist Party. She returned to Spain in 1977 after Franco's death and was re-elected to the Cortes (at the age of 81) in the first parliamentary elections for 40 years.

She joined the Spanish Socialist Party in 1917 and wrote for a workers' newspaper under the pen name La Pasionaria.

Ibert Jacques François Antoine (1890–1962). French composer. Although writing in a variety of genres and styles, his music is generally considered light, due in large part to his seven often witty operas. However, his music reflects its subject matter: in his symphonic poem *La Ballade de la geôle de Reading* (1922) he captures the horror of Oscar Wilde's poem, while in his Flute Concerto 1934 he involves the full technical range of the solo instrument.

Iberville Pierre Le Moyne, Sieur d' (1661–1706). French colonial administrator and explorer in America. Born in Montreal, Canada, Iberville joined the French navy and saw action against the English in the struggle for Canada 1686–97. With his brother, the Sieur de Bienville, he led an expedition from France and established a colony at the mouth of the Mississippi river in America. In 1699–1700 they established settlements at the later sites of Biloxi and New Orleans.

Ibn al-'Arabi (Abu Bakr Muhammad bin Ali Muhyi al-Din) (1165–1240). Andalusian-born mystic and teacher who settled in Damascus. To Ibn 'Arabi love was more important than knowledge, a theory that is totally rejected by traditional Muslim lawyers. A prolific writer, he combined inner devotion with an analytical mind, concluding the unity of faiths despite their apparent divergency. He wrote an estimated 400 books and treatises, including *al-Futuhat al-Makiyya/The Makkan Inspirations*.

Ibn Battuta (1304–1368). Arab traveller born in Tangier. In 1325, he went on an extraordinary 120,675-km/75,000-mi journey via Mecca to Egypt, E Africa, India, and China, returning some 30 years later. During this journey he also visited Spain and crossed the Sahara to Timbuktu. The narrative of his travels, *The Adventures of Ibn Battuta*, was written with an assistant, Ibn Juzayy.

Ibn Hanbal Ahmad (780–855). Founder of the last of the four main schools of Sunni Islamic law. He was an expert on the Hadith of the prophet Muhammad (traditions concerning his life and sayings). Modern Wahabis adhere to his teachings.

Ibn Hanbal was born in Baghdad and instructed by Imam Shafi'i. His main work, the *Musnad/The Reliable*, contained 30,000 Hadith.

Ibn Saud Abdul Aziz (1880–1953). First king of Saudi Arabia from 1932. His father was the son of the sultan of Nejd, at whose capital, Riyadh, Ibn Saud was born. In 1891 a rival group seized Riyadh, and Ibn Saud went into exile with his father, who resigned his claim to the throne in his son's favour. In 1902 Ibn Saud recaptured Riyadh and recovered the kingdom, and by 1921 he had brought all central Arabia under his rule. In 1924 he invaded the Hejaz, of which he was proclaimed king in 1926.

Nejd and the Hejaz were united 1932 in the kingdom of Saudi Arabia. Ibn Saud introduced programmes for modernization with revenue from oil, which was discovered 1936.

Ibn Sina Arabic name of ◊Avicenna, scholar, and translator.

Ibrahim Abdullah. Adopted name of 'Dollar' Brand (1934–1990). South African pianist and composer. He first performed in the USA 1965 and had a great influence on the fusion of African rhythms with American jazz. His compositions range from songs to large works for orchestra.

Ibsen Henrik Johan (1828–1906). Norwegian dramatist and poet. His realistic and often controversial plays revolutionized European theatre. Driven into exile 1864–91 by opposition to the satirical *Love's Comedy* 1862, he wrote the verse dramas *Brand* 1866 and *Peer Gynt* 1867, followed by realistic plays dealing with social issues, including *Pillars of Society* 1877, *A Doll's House* 1879, *Ghosts* 1881, *An Enemy of the People* 1882, and *Hedda Gabler* 1891. By the time he returned to Norway, he was recognized as the country's greatest living writer.

His later plays, which are more symbolic, include *The Master Builder* 1892, *Little Eyolf* 1894, *John Gabriel Borkman* 1896, and *When We Dead Awaken* 1899. His influence on European and American theatre in the 20th century has been profound.
Suggested reading
Beyer, Edward *Ibsen: The Man and His Work* (1980)
Clurman, Harold *Ibsen: The Man and the Dramatist* (1977)
Lyons, Charles *Henrik Ibsen: The Divided Consciousness* (1972)
Meyer, Michael *Henrik Ibsen* (1967–71)

Ibuse Masuji (1898–1993). Japanese novelist and poet, considered one of the most important Japanese writers of this century. His best-known novel is *Kuroit Ame/Black Rain* 1966, a powerful and moving account of the devastating effects of nuclear war, and other works include *Tomonotsu Chakai Ki/Recordings of the Tea Ceremonies at Tomonotsu* 1984, an account, in the form of diary records, of events at thirteen 16th-century tea ceremonies.

Ibuse was born in Hiroshima Province. After leaving school he first studied French at Waseda University, and then entered Nihon Bijutsu Gakko, Tokyo's leading art school. His poetry during this time shows an artist's attention to visual detail. A short story in fable form, 'Koi/Carp' 1928, was followed by others such as 'Sanshō Uo/Salamander' 1929, and his first novel, *Shigoto Beya/A Room to Work In* appeared 1931. After this came a novella, *Kawa/River* 1932, some essays on fishing, his favourite hobby, and a satirical second novel, *Shūkin Ryokō/Travel to Collect Money* 1936, which was later made into a successful film. He won the Naoki Prize 1938 for *Jon Manjirō Hyōryūki/Jon Manjiro Castaway: his life and adventures*, a true account of a man whose boat was swept across the Pacific by a storm.

Ickes Harold LeClair (1874–1952). US public official. A liberal Republican, he was appointed secretary of the interior by F D Roosevelt 1933. As director of the Public Works Administration (PWA, established 1935), he administered Roosevelt's New Deal development projects. In World War II, he was administrator of solid fuels, petroleum, fisheries, and coal mines. He served briefly under President Truman, but resigned from the cabinet 1946.

Born in Blair County, Pennsylvania, USA, Ickes was educated at the University of Chicago and was admitted to the bar 1907. After resigning from his political post, Ickes wrote a newspaper column and published several autobiographical works. *The Secret Diary of Harold L Ickes* appeared 1953.

Iglesias Pablo (1850–1925). Spanish politician, founder of the Spanish Socialist Party (Partido Socialista Obrero Español, PSOE) in 1879. In 1911 he became the first socialist deputy to be elected to the *Cortes* (Spanish parliament).

Ignatius Loyola, St (born Iñigo López de Recalde) (1491–1556). Spanish noble who founded the Jesuit order 1534, also called the Society of Jesus. Canonized 1622.

His deep interest in the religious life began in 1521, when reading the life of Jesus while recuperating from a war wound. He visited the Holy Land in 1523, studied in Spain and Paris, where he took vows with St Francis Xavier, and was ordained 1537. He then moved to Rome and with the approval of Pope Paul III began the Society of Jesus, sending missionaries to Brazil, India, and Japan, and founding Jesuit schools. Feast day 31 July.

Let me be eaten by wild beasts, through whom I can attain to God. I am God's wheat, and I am ground by the teeth of wild beasts that I may be found to be the pure bread of Christ.

ST IGNATIUS OF ANTIOCH
Letter to the Romans 4:1

Ignatius of Antioch, St (died *c.* 110). Christian martyr. Traditionally a disciple of St John, he was bishop of Antioch, and was thrown to the wild beasts in Rome. He wrote seven epistles, important documents of the early Christian church. Feast day 1 Feb.

Ikhnaton another name for ◊Akhenaton, pharaoh of Egypt.

Iliescu Ion (1930–   ). Romanian president from 1990. A former member of the Romanian Communist Party (PCR) and of Nicolae Ceausescu's government, Iliescu swept into power on Ceausescu's fall as head of the National Salvation Front.

Iliescu was elected a member of the PCR central committee 1968, becoming its propaganda secretary 1971. Conflict over the launching of a 'cultural revolution' and the growth of Ceausescu's personality cult led to Iliescu's removal from national politics: he was sent to Timisoara as chief of party propaganda. At the outbreak of the 'Christmas revolution' 1989, Iliescu was one of the first leaders to emerge, becoming president of the Provisional Council of National Unity Feb 1990. He won an overwhelming victory in the presidential elections May 1990, despite earlier controversy over his hard line.

Illich Ivan (1926–   ). US radical philosopher and activist, born in Austria. His works, which include *Deschooling Society* 1971, *Towards a History of Need* 1978, and *Gender* 1983, are a critique of contemporary economic development, especially in the Third World.

Illich was born in Vienna and has lived in the USA and Latin America. He believes that modern technology and bureaucratic institutions are destroying peasant skills and self-sufficiency and creating a new form of dependency: on experts, professionals, and material goods. True liberation, he believes, can only be achieved by abolishing the institutions on which authority rests, such as schools and hospitals.

Imhotep (lived *c.* 2800 BC). Egyptian physician and architect, adviser to King Zoser (3rd dynasty). He is thought to have designed the step pyramid at Sakkara, and his tomb (believed to be in the N Sakkara cemetery) became a centre of healing. He was deified as the son of Ptah and was identified with Aesculapius, the Greek god of medicine.

Immelmann Max (1890–1916). German fighter ace in World War I. He developed the 'Immelmann Turn', a manoeuvre in which, pursued, he would climb suddenly in a half-loop, roll, and then dive back at his pursuer. Decorated by the Kaiser Jan 1915, he was shot down and killed near Lens by Lt George McCubbin 18 June 1916.

Ince Thomas Harper (1882–1924). US film director and producer. He is noted for bringing realism into the silent Western genre, notably in a series of films featuring William S Hart. In 1915 he joined Mack Sennett and D W Griffith to form Triangle Film Corporation, subsequently functioning mainly as a producer. His most ambitious film as producer was *Civilization* 1916.

Inchbald Elizabeth (born Simpson) (1753–1821). English author and actress. She wrote *A Simple Story* 1791 and *Nature and Art* 1796, both romances in which gifted, high-spirited heroines struggle against society's restraints on women. She also wrote plays including *I'll Tell You What* 1786 and *Lovers Vows* 1798.

India Sigismondo d' (*c.* 1582–1629). Italian composer whose highly chromatic madrigals (in eight books 1606–24) have been valued as second only to those of Monteverdi. He left his native Sicily to work at the Turin court 1611–23.

Indy (Paul Marie Théodore) Vincent d' (1851–1931). French composer. He studied under César Franck, and was one of the founders of the *Schola Cantorum*. His works include operas (*Fervaal* 1897), symphonies, tone poems (*Istar* 1896), and chamber music.

Inge William Ralph (1860–1954). English philosopher and dean of St Paul's in London 1911–1934. As a Christian Platonist and an expert on Plotinus, he believed that self-disciplined prayer admitted the individual to an eternal world of light and peace. As a social commentator, he inclined to rather pessimistic and politically conservative views, and he became known as 'the gloomy dean'.

Inge was born in Crayke, North Yorkshire. He taught at Eton public school and at Oxford University before joining the church. His works include *Christian Mysticism* 1899, *Christian Ethics and Modern Problems* 1930, and *The End of an Age* 1948.

A man may build himself a throne of bayonets, but he cannot sit on it.

WILLIAM INGE
quoted in Sir James Marchant (ed) *Wit and Wisdom of Dean Inge*

Ingenhousz Jan (1730–1799). Dutch physician and plant physiologist who established in 1779 that in sunlight plants absorb carbon dioxide and give off oxygen. He found that plants, like animals, respire all the time and that respiration occurs in all the parts of plants.

Ingenhousz was born in Breda and studied at Louvain and Leiden and abroad at Paris and Edinburgh, after which he set up a private medical practice in Breda. In 1765, he left for England, going to work at the Foundling Hospital, London, where he successfully inoculated patients against smallpox (using the hazardous live virus). In 1768 he was sent to the Austrian court by George III, to inoculate the royal family, and became court physician there 1772–79. He then returned to England.

Apart from studying plants, Ingenhousz developed in 1776 an improved apparatus for generating large amounts of electricity; he also invented a hydrogen-fuelled lighter to replace the tinderbox, and investigated the use of an air and ether vapour mixture as a propellant for an electrically fired pistol. Ingenhousz's work *Experiments On Vegetables, Discovering their Great Power of Purifying the Common Air in Sunshine, and of Injuring it in the Shade or at Night* 1779 laid the foundations for the study of photosynthesis.

Ingold Christopher Kelk (1893–1970). English organic chemist who specialized in the concepts, classification, and terminology of theoretical organic chemistry. He explained the mechanisms of organic reactions in terms of the behaviour of electrons in the molecules concerned. His *Structure and Mechanisms in Organic Chemistry* 1953 is a classic reference book. Knighted 1958.

Ingold was born in London and studied at Southampton. He became professor at Leeds 1924, moving 1930 to University College, London.

Ingres Jean-Auguste-Dominique (1780–1867). French painter. He was a student of David and a leading exponent of the Neo-Classical style. He studied and worked in Rome about 1807–20, where he began the *Odalisque* series of sensuous female nudes, then went to Florence, and returned to France 1824. His portraits painted in the 1840s–50s are meticulously detailed and highly polished.

Ingres' style developed in opposition to Romanticism. Early works include portraits of Napoleon. Later he painted huge ceilings for the Louvre and for Autun Cathedral. His quarrel with the Romantics and the nature of his own Classicism could be simply stated as a preference for drawing rather than colour. His pencil portraits, many executed during his first Italian stay, display his drawing skill. In the painted portrait, such as those of M de Norvins (National Gallery, London) or Mme de Sennones (Musée de Nantes), he could produce masterpieces. The paintings of the nude of his later years have a sensuous beauty. It would be easy to call him academic and reactionary on the strength of prejudices obstinately maintained to the end of his long life, yet his realistic genius outweighs his defects. The Musée Ingres, Montauban, founded 1843, received the contents of his studio by bequest, including 4,000 of his drawings and numerous paintings.

Suggested reading
Friedlaender, Walter *David to Delacroix* (trs 1952)
Picon, Gaeton *Ingres* (trs 1980)
Rosenblum, Robert *Jean-Auguste-Dominique Ingres* (1967)

Innes-Ker family name of dukes of Roxburghe; seated at Floors Castle, Roxburghshire, Scotland.

Inness George (1825–1894). US landscape painter. He was influenced by the Hudson River School. His early works, such as *The Delaware Valley* 1865 (Metropolitan Museum of Art, New York), are on a grand scale and show a concern for the natural effects of light. Later he moved towards Impressionism.

Inness was largely self-taught, though he profited by the study of Corot and the Barbizon painters on his frequent visits to Europe. This influence seems to have directed him away from the spacious panoramas of American Romantic landscape to a more intimate naturalistic approach. *The Lackawanna Valley*, 1855 (Washington, National Gallery), and *Peace and Plenty*, 1865 (New York, Metropolitan Museum), are among his best works. He died during a visit to Scotland.

Innocent thirteen popes including:

Greediness closed Paradise; it beheaded John the Baptist.
INNOCENT III
De Contemptu Mundi

Innocent III (c. 1161–1216). Pope from 1198 who asserted papal power over secular princes, in particular over the succession of Holy Roman emperors. He also made King John of England his vassal, compelling him to accept Stephen Langton as archbishop of Canterbury. He promoted the fourth Crusade and crusades against the non-Christian Livonians and Letts, and the Albigensian heretics of S France.

Suggested reading
Packard, S R *Europe and the Church Under Innocent III* (1968)
Sayers, Jane *Innocent III: Leader in Europe, 1198–1216* (1994)
Smith, C E *Innocent III, Church Defender* (1951)
Tillman, H *Pope Innocent III* (trs 1980)

Inönü Ismet (1884–1973). Turkish politician and soldier, president 1938–50 and prime minister 1923–38 and 1961–65. He continued the modernization and westernization of Turkey begun by the republic's founder Kemal Atatürk, and kept his country out of World War II. After 1945 he attempted to establish democratic institutions.

He was born in Smyrna, in Asia Minor, and pursued a career as an army officer before and during World War I. During the Turkish War of Independence 1919–22 he was Atatürk's Chief of Staff of the army, and stopped the Greek advance in Anatolia at the first and second battles of Inönü 1921 (from which he later took his name). Representing Turkey at the peace conference, he signed the Treaty of Lausanne 1923. He was the first prime minister of Turkey and was elected president after the death of Atatürk 1938. Despite the efforts of the British prime minister Winston Churchill to bring Turkey into World War II, Inönü managed to keep the country neutral until 1945. Although a supporter of one-party rule between 1939 and 1946, he later became a champion of democracy. Losing power to Adnan Menderes (1899–1961) in the first free elections 1950, Inönü was leader of the opposition until he became prime minister 1961 after the military coup 1960 and execution of Menderes 1961. He lost power to the pro-Western Suleyman Demirel 1965.

Inoue Yasushi (1907–1991). Japanese writer (fiction, travel essays, art history). His interest in China and central Asia is evident in many stories and historical novels. The novels feature isolated protagonists at dramatic moments of Asian history. Examples are *Tempyō no iraka/The Roof Tile of Tempyo* 1957, translation 1976, *Koshi*, based on the life of Confucius, and *Shirobama*, describing a childhood in old Japan.

A work of art is above all an adventure of the mind.
EUGÈNE IONESCO
Notes and Counter-Notes pt 2, 'An Address Delivered
to a Gathering of French and German Writers' 1964

Ionesco Eugène (1912–1994). Romanian-born French dramatist. He was a leading exponent of the Theatre of the Absurd. Most of his plays are in one act and concern the futility of language as a means of communication. These include *La Cantatrice chauve/The Bald Prima Donna* 1950, and *La Leçon/The Lesson* 1951. Later full-length plays include *Rhinocéros* 1958 and *Le Roi se meurt/Exit the King* 1961.

He was born Eugen Ionescu in Slatina, Romania. His father, a lawyer, was Romanian, his mother French. The family moved to Paris, where Ionesco grew up, while his father returned to Romania 1917. Ionesco was taken back to Romania at the age of 14 to stay with his father, now divorced. He ran away from home when he was 17 and entered the University of Bucharest to study French.

He started writing seriously, producing a small book of poems 1931 and several newspaper articles. In 1934 he published *Nu*, a collection of essays on the leading Romanian writers of the time. He became a drama critic for the magazine *Facla*, and taught French until 1938, when he returned to Paris to do research at the Sorbonne. He spent the war years mainly in Marseille. Back in Paris after the war, he worked as a proofreader and began to learn English with the aid of a teach-yourself manual; this experience led him to write the 'anti-play' *La Cantatrice Chauve*, which has played in Paris virtually without a break since its first performance 1950, and the Theatre of the Absurd came into being. Ionesco was the most characteristic practitioner, more perhaps than Arthur Asimov and Samuel Beckett.

About a dozen plays followed, including *La Leçon/The Lesson*, *Les Chaises/The Chairs* 1952, and *Tueur sans gages/The Killer* 1959. In 1960 Jean-Louis Barrault produced *Le Rhinocéros* at the Théâtre de France. In this play, all except one of the inhabitants of a provincial town turn into a herd of lethal rhinoceroses, symbolizing an authoritarian society. Ionesco's next play, *La soif et la faim/Hunger and Thirst* 1966, was commissioned by the Comédie Française. However, his later work lacks the brilliance of the earlier. He was elected to the Académie Française 1971 and received many other honours, among them the Légion d'Honneur and the Grand Prix National du Théâtre.

Ipatieff Vladimir Nikolayevich (1867–1952). Russian-born US organic chemist who developed catalysis in organic chemistry, particularly in reactions involving hydrocarbons.

Ipatieff was born in Moscow, became an officer in the Imperial Russian Army, and studied at the Mikhail Artillery Academy in St Petersburg and in Germany at Munich, as well as spending a brief period in France studying explosives. He returned to Russia 1899 as professor of chemistry and explosives at the Mikhail Artillery Academy. During World War I and the Russian Revolution, he held various administrative and advisory appointments. At the age of 64, he defected to the USA. From 1931 to 1935 he was professor at Northwestern University, Illinois, and consultant to the Universal Oil Products Company, Chicago, which funded the building of the Ipatieff High Pressure Laboratory at Northwestern 1938.

In 1900 Ipatieff discovered the specific nature of catalysis in high-temperature organic gas reactions, and how using high pressures the method could be extended to liquids. He developed an autoclave called the Ipatieff bomb for heating liquid compounds to above their boiling points under high pressure. He synthesized methane and produced polyethylene by polymerizing ethylene (ethene). In Chicago, Ipatieff began to apply his high-temperature catalysis reactions to petrol to give it a higher octane rating. Important for the production of aviation fuel during World War II, the method is still used.

Ipoustéguy Jean Robert (1920–). French sculptor, painter, and draughtsperson. He is known for his innovative combination of figurative and abstract traditions in sculpture. Typically, his work symbolizes the trials of modern life, generally in the form of an upright male figure both supported and entrapped by rigid armatures, with limbs partially lacerated or eroded, as in *Val de Grâce* 1977 (Galerie Claude Bernard, Paris).

Ipoustéguy turned from painting to three-dimensional form 1949–50, translating the rocky landscapes of 15th-century Italian frescoes into large sculptures with figures emerging. Brancusi was an early influence.

Iqbāl Muhammad (1876–1938). Islamic poet and thinker. His literary works, in Urdu and Persian, were mostly verse in the classical style, suitable for public recitation. He sought through his writings to arouse Muslims to take their place in the modern world. Knighted 1922.

His most celebrated work, the Persian *Asrā-e khŭdī/Secrets of the Self* 1915, put forward a theory of the self that was opposite to the traditional abnegation found in Islam. He was an influence on the movement that led to the creation of Pakistan.

Ireland John Nicholson (1879–1962). English composer. His works include the mystic orchestral prelude *The Forgotten Rite* 1917 and the piano solo *Sarnia* 1941. Benjamin Britten was his pupil.

Irene, St (*c.* 752–*c.* 803). Byzantine empress 797–802. The wife of Leo IV (750–80), she became regent for their son Constantine (771–805) on Leo's death. In 797 she deposed her son, had his eyes put out, and assumed the full title of *basileus* ('emperor'), ruling in her own right until deposed and exiled to Lesvos by a revolt in 802. She was made a saint by the Greek Orthodox church for her attacks on iconoclasts.

No man could prevail so much, nor order Cromwell so far, as Ireton could.

Bulstrode Whitelocke on HENRY IRETON
in *Memorials of English Affairs* 1625–60

Ireton Henry (1611–1651). English Civil War general. He joined the parliamentary forces and fought at Edgehill 1642, Gainsborough 1643, and Naseby 1645. After the Battle of Naseby, Ireton, who was opposed to both the extreme republicans and Levellers, strove for a compromise with Charles I, but then played a leading role in his trial and execution. He married his leader Cromwell's daughter in 1646. Lord Deputy in Ireland from 1650, he died after the capture of Limerick.

Irons Jeremy (1948–). English actor. His aristocratic bearing, immaculate grooming, and precise diction have led to frequent

casting as a repressed, upper-class character. A hint of ambiguity under this surface sheen has made him perfect for such film roles as Claus von Bulow in *Reversal of Fortune* 1990 (Academy Award) and the twin brothers in *Dead Ringers* 1988. Other key films include *The French Lieutenant's Woman* 1981, *The Mission* 1986, and *Damage* 1992.

He came to prominence in a television adaptation of Evelyn Waugh's *Brideshead Revisited* 1981. His other screen appearances include *Moonlighting* 1982, *Un Amour de Swann/Swann in Love* 1984, and *The House of the Spirits* and *M. Butterfly* both 1993.

Ironside (William) Edmund, 1st Baron Ironside (1880–1959). British field marshal. Ironside served in the South African War 1899–1902 and World War I. In World War II, he replaced Gort as Chief of the Imperial General Staff 1939 because the minister of war, Leslie Hore-Belisha (1893–1957), found him more congenial. In May 1940 he sided with Gort against Churchill in a disagreement over the possibility of the British Expeditionary Force breaking out to the south. Churchill transferred Ironside to the Home Forces, but Ironside handed the post over to Alanbrooke July 1940 and retired. KCB 1919, baron 1941.

Irvine Andrew Robertson (1951–). British rugby union player who held the world record for the most points scored in senior international rugby with 301 (273 for Scotland, 28 for the British Lions) between 1972 and 1982.

In character he was ambitious, proud, lonely and self-centred ('an egoist of the great type' is Miss Terry's phrase for him).

H H Child on HENRY IRVING
in *Dictionary of National Biography*

Irving Henry. Stage name of John Henry Brodribb (1838–1905). English actor. He established his reputation from 1871, chiefly at the Lyceum Theatre in London, where he became manager 1878. He staged a series of successful Shakespearean productions, including *Romeo and Juliet* 1882, with himself and Ellen Terry playing the leading roles. He was the first actor to be knighted, 1895.

A writer's sense of immortality: if you're in print and on the shelves, you're alive.

JOHN IRVING
The World According to Garp ch 19 1978

Irving John Winslow (1942–). US novelist. His bizarre and funny novels include his bestseller, *The World According to Garp* 1978, a vivid comic tale about a novelist killed by a disappointed reader; *A Prayer for Owen Meany* 1988, about the events that follow the killing by a young boy of his best friend's mother in a baseball accident; and *A Son of the Circus* 1994.

Irving Washington (1783–1859). US essayist and short-story writer. He published a mock-heroic *History of New York* 1809, supposedly written by the Dutchman 'Diedrich Knickerbocker'. In 1815 he went to England where he published *The Sketch Book of Geoffrey Crayon, Gent.* 1820, which contained such stories as 'Rip Van Winkle' and 'The Legend of Sleepy Hollow'. His other works include *The Alhambra* 1832, sketches about Spanish subjects, and *Tour of the Prairies* 1835, about the American West. His essays and tales remain popular.

Suggested reading
Hedges, William *Washington Irving: An American Study, 1802–1832* (1965)

I am always at a loss to know how much to believe of my own stories.

WASHINGTON IRVING
Tales of a Traveller 1824

Johnston, J *Heart That Would Not Hold: A Biography of Washington Irving* (1971)

Myers, Andrew (ed) *Washington Irving: A Tribute* (1972)

Isaac in the Old Testament, a Hebrew patriarch, son of Abraham and Sarah, and father of Esau and Jacob.

Isaacs Alick (1921–1967). Scottish virologist who, with Swiss colleague Jean Lindemann, in 1957 discovered interferon, a naturally occurring antiviral substance produced by cells infected with viruses. The full implications of this discovery are still being investigated.

Isaacs was born and educated in Glasgow. From 1951 he worked at the World Influenza Centre, London, becoming its director 1961.

Isaacs Jorge (1837–1895). Colombian writer. Son of an English Jew, he settled in Bogotá 1864 and began to publish poetry and fiction. Despite a career in public life, he is chiefly remembered for the famous romantic novel *María* 1867, an idyllic picture of life in his native Cauca Valley.

Isaacs Rufus Daniel, 1st Marquess of Reading (1860–1935). British Liberal lawyer and politician. As Lord Chief Justice he tried the Irish nationalist Roger Casement in 1916. Viceroy of India 1921–26; foreign secretary 1931. KCVO 1911, baron 1914, viscount 1916, earl 1917, marquess 1926.

What attracts me in him is his untirable capacity for simple enjoyment, his gravity and insight, and a critical faculty that never cuts.

Margot Asquith on RUFUS ISAACS
in her *Autobiography* 1920

Isaacs Susan (1943–). US novelist and screenwriter. The plots of her popular mysteries and adventure stories put women, usually suburban housewives, in the leading roles. Her novels *Compromising Positions* 1978 and *Shining Through* 1988 were best sellers and were made into films, for which she wrote the screenplays.

Her other novels include *Close Relations* 1980 *Almost Paradise* 1984, *Magic Hour* 1991, and *After All These Years* 1993. She wrote the screenplay for *Hello Again* 1987.

Isabella two Spanish queens:

Isabella (I) the Catholic (1451–1504). Queen of Castile from 1474, after the death of her brother Henry IV. By her marriage with Ferdinand of Aragon 1469, the crowns of two of the Christian states in the Moorish-held Spanish peninsula were united. Her youngest daughter was Catherine of Aragon, first wife of Henry VIII of England.

She introduced the Inquisition into Castile, expelled the Jews and the Moors, and gave financial encouragement to Columbus. The Catholic church proposed to beatify Isabella in 1992, an announcement which aroused the indignation of Jewish groups.

Suggested reading

Fernández-Armesto, Felipe *Ferdinand and Isabella* (1975)

Mariéjol, J H *The Spain of Ferdinand and Isabella* (trs 1961)

Isabella II (1830–1904). Queen of Spain from 1833, when she succeeded her father Ferdinand VII (1784–1833). The Salic Law banning a female sovereign had been repealed by the Cortes (parliament), but her succession was disputed by her uncle Don Carlos de Bourbon (1788–1855). After seven years of civil war, the Carlists were defeated. She abdicated in favour of her son Alfonso XII in 1868.

Isabella of France (1292–1358). Daughter of King Philip IV of France, she married King Edward II of England 1308, but he slighted and neglected her for his favourites, first Piers Gaveston (died 1312) and later the Despenser family. Supported by her lover, Roger Mortimer, Isabella conspired to have Edward deposed and murdered.

She is known to history as the 'she-wolf of France'.

Isaiah (lived 8th century BC). In the Old Testament, the first major Hebrew prophet. The Book of Isaiah in the Old Testament was traditionally believed to be written by him, but it is now thought that large parts of it are the work of at least two other writers. Isaiah was the son of Amos, probably of high rank, and lived largely in Jerusalem. He was influential in the court of ancient Judah until the Assyrian invasion of 701 BC.

Isaurian 8th-century Byzantine imperial dynasty, originating in Asia Minor. Members of the family had been employed as military leaders by the Byzantines, and they gained great influence and prestige as a result. Leo III acceded in 717 as the first Isaurian emperor, and was followed by Constantine V (718–75), Leo IV (750–80), and Leo's widow Irene, who acted as regent for their son before deposing him 797 and assuming the title of emperor herself. She was deposed 802. The Isaurian rulers maintained the integrity of the empire's borders. With the exception of Irene, they attempted to suppress the use of religious icons.

I am a camera; with its shutter open, quite passive, recording, not thinking.

CHRISTOPHER ISHERWOOD
Goodbye to Berlin 'Berlin Diary' 1939

Isherwood Christopher William Bradshaw (1904–1986). English novelist. He lived in Germany 1929–33 just before Hitler's rise to power, a period that inspired *Mr Norris Changes Trains* 1935 and *Goodbye to Berlin* 1939, creating the character of Sally Bowles (the basis of the musical *Cabaret* 1968). Returning to England, he collaborated with W H Auden in three verse plays. Later novels include *Prater Violet* 1945 and *Meeting by the River* 1967.

Suggested reading

Finney, Brian *Christopher Isherwood* (1979)

Lehmann, John *Christopher Isherwood: A Personal Memoir* (1987)

Parker, Peter *Christopher Isherwood* (1996)

Summers, Claude *Christopher Isherwood* (1980)

Ishiguro Kazuo (1954–). Japanese-born British novelist. His novel *An Artist of the Floating World* won the 1986 Whitbread Prize, and *The Remains of the Day* won the 1989 Booker Prize. His work is characterized by a sensitive style and subtle structure.

Ishiguro's first novel, *A Pale View of Hills*, takes place mainly in his native Nagasaki, dealing obliquely with the aftermath of the atom bomb. *An Artist of the Floating World* is set entirely in Japan but thematically linked to *The Remains of the Day* (filmed 1993), which is about an English butler coming to realize the extent of his self-sacrifice and self-deception. All three have in common a melancholy reassessment of the past. His *The Unconsoled* 1995 was a departure from his usual style.

Ishmael in the Old Testament, the son of Abraham and his wife Sarah's Egyptian maid Hagar; traditional ancestor of Muhammad and the Arab people. He and his mother were driven away by Sarah's jealousy. Muslims believe that it was Ishmael, not Isaac, whom God commanded Abraham to sacrifice, and that Ishmael helped Abraham build the Kaaba in Mecca.

Every word we speak, every pulsation of our veins, is related by musical rhythms to the powers of harmony.

ISIDOR OF SEVILLE
Etymologiae 622–633

Isidore of Seville (*c.* 560–636). Writer and missionary. His *Ethymologiae* was the model for later medieval encyclopedias and helped to preserve classical thought during the Middle Ages; his *Chronica Maiora* remains an important source for the history of Visigothic Spain. As bishop of Seville from 600, he strengthened the church in Spain and converted many Jews and Aryan Visigoths.

Iskander Fazil Abdulovich (1929–). Georgian satirical writer. He attracted attention with *Sozvezdie kozlotura/The Goatibex Constellation* 1966, an effective satire on the bureaucratic control of agriculture. *Sandro iz Chegema/Uncle Sandro of Chegem* 1973 sardonically explores Stalinist politics and the cultural contrast between the distinctive traditions of his native region of Abkhazia and Soviet importations.

Ismail (1830–1895). Khedive (governor) of Egypt 1866–79. A grandson of Mehmet Ali, he became viceroy of Egypt in 1863 and in 1866 received the title of khedive from the Ottoman sultan. He amassed huge foreign debts and in 1875 Britain, at Prime Minister Disraeli's suggestion, bought the khedive's Suez Canal shares for nearly £4 million, establishing Anglo-French control of Egypt's finances. In 1879 the UK and France persuaded the sultan to appoint Tewfik, his son, khedive in his place.

Ismail I (1486–1524). Shah of Persia from 1501, founder of the Safavi dynasty, who established the first national government since the Arab conquest and Shi'ite Islam as the national religion.

I maintain that we Athenians should make peace with all mankind.

ISOCRATES
Orations 8.16

Isocrates (436–338 BC). Athenian orator. He may have been a friend of the philosopher Socrates when a young man. He was a professional speechwriter and teacher of rhetoric, and a persistent advocate of Greek unity and supremacy.

Isozaki Arata (1931–). Japanese architect. One of Kenzo Tange's team 1954–63, he has tried to blend Western Post-Modernist with elements of traditional Japanese architecture. His works include Ochanomizu Square, Tokyo (retaining the existing façades), the Museum of Contemporary Art, Los Angeles (begun 1984), and buildings for the 1992 Barcelona Olympics.

Israëls Jozef (1824–1911). Dutch painter. In 1870 he settled in The Hague and became a leader of the Hague School of landscape painters, who shared some of the ideals of the Barbizon School in France. His low-keyed and sentimental scenes of peasant life recall the work of Millet.

Issigonis Alec (Alexander Arnold Constantine) (1906–1988). Turkish-born British engineer who designed the Morris Minor 1948 and the Mini-Minor 1959 cars, comfortable yet cheaper to run than their predecessors. Overseeing the separate approaches of styling, interior packaging, body engineering, and chassis layout, Issigonis conceived the overall vehicle; specialists in his team then designed and engineered the subsystems of the car. His designs gave much greater space for the occupants together with greatly increased dynamic handling stability. He is credited with adding the word 'mini' to the English language. Knighted 1969.

Itagaki Taisuke (1837–1919). Japanese military and political leader, the founder of Japan's first political party, the Jiyūō (Liberal Party) 1875–81. Involved in the overthrow of the Tokugawa shogunate and the Meiji restoration 1866–68, Itagaki became a champion of democratic principles while continuing to serve in the government for short periods.

After ennoblement in 1887 he retained the leadership of the party and co-operated with Itō Hirobumi in the establishment of parliamentary government in the 1890s.

Itō Hirobumi. Prince (1841–1909). Japanese politician, prime minister 1887, 1892–96, 1898, 1900–01. He was a key figure in the modernization of Japan and was involved in the Meiji restoration 1866–68 and in official missions to study forms of government in the USA and Europe in the 1870s and 1880s. As minister for home affairs, he helped draft the Meiji constitution of 1889.

Itō was a samurai from Chōshū, a feudal domain that rebelled against the shogunate in the 1850s–60s. In 1863 he became one of the first Japanese to study in England, and in 1871–73 he was a member of a diplomatic mission to Europe and the USA. Given responsibility for drafting the constitution, he went abroad again

1882–83 to study European models. He was appointed a government adviser 1885 and went on to become prime minister many times. While resident-general in Korea, he was assassinated by Korean nationalists, which led to Japan's annexation of that country.

Politically Itō was a moderate, favouring negotiation and compromise.

Iturbide Agustín de (1783–1824). Mexican military leader (*caudillo*) who led the conservative faction in the nation's struggle for independence from Spain. In 1822 he crowned himself Emperor Agustín I. His extravagance and failure to restore order led all other parties to turn against him, and he reigned for less than a year.

Ivan six rulers of Russia, including:

Ivan (III) the Great (1440–1505). Grand duke of Muscovy from 1462, who revolted against Tatar overlordship by refusing tribute to Grand Khan Ahmed 1480. He claimed the title of tsar, and used the double-headed eagle as the Russian state emblem.

Ivan (IV) the Terrible (1530–1584). Grand duke of Muscovy from 1533; he assumed power 1544 and was crowned as first tsar of Russia 1547. He conquered Kazan 1552, Astrakhan 1556, and Siberia 1581. He reformed the legal code and local administration 1555 and established trade relations with England. In his last years he alternated between debauchery and religious austerities, executing thousands and, in rage, his own son.

Ivan attempted to centralize his rule in Muscovy. He campaigned against the Tatars of Kazan, Astrakhan, and elsewhere, but his policy of forming Russia into an empire led to the fruitless 24-year Livonian war. His regime was marked by brutality, evidenced by the destruction (sacking) of Novgorod.
Suggested reading
Bobrick, Benson *Ivan the Terrible* (1987)
Payne, R and Romanoff, N *Ivan the Terrible* (1975)
Troyat, H *Ivan the Terrible* (1984)

Did I ascend the throne by robbery or armed bloodshed? I was born to rule by the grace of God ... I grew up upon the throne.

IVAN (IV) THE TERRIBLE
Letter to Prince Kurbsky Sept 1577

Ives Burl. Stage name of Charles Icle Ivanhoe Ives (1909–1995). US actor and singer. First established as a popularizer of American folk music, then, with his heavy build and goatee beard, as an imposing character actor, he created the role of the dying Southern patriarch Big Daddy in Tennessee Williams's *Cat on a Hot Tin Roof* on stage in 1955, and reprised in the 1958 screen version. He took a variety of important screen roles, including the vicious land baron in *The Big Country* 1958, for which he won an Oscar as best supporting actor, and the enigmatic German doctor in *Our Man in Havana* 1959, his own favourite role. As a singer, he had several minor pop and country-and-western hits, including a version of 'Ghost Riders in the Sky' 1949, 'Wild Side of Life' 1952, and 'A Little Bitty Tear' 1962.

Ives Charles Edward (1874–1954). US composer. He experimented with atonality, quarter tones, clashing time signatures, and quotations from popular music of the time. He wrote five symphonies, including *Holidays Symphony* 1904–13; chamber music, including the *Concord Sonata*; and the orchestral works *Three Places in New England* 1903–14 and *The Unanswered Question* 1908.
Suggested reading
Bloack, G H *Charles Ives* (1988)
Burkholder, J P *Charles Ives* (1985)

Please don't try to make things nice! All the wrong notes are right. Just copy as I have – I want it that way.

CHARLES IVES
MS note to copyist on the score of *The Fourth of July*

Hitchcock, H W *Ives* (1977)
Perry, R S *Charles Ives and the American Mind* (1974)
Rossiter, Frank R *Charles Ives and His America* (1976)
Wooldridge, D *From the Steeples to the Mountains: A Study of Charles Ives* (1974)

Ives Frederic Eugene (1856–1937). US inventor who developed the halftone process of printing photographs in 1878. The process uses a screen to break up light and dark areas into dots. By 1886 he had evolved the halftone process now generally in use. Among his many other inventions was a three-colour printing process (similar to the four-colour process).

Ivory James Francis (1928–). US film director. He established his reputation with the Indian-made *Shakespeare Wallah* 1965, which began collaborations with Ishmail Merchant and writer Ruth Prawer Jhabvala. Ivory subsequently directed films in various genres in India, the USA and Europe, but became associated with adaptations of classic literature, including *The Bostonians* 1984, *A Room with a View* 1987, *Maurice* 1987, and *Howards End* 1992. He directed *The Remains of the Day* 1993, and *Jefferson in Paris* 1995.

Izetbegović Alija (1925–). Bosnia-Herzegovinan politician, president from 1990. A lifelong opponent of communism, he founded the Party of Democratic Action (PDA) 1990, ousting the communists in the multiparty elections that year. Adopting a moderate stance during the civil war in Bosnia-Herzegovina, he sought an honourable peace for his country in the face of ambitious demands from Serb and Croat political leaders, and signed the Dayton peace accord Nov 1995.

A former legal adviser, he was imprisoned for 'pan-Islamic activity' 1946–48 and 1983–88.

J

Jackson Alexander Young (1882–1974). Canadian landscape painter. He was a leading member of the 'Group of Seven', who aimed to create a specifically Canadian school of landscape art.

Jackson Andrew (1767–1845). 7th president of the USA 1829–37, a Democrat. A major general in the War of 1812, he defeated a British force at New Orleans in 1815 (after the official end of the war in 1814) and was involved in the war that led to the purchase of Florida in 1819.

Jackson was born in South Carolina and spent his early life in poverty. After an unsuccessful attempt in 1824, he was elected president in 1829. This was the first election in which electors were chosen directly by voters rather than state legislators. He demanded and received absolute loyalty from his cabinet members and made wide use of his executive powers. The political organization he built as president, with Martin Van Buren (1782–1862), was the basis for the modern Democratic Party.

In 1832 he vetoed the renewal of the US bank charter and was re-elected, whereupon he continued his struggle against the power of finance. His administration is said to have initiated the spoils system.
Suggested reading
Davis, B *Old Hickory: A Life of Andrew Jackson* (1977)
Latner, R *The Presidency of Andrew Jackson* (1979)
Rimini, Robert (ed) *The Age of Jackson* (1972)
Sellers, Charles *Andrew Jackson: A Profile* (1971)

Jackson Betty (1947–). English fashion designer. She produced her first collection 1981 and achieved an international reputation as a designer of young, up-to-the-minute clothes. She has produced simple shaped separates, generously cut, in solid colours and some bold printed fabrics.

Jackson Charles Reginald (1903–1968). US novelist. He wrote the acclaimed *The Lost Weekend* 1944, a powerful and atmospheric psychological study of alcoholism set in Manhattan, which was made into an Academy Award-winning film 1945. His other novels include *The Fall of Valor* 1946, dealing with homosexuality, and *The Outer Edges* 1948, concerning the effects of a newspaper story.

Jackson Glenda (1936–). English actress and politician, Labour member of Parliament from 1992. She has made many stage appearances for the Royal Shakespeare Company, including *Marat/Sade* 1966, Hedda in *Hedda Gabler* 1975, and Cleopatra in *Antony and Cleopatra* 1978. Her films include the Oscar-winning *Women in Love* 1969, *Sunday Bloody Sunday* 1971, and *A Touch of Class* 1973. On television she played Queen Elizabeth I in *Elizabeth R* 1971.

In 1990 she was chosen by the Labour Party as a candidate for Parliament and was elected member for Hampstead and Highgate in N London April 1992.

Jackson Howell Edmunds (1832–1895). US jurist. Elected to the US Senate 1880, he was named federal district judge 1886 by Grover Cleveland and chief judge of the circuit court of appeals 1891 by Benjamin Harrison. In 1893 Jackson was appointed to the US Supreme Court, but illness prevented him from carrying out his duties.

Born in Paris, Tennessee, Jackson received his law degree from Cumberland University 1856. During the American Civil War 1861–65, he served as an official in Tennessee's Confederate government.

Jackson Jesse Louis (1941–). US Democratic politician, a cleric and campaigner for minority rights. He contested his party's 1984 and 1988 presidential nominations in an effort to increase voter registration and to put black issues on the national agenda. He is an eloquent public speaker.

Born in North Carolina and educated in Chicago, Jackson emerged as a powerful Baptist preacher and black activist politician, working first with the civil-rights leader Martin Luther King, Jr, then on building the political machine that gave Chicago a black mayor 1983. Jackson sought to construct what he called a *rainbow coalition* of ethnic-minority and socially deprived groups. He took the lead in successfully campaigning for US disinvestment in South Africa 1986.

Jackson John Hughlings (1835–1911). English neurologist and neurophysiologist. As a result of his studies of epilepsy, Jackson demonstrated that specific areas of the cerebral cortex (outer mantle of the brain) control the functioning of particular organs and limbs. He also demonstrated that Helmholtz's ophthalmoscope is a crucial diagnostic tool for disorders of the nervous system.

Jackson Lady. Title of British economist Barbara ◊Ward.

Jackson Mahalia (1911–1972). US gospel singer. She made her first recording 1934, and her version of the gospel song 'Move on Up a Little Higher' was a commercial success 1945. Jackson became a well-known radio and television performer in the 1950s and was invited to sing at the presidential inauguration of John F Kennedy.

Jackson Marjorie (1932–). Australian athlete, born in Lithgow, New South Wales. She won the gold medals for the 100 metres and 200 metres events at the 1952 Olympics and set ten world record times during her career, becoming known as the 'Lithgow Flash'.

The thing that touches me is very special. It's a message I have to tell. I start crying, and the pain is wonderful. It's amazing. It's like God.

MICHAEL JACKSON
in *Newsweek* 1983

Jackson Michael Joseph (1958–). US rock singer and songwriter. His videos and live performances are meticulously choreographed. His first solo hit was 'Got to Be There' 1971; his worldwide popularity peaked with the albums *Thriller* 1982, *Bad* 1987, and *Dangerous* 1991. Jackson's career faltered after allegations of child abuse, but he returned with the album *History* 1995.

He turned professional 1969 as the youngest member of *the Jackson Five*, who had several hits on Motown Records, beginning with their first single, 'I Want You Back'. The group left Motown 1975 and changed its name to *the Jacksons*. Michael was the lead singer, but soon surpassed his brothers in popularity as a solo performer. From *Off the Wall* 1979 to *Bad*, his albums were produced by Quincy Jones. *Thriller* sold 41 million copies, a world record, and yielded an unprecedented number of hit singles, among them 'Billie Jean' 1983.

Jackson 'Stonewall' (Thomas Jonathan) (1824–1863). US Confederate general in the American Civil War. He acquired his nickname and his reputation at the Battle of Bull Run, from the firmness with which his brigade resisted the Northern attack. In 1862 he organized the Shenandoah Valley campaign and assisted Robert E Lee's invasion of Maryland. He helped to defeat General Joseph E Hooker's Union army at the battle of Chancellorsville, Virginia, but was fatally wounded by one of his own soldiers in the confusion of battle.
Suggested reading
Chambers, Lenoir *Stonewall Jackson* (1959)
Douglas, H K *I Rode with Stonewall* (1940)

Fritz, Jean *Stonewall* (1979)
Tate, Allen *Stonewall Jackson* (1957)

Jack the Ripper popular name for the unidentified mutilator and murderer of at least five women prostitutes in the Whitechapel area of London in 1888. The murders understandably provoked public outrage; the police were heavily criticized, which later led to a reassessment of police procedures. Jack the Ripper's identity has never been discovered, although several suspects have been proposed, including members of the royal household.

Jacob François (1920–   ). French biochemist who, with Jacques Monod and André Lwoff, pioneered research into molecular genetics and showed how the production of proteins from DNA is controlled. They shared the Nobel Prize for Physiology or Medicine 1965.

In 1950 Jacob joined the Pasteur Institute in Paris as a research assistant, becoming head of the Department of Cellular Genetics 1964 and also professor of cellular genetics at the Collège de France.

Jacob Joseph (1854–1916). Australian-born US folklorist and collector of fairy tales. He published collections of vividly re-told fairy stories such as *English Fairy Tales* 1890, *Celtic Fairy Tales* 1892 and 1894, and *Indian Fairy Tales* 1892.

Jacobi Carl Gustav Jacob (1804–1851). German mathematician and mathematical physicist, much of whose work was on the theory of elliptical functions, mathematical analysis, number theory, geometry, and mechanics.

Jacobi was born in Potsdam. A child prodigy, he went to Berlin University in 1821 and graduated in the same year. In 1826 he joined the staff at Königsberg (now Kaliningrad) University, becoming professor 1832.

Jacquard Joseph-Marie Jaquard demonstrating his loom that was able to weave complicated patterns when 'programmed' with punched cards. (Image Select)

Jacobi invented a functional determinant – now called the *Jacobian determinant* – which has been of considerable use in later analytical investigations, and was even supportive in the development of quantum mechanics. He advanced the theory of the configurations of rotating liquid masses by showing that the ellipsoids now known as *Jacobi's ellipsoids* are figures of equilibrium.

Jacobi was always trying to link together different mathematical disciplines. For instance, he introduced elliptic functions into number theory and into the theory of integration, which in turn connected with the theory of differential equations and his own principle of the last multiplier. His book *Fundamenta nova theoriae functionum ellipticarum* 1829 introduced his own concept of hyperelliptic functions.

Jacobi Derek George (1938–   ). English actor. His powerful and sensitive talent has ensured a succession of leading roles in Shakespearean and other mainly serious drama on stage, television, and film. In the theatre he has several times played the title role in *Hamlet*, notably in 1979 in the newly reformed Old Vic production in London. Television appearances include the acclaimed title role in *I, Claudius* 1976 (BAFTA award).

Other stage work includes *The Tempest* and *Peer Gynt* 1982, *Cyrano de Bergerac* 1983, *Much Ado About Nothing* 1985, *Richard II* 1988, *Richard III* 1989, *Becket* 1991, and *Macbeth* 1993–94. Films include *Day of the Jackal* 1973, *Little Dorrit* 1987, *Henry V* 1989, and *Dead Again* 1991.

> *'Sailor men 'ave their faults,' said the night-watchman frankly ... 'I used to 'ave myself when I was at sea.'*
> W W JACOBS
> *Lady of the Barge* 'Bill's Paper Chase' 1902

Jacobs W(illiam) W(ymark) (1863–1943). English author. He used his childhood knowledge of London's docklands in amusing short stories such as 'Many Cargoes' 1896. He excelled in the macabre, for example 'The Monkey's Paw' 1902.

Jacobsen Arne (1902–1971). Danish architect. He introduced the ideas of the Modernist pioneers Le Corbusier and Mies van der Rohe into Denmark. As architect of St Catherine's College, Oxford, UK, 1959, he also designed the furniture and cutlery.

Jacobsen designed the Bellavista housing estate near Copenhagen, and the Bellevue Theatre 1933. Other works include the Scandinavian Airlines System building in Copenhagen 1959.

Jacquard Joseph Marie (1752–1834). French textile manufacturer who invented a punched-card system for programming designs on a carpetmaking loom. In 1801 he constructed looms that used a series of punched cards to control the pattern of longitudinal warp threads depressed before each sideways passage of the shuttle. On later machines the punched cards were joined to form an endless loop that represented the 'program' for the repeating pattern of a carpet. By 1812 there were 11,000 Jacquard looms working in France, and they were introduced into many other countries.

Jacquard-style punched cards were used in the early computers of the 1940s–1960s.

Jacuzzi Candido (1903–1986). Italian-born US engineer who invented the Jacuzzi, a pump that produces a whirlpool effect in a bathtub. The Jacuzzi was commercially launched as a health and recreational product in the mid-1950s.

Jagan Cheddi Berrat (1918–   ). Guyanese left-wing politician, president from 1992. He led the People's Progressive Party (PPA) from 1950, and was the first prime minister of British Guyana 1961–64. As candidate for president Aug 1992, he opposed privatization as leading to 'recolonization'. The PPA won a decisive victory, and Jagan as veteran leader replaced Desmond Hoyte.

Jagan Janet (1920–   ). Guyanese left-wing politician, wife of Cheddi Jagan. She was general secretary of the People's Progressive Party 1950–70.

Jahangir ('Holder of the World') adopted name of Salim (1569–1627). Third Mogul emperor of India 1605–27, succeeding his father Akbar the Great. The first part of his reign was marked by peace, prosperity and a flowering of the arts, but the latter half by rebellion and succession conflicts. In 1622 he lost Kandahar province in Afghanistan to Persia. His rule was marked by the influence of his Persian wife Nur Jahan and her conflict with Prince Khurran (later Shah Jahan). Jahangir designed the Shalimar Gardens in Kashmir and buildings and gardens in Lahore.

Suggested reading
Gascoigne, Bamber and Christina *The Great Moghuls* (1971)
Hansen, Waldemar *The Peacock Throne: The Drama of Mogul India* (1972)
Prasad, Beni *History of Jahangir* (1922)

Jakeš Miloš (1922–). Czech communist politician, a member of the Politburo from 1981 and party leader 1987–89. A conservative, he supported the Soviet invasion of Czechoslovakia in 1968.

Jakeš, an electrical engineer, joined the Communist Party of Czechoslovakia (CCP) in 1945 and studied in Moscow 1955–58. As head of the CCP's central control commission, he oversaw the purge of reformist personnel after the suppression of the 1968 Prague Spring. In Dec 1987 he replaced Gustáv Husák as CCP leader. He was forced to resign Nov 1989 following a series of pro-democracy mass rallies.

Although he enjoyed close relations with the Soviet leader Gorbachev, Jakeš was a cautious reformer who was unpopular with the people.

Jakobson Roman Osipovic (1896–1982). Russian-born American linguist, member of the Prague school. He co-founded the Prague Linguistic Circle, the 'cradle of the structuralist movement in modern linguistics', and with the Russian linguist Nikolai Trubetzkoy, produced a structural theory of phonology (the study of language sounds).

James Elmore, adopted name of Elmore Brooks (1918–1963). US blues guitarist, singer, and songwriter. His electric slide-guitar style had great impact on rock music. He is particularly associated with the song 'Dust My Broom' (written by Robert Johnson, his main influence) 1952, as well as 'It Hurts Me Too' 1952, 'The Sky Is Crying' 1960, and 'Shake Your Money Maker' 1961.

James was born in Mississippi but active mainly in Chicago from 1952.

Experience ... is an immense sensibility, a kind of huge spiderweb of the finest silken threads suspended in the chamber of consciousness, and catching every air-born particle in its tissue.

HENRY JAMES
The Art of Fiction

James Henry (1843–1916). US novelist. He lived in Europe from 1875, a naturalized British subject 1915. His novels deal with the social, moral, and aesthetic issues arising from the complex relationship of European to American culture. Initially a master of psychological realism, noted for the complex subtlety of his prose style, James became increasingly experimental, writing some of the essential works of early Modernism. His major novels include *The Portrait of a Lady* 1881, *The Bostonians* 1886, *What Maisie Knew* 1887, *The Ambassadors* 1903, and *The Golden Bowl* 1904. He also wrote more than a hundred shorter works of fiction, notably the novella *The Aspern Papers* 1888 and the supernatural/psychological riddle *The Turn of the Screw* 1898.

Other major works include *Roderick Hudson* 1876, *The American* 1877, *Washington Square* 1881, *The Tragic Muse* 1890, *The Spoils of Poynton* 1897, *The Awkward Age* 1899, and *The Wings of the Dove* 1902.

Suggested reading
Edel, Leon *Henry James* ((5 vols 1953–72))
Edel, Leon *Henry James: A Life* (1985, abr of above)
Putt, S G *Henry James: A Reader's Guide* (1966)

James Jesse Woodson (1847–1882). US bank and train robber, born in Missouri and a leader, with his brother Frank (1843–1915), of the Quantrill raiders, a Confederate guerrilla band in the Civil War. Frank later led his own gang. Jesse was killed by Bob Ford, an accomplice; Frank remained unconvicted and became a farmer.

'I heard one cry in the night, and ... one laugh afterwards. If I cannot forget that, I shall not be able to sleep.'

M R JAMES
Ghost Stories of an Antiquary 'Count Magnus' 1904

James M(ontague) R(hodes) (1862–1936). English writer, theologian, linguist, and medievalist. He wrote *Ghost Stories of an Antiquary* 1904 and other supernatural tales.

God gives every bird his worm, but He does not throw it into the nest.

P D JAMES
Devices and Desires ch 40 1989

James P(hyllis) D(orothy), Baroness James of Holland Park (1920–). English detective novelist. She created the characters Superintendent Adam Dalgliesh and private investigator Cordelia Gray. She was a tax official, hospital administrator, and civil servant before turning to writing. Her books include *Death of an Expert Witness* 1977, *The Skull Beneath the Skin* 1982, *A Taste for Death* 1986, and *Original Sin* 1994. Baroness 1991.

All her life she had fabricated mysteries, exploited coincidence, arranged facts to conform to theory, manipulated her characters, relished the self-importance of vicarious power.

P D JAMES
Original Sin 1994

James William (1842–1910). US psychologist and philosopher. He was among the first to take an approach emphasizing the ends or purposes of behaviour and to advocate a scientific, experimental psychology. His *Varieties of Religious Experience* 1902 is one of the most important works on the psychology of religion.

In his classic *Principles of Psychology* 1890, James introduced the notion of the 'stream of consciousness' (thought, consciousness, or subjective life regarded as a flow rather than as separate bits), and propounded the theory of emotions now known as the James–Lange theory. James wrote extensively on abnormal psychology and had much to contribute to the study of the paranormal.

He was the brother of the novelist Henry James. He turned from medicine to psychology and taught at Harvard 1872–1907. Although on his own admission unsuited to experimental work, he established one of the first psychological laboratories at Harvard in 1875.

James's main philosophical ideas are set out in *Pragmatism, a New Name for Some Old Ways of Thinking* 1907, an attempt to give an account of truth in terms of its satisfactory outcomes that owes much to the US philosopher C S Peirce's ideas on pragmatism, and *Essays in Radical Empiricism* 1912, in which he proposed that ultimate reality consists of 'pure experience', defining this as 'the immediate flux of life which furnishes the material to our later reflection'.

The art of being wise is the art of knowing what to overlook.

WILLIAM JAMES
Principles of Psychology 1890

Suggested reading

Allen, G *William James: A Biography* (1967)
Ayer, A J *The Origins of Pragmatism* (1968)
Barzun, Jacques *A Stroll with William James* (1984)
Reck, A *Introduction to William James* (1967)

He [William James] is so concrete, so living; I, a mere table of contents, so abstract, a very snarl of twine.

Charles Peirce on WILLIAM JAMES
in J Passmore *A Hundred Years of Philosophy* 1957

James (I) the Conqueror (1208–1276). King of Aragon from 1213, when he succeeded his father. He conquered the Balearic Islands and took Valencia from the Moors, dividing it with Alfonso X of Castile by a treaty of 1244. Both these exploits are recorded in his autobiography *Libre dels feyts/Chronicle*. He largely established Aragon as the dominant power in the Mediterranean.

James two kings of Britain:

James I (1566–1625). King of England from 1603 and Scotland (as James VI) from 1567. The son of Mary Queen of Scots and Lord Darnley, he succeeded on his mother's abdication from the Scottish throne, assumed power 1583, established a strong centralized authority, and in 1589 married Anne of Denmark (1574–1619).

As successor to Elizabeth I in England, he alienated the Puritans by his High Church views and Parliament by his assertion of divine right, and was generally unpopular because of his favourites, such as Buckingham, and his schemes for an alliance with Spain. He was succeeded by his son Charles I.

Suggested reading

Bingham, Caroline *The Making of a King: The early Years of James VI and I* (1968)
Durston, Christopher *James I* (1993)
Fraser, Antonia *King James VI of Scotland, I of England* (1974)
Kenyon, J P *The Stuarts* (1967)
Willson, D H *King James VI and I* (1956)

A custom loathsome to the eye, hateful to the nose, harmful to the brain, dangerous to the lungs.

JAMES I
on tobacco smoking in *A Counterblast to Tobacco* 1604

James II (1633–1701). King of England and Scotland (as James VII) from 1685, second son of Charles I. He succeeded Charles II. James married Anne Hyde 1659 (1637–1671, mother of Mary II and Anne) and Mary of Modena 1673 (mother of James Edward Stuart). He became a Catholic 1671, which led first to attempts to exclude him from the succession, then to the rebellions of Monmouth and Argyll, and finally to the Whig and Tory leaders' invitation to William of Orange to take the throne in 1688. James fled to France, then led an uprising in Ireland 1689, but after defeat at the Battle of the Boyne 1690 remained in exile in France.

Suggested reading

Ashley, Maurice *James II* (1978)
Childs, John *The Army, James II and the Glorious Revolution* (1981)
Kenyon, J P *The Stuarts* (1967)
Miller, J *James II: A Study of Kingship* (1978)
Mullett, Michael *James II and English Politics, 1678–1688* (1994)
Trevor, M *The Shadow of a Crown: The Life of James II of England and VII of Scotland* (1988)

His religion suits well with his temper; heady, violent and bloody, who easily believes the rashest and worst of counsels to be most sincere and hearty.

Anon report on JAMES II drawn up for the Earl of Shaftesbury *c.* 1680

James seven kings of Scotland:

God gives not kings the style of Gods in vain ... So kings should fear and serve their God again.

JAMES I
'Sonnet Addressed to His Son, Prince Henry'

James I (1394–1437). King of Scotland 1406–37, who assumed power 1424. He was a cultured and strong monarch whose improvements in the administration of justice brought him popularity among the common people. He was assassinated by a group of conspirators led by the Earl of Atholl.

[He was] a vigorous, politic, and singularly successful king ... popular with the commons, with whom ... he mingled freely ... in peace and war.

A J G Mackay on JAMES II
in *Dictionary of National Biography*

James II (1430–1460). King of Scotland from 1437, who assumed power 1449. The only surviving son of James I, he was supported by most of the nobles and parliament. He sympathized with the Lancastrians during the Wars of the Roses, and attacked English possessions in S Scotland. He was killed while besieging Roxburgh Castle.

James III (1451–1488). King of Scotland from 1460, who assumed power 1469. His reign was marked by rebellions by the nobles, including his brother Alexander, Duke of Albany. He was murdered during a rebellion supported by his son, who then ascended the throne as James IV.

James IV (1473–1513). King of Scotland from 1488, who married Margaret (1489–1541, daughter of Henry VII) in 1503. He came to the throne after his followers murdered his father, James III, at Sauchieburn. His reign was internally peaceful, but he allied himself with France against England, invaded 1513 and was defeated and killed at the Battle of Flodden. James IV was a patron of poets and architects as well as a military leader.

As king he was vigorous, imposing and popular, if extravagant and pleasure-bent.

E N Williams on JAMES IV
in *Penguin Dictionary of English and European History 1485–1789* 1980

James V (1512–1542). King of Scotland from 1513, who assumed power 1528. During the long period of his minority, he was caught in a struggle between pro-French and pro-English factions. When he assumed power, he allied himself with France and upheld Catholicism against the Protestants. Following an attack on Scottish territory by Henry VIII's forces, he was defeated near the border at Solway Moss 1542.

God's will be done. It came with a lass and will go with a lass.

JAMES V
on the Stuart tenure of the Scottish crown: when informed of the birth of a daughter (Mary Queen of Scots) Dec 1542 on his deathbed after defeat by the English at the Battle of Solway Moss

---

James VI of Scotland. See ◊James I of England.

James VII of Scotland. See ◊James II of England.

James Francis Edward Stuart (1688–1766). British prince, known as the Old Pretender (for the Jacobites, he was James III). Son of James II, he was born at St James's Palace and after the revolution of 1688 was taken to France. He landed in Scotland in 1715 to head a Jacobite rebellion but withdrew through lack of support. In his later years he settled in Rome.

Suggested reading
Bevan, B *King James III of England: A Study of Kingship in Exile* (1972)
Lees-Milne, James *The Last Stuarts* (1984)

We saw nothing in him that looked like spirit.
Jacobite writer on JAMES FRANCIS EDWARD STUART
in *True Account of the Proceedings at Perth, written by a Rebel 1716*

James, St several Christian saints, including:

James, St (called the Great) (lived 1st century AD). New Testament apostle, originally a Galilean fisher. He was the son of Zebedee and brother of the apostle John. He was put to death by Herod Agrippa. James is the patron saint of Spain. Feast day 25 July.

Lord, may we call down fire from heaven to burn them up?
ST JAMES
Response to the Samaritans' refusal to admit Jesus. The Bible, Luke 9:53–4

James, St (called the Little) (lived 1st century AD). In the New Testament, a disciple of Christ, son of Alphaeus. Feast day 3 May.

James, St (called the Just) (lived 1st century AD). The New Testament brother of Jesus, to whom Jesus appeared after the Resurrection. Leader of the Christian church in Jerusalem, he was the author of the biblical Epistle of James.

As I have not succeeded [in the Jameson Raid] the natural thing has happened [trial and imprisonment] … if I had succeeded I should have been forgiven.
LEANDER STARR JAMESON
in giving evidence before a parliamentary select committee inquiring into the Jameson Raid 1897

Jameson Leander Starr (1853–1917). British colonial administrator. In South Africa, early in 1896, he led the Jameson Raid from Mafeking into Transvaal to support the non-Boer colonists there, in an attempt to overthrow the government (for which he served some months in prison). Returning to South Africa, he succeeded Cecil Rhodes as leader of the Progressive Party of Cape Colony, where he was prime minister 1904–08. 1st baronet 1911.

I do not play about with empty melodies. I dip them in life and nature. I find work very difficult and serious – perhaps for this reason.
LEOŠ JANÁČEK
in letter to K E Sokol, 1925

Janáček Leoš (1854–1928). Czech composer. He became director of the Conservatoire at Brno 1919 and professor at the Prague Conservatoire 1920. His music, highly original and influenced by Moravian folk music, includes arrangements of folk songs, operas (*Jenůfa* 1904, *The Cunning Little Vixen* 1924), and the choral *Glagolitic Mass* 1926.

Suggested reading
Chisholm, Erik *The Operas of Janáček* (1971)
Hollander, Hans *Leos Janáček: His Life and Work* (trs 1963)
Horsbrugh, I *Leos Janáček* (1982)

Janequin Clément (c. 1472–c. 1560). French composer of chansons and psalms. He was choirmaster of Angers Cathedral 1534–37 and then based in Paris from 1549. His songs of the 1520s–30s are witty and richly textured in imitative effects, for example 'Le Chant des oiseaux'/'Birdsong', 'La Chasse'/'The Hunt', and 'Les Cris de Paris'/'Street Cries of Paris'.

'La Bataille de Marignan'/'The Battle of Marignan' 1515 incorporates the sounds of warriors fighting.

Janet Pierre Marie Félix (1859–1947). French psychiatrist. He is known for his detailed work on neurosis. His early work focused on the psychasthenias, a term he coined to describe anxiety, phobias, and obsessional disorders. He went on to formulate a comprehensive theory of development, in which abnormal behaviour and neuroses were seen to result from an individual's failure to fully integrate psychological functions associated with a given developmental stage.

It was as a student of Jean-Martin Charcot that Janet first became interested in the study of neurosis and its treatment by hypnosis. From 1895 he was director of studies in experimental psychology at the Sorbonne before being appointed professor of experimental and comparative psychology at the Collège de France 1902, a post he held until 1936. His major works, as yet not fully translated into English, include *Névroses et idées fixes* 1898, *Les Obsessions et la psychasthenie* 1903, and *Les Névroses* 1905.

Jannings Emil, stage name of Theodor Friedrich Emil Jarenz (1886–1950). German actor in films from 1914. In *Der Blaue Engel/The Blue Angel* 1930 he played a schoolteacher who becomes disastrously infatuated with Marlene Dietrich. His other films include *Der Letzte Mann/The Last Laugh* 1924, *Faust* 1926, and *The Last Command* 1928.

Jansen Cornelius Otto (1585–1638). Dutch Roman Catholic theologian, founder of *Jansenism* with his book *Augustinus* 1640. He became professor at Louvain, Belgium, 1630, and bishop of Ypres, Belgium, 1636.

Jansen held that the performance of God's commandments is impossible for human beings without special grace from God. Since the operation of God's grace is irresistible, the destiny of all humans is therefore predetermined.

Jansky Karl Guthe (1905–1950). US radio engineer who in 1932 discovered that the Milky Way galaxy emanates radio waves; he did not follow up his discovery, but it marked the birth of radioastronomy.

In 1928 he joined the Bell Telephone Laboratories, New Jersey, where he investigated causes of static that created interference on radio-telephone calls.

Janssen (Pierre) Jules César (1824–1907). French astronomer who studied the solar spectrum; he developed a spectrohelioscope 1868. In 1867 he concluded that water vapour was present in the atmosphere of Mars.

Jansky Radio engineer Karl Jansky pictured with an aerial array. The photograph was taken in 1928 in New Jersey. Jansky became the first radio astronomer when he detected radio waves originating in the Milky Way. (Image Select)

Janssen was born and educated in Paris, and built an observatory on the flat roof of his house there. He was made professor of physics at the Ecole Spéciale d'Architecture 1865, established an observatory on Mont Blanc in the Alps, and in 1875 became director of the new astronomical observatory at Meudon, near Paris. Scientific expeditions took him to many parts of the world, including Peru and Japan; during the Franco-Prussian War he travelled to Algeria by balloon to observe an eclipse. *Atlas de photographies solaires* 1904 contained Janssen's photographs of the Sun, taken from 1876 onwards.

Jaques-Dalcroze Emile (1865–1950). Swiss composer and teacher. He is remembered for his system of physical training by rhythmical movement to music (eurhythmics), and founded the Institut Jaques-Dalcroze in Geneva 1915.

Jarman Derek (1942–1994). English avant-garde film director. Jarman made several low-budget, highly innovative features, often with homo-erotic associations. His homosexuality was a dominant refrain in his work and he was a committed campaigner for gay rights. His films include *Sebastiane* 1975, with dialogue spoken in Latin, *Caravaggio* 1986, *Edward II* 1991, a free adaptation of Christopher Marlowe's play, and his biography of the philosopher *Wittgenstein* 1993.

Jarman's films often deal with historical subjects using deliberate elements of anachronism and contemporary comment, to provocative effect. His work provoked strong reactions, ranging from admiration for his formal daring, to rejection for what was seen as wilful obscurity.

Jarmusch Jim (1953–). US independent film director and screenwriter. As a maker of low-cost experimental films, Jarmusch established a reputation with *Stranger Than Paradise* 1984. The film was marked by the hip urban humour and minimalist form that would recur in *Down By Law* 1986, a comedy set in the Louisiana bayou. His other films include *Mystery Train* 1989, about one night spent in a Memphis low-rent hotel by disparate characters, and *Night On Earth* 1992.

Night on Earth is divided into five segments, each conducted in the back of a cab in different cities at different times during the same night. Although the film has the benefit of a larger budget than Jarmusch's previous movies, it still retains much of its maker's quirky personality.

Jarnach Philipp (1892–1982). German composer of Catalan/French descent. After studies in Paris he met Busoni in Zurich 1915 and remained to complete the latter's opera *Doktor Faust* 1925 after Busoni's death. His own works, in Italianate Neo-Classical style, include orchestral and chamber music.

Järnefelt (Edvard) Armas (1869–1958). Finnish composer. He is chiefly known for his 'Praeludium' 1907 and the lyrical 'Berceuse' 1909 for small orchestra, from music for the drama *The Promised Land*.

Jarrett Keith (1945–). US jazz pianist and composer. An eccentric innovator, he performs both alone and with small groups. Jarrett was a member of the rock-influenced Charles Lloyd Quartet 1966–67, and played with Miles Davis 1970–71. *The Köln Concert* 1975 is a characteristic solo live recording.

We believe ... that the applause of silence is the only kind that counts.

ALFRED JARRY
'Twelve Theatrical Topics' Topic 12

Jarry Alfred (1873–1907). French satiric dramatist. His grossly farcical *Ubu Roi* 1896 foreshadowed the Theatre of the Absurd and the French Surrealist movement in its freedom of staging and subversive humour.

Jaruzelski Wojciech Witold (1923–). Polish general, communist leader from 1981, president 1985–90. He imposed martial law for the first year of his rule, suppressed the opposition, and banned trade-union activity, but later released many political prisoners. In 1989, elections in favour of the free trade union Solidarity forced Jaruzelski to speed up democratic reforms, overseeing a transition to a new form of 'socialist pluralist' democracy and stepping down as president 1990.

Jaruzelski, who served with the Soviet army 1939–43, was defence minister 1968–83 and entered the Politburo 1971. At the height of the crisis of 1980–81 he assumed power as prime minister and PUWP first secretary; in 1985 he resigned as prime minister to become president, but remained the dominant political figure in Poland. His attempts to solve Poland's economic problems were unsuccessful. He apologized for the 'pain and injustice' suffered by Poles during his term as head of state in his leaving speech of Dec 1990.

Jaspers Karl Theodor (1883–1969). German philosopher, often described as an existentialist. His voluminous writings are filled with highly subjective paraphrases of the great philosophers, followed by appeals to the readers to be concerned with their own existence. He believed that apes are degenerate humans.

Jaspers was born in Oldenburg, studied medicine and psychology, and in 1921 became professor of philosophy at Heidelberg. His works include *General Psychopathology* 1913 and *Philosophy* 1932.

There is ... over the affairs of the army a universal conspiracy of silence, of childlike mysteries, of clannishness, routine and intrigue.

JEAN JAURÈS
L'Armee Nouvelle 1910

Jaurès (Auguste Marie Joseph) Jean (Léon) (1859–1914). French socialist politician and advocate of international peace. He was a lecturer in philosophy at Toulouse until his election 1885 as a deputy (member of parliament). In 1893 he joined the Socialist Party, established a united party, and in 1904 founded the newspaper *L'Humanité*, becoming its editor until his assassination.

Jawlensky Alexei von (1864–1941). Russian painter. He was a major figure in the German revolutionary art movements of the early 1900s. Like his close friend Kandinsky, he was influenced by Fauvism and Russian folk art. He reached his most abstract style 1908–10 with paintings such as *Murnau* 1910 (National Gallery of Art, Washington, DC), but is best-known for his Expressionist portraits of women, for example *Helene with Red Turban* 1910 (Solomon R Guggenheim Museum, New York). In the 1920s he produced a series of unusual, Cubist-style heads, in which his subjects were abstracted to flat shapes with slit eyes, as in *Head: Red Light* 1926 (San Francisco Museum of Modern Art, San Francisco).

Jay John (1745–1829). US diplomat and jurist, a member of the Continental Congress 1774–89 and its president 1779. With Benjamin Franklin and John Adams, he negotiated the Peace of Paris 1783, which concluded the American Revolution. President Washington named him first chief justice of the US 1789. He negotiated Jay's Treaty with England 1795, averting another war. He was governor of New York 1795–1801.

Born in New York City, Jay was admitted to the bar 1768. He became first chief justice of New York 1778. He was US minister to Spain 1779–82 and later served as foreign secretary for the Continental Congress 1783–89. A strong supporter of the federal constitution, he collaborated with Alexander Hamilton and James Madison on the *Federalist Papers* 1787–88, aiding ratification of the US constitution.

Suggested reading
Monaghan, Frank *John Jay* (1935, rep 1972)
Morris, Richard *John Jay: The Nation and the Court* (1967)
Morris, Richard *John Jay: Witness at the Creation* (1989)

Jayawardene Junius Richard (1906–1996). Sri Lankan politician. Leader of the United Nationalist Party from 1973, he became prime minister 1977 and the country's first president 1978–88. Jayawardene embarked on a free-market economic strategy, but was confronted with increasing Tamil-Sinhalese ethnic unrest, forcing the imposition of a state of emergency 1983.

Life exists in the universe only because the carbon atom possesses certain exceptional properties.

JAMES JEANS
Mysterious Universe 1930

Jeans James Hopwood (1877–1946). British mathematician and scientist. In physics he worked on the kinetic theory of gases, and on forms of energy radiation; in astronomy, his work focused on giant and dwarf stars, the nature of spiral nebulae, and the origin of the cosmos. He did much to popularize astronomy. Knighted 1928.

Jeans was born in Ormskirk, Lancashire, and studied at Cambridge. From 1905 to 1909 he was professor of applied mathematics at Princeton University in the USA, and lectured at Cambridge 1910–12. Thereafter he devoted himself to private research and writing, although he was a research associate at Mount Wilson Observatory, California, 1923–44.

In 1905 Jeans formulated the Rayleigh–Jeans law, which describes the spectral distribution of black-body radiation (previously studied by English physicist Lord Rayleigh) in terms of wavelength and temperature. For some time thereafter Jeans investigated various problems in quantum theory, but in about 1912 he turned his attention to astrophysics. In 1928 he stated his belief that matter was continuously being created in the universe (a forerunner of the steady-state theory). His *Dynamical Theory of Gases* 1904 became a standard text.

Jefferies (John) Richard (1848–1887). English naturalist and writer. His books on the countryside include *Gamekeeper at Home* 1878, *Wood Magic* 1881, and *Story of My Heart* 1883.

Jeffers (John) Robinson (1887–1962). US poet. He wrote free verse and demonstrated an antagonism to human society. His collected volumes include *Tamar and Other Poems* 1924, *The Double Axe* 1948, and *Hungerfield and Other Poems* 1954.

Jefferson Thomas (1743–1826). 3rd president of the USA 1801–09, founder of the Democratic Republican Party. He published *A Summary View of the Rights of America* 1774 and as a member of the Continental Congresses of 1775–76 was largely responsible for the drafting of the Declaration of Independence. He was governor of Virginia 1779–81, ambassador to Paris 1785–89, secretary of state 1789–93, and vice president 1797–1801.

Jefferson was born in Virginia into a wealthy family. His interests included music, painting, architecture, and the natural sciences; he was very much a product of the 18th-century Enlightenment. His political philosophy of 'agrarian democracy' placed responsibility for upholding a virtuous American republic mainly upon a citizenry of independent yeoman farmers. Ironically, his two terms as president saw the adoption of some of the ideas of his political opponents, the Federalists.

He was supportive of the French Revolution and spent four years in France while dispatching advice through his ally James Madison on the proposals for a Constitutional Convention. Upon his return to the political scene, he carried on his battle with Alexander Hamilton, who held views of America directly opposed to his own agrarian, democratic inclinations.

Suggested reading
Binger, Carl *Thomas Jefferson: A Well-Tempered Mind* (1970)
Brodie, F M *Thomas Jefferson: An Intimate History* (1974)
Jefferson, Thomas *Autobiography* (many editions)
Lehmann, Karl *Thomas Jefferson, American Humanist* (1947)
Peterson, M *Thomas Jefferson: A Profile* (1967)
Randall, W S *Thomas Jefferson: A Life* (1993)

Jeffrey Francis, Lord (1773–1850). Scottish lawyer and literary critic. Born in Edinburgh, he was a founder and editor of the

Edinburgh Review 1802–29. In 1830 he was made Lord Advocate, and in 1834 a Scottish law lord. He was hostile to the Romantic poets, and wrote of Wordsworth's *Excursion*: 'This will never do.'

Jeffreys Alec John (1950–). British geneticist who discovered the DNA probes necessary for accurate genetic fingerprinting so that a murderer or rapist could be identified by, for example, traces of blood, tissue, or semen.

Jeffreys of Wem George, 1st Baron Jeffreys of Wem (1644–1689). Welsh judge, popularly known as 'the hanging judge'. He became Chief Justice of the King's Bench in 1683, and presided over many political trials, notably those of Philip Sidney, Titus Oates, and Richard Baxter, becoming notorious for his brutality. Knighted 1677, baron 1685.

Jeffreys was born in Denbighshire. In 1685 he was made Lord Chancellor and, after Monmouth's rebellion, conducted the 'bloody assizes' during which 320 rebels were executed and hundreds more flogged, imprisoned, or transported. He was captured when attempting to flee the country after the revolution of 1688, and died in the Tower of London. *See illustration on page 448.*

Here lies the preacher, judge, and poet, Peter / Who broke the laws of God, and man, and metre.

FRANCIS, LORD JEFFREY
'On Peter Robinson'

Jehosophat 4th king of Judah *c.* 873–*c.* 849 BC; he allied himself with Ahab, king of Israel, in the war against Syria.

Jehu (*c.* 842–815 BC). King of Israel. He led a successful rebellion against the family of Ahab and was responsible for the death of Jezebel.

Jekyll Gertrude (1843–1932). English landscape gardener and writer. She created over 200 gardens, many in collaboration with the architect Edwin Lutyens. In her books, she advocated natural gardens of the cottage type, with plentiful herbaceous borders.

Jefferson 3rd US president and great liberal statesman, Thomas Jefferson. He was the first president to be inaugurated in Washington (a city which he helped to plan). Among the important events of his presidency were the Louisiana Purchase 1803 of the French territories in the Mississippi Basin, and the abolition of the slave trade 1808.

Jeffreys of Wem *Judge Jeffreys was appointed Lord Chancellor by James II as a reward for his support for the crown, such as his brutal punishment of those who had supported Monmouth's rebellion in the 'bloody assizes' 1685. After the accession of William and Mary 1688 he was imprisoned in the Tower of London where he died the following year.*

Originally a painter and embroiderer, she took up gardening at the age of 48 because of worsening eyesight. Her home at Munstead Wood, Surrey, was designed for her by Lutyens.

Jellicoe Geoffrey Alan (1900–1996). English architect, landscape architect, and historian. His contribution to 20th-century thinking on landscapes and gardens was mainly through his writings, notably *Landscape of Man* 1975. However, he also made an impact as a designer, working in a contemplative and poetic vein and frequently incorporating water and sculptures. Representative of his work are the Kennedy Memorial at Runnymede, Berkshire, 1965 (a granite path winds uphill to the memorial stone, which stands beside an American Scarlet oak), and the gardens at Sutton Place, Sussex, 1980–84. Knighted 1979.

Jellicoe studied at the Architectural Association in London and as early as 1925 co-authored an extensively researched publication *Italian Gardens of the Renaissance*. His designs show the influence of modern artists, such as Paul Klee and Ben Nicholson, while his information centre and restaurant at Cheddar Gorge, Somerset 1934, reflects the work of German architect Erich Mendelsohn. Other examples of his work are at St Pauls Walden Bury, Hertfordshire 1936–89, and at Schute House garden, Wiltshire 1970–89.

Jellicoe John Rushworth, 1st Earl Jellicoe (1859–1935). British admiral who commanded the Grand Fleet 1914–16 during World War I; the only action he fought was the inconclusive battle of Jutland. He was First Sea Lord 1916–17, when he failed to push the introduction of the convoy system to combat U-boat attacks. KCVO 1907, viscount 1918, 1st earl 1925.

Jencks Charles (1939–). US architectural theorist, living in Britain. He coined the term 'Post-Modern architecture' and wrote *The Language of Post-Modern Architecture* 1984.

Jenkins Roy Harris, Baron Jenkins of Hillhead (1920–). British politician. He became a Labour minister of aviation 1964, was home secretary 1965–67 and 1974–76, and chancellor of the Exchequer

1967–70 under Harold Wilson. In 1970 he became deputy leader of the Labour Party, but resigned 1972 because of disagreement with Wilson on the issue of UK entry to the European Community (now the European Union). He was president of the European Commission 1977–81. In 1981 he became one of the founders of the Social Democratic Party and was elected 1982, but lost his seat 1987. In the same year, he was elected chancellor of Oxford University and made a life peer.

Suggested reading
Campbell, John *Roy Jenkins: A Biography* (1983)

Jenner Edward (1749–1823). English physician who pioneered vaccination. In Jenner's day, smallpox was a major killer. Jenner observed that people who worked with cattle and contracted cowpox from them never subsequently caught smallpox. In 1798 he published his findings that a child inoculated with cowpox, then two months later with smallpox, did not get smallpox. He coined the word 'vaccination' from the Latin word for cowpox, *vaccinia*.

Jenner Henry (Gwas Myhal) (1849–1934). English poet. He attempted to revive Cornish as a literary language, and in 1904 published a handbook of the Cornish language.

Jennings (Frank) Humphrey (Sinkler) (1907–1950). English documentary film maker. He introduced a poetic tone and subjectivity to factually based material. He was active in the General Post Office Film Unit from 1934 and his wartime films vividly portrayed London in the Blitz: *London Can Take It* 1940, *This Is England* 1941, and *Fires Were Started* 1943.

Jennings Pat (Patrick) (1945–). Irish footballer. In his 21-year career he was an outstanding goalkeeper. He won a British record 119 international caps for Northern Ireland 1964–86 (now surpassed by Peter Shilton), and played League football for Watford, Tottenham Hotspur, and Arsenal.

Jensen (Johannes) Hans (Daniel) (1907–1973). German physicist who shared the 1963 Nobel Prize for Physics with Maria Goeppert-Mayer and Eugene Wigner for work on the detailed characteristics of atomic nuclei.

He became professor at the Institute of Technology in Hanover 1941 and at Heidelberg 1949. Jensen proposed in 1949 the theory that a nucleus has a structure of shells or spherical layers, each filled with neutrons and protons. He explained it in *Elementary Theory of Nuclear Shell Structure* 1955, written with Goeppert-Mayer, who had developed the shell theory independently. Jensen and his colleagues also suggested that there is a very strong interaction between the spin and the orbit of a particle and that the lower of two states is always the one with angular momentum parallel rather than antiparallel. This may account for magic numbers, certain numbers of neutrons or protons that fill the shells of particularly stable elements.

Jeremiah (lived 7th–6th century BC). Old Testament Hebrew prophet, whose ministry continued 626–586 BC. He was imprisoned during Nebuchadnezzar's siege of Jerusalem on suspicion of intending to desert to the enemy. On the city's fall, he retired to Egypt.

Jerne Niels Kaj (1911–1994). British-born Danish microbiologist and immunologist, who profoundly influenced the development of modern immunology by establishing its cellular basis, and shared the 1984 Nobel Prize for Physiology or Medicine.

In 1956 he published his paper 'Natural Selection Theory of Antibody Formation' proposing that antibodies pre-exist in the body before the presence of the foreign substance, when the antibody with the best fit is selected. It was previously believed that antibodies were flexible, nonspecific molecules that adopted different shapes to wrap round foreign molecules.

As Chief Medical Officer for WHO (1956–62), Jerne built up a network of distinguished immunologists before returning to academic life 1962 with a professorship in microbiology at Pittsburgh University. In 1969 he founded and built up the Basel Institute of Immunology, funded by Roche, of which he was also director until his retirement in 1980.

Jeroboam (lived 10th century BC). First king of Israel *c.* 922–901 BC after it split away from the kingdom of Judah.

Love is like the measles; we all have to go through it.

JEROME K JEROME
Idle Thoughts of an Idle Fellow, 'On Being in Love' 1889

Jerome Jerome K(lapka) (1859–1927). English journalist and writer. His works include the humorous essays *Idle Thoughts of an Idle Fellow* 1889, the novel *Three Men in a Boat* 1889, and the play *The Passing of the Third Floor Back* 1907.

It is impossible to enjoy idling thoroughly unless one has plenty of work to do.

JEROME K JEROME
Idle Thoughts of an Idle Fellow 'On Being Idle' 1889

Jerome, St (*c.* 340–420). One of the early Christian leaders and scholars known as the Fathers of the Church. His Latin versions of the Old and New Testaments form the basis of the Roman Catholic Vulgate. He is usually depicted with a lion. Feast day 30 Sept.

Love is not to be purchased, and affection has no price.

ST JEROME
Letter no 3

Jervis John, 1st Earl of St Vincent (1735–1823). English admiral who secured the blockage of Toulon, France, 1795 in the Revolutionary Wars, and the defeat of the Spanish fleet off Cape St Vincent 1797, in which Admiral Nelson played a key part. Jervis was a rigid disciplinarian. KB 1782, earl 1797.

My old oak.

Attributed remark by George IV on JOHN JERVIS

Jeschonneck Hans (1899–1943). German air force general. Selected by Goering to help establish the Luftwaffe in the 1930s, he became Chief of Air Staff 1939, but turned out to have been over-promoted. A sound enough pilot and administrator, he was out of his depth trying to plan the air defences of Germany. His final mistake was to order his nightfighters to Berlin, where they were shot at by their own artillery, while the RAF were raiding Peenemunde Aug 1943. He shot himself the next day.

Jespersen (Jens) Otto (Harry) (1860–1943). Danish linguist. At the beginning of his career he was concerned with phonetics and comparative philology. Later his enormous contribution to the study of English occupied much of his time, but he also worked on general linguistic theory and on syntax (the rules governing the way words are put together in sentences). He is the author of the classic seven-volume *Modern English Grammar* 1909–49.

He wrote, for example, on traditional 'notional' grammar, which assumes that there are universal categories of grammar that apply to all languages, such as the parts of speech – nouns, verbs, and so on, and tense and mood. His other works include *Language* 1922 and *The Philosophy of Grammar* 1924. He was professor of English at Copenhagen University 1893–1925.

Jessop William (1745–1814). British canal engineer who built the first canal in England entirely dependent on reservoirs for its water supply (the Grantham Canal 1793–97), and designed (with Thomas Telford) the 300-m/1,000-ft-long Pontcysyllte aqueduct over the river Dee. Jessop also designed the forerunner of the iron rail that later became universally adopted for railways.

Jessop's first tunnel was the 2.8-km/1.7-mi-long Butterley Tunnel on the Cromford Canal he built in Derbyshire, and this led to the forming of the Butterley Iron Works in 1790, making rails and bridges.

Jessop was chief engineer 1793–1805 of the Grand Union Canal, linking London and the Midlands over a distance of 150 km/95 mi. He was also responsible for the Barnsley, Rochdale, and Trent navigation, and the Nottingham and Ellesmere canals. Jessop was also chief engineer of the Surrey Iron Railway, built 1801–02. He worked on the construction of a large wet dock area on the Avon at Bristol, on the West India Docks and the Isle of Dogs Canal in London, on the harbours at Shoreham and Littlehampton, and on many other projects.

Jesus (*c.* 4 BC–AD 29 or 30). Hebrew preacher on whose teachings Christianity was founded. According to the accounts of his life in the four Gospels, he was born in Bethlehem, Palestine, son of God and the Virgin Mary, and brought up by Mary and her husband Joseph as a carpenter in Nazareth. After adult baptism, he gathered 12 disciples, but his preaching antagonized the Roman authorities and he was executed by crucifixion. Three days later there came reports of his resurrection and, later, his ascension to heaven.

Through his legal father Joseph, Jesus belonged to the tribe of Judah and the family of David, the second king of Israel, a heritage needed by the Messiah for whom the Hebrew people were waiting. In AD 26 or 27 his cousin John the Baptist proclaimed the coming of the promised Messiah and baptized Jesus, who then made two missionary journeys through the district of Galilee. His teaching, summarized in the Sermon on the Mount, aroused both religious opposition from the Pharisees and secular opposition from the party supporting the Roman governor Herod Antipas. When Jesus returned to Jerusalem (probably in AD 29), a week before the Passover festival, he was greeted by the people as the Messiah, and the Hebrew authorities (aided by the apostle Judas) had him arrested and condemned to death, after a hurried trial by the Sanhedrin (supreme Jewish court). The Roman procurator, Pontius Pilate, confirmed the sentence, stressing the threat posed to imperial authority by Jesus' teaching.

Suggested reading
Crossan, J D *The Historical Jesus* (1991)
Dodd, C H *The Founder of Christianity* (1970)
Dunn, J D G *The Evidence for Jesus* (1985)
Kee, Howard *Jesus in History* (1977)
Mackey, J P *Jesus: The Man and the Myth* (1979)
Wilson, A N *Jesus* (1993)

Jevons William Stanley (1835–1882). British economist who introduced the concept of marginal utility: the increase in total utility (satisfaction or pleasure of consumption) relative to a unit increase of the goods consumed.

He became professor of logic and political economy at Owens College, Manchester, 1866, and taught at University College, London, 1876–81.

Jhabvala Ruth Prawer (1927–). Adoptively Indian novelist. Born in Cologne of Polish parents and educated in England, she went to live in India when she married 1951. Her novels explore the idiosyncratic blend of East and West in the Indian middle class, as in *Esmond in India* 1957. She has also written terse short stories about urban India and successful film scripts for Merchant Ivory, including a treatment of her own novel *Heat and Dust*, awarded the Booker Prize 1975. Her film scripts for *A Room with a View* 1987 and *Howards End* 1992 both received Academy awards. She also wrote the scripts for *The Remains of the Day* 1993 and *Jefferson in Paris* 1995.

Jiang Jie Shi alternate transcription of ◊Chiang Kai-shek.

Jiang Qing or Chiang Ching (1914–1991). Chinese communist politician, third wife of the party leader Mao Zedong. In 1960 she became minister for culture, and played a key role in the 1966–69 Cultural Revolution as the leading member of the Shanghai-based Gang of Four, who attempted to seize power 1976. Jiang was imprisoned 1981.

Jiang was a Shanghai actress when in 1937 she met Mao Zedong at the communist headquarters in Yan'an; she became his wife 1939.

She emerged as a radical, egalitarian Maoist. Her influence waned during the early 1970s and her relationship with Mao became embittered. On Mao's death Sept 1976, the Gang of Four sought to seize power by organizing military coups in Shanghai and Beijing. They were arrested for treason by Mao's successor Hua Guofeng and tried 1980–81. The Gang were blamed for the excesses of the Cultural Revolution, but Jiang asserted during her trial that she had only followed Mao's orders as an obedient wife. This was rejected, and Jiang received a death sentence Jan 1981, which was subsequently commuted to life imprisonment.

Jiang Zemin (1926–   ). Chinese political leader, state president from 1993. He succeeded Zhao Ziyang as Communist Party leader after the Tiananmen Square massacre of 1989. Jiang is a cautious proponent of economic reform who has held with unswerving adherence to the party's 'political line'.

The son-in-law of Li Xiannian, Jiang joined the Chinese Communist Party's politburo in 1967 after serving in the Moscow embassy and as mayor of Shanghai. He subsequently succeeded Deng Xiaoping as head of the influential central military commission and replaced Yang Shangkun as state president March 1993.

Jiménez Juan Ramón (1881–1958). Spanish lyric poet. Born in Andalusia, he left Spain during the civil war to live in exile in Puerto Rico. Nobel prize 1956.

Jin dynasty or Chin dynasty (960–1279). Hereditary rulers of N China, including Manchuria and part of Mongolia, 1122–1234, during the closing part of the Song era. The dynasty was founded by Juchen (Jurchen) nomad hunters, who sacked the northern Song capital Kaifeng 1126, forcing the Song to retreat south to Hangzhou. The Jin eventually ruled N China as far south as the Huai River. Over time, the Juchen became Sinicized, but from 1214 lost much of their territory to the Mongols led by Genghis Khan.

Jinnah Muhammad Ali (1876–1948). Indian politician, Pakistan's first governor-general from 1947. He was president of the Muslim League 1916, 1934–48, and by 1940 was advocating the need for a separate state of Pakistan; at the 1946 conferences in London he insisted on the partition of British India into Hindu and Muslim states.
Suggested reading
Bolitho, H *Jinnah* (1954)
McDonagh, S *Mohammed Ali Jinnah, Maker of Modern Pakistan* (1971)

Jiricna Eva (1939–   ). Czech architect who has worked in the UK since 1968. Her fashion shops, bars, and cafés for the Joseph chain are built in a highly refined Modernist style.

Joachim Joseph (1831–1907). Austro-Hungarian violinist and composer. He studied under Mendelssohn and founded the Joachim Quartet (1869–1907). Joachim played and conducted the music of his friend Brahms. His own compositions include pieces for violin and orchestra, chamber, and orchestral works.

Joachim of Fiore (c. 1132–1202). Italian mystic, born in Calabria. In his mystical writings he interpreted history as a sequence of three ages, that of the Father, Son, and Holy Spirit, the last of which, the age of perfect spirituality, was to begin 1260. His messianic views were taken up enthusiastically by many followers.

He was a Cistercian monk, and abbot of Corazzo from 1177. He founded his own order at San Giovanni in Fiore.

Joannitius Hunayn ibn Ishaq al Ibadi (809–873). Arabic translator, a Nestorian Christian, who translated Greek learning – including Ptolemy, Euclid, Hippocrates, Plato, and Aristotle – into Arabic or Syrian for the Abbasid court in Baghdad.

Joan of Arc, St (French Jeanne d'Arc) (c. 1412–1431). French military leader. In 1429 she persuaded the future Charles VII that she had a divine mission to expel the occupying English from N France and secure his coronation. She raised the siege of Orléans, defeated the English at Patay, north of Orléans, and Charles was crowned in Reims. However, she failed to take Paris and was captured in May 1430 by the Burgundians, who sold her to the English.

Joan was born at Domrémy in Lorraine, daughter of a prosperous farmer. She sought out Charles VII, then dauphin, at Chinon, NW France, and assembled a large army. After her success in relieving Orléans, she became known as the Maid of Orléans. She was captured when helping to raise the siege of Compiègne, and imprisoned for four months by the English. Found guilty of witchcraft and heresy by a tribunal of French ecclesiastics who supported the English, she was burned to death at the stake in Rouen 30 May 1431. In 1920 she was canonized.
Suggested reading
Gies, F *Joan of Arc: The Legend and the Reality* (1981)
Lucie-Smith, E *Joan of Arc* (1977)
Sackville-West, V *Joan of Arc* (1936)
Warner, M *Joan of Arc, the Image of Female Heroism* (1981)

Joan of Kent (1328–1385). Countess of Kent. She married Edward the Black Prince 1361 and their younger son became Richard II. John of Gaunt took refuge at her home in Kennington when his palace was besieged by Londoners 1376. Her beauty and gentleness earned her the nickname 'Fair Maid of Kent'.

Job (lived c. 5th century BC). In the Old Testament, Hebrew leader who in the Book of Job questioned God's infliction of suffering on the righteous while enduring great sufferings himself. Although Job comes to no final conclusion, his book is one of the first attempts to explain the problem of human suffering in a world believed to be created and governed by a God who is all-powerful and all-good.

The generals ... are arrogant ... They still look on [Hitler] as the Corporal of the World War instead of the greatest statesman since Bismarck.

ALFRED JODL
in his Diary 13 Sept 1938

Jodl Alfred (1890–1946). German general. In World War II he was in effect responsible for most German operations outside the USSR and he drew up the Nazi government's plan for the attack on Yugoslavia, Greece, and the USSR. In Jan 1945 he became Chief of Staff and headed the delegation that signed Germany's surrender in Reims 7 May 1945. He was tried for war crimes in Nuremberg 1945–46 and hanged.

I have not done much evil in my life and I have sincerely loved my wife.

JOSEPH, MARSHAL JOFFRE
Last confession 1931

Joffre Joseph Jacques Césaire (1852–1931). Marshal of France during World War I. He was chief of general staff 1911. The German invasion of Belgium 1914 took him by surprise, but his stand at the Battle of the Marne resulted in his appointment as supreme commander of all the French armies 1915. His failure to make adequate preparations at Verdun 1916 and the military disasters on the Somme led to his replacement by Nivelle Dec 1916.

John Augustus Edwin (1878–1961). Welsh painter. He is known for his portraits, including *The Smiling Woman* 1910 (Tate Gallery, London) of his second wife, Dorelia McNeill. His sitters included such literary and society figures as Thomas Hardy, Dylan Thomas, W B Yeats, and Cecil Beaton.

He led a bohemian and nomadic life and was the brother of the artist Gwen John.

John studied at the Slade School, taught art at the University College, Liverpool, 1901–03, and began to exhibit at the New English Art Club in 1903. He led a nomadic existence 1910–19 in Ireland, Dorset, and Wales, when he produced many poetic small oil paintings of figures in landscape. He was an official artist to the Canadian Corps in World War I, and RA 1928, resigning 1938 because of the Academy's rejection of a sculpture by Epstein, but accepting re-election 1940. He received the Order of Merit 1942. His portraits are outstanding in their combined certainty of drawing and temperamental handling of paint. His sense of colour and a modified Post-Impressionism appear in his landscapes of the south of France and his flower pieces. His cartoon for a mural decoration, *Galway*, 1916 (Tate, London), shows an inclination for large-scale work of this kind, which was never fully realized. He produced beautiful drawings of the figure at every stage of his career, and also some etchings. His autobiography, *Chiaroscuro*, appeared 1952.

John Elton. Stage name of Reginald Kenneth Dwight (1947–). English pop singer, pianist, and composer. His best-known album, *Goodbye Yellow Brick Road* 1973, includes the hit 'Bennie and the Jets'. Among his many other highly successful songs are 'Rocket Man', 'Crocodile Rock', and 'Daniel' all 1972, 'Candle in the Wind' 1973, 'Pinball Wizard' 1975, 'Blue Eyes' 1982, 'Nikita' 1985 and 'Sacrifice' 1989, the latter from his album *Sleeping with the Past*. His output is prolific and his hits have continued intermittently into the 1990s.

He enjoyed his greatest popularity, especially in the USA, from his second album, *Elton John* 1970 to *Blue Moves* 1976, working exclusively with the lyricist Bernie Taupin (1950–).

John Gwen(dolen Mary) (1876–1939). Welsh painter. She lived in France for most of her life. Many of her paintings depict young women or nuns (she converted to Catholicism 1913), but she also painted calm, muted interiors.

Her style was characterized by a sensitive use of colour and tone.

He had the mental abilities of a great king, but the inclinations of a petty tyrant.

W C Warren on JOHN (I) LACKLAND
in *King John* 1964

John (I) Lackland (1167–1216). King of England from 1199 and acting king from 1189 during his brother Richard the Lion-Heart's absence on the third Crusade.

He lost Normandy and almost all the other English possessions in France to Philip II of France by 1205. His repressive policies and excessive taxation brought him into conflict with his barons, and he was forced to seal the Magna Carta 1215. Later repudiation of it led to the first Barons' War 1215–17, during which he died.

John's subsequent bad reputation was only partially deserved. It resulted from his intrigues against his brother Richard I, his complicity in the death of his nephew Prince Arthur of Brittany, a rival for the English throne, and the effectiveness of his ruthless taxation policy, as well as his provoking Pope Innocent III to excommunicate England 1208–13. John's attempt to limit the papacy's right of interference in episcopal elections, which traditionally were the preserve of English kings, was resented by monastic sources, and these provided much of the evidence upon which his reign was later judged.

Suggested reading
Curren-Aquino, D T (ed) *King John: New Perspectives* (1988)
Holt, J C *King John* (1963)
Warren, W L *King John* (1961)

John two kings of France, including:

John II (1319–1364). King of France from 1350. He was defeated and captured by the Black Prince at Poitiers 1356 and imprisoned in England. Released 1360, he failed to raise the money for his ransom and returned to England 1364, where he died.

John name of 23 popes, including:

John XXII (born Jacques Duese) (1249–1334). Pope 1316–34. He spent his papacy in Avignon, France, engaged in a long conflict with the Holy Roman emperor, Louis of Bavaria, and the Spiritual Franciscans, a monastic order who preached the absolute poverty of the clergy.

John XXIII (Angelo Giuseppe Roncalli) (1881–1963). Pope from 1958. He improved relations with the USSR in line with his encycli-

cal *Pacem in Terris/Peace on Earth* 1963, established Roman Catholic hierarchies in newly emergent states, and summoned the Second Vatican Council, which reformed church liturgy and backed the ecumenical movement.

Suggested reading
John XXIII *Journal of a Soul* (memoirs) (trs 1964)
Johnson, Paul *Pope John XXIII* (1974)
Zizola, G *The Utopia of John XXIII* (trs 1978)

'John XXIII' (Baldassare Costa) (*c.* 1370–1419). Antipope 1410–15. In an attempt to end the Great Schism he was elected pope by a council of cardinals in Bologna, but was deposed by the Council of Constance 1415, together with the popes of Avignon and Rome. His papacy is not recognized by the church.

John three kings of Poland, including:

John III Sobieski (1624–1696). King of Poland from 1674. He became commander in chief of the army 1668 after victories over the Cossacks and Tatars. A victory over the Turks 1673 helped to get him elected to the Polish throne, and he saved Vienna from the besieging Turks 1683.

John six kings of Portugal, including:

John I (1357–1433). King of Portugal from 1385. An illegitimate son of Pedro I, he was elected by the Cortes (parliament). His claim was supported by an English army against the rival king of Castile, thus establishing the Anglo-Portuguese Alliance 1386.

He married Philippa of Lancaster, daughter of John of Gaunt.

John IV (1604–1656). King of Portugal from 1640. Originally duke of Braganza, he was elected king when the Portuguese rebelled against Spanish rule. His reign was marked by a long war against Spain, which did not end until 1668.

John VI (1769–1826). King of Portugal and regent for his insane mother Maria I from 1799 until her death 1816. He fled to Brazil when the French invaded Portugal 1807 and did not return until 1822. On his return Brazil declared its independence, with John's elder son Pedro as emperor.

John, St (lived 1st century AD). New Testament apostle. Traditionally, he wrote the fourth Gospel and the Johannine Epistles (when he was bishop of Ephesus), and the Book of Revelation (while exiled to the Greek island of Patmos). His emblem is an eagle; his feast day 27 Dec.

St John is identified with the unnamed 'disciple whom Jesus loved'. Son of Zebedee, born in Judaea, he and his brother James were Galilean fishermen. Jesus entrusted his mother to John at the Crucifixion, where John is often shown dressed in red, with curly hair. Another of his symbols is a chalice with a little snake in it.

John Chrysostom, St (*c.* 345–407). Christian scholar, hermit, preacher, and Eastern Orthodox bishop of Constantinople 398–404. He was born in Antioch (now Antakya, Turkey). Feast day 13 Sept. He was given the name Chrysostom ('Golden Mouth') because of his eloquence.

John of Austria Don (1547–1578). Spanish soldier, the illegitimate son of the Holy Roman emperor Charles V. He defeated the Turks at the Battle of Lepanto 1571.

John captured Tunis 1573 but quickly lost it. He was appointed governor-general of the Netherlands 1576 but discovered that real power lay in the hands of William of Orange. John withdrew 1577 and then attacked and defeated the patriot army at Gemblours 31 Jan 1578 with the support of reinforcements from Philip II of Spain. Lack of money stopped him from going any farther. He died of fever.

An attractive and glamorous hero ... he was out to compensate for his illegitimacy by winning a throne.

E N Williams on DON JOHN OF AUSTRIA in *Penguin Dictionary of English and European History 1485–1789* 1980

John of Damascus, St (*c.* 676–*c.* 754). Eastern Orthodox theologian and hymn writer, a defender of image worship against the iconoclasts (image-breakers). Contained in his *The Fountain of Knowledge* is 'An Accurate Exposition of the Orthodox Faith', an important chronicle of theology from the 4th to 7th centuries.

He was born in Damascus, Syria. Feast day 4 Dec.

Old John of Gaunt, time-honoured Lancaster.

William Shakespeare on JOHN OF GAUNT
in *Richard II* I i

John of Gaunt (1340–1399). English nobleman and politician, born in Ghent, fourth son of Edward III, Duke of Lancaster from 1362. He distinguished himself during the Hundred Years' War. During Edward's last years, and the years before Richard II attained the age of majority, he acted as head of government, and Parliament protested against his corrupt rule.

Suggested reading
Armitage-Smith, S *John of Gaunt* (1904)
Goodman, Anthony *John of Gaunt: The Exercise of Princely Power in Fourteenth Century Europe* (1992)

John of Lancaster Duke of Bedford (1389–1435). English prince, third son of Henry IV. He was regent of France 1422–31 during the minority of Henry VI, his nephew, and protector of England 1422–35. He mostly left English affairs to his brother, Humphrey, Duke of Gloucester. He allowed Joan of Arc to be burnt as a witch 1431 and had Henry VI crowned king of France 1431. KG 1400, duke 1414.

Gaming is the mother of lies and perjuries.

JOHN OF SALISBURY
Policraticus bk i 1175

John of Salisbury (*c.* 1115–1180). English philosopher and historian. His *Policraticus* portrayed the church as the guarantee of liberty against the unjust claims of secular authority.

He studied in France 1130–1153, in Paris with Abelard and at Chartres. He became secretary to Thomas à Becket and supported him against Henry II, and fled to France after Becket's murder, becoming bishop of Chartres 1176.

John of the Cross, St (1542–1591). Spanish Roman Catholic Carmelite friar from 1564, who was imprisoned several times for attempting to impose the reforms laid down by St Teresa. His verse describes spiritual ecstasy. Feast day 24 Nov.

He was persecuted and sent to the monastery of Ubeda until his death. He was beatified 1674 and canonized 1726.

John the Baptist, St (*c.* 12 BC–*c.* AD 27). In the New Testament, an itinerant preacher. After preparation in the wilderness, he proclaimed the coming of the Messiah and baptized Jesus in the river Jordan. He was later executed by Herod Antipas at the request of Salome, who demanded that his head be brought to her on a platter.

John was the son of Zacharias and Elizabeth (a cousin of Jesus' mother), and born in Nazareth, Galilee. He and Jesus are often shown together as children.

John Paul two popes:

John Paul I (Albino Luciani) (1912–1978). Pope 26 Aug–28 Sept 1978. His name was chosen as the combination of his two immediate predecessors.

John Paul II (Karol Jozef Wojtyla) (1920–). Pope from 1978, the first non-Italian to be elected pope since 1522. He was born near Kraków, Poland. He has upheld the tradition of papal infallibility and has condemned artificial contraception, women priests, married priests, and modern dress for monks and nuns – views that have aroused criticism from liberalizing elements in the church.

In a March 1995 encyclical, the pope stated in unequivocal terms his opposition to abortion, birth control, in vitro fertilization, genetic manipulation, and euthanasia, and employed the church's strongest language to date against capital punishment.

In 1939, at the beginning of World War II, Wojtyla was conscripted for forced labour by the Germans, working in quarries and a chemical factory, but from 1942 studied for the priesthood illegally in Kraków. After the war he taught ethics and theology at the universities of Lublin and Kraków, becoming archbishop of Kraków 1964. In 1967 he was made a cardinal. He was shot and wounded by a Turk in an attempt on his life 1981. Although he has warned against the involvement of priests in political activity, he opposed the Gulf War 1991 and has condemned arms manufacturers as sinful.

Suggested reading
Johnson, Paul *Pope John Paul II and the Catholic Restoration* (1982)
Thomas, Gordon and Morgan-Witts, Max *Pontiff* (1983)
Williams, G H *The Mind of John Paul II* (1981)

Johns Jasper (1930–). US painter, sculptor, and printmaker. He was one of the foremost exponents of Pop art. He rejected abstract art, favouring such mundane subjects as flags, maps, and numbers as a means of exploring the relationship between image and reality. His work employs pigments mixed with wax (encaustic) to create a rich surface with unexpected delicacies of colour. He has also created collages and lithographs. One of his best-known works is the bronze *Ale Cans* 1960 (Kunstmuseum, Basel).

Born in Augusta, Georgia, he moved to New York City in 1952. In the 1960s his works became more abstract before veering toward Abstract Expressionism in the mid-1970s. He was also influenced by Marcel Duchamp.

Suggested reading
Crichton, Michael *Jasper Johns* (1994)
Kozloff, Max *Jasper Johns* (1969)
Orton, Fred *Figuring Jasper* (1994)

Johns W(illiam) E(arl), 'Captain' (1893–1968). English author. From 1932 he wrote popular novels about World War I flying ace 'Biggles', now sometimes criticized for chauvinism, racism, and sexism. Johns was a flying officer in the RAF (there is no rank of captain) until his retirement 1930.

Johnson Alvin Saunders (1874–1971). US social scientist and educator. He was a founder and an editor of the *New Republic* 1917. Joining with some of America's greatest scholars, Johnson was one of the founders of the New School for Social Research in New York City, serving as its director 1923–45. Johnson's memoir, *Progress: An Autobiography*, was published 1952.

Had I been a man I might have explored the Poles or climbed Mount Everest ... my spirit found outlet in the air.

AMY JOHNSON
quoted in Margot Asquith *Myself When Young*

Johnson Amy (1903–1941). English aviator. She made a solo flight from England to Australia 1930, in $9\frac{1}{2}$ days, and in 1932 made the fastest ever solo flight from England to Cape Town, South Africa. Her plane disappeared over the English Channel in World War II while she was serving with the Air Transport Auxiliary.

Suggested reading
Babington-Smith, Constance *Amy Johnson* (1967)

Johnson Andrew (1808–1875). 17th president of the USA 1865–69, a Democrat. He was a congressman from Tennessee 1843–53, governor of Tennessee 1853–57, senator 1857–62, and vice president 1865. He succeeded to the presidency on Lincoln's assassination (15 April 1865). His conciliatory policy to the defeated South after the Civil War involved him in a feud with the Radical Republicans, culminating in his impeachment 1868 before the Senate, which failed to convict him by one vote.

Johnson was born in Raleigh, North Carolina. Among his achievements was the purchase of Alaska from Russia 1867. When he tried to dismiss Edwin Stanton, a cabinet secretary, his political opponents seized on the opportunity to charge him with 'high crimes and misdemeanours' and attempted to remove him from office; it was this battle that ended in his impeachment. Jackson's tenure as president was characterized by his frustration and political stalemate. He presided over the re-entry of the Southern states into the Union. He was returned to the Senate from Tennessee 1875, but died shortly afterwards.

Suggested reading
Castel, A *The Presidency of Andrew Johnson* (1979)
Gerson, N B *The Trial of Andrew Johnson* (1977)
Lomask, M *Andrew Johnson: President on Trial* (1960)
McKitrick, E L *Andrew Johnson: A Profile* (1969)

[He] reduced the presidency to the level of a grog shop.

John Sherman on ANDREW JOHNSON
quoted in W B Hesseltine *Ulysses S Grant* 1935

Johnson Celia (1908–1982). English actress. She was perceived as quintessentially English. She starred with Trevor Howard in the romantic film *Brief Encounter* 1946; later films include *The Captain's Paradise* 1953 and *The Prime of Miss Jean Brodie* 1968. DBE 1981.

We're neither of us free to love each other ... there's too much in the way ... There's still time ... if we control ourselves ... and behave like sensible human beings.

CELIA JOHNSON
in the film *Brief Encounter* 1945

Johnson Earvin ('Magic') (1959–   ). US basketball player. He played for the Los Angeles Lakers 1979–91 and 1992–   , a team that won the National Basketball Association (NBA) championship 1980, 1982, 1985, 1987, and 1988. He played in the victorious 1992 US Olympic basketball team in Barcelona, Spain.

In 1991, he announced that he had contracted the HIV virus and would retire from basketball to devote his time to AIDS awareness and prevention programmes. However, he made a comeback in 1996.

Johnson Eastman (1824–1906). US painter. Born in Germany, he trained in Düsseldorf, The Hague, and Paris. Painting in the open air, he developed a fresh and luminous landscape style.

He studied art at Düsseldorf and worked for some years as a young man at The Hague. Returning to America 1855 he painted some scenes of Native American and frontier life in Wisconsin, made drawings of the Union Army during the Civil War and settled in New York, as a portrait painter mainly, though also painting genre scenes of American life.

Johnson had his first success with a nostalgic naturalist scene, *Old Kentucky Home* 1859 (New York Historical Society).

Johnson Hiram Warren (1866–1945). US politician. He was the 'Bull Moose' party candidate for vice president in Theodore Roosevelt's unsuccessful bid to regain the presidency 1912. Elected to the US Senate 1917, Johnson served there until his death. He was an unyielding isolationist, opposing US involvement in World War I as well as membership in the League of Nations and World Court.

Born in Sacramento, California, USA, Johnson attended the University of California and was admitted to the bar 1888. In 1902 he established a law practice in San Francisco before entering politics and serving as governor of California 1911–17.

Johnson Jack (John Arthur) (1878–1946). US heavyweight boxer. He overcame severe racial prejudice to become the first black heavyweight champion of the world 1908 when he travelled to Australia to challenge Tommy Burns. The US authorities wanted Johnson 'dethroned' because of his colour but could not find suitable challengers until 1915, when he lost the title in a dubious fight decision to the giant Jess Willard.

Johnson, Andrew *Andrew Johnson who became 17th US president on the assassination of Abraham Lincoln. He sought to execute Lincoln's plan to readmit seceded states of the Union after the American Civil War, but was blocked by the Radical Republicans who insisted on keeping the southern states under military government until they fully accepted antislavery laws.*

Johnson James Weldon (1871–1938). US writer, lawyer, diplomat, and social critic. He was a strong supporter of Theodore Roosevelt and served him and Taft as US consul in Venezuela and Nicaragua 1906–12. He was editor of *New York Age* 1912–22 and was active in the National Association for the Advancement of Colored People (NAACP). As poet and anthropologist, he became one of the chief figures of the Harlem Renaissance of the 1920s. His autobiography *Along This Way* was published 1933.

Born in Jacksonville, Florida, USA, and educated at Atlanta University, Johnson became the first black American admitted to the Florida bar 1897.

Johnson Lyndon Baines (1908–1973). 36th president of the USA 1963–69, a Democrat. He was elected to Congress 1937–49 and the Senate 1949–60. Born in Texas, he brought critical Southern support as J F Kennedy's vice-presidential running mate 1960, and became president on Kennedy's assassination.

Following Kennedy's assassination, Johnson pushed civil rights legislation through Congress. However, his foreign policy met with considerably less success. After the Tonkin Gulf Incident, which escalated US involvement in the Vietnam War, support won by Johnson's Great Society legislation (civil rights, education, alleviation of poverty) dissipated, and he declined to run for re-election 1968.

Suggested reading
Dallek, Robert *Lone Star Rising: Lyndon Johnson and His Times* (1991)
Divine, R A *The Johnson Years* (1987)
Heath, J F *Decade of Disillusionment: The Kennedy–Johnson Years* (1975)
Johnson, Lyndon Baines *The Vantage Point* (1971)
Miller, Merle *Lyndon: An Oral Biography* (1980)

Johnson Pamela Hansford, Lady Snow (1912–1981). British novelist, who in 1950 married C P Snow; her novels include *Too Dear for my Possessing* 1940 and *The Honours Board* 1970.

Johnson Philip Cortelyou (1906–   ). US architect. He coined the term 'International Style' 1932. Originally designing in the style of Mies van der Rohe, he later became an exponent of Post-

Johnson, Lyndon B *Lyndon B Johnson became president of the USA 1963 after the assassination of John F Kennedy. He introduced a broad range of social reforms, including major advances in black civil rights, but his extension of Kennedy's policy of US involvement in Vietnam led to riots on university campuses and made his administration deeply unpopular.*

Modernism. He designed the giant AT&T building in New York 1978, a pink skyscraper with a Chippendale-style cabinet top. He was director of architecture and design at the Museum of Modern Art, New York 1932–54, where he built the annexe and sculpture court.

Suggested reading
Jacobus, John *Philip Johnson* (1962)
Knight III, Carleton *Philip Johnson/John Burgee: Architecture* (1985)
Noble, C *Philip Johnson* (1968)

Johnson Robert (*c.* 1912–1938). US blues guitarist, songwriter, and singer. His intense, eerie playing and short, mysterious life made him a legend. His work has been studied by countless guitar players and his songs include 'Love in Vain', 'Terraplane Blues', 'Crossroads', and 'Hellhound on My Trail' (all 1936–37).

Born in rural Mississippi, Johnson was an exponent of acoustic delta blues, though his style, with distinctive bottleneck slide playing, foreshadowed the development of urban blues. He worked intermittently on a plantation, but also spent time on the road and performed with the blues musicians Howlin' Wolf and Sonny Boy Williamson II (1899–1965), among others. All his 29 recordings were made in Texas 1936 and 1937; he was murdered 1938.

Johnson Samuel, known as 'Dr Johnson' (1709–1784). English lexicographer, author, and critic. He was also a brilliant conversationalist and the dominant figure in 18th-century London literary society. His *Dictionary*, published 1755, remained authoritative for over a century, and is still remarkable for the vigour of its definitions. In 1764 he founded the Literary Club, whose members included the painter Joshua Reynolds, the political philosopher Edmund Burke, the dramatist Oliver Goldsmith, the actor David Garrick, and James Boswell.

Johnson's first meeting with Boswell was in 1763. A visit with Boswell to Scotland and the Hebrides 1773 was recorded in *Journey to the Western Isles of Scotland* 1775. Other works include a satire imitating Juvenal, *The Vanity of Human Wishes* 1749, the philosophical romance *Rasselas* 1759, an edition of Shakespeare 1765, and the classic *Lives of the Most Eminent English Poets* 1779–81. He was buried in Westminster Abbey and his house in Gough Square,

London, is preserved as a museum. His wit and humanity are documented in Boswell's classic *Life of Samuel Johnson* 1791.

Suggested reading
Bate, W *Samuel Johnson* (1977)
Boswell, James *The Life of Samuel Johnson* (1791; several recent editions)
Greene, D *Samuel Johnson* (1970)
Irwin, G *Samuel Johnson: A Personality in Conflict* (1971)
Wain, J *Samuel Johnson: A Biography* (1975)

Johnson Uwe (1934–1984). German novelist who left East Germany for West Berlin 1959, and wrote of the division of Germany in, for example, *Anniversaries* 1977.

Johnston Brian Alexander (1912–1994). English broadcaster, writer, and entertainer. Considered the 'voice of cricket' for nearly half a century, Johnston began commentating for the BBC 1946, but was perhaps best known for his commentary on Radio 3's *Test Match Special* from 1970. His genuine love of cricket and cheerful, friendly manner made him a popular broadcaster. Despite his finely tuned professionalism, Johnston fell prone to numerous broadcasting gaffes, as at the Oval 1976, when he tersely announced: 'The bowler's Holding, the batsman's Willey.'

Johnston Joseph Eggleston (1807–1891). US military leader during the American Civil War 1861–65. Joining the Confederacy, he commanded the Army of Tennessee 1863. After the war, Johnston returned to private life, later serving in the US House of Representatives 1879–81 and as federal railroad commissioner 1887–91.

Born near Farmville, Virginia, Johnston graduated from West Point military academy 1829. As a military engineer, he served with distinction during the Mexican War 1846–48.

Johnson, Samuel *An etching of Samuel Johnson based on a portrait by Joshua Reynolds. Writer, critic, lexicographer, and renowned conversationalist and wit, Doctor Johnson dominated 18th-century English literature. It took him seven years to complete the two volumes of his massive* Dictionary of the English Language *1755, in which he wryly defined a lexicographer as a 'harmless drudge'.*

Like the author of a chanson de gest, he looks back to a better and nobler time.

Michael Clanchy on JEAN, SIRE DE JOINVILLE
in *Blackwell's Dictionary of Historians* 1988

Joinville Jean, Sire de Joinville (*c.* 1224–*c.* 1317). French historian, born in Champagne. He accompanied Louis IX on the crusade of 1248–54, which he described in his *History of St Louis.*

Joliet (or Jolliet) Louis (1645–1700). French-born Canadian explorer. He and Jesuit missionary Jacques Marquette were the first to successfully chart the course of the Mississippi river down to its junction with the Arkansas river. They returned to Canada by way of the Illinois territory.

Born in Quebec, Canada, Joliet was sent by the Canadian governor on an extensive exploration of the Great Lakes 1669. After his expedition along the Mississippi, he later explored Labrador and Hudson Bay.

Suggested reading
Eifert, Virginia *Louis Jolliet, Explorer of Rivers* (1961)
Hamilton, R N *Marquette's Explorations: The Narratives Reexamined* (1970)
Scanlon, M S *Trails of the French Explorers* (1956)

Joliot-Curie Frédéric (Jean) Joliot (1900–1958) and Irène (born Curie) (1897–1956). French physicists who made the discovery of artificial radioactivity, for which they were jointly awarded the 1935 Nobel Prize for Chemistry.

Irène was the daughter of Marie and Pierre Curie and began work at her mother's Radium Institute 1921. In 1926 she married Frédéric, a pupil of her mother's, and they began a long and fruitful collaboration. In 1934 they found that certain elements exposed to radiation themselves become radioactive. She died of leukaemia caused by overexposure to radioactivity.

Frédéric Joliot was born in Paris and graduated from the Ecole Supérieure de Physique et de Chimie Industrielle. He joined the Radium Institute 1925. In 1937 he became professor of nuclear physics at the Collège de France. He succeeded his wife as director of the Radium Institute 1956.

You ain't heard nuttin' yet!

AL JOLSON
quoted in Martin Abramson *The Real Story of Al Jolson*

Jolson Al, stage name of Asa Yoelson (1886–1950). Russian-born US singer and entertainer. Popular in Broadway theatre and vaudeville, he was chosen to star in the first talking picture, *The Jazz Singer* 1927. Jolson, who got his start in vaudeville, was also a popular recording star.

Jonah (lived 7th century BC). Hebrew prophet whose name is given to a book in the Old Testament. According to this, he fled by ship to evade his mission to prophesy the destruction of Nineveh. The crew threw him overboard in a storm, as a bringer of ill fortune, and he spent three days and nights in the belly of a whale before coming to land.

Jonathan (Joseph) Leabua, Chief (1914–1987). Lesotho politician. A leader in the drive for independence, Jonathan became prime minister of Lesotho 1965. His rule was ended by a coup 1986.

As prime minister, Jonathan played a pragmatic role, allying himself in turn with the South African government and the Organization of African Unity.

Jones Allen (1937–). English painter, sculptor, and printmaker. He was a leading exponent of Pop art. His colourful paintings are executed in the style of commercial advertising, and unabashedly celebrate the female form, for example, *Perfect Match* 1966–67 (Wallraf-Richartz Museum, Cologne).

His witty, abbreviated imagery of women clad in bustiers, garterbelts, stocking tops, and stiletto-heeled shoes is intended as a comment on male fantasies and sexual fetishes.

Jones Bobby (Robert Tyre) (1902–1971). US golfer. He was the game's greatest amateur player, who never turned professional but won 13 major amateur and professional tournaments, including the Grand Slam of the amateur and professional opens of both the USA and Britain 1930. Born in Atlanta, Georgia, Jones finished playing competitive golf 1930 and concentrated on his law practice. He maintained his contacts with the sport and was largely responsible for inaugurating the US Masters.

Jones 'Casey' (John Luther) (1864–1900). US railroad engineer and folk hero. His death on the 'Cannonball Express', while on an overnight run 1900, is the subject of popular legend. Colliding with a stalled freight train, he ordered his fireman to jump to safety and rode the 'Cannonball' to his death. The folk song 'Casey Jones' is an account of the event.

Jones Chuck (Charles Martin) (1912–). US film animator and cartoon director. He worked at Warner Bros with characters such as Bugs Bunny, Daffy Duck, Wile E Coyote, and Elmer Fudd.

Jones George (1931–). US country singer, one of the genre's most popular male vocalists. His expressive vocal technique is usually employed on sentimental ballads ('Good Year for the Roses' 1970, 'The Grand Tour' 1974) or honky-tonk (dance-hall) numbers ('The Race Is On' 1964), often in duets.

Jones was born in Texas and first recorded 1954. During and after his marriage to singer Tammy Wynette (1942–), they made many records together, including the hits 'We're Gonna Hold On' 1973 and 'Golden Ring' 1976.

Jones Gwyneth (1936–). Welsh soprano. She has performed as Sieglinde in *Die Walküre* and Desdemona in *Otello.*

O God! Put back thy universe and give me yesterday.

HENRY ARTHUR JONES
The Silver King 1882

Jones Henry Arthur (1851–1929). English dramatist. Among some 60 of his melodramas, *Mrs Dane's Defence* 1900 is most notable as an early realist problem play.

Jones Inigo (1573–1652). English Classical architect. He introduced the Palladian style to England. Born in London, he studied in Italy where he encountered the works of Palladio. He was employed by James I to design scenery for Ben Jonson's masques and appointed Surveyor of the King's Works 1615–42. He designed the Queen's House, Greenwich, 1616–35, and his English Renaissance masterpiece, the Banqueting House in Whitehall, London, 1619–22. His work was to provide the inspiration for the Palladian Revival a century later.

Suggested reading
Harris, J, Orgel, S and Strong, R *The King's Arcadia: Inigo Jones and the Stuart Court* (1973)
Lees-Milne, J *The Age of Inigo Jones* (1953)
Summerson, John *Inigo Jones* (1966)

Jones John Paul (1747–1792). Scottish-born American naval officer in the American Revolution 1775. Heading a small French-sponsored squadron in the *Bonhomme Richard*, he captured the British warship *Serapis* in a bloody battle off Scarborough 1799.

Jones was born in Kirkcudbright, Scotland. He was originally a trader and slaver but became a privateer 1775, and then a commodore. After the War of Independence, he joined the Russian navy as a rear admiral 1788, fighting against Turkey, but lost the Empress Catherine's favour and died in France.

I have not yet begun to fight.

JOHN PAUL JONES
On being asked during a sea battle 1779,
if he would surrender, as his ship was sinking

Suggested reading
Abbazia, P *John Paul Jones: America's First Naval Hero* (1976)
Morison, Samuel Eliot *John Paul Jones* (1959)

Jones Quincy (Delight) (1933–). US musician, producer, composer, and arranger. He has worked in jazz, rock, and pop. By 1991 he had won 19 Grammy awards and composed scores for 37 films. Among his production credits is Michael Jackson's *Thriller* 1982; his own albums include *Walking in Space* 1969 and *Back on the Block* 1990.

Jones Thomas (1870–1955). Welsh politician who gave up an academic career as professor of economics at Queens University, Belfast, 1909 to become a political adviser. He acted first for Lloyd George, as assistant secretary of the War Cabinet 1916, and then successively for Bonar Law, Baldwin, and MacDonald. He was also highly successful as a fundraiser.

In every woman's heart there is a god of the woods, and this god is not available for marriage or for home improvement or for parenthood.
ERICA JONG
Fear of Fifty 1994

Jong Erica Mann (1942–). US novelist and poet. She won a reputation as a feminist poet with her first collection *Fruits & Vegetables* 1971. Her novel *Fear of Flying* 1973, depicted a liberated woman's intense sexual adventures and became an instant best seller. It was followed by two sequels *How To Save Your Own Life* 1977 and *Parachutes and Kisses* 1984. Other works include her non-fictional *Witches* 1981, and a portrait of Henry Miller *The Devil at Large* 1993.

Jongkind Johan Barthold (1819–1891). Dutch painter. He left Holland early, going first to Düsseldorf, then to Paris, afterwards leading a wandering career spent mainly in France, though he returned to Holland from time to time. His favourite painting grounds were Paris and the region round Le Havre, where he met and greatly impressed both Boudin and Monet. His atmospheric landscapes and fresh and broken colour (in watercolours as well as oils) heralded the spirit and technique of Impressionism. The Barbizon painters and some critics, notably the de Goncourts, were quick to see his merits, but he lived in poverty, eventually becoming subject to persecution mania. His studies of the Normandy coast show a keen observation of the natural effects of light. He is often considered to belong to the French School.

Drink to me only with thine eyes, / And I will pledge with mine; / Or leave a kiss but in the cup, / And I'll not look for wine.
BEN JONSON
'To Celia'

Jonson Ben(jamin) (1572–1637). English dramatist, poet, and critic. *Every Man in his Humour* 1598 established the English 'comedy of humours', in which each character embodies a 'humour', or vice, such as greed, lust, or avarice. This was followed by *Cynthia's Revels* 1600 and *Poetaster* 1601. His first extant tragedy is *Sejanus* 1603, with Burbage and Shakespeare as members of the original cast. His great comedies are *Volpone, or The Fox* 1606, *The Alchemist* 1610, and *Bartholomew Fair* 1614. He wrote extensively for court entertainment with the masques he produced with scenic designer Inigo Jones.

Jonson was born in Westminster, London, and entered the theatre as an actor and dramatist 1597. In 1598 he narrowly escaped the gallows for killing a fellow player in a duel. He collaborated with Marston and Chapman in *Eastward Ho!* 1605, and shared their imprisonment when official exception was taken to the satirization of James I's Scottish policy.

Suggested reading
Chute, Marchette *Ben Jonson of Westminster* (1954)
Linklater, E *Ben Johnson and King James* (1931)
Miles, Rosaline *Ben Jonson* (1986)
Riggs, David *Ben Jonson* (1989)

Jooss Kurt (1901–1979). German choreographer and teacher. He attempted to synthesize ballet with modern dance by stripping the former of its decadent mannerisms whilst retaining its rigorous discipline and precision. His socially conscious works, such as the acclaimed antiwar *The Green Table* 1932, strove to express his ideal of dance as a voice for the common man.

He founded the Folkwang School and company 1927 in Essen, Germany. Forced out by the Nazis, Jooss established a base at Dartington Hall, Devon, England, 1934. In 1949 he returned to his Essen school, where he worked until he retired 1968.

Although not beautiful in the usual sense, she sure projects. Janis is a sex symbol in an unlikely package.
Village Voice on JANIS JOPLIN
22 Feb 1968

Joplin Janis (1943–1970). US blues and rock singer. She was lead singer with the San Francisco group Big Brother and the Holding Company 1966–68. Her biggest hit, Kris Kristofferson's 'Me and Bobby McGee', was released on the posthumous *Pearl* album 1971.
Suggested reading
Dalton, David *Janis* (1971)
Friedman, Myra *Buried Alive: The Biography of Janis Joplin* (1973)

Joplin Scott (1868–1917). US ragtime pianist and composer. He was active in Chicago. His 'Maple Leaf Rag' 1899 was the first instrumental sheet music to sell a million copies, and 'The Entertainer', as the theme tune of the film *The Sting* 1973, revived his popularity. He was an influence on Jelly Roll Morton and other early jazz musicians.
Suggested reading
Gammond, Peter *Scott Joplin and the Ragtime Era* (1975)
Haskins, J and Benson, K *Scott Joplin: The Man Who Made Ragtime* (1978)

Jordaens Jacob (1593–1678). Flemish painter. His style follows Rubens, whom he assisted in various commissions. Much of his work is exuberant and on a large scale, including scenes of peasant life and mythological subjects, as well as altarpieces and portraits.

He was the pupil of Adam van Noort, whose daughter he married, and his development is parallel with that of Rubens, in whose studio he worked. He painted with immense gusto and might be called a coarser Rubens. After the latter's death he was the leading figure of Flemish Baroque painting. Though he never went to Italy, he strongly reflects in some works not only the Flemish spirit but the lighting and gesture of Caravaggio, as in the *Meleager and Atalanta* (Antwerp). His vivacious earthy manner (in which Sir Joshua Reynolds found 'neither grace nor dignity') is well illustrated by *The Royal Toast* (Brussels).

Jordan (Marie Ennemond) Camille (1838–1922). French mathematician, the greatest exponent of algebra in his day. He concentrated on research in topology, analysis, and particularly group theory, publishing *Traité des substitutions et des equations algébriques* 1870.

Jordan was born in Lyon and studied engineering at the Ecole Polytechnique in Paris, but it was as a mathematician that he joined its staff in 1873. He also gave lectures at the Collège de France.

Influenced by the work of French mathematician Evariste Galois, Jordan systematically developed the theory of finite groups and arrived at the concept of infinite groups. He also developed three theorems of finiteness.

In topology, Jordan developed an entirely new approach by investigating symmetries in polyhedra from an exclusively combinatorial viewpoint. Moreover, he formulated the proof for the 'decomposition' of a plane into two regions by a simple closed curve. Much of

Jordan's later work was concerned with the theory of functions, and he applied the theory of functions of bounded variation to the particular curve that bears his name.

Jordan Dorothea (born Bland) (1762–1816). Irish actress. She made her debut 1777, and retired 1815. She was a mistress of the Duke of Clarence (later William IV); they had ten children with the name FitzClarence.

Jordan Michael Jeffrey (1963–). US basketball player. Widely considered to be the greatest basketball player of all time, he played for the Chicago Bulls from 1984, and led them to National Basketball Association (NBA) championship wins 1991, 1992, and 1993. As a rookie he led the NBA in points scored (2,313). During the 1986–87 season he scored 3,000 points, only the second player in NBA history to do so. He retired from professional basketball Oct 1993, but returned to the game March 1995.

Jordan Neil (1950–). Irish film director, screenwriter, and novelist. Jordan made his first film, the fantasy-tinged thriller *Angel* 1982, in Ireland, followed by the fantasy-dominated *The Company of Wolves* 1984, and the gritty crime thriller *Mona Lisa* 1986 in England. *The Crying Game* 1992, a subtle story involving an IRA provisional, won Jordan an Academy Award for best screenplay. He subsequently made *Interview with the Vampire* 1994. Jordan has published several books including a short-story collection *Night in Tunisia* 1978.

Jörgensen Jörgen (1779–1845). Danish sailor who in 1809 seized control of Iceland, announcing it was under the protection of Britain. His brief reign of corruption ended later the same year when he was captured by a British naval ship. After long imprisonment, in about 1823 he was transported to Van Diemen's Land (Tasmania), where he was pardoned. He wrote a dictionary of Australian Aboriginal dialect.

Joseph in the New Testament, the husband of the Virgin Mary, a descendant of King David of the Tribe of Judah, and a carpenter by trade. Although Jesus was not the son of Joseph, Joseph was his legal father. According to Roman Catholic tradition, he had a family by a previous wife, and was an elderly man when he married Mary.

Joseph in the Old Testament, the 11th and favourite son of Jacob, sold into Egypt by his jealous half-brothers. After he had risen to power there, they and his father joined him to escape from famine in Canaan.

Joseph Chief (c. 1840–1904). American Indian chief of the Nez Percé people. After initially agreeing to leave tribal lands 1877, he later led his people in armed resistance. Defeated, Joseph ordered a mass retreat to Canada, but the Nez Percé were soon caught by General Nelson Miles. They were sent to the Colville Reservation, Washington 1885.

Born in the Wallowa Valley of Oregon, Joseph was the son of a Nez Percé leader who resisted territorial encroachment by the US government. At his father's death 1873, Joseph assumed the title of chief and was originally an advocate of passive resistance.

Joseph Helen (1905–1992). British-born South African teacher and anti-racist campaigner. A fearless fighter for racial tolerance and equality, she became a close friend of the leading figures in the African National Congress (ANC), including Nelson Mandela and Walter Sisulu. For her work with the ANC, she was awarded its highest honour, Isithwalandwe-Seaparankoe.

Joseph Keith Sinjohn, Baron Joseph (1918–1994). British Conservative politician. A barrister, he entered Parliament 1956. He held ministerial posts 1962–64, 1970–74, 1979–81, and was secretary of state for education and science 1981–86. He was made a life baron 1987.

He served in the governments of Harold Macmillan, Alec Douglas-Home, and Edward Heath during the 1960s and 1970s, but it was not until Margaret Thatcher came to office 1979 that he found a prime minister truly receptive to his views and willing to translate them into policies. With her, he founded the right-wing Centre for Policy Studies, which sought to discover and apply the secrets of the successful market economies of West Germany and Japan.

Joseph Père. Religious name of François Joseph Le Clerc du Tremblay (1577–1638). French Catholic Capuchin monk. He was the influential secretary and agent to Louis XIII's chief minister Cardinal Richelieu, and nicknamed *L'Eminence Grise* ('the Grey Eminence') in reference to his grey habit.

Joseph two Holy Roman emperors:

> *More cheerful and worldly and less Jesuit-ridden than most Hapsburgs.*
>
> E N Williams on JOSEPH I
> in *Penguin Dictionary of English and European History 1485–1789* 1980

Joseph I (1678–1711). Holy Roman emperor from 1705 and king of Austria, of the house of Habsburg. He spent most of his reign involved in fighting the War of the Spanish Succession.

> *Here lies Joseph, who failed in everything he undertook.*
>
> JOSEPH II
> suggesting his own epitaph when reflecting
> upon disappointment of his hopes for reform

Joseph II (1741–1790). Holy Roman emperor from 1765, son of Francis I (1708–1765).

The reforms he carried out after the death of his mother, Maria Theresa, in 1780, provoked revolts from those who lost privileges.

Joseph of Arimathaea, St (lived 1st century AD). In the New Testament, a wealthy Hebrew, member of the Sanhedrin (supreme court), and secret supporter of Jesus. On the evening of the Crucifixion he asked the Roman procurator Pilate for Jesus' body and buried it in his own tomb. Feast day 17 March.

According to tradition, Joseph brought the Holy Grail to England about AD 63 and built the first Christian church in Britain, at Glastonbury.

> *Napoleon! Elba! Marie Louise!*
>
> JOSEPHINE
> Last words 1814

Josephine Marie Josèphe Rose Tascher de la Pagerie (1763–1814). As wife of Napoleon Bonaparte, she was empress of France 1804–1809. Born on Martinique, she married in 1779 Alexandre de Beauharnais, who played a part in the French Revolution, and in 1796 Napoleon, who divorced her 1809 because she had not produced children.

Suggested reading
Epton, Nina *Josephine and Her Children* (1976)

Josephs Wilfred (1927–). English composer. As well as film and television music, he has written nine symphonies, concertos, and chamber music. His works include the *Jewish Requiem* 1969 and the opera *Rebecca* 1983.

Josephson Brian David (1940–). Welsh physicist, a leading authority on superconductivity. In 1973 he shared a Nobel prize for his theoretical predictions of the properties of a supercurrent through a tunnel barrier (the *Josephson effect*), which led to the development of the *Josephson junction*. The Josephson junction is a device used in superchips (large and complex integrated circuits) to speed the passage of signals by electron tunnelling. These chips respond a thousand times faster than silicon chips, but the components of the Josephson junction operate only at temperatures close to absolute zero.

Josephus Flavius (AD 37–c. 100). Jewish historian and general, born in Jerusalem. He became a Pharisee and commanded the

Jewish forces in Galilee in their revolt against Rome from AD 66 (which ended with the mass suicide at Masada). When captured, he gained the favour of the Roman emperor Vespasian and settled in Rome as a citizen. He wrote *Antiquities of the Jews*, an early history to AD 66; *The Jewish War*; and an autobiography.

There is no place of toil, no burning heat, no piercing cold, nor any briars there ... the Bosom of Abraham.

FLAVIUS JOSEPHUS
Discourse to the Greeks concerning Hades

Joshua (lived 13th century BC). In the Old Testament, successor of Moses, who led the Jews in their return to and conquest of the land of Canaan. The city of Jericho was the first to fall – according to the Book of Joshua, the walls crumbled to the blast of his trumpets.

Josiah (*c.* 647–609 BC). King of Judah. Grandson of Manasseh and son of Amon, he succeeded to the throne at the age of eight. The discovery of a Book of Instruction (probably Deuteronomy, a book of the Old Testament) during repairs of the Temple 621 BC stimulated thorough reform, which included the removal of all sanctuaries except that of Jerusalem. He was killed in a clash at Megiddo with Pharaoh-nechoh, king of Egypt.

Josquin Desprez or des Prés (1440–1521). Franco-Flemish composer. His synthesis of Flemish structural counterpoint and Italian harmonic expression, acquired in the service of the Rome papal chapel 1484–1503, marks a peak in Renaissance vocal music. In addition to masses on secular as well as sacred themes, including the *Missa 'L'Homme armé'*/*Mass on 'The Armed Man'* 1504, he also wrote secular chansons such as 'El Grillo'/'The Cricket' employing imitative vocal effects.

Joubert Piet (Petrus Jacobus) (1831–1900). Boer general in South Africa. He opposed British annexation of the Transvaal 1877, proclaimed its independence 1880, led the Boer forces in the First South African War against the British 1880–81, defeated Jameson 1896, and fought in the Second South African War.

Joule James Prescott (1818–1889). English physicist whose work on the relations between electrical, mechanical, and chemical effects led to the discovery of the first law of thermodynamics.

He determined the mechanical equivalent of heat (Joule's equivalent) 1843, and the SI unit of energy, the joule, is named after him. He also discovered Joule's law, which defines the relation between heat and electricity; and with Irish physicist Lord Kelvin in 1852 the Joule–Kelvin (or Joule–Thomson) effect. The Joule-Kelvin effect produces cooling in a gas when the gas expands through a narrow jet. It can be felt when, for example, compressed air escapes through the valve of a bicycle tyre. The effect is caused by the conversion of heat into work done by the molecules in overcoming attractive forces between them as they move apart.

Jovian (Flavius Claudius Jovianus) (*c.* 331–364). Roman emperor from 363. Captain of the imperial bodyguard, he was chosen as emperor by the troops after Julian's death. He concluded an unpopular peace with the Sassanian Empire and restored Christianity as the state religion.

Jowett Benjamin (1817–1893). English scholar. He promoted university reform, including the abolition of the theological test for degrees, and translated classical Greek works by Plato, Aristotle, and Thucydides.

Jowett was ordained in 1842. He became professor of Greek at Oxford University 1855, and master of Balliol College 1870.

Joy Alfred Harrison (1882–1973). US astronomer who worked on stellar distances and the radial motions of stars. He observed variable stars and classified them according to their spectra; he also determined the distance and direction of the centre of the Galaxy and attempted to calculate its rotation period. From 1904 to 1914 he worked at the American University of Beirut, Lebanon, becoming professor of astronomy and director of the observatory. He returned to the USA 1914, and worked at the Mount Wilson Observatory 1915–52.

Joy later became interested in the parts of the Galaxy where dark, absorbing clouds of gas and dust exist, and in these areas he found examples of a particular kind of variable star, called a T Tauri star. Such stars appear to be in an early stage of their evolutionary history.

Joyce Eileen Alannah (1912–1991). Australian concert pianist. Her playing combined subtlety with temperamental fire. Her immense repertoire included over 70 works for piano and orchestra. She made her UK debut 1930 and retired in the early 1960s.

Joyce James Augustine Aloysius (1882–1941). Irish writer. He revolutionized the form of the English novel with his 'stream of consciousness' technique. His works include *Dubliners* 1914 (short stories), *Portrait of the Artist as a Young Man* 1916, *Ulysses* 1922, and *Finnegans Wake* 1939.

Ulysses, which records the events of a single Dublin day, experiments with language and combines direct narrative with the unspoken and unconscious reactions of the characters. Banned at first for obscenity in the USA and the UK, it enjoyed great impact. It was first published in Paris, where Joyce settled after World War I. *Finnegans Wake* continued Joyce's experiments with language, attempting a synthesis of all existence.

Suggested reading

Burgess, A *Joysprick: An Introduction to the Language of James Joyce* (1975)
Deming, R H *James Joyce* (1987)
Ellmann, R *James Joyce* (1982)
Hodgart, M J *James Joyce: A Student's Guide* (1978)
Joyce, S *My Brother's Keeper* (1958)
Kenner, H *Dublin's Joyce* (1987)
Levin, H *James Joyce: A Critical Introduction* (1960)
Maddox, B *Nora* (1988)

All moanday, tearsday, wailsday, thumpsday, frightday, shatterday till the fear of the Law.

JAMES JOYCE
Finnegans Wake pt 2 1939

Joyce William (1906–1946). Born in New York, son of a naturalized Irish-born American, he carried on fascist activity in the UK as a 'British subject'. During World War II he made propaganda broadcasts from Germany to the UK, his upper-class accent earning him the nickname Lord Haw Haw. He was hanged for treason.

Germany calling! Germany calling!

WILLIAM JOYCE
Habitual introduction to propaganda broadcasts
by Joyce to Britain during the Second World War.

Juan Carlos (1938–). King of Spain. The son of Don Juan, pretender to the Spanish throne, he married Princess Sofia in 1962, eldest daughter of King Paul of Greece. In 1969 he was nominated by Franco to succeed on the restoration of the monarchy intended to follow Franco's death; his father was excluded because of his known liberal views. Juan Carlos became king 1975.

Juárez Benito Pablo (1806–1872). Mexican politician, president 1861–65 and 1867–72. In 1861 he suspended repayments of Mexico's foreign debts, which prompted a joint French, British, and Spanish expedition to exert pressure. French forces invaded and created an empire for Maximilian, brother of the Austrian emperor. After their withdrawal in 1867, Maximilian was executed, and Juárez returned to the presidency.

Judah Ha-Nasi 'the Prince' (*c.* 135–*c.* 220). Jewish scholar who with a number of colleagues edited the collection of writings known as the *Mishnah*, which formed the basis of the *Talmud*, in the 2nd century AD. He was a rabbi and president of the Sanhedrin (supreme religious court).

Judas Iscariot (lived 1st century AD). In the New Testament, the disciple who betrayed Jesus. The story of Judas differs slightly in the four gospels. Just before Passover he went to the chief priests to arrange to betray Jesus and was offered 30 pieces of silver. During the last supper, Jesus foretold his betrayal by one of his disciples. Matthew's gospel tells how Judus later repented his action and hanged himself.

There are some doubting souls who need your pity; snatch them from the flames and save them. There are others for whom pity must be mixed with fear; hate the very clothing of those who are contaminated with sensuality.

ST JUDE
The Bible, 'Letter of Jude' 22–3

Jude, St (lived 1st century AD). Supposed half-brother of Jesus and writer of the Epistle of Jude in the New Testament; patron saint of lost causes. Feast day 28 Oct.

Judith of Bavaria (800–843). Empress of the French. The wife of Louis the Pious (Louis I of France) from 819, she exercised power over her husband to the benefit of their son Charles the Bold.

Judson Edward Zane Carroll, better known by his pen name 'Ned Buntline' (1823–1886). US author. Specializing in short adventure stories, he developed a stereotyped frontier hero in the pages of his own periodicals *Ned Buntline's Magazine* and *Buntline's Own*. In his dime novels in the 1870s, he immortalized Buffalo Bill Cody.

Born in Stamford, New York, Judson served in the US Navy, and became an editor and writer in Cincinnati, eventually moving to New York. A violent racist, Judson was one of the founders of the antiforeign 'Know-Nothing' party in the 1850s.

Jugurtha (died 104 BC). King of Numidia, N Africa, who, after a long resistance, was betrayed to the Romans and put to death.

Juin Alphonse Pierre (1888–1967). French general. A fellow-student of de Gaulle at the St Cyr military academy, in World War II he was captured by the Germans May 1940. He was released July and offered the post of war minister in the Vichy government. He refused and instead became commander in chief N Africa, succeeding General Weygand. When the Allies invaded Africa 1942 he promptly joined them and later led French forces against the Germans in Tunisia and Italy. He became Chief of Staff of the Free French and took part in the liberation of France 1944. He was posthumously appointed Marshal of France by de Gaulle.

Julia (39 BC–AD 14). Roman noblewoman, daughter of Augustus, the Roman emperor, wife of Agrippa, and mother of Caligula and Agrippina the Younger. Her later marriage to Tiberius proved a failure, and in 2 BC Augustus banished her for alleged immorality.

Juliana (1909–). Queen of the Netherlands 1948–80. The daughter of Queen Wilhelmina (1880–1962), she married Prince Bernhard of Lippe-Biesterfeld in 1937. She abdicated 1980 and was succeeded by her daughter Beatrix.

Julian of Norwich (c. 1342–after 1413). English mystic. She lived as a recluse, and recorded her visions in *The Revelation of Divine Love* 1403, which shows the influence of neo-Platonism.

Thou hast conquered, O Galilean.

JULIAN THE APOSTATE
Last words

Julian the Apostate (332–363). Roman emperor. Born in Constantinople, the nephew of Constantine the Great, he was brought up as a Christian but early in life became a convert to paganism. Sent by Constantius to govern Gaul in 355, he was proclaimed emperor by his troops 360, and in 361 was marching on Constantinople when Constantius' death allowed a peaceful succession. He revived pagan worship and refused to persecute heretics. He was killed in battle against the Persians of the Sassanian Empire.

Julius three popes, including:

Julius II (Giuliano della Rovere) (1443–1513). Pope 1503–13. A politician who wanted to make the Papal States the leading power in Italy, he formed international alliances first against Venice and then against France. He began the building of St Peter's Church in Rome 1506 and was a patron of the artists Michelangelo and Raphael.

Nay, give me a sword, for I am no scholar.

JULIUS II
to Michelangelo who, while carving a statue at
Bologna to commemorate Julius's capture of the city,
asked the Pope what he should place in his hand, 1506

Junayd (al-) bin Muhammad al-Baghdadi (c. 825–c. 910). Eminent Muslim mystic Sufi who advocated the integration of mysticism into ordinary life. His family was originally from Nahawand (S Iran), although he lived and taught in Baghdad. He disapproved of ecstatic mysticism and of seeking union with God, advocating instead a settled, sober way of life and a constant awareness of God. His distinctive Sufi personality stems from the ability to combine his knowledge of Islamic law learned from Imam Shafi with his Sufi commitment developed with his Sufi master al-Saqati.

Jung Carl Gustav (1875–1961). Swiss psychiatrist who collaborated with Sigmund Freud from 1907 until their disagreement in 1914 over the importance of sexuality in causing psychological problems. Jung studied myth, religion, and dream symbolism, saw the unconscious as a source of spiritual insight, and distinguished between introversion and extroversion.

Jung devised the word-association test in the early 1900s as a technique for penetrating a subject's unconscious mind. He also

Jung *Swiss psychiatrist Carl Gustav Jung. He was a contemporary of Sigmund Freud and they both believed that the unconscious mind plays an important role in determining the psychological health of an individual. Jung disagreed with Freud's theory that sexuality was heavily involved in this.* (Image Select)

developed his theory concerning emotional, partly repressed ideas which he termed 'complexes'. In place of Freud's emphasis on infantile sexuality, Jung introduced the idea of a 'collective unconscious' which is made up of many archetypes or 'congenital conditions of intuition'.

Jung was born near Basel and studied there and at Zürich.

He worked at the Burghölzli Psychiatric Clinic in Zürich 1902–09. In 1907 he met Freud and became his chief disciple, appointed president of the International Psychoanalytic Association on its foundation 1910. But in 1914 he resigned from the association and set up his own practice in Zürich. In 1933 he became professor at the Zürich Federal Institute of Technology.

Every form of addiction is bad, no matter whether the narcotic be alcohol or morphine or idealism.

CARL JUNG
Memories, Dreams, Reflections ch 12 1963

The book that provoked his split with Freud was *Wandlungen und Symbole de Libido/The Psychology of the Unconscious* 1912. Jung introduced the concept of introverts and extroverts in *Psychologische Typen/Psychological Types* 1921. This work also contained his theory that the mind has four basic functions: thinking, feeling, sensations, and intuition. Any particular person's personality can be ascribed to the predominance of one of these functions.

Suggested reading
Bennet, E A *What Jung Really Said* (1971)
Brome, V *Jung* (1978)
Fordham, F *An Introduction to Jung's Psychology* (1966)
Hall, C S and Nordby, V J *A Primer of Jungian Psychology* (1973)
Jung, C G *Memories, Dreams, Reflections* (1961)
Stern, P *C G Jung: The Haunted Prophet* (1976)
Storr, Anthony *Jung* (1973)

Junkers Hugo (1859–1935). German aeroplane designer. In 1919 he founded in Dessau the aircraft works named after him. Junkers planes, including dive bombers, night fighters, and troop carriers, were used by the Germans in World War II.

Juppé Alain Marie (1945–   ). French neo-Gaullist politician, foreign minister 1993–95 and prime minister from 1995. In 1976, as a close lieutenant of Jacques Chirac, he helped to found the right-of-centre Rally for the Republic (RPR) party, of which he later became secretary-general. He was appointed premier by newly elected president Chirac May 1995 but, within months, found his position under threat as a result of a housing scandal. Opposition to his government's economic programme provoked a general strike Nov 1995.

The son of a Gascony farmer, Juppé was educated at the prestigious Ecole d'Administration and his early career was as a 'fast-track' civil servant. He was first elected to the French National Assembly, for a Paris constituency, 1983. Nicknamed 'Amstrad' for his lightning intellect, he became a budget minister in the 1986–88 Chirac administration and was an outstanding foreign minister in the Balladur government of 1993–95. A pro-European technocrat,

he became prime minister when Chirac was elected president May 1995. Juppé was re-elected mayor of Bordeaux June 1995.

Jurgens Curt (born Curd Jürgens) (1912–1982). German film and stage actor. He was well established in his native country before moving into French and then Hollywood films in the 1960s. His films include *Operette/Operetta* 1940, *Et Dieu créa la femme/And God Created Woman* 1956, *Lord Jim* 1965, and *The Spy Who Loved Me* 1977.

Just Ernest Everett (1833–1941). US biologist whose research focused on cell physiology and experimental embryology, particularly fertilization and experimental parthenogenesis in marine eggs.

Just was born in Charleston, South Carolina, and educated at Dartmouth College, New Hampshire. He was professor of zoology at Howard University 1912–29, and spent his summers conducting research at the Marine Biological Laboratories at Woods Hole, Massachusetts. In 1929, frustrated with the limitations imposed on him by racists, Just went to Europe to conduct research in German laboratories and at French and Italian marine stations. With the German occupation of France, Just returned to his former post at Howard in 1940.

Just became the leading authority on the embryological resources of the marine group of animals. His focus of attention was the cell and in particular the ectoplasm, which, contrary to popular belief, he stated was just as important as the nucleus, and was primarily responsible for the individuality and development of the cell. He was a co-author of *General Cytology* 1924 and published *Biology of the Cell Surface* 1939.

We have good hope that God will grant us to rule over the rest of what was subject to the ancient Romans, but which they lost through indolence.

JUSTINIAN I
Novel 30

Justinian I (c. 483–565). Byzantine emperor from 527. He recovered N Africa from the Vandals, SE Spain from the Visigoths, and Italy from the Ostrogoths, largely owing to his great general Belisarius. He ordered the codification of Roman law, which has influenced European jurisprudence; he built the church of Sta Sophia in Constantinople, and closed the university in Athens 529.

Justin, St (c. 100–c. 163). One of the early Christian leaders and writers known as the Fathers of the Church. Born in Palestine of a Greek family, he was converted to Christianity and wrote two *Apologies* in its defence. He spent the rest of his life as an itinerant missionary, and was martyred in Rome. Feast day 1 June.

Juvenal (c. AD 60–140). Roman satirical poet. His 16 surviving satires give an explicit and sometimes brutal picture of the corrupt Roman society of his time. He may have lived in exile under the emperor Domitian, and remained very poor.

K

Kabelevsky Dmitri Borisovich (1904–1987). Russian composer and pianist. Known in the West for his keyboard and instrumental works, his reputation in the USSR was based upon vocal works, including the opera *The Taras Family* 1947. Kabelevsky's work mirrored the Soviet authorities' policy of 'Socialist Realism' in his transparent Neo-Classical style. As a result, it is more immediately accessible than the music of his contemporaries Prokofiev and Shostakovich, who were frequently criticized by the government. He helped guide the official course of music in the USSR after World War II.

Kádár János (1912–1989). Hungarian communist leader, in power 1956–88, after suppressing the national uprising. As Hungarian Socialist Workers' Party (HSWP) leader and prime minister 1956–58 and 1961–65, Kádár introduced a series of market-socialist economic reforms, while retaining cordial political relations with the USSR.

Kádár was a mechanic before joining the outlawed Communist Party and working as an underground resistance organizer in World War II. After the war he was elected to the National Assembly, served as minister for internal affairs 1948–50, and became a prominent member of the Hungarian Workers' Party (HSP). Imprisoned 1951–53 for deviation from Stalinism, Kádár was rehabilitated 1955, becoming party leader in Budapest, and in Nov 1956, at the height of the Hungarian national rising, he was appointed head of the new HSWP. With the help of Soviet troops, he suppressed the revolt. He was ousted as party general secretary May 1988, and forced into retirement May 1989.

You may object that it is not a trial at all; you are quite right, for it is only a trial if I recognize it as such.

FRANZ KAFKA
The Trial ch 2 1925

Kafka Franz (1883–1924). Czech novelist. He wrote in German. His three unfinished allegorical novels *Der Prozess/The Trial* 1925, *Der Schloss/The Castle* 1926, and *Amerika/America* 1927 were posthumously published despite his instructions that they should be destroyed. His short stories include 'Die Verwandlung/The Metamorphosis' 1915, in which a man turns into a huge insect. His vision of lonely individuals trapped in bureaucratic or legal labyrinths can be seen as a powerful metaphor for modern experience.

Suggested reading
Haymon, R *Kafka* (1982)
Heller, E *Franz Kafka* (1975)
Pawel, E *The Nightmare of Reason: A Life of Franz Kafka* (1984)
Robert, M *Kafka's Loneliness* (1982)

Kahlo Frida (1907–1954). Mexican painter. Combining the folk arts of South America with Classical and Modern styles, she concentrated on surreal self-portraits in which she explored both her own physical disabilities (she was crippled in an accident when 15) and broader political and social issues. Her work became popular during the 1980s. She was the wife of the painter Diego Rivera.

Suggested reading
Herrera, Hayden *Frida* (1983)
Kahlo, Frida *The Diary of Frida Kahlo: An Intimate Self-Portrait* (1995)
Kahlo, Frida *Letters* (trs 1995)

Kahn Louis Isadore (1901–1974). US architect. A follower of Mies van der Rohe, he developed a classically romantic style, in which

functional service areas such as stairwells and air ducts feature prominently, often as towerlike structures surrounding the main living and working, or 'served', areas. Khan's projects are characterized by an imaginative use of concrete and brick and include the Yale Art Gallery 1953, for which he gained instant renown, the Richards Medical Research Building, University of Pennsylvania, 1957–61, and the Centre for British Art and Studies, Yale University 1969–74.

Kahn taught at the Yale School of Architecture from 1947 and was an important influence on urban planning. It was not until he was in his 50s that his first major work was completed, being previously more concerned with theory. His other designs include the Salk Institute for Biological Studies, La Jolla, California 1959–65, and the Kimbell Art Museum, Fort Worth, Texas 1966–72, which is now seen as exemplary in its use and control of daylight in a gallery setting.

Kaifu Toshiki (1932–). Japanese conservative politician, prime minister 1989–91. A protégé of former premier Takeo Miki, he was selected as a compromise choice as Liberal Democratic Party (LDP) president and prime minister Aug 1989, following the resignation of Sosuke Uno. Kaifu resigned Nov 1991, having lost the support of important factional leaders in the LDP, and was replaced by Kiichi Miyazawa. In Dec 1994, Kaifu became leader of the Shinshinto (New Frontier Party) opposition coalition.

Kaifu entered politics 1961, was deputy chief secretary 1974–76 in the Miki cabinet, and was education minister under Nakasone. He is a member of the minor Komoto faction. In 1987 he received what he claimed were legitimate political donations amounting to £40,000 from a company later accused of bribing a number of LDP politicians. His popularity as prime minister was dented by the unconstitutional proposal, defeated in the Diet, to contribute Japanese forces to the UN coalition army in the Persian Gulf area after Iraq's annexation of Kuwait 1990. His lack of power led to his replacement as prime minister 1991.

Kaiser Georg (1878–1945). German playwright. He was the principal exponent of German Expressionism. His large output includes *Die Bürger von Calais/The Burghers of Calais* 1914 and *Gas* 1918–20.

Kaiser Henry John (1882–1967). US industrialist. He developed steel and motor industries, and his shipbuilding firms became known for the mass production of vessels, including the 'Liberty ships' – cheap, quickly produced transport ships – built for the UK in World War II.

Kaldor Nicholas, Baron Kaldor (1908–1986). British economist, born in Hungary, special adviser 1964–68 and 1974–76 to the UK government. He was a firm believer in long-term capital gains tax and selective employment tax, and a fierce critic of monetarism. He advised several Third World governments on economic and tax reform. He was professor of economics at the University of Cambridge. Baron 1974.

Kalecki Michal (1899–1970). Polish-born economist who settled in England in the 1930s. In the late 1940s, he moved to the USA to work in the United Nations secretariat. In 1955 he resigned in protest against the communist witch-hunts started by Senator Joe McCarthy and returned to Poland. Independently of John Maynard Keynes, he analysed the failure of market forces to bring about full employment in his book *Essays on Business Cycle Theory* 1933 and in an article in the *Political Quarterly* 1943. He also analysed the effects of uncertainty on economic activity in *Studies in Economic Dynamics* 1943.

Kaledin Alexander Maximovich (1861–1918). Russian soldier. Kaledin joined the Trans-Baikal Cossack horse artillery 1879 and by the outbreak of World War I was a general commanding a cavalry division. He succeeded General Brusilov in command of the 8th Russian army 1916 and led this army during the Brusilov Offensive. After the Russian Revolution March 1917 he supported the attempts to reorganize the army and was appointed *Hetman* of the Cossacks Sept 1917. Following the November revolution, Kaledin joined the counter-revolutionary 'Whites' but committed suicide 1918.

Kalf Willem (1619–1693). Dutch painter. He was active in Amsterdam from 1653. He specialized in still lifes set against a dark background. These feature arrangements of glassware, polished metalwork, decorated porcelain, and fine carpets, with the occasional half-peeled lemon (a Dutch still-life motif).

Kālidāsa (lived 5th century AD). Indian epic poet and dramatist. His works, in Sanskrit, include the classic drama *Sakuntalā,* the love story of King Dushyanta and the nymph Sakuntala.

Kalinin Mikhail Ivanovich (1875–1946). Soviet politician, founder of the newspaper *Pravda*. He was prominent in the 1917 October Revolution, and in 1919 became head of state (president of the Central Executive Committee of the Soviet government until 1937, then president of the Presidium of the Supreme Soviet until 1946).

Kaltenbrunner Ernst (1903–1946). Austrian Nazi leader. After the annexation of Austria 1938 he joined police chief Himmler's staff, and as head of the Security Police (SD) from 1943 was responsible for the murder of millions of Jews and Allied soldiers in World War II. After the war, he was tried at Nuremberg for war crimes and hanged Oct 1946.

Liked and respected for his talents as a clear-headed writer and speaker, especially as a chairman.

Alan Bullock on LEV BORISOVICH KAMENEV
in *Hitler and Stalin* 1991

Kamenev Lev Borisovich (born Rosenfeld) (1883–1936). Russian leader of the Bolshevik movement after 1917 who, with Stalin and Zinoviev, formed a ruling triumvirate in the USSR after

Kant German philosopher Immanuel Kant. He revolutionized philosophy by asserting that actions are motivated by rational rather than emotional considerations. (Image Select)

Lenin's death 1924. His alignment with the Trotskyists led to his dismissal from office and from the Communist Party by Stalin 1926. Arrested 1934 after Kirov's assassination, Kamenev was secretly tried and sentenced, then retried, condemned, and shot 1936 for allegedly plotting to murder Stalin.

Kamerlingh Onnes Heike (1853–1926). Dutch physicist who worked mainly in the field of low-temperature physics. In 1911, he discovered the phenomenon of superconductivity (enhanced electrical conductivity at very low temperatures), for which he was awarded the 1913 Nobel prize. Kamerlingh Onnes made a particular study of the effects of low temperature on the conductivity of mercury, lead, nickel, and manganese–iron alloys. He found that the imposition of a magnetic field eliminated superconductivity even at low temperatures.

He was professor of experimental physics at the University of Leiden 1882–1924, and in 1894 he founded the cryogenic laboratories at Leiden, which became a world centre of low-temperature physics.

Kandinsky Vasily (1866–1944). Russian-born painter, a pioneer of abstract art. Between 1910 and 1914 he produced the series *Improvisations* and *Compositions*, the first known examples of purely abstract work in 20th-century art. He was an originator of the *Blaue Reiter* movement 1911–12, and taught at the Bauhaus school of design in Germany 1921–33. Kandinsky originally experimented with Post-Impressionist styles and Fauvism. His highly coloured works had few imitators, but his theories on composition, published in *Concerning the Spiritual in Art* 1912, were taken up by the abstractionists.

Kandinsky was born in Moscow and travelled widely, settling in Munich, Germany, 1896. He moved to Paris 1933, becoming a French citizen 1939.

Further theories were published in *Reminiscences* 1913 and *Point and Line to Plane* 1926.
Suggested reading
Grohmann, W *Wassily Kandinsky: Life and Work* (1958)
Lindsay, K and Vergo, P (eds) *Kandinsky: Complete Writings on Art* (1982)
Overy, P *Kandinsky: The Language of the Eye* (1969)
Roethel, H and Benjamin, J *Kandinsky* (1979)

Kane Sheikh Hamidou (1928–   ). Senegalese novelist, writing in French. His first novel, *L'Aventure ambiguë/Ambiguous Adventure* 1961, is an autobiographical account of a young African alienated from the simple faith of his childhood and initiated into an alien Islamic mysticism, before being immersed in materialist French culture.

He studied law and philosophy in France before returning to Senegal as a French civil servant.

Kant Immanuel (1724–1804). German philosopher who believed that knowledge is not merely an aggregate of sense impressions but is dependent on the conceptual apparatus of the human understanding, which is itself not derived from experience. In ethics, Kant argued that right action cannot be based on feelings or inclinations but conforms to a law given by reason, the *categorical imperative*.

It was in his *Kritik der reinen Vernunft/Critique of Pure Reason* 1781 that Kant inaugurated a revolution in philosophy by turning attention to the mind's role in constructing our knowledge of the objective world. He also argued that God's existence could not be proved theoretically. His other main works are *Kritik der praktischen Vernunft/Critique of Practical Reason* 1788 and *Kritik der Urteilskraft/Critique of Judgement* 1790.
Suggested reading
Beck, L W *Studies in the Philosophy of Kant* (1965)

Two things fill the mind with ever-increasing wonder and awe ... the starry heavens above me and the moral law within me.

IMMANUEL KANT
Critique of Practical Reason, conclusion 1788

Ewing, A C *A Short Commentary on Kant's Critique of Pure Reason* (1950)
Hartnack, Justus *Immanuel Kant* (1974)
Körner, Stephan *Kant* (1955)
Wilkerson, T E *Kant's Critique of Pure Reason: A Commentary for Students* (1976)

Kantor Tadeusz (1915–1990). Polish theatre director and scene designer. He founded his experimental theatre Cricot 2 in 1955, and produced such plays as *Dead Class* 1975, with which he became internationally known. Later productions include *Wielopole, Wielopole* 1980, *Let the Artists Die* 1985, and *I Shall Never Return* 1988.

First involved with the puppet theatre, Kantor started directing in 1942, and designed many productions in Cracow 1944–55. He also produced several plays by dramatist Stanislaw Witkiewicz.

Kantorovich Leonid Vitaliyevich (1912–1986). Soviet mathematical economist whose theory that decentralization of decisions in a planned economy could only be made with a rational price system earned him a share of the 1975 Nobel Prize for Economics.

Kapitza Peter (Pyotr Leonidovich) (1894–1984). Soviet physicist who in 1978 shared a Nobel prize for his work on magnetism and low-temperature physics. He worked on the superfluidity of liquid helium and also achieved the first high-intensity magnetic fields. In 1939, Kapitza built apparatus for producing large quantities of liquid oxygen, used in steel production. He also invented a turbine for producing liquid air cheaply in large quantities.

Kapitza was born near St Petersburg and studied at Petrograd Polytechnical Institute, after which he went to the UK and worked at the Cavendish Laboratory, Cambridge, with nuclear physicist Ernest Rutherford. In 1930, Kapitza became director of the Mond Laboratory at Cambridge, which had been built for him. But when in 1934 he went to the USSR for a professional meeting, dictator Josef Stalin did not allow him to return. The Mond Laboratory was sold to the Soviet government at cost and transported to the Soviet Academy of Sciences for Kapitza's use. In 1946, he refused to work on the development of nuclear weapons and was put under house arrest until after Stalin's death 1953.

Kaplan Viktor (1876–1934). Austrian engineer who invented a water turbine with adjustable rotor blades. In the machine, patented 1920, the rotor was on a vertical shaft and could be adjusted to suit any rate of flow of water. Horizontal Kaplan turbines are used at the installation on the estuary of the river Rance in France, the world's first tidal power station, which opened 1966.

After working in industry, he became professor at the Technische Hochschule in Brunn 1903. Kaplan published his first paper on turbines in 1908, and set up a propeller turbine for the lowest possible fall of water. In 1913 the first prototype of the turbine was completed.

Kapteyn Jacobus Cornelius (1851–1922). Dutch astronomer who analysed the structure of the universe by studying the distribution of stars using photographic techniques. To achieve more accurate star counts he introduced the technique of statistical astronomy.

After working at the observatory at Leiden, he was professor at Groningen 1875–1921.

In 1906 he selected 206 specific stellar zones, aiming to ascertain the magnitudes of all the stars within these zones, as well as to collect data on their spectral type, radial velocity, proper motion, and so on. This enormous project was the first co-ordinated statistical analysis in astronomy and involved the co-operation of over 40 different observatories.

Karadžić Radovan (1945–). Montenegrin-born leader of the Bosnian Serbs, leader of the community's unofficial government from 1992. He cofounded the Serbian Democratic Party of Bosnia-Herzegovina (SDS-BH) 1990 and launched the siege of Sarajevo 1992, plunging the country into a prolonged and bloody civil war. A succession of peace initiatives for the region failed due to his ambitious demands for Serbian territory, and he was subsequently implicated in war crimes allegedly committed in Bosnia-Herzegovina. In the

autumn of 1995, in the wake of a sustained NATO bombardment of Bosnian Serb positions around Sarajevo, Karadžić agreed to enter peace negotiations, and in Nov signed the US-sponsored Dayton peace accord. This divided Bosnia into separate Moslem, Croat, and Serb areas and effectively excluded him from further power. He was charged with genocide and crimes against humanity at the Yugoslav War Crimes Tribunal in The Hague, Netherlands, Nov 1995.

Distrusted in the West and viewed as an intransigent figure, for many Bosnian Serbs he is a moderate.

Karadžić Vuk Stefanović (1787–1864). Serbian linguist and translator. He collected folk songs and popular stories, compiled a Serbian grammar 1815 and dictionary 1818 and 1852, and translated the New Testament 1847.

A kind of musical Malcolm Sargent.

Thomas Beecham on HERBERT VON KARAJAN
quoted in Harold Atkins and Archie Newman *Beecham Stories* 1978

Karajan Herbert von (1908–1989). Austrian conductor. He dominated European classical music performance after 1947. He was principal conductor of the Berlin Philharmonic Orchestra 1955–89, artistic director of the Vienna State Opera 1957–64, and of the Salzburg Festival 1956–60. A perfectionist, he cultivated an orchestral sound of notable smoothness and transparency; he also staged operas and directed his own video recordings. He recorded the complete Beethoven symphonies three times, and had a special affinity with Mozart and Bruckner, although his repertoire extended from Bach to Schoenberg.

Karamanlis Konstantinos (1907–). Greek politician of the New Democracy Party. A lawyer and an anticommunist, he was prime minister Oct 1955–March 1958, May 1958–Sept 1961, and Nov 1961–June 1963 (when he went into self-imposed exile because of a military coup). He was recalled as prime minister on the fall of the regime of the 'colonels' in July 1974, and was president 1980–85.

Karan Donna (1948–). US fashion designer. She has had her own label since 1984. As well as trendy, wearable sportswear in bright colours, and tight, clingy clothes such as the bodysuit, she produces executive workwear. In 1989 she launched a ready-to-wear line, DKNY. In 1992–93 she moved away from the structured look of the 1980s to produce lighter, casual, and more fluid outfits.

Karg-Elert Sigfrid (1877–1933). German composer. After studying at Leipzig he devoted himself to the European harmonium. His numerous concert pieces and graded studies, including *66 Choral Improvisations* 1908–10, exploit a range of impressionistic effects such as the 'endless chord'.

The Monster was the best friend I ever had.

BORIS KARLOFF
speaking of Frankenstein's monster character

Karloff Boris. Stage name of William Henry Pratt (1887–1969). English-born US actor. He is best known for his work in the USA. He achieved Hollywood stardom with his role as the monster in the film *Frankenstein* 1931. Several popular sequels followed as well as starring appearances in other films including *Scarface* 1932, *The Lost Patrol* 1934, and *The Body Snatcher* 1945. In 1941 Karloff gained acclaim on Broadway in *Arsenic and Old Lace*. He continued in television and films until *Targets* 1967.

Karmal Babrak (1929–1996). Afghani communist politician, president 1979–86. In 1965 he formed what became the banned People's Democratic Party of Afghanistan (PDPA) 1977. As president, with Soviet backing, he sought to broaden the appeal of the PDPA but encountered wide resistance from the Mujaheddin (Muslim guerrillas).

Karmal was imprisoned for anti-government activity in the early 1950s. He was a member of the government 1957–62 and of the national assembly 1965–72. In Dec 1979 he returned from brief exile in E Europe with Soviet support to overthrow President Hafizullah Amin and was installed as the new head of state. Karmal was persuaded to step down as president and PDPA leader May 1986 as the USSR began to search for a compromise settlement with opposition groupings and to withdraw troops. In July 1991, he returned to Afghanistan from exile in Moscow.

The scientist describes what is: the engineer creates what never was.

THEODOR VON KÁRMÁN
Biogr. Mem. FRS 26 110 1980

Kármán Theodore von (1881–1963). Hungarian-born US aerodynamicist who enabled the USA to acquire a lead in rocket research. The research establishments he helped create include the Jet Propulsion Laboratory in Pasadena, California.

Kármán was born and educated in Budapest. In 1908 he went to France and witnessed an early aeroplane, which inspired him to concentrate on aeronautical engineering. Between 1913 and 1930, with the exception of the years of World War I, when he directed aeronautical research in the Austro-Hungarian army, Kármán built the new Aachen Institute, Germany, into a world-recognized research establishment. From 1928 he divided his time between the Aachen Institute and the Guggenheim Aeronautical Laboratory of the California Institute of Technology, USA.

Studying the flow of fluids round a cylinder, Kármán discovered that the wake separates into two rows of vortices which alternate like street lights. This phenomenon is called the Kármán vortex street, or Kármán vortices, and it can build up destructive vibrations. The Tacoma Narrows suspension bridge was destroyed in 1940 by such vortices.

Kármán prompted the first research and development programme on long-range rocket-propelled missiles. He also worked on boundary layer and compressibility effects, supersonic flight, propeller design, helicopters, and gliders.

Karpov Anatoly Yevgenyevich (1951–). Russian chess player. He succeeded Bobby Fischer of the USA as world champion 1975, and held the title until losing to Gary Kasparov 1985. He lost to Kasparov again in 1990.
Suggested reading
Byrne, Robert *Anatoly Karpov* (1976)
Karpov, Anatoly *Chess is My Life* (autobiography) (trs 1980)

Karrer Paul (1889–1971). Swiss organic chemist who synthesized various vitamins and determined their structural formulas, for which he shared the 1937 Nobel Prize for Chemistry. He also worked on vegetable dyes.

Karrer was born in Moscow but grew up in Switzerland. He studied at Zürich, was professor at the Zürich Chemical Institute from 1918 and its director 1919–59.

Karrer's early work concerned vitamin A and its chief precursor, carotene. Karrer worked out its correct constitutional formula in 1930, although he was not to achieve a total synthesis until 1950. He showed in 1931 that vitamin A is related to the carotenoids, substances that give a yellow, orange, or red colour to many foodstuffs. There are in fact two A vitamins. Karrer proved that there are several isomers of carotene, and that vitamin A_1 is equivalent to half a molecule of its precursor β-carotene.

In 1935, he solved the structure of vitamin B_2 (riboflavin). He also investigated vitamin E (tocopherol), which is a group of closely related compounds, and in 1938 he solved the structure of α-tocopherol, the most biologically active component.

In 1927, Karrer published *Lehrbuch der organischen Chemie/ Textbook of Organic Chemistry*.

Karsh Yousuf (1908–). Canadian portrait photographer, born in Armenia. He is known for his formal and dramatically lit studies of the famous, in which he attempts to capture their 'inward power'.

His most notable picture is the defiant portrait of Winston Churchill which appeared on the cover of *Life* magazine 1941.

Kasparov Gary Kimovich (born Garri Weinstein) (1963–). Russian chess player. When he beat his compatriot Anatoly Karpov to win the world title 1985, he was the youngest-ever champion at 22 years 210 days.

Kassem Abdul Karim (1914–1963). Iraqi politician, prime minister from 1958; he adopted a pro-Soviet policy. Kassem pardoned the leaders of the pro-Egyptian party who tried to assassinate him 1959. He was executed after the 1963 coup.

Katō Kiyomasa (1562–1611). Japanese warrior and politician who was instrumental in the unification of Japan and the banning of Christianity in the country. He led the invasion of Korea 1592, and helped Toyotomi Hideyoshi and Tokugawa Ieyasu in their efforts to unify Japan.

Katō Taka-akira (1860–1926). Japanese politician, prime minister 1924–26. After a long political career with several terms as foreign minister, Katō led probably the most democratic and liberal regime of the Japanese Empire.

Katsura Tarō (1847–1913). Prince of Japan, army officer, politician, and prime minister (1901–06, 1908–11, 1912–13). He was responsible for the Anglo-Japanese treaty of 1902 (an alliance against Russia), the successful prosecution of the Russo-Japanese war 1904–05, and the annexation of Korea 1910.

Having assisted in the Meiji restoration 1866–68, Katsura became increasingly involved in politics. His support for rearmament, distaste for political parties, and oligarchic rule created unrest; his third ministry Dec 1912–Jan 1913 lasted only seven weeks.

Katz Bernard (1911–). British biophysicist. He shared the 1970 Nobel Prize for Physiology or Medicine for work on the biochemistry of the transmission and control of signals in the nervous system, vital in the search for remedies for nervous and mental disorders. Knighted 1969.

Katz was born in Leipzig, studied medicine at the university there, and then did postgraduate work at University College, London. Having done research in Australia 1939–42, he then served in the Royal Australian Air Force until the end of World War II, after which he returned to the UK. He spent the rest of his academic career at University College, London, becoming professor 1952.

In the 1940s, Katz joined in the Nobel-prizewinning research of Alan Hodgkin on the electrochemical behaviour of nerve membranes.

Kauffer Edward McKnight (1890–1954). US poster artist. He lived in the UK 1914–41.

Kauffmann (Maria Anna Catherina) Angelica (1741–1807). Swiss Neo-Classical painter. She worked extensively in England, with the keen support of Joshua Reynolds. She was in great demand as a portraitist, but also painted mythological scenes for large country houses.

The daughter of a painter who gave her lessons in both music and visual art, she lived in Italy for three years as a child, painting precociously. On a second visit, 1763–66, she painted the portrait of Winckelmann and was no doubt strongly influenced by his Neo-Classicism. She came to London 1786, was befriended by Reynolds, and became popular as a portraitist and for classical and allegorical subjects.
Suggested reading
Mayer, Dorothy *Angelika Kauffmann RA, 1741–1807* (1972)
Roworth, Wendy W *Kauffmann: A Continental Artist in Georgian England* (1992)

Kaufman George S(imon) (1889–1961). US dramatist. He is the author (often in collaboration with others) of many Broadway hits, including *Of Thee I Sing* 1931, a Pulitzer prize-winning satire on US politics; *You Can't Take It with You* 1936; *The Man Who Came to Dinner* 1939; and *The Solid Gold Cadillac* 1952. Many of his plays became classic Hollywood films.

Kaunda Kenneth David (1924–). Zambian politician, president 1964–91. Imprisoned 1958–60 as founder of the Zambia African National Congress, he became in 1964 the first prime minister of Northern Rhodesia, then the first president of independent Zambia. In 1973 he introduced one-party rule. He supported the nationalist movement in Southern Rhodesia, now Zimbabwe, and survived a coup attempt 1980 thought to have been promoted by South Africa. He was elected chair of the Organization of African Unity 1970 and 1987. He lost the first multiparty elections, Nov 1991, to Frederick Chiluba.

Suggested reading
Kaunda, Kenneth *The Riddle of Violence* (memoirs) (1981)
MacPherson, Fergus *Kaunda of Zambia* (1975)

Kautsky Karl Johann (1854–1938). German socialist theoretician who opposed the reformist ideas of Edouard Bernstein from within the Social Democratic Party. In spite of his Marxist ideas he remained in the party when its left wing broke away to form the German Communist Party (KPD).

Kawabata Yasunari (1899–1972). Japanese novelist. He translated Lady Murasaki, and was the author of *Snow Country* 1947 and *A Thousand Cranes* 1952. His novels are characterized by melancholy and loneliness. He was the first Japanese to win the Nobel Prize for Literature, 1968.

Kawakubo Rei (1943–). Japanese fashion designer. She graduated 1964 in fine art from Keio University, Tokyo, and in 1967 began working as a freelance stylist. In 1973 she established Comme des Garçons, and her first women's collection was shown in Tokyo 1975. She launched her Homme line 1978, promoting it by a series of photographs of artists wearing her designs.

Kay John (1704–*c*. 1780). English inventor who developed the flying shuttle, a machine to speed up the work of hand-loom weaving. He patented his invention 1733.

Kay was born near Bury, Lancashire, and may have been educated in France. He invented many kinds of improved textile machinery, but was ruined by lawsuits in defence of his flying-shuttle patent. In 1753 his house in Bury was wrecked by a mob, who feared the use of machinery would cause unemployment. Kay left the country, and had some success introducing the flying shuttle to France, but is believed to have died there in poverty.

In 1730 he was granted a patent for an 'engine' for twisting and carding mohair, and for twining and dressing thread. At about the same time he improved the reeds for looms by manufacturing the 'darts' of thin polished metal instead of cane.

Up to that time the shuttle had been passed by hand from side to side through alternate warp threads. In weaving broadcloth two workers had to be employed to throw the shuttle from one end to the other. With Kay's flying shuttle, the amount of work a weaver could do was more than doubled, and the quality of the cloth was also improved.

I am a wife-made man.

DANNY KAYE
referring to his lyricist, Sylvia Fine, who was also
his wife, in Leslie Halliwell *Filmgoer's Companion* 1965

Kaye Danny. Stage name of David Daniel Kaminski (1913–1987). US actor, comedian, and singer. He appeared in many films, including *Wonder Man* 1944, *The Secret Life of Walter Mitty* 1946, and *Hans Christian Andersen* 1952. He achieved success on Broadway in *Lady in the Dark* 1940. He also starred on television, had his own show 1963–67, toured for UNICEF, and guest-conducted major symphony orchestras in later years.

Kazan Elia (born Kazanjoglous) (1909–). US stage and film director. He was a founder of the Actors Studio 1947. Plays he directed include *The Skin of Our Teeth* 1942, *A Streetcar Named Desire* 1947 (filmed 1951), *Death of a Salesman* 1949, and *Cat on a Hot Tin Roof* 1955; films include *Gentleman's Agreement* 1947 (Academy Award), *On the Waterfront* 1954, *East of Eden* 1955, and *The Visitors* 1972.

Kazantzakis Nikos (1885–1957). Greek writer. His works include the poem *I Odysseia/The Odyssey* 1938 (which continues Homer's *Odyssey*), and the novels *Zorba the Greek* 1946, *The Greek Passion*, and *The Last Temptation of Christ*, both 1951. *Zorba the Greek* was filmed 1964 and *The Last Temptation of Christ* (controversially) 1988.

Kean Edmund (1787–1833). English tragic actor. He was noted for his portrayal of villainy in the Shakespearean roles of Shylock, Richard III, and Iago. He died on stage, playing Othello opposite his son as Iago.

His life story was turned into a romantic myth and dramatized by both the elder Dumas and Jean-Paul Sartre.

Keane Molly (Mary Nesta) (1905–1996). Irish novelist. Her comic novels of Anglo-Irish life include *Good Behaviour* 1981, *Time After Time* 1983, and *Loving and Giving* 1988. She also wrote under the name M J Farrell.

Kearny Philip (1814–1862). US military leader. In 1859 he served in the army of Napoleon III in Italy and received the French Croix de Guerre for his actions. With the outbreak of the American Civil War 1861, Kearny returned to the USA and was named brigadier general of the New Jersey militia. He was killed in action near Chantilly, Virginia.

Kearny, born in New York, received a law degree from Columbia University 1833. Choosing a career in the military, he obtained a commission in the US Dragoons 1837. He was trained in cavalry techniques in France and saw action in the Mexican War 1846–48, where he lost an arm. He was the nephew of Stephen W Kearny.

Kearny Stephen Watts (1794–1848). US military leader. As brigadier general he was given command of the Army of the West 1846. During the Mexican War 1846–48, he was the military governor of New Mexico and joined in the conquest of California 1847 becoming military governor.

Kearny was born in Newark, New Jersey, and attended Columbia University. He first saw action in the Anglo-American War of 1812. In 1848 he served as governor-general of occupied Veracruz and Mexico City. He died of a tropical fever acquired there.

Keating Paul John (1944–). Australian politician, Labor Party (ALP) leader and prime minister from 1991. He was treasurer and

Keating *Paul Keating, Australian prime minister from 1991 and a committed republican. As Labor finance minister under Bob Hawke, Keating was unpopular for his harsh financial measures, but he successfully displaced Hawke as leader of the party 1991.*

deputy leader of the ALP 1983–91. In 1993 he announced plans for Australia to become a federal republic by the year 2001, inciting a mixed reaction among Australians.

Keating was active in ALP politics from the age of 15. He held several posts in Labor's shadow ministry 1976–83. As finance minister 1983–91 under Bob Hawke, Keating was unpopular with the public for his harsh economic policies. He successfully challenged Hawke for the ALP party leadership Dec 1991 and his premiership was confirmed by the March 1993 general election victory of the ALP, for an unprecedented fifth term of office.

If there's a way of saying 'I love you' without saying it – that's film.

BUSTER KEATON
quoted by Dustin Hoffman in *Films Illustrated* May–June 1980

Keaton Buster (Joseph Francis) (1896–1966). US comedian, actor, and film director. After being a star in vaudeville, he became one of the great comedians of the silent film era, with an inimitable deadpan expression (the 'Great Stone Face') masking a sophisticated acting ability. His films include *One Week* 1920, *The Navigator* 1924, *The General* 1927, and *The Cameraman* 1928.

He rivalled Charlie Chaplin in popularity until studio problems ended his creative career. He then made only shorts and guest appearances, as in Chaplin's *Limelight* 1952 and *A Funny Thing Happened on the Way to the Forum* 1966.
Suggested reading
Dardis, Tom *Keaton: The Man Who Wouldn't Lie Down* (1979)
Keaton, Buster *My Wonderful World of Slapstick* (memoirs) (1960)
Robinson, David *Buster Keaton* (1969)

He passes into the universe folk-heritage as the supreme clown-poet.

David Robinson on BUSTER KEATON 1968

Keaton *US comedy star Buster Keaton in a scene from* The General *1927, a film set in the American Civil War. He became one of the stars of silent films and, because of his distinctive deadpan expression, was nicknamed the 'Great Stone Face'.*

Keats John (1795–1821). English Romantic poet. He produced work of the highest quality and promise before dying at the age of 25. *Poems* 1817, *Endymion* 1818, the great odes (particularly 'Ode to a Nightingale' and 'Ode on a Grecian Urn' written 1819, published 1820), and the narratives 'Lamia', 'Isabella', and 'The Eve of St Agnes' 1820, show his lyrical richness and talent for drawing on both classical mythology and medieval lore.

Born in London, Keats studied at Guy's Hospital 1815–17, but then abandoned medicine for poetry. *Endymion* was harshly reviewed by the Tory *Blackwood's Magazine* and *Quarterly Review*, largely because of Keats' friendship with the radical writer Leigh Hunt (1784–1859). In 1819 he fell in love with Fanny Brawne (1802–1865). Suffering from tuberculosis, he sailed to Italy 1820 in an attempt to regain his health, but died in Rome. Valuable insight into Keats' poetic development is provided by his *Letters,* published 1848.
Suggested reading
Barnard, J K *Keats* (1987)
Gittings, R *John Keats* (1968)
Walsh, W *Introduction to Keats* (1981)
Watts, C *Preface to Keats* (1985)

A thing of beauty is a joy for ever: / Its loveliness increases.

JOHN KEATS
Endymion 1818

Keble John (1792–1866). Anglican priest and religious poet. His sermon on the decline of religious faith in Britain, preached 1833, heralded the start of the Oxford Movement, a Catholic revival in the Church of England. Keble College, Oxford, was founded 1870 in his memory.

Keble was professor of poetry at Oxford 1831–41. He wrote four of the *Tracts for the Times* (theological treatises in support of the Oxford Movement), and from 1835 was vicar of Hursley in Hampshire.

Keegan (Joseph) Kevin (1951–   ). English footballer and football manager. He played for Scunthorpe United 1968–71, Liverpool 1971–77, SV Hamburg (Germany) 1977–80, Southampton 1980–82, and Newcastle United 1982–84, winning 63 full England caps and captaining his country. He was Footballer of the Year and PFA Player of the Year 1976, European Footballer of the Year 1978 and 1979, and PFA Player of the Year 1982. He became manager of Newcastle United 1992.

Keeler Christine (1942–   ). British prostitute of the 1960s. She became notorious in 1963 after revelations of affairs with both a Soviet attaché and the war minister John Profumo, who resigned after admitting lying to the House of Commons about their relationship. Her patron, the osteopath Stephen Ward, convicted of living on immoral earnings, committed suicide and Keeler was subsequently imprisoned for related offences.

Keeler James Edward (1857–1900). US astrophysicist who studied the rings of Saturn and the abundance and structure of nebulae. He demonstrated 1888 that nebulae resembled stars in their pattern of movement.

Keeler was born in La Salle, Illinois, and studied at Johns Hopkins University and in Germany at Heidelberg and Berlin. He was appointed astronomer at the Lick Observatory on its completion 1888; became professor and director of the Allegheny Observatory 1891; and returned to the Lick as director 1898.

In 1895, Keeler made a spectroscopic study of Saturn and its rings, in order to examine the planet's period of rotation. He found that the rings did not rotate at a uniform rate, thus proving for the first time that they could not be solid and confirming Scottish scientist James Clerk Maxwell's theory that the rings consist of meteoritic particles.

After 1898, Keeler devoted himself to a study of all the nebulae that William Herschel had catalogued a hundred years earlier. He succeeded in photographing half of them, and in the course of his work he discovered many thousands of new nebulae.

Kefauver (Carey) Estes (1903–1963). US Democratic politician. He was elected to the US House of Representatives 1939 and served in the US Senate 1948 until his death. He was an unsuccessful candidate for the Democratic presidential nomination 1952 and 1956.

Born near Madisonville, Tennessee, USA, Kefauver was educated at the University of Tennessee, received a law degree from Yale University 1927 and established a private law practice in Chattanooga, Tennessee. As chair of the Senate Judiciary Committee, he held widely publicized, televised hearings on organized crime 1950–51.

Keillor Garrison Edward (1942–   ). US writer and humorist. His hometown Anoka, Minnesota, in the American Midwest, inspired his popular, richly comic stories about Lake Wobegon, including *Lake Wobegon Days* 1985 and *Leaving Home* 1987, which often started as radio monologues about 'the town that time forgot, that the decades cannot improve'. Later works include *We Are Still Married* 1989, *Radio Romance* 1991, and *The Book of Guys* 1993.

Keïta Salif (1949–   ). Malian singer and songwriter. His combination of traditional rhythms and vocals with electronic instruments made him popular in the West in the 1980s; in Mali he worked 1973–83 with the band Les Ambassadeurs and became a star throughout W Africa, moving to France 1984. His albums include *Soro* 1987 and *Amen* 1991.

Keitel Wilhelm (1882–1946). German field marshal in World War II, chief of the supreme command from 1938 and Hitler's chief military adviser. He dictated the terms of the French armistice 1940 and was a member of the court which sentenced many officers to death for their part in the July Plot 1944. He signed Germany's unconditional surrender in Berlin 8 May 1945. Tried at Nuremberg for war crimes, he was hanged.

Kekulé von Stradonitz Friedrich August (1829–1896). German chemist whose theory 1858 of molecular structure revolutionized organic chemistry. He proposed two resonant forms of the benzene ring.

In 1865 Kekulé announced his theory of the structure of benzene, which he envisaged as a hexagonal ring of six carbon atoms connected by alternate single and double bonds. In 1867 he proposed the tetrahedral carbon atom, which was to become the cornerstone of modern structural organic chemistry.

Kekulé was born in Darmstadt and studied at Giessen and Paris. After working in Switzerland, he went in 1854 to London, where he met many leading chemists of the day. When he returned to Germany 1855, he opened a small private laboratory in Heidelberg. In 1858 he became professor at Ghent; in 1865 at Bonn.

In 1858, Kekulé published a paper in which, after giving reasons why carbon should be regarded as a four-valent element, he set out the essential features of his theory of the linking of atoms.

Keller Gottfried (1819–1890). Swiss poet and novelist. His books include *Der Grüne Heinrich/Green Henry* 1854–55. He also wrote short stories, of which the collection *Die Leute von Seldwyla/The People of Seldwyla* 1856–74 describes small-town life.

Science may have found a cure for most evils; but it has found no remedy for the worst of them all – the apathy of human beings.

HELEN KELLER
My Religion 1927

Keller Helen Adams (1880–1968). US author and campaigner for the blind. She became blind and deaf after an illness when she was only 19 months old, but the teaching of Anne Sullivan, her lifelong companion, enabled her to learn the names of objects and eventually to speak. Keller graduated with honours from Radcliffe College 1904; published several books, including *The Story of My Life* 1902;

and toured the world, lecturing to raise money for the blind. She was born in Alabama.

Suggested reading
Keller, Helen *The Story of My Life* (1903, several later editions)
Lash, J P *Helen and Teacher* (1980)
Weiner, M *Helen Keller* (1970)

Kellogg Frank Billings (1856–1937). US political leader and diplomat. Elected to the US Senate 1916, he was appointed US ambassador to Great Britain by President Harding 1922 and secretary of state 1925. He formulated the Kellogg–Briand Pact 1927, the international antiwar resolution, for which he was awarded the Nobel Peace Prize 1929.

Born in Potsdam, New York, Kellogg studied law in Minnesota and was admitted to the bar 1877. He served as a prosecutor of federal antitrust cases before being elected to the US Senate. He later served as judge on the World Court 1930–35.

Kelly Emmett (1898–1979). US clown and circus performer. He created his 'Weary Willie' clown character while with the Hagenbeck-Wallace circus 1931. Joining the Ringling Brothers and Barnum and Bailey Circus 1942, he made 'Weary Willie' into one of the most famous clowns in the world.

I never wanted to be a dancer. It's true! I wanted to be a short-stop for the Pittsburg Pirates.

GENE KELLY
Variety 12 Nov 1985

Kelly Gene (Eugene Curran) (1912–1996). US film actor, dancer, choreographer, and director. He was a major star of the 1940s and

Keller Helen Keller, US writer and campaigner for the blind. Keller's life was documented in a book, The Miracle Worker, by William Gibson, which won the Pulitzer Prize and was made into a film 1962. (Image Select)

Kelly, Grace *US film actress Grace Kelly, later Princess of Monaco, in Alfred Hitchcock's* Rear Window *1954. Her portrayal of cool blonde innocence made her a perfect Quaker bride in* High Noon *1952, and provided a counterpoint for Alfred Hitchcock's macabre suspense scenarios.*

1950s in a series of MGM musicals, including *On the Town* 1949, *Singin' in the Rain* 1952 (both of which he co-directed), and *An American in Paris* 1951. He also directed *Hello Dolly* 1969.

Kelly Grace Patricia (1929–1982). US film actress. She starred in *High Noon* 1952, *The Country Girl* 1954, for which she received an Academy Award, and *High Society* 1955. She also starred in three Hitchcock films – *Dial M for Murder* 1954, *Rear Window* 1954, and *To Catch a Thief* 1955. She retired from acting after marrying Prince Rainier III of Monaco 1956. After her marriage she devoted herself to the principality, raised three children, and was active in charities until she died in a car accident.

Kelly Ned (Edward) (1855–1880). Australian bushranger. The son of an Irish convict, he wounded a police officer in 1878 while resisting the arrest of his brother Daniel for horse-stealing. The two brothers escaped and carried out bank robberies. Kelly wore a distinctive home-made armour. In 1880 he was captured and hanged.

Such is life.

NED KELLY
Last words before being hanged 1880

Suggested reading

Brown, M *Ned Kelly: Australian Son* (1980)
Jennings, M J *Ned Kelly: The Legend and the Man* (1968)
Osborne, Charles *Ned Kelly* (1970)

Kelly Petra (1947–1992). German politician and activist. She was a vigorous campaigner against nuclear power and other environmental issues and founded the German Green Party 1972. She was a member of the Bundestag (parliament) 1983–90, but then fell out with her party.

Born in Germany, Kelly was brought up in the USA and was influenced by the civil-rights movement there. She worked briefly in the office of lawyer and politician Robert Kennedy and, returning to Germany, she joined the European Economic Community as a civil servant 1972. Her goal, to see the ecological movement as a global organization, became increasingly frustrated by the provincialism of the German Green Party. She died at the hands of her lover, the former general Gert Bastian, who then committed suicide.

Kelly William (1811–1888). US metallurgist, arguably the original inventor of the 'air-boiling process' for making steel, known universally as the Bessemer process.

Kelly was born in Pittsburgh, Pennsylvania. Having bought iron-ore lands and a furnace in Eddyville, Kentucky, he developed his steel-making process in the 1850s. Steel under the Kelly patent was first produced commercially 1864, but by then Kelly had sold his patent. He founded an axemaking business in Louisville, Kentucky, and remained in relative obscurity in spite of his invention, which became known under Henry Bessemer's name.

Experimenting, Kelly found that contrary to all ironmakers' beliefs, molten iron containing sufficient carbon became much hotter when air was blown on to it. An air blast can burn out 3–5% of carbon contained in molten cast iron. Here the carbon itself is acting as a fuel. When he heard that Bessemer had been granted a US patent on the same process, Kelly immediately applied for a patent and managed 1857 to convince the Patent Office that he was the original inventor.

After he had sold the patent, Kelly built a tilting type of converter, which produced soft steel cheaply for the first time and in large quantities. It was used for rails, bars, and structural shapes.

Kelman James (1946–). Scottish novelist and short-story writer. His works are angry, compassionate, and ironic, and make effective use of the trenchant speech patterns of his native Glasgow. These include the novels *The Busconductor Hines* 1984, *A Disaffection* 1989, and *How Late It Was, How Late* 1994 (Booker Prize); the short-story collections *Greyhound for Breakfast* 1987 and *The Burn* 1991; and the play *The Busker* 1985.

Kelsen Hans (1881–1973). Austrian-American jurist and philosopher. In analysing the structure of law, he argued that a legal system was a hierarchy of norms. Each norm, or legal proposition, was validated by a previous norm leading back to a fundamental postulate, or *Grundnorm*; for example, the will of the queen in Parliament. Thus the law and the state were essentially the same. This he called the pure theory of law; pure because it was free from any ethical, ideological, or sociological considerations.

Do not imagine that mathematics is hard and crabbed, and repulsive to common sense. It is merely the etherealization of common sense.

WILLIAM KELVIN
In S P Thomson *Life of Lord Kelvin* 1910

Kelvin William Thomson, 1st Baron Kelvin (1824–1907). Irish physicist who introduced the kelvin scale, the absolute scale of temperature. His work on the conservation of energy 1851 led to the second law of thermodynamics. Knighted 1866, baron 1892.

Kelvin's knowledge of electrical theory was largely responsible for the first successful transatlantic telegraph cable. In 1847 he concluded that electrical and magnetic fields are distributed in a manner analogous to the transfer of energy through an elastic solid. From 1849 to 1859, Kelvin also developed the work of English scientist Michael Faraday into a full theory of magnetism, arriving at an expression for the total energy of a system of magnets.

He was professor of natural philosophy at Glasgow 1846–99, and there created the first physics laboratory in a British university.

Suggested reading
MacDonald, D K C *Faraday, Maxwell and Kelvin* (1965)
Sharlin, H and T *Lord Kelvin: The Dynamic Victorian* (1978)
Thompson, S P *The Life of Lord Kelvin* (1977)

Kemal Yashar. Adopted name of Yashar Kemal Gokceli (1923–). Turkish novelist and journalist. Renowned for his progressive and politically conscious writings, Kemal has been jailed repeatedly for his socialist convictions. He has published over thirty works, including novels and plays; thirteen of his novels have appeared in English translation, and include *Anatolian Tales* 1967 (translated 1968) and *The Legend of the Thousand Bulls* 1971 (translated 1976). His work often portrays the essential decency of peasants and the difficulty of their struggle for existence.

Many of Kemal's novels are intensely political, and characterized by elements of folklore and fairy tale. In his first, *Ince Memed* 1955–73 (two of the four volumes have been translated as *Memed, My Hawk* 1961 and *They Burn the Thistles* 1977), the hero is a kind of Turkish Robin Hood. Another peasant hero, Long Ali, is featured in *The Wind from the Plain* 1960 (translated 1963), *Iron Earth, Copper Sky* 1963 (translated 1974), and *The Undying Grass* 1968 (translated 1977). Other works include *The Saga of a Seagull* 1976 (translated 1981), and *The Birds Have Also Gone* 1978 (translated 1987).

Kemal Atatürk Mustafa. Turkish politician; see ◊Atatürk.

Kemble Charles (1775–1854). English actor and theatre manager, younger brother of Philip Kemble. His greatest successes were in romantic roles with his daughter Fanny Kemble.

Kemble Fanny (Frances Anne) (1809–1893). English actress. She first appeared as Shakespeare's Juliet 1829. In 1834, on a US tour, she married a Southern plantation owner and remained in the USA until 1847. Her *Journal of a Residence on a Georgian Plantation* 1835 is a valuable document in the history of slavery. She was the daughter of Charles Kemble.

Kemble (John) Philip (1757–1823). English actor and theatre manager. He excelled in tragedy, including the Shakespearean roles of Hamlet and Coriolanus. As manager of Drury Lane 1788–1803 and Covent Garden 1803–17 in London, he introduced many innovations in theatrical management, costume, and scenery.

He was the son of the strolling player Roger Kemble (1721–1802), whose children included the actors Charles Kemble and Mrs Siddons.

Kemp Will (died 1603). English clown. A member of several Elizabethan theatre companies, he joined the Chamberlain's Men 1594, acting in the roles of Dogberry in Shakespeare's *Much Ado About Nothing* and Peter in *Romeo and Juliet*. He published *Kempe's Nine Days' Wonder* 1600, an account of his nine-day dance to Norwich from London.

Kempe Margerie (born Brunham) (c. 1373–c. 1439). English Christian mystic. She converted to religious life after a period of mental derangement, and travelled widely as a pilgrim. Her *Boke of Margery Kempe* about 1420 describes her life and experiences, both religious and worldly. It has been called the first autobiography in English.

Suggested reading
Cholmeley, K *Margery Kempe: Genius and Mystic* (1947)
Collis, L *Margery Kempe* (1964)
Kempe, Margery *The Book of Margery Kempe* (trs by B Windeatt 1985)
Thornton, Martin *Margery Kempe* (1961)

Kempe Rudolf (1910–1976). German conductor. Renowned for the clarity and fidelity of his interpretations of the works of Richard Strauss and Wagner's *Ring* cycle, he conducted Britain's Royal Philharmonic Orchestra 1961–75 and was musical director of the Munich Philharmonic from 1967.

Kempff Wilhelm Walter Friedrich (1895–1991). German pianist and composer. He excelled at the 19th-century classical repertory of Beethoven, Brahms, Chopin, and Liszt. He resigned as director of the Stuttgart Conservatory when only 35 to concentrate on performing; later he played with Pablo Casals, Yehudi Menuhin, and Pierre Fournier.

Oh how quickly the glory of the world passes away!
THOMAS À KEMPIS
Imitatio Christi

Kempis Thomas à. Medieval German monk and religious writer; see ◊Thomas à Kempis.

Kendall Edward Calvin (1886–1972). US biochemist. In 1914 he isolated the hormone thyroxine, the active compound of the thyroid gland. He went on to work on secretions from the adrenal gland, among which he discovered the steroid cortisone. For this Kendall shared the 1950 Nobel Prize for Physiology or Medicine with Philip Hench and Tadeus Reichstein.

From 1914 he worked at the Mayo Foundation, Minnesota, USA, becoming professor there 1921.

Kendrew John Cowdery (1917–). English biochemist who determined the structure of the muscle protein myoglobin. For this work Kendrew shared the 1962 Nobel Prize for Chemistry with his colleague Max Perutz. Knighted 1974.

Kendrew was born in Oxford and studied at Cambridge, where he spent most of his academic career. In 1975 he became director of the European Molecular Biology Laboratory at Heidelberg, Germany.

In 1946 at Cambridge Kendrew began working with Perutz. Their research centred on the fine structure of various protein molecules; Kendrew was assigned the task of studying myoglobin, a globular protein which occurs in muscle fibres (where it stores oxygen). He used X-ray diffraction techniques to elucidate the amino acid sequence in the peptide chains that form the myoglobin molecule. Early computers were programmed to analyse the X-ray photographs. By 1960, Kendrew had determined the spatial arrangement of all 1,200 atoms in the molecule, showing it to be a folded helical chain of amino acids with an amino ($-NH_2$) group at one end and a carboxylic ($-COOH$) group at the other. It involves an iron-containing haem group, which allows the molecule to absorb oxygen.

Keneally Thomas Michael (1935–). Australian novelist. He won the Booker Prize with *Schindler's Ark* 1982, a novel based on the true account of Polish Jews saved from the gas chambers in World War II by a German industrialist. Other works include *Woman of the Inner Sea* 1992.

Among his other books are *The Chant of Jimmie Blacksmith* 1972 (filmed 1978), based on the life of the Aboriginal bushranger Jimmy Governor, *Confederates* 1980, *A Family Madness* 1986, *The Playmaker* 1987, *To Asmara* 1989, and *A River Town* 1995.

Keneally was born in Sydney. He studied for the Catholic priesthood but left before ordination. He has won the Miles Franklin Award on two occasions with *Bring Larks and Heroes* 1967, set amid the brutality and corruption of a penal colony, and *Three Cheers for the Paraclete* 1968, which deals with a young priest's conflict with his superiors. His other works include *A Dutiful Daughter* 1971, *Blood Red, Sister Rose* 1974, about Joan of Arc, and *Towards Africa* 1989, dealing with the conflict in Eritrea.

Kennedy Anthony (1936–). US jurist, appointed associate justice of the US Supreme Court 1988. A conservative, he wrote the majority opinion in *Washington* v *Harper* 1990 that the administration of medication for mentally ill prisoners, without the prisoner's consent, is permissible.

He established a private law practice in California 1962–75. He taught constitutional law at McGeorge School of Law of the

University of the Pacific 1965–88 and was appointed judge of the US Court of Appeals for the Seventh Circuit 1976. He was appointed to the Supreme Court by President Reagan.

He supported the majority opinion in the 1989 case, *Texas v Johnson*, that ruled that the burning of the US flag in protest was protected by the First Amendment. In *Saffle v Parks* 1990 he wrote the opinion that a writ of habeas corpus may be obtained only according to the laws in force at the time of a prisoner's conviction.

Kennedy Edward Moore ('Ted') (1932–). US Democratic politician. He aided his brothers John and Robert Kennedy in their presidential campaigns of 1960 and 1968 respectively, and entered politics as a senator for Massachusetts 1962. He failed to gain the presidential nomination 1980, largely because of questions about his delay in reporting a car crash at Chappaquiddick Island, near Cape Cod, Massachusetts, in 1969, in which his passenger, Mary Jo Kopechne, was drowned.

Kennedy John F(itzgerald) ('Jack') (1917–1963). 35th president of the USA 1961–63, a Democrat; the first Roman Catholic and the youngest person to be elected president.

Son of financier Joseph Kennedy, John was born in Brookline, Massachusetts, educated at Harvard and briefly at the London School of Economics, and served in the navy in the Pacific during World War II, winning the Purple Heart and the Navy and Marine Corps medal.

After a brief career in journalism he was elected to the House of Representatives 1946. At this point he was mainly concerned with domestic politics and showed few signs of the internationalism for

Kennedy, John F *US president John F Kennedy. Kennedy, a Democrat, defeated Richard Nixon in the election of 1960, to become the 35th president of the USA, and the first Roman Catholic president. He was assassinated 1963.* (Image Select)

which he later became famous. In 1952 he was elected to the Senate from Massachusetts, defeating Republican Henry Cabot Lodge, Jr, one of Eisenhower's leading supporters. In 1953 he married socialite Jacqueline Lee Bouvier (1929–1995).

Kennedy made his name as a supporter of civil rights' legislation and as a prominent internationalist, but his youth and his Roman Catholicism were considered serious barriers to the White House. His victory in all seven primaries that he entered, however, assured his place as Democratic candidate for the presidency 1960. His programme was a radical one, covering promises to deal with both civil rights and social reform. On television Kennedy debated well against the Republican candidate Richard Nixon, yet went on to win the presidency by one of the narrowest margins ever recorded.

Critics suggest style was more important than substance in the Kennedy White House, but he inspired a generation of idealists and created an aura of positive activism. He brought academics and intellectuals to Washington as advisers, and his wit and charisma combined with political shrewdness disarmed many critics. His inaugural address, with its emphasis on the 'new frontier', was reminiscent of Roosevelt. In fact Kennedy did not succeed in carrying through any major domestic legislation, though, with the aid of his brother Robert Kennedy, the Attorney-General, desegregation continued and the Civil Rights Bill was introduced. He created the Peace Corps, volunteers who give various types of health, agricultural, and educational aid overseas, and he proposed the Alliance for Progress for aid to Latin America.

It was in foreign affairs that Kennedy's presidency was most notable. Early in 1961 came the fiasco of the Bay of Pigs, which, though partially carried over from the previous administration, was undoubtedly Kennedy's responsibility. This was redeemed by his masterly handling of the Cuban missile crisis 1962, where his calm and firm approach had a prolonged effect on US–Soviet relations. The Nuclear Test Ban Treaty 1963, achieved a further lessening of tension. Kennedy's internationalism won him a popular European reputation not attained by any of his predecessors. He visited W Europe 1961 and 1963, and was tumultuously received on each occasion. The US involvement in the Vietnam War began during Kennedy's administration.

On 22 Nov, while on a tour of Texas, Kennedy was shot while driving through Dallas and died shortly afterwards. His presumed assassin, Lee Harvey Oswald, was himself shot 24 Nov while under arrest. Kennedy's death caused worldwide grief and his funeral was attended by heads of state and their representatives from all over the world. He was buried in Arlington National Cemetery.

Suggested reading

Gadney, R *Kennedy* (1983)
Lane, Mark *Rush to Judgement: A Critique of the Warren Commission Enquiry* (1966)
Longford, Lord *Kennedy* (1976)
Manchester, William *Death of a President* (1967)
Schlesinger, Arthur M, Jr *A Thousand Days: John F Kennedy in the White House* (1965)
Sorenson, Theodore *Kennedy* (1965)
White, T H *The Making of the President 1960* (1961)

When the going gets tough, the tough get going.

J H Cutler on JOSEPH P KENNEDY
in *Honey Fitz* 1962

Kennedy Joseph Patrick (1888–1969). US industrialist and diplomat; ambassador to the UK 1937–40. A self-made millionaire, he ventured into the film industry, then set up the Securities and Exchange Commission (SEC) for F D Roosevelt. He groomed each of his sons – Joseph Patrick Kennedy, Jr (1915–1944), John F Kennedy, Robert Kennedy, and Edward Kennedy – for a career in politics. His eldest son, Joseph, was killed in action with the naval air force in World War II.

Kennedy Nigel Paul (1956–). English violinist. He is credited with expanding the audience for classical music. His 1986 recording of Vivaldi's *Four Seasons* sold more than 1 million copies. He retired from the classical concert platform 1992.

Kennedy was educated at the Yehudi Menuhin School, Surrey, England, and the Juilliard School of Music, New York. He has allied Menuhin's ethic of openness and populism to modern marketing techniques. By cultivating a media image that challenges conventional standards of dress and decorum, he has succeeded in attracting young audiences to carefully understated performances of J S Bach, Max Bruch, and Alban Berg. His repertoire of recordings also includes jazz.

The free way of life proposes ends, but it does not prescribe means.

ROBERT KENNEDY
The Pursuit of Justice pt 5

Kennedy Robert Francis (1925–1968). US Democratic politician and lawyer. He was presidential campaign manager for his brother John F Kennedy 1960, and as attorney general 1961–64 pursued a racket-busting policy and promoted the Civil Rights Act of 1964. He was also a key aide to his brother. When John Kennedy's successor, Lyndon Johnson, preferred Hubert H Humphrey for the 1964 vice-presidential nomination, Kennedy resigned and was elected senator for New York. In 1968 he campaigned for the Democratic Party's presidential nomination, but during a campaign stop in California was assassinated by Sirhan Bissara Sirhan (1944–   ), a Jordanian.
Suggested reading
Guthman, Edwin and Shulman, Jeffrey *Robert Kennedy: In His Own Words* (1988)
Newfield, Jack *Robert Kennedy: A Memoir* (1969)
Schlesinger, Arthur *Robert Kennedy and his Times* (1978)
Shannon, William *The Heir Apparent* (1967)

Kennedy William Joseph (1928–   ). US novelist. He wrote the *Albany Trilogy* consisting of *Legs* 1976, about the gangster 'Legs' Diamond; *Billy Phelan's Greatest Game* 1983, about a pool player; and *Ironweed* 1984 (Pulitzer Prize), about a baseball player's return to the city of Albany, New York State. He also wrote *Quinn's Book* 1988, and *Very Old Bones* 1992.

Kennelly Arthur Edwin (1861–1939). US engineer who gave his name to the Kennelly–Heaviside layer (now the E layer) of the ionosphere. He verified in 1902 the existence of an ionized layer in the upper atmosphere, predicted by Heaviside.

Kenneth two kings of Scotland:

Kenneth I (called MacAlpin) (died 860). King of Scotland from about 844. Traditionally, he is regarded as the founder of the Scottish kingdom (Alba) by virtue of his final defeat of the Picts about 844. He invaded Northumbria six times, and drove the Angles and the Britons over the river Tweed.

Kenneth II (died 995). King of Scotland from 971, son of Malcolm I. He invaded Northumbria several times, and his chiefs were in constant conflict with Sigurd the Norwegian over the area of Scotland north of the river Spey. He is believed to have been murdered by his subjects.

Kent Bruce (1929–   ). British peace campaigner who was general secretary of the Campaign for Nuclear Disarmament 1980–85. He has published numerous articles on disarmament, Christianity, and peace. He was a Catholic priest until 1987.

Kent Edward Augustus, Duke of Kent and Strathearn (1767–1820). British general. The fourth son of George III, he married Victoria Mary Louisa (1786–1861), widow of the Prince of Leiningen, in 1818, and had one child, the future Queen Victoria.

Kent Edward George Nicholas Paul Patrick, 2nd Duke of Kent (1935–   ). British prince, grandson of George V. His father, George (1902–1942), was created Duke of Kent just before his marriage in 1934 to Princess Marina of Greece and Denmark (1906–1968). The second duke succeeded when his father (George Edward Alexander

Edmund) was killed in an air crash on active service with the RAF.

He was educated at Eton public school and Sandhurst military academy, and then commissioned in the Royal Scots Greys. In 1961 he married Katharine Worsley (1933–   ) and his heir is George (1962–   ), Earl of St Andrews. His brother, Prince Michael (1942–   ), became an officer with the Hussars in 1962. His sister, Princess Alexandra (1936–   ), married in 1963 Angus Ogilvy (1928–   ), younger son of the 12th Earl of Airlie; they have two children, James (1964–   ) and Marina (1966–   ).

Kent William (1684–1748). English architect, landscape gardener, and interior designer. Working closely with Burlington, he was foremost in introducing the Palladian style to Britain from Italy, excelling in richly carved, sumptuous interiors and furnishings, as at Holkham Hall, Norfolk (begun 1734). Immensely versatile, he also worked in a Neo-Gothic style, and was a pioneer in Romantic landscape gardening, for example, the grounds of Stowe House in Buckinghamshire. Horace Walpole called him 'the father of modern gardening'.

Kentigern, St (also called Mungo) (c. 518–603). First bishop of Glasgow, born at Culross, Scotland. Anti-Christian factions forced him to flee to Wales, where he founded the monastery of St Asaph. In 573 he returned to Glasgow and founded the cathedral there. Feast day 14 Jan.

Kenton Stan(ley Newcomb) (1912–1979). US exponent of progressive jazz. He broke into West Coast jazz 1941 with his 'wall of brass' sound. He helped introduce Afro-Cuban rhythms to US jazz, and combined jazz and classical music in compositions like 'Artistry in Rhythm' 1943.

Kenyatta Jomo. Assumed name of Kamau Ngengi (c. 1894–1978). Kenyan nationalist politician, prime minister from 1963, as well as the first president of Kenya from 1964 until his death. He led the Kenya African Union from 1947 (KANU from 1963) and was active in liberating Kenya from British rule.

A member of the Kikuyu ethnic group, Kenyatta was born near Fort Hall, son of a farmer. Brought up at a Church of Scotland mission, he joined the Kikuyu Central Association (KCA), devoted to recovery of Kikuyu lands from white settlers, and became its president. He spent some years in Britain, returning to Kenya in 1946. He became president of the Kenya African Union (successor to the banned KCA 1947). In 1953 he was sentenced to seven years' imprisonment for his management of the guerrilla organization Mau Mau, though some doubt has been cast on his complicity. Released to exile in N Kenya in 1958, he was allowed to return to Kikuyuland 1961 and in 1963 became prime minister (also president from 1964) of independent Kenya. His slogans were *'Uhuru na moja'* (Freedom and unity) and *'Harambee'* (Pull together).
Suggested reading
Gertzel, C *The Politics of Independent Kenya* (1970)
Kenyatta, Jomo *Suffering Without Bitterness* (memoirs) (1968)
Murray-Brown, Jeremy *Kenyatta* (1973)

Kenyon Joseph (1885–1961). English organic chemist who studied optical activity, particularly of secondary alcohols.

Working as a laboratory assistant at Blackburn Technical College, he won a scholarship and went on to become a lecturer there. He worked on photographic developers and dyes at the British Dyestuffs Corporation, Oxford, 1916–20, and was head of the Chemistry Department at Battersea Polytechnic, London, 1920–50.

Kenyon published his research on secondary alcohols in 1911. He resolved the optically active stereoisomers of secondary octyl alcohol (octan-2-ol), and went on to obtain an optically pure series of secondary alcohols. Kenyon put forward the 'obstacle' theory for the cause of optical activity in certain substituted diphenic acids. He synthesized and attempted to resolve some selenoxides, confirming differences between these and sulphoxides, and investigated the geometric and optical isomerism of the methylcyclohexanols.

Kenyon Kathleen Mary (1906–1978). British archaeologist whose all-female dig in Jericho 1952 uncovered remains of a New Stone Age (Neolithic) settlement dated to about 6800 BC. DBE 1973.

Kenzo trade name of Kenzo Takada (1940–). Japanese fashion designer. He has been active in France from 1964. He opened his shop Jungle JAP 1970, and by 1972 he was well established, known initially for unconventional designs based on traditional Japanese clothing. His fabrics are characterized by rich pattern and colour combinations.

Kepler Johannes (1571–1630). German mathematician and astronomer. He formulated what are now called Kepler's laws of planetary motion: (1) the orbit of each planet is an ellipse with the Sun at one of the foci; (2) the radius vector of each planet sweeps out equal areas in equal times; (3) the squares of the periods of the planets are proportional to the cubes of their mean distances from the Sun.

Kepler became assistant to Danish astronomer Tycho Brahe 1600, and succeeded him 1601 as imperial mathematician to Holy Roman Emperor Rudolph II. Kepler observed in 1604 a supernova, the first visible since the one discovered by Brahe 1572. Kepler completed and published the *Rudolphine Tables* 1627, the first modern astronomical tables, based on Brahe's observations. His analysis of these data led to the discovery of his three laws, the first two of which he published in *Astronomia nova* 1609 and the third in *Harmonices mundi* 1619.
Suggested reading
Beer, Arthur (ed) *Kepler: Four Hundred Years* (1974)
Caspar, Max *Johannes Kepler* (trs 1959)
Koestler, Arthur *The Watershed* (1960)

Where there is matter, there is geometry.

JOHANNES KEPLER
Attributed

Kerekou Mathieu Ahmed (1933–). Benin socialist politician and soldier, president 1980–91. In 1972, when deputy head of the Dahomey army, he led a coup to oust the ruling president and establish his own military government. He embarked on a programme of 'scientific socialism', changing his country's name to Benin to mark this change of direction. In 1987 he resigned from the army and confirmed a civilian administration. He was re-elected president 1989, but lost to Nicéphore Soglo in the 1991 presidential elections.

Kerensky Alexandr Feodorovich (1881–1970). Russian revolutionary politician, prime minister of the second provisional government before its collapse Nov 1917, during the Russian Revolution. He was overthrown by the Bolshevik revolution and fled to France 1918 and to the USA 1940.

I am trying to do something for the future of American music, which today has no class whatsoever and is mere barbaric mouthing.

JEROME KERN
quoted in *New York Times*, 1920

Kern Jerome David (1885–1945). US composer. Many of Kern's songs have become classics, notably 'Smoke Gets in Your Eyes' from his musical *Roberta* 1933. He wrote the operetta *Show Boat* 1927, which includes the song 'Ol' Man River'.

Based on Edna Ferber's novel, *Show Boat* was the first example of serious musical theatre in the USA. Kern wrote dozens of hit songs and musicals from 1904 and Hollywood movies from the beginning of the sound era 1927. He worked mainly with lyricist Otto Harbach but also with Ira Gershwin, Oscar Hammerstein II, Dorothy Fields, and Johnny Mercer.

Kerouac Jack (Jean Louis) (1922–1969). US novelist. He named and epitomized the Beat Generation of the 1950s. The first of his autobiographical, myth-making books, *The Town and the City* 1950, was followed by the rhapsodic *On the Road* 1957. Other works written with similar free-wheeling energy and inspired by his interests in jazz and Buddhism include *The Dharma Bums* 1958, *Doctor Sax* 1959, and *Desolation Angels* 1965. His major contribution to poetry was *Mexico City Blues* 1959.

I had nothing to offer anybody except my own confusion.

JACK KEROUAC
On the Road 1957

He became a legendary symbol of youthful rebellion from the late 1950s, but before Kerouac's early death from alcoholism, he had become a semi-recluse, unable to cope with his fame.
Suggested reading
Charters, A *Kerouac: A Biography* (1973)
Gifford, Barry and Lee, Lawrence *Jack's Book: An Oral History of Jack Kerouac* (1978)
Nicosia, Gerald *Memory Babe* (1983)

Kerr Deborah Jane (1921–). Scottish actress. She often played genteel, ladylike roles. Her performance in British films such as *Major Barbara* 1940 and *Black Narcissus* 1946 led to starring parts in Hollywood: *Quo Vadis* 1951, *From Here to Eternity* 1953, and *The King and I* 1956. She retired 1969, but made a comeback with *The Assam Garden* 1985.

Kerr John (1824–1907). Scottish physicist who discovered the Kerr effect 1875, which produces double refraction in certain media on the application of an electric field.

He was lecturer in mathematics at the Free Church Training College for Teachers, Glasgow, 1857–1901, and set up a modest laboratory there.

Kerr John Robert (1914–1990). Australian lawyer who as governor-general 1974–77 controversially dismissed the prime minister, Gough Whitlam, and his government 1975. KCMG 1974.

Kertész André (1894–1986). Hungarian-born US photographer. His spontaneity had a great impact on photojournalism. A master of the 35-mm-format camera, he recorded his immediate environment with wit and style.

He lived in Paris 1925–36, where he befriended and photographed many avant-garde artists and writers, and in New York City 1936–86, where he did commercial photography for major US magazines as well as creative photography.
Suggested reading
Borhan, Pierre *André Kertész: His Life and Work* (1994)
Kertész, André *Kertész on Kertész: A Self-Portrait* (1985)
Kismaric, Carole *André Kertész* (1977)
Phillips, Sandra S and Travis, David *Kertész* (1985)

Kesey Ken Elton (1935–). US writer. He used his experience of working in a mental hospital as the basis for his best-selling first novel *One Flew Over the Cuckoo's Nest* 1962 (filmed 1975). This was followed by his Oregon-set novel *Sometimes a Great Notion* 1964. In the mid-1960s he gave up writing and became one of the leaders of the hippie movement.

He returned to writing with *Kesey's Garage Sale* 1973 and *Demon Box* 1988, collections of less energetic, sometimes folksy material. *Last Go Round* was published 1994. Kesey's life as a hippie was described by Tom Wolfe in his *Electric Kool-Aid Acid Test*.

Kesselring Albert (1885–1960). German field marshal in World War II, commander of the Luftwaffe (air force) 1939–40, during the invasions of Poland and the Low Countries and the early stages of the Battle of Britain. He later served under Field Marshal Rommel in N Africa, took command in Italy 1943, and was commander in chief on the western front March 1945. His death sentence for war crimes at the Nuremberg trials 1947 was commuted to life imprisonment, but he was released 1952.

Ketch Jack (died 1686). English executioner who included Monmouth in 1685 among his victims; his name was once a common nickname for an executioner.

He did not dispose himself for receiving the fatal stroke in such a position as was most suitable.

JACK KETCH
Excuse for bungling the execution of Lord Russell
21 July 1683 in *The Apologie of John Ketch Esquire*

Kettlewell Henry Bernard David (1907–1979). English geneticist and lepidopterist who carried out important research into the influence of industrial melanism on natural selection in moths, showing why moths are darker in polluted areas.

Kettlewell was born in Howden, Yorkshire, and studied medicine at Cambridge and at St Bartholomew's Hospital, London. He was based at Cape Town University, South Africa, 1949–52, investigating methods of locust control and going on expeditions. Returning to the UK, he spent the rest of his career at Oxford as a genetics researcher.

Kettlewell's research into industrial melanism focused on the peppered moth *Biston betularia*. He demonstrated experimentally the efficiency of natural selection as an evolutionary force: light-coloured moths are more conspicuous than dark-coloured ones in industrial areas, where the vegetation is darkened by pollution, and are therefore easier prey for birds, but are less conspicuous in unpolluted rural areas, where the vegetation is lighter in colour, and therefore survive predation better.

'Tis the star-spangled banner; O long may it wave / O'er the land of the free, and the home of the brave!

FRANCIS SCOTT KEY
'The Star-Spangled Banner'

Key Francis Scott (1779–1843). US lawyer and poet. He wrote the song 'The Star-Spangled Banner' while Fort McHenry, Baltimore, was besieged by British troops 1814; since 1931 it has been the national anthem of the USA.

But this long run is a misleading guide to current affairs. In the long run we are all dead.

JOHN MAYNARD KEYNES
Tract on Monetary Reform 1923

Keynes John Maynard, 1st Baron Keynes (1883–1946). English economist whose *General Theory of Employment, Interest, and Money* 1936 proposed the prevention of financial crises and unemployment by adjusting demand through government control of credit and currency. He is responsible for that part of economics now known as macroeconomics. Baron 1942.

Keynes was a fellow of King's College, Cambridge. He worked at the Treasury during World War I, and took part in the peace conference as chief Treasury representative, but resigned in protest against the financial terms of the treaty. He justified his action in *The Economic Consequences of the Peace* 1919. His later economic works aroused much controversy.

Keynes led the British delegation at the Bretton Woods Conference 1944, which set up the International Monetary Fund. His theories were widely accepted in the aftermath of World War II, and he was one of the most influential economists of the 20th century. His ideas are today often contrasted with those of monetarism.

Suggested reading
Fletcher, G *The Keynesian Revolution and its Critics* (1987)
Harrod, R *The Life of John Maynard Keynes* (1952)
Lekachman, R *Marx and Keynes: The Limits of the Mixed Economy* (1969)
Skidelsky, Robert *John Maynard Keynes: Hopes Betrayed* (1983)
Skidelsky, Robert *John Maynard Keynes: the Economist as Saviour* (1992)

Khachaturian Aram Il'yich (1903–1978). Armenian composer.

His use of folk themes is shown in the ballets *Gayaneh* 1942, which includes the 'Sabre Dance', and *Spartacus* 1956.

Khaddhafi Moamer al, or Gaddafi or Qaddafi (1942–). Libyan revolutionary leader. Overthrowing King Idris 1969, he became virtual president of a republic, although he nominally gave up all except an ideological role 1974. He favours territorial expansion in N Africa reaching as far as Zaire, has supported rebels in Chad, and has proposed mergers with a number of countries. During the Gulf War, however, he advocated diplomacy rather than war. His theories, based on those of the Chinese communist leader Mao Zedong, are contained in a *Green Book*.

Khaddhafi's alleged complicity in international terrorism led to his country's diplomatic isolation during the 1980s and in 1992 United Nations sanctions were imposed against Libya after his refusal to allow extradiction of two suspects in the Lockerbie and Union de Transport Ariens bombings.

In 1995 Khaddhafi faced an escalating campaign of violence by militant Islamicists, the strongest challenge to his regime to date.
Suggested reading
Blundy, David and Lycett, Andrew *Quaddafi and the Libyan Revolution* (1987)
Cooley, John K *Libyan Sandstorm* (1982)
Wright, J *Libya* (1982)

Khalaf Salah, also known as Abu Iyad (1933–1991). Palestinian nationalist leader. He became a refugee in 1948 when Israel became independent, and was one of the four founder members – with Yassir Arafat – of the PLO in the 1960s. One of its most senior members, he was involved with the Black September group, and is believed to have orchestrated their campaign of terrorist attacks such as the 1972 killing of 11 Israeli athletes at the Munich Olympics. He later argued for a diplomatic as well as a terrorist campaign.

He was assassinated by an Arab dissident follower of Abu Nidal.

Khalifa Sudanese leader ◊Abd Allah.

Khama Seretse (1921–1980). Botswanan politician, prime minister of Bechuanaland 1965, and first president of Botswana from 1966 until his death.

Son of the Bamangwato chief Sekoma II (died 1925), Khama studied law in Britain and married an Englishwoman, Ruth Williams. This marriage was strongly condemned by his uncle Tshekedi Khama, who had been regent during his minority, as contrary to tribal custom, and Seretse Khama was banished 1950. He returned 1956 on his renunciation of any claim to the chieftaincy. KBE 1966.

Khan Imran Niazi (1952–). Pakistani cricketer, an all-rounder who played cricket in England for Worcestershire and Sussex and made his test debut 1971. He played 88 test matches for Pakistan, of which 48 were as captain. In 1992 he captained his country to victory in the World Cup. He scored 17,771 first-class runs at an average of 36.87, and took 1,287 wickets at an average of 22.32. He retired in 1992.

Khan Jahangir (1963–). Pakistani squash player who won the world open championship a record six times 1981–85 and 1988, and was World Amateur champion 1979, 1983, and 1985. He announced his retirement 1993.

Khan was ten times British Open champion 1982–91. After losing to Geoff Hunt (Australia) in the final of the 1981 British Open, he did not lose again until Nov 1986 when he lost to Ross Norman (New Zealand) in the World Open final.

Khan, Aga Islamic leader, see ◊Aga Khan.

Khasbulatov Rusian (1943–). Russian politician, chair of the Supreme Soviet 1991–93. As Russian first vice president, he was a strong supporter of Boris Yeltsin, but from 1991 relations between the two deteriorated and Khasbulatov repeatedly tried to block the Russian leader's economic and political reforms. His critics accused him of shifting his ideological ground to pursue his personal ambitions. In Sept 1993 he was arrested and imprisoned after leading a rebellion against Yeltsin, but was granted an amnesty and released Feb 1994. He subsequently announced his retirement from national politics, but in Dec 1995 contested the leadership elections in his native Chechnya.

Khasbulatov was expelled as a child during one of Stalin's purges from western USSR to Kazakhstan.

Khashoggi Adnan (1935–). Saudi entrepreneur and arms dealer who built up a large property company, Triad, based in Switzerland, and through ownership of banks, hotels, and real estate became a millionaire. In 1975 he was accused by the USA of receiving bribes to secure military contracts in Arab countries, and in 1986 he was financially disadvantaged by the slump in oil prices and political problems in Sudan. In April 1989 he was arrested in connection with illegal property deals. He successfully weathered all three setbacks.

Khomeini Ayatollah Ruhollah (1900–1989). Iranian Shi'ite Muslim leader. He was born in Khomein, central Iran. Exiled for opposition to Shah Pahlavi from 1964, he returned when the shah left the country 1979, and established a fundamentalist Islamic republic. His rule was marked by a protracted war with Iraq, and suppression of opposition within Iran, executing thousands of opponents. Khomeini was hostile toward both superpowers, held US embassy hostages 1979–81, and supported terrorist groups
Suggested reading
Bakhash, S *The Reign of the Ayatollahs* (1986)
Keddie, N R *Religion and Politics in Iran* (1983)

Khorana Har Gobind (1922–). Indian-born US biochemist who in 1976 led the team that first synthesized a biologically active gene. He showed that a pattern of three nucleotides, called a triplet, specifies a particular amino acid (the building blocks of proteins). He further discovered that some of the triplets provided punctuation marks in the code, marking the beginning and end points of protein synthesis. In 1968 he shared the Nobel Prize for Physiology or Medicine for research on the chemistry of the genetic code and its function in protein synthesis. Khorana's work provides much of the basis for gene therapy and biotechnology.

Khorana was born in Raipur in the Punjab, now in Pakistan. He studied at Punjab University; in the UK at Liverpool; and in Switzerland at Zürich; returning to Britain 1950 to work at Cambridge. He has held academic posts in the USA and Canada, becoming professor at the University of Wisconsin 1962 and at the Massachusetts Institute of Technology 1970.

Comrades! We must abolish the cult of the individual decisively, once and for all.

NIKITA KHRUSHCHEV
Speech to the secret session of the
20th Congress of the Communist Party 25 Feb 1956

Khrushchev Nikita Sergeyevich (1894–1971). Soviet politician, secretary general of the Communist Party 1953–64, premier 1958–64. He emerged as leader from the power struggle following Stalin's death and was the first official to denounce Stalin, in 1956. His de-Stalinization programme gave rise to revolts in Poland and Hungary 1956. Because of problems with the economy and foreign affairs (a breach with China 1960; conflict with the USA in the Cuban missile crisis 1962), he was ousted by Leonid Brezhnev and Alexei Kosygin.

Born near Kursk, the son of a miner, Khrushchev fought in the post Revolutionary civil war 1917–20, and in World War II organized the guerrilla defence of his native Ukraine. He denounced Stalinism in a secret session of the party Feb 1956.

Many victims of the purges of the 1930s were either released or posthumously rehabilitated, but when Hungary revolted in Oct against Soviet domination, there was immediate Soviet intervention. In 1958 Khrushchev succeeded Bulganin as chair of the council of ministers (prime minister). His policy of competition with capitalism was successful in the space programme, which launched the world's first satellite (*Sputnik*).

Suggested reading
Ebon, Martin *Nikita Khrushchev* (1986)
Khrushchev, Nikita *Khrushchev Remembers* (memoirs) (trs 1970–74)
Medvedev, Roy A *Khrushchev* (1982)

Khufu (lived *c.* 2550 BC). Egyptian king of Memphis, who built the largest of the pyramids, known to the Greeks as the pyramid of Cheops (the Greek form of Khufu).

Khwārizmī, al- Muhammad ibn-Mūsā (*c.* 780–*c.* 850). Persian mathematician who wrote a book on algebra, from part of whose title (*al-jabr*) comes the word 'algebra', and a book in which he introduced to the West the Hindu–Arabic decimal number system. The word 'algorithm' is a corruption of his name.

He was born in Khwarizm (now Khiva, Uzbekistan), but lived and worked in Baghdad. He compiled astronomical tables and was responsible for introducing the concept of zero into Arab mathematics.

This is a very false and faithless generation.

'CAPTAIN' WILLIAM KIDD
Last words before being hanged 1702. He had
only surrendered on the sure promise of a free pardon.

Kidd William, 'Captain' (*c.* 1645–1701). Scottish pirate. He spent his youth privateering for the British against the French off the North American coast, and in 1695 was given a royal commission to suppress piracy in the Indian Ocean. Instead, he joined a group of pirates in Madagascar. On his way to Boston, Massachusetts, he was arrested 1699, taken to England, and hanged. His execution marked the end of some 200 years of semi-official condoning of piracy by the British government.

Kiefer Anselm (1945–). German Neo-Expressionist painter. He studied under Joseph Beuys and his works include monumental landscapes on varied surfaces, often with the paint built up into heavily textured impasto with other substances. Much of his Neo-Expressionist work deals with recent German history.

Kierkegaard Søren Aabye (1813–1855). Danish philosopher and theologian, often considered to be the founder of existentialism. He argued that no system of thought could explain the unique experience of the individual. He defended Christianity, suggesting that God cannot be known through reason, but only through a 'leap of faith'. His chief works are *Enten-Eller/Either-Or* 1843 and *Begrebet Angest/Concept of Dread* 1844.

Kierkegaard was born in Copenhagen, where he spent most of his life. The son of a Jewish merchant, he converted to Christianity in 1838, although he became hostile to the established church and his beliefs caused much controversy. He stressed pure choice and the absurdity of the Christian faith, and believed that God and exceptional individuals were above moral laws. *Efterskrift/Postscript* 1846 summed up much of his earlier writings.
Suggested reading
Hannay, A *Kierkegaard* (1981)
Lebowitz, Naomi *Kierkegaard: A Life of Allegory* (1985)
Mullen, John Douglas *Kierkegaard's Philosophy* (1981)
Rohde, P *Søren Kierkegaard: An Introduction to his Life and Philosophy* (1963)
Walker, Jeremy *Kierkegaard* (1985)

Killy Jean-Claude (1943–). French skier. He won all three gold medals (slalom, giant slalom, and downhill) at the 1968 Winter Olympics in Grenoble.

The first World Cup winner 1967, he retained the title 1968 and also won three world titles.

Kilmer Joyce (1886–1918). US poet. His first collection of poems *Summer of Love* was published 1911. He later gained an international reputation with the title work of *Trees and Other Poems* 1914. At the outbreak of World War I, Kilmer joined the 165th Regiment and was killed in action in France

I think that I shall never see / A poem lovely as a tree.

JOYCE KILMER
'Trees'

Kilmuir David Patrick Maxwell Fyfe, 1st Earl of Kilmuir (1900–1967). British lawyer and Conservative politician. He was solicitor-general 1942–45 and attorney-general in 1945 during the Churchill governments. He was home secretary 1951–54 and lord chancellor 1954–62. Knighted 1942, viscount 1954, earl 1962.

Loyalty was the Tories' secret weapon.

DAVID MAXWELL FYFE, 1ST EARL OF KILMUIR
quoted in Anthony Sampson *Anatomy of Britain* ch 6 1962

Kilvert (Robert) Francis (1840–1879). English cleric. He wrote a diary recording social life on the Welsh border 1870–79, published 1938–39. He delineated landscape and human experience with great sensitivity and vividness.

Of all noxious animals ... the most noxious is a tourist.

FRANCIS KILVERT
Diary 5 April 1870

Kim Dae Jung (1924–). South Korean social-democratic politician. As a committed opponent of the regime of General Park Chung Hee, he suffered imprisonment and exile.

A Roman Catholic, born in the poor SW province of Cholla, Kim was imprisoned by communist troops during the Korean War. He rose to prominence as an opponent of Park and was only narrowly defeated when he challenged Park for the presidency in 1971. He was imprisoned 1976–78 and 1980–82 for alleged 'anti-government activities' and lived in the USA 1982–85. On his return to South Korea he spearheaded a fragmented opposition campaign for democratization, but, being one of several opposition candidates, was defeated by the government nominee, Roh Tae Woo, in the presidential election of Dec 1987.

A political firebrand, Kim enjoyed strong support among blue-collar workers and fellow Chollans, but was feared and distrusted by the country's business and military elite. He was again defeated in the presidential elections 1992 by Kim Young Sam and subsequently announced his retirement from active politics.

Kim Il Sung (1912–1994). North Korean communist politician and marshal. He became prime minister 1948 and president 1972, retaining the presidency of the Communist Workers' party. He liked to be known as the 'Great Leader' and campaigned constantly for the reunification of Korea. His son Kim Jong Il (1942–), known as the 'Dear Leader', succeeded him.

Kim Jong Il (1942–). North Korean communist politician, national leader from 1994, when he succeeded his father, Kim Il Sung. Despite his official designation 'Dear Leader', he lacked his father's charisma and did not automatically inherit the public adulation accorded to him.

Kim Jong Il held a succession of senior party posts from the early 1960s. He was a member of the politburo from 1974 and its controlling inner presidium from 1980 and, although he had received no military training, was made commander in chief of the armed forces in 1991. The belief that he masterminded terrorist activities in the 1970s and 1980s made the West apprehensive about the succession.

Kim Young Sam (1927–). South Korean democratic politician, president from 1993. A member of the National Assembly from 1954 and president of the New Democratic Party (NDP) from 1974, he lost his seat and was later placed under house arrest because of his opposition to President Park Chung Hee. In 1983 he led a prodemocracy hunger strike but in 1987 failed to defeat Roh Tae-Woo in the presidential election. In 1990 he merged the NDP with the ruling party to form the new Democratic Liberal Party (DLP).

In the Dec 1992 presidential election he captured 42% of the national vote, assuming office Feb 1993. As president, he encouraged greater political openness, some deregulation of the economy, and a globalization (segyehwa) initiative.

Kimmel Husband E (1882–1968). US admiral; commander in chief of the US Pacific Fleet at Pearl Harbor Dec 1941. Severely criticized after the success of the Japanese attack, Kimmel complained that he had not been warned by Washington and that he had taken all the preventive measures laid down by regulations. His only positive action, sending his carriers out on a routine exercise, at least saved a crucial portion of the fleet. Nevertheless, he was relieved of his duties ten days after the attack and held no active post thereafter.

Kimura Motō (1924–). Japanese biologist who, as a result of his work on population genetics and molecular evolution, has developed a theory of neutral evolution that opposes the conventional neo-Darwinistic theory of evolution by natural selection.

Kimura was born in Okazaki, near Nagoya, and studied at Kyoto and in the USA at Iowa State and Wisconsin universities. He spent most of his career at the National Institute of Genetics in Mishima, starting 1949 and becoming head of the Department of Population Genetics 1964.

Kimura began in 1968 the work that was to lead to the theory of neutral evolution. Comparing the amino acid compositions of the alpha and beta chains of the haemoglobin molecules in humans with those in carp, he found that the alpha chains have evolved in two distinct lineages, accumulating mutations independently and at about the same rate over a period of some 400 million years. According to Kimura's theory, evolutionary rates are determined by the structure and function of molecules, and most variability and evolutionary change within a species is caused by the random drift of mutant genes that are all selectively equivalent and selectively neutral. Kimura's theory denies that the environment influences evolution and that mutant genes confer either advantageous or disadvantageous traits.

King Albert. Adopted name of Albert Nelson (1923–1992). US blues guitarist and singer. His ringing style influenced numerous rock guitarists. His recordings for the Stax label, such as 'Born Under a Bad Sign' and 'Crosscut Saw' (both 1967), became classics and made him popular beyond the blues circuit. His playing also shows psychedelic and funk influences.

Horn sections added a funk element to King's music in the 1970s, both before and after the demise of Stax; later he returned to a purer blues sound, as on the album *I'm in a Phone Booth, Baby* 1986, with its title track written by the younger blues musician Robert Cray.

King B B (Riley) (1925–). US blues guitarist, singer, and songwriter. One of the most influential electric-guitar players, he became an international star in the 1960s. His albums include *Blues Is King* 1967, *Lucille Talks Back* 1975, and *Blues 'n' Jazz* 1983.

King Billie Jean (born Moffitt) (1943–). US tennis player. She won a record 20 Wimbledon titles 1961–79 and 39 Grand Slam titles. She won the Wimbledon singles title six times, the US Open singles title four times, the French Open once, and the Australian Open once.

Her first Wimbledon title was the doubles with Karen Hantze 1961, and her last, also doubles, with Martina Navratilova 1979. Her 39 Grand Slam wins at singles and doubles are third only to Navratilova and Margaret Court.

King Ernest Joseph (1878–1956). US admiral. Commander in chief of the US Fleet Dec 1941, in March 1942 he also became chief of naval operations and was later a member of the Joint Chiefs of Staff and the Anglo-US Combined Chiefs of Staff. Promoted to fleet admiral 1944, he organized and directed the naval forces in the Pacific; he was always reluctant to divert any resources to any other theatre and his efforts to obtain the most supplies for his Pacific Forces often caused problems in the European theatre.

King Martin Luther (1929–1968). US civil-rights campaigner, black leader, and Baptist minister. He first came to national attention as leader of the Montgomery, Alabama, bus boycott 1955, and was one of the organizers of the march of 200,000 people on Washington DC 1963 to demand racial equality. An advocate of nonviolence, he was awarded the Nobel Peace Prize 1964. He was assassinated in Memphis, Tennessee, by James Earl Ray (1928–   ).

I have a dream that my four little children will one day live in a nation where they will not be judged by the colour of their skin but by the content of their character.

MARTIN LUTHER KING
Speech at a civil-rights march in Washington 28 Aug 1963

Born in Atlanta, Georgia, son of a Baptist minister, King founded the Southern Christian Leadership Conference 1957. A brilliant and moving speaker, he was the symbol of, and leading figure in, the campaign for integration and equal rights in the late 1950s and early 1960s. In the mid-1960s his moderate approach was criticized by black militants. He was the target of intensive investigation by the federal authorities, chiefly the FBI under J Edgar Hoover. His personal life was scrutinized and criticized by those opposed to his policies. King's birthday (15 Jan) is observed on the third Monday in Jan as a public holiday in the USA.

James Earl Ray was convicted of the murder, but there is little evidence to suggest that he committed the crime. Various conspiracy theories concerning the FBI, the CIA, and the Mafia have been suggested.

King, Martin Luther *US civil rights leader Martin Luther King. His famous 'I have a dream ... ' speech, delivered at the end of the civil rights march on Washington 28 Aug 1963, epitomised the aims of the US civil rights movement in the early 1960s. (Image Select)*

Suggested reading
Fairclough, A *To Redeem the Soul of America* (1987)
Lewis, D L *Martin Luther King: A Critical Biography* (1970)
Oates, S B *Let the Trumpet Sound: A Life of Martin Luther King Jr* (1982)

King Philip Gidley (1758–1808). English naval officer and colonial administrator in Australia, governor of New South Wales 1800–06. He was appointed second lieutenant on the First Fleet flagship, HMS *Sirius*, in 1796 and after the arrival in New South Wales was commandant of Norfolk Island 1788–90. He succeeded Hunter as governor, continuing his work of controlling the liquor traffic and quelling disturbances caused by Irish political prisoners. Settlements at Newcastle, Hobart, and Launceston were established during his governorship and Port Phillip was discovered. In 1803 he allowed the government printer to publish the *Sydney Gazette*. He retired because of friction with the military.

King Stephen Edwin (1947–   ). US writer of best-selling horror novels with small-town or rural settings. Many of his works have been filmed, including *Carrie* 1974, *The Shining* 1978, and *Christine* 1983. His recent novels include *It* and *The Tommyknockers* (both 1987), *The Dark Half* 1989, and *Dolores Claiborne* 1992. He has also published three volumes of short stories, several screenplays, and a number of novels under the pseudonym Richard Bachman.

[He was] always careful [in his speeches] to leave himself a way of retreat, if only by the breadth of a hair for subsequent splitting.

B K Sandwell on W L MACKENZIE KING
in *Dictionary of National Biography*

King W(illiam) L(yon) Mackenzie (1874–1950). Canadian Liberal prime minister 1921–26, 1926–30, and 1935–48. He maintained the unity of the English- and French-speaking populations, and was instrumental in establishing equal status for Canada with Britain. He took part in the 1926 imperial conference which recognized the dominion's equal status with Britain, and his proposals, that self-governing countries maintain close co-operation with, but be linked only by allegiance to the British crown, were included in the Statute of Westminster.

The spruce beauty of the slender red line ... though the line was slender, it was very rigid and exact.

ALEXANDER WILLIAM KINGLAKE
Invasion of the Crimea vol iii 1868

Kinglake Alexander William (1809–1891). British historian of the Crimean War who also wrote a Middle East travel narrative *Eothen* 1844.

I love British Cinema like a doctor loves his dying patient.

BEN KINGSLEY
Remark at Dinard 29 Sept 1990

Kingsley Ben (Krishna Banji) (1943–   ). British film actor of Indian descent. He usually plays character parts. He played the title role of *Gandhi* 1982, for which he won an Academy Award, and appeared in *Betrayal* 1982, *Testimony* 1987, and *Pascali's Island* 1988.

Kingsley Charles (1819–1875). English author. A rector, he was known as the 'Chartist clergyman' because of such social novels as *Alton Locke* 1850. His historical novels include *Westward Ho!* 1855. He also wrote, for children, *The Water Babies*. 1863.

Be good, sweet maid, and let who will be clever.

CHARLES KINGSLEY
'A Farewell'

Kingsley Henry (1830–1876). English novelist and younger brother of Charles Kingsley. He wrote two novels with Australian settings – *The Recollections of Geoffry Hamlyn* 1859 and *The Hillyars and the Burtons* 1865, both emigrant success stories – and used Australian material in several others.

Kingsley Mary Henrietta (1862–1900). English ethnologist. She made extensive expeditions in W Africa and published lively accounts of her findings, for example *Travels in West Africa* 1897. She died while nursing Boer prisoners during the South African War. She was the niece of the writer Charles Kingsley.

For men must work, and women must weep, / And there's little to earn, and many to keep.

MARY KINGSLEY
'The Three Fishers'

Kingston Maxine Hong (1940–   ). US writer. A major voice of Chinese-American culture, her semi-fictional *The Woman Warrior: Memoirs of a Girlhood Among Ghosts* 1976 was followed by *China Men* 1980, which continued her imaginative chronicling of family history and cultural folklore. Her work documents the Oriental experience, dealing with alienation, exploitation, and the problems of both national and racial identity in a prose of delicate precision and vivid power.

Kinnock Neil Gordon (1942–   ). British Labour politician, party leader 1983–92. Born and educated in Wales, he was elected to represent a Welsh constituency in Parliament 1970 (Islwyn from 1983). He was further left than prime ministers Wilson and Callaghan, but as party leader (in succession to Michael Foot) adopted a moderate position, initiating a major policy review 1988–89. He resigned as party leader after Labour's defeat in the 1992 general election. In 1994 he left parliament to become a European commissioner.
Suggested reading
Harris, Robert *The Making of Neil Kinnock* (1984)
Jones, Eileen *Neil Kinnock* (1994)

Kino Eusebio Francisco (*c.* 1644–1711). Italian-born Jesuit missionary in America. Kino entered the Jesuit order 1665. After teaching at the University of Ingolstadt, he was sent as a missionary to New Spain 1678. He arrived in Mexico City 1681 and joined a short-lived colony in Baja California. In 1687 he began exploration of Pimería Alta, now modern Sonora, Mexico, and S Arizona. There he established the missions of Tumacacori and San Xavier del Bac near modern Tucson. Kino later explored the Colorado Valley and discovered the massive prehistoric Indian ruins of Casa Grande.

Kinsella Thomas (1928–   ). Irish poet and translator. Collections like *Fifteen Dead* 1979 confront the violence and moral vacuum in contemporary Ireland. Later poems are more experimental than accessible. His translations from Irish Gaelic into English show a keen awareness of Gaelic tradition.

Kinsella is a prolific and highly regarded poet, whose publications range from *Poems* 1956 to *From Centre City* 1994. Early work tended to be personal and lyrical, dealing with the difficulties of love, family illness, and the almost ghostly calm of an unpopulated countryside.

Kinsey Alfred Charles (1894–1956). US researcher whose studies of male and female sexual behaviour 1948–53, based on questionnaires, were the first serious published research on this topic. Many misconceptions, social-class differences, and wide variations in practice and expectations have been discovered as a result of Kinsey's work.

The Institute for Sex Research at Indiana University, founded 1947, continues the objective study of human sexual behaviour.

Kinski Klaus (1926–1991). German actor. He featured in Werner Herzog's films *Aguirre the Wrath of God* 1972, *Nosferatu: Phantom of the Night* 1979, and *Fitzcarraldo* 1982. His other films include *For a Few Dollars More* 1965, *Dr Zhivago* 1965, and *Venom* 1982. He was the father of the actress Nastassja Kinski (1961–   ).

I make movies for money. Exclusively for money. So I sell myself at the highest prices. Exactly like a prostitute.

KLAUS KINSKI
in *Playboy* Nov 1985

Kipling (Joseph) Rudyard (1865–1936). English writer, born in India. *Plain Tales from the Hills* 1888, about Anglo-Indian society, contains the earliest of his masterly short stories. His books for children, including *The Jungle Book* 1894–95, *Just So Stories* 1902, *Puck of Pook's Hill* 1906, and the novel *Kim* 1901, reveal his imaginative identification with the exotic. Poems such as 'Danny Deever', 'Gunga Din', and 'If–' express an empathy with common experience, which contributed to his great popularity, together with a vivid sense of 'Englishness' (sometimes denigrated as a kind of jingoist imperialism). His work is increasingly valued for its complex characterization and subtle moral viewpoints. Nobel prize 1907.

Born in Bombay, Kipling was educated at the United Services College at Westward Ho!, England, which provided the background for *Stalky and Co* 1899. He worked as a journalist in India 1882–89; during these years he wrote *Plain Tales from the Hills*, *Soldiers Three* 1890, *Wee Willie Winkie* 1890, and others. Returning to London he published *The Light that Failed* 1890 and *Barrack-Room Ballads* 1892. He lived largely in the USA 1892–96, where he produced the two *Jungle Books* and *Captains Courageous* 1897. Settling in Sussex, SE England, he published *Kim* (set in India), the *Just So Stories*, *Puck of Pook's Hill*, and *Rewards and Fairies* 1910.
Suggested reading
Amis, Kingsley *Rudyard Kipling and his World* (1975)
Harrison, James *Rudyard Kipling* (1982)
Kipling, Rudyard *Something of Myself* (1937)
Laski, M *From Palm to Pine* (1987)
Mason, Philip *Kipling: The Glass, the Shadow and the Fire* (1975)
Wilson, Angus *The Strange Ride of Rudyard Kipling: His Life and Works* (1977)

Oh, East is East, and West is West, and never the twain shall meet.

RUDYARD KIPLING
'The Ballad of East and West'

Kipping Frederic Stanley (1863–1949). English chemist who pioneered the study of the organic compounds of silicon; he invented the term 'silicone', which is now applied to the entire class of oxygen-containing polymers.

Kipping was professor at University College, Nottingham (later Nottingham University), 1897–1936. In his early research Kipping investigated the preparation and properties of optically active camphor derivatives and nitrogen compounds. In 1899 he began to look for stereoisomerism among the organic compounds of silicon, preparing them using the newly available Grignard reagents. He prepared condensation products – the first organosilicon polymers – which he called silicones. To Kipping these were chemical curiosities and it was not until World War II that they found application as substitutes for oils and greases. Kipping and Perkin co-wrote *Organic Chemistry* 1894, a standard work for the next 50 years.

Kirchhoff Gustav Robert (1824–1887). German physicist who with R W von Bunsen developed spectroscopic analysis in the 1850s and showed that all elements, heated to incandescence, have their individual spectra.

In 1850 he was appointed professor at Breslau, where he was joined by Bunsen the following year. In 1852 Bunsen moved to Heidelberg and Kirchhoff followed him 1854. He moved to Berlin 1875.

In 1845 and 1846 he derived the laws known as Kirchhoff's laws that determine the value of the electric current and potential at any point in a network. He went on to show that electrostatic potential is identical to tension, thus unifying static and current electricity. In 1859 Kirchhoff announced a law stating that the ratio of the emission and absorption powers of all material bodies is the same at a given temperature and a given wavelength of radiation produced. From this, Kirchhoff went on in 1862 to derive the concept of a perfect black body – one that would absorb and emit radiation at all wavelengths.

Kirchner Ernst Ludwig (1880–1938). German Expressionist artist. He was a leading member of the *die Brücke* group in Dresden from 1905 and in Berlin from 1911. His Dresden work, which includes paintings and woodcuts, shows the influence of African and medieval art. In Berlin he turned to city scenes and portraits, using lurid colours and bold diagonal paint strokes recalling woodcut technique. He suffered a breakdown during World War I and settled in Switzerland, where he committed suicide.

Kirckman Jacob (1710–1792). German-born organist and composer. He settled in London about 1730 and founded a family firm of harpsichord makers which dominated the British market during the late 18th century and moved into piano manufacture 1809.

A complex man. Possessed of tremendous drive for self-improvement, of a capacity to listen, to reflect, and to judge … he could also be prickly, petty-minded and prejudiced.

T H Beaglehole on NORMAN KIRK
in *Dictionary of National Biography*

Kirk Norman Eric (1923–1974). New Zealand Labour politician, prime minister 1972–74. He entered parliament 1957 and led the Labour Party from 1964. During his office as prime minister he withdrew New Zealand troops from the Vietnam War and attempted to block French nuclear tests in the Pacific.

Kirkland Gelsey (1953–). US ballerina. She danced with effortless technique and innate musicality. She joined the New York City Ballet 1968, where George Balanchine staged a new *Firebird* for her 1970 and Jerome Robbins chose her for his *Goldberg Variations* 1971 and other ballets. In 1974 Mikhail Baryshnikov sought her out and she joined the American Ballet Theater 1975, where they danced in partnership, for example in *Giselle*.

She was, however, plagued by personal and emotional problems, including cocaine addiction, documented in her autobiography, *Dancing on my Grave* 1986, and her career nosedived after 1976. She has been with the American Ballet Theater on and off since then and has also made several appearances for the Royal Ballet, London, as in *Romeo and Juliet* 1986.

Kirkpatrick Jeane Duane Jordan (1926–). US politician and professor of political science. She served as US ambassador to the United Nations 1981–85. Originally a Democrat, she often spoke out against communism and left-wing causes. She joined the Republican Party 1985.

Kirkwood Daniel (1814–1895). US astronomer who identified and explained the Kirkwood gaps, asteroid-free zones in the Solar System. He used the same theory to explain the nonuniform distribution of particles in the ring system of Saturn.

In 1851 he became professor of mathematics at the University of Delaware; later at Indiana and at Jefferson College, Pennsylvania. From 1891 he lectured in astronomy at the University of Stanford, California.

In 1857 Kirkwood first noticed that three regions of the minor planet zone, sited at 2.5, 2.95, and 3.3 astronomical units from the Sun, lacked asteroids completely. In 1866, he proposed that the gaps arose as a consequence of perturbations caused by the planet Jupiter. The effect of Jupiter's mass would be to force any asteroid that appeared in one of the asteroid-free zones into another orbit, with the result that it would immediately leave the zone.

Kirov Sergei Mironovich (1886–1934). Russian Bolshevik leader who joined the party 1904 and played a prominent part in the 1918–20 civil war. As one of Stalin's closest associates, he became

first secretary of the Leningrad Communist Party. His assassination, possibly engineered by Stalin, led to the political trials held during the next four years as part of the purge.

Kishi Nobusuke (1896–1987). Japanese politician and prime minister 1957–60. A government minister during World War II and imprisoned 1945, he was never put on trial and returned to politics 1953. During his premiership, Japan began a substantial rearmament programme and signed a new treaty with the USA that gave greater equality in the relationship between the two countries.

There cannot be a crisis next week. My schedule is already full.

HENRY KISSINGER
in *New York Times Magazine* 1 June 1969

Kissinger Henry Alfred (1923–). German-born US diplomat. After a brilliant academic career at Harvard University, he was appointed national security adviser 1969 by President Nixon, and was secretary of state 1973–77. His missions to the USSR and China improved US relations with both countries, and he took part in negotiating US withdrawal from Vietnam 1973 and in Arab-Israeli peace negotiations 1973–75.

Born in Bavaria, Kissinger emigrated to the USA 1938. After work in Germany for army counter-intelligence, he won a scholarship to Harvard, and subsequently became a government consultant. His secret trips to Beijing and Moscow led to Nixon's visits to both countries and a general détente. In 1973 he shared the Nobel Peace Prize with Le Duc Tho, the North Vietnamese Politburo member, for his part in the Vietnamese peace negotiations, and in 1976 he was involved in the negotiations in Africa arising from the Angola and Rhodesia crises. In 1983, President Reagan appointed him to head a bipartisan commission on Central America. He was widely regarded as the most powerful member of Nixon's administration.

Suggested reading
Isaacson, Walter *Kissinger: A Biography* (1992)
Kissinger, Henry *White House Years* (memoirs) (1979)
Kissinger, Henry *Years of Upheaval* (memoirs) (1982)
Starr, H *Henry Kissinger* (1984)

Kitaj R(onald) B(rooks) (1932–). US painter and graphic artist, active in Britain. His work is mainly figurative, and employs a wide range of allusions to art, history, and literature. *The Autumn of Central Paris (After Walter Benjamin)* 1972–74 is a typical work. His distinctive use of colour was in part inspired by studies of the Impressionist painter Degas. Much of Kitaj's work is outside the predominant avant-garde trend and inspired by diverse historical styles. Some compositions are in triptych form.

Kitasato Shibasaburō (1852–1931). Japanese bacteriologist who discovered the bubonic plague bacillus while investigating an outbreak of plague in Hong Kong. He was the first to grow the tetanus bacillus in pure culture. He and German bacteriologist Emil von Behring discovered that increasing nonlethal doses of tetanus toxin give immunity to the disease. Having made the discovery of antitoxic immunity 1890, Kitasato and von Behring rapidly developed a serum for treating anthrax. Kitasato also isolated the causative organism of dysentery in 1898 and studied the method of infection in tuberculosis.

In 1885 he was sent by the government to study bacteriology in Germany and went to work in the laboratory of Robert Koch in Berlin. On his return 1891, Kitasato set up a small private institute of bacteriology. When this was incorporated into Tokyo University against Kitasato's wishes 1915, he resigned and founded the Kitasato Institute, which he headed for the rest of his life.

Kitchener Horatio Herbert, 1st Earl Kitchener of Khartoum (1850–1916). British soldier and administrator. He defeated the Sudanese dervishes at Omdurman 1898 and reoccupied Khartoum.

Kitchener was born in County Kerry, Ireland. He was commissioned 1871, and transferred to the Egyptian army 1882. Promoted to commander in chief 1892, he forced a French expedition to withdraw in the Fashoda Incident. During the South African War he acted as Lord Roberts's Chief of Staff 1900–02. He conducted war by scorched-earth policy and created the earliest concentration camps for civilians. Subsequently he commanded the forces in India 1902–09 and acted as British agent in Egypt, and in 1914 received an earldom. As British secretary of state for war from 1914, he modernized the British forces. He was one of the first to appreciate that the war would not be 'over by Christmas' and planned for a three-year war for which he began raising new armies. He bears some responsibility for the failure of the Gallipoli campaign, having initially refused any troops for the venture, and from then on his influence declined. He was drowned when his ship was sunk on the way to Russia. KCMG 1894, baron 1898, viscount 1902, earl 1914.

Suggested reading
Cassar, G H *Kitchener: Architect of Victory* (1977)
Royle, T *The Kitchener Enigma* (1985)
Warner, Phillip *Kitchener: The Man Behind the Legend* (1986)

I don't mind your being killed, but I object to your being taken prisoner.

EARL KITCHENER
to the Prince of Wales (later Edward VIII) when he asked to go to the Front in World War I, quoted in Viscount Esher *Journal* 18 Dec 1914

Klammer Franz (1953–). Austrian skier who won a record 35 World Cup downhill races between 1974 and 1985. Olympic gold medallist 1976. He was the combined world champion 1974, and the World Cup downhill champion 1975–78 and 1983.

Klaproth Martin Heinrich (1743–1817). German chemist who first identified the elements uranium and zirconium, in 1789. He was a pioneer of analytical chemistry.

Klaproth was born in Wernigerode, Saxony, apprenticed to an apothecary when he was 16, and in 1771 became manager of a pharmacy in Berlin. He lectured in chemistry at the Berlin School of Artillery from 1792, and when the University of Berlin was founded in 1810 he became its first professor of chemistry.

Klaproth distinguished strontia (strontium oxide) from baryta (barium oxide) and in 1795 rediscovered and named titanium. He isolated chromium in 1797 independently of French chemist Louis Vauquelin, but credited Franz Müller (1740–1825) with the priority for the discovery of tellurium, which Klaproth extracted in 1798 and named. In 1803, Klaproth identified cerium oxide and confirmed the existence of cerium, discovered by Swedish chemist Jöns Berzelius in the same year. He also studied the rare earth minerals.

Klaus Václav (1941–). Czech politician and economist, prime minister of the Czech Republic from 1993.

Klaus was born and educated in Prague and went on to hold a number of academic posts 1971–87. He became politically active in the events that led to the 'velvet revolution' in Czechoslovakia Nov 1989. He was federal finance minister in the government of Václav Havel and was then elected chair of Civic Forum Oct 1990. Moving to the right of the political spectrum, he established the Civic Democratic Party (CDP) 1991, as deputy prime minister. When the new independent republic was created, January 1993, Klaus became its first prime minister. The architect of Eastern Europe's most successful economic reform programme, he has been a keen promoter of membership of the European Union.

Standing at his appointed place, at the trunk of the tree, he does nothing other than gather and pass on what comes to him from the depths. He neither serves nor rules – he transmits … . And the beauty at the crown is not his own. He is merely a channel.

PAUL KLEE
On Modern Art 1948

Kitchener *British commander of forces and imperialist governor Lord Kitchener. As war minister during World War I, he was a source of inspiration to British soldiers, driving a successful recruitment campaign with the slogan 'Your country needs YOU'.* (Image Select)

Klee Paul (1879–1940). Swiss artist. He was one of the most original and prolific artists of the 20th century, painting over 760 panel paintings and 9,000 works. A talented violinist, he played for Berne Symphony Orchestra until 1906, when he settled in Munich, and joined the *Blaue Reiter* group 1912. He taught at the Bauhaus school of design 1921–31, when he took up a professorship at the Dusseldorf Art Academy, from which post he was dismissed by the Nazis 1933, when he returned to Switzerland. Endlessly inventive and playful, his many works are an exploration of the potential of line, plane, and colour. Suggesting a childlike innocence, they are based on the belief in a reality beyond appearances as in *Twittering Machine* 1922 (Museum of Modern Art, New York).

Klee travelled with the painter August Macke to Tunisia 1914, a trip that transformed his sense of colour. His influential views on art were presented in *Pedagogical Sketchbook* 1925. The Klee Foundation, Berne, has a large collection of his work. Other publications include *On Modern Art* 1948.

Suggested reading
Franciscono, M *Paul Klee: His Work and Thought* (1991)
Grohmann, W *Paul Klee* (1967)
Klee, Paul *Pedagogical Sketchbooks* (1944)
Klee, Paul *The Thinking Eye* (1961)
Lanchner, C (ed) *Paul Klee* (1987)
Lynton, N *Klee* (1975)

Klein Calvin Richard (1942–). US fashion designer. His collections are characterized by the smooth and understated, often in natural fabrics such as mohair, wool, and suede, in subtle colours. He set up his own business 1968, specializing in designing coats and suits, and expanded into sportswear in the mid-1970s. His designer jeans became a status symbol during the same period.

Klein (Christian) Felix (1849–1925). German mathematician and mathematical physicist who unified the various Euclidean and non-Euclidean geometries.

He was professor at Erlangen 1872–75, at the Technische Hochschule in Munich 1875–80, and then took up a similar post in Leipzig. From 1886 he was at Göttingen, and helped make it Germany's main centre for all the exact sciences.

Klein announced 1872 what he called the Erlangen *Programm* on the unification of geometries. He showed that each of the different geometries devised during the 19th century is associated with a separate 'collection', or 'group', of tranformations. Seen in this way, the geometries could all be treated as members of one family. In his work on number theory, group theory, and the theory of differential equations, Klein was greatly influenced by German mathematician Bernhard Riemann, and redefined a Riemann surface so that it came to be regarded as an essential part of function theory.

Klein initiated 1895 the writing of an encyclopedia of mathematics. He published books on the historical development of mathematics in the 19th century, and a textbook (with his colleague Arnold Sommerfeld) on the theory of the gyroscope.

Klein Melanie (born Reizes) (1882–1960). Austrian child psychoanalyst. She pioneered child psychoanalysis and play studies, and was influenced by Sigmund Freud's theories. She published *The Psychoanalysis of Children* 1960.

Klein intended to follow a medical career. She gave this up when she married, but after the birth of her three children became interested in psychoanalysis. In 1919 she published her first paper on the psychoanalysis of young children. She moved to London 1926, where the main part of her work was done. In 1934 Klein extended her study to adult patients, and her conclusions, based on her observations of infant and childhood anxiety, were published in her book *Envy and Gratitude* 1957.

Suggested reading
Grosskurth, P *Melanie Klein* (1987)
Klein, Melanie *Love, Guilt and Reparation, and Other Writings 1921-45* (1975)
Segal, Hanna *Introduction to the Work of Melanie Klein* (1979)

Klein Roland (1938–). French fashion designer, active in the UK from 1965. He opened his own-label shop 1979 and from 1991 designed menswear for the Japanese market.

Klein Yves (1928–1962). French painter and leading exponent of the Neo-Dada movement. He painted bold abstracts and devised provocative experimental works, including imprints of nude bodies.

Kleist (Bernd) Heinrich (Wilhelm) von (1777–1811). German dramatist. His comedy *Der zerbrochene Krug/The Broken Pitcher* 1808 (published 1812) and drama *Prinz Friedrich von Homburg/The Prince of Homburg* 1810 (published 1821) achieved success only after his suicide. His dominant themes are corruption, duty, and obsessional feelings.

Kleist entered the Prussian army at the age of 14, remaining for five years. His novella *Michael Kohlhaas* 1808 describes a righteous schoolmaster led to carry out robbery and murder for political ends. His tragedy *Penthesilea* 1808 has the love of the Amazon queen for the Greek warrior Achilles as its subject.

Kleist (Paul Ludwig) Ewald von (1881–1954). German field marshal. Commissioned into the cavalry 1902, he was a lieutenant-general by 1935 and retired 1938. He was recalled 1939 and given command of XXII Army Corps in Poland, then led Panzer Group Kleist in France 1940. He then led 1 Panzer Group in the Balkans and 1 Panzer Army in the invasion of the USSR. Promoted to field marshal Nov 1942, he commanded Army Group A in the Ukraine. He retired for the second time 30 March 1944, but when the Soviets occupied Germany he was captured and remained a prisoner until he died.

Klemperer Otto (1885–1973). German conductor. He was celebrated for his interpretation of contemporary and Classical music (especially Beethoven and Brahms). He conducted the Los Angeles Orchestra 1933–39 and the Philharmonia Orchestra, London, from 1959.

Kliegl John H (1869–1959) and Anton T (1872–1927). German-born US brothers who in 1911 invented the brilliant carbon-arc (klieg) lights used in television and films. They also created scenic effects for theatre and film. John emigrated to the USA 1888, Anton 1892, and in 1896 in New York they formed the Kliegl Brothers Universal Electric Stage Lighting Company.

Klimt Gustav (1862–1918). Austrian painter. He was influenced by Jugendstil (Art Nouveau) and Symbolism and was a founding member of the Vienna Sezession group 1897. His paintings have a jewelled effect similar to mosaics, for example *The Kiss* 1909 (Musée des Beaux-Arts, Strasbourg). His many portraits include *Judith I* 1901 (Österreichische Galerie, Vienna).

Suggested reading
Novotny, Fritz and Dobai, Johannes *Gustav Klimt* (trs 1968)
Partsche, Susanna *Gustav Klimt: Painter of Women* (1994)
Whitford, Frank *Klimt* (1990)

Kline Franz Joseph (1910–1962). US Abstract Expressionist painter. He created large, graphic compositions in black and white using angular forms, like magnified calligraphic brushstrokes. He did not introduce colour into his work until the late 1950s.

Klippel Roger (1920–). Australian contemporary sculptor noted for his junk sculpture. In the early 1950s his linear, flowing constructions influenced the development of Abstract painting in Australia.

Klopstock Friedrich Gottlieb (1724–1803). German poet. His religious epic *Der Messias/The Messiah* 1748–73 and *Oden/Odes* 1771 anticipated Romanticism.

He was born in Quedlinburg. In 1746 he moved to Leipzig, where he anonymously published the first three cantos of *Der Messias* in *Bremer Beiträge* 1748. Invited by Frederick V of Denmark, he lived in Copenhagen 1751–70 and was given an annuity to complete *Der Messias*. In 1775, he spent a year at the court of the margrave of Baden at Karlsruhe, and received a pension with which he retired to Hamburg for the rest of his life. His plays include *Der Tod Adams* 1757, *Salomo* 1764, *Hermanns Schlacht* 1769, and *Hermann und die Fürsten* 1784. His non-fiction concerning literature, philology, and the history of German poetry includes *Die Gelehrtenrepublik* 1774, *Fragmente über Sprache und Dichtkunst* 1779, and *Grammatische Gespräche* 1794.

Kluck (Heinrich Rudolph) Alexander von (1846–1934). German soldier. He commanded the German 1st Army which invaded Belgium at the start of World War I. After taking Brussels and outflanking Antwerp, he advanced on Mons, driving out the British army, and then advanced on Paris. He was attacked by the combined British and French armies in the Battle of the Marne Sept 1914 which led to a general retreat of the German line to the river Aisne where he made a successful stand. He was wounded at Soissons 1915 and retired 1916.

Kluge (Hans) Gunther von (1882–1944). German field marshal. He served in the invasions of Poland and France and was promoted to field marshal July 1940. He led the 4th Army in the invasion of the USSR, later succeeding von Bock as commander of Army Group Centre. He replaced von Rundstedt as commander in chief in the West July 1944, with orders to throw the Allies back into the sea. After the disaster at the Falaise Gap he was relieved and replaced by Model. He was caught up in the aftermath of the failed July Plot against Hitler, although not involved in it himself and was 'invited' to commit suicide.

Kneller Godfrey (born Gottfried Kniller) (1646–1723). German-born portrait painter who lived in England from 1674. He was court painter to Charles II, James II, William III, and George I. Among his paintings are the series *Hampton Court Beauties* (Hampton Court,

Richmond, Surrey, a sequel to Peter Lely's *Windsor Beauties*), and 48 portraits of the members of the Whig Kit Cat Club 1702–17 (National Portrait Gallery, London). He was knighted 1692 and made a baronet in 1715.

Knight Laura (born Johnson) (1877–1970). English painter. She focused on detailed, narrative scenes of Romany, fairground, and circus life, and the ballet. She was an official war artist during World War II. DBE 1929.

Knipper Lev Konstantinovich (1898–1974). Soviet composer. His early work shows the influence of Stravinsky, but after 1932 he wrote in a more popular idiom, as in the symphony *Poem of Komsomol Fighters* 1933–34 with its mass battle songs. He is known in the West for his song 'Cavalry of the Steppes'.

Knopf Eleanora Frances (born Bliss) (1883–1974). US geologist who studied metamorphic rocks.

She spent most of her career working for the US Geological Survey. During the 1930s she was also a visiting lecturer at Yale and at Harvard.

In 1913 in Pennsylvania, she discovered the mineral glaucophane, previously unsighted in America east of the Pacific. In the 1920s Knopf studied the Pennsylvania and Maryland piedmont and the geologically complex mountain region along the New York–Connecticut border.

She introduced the technique of petrofabrics to the USA. The technique had been developed in Austria at Innsbruck University. Knopf applied it to the study of metamorphic rocks and wrote about it in *Structural Petrology* 1938.

The First Blast of the Trumpet Against the Monstrous Regiment of Women.

JOHN KNOX
Pamphlet title 1558

Knox John (*c.* 1505–1572). Scottish Protestant reformer, founder of the Church of Scotland. He spent several years in exile for his beliefs, including a period in Geneva where he met John Calvin.

Originally a Roman Catholic priest, Knox is thought to have been converted by the reformer George Wishart. When Wishart was burned for heresy, Knox went into hiding, but later preached the reformed doctrines.

Captured by French troops in Scotland 1547, he was imprisoned in France, sentenced to the galleys, and released only by the intercession of the British government 1549. In England he assisted in compiling the Prayer Book, as a royal chaplain from 1551. On Mary's accession 1553 he fled the country and in 1557 was, in his absence, condemned to be burned. In 1559 he returned to Scotland. He was tried for treason but acquitted 1563. He wrote a *History of the Reformation in Scotland* 1586 and *First Blast of the Trumpet Against the Monstrous Regiment of Women* 1558.

Suggested reading

Reid, W S *Trumpeter of God: A Biography of John Knox* (1974)

Ridley, Jasper *John Knox* (1968)

Smith, G B and Martin, D *John Knox: Apostle of the Scottish Reformation* (1982)

Knox Ronald Arbuthnott (1888–1957). British Roman Catholic scholar whose translation of the Bible 1945–49 was officially approved by the Roman Catholic Church. He became Anglican chaplain to the University of Oxford on his ordination 1912, but resigned 1917 on his conversion, and was Catholic chaplain 1926–39.

There once was a man who said, 'God / Must think it exceedingly odd / If he finds that this tree / Continues to be / When there's no one about in the Quad.'

RONALD KNOX
quoted in Langford Reed *Complete Limerick Book* 1924

Koch Ed(ward Irving) (1924–   ). US politician, mayor of the city of New York 1979–89. A Democrat, he was a member of Congress 1969–79. As mayor, he faced a budget deficit and the deterioration of the inner city. He handled these problems skilfully and saved the city from bankruptcy. Defeated as a mayoral candidate 1989, he returned to his law practice.

Koch was born in New York City, the son of Polish Jewish immigrants. He practised as a lawyer 1949–69, helping to found a Wall Street law firm, before being elected to the House of Representatives, serving five terms. His books include *His Eminence and Hizzoner* 1989, *All the Best, Letters from a Feisty Mayor* 1990, *Citizen Koch* 1992, and *Ed Koch on Everything* 1994.

Koch (Heinrich Hermann) Robert (1843–1910). German bacteriologist. Koch and his assistants devised the techniques for culturing bacteria outside the body, and formulated the rules for showing whether or not a bacterium is the cause of a disease. Nobel Prize for Physiology or Medicine 1905. His techniques enabled him to identify the bacteria responsible for tuberculosis (1882), cholera (1883), and other diseases. He investigated anthrax bacteria in the 1870s and showed that they form spores which spread the infection. Koch also showed that rats are vectors of bubonic plague and that sleeping sickness is transmitted by the tsetse fly.

Koch was born near Hanover and studied at Göttingen. He began research in the 1870s while working as a district medical officer. In 1879 he was appointed to the Imperial Health Office in Berlin to advise on hygiene and public health. He was professor at Berlin 1885–91, when he became director of the newly established Institute for Infectious Diseases, but he resigned 1904 and spent much of the rest of his life advising foreign countries on ways to combat various diseases.

Koch, Robert German physician and pioneer bacteriologist Robert Koch, who recieved the Nobel Prize for Physiology or Medicine 1905 for his work on tuberculosis. Koch identified and isolated the cholera germ and showed that the tsetse fly was the carrier of sleeping sickness. He also formulated a series of systematic principles, 'Koch postulates', for analysing and identifying new infectious diseases that are still used today. (Image Select)

Suggested reading
Knight, David *Robert Koch: Father of Bacteriology* (1961)
Reid, Robert *Microbes and Men* (1975)

Kodály Zoltán (1882–1967). Hungarian composer and educationist. With Béla Bartók, he recorded and transcribed Magyar folk music, the scales and rhythm of which he incorporated in a deliberately nationalist style. His works include the cantata *Psalmus Hungaricus* 1923, a comic opera *Háry János* 1925–27, and orchestral dances and variations. His 'Kodály method' of school music education is widely practised.

There must be a strenuous attempt to replace music that comes from the fingers and the mechanical playing of instruments with music that comes from the soul and is based on singing.

ZOLTÁN KODÁLY
Fifty-five Two-part Exercises 1954

Koenig Marie-Pierre Joseph Francis (1898–1970). French general. He fought in Norway and France 1940 then escaped to the UK to join de Gaulle. He commanded the French Brigade in the Libyan desert, defending Bir Hachiem before being evicted by Rommel 1942. He later served on Eisenhower's staff to co-ordinate the French resistance with the invasion 1944 and after 6 June took command of the French Forces of the Interior. After the surrender of Paris he became military governor of the city and commanded the French forces of occupation in Germany 1945–49.

Koestler Arthur (1905–1983). Hungarian-born British writer. Imprisoned by the Nazis in France 1940, he escaped to England. His novel *Darkness at Noon* 1940, regarded as his masterpiece, is a fictional account of the Stalinist purges, and draws on his experiences as a prisoner under sentence of death during the Spanish Civil War. He also wrote extensively about creativity, science, parapsychology, politics, and culture.

Koestler's other novels include *Thieves in the Night* 1946, *The Lotus and the Robot* 1960, and *The Call Girls* 1972. His nonfiction includes *The Yogi and the Commissar* 1945, *The Sleepwalkers* 1959, *The Act of Creation* 1964, *The Ghost in the Machine* 1967, *The Roots of Coincidence* 1972, *The Heel of Achilles* 1974, and *The Thirteenth Tribe* 1976. Autobiographical works include *Arrow in the Blue* 1952 and *The Invisible Writing* 1954. He was a member of the Voluntary Euthanasia Society and committed suicide with his wife after suffering for a long time from Parkinson's disease.

Koestler was born in Budapest and educated as an engineer in Vienna, Austria; he then became a journalist in Palestine and the USSR. He joined the Communist Party in Berlin 1931, but left it 1938 (he recounts his disillusionment with communism in *The God That Failed* 1950). His account of being held by the Nazis is contained in *Scum of the Earth* 1941. He endowed Britain's first chair of parapsychology at Edinburgh, established 1984.

Suggested reading
Calder, Jenni *Chronicles of Conscience* (1968)
Hamilton, Iain *Koestler: A Life* (1982)
Harris, H (ed) *Astride Two Cultures: Arthur Koestler at Seventy* (1975)
Inglis, Brian *Arthur Koestler and Parapsychology* (1984)
Koestler, Arthur *Spanish Testament* (1937) *Arrow in the Blue* (1952)
  The Invisible Writing (1954) (autobiographies)
Mikes, George *Arthur Koestler* (1983)

Koga Mineichi (1885–1943). Japanese admiral of World War II. He succeeded Yamamoto as commander in chief of the Japanese fleet 1943 and followed the same policy of defending the Pacific islands. He frequently suffered defeats at the hands of the US fleets, particularly at Rabaul 1943. He eventually moved to Singapore with the intention of assembling the Japanese fleet there for a final battle with the US fleet, but was killed in an aircraft accident March 1944.

Kohl Helmut (1930–). German conservative politician, leader of the Christian Democratic Union (CDU) from 1976, West German chancellor (prime minister) 1982–90. He oversaw the reunification of East and West Germany 1989–90 and in 1990 won a resounding victory to become the first chancellor of reunited Germany. His miscalculation of the true costs of reunification and their subsequent effects on the German economy led to a dramatic fall in his popularity, but as the economy recovered, so did his public esteem, enabling him to achieve a historic fourth electoral victory 1994.

Kohl studied law and history before entering the chemical industry. Elected to the Rhineland-Palatinate *Land* (state) parliament 1959, he became state premier 1969. After the 1976 Bundestag (federal parliament) elections Kohl led the CDU in opposition. He became federal chancellor 1982, when the Free Democratic Party (FDP) withdrew support from the socialist Schmidt government, and was elected at the head of a new coalition that included the FDP. From 1984 Kohl was implicated in the Flick bribes scandal over the illegal business funding of political parties, but he was cleared of all charges 1986, and was re-elected chancellor Jan 1987, Dec 1990, and Oct 1994.

Köhler Georges Jean Franz (1946–1995). German immunologist who helped revolutionize medical research through the development of monoclonal antibodies, for which he shared the 1984 Nobel Prize for Physiology or Medicine.

Köhler was born in Munich and educated at Freiburg University. In 1971 he moved to the Basel Institute in Switzerland, where he gained his PhD and began to develop his interest in antibodies and their production as part of the normal immune response. In particular, he became fascinated with the enormous range of antibodies a single animal can produce.

Köhler moved to Cambridge, England 1974 where he began his collaboration with Milstein. Within a year, the work for which they were to share the Nobel prize had been completed. Köhler revolutionized the method by which antibodies for research were produced, a process which had previously been slow and unreliable, and requiring large numbers of animals. He took lymphocytes from an immunized mouse and fused them to tumour cells, resulting in a limitless population of cloned cells that could produce a pure 'monoclonal' antibody of known specificity.

By 1980 the monoclonal antibody technique was being used in laboratories around the world. In 1985 Köhler became director of the Max Planck Institute for Immune Biology, in Freiburg, where he continued his research until his death.

Köhler Wolfgang (1887–1967). Estonian-born German psychologist, cofounder with Max Wertheimer and Kurt Koffka (1886–1941) of the Gestalt school of psychology. Based on his study of the behaviour of apes in a colony on Tenerife, he developed the controversial hypothesis that problem-solving is dependent on a process of insight – a concept central to Gestalt theory – rather than on trial-and-error learning, as was more commonly believed. He published his experiments and observations from this period in *The Mentality of Apes* 1925.

Köhler was appointed to the chair of psychology at Berlin 1921, largely on the basis of work done in the field of physics – which he believed to be vital to the future of psychology – but emigrated to the USA 1934. Other important works inspired by Gestalt principles include *Gestalt Psychology* 1929, *The Place of Value in the World of Facts* 1938, and *Dynamics in Psychology* 1940.

Koivisto Mauno Henrik (1923–). Finnish politician, prime minister 1968–70 and 1979–82, and president 1982–94. He was finance minister 1966–67 and led a Social Democratic Party coalition as prime minister 1968–70. He became interim president 1981 after the resignation of Urho Kekkonen, and was elected president the following year. As president he shared power with Centre Party prime minister Esko Aho in Finland's unusual 'dual executive'.

Kok Wim (1938–). Dutch trade unionist and politician, leader of the Labour Party (PvdA) and prime minister from 1994. After an inconclusive general election May 1994, Kok eventually succeeded in forming a broad-based three-party coalition of the PvdA with the People's Party of Freedom and Democracy (VVD) and Democrats 66, both centrist parties.

Kok spent over 20 years in the trade union movement before winning a parliamentary seat for the PvdA 1986. He became its leader and served as deputy prime minister 1989–94 in the centre-left coalition of Ruud Lubbers, before accepting the challenge of succeeding him.

Kokhba Bar. Adopted name of Simeon bar Koziba (lived 2nd century AD). Hebrew leader of the revolt against the Hellenization campaign of Emperor Hadrian 132–35, when Palestine was a province of the Roman Empire. The uprising resulted in the razing of Jerusalem and Kokhba's death in battle.

Kokoschka Oskar (1886–1980). Austrian Expressionist painter and writer who lived in England from 1938. Initially influenced by the Vienna Sezession painters, he painted vivid seascapes and highly charged portraits. His writings include several plays.

He studied at the School of Arts and Crafts in Vienna, went to Berlin 1907 and then travelled to Switzerland and Italy. A strong prejudice against formal and academic rules already appeared in his work, and after World War I, in which he was wounded, he violently conveyed in pictures and writings a sense of human suffering and cruelty. This Expressionism led eventually to his being banned by the Nazis. Before that he had spent a period as a teacher at Dresden, 1920–24, and in Mediterranean travel. He moved to Vienna 1931, to Prague 1934, and to London 1938, becoming a naturalized British subject 1947. He later lived in Switzerland. In portraits, landscape and still life he showed a restless and romantic vigour. *The Tempest*, 1914 (Basel, Kunstmuseum), is a notable work, and his views of the Thames are outstanding among modern landscapes.
Suggested reading
Gombrich, E H *Homage to Kokoschka* (1984)
Hodin, J P *Kokoschka* (1966)
Kokoschka, Oskar *My Life* (trs 1974)
Whitford, Frank *Oskar Kokoschka* (1986)

Kolbe (Adolf Wilhelm) Hermann (1818–1884). German chemist, generally regarded as the founder of modern organic chemistry with his synthesis of acetic acid (ethanoic acid) – an organic compound – from inorganic starting materials. (Previously organic chemistry had been devoted to compounds that occur only in living organisms.)

Kolbe was born near Göttingen and educated there. He worked in the UK 1845–47, at the London School of Mines. In 1851 he was appointed professor at Marburg; by 1865 he had moved to Leipzig and had begun to set up the largest and best-equipped laboratory of the time.

Kolchak Alexander Vasilievich (1874–1920). Russian admiral, commander of the White forces in Siberia after the Russian Revolution. In 1914 he was rear-admiral of the Black Sea fleet and was appointed vice-admiral 1916. In June 1917 his sailors mutinied in Sevastopol and arrested him, together with most of his officers, only releasing him when he resigned his post. In the winter of 1917 he organized a force of White Russians in E Siberia and established an anti-Bolshevik government in Omsk 1918. In 1918–19, at the head of a sizeable army, he marched west to the Urals and inflicted defeats on several Bolshevik forces, but late in 1919 he was captured by Bolsheviks at Irkutsk and shot 7 Feb 1920.

Koller Carl (1857–1944). Austrian ophthalmologist who introduced local anaesthesia 1884, using cocaine. When psychoanalyst Sigmund Freud discovered the painkilling properties of cocaine, Koller recognized its potential as a local anaesthetic. He carried out early experiments on animals and on himself, and the technique quickly became standard in ophthalmology, dentistry, and other areas in cases where general anaesthesia exposes the patient to needless risk.

Kollontai Alexandra Mikhailovna (born Domontovich) (1872–1952). Russian revolutionary, politician, and writer.

In 1896, while on a tour of a large textile factory, she saw the appalling conditions endured by factory workers in Russia. Thereafter she devoted herself to improving conditions for working women. In 1905 she published *On the Question of the Class Struggle.*

She was harassed by the police for her views and went into exile in Germany 1914. On her return to the USSR 1917 she joined the Bolsheviks, and, as commissar for public welfare, was the only female member of the first Bolshevik government. She campaigned for domestic reforms such as acceptance of free love, simplification of divorce laws, and collective child care. She toured the USA to argue against its involvement in World War I and organized the first all-Russian Congress of Working and Peasant Women 1918. In 1923 she published *The Love of Worker Bees,* a collection of short stories. She was sent abroad by Stalin, first as trade minister, then as ambassador to Sweden 1943. Kollontai took part in the armistice negotiations ending the Soviet-Finnish War 1944.
Suggested reading
Clements, Barbara *Bolshevik Feminist* (1979)
Kollontai, Alexandra *Autobiography of a Sexually Emancipated Woman* (trs 1972)
Porter, C *Alexandra Kollontai* (1981)

Kollwitz Käthe (born Schmidt) (1867–1945). German graphic artist and sculptor, noted for the powerful drawings, woodcuts, etchings and lithographs in which she expressed proletarian and pacifist sympathies. Her father, Karl Schmidt, was an ardent radical, and her husband, Dr Karl Kollwitz, worked among the poor of Berlin, both influencing the trend of her thought and the subject matter of her art. Among her principal works were the *Peasants' War* series, 1902–08, and her poster *Never Again War* after World War I.

Both the Kaiser Government and the Nazis regarded her with suspicion. Her house in Berlin was hit in the bombing of 1943 and much of her work was then destroyed, though a number of drawings have found their way into American collections.
Suggested reading
Keans, M *Käthe Kollwitz: Woman and Artist* (1976)
Klein, M D *Käthe Kollwitz: Life in Art* (1972)

Komensky Jan Amos, known as Comenius (1592–1670). Moravian pastor and educationist. He believed that a universal Christian brotherhood could be achieved through the improvement of education. He thought that understanding and not coercion was the key to learning and that teaching should build on the sense experiences of the child. His major work *Didactica Magna/The Great Didactic* 1657 had a lasting influence throughout Europe.
Suggested reading
Sadler, J (ed) *Comenius* (1969)

Kondo Nobutaki (1856–1953). Japanese admiral of World War II. Kondo was the commander of the Southern Sea Force which sank the British battleships *Prince of Wales* and *Repulse* off the coast of Malaya 10 Dec 1941. He took part in the Battle of Midway 1942, though he withdrew without engaging the US fleet, and was also involved in the naval battles off Guadalcanal and in the Battle of the Eastern Solomons.

Kong Zi Pinyin form of ◊Confucius, Chinese philosopher.

Koniev Ivan Stepanovich (1898–1973). Soviet marshal who in World War II liberated Ukraine from the invading German forces 1943–44 and then 1945 advanced from the south to Berlin to link up with the British-US forces. He commanded all Warsaw Pact forces 1955–60.

Konoe Fumimaro, Prince (1891–1946). Japanese politician and prime minister 1937–39 and 1940–41. Entering politics in the 1920s, Konoe was active in trying to curb the power of the army in government and preventing an escalation of the war with China. He helped to engineer the fall of the Tōjō government 1944 but committed suicide after being suspected of war crimes.

Koolhaas Rem (1934–). Dutch architect, a Post-Modernist. His work includes Eurolille (railway station, conference, and exhibition centre), Lille, France, 1994; the National Dance Theatre, The Hague, Netherlands, 1987; and the Kunsthal (art gallery) in Rotterdam, Netherlands, 1992.

Koolhaas was born in Amsterdam and studied in the UK at the Architectural Association in London, where he was influenced by the Archigram group. He became professor at Harvard in the USA and set up a practice in Rotterdam, the Office of Metropolitan Architecture. He has published *Delirious New York* 1978, and *S, M, L, XL* 1995.

Korbut Olga Valentinovna (1955–). Soviet gymnast who attracted world attention at the 1972 Olympic Games with her lively floor routine, winning three gold medals for the team, beam, and floor exercises.

Korda Alexander Laszlo (1893–1956). Hungarian-born British film producer and director. He was a dominant figure in the British film industry during the 1930s and 1940s. His films include *The Private Life of Henry VIII* 1933, *The Third Man* 1949, and *Richard III* 1956. Knighted 1942.

Koresh David. Adopted name of Vernon Wayne Howell (1959–1993). US Christian religious leader of the Branch Davidians, an offshoot of the Seventh-Day Adventist Church that believes in the literal apocalyptic end of history, as described in the biblical Book of Revelation, prior to the second coming of Christ. With a number of co-religionists, he died in a fire at the cult's headquarters in Waco, Texas, as a result of military intervention.

Kōrin Ogata (*c.* 1660–1716). Japanese artist; see ◊Ogata.

Kornberg Arthur (1918–). US biochemist. He discovered the enzyme DNA-polymerase 1956, which enabled molecules of the genetic material DNA to be synthesized for the first time. For this work he shared the 1959 Nobel Prize for Physiology or Medicine. By 1967 he had synthesized a biologically active artificial viral DNA.

He held senior appointments at the Washington University School of Medicine (1953) and the Stamford University School of Medicine, Palo Alto, California (1959), before becoming head of the Biochemistry Department at Stamford.

Kornberg Hans Leo (1928–). German-born British biochemist who investigated metabolic pathways and their regulation, especially in microorganisms. He studied the way in which the cellular economy is balanced to prevent overproduction or waste, and introduced the concept of anaplerotic reactions, whereby metabolic processes are maintained by special enzymes that replenish materials syphoned off for anabolic purposes. Knighted 1978.

Kornberg was born in Herford, Westphalia, and went to Britain in 1939 as a refugee from Nazi persecution. He studied at Sheffield under biochemist Hans Krebs, and in the USA at Yale and the University of California. On his return to the UK he joined the Medical Research Council Cell Metabolism Unit headed by Krebs in Oxford. In 1960 he became professor at Leicester, and in 1975 at Cambridge.

There was a review by Irving Kolodin which noted that Korngold's Violin Concerto had more corn than gold.

Nicolas Slonimsky on ERICH KORNGOLD
in *A Thing or Two About Music*, 1948

Korngold Erich Wolfgang (1897–1957). Austrian-born US composer. He began composing while still in his teens and achieved early recognition when his opera *Die tote Stadt/Dead City* was premiered simultaneously in Hamburg and Cologne 1920. In 1934 he moved to Hollywood to become a composer for Warner Brothers. His film scores, in richly orchestrated and romantic style, include *The Adventures of Robin Hood* 1938 and *Of Human Bondage* 1945.

Kornilov Lavr Georgyevich (1870–1918). Russian general, commander in chief of the army, who in Aug 1917 launched an attempted coup, backed by officers, against the revolutionary prime minister, Kerensky. The coup failed, but brought down the provisional government, clearing the way for the Bolsheviks to seize power.

Korolev Sergei Pavlovich (1906–1966). Russian designer of the first Soviet intercontinental missile, used to launch the first Sputnik satellite 1957 and the Vostok spacecraft, also designed by Korolev, in which Yuri Gagarin made the world's first space flight 1961.

Korolev and his research team built the first Soviet liquid-fuel rocket, launched 1933. His innovations in rocket and space technology include ballistic missiles, rockets for geophysical research, launch vehicles, and crewed spacecraft. Korolev was also responsible for the *Voskhod* spaceship, from which the first space walks were made.

Korolev was born in Zhitomir, Ukraine, and trained as an aircraft designer. He was a member of the Institute for Jet Research from its foundation 1933, and worked as an engine designer 1924–46. Later he was appointed head of the large team of scientists who developed high-powered rocket systems.

Korsch Karl (1886–1961). German Marxist philosopher. In *Marxism and Philosophy* 1923 he argued against the dialectical materialism of Friedrich Engels. Always critical of the Soviet variety of Marxism, Korsch also criticized, in *Karl Marx* 1938, the early, or 'Hegelian', Marxism of Theodor Adorno and Herbert Marcuse. Korsch believed that the wellbeing of theory and practice depended on the continued reinterpretation of Marxism. His 'ultra-leftism' led to his expulsion from the Communist Party 1926.

He studied at the University of Jena and taught philosophy there until the Nazis came to power, when he emigrated to the USA. He returned to Europe 1950 and lectured in Germany and Switzerland.

Kościuszko Tadeusz Andrzej (1746–1817). Polish general and nationalist who served with George Washington in the American Revolution (1776–83). He returned to Poland 1784, fought against the Russian invasion that ended in the partition of Poland, and withdrew to Saxony. He returned 1794 to lead the revolt against the occupation, but was defeated by combined Russian and Prussian forces and imprisoned until 1796.

Kosinski Jerzy Nikodem (1933–1991). Polish-born US author, in the USA from 1957. His childhood experiences as a Jew in Poland during World War II are recounted in *The Painted Bird* 1965, a popular success. The novel that established his cult status, the comic media satire *Being There* 1971 (filmed 1979), was followed by increasingly violent works such as *The Devil Tree* 1974, *Pinball* 1982, and *The Hermit of 69th Street* 1987.

Despotism and oppression never yet were beaten except by heroic resistance.

LAJOS KOSSUTH
Speech on landing in the USA, Staten Island 5 Dec 1851

Kossuth Lajos (1802–1894). Hungarian nationalist and leader of the revolution of 1848. He proclaimed Hungary's independence of Habsburg rule, became governor of a Hungarian republic 1849, and, when it was defeated by Austria and Russia, fled first to Turkey and then to exile in Britain and Italy.

Suggested reading
Deak, Istvan *The Lawful Revolution* (1979)
Headley, P C *Kossuth* (1971)
Lengyel, Emil *Lajos Kossuth: Hungary's Great Patriot* (1969)

An able, hard, hard-working but unimaginative official ... very much afraid of his own inadequacies if he went outside his brief.

George Brown on KOSYGIN
in *In My Way* 1970

Kosygin Alexei Nikolaievich (1904–1980). Soviet politician, prime minister 1964–80. He was elected to the Supreme Soviet 1938, became a member of the Politburo 1946, deputy prime minister 1960, and succeeded Khrushchev as premier (while Brezhnev succeeded him as party secretary). In the late 1960s Kosygin's influence declined.

Kosztolányi Deszö (1885–1936). Hungarian poet, novelist, and critic. He was associated with the literary magazine *Nyugat/The*

West, founded 1908, but unlike others in that circle he was more interested in aesthetic than social questions. His sympathetic observation of human weakness is apparent in his poem cycle *A szegeny kisgyermek panaszai/The Complaints of a Poor Little Child* 1910 and his novel *Edes Anna/Wonder Maid* 1926, a tale of a servant girl.

Koudelka Josef (1939–). Czech photographer. He is best known for his photographs of East European gypsies whose vanishing way of life he has recorded. He also photographed the Russian invasion of Czechoslovakia 1968 and the inauguration of Václav Havel as president of Czechoslovakia 1989.

Ven my stick touches the air, you play.

> SERGE KOUSSEVITSKY
> quoted in Charles N Gattey *Peacocks on the Podium* 1982

Koussevitsky Serge (1874–1951). Russian musician and conductor. He is well known for his work in the USA. He established his own orchestra in Moscow 1909, introducing works by Prokofiev, Rachmaninov, and Stravinsky. Although named director of the State Symphony after the Bolshevik Revolution 1917, Koussevitsky left the USSR for the USA, becoming director of the Boston Symphony Orchestra 1924.

Koussevitsky was trained at a conservatory in Moscow, becoming a recognized virtuoso on the double bass. He first appeared as a conductor in Berlin 1908. In 1934 he founded the annual Tanglewood summer music festival in W Massachusetts.

Kovac Michal (1930–). Slovak politician, president from 1993, when Czechoslovakia split in two to become the Czech and Slovak republics. He was known to favour some confederal arrangement with the Czech Republic and, in consequence, his election was welcomed by the Czech government.

After a career as an academic economist and banker, he served as Slovak minister of finance in the post-communist administration between 1989 and 1991. A member of the centre-left nationalist Movement for a Democratic Slovakia (HZDS), he was the speaker of Czechoslovakia's federal assembly from 1992 and, after the 'velvet divorce' of Jan 1993, became the Slovak Republic's first president. Immediately after his election as president Kovac said he would resign his membership of the HZDS 'as a signal that we are ready to put the general interests of the country above partisan interests'. During 1995 Kovac's relations with Vladimir Meciar became strained over allegations of Meciar's intent to oust him.

Kovalevskaia Sofya Vasilevna (1850–1891). Russian mathematician and novelist who worked on partial differential equations and Abelian integrals. In 1886 she won the Prix Bordin of the French Academy of Sciences for a paper on the rotation of a rigid body about a point, a problem the 18th-century mathematicians Euler and Lagrange had both failed to solve.

She was born in Moscow and studied in Germany at Heidelberg, Berlin, and Göttingen. Excluded from most European academic posts because of her sex, she finally obtained a lectureship in Sweden and became professor at Stockholm 1889. In addition to her mathematical work, she wrote plays and novels, including *Vera Brantzova* 1895.

Krafft-Ebing Richard, Baron von (1840–1902). German pioneer psychiatrist and neurologist. He published *Psychopathia Sexualis* 1886.

Educated in Germany, Krafft-Ebing became professor of psychiatry at Strasbourg 1872. His special study was the little-understood relationship between minor paralysis and syphilis, a sexually transmitted disease. In 1897 he performed an experiment which conclusively showed that his paralysed patients must previously have been infected with syphilis. He also carried out a far-reaching study of sexual behaviour.

Kramer Josef (1907–1945). German SS officer, commandant of Belsen concentration camp Nov 1944 until its liberation by British

troops April 1945. Film of the camp shocked cinema audiences across Britain and the USA and Kramer was named the 'Beast of Belsen'. He was convicted of war crimes at Nuremberg and was hanged.

A concentration camp guard from 1932, he gradually worked his way up, commanding at Natzweiler, where he inaugurated the first gas chambers, then at Auschwitz May 1944, before finally becoming commandant at Belsen.

Krasiński Zygmunt Hrabia (1812–1859). Polish dramatist and Romantic poet. He lived and wrote in exile but his messianic vision of Polish sacrifice and resurrection in poems such as 'Przedświt/The Moment Before Dawn' 1843 inspired his countrymen.

Kravchuk Leonid (1934–). Ukrainian politician, president 1990–94. Formerly a member of the Ukrainian Communist Party (UCP), he became its ideology chief in the 1980s. After the suspension of the UCP Aug 1991, Kravchuk became an advocate of independence and market-centred economic reform. Faced with a rapidly deteriorating economic situation 1993, he assumed direct control of government, eliminating the post of prime minister. He was, however, defeated by former prime minister Leonid Kuchma in the July 1994 presidential elections.

Krebs Hans Adolf (1900–1981). German-born British biochemist who discovered the citric acid cycle, also known as the Krebs cycle, the final pathway by which food molecules are converted into energy in living tissues. For this work he shared the 1953 Nobel Prize for Physiology or Medicine. Knighted 1958.

Krebs first became interested in the process by which the body degrades amino acids. He discovered that nitrogen atoms are the first to be removed (deamination) and are then excreted as urea in the urine. Krebs then investigated the processes involved in the production of urea from the removed nitrogen atoms, and by 1932 he had worked out the basic steps in the urea cycle.

Krebs was born in Hildesheim and studied at the universities of Göttingen, Freiburg, Munich, Berlin, and Hamburg. In 1933, with the rise to power of the Nazis, he moved to the UK, initially to Cambridge and in 1935 to Sheffield. He was professor at Sheffield 1945–54, and at Oxford 1954–67.

Kreisler plays as the thrush sings in Thomas Hardy's poem, hardly conscious of his own lovely significance.

> Neville Cardus on FRITZ KREISLER
> in *The Delights of Music* 1966

Kreisler Fritz (1875–1962). Austrian violinist and composer. He was a US citizen from 1943. His prolific output of recordings in the early 20th century introduced a wider public to classical music from old masters such as J S Bach and Couperin to moderns such as de Falla and Rachmaninov. He also composed and recorded romantic pieces in the style of the classics, often under a pseudonym. He gave the first performance of Elgar's Violin Concerto 1910, dedicated to him by the composer.

Krenek Ernst (1900–). Austrian-born US composer and theorist. Following early popular success with jazz-influenced operas *Jonny spielt auf/Johnny Strikes Up* 1926 and *Leben des Orest/Life of Orestes* 1930, he supported himself as a critic while working on the ambitious twelve-tone opera *Karl V/Charles V* 1938. He moved to teaching posts in the USA 1939 but remained in contact with postwar developments in extended serialism and aleatoric music with *Quaestio Temporis/In Search of Time* 1957, and with electronic music in *Spiritus intelligentiae sanctus* 1956. His writings include the study *Johannes Ockeghem* 1953 and *Horizon Circled* 1974.

Krenz Egon (1937–). East German communist politician. A member of the East German Socialist Unity Party (SED) from 1955, he joined its politburo 1983 and was a hardline protégé of Erich Honecker, succeeding him as party leader and head of state 1989 after widespread prodemocracy demonstrations. Pledging a 'new course', Krenz opened the country's western border and promised more open elections, but his conversion to pluralism proved weak in the face of popular protest and he resigned Dec 1989 after only a few weeks as party general secretary and head of state. In 1995 he was charged in connection with the deaths of East Germans who had attempted to flee to the West during the period of communist rule.

To my knowledge I am the only composer of my generation who has thoroughly and consistently practiced what is called 'serialism', and I have been blamed (a) for doing it at all, (b) for doing it too late, and (c) for still being at it.

ERNST KRENEK
Horizons Circled 1974

Kretschmer Otto (1912–). German U-boat commander; highly successful, he was awarded the Knights Cross for sinking seven ships on a single patrol. He is generally credited with sinking about 300,000 tons of Allied shipping in 18 months of patrolling until he was trapped by British destroyers 27 March 1941. He scuttled his boat and both he and his crew were taken prisoner.

Kreutzer Rodolphe (1766–1831). French violinist and composer of German descent. Beethoven dedicated his violin sonata Opus 47 to him, known as the *Kreutzer* Sonata.

Krier Leon (1946–). Luxembourg architect who settled in Britain 1968. He has built little but his anti-Modernist arguments have helped to revive vernacular traditions and 19th-century Neo-Classicism. From 1968 to 1970 Krier assisted James Stirling with significant projects such as the Derby Civic Centre 1970 competition. Prince Charles commissioned him 1988 to design a model village, Poundbury, adjoining Dorchester, Dorset.

Kristeva Julia (1941–). Bulgarian-born French psychoanalyst and literary theorist. Drawing on Freudian psychoanalysis and structuralist linguistics, she has analysed the relationship between language, society, and the self. In *Semeiotiké* 1969 she argues that the self is not a stable, autonomous entity, but the product of language.

Consequently, those elements that are repressed in the well-ordered language of bourgeois society (the 'dominant social discourse') become the repressed elements (the unconscious) of the self. She examines the political and cultural implications of this position in *The Revolution in Poetic Language* 1974, in which she claims that poetry is essentially an expression of the irrational, of those repressed elements that form the unconscious. Poetry (and such disruptors as laughter and pleasure) challenges the order, rationality, and repressive control of the dominant social discourse, and so shows that revolution is possible at both the personal and political level.

Polylogue 1977 and *Love Stories* 1983 express her growing interest in the relationship between language, the body, and the limits of personal identity with her analyses of sexuality and the 'feminine' becoming an important part of feminist debates. Among her more accessible books are *About Chinese Women* 1974, a feminist study of the Cultural Revolution, and *Les Samourais* 1991, a novel containing thinly disguised portraits of several figures who have recently dominated French intellectual life.

Kristiansen Ingrid (1956–). Norwegian athlete, an outstanding long-distance runner of 5,000 metres, 10,000 metres, marathon, and cross-country races. She has won all the world's leading marathons. In 1986 she knocked 45.68 seconds off the world 10,000 metres record. She was the world cross-country champion 1988 and won the London marathon 1984–85 and 1987–88.

Kroeber Alfred Louis (1876–1960). US anthropologist. His extensive research into and analysis of the culture of California,

Plains, Mexican, and South American Indians dramatically broadened the scope of anthropological studies. His textbook *Anthropology* 1923 remains a classic and influential work.

Born in Hoboken, New Jersey, USA, Kroeber was the first student of Franz Boas to receive a PhD from Columbia University 1901. After establishing a department of anthropology at the University of California at Berkeley, he led archaeological expeditions to New Mexico beginning 1915.

Kroger Helen. Adopted name of Leoninta Cohen (1913–1992). Communist sympathizer and Soviet spy. Convicted in the UK of espionage 1961, with her husband Morris Cohen, she was imprisoned and then released eight years later in a spy-swap deal, allowing her and her husband to settle in Moscow.

God made the integers, man made the rest.

LEOPOLD KRONECKER
Jahresberichte der deutschen Mathematiker Vereinigung
bk 2 in F Cajori *A History of Mathematics* 1919

Kronecker Leopold (1823–1891). German mathematician who devised the Kronecker delta in linear algebra. He attempted to unify analysis, algebra, and elliptical functions.

Kronecker was born at Liegnitz (now Legnica, Poland), and studied at Berlin, Bonn, and Breslau. Financially independent, he devoted himself to research and lectured at Berlin from 1861. In 1883 he became professor there.

Kronecker was obsessed with the idea that all branches of mathematics (apart from geometry and mechanics) should be treated as parts of arithmetic. He also believed that whole numbers were sufficient for the study of mathematics. Kronecker published a system of axioms 1870, later shown to govern finite Abelian groups.

Kropotkin Peter Alexeivich, Prince Kropotkin (1842–1921). Russian anarchist. Imprisoned for revolutionary activities 1874, he escaped to the UK 1876 and later moved to Switzerland. In 1879 he launched an anarchist journal, *Le Révolté*. Expelled from Switzerland 1881, he went to France, where he was imprisoned 1883–86. He lived in Britain until 1917, when he returned to Moscow. Unsympathetic to the Bolsheviks, he retired from politics after the Russian Revolution. Among his works are *Memoirs of a Revolutionist* 1899, *Mutual Aid* 1902, and *Modern Science and Anarchism* 1903.

Kropotkin was also a noted geologist and geographer.
Suggested reading
Kropotkin, Pyotr *Memoirs of a Revolutionary* (1899, rep 1989)
Miller, Martin *Kropotkin* (1976)
Woodcock, George and Avakumović, Ivan *The Anarchist Prince* (1950)

Krueger Walter (1881–1967). US general. After building his reputation as a trainer, Krueger took command of 6th US Army in Australia 1943, under MacArthur. He soon made it into a highly efficient force which served in New Guinea, New Britain, and the Admiralty Islands. He invaded the Philippines Oct 1944, finally taking Manila after a month of house-to-house fighting.

Kruger (Stephanus Johannes) Paul(us) (1825–1904). President of the Transvaal 1883–1900. He refused to remedy the grievances of the Uitlanders (English and other non-Boer white residents) and so precipitated the Second South African War.
Suggested reading
Kruger, D W *Paul Kruger* (1961–63)
Kruger, Paul *The Memoirs of Paul Kruger* (1902, rep 1969)

Krupp Alfred (1812–1887). German metallurgist who became known as the 'Cannon King' because of the cast-steel guns he manufactured.

Krupp was born in Essen and left school at 14 to join the family steel works. With the advent of the railways, the firm developed into a vast industrial empire. Despite Krupp's reputation, the output of goods – even in wartime – was predominantly for peaceful purposes.

From a staff of seven, Krupp's enterprise had grown to employ 21,000 by his death.

Krupp designed and developed new machines. He invented the first weldless steel tyre for railway vehicles. He also invented the spoon roll for making spoons and forks, and manufactured rolling mills for use in government mints. In 1847 the firm cast its first steel cannon, but it still specialized in making fine steel suitable for dies, rolls, and machine-building. Krupp introduced the Bessemer and open-hearth steelmaking processes 1852.

Krupp created a comprehensive welfare scheme for his workers, with a sickness fund, low-cost housing, and pension schemes for all his employees. Medical care and consumer co-operatives enjoyed company backing. These institutions acted as models for the social legislation enacted in Germany in the 1880s.

Suggested reading
Batty, Peter *The House of Krupp* (1966)
Klass, Gert von *Krupps: The Story of an Industrial Empire* (trs 1954)
Manchester, William *The Arms of Krupp* (1959)

Kryukov Fyodor (1870–1920). Russian writer. He was alleged by Alexander Solzhenitsyn to be the real author of *And Quiet Flows the Don* by Mikhail Sholokhov.

Kubelik Jan (1880–1940). Czech violinist and composer. He performed in Prague at the age of eight, and became one of the world's greatest virtuosos; he also wrote six violin concertos.

Kubelik (Jeronym) Rafael (1914–1996). Czech conductor and composer. He was the son of violinist Jan Kubelik. His works include

Kruger South African politician Paul Kruger, leader of the Boers in their fight against the British. He took part in the 'Great Trek' of the Boers into the hinterland of South Africa 1836–40 and helped found the Transvaal Republic. He was known affectionately to Boers as 'Oom [Uncle] Paul'. (Image Select)

symphonies and operas, such as *Veronika* 1947. He was musical director of the Royal Opera House, Covent Garden, London, 1955–58.

Kubitschek Juscelino (1902–1976). Brazilian president 1956–61. His term as president saw political peace, civil liberty, and rapid economic growth at the cost of high inflation and corruption. He had a strong commitment to public works and the construction of Brasília as the nation's capital.

Kubitschek entered congress 1934, and was governor of Minas Gerais 1951–55, pursuing an active policy of road building, electrification, and industrial development.

Kublai Khan (c. 1216–1294). Mongol emperor of China from 1259. He completed his grandfather Genghis Khan's conquest of N China from 1240, and on his brother Mungo's death 1259 established himself as emperor of China. He moved the capital to Beijing and founded the Yuan dynasty, successfully expanding his empire into Indochina, but was defeated in an attempt to conquer Japan 1281.

Suggested reading
Morgan, D *The Mongols* (1987)
Rossabi, M *Khublai Khan* (1988)

Kubrick Stanley (1928–). US film director, producer, and screenwriter. His films include *Paths of Glory* 1957, *Dr Strangelove* 1964, *2001: A Space Odyssey* 1968, *A Clockwork Orange* 1971, and *The Shining* 1979. More than any of his American contemporaries, Kubrick achieved complete artistic control over his films, which have been eclectic in subject matter and ambitious in both scale and technique. His other films include *Lolita* 1962 and *Full Metal Jacket* 1987.

Suggested reading
Nelson, Thomas *Kubrick: Inside a Film Artist's Maze* (1982)
Phillips, Gene *Kubrick* (1975)

Truth is too multi-faceted to be contained in a five line summary.

STANLEY KUBRICK
in *Rolling Stone* 27 Aug 1982

Kuchma Leonid (1938–). Ukrainian politician, prime minister 1992–93 and president from 1994. A traditional Soviet technocrat, he worked his way up the hierarchy of the Communist Party (CPSU) and, when the USSR was dissolved and Ukraine gained independence 1991, was well placed to assume senior positions within the Ukrainian administration. As prime minister, he established himself as a moderate reformer and, in June, after he had beaten the incumbent Leonid Kravchuk for the presidency, promised to continue a policy of gradual reforms.

Kuchma campaigned for closer ties with Russia and received around 90% of the vote in Russian-speaking regions of E Ukraine and in Crimea.

Kuhn Richard (1900–1967). Austrian-born German chemist who determined the structures of vitamins A, B_2, and B_6 in the 1930s, having isolated them from cow's milk. He was awarded the 1938 Nobel Prize for Chemistry.

In 1929 he became professor at Heidelberg and director of the Kaiser Wilhelm (later Max Planck) Institute for Medical Research. He remained there until the late 1930s, when he was caught in a Nazi roundup of Jews and imprisoned in a concentration camp. He was unable to receive his Nobel prize until the end of World War II in 1945, when he returned to work in Heidelberg.

Kuhn's early research concerned the carotenoids, the fat-soluble yellow pigments found in plants which are precursors of vitamin A. In the 1940s, Kuhn continued to carry out research on carbohydrates, studying alkaloid glycosides such as those that occur in tomatoes, potatoes, and other plants of the genus *Solanum*. In 1952, he returned to experiments with milk, extracting carbohydrates from thousands of litres of milk using chromatography. This work led in the 1960s to the investigation of similar sugar-type substances in the human brain.

Kuhn Thomas Samuel (1922–1996). US historian and philosopher of science, who showed that social and cultural conditions affect the directions of science. *The Structure of Scientific Revolutions* 1962 argued that even scientific knowledge is relative, dependent on the *paradigm* (theoretical framework) that dominates a scientific field at the time. Such paradigms (for example, Darwinism and Newtonian theory) are so dominant that they are uncritically accepted as true, until a 'scientific revolution' creates a new orthodoxy. Kuhn's ideas have also influenced ideas in the social sciences.

Kuiper Gerard Peter (1905–1973). Dutch-born US astronomer who made extensive studies of the Solar System. His discoveries included the atmosphere of the planet Mars and that of Titan, the largest moon of the planet Saturn. Kuiper was adviser to many NASA exploratory missions, and pioneered the use of telescopes on high-flying aircraft. The Kuiper Airborne Observatory, one such telescope, is named after him; it was permanently grounded Oct 1995.

Kuiper was born in Harenkarspel and educated at Leiden, emigrating to the USA 1933. He joined the staff of the Yerkes Observatory (affiliated to the University of Chicago) and was its director 1947–49 and 1957–60. From 1960 he held a similar position at the Lunar and Planetary Laboratory at the University of Arizona.

In 1948, Kuiper correctly predicted that carbon dioxide was one of the chief constituents of the Martian atmosphere. He discovered the fifth moon of Uranus, which he called Miranda, also in 1948; and in 1949 he discovered the second moon of Neptune, Nereid. Kuiper's spectroscopic studies of Uranus and Neptune led to the discovery of features subsequently named Kuiper bands, which indicate the presence of methane.

Kulpe Oswald (1862–1915). German psychologist and philosopher. In philosophy, he was attacked by the followers of Immanuel Kant for believing that metaphysics was possible. His psychology is similar to the phenomenology of Edmund Husserl.

Kulpe was a disciple of German physiologist Wilhelm Wundt, and was professor at Würzburg 1894–1909, Bonn 1909–1912, and Munich 1912–1923. His psychological research concerned perception, judgement, and thought, and his works include *Grundriss der Psychologie/Outline of Psychology* 1893.

Kummer Ernst Eduard (1810–1893). German mathematician who introduced 'ideal numbers' in the attempt to prove Fermat's last theorem. His research into systems of rays led to the discovery of the fourth-order surface known as the Kummer surface.

He was professor at Breslau 1842–55, when he was appointed to professorships at the University of Berlin and the Berlin War College.

Ideal numbers is one of the most creative and influential ideas in the history of mathematics. With their aid Kummer was able to prove, in 1850, that the equation: $x^l + y^l + z^l = 0$ was impossible in non-zero integers for all regular prime numbers (a special type of prime number related to Bernoulli numbers). He was then able to determine that the only primes less than 100 that are not regular are 37, 59, and 67. For many years Kummer continued to work on the problem and he was eventually able to prove that the equation is impossible for all primes $l < 100$. The Kummer surface can be described as the quartic which is the singular surface of the quadratic line complex and involves the very sophisticated and complicated concept of this surface as the wave surface in space of four dimensions. Kummer also made an important contribution to function theory by his investigations into hypergeometric series.

Despite his organizational talents, he was unable to master the complexities of actual government or the tactics of power struggles within the international Communist movement.

Encyclopaedia Britannica on BÉLA KUN
vol 7

Kun Béla (1886–1937). Hungarian politician who created a Soviet republic in Hungary March 1919, which was overthrown Aug 1919 by a Western blockade and Romanian military actions. The succeeding regime under Admiral Horthy effectively liquidated both socialism and liberalism in Hungary.

Suggested reading
Tokés, R *Bela Kun and the Hungarian Soviet Revolution* (1967)

Kundera Milan (1929–). Czech writer. His first novel, *The Joke* 1967, brought him into official disfavour in Prague, and, unable to publish further works, he moved to France. Other novels include *The Book of Laughter and Forgetting* 1979 and *The Unbearable Lightness of Being* 1984 (filmed 1988).

Kundt August Adolph Eduard Eberhard (1839–1894). German physicist who in 1866 invented Kundt's tube, a simple device for meas-uring the velocity of sound in gases and solids. Kundt's tube is a glass tube containing some dry powder and closed at one end. Into the open end, a disc attached to a rod is inserted. When the rod is sounded, the vibration of the disc sets up sound waves in the air in the tube and a position is found in which standing waves occur, causing the dust to collect at the nodes of the waves. By measuring the length of the rod and the positions of the nodes in the tube, the velocity of sound in either the rod or air can be found, provided one of these quantities is known. By using rods made of various materials and different gases in the tube, the velocity of sound in a range of solids and gases can be determined. His later work entailed the demonstration of the dispersion of light in liquids, vapours, and metals.

Kundt was born in Schwerin, Mecklenburg, and educated at Leipzig and Berlin. He was professor at the Polytechnic in Zürich, Switzerland, 1868, at Würzburg from 1869, and was one of the founders of the Strasbourg Physical Institute 1872. He ended his career as director of the Berlin Physical Institute from 1888.

Küng Hans (1928–). Swiss Roman Catholic theologian who was barred from teaching by the Vatican 1979 'in the name of the Church' because he had cast doubt on papal infallibility and on whether Christ was the son of God. He was professor at Tübingen University, Germany, from 1963.

Suggested reading
Nowell, Robert *A Passion for Truth: Hans Küng* (1981)
Scheffczyk, L *On Being a Christian: The Hans Küng Debate* (1982)

Kuniyoshi Utagawa (1797–1861). Japanese printmaker. His series *108 Heroes of the Suikoden* depicts heroes of the Chinese classic novel *The Water Margin*. Kuniyoshi's dramatic, innovative style lent itself to warriors and fantasy, but his subjects also include landscapes and cats.

Kupka Frank (František) (1871–1957). Czech painter and illustrator. He was a pioneer of non-representational art. He studied in Prague, Vienna, and Paris, where he lived from 1895. His *Amorpha, Fugue in Two Colours: Red and Blue* 1912 (Národni Galerie, Prague) is thought to be the earliest example of an entirely abstract painting.

Prompted by the theories of Seurat, he explored the expressive power of colour and the spiritual significance of forms, arriving like Kandinsky at an abstract language of 'signs'. Kupka's multiple coloured spheres and 'linear rhythms' were intended to provide the visual equivalent of music. His work, together with that of Robert Delaunay, has been dubbed Orphism.

Kureishi Hanif (1954–). English dramatist, film maker, and novelist. His work concentrates on the lives of Asians living in Britain. His early plays *Outskirts* 1981 and *Birds of Passage* 1983 were followed by the screenplays for the films *My Beautiful Laundrette* 1984 and *Sammy and Rosie Get Laid* 1987, both directed by Stephen Frears. He wrote and directed the film *London Kills Me* 1991. *The Buddha of Suburbia* 1990 was followed by another novel, *The Black Album* 1995.

Kuribyashi Todomichi (1885–1945). Japanese general of World War II; commander of Japanese forces on Iwo Jima. He constructed a powerful series of defensive positions held by some 23,000 troops. The US invasion of the island 1945 was not made any easier by Kuribyashi issuing orders to his men that each had to kill 10 enemy troops before they died. He signalled 'Goodbye' to his surviving troops 23 March 1945 and went into the front line to his death.

Kuropatkin Alexei Nikolaievich (1848–1921). Russian general. He distinguished himself as Chief of Staff during the Russo-Turkish War 1877–78, was commander in chief in Manchuria 1903, and resigned after his defeat at Mukden 1905 in the Russo-Japanese War. During World War I he commanded the armies on the northern front until 1916.

To be an artist means never to look away.

AKIRA KUROSAWA
in *Guardian* 1980

Kurosawa Akira (1910–   ). Japanese director. His film *Rashōmon* 1950 introduced Western audiences to Japanese cinema. Epics such as *Shichinin no samurai/Seven Samurai* 1954 combine spectacle with intimate human drama. Kurosawa's films with a contemporary setting include *Drunken Angel* 1948 and *Ikiru/Living* 1952, both using illness as metaphor. *Yōjimbō* 1961, *Kagemusha* 1981, and *Ran* 1985 (loosely based on Shakespeare's *King Lear*) are historical films with an increasingly bleak outlook.

Suggested reading
Kurosawa, Akira *Something Like an Autobiography* (1982)
Richie, D *The Films of Akira Kurosawa* (1984)
Richie, D *Japanese Cinema: Film Style and National Character* (1971)

Kusana dynasty or Yueh-chih dynasty. N Indian family ruling between the 1st and 2nd centuries AD. The greatest Kusana king was Kaniska (ruled *c.* 78–102). A devout Buddhist and liberal patron of the arts, he extended the empire across central and E India. In decline by 176, the dynasty was overthrown by the Sassanians about 240.

An Indo-European-speaking nomadic people of central Asian descent, the Kusana were forced from China when the Great Wall was extended W by the Han dynasty. Under chief Kujula Kadphises (reigned 15–55), one group of Kusanas secured control over NW India, establishing a capital city at Purushapura (modern Peshawar).

Kuti Fela Anikulapo (1938–   ). Nigerian singer, songwriter, and musician. He is a strong proponent of African nationalism and ethnic identity. His albums of big-band African funk include *Coffin for Head of State* 1978, *Teacher Don't Teach Me Nonsense* 1987, and *Underground System* 1993.

Kuti had his first local hit 1971 and soon became a W African star. His political protest songs (in English) caused the Nigerian army to attack his commune 1974 and again 1977, and he has been a political prisoner. Unsparing in his attacks on neocolonialism and corruption, he holds up Idi Amin as a role model.

Kutuzov Mikhail Illarionovich, Prince of Smolensk (1745–1813). Commander of the Russian forces in the Napoleonic Wars. He commanded an army corps at Austerlitz and the army in its retreat 1812. After the burning of Moscow that year, he harried the French throughout their retreat and later took command of the united Prussian armies.

Kuznets Simon Smith (1901–1985). Russian-born US economist. He developed theories of national income and economic growth, used to forecast the future, in *Economic Growth of Nations* 1971. He won the Nobel Prize for Economics 1971.

He emigrated to the USA 1922, and taught at the University of Pennsylvania 1930–54, Johns Hopkins 1954–60, and Harvard 1960–71.

Kuznetsov Anatoly Vasilyevich (1929–1979). Russian writer. His novels *Babi Yar* 1966, describing the wartime execution of Jews at Babi Yar, near Kiev, and *The Fire* 1969, about workers in a large metallurgical factory, were seen as anti-Soviet. He lived in Britain from 1969, adopting the pseudonym A Anatoli.

Kuznetsov Vasily (1894–1964). Soviet general of World War II. A young general when he defended Kiev 1941, he was afterwards made a scapegoat for its loss, though General Budenny was really at fault. Remarkably, Kuznetsov survived and was given a command at Stalingrad, where he performed well, and then became deputy commander of the Southwest Front, fighting from the Don to Berlin.

Kyd Thomas (*c.* 1557–1595). English dramatist. He was the author of a bloody revenge tragedy, *The Spanish Tragedy c.* 1588, which anticipated elements present in Shakespeare's *Hamlet.*

Kyprianou Spyros (1932–   ). Cypriot politician, president 1977– 88. Foreign minister 1961–72, he founded the federalist, centre-left Democratic Front 1976.

Educated in Cyprus and the UK, he became a barrister in England 1954. He became secretary to Archbishop Makarios in London 1952 and returned with him to Cyprus 1959. On the death of Makarios 1977 he became acting president and was then elected president. He was defeated in the 1988 presidential elections.

L

Laban Rudolf von (1879–1958). Hungarian dance theoretician. He is known as the leader of modern dance theory. He invented Labanotation, an accurate, detailed system of recording steps and movements. He also tried to order the principles of human motion into specific systems, such as choreutics (the relationship of the body to the space it occupies) and eukinetics (formulation of all possible types and directions of body movements). He researched the connection between psychology and motion in his theoretical work.

Laban was the founder of various schools, companies, and institutions in Germany from 1910. In the 1920s he pioneered the amateur movement of Bewegungschöre ('movement choirs') to promote 'community dance'. He emigrated to England 1937 where he continued to work mostly in the field of dance education. Among his pupils were Karl Jooss and Mary Wigman.

Labèque Katia (1950–) and Marielle (1952–) French duo-pianists, sisters. In a joint career that began 1961, their repertoire has encompassed works by classical composers (Bach, Mozart, Brahms) as well as modern pieces (Stravinsky, Messiaen, Boulez). They also play ragtime.

Labrouste (Pierre François) Henri (1801–1875). French architect. He was a pioneer in his use of such materials as iron. His Library of Ste Geneviève, Paris, 1843–50, has a slender and elegant ironwork frame supporting a vaulted ceiling. The severity of its flat stone façade, punctuated by round-headed windows, is in stark contrast to the decorative Beaux Arts style, which was dominant at the time of its conception.

Party loyalty lowers the greatest of men to the petty level of the masses.

JEAN DE LA BRUYÈRE
The Characters 1688

La Bruyère Jean de (1645–1696). French essayist. He was born in Paris, studied law, took a post in the revenue office, and in 1684 entered the service of the French commander the Prince of Condé. His 'Caractères/The Characters' 1688, satirical portraits of his contemporaries, made him many enemies.

Lacaille Nicolas Louis de (1713–1762). French astronomer who determined the positions of nearly 10,000 stars of the southern hemisphere 1750–54. He also performed a number of geodetic investigations; in particular, he made the first measurement of the arc of meridian in the southern hemisphere. *Coelum australe stelliferum* 1763 catalogued all Lacaille's data from the southern hemisphere.

Lacaille was born in Rumigny, near Rheims, and studied theology in Paris. He began to make astronomical observations in 1737 and participated in two Academy of Sciences projects, in 1738 and 1739. At the age of 26 he became professor of mathematics at the Collège Mazarin (now the Institut de France), Paris. He was subsequently given an observatory.

Lacan Jacques (1901–1981). French psychoanalyst and theorist. His attempt to reinterpret Sigmund Freud in terms of the structural linguistics of Ferdinand de Saussure has influenced studies in literature, social ideology, aesthetics, and philosophy, but has had little effect on the practice of psychoanalysis. His main work is *Ecrits/Writings* 1966.

Lacan rejects the notion of a stable, coherent, autonomous self and argues that the self is formed in a complex network (the 'symbolic order') of language and social customs. It follows that the self is inherently unstable and 'neurotic'. In Lacan's theories, Freud's Oedipal stage is replaced by the child's entry in to language and society, the secure sense of narcissistic self-sufficiency giving way to a realization of difference, alienation, and loss.

Laccnaire Pierre-François (1803–1836). French criminal, guillotined for murder. A petty criminal and army deserter, he became a dandy in the 1830s. In his memoirs 1835, he chillingly describes how he financed his high life by killing. His trial and execution made him a celebrity.

Have you not as yet observed that pleasure, which is undeniably the sole motive force behind the union of the sexes, is nevertheless not enough to form a bond between them? And that, if it is preceded by desire which impels, it is succeeded by disgust which repels? That is a law of nature which love alone can alter.

PIERRE CHODERLOS DE LACLOS
Les Liaisons Dangereuses letter 131 1782

Laclos Pierre Ambroise François Choderlos de (1741–1803). French author. An army officer, he wrote a single novel in letter form, *Les Liaisons dangereuses/Dangerous Liaisons* 1782, an analysis of moral corruption. It was adapted as a play 1985 by Christopher Hampton (1946–) and as a film 1988, directed by Stephen Frears (1941–).

La Condamine Charles Marie de (1701–1774). French soldier and geographer who was sent by the French Academy of Sciences to Peru 1735–43 to measure the length of an arc of the meridian. On his return journey he travelled the length of the Amazon, writing about the use of the nerve toxin curare, india rubber, and the advantages of inoculation.

Lacroix Christian Marie Marc (1951–). French fashion designer. He opened his couture and ready-to-wear business 1987, after working with Jean Patou 1981–87. He made headlines with his fantasy creations, including the short puffball skirt, rose prints, and low décolleté necklines. Lacroix uses experimental fabrics, sometimes handwoven by traditional rural and community workshops.

A small boy's idea of a tough guy.

Raymond Chandler on ALAN LADD
quoted in Leslie Halliwell *Filmgoer's Companion* 1965

Ladd Alan (1913–1964). US actor. His first leading role, as the professional killer in *This Gun for Hire* 1942, made him a star. His most famous role was as the gunslinging stranger in *Shane* 1953, but his career declined after the mid-1950s. His last role was in *The Carpetbaggers* 1964.

Laënnec René Théophile Hyacinthe (1781–1826). French physician, inventor of the stethoscope 1816. He introduced the new diagnostic technique of auscultation in his book *Traité de l'auscultation médiaté* 1819, which quickly became a medical classic.

He was appointed personal physician to Cardinal Fesch, uncle of Napoleon I. In 1812–13, with France at war, Laënnec took charge of the wards in the Salpetrière Hospital reserved for Breton soldiers. On the restoration of the monarchy, he became physician to the Necker Hospital, retiring 1818. In 1822 he was appointed professor at the Collège de France.

Laënnec was interested in emphysema, tuberculosis, and physical signs of chest diseases. Although auscultation had been known since the days of Hippocrates, it was always done by the 'direct' method, which was often inconvenient. Laënnec introduced the 'mediate' method by using a hollow wooden tube for listening to the lungs, and a solid wooden rod to listen to the heart. He called it a stethoscope from the Greek *stethos* 'chest'.

Lafarge John (1835–1910). US painter and ecclesiastical designer. He is credited with the revival of stained glass in America and also created woodcuts, watercolours, and murals. Lafarge visited Europe 1856 and the Far East 1886. In the 1870s he turned from landscape painting (inspired by the French painter Corot) to religious and still-life painting. Decorating the newly built Trinity Church in Boston, Massachusetts, he worked alongside the sculptor Augustus Saint-Gaudens.

Life is like the flame of a lamp; when there is no more oil ... zest! It goes out and all is over.

LAFAYETTE
commenting on the inevitability of death 1834

Lafayette Marie Joseph Paul Yves Roch Gilbert de Motier, Marquis de (1757–1834). French soldier and politician. He fought against Britain in the American Revolution 1777–79 and 1780–82. During the French Revolution he sat in the National Assembly as a constitutional royalist and in 1789 presented the Declaration of the Rights of Man. After the storming of the Bastille, he was given command of the National Guard. In 1792 he fled the country after attempting to restore the monarchy and was imprisoned by the Austrians until 1797. He supported Napoleon Bonaparte in 1815, sat in the chamber of deputies as a Liberal from 1818, and played a leading part in the revolution of 1830.

He was a popular hero in the USA, and the cities of Lafayette in Louisiana and Indiana are named after him, as was the Lafayette Escadrille – American aviators flying for France during World War I, before the USA entered 1917.

Suggested reading
Bernier, O *Lafayette: Hero of Two Worlds* (1983)
Buckmann, Peter *Lafayette* (1977)
Gottschalk, Louis *Lafayette*, 5 vols (1935–69)

Lafayette Marie-Madeleine, Comtesse de (1634–1693). French author. Her *Mémoires* of the French court are keenly observed, and her *La Princesse de Clèves* 1678 is the first French psychological novel and *roman à clef* ('novel with a key'), in that real-life characters (including the writer François de La Rochefoucauld, who was for many years her lover) are presented under fictitious names.

Lafitte Jean (*c.* 1780–*c.* 1825). Pirate in America. Suspected of complicity with the British, he was attacked by American forces soon after the outbreak of the Anglo-American War 1812. He proved his loyalty to General Andrew Jackson by his heroic participation in the Battle of New Orleans 1815.

Reportedly born in France, Lafitte settled in New Orleans, where he became a smuggler and privateer. Gathering a band of followers around him, he set up headquarters in nearby Barataria Bay and spent several years raiding Spanish shipping in the Gulf of Mexico. After the war with England 1814 Lafitte established headquarters in Galveston Bay.

La Follette Robert Marion (1855–1925). US political leader. A US senator 1906–25, he was a leader of the national progressive reform movement and unsuccessfully ran for president on the Progressive ticket 1924. His *Autobiography, A Personal Narrative of Political Experiences* appeared in 1913.

Born in Primrose, Wisconsin, USA, La Follette was educated at the state university and was admitted to the bar 1880. Entering politics, he served as district attorney 1880–94 and as a member of the US House of Representatives 1885–91. He was elected Wisconsin governor 1900.

La Fontaine Jean de (1621–1695). French poet. He was born at Château-Thierry, and from 1656 lived largely in Paris, the friend of the playwrights Molière and Racine, and the poet Boileau. His works include *Fables* 1668–94 and *Contes* 1665–74, a series of witty and bawdy tales in verse.

Lafontaine Oskar (1943–). German socialist politician, federal deputy chair of the Social Democrat Party (SPD) from 1987 and chair from 1995. Leader of the Saar regional branch of the SPD from 1977 and former mayor of Saarbrucken, he was nicknamed 'Red Oskar' because of his radical views on military and environmental issues. His attitude became more conservative once he had become minister-president of Saarland 1985.

He was the SPD's unsuccessful chancellor-candidate in the first all-German general election 1990, surviving a serious knife attack during the campaign, in which he warned of the economic cost of unification. In Nov 1995 he toppled Rudolph Scharping at the SPD conference to become party leader. He is opposed to the Maastricht Treaty on European union, viewing it as insufficiently federalist, and has indicated that he may seek to construct an SPD–Green–Reformed Communist 'broad centre-left' coalition to replace the dominant Christian Democrats.

Laforgue Jules (1860–1887). French poet. He pioneered free verse and inspired later French and English writers.

Lagerfeld Karl Otto (1938–). German-born fashion designer. He has been a leading figure on the fashion scene from the early 1970s. As design director at Chanel for both the couture and ready-to-wear collections from 1983, he updated the Chanel look. He showed his first collection under his own label 1984.

Lagerkvist Pär Fabian (1891–1974). Swedish writer. His work includes lyric poetry, dramas (including *The Hangman* 1935), and novels, such as *Barabbas* 1950. He was awarded the 1951 Nobel Prize for Literature.

Lagerlöf Selma Ottiliana Lovisa (1858–1940). Swedish novelist. Her first work was the romantic historical novel *Gösta Berling's Saga* 1891. The children's fantasy *Nils Holgerssons underbara resa/The Wonderful Voyage of Nils Holgersson* 1906–07 grew from her background as a schoolteacher. She was the first woman to receive a Nobel prize, 1909.

I do not know.

JOSEPH LAGRANGE
Lagrange summarizing his life's work

Lagrange Joseph Louis (1736–1813). Italian-born French mathematician. His *Mécanique analytique* 1788 applied mathematical analysis, using principles established by Isaac Newton, to such problems as the movements of planets when affected by each other's gravitational force. In 1755, advancing beyond Newton's theory of sound, Lagrange settled a dispute on the nature of a vibrating string. Later he proved some of Pierre de Fermat's theorems, which had remained unproven for a century. He presided over the commission that introduced the metric system in 1793.

Lagrange was born in Turin and appointed professor of mathematics at the Royal Artillery School there when he was just 19. In 1766 Frederick the Great of Prussia invited him to become director of the Berlin Academy of Sciences, and in 1787, on the invitation of Louis XVI, Lagrange moved to Paris as a member of the French Royal Academy. He was professor at the Ecole Polytechnique from 1797.

La Guardia Fiorello Henry (1882–1947). US Republican politician; congressman 1917, 1919, 1923–33; mayor of New York 1933–45. Elected against the opposition of the powerful Tammany Hall Democratic Party organization, he improved the administration, suppressed racketeering, and organized unemployment relief, slum-clearance schemes, and social services. Although nominally a Republican, he supported the Democratic president F D Roosevelt's New Deal. La Guardia Airport, in New York City, is named after him.

Suggested reading
Heckscher, A and Robinson, P *When La Guardia was Mayor: New York's Legendary Years* (1978)
Kessner, Thomas *Fiorello H La Guardia and the Making of Modern New York* (1989)

Laing R(onald) D(avid) (1927–1989). Scottish psychoanalyst, originator of the social theory of mental illness; for example, that schizophrenia is promoted by family pressure for its members to conform to standards alien to themselves. By investigating the personal interactions within the families of diagnosed schizophrenics, he found that the seemingly bizarre behaviour normally regarded as indicating the illness began to make sense. His books include *The Divided Self* 1960 and *The Politics of the Family* 1971.

Suggested reading
Boyars, Robert (ed) *R D Laing and Anti-Psychiatry* (1974)
Collier, Andrew *R D Laing: The Philosophy and Politics of Psychotherapy* (1977)
Laing, Adrian (ed) *R D Laing: A Biography* (1974)
Laing, R D *The Making of a Psychiatrist* (autobiography) (1985)

Laithwaite Eric Roberts (1921–). English electrical engineer who developed the linear motor. The idea of a linear induction motor had been suggested in 1895, but Laithwaite discovered that it is possible to arrange two linear motors back to back, so as to produce continuous oscillation without the use of any switching device. The important feature of the linear motor is that it is a means of propulsion without the need for wheels.

He studied at the University of Manchester and, with the interruption of World War II, remained there until 1964, when he became professor of heavy electrical engineering at the Imperial College of Science and Technology at the University of London, moving to the Royal Institution 1967–76. He made many popular radio and television broadcasts.

You could put all the talent I had into your left eye and still not suffer from impaired vision.

VERONICA LAKE
quoted in Leslie Halliwell *Filmgoer's Companion* 1965

Lake Veronica. Stage name of Constance Frances Marie Ockelman (1919–1973). US film actress. She was almost as celebrated for her much imitated 'peekaboo' hairstyle as for her acting. She co-starred with Alan Ladd in several films during the 1940s, including *This Gun for Hire* and *The Glass Key* both 1942, and *The Blue Dahlia* 1946. She also appeared in *Sullivan's Travels* 1942 and *I Married a Witch* 1942.

Lake (William) Anthony (Kirsopp) (1939–). US government official, national security adviser from Jan 1993. He has helped to shape President Bill Clinton's foreign policy of support for the new market-based democracies in Eastern Europe and elsewhere.

Having joined the foreign service, Lake was sent to South Vietnam 1963. As special assistant to Henry Kissinger, President Nixon's national security adviser, 1969–70, Lake tried to persuade Kissinger to urge Nixon to withdraw US troops from SE Asia. He resigned 1970 after the US invasion of Cambodia. Under President Carter he was director of policy planning for Secretary of State Cyrus Vance 1976–80.

Lake became a professor of international relations at Mount Holyoke College 1981 after the defeat of Carter in the presidential election. Lake's books include *Our Own Worst Enemy: The Unmaking of American Foreign Policy* 1984 and *Somoza Falling* 1989.

Lalande Joseph Jérome le Français de (1732–1807). French astronomer who observed the transit of Venus and helped to calculate the size of the Solar System. Such transits occur twice within a period of eight years only every 113 years. During the transit, which takes approximately five hours, Venus can be seen silhouetted across the face of the Sun; the distance of the Earth from the Sun can be deduced by measuring the different times that the planet takes to cross the face of the Sun when seen from different latitudes on Earth. He compiled a catalogue of 47,000 stars.

He was appointed professor at the Collège de France in 1762 and during his tenure there he published *Treatise of Astronomy* 1764. In 1795 he was made director of the Paris Observatory.

Lalique René (1860–1945). French designer and manufacturer of Art Nouveau glass, jewellery, and house interiors. The Lalique factory continues in production at Wingen-sur-Moder, Alsace, under his son Marc and granddaughter Marie-Claude.

Lalo (Victor Antoine) Edouard (1823–1892). French composer. His Spanish ancestry and violin training are evident in the *Symphonie Espagnole* 1873 for violin and orchestra, and Concerto for Cello and Orchestra 1877. He also wrote an opera, *Le Roi d'Ys/The King of Ys*, 1887.

Lam Wifredo (1902–1982). Cuban painter. Influenced by Surrealism in the 1930s (he lived in Paris 1937–41), he created a semi-abstract style using mysterious and sometimes menacing images and symbols, mainly taken from Caribbean traditions. His *Jungle* series, for example, contains voodoo elements. He visited Haiti and Martinique in the 1940s, Paris 1952, and also made frequent trips to Italy.

Lamar Lucius Quintus Cincinnatus (1825–1893). US jurist and public official. After teaching at the University of Mississippi, he was elected to the US House of Representatives, serving 1857–60. During the American Civil War 1861–65 he served briefly in the Confederate army and was named Confederate envoy to Russia. After the war Lamar returned to the University of Mississippi and sat in the US House of Representatives 1873–77. He was a member of the US Senate 1877–85 and served as President Cleveland's secretary of the interior 1885–87. He sat on the US Supreme Court 1888–93.

Lamarck Jean Baptiste de (1744–1829). French naturalist whose theory of evolution, known as Lamarckism, was based on the idea that acquired characteristics (changes acquired in an individual's lifetime) are inherited by the offspring, and that organisms have an intrinsic urge to evolve into better-adapted forms. *Philosophie zoologique/Zoological Philosophy* 1809 outlined his 'transformist' (evolutionary) ideas. It tried to show that various parts of the body developed because they were necessary, or disappeared because of disuse when variations in the environment caused a change in habit. If these body changes were inherited over many generations, new species would eventually be produced.

Lamarck was the first to distinguish vertebrate from invertebrate animals by the presence of a bony spinal column. He was also the first to establish the crustaceans, arachnids, and annelids among the invertebrates. It was Lamarck who coined the word 'biology'.

He studied medicine, meteorology, and botany, and travelled across Europe as botanist to King Louis XVI from 1781. In 1793 he was made professor of zoology at the Museum of Natural History in Paris.

To love for the sake of being loved is human, but to love for the sake of loving is angelic.

ALPHONSE DE LAMARTINE
Graziella pt 4 ch 5 1929

Lamartine Alphonse Marie Louis de (1790–1869). French poet. He wrote romantic poems, including *Méditations poétiques* 1820, followed by *Nouvelles méditations/New Meditations* 1823, and *Harmonies* 1830. His *Histoire des Girondins/History of the Girondins* 1847 helped to inspire the revolution of 1848.

He entered the Chamber of Deputies 1833.

Lamb Charles (1775–1834). English essayist and critic. He collaborated with his sister *Mary Lamb* (1764–1847) on *Tales from Shakespeare* 1807, and his *Specimens of English Dramatic Poets* 1808 helped to revive interest in Elizabethan plays. As 'Elia' he contributed essays to the *London Magazine* from 1820 (collected 1823 and 1833).

He was a contemporary of Coleridge, with whom he published some poetry 1796. He was a clerk at India House 1792–1825, when he retired to Enfield. His sister Mary stabbed their mother to death in a fit of insanity 1796, and Charles cared for her between her periodic returns to an asylum.

Suggested reading
Barnett, George *Charles Lamb* (1976)
Cecil, David *A Portrait of Lamb* (1983)
Randel, Fred *The World of Elia: Charles's Lamb's Essayistic Romanticism* (1975)

I love to lose myself in other men's minds. When I am not walking, I am reading; I cannot sit and think. Books think for me.

         CHARLES LAMB
Last Essays of Elia, 'Detached Thoughts on Books and Reading' 1823

Lamb Horace (1849–1934). English applied mathematician. His chief work is *Treatise on the Motion of Fluids* 1879, revised and updated as *Hydrodynamics* 1895–1932, but he also wrote on elasticity, sound, and mechanics. Knighted 1931.

He went to Australia 1875 to take up the chair of mathematics at the University of Adelaide. In 1885 he returned to Manchester as professor at Owens College.

Lamb was particularly adept at applying the solution of a problem in one field to problems in another. A paper of 1882, which analysed the modes of oscillation of an elastic sphere, achieved its true recognition in 1960, when free Earth oscillations during an earthquake behaved in the way he had described. A paper of 1904 gave an analytical account of propagation over the surface of an elastic solid of waves generated by given initial disturbances, and the analysis he provided is now regarded as one of the seminal contributions to theoretical seismology.

Lamb Willis Eugene (1913–). US physicist who revised the quantum theory of Paul Dirac. The hydrogen atom was thought to exist in either of two distinct states carrying equal energies. More sophisticated measurements by Lamb in 1947 demonstrated that the two energy levels were not equal. This discrepancy, since known as the Lamb shift, won him the 1955 Nobel Prize for Physics.

Lambert George Washington Thomas (1873–1930). Australian painter and sculptor. In Sydney he studied with Julian Ashton. In 1917 he was appointed official war artist with the Australian Light Horse in Palestine, resulting in a series of paintings, drawings and sculptures, many of which are in the Australian War Memorial, Canberra. He is also known for his landscapes and portraits.

A realist in outlook and often a cynic in speech, he spent a good deal of money on tulips.

         C P Hill on JOHN LAMBERT
in *Who's Who in History* vol iii 1965

Lambert John (1619–1684). English general, a cavalry commander in the Civil War under Cromwell (at the battles of Marston Moor, Preston, Dunbar, and Worcester). Lambert broke with Cromwell over the proposal to award him the royal title. After the Restoration he was imprisoned for life.

Lamburn Richmal Crompton. Full name of English writer Richmal ◊Crompton.

Lamming George William (1927–). Barbadian novelist and poet. The autobiographical *In the Castle of my Skin* 1953 describes his upbringing in the small village where he was born. His imaginative explorations of Caribbean history and society sustain a political vision of a future resting with the common people and depending on the creative union of the minds of the artist and the politician. His *Conversations: Essays, Addresses and Interviews* was published 1992.

Lamont Norman Stewart Hughson (1942–). UK Conservative politician, chief secretary of the Treasury 1989–90, chancellor of the Exchequer 1990–93.

Born in the Shetland Islands and educated at Cambridge, Lamont was elected to Parliament 1972 as member for Kingston upon Thames. He masterminded John Major's leadership campaign. As chancellor of the Exchequer, he firmly backed Britain's membership of the ERM and, despite signs that the pound was in trouble, specifically ruled out devaluation 10 Sept 1992. A week later, in the face of mounting international pressure on the pound, he was forced to devalue and withdraw from the ERM, inciting fierce criticism and calls for his resignation. He was replaced as chancellor by Kenneth Clarke May 1993, after which he became a fierce right-wing critic of the Major administration.

If we want everything to remain as it is, it will be necessary for everything to change.

         GIUSEPPE DI LAMPEDUSA
The Leopard ch 1 1960

Lampedusa Giuseppe Tomasi di (1896–1957). Italian aristocrat. He was the author of *Il gattopardo/The Leopard* 1958 (translated into English 1960), a novel set in his native Sicily during the period following its annexation by Garibaldi 1860. It chronicles the reactions of an aristocratic family to social and political upheavals.

Lancaster Burt(on Stephen) (1913–1994). US film actor, formerly a circus acrobat. A star from his first film, *The Killers* 1946, he proved himself adept both at action roles and more complex character parts as in such films as *From Here to Eternity* 1953, *Elmer Gantry* 1960 (Academy Award), *The Leopard/Il Gattopardo* 1963, *The Swimmer* 1968, and *Atlantic City* 1980.

Lancaster was spotted by a Hollywood agent in his first Broadway acting role 1945. Following his successful screen debut and several further underworld films, he switched to swashbuckling in *The Flame and the Arrow* 1950 and *The Crimson Pirate* 1952, taking pride in performing his own stunts. In a different vein, he took on the role of a down-at-heel ex-alcoholic in *Come Back Little Sheba* 1953. He continued to alternate heroic roles with offbeat characterizations like the odious gossip columnist of *Sweet Smell of Success* 1957. In 1948 he became one of the first Hollywood stars to form his own production company, Hecht-Hill-Lancaster.

Lancaster Osbert (1908–1986). English cartoonist and writer. In 1939 he began producing daily 'pocket cartoons' for the *Daily Express*, in which he satirized current social mores through such characters as Maudie Littlehampton. He was originally a book illustrator and muralist.

In the 1930s and 1940s he produced several tongue-in-cheek guides to architectural fashion (such as *Homes, Sweet Homes* 1939 and *Drayneflete Revisited* 1949), from which a number of descriptive terms, such as Pont Street Dutch and Stockbroker Tudor, have entered the language. He was knighted 1975.

Lancaster, House of English royal house, a branch of the Plantagenets. It originated in 1267 when Edmund (died 1296), the younger son of Henry III, was granted the earldom of Lancaster. Converted to a duchy for Henry of Grosmont (died 1361), it passed to John of Gaunt in 1362 by his marriage to Blanche, Henry's daughter. John's son, Henry IV, established the royal dynasty of Lancaster in 1399, and he was followed by two more Lancastrian kings, Henry V and Henry VI.

Lanchester Frederick William (1868–1946). English engineer who began producing motorcars 1896. Lanchester's first motorcar had a single cylinder 4-kW/5-hp engine and chain drive. His second completed a 1,600-km/1,000-mi tour in 1900. From early on, Lanchester manufactured his cars with interchangeable parts.

He joined the Forward Gas Engine Company of Birmingham 1889, and in 1893 set up his own workshop. The Lanchester Engine Company built some 350 cars between 1900 and 1905, before going bankrupt. In 1909 he was appointed consultant to the Daimler company. He founded Lanchester's Laboratories Ltd in 1925 to provide research and development services.

In the early 1890s Lanchester turned his attention to the theory and practice of crewed flight. His work on stability was fundamental to aviation and he formulated the first comprehensive theory of lift and drag. He published *Aerial Flight* 1907–08 and was invited to join Prime Minister Asquith's advisory committee for aeronautics on its formation 1909. An experimental aircraft codesigned by Lanchester did not survive its trial flight 1911, and he abandoned the practical side of aviation. However, planes that incorporated many of his ideas took to the air in the next few years. Lanchester was also interested in radio and patented a loudspeaker and other audio equipment.

Lancret Nicolas (1690–1743). French painter. He illustrated amorous scenes from the *Fables* of La Fontaine. The fellow pupil with Watteau of Claude Gillot, like Watteau he painted the characters of Italian comedy and numerous *fêtes galantes* (festive groups of courtly figures in fancy dress), though he lacked Watteau's poetry of colour and design. He introduced several personalities of the stage into his pictures, among them the celebrated dancer Mlle Camargo. Typical examples of his works are in the Louvre and the Wallace Collection.

Land Edwin Herbert (1909–1991). US inventor of the Polaroid Land camera 1947. The camera developed the film in one minute inside the camera and produced an 'instant' photograph.

Landau Lev Davidovich (1908–1968). Russian theoretical physicist. He was awarded the 1962 Nobel Prize for Physics for his work on liquid helium.

Landé Alfred (1888–1975). German-born US quantum physicist. In 1923 he published a formula expressing a factor, now known as the Landé splitting factor, for all multiplicities as a function of the quantum numbers of the stationary state of the atom.

From 1922 he was on the staff at Tübingen, the main centre of atomic spectroscopy in Germany. He emigrated to the USA 1931, because of the rise of the Nazi regime, to settle in Columbus, Ohio, as professor of theoretical physics at Ohio State University.

In collaboration with German physicist Max Born, Landé published a paper 1918 on their conclusion that Danish physicist Niels Bohr's model of coplanar electronic orbits must be wrong, and that they must be inclined to each other. Later Landé visited Bohr in Copenhagen to discuss the Zeeman effect (the splitting of spectral lines in a magnetic field), which pointed him towards the discovery of the Landé splitting factor. This is the ratio of an elementary magnetic moment to its causative angular momentum when the angular momentum is measured in quantized units.

Landon Alf(red Mossman) (1887–1987). US public official. After a successful career in business, he entered politics and was elected governor of Kansas 1932. As a popular liberal Republican, Landon ran for president against the incumbent F D Roosevelt 1936 but was overwhelmingly defeated. He later accepted a presidential appointment as US delegate to the 1938 Pan-American Conference. After World War II, Landon became a voice for the elimination of trade barriers and for international development.

I strove with none; for none was worth my strife; / Nature I loved, and next to Nature, Art; / I warmed both hands before the fire of life; / It sinks, and I am ready to depart.

WALTER SAVAGE LANDOR
'Finis'

Landor Walter Savage (1775–1864). English poet and essayist. He lived much of his life abroad, dying in Florence, where he had fled after a libel suit 1858. His works include the epic *Gebir* 1798 and *Imaginary Conversations of Literary Men and Statesmen* 1824–29.

Landowska Wanda Louise (1877–1959). Polish harpsichordist and scholar. She founded a school near Paris for the study of early music, and was for many years one of the few artists regularly performing on the harpsichord. In 1941 she moved to the USA.

Landsbergis Vytautas (1932–). President of Lithuania 1990–93. He became active in nationalist politics in the 1980s, founding and eventually chairing the anticommunist Sajudis independence movement 1988. When Sajudis swept to victory in the republic's elections March 1990, Landsbergis chaired the Supreme Council of Lithuania, becoming, in effect, president. He immediately drafted the republic's declaration of independence from the USSR which, after initial Soviet resistance, was recognized Sept 1991.

Landseer Edwin Henry (1802–1873). English painter, sculptor, and engraver of animal studies. Much of his work reflects the Victorian taste for sentimental and moralistic pictures, for example *Dignity and Impudence* 1839 (Tate Gallery, London). The *Monarch of the Glen* 1850 (John Dewar and Sons Ltd), depicting a highland stag, was painted for the House of Lords. His sculptures include the lions at the base of Nelson's Column in Trafalgar Square, London, 1857–67. Knighted 1850.

Landsteiner Karl (1868–1943). Austrian-born US immunologist who discovered the ABO blood group system 1900–02, and aided in the discovery of the Rhesus blood factors 1940. He also discovered the polio virus. Nobel prize 1930.

In 1927 Landsteiner found that, in addition to antigens A and B, human blood cells contain one or other or both of two heritable antigens, M and N. These are of no importance in transfusions, because human serum does not contain the corresponding antibodies, but they are of value in resolving paternity disputes. His book *The Specificity of Serological Reactions* 1936 helped establish the science of immunology. He also developed a test for syphilis.

He worked at the Vienna Pathology Laboratory 1898–1908, became professor at a Vienna hospital, and left Austria 1919 for the Netherlands, moving 1922 to the USA and the Rockefeller Institute for Medical Research, New York.

Landy John Michael (1930–). Australian athlete, the second runner after England's Roger Bannister to break the four-minute mile. He did this in 3 minutes 58 seconds in 1954.

Lane Edward William (1801–1876). English traveller and translator. He was one of the earliest English travellers to Egypt to learn Arabic; his pseudo-scholarly writings, including *Manners and Customs of the Modern Egyptians* 1836 and an annotated translation of the *Arabian Nights* 1838–40, propagated a stereotyped image of the Arab world.

Lane William (1861–1917). Australian radical political journalist and union activist, born in England, who established New Australia in Paraguay 1893. His writings include the novel *The Workingman's Paradise* 1892.

Lanfranc (c. 1010–1089). Italian archbishop of Canterbury from 1070; he rebuilt the cathedral, replaced English clergy by Normans, enforced clerical celibacy, and separated the ecclesiastical from the secular courts. His skill in theological controversy did much to secure the church's adoption of the doctrine of transubstantiation. He came over to England with William the Conqueror, whose adviser he was.

Lanfranc was born in Pavia, Italy. He entered the monastery of Bec, Normandy, in 1042, where he opened a school; St Anselm, later his successor, was his pupil there.

They hear like ocean on a western beach/ The surge and thunder of the Odyssey.

ANDREW LANG
'As One that for a Weary Space has Lain'

Lang Andrew (1844–1912). Scottish historian and folklore scholar. His writings include historical works; anthropological essays, such as

'Myth, Ritual and Religion' 1887 and 'The Making of Religion' 1898, which involved him in controversy with the anthropologist James G Frazer; novels; and a series of children's books, beginning with *The Blue Fairy Tale Book* 1889.

Lang Fritz (1890–1976). Austrian film director. His films are characterized by a strong sense of fatalism and alienation. His German films include *Metropolis* 1927, the sensational *M* 1931, in which Peter Lorre starred as a child-killer, and the series of Dr Mabuse films, after which he fled from the Nazis to Hollywood 1935. His US films include *Fury* 1936, *You Only Live Once* 1937, *Scarlet Street* 1945, *Rancho Notorious* 1952, and *The Big Heat* 1953. He returned to Germany and directed a third picture in the Dr Mabuse series 1960.

Suggested reading
Eisner, Lotte *Fritz Lang* (1977)
Jenkins, S *Fritz Lang* (1981)
Jensen, Paul *The Cinema of Fritz Lang* (1969)

Lang Jack (John Thomas) (1876–1975). Australian Labor politician, premier of New South Wales 1925–27, 1930–32. His first government introduced social reforms such as child endowment, widows' pensions, and reduced working hours. His second term of government was at the height of the Depression. At this time the New South Wales Labor Party split from the national Labor Party and Lang was instrumental in the fall of the Scullin government. Lang's plan for combating the economic problems of the time by non-payment or reduction of interest on loans led to his dismissal in May 1932 by the governor, Sir Philip Game, and his defeat at the subsequent election. He remained a powerful figure in Australian politics with an electoral following despite his rejection by the federal Labor Party and his propensity for faction fighting. Finally expelled from the New South Wales Labor Party, he entered federal parliament in 1946 representing his 'non-communist' Labor Party but lost the seat three years later. His turbulent career had seen him move from the far left to the far right of the Australian Labor movement.

lang k d (1961–). Canadian singer. Her mellifluous voice and androgynous image gained her a wide following beyond the country-music field where she first established herself. Her albums include *Angel With a Lariat* 1987, *Shadowland* 1988, *Absolute Torch and Twang* 1989, the mainstream *Ingénue* 1992, and *Even Cowgirls get the Blues* 1993. She made her debut as an actress 1992 starring in the film *Salmonberries* by Percy Adlon.

Langdon Harry Philmore (1884–1944). US silent film comedian. With his baby face and unflagging optimism, Langdon's persona was that of the innocent, childlike man grappling with grown-up problems. His career briefly flourished under the guidance of the director Frank Capra, who directed Langdon's three most successful films – *The Strong Man* and *Tramp, Tramp, Tramp* both 1926, and *Long Pants* 1927. Langdon's attempts to direct his own films proved abortive, and after the coming of sound, he was reduced to playing secondary roles in minor productions.

Lange David Russell (1942–). New Zealand Labour politician, prime minister 1983–89. Lange, a barrister, was elected to the House of Representatives 1977. Labour had a decisive win in the 1984 general election on a non-nuclear military policy, which Lange immediately put into effect, despite criticism from the USA. He introduced a free-market economic policy and was re-elected 1987. He resigned Aug 1989 over a disagreement with his finance minister.

Lange Dorothea (born Nutzhorn) (1895–1965). US photographer. She was hired 1935 by the federal Farm Security Administration to document the westward migration of farm families from the Dust Bowl of the southern central USA. Her photographs, characterized by a gritty realism, were widely exhibited and subsequently published as *An American Exodus: A Record of Human Erosion* 1939.

Lange Jessica (1949–). US actress of cool blonde looks. Lange made a notable screen debut as heroine of the remake of *King Kong* 1976 and went on to attract attention in the explicit love scenes with

Jack Nicholson in *The Postman Always Rings Twice* 1981. She received the Academy Award for best supporting actress in *Tootsie* 1982. Other roles include *Music Box* 1989 and *Cape Fear* 1991.

Langer Bernhard (1957–). German golfer who came to prominence in 1981 when he became Europe's leading money winner and made his Ryder Cup debut. In 1985 he won the US Masters. Germany's first international golfing star, he may sadly be remembered for missing a putt on the final green that would have retained the 1991 Ryder Cup.

Langevin Paul (1872–1946). French physicist who contributed to the studies of magnetism and X-ray emissions, especially para-magnetic (weak attractive) and diamagnetic (weak repulsive) phenomena in gases. During World War I he invented an apparatus for locating enemy submarines, which is the basis of modern echo-location techniques.

Langevin was born and educated in Paris and also studied in the UK at the Cavendish Laboratories, Cambridge. He was professor at the Collège de France 1904–09 and from 1909 at the Sorbonne. In 1940, after the start of World War II and the German occupation of France, Langevin became director of the Ecole Municipale de Physique et de Chimie Industrielles, where he had been teaching since 1902, but he was soon arrested by the Nazis for his antifascist views. He escaped to Switzerland in 1944, returning after the liberation of Paris.

Langevin suggested 1905 that the alignment of molecular moments in a paramagnetic substance would be random except in the presence of an externally applied magnetic field. He extended his description of magnetism in terms of electron theory to account for diamagnetism, and showed how a magnetic field would affect the motion of electrons in the molecules to produce a moment that is opposed to the field. He was an early supporter of Albert Einstein's theories, and the nuclear institute in Grenoble is named after him.

Langland William (c. 1332–c. 1400). English poet. His alliterative *The Vision of William Concerning Piers the Plowman* appeared in three versions between about 1367 and 1386, but some critics believe he was only responsible for the first of these. The poem forms a series of allegorical visions, in which Piers develops from the typical poor peasant to a symbol of Jesus, and condemns the social and moral evils of 14th-century England.

Langley Samuel Pierpoint (1834–1906). US astronomer, scientist, and inventor of the bolometer, an instrument that measures radiation. His steam-driven aeroplane flew for 90 seconds in 1896 – the first flight by an engine-equipped aircraft.

He was professor of physics and astronomy at the Western University of Pennsylvania 1866–87, and studied the infrared portions of the solar system.

From 1887 he was secretary of the Smithsonian Institution in Washington DC. He founded the Smithsonian Astrophysical Observatory in 1890 and turned to pioneering work in aerodynamics, contributing greatly to the design of early aircraft. He built and tested the first successful (but uncrewed) heavier-than-air craft (aeroplane), which he launched by catapult and which flew over the Potomac River in 1896. The subsequent catapult-launched flights of the Wright brothers at Kitty Hawk owed much to Langley's principles as well as to the more powerful engines available by the early 1900s. The Langley design was tested in later years by using a model with a modern engine; it flew successfully with a pilot aboard.

Langmuir Irving (1881–1957). US scientist who invented the mercury vapour pump for producing a high vacuum, and the atomic hydrogen welding process; he was also a pioneer of the thermionic valve. In 1932 he was awarded a Nobel prize for his work on surface chemistry. He worked at the research laboratories of the General Electric Company 1909–50.

Langmuir's research on electric discharges in gases at very low pressures led to the discovery of the space-charge effect: the electron current between electrodes of any shape in vacuum is proportional to the 3/2 power of the potential difference between the electrodes. He also studied the mechanical and electrical properties of tungsten lamp filaments. Langmuir's introduction of nitrogen into light bulbs prevented them from blackening on the inside but increased heat loss, which was overcome by coiling the tungsten filament. Langmuir was the first to use the terms 'electrovalency' (for ionic bonds between metals and nonmetals) and 'covalency' (for shared-electron bonds between nonmetals). During the 1920s, Langmuir became particularly interested in the properties of liquid surfaces. He went on to propose his general adsorption theory for the effect of a solid surface during a chemical reaction.

Any service rendered to the temporal king to the prejudice of the eternal King is ... an act of treachery.

STEPHEN LANGTON
Letter from exile to the baronage of England during
the period of papal interdict imposed on King John.

Langton Stephen (*c.* 1150–1228). English priest who was mainly responsible for drafting the charter of rights, the Magna Carta.

He studied in Paris, where he became chancellor of the university, and in 1206 was created a cardinal. When in 1207 Pope Innocent III secured Langton's election as archbishop of Canterbury, King John refused to recognize him, and he was not allowed to enter England until 1213. He supported the barons in their struggle against John and worked for revisions to both church and state policies.

Langtry Lillie. Stage name of Emilie Charlotte le Breton (1853–1929). English actress. She was the mistress of the future Edward VII. She was known as the 'Jersey Lily' from her birthplace in the Channel Islands and considered to be one of the most beautiful women of her time.

She was the daughter of a rector, and married Edward Langtry (died 1897) in 1874. She first appeared professionally in London 1881, and had her greatest success as Rosalind in Shakespeare's *As You Like It*. In 1899 she married Sir Hugo de Bathe.

Suggested reading
Birkett, J *Lillie Langtry* (1979)
Langtry, Lillie *The Days I Knew* (memoirs) (1925)
Sichel, Pierre *The Jersey Lily* (1958)

Lanier Sidney (1842–1881). US flautist and poet. His *Poems* 1877 contain interesting metrical experiments, in accordance with the theories expounded in his *Science of English Verse* 1880, on the relation of verse to music.

Lanrezac Charles Louis Marie (1852–1925). French soldier. He saw action in the Franco-Prussian War and Tunisia. At the start of World War I, he commanded the 5th Army which was driven back from the Sambre, precipitating the retreat from Mons. He showed no tendencies toward the offensive and was incapable of liaising with the British, and so was relieved of his command Oct 1914 and appointed inspector of military schools.

The most lovable figure in modern politics.

A J P Taylor on GEORGE LANSBURY
in *English History 1914–1945* 1965

Lansbury George (1859–1940). British Labour politician, leader in the Commons 1931–35. He was a member of Parliament for Bow 1910–12 – when he resigned to force a by-election on the issue of votes for women, which he lost – and again 1922–40. In 1921, while mayor of the London borough of Poplar, he went to prison with most of the council rather than modify their policy of more generous unemployment relief.

Lansbury was editor of the *Daily Herald* 1912, carried it on as a weekly through World War I, and again as a daily until 1922. He was the leader of the parliamentary Labour party 1931–35, but resigned (as a pacifist) in opposition to the party's militant response to the Italian invasion of Abyssinia (present-day Ethiopia).

Suggested reading
Holman, Robert *George Lansbury* (1990)

Lansbury, George *Looking Backwards – And Forwards* (autobiography) (1935)
Postgate, R *The Life of George Lansbury* (1951)

Lansdowne Henry Charles Keith Petty-Fitzmaurice, 5th Marquis of Lansdowne (1845–1927). British Liberal Unionist politician, governor-general of Canada 1883–88, viceroy of India 1888–93, war minister 1895–1900, and foreign secretary 1900–06. While at the Foreign Office he abandoned Britain's isolationist policy by forming an alliance with Japan and an entente cordiale with France. His letter of 1917 suggesting an offer of peace to Germany created a controversy. Marquess 1866.

Lantz Walter (1900–1994). US animator and cartoon-film producer. His best-remembered contribution to popular culture is Woody Woodpecker, a disruptive bird with a piercing laugh, who featured in a total of 194 cartoons made by Lantz's studio 1940–72.

As a teenager, he worked for press magnate William Randolph Hearst, who had opened an animation studio to promote the characters in his newspapers' comic strips. Lantz moved on to Bray Studios, working among other projects on a Mutt and Jeff series, then moved to Hollywood, where he was briefly a 'gag man' for the slapstick-film producer Mack Sennett. Lantz worked for Walt Disney and Universal Studios before founding his own animation studio. His *Swing Symphonies*, using well-known vocalists on the soundtrack, were popular during World War II, but his greatest success came with Woody, who first appeared as an incidental character in a cartoon featuring an earlier Lantz figure, Andy Panda. The woodpecker was the brainchild of Ben Hardaway, who before joining Lantz's staff had created Daffy Duck for Warner Brothers. Woody's voice, initially by Mel Blanc, was subsequently provided by Grace Stafford, Lantz's second wife.

Lantz received an honorary Academy Award for his contribution to animation 1979.

Lanvin Jeanne (1867–1946). French fashion designer. She is known for her mother-and-daughter ensembles, which she began making in the early 1900s. The influence of Oriental patterns 1910 led her to create Eastern-style evening wear in velvet and satin, and she became well known for her chemise-style designs just before World War I. Her work was characterized by fine craft and embroidery and her label became a prosperous couture business.

Trained as a dressmaker and milliner, she opened a millinery shop in Paris 1890. After her death her business continued under her daughter, creating couture and ready-to-wear clothing.

A journey of a thousand miles must begin with a single step.

LAO ZI
Tao Tê Ching

Lao Zi or Lao Tzu (*c.* 604–531 BC). Chinese philosopher, commonly regarded as the founder of Taoism, with its emphasis on the Tao, the inevitable and harmonious way of the universe. Nothing certain is known of his life. The *Tao Tê Ching*, the Taoist scripture, is attributed to him but apparently dates from the 3rd century BC.

Suggested reading
Girardot, N J *Myth and Meaning in Early Taoism* (trs 1983)
Kaltenmark, Max *Lao-Tzu and Taoism* (trs 1969)
Lao Tzu *Tao Tê Ching* (trs by D Lau 1963)

La Pérouse Jean François de Galaup, Comte de (1741–1788). French explorer and navigator. In 1785 he was sent by Louis XVI on an exploratory voyage to the N and S Pacific, also with the aim of annexing the part of Australia not taken possession of by Capt Cook. In Dec 1787 he arrived in Botany Bay just days after the arrival of the First Fleet, and spent six weeks there repairing and refitting. On 24 Jan 1788 he established a camp on the N of Botany Bay. He sailed again in March and was not seen again. It is likely that his ships were wrecked on Vanikoro Island in the Santa Cruz group.

The northern shore of Botany Bay near where his ships were anchored is named after him.

Laplace Pierre Simon, Marquis de (1749–1827). French astronomer and mathematician. In 1796, he theorized that the solar system originated from a cloud of gas (the nebular hypothesis). He studied the motion of the Moon and planets, and published a five-volume survey of celestial mechanics, *Traité de méchanique céleste* 1799–1825. Among his mathematical achievements was the development of probability theory.

Traité de mécanique céleste contained the law of universal attraction – the law of gravity as applied to the Earth – and explanations of such phenomena as the ebb and flow of tides and the precession of the equinoxes. Marquis 1817.

He became professor of mathematics at the Paris Ecole Militaire 1767. In 1799 Napoleon briefly appointed Laplace minister of the interior before elevating him to the senate. From 1814, Laplace supported the Bourbon monarchy, and in 1826 refused to sign a declaration of the French Academy supporting the freedom of the press.

Lapworth Arthur (1872–1941). British chemist, one of the founders of modern physical-organic chemistry.

He became head of the Chemistry Department at Goldsmiths' College, London, in 1900. In 1909 he moved to Manchester, where he spent the rest of his life, becoming professor 1922.

Lapworth was one of the first to emphasize that organic compounds can ionize, and that different parts of an organic molecule behave as though they bear electrical charges, either permanently or at the moment of reaction.

With the development of theories of valency based on the electronic structure of the atom, Lapworth was able to refine some speculations about 'alternative polarities' in organic compounds into a classification of reaction centres as either anionoid or cationoid, the changes being determined by the influence of a key atom such as oxygen. He collaborated on these concepts with Robinson in the mid-1920s. A different terminology (nucleophilic for anionoid and electrophilic for cationoid), introduced by English chemist Christopher Ingold, eventually gained general acceptance.

Lara Brian (1969–). Trinidadian cricket player, a left-handed batsman who plays first-class cricket for Trinidad and Tobago and for Warwickshire. In April 1994 he broke the world individual test batting record with an innings of 375 against England, and 50 days later he broke the world record for an individual innings in first-class cricket with an unbeaten 501 for Warwickshire against Durham. Lara's innings of 501 contained a world record 72 boundaries – 10 sixes and 62 fours – and was part of a sequence of seven centuries in eight innings starting with his test record score.

Lardner Ring(gold) Wilmer (1885–1933). US short-story writer. A sports reporter, he based his characters on the people he met professionally. His collected volumes of short stories include *You Know Me, Al* 1916, *Round Up* 1929, and *Ring Lardner's Best Short Stories* 1938, all written in colloquial language.

He tended to give way to the revolutionary impatience of the masses, although his rhetoric, which they cheered to the echo, was unspecific and consisted largely of Marxist platitudes.

Paul Preston on FRANCISCO LARGO CABALLERO
in *The Spanish Civil War* 1986

Largo Caballero Francisco (1869–1946). Spanish socialist and leader of the Spanish Socialist Party (PSOE). He became prime minister of the Popular Front government elected in Feb 1936 and remained in office for the first ten months of the Civil War before being replaced in May 1937 by Juan Negrin (1887–1956).

Larionov Mikhail Fedorovich (1881–1964). Russian painter. He was active in Paris from 1919. With his wife Natalia Goncharova, he pioneered a semi-abstract style known as Rayonnism in which subjects appear to be deconstructed by rays of light from various sources. He is best remembered for his childlike *Soldier* series

1908–11, which was heavily influenced by Russian folk art. Larionov also produced stage sets for Diaghilev's Ballets Russes from 1915. In Paris he continued to work as a theatrical designer and book illustrator.

Deprivation is for me what daffodils were for Wordsworth.

PHILIP LARKIN
Observer 1979

Larkin Philip Arthur (1922–1985). English poet. His perfectionist, pessimistic verse includes *The North Ship* 1945, *The Whitsun Weddings* 1964, and *High Windows* 1974. He edited *The Oxford Book of 20th-Century English Verse* 1973. After his death, his letters and writings revealed an intolerance and misanthropy not found in his published material.

Born in Coventry, Larkin was educated at Oxford, and from 1955 was librarian at Hull University. He also wrote two novels.

Suggested reading
Kuby, L *An Uncommon Poet for the Common Man* (1974)
Motion, Andrew *Philip Larkin: A Writer's Life* (1993)
Thwaite, A *Larkin at Sixty* (1982)

If grief could burn out/ Like a sunken coal / The heart would rest quiet.

PHILIP LARKIN
'If Grief Could Burn Out' *Collected Poems* 1988

La Rochefoucauld François, Duc de (1613– 1680). French writer. His *Réflexions, ou sentences et maximes morales/Reflections, or Moral Maxims* 1665 is a collection of brief, epigrammatic, and cynical observations on life and society, with the epigraph 'Our virtues are mostly our vices in disguise'.

Born in Paris, he became a soldier, and took part in the *Fronde* revolts. His later years were divided between the court and literary society. He was a lover of Mme de Lafayette.

Larousse Pierre Athenase (1817–1875). French grammarian and lexicographer. His encyclopedic dictionary, the *Grand dictionnaire universel du XIXème siècle/Great Universal 19th-Century Dictionary* 1865–76, continues to be published in revised form.

Larsen Henning (1925–). Danish architect. His works include the Saudi Ministry of Foreign Affairs at Riyadh (said to be his masterpiece) and the opera house at Compton Verney, Warwickshire, England. He has been commissioned to design the new conference centre at Churchill College, Cambridge.

He was made professor of architecture at the Danish Royal Academy of Fine Arts 1968.

Larsson Carl (1853–1919). Swedish painter, engraver, and illustrator. His watercolours of domestic life, subtly coloured and full of detail, were painted for his book *Ett Hem/A Home* 1899.

Larsson Lars-Erik (1908–1986). Swedish composer, conductor, and critic. His works vary between traditional and more modern styles. For instance, the ten *Two-Part Piano Pieces* 1932 introduced the twelve-tone system to Swedish music, while his *Sinfonietta*, composed in the same year, is contrapuntal and Neo-Baroque in style. However, despite the dichotomy in his work, the characteristic that threads Larsson's music together is his gift of lyricism.

Lartigue Jacques-Henri Charles Auguste (1894–1986). French photographer. He began taking photographs of his family at the age of seven, and went on to make autochrome colour prints of women. During his lifetime he took over 40,000 photographs, documenting everyday people and situations.

la Salle René Robert Cavelier, Sieur de (1643–1687). French explorer. He made an epic voyage through North America, exploring the Mississippi River down to its mouth, and in 1682 founded

Louisiana. When he returned with colonists, he failed to find the river mouth again, and was eventually murdered by his mutinous men.

Las Casas Bartolomé de (1474–1566). Spanish missionary, historian, and colonial reformer, known as the Apostle of the Indies. He was one of the first Europeans to call for the abolition of Indian slavery in Latin America. He took part in the conquest of Cuba in 1513, but subsequently worked for Native American freedom in the Spanish colonies. *Apologetica historia de las Indias* (first published 1875–76) is his account of Indian traditions and his witnessing of Spanish oppression of the Indians.

Las Casas sailed to Hispaniola in the West Indies in 1502 and was ordained priest there in 1512. From Cuba he returned to Spain in 1515 to plead for the Indian cause, winning the support of the Holy Roman emperor Charles V. In what is now Venezuela he unsuccessfully attempted to found a settlement of free Indians. In 1530, shortly before the conquest of Peru, he persuaded the Spanish government to forbid slavery there. In 1542 he became bishop of Chiapas in S Mexico. He returned finally to Spain in 1547.

Lasdun Denys Louis (1914–). English Modernist architect. Many of his designs emphasize the horizontal layering of a building, creating the effect of geological strata extending into the surrounding city or landscape. This effect can be seen in his designs for the University of East Anglia, Norwich, 1962–68, and the National Theatre on London's South Bank 1967–76. Knighted 1976.

Lasdun trained at the Architectural Association, London, worked in partnership with Wells Coates (1895–1958) 1935–37 and from 1938 was a member of Berthold Lubetkin's Tecton Group until its dissolution 1948. His first significant work, Hallfield Housing Estate, Paddington, London 1951–59, shows Tecton influence. Other works of note include Keeling House council flats, Bethnal Green, London, 1952–55 and the Royal College of Physicians in Regent's Park, London, 1960–64.

Laski Harold Joseph (1893–1950). British political theorist. Professor of political science at the London School of Economics from 1926, he taught a modified Marxism and published *A Grammar of Politics* 1925 and *The American Presidency* 1940. He was chair of the Labour Party 1945–46.

Lassalle Ferdinand (1825–1864). German socialist. He was imprisoned for his part in the revolutions of 1848, during which he met the philosopher Karl Marx, and in 1863 founded the General Association of German Workers (later the Social-Democratic Party). His publications include *The Working Man's Programme* 1862 and *The Open Letter* 1863. He was killed in a duel arising from a love affair.

Lassus Roland de, also known as Orlando di Lasso (*c.* 1532–1594). Franco-Flemish composer. His works include polyphonic sacred music, songs, and madrigals, including settings of poems by his friend Ronsard such as 'Bonjour mon coeur/Good day my heart' 1564.

Latimer Hugh (*c.* 1485–1555). English Christian church reformer and bishop. After his conversion to Protestantism in 1524 he was imprisoned several times but was protected by Cardinal Wolsey and Henry VIII.

Latimer was appointed bishop of Worcester in 1535, but resigned in 1539. Under Edward VI his sermons denouncing social injustice won him great influence, but he was arrested in 1553, once the Catholic Mary was on the throne, and two years later he was burned at the stake in Oxford.

Suggested reading
Chester, A G *Hugh Latimer: Apostle to the English* (1954)
Darby, H S *Hugh Latimer* (1953)

Latimer Louis Howard (1848–1928). US inventor of improvements to electric lighting. He was a member of the Edison Pioneers, an organization of scientists who worked with Thomas Edison. He also supervised the installation of electric lights in New York, Philadelphia, Canada, and London.

Latimer was born in Chelsea, Massachusetts, and left school to help support the family by selling copies of the anti-slavery journal *The Liberator*. Working at a firm of patent solicitors, he learned mechanical drawing and assisted Scottish inventor Alexander Graham Bell with his application for the telephone patent. In 1880, Latimer was employed by Hiram Maxim at the US Electric Lighting Company, moving 1883 to the Edison Electric Light Company (later the General Electric Company). Between 1896 and 1911 he served as expert witness for the Board of Patent Control formed by the General Electric and Westinghouse companies to protect their patents.

After co-inventing an electric lamp 1881, Latimer went on to invent a cheap method for producing long-lasting carbon light-bulb filaments 1882. Other Latimer patents included a 'Water Closet for Railroad Cars' 1874, 'Apparatus for Cooling and Disinfecting' 1886, and 'Locking Rack for Hats, Coats, and Umbrellas' 1896.

La Tour Georges de (1593–1652). French painter. He was active in Lorraine, patronized by the duke of Lorraine, Richelieu, and perhaps also by Louis XIII. Many of his pictures are illuminated by a single source of light, with deep contrasts of light and shade, as in *Joseph the Carpenter* about 1645 (Louvre, Paris). They range from religious paintings to domestic genre scenes.

Although famous during his lifetime, La Tour was long a forgotten master and it is only in the 20th century that he has been acclaimed as one of the greatest 17th-century French painters. Since much of his work was unsigned, many 20th-century scholars have argued about the attribution of his work. Nothing is known of his training, but his work suggests acquaintance with the work of the Dutch 'candlelight' painters, for example Honthorst, and he probably visited Italy. The style of Caravaggio and the Netherlandish practice of illuminating a scene by artificial light are transformed in his paintings into a grave and simplified beauty, *The New-born Child* (Musée de Rennes) being a famous example. Other masterpieces are *The Hurdy-gurdy Player* (Nantes), an early work, and the *St Sebastian mourned by St Irene* (Berlin).

That beautiful region [Kentucky] which was soon to verify its Indian appellation of the dark and bloody ground.

CHARLES JOSEPH LA TROBE
The Rambler in North America i 90 1835

La Trobe Charles Joseph (1801–1875). Australian administrator. He was superintendent of Port Phillip district 1839–51 and first lieutenant governor of Victoria 1851–54. The Latrobe River in Victoria is named after him.

Latsis John (1910–). Greek multimillionaire shipping tycoon who, in addition to a tanker and cargo fleet, has oil and construction interests. His donation of £2 million to the UK Conservative Party drew renewed attention to his support for the right-wing military junta that ruled Greece 1967–74.

Lattre de Tassigny Jean de (1889–1952). French general. He served in World War I, and in World War II commanded the 14th Division during the German invasion 1940. He was imprisoned by the Germans after the armistice but escaped to the UK 1943 and joined General de Gaulle's Free French forces. He was the French signatory to the German surrender in Berlin 9 May 1945. Following the war he commanded NATO Land Forces Europe 1948 and was commander in chief Indo-China (now Vietnam) 1950–52.

Latynina Larissa Semyonovna (1935–). Soviet gymnast, winner of more Olympic medals than any person in any sport. She won 18 between 1956 and 1964, including nine gold medals. She won a total of 12 individual Olympic and world championship gold medals.

Laud William (1573–1645). English priest; archbishop of Canterbury from 1633. Laud's High Church policy, support for

Charles I's unparliamentary rule, censorship of the press, and persecution of the Puritans all aroused bitter opposition, while his strict enforcement of the statutes against enclosures and of laws regulating wages and prices alienated the propertied classes. His attempt to impose the use of the Prayer Book on the Scots precipitated the English Civil War. Impeached by Parliament 1640, he was imprisoned in the Tower of London, summarily condemned to death, and beheaded.

Suggested reading
Carlton, Charles *Archbishop Laud* (1987)
Trevor-Roper, Hugh *Archbishop Laud* (1963)

All that I laboured for ... was that the external worship of God ... might be kept up in uniformity ... decency and some beauty of holiness.

WILLIAM LAUD
Answer to articles brought against him in Parliament Feb 1641

Lauda Niki (Nikolas Andreas) (1949–). Austrian motor-racing driver who won the Formula One World Championship 1975, 1977, and 1984. He was also runner-up 1976, just six weeks after having a serious accident at Nurburgring, Germany.

Lauda was Formula Two champion 1972, and drove for March, BRM, Ferrari, and Brabham before his retirement 1978. He returned to the sport 1984 and won his third world title in a McLaren before eventually retiring 1985 to concentrate on his airline business, Lauda-Air. He now also acts as an adviser to the Ferrari team.

Keep right on to the end of the road / Keep right on to the end.

HARRY LAUDER
'The End of the Road'

Lauder Harry (Hugh MacLennan) (1870–1950). Scottish music-hall comedian and singer. He began his career as an 'Irish' comedian. Knighted 1919.

He was originally a millworker and miner, remembered for such songs as 'I love a lassie'.

The coldest friend and the violentest enemy I ever knew – I felt it too much not to know it.

Gilbert Burnet on JOHN MAITLAND, 1ST DUKE OF LAUDERDALE
in *History of His Own Times* 1723–34

Lauderdale John Maitland, 1st Duke of Lauderdale (1616–1682). Scottish politician. Formerly a zealous Covenanter, he joined the Royalists 1647, and as high commissioner for Scotland 1667–79 persecuted the Covenanters. He was created duke of Lauderdale 1672, and was a member of the Cabal ministry 1667–73.

Laue Max Theodor Felix von (1879–1960). German physicist who was a pioneer in measuring the wavelength of X-rays by their diffraction through the closely spaced atoms in a crystal. His work led to the techniques of X-ray spectroscopy, used in nuclear physics, and X-ray diffraction, used to elucidate the molecular structure of complex biological materials. Nobel prize 1914.

He was assistant to Max Planck at the Institute of Theoretical Physics in Berlin 1905–09, and worked at the Institute of Theoretical Physics in Munich 1909–14, when he became professor at Frankfurt. After World War I he became director of the Institute of Theoretical Physics in Berlin, resigning 1943 in protest against Nazi policies. Although Laue had refused to participate in the German atomic-energy project, he was interned in Britain by the Allies after the war. He returned to Germany 1946, and in 1951 became director of the Max Planck Institute for Research in Physical Chemistry.

Laughton English stage and film actor Charles Laughton. One of the finest character actors of the 1930s, he played the leading roles in the films The Private Life of Henry VIII *1933,* Mutiny on the Bounty *1935, and* The Hunchback of Notre Dame *1939.*

Laughton Charles (1899–1962). English actor who became a US citizen 1950. Initially a classical stage actor, he joined the Old Vic 1933. His films include such roles as the king in *The Private Life of Henry VIII* 1933 (Academy Award), Captain Bligh in *Mutiny on the Bounty* 1935, and Quasimodo in *The Hunchback of Notre Dame* 1939. In 1955 he directed *Night of the Hunter* and in 1962 appeared in *Advise and Consent*.

Here's another fine mess you've gotten me into.

OLIVER HARDY
The Laurel and Hardy Murder Case 1930

Laurel and Hardy Stan Laurel (stage name of Arthur Stanley Jefferson) (1890–1965) and Oliver Hardy (1892–1957). US film comedians. They were one of the most successful comedy teams in film history (Stan was slim, Oliver rotund). Their partnership began 1927, survived the transition from silent films to sound, and resulted in more than 200 short and feature-length films. Among these are *Pack Up Your Troubles* 1932, *Our Relations* 1936, and *A Chump at Oxford* 1940.

Suggested reading
Everson, W *The Films of Laurel and Hardy* (1983)
Guiles, Fred *Stan: The Life of Stan Laurel* (1980)
McCabe, John *Mr Laurel and Mr Hardy* (1961)

Lauren Ralph. Adopted name of Ralph Lipschitz (1939–). US fashion designer. He has produced menswear under the Polo label from 1968, women's wear from 1971, children's wear, and home furnishings from 1983. He also designed costumes for the films *The Great Gatsby* 1973 and *Annie Hall* 1977. Many of his designs are based on uniforms and traditional British sporting and country clothing.

Laurence (Jean) Margaret (born Wemyss) (1926–1987). Canadian writer. Her novels include *The Stone Angel* 1964 and *A Jest of God* 1966, both set in the Canadian prairies, and *The Diviners* 1974. She also wrote short stories set in Africa, where she lived for a time. She is particularly adept at demonstrating the interactions of character and environment and tracing the mental processes of suspicion and defensive deviousness.

Suggested reading
Laurence, Margaret *Dance on the Earth: A Memoir* (1989)
New, William (ed) *Margaret Laurence* (1977)
Thomas, Clara *The Manawaka World of Margaret Laurence* (1975)

Laurier Wilfrid (1841–1919). Canadian politician, leader of the Liberal Party 1887–1919 and prime minister 1896–1911. The first French-Canadian to hold the office, he encouraged immigration into Canada from Europe and the USA, established a separate Canadian navy, and sent troops to help Britain in the Boer War. GCMG 1897.

Whether splendidly isolated or dangerously isolated – this isolation of England comes from her superiority.

WILFRID LAURIER
Speech in the Canadian House of Commons 5 Feb 1896

Laval Carl Gustaf Patrik de (1845–1913). Swedish engineer who made a pioneering contribution to the development of high-speed steam turbines. He invented the special reduction gearing that allows a turbine rotating at high speed to drive a propeller or machine at comparatively slow speed, a principle having universal application in marine engineering.

In 1887, de Laval developed a small, high-speed turbine with a speed of 42,000 revolutions per minute. He is credited with being the first to use a convergent–divergent type of nozzle in a steam turbine in order to realize the full potential energy of the expanding steam in a single-stage machine, completed 1890. He also invented various devices for the dairy industry, including a high-speed centrifugal cream separator 1878 and a vacuum milking machine, perfected 1913.

De Laval's other interests ranged from electric lighting to electrometallurgy in aerodynamics. In the 1890s he employed more than 100 engineers in developing his devices and inventions, which are exactly described in the 1,000 or more diaries he kept.

Laval Pierre (1883–1945). French right-wing politician. He was prime minister and foreign secretary 1931–32, and again 1935–36.

Laval, born near Vichy, entered the chamber of deputies in 1914 as a socialist, but after World War I moved towards the right. His second period as prime minister was marked by the Hoare–Laval Pact for concessions to Italy in Abyssinia (now Ethiopia). In World War II he joined Pétain's Vichy government as vice-premier in June 1940; dismissed in Dec 1940, he was reinstated by Hitler's orders as head of the government and foreign minister in 1942. His part in the deportation of French labour to Germany during World War II made him universally hated. When the Allies invaded, he fled the country but was arrested in Austria, tried for treason, and shot after trying to poison himself.

Suggested reading
Cole, H *Laval* (1963)
Thompson, David *Two Frenchmen: Pierre Laval and Charles de Gaulle* (1951)
Warner, Geoffrey *Pierre Laval and the Eclipse of France* (1968)

La Vallière Louise Françoise de la Baume le Blanc, Duchesse (1644–1710). Mistress of the French king Louis XIV; she gave birth to four children 1661–74. She retired to a convent when superseded in his affections by the Marquise de Montespan.

Laver Rod(ney George) (1938–   ). Australian lawn-tennis player. He was one of the greatest left-handed players, and the only player to win the Grand Slam twice (1962 and 1969). He won four Wimbledon singles titles, the Australian title three times, the US Open twice, and the French Open twice. He turned professional after winning Wimbledon in 1962 but returned when the championships were opened to professionals in 1968.

Laveran (Charles Louis) Alphonse (1845–1922). French physician who discovered that the cause of malaria is a protozoan, the first time that protozoa were shown to be a cause of disease. For this work

and later discoveries of protozoan diseases he was awarded the 1907 Nobel Prize for Physiology or Medicine.

When the Franco-Prussian war broke out he became an army surgeon, and in 1874 he was appointed professor of military medicine at the Ecole du Val-de-Grâce. Between 1878 and 1883 he was posted to Algeria. He left the army 1896 to join the Pasteur Institute in Paris, and in 1907 he used the money from his Nobel prize to open the Laboratory of Tropical Diseases at the institute.

In 1880, Laveran examined blood samples from malarial patients and discovered amoebalike organisms growing within red blood cells. They divided and formed spores, which invaded unaffected blood cells. He noted that the spores were released in each affected red cell at the same time and corresponded with a fresh attack of fever in the patient. Laveran's studies of protozoan diseases included leishmaniasis and trypanosomiasis. His publications included *Traité des maladies et épidemies des armées/Treatise on Army Sicknesses and Epidemics* 1875 and *Trypanosomes et trypanosomiasis* 1904.

Lavery John (1856–1941). Irish portrait-painter of Edwardian society. He studied in Glasgow, London, and Paris and was influenced by the Impressionists and Whistler. Knighted 1918.

It took them only an instant to cut off that head, and a hundred years may not produce another like it.

J L Lagrange on the morrow of ANTOINE LAVOISIER's execution 1794

Lavoisier Antoine Laurent (1743–1794). French chemist. He proved that combustion needs only a part of the air, which he called oxygen, thereby destroying the theory of phlogiston (an imaginary 'fire element' released during combustion). With astronomer and mathematician Pierre de Laplace, he showed 1783 that water is a compound of oxygen and hydrogen. In this way he established the basic rules of chemical combination.

Lavoisier established that organic compounds contain carbon, hydrogen, and oxygen. From quantitative measurements of the changes during breathing, he showed that carbon dioxide and water are normal products of respiration.

He worked as a tax collector and became director of the Academy of Sciences 1785. Two years later he became a member of the provincial assembly of Orléans. During the French Revolution, left-wing leader Jean-Paul Marat, whose membership of the Academy of Sciences had been blocked by Lavoisier, accused him of imprisoning Paris and preventing air circulation because of the wall he had built round the city in 1787. He fled from his home and laboratory in 1792 but was later arrested, tried, and guillotined.

Suggested reading
Guerlac, Henry *Antoine-Laurent Lavoisier: Chemist and Revolutionary* (1975)
Holmes, Frederic *Lavoisier and the Chemistry of Life* (1985)
McKie, D *Antoine Lavoisier: Scientist, Economist, Social Reformer* (1952)

Lavrentiev Mikhail (1900–   ). Soviet scientist who developed the Akademgorodok ('Science City') in Novosibirsk, Russia from 1957.

It is fitting that we should have buried the Unknown Prime Minister by the side of the Unknown Soldier.

Herbert Asquith on ANDREW BONAR LAW
after Law's funeral in Westminster Abbey.
Quoted in Robert Skidelsky *Oswald Mosley* ch 27 1975

Law Andrew Bonar (1858–1923). British Conservative politician. Law was born in New Brunswick, Canada. He made a fortune in Scotland as a banker and iron-merchant before entering Parliament 1900. Elected leader of the opposition 1911, he became colonial secretary in Asquith's coalition government 1915–16, chancellor of the Exchequer 1916–19, and Lord Privy Seal 1919–21 in Lloyd

George's coalition. He formed a Conservative Cabinet 1922, but resigned on health grounds.

Suggested reading

Blake, Robert *The Unknown Prime Minister: The Life and Times of Andrew Bonar Law* (1955)

Ramsden, John *The Age of Balfour and Baldwin* (1978)

Law William (1686–1761). English cleric. His Jacobite opinions caused him to lose his fellowship at Emmanuel College, Cambridge, in 1714. His work *A Serious Call to a Devout and Holy Life* 1728 influenced John Wesley, the founder of Methodism.

Lawes Henry (1596–1662). English composer. His works include music for Milton's masque *Comus* 1634. His brother William Lawes (1602–1645) was also a composer, notably for viol consort.

Lawes John Bennet (1814–1900). English agriculturist who patented the first artificial 'super-phosphate' fertilizer. In 1843 he established the Rothamsted Experimental Station (Hertfordshire) at his birthplace. Baronet 1882.

Lawler Ray(mond Evenor) (1921–). Australian actor and dramatist. His work includes *The Summer of the Seventeenth Doll* 1955, a play about sugar-cane cutters, in which he played the lead role in the first production in Melbourne.

Lawrence D(avid) H(erbert) (1885–1930). English writer whose work expresses his belief in emotion and the sexual impulse as creative and true to human nature. His writing first received attention after the publication of the semi-autobiographical *Sons and Lovers* 1913. Other novels include *The Rainbow* 1915, *Women in Love* 1921, and *Lady Chatterley's Lover* 1928. Lawrence also wrote short stories (for example, 'The Woman Who Rode Away') and poetry.

The Rainbow was suppressed for obscenity, and *Lady Chatterley's Lover* was banned as obscene in the UK until 1960.

Law British Conservative politician Andrew Bonar Law. He made his fortune in the iron business in Glasgow before entering politics. He was one of the British representatives in the negotiations over the terms of settlement at the end of World War I and was a signatory to the Treaty of Versailles. (Image Select)

The son of a Nottinghamshire miner, Lawrence studied at University College, Nottingham, and became a teacher. In 1914 he married Frieda von Richthofen, ex-wife of his university professor, with whom he had run away 1912. Frieda was the model for Ursula Brangwen in *The Rainbow* and its sequel, *Women in Love*; *Sons and Lovers* includes a portrayal of his mother (died 1911). Lawrence's travels in search of health (he suffered from tuberculosis, from which he eventually died near Nice, France) prompted books such as *Mornings in Mexico* 1927.

Suggested reading

Aldington, R *D H Lawrence: Portrait of a Genius, But...* (1950)

Burgess, A *Flame Into Being: The Life and Work of D H Lawrence* (1985)

Leavis, F R *D H Lawrence, Novelist* (1955)

Meyers, J *D H Lawrence* (1990)

Nehls, E *D H Lawrence: A Composite Biography* (1957–59)

Sagar, K *D H Lawrence: Life into Art* (1985)

Lawrence Ernest O(rlando) (1901–1958). US physicist. His invention of the cyclotron particle accelerator pioneered the production of artificial radioisotopes and the synthesis of new transuranic elements. Nobel prize 1939.

He was professor of physics at the University of California, Berkeley, from 1930 and director from 1936 of the Radiation Laboratory, which he built into a major research centre for nuclear physics. During World War II, Lawrence was involved with the separation of uranium-235 and plutonium for the development of the atomic bomb, and he organized the Los Alamos Scientific Laboratories at which much of the work on this project was carried out. After the war, he continued as a believer in nuclear weapons and advocated the acceleration of their development.

The first cyclotrons were made in 1930 and were only a few centimetres in diameter. Each larger and improved design produced particles of higher energy than its predecessor, and a 68-cm/27-in model was used to produce artificial radioactivity. Among the results obtained from the use of the accelerated particles in nuclear transformations was the disintegration of the lithium nucleus to produce helium nuclei.

Lawrence Gertrude Alexandra Dagma (born Klasen) (1898–1952). English actress. She began as a dancer in the 1920s and later took leading roles in musical comedies. Her greatest successes were in the play *Private Lives* 1930–31, written especially for her by Noël Coward, with whom she co-starred, and *The King and I* 1951.

> *[He had] a self-will of heroic, even of Titanic, proportions; and one has the impression that he lived for the most part in one of the more painful corners of the inferno. He is one of those great men for whom one feels intensely sorry, because he was nothing but a great man.*
>
> Aldous Huxley on T E LAWRENCE
> in a letter to Victoria Ocampo 12 Dec 1946

Lawrence T(homas) E(dward), known as Lawrence of Arabia (1888–1935). British soldier, scholar, and translator. Appointed to the military intelligence department in Cairo, Egypt, during World War I, he took part in negotiations for an Arab revolt against the Ottoman Turks, and in 1916 attached himself to the emir Faisal. He became a guerrilla leader of genius, combining raids on Turkish communications with the organization of a joint Arab revolt, described in *The Seven Pillars of Wisdom* 1926.

Lawrence was born in Wales, studied at Oxford, and during 1910–14 took part in archaeological expeditions to Syria and Mesopotamia. On the outbreak of war he was recalled to England and employed producing maps of the Arab regions. When the sheriff of Mecca revolted against the Turks 1916 Lawrence was given the rank of colonel and went with the British Mission to King Hussein. There he reorganized the Arab army, which he practically commanded, and conducted guerrilla operations on the flank of the

British Army 1916–18. In 1918 he led his successful Arabs into Damascus. At the end of the war he was awarded the DSO for his services, and became adviser to the Foreign Office on Arab affairs. Disappointed by the Paris Peace Conference's failure to establish Arab independence, he joined the Royal Air Force in 1922 as an aircraftman under the name Ross, transferring to the tank corps under the name T E Shaw in 1923 when his identity became known. In 1935 he was killed in a motorcycle accident.

Suggested reading
Clements, F *T E Lawrence: A Reader's Guide* (1973)
Lawrence, T E *The Seven Pillars of Wisdom* (1935, several recent editions)
Lawrence, T E *The Mint* (1955)
Stewart, D *T E Lawrence* (1977)
Tabachnick, S *The T E Lawrence Puzzle* (1984)
Yardley, M *Backing into the Limelight: A Biography of T E Lawrence* (1985)

Lawrence Thomas (1769–1830). English painter. He was the leading portraitist of his day. He became painter to George III 1792 and president of the Royal Academy 1820–30. *Queen Charlotte* 1789 (National Gallery, London) is one of his finest portraits.

An infant prodigy, he was already successful and celebrated for his likenesses at Bath before he was twelve, and with little instruction he quickly became accomplished in oil painting, receiving the homage of society as the heir of the 18th-century tradition. After the Napoleonic wars he was commissioned by the Prince Regent to paint the allied sovereigns and dignitaries, travelling in state for this purpose to Aix-la-Chapelle, Vienna and Rome; the portraits are now in the Waterloo Room, Windsor, and include some of his most brilliant works, for example the *Pope Pius VII*.

He belongs to the Romantic period in the restless glitter of his style, which interested both Géricault and Delacroix, though it descends in a number of paintings into a superficial showiness. A man of cultivated and discerning taste, Lawrence has a secondary celebrity for his great collection of old master drawings, especially rich in Michelangelos and Raphaels. It realized £20,000 in the sale after his death, and though not acquired entire by the nation as he had wished, part of it went to Oxford University and is in the Ashmolean Museum. Knighted 1815.

Lawrence, St Christian martyr. Probably born in Spain, he became a deacon of Rome under Pope Sixtus II and, when summoned to deliver the treasures of the church, displayed the beggars in his charge, for which he was broiled on a gridiron. Feast day 10 Aug.

Lawson Henry (1867–1922). Australian short-story writer. First noted for verse about bush life and social and political protest, he is now remembered chiefly for his stories. Direct experience of travelling in the outback in a severe drought 1892 reinforced the grim realism of his vision of Australian rural life. His best work, represented by the collections *While the Billy Boils* 1896 and *Joe Wilson and his Mates* 1901, is sharply detailed, colloquial, and ironically understated.

Lawson Nigel, Baron Lawson of Blaby (1932–). British Conservative politician. A former financial journalist, he was financial secretary to the Treasury 1979–81, secretary of state for energy 1981–83, and chancellor of the Exchequer from 1983. He resigned 1989 after criticism by government adviser Alan Walters over his policy of British membership of the European Monetary System. Baron 1992.

Lawson William (1774–1850). English-born pastoralist and explorer of Australia who, with Blaxland and Wentworth, made the first successful crossing of the Blue Mountains, New South Wales, in 1813.

Laxness Halldór Gudjónsson (1902–). Icelandic novelist. He wrote about Icelandic life in the style of the early sagas. His novel *Salka Valka* 1931–32 is a vivid, realistic portrayal of a small fishing community and centres on a strong female character. He was awarded a Nobel prize 1955.

Layamon (lived *c.* 1200). English poet. He was the author of the *Brut*, a chronicle of about 30,000 alliterative lines on the history of Britain from the legendary Brutus onwards, which gives the earliest version of the Arthurian legend in English.

Layard Austen Henry (1817–1894). British archaeologist. He travelled to the Middle East in 1839, conducted two expeditions to Nineveh and Babylon 1845–51, and sent to the UK the specimens forming the greater part of the Assyrian collection in the British Museum. GCB 1878.

Send these, the homeless, tempest-tossed to me: / I lift my lamp beside the golden door.

EMMA LAZARUS
'The New Colossus' (Inscription on the Statue of Liberty)

Lazarus Emma (1849–1887). US poet. She was the author of the poem on the base of the Statue of Liberty that begins: 'Give me your tired, your poor/Your huddled masses yearning to breathe free.'

Leach Bernard Howell (1887–1979). English potter. His simple designs, inspired by a period of study in Japan, pioneered a revival of the art. He established the Leach Pottery at St Ives, Cornwall, 1920.

The North alone is silent and at peace. Give man time and he will spoil that too.

STEPHEN LEACOCK
My Discovery of the West 1937

Leacock Stephen Butler (1869–1944). Canadian political scientist, historian, and humorist. His humour has survived his often rather conservative political writings. His butts include the urban plutocracy and (in the parodies of *Frenzied Fictions* 1918) popular fiction, as well as human folly generally. His other humorous works include *Literary Lapses* 1910 and the controversial because recognizable *Sunshine Sketches of a Little Town* 1912.

Born in Hampshire, England, Leacock lived in Canada from 1876 and was head of the department of economics at McGill University, Montreal, 1908–36. He published studies of Mark Twain and Charles Dickens.

Suggested reading
Davies, Robertson *The Feast of Stephen* (1970)
Leacock, Stephen *The Boy I Left Behind Me* (autobiography) (1946)
Legate, David *Stephen Leacock* (1970)

Leadbelly Stage name of Huddie William Ledbetter (*c.* 1889–1949). US blues and folk singer, songwriter, and guitarist. He was a source of inspiration for the urban folk movement of the 1950s. He was 'discovered' in prison by folklorists John Lomax (1875–1948) and Alan Lomax (1915–), who helped him begin a professional concert and recording career 1934. His songs include 'Rock Island Line' and 'Good Night, Irene'.

Leakey Louis Seymour Bazett (1903–1972). East African archaeologist, anthropologist, and palaeontologist. Leakey was born in Kabete, Kenya, and studied in the UK at Cambridge. Between 1926 and 1937 he led a series of archaeological research expeditions to E Africa. He was curator of the Coryndon Museum, Nairobi, Kenya, 1945–61, and one of the founder trustees of the Kenya National Parks and Reserves. In 1961 he founded the National Museum Centre for Prehistory and Palaeontology.

Leakey began excavations at Olduvai Gorge in 1931. With Mary Leakey, he discovered a site in the Rift Valley of the Acheulian culture, which flourished between 1.5 million and 150,000 years ago. The Leakeys also found the remains of 20-million-year-old apes on an island in Lake Victoria. In 1960 they discovered the remains of *Homo habilis*, 1.7 million years old, and the skull of an Acheulian hand-axe user, *Homo erectus*, which Leakey maintained was on the direct evolutionary line of *Homo sapiens*, the modern human. In

1961 at Fort Ternan, Kenya, he found jawbone fragments of another early primate, believed to be 14 million years old.

His books for a general readership include *Stone Age Africa* 1936 and *White African* 1937.

Leakey Mary Douglas (born Nicol) (1913–1996). British archaeologist and anthropologist. In 1948 she discovered, on Rusinga Island, Lake Victoria, E Africa, the prehistoric ape skull known as *Proconsul*, about 20 million years old; and human footprints at Laetoli, to the south, about 3,750,000 years old.

She was born in London and became assistant to an archaeologist. Her collaboration with Louis Leakey began when she illustrated a book he was working on. In 1936, Mary Leakey began excavating a Late Stone Age site north of Nairobi, and with her husband discovered the remains of an important Neolithic settlement.

The Leakeys together and separately carried out excavations in Kenya, and accumulated evidence that E Africa was the possible cradle of the human race. By the middle of the 1960s Mary was living almost continuously at the permanent camp they had established at the Olduvai Gorge. She described her work in the book *Olduvai Gorge: My Search for Early Man* 1979.

Leakey Richard Erskine Frere (1944–). Kenyan palaeo-anthropologist. In 1972 he discovered at Lake Turkana, Kenya, an apelike skull, estimated to be about 2.9 million years old; it had some human characteristics and a brain capacity of 800 cu cm. In 1984 his team found an almost complete skeleton of *Homo erectus* some 1.6 million years old. He is the son of Louis and Mary Leakey.

He was appointed director of the Kenyan Wildlife Service 1988, waging a successful war against poachers and the ivory trade, but was forced to resign 1994 in the face of political interference. He lost both legs in a plane crash 1993. Since resigning, he has co-founded 1995 the Kenyan political party Safina (Swahili for Noah's Ark), which aims to clean up Kenya. The party was accused of racism and colonialism by President Daniel arap Moi.

His wife Meave continues the search for fossil humans, and in 1995 announced the discovery of bones of *Australopithecus anamensis*, an upright hominid of about 4 million years ago.

> *No one caught on that Ryan's Daughter was actually an adaptation of Madame Bovary.*
> DAVID LEAN
> in *Film Yearbook* 1986

Lean David (1908–1991). English film director. His films, noted for their painstaking craftsmanship, include early work codirected with playwright Noël Coward. *Brief Encounter* 1946 established Lean as a leading talent. Among his later films are such accomplished epics as *The Bridge on the River Kwai* 1957 (Academy Award), *Lawrence of Arabia* 1962 (Academy Award), and *Dr Zhivago* 1965. The unfavourable reaction to *Ryan's Daughter* 1970 caused him to withdraw from film making for over a decade, but *A Passage to India* 1984 represented a return to form. Knighted 1984.

Lear Edward (1812–1888). English artist and humorist. His *Book of Nonsense* 1846 popularized the limerick (a five-line humorous verse). He first attracted attention by his paintings of birds, and later turned to landscapes. He travelled to Italy, Greece, Egypt, and India, publishing books on his travels with his own illustrations, and spent most of his later life in Italy.

Born in Holloway, London of Danish descent, Lear was the 20th of 21 children and was brought up by an elder sister. His father was declared bankrupt when he was 4, he had only 5 years of schooling, and he was both epileptic and asthmatic. As a young man he was for a time art master to Queen Victoria. He made ornithological drawings 1832–36 as draughtsman for the zoologist John Gould, and later exhibited at the Royal Academy.

His *Book of Nonsense* was produced for the grandchildren of his patron, the Earl of Derby. It was this book in particular which gained him fame. His other works are *Journal of a Landscape Painter in Albania* 1851, *Journal of a Landscape Painter in Southern Calabria*

1852, *In Corsica* 1870, *More Nonsense Rhymes* 1872, and *Laughable Lyrics* 1877.
Suggested reading
Chitty, Susan *That Singular Person Called Lear* (1988)
Lehmann, John *Edward Lear and His World* (1977)
Levi, Peter *Edward Lear* (1995)
Noakes, Vivien *Edward Lear: The Life of a Wanderer* (1968)

Leavis F(rank) R(aymond) (1895–1978). English literary critic. With his wife Q D Leavis (1906–1981), he cofounded and edited the review *Scrutiny* 1932–53. He championed the work of D H Lawrence and James Joyce and in 1962 attacked C P Snow's theory of 'the two cultures' (the natural alienation of the arts and sciences in intellectual life). His other works include *New Bearings in English Poetry* 1932 and *The Great Tradition* 1948. He was a lecturer at Cambridge University.

> *The few really great – the major novelists ... are significant in the terms of the human awareness they promote.*
> F R LEAVIS
> *The Great Tradition* 1948

Leavitt Henrietta Swan (1868–1921). US astronomer who in 1912 discovered the period–luminosity law, which links the brightness of a Cepheid variable star to its period of variation. This law allows astronomers to use Cepheid variables as 'standard candles' for measuring distances in space.

She joined the Harvard College Observatory 1902, and was ultimately appointed head of the department of photographic stellar photometry.

Lebedev Peter Nikolaievich (1866–1912). Russian physicist. He proved by experiment that light exerts a minute pressure upon a physical body, thereby confirming James Maxwell's theoretic prediction.

He was professor at Moscow University 1892–1911, resigning on political grounds.

Lebedev also investigated the effects of electromagnetic, acoustic, and hydrodynamic waves on resonators; demonstrated the behavioural similarities between light and (as they are now known to be) other electromagnetic radiations; detected electromagnetic waves of higher frequency than had previously been studied; and researched into the Earth's magnetic field.

Lebesgue Henri Léon (1875–1941). French mathematician who developed a new theory of integration, now named after him. He also made contributions to set theory, the calculus of variations, and function theory.

He was professor at the University of Poitiers 1906–10, when he was appointed lecturer in mathematics at the Sorbonne. In 1920 he was promoted to the chair of the application of geometry to analysis, but he left the Sorbonne 1921 to take up his final academic post as professor of mathematics at the Collège de France.

Leblanc Nicolas (1742–1806). French chemist who in the 1780s developed a process for making soda ash (sodium carbonate, Na_2CO_3) from common salt (sodium chloride, NaCl). Soda ash was widely used industrially in making glass, paper, soap, and various chemicals. In the Leblanc process, salt was first converted into sodium sulphate by the action of sulphuric acid, which was then roasted with chalk or limestone (calcium carbonate) and coal to produce a mixture of sodium carbonate and sulphide. The carbonate was leached out with water and the solution crystallized. The process was adopted throughout Europe.

He studied medicine and became physician and assistant in 1780 to Louis Philippe Joseph (who, as duke of Orléans, would be guillotined 1793). Leblanc devised his method of producing soda ash to win a prize offered 1775 by the French Academy of Sciences, but the Revolutionary government granted him only a patent (1791), which they seized along with his factory three years later. He had no money left to re-establish the process when the factory was handed back to him by Napoleon in 1802. A broken man, Leblanc committed suicide.

Lebon Phillipe (1767–1804). French engineer who in 1801 became the first person successfully to use 'artificial' gas as a means of illumination on a large scale.

He studied at the Ecole des Ponts et Chaussées, where he later taught mechanics. He also made some attempts at perfecting the steam engine.

In about 1797, Lebon became interested in extracting gas from wood for heating and lighting purposes. He placed some sawdust in a glass tube and held it over a flame. The gas given off caught alight as it emerged from the tube, but it smoked badly and smelled. Persevering, he patented in 1799 the Thermolampe (heat lamp). For several months in 1801, he exhibited a large version of the lamp in Paris. It attracted huge crowds, but, because he had been unable to eliminate the repulsive odour given off by the gas, the public decided that his invention was not a practical one. It was left to William Murdoch (working independently at about the same time in Scotland) to succeed where Lebon had failed, and Murdoch has received the credit for the invention of gas lighting.

A man little fitted to be a national leader in an emergency.

JAMES JOLL on ALBERT LEBRUN
in *Europe Since 1870* 2nd ed 1976

Lebrun Albert (1871–1950). French politician. He became president of the senate in 1931 and in 1932 was chosen as president of the republic. In 1940 he handed his powers over to Marshal Pétain.

Le Brun Charles (1619–1690). French artist, court painter to Louis XIV from 1662. He became director 1663 of the French Academy and of the Gobelins factory, which produced art, tapestries, and furnishings for the new palace of Versailles.

The son of a sculptor, he showed precocious talent, studied under Vouet and at Rome, learning much from Poussin, was a painter to the king at 19 and was a founder member of the Académie 1648. He was patronized by Fouquet, for whom he decorated the Château de Vaux, then by Colbert, who found in him the perfect instrument for creating a comprehensive system of art and manufacture, ultimately glorifying the absolutism of the Grand Monarque. He became the first painter to the king 1662, director of the Manufacture Royale des Meubles 1663, turned the Académie into a monopoly under his dictatorship, directed the decoration of Versailles, his chief work (notably the Staircase of the Ambassadors and the *Galerie des Glaces*), and made the Gobelins into a great centre of art industry employing painters, sculptors, weavers, dyers, goldsmiths and other craftsmen. His prodigious output included religious and history paintings, for example the *History of Alexander* series (Louvre) designed for tapestry, portraiture such as the group of the banker Jabach and his family (Berlin), and countless designs for decorative projects. After the death of Colbert 1683 he was replaced in authority by his enemy Mignard, though Louis XIV remained his loyal admirer.

A committee is an animal with four back legs.

JOHN LE CARRÉ
Tinker, Tailor, Soldier, Spy 1974

Le Carré John. Pen name of David John Moore Cornwell (1931–). English writer of thrillers. His low-key realistic accounts of complex espionage include *The Spy Who Came in from the Cold* 1963, *Tinker Tailor Soldier Spy* 1974, *Smiley's People* 1980, *The Russia House* 1989, *The Night Manager* 1993, and *Our Game* 1995. He was a member of the Foreign Service 1960–64.

Le Châtelier Henri Louis (1850–1936). French physical chemist who formulated the principle now named after him, which states

that if any constraint is applied to a system in chemical equilibrium, the system tends to adjust itself to counteract or oppose the constraint.

He was professor of chemistry at the École des Mines 1877–98, moving first to the Collège de France and then in 1908 to the Sorbonne.

Le Châtelier's principle, formulated 1884–88, is particularly relevant in predicting the effects of changes in temperature and pressure on chemical reactions. It also agreed with the new thermodynamics being worked out in the USA by Josiah Gibbs. Le Châtelier was largely responsible for making Gibbs's researches known in Europe.

In 1895 Le Châtelier put forward the idea of the oxyacetylene torch for cutting and welding steel.

Leclair Jean-Marie (1697–1764). French violinist and composer. Originally a dancer and ballet-master, he composed ballet music, an opera, *Scilla et Glaucus*, and violin concertos.

Leclanché Georges (1839–1882). French engineer. In 1866 he invented a primary electrical cell, the Leclanché cell, which is still the basis of most dry batteries.

A Leclanché cell consists of a carbon rod (the anode) inserted into a mixture of powdered carbon and manganese dioxide contained in a porous pot, which sits in a glass jar containing an electrolyte (conducting medium) of ammonium chloride solution, into which a zinc cathode is inserted. The cell produces a continuous current, the carbon mixture acting as a depolarizer; that is, it prevents hydrogen bubbles from forming on the anode and increasing resistance. In a dry battery, the electrolyte is made in the form of a paste with starch.

Leclerc Phillipe. Assumed name of Jacques Philippe de Hautecloque (1902–1947). General in the Free French forces of World War II. A captain in the 4th French Infantry Division, he deserted 1940 to avoid surrendering to the Germans. He was captured but escaped to the UK. He was appointed general officer commanding French Equatorial Africa and governor of Chad and Cameroun for the Free French, and changed his name to avoid repercussions against his family in France. Leclerc's troops joined the British in N Africa and the US 3rd Army under Patton for the D-Day landings 6 June 1944. Leclerc received the German surrender of Paris 25 Aug 1945, and then took his division to Alsace to liberate Strasbourg.

Leconte de Lisle Charles Marie René (1818–1894). French poet. He was born on the Indian Ocean Island of Réunion, settled in Paris 1846, and headed the anti-Romantic group *Les Parnassiens* 1866–76. His work drew inspiration from the ancient world, as in *Poèmes antiques/Antique Poems* 1852, *Poèmes barbares/Barbaric Poems* 1862, and *Poèmes tragiques/Tragic Poems* 1884.

Le Corbusier Assumed name of Charles-Edouard Jeanneret (1887–1965). Swiss-born French architect. He was an early and influential exponent of the Modern Movement and one of the most innovative of 20th-century architects. His distinct brand of Functionalism first appears in his town-planning proposals of the early 1920s, which advocate 'vertical garden cities' with zoning of living and working areas and traffic separation as solutions to urban growth and chaos. From the 1940s several of his designs for multistorey villas were realized, notably his Unité d'hàbitation, Marseilles, 1947–52 (now demolished), using his Modulor system of standard-sized units mathematically calculated according to the proportions of the human figure.

His white-stuccoed, Cubist-style villas of the 1920s were designed as 'machines for living in', making the most of space and light through open-plan interiors, use of *pilotis* (stilts carrying the building), and roof gardens. He moved on to a more expressive mode (anticipating Brutalism) with rough, unfinished exteriors, as in the Ministry of Education, Rio de Janeiro, 1936–45, designed with Lucio Costa (1902–) and Oscar Niemeyer. In the reconstruction period after World War II, Le Corbusier's urbanization theories were highly influential, disseminated through the work of the urban planning body CIAM, although only in the gridlike layout of the new city of Chandigarh, India, 1951–56, was he able to see his visions of urban zoning fully realized. His sculptural design for the church of

Notre-Dame du Haut du Ronchamp 1950–54, worked out in the minutest detail, is a supreme example of aesthetic Functionalism.

Le Corbusier was originally a painter and engraver, but turned his attention to the problems of contemporary industrial society. His books *Vers une Architecture/Towards a New Architecture* 1923 and *Le Modulor* 1948 have had worldwide significance for town planning and building design.

Suggested reading
Blake, Peter *Le Corbusier: Architecture and Form* (1963)
Curtis, W *Le Corbusier: Ideas and Forms* (1986)
Serenyi, Peter (ed) *Le Corbusier in Perspective* (1975)

Lecouvreur Adrienne (1692–1730). French actress. She performed at the Comédie Française national theatre, where she first appeared 1717. Her many admirers included the philosopher Voltaire and the army officer Maurice de Saxe; a rival mistress of the latter, the Duchesse de Bouillon, is thought to have poisoned her.

You have made possible the advance of research to the structure of the actual genetic material.

Nobel prize citation on JOSHUA LEDERBERG 1958

Lederberg Joshua (1925–). US geneticist who showed that bacteria can reproduce sexually, combining genetic material so that offspring possess characteristics of both parent organisms. In 1958 he shared the Nobel Prize for Physiology or Medicine with George Beadle and Edward Tatum.

Lederberg is a pioneer of genetic engineering, a science that relies on the possibility of artificially shuffling genes from cell to cell. He realized 1952 that bacteriophages, viruses which invade bacteria, can transfer genes from one bacterium to another, a discovery that led to the deliberate insertion by scientists of foreign genes into bacterial cells.

He was at the University of Wisconsin 1947–59, rising to professor, and moved 1959 to Stanford University, California, becoming director of the Kennedy Laboratories of Molecular Medicine 1962.

Ledoux Claude-Nicolas (1736–1806). French Neo-Classical architect. He is stylistically comparable to E L Boullée in his use of austere, geometric forms, exemplified in his series of 44 toll houses surrounding Paris (of which only four remain), notably the Barrière de la Villette in the Place de Stalingrad, Paris, 1785–89.

Let me pass, I have to follow them, I am their leader.

ALEXANDRE LEDRU-ROLLIN
as he tried to force his way through a mob during
the 1848 Revolution, of which he was one of the chief
instigators, quoted in L Harris *The Fine Art of Political Wit* 1965

Ledru-Rollin Alexandre Auguste (1807–1874). French politician and contributor to the radical and socialist journal *La Réforme*. He became minister for home affairs in the provisional government formed in 1848 after the overthrow of Louis Philippe and the creation of the Second Republic, but he opposed the elected president Louis Napoleon.

Le Duc Anh (1920–). Vietnamese soldier and communist politician, president from 1992. A member of the politburo's military faction, he is regarded as a conservative, anxious to maintain tight party control over domestic policies.

A long-standing member of the Vietnamese Communist Party, he led Vietcong combat units during the Vietnam War. Later, as a politburo member, he held a succession of government posts, including internal security, foreign policy, and defence, before being elected to the new post of state president, replacing a collective presidency, Sept 1992.

Le Duc Tho (1911–1990). North Vietnamese diplomat who was joint winner (with US secretary of state Kissinger) of the 1973 Nobel Peace Prize for his part in the negotiations to end the Vietnam War. He indefinitely postponed receiving the award.

Ledyard John (1751–1789). American explorer and adventurer. As a British marine, he was sent to Long Island during the American Revolution 1775, but, refusing to fight against his own countrymen, he deserted in 1782. After an ill-fated journey through Siberia, he died in Cairo on his way to find the source of the Niger river.

Lee Bruce. Stage name of Lee Yuen Kam (1941–1973). US 'Chinese Western' film actor. He was an expert in kung fu, who popularized the oriental martial arts in the West with pictures such as *Fists of Fury* 1972 (made in Hong Kong) and *Enter the Dragon* 1973, his last film.

In Britain any degree of success is met with envy and resentment.

CHRISTOPHER LEE
in *Film Illustrated* 1978

Lee Christopher Frank Carandini (1922–). English film actor. His gaunt figure was memorable in the title role of *Dracula* 1958 and several of its sequels. He has not lost his sinister image in subsequent Hollywood productions. His numerous other films include *Hamlet* 1948, *The Mummy* 1959, *Julius Caesar* 1970, and *The Man with the Golden Gun* 1974.

Lee Gypsy Rose (born Rose Louise Hovick) (1914–1970). US entertainer. An 'elegant lady' in striptease routines, she was popular in literary circles. Also a published author, she wrote two mystery novels, *The G-String Murders* 1941 and *Mother Finds a Body* 1942. Her autobiography *Gypsy: A Memoir* 1957 was adapted for stage 1959 and film 1962.

Lee Henry (1756–1818). American military and political leader. In the cavalry during the American Revolution 1775–83, he rose to the rank of major, winning the nickname 'Light-Horse Harry' for his lightning attacks. After the war, he entered politics and served in the Continental Congress 1785–88, as governor of Virginia 1792–95, and as a member of the US House of Representatives 1799–1801.

Born in Leesylvania, Virginia, Lee was educated at Princeton University. He was a close friend of George Washington and helped suppress the Whiskey Rebellion 1794. He was the father of Robert E Lee.

Lee Jennie (Janet), Baroness Lee of Asheridge (1904–1988). British socialist politician. She became a member of Parliament for the Independent Labour Party at the age of 24, and in 1934 married Aneurin Bevan. On the left wing of the Labour Party, she was on its National Executive Committee 1958–70 and was minister of education 1967–70, during which time she was responsible for founding the Open University in 1969. She was made a baroness in 1970.

Lee Laurie (1914–). English writer. His works include the autobiographical novel *Cider with Rosie* 1959, a classic evocation of childhood; nature poetry such as *The Bloom of Candles* 1947; and travel writing including *A Rose for Winter* 1955.

See the conquering hero comes, / Sound the trumpets, beat the drums.

NATHANIEL LEE
The Rival Queens 1677

Lee Nathaniel (*c.* 1653–1692). English dramatist. From 1675 on, he wrote a number of extravagant tragedies, such as *The Rival Queens* 1677, about the two wives of Alexander the Great.

Lee Robert E(dward) (1807–1870). US Confederate general in the American Civil War, a military strategist. As military adviser to Jefferson Davis, president of the Confederacy, and as commander of

Lee, Robert *US Confederate general Robert E Lee. In the American Civil War, Lee was commander of the army of N Virginia, and military adviser to Jefferson Davis, president of the Confederacy. He surrendered 1865.*
(Image Select)

the army of N Virginia, he made several raids into Northern territory, but was defeated at Gettysburg and surrendered 1865 at Appomattox.

Lee, born in Virginia, was commissioned 1829 and served in the Mexican War. In 1859 he suppressed John Brown's raid on Harper's Ferry. On the outbreak of the Civil War 1861 he joined the Confederate army of the Southern States, and in 1862 received the command of the army of N Virginia and won the Seven Days' Battle defending Richmond, Virginia, the Confederate capital, against General McClellan's Union forces.

In 1863 Lee won victories at Fredericksburg and Chancellorsville, and in 1864 at Cold Harbor, but was besieged in Petersburg, June 1864–April 1865. He surrendered to General Grant 9 April 1865 at Appomattox courthouse.

Suggested reading
Dowdey, Clifford *Lee* (1965)
Dowdey, Clifford *The Death of a Nation: The Story of Lee and His Men at Gettysburg* (1988)
Fishwick, M W *Lee and the War* (1963)
Fuller, J F *Grant and Lee* (1982)
Sanborn, Margaret *Robert E Lee* (1966–67)

Lee Spike (Shelton Jackson) (1957–). US film director, actor, and writer. His work presents the bitter realities of contemporary African-American life in an aggressive, often controversial manner. His films, in which he sometimes appears, include *She's Gotta Have It* 1986, *Do The Right Thing* 1989, *Jungle Fever* 1991, and *Malcolm X* 1992.

Lee Kuan Yew (1923–). Singapore politician, prime minister 1959–90. Lee founded the anticommunist Socialist People's Action Party 1954 and entered the Singapore legislative assembly 1955. He was elected the country's first prime minister 1959, and took Singapore out of the Malaysian federation 1965. He remained in power until his resignation 1990, and was succeeded by Goh Chok Tong. Until 1992 he held on to the party leadership.

Leech John (1817–1864). English caricaturist. He illustrated many books, including Dickens' *A Christmas Carol*, and during 1841–64 contributed about 3,000 humorous drawings and political cartoons to *Punch* magazine.

Leese Oliver William Hargreaves (1894–1978). British general. He served with the British Expeditionary Force in France 1940, then took command of XXX Corps of the 8th Army in N Africa shortly before El Alamein 1942. He remained one of Montgomery's most trusted corps commanders, serving with him through the desert, Sicily, and Italy, and succeeding to the command of 8th Army when Montgomery left. He was appointed commander in chief Allied Land Forces Southeast Asia (ALFSEA) 1944 and held this post until succeeded by Field Marshal Slim 1945. Succeeded to baronetcy 1937.

Lee Teng-hui (1923–). Taiwanese right-wing politician, vice president 1984–88, president and Kuomintang party leader from 1988. Lee, the country's first island-born leader, is viewed as a reforming technocrat.

Born in Tamsui, Taiwan, Lee taught for two decades as professor of economics at the National Taiwan University before becoming mayor of Taipei in 1979. A member of the Kuomintang party and a protégé of Chiang Ching-kuo, he became vice president of Taiwan in 1984 and succeeded to both the state presidency and Kuomintang leadership on Chiang's death in Jan 1988. He has significantly accelerated the pace of liberalization and Taiwanization in the political sphere.

Lee Tsung-Dao (1926–). Chinese physicist whose research centred on the physics of weak nuclear forces. In 1956 Lee proposed that weak nuclear forces between elementary particles might disobey certain key assumptions; for instance, the conservation of parity. He shared the 1957 Nobel Prize for Physics with his colleague Yang Chen Ning (1922–).

Lee trained in China; a scholarship sent him to the USA in 1946, working mostly on particle physics at the Princeton Institute of Advanced Study and at the University of California.

Leeuwenhoek Anton van (1632–1723). Dutch pioneer of microscopic research. He ground his own lenses, some of which magnified up to 300 times. With these he was able to see individual red blood cells, sperm, and bacteria, achievements not repeated for more than a century.

Leeuwenhoek was born in Delft and apprenticed to a cloth merchant. From 1660, having obtained the sinecure of chamberlain to the sheriffs of Delft, he devoted much of his time to lens grinding and microscopy. From 1672 to 1723 he described and illustrated his observations in more than 350 letters to the Royal Society of London. His fame was such that he was visited by several reigning monarchs, including Frederick I of Prussia and Tsar Peter the Great.

Leeuwenhoek ground more than 400 lenses, which he mounted in various ways in single-lens microscopes. Most of them were very small (some were about the size of a pinhead). In 1674 he discovered protozoa, which he called 'animalicules', and calculated their sizes. He also studied the structure of the lens in the eye, muscle striations, insects' mouthparts, the fine structure of plants, and discovered parthenogenesis in aphids.

It is difficult to deny, or even to doubt the existence of such a phenomenon as the vampire.

SHERIDAN LE FANU
Carmilla ch 15 1970 ed

Le Fanu (Joseph) Sheridan (1814–1873). Irish writer. He wrote mystery novels and short stories, such as *The House by the Churchyard* 1863, *Uncle Silas* 1864, and *In a Glass Darkly* 1872.

Lefebvre Marcel François (1905–1991). French Catholic priest in open conflict with the Roman Catholic Church. In 1976, he was suspended by Pope Paul VI for the unauthorized ordination of priests at his Swiss headquarters. He continued and in June 1988 he was excommunicated by Pope John Paul II, in the first formal schism within the church since 1870.

Ordained in 1929, Lefebvre was a missionary and an archbishop in W Africa until 1962. He opposed the liberalizing reforms of the Second Vatican Council 1962–65 and formed the 'Priestly Cofraternity of Pius X'.

Legendre Adrien-Marie (1752–1833). French mathematician who was particularly interested in number theory, celestial mechanics, and elliptic functions. In 1783–84 he introduced to celestial mechanics what are now known as Legendre polynomials. These are solutions to a second-order differential equation.

During the French Revolution, he became head of the government department established to standardize French weights and measures 1794, as well as professor at the Institut de Marat. From 1813 he was chief of the Bureau de Longitudes.

Léger Fernand (1881–1955). French painter and designer. He was associated with Cubism. From around 1909 he evolved a characteristic style of simplified forms, clear block outlines, and bold colours. Mechanical forms are constant themes in his work, which includes designs for the Swedish Ballet 1921–22, murals, and the abstract film *Ballet mécanique/Mechanical Ballet* 1924.

Originally trained as an architect, he turned to painting 1903, studying at the École des Beaux Arts, the Académie Julian and in the Louvre. At first attracted by Impressionism, he came under the Cubist influence 1909–14, and during a period of war service took an interest in machine forms which became an important factor in his work from 1917. He made use of such things as railway signal boxes and street signs in 'mechanized' composition, though in his later work he returned to human themes – always, however, with a strongly simplified decorative element. He was in the USA 1940–45, but returned to Paris 1945. In addition to paintings he produced a number of lithographs and book illustrations, and designs for wall decoration, mosaic and stained glass.

Suggested reading
De Francia, Peter *Ferdnand Léger* (1983)
Green, Christopher *Léger and the Avant-Garde* (1976)
Néret, Gilles *F. Léger* (trs 1993)

Le Gray Gustave (1820–1882). French photographer. In 1850 he invented the waxed paper negative, a more efficient version of the calotype where the paper is waxed before being coated with silver iodide. He also experimented with printing images using more than one negative, notably in his detailed seascapes which use a separate negative for sea and sky.

Le Guin Ursula K(roeber) (1929–). US writer of science fiction and fantasy. Her novels include *The Left Hand of Darkness* 1969, which questions sex roles; the *Earthsea* series 1968–91; *The Dispossessed* 1974, which compares an anarchist and a capitalist society; and *Always Coming Home* 1985.

Lehár Franz (1870–1948). Hungarian composer. He wrote many operettas, among them *The Merry Widow* 1905, *The Count of Luxembourg* 1909, *Gypsy Love* 1910, and *The Land of Smiles* 1929. He also composed songs, marches, and a violin concerto.

Lehman Herbert Henry (1878–1963). US political leader. In 1932 he became governor of New York, and his subsequent support of F D Roosevelt's reform policies earned his own administration the name 'Little New Deal'. In 1942 Lehman was appointed director of the federal Office of Foreign Relief and Rehabilitation. He served in the US Senate 1949–57.

Lehmann Lotte (1888–1976). German soprano. She excelled in Wagnerian operas and was an outstanding Marschallin in Richard Strauss' *Der Rosenkavalier*.

Lehmann Rosamond Nina (1901–1990). English novelist. Her books include *Dusty Answer* 1927, *The Weather in the Streets* 1936,

The Echoing Grove 1953, and, following a long silence, *A Sea-Grape Tree* 1976. Once neglected as too romantic, her novels have regained popularity in the 1980s because of their sensitive portrayal of female adolescence.

One can present people with opportunities. One cannot make them equal to them.

ROSAMOND LEHMANN
The Ballad and the Source 1944

Lehmbruck Wilhelm (1881–1919). German sculptor, painter, and printmaker. He was a leading Expressionist of the early 1900s, whose elongated, sorrowing figures carry great emotional power. His principal works are a distillation of archaic and classical forms, their pathos derived from the artist's innate melancholy and his impressions of the chaos of war. *The Fallen* 1915–16 (Lehmbruck Estate, Duisburg) is a late masterpiece in cast stone.

Lehmbruck executed his major works 1910–19, initially in Paris 1910–14 under the influence of Rodin and Aristide Maillol and stimulated by his friendships with Brancusi, Archipenko, and Modigliani.

Lehrer Tom (Thomas Andrew) (1928–). US humorist and mathematician. During the 1950s and 1960s he wrote and performed satirical songs, accompanying himself on the piano. Sometimes political, mainly characterized by black humour, songs like 'Poisoning Pigeons in the Park' won a following throughout the world.

Lehrer's music was full of quotations from popular songs of the past; such numbers as 'My Home Town', 'The Old Dope Peddler', and 'I Hold Your Hand in Mine' parodied old sentimental songs, while the rousing march 'We Will All Go Together When We Go' anticipated a nuclear holocaust. His albums include the live *An Evening Wasted with Tom Lehrer* 1959 and *That Was the Year That Was* 1965.

Lehrer was born in New York. He began writing songs as a graduate student at Harvard, and performed professionally from 1953. After returning to teach mathematics at Harvard 1960, he continued to write songs until 1967, and performed occasionally. In 1972 he joined the faculty of Cowell College, University of California at Santa Cruz, to teach both mathematics and the history of American musical comedy.

Leiber and Stoller Jerry Leiber (1933–) and Mike Stoller (1933–) US songwriters and record producers. They wrote classic pop and rock songs of the 1950s and early 1960s, including hits for vocal group the Coasters ('Riot in Cell Block Number Nine' 1953, 'Searchin'' 1957, 'Poison Ivy' 1959) and songs for early Elvis Presley films such as 'Jailhouse Rock' 1957. Storytelling and tongue-in-cheek humour characterize their work, ranging from 'Love Potion Number Nine' (a 1959 hit for vocal group the Clovers) to 'Is That All There Is?' (a 1969 hit for jazz singer Peggy Lee (1920–)).

The imaginary number is a fine and wonderful recourse of the divine spirit, almost an amphibian between being and not being.

GOTTFRIED WILHELM LEIBNIZ
Attributed remark

Leibniz Gottfried Wilhelm (1646–1716). German mathematician, philosopher, and diplomat. Independently of, but concurrently with, English scientist Isaac Newton he developed the branch of mathematics known as calculus. In his metaphysical works, such as *The Monadology* 1714, he argued that everything consisted of innumerable units, monads, the individual properties of which determined each thing's past, present, and future.

Monads, although independent of each other, interacted predictably; this meant that Christian faith and scientific reason need not be in conflict and that 'this is the best of all possible worlds'. Leibniz's optimism is satirized in French philosopher Voltaire's novel *Candide*.

Leibniz was born in Leipzig and studied there and at Jena. From 1866 he was in the service of the archbishop and elector of Mainz, his special task being to devise plans to preserve the peace of Europe, just then emerging from the Thirty Years' War. This took him to France for three years. On the death of the elector of Mainz in 1673, Leibniz went to London, and there became acquainted with the work of Newton. The last 15 years of his life would be marred by dispute with Newton over which of them first invented the calculus. From 1676, Leibniz was librarian to the duke of Brunswick in Hanover, and often charged with diplomatic missions. From 1712 to 1714 he was an imperial privy councillor in Vienna. In 1714 the duke of Brunswick acceded to the English throne as George I, but Leibniz was denied permission to accompany him to London.

Leibniz designed a calculating machine, completed about 1672, which was able to multiply, divide, and extract roots. He worked intermittently throughout his life at devising what he called a Universal Characteristic, a language that would be accessible to everyone.

Suggested reading
Broad, C D and Lewy, C *Leibniz: An Introduction* (1975)
Brown, Stuart *Leibniz* (1984)
Saw, Ruth *Leibniz* (1956)

Leibovitz Annie (1950–). US photographer. Her elaborately staged portraits of American celebrities appeared first in *Rolling Stone* magazine and later in *Vanity Fair*. The odd poses in which her sitters allow themselves to be placed suggest an element of self-mockery.

Leicester Robert Dudley, Earl of Leicester (*c.* 1532–1588). English courtier. Son of the Duke of Northumberland, he was created Earl of Leicester 1564. Queen Elizabeth I gave him command of the army sent to the Netherlands 1585–87 and of the forces prepared to resist the threat of Spanish invasion 1588. His lack of military success led to his recall, but he retained Elizabeth's favour until his death.

Leicester's good looks attracted Queen Elizabeth, who made him Master of the Horse 1558 and a privy councillor 1559. But his poor performance in the army ended any chance of marrying the queen. He was a staunch supporter of the Protestant cause.

Leichhardt (Friedrich Wilhelm) Ludwig (1813–1848). Prussian-born Australian explorer. In 1843, he walked 965 km/600 mi from Sydney to Moreton Bay, Queensland, and in 1844 walked from Brisbane to Arnhem Land; he disappeared during a further expedition from Queensland in 1848. Patrick White used the character of Leichhardt in his book *Voss* 1957.

Leif Ericsson Norse explorer; see ◊Ericsson, Leif.

Leigh Mike (1943–). English dramatist and filmmaker. He is noted for his sharp, carefully improvised social satires. He directs his own plays, which evolve through improvisation before they are scripted. His work for television includes *Nuts in May* 1976 and *Abigail's Party* 1977; his films include *High Hopes* 1989, *Life Is Sweet* 1991, and *Naked* 1993, a bleak depiction of a Homeric journey through modern London.

Leigh Vivien. Stage name of Vivien Mary Hartley (1913–1967). Indian-born English actress. She appeared on the stage in London and New York, and won Academy Awards for her performances as Scarlett O'Hara in *Gone with the Wind* 1939 and as Blanche du Bois in *A Streetcar Named Desire* 1951. She was married to Laurence Olivier 1940–60, and starred with him in the play *Antony and Cleopatra* 1951. Her other films include *Lady Hamilton* 1941, *Anna Karenina* 1948, and *Ship of Fools* 1965.

Leigh-Mallory Trafford Leigh (1892–1944). British air chief marshal in World War II. He took part in the Battle of Britain and was commander in chief of Allied air forces during the invasion of France. He ensured complete Allied air superiority during the

invasion and his plan to destroy German road and rail links was crucial in isolating most of the German defence forces. KCB 1943.

Leighton Frederic Stretton, 1st Baron Leighton of Stretton (1830–1896). English painter and sculptor. He specialized in Classical Greek subjects such as his *Captive Andromache* 1888 (Manchester City Art Gallery). He became president of the Royal Academy 1878. His house and studio near Holland Park, London, are now a museum.

Comprehensively trained in Italy, Germany and France, he became the main representative of classicism in its late-Victorian form, that is, in subject pictures inspired by ancient Greece and the Parthenon frieze. Many landscapes also resulted from his extensive travels, and his visits to the Middle East suggested the *décor* of the famous Arab Hall at his house in London. His decorative art in fresco and mosaic can be studied in the Victoria and Albert Museum; his bronzes *The Sluggard* and *Athlete struggling with Python* are in the Tate Gallery, London. His varied talents, learning and personal charm contributed to make him a great success as president of the Royal Academy. Knighted 1878, baron 1896.

Leishman William Boog (1865–1926). Scottish army physician who discovered the protozoan parasite that causes the group of diseases now known as leishmaniasis. Knighted 1909.

Leishman was born and educated in Glasgow, and spent his entire career in the Royal Army Medical Corps. He was posted to India 1890–97. From 1903 he was professor at the Army Medical School. In 1914 he began advising the War Office on tropical diseases, and he became the first director of pathology at the War Office in 1919. He was director-general of the Army Medical Service from 1923.

Leisler Jacob (1640–1691). German-born colonial administrator in America. Taking advantage of the political instability caused by England's Glorious Revolution of 1688, he took command of New York in the name of William and Mary. Deposed in 1691 by troops dispatched from England, Leisler was tried and hanged for treason.

Born in Frankfurt, Germany, Leisler arrived in New Amsterdam (New York from 1664) as a mercenary for the Dutch West India Company 1660, becoming a successful merchant when the colony passed to English rule.

Lejeune Jérôme Jean Louis Marie (1926–1994). French medical geneticist. Although the congenital condition known now as Down's syndrome was named after English physician J L H Down who studied it, it was Lejeune who discovered that Down's syndrome is the result of having an additional chromosome.

He believed chromosome deviations would in the future be treated by gene therapy, and vigorously opposed prenatal screening with a view to terminating Down's syndrome fetuses.

In 1964 Lejeune was appointed professor of fundamental genetics in the Faculty of Medicine in Paris. He firmly believed in the 'brotherhood' of humanity; that the chromosome pattern of modern humans must have originated in a very small group of people – even one pair.

Leland John (*c.* 1506–1552). English antiquary whose manuscripts have proved a valuable source for scholars. He became chaplain and librarian to Henry VIII, and during 1534–43 toured England collecting material for a history of English antiquities. The *Itinerary* was published in 1710.

Lely Peter. Adopted name of Pieter van der Faes (1618–1680). Dutch painter. He was active in England from 1641, painting fashionable portraits in the style of van Dyck. His subjects included Charles I, Cromwell, and Charles II. He painted a series of admirals, *Flagmen* (National Maritime Museum, London), and one of *The Windsor Beauties* (Hampton Court, Richmond), fashionable women of Charles II's court. Knighted 1679.

Lemaître Georges Edouard (1894–1966). Belgian cosmologist who in 1933 proposed the Big Bang theory of the origin of the universe. US astronomer Edwin Hubble had shown that the universe was expanding, but it was Lemaître who suggested that the expansion had been started by an initial explosion, the Big Bang, a theory that is now generally accepted. Lemaître visualized a 'primal atom', an incredibly dense 'egg' containing all the material for the universe within a sphere about 30 times larger than the Sun. Somewhere between 20,000 and 60,000 million years ago, in his view, this atom exploded. Lemaître was made professor of astrophysics at the University of Louvain 1927.

Leman Gerart Matheu Joseph Georges (1851–1920). Belgian general. He was director of studies at the Belgian military academy 1899 and commandant 1905. He was commandant of the fortress at Liège 1914 and directed its defence when the Germans attacked at the start of World War I. He was wounded and captured Aug 1914. After a period in a prison camp his health deteriorated and he was permitted to go into internment in Switzerland 1917 and to return to Belgium Jan 1918, where he died 17 Oct 1920.

Le May Curtis E(merson) (1906–   ). US air force general. He commanded 305 Bomber Group, one of the first US units to arrive in the UK in World War II, and devised most of the tactics employed by the 8th Air Force. He took charge of 20th Bomber Command in the India-Burma-China theatre 1944 and carried out long-range B-29 raids against Formosa and W Japan. He then moved to 21 Bomber Command in the Marianas Jan 1945, and began a strong offensive against Japanese cities. The B-29 bombers which dropped the atom bombs Aug 1945 were under Le May's command.

I'd like to spend the rest of my life doing nothing but Billy Wilder films.

JACK LEMMON
in *Film and Filming* Nov 1969

Lemmon Jack (John Uhler III) (1925–   ). US character actor. He has often been cast as the lead in comedy films, such as *Some Like It Hot* 1959, but is equally skilled in serious roles, as in *The China Syndrome* 1979, *Save the Tiger* 1973 (Academy Award), and *Missing* 1982.

LeMond Greg (1961–   ). US racing cyclist, the first American to win the Tour de France 1986. Although his career received a setback in 1987 through injury, he recovered sufficiently to regain his Tour de France title in 1989 by seven seconds, the smallest margin ever. He won it again in 1990. He also won the World Professional Road Race in 1983 and 1989.

Le Nain three 17th-century French painters, all born at Laon and active in Paris: Antoine, the eldest (*c.* 1588–1648), Louis (*c.* 1593–1648) and Mathieu, the youngest (*c.* 1607–1677). Nothing is known of their training, though all became members of the Académie 1648. They seem to have collaborated, in some works at least, though the signature on pictures, 'Le Nain', without initial, does not distinguish them.

The paintings have been divided into three (not very determinate) groups: 'Antoine', small figures painted on copper; 'Louis', larger in scale and subdued in colour; 'Mathieu', subjects reflecting a higher social level than the peasant scenes of the other two. From this classification Louis emerges as the main representative of the family genius and one of the great French artists of the early 17th century in the sympathetic realism and beauty of painting in his compositions drawn from peasant life, such as the *Peasants' Meal* (Louvre).

Lenard Philipp Eduard Anton (1862–1947). Hungarian-born German physicist who investigated the photoelectric effect and

No entry to Jews and Members of the German Physical Society

Notice on PHILIPP LENARD's office door

cathode rays (the stream of electrons emitted from the cathode in a vacuum tube). Nobel prize 1905.

In 1898 he became professor of experimental physics at Kiel, and held the same post at Heidelberg 1907–31. In 1924 Lenard became a Nazi. Obsessed with the idea of producing a purely 'Aryan' physics, he spent his later years reviling Albert Einstein and other Jewish physicists.

Lenard's work on cathode rays began 1892, and led him to the conclusion that an atom is mostly empty space. He also suggested that the part of the atom where the mass was concentrated consisted of neutral doublets or 'dynamids' of negative and positive electricity. This preceded by ten years the classic model of the atom proposed by Ernest Rutherford 1911.

Lenard devised the grid in the thermionic valve that controls electron flow. He showed that an electron must have a certain minimum energy before it can produce ionization in a gas. He also studied luminescent compounds and, from 1902 onwards, discovered several fundamental effects in photoelectricity.

Love never dies of starvation, but often of indigestion.

NINON DE LENCLOS
L'Esprit des Autres 3

Lenclos Ninon (Anne) de (1615–1705). French courtesan. As the recognized leader of Parisian society, she was the mistress of many highly placed men, including General Condé and the writer La Rochefoucauld.

Lendl Ivan (1960–   ). Czech-born American lawn-tennis player. He has won eight Grand Slam singles titles, including the US and French titles three times each. He has won more than $15 million in prize money. He retired from the game Dec 1994, citing a degenerative spinal condition.

L'Enfant Pierre Charles (1754–1825). French-born US architect and engineer. He is remembered for his survey and plan for the city of Washington 1791–92. Although he was dismissed from the project before he was able to design any major buildings, the constructed layout is much as he conceived it, clearly reflecting the plan of his native Versailles. After having served on the American side in the War of Independence, L'Enfant received several important commissions, notably Federal House, Philadelphia.

Leng Virginia Helen Antoinette (1955–   ). British three-day eventer (rider in horse trials), born in Malta. She has won world, European, and most major British championships. She was a member of the British team at two world championships (1982 and 1986) and was the individual champion in 1986 on Priceless. She won the European individual title twice (1985 and 1989), the Badminton horse trials in the same years, and Burghley Horse Trials in 1983, 1984, and 1986.

Lenglen Suzanne (1899–1938). French tennis player, Wimbledon singles and doubles champion 1919–23 and 1925, and Olympic champion 1921. She became professional in 1926. She also popularized sports clothes designed by Jean Patou.

It is true that liberty is precious – so precious that it must be rationed.

VLADIMIR LENIN
quoted in S and B Webb *Soviet Communism* 1941

Lenin Vladimir Ilyich. Adopted name of Vladimir Ilyich Ulyanov (1870–1924). Russian revolutionary, first leader of the USSR, and communist theoretician. Active in the 1905 Revolution, Lenin had to leave Russia when it failed, settling in Switzerland in 1914. He returned to Russia after the February revolution of 1917. He led the Bolshevik revolution in Nov 1917 and became leader of a Soviet government, concluded peace with Germany, and organized a successful resistance to White Russian (pro-tsarist) uprisings and foreign intervention 1918–20. His modification of traditional Marxist doctrine to fit conditions prevailing in Russia became known as Marxism-Leninism, the basis of communist ideology.

Lenin was born on 22 April, 1870 in Simbirsk (now renamed Ulyanovsk), on the river Volga, and became a lawyer in St Petersburg. His brother was executed in 1887 for attempting to assassinate Tsar Alexander III. A Marxist from 1889, Lenin was sent to Siberia for spreading revolutionary propaganda 1895–1900. He then edited the political paper *Iskra* ('The Spark') from abroad, and visited London several times. In *What Is to be Done?* 1902, he advocated that a professional core of Social Democratic Party activists should spearhead the revolution in Russia, a suggestion accepted by the majority (*bolsheviki*) at the London party congress 1903. From Switzerland he attacked socialist support for World War I as aiding an 'imperialist' struggle, and wrote *Imperialism* 1917.

After the renewed outbreak of revolution in Feb/March 1917, he was smuggled back into Russia in April by the Germans so that he could take up his revolutionary activities and remove Russia from the war, allowing Germany to concentrate the war effort on to the Western Front. On arriving in Russia Lenin established himself at the head of the Bolsheviks, against the provisional government of Kerensky; a complicated power struggle ensued, but eventually Lenin triumphed 8 Nov 1917; a Bolshevik government was formed, and peace negotiations with Germany were begun leading to the signing of the Treaty of Brest Litovsk 3 March 1918.

From the overthrow of the provisional government in Nov 1917 until his death, Lenin effectively controlled the Soviet Union, although an assassination attempt in 1918 injured his health. He founded the Third (Communist) International in 1919. With communism proving inadequate to put the country on its feet, he introduced the private-enterprise New Economic Policy 1921.

Lenin's embalmed body is in a mausoleum in Red Square, Moscow. In 1898 he married Nadezhda Konstantinova Krupskaya (1869–1939), who shared his work and wrote *Memories of Lenin*.

Suggested reading
Conquest, Robert *Lenin* (1972)
Hill, Christopher *Lenin and the Russian Revolution* (1978)
Schapiro, Leonard and Reddaway, Peter (eds) *Lenin* (1987)
Shub, D *Lenin* (1966)
Ulam, Adam *Lenin and the Bolsheviks* (1965)
Volkogonov, Dmitri *Lenin: Life and Legacy* (trs 1994)

Give Peace a Chance.

JOHN LENNON
Song title

Lennon John Winston (1940–1980). UK rock singer, songwriter, and guitarist; a founder member of the Beatles. He lived in the USA from 1971. Both before the band's break-up 1970 and in his solo career, he collaborated intermittently with his wife Yoko Ono (1933–   ). 'Give Peace a Chance', a hit 1969, became an anthem of the peace movement. His solo work alternated between the confessional and the political, as on the album *Imagine* 1971. He was shot dead by a fan.

Lennon is regarded as having tempered with cynicism and acerbic wit the tendency to sentimentality of his Beatle co-writer Paul McCartney, but idealism was evident in Lennon's life outside the Beatles, with publicity stunts like the 1969 'bed-in for peace' (he and Ono stayed in bed in an Amsterdam hotel for a week, receiving the press). His first solo album, *John Lennon/Plastic Ono Band* 1970, contained deeply personal songs like 'Mother' and 'Working Class Hero'; subsequent work, though uneven, included big hits like 'Whatever Gets You Through the Night' 1974. He often worked with producer Phil Spector. On *Rock 'n' Roll* 1975 Lennon covered non-original songs that the Beatles had played in the early 1960s. *Double Fantasy* 1980, made in collaboration with Ono, reached number one in the album charts after his death.

At the height of Beatlemania, Lennon published two small books of his drawings and nonsense writings, *In His Own Write* 1964 and *A Spaniard in the Works* 1965.

Suggested reading
Coleman, Ray *John Winston Lennon* (1984)
Goldman, Albert *The Lives of John Lennon* (1988)
Shevey, Sandra *The Other Side of Lennon* (1990)

Lennox Charlotte (born Ramsay) (1720–1804). American-born English novelist. Her popular novel *The Female Quixote* 1752 describes how the beautiful and intelligent Arabella creates comic misunderstandings through interpreting real life as if it were a French romance. Lennox died penniless in spite of producing *Shakespear Illustrated* 1753–54 (an anthology of Shakespearean sources), and the novels *Henrietta* 1753, *Sophia* 1761, and *Euphemia* 1790.

Ah what is man? Wherefore does he why? Whence did he whence? Whither is he withering?

DAN LENO
From Dan Leno's own stage material

Leno Dan. Stage name of George Galvin (1860–1904). English comedian. A former acrobat, he became the idol of the music halls, and was considered the greatest of pantomime 'dames'.

Lenoir (Jean Joseph) Etienne (1822–1900). Belgian-born French engineer and inventor who in the early 1860s produced the first practical internal-combustion engine and a car powered by it. He also developed a white enamel 1847, an electric brake 1853, and an automatic telegraph 1865.

Several people had claimed to have invented an internal-combustion engine, but not until Lenoir in 1859 did a practical model become a reality. His engine consisted of a single cylinder with a storage battery (accumulator) for the electric ignition system. Its two-stroke cycle was provided by slide valves, and it was fuelled by coal gas.

Lenoir built a small car around one of his prototypes in 1863, but it had an efficiency of less than 4% and although he claimed it was silent, this was only true when the vehicle was not under load. The real value of his engine was for powering small items of machinery, and by 1865 more than 400 were in use, driving printing presses, lathes, and water pumps. Its use for vehicles was restricted by its size.

Le Nôtre André (1613–1700). French landscape gardener. He created the gardens at Versailles 1662–90 and les Tuileries, Paris. His grandiose scheme for Versailles complemented Le Vau's original design for the palace façade, extending its formal symmetry into the surrounding countryside with vast *parterres* (gardens having beds and paths arranged to form a pattern), radiating avenues, and unbroken vistas. His earlier work at Vaux-le-Viscomte, outside Paris, 1657–61, anticipates the Versailles plan, but on a smaller scale.

Lentaigne Walter (1899–1955). British general. He raised and trained the 111th Indian Infantry Brigade which became part of the Chindits. When Wingate was killed March 1944 he took over command of the Chindit operations and carried them to a successful conclusion.

I have neither eye to see, nor tongue to speak here, but as the House is pleased to direct me.

WILLIAM LENTHALL
refusing to answer King Charles I's demand concerning the five MPs whom the king wished to arrest 4 Jan 1642

Lenthall William (1591–1662). English lawyer. Speaker of the House of Commons in the Long Parliament of 1640–60, he played an active part in the Restoration of Charles II.

Lenya Lotte. Adopted name of Karoline Wilhelmine Blamauer (1898–1981). Austrian actress and singer. She was married five times, twice to the composer Kurt Weill, first in 1926, with whom she emigrated to the USA 1935. She appeared in several of the Brecht–Weill operas, notably *Die Dreigroschenoper/The Threepenny Opera* 1928. Her plain looks and untrained singing voice brought added realism to her stage roles.

Lenz Heinrich Friedrich Emil (1804–1865). Russian physicist who in 1833 formulated Lenz's law, a fundamental law of electromagnetism. He also found that the strength of a magnetic field is proportional to the strength of the magnetic induction.

As geophysical scientist, he accompanied Otto von Kotzebue (1787–1846) on his third expedition around the world 1823–26. On his return, Lenz joined the St Petersburg Academy of Science, and from 1840 held posts at the University of St Petersburg.

On his voyage with Kotzebue, Lenz studied climatic conditions such as barometric pressure, and made extremely accurate measurements of the salinity, temperature, and specific gravity of sea water. On a later expedition he measured the level of the Caspian Sea.

Lenz's studies of electromagnetism date from 1831. Lenz's law is in fact a special case of the law of conservation of energy. If the induced current were to flow in the opposite direction, it would assist the motion of the magnet or wire and energy would increase without any work being done, which is impossible.

Lenz also studied the relationship between heat and current and discovered, independently of English physicist James Joule, the law now known as Joule's law.

Leo (III) the Isaurian (*c.* 680–741). Byzantine emperor and soldier. He seized the throne in 717, successfully defended Constantinople against the Saracens 717–18, and attempted to suppress the use of images in church worship.

Leo thirteen popes, including:

Leo (I) the Great (St Leo) (*c.* 390–461). Pope from 440 who helped to establish the Christian liturgy. Leo summoned the Chalcedon Council where his Dogmatical Letter was accepted as the voice of St Peter. Acting as ambassador for the emperor Valentinian III (425–455), Leo saved Rome from devastation by the Huns by buying off their king, Attila.

Leo III (*c.* 750–816). Pope from 795. After the withdrawal of the Byzantine emperors, the popes had become the real rulers of Rome. Leo III was forced to flee because of a conspiracy in Rome and took refuge at the court of the Frankish king Charlemagne. He returned to Rome in 799 and crowned Charlemagne emperor on Christmas Day 800, establishing the secular sovereignty of the pope over Rome under the suzerainty of the emperor (who became the Holy Roman emperor).

Leo X (Giovanni de' Medici) (1475–1521). Pope from 1513. The son of Lorenzo the Magnificent of Florence, he was created a cardinal at 13. He bestowed on Henry VIII of England the title of Defender of the Faith. A patron of the arts, he sponsored the rebuilding of St Peter's Church, Rome. He raised funds for this by selling indulgences (remissions of punishment for sin), a sale that led the religious reformer Martin Luther to rebel against papal authority. Leo X condemned Luther in the bull *Exsurge domine* 1520 and excommunicated him in 1521.

Suggested reading
Chamberline, E R *The Bad Popes* (1969)
Hibbert, Christopher *The House of the Medici* (1980)

Leo XIII (Vincenzo Gioacchino Pecci) (1810–1903). Pope from 1878. After a successful career as a papal diplomat, he established good relations between the papacy and European powers, the USA, and Japan. He remained intransigent in negotiations with the Italian government over the status of Rome, insisting that he keep control over part of it. He was the first pope to emphasize the duty of the church in matters of social justice. His encyclical *Rerum novarum* 1891 pointed out the moral duties of employers towards workers.

Suggested reading
Burton, Katherine *Leo XIII: The First Modern Pope* (1962)
Gargan, E T (ed) *Leo XIII and the Modern World* (1961)

Leonard Elmore John, Jr (1925–). US author of Westerns and thrillers. His writing is marked by vivid dialogue, as in *City Primeval* 1980, *La Brava* 1983, *Stick* 1983, *Glitz* 1985, *Freaky Deaky* 1988, and *Get Shorty* 1990.

Leonard Sugar Ray (Charles) (1956–). US boxer. In 1988 he became the first man to have won world titles at five officially recognized weights. In 1976 he was Olympic light-welterweight champion; he won his first professional title in 1979 when he beat Wilfred Benitez for the World Boxing Council (WBC) welterweight title. He later won titles at junior middleweight (World Boxing Association; WBA version) 1981, middleweight (WBC) 1987, light-heavyweight (WBC) 1988, and super-middleweight (WBC) 1988. In 1989 he drew with Thomas Hearns. He retired 1992.

Leonardo da Vinci (1452–1519). Italian painter, sculptor, architect, engineer, and scientist. He was the son of Ser Piero da Vinci, a Florentine lawyer, and his mother, Catarina, was of humble birth and unmarried. The child was brought up in his father's household and showed unusual gifts from his earliest years, youthful pursuits being music, modelling, and drawing. His father placed him in the studio of Andrea del Verrocchio, where he was the fellow pupil of Botticelli, Perugino and Lorenzo di Credi. It is probable that he painted the kneeling angel in Verrocchio's *Baptism* (Uffizi), in which according to legend the master recognized the pupil's superiority. He was enrolled in the painters' guild at Florence 1472, and Lorenzo the Magnificent took him under his protection 1477. Before 1481 he began to devote himself to those projects and studies in architecture, hydraulics, mechanics, engineering, astronomy, geology, and anatomy, whose diverse nature still arouses wonder. To this period belong the *Virgin and Child* (Munich), doubtfully regarded by some authorities but containing many Leonardesque details, the portrait of Ginevra de Benci (Liechtenstein Collection) and the unfinished *Adoration of the Magi* (Uffizi).

He left Florence for Milan about 1482, offering his services to Lodovico Sforza, primarily as a military and naval engineer, as a sculptor next and as a painter incidentally. Soon after his arrival he painted Lodovico's mistress, Cecilia Gallerani (the *Lady with an Ermine*, Cracow, Czartoryski Collection), and, in partnership with Ambrogio da Predis 1483, the altarpiece to which Leonardo contributed the central panel, *The Virgin of the Rocks*. The existence of two versions, one in the Louvre and one in the National Gallery, London, may be explained by the revision of the altarpiece 1506 after a long period of haggling, when presumably a first version of the panel was sent to France and the other was finally accepted by the confraternity of the Immaculate Conception. Other great undertakings were the bronze equestrian monument to Francesco Sforza, of which only the model was completed, and the world-famous fresco of the *Last Supper* in the refectory of Santa Maria dell Grazie. This masterpiece, in which he used an experimental oil medium, suffered also from the damp wall on which it was painted; modern restoration by Cavaliere Cavenaghi has restored, as far as it was possible, a painting which lives always as a great conception.

In 1500 Leonardo was in Venice, where he may have met Giorgione, who was greatly impressed by his treatment of light and shade. He was in the employ of Caesar Borgia 1502, mapping out the country and planning canals, harbours and other works, and 1503 was commissioned by the Signory of Florence to produce a battle scene on the walls of the Council Hall, Michelangelo being at the same time commissioned for a similar work. The cartoons of both aroused the greatest admiration, Leonardo's cartoon of the *Battle of Anghiari* being finished in two years and exhibited with that of Michelangelo. Raphael, aged 19, saw them both at work. As so often, however, Leonardo left the work unfinished, an experimental technique again destroying what he had done. The portrait of Mona Lisa (*La Gioconda*), the wife of Francesco Zanobi del Giocondo, that mysterious smiling picture with all the subtle elusiveness of expression that Leonardo loved, was finished 1504. Francis I later bought it for 4,000 gold florins and it was placed in the Louvre. The picture was stolen 1911, but eventually recovered. In 1506 Leonardo returned to Milan, now under French domination, later spent some unsatisfactory years in Rome and then accepted Francis I's invitation to France, spending his last years in the small castle of Cloux near the royal residence of Amboise on the Loire. His last painting was the St John the Baptist, *c.* 1514–15, now in the Louvre.

The fame of Leonardo rests on an imagination which variously inspired all his undertakings. His voluminous notebooks and diagrammatic drawings, of which the Royal Library, Windsor Castle, contains the greatest collection, show a profound research into general scientific laws demonstrable by observation and experiment. In applied science he had all the equipment of a great inventor, anticipating the aeroplane, the armoured vehicle, and the submarine. On the subject of architecture and town planning he had a modern attitude towards acoustics, light and space, and conceived two-level highways. His notes for a treatise on painting and his remarks on the observation of accidental effects in nature are still stimulating to artists. Superb examples of his powers as a draughtsperson, apart from his scientific and anatomical studies, are his drawings of horses and warriors for the *Battle of Anghiari*, his silverpoint bust of a warrior (British Museum) and his self-portrait in sanguine (Turin), while his cartoon for the *Virgin and St Anne* (Royal Academy) is a monochrome masterpiece. Another aspect of his imagination is seen in the paintings, which have so much of mystery and subtlety that they have never ceased to inspire the world's wonder. The work of his pupil Boltraffio shows how little of his magic was directly communicable, though Correggio and Giorgione demonstrate what could be learnt from his mastery of light and shade.

Suggested reading
Clark, Kenneth *Leonardo da Vinci* (1959)
Franzer, Carlo *Leonardo* (1969)
Gould, C *Leonardo: The Artists and the Non-Artists* (1975)
Payne, Robert *Leonardo* (1978)
Rosci, Marco *The Hidden Leonardo* (1977)
Wallace, Robert *The World of Leonardo* (1966)
Wasserman, L *Leonardo de Vinci* (1975)

Leoncavallo Ruggero (1858–1919). Italian operatic composer. He played in restaurants, composing in his spare time, until the success of *I Pagliacci/The Strolling Players* 1892. His other operas include *La Bohème/Bohemian Life* 1897 (contemporary with Puccini's version) and *Zaza* 1900.

Leone Sergio (1921–1989). Italian film director, responsible for popularizing 'spaghetti' Westerns (Westerns made in Italy and Spain, usually with a US leading actor and a European supporting cast and crew) and making a world star of Clint Eastwood. His films include *Per un pugno di dollari/A Fistful of Dollars* 1964, *C'era una volta il West/Once Upon a Time in the West* 1968, and *C'era una volta il America/Once Upon a Time in America* 1984.

Go tell the Spartans, you who read / We took their orders and are dead.

Herodotus' epitaph for
LEONIDAS and the 300 Spartans
at Thermopylae in *History* bk 8, ch 228

Leonidas (died *c.* 480 BC). Greek epigrammatist from Taranto. About 100 of his poems are included in the collection called the *Greek Anthology*.

Leonov Aleksei Arkhipovich (1934–). Soviet cosmonaut. In 1965 he was the first person to walk in space, from the spacecraft *Voskhod 2*.

Leonov Leonid Maksimovich (1899–). Russian novelist and playwright. His works include the novels *The Badgers* 1925 and *The Thief* 1927, and the drama *The Orchards of Polovchansk* 1938.

Leontief Wassily (1906–). US economist, born in the USSR. He is one of the major contributors to the development of input-

output analysis, which relates the output of products to the inputs required to produce them. Leontief is associated in particular with the coefficients relating output to the quantity of inputs.

Leopardi Giacomo, Count Leopardi (1798–1837). Italian romantic poet. The first collection of his uniquely pessimistic poems, *I Versi/Verses*, appeared 1824 and was followed by his philosophical *Operette morali/Minor Moral Works* 1827, in prose, and *I Canti/Lyrics* 1831.

Born at Recanati of a noble family, Leopardi wrote many of his finest poems, including his patriotic odes, before he was 21. Throughout his life he was tormented by ill health, by the consciousness of his deformity (he was hunchbacked), by loneliness and a succession of unhappy love affairs, and by his 'cosmic pessimism' and failure to find consolation in any philosophy.

Suggested reading
Barricelli *Leopardi* (1986)
Origo, Iris *Leopardi: A Study in Solitude* (1953)

Leopold three kings of the Belgians:

Pious, virtuous, artistic and musical, he was more suited to the Church than the State.

E N Williams on LEOPOLD I
in *Penguin Dictionary of English and European History* 1980

Leopold I (1790–1865). King of the Belgians from 1831, having been elected to the throne on the creation of an independent Belgium. Through his marriage, when prince of Saxe-Coburg, to Princess Charlotte Augusta, he was the uncle of Queen Victoria of Great Britain and had considerable influence over her.

A constitutional king must learn to stoop.

LEOPOLD II
instructing Prince Albert, heir-apparent, to pick up some papers
that had fallen on the floor, quoted in Betty Kelen *The Mistress*

Leopold II (1835–1909). King of the Belgians from 1865, son of Leopold I. He financed the US journalist Henry Stanley's explorations in Africa, which resulted in the foundation of the Congo Free State (now Zaire), from which he extracted a huge fortune by ruthless exploitation.

Leopold III (1901–1983). King of the Belgians 1934–51. He surrendered to the German army in World War II 1940. Postwar charges against his conduct led to a regency by his brother Charles and his eventual abdication 1951 in favour of his son Baudouin.

Leopold two Holy Roman emperors:

Leopold I (1640–1705). Holy Roman emperor from 1658, in succession to his father Ferdinand III. He warred against Louis XIV of France and the Ottoman Empire.

Leopold II (1747–1792). Holy Roman emperor in succession to his brother Joseph II. He was the son of Empress Maria Theresa of Austria. His hostility to the French Revolution led to the outbreak of war a few weeks after his death.

The left doesn't have a monopoly on ecology. We at the National Front respect life and love animals. I myself have a white rat whom I kiss every day on the mouth.

JEAN-MARIE LE PEN
on environmentalism, Nov 1991

Le Pen Jean-Marie (1928–). French extreme right-wing politician. In 1972 he formed the French National Front, supporting immigrant repatriation and capital punishment; the party gained

14% of the national vote in the 1986 election. Le Pen was elected to the European Parliament 1984.

Le Pen served as a paratrooper in French Indochina and Algeria during the 1950s. He became a right-wing National Assembly deputy 1956. During the 1960s, he was connected with the extremist *Organisation de l'Armée Secrète* (OAS), devoted to perpetuating French rule in Algeria. The National Front has considerable support among underprivileged white youth but Le Pen's openly fascist statements caused his bid for the presidency 1988 to founder. He again unsuccessfully contested the presidency 1995.

Le Play (Pierre Guillaume) Frédéric (1806–1882). French mining engineer and social scientist. His comprehensive reports for the mining industry, which covered the social conditions of workers as well as manufacturing and management methods, provided the basis for empirical sociology.

He believed that the family was the basic social unit and that its condition of well-being and stability was the best way of judging the state of society in general.

Leppard Raymond John (1927–). English conductor and musicologist. His imaginative reconstructions of Monteverdi and Cavalli operas did much to generate popular interest in early opera and to stimulate academic investigation of the performance implications of early music manuscript scores.

The love of savages isn't much better than the love of noble ladies; ignorance and simple-heartedness can be as tiresome as coquetry.

MIKHAIL LERMONTOV
A Hero of Our Time, 'Bella' 1840

Lermontov Mikhail Yurevich (1814–1841). Russian Romantic poet and novelist. In 1837 he was sent into active military service in the Caucasus for writing a revolutionary poem on the death of Pushkin, which criticized court values, and for participating in a duel. Among his works are the psychological novel *A Hero of Our Time* 1840 and a volume of poems *October* 1840.

Why can't a woman be more like a man?

ALAN JAY LERNER
'A Hymn to Him'

Lerner Alan Jay (1918–1986). US lyricist. He collaborated with Frederick Loewe on musicals including *Brigadoon* 1947, *Paint Your Wagon* 1951, *My Fair Lady* 1956, *Gigi* 1958, and *Camelot* 1960.

Le Roy Ladurie Emmanuel Bernard (1929–). French historian. He was a pupil of Fernand Braudel and, like him, a leading member of the Annales school. The importance he attaches to customs, rituals, and symbols is seen in *Le Carneval de Romans/Carnival in Romans* 1979, a study of a riot in a small French town 1579–80.

His doctoral thesis *Les Paysans de Languedoc/The Peasants of Languedoc* 1966 dealt with economic and social changes in a region of S France in the 15th to 18th centuries and especially with 'the activities, the struggles, and the thoughts of the people themselves'. *Montaillou: village occitan de 1294 à 1324/Montaillou: Cathars and Catholics in a French Village* 1978 was a bestseller in both France and Britain. His belief that ecological and demographic factors determined the conditions of life in rural Europe is supported at length in *Le Territoire de l'historien* 1973 (selections from Vol 1 translated 1979 as *The Territory of the Historian*; selections from Vol 2 translated 1981 as *The Mind and Method of the Historian*).

Le Sage Alain-René (1668–1747). French novelist and dramatist. His novels include *Le Diable boîteux/The Devil upon Two Sticks* 1707 and his picaresque masterpiece *Gil Blas de Santillane* 1715–35, which is much indebted to Spanish originals.

Lesseps Ferdinand Marie, Vicomte (1805–1894). French engineer who designed and built the Suez Canal 1859–69. He began work on the Panama Canal in 1881, but withdrew after failing to construct it without locks.

Lesseps was born in Versailles and became a diplomat. From 1825 he held posts in various capitals, including Lisbon, Tunis, and Cairo. Interested in engineering and construction, he suggested in 1854 that a passage should be cut to link the Mediterranean with the Red Sea, and was put in charge of the work. The canal was successfully completed 1869, shortening the route between Britain and India by 9,700 km/6,000 mi.

The Panama Canal project, undertaken when he was in his 70s, met with failure and bankruptcy. Lesseps was sentenced to five years' imprisonment for breach of trust, but was too ill to leave his house.

Lessing Doris May (born Tayler) (1919–). English novelist, brought up in Rhodesia. Concerned with social and political themes, particularly the place of women in society, her work includes *The Grass is Singing* 1950, the five-novel series *Children of Violence* 1952–69, *The Golden Notebook* 1962, *The Good Terrorist* 1985, *The Fifth Child* 1988, and *London Observed* 1990. She has also written an 'inner space fiction' series *Canopus in Argus: Archives* 1979–83, and under the pen name 'Jane Somers', *The Diary of a Good Neighbour* 1981.

Suggested reading
King, J *Doris Lessing* (1989)
Maslen, E *Doris Lessing* (1983)
Sage, L *Doris Lessing* (1983)
Taylor, J (ed) *Notebooks, Memoirs, Archives: Reading and Rereading Doris Lessing* (1982)

Lessing Gotthold Ephraim (1729–1781). German dramatist and critic. His plays include *Miss Sara Sampson* 1755, *Minna von Barnhelm* 1767, *Emilia Galotti* 1772, and the verse play *Nathan der Weise* 1779. His works of criticism *Laokoon* 1766 and *Hamburgische Dramaturgie* 1767–68 influenced German literature. He also produced many theological and philosophical writings.

Laokoon analysed the functions of poetry and the plastic arts; *Hamburgische Dramaturgie* reinterpreted Aristotle and attacked the restrictive form of French classical drama in favour of the freer approach of Shakespeare.

Yesterday I loved, today I suffer, tomorrow I die: but I still think fondly, today and tomorrow, of yesterday.

GOTTHOLD LESSING
'Lied aus dem Spanischen'

Lethaby William Richard (1857–1931). English architect. An assistant to Norman Shaw, he embraced the principles of William Morris and Philip Webb in the Arts and Crafts movement, and was cofounder and first director of the Central School of Arts and Crafts from 1894. He wrote a collection of essays entitled 'Form in Civilization' 1922.

Letterman David (1947–). US television talk-show presenter. He was host of *Late Night with David Letterman* for the NBC network 1983–93, then moved to CBS to present *The Late Show with David Letterman*.

Letterman was born in Indianapolis, Indiana. He was spotted by talent scouts for Johnny Carson's NBC *Tonight Show* 1978, and became a guest host. *The David Letterman Show* 1980 ran for only 18 weeks before it was cancelled because of poor ratings.

Lettow-Vorbeck Paul Emil von (1870–1964). German general. He served in the Boxer Rebellion in China 1900 and afterwards in German East Africa. In World War I, he was military commander in German East Africa (now Tanzania) where he kept the Allies at bay for most of the war despite being vastly outnumbered .

Le Vau Louis (1612–1670). French architect. He was a leading exponent of the Baroque style. His design for the château of Vaux-le-Viscomte outside Paris (begun 1657) provided the inspiration for the remodelling of Versailles, on which he worked from 1669. Many of Le Vau's additions to the palace, notably the elegantly symmetrical garden façade, were altered by later enlargements under Hardouin-Mansart. Le Vau also contributed to the east front of the Louvre 1667 and designed les Tuileries, Paris.

> *In person ... little and crooked, but his wise exercise of authority won universal respect.*
>
> Henry Patton on ALEXANDER LEVEN
> in *Dictionary of National Biography*

Leven Alexander Leslie, 1st Earl of Leven (*c.* 1580–1661). Scottish general in the English Civil War. He led the Covenanters' army which invaded England in 1640, commanded the Scottish army sent to aid the English Puritans in 1643–46, and shared in the Parliamentarians' victory over the Royalists in the Battle of Marston Moor. Earl 1641.

Lever Charles James (1806–1872). Irish novelist. He wrote novels of Irish and army life, such as *Harry Lorrequer* 1837, *Charles O'Malley* 1840, and *Tom Burke of Ours* 1844.

Leverrier Urbain Jean Joseph (1811–1877). French astronomer who predicted the existence and position of the planet Neptune, discovered in 1846.

The possibility that another planet might exist beyond Uranus, influencing its orbit, had already been suggested. Leverrier calculated the orbit and apparent diameter of the hypothetical planet, and wrote to a number of observatories, asking them to test his prediction of its position. Johann Galle at the Berlin Observatory found it immediately, within 1° of Leverrier's coordinates.

Leverrier was born in St Lô, Normandy, and studied in Paris at the Ecole Polytechnique, joining the staff 1837. He became professor 1847, and in 1849 a chair of celestial mechanics was established for him at the Sorbonne. He was politically active in the revolutions of 1848, serving as a member of the legislative assembly in 1849 and as senator in 1852. In 1854 he became director of the Paris Observatory.

Levertov Denise (1923–). English-born US poet. She published her first volume of poetry *The Double Image* 1946, after which she moved to America. In the 1950s she was associated with the Black Mountain poets, and in the 1960s campaigned for civil rights. Poetry collections include *Here and Now* 1957, *Candles in Babylon* 1982, and *A Door in the Hive* 1993; her essays on political, feminist, and creative issues appeared in 'O Taste and See' 1964 and 'The Poet in the World' 1973.

Leveson-Gower Granville George, 2nd Earl Granville (1815–1891). English politician. He held several cabinet posts 1851–86, including that of foreign secretary 1870–74 and 1880–85 under Gladstone. He supported Gladstone's Home Rule policy and played a leading part in the decision to send General Gordon to Khartoum 1884. Earl 1846.

Lévesque René (1922–1987). French-Canadian politician. In 1968 he founded the Parti Québecois, with the aim of an independent Quebec, but a referendum rejected the proposal in 1980. He was premier of Quebec 1976–85.

Levi Primo (1919–1987). Italian novelist. He joined the anti-Fascist resistance during World War II, was captured, and sent to the concentration camp at Auschwitz. He wrote of these experiences in *Se questo è un uomo/If This is a Man* 1947. His other books, all based on his experience of the war, include *Period Tables* 1975 and *Moments of Reprieve* 1981.

Levi-Civita Tullio (1873–1941). Italian mathematician who developed, in collaboration with Gregorio Ricci-Curbastro, the absolute differential calculus, published 1900. Levi-Civita also introduced the concept of parallelism in curved space 1917.

He was professor at the Engineering School in Padua 1897–1918, when he became professor of higher analysis at Rome. In 1938, the anti-Semitic laws promulgated by the Fascist government forced him to leave the university; he was also expelled from all Italian scientific societies.

The absolute differential calculus was a completely new calculus, applicable to both Euclidean and non-Euclidean spaces. Most significantly, it could be applied to Riemannian curved spaces, and would be fundamental to Albert Einstein's development of the general theory of relativity. Levi-Civita's idea of parallel displacement later developed into tensor calculus.

Levi-Montalcini Rita (1909–). Italian neurologist who discovered nerve-growth factor, a substance that controls how many cells make up the adult nervous system. She shared the 1986 Nobel Prize for Physiology or Medicine with her co-worker, US biochemist Stanley Cohen (1922–).

Levi-Montalcini was born and educated in Turin and began her research there. When the Fascist anti-Semitic laws forced her to leave the university 1939, she constructed a home laboratory. After World War II she moved to the USA and was at the Washington University in St Louis 1947–81, becoming professor 1958. In 1981 she went to Rome.

Levi-Montalcini first discovered nerve-growth factor in the salivary glands of developing mouse embryos, and later in many tissues. She established that it was chemically a protein, and analysed the mechanism of its action. Her work has contributed to the understanding of some neurological diseases, tissue regeneration, and cancer mechanisms.

Levinson Barry (1932–). US film director and screenwriter. Levinson began his career as a scriptwriter for television comedy programmes such as *The Carol Burnett Show*. Later, he turned to writing feature films such as *High Anxiety* 1977 (with Mel Brooks), *And Justice For All* 1979, and *Unfaithfully Yours* 1983. Working in Hollywood's mainstream, he has been responsible for some of the best adult comedy films of the 1980s and 1990s. Winning cult status for the offbeat realism of *Diner* 1982, Levinson went on to make such large-budget movies as *Good Morning Vietnam* 1987, *Tin Men* 1987, *Rain Man* 1988 (Academy Awards for best picture and best director), *Bugsy* 1991, and *Toys* 1992.

Lévi-Strauss Claude (1908–). French anthropologist who helped to formulate the principles of structuralism by stressing the interdependence of cultural systems and the way they relate to each other. In his analyses of kinship, myth, and symbolism, Lévi-Strauss argued that, though the superficial appearance of these factors might vary between societies, their underlying structures were universal and could best be understood in terms of binary oppositions: left and right, male and female, nature and culture, the raw and the cooked, and so on. His works include *Tristes Tropiques* 1955 – an intellectual autobiography – and *Mythologiques/Mythologies* 1964–71.

Lévi-Strauss was born in Belgium and studied philosophy at Paris. He taught in Brazil at the University of São Paolo 1935–39 and later at academic institutions in New York, where he was a cultural attaché at the French embassy 1946–47. He taught at the Sorbonne 1948–58 and became professor of social anthropology at the Collège de France 1958.

Suggested reading
Leach, Edmund *Claude Lévi-Strauss* (1970)
Pace, David *Claude Lévi-Strauss* (1983)
Paz, Octavio *Claude Lévi-Strauss* (tr 1970)

Lévy-Bruhl Lucien (1857–1939). French anthropologist and philosopher who was mainly concerned with analysing the differences between modern and primitive mentalities. In *How Natives Think* 1910, he argued that primitive thought operated through its own system of rules. This he described as 'pre-logical' because it ignored logic and accepted contradiction. He significantly revised his views towards the end of his life.

Lewes George Henry (1817–1878). English philosopher and critic. Originally an actor, he turned to literature and philosophy; his works include a *Biographical History of Philosophy* 1845–46, and *Life and Works of Goethe* 1855. He married 1840, but left his wife 1854 to live with the writer Mary Ann Evans (George Eliot), whom he had met 1851.

The pen, in our age, weighs heavier in the social scale than the sword of a Norman Baron.

GEORGE LEWES
Ranthorpe epilogue 1845

Lewis Carl (Frederick Carlton) (1961–). US track and field athlete who won eight gold medals and one silver in three successive Olympic Games. At the 1984 Olympic Games he equalled the performance of Jesse Owens, winning gold medals in the 100 and 200 metres, 400-metre relay, and long jump. In the 1988 Olympics, he repeated his golds in the 100 metres and long jump, and won a silver in the 200 metres. Although in the 1992 Olympics he failed to make the USA's 100-metre and 200-metre squads, he repeated his success in the long jump and anchored the USA's record-breaking 400-metre relay team.

Lewis Cecil Day. Irish poet; see ◊Day Lewis.

The safest road to Hell is the gradual one.

C S LEWIS
The Screwtape Letters 1942

Lewis C(live) S(taples) (1898–1963). British academic and writer, born in Belfast. His books include the medieval study *The Allegory of Love* 1936 and the space fiction *Out of the Silent Planet* 1938. He was a committed Christian and wrote essays in popular theology such as *The Screwtape Letters* 1942 and *Mere Christianity* 1952, the autobiographical *Surprised by Joy* 1955, and a series of books of Christian allegory for children, set in the magic land of Narnia, including *The Lion, the Witch, and the Wardrobe* 1950.
Suggested reading
Christopher, J R *C S Lewis* (1987)
Griffin, W *Clive Staples Lewis: A Dramatic Life* (1986)
Sayer, G *Jack: C S Lewis and His Times* (1985)
Wilson, A N *C S Lewis* (1990)

Lewis Gilbert Newton (1875–1946). US theoretical chemist who defined a base as a substance that supplies a pair of electrons for a chemical bond, and an acid as a substance that accepts such a pair. He also set out the electronic theory of valency and in thermodynamics listed the free energies of 143 substances.

He worked at the Massachusetts Institute of Technology (MIT) 1905–12, and spent the rest of his career at the University of California, Berkeley. Lewis's main works were both published 1923: *Valence and the Structure of Atoms and Molecules* and (with Merle Randall) *Thermodynamics and the Free Energy of Chemical Substances*.

Lewis (Harry) Sinclair (1885–1951). US novelist. He made a reputation with satirical, but sentimental, social documentary novels, principally *Main Street* 1920, depicting American small-town life; and *Babbitt* 1922, the story of a real-estate dealer of the Midwest caught in the conventions of his milieu. These were followed by *Arrowsmith* 1925, a study of the pettiness in medical science; *Elmer Gantry* 1927, a satiric portrayal of evangelical religion; and *Dodsworth* 1929, about a US industrialist. He was the first American to be awarded the Nobel Prize for Literature, 1930. His other works include *It Can't Happen Here* 1935, *Cass Timberlane* 1945, *Kingsblood Royal* 1947, and *The God-Seeker* 1949.
Suggested reading
Lundquist, James *Sinclair Lewis* (1973)
Schorer, Mark *Sinclair Lewis: An American Life* (1961)

To George F Babbitt, as to most prosperous citizens of Zenith, his motor-car was poetry and tragedy, love and heroism.

SINCLAIR LEWIS
Babbitt ch 3 1923

Lewis Jerry. Stage name of Joseph Levitch (1926–). US comic actor and director. He worked in partnership with Dean Martin 1946–56; their film debut was in *My Friend Irma* 1949. He was revered as a solo performer by French critics ('Le Roi du Crazy'), but films that he directed such as *The Nutty Professor* 1963 were less well received in the USA. He appeared in a straight role opposite Robert De Niro in *The King of Comedy* 1982.

Lewis Jerry Lee (1935–). US rock-and-roll and country singer and pianist. His trademark was the boogie-woogie-derived 'pumping piano' style in hits such as 'Whole Lotta Shakin' Going On' and 'Great Balls of Fire' 1957; later recordings include 'What Made Milwaukee Famous' 1968.

Lewis John L(lewellyn) (1880–1969). US labour leader. President of the United Mine Workers (UMW) 1920–60, he was largely responsible for the adoption of national mining safety standards in the USA. His militancy and the miners' strikes during and after World War II led to President Truman's nationalization of the mines in 1946.

Born in Lucas, Iowa, USA, Lewis worked in the coal mines from an early age. He became a regional officer of the United Mine Workers (UMW) and served as its liaison with the American Federation of Labor (AFL) 1911. He helped found the AFL's offshoot, the Congress of Industrial Organizations 1935, which unionized workers in mass-production industries.

Lewis Lennox (1966–). British-born boxer who won the world heavyweight title 1992, becoming the first British boxer to do so this century. He was awarded the title when the reigning champion, Riddick Bowe, refused to fight him. After defending the title successfully for nearly 2 years, he lost to Oliver McCall in Sept 1994. Lewis turned professional in 1989, won the European title 1990, and the British title 1991.

Lewis Matthew Gregory (1775–1818). English writer. He was known as 'Monk' Lewis from his gothic horror romance *The Monk* 1795.

Lewis Mortimer William (1796–1879). English-born architect in Australia who, as colonial architect (1835–49), designed many official buildings and court houses in New South Wales. His works, favouring Greek Revival style, include Darlinghurst Court House, East Sydney 1836, Hartley Court House 1837 and Berrima Court House 1838.

Angels in jumpers.

WYNDHAM LEWIS
attributed. Referring to figures in Stanley Spencer's paintings

---

Lewis (Percy) Wyndham (1882–1957). English writer and artist. He pioneered Vorticism, which with its feeling of movement sought to reflect the age of industry. He had a hard and aggressive style in both his writing and his painting. His literary works include the novels *Tarr* 1918 and *The Childermass* 1928, the essay 'Time and Western Man' 1927, and autobiographies. In addition to works of a semi-abstract kind he painted a number of portraits, including those of Edith Sitwell, Ezra Pound and T S Eliot.

He was born off Maine, on his father's yacht, and studied art at the Slade School and in Paris. He invented the variant of Cubist and Futurist ideas known as Vorticism, opposing the 'everyday visual real' and favouring machinelike forms, and edited *Blast* 1914–15, a literary and artistic magazine proclaiming its principles. Both in numerous written works and in his paintings he was an intellectual independent, and one of his later literary products, *The Demon of Progress in the Arts*, 1954, was an attack on formalized extremism. *The Surrender of Barcelona*, 1936 (Tate, London), applies mechanistic treatment to an imagined scene of the past.

Suggested reading

Meyers, Geoffrey *The Enemy: A Biography of Wyndham Lewis* (1980)
Pritchard, William *Wyndham Lewis* (1968)

Lewis (William) Arthur (1915–). British economist born on St Lucia, West Indies. He specialized in the economic problems of developing countries and created a model relating the terms of trade between less developed and more developed nations to their respective levels of labour productivity in agriculture. He shared the Nobel Prize for Economics with an American, Theodore Schultz, 1979. He wrote many books, including the *Theory of Economic Growth* 1955. Knighted 1963.

Lewis and Clark Meriwether Lewis (1774–1809) and William Clark (1770–1838). US explorers. Lewis was commissioned in 1803 by his friend president Thomas Jefferson to find a land route to the Pacific, and chose Clark to accompany him. They followed the Missouri river to its source, crossed the Rocky Mountains (aided by an Indian woman, Sacajawea) and followed the Columbia River to the Pacific, then returned overland to St Louis 1804–06. The expedition was an important success, as it opened up a large amount of new land to the USA. Clark's detailed journals and maps of the expedition added to an understanding of the region and facilitated westward expansion.

Formerly private secretary to President Jefferson, Lewis was rewarded for his expedition with the governorship of the Louisiana Territory. His sudden death, near Nashville, Tennessee, has been ascribed to suicide or more probably murder.

Clark was made superintendent of Indian affairs in 1807, and was governor of Missouri Territory 1813–21.

Suggested reading

Allen, John *Passage Through the Garden: Lewis and Clark and the Image of the American Northwest* (1975)
Cutright, P R *Lewis and Clark: Pioneering Naturalists* (1969)

Lewton Val. Stage name of Vladimir Ivan Leventon (1904–1951). Russian-born US film producer. He was responsible for a series of atmospheric B horror films made for RKO in the 1940s, including *Cat People* 1942 and *The Body Snatcher* 1946. He co-wrote several of his films under the adopted name of Carlos Keith.

Leyden Lucas van. See ◊Lucas van Leyden, Dutch painter.

Lhôte André (1885–1962). French painter, art teacher, and critic. He opened the Académie Montparnasse 1922 and founded a South American branch of the school in Rio de Janeiro 1952. He also wrote treatises on landscape painting and figure painting. Inspired by Cubism, his own paintings are complex compositions of geometrical forms painted in pure colours, for example *Rugby* 1917 (Museum of Modern Art, Paris).

Liao dynasty family that ruled part of NE China and Manchuria 945–1125 during the Song era. It was founded by cavalry-based Qidan (Khidan) people, Mongolian-speakers who gradually became Sinicized. They were later defeated by the nomadic Juchen (Jurchen) who founded the Jin dynasty.

The dynasty had five capitals, and cabinets for the northern and southern regions. It adopted Chinese ceremonies and writing, but maintained Qidan speech, food, and clothing. The success of barbarian rule over a Chinese population influenced later invaders such as the Mongols and Manchu.

Liaquat Ali Khan Nawabzada (1895–1951). Indian politician, deputy leader of the Muslim League 1940–47, first prime minister of Pakistan from 1947. He was assassinated by objectors to his peace policy with India.

Libby Willard Frank (1908–1980). US chemist whose development in 1947 of radiocarbon dating as a means of determining the age of organic or fossilized material won him a Nobel prize in 1960.

During World War II he worked on the development of the atomic bomb (the Manhattan Project). In 1945 he became professor at the University of Chicago's Institute for Nuclear Studies. He was a member of the US Atomic Energy Commission 1954–59, and then became director of the Institute of Geophysics at the University of California.

Having worked on the separation of uranium isotopes for producing fissionable uranium-238 for the atomic bomb, he turned his attention to carbon-14, a radioactive isotope that occurs in the tissues of all plants and animals, decaying at a steady rate after their death. He and his co-workers accurately dated ancient Egyptian relics by measuring the amount of radiocarbon they contained, using a sensitive Geiger counter. By 1947 they had developed the technique so that it could date objects up to 50,000 years old.

Liberace Wladziu Valentino (1919–1987). US pianist. He performed popular classics in a flamboyant style (for example, Beethoven's *Moonlight Sonata* reduced to four minutes). His playing was overshadowed by his extravagant outfits and the candelabra always adorning his piano. *The Liberace Show* had a regular slot on US television in the 1950s.

Liberator, the title given to Simón ◊Bolívar, South American revolutionary leader; also a title given to Daniel ◊O'Connell, Irish political leader; and to Bernardo ◊O'Higgins, Chilean revolutionary.

Liberty Arthur Lasenby (1843–1917). English shopkeeper and founder of a shop of the same name in London 1875. Originally importing Oriental goods, it gradually started selling British Arts and Crafts and Art Nouveau furniture, tableware, and fabrics. Art Nouveau is sometimes still called *stile Liberty* in Italy. Knighted 1913.

Lichfield Patrick Anson, 5th Earl of Lichfield (1939–). British photographer. Since 1981 he has been known for his travel and publicity shots as well as his royal portraits.

Li Cho Hao (1913–). Chinese-born US biochemist who discovered in 1966 that human pituitary growth hormone (somatotropin) consists of a chain of 256 amino acids. In 1970 he succeeded in synthesizing this hormone, the largest protein molecule synthesized up to that time.

Li was born in Guangzhu and educated at the University of Nanjing. In 1935 he emigrated to the USA, where he took up postgraduate studies at the University of California at Berkeley and later joined the staff. He became professor 1950.

Lichtenstein Roy (1923–). US Pop artist. He uses advertising imagery and comic-strip techniques, often focusing on popular ideals of romance and heroism, as in *Whaam!* 1963 (Tate Gallery, London). He has also produced sculptures in brass, plastic, and enamelled metal.

Liddell Hart Basil Henry (1895–1970). British military strategist. He was an exponent of mechanized warfare, and his ideas were adopted in Germany in 1935 in creating the 1st Panzer Division, combining motorized infantry and tanks. From 1937 he advised the UK War Office on army reorganization. Knighted 1966.

Lie (Marius) Sophus (1842–1899). Norwegian mathematician who provided the foundations for the science of topology in transformation groups known as the Lie groups. He was one of the first mathematicians to emphasize the importance of the notion of groups in geometry.

He was professor at Christiania 1873–86 and 1898–99 and at Leipzig, Germany, 1886–98.

Lie's first great discovery, made in 1870, was that of his contact transformation, which mapped straight lines with spheres and principal tangent curves into curvature lines. In his theory of tangential transformations occurs the particular transformation that makes a sphere correspond to a straight line. By 1873 Lie had begun to investigate transformation groups. In this work on group theory he chose a new space element, the contact element, which is an incidence pair of point and line or of point and hyperplane. This led him to the discovery of Lie groups, one of the basic notions of which is that of infinitesimal transformation.

The Lie integration theorem, which he developed, made it possible to classify partial differential equations in such a way as to make most of the classical methods of solving such equations reducible to a single principle.

Now we are in a period which I can characterize as a period of cold peace.

TRYGVE LIE
in *Observer* 21 Aug 1949

Lie Trygve Halvdan (1896–1968). Norwegian Labour politician and diplomat. He became secretary of the Labour Party in 1926. During the German occupation of Norway in World War II he was foreign minister in the exiled government 1941–46, when he helped retain the Norwegian fleet for the Allies. He became the first secretary general of the United Nations 1946–53, but resigned over Soviet opposition to his handling of the Korean War.

God has ordered all his creation by Weight and Measure.

JUSTUS VON LIEBIG
Notice above entrance to Liebig's laboratory

Liebig Justus, Baron von (1803–1873). German chemist, a major contributor to agricultural chemistry. He introduced the theory of compound radicals and discovered chloroform and chloral. Many new methods of organic analysis were introduced by Liebig, and he devised ways of determining hydrogen, carbon, and halogens in organic compounds. He demonstrated that plants absorb minerals (and water) from the soil and postulated that the carbon used by plants comes from carbon dioxide in the air rather than from the soil.

Liebig was born in Darmstadt, Hesse, and studied at Bonn (where he was arrested for his liberalist political activity), Erlangen, and Paris. At the age of 21 he became professor at Giessen, moving to Munich 1852.

Liebig studied fermentation (but would not acknowledge that yeast is a living substance), and analysed various body fluids and urine. He calculated the calorific values of foods, emphasizing the role of fats as a source of dietary energy, and even developed a beef extract – long marketed as Liebig extract.

We are fighting for the gates of heaven.

KARL LIEBKNECHT
quoted in Albert Camus *The Rebel* ch 3 1971. Said during the abortive German revolution of 1918–19.

Liebknecht Karl (1871–1919). German socialist, son of Wilhelm Liebknecht. A founder of the German Communist Party, originally known as the Spartacus League 1918, he was one of the few socialists who refused to support World War I. He led an unsuccessful revolt with Rosa Luxemburg in Berlin in 1919 and both were murdered by army officers.

Liebknecht practised as a barrister in Berlin and did his military service in the Prussian Guard, but turned to socialism while defending a group of agitators in Konigsberg 1904. Imprisoned for sedition 1907, he was eventually elected to the Reichstag 1912 but was expelled 1916 and again imprisoned.

Liebknecht Wilhelm (1826–1900). German socialist. A friend of the communist theoretician Karl Marx, with whom he took part in the revolutions of 1848, he was imprisoned for opposition to the Franco-Prussian War 1870–71. He was one of the founders of the Social Democratic Party 1875. He was the father of Karl Liebknecht.

Lifar Serge (1905–1986). Ukrainian dancer and choreographer. Born in Kiev, he studied under Nijinsky, joined the Diaghilev company 1923, and was artistic director and principal dancer of the Paris Opéra 1929–44 and 1947–59. He completely revitalized the

company and in so doing, reversed the diminished fortunes of French ballet. A great experimenter, he produced his first ballet without music, *Icare* 1935. He developed the role of the male dancer in his *Prometheus* 1929 and *Romeo and Juliet* (music by Prokofiev) 1955.

Ligachev Egor Kuzmich (1920–   ). Soviet politician. He joined the Communist Party 1944, and became a member of the Politburo 1985. He was replaced as the party ideologist in 1988 by Vadim Medvedev. Ligachev was regarded as the chief conservative ideologist, and the leader of conservative opposition to President Gorbachev. In July 1990 he failed to secure election to the CPSU Politburo or Central Committee and also failed in his bid to become elected as party deputy general secretary.

Ligeti György Sándor (1923–   ). Hungarian-born Austrian composer. He developed a dense, highly chromatic, polyphonic style in which melody and rhythm are sometimes lost in shifting blocks of sound. He achieved international prominence with *Atmosphères* 1961 and *Requiem* 1965, which achieved widespread fame as background music for Stanley Kubrick's film epic *2001: A Space Odyssey* 1968. Other works include an opera *Le Grand Macabre* 1978, and *Poème symphonique* 1962, for 100 metronomes.

Ligget Hunter (1857–1935). US general. Joined the army 1879 and saw service in Cuba and the Philippines, later becoming president of the Army War College. He succeeded General Pershing as commander of the US Army in France 1918 and conducted the successful campaign in the Argonne.

Light William (1786–1839). English soldier, naval officer, and surveyor in Australia, born in Malaya. He was appointed surveyor-general of the new colony of South Australia in 1836 and departed ahead of the main party. He chose the site for Adelaide on the banks of the Torrens River and stood firm against the attempts of Governor Hindmarsh to have it moved to the coast. He also laid out the plan for the settlement's centre and is regarded as the founder of Adelaide.

Lighthill (Michael) James (1924–   ). British mathematician who specialized in the application of mathematics to high-speed aerodynamics and jet propulsion. He was Lucasian professor at Cambridge 1969-79 and provost of University College, London (1979-   ). He received a knighthood 1971.

Li Hongzhang or Li Hung-chang (1823–1901). Chinese politician, promulgator of Western ideas and modernization. He was governor general of Zhili (or Chihli) and high commissioner of the Northern Ports 1870–95, responsible for foreign affairs. He established a modern navy, the Beiyang fleet, 1888, which was humiliatingly destroyed in the Sino-Japanese War.

Li became aware of the need to 'learn from the West' from his association with British general Charles Gordon during the Taiping Rebellion 1850–64, which his regional Anhui army helped to suppress. He also negotiated the Boxer protocol with Western powers 1900.

So suddenly addicted still / To's only Principle, his will – / And rather on a gibbet dangle, / Than miss his clear Delight, to wrangle.

Samuel Butler on JOHN LILBURNE
Hudibras pt III 1678

Lilburne John (*c.* 1614–1657). English republican agitator. He was imprisoned 1638–40 for circulating Puritan pamphlets, fought in the Parliamentary army in the Civil War, and by his advocacy of a democratic republic won the leadership of the Levellers, the democratic party in the English Revolution.

In 1640, Oliver Cromwell made a speech in favour of Lilburne to get him released, and in 1641, Lilburne received an indemnity of £3,000. He rose to the rank of lieutenant colonel in the army, but resigned in 1645 because of the number of Presbyterians. In 1647 he

Lilienthal *German aviator Otto Lilienthal, in one of his gliders. Lilienthal studied bird flight, and used his findings as a basis for the construction of gliders. He made over 2,000 flights before being killed in a crash.* (Image Select)

as broadcasting, he tours cities where his radio programme is heard, doing solo shows. His book *The Way Things Ought to Be* 1992 was a best seller.

Limbourg brothers Paul (Pol), Herman, and Jan (Hennequin, Janneken), Franco-Flemish painters, (active late 14th and early 15th centuries) working in Paris, then at the ducal court of Burgundy. They produced richly detailed manuscript illuminations, including two Books of Hours.

Patronized by Jean de Berry, Duke of Burgundy, from about 1404, they illustrated two Books of Hours that are masterpieces of the International Gothic style, the *Belles Heures* about 1408 (Metropolitan Museum of Art, New York), and *Les Très Riches Heures du Duc de Berry* about 1413–15 (Musée Condé, Chantilly). Their miniature paintings include a series of scenes representing the months, presenting an almost fairytale world of pinnacled castles with lords and ladies, full of detail and brilliant decorative effects. All three brothers were dead by 1416.

Linacre Thomas (*c.* 1460–1524). English humanist, physician to Henry VIII, from whom he obtained a charter in 1518 to found the Royal College of Physicians, of which he was first president.

Lin Biao or Lin Piao (1908–1971). Chinese politician and general. He joined the communists in 1927, became a commander of Mao Zedong's Red Army, and led the Northeast People's Liberation Army in the civil war after 1945. He became defence minister in 1959, and as vice chair of the party in 1969 he was expected to be Mao's successor. But in 1972 the government announced that Lin had been killed in an aeroplane crash in Mongolia on 17 Sept 1971 while fleeing to the USSR following an abortive coup attempt.

That we here highly resolve that the dead shall not have died in vain, that this nation, under God, shall have a new birth of freedom; and that government of the people, by the people, and for the people, shall not perish from the earth.

ABRAHAM LINCOLN
Gettysburg Address 19 Nov 1863

---

was put in the Tower of London for accusations against Cromwell. He was banished in 1652 and arrested again on his return in 1653. He was acquitted, but still imprisoned until 1655 for 'the peace of the nation'.

Lilienthal Otto (1848–1896). German aviation pioneer who inspired US aviators Orville and Wilbur Wright. From 1891 he made and successfully flew many gliders, including two biplanes, before he was killed in a glider crash.

Lilienthal demonstrated the superiority of cambered wings over flat wings – the principle of the aerofoil. In his planes the pilot was suspended by the arms, as in a modern hang-glider. He achieved glides of more than 300 m/1,000 ft, and gliding began to catch on as a sport. Lilienthal's book *Der Vogelflug als Grundlage der Fliegekunst/Bird Flight as a Basis for Aviation* 1889 greatly influenced other aviation pioneers.

Lillee Dennis Keith (1949–). Australian cricketer regarded as the best fast bowler of his generation. He made his Test debut in the 1970–71 season and subsequently played for his country 70 times. Lillee was the first to take 300 wickets in Test cricket. He played Sheffield Shield cricket for Western Australia and at the end of his career made a comeback with Tasmania.

Liman von Sanders Otto (1855–1929). German general assigned to the Turkish army to become inspector-general and a Turkish field marshal in Dec 1913. This link between the Turks and the Germans caused great suspicion on the part of the French and Russians. He commanded the Turkish forces at Gallipoli and then took command of all Turkish forces in the Middle East.

Limbaugh Rush (1951–). US right-wing political commentator and broadcaster. His daily three-hour radio talk show *The Rush Limbaugh Show*, articulating popular prejudices, was launched 1988 and was by 1996 syndicated to 600 radio stations throughout the USA. He has no guests on his show, doing all the talking himself.

He stands for conservative views, believing in 'less government', and particularly likes to attack President Bill Clinton and Hillary Clinton.

Limbaugh was born in Cape Girardeau, Missouri. He first ran a talk show on KFBK radio in Sacramento, California, 1984. As well

Lincoln Abraham (1809–1865). 16th president of the USA 1861–65, a Republican. In the American Civil War, his chief concern was the preservation of the Union from which the Confederate (Southern) slave states had seceded on his election. In 1863 he announced the freedom of the slaves with the Emancipation Proclamation. He was re-elected in 1864 with victory for the North in sight, but was assassinated at the end of the war.

Lincoln was born in a log cabin in Kentucky. Self-educated, he practised law from 1837 in Springfield, Illinois. He was a member of the state legislature 1832–42, during which period he was known as Honest Abe, and in 1846 sat in Congress, although his law practice remained his priority. The repeal of the Missouri Compromise 1854 and the reopening of the debate on the extension of slavery in the new territories of the USA drew him back into politics. He joined the new Republican Party 1856 and two years later was chosen as their candidate for senator in Illinois, opposing the incumbent Stephen Douglas, who had been largely responsible for repeal of the Compromise. In the ensuing debate, Lincoln revealed his power as an orator, but failed to wrest the post from Douglas. However, he had established a national reputation and in 1860 was chosen by the Republicans, now pledged to oppose the extension of slavery, as their presidential candidate. He was elected on a minority vote, defeating Douglas and another Democratic Party candidate.

Prior to Lincoln's inauguration, seven Southern states proclaimed their formal secession from the Union. Lincoln's inaugural address March 1861 was conciliatory: he declared he had no intention of interfering with slavery where it already existed, but pronounced the Union indissoluble, declaring that no state had the right to secede from it. His refusal to concede to Confederate demands for the evacuation of the federal garrison at Fort Sumter, Charleston, South Carolina the following month, precipitated the first hostilities of the Civil War.

In 1862, following an important Union victory at Antietam, Lincoln proclaimed the emancipation of all slaves in states engaged in rebellion, thereby surpassing the limits of the constitution he had gone to war to maintain. In the Gettysburg Address 1863, he declared the aims of preserving a 'nation conceived in liberty, and dedicated to the proposition that all men are created equal'. With the war turning in favour of the North, he was re-elected 1864 with a large majority on a National Union ticket, having advocated a reconciliatory policy towards the South 'with malice towards none, with charity for all'.

Five days after General Lee's surrender, Lincoln was shot in a theatre audience by an actor and Confederate sympathizer, John Wilkes Booth.

Suggested reading
Longford, Lord *Abraham Lincoln* (1974)
Neely, Mark, Jr *The Abraham Lincoln Encyclopedia* (1981)
Oates, Stephen *With Malice Towards None: The Life of Abraham Lincoln* (1977)
Sandburg, Carl *Abraham Lincoln: The Prairie Years* (1926)
Sandburg, Carl *Abraham Lincoln: The War Years* (1939)
Thomas, B P *Portrait for Posterity: Lincoln and his Biographers* (1947)

Lincoln Benjamin (1733–1810). American military and political leader. As brigadier general in the Continental army during the American Revolution 1775–83, he aided the victory at Saratoga 1777 but was forced to surrender to the British at Charleston 1780. He was secretary of war for the Continental Congress 1781–83, and led the suppression of Shays' Rebellion 1787.

Lind Jenny (Johanna Maria) (1820–1887). Swedish soprano. She had a remarkable range, and was nicknamed the 'Swedish nightingale'. She toured the USA 1850–52 under the management of circus promoter P T Barnum.

The tragedy of a scientific man is that he has found no way to guide his own discoveries to a constructive end.

CHARLES A LINDBERGH
Attributed remark

Lindbergh Charles A(ugustus) (1902–1974). US aviator who made the first solo nonstop flight in 33.5 hours across the Atlantic (Roosevelt Field, Long Island, New York, to Le Bourget airport, Paris) 1927 in the *Spirit of St Louis*, a Ryan monoplane designed by him.

Lindbergh was born in Detroit, Michigan. He was a barnstorming pilot before attending the US Army School in Texas 1924 and becoming an officer in the Army Air Service Reserve 1925. His son Charles Jr (1930–1932) was kidnapped and killed; ensuing legislation against kidnapping was called the Lindbergh Act. Although he admired the Nazi air force and championed US neutrality in the late 1930s, he flew 50 combat missions in the Pacific theatre in World War II. He wrote *The Spirit of St Louis* 1953 (Pulitzer prize).

Suggested reading
Davis, K S *The Hero: Charles A Lindbergh and the American Dream* (1959)
Lindbergh, Charles *The Spirit of St Louis* (autobiography) (1953)
Mosley, Leonard *Lindbergh* (1976)

Lindblad Bertil (1895–1965). Swedish astronomer who demonstrated the rotation of our Galaxy. He went on to stipulate that the speed of rotation of the stars in the Galaxy was a function of their distance from the centre (the 'differential rotation theory').

He was appointed director of the new Stockholm Observatory in 1927, and made professor of astronomy at the Royal Swedish Academy of Sciences.

Lindemann (Carl Louis) Ferdinand (1852–1939). German mathematician whose discussion of the nature of π in 1882 laid to

Lincoln, Abraham *US president Abraham Lincoln. A Republican, he was the 16th president of the USA. He was assassinated 1865, five days after the surrender of the Confederate forces in the American Civil War. (Image Select)*

rest the old question of 'squaring the circle'. The question whether π was a transcendental (nonalgebraic) number had never received a satisfactory answer until Lindemann proved it in his 1882 paper. He was professor at Würzburg 1879-83, and at Königsberg 1883-93; from 1893 until his death, he taught at Munich.

The perfectly designed machine is one in which all its working parts wear out simultaneously. I am that machine.

FREDERICK LINDEMANN, LORD CHERWELL
Letter from Lindemann to Lord De L'Isle 1957, shortly before he died.

Lindemann Frederick Alexander. Original name of Viscount ◊Cherwell, British physicist.

Lindrum Walter Albert (1898–1960). Australian billiards player. In 1933 he took the world title from England's Joe Davis and defended it successfully in 1934. No further world championships were held until the 1950s by which time he had retired undefeated. In 1932 he scored a world record break of 4,137 and altogether scored 711 breaks of more than 1,000. His nephew, Horace, (1912–1974) was world professional snooker champion 1952.

Lindsay (Nicholas) Vachel (1879–1931). US poet. He wandered the country, living by reciting his balladlike verse, collected in volumes

Linnaeus *Naturalist and physician Carolus Linnaeus. During the eighteenth century Linnaeus described the classification of plants into groups with shared characteristics. This system has given a unique and concise name that can be recognized throughout the world, for every organism identified.*(Image Select)

including *General William Booth Enters into Heaven* 1913, *The Congo* 1914, and *Johnny Appleseed* 1928.

Lindsay Jack (1900–1990). Australian writer, based in London. His enduring leftist sympathies pervade an enormous and varied literary output; he published over 100 books, including poems and classical translations, notably his *Catullus* 1929, political studies, historical novels with settings ranging from ancient Pompeii to 19th-century England, and biographies of Helen of Troy, Blake, Turner, and William Morris.

The son and, for a time, disciple of the influential artist and writer Norman Lindsay (1879–1969), he developed a more independent vision in response to Marxist and European influences in the 1930s.

Lindsay Norman Alfred William (1879–1969). Australian artist and writer. In his long career he worked as an illustrator on the *Bulletin*, produced water colours, pen drawings, oil paintings, etchings, sculptures and models, illustrated classic erotic works, was a prolific writer of fiction, nonfiction, and critical reviews and was involved in magazine publishing ventures. His many works include *Redheap* and *The Cautious Amorist*, both banned in Australia until 1958, *The Age of Consent* 1938, *The Cousin from Fiji*, and the children's novels *The Magic Pudding* 1918 and *The Flyaway Highway* 1936.

Lindwall Ray(mond Russell) (1921–1996). Australian cricketer noted as a fast bowler and all-rounder. He played in 61 tests 1946–60.

Lineker Gary (1960–). English footballer who scored over 250 goals in 550 games for Leicester, Everton, Barcelona, and Tottenham. With 48 goals in 80 internationals he failed by one goal to equal Bobby Charlton's record of 49 goals for England. Lineker was elected Footballer of the Year in 1986 and 1992, and was leading scorer at the 1986 World Cup finals. In 1993 he moved to Japan to play for Nagoya Grampus Eight.

Linlithgow John Adrian Louis Hope, 1st Marquess Linlithgow (1860–1908). British administrator, son of the 6th earl of Hopetoun, first governor general of Australia 1900–02. Earl 1873, marquess 1902.

His son Victor Alexander John Hope (1887–1952) was viceroy and governor general of India 1936–43; marquess 1908.

Nature does not make jumps.

CAROLUS LINNAEUS
Philosophia Botanica

Linnaeus Carolus (Latinized form of Carl von Linné) (1707–1778). Swedish naturalist and physician. His botanical work *Systema naturae* 1735 contained his system for classifying plants into groups depending on shared characteristics (such as the number of stamens in flowers), providing a much-needed framework for identification. He also devised the concise and precise system for naming plants and animals, using one Latin (or Latinized) word to represent the genus and a second to distinguish the species.

For example, in the Latin name of the daisy, *Bellis perennis*, *Bellis* is the name of the genus to which the plant belongs, and *perennis* distinguishes the species from others of the same genus. By tradition the generic name always begins with a capital letter. The author who first described a particular species is often indicated after the name, for example, *Bellis perennis Linnaeus*, showing that the author was Linnaeus. Linnaeus's system of nomenclature was introduced in *Species plantarum* 1753 and the fifth edition of *Genera plantarum* 1754 (first edition 1737). In 1758 he applied his binomial system to animal classification.

He practised as a physician and was appointed professor of medicine at Uppsala 1741, but changed this position in 1742 for the chair of botany.

Suggested reading
Blunt, W *The Complete Naturalist: A Life of Linnaeus* (1971)
Gourlie, N *The Prince of Botanists: Carl Linnaeus* (1953)
Weinstock, J *Contemporary Perspectives on Linnaeus* (1985)

Linnett John Wilfrid (1913–1975). English chemist who studied molecular force fields, spectroscopy, the measurement of burning velocities in gases, the recombination of atoms at surfaces, and theories of chemical bonding.

His career was spent at Oxford and then at Cambridge, where he became professor 1965 and was vice chancellor 1973–75.

His work on explosion limits concentrated on the reaction between carbon monoxide, hydrogen, and oxygen, which led to the study of atomic reactions on surfaces of metal alloys.

In 1960, Linnett originated a modification to the octet rule concerning valency electrons. He proposed that the octet should be considered as a double quartet of electrons rather than as four pairs, and in this way he was able to explain the stability of 'odd electron' molecules such as nitric oxide.

Linnett published more than 250 scientific papers and two textbooks, in one of which (*Wave Mechanics and Valency*) he explains the processes and techniques involved in the application of wave mechanics to the electronic structures of atoms and molecules.

Lin Piao alternative transliteration of ◊Lin Biao.

Liouville Joseph (1809–1882). French mathematician whose main influence was as the founder and first editor 1836–74 of the *Journal* *de Mathématiques Pures et Appliqués*, which became known as the *Journal de Liouville*.

From 1831 for 50 years, he taught mathematics at all the leading institutions of higher learning in Paris, becoming professor 1838 at the Ecole Polytechnique. He was also for a time the director of the Bureau de Longitudes. During the revolutions of 1848, he was elected as a moderate republican to the constituent assembly, but lost his seat the following year.

The chief mathematical interest of his career was in analysis. In that field he published more than 100 papers between 1832 and 1857. In collaboration with Charles-François Sturm (1803–1855), Liouville published papers in 1836 on vibration, which laid the foundations of the theory of linear differential equations. He also provided the first proof of the existence of transcendental functions.

Lipatti Dinu (1917–1950). Romanian pianist. He perfected a small repertoire, notably of the works of Chopin.

Lipchitz Jacques (1891–1973). Lithuanian-born sculptor. He was active in Paris from 1909 and emigrated to the USA 1941. He was one of the first Cubist sculptors, his best-known piece being *Man with a Guitar* 1916 (Museum of Modern Art, New York). In the 1920s he experimented with small open forms he called 'transparents'. His later works, often political allegories, were characterized by heavy, contorted forms.

Li Peng (1928–   ). Chinese communist politician, a member of the Politburo from 1985, and head of government from 1987. During the prodemocracy demonstrations of 1989 he supported the massacre of students by Chinese troops and the subsequent execution of others. He sought improved relations with the USSR before its demise, and has favoured maintaining firm central and party control over the economy.

Li was born at Chengdu in Sichuan province, the son of the writer Li Shouxun (who took part in the Nanchang rising 1927 and was executed 1930), and was adopted by the communist leader Zhou Enlai. He studied at the communist headquarters of Yan'an 1941–47 and trained as a hydroelectric engineer at the Moscow Power Institute from 1948. He was appointed minister of the electric power industry 1981, a vice premier 1983, and prime minister 1987. In 1989 he launched the crackdown on demonstrators in Beijing that led to the massacre in Tiananmen Square.

Lipmann Fritz Albert (1899–1986). German-born US biochemist. He investigated the means by which the cell acquires energy and highlighted the crucial role played by the energy-rich phosphate molecule adenosine triphosphate (ATP). For this and further work on metabolism, Lipmann shared the 1953 Nobel Prize for Physiology or Medicine with Hans Krebs.

Li Po (*c.* 705–762). Chinese poet. He used traditional literary forms, but his exuberance, the boldness of his imagination, and the intensity of his feeling have won him recognition as perhaps the greatest of all Chinese poets. Although he was mostly concerned with higher themes, he is also remembered for his celebratory verses on drinking.

Lippershey Hans (*c.* 1570–*c.* 1619). Dutch lensmaker, credited with inventing the telescope in 1608.

Lippi Filippino (*c.* 1457–1504). Italian painter of the Florentine school. He was the son of Filippo Lippi. His frescoes, typical of late 15th-century Florentine work, can be found in Sta Maria sopra Minerva, Rome, in Sta Maria Novella, Florence, and elsewhere.

He studied under Fra Diamante, his father's pupil, and Botticelli, being the latter's most distinguished pupil. He painted many altarpieces and frescoes in a graceful and delicate style, both as regards the human types represented and in the treatment of fluttering draperies and other accessories. His earlier works include the *Vision of St Bernard*, an altarpiece in the chapel of the Badia, Florence, the famous *Madonna and Child with Sts Victor, John the Baptist, Bernard and Zenobius*, 1485 (Uffizi), and the *Virgin and Child with Sts Jerome and Dominic*, 1485 (National Gallery, London). In 1484 he completed the frescoes left unfinished by Masaccio in Santa Maria del Carmine. He was in Rome for some years from 1488 and painted frescoes of scenes from the life of St Thomas Aquinas for a chapel in Santa Maria sopra Minerva. Frescoes for the Strozzi Chapel in Santa Maria Novella, Florence, 1500–02, were his last important undertaking. A notable altarpiece of the later Florentine period is *The Adoration of the Magi*, 1496 (Uffizi).

Lippi Fra Filippo (*c.* 1406–1469). Italian painter. His works include frescoes depicting the lives of St Stephen and St John the Baptist in Prato Cathedral 1452–66. He also painted many altarpieces of Madonnas and groups of saints.

Lippi was born in Florence. A Carmelite monk in early life, he is first mentioned as a painter 1431 and in his early work formed his style on that of Masaccio. He was much patronized by the Medici family, but lost two church offices after being convicted of forgery. Though pardoned and made chaplain of the convent of Santa Margherita in Prato, he again distinguished himself by eloping with a nun, Lucrezia Buti, by whom he had two children, one of them the painter Filippino Lippi. A dispensation arranged by the Medici sanctioned their marriage. Of his frescoes in the choir of Prato Cathedral, 1452–64, depicting events in the lives of St John the Baptist and St Stephen, the most important are the *Death of St Stephen*, in the background of which he introduced a portrait of himself, and that of Salome dancing. His last years were spent at Spoleto, where with his pupil, Fra Diamante, he worked on frescoes of the life of the Virgin for the cathedral. He also painted many panel pictures and created that wistful type of beauty in his Madonnas (owing something to Fra Angelico) which was to be an ideal pursued by many Florentine masters of the 15th century.

Lippmann Gabriel (1845–1921). French doctor. He invented the direct colour process in photography. He was awarded the Nobel Prize for Physics in 1908.

The final test of a leader is that he leaves behind him in other men the conviction and the will to carry on.
WALTER LIPPMANN
in *New York Herald Tribune* 14 Apr 1945

Lippmann Walter (1889–1974). US liberal political commentator. From 1921 Lippmann was the chief editorial writer for the *New York World* and from 1931 wrote the daily column 'Today and Tomorrow', which was widely syndicated through the *New York Herald Tribune*. Among his books are *A Preface to Morals* 1929, *The Good Society* 1937, and *The Public Philosophy* 1955.

He was one of the founders of the *New Republic* magazine 1914. After service in army intelligence during World War I, he became an adviser to President Wilson at the Versailles Peace Conference.

Lipschitz Rudolf Otto Sigismund (1832–1903). German mathematician who developed a hypercomplex system of number theory, which became known as Lipschitz algebra. His work in basic analysis provided a condition for the continuity of a function, now known as the Lipschitz condition, subsequently of great importance in proofs of existence and uniqueness, as well as in approximation theory and constructive function theory. From 1864 he was professor at the University of Bonn.

Lipschitz's book *Grundlagen der Analysis* 1877–80 was a synthetic presentation of the foundations of mathematics and their applications. The work provided a comprehensive survey of what was then known of the theory of rational integers, differential equations, and function theory.

Lipscomb William Nunn (1919–   ). US chemist who studied the relationships between the geometric and electronic structures of molecules and their chemical and physical behaviour. He became professor at Harvard 1959.

Lipscomb studied the boron hydrides and their derivatives and put forward bonding theories to explain the structures of electron-deficient compounds in general. He developed low-temperature X-ray diffraction methods to study simple crystals of nitrogen, oxygen, fluorine, and other substances that are solid only below liquid nitrogen temperatures.

Lipscomb went on to investigate the carboranes and the sites of electrophilic attack on these compounds, using nuclear magnetic resonance spectroscopy (NMR). This work led to the theory of chemical shifts. The calculations provided the first accurate values for the constants that describe the behaviour of several types of molecules in magnetic or electric fields. They also gave a theoretical basis for applying quantum mechanics to complex molecules.

Lispector Clarice (1925–1977). Brazilian writer. She was particularly concerned with the themes of adolescence, femininity, alienation, and self-awareness. Her acclaimed first novel *Perto do Coração Selvagem/Near to the Savage Heart* 1944, published when she was 19, was followed by other novels and distinguished short stories, including *A Legião Estrangeira/The Foreign Legion* 1964.

Lissajous Jules Antoine (1822–1880). French physicist who from 1855 developed *Lissajous figures* as a means of visually demonstrating the vibrations that produce sound waves. He became rector of the Academy of Chambéry in 1874, and then took up the same position at Besançon in 1875.

Lissajous first reflected a light beam from a mirror attached to a vibrating object such as a tuning fork to another mirror that rotated. The light was then reflected onto a screen, where the spot traced out a curve whose shape depended on the amplitude and frequency of the vibration. He then refined this method by using two mirrors mounted on vibrating tuning forks at right angles, and produced a wider variety of figures. By making one of the forks a standard, the acoustic characteristics of the other fork could be determined by the shape of the Lissajous figure produced.

Lissitzky El (Eliezer Markowich) (1890–1941). Russian painter, designer, printmaker, typographer, and illustrator. He was a pioneer of non-objective art. In his *Prouns* series of lithographs and works on paper, he plays with the illusion of perspective, floating precise, geo-

Liszt The composer and pianist Franz Liszt (1811–1886). He was the leading virtuoso pianist of the 19th century, and perhaps of all time. In later years he retired from the concert platform, turning increasingly to composition and religion. (Image Select)

metric forms against an infinite white ground, as in *Proun 7A, Moscow* 1919–20 (Kunstmuseum, Basel).

A trained architect and engineer, Lissitzky taught with Chagall and Malevich at the art school in Vitebsk 1919 and, inspired by the latter's use of pure geometric form, swiftly turned to abstract art. Travelling between Russia, Germany, and Switzerland, he spread the ideas of the Russian avant-garde through his art, lectures, and radical designs for typography and exhibition displays. His theories influenced Dutch De Stijl and German Bauhaus teaching, and were later transmitted to the USA.

List Wilhelm (1880–1971). German field marshal. In World War II, he commanded the 14th German Army in Poland 1939 and the 12th Army in France 1940, and was then promoted to field marshal. He led the southern wing of the invasion of Greece and Yugoslavia 1941. Moving to the Eastern Front, he commanded Army Group A in the Caucasus 1942 but was dismissed Sept 1942 for failing to obey Hitler's directives. He was convicted of war crimes at Nuremberg 1945 and served 5 years of a life sentence.

Lister Joseph, 1st Baron Lister (1827–1912). English surgeon and founder of antiseptic surgery, influenced by Louis Pasteur's work on bacteria. He introduced dressings soaked in carbolic acid and strict rules of hygiene to combat wound sepsis in hospitals. Baronet 1883, baron 1897. The number of surgical operations greatly increased following the introduction of anaesthetics, but death rates were more than 40%. Under Lister's regime they fell dramatically.

He was professor of surgery at Glasgow 1860–69, at Edinburgh 1869–77, and at King's College, London, 1877–92. In 1891 he became chair of the newly formed British Institute of Preventive Medicine (later the Lister Institute).

Sepsis was at this time thought to be a kind of combustion caused by exposing moist body tissues to oxygen. Learning of Pasteur's discovery of microorganisms, however, Lister began to use carbolic acid as a disinfectant. In 1867 he announced that his wards in the Glasgow Royal Infirmary had remained clear of sepsis for nine months. Later he adopted the method developed by Robert Koch in Germany of using steam to sterilize surgical instruments and dressings.

Suggested reading
Fisher, Richard *Joseph Lister, 1827–1912* (1977)
Goldman, Martin *Lister Ward* (1987)

Liszt Franz (1811–1886). Hungarian pianist and composer. An outstanding virtuoso of the piano, he was an established concert artist by the age of 12. His expressive, romantic, and frequently chromatic works include piano music (*Transcendental Studies* 1851), masses and oratorios, songs, organ music, and a symphony. Much of his music is programmatic; he also originated the symphonic poem. Liszt was taught by his father, then by Carl Czerny (1791–1857). He travelled widely in Europe, producing an operetta *Don Sanche* in Paris at the age of 14. As musical director and conductor at Weimar 1848–59, he championed the music of Berlioz and Wagner.

Retiring to Rome, he turned again to his early love of religion, and in 1865 became a secular priest (adopting the title Abbé), while continuing to teach and give concert tours for which he also made virtuoso piano arrangements of orchestral works by Beethoven, Schubert, and Wagner. He died at Bayreuth in Germany.

Suggested reading
Taylor, Ronald *Franz Liszt* (1986)
Walker, Alan *Liszt* (1983–87)
Williams, Adrian *Portrait of Liszt* (1990)

Little Richard stage name of Richard Wayne Penniman (1932–). US rock singer and pianist. He was one of the creators of rock and roll with his wildly uninhibited renditions of 'Tutti

---

I am the real King of rock'n'roll. I was singing before anybody knew what rock was ... People like Elvis Presley were the builders of rock'n'roll, but I was the architect.

LITTLE RICHARD
in *Los Angeles Times* 1984

Frutti' 1956, 'Long Tall Sally' 1956, and 'Good Golly Miss Molly' 1957. His subsequent career in soul and rhythm and blues was interrupted by periods as a Seventh-Day Adventist cleric.

Littlewood Joan Maud (1914–). English theatre director. She established the Theatre Workshop 1945 and was responsible for many vigorous productions at the Theatre Royal, Stratford, London 1953–75, such as *A Taste of Honey* 1959, Brendan Behan's *The Hostage* 1959–60, and *Oh, What a Lovely War* 1963.

Peace is indivisible.

MAXIM LITVINOV
Speech to the League of Nations July 1936

Litvinov Maxim. Adopted name of Meir Walach (1876–1951). Soviet politician, commissioner for foreign affairs under Stalin from Jan 1931 until his removal from office in May 1939.

Litvinov believed in cooperation with the West and obtained US recognition of the USSR in 1934. In the League of Nations he advocated action against the Axis (the alliance of Nazi Germany and Fascist Italy); he was therefore dismissed just before the signing of the Hitler–Stalin nonaggression pact 1939. After the German invasion of the USSR, he was ambassador to the USA 1941–43.

Liu Shaoqi or Liu Shao-chi (1898–1969). Chinese communist politician, in effective control of government 1960–65. A Moscow-trained labour organizer, he was a firm proponent of the Soviet style of government based around disciplined one-party control, the use of incentive gradings, and priority for industry over agriculture. This was opposed by Mao Zedong, but began to be implemented by Liu while he was state president 1960–65.

Liu was brought down during the Cultural Revolution.

The son of a Hunan peasant farmer, Liu attended the same local school as Mao. As a member of the Chinese Communist Party (CCP), he was sent to Moscow to study communism, and returned to Shanghai in 1922. Mao yielded the title of president to him in 1960, and after the failure of the Great Leap Forward to create effective agricultural communes, Liu introduced a recovery programme. This was successful, but was seen as a return to capitalism. He was stripped of his post and expelled from the CCP in April 1969 and banished to Kaifeng in Henan province, where he died in Nov 1969 after being locked in a disused bank vault. He was rehabilitated posthumously ten years later.

Lively Penelope Margaret (1933–). British writer. She has written many novels for children (*A Stitch in Time* 1976 won the Whitbread Literary Award) and, from 1977, for adults (*Moon Tiger* 1987 won the Booker Prize). Her fiction is characterized by an absorption in the influence of the past on the present.

The childhood memoir *Oleander Jacaranda* recalls her early days in Egypt (she was born in Cairo), but her fiction is often set in Oxfordshire, where she has long lived. Her children's novels often have a supernatural element; for example, *The Ghost of Thomas Kempe* 1973 wittily explored the clash between the 17th and 20th centuries. Her adult novels pursue the influence of surviving memory – architectural, topographical, pictorial. They include *Cleopatra's Sister* 1993.

The Arch-Mediocrity.

Benjamin Disraeli on ROBERT JENKINSON, 2ND EARL LIVERPOOL
in *Coningsby* 1844

Liverpool Robert Banks Jenkinson, 2nd Earl Liverpool (1770–1828). British Tory politician. He entered Parliament 1790 and was foreign secretary 1801–03, home secretary 1804–06 and 1807–09, war minister 1809–12, and prime minister 1812–27. His government conducted the Napoleonic Wars to a successful conclusion, but its ruthless suppression of freedom of speech and of the press aroused such opposition that during 1815–20 revolution frequently seemed imminent. Earl 1808.

Livia Drusilla (58 BC–AD 29). Roman empress, wife of Augustus from 39 BC. She was the mother by her first husband of Tiberius and engaged in intrigue to secure his succession to the imperial crown. She remained politically active to the end of her life.

Live mindful of our marriage, Livia, and farewell.

Augustus on LIVIA DRUSILLA
Augustus' dying words, quoted by Suetonius in *Augustus* ch 99.1

Livingston Robert R (1746–1813). American public official and diplomat. As secretary for foreign affairs 1781, he directed negotiations for the Paris Peace Treaty 1783. In 1801 he was named minister to France by President Jefferson. With James Monroe, Livingston secured the purchase of the Louisiana Territory 1803, acquiring a large part of North America from the French.

Born in New York and educated at King's College (now Columbia University), Livingston was admitted to the bar 1770. After service in the Continental Congress 1775 he helped write the New York Constitution and served as state chancellor 1776–1801. He returned to the Continental Congress 1779.

Livingstone David (1813–1873). Scottish missionary explorer. In 1841 he went to Africa, reached Lake Ngami 1849, followed the Zambezi to its mouth, saw the Victoria Falls 1855, and went to East and Central Africa 1858–64, reaching Lakes Shirwa and Malawi. From 1866, he tried to find the source of the river Nile, and reached Ujiji in Tanganyika in Nov 1871. British explorer Henry Stanley joined Livingstone in Ujiji. Livingstone not only mapped a great deal of the African continent but also helped to end the Arab slave trade.

He died in Old Chitambo (now in Zambia) and was buried in Westminster Abbey, London.

Livingstone, David *Scottish missionary and explorer David Livingstone. After taking a medical degree at Glasgow University, he became a missionary and went to Africa 1841. He was responsible for mapping much of the African continent. (Image Select)*

Suggested reading
Helly, D *Livingstone's Legacy* (1986)
Ransford, O *David Livingstone: The Dark Interior* (1978)
Seaver, G *David Livingstone, His Life and Letters* (1957)

Livingstone Ken(neth) (1945–). British left-wing Labour politician. He was leader of the Greater London Council (GLC) 1981–86 and a member of Parliament from 1987. He stood as a candidate for the Labour Party leadership elections 1992.

Livingstone joined the Labour Party in 1968, and was active in London politics from 1971. As leader of the GLC until its abolition in 1986, he displayed outside GLC headquarters current unemployment figures so that they were clearly visible to MPs in the Palace of Westminster across the river Thames. He was elected to Parliament representing the London constituency of Brent East in 1987.

Part of the problem is that many MPs never see the London that exists beyond the wine bars and brothels of Westminster.

KEN LIVINGSTONE
quoted in *Observer* 22 Feb 1987

Livy (Titus Livius) (59 BC–AD 17). Roman historian. He was the author of a *History of Rome* from the city's foundation to 9 BC, based partly on legend. It was composed of 142 books, of which 35 survive, covering the periods from the arrival of Aeneas in Italy to 293 BC and from 218 to 167 BC.

Woe to the vanquished.

LIVY
History V 48

Li Xiannian (1909–1992). Chinese politician, member of the Chinese Communist Party (CCP) Politburo from 1956. He fell from favour during the 1966–69 Cultural Revolution, but was rehabilitated as finance minister in 1973, supporting cautious economic reform. He was state president 1983–88.

Li, born into a poor peasant family in Hubei province, joined the CCP in 1927 and served as a political commissar during the Long March of 1934–36. During the 1950s and early 1960s Li was vice premier to the State Council and minister for finance and was inducted into the CCP Politburo and secretariat in 1956 and 1958 respectively.

Llewellyn Richard. Pen name of Richard Dafydd Vivian Llewellyn Lloyd (1906–1983). Welsh writer. *How Green Was My Valley* 1939, a novel about a S Wales mining family, was made into a play and a film. He also wrote two sequels, plays, and the novels *None but the Lonely Heart* 1943 and *A Few Flowers for Shiner* 1950.

Llewelyn two princes of Wales:

He gave good justice to all men, and attracted all men to his service.

Annales Cambriae on LLEWELYN I

Llewelyn I (1173–1240). Prince of Wales from 1194 who extended his rule to all Wales not in Norman hands, driving the English from N Wales 1212, and taking Shrewsbury 1215. During the early part of Henry III's reign, he was several times attacked by English armies. He was married to Joanna, illegitimate daughter of King John.

The last champion of Welsh liberty ... Brave, active and strenuous ... perhaps, better able to conceive than to carry out an elaborate policy.

T F Tout on LLEWELYN II AP GRUFFYDD
in *Dictionary of National Biography*

Llewelyn II ap Gruffydd (*c.* 1225–1282). Prince of Wales from 1246, grandson of Llewelyn I. In 1277 Edward I of England compelled Llewelyn to acknowledge him as overlord and to surrender S Wales. His death while leading a national uprising ended Welsh independence.

Lloyd Harold Clayton (1893–1971). US film comedian. He wore thick horn-rimmed glasses and straw hat, and performed daring stunts in his cliff-hangers. He appeared from 1913 in silent and talking films. His silent films include *Grandma's Boy* 1922, *Safety Last* 1923, and *The Freshman* 1925. His first talkie was *Movie Crazy* 1932. He produced films after 1938, including the anthologies *Harold Lloyd's World of Comedy* 1962 and *Funny Side of Life* 1964.

'Master comedian and good citizen.'

Citation of a special American Academy of Motion Picture
Arts and Sciences award for HAROLD LLOYD 1952

Lloyd John, known as John Scolvus, 'the skilful' (lived 15th century). Welsh sailor who carried on an illegal trade with Greenland and is claimed to have reached North America, sailing as far south as Maryland, in 1477 (15 years before the voyage of Columbus).

Lloyd Marie. Stage name of Matilda Alice Victoria Wood (1870–1922). English music-hall artist. Her Cockney songs embodied the music-hall traditions of 1890s comedy.

Lloyd Selwyn. See ◊Selwyn Lloyd, British Conservative politician.

Lloyd George David, 1st Earl Lloyd George of Dwyfor (1863–1945). Welsh Liberal politician, prime minister of Britain 1916–22. A pioneer of social reform, as chancellor of the Exchequer 1908–15 he introduced old-age pensions 1908 and health and unemployment insurance 1911. High unemployment, intervention in the Russian Civil War, and use of the military police force, the Black and Tans, in Ireland eroded his support as prime minister, and the creation of the Irish Free State in 1921 and his pro-Greek policy against the Turks caused the collapse of his coalition government. Earl 1945.

Lloyd George was born in Manchester, became a solicitor, and was member of Parliament for Caernarvon Boroughs from 1890. During the Boer War, he was prominent as a pro-Boer. His 1909 budget (with graduated direct taxes and taxing land values) provoked the Lords to reject it, and resulted in the Act of 1911 limiting their powers. He held ministerial posts during World War I until 1916 when there was an open breach between him and Prime Minister Asquith, and he became prime minister of a coalition government. Securing a unified Allied command, he enabled the Allies to withstand the last German offensive and achieve victory. After World War I he had a major role in the Versailles peace treaty. In the 1918 elections, he achieved a huge majority over Labour and Asquith's followers. He had become largely distrusted within his own party by 1922, and never regained power.

Suggested reading
Beaverbrook, Lord *The Decline and Fall of Lloyd George* (1963)
Constantine, Stephen *Lloyd George* (1992)
George, W R P *Lloyd George: Backbencher* (1983)
Grigg, John *Lloyd George* (1978–84)
Woodward, David *Lloyd George and the Generals* (1983)

Lloyd Webber Andrew (1948–). English composer. His early musicals, with lyrics by Tim Rice, include *Joseph and the Amazing Technicolor Dreamcoat* 1968, *Jesus Christ Superstar* 1970, and *Evita* 1978, based on the life of the Argentine leader Eva Perón. He also wrote *Cats* 1981, based on T S Eliot's *Old Possum's Book of Practical Cats*, *Starlight Express* 1984, *The Phantom of the Opera* 1986, and *Aspects of Love* 1989.

Other works include *Variations for Cello* 1978, written for his brother Julian Lloyd Webber (1951–) who is a solo cellist, and a *Requiem Mass* 1985.

Llull Ramon See ◊ Lully, Raymond.

Loach Ken(neth) (1936–   ). British film and television director. Loach became known for his trenchantly realistic treatment of social issues with television dramas such as *Cathy Come Home* 1966, concerning the plight of homeless people.

His first film was *Poor Cow* 1967; its successor, *Kes* 1971, dealing with working-class life in the north of England, was more favourably received. During the 1970s he was mainly active in television but returned to the cinema in the early 1990s, directing *Hidden Agenda* 1990, about the Northern Ireland troubles, the comedy *Riff Raff* 1991, and *Raining Stones* 1993.

Non-Euclidean geometry might find application in the intimate sphere of molecular attraction.

NIKOLAI IVANOVICH LOBACHEVSKY
Complete Geometrical Works 1883–1886

Lobachevsky Nikolai Ivanovich (1792–1856). Russian mathematician who founded non-Euclidean geometry, concurrently with, but independently of, Karl Gauss in Germany and János Bolyai in Hungary. Lobachevsky published the first account of the subject in 1829, but his work went unrecognized until Georg Riemann's system was published.

In Euclid's system, two parallel lines will remain equidistant from each other, whereas in Lobachevskian geometry, the two lines will approach zero in one direction and infinity in the other. In Euclidean geometry the sum of the angles of a triangle is always equal to the sum of two right angles; in Lobachevskian geometry, the sum of the angles is always less than the sum of two right angles. In Lobachevskian space, also, two geometric figures cannot have the same shape but different sizes. The clearest statement of Lobachevsky's geometry was made in the book *Geometrische Untersuchungen zur Theorie der Parallellinien*, published in Berlin 1840. His last work was *Pangéométrie* 1855.

Lobachevsky was born at Nizhni-Novgorod and studied at the University of Kazan, Tatarstan. He taught there from 1814, becoming professor 1822 and rector of the university 1827–47. He also took on administrative work for the government.

Lobengula (1836–1894). King of Matabeleland (now part of Zimbabwe) 1870–93.

After accepting British protection from internal and external threats to his leadership in 1888, Lobengula came under increasing pressure from British mining interests to allow exploitation of goldfields near Bulawayo. This led to his overthrow by a British military expedition organized by Cecil Rhodes's South African Company in 1893.

Lochner Stephan (*c.* 1400–1451). German painter. Active in Cologne from 1442, he was a master of the International Gothic style. Most of his work is still in Cologne, notably the *Virgin in the Rose Garden* about 1440 (Wallraf-Richartz Museum) and *Adoration of the Magi* 1448 (Cologne Cathedral). His work combines the delicacy of the International Gothic style with the naturalism of Flemish painting.

Nothing was made by God for man to spoil or destroy.

JOHN LOCKE
Second Treatise on Government iv 31

Locke John (1632–1704). English philosopher. His *Essay concerning Human Understanding* 1690 maintained that experience was the only source of knowledge (empiricism), and that 'we can have knowledge no farther than we have ideas' prompted by such experience. *Two Treatises on Government* 1690 helped to form contemporary ideas of liberal democracy. For Locke, the physical universe was a mechanical system of material bodies, composed of corpuscles, or 'invisible particles'. He believed that at birth the mind was a blank, and that all ideas came from sense impressions.

His *Two Treatises on Government* supplied the classical statement of Whig theory and enjoyed great influence in America and France.

It supposed that governments derive their authority from popular consent (regarded as a 'contract'), so that a government may be rightly overthrown if it infringes such fundamental rights of the people as religious freedom.

Locke was born in Somerset and studied at Oxford. He practised medicine, and in 1667 became secretary to the Earl of Shaftesbury. He consequently fell under suspicion as a Whig and in 1683 fled to Holland, where he lived until the 1688 revolution brought William of Orange to the English throne. In later life he published many works on philosophy, politics, theology, and economics; these include *Letters on Toleration* 1689–92 and *Some Thoughts concerning Education* 1693.

Suggested reading
Cranston, Maurice *John Locke: A Biography* (1957)
Dunn, John *The Political Thought of John Locke* (1969)
Grant, R W *John Locke's Liberalism* (1987)
Mabbott, J D *John Locke* (1973)
Yolton, John *John Locke and the Way of Ideas* (1956)

Locke Joseph (1805–1860). English railway engineer, an associate of railway pioneers Isambard Kingdom Brunel and George and Robert Stephenson. He built many railway lines in the UK and France.

Locke was born near Sheffield, Yorkshire, and left school at 13. In 1823 he went to work for George Stephenson, and learned much about surveying, railway engineering, and construction. From 1847 he was Liberal member of Parliament for Honiton, Devon.

Locke's first task undertaken alone was the construction of a railway line from the Black Fell colliery to the river Tyne. He then began surveys for lines running between Leeds and Hull, Manchester and Bolton, and Canterbury and Whitstable. Locke built as straight as possible, used the terrain, and avoided the expense of tunnels whenever he could. Building the London to Southampton line, which opened 1840, he cut through the chalk Downs. He also built the Sheffield-to-Manchester route through the millstone grit of the Pennines. In 1841 he began work as chief engineer on the Paris-to-Rouen line, the first of several contracts in France.

Lockwood Margaret Mary (1916–1990). English actress. Between 1937 and 1949 she acted exclusively in the cinema, appearing in Alfred Hitchcock's *The Lady Vanishes* 1938 and in *The Wicked Lady* 1945. After 1955 she made only one film, *The Slipper and the Rose* 1976, although she periodically appeared on stage and on television until her retirement 1980.

Lockwood attended the Royal Academy of Dramatic Art (RADA), and made her stage and film debut 1934. During the war years she starred in several of the melodramas made by the Gainsborough studio (a British film company of the 1930s), including her role as the female highwayman of *The Wicked Lady*. She later played the role of a barrister in the television courtroom series *Justice* 1972–73. The last years of her life were spent as a virtual recluse. She published an autobiography, *Lucky Star*, 1955. Her daughter is the actress Julia Lockwood (1941–   ).

Lockyer (Joseph) Norman (1836–1920). English scientist who studied the spectra of solar prominences and sunspots. Through his pioneering work in spectroscopy, he discovered the existence of helium. KCB 1897.

Lockyer was born in Rugby, the Midlands, and began as an amateur astronomer. In 1869 he founded the scientific journal *Nature*, which he was to edit for 50 years. He was director of the Solar Physics Observatory in South Kensington, London, 1890–1911.

In 1869 Lockyer attached a spectroscope to a 15-cm/6-in telescope and used it to observe solar prominences at times other than during a total solar eclipse. Although Lockyer had been the first to think of it, the same idea had occurred to French astronomer Pierre Janssen, then working in India, and they simultaneously notified the French Academy of Sciences of the same result. Later they worked together, Janssen providing the observations of the Sun's spectrum that led to the discovery of helium.

Lockyer also developed the theory that Stonehenge is oriented towards the direction in which the Sun rises at the time of the summer solstice. From the gradual change in position of the solstitial sunrise, he calculated that the monument must date from 1840 BC, plus or minus 200 years – later confirmed by radiocarbon dating.

Literature is mostly about having sex and not much about having children. Life is the other way round.
DAVID LODGE
The British Museum is Falling Down 1965

Lodge David John (1935–   ). English novelist, short-story writer, dramatist, and critic. Much of his fiction concerns the role of Catholicism in mid-20th-century England, exploring the situation both through broad comedy and parody, as in *The British Museum is Falling Down* 1967, and realistically, as in *How Far Can You Go?* 1980. *Nice Work* 1988 was short-listed for the Booker Prize.

His other works include *Changing Places* 1975 and its sequel *Small World* 1984, both satirical 'campus' novels; the play, *The Writing Game* 1990; and *Paradise News* 1991.

Lodge Henry Cabot (1850–1924). US politician, Republican senator from 1893, and chair of the Senate Foreign Relations Committee after World War I. He supported conservative economic legislation at home but expansionist policies abroad. Nevertheless, he influenced the USA to stay out of the League of Nations 1920 as a threat to US sovereignty.

As an advocate of American pursuit of empire, he joined President T Roosevelt in calling for war against Spain 1898. He insisted on modifications to the Treaty of Versailles with its provisions for the League of Nations. President Wilson refused to accede, and the Senate was deadlocked, finally refusing to ratify the treaty.

Lodge Henry Cabot, II (1902–1985). US diplomat. He was Eisenhower's presidential campaign manager and the US representative at the United Nations 1953–60. Ambassador to South Vietnam 1963–64 and 1965–67, he replaced W A Harriman as President Nixon's negotiator in the Vietnam peace talks 1969. He was a grandson of Henry Cabot Lodge.

Lodge Oliver Joseph (1851–1940). British physicist. He developed a system of wireless communication in 1894, and his work was instrumental in the development of radio receivers. He also proved that the ether does not exist, a discovery fundamental to the theory of relativity. After his son was killed in 1915, Lodge became interested in psychic research. Knighted 1902.

He became professor of physics at the University of Liverpool on its founding 1881; in 1900, he moved to the University of Birmingham to become its first principal.

Lodge invented a coherer, a device consisting of a container packed with metal granules whose electrical resistance varies with the passage of electromagnetic radiation. Designed to detect electromagnetic waves, this was developed into a detector of radio waves in the early investigations of radio communication, with which Lodge was closely involved.

Love in my bosom like a bee / Doth suck his sweet; / Now with his wings he plays with me, / Now with his feet. / Within mine eyes he makes his nest, / His bed amidst my tender breast; / My kisses are his daily feast, / And yet he robs me of my rest. / Ah, wanton, will ye?
THOMAS LODGE
'Love in my bosom like a bee'

Lodge Thomas (c. 1558–1625). English author. His romance *Rosalynde* 1590 was the basis of Shakespeare's play *As You Like It*.

Lody Carl (died 1914). German spy operating in the UK during World War I. He was arrested in Ireland and shot in the Tower of London 6 Nov 1914, the first German spy to be executed in the war.

As a lieutenant in the German Naval reserve, Lody frequently visited British ports prior to 1914 in the guise of a travel guide, and on the outbreak of war he was selected by German spymaster Boy-Ed as his UK agent. He was given a stolen US passport, went to England, reported on air raid protection in London, then went to the naval base at Rosyth, to Liverpool, and finally to Ireland. When arrested at Killarney, he was found to be in possession of incriminating documents and later discovered to have been responsible for the sinking of a British cruiser by reporting its sailing to the German Navy.

Loeb James (1867–1933). German banker, born in New York, who financed the Loeb Classical Library of Greek and Latin authors, which gives the original text with a parallel translation.

Loewe Frederick (1904–1988). US composer of musicals. In 1942 he joined forces with the lyricist Alan Jay Lerner, and their joint successes include *Brigadoon* 1947, *Paint Your Wagon* 1951, *My Fair Lady* 1956, *Gigi* 1958, and *Camelot* 1960.

Born in Berlin, the son of an operatic tenor, he studied under Ferruccio Busoni, and in 1924 went with his father to the USA.

Loewi Otto (1873–1961). German physiologist whose work on the nervous system established that a chemical substance is responsible for the stimulation of one nerve cell (neuron) by another. The substance was shown by the physiologist Henry Dale to be acetylcholine, now known to be one of the most vital neurotransmitters. For this work Loewi and Dale were jointly awarded the 1936 Nobel Prize for Physiology or Medicine.

Loewy Raymond Fernand (1893–1986). French-born US designer. His work includes the S-I steam engine 1937, the Lucky Strike cigarette packet, the Silversides Greyhound bus 1940–54, and the Avanti Studebaker car 1962.

Loewy began as a fashion illustrator, and became one of the first designers to work as a freelance consultant, as well as the most famous. Most of his work was done by technical support staff – Loewy was a stylist rather than an engineering draughtsperson.

Lofting Hugh John (1886–1947). English writer and illustrator of children's books. His best-known work is the 'Dr Dolittle' series, in which the hero can talk to animals. Born in Maidenhead, Berkshire, Lofting was originally a civil engineer. He went to the USA 1912.

I live by a man's code designed to fit a man's world, yet at the same time I never forget that a woman's first job is to choose the right shade of lipstick.
CAROLE LOMBARD
in Leslie Halliwell Filmgoer's Companion 1965

Lombard Carole. Stage name of Jane Alice Peters (1908–1942). US comedy film actress. A warm and witty actress, she starred in several celebrated comedies of the 1930s and early 1940s: *Twentieth Century* 1934, *My Man Godfrey* 1936, and *To Be or Not to Be* 1942. She was married to Clark Gable from 1939 until her death in a plane crash.

Lombardi Vince(nt Thomas) (1913–1970). US football coach. As head coach of the Green Bay Packers 1959, he transformed a losing team into a major power, winning the first two Super Bowls 1967 and 1968. His last coaching position was with the Washington Redskins 1969–70.

Born in Brooklyn, New York, USA, Lombardi was educated at Fordham University. He was an assistant coach at Fordham 1947–48 and West Point 1949–54, after which he entered professional football as offensive coach with the New York Giants.

Lombroso Cesare (1835–1909). Italian criminologist. His chief work is *L'uomo delinquente/The Delinquent Man* 1889. He held the now discredited idea that there was a physically distinguishable 'criminal type'.

He became a professor of mental diseases at Pavia in 1862. Subsequently he held professorships in forensic medicine, psychiatry, and criminal anthropology at Turin.

London Jack (John Griffith Chaney) (1876–1916). US novelist. He was a prolific author of naturalistic novels, adventure stories, and socialist reportage. His works, which are often based on his own life, typically concern the human struggle for survival against extreme natural forces, as dramatized in such novels as *The Call of the Wild* 1903, *The Sea Wolf* 1904, and *White Fang* 1906. By 1906 he was the most widely read writer in the USA and had been translated into 68 languages.

London was an adventurer himself, at various times a sailor, a hobo riding freight trains, and a gold prospector in the Klondike. His many short stories are collected in *The Son of the Wolf* 1900, *The God of His Fathers* 1901, *Children of the Frost* 1902, *Love of Life* 1907, and *Smoke Bellew* 1912. Among his other novels are *The People of the Abyss* 1903, *The Road* 1907, *The Iron Heel* 1907, and *Martin Eden* 1909.

Long Huey Pierce (1893–1935). US Democratic politician, nicknamed 'the Kingfish', governor of Louisiana 1928–31, US senator for Louisiana 1930–35, legendary for his political rhetoric. He was popular with poor white voters for his programme of social and economic reform, which he called the 'Share Our Wealth' programme. It represented a significant challenge to F D Roosevelt's New Deal economic programme. Long's scheme called for massive redistribution of wealth through high inheritance taxes and confiscatory taxes on high incomes. His own extravagance, including the state capitol building at Baton Rouge built of bronze and marble, was widely criticized. Although he became a virtual dictator in the state, his slogan was 'Every man a king, but no man wears a crown'. He was assassinated.

Suggested reading
Liebling, A J *The Earl of Louisiana* (1961)
Sindler, A P *Huey Long's Louisiana* (1972)
Williams, T Harry *Huey Long* (1969)

Long Richard (1945–). English Conceptual artist. In the vanguard of 1960s young artists wishing to break away from studio-created art, he has worked both outdoors and on the spot in galleries. He has used natural materials such as stone, slate, wood, and mud to represent the ritualized traces of early peoples, notably in *River Avon Driftwood* 1977 (Museum of Contemporary Art, Ghent). Only photographic records remain of much of his work.

He created his celebrated stone circles and rivers of sticks during walks in remote areas of Ireland, the Himalayas, Africa, and Iceland.

Long Sydney (1871–1955). Australian painter and etcher known particularly for his Australian landscapes populated with figures from classical mythology. His *Spirit of the Plains* 1897 (Art Gallery of Queensland, Brisbane), in which dancing brolgas follow a naked piper across a fantasy landscape, shows the influence of the Art Nouveau style which characterized his later work.

Longfellow Henry Wadsworth (1807–1882). US poet. He is remembered for his ballads ('Excelsior', 'The Village Blacksmith', 'The Wreck of the Hesperus') and the mythic narrative epics *Evangeline* 1847, *The Song of Hiawatha* 1855, and *The Courtship of Miles Standish* 1858.

Longfellow was born in Portland, Maine. He graduated from Bowdoin College and taught modern languages there and at Harvard University 1835–54, after which he travelled widely. The most popular US poet of the 19th century, Longfellow was also an adept translator. His other works include six sonnets on Dante, a translation of Dante's *Divine Comedy*, and *Tales of a Wayside Inn* 1863, which includes the popular poem 'Paul Revere's Ride'.

Suggested reading
Arvin, N *Longfellow: His Life and Work* (1963)
Wagenknecht, E *Henry Wadsworth Longfellow: Portrait of an American Humanist* (1985)
Wagenknecht, E *Henry Wadsworth Longfellow: His Poetry and Prose* (1986)

Longford Elizabeth Pakenham, Countess of Longford (born Harman) (1906–). English historical writer whose books include *Victoria RI* 1964. She is married to Lord Longford; their eldest daughter is Lady Antonia Fraser.

Biography is too important to become a playground for fantasies, however ingenious.
ELIZABETH, COUNTESS OF LONGFORD
The Pebbled Shore epilogue 1986

Longford Frank (Francis Aungier) Pakenham, 7th Earl of Longford (1905–). Anglo-Irish Labour politician. He was brought up a Protestant but is now a leading Catholic. He is an advocate of penal reform. Earl 1961.

He worked in the Conservative Party Economic Research Department 1930–32, yet became a member of the Labour Party and held ministerial posts 1948–51 and 1964–68.

The male sex still constitute in many ways the most obstinate vested interest one can find.
FRANK PAKENHAM, 7TH EARL OF LONGFORD
Speech in House of Lords 23 June 1963

Longford Raymond John Walter Hollis (1878–1959). Australian actor, film director, and producer. He is best known for the screen classic *The Sentimental Bloke* 1919 which starred Lottie Lyell, his partner and close associate. His other films include *Ginger Mick* 1920, *On Our Selection* 1920, and *The Blue Mountains Mystery* 1921. The only sound film he made was *The Man They Could Not Hang*, 1934, which was not well received and was his last as a director.

Longhena Baldassare (1598–1682). Venetian Baroque architect. He designed the striking, scenographic church of Sta Maria della Salute at the entrance to the Grand Canal, Venice, 1630–87. This Baroque masterpiece is of octagonal plan, with a massive dome anchored to its base by giant scrolls. His other Venetian works include the Palazzo Rezzonico (begun 1667) and the Palazzo Pesaro (begun 1676).

Longinus Cassius (AD 213–273). Greek philosopher. He taught in Athens for many years. As adviser to Zenobia of Palmyra, he instigated her revolt against Rome and was put to death when she was

Longfellow US poet Henry Wadsworth Longfellow, photographed shortly before his death 1882. He was the most famous American poet of the 19th century and the first to be commemorated in Poets' Corner, Westminster Abbey, London. His best-known works are his long narrative poems such as The Song of Hiawatha.

captured. He was formerly thought to be the author of the famous literary critical treatise *On the Sublime*, which influenced the English poets John Dryden and Alexander Pope.

Longuet-Higgins Hugh Christopher (1923–). English theoretical chemist whose main contributions have involved the application of precise mathematical analyses, particularly statistical mechanics, to chemical problems.

He was professor of theoretical physics at King's College, London, 1952–54, and professor of theoretical chemistry at Cambridge 1954–67. He then went to Edinburgh University to study artificial intelligence and information-processing systems, which he thought had a closer bearing on true biology than purely physiochemical studies. In 1974 he moved to Sussex University, where he expanded this field into studies of the mechanisms of language and the perception of music.

Longuet-Higgins successfully predicted the structures of boron hydrides and the then unknown beryllium hydride, and the existence of the ion $(B_{12}H_{12})^{2-}$.

In 1947 Longuet-Higgins developed the orbital theory of conjugated organic molecules, deriving theoretically results that had been known experimentally for decades. He showed how the properties of conjugated systems can be derived by combining into molecular orbital theory a study of nonbonding orbitals.

He formulated a theory to describe the thermodynamic properties of mixtures, which he later extended to polymer solutions. He also investigated the optical properties of helical molecules and worked on electronic spectra.

Longus (lived 2nd or 3rd century AD). Greek author. He was the author of the first pastoral romance *Daphnis and Chloe*.

Lonsdale Hugh Cecil Lowther, 5th Earl of Lonsdale (1857–1944). British sporting enthusiast. Lonsdale Belts in boxing, first presented in 1909, are named after him. Any fighter who wins three British title fights in one weight division retains a Lonsdale Belt. A former president of the National Sporting Club, he presented his first belt to the club in 1909, and it was won by Freddie Welsh (lightweight) later that year. Earl 1882.

Lonsdale was an expert hunter, steeplechaser, boxer, and sailor. Notorious for extramarital affairs, he was ordered to leave Britain by Queen Victoria after a scandal with the actress Violet Cameron. As a result, he set off to the Arctic in 1888 for 15 months, travelling by boat and sleigh through N Canada to Alaska. The collection of Inuit artefacts he brought back is now in the Museum of Mankind, London.

Lonsdale Kathleen (born Yardley) (1903–1971). Irish X-ray crystallographer who was among the first to determine the structures of organic molecules. She derived the structure factor formulas for all space groups. DBE 1956.

After graduating from Bedford College for Women in London, she joined the research team of W H Bragg at University College, London, and later at the Royal Institution. Between 1927 and 1931 she worked at Leeds and then returned to the Royal Institution. As a pacifist, she was imprisoned for a month during World War II. In 1946 she became professor of chemistry and head of the Department of Crystallography at University College, London.

At Leeds she used a grant from the Royal Society to buy an ionization spectrometer and electroscope and solved the structure of crystals of hexamethylbenzene.

Lonsdale was interested in X-ray work at various temperatures and thermal motion in crystals. She also used divergent beam X-ray photography to investigate the textures of crystals. She studied solid-state reactions, the pharmacological properties and crystal structures of methonium compounds, and the composition of bladder and kidney stones.

Lonsdale William (1799–1864). English army officer and colonial administrator in Australia. In 1836 he was appointed the first police magistrate and commandant of the new settlement at Port Phillip, then still part of New South Wales. When La Trobe arrived as superintendent in 1839, Lonsdale continued as police magistrate,

then subtreasurer and acting superintendent. In 1851 Victoria was separated from New South Wales and he was appointed colonial secretary to the new colony.

Loos Adolf (1870–1933). Austrian architect. His buildings include private houses on Lake Geneva 1904 and the Steiner House in Vienna 1910. In his article 'Ornament and Crime' 1908 he rejected the ornamentation and curved lines of the Viennese Jugendstil movement.

So this gentleman said a girl with brains ought to do something with them besides think.

ANITA LOOS
Gentlemen Prefer Blondes 1966

Loos Anita (1893–1981). US writer. She was the author of the humorous fictitious diary *Gentlemen Prefer Blondes* 1925. She became a screenwriter 1912 and worked on more than 60 films, including D W Griffith's *Intolerance* 1916.

Lope de Vega (Carpio) Felix. Spanish poet and dramatist; see ◊Vega, Lope de.

First and greatest of the Portuguese royal chroniclers and the most accomplished writer of fifteenth century Portuguese prose.

Encyclopaedia Britannica on FERNÃO LOPES
1990

Lopes Fernão (*c.* 1380–1460). Portuguese historian, whose *Crónicas/Chronicles* (begun 1434) relate vividly the history of the Portuguese monarchy between 1357 and 1411.

López Carlos Antonio (1790–1862). Paraguayan dictator (in succession to his uncle José Francia) from 1840. He achieved some economic improvement, and he was succeeded by his son Francisco López.

López Francisco Solano (1827–1870). Paraguayan dictator in succession to his father Carlos López. He involved the country in a war with Brazil, Uruguay, and Argentina, during which approximately 80% of the population died.

Lopez Nancy (1957–). US golfer who turned professional in 1977 and in 1979 became the first woman to win $200,000 in a season. She has won the US LPGA title three times and has won more than 35 tour events, and $3 million in prize money.

Lorca Federico García (1898–1936). Spanish poet and playwright. His plays include *Bodas de sangre/Blood Wedding* 1933 and *La casa de Bernarda Alba/The House of Bernarda Alba* 1936. His poems include 'Lament', written for the bullfighter Mejías. Lorca was shot by the Falangists during the Spanish Civil War.

Lorca was born in Granada, and *Romancero gitano/Gipsy Balladbook* 1928 shows the influence of the Andalusian songs of the area. In 1929–30 Lorca visited New York, and his experiences are reflected in *Poeta en Nuevo York/Poet in New York* 1940. Returning to Spain, he founded a touring theatrical company and began to write plays.

Suggested reading
Campbell, Roy *Lorca: An Appreciation of His Poetry* (1952)
García Lorca, Francisco *In the Green Morning: Memories of Federico* (trs 1986)
Gibson, Ian *The Death of Lorca* (1973)

Lord Haw Haw nickname of William ◊Joyce, who made propaganda broadcasts during World War II.

Loren Sophia. Stage name of Sofia Scicolone (1934–). Italian film actress. Her boldly sensual appeal was promoted by her husband, producer Carlo Ponti. Her work includes *Aida* 1953, *The Key* 1958, *La Ciociara/Two Women* 1960, *Judith* 1965, and *Firepower* 1979.

Everything you see, I owe to spaghetti.

SOPHIA LOREN
quoted in Leslie Halliwell *Filmgoer's Companion* 1965

Lorentz Hendrik Antoon (1853–1928). Dutch physicist, winner (with his pupil Pieter Zeeman) of a Nobel prize in 1902 for his work on the Zeeman effect, in which a magnetic field splits spectral lines.

Lorentz spent most of his career trying to develop and improve Scottish scientist James Clerk Maxwell's electromagnetic theory. He also attempted to account for the anomalies of the Michelson–Morley experiment by proposing (independently of Irish physicist George Fitzgerald) that moving bodies contracted in their direction of motion. He took the matter further with his method of transforming space and time coordinates, later known as Lorentz transformations, which prepared the way for Albert Einstein's theory of relativity.

Lorentz was born in Arnhem and studied at Leiden, where he became professor of theoretical physics at the age of 24. In 1912 he became director of the Teyler Institute in Haarlem.

Historians will have to face the fact that natural selection determined the evolution of culture in the same manner as it did that of species.

KONRAD LORENZ
On Aggression 1966

Lorenz Konrad Zacharias (1903–1989). Austrian ethologist who studied the relationship between instinct and behaviour, particularly in birds, and described the phenomenon of imprinting 1935. His books include *King Solomon's Ring* 1952 (on animal behaviour) and *On Aggression* 1966 (on human behaviour). In 1973 he shared the Nobel Prize for Physiology or Medicine with Nikolaas Tinbergen and Karl von Frisch.

In 1940 he was appointed professor of general psychology at the Albertus University in Königsberg, Germany. Lorenz sympathized with Nazi views on eugenics, and in 1938 applied to join the Nazi party. From 1942 to 1944 he was a physician in the German army, and then spent four years in the USSR as a prisoner of war. Returning to Austria, he successively headed various research institutes.

Together, Lorenz and Tinbergen discovered how birds of prey are recognized by other birds. All birds of prey have short necks, and the sight of any bird – or even a dummy bird – with a short neck causes other birds to fly away.

Lorenz Ludwig Valentine (1829–1891). Danish mathematician and physicist. He developed mathematical formulae to describe phenomena such as the relation between the refraction of light and the density of a pure transparent substance, and the relation between a metal's electrical and thermal conductivity and temperature.

Lorenz became professor at the Military Academy in Copenhagen 1876. From 1887, his research was funded by the Carlsberg Foundation.

He investigated the mathematical description for light propagation through a single homogeneous medium and described the passage of light between different media. The formula for the mathematical relationship between the refractive index and the density of a medium was published by Lorenz in 1869 and by Hendrick Lorentz (who discovered it independently) in 1870 and is therefore called the Lorentz–Lorenz formula. Using his electromagnetic theory of light, Lorenz was able to derive a correct value for the velocity of light.

Lorenzetti Ambrogio (active 1319–1348). Italian painter. He worked in Siena and Florence. His allegorical frescoes *Good and Bad Government* 1337–39 (Town Hall, Siena) include a detailed panoramic landscape and a view of the city of Siena which shows an unusual mastery of spatial effects.

Lorenzetti Pietro (active 1320–1348). Italian painter. Of the Sienese school he worked in Assisi. His frescoes in the Franciscan basilica, Assisi, reflect the Florentine painter Giotto's concern with mass and weight, as in his *Birth of the Virgin* 1342 (Cathedral Museum, Siena). He was the brother of Ambrogio Lorenzetti.

Lorimer Robert Stodart (1864–1929). Scottish architect. The most prolific architect representative of the Scottish Arts and Crafts movement, Lorimer drew particularly from Scottish vernacular buildings of the 16th and 17th centuries to create a series of mansions and houses, practically planned with picturesque, turreted exteriors. Examples of his work include Ardkinglas House, Argyll, 1906, and Ruwallan House, Ayrshire, 1902. Knighted 1911.

Lorrain Claude. French painter; see ◊Claude Lorrain.

Lorre Peter. Stage name of Lazlo Löwenstein (1904–1964). Hungarian character actor. He made several films in Germany before moving to Hollywood 1935. He appeared in *M* 1931, *Mad Love* 1935, *The Maltese Falcon* 1941, *Casablanca* 1942, *Beat the Devil* 1953, and *The Raven* 1963. He directed one film *Der Verlorene/The Lost One* 1953.

Los Angeles Victoria de (1923–). Spanish soprano. She is renowned for her elegantly refined interpretations of Spanish songs and for the roles of Manon and Madame Butterfly in Puccini's operas.

Losey Joseph Walton (1909–1984). US film director. Blacklisted as a former communist in the McCarthy era, he settled in England, where his films included *The Servant* 1963, *Accident* 1967, and *The Go-Between* 1971.

Suggested reading
Caute, David *Joseph Losey: A Revenge on Life* (1994)
Ciment, Michael *Conversations with Losey* (1985)
Rham, Edith de *Joseph Losey* (1991)

Lothair (825–869). King of Lotharingia from 855, when he inherited the region from his father, the Holy Roman emperor Lothair I.

Lothair two Holy Roman emperors:

Lothair I (795–855). Holy Roman emperor from 817 in association with his father Louis I. On Louis's death in 840, the empire was divided between Lothair and his brothers; Lothair took N Italy and the valleys of the rivers Rhône and Rhine.

Lothair II (c. 1070–1137). Holy Roman emperor from 1133 and German king from 1125. His election as emperor, opposed by the Hohenstaufen family of princes, was the start of the feud between the Guelph and Ghibelline factions, who supported the papal party and the Hohenstaufens' claim to the imperial throne respectively.

Loti Pierre. Pseudonym of (Louis Marie) Julien Viaud (1850–1923). French novelist. He depicted the lives of Breton sailors in novels such as *Pêcheur d'Islande/The Iceland Fisherman* 1886. His extensive experience of the East as a naval officer was transmuted into very popular exotic fictions such as *Aziyadé* 1879 and *Madame Chrysanthème* 1887 and sometimes melancholy travel books and reminiscences such as *Un jeune Officier pauvre/A Poor Young Officer* 1923.

Lotto Lorenzo (c. 1480–1556). Italian painter. Born in Venice, he was active in Bergamo, Treviso, Venice, Ancona, and Rome. His early works were influenced by Giovanni Bellini; his mature style belongs to the High Renaissance. He painted religious works but is best known for his portraits, which often convey a sense of unease or an air of melancholy.

He evolved a rich and imaginative style, and in portraiture approached greatness, as in the *Prothonotary Apostolic, Giuliano* (National Gallery). *A Lady as Lucretia* (also National Gallery) well represents a type of his work which inspired the young Caravaggio. His most celebrated altarpieces are in the churches of the Carmine and SS Giovanni e Paolo, Venice, the cathedral at Asola and at Monte San Giusto near Ancona, where the church contains a *Crucifixion* with 23 life-size figures. The last two years of his life were spent in monastic retreat in the Santa Casa monastery at Loreto.

Loudon John Claudius (1783–1843). Scottish landscape gardener, writer, and architect. He followed and developed Humphrey Repton's ideas and theories, giving them fresh currency 1840 by reprinting all Repton's works in one volume. His work is typified by his unadorned, utilitarian style; the best known example is the park at Derby Arboretum. Loudon also published Encyclopedias of: Gardening (1822), Agriculture (1825), Plants (1829), Architecture (1832), and Trees (1838).

He can run, but he can't hide.

JOE LOUIS
of his opponent Billy Conn, in *New York Herald Tribune* 9 June 1946

Louis Joe. Assumed name of Joseph Louis Barrow (1914–1981). US boxer, nicknamed 'the Brown Bomber'. He was world heavyweight champion between 1937 and 1949 and made a record 25 successful defences (a record for any weight). Louis was the longest reigning world heavyweight champion at 11 years and 252 days before announcing his retirement in 1949. He made a comeback and lost to Ezzard Charles in a world title fight in 1950.

Suggested reading
Louis, Joe *Joe Louis: My Life* (1978)
Mead, Chris *Champion* (1985)
Nagler, Barney *Brown Bomber* (1972)

Louis Morris. Adopted name of Morris Bernstein (1912–1962). US abstract painter. From Abstract Expressionism he turned to the colour-staining technique developed by Helen Frankenthaler, using thinned-out acrylic paints poured on rough canvas to create the illusion of vaporous layers of colour. The series *Veils* 1959–60 and *Unfurleds* 1960–61 are examples.

Louis eighteen kings of France, including:

Louis (I) the Pious (788–840). Holy Roman emperor from 814, when he succeeded his father Charlemagne.

Louis (II) the Stammerer (846–879). King of France from 877, son of Charles II the Bald. He was dominated by the clergy and nobility, who exacted many concessions from him.

Louis III (*c.* 863–882). King of N France from 879, while his brother Carloman (866–884) ruled S France. He was the son of Louis II. Louis countered a revolt of the nobility at the beginning of his reign, and his resistance to the Normans made him a hero of epic poems.

Louis IV (d'Outremer) (*c.* 921–954). King of France from 936. His reign was marked by the rebellion of nobles who refused to recognize his authority. As a result of his liberality they were able to build powerful feudal lordships.

He was raised in England after his father Charles III the Simple, had been overthrown in 922 by Robert I. After the death of Raoul, Robert's brother-in-law and successor, Louis was chosen by the nobles to be king. He had difficulties with his vassal Hugh the Great, and skirmishes with the Hungarians, who had invaded S France.

Louis V (*c.* 966–987). King of France from 986, last of the Carolingian dynasty (descendants of Charlemagne).

Louis (VI) the Fat (1081–1137). King of France from 1108. He led his army against feudal brigands, the English (under Henry I), and the Holy Roman Empire, temporarily consolidating his realm and extending it into Flanders. He was a benefactor to the church, and his advisers included Abbot Suger.

Louis VII (*c.* 1120–1180). King of France from 1137, who led the Second Crusade. He annulled his marriage to Eleanor of Aquitaine 1152, whereupon Eleanor married Henry of Anjou, later Henry II of England. Louis was involved in a bitter struggle with Henry 1152–74.

Louis VIII (1187–1226). King of France from 1223, who was invited to become king of England in place of John by the English

barons, and unsuccessfully invaded England 1215–17.

Louis IX St (1214–1270). King of France from 1226, leader of the seventh and eighth Crusades. He was defeated in the former by the Muslims, spending four years in captivity. He died in Tunis. He was canonized in 1297.

Louis (X) the Stubborn (1289–1316). King of France who succeeded his father Philip IV in 1314. His reign saw widespread discontent among the nobles, which he countered by granting charters guaranteeing seignorial rights, although some historians claim that by using evasive tactics, he gave up nothing.

Louis XI (1423–1483). King of France from 1461. He broke the power of the nobility (headed by Charles the Bold) by intrigue and military power.

Louis XII (1462–1515). King of France from 1498. He was duke of Orléans until he succeeded his cousin Charles VIII to the throne. His reign was devoted to Italian wars.

Monsieur le Grand is about to pass a bad quarter of an hour.

LOUIS XIII
quoted in Lady Jackson *Old Paris* vol i. On the execution of the Marquis de Cinq-Mars 1642.

Louis XIII (1601–1643). King of France from 1610 (in succession to his father Henry IV), he assumed royal power in 1617. He was under the political control of Cardinal Richelieu 1624–42.

I am the State (L'Etat c'est moi).

LOUIS XIV
Attributed remark before the Parlement of Paris 13 April 1655

Louis XIV (called the Sun King) (1638–1715). King of France from 1643, when he succeeded his father Louis XIII; his mother was Anne of Austria. Until 1661 France was ruled by the chief minister, Jules Mazarin, but later Louis took absolute power, summed up in his saying *L'Etat c'est moi* ('I am the state'). Throughout his reign he was engaged in unsuccessful expansionist wars – 1667–68, 1672–78, 1688–97, and 1701–13 (the War of the Spanish Succession) – against various European alliances, always including Britain and the Netherlands. He was a patron of the arts.

His reign was one of prosperity and increase for France: under chief minister Jean Baptiste Colbert the finances of the kingdom were reformed, trade was increased, and there was a strong colonial policy. Under his war minister, Louvois, the armies were re-formed, and under his generals, Turenne and Condé, the French army became the finest fighting machine in Europe.

At home his power was absolute. The courts were entirely under his control, and his principle of embodying the state personally was all but true. Louis had a large number of mistresses, and many illegitimate children.

Following the death of his father-in-law, Philip II of Spain, Louis claimed the Spanish Netherlands and attempted 1667–68 to annex the territory, but was frustrated by an alliance of the Netherlands, Britain, and Sweden. Having detached Britain from the alliance, he invaded the Netherlands 1672, but the Dutch stood firm (led by William of Orange) and despite the European alliance formed against France, achieved territorial gains at the Peace of Nijmegen 1678.

War was renewed in the war of the League of Augsburg 1688–97 between Louis and the Grand Alliance (including Britain), formed

---

The function of kings consists primarily of using good sense, which always comes naturally and easily.

LOUIS XIV
Mémoires for the Instruction of the Dauphin 1661

by William of Orange. The French were everywhere victorious on land, but the French fleet was almost destroyed at the Battle of La Hogue 1692 and the Treaty of Ryswick forced Louis to give up all his conquests since 1678. The acceptance by Louis of the Spanish throne in 1700 (for his grandson) precipitated the War of the Spanish Succession, with England encouraged to join against the French by Louis' recognition of the Old Pretender as James III. Although the Treaty of Utrecht 1713 gave Spain to Louis' grandson, the war effectively ended French supremacy in Europe, and left France virtually bankrupt.

In 1660 Louis married the Infanta Maria Theresa of Spain, but he was greatly influenced by his mistresses, including Louise de La Vallière, Madame de Montespan, and Madame de Maintenon whom he married 1684 after Maria Theresa's death. She was greatly influenced by the Jesuits and played a great part in persuading Louis to revoke the Edict of Nantes 1685.

Suggested reading
Cronin, V *Louis XIV* (1964)
Hatton, R *Louis XIV and his World* (1972)
Mitford, N *The Sun King* (1966)
Wolf, J B *Louis XIV* (1968)

The last argument of kings.

LOUIS XV
ordered this to be engraved on his cannon (its use
as a motto for cannon dates back to 1613).

Louis XV (1710–1774). King of France from 1715, with the Duke of Orléans as regent until 1723. He was the great-grandson of Louis XIV. Indolent and frivolous, Louis left government in the hands of his ministers, the Duke of Bourbon and Cardinal Fleury (1653–1743). On the latter's death he attempted to rule alone but became entirely dominated by his mistresses, Madame de Pompadour and Madame du Barry. His foreign policy led to French possessions in Canada and India being lost to England.

Suggested reading
Gooch, G P *Louis XV: The Monarchy in Decline* (1956)

May my blood cement your happiness!

LOUIS XVI
Spoken on the scaffold 21 Jan 1793

Louis XVI (1754–1793). King of France from 1774, grandson of Louis XV, and son of Louis the Dauphin. He was dominated by his queen, Marie Antoinette, and French finances fell into such confusion that in 1789 the States General (parliament) had to be summoned, and the French Revolution began. Louis lost his personal popularity in June 1791 when he attempted to flee the country, and in Aug 1792 the Parisians stormed the Tuileries palace and took the royal family prisoner. Deposed in Sept 1792, Louis was tried in Dec, sentenced for treason in Jan 1793, and guillotined.

Suggested reading
Cronin, Vincent *Louis and Antoinette* (1974)
Hardman, John *Louis XVI* (1983)
Padover, S K *The Life and Death of Louis XVI* (1963)

The music is so beautiful. Listen, listen, in the midst of all those voices I recognize my mother's.

LOUIS XVII
Last words in prison, 1795

Louis XVII (1785–1795). Nominal king of France, the son of Louis XVI. During the French Revolution he was imprisoned with his parents in 1792 and probably died in prison.

Louis XVIII (1755–1824). King of France 1814–24, the younger brother of Louis XVI. He assumed the title of king in 1795, having fled into exile in 1791 during the French Revolution, but became king only on the fall of Napoleon I in April 1814. Expelled during

Napoleon's brief return (the 'hundred days') in 1815, he resumed power after Napoleon's final defeat at Waterloo, pursuing a policy of calculated liberalism until ultra-royalist pressure became dominant after 1820.

Punctuality is the politeness of kings.

Attributed to LOUIS XVIII in *Souvenirs de J Lafitte* bk 1 ch 3 1844

Louis-Napoleon name by which ◊Napoleon III was known.

Louis Philippe (1773–1850). King of France 1830–48. Son of Louis Philippe Joseph, Duke of Orléans 1747–93; both were known as Philippe Egalité from their support of the 1792 Revolution. Louis Philippe fled into exile 1793–1814, but became king after the 1830 revolution with the backing of the rich bourgeoisie. Corruption discredited his regime, and after his overthrow, he escaped to the UK and died there.

The friendly understanding that exists between my government and hers.

LOUIS PHILIPPE
Speech 27 Dec 1843, referring to an informal understanding
reached between Britain and France in 1843. The more
familiar phrase *entente cordiale* was first used in 1844

Lovat Simon Fraser, 12th Baron Lovat (*c.* 1667–1747). Scottish Jacobite. Throughout a political career lasting 50 years he constantly intrigued with both Jacobites and Whigs, and was beheaded for supporting the 1745 rebellion. Baron 1733.

He curiously united the peculiarities of a wild highland chief with those of a cultivated gentleman.

T F Henderson on SIMON FRASER LOVAT
in *Dictionary of National Biography*

Lovecraft H(oward) P(hillips) (1890–1937). US writer of horror fiction. His stories of hostile, supernatural forces have lent names and material to many other writers in the genre. Much of his work on this theme was collected in *The Outsider and Others* 1939.

Lovejoy Arthur Oncken (1873–1963). US philosopher who advocated identifying the implicit ideas of a period in history, and then subjecting them to logical analysis. One of his techniques was what he called philosophical semantics – the investigation of recurrent terms and phrases in the literature of a period.

Lovejoy taught for some 40 years at Johns Hopkins University, Baltimore, Maryland. His works include the classic study *The Great Chain of Being* 1936, *Essays in the History of Ideas* 1948, and *Revolt against Dualism* 1930.

Stone walls do not a prison make / Nor iron bars a cage.

RICHARD LOVELACE
'To Althea from Prison'

Lovelace Richard (1618–1658). English poet. Imprisoned 1642 for petitioning for the restoration of royal rule, he wrote 'To Althea from Prison', and in a second term in jail 1648 revised his collection *Lucasta* 1649.

Lovell (Alfred Charles) Bernard (1913–). English radio astronomer, director 1951–81 of Jodrell Bank Experimental Station (now Nuffield Radio Astronomy Laboratories). During World War II Lovell worked on developing a radar system to improve the aim of bombers in night raids. After the war he showed that radar could be a useful tool in astronomy, and lobbied for the setting-up of a radio-astronomy station. Jodrell Bank was built near Manchester 1951–57. Although its high cost was criticized, its public success after tracking the Soviet satellite *Sputnik I* 1957 assured its future. Knighted 1961.

Lovell was born in Gloucestershire and studied at Bristol. His academic career was spent at Manchester, where he became the first professor of radio astronomy 1951. His books include *Radio Astronomy* 1951 and *The Exploration of Outer Space* 1961.

Lovelock James Ephraim (1919–). British scientist who began the study of CFCs in the atmosphere in the 1960s (though he did not predict the damage they cause to the ozone layer) and who later elaborated the Gaia hypothesis. Lovelock invented the electron capture detector in the 1950s, a device for measuring minute traces of atmospheric gases. In the 1970s he worked as a consultant to NASA.

Low David Alexander Cecil (1891–1963). New Zealand-born British political cartoonist, creator (in newspapers such as the London *Evening Standard*) of Colonel Blimp, the TUC carthorse, and others.
Suggested reading
Low, David *Autobiography* (1956)

Low Juliette Gordon (1860–1927). Founder of the Girl Scouts in the USA. She formed a troop of 16 'Girl Guides' in Savannah 1912, based on UK scouting organizations founded by Robert Baden-Powell. Establishing national headquarters in Washington DC 1913, she changed the name of the organization to the Girl Scouts of America (GSA).

Born in Savannah, Georgia, USA and educated in New York, Low moved temporarily to England. She served as president of the GSA 1915–20 and worked tirelessly to establish Girl Scout troops throughout the USA.

Lowe John (1947–). English darts player. He has won most of the major titles including the world championships in 1979 and 1987. In 1986 he achieved the first televised nine-dart finish at the MFI Championship at Reading.

Lowell Amy Lawrence (1874–1925). US poet. She began her career by publishing the conventional *A Dome of Many-Colored Glass* 1912 but eventually succeeded Ezra Pound as leader of the Imagists. Her works, in free verse, include *Sword Blades and Poppy Seed* 1916.

Lowell Francis Cabot (1775–1817). US industrialist who imported the new technology of English textile mills to America. On a trip to England 1810–12 he was impressed by the country's mechanized mills and returned to the USA to build his own, similar mills. With the cutoff of international trade during the Anglo-American War of 1812, Lowell established the Boston Manufacturing Company, a mechanized textile mill at Waltham, Massachusetts. After the war he campaigned for tariff protection for the US textile industry. In 1822 the mill town of Lowell, Massachusetts, was established and named after him.

Lowell J(ames) R(ussell) (1819–1891). US poet. His works range from the didactic *The Vision of Sir Launfal* 1848 to such satirical poems as *The Biglow Papers* 1848. As a critic, he developed a deep awareness of the US literary tradition. He was also a diplomat and served as minister to Spain 1877–80 and England 1880–85.

His early poetry, complex and tightly structured, focused on spiritual crises. His later poetry (from the 1850s) was looser and drew freely on his personal relationships, his involvement in left-wing politics, and his periods of mental instability.

He taught at Harvard and was editor 1857–61 of *The Atlantic Monthly* and coeditor 1863–72 of *The North American Review*. Among his critical works are essays on great masters, including Shakespeare, Dante, and Coleridge. Lowell was active in the abolitionist movement, publishing more than 50 antislavery articles between 1845 and 1850. Other works include *Leaves from My Italian Journal* 1854.

Lowell Percival (1855–1916). US astronomer who predicted the existence of a planet beyond Neptune, starting the search that led to the discovery of Pluto 1930. In 1894 he founded the Lowell Observatory in Flagstaff, Arizona, where he reported seeing 'canals' (now known to be optical effects and natural formations) on the surface of Mars.

He spent 16 years in business and diplomacy, mainly in the Far East, before taking up astronomy, becoming professor at the Massachusetts Institute of Technology 1902.

If we see light at the end of the tunnel, / It's the light of the oncoming train.

ROBERT LOWELL
'Since 1939'

Lowell Robert Traill Spence (1917–1977). US poet. His brutal yet tender verse stressed the importance of individualism, especially during times of war. His works include *Lord Weary's Castle* 1946 (Pulitzer prize), *Life Studies* 1959, and *For the Union Dead* 1964.

Much of his poetry is confessional. During World War II he was imprisoned for five months for conscientious objection. Several of his poems, notably 'Memories of West Street and Lepke', reflect on this experience. 'Skunk Hour', included in the acclaimed volume *Life Studies*, is another example of his autobiographical poetry. In the 1960s he was again a war protester and also a civil-rights activist.

Other works include *Land of Unlikeness* 1944, *The Mills of the Kaanaughs* 1951, *The Old Glory* 1965, *Near the Ocean* 1967, *Notebook* 1969, *The Dolphin* 1973 (Pulitzer prize), and *Day by Day* 1977.
Suggested reading
Axelrod, S G *Robert Lowell: Life and Art* (1978)
Hobsbaum, P *A Reader's Guide to Robert Lowell* (1988)
Mazzaro, J *The Poetic Themes of Robert Lowell* (1965)

Lowry (Clarence) Malcolm (Boden) (1909–1957). English novelist. Mexico is the setting for his inventive masterpiece *Under the Volcano* 1947, which follows the last day of an alcoholic British consul.

After a rebellious youth and a voyage to China as a deck hand (which resulted in *Ultramarine* 1933, his first novel), he became an itinerant alcoholic who periodically wrote. He was deported from Mexico and lived mainly in Canada until in 1954 returning to the UK, where he committed suicide. The posthumous publication of much of his unfinished work (for example, *Lunar Caustic* 1968) was not entirely successful.

Lowry L(aurence) S(tephen) (1887–1976). English painter. Born in Manchester, he lived mainly in nearby Salford and painted northern industrial townscapes. In the 1920s he developed a naive style characterized by matchstick figures and an almost monochrome palette. Although a legend in his lifetime, he remained an elusive, retiring figure.

Loy Myrna. Stage name of Myrna Williams (1905–1993). US film actress, a Hollywood star of the 1930s. A self-confident, independent woman as well as a glamorous comedienne, she brought a new kind of personality to US cinema. She played Nora Charles in the *Thin Man* series 1934–47 co-starring William Powell. Her other films include *The Mask of Fu Manchu* 1932 and *The Rains Came* 1939.

Loy devoted the World War II years to working for the Red Cross, and made a noteworthy return to the screen, in somewhat more matronly guise, in *The Best Years of Our Lives* 1946. Her subsequent film appearances were relatively infrequent, because she devoted much of her time to working for UNESCO. *Midnight Lace* 1960 was her last substantial screen role, though she later made occasional cameo appearances, and appeared on the Broadway stage in New York in a revival of *The Women* 1973.

Loyola founder of the Jesuits. See ◊Ignatius Loyola.

Lubbers Rudolph Franz Marie ('Ruud') (1939–). Dutch politician, prime minister of the Netherlands 1982–94. Leader of the right-of-centre Christian Democratic Appeal (CDA), he became minister for economic affairs 1973.

In 1995 he was widely tipped to succeed Willy Claes as secretary-general of NATO, but his candidature was blocked by the USA.

Lubetkin Berthold Romanovitch (1901–1990). Russian-born architect. He settled in the UK 1930 and formed, with six young architects, a group called Tecton. His pioneering designs include Highpoint I, a block of flats in Highgate, London, 1933–35, and the curved lines of the Penguin Pool 1933 at London Zoo, which employ reinforced concrete to sculptural effect.

During the 1930s, Tecton was responsible for many buildings erected in England in the International Style then flourishing elsewhere in Europe, including the Gorilla House 1937 at the London Zoo and a health centre for the London borough of Finsbury 1938. The group was also a training ground for the avant-garde architects of the next generation, such as Denys Lasdun.

Lubitsch Ernst (1892–1947). German film director. He worked in the USA from 1921. Known for his stylish comedies, his sound films include *Trouble in Paradise* 1932, *Design for Living* 1933, *Ninotchka* 1939, and *To Be or Not to Be* 1942.

Starting as an actor in silent films in Berlin, he turned to writing and directing, including *Die Augen der Mummie Ma/The Eyes of the Mummy* 1918 and *Die Austernprinzessin/The Oyster Princess* 1919. In the USA he directed the silent films *The Marriage Circle* 1924 and *The Student Prince* 1927.

Lubovitch Lar (1943–). US modern-dance choreographer. He founded the Lar Lubovitch Dance Company 1976. He was the first to use Minimalist music, for which he created a new style of movement in works like *Marimba* 1977 and *North Star* 1978.

Lucan (Marcus Annaeus Lucanus) (AD 39–65). Latin poet. Born in Córdoba, Spain, he was a nephew of the writer Seneca and favourite of Nero until the emperor became jealous of his verse. Lucan then joined a republican conspiracy and committed suicide on its failure. His epic poem *Pharsalia* deals with the civil wars of Caesar and Pompey, and was influential in the Middle Ages and Renaissance.

Lucan Richard John Bingham, 7th Earl of Lucan (1934–). British aristocrat and professional gambler. On 7 Nov 1974 his wife was attacked and their children's nanny murdered. No trace of Lucan has since been found, and there has been no solution to the murder. Earl 1964.

May the force be with you.

GEORGE LUCAS
Star Wars: from the Adventures of Luke Skywalker 1976

Lucas George (1944–). US film director and producer. His imagination was fired by the comic books in his father's store. He wrote and directed *Star Wars* 1977 and wrote and produced *The Empire Strikes Back* 1980 and *Return of the Jedi* 1983. His other films as director are *THX 1138* 1971 and *American Graffiti* 1973. Later works as a producer include *Raiders of the Lost Ark* 1981, *Indiana Jones and the Temple of Doom* 1984, *Willow* 1988, and *Indiana Jones and the Last Crusade* 1989.

Lucas Robert (1937–). US economist, leader of the University of Chicago school of 'new classical' macroeconomics, which contends that wage and price adjustment is almost instantaneous and that the level of unemployment at any time must be the natural rate (it cannot be reduced by government action except in the short term and at the cost of increasing inflation).

Lucas van Leyden (1494–1533). Dutch painter and engraver. Active in Leiden and Antwerp, he was a pioneer of Netherlandish genre scenes, for example *The Chess Players* (Staatliche Museen, Berlin). His woodcuts and engravings were inspired by Albrecht Dürer.

Lucas was a pupil of Cornelisz Engelbrechts. He settled at Antwerp, where he met Dürer 1521, and the engravings and woodcuts by which he won early fame show Dürer's influence though possessing a decorative charm of their own which is characteristic in

all his work. His unusual colour and pictorial imagination are well exemplified in the painting *Lot and his Daughters* (Louvre).

There's nothing like a good dose of another woman to make a man appreciate his wife.

CLARE BOOTHE LUCE
quoted in L and M Cowan *The Wit of Women* 1969

Luce (Ann) Clare Boothe (1903–1987). US journalist, playwright, and politician. She was managing editor of *Vanity Fair* magazine 1933–34, and wrote several successful plays, including *The Women* 1936 and *Margin for Error* 1940, both of which were made into films. She served as a Republican member of Congress 1943–47 and as ambassador to Italy 1953–57.

Luce Henry Robinson (1898–1967). US publisher, founder of Time, Inc, which published the weekly news magazine *Time* 1923, the business magazine *Fortune* 1930, the pictorial magazine *Life* 1936, and the sports magazine *Sports Illustrated* 1954. He married Clare Boothe Luce in 1935.

Lucian (*c.* 125–*c.* 190). Greek writer. In his satirical dialogues, he pours scorn on religions and mocks human pretensions. He was born at Samosata in Syria and for a time was an advocate at Antioch, but later travelled before settling in Athens about 165. He occupied an official post in Egypt, where he died.

Lucilius Gaius (*c.* 180–*c.* 102 BC). Roman satirical poet, associated with the literary circle of Scipio Aemilianus (184–129 BC). He first established the literary form of satire, later perfected by Horace and Juvenal. Only fragments of his work survive.

Lucretia Roman woman, the wife of Collatinus, said to have committed suicide after being raped by Sextus, son of Tarquinius Superbus, the last king of Rome. According to tradition, this incident led to the dethronement of Tarquinius and the establishment of the Roman Republic in 509 BC.

And like runners they hand on the torch of life.

LUCRETIUS
De Rerum Natura

Lucretius (Titus Lucretius Carus) (*c.* 99–55 BC). Roman poet and Epicurean philosopher whose *De Rerum natura/On the Nature of The Universe* envisaged the whole universe as a combination of atoms, and had some concept of evolutionary theory. According to Lucretius, animals were complex but initially quite fortuitous clusters of atoms, only certain combinations surviving to reproduce.

Lucullus Lucius Licinius (*c.* 110–*c.* 56 BC). Roman general and consul. As commander against Mithridates of Pontus 74–66 he proved to be one of Rome's ablest generals and administrators, until superseded by Pompey. He then retired from politics. The eastern booty accumulated by Lucullus enabled him to live a life of luxury, and Lucullan feasts became legendary.

Did you not know that today Lucullus is dining with Lucullus?

LUCULLUS
Reaction to presentation of an ordinary meal,
quoted in Plutarch *Life of Lucullus* ch 41.2

Ludendorff Erich von (1865–1937). German general, chief of staff to Hindenburg in World War I, and responsible for the eastern-front victory at the Battle of Tannenberg in 1914. After Hindenburg's appointment as chief of general staff and Ludendorff's as quartermaster-general in 1916, he was also politically influential and the two were largely responsible for the conduct of the war from then on.

Following his successes of 1915, he accompanied Hindenburg to the Western Front where they carried out the attack on Verdun 1916. He reorganized the German Army, devising the strategy of advancing the Eastern Front while holding the French and British in check in the west. He planned the German Spring Offensive of 1918 but the collapse of the Hindenburg Line under British attack in Sept and the collapse of Bulgaria shortly after caused him to lose confidence and he called for peace negotiations. When talks were opened he changed his mind, refused to cooperate, and was dismissed by the Kaiser 26 Oct 1918. He took part in the Nazi rising in Munich in 1923 and sat in the Reichstag (parliament) as a right-wing Nationalist.

Suggested reading
Goodspeed, D J *Ludendorff* (1966)
Ludendorff, Erich *Ludendorff's Own Story* (autobiography) (trs 1919)
Parkinson, Roger *Tormented Warrior* (1979)

The Army had been fought to a standstill and was utterly worn out.

ERICH VON LUDENDORFF
On the Battle of the Somme

Ludwig Carl Friedrich Wilhelm (1816–1895). German physiologist who invented graphic methods of recording events within the body. He demonstrated that the circulation of the blood is purely mechanical in nature and involves no occult vital forces.

In 1847 Ludwig invented the kymograph, a rotating drum on which a stylus charts a continuous record of blood pressure and temperature. This was a forerunner of today's monitoring systems.

He was professor at Marburg 1841–49, and then held posts at Zürich, Switzerland, and in Vienna at the Austrian military medical academy. From 1865 he was professor at Leipzig.

Ludwig devised a system of measuring the level of nitrogen in urine to quantify the rate of protein metabolism in the human body. In 1859 he described his mercurial blood-gas pump, which enabled him to separate gases from a given quantity of blood. He also invented the *Stromuhr*, a flowmeter which measures the rate of the flow of blood in the veins. Ludwig published *Das Lehrbuch der Physiologie/A Physiology Textbook* 1852–56, the first modern text on physiology.

Ludwig three kings of Bavaria, including:

Ludwig I (1786–1868). King of Bavaria 1825–48, succeeding his father Maximilian Joseph I. He made Munich an international cultural centre, but his association with the dancer Lola Montez, who dictated his policies for a year, led to his abdication in 1848.

He concerned himself only intermittently with affairs of state, preferring a life of increasingly morbid seclusion and developing a mania for extravagant building projects.

Encyclopaedia Britannica on LUDWIG II
1990

Ludwig II (1845–1886). King of Bavaria from 1864, when he succeeded his father Maximilian II. He supported Austria during the Austro-Prussian War 1866, but brought Bavaria into the Franco-Prussian War as Prussia's ally and in 1871 offered the German crown to the king of Prussia. He was the composer Richard Wagner's patron and built the Bayreuth theatre for him. Declared insane 1886, he drowned himself soon after.

Suggested reading
Blunt, W *The Dream King: Ludwig II of Bavaria* (1970)
Chapman-Huston, Desmond *Bavarian Fantasy* (1955)

Ludwig III (1845–1921). King of Bavaria 1913–18, when he abdicated upon the formation of a republic.

Luening Otto (1900–). US composer. He studied in Zurich with Philipp Jarnach, and privately with Feruccio Busoni. He was appointed to Columbia University 1949, and in 1951 began a series of pioneering compositions for instruments and tape, some in partnership with Vladimir Ussachevsky (1911–) (*Incantation* 1952, *A Poem in Cycles and Bells* 1954). In 1959 he became co-director, with Milton Babbitt and Ussachevsky, of the Columbia-Princeton Electronic Music Center.

His ultimate objective was to prepare the African people for self-rule under ... their own characteristic institutions without premature modernization by European influences.

Lord Hailey on FREDERICK LUGARD
in *Dictionary of National Biography*

Lugard Frederick John Dealtry, 1st Baron Lugard (1858–1945). British colonial administrator. He served in the army 1878–89 and then worked for the British East Africa Company, for whom he took possession of Uganda in 1890. He was high commissioner for N Nigeria 1900–07, governor of Hong Kong 1907–12, and governor general of Nigeria 1914–19. His *Dual Mandate* 1922 was an influential plea for development through the existing African system of chieftainship, rather than Western democracy. KCMG 1901, baron 1928.

Lugosi Bela. Stage name of Bela Ferenc Denzso Blasko (1884–1956). Hungarian-born US film actor. Acclaimed for his performance in *Dracula* on Broadway 1927, Lugosi began acting in feature films 1930. His appearance in the film version of *Dracula* 1931 marked the start of Lugosi's long career in horror films – among them, *Murders in the Rue Morgue* 1932, *The Raven* 1935, and *The Wolf Man* 1941. His career subsequently declined due to the effects of drug addiction.

Lu Hsün alternative transliteration of Chinese writer ◊Lu Xun.

Lukács Georg (1885–1971). Hungarian philosopher and literary critic, one of the founders of 'Western' or 'Hegelian' Marxism, a philosophy opposed to the Marxism of the official communist movement. He also wrote on aesthetics and the sociology of literature.

In *History and Class Consciousness* 1923, he discussed the process of reification, reintroducing alienation as a central concept, and argued that bourgeois thought was 'false consciousness'. Rejected by official socialist literati, he was also an outsider to the dominant literary movements of the West. He repudiated the view held by both, according to him, that 'literature and art really can be manipulated according to the needs of the day'. He argued for realism in literature and opposed modernism, particularly the work of James Joyce and Franz Kafka.

Lukács joined the Hungarian Communist Party in 1918 and was deputy minister of education during the short-lived Hungarian Soviet Republic in 1919. When the Hungarian communist uprising was put down 1919, he emigrated first to Germany and then, in 1930, to the USSR. His Marxist views were considered unorthodox by the Soviet leaders and he had to make a humiliating public retraction of his 'errors' in Moscow 1930. He consistently protested against demands that literature should support Stalin's policies and misdeeds. In 1945 Lukács returned to Hungary. He was a member of the short-lived Hungarian revolutionary government of 1956 and was briefly imprisoned when it was ended with the arrival of Soviet tanks.

Influenced by the German sociologists Georg Simmel and Max Weber, Lukács wrote two of his best books on literature, *Soul and Form* 1910 and *The Theory of the Novel* 1916, before he became a communist.

Suggested reading
Congdon, Lee *Young Lukács* (1983)
Lichtheim, George *Lukács* (1970)
Parkinson, George *Georg Lukács: The Man, His Works, and His Ideas* (1970)

Luke, St (lived 1st century AD). Traditionally the compiler of the third Gospel and of the Acts of the Apostles in the New Testament.

He is the patron saint of painters; his emblem is a winged ox, and his feast day is 18 Oct.

Luke is supposed to have been a Greek physician born in Antioch (Antakiyah, Turkey) and to have accompanied Paul after the ascension of Jesus.

Luks George Benjamin (1867–1933). US painter and graphic artist. A member of the Ashcan School, his paintings capture the excitement and colour of life in New York City's slums.

Lully Jean-Baptiste. Adopted name of Giovanni Battista Lulli (1632–1687). French composer of Italian origin. He was court composer to Louis XIV. He composed music for the ballet, for Molière's plays, and established French opera with such works as *Alceste* 1674 and *Armide et Rénaud* 1686. He was also a ballet dancer.
Suggested reading
Scott, Ralph *Jean-Baptiste Lully* (1973)

Lully Raymond (c. 1232–1316). Catalan scholar and mystic. He began his career at the court of James I of Aragon (1212–1276) in Majorca. He produced treatises on theology, mysticism, and chivalry in Catalan, Latin, and Arabic. His *Ars magna* was a mechanical device, a kind of prototype computer, by which all problems could be solved by manipulating fundamental Aristotelian categories. He also wrote the prose romance *Blanquerna* in his native Catalan, the first novel written in a Romance language. In later life he became a Franciscan.

He is known for his desire to convert Muslims, which led to his being stoned to death in Algeria. He also invented a mechanistic method of learning and of solving all problems by application of key fundamental notions. His followers, known as Lullists, continued this methodology and spirituality, and were accused of mixing religious mysticism with alchemy.

Lumet Sidney (1924–   ). US film director. His prolific and eclectic body of work covers such powerful, intimate dramas as *Twelve Angry Men* 1957, or intense, urban dramas such as *Serpico* 1973, and *Dog Day Afternoon* 1975. Among his other films are *Fail Safe* 1964, *Equus* 1977, and *Running on Empty* 1988.

Lumière Auguste Marie Louis Nicolas (1862–1954) and Louis Jean (1864–1948). French brothers who pioneered cinematography. In 1895 they patented their cinematograph, a combined camera and projector operating at 16 frames per second, and opened the world's first cinema in Paris to show their films.

The Lumières' first films were short static shots of everyday events such as *La Sortie des usines Lumière* 1895 about workers leaving a factory and *L'Arroseur arrosé* 1895, the world's first fiction film. Production was abandoned in 1900. Auguste went on to do medical research. Louis invented a photorama for panoramic shots and in 1907 a colour-printing process using dyed starch grains. Later he experimented with stereoscopy and three-dimensional films.

Lummer Otto Richard (1860–1925). German physicist who specialized in optics and thermal radiation. His investigations led directly to the radiation formula of Max Planck, which marked the beginning of quantum theory.

He became an assistant to Hermann Helmholtz at Berlin 1884 and moved with him to the newly established Physikalische Technische Reichsanstalt in Berlin 1887. In 1894 Lummer was made professor there. From 1904 he was professor at Breslau (now Wroclaw, Poland).

In collaboration with Eugen Brodhun, he designed a photometer (the Lummer–Brodhun cube) and worked towards the establishment of an international standard of luminosity. Lummer and Wilhelm Wien made the first practical black-body radiator by making a small aperture in a hollow sphere. When heated to a particular temperature, it behaved like an ideal black body. Studying emission from black bodies, Lummer later confirmed Wien's displacement law but found an anomaly in Wien's radiation law.

Lummer designed a mercury vapour lamp for use when monochromatic light is required, for instance in fluorescence microscopy, and in 1902 designed a high-resolution spectroscope.

Lumumba Patrice Emergy (1925–1961). Congolese politician, prime minister of Zaire 1960. Imprisoned by the Belgians, but released in time to attend the conference giving the Congo independence in 1960, he led the National Congolese Movement to victory in the subsequent general election. He was deposed in a coup d'état, and murdered some months later.

Lunardi Vincenzo (1759–1806). Italian balloonist. He came to London as secretary to the Neapolitan ambassador, and made the first balloon flight in England from Moorfields in 1784.

Lunt Alfred (1893–1977). US actor. He went straight from school into the theatre, and in 1922 married the actress Lynn Fontanne with whom he subsequently co-starred in more than 30 plays. They formed a sophisticated comedy duo, and the New York Lunt–Fontanne Theatre was named after them. Their shows included *Design for Living* by Noël Coward 1933, *There Shall Be No Night* 1940–41, and *The Visit* 1960.

Luo Guan Zhong or Luo Kuan-chung (lived 14th century). Chinese novelist who reworked popular tales into *The Romance of the Three Kingdoms* and *The Water Margin*.

Luo Kuan-chung alternative transliteration of Chinese writer ◊Luo Guan Zhong.

Lupino Ida (1918–   ). English-born US actress and film director. As an actress, Lupino won fame playing tough and determined women in thrillers such as *High Sierra* 1941. Later, while continuing to act, she set up an independent production company 1949, for which she directed several low-budget films during the 1950s, including *The Hitch Hiker* 1953, an all-male suspense story, and the domestic drama *The Bigamist* 1953. She was the only woman directing feature films in Hollywood during the 1950s.

Lupu Radu (1945–   ). Romanian pianist. He favours the standard 19th-century repertoire, from Schubert to Brahms, and plays with a lyrical and expressive tone.

Lupu The pianist Radu Lupu is a soloist with the world's leading orchestras. He concentrates on the standard 18th- and 19th- century repertory, and has recorded the complete set of Beethoven concertos with Zubin Mehta and the Israel Philharmonic. He makes frequent tours of Britain.

Lurçat Jean (1892–1966). French artist. He revived tapestry design, as in *Le Chant du Monde* 1957–63. Inspired by Cubism and later Surrealism, his work is characterized by strong colours and bold stylization.

Cézanne and Picasso were influences on his early work. In the 1920s he travelled extensively, and his acquaintance with Spain and the Sahara led him to produce a number of paintings evoking the poetry of barren landscape. Better known for his tapestry designs, he has been largely responsible for the modern French revival of tapestry as an art.

Luria Salvador Edward (1912–1991). Italian-born US physician who was a pioneer in molecular biology, especially the genetic structure of viruses. Luria was a pacifist and was identified with efforts to keep science humanistic. He shared the Nobel Prize for Physiology or Medicine 1969.

Luria was born in Turin. He left Fascist Italy 1938, going first to France, where he became a research fellow at the Institut du Radium in Paris, and then to the USA 1940. From 1943 he taught at a number of universities and in 1959 became a professor at the Massachusetts Institute of Technology (MIT). He founded the MIT Center for Cancer Research, which he directed 1972–85. For some time he taught a course in world literature to graduate students at MIT and at Harvard Medical School to ensure their involvement in the arts.

Lurie Alison (1926–   ). US novelist and critic. Her subtly written and satirical novels include *Imaginary Friends* 1967; *The War Between the Tates* 1974; *Foreign Affairs* 1985, a tale of transatlantic relations that won the Pulitzer Prize; *The Truth About Lorin Jones* 1988; and *Women and Children* 1994.

Luther Martin (1483–1546). German Christian church reformer, a founder of Protestantism. While he was a priest at the University of Wittenberg, he wrote an attack on the sale of indulgences (remissions of punishment for sin). The Holy Roman emperor Charles V summoned him to the Diet (meeting of dignitaries of the Holy Roman Empire) of Worms in Germany, in 1521, where he refused to retract his objections. Originally intending reform, his protest led to schism, with the emergence, following the Augsburg Confession 1530 (a statement of the Protestant faith), of a new Protestant church. Luther is regarded as the instigator of the Protestant revolution, and Lutheranism is now the predominant religion of many N European countries, including Germany, Sweden, and Denmark.

Luther was born in Eisleben, the son of a miner; he studied at the University of Erfurt, spent three years as a monk in the Augustinian convent there, and in 1507 was ordained priest. Shortly afterwards he attracted attention as a teacher and preacher at the University of Wittenberg; and in 1517, after returning from a visit to Rome, he attained nationwide celebrity for his denunciation of the Dominican monk Johann Tetzel (1455–1519), one of those sent out by the pope to sell indulgences as a means of raising funds for the rebuilding of St Peter's Basilica in Rome.

> *My conscience is taken captive by God's word, I cannot and will not recant anything. ... Here I stand. I can do no other. God help me. Amen.*
> MARTIN LUTHER
> Speech at the Diet of Worms 18 Apr 1521

On 31 Oct 1517, Luther nailed on the church door in Wittenberg a statement of 95 theses concerning indulgences, and the following year he was summoned to Rome to defend his action. His reply was to attack the papal system even more strongly, and in 1520 he publicly burned in Wittenberg the papal bull (edict) that had been launched against him. On his way home from the imperial Diet of Worms he was taken into 'protective custody' by the elector of Saxony in the castle of Wartburg. Later he became estranged from the Dutch theologian Erasmus, who had formerly supported him in his attacks on papal authority, and engaged in violent controversies with political and religious opponents. After the Augsburg Confession 1530, Luther gradually retired from the Protestant leadership. His translation of the scriptures marks the emergence of modern German.

Suggested reading
Atkinson, J *Luther and the Birth of Protestantism* (1968)
Bainton, R *Here I Stand* (1951)
Erikson, E H *Young Martin Luther* (1958)
Green, V H H *Luther and the Reformation* (1964)
Koenigsberger, G *Luther: A Profile* (1973)
Oberman, H A *Luther* (1990)
Schwiebert, E G *Luther and his Times* (1950)

Luthuli Albert John, or Lutuli (*c.* 1898–1967). South African politician, president of the African National Congress 1952–67. Luthuli, a Zulu tribal chief, preached nonviolence and multiracialism. Arrested in 1956, he was never actually tried for treason, although he suffered certain restrictions from 1959. He was under suspended sentence for burning his pass (an identity document required of non-white South Africans) when awarded the 1960 Nobel Peace Prize.

> *Each musician performs his part as freely as if he were the only player: the rhythmic values serve only as a guide.*
> WITOLD LUTOSLAWSKI
> Instruction to musicians playing *Jeux Venitiens* 1961

Lutoslawski Witold (1913–1994). Polish composer and conductor. His output includes three symphonies, *Paroles tissées/Teased Words* 1965 for tenor and chamber orchestra, dedicated to Peter Pears, and *Chain I* for orchestra 1981. For 30 years he conducted most of the world's leading orchestras in his own compositions, and was greatly influential both within and beyond his native land.

His early major compositions, such as *Variations on a Theme of Paganini* 1941 for two pianos and *First Symphony* 1947, drew some criticism from the communist government. After 1956, under a

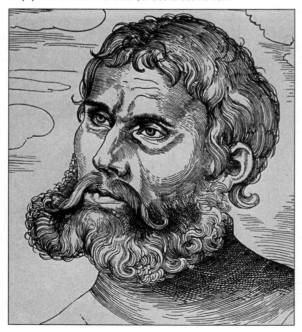

Luther *The German Christian church reformer Martin Luther in about 1522. Luther's criticisms of the Roman Catholic Church initiated the Protestant Reformation. He was excommunicated 1520, but publicly burned the papal bull of excommunication, and continued his work.*

more liberal regime, he adopted avant-garde techniques, including improvisatory and aleatoric forms, in *Venetian Games* 1961.

Lutoslawski was born in Warsaw while it was part of the Russian Empire. He spent part of his early childhood in Moscow – the family moved there 1915 to escape from the German Army – where his father was arrested by the Bolsheviks and summarily executed 1918. He returned to Warsaw and began piano and violin lessons. From the age of 15 he also studied composition with Witold Maliszewski, who was teaching at the Warsaw Conservatory. Military service 1937 and World War II interrupted his career.

Lutyens (Agnes) Elizabeth (1906–1983). English composer. Her works, using the twelve-tone system, are expressive and tightly organized, and include chamber music, stage, and orchestral works. Her choral and vocal works include a setting of the Austrian philosopher Ludwig Wittgenstein's *Tractatus* and a cantata *The Tears of Night*. She also composed much film and incidental music.

The youngest daughter of architect Sir Edwin Lutyens, she married BBC director of music Edward Clark. Her autobiography *A Goldfish Bowl* was published 1973.

Lutyens Edwin Landseer (1869–1944). English architect. His designs ranged from the picturesque, such as Castle Drogo, Devon, 1910–30, to Renaissance-style country houses, and ultimately evolved into a Classical style as seen in the Cenotaph, London, 1919, and the Viceroy's House, New Delhi, India, 1912–31. His complex use of space, interest in tradition, and distorted Classical language have proved of great interest to a number of Post-Modern architects, especially Robert Venturi. Knighted 1918.

Suggested reading
Butler, A S G and Hussey, C *The Architecture of Edwin Lutyens*
Hussey, C *The Life of Edwin Lutyens* (1950)
Irving, R *Indian Summer: Lutyens, Baker and Imperial Delhi* (1981)

Luxemburg Rosa (1870–1919). Polish-born German communist. She helped found the Polish Social Democratic Party in the 1890s (which later became the Polish Communist Party). She was a leader of the left wing of the German Social Democratic Party from 1898 and collaborator with Karl Liebknecht in founding the communist Spartacus League 1918. She was murdered with him by army officers during the Jan 1919 Berlin workers' revolt.

Suggested reading
Ettinger, E *Rosa Luxemburg: A Life* (1986)
Frölich, Paul *Rosa Luxemburg* (trs 1970)
Nettl, J P *Rosa Luxemburg: A Biography* (1966)

Freedom is always and exclusively freedom for the one who thinks differently.

ROSA LUXEMBURG
The Russian Revolution 1961

Lu Xun pen name of Chon Shu-jêu (1881–1936). Chinese short-story writer. His three volumes of satirically realistic stories, *Call to Arms*, *Wandering*, and *Old Tales Retold*, reveal the influence of the Russian writer Nicolai Gogol. He was also an important polemical essayist and literary critic.

Lwoff André Michel (1902–). French microbiologist who proved that enzymes produced by some genes regulate the functions of other genes. He shared the 1965 Nobel Prize for Physiology or Medicine with his fellow researchers Jacques Lucien Monod and François Jacob.

Lwoff was born in Ainy-le-Château, Allier. From 1921 he worked at the Pasteur Institute. During World War II he was active in the French Resistance. He was professor at the Sorbonne 1959–68 and head of the Cancer Research Institute in Villejuif 1968–72.

In the 1920s, Lwoff demonstrated the coenzyme nature of vitamins. He also discovered the extranuclear genetic control of some characteristics of protozoa.

In the late 1940s, Lwoff worked out the mechanism of lysogeny in bacteria, in which the DNA of a virus becomes attached to the chromosome (DNA) of a bacterium, behaving almost like a bacterial gene. It is therefore replicated as part of the host's DNA and so multiplies at the same time. But certain agents (such as ultraviolet radiation) can turn the 'latent' viral DNA, called the prophage, into a vegetative form which multiplies, destroys its host, and is released to infect other bacteria.

Lycett Joseph (*c.* 1774–1825). Australian landscape painter, born in England and transported to New South Wales in 1814 for forgery. He is known for his paintings of houses and scenic views in and around Sydney, such as *Warragamba River* 1824 (Dixson Galleries, Sydney). In 1822 he returned to London and there published *Views in Australia or New South Wales, and Van Diemen's Land* which was issued in 13 monthly parts 1824–25.

Lycurgus Spartan lawgiver. He was believed to have been a member of the royal house of the ancient Greek city-state of Sparta, who, while acting as regent, gave the Spartans their constitution and system of education. Many modern scholars believe him to be purely mythical.

Lydgate John (*c.* 1370–*c.* 1450). English poet. Lydgate was probably born at Lydgate, Suffolk; he entered the Benedictine abbey of Bury St Edmunds, was ordained 1397, and was prior of Hatfield Broadoak 1423–34. He was a friend of the poet Geoffrey Chaucer. His numerous works were often translations or adaptations, such as *Troy Book* and *Falls of Princes*.

Lyell Charles (1797–1875). Scottish geologist. In his *Principles of Geology* 1830–33, he opposed the French anatomist Georges Cuvier's theory that the features of the Earth were formed by a series of catastrophes, and expounded the Scottish geologist James Hutton's view, known as uniformitarianism, that past events were brought about by the same processes that occur today – a view that influenced Charles Darwin's theory of evolution. Knighted 1848.

Luxemburg *Rosa Luxemburg, German political activist and co-founder of the radical Spartacists, a group that subsequently became the German Communist Party. An effective orator and writer, she wrote* Sozialreform oder Revolution/Social Reform or Revolution *1889.*

Lyell suggested that the Earth was as much as 240 million years old (in contrast to the 6,000 years of prevalent contemporary theory), and provided the first detailed description of the Tertiary period, dividing it into the Eocene, Miocene, and older and younger Pliocene periods. Darwin simply applied Lyell's geological method – explaining the past through what is observable in the present – to biology. In 1831 he became professor of geology at King's College, London.

Lyell Lottie Edith (1890–1925). Australian actress, film director, producer, and writer. She was Australia's first movie star and was noted for her skill with horses which was seen in many of her films. She was long associated with director and producer Raymond Longford and played an important part in the production of films usually credited to him. Her films include *Mutiny on the Bounty* 1916 which she also co-wrote, *The Sentimental Bloke* 1919, *Ginger Mick* 1920, which she also co-wrote and *The Dinkum Bloke* 1923 of which she was also co-producer and assistant director.

Lyle Sandy (Alexander Walter Barr) (1958–). Scottish golfer who came to prominence in 1978 when he won the Rookie of the Year award. He won the British Open in 1985 and added the Masters and World Match-Play titles 1988. He was Europe's leading money winner in 1979, 1980, and 1985 and has played in five Ryder Cups.

Night hath a thousand eyes.

JOHN LYLY
The Maydes Metamorphosis 1600

Lyly John (c. 1553–1606). English dramatist and author. His romance *Euphues, or the Anatomy of Wit* 1578, with its elaborate stylistic devices, gave rise to the word 'euphuism' for an affected rhetorical style.

Lyman Theodore (1874–1954). US physicist whose work was confined to the spectroscopy of the extreme ultraviolet region. His working life was spent at Harvard, where he became professor 1921.

When Lyman began his research, the ultraviolet end of the spectrum had been observed by enclosing the spectroscope in a vacuum with fluorite windows. Using a concave ruled grating instead of a fluorite prism, Lyman discovered false lines in the ultraviolet due to light in the visible region, and these came to be called Lyman ghosts. A series of lines in the hydrogen spectrum discovered by Lyman 1914 was named the Lyman series. He correctly predicted that the first line would be present in the Sun's spectrum. In the 1920s Lyman began to examine spectra in the ultraviolet region of helium, aluminium, magnesium, and neon. His last paper was published in 1935 on the transparency of air between 1,100 and 1,300 Å.

Lyman was also a traveller and naturalist. From the Altai mountains of China and Mongolia, he brought back the first specimen of a gazelle *Procapra altaica* and 13 previously unknown smaller mammalian species. A stoat became known as Lyman's stoat, *Mustela lymani*.

Lynagh Michael (1963–). Australian rugby union player who holds the world record of 689 points (as at 1 May 1992) in internationals. He is Australia's most capped stand-off and, with Nicholas Farr-Jones, holds the world record of over 40 appearances as an international halfback partnership. A key member of Australia's 1991 World Cup winning team, he plays for Queensland University and Queensland.

Lynch David (1946–). US film director. He first came to prominence with the nightmarish and macabre stream-of-consciousness film *Eraserhead* 1976. Continuing his obsession with social misfits, Lynch made *The Elephant Man* 1980, about the celebrated Victorian 'freak' John Merrick. His penchant for contemporary surrealism has since been demonstrated in *Blue Velvet* 1987 and *Wild At Heart* 1990, and in the cult television series *Twin Peaks* 1990.

Lynch Jack (John Mary) (1917–). Irish politician, prime minister 1966–73 and 1977–79. A Gaelic footballer and a barrister, in 1948 he entered the parliament of the republic as a Fianna Fáil member.

Lynden-Bell Donald (1935–). English astrophysicist whose theories on the structure and dynamics of galaxies predicate black holes at the centre. Lynden-Bell was born in Dover, Kent, and studied at Cambridge. After two years at the California Institute of Technology and Hale Observatories, he returned to Cambridge, where in 1972 he became professor and director of the Institute of Astronomy.

In 1969 Lynden-Bell proposed that quasars were powered by massive black holes. Later, continuing this line of thought, he postulated the existence of black holes of various masses in the nuclei of individual galaxies. The presence of these black holes would account for the large amounts of infrared energy that emanate from a galactic centre. Lynden-Bell further argued that in the dynamic evolution of star clusters, the core of globular star clusters evolves independently of outer parts, and that only a dissipative collapse of gas would account for that evolution.

Lynen Feodor Felix Konrad (1911–1979). German biochemist who investigated the synthesis of cholesterol in the human body and the metabolism of fatty acids. For this work he shared the 1964 Nobel Prize for Physiology or Medicine with Konrad Bloch.

Lynen was born and educated in Munich, where he spent his whole career, becoming professor 1953 and director of the Max Planck Institute for Cell Chemistry (later Biochemistry) 1954.

Lynen in Munich and Bloch in the USA corresponded and worked out the 36 steps involved in the synthesis of cholesterol. Bloch found that the basic unit is the simple acetate (ethanoate) ion, a chemical fragment containing only two carbon atoms. In 1951, Lynen found the carrier of this fragment. Bloch then found an intermediate compound, squalene – a long hydrocarbon containing 30 carbon atoms. The final stage was the transformation of the carbon chain of squalene into the four-ring molecule of cholesterol.

Lynn Vera Margaret Lewis (1917–). English singer. Known during World War II as the 'Forces' Sweetheart', she became famous with such songs as 'We'll Meet Again', 'White Cliffs of Dover', and in 1952 'Auf Wiederseh'n, Sweetheart'. DBE 1975.

He reassured people and conciliated temperamental colleagues with such geniality that cartoonists liked to depict him as the 'koala bear' of politics.

Alan Palmer on JOSEPH LYONS
in *Penguin Dictionary of Twentieth Century History* 1979

Lyons Joseph Aloysius (1879–1939). Australian politician, founder of United Australia Party 1931, prime minister 1931–39. Lyons followed the economic orthodoxy of the time, drastically cutting federal spending.

He was born in Tasmania and first elected to parliament in 1929. His wife Enid Muriel Lyons (1897–1981) was the first woman member of the House of Representatives and of the federal cabinet. She became GBE 1937.

Lyons Joseph Nathaniel (1848–1917). British entrepreneur, founder of the catering firm of J Lyons in 1894. He popularized teashops, and the 'Corner Houses' incorporating several restaurants of varying types were long a feature of London life. Knighted 1911.

Lyot Bernard Ferdinand (1897–1952). French astronomer who also designed and constructed optical instruments. He concentrated on the study of the solar corona, for which he devised the coronagraph 1930 and the photoelectric polarimeter, and he proved that some of the Fraunhofer lines in the solar spectrum represent ionized forms of known metals rather than undiscovered elements. From 1920 he worked at the Meudon Observatory, becoming chief astronomer 1943.

Most of Lyot's research during the 1920s was devoted to the study of polarized light, reflected to the Earth from the Moon and from other planets. In addition to designing a polariscope of greatly improved sensitivity, Lyot reported 1924 that the Moon was probably covered by a layer of volcanic ash and that duststorms were a common feature of the Martian surface.

By making it possible to observe the Sun's corona in broad daylight rather than only during eclipses, the coronagraph also permitted the observation of continuous changes in the corona. This meant that the corona could be filmed, as Lyot demonstrated for the first time in 1935. He also reported the rotation of the corona in synchrony with the Sun.

Lyotard Jean François (1924–   ). French philosopher, one of the leading theorists of Post-Modernism. His central concern is the role of knowledge in contemporary society. A member of Marxist groups in the 1950s and 1960s, he became disillusioned with the ideology of revolution, and developed a radical scepticism towards all attempts to make sense of history and society.

Cheat boys with knucklebones but men with oaths.

LYSANDER
quoted in Plutarch *Life of Lysander* ch 8.4

Lysander (died 395 BC). Spartan general, politician and admiral. He brought the Peloponnesian War between Athens and Sparta to a successful conclusion by capturing the Athenian fleet at Aegospotami 405 BC, and by starving Athens into surrender in the following year. He set up puppet governments in Athens and its former allies, and tried to secure for himself the Spartan kingship, but was killed in battle with the Thebans 395 BC.

The Party, the Government, and J V Stalin personally have taken an unflagging interest in the further development of the Michurian teaching.

LYSENKO
condemning Mendelism, Moscow 1948

Lysenko Trofim Denisovich (1898–1976). Soviet biologist who believed in the inheritance of acquired characteristics (changes acquired in an individual's lifetime) and used his position under Joseph Stalin officially to exclude Gregor Mendel's theory of inheritance. He was removed from office after the fall of Nikita Khrushchev in 1964.

As leader of the Soviet scientific world, Lysenko encouraged the defence of mechanistic views about the nature of heredity and speciation. This created an environment conducive to the spread of unverified facts and theories, such as the doctrine of the noncellular 'living' substance and the transformation of viruses into bacteria. Research in several areas of biology came to a halt.

From 1929 to 1938 he held senior positions at the Ukrainian All-Union Institute of Selection and Genetics in Odessa, becoming director of the Institute of Genetics of the USSR Academy of Sciences in 1940.

By advocating vernalization (a method of making seeds germinate quickly in the spring), Lysenko achieved considerable increases in crop yields, and this was the basis of his political support. As his influence increased, he enlarged the scope of his theories, using his authority to remove any opposition.

Lysias (c. 459–c. 380 BC). Greek orator, born in Syracuse, Sicily. He settled in Athens 412 BC, escaping from the city into exile under the Thirty Tyrants 404 BC, and returning when democracy was restored a year later to impeach one of the tyrants in his speech *Against Eratosthenes*. His speeches were expressed in a plain, clear

style and provide evidence of the political and social upheaval following the coup. Of the 800 speeches known in antiquity, 23 survive intact.

The appearance of Alexander is best represented by Lysippus' statues, and it is by this artist alone that Alexander himself thought he should be modelled.

Plutarch on LYSIPPUS
in *Life of Alexander* ch 4.1

Lysippus or Lysippos (lived 4th century BC). Greek sculptor. He made a series of portraits of Alexander the Great (Roman copies survive, including examples in the British Museum and the Louvre) and also sculpted the *Apoxyomenos*, an athlete (copy in the Vatican), and a colossal *Hercules* (lost).

Lyte Henry Francis (1793–1847). British cleric, author of the hymns 'Abide with me' and 'Praise, my soul, the King of Heaven'.

Abide with me; fast falls the eventide; / The darkness deepens; Lord, with me abide.

HENRY LYTE
'Abide with Me'

Lyttleton Raymond Arthur (1911–1995). English astronomer and theoretical physicist who focused on stellar evolution and composition, as well as the nature of the Solar System.

Lyttleton was born near Birmingham and studied at Cambridge and at Princeton in the USA. He returned to Cambridge in 1937, and together with Fred Hoyle he established a research school there in theoretical astronomy. He held a number of scientific posts, including a position at the Jet Propulsion Laboratory in California 1960.

In 1939 Lyttleton and Hoyle demonstrated the presence of interstellar hydrogen on a large scale, at a time when most astronomers believed space to be devoid of interstellar gas. In the early 1940s they applied the new advances in nuclear physics to the problem of energy generation in stars.

Lyttleton published 1953 a monograph on the stability of rotating liquid masses, and later postulated that the Earth's liquid core was produced by a phase change resulting from the combined effects of intense pressure and temperature. He also stressed the hydrodynamic significance of the liquid core in the processes of precession and nutation.

In 1959 with cosmologist Hermann Bondi he proposed the electrostatic theory of the expanding universe.

Lytton Edward George Earle Lytton Bulwer, 1st Baron Lytton (1803–1873). English writer. His novels successfully followed every turn of the public taste of his day and include the Byronic *Pelham* 1828, *The Last Days of Pompeii* 1834, and *Rienzi* 1835. His plays include *Richelieu* 1838. He was Colonial Secretary 1858–59. He entered Parliament as a Liberal 1831–41, and as a Conservative 1852–66. Baronet 1838, baron 1866.

Lytton (Edward) Robert Bulwer, 1st Earl of Lytton (1831–1891). British diplomat, viceroy of India 1876–80, where he pursued a controversial 'Forward' policy. Only son of the novelist, he was himself a poet under the pseudonym *Owen Meredith*, writing *King Poppy* 1892 and other poems. Earl 1870.

✧ M ✧

Maazel Lorin Varencove (1930–   ). US conductor and violinist. He became musical director of the Pittsburgh Symphony Orchestra 1986. A wide-ranging repertoire includes opera, from posts held at Berlin, Vienna, Bayreuth, and Milan, in addition to the symphonic repertoire, in particular Sibelius and Tchaikovsky. His orchestral preparation is noted for its inner precision and dynamic range.

He recorded the *Requiem Mass* 1985 and *Variations for Cello and Six-Piece Rock Bank* 1978, orchestrated 1986 (after Paganini) by Andrew Lloyd Webber.

Mabuse Jan. Adopted name of Jan Gossaert (*c.* 1478–*c.* 1533). Flemish painter. He was active chiefly in Antwerp. His common name derives from his birthplace, Maubeuge. His visit to Italy 1508 with Philip of Burgundy started a new vogue in Flanders for Italianate ornament and Classical detail in painting, including sculptural nude figures, as in his *Neptune and Amphitrite* about 1516 (Staatliche Museen, Berlin).

His works include *The Adoration of the Magi* (National Gallery, London).

McAdam John Loudon (1756–1836). Scottish engineer, inventor of the *macadam* road surface. McAdam introduced a method of road building that raised the road above the surrounding terrain, compounding a surface of small stones bound with gravel on a firm base of large stones. Today, it is bound with tar or asphalt.

A camber, making the road slightly convex in section, ensured that rainwater rapidly drained off the road and did not penetrate the foundation. By the end of the 19th century, most of the main roads in Europe were built in this way.

He was appointed paving commissioner in Bristol in 1806; ten

McAdam *Scottish civil engineer John McAdam. McAdam developed a procedure for the construction of roads, the principles of which are still used today. Roads are raised above the countryside and are prepared by compacting small gravel on top of larger stones to allow easy drainage. (Image Select)*

MacArthur, Douglas *US general Douglas MacArthur signing Japan's surrender documents on board USS* Missouri *in Tokyo Bay, 2 Sept 1945. As Allied commander in the SW Pacific since 1942, he masterminded the defeat of Japan.*

years later he became surveyor-general of the roads in that region, and of all the roads in Britain 1827. McAdam was also responsible for reforms in road administration, and advised many turnpike trusts. He ensured that public roads became the responsibility of the government, financed out of taxes for the benefit of everyone.

MacArthur Douglas (1880–1964). US general in World War II, commander of US forces in the Far East and, from March 1942, of the Allied forces in the SW Pacific.

The son of an army officer, born in Arkansas, MacArthur became Chief of Staff 1930–35. He defended the Philippines against the Japanese forces 1941–42 and escaped to Australia, where he based his headquarters. He was responsible for the reconquest of New Guinea 1942–45 and of the Philippines 1944–45, being appointed general of the army 1944. As commander of the UN forces in the Korean War, he invaded the North 1950 until beaten back by Chinese troops; his threats to bomb China were seen as liable to start World War III and he was removed from command, but received a hero's welcome on his return to the USA.

Suggested reading

Clayton, J D *The Years of MacArthur* (1970–85)
Manchester, W *American Caesar: Douglas MacArthur, 1880–1964* (1978)

MacArthur John (1767–1834). Australian colonist, a pioneer of sheep breeding and vine growing. He quarrelled with successive governors of New South Wales, and, when arrested by William Bligh, stirred up the Rum Rebellion 1808, in which Bligh was himself arrested and deposed.

Born in Devon, England, MacArthur went to Sydney 1790, and began experiments in sheep breeding 1794, subsequently importing from South Africa the merino strain. In later years he studied viticulture and planted vines from 1817, establishing the first commercial vineyard in Australia.

MacArthur Robert Helmer (1930–1972). Canadian-born US ecologist who did much to change ecology from a descriptive discipline to a quantitative, predictive science. For example, his index of vegetational complexity (foliage height diversity) 1961 made it possible to compare habitats and predict the diversity of their species in a definite equation. From 1965 he was professor of biology at Princeton.

He studied the relationship between five species of warbler that coexist in the New England forests; these species are now known as MacArthur's warblers.

Investigating population biology, MacArthur examined how the diversity and relative abundance of species fluctuate over time and how species evolve. In particular, he managed to quantify some of the factors involved in the ecological relationships between species.

'Take my camel, dear', said my Aunt Dot.

ROSE MACAULAY
Just a Smack at Auden

Macaulay (Emilie) Rose (1881–1958). English novelist. The serious vein of her early novels changed to light satire in *Potterism* 1920 and *Keeping up Appearances* 1928. Her later books include *The Towers of Trebizond* 1956. DBE 1958.

Now who will stand on either hand, / And keep the bridge with me?

THOMAS BABINGTON MACAULAY
Lays of Ancient Rome, 'Horatius' 29 1842

Macaulay Thomas Babington, 1st Baron Macaulay (1800–1859). English historian, essayist, poet, and politician, secretary of war 1839–41. His *History of England* in five volumes 1849–61 celebrates the Glorious Revolution of 1688 as the crowning achievement of the Whig party. Baron 1857.

His works include an essay on Milton 1825 published in the *Edinburgh Review*; a volume of verse, *Lays of Ancient Rome* 1842; and the *History of England* covering the years up to 1702.

He entered Parliament as a liberal Whig 1830. In India 1834–38, he redrafted the Indian penal code. He sat again in Parliament 1839–47 and 1852–56, and in 1857 accepted a peerage.

Suggested reading
Clive, John *Thomas Babington Macaulay* (1973)
Edwards, Owen Dudley *Macaulay* (1988)
Millgate, Jane *Macaulay* (1973)

I wish I was as cocksure of anything as Tom Macaulay is of everything.

Remark by the 2nd Viscount Melbourne on THOMAS BABINGTON MACAULAY

McAuley Dave (1961–). Irish boxer who won the International Boxing Federation (IBF) flyweight championship in 1989, and has made more successful defences of a world title than any other boxer. McAuley won the British title in 1986.

McAuliffe Anthony Clement (1898–1975). US brigadier general. He organized a stubborn defence of Bastogne 18–26 Dec 1944 during the Battle of the Bulge, before his unit, the 101st US Airborne Division, was relieved by the US 3rd Army under General Patton.

McBain James William (1882–1953). Canadian physical chemist whose main researches were concerned with colloidal solutions, particularly soap solutions.

From 1906 he worked in the UK at the University of Bristol, becoming professor 1919. In 1926, he went to the USA to become professor at Stanford, California.

As early as 1910 he showed that aqueous solutions of soaps such as sodium palmitate are good electrolytic conductors. He postulated the existence of a highly mobile carrier of negative electricity – the 'association ion' or 'ionic micelle'. To determine the thermodynamic properties of soap solutions, he developed his own method based on the lowering of the dew point. McBain proved that the surface phase in simple solutions is not just one monolayer thick: oriented underlayers exist beneath the monolayers of soap, and he devised an ingenious apparatus for determining their composition.

In the adsorption of gases and vapours by solids, various processes can take place simultaneously: physical sorption, chemisorption, and permeation of the solid by the gas or vapour. McBain introduced the generalized term 'sorption' to include all such cases. The McBain–Bakr spring balance provides a continuous record of the quantities and rate of sorption.

His evil reputation is owed entirely to the imagination of fourteenth and fifteenth century chroniclers.

Richard Fletcher on MACBETH
in Who's Who in Roman Britain and Anglo-Saxon England 1989

Macbeth (died 1057). King of Scotland from 1040. The son of Findlaech, hereditary ruler of Moray, he was commander of the forces of Duncan I, King of Scotia, whom he killed in battle 1040. His reign was prosperous until Duncan's son Malcolm III led an invasion and killed him at Lumphanan.

Macbeth George Mann (1932–1992). Scottish poet and novelist. His early poetry, such as *A Form of Words* 1954, often focused on violent or macabre events. *The Colour of Blood* 1967 and *Collected Poems 1958–1970* published 1971 show mastery of both experimental and traditional styles and a playful wit. Committed to performance poetry, he produced poetry programmes for BBC radio 1955–76. There are strong erotic elements in his eight novels, which include *The Seven Witches* 1978 and *Dizzy's Woman* 1986.

McBride Willie John (William James) (1940–). Irish Rugby Union player. He was capped 63 times by Ireland, and won a record 17 British Lions caps. He played on five Lions tours, 1962, 1966, 1968, 1971, and in 1974 as captain when they returned from South Africa undefeated.

McCabe John (1939–). English pianist and composer. His works include three symphonies, two violin concertos, an opera *The Play of Mother Courage* 1974, and orchestral works including *The Chagall Windows* 1974 and *Concerto for Orchestra* 1982. He was director of the London College of Music 1983–90.

Maccabee or Hasmonaean. Member of an ancient Hebrew family founded by the priest Mattathias (died 166 BC) who, with his sons, led the struggle for independence against the Syrians in the 2nd century BC. Judas (died 161) reconquered Jerusalem 164 BC, and Simon (died 135) established its independence 142 BC. The revolt of the Maccabees lasted until the capture of Jerusalem by the Romans 63 BC. The story is told in four books of the Apocrypha.

McCarran Patrick (1876–1954). US Democrat politician. He became senator for Nevada 1932, and as an isolationist strongly opposed lend-lease during World War II. He sponsored the McCarran–Walter Immigration and Nationality Act of 1952, which severely restricted entry and immigration to the USA; the act was amended 1965.

McCarthy (Charles) Cormac (1933–). US novelist. McCarthy grew up in Tennessee, which is reflected in his work. His work is full of black humour and explosive revelation, especially the sanguinary

Blood Meridian 1985. Despite his difficult, unpunctuated prose, he is a cult figure in some circles.

Outer Dark 1968 and *Child of God* 1973 have an almost scriptural concentration on vengeful justice; the somewhat autobiographical *Suttree* 1979 explores a subterranean world of drunks and vagabonds. *All the Pretty Horses* 1992 and *The Crossing* 1994 were the first two of an intended USA-Mexico Border trilogy.

McCarthy Eugene Joseph (1916–). US politician. He was elected to the US House of Representatives 1948 and to the US Senate 1958. An early opponent of the Vietnam War, he ran for president 1968. Although his victory in the New Hampshire primary forced incumbent L B Johnson out of the race, McCarthy lost the Democratic nomination to Hubert Humphrey.

Born in Watkins, Minnesota, USA, McCarthy received a master's degree in economics from the University of Minnesota and became active in the Democratic-Farmer-Labor party. After another unsuccessful bid for the presidency in 1972, he returned to private life, concentrating on writing and lecturing.

McCarthyism is Americanism with its sleeves rolled.
JOE MCCARTHY
Speech in Wisconsin 1952

McCarthy Joe (Joseph Raymond) (1908–1957). US right-wing Republican politician. His unsubstantiated claim 1950 that the State Department and US army had been infiltrated by communists started a wave of anticommunist hysteria, wild accusations, and blacklists, which continued until he was discredited 1954. He was censured by the US Senate for misconduct.

A lawyer, McCarthy became senator for his native Wisconsin 1946, and in Feb 1950 caused a sensation by claiming to hold a list of about 200 Communist Party members working in the State Department. This was in part inspired by the Alger Hiss case. McCarthy continued a witch-hunting campaign against, among others, members of the Truman administration. When he turned his attention to the army, and it was shown that he and his aides had been falsifying evidence, President Eisenhower renounced him and his tactics. By this time, however, many people in public life and the arts had been unofficially blacklisted as suspected communists or fellow travellers (communist sympathizers). *McCarthyism* came to represent the practice of using innuendo and unsubstantiated accusations against political adversaries.

Suggested reading
Landis, M *Joseph McCarthy* (1987)
Oshinsky, D M *A Conspiracy So Immense: The World of Joe McCarthy* (1983)
Reeves, T C *The Life and Times of Joe McCarthy* (1981)

If someone tells you he is going to make a 'realistic decision', you immediately understand that he has resolved to do something bad.
MARY MCCARTHY
'American Realist Playwrights'

McCarthy Mary Therese (1912–1989). US novelist and critic. Much of her work looks probingly at US society, for example, the novel *The Groves of Academe* 1952, which describes the anti-Communist witch-hunts of the time, and *The Group* 1963 (filmed 1966), which follows the post-college careers of eight women.

Suggested reading
Brightman, Carol *Writing Dangerously* (1992)
Gelderman, Carol *Mary McCarthy: A Life* (1988)
McCarthy, Mary *Memories of a Catholic Girlhood* (autobiography) (1957)
McCarthy, Mary *How I Grew* (autobiography) (1985)

McCartney (James) Paul (1942–). UK rock singer, songwriter, and bass guitarist. He was a member of the Beatles, and leader of the

pop group Wings 1971–81. His subsequent solo hits have included collaborations with Michael Jackson and Elvis Costello. Together with composer Carl Davis, McCartney wrote the *Liverpool Oratorio* 1991, his first work of classical music.

Suggested reading
Coleman, Ray *McCartney: Yesterday and Tomorrow* (1995)
Davies, Hunter *The Beatles* (1985)
Lozinn, Allan *The Beatles* (1995)

Some people say: 'don't talk too much about The Beatles ... talk about your new album'. But I don't mind.
PAUL MCCARTNEY
quoted by Irwin Stambler in *The Encyclopedia of Rock, Pop and Soul* 1989

McCauley Mary Ludwig Hays ('Molly Pitcher') (1754–1832). American war heroine. During the American Revolution, she accompanied her husband to the Battle of Monmouth 1778 and brought water in a pitcher to the artillerymen during the heat of the battle, thus gaining her nickname.

Born in Trenton, New Jersey, McCauley worked as a domestic servant and married a local man, John Hays.

McClellan George Brinton (1826–1885). US Civil War general, commander in chief of the Union forces 1861–62. He was dismissed by President Lincoln when he delayed five weeks in following up his victory over the Confederate General Lee at Antietam. He was the unsuccessful Democrat presidential candidate against Lincoln 1864.

McClintock Barbara (1902–1992). US geneticist who discovered jumping genes (genes that can change their position on a chromosome from generation to generation). This would explain how originally identical cells take on specialized functions as skin, muscle, bone, and nerve, and also how evolution could give rise to the multiplicity of species. She was awarded a Nobel prize 1983.

McClintock's discovery that genes are not stable overturned one of the main tenets of heredity laid down by Gregor Mendel, the 19th-century Moravian monk who founded genetics. It had enormous implications and explained, for example, how resistance to antibiotic drugs can be transmitted between entirely different bacterial types.

She utilized X-rays to induce chromosomal aberrations and rearrangements and examined the ways in which chromosomes repair such damage. This information helped other scientists understand the problems of radiation sickness after the explosion of the atom bomb at Hiroshima, Japan.

McClintock Francis Leopold (1819–1907). Irish polar explorer and admiral. He discovered the fate of the John Franklin expedition and further explored the Canadian Arctic. Knighted 1860.

McClure Robert John le Mesurier (1807–1873). Irish-born British admiral and explorer. While on an expedition 1850–54 searching for John Franklin, he was the first to pass through the Northwest Passage. Knighted 1854.

McColgan Elizabeth (1964–). Scottish long-distance runner who became the 1992 world 10,000 metres champion. She won consecutive gold medals at the Commonwealth games in 1986 and 1990 at the same distance.

McCollum Elmer Verner (1879–1967). US biochemist and nutritionist who originated the letter system of naming vitamins. He also researched into the role of minerals in the diet. His choice of the albino rat as a laboratory animal was to make it one of the most used animals for research.

He worked at the University of Wisconsin 1907–17. From 1917 he was professor at the School of Hygiene and Public Health at Johns Hopkins University.

McCollum discovered in the early 1910s that growth retardation results from a diet deficient in certain fats and that such deficiencies can be compensated for by providing a specific extract from either butter or eggs. He called this essential component 'fat-soluble A', because it dissolves in lipids. He then showed that there is another essential dietary component, which he called 'water-soluble B'. Later he found that they are not single compounds but complexes. At Johns Hopkins, McCollum collaborated in the discovery of vitamin D.

McCone John Alex (1902–1991). US industrialist, head of the Central Intelligence Agency (CIA) in the 1960s. A devout Catholic and a fervent opponent of communism, he declined to use extreme measures to secure some of the political ends his political masters sought.

Early successes in the steel and construction industries made McCone a multimillionaire on the strength of winning several government contracts. He became chair of the US Atomic Energy Commission 1958, and was chosen by President Kennedy to succeed Allen Dulles as director of the CIA 1961. He was eventually removed from his post by President Johnson, and returned to his business career as a director of the International Telephone and Telegraph Corporation (ITT).

MacCormac Richard Cornelius (1938–). English architect. His work shows a clear geometric basis with a concern for the well-made object reminiscent of the Arts and Crafts tradition. The residential building at Worcester College, Oxford, 1983 epitomizes his approach: the student rooms are intricately related in a complex geometric plan and stepped section. He became president of the Royal Institute of British Architects 1991. His other works include Coffee Hall flat, Milton Keynes, 1974; housing in Duffryn, Wales 1974; and Fitzwilliam College, Cambridge, 1986.

McCormick Cyrus Hall (1809–1884). US inventor of the reaping machine 1831, which revolutionized 19th-century agriculture.

McCormick was born in Virginia. Encouraged by his father, who was an inventor, he produced in 1831 a hillside plough as well as the prototype for his reaping machine, which took nine years to perfect. He began manufacturing it in Chicago 1847. But in 1848, when his patent expired, he faced strong competition and only his good business sense kept him from being overwhelmed by other manufacturers who had been waiting to encroach on his markets. He survived and prospered, and successfully introduced his reaping machine into Europe.

It was estimated that a McCormick reaper operated by a two-person crew and drawn by a single horse could cut as much corn as could 12 to 16 people with reap hooks.

McCowen Alec (Alexander Duncan) (1925–). English actor. His Shakespearean roles include Richard II and the Fool in *King Lear*; he is also known for his dramatic one-man shows.

McCrea Joel (1905–1991). US film actor. He rapidly graduated to romantic leads in the 1930s and played in several major 1930s and 1940s productions, such as *Dead End* 1937 and *Sullivan's Travels* 1941. In later decades he was associated almost exclusively with the Western genre, notably *Ride the High Country* 1962, now recognized as a classic Western film.

McCrea William Hunter (1904–). Irish theoretical astrophysicist and mathematician who particularly studied the evolution of galaxies and planetary systems. He also considered the formation of molecules in interstellar matter and the composition of stellar atmospheres. Knighted 1985.

He was professor of mathematics at Queen's University, Belfast, 1936–44, and at the University of London 1945–66, when he was appointed professor of theoretical astronomy at the University of Sussex.

Studying the factors that would influence the earliest stages of the evolution of stars, McCrea focused on what might happen if the condensing material encountered interstellar matter that was itself in a state of turbulence.

Together with English astrophysicist Edward Milne, McCrea found that Newtonian dynamics could be advantageously applied to the analysis of the primordial gas cloud. The model relied on the assumption that the gas cloud would be 'very large' rather than of infinite size, although for the purposes of observation it would be 'infinite'.

In physics, McCrea worked on forbidden (low-probability) transitions of electrons between energy states, analyses of penetration of potential barriers (for instance by 'tunnelling'), and relativity theory.

MacCready Paul Beattie (1925–). US designer of the *Gossamer Condor* aircraft, which made the first controlled flight by human power alone 1977. His *Solar Challenger* flew from Paris to London under solar power, and in 1985 he constructed a powered model of a giant pterosaur, an extinct flying animal.

McCubbin Frederick (1885–1917). Australian artist, noted for his portrayal of Australian bush scenes. With Tom Roberts he founded the artist's camp which grew into the Heidelberg School. Many of his paintings depict themes from Australian social history, are sombre in tone and concerned more with creating a mood than with the effects of light and shadow. They are characterized by large scale compositions of carefully posed figures set against a sunless bush, such as in the triptych *The Pioneer* 1904 (National Gallery of Victoria, Melbourne). His later works such as *The Pool, London* 1907 (Jack Manton Collection, Victoria) show a greater interest in atmospheric effects.

McCudden James Thomas Byford (1895–1918). British fighter pilot in World War I. McCudden was credited with shooting down at least 54 enemy aircraft by the time of his death in a flying accident 8 July 1918 and was extensively decorated throughout the war. He won the Victoria Cross 1918.

There's nothing that makes you so aware of the improvisation of human existence as a song unfinished.

CARSON MCCULLERS
The Ballad of the Sad Cafe, 'The Sojourner' 1951

McCullers (Lula) Carson (born Smith) (1917–1967). US novelist. Most of her writing, including the novels *The Heart is a Lonely Hunter* 1940 and *Reflections in a Golden Eye* 1941, is set in her native South. Her work, like that of Flannery O'Connor, has been characterized as 'Southern Gothic' for its images of the grotesque, using physical abnormalities to project the spiritual and psychological distortions of Southern experience. Her other works include her novel, *The Member of the Wedding* 1946, which was also a stage success, and the novella *The Ballad of the Sad Café* 1951.

McCullin Don(ald) (1935–). English war photographer. He started out as a freelance photojournalist for the Sunday newspapers. His coverage of hostilities in the Congo 1967, Vietnam 1968, Biafra 1968 and 1970, and Cambodia 1970 are notable for their pessimistic vision. He has published several books of his work, among them *Destruction Business*.

McCulloch Warren Sturgis (1899–1969). US neurophysiologist who developed cybernetic and computational models of the brain. His papers include 'What the Frog's Eye Tells the Frog's Brain' 1959, which detailed the way in which information is transmitted from the retina to the brain to detect significant features or events in the frog's environment.

His initial work, conducted at Yale in the 1930s, concentrated on primate physiology; his work on brain models was undertaken initially at the University of Illinois and later, from 1952, at the Massachusetts Institute of Technology.

McCullough David Gaub (1933–). US writer and television presenter specializing in American history. His *Truman* 1992 won the Pulitzer Prize for biography. He was host of the television series *Smithsonian World* 1984–88, and narrated the television documentary series *The Civil War* 1990.

McCullough was born in Pittsburgh, Pennsylvania. He writes history as a narrative rather than as analysis. Many of his books have won awards, including *The Great Bridge* 1972 about the construction of the Brooklyn Bridge, *The Path Between the Seas: The Creation of the Panama Canal 1870–1914* 1977, and *Mornings on Horseback* 1981, about the early life of Theodore Roosevelt.

Macdonald, John Alexander *Canadian politician John Alexander Macdonald, the first prime minister of the Dominion of Canada. He campaigned throughout the 1860s for the remaining British colonies in North America to be united and as prime minister of the new dominion expanded it to include Rupert's Land, Northwestern Territory, and British Columbia.* (Image Select)

MacDermot Galt (1928–). US composer. He wrote the rock musical *Hair* 1967, with lyrics by Gerome Ragni and James Rado. It challenged conventional attitudes about sex, drugs, and the war in Vietnam. In the UK, the musical opened in London 1968, on the same day stage censorship ended.

I'll ha'e nae hauf-way hoose, but aye be whaur /
Extremes meet.

HUGH MACDIARMID
'A Drunk Man Looks at the Thistle'

MacDiarmid Hugh. Pen name of Christopher Murray Grieve (1892–1978). Scottish poet. A nationalist and Marxist, his works include *A Drunk Man looks at the Thistle* 1926 and two *Hymns to Lenin* 1930 and 1935.

Macdonald Flora (1722–1790). Scottish heroine who rescued Prince Charles Edward Stuart, the Young Pretender, after his defeat at Culloden 1746. Disguising him as her maid, she escorted him from her home in the Hebrides to France. She was arrested, but released 1747.

MacDonald George (1824–1905). Scottish novelist and children's writer. *David Elginbrod* 1863 and *Robert Falconer* 1868 are characteristic novels but his children's stories, including *At the Back of the North Wind* 1871 and *The Princess and the Goblin* 1872, are today more often read.

Mystical imagination pervades all his books and this inspired later writers including G K Chesterton, C S Lewis, and J R R Tolkien.

MacDonald (James) Ramsay (1866–1937). British politician, first Labour prime minister Jan–Oct 1924 and 1929–31. Failing to deal

---

He had sufficient conscience to bother him but not
sufficient to keep him straight.

Lloyd George on RAMSEY MACDONALD
quoted in A J Sylvester *Life with Lloyd George*

---

with worsening economic conditions, he left the party to form a coalition government 1931, which was increasingly dominated by Conservatives, until he was replaced by Stanley Baldwin 1935.

MacDonald was born in Scotland, the son of a labourer. He joined the Independent Labour Party 1894, and became first secretary of the new Labour Party 1900. He was elected to Parliament 1906, and led the party until 1914, when his opposition to World War I lost him the leadership. This he recovered 1922, and in Jan 1924 he formed a government dependent on the support of the Liberal Party. When this was withdrawn in Oct the same year, he was forced to resign. He returned to office 1929, again as leader of a minority government, which collapsed 1931 as a result of the economic crisis. MacDonald left the Labour Party to form a national government with backing from both Liberal and Conservative parties. He resigned the premiership 1935.

Suggested reading
Mackintosh, John P *British Prime Ministers in the Twentieth Century* (1977)
Marquand, David *Ramsay MacDonald* (1977)
Sacks, B *Ramsay MacDonald in Thought and Action* (1952)

Macdonald John Alexander (1815–1891). Canadian Conservative politician, prime minister 1867–73 and 1878–91. He was born in Glasgow but taken to Ontario as a child. In 1857 he became prime minister of Upper Canada. He took the leading part in the movement for federation, and in 1867 became the first prime minister of Canada. He was defeated 1873 but returned to office 1878 and retained it until his death. KCB 1867.

Suggested reading
Creighton, D G *John A Macdonald: The Young Politician* (1952)
Creighton, D G *John A Macdonald: The Old Chieftain* (1955)
Swainson, Donald *John A Macdonald: The Man and the Politician* (1971)

If we can obtain ... a vigorous general government we shall not be ... Nova Scotians, nor Canadians, but British Americans under ... the British sovereign.

JOHN ALEXANDER MACDONALD
Speech of 1864 at a dinner in Halifax, Nova Scotia at the time of his pursuit of a federal government for Canada

---

MacDonnell Richard Graves (1814–1881). British lawyer and colonial administrator, born in Ireland. He was governor of South Australia 1855–62 during which time he oversaw the development of roads and railways, and greatly encouraged the agricultural and pastoral industries, correctly predicting a good future for wine growing in the colony. Knighted 1856.

MacDowell Edward Alexander (1860–1908). US Romantic composer. He was influenced by Liszt. His works include the *Indian Suite* 1896 and piano concertos and sonatas. He was at his best with short, lyrical piano pieces, such as 'To a Wild Rose' from *Woodland Sketches* 1896. Returning to the USA after several years in Germany, he played his *Second Piano Concerto in D Minor* 1889, his most successful longer work, in New York City. He was one of the first US composers to receive international acclaim.

McDowell Malcolm Taylor (1943–). English actor. He played the rebellious hero in Lindsay Anderson's film *If...* 1969 and confirmed his acting abilities in Stanley Kubrick's *A Clockwork Orange* 1971. Other films include *O Lucky Man* 1973, *Caligula* 1979, and *Blue Thunder* 1983.

McEnroe John Patrick (1959–). US tennis player whose brash behaviour and fiery temper on court dominated the men's game in the early 1980s. He was three times winner of Wimbledon 1981 and 1983–84. He also won three successive US Open titles 1979–81 and again in 1984. A fine doubles player, McEnroe also won ten Grand Slam titles, seven in partnership with Peter Flemming.

McEvoy (Arthur) Ambrose (1878–1927). Irish painter, a contemporary of Augustus John at the Slade School. He painted interiors with figures and portraits, being especially noted for portraits of women.

McEwan Ian Russell (1948–). English novelist and short-story writer. His works often have sinister or macabre undertones and contain elements of violence and bizarre sexuality, as in the short stories in *First Love, Last Rites* 1975. His novels include *The Comfort of Strangers* 1981 and *The Child in Time* 1987, and a collection of short stories *The Daydreamer* 1994. *Black Dogs* 1992 was short-listed for the Booker Prize.

McEwen Jack (John) (1900–1980). Australian Country Party politician, prime minister 1967–68. He entered federal parliament in 1934 and was minister for commerce and agriculture in coalition governments after 1949. In 1956 he reorganized his portfolio into the Department of Trade and used it as a powerful base from which to influence government policy on primary and secondary industries. From 1958 he was leader of the Country Party and deputy prime minister. After the death of Harold Holt in 1967 he was caretaker prime minister for three weeks until the Liberal Party chose a new leader. He influenced this choice by vetoing deputy Liberal leader William McMahon as a candidate. He retired in 1971. Knighted 1971.

McGahern John (1934–). Irish novelist. He won early acclaim for *The Barracks* 1963, a study of the mind of a dying woman. His books explore Irish settings and issues as in *Amongst Women* 1991, about an ageing member of the IRA. His other works include *The Dark* 1965, *Nightlines* 1970, *The Leavetaking*, and *The High Ground* 1985.

McGill Linda (1945–). Australian long-distance swimmer, the first Australian to swim the English Channel 1965. Other firsts include swimming across Port Phillip Bay, Victoria; from Townsville to Magnetic Island, Queensland; and around the island of Hong Kong.

McGinley Phyllis (1905–1978). Canadian-born US writer of light verse. She was a contributor to the *New Yorker* magazine and published many collections of social satire. Her works include *One More Manhattan* 1937 and *The Love Letters of Phyllis McGinley* 1954.
Suggested reading
Wagner, Linda *Phyllis McGinley* (1971)

McGonagall William (1830–1902). Scottish poet. He is noted for the unintentionally humorous effect of his extremely bad serious verse: for example, his poem on the Tay Bridge disaster of 1879.

The man that gets drunk is little more than a fool, / And is in the habit, no doubt, of advocating Home Rule.

WILLIAM MCGONAGALL
'The Demon Drink'

McGovern George Stanley (1922–). US politician. A Democrat, he was elected to the US House of Representatives 1956, served as an adviser to the Kennedy administration, and was a US senator 1962–80. He won the presidential nomination 1968, but was soundly defeated by the incumbent Richard Nixon.

Born in Avon, South Dakota, USA, McGovern served as a combat pilot during World War II and received a PhD in history from Northwestern University 1953. He was defeated for re-election to the Senate 1980 and retired to a career of lecturing and writing.

McGrath John Peter (1935–). Scottish dramatist and director. He founded the socialist 7:84 Theatre Companies in England 1971 and Scotland 1973, and is the author of such plays as *Events Guarding the Bofors Gun* 1966; *The Cheviot, the Stag, and the Black, Black Oil* 1973, a musical account of the economic exploitation of the Scottish highlands; and *The Garden of England* 1985.

McGrath has published two books arguing the case for popular and radical theatre: *A Good Night Out* 1981 and *The Bone Won't Break* 1990.

McGraw John Joseph (1873–1934). US baseball manager. He became player-manager of the New York Giants 1902, and in this dual capacity led the team to two National League pennants and a World Series championship. After retiring as a player 1906, he managed the Giants to eight more pennants and two world championships.

Born in Truxton, New York, McGraw began his career 1891 as an infielder with the Baltimore Orioles, which joined the National League 1892, becoming the team's manager 1899.

McGregor Douglas (1906–1964). US social psychologist. He is known for his motivational theory of work and management based on the concept of 'Theory X' and 'Theory Y' set out in *The Human Side of Enterprise* 1960. These two theories describe two different ways that managers view their workforces. Theory X managers assume that humans are naturally lazy, dislike work, and shun responsibility and so have to be coerced through a system of rewards, threats, and punishment to perform their allotted task. Theory Y, however, assumes that people want to work and take on responsibility, and indeed have an innate psychological need to do so. Work and responsibility provide not only financial but also emotional security and self-esteem, thereby satisfying many other higher-order needs than allowed by Theory X. Obviously each has implications for managerial practice across a broad spectrum of organizations.

McGuffey William Holmes (1800–1873). US educator. He is best remembered for his series the *Eclectic Readers*, which became standard reading textbooks throughout the USA in the 19th century. He was president of Cincinnati College 1836–39 and Ohio University 1839–45.

In 1825 he joined the faculty of Miami University, where he lectured on philosophy and became interested in the issue of public-school reform. He was professor at the University of Virginia 1845–73.

Every statement in physics has to state relations between observable quantities.

ERNST MACH
Mach's Principle

Mach Ernst (1838–1916). Austrian philosopher and physicist. He was an empiricist, believing that science is a record of facts perceived by the senses, and that acceptance of a scientific law depends solely on its standing the practical test of use; he opposed concepts such as Isaac Newton's 'absolute motion'. Mach numbers are named after him. The Mach number is the ratio of the speed of a body to the speed of sound in the undisturbed medium through which the body travels. An aircraft flying at Mach 2 is flying at twice the speed of sound in air at that particular height.

He was professor at Graz 1864–67, Prague 1867–95, and Vienna 1895–1901. He was then appointed to the upper chamber of the Austrian parliament.

Mach studied physiological phenomena such as vision, hearing, our sense of time, and the kinesthetic sense. He investigated stimulation of the retinal field with spatial patterns and discovered a strange visual effect called Mach bands. This was subsequently forgotten, and was rediscovered in the 1950s.

Mach's book *Die Mechanik* 1863 gave rise to debate on Mach's principle, which states that a body could have no inertia in a universe devoid of all other mass as inertia depends on the reciprocal interaction of bodies, however distant. This principle influenced Einstein.
Suggested reading
Blackmore, John *Ernst Mach: His Life, Work and Influence* (1972)

Mácha Karel Hynek (1810–1836). Czech romantic poet. He is chiefly remembered for his patriotic and influential lyrical epic *Máj*/*May* 1836.

Machado Antonio (1875–1939). Spanish poet and dramatist. Born in Seville, he was inspired by the Castilian countryside in his lyric verse, contained in *Campos de Castilla*/*Countryside of Castile* 1912.

Machado de Assis Joaquim Maria (1839–1908). Brazilian writer and poet. He is generally regarded as the greatest Brazilian novelist. His sceptical, ironic wit is well displayed in his 30 volumes of novels and short stories, including *Epitaph for a Small Winner* 1880 and *Dom Casmurro* 1900.

Machaut Guillaume de (1300–1377). French poet and composer. Born in Champagne, he was in the service of John of Bohemia for 30 years and, later, of King John the Good of France. He gave the ballade and rondo forms a new individuality and ensured their lasting popularity. His *Messe de Nostre Dame* about 1360, written for Reims Cathedral, is an early masterpiece of *ars nova*, 'new (musical) art', exploiting unusual rhythmic complexities.

Machel Samora Moises (1933–1986). Mozambique nationalist leader, president 1975–86. Machel was active in the liberation front Frelimo from its conception 1962, fighting for independence from Portugal. He became Frelimo leader 1966, and Mozambique's first president from independence 1975 until his death in a plane crash near the South African border.

Machen Arthur. Pen name of Arthur Llewellyn Jones (1863–1947). Welsh author. His stories of horror and the occult include *The Great God Pan* 1894 and *House of Souls* 1906. *The Hill of Dreams* 1907 is partly autobiographical.

One of the most powerful safeguards a prince can have against conspiracies is to avoid being hated by the populace.

NICCOLÒ MACHIAVELLI
The Prince 1513

Machiavelli Niccolò (1469–1527). Italian politician and author. His name is synonymous with cunning and cynical statecraft. In his chief political writings, *Il principe/The Prince* 1513 and *Discorsi/Discourses* 1531, he discussed ways in which rulers can advance the interests of their states (and themselves) through an often amoral and opportunistic manipulation of other people.

Machiavelli was born in Florence and was second chancellor to the republic 1498–1512. On the accession to power of the Medici family 1512, he was arrested and imprisoned on a charge of conspiracy, but in 1513 was released to exile in the country. *The Prince*, based on his observations of Cesare Borgia, is a guide for the future prince of a unified Italian state (which did not occur until the Risorgimento in the 19th century). In *L'Arte della guerra/The Art of War* 1520, Machiavelli outlined the provision of an army for the prince, and in *Historie fiorentine/History of Florence* he analysed the historical development of Florence until 1492. Among his later works are the comedies *Clizia* 1515 and *La Mandragola/The Mandrake* 1524.

Suggested reading
Anglo, Sydney *Machiavelli* (1970)
Curry, Patrick and Zarate, Oscar *Machiavelli for Beginners* (1995)
Grazia, Sebastian de *Machiavelli in Hell* (1989)
Hale, J R *Machiavelli and Renaissance History* (1961)
Ridolfi, R *The Life and Times of Niccolo Machiavelli* (trs 1963)
Skinner, Quentin *Machiavelli* (1981)

McInerney Jay (1955–). US novelist. His first novel, *Bright Lights, Big City* 1984, was a richly comic portrait of a bright young man in Manhattan society. It was followed by *Ransom* 1985 and *Story of My Life* 1988.

McIndoe Archibald Hector (1900–1960). New Zealand plastic surgeon. He became known in the UK during World War II for his remodelling of the faces of badly burned pilots. Knighted 1947.

MacInnes Colin (1914–1976). English novelist. His work is characterized by sharp depictions of London youth and subcultures of the 1950s, as in *City of Spades* 1957 and *Absolute Beginners* 1959. He is the son of the novelist Angela Thirkell.

Macintosh Charles (1766–1843). Scottish manufacturing chemist who invented a waterproof fabric, lined with rubber, that

was used for raincoats – hence *mackintosh*. Other waterproofing processes have now largely superseded this method.

Mack Connie. Adopted name of Cornelius Alexander McGillicuddy (1862–1956). US baseball manager. With the establishment of the American League 1901, he invested his own money in the Philadelphia Athletics ('A's') and became the team's first manager. In his record 50 years with the team 1901–51, he led them to nine American League pennants and five World Series championships.

Born in East Brookfield, Massachusetts, USA, Mack began his professional baseball career as a catcher 1883 and became player-manager of the Pittsburgh Pirates 1894.

McKay Heather Pamela (born Blundell) (1941–). Australian squash player. She won 14 consecutive Australian titles 1960–73 and was twice World Open champion (inaugurated 1976). Between 1962 and 1980 she was unbeaten. She moved to Canada 1975 and became the country's outstanding racquetball player. She won the British Open title an unprecedented 16 years in succession 1962–77.

Mackay of Clashfern James Peter Hymers Mackay, Baron Mackay of Clashfern (1927–). Scottish lawyer and Conservative politician. He became Lord Chancellor 1987 and in 1989 announced a reform package to end legal restrictive practices.

He became a QC 1965 and 1979 was unexpectedly made Lord Advocate for Scotland and a life peer. His reform package included ending the barristers' monopoly of advocacy in the higher courts; promoting the combination of the work of barristers and solicitors in 'mixed' practices; and allowing building societies and banks to do property conveyancing, formerly limited to solicitors. The plans met with fierce opposition.

Macke August (1887–1914). German Expressionist painter. He was a founding member of the *Blaue Reiter* group in Munich. With Franz Marc he developed a semi-abstract style derived from Fauvism and Orphism.

He first met Marc and Kandinsky 1909, and in 1912 he and Marc went to Paris, where they encountered the abstract style of Robert Delaunay. In 1914 Macke visited Tunis with Paul Klee, and was inspired to paint a series of brightly coloured watercolours largely composed of geometrical shapes but still representational. He was killed in World War I.

McKell William John (1891–1985). Australian Labor politician, premier of New South Wales 1941–47, governor-general of Australia 1947–53. He was an official of the Boilermakers' Union before entering the New South Wales Legislative Assembly in 1917. He held several portfolios up to 1932, also studying law and practising at the bar. In 1939 he defeated Lang for the leadership of the Labor Party and became premier in 1941. In government he combined a vigorous programme of social reform with the war effort, his moderate, popular style laying the groundwork for the Labor governments that held power in New South Wales up to 1965. He was appointed governor-general on the recommendation of Chifley. GCMG 1951.

McKellen Ian Murray (1939–). English actor. Acclaimed as the leading Shakespearean player of his generation, his stage roles include Richard II 1968, Macbeth 1977, Max in Martin Sherman's *Bent* 1979, Platonov in Chekhov's *Wild Honey* 1986, Iago in *Othello* 1989, and Richard III 1990. His films include *Priest of Love* 1982 and *Plenty* 1985.

Mackendrick Alexander (1912–1993). US-born Scottish film director and teacher. He was responsible for some of Ealing Studios' finest films, including *Whisky Galore!* 1949, *The Man in the White Suit* 1951, and *Mandy* 1952. *The Ladykillers* 1955, which proved to be Ealing's last major film, possesses a macabre eccentricity that places it in the front rank of British comedy. Mackendrick went to Hollywood to direct *Sweet Smell of Success* 1957, an acerbic portrayal of a powerful New York gossip columnist. Although critically acclaimed, the film was a box-office failure, and Mackendrick's problems with Burt Lancaster, the film's producer and star, undermined Mackendrick's subsequent career. He directed three more films, of which the most accomplished was *A High Wind in Jamaica* 1965, but all were variously troubled, and Mackendrick was happy to abandon active filmmaking for teaching film at the California Institute of Fine Arts.

Mackennal (Edgar) Bertram (1863–1931). Australian sculptor who worked mainly in London and Europe. His Australian works include the Cenotaph, Martin Place, Sydney, the statue of King George V, Parliament House, Canberra, and the life-size figure *Circe* 1892 (National Gallery of Victoria, Melbourne). He was knighted (KCVO) in 1921, the first Australian artist to be so honoured.

Mackensen August von (1849–1945). German field marshal. During World War I he achieved the breakthrough at Gorlice and the conquest of Serbia 1915, and in 1916 played a major role in the overthrow of Romania.

He first came to prominence in the second battle for Warsaw 1914, became the supreme commander of Austro-German forces in Galicia 1915, then advanced into SE Poland and helped drive the Russians from Warsaw. He was promoted to field-marshal and over-ran Serbia late 1915. Following Romania's entry into the war he occupied first Dobruja Aug 1916 then Romania itself. After the collapse of Russia, he was able to consolidate his position in Romania and became de facto ruler of the country until the armistice. After the war Mackensen retained his popularity to become a folk hero of the German army.

Mackenzie Alexander (1764–1820). British explorer and fur trader. In 1789, he was the first European to see the river, now part of N Canada, named after him. In 1792–93 he crossed the Rocky Mountains to the Pacific coast of what is now British Columbia, making the first known crossing north of Mexico. Knighted 1807.

Women do not find it difficult nowadays to behave like men, but they often find it extremely difficult to behave like gentlemen.

COMPTON MACKENZIE
Literature in My Time 1933

Mackenzie (Edward Montague) Compton (1883–1972). Scottish author. He published his first novel *The Passionate Elopement* 1911. Later works were *Carnival* 1912, *Sinister Street* 1913–14 (an autobiographical novel), and the comic *Whisky Galore* 1947. He published his autobiography in ten 'octaves' (volumes) 1963–71. Knighted 1952.

Mackenzie William Lyon (1795–1861). Canadian politician, born in Scotland. He emigrated to Canada 1820, and led the rebellion of 1837–38, an unsuccessful attempt to limit British rule and establish more democratic institutions in Canada. After its failure he lived in the USA until 1849, and in 1851–58 sat in the Canadian legislature as a Radical. He was grandfather of W L Mackenzie King, the Liberal prime minister.

McKern (Reginald) Leo (1920–). Australian character actor. Active in the UK, he is probably best known for his portrayal of the barrister Rumpole in the television series *Rumpole of the Bailey*. His films include *Moll Flanders* 1965, *A Man for All Seasons* 1966, and *Ryan's Daughter* 1970.

Mackerras (Alan) Charles (MacLaurin) (1925–). Australian conductor. He has helped to make the music of the Czech composer Leoš Janáček more widely known. He was conductor of the English National Opera 1970–78. Knighted 1979.

McKillop Mary Helen (Mother Mary of the Cross) (1842–1909). Australian nun and teacher. She was co-founder of the Sisters of St Joseph of the Sacred Heart and established schools for poor children in remote areas. Her beatification by Pope John Paul II Jan 1995 made her Australia's first saint.

McKinley William (1843–1901). 25th president of the USA 1897–1901, a Republican. His term as president was marked by the USA's adoption of an imperialist policy, as exemplified by the Spanish-American War 1898 and the annexation of the Philippines. He was first elected to Congress 1876. He was assassinated.

McKinley was born in Niles, Ohio, and became a lawyer. Throughout his political life, he was a trusted friend of business interests, supporting high tariffs for fledgling US industries. He sat in the House of Representatives 1877–83 and 1885–91, and was governor of Ohio 1892–96. As president he presided over a period of prosperity and was drawn into foreign conflicts largely against his will.

Suggested reading
Gould, Lewis *The Presidency of William McKinley* (1981)
Leech, M *In the Days of McKinley* (1959)

Mackintosh Charles Rennie (1868–1928). Scottish architect, designer, and painter. He worked initially in the Art Nouveau idiom but later developed a unique style, both rational and expressive.

Influenced by the Arts and Crafts movement, he designed furniture and fittings, cutlery, and lighting to go with his interiors. Although initially influential, particularly on Austrian architects such as J M Olbrich and Josef Hoffman, Mackintosh was not successful in his lifetime and has only recently come to be regarded as a pioneer of modern design.

His chief works include the Glasgow School of Art 1896, various Glasgow tea rooms 1897–*c*. 1911, and Hill House, Helensburgh 1902–03.

Suggested reading
Howarth, Thomas *Charles Rennie Mackintosh and the Modern Movement* (1977)
Macleod, Robert *Charles Rennie Mackintosh* (1968)

Mackenzie, Compton *Scottish writer Compton Mackenzie. His best known novel* Whisky Galore, *was turned into a very successful film.* (Image Select)

Mackmurdo Arthur Heygate (1851–1942). English designer and architect. He founded the Century Guild 1882, a group of architects, artists, and designers inspired by William Morris and John Ruskin. His textile designs are forerunners of Art Nouveau.

In America, the buck is God.

SHIRLEY MACLAINE
in *Evening Standard* 1965

MacLaine Shirley. Stage name of Shirley MacLean Beatty (1934–). US actress. A versatile performer, her films include Alfred Hitchcock's *The Trouble with Harry* 1955 (her debut), *The Apartment* 1960, and *Terms of Endearment* 1983, for which she won an Academy Award.

MacLaine trained as a dancer and has played in musicals, comedy, and dramatic roles. Her many offscreen interests (politics, writing) have limited her film appearances. She is the sister of Warren Beatty.

Maclaurin Colin (1698–1746). Scottish mathematician who played a leading part in establishing the hegemony of Isaac Newton's calculus in the UK. Maclaurin was the first to present the correct theory for distinguishing between the maximum and minimum values of a function.

At the age of 19, he was appointed professor at the Marischal College of Aberdeen. On a visit to London in 1719 he first met Isaac Newton. Maclaurin left Aberdeen 1722 to become travelling tutor to the son of an English diplomat, returning to Scotland 1724 to become professor at Edinburgh. He won the admiration of Edinburgh society for his public lectures and demonstrations in experimental physics and astronomy. In 1745, during the Jacobite rebellion, he organized the defence of Edinburgh.

Maclaurin's *Treatise of Fluxions* 1742 was an attempt to prove Newton's doctrine of prime and ultimate ratios and to provide a geometrical framework to support Newton's fluxional calculus. So influential was the treatise that it contributed to the ascendancy of Newtonian mathematics which cut off Britain from developments in the rest of the world.

Maclean Alistair (1922–1987). Scottish adventure novelist. His first novel, *HMS Ulysses* 1955, was based on wartime experience. It was followed by *The Guns of Navarone* 1957 and other adventure novels. Many of his books were made into films.

Maclean Donald Duart (1913–1983). British spy who worked for the USSR while in the UK civil service. He defected to the USSR 1951 together with Guy Burgess.

Maclean, brought up in a strict Presbyterian family, was educated at Cambridge, where he was recruited by the Soviet KGB. He worked for the UK Foreign Office in Washington 1944 and then Cairo 1948 before returning to London, becoming head of the American Department at the Foreign Office 1950.

Maclean Fitzroy Hew (1911–1996). Scottish writer and diplomat whose travels in the USSR and Central Asia inspired his *Eastern Approaches* 1949 and *A Person from England* 1958. His other books include *To the Back of Beyond* 1974, *Holy Russia* 1979, and *Bonnie Prince Charlie* 1988. Baronet 1957.

During 1943–45 he commanded a unit giving aid to partisans in Yugoslavia and advised that Allied support be switched from the Chetniks to the communist partisans under Tito. He was an MP 1941–74, and Parliamentary Under Secretary of State at the War Office 1954–57. Between 1964 and 1974 he chaired a military committee of the United Nations delegation to the North Atlantic Assembly.

McLean John (1785–1861). US jurist. In 1829 he was appointed to the US Supreme Court by President Jackson. During his Court tenure, McLean was an outspoken advocate of the abolition of slavery, writing a passionate dissent in the Dred Scott case 1857.

Born in Morris County, New Jersey, USA, and raised in Ohio, McLean studied law in Cincinnati and was admitted to the bar 1807.

After editing a local newspaper, he served in the US Congress 1813–16 and as a judge on the Ohio Supreme Court 1816–22.

MacLeish Archibald (1892–1982). US poet. He made his name with the long narrative poem *Conquistador* 1932, which describes Cortés' march to the Aztec capital, but his later plays in verse, *Panic* 1935 and *Air Raid* 1938, deal with contemporary problems.

He was born in Illinois, was assistant secretary of state 1944–45, and helped to draft the constitution of UNESCO. From 1949 to 1962 he was Boylston Professor of Rhetoric at Harvard, and his essays in *Poetry and Opinion* 1950 reflect his feeling that a poet should be committed to expressing his outlook in his verse.

MacLennan (John) Hugh (1907–1990). Canadian novelist and essayist. He has explored the theme of an emerging Canadian identity in realist novels such as *Barometer Rising* 1941 and *Two Solitudes* 1945, which confronts the problems of cooperation between French-and English-speaking Canadians. Later works include *The Watch that Ends the Night* 1959 and *Voices in Time* 1981, bleakly imagining Montréal after a nuclear holocaust.

Suggested reading

Cameron, E *Hugh MacLennan: A Writer's Life* (1981)
Cockburn, Robert *The Novels of Hugh MacLennan* (1973)

MacLennan Robert Adam Ross (1936–). Scottish centrist politician; member of Parliament for Caithness and Sutherland from 1966. He left the Labour Party for the Social Democrats (SDP) 1981, and was SDP leader 1988 during merger negotiations with the Liberals. He then became a member of the new Social and Liberal Democrats.

MacLennan was educated in Scotland, England, and the USA, and called to the English Bar 1962. When David Owen resigned the SDP leadership 1988, MacLennan took over until the merger with the Liberal Party had been completed. He took a leading part in the negotiations.

History is too serious to be left to historians.

IAIN MACLEOD
in *Observer* 16 July 1961

Macleod Iain Norman (1913–1970). British Conservative politician. As colonial secretary 1959–61, he forwarded the independence of former British territories in Africa; he died in office as chancellor of the Exchequer.

Maclise Daniel (1806–1870). Irish painter of historical subjects. He is remembered mainly by his series of portrait drawings of eminent literary men and women, 1830–38, and the two frescoes in the House of Lords, *The Interview between Wellington and Blücher* and *The Death of Nelson*, on which he lavished immense effort.

McLuhan (Herbert) Marshall (1911–1980). Canadian theorist of communication who emphasized the effects of technology on modern society. He coined the phrase 'the medium is the message', meaning that the form rather than the content of information has become crucial. His works include *The Gutenberg Galaxy* 1962 (in which he coined the phrase 'the global village' for the worldwide electronic society then emerging), *Understanding Media* 1964, and *The Medium Is the Massage* (sic) 1967.

Suggested reading

Miller, Jonathan *Marshall McLuhan* (1971)
Theall, Donald *The Medium is the Rear View Mirror: Understanding McLuhan* (1971)

MacMahon Marie Edmé Patrice Maurice, Comte de (1808–1893). Marshal of France. Captured at Sedan 1870 during the

Here I am and here I stay.

Comment by COMTE DE MACMAHON
after he had taken the Malakof fortress at the siege of Sebastopol
8 Sept 1855 and had been warned that it might be blown up.

Franco-Prussian War, he suppressed the Paris Commune after his release, and as president of the republic 1873–79 worked for a royalist restoration until forced to resign.

McMahon William (1908–1988). Australian Liberal politician, prime minister 1971–72. Elected to the House of Representatives in 1949, he held a number of portfolios, becoming deputy leader of the Liberal Party and treasurer in 1966. He gained a reputation as a hard-working and well-prepared minister. After the death of prime minister Holt in 1967, Country Party leader John McEwen vetoed McMahon as coalition leader and he continued as treasurer up to 1969 and minister for external affairs 1969–71 under Gorton. In 1971 the Country Party lifted its embargo on McMahon and he replaced Gorton as prime minister. However, he was no match for opposition leader Whitlam and lost the election of 1972. He retired from politics in 1982. GCMG 1977.

McMillan Edwin Mattison (1907–1991). US physicist. In 1940 he discovered neptunium, the first transuranic element, by bombarding uranium with neutrons. He shared a Nobel prize with Glenn Seaborg 1951.

In 1943 McMillan developed a method of overcoming the limitations of the cyclotron, the first accelerator, for which he shared, 20 years later, an Atoms for Peace award with I Veksler, director of the Soviet Joint Institute for Nuclear Research, who had come to the same discovery independently.

From 1932 he was on the staff at the University of California, as professor 1946–73, except during World War II when he worked on radar and Seaborg took up his work at Berkeley. The discovery of plutonium facilitated the construction of the first atom bomb, in which McMillan also took part.

Most of our people have never had it so good.

HAROLD MACMILLAN
Speech in Bedford 20 July 1957

Macmillan (Maurice) Harold, 1st Earl of Stockton (1894–1986). British Conservative politician, prime minister 1957–63; foreign secretary 1955 and chancellor of the Exchequer 1955–57. In 1963 he attempted to negotiate British entry into the European Economic Community, but was blocked by French president de Gaulle. Much of his career as prime minister was spent defending the retention of a UK nuclear weapon, and he was responsible for the purchase of US Polaris missiles 1962. Earl 1984.

Macmillan was MP for Stockton 1924–29 and 1931–45, and for Bromley 1945–64. As minister of housing 1951–54 he achieved the construction of 300,000 new houses a year. He became prime minister on the resignation of Anthony Eden after the Suez crisis, and led the Conservative Party to victory in the 1959 elections on the slogan 'You've never had it so good' (the phrase was borrowed from a US election campaign). Internationally, his realization of the 'wind of change' in Africa advanced the independence of former colonies. Macmillan's nickname Supermac was coined by the cartoonist Vicky.
Suggested reading
Fisher, Nigel *Harold Macmillan: A Biography* (1982)
Horne, Alistair *Macmillan, 1894–1956* (1988)
Horne, Alistair *Macmillan, 1957–1986* (1988)
Sampson, Anthony *Macmillan: A Study in Ambiguity* (1967)

MacMillan Kenneth (1929–1992). Scottish choreographer. After studying at the Sadler's Wells Ballet School he was director of the Royal Ballet 1970–77 and then principal choreographer 1977–92. He was also director of Berlin's German Opera ballet company 1966–69. A daring stylist, he often took risks with his choreography, expanding the ballet's vocabulary with his frequent use of historical sources, religious music, and occasional use of dialogue. His works include *Romeo and Juliet* 1965 (filmed 1966) for Margot Fonteyn and Rudolf Nureyev.

He is also renowned for his work with the Canadian dancer Lynn Seymour, including *Le Baiser de la fée* 1960 and *The Invitation* 1960. In *Anastasia* 1967, based on the case of the mental patient who claimed to be the Romanovs' missing heir, MacMillan contrasted different eras, musical styles, and incorporated newsreel footage. Other works include *The Song of the Earth* 1965, *Elite Syncopations* 1974, *Mayerling* 1978, *Orpheus* 1982, and *The Prince of the Pagodas* 1989 (originally choreographed by John Cranko 1957 to music by Benjamin Britten). Knighted 1983.

MacMillan Kirkpatrick (1813–1878). Scottish blacksmith who invented the bicycle 1839. His invention consisted of a 'hobbyhorse' that was fitted with treadles and propelled by pedalling.

McMurtry Larry ('Jeff') (1936–). US writer. Many of his works were made into films, including *Terms of Endearment* 1975, the film of which won the 1983 Academy Award for Best Picture.

Born in Wichita Falls, Texas, USA, McMurtry mostly wrote about the Southwest and about his home state of Texas in particular. Among his many other titles are *Horseman, Pass By* 1961 (film *Hud* 1963), *Leaving Cheyenne* 1963 (film *Lovin' Molly* 1963), and *The Last Picture Show* 1966 (film 1971). He also wrote *The Desert Rose* 1983, *Lonesome Dove* 1986 (Pulitzer prize), *Texasville* 1987, and *Buffalo Girls* 1990.

McNaught William (1813–1881). Scottish mechanical engineer who invented the compound steam engine 1845. This type of engine extracts the maximum energy from the hot steam by effectively using it twice – once in a high-pressure cylinder (or cylinders) and then, when exhausted from this, in a second, low-pressure cylinder. Three types of new engine were to emerge using McNaught's principle. The first used cylinders mounted side by side, the second had cylinders in a line (a tandem compound), and the third and rarest type had the high-pressure cylinder enclosed by the low-pressure one.

The sunlight on the garden / Hardens and grows cold, /
We cannot cage the minute / Within its net of gold, /
When all is told / We cannot beg for pardon.

LOUIS MACNEICE
'Sunlight on the Garden'

MacNeice (Frederick) Louis (1907–1963). Northern Irish poet. He made his debut with *Blind Fireworks* 1929 and developed a polished ease of expression, reflecting his classical training, as in *Autumn Journal* 1939. He is noted for his low-key, socially committed but politically uncommitted verse.

Later works include the play *The Dark Tower* 1947, written for radio, for which medium he also wrote features 1941–49; a verse translation of Goethe's *Faust*; and the radio play *The Administrator* 1961. He also translated Aeschylus' *Agamemnon* 1936.

McPartland Jimmy (James Duigald) (1907–1991). US cornet player. He was one of the founders of the Chicago school of jazz in the 1920s. He was influenced by Louis Armstrong and Bix Beiderbecke, whom he replaced in a group called the Wolverines 1924. He also recorded with guitarist Eddie Condon, and from the late 1940s often worked with his wife, British pianist Marian McPartland (1920–).

McPhee Colin (1900–1964). US composer. His studies of Balinese music 1934–36 produced two works, *Tabuh-tabuhan* for two pianos and orchestra 1936 and *Balinese Ceremonial Music* for two pianos 1940, which influenced Benjamin Britten, John Cage, and later generations of US composers.

McPherson Aimee Semple (born Kennedy) (1890–1944). Canadian-born US religious leader. As a popular preacher, 'Sister Aimee' reached millions through radio broadcasts of her weekly sermons, in which she emphasized the power of faith. She established the Church of the Four-Square Gospel in Los Angeles 1918.

Born in Ingersoll, Ontario, USA, McPherson worked as a missionary to China before becoming an itinerant evangelist in the USA, gaining a large following through her revival tours. Her brief but suspicious 1926 'disappearance' tarnished her reputation. She committed suicide 1944.

Madison *4th US president James Madison, whose proposals at the Constitutional Convention 1787 earned him the title of 'father of the US Constitution'. His second term was marked by the war with Britain 1812–14, known as 'Madison's War', in which Washington was captured and the White House burned.*

Macpherson James (1736–1796). Scottish writer and literary forger. He was the author of *Fragments of Ancient Poetry collected in the Highlands of Scotland* 1760, followed by the epics *Fingal* 1761 and *Temora* 1763, which he claimed as the work of the 3rd-century bard Ossian. After his death they were shown to be forgeries.

When challenged by Dr Samuel Johnson, Macpherson failed to produce his originals, and a committee decided 1797 that he had combined fragmentary materials with oral tradition. Nevertheless, the works of 'Ossian' influenced the development of the Romantic movement in Britain and in Europe.

He laid out Sydney as it now exists.

C A Harris on LACHLAN MACQUARIE
in *Dictionary of National Biography*

Macquarie Lachlan (1762–1824). Scottish administrator in Australia. He succeeded Admiral Bligh as governor of New South Wales 1809, raised the demoralized settlement to prosperity, and did much to rehabilitate ex-convicts. In 1821 he returned to Britain in poor health, exhausted by struggles with his opponents. Lachlan river and Macquarie river and island are named after him.

In my own mind, I'm not sure that acting is something a grown man should be doing.

STEVE MCQUEEN
in Leslie Halliwell *Filmgoer's Companion* 1965

McQueen Steve (Terrence Steven) (1930–1980). US film actor. He was admired for his portrayals of the strong, silent loner, and noted for performing his own stunt work. After television success in the 1950s, he became a film star with *The Magnificent Seven* 1960. His films include *The Great Escape* 1963, *Bullitt* 1968, *Papillon* 1973, and *The Hunter* 1980.

Macready William Charles (1793–1873). English actor. He made his debut at Covent Garden, London, 1816. Noted for his roles as Shakespeare's tragic heroes (Macbeth, Lear, and Hamlet), he was partly responsible for persuading the theatre to return to the original texts of Shakespeare and abandon the earlier, bowdlerized versions.

He was manager of Drury Lane Theatre, London, 1841–43.

McTaggart John McTaggart Ellis (1866–1925). English philosopher. A follower of Hegel, he argued for atheism, the immortality of the soul, and the unreality of time. McTaggart's ingenious arguments give his work lasting interest. His great work is *The Nature of Existence* 1927. He was a fellow of Trinity College, Cambridge.

MacWhirter John (1839–1911). Scottish landscape painter. His works include *June in the Austrian Tyrol, Spindrift* and various watercolours.

McWhirter Norris Dewar (1925–   ). British editor and compiler, with his twin brother, Ross McWhirter (1925–1975), of the *Guinness Book of Records* from 1955.

Maderna Bruno (1920–1973). Italian composer and conductor. He collaborated with Luciano Berio in setting up an electronic studio in Milan. His compositions combine aleatoric and graphic techniques with an elegance of sound. They include a pioneering work for live and pre-recorded flute, *Musica su due dimensioni* 1952, numerous concertos, and *Hyperion* 1964, a 'mobile opera', consisting of a number of composed scenes that may be combined in several ways.

Madison James (1751–1836). 4th president of the USA 1809–17. In 1787 he became a member of the Philadelphia Constitutional Convention and took a leading part in drawing up the US Constitution and the Bill of Rights. He allied himself firmly with Thomas Jefferson against Alexander Hamilton in the struggle between the more democratic views of Jefferson and the aristocratic, upper-class sentiments of Hamilton. As secretary of state in Jefferson's government 1801–09, Madison completed the Louisiana Purchase negotiated by James Monroe. During his period of office the War of 1812 with Britain took place.
Suggested reading
Ketcham, Ralph *James Madison* (1971)
Koch, A *Jefferson and Madison: The Great Collaboration* (1950)
Rutland, Robert *James Madison and the Search for Nationhood* (1981)

Madonna Italian name for the Virgin ◊Mary, meaning 'my lady'.

Madonna stage name of Madonna Louise Veronica Ciccone (1958–   ). US pop singer and actress who presents herself on stage and in videos with an exaggerated sexuality. Her first hit was 'Like a Virgin' 1984; others include 'Material Girl' 1985 and 'Like a Prayer' 1989. Her films include *Desperately Seeking Susan* 1985, *Dick Tracy* 1990, the documentary *In Bed with Madonna* 1991, and *A League of Their Own* 1992.

In the early years of her career she frequently employed Catholic trappings in her dress and stage show. Her book *Sex*, a collection of glossy, erotic photographs interspersed with explicit fantasies in the form of short stories, was published 1992, coinciding with the release of the dance album *Erotica*.

Maecenas Gaius Cilnius (*c.* 69–8 BC). Roman patron of the arts, and close friend and diplomatic agent of Augustus. He was influential in providing encouragement and material support for the Augustan poets Horace and Virgil.

Maelzel Johann Nepomuk (1772–1838). German inventor. His name is invariably linked to the metronome. He did not invent the machine, but appropriated the idea, developing it 1814.

Maeterlinck Maurice Polydore Marie Bernard, Count (1862–1949). Belgian poet and dramatist. His plays include *Pelléas et Mélisande* 1892, *L'Oiseau bleu/The Blue Bird* 1908, and *Le Bourgmestre de Stilmonde/The Burgomaster of Stilemonde* 1918. This last celebrates Belgian resistance in World War I, a subject that led to his exile in the USA 1940. Nobel prize 1911.

We possess only the happiness we are able to understand.
MAURICE MAETERLINCK
Wisdom and Destiny 1898

Magellan Ferdinand (*c.* 1480–1521). Portuguese navigator. In 1519 he set sail in the *Victoria* from Seville with the intention of reaching the East Indies by a westerly route. He sailed through the *Strait of Magellan* at the tip of South America, crossed an ocean he named the Pacific, and in 1521 reached the Philippines, where he was killed in a battle with the islanders. His companions returned to Seville 1522, completing the voyage under del Cano.

Magellan was brought up at court and entered the royal service, but later transferred his services to Spain. He and his Malay slave, Enrique de Malacca, are considered the first circumnavigators of the globe, since they had once sailed from the Philippines to Europe.
Suggested reading
Cameron, Ian *The First Circumnavigation of the World* (1973)
Guallemard, F H H *The Life of Ferdinand Magellan, 1480–1521* (1890, rep 1971)
Parr, Charles M *Ferdinand Magellan, Circumnavigator* (1964)
Pigafetta, Antonio *Magellan's Voyages Around the World* (trs 1969)

Magendie François (1783–1855). French physician, a pioneer of modern experimental physiology. He helped to introduce into medicine the range of plant-derived compounds known as alkaloids as well as strychnine, morphine and codeine, and quinine.

Magendie was born in Bordeaux and studied at Paris, where he became physician to the Hôtel Dieu. Elected a member of the Académie des Sciences 1821, he became its president 1837. In 1831, he was appointed professor of anatomy at the Collège de France.

Using extensive vivisection and a certain amount of self-experimentation, Magendie conducted trials on plant poisons, deploying animals to track precise physiological effects. He demonstrated that the stomach's role in vomiting is essentially passive, and analysed emetics. He investigated the role of proteins in human diet; he was interested in olfaction; and he studied the white blood cells. He worked protractedly on the nerves of the spine and the skull – a canal leading from the fourth ventricle is now known as the 'foramen of Magendie'.

His numerous works include *Elements of Physiology* 1816–17.

Magistretti Vico (1920–). Italian architect and furniture designer. Active in Milan from 1945, he was a member of the generation which created the postwar modern Italian design movement. He has worked closely with the Arflex and Cassina companies, among others, to create many lasting furniture designs in the modern style.

Examples from the 1960s include chairs and tables in brightly coloured plastics, while more recently his 'Sindbad' sofa for Cassina 1981 has shown that Italy could still lead the way in elegant modern design.

Magritte René François Ghislain (1898–1967). Belgian Surrealist painter. His work focuses on visual paradoxes and everyday objects taken out of context. Recurring motifs include bowler hats, apples, and windows, for example *Golconda* 1953 (private collection), in which men in bowler hats are falling from the sky to a street below.

Magritte joined the other Surrealists in Paris 1927, returning to Brussels 1930. His most influential works are those that question the relationship between image and reality, as in *The Treason of Images* 1928–29 (Los Angeles County Museum of Art), in which a picture of a smoker's pipe appears with the words 'Ceci n'est pas une pipe' ('This is not a pipe').
Suggested reading
Gablik, S *Magritte* (1970)
Hammacher, A M *Magritte* (1986)
Noel, B *Magritte* (1977)

Mahan Alfred Thayer (1840–1914). US naval officer and military historian, author of 'The Influence of Sea Power upon History' 1890–92, in which he propounded a global strategy based on the importance of sea power. It deeply influenced President Theodore Roosevelt and Wilhelm II of Germany to expand their respective nations' fleets.

Mahan argued that Britain held a strategic advantage over the central powers and predicted the defeat of the German navy in World War I.

The maritime Clausewitz, the Schlieffen of the sea.
Barbara W Tuchman on ALFRED THAYER MAHAN
in *The Guns of August*

Mahathir bin Mohamed (1925–). Prime minister of Malaysia from 1981. Leader of the New United Malays' National Organization (UMNO Baru), his 'look east' economic policy, which emulates Japanese industrialization, has met with considerable success.

Mahathir bin Mohamed was elected to the House of Representatives 1964 and gained the support of the radical youth wing of the then dominant United Malay's National Organization (UMNO) as an advocate of economic help to *bumiputras* (ethnic Malays) and as a proponent of a more Islamic social policy. Mahathir held a number of ministerial posts from 1974 before being appointed prime minister and UMNO leader 1981. He was re-elected 1986, but alienated sections of UMNO by his authoritarian leadership and from 1988 led a reconstituted UMNO Baru (New UMNO). In 1994 he temporarily suspended all forthcoming trade deals with the UK after allegations in the British press that aid for Malaysia's Pergau dam had been given in exchange for an arms contract 1988. In the 1995 elections, his UMNO-Baru-led coalition achieved a landslide victory.

Mahatma (Sanskrit 'great soul') title conferred on Mohandas ◊Gandhi by his followers as the first great national Indian leader.

Mahavira (*c.* 599–527 BC). Indian sage from whose teachings the Jain faith arose. At the age of 30 he turned from a life of comfort to asceticism which he practised for 12 years. At the end of this time he began to bring together a group of followers who were to be the bridge-builders who would pass on right knowledge and right conduct to others.

A contemporary of the Buddha, Mahavira lived in N India and is believed by the Jains to be the 24th *tirthankara* or bridge builder. The *tirthankara*s come to each era of time and preach the way to right knowledge and right conduct. After 30 years of building his community, he died in the town of Pava.

Mahdi (Arabic 'he who is guided aright') in Islam, the title of a coming messiah who will establish a reign of justice on Earth. The title has been assumed by many Muslim leaders, notably the Sudanese sheikh Muhammad Ahmed (1848–1885), who headed a revolt 1881 against Egypt and 1885 captured Khartoum.

His great-grandson Sadiq el Mahdi (1936–), leader of the Umma party in Sudan, was prime minister 1966–67. He was imprisoned 1969–74 for attempting to overthrow the military regime.

Mahfouz Naguib (1911–). Egyptian novelist and playwright. His novels, which deal with the urban working class, include the semi-autobiographical *Khan al-Kasrain/The Cairo Trilogy* 1956–57. His *Children of Gebelawi* 1959 was banned in Egypt because of its treatment of religious themes. He won the Nobel Prize for Literature 1988. He was seriously wounded in a knife attack by Islamic militants outside his home in Cairo in Oct 1994.

Mahler Alma (born Schindler) (1879–1964). Austrian pianist and composer of lieder (songs). She was the daughter of the artist Anton Schindler and abandoned composing when she married the composer Gustav Mahler 1902. After Mahler's death she lived with the architect Walter Gropius; their daughter Manon's death inspired Berg's *Violin Concerto*. She later married the writer Franz Werfel.

Mahler Gustav (1860–1911). Austrian composer and conductor. His epic symphonies express a world-weary Romanticism in visionary tableaux incorporating folk music and pastoral imagery. He composed nine large-scale symphonies, many with voices, including *Symphony No 2 'Resurrection'* 1884–86, revised 1893–96, and left a tenth unfinished. He also composed orchestral lieder (songs) including *Das Lied von der Erde/The Song of the Earth* 1909 and *Kindertotenlieder/Dead Children's Songs* 1901–04.

The *Symphony No 2* second movement, based on a *ländler* (folk dance in three time), is reinterpreted in stream-of-consciousness mode by Berio in *Sinfonia* 1968, into which Berio inserts a history of musical references from J S Bach to Stockhausen. The *Adagietto* slow movement from *Symphony No 5* provided a perfect foil for Luchino Visconti's film *Death in Venice* 1971.

Mahler was born in Bohemia (now the Czech Republic); he studied at the Vienna Conservatoire, and conducted in Prague, Leipzig, Budapest, and Hamburg 1891–97. He was director of the Vienna Court Opera from 1897 and conducted the New York Philharmonic from 1910.

Suggested reading
Cooke, D *Gustav Mahler: An Introduction to his Music* (1980)
James, B *The Music of Gustav Mahler* (1985)
Mitchell, D *Mahler* (1958–85)
Walter, B *Gustav Mahler* (1941)

Mahmud two sultans of the Ottoman Empire:

Mahmud I (1696–1754). Ottoman sultan from 1730. After restoring order to the empire in Istanbul 1730, he suppressed the janissary rebellion 1731 and waged war against Persia 1731–46. He led successful wars against Austria and Russia, concluded by the Treaty of Belgrade 1739. He was a patron of the arts and also carried out reform of the army.

Mahmud II (1785–1839). Ottoman sultan from 1808 who attempted to westernize the declining empire, carrying out a series of far-reaching reforms in the civil service and army. The pressure for Greek independence after 1821 led to conflict with Britain, France, and Russia, and he was forced to recognize Greek independence 1830.

In 1826 Mahmud destroyed the elite janissary army corps. Wars against Russia 1807–12 resulted in losses of territory. The Ottoman fleet was destroyed at the Battle of Navarino 1827, and the Ottoman forces suffered defeat in the Russo-Turkish war 1828–29. There was further disorder with the revolt in Egypt of Mehmet Ali 1831–32, which in turn led to temporary Ottoman-Russian peace. Attempts to control the rebellious provinces failed 1839, resulting in effect in the granting of Egyptian autonomy.

Mahomed Ismail (1931–). South African lawyer, appointed the country's first non-white judge 1991. As legal adviser to SWAPO, he was the author of Namibia's constitution, which abolished capital punishment. He has defended many anti-apartheid activists in political trials.

Mahomed, born in Pretoria, became a barrister 1957. Classified as Indian under the apartheid system, he was hampered by restrictions on his movements, but went on to become president of Lesotho's Court of Appeal and a member of Swaziland's Appellate Division, and as a member of the Namibian Supreme Court he ruled corporal punishment unconstitutional. He is an eloquent speaker.

Alimony is the curse of the writing classes.

NORMAN MAILER
Attributed remark 1980

Mailer Norman Kingsley (1923–). US writer and journalist. One of the most prominent figures of postwar American literature, he gained wide attention with his first, bestselling book *The Naked and the Dead* 1948, a naturalistic war novel. His later works, which use sexual and scatological material, show his personal engagement with history, politics, and psychology. Always a pugnacious and controversial writer, his polemics on the theory and practice of violence-as-sex brought him into direct conflict with feminist Kate Millett in a series of celebrated debates during the 1970s.

His essay 'White Negro' in *Advertisements for Myself* 1959, defining the 'hipster' hero, was a seminal statement of the artistic need to rebel against cultural conformity. His other books include his dark thriller of sex and power, *An American Dream* 1965, the fictionalized antiwar journalism of *The Armies of the Night* 1968 (Pulitzer prize), *The Executioner's Song* 1979 (Pulitzer prize), about convicted murderer Gary Gilmore, and two massive novels, *Ancient Evenings* 1983, dealing with Egyptian life and mythologies, and *Harlot's Ghost* 1991, about the CIA. A combative public figure, Mailer cofounded the magazine *Village Voice* in the 1950s, edited *Dissent*, and in 1969 ran for mayor of New York City. *Pablo and Fernande* appeared 1994.

Suggested reading
Manso, Peter *Mailer: His Life and Times* (1985)
Mills, Hilary *Mailer: A Biography* (1982)
Poirier, Richard *Norman Mailer* (1972)

Maillart Ella Kini (1903–). Swiss explorer, skier, and Olympic sailor whose six-month journey into Soviet Turkestan was described in *Turkestan Solo* 1934. Her expedition across the Gobi Desert with Peter Fleming is recounted in *Forbidden Journey* 1937.

Maillol Aristide Joseph Bonaventure (1861–1944). French artist who turned to sculpture in the 1890s. His work, which is mainly devoted to the female nude, shows the influence of classical Greek art but tends towards simplified rounded forms. Maillol was influenced by *les Nabis*. A typical example of his work is *Fame* for the Cézanne monument in Aix-en-Provence.

Maiman Theodore Harold (1927–). US physicist who in 1960 constructed the first working laser. From 1955 to 1961 he worked at the Hughes Research Laboratories. In 1962 he founded the Korad Corporation to manufacture lasers; in 1968 he founded Maiman Associates, a laser and optics consultancy; he cofounded the Laser Video Corporation 1972. In 1975 he joined the TRW Electronics Company, Los Angeles.

In 1955, Maiman began improving the maser (microwave amplifier), first designed in 1953 by US physicist Charles Townes. Townes had also demonstrated the theoretical possibility of constructing an optical maser, or laser, but Maiman was the first to build one. His laser consisted of a cylindrical, synthetic ruby crystal with parallel, mirror-coated ends, the coating at one end being semitransparent to allow the emission of the laser beam. A burst of intense white light stimulated the chromium atoms in the ruby to emit noncoherent red light. This red light was then reflected back and forth by the mirrored ends until eventually some of the light emerged as an intense beam of coherent red light – laser light. Maiman's apparatus produced pulses; the first continuous-beam laser was made in 1961 at the Bell Telephone Laboratories.

Maimonides Moses (Moses Ben Maimon) (1135–1204). Spanish-born Jewish rabbi and philosopher, one of the greatest Hebrew scholars. He attempted to reconcile faith and reason. His codification of Jewish law is known as the *Mishneh Torah/Torah Reviewed* 1180; he also formulated the Thirteen Principles, which summarize the basic beliefs of Judaism.

Maimonides was born in Córdoba, but left Spain 1160 to escape the persecution of the Jews and settled in Fez, and later in Cairo, where he was personal physician to Sultan Saladin. His philosophical classic *More nevukhim/The Guide to the Perplexed* 1176–91 helped to introduce Aristotelian thought into medieval philosophy. He also wrote ten books on medicine.

Maine de Biran Marie-François-Pierre (1766–1824). French thinker and politician. He speculated that the self is an active power developed through experience, and developed a philosophy in which the will was the source of human freedom. He was councillor of state 1816.

Maine de Biran was a member and treasurer of the chamber of deputies (national assembly) 1814. His main works include *L'Influence d'habitude/The Influence of Habit* 1802 and *Essai sur les fondements de la psychologie/Essay on the Foundations of Psychology* 1812.

Maintenon Françoise d'Aubigné, Marquise de (1635–1719). Second wife of Louis XIV of France from 1684, and widow of the writer Paul Scarron (1610–1660). She was governess to the children of Mme de Montespan by Louis, and his mistress from 1667. She secretly married the king after the death of Queen Marie Thérèse 1683. Her political influence was considerable and, as a Catholic convert from Protestantism, her religious opinions were zealous.

> *You must make use of people according to their abilities, and realize that absolutely no one is perfect.*
> FRANÇOISE D'AUBIGNÉ, MARQUISE DE MAINTENON
> Letter to Count d'Aubigné 25 Sept 1679

Maizière Lothar de (1940–   ). German conservative politician, see Ọde Maizière.

Major John (1943–   ). British Conservative politician, prime minister from 1990.

He was foreign secretary 1989 and chancellor of the Exchequer 1989–90. His initial positive approach to European Community matters was hindered from 1991 by divisions within the Conservative Party. Despite continuing public dissatisfaction with the poll tax, the National Health Service, and the recession, Major was returned to power in the April 1992 general election. His subsequent handling of a series of domestic crises called into question his ability to govern the country effectively, but he won backing for his launch of a joint UK-Irish peace initiative on Northern Ireland 1993, which led to a general cease-fire 1994. On the domestic front, local and European election defeats and continuing divisions within the Conservative Party led to his dramatic and unexpected resignation of the party leadership June 1995 in a desperate bid for party unity. He was narrowly re-elected to the post the following month.

Formerly a banker, he became MP for Huntingdonshire 1979 and become deputy to Chancellor Nigel Lawson 1987. In 1989 Major was appointed foreign secretary and, after Lawson's resignation, chancellor, within the space of six months. As chancellor he led Britain into the European Exchange Rate Mechanism (ERM) Oct 1990. The following month he became prime minister on winning the Conservative Party leadership election in a contest with Michael Heseltine and Douglas Hurd, after the resignation of Margaret Thatcher. Although victorious in the 1992 general election, he subsequently faced mounting public dissatisfaction over a range of issues, including the sudden withdrawal of the pound from the ERM, a drastic pit-closure programme, and past sales of arms to Iraq. In addition, Major had to deal with 'Euro-sceptics' within his own party who fiercely opposed any moves which they saw as ceding national sovereignty to Brussels. His success in negotiating a Northern Ireland cease-fire 1994 did much to improve his standing, but delay in progressing peace talks resulted in criticism of his cautious approach.

Suggested reading
Anderson, Bruce *John Major* (1991)
Junor, Penny *The Major Enigma* (1993)

Makarenko Anton Semyonovitch (1888–1939). Russian educationist. In his work with homeless orphans and delinquents after the Russian Revolution, he encouraged children to take responsibility not just for themselves but, more importantly, for the good of the community as a whole. His ideas have been criticized for being implicitly totalitarian.

> *A national hero to the Greeks ... too large a hero for his small island to accommodate.*
> C M Woodhouse on MAKARIOS III
> in *Dictionary of National Biography*

Makarios III (born Mikhail Christodoulou Mouskos) (1913–1977). Cypriot politician, Greek Orthodox archbishop 1950–77. A leader of the Greek-Cypriot resistance organization EOKA, he was exiled by the British to the Seychelles 1956–57 for supporting armed action to achieve union with Greece (*enosis*). He was president of the republic of Cyprus 1960–77 (briefly deposed by a Greek military coup July–Dec 1974).

> *Mirrors are the big enemy. When you don't like your image, it's very depressing, but you try to work it out.*
> NATALIA MAKAROVA
> quoted in L Shaw *Where are the Women in Ballet Today?* 1989

Makarova Natalia Romanovna (1940–   ). Russian ballerina. She danced with the Kirov Ballet 1959–70, then sought political asylum in the West, becoming one of the greatest international dancers of the ballet boom of the 1960s and 1970s. A dancer of exceptional musicality and heightened dramatic sense, her roles include the title role in *Giselle* and Aurora in *The Sleeping Beauty*. She has also danced modern works including Jerome Robbins' *Other Dances* 1976, which he created for her. She has also produced ballets, such as *La Bayadère* 1974, for the American Ballet Theater, and *Swan Lake* 1988, for the London Festival Ballet.

Makeba Miriam Zenzile (1932–   ). South African singer. In political exile 1960–90, she was one of the first world-music performers to make a name in the West, and is particularly associated with 'The Click Song', which features the glottal clicking sound of her Xhosa language. She was a vocal opponent to apartheid, and South Africa banned her records.

Makeba sang with a group called the Skylarks 1956–59. Introduced to US audiences 1960 when folk music was popular, she performed many traditional songs as well as South African pop songs, such as 'Pata Pata' and 'Mbube', with jazz stylings.

Her first two marriages were to trumpeter Hugh Masekela and Black Power leader Stokeley Carmichael.

> *The past exudes legend: one can't make pure clay of time's mud.*
> BERNARD MALAMUD
> *Dubin's Lives* 1979

Malamud Bernard (1914–1986). US novelist and short-story writer. He first attracted attention with *The Natural* 1952, a mythic story about a baseball hero. It established Malamud's central concern of moral redemption and transcendence, which was more typically dealt with in books set in Jewish immigrant communities. These drew on the magical elements and mores of the European Yiddish tradition and include such novels as *The Assistant* 1957, *The Fixer* 1966, *Dubin's Lives* 1979, and *God's Grace* 1982.

Short story collections include *The Magic Barrel* 1958, *Rembrandt's Hat* 1973, and *The Stories of Bernard Malamud* 1983.

Malan Daniel François (1874–1959). South African right-wing politician, prime minister 1948–54. He founded the Purified National Party 1934. His policy of apartheid was implemented in a series of acts of Parliament including the Group Areas Act, the Mixed Marriages Act, and the Immorality Act.

Born near Riebeeck West, Cape Province, Malan was a neighbour and school friend of Jan Smuts, who was to precede him as prime minister. Malan studied in the Netherlands and became a minister of the Dutch Reformed Church. He helped to launch the Nationalist Party in the Cape 1915, and started the first official newspaper of the party, *Die Burger* 1915, working as editor until 1924. Elected to Parliament 1919, he joined the government as minister of the interior 1924. When he became prime minister 1948, as well as minister of external affairs, he formed an exclusively Afrikaner government.

Malcolm four kings of Scotland, including:

Malcolm III called 'Canmore' (*c.* 1031–1093). King of Scotland from 1058, the son of Duncan I (murdered by Macbeth 1040). He fled to England when the throne was usurped by Macbeth, but recovered S Scotland and killed Macbeth in battle 1057. He was killed at Alnwick while invading Northumberland, England.

The first king of Scotland who is more than a name.

A J G Mackay on MALCOLM III
in *Dictionary of National Biography*

Malcolm X adopted name of Malcolm Little (1926–1965). US black nationalist leader. While serving a prison sentence for burglary 1946–53, he joined the Black Muslims sect. On his release he campaigned for black separatism, condoning violence in self-defence, but 1964 modified his views to found the Islamic, socialist Organization of Afro-American Unity, preaching racial solidarity.

He was born in Omaha, Nebraska, but grew up in foster homes in Michigan, Massachusetts, and New York. In 1952 he officially changed his name to Malcolm X to signify his rootlessness in a racist society. Having become an influential national and international leader, Malcolm X publicly broke with the Black Muslims 1964. A year later he was assassinated by Black Muslim opponents while addressing a rally in Harlem, New York City. His *Autobiography of Malcolm X* was published 1964.

Suggested reading
Malcolm X and Haley, Alex *The Autobiography of Malcolm X* (1965)
Goldman, Peter *The Life and Death of Malcolm X* (1979)
Green, Cheryll Y (ed) *Malcolm X: Make it Plain* (oral biography) (1994)
Wolfenstein, Victor *The Victims of Democracy* (1981)

Malebranche Nicolas (1638–1715). French philosopher. His *De la Recherche de la vérité/Search after Truth* 1674–78 was inspired by René Descartes; he maintained that exact ideas of external objects are obtainable only through God.

Malenkov Georgi Maximilianovich (1902–1988). Soviet prime minister 1953–55, Stalin's designated successor but abruptly ousted as Communist Party secretary within two weeks of Stalin's death by Khrushchev, and forced out as prime minister 1955 by Bulganin. Malenkov subsequently occupied minor party posts. He was expelled from the Central Committee 1957 and from the Communist Party 1961.

Malevich Kasimir Severinovich (1878–1935). Russian abstract painter. In 1912 he visited Paris where he was influenced by Cubism, and in 1913 launched his own abstract style, *Suprematism*. He reached his most abstract in *White on White* about 1918 (Museum of Modern Art, New York), a white square painted on a white background, but later returned to figurative themes treated in a semi-abstract style.

He studied at Kiev and went to Moscow, *c.* 1900, where he was impressed by the modern French paintings then being collected there by wealthy merchants. He passed through Fauve, Cubist and Futurist phases, but in 1915 turned dramatically to simple geometric forms. His *White on White* is a celebrated product of his theories, which he vigorously propagated in the early years after the Bolshevik Revolution. The return to conservatism in art in the then USSR, *c.* 1930, marked the end of his influence, but he was a gifted artist and played a leading role in the history of abstraction.

Malherbe François de (1555–1628). French poet and grammarian. He became court poet about 1605 under Henry IV and Louis XIII. He advocated reform of language and versification, and established the 12-syllable alexandrine as the standard form of French verse.

Malik Abu Abdallah Malik ibn Anas (716–795). Founder of the Maliki School of Sunni Islamic law, which dominates in N Africa. His main work was *Muwatta/The Simplified*, a book about Islamic law which was intended to be a bridge between the complexity of scholars and the simplicity of ordinary people, giving a guide for Muslims to follow.

He was born in Medina; his first teacher was Sahl ibn Sa'd, a companion of the prophet Muhammad. Malik was a close acquaintance of the jurist Abu Hanifah. His main pupil was al-Shafi'i.

Malik Yakob Alexandrovich (1906–1980). Soviet diplomat. He was permanent representative at the United Nations 1948–53 and 1968–76, and it was his walkout from the Security Council in Jan 1950 that allowed the authorization of UN intervention in Korea.

Malinovsky Rodion Yakovlevich (1898–1967). Russian soldier and politician. In World War II he fought at Stalingrad, commanded in the Ukraine, and led the Soviet advance through the Balkans to capture Budapest 1945 before going east to lead the invasion of Manchuria. He was minister of defence 1957–67.

Malinowski Bronislaw Kasper (1884–1942). Polish-born British anthropologist, one of the founders of the theory of functionalism in the social sciences. During expeditions to the Trobriand Islands (now part of Papua New Guinea) 1915–16 and 1917–18, his detailed studies of the islanders led him to see customs and practices in terms of their function in creating and maintaining social order.

His fieldwork involved a revolutionary system of 'participant observation' whereby the researcher became completely involved in the life of the people he studied. He wrote several influential monographs on the islanders, including *Argonauts of the Pacific*.

Suggested reading
Firth, Raymond *Man and Culture: An Evaluation of the Work of Bronislaw Malinowski* (1957)

Malipiero Gian Francesco (1882–1973). Italian composer and editor of Monteverdi and Vivaldi. His own works include operas in a Neo-Classical style, based on Shakespeare's *Julius Caesar* 1934–35 and *Antony and Cleopatra* 1936–37.

Mallarmé Stéphane (1842–1898). French poet. He founded the Symbolist school with Paul Verlaine. His belief that poetry should be evocative and suggestive was reflected in *L'Après-midi d'un faune/Afternoon of a Faun* 1876, which inspired the composer Debussy. Later works are *Poésies complètes/Complete Poems* 1887, *Vers et prose/Verse and Prose* 1893, and the prose *Divagations/ Digressions* 1897.

Suggested reading
Bowie, M *Mallarmé and the Art of Being Difficult* (1978)
Fowlie, Wallace *Mallarmé* (1953)
Millan, Gordon *Mallarmé: A Throw of the Dice: The Life of Stéphane Mallarmé* (1994)
Morris, D *Stéphane Mallarmé* (1977)

It takes a long time to learn simplicity.

LOUIS MALLE
in *Film Illustrated* March 1981

Malle Louis (1932–1995). French film director. After a period as assistant to director Robert Bresson, he directed *Les Amants/The Lovers* 1958, audacious for its time in its explicitness. His subsequent films, made in France and the USA, include *Zazie dans le métro* 1961, *Viva Maria* 1965, *Pretty Baby* 1978, *Atlantic City* 1980, *Au Revoir les Enfants* 1988, *Milou en mai* 1989, and *Damage* 1993.

The joy of love is too short, and the sorrow thereof, and what cometh thereof, dureth over long.

THOMAS MALORY
Le Morte d'Arthur bk 10 ch 56 1469–70

Malory Thomas (lived 15th century). English author. He is known for the prose romance *Le Morte d'Arthur* about 1470, a translation from the French, modified by material from other sources. It deals with the exploits of King Arthur's knights of the Round Table and the quest for the Holy Grail. Knight of the shire 1445.

Malory's identity is uncertain. He is thought to have been the Warwickshire landowner of that name who was member of Parliament for Warwick 1445 and was charged with rape, theft, and attempted murder 1451 and 1452. If that is so, he must have compiled *Le Morte d'Arthur* during his 20 years in Newgate prison.

Suggested reading
Matthews, William *The Ill-Famed Knight* (1966)
Reiss, E *Sir Thomas Malory* (1966)

Malouf David George Joseph (1934–). Australian poet, novelist, and short-story writer. He is of Lebanese and English extraction. His poetry collections include *Neighbours in a Thicket* 1974, which won several awards, *Wild Lemons* 1980, and *First Things Last* 1980. Malouf's first novel *Johnno* 1975 deals with his boyhood in Brisbane. It was followed by *An Imaginary Life* 1978 and other novels, including *Fly Away Peter* 1982, *The Great World* 1990, and *Remembering Babylon* 1993.

He has also written opera librettos for *Voss* 1986, from the novel of Patrick White, and *La Mer de Glace* 1991.

Malpighi Marcello (1628–1694). Italian physiologist who made many anatomical discoveries in his pioneering microscope studies of animal and plant tissues. For example, he discovered blood capillaries and indentified the sensory receptors (papillae) of the tongue, which he thought could be nerve endings.

He first lectured in logic at Bologna, and although he was professor of theoretical medicine at Pisa 1656–59 and at Messina 1662–66, he returned to Bologna in between. In 1667, the Royal Society in England made him an honorary member and supervised the printing of his later works. In 1691, Malpighi moved to Rome and retired there as chief physician to Pope Innocent XII.

Studying the lungs of a frog, Malpighi found them to consist of thin membranes containing fine blood vessels covering vast numbers of small air sacs. This discovery made it easier to explain how air (oxygen) seeps from the lungs to the blood vessels and is carried around the body. He also investigated the anatomy of insects and found the tracheae, the branching tubes that open to the outside in the abdomen and supply the insect with oxygen for respiration.

Malraux André Georges (1901–1976). French writer. An active antifascist, he gained international renown for his novel *La Condition humaine/Man's Estate* 1933, set during the Nationalist/Communist Revolution in China in the 1920s. *L'Espoir/Days of Hope* 1937 is set in Civil War Spain, where he was a bomber pilot in the International Brigade. In World War II he supported the Gaullist resistance, and was minister of cultural affairs 1960–69.

Suggested reading
Hewitt, James *André Malraux* (1978)
Lewis, R W B (ed) *Malraux: A Collection of Critical Essays* (1964)
Madsen, A *Malraux* (1977)
Malraux, André *Antimemoirs* (autobiography) (trs 1968)
Righter, William *The Rhetorical Hero* (1964)

Malthus Thomas Robert (1766–1834). English economist. His *Essay on the Principle of Population* 1798 (revised 1803) argued for population control, since populations increase in geometric ratio and food supply only in arithmetic ratio, and influenced Charles Darwin's thinking on natural selection as the driving force of evolution. Malthus's main books on economics are *An Inquiry into the Nature and Progress of Rent* 1815 and *Principles of Political Economy* 1820.

In 1805 he became professor of history and political economy at Haileybury College.

Malthus saw war, famine, and disease as necessary checks on population growth. Later editions of his work suggested that 'moral restraint' (delaying marriage, with sexual abstinence before it) could also keep numbers from increasing too quickly, a statement seized on by later birth-control pioneers (the 'neo-Malthusians').

Suggested reading
Boner, H A *Hungry Generations* (1955)
Nickerson, Jane *Homage to Malthus* (1975)
Paglin, M *Malthus and Lauderdale: The Anti-Ricardian Traditions* (1956)
Turner, M (ed) *Malthus and his Time* (1986)

Malus Etienne Louis (1775–1812). French physicist who discovered the polarization of light by reflection from a surface. He also found the law of polarization that relates the intensity of the polarized beam to the angle of reflection.

From 1796 he was in the army, taking part in Napoleon's campaign in Egypt and Syria in 1798 and eventually rising to major, but he was also an examiner for the Ecole Polytechnique.

Malus began doing experiments on double refraction in 1807. This phenomenon causes a light beam to split in two on passing through Iceland spar and certain other crystals. An empirical description had been given by Dutch physicist Christiaan Huygens, based on the assumption that light is wavelike in character, and Malus's results confirmed Huygens's laws.

Mamet David Alan (1947–). US dramatist, film screenwriter, and director. His plays, with their vivid, freewheeling language and urban settings, are often compared with those of Harold Pinter. His *American Buffalo* 1975, about a gang of hopeless robbers, was his first major success. It was followed by *Sexual Perversity in Chicago* 1978 and *Glengarry Glen Ross* 1983, a dark depiction of American business ethics. His film work has included screenplays for *The Postman Always Rings Twice 1981*, *The Verdict* 1982, and *The Untouchables* 1987.

He made his directorial debut with *House of Games* 1987, which used gambling as a metaphor for the bluff and double-bluff of relationships. Among his other works are the plays *Speed-the-Plow* 1988, *Oleanna* 1992, about a sexual harassment case, and *Cryptogram* 1994, about childhood uncertainty; and the film *Things Change* 1987, which he directed and scripted.

Mamoulian Rouben (1897–1987). Armenian stage and film director. He lived in the USA from 1923. After several years on Broadway he turned to films, making the first sound version of *Dr Jekyll and Mr Hyde* 1932 and *Queen Christina* 1933. His later work includes *The Mark of Zorro* 1940 and *Silk Stockings* 1957.

Manchu or Qing. Last ruling dynasty in China, from 1644 until its overthrow 1912; its last emperor was the infant P'u-i. Originally a nomadic people from Manchuria, they established power through a

Malthus *English cleric and economist Thomas Robert Malthus, whose work on the principles of population had a major effect on the formulation of the theory of evolution. Malthus was an advocate of population control and argued that population increased faster than the supply of food and natural resources needed to sustain it. (Ann Ronan/Image Select)*

series of successful invasions from the north, then granted trading rights to the USA and Europeans, which eventually brought strife and the Boxer Rebellion.

Mancini Henry (1924–1994). US composer. A four-time Oscar winner for film music, he was perhaps most famous for the song 'Moon River' from *Breakfast at Tiffany's* 1961, and for the theme to *The Pink Panther* 1963 and its numerous sequels. Mancini wrote and conducted the music for more than 80 films.

Born in Cleveland, Ohio, he grew up in a steel-producing town, where his father taught him to play the flute when he was eight. He also took up the piano, and began arranging music while in his teens. World War II interrupted his studies at the Juilliard School of Music in New York.

He became an arranger for the postwar Glenn Miller Orchestra and worked on the film *The Glenn Miller Story* 1954. One of his most striking early scores was the jazz-tinged music for *Touch of Evil* 1958, and he achieved wider attention with the music for the TV series *Peter Gunn* 1958–60. He later scored all the films of Blake Edwards, maker of the *Pink Panther* series, and for TV assignments as well as features. Mancini was also a prolific recording artist, collecting 20 Grammy awards and six gold albums.

Mandela Nelson (Rolihlahia) (1918–). South African politician and lawyer, president from 1994. He became president of the African National Congress (ANC) 1991. Imprisoned from 1964, as organizer of the then banned ANC, he became a symbol of unity for the worldwide anti-apartheid movement.

Mandela was born near Umbata, S of Lesotho, the son of a local chief. In a trial of several ANC leaders, he was acquitted of treason 1961, but was once more arrested 1964 and given a life sentence on charges of sabotage and plotting to overthrow the government. In Feb 1990 he was released from prison on the orders of state president F W de Klerk and in July 1991 was elected, unopposed, to the presidency of the ANC. In Dec 1991 the ANC began constitutional negotiations with the government and in Feb 1993 Mandela and President de Klerk agreed to the formation of a government of national unity after free, nonracial elections (later scheduled for April 1994). In May 1994 he was sworn in as South Africa's first post-apartheid president after the ANC won 62.65% of the vote in universal-suffrage elections. He shared the Nobel Prize for Peace 1993 with South African president F W de Klerk.

Mandela married the South African civil-rights activist Winnie Mandela 1955 (the couple separated 1992 and were divorced 1996).
Suggested reading
Benson, M *Nelson Mandela* (1986)
Mandela, Nelson *Long Walk to Freedom: The Autobiography of Nelson Mandela* (1994)
Meer, F *Higher than Hope* (1990)

Mandela Winnie (Nomzamo) (1934–). Civil-rights activist in South Africa, wife of Nelson Mandela.

Actively involved in promoting the ANC's cause during her husband's long imprisonment, Winnie Mandela was jailed for a year and put under house arrest several times. In 1989 she was involved in the abduction of four youths, one of whom, Stompie Seipei, was later murdered. She was convicted of kidnapping and assault, and given a six-year jail sentence May 1991, with the right to appeal. In April 1992 she and Nelson Mandela separated after 33 years of marriage. In the same year she resigned from her ANC leaderships posts, including her seat on the ANC National Executive Committee. Her sentence was waived by South Africa's highest court 1993, and she was later nominated an ANC candidate for the April 1994 elections. She was appointed minister for arts, culture, science, and technology May 1994, but after allegations of corruption, including the handing out of government contracts in return for kickbacks, she was relieved of her post 1995. She and her husband were divorced 1996.

Mandelbrot Benoit B (1924–). Polish-born French mathematician who coined the term 'fractal' to describe geometrical figures in which an identical motif repeats itself on an ever-diminishing scale.

The concept is associated with chaos theory. Another way of describing a fractal is as a curve or surface generated by the repeated subdivision of a mathematical pattern.

Mandelbrot was born in Warsaw and studied at the Ecole Polytechnique and the Sorbonne, Paris, and the California Institute of Technology. His academic career was divided mainly between France and the USA. In 1958 he began an association with IBM's research laboratories in New York. In 1987, he became professor at Yale.

Mandelbrot's research has provided mathematical theories for erratic chance phenomena and self-similarity methods in probability. He has also carried out research on sporadic processes, thermodynamics, natural languages, astronomy, geomorphology, computer art and graphics, and the fractal geometry of nature.

His books include *Logique, Langage et Théorie de l'Information* (with L Apostel and A Morf) 1957, *Fractals: Form, Chance and Dimension* 1977, and *The Fractal Geometry of Nature* 1982.

Mandelstam Osip Emilevich (1891–1938). Russian poet. He was a leader of the Acmeist movement. The son of a Jewish merchant, he was sent to a concentration camp by the communist authorities in the 1930s, and died there. His posthumously published work, with its classic brevity, established his reputation as one of the greatest 20th-century Russian poets.

His wife Nadezhda's memoirs of her life with her husband, *Hope Against Hope*, were published in the West 1970, but not until 1988 in the USSR.

Mandeville John (died *c.* 1372). Supposed author of a 14th-century travel manual for pilgrims to the Holy Land. Originally written in French, it was probably the work of Jean d'Outremeuse of Liège. As well as references to real marvels, such as the pyramids, there are tales of headless people with eyes in their shoulders and other such fantastic inventions. He was knighted.

Manet Edouard (1832–1883). French painter. Active in Paris, he was one of the foremost French artists of the 19th century. Rebelling against the academic tradition, he developed a clear and unaffected realist style.

Born in Paris, he trained under a history painter, Thomas Couture, and was inspired by Goya and Velázquez and also by Courbet. The first picture he sent to the Salon, the *Buveur d'Absinthe*, 1859, was refused, inaugurating a long series of sensational rejections. He brilliantly succeeded in his aim of handling an old master subject in contemporary fashion in the two celebrated pictures of the 1860s, *Le Déjeuner sur l'Herbe*, 1863 (translating Giorgione's *Concert Champêtre* into modern terms), and *Olympia*, 1865 (Titian's Venus brought up to date), but both pictures (now at the Musée d' Orsay, Paris) were misunderstood, their unconventional nudities causing a scandal. Exhibited in the Salon des Refusés 1863, the *Déjeuner* became the symbol of revolt against academic and Philistine prejudice, and Manet, though no rebel by nature, became the centre of the group of younger artists whose meetings and discussions at the Café Guerbois were the seeding-ground of Impressionism. For political rather than aesthetic reasons his *Execution of Maximilian*, 1867 (of which there are four versions, at Boston, Mannheim and Copenhagen, with fragments of the second version in the National Gallery), was barred from his one-man show of that year. After the Franco-Prussian War, in which he served as an officer in the National Guard, he took to *plein-air* painting under the influence of Monet and Berthe Morisot, his pupil and sister-in-law. He worked at Argenteuil with Monet and Renoir 1874, but abstained from exhibiting at the Impressionist exhibitions. His colour freshened, though he was Impressionistic rather in giving the vividness of the first sketch than in systematic division of colour. The cabaret and its frequenters figure largely in his later work (as in that of Degas), the *Bon Bock*, a success of 1873, being followed by *La Servante de Bocks*, 1878–79, and the famous masterpiece (executed after the first onset of fatal illness) *Un Bar aux Folies-Bergère*, 1881–82 (London, Courtauld Institute Gallery).
Suggested reading
Hamilton, George *Manet and his Circle* (1954)
Reff, T *Manet and Modern Paris* (1982)
Schneider, P *The World of Manet* (1968)

Mangin Charles Marie Emmanuel (1866–1925). French general. At the outbreak of World War I he returned from Morocco to command a division in the first Battle of the Marne, then recaptured the forts of Douaumont and Vaux-Fossoy in the action at Verdun 1916. His part in General Nivelle's offensive in the Champagne sector 1917 was disastrous and was one of the factors which led to the serious mutiny in the French army later in the year. He played a leading role in the counter-offensive to drive the Germans from the Aisne and the Marne 1918, and following the war commanded the French Army of Occupation in Germany.

Whatever you do, you lose a lot of men.

CHARLES MANGIN
Remark on comparing casualty figures from each division at Verdun 1916

Mankiewicz Joseph L(eo) (1909–1993). US film writer and director. He is celebrated as the writer–director of one of the wittiest films ever to come out of Hollywood *All About Eve* 1950 (Academy Award), a satirical melodrama about theatre people. He made his name with the social comedy *A Letter to Three Wives* 1949 (Academy Award).

Born in Wilkes Barr, Pennsylvania, Mankiewicz was the younger brother of Herman (co-author of *Citizen Kane*), and through his brother's good offices entered films 1929 as a staff writer at Paramount studios. He moved to MGM, where he subsequently became a producer and was responsible for Fritz Lang's first American film *Fury* 1936 and for *Three Comrades* 1938, partly scripted by Scott Fitzgerald. After moving to Fox, he began directing with *Dragonwyck* 1946, and directed films in several genres before making his name with *A Letter to Three Wives* and *All About Eve*.

Back at MGM, he directed an acclaimed film of *Julius Caesar* 1953, and in Europe as an independent producer made *The Barefoot Contessa* 1954, which offered an acerbic view of the film industry, but was somewhat compromised by the requirements of censorship. His involvement with the epic *Cleopatra* 1963, though profitable, was unhappy, and he made only three subsequent films. His last was *Sleuth* 1972, an ingeniously theatrical thriller with only two performers, Laurence Olivier and Michael Caine.

Manley Michael Norman (1923–   ). Jamaican politician, leader of the socialist People's National Party from 1969, and prime minister 1972–80 and 1989–92.

He resigned the premiership because of ill health March 1992 and was succeeded by P J Patterson. Manley left parliament April 1992. His father, Norman Manley (1893–1969), was the founder of the People's National Party and prime minister 1959–62.

Mann Anthony. Stage name of Emil Anton Bundmann (1906–1967). US film director. He made a series of violent but intelligent 1950s Westerns starring James Stewart, such as *Winchester '73* 1950. He also directed the epic *El Cid* 1961. His other films include *The Glenn Miller Story* 1954 and *A Dandy in Aspic* 1968.

Mann Heinrich (1871–1950). German novelist. He fled to the USA 1937 with his brother Thomas Mann. His books include *Im Schlaraffenland/In the Land of Cockaigne* 1901; *Professor Unrat/The Blue Angel* 1904, depicting the sensual downfall of a schoolmaster; a scathing trilogy dealing with the Kaiser's Germany *Das Kaiserreich/The Empire* 1918–25; and two volumes on the career of Henry IV of France 1935–38.

Mann Horace (1796–1859). US political leader and education reformer. Resigning from the Massachusetts state legislature 1937, he served as secretary of the state school board 1837–48. In that position he helped raise the level of funding and instruction for public education.

Born in Franklin, Massachusetts, Mann was educated at Brown University and was admitted to the bar 1823. After serving in the US House of Representatives 1848–53, he became president of Antioch College 1853–59. He served in the Massachusetts House of Representatives 1827–33 and Massachusetts Senate 1835–37.

Logically considered, freedom and equality are mutually exclusive, just as society and the individual are mutually exclusive.

THOMAS MANN
Order of the Day, 'The War and the Future' 1942

Mann Thomas (1875–1955). German novelist and critic. He was concerned with the theme of the artist's relation to society. His first novel was *Buddenbrooks* 1901, which, followed by *Der Zauberberg/ The Magic Mountain* 1924, led to a Nobel prize 1929. Notable among his works of short fiction is 'Der Tod in Venedig/ Death in Venice' 1913.

Mann worked in an insurance office in Munich and on the staff of the periodical *Simplicissimus*. His opposition to the Nazi regime forced him to leave Germany and in 1940 he became a US citizen. Among his other works are a biblical tetralogy on the theme of Joseph and his brothers 1933–44, *Dr Faustus* 1947, *Die Bekenntnisse des Hochstaplers Felix Krull/ Confessions of Felix Krull, Confidence Trickster* 1954, and a number of short stories, including 'Tonio Kröger' 1903.

Suggested reading
Bürgin, H and Mayer, H O *Thomas Mann: A Chronicle of his Life* (1969)
Feuerlicht, I *Thomas Mann* (1968)
Heller, E *The Ironic German* (1958)
Mann, Thomas *Sketch of My Life* (1960)
Swales, M *Thomas Mann: A Study* (1980)

Mannerheim Carl Gustav Emil von (1867–1951). Finnish general and politician, leader of the conservative forces in the civil war 1917–18 and regent 1918–19. He commanded the Finnish army 1939–40 and 1941–44, and was president of Finland 1944–46.

After the Russian Revolution 1917, a Red (socialist) militia was formed in Finland with Russian backing, and independence was declared in Dec. The Red forces were opposed by a White (counter-revolutionary) army led by Mannerheim, who in 1918 crushed the socialists with German assistance. He was recalled from retirement 1939 to defend Finland against Soviet invasion, and gave the Soviets a hard fight before yielding. In 1941 Finland allied itself with Germany against the USSR but by 1944 it was obvious the Germans were losing. After leading the defence against Soviet invasion in two wars, he negotiated the peace settlement with the USSR and became president.

Manners family name of dukes of Rutland; seated at Belvoir Castle, Lincolnshire, England.

Mannesmann Reinhard (1856–1922). German ironfounder who invented a method of making seamless steel tubes, patented 1891.

Mannesmann was born in Remscheid, Westphalia, and joined the family ironworks. The idea behind the seamless tube had been conceived by his father in 1860. One of the first Mannesmann plants was installed in Swansea, South Wales, 1887. In 1893 the Mannesmannröhrenwerke Aktiengesellschaft was formed. Mannesmann also formed a company 1908 to exploit mineral resources in Morocco, but was forced by the French to withdraw.

The Mannesmann process involved the passing of a furnace-heated bar between two rotating rolls. Because of their geometrical configuration, the rolls drew the bar forward and at the same time produced tensions in the hot metal that caused it to tear apart at the centre. A stationary, pointed mandrel caused the ingot of metal to open out and form a tube.

Mannheim Karl (1893–1947). Hungarian sociologist who settled in the UK 1933. In *Ideology and Utopia* 1929 he argued that all knowledge, except in mathematics and physics, is ideological, a reflection of class interests and values; that there is therefore no such thing as objective knowledge or absolute truth.

Mannheim distinguished between ruling-class ideologies and those of utopian or revolutionary groups, arguing that knowledge is created by a continual power struggle between rival groups and ideas. Later works such as *Man and Society* 1940 analysed contemporary mass society in terms of its fragmentation and susceptibility to extremist ideas and totalitarian governments.

Manning Henry Edward (1808–1892). English priest, one of the leaders of the Oxford Movement. In 1851 he was converted from the Church of England to Roman Catholicism, and in 1865 became archbishop of Westminster. He was created a cardinal 1875.

Manning left the Colonial Office for the Church of England, becoming archdeacon of Chichester 1840. He founded in 1857 the congregation of the Oblates of St Charles Borromeo. In 1875 he held an ardent dispute with the Liberal leader W E Gladstone on the question of papal infallibility.

'This,' she thought, 'is marriage: knowing too much about each other.'

OLIVIA MANNING
Battle Lost and Won ch 3 1978

Manning Olivia Mary (1908–1980). English novelist. Among her books are the semi-autobiographical series set during World War II. These include *The Great Fortune* 1960, *The Spoilt City* 1962, and *Friends and Heroes* 1965, forming the 'Balkan trilogy', and a later 'Levant trilogy'.

Mannix Daniel (1864–1963). Australian Roman Catholic prelate, born in Ireland. He was noted for his spirited demands that Catholics be given a greater share of wealth and political power in Australia, for his opposition to mixed marriages and birth control, and for his support of the Easter rebellion in Ireland. He was outspoken in his opposition to conscription during the referenda of 1916 and 1917 and held huge public rallies attracting up to 100,000 people. Mannix was archbishop of Melbourne 1917–63.

Manning *English novelist Olivia Manning. Her experiences in Bucharest, Greece, and Egypt inspired the Balkan and Levant trilogies, which were adapted for television under the title* Fortunes of War.

Manoel two kings of Portugal:

Manoel I (1469–1521). King of Portugal from 1495, when he succeeded his uncle John II (1455–1495). He was known as 'the Fortunate', because his reign was distinguished by the discoveries made by Portuguese navigators and the expansion of the Portuguese empire.

Manoel II (1889–1932). King of Portugal 1908–10. He ascended the throne on the assassination of his father, Carlos I, but was driven out by a revolution 1910, and lived in England.

Man Ray see ◊Ray.

Mansart Jules Hardouin. See ◊Hardouin-Mansart, Jules.

Mansell Nigel (1954–   ). English motor-racing driver. He started his Formula One career with Lotus 1980. Runner-up in the world championship on two occasions, he became world champion 1992 and in the same year announced his retirement from Formula One racing, having won a British record of 30 Grand Prix races.

He joined the Newman-Haas team 1993 to compete in the PPG IndyCar championship series and won the championship in his debut season. He returned to Formula One racing in selected races 1994, and signed for Mercedes-McLaren 1995. However, after experiencing problems with Mercedes-McLaren cars during the 1995 season, he parted company with the team.

Mansfield Jayne. Stage name of Vera Jayne Palmer (1933–1967). US actress. She had a short career as a kind of living parody of Marilyn Monroe in films including *The Girl Can't Help It* 1956 and *Will Success Spoil Rock Hunter?* 1957.

Whenever I prepare for a journey I prepare as though for death. Should I never return, all is in order.

KATHERINE MANSFIELD
Journal 29 January 1922

Mansfield Katherine. Pen name of Kathleen Beauchamp (1888–1923). New Zealand writer. She lived most of her life in England. Her delicate artistry emerges not only in her volumes of short stories – such as *In a German Pension* 1911, *Bliss* 1920, and *The Garden Party* 1923 – but also in her 'Letters' and *Journal*.

Born near Wellington, New Zealand, she was educated in London, to which she returned after a two-year visit home, where she published her earliest stories. She married the critic John Middleton Murry 1913.

Suggested reading
Alpers, Antony *The Life of Katherine Mansfield* (1980)
Boddy, Gillian *Katherine Mansfield: The Woman and the Writer* (1988)
Mansfield, Katherine *The Letters and Journals of Katherine Mansfield: A Selection* (edited by C K Stead 1977)
Tomalin, Claire *Katherine Mansfield: A Secret Life* (1987)

Manson Patrick (1844–1922). Scottish physician who showed that insects are responsible for the spread of diseases like elephantiasis and malaria. KCMG 1903. He spent 23 years in practice in the Far East. Returning to the UK 1892, he founded the School of Tropical Medicine in London 1899, and taught there until 1914.

In 1876 Manson began studying filariasis infection in humans. Having gained a clear idea of the life history of the invading parasite, he correctly conjectured that the disease was transmitted by an insect, a common brown mosquito. He went on to study other parasitic infections; for instance, the fluke parasite, ringworms, and guinea worm. He developed the thesis that malaria was also spread by a mosquito 1894; the work that proved this was carried out by Manson and British physician Ronald Ross.

Mansoor Mallikarjun (1910–1992). Indian classical singer. He dominated Indian vocal music for almost 50 years, singing a combination of Hindustani (north Indian) and Carnatic (south Indian) music.

He made his first recording in 1933, for HMV, and by the 1940s his fame had spread across the whole of India. He became a music adviser to All India Radio 1960. In 1962 he won the Karnataka Sangeet Natak Academy Award, which he was to win on three further occasions. A few months before he died he received the Padma Vibhushana, one of India's highest decorations.

Manstein Erich von ('Fritz'). Adopted name of Erich von Lewinski (1887–1973). German field marshal. He served as Chief of Staff to von Rundstedt in the Polish and French campaigns 1939–40 and commanded a Panzer corps in the invasion of the USSR 1941. He was given the task of capturing Leningrad Aug 1942, but was then moved to Army Group Don and ordered to relieve the German 6th Army trapped in Stalingrad. He was unable to help the trapped army but dealt with the subsequent Soviet offensive and captured Kharkov. He fought at the Battle of Kursk July 1943, after which he conducted the withdrawal of Army Group South. After a series of arguments with Hitler over this withdrawal he was dismissed and took no further part in the war. He was imprisoned as a war criminal 1945–53.

Mantegna Andrea (*c.* 1431–1506). Italian Renaissance painter and engraver, active chiefly in Padua and Mantua, where some of his frescoes remain. Paintings such as *The Agony in the Garden* about 1455 reveal a dramatic, linear style, mastery of perspective, and strongly Classical architectural detail.

Mantegna was born in Vicenza. He was brought up and trained by Francesco Squarcione at Padua, his master entering him in the guild of painters before he was eleven. Like Squarcione, and indeed all the north Italian artists who saw Donatello's work at Padua, he was later impressed by the great sculptor's achievement as well as by the paintings of the Florentines, Uccello and Filippo Lippi. The spirit of Florence is joined with that of Venice in Mantegna, for he was also influenced in style by Jacopo Bellini, whose daughter Lodovisia he married 1453.

Early paintings which won him fame were his frescoes in the Eremitani church at Padua, 1449–54. These were mainly destroyed in World War II, though two sections moved to Venice remain. The nature of his art about this period can be intimately studied in the panel *The Agony in the Garden* (National Gallery, London), splendidly designed as a formal composition. The background was probably taken in essentials from a drawing by Jacopo Bellini, but the sculptural quality, the effects of perspective and foreshortening, and the austerity of form, were Mantegna's own.

Principal later pictures were the *Lamentation* (Milan, Brera), with its dramatic foreshortening of the body of the dead Christ, the *Madonna della Vittoria* (Louvre), celebrating a Mantuan victory over the French, and two paintings intended for the boudoir of Isabella d'Este at Mantua, the *Parnassus* and *Virtue triumphant over Vice* (Louvre), in which Mantegna shows a graceful fancy strikingly different from his usual austerity. They show how little he was a man of set formulas. As an engraver he was highly original in the style and straight-line shading of his religious and mythological copperplates.

Mantle Mickey Charles (1931–1995). US baseball player. Signed by the New York Yankees, he broke into the major leagues 1951. A powerful switch-hitter (able to bat with either hand), he also excelled as a centre-fielder. In 1956 he won baseball's Triple Crown, leading the American League in batting average, home runs, and runs batted in. He retired 1969 after 18 years with the Yankees and seven World Series championships.

Manutius or Manuzio, Aldus (1449–1515). Italian printer, established in Venice (which he made the publishing centre of Europe) from 1490; he introduced italic type and was the first to print books in Greek.

Manzoni Alessandro, Count (1785–1873). Italian poet and novelist. He was the author of the historical romance *I promessi sposi/The Betrothed* 1825–27, set in Spanish-occupied Milan during the 17th century. He is regarded as the greatest Italian novelist although later writers have often avoided his extreme romanticism. Verdi's *Requiem* commemorates him.

Manzù Giacomo (1908–1991). Italian sculptor. From the 1930s, he worked mostly in bronze. Although a left-wing agnostic, he received many religious commissions, including the *Door of Death* 1964 for St Peter's basilica, Rome, and a portrait bust of Pope John XXIII 1963. His figures reveal a belief in the innate dignity of the human form.

Mao Tse-tung alternative transcription of ◊Mao Zedong.

Mao Zedong or Mao Tse-tung (1893–1976). Chinese political leader and Marxist theoretician. A founder of the Chinese Communist Party (CCP) 1921, Mao soon emerged as its leader. He organized the Long March 1934–35 and the war of liberation 1937–49, following which he established a People's Republic and communist rule in China; he headed the CCP and government until his death. His influence diminished with the failure of his 1958–60 Great Leap Forward, but he emerged dominant again during the 1966–69 Cultural Revolution.

Mao adapted communism to Chinese conditions, as set out in the *Little Red Book*.

Mao, son of a peasant farmer in Hunan province, was once library assistant at Beijing University and a headteacher in Changsha. He became chief of CCP propaganda under the Guomindang (nationalist) leader Sun Yat-sen (Sun Zhong Shan) until dismissed by Sun's successor Chiang Kai-shek (Jiang Jie Shi). In 1931–34 Mao set up a communist republic in Jiangxi and, together with Zhu De, marshalled the Red Army in the Long March to Shaanxi to evade Guomindang suppressive tactics. In Yan'an 1936–47, he built up a people's republic and married his third wife Jiang Qing 1939. CCP head from 1935, Mao set up an alliance with the nationalist forces 1936–45 aimed at repelling the Japanese invaders. Civil war with the Guomindang was renewed from 1946 to 1949, when Mao defeated them at Nanjing and established the People's Republic and CCP rule under his leadership. During the civil war, he successfully employed mobile, rural-based guerrilla tactics. Mao served as party head until his death Sept 1976 and as state president until 1959. After the damages of the Cultural Revolution, the Great Helmsman, as he was called, worked with his prime minister Zhou Enlai to oversee reconstruction.

Mao's writings and thoughts dominated the functioning of the People's Republic 1949–76. He wrote some 2,300 publications, comprising 3 million words; 740 million copies of his *Quotations* have been printed. Adapting communism to Chinese conditions, he stressed the need for rural rather than urban-based revolutions in Asia, for reducing rural–urban differences, and for perpetual revolution to prevent the emergence of new élites. Mao helped precipitate the Sino-Soviet split 1960 and was a firm advocate of a nonaligned Third World strategy. After 1978, the leadership of Deng Xiaoping reinterpreted Maoism and criticized its policy excesses, but many of Mao's ideas remain valued.

Suggested reading

Garfinkel, B *Mao Tse-tung* (1985)
Li, Zhisui *The Private Life of Chairman Mao* (1994)
Rule, P *Mao Zedong* (1984)
Salisbury, H *The Long March* (1984)
Terrill, R *Mao: A Biography* (1980)
Wilson, D *Mao, the People's Emperor* (1979)

Map Walter (*c.* 1140–*c.* 1209). Welsh cleric and satirist in the service of Henry II as an itinerant justice in England; envoy to Alexander III of Scotland. His *De Nugis Curialium* was a collection of gossip and scandal from royal and ecclesiastical courts.

Mapplethorpe Robert (1946–1989). US art photographer. He was known for his use of racial and homo-erotic imagery in chiefly fine platinum prints. He developed a style of polished elegance in his gallery art works, whose often culturally forbidden subject matter caused controversy.

Suggested reading

Danto, Arthur C *Playing with the Edge: The Photographic Achievement of Robert Mapplethorpe* (1996)
Morriscoe, Patricia *Mapplethorpe* (1995)

Maradona Diego Armando (1960–). Argentine footballer. One of the outstanding players of the 1980s, he won over 80 international caps, and helped his country to three successive World Cup finals. He was South American footballer of the year 1979 and 1980. Despite his undoubted talent, his career was dogged by a series of drugs scandals, notably his disqualification from the 1994 World Cup after failing a drugs test.

Maradona played for Argentinos Juniors and Boca Juniors before leaving South America for Barcelona, Spain, 1982 for a transfer fee of approximately £5 million. He moved to Napoli, Italy, for £6.9 million 1984, and contributed to their first Italian League title. In the 1986 World Cup he appeared illegally to use his hand to score a winning goal – his infamous 'hand of God' incident. His Italian league career ended in disgrace in March 1991 when he was tested positive for cocaine after a match and banned from football for 15 months. He joined Seville, Spain, 1992 and returned to Argentina 1993 to play for Newell's Old Boys. Recalled to the national team for the 1994 World Cup, he failed a drug test halfway through the tournament and was immediately withdrawn from the team and suspended from all football pending a FIFA hearing.

The goal was scored a little bit by the hand of God, another bit by the head of Maradona.

DIEGO MARADONA
after scoring a doubtful goal in the World Cup 1986

Marat Jean Paul (1743–1793). French Revolutionary leader and journalist. He was elected to the National Convention 1792, where he carried on a long struggle with the right-wing Girondins, ending in their overthrow May 1793. In July he was murdered by Charlotte Corday, a member of the Girondins.
Suggested reading
Censer, J *Prelude to Power* (1976)
Gottschalk, Louis *Jean Paul Marat: A Study in Radicalism* (1927, rep 1967)
Schama, Simon *Citizens: A Chronicle of the French Revolution* (1989)

Marc Franz (1880–1916). German Expressionist painter. He was associated with Wassily Kandinsky in founding the *Blaue Reiter* movement. Animals played an essential part in his view of the world, and bold semi-abstracts of red and blue animals, particularly horses, are characteristic of his work.

Marconi Italian physicist and inventor Guglielmo Marconi shown working on one of his wireless telegraphy sets. The apparatus shown consists of a 10 in induction coil spart transmitter (right), a morse inker and a 'grasshopper' key (centre). Marconi spent the last sixteen years of his life living and working on his private yacht, the Elettra, and was a staunch supporter of Mussolini during the 1930s. (Image Select)

He studied at Munich, and after travel to Italy and Paris was influenced by Post-Impressionist art, applying its lessons of colour and design to animal painting and in particular a series of horses. Acquaintance with Kandinsky and Macke 1910 led to his adopting their free use of brilliant colour, and in 1912 a meeting with Delaunay in Paris added a Cubist influence, as in his *Roes in the Wood*, 1913–14 (Karlsruhe). His animals were subjective and symbolic creations rather than studies of nature and in this sense he was an Expressionist. The trend of his development, cut short by war, was towards abstraction. He was killed at Verdun in World War I.

Marceau Marcel (1923–). French mime artist. He is the creator of the clown-harlequin Bip and mime sequences such as 'Youth, Maturity, Old Age, and Death'.

Marchais Georges René Louis (1920–). Leader of the French Communist Party (PCF) 1972–94. Under his leadership, the party committed itself to a 'transition to socialism' by democratic means and entered into a union of the left with the Socialist Party (PS). This was severed 1977, and the PCF returned to a more orthodox pro-Moscow line, after which its share of the vote decreased.

Marchais joined the PCF 1947 (having worked for much of World War II in the Messerschmidt armaments factory in Germany) and worked his way up through the party organization to become its general secretary. He was a presidential candidate 1981, and sanctioned the PCF's participation in the Mitterrand government 1981–84. He remained leader of the PCF despite a fall in its national vote from 21% 1973 to 10% 1986. In Jan 1994 he resigned and was replaced by his protegé, Robert Hue.

Marchand Jean Baptiste (1863–1934). French general and explorer. In 1898, he headed an expedition in Africa from the French Congo, which occupied the town of Fashoda (now Kodok) on the White Nile. The subsequent arrival of British troops under Kitchener resulted in a crisis that nearly led to war between Britain and France.

Marcian considered wealth to be the ability to provide for the needy and to safeguard the possessions of those with property.

Evagrius on MARCIAN
in *Church History* bk 2, ch 1

Marcian (396–457). Eastern Roman emperor 450–457. He was a general who married Pulcheria, sister of Theodosius II; he became emperor on Theodosius' death. He convened the Council of Chalcedon (the fourth Ecumenical Council of the Christian Church) 451 and refused to pay tribute to Attila the Hun.

Marciano Rocky (Rocco Francis Marchegiano) (1923–1969). US boxer, world heavyweight champion 1952–56. He retired after 49 professional fights, the only heavyweight champion to retire undefeated.

Born in Brockton, Massachussetts, he was known as the 'Brockton Blockbuster'. He knocked out 43 of his 49 opponents. Marciano was killed in a plane crash.
Suggested reading
Libby, Bill *Rocky: The Story of a Champion* (1971)
Skehan, Everett *Rocky Marciano* (1977)

Marconi Guglielmo (1874–1937). Italian electrical engineer and pioneer in the invention and development of radio. In 1895 he achieved radio communication over more than a mile, and in England 1896 he conducted successful experiments that led to the formation of the company that became Marconi's Wireless Telegraph Company Ltd. He shared the Nobel Prize for Physics 1909.

After reading about radio waves, Marconi built a device to convert them into electrical signals. He then tried to transmit and receive radio waves over increasing distances. In 1898 he successfully transmitted signals across the English Channel, and in 1901 established communication with St John's, Newfoundland, from Poldhu in

Cornwall, and in 1918 with Australia. Marconi's later inventions included the magnetic detector 1902, horizontal direction telegraphy 1905, and the continuous wave system 1912. During World War I he worked on the development of very short wavelength beams. Marconi was an Italian delegate to the Versailles peace conference 1919 after World War I.

Marco Polo see ◊Polo, Marco.

Marcos Ferdinand Edralin (1917–1989). Filipino right-wing politician, president from 1965 to 1986. He was backed by the USA when in power, but in 1988 US authorities indicted him and his wife Imelda Marcos for racketeering and embezzlement.

Marcos was convicted while a law student 1939 of murdering a political opponent of his father, but eventually secured his own acquittal. In World War II he was a guerrilla fighter, survived the Japanese prison camps, and became president 1965.

His regime became increasingly repressive, with secret pro-Marcos groups terrorizing and executing his opponents. He was overthrown and exiled 1986 by a nonviolent 'people's power' movement, led by Corazon Aquino, widow of a murdered opposition leader, which obtained international and army support. A US grand jury investigating Marcos and his wife alleged that they had embezzled over $100 million from the government of the Philippines, received bribes, and defrauded US banks. Marcos was too ill to stand trial.

Marcos Imelda Romualdez (1930–). Filipino politician and socialite, wife of Ferdinand Marcos, in exile 1986–91. She was acquitted 1990 of defrauding US banks. Under indictment for misuse of Philippine state funds, she returned to Manila in Nov 1991 and was an unsuccessful candidate in the 1992 presidential elections. She was convicted of corruption and sentenced to 18–24 years imprisonment 1993, but remained free on bail. In May 1995 she was elected to the Phillipines' House of Representatives by a landslide majority.

After her husband's death 1989, Imelda Marcos stood trial in New York City in answer to charges of concealing ownership of US property and other goods, purchased with stolen Philippine-government funds. She was acquitted, her lawyer claiming the responsibility had lain solely with her husband. In 1991, the government of the Philippines lifted its ban on Imelda Marcos returning to her homeland in the hope of recouping an estimated $350 million from frozen Marcos accounts in Swiss banks. Simultaneously, they filed 11 charges of tax evasion against her and 18 against her children.

Marcus Aurelius Antoninus adopted name of Marcus Annius Verus (AD 121–180). Roman emperor from 161 and Stoic philosopher. He wrote the philosophical *Meditations*. Born in Rome, he was adopted by his uncle, the emperor Antoninus Pius, whom he succeeded in 161. He conceded an equal share in the rule to Lucius Verus (died 169). Marcus Aurelius spent much of his reign warring against the Germanic tribes and died in Pannonia, where he had gone to drive back the invading Marcomanni.

Suggested reading
Birley, A R *Marcus Aurelius* (1987)
Rist, J M *The Stoics* (1978)

Marcuse Herbert (1898–1979). German political philosopher, in the USA from 1934; his theories combining Marxism and Freudianism influenced radical thought in the 1960s. His books include *One-Dimensional Man* 1964.

Marcuse preached the overthrow of the existing social order by using the system's very tolerance to ensure its defeat; he was not an advocate of violent revolution. A refugee from Hitler's Germany, he became professor at the University of California at San Diego 1965.

Suggested reading
Bleich, Harold *The Philosophy of Herbert Marcuse* (1977)
Lind, Peter *Marcuse and Freedom* (1985)
MacIntyre, Alasdair *Herbert Marcuse: An Exposition and a Polemic* (1970)

Margaret (called 'the Maid of Norway') (1283–1290). Queen of Scotland from 1285, the daughter of Eric II, King of Norway, and

Princess Margaret of Scotland. When only two years old she became queen of Scotland on the death of her grandfather, Alexander III, but died in the Orkneys on the voyage from Norway to her kingdom.

Her great-uncle Edward I of England arranged her marriage to his son Edward, later Edward II. Edward declared himself overlord of Scotland by virtue of the marriage treaty, and 20 years of civil war and foreign intervention followed.

Margaret Rose (1930–). Princess of the UK, younger daughter of George VI and sister of Elizabeth II. In 1960 she married Anthony Armstrong-Jones, later created Lord Snowdon, but they were divorced 1978. Their children are David, Viscount Linley (1961–) and Lady Sarah Armstrong-Jones (1964–).

She never learnt to play the part of mediator, or to raise the crown above the fierce faction fight that constantly raged round Henry VI's court.
R F Henderson on MARGARET OF ANJOU
Dictionary of National Biography

Margaret of Anjou (1430–1482). Queen of England from 1445, wife of Henry VI of England. After the outbreak of the Wars of the Roses 1455, she acted as the leader of the Lancastrians, but was defeated and captured at the battle of Tewkesbury 1471 by Edward IV.

Her one object had been to secure the succession of her son, Edward (born 1453), who was killed at Tewkesbury. After five years' imprisonment Margaret was allowed in 1476 to return to her native France, where she died in poverty.

Margaret, St (c. 1045–1093). Queen of Scotland, the granddaughter of King Edmund Ironside of England. She went to Scotland after the Norman Conquest, and soon after married Malcolm III. The marriage of her daughter Matilda to Henry I united the Norman and English royal houses.

Through her influence, the Lowlands, until then purely Celtic, became largely anglicized. She was canonized 1251 in recognition of her benefactions to the church.

Margrethe II (1940–). Queen of Denmark from 1972, when she succeeded her father Frederick IX. In 1967, she married the French diplomat Count Henri de Laborde de Monpezat, who took the title Prince Hendrik. Her heir is Crown Prince Frederick (1968–).

Marguerite of Navarre also known as Margaret d'Angoulême (1492–1549). Queen of Navarre from 1527, French poet, and author of the *Heptaméron* 1558, a collection of stories in imitation of Boccaccio's *Decameron*. The sister of Francis I of France, she was born in Angoulême. Her second husband 1527 was Henri d'Albret, king of Navarre.

I want to meet my God awake.
MARIA THERESA
Refusing to take a drug when dying 1780

Maria Theresa (1717–1780). Empress of Austria from 1740, when she succeeded her father, the Holy Roman emperor Charles VI; her claim to the throne was challenged and she became embroiled, first in the War of the Austrian Succession 1740–48, then in the Seven Years' War 1756–63; she remained in possession of Austria but lost Silesia.

She married her cousin Francis of Lorraine 1736, and on the death of her father became archduchess of Austria and queen of Hungary and Bohemia. Her claim was challenged by Charles of Bavaria, who was elected emperor 1742, while Frederick of Prussia occupied Silesia. The War of the Austrian Succession followed, in which Austria was allied with Britain, and Prussia with France; when it ended 1748, Maria Theresa retained her heritage, except that Frederick kept Silesia, while her husband had succeeded Charles as emperor 1745. Intent on recovering Silesia, she formed an alliance with France and Russia against Prussia; the Seven Years' War, which resulted, exhausted Europe and left the territorial position as before. After 1763 she pursued a consistently peaceful policy, concentrating on internal reforms; although her methods were despotic, she fostered education, codified the laws, and abolished torture. She also expelled the Jesuits. In these measures she was assisted by her son, Joseph II, who became emperor 1765, and succeeded her in the Habsburg domains.

Suggested reading

Crankshaw, Edward *Maria Theresa* (1970)

Pick, Robert *Maria Theresa: The Earlier Years* (1966)

Marie (1875–1938). Queen of Romania. She was the daughter of the duke of Edinburgh, second son of Queen Victoria of England, and married Prince Ferdinand of Romania in 1893 (he was king 1922–27). She wrote a number of literary works, notably *Story of My Life* 1934–35. Her son Carol became king of Romania, and her daughters, Elisabeth and Marie, queens of Greece and Yugoslavia respectively.

Let them eat cake.

MARIE ANTOINETTE
Attributed remark, on being told that the poor had no bread

Marie Antoinette (1755–1793). Queen of France from 1774. She was the daughter of Empress Maria Theresa of Austria, and married Louis XVI of France 1770. Her reputation for extravagance helped provoke the French Revolution of 1789. She was tried for treason Oct 1793 and guillotined.

Marie Antoinette influenced her husband to resist concessions in the early days of the Revolution – for example, Mirabeau's plan for a constitutional settlement. She instigated the disastrous flight to Varennes, which discredited the monarchy, and welcomed foreign intervention against the Revolution, betraying French war strategy to the Austrians 1792.

Suggested reading

Haslip, J *Marie Antoinette* (1988)

Hearsey, J *Marie Antoinette* (1969)

Kamroff, O *Marie Antoinette* (1972)

Seward, D *Marie Antoinette* (1982)

Marie de France (*c.* 1150–1215). French poet. She is thought to have been the half-sister of Henry II of England, and abbess of Shaftesbury 1181–1215. She wrote *Lais* (verse tales that dealt with Celtic and Arthurian themes) and *Ysopet*, a collection of fables.

Marie de' Medici (1573–1642). Queen of France, wife of Henry IV from 1600, and regent (after his murder) for their son Louis XIII. She left the government to her favourites, the Concinis, until Louis XIII seized power and executed them 1617. She was banished but, after she led a revolt 1619, Richelieu effected her reconciliation with her son. When she attempted to oust him again 1630, she was exiled.

Marie Louise (1791–1847). Queen consort of Napoleon I from 1810 (after his divorce from Josephine), mother of Napoleon II. She was the daughter of Francis I of Austria and on Napoleon's fall returned with their son to Austria, where she was granted the duchy of Parma 1815.

Mariette Auguste Ferdinand François (1821–1881). French Egyptologist whose discoveries from 1850 included the 'temple' between the paws of the Sphinx. He founded the Egyptian Museum in Cairo.

Marin John (1870–1953). US painter. His seascapes in watercolour and oil were influenced by Impressionism. He visited Europe 1905–11 and began his paintings of the Maine coast 1914.

He is especially noted for his watercolours, in which the feeling of landscape or seascape is conveyed by forceful, cubistically broken shapes and patterns of colour. He began his career as an architect, studied painting in Philadelphia and New York and travelled much in Europe, 1905–11, subsequently settling in New Jersey. Many of his original inventions in watercolour were inspired by the coast of Maine and the streets of Manhattan.

Marinetti Filippo Tommaso Emilio (1876–1944). Italian author. In 1909 he published the first manifesto of Futurism, which called for a break with tradition in art, poetry, and the novel, and glorified the machine age.

Marinetti illustrated his theories in *Mafarka le futuriste: Roman africaine/Mafarka the Futurist: African novel* 1909. His best-known work is *Manifesto technico della letteratura futuristica/Technical Manifesto of Futurist Literature* 1912 (translated 1971). He also wrote plays, a volume on theatrical practice 1916, and a volume of poems *Guerra sola igiene del mondo/War the Only Hygiene of the World* 1915.

Marini Marino (1901–1980). Italian sculptor. Inspired by ancient art, he developed a distinctive horse-and-rider theme, reducing the forms to an elemental simplicity. He also produced fine portraits in bronze.

Marion Francis (*c.* 1732–1795). American military leader. He waged a successful guerrilla war against the British after the fall of Charleston 1780 during the American Revolution. Establishing his field headquarters in inaccessible areas, he became popularly known as the 'Swamp Fox'. He played a major role in the American victory at Eutaw Springs 1781.

Mariotte Edme (1620–1684). French physicist and priest known for his recognition in 1676 of Boyle's law about the inverse relationship of volume and pressure in gases, formulated by Irish physicist Robert Boyle 1672. He had earlier, in 1660, discovered the eye's blind spot.

We don't love qualities, we love persons; sometimes by reason of their defects as well as of their qualities.

JACQUES MARITAIN
Reflections on America ch 3 1958

Maritain Jacques (1882–1973). French philosopher. Originally a disciple of Henri Bergson, he later became the best-known of the neo-Thomists, applying the methods of Thomas Aquinas to contemporary problems.

Maritain distinguished three types of knowledge: scientific, metaphysical, and mystical. His works include *La philosophie bergsonienne/Bergsonian Philosophy* 1914 and *Introduction à la philosophie/Introduction to Philosophy* 1920.

Man, would you dare to kill Gaius Marius?

GAIUS MARIUS'
challenge to his German executioner.
Quoted in Plutarch *Life of Marius* ch 39.2

Marius Gaius (*c.* 157–86 BC). Roman general and politician. He was elected consul seven times, the first time in 107 BC. He defeated the Cimbri and the Teutons (Germanic tribes attacking Gaul and Italy) 102–101 BC. Marius tried to deprive Sulla of the command in the east against Mithridates and, as a result, civil war broke out 88 BC. Sulla marched on Rome, and Marius fled to Africa, but later returned and created a reign of terror in Rome.

Marivaux Pierre Carlet de Chamblain de (1688–1763). French novelist and dramatist. His sophisticated comedies include *Le Jeu de l'amour et du hasard/The Game of Love and Chance* 1730 and *Les Fausses Confidences/False Confidences* 1737; his novel *La Vie de Marianne/The Life of Marianne* 1731–41 has autobiographical elements. Marivaux gave the word *marivaudage* (oversubtle lovers' conversation) to the French language.

He was born and lived for most of his life in Paris, writing for both of the major Paris theatre companies, the Comédie Française and the Comédie Italienne, which specialized in commedia dell'arte.

Mark, St (lived 1st century AD). In the New Testament, Christian apostle and evangelist whose name is given to the second Gospel. It was probably written AD 65–70, and used by the authors of the first and third Gospels. He is the patron saint of Venice, and his emblem is a winged lion; feast day 25 April.

His first name was John, and his mother, Mary, was one of the first Christians in Jerusalem. He was a cousin of Barnabas, and accompanied Barnabas and Paul on their first missionary journey. He was a fellow worker with Paul in Rome, and later became Peter's interpreter after Paul's death. According to tradition he was the founder of the Christian church in Alexandria, and St Jerome says that he died and was buried there.

Pick up Mark and bring him with you, for I find him a useful assistant.

St Paul on ST MARK
the Bible, 2 Timothy 5:11

Mark Antony (Marcus Antonius) (c. 83–30 BC). Roman politician and soldier. He served under Julius Caesar in Gaul, and was consul with him in 44, when he tried to secure for Caesar the title of king. After Caesar's assassination, he formed the Second Triumvirate with Octavian (later Augustus) and Lepidus. In 42 he defeated Brutus and Cassius at Philippi. He took Egypt as his share of the empire and formed a liaison with Cleopatra, but in 40 he returned to Rome to marry Octavia, the sister of Octavian. In 32 the Senate declared war on Cleopatra, and Antony, who had combined forces with Cleopatra, was defeated by Octavian at the battle of Actium 31 BC. He returned to Egypt and committed suicide.

Cleopatra, I am grieved that such a commander as I should be found inferior to a woman in courage.

MARK ANTONY'S
reaction to the false news of Cleopatra's suicide.
Quoted in Plutarch *Antonius* ch 66.3

Markevich Igor (1912–1983). Russian-born conductor and composer. His austere ballet *L'Envol d'Icare/The Flight of Icarus* 1932 influenced Bartók. After World War II he concentrated on conducting, specializing in Russian and French composers 1880–1950.

Markham Beryl (1903–1986). British aviator who made the first solo flight from east to west across the Atlantic 1936. Her book about her Kenya childhood, *West With The Night* 1942 was a bestseller.

Markievicz Constance Georgina, Countess Markievicz (born Gore Booth) (1868–1927). Irish nationalist who married the Polish Count Markievicz 1900. Her death sentence for taking part in the Easter Rising of 1916 was commuted, and after her release from prison 1917 she was elected to the Westminster Parliament as a Sinn Féin candidate 1918 (technically the first British woman member of Parliament), but did not take her seat.

Markov Andrei Andreyevich (1856–1922). Russian mathematician, formulator of the Markov chain, an example of a stochastic (random) process.

Markov was born in Ryazan, near Moscow, and studied at St Petersburg, where he became professor 1893. At the same time he became involved in liberal political movements. He refused to accept tsarist decorations and in 1907 renounced his membership of the electorate when the government dissolved the fledgling representative *duma*, or parliament.

A Markov chain may be described as a chance process that possesses a special property, so that its future may be predicted from the present state of affairs just as accurately as if the whole of its past history were known. Markov believed that the only real examples of his chains were to be found in literary texts, and he illustrated his discovery by calculating the alteration of vowels and consonants in Pushkin's *Eugene Onegin*. Markov chains are now used in the social sciences, atomic physics, quantum theory, and genetics.

Markov Georgi (1929–1978). Bulgarian playwright and novelist

who fled to the UK 1971; he was assassinated by being jabbed with a poisoned umbrella.

When I joined Diaghilev I was in socks, and very naive and somehow he wanted to keep me that way.

ALICIA MARKOVA
quoted in 'Prima Alicia' in *Guardian* 5 Feb 1989

Markova Alicia. Adopted name of Lilian Alicia Marks (1910–   ). English ballet dancer. She danced with Diaghilev's company 1925–29, was the first resident ballerina of the Vic-Wells Ballet 1933–35, partnered Anton Dolin in their own Markova–Dolin Ballet Company 1935–38, and danced with the Ballets Russes de Monte Carlo 1938–41, American Ballet Theater, USA, 1941–46, and the London Festival Ballet 1950–52. A dancer of delicacy and lightness, she is associated with the great classical ballets such as *Giselle*.

She created a number of roles in Frederick Ashton's early ballets, such as *Façade* 1931. DBE 1963.

Marks Simon, 1st Baron Marks of Broughton (1888–1964). English chain-store magnate. His father, Polish immigrant Michael Marks, had started a number of 'penny bazaars' with Yorkshireman Tom Spencer 1887; Simon Marks entered the business 1907 and built up a national chain of Marks and Spencer stores. Knighted 1944, baron 1961.

He never fought a battle that he did not win, and never besieged a place he did not take.

Edward Creasy on JOHN CHURCHILL, 1ST DUKE OF MARLBOROUGH
The Fifteen Decisive Battles of the World 1851

Marlborough John Churchill, 1st Duke of Marlborough (1650–1722). English soldier, created a duke 1702 by Queen Anne. He was granted land in Oxfordshire in recognition of his services, which included defeating the French army outside Vienna in the Battle of Blenheim 1704, during the War of the Spanish Succession. Blenheim Palace was built on the Oxfordshire estate.

In 1688 he deserted his patron, James II, for William of Orange, but in 1692 fell into disfavour for Jacobite intrigue.

He had married Sarah Jennings (1660–1744), confidante of the future Queen Anne, who created him a duke on her accession. He achieved further victories in Belgium at the battles of Ramillies 1706 and Oudenaarde 1708, and in France at Malplaquet 1709. However, the return of the Tories to power and his wife's quarrel with the queen led to his dismissal 1711 and his flight to Holland to avoid charges of corruption. He returned 1714.

Marley Bob (Robert Nesta) (1945–1981). Jamaican reggae singer and songwriter. A Rastafarian, his songs, many of which were topical and political, popularized reggae worldwide in the 1970s. They include 'Get Up, Stand Up' 1973 and 'No Woman No Cry' 1974; his albums include *Natty Dread* 1975 and *Exodus* 1977.

The core of Marley's band the Wailers was formed around 1960, and they began making local hits – 'Simmer Down' 1963, 'Rude Boy' 1965, 'Stir It Up' 1967, 'Trench Town Rock' 1971 – combining rock steady (a form of ska), soul, and rock influences. *Catch a Fire* 1972 was a seminal reggae album, but the international breakthrough came with *Burnin'* 1973, containing the song 'I Shot the Sheriff'. *Punky Reggae Party* 1977 was a nod to their British punk fans. Marley toured Africa 1978 and began to incorporate African elements in his music. His last album was *Uprising* 1980.

Oh it's a disgrace to see the human race / In a rat race / You got the horse race / You got the dog race / You got the human race.

Lyrics to BOB MARLEY's soul classic 'Rat Race'

Suggested reading
Boot, Adrian and Salewicz, Chris *Bob Marley: Songs of Freedom: A Biography* (1995)
White, Timothy *Catch a Fire* (1983)

Marlowe Christopher (1564–1593). English poet and dramatist. His work includes the blank-verse plays *Tamburlaine the Great c.* 1587, *The Jew of Malta c.* 1589, *Edward II* and *Dr Faustus*, both *c.* 1592, the poem *Hero and Leander* 1598, and a translation of Ovid's *Amores*.

Marlowe was born in Canterbury and educated at Cambridge University, where he is thought to have become a government agent. His life was turbulent, with a brief imprisonment in connection with a man's death in a brawl (of which he was cleared), and a charge of atheism (following statements by the dramatist Thomas Kyd under torture). He was murdered in a Deptford tavern, allegedly in a dispute over the bill, but it may have been a political killing.

Suggested reading
Knoll, R E *Christopher Marlowe* (1969)
Kocher, P H *Christopher Marlowe: A Study of His Thought, Learning and Character* (1962)
Leech, C *Christopher Marlowe* (1988)
Nicholl, Charles *The Murder of Christopher Marlowe* (1992)
Princiss, G *Christopher Marlowe* (1984)
Wraight, A D *In Search of Christopher Marlowe* (1993)

Was this the face that launch'd a thousand ships, / And burnt the topless towers of Ilium?

CHRISTOPHER MARLOWE
Doctor Faustus V i c. 1592

Marmontel Jean François (1723–1799). French novelist and dramatist. He wrote tragedies and libretti, and contributed to the *Encyclopédie*. In 1758 he obtained control of the journal *Le Mercure/ The Mercury*, in which his *Contes moraux/Moral Studies* 1761 appeared. Other works include *Bélisaire/Belisarius* 1767 and *Les Incas/The Incas* 1777.

Marmontel was appointed historiographer of France 1771, secretary to the Académie 1783, and professor of history at the Lycée 1786, but retired 1792 to write his *Mémoires d'un père/Memoirs of a Father* 1804.

Marot Clément (*c.* 1496–1544). French poet. He is known for his translation of the *Psalms* 1539–43. His graceful, witty style became a model for later writers of light verse.

Born at Cahors, he accompanied Francis I to Italy 1524 and was taken prisoner at Pavia; he was soon released, and by 1528 was a salaried member of the royal household. Suspected of heresy, he fled to Turin, where he died.

Marquand J(ohn) P(hillips) (1893–1960). US writer. Author of a series of stories featuring the Japanese detective Mr Moto, he later made his reputation with gently satirical novels of Boston society, including *The Late George Apley* 1937 (Pulitzer prize) and *H M Pulham, Esq* 1941.

Marquet Pierre Albert (1875–1947). French painter. His subjects were landscapes and Parisian scenes, chiefly the river Seine and its bridges. He was associated with Fauvism but soon developed a more conventional, naturalistic style.

He went to Paris 1890 and studied at the école des Beaux-Arts, later meeting Matisse, with whom he often painted on the banks of the Seine. In his many paintings of towns, harbours and rivers he showed a particular gift of simplification which seized unerringly upon the essentials in the scene before him.

Marquette Jacques (1637–1675). French Jesuit missionary and explorer. He went to Canada 1666, explored the upper lakes of the St Lawrence river, and in 1673 with Louis Jolliet (1645–1700), set out on a voyage down the Mississippi on which they made the first accurate record of its course. In 1674 he and two companions camped near the site of present-day Chicago, making them the first Europeans to live there.

Márquez Gabriel García. See ◊García Márquez, Colombian novelist.

Marquis Don(ald Robert Perry) (1878–1937). US author. He is chiefly known for his humorous writing, including *Old Soak* 1921, which portrays a hard-drinking comic, and *archy and mehitabel* 1927, verse adventures typewritten by a literary cockroach.

Marr David Courtenay (1945–1980). English psychologist who developed computer-based models of the visual system. Drawing on neurophysiology and psychology of vision, he applied his models to a number of issues, notably the problem of how objects in the perceptual field are represented within the brain. His findings are summarized in *Vision* 1982, published posthumously.

From 1975 he worked in the USA at the artificial-intelligence laboratory of the Massachusetts Institute of Technology.

Marriner Neville (1924–). English conductor and violinist. He founded the chamber orchestra known as the Academy of St Martin-in-the-Fields 1956. He is an authority on 17th- and 18th-century music, forming the Jacobean Ensemble with Thurston Dart to perform early music. Knighted 1985.

Marriott Steve (1947–1991). UK pop singer and guitarist. He was successful in the mid-1960s as lead singer with the Small Faces, a mod group; less successful with Humble Pie 1969–75; and subsequently reduced to playing the pub circuit. The Small Faces had a number-one hit in 1966 with 'All or Nothing'.

Marriott's show-business career began with the part of the Artful Dodger in the musical *Oliver!* His first recordings imitated Buddy Holly, and he was briefly in a band called the Moments before forming the Small Faces 1965 with Ronnie Lane, Ian McLagen, and Kenny Jones. They were popular on the London mod scene and soon had a hit with 'Whatcha Gonna Do About It?' 1965, followed by TV appearances on *Ready Steady Go!*, *Sha La La La Lee*, and *My Mind's Eye*. The band came third in a 1966 popularity poll after the Beatles and the Rolling Stones.

If you please, ma'am, it was a very little one.

FREDERICK MARRYAT
Mr Midshipman Easy (a servant's excuse for her illegitimate baby) 1836

Marryat Frederick 'Captain' (1792–1848). English naval officer and writer. Born in London, he entered the Royal Navy in 1806. He resigned from the Royal Navy in 1830 after the success of his first novel, *Frank Mildmay*. His adventure stories include *Peter Simple* 1834 and *Mr Midshipman Easy* 1836; he also wrote a series of children's books, including *Children of the New Forest* 1847.

Marsalis Branford (1960–). US saxophonist. Born in New Orleans, he was taught by his father Ellis Marsalis, and played alto in Art Blakey's Jazz Messengers 1981, alongside his brother Wynton Marsalis. He was tenor/soprano lead saxophonist on Wynton's 1982 world tour, and has since recorded with Miles Davis, Tina Turner, and Dizzy Gillespie. His first solo recording was *Scenes in the City* 1983.

Marsalis Wynton (1961–). US trumpet player. He has recorded both classical and jazz music. He was a member of Art Blakey's Jazz Messengers 1980–82 and also played with Miles Davis before forming his own quintet. At one time this included his brother Branford Marsalis on saxophone.

Marsh (Edith) Ngaio (1899–1982). New Zealand detective fiction writer. Her first detective novel *A Man Lay Dead* 1934 introduced her protagonist Chief Inspector Roderick Alleyn. DBE 1966.

Originally an actress, and later a theatre producer, she went to England 1928 and worked as an interior decorator.

Suggested reading
Lewis, Margaret *Ngaio Marsh* (1991)
Marsh, Ngaio *Black Beech and Honeydew* (autobiography) (1965)

Marsh Othniel Charles (1831–1899). US palaeontologist. As official palaeontologist for the US Geological Survey from 1882, he identified many previously unknown fossil species and was an early devotee of Charles Darwin. He wrote *Odontornithes* 1880, *Dinocerata* 1884, and *Dinosaurs of North America* 1896.

As first professor of palaeontology in the USA at the Yale faculty, he mounted fossil-hunting expeditions to the West from 1870. He served as president of the American Academy of Sciences 1883–95.

Marsh Rodney William (1947–   ). Australian cricketer who holds the world record for a wicket-keeper with 355 dismissals in Test cricket. A Western Australian, he originally played for his state as a batsman. As wicket-keeper, he claimed 355 victims in 96 tests from 1970 to 1984, many from the bowling of Dennis Lillee. He was the first player to reach a Test double of 3,000 runs and 300 dismissals.

Marshall Alan (1902–1984). Australian novelist and short-story writer. He is best known for his childhood autobiography *I Can Jump Puddles* 1955, the story of his adjustment as a young boy to paralysis after he was crippled by polio at the age of six. The book has sold more than three million copies, was produced as an award-winning film in Czechoslovakia in 1970 and as a television series in Australia in 1980. His collections of short stories include 'Tell Us About the Turkey Jo' 1946 and 'How's Andy Going?' 1956.

Marshall Alfred (1842–1924). English economist, a pioneer of neoclassical economics. He stressed the importance of supply and demand for the determination of prices in markets, introducing the concept of elasticity of demand relative to price. His ideas are set out in *Principles of Economics* 1890.

Marshall derived the relationship between demand for a product and its price from the concept of marginal utility, the extra satisfaction gained by a consumer from an additional purchase.

Marshall suggested that consumers will stop increasing consumption of a product when the price they have to pay is greater than the marginal utility derived from it. Since marginal utility declines as more is consumed, the demand for a product falls as price rises. From this a graph of the demand curve could be drawn, showing how quantity demanded varies with price. The term 'elasticity' was used by Marshall to denote the response of demand to changes in price. On the supply side, higher prices are needed to persuade firms to increase output. The market price is determined where the

demand curve and supply curve intersect. Marshall was professor of economics at Cambridge 1885–1908.
Suggested reading
Reisman, D *Alfred Marshall* (1987)

Marshall George Catlett (1880–1959). US general and diplomat. He was army Chief of Staff in World War II, secretary of state 1947–49, and secretary of defence Sept 1950–Sept 1951. He foresaw the inevitability of US involvement in the war and prepared the army well for it. He initiated the *Marshall Plan* 1947 and received the Nobel Peace Prize 1953.

Marshall John (1755–1835). US politician and jurist. Born in Prince William (now Faquier) County, Virginia, Marshall served intermittently in the Continental Army until 1780 and then studied law. As a Federalist, he served in the Virginia state legislature and 1797 became a minister to France. He held office in the US House of Representatives 1799–1800 and was secretary of state 1800–01. As chief justice of the US Supreme Court 1801–35, he established the independence of the Court and the supremacy of federal over state law, and his opinions became universally accepted interpretations of the US Constitution.

Marshall John Ross (1912–1988). New Zealand National Party politician, notable for his negotiations of a free-trade agreement with Australia. He was deputy to K J Holyoake as prime minister and succeeded him Feb–Nov 1972. GBE 1974.

Marshall Thurgood (1908–1993). US jurist and civil-rights leader. As US Supreme Court justice from 1967, he frequently presided over landmark civil rights cases such as *Brown* v *Board of Education* 1954. In 1954, he led the Supreme Court to abandon the 'separate but equal' doctrine and forbid states from establishing separate schooling for black and white pupils. The first black associate justice, he was a strong voice for civil and individual rights throughout his career.

Born in Baltimore, Maryland, USA, Marshall received a law degree from Howard University 1933. Active in civil rights, he was named director of the National Association for the Advancement of Colored People (NAACP) Legal Defense and Education Fund 1940. He was named to the US Court of Appeals 1961 and served as US solicitor general 1965–67. In 1967 President Johnson appointed him to the US Supreme Court.

Marshall William Raine (1865–1939). British general. He served in India 1897–98, and in the South African war 1899–1902 where he was wounded. In 1915 he was given command of the 87th Brigade which he led at Gallipoli. He later commanded a division, and was made a corps commander in Mesopotamia Sept 1916. On the sudden death of General Maude Nov 1917, he assumed overall command in the area and successfully completed the campaign. KCB 1917.

Marsilius of Padua (*c.* 1270–*c.* 1342). Italian scholar and jurist. Born in Padua, he studied and taught at Paris and in 1324 collaborated with John of Jandun (*c.* 1286–1328) in writing the *Defensor pacis/Defender of the Peace*, a plea for the subordination of the ecclesiastical to the secular power and for the right of the people to choose their own government. He played a part in the establishment of the Roman republic 1328 and was made archbishop of Milan.

Marston John (1576–1634). English satirist and dramatist. His early plays *Antonio and Mellida* and the tragic *Antonio's Revenge* 1599 were followed by the comedies *The Malcontent* 1604 and *The Dutch Courtesan* 1605. Marston also collaborated with dramatists George Chapman and Ben Jonson in *Eastward Ho!* 1605, which satirized the Scottish followers of James I, and for which the authors were imprisoned.

Martens Conrad (1801–1878). Australian landscape painter. In 1832–34 he was topographer on the *Beagle* with Charles Darwin. He settled in Sydney 1835 and there produced a large number of drawings, watercolours, and oil paintings, mostly of the harbour, such as *Sydney from Vaucluse* 1864 (Dixson Galleries, Sydney) but also of

Marsalis US virtuoso saxophonist Branford Marsalis. He has recorded with jazz greats Miles Davis and Dizzy Gillespie as well as pop stars Sting and Tina Turner. He has recorded arrangements of classical pieces by French and Russian composers with the English Chamber Orchestra.

the Blue Mountains, Illawarra and south coast regions of New South Wales and of the Darling Downs in Queensland.

Martens Wilfried (1936–). Prime minister of Belgium 1979–92, member of the Social Christian Party (CVP). He was president of the Dutch-speaking CVP 1972–79 and, as prime minister, headed several coalition governments in the period 1979–92, when he was replaced by Jean-Luc Dehaene heading a new coalition.

Martí José Julian (1853–1895). Cuban revolutionary. Active in the Cuban independence movement from boyhood, he was deported to Spain 1871, returning 1878. Exiled again for continued opposition, he fled to the USA 1880, from where he organized resistance to Spanish rule. Martí was chief of the Cuban Revolutionary Party formed 1892, and united Cubans in exile. He was killed in battle at Dos Ríos, soon after proclaiming the uprising which led to Cuban independence. In 1959 Fidel Castro cited him as the 'intellectual author' of the revolution, and he remains a national hero.

Martial (Marcus Valerius Martialis) (*c.* AD 41–*c.* 104). Latin poet and epigrammatist. Born in Bilbilis, Spain, Martial settled in Rome AD 64, where he lived a life of poverty and dependence. His poetry, often obscene, is keenly observant of all classes in contemporary Rome.

Martin destroyed pagan temples, suppressed heresy, built churches, and secured great renown because of his many miracles, crowning his claim to fame by restoring three dead men to life.

St Gregory of Tours on ST MARTIN
in *Histories* bk 1, ch 39

Martin, St (*c.* 316–*c.* 400). Bishop of Tours, France, from about 371, and founder of the first monastery in Gaul. He is usually represented as tearing his cloak to share it with a beggar. His feast day is Martinmas, 11 Nov.

Born in Pannonia, SE Europe, a soldier by profession, Martin was converted to Christianity, left the army, and lived for ten years as a recluse. After being elected bishop of Tours, he worked for the extinction of idolatry and the extension of monasticism in France.

Martin Archer John Porter (1910–). British biochemist who received the 1952 Nobel Prize for Chemistry for work with Richard Synge on paper chromatography in 1944.

He has held both commercial and academic research posts; he worked at the Wool Industries Research Association in Leeds 1938–46, at the National Institute for Medical Research 1952–59, was director of the Abbotsbury Laboratory 1959–70, and taught at the University of Sussex 1973–78.

Martin and Synge began in 1941 the development of partition chromatography for separating the components of complex mixtures. A drop of the solution to be analysed is placed at one end of a strip of filter paper and allowed to dry. That end of the strip is then immersed in a solvent, which deposits the various components of the mixture as it permeates the strip of paper. The dried strip is sprayed with a reagent that produces a colour change with the components; Martin and Synge used ninhydrin to reveal the positions of amino acids. The developed strip is called a chromatogram.

In 1953, Martin began working on gas chromatography, which separates chemical vapours by differential adsorption on a porous solid.

Martin Frank (1890–1974). Swiss composer, pianist, and harpsichordist. His works are characterized by delicate colouring in instrumentation and an expressive quality combined in later works with a loosely interpreted twelve-tone system. Composing for both large-and small-scale forces, from orchestra to chamber music, his best known works are the operas *Der Sturm/The Tempest* 1956 and *Monsieur de Pourceaugnac* 1962.

Martin James (1893–1981). Northern Irish aeronautical engineer who designed and manufactured ejection seats. At the time of his death about 35,000 ejection seats were in service with the air forces

and navies of 50 countries. Knighted 1965.

In his early 20s he designed a three-wheeled car, and then set up a business in London. In the early 1930s he built a two-seater monoplane made of round-section, thin-gauge steel tubing. The design of this machine, Martin-Baker MB-1, marked the start of a partnership between Martin and Captain Valentine Henry Baker, the company's chief test pilot. During the next ten years to 1944, Martin designed three fighter aircraft that performed well and could be produced cheaply, but he received no orders.

The ejection seat was invented during World War II to improve the Spitfire pilot's chances of escape by parachute. Martin-Baker seats were fitted in new British military jet aircraft from 1947. Martin continued to develop the ejection seat for use at higher speeds, greater altitudes, vertical takeoff, multiple crew escape, and underwater ejection.

Martin John (1789–1854). English Romantic painter. He depicted grandiose landscapes and ambitious religious subjects, such as *Belshazzar's Feast* (several versions). He began his career as heraldic coach painter in Newcastle but, settling in London, made his mark by scenes of fantasy, of doomed cities and supernal wrath, stupendous in the theatrical effect attained by placing small figures in vast settings with tunnel-like effects of perspective. The Bible and Milton suggested many of his themes. Other examples of his work are *The Plains of Heaven* 1851–53 and the apocalyptic *The Last Judgement* 1853 (both Tate Gallery, London). Martin often made mezzotint engravings from his own work; he also illustrated Milton's *Paradise Lost.*

Martin (Basil) Kingsley (1897–1969). English journalist who edited the *New Statesman* 1931–60 and made it the voice of controversy on the left.

Martin (John) Leslie (1908–). English architect. He was co-editor (with Naum Gabo and Ben Nicholson) of the review *Circle*, which helped to introduce the Modern Movement to England. With Peter Moro (1911–) and Robert Matthew (1905–1975), he designed the Royal Festival Hall, London, 1951. In 1991 he received a RIBA award for his series of buildings for the Gulbenkian Foundation, Lisbon (completed 1984), which span a period of 30 years. Knighted 1957.

Martin was professor of architecture at Cambridge University from 1956–72, during which period the department's Centre for Land Use and Built Form Studies exercised considerable influence over the development of architectural theory.

Martin Richard (1754–1834). Irish landowner and lawyer known as 'Humanity Martin'. He founded the British Royal Society for Prevention of Cruelty to Animals 1824.

Martin Violet Florence (1862–1915). Irish novelist. She wrote under the pen name Martin Ross. She collaborated with her cousin Edith Somerville on tales of Anglo-Irish provincial life – for example, *Some Experiences of an Irish RM* 1899.

Martin five popes, including:

Martin V (born Oddone Colonna) (1368–1431). Pope from 1417. A member of the Roman family of Colonna, he was elected during the Council of Constance, and ended the Great Schism between the rival popes of Rome and Avignon.

Martin du Gard Roger (1881–1958). French novelist. He realistically recorded the way of life of the bourgeoisie in the eight-volume *Les Thibault/The World of the Thibaults* 1922–40. Nobel prize 1937.

Martineau Harriet (1802–1876). English journalist, economist, and novelist who wrote popular works on economics, children's

---

Any one must see at a glance that if men and women marry those whom they do not love, they must love those whom they do not marry.

HARRIET MARTINEAU
Society in America vol iii 'Marriage' 1837

stories, and articles in favour of the abolition of slavery.

Suggested reading
Martineau, Harriet *Autobiography* (1877, rep 1983)
Pichanick, Valerie *Harriet Martineau and Her Work, 1802–1876* (1980)
Webb, R K *Harriet Martineau: A Radical Victorian* (1960)
Wheatley, Vera *The Life and Work of Harriet Martineau* (1957)

Martineau James (1805–1900). British Unitarian minister and philosopher. A great orator, he anticipated Anglican modernists in his theology.

Martinez Conchita (1972–). Spanish tennis player. Seeded third in the Wimbledon women's championships 1994, she defeated Martina Navratilova (herself champion nine times) to win her first Grand Slam title.

Born in Monzon, Spain, Martinez turned professional 1988 and reached the Wimbledon semi-finals 1993. A clay-court specialist, she has been described as a 'base liner' who comes to the net on grass only when necessary, compensating with winning passes from the base line and her solid consistency.

Martinez Maria Montoya (1890–1980). Pueblo Indian potter. She revived the traditional silvery black-on-black ware (made without the wheel) at San Ildefonso Pueblo, New Mexico, USA.

Martínez Ruiz José. Real name of ◊Azorín, Spanish author.

Martini Simone. Sienese painter; see ◊Simone Martini.

Martins Peter (1946–). Danish-born US dancer, choreographer, and ballet director. He was principal dancer with the New York City Ballet (NYCB) from 1969, its joint ballet master (with Jerome Robbins) from 1983, and its director from 1990. He is especially noted for his partnership with Suzanne Farrell, with whom he danced Balanchine's *Jewels* 1967. He retired from performing 1983, after partnering Farrell in *The Nutcracker*, to concentrate on choreography.

Martins trained at the Royal Danish Ballet School, joining the company 1965. He created roles in, among others, Robbins' *Goldberg Variations* 1971 and Balanchine's *Stravinsky Violin Concerto* and *Duo Concertante* both 1972, and has choreographed many ballets, for example, *Calcium Night Light* 1978.

I do not perform any miracles. I am merely exact.

BOHUSLAV MARTINU
quoted in Safránek, *Bohuslav Martinu*, 1946

Martinu Bohuslav Jan (1890–1959). Czech composer. He settled in New York after the Nazi occupation of Czechoslovakia 1939. His music is voluble, richly expressive, and has great vitality. His works include the operas *Julietta* 1937 and *The Greek Passion* 1959, symphonies, and chamber music.

Marvell Andrew (1621–1678). English metaphysical poet and satirist. His poems include 'To His Coy Mistress' and 'Horatian Ode upon Cromwell's Return from Ireland'. He was committed to the parliamentary cause, and was member of Parliament for Hull from 1659. He devoted his last years mainly to verse satire and prose works attacking repressive aspects of government.

Suggested reading
Hunt, John Dixon *Andrew Marvell: His Life and Writings* (1978)
Hyman, L W *Andrew Marvell* (1964)
Sackville-West, Vita *Andrew Marvell* (1929, rep 1971)
Wallace, J M *Destiny His Choice* (1968)
Wilcher, R *Andrew Marvell* (1985)

Marvin Lee (1924–1987). US film actor. He began his career playing violent, often psychotic villains and progressed to playing violent, occasionally psychotic heroes. His work includes *The Big Heat* 1953, *The Killers* 1964, and *Cat Ballou* 1965.

Marx Karl Heinrich (1818–1883). German philosopher, economist, and social theorist whose account of change through conflict is known as historical, or dialectical, materialism. His *Das Kapital/Capital* 1867–95 is the fundamental text of Marxist economics, and his systematic theses on class struggle, history, and the importance of economic factors in politics have exercised an enormous influence on later thinkers and political activists.

Marx was born in Trier, the son of a lawyer, and studied law and philosophy at Bonn and Berlin. During 1842–43, he edited the *Rheinische Zeitung/Rhineland Newspaper* until its suppression, and during the revolution of 1848 he edited the *Neue Rheinische Zeitung/New Rhineland Newspaper*. In 1844 Marx began his lifelong collaboration with Friedrich Engels, with whom he developed the Marxist philosophy, first formulated in their joint works *Die heilige Familie/The Holy Family* 1844 and *Die deutsche Ideologie/German Ideology* 1846 (which contains the theory demonstrating the material basis of all human activity: 'Life is not determined by consciousness, but consciousness by life'). Both joined the Communist League, a German refugee organization, and in 1847–48 they prepared its programme, *The Communist Manifesto*. In the wake of the 1848 revolution, Marx was expelled from Prussia 1849.

He then settled in London, where he wrote *Die Klassenkämpfe in Frankreich/Class Struggles in France* 1849, *Die Achtzehnte Brumaire des Louis Bonaparte/The 18th Brumaire of Louis Bonaparte* 1852, *Zur Kritik der politischen ökonomie/Critique of Political Economy* 1859, and his monumental work *Das Kapital/Capital*. In 1864 the International Working Men's Association was formed, whose policy Marx, as a member of the general council, largely controlled. Although he showed extraordinary tact in holding together its diverse elements, it collapsed 1872 owing to Marx's disputes with the anarchists, including the Russian Bakunin.

Marx's philosophical work owes much to the writings of the German G W F Hegel, though he rejected Hegel's idealism. It includes *Misère de la philosophie/Poverty of Philosophy* 1847. The second and third volumes of *Das Kapital* were edited from his notes by Engels and published posthumously.

Suggested reading
Kerr, C *Marshall, Marx and the Modern Times* (1969)
Berlin, Isaiah *Karl Marx* (1939)
Carver, Terrell *Marx and Engels* (1983)
McLellan, David *Karl Marx: His Life and Thought* (1973)
Padover, S *Karl Marx: An Intimate Biography* (1978)

I never forget a face but in your case I'll be glad to make an exception.

GROUCHO MARX
quoted by Leo Rosten in *People I have Loved, Known or Admired*

Marx Brothers team of US film comedians: Leonard 'Chico', from the 'chicks' – women – he chased (1891–1961); Adolph, the silent 'Harpo', from the harp he played (1888–1964); Julius 'Groucho', from his temper (1890–1977); Milton 'Gummo' from his gumshoes, or galoshes (*c.* 1892–1977), who left the team before they began making films; and Herbert 'Zeppo', born at the time of the first zeppelins (1901–1979), part of the team until 1935. They made a total of 13 zany films (1929–49) including *Animal Crackers* 1930, *Monkey Business* 1931, *Duck Soup* 1933, *A Day at the Races* 1937, *A Night at the Opera* 1935, and *Go West* 1940.

They made their reputation on Broadway in *Cocoanuts* 1926 (later filmed). After the team disbanded 1948, Groucho continued to make films and appeared on his own television quiz show, *You Bet Your Life* 1947–62.

Suggested reading
Adamson, Joseph *Groucho, Harpo, Chico and Sometimes Zeppo* (1973)
Chandler, Charlotte *Hello, I Must Be Going* (1978)
Crichton, K *The Marx Brothers* (1950)

Mary Queen of Scots (1542–1587). Queen of Scotland 1542–67. Also known as Mary Stuart, she was the daughter of James V. Mary's connection with the English royal line from Henry VII made her a threat to Elizabeth I's hold on the English throne, especially as she represented a champion of the Catholic cause.

Mary's mother was the French Mary of Guise. Born in Linlithgow (now in Lothian region, Scotland), Mary was sent to France, where she married the dauphin, later Francis II. After his death she returned to Scotland 1561, which, during her absence, had become Protestant. She married her cousin, the Earl of Darnley, 1565, but they soon quarrelled, and Darnley took part in the murder of Mary's secretary, Rizzio. In 1567 Darnley was assassinated as the result of a conspiracy formed by the Earl of Bothwell, possibly with Mary's connivance, and shortly after Bothwell married her. A rebellion followed; defeated at Carberry Hill, Mary abdicated and was imprisoned. She escaped 1568, raised an army, and after its defeat at Langside fled to England, only to be imprisoned again. A plot against Elizabeth I devised by Anthony Babington led to her trial and execution at Fotheringay Castle 1587.

Suggested reading
Donaldson, Gordon *Mary, Queen of Scots* (1973)
Fraser, Antonia *Mary, Queen of Scots* (1969)
Landon-Davies, J *Mary Queen of Scots* (1966)
Strong, Roy and Oman, Julia *Mary, Queen of Scots* (1973)

O Lord my God, I have trusted in thee; / O Jesu my dearest one, now set me free. / In prison's oppression, in sorrow's obsession, / I weary for thee.

MARY QUEEN OF SCOTS
Written in her Book of Devotion before her execution,
quoted in Algernon Swinburne (tr) *Mary Stuart* V i 1881

Mary in the New Testament, the mother of Jesus through divine intervention (the Annunciation), wife of Joseph. The Roman Catholic Church maintains belief in her Immaculate Conception and bodily assumption into heaven, and venerates her as a mediator. Feast day of the Assumption is 15 Aug.

Traditionally her parents were elderly and named Joachim and Anna. Mary (Hebrew Miriam) married Joseph and accompanied him to Bethlehem. Roman Catholic doctrine assumes that the brothers of Jesus were Joseph's sons by an earlier marriage, and that she remained a virgin. Pope Paul VI proclaimed her 'Mother of the Church' 1964.

Suggested reading
Graef, Hilda *Mary: A History of Doctrine and Devotion* (1963–65)
Patsch, Joseph *Our Lady in the Gospels* (1958)
Warner, Marina *Alone of All Her Sex: The Myth and Cult of the Virgin Mary* (1976)

Mary Duchess of Burgundy (1457–1482). Daughter of Charles the Bold, Duke of Burgundy. She married Maximilian of Austria 1477, thus bringing the Low Countries into the possession of the Habsburgs and, ultimately, of Spain.

So that's what hay looks like.

QUEEN MARY
quoted by James Pope-Hennessy *Life of Queen Mary* ch 8 1959

Mary Queen (1867–1953). Consort of George V of the UK. The daughter of the Duke and Duchess of Teck, the latter a granddaughter of George II, in 1891 she became engaged to the Duke of Clarence, eldest son of the Prince of Wales (later Edward VII). After his death 1892, she married 1893 his brother George, Duke of York, who succeeded to the throne 1910.

Mary two queens of England:

Mary I (called 'Bloody Mary') (1516–1558). Queen of England from 1553. She was the eldest daughter of Henry VIII by Catherine of Aragon. When Edward VI died, Mary secured the crown without difficulty in spite of the conspiracy to substitute Lady Jane Grey. In 1554 Mary married Philip II of Spain, and as a devout Roman Catholic obtained the restoration of papal supremacy and sanctioned the persecution of Protestants. She was succeeded by her half-sister Elizabeth I.

Suggested reading
Erickson, C *Bloody Mary* (1978)
Ridley, Jasper *The Life and Times of Mary Tudor* (1973)

When I am dead and opened, you shall find 'Calais' lying in my heart.

MARY I
Attributed remark in Holinshed's *Chronicles*

Mary II (1662–1694). Queen of England, Scotland, and Ireland from 1688. She was the Protestant elder daughter of the Catholic James II, and in 1677 was married to her cousin William of Orange. After the 1688 revolution she accepted the crown jointly with William. During his absences from England she took charge of the government, and showed courage and resource when invasion seemed possible 1690 and 1692.

Suggested reading
Hamilton, Elizabeth *William's Mary* (1972)
MacCubbin, R P and Hamilton-Phillips, M (eds) *The Age of William and Mary* (1988)
Van Der See, B and H A *William and Mary* (1973)

Her understanding, though very imperfectly cultivated, was quick, ... and her letters were so well expressed that they deserved to be well spelt.

T B Macaulay on MARY II
in *History of England* 1839

Mary Magdalene, St (lived 1st century AD). In the New Testament, a woman whom Jesus cured of possession by evil spirits. She was present at the Crucifixion and burial, and was the first to meet the risen Jesus. She is often identified with the woman of St Luke's gospel who anointed Jesus' feet, and her symbol is a jar of ointment; feast day 22 July.

Mary of Guise (or Mary of Lorraine) (1515–1560). French wife of James V of Scotland from 1538, and from 1554 regent of Scotland for her daughter Mary Queen of Scots. A Catholic, she moved from reconciliation with Scottish Protestants to repression, and died during a Protestant rebellion in Edinburgh.

Quick-witted rather than intelligent ... she remained proud, dignified and increasingly devout, a far more spirited figure than the apathetic James II [her husband].

C P Hill on MARY OF MODENA
in *Who's Who in History* vol iii 1965

Mary of Modena (born Marie Beatrice d'Este) (1658–1718). Queen consort of England and Scotland. She was the daughter of the Duke of Modena, Italy, and married James, Duke of York, later James II, 1673. The birth of their son James Francis Edward Stuart was the signal for the revolution of 1688 that overthrew James II. Mary fled to France.

Masaccio (Tommaso di Giovanni di Simone Guidi) (1401–*c.* 1428). Florentine painter. He was a leader of the early Italian Renaissance. His frescoes in Sta Maria del Carmine, Florence, 1425–28, which he painted with Masolino da Panicale, show a decisive break with Gothic conventions. He was the first painter to apply the scientific laws of perspective, newly discovered by the architect Brunelleschi, and achieved a remarkable sense of space and volume.

Masaccio's frescoes in the Brancacci Chapel of Sta Maria del Carmine include scenes from the life of St Peter, notably *The Tribute Money*, and a moving account of *Adam and Eve's Expulsion from Paradise*. They have a monumental grandeur, without trace of Gothic decorative detail, unlike the work of his colleague and teacher Masolino. Masaccio's figures have solidity and weight and are clearly set in three-dimensional space. Other works are the *Trinity* about 1428 (Sta Maria Novella, Florence) and the polyptych for the Carmelite church in Pisa 1426 (National Gallery, London/Staatliche Museen, Berlin/Museo di Capodimonte, Naples). Although his career marks a turning point in Italian art, he attracted few imitators.

Suggested reading
Berti, Luciano *Masaccio* (1967)
Cole, Bruce *Masaccio and the Art of Early Renaissance Florence* (1980)

Masaryk Jan Garrigue (1886–1948). Czechoslovak politician, son of Tomáš Masaryk. He was foreign minister from 1940, when the Czechoslovak government was exiled in London in World War II. He returned 1945, retaining the post, but as a result of political pressure by the communists committed suicide.

Our whole history inclines us towards ... the democracies of the West.

TOMÁŠ MASARYK
Inaugural presidential message 23 Dec 1918

Masaryk Tomáš Garrigue (1850–1937). Czechoslovak nationalist politician. He directed the revolutionary movement against the Austrian Empire, founding with Eduard Beneš and Stefanik the Czechoslovak National Council, and in 1918 was elected first president of the newly formed Czechoslovak Republic. Three times re-elected, he resigned 1935 in favour of Beneš.

After the communist coup 1948, Masaryk was systematically removed from public memory in order to reverse his semi-mythological status as the forger of the Czechoslovak nation.

What a pity! What a pity! He is a young man, whose feeling for music exceeds his knowledge of it.

Guiseppe Verdi on PIETRO MASCAGNI
quoted in Gino Monaldi, *Verdi* 1889

Mascagni Pietro (1863–1945). Italian composer. His one-act opera *Cavalleria rusticana/Rustic Chivalry* was first produced in Rome 1890 in the new verismo or realistic style.

Masefield John (1878–1967). English poet and novelist. His early years in the navy inspired *Salt Water Ballads* 1902 and several adventure novels; he also wrote children's books, such as *The Box of Delights* 1935, and plays. He was poet laureate from 1930.

The Everlasting Mercy 1911, characterized by its forcefully colloquial language, and *Reynard the Fox* 1919 are long verse narratives. His other works include the novel *Sard Harker* 1924 and the critical work *Badon Parchments* 1947.

I must go down to the seas again, to the lonely sea and the sky, / And all I ask is a tall ship and a star to steer her by.

JOHN MASEFIELD
'Sea Fever'

Masekela Hugh (1939–). South African trumpet player. Exiled from his homeland 1960–90, he has recorded jazz, rock, and mbaqanga (township jive).

His albums include *Techno-Bush* 1984. An opponent of apartheid, he left South Africa with his wife, singer Miriam Makeba.

Masina Giulietta. Stage name of Giulia Anna Masina (1921–1994). Italian actress. The wife from 1943 of director Federico Fellini, she appeared in several of his most celebrated films, notably *La strada/The Street* 1954, in which the pathos and comedy of her portrayal of a put-upon waif was widely described as Chaplinesque, and *Le notti di Cabiria/Nights of Cabiria* 1957, in which she won acclaim for her portrayal of a naive prostitute. In 1985 she returned to the screen in her husband's *Ginger e Fred/Ginger and Fred*, appropriately in the guise of a show-business veteran making a comeback.

Masaryk *Czechoslovak independence campaigner and statesman Tomáš Masaryk. Before being elected president of the new Czechoslovakian Republic, he was professor of philosophy at the Czech University in Prague, and was highly respected at home and abroad.* (Image Select)

Masire Quett Ketumile Joni (1925–). President of Botswana from 1980. In 1962, with Seretse Khama, he founded the Botswana Democratic Party (BDP) and in 1965 was made deputy prime minister. After independence 1966, he became vice president and, on Khama's death 1980, president, continuing a policy of nonalignment.

Masire was a journalist before entering politics, sitting in the Bangwaketse Tribal Council and then the Legislative Council before co-founding the BDP. A centrist, he has helped Botswana become one of the most stable states in Africa.

Maskell Dan (1908–1992). British tennis broadcaster, player, and coach. He was BBC Television's chief tennis commentator for 43 years and remembered as the 'voice of Wimbledon'.

Maskell became world professional champion 1927, and in 1929 he moved to the All England Lawn Tennis and Croquet Club at Wimbledon as their first professional coach. During that time he coached the Davis Cup team to victory, in the great years of the tennis champion Fred Perry. By 1951 Maskell had won the British Professional Championships 16 times. Between 1947 and 1973 he was also the Lawn Tennis Association training manager, devoting himself to the transformation of its coaching and development work.

Maskell's broadcasting career began 1949 when he became a radio commentator at Wimbledon. Two years later he moved into television coverage of the tournament. It was not long before his distinguished style of commentary became as much a part of Wimbledon as its strawberries and cream.

Maskelyne Nevil (1732–1811). English astronomer who made observations to investigate the reliability of the lunar distance method for determining longitude at sea. In 1774 he estimated the mass of the Earth by noting the deflection of a plumb line near Mount Schiehallion in Scotland. Maskelyne, the fifth Astronomer Royal 1765–1811, began publication 1766 of the *Nautical Almanac*. This contained astronomical tables and navigational aids, and was probably his most enduring contribution to astronomy.

Masolino (Tommaso da Panicale) (*c.* 1383–*c.* 1447). Florentine painter. He worked with Masaccio on the fresco cycle in the Brancacci Chapel of Sta Maria del Carmine, Florence, about 1425. He shared Masaccio's enthusiasm for the newly discovered technique of perspective but reverted, after the younger man's death, to his own preferred decorative style, in the tradition of International Gothic. An example is his fresco work at Castiglione d'Olona, near Como, about 1435.

A goldsmith in youth, he is believed to have worked under Ghiberti on the baptistery doors at Florence, 1403–07, before turning to painting. Other works besides the Brancacci Chapel include a Madonna, dated 1423 (Bremen), frescoes at Castiglione d'Olona, and an altarpiece, parts of which are in the galleries of Naples, Philadelphia and London.

Mason A(lfred) E(dward) W(oodley) (1865–1948). English novelist. He was the author of a tale of cowardice redeemed in the Sudan, *The Four Feathers* 1902, and a series featuring the detective Hanaud of the Sûreté, including *At the Villa Rose* 1910.

Mason Bobbie Ann (1940–). US writer. Her novel *In Country* 1985 was acclaimed for its portrayal of the impact of the Vietnam War on rural lives. It was followed by *Spence + Lila* 1988 and a collection of stories *Love Life* 1989.

Mason James Neville (1909–1984). English film actor. He portrayed romantic villains in British films of the 1940s. After *Odd Man Out* 1947 he worked in the USA, often playing intelligent but troubled, vulnerable men, notably in *A Star Is Born* 1954. He returned to Europe 1960, where he made *Lolita* 1962, *Georgy Girl* 1966, and *Cross of Iron* 1977. Other films include *The Wicked Lady* 1946, *Five Fingers* 1952 and *North by Northwest* 1959. His final role was in *The Shooting Party* 1984.

Mason Ronald Alison Kells (1905–1971). New Zealand poet and dramatist. Classical studies influenced his characteristic stripped language, tense rhythms, and strict verse forms. These features, in combination with a sombre, sometimes macabre intensity of feeling were all apparent even in his precocious early collection *The Beggar* 1924, followed by *No New Thing* 1934. A more buoyant vision emerged in *This Dark Will Lighten* 1941. An active trade unionist, he also wrote political journalism and 'committed' plays such as *Refugee* 1945.

Massasoit also known as Ousamequin, 'Yellow Feather' (*c.* 1590–1661). American chief of the Wampanoag, a people inhabiting the coasts of Massachusetts Bay and Cape Cod. He formed alliances with Plymouth Colony 1621 and Massachusetts Bay Colony 1638. After his death, his son Metacomet, known to the English as 'King Philip', took over his father's leadership.

Masséna André (1758–1817). Marshal of France. He served in the French Revolutionary Wars and under the emperor Napoleon was created marshal 1804, duke of Rivoli 1808, and prince of Essling 1809. He was in command in Spain 1810–11 in the Peninsular War and was defeated by British troops under Wellington.

Massenet feels it as a Frenchman, with powder and minuets: I shall feel it as an Italian, with desperate passion.

Giacomo Puccini on JULES MASSENET
on Jules Massenet's *Manon*, quoted in Mosco Carner *Puccini* 1974

Massenet Jules Emile Frédéric (1842–1912). French composer of operas. His work is characterized by prominent roles for females, sincerity, and sentimentality. Notable works are *Manon* 1884, *Le Cid* 1885, and *Thaïs* 1894; among other works is the orchestral suite *Scènes pittoresques* 1874.

Massenet was born at Montaud, St Etienne, and studied at the Paris Conservatoire, where he subsequently became professor of composition. His long and successful career included no fewer than 27 operas, mainly for the Paris Opéra and Opéra-Comique, and the Monte Carlo Opera. There have been revivals of some of his lesser-known work since the 1980s.

Massey (Charles) Vincent (1887–1967). Canadian Liberal Party politician. He was the first Canadian to become governor-general of Canada (1952–59). He helped to establish the Massey Foundation 1918 which funded the building of Massey College and the University of Toronto. His brother Raymond Massey (1896–1983), an actor, became a US citizen in 1944: his films include *Things to Come* 1936 and *Mourning Becomes Electra*. Raymond's son Daniel Massey (1933–) and daughter Anna Massey (1937–) are also actors.

A strong, purposeful man, who, once having come to a decision, never faltered.

T M Wilford on WILLIAM FERGUSON MASSEY
in *Dictionary of National Biography*

Massey William Ferguson (1856–1925). New Zealand politician, born in Ireland; prime minister 1912–25. He led the Reform Party, an offshoot of the Conservative Party, and as prime minister before World War I concentrated on controlling militant unions and the newly formed Federation of Labour. During the war he governed at the head of a coalition with the Liberals. Afterwards he promoted migration and liberalization of agrarian policy while opposing the movement for a more independent status within the Empire.

Massine Léonide. Adopted name of Leonid Fyodorovich Miassin (1895–1979). Russian choreographer and dancer with the Ballets Russes. He was a creator of comedy in ballet and also symphonic ballet using concert music. His works include the first Cubist-inspired ballet, *Parade* 1917, *La Boutique fantasque* 1919, and *The Three-Cornered Hat* 1919.

He succeeded Mikhail Fokine at the Ballets Russes and continued with the company after Sergei Diaghilev's death, later working in both the USA and Europe.

Massinger Philip (1583–1640). English dramatist. He was the author of *A New Way to Pay Old Debts c.* 1625. He collaborated with John Fletcher and Thomas Dekker, and has been credited with a share in writing Shakespeare's *Two Noble Kinsmen* and *Henry VIII*.

Masson André Aimé René (1896–1987). French artist and writer. He was a leader of Surrealism until 1929 when he quarrelled with André Breton. His interest in the unconscious mind led him to experiment with automatic drawing – simple pen-and-ink work – and later textured accretions of pigment, glue, and sand. His automatic drawings influenced Gorky and the Expressionists.

During World War II he moved to the USA, then returned to France and painted landscapes.

Masters Edgar Lee (1869–1950). US poet. In *Spoon River Anthology* 1915, a collection of free-verse epitaphs, the people of a small town tell of their frustrated lives.

The magic mountain is always the one beyond the one you have climbed ... If it were not so ... man could only dream, or only do – but never both.

JOHN MASTERS
Coromandel ch 5 1955

Masters John (1914–1983). British novelist. Born in Calcutta, he served in the Indian army 1934–47. He wrote a series of books dealing with the Savage family throughout the period of the Raj – for example, *Nightrunners of Bengal* 1951, *The Deceivers* 1952, and *Bhowani Junction* 1954.

Masterson Bat (William Barclay) (1853–1921). US marshal and sportswriter. In 1878 he succeeded his murdered brother, Edward, as marshal in Dodge City, Kansas, and gunned down his brother's killers in the famous gunfight at the OK Corral 1881 at Tombstone in Arizona. He moved to New York 1902, where he became a sports-writer for the *Morning Telegraph*.

Born in Iroquois County, Illinois, and raised in Kansas, Masterson worked in his early adult years as a buffalo hunter and scout before becoming a deputy marshal in Dodge City 1876.

He briefly served with Wyatt Earp 1880 before moving to Kansas City.

Mästlin Michael (1550–1631). German astronomer and mathematician who was one of the first scholars to accept and teach Polish astronomer Copernicus's observation that the Earth orbits the Sun. One of Mästlin's pupils was German mathematician Johannes Kepler.

In 1580 he became professor of mathematics at Heidelberg and in 1584 at Tübingen, where he taught for 47 years.

In 1573, Mästlin published an essay concerning the nova that had appeared the previous year. Its location in relation to known stars convinced him that the nova was a new star – which implied, contrary to traditional belief, that things could come into being in the spheres beyond the Moon. Observation of the comets of 1577 and 1580 convinced Mästlin that they also were located beyond the Moon. Together with other observations, this led him explicitly to argue against the traditional cosmology of Aristotle. However, Mästlin's *Epitome of Astronomy* 1582, a popular introduction to the subject, propounded a traditional cosmology because this was easier to teach.

Mastroianni Marcello (1924–1997). Italian film actor. He was popular for his carefully understated roles as an unhappy romantic lover in such films as Antonioni's *La notte/The Night* 1961. He starred in several films with Sophia Loren, including *Una giornata speciale/A Special Day* 1977, and worked with Fellini in *La dolce vita* 1960, *8½* 1963, and *Ginger and Fred* 1986.

Masur Kurt (1927–). German conductor. He has been music director of the New York Philharmonic from 1990. His speciality is late Romantic and early 20th-century repertoire, in particular Mendelssohn, Liszt, Bruch, and Prokofiev.

He was conductor of the Dresden Philharmonic Orchestra 1955–58 and 1967–72, before making his London debut 1973 with the New Philharmonia. He was prominent in the political campaigning that took place prior to German unification.

Masursky Harold (1923–). US geologist who has conducted research into the surface of the Moon and the planets. Working for the US space agency NASA from 1962, he participated in the Mariner, Apollo, Viking, Pioneer, and Voyager programmes.

After 11 years with the US Geological Survey, he transferred to the branch for astrogeological studies and began work at the National Aeronautics and Space Administration (NASA).

Masursky was responsible for the surveying of lunar and planetary surfaces, particularly in regard to the choice of landing sites. He was a member of the working groups that monitored and guided the Moon landing 1969 and analysed the data afterwards. He led the team that monitored observations of Mars made by *Mariner 9* 1971, then selected landing sites on Mars for the Viking probes 1975. In 1978, Masursky joined the Venus Orbiter Imaging Radar Science Working Group. The surface of Venus, hidden from visual or televisual observation by its thick layer of cloud, was mapped on the basis of radar readings taken from the orbiting Pioneer probe.

Mata Hari Stage name of Margaretha Geertruida Zelle (1876–1917). Dutch courtesan, dancer, and probable spy. In World War I she had affairs with highly placed military and government officials on both sides and told Allied secrets to the Germans. She may have been a double agent, in the pay of both France and Germany. She was shot by the French on espionage charges.

Suggested reading
Howe, Russell Warren *Mata Hari: The True Story* (1986)
Waagenaar, Sam *The Murder of Mata Hari* (1964)

Mather Cotton (1663–1728). American theologian and writer. He was a Puritan minister in Boston, and wrote over 400 works of history, science, annals, and theology, including *Magnalia Christi Americana/The Great Works of Christ in America* 1702, a vast compendium of early New England history and experience. Mather appears to have supported the Salem witch-hunts.

Suggested reading
Levin, David *Cotton Mather, 1663–1703* (1978)
Middlekauff, Robert *The Mathers: Three Generations of Puritan Intellectuals, 1596–1728* (1971)

Mather Increase (1639–1723). American colonial and religious leader. As a defender of the colonial right to self-government, he went to England 1688 to protest revocation of the Massachusetts charter. However, his silence during the Salem witch trials of 1692 lessened his public influence.

Born in Dorchester, Massachusetts, and educated at Harvard University, Mather served as a cleric in England during the Puritan Commonwealth, returning to Massachusetts 1661 where he was named teacher of Boston's Second Church 1664. He was president of Harvard 1685–1701.

Mathewson Christy (Christopher) (1880–1925). US baseball player. He was signed by the New York Giants of the National League 1900 and during a 17-year major-league career, he amassed an impressive record of 373 wins and 188 losses. He retired from play 1916, becoming manager of the Cincinnati Reds 1916–18.

Mathis Johnny (John Royce) (1935–). US singer. A crooner of romantic ballads, he made his breakthrough in 1957 with four hit singles, including 'Chances Are'. By 1996 he had made more than 75 albums and sold over 100 million records.

Mathis was born in San Francisco and was a successful athlete before turning to singing. Influenced by popular jazz and ballad singers, he made his first recordings 1956, resulting in the hit 'Wonderful! Wonderful!'. Other favourites include 'Misty' 1959, 'Raindrops Keep Fallin' on My Head' 1970, and 'Too Much, Too Little, Too Late' (a duet with Deniece Williams) 1978. He played the role of a nightclub singer and sang the title song in the film *A Certain Smile* 1958.

Here lies Henry's daughter [Henry I], wife [Henry V of Germany] and mother [of Henry II]. Great by birth, greater by marriage but greatest by motherhood.

Epitaph on the Empress Maud (MATILDA) in the Abbey of Bec

Matilda the Empress Maud (1102–1167). Claimant to the throne of England. On the death of her father, Henry I, 1135, the barons elected her cousin Stephen to be king. Matilda invaded England 1139, and was crowned by her supporters 1141. Civil war ensued until Stephen was finally recognized as king 1153, with Henry II (Matilda's son) as his successor.

Matilda was recognized during the reign of Henry I as his heir. She married first the Holy Roman emperor Henry V and, after his death, Geoffrey Plantagenet, Count of Anjou (1113–1151).

Matisse Henri Emile Benoît (1869–1954). French painter, sculptor, illustrator, and designer. He was one of the most original creative forces in early 20th-century art. Influenced by Impressionism, Post-Impressionism, and later Cubism, he developed a style characterized by surface pattern, strong, sinuous line, and brilliant colour. Among his favoured subjects were odalisques (women of the harem), bathers, and dancers; for example, *The Dance* 1910 (The Hermitage, St Petersburg). The luxurious

There is nothing more difficult for a truly creative painter than to paint a rose, because before he can do so he has first to forget all the roses that were ever painted.

HENRI MATISSE
Remark recalled in obituaries after his death 5 Nov 1954

subtleties of Persian art attracted him about 1910, and in developing a related sense of colour and in a decorative simplification of line and mass, he diverged from the movement which succeeded Fauvism in the limelight, Cubism, for which he had little sympathy. For some years he travelled about the world, but settled at Nice 1917, devoting himself to paintings of Mediterranean interiors, still life and odalisques, characterized by great economy of means, brilliant colour and the free use of textile patterns as a subsidiary decorative element. Later works include pure abstracts, as in his collages of coloured paper shapes (*gouaches découpées*) and the designs 1949–51 for the decoration of a chapel for the Dominican convent in Vence, near Nice. He also designed sets and costumes for Diaghilev's Ballets Russes. Matisse's work figures in most of the principal collections of modern art, the largest number of his paintings being in the Moscow Museum of Western Art (enriched by the collections of the Moscow merchants) and the Barnes Foundation, Pennsylvania.

Suggested reading
Barr, A *Matisse: His Art and his Public* (1951)
Brill, F *Matisse* (1966)
Flam, J (ed) *Matisse on Art* (1973)
Gowing, L *Matisse* (1979)
Watkins, N *Matisse* (1984)

Matsudaira Tsuneo (1877–1949). Japanese diplomat and politician who became the first chair of the Japanese Diet (parliament) after World War II. He negotiated for Japan at the London Naval Conference of 1930 and acted as imperial household minister 1936–45, advising the emperor, but was unsuccessful in keeping Japan out of a war with the Western powers.

Matsukata Masayoshi, Prince (1835–1924). Japanese politician, premier 1891–92 and 1896–98. As minister of finance 1881–91 and 1898–1900, he paved the way for the modernization of the Japanese economy.

Matsuoka Yosuke (1880–1946). Japanese politician, foreign minister 1940–41. A fervent nationalist, Matsuoka led Japan out of the League of Nations when it condemned Japan for the seizure of Manchuria. As foreign minister, he allied Japan with Germany and Italy. At the end of World War II, he was arrested as a war criminal but died before his trial.

Matsys Quentin, (also Massys or Metsys) (c. 1465–1530). Flemish painter. Born in Louvain, he was active in Antwerp. He painted religious subjects such as the *Lamentation over Christ* 1511 (Musées Royaux, Antwerp) and portraits set against landscapes or realistic interiors.

He was the son of a metalworker and clockmaker at Louvain and trained there and perhaps in the studio of Dirck Bouts. His art represents two phases of transition, from the later period of early Netherlandish art, represented by Memlinc and Gerard David, to that of Italian influence, and from declining Bruges to the newly flourishing city of Antwerp, where he became a member of the Painters' Guild 1491. He is noted for the refinement and delicacy of his female types, in which he seems to show acquaintance with the work of Leonardo, and for landscape backgrounds related in character to those of his contemporary at Antwerp, Patenier. He branched out also in the vein of *The Moneychanger and his Wife* (Louvre), which he made a popular subject among painters such as van Reymerswael. His sons Cornelis (c. 1508–c. 1580) and Jan (c. 1509–1575) were also painters and pupils of Quinten. Other works include the *St Anne Altarpiece* 1509 (Musées Royaux, Brussels) and a portrait of *Erasmus* 1517 (Museo Nazionale, Rome).

Matta (Roberto Sebastien Antonio Matta Echaurren) (1911–). Chilean-born French painter. He was a leading figure, along with André Masson, of Surrealist-inspired automatic painting, in which images are allowed to flow from the unconscious through the hand directly onto paper or canvas. His expressed intention in much of his work is an attempt to define the anxieties of the age through the force and motion of forms, as in *Years of Fear* 1942 (Solomon R Guggenheim Museum, New York).

Trained as an architect, Matta spent World War II in New York where he met and was influenced by Marcel Duchamp. His first mature work of the 1940s explodes with bursts of colour and skeins of indefinable organic or mechanistic form, generally hurtling or floating in cosmic space. His style became more figurative and calligraphic in the 1980s.

> *The more success you have, the less you use the things that got you there in the first place. You end up doing what I call Retirement Acting – merely exhibiting your former skills.*
>
> WALTER MATTHAU
> in *Sunday Express* 1979

Matthau Walter. Stage name of Walter Matuschanskavasky (1920–). US character actor. He was impressive in both comedy and dramatic roles. He gained film stardom in the 1960s after his stage success in *The Odd Couple* 1965. His many films include *Kotch* 1971, *Charley Varrick* 1973, and *The Sunshine Boys* 1975.

Matthew, St (lived 1st century AD). Christian apostle and evangelist, the traditional author of the first Gospel. He is usually identified with Levi, who was a tax collector in the service of Herod Antipas, and was called by Jesus to be a disciple as he sat by the Lake of Galilee receiving customs dues. His emblem is a man with wings; feast day 21 Sept.

Matthews Stanley (1915–). English footballer who played for Stoke City, Blackpool, and England. He played nearly 700 Football League games, and won 54 international caps. He was the first Footballer of the Year 1948 (again 1963), the first European Footballer of the Year 1956, and the first footballer to be knighted for services to the game 1965.

An outstanding right-winger, he had the nickname 'the Wizard of the Dribble' because of his ball control. At the age of 38 he won an FA Cup Winners' medal when Blackpool beat Bolton Wanderers 4–3, Matthews laying on three goals in the last 20 minutes. He continued to play first-division football after the age of 50.

Matthews Stanley (1824–1889). US jurist. Appointed by President Garfield as associate justice of the US Supreme Court 1881–99, his most important decision, *Hurtado* v *California* 1888, was an important constitutional definition of due process of law.

Born in Cincinnati, Ohio, USA, Matthews graduated from Kenyon College and studied law in Cincinnati. He served in the Ohio Senate 1855–57 and as a US attorney for the southern district of Ohio 1858–61. After the American Civil War (1861–65), he sat as a judge of the Cincinnati Superior Court and then returned to private practice.

Matthias Corvinus (c. 1440–1490). King of Hungary from 1458. His aim of uniting Hungary, Austria, and Bohemia involved him in long wars with Holy Roman emperor Frederick III and the kings of Bohemia and Poland, during which he captured Vienna (1485) and made it his capital. His father was János Hunyadi.

Mattox Matt (1921–). US jazz dancer and teacher. He pioneered jazz dance in the USA and appeared in many films; for example, *Seven Brides for Seven Brothers* 1954. From 1970 he taught at the Dance Centre, London, and later in Paris.

Matura Mustapha (1939–). Trinidad-born British dramatist. Co-founder of the Black Theatre Cooperative 1978, his plays deal with problems of ethnic diversity and integration. These include *As Time Goes By* 1971, *Play Mas* 1974, and *Meetings* 1981. Other works include *Playboy of the West Indies* 1984 and *Trinidad Sisters* 1988 (adaptations of plays by Synge and Chekhov respectively), and *The Coup* 1991.

Mature Victor (1915–). US film actor. He was a star of the 1940s and early 1950s. He gave strong performances in, among others, *My Darling Clementine* 1946, *Kiss of Death* 1947, and *Samson and Delilah* 1949.

Mauchly John William (1907–1980). US physicist and engineer who, in 1946, constructed the first general-purpose computer, the ENIAC, in collaboration with John Eckert. Their company was bought by Remington Rand 1950, and they built the UNIVAC 1 computer 1951 for the US census.

The work on ENIAC was carried out by the two during World War II, and was commissioned to automate the calculation of artillery firing tables for the US Army. In 1949 Mauchly and Eckert designed a small-scale binary computer, BINAC, which was faster and cheaper to use. Punched cards were replaced with magnetic tape, and the computer stored programs internally.

Mauchly was born in Cincinnati, Ohio, and studied at Johns Hopkins University, becoming professor of physics at Ursinus College in Collegeville, Pennsylvania. In 1941 he moved to the Moore School of Electrical Engineering of the University of Pennsylvania, and became principal consultant on the ENIAC project. A dispute over patent policy with the Moore School caused Mauchly and Eckert to leave and set up a partnership 1948. Mauchly was a consultant to Remington Rand (later Sperry Rand) 1950–59 and again from 1973, after setting up his own consulting company 1959.

Maude (Frederick) Stanley (1864–1917). British general in World War I. Maude served in the Sudan and then in the South African War 1899–1902, where he won the DSO. He went to France as a staff officer Aug 1914 and commanded a brigade Oct 1914, but was wounded and returned to the UK. He then went to the Middle East and was given command of the forces in Mesopotamia Aug 1916. He drove the Turks from Kut-al-Imara and captured Baghdad. He successfully carried out follow-up operations but then contracted cholera and died Nov 1917. Well-liked and skilful, Maude was an effective general and his sudden death was a great loss to the army. KCB 1916.

There comes a time in every man's life when he must make way for older men.

Remark made by REGINALD MAUDLING in the Smoking Room of the House of Commons on being replaced in the Shadow Cabinet by John Davies, his elder by four years, in *Guardian* 20 Nov 1976

Maudling Reginald (1917–1979). British Conservative politician, chancellor of the Exchequer 1962–64, contender for the party leadership 1965, and home secretary 1970–72. He resigned when referred to during the bankruptcy proceedings of the architect John Poulson, since (as home secretary) he would have been in charge of the Metropolitan Police investigating the case.

Maudslay Henry (1771–1831). English engineer and toolmaker who improved the metalworking lathe so that it could be employed for precise screw cutting. He also designed a bench micrometer, the forerunner of the modern instrument.

Maudslay was born in London and went to work at the Woolwich Arsenal at the age of 12, apprenticed to the metalworking shop. For a time he worked for inventor Joseph Bramah, and then started his own business.

Maudslay's new screw-cutting lathe gave such precision as to allow previously unknown interchangeability of nuts and bolts and standardization of screw threads. He was also able to produce sets of taps and dies. In 1801–08, in conjunction with engineer Marc Brunel, he constructed machines for making wooden pulley blocks at Portsmouth dockyard. Maudslay's firm went on to produce marine steam engines.

Maufe Edward Brantwood (1883–1974). English architect. His works include the Runnymede Memorial and Guildford Cathedral. Knighted 1954.

Mauger Ivan Gerald (1939–). New Zealand speedway star. He won the world individual title a record six times 1968–79.

Maugham (William) Somerset (1874–1965). English writer. His work includes the novels *Of Human Bondage* 1915, *The Moon and*

Sixpence 1919, and *Cakes and Ale* 1930; the short-story collections *The Trembling of a Leaf* 1921 and *Ashenden* 1928; and the plays *Lady Frederick* 1907 and *Our Betters* 1923.

Maugham was born in Paris and studied medicine at St Thomas's, London. During World War I he was a secret agent in Russia; his *Ashenden* spy stories are based on this experience.
Suggested reading
Calder, Robert *Willie: The Life of W Somerset Maugham* (1989)
Morgan, Ted *Maugham* (1980)
Raphael, Frederic *Somerset Maugham and His World* (1989)

Money is like a sixth sense without which you cannot make a complete use of the other five.

SOMERSET MAUGHAM
Of Human Bondage ch 51 1915

Maupassant (Henry René Albert) Guy de (1850–1893). French author. He established a reputation with the short story 'Boule de suif/Ball of Fat' 1880 and wrote some 300 short stories in all. His novels include *Une Vie/A Woman's Life* 1883 and *Bel-Ami* 1885. He was encouraged as a writer by Gustave Flaubert.
Suggested reading
Lerner, Michael *Maupassant* (1975)
Steegmuller, Francis *Maupassant: A Lion in the Path* (1949)
Mallace, Albert *Maupassant* (1974)

It is love that is sacred. ... Marriage and love have nothing in common. ... We marry only once ... but we may love twenty times. ... Marriage is law, and love is instinct.

GUY DE MAUPASSANT
'Love of Long Ago'

Maupin Armistead (1944–). US novelist and dramatist. His first six novels, from *Tales of the City* 1978 to *Sure of You* 1990, were revisions of a daily fiction serial in two newspapers in San Francisco, where they are set.

Through the characters in a run-down rooming house, Maupin gives a sharply delineated and ingeniously entertaining picture of urban life, especially gay life, that remains broadly optimistic even with the sad portrayal of AIDS in later volumes. He has also written the long-running play *Beach Blanket Babylon* 1975 and the words for the musical *Heart's Desire* 1990. *Tales of the City* was adapted into a drama series by Channel 4 TV in the UK 1994.

Mauriac François (1885–1970). French novelist. His novel *Le Baiser au lépreux/A Kiss for the Leper* 1922 describes the conflict of an unhappy marriage. The irreconcilability of Christian practice and human nature is examined in *Fleuve de feu/River of Fire* 1923, *Le Désert de l'amour/The Desert of Love* 1925, and *Thérèse Desqueyroux* 1927. Nobel Prize for Literature 1952.

Maurice (John) F(rederick) D(enison) (1805–1872). Anglican cleric from 1834, co-founder with Charles Kingsley of the Christian Socialist movement. He was deprived of his professorships in English history, literature, and divinity at King's College, London, because his *Theological Essays* 1853 attacked the doctrine of eternal punishment; he became professor of moral philosophy at Cambridge 1866.

Maurois André. Pen name of Emile Herzog (1885–1967). French novelist and writer. His works include the semi-autobiographical *Bernard Quesnay* 1926 and fictionalized biographies, such as *Ariel* 1923, a life of Shelley.

A marriage without conflicts is almost as inconceivable as a nation without crises.

ANDRÉ MAUROIS
The Art of Living 1940

In World War I he was attached to the British Army, and the essays in *Les Silences du Colonel Bramble* 1918 offer humorously sympathetic observations on the British character.

Mauroy Pierre (1928–). French socialist politician, prime minister 1981–84. He oversaw the introduction of a radical reflationary programme. He was first secretary (leader) of the Socialist Party 1988–1992.

Mauroy worked for the FEN teachers' trade union and served as national secretary for the Young Socialists during the 1950s, rising in the ranks of the Socialist Party in the NE region. He entered the National Assembly 1973 and was prime minister in the Mitterrand government of 1981, but was replaced by Laurent Fabius in July 1984.

Maury Antonia Caetana de Paiva Pereira (1866–1952). US expert in stellar spectroscopy who specialized in the detection of binary stars. She became an assistant at the Harvard College Observatory, under the direction of Edward Pickering, even before she graduated in 1887. Later she lectured in astronomy in various US cities, and taught privately. In 1908 she returned to Harvard to study the complex spectrum of Beta Lyrae.

Having assisted Pickering in establishing that the star Mizar (Zeta Ursae Majoris) is a binary star, with two distinct spectra, Maury was the first to calculate the 104-day period of this star. In 1889, she discovered a second such star, Beta Aurigae, and established that it has a period of only four days.

Studying the spectra of bright stars, Maury found three major divisions among spectra, depending upon the width and distinctness of the spectral lines. In 1896 she published her new classification scheme for spectral lines, based on the examination of nearly 5,000 photographs and covering nearly 700 bright stars in the northern sky.

Maury Matthew Fontaine (1806–1873). US naval officer, founder of the US Naval Oceanographic Office. His system of recording oceanographic data is still used today.

Maury, Matthew US naval officer and oceanographer Matthew Maury. He wrote Navigation *after a voyage around the world 1830, and* The Physical Geography of the Sea *1855.*

Mauryan dynasty Indian dynasty *c.* 321–*c.* 185 BC, founded by Chandragupta Maurya (321–*c.* 279 BC). Under Emperor Asoka most of India was united for the first time, but after his death in 232 the empire was riven by dynastic disputes. Reliant on a highly organized aristocracy and a centralized administration, it survived until the assassination of Emperor Brihadratha 185 BC and the creation of the Sunga dynasty.

The empire's core lay in the former janapada of Magadha, situated in the Ganges valley of N India, near plentiful iron ore supplies and with its capital at Pataliputra (now Patna). Chandragupta and his son Bindusara (ruled *c.* 268–231 BC) expanded it to the W and S, and there was consolidation under Asoka. Divided into four provinces, each headed by a prince, the empire was noted for its comparatively advanced bureaucracy, and its encouragement of cultivation and commerce through public works and fiscal measures.

Mauss Marcel (1872–1950). French sociologist and anthropologist. In *The Gift* 1954, he argues that the exchange of gifts creates a system of reciprocity which is fundamental to the ordering of society. His initial studies concentrated on religion, especially the nature and function of sacrifice.

Mavor O H. Real name of the Scottish dramatist James ◊Bridie.

Mawson Douglas (1882–1958). Australian explorer who reached the magnetic South Pole on Shackleton's expedition of 1907–09. Knighted 1914. Mawson led Antarctic expeditions 1911–14 and 1929–31. Australia's first permanent Antarctic base was named after him. He was professor of mineralogy at the University of Adelaide 1920–53.
Suggested reading
Mawson, P *Mawson of the Antarctic* (1964)
Price, A G *The Winning of the Australian Antarctic* (1962)

Maxim Hiram Stevens (1840–1916). US-born British inventor of the first fully automatic machine gun, in 1884. Its efficiency was further improved by Maxim's development of a cordlike propellant explosive, cordite. Knighted 1901.

While working as chief engineer for the US Electric Lighting Company, he came up with a way of manufacturing carbon-coated filaments for the early light bulbs that ensured that each filament was evenly coated. Deciding to concentrate on arms manufacture, he settled in Britain and set up a small laboratory in London. The company created to produce the Maxim gun soon became absorbed into Vickers Limited. By 1889, the British Army had adopted the gun for use.

The Maxim gun of 1884 used the recoil from the shots to extract, eject, load, and fire cartridges. With a water-cooled barrel, it could fire ten rounds per second.

Maximilian (1832–1867). Emperor of Mexico 1864–67. He accepted that title when the French emperor Napoleon III's troops occupied the country, but encountered resistance from the deposed president Benito Juárez. In 1866, after the French troops withdrew on the insistence of the USA, Maximilian was captured by Mexican republicans and shot. Brother of Emperor Franz Joseph of Austria, he was given command of the Austrian navy in 1854, and was governor of Lombardy and Venetia 1857–59. He married Princess Charlotte of Belgium in 1857.

Unstable, easily tempted by wild plans, usually without patience, and always without money.

K Brandi on MAXIMILIAN I
The Emperor Charles V 1939

Maximilian I (1459–1519). Holy Roman emperor from 1493, the son of Emperor Frederick III. He had acquired the Low Countries through his marriage to Mary of Burgundy 1477.

He married his son Philip I (the 'Handsome') to the heiress to the Spanish throne, and undertook long wars with Italy and Hungary in attempts to extend Habsburg power. He was the patron of the artist Dürer.

Maxwell (Ian) Robert (born Jan Ludvik Hoch) (1923–1991). Czech-born British publishing and newspaper proprietor who owned several UK national newspapers, including the *Daily Mirror*, the Macmillan Publishing Company, and the New York *Daily News*. At the time of his death the Maxwell domain carried debts of some $3.9 billion.

Born into a poor Jewish family in Czechoslovakia, he escaped to Romania 1939 and later to Britain. His father was shot and his mother and other members of his family died in Auschwitz. As a young man, he had a distinguished wartime army career, and was awarded the Military Cross.

He founded two major organizations: the family-owned Liechtenstein-based Maxwell Foundation, which owned 51% of Mirror Group Newspapers; and Maxwell Communication Corporation, 67% owned by the Maxwell family, which had shares in publishing, electronics, and information companies.

He was also the publisher of the English edition of *Moscow News* from 1988, and had private interests (not connected with the Maxwell Corporation) in the Hungarian newspapers *Esti Hirlap* and *Magyar Hirlap* (he owned 40% of the latter, from 1989), the German *Berliner Verlag*, and the Israeli *Maariv*.

Maxwell was Labour member of Parliament for Buckingham 1964–70. Acquiring the Mirror Group of newspapers from Reed International 1984, he introduced colour and made it profitable. In 1990 he bought the US book publisher Macmillan and in 1991 the New York *Daily News*, which was on the verge of closure after a bitter labour dispute. In the UK the national newspapers owned by the Maxwell Foundation 1984–91 were the *Daily Mirror*, *Sunday Mirror*, and *People* (all of which support the Labour party); in 1990 the weekly *European* was launched.

In late 1991 Maxwell, last seen on his yacht off the Canary Islands, was found dead at sea. His sons Kevin and Ian were named as his successors. After his death it was revealed that he had been involved in fraudulent practices for much of his career. In 1991 the Serious Fraud Office started an investigation into pension fund losses following reports of transfers of over £400 million from the Maxwell pension funds to the private Maxwell firms, to offset mounting company losses, affecting more than 30,000 current and future pensioners. Kevin and Ian Maxwell and Larry Trachtenberg (financial adviser) were arrested and charged 1992. In May 1995 Kevin and Ian Maxwell went on trial, charged with conspiring to commit fraud. In Jan 1996 they were cleared of all charges to defraud the Maxwell pension funds, following an eight-month trial that cost £25 million, although Kevin has to face a further trial.

Suggested reading
Bower, Tim *Maxwell* (1992)
Greenslade, Roy *Maxwell* (1992)
Haines, Joe *Maxwell* (1988)

The only laws of matter are those which our minds must fabricate, and the only laws of mind are fabricated by matter.

JAMES CLERK MAXWELL
Attributed remark

Maxwell James Clerk (1831–1879). Scottish physicist. His main achievement was in the understanding of electromagnetic waves: Maxwell's equations bring together electricity, magnetism, and light in one set of relations. He studied gases, optics, and the sensation of colour, and his theoretical work in magnetism prepared the way for wireless telegraphy and telephony.

In developing the kinetic theory of gases, Maxwell gave the final proof that heat resides in the motion of molecules. Studying colour vision, Maxwell explained how all colours could be built up from mixtures of the primary colours red, green, and blue. Maxwell confirmed English physicist Thomas Young's theory that the eye has three kinds of receptors sensitive to the primary colours, and showed that colour blindness is due to defects in the receptors. In 1861 he produced the first colour photograph to use a three-colour process.

He was professor of natural philosophy at Aberdeen 1856–60, and of natural philosophy and astronomy at London 1860–65. From 1871 he was professor of experimental physics at Cambridge, where he set up the Cavendish Laboratory 1874. Maxwell's works include *Perception of Colour* 1860, *Theory of Heat* 1871, *Treatise on Electricity and Magnetism* 1873, and *Matter and Motion* 1876.

Suggested reading
Everitt, C W F *James Clerk Maxwell: Physicist and Natural Philosopher* (1975)
Tolstoy, Ivan *James Clerk Maxwell* (1982)

May Thomas Erskine, 1st Baron Farnborough (1815–1886). English constitutional jurist. He was Clerk of the House of Commons from 1871 until 1886, when he was created Baron Farnborough. He wrote a practical *Treatise on the Law, Privileges, Proceedings, and Usage of Parliament* 1844, the authoritative work on parliamentary procedure. KCB 1866.

The love boat has crashed against the everyday. You and I, we are quits, and there is no point in listing mutual pains, sorrows, and hurts.

VLADIMIR MAYAKOVSKY
Unfinished poem written at the time of his suicide 1930

Mayakovsky Vladimir Vladimirovich (1893–1930). Russian Futurist poet. He combined revolutionary propaganda with efforts to revolutionize poetic technique in his poems '150,000,000' 1920 and 'V I Lenin' 1924. His satiric play *The Bedbug* 1928 was taken in the West as an attack on philistinism in the USSR.

Maybach Wilhelm (1846–1929). German engineer and inventor who worked with Gottlieb Daimler on the development of early motorcars. Maybach invented the float-feed carburettor, which allowed petrol to be used as a fuel for internal-combustion engines, most of which up to that time had been fuelled by gas.

Maybach and Daimler went into partnership 1882 in Stuttgart, where they produced one of the first petrol engines. In 1895, Maybach became technical director of the Daimler Motor Company. He left Daimlers in 1907 to set up his own factory for making engines for Zeppelin's airships.

In 1901, Maybach designed the first Mercedes car. He invented the spray-nozzle or float-feed carburettor in 1893. It made the fuel enter through a jet as a fine spray. The vaporized fuel mixed with air to produce a combustible mixture for the engine's cylinders. Maybach's other inventions include the honeycomb radiator, an internal expanding brake 1901, and an axle-locating system for use with independent suspensions.

Mayer Christian (1719–1783). Austrian astronomer, mathematician, and physicist. He was the first to investigate and catalogue double stars, though his equipment was unable to distinguish true binary stars (in orbit round each other) from separate stars seen together only by the coincidence of Earth's viewpoint.

Mayer was born in Moravia. He became a Jesuit priest and in 1752 professor of mathematics and physics at Heidelberg. When the elector palatine Karl Theodor built an observatory at Schwetzingen, and then a larger one at Mannheim, Mayer was appointed court astronomer. He lost this post with the pope's dissolution of the Jesuit order in 1773, although he managed to continue his astronomical studies.

Mayer measured the degree of the meridian, based on work conducted in Paris and in the Rhineland Palatinate, and observed the transits of Venus in 1761 and 1769. The latter observation was conducted in Russia at the invitation of Catherine II.

Mayer Johann Tobias (1723–1762). German cartographer, astronomer, and physicist who improved standards of observation and navigation. He produced a map of the Moon's surface and concluded that it had no atmosphere.

In 1746 he began work for the Homann Cartographic Bureau in Nuremberg, and he ended his career as professor at the Georg August Academy in Göttingen.

At the Homann Cartographic Bureau, Mayer drew up some 30 maps of Germany. These established exacting new standards for using geographical data in conjunction with astronomical details to determine latitudes and longitudes on Earth. To obtain some of the astronomical details, he observed lunar oscillations and eclipses using a telescope of his own design. *Mayer's Lunar Tables* 1753 were correct to one minute of arc.

Mayer also invented a simple and accurate method for calculating solar eclipses, compiled a catalogue of zodiacal stars, and studied stellar proper motion.

Mayer Julius Robert von (1814–1878). German physicist who in 1842 anticipated James Joule in deriving the mechanical equivalent of heat, and Hermann von Helmholtz in the principle of conservation of energy.

In 1845, Mayer extended the principle to show that living things are powered solely by physical processes utilizing solar energy and not by any kind of innate vital force. He described the energy conversions that take place in living organisms, realizing that plants convert the Sun's energy into food that is consumed by animals to provide a source of energy to power their muscles and provide body heat.

Mayer Louis B(urt). Adopted name of Eliezer Mayer (1885–1957). Russian-born US film producer. He immigrated with his parents to Canada 1888. Inheriting his father's scrap-metal business, he settled in Massachussetts 1907. Attracted to the entertainment industry, he became a successful theatre-owner in New England and in 1914 began to buy the distribution rights to feature films. Mayer was soon involved in film production, moving to Los Angeles 1918 and becoming one of the founders of Metro-Goldwyn-Mayer (MGM) studios 1924. It was Mayer who was largely responsible for MGM's lavish style. He retired 1951.

Mayer Robert (1879–1985). German-born British philanthropist. He founded the Robert Mayer Concerts for Children and the Transatlantic Foundation Anglo-American Scholarships. KCVO 1979.

Mayhew Patrick Barnabas Burke (1929–). British lawyer and Conservative politician, Northern Ireland secretary from 1992. He was appointed Solicitor General 1983 and four years later Attorney General, becoming the government's chief legal adviser. His appointment as Northern Ireland secretary came at a propitious time and within two years he had witnessed the voluntary cessation of violence by both Republicans and Loyalists.

After embarking on a successful legal career, Mayhew entered the House of Commons 1974, winning the safe seat of Royal Tunbridge Wells, and five years later began his ministerial ascent in the Department of Employment. Knighted 1983.

Maynard Smith John (1920–). British biologist. He applied game theory to animal behaviour and developed the concept of the evolutionary stable strategy as a mathematical technique for studying the evolution of behaviour. His books include *The Theory of Evolution* 1958 and *Evolution and the Theory of Games* 1982.

Mayo William James (1861–1939). US surgeon, founder, with his brother Charles Horace Mayo (1865–1939), of the Mayo Clinic for medical treatment 1889 in Rochester, Minnesota.

Mays Willie Howard, Jr (1931–). US baseball player who played with the New York (later San Francisco) Giants 1951–72 and the New York Mets 1973. He hit 660 career home runs, third best in baseball history, and was also an outstanding fielder and runner. He was the National League's Most Valuable Player 1954 and 1965.

Ma Yuan (*c.* 1190–1224). Chinese landscape painter. He worked in the lyrical tradition of the southern Song court. His paintings show a subtle use of tone and gentler brushwork than those of his contemporary Hsia Kuei.

Mazarin Jules (born Giulio Raimondo Mazzarini) (1602–1661). French politician who succeeded Richelieu as chief minister of France 1642. His attack on the power of the nobility led to the Fronde and his temporary exile, but his diplomacy achieved a successful conclusion to the Thirty Years' War, and, in alliance with

Oliver Cromwell during the British protectorate, he gained victory over Spain.

Suggested reading
Church, W F *The Impact of Absolutism in France* (1969)
Gowan, C D'O *The Background of the French Classics* (1960)
Hassall, A *Mazarin* (1973)
Treasure, Geoffrey *Mazarin: The Crisis of Absolutism in France* (1995)

The French are nice people. I allow them to sing and to write, and they allow me to do whatever I like.

Attributed to MAZARIN by Elizabeth Charlotte, Duchess of Orleans in a letter of 25 Oct 1715

Mazowiecki Tadeusz (1927–). Polish politician, founder member of Solidarity, and Poland's first postwar noncommunist prime minister 1989–90. Forced to introduce unpopular economic reforms, he was knocked out in the first round of the Nov 1990 presidential elections, resigning in favour of his former colleague Lech Walesa. In April 1994 he formed the centrist Freedom Union (UW).

A former member of the Polish parliament 1961–70, he was debarred from re-election by the authorities after investigating the police massacre of Gdańsk strikers. He became legal adviser to Lech Walesa and, after a period of internment, edited the Solidarity newspaper *Tygodnik Solidarność*. In 1989 he became prime minister after the elections denied the communists their customary majority. A devout Catholic, he is a close friend of Pope John Paul II.

Nations are the citizens of humanity, as individuals are the citizens of the nation.

GIUSEPPE MAZZINI
On the Duties of Man, printed in E A Venturi *Joseph Mazzini* 1875

Mazzini Giuseppe (1805–1872). Italian nationalist. He was a member of the revolutionary society, the Carbonari, and founded in exile the nationalist movement Giovane Italia (Young Italy) 1831. He acted as a focus for the movement for Italian unity.

Mazzini, born in Genoa, studied law. For his subversive activity with the Carbonari he was imprisoned 1830, then went to France, founding in Marseille the Young Italy movement, followed by an international revolutionary organization, Young Europe, 1834. For many years he lived in exile in France, Switzerland, and the UK, and was condemned to death in his absence by the Sardinian government, but returned to Italy for the revolution of 1848. He conducted the defence of Rome against French forces and, when it failed, he refused to join in the capitulation and returned to London, where he continued to agitate until his death in Geneva, Switzerland.

Suggested reading
Griffith, Gwilym *Mazzini: Prophet of Modern Europe* (1932, rep 1970)
Salvemini, Gaetano *Mazzini* (1956)
Smith, Denis M *Mazzini* (1994)

Mbeki Thabo (1942–). South African politician, first executive deputy president from 1994. As chair of the African National Congress (ANC) from 1989, he played an important role in the constitutional talks with the de Klerk government which eventually led to the adoption of a nonracial political system.

An active member of the ANC from an early age, Mbeki led its student and, later, youth branches, and was, in consequence, detained for six weeks by the South African authorities 1962. After his release he worked for the ANC in their London offices 1967–70 and subsequently underwent several months military training in the Soviet Union. As a leading member of the ANC, he represented it in Swaziland 1975–76 and Nigeria 1976–78. He was director of information and publicity 1984–89 and then national chairman.

Mboya Tom (Thomas Joseph) (1930–1969). Kenyan politician, a founder of the Kenya African National Union (KANU), and minister of economic affairs from 1964 until his assassination.

Mead George Herbert (1863–1931). US philosopher and social psychologist who helped to found the philosophy of pragmatism. He taught at the University of Chicago during its prominence as a centre of social scientific development in the early 20th century, and is regarded as the founder of symbolic interactionism. His work on group interaction had a major influence on sociology, stimulating the development of role theory, phenomenology, and ethnomethodology.

Suggested reading
Baldwin, J D *George Herbert Mead* (1986)
Miller, D *George Herbert Mead* (1973)
Mead, George Herbert *Mind, Self and Society* (1934)

Human beings do not carry civilization in their genes.
MARGARET MEAD
New York Times Magazine April 1964

Mead Margaret (1901–1978). US anthropologist who popularized cultural relativity and challenged the conventions of Western society with *Coming of Age in Samoa* 1928 and subsequent works. Her fieldwork was later criticized. She was a popular speaker on civil liberties, ecological sanity, feminism, and population control.

Coming of Age in Samoa was a study of differences in temperament between males and females in Samoan and Western societies caused by child-rearing practices. She expanded on this same subject in *Growing Up in New Guinea* 1930 and *Sex and Temperament in Three Primitive Societies* 1935. She also wrote *And Keep Your Powder Dry* 1942, about the US national character, and *Soviet Attitudes Toward Authority* 1951. Her autobiographical works include *Blackberry Winter: My Earlier Years* 1972 and *Letters from the Field, 1925–1975* 1977.

Suggested reading
Freeman, D *Margaret Mead and Samoa* (1983)
Gordon, Joan *Margaret Mead: The Complete Biography 1925–1975* (1977)
Mead, Margaret *Culture and Commitment* (1970)
Mead, Margaret *Blackberry Winter: My Earlier Years* (1972)

Meade George Gordon (1815–1872). US military leader. During the American Civil War, he commanded the Pennsylvania volunteers at the Peninsular Campaign, Bull Run, and Antietam 1862. He led the Army of the Potomac, and the Union forces at Gettysburg 1863. After the war, he served as military governor of Georgia, Alabama, and Florida 1868–69.

Born in Cadiz, Spain, Meade graduated from West Point military academy 1835. After working on private railroad and surveying projects 1836–42, he returned to the army, serving in the Mexican War 1846–48.

Meade James Edward (1907–). British Keynesian economist. He shared a Nobel prize in 1977 for his work on trade and capital movements, and published a four-volume *Principles of Political Economy* 1965–76.

Meade Richard John Hannay (1938–). British equestrian in three-day events. He won three Olympic gold medals 1968 and 1972, and was twice a world champion. He is associated with horses such as Cornishman, Laureston, and The Poacher, and has won all the sport's major honours.

Mechnikov Ilya Ilich (1845–1916). Russian-born French zoologist who discovered the function of white blood cells and phagocytes (amoebalike blood cells that engulf foreign bodies). He also described how these 'scavenger cells' can attack the body itself (auto-immune disease). He shared the Nobel Prize for Physiology or Medicine 1908.

He was professor of zoology and anatomy at Odessa 1867–82, when he moved to Messina in Italy to continue his research. He briefly returned to Odessa, but left Russia 1888 to join the Pasteur Institute in Paris, becoming director on Louis Pasteur's death 1895.

While studying the transparent larvae of starfish, Mechnikov observed that certain cells surrounded and engulfed foreign particles that entered the bodies of the larvae. Later he demonstrated that phagocytes exist in higher animals, and form the first line of defence against acute infections. Mechnikov spent the last decade of his life trying to demonstrate that lactic acid-producing bacteria in the intestine increase a person's lifespan.

Meciar Vladimir (1942–). Slovak politician, prime minister of the Slovak Republic Jan 1993–March 1994 and again from Oct 1994. He held a number of posts under the Czechoslovak communist regime until, as a dissident, he was expelled from the party 1970. He joined the Public Against Violence (PAV) movement 1989, campaigning for a free Czechoslovakia, then, as leader of the Movement for a Democratic Slovakia (HZDS) from 1990, sought an independent Slovak state. With his Czech counterparts Meciar played an important role in ensuring that the 'velvet revolution' of 1989 was translated into a similarly bloodless 'velvet divorce'. Under the federal system, Meciar became prime minister of the Slovak Republic 1990 and the new state's first prime minister Jan 1993.

His resignation from the post of premier March 1994 followed a confrontation with President Kovac over Meciar's handling of the privatization programme. The HZDS's election victory Oct 1994 returned Meciar to power.

A nationalist populist, he pledged to halt voucher privatization and to curb the growing influence of the republic's ethnic-Hungarian minority.

Medawar Peter Brian (1915–1987). British immunologist who, with Macfarlane Burnet, discovered that the body's resistance to grafted tissue is undeveloped in the newborn child, and studied the way it is acquired. They shared a Nobel prize 1960. Knighted 1965.

He was professor of zoology at Birmingham University 1947–51 and at University College, London, 1951–62; he was director of the National Institute for Medical Research 1962–75. In 1977 he was appointed professor of experimental medicine at the Royal Institution.

Acting on Burnet's hypothesis that an animal's ability to produce a specific antibody is not inherited, Medawar inoculated mouse embryos of one strain with cells from mice of another strain, and found that the embryos did not produce antibodies against the cells of the other strain. Medawar's work has been vital in understanding the phenomenon of tissue rejection following transplantation.

Medawar wrote essays for the general reader, collected in, for example, *The Hope of Progress* 1972, *The Art of the Soluble* 1967, and *The Limits of Science* 1985.

Medici noble family of Florence, the city's rulers from 1434 until they died out 1737. Family members included ◊Catherine de' Medici, Pope ◊Leo X, Pope ◊Clement VII, and ◊Marie de' Medici.

Suggested reading
Brion, M *The Medici: A Great Florentine Family* (1969)
Hale, J R *Florence and the Medici* (1977)
Hibbert, C *The House of Medici* (1974)

Medici Cosimo de' (1389–1464). Italian politician and banker. Regarded as the model for Machiavelli's *The Prince*, he dominated the government of Florence from 1434 and was a patron of the arts. He was succeeded by his inept son Piero de' Medici (1416–1469).

We read that we ought to forgive our enemies, but we do not read that we ought to forgive our friends.
COSIMO DE' MEDICI (1389–1464)
quoted by Francis Bacon in *Apophthegms* 206 1624

Medici Cosimo de' (1519–1574). Italian politician, ruler of Florence; duke of Florence from 1537 and 1st grand duke of Tuscany from 1569.

Medici Ferdinand de' (1549–1609). Italian politician, grand duke of Tuscany from 1587.

Medici Giovanni de' (1360–1429). Italian entrepreneur and banker, with political influence in Florence as a supporter of the popular party. He was the father of Cosimo de' Medici.

Medici Lorenzo de', 'the Magnificent' (1449–1492). Italian politician, ruler of Florence from 1469. He was also a poet and a generous patron of the arts.

Whoever wants to be happy, let him be so: about tomorrow there's no knowing.

LORENZO DE' MEDICI 'THE MAGNIFICENT'
Trionfo di Bacco ed Arianna

Medvedev Vadim Andreyevich (1925–). Soviet communist politician. He was deputy chief of propaganda 1970–78, was in charge of party relations with communist countries 1986–88, and in 1988 was appointed by the Soviet leader Gorbachev to succeed the conservative Ligachev as head of ideology. He adhered to a firm Leninist line.

Mee Margaret Ursula (1909–1988). English botanical artist. In the 1950s she went to Brazil, where she accurately and comprehensively painted many plant species of the Amazon basin. She is thought to have painted more species than any other botanical artist.

Meegeren Hans, or Henricus, van (1889–1947). Dutch forger, mainly of Vermeer's paintings. His 'Vermeer' *Christ at Emmaus* was bought for Rotterdam's Boymans Museum 1937. He was discovered when a 'Vermeer' sold to the Nazi leader Goering was traced back to him after World War II. Sentenced to a year's imprisonment, he died two months later.

Mehmet Ali or Muhammad Ali (1769–1849). Pasha (governor) of Egypt from 1805, and founder of the dynasty that ruled until 1953. An Albanian in the Ottoman service, he had originally been sent to Egypt to fight the French. As pasha, he established a European-style army and navy, fought his Turkish overlord 1831 and 1839, and conquered Sudan.

Suggested reading
Dodwell, H H *The Founder of Modern Egypt: A Study of Muhammad Ali* (1913, rep 1974)
Holt, P M *Egypt and the Fertile Crescent, 1566–1922* (1966)
Vatikiotis, P J *The History of Modern Egypt* (1991)

Mehta Ved Parkash (1934–). Indian journalist. He was educated at blind schools in Bombay and the USA, and later at Oxford and Harvard. A staff writer for the *New Yorker* since 1960 (he took US citizenship 1975), he has written family and personal chronicles such as *Daddyji* 1971 and *The Ledge between the Streams* 1984 and humane but deceptively mild-mannered essays on philosophical, theological, and historical issues collected in volumes such as *Fly and the Fly-Bottle* 1963.

Mehta Zubin (1936–). Indian-born US conductor. He was appointed music director of the Montreal Symphony 1961–67 and of the Los Angeles Philharmonic 1962–78, thus becoming the first person to direct two North American symphony orchestras simultaneously. He has been music director of the New York Philharmonic from 1978. He specializes in robust, polished interpretations of 19th- and 20th-century repertoire, including contemporary US composers.

Meier Richard Alan (1934–). US architect. His white designs spring from the poetic Modernism of the Le Corbusier villas of the 1920s. Originally one of the New York Five, Meier has remained closest to its purist ideals. His abstract style is at its most mature in the Museum für Kunsthandwerk (Museum of Arts and Crafts), Frankfurt, Germany, which was completed 1984.

Earlier schemes are the Bronx Developmental Centre, New York, 1970–76, and the Athenaeum–New Harmony, Indiana, 1974. He is the architect for the Getty Museum, Los Angeles, due to open 1996.

Meiji Mutsuhito (1852–1912). Emperor of Japan from 1867, under the regnal era name Meiji ('enlightened'). During his reign Japan became a world industrial and naval power. His ministers abolished the feudal system and discrimination against the lowest caste, established state schools, reformed the civil service, and introduced conscription, the Western calendar, and other measures to modernize Japan, including a constitution 1889.

He took the personal name Mutsuhito when he became crown prince 1860. He was the son of Emperor Kōmei (reigned 1846–67), who was a titular ruler in the last years of the Tokugawa shogunate.

Meikle Andrew (1719–1811). Scottish millwright who in 1785 designed and built the first practical threshing machine for separating cereal grains from the husks.

Meinecke Friedrich (1862–1954). German historian who endeavoured to combine intellectual and political history and produce a synthesis of cultural and political values. His book *Cosmopolitanism and the National State* 1908 is an account of how the Enlightenment's ideals gave way to the nationalism of the romantics.

Meinecke worked in the Prussian State Archives for 14 years before becoming a professional historian. His works include *Machiavellism* 1924, concerned with the ideas of statecraft and their development from the 15th century to the time of Frederick the Great, and *Historicism* 1936, which deals with the beginnings and development of historicism from the Italian philosopher Giambattista Vico onwards. Meinecke's critical reaction and opposition to the Nazi state are explained in his book *The German Catastrophe* 1946.

Meinhof Ulrike Marie (1934–1976). West German urban guerrilla, member of the Baader-Meinhof gang in the 1970s. A left-wing journalist, Meinhof was converted to the use of violence to achieve political change by the imprisoned Andreas Baader. She helped free Baader and they became joint leaders of the urban guerrilla organization the Red Army Faction. As the faction's chief ideologist, Meinhof was arrested in 1972 and, in 1974, sentenced to eight years' imprisonment. She committed suicide 1976 in the Stammheim high-security prison.

Meinong Alexius (1853–1920). Austrian philosopher who held that non-existents – like the golden mountain, the round square, or dragons – have classifiable natures. He also distinguished many different types of existence, most notably subsistence, which he believed to be the type of existence possessed by states of mind.

Meinong was professor of philosophy at Graz from 1889 until his death. His works include *Über Annahmen/On Assumptions* 1902. His philosophical psychology influenced English philosophers Bertrand Russell and G E Moore.

Meir Golda (born Mabovitch, later Myerson) (1898–1978). Israeli Labour (*Mapai*) politician. Born in Russia, she emigrated to the USA 1906, and in 1921 went to Palestine. She was foreign minister 1956–66 and prime minister 1969–74. Criticism of the Israelis' lack of preparation for the 1973 Arab-Israeli War led to election losses for Labour and, unable to form a government, she resigned.

Suggested reading
McAuley, K *Golda Meir* (1985)
Meir, Golda *My Life* (1975)

Meiselas Susan (1948–). US freelance war photographer. She has covered conflicts in Nicaragua and El Salvador. Her brilliant Cibachrome prints seem anti-heroic in their intention.

Meitner Lise (1878–1968). Austrian-born Swedish physicist who worked with German radiochemist Otto Hahn and was the first to realize that they had inadvertently achieved the fission of uranium. They also discovered protactinium 1918. She refused to work on the atom bomb.

Meitner become an assistant to Max Planck at the Berlin Institute of Theoretical Physics, and she was made professor at Berlin 1926. But in 1938 she was forced to leave Nazi Germany, and soon found a post at the Nobel Physical Institute in Stockholm. In 1947, a laboratory was established for her by the Swedish Atomic Energy Commission, and she later worked on an experimental nuclear reactor.

In 1934 Meitner began to study the effects of neutron bombardment on uranium with Hahn. It was not found until after Meitner had fled from Germany that the neutron bombardment had produced not transuranic elements, as they expected, but three isotopes of barium. Meitner and her nephew Otto Frisch realized that the uranium nucleus had been split; they called it fission. A paper describing their analysis appeared 1939.

Meitner continued to study the nature of fission products. Her later research concerned the production of new radioactive species using the cyclotron, and also the development of the shell model of the nucleus.

Melanchthon Philip. Assumed name of Philip Schwarzerd (1497–1560). German theologian who helped Martin Luther prepare a German translation of the New Testament. In 1521 he issued the first systematic formulation of Protestant theology, reiterated in the *Confession of Augsburg* 1530.

He adopted the name Melanchthon as the Greek form of his family name, meaning 'black earth'. He was a humanist, and was professor of Greek at Wittenberg from 1518. There he came under Luther's influence and became an evangelical theologian. He also translated and wrote commentaries on the Bible.

Suggested reading
Manschrek, C *Philip Melanchthon: The Quiet Reformer* (1958)
Pauck, W (ed) *Melanchthon and Bucer* (1969)

Madame Melba has the voice of a lark and, so far as her acting is evidence, the soul of one also.

The *New York Times* on NELLIE MELBA as Manon,
quoted in Joseph Wechsberg *The Opera* 1972

Melba Nellie. Adopted name of Helen Porter Mitchell (1861–1931). Australian soprano. She studied in Paris under Marchesi 1886, and made her opera debut 1887. Her recordings of Italian and French romantic opera, including a notable *Lucia di Lammermoor*, are distinguished by a radiant purity and technical finesse. DBE 1918.

Peach melba (half a peach plus vanilla ice cream and melba sauce, made from sweetened, fresh raspberries) and melba toast (crisp, thin toast) are named after her.

Suggested reading
Hetherington, John *Melba* (1968)
Melba, Dame Nellie *Melodies and Memories* (memoirs) (1925)
Welchsberg, Joseph *Red Plush and Black Velvet* (1961)

Melbourne (Henry) William Lamb, 2nd Viscount Melbourne (1779–1848). British Whig politician. Home secretary 1830–34, he was briefly prime minister in 1834 and again 1835–41. Accused in 1836 of seducing Caroline Norton, he lost the favour of William IV. Viscount 1829.

Melbourne was married 1805–25 to Lady Caroline Ponsonby (novelist Lady Caroline Lamb, 1785–1828). He was an adviser to the young Queen Victoria.

Meldrum (Duncan) Max (1875–1955). Australian artist, born in Scotland. His firmly held belief was that art was 'the science of exact optical analysis', concentrating on tonal quality rather than drawing. He lived and painted in Paris 1899–1913. His *Portrait of the Artist's Mother* 1913 (National Gallery of Victoria, Melbourne), painted shortly after his return to Melbourne, is probably his best-known work.

Meleager (*c.* 140–*c.* 170 BC). Greek philosopher and epigrammatist. He compiled an anthology of epigrams, known as the *Garland*, for which he wrote an introduction, comparing each poet to an appropriate flower. His own epigrams are mostly erotic, and successfully combine sophistication with feeling.

Melgarejo Mariano (*c.* 1820–1871). Bolivian dictator and most notorious of the caudillos who dominated 19th-century Bolivia. Melgarejo seized power 1864 and survived a series of rebellions before he was overthrown by the last in a series of military uprisings seven years later.

Melgarejo sold disputed land to Brazil, allowed Chilean businessmen to exploit Bolivian nitrate deposits, and seized large tracts of Indian land in the Altiplano (high plateau) to be sold to the highest bidder. This policy deprived virtually all Indians in the area of their land within a few decades.

Méliès Georges (1861–1938). French film pioneer. Beginning his career as a stage magician, Méliès' interest in cinema was sparked by the Lumière brothers' cinematograph, premiered 1895. He constructed a camera and founded a production company, Star Film. From 1896 to 1912 he made over 1,000 films, mostly fantasies (including *Le Voyage dans la lune/A Trip to the Moon* 1902). He developed trick effects, slow motion, double exposure, and dissolves, and in 1897 built Europe's first film studio at Montreuil. Méliès failed to develop as a film maker and he went bankrupt 1913.

Mellanby Kenneth (1908–). British ecologist and entomologist who in the 1960s drew attention to the environmental effects of pollution, particularly by pesticides. He advocated the use of biological control methods, such as introducing animals that feed on pests.

On the staff of the London School of Hygiene and Tropical Medicine 1930–45, he went to E Africa to study the tsetse fly; while doing his World War II military service, he investigated scrub typhus in Burma (now Myanmar) and New Guinea. In 1947 he became the principal of University College, Ibadan, Nigeria's first university, which he played a part in creating. He was head of the Entomology Department at Rothamsted Experimental Station 1955–61, when he founded and became director of the Monks Wood Research Station (now called the Institute of Terrestrial Ecology) in Huntingdon, Cambridgeshire.

Mellon Andrew William (1855–1937). US financier who donated his art collection to found the National Gallery of Art, Washington DC, in 1937. His son, Paul Mellon (1907–) was its president 1963–79. He funded Yale University's Center for British Art, New Haven, Connecticut, and donated major works of art to both collections.

Melnikov Konstantin Stepanovich (1890–1974). Soviet architect. He was noted for his imaginative interpretations of the Constructivist ethic. His design for the Rusakov Workers Club, Moscow, 1927–28,

Melbourne English Whig politician, a supporter of Parliamentary reform. He was prime minister when Queen Victoria came to the throne and showed tact and benevolence in guiding her through her early years of rule.

leans towards Expressionism, with its interior dominated by cantilevered segments from the highest of three auditoria that extend over the open ground-floor plan. The Club was later to influence James Stirling in his Leicester University Engineering Building 1959–63.

He is indebted to his memory for his jests, and to his imagination for his facts.

R B Sheridan on HERMAN MELVILLE
in reply to Dundas in the House of Commons

Melville Herman (1819–1891). US writer. His novel *Moby-Dick* 1851 was inspired by his whaling experiences in the South Seas and is considered to be one of the masterpieces of American literature. These experiences were also the basis for earlier fiction, such as the adventure narratives of *Typee* 1846 and *Omoo* 1847. *Billy Budd, Sailor* was completed just before his death and published 1924. Although most of his works were unappreciated during his lifetime, today he is one of the most highly regarded of US authors.

Melville was born in Albany, New York. His family was left destitute when his father became bankrupt and died when Melville was 12. He went to sea as a cabin boy 1839. His love for the sea was inspired by this and later voyages. He published several volumes of verse, as well as short stories (*The Piazza Tales* 1856). He worked in the New York customs office 1866–85, writing no prose from 1857 until *Billy Budd*. A friend of Nathaniel Hawthorne, he explored the dark, troubled side of American experience in novels of unusual form and great philosophical power.

Billy Budd was the basis of an opera by Benjamin Britten 1951, and was made into a film 1962.

Mendel *Austrian monk and botanist Gregor Johann Mendel, who, by characteristically breeding pea plants in a monastery garden, discovered the basic laws of heredity. Mendel published his findings in 1865, but the importance of his results were not recognized at the time. It was not until 1900, sixteen years after his death, that his work was rediscovered and became the basis of modern genetics. (Ann Ronan/Image Select)*

Suggested reading
Hillway, N *Herman Melville* (1979)
Rosenberry, E H *Melville* (1979)
Samson, J *White Lies: Melville's Narratives of Facts* (1989)

Memling (or Memlinc) Hans (*c.* 1430–1494). Flemish painter. He was born near Frankfurt-am-Main, Germany, but worked in Bruges. Memling is said to have been a pupil of van der Weyden, but his style is calmer and softer. He painted religious subjects and portraits.

He settled at Bruges, *c.* 1466, where he had a prosperous career, producing religious paintings of great beauty and portraits of dignified reticence, anticipating those of Holbein in quality. His landscape backgrounds have singular charm. Though taking elements of style from van Eyck, Dirck Bouts, and van der Weyden, and showing little development in his work (save in his later years the introduction of some Italian decorative motives), his delicate sense of beauty makes him an outstanding master. Notable works are the *Mystic Marriage of St Catherine* (Hospital of St John, Bruges); the *Donne Triptych* (National Gallery, London), which includes a self-portrait; *Bathsheba* (Stuttgart), a life-sized nude; and such fine portraits as that of Guillaume Moreel and his wife (Brussels). His portraits include *Tommaso Portinari and His Wife* about 1480 (Metropolitan Museum of Art, New York), and he decorated the *Shrine of St Ursula* 1489 in the Hospital of St John, Bruges, which is now the Memling Museum.

Evil communications corrupt good manners.

MENANDER
in *Oxford Book of Greek Verse* 1930

Menander (*c.* 342–291 BC). Greek comic dramatist. Previously only known by reputation and some short fragments, Menander's comedy *Bad-Tempered Man* 316 BC, was discovered 1957 on Egyptian papyrus. Substantial parts of *The Samian Woman*, *The Arbitration*, *The Unkindest Cut*, and *The Shield* are also extant. His comedies, with their wit and ingenuity of plot often concerning domestic intrigue, were adapted by the Roman comic dramatists Plautus and Terence.

Mencius latinized name of Mengzi (*c.* 372–*c.* 289 BC). Chinese philosopher and moralist in the tradition of orthodox Confucianism. He considered human nature innately good, although this goodness required cultivation, and based his conception of morality on this conviction.

Mencius was born in Shantung (Shandong) province, and founded a Confucian school. After 20 years' unsuccessful search for a ruler to put into practice his enlightened political programme, based on people's innate goodness, he retired. His teachings are preserved as the *Book of Mengzi*.

Mencken H(enry) L(ouis) (1880–1956). US essayist and critic. He was known as 'the sage of Baltimore'. His unconventionally phrased, satiric contributions to the periodicals *The Smart Set* and *American Mercury* (both of which he edited) aroused controversy.

His critical reviews and essays were gathered in *Prejudices* 1919–27, comprising six volumes. He did not restrict himself to literary criticism, but took nearly every US institution to task in his writings. His book, *The American Language* 1918, is often revised.

Mendel Gregor Johann (1822–1884). Austrian biologist, founder of genetics. His experiments with successive generations of peas gave the basis for his theory of particulate inheritance rather than blending, involving dominant and recessive characters. His results, published 1865–69, remained unrecognized until the early 20th century. From his findings Mendel formulated his law of segregation and law of independent assortment of characters, which are now recognized as two of the fundamental laws of heredity.

Mendel was born in Heinzendorf (now Hyncice in the Czech Republic), and entered the Augustinian monastery in Brünn, Moravia (now Brno, Czech Republic) 1843. Later he studied at Vienna. In 1868 he became abbot of the monastery.

Suggested reading
Iltis, Hugo *Life of Mendel* (trs 1932, rep 1966)
Orel, V *Mendel* (1984)

Mendeleyev Dmitri Ivanovich (1834–1907). Russian chemist who framed the periodic law in chemistry 1869, which states that the chemical properties of the elements depend on their relative atomic masses. This law is the basis of the periodic table of the elements, in which the elements are arranged by atomic number and organized by their related groups.

Mendeleyev was the first chemist to understand that all elements are related members of a single ordered system. From his table he predicted the properties of elements then unknown, of which three (gallium, scandium, and germanium) were discovered in his lifetime. Meanwhile Lothar Meyer in Germany presented a similar but independent classification of the elements.

He became professor at the Technical Institute in St Petersburg 1864. But in 1890, for supporting a student rebellion, he was retired from the university and became controller of the Bureau for Weights and Measures.

His textbook *Principles of Chemistry* 1868–70 was widely adopted.

There will come a time, when the world will be filled with one science, one truth, one industry, one brotherhood, one friendship with nature ... this is my belief, it progresses, it grows stronger, this is worth living for, this is worth waiting for.

DMITRI IVANOVICH MENDELEYEV
In Y A Urmantsev *The Symmetry of Nature and the Nature of Symmetry* p 49 1974

Mendelsohn Erich (1887–1953). German Expressionist architect. He caused a sensation with his sculptural curved design for the Einstein Tower, Potsdam, 1919–20. His later work fused Modernist and Expressionist styles; in Britain he built the de la Warr Pavilion 1935–36 in Bexhill-on-Sea, East Sussex. In 1941 he settled in the USA, where he designed the Maimonides Hospital, San Francisco, 1946–50.

Mendelssohn (-Bartholdy) (Jakob Ludwig) Felix (1809–1847). German composer, also a pianist and conductor. His music has the lightness and charm of Classical music, applied to Romantic and descriptive subjects. Among his best-known works are *A Midsummer Night's Dream* 1827; the *Fingal's Cave* overture 1832; and five symphonies, which include the 'Reformation' 1830, the 'Italian' 1833, and the 'Scottish' 1842. He was instrumental in promoting the revival of interest in J S Bach's music. Mendelssohn wrote chamber music; two violin concertos, including the renowned E minor 1844; operas, including *Son and Strangers* 1829; piano works; choral works; and songs.

Suggested reading
Blunt, Wilfred *On the Wings of a Song: A Biography of Felix Mendelssohn* (1974)
Jacob, H *Felix Mendelssohn and his Times* (1963)
Kupferberg, Herbert *Felix Mendelssohn: His Life, His Family, His Music* (1972)
Marek, George R *Gentle Genius* (1972)
Werner, E *Mendelssohn* (1973)

Mendes Chico (Filho Francisco) (1944–1988). Brazilian environmentalist and labour leader. Opposed to the destruction of Brazil's rainforests, he organized itinerant rubber tappers into the Workers' Party (PT) and was assassinated by Darci Alves, a cattle rancher's son. Of 488 similar murders in land conflicts in Brazil 1985–89, his was the first to come to trial.

No French Radical leader since Gambetta in 1881 has enjoyed such wide esteem while having so little opportunity to shape policy.

Alan Palmer on PIERRE MENDÈS-FRANCE
in *Penguin Dictionary of Twentieth Century History* 1979

Mendès-France Pierre (1907–1982). French prime minister and foreign minister 1954–55. He extricated France from the war in Indochina, and prepared the way for Tunisian independence.

Mendoza Antonio de (c. 1490–1552). First Spanish viceroy of New Spain (Mexico) 1535–51. He attempted to develop agriculture and mining and supported the church in its attempts to convert the Indians. The system he established lasted until the 19th century. He was subsequently viceroy of Peru 1551–52.

Menelik II (1844–1913). Negus (emperor) of Abyssinia (now Ethiopia) from 1889. He defeated the Italians 1896 at Aduwa and thereby retained the independence of his country.

Menem Carlos Saul (1935–). Argentine politician, president from 1989. As president, he introduced sweeping privatization and public spending cuts, released hundreds of political prisoners jailed under the Alfonsín regime, and sent two warships to the Gulf to assist the USA against Iraq in the 1992 Gulf War (the only Latin American country to offer support to the USA). He also improved relations with the UK.

The son of Syrian immigrants to La Rioja province in the 1920s, Menem joined the Justicialist Party while training to be a lawyer. In 1963 he was elected president of the party in La Rioja and in 1983 became governor. In 1989 he defeated the Radical Civic Union Party candidate and became president of Argentina. Despite anti-British speeches during the election campaign, President Menem soon declared a wish to resume normal diplomatic relations with the UK and to discuss the future of the Falkland Islands in a spirit of compromise. He was re-elected 1995.

Menéndez de Avilés Pedro (1519–1574). Spanish colonial administrator in America. Philip II of Spain granted him the right to establish a colony in Florida to counter the French presence there. In 1565 he founded St Augustine and destroyed the French outpost at Fort Caroline.

Born in Avilés, Spain, he saw service in the navy of Charles V and was named to the vital post of captain general of the Indies fleet 1554. His later attempts to establish colonies in the Chesapeake region were unsuccessful but Menéndez maintained a firm Spanish claim on the Florida peninsula.

Menes (lived c. 3050 BC). Traditionally, the first king (pharaoh) of the first dynasty of ancient Egypt. He is said to have founded Memphis and organized worship of the gods.

Mengistu Haile Mariam (1937–). Ethiopian soldier and socialist politician, head of state 1977–91 (president 1987–91). He seized power in a coup, and instituted a regime of terror to stamp out any effective opposition. Confronted with severe problems of drought and secessionist uprisings, he survived with help from the USSR and the West until his violent overthrow by rebel forces.

As an officer in the Ethiopian army, Mengistu took part in the overthrow in 1974 of Emperor Haile Selassie and in 1977 led another coup, becoming head of state. In 1987 civilian rule was formally reintroduced, but with the Marxist-Leninist Workers' Party of Ethiopia the only legally permitted party. In May 1991, two secessionist forces closed in on the capital of Addis Ababa, and Mengistu fled the country. He was eventually granted asylum in Zimbabwe. In 1995 he was tried in absentia on charges of mass murder, relating to the assassination of Emperor Selassie and the deaths of thousands of his political opponents during the period known as the 'Red Terror' 1977–79.

Mengs Anton Raffael (1728–1779). German Neo-Classical painter. He was court painter in Dresden 1745 and in Madrid 1761; he then worked alternately in Rome and Spain.

He was the son of Ismael Mengs, court painter at Dresden. He was taken to Rome as a boy and had an early success with pastel portraits, later rivalling Batoni in portraiture. He married an Italian and lived and worked mainly in Italy, though also executing some commissions in Madrid. His friendship with the art historian Winckelmann and the ideas he expressed in writing gave him a certain importance in the Neo-Classic development, but his *Parnassus*

Menuhin *The violinist and conductor Yehudi Menuhin in 1991. At the age of 16 he played Elgar's Violin Concerto with the 75-year-old composer as conductor, and since then has inspired several composers to write for him. During recent years he has turned increasingly to conducting.*

(Villa Albani, Rome) has been generally considered a poor piece of eclecticism and his emptiness of style was severely criticized by Goethe.

Menninger Karl Augustus (1893–1990). US psychiatrist, instrumental in reforming public mental-health facilities. With his father, psychiatrist Charles Menninger, he founded the Menninger Clinic in Topeka 1920 and with his brother William, also a psychiatrist, established the Menninger Foundation 1941. Among his influential books were *The Human Mind* 1930, *Man Against Himself*, and *The Vital Balance* 1963.

Menon (Vengalil Krishnan Kunji-) Krishna (1897–1974). Indian politician who was a leading light in the Indian nationalist movement. He was barrister of the Middle Temple in London, and Labour member of St Pancras Borough Council 1934–47. He was secretary of the India League in the UK from 1929, and in 1947 was appointed Indian high commissioner in London. He represented India at the United Nations 1952–62. He became a member of the Indian parliament 1953, minister without portfolio 1956, and defence minister 1957–62. He was dismissed by Nehru 1962 when China invaded India after Menon's assurances to the contrary.
Suggested reading
Brecher, M *India and World Politics: Krishna Menon's View of the World* (1968)
George, T J S *Krishna Menon* (1964)

Menotti Gian Carlo (1911–). Italian-born US composer. He created small-scale realist operas in tonal idiom, including *The Medium* 1946, *The Telephone* 1947, *The Consul* 1950, *Amahl and the*

Theatre music must make its point and communicate its emotion at the same moment the action develops: It cannot wait to be understood until after the curtain comes down.

GIAN CARLO MENOTTI
quoted in David Ewen *American Composers* 1982

Night Visitors 1951 (the first opera to be written for television), and *The Saint of Bleecker Street* 1954. He has also written orchestral and chamber music. He was co-librettist with Samuel Barber for the latter's *Vanessa* and *A Hand of Bridge*.

Improvisation is not the expression of accident but rather of the accumulated yearnings, dreams and wisdom of our very soul.

YEHUDI MENUHIN
Theme and Variations 1972

Menuhin Yehudi, Baron Menuhin (1916–). US-born violinist and conductor. His solo repertoire extends from Vivaldi to Enescu. He recorded the Elgar *Violin Concerto* 1932 with the composer conducting, and commissioned the *Sonata* for violin solo 1944 from an ailing Bartók. He has appeared in concert with sitar virtuoso Ravi Shankar, and with jazz violinist Stephane Grappelli. KBE 1965, baron 1993.

He made his debut with an orchestra at the age of 11 in New York. A child prodigy, he achieved great depth of interpretation, and was often accompanied on the piano by his sister Hephzibah (1921–1981). In 1959 he moved to London, becoming a British subject 1985. He founded the Yehudi Menuhin School of Music, Stoke d'Abernon, Surrey, 1963.

Menzel Donald Howard (1901–1976). US physicist and astronomer whose work on the spectrum of the solar chromosphere revolutionized much of solar astronomy. He was one of the first scientists to combine astronomy with atomic physics.

In 1932, Menzel joined Harvard University Observatory, where he was to become director some 30 years later. The coronagraph he constructed there was the beginning of High Altitude Observatory for solar physics research. During his career Menzel took part in the setting-up or development of several observatories in the USA. He retired from Harvard 1971 to become scientific director of a company manufacturing antennae for communications and radioastronomy.

In addition to this work, Menzel devised a technique for computing the temperature of planets from measurements of water cell transmissions and he made important contributions to atmospheric geophysics, radio propagation, and even lunar nomenclature. He also held patents on the use of gallium in liquid ball bearings and on heat transfer in atomic plants.

He had a better mind than anyone else in and around Australia ... [and] was a statesman singularly free from over-confidence, petty vanity and vexation of spirit.

Paul Hasluck on ROBERT GORDON MENZIES
in *Dictionary of National Biography*

Menzies Robert Gordon (1894–1978). Australian politician, leader of the United Australia (now Liberal) Party and prime minister 1939–41 and 1949–66.

A Melbourne lawyer, he entered politics 1928, was attorney-general in the federal parliament 1934–39, and in 1939 succeeded Joseph Lyons as prime minister and leader of the United Australia Party, resigning 1941 when colleagues were dissatisfied with his leadership of Australia's war effort. In 1949 he became prime minister of a Liberal-Country Party coalition government, and was re-elected 1951, 1954, 1955, 1958, 1961, and 1963; he followed America's lead in committing Australia to the Vietnam War and retired soon after, in 1966. His critics argued that he did not show enough interest in Asia, and supported the USA and white African regimes too uncritically. His defenders argued that he provided stability in domestic policy and national security. KT 1963.
Suggested reading
Menzies, Robert Gordon *Afternoon Light: Some Memories of Men and Events* (1967)
Perkins, Kevin *Menzies: Last of the Queen's Men* (1968)

Menzies William Cameron (1896–1957). US art director of films, later a director and producer. He was one of Hollywood's most imaginative and talented designers. He was responsible for the sets of such classics as *Gone with the Wind* (Academy Award for best art direction) 1939 and *Foreign Correspondent* 1940. His films as director include *Things to Come* 1936 and *Invaders from Mars* 1953.

Mercator Gerardus. Latinized form of Gerhard Kremer (1512–1594). Flemish map-maker who devised the first modern atlas, showing *Mercator's projection* in which the parallels and meridians on maps are drawn uniformly at 90°. It is often used for navigational charts, because compass courses can be drawn as straight lines, but the true area of countries is increasingly distorted the further north or south they are from the equator.

He was a disillusioned Marxist.

Phyllis Hartnoll on DAVID MERCER
in *Oxford Companion to the Theatre* 1983

Mercer David (1928–1980). English dramatist. He first became known for his television plays, including *A Suitable Case for Treatment* 1962, filmed as *Morgan, A Suitable Case for Treatment* 1966; stage plays include *After Haggerty* 1970.

Merchant Ismail (1936–). Indian film producer, known for his stylish collaborations with James Ivory on films including *Shakespeare Wallah* 1965, *The Europeans* 1979, *Heat and Dust* 1983, *A Room with a View* 1987, *Maurice* 1987, *Howards End* 1992, and *The Remains of the Day* 1993.

Merckx Eddie (1945–). Belgian cyclist known as 'the Cannibal'. He won the Tour de France a joint record five times 1969–74.

Merckx turned professional 1966 and won his first classic race, the Milan-San Remo, the same year. He went on to win 24 classics as well as the three major tours (of Italy, Spain, and France) a total of 11 times. He was world professional road-race champion three times and in 1971 won a record 54 races in the season. He rode 50 winners in a season four times. He retired in 1977.

Mercouri Melina. Professional name of Maria Amalia Mercouris (1925–1994). Greek actress and politician. As minister of culture 1981–89 and 1993–94, she was a tireless campaigner for the arts both at home and within the European Community, and campaigned in particular for the return of the Elgin Marbles to Greece from the UK. As an actress she gained international recognition in the film *Never on Sunday* 1960, in which she played an exuberantly cheerful prostitute. Fittingly, the film was set in Piraeus, the constituency which she represented in the Greek parliament from 1977 until her death.

Mercouri was in the USA at the time of the 1967 military coup in Greece and was stripped of her nationality. She campaigned vocally against the colonels' regime, and in 1977, three years after their fall, was elected to parliament for Andreas Papandreou's PASOK party. When PASOK took power, she was appointed culture minister, and took up in particular the cause of seeking the return to Greece from the UK of the Elgin Marbles – or, as she preferred to term them, the Parthenon Marbles.

Meredith George (1828–1909). English novelist and poet. His realistic psychological novel, *The Ordeal of Richard Feverel* 1859, engendered both scandal and critical praise. His best-known novel *The Egoist* 1879, is superbly plotted and dissects the hero's self-centredness with merciless glee. The sonnet sequence, *Modern Love* 1862, reflects the failure of his own marriage to the daughter of Thomas Love Peacock. His other works include *Evan Harrington* 1861, *Diana of the Crossways* 1885, and *The Amazing Marriage* 1895. His verse includes *Poems and Lyrics of the Joy of Earth* 1883.

Mergenthaler Ottmar (1854–1899). German-born US inventor of the Linotype machine 1884–86. Casting hot-metal type in complete lines, this greatly speeded typesetting and revolutionized printing and publishing.

He emigrated to the USA in 1872 and settled in Baltimore 1876, working for James O Clephane. They tried to develop a writing machine but abandoned the idea and in 1884 produced a prototype of the Linotype machine. By 1886, the first machines were in use and a company was formed for their production. Over the years, Mergenthaler contributed as many as 50 modifications to the original design.

The machine was like a large typewriter, with a store of letter matrices (moulds) at the top. The keyboard operator caused the matrices to drop into position in a line. As each line was completed, a cast was made to form a metal 'slug' with the letters in relief on one side. The slug fitted into a page of type for printing, while the matrices were returned for re-use. A person operating one of Mergenthaler's keyboards could set type up to three or four times faster than by hand. Books became cheaper and newspapers more up to date, for the Linotype made it possible to change and reset copy within minutes of going to press.

Mérimée Prosper (1803–1870). French author. Among his works are the short novels *Colomba* 1841, *Carmen* 1846 (the basis for Bizet's opera), and the *Lettres à une inconnue/Letters to an Unknown Girl* 1873.

Born in Paris, he entered the public service and under Napoleon III was employed on unofficial diplomatic missions.

Merleau-Ponty Maurice (1908–1961). French philosopher, one of the most significant contributors to phenomenology after Edmund Husserl. He attempted to move beyond the notion of a pure experiencing consciousness, arguing in *The Phenomenology of Perception* 1945 that perception is intertwined with bodily awareness and with language. In his posthumously published work *The Visible and the Invisible* 1964, he argued that our experience is inherently ambiguous and elusive and that the traditional concepts of philosophy are therefore inadequate to grasp it.

Merovingian dynasty Frankish dynasty, named after its founder, Merovech (5th century AD). His descendants ruled France from the time of Clovis (481–511) to 751.

Merrill Frank (1903–1955). US brigadier general. He became assistant military attaché in Tokyo 1938 and studied the Japanese language and military system. He served with Stilwell in the retreat from Burma and Jan 1944 was given command of 5307 Composite Unit (Provisional), a US group formed for long-range penetration behind the Japanese lines, later known as 'Merrill's Marauders'.

The 'Marauders' fought in the Hukawng Valley and Myitkyina but due to Stilwell's neglect of their supply line and his insistence on continuing in action too long, the unit was virtually destroyed by overstress and disease. Merrill, together with most of his men, was hospitalized but later became deputy US Commander in Burma and then Chief of Staff to the 10th Army in the Pacific.

Mersenne Marin (1588–1648). French mathematician and philosopher who, from his base in Paris, did much to disseminate throughout Europe the main advances of French science. In mathematics he defined a particular form of prime number, since referred to as a *Mersenne prime*.

Merton Louis Thomas (1915–1968). US Trappist Christian monk. He felt that contemporary society was suffering an inward crisis and stood in need of contemplative reflection. His poetic and spiritual writings include an autobiography, *The Seven Storey Mountain* 1946. His writings were directed to those living a monastic life, but his influence is much wider.

Merton Robert King (1910–). US sociologist. He undertook studies of deviance and anomie, role theory, the sociology of knowledge, and historical sociology. His book *Science, Technology and Society in 17th-Century England* 1938 had a considerable influence on historians of science.

Merton continued the German sociologist Max Weber's work on the link between Protestantism and capitalism by considering the enormous amount of scientific inquiry carried out during the 17th century in terms of social and cultural change. In *Social Theory and*

Social Structure 1951, Merton accepted that the task of sociology is to discover 'systematic regularity' in social phenomena, but was doubtful about grand, all-inclusive theories. Instead he preferred 'middle-range theories', a few careful theories explaining a limited number of phenomena.

Merton taught at Columbia University, New York, where, from 1941, he co-directed the Bureau of Applied Social Research with the Austrian-born US sociologist Paul F Lazarsfeld (1901–1976).

Meselson Matthew Stanley (1930–   ). US molecular biologist who, with Franklin Stahl, confirmed that replication of the genetic material DNA is semiconservative (that is, the daughter cells each receive one strand of DNA from the original parent cell and one newly replicated strand).

Meselson was born in Denver, Colorado, and studied physical chemistry at the California Institute of Technology. He remained at Caltech, rising to professor of biology, until 1976, when he moved to Harvard. In 1963 he became a consultant to the US Arms Control and Disarmament Agency.

Meselson has also investigated the molecular biology of nucleic acids, the mechanisms of DNA recombination and repair, and the processes of gene control and evolution.

Mesmer Friedrich Anton (or Franz) (1734–1815). Austrian physician, an early experimenter in hypnosis, which was formerly (and popularly) called 'mesmerism' after him. He claimed to reduce people to trance state by consciously exerted 'animal magnetism', their willpower being entirely subordinated to his. Expelled by the police from Vienna, he created a sensation in Paris in 1778, but was denounced as a charlatan in 1785.

Mesrine Jacques (1937–1979). French criminal. From a wealthy family, he became a burglar celebrated for his glib tongue, sadism, and bravado, and for his escapes from the police and prison. Towards the end of his life he had links with left-wing guerrillas. He was shot dead by the police.

Messager André Charles Prosper (1853–1929). French composer and conductor. He studied under Saint-Saëns. Messager composed light operas, such as *La Béarnaise* 1885 and *Véronique* 1898.

Messalina was unenthusiastic, not because she loved her husband Claudius, but because she feared that her lover, once in power, might despise his mistress.

Tacitus on VALERIA MESSALINA
Annals bk 11, ch 26

Messalina Valeria (*c.* AD 25–48). Third wife of the Roman emperor Claudius. She was notorious for her immorality, forcing a noble to marry her AD 48, although still married to Claudius, who then had her executed.

Messerschmitt Willy (Wilhelm Emil) (1898–1978). German aeroplane designer whose Me-109 was a standard Luftwaffe fighter in World War II, and whose Me-262 (1944) was the first mass-produced jet fighter.

Messerschmitt aeroplanes were characterized by simple concept, minimum weight and aerodynamic drag, and the possibility of continued development. He designed cantilever monoplanes from the early 1920s when the market still looked for biplanes with visible struts and bracing wires. The Me-109 held the world speed record of 610 kph/379 mph from 1937.

Messerschmitt was born in Frankfurt-am-Main and studied at the Technische Hochschule in Munich. A glider he designed with gliding pioneer Friedrich Harth achieved an unofficial world duration record in 1921. The following year they set up a flying school and in 1923, while still a student, Messerschmitt formed his own company in Bamberg. Its first product was the S-14 cantilever monoplane glider. He produced his first powered aircraft in 1925, the ultralight sports two-seater Me-17. In 1926 came the Me-18 small transport.

The Me-37 1934 was the archetypal low-wing four-seater cabin monoplane, with retractable landing gear and flaps.

By 1938, Messerschmitt was appointed chair and general director of the company manufacturing his designs, Bayerische Flugzeugwerke, renamed Messerschmitt Aktiengesellschaft. He and his company went on to produce numerous designs for fighter, bomber, and transport aircraft. From the end of World War II Messerschmitt was held prisoner for two years by the Allies, and was then banned from manufacturing aircraft in Germany. Instead, he designed and produced a two-seater bubble car.

Messerschmitt took up aircraft design again in 1952 under contract with Spanish manufacturer Hispano. Between 1956 and 1964 he worked in association with the German Bolkow and Heinkel companies and developed the VJ-101 supersonic V/STOL (vertical/short takeoff and landing) combat aircraft. His company merged with Bolkow in 1963 and they were later joined by Hamburger Flugzeugbau. In 1969, Messerschmitt became chair of the resulting Messerschmitt Bolkow Blohm (MBB) group.

Messiaen Olivier Eugène Prosper Charles (1908–1992). French composer, organist, and teacher. His music is mystical in character, vividly coloured, and incorporates transcriptions of birdsong. Among his works are the *Quartet for the End of Time* 1941, the large-scale *Turangalîla Symphony* 1949, and solo organ and piano pieces. As a teacher at the Paris Conservatoire from 1942, he influenced three generations of composers. His theories of melody, harmony, and rhythm, drawing on medieval and oriental music, have inspired contemporary composers such as Boulez and Stockhausen.

He was born in Avignon, and spent most of his life in Paris, where he was appointed organist at La Trinité church 1931. He was a devout Christian.

Suggested reading
Messiaen, Olivier *Technique of My Mystical Language* (tr 1957)
Nichols, R *Messiaen* (1975)
Samuel, C *Conversations with Olivier Messiaen* (1976)

Messier Charles (1730–1817). French astronomer who discovered 15 comets and in 1784 published a list of 103 star clusters and nebulae. Objects on this list are given M (for Messier) numbers, which astronomers still use today, such as M1 (the Crab nebula) and M31 (the Andromeda galaxy).

Messier was born in Badonviller, Lorraine, and joined the Paris Observatory. Watching for the predicted return of Halley's comet, he was one of the first people to spot it, an experience that inspired him with the desire to go on discovering new comets for the rest of his life. Louis XV nicknamed him the 'Comet Ferret'.

But Messier's search was continually hampered by rather obscure forms which he came to recognize as nebulae. During the period 1760–84, therefore, he compiled a list of these nebulae and star clusters, so that he and other astronomers would not confuse them with possible new comets.

Meštrović Ivan (1883–1962). Yugoslav sculptor. He became a US citizen 1954. His works include portrait busts of the sculptor Rodin (with whom he is often compared), President Hoover, Pope Pius XI, and many public monuments.

Metacomet Wampanoag leader better known as King ◊Philip.

Metalious Grace (born Repentigny) (1924–1964). US novelist. She wrote many short stories but made headlines with *Peyton Place* 1956, an exposé of life in a small New England town, which was made into a film 1957 and a long-running television series.

Metastasio Pen name of Pietro Armando Dominico Trapassi (1698–1782). Italian poet and the leading librettist of his day, creating 18th-century Italian *opera seria* (serious opera).

Metaxas Ioannis (1870–1941). Greek general and politician, born in Ithaca. He restored George II (1890–1947) as king of Greece, under whom he established a dictatorship as prime minister from 1936, and introduced several necessary economic and military reforms. He led resistance to the Italian invasion of Greece in 1941, refusing to abandon Greece's neutral position.

His powers of personal application to work were phenomenal but tended to produce dutiful servants rather than men of initiative.

Alan Palmer on IOANNIS METAXAS
in *Penguin Dictionary of Twentieth Century History* 1979

Methodius, St (*c.* 825–884). Greek Christian bishop, who with his brother Cyril translated much of the Bible into Slavonic. Feast day 14 Feb.

Metsu Gabriel (1629–1667). Dutch painter, a pupil of Gerard Dou. He settled at Amsterdam as a painter of genre pictures, being among the foremost of those who depicted interiors and scenes from well-to-do Dutch family life, sometimes attempting to emulate Vermeer and sometimes recalling the polish of Terborch. A masterpiece, personal in style, is the famous *The Sick Child* (Rijksmuseum).

For great evils drastic remedies are necessary and whoever has to treat them should use the instrument which cuts the best.

Report by METTERNICH as ambassador in
Paris to the Austrian foreign minister 24 Sept 1808

Metternich Klemens Wenzel Nepomuk Lothar, Prince von (1773–1859). Austrian politician, the leading figure in European diplomacy after the fall of Napoleon. As foreign minister 1809–48 (as well as chancellor from 1821), he tried to maintain the balance of power in Europe, supporting monarchy and repressing liberalism.

At the Congress of Vienna 1815, Metternich advocated cooperation by the great powers to suppress democratic movements. The revolution of 1848 forced him to flee to the UK; he returned 1851 as a power behind the scenes.

Suggested reading

Kraehe, Enno (ed) *The Metternich Controversy* (1971)
May, Arthur J *The Age of Metternich* (1963)
Palmer, Alan *Metternich: Councillor of Europe* (1972)

Meyer Alfred (1895–1990). German-born British neuropathologist. His most significant work was on the anatomical aspects of frontal leucotomy, and the nature of the structural abnormalities in the brain associated with temporal-lobe epilepsy.

Meyer was born in Krefeld. His successful early career was threatened by the rise of the Nazis, and he escaped to the UK in 1933, beginning work at the Maudsley Hospital, London. His study of frontal leucotomy led to a classic book on the subject with Elizabeth Beck, published 1954; and he undertook pioneering work on the pathology of epilepsy while professor of neuropathology at the Institute of Psychiatry.

Meyer (Julius) Lothar (1830–1895). German chemist who, independently of his Russian contemporary Dmitri Mendeleyev, produced a periodic law describing the properties of the chemical elements.

He was professor of chemistry at Karlsruhe Polytechnic 1868–76, and at Tübingen University for the rest of his life.

In his book *Die modernen Theorien der Chemie*/*Modern Chemical Theory* 1864, Meyer drew up a table presenting all the elements according to their atomic weights (relative atomic masses), relating the weights to chemical properties. In 1870 he published a graph of atomic volume (atomic weight divided by density) against atomic weight, which demonstrated the periodicity in the variation of the elements' properties. He showed that each element will not combine with the same numbers of hydrogen or chlorine atoms, establishing the concept of valency and grouping elements as univalent, bivalent, trivalent, and so on.

Meyer never claimed priority for his findings and, unlike Mendeleyev, he made no predictions about the composition and properties of any elements still to be discovered.

Meyer Viktor (1848–1897). German organic chemist who invented an apparatus for determining vapour densities (and hence molecular weights), now named after him. He was also the discoverer of the heterocyclic compound thiophene.

At the age of 22 he was appointed professor at Stuttgart Polytechnic, in 1885 at Göttingen, and in 1889 at Heidelberg.

In 1871, Meyer experimentally proved Avogadro's hypothesis by measuring the vapour densities of volatile substances (molecular weight, or relative molecular mass, is twice the vapour density). He went on to determine the vapour densities of inorganic substances at high temperatures.

From benzene obtained from petroleum, Meyer in 1883 isolated thiophene, a heterocyclic compound containing sulphur, which much later was to become an important component of various synthetic drugs.

Meyer published *Textbook of Organic Chemistry* 1883–96 and, with his brother Karl, *Pyrotechnical Research* 1885.

Meyerbeer Giacomo. Adopted name of Jakob Liebmann Meyer Beer (1791–1864). German composer. His spectacular operas include *Robert le Diable* 1831 and *Les Huguenots* 1836. From 1826 he lived mainly in Paris, returning to Berlin after 1842 as musical director of the Royal Opera.

Meyerhof Otto (1884–1951). German-born US biochemist who carried out research into the metabolic processes involved in the action of muscles. For this work he shared the 1922 Nobel Prize for Physiology or Medicine.

From 1912 he worked at the University of Kiel, becoming professor 1918. He headed a department specially created for him at the Kaiser Wilhelm Institute for Biology in Berlin 1924–29, when he moved to Heidelberg. As a result of Adolf Hitler's rise to power in the 1930s, Meyerhof left Germany 1938 and went to Paris, where he became director of research at the Institut de Biologie Physiochimique. In 1940, when France fell to Germany in the early part of World War II, he fled to the USA, and was given a professorship at the University of Pennsylvania.

In 1920 Meyerhof showed that, in anaerobic conditions, the amounts of glycogen metabolized and of lactic acid produced in a contracting muscle are proportional to the tension in the muscle. He also demonstrated that 20–25% of the lactic acid is oxidized during the muscle's recovery period and that energy produced by this oxidation is used to convert the remainder of the lactic acid back to glycogen. Meyerhof introduced the term glycolysis to describe the anaerobic degradation of glycogen to lactic acid, and showed the cyclic nature of energy transformations in living cells. The complete metabolic pathway of glycolysis is known as the Embden–Meyerhof pathway after Meyerhof and Gustav George Embden (1874–1933).

Meyerhold Vsevolod Yemilyevich (1874–1940). Russian actor and director. He developed a system of actor training known as biomechanics, which combined insights drawn from sport, the circus, and modern studies of time and motion. He produced the Russian poet Mayakovsky's futurist *Mystery-Bouffe* 1918 and 1921, and his *The Bed Bug* 1929.

A member of the Moscow Art Theatre, Meyerhold was briefly director of its Studio Theatre under Stanislavsky 1905. Before the revolution of 1917 he developed a strong interest in *commedia dell'arte* and stylized acting. He received state support from 1920, but was arrested 1938 and shot under the Stalinist regime.

Meynell Alice Christiana Gertrude (born Thompson) (1847–1922). English poet. She published *Preludes* 1875 and her collected poems appeared 1923. She married the author and journalist Wilfrid Meynell (1852–1948).

Miandad Javed (1957–). Pakistani Test cricketer, his country's leading run-maker. He scored a century on his Test debut in 1976 and has since become one of a handful of players to make 100 Test appearances. He has captained his country and helped Pakistan to win the 1992 World Cup. His highest score of 311 was made when he was aged 17.

Micah (lived 8th century BC). In the Old Testament, a Hebrew prophet whose writings denounced the oppressive ruling class of Judah and demanded justice.

Michael Mikhail Fyodorovich Romanov (1596–1645). Tsar of Russia from 1613. He was elected tsar by a national assembly, at a time of chaos and foreign invasion, and was the first of the Romanov dynasty, which ruled until 1917.

Michael (1921–   ). King of Romania 1927–30 and 1940–47. The son of Carol II, he succeeded his grandfather as king 1927 but was displaced when his father returned from exile 1930. In 1940 he was proclaimed king again on his father's abdication, overthrew 1944 the fascist dictatorship of Ion Antonescu (1882–1946), and enabled Romania to share in the victory of the Allies at the end of World War II. He abdicated and left Romania 1947.

On 25 Dec 1990 King Michael, with his wife Anne and daughter Sophia, attempted to return to Romania, but he was expelled early the following day.

Michaux André (1746–1802). French botanist and explorer. As manager of a royal farm, he was sent by the French government 1782 and 1785 on expeditions to collect plants and select timber for shipbuilding. Together with his son François (1770–1852), he travelled to Carolina, Florida, Georgia, and, in 1792, to Hudson's Bay. On his return to France, he compiled the first guide to the flora of E America.

François Michaux wrote the first book on American forest trees 1810–13.

Michelangelo properly Michelangelo di Lodovico Buonarroti (1475–1564). Italian sculptor, painter, architect, and poet. He was active in his native Florence and in Rome. His giant talent dominated the High Renaissance. The marble *David* 1501–04 (Accademia, Florence) set a new standard in nude sculpture. His massive figure style was translated into fresco in the Sistine Chapel 1508–12 and 1536–41 (Vatican). Other works in Rome include the dome of St Peter's basilica. His influence, particularly on the development of Mannerism, was profound.

At 13 he was allowed to become apprentice to the successful painter Domenico Ghirlandaio. He also studied Giotto and the frescoes of Masaccio in the Brancacci Chapel. Chosen as one of the young artists whom Lorenzo allowed to work in the school and the collection of classical sculpture in the Medici gardens, under the custodian, Bertoldo, he was encouraged to develop his natural gift and liking for sculpture. In rivalry with the antique, he produced the *Head of a Faun* that delighted his patron and the relief, *Battle of Centaurs and Lapiths* (Florence, Casa Buonarotti).

He went to Rome 1496, aged 21, where a Cupid in which he had counterfeited the antique attracted notice, and during five years' stay he produced two famous works of sculpture, strangely contrasting in style and spirit, his *Bacchus* (Florence, Museum) and *Pietà* (St Peter's, Rome). He returned to Florence 1501 at the family's request, and was next occupied by the famous and colossal *David*, carved from a block of Carrara marble that had been discarded as spoilt. Michelangelo had not abandoned painting altogether. The *Entombment* and *Madonna and Child with St John and Angels* (National Gallery) have been regarded as works of about his 20th year; the Holy Family (Uffizi) of 1503 was a masterpiece executed for his and Raphael's patron Angelo Doni; and in 1504 he was commissioned to paint a large fresco in the council hall of the new Florentine Republic as a companion piece to the *Battle of Anghiari* by Leonardo da Vinci. He was, however, summoned to Rome by Julius II to work on the famous tomb on which he was to toil at intervals during 40 years.

A fresh project of the impetuous pope was among the circumstances first diverting him from the task: the decoration of the vaulting of the Sistine Chapel. The architect, Bramante, suggested that the commission should be given to Michelangelo, out of jealousy, it was presumed, in the belief that he would fail in the

undertaking or produce a minor work. Though reluctant, Michelangelo accepted the challenge, and in an astonishingly short space of time, working without assistants and under difficult conditions, painted the famous ceiling. A tremendous biblical symphony, it interprets the Creation of the World and of Man, the Fall, and the Flood in nine great compositions flanked by the figures of prophets and sibyls, and with supporting 'slaves' or 'atlases'. The conception is conveyed with the utmost force and lucidity by the human figure and gesture alone, as in the magnificent *Creation of Adam*. Michelangelo was then 37.

He went back to sculpture to become again involved in the 'tragedy of the tomb'. It was not until 1545 that it was finished, on a less ambitious scale than had been planned, only the figure of Moses being the artist's own work. He was commissioned 1520 by Clement VII, to design the Medici supulchral chapel in San Lorenzo, Florence. This, with its famous figures of Day and Night, Morning and Evening, was finished 1535. In 1534 he was required by Clement VII to devote himself to painting the altar wall of the Sistine Chapel, which had previously been decorated by Perugino, a commission urgently affirmed by Clement's successor, Paul III. He took the Last Judgment as his subject and in six years produced his overwhelming masterpiece. It was in a different key from either the wall frescoes of other painters in the chapel or Michelangelo's own earlier work on the ceiling.

Suggested reading

Brandes, Georg *Michelangelo: His Life, His Times, His Era* (1963)
Einem, H von *Michelangelo* (1973)
Hartt, Frederick *Michelangelo* (1965)
Hibbard, Howard *Michelangelo: Painter, Sculptor, Architect* (1978)
Murray, Linda *Michelangelo: His Life, Work and Times* (1984)
Tolnay, Charles de *Michelangelo* (1943–60)

You are one of the forces of nature.

JULES MICHELET
Letter to Alexandre Dumas, quoted in
Dumas *Memoirs* vol VI ch 138 1852–54

Michelet Jules (1798–1874). French historian, author of a 17-volume *Histoire de France/History of France* 1833–67, in which he immersed himself in the narrative and stressed the development of France as a nation. He also produced a number of books on nature, including *L'Oiseau/The Bird* 1856 and *La Montagne/The Mountain* 1868.

Michell Keith (1928–   ). Australian actor, director, singer, and theatre administrator in England. He played McDuff to Laurence Olivier's Macbeth (1955) and is known particularly for the role of Henry VIII in the BBC television series *The Six Wives of Henry VIII* 1969.

Michelozzo di Bartolomeo (1396–1472). Italian sculptor and architect. He worked with Ghiberti and Donatello. Although overshadowed by such contemporaries as Brunelleschi and Alberti, he was the chosen architect of Cosimo de' Medici and was commissioned by him to design the Palazzo de' Medici (now Palazzo Medici-Riccardi, Florence), begun in the 1440s, and the library of the monastery of San Marco, about 1436.

Michels Robert (1876–1936). German social and political theorist. In *Political Parties* 1911, he propounded the 'iron law of oligarchy', arguing that in any organization or society, even a democracy, there is a tendency towards rule by the few in the interests of the few, and that ideologies such as socialism and communism were merely propaganda to control the masses.

Originally a radical, he became a critic of socialism and Marxism, and in his last years supported the dictators Hitler and Mussolini. Michels believed that the rise of totalitarian governments – both fascist and communist – in the 1930s confirmed his analysis and proved that the masses were incapable of asserting their own interests.

Michelson Albert Abraham (1852–1931). German-born US physicist. With his colleague Edward Morley, he performed in 1887 the Michelson–Morley experiment to detect the motion of the Earth through the postulated ether (a medium believed to be necessary for the propagation of light). The failure of the experiment indicated the non-existence of the ether, and led Albert Einstein to his theory of relativity. Michelson was the first American to be awarded a Nobel prize, in 1907.

He invented the Michelson interferometer to detect any difference in the velocity of light in two directions at right angles. In the Michelson interferometer, a light beam is split into two by a semi-silvered mirror. The two beams are then reflected off fully silvered mirrors and recombined to form an interference pattern of dark and light bands. The negative result of the Michelson–Morley experiment demonstrated that the velocity of light is constant whatever the motion of the observer. Michelson also made a precise measurement of the speed of light.

Michelucci Giovanni (1891–1990). Italian architect. A leading exponent of Rationalism in the 1930s, he produced numerous urban projects characterized by a restrained Modernism, for example, the Sta Maria Novella Station in Florence 1934–37. He departed from his Rationalist principles in his design for the church of San Giovanni 1961 by the Autostrada del Sole near Florence, a fluid, sculptural composition in poured concrete.

Michotte Albert (1881–1965). Belgian experimental psychologist. He is known for his investigations of perceptual causality. By means of ingenious and careful experimentation, he studied the dynamic organization of the perceptual world and was particularly concerned with the role of language in the analysis of perceptual phenomena. His book *La Perception de la causalité/The Perception of Causality* 1946 has become a classic.

In his experiments, subjects looking through a slit saw what appeared to them as two small rectangular spots in motion. Alternatively, they looked at a screen on which small moving shapes were projected. When one object A was seen to bump into another B, A appeared to give B a push or set it in motion, which Michotte termed the launching effect. If object A on reaching object B was seen to move with it and at the same speed, A appeared to carry B, which he termed the entraining effect. Michotte observed these phenomena, and others, under various experimental conditions. His work is important not least because it is a scientific investigation of a topic that has mainly been the province of philosophers.

Mickiewicz Adam Bernard (1798–1855). Polish revolutionary poet. His *Pan Tadeusz* 1832–34 is Poland's national epic. He died in Constantinople while raising a Polish corps to fight against Russia in the Crimean War.

Middleton Thomas (c. 1570–1627). English dramatist. He produced numerous romantic plays, tragedies, and realistic comedies, both alone and in collaboration, including *A Fair Quarrel* and *The Changeling* 1622 with William Rowley; *The Roaring Girl* with Dekker; and *Women Beware Women* 1621.

His political satire *A Game at Chess* 1624 was concerned with the plots to unite the royal houses of England and Spain, and caused a furore with the authorities.

Midgley Mary (1919–). English moral philosopher who used studies of animal behaviour (ethology) to support broadly Aristotelian ethics. She has also argued that our moral concern should extend to animals. Midgley taught at the University of Newcastle-upon-Tyne from 1963 until her retirement. Her publications include *Beast and Man: The Roots of Human Nature* 1978, *Animals and Why They Matter* 1983, and *Wickedness: a Philosophical Enquiry* 1984.

Midgley Thomas (1889–1944). US industrial chemist and engineer whose two main discoveries, universally adopted, were later criticized as damaging to the environment. He found in 1921 that tetraethyl lead is an efficient antiknock additive to petrol (preventing pre-ignition in car engines), and in 1930 introduced Freons (a group of chlorofluorocarbons) as the working gases in refrigerators, freezers, and air-conditioning units.

From 1916 he worked for the Dayton Engineering Laboratories Company, Ohio, later taken over by General Motors. He became a vice president of the Ethyl Corporation 1923 and ten years later a director of the Ethyl-Dow Chemical Company.

Mies van der Rohe Ludwig (1886–1969). German architect. A leading exponent of the International Style, he practised in the USA from 1937. He succeeded Walter Gropius as director of the Bauhaus 1929–33. He designed the bronze-and-glass Seagram building in New York City 1956–59 and numerous apartment buildings.

He became professor at the Illinois Technical Institute 1938–58, for which he designed a new campus on characteristically functional lines from 1941. He also designed the National Gallery, Berlin, 1963–68.

Suggested reading
Blake, Peter *Mies van der Rohe: Architecture and Structure* (1960)
Drexler, A *Ludwig Mies van der Rohe* (1960)
Johnson, Philip C *Mies van der Rohe* (1947)

Mifune Toshiro (1920–). Japanese film actor. He appeared in many films directed by Akira Kurosawa, including *Rashōmon* 1950, *Shichinin no samurai/Seven Samurai* 1954, and *Throne of Blood* 1957. He has occasionally appeared in European and American films: *Grand Prix* 1966, *Hell in the Pacific* 1969.

Migne Jacques Paul (1800–1875). French curate and religious publisher. Migne published a gigantic series of essential texts of the Catholic Faith, including *Patrologia latin* 1844–55 in 218 volumes, and *Patrologia graeca* 1857–66 in 166 volumes. In all, he published over 1,000 volumes. At the peak of his activity, he employed some 600 staff, and used innovative methods to achieve high sales, including special subscription offers. It took 49 editors to compile the index to his Patrologies.

Migne was ordained 1824 but resigned after being censured by his bishop for publishing a pamphlet denouncing anticlericals.

He set up several newspapers, many of which did little more than recycle others' material, before devoting himself to publishing.

I wanted much, I began much, but the gale of the world carried away me and my work.

DRAZA MIHAILOVIĆ
Final defence plea at his trial. Belgrade 15 July 1946

Mihailović Draza (Dragoljub) (1893–1946). Yugoslav soldier, leader of the guerrilla Chetniks of World War II, a nationalist resistance movement against the German occupation. His feud with Tito's communists led to the withdrawal of Allied support and that of his own exiled government from 1943. He turned for help to the Italians and Germans, and was eventually shot for treason.

Milarepa (1040–1123). The greatest of all Tibetan Buddhist sages, seen as the founder of one of the four main schools of Lamaism, the Kagyu school, whose central purpose is meditation. Milarepa's life is told in a classic of Buddhist spirituality written down in the 15th century. After an early life of hardship and of powerful evil magic, Milarepa repented and went to study Buddhism under the master Marpa. From him he learned the importance of solitary meditation, even walling himself up for years at a time. Milarepa is not just beloved by the Kagyu school, which he founded; he stands as the paragon of the Tibetan mystic and hermit and is a popular figure of devotion.

Milch Erhard (1893–1972). German field marshal in World War II. Although not a pilot he commanded a fighter group during World War I and 1926 became chairman of Lufthansa, the German national airline. Using this cover, he trained pilots and developed equipment for the future Luftwaffe air force. In 1936 he became General der Flieger of the Luftwaffe and 1941 took over responsibility for aircraft production. Imprisoned as a war criminal, he was released in 1955.

Miles Bernard James, Baron Miles (1907–1991). English actor and producer. He appeared on stage as Briggs in *Thunder Rock* 1940 and

Iago in *Othello* 1942, and his films include *Great Expectations* 1947. He founded a trust that in 1959 built the City of London's first new theatre for 300 years, the Mermaid, which presents a mixed classical and modern repertoire. Knighted 1969, baron 1979.

Milford Haven Marquess of. Title given in 1917 to Prince Louis of ◊Battenberg (1854–1921).

The indifference of the public is what's depressing. Enthusiasm, or vehement protest, shows that your work really lives.

DARIUS MILHAUD
quoted in James Harding, *The Ox on the Roof* 1972

Milhaud Darius (1892–1974). French composer and pianist. A member of the group of composers known as *Les Six*, he was extremely prolific in a variety of styles and genres, influenced by jazz, the rhythms of Latin America, and electronic composition. He is noted for his use of polytonality (the simultaneous existence of two or more keys), as in the *Saudades do Brasil* 1921 for orchestra and *L'Homme et son désir* 1918. Other works include the operas *Christophe Colombe/Christopher Columbus* 1928 and *Bolívar* 1943, and the jazz ballet *La Création du monde* 1923. He lived in both France and the USA.

A pastoral element also runs through many of his works, as in his first string quartet 1912 and six chamber symphonies 1917–22. His Jewish ancestry is evident in the cantata *Ani maamiu* written for the Festival of Israel 1973.

Mill James (1773–1836). Scottish philosopher and political thinker who developed the theory of utilitarianism. He is remembered for his political articles, and for the rigorous education he gave his son John Stuart Mill.

Millais British painter John Millais from a lithograph c. 1880. A founder member of the Pre-Raphaelite Brotherhood, he later left the group, although some of his best works were painted in the Pre-Raphaelite manner, for example Ophelia 1852, and Autumn Leaves 1856. (Image Select)

Born near Montrose on the east coast, Mill moved to London 1802. Associated for most of his working life with the East India Company, he wrote a vast *History of British India* 1817–18. He was one of the founders of University College, London, together with his friend and fellow utilitarian Jeremy Bentham.

The liberty of the individual must be thus far limited; he must not make himself a nuisance to other people.

JOHN STUART MILL
Essay on Liberty ch 3 1859

Mill John Stuart (1806–1873). English philosopher and economist who wrote *On Liberty* 1859, the classic philosophical defence of liberalism, and *Utilitarianism* 1863, a version of the 'greatest happiness for the greatest number' principle in ethics. His progressive views inspired *On the Subjection of Women* 1869.

He was born in London, the son of James Mill. In 1822 he entered the East India Company, where he remained until retiring in 1858. In 1826, as described in his *Autobiography* 1873, he passed through a mental crisis; he found his father's bleakly intellectual Utilitarianism emotionally unsatisfying and abandoned it for a more human philosophy influenced by the poet Samuel Taylor Coleridge. Mill sat in Parliament as a Radical 1865–68 and introduced a motion for women's suffrage.

In *Utilitarianism*, he states that actions are right if they bring about happiness and wrong if they bring about the reverse of happiness. *On Liberty* moved away from the Utilitarian notion that individual liberty was necessary for economic and governmental efficiency and advanced the classical defence of individual freedom as a value in itself and the mark of a mature society; this change can be traced in the later editions of *Principles of Political Economy* 1848. His philosophical and political writings include *A System of Logic* 1843 and *Considerations on Representative Government* 1861.

Suggested reading

August, E (ed) *John Stuart Mill: A Mind at Large* (1975)
Britton, K W *John Stuart Mill: His Life and Thought* (1969)
Cowling, Maurice *Mill and Liberalism* (1963)
Packe, Michael *The Life of John Stuart Mill* (1954)
Robson, J M *The Improvement of Mankind: The Social and Political Philosophy of John Stuart Mill* (1968)

Millais John Everett (1829–1896). English painter. He was a founder member of the Pre-Raphaelite Brotherhood (PRB) 1848. By the late 1850s he had left the PRB, and his style became more fluent and. less detailed. Baronet 1885.

He was precocious in talent and a student at the Royal Academy Schools at the age of 11. Youthful acquaintance with Holman Hunt and Rossetti led to his joining them in the formation of the Pre-Raphaelite Brotherhood, 1848, and producing some of the best works inspired by its doctrine of 'truth to nature' during the 1850s, among them *Christ in the House of His Parents*, 1850 (Tate Gallery) (which caused an outcry on its first showing, since its realistic detail was considered unfitting to a sacred subject) and the painting of Miss Siddal as Ophelia, 1852 (National Gallery). His marriage to Euphemia Gray 1855 after the annulment of her marriage with Ruskin estranged him from that early mentor and the milieu of Pre-Raphaelite idealism. His original style and quality disappeared from the popular subject pictures and portraits of an academically successful career, of which *Bubbles* 1885 was one of the sensations. His illustrations to the Moxon Tennyson of 1857 and for Trollope's *Orley Farm*, 1863, show the change from Pre-Raphaelite to mid-Victorian.

Suggested reading

Gaunt, William *The Pre-Raphaelite Tragedy* (1942)
Hinton, Timothy *The Pre-Raphaelites* (1970)
Millais, John *The Life and Letters of John Everett Millais* (1899, rep 1973)

Millay Edna St Vincent (1892–1950). US poet. She wrote romantic, emotional verse, including *Renascence and Other Poems* 1917 and *The Harp-Weaver and Other Poems* 1923 (Pulitzer prize 1924).

She was a favourite of the free-spirited youth of the 1920s. Born in Rockland, Maine, she moved to New York City's Greenwich Village and became a voice for political and social causes through such works as *A Few Figs from Thistles* 1920 and *Second April* 1921. Her other works include the sonnet sequence *Fatal Interview* 1931, *Make Bright the Arrows*, and several verse plays.

I only know that summer sang in me / A little while, that in me sings no more.

EDNA ST VINCENT MILLAY
Harp-Weaver and Other Poems sonnet 19 1923

Miller (Alton) Glenn (1904–1944). US trombonist and bandleader. He was an exponent of the big-band swing sound from 1938. He composed his signature tune 'Moonlight Serenade' (a hit 1939). Miller became leader of the US Army Air Force Band in Europe 1942, made broadcasts to troops throughout the world during World War II, and disappeared without trace on a flight between England and France.
Suggested reading
Fowler, John *Moonlight Serenade* (1972)
Simon, George *Glenn Miller and His Orchestra* (1980)

A good newspaper, I suppose, is a nation talking to itself.

ARTHUR MILLER
Observer 26 Nov 1962

Miller Arthur (1915–   ). US dramatist. His plays deal with family relationships and contemporary American values, and include *Death of a Salesman* 1949 and *The Crucible* 1953, based on the Salem witch trials and reflecting the communist witch-hunts of Senator Joe McCarthy. He was married 1956–61 to the film star Marilyn Monroe, for whom he wrote the film *The Misfits* 1960.

Among other plays are *All My Sons* 1947, *A View from the Bridge* 1955, *After the Fall* 1964, based on his relationship with Monroe. More recent work includes *The American Clock* 1979 on the 1930s depression, *The Ride Down Mount Morgan* 1991, and *Broken Glass* 1994, on anti-semitism in the 1930s.
Suggested reading
Hogan, Robert *Arthur Miller* (1967)
Roudane, M C *Conversations with Arthur Miller* (1987)
Schlueter, J and Flanagan, J K *Arthur Miller* (1987)

Miller Godfrey Clive (1893–1964). Australian painter and art teacher, born in New Zealand. His lifetime concern was to find a pictorial technique able to suggest permanence and change at the same time. His work, in which tiny facets of colour are fixed in intricate interweaving grids, shows reference to Pointillism and Cubism. His *Nude and the Moon* 1954–58 (Art Gallery of New South Wales, Sydney) is typical of his style.

The aim of life is to live, and to live means to be aware, joyously, drunkenly, serenely, divinely aware.

HENRY MILLER
The Wisdom of the Heart, 'Creative Death' 1941

Miller Henry Valentine (1891–1980). US writer. From 1930 to 1940 he lived a bohemian life in Paris, where he wrote his fictionalized, sexually explicit, autobiographical trilogy *Tropic of Cancer* 1934, *Black Spring* 1936, and *Tropic of Capricorn* 1938. They were banned in the USA and England until the 1960s.

Born in New York City, Miller settled in Big Sur, California, in 1944 and wrote the autobiographical *The Rosy Crucifixion* trilogy, consisting of *Sexus* 1949, *Plexus* 1949, and *Nexus* 1957 (published as a whole in the USA 1965). Inspired by Surrealism, Miller was a writer of exuberant and comic prose fuelled by anarchist passion, and was later adopted as a guru by the followers of the Beat

Generation. His other works include *The Colossus of Maroussi* 1941, *The Air-Conditioned Nightmare* 1945, a vitriolic and apocalyptic vision of American culture, and *The Time of the Assassins* 1956, a portrait of the French poet Rimbaud.
Suggested reading
Brown, J D *Henry Miller* (1986)
Ferguson, Robert *Henry Miller: A Life* (1991)
Mailer, Norman *Black Messiah* (1981)
Miller, Henry *My Life and Times* (1971)

Miller Keith Ross (1919–   ). Australian cricketer. An aggressive all-rounder, he played in 55 tests 1946–57.

Miller Stanley Lloyd (1930–   ). US chemist. In the early 1950s, under laboratory conditions, he tried to recreate the formation of life on Earth. To water under a gas mixture of methane, ammonia, and hydrogen, he added an electrical discharge. After a week he found that amino acids, the ingredients of protein, had been formed.

From 1960 he held appointments at the University of California in San Diego, rising to professor of chemistry.

Miller made his experiment while working for his PhD under Harold Urey, using the components that had been proposed for the Earth's primitive atmosphere by Urey and Russian biochemist Alexandr Oparin. The electrical discharge simulated the likely type of energy source.

Miller William (1801–1880). Welsh crystallographer, developer of the Miller indices, a coordinate system of mapping the shapes and surfaces of crystals.

Miller William Hallowes (1782–1849). US religious leader. Ordained as a Baptist minister 1833, Miller predicted that the Second Advent would occur 1844. Many of his followers sold their property in expectation of the end of the world. Although Miller's

Miller, Arthur *One of the most acclaimed US playwrights of the 20th century, Arthur Miller has sought to find an authentic form of modern tragedy – an engaged and committed drama which does justice both to social themes and to the moral and psychological complexity of the individual.*

movement disbanded soon after, his teachings paved the way for later Adventist sects.

Born in Pittsfield, Massachusetts, and raised in New York, Miller later settled in Vermont. Convinced that the Second Coming of Jesus was imminent, he began to preach about the millennium.

Millet Jean François (1814–1875). French artist. A leading member of the Barbizon School, he painted scenes of peasant life and landscapes. *The Angelus* 1859 (Musée d'Orsay, Paris) was widely reproduced in his day.

After a long struggle to earn a living by painting shepherdesses and nude bathers in the 18th-century *style galant*, he found his true vein in *The Winnower* of 1848. He settled at the village of Barbizon 1849, with his second wife and growing family, and there, still in poverty, devoted himself exclusively to the paintings of peasant life for which he is famous, such as *The Gleaners*, 1857, and *The Angelus*. In the sombre melancholy of his pictures he may be called a realist, though the ethical or emotional element is often prominent. Millet was also a faulty technician in oils, his paint often being lifeless and muddled in texture, but in pastels, drawings, and etchings his great powers were fully displayed. He is distinct from his colleagues of the Barbizon School in the equal importance he attached to figure and landscape, and that he conveyed an essential harmony between them is one of his achievements.

Millett Kate (1934–). US radical feminist lecturer, writer, and sculptor whose book *Sexual Politics* 1970 was a landmark in feminist thinking. She was a founding member of the *National Organization of Women* (NOW). Later books include *Flying* 1974, *The Prostitution Papers* 1976, *Sita* 1977, and *The Loony Bin Trip* 1991, describing a period of manic depression and drug therapy.

Millikan Robert Andrews (1868–1953). US physicist, awarded a Nobel prize 1923 for his determination of Planck's constant (a fundamental unit of quantum theory) 1916 and the electric charge on an electron 1913.

His experiment to determine the electronic charge, which took five years to perfect, involved observing oil droplets, charged by external radiation, falling under gravity between two horizontal metal plates connected to a high-voltage supply. By varying the voltage, he was able to make the electrostatic field between the plates balance the gravitational field so that some droplets became stationary and floated. If a droplet of weight W is held stationary between plates separated by a distance d and carrying a potential difference V, the charge, e, on the drop is equal to Wd/V. Millikan also carried out research into cosmic rays, a term that he coined in 1925, when he proved that the rays do come from space. He worked at the University of Chicago 1896–21, becoming professor 1910, and at the California Institute of Technology 1921–45.

Millin Sarah Gertrude (born Liebson) (1889–1968). South African novelist. She was an opponent of racial discrimination, as seen in, for example, *God's Step-Children* 1924.

Mills C(harles) Wright (1916–1962). US sociologist whose concern for humanity, ethical values, and individual freedom led him to criticize the US establishment. Originally in the liberal tradition, Mills later adopted Weberian and even Marxist ideas. He aroused considerable popular interest in sociology with such works as *White Collar* 1951; *The Power Elite* 1956, depicting the USA as ruled by businessmen, military experts, and politicians; and *Listen, Yankee* 1960.

Mills John Lewis Ernest Watts (1908–). English actor. A very versatile performer, he appeared in films such as *In Which We Serve* 1942, *The Rocking Horse Winner* 1949, *The Wrong Box* 1966, and *Oh! What a Lovely War* 1969. He received an Academy Award for *Ryan's Daughter* 1970. He is the father of the actresses Hayley Mills and Juliet Mills. Knighted 1976.

Mills William Hobson (1873–1959). English organic chemist who worked mainly on stereochemistry and the synthesis of cyanine dyes.

Mills was born in London and studied at Cambridge, where he was professor from 1912. He also collected 2,200 specimens of the British bramble plant *Rubus fructiosus* for the university.

Mills and his co-workers investigated cyanine dyestuffs for preparing photographic emulsions, mainly for use by the military in World War I. Other early research concerned stereochemistry, particularly optical isomerism – the phenomenon in which pairs of (usually organic) compounds differ only in the arrangements of their atoms in space. In the 1920s he investigated substituted derivatives of naphthalene, quinolene, and benzene.

Mills Brothers US vocal group that specialized in close-harmony vocal imitations of instruments, comprising Herbert Mills (1912–), Harry Mills (1913–1982), John Mills (1889–1935), and Donald Mills (1915–). Formed 1922, the group first broadcast on radio 1925, and continued to perform until the 1950s. Their 70 hits include 'Lazy River' 1948 and 'You Always Hurt the One You Love' 1944.

Isn't it funny / How a bear likes honey? / Buzz! Buzz! Buzz! / I wonder why he does?

A A MILNE
Winnie-the-Pooh ch 2 1926

Milne A(lan) A(lexander) (1882–1956). English writer. His books for children were based on the teddy bear and other toys of his son Christopher Robin (*Winnie-the-Pooh* 1926 and *The House at Pooh Corner* 1928). He also wrote children's verse (*When We Were Very Young* 1924 and *Now We Are Six* 1927) and plays, including an adaptation of Kenneth Grahame's *The Wind in the Willows* as *Toad of Toad Hall* 1929.

Milne was educated at Westminster and Cambridge, where he studied mathematics. At the age of 24 he was assistant editor of *Punch* magazine. Some critics have seen in the Pooh series a parallel with Milne's rejection of Christianity, in that Pooh and Piglet take comfort by belief in a god, Christopher Robin, who the reader knows to be a thoughtless child who cannot even spell.

… you can't help respecting anybody who can spell TUESDAY even if he doesn't spell it right.

A A MILNE
House at Pooh Corner ch 5 1928

Milne Edward Arthur (1896–1950). English astrophysicist and mathematician who formulated a theory of relativity which he called kinematic relativity, parallel to Albert Einstein's general theory.

Milne was born in Hull, Yorkshire, and studied at Cambridge, where he spent his academic career until 1925. He then moved to Manchester as professor of mathematics. From 1929 he was professor at Oxford.

Studying stellar structure, Milne suggested that a decrease in luminosity might cause the collapse of a star, and that this would be associated with nova formation. Some of his cosmological theories were developed with Irish astrophysicist William McCrea.

In 1932, Milne began his attempt to explain the properties of the universe by kinematics (the movement of bodies). Basing his theory on Euclidean space and on Einstein's special theory of relativity alone, Milne was able to formulate systems of theoretical cosmology, dynamics, and electrodynamics. He also gave a more acceptable estimate for the overall age of the universe (10,000 million years) than that provided by the general theory of relativity.

Milne George Francis, 1st Baron Milne (1866–1948). British soldier. Milne served in both the Sudan campaign and the South African war, winning the DSO. In World War I he took command of British troops in Salonika May 1916 where he was responsible for the defensive operations against the Bulgarian army 1917 and for the offensive which led to the collapse of Bulgaria 1918. He was promoted to general 1920. He retired Sept 1920 to become lieutenant of the Tower of London. KCB 1918, baron 1933.

Milner Alfred, 1st Viscount Milner (1854–1925). British colonial administrator. As governor of Cape Colony 1897–1901, he negotiated with Kruger but did little to prevent the second South African War; and as governor of the Transvaal and Orange River colonies 1902–05 after their annexation, he reorganized their administration. In 1916 he became a member of Lloyd George's war cabinet. He emphasized the 'organic union' of the Empire, rather than the need for independence for its members. As secretary for war 1918–19 he was largely responsible for creating a unified Allied command under Foch. KCB 1895, baron 1901, viscount 1902.

If we believe a thing to be bad, and if we have a right to prevent it, it is our duty to try to prevent it, and to damn the consequences.

ALFRED, VISCOUNT MILNER
Speech in Glasgow 26 Nov 1909 on the House of Lords and the budget

Milošević Slobodan (1941–). Serbian communist politician, party chief and president of Serbia from 1986; re-elected Dec 1990 in multiparty elections and again Dec 1992. Milošević wielded considerable influence over the Serb-dominated Yugoslav federal army during the 1991–92 civil war and continued to back Serbian militia in Bosnia-Herzegovina 1992–94, although publicly disclaiming any intention to 'carve up' the newly independent republic. Widely believed to be the instigator of the conflict, Milošević changed tactics from 1993, adopting the public persona of peacemaker and putting pressure on his allies, the Bosnian Serbs, to accept negotiated peace terms; this contributed to the Dayton peace accord for Bosnia-Herzegovina Nov 1995.

Milošević was educated at Belgrade University and rapidly rose through the ranks of the Yugoslavian Communist Party (LCY) in his home republic of Serbia, helped by his close political and business links to Ivan Stambolic, his predecessor as local party leader. He won popular support within Serbia for his assertive nationalist stance, encouraging street demonstrations in favour of the reintegration of Kosovo and Vojvodina autonomous provinces into a 'greater Serbia'. Serbia's formal annexation of Kosovo Sept 1990 gave him a landslide majority in multiparty elections Dec 1990, but in March 1991 there were 30,000-strong riots in Belgrade, calling for his resignation. Despite this, in Dec 1992 he won a 55% share of the vote in a direct presidential election, defeating the Serbian-born US businessman Milan Panic. In Oct 1994 Milošević imposed a border blockade of the Bosnian Serbs, as a result of which international sanctions against Yugoslavia were eased.

Mi ́osz Czes ́aw (1911–). Polish-American writer. He became a diplomat before defecting and becoming a US citizen. His poetry in English translation, classical in style, includes *Selected Poems* 1973 and *Bells in Winter* 1978. His collection of essays *The Captive Mind* 1953 concerns the impact of communism on Polish intellectuals. Among his novels are *The Seizure of Power* 1955, *The Issa Valley* 1981, and *The Land of Ulro* 1984. Nobel Prize for Literature 1980.

Milstein César (1927–). Argentine-born British molecular biologist who developed monoclonal antibodies, giving immunity against specific diseases. He shared the Nobel Prize for Physiology or Medicine 1984 with Georges Köhler and Niels Jerne.

Monoclonal antibodies are cloned cells that can be duplicated in limitless quantities and, when introduced into the body, can be targeted to seek out sites of disease. Milstein and his colleagues had thus devised a means of accessing the immune system for purposes of research, diagnosis, and treatment.

From 1963 he worked in the UK at the Laboratory of Molecular Biology, Cambridge, and later became joint head of its Protein Chemistry Division.

Milstein and his colleagues were among the first to determine the complete sequence of the short, low-molecular-weight part of the immunoglobulin molecule (known as the light chain). He then determined the nucleotide sequence of a large portion of the messenger RNA for the light chain. His findings led him to the technique for preparing monoclonal antibodies.

Miltiades the Younger (*c.* 550–489 BC). Athenian general, ruler of part of Thrace near the Hellespont. He was largely responsible for defeating the Persians at Marathon in 490 BC. He was the father of Cimon.

As good almost kill a man as kill a good book; who kills a man kills a reasonable creature, God's image; but he who destroys a good book, kills reason itself, kills the image of God, as it were in the eye.

JOHN MILTON
Areopagitica 1644

Milton John (1608–1674). English poet. His epic *Paradise Lost* 1667 is one of the landmarks of English literature. Early poems, including *Comus* (a masque performed 1634) and *Lycidas* (an elegy 1638), showed Milton's superlative lyric gift. Latin secretary to Oliver Cromwell during the Commonwealth period, he also wrote many pamphlets and prose works, including *Areopagitica* 1644, which opposed press censorship.

Born in London and educated at Christ's College, Cambridge, Milton was a scholarly poet, ambitious to match the classical epics, and with strong theological views. Of polemical temperament, he published prose works on republicanism and church government. His middle years were devoted to the Puritan cause and writing pamphlets, including *The Doctrine and Discipline of Divorce* 1643, which was based on his own experience of marital unhappiness. From 1649 he was (Latin) secretary to the Council of State. His assistants, as his sight failed, included Andrew Marvell. *Paradise Lost* 1667 and the less successful sequel *Paradise Regained* 1671 were written when he was blind and in some political danger (after the restoration of Charles II), as was *Samson Agonistes* 1671, a powerful if untheatrical play.

Suggested reading
Graves, R *Wife to Mr Milton* (1943)
Hanford, J H and Taffe, V G *A Milton Handbook* (1970)
Hill, Christopher *Milton and the Puritan Revolution* (1977)
Parker, W R *Milton: A Biography* (1968)
Potter, L *A Preface to Milton* (1972)
Tillyard, E M W *Milton* (1966)
Wilson, A N *The Life of John Milton* (1983)

Mimnermus (lived 7th century BC). Greek poet from Ionia. The surviving fragments of his work deal with love, old age, and war. The collection *Nanno*, the name of a beloved flute-player, contains reflections on the short-lived joys of youth.

Minamoto or Genji. Ancient Japanese clan, the members of which were the first ruling shoguns 1192–1219. Their government was based in Kamakura, near present-day Tokyo. After the death of the first shogun, Minamoto Yoritomo (1147–1199), the real power was exercised by the regent for the shogun; throughout the Kamakura period (1192–1333), the regents were of the Hōjō family, a branch of the Taira.

The Minamoto claimed descent from a 9th-century emperor. Minamoto Yoriyoshi (988–1075) was a warlord who built up a power base in the Kanto region when appointed by the court to put down a rebellion there. During the 11th and 12th centuries the Minamoto and the Taira were rivals for power at the court and in the country. The Minamoto emerged victorious in 1185 and Yoritomo received the patent of shogun 1192. Zen teaching and Buddhist sculpture flourished during their shogunate.

Mindszenty József (born József Pehm) (1892–1975). Roman Catholic primate of Hungary. He was imprisoned by the communist government 1949, but escaped 1956 to take refuge in the US legation. The pope persuaded him to go into exile in Austria 1971, and he was 'retired' when Hungary's relations with the Vatican improved 1974. His remains were returned to Hungary from Austria and re-interred at Esztergom 1991.

Ming dynasty Chinese dynasty 1368–1644, based in Nanjing. During the rule 1402–24 of Yongle (or Yung-lo), there was territorial expansion into Mongolia and Yunnan in the SW. The administrative system was improved, public works were carried out, and foreign trade was developed. Art and literature flourished and distinctive blue and white porcelain was produced.

The Ming dynasty was founded by Zhu Yuanzhang (or Chu Yuan-chang) (1328–1398), a rebel leader who captured the Yuan capital Khanbaligh (modern Beijing) 1368. He set up his headquarters in Nanjing and proclaimed himself Emperor Hong Wu. From the late 16th century, the Ming faced the threat of attack from the NE by Japan, which invaded its tributary Korea 1592. Population pressure also led to peasant rebellions, and decline came with the growth of eunuch power, pressure from Mongols in the N, and an increasing burden of taxes.

Mingus Charles (1922–1979). US jazz bassist and composer. He played with Louis Armstrong, Duke Ellington, and Charlie Parker. His experimentation with atonality and dissonant effects opened the way for the new style of free collective jazz improvisation of the 1960s.

Based on the West Coast until 1951, Mingus took part in the development of cool jazz. Subsequently based in New York, he worked with a number of important musicians and expanded the scope of the bass as a lead instrument. Recordings include *Pithecanthropus Erectus* 1956 and *Mingus at Monterey* 1964.

Minkowski Hermann (1864–1909). Russian-born German mathematician whose introduction of the concept of space-time was essential to the genesis of the general theory of relativity.

Minkowski was born near Kaunas and studied at Königsberg, Germany (now Kaliningrad, Russia). In 1896 he became professor at the Federal Institute of Technology in Zurich, Switzerland, returning to Germany 1902 as professor at Göttingen.

Minkowski's concept of the geometry of numbers constituted an important addition to number theory, and his research into that topic led him to consider certain geometric properties in a space of *n* dimensions and so to hit upon his notion of the space-time continuum. The principle of relativity, already put forward by Jules Poincaré and Albert Einstein, led Minkowski to the view that space and time were interlinked. In *Raum und Zeit/Space and Time* 1909, he proposed a four-dimensional manifold in which space and time became inseparable. The central idea was, as Einstein allowed, necessary for the working-out of the general theory of relativity.

Minkowski Rudolph Leo (1895–1976). German-born US astrophysicist, responsible for the compilation of a set of photographs now found in every astronomical library, the National Geographic Society Palomar Observatory Sky Survey. A leading authority on novae and planetary nebulae, he was a pioneer in the science of radioastronomy.

He became professor of physics at Hamburg 1922, but the rise of Nazism in Germany caused him to emigrate to the USA 1935. He worked at the Mount Wilson and Palomar observatories in California until 1959, and at the University of California at Berkeley 1960–65.

Minkowski divided supernovae into two principal types, and more than doubled the number of known planetary nebulae. In collaboration with Walter Baade, who had also been his colleague at Hamburg, Minkowski identified a discrete radio source, Cygnus A, in 1951. This was the first time an extragalactic radio source was optically identified. Minkowski determined the optical red shift of the radio source 3C 295, which was then the farthest point on the velocity–distance diagram of cosmology, in his last observing run at the Palomar 500-cm/200-in telescope.

Minnelli Liza May (1946–). US actress and singer. The daughter of Judy Garland and the director Vincente Minnelli, she achieved stardom in the Broadway musical *Flora, the Red Menace* 1965 and in the film *Cabaret* 1972. Her subsequent films include *New York, New York* 1977 and *Arthur* 1981.

Minnelli Vincente (1910–1986). US film director. He specialized in musicals and occasional melodramas. His most successful films,

such as *Meet Me in St Louis* 1944 and *Lust for Life* 1956, display great visual flair.

Minto Gilbert John Murray Kynynmond, 4th Earl of (1845–1914). British colonial administrator who succeeded Curzon as viceroy of India, 1905–10. With John Morley, secretary of state for India, he co-sponsored the Morley Minto reforms of 1909. The reforms increased Indian representation in government at provincial level, but also created separate Muslim and Hindu electorates which, it was believed, helped the British Raj in the policy of divide and rule. Earl 1891.

Mintoff Dom(inic) (1916–). Labour prime minister of Malta 1971–84. He negotiated the removal of British and other foreign military bases 1971–79 and made treaties with Libya.

Minton Thomas (1765–1836). English potter. He first worked under the potter Josiah Spode, but in 1789 established himself at Stoke-on-Trent as an engraver of designs (he originated the 'willow pattern') and in the 1790s founded a pottery there, producing high-quality bone china, including tableware.

Minuit Peter (*c.* 1580–1638). Dutch colonial administrator in America. As a founder of New Amsterdam on Manhattan Island 1626 and its director general, he negotiated with the local Indians and supervised the construction of Fort Amsterdam. Ousted from his post 1631 by the Dutch Reformed Church, he helped found the Swedish colony of Fort Christina at the modern site of Wilmington, Delaware, 1638.

Born in Prussia, Minuit took part in the colonization activities of the Dutch West India Company in America. He was lost in a hurricane in the West Indies.

To administer is to govern; to govern is to reign.

COMTE DE MIRABEAU
Memorandum 3 July 1790

Mirabeau Honoré Gabriel Riqueti, Comte de (1749–1791). French politician, leader of the National Assembly in the French Revolution. He wanted to establish a parliamentary monarchy on the English model. From May 1790 he secretly acted as political adviser to the king.

Mirabeau was from a noble Provençal family. Before the French Revolution he had a stormy career, was three times imprisoned, and spent several years in exile. In 1789 he was elected to the States General. His eloquence won him the leadership of the National Assembly; nevertheless, he was out of sympathy with the majority of the deputies, whom he regarded as mere theoreticians.

Miranda Carmen. Stage name of Maria de Carmo Miranda da Cunha (1909–1955). Portuguese dancer and singer. She lived in Brazil from childhood, moving to Hollywood 1939. Her Hollywood musicals include *Down Argentine Way* 1940 and *The Gang's All Here* 1943. Her hallmarks were extravagant costumes and headgear adorned with tropical fruits, a staccato singing voice, and fiery temperament.

Mirandola Italian 15th-century philosopher. See ◊Pico della Mirandola.

Mirman Sophie (1956–). British entrepreneur, founder of the Sock Shop, launched on the US market in 1987. After the collapse of Sock Shop in 1990, she launched an upmarket children's shop, Trotters.

Miró Joan (1893–1983). Spanish Surrealist painter. In the mid-1920s he developed an abstract style, lyrical and often witty, with amoeba shapes, some linear, some highly coloured, generally floating on a plain background.

During the 1930s his style became more sober and after World War II he produced larger abstracts. He experimented with sculpture and printmaking and produced ceramic murals (including two in the UNESCO building, Paris, 1958). He also designed stained glass and sets for the ballet impresario Sergei Diaghilev.

Suggested reading
Krauss, Rosalind and Rowell, Margit *Joan Miró: Magnetic Fields* (1972)
Lanchner, Carolyn *Joan Miró* (1993)
Penrose, Roland *Miró* (1970)
Rowell, Margit *Joan Miró: Selected Writings and Interviews* (1986)

Mirren Helen (1945–). English actress. She has played both modern and classical stage roles. Her Shakespearean roles include Lady Macbeth and Isabella in *Measure for Measure*. Her films include *The Long Good Friday* 1981 and *Cal* 1984; and *Prime Suspect* 1990 for television.

Mirrlees Hope (1887–1978). British writer whose fantasy novel *Lud-in-the-Mist* 1926 contrasts the supernatural with the real world.

Mises Richard von (1883–1953). Austrian mathematician and aerodynamicist who made valuable contributions to statistics and the theory of probability, in which he emphasized the idea of random distribution.

Von Mises was born in Lemberg (now Lvov, Ukraine), and educated at Vienna. He was professor at the University of Strassburg (now Strasbourg, France) 1909–18. In 1920 he was appointed director of the Institute for Applied Mathematics at Berlin, but with the coming to power of Adolf Hitler in 1933, von Mises emigrated to Turkey and taught at the University of Istanbul. In 1939 he went to the USA to join the faculty of Harvard, where he was professor from 1944.

Von Mises's first interest was fluid mechanics, especially in relation to aerodynamics and aeronautics. He learned to fly and in 1913 gave the first university course in the mechanics of powered flight. He made significant improvements in boundary-layer-flow theory and aerofoil design and, in 1915, built an aeroplane for the Austrian military. During World War I he served as a pilot.

Von Mises was drawn into the field of probability theory and statistics by his association (from 1907 until the 1920s) with the Viennese school of logical positivism. He came to the conclusion that a probability cannot be simply the limiting value of a relative frequency, and added the proviso that any event should be irregularly or randomly distributed in the series of occasions in which its probability is measured.

Von Mises's ideas were contained in two papers which he published in 1919. Little noticed at the time, they have come to influence all modern statisticians.

Mishich Zivoyin (1855–1921). Serbian field marshal. He fought in the Serbo-Turkish wars and the war against Bulgaria 1885–86, and was chief of the general staff during the Balkan Wars 1912–13. In World War I he commanded the Serbian 2nd Army and played a major role in resisting the Austrian invasions. Appointed field-marshal 1914, he commanded the Serbian forces which played a part in the subjugation of Bulgaria Sept 1918.

Mishima Yukio. Pen name of Hiraoka Kimitake (1925–1970). Japanese novelist. His work often deals with sexual desire and perversion, as in *Confessions of a Mask* 1949 and *The Temple of the Golden Pavilion* 1956. He committed hara-kiri (ritual suicide) as a protest against what he saw as the corruption of the nation and the loss of the samurai warrior tradition.

Suggested reading
Nathan, J *Mishima* (1974)
Scott-Stokes, H *The Life and Death of Yukio Mishima* (1974)

Mistinguett ... Queen of the Paris Night.
Title of MISTINGUETT's autobiography 1954

Mistinguett Stage name of Jeanne Marie Bourgeois (1875–1956). French actress and dancer. A leading music-hall artist in Paris from 1899, she appeared in revues at the Folies-Bergère, Casino de Paris, and Moulin Rouge. She was known for the song 'Mon Homme' and her partnership with Maurice Chevalier.

Mistral Gabriela. Pen name of Lucila Godoy de Alcayaga (1889–1957). Chilean poet. She wrote *Sonnets of Death* 1915 and was awarded the Nobel Prize for Literature 1945. She was consul of Chile in Spain, and represented her country at the League of Nations and the United Nations.

Arthur Mitchell's goals were to disprove the idea that classical ballet cannot be danced by black performers.
Christy Adair on ARTHUR MITCHELL
in *Woman and Dance; Sylphs and Sirens* 1992

Mitchell Arthur (1934–1990). US dancer. He was director of the Dance Theater of Harlem, which he founded 1968 with Karel Shook (1920–). Mitchell was a principal dancer with the New York City Ballet 1956–68, creating many roles in Balanchine's ballets, such as *Agon* 1967.

Don't it always seem to go / That you don't know what you've got till it's gone / They paved paradise and put up a parking lot.
JONI MITCHELL
'Big Yellow Taxi' 1970

Mitchell Joni. Adopted name of Roberta Joan Anderson (1943–). Canadian singer, songwriter, and guitarist. She began in the 1960s folk style and subsequently incorporated elements of rock and jazz with confessional, sophisticated lyrics. Her albums include *Blue* 1971 and *Hejira* 1976.

Mitchell Juliet (1940–). British psychoanalyst and writer. Her article in *New Left Review* 1966 entitled 'Women: The Longest Revolution' was one of the first attempts to combine socialism and feminism, using Marxist theory to explain the reasons behind women's oppression. She published *Women's Estate* 1971 and *Psychoanalysis and Feminism* 1974.

Death and taxes and childbirth! There's never any convenient time for any of them.
MARGARET MITCHELL
Gone with the Wind ch 38 1936

Mitchell Margaret (1900–1949). US novelist. She was born in Atlanta, Georgia, which is the setting for her one book, the bestseller *Gone with the Wind* 1936 (Pulitzer prize), a story of the US Civil War.

It was filmed 1939 starring Vivien Leigh and Clark Gable.

Mitchell Peter Dennis (1920–1992). English chemist. He received a Nobel prize in 1978 for work on the conservation of energy by plants during respiration and photosynthesis. He showed that the transfer of energy during life processes is not random but directed.

He worked at the Chemical Biology Unit in the Department of Zoology at Edinburgh 1955–63, and then established the privately run Glynn Research Institute at Bodmin, Cornwall.

It had been believed that the energy absorbed by animals from food and by plants from sunlight was utilized in cells by purely chemical means. The cell was seen as a bag of enzymes in which random and directionless processes took place. Mitchell proved that currents of protons pass through cell walls, which, instead of being simple partitions between cells, are, in fact, full of directional pathways. This discovery demonstrated the existence of a reverse kind of electricity (Mitchell called it 'proticity'), which he successfully used to run an engine.

Mitchell R(eginald) J(oseph) (1895–1937). English aircraft designer whose Spitfire fighter was a major factor in winning the Battle of Britain during World War II.

From 1916 he worked for the Supermarine Aviation Company, which specialized in flying boats. His first aeroplane, the Sea Lion 1919, was adapted from a standard design; faster models of Sea Lion followed. In 1924, Mitchell was allowed to design his own aeroplane, the Supermarine S-4. It was a monoplane and the whole wing section was made in one piece. He won speed records with several of the S-model planes in the 1920s.

The single-engined Spitfire prototype was produced 1936. More than 19,000 Spitfires were eventually built. The manoeuvrability and adaptability of the Spitfire accounted for its success.

Mitchell Thomas Livingstone (1792–1855). Scottish-born surveyor and explorer in Australia who led expeditions through New South Wales 1831–32 and 1835–36, Victoria 1836, and Queensland 1846. He established that the Darling River joined the Murray, and helped to open the Maranoa region, Queensland, to pastoralism. Knighted 1839.

Mitchison Naomi Mary Margaret (born Haldane) (1897–   ). Scottish writer. Her more than 70 books include *The Conquered* 1923 and *The Corn King and the Spring Queen* 1931, novels evoking ancient Greece and Rome. A socialist activist, she also campaigned for birth control.

The settings of other novels range from prehistoric Scotland and the Holy Roman Empire to Africa (she was made a tribal adviser in Botswana 1963) and distant galaxies (*Memoirs of a Spacewoman* 1962). She has also written short stories, plays, poetry, and five volumes of autobiography, culminating in *As It Was* 1988.

She was born in Edinburgh, the sister of the geneticist J B S Haldane, and brought up in Oxford; from 1937 she lived in W Scotland, where she was active in local politics. For her historical novels, although she had little formal classical knowledge, she made great use of histories and translations to produce a clear, direct, unsentimental narrative; she also wrote a biography of the Byzantine princess *Anna Comnena* 1928. Mitchison went on publishing novels into her nineties.

People think I have an interesting walk. Hell, I'm just trying to keep my gut in.

ROBERT MITCHUM
in Leslie Halliwell *Filmgoer's Companion* 1965

Mitchum Robert Charles Duran (1917–   ). US film actor. A star for more than 30 years, he was equally at home as the relaxed mod-

Mitterrand French socialist politician and former president François Mitterrand.

ern hero or psychopathic villain. His films include *Out of the Past* 1947, *The Night of the Hunter* 1955, and *The Friends of Eddie Coyle* 1973.

Mitford Mary Russell (1787–1855). English author. She is remembered for her sketches in *Our Village* 1824–32 describing Three Mile Cross, near Reading, where she lived.

Mitford sisters the six daughters of British aristocrat Lord Redesdale, including: Nancy (1904–1973), author of the semi-autobiographical *The Pursuit of Love* 1945 and *Love in a Cold Climate* 1949, and editor and part author of *Noblesse Oblige* 1956 elucidating 'U' (upper-class) and 'non-U' behaviour; Diana (1910–   ), who married Oswald Mosley; Unity (1914–1948), who became an admirer of Hitler; and Jessica (1917–1996), author of the autobiographical *Hons and Rebels* 1960 and *The American Way of Death* 1963.

Though I have taken precautions against all other poisons, I have not against the most deadly of all which constantly resides with rulers, namely treachery of army, children and friends.

MITHRIDATES
Dying words, quoted in Appian *History of Mithridatic Wars* bk 12, ch 111

Mithridates VI Eupator (called 'the Great') (c. 120–63 BC). King of Pontus (on the Black Sea coast of modern Turkey), who became the greatest obstacle to Roman expansion in the E. He massacred 80,000 Romans in overrunning the rest of Asia Minor and went on to invade Greece. He was defeated by Sulla in the First Mithridatic War 88–84; by Lucullus in the Second 83–81; and by Pompey in the Third 74–64. He was killed by a soldier at his own order.

Mitre Bartólomé (1821–1906). Argentine president 1862–68. In 1852 he helped overthrow the dictatorial regime of Juan Manuel de Rosas, and in 1861 helped unify Argentina. Mitre encouraged immigration and favoured growing commercial links with Europe. He is seen as a symbol of national unity.

Mitscherlich Eilhard (1794–1863). German chemist who discovered isomorphism (the phenomenon in which substances of analogous chemical composition crystallize in the same crystal form). He also synthesized many organic compounds for the first time.

Mitscherlich was born in Jever, Lower Saxony, and entered Heidelberg University to study Oriental languages, later continuing this study at Paris, but having to abandon it with the fall of Napoleon. He instead studied science at Göttingen and then worked with Swedish chemist Jöns Berzelius in Stockholm for two years. Mitscherlich became professor at Berlin 1825.

Mitscherlich began studying crystals in 1818. Observing that crystals of potassium phosphate and potassium arsenate appear to be nearly identical in form, he learned exact crystallographic methods and then applied spherical trigonometry to the data he obtained. He extended his researches to phosphates, arsenates, and carbonates, publishing the results 1822 and introducing the term isomorphism.

In 1834, Mitscherlich synthesized benzene, which he termed *Benzin*. He showed that yeast (which in 1842 he identified as a microorganism) can invert sugar in solution. Mitscherlich published his influential *Lehrbuch der Chemie/Textbook of Chemistry* 1829.

Mitsotakis Constantine (1918–   ). Greek politician, leader of the conservative New Democracy Party (ND) 1984–93, prime minister 1990–93. Minister for economic coordination 1965 (a post he held again 1978–80), he was arrested by the military junta 1967, but escaped from house arrest and lived in exile until 1974. In 1980–81 he was foreign minister. He resigned the leadership of the ND after its 1993 election defeat.

Mitterrand François Maurice Marie (1916–1996). French socialist politician, president 1981–95. He held ministerial posts in 11 governments 1947–58, and founded the French Socialist Party (PS) 1971. In 1985 he introduced proportional representation, allegedly to weaken the growing opposition from left and right. From 1982 his administrations combined economic orthodoxy with social reform.

Mitterrand studied law and politics in Paris. During World War II he was prominent in the Resistance after initially being a supporter of Marshal Pétain's Vichy regime. He entered the National Assembly as a centre-left deputy for Nièvre. Opposed to General de Gaulle's creation of the Fifth Republic 1958, he formed the centre-left anti-Gaullist Federation of the Left in the 1960s. In 1971 he became leader of the new PS. An electoral union with the Communist Party 1972–77 established the PS as the most popular party in France.

Mitterrand was elected president 1981. His programme of reform was hampered by deteriorating economic conditions after 1983. When the socialists lost their majority March 1986, he was compelled to work with a right-wing prime minister, Jacques Chirac, and grew in popularity. He defeated Chirac to secure a second term in the presidential election May 1988. In 1993 he entered a second term of 'cohabitation' with the conservative prime minister Edouard Balladur. However, whereas he was able to enhance his reputation when 'cohabiting' with Chirac, his popularity waned and his influence weakened in contrast with the successful premiership of Balladur. Towards the end of his presidency his failing health further weakened his hold on power.

Suggested reading

Cole, A *François Mitterrand: A Study in Political Leadership* (1994)

Friend, J W *Seven Years in France* (1989)

Mazly, Sonya and Newman, Michael (eds) *Mitterrand's France* (1987)

Mitterrand, François *The Wheat from the Chaff* (memoirs) (trs 1982)

Nay, Catherine *The Black and the Red* (trs 1987)

Tom was as elegant on a horse as Fred Astaire on a dance floor, and that's the elegantist there is.

Adela Rogers St John, on TOM MIX
in *The Honeycomb*

Mix Tom (Thomas) (1880–1940). US film actor. He was the most colourful cowboy star of silent films. At their best, his films, such as *The Range Riders* 1910 and *King Cowboy* 1928, were fast-moving and full of impressive stunts. His talkies include *Destry Rides Again* 1932 and *The Miracle Rider* 1935.

Miyake Issey (1938–). Japanese fashion designer. Active in Paris from 1965, he showed his first collection in New York and Tokyo 1971, and has been showing in Paris since 1973. His 'anti-fashion' looks combined Eastern and Western influences: a variety of textured and patterned fabrics were layered and wrapped round the body to create linear and geometric shapes. His inspired designs have had a considerable influence on the fashion scene.

Miyamoto Musashi (c. 1584–1645). Japanese samurai. His manual on military strategy and sword fighting, *Gorinsho/The Book of Five Rings* 1645, became popular in English translation 1974 in the USA as a guide to business success.

In Japan, Miyamoto Musashi is popular as the hero of a long historical novel that glamorizes his martial-arts exploits and has been the basis for a series of films and comic books. The historical Miyamoto was a painter as well as a fencer, and spent his life travelling Japan in search of Zen enlightenment.

Miyazawa Kiichi (1919–). Japanese right-wing politician, prime minister 1991–93. After holding a number of key government posts, he became leader of the ruling Liberal Democratic Party (LDP) and prime minister Nov 1991. Defeated June 1993 on a vote of confidence (triggered by demand for electoral reform), he called a general election for July. He resigned after the LDP failed to hold its majority (the party's first defeat in 38 years).

Mizoguchi Kenji (1898–1956). Japanese film director. *Ugetsu Monogatari* 1953 confirmed his international reputation. Notable for his sensitive depiction of female psychology, he also directed *The*

Poppies 1935, *Sansho daiyu/Sansho the Bailiff* 1954, and *Street of Shame* 1956.

Mladenov Peter Toshev (1936–). Bulgarian Communist politician, secretary general of the Bulgarian Communist Party from Nov 1989, after the resignation of Zhivkov, until Feb 1990. He was elected state president in April 1990 but was replaced four months later.

Mladic Ratko (1943–). Bosnian general, leader of the Bosnian Serb army from 1992. He was charged with genocide and other war crimes by a United Nations tribunal 1995.

Mladic was born in Kalnovik, Herzegovina. He graduated from a military academy and joined the Yugoslav Communist Party 1965.

He took part in the 1994 peace talks.

Mnouchkine Ariane (1939–). French theatre director. She founded the Théâtre du Soleil 1964, which established a reputation with a vigorous production of Arnold Wesker's *The Kitchen* 1967. After 1968, the company began to devise its own material, firstly with *The Clowns* 1969, which was followed by *1789* 1970, an exploration of the French Revolution, and *L'Age d'or* 1975, concerning the exploitation of immigrant workers. She has also directed *Les Atrides* 1992, a version of Aeschylus' *Oresteia*.

Mnouchkine adapted *Mephisto* 1979 from Klauss Mann's novel; directed a series of Shakespeare's plays (*Richard II* 1981, *Twelfth Night* 1982) inspired by Japanese theatrical conventions; and collaborated with the writer Helene Cixous on *Sihanouk* 1985, a production about Cambodia, and *L'Indiade* 1987.

Mo Timothy (1950–). British novelist. His works are mainly set in Hong Kong (where he was born) and the East Indies, though *Sour Sweet* 1982 describes a Triad-threatened Chinese family of restaurateurs in London, and is full of realistic detail and brisk humour.

An Insular Possession 1986 is an enormously comprehensive historical novel about the Opium Wars; *The Redundancy of Courage* 1991 deals with guerrillas in East Timor; and *Brownout on Breadfruit Boulevard* 1995 (which he published himself) is a political comedy with a coprophiliac sideline.

Möbius August Ferdinand (1790–1868). German mathematician and theoretical astronomer, discoverer of the Möbius strip and considered one of the founders of topology.

Möbius formulated his barycentric calculus in 1818, a mathematical system in which numerical coefficients were assigned to points. The position of any point in the system could be expressed by varying the numerical coefficients of any four or more non-coplanar points.

Möbius was born near Naumburg and studied at Leipzig and Göttingen. From 1815 he was on the staff at Leipzig, where he became professor of astronomy and higher mechanics 1844 and director of the observatory 1848.

In addition to the Möbius strip, he discovered the Möbius net, later of value in the development of projective geometry; the Möbius tetrahedra, two tetrahedra that mutually circumscribe and inscribe each other, which he described 1828; and the Möbius function in number theory, published 1832.

During a lecture of 1840, Möbius set the problem to find the least number of colours required on a plane map to distinguish political regions, given that each boundary line should separate two differently coloured regions. It has now been proved by computer analysis that four colours will always suffice.

Mobutu Sese Seko Kuku Ngbendu Wa Za Banga (1930–). Zairean president from 1965. He assumed the presidency in a coup, and created a unitary state under a centralized government. The harshness of some of his policies and charges of corruption attracted widespread international criticism. In 1991 opposition leaders forced Mobutu to agree formally to give up some of his powers, but the president continued to oppose constitutional reform initiated by his prime minister, Etienne Tshisekedi. Despite his opposition, a new transitional constitution was adopted 1994.

Mobutu abolished secret voting in elections 1976 in favour of a system of acclamation at mass rallies. His personal wealth is estimated at $3–4 billion, and more money is spent on the presidency than on the entire social-services budget.

Model Walter (1891–1945). German field marshal in World War II. He commanded Panzer units in France and on the Eastern Front before moving to the West to shore up the German defences following the Allied invasion of Europe.

He became commander in chief in the West Aug 1944, too late to stop the Allied advances in Normandy after the D-Day landings. Replaced by von Rundstedt, he was then responsible for defeating the British airborne landing at Arnhem and launching the German offensive in the Battle of the Bulge. In April 1945 his army was trapped in the Ruhr pocket and, declaring that no German field marshal should permit himself to be captured, he shot himself.

Modersohn-Becker Paula (born Becker) (1876–1907). German painter and graphic artist. She was a member of the artists' colony at Worpswede from 1898. She painted still lifes and scenes of peasant life, but is best-known for her self-portraits and portraits of mothers and children. In her concern with expressing inner emotions and her sensitive use of shape and colour (influenced by Gauguin and the Fauves), she anticipated German Expressionism.
Suggested reading
Perry, G *Paula Modersohn-Becker* (1978)
Tufts, E *Our Hidden Heritage: Five Centuries of Women Artists* (1974)

Modigliani Amedeo (1884–1920). Italian artist. He was active in Paris from 1906. He painted and sculpted graceful nudes and portrait studies. His paintings – for example, the portrait of his mistress Jeanne Hébuterne, painted 1919 (Guggenheim Museum, New York) – have a distinctive style, the forms elongated and sensual.

Born in Livorno of an Italian-Jewish family, he first studied art in Florence and Venice, but settled in Paris 1906. It is usual to associate him with the School of Paris, though he had in fact no place in its *avant-garde* movements except that he shared the Cubist interest in primitive and African sculpture. He was encouraged to sculpt by Constantin Brancusi, and his series of strictly simplified heads reflects a shared interest in archaic sculptural styles. The study of Negro masks suggested the bold elongation and simplification of his sculptured heads, though these remained entirely European in character, while his paintings – portraits and nudes – despite similar exaggerations, were fundamentally Italian in colour with a sense of linear beauty that showed his sympathy with the School of Siena and with Botticelli. His drawings, of which he made a great number (often selling them for a few francs or a drink in a cafe), had equal distinction. After years of poverty he had some little success towards 1918, but privations, drugs, alcohol and tuberculosis combined to cut short his life.
Suggested reading
Fifield, William *Modigliani* (1976)
Mann, Carol *Modigliani* (1980)
Modigliani, Jeanne *Modigliani: Man and Myth* (memoir by his daughter) (trs 1958)
Rose, June *Modigliani: The Pure Bohemian* (1990)

Modotti Tina (1896–1942). Italian photographer. She studied with Edward Weston and went to Mexico with him 1923. As well as her sensitive studies of Mexican women, she recorded the work of the Mexican muralists and made near-abstract prints of stairs and flowers.

Mogul dynasty N Indian dynasty (1526–1858), established by Babur, Muslim descendant of Tamerlane, the 14th-century Mongol leader. The Mogul emperors ruled until the last one, Bahadur Shah II, was dethroned and exiled by the British; they included Akbar, Aurangzeb, and Shah Jahan. The Moguls established a more extensive and centralized empire than their Delhi sultanate forebears, and the Mogul era was one of great artistic achievement as well as urban and commercial development.

When Akbar died 1605 the Mogul empire had a population of 70–100 million, but it was at its largest under Aurangzeb (ruled 1658–1707), who briefly subdued the Deccan and the south-central states of Bijapur and Golconda. However, Mogul authority never

extended into the far south and, although more bureaucratized than the Delhi sultanate, power waxed and waned between central and local rulers. As the Dutch trader Francisco Pelsaert (1595–1630) commented, while Mogul emperors were 'kings of the plains and open roads', they effectively ruled barely a half of the dominions over which they claimed sovereignty, there being 'nearly as many rebels as subjects'.

Mohammed Alternative form of ◊Muhammad, founder of Islam.

Moholy-Nagy Laszlo (1895–1946). US photographer. Born in Hungary, he lived in Germany 1923–29, where he was a member of the Bauhaus school, and fled from the Nazis 1935. Through the publication of his illuminating theories and practical experiments, he had great influence on 20th-century photography and design.

Mohs Friedrich (1773–1839). German mineralogist who 1812 devised Mohs' scale of minerals, classified in order of relative hardness.

Mohs was born in the Saxon Hartz Mountains. He studied at Halle and at the Freiberg Mining Academy, and was appointed professor of mineralogy at Graz 1812, and later at Freiberg. He ended his career in Austria as professor at Vienna from 1826.

Mohs achieved eminence for his system of the classification of minerals, dividing these into genera and species in the manner of Swedish botanist Linnaeus. Although recognized as useful, the strategy was widely criticized for failing to take sufficient account of chemical composition, and it is no longer used. He also classified crystals on the basis of the orientation of their axes.

Moi Daniel arap (1924–). Kenyan politician, president from 1978. Leader of the Kenya African National Union (KANU), he became minister of home affairs 1964, vice president 1967, and succeeded Jomo Kenyatta as president. He enjoys the support of Western governments but has been widely criticized for Kenya's poor human-rights record. Since 1988 his rule has become increasingly authoritarian. In 1991, in the face of widespread criticism, he promised an eventual introduction of multiparty politics. In 1992 he was elected president in the first free elections amid widespread accusations of vote rigging.

Moissan (Ferdinand Frédéric) Henri (1852–1907). French chemist. For his preparation of pure fluorine 1886, Moissan was awarded the 1906 Nobel Prize for Chemistry. He also attempted to create artificial diamonds by rapidly cooling carbon heated to high temperatures. His claims of success were treated with suspicion.

Moivre Abraham de (1667–1754). French mathematician who pioneered the development of analytical trigonometry, for which he formulated his theorem regarding complex numbers. He also devised a means of research into the theory of probability.

Abraham de Moivre was born in Vitry-le-François, Champagne, and studied in Paris. With the revocation of the Edict of Nantes 1685, he was imprisoned as a Protestant for 12 months; on his release he went immediately to England. In London he became a close friend of Isaac Newton and Edmund Halley, but he never obtained a permanent position; he eked out a precarious living by tutoring and acting as a consultant for gambling syndicates and insurance companies.

His *The Doctrine of Chances* was published first in Latin and then in expanded English versions 1718, 1738, and 1758. It was one of the first books on probability, and made an approximation to the normal or Gaussian distribution, which was incorporated into statistical studies for the next 200 years. De Moivre was the first to derive an exact formulation of how 'chances' and stable frequency are related.

Analysing mortality statistics, de Moivre laid the mathematical foundations of the theory of annuities, for which he devised formulae based on a postulated law of mortality and constant rates of interest on money. First published 1725, his work became standard in textbooks of all subsequent commercial applications.

Molière pen name of Jean-Baptiste Poquelin (1622–1673). French satirical dramatist and actor. Modern French comedy developed from his work. After the collapse of the Paris Illustre Théâtre (of which he was one of the founders), Molière performed in the provinces 1645–58. In 1655 he wrote his first play, *L'Etourdi/ The Blunderer*, and on his return to Paris produced *Les Précieuses ridicules/ The Affected Ladies* 1659. His satires include *L'Ecole des femmes/ The School for Wives* 1662, *Le Misanthrope* 1666, *Le Bourgeois Gentilhomme/ The Would-Be Gentleman* 1670, and *Le Malade imaginaire/ The Imaginary Invalid* 1673. Other satiric plays include *Tartuffe* 1664 (banned until 1697 for attacking the hypocrisy of the clergy), *Le Médecin malgré lui/ The Doctor in Spite of Himself* 1666, and *Les Femmes savantes/ The Learned Ladies* 1672.

Molière's comedies, based on the exposure of hypocrisy and cant, made him vulnerable to many attacks (from which he was protected by Louis XIV) and marked a new departure in the French theatre away from reliance on classical Greek themes.

Suggested reading
Fernandez, R *Molière: The Man Seen Through His Plays* (1958)
Gowan, C D'O *The Background of the French Classics* (1960)
Lawrence, F L *Molière: The Comedy of Unreason* (1968)
Moore, W G *Molière: A New Criticism* (1962)

I assure you that a learned fool is more foolish than an ignorant fool.

MOLIÈRE
Les Femmes Savantes iv iii 1672

Molinos Miguel de (1640–1697). Spanish mystic and Roman Catholic priest. He settled in Rome and wrote several devotional works in Italian, including the *Guida spirituale/Spiritual Guide* 1675, which aroused the hostility of the Jesuits. In 1687 he was sentenced to life imprisonment. His doctrine is known as quietism.

Molnár Ferenc (1878–1952). Hungarian novelist and playwright. His play *Liliom* 1909 is a study of a circus barker (a person who calls out to attract the attention of members of the public), adapted as the musical *Carousel*. His novels include *Paul Street Boys* 1907.

To Soviet patriots the homeland and communism become fused in one inseparable whole.

MOLOTOV
Speech to the Supreme Soviet 6 Nov 1939

Molotov Vyacheslav Mikhailovich. Assumed name of V M Skriabin (1890–1986). Soviet communist politician. He was chair of the Council of People's Commissars (prime minister) 1930–41 and foreign minister 1939–49 and 1953–56. He negotiated the 1939 nonaggression treaty with Germany (the Ribbentrop–Molotov pact), and, after the German invasion 1941, the Soviet partnership with the Allies. His postwar stance prolonged the Cold War and in 1957 he was expelled from the government for Stalinist activities.

Everlasting peace is a dream, and not even a pleasant one ... war is a necessary part of God's arrangement of the world.

HELMUTH, COUNT VON MOLTKE
Letter to Dr J K Bluntschli 11 Dec 1880

Moltke Helmuth Carl Bernhard, Count von (1800–1891). Prussian general. He became chief of the general staff 1857, and was responsible for the Prussian strategy in the wars with Denmark 1863–64, Austria 1866, and France 1870–71. He was created count 1870 and field marshal 1871.

Moltke Helmuth Johannes Ludwig von (1848–1916). German general (nephew of Count von Moltke, the Prussian general), chief of the German general staff 1906–14. His use of General Alfred von Schlieffen's (1833–1913) plan for a rapid victory on two fronts failed and he was relieved of command after the defeat at the Marne.

Despite warnings from other staff officers, he made several modifi-

cations to the Schlieffen Plan which severely diluted its effect. Once operations had begun he failed to keep in contact with the various formations, delayed decisions, shifted troops from one flank to another, withdrew others to reinforce the Eastern Front, and in general showed himself to be incapable of discharging the duties of his office.

Molvig Jon (1923–1970). Australian landscape and portrait painter. Molvig's art shows links with the European Expressionist movement and artists Nolde and Kokoschka in works such as his *Ballad of a Dead Stockman* 1959 (Art Gallery of New South Wales, Sydney). He won the 1966 Archibald Prize.

Molyneaux Jim (James Henry) (1920–). Northern Ireland Unionist politician, leader of the Official Ulster Unionist Party (the largest Northern Ireland party) 1979–95. A member of the House of Commons from 1970, he temporarily relinquished his seat 1983–85 in protest at the Anglo-Irish Agreement. He resigned as party leader 1995. Although a fervent supporter of the union between Britain and Northern Ireland, he is regarded as one of the more moderate Loyalists.

Momaday N(avarre) Scott (1934–). US writer of Kiowa descent. He won a Pulitzer prize for his novel *House Made of Dawn* 1968, about a young American Indian at home in neither white nor his ancestral society. He was professor of English at Stanford University 1972–81.

Mommsen (Christian Matthias) Theodor (1817–1903). German historian who specialized in Roman history and held chairs at Leipzig 1848, Zürich 1852, and Breslau 1854. During this period he published a three-volume work on Roman history and then a series of extensive works on Roman law 1871–99. A political Liberal, he was highly critical of Bismarck's policies and served in the Prussian parliament 1863–66 and 1873–79 and in the Reichstag 1881–84, contributing to major political journals.

In 1902, he was awarded the Nobel Prize for Literature, the first German to be honoured in this way.

Momoh Joseph Saidu (1937–). Sierra Leone soldier and politician, president 1985–92. An army officer who became commander

Molotov *For over 40 years Molotov was at the heart of Soviet political life. He was responsible for the nationalization of Soviet industry, for the suppression of opponents of Bolshevism, and, especially during World War II and the Cold War, for determining Soviet foreign policy. Falling into disfavour in the 1950s, he was appointed ambassador to Outer Mongolia.*

1983, with the rank of major-general, he succeeded Siaka Stevens as president when he retired; Momoh was endorsed by Sierra Leone's one political party, the All-People's Congress. He dissociated himself from the policies of his predecessor, pledging to fight corruption and improve the economy. In April 1992 he fled to neighbouring Guinea after a military takeover.

Monagas José Tadeo (1784–1868). Venezuelan president 1847–51 and 1855–58, a hero of the independence movement. Monagas wanted to create a separate state in E Venezuela called Oriente, leading an uprising against President José Antonio Páez 1831. He called it off in return for a pardon for his rebels. The Liberal Monagas clan gained power after the fall 1847 of Páez's Conservative oligarchy. Monagas's brother José Gregorio was president 1851–55, and their 'Liberal oligarchy' was marked by a series of revolts led by Páez's supporters and by the disillusionment of their Liberal backers. José Tadeo was forced to resign 1858.

Monash John (1865–1931). Australian civil engineer, army officer, and administrator. He was a colonel at the outbreak of World War I and commanded the 4th Infantry Brigade through the Gallipoli campaign. He then established a reputation as a commander in France 1916 and in 1918 succeeded Birdwood in command of the Australian Corps, becoming recognized as one of the most capable of the British corps commanders in battles such as Amiens, Mont St Quentin, and the breaking of the Hindenburg Line. KCB 1918.

After the war he was chairman of the State Electricity Commission of Victoria, as well as holding several other public positions. He was also a Jewish spokesperson and active Zionist.

The blockhead Albemarle hath strange luck to be loved, though he be ... the heaviest man in the world, but stout and honest to his country.

GEORGE MONCK, 1ST DUKE OF ALBEMARLE
Samuel Pepys *Diary* 24 Oct 1667

Monck or Monk George, 1st Duke of Albemarle (1608–1670). English soldier. During the English Civil War he fought for King Charles I, but after being captured changed sides and took command of the Parliamentary forces in Ireland. Under Oliver Cromwell he became commander in chief in Scotland, and in 1660 he led his army into England and brought about the restoration of Charles II. Duke 1660.

Moncrieff Gladys (1892–1976). Australian musical comedy performer and singer of light opera; known affectionately as 'Our Glad'. She is best remembered for her performance of Teresa in *Maid of the Mountains*, a role which she played more than 3,000 times between 1921 and 1952.

Mond Ludwig (1839–1909). German-born British chemist who invented a process for recovering sulphur during the manufacture of alkali. He gave his name to a method of extracting nickel from nickel carbonyl, one of its volatile organic compounds. His son Alfred Mond, 1st Baron Melchett (1868–1930), was a founder of Imperial Chemical Industries (ICI).

Mond was born in Kassel and studied chemistry at Marburg and Heidelberg. In 1859, working in a small soda works near Kassel, he initiated the new process for the recovery of sulphur. This gained him an invitation from a Lancashire industrial chemist, and Mond moved to the UK 1862. In 1873, he helped to found the firm of Brunner, Mond, and Company, which pioneered the British chemical industry.

In 1879, Mond became interested in the production of ammonia. One outcome was the development of the Mond producer gas process, in which carbon monoxide and hydrogen are produced by alternately passing air and steam over heated coal or coke (and the hydrogen used to convert nitrogen into ammonia). By the early 1900s, Mond's Dudley Port Plant in Staffordshire was using 3 million tonnes of coal each year to make producer gas (Mond gas).

Mondale Walter Frederick (1928–   ). US Democrat politician, unsuccessful presidential candidate 1984. He was a senator 1964–76 from his home state of Minnesota, and vice president to Jimmy Carter 1977–81. After losing the 1984 presidential election to Ronald Reagan, Mondale retired from national politics to resume his law practice.

Mondrian Piet (Pieter Cornelis Mondriaan) (1872–1944). Dutch painter. In Paris from 1911 Mondrian was inspired by Cubism. He returned to the Netherlands during World War I, where he executed a series of still lifes and landscapes to refine his ideas, ultimately developing a pure abstract style. He again lived in Paris 1919–38, then in London, and from 1940 in New York. He was a founder member of the De Stijl movement and chief exponent of Neo-Plasticism, a rigorous abstract style based on the use of simple geometric forms and pure colours. He typically created a framework using vertical and horizontal lines, and filled the rectangles with primary colours, mid-grey, or black, others being left white. His *Composition in Red, Yellow and Blue* 1920 (Stedelijk, Amsterdam) is typical.

His aesthetic theories were published in the journal *De Stijl* from 1917, in *Neoplasticism* 1920, and in the essay 'Plastic Art and Pure Plastic Art' 1937. From the New York period his *Broadway Boogie-Woogie* 1942–43 (Museum of Modern Art, New York) reflects a late preoccupation with jazz rhythms.

Suggested reading
Holtzman, H and Martin, J (eds) *The New Art, The New Life: The Collected Writings of Piet Mondrian* (1986)
Jaffé, H *Piet Mondrian* (1970)
Lemoine, S *Mondrian and De Stijl* (1987)
Milner, J *Mondrian* (1992)
Welsh, R *Mondrian* (1966)

Monet Claude (1840–1926). French painter. He was a pioneer of Impressionism and a lifelong exponent of its ideals; his painting *Impression, Sunrise* 1872 gave the movement its name. In the 1870s he began painting the same subjects at different times of day to explore the ever-changing effects of light on colour and form; the *Haystacks* and *Rouen Cathedral* series followed in the 1890s, and from 1899 he painted a series of *Water Lilies* in the garden of his house at Giverny, Normandy (now a museum).

He spent his youth at Le Havre, where he was diverted from boyish caricature to open-air landscape painting by the encouragement of Boudin. Boudin and Jongkind, with whom Monet became friendly 1860, had taught him much about atmosphere before he went 1862 to Gleyre's studio in Paris, where he met Renoir, Sisley, and Bazille. He painted with them in the forest of Fontainebleau and until 1870 was engaged in perfecting a new approach to which the realism of Courbet and the direct method of Manet both contributed, as may be seen in the beautiful *Femmes au Jardin*, 1867 (Louvre), and the Manetesque *Plage à Trouville*, 1870 (Tate). A wartime interlude followed, spent in Holland and London, where he admired the works of Turner. He worked at Argenteuil 1872–78, where he had a floating studio, his mature method of rendering light in colour being now fully developed. His *Impression* in the exhibition of 1874, in which he and his friends appeared as a fairly homogeneous group, brought the term 'Impressionism' into currency for the first time. He painted at Vétheuil, 1878–83, and afterwards settled at Giverny, where in the garden of his house he painted his last remarkable studies of water lilies. Almost abstract visions of colour, these studies were long regarded dubiously as the most formless of his works, but have been hailed in recent years as outstanding examples of pure painting.

Suggested reading
Gordon, R and Forge, A *Monet* (1983)
House, J *Monet: Nature into Art* (1986)
Isaacson, J *Monet: Observation and Reflection* (1978)
Petrie, B *Claude Monet, the First of the Impressionists* (1979)

Monge Gaspard (1746–1818). French mathematician and chemist, the founder of descriptive geometry. His application of analysis to infinitesimal geometry also paved the way for later developments.

In 1771 he was drawn into the scientific circle attached to the Academy of Sciences in Paris, and in 1780 he was given official duties as assistant geometer to the Academy. By the time the French Revolution broke out in 1789, Monge was an active supporter of the radicals. He was appointed minister of the navy 1792, but was forced to resign the following year. As a member of the Committee on Arms 1793–94, he supervised the Paris armaments workshops and helped to develop military balloons. He also served on the commission to standardize weights and measures. He was instrumental in establishing the institution that became the Ecole Polytechnique, was briefly its director, and taught there until 1809.

In 1796, Monge's friendship with Napoleon began. He was sent to the newly conquered Italy as a member of various commissions. In 1798 he assisted in the preparation for the Egyptian campaign; he then accompanied Napoleon and was appointed president of the Institut d'Egypte established in Cairo. Monge also went with Napoleon on expeditions to the Suez region and Syria in 1799. Subsequently Napoleon appointed him a senator. When Napoleon was overthrown in 1815, Monge was discredited.

Moniz Antonio Egas (1874–1955). Portuguese neurologist, pioneer of prefrontal leucotomy (surgical separation of white fibres in the prefrontal lobe of the brain) to treat schizophrenia and paranoia; the treatment is today considered questionable. He shared the 1949 Nobel Prize for Physiology or Medicine.

Monk Thelonious Sphere (1917–1982). US jazz pianist and composer. He took part in the development of bebop. He had a highly idiosyncratic style, but numbers such as 'Round Midnight' and 'Blue Monk' have become standards. Monk worked in Harlem, New York, during the Depression, and became popular in the 1950s.

Do not hack me as you did my Lord Russell.

JAMES, DUKE OF MONMOUTH
To his executioner 15 July 1685

Monmouth James Scott, 1st Duke of Monmouth (1649–1685). Claimant to the English crown, the illegitimate son of Charles II and Lucy Walter. After James II's accession 1685, Monmouth landed in England at Lyme Regis, Dorset, claimed the crown, and raised a rebellion, which was crushed at Sedgemoor in Somerset. He was executed with 320 of his accomplices. Duke 1663.

When James II converted to Catholicism, the Whig opposition attempted unsuccessfully to secure Monmouth the succession to the crown by the Exclusion Bill, and having become implicated in a Whig conspiracy, the Rye House Plot 1683, he fled to Holland.
Suggested reading
Bevan, B *James, Duke of Monmouth* (1973)
Wigfield, W M *The Monmouth Rebels, 1685* (1985)

Monnet Jean (1888–1979). French economist. The originator of Winston Churchill's offer of union between the UK and France 1940, he devised and took charge of the French modernization programme under Charles de Gaulle 1945. In 1950 he produced the 'Schuman Plan' initiating the coordination of European coal and steel production in the European Coal and Steel Community, which developed into the Common Market, the forerunner of the European Union.

There are living systems; there is no 'living matter'.

JACQUES MONOD
Lecture Nov 1967

Monod Jacques Lucien (1910–1976). French biochemist who shared the 1965 Nobel Prize for Physiology or Medicine with his coworkers André Lwoff and François Jacob for research in genetics and microbiology.

From 1945 he worked at the Pasteur Institute, where he collaborated with Lwoff and Jacob. In 1953, Monod became director of the Department of Cellular Biochemistry at the Pasteur Institute and

Monroe James Monroe, remembered for the Monroe Doctrine, his warning to European nations not to interfere with the countries of the Americas.

also a professor at the University of Paris. In 1971, he was appointed director of the entire Pasteur Institute.

Working on the way in which genes control intracellular metabolism in microorganisms, Monod and his colleagues postulated the existence of a class of genes (which they called operons) that regulate the activities of the genes that actually control the synthesis of enzymes within the cell. They further hypothesized that the operons suppress the activities of the enzyme-synthesizing genes by affecting the synthesis of messenger RNA.

In his book *Chance and Necessity* 1971, Monod summoned contemporary biochemical discoveries to support the idea that all forms of life result from random mutation (chance) and Darwinian selection (necessity).

Monroe James (1758–1831). 5th president of the USA 1817–25, a Democratic Republican. He served in the American Revolution, was minister to France 1794–96, and in 1803 negotiated the Louisiana Purchase. He was secretary of state 1811–17. His name is associated with the Monroe Doctrine.

Monroe was born in Westmoreland County, Virginia. He attended the College of William and Mary and studied law under his lifelong friend Thomas Jefferson. Monroe served in the Virginia legislature 1782, in the US Senate 1790–94, and as governor of Virginia 1799–1802. During the Constitutional Convention he opposed ratification, fearing a central government with excessive power. As president, he presided over the so-called Era of Good Feeling, a period of domestic tranquillity. He took no firm stand on the question of slavery, making his mark in foreign policy.
Suggested reading
Ammon, H *James Monroe: The Quest for National Identity* (1971)
Wilmerding, Lucius *James Monroe* (1960)

Monroe Marilyn. Stage name of Norma Jean Mortenson or Baker (1926–1962). US film actress. The voluptuous blonde sex symbol of the 1950s, she made adroit comedies such as *Gentlemen Prefer Blondes* 1953, *How to Marry a Millionaire* 1953, *The Seven Year Itch* 1955, *Bus Stop* 1956, and *Some Like It Hot* 1959.

Monroe US film actress Marilyn Monroe in the film Gentlemen Prefer Blondes 1953. An orphan, she married a local policeman at 16, before her astonishing rise to stardom in such films as Some Like it Hot 1959. From that point her life, and tragic death, became a public spectacle.

Born in Los Angeles to a single mother often confined in mental institutions, she had a wretched childhood and married for the first time at the age of 16. Her second husband was baseball star Joe DiMaggio, and her third was playwright Arthur Miller, who wrote *The Misfits* 1960 for her, a serious film that became her last. She committed suicide, taking an overdose of sleeping pills.

Suggested reading
Jordan, Ted *Marilyn Monroe: A Hollywood Love Story* (1989)
Mailer, Norman *Marilyn* (1973)
McCann, Graham *Marilyn Monroe* (1988)
Steinem, Gloria *Marilyn* (1986)
Spoto, Donald *Marilyn Monroe: The Biography* (1993)

I always say a kiss on the hand might feel very good, but a diamond tiara lasts forever.

MARILYN MONROE
Parodying her own image in the film *Gentlemen Prefer Blondes* 1953

Monsarrat Nicholas John Turney (1910–1979). English novelist. He served with the navy in the Battle of the Atlantic, the subject of his book *The Cruel Sea* 1951.

Montagu Edward John Barrington Douglas Scott, 3rd Baron Montagu of Beaulieu (1926–). British car enthusiast, founder of the Montagu Motor Museum at Beaulieu, Hampshire, and chair of English Heritage (formerly Historic Buildings and Monuments Commission) 1983–92. Baron 1929.

General notions are generally wrong.

LADY MARY WORTLEY MONTAGU
Letter to her husband, 28 March 1701 in *Complete Letters* vol i 1763

Montagu Lady Mary Wortley (born Pierrepont) (1689–1762). English society hostess. She was well known in literary circles, associating with writers such as English poet Alexander Pope, with whom she later quarrelled. Her witty and erudite letters were renowned. She introduced inoculation against smallpox into Britain.

Suggested reading
Halsband, Robert *The Life of Lady Montagu Wortley* (1956)
Halsband, Robert *The Complete Letters of Lady Mary Wortley Montagu* (1965-67)

Montagu (Montague Francis) Ashley (born Ehrenburg) (1905–). British-born US anthropologist. As a critic of theories of racial determinism, he was a forceful defender of human rights and wrote such important works as *Man's Most Dangerous Myth: The Fallacy of Race* 1942. In 1950 he helped draft the definitive UNESCO 'Statement on Race'.

Montagu-Douglas-Scott family name of the dukes of Buccleuch; seated at Bowhill, Selkirk, Scotland; Boughton House, Northamptonshire, England; and Drumlanrig, Dumfriesshire, Scotland; descended from the Duke of Monmouth.

How many things served us but yesterday as articles of faith, which today we deem but fables?

MONTAIGNE
Essays bk 1 ch 26 1580

Montaigne Michel Eyquem de (1533–1592). French writer. He is regarded as the creator of the essay form. In 1580 he published the first two volumes of his *Essais*; the third volume appeared 1588. Montaigne deals with all aspects of life from an urbanely sceptical viewpoint. Through the translation by John Florio 1603, he influenced Shakespeare and other English writers.

He was born at the Château de Montaigne near Bordeaux, studied law, and in 1554 became a counsellor of the Bordeaux *parlement*. Little is known of his earlier life, except that he regularly visited Paris and the court of Francis II. In 1571 he retired to his estates, relinquishing his magistracy. He toured Germany, Switzerland, and Italy 1580–81, returning upon his election as mayor of Bordeaux, a post he held until 1585.

Suggested reading
Brush, C B *Montaigne and Bayle* (1966)
Burke, Peter *Montaigne* (1981)
Frame, Donald *Montaigne: A Biography* (1965)

Montale Eugenio (1896–1981). Italian poet and writer. His pessimistic poetry, for which he was awarded a Nobel prize 1975, includes *Ossi di seppia/Cuttlefish Bones* 1925, *Le Occasioni/Occasions* 1939, and (showing a greater warmth and approachability) *La bufera e altro/The Storm and Other Poems* 1956. He was also an important critic and translator.

Montana Claude (1949–). French fashion designer who promoted the broad-shouldered look. He established his own business 1976 and launched his first collection 1977.

He began as a jewellery designer in London, returning to Paris 1971, and becoming an assistant designer in a leather manufacturing company 1973. His first collections shook the ready-to-wear market, showing wide-shouldered outfits, in black, red, and grey leather, which narrowed sharply at the waist, with slim-fitting skirts or trousers or helmets and chains. In 1984 he moved away from the 'powerful' look to design garments in soft, rounded shapes and silk pyjamas which were topped by long satin and velvet robes in bright colours such as coral, absinthe green, lavender, aqua, and rose.

Montana Joe (1956–). US football player who has appeared in four winning Super Bowls as quarterback for the San Francisco 49ers 1982, 1985, 1989, and 1990, winning the Most Valuable Player award in 1982, 1985, and 1990. He threw a record five touchdown passes in the 1990 Super Bowl. He joined the Kansas City Chiefs 1993.

He graduated from Notre Dame University, where he led his team to the national college championship 1978. He was the leading passer in the National Football Conference 1981, 1984, and 1985. He recovered from a serious back injury in 1986 to become the leading passer in the National Football League 1987, setting league records for touchdowns thrown (31) and consecutive completions

(22). In the 1989 Super Bowl, he set a record for passing yardage and the most passes without an interception (33).

Montand Yves. Stage name of Ivo Livi (1921–1991). Italian-born French actor and singer who became known for his music-hall performances, and who later achieved fame in the thriller *Le Salaire de la peur/The Wages of Fear* 1953 and continued to be popular in French and American films, including *Let's Make Love* 1960 (with Marilyn Monroe), *Z* 1968, *Le Sauvage/The Savage* 1976, *Jean de Florette* 1986, and *Manon des sources* 1986.

Montcalm-Gozon Louis-Joseph de, Marquis de (1712–1759). French general, appointed military commander in Canada 1756. He won a succession of victories over the British during the French and Indian War, but was defeated in 1759 by James Wolfe at Quebec on the Plains of Abraham, where both he and Wolfe were killed; this battle marked the end of French rule in Canada.

So much the better. I shall not then live to see the surrender of Quebec.
LOUIS-JOSEPH DE MONTCALM-GOZON
Last words when told he was about to die in battle at Quebec 1759.

Montespan Françoise-Athénaïs de Rochechouart, Marquise de (1641–1707). Mistress of Louis XIV of France from 1667. They had seven children, for whom she engaged as governess the future Madame de Maintenon, who later supplanted her. She retired to a convent in 1691.

Montesquieu Charles Louis de Secondat, Baron de la Brède (1689–1755). French philosophical historian, author of *Lettres persanes/Persian Letters* 1721. After the success of *Lettres persanes*, which satirizes French legal and political institutions, he adopted a literary career, writing *Considérations sur les causes de la grandeur des Romains et de leur décadence/Considerations on the Greatness and Decadence of the Romans* 1734. *De l'Esprit des lois/The Spirit of the Laws* 1748, a 31-volume philosophical disquisition on politics and sociology as well as legal matters, advocated the separation of powers within government, a doctrine that became the basis of liberal constitutions.
Suggested reading
Richter, M (ed) *Political Theory of Montesquieu* (1969)
Shklar, Judith *Montesquieu* (1987)

An empire founded by war has to maintain itself by war.
CHARLES MONTESQUIEU
Considérations sur les causes de la grandeur des Romains et de leur décadence ch 8 1734

Montessori Maria (1870–1952). Italian educationist. In 1894, she became the first woman in Italy to take a medical degree. She specialized in paediatric medicine and psychiatry. Working with mentally disabled children, she developed the *Montessori method*, an educational system for all children based on an informal approach, incorporating instructive play and allowing children to develop at their own pace.

The Montessori method also emphasizes the value of work. Children are given a wide variety of materials carefully graded to permit repetition, self-correction, and self-education. She wrote *The Montessori Method* 1912 and *The Secret of Childhood* 1936.
Suggested reading
Kramer, R *Maria Montessori: A Biography* (1983)
Lillard, P P *Maria Montessori: A Modern Approach* (1972)
Orem, R *Montessori: Her Method and the Movement* (1974)
Standing, E M *Maria Montessori* (1958)
Standing, E M *The Montessori Revolution* (1966)

Monteux Pierre (1875–1964). French conductor. Ravel's *Daphnis and Chloe* and Stravinsky's *The Rite of Spring* were first performed under his direction. He conducted Diaghilev's Ballets Russes 1911–14 and 1917, and the San Francisco Symphony Orchestra 1935–52.

Monteverdi Claudio Giovanni Antonio (1567–1643). Italian composer. He contributed to the development of the opera with *La favola d'Orfeo/The Legend of Orpheus* 1607 and *L'incoronazione di Poppea/The Coronation of Poppea* 1642. He also wrote madrigals, motets, and sacred music, notably the *Vespers* 1610.

Born in Cremona, he was in the service of the Duke of Mantua about 1591–1612, and was director of music at St Mark's, Venice, from 1613. He was first to use an orchestra and to reveal the dramatic possibilities of the operatic form. His first opera *Orfeo* was produced for the carnival at Mantua 1607.
Suggested reading
Arnold, D *Claudio Monteverdi* (1975)
Arnold, D and Fortune, N (eds) *The Monteverdi Companion* (1968)

Let the word be master of the melody, not its slave.
CLAUDIO MONTEVERDI
quoted in Sam Morgenstern *Composers on Music* 1958

Montez Lola. Stage name of Maria Dolores Eliza Rosanna Gilbert (1818–1861). Irish actress and dancer. She appeared on the stage as a Spanish dancer, and in 1847 became the mistress of King Ludwig I of Bavaria, whose policy she dictated for a year. Her liberal sympathies led to her banishment through Jesuit influence in 1848. She died in poverty in the USA.

Montezuma II (1466–1520). Aztec emperor 1502–20. When the Spanish conquistador Cortés invaded Mexico, Montezuma was imprisoned and killed during the Aztec attack on Cortés's force as it tried to leave Tenochtitlán, the Aztec capital city.
Suggested reading
Burland, C A *Montezuma: Lord of the Aztecs* (1973)
Davies, Nigel *The Aztecs: A History* (1973)
Lincoln, J D *Montezuma* (1977)

Commend your souls to God, for our bodies are the foe's.
SIMON DE MONTFORT
Last words to his supporters at the Battle of Evesham 1265, where he was killed.

Montfort Simon, 1st Earl of Leicester (c. 1208– 1265). English politician and soldier. From 1258 he led the baronial opposition to Henry III's misrule during the second Barons' War and in 1264 defeated and captured the king at Lewes, Sussex. In 1265, as head of government, he summoned the first parliament in which the towns were represented; he was killed at the battle of Evesham during the last of the Barons' Wars.

Born in Normandy, the son of Simon de Montfort (c. 1160–1218) who led a crusade against the Albigenses, he arrived in England in 1230, married Henry III's sister, and was granted the earldom of Leicester.
Suggested reading
Knowles, C H *Simon de Montfort* (1965)
Labarge, Margaret *Simon de Montfort* (1962)

Montgolfier Joseph Michel (1740–1810) and Jacques Etienne (1745–1799). French brothers whose hot-air balloon was used for the first successful human flight 21 Nov 1783. On 5 June 1783 they first sent up a balloon filled with hot air, launched in the marketplace of Annonay. Next, they took their invention to the palace of Versailles, where, before a large audience (which included Louis XVI and Marie Antionette), their balloon ascended, carrying a sheep, a cock, and a duck, and made an eight-minute flight of approximately 3 km/2 mi. After further experiments with wood-fuelled fabric-and-paper balloons, and one crewed ascent in a tethered ballon, they sent up two people who travelled for 20 minutes above Paris, a journey of 9 km/6 mi. The Montgolfier experiments greatly stimulated scientific interest in aviation.

The Montgolfier brothers were papermakers of Annonay, near Lyon. Jacques invented vellum paper. Joseph Montgolfier later developed a type of parachute, a calorimeter, and a hydraulic ram and press.

Montgomery Bernard Law, 1st Viscount Montgomery of Alamein (1887–1976). British field marshal. In World War II he commanded the 8th Army in N Africa in the Second Battle of El Alamein 1942. As commander of British troops in N Europe from 1944, he received the German surrender 1945. KCB 1942, viscount 1946.

At the start of World War II he commanded part of the British Expeditionary Force in France 1939–40 and took part in the evacuation from Dunkirk. In Aug 1942 he took command of the 8th Army, then barring the German advance on Cairo; the victory of El Alamein in Oct turned the tide in N Africa and was followed by the expulsion of Field Marshal Rommel from Egypt and rapid Allied advance into Tunisia. In Feb 1943 Montgomery's forces came under US general Eisenhower's command, and they took part in the conquest of Tunisia and Sicily and the invasion of Italy. Montgomery was promoted to field marshal in 1944. Montgomery commanded the Allied armies during the opening phase of the invasion of France in Jun 1944, and from Aug the British and imperial troops that liberated the Netherlands, overran N Germany, and entered Denmark. At his 21st Army Group headquarters on Lüneburg Heath, he received the German surrender on 4 May 1945. He was in command of the British occupation force in Germany until Feb 1946, when he was appointed chief of the Imperial General Staff. In 1948 he became permanent military chair of the Commanders-in-Chief Committee for W European defence, and 1951–58 was deputy Supreme Commander Europe.

Suggested reading
Hamilton, N *Monty: The Making of a General* (1981)
Hamilton, N *Monty: Master of the Battlefield* (1983)
Hamilton, N *Monty: The Field-Marshal* (1986)
Lewin, R *Montgomery as Military Commander* (1971)
Thompson, R *The Montgomery Legend* (1967)

Montgomery Robert Henry (1904–1981). US film actor. He starred in films of the 1930s and 1940s such as *Night Must Fall* 1937 and *Mr and Mrs Smith* 1941. He directed some of his later films, such as *Lady in the Lake* 1947, before turning to television and Republican politics.

Montgomery, Bernard *British general Bernard Montgomery in Nov 1942, after he had taken command of the British 8th Army in N Africa. A month later the 8th Army defeated Rommel's army at El Alamein.*

Montherlant Henri Marie Joseph Millon de (1896–1972). French author. His novels, which are marked by an obsession with the physical, include *Aux Fontaines du désir*/*To the Fountains of Desire* 1927 and *Pitié pour les femmes*/*Pity for Women* 1936. His most critically acclaimed work is *Le Chaos et la nuit*/*Chaos and Night* 1963.

> *The man who marries always makes the woman a present because she needs marriage and he does not ... woman is made for man, man is made for life.*
> HENRI DE MONTHERLANT
> *Girls* 1959

Monti Eugenio (1928–). Italian bobsleigh driver who won Olympic gold medals in two-and four-crew bobs in 1968, and between 1957 and 1968 won 11 world titles. His two-person successes were shared with the brakemen Renzo Alvera and Sergio Siorpaes, both Italian. On his retirement in 1968 Monti became manager to the Italian team.

Montrose James Graham, 1st Marquess and 5th Earl of Montrose (1612–1650). Scottish soldier, son of the 4th Earl of Montrose. He supported the Covenanters against Charles I, but after 1640 changed sides. Defeated in 1645 at Philiphaugh, he escaped to Norway. Returning in 1650 to raise a revolt, he survived shipwreck only to have his weakened forces defeated, and (having been betrayed to the Covenanters) was hanged in Edinburgh. Marquess 1644, earl 1626.

Montt Manuel (1809–1900). Chilean president 1851–61. He was a hardliner who promoted economic development, especially railway building, the telegraph, postal services, and gas lighting. His final years in office saw economic recession and political turmoil, including clashes between church and state.

Partly self-educated, Montt became rector of the Instituto Nacional 1835, and while serving as minister of education 1841–45 he offered support to the great reformer Domingo Faustino Sarmiento, then in exile.

Moody Dwight Lyman (1837–1899). US evangelist. During the American Civil War 1861–65, he provided medical and moral support to the troops. In the 1870s he became a popular evangelist and founded the Northfield Seminary (now School) for girls 1879 and the Mount Hermon School for boys 1881, both in Massachusetts.

Born in East Northfield, Massachusetts, USA, Moody moved to Boston as a young man and joined the Congregational Church 1856. Later settling in Chicago, he devoted himself to preaching among the poor. In 1889 he founded the Chicago (later Moody) Bible Institute.

Moody Helen Wills. Married name of US tennis player Helen Newington ◊Wills.

Moon Sun Myung (1920–). Korean industrialist and founder of the Unification Church (Moonies) 1954. From 1973 he launched a major mission in the USA and elsewhere. The church has been criticized for its manipulative methods of recruiting and keeping members. He was convicted of tax fraud in the USA 1982. Moon has allegedly been associated with extreme right-wing organizations, arms manufacture, and the Korean Central Intelligence Agency.

Moon William (1818–1894). English inventor of the Moon alphabet for the blind. Devised in 1847, it uses only nine symbols in different orientations. From 1983 it has been possible to write it with a miniature typewriter.

Moorcock Michael John (1939–). English writer. Associated with the 1960s new wave in science fiction, he was editor of the magazine *New Worlds* 1964–69. He wrote the Jerry Cornelius novels, collected as *The Cornelius Chronicles* 1977, and *Gloriana* 1978. Among later novels are *The Revenge of the Rose* 1989 and *Blood* 1994.

Moore (John) Jeremy (1928–). British major general of the Commando Forces, Royal Marines, 1979–82. He commanded the land forces in the UK's conflict with Argentina over the Falklands 1982. KCB 1982.

Moore Bobby (Robert Frederick) (1941–1993). English footballer who led the England team to victory against West Germany in the 1966 World Cup final. A superb defender, he played 108 games for England 1962–70 (until 1978, a world-record number of international appearances) and was captain 90 times. His Football League career, spent at West Ham 1968–74 and Fulham 1974–77, spanned 19 years and 668 matches.

Moore Brian (1921–). Irish-born novelist. He emigrated to Canada 1948 and then to the USA 1959. His books include *Judith Hearne* 1955, *The Temptation of Eileen Hughes* 1981, *Black Robe* 1985, *The Colour of Blood* 1987, and *No Other Life* 1993. Catholicism, obsession, and the contrast between dreams and reality are recurrent and powerful themes, depicted with stylistic economy and realism.

Other works include *The Luck of Ginger Coffey* 1960 and *The Emperor of Ice Cream* 1966. His earliest books were published under the pen name of Michael Bryan.

Moore Charles (1925–1993). US architect with an eclectic approach to design. He was an early exponent of Post-Modernism in, for example, his students' housing for Kresge College, University of California at Santa Cruz, 1973–74, and the Piazza d'Italia in New Orleans, 1975–78, which is one of the key monuments of Post-Modernism.

Sea Ranch, California 1964–65, one of his earliest projects, is in the vernacular timber tradition. At Kresge College he created a stage set of streets and forums. The Piazza d'Italia was built for the local Italian community and has a fountain in the shape of Italy.

A grubby cherub.

Jonathan Miller on DUDLEY MOORE
quoted in Leslie Halliwell *Filmgoer's Companion* 1965

Moore Dudley Stuart John (1935–). English actor, comedian, and musician. He was formerly teamed with the comedian Peter Cook. Moore became a Hollywood star after appearing in *'10'* 1979. His other films, mostly comedies, include *Bedazzled* 1968, *Arthur* 1981, *Santa Claus* 1985, and *Blame it on the Bellboy* 1992. He is also an accomplished musician and has given classical piano concerts.

I ... use the word 'beautiful' to denote that of which the admiring contemplation is good in itself.

G E MOORE
Principia Ethica ch 6 1903

Moore G(eorge) E(dward) (1873–1958). British philosopher who generally defended common-sense views of the world and what is said about it in ordinary language. In ethics, he held that any attempt to identify goodness with another concept, such as happiness, was a fallacy – the 'naturalistic fallacy'.

Educated at Cambridge, he was professor of philosophy at the university 1925–39, and edited the journal *Mind*, to which he contributed 1921–47. His books include *Principia Ethica* 1903, in which he attempted to analyse the moral question 'What is good?', and *Some Main Problems of Philosophy* 1953.

Moore George (1923–). Australian jockey. Apprenticed in Brisbane, he moved to Sydney and had his first big win on Cordale in the 1946 Metropolitan. He rode winners in most Australian classic races, except the Melbourne Cup. From 1960 he spent time in France and England, riding winners in both the English and French Derbies. In his total career he rode 2,278 winners in seven countries.

Moore George Augustus (1852–1933). Irish novelist. Born in County Mayo, he studied art in Paris 1870, and published two volumes of poetry there. His first novel, *A Modern Lover* 1883, was sexually frank for its time and banned in some quarters. It was

followed by others, including *Esther Waters* 1894 and *The Brook Kerith* 1916

A man travels the world in search of what he needs and returns home to find it.

GEORGE MOORE
The Brook Kerith

Moore Gerald (1899–1987). English pianist. He was renowned as an accompanist to Elizabeth Schwarzkopf, Kathleen Ferrier, Heddle Nash, and other singers, a role he raised to equal partnership.

Moore Henry Spencer (1898–1986). English sculptor. His subjects include the reclining nude, mother and child groups, the warrior, and interlocking abstract forms. Many of his post-1945 works are in bronze or marble, including monumental semi-abstracts such as *Reclining Figure* 1957–58 (outside the UNESCO building, Paris), and often designed to be placed in landscape settings.

Moore claimed to have learned much from archaic South and Central American sculpture, and this is reflected in his work from the 1920s. By the early 1930s most of his main themes had emerged, and the Surrealists' preoccupation with organic forms in abstract works proved a strong influence; Moore's hollowed wooden shapes strung with wires date from the late 1930s. Semi-abstract work suggesting organic structures recurs after World War II, for example in the interwoven bonelike forms of the *Hill Arches* and the bronze *Sheep Pieces* 1970s, set in fields by his studio in Hertfordshire.

Born in Yorkshire, Moore studied at Leeds and the Royal College of Art, London. As an official war artist during World War II, he made a series of drawings of people in London's air-raid shelters. Many of his works are now exhibited in the garden and fields overlooking his home in Perry Green, Hertfordshire, looked after by the Henry Moore Foundation (set up by the artist, his wife and daughter 1977). In 1995 the Foundation turned over £3.2 million.

Suggested reading
Berthoud, W *The Life of Henry Moore* (1987)
Packer, W *Henry Moore* (1985)
Read, H *Henry Moore: A Study of his Life and Work* (1965)
Russell, J *Henry Moore* (1968)
Sylvester, D *Henry Moore* (1968)

Moore John (1761–1809). Scottish-born British general. He entered the army in 1776, serving in the American and French Revolutionary Wars and against the Irish rebellion of 1798. In 1808 he commanded the British army sent to Portugal in the Peninsular War. After advancing into Spain he had to retreat to Corunna in the NW, and was killed in the battle fought to cover the embarkation. KB 1804.

My father used to say, 'Superior people never make long visits'.

MARIANNE MOORE
'Silence'

Moore Marianne Craig (1887–1972). US poet. She edited the literary magazine *The Dial* 1925–29, and published several volumes of witty and intellectual verse, including *Observations* 1924, *What are Years* 1941, and *A Marianne Moore Reader* 1961. She also published translations and essays. Her work is noted for its observation of detail. T S Eliot was an admirer of her poetry.

Suggested reading
Engel, B F *Marianne Moore* (1964)
Hall, D *Marianne Moore: The Cage and the Animals* (1970)
Philips, E *Marianne Moore* (1982)

Moore Patrick Alfred Caldwell (1923–). British broadcaster, writer, and popularizer of astronomy. He began presenting the BBC television series *The Sky at Night* 1968.

Moore served with the Royal Air Force during World War II, and for seven years after the war he assisted at a training school for pilots. From 1965 to 1968 he was director of the Armagh Planetarium, Northern Ireland. He has never worked as an astronomer. His many books include *Atlas of the Universe* 1970, *Guide to the Planets* 1976, *Guide to the Stars* 1977, and *Can You Speak Venusian?* 1977.

You're not a star till they can spell your name in Vladivostok.

ROGER MOORE
Attributed remark

Moore Roger George (1927–). English actor. He starred in the television series *The Saint* 1962–70, and assumed the film role of James Bond 1973 in *Live and Let Die*. His last appearance as Bond was in *A View to a Kill* 1985.

'Tis the last rose of summer / Left blooming alone; / All her lovely companions / Are faded and gone.

THOMAS MOORE
'Tis the Last Rose'

Moore Thomas (1779–1852). Irish poet. Among his works are the verse romance *Lalla Rookh* 1817 and the *Irish Melodies* 1807–35. These were set to music by John Stevenson 1807–35 and include 'The Minstrel Boy' and 'The Last Rose of Summer'.

Moorhouse Adrian (1964–). English swimmer who won the 100 metres breaststroke at the 1988 Seoul Olympics. He has won gold medals at both the Commonwealth Games and the European Championships but was disqualified from first place for an illegal turn during the 1986 world championships.

Moorhouse Frank (1938–). Australian short-story writer. His work includes 'The Americans, Baby' 1972, 'The Electrical Experience' 1974, 'Conference-ville' 1976, 'The Everlasting Secret Family and Other Secrets' 1980, 'Room Service' 1985, and 'Woman of High Direction' 1993. He has also written film scripts, including *Between Wars* 1974.

Moorhouse Geoffrey (1931–). British travel writer. His books include *The Fearful Void* 1974, and (on cricket) *The Best-Loved Game* 1979.

Mor Anthonis (Anthonis Mor van Dashorst/Antonio Moro) (*c*. 1517–1577). Dutch portraitist. He became court painter to the Spanish rulers in the Netherlands. Suitably formal and austere, his portraits of contemporary European royalty greatly influenced development of the genre. Knighted *c*. 1553. He visited Italy, Spain, Portugal, and England, where he painted a portrait of Mary I 1554 (Prado, Madrid) at the time of her marriage to Philip II of Spain. He was influenced by, and borrowed freely, from Titian.

Morandi Giorgio (1890–1964). Italian still-life painter and etcher. He was influenced by Metaphysical Painting. His subtle studies of bottles and jars convey a sense of calm and repose, as in *Still Life* 1946 (Tate Gallery, London).

Early influences on his work were the still life of Cézanne and the 'metaphysical' painting of Chirico and Carrà, 1918–20, but he evolved a personal style in the treatment of a narrow range of subjects – especially simple still-life objects in a variety of subtly designed and abstract arrangements.

Morant Harry Harbord (1865–1902). English-born Australian soldier and balladist, known as 'Breaker' Morant from the pen-name he used while writing verse for the *Bulletin* in the 1890s. During the Boer War he was court-martialled and hanged by the British military authorities for the murder of a Boer prisoner. The strength of Australian protest ensured that in subsequent wars Australians were exempt from being sentenced to death by British military jurisdiction.

Moravia Alberto. Pen name of Alberto Pincherle (1907–1991). Italian novelist. His first successful novel was *Gli indifferenti/The Time of Indifference* 1929, but its criticism of Mussolini's regime led to the government censoring his work until after World War II. Later books include *La romana/Woman of Rome* 1947, *La ciociara/Two Women* 1957, and *La noia/The Empty Canvas* 1961, a study of an artist's obsession with his model.

Moray Another spelling of ◊Murray, regent of Scotland 1567–70.

Morazán Francisco (1792–1842). Central American politician, born in Honduras. He was elected president of the United Provinces of Central America in 1830. In the face of secessions he attempted to hold the union together by force but was driven out by the Guatemalan dictator Rafael Carrera. Morazán was eventually captured and executed in 1842.

More Henry (1614–1687). English philosopher, theologian, and member of the Cambridge Platonists. He denied René Descartes's division of mind and matter (Cartesian dualism), maintaining that mind or spirit had extension in space. Mind or spirit could penetrate material objects, and was the only cause of motion in things, and the only cause (as the soul) of actions by people.

More was born in Grantham and educated at Cambridge. He took orders, but declined all preferment (including two deaneries and a bishopric), devoting himself instead to the study of Plato and his followers.

His works include *Philosophical Poems* 1647 and *Divine Dialogues* 1660.

More Kenneth Gilbert (1914–1982). English actor. A wholesome film star of the 1950s, he was cast as leading man in adventure films and light comedies such as *Genevieve* 1953, *Doctor in the House* 1954, and *Northwest Frontier* 1959. He played war hero Douglas Bader in *Reach for the Sky* 1956.

More (St) Thomas (1478–1535). English politician and author. From 1509 he was favoured by Henry VIII and employed on foreign embassies. He was a member of the privy council from 1518 and Lord Chancellor from 1529.

Son of a London judge, More studied Greek, Latin, French, theology, and music at Oxford, and law at Lincoln's Inn, London, and was influenced by the humanists John Colet and Erasmus, who became a friend. In Parliament from 1504, he was made Speaker of the House of Commons in 1523. He was knighted in 1521, and on the fall of Cardinal Wolsey became Lord Chancellor, but resigned in 1532 because he could not agree with the king on his ecclesiastical policy and marriage with Anne Boleyn. In 1534 he refused to take the oath of supremacy to Henry VIII as head of the church, and after a year's imprisonment in the Tower of London he was executed.

Among Thomas More's writings are the Latin *Utopia* 1516, sketching an ideal commonwealth; the English *Dialogue* 1528, a theological argument against the Reformation leader Tyndale; and a *History of Richard III*. He was also a patron of artists, including Holbein. More was canonized in 1935. The title of his political book *Utopia* has come to mean any supposedly perfect society.

Suggested reading
Kenny, Anthony *Thomas More* (1983)
Marius, Richard *Thomas More: A Biography* (1984)
Reynolds, Ernest *The Field is Won: The Life and Death of Saint Thomas More* (1968)
Ridley, Jasper *The Statesman and the Fanatic: Thomas Wolsey and Thomas More* (1982)

Your sheep that were wont to be so meek and tame ... now ... eat up and swallow down the very men themselves.

THOMAS MORE
Utopia bk 1

Moreau Gustave (1826–1898). French Symbolist painter. His atmospheric works depict biblical, mythological, and literary scenes and are richly coloured and detailed; for example, *Salome Dancing Before Herod* 1876 (Musée Moreau, Paris).

He was academic in style, but a passionate and 'decadent' quality in his *Salome* led Huysmans to admire and describe it in his novel *à Rebours*, and his work has points of resemblance to that of Odilon Redon. Towards the end of his life he became an influential teacher at the Ecole des Beaux-Arts in Paris, Matisse, Marquet and Rouault being among his pupils. He left 8,000 paintings and drawings to the nation, his house being converted into a museum.

Say to the Emperor that I go to the tomb with the same feelings of veneration, respect and devotion that he inspired in me the first time I saw him.

JEAN MOREAU
Last words, sent to Napoleon from exile, 1813

Moreau Jean Victor Marie (1763–1813). French general in the Revolutionary Wars who won a brilliant victory over the Austrians at Hohenlinden 1800; as a republican he intrigued against Napoleon and, when banished, joined the Allies and was killed at the Battle of Dresden.

I expose myself in an interview – and I assume the interviewer is exposing himself, too.

JEANNE MOREAU
Radio Times 1977

Moreau Jeanne (1928–　). French actress. She has appeared in international films, often in passionate, intelligent roles. Her work includes *Les Amants/The Lovers* 1958, *Jules et Jim/Jules and Jim* 1961, *Chimes at Midnight* 1966, and *Querelle* 1982.

Morelos José María (1765–1815). Mexican priest and revolutionary. A mestizo (person with Spanish American and American Indian parents), Morelos followed independence campaigner Miguel Hidalgo y Costilla, intending to be an army chaplain, but he displayed military genius and came to head his own forces. The independence movement was stalled for five years after his death.

He sought to rescue the revolution from chaos and violence, and to widen its political base. However, the Creoles failed to respond. After four major campaigns against the Spaniards, he was captured, stripped of the priesthood by the Inquisition, and executed.

Moresby John (1830–1922). British naval explorer and author. He was the first European to visit the harbour in New Guinea, now known as Port Moresby.

Morgagni Giovanni Battista (1682–1771). Italian anatomist who developed the view that disease was not an imbalance of the body's humours but a result of alterations in the organs. His work *De sedibus et causis morborum per anatomen indagatis/On the Seats and Causes of Diseases as Investigated by Anatomy* 1761 formed the basis of pathology.

As professor of anatomy at Padua, he carried out more than 400 autopsies. He did not use a microscope and he regarded each organ of the body as a composite of minute mechanisms.

Morgagni was the first to delineate syphilitic tumours of the brain and tuberculosis of the kidney. He grasped that where only one side of the body is stricken with paralysis, the lesion lies on the opposite side of the brain. His explorations of the female genitals, of the glands of the trachea, and of the male urethra also broke new ground.

Morgan Ann Haven (1882–1966). US zoologist who promoted the study of ecology and conservation. She particularly studied the zoology of aquatic insects and the comparative physiology of hibernation.

From 1912 to 1947 she taught at Mount Holyoke College, becoming professor 1918. She spent her summers at a variety of research laboratories, including the Marine Biological Laboratory at Woods Hole in Massachusetts, and also worked at the Tropical Research Laboratory of British Guiana (now Guyana). She was a member of the National Committee on Policies in Conservation Education.

Her *Field Book of Ponds and Streams: An Introduction to the Life of Fresh Water* 1930 attracted amateur naturalists as well as providing an authoritative taxonomic guide for professionals.

Morgan Conwy Lloyd (1852–1936). English psychologist. Of immense influence in the field of contemporary comparative psychology, he is renowned for his observational studies of animals in natural settings. In 1894 he was the first to describe trial-and-error learning in animals.

In trial-and-error learning an animal learns a trick, for example, how to lift a latch to open a gate, by making several attempts without any insights into what the trick involves. Eventually it lifts the latch, an act that is immediately reinforced by the freedom that follows.

Morgan was appointed professor of geology and zoology at the University College of Bristol (later the University of Bristol). In 1899, following the publication of two influential books *Animal Life and Intelligence* 1890 and *An Introduction to Comparative Psychology* 1894, he was elected a Fellow of the Royal Society, the first to be elected for research in psychology. Recognizing the tendency of previous researchers, notably G J Romanes (1848–1894), to attribute human characteristics to animals, he developed rigorous procedures of control and analysis in order to avoid such prejudice.

Morgan Frederick Edgworth (1894–1967). British general in World War II. He was appointed Chief of Staff to plan the future invasion of Europe Jan 1943. His plan was accepted July and with some modifications became the plan for Operation Overlord. He and his staff spent the following year working out the plan in minute detail. KCB 1944.

Morgan Garrett A (1875–1963). US inventor who patented the gas mask 1914 and the automatic three-way traffic signal 1923. From 1895 he lived in Cleveland, doing repairs, then opening a tailoring shop 1909, and went on to establish the G A Morgan Hair Refining Company in 1913 as a result of discovering a human hair-straightening process. In 1916 he set up a company to manufacture and sell the safety hood, as he called the gas mask. During World War I the design of the gas mask was improved and it became part of the standard field equipment of US soldiers.

In 1920 Morgan started his own newspaper, the *Cleveland Call*, later the *Call and Post*. He sold the right to the traffic signal to the General Electric Corporation for $40,000. He also invented a friction-drive clutch.

Morgan served as treasurer of the Cleveland Association of Colored Men from 1914 until it merged with the National Association for the Advancement of Colored People, of which he remained an active member all his life.

An intrepid and ingenious leader ... he was also a mean and treacherous scoundrel who even cheated his own men out of ... the ... loot.

C P Hill on HENRY MORGAN in *Who's Who in History* vol III 1965

Morgan Henry (*c.* 1635–1688). Welsh buccaneer in the Caribbean. He made war against Spain, capturing and sacking Panama 1671. In 1675 he was knighted and appointed lieutenant governor of Jamaica.

Morgan J(ohn) P(ierpont) (1837–1913). US financier and investment banker whose company (sometimes criticized as 'the money trust') became the most influential private banking house after the Civil War, being instrumental in the formation of many trusts to stifle competition. He set up the US Steel Corporation 1901 and International Harvester 1902.

Morgan Lewis Henry (1818–1881). US anthropologist who pioneered the study of NE Native American culture and was adopted by the Iroquois.

Morgan Thomas Hunt (1866–1945). US geneticist who helped establish that the genes are located on the chromosomes, discovered sex chromosomes, and invented the techniques of genetic mapping. He was the first to work on the fruit fly *Drosophila*, which has since become a major subject of genetic studies. Nobel Prize for Physiology or Medicine 1933.

He was professor of experimental zoology at Columbia University 1904–28, when he was appointed director of the Laboratory of Biological Sciences at the California Institute of Technology.

Following the rediscovery of Austrian scientist Gregor Mendel's work, Morgan's interest turned from embryology to the mechanisms involved in heredity, and in 1908 he began his research on the genetics of *Drosophila*. From his findings he postulated that certain characteristics are sex-linked, that the X-chromosome carries several discrete hereditary units (genes), and that the genes are linearly arranged on chromosomes. He also demonstrated that sex-linked characters are not invariably inherited together, from which he developed the concept of crossing-over and the associated idea that the extent of crossing-over is a measure of the spatial separation of genes on chromosomes.

Morgan published a summary of his work in *The Mechanism of Mendelian Heredity* 1915.

Móricz Zsigismond (1879–1942). Hungarian novelist. Calvinist by upbringing, the leading Hungarian realist of his generation, he wrote about social decay, collision, and conflict within and beyond the family. His first novel *Sárarany/Golden Mud* 1910 ruthlessly dissects the frustration and bleakness of village life. Later work included monumental historical novels such as the trilogy *Erdély/Transylvania* 1922–35 and the love story *Légy jó mindhalálig/Be Good Till Death* 1920.

Mori Ōgai pen name of Mori Rintarō (1862–1922). Japanese novelist, poet, and translator. From an aristocratic samurai family, he initiated the Japanese vogue for autobiographical revelation with works such as his story of unhappy love *Maihime/The Dancing Girl* 1890 and the popular novel *Gan* 1911–13. His later work is more impersonal, consisting of historical depictions of the samurai code.

Morisot Berthe Marie Pauline (1841–1895). French Impressionist painter. She specialized in sensitive pictures of women and children. Taught by Corot, she was also much influenced by Manet and, in the 1880s, Renoir. She exhibited in most of the Impressionist shows. She was the granddaughter of the artist Fragonard.

Morland George (1763–1804). English painter. His picturesque rural subjects were widely reproduced in engravings. He was an admirer of Dutch and Flemish painters of rustic life.

He was a pupil of his father, Henry Robert Morland (1730–1797), also a painter of genre. He exhibited drawings at the Royal Academy when ten years old, studied art at the Royal Academy Schools and learned also by copying Flemish and Dutch masters, though his alehouses, cottages and farmyards are essentially English. He was a natural painter in a fluent easy style, his pictures popular in engravings by William and James Ward (whose sister he married), but many seem to have been dashed off to pay a debt. His careless mode of living caused him to be imprisoned for debt 1799–1802, and again 1804. Many of his rural scenes were painted at Kensal Green, and some coastal ruins resulted from visiting the Isle of Wight. *Inside of a Stable*, exhibited at the Academy 1791 (National Gallery, London), shows him at his best.

Morley Edward Williams (1838–1923). US physicist who collaborated with Albert Michelson on the *Michelson–Morley experiment* 1887. In 1895 he established precise and accurate measurements of the densities of oxygen and hydrogen.

He spent his career at Adelbert College, Cleveland, Ohio, becoming professor 1869. From 1873 to 1888, he was simultaneously professor at Cleveland Medical College.

All Morley's research involved the use of precision instruments. Using a eudiometer he had made accurate to within 0.0025%, he was able to confirm on the basis of the oxygen content of the air and meteorological data that, under certain conditions, cold air derives from the downward movement of air from high altitudes rather than from the southward movement of northerly cold air.

Morley John, 1st Viscount Morley of Blackburn (1838–1923). British Liberal politician and writer. He entered Parliament in 1883, and was secretary for Ireland in 1886 and 1892–95. As secretary for India 1905–10, he prepared the way (with Viceroy Gilbert Minto) for more representative government. He was Lord President of the Council 1910–14, but resigned in protest against the declaration of war. He published lives of the philosophers Voltaire and Rousseau and the politicians Burke and Gladstone. Viscount 1908.

Morley Malcolm (1931–). English painter. He was active in New York from 1964. He coined the term 'Superrealism' for his work in the 1960s. In 1984 he was awarded the first Turner Prize.

It is a great help for a man to be in love with himself. For an actor it is absolutely essential.
ROBERT MORLEY
in Leslie Halliwell *Filmgoer's Companion* 1965

Morley Robert (1908–1992). English actor and playwright. He was active both in Britain and the USA. His film work consisted mainly of character roles, in such movies as *Marie Antoinette* 1938, *The African Queen* 1952, and *Oscar Wilde* 1960.

If therefore you will compose in this kind, you must possess yourself of an amorous humour ... so that you must in your music be wavering like the wind, sometimes wanton, sometimes drooping, sometimes grave and staid, otherwise effeminate.
THOMAS MORLEY
A Plain and Easy Introduction to Practical Music 1597

Morley Thomas (*c.* 1557–*c.* 1602). English composer. He wrote consort music, madrigals, and airs including the lute song 'It was a lover and his lass' for Shakespeare's play *As You Like It* 1599. He edited a collection of Italian madrigals *The Triumphs of Oriana* 1601, and published an influential keyboard tutor *A Plaine and Easie Introduction to Practicall Musicke* 1597. He was also organist at St Paul's Cathedral, London.

Moro Aldo (1916–1978). Italian Christian Democrat politician. Prime minister 1963–68 and 1974–76, he was expected to become Italy's president, but he was kidnapped and shot by Red Brigade urban guerrillas.

Morphett John (1809–1892). Australian pioneer and politician, born in England. He sailed to South Australia with the main survey party in 1836, assisted William Light in laying out Adelaide and helped found the *South Australian* newspaper. In 1857 he was elected to the newly constituted Legislative Council and was its president 1865–73. Knighted 1870.

Morricone Ennio (1928–). Italian composer of film music. His atmospheric scores for 'spaghetti Westerns', notably the Clint Eastwood movies *A Fistful of Dollars* 1964 and *The Good, the Bad, and the Ugly* 1966, were widely imitated. His highly ritualized, incantatory style pioneered the use of amplified instruments and solo voices, using studio special effects.

Every question we answer leads on to another question. This has become the greatest survival trick of our species.
DESMOND MORRIS
The Naked Ape ch 5 1967

Morris Desmond John (1928–). British zoologist, a writer and broadcaster on animal and human behaviour. His book *The Naked Ape* 1967 was a best seller.

Morris studied at Birmingham and at Oxford, working on animal behaviour under Nikolaas Tinbergen. He became head of the Granada Television and Film Unit at the Zoological Society in London in 1956. Three years later he was appointed Curator of Mammals at London Zoo and from 1967 to 1968 served as director of the Institute of Contemporary Arts in London.

In his book *The Human Zoo* 1969, Morris scrutinizes the society that the naked ape has created for itself. He compares civilized humans with their captive animal counterparts and shows how confined animals seem to demonstrate the same neurotic behaviour patterns as human beings often do in crowded cities. He believes the urban environment of the cities to be the human zoo.

Morris Henry (1889–1961). British educationalist. He inspired and oversaw the introduction of the 'village college' and community school/education, which he saw as regenerating rural life. His ideas were also adopted in urban areas.

Morris emphasized the value of providing single-site centres of continuing education and leisure activity for both adults and children alike. He persuaded Walter Gropius, together with Maxwell Fry, to design the Village College at Impington, near Cambridge, 1939. He was chief education officer for Cambridgeshire 1922–54.

Morris Jan (1926–). English travel writer and journalist. Her books display a zestful, witty, and knowledgeable style and offer vivid sense impressions combined with deftly handled historical perspectives. These books include *Coast to Coast* 1956, *Venice* 1960, *Oxford* 1965, *Farewell the Trumpets* 1978, and *Among the Cities* 1985. Born James Morris, her adoption of female gender is described in *Conundrum* 1974.

As a young journalist with the British Everest expedition in 1953 James Morris was the first to send news that the mountain had been conquered.

Morris Mark (1956–). US choreographer and dancer. His ballets merge various styles ranging from avant-garde, ballet, folk, and jazz dance. He was artistic director of the Théâtre de la Monnaie in Brussels 1988–91. He is the director of his own company in New York.

Morris Robert (1734–1806). American political leader. A signatory of the Declaration of Independence 1776, he served in the Continental Congress 1775–78. In 1781 he was appointed superintendent of finance and dealt with the economic problems of the new nation. He served as one of Pennsylvania's first US senators 1789–95.

Born in Liverpool, England, Morris emigrated to America 1747, joining a merchant firm in Philadelphia. He became a cautious supporter of American independence. He attended the Constitutional Convention 1787.

Morris Thomas, Jr (1851–1875). British golfer, one of the first great champions. He was known as 'Young Tom' to distinguish him from his father (known as 'Old Tom'). Morris Jr won the British Open four times between 1868 and 1872.

Morris William (1834–1896). English designer, socialist, and writer. Morris was born in London and educated at Oxford, where he formed a lasting friendship with the Pre-Raphaelite artist Edward Burne-Jones and was influenced by the art critic John Ruskin and the painter and poet Dante Gabriel Rossetti. He shared the Pre-Raphaelite painters' fascination with medieval settings. In 1861 he cofounded a firm that designed and produced furniture, carpets, and decorative wallpapers, many of which are still produced today. His Kelmscott Press, set up 1890 to print beautifully designed books, influenced printing and book design. The prose romances *A Dream of John Ball* 1888 and *News from Nowhere* 1891 reflect his socialist ideology. He also lectured on socialism.

Morris abandoned his first profession, architecture, to study painting, but had a considerable influence on such architects as William Lethaby and Philip Webb. As a founder of the Arts and Crafts movement, Morris did much to raise British craft standards. His first book of verse was *The Defence of Guenevere* 1858. Morris

published several verse romances, notably *The Life and Death of Jason* 1867 and *The Earthly Paradise* 1868–70; a visit to Iceland 1871 inspired the epic poem *Sigurd the Volsung* 1876 and general interest in the sagas. He joined the Social Democratic Federation 1883, but left it 1884 because he found it too moderate, and set up the Socialist League. To this period belong the critical and sociological studies *Signs of Change* 1888 and *Hopes and Fears for Art* 1892, and the narrative poem 'The Pilgrims of Hope' 1885.

Suggested reading

Harvey, C *William Morris: Design and Enterprise in Victorian England* (1991)
Henderson, P *William Morris: His Life, Work and Friends* (1967)
Lindsay, J *William Morris* (1975)
Thompson, E *William Morris: Romantic to Revolutionary* (1977)
Watkinson, R *William Morris as Designer* (1967)

War is an endurance test and we, who know that right is on our side, will last out longest.

HERBERT MORRISON
Broadcast message as minister of supply 9 Aug 1940

Morrison Herbert Stanley, Baron Morrison of Lambeth (1888–1965). British Labour politician. He was a founder member and later secretary of the London Labour Party 1915–45, and a member of the London County Council 1922–45. He entered Parliament in 1923, and organized the Labour Party's general election victory in 1945. He was twice defeated in the contest for leadership of the party, once by Clement Attlee in 1932, and then by Hugh Gaitskell 1955. A skilful organizer, he lacked the ability to unite the party. Baron 1959.

He was minister of transport 1929–31, home secretary 1940–45, Lord President of the Council and leader of the House of Commons 1945–51, and foreign secretary March–Oct 1951.

Morrison Toni (Chloe Anthony, born Wofford) (1931–). US novelist. Her fiction records black life in the South, including *Song of Solomon* 1978, *Tar Baby* 1981, *Beloved* 1987, based on a true story about infanticide in Kentucky, which won the Pulitzer Prize 1988, and *Jazz* 1992. Nobel Prize for Literature 1993.

Hearing Morrison is hearing contemporary vernacular pop music at it's best ... always has been.

Philip Elwood on VAN MORRISON in *San Francisco Examiner* 6 Oct 1978

Morrison Van (George Ivan) (1945–). Northern Irish singer and songwriter. His jazz-inflected Celtic soul style was already in evidence on *Astral Weeks* 1968 and has been highly influential. Among other albums are *Tupelo Honey* 1971, *Veedon Fleece* 1974, and *Avalon Sunset* 1989.

Morrison began in the beat-music era by forming the group Them 1964–66, which had two hits, 'Here Comes the Night' and 'Gloria'; the latter became a standard.

I was looking for a job, and then I found a job / And heaven knows I'm miserable now.

MORRISSEY
'Heaven Knows I'm Miserable Now'

Morrissey stage name of Steven Patrick Morrissey (1959–). English rock singer and lyricist. He was a founder member of the Smiths 1982–87 and subsequently a solo artist. His lyrics reflect on everyday miseries or glumly celebrate the England of his childhood. Solo albums include *Viva Hate* 1987 and *Your Arsenal* 1992.

As the front person of the Smiths, Morrissey developed an image of flippant asceticism. Claiming to be socially inept and celibate, he embodied the anxieties of an adolescent audience.

Morse Samuel Finley Breese (1791–1872). US inventor. In 1835 he produced the first adequate electric telegraph, and in 1843 was granted $30,000 by Congress for an experimental line between Washington DC and Baltimore. With his assistant Alexander Bain (1810–1877) he invented the Morse code.

After graduating from Yale, he went to the UK and studied art at the Royal Academy in London. He became professor of the art of design at New York University.

Between 1832 and 1836 he developed his idea that an electric current could be made to convey messages. The signal current would be sent in an intermittent coded pattern and would cause an elctromagnet to attract intermittently to the same pattern on a piece of soft iron to which a pencil or pen would be attached and which in turn would make marks on a moving strip of paper.

What hath God wrought?

SAMUEL MORSE
First message sent on his electric telegraph May 1844

Mort Thomas Sutcliffe (1816–1878). Australian merchant, born in England. He is best remembered for his pioneering refrigeration experiments directed at freezing meat for export. He successfully operated refrigerated railway transport of country milk and meat to Sydney, but died before the first cargo of frozen meat left Australia in 1879.

Mortimer, John *English writer and lawyer John Mortimer produces popular novels and plays evoking an English middle class in moral decline. His television screenplays include* I Claudius *1976 and* Brideshead Revisited *1981. His autobiography,* Clinging to the Wreckage, *appeared 1982.*

Morse *US artist and inventor Samuel Morse, shown next to a printing telegraph. Backed by $30,000 from Congress, Morse erected the first telegraph line between Baltimore and Washington and sent the first message May 1844. His invention was such a success that within four years of Morse's first public demonstration, America had five thousand miles of telegraph wire. (Ann Ronan/Image Select)*

Mortensen Stanley (1921–1991). English footballer. He was centre forward for the Blackpool Football Club 1946–55, and won 25 international caps while playing for the England team.

Mortimer John Clifford (1923–). English barrister and writer. His works include the plays *The Dock Brief* 1958 and *A Voyage Round My Father* 1970, the novel *Paradise Postponed* 1985, and the television series *Rumpole of the Bailey*, from 1978, centred on a fictional barrister.

Matrimony and murder both carry a mandatory life sentence.

JOHN MORTIMER
Rumpole for the Defence, 'Rumpole and the Boat People' 1982

Mortimer Roger de, 8th Baron of Wigmore and 1st Earl of March (c. 1287–1330). English politician and adventurer. Knighted 1306, earl 1328. A rebel, he was imprisoned by Edward II for two years before making his escape from the Tower of London to France. There he joined with the English queen, Isabella, who was conducting negotiations at the French court, and returned with her to England in 1326. Edward fled when they landed with their followers, and Mortimer secured Edward's deposition by Parliament. From 1327 Mortimer ruled England as the queen's lover. In 1328 he was created Earl of March. He was popularly supposed responsible for Edward II's murder, and when the young Edward III had him seized while with the Queen at Nottingham Castle, he was hanged, drawn, and quartered at Tyburn, London.

Contemporaries remarked on his pride and arrogance, and found him as insufferable as the Despensers whom he had destroyed.

Michael Hicks on ROGER DE MORTIMER
in *Who's Who in Late Medieval England* 1991

Morton Henry Vollam (1892–1979). English journalist and travel writer, author of the *In Search of...* series published during the 1950s. His earlier travel books include *The Heart of London* 1925, *In the Steps of the Master* 1934, and *Middle East* 1941.

Morton J(ohn) B(ingham), (full name John Cameron Andrieu Bingham Michael Morton) (1893–1979). British journalist who contributed a humorous column to the *Daily Express* 1924–76 under the pen name *Beachcomber*.

Morton Jelly Roll. Stage name of Ferdinand Joseph La Menthe Morton (1885–1941). US New Orleans-style jazz pianist, singer, and composer. Influenced by Scott Joplin, he was a pioneer in the development of jazz from ragtime to swing by improvising and imposing his own personality on the music. His 1920s band was called the Red Hot Peppers.

Morton William Thomas Green (1819–1868). US dentist who in 1846, with Charles Thomas Jackson (1805–1880), a chemist and physician, introduced ether as an anaesthetic. They were not the first to use it but they patented the process and successfully publicized it.

Morton was born in Massachusetts. He set up his own dental practice in Boston in 1844 and began investigating ways to deaden pain during dental surgery. Jackson advised him to try ether. Later, Morton attempted to claim sole credit as its discoverer and spent the rest of his life in costly litigation with Jackson.

In 1846, Morton extracted a tooth from a patient under ether and later in the same year staged a public demonstration of ether anaesthesia in an operation at the Massachusetts General Hospital to remove a facial tumour. Morton's contribution to medicine lay in making the value of anaesthesia generally known and appreciated. Crawford Long (1815–1878) had in 1842 successfully used ether anaesthesia during an operation, although he did not publish this work until 1849.

Moschino Franco (1950–1995). Italian fashion designer. He became known for his irreverent clothing after opening his own business 1983. His tailored and classic designed outfits are decorated with slogans, peace symbols, diamanté anarchy signs, and other accessories such as heart-shaped buttons. His printed scarf designs include trompe l'oeil necklaces, handbags, and other accessories.

Moseley, as it were, called the role of the elements.

Frederick Soddy commenting on HENRY MOSELEY 1920

Moseley Henry Gwyn Jeffreys (1887–1915). English physicist. From 1913 to 1914 he devised the series of atomic numbers (reflecting the charges of the nuclei of different elements) that led to the revision of Russian chemist Dmitri Mendeleyev's periodic table of the elements.

He worked in the Manchester laboratory of Ernest Rutherford, the pioneer of atomic science, 1910–13, and then at Oxford. Moseley was killed during the Gallipoli campaign of World War I.

In 1913 Moseley introduced X-ray spectroscopy and found that the X-ray spectra of the elements were similar but with a deviation that changed regularly through the series. A graph of the square root of the frequency of each radiation against the number representing the element's position in the periodic table gave a straight line. He called this number the atomic number of the element; the equation is known as Moseley's law. When the elements are arranged by atomic number instead of atomic mass, problems appearing in the Mendeleyev version are resolved. The numbering system also enabled Moseley to predict correctly that several more elements would be discovered.

Moses (lived *c.* 13th century BC). Hebrew lawgiver and judge who led the Israelites out of Egypt to the promised land of Canaan. On Mount Sinai he claimed to have received from Jehovah the oral and written Law, including the Ten Commandments engraved on tablets of stone. The first five books of the Old Testament – in Judaism, the Torah – are ascribed to him.

According to the Torah, the infant Moses was hidden among the bulrushes on the banks of the Nile when the pharaoh commanded that all newborn male Hebrew children should be destroyed. He was found by a daughter of Pharaoh, who reared him. Eventually he became the leader of the Israelites in their Exodus from Egypt and their 40 years' wandering in the wilderness. He died at the age of 120, after having been allowed a glimpse of the Promised Land from Mount Pisgah.

Suggested reading
Auerbach, Elias *Moses* (1975)
Coats, G W *Moses* (1988)
Daiches, David *Moses: The Man and His Vision* (1975)

Moses 'Grandma' (born Anna Mary Robertson) (1860–1961). US painter. She was self-taught, and began full-time painting about 1927, after many years as a farmer's wife. She painted naive and colourful scenes from rural American life.

Moses Ed(win Corley) (1955–). US track athlete and 400 metres hurdler. Between 1977 and 1987 he ran 122 races without defeat. He first broke the world record in 1976, and set a time of 47.02 seconds 1983. He was twice Olympic champion and twice world champion.

Moses Robert (1888–1981). US public official and urban planner. As parks commissioner for New York State 1924–64 and New York City 1934–60, he oversaw the development of bridges, highways, and public facilities. Serving as New York secretary of state 1927–28, he was the unsuccessful Republican candidate for New York governor 1934. Known as a power broker, he held tremendous power in the USA for more than 40 years.

While the right hand dealt with grandiose ideas and glory, the left hand let the rat out of the sewer.

Nicholas Mosley on his father OSWALD MOSLEY
quoted in Robert Skidelsky *Oswald Mosley* 1975

Mosley Oswald Ernald (1896–1980). British politician, founder of the British Union of Fascists (BUF) 1932. He was a member of Parliament 1918–31, then led the BUF until his internment 1940–43 during World War II. In 1946 Mosley was denounced when it became known that Italy had funded his pre-war efforts to establish fascism in Britain, but in 1948 he resumed fascist propaganda with his Union Movement, the revived BUF. 6th baronet 1928.

His first marriage was to a daughter of the Conservative politician Lord Curzon, his second to Diana Freeman-Mitford, one of the Mitford sisters.

Mosquera Tomás Cipriano de (1798–1878). Colombian general and political thinker. Active in the struggle for independence, Mosquera was made intendant of Guayaquil 1826 by Simón Bolívar. In his first term as president of New Granada 1845–49 he promoted educational, taxation, and political reforms, but split the ruling class. He called the assembly which created the United States of Colombia 1863. Later he took on the Catholic church with a series of anti-clerical policies.

He served in the administration of President José Ignacio de Márquez (1837–41). Exiled 1867 to Peru he returned 1870 and served as governor of Cauca 1871–73, continuing to argue for economic development.

There are only two things no man will admit he can't do well: drive and make love.

STIRLING MOSS
Attributed remark 1963

Moss Stirling (1929–). English racing-car driver. Despite being one of the best-known names in British motor racing, Moss never won the world championship. He was runner-up on four occasions, losing to Juan Manuel Fangio in 1955, 1956, and 1957, and to fellow Briton Mike Hawthorn (1929–1959) in 1958.

In his early days he drove solely for British manufacturers before moving to the Italian firm Maserati, and then to the German Mercedes team, returning once more to British firms such as Vanwall in 1958 and later to Lotus. A bad accident at Goodwood in 1962 ended his career but he maintained contact with the sport and in recent years has taken part in sports-car races.

Mossadeq Muhammad (1880–1967). Iranian prime minister 1951–53. A dispute arose with the Anglo-Iranian Oil Company when he called for the nationalization of Iran's oil production, and when he failed in his attempt to overthrow the shah, he was arrested by loyalist forces with support from the USA. From 1956 he was under house arrest.

Mössbauer Rudolf Ludwig (1929–). German physicist who discovered in 1958 that under certain conditions an atomic nucleus can be stimulated to emit very sharply defined beams of gamma rays – a phenomenon that became known as the Mössbauer effect. For this work he shared the 1961 Nobel Prize for Physics.

In 1960 he went to the USA and a year later became professor of physics at the California Institute of Technology, Pasadena. He remained in this position while simultaneously holding a professorship at Munich.

Mössbauer began research into the effects of gamma rays on matter in 1953. The absorption of a gamma ray by an atomic nucleus usually causes it to recoil, so affecting the wavelength of the re-emitted ray. Mössbauer found that at low temperatures crystals will absorb gamma rays of a specific wavelength and resonate, so that the crystal as a whole recoils while the nuclei do not because they are tightly bound in the crystal lattice. This recoilless nuclear resonance absorption became known as the Mössbauer effect. The effect is exploited in Mössbauer spectroscopy, a useful tool in the study of the structure of solids.

He who hesitates is poor.

ZERO MOSTEL
in *The Producers* 1968

Mostel Zero (Samuel Joel) (1915–1977). US comedian and actor. Although he worked mainly in the theatre, his films include *Panic in the Streets* 1950, *A Funny Thing Happened on the Way to the Forum* 1966, *The Producers* 1967, and *The Front* 1976.

Motherwell Robert Burns (1915–1991). US painter. He was associated with the New York school of action painting. Borrowing from Picasso, Matisse, and the Surrealists, Motherwell's style of Abstract Expressionism retained some suggestion of the figurative. His works include the *Elegies to the Spanish Republic* 1949–76, a series of over 100 paintings devoted to the Spanish Civil War. He edited the *Documents of Modern Art* series and was a teacher at the Hunter College, New York.

Motion Andrew (1952–). English poet, biographer, and novelist. His volumes of poetry include *The Price of Everything* 1994, and he published the authorized biography of the poet Philip Larkin 1993.

Motion's poems show the influence of Larkin and Edward Thomas. They are clear and candidly personal, dealing with the family, marriage, platonic and romantic friendship. He has published critical works on Thomas 1981 and Larkin 1982, as well as a three-generation biography, *The Lamberts* 1986. His novels *The Pale Companion* 1989 and *Famous for the Creatures* 1991 were less successful.

Mott Nevill Francis (1905–1996). English physicist who researched the electronic properties of metals, semiconductors, and noncrystalline materials. He shared the Nobel Prize for Physics 1977. Knighted 1962.

He was at Bristol 1933–54, first as professor of theoretical physics and then as director of the Henry Herbert Wills Physical Laboratories. From 1954 to 1971, he was professor at Cambridge.

Mott initially studied dislocations and other defects in crystalline structure. He was the first to put forward a comprehensive theory of the process involved when a photographic film is exposed to light.

Mott and his colleagues discovered special electrical characteristics in glassy semiconductors and laid down fundamental laws of behaviour for their materials. As a result of this work, more efficient photovoltaic cells can now be produced, and the memory capacity of computers increased.

Mottelson Ben(jamin Roy) (1926–). US-born Danish physicist who with Aage Bohr and James Rainwater shared the 1975 Nobel Prize for Physics for their work on the structure of the atomic nucleus.

Mottelson was born in Chicago, Illinois, and educated at Purdue University. Based in Copenhagen from 1950, he was at the Institute of Theoretical Physics to 1953, then held a position at CERN (European Centre for Nuclear Research), and became professor at Nordita 1957.

In the early 1950s, Mottelson and Bohr together confirmed experimentally the theory worked out by Rainwater about the structure of the nucleus. Mottelson published several books and many scientific papers jointly with Bohr.

Mo Tzu (c. 470–c. 391 BC). Chinese philosopher. His pragmatism and anti-Confucian teachings are summarized in a book also called *Mo Tzu*. His followers formed a group known as the Mohists. The core of Mo Tzu's teaching was frugality, universal love, and the rejection and condemnation of warfare.

Mo Tzu attacked what he saw as the empty formulas of the Confucians by stating that nothing should be undertaken unless it was of clear benefit to the people. He saw this as the necessary guiding principle that governments should follow. He held that if universal love was the norm, nations would not go to war with each other, people would not harm each other, and the wastefulness of dispute and warfare would thus be avoided, benefiting everyone.

I can't think of a more wonderful thanksgiving for the life I have had than that everyone should be jolly at my funeral.

LOUIS MOUNTBATTEN
quoted in R Hough *Mountbatten* 1980

Mountbatten Louis Francis Albert Victor Nicholas, 1st Earl Mountbatten of Burma (1900–1979). British admiral and administrator. In World War II he became chief of combined operations 1942 and commander in chief in SE Asia 1943. As chief of combined operations 1942 he was criticized for the heavy loss of Allied lives in the disastrous Dieppe raid. In SE Asia he concentrated on the reconquest of Burma, although the campaign was actually conducted by General Slim. Mountbatten accepted the surrender of 750,000 Japanese troops in his area of command at a formal parade in Singapore Sept 1945. As last viceroy and governor-general of India 1947–48, he oversaw that country's transition to independence. He was chief of UK Defence Staff 1959–65. He was killed by an Irish Republican Army bomb aboard his yacht in the Republic of Ireland. KCVO 1922, viscount 1945, earl 1947.

Suggested reading

Butler, David *Lord Mountbatten: The Last Viceroy* (1986)
Hough, Richard *Mountbatten* (1981)
Lambton, Antony *The Mountbattens: The Battenbergs and Young Mountbatten* (1989)
Ziegler, Philip *Mountbatten: The Official Biography* (1985)

Moya Jacko (John Hidalgo) (1920–1994). US-born British architect. His Modernist work, in partnership with others, includes housing estates, Oxbridge college buildings, and the Skylon 1951, an elegant, lightweight, pointed structure suspended vertically on balancing wires above the Thames riverside walkways, the most visible landmark of the Festival of Britain in London.

Moynihan Daniel Patrick (1927–). US Democrat politician and diplomat. Moynihan was ambassador to India 1973–75 and to the United Nations 1975–76. Senator from New York from 1977, he became chair of the Senate Finance Committee Jan 1993. He has concerned himself with the problem of poverty among urban black families, and was one of the authors of *The Negro Family: A Case for National Action* 1965, which came to be known as the Moynihan Report.

Moynihan was born in Tulsa, Oklahoma. He embarked on an academic career before his appointment to the Department of Labor 1961. He was a member of the Joint Center for Urban Studies of the Massachusetts Institute of Technology and Harvard 1960–65 and its director 1966–69. Assistant to the president for urban affairs 1969–73, he was the architect of President Nixon's family-assistance programme, which was rejected by Congress. In *Family and Nation* 1985, he lays out a taxation policy to encourage two-parent families, in an attempt to check the emergence of an underclass. His *Pandemonium: Ethnicity in International Politics* was published 1993.

Moyse Marcel (1889–1984). French flautist. Trained at the Paris Conservatoire, he made many recordings and was an eminent teacher.

Mozart (Johann Chrysostom) Wolfgang Amadeus (1756–1791). Austrian composer and performer who showed astonishing precocity as a child and was an adult virtuoso. He was trained by his father, Leopold Mozart (1719–1787). From an early age he composed prolifically, his works including 27 piano concertos, 23 string quartets, 35 violin sonatas, and 41 symphonies including the E flat K543, G minor K550, and C major K551 ('Jupiter') symphonies, all composed 1788. His operas include *Idomeneo* 1780, *Entführung aus dem Serail/The Abduction from the Seraglio* 1782, *Le Nozze di Figaro/The Marriage of Figaro* 1786, *Don Giovanni* 1787, *Così fan tutte/Thus Do All Women* 1790, and *Die Zauberflöte/The Magic Flute* 1791. Together with Haydn, Mozart's music marks the height of the Classical age in its purity of melody and form.

Mubarak *Hosni Mubarak, president of Egypt, addressing the United Nations General Assembly 1989. Mubarak has pursued an even-handed approach to international relations, remaining friendly with the USA while improving relationships with other Arab states, which had been damaged by the signing of the Egypt-Israeli peace treaty of 1979.*

Mozart *The young musical genius Wolfgang Amadeus Mozart playing at a recital for the French aristocracy, c. 1763. Mozart began composing at the age of 5 and by the end of his life had produced an astonishing range of masterpieces.*

Mozart's career began when, with his sister, Maria Anna, he was taken on a number of tours 1762–79, visiting Vienna, the Rhineland, Holland, Paris, London, and Italy. He had already begun to compose. In 1772 he was appointed master of the archbishop of Salzburg's court band but he found the post uncongenial and in 1781 was suddenly dismissed. He married Constanze Weber 1782, settled in Vienna, and embarked on a punishing freelance career as concert pianist, composer, and teacher that brought lasting fame but only intermittent financial security. His *Requiem*, unfinished at his death, was completed by a pupil.

His works were catalogued chronologically 1862 by the musicologist Ludwig von Köchel (1800–1877) whose system of numbering – giving each work a 'Köchel number', for example K354 – remains in use in modified form.

Suggested reading

Biancolli, L L *The Mozart Handbook: A Guide to the Man and his Music* (1954)
Blom, E *Mozart* (1985)
Deutsch, O E *Mozart: A Documentary Biography* (1966)
Einstein, A *Mozart: His Character, His Work* (1959)
Hildesheimer, W *Mozart* (1982)
Liebner, J *Mozart on Stage* (1972)
Sadie, S *The New Grove Mozart* (1982)

Mphahlele Es'kia (Ezekiel) (1919–). South African literary critic, journalist, and novelist. He is best known for his influential autobiography *Down Second Avenue* 1959.

Mubarak (Muhammad) Hosni (1928–). Egyptian politician, president from 1981. Vice president to Anwar Sadat from 1975, Mubarak succeeded him on his assassination. He has continued to pursue Sadat's moderate policies, and has significantly increased the freedom of the press and of political association, while trying to repress the growing Islamic fundamentalist movement. He was re-elected (uncontested) 1987 and 1993. He survived an assassination attempt 1995.

Mubarak commanded the air force 1972–75 and was responsible for the initial victories in the Egyptian campaign of 1973 against Israel. He led Egypt's opposition to Iraq's 1990 invasion of Kuwait and played an instrumental role in arranging the Middle East peace conference Nov 1991.

Mucha Alphonse Maria (1860–1939). Czech painter and designer. His Art Nouveau posters and decorative panels brought him international fame, presenting idealized images of young women with long, flowing tresses, within a patterned flowered border. His early theatre posters were done for the actress Sarah Bernhardt, notably the lithograph *Gismonda* 1894.

Trained in Munich, Mucha went to Paris 1888 where he worked intermittently as a graphic artist. The Art Nouveau theatre posters for Bernhardt, for whom he also designed costumes and jewellery, helped both to launch his career and popularize the style. He also designed textiles, furniture, ceramic plaques, and exhibition displays, and in 1900–01 a jewellery boutique for Georges Fouquet in Paris (now demolished).

Mu-Chi (Muqi) (*c.* 1180–*c.* 1270). Chinese painter of the Song dynasty. A Chan Buddhist, he employed a technique based on intuition and spontaneity. One of his best-known works is *Six Persimmons* early 13th century (Daitoku-ji, Kyoto), illustrating his ability to depict an object with a few deft brush strokes.

Mugabe Robert Gabriel (1924–). Zimbabwean politician, prime minister from 1980 and president from 1987. He was in detention in Rhodesia for nationalist activities 1964–74, then carried on guerrilla warfare from Mozambique. As leader of ZANU he was in an uneasy alliance with Joshua Nkomo of ZAPU (Zimbabwe African People's Union) from 1976.

Mugabe is a member of the Shona people, and was educated at Fort Hare University, South Africa. In 1985 he postponed the introduction of a multiparty state for five years. His failure to anticipate and respond to the 1991–92 drought in southern Africa adversely affected his popularity.

The world is so overflowing with absurdity that it is difficult for the humorist to compete.

MALCOLM MUGGERIDGE
on becoming editor of *Punch*

Muggeridge (Thomas) Malcolm (1903–1990). English journalist and author. He worked for the *Guardian*, the *Calcutta Statesman*, the London *Evening Standard*, and the *Daily Telegraph* before becoming editor of *Punch* 1953–57. He contributed regularly to television

Muir, Jean British fashion designer Jean Muir describes her work as having three sources: intuition, esthetic appreciation, and technical expertise.

programmes after 1953, and wrote an autobiography, *Chronicles of Wasted Time* 1982. In later life he abjured his misspent youth and became a Roman Catholic.

Mugler Thierry (1946–). French fashion designer. He launched his first collection 1971 under the label Café de Paris. By 1973 he was designing under his own label. Strongly influenced by 1940s and 1950s fashion, his designs had broad shoulders and well-defined waists. His catwalk shows are often spectacular.

Muhammad (Arabic 'praised') or Mohammed, Mahomet (*c.* 570– 632). Founder of Islam, born in Mecca on the Arabian peninsula. In about 616 he began to preach the worship of one God, who allegedly revealed to him the words of the Koran (it was later written down by his followers) through the angel Jibra'el (Gabriel). Muhammad fled from persecution to the town now known as Medina in 622: the flight, *Hijrah* or *Hegira*, marks the beginning of the Islamic era.

Muhammad was originally a shepherd and trader. He married Khadija, a widow, in 595, spent time in meditation, and received his first revelation in 610. The series of revelations continued throughout his life. At first he doubted their divine origin but later began to teach others, who wrote down the words of his revelations; they were collected after his death to form the Koran.

The move to Medina resulted in the first Islamic community, which for many years fought battles against fierce opposition from Mecca and from neighbouring tribes. In 630 the Muslim army defeated that of Mecca and the city came under Muslim rule. By the time of Muhammad's death in 632, Islam had spread throughout the Arabian peninsula. After his death, the leadership of the Muslims was disputed.

Muslims believe that Muhammad was the final prophet, although they recognize other, earlier prophets, including Ibrahim (Abraham) and Isa (Jesus). Muhammad is not worshipped, but honoured by the words 'Peace be upon him' whenever Muslims mention his name.
Suggested reading
Cook, Michael *Muhammad* (1983)
Schimmel, A *And Muhammad is His Messenger* (1985)
Watt, W M *Mohammed: Prophet and Statesman* (1961)

Muir Edwin (1887–1959). Scottish poet. He drew mystical inspiration from his Orkney childhood. *First Poems* 1925 were published after a period of residence in Prague, which also resulted in translations of Kafka, in collaboration with his wife, Willa. Dreams, myths, and menaces coexist in his poetry. His notable *Autobiography* 1954, explores similar themes.

Muir Jean Elizabeth (1933–1996). English fashion designer. She worked for Jaeger 1956–61 and set up her own fashion house 1961. In 1991 she launched a knitwear collection. Her clothes are characterized by soft, classic, tailored shapes in leathers and soft fabrics.

Muir John (1838–1914). Scottish-born US conservationist. Muir emigrated to the USA with his family 1849. After attending the University of Wisconsin, he travelled widely and compiled detailed nature journals of his trips. He moved to California 1868 and later explored Glacier Bay in Alaska and mounted other expeditions to Australia and South America. From 1880 he headed a campaign that led to the establishment of Yosemite National Park. He was named adviser to the National Forestry Commission 1896 and continued to campaign for the preservation of wilderness areas for the rest of his life.

Muir Thomas (1844–1934). Scottish mathematician whose five-volume treatise on the history of determinants 1906–30 made the work of other mathematicians accessible to scholars. Knighted 1915.

In 1874 he resigned a position as assistant professor at Glasgow to become head of the Mathematics and Science Department at Glasgow High School. From 1892 he was superintendent-general of education in South Africa and vice chancellor of the University of Cape Town.

Although not himself a creative mathematician, Muir published 307 papers, most of them on determinants and allied subjects. His books include *A Treatise on the Theory of Determinants* 1882 and *The Theory of Determinants in its Historical Order of Development* 1890.

Muldoon Robert David (1921–1992). New Zealand National Party politician, prime minister 1975–84. He pursued austere economic policies such as a wage-and-price policy to control inflation. GCMG 1984.

A chartered accountant, he was minister of finance 1967–72, and in 1974 replaced John Marshall as leader of the National Party, after the latter had been criticized as insufficiently aggressive in opposition. He became prime minister in 1975; he sought to introduce curbs on trade unions, was a vigorous supporter of the Western alliance, and a proponent of reform of the international monetary system. He was defeated in the general election of 1984 and was succeeded as prime minister by the Labour Party's David Lange. Muldoon announced his retirement from politics 1992.

Suggested reading
Muldoon, Robert *The Rise and Fall of a Young Turk* (autobiography) (1974)

Müller Heiner (1929–). German dramatist. His scripts have played a leading role in contemporary avant-garde theatre in Germany and abroad. Early political works, showing the influence of Brecht, (*The Scab* 1950, *The Correction* 1958) were followed by *Mauser* 1970, *Cement* 1972 (on the Russian revolution), *Hamletmachine* 1977, and *Medea-material* 1982. He collaborated closely with the American director Robert Wilson during the 1980s.

Muller Hermann Joseph (1890–1967). US geneticist who discovered 1926 that mutations can be artificially induced by X-rays. This showed that mutations are nothing more than chemical changes. He was awarded the Nobel Prize for Physiology or Medicine 1946.

Muller campaigned against the needless use of X-rays in diagnosis and treatment, and pressed for safety regulations to ensure that people who were regularly exposed to X-rays were adequately protected. He also opposed nuclear-bomb tests.

In 1920 he joined the University of Texas, Austin, later becoming professor of zoology. The constraints on his freedom to express his socialist political views caused him to leave the USA 1932, and from 1933 he worked at the Institute of Genetics in the USSR. But the false ideas of Trofim Lysenko began to dominate Soviet biological research; openly critical of Lysenkoism, Muller was forced to leave in 1937. After serving in the Spanish Civil War, he worked at the Institute of Animal Genetics in Edinburgh. In 1940 he returned to the USA, becoming professor at Indiana University 1945.

In 1919 Muller found that the mutation rate was increased by heat, and that heat did not always affect both of the chromosomes in a chromosome pair. From this he concluded that mutations involved changes at the molecular or submolecular level. Next he experimented with X-rays as a means of inducing mutations, and by 1926 he had proved the method successful.

Muller's research convinced him that almost all mutations are deleterious. In the normal course of evolution, deleterious mutants die out and the few advantageous ones survive, but he believed that if the mutation rate is too high, the number of imperfect individuals may become too large for the species as a whole to survive.

Müller Johannes. German astronomer, see ◊Regiomontanus.

Müller Johannes Peter (1801–1858). German comparative anatomist whose studies of nerves and sense organs opened a new chapter in physiology by demonstrating the physical nature of sensory perception. His name is associated with a number of discoveries, including the Müllerian ducts in the mammalian fetus and the lymph heart in frogs.

Müller Paul Herman (1899–1965). Swiss chemist who discovered the first synthetic contact insecticide, DDT, 1939. For this he was awarded a Nobel prize 1948.

Müller was born in Olten, Solothurn, and studied at Basel. He went to work for the chemical firm of J R Geigy, researching principally into dyestuffs and tanning agents; he subsequently joined the staff of Basel University.

In 1935, Müller started the search for a substance that would kill insects quickly but have little or no poisonous effect on plants and animals, unlike the arsenical compounds then in use. He concentrated his search on chlorine compounds and in 1939 synthesized DDT.

The Swiss government successfully tested DDT against the Colorado potato beetle in 1939 and by 1942 it was in commercial production. Its first important use was in Naples, Italy, where a typhus epidemic 1943–44 was ended when the population was sprayed with DDT to kill the body lice that are the carriers of typhus.

DDT (dichloro-diphenyl-trichloroethane) was to have a profound effect on the health of the world, killing insect vectors such as mosquitoes that spread malaria and yellow fever and by combating insect pests that feed on food crops. Gradually the uses of DDT in public hygiene and in agriculture became limited by increasing DDT-resistance in insect species. DDT is highly toxic and persists in the environment and in living tissue, disrupting food chains and presenting a hazard to animal life. Its use is now banned in most countries.

Mulligan Gerry (Gerald) (1927–1996). US jazz saxophonist, arranger, and composer. Spanning the bebop and cool jazz movements, he worked with trumpeter Miles Davis on the seminal *Birth of the Cool* album 1950 and led his own quartet from 1951, which briefly featured Chet Baker on trumpet.

Born in New York but based in Los Angeles from 1952, Mulligan is chiefly associated with the West Coast jazz style. An outstanding baritone-sax player, he worked with many great names in jazz, including bandleader Stan Kenton (for whom he wrote arrangements) and pianist Thelonius Monk.

Mulliken Robert Sanderson (1896–1986). US chemist and physicist who received the 1966 Nobel Prize for Chemistry for his development of the molecular orbital theory. He was professor at the University of Chicago 1931-61.

Mulock unmarried name of English novelist Dinah ◊Craik.

Mulready William (1786–1863). Irish painter. Active in England, he depicted rural scenes. In 1840 he designed the first penny-postage envelope, known as the Mulready envelope.

Mulroney (Martin) Brian (1939–). Canadian politician, Progressive Conservative Party leader 1983–93, prime minister 1984–93. He achieved a landslide in the 1984 election, and won the 1988 election on a platform of free trade with the USA, but with a reduced majority. Opposition within Canada to the 1987 Meech Lake agreement, a prerequisite to signing the 1982 Constitution, continued to plague Mulroney in his second term. A revised reform package Oct 1992 failed to gain voters' approval, and in Feb 1993 he was forced to resign the leadership of the Conservative Party, though he remained prime minister until Kim Campbell was appointed his successor in June.

Muluzi Bakili (1943–). Malawi politician, president from 1994. Muluzi formed the United Democratic Front (UDF) 1992 when President Banda agreed to end one-party rule, and went on to win almost half of the presidential votes. Since taking office, he has applied his business experience to the task of liberalizing trade and reviving the economy.

Born in Machinga, southern Malawi, he used his entrepreneurial skills to become a wealthy businessman. Entering politics, he became close to President Hastings Banda and served in his government as well as being secretary-general of the ruling Malawi Congress Party (MCP). In 1982 a rift developed when he was accused of stealing party funds and replaced as secretary general. He then joined the underground opposition and when, in 1992, the president conceded to demands for an end to one-party rule, Muluzi formed the UDF to fight the impending presidential and assembly elections. In May 1994 the UDF won 84 of the 175 assembly seats and Muluzi 47% of the votes for the presidency.

Banda accepted that his rival was a 'clear winner' and promised to work with him in 'building a better democratic Malawi'.

Mumford Lewis (1895–1990). US urban planner and social critic, concerned with the adverse effect of technology on contemporary society. His books, including *Technics and Civilization* 1934 and *The Culture of Cities* 1938, discussed the rise of cities and proposed the creation of green belts around large conurbations. His view of the importance of an historical perspective in urban planning for the future is reflected in his major work *The City in History* 1961.

Suggested reading
Miller, Donald *Lewis Mumford* (1992)
Mumford, Lewis *Sketches from Life* (autobiography) (1982)

Every generation revolts against its fathers and makes friends with its grandfathers.

LEWIS MUMFORD
The Brown Decades 1931

Munch Edvard (1863–1944). Norwegian painter and printmaker. He studied in Paris and Berlin, and his major works date from the period 1892–1908, when he lived mainly in Germany. His paintings often focus on neurotic emotional states. The *Frieze of Life* 1890s, a sequence of highly charged, symbolic paintings, includes some of his most characteristic images, such as *Skriket/The Scream* 1893. He later reused these in etchings, lithographs, and woodcuts.

Munch was influenced by van Gogh and Gauguin but soon developed his own expressive style, reducing his compositions to broad areas of colour with sinuous contours emphasized by heavy brushstrokes, distorting faces and figures. His first show in Berlin 1892 made a great impact on young German artists. In 1908 he suffered a nervous breakdown and returned to Norway. Later works include a series of murals 1910–15 in the assembly halls of Oslo University.

Suggested reading
Benesch, Otto *Edvard Munch* (1960)
Hodin, J P *Edvard Munch* (1972)
Selz, J *Edvard Munch* (1974)
Stang, R *Edvard Munch: The Man and his Art* (1979)

Münchhausen Karl Friedrich Hieronymus, Freiherr (Baron) von (1720–1797). German soldier. He served with the Russian army against the Turks, and after his retirement 1760 told exaggerated stories of his adventures. This idiosyncrasy was utilized by the German writer Rudolf Erich Raspe (1737–1794) in his extravagantly fictitious *Adventures of Baron Munchausen* 1785, which he wrote in English while living in London.

Mungo, St another name for St ◊Kentigern, first bishop of Glasgow.

Munkácsi Martin (1896–1963). Hungarian-born US photographer. After a successful career in Budapest and then Berlin, where he was influenced by the New Photography movement, he moved to the USA 1934. There he worked as a fashion photographer pioneering a more lively and natural style of photograph for such magazines as *Harper's Bazaar* and *Ladies' Home Journal*.

Munnings Alfred James (1878–1959). English painter. He excelled in racing and hunting scenes, and painted realistic everyday scenes featuring horses, such as horsefairs or horses grazing. As president of the Royal Academy 1944–49 he was outspoken in his dislike of 'modern art'.

Munro Alice (1931–). Canadian author. She is known for her short stories in which she is remarkably sensitive to suppressed or unrecognized feeling in small-town life. Collections of her work include *Dance of the Happy Shades* 1968, *The Progress of Love* 1987, and *Open Secrets* 1994. She has written only one novel, *Lives of Girls and Women* 1971.

Munro H(ugh) H(ector). English author who wrote under the pen name ◊Saki.

Murakami Haruki (1949–). Japanese novelist and translator. He is one of Japan's best-selling writers, influenced by 20th-century US writers and popular culture. His dreamy, gently surrealist novels include *A Wild Sheep Chase* 1982 and *Norwegian Wood* 1987.

Murasaki Shikibu (*c.* 978–*c.* 1015). Japanese writer. She was a lady at the court. Her masterpiece of fiction, *The Tale of Genji* c. 1010, is one of the classic works of Japanese literature, and may be the world's first novel.

She was a member of the Fujiwara clan, but her own name is not known; scholars have given her the name Murasaki after a character in the book. It deals with upper-class life in Heian Japan, centring on the affairs of Prince Genji. A portion of her diary and a number of poems also survive.

Murat Joachim (1767–1815). King of Naples 1808–15. An officer in the French army, he was made king by Napoleon, but deserted him in 1813 in the vain hope that Austria and Great Britain would recognize him. In 1815 he attempted unsuccessfully to make himself king of all Italy, but when he landed in Calabria in an attempt to gain the throne he was captured and shot.

Suggested reading
Cole, Hubert *The Murats* (1972)
Connelly, Owen *Napoleon's Satellite Kingdoms* (1965)

I have too often braved death to fear it.

JOACHIM MURAT
Spoken on the scaffold 13 Oct 1815

Murayama Tomiichi (1924–). Japanese trade unionist and politician, leader of the Social Democratic Party (SDPJ) from 1993, prime minister from 1994. At the age of 70, Murayama, who had held no previous political office, became Japan's first socialist prime minister for more than 30 years. His emergence as a major figure followed months of virtual chaos in Japanese politics, during which two prime ministers resigned. Despite losses for the SDPJ in upper house elections 1995, his administration survived.

A student of economics, Murayama joined the SDPJ immediately on graduating. In Sept 1993 he succeeded Sadao Yamahana as leader of the SDPJ. In April 1994 Premier Morohiro Hosokawa resigned, charged with financial misconduct, and was succeeded by Tsutomu Hata, heading a seven-party coalition backed by the SDPJ. Murayama's withdrawal of his party's support, which occurred within hours of the new government taking office, forced Hata's eventual resignation. Murayama succeeded him in June.

Murchison Roderick Impey (1792–1871). Scottish geologist responsible for naming the Silurian period (in his book *The Silurian System* 1839). Expeditions to Russia 1840–45 led him to define another worldwide system, the Permian, named after the strata of the Perm region. Knighted 1846, baronet 1866.

Murchison was born in Ross-shire. He entered the army at 15 and fought in the Peninsular War. Often accompanied by geologists Adam Sedgwick or Charles Lyell, Murchison made field explorations in Scotland, France, and the Alps. In 1855 he became director-general of the UK Geological Survey. An ardent imperialist, for many years he was also president of the Royal Geographical Society, encouraging African exploration and annexation.

Murchison believed in a universal order of the deposition of strata, indicated by fossils rather than solely by lithological features. Fossils showed a clear progression in complexity. The Silurian system contained, in his view, remains of the earliest life forms. He based it on studies of slate rocks in South Wales.

With Sedgwick's cooperation, Murchison also established the Devonian system in SW England.

Murcutt Glenn Marcus (1936–). Australian architect noted for his innovative of use of building materials to produce structures in harmony with the landscape of rural and outback Australia. A pair of farmhouses at Mount Irvine, New South Wales 1980, employ galvanized iron, external venetian blinds and local pine.

Murdoch (Jean) Iris (1919–). English novelist, born in Dublin. Her novels combine philosophical speculation with often outrageous situations and tangled human relationships. They include *The Sandcastle* 1957, *The Sea, The Sea* 1978 (Booker Prize), *The Message to the Planet* 1989, and *The Green Knight* 1993. DBE 1987.

A lecturer in philosophy, she became a fellow of St Anne's College, Oxford University, 1948, and published *Sartre, Romantic Rationalist* 1953. Her novel *A Severed Head* 1961 was filmed 1983.

Suggested reading
Conradi, P J *Iris Murdoch: The Saint and the Artists* (1986)
Dipple, E *Iris Murdoch: Work for the Spirit* (1982)
Johnson, D *Iris Murdoch* (1987)

Murdoch (Keith) Rupert (1931–). Australian-born US media magnate with worldwide interests. His UK newspapers, generally right-wing, include the *Sun*, the *News of the World*, and *The Times*; in the USA, he has a 50% share of 20th Century Fox, six Metromedia TV stations, and newspaper and magazine publishing companies. He purchased a 50% stake in a Hungarian tabloid, *Reform*, from 1989.

His newspapers (which also include *Today* and the *Sunday Times*) and 50% of Sky Television, the UK's first satellite television service, are controlled by News International, a wholly owned subsidiary of the Australian-based News Corporation. In Nov 1990 Sky Television and its rival company British Satellite Broadcasting merged to form British Sky Broadcasting (BSkyB). Over 70% of newspapers sold in Australia are controlled by Murdoch.

Suggested reading
Leapman, Michael *Barefaced Cheek: The Apotheosis of Rupert Murdoch* (1984)
Munster, George *Rupert Murdoch: A Paper Prince* (1985)
Regan, Simon *Murdoch* (1976)

Murdock William (1754–1839). Scottish inventor and technician. Employed by James Watt and Matthew Boulton to build steam engines, he was the first to develop gas lighting on a commercial scale, holding the gas in gasometers, from the 1790s.

Murdock was born in Auchinleck, Ayrshire. Between 1777 and 1830 he worked for Boulton and Watt, mainly in Birmingham and Cornwall.

In 1792, Murdock lighted his house in Redruth, Cornwall, by gases produced by distilling coal or wood, but it was not until about 1799 that he perfected methods for making, storing, and purifying gas. Watt and Boulton's Birmingham factory was lit by gas from 1802–03, and the manufacture of gasmaking plant seems to have begun about this period, probably in connection with apparatus for producing oxygen and hydrogen for medical purposes. A paper Murdock read before the Royal Society 1808 is the earliest practical essay on the subject.

Murdock made improvements to the steam engine, though he failed to persuade Boulton and Watt that a steam carriage was a practical idea. He was the first to devise an oscillating engine, about 1784. He also experimented with compressed air, and in 1803 constructed a steam gun.

Murger (Louis) Henri (1822–1861). French writer. In 1848 he published *Scènes de la vie de bohème*/*Scenes of Bohemian Life* which formed the basis of Puccini's opera *La Bohème*.

Murillo Bartolomé Esteban (1618–1682). Spanish painter. Active mainly in Seville, he painted sentimental pictures of the Immaculate Conception, and also specialized in studies of street urchins. His *Self-Portrait* about 1672 (National Gallery, London) is generally considered to be one of his finest works.

Born in Seville, he studied art under Juan Castillo and, having saved a little money by hawking pictures at fairs and painting church pictures for export to South America, seems to have gone to Madrid, where he benefited by the study of the works of Titian, Rubens and van Dyck in the royal palaces, and received some encouragement from Velazquez. He married a woman of wealth in Seville 1645 and gained a fortune by his own efforts, receiving a vast number of commissions. The Academy of Seville was founded by him 1660, and he remained in the city during his years of success, declining the honour of becoming court painter to Charles II 1670. In early days he

Murdoch, Iris *Irish-born English novelist and philosopher Iris Murdoch. Her novels are noted for their complex plots adroitly handled and the subtle, ever changing relationships of the characters. Though their incidents are often comic and bizarre, their underlying concern is how love, freedom, and goodness can survive moral and intellectual blindness. These themes are analysed formally in her philosophical works, which include studies of Sartre and Plato.*

painted many pictures of peasant and street urchin types, but his later works were mainly religious and executed in his soft and melting *estilo vaporoso*, as in the *Immaculate Conception* (Prado), a favoured theme, of which there are many versions. The *Melon Eaters* (Munich) and *Two Peasant Boys* (Dulwich) are notable examples of his naturalism, traceable to Ribera and Velazquez but not free from the sentimentality which makes his religious works unpalatable to modern taste. Placed among the greatest masters until the 19th century, he has since been looked on with disfavour as the originator of much that was mawkish and empty in art. The dramatized genre of his *Prodigal Son* series shows his later work at its best. He employed a number of assistants, and many works still ascribed entirely to his hand may have been their work.

Murnau F W. Adopted name of Friedrich Wilhelm Plumpe (1889–1931). German silent-film director. He was known for his expressive images and 'subjective' use of a moving camera in *Der letzte Mamm*/*The Last Laugh* 1924. Other films include *Nosferatu* 1922 (a version of the Dracula story), *Sunrise* 1927, and *Tabu* 1931.

Murphy Audie (1924–1971). US actor and war hero. He starred mainly in low-budget Westerns. His more prestigious work includes *The Red Badge of Courage* 1951, *The Quiet American* 1958, and *The Unforgiven* 1960. He was the most decorated American soldier of World War II and played himself in the film story of his war years *To Hell and Back* 1955.

Murphy Dervla Mary (1931–). Irish travel writer. Her books include *Full Tilt* 1965, *Tibetan Foothold* 1966, *In Ethiopia with a Mule* 1968, *Cameroon with Egbert* 1989, and *The Ukimwi Road* 1993. Travelling with minimal resources in the UK as well as in Asia,

Africa, and South America, her responses to both people and landscapes are reported with warmth and a naive originality.

Rape must be exceedingly disagreeable yet at least one is still among those present next morning.

DERVIA MURPHY
quoted in Mary Russell *The Blessings of a Good Thick Skirt* ch 10 1986

Murphy Eddie (Edward Regan) (1951–). US film actor and comedian. His first film, *48 Hours* 1982, introduced the street-wise, cocksure character that has become his speciality. Its great success, and that of his next two films, *Trading Places* 1983 and *Beverly Hills Cop* 1984, made him one of the biggest box-office draws of the 1980s.

Murphy began his career at 15 as a stand-up comedian before appearing regularly on the US television show *Saturday Night Live*. Other films include *Beverly Hills Cop II* 1987, his filmed live show *Eddie Murphy Raw* 1987, *Coming to America* 1988, which he cowrote, *Harlem Nights* 1989, which he produced and directed, and *Boomerang* and *The Distinguished Gentleman* both 1992.

Murray family name of dukes of Atholl; seated at Blair Castle, Perthshire, Scotland.

Murray Archibald James (1860–1945). British general. At the start of World War I, he went to France as Chief of Staff but returned to Britain Oct 1915 to become Chief of the Imperial General Staff. He was appointed to command the Mediterranean Expeditionary Force and went to Egypt where he organized the country's defences. He led the British advance into Palestine but failed to capture Gaza. He returned to Britain 1917 to take over the prestigious Aldershot command which he retained until 1919. KCB 1911.

Murray (George) Gilbert (Aimé) (1866–1957). Australian-born British scholar. Author of *History of Ancient Greek Literature* 1897, he became known for verse translations of the Greek dramatists, notably of Euripides, which rendered the plays more accessible to readers.

He was taken to England 1877, and was professor of Greek at Glasgow University 1889–99 and at Oxford 1908–36.
Suggested reading
Smith, Jean and Toynbee, Arnold (eds) *Gilbert Murray: An Unfinished Autobiography* (1960)
West, Francis *Gilbert Murray: A Life* (1960)
Wilson, Duncan *Gilbert Murray OM* (1987)

Murray James Augustus Henry (1837–1915). Scottish philologist. He was the first editor of the *Oxford English Dictionary* (originally the *New English Dictionary*) from 1878 until his death; the first volume was published 1884. He edited more than half the dictionary singlehanded, working in a shed (nicknamed the Scriptorium) in his back garden. Knighted 1908.

Whether acting avowedly as leader or remaining carefully in the background, he was the dominant political personality in Scotland.

T F Henderson on JAMES STUART, 1ST EARL OF MURRAY
in *Dictionary of National Biography*

Murray James Stuart, 1st Earl of Murray, or Moray (1531–1570). Regent of Scotland from 1567, an illegitimate son of James V. He was one of the leaders of the Scottish Reformation, and after the deposition of his half-sister Mary Queen of Scots, he became regent. He was assassinated by one of her supporters. Earl 1562.

Murray (John) Hubert (Plunkett) (1861–1940). Australian administrator in New Guinea. He became first lieutenant governor 1908 when New Guinea was renamed Papua and possession transferred from Britain to Australia. He was still in office when he died but had been in the main frustrated in his aim of developing Papua by European enterprise. KCMG 1925.

Murray Joseph Edward (1919–). US surgeon whose work in the field of controlling rejection of organ transplants earned him a shared Nobel Prize for Physiology or Medicine 1990.

Murray Les(lie) A(llan) (1938–). Australian poet. His poetry, adventurous, verbally inventive, deeply serious, has appeared in collections such as *The Vernacular Republic: Poems 1961–1981* 1982, *The People's Otherworld* 1983, *The Australian Seasons* 1985, and *Translations from the Natural World* 1993. He has emerged as a determined advocate of the virtues and values of rural life.

Born in a rural area on the coast of New South Wales, he was lured to the city as a student at Sydney University and an academic translator in Canberra.

Murrow Edward R(oscoe) (1908–1965). US broadcast journalist who covered World War II from London for the Columbia Broadcasting System (CBS).
Suggested reading
Smith, Robert F *Edward Murrow: The War Years* (1978)
Kendrick, Alexander *Prime Time* (1969)
Sperber, A M *Murrow* (1986)

Murry John Middleton (1889–1957). English writer. He produced studies of Dostoevsky, Keats, Blake, and Shakespeare; poetry; and an autobiographical novel, *Still Life* 1916. In 1913 he married the writer Katherine Mansfield, whose biography he wrote. He was a friend of the writer D H Lawrence.

Musashi Miyamoto. See ◊Miyamoto Musashi, Japanese samurai.

Museveni Yoweri Kaguta (1944–). Ugandan general and politician, president from 1986. He entered the army, eventually rising to the rank of general. He led the opposition to Idi Amin's regime 1971–78 and was minister of defence 1979–80 but, unhappy with Milton Obote's autocratic leadership, formed the National Resistance Army (NRA). When Obote was ousted in a coup in 1985, Museveni entered into a brief power-sharing agreement with his successor, Tito Okello, before taking over as president. Museveni leads a broad-based coalition government, and in 1993 reinstated the country's four tribal monarchies.

Musgrave Thea (1928–). Scottish composer. Her works, in a conservative modern idiom, include concertos for horn, clarinet, and viola; string quartets; and operas, including *Mary, Queen of Scots* 1977.

Musial Stan(ley Frank). Nicknamed 'Stan the Man' (1920–). US baseball player. During his playing career of 22 years, he led the National League 6 times in hits, 8 times in doubles, 5 times in triples, and 7 times in batting average. He played his last season 1963 and was hired by the Cardinals as an executive.

Born in Donora, Pennsylvania, USA, Musial was an outstanding high-school athlete and was signed by the St Louis Cardinals 1938 and played as a Cardinal outfielder and first baseman from 1941.

Musil Robert (1880–1942). Austrian novelist. He was the author of the unfinished *Der Mann ohne Eigenschaften/The Man without Qualities* (three volumes, 1930–43). Its hero shares the author's background of philosophical study and scientific and military training, and is preoccupied with the problems of the self viewed from a mystic but agnostic viewpoint.

Muskie Edmund S(ixtus) (1914–1996). US Democrat politician. A moderate by ideology and nature, he was a senator from Maine 1959–81 and secretary of state 1980–81. As a senator he concentrated on the environment, specializing in legislation on clean air and clean water. In the 1968 presidential election he was Hubert Humphrey's vice-presidential candidate. He entered the state legislature 1947, and was governor of Maine 1955–59.

Musset (Louis Charles) Alfred de (1810–1857). French poet and playwright. Born in Paris, he abandoned the study of law and medicine to join the circle of Victor Hugo. He achieved success with the volume of poems *Contes d'Espagne et d'Italie/Stories of Spain and Italy* 1829. His *Confessions d'un enfant du siècle/Confessions of a Child of the Century* 1835 recounts his broken relationship with George Sand. Typical of his work are the verse in *Les Nuits/Nights* 1835–37 and the short plays *Comédies et proverbes/Comedies and Proverbs* 1840. In 1833 he accompanied the writer George Sand to Italy as her lover.

Mussolini Benito Amilcare Andrea (1883–1945). Italian dictator 1925–43. As founder of the Fascist Movement 1919 and prime minister from 1922, he became known as *Il Duce* ('the leader'). He invaded Ethiopia 1935–36, intervened in the Spanish Civil War 1936–39 in support of Franco, and conquered Albania 1939. In June 1940 Italy entered World War II supporting Hitler. Forced by military and domestic setbacks to resign 1943, Mussolini established a breakaway government in N Italy 1944–45, but was killed trying to flee the country.

Mussolini was born in the Romagna, the son of a blacksmith, and worked in early life as a teacher and journalist. He became active in the socialist movement, from which he was expelled 1914 for advocating Italian intervention in World War I. In 1919 he founded the Fascist Movement, whose programme combined violent nationalism with demagogic republican and anticapitalist slogans, and launched a campaign of terrorism against the socialists. This movement was backed by many landowners and industrialists and by the heads of the army and police, and in Oct 1922 Mussolini was in power as prime minister at the head of a coalition government. In 1925 he assumed dictatorial powers, and in 1926 all opposition parties were banned. During the years that followed, the political, legal, and education systems were remodelled on Fascist lines.

If I advance, follow me; if I retreat, kill me; if I die, avenge me.

BENITO MUSSOLINI
to Fascist officials after an assassination attempt 6 Apr 1926

Mussolini's Blackshirt followers were the forerunners of Hitler's Brownshirts, and his career of conquest drew him into close cooperation with Nazi Germany. Italy and Germany formed the Axis alliance 1936. During World War II, Italian defeats in N Africa and Greece, the Allied invasion of Sicily, and discontent at home destroyed Mussolini's prestige, and in July 1943 he was compelled to resign by his own Fascist Grand Council. He was released from prison by German parachutists Sept 1943 and set up a 'Republican Fascist' government in N Italy. In April 1945 he and his mistress, Clara Petacci, were captured by partisans at Lake Como while heading for the Swiss border, and shot. Their bodies were taken to Milan and hung upside down in a public square.

Mussolini *Benito Mussolini addressing supporters c. 1936. Mussolini was an Italian dictator who founded the Fascist Movement 1919, and became prime minister 1922. Under Mussolini, Italy formed the Axis alliance with Nazi Germany 1936, and entered World War II in support of Germany 1940.* (Image Select)

Suggested reading
Collier, Richard *Duce!* (1971)
Fermin, Laura *Mussolini* (1961)
Kirkpatrick, I *Mussolini: A Study in Power* (1964)
Smith, Denis M *Mussolini* (1981)

Mussorgsky Modest Petrovich (1839–1881). Russian nationalist composer. Born in Karevo (Pskov, Russia), he resigned his commission in the army 1858 to concentrate on music while working as a government clerk. He was influenced by both folk music and literature. He was a member of the group of five composers 'The Five'. His opera masterpiece *Boris Godunov* 1869, revised 1871–72, touched a political nerve and employed realistic transcriptions of speech patterns. Many of his works, including *Pictures at an Exhibition* 1874 for piano, were 'revised' and orchestrated by others, including Rimsky-Korsakov, Ravel, and Shostakovich, and some have only recently been restored to their original harsh beauty. Among his other works are the incomplete operas *Khovanshchina* and *Sorochintsy Fair*, the orchestral *Night on the Bare Mountain* 1867, and many songs. He died in poverty, from alcoholism.

Suggested reading
Calvocoressi, M (revised by Gerald Abraham) *Mussorgsky* (1974)
Leyda, Jay and Bertensson, Sergei *The Mussorgsky Reader* (1974)
Seroff, Victor *Modest Mussorgsky* (1968)

Mustafa Kemal Pasha Turkish leader who assumed the name of ◊Atatürk.

Mutaguchi Renya (1888–1966). Japanese general in World War II. An ambitious and hot-tempered man, he commanded the Japanese force which captured Malaya and Singapore 1941, then went to command the 15th Japanese Army in Burma (now Myanmar) where he planned and commanded the disastrous offensives against Imphal and Kohima 1944. Following his failure, he was dismissed and was employed in administrative jobs thereafter.

Muti Riccardo (1941–). Italian conductor. Artistic director of La Scala, Milan, from 1986, he was previously conductor of the

Muti *The Italian conductor Riccardo Muti. He won the Guido Cantelli conducting prize 1967 and became principal conductor 1969 and musical director 1977 of the Florence Music Festival, Maggio Musicale. He made his operatic debut at Covent Garden 1977 with Aida, and since then has worked with many leading orchestras and opera companies.*

Philharmonia Orchestra, London, 1973–82 and the Philadelphia Orchestra from 1981. He is equally at home with opera or symphonic repertoire performed with bravura, energy, and scrupulous detail, and is known as a purist.

Mutsuhito personal name of the Japanese emperor Meiji.

Muybridge Eadweard. Adopted name of Edward James Muggeridge (1830–1904). English-born US photographer. He made a series of animal locomotion photographs in the USA in the 1870s and proved that, when a horse trots, there are times when all its feet are off the ground. He also explored motion in birds and humans.

Muzorewa Abel Tendekayi (1925–). Zimbabwean politician and Methodist bishop. Muzorewa was educated at Methodist colleges in Rhodesia and Nashville, Tennessee. He was president of the African National Council 1971–85 and prime minister of Rhodesia/Zimbabwe 1979–80. He was detained for a year in 1983–84. He was leader of the minority United Africa National Council, which merged with the Zimbabwe Unity Movement (ZUM) 1994.

Mwinyi Ali Hassan (1925–). Tanzanian socialist politician, president from 1985, when he succeeded Julius Nyerere. He began a revival of private enterprise and control of state involvement and spending, and instituted a multi-party political system 1995.

Myers F(rederic) W(illiam) H(enry) (1843–1901). English psychic researcher and classical scholar who coined the word 'telepathy'. He was a founder 1882 and one of the first presidents, 1900, of the Society for Psychical Research.

Myers became an indefatigable investigator of the paranormal. He collaborated with Edmund Gurney (1847–1888) and Frank Podmore (1856–1910) on *Phantasms of the Living* 1886, the first thorough study of 'crisis' apparitions – cases in which a relevant apparition is 'seen' by someone roughly 12 hours either side of another's death or encounter with danger. His *Human Personality and its Survival of Bodily Death*, published posthumously 1903, is an account of 19th-century psychical reseach, dealing with, among other topics, sleep, hypnotism, genius, automatism, and telepathy.

Myrdal (Karl) Gunnar (1898–1987). Swedish economist, author of many works on development economics. He shared a Nobel prize in 1974.

Myron (c. 500–440 BC). Greek sculptor. His *Discobolus/Discus-Thrower* and *Athene and Marsyas*, much admired in his time, are known through Roman copies. They confirm his ancient reputation for brilliant composition and naturalism.

Myron was the first sculptor to enlarge the scope of realism, having great rhythm in his art and being careful in proportions.

Pliny the Elder on MYRON
in *Natural History* bk 34, ch 58

N

Nabokov Vladimir Vladimirovich (1899–1977). US writer. He left his native Russia 1917 and began writing in English in the 1940s. He settled in the USA 1940, and became a US citizen 1945. He was professor of Russian literature at Cornell University 1948–59, producing a translation and commentary on Pushkin's *Eugene Onegin* 1963. His most widely known book is *Lolita* 1955, the story of the middle-aged Humbert Humbert's infatuation with a precocious girl of 12. His other books, remarkable for their word play and ingenious plots, include *Laughter in the Dark* 1938, *The Real Life of Sebastian Knight* 1945, *Pnin* 1957, and his memoirs *Speak, Memory* 1947. He was also a lepidopterist (a collector of butterflies and moths), a theme used in his book *Pale Fire* 1962.

Suggested reading
Clancy, Laurie *The Novels of Vladimir Nabokov* (1984)
Rampton, David *Vladimir Nabokov: A Critical Study of the Novels* (1984)
Sharpe, Tony *Vladimir Nabokov* (1991)
Wood, Michael *The Magician's Doubts: Nabokov and the Risks of Fiction* (1994)

Nadar adopted name of Gaspard-Félix Tournachon (1820–1910). French portrait photographer and caricaturist. He took the first aerial photographs (from a balloon 1858) and was the first to take flash photographs (using magnesium bulbs).

Nadelman Elie (1882–1946). Polish-born sculptor, a US citizen from 1927. He is celebrated for his stylish, 'tubular' figures with doll-like faces and body parts that melt into flowing contours, as in *Man in the Open Air* about 1914–15 (Museum of Modern Art, New York).

Nadelman's first sculpture exhibitions, in Paris 1909 and New York 1914, caused a sensation in their espousal of a Modernist approach. He evolved his 'mannikins' of burlesque queens, dancers, circus performers, and society ladies in the USA from 1914. Frequently satirical in tone, the figures derived from the artist's interest in paring down the human figure to a smooth, almost boneless, curvilinear essence. His work influenced Art Deco design and such US painters as Guy Pène du Bois (1884–1958).

Nader Ralph (1934–). US lawyer and consumer advocate. Called the 'scourge of corporate morality', he led many major consumer campaigns. He investigated the lack of safety of color televisions, nuclear plants, and X-rays, as well as the procedures used by food and drug companies, overall job safety standards, and environmental pollution. The people who worked with and for him became known as 'Nader's Raiders.' Nader also co-wrote *Who's Poisoning America: Corporate Polluters and Their Victims in the Chemical Age* 1981 and *The Big Boys: Styles of Corporate Power* 1986. His book *Unsafe at Any Speed* 1965 led to US car-safety legislation.

Nadir Asil (1940–). Turkish Cypriot entrepreneur whose business interests in the UK and Cyprus made him one of Britain's 50 wealthiest people. He was declared bankrupt 1990 with estimated debts of £100 million. He was charged with theft and false accounting but jumped bail 1993 and returned to Cyprus. He was a major supporter of the Conservative Party, to which he donated over £400,000 in the 1990s.

Nadir Shah (Khan) (*c.* 1880–1933). King of Afghanistan from 1929. Nadir played a key role in the 1919 Afghan War, but was subsequently forced into exile in France. He returned to Kabul in 1929 to seize the throne and embarked on an ambitious modernization programme. This alienated the Muslim clergy and in 1933 he was assassinated by fundamentalists. His successor as king was his son Zahir Shah.

Nagel Ernest (1901–1985). Czech-born US philosopher who specialized in the philosophy of science and logic. He analysed the logical structure of scientific enquiries; and, in particular, he argued that the social sciences are capable of making useful general laws and explanations. His *The Structure of Science: Problems in the Logic of Scientific Explanation* 1961 is a classic in this field. He also held that the world contains no ultimate ingredients beyond matter. He was professor of philosophy at Columbia University.

Nagell Trygve (1895–). Norwegian mathematician whose most important work was in the fields of abstract algebra and number theory.

Nagell was born and educated in Oslo, and remained at Oslo university until 1931, when he became professor at Uppsala, Sweden, retiring 1962.

Nagell first made his name with a series of papers in the early 1920s on indeterminate equations, investigations which led to the publication of a treatise on indeterminate analysis in 1929. He also published papers and books, in Swedish and English, on number theory. From the late 1920s onwards his chief interest was the study of algebraic numbers, and his 1931 study of algebraic rings was perhaps his most important contribution to abstract algebra.

Nagumo Chuichi (1886–1944). Japanese admiral in World War II, commander of the Fast Carrier Striking Force which attacked Pearl Harbor Dec 1941. A cautious man, after his aircraft had made two raids against Pearl Harbor he refused to mount a third, as urged by his air commanders, which ensured the survival of the vast US Navy oil stores. Had these been destroyed, the US fleet would have been forced to retire to the US Pacific coast.

Nagumo entered the Indian Ocean April 1942, attacked British naval bases in Ceylon, and sank several British warships. He was decisively defeated at the Battle of Midway May 1942, but fared better in the Solomons and at Santa Cruz, although he lost much of his aircraft strength. He was relieved and sent to command the defences of Saipan, committing suicide when the island was successfully invaded by US forces July 1944.

Nagy Imre (1895–1958). Hungarian politician, prime minister 1953–55 and 1956. He led the Hungarian revolt against Soviet domination in 1956, for which he was executed.

Nagy, an Austro-Hungarian prisoner of war in Siberia during World War I, became a Soviet citizen after the Russian Revolution, and lived in the USSR 1930–44. In 1953, after Stalin's death, he became prime minister, introducing liberal measures such as encouraging the production of consumer goods, but was dismissed 1955 by hardline Stalinist premier Rákosi. Reappointed Oct 1956 during the Hungarian uprising, he began taking liberalization further than the Soviets wanted; for example, announcing Hungarian withdrawal from the Warsaw Pact. Soviet troops entered Budapest, and Nagy was dismissed Nov 1956. He was captured by the KGB and shot. In 1989 the Hungarian Supreme Court recognized his leadership of a legitimate government and quashed his conviction for treachery.

Nahayan Sheik Sultan bin Zayed al- (1918–). Emir of Abu Dhabi from 1969, when he deposed his brother, Sheik Shakhbut. He was elected president of the supreme council of the United Arab Emirates 1971. In 1991 he was implicated, through his majority ownership, in the international financial scandals associated with the Bank of Commerce and Credit International (BCCI), and in 1994 approved a payment by Abu Dhabi of $1.8 billion to BCCI creditors.

Before 1969 Sheik Nahayan was governor of the eastern province of Abu Dhabi, one of seven Trucial States in the Persian Gulf and Gulf of Oman, then under British protection. An absolute ruler, he was unanimously re-elected emir 1986 by other UAE sheiks, among whom he enjoys considerable popularity.

Nāhum (lived 7th century BC). In the Old Testament, a Hebrew prophet, possibly born in Galilee, who forecast the destruction of Nineveh, the Assyrian capital, by the Medes 612 BC.

I'm the kind of writer that people think other people are reading.

V S NAIPAUL
in *Radio Times* 1979

Naipaul V(idiadhar) S(urajprasad) (1932–). Trinidadian novelist living in Britain. His novels include *A House for Mr Biswas* 1961, *The Mimic Men* 1967, *A Bend in the River* 1979, *Finding the Centre* 1984, and *A Way in the World* 1994. His brother Srinivasa ('Shiva') Naipaul (1945–1985) was also a novelist (*Fireflies* 1970) and journalist.

Naismith James (1861–1939). Canadian-born inventor of basketball. He invented basketball as a game to be played indoors during the winter, while attending the Young Men's Christian Association (YMCA) Training School in Springfield, Massachusetts, USA, 1891. Among his books is *Basketball, Its Origin and Development*, published posthumously 1941.

Najibullah Ahmadzai (1947–1996). Afghan communist politician, leader of the People's Democratic Party of Afghanistan (PDPA) from 1986, and state president 1986–92. His government initially survived the withdrawal of Soviet troops Feb 1989, but continuing pressure from the Mujaheddin forces resulted in his overthrow.

A Pathan, Najibullah joined the communist PDPA 1965, allying with its gradualist Parcham (banner) faction, and was twice imprisoned for anti-government political activities during the 1960s and 1970s. After the Soviet invasion Dec 1979, Najibullah became head of the KHAD secret police and entered the PDPA Politburo 1981. He replaced Babrak Karmal as leader of the PDPA, and thus the nation, May 1986. His attempts to broaden the support of the PDPA regime had little success, and his hold on power became imperilled 1989 following the withdrawal of the Soviet military forces. The Mujaheddin continued to demand his resignation and resisted any settlement under his regime. In the spring of 1992, he was captured while attempting to flee the country and placed under United Nations protection, pending trial by an Islamic court. He was executed 1996 by the Talibaan government.

Nakasone Yasuhiro (1918–). Japanese conservative politician, leader of the Liberal Democratic Party (LDP) and prime minister 1982–87. He stepped up military spending and increased Japanese participation in international affairs, with closer ties to the USA. He encouraged a less paternalist approach to economic management. Although embarrassed by the conviction of one of his supporters in the 1983 Lockheed corruption scandal, he was re-elected 1986 by a landslide. He was forced to resign his party post May 1989 as a result of having profited from insider trading in the Recruit scandal. After serving a two-year period of atonement, he rejoined the LDP April 1991.

Nakian Reuben (1897–). US sculptor. His rough, freely improvised work of the 1950s linked him to action painting, though figurative references (usually to mythology) remain. From the 1960s he produced more abstract, generally monumental sculptures, cast in bronze from plaster and chicken-wire maquettes, for example, *Goddess of the Golden Thighs* 1964–65 (Detroit Institute of Arts, Detroit).

Namath Joe (Joseph William) (1943–). US football player. Born in Beaver Falls, Pennsylvania, Namath played quarterback for the University of Alabama, leading his team to victory in the 1965 Orange Bowl. In 1965 he signed with the New York Jets of the newly established American Football League and in 1969 led the team to a historic upset victory over the Baltimore Colts in Super Bowl III. After leaving the Jets 1977, he briefly played with the Los Angeles Rams. Knee injuries forced his retirement as a player 1978.

Namatjira Albert (1902–1959). Australian Aboriginal painter. He created watercolour landscapes of the Australian interior. Acclaimed after an exhibition in Melbourne 1938, he died destitute.

Namier Lewis Bernstein (Ludwik Bernsztajn vel Niemirowski) (1888–1960). Polish-born British historian. After arriving in Britain 1906, Namier studied at Oxford. During World War I he worked in the Foreign Office, and thereafter in business, while preparing his two major studies of 18th-century British politics. Their success led to his appointment as professor of history at Manchester University 1931–53. His chief works, *The Structure of Politics at the Accession of George III* 1929 and *England in the Age of the American Revolution* 1930, challenged accepted interpretations of 18th-century British history in terms of Whig–Tory rivalry. Knighted 1952.

He also made contributions to the study of 19th-century European history, in particular with *1848: The Revolution of the Intellectuals* 1946, and wrote many essays and reviews collected in *Avenues of History* 1952, *Personalities and Powers* 1955, and *Vanished Supremacies* 1958.

Namuth Hans (1915–1990). German-born US photographer. He specialized in portraits and documentary work. He began as a photojournalist in Europe in the 1930s and opened a portrait studio in New York 1950. His work includes documentation of the Guatemalan Mam Indians (published as *Los Todos Santeros* 1989) and of US artists from the 1950s (published as *Artists 1950–1981*). He also carried out assignments for magazines.

Nanak (1469–c. 1539). Indian guru and founder of Sikhism, a religion based on the unity of God and the equality of all human beings. He was strongly opposed to caste divisions.

Greatly influenced by Islamic mysticism (Sufism), Nanak preached a new path of release from the Hindu cycle of rebirth and caste divisions through sincere meditation on the name of God. He is revered by Sikhs ('disciples') as the first of their ten gurus (religious teachers). At 50, after many years travelling and teaching, he established a new town in the Punjab called Kartarpur, where many people came to live as his disciples. On his deathbed, Guru Nanak announced his friend Lehna as his successor, and gave him the name Angad ('part of me').

Nana Sahib popular name for Dandhu Panth (1820–c. 1859). The adopted son of a former peshwa (chief minister) of the Maratha people of central India, he joined the rebels in the Indian Mutiny 1857–58, and was responsible for the massacre at Kanpur when safe conducts given to British civilians were broken and many women and children massacred. After the failure of the mutiny he took refuge in Nepal.

Nancarrow Conlon (1912–). US composer. He settled in Mexico 1940. Using a player-piano as a form of synthesizer, punching the rolls by hand, he experimented with mathematically derived combinations of rhythm and tempo in *37 Studies for Piano-Player* 1950–68, works of a hypnotic persistence that aroused the admiration of a younger generation of minimalist composers.

Nanni di Banco (c. 1384–1421). Florentine sculptor. He worked on several of the great civic commissions of 15th-century Florence. He remained independent of Donatello's sculptural innovations, using conservative techniques to create classical imagery. His major work, commissioned for a niche at Orsanmichele, is *Quattro Santi Coronati* about 1413, a group of four Roman sculptors who were also Christian martyrs. His relief *Assumption* 1414–21 over the Porta della Mandorla of Florence Cathedral prefigures Baroque style. But for an early death, his career might have rivalled Donatello's.

Nansen Fridtjof (1861–1930). Norwegian explorer and scientist. He made his first voyage to Greenland waters in a sealing ship 1882, and in 1888–89 attempted to cross the Greenland icefield. In 1893, he sailed to the Arctic in the *Fram*, which was deliberately allowed to drift north with an iceflow. Nansen, accompanied by F Hjalmar Johansen (1867–1923), continued north on foot and reached 86° 14′ N, the highest latitude then attained. He was professor of zoology and oceanography at the University of Christiania (now Oslo) and Norwegian ambassador in London 1906–08. After World War I, Nansen became League of Nations high commissioner for refugees. Nobel Peace Prize 1923. The *Nansen passport* issued to stateless persons is named after him.

Suggested reading
Scott, James *Fridtjof Nansen* (1971)
Shackleton, Edward *Nansen the Explorer* (1959)
Vogt, Per and others *Nansen: Explorer, Scientist, Humanitarian* (1962)

Naoroji Dadabhai (1825–1917). Indian-born British politician. A founder-member of the Indian National Congress, he left India 1886 to seek a seat in Parliament, which he achieved as Liberal for Finsbury Central 1892, the first black British MP. A Parsee, he was a teacher of mathematics in Bombay prior to leaving for the UK.

Peccavi [I have Sind].

CHARLES JAMES NAPIER
Punning message announcing his victory at Hyderabad
1843 which meant the capture of the Indian province of Sind

Napier Charles James (1782–1853). British general. He conquered Sind in India (now a province of Pakistan) 1841–43 with a very small force and governed it until 1847. He was the first commander to mention men from the ranks in his dispatches. KCB 1838.

Napier John, 8th Laird of Merchiston (1550–1617). Scottish mathematician who invented logarithms 1614 and 'Napier's bones', an early mechanical calculating device for multiplication and division. It was Napier who first used and then popularized the decimal point to separate the whole number part from the fractional part of a number.

Napier was born in Merchiston Castle, near Edinburgh, and studied at St Andrews. He never occupied any professional post.

English mathematician Henry Briggs went to Edinburgh in 1616 and later to discuss the logarithmic tables with Napier. Together they worked out improvements, such as the idea of using the base ten.

Napier also made advances in scientific farming, especially by the use of salt as a fertilizer. In 1597 he patented a hydraulic screw by means of which water could be removed from flooded coal pits.

Napier published a denunciation of the Roman Catholic Church, *A Plaine Discovery of the Whole Revelation of St John* 1593, as well as *Mirifici logarithmorum canonis descriptio/Description of the Marvellous Canon of Logarithms* 1614 and *Mirifici logarithmorum canonis constructio* 1619. In *Rabdologiae* ('numeration by little rods') 1617 he explained his mechanical calculating system and showed how square roots could be extracted by the manipulation of counters on a chessboard.

Napier Robert Cornelis, 1st Baron Napier of Magdala (1810–1890). British field marshal. Knighted for his services in relieving Lucknow during the Indian Mutiny, he took part in capturing Peking (Beijing) during the war against China in 1860. He was commander in chief in India 1870–76 and governor of Gibraltar 1876–82. KCB 1859, baron 1868.

Napoleon I (Napoleon Bonaparte) (1769–1821). Emperor of the French 1804–14 and 1814–15. A general from 1796 in the Revolutionary Wars, in 1799 he overthrew the ruling Directory and made himself dictator. From 1803 he conquered most of Europe

---

England is a nation of shopkeepers.

NAPOLEON I
Attributed remark

(the Napoleonic Wars) and installed his brothers as puppet kings. After the Peninsular War and retreat from Moscow 1812, he was forced to abdicate 1814 and was banished to the island of Elba. In March 1815 he reassumed power but was defeated by British and Prussian forces at the Battle of Waterloo and exiled to the island of St Helena. His internal administrative reforms and laws are still evident in France.

Napoleon, born in Ajaccio, Corsica, received a commission in the artillery 1785 and first distinguished himself at the siege of Toulon 1793. Having suppressed a royalist uprising in Paris 1795, he was given command against the Austrians in Italy and defeated them at Lodi, Arcole, and Rivoli 1796–97. Egypt, seen as a halfway house to India, was overrun and Syria invaded, but his fleet was destroyed by the British admiral Nelson at the Battle of the Nile. Napoleon returned to France and carried out a coup against the government of the Directory to establish his own dictatorship, nominally as First Consul. The Austrians were again defeated at Marengo 1800 and the coalition against France shattered, a truce being declared 1802. A plebiscite the same year made him consul for life. In 1804 a plebiscite made him emperor.

My dear general, you are certainly an excellent soldier; but, in regard to music, you must excuse me if I don't think it necessary to adapt my compositions to your comprehension.

Luigi Cherubini to NAPOLEON I
quoted in Edward Bellasis *Cherubini* 1874

While retaining and extending the legal and educational reforms of the Jacobins, Napoleon replaced the democratic constitution established by the Revolution with a centralized despotism, and by his concordat with Pius VII conciliated the Catholic church. The Code Napoléon remains the basis of French law.

War was renewed by Britain 1803, aided by Austria and Russia from 1805 and Prussia from 1806. Prevented by the British navy from invading Britain, Napoleon drove Austria out of the war by victories at Ulm and Austerlitz 1805, and Prussia by the victory at Jena 1806. Then, after the battles of Eylau and Friedland, he formed an alliance with Russia at Tilsit 1807. Napoleon now forbade entry of British goods to Europe, attempting an economic blockade known as the Continental System, occupied Portugal, and in 1808 placed his brother Joseph on the Spanish throne. Both countries revolted, with British aid, and Austria attempted to re-enter the war but was defeated at Wagram. In 1796 Napoleon had married Josephine de Beauharnais, but in 1809, to assert his equality with the Habsburgs, he divorced her to marry the Austrian emperor's daughter, Marie Louise.

When Russia failed to enforce the Continental System, Napoleon marched on and occupied Moscow, but his army's retreat in the bitter winter of 1812 encouraged Prussia and Austria to declare war again 1813. He was defeated at Leipzig and driven from Germany. Despite his brilliant campaign on French soil, the Allies invaded Paris and compelled him to abdicate April 1814; he was banished to the island of Elba, off the west coast of Italy. In March 1815 he escaped and took power for a hundred days, with the aid of Marshal Ney, but Britain and Prussia led an alliance against him at Waterloo, Belgium, in June. Surrendering to the British, he again abdicated, and was exiled to the island of St Helena, 1,900 km/1,200 mi west of Africa, where he died. His body was brought back 1840 to be interred in the Hôtel des Invalides, Paris.

Suggested reading
Castelot, A *Napoleon* (1971)
Chandler, D *Napoleon* (1973)
Connelly, O *Blundering to Glory: Napoleon's Military Campaigns* (1987)
Geyl, P *Napoleon, For and Against* (1965)
Jones, R B *Napoleon: Man and Myth* (1977)
Kafker, F and Laux, J *Napoleon and his Times* (1988)
Lachouque, H *The Anatomy of Glory: Napoleon and his Guard* (1978)

Napoleon II (born François Charles Joseph Bonaparte) (1811–1832). Title given by the Bonapartists to the son of Napoleon I and Marie Louise; until 1814 he was known as the king of Rome and after 1818 as the duke of Reichstadt. After his father's abdication 1814 he was taken to the Austrian court, where he spent the rest of his life.

We must not seek to fashion events, but let them happen of their own accord.

NAPOLEON III
to Bismarck at Biarritz 4 Oct 1865

Napoleon III (born Charles Louis Napoleon Bonaparte) (1808–1873). Emperor of the French 1852–70, known as Louis-Napoleon. After two attempted coups (1836 and 1840) he was jailed, then went into exile, returning for the revolution of 1848, when he became president of the Second Republic but proclaimed himself emperor 1852. In 1870 he was manoeuvred by the German chancellor Bismarck into war with Prussia; he was forced to surrender at Sedan, NE France, and the empire collapsed.

The son of Louis Bonaparte and Hortense de Beauharnais, brother and step-daughter respectively of Napoleon I, he led two unsuccessful revolts against the French king Louis Philippe, at Strasbourg 1836 and at Boulogne 1840. After the latter he was imprisoned. Escaping in 1846, he lived in London until 1848. He was elected president of the newly established French republic in Dec, and set himself to secure a following by posing as the champion of order and religion against the revolutionary menace. He secured his re-election by a military coup d'état 1851, and a year later was proclaimed emperor. Hoping to strengthen his regime by military triumphs, he joined in the Crimean War 1854–55, waged war with Austria 1859, winning the Battle of Solferino, annexed Savoy and Nice 1860, and attempted unsuccessfully to found a vassal empire in Mexico 1863–67. In so doing he aroused the mistrust of Europe and isolated France.

At home, his regime was discredited by its notorious corruption; republican and socialist opposition grew, in spite of severe repression, and forced Napoleon, after 1860, to make concessions in the direction of parliamentary government. After losing the war with Prussia he withdrew to England, where he died. His son by Empress Eugénie, Eugène Louis Jean Joseph Napoleon, Prince Imperial (1856–79), was killed fighting with the British army against the Zulus in Africa.

Narayan Jaya Prakash (1902–1979). Indian politician. A veteran socialist, he was an associate of Vinobha Bham in the Bhoodan movement for rural reforms that took place during the last years of the Raj. He was prominent in the protest movement against Indira Gandhi's emergency regime 1975–77, and acted as umpire in the Janata party leadership contest that followed Indira Gandhi's defeat in 1977.

Narayan R(asipuram) K(rishnaswamy) (1906–   ). Indian novelist. He was brought up (in Mysore) on classical Indian tales and Vedic poetry. His immensely popular novels, notably *Swami and Friends* 1935, his first, and *The Man-Eater of Malgudi* 1962, successfully combine Realism with mythic and grotesque elements. They are comedies of sadness, of the family and middle-class life, set in 'Malgudi', intensely local yet representative of India and indeed of humanity. A more recent work is *The Grandmother's Tale* 1992. His vivid autobiographical sketches 'My Days' were published 1974.

Nares George Strong (1831–1915). Scottish vice-admiral and explorer who sailed to the Canadian Arctic on an expedition in search of English explorer John Franklin 1852, and again in 1876 when he discovered the Challenger Mountains. During 1872–76 he commanded the Challenger Expedition. His Arctic explorations are recounted in *Voyage to the Polar Seas* 1878. KCB 1876.

Narses (c. 478–c. 573). Byzantine general. Originally a eunuch slave, he later became an official in the imperial treasury. He was joint commander with the Roman general Belisarius in Italy 538–39, and in 552 destroyed the Ostrogoths at Taginae in the Apennines.

Narses so venerated God that the Virgin Mary commanded him when to fight.

Evagrius on NARSES
in *Ecclesiastical History* 4.24.

Narváez Pánfilo de (c. 1480–1525). Spanish conquistador and explorer. Narváez was largely responsible for bringing Cuba under Spanish control 1511. The governor of Cuba sent him to Mexico 1520 to reassert authority over Hernán Cortés. Defeated, he was held captive for two years. He drowned during an expedition to Florida after a fruitless detour for gold split his party.

Nash 'Beau' (Richard) (1674–1762). British dandy. As master of ceremonies at Bath from 1705, he made the town a fashionable spa resort, and introduced a polished code of manners into polite society.

Candy / Is dandy / But liquor / Is quicker.

OGDEN NASH
'Reflections on Ice-breaking'

Nash (Frederic) Ogden (1902–1971). US poet and wit. He published numerous volumes of humorous, quietly satirical light verse, characterized by unorthodox rhymes and puns. They include *I'm a Stranger Here Myself* 1938, *Versus* 1949, and *Bed Riddance* 1970. Most of his poems first appeared in the *New Yorker* magazine, where he held an editorial post and did much to establish the magazine's tone.

Nash John (1752–1835). English architect. In the first phase of his career he was best known for designing country houses, using a wide variety of styles. Later he laid out Regent's Park, London, and its approaches, a vast grandiose scheme of terraces and crescents and palatial-style houses with ornate stucco façades. He also laid out Trafalgar Square and St James's Park. Between 1811 and 1821 he planned Regent Street (later rebuilt), repaired and enlarged Buckingham Palace (for which he designed Marble Arch), and rebuilt the Royal Pavilion, Brighton, in flamboyant oriental style.

Nash John Northcote (1893–1977). English illustrator, landscape artist, and engraver. He was the brother of the artist Paul Nash.

Nash Paul (1889–1946). English painter. He was an official war artist in World Wars I and II. In his pictures of World War I, such as *The Menin Road*, in the Imperial War Museum, he created strange patterns out of the scorched landscape of the Western Front. In the 1930s he was one of a group of artists promoting avant-garde style, and was deeply influenced by Surrealism. Two works which illustrate the visionary quality of his paintings are *Totes Meer/Dead Sea* 1940–41 (Tate Gallery, London) and *Solstice of the Sunflower* 1945 (National Gallery of Canada, Ottawa). 'Structural purpose' was an aim which led him into many forms of design, for textiles, ceramics, the stage and the book, but the Surrealist trend of the 1930s and the exhibition of 1936 brought out an imaginative and poetic feeling already apparent in his oils and watercolours.

Although quite extraordinarily energetic, he was almost equally dilatory in making decisions ... he seemed too absorbed in details rather than in broad policy decisions.

Keith Sinclair on WALTER NASH
in *Dictionary of National Biography*

Nash Walter (1882–1968). New Zealand Labour politician. He was born in England, and emigrated to New Zealand 1909. He held ministerial posts 1935–49, was prime minister 1957–60, and leader of the Labour Party until 1963. GCMG 1965.

Nashe Thomas (1567–1601). English poet, satirist, and anti-Puritan pamphleteer. Born in Suffolk, he settled in London about 1588, where he was rapidly drawn into the Martin Marprelate controversy (a pamphleteering attack on the clergy of the Church of England by Puritans), and wrote at least three attacks on the Martinists. Among his later works are the satirical *Pierce Pennilesse* 1592 and the religious *Christes Teares over Jerusalem* 1593; his *The Unfortunate Traveller* 1594 is a picaresque narrative mingling literary parody and mock-historical fantasy.

Brightness falls from the air; | Queens have died young and fair; | Dust hath closed Helen's eye.

THOMAS NASHE
'In Time of Pestilence'

Nasmyth Alexander (1758–1840). Scottish portrait and landscape painter. He is regarded as the creator of the Scottish landscape-painting tradition. Born in Edinburgh, he concentrated from 1806 on landscapes, usually Classical and Italianate. Alexander settled in London, *c.* 1797, and his landscapes of southern England earned him the title of the 'English Hobbema'. His portrait of the poet Robert Burns hangs in the Scottish National Gallery. His son, Patrick (1787–1831), was also a painter.

Nasmyth James (1808–1890). Scottish engineer and machine-tool manufacturer whose many inventions included the steam hammer 1839 for making large steel forgings.

Nasmyth was born in Edinburgh and left school at the age of 12. As assistant to English toolmaker Henry Maudslay, he devised a flexible shaft of coiled spring steel for drilling holes in awkward places. After the death of Maudslay 1831, Nasmyth set up his own workshop, first in Edinburgh, then in Manchester, manufacturing machine tools, locomotives, and other machinery. His steam hammer was first used to make the propeller shaft for Isambard Kingdom Brunel's steamship *Great Britain*.

Nasmyth devised many other tools, including a vertical cylinder-boring machine which speeded up the production of steam engines, and all manner of lateral, transverse, and rotating cutting machines.

Nasrin Tashima (1962–). Bangladeshi writer and feminist, in exile from 1994. Accused of blasphemy, and charged with insulting religious sentiments, she has been subject to death threats and mass demonstrations since the publication 1993 of her novel *Lajja/Shame*, dealing with Muslim–Hindu conflict. The book has been banned in Sri Lanka. In 1993–94 'fatwa' calls for her death were issued, and a price put on her head. She has also criticised Sharia law.

Born in Myrmensingh, she trained as an anaesthetist, and began writing a syndicated newspaper column 1990 about religious intolerance and the oppression of women. She has also published several volumes of poetry.

Nasser Gamal Abdel (1918–1970). Egyptian politician, prime minister 1954–56 and from 1956 president of Egypt (the United Arab Republic 1958–71). Nasser entered the army from Cairo Military Academy, and was wounded in the Palestine War of 1948–49. In 1952 he was the driving power behind the Neguib coup, which ended the monarchy. Initially unpopular after the coup, he took advantage of demands for change by initiating land reform and depoliticizing the army. His position was secured by an unsuccessful assassination attempt 1954. His nationalization of the Suez Canal 1956 led to an Anglo-French invasion and the Suez Crisis, and his ambitions for an Egyptian-led union of Arab states led to disquiet in the Middle East (and in the West). Nasser was also an early and influential leader of the nonaligned movement.

Suggested reading
Baker, R W *Egypt's Uncertain Revolution Under Nasser and Sadat* (1978)
Hasou, T Y *The Struggle for the Arab World: Egypt's Nasser and the Arab League* (1985)
Vatikiotis, P J *Nasser and His Generation* (1978)

Nast Thomas (1840–1902). German-born US illustrator and cartoonist. During the American Civil War, Nast served as a staff artist for *Harper's Weekly* and later drew its editorial cartoons. His vivid caricatures helped bring down New York's Boss Tweed and established the donkey and the elephant as the symbols of Democrats and Republicans, respectively.

Nastase Ilie (1946–). Romanian lawn-tennis player who won the US Open singles title in 1972 and the French Open in 1973. He also won five Grand Slam doubles titles.

Nathans Daniel (1928–). US microbiologist who shared the 1978 Nobel Prize for Physiology or Medicine with his colleague Hamilton Smith for their work on restriction enzymes, special enzymes that can cleave genes into fragments.

From 1962 he worked at Johns Hopkins University, Baltimore, becoming director of the Department of Microbiology 1972.

In addition to the work done with Smith, Nathans also performed much original research of his own in this field. Using the carcinogenic SV40 virus, he showed in 1971 that it could be cleaved into 11 specific fragments, and in the following year he determined the order of these fragments.

Nation Carrie Amelia Moore (1846–1911). US Temperance Movement crusader during the Prohibition 1920–33. Born in Kentucky, she briefly worked as a teacher in Missouri. After the death of her alcoholic first husband, she became the country's most outspoken prohibitionist. She circulated *Smasher's Mail* as part of her campaign. Protesting against Kansas state's flagrant disregard for the prohibition law, she marched into illegal saloons with a hatchet, lecturing the patrons on the abuses of alcohol and smashing bottles and bar.

Natsume Sōseki pen name of Natsume Kinnosuke (1867–1916). Japanese novelist. A brilliant student and teacher of English, he responded discerningly to the pervasive new European influences of his era, depicted the plight of the alienated Japanese intellectual, and ushered in the modern Japanese novel. He explored the isolation and frustration of well-educated protagonists in works such as *Mon/The Gate* 1910, *Kojin/The Wayfarer* 1912–13, and *Kokoro* 1914.

Natta Giulio (1903–). Italian chemist who worked on the production of polymers. He shared a Nobel prize 1963 with German chemist Karl Ziegler. Natta's early work on heterogeneous catalysts formed the basis for many important industrial syntheses.

After holding professorships at Pavia, Rome, and Turin, he returned to Milan Polytechnic 1938 as director of the Industrial Chemistry Research Institute, to work on artificial rubber. In 1953 he became a consultant to Montecatini, a company that had a licence arrangement with Ziegler.

Navratilova Martina (1956–). Czech tennis player who became a naturalized US citizen 1981. The most outstanding woman player of the 1980s, she had 55 Grand Slam victories by 1991, including 18 singles titles. She won the Wimbledon singles title a record nine times, including six in succession 1982–87. She was defeated by Conchita Martinez in the final of her last Wimbledon as a singles player 1994.

Navratilova won her first Wimbledon title in 1976 (doubles with Chris Evert). Between 1974 and 1988 she won 52 Grand Slam titles (singles and doubles), second only to Margaret Court. Her first Grand Slam win was mixed doubles at the 1974 French Championship (with Ivan Molina, Colombia).

Nazarbaev Nursultan Abishevich (1940–). President of Kazakhstan from 1990. In the Soviet period he was prime minister of the republic 1984–89 and leader of the Kazakh Communist Party 1989–91, which established itself as the independent Socialist Party of Kazakhstan Sept 1991. He is an advocate of free-market policies, and yet also enjoys the support of the environmentalist lobby. He joined the Communist Party at 22 and left it after the failed Soviet coup 1991.

N'Dour Youssou (1959–). Senegalese singer, songwriter, and musician. His fusion of traditional *mbalax* percussion music with bluesy Arab-style vocals, accompanied by African and electronic instruments, became popular in the West in the 1980s on albums such as *Immigrés* 1984 with the band Le Super Etoile de Dakar.

Neagle Anna (born (Florence) Marjorie Robertson) (1904–1986). English actress. She was made a star by her producer-director husband Herbert Wilcox (1890–1977). Her films include *Nell Gwyn* 1934, *Victoria the Great* 1937, and *Odette* 1950. DBE 1969.

Neale John Mason (1818–1866). Anglican cleric. He translated ancient and medieval hymns, including 'Jerusalem, the Golden'.

> *He expected his friends to live up to his own high standards of integrity. He would always say when he did not know.*
>
> John Tilney on AIREY NEAVE
> in *Dictionary of National Biography*

Neave Airey Middleton Sheffield (1916–1979). British intelligence officer and Conservative member of Parliament 1953–79, a close adviser to former prime minister Margaret Thatcher. During World War II he escaped from Colditz, a German high-security prison camp. As shadow undersecretary of state for Northern Ireland from 1975, he became a target for extremist groups and was assassinated by an Irish terrorist bomb.

> *Is not this Babylon the great, which I have built as a royal residence by my own mighty power and for the honour of my majesty.*
>
> NEBUCHADNEZZAR
> in the Bible, Daniel 4:30

Nebuchadnezzar or Nebuchadrezzar II (*c.* 630–*c.* 562 BC). King of Babylonia from 604 BC. Shortly before his accession he defeated the Egyptians at Carchemish and brought Palestine and Syria into his empire. Judah revolted, with Egyptian assistance, 596 and 587–586 BC; on both occasions he captured Jerusalem and took many Hebrews into captivity. He largely rebuilt Babylon and constructed the hanging gardens.

Necker Jacques (1732–1804). French politician. As finance minister 1776–81, he attempted reforms, and was dismissed through Queen Marie Antoinette's influence. Recalled 1788, he persuaded

Nehru The Indian politician and prime minister Jawaharlal Nehru, with his daughter Indira Gandhi 1940. Nehru played an important part in the negotiations for an independent India, and became its first prime minister 1947. (Image Select)

Louis XVI to summon the States General (parliament), which earned him the hatred of the court, and in July 1789 he was banished. The outbreak of the French Revolution with the storming of the Bastille forced his reinstatement, but he resigned Sept 1790.

> *Chinese civilization has the overpowering beauty of the wholly other, and only the wholly other can inspire the deepest love and the profoundest desire to learn.*
>
> JOSEPH NEEDHAM
> *The Grand Titration* 1970

Needham Joseph (1900–1995). English biochemist and sinologist, historian of Chinese science. He worked first on problems in embryology. In the 1930s he learned Chinese and began to collect material. The first volume of his *Science and Civilization in China* was published 1954 and by 1990 sixteen volumes had appeared.

Needham was born in London and studied at Cambridge, where he spent his academic career. The arrival of some Chinese biochemists 1936 prompted him to learn their language, and in 1942–46 he travelled through China as head of the British Scientific Mission. From 1946 to 1948 he was head of the Division of Natural Sciences at the United Nations, after which he returned to Cambridge.

In *Chemical Embryology* 1931, Needham concluded that embryonic development is controlled chemically. The discovery of morphogenetic hormones and later of the genetic material DNA confirmed this view.

Needham became increasingly interested in the history of science, particularly of Chinese science, and he progressively reduced his biochemical investigations. *Science and Civilization in China* is a huge synthesis of history, science, and culture in China.

Nefertiti or Nofretete (14th century BC). Queen of Egypt and wife of the pharaoh Akhenaton.

She disappeared from the records about 12 years after the marriage, and her name was defaced on monuments at some later date. A small gold scarab bearing her name, inscribed within the royal cartouche that marks the name of a pharaoh, was recovered in 1986 from an ancient wreck and suggests that she briefly ruled in her own right.

Nègre Charles (1820–1880). French photographer. Originally a painter, he turned to photography after learning the waxed paper process from Gustave Le Gray 1851. He began by producing everyday street scenes as studies for his paintings but soon embarked on a series of documentary projects which included studies of Chartres Cathedral, Provence, and the Imperial Asylum at Vincennes.

Nehemiah (5th century BC). Hebrew governor of Judaea under Persian rule. He rebuilt Jerusalem's walls 444 BC, and made religious and social reforms.

Nehru Jawaharlal (1889–1964). Indian nationalist politician, prime minister from 1947. Before the partition (the division of British India into India and Pakistan), he led the socialist wing of the nationalist Congress Party, and was second in influence only to Mahatma Gandhi. He was imprisoned nine times by the British 1921–45 for political activities. As prime minister from the creation of the dominion (later republic) of India in Aug 1947, he originated the idea of nonalignment (neutrality towards major powers). His daughter was Prime Minister Indira Gandhi. His sister, Vijaya Lakshmi Pandit (1900–1990) was the UN General Assembly's first female president (1953–54).

Suggested reading
Ali, Tariq *Nehru and the Gandhis* (1985)
Gopal, Sarvepalli *Jawaharlal Nehru: A Biography* (1975)
Gorev, A *Jawaharlal Nehru* (1982)
Nanda, B *The Nehrus* (1962)

Neill A(lexander) S(utherland) (1883–1973). Scottish educationist. In 1924, partly in reaction to his own repressive upbringing, he founded a school, Summerhill, where liberal and progressive ideas such as self-government by pupils and the voluntary attendance of lessons achieved remarkable results, especially with problem children.

Neizvestny Ernst Iosifovich (1925–). Russian artist and sculptor. He argued with the Soviet premier Khrushchev 1962 and eventually left the country 1976. His works include a vast relief in the Moscow Institute of Electronics and the Aswan monument in Egypt, the tallest sculpture in the world.

Nekrasov Nikolai Alekseevich (1821–1878). Russian poet and publisher. He espoused the cause of the freeing of the serfs and identified himself with the peasants in such poems as 'Who Can Live Happy in Russia?' 1876.

Nelson Azumah (1958–). Ghanaian featherweight boxer, world champion from 1984 to 1987. Nelson won the 1978 Commonwealth Games at featherweight, the World Boxing Championship (WBC) featherweight title in 1984, beating Wilfredo Gomez, and in 1988 captured the super-featherweight title by beating Mario Martinez.

You must hate a Frenchman as you hate the devil.

Said by NELSON to a midshipman under his command on HMS *Agamemnon* in the western Mediterranean 1793 and quoted in Robert Southey *Life of Nelson* ch 3 1813

Nelson Horatio, 1st Viscount Nelson (1758–1805). English admiral. He joined the navy in 1770. In the Revolutionary Wars against France he lost the sight in his right eye 1794 and lost his right arm 1797. He became a national hero, and rear admiral, after the victory off Cape St Vincent, Portugal. In 1798 he tracked the French fleet to Aboukir Bay where he almost entirely destroyed it.

Nelson was almost continuously on active service in the Mediterranean 1793–1800, and lingered at Naples for a year, during which he helped to crush a democratic uprising and fell completely under the influence of Lady Hamilton. In 1800 he returned to England and soon after separated from his wife, Frances Nisbet (1761–1831). He was promoted to vice admiral 1801, and sent to the Baltic to operate against the Danes, nominally as second in command; in fact, it was Nelson who was responsible for the victory of Copenhagen and for negotiating peace with Denmark. In 1803 he received the Mediterranean command and for nearly two years blockaded Toulon. When in 1805 his opponent, the French admiral Pierre de Villeneuve (1763–1806), eluded him, Nelson pursued him to the West Indies and back, and on 21 Oct defeated the combined French and Spanish fleets off Cape Trafalgar, 20 of the enemy ships being captured. Nelson himself was mortally wounded. He is buried in St Paul's Cathedral, London. KB 1797, baron 1798, viscount 1801.
Suggested reading
Hattersley, Roy *Nelson* (1974)
Hibbert, Christopher *Nelson: A Personal History* (1994)
Howarth, D and S *Lord Nelson: The Immortal Hero* (1989)
Lloyd, C *Nelson and Sea Power* (1973)
Pocock, T *Horatio Nelson* (1987)
Warner, O *A Portrait of Lord Nelson* (1988)

Nelson Willie (1933–). US country and western singer, songwriter, and guitarist. He first made an impact in the mid-1970s as a pioneer of the Texas 'outlaw' school of country music that rejected string overdubs, suits, and surface gloss. His albums include *Shotgun Willie* 1973, *Always On My Mind* 1982, and *Across the Borderline* 1993. He also had many joint successes with Waylon Jennings (1937–), including 'Mamas, Don't Let Your Babies Grow Up to Be Cowboys' 1978.

Nemerov Howard Stanley (1920–). US poet, critic, and novelist. He published his poetry collection *Guide to the Ruins* 1950, a short-story collection *A Commodity of Dreams* 1959, and *Collected Poems* 1977, which won both the National Book Award and the Pulitzer Prize 1978. Later poetry includes *Trying Conclusions* 1991.

Nennius (lived *c.* 800). Welsh historian, believed to be the author of a Latin *Historia Britonum*, which contains the earliest reference to King Arthur's wars against the Saxons.

The Historia Britonum is of interest as presenting a distinctively British perspective on the events of the fourth to the seventh centuries.

Richard Fletcher on NENNIUS
in *Who's Who in Roman Britain and Anglo-Saxon England* 1989

Nernst (Walther) Hermann (1864–1941). German physical chemist who won a Nobel prize 1920 for work on heat changes in chemical reactions. He proposed in 1906 the principle known as the *Nernst heat theorem* or the third law of thermodynamics: chemical changes at the temperature of absolute zero involve no change of entropy (disorder).

He became professor of chemistry at Göttingen 1894, moving to Berlin 1905. During World War I, he was the first scientist to propose using chemical agents as a weapon.

In solution chemistry, every pH measurement depends on theories Nernst presented in the 1880s, as does the use and theory of indicators and buffer solutions.

In 1911, with British physicist Frederick Lindemann (later Lord Cherwell), Nernst constructed a special calorimeter for measuring specific heats at low temperatures.

With German chemist Fritz Haber he studied equilibria in commercially important gas reactions, such as the reversible reaction between hydrogen and carbon dioxide to form water and carbon monoxide. In 1918, Nernst investigated reactions that are initiated by light.

Having invented a substitute for the carbon filament in an electric lamp 1897, Nernst used the money from his patent to become a pioneer motorist. Many early automobiles had difficulty climbing hills, but Nernst devised a method of injecting nitrous oxide (dinitrogen monoxide) into the cylinders when the engine got into difficulties. In the 1920s he invented a 'Neo-Bechstein' piano which amplified sounds produced at low amplitudes.

His *Theoretische Chemie/Theoretical Chemistry* 1895 became a standard textbook.

But above all he was carried away by a craze for popularity and he was jealous of all who in any way stirred the feeling of the mob.

Suetonius on NERO
in *Nero* ch 53

Nero adopted name of Lucius Domitius Ahenobarbus (AD 37–68). Roman emperor from 54. Son of Domitius Ahenobarbus and Agrippina, Nero was adopted by Claudius, and succeeded him as emperor. He was a poet and connoisseur of art, and performed publicly as an actor and a singer. In 59 he had his mother Agrippina and his wife Octavia put to death. The great fire at Rome 64 was blamed on the Christians, whom he subsequently persecuted. In 65 a plot against Nero was discovered. Further revolts followed 68, and he committed suicide.
Suggested reading
Grant, Michael *Nero: Emperor in Revolt* (1970)
Griffin, Miriam *Nero: The End of a Dynasty* (1985)

Neruda Pablo. Pen name of Neftalí Ricardo Reyes y Basualto (1904–1973). Chilean poet and diplomat. After World War II he entered political life in Chile as a communist, and was a senator 1945–48. He went into exile in 1948 but returned in 1952. His work includes lyrics and the epic poem of the American continent *Canto General* 1950. He was awarded the Nobel Prize for Literature 1971. He served as consul and ambassador to many countries.
Suggested reading
Agosin, M *Pablo Neruda* (1986)
Costa, R de *The Poetry of Pablo Neruda* (1979)

Durán, Manuel and Safir, Margery *Earth Tones* (1981)
Neruda, Pablo *Memoirs* (trs 1977)

A good ruler should not have to give evidence of his
intentions when they can be clearly understood.

NERVA's proclamation at his accession.
Quoted in Pliny *Letters* bk 10.58

Nerva (Marcus Cocceius Nerva) (AD c. 30–98). Roman emperor. He was proclaimed emperor on Domitian's death AD 96, and introduced state loans for farmers, family allowances, and allotments of land to poor citizens in his sixteen-month reign.

Nerval Gérard de. Pen name of Gérard Labrunie (1808–1855). French writer and poet. He was a precursor of French Symbolism and Surrealism. His writings include the travelogue *Voyage en Orient* 1851; short stories, including the collection *Les Filles du feu* 1854; poetry; a novel *Aurélia* 1855, containing episodes of visionary psychosis; and drama. He lived a wandering life, and suffered from periodic insanity, finally taking his own life.

Nervi Pier Luigi (1891–1979). Italian engineer. He used soft steel mesh within concrete to give it flowing form; for example, the Turin exhibition hall 1948–49, consisting of a single undulating large-span roof, the UNESCO building in Paris 1953–58, with Marcel Breuer and Bernard-Louis Zehrfuss (1911–), and the cathedral at New Norcia, near Perth, Australia, 1960. He was the structural engineer on Gio Ponti's Pirelli skyscraper project in Milan 1958.

Nesbit E(dith) (1858–1924). English author of children's books. She wrote *The Story of the Treasure Seekers* 1899 and *The Railway Children* 1906. Her stories often have a humorous magical element, as in *Five Children and It* 1902. *The Treasure Seekers* is the first of several books about the realistically squabbling Bastable children. Nesbit was a Fabian socialist and supported her family by writing.

Netanyahu Bibi (Binjamin) (1949–). Israeli right-wing politician and diplomat, leader of the Likud (Consolidation Party) from 1993 and prime minister from 1996. He served in the Israeli embassy in Washington 1982–84 and was a principal representative at the United Nations in New York 1984–88. As deputy foreign minister in the Likud-led government of Shamir, he was the chief Israeli spokesperson in the 1991–92 Middle East peace talks. A hard-line politician, he succeeded Yitzak Shamir to the Likud leadership in March 1993 following the party's 1992 electoral defeat.

Neugebauer Gerald (1932–). German-born US astronomer whose work has been crucial in establishing infrared astronomy. He has been closely involved with the space agency NASA's interplanetary missions and the design of new infrared telescopes.

Neugebauer was born in Göttingen, Germany, and studied at Cornell University and at the California Institute of Technology, where he spent his academic career from 1962. He became professor 1970 and director of the Palomar Observatory 1981. His involvement with NASA began 1969 and included work on the infrared radiometers carried aboard the Mariner missions to Mars. In 1976 he became the US principal scientist on the Infrared Astronomical Satellite.

During the mid-1960s Neugebauer and his colleagues began to establish the first infrared map of the sky. Some 20,000 new infrared sources were detected and most of these did not coincide with known optical sources. Among the brightest and strangest of these sources is in the Orion nebula, and is known as the Becklin–Neugebauer object after its discoverers. Carbon monoxide is blowing outwards from it at a high velocity. The object is thought to be a very young star.

Neumann (Johann) Balthasar (1687–1753). German Rococo architect and military engineer. He designed the bishop's palace in Würzburg (begun 1719; structurally complete 1744). As in his other palace designs, the centrepiece was a magnificent ceremonial staircase, its ceiling decorated by Tiepolo.

Neutra Richard Joseph (1892–1970). Austrian-born architect, a US citizen from 1929. Influenced by Adolf Loos and Erich Mendelsohn, he worked with Rudolph Schindler in Los Angeles from 1926 and became a leading exponent of the International Style. His works, often in impressive landscape settings, include Lovell Health House, Los Angeles, 1929, and the Kaufmann Desert House, Palm Springs, 1947.

Nevelson Louise (born Berliawsky) (1900–1988). Russian-born US sculptor and printmaker. A major exponent of assemblage sculpture, she was renowned for her room-sized wall-like reliefs consisting of stacked tiers of shallow open boxes filled with abstract arrangements in wood, as in *Black Majesty* 1956 (Whitney Museum of American Art, New York). From the 1960s she worked with other materials, for example plexiglass in *Ice Palace* 1967 (private collection, New York), and later produced outdoor works in steel and aluminium.

Nevelson's early work, small sculptures of found objects produced in the 1940s, has primitive and Surrealist overtones. The environmental 'walls', or 'cathedrals', for which she is best known date from the early 1950s. Painted a uniform black or (in later models) white or gold, the 'walls' consist of stacked tiers of shallow open boxes filled with abstract arrangements in wood.

Neville Brothers, the US rhythm-and-blues group, exponents of the New Orleans style, internationally successful from the 1980s. There are four Neville brothers, the eldest of whom has been active from the 1950s in various musical ventures. Albums include *Yellow Moon* 1989.

Aaron Neville (1941–) had hits as a vocalist in the 1960s, for example 'Tell It Like It Is' 1966. Two of the brothers – Art (1938–) and Cyril (1950–) – were in the Meters, a critically acclaimed group formed in the late 1960s, whose albums include *The Wild Tschoupitoulas* 1976. The Neville Brothers line-up comprising all four brothers, plus other musicians, was formed 1978.

There's a breathless hush in the Close to-night – / Ten to
make and the match to win.

HENRY NEWBOLT
'Vitaï Lampada'

Newbolt Henry John (1862–1938). English poet and naval historian. His works include *The Year of Trafalgar* 1905 and *A Naval History of the War* 1920 on World War I. His *Songs of the Sea* 1904 and *Songs of the Fleet* 1910 were set to music by Irish composer Charles Villiers Stanford. Knighted 1915.

The windows on the corridor side next to the platform
were all locked, presumably to prevent foreigners escaping
into the USSR.

ERIC NEWBY
Big Red Train Ride ch 2 1978

Newby (George) Eric (1919–). English travel writer and sailor. His books include *A Short Walk in the Hindu Kush* 1958, *The Big Red Train Ride* 1978, *Slowly Down the Ganges* 1966, and *A Traveller's Life* 1985.

He was a living, moving, talking caricature ... always in
a hurry, he was never in time.

T B Macaulay on THOMAS PELHAM-HOLLES, 1ST DUKE OF NEWCASTLE
Essays 'Horace Walpole's Letters' 1843

Newcastle Thomas Pelham-Holles, 1st Duke of Newcastle (1693–1768). British Whig politician, prime minister 1754–56 and 1757–62. He served as secretary of state for 30 years from 1724, then succeeded his younger brother, Henry Pelham, as prime minister 1754. In 1756 he resigned as a result of setbacks in the Seven

Years' War, but returned to office 1757 with Pitt the Elder (1st Earl of Chatham) taking responsibility for the conduct of the war. Earl 1714, duke 1715.

Newcomb Simon (1835–1909). Canadian-born US mathematician and astronomer who compiled charts and tables of astronomical data with phenomenal accuracy. His calculations of the motions of the bodies in the Solar System were in use as daily reference all over the world for more than 50 years, and the system of astronomical constants for which he was most responsible is still the standard.

In 1861 he joined the navy, where he was assigned to the US Naval Observatory at Washington DC, and in 1877 put in charge of the American Nautical Almanac office. From 1884 he was also professor of mathematics and astronomy at Johns Hopkins University. He retired with the rank of rear admiral.

At the Nautical Almanac office, Newcomb started the great work that was to occupy the rest of his life: the calculation of the motions of the bodies in the Solar System. The results were published in *Astronomical Papers Prepared for the Use of the American Ephemeris and Nautical Almanac*, a series that he founded 1879.

With his British counterpart Arthur Matthew Weld Downing (1850–1917), Newcomb established a universal standard system of astronomical constants. This was adopted at an international conference 1896, and again 1950.

Newcomen Thomas (1663–1729). English inventor of an early steam engine. His 'fire engine' 1712 was used for pumping water from mines until James Watt invented one with a separate condenser.

Newcomen was born in Dartmouth, Devon, and set up a blacksmith's shop there, assisted by a plumber called John Calley (died 1717). The first authenticated Newcomen engine was erected in 1712 near Dudley Castle, Wolverhampton, but a number of earlier machines must have been operated to develop the engine to this point. The whole situation is confused by a patent granted to Thomas Savery to 'raise water by the force of fire'; in later years Newcomen paid royalties to Savery.

Newcomen's engine consumed an enormous amount of coal because fresh hot steam had to be raised for each piston stroke. The early engines were very expensive because the cylinder was made of brass; later, iron cylinders were produced, but they were thick-walled and consequently even less efficient in terms of coal consumed. However, they were mostly used in coal mines.

It was with the Newcomen engine that the age of steam began.

Ne Win ('Brilliant Sun') adopted name of Maung Shu Maung (1911–). Myanmar (Burmese) politician, prime minister 1958–60, ruler from 1962 to 1974, president 1974–81, and chair until 1988 of the ruling Burma Socialist Programme Party (BSPP). His domestic 'Burmese Way to Socialism' policy programme brought the economy into serious decline.

Active in the nationalist movement during the 1930s, Ne Win joined the Allied forces in the war against Japan in 1945 and held senior military posts before becoming prime minister in 1958. After leading a coup in 1962, he ruled the country as chair of the revolutionary council until 1974, when he became state president. Although he stepped down as president 1981, he continued to dominate political affairs, but was forced to resign as BSPP leader 1988 after riots in Rangoon (now Yangon).

Newlands John Alexander Reina (1837–1898). English chemist who worked as an industrial chemist; he prepared in 1863 the first periodic table of the elements arranged in order of relative atomic masses, and pointed out 1865 the 'law of octaves' whereby every eighth element has similar properties. He was ridiculed at the time, but five years later Russian chemist Dmitri Mendeleyev published a more developed form of the table, also based on atomic masses, which forms the basis of the one used today (arranged by atomic number).

He set up in practice as an analytical chemist 1864, and in 1868 became chief chemist in a sugar refinery, where he introduced a number of improvements in processing. Later he left the refinery and again set up as an analyst.

Like many of his contemporaries, Newlands first used the terms 'equivalent weight' and 'atomic weight' without any distinction in meaning, and in his first paper 1863 he used the values accepted by his predecessors. The incompleteness of a table he drew up 1864 he attributed to the possible existence of additional, undiscovered elements; for example, he predicted the existence of germanium.

Newman Alfred (1901–1970). US film composer. From the 1930s to the late 1960s, Newman worked prolifically on virtually every genre of film, spending some 20 years in mid-career at the 20th Century-Fox studio. His many Academy Awards include those for *Song of Bernadette* 1943 and *Love Is a Many Splendored Thing* 1955.

Newman's plangent theme from *Street Scene* 1931 became a leit-motif in several Fox crime movies of the 1940s, notably *Kiss of Death* 1947. His 'Ann Rutledge theme' from *Young Mr Lincoln* 1939 was reused by director John Ford for his *The Man Who Shot Liberty Valance* 1962.

Newman Barnett (1905–1970). US painter, sculptor, and theorist. His paintings are solid-coloured canvases with a few sparse vertical stripes. They represent a mystical pursuit of simple or elemental art. His sculptures, such as *Broken Obelisk* 1963–67, consist of geometric shapes, each mounted on top of the other.

We can believe what we choose. We are answerable for what we choose to believe.

JOHN HENRY NEWMAN
Letter to Mrs Froude 27 June 1848

Newman John Henry (1801–1890). English Roman Catholic theologian. While still an Anglican, he wrote a series of *Tracts for the Times*, which gave their name to the Tractarian Movement (subsequently called the Oxford Movement) for the revival of Catholicism. He became a Catholic 1845 and was made a cardinal 1879. In 1864 his autobiography, *Apologia pro vita sua*, was published.

Newman, born in London, was ordained in the Church of England 1824, and in 1827 became vicar of St Mary's, Oxford. There he was influenced by the historian R H Froude and the Anglican priest Keble, and in 1833 published the first of the *Tracts for the Times*. They culminated in *Tract 90* 1841 which found the Thirty-Nine Articles of the Anglican church compatible with Roman Catholicism, and Newman was received into the Roman Catholic Church in 1845. He was rector of Dublin University 1854–58 and published his lectures on education as *The Idea of a University* 1873. His poem *The Dream of Gerontius* appeared in 1866, and *The Grammar of Assent*, an analysis of the nature of belief, in 1870. He wrote the hymn 'Lead, kindly light' 1833.

Suggested reading
Bouyer, Louis *Newman: His Life and Spirituality* (1958)
Capuchin, Z *John Henry Newman: His Inner Life* (1987)
Ker, Ian *John Henry Newman: A Biography* (1988)
Martin, Brian *John Henry Newman: His Life and Works* (1982)

Why have hamburger out when you've got steak at home? That doesn't mean it's always tender.

PAUL NEWMAN
Attributed remark, March 1984

Newman Paul (1925–). US actor and director. He was one of Hollywood's leading male stars of the 1960s and 1970s, initially often as an alienated figure, and later in character roles of many kinds. His films include *Somebody Up There Likes Me* 1956, *Cat on a Hot Tin Roof* 1958, *The Hustler* 1961, *Sweet Bird of Youth* 1962, *Hud* 1963, *Cool Hand Luke* 1967, *Butch Cassidy and the Sundance Kid* 1969, *The Sting* 1973, *The Verdict* 1983, *The Color of Money* 1986 (for which he won an Academy Award), *Mr and Mrs Bridge* 1991, and *The Hudsucker Proxy* 1994.

He directed his wife Joanne Woodward in *Rachel, Rachel* 1968 and other films and is noted as a racing-car driver and for his philanthropic activities. The profits from his Newman's Own speciality foods are donated to charity.

Suggested reading
Godfrey, Lionel *Paul Newman* (1979)
Quirk, L J *The Films of Paul Newman* (1981)

Newman Randy Gary (1944–). US pop singer, songwriter, and pianist. His mordantly satirical songs have earned him a cult following and occasionally, as with the single 'Short People' from the album *Little Criminals* 1977, mass appeal. Born in Louisiana, he devoted an album *Good Old Boys* 1974 to controversial governor Huey Long. Later albums include *Land of Dreams* 1988.

The nephew of the film composer Alfred Newman, he has written the soundtracks to several films, including *The Three Amigos* 1986.

Newson Lloyd (1954–). Australian choreographer and dancer. He is an exponent of avant-garde dance in Britain and his work often explores psychological and social issues. Frequently provocative, Newson challenges conventional conceptions of gender stereotypes in his ballets, for example, *My Body, Your Body* 1987. His choreographic methods make use of contact improvisation and are strongly influenced by Pina Bausch. He is the cofounder and director of the DV8 Physical Theatre 1986.

Newton Isaac (1642–1727). English physicist and mathematician who laid the foundations of physics as a modern discipline. During 1665–66, he discovered the binomial theorem, differential and integral calculus, and that white light is composed of many colours. He developed the three standard laws of motion and the universal law of gravitation, set out in *Philosophiae naturalis principia mathematica* 1687 (usually referred to as the *Principia*). Newton's laws of motion are: (1) Unless acted upon by an unbalanced force, a body at rest stays at rest, and a moving body continues moving at the same speed in the same straight line. (2) An unbalanced force applied to a body gives it an acceleration proportional to the force and in the direction

Newton *An engraving of English scientist and mathematician Isaac Newton, who developed the theory of gravitation and the three laws of motion that bear his name. (Ann Ronan/Image Select)*

of the force. (3) When a body A exerts a force on body B, B exerts an equal and opposite force on A; that is, to every action there is an equal and opposite reaction.

Newton developed his general theory of gravitation as a universal law of attraction between any two objects, stating that the force of gravity is proportional to the masses of the objects and decreases in proportion to the square of the distance between the two bodies.

In 1679 Newton calculated the Moon's motion on the basis of his theory of gravity and also found that his theory explained the laws of planetary motion that had been derived by German astronomer Johannes Kepler on the basis of observations of the planets.

Newton was born at Woolsthorpe Manor, Lincolnshire, and studied at Cambridge, where he became professor at the age of 26. He resisted James II's attacks on the liberties of the universities, and sat in the parliaments of 1689 and 1701–02 as a Whig. Appointed warden of the Royal Mint in 1696, and master in 1699, he carried through a reform of the coinage. Most of the last 30 years of his life were taken up by studies of theology and chronology, and experiments in alchemy.

Newton and German mathematician Gottfried Leibniz worked independently on the development of a differential calculus, both making significant advances, but Newton claimed to be its sole inventor. When Leibniz appealed to the Royal Society for a fair hearing, Newton appointed a committee of his own supporters and even wrote their report himself. The result of this controversy was to isolate English mathematics and to set it back many years, for it was Leibniz's terminology that came to be used. A similar dispute arose between Newton and English scientist Robert Hooke, who claimed prior discovery of the inverse square law of gravitation.

Newton began to investigate the phenomenon of gravitation in 1665, inspired, legend has it, by seeing an apple fall from a tree. But he was also active in algebra and number theory, classical and analytical geometry, computation, approximation, and even probability.

A by-product of his experiments with light and prisms was the development of the reflecting telescope. Newton investigated many other optical phenomena, including thin film interference effects, one of which, 'Newton's rings', is named after him.

De motu corporum in gyrum/On the Motion of Bodies in Orbit was written in 1684. The publication of the *Principia* was financed by his friend Edmond Halley. In 1704, Newton summed up his life's work on light in *Opticks*.

Suggested reading
Christianson, G E *In the Presence of the Creator: Isaac Newton and His Times* (1984)
Gjertson, Derek *The Newton Handbook* (1987)
Stayer, Marcia *Newton's Dream* (1988)
Westfall, R S *Never at Rest: A Biography of Isaac Newton* (1981)

The bravest of the brave.

MICHEL, PRINCE OF NEY
Title won by Ney at the Battle of Friedland 1807

Ney Michel, Duke of Elchingen, Prince of (1769–1815). Marshal of France under Napoleon I, who commanded the rearguard of the French army during the retreat from Moscow, and for his personal courage was called 'the bravest of the brave'. When Napoleon returned from Elba, Ney was sent to arrest him, but instead deserted to him and fought at Waterloo. He was subsequently shot for treason.

The son of a cooper, he joined the army in 1788, and rose from the ranks. He served throughout the Revolutionary and Napoleonic Wars.

Suggested reading
Foster, John *Napoleon's Marshal* (1968)
Lawford, James *Napoleon: The Last Campaigns, 1813–1815* (1978)
Morton, J B *Marshal Ney* (1958)

Ngugi wa Thiong'o (born James Ngugi) (1938–). Kenyan writer. His work includes essays, plays, short stories, and novels. Imprisoned after the performance of the play *Ngaahika Ndeenda/I Will Marry When I Want* 1977, he lived in exile from 1982. His novels, written in English and Kikuyu, include *The River Between* 1965, *Petals of Blood* 1977, *Caitaani Mutharaba-ini/Devil on the Cross* 1982, and *Matigari* 1989, and deal with colonial and post-independence oppression.

Nguyen Van Linh (1913–   ). Vietnamese communist politician, member of the Politburo 1976–81 and from 1985; leader of the Communist Party of Vietnam (CPV) 1986–91. He began economic liberalization and troop withdrawal from Cambodia and Laos.

Nguyen, born in North Vietnam, joined the anti-colonial Thanh Nien, a forerunner of the current CPV, in Haiphong 1929. He spent much of his subsequent party career in the South as a pragmatic reformer. He was a member of CPV's Politburo and secretariat 1976–81, suffered a temporary setback when party conservatives gained the ascendancy, and re-entered the Politburo in 1985, becoming CPV leader in Dec 1986 and resigning from the post June 1991.

Nice Margaret (born Morse) (1883–1974). US ornithologist who made an extensive study of the life history of the sparrow. She also campaigned against the indiscriminate use of pesticides.

Morse was born in Amherst, Massachusetts, and studied at Mount Holyoke College and Clark University in Worcester, Massachusetts, graduating in child psychology. She never had an academic appointment.

Her first ornithological research was a detailed study of the birds of Oklahoma. In 1927 she moved to Ohio, where she carried out the study of sparrows that established her as one of the leading ornithologists in the world, recording the behaviour of individual birds over a long period of time. A family move to Chicago provided fewer opportunities for Nice to study living birds, so she spent more of her time writing, and became involved in conservation issues.

Nichiren (1222–1282). Japanese Buddhist monk, founder of the sect that bears his name. The sect bases its beliefs on the *Lotus Sūtra*, which Nichiren held to be the only true revelation of the teachings of Buddha, and stresses the need for personal effort to attain enlightenment.

Nicholas two tsars of Russia:

Nicholas I (1796–1855). Tsar of Russia from 1825. His Balkan ambitions led to war with Turkey 1827–29 and the Crimean War 1853–56.

Ney French marshal under Napoleon I, Michel Ney. Retained in Louis XVIII's army during Napoleon's exile on Elba, Ney deserted the king and rejoined the emperor to fight at the Battle of Waterloo.

Russia has two generals in whom she can confide – Generals Janvier (January) and Fevrier (February).
NICHOLAS I
Nicholas I referring to the Russian winter, the subject of famous *Punch* cartoon ' General Fevrier turned traitor' 10 March 1853

Nicholas II (1868–1918). Tsar of Russia 1894–1917. He was dominated by his wife, Tsarina Alexandra, who was under the influence of the religious charlatan Rasputin. His mismanagement of the Russo-Japanese War and of internal affairs led to the revolution of 1905, which he suppressed, although he was forced to grant limited constitutional reforms. He took Russia into World War I in 1914, was forced to abdicate in 1917 after the Russian Revolution, and was executed with his family.
Suggested reading
Cowles, V *The Last Tsar* (1977)
Grey, I *The Romanovs* (1970)
Massie, R *Nicholas and Alexandra* (1967)
Vogt, G *Nicholas II* (1987)

I shall maintain the principle of autocracy just as firmly and unflinchingly as it was upheld by my ... father.
NICHOLAS II
Declaration to representatives of the Zemstvo of Tver 17 Jan 1896

Nicholas of Cusa or Nicolaus Cusanus (1401–1464). German philosopher, involved in the transition from scholasticism to the philosophy of modern times. He argued that knowledge is learned ignorance (*docta ignorantia*) since God, the ultimate object of knowledge, is above the opposites by which human reason grasps the objects of nature. He also asserted that the universe is boundless and has no circumference, thus breaking with medieval cosmology.

Nicholas, St also known as Santa Claus (lived 4th century AD). In the Christian church, patron saint of Russia, children, merchants, sailors, and pawnbrokers; bishop of Myra (now in Turkey). His legendary gifts of dowries to poor girls led to the custom of giving gifts to children on the eve of his feast day, 6 Dec, still retained in some countries, such as the Netherlands; elsewhere the custom has been transferred to Christmas Day. His emblem is three balls.

Nicholls Douglas Ralph (1906–1988). Australian Aboriginal spokesman, pastor of the Church of Christ, and administrator. He was the first Aborigine to be knighted 1972 and was governor of South Australia 1976–77.

Nichols Peter Richard (1927–   ). English dramatist. His first stage play, *A Day in the Death of Joe Egg* 1967, explored the life of a couple with a paraplegic child, while *The National Health* 1969 dramatized life in the face of death from cancer. *Privates on Parade* 1977, about the British army in Malaya, was followed by the middle-class comedy *Passion Play* 1981.

Nicholson Ben(jamin Lauder) (1894–1982). English abstract artist. After early experiments influenced by Cubism and the Dutch De Stijl group, Nicholson developed an elegant style of geometrical reliefs, notably a series of white reliefs (from 1933).

Son of artist William Nicholson, he studied at the Slade School of Art, London, as well as in Europe and in California. He married the sculptor Barbara Hepworth and was a leading member of the St Ives School.

If there's any realistic deterrent to marriage, it's the fact that you can't afford divorce.
JACK NICHOLSON
quoted in *Playboy* 1972

Nicholson Jack (1937–   ). US film actor. In the late 1960s, he captured the mood of nonconformist, uncertain young Americans

Nicholson, Jack *US actor Jack Nicholson as the Joker in* Batman. *Nicholson rose to fame after starring in the films* Easy Rider *1969 and* Five Easy Pieces *1970.* (Image Select)

in such films as *Easy Rider* 1969 and *Five Easy Pieces* 1970. He subsequently became a mainstream Hollywood star, appearing in *Chinatown* 1974, *One Flew over the Cuckoo's Nest* (Academy Award) 1975, *The Shining* 1979, *Terms of Endearment* (Academy Award) 1983, *Batman* 1989, and *A Few Good Men* 1992. He has directed several films, including *The Two Jakes* 1990, a sequel to *Chinatown*.

Nicholson John (1821–1857). British general and colonial administrator in India, born in Ireland. He was administrative officer at Bannu in the Punjab 1851–56, and was highly regarded for the justness of his rule. Promoted to brigadier general 1857 on the outbreak of the Indian Mutiny, he defeated resistance in the Punjab, but was killed during the storming of Delhi.

Nicholson William Newzam Prior (1872–1949). English artist. He studied art in Paris, and he and his brother-in-law won early fame for posters that simplified cut-paper design with striking effect. Another early graphic achievement was his series of woodcuts in colour, for example his *Queen Victoria*. He subsequently painted in oils, producing portraits, landscapes, and still lifes with a fine technical quality. He was especially noted for the latter. He also developed the art of poster design in partnership with his brother-in-law, James Pryde. They were known as 'the Beggarstaff Brothers'. He was the father of Ben Nicholson. Knighted 1936.

Nicias (c. 470–413 BC). Athenian politician and general. During the Peloponnesian War he negotiated the short-lived Peace of Nicias between Sparta and Athens 421 BC. He was placed in command of the Sicilian expedition 415 BC and, although opposed to it, laid siege to Syracuse. He was captured by the Syracusans and executed. His lack of confidence and indecisiveness played a large part in the failure of the Sicilian expedition.

Nicklaus Jack William (1940–). US golfer, nicknamed 'the Golden Bear'. He won a record 20 major titles, including 18 professional majors between 1962 and 1986. Nicklaus played for the US Ryder Cup team six times 1969–81 and was nonplaying captain

1983 and 1987 when the event was played over the course he designed at Muirfield Village, Ohio. He was voted the 'Golfer of the Century' 1988.

Nicol William (1768–1851). Scottish physicist and geologist who invented the first device for obtaining plane-polarized light – the Nicol prism – in 1828. Nicol was born in Edinburgh and lectured at the university there. He did not publish any of his research findings until 1826.

Nicol made his prism by bisecting a parallelepiped of Iceland spar (a naturally occurring, transparent crystalline form of calcium carbonate) along its shortest diagonal, then cementing the two halves together with Canada balsam. Light entering the prism is refracted into two rays, one of which emerges as plane-polarized light. Nicol prisms greatly facilitated the study of refraction and polarization, and were later used to investigate molecular structures and optical activity of organic compounds.

In 1815, Nicol developed a method of preparing extremely thin sections of crystals and rocks for microscopical study. His technique (which involved cementing the specimen to a glass slide and then carefully grinding until it was extremely thin) made it possible to view mineral samples by transmitted rather than reflected light and therefore enabled the minerals' internal structures to be seen.

Nicolle Charles Jules Henri (1866–1936). French bacteriologist whose discovery in 1909 that typhus is transmitted by the body louse made the armies of World War I introduce delousing as a compulsory part of the military routine. His original observation was that typhus victims, once admitted to hospitals, did not infect the staff; he speculated that transmission must be via the skin or clothes, which were washed as standard procedure for new admissions. The experimental evidence was provided by infecting a healthy monkey using a louse recently fed on an infected chimpanzee. Nobel Prize for Physiology or Medicine 1928.

He became director of the Pasteur Institute in Tunis 1902. From 1932 he was professor at the Collège de France. He was also a novelist.

Nicolson Harold George (1886–1968). English author and diplomat. His works include biographies (*Lord Carnock* 1930; *Curzon: The Last Phase* 1934; and *King George V* 1952) and studies such as *Monarchy* 1962, as well as the *Diaries and Letters* 1930–62 for which he is best known. He married Vita Sackville-West 1913.

Their relationship was described by their son, Nigel Nicolson, in *Portrait of a Marriage* 1973. KCVO 1953.

It was like playing squash with a dish of scrambled eggs.
HAROLD NICOLSON
Diaries and Letters 1939–1945 18 March 1943 (replying to Lady Astor in the House of Commons) 1966–68

Niebuhr Barthold Georg (1776–1831). German historian. He was Prussian ambassador in Rome 1816–23, and professor of Roman history at Bonn until 1831. His three-volume *History of Rome* 1811–32 critically examined original sources.

Niebuhr Carsten (1733–1815). Danish map-maker, surveyor, and traveller, sent by the Danish government to explore the Arabian peninsula 1761–67.

Niebuhr Reinhold (1892–1971). US Protestant theologian, a Lutheran minister. His *Moral Man and Immoral Society* 1932 attacked depersonalized modern industrial society but denied the

---

God, give us the serenity to accept what cannot be changed; Give us the courage to change what should be changed; Give us the wisdom to distinguish one from the other.
REINHOLD NIEBUHR
quoted in Richard Wightman Fox *Reinhold Niebuhr* 1985

possibility of fulfilling religious and political utopian aspirations, a position that came to be known as Christian Realism. Niebuhr was a pacifist, activist, and socialist but advocated war to stop totalitarianism in the 1940s.

Niebuhr taught for more than 30 years at the Union Theological Seminary in New York City. Originally a strong exponent of Christian socialism, he became increasingly pessimistic about the possibility of achieving it, given humanity's irreducible egoistic pride, which he identified with original sin. He came to believe that liberal democracy must be sustained not because it can bring about human perfection but as a way of avoiding the systematic cruelty that comes with unrestrained power. From 1945 he founded Americans for Democratic Action and became an adviser to the State Department.

Suggested reading
Fox, Richard *Reinhold Niebuhr* (1987)
Harland, G *The Thought of Reinhold Niebuhr* (1960)
Kegley, C W and Bretall, R W *Reinhold Niebuhr: His Religious, Social and Political Thought* (1984)
Scott, Nathan (ed) *The Legacy of Reinhold Niebuhr* (1975)

I think through the instruments themselves, almost as if I had crept inside them.

CARL NIELSEN
Politiken 1925

Nielsen Carl August (1865–1931). Danish composer. His works combine an outward formal strictness with an inner waywardness of tonality and structure. They include the Neo-Classical opera *Maskarade/Masquerade* 1906, a wind quintet 1922, six programmatic symphonies, numerous songs, and incidental music on Danish texts. He also composed concertos for violin 1911, flute 1926, and clarinet 1928; chamber music; and piano works.

Niemeyer (Soares Filho) Oscar (1907–). Brazilian architect. He was joint designer of the United Nations headquarters in New York 1947 and from 1957 architect of many public buildings in the capital, Brasília. His idiosyncratic interpretation of the Modernist idiom uses symbolic form to express the function of a building; for example, the Catholic Cathedral in Brasília.

Niemöller (Friedrich Gustav Emil) Martin (1892–1984). German Christian Protestant pastor. He was imprisoned in a concentration camp 1938–45 for campaigning against Nazism in the German church. In 1946 he proclaimed Germany's war guilt at the International Missionary Council in Geneva, and was first bishop of the newly formed Evangelical Church of Hesse-Nassau 1947–64. He was president of the World Council of Churches 1961–68.

Niepce Joseph Nicéphore (1765–1833). French pioneer of photography. Niepce was born in Chalon-sur-Saône and became administrator of Nice 1795. From 1801 he devoted himself to research. Niepce invented heliography, a precursor of photography that fixed images onto pewter plates coated with pitch and required eight-hour exposures. He produced the world's first photograph from nature 1826 and later collaborated with Daguerre on the faster daguerreotype process. The first photograph was a positive image, a view from Niepce's attic bedroom. The image was captured, after an eight-hour exposure, in a camera obscura on a metal plate coated with light-sensitive bitumen. The plate has survived and is to be found in the University of Texas.

Nietzsche Friedrich Wilhelm (1844–1900). German philosopher who rejected the accepted absolute moral values and the 'slave morality' of Christianity. He argued that 'God is dead' and therefore people were free to create their own values. His ideal was the *übermensch*, or 'Superman', who would impose his will on the weak and worthless. Nietzsche claimed that knowledge is never objective but always serves some interest or unconscious purpose.

His insights into the relation between thought and language were a major influence on philosophy. Although he has been claimed as a precursor by Nazism, many of his views are incompatible with totalitarian ideology. He is a profoundly ambivalent thinker whose philosophy can be appropriated for many purposes.

He published *Morgenröte/The Dawn* 1880–81, *Die fröhliche Wissenschaft/The Gay Science* 1881–82, *Also sprach Zarathustra/Thus Spoke Zarathustra* 1883–85, *Jenseits von Gut und Böse/Between Good and Evil* 1885–86, *Zur Genealogie der Moral/Towards a Genealogy of Morals* 1887, and *Ecce Homo* 1888.

Suggested reading
Bergmann, P *Nietzsche* (1987)
Heller, E *The Importance of Nietzsche* (1989)
Kaufmann, W *Nietzsche: Philosopher, Psychologist, Antichrist* (1974)
Stern, J P *Nietzsche* (1978)

To understand God's thoughts we must study statistics, for these are the measure of his purpose.

FLORENCE NIGHTINGALE
quoted in K Pearson *Life and Letters of Francis Galton* vol II ch 13 1 1900

Nightingale Florence (1820–1910). English nurse, the founder of nursing as a profession. She took a team of nurses to Scutari (now Üsküdar, Turkey) in 1854 and reduced the Crimean War hospital death rate from 42% to 2%. In 1856 she founded the Nightingale School and Home for Nurses in London.

Born in Florence, Italy, she trained in Germany and France. She was the author of the classic *Notes on Nursing*; she was awarded the Order of Merit 1907.

Suggested reading
Dengler, S *Florence Nightingale* (1988)
Huxley, E *Florence Nightingale* (1975)

Nightingale *Although nursing was thought to be totally unsuitable work for a woman of the Victorian middle classes, Florence Nightingale (seen in this 1859 photograph) was unwavering in her determination to transform both the standard of care that nurses provided and their professional status. The publicity surrounding her work in the Crimean War as 'the Lady with the Lamp' allowed her to achieve both aims.*

Smith, F *Florence Nightingale: Reputation and Power* (1982)
Strachey, L *Eminent Victorians* (1918, several reprints)
Woodham-Smith, C *Florence Nightingale, 1820–1910* (1951)

Nijinksa Bronislava (1891–1972). Russian choreographer and dancer. Nijinksa was the first major female choreographer to work in classical ballet, creating several dances for Diaghilev's Ballets Russes, including *Les Noces* 1923, a landmark in 20th-century modernist dance. She was the sister of Vaslav Nijinsky, continuing his revolutionary ideas of kinetic movement in dance. Other pieces include *Les Biches* 1924.

She joined the Ballets Russes as a dancer 1909, leaving when her brother was fired, to return as choreographer 1921. She staged the fairy dances in Max Reinhardt's film *A Midsummer Night's Dream* 1935.

It just happens. I go up, pause a little and then come down.

VASLAV NIJINSKY on his incredible elevation
quoted in Christy Adair *Woman and Dance; Sylphs and Sirens* 1992

Nijinsky Vaslav Fomich (1890–1950). Russian dancer and choreographer. Noted for his powerful but graceful technique, he was a legendary member of Diaghilev's *Ballets Russes,* for whom he choreographed Debussy's *Prélude à l'après-midi d'un faune* 1912 and *Jeux* 1913, and Stravinsky's *Le Sacre du printemps/The Rite of Spring* 1913.

Nijinsky also took lead roles in ballets such as *Petrushka* 1911. He rejected conventional forms of classical ballet in favour of free expression. His sister was the choreographer Bronislava Nijinska.

Suggested reading
Beaumont, C W *Nijinsky* (1974)
Kirstein, L *Nijinsky Dancing* (1975)
Nijinsky, V *The Diary of Vaslav Nijinsky* (1968)

Niland D'Arcy Francis (1917–1967). Australian writer. He is best known for the internationally successful novel *The Shiralee* 1955, later made into a film starring Peter Finch, which drew on his experiences as an itinerant worker in rural Australia. His other works include *Call Me When the Cross Turns Over* 1957 and *Dead Men Running* 1969, which was produced as an ABC television serial.

Nilsson Harry. Stage name of Harry Edward Nelson III (1941–1994). US singer and songwriter, best known for his contributions to the soundtrack of the John Schlesinger film *Midnight Cowboy* 1969, most notably the hit single 'Everybody's Talkin'', which earned him the first of several Grammy awards. His albums include *Nilsson Schmilsson* 1971 and *Son of Schmilsson* 1972. Nilsson collaborated with ex-Beatles John Lennon (who produced his album *Pussy Cats* 1974) and Ringo Starr (on a film score the same year). He also wrote the script and music of a full-length animated TV film, *The Point* 1971. He was said to have perfect phrasing and a three-octave range, but disliked performing.

Nilsson (Märta) Birgit (born Svennsson) (1918–). Swedish soprano. One of the greatest singers of Wagner, she is best remembered for her roles in his operas: Brünhilde in *Der Ring des Nibelungen/The Ring of the Nibelung* and Isolde in *Tristan und Isolde.* Her voice was pure and perfect in intonation, with a phenomenal range which was consistently smooth.

Nimitz Chester William (1885–1966). US admiral, commander in chief of the US Pacific fleet. He reconquered the Solomon Islands 1942–43, Gilbert Islands 1943, the Mariana Islands and the Marshall Islands 1944, and signed the Japanese surrender 1945 as the US representative.

Nin Anaïs (1903–1977). French-born US novelist and diarist. Born in Paris, she started out as a model and dancer, but later took up the study of psychoanalysis. She emigrated to the USA 1940, becoming a prominent member of Greenwich Village literary society in New York. Her extensive and impressionistic diaries, published 1966–76,

reflect her interest in dreams, which along with psychoanalysis are recurring themes of her gently erotic novels (such as *House of Incest* 1936 and *A Spy in the House of Love* 1954). Her correspondence with Henry Miller was published 1985.

Suggested reading
Bair, Deidre *Anaïs Nin* (1995)
Nin, Anaïs *Diaries* (1966–85)
Nin, Anaïs *A Literate Passion: Letters on Anaïs Nin and Henry Miller, 1932–1953* (1985)

Nirenberg Marshall Warren (1927–). US biochemist who shared the 1968 Nobel Prize for Physiology or Medicine for his work in deciphering the chemistry of the genetic code. From 1957 he worked at the National Institute of Health, later moving to the Laboratory of Biochemical Genetics at the National Heart, Lung, and Blood Institute in Bethesda, Maryland.

Nirenberg was interested in the way in which the nitrogen bases – adenine (A), cytosine (C), guanine (G), and thymine (T) – specify a particular amino acid. To simplify the task of identifying the RNA triplet (codon) responsible for each amino acid, he used a simple synthetic RNA polymer. He found that certain amino acids could be specified by more than one codon, and that some triplets did not specify an amino acid at all. These 'nonsense' triplets signified the beginning or the end of a sequence. He then worked on finding the orders of the letters in the triplets, and obtained unambiguous results for 60 of the possible codons.

Nithsdale William Maxwell, 5th Earl of Nithsdale (1676–1744). English Jacobite leader who was captured at Preston, brought to trial in Westminster Hall, London, and condemned to death 1716. With his wife's assistance he escaped from the Tower of London in women's dress, and fled to Rome. Earl 1696.

Nivelle Robert Georges (1856–1924). French general. In World War I, he planned a massive offensive in the Craonne-Reims area for April 1917, but his public boasting forewarned the Germans and the offensive was a disaster, with enormous French casualties which precipitated the mutinies in the French army later that year. Nivelle was removed, replaced by General Pétain, and sent back to command the troops in North Africa.

Nivelle's record until 1917 had been good: he had served in Algeria, Tunisia, and China before World War I and had served creditably in the invasion of Alsace and the Battle of Aisne 1914. He had also played an important part at the Battle of Verdun 1916; it was as a result of this success that he replaced Marshal Joffre as commander in chief of the armies of the north and northeast 12 Dec 1916.

Actors never retire. They're just offered smaller parts.

DAVID NIVEN
Evening Standard 29 Oct 1976

Niven (James) David (Graham) (1910–1983). Scottish-born US film actor. In Hollywood from the 1930s, his films include *Wuthering Heights* 1939, *Around the World in 80 Days* 1956, *Separate Tables* 1958 (Academy Award), *The Guns of Navarone* 1961, and *The Pink Panther* 1964. He published two best-selling volumes of autobiography, *The Moon's a Balloon* 1972 and *Bring on the Empty Horses* 1975.

There can be no whitewash at the White House.

RICHARD NIXON
Television speech on Watergate 30 Apr 1973

Nixon Richard Milhous (1913–1994). 37th president of the USA 1969–74, a Republican. He attracted attention as a member of the Un-American Activities Committee 1948, and was vice president to Eisenhower 1953–61. As president he was responsible for US withdrawal from Vietnam, and the normalization of relations with communist China, but at home his culpability in the cover-up of the Watergate scandal and the existence of a 'slush fund' for political

machinations during his re-election campaign 1972 led to his resignation 1974 when threatened with impeachment.

Born at Yorba Linda, California, of a lower middle-class Quaker
family that had migrated from the midwest, he grew up in Whittier,
California and practised law there 1937–42, then served in the navy
1942–46.

Nixon entered Congress 1947, and rose to prominence during the
McCarthyite era of the 1950s. As a member of the Un-American
Activities Committee, he pressed for the investigation of Alger Hiss,
accused of being a spy. Nixon was senator for California from 1951
until elected vice president. He played a more extensive role in government than previous vice presidents, in part because of the poor
health of President Eisenhower. He lost the 1960 presidential election to J F Kennedy, partly because televised electoral debates put
him at a disadvantage.

He did not seek presidential nomination 1964, but in a 'law and
order' campaign defeated vice president Humphrey 1968 in one of
the most closely contested elections in US history. Facing a
Democratic Congress, Nixon sought to extricate the US from the
war in Vietnam. He formulated the Nixon Doctrine 1969, abandoning close involvement with Asian countries, but escalated the war in
Cambodia by massive bombing.

Nixon was re-elected 1972 in a landslide victory over George
McGovern, and immediately faced allegations of irregularities and
illegalities conducted on his behalf in his re-election campaign and
within the White House. Despite his success in extricating the US
from Vietnam, congressional and judicial investigations, along with
press exposures of the Watergate affair – the bungling, Republican-
sponsored campaign break-in of the Democrats' headquarters 1972
and the sleazy cover-up which followed – undermined public support. He resigned 1974, the first and only US president to do so,
under threat of impeachment on three counts: obstruction of the
administration of justice in the investigation of Watergate; violation
of constitutional rights of citizens, for example attempting to use the
Internal Revenue Service, Federal Bureau of Investigation, and
Central Intelligence Agency as weapons against political opponents;
and failure to produce 'papers and things' as ordered by the Judiciary
Committee.

He was granted a pardon 1974 by President Ford and turned to
lecturing and writing.

Suggested reading

Aitken, Jonathan *Nixon: A Life* (1993)
Ambrose, S *Nixon* (1987)
McGinnis, J *The Selling of the President* (1988)
Parmet, Herbert S *Nixon and His America* (1990)
Sulzberger, C L *The World and Richard Nixon* (1987)
Woodward, Bob and Bernstein, Carl *All the President's Men* (1975)
Woodward, Bob and Bernstein, Carl *The Final Days* (1987)

Nizzoli Marcello (1887–1969). Italian industrial designer. He is
best known for his innovative designs for office machines for the
Olivetti company. A member of the pre-World War II generation of
Italian designers, Nizzoli moved through painting and exhibition
and graphic design before being brought in by Adriano Olivetti, son
of the founder, 1938 to work on the company's machines.

Notable designs include the 'Lexicon 80' typewriter 1948 which
was among the first objects to be recognized internationally as representing the emergence of a new modern design movement in
postwar Italy.

Nkomo Joshua Mqabuko Nyongolo (1917–). Zimbabwean
politician, vice president from 1988. After completing his education
in South Africa, Joshua Nkomo became a welfare officer on
Rhodesian Railways and later organizing secretary of the Rhodesian
African Railway Workers' Union. He entered politics 1950, and was
president of the ANC in S Rhodesia 1957–59. As president of
ZAPU (Zimbabwe African People's Union) from 1961, he was a
leader of the black nationalist movement against the white
Rhodesian regime. Arrested along with other black African politicians, he was kept in detention 1963–74. After his release he joined
forces with Robert Mugabe as a joint leader of the Patriotic Front

Nixon *37th US president Richard Milhous Nixon, the only president ever
to resign from office. During his presidency Nixon began the gradual
withdrawal of US troops from Vietnam and improved relations with the
Eastern bloc. He resigned 9 Aug 1974, over his involvement in the
Watergate scandal.*

1976, opposing the white-dominated regime of Ian Smith. Nkomo
took part in the Lancaster House Conference, which led to
Rhodesia's independence as the new state of Zimbabwe. He was a
member of Robert Mugabe's cabinet 1980–82 and from 1987.

Nkosi Lewis (1936–). South African writer and broadcaster. He
is particularly noted for his play about Johannesburg *The Rhythms of
Violence* 1964 and his influential essays 'Home and Exile' 1965.

Nkrumah Kwame (1909–1972). Ghanaian nationalist politician,
prime minister of the Gold Coast (Ghana's former name) 1952–57
and of newly independent Ghana 1957–60. He became Ghana's first
president 1960 but was overthrown in a coup 1966. His policy of
'African socialism' led to links with the communist bloc.

Originally a teacher, he studied later in both Britain and the USA,
and on returning to Africa formed the Convention People's Party
(CPP) 1949 with the aim of immediate self-government. He was
imprisoned in 1950 for incitement of illegal strikes, but was released
the same year. As president he established an authoritarian regime
and made Ghana a one-party (CPP) state 1964. He then dropped
his stance of nonalignment and drew closer to the USSR and other
communist countries. Deposed from the presidency while on a visit
to Beijing (Peking) 1966, he remained in exile in Guinea, where he
was made a co-head of state until his death, but was posthumously
'rehabilitated' 1973. *See illustration on page 634.*

Suggested reading

Bretton, Henry *The Rise and Fall of Kwame Nkrumah* (1967)
Davidson, Basil *Black Star: A View of the Life and Times of Kwame
Nkrumah* (1973)
Kellner, Douglas *Nkrumah* (1987)
Nkrumah, Kwame *Ghana: The Autobiography of Kwame Nkrumah*
(1957)

Nobel Alfred Bernhard (1833–1896). Swedish chemist and engineer. He invented dynamite in 1867, gelignite 1875, and ballistite, a

Nkrumah *Kwame Nkrumah, seen here addressing the United Nations General Assembly 1961, led Ghana to independence 1957 and became the country's first president. Called 'the Gandhi of Africa', he was prominent in the anticolonial and Pan African movements of the 1950s and 1960s.*

smokeless gunpowder, in 1887. Having amassed a large fortune from the manufacture of explosives and the exploitation of the Baku oilfields in Azerbaijan, near the Caspian Sea, he left this in trust for the endowment of five Nobel prizes.

Nobel was born in Stockholm and studied in Europe and North America. During the Crimean War 1853–56, Nobel worked in St Petersburg, Russia, in his father's company, which produced large quantities of munitions. After the war his father went bankrupt, and in 1859 the family returned to Sweden. During the next few years Nobel developed several new explosives and factories for making them. In 1864, a nitroglycerine factory blew up, killing Nobel's younger brother and four other people.

In 1863 Nobel invented a mercury fulminate detonator for use with nitroglycerine. Dynamite was invented to make the handling of nitroglycerine safer, by mixing it with kieselguhr, a porous diatomite mineral. Gelignite, a colloidal solution of nitrocellulose (gun cotton) in nitroglycerine, was safer still: less sensitive to shock and strongly resistant to moisture.

Nobel also worked in electrochemistry, optics, biology, and physiology, and helped to solve many problems in the manufacture of artificial silk, leather, and rubber.

He did not endow a prize for mathematics after his wife ran off with a mathematician.

His uncompromising stand on disarmament prevented him from achieving the very high office to which his intelligence and political skills might otherwise have propelled him.

Roger Bannister on PHILIP NOEL-BAKER
in *Dictionary of National Biography*

Noel-Baker Philip John, Baron Noel-Baker (1889–1982). British Labour politician. He was involved in drafting the charters of both the League of Nations and the United Nations. He published *The*

Arms Race 1958, and was awarded the 1959 Nobel Peace Prize. Baron 1977.

Noether (Amalie) Emmy (1882–1935). German mathematician who became one of the leading figures in abstract algebra. Modern work in the field of a general theory of ideals dates from her papers of the early 1920s.

Noether was born in Erlangen, the daughter of mathematician Max Noether. Despite a rule barring women from university study, she was awarded a doctorate from Erlangen in 1907 for a thesis on algebraic invariants. But as a woman she could not hold a post in the university faculty. She persisted with her research independently and at the request of mathematician David Hilbert was invited to lecture at Göttingen 1915. There she worked with Hilbert on problems arising from Albert Einstein's theory of relativity, and in 1922 became associate professor. She remained at Göttingen until the Nazi purge of Jewish university staff in 1933. The rest of her life was spent as professor of mathematics at Bryn Mawr College in Pennsylvania, USA.

Noether first made her mark as a mathematician with a paper 1920 on noncommutative fields (where the *order* in which the elements are combined affects the result). For the next few years she worked on the establishment and systematization of a theory of ideals, and introduced the concept of primary ideals. After 1927 she returned to the subject of noncommutative algebras, her chief investigations being conducted into linear transformations of noncommutative algebras and their structure.

Noether Max (1844–1921). German mathematician who contributed to the development of algebraic geometry and the theory of algebraic functions.

Noether was born in Mannheim and studied at Heidelberg. He spent his career there and at Erlangen, where he became professor 1888. His daughter Emmy Noether became a notable mathematician.

Nofretete alternative name for ◊Nefertiti, queen of Egypt.

Nobel *Swedish chemist and industrialist Alfred Nobel spent most of his working life developing explosives, particularly dynamite and gelignite. On his death in 1896, Nobel left all his considerable fortune to a foundation that funds the annual awards that bear his name. The first Nobel prizes – for physics, physiology or medicine, chemistry, literature, and contributions to peace – were awarded 1901. (Ann Ronan/Image Select)*

Noguchi Hideyo (born Noguchi Seisaku) (1876–1928). Japanese bacteriologist who studied syphilitic diseases, snake venoms, trachoma, and poliomyelitis. He discovered the parasite of yellow fever, a disease from which he died while working in British W Africa.

Noguchi Isamu (1904–1988). US sculptor and designer. He was recognized for the serene, expressive power of his abstracted, organic forms, for example *Khmer* 1962 (Garden of National Museum, Jerusalem). Noguchi has also designed stage sets, notably for the Martha Graham Dance Company 1935–66, and sculpture gardens in such major cities as New York and Tokyo.

The son of a Japanese father and American mother, Noguchi spent his childhood in Japan and made frequent return visits. He went to Paris in the 1920s and from 1927–29 was assistant to Brancusi, whose example made a lasting impact on his work. From early sculptures in lively, biomorphic shapes cut from sheet metal, he turned to carving in stone in the 1940s and also worked in bronze and marble. His sculpture gardens display a sure grasp of his Western/Oriental heritage.

Nolan Sidney Robert (1917–1992). Australian artist. Largely self-taught, he created atmospheric paintings of the outback, exploring themes from Australian history such as the life of the outlaw Ned Kelly and the folk heroine Mrs Fraser.

Nolan was born in Carlton, a suburb of Melbourne, Australia. His family was poor, and he left school at 14 to work in the art studio of a hat firm, where he acquired useful skills in mixed media and paint spraying. He attended art evening classes at the Melbourne Gallery's school. His interest in European art developed during his early twenties and in 1938 he came to the notice of art patrons John and Sunday Reed, who supported him for several years.

He took up landscape painting to relieve boredom while serving in the army from 1942. At the end of the war he began the first series of paintings on the life and exploits of Ned Kelly, depicting him in scrap-metal armour and a grotesque square helmet.

Nolan's other works include the *Leda and the Swan* series 1960, and many paintings from his travels in Africa, America, Antartica, and China. His non-Australian paintings failed to excite the critics, and he suffered some neglect for 20 years or more until the showing of his famous earlier paintings at the *Angry Penguins* exhibition 1988 at the Hayward Gallery, London, revived interest in his work.
Suggested reading
Clark, J *Sidney Nolan* (1988)

Noland Kenneth Clifton (1927–   ). US painter. He is associated with the colour-stain painters Helen Frankenthaler and Morris Louis. In the 1950s and early 1960s he painted targets, or concentric circles of colour, in a clean, hard-edged style on unprimed canvas. His work centred on geometry, colour, and symmetry. His paintings of the 1960s experimented with the manipulation of colour vision and afterimages, pioneering the field of Op art.

Nolde Emil. Adopted name of Emil Hansen (1867–1956). German Expressionist painter and graphic artist. Nolde studied in Paris and Dachau, joined the group of artists known as *die Brücke* 1906–07, and visited Polynesia 1913; he then became almost a recluse in NE Germany.

He painted biblical subjects marked by a barbaric intensity of colour, still lifes, and studies of the landscape of his native region on the German–Danish border. His work includes brilliant water-colours.

Nollekens Joseph (1737–1823). English Neo-Classical sculptor. He specialized in portrait busts and memorials. He worked in Rome 1759–70 and on his return to London enjoyed great success, executing busts of many eminent people including George III, the Prince of Wales (later George IV), the politicians Pitt the Younger and Fox, and the actor David Garrick.

Nono Luigi (1924–1990). Italian composer. He wrote attenuated pointillist works such as *Il canto sospeso/Suspended Song* 1955–56 for soloists, chorus, and orchestra, in which influences of Webern and

Nordenskjöld Swedish polar explorer Nils Nordenskjöld, leader of the expedition that discovered the Northeast Passage from the Atlantic to the Pacific along the north coast of Asia 1878–79. He also explored and mapped the island of Spitsbergen.

Gabrieli are applied to issues of social conscience. After the opera *Intolleranza 1960/Intolerance 1960* his style became more richly expressionist, and his causes more overtly polemical.

Nordenskjöld Nils Adolf Erik (1832–1901). Swedish explorer. He made voyages to the Arctic with the geologist Torell and in 1878–79 discovered the Northeast Passage. He published the results of his voyages in a series of books, including *Voyage of the Vega round Asia and Europe* 1881.

Norfolk Miles Francis Stapleton Fitzalan-Howard, 17th Duke of Norfolk (1915–   ). Earl marshal of England, and premier duke and earl; seated at Arundel Castle, Sussex, England. As earl marshal, he is responsible for the organization of ceremonial on major state occasions. Baron 1971, duke 1975.

Noriega Manuel Antonio Morena (1940–   ). Panamanian soldier and politician, effective ruler of Panama from 1982, as head of the National Guard, until deposed by the USA 1989. An informer for the US Central Intelligence Agency, he was known to be involved in drug trafficking as early as 1972. He enjoyed US support until 1987. In the 1989 US invasion of Panama, he was forcibly taken to the USA. He was tried and convicted of trafficking 1992.

Noriega was commissioned in the National Guard 1962, and received US counter-intelligence training. He became intelligence chief 1970 and Chief of Staff 1982. He wielded considerable political power behind the scenes, which led to his enlistment by the CIA, and he was seen as an ally against Nicaragua until the Irangate scandal limited US covert action there. In the 1984 and 1989 presidential elections, Noriega claimed a fraudulent victory for his candidate. Bribes accepted by Noriega for tacitly permitting money laundering and the transhipment of cocaine are estimated at $15 million, but after 1985 he co-operated with the US Drug Enforcement Administration. However, relations between Panama and the USA deteriorated and in Dec 1989 President Bush ordered an invasion of

Norman, Jessye *The soprano Jessye Norman in 1992. Since her debut as Elisabeth (Tannhäuser) in 1969, she has applied her beautiful, flexible voice to a variety of works ranging from Mozart to Verdi and Wagner. She has also pursued a highly successful concert career.*

the country by 24,000 US troops. Noriega was seized and taken to the USA for trial. In April 1992 he was given a 40-year prison sentence for drug trafficking and racketeering.

Norman Greg (1955–). Australian golfer, nicknamed 'the Great White Shark'. After many wins in his home country, he enjoyed success on the European PGA Tour before joining the US Tour. He has won the World Match-Play title three times.

Norman Jessye (1945–). US soprano. She is acclaimed for majestically haunting interpretations of German opera and *lieder* (songs), notably Wagner, Mahler, and Richard Strauss, but is equally at home with Ravel and Chausson songs and gospel music.

She was born in Augusta, Georgia, and made her operatic debut at the Deutsche Oper, Berlin, 1969.

Norman Montagu Collet, 1st Baron Norman (1871–1950). British banker. Governor of the Bank of England 1920–44, he handled German reparations (financial compensation exacted by the Allies) after World War I, and, by his advocacy of a return to the gold standard in 1925 and other policies, was held by many to have contributed to the economic depression of the 1930s. Baron 1944.

Norrington Roger Arthur Carver (1934–). English conductor. An early music enthusiast, he has promoted the use of period instruments in his many recordings. He is noted for his interpretations of the Mozart and Beethoven symphonies, which he often takes at unusually fast tempos, drawing criticism from some that the expressive intensity of the music is thereby lost.

Norris Frank (Benjamin Franklin) (1870–1902). US novelist. A naturalist writer, he wrote *McTeague* 1899, about a brutish San Francisco dentist and the love of gold (filmed as *Greed* 1923). He

completed only two parts of his projected trilogy, the *Epic of Wheat*: *The Octopus* 1901, dealing with the struggles between wheat farmers, and *The Pit* 1903, describing the Chicago wheat exchange.

Norrish Ronald George Wreyford (1897–1978). English physical chemist who studied fast chemical reactions, particularly those initiated by light. He shared the 1967 Nobel Prize for Chemistry with his co-worker George Porter. Norrish was largely responsible for the advance of reaction kinetics to a distinct discipline within physical chemistry.

Norrish was born and educated in Cambridge and spent his academic career there, becoming professor 1937.

Norrish began working in photochemistry in 1923. His interest in using intense flashes of light to initiate photochemical reactions seems to have been stimulated by his work during World War II with his student George Porter, investigating methods of suppressing the flash from guns and developing incendiary materials. By varying the time delay between two flashes, Norrish was able to study the kinetics of the formation and decay of very shortlived radicals or ions.

Norrish went on to apply these techniques to the study of chain reactions. He also made pioneering studies of the kinetics of polymerization. He and his co-workers discovered the gel effect, which occurs in the later stages of free-radical polymerization.

I was the creature of Parliament in my rise; when I fell I was its victim.

LORD NORTH
in W Baring Pemberton *Lord North* 1938

North Frederick, 2nd Earl of Guilford, known as Lord North (1732–1792). British Tory politician. He entered Parliament in 1754, became chancellor of the Exchequer in 1767, and was prime minister in a government of Tories and 'king's friends' from 1770. His hard line against the American colonies was supported by George III, but in 1782 he was forced to resign by the failure of his policy. In 1783 he returned to office in a coalition with Charles Fox. After its defeat, he retired from politics. Earl 1790.

North Oliver (1943–). US Marine lieutenant colonel. In 1981 he joined the staff of the National Security Council (NSC), where he supervised the mining of Nicaraguan harbours 1983, an air-force bombing raid on Libya 1986, and an arms-for-hostages deal with Iran 1985, which, when uncovered 1986 (Irangate), forced his dismissal and trial.

North was born into a San Antonio, Texas, military family and was a graduate of the US Naval Academy. He led a Marine platoon in the Vietnam War 1968–69. After working as a Marine instructor, as well as participating in a number of overseas secret missions, he became the NSC deputy director for political military affairs.

After Irangate, North was convicted on felony charges of obstructing Congress, mutilating government documents, and taking an illegal gratuity. In Sept 1991, all charges against him were dropped on the grounds that, since his evidence before Congressional committees July 1987 had been widely televised, it was impossible to give him a fair trial. He was unsuccessful as Virginia's Republican candidate for the Senate in the 1994 midterm elections.

North Thomas (*c.* 1535–*c.* 1601). English translator. His version of Plutarch's *Lives* 1579 was the source for Shakespeare's Roman plays. Knighted 1591.

Northcliffe Alfred Charles William Harmsworth, 1st Viscount Northcliffe (1865–1922). British newspaper proprietor, born in Dublin. Founding the *Daily Mail* 1896, he revolutionized popular journalism, and with the *Daily Mirror* 1903 originated the picture paper. In 1908 he also obtained control of *The Times*. Baron 1905, viscount 1917.

His brother Harold Sidney Harmsworth, 1st Viscount Rothermere (1868–1940), was associated with him in many of his newspapers; baron 1914, viscount 1919.

Suggested reading
Ferris, Paul *The House of Northcliffe* (1972)
Greenwall, H J *Northcliffe: Napoleon of Fleet Street* (1957)
Pound, Reginald and Harmsworth, Geoffrey *Northcliffe* (1959)

Northern Wei dynasty (386–535) hereditary Chinese rulers, in one of the Three Kingdoms.

Northrop John Howard (1891–1987). US chemist. In the 1930s he crystallized a number of enzymes, including pepsin and trypsin, showing conclusively that they were proteins. He shared the 1946 Nobel Prize for Chemistry with Wendell Stanley and James Sumner.

Northumberland John Dudley, Duke of Northumberland (*c.* 1502–1553). English politician, son of the privy councillor Edmund Dudley (beheaded 1510), and chief minister until Edward VI's death 1553. Knighted 1523, earl 1547.

He tried to place his daughter-in-law Lady Jane Grey on the throne, and was executed on Mary I's accession.

And all our calm is in that balm – / Not lost but gone before.

CAROLINE NORTON
'Not Lost but Gone Before'

Norton Caroline Elizabeth Sarah (born Sheridan) (1808–1877). British writer, granddaughter of R B Sheridan. Her works include *Undying One* 1830 and *Voice from the Factories* 1836, attacking child labour.

In 1836 her husband falsely accused Lord Melbourne of seducing her, obtained custody of their children, and tried to obtain the profits from her books. Public reaction to this prompted changes in the laws of infant custody and married women's property rights.

Nostradamus Latinized name of Michel de Nôtredame (1503–1566). French physician and astrologer who was consulted by Catherine de' Medici and Charles IX of France. His book of prophecies in verse, *Centuries* 1555, makes cryptic predictions about world events up to the year 3797. His books were banned by the Roman Catholic Church.

Suggested reading
Hogue, John *Nostradamus and the Millennium: Last Predictions* (1987)
Leoni, Edgar *Nostradamus and His Prophecies* (1982)

Nott John William Frederick (1932–). British Conservative politician, minister for defence 1981–83 during the Falkland Islands conflict with Argentina. KCB 1983.

Nouvel Jean (1945–). French architect. He uses the language of High Tech building in novel and highly distinctive ways. His celebrated Institut du Monde Arabe, Paris, 1981–87, adapts traditional Islamic motifs to technological ends: mechanized irises, for instance, control the penetration of daylight.

In his design for the Nemausus building in Nîmes 1983–87, he takes industrial materials and robs them of their functional role, incorporating them into a jagged, precarious assemblage.

Novak Kim (Marilyn Pauline) (1933–). US film actress of ethereal beauty. She starred in such films as *Pal Joey* 1957, *Bell, Book and Candle* 1958, *Vertigo* 1958, *Kiss Me Stupid* 1964, and *The Legend of Lylah Clare* 1968.

Novalis pen name of Friedrich Leopold von Hardenberg (1772–1801). Pioneer German Romantic poet. He wrote *Hymnen an die Nacht/Hymns to the Night* 1800, prompted by the death of his fiancée Sophie von Kühn. He left two unfinished romances, *Die Lehrlinge zu Sais/The Novices of Sais* and *Heinrich von Ofterdingen*.

Novello Ivor. Stage name of Ivor Novello Davies (1893–1951). Welsh composer and actor-manager. He wrote popular songs, such as 'Keep the Home Fires Burning', in World War I, and musicals in which he often appeared as the romantic lead, including *Glamorous Night* 1925, *The Dancing Years* 1939, and *Gay's the Word* 1951.

Novello Vincent (1781–1861). English publisher and organist of Italian origin. He established the firm Novello and Co 1811, originally to publish sacred music in order to facilitate his duties as a choirmaster. He later published the music of Purcell, Mozart, Haydn, and Beethoven and handed the firm to his eldest son Alfred (1810–1896).

Noverre Jean-Georges (1727–1810). French choreographer, writer, and ballet reformer. He promoted *ballet d'action* (with a plot) and simple, free movement, and is often considered the creator of modern classical ballet. *Les Petits Riens* 1778 was one of his works.

Nowra Louis (1950–). Australian dramatist and novelist. He is best known for his plays which include *Inner Voices* 1977, set in Russia in 1794, *Visions* 1979, set in Paraguay of the 1860s, *The Precious Woman* 1981, set in China of the 1920s, and *Byzantine Flowers* which opened in Sydney 1989.

Noyce Robert Norton (1927–1990). US scientist and inventor, with Jack Kilby, of the integrated circuit (chip), which revolutionized the computer and electronics industries in the 1970s and 1980s. In 1968 he and six colleagues founded Intel Corporation, which became one of the USA's leading semiconductor manufacturers.

Noyce was awarded a patent for the integrated circuit 1959. In 1961 he founded his first company, Fairchild Camera and Instruments Corporation, around which Silicon Valley was to grow. The company was the first in the world to understand and exploit the commercial potential of the integrated circuit. It quickly became the basis for such products as the personal computer, the pocket calculator, and the programmable microwave oven. At the time of his death, he was president of Sematech Incorporated, a government–industry research consortium created to help US firms regain a lead in semiconductor technology that they had lost to Japanese manufacturers.

Go down to Kew in lilac-time (it isn't far from London!)

ALFRED NOYES
'Barrel Organ'

Noyes Alfred (1880–1958). English poet. He wrote poems about the sea and the anthology favourites 'The Highwayman', 'Barrel Organ', and 'Go down to Kew in lilac-time...'.

Watch for me by moonlight; / I'll come to thee by moonlight though hell should bar the way!

ALFRED NOYES
'Highwayman'

Noyes Eliot (1910–1977). US architect and industrial designer, retained as a consultant by the IBM company from 1947 and responsible for the company's high design profile until 1977. In addition to his typewriters for IBM, his own notable work includes a design for a filling station for Mobil 1964. He was the first director of design at New York's Museum of Modern Art 1940–42.

Throughout his career he remained committed to a principle of 'good design' which shunned vulgarity and espoused principles which had been established in Europe.

Noyes John Humphrey (1811–1886). US religious and communal leader. He formulated the 'doctrine of free love' 1837 and in 1848 founded the Oneida Community in central New York which served as a forum for his social experiments. In 1879 Noyes was forced to move to Canada to avoid legal action against him. The former community, which made silverware and steel traps, became a joint stock company 1881.

Nozick Robert (1938–). US political philosopher. He argues that the state's existence can be justified only when it is limited to the narrow function of protection against force, theft, and fraud, and to the enforcement of contracts. Any more extensive activities by the state will inevitably violate individual rights. His main work is *Anarchy, State and Utopia* 1974.

Nu U Thakin (1907–1995). Myanmar politician, prime minister of Burma (now Myanmar) for most of the period from 1947 to the military coup of 1962. He was the country's first democratically elected prime minister. Exiled from 1966, U Nu returned to the country 1980 and, in 1988, helped found the National League for Democracy opposition movement.

U Nu oversaw the transition to independence in 1948, and sought

Nuffield *English car manufacturer and philanthropist Lord Nuffield. He began his career manufacturing bicycles 1895 with just £5 of capital.*

to promote democracy and preserve unity in a nation faced by insurgencies by the Burmese Communist Party and the separatist Karen community. A devout Buddhist who took vows of celibacy and teetotalism in 1948, he sought to govern as a *rajarsi* (ruler-sage) and promoted Theravāda Buddhism, sponsoring the construction of the Kaba-Aye peace pagoda. Despite leading the fractious AFPFL to successive electoral victories in 1952, 1956, and 1960, U Nu stepped down as prime minister temporarily in 1956–57 and 1958–60. He was overthrown in March 1962 by a military coup led by General Ne Win. He was placed under house arrest for five years, before living in exile in Thailand and India, where he resided near a Buddhist monastery.

On his return to Myanmar in 1980, he abandoned politics and concentrated on translating classic Buddhist texts from Burmese to English. However, moved by the prodemocracy uprising during 1988, he formed the National League for Democracy and declared himself prime minister. He was placed under house arrest in Nov 1988 by the new military junta which had recently seized power, and in 1991 his party was outlawed.

U Nu remained under detention until April 1992.

Nuffield William Richard Morris, 1st Viscount Nuffield (1877–1963). English manufacturer and philanthropist. Starting with a small cycle-repairing business, in 1910 he designed a car that could be produced cheaply, and built up Morris Motors Ltd at Cowley, Oxford.

He endowed Nuffield College, Oxford, 1937 and the Nuffield Foundation 1943. Baronet 1929, baron 1934, viscount 1938.

Nujoma Sam Daniel (1929–   ). Namibian left-wing politician, founder and leader of SWAPO (the South-West Africa People's Organization) from 1959, president from 1990. He was exiled in 1960 and controlled guerrillas from Angolan bases until the first free elections were held 1989, taking office early the following year.

Núñez Rafael (1825–1894). Colombian president 1880–82 and 1884–94, responsible for a new, authoritarian constitution 1886. A doctrinaire Liberal in the 1850s, he held several government posts, and was a foreign diplomat 1863–74. During his terms in office he restored the church's influential position and tried to stimulate economic development with a protective tariff. He also established a central bank, and concluded a concordat with the Vatican 1887.

Nunn Trevor Robert (1940–   ). English stage director. He was artistic director of the Royal Shakespeare Company 1968–86. He received a Tony award (with John Caird (1948–   )) for his production of *Nicholas Nickleby* 1982 and for the musical *Les Misérables* 1985.

Nureyev Rudolf Hametovich (1938–1993). Russian dancer and choreographer. A soloist with the Kirov Ballet, he defected to the West during a visit to Paris 1961. Mainly associated with the Royal Ballet (London) and as Margot Fonteyn's principal partner, he was one of the most brilliant dancers of the 1960s and 1970s. Nureyev danced in such roles as Prince Siegfried in *Swan Lake* and Armand in *Marguerite and Armand*, which was created especially for Fonteyn and Nureyev. He also danced and acted in films and on television and choreographed several ballets. It was due to his enormous impact on the ballet world that the male dancer's role was elevated to the equivalent of the ballerina's.

Nureyev was a Tatar. He was born near Lake Baikal, on a train journey, and grew up in Ufa in extreme poverty. A love of folk dancing and the sight of professional dancers at the town's small opera house led to lessons with Anna Udeltsova, who had been a member of the Diaghilev Ballet. At the age of 17 he entered the famous Vaganova Institute (also known as the Kirov Ballet School) in St Petersburg in the class of Aleksandr Pushkin, a brilliant teacher. Just three years later he joined the Kirov Ballet as a soloist, dancing with Natalya Dudinskaya, its top prima ballerina, for his first engagement.

In 1961 the Kirov Ballet was in Paris on its first important tour of the West. Nureyev was highly praised but his socializing with French friends incurred the displeasure of the Soviet officials, who told him he had to return. Sensing that he would never again be allowed to leave the Soviet Union, he slipped his escort at Le Bourget Airport and sought political asylum – and a new career. In Nov 1961 he made his London debut at a gala in aid of the Royal Academy of Dancing with *Poème Tragique*, a short solo composed for him by Frederick Ashton, the director of the Royal Ballet, and this led to an invitation to partner Margot Fonteyn, the academy's president, in *Giselle* at Covent Garden. Thus began the legendary partnership and a new lease of artistic life for Fonteyn, who was 19 years his senior.

As well as dancing in the classics of the 19th century, he created many roles in modern works, most notably with Fonteyn in Ashton's *Marguerite and Armand*, first performed at Covent Garden 1963. He choreographed and staged ballets for nearly all the major companies, reviving works from the Russian repertoire like *The Sleeping Beauty*, *The Nutcracker*, and *Raymonda*. In 1983 he was appointed director of the Ballet at the Opéra in Paris, revitalized it, and gave much encouragement to young dancers. He appeared many times on TV and in films, including the feature *I Am a Dancer*, shown first in 1972. As a result of his becoming a victim of AIDS, his physical powers inevitably declined but he was determined to continue working. He took up the new challenge of conducting in his last years and conducted (with considerable success) orchestras in Europe and the USA. His last appearance was a very emotional one at the Paris Opéra where he had been staging *La Bayadère*.

Suggested reading
Barnes, Clive *Nureyev* (1982)
Nureyev, R *Nureyev* (1962)
Percival, John *Fonteyn and Nureyev* (1962)

Nutter Tommy (1943–1992). English tailor. His trend-setting suits became famous in the 1960s–70s. Although employing conventional techniques, he made a distinct break with many traditions of tailoring when he produced suits with wide lapels and flared trousers and experimented with fabrics, for example cutting pinstripes on the horizontal and mixing gamekeeper tweeds in three-piece suits.

In 1969 he opened his own tailoring shop in Savile Row, London, where he attracted many celebrity clients such as the Beatles, Mick and Bianca Jagger, Elton John, and the fashion designer Hardy Amies. Despite financial difficulties in the early 1970s he launched his first ready-to-wear line for Austin Reed 1978, and in 1980 signed a five-year contract to design fabrics for a cloth manufacturer in Japan.

Nyerere Julius Kambarage (1922–). Tanzanian socialist politician, president 1964–85. He devoted himself from 1954 to the formation of the Tanganyika African National Union and subsequent campaigning for independence. He became chief minister 1960, was prime minister of Tanganyika 1961–62, president of the newly formed Tanganyika Republic 1962–64, and first president of Tanzania 1964–85. He attempted to establish collective farms, but his policies ultimately failed. He was head of the Organization of African Unity 1984.

Nyers Rezso (1923–). Hungarian socialist leader. In 1940 Nyers joined the Hungarian Social Democratic Party, which in 1948 was forcibly merged with the communists. He became secretary of the ruling Hungarian Socialist Worker's Party's central committee 1962. A member of the politburo from 1966 and the architect of Hungary's liberalizing economic reforms in 1968, he was ousted from power by hardliners 1974. In 1988 he was brought back into the politburo, and was head of the newly formed Hungarian Socialist Party 1989–90.

Nyholm Ronald Sydney (1917–1971). Australian inorganic chemist who worked on the coordination compounds (complexes) of the transition metals. Knighted 1967.

Nureyev *Russian-born ballet dancer and choreographer Rudolf Nureyev, whose skill and versatility brought him international acclaim. He revised the choreography of some ballets to satisfy the demands of his skill, agility, and strength; in 1964 he reworked* Swan Lake, *giving the male dancer the dominant role, following a precedent set by Nijinsky.*

Nyholm was born in Broken Hill, New South Wales, and studied at Sydney and, after World War II, at University College, London, where he became professor 1955. As chair of the Chemistry Consultative Committee, he was largely responsible for the Nuffield chemistry course taught in British schools and for changes to the examination syllabuses. He advocated an integrated approach to the teaching of chemistry.

Nyholm systematically exploited physical methods to study the structures and properties of coordination compounds. He employed X-ray crystallography and nuclear magnetic resonance spectroscopy, and found that magnetic moment seemed to give the closest connection between electronic structure, chemical structure, and stereochemistry.

Nykvist Sven (1924–). Swedish director of photography. He was associated with the director Ingmar Bergman. From the mid-1970s onwards he worked frequently in the USA. His films include *The Virgin Spring* 1960 (for Bergman), *Pretty Baby* 1978 (for Louis Malle), and *Fanny and Alexander* 1982 (for Bergman). He directed *Oxen/The Ox* 1992.

Nyman Michael (1944–). English composer. Born in London, Nyman studied musicology at University College, London, and wrote a monograph on avant-garde music, *Experimental Music* 1974, before he began composing in mid-1980s. His highly stylized music is characterized by processes of gradual modification by repetition of complex musical formulae (known as minimalism). His compositions include scores for English film maker Peter Greenaway and New Zealand film maker Jane Campion (*The Piano* 1993); a chamber opera, *The Man Who Mistook His Wife for a Hat* 1989; and three string quartets.

Oakeshott Michael Joseph (1901–1990). British political philosopher, author of *On Civilization* 1969. A conservative, he was praised by the right for emphasizing experience over ideals, summed up as 'Tory anarchism'. He was professor of politics at the London School of Economics 1951–69. His other books include *A Guide to the Classics* 1936 on picking winners in horseracing.

Anyone who has had a glimpse of the range and subtlety of the thought of Plato or of Hegel will long ago have despaired of becoming a philosopher.

MICHAEL OAKESHOTT
Experience and its Modes ch 1 1933

Oakley Annie, (Phoebe Anne Oakley Mozee) (1860–1926). US sharpshooter, member of Buffalo Bill's Wild West Show. Even though she was partially paralysed in a train crash 1901, she continued to astound audiences with her ability virtually until her death. Kaiser Wilhelm of Germany had such faith in her talent that he allowed her to shoot a cigarette from his mouth.

His violence of language ultimately did his cause harm, but [earlier] nothing short of sensational and denunciatory statements would have served to excite opinion.

E L Woodward on RICHARD OASTLER
in *The Age of Reform 1815–1870* 1938

Oastler Richard (1789–1861). English social reformer. He opposed child labour and the poor law 1834, which restricted relief, and was largely responsible for securing the Factory Act 1833 and the Ten Hours Act 1847. He was given the nickname of the 'Factory King' for his achievements on behalf of workers.

Our enemy is by tradition our savior, in preventing us from superficiality.

JOYCE CAROL OATES
quoted in 'Master Race', *Partisan Review 50th Anniversary Edition*

Oates Joyce Carol (1938–). US writer. Her novels are often aggressive, realistic descriptions of the forces of darkness and violence in modern culture. A prolific writer, she uses a wide range of genres and settings including the comedy *Unholy Loves* 1979, the Gothic horror of *A Bloodsmoor Romance* 1982, and the thriller *Kindred Passions* 1987. Her other novels include *A Garden of Earthly Delights* 1967, *them* 1969, *Because It Is Bitter, and Because It Is My Heart* 1990, and *Zombie* 1995.

Oates Laurence Edward Grace (1880–1912). British Antarctic explorer who accompanied Robert Falcon Scott on his second expedition to the South Pole. On the return journey, suffering from frostbite, he went out alone into the blizzard to die rather than delay the others.

Oates Titus (1648–1705). English conspirator. A priest, he entered the Jesuit colleges at Valladolid, Spain, and St Omer, France, as a spy 1677–78, and on his return to England announced he had discovered a 'Popish Plot' to murder Charles II and re-establish Catholicism. Although this story was almost entirely false, many

innocent Roman Catholics were executed during 1678–80 on Oates's evidence. In 1685 Oates was flogged, pilloried, and imprisoned for perjury. He was pardoned and granted a pension after the revolution of 1688.

Such a man's Testimonie should not be taken against the life of a dog.

John Evelyn on TITUS OATES
at the trial of Lord Stafford in his *Diary* 6 Dec 1680

Oberon Merle. Stage name of Estelle Merle O'Brien Thompson (1911–1979). Indian-born British actress. (She claimed to be Tasmanian.) She starred in several films by Alexander Korda (to whom she was briefly married 1939–45), including *The Scarlet Pimpernel* 1935. She played Cathy to Laurence Olivier's Heathcliff in *Wuthering Heights* 1939, and after 1940 worked in the USA.

Obote (Apollo) Milton (1924–). Ugandan politician who led the independence movement from 1961. He became prime minister 1962 and was president 1966–71 and 1980–85, being overthrown by first Idi Amin and then by Lt-Gen Tito Okello.

Obraztsov Sergei Vladimirovich (1901–). Russian puppeteer. He was head of the Moscow-based State Central Puppet Theatre, the world's largest puppet theatre (with a staff of 300). The repertoire was built up from 1923.

Obrecht Jacob (c. 1450–1505). Flemish composer. One of the outstanding composers of his day, his mostly polyphonic sacred music (which in style predates that of Josquin Desprez) centred on the Mass, for which he wrote 24 compositions. He was innovative, developing borrowed material, and using a secular fixed *cantus firmus* (Latin 'fixed song') in his *Missa super Maria zart*. He also wrote motets and secular works. He worked as a kapellmeister (choirmaster) in Utrecht, Antwerp, and Bruges. He died of the plague.

Obrenovich Serbian dynasty that ruled 1816–42 and 1859–1903. The dynasty engaged in a feud with the rival house of Karageorgevich, which obtained the throne by the murder of the last Obrenovich 1903.

O'Brien Flann. Pen name of Brian O'Nolan (1911–1966). Irish humorist, novelist, and essayist who wrote in Irish Gaelic and English. For 30 years he was a brilliant columnist on the *Irish Times* under the pen name *Myles na Gopaleen*. His first novel, the ambitious, exploratory *At Swim-Two-Birds* 1939, was influenced by James Joyce. His novel *The Third Policeman* 1967 (written 1940) is an experimental detective work grimly reminiscent of Samuel Beckett.

O'Brien was born in County Tyrone and worked as a civil servant. He wrote one novel in Gaelic, *An Béal Bocht/The Poor Mouth* 1941. A selection of his newspaper columns appeared posthumously in *The Best of Myles* 1968.

O'Brien James Bronterre (1805–1864). Irish Chartist. He moved from Ireland to London 1829 where he became leader of the Chartist working class movement. He was editor of the *Poor Man's Guardian* 1831–35 and was imprisoned for his seditious speeches 1840–41. He helped found the socialist National Reform League 1850.

O'Brien (Josephine) Edna (1930–). Irish writer. Her first novel, *The Country Girls* 1960, began a trilogy about two girls who flee restrictive rural Ireland for excitement in Dublin and London, ending in bleak disillusionment. Much of her work was banned by the Irish censors. Loneliness, guilt, and loss tend to dominate her work, though she has a lyrical prose style and there are moments of joyful self-fulfilment. Her lack of inhibition has led to comparison with the French writer Colette.

O'Brien published four volumes of short stories 1968–86, plays (including *Virginia* 1981 about Virginia Woolf), and *Northern Ireland* 1976, a nostalgic tribute. A recent novel is *House of Splendid Isolation* 1994.

O'Brien Margaret Angela Maxine (1937–   ). US child actress, a star of the 1940s. She received a special Academy Award 1944, but her career, which included leading parts in *Lost Angel* 1943, *Meet Me in St Louis* 1944, and *The Secret Garden* 1949, did not survive beyond adolescence.

O'Brien Willis H (1886–1962). US film animator and special-effects creator. He was responsible for one of the cinema's most memorable monsters, the giant ape in *King Kong* 1933.

O'Casey Sean. Adopted name of John Casey (1884–1964). Irish dramatist. His early plays are tragicomedies, blending realism with symbolism and poetic with vernacular speech: *The Shadow of a Gunman* 1922, *Juno and the Paycock* 1925, and *The Plough and the Stars* 1926. Later plays include *Red Roses for Me* 1946 and *The Drums of Father Ned* 1960. He also wrote the antiwar drama *The Silver Tassie* 1929, *The Star Turns Red* 1940, *Oak Leaves and Lavender* 1947, and a six-volume autobiography.

Suggested reading
Ayling, R and Durkan, M J *Sean O'Casey: A Biography* (1978)
Kenneally, Michael *Portraying the Self: Sean O'Casey and the Art of Autobiography* (1988)
O'Connor, Garry *Sean O'Casey: A Life* (1988)
O'Riordan, John *A Guide to O'Casey's Plays* (1985)

Occam or Ockham, William of (c. 1300–1349). English philosopher and scholastic logician who revived the fundamentals of nominalism. As a Franciscan monk he defended evangelical poverty against Pope John XXII, becoming known as the Invincible Doctor. He was imprisoned in Avignon, France, on charges of heresy 1328 but escaped to Munich, Germany, where he died. The principle of reducing assumptions to the absolute minimum is known as *Occam's razor*.

Ochoa Severo (1905–1993). Spanish-born US biochemist who discovered an enzyme able to assemble units of the nucleic acid RNA 1955. For his work towards the synthesis of RNA, Ochoa shared the 1959 Nobel Prize for Physiology or Medicine.

Ochoa was one of the pioneers in molecular biology and genetic engineering. His early work concerned biochemical pathways in the human body, especially those involving carbon dioxide, but his main research was into nucleic acids and how their nucleotide units are linked, either singly (as in RNA) or to form two helically wound strands (as in DNA). In 1955 Ochoa obtained an enzyme from bacteria that was capable of joining together similar nucleotide units to form a nucleic acid, a type of artificial RNA. Nucleic acids containing exactly similar nucleotide units do not occur naturally, but the method of synthesis used by Ochoa was the same as that employed by a living cell.

He lectured at Madrid 1931–35, until the threat of the Spanish Civil War forced him to flee Spain for Germany, where he worked at the University of Heidelberg. With the rise of Hitler, he fled again 1937, this time to Britain, where he worked at Oxford University. He moved to the USA 1940, and worked at Washington University 1941–42, before moving to New York University, first as a research associate in the college of medicine, and then 1954–75 as a professor in the department of biochemistry. He joined the Roche Institute of Molecular Biology 1975, and became a US citizen 1956.

Ochoa, who counted Dali and Lorca among his friends, was a very dedicated world citizen and a music lover. He was president of the International Union of Biochemistry, and a member of the Soviet Academy of Sciences. He returned to Spain permanently 1985, where his fame is attested by the fact that most cities have a street named after him.

Ochs Adolph Simon (1858–1935). US newspaper publisher. In 1896 he gained control of the then faltering *New York Times* and transformed it into a serious, authoritative publication. Among Ochs's innovations were a yearly index and a weekly book-review section.

Ockham William of. English philosopher; see ◊Occam.

O'Connell Daniel (1775–1847). Irish politician, called 'the Liberator'. In 1823 O'Connell founded the Catholic Association to press Roman Catholic claims. His reserved and vacillating leadership and conservative outlook on social questions alienated his most active supporters, who broke away and formed the nationalist Young Ireland movement. Although ineligible, as a Roman Catholic, to take his seat, he was elected member of Parliament for County Clare 1828 and so forced the government to grant Catholic emancipation. In Parliament he co-operated with the Whigs in the hope of obtaining concessions until 1841, when he launched his campaign for repeal of the union.

He had the qualities of a successful demagogue; he was ... big, heavily-built ... with a tremendous voice, a rough humour, and a quick power of epigram and repartee.

E L Woodward on FERGUS O'CONNOR
in *The Age of Reform 1815–1870* 1938

O'Connor Feargus Edward (1794–1855). Irish parliamentarian, a follower of Daniel O'Connell. He sat in Parliament 1832–35, and as editor of the *Northern Star* became an influential figure of the radical working-class Chartist movement.

O'Connor (Mary) Flannery (1925–1964). US novelist and short-story writer. Her works have a great sense of evil and sin, and often explore the religious sensibility of the Deep South, as in her novels *Wise Blood* 1952 and *The Violent Bear It Away* 1960. Her work exemplifies the postwar revival of the Gothic novel in Southern US fiction.

Her collections of short stories include *A Good Man Is Hard to Find* 1955, *Everything That Rises Must Converge* 1965, *The Habit of Being* 1979, and *Flannery O'Connor: Collected Works* 1988.

Suggested reading
O'Connor, Flannery *The Habit of Being* (letters) (edited by S Fitzgerald 1979)
Paulson, Suzanne *Flannery O'Connor: A Study of Her Short Fiction* (1988)

O'Connor Richard Nugent (1889–1981). British general in World War II. In 1940 he became commander of the Western Desert Force in Egypt, defeating the Italians at Sidi Barrani Dec 1940. He went on to capture Bardia and destroyed the Italian 10th Army at Beda Fomm. He was captured by the Germans April 1942, but escaped two years later and returned to the UK. He commanded VIII Corps in the Normandy campaign. KCB 1941.

O'Connor Sandra Day (1930–   ). US jurist and the first female associate justice of the US Supreme Court 1981–   . Considered a moderate conservative, she dissented in *Texas v Johnson* 1990, a decision that ruled that the legality of burning the US flag in protest was protected by the First Amendment. In 1965 she became an assistant Arizona attorney general and in 1969 was appointed to a vacancy in the state senate, to which she was later elected and of which she became majority leader 1972. In 1974 she was elected a county court judge and in 1979 was appointed to the state court of appeals. In 1981 President Reagan appointed her to the US Supreme Court, where she generally espoused a conservative position.

Octavia (AD 40–62). Roman noblewoman, daughter of the Roman emperor Claudius and Messalina. She married Nero AD 53 but was divorced by him and placed under house arrest in AD 62. She was subsequently banished to the island of Pandateria where she was executed on a false charge of treason. Her story forms the subject of the only surviving Latin play on a contemporary subject, *Octavia*, which is often attributed to Seneca.

Probably the victim of papal intrigues, he was imprisoned until after William's death 1087, and then banished 1088 after supporting the revolt against William II. Odo settled in Normandy, where he devoted himself to rebuilding Bayeux cathedral. In 1096 he set off with Duke Robert II on the First Crusade, but died on the way at Palermo, Italy. He probably commissioned the Bayeux Tapestry for the dedication of Bayeux Cathedral 1077. The tapestry shows him armed with a mace, supposedly to conform to the prohibition against clerics spilling blood.

Odoacer (*c.* 433–493). King of Italy from 476, when he deposed Romulus Augustulus, the last Roman emperor. He was a leader of the barbarian mercenaries employed by Rome. He was overthrown and killed by Theodoric the Great, king of the Ostrogoths.

Odoyevsky Vladimir (1804–1869). Russian writer whose works include tales of the supernatural, science fiction, satires, children's stories, and music criticism.

Ōe Kenzaburō (1935–). Japanese novelist. Involved in leftist politics in Japan, he has explored the situation of culturally disinherited postwar youth. His works include *Kojinteki-na taiken/A Personal Matter* 1964, describing from direct experience the development of an abnormal baby, seen by some as a metaphor for the contemporary Japanese situation. His earlier novel *Shiiku/The Catch* 1958 was awarded the Akutagawa Prize. He was awarded the Nobel Prize for Literature 1994.

Oersted Hans Christian (1777–1851). Danish physicist who founded the science of electromagnetism. In 1820 he discovered the magnetic field associated with an electric current.

He worked as a pharmacist before making a tour of Europe 1801–03 to complete his studies in science. On his return, Oersted gave public lectures with great success, and was professor of physics at Copenhagen 1806–29, when he became director of the Polytechnic Institute in Copenhagen.

Believing that all forces must be interconvertible, Oersted had predicted in 1813 that an electric current would produce magnetism when it flowed through a wire, just as it produced heat and light. His 1820 experiment involved a compass needle placed beneath a wire connected to a battery. He found that a circular magnetic field is produced around a wire carrying a current.

In 1822, Oersted turned to the compressibility of gases and liquids, devising a useful apparatus to determine compressibility. He also investigated thermoelectricity, in 1823.

O'Faolain Sean (Gaelic name adopted by John Francis Whelan) (1900–1991). Irish novelist, short-story writer, and biographer. His first novel, *A Nest of Simple Folk* 1933, was followed by an edition of translated Gaelic, *The Silver Branch* 1938. His many biographies include *Daniel O'Connell* 1938 and *De Valera* 1939, about the nationalist whom he had fought beside in the Irish Republican Army.

O'Farrell Henry James (1833–1868). Australian Fenian supporter, born in Ireland, who made an assassination attempt on Prince Alfred, Duke of Edinburgh, second son of Queen Victoria, during a visit to Australia in 1868. He shot the prince at Clontarf, Sydney. This was an isolated incident rather than part of a Fenian plot as claimed by anti-Irish elements. O'Farrell was convicted of attempted murder and hanged.

Oersted *Danish physicist Hans Christian Oersted shown discovering the effect of an electric current on a magnetic needle during a lecture at the University of Copenhagen 1820. As well as his pioneering work on the electromagnetic effect, Oersted was also the first scientist to isolate the element aluminium.* (Ann Ronan/Image Select)

Octavian original name of ◊Augustus, the first Roman emperor.

Oddsson David (1948–). Icelandic politician, prime minister from 1991. Oddsson began his career in local politics, becoming mayor of Reykjavík 1982. A member of the right-of-centre Independence Party, he was made vice chairman of the party 1989 and chairman 1991, when he succeeded Thorsteinn Pálsson as premier. Outside of politics, he has an established reputation as a stage and TV dramatist.

Go out and fight so life shouldn't be printed on dollar bills.
CLIFFORD ODETS
Awake and Sing! 1935

Odets Clifford (1906–1963). US dramatist. He was associated with the Group Theatre and the most renowned of the social-protest dramatists of the Depression era. His plays include *Waiting for Lefty* 1935, about a taxi drivers' strike, *Awake and Sing* 1935, *Golden Boy* 1937, and *The Country Girl* 1950. In the late 1930s he went to Hollywood and became a successful film writer and director, but he continued to write plays.

Suggested reading
Brenman-Gibson, Margaret *Clifford Odets: A Biography* (1981)
Cantor, Harold *Clifford Odets: Playwright-Poet* (1978)

Odo of Bayeux (*c.* 1030–1097). French bishop, co-regent of England, who probably commissioned the Bayeux Tapestry. He was the son of Duke Robert the Devil of Normandy and half-brother of William the Conqueror, from whom he received his bishopric 1049. His service at the Battle of Hastings won him the earldom of Kent 1067 and vast English estates, making him one of the richest men in Europe. During William's absence in Normandy 1067 he shared the regency of England with William Fitzosborne and remained prominent in the royal administration until 1082. Earl of Kent 1066.

No other Anglo-Saxon king ever regarded the world at large with so secular a mind or so acute a political sense.
F M Stenton on OFFA
in Anglo-Saxon England 2nd ed 1947

Offa (died *c.* 796). King of Mercia, England, from 757. He conquered Essex, Kent, Sussex, and Surrey; defeated the Welsh and the West Saxons; and established Mercian supremacy over all England south of the river Humber.

Offenbach Jacques (1819–1880). French composer. He wrote light opera, initially for presentation at the Bouffes parisiens. Among his works are *Orphée aux enfers/Orpheus in the Underworld* 1858, revised 1874, *La Belle Hélène* 1864, and *Les Contes d'Hoffmann/The Tales of Hoffmann* 1881.
Suggested reading
Faris, Alexander *Jacques Offenbach* (1980)
Harding, James *Jacques Offenbach* (1980)

Offenbach's music is wicked. It is abandoned stuff: every accent is a snap of the fingers in the face of moral responsibility.

George Bernard Shaw on JACQUES OFFENBACH
quoted in Alexander Faris *Jacques Offenbach* 1980

O'Flaherty Liam (1896–1984). Irish author. He is best known for his short stories published in volumes such as *Spring Sowing* 1924, *The Tent* 1926, and *Two Lovely Beasts* 1948. His novels, set in County Mayo, include *The Neighbour's Wife* 1923, *The Informer* 1925, and *Land* 1946.

Ogata Kōrin (1658–1716). Japanese painter and designer. His style is highly decorative, typically combining brightly coloured, naturalistic and stylized elements against a gold background. *Iris Screen* from the early 18th century (Nezu Art Museum, Tokyo) is one of his best-known works.

The son of a rich silk merchant of Kyoto, he was related to the painters Kōetsu and Sōtatsu and admired and was influenced by their work. Trained in the classic Kano style, he diverged from it in a bold and simplified style of his own. His vigour and breadth of design are shown in his lacquer screens. In smaller paintings he showed great mastery of calligraphic brushwork. His art was forgotten for some time after his death but was re-established in esteem by his follower Sakai Hōitsu (1771–1828), who published his paintings and designs in woodcut books.

Ogden C(harles) K(ay) (1889–1957). English writer and scholar. With I A Richards he developed the simplified form of English known as Basic English, built on a vocabulary of just 850 words. Together they wrote *Foundations of Aesthetics* 1921 and *The Meaning of Meaning* 1923.

Ogdon John Andrew Howard (1937–1989). English pianist and composer. A contemporary of Alexander Goehr and Peter Maxwell Davies at Manchester University, he won early recognition at the Moscow Tchaikovsky Piano Competition 1962 and went on to become an ebullient champion of neglected virtuoso repertoire by Alkan, Bartók, Busoni, and Sorabji. For a number of years unable to perform as a result of depression, he recovered to make a successful return to the concert hall shortly before his death.

Ogino Ginko (1851–1913). Japan's first woman doctor. She left her husband after a year of marriage because he infected her with gonorrhoea. Finding it intolerable to be treated by a male doctor, she decided to become a doctor herself. As a woman she could not enrol in medical school but after eight years, aged 28, she was allowed to study privately. She dedicated her life to treating the sick.

Oglethorpe James Edward (1696–1785). English soldier and colonizer of Georgia. He served in parliament for 32 years and in 1732 obtained a charter for the colony of Georgia, USA, intended as a refuge for debtors and for European Protestants. The colony was also intended by the British to act as a buffer against Spanish Florida. The colonists were selected carefully, and every aspect of life was planned and supervised.

Oglethorpe served as Georgia's first colonial governor 1733–34. In 1743, frustrated by settlers' complaints, he returned to England.

O'Hara Frank (1926–1966). US poet and art critic. He was the leading member of the New York School of poets (others include John Ashbery, Kenneth Koch (1925–), and James Schuyler (1923–)), whose work was based on an immediate and autobiographical relationship to city life. His work includes *Lunch Poems* 1964.

Offenbach *The German-born composer Jacques Offenbach, from a chromolithograph. After moving to Paris as a teenager, he later became a leading composer of opéras-comiques. Wagner, never renowned for his humour, did not appreciate being parodied in* Le Carnaval des revues. (Image Select)

A curator at the Museum of Modern Art, he was associated, both personally and artistically, with the Abstract Expressionist painters. O'Hara also wrote essays and criticism collected in *Standing Still in New York* and *Art Chronicles* both 1975.

O'Hara John Henry (1905–1970). US novelist. His *Appointment in Samarra* 1934 was a work of tough social realism and dealt with the world of the country-club set. This was followed by *Butterfield 8* 1935, which was based on a murder case and sharply observed the sordid reality and bourgeois anxiety of the Depression years.

O'Higgins Bernardo (1778–1842). Chilean revolutionary, known as 'the Liberator of Chile'. He was a leader of the struggle for independence from Spanish rule 1810–17 and head of the first permanent national government 1817–23.

Ohm Georg Simon (1789–1854). German physicist who studied electricity and discovered the fundamental law that bears his name. Ohm's law states that the steady electrical current in a metallic circuit is directly proportional to the constant total electromotive force in the circuit. The SI unit of electrical resistance, the *ohm*, is named after him, and the unit of conductance (the inverse of resistance) was formerly called the *mho*, which is 'ohm' spelled backwards.

He worked as a schoolteacher until 1833, when he became professor of physics at the Polytechnic Institute, Nuremberg, moving to Munich University 1849.

Ohm began the work that led him to his law of electricity in 1825. He investigated the amount of electromagnetic force produced in a wire carrying a current, expecting it to decrease with the length of the wire in the circuit. Using a thermocouple because it produced a constant electric current, he employed an electroscope to measure how the tension varied at different points along a conductor to verify his law, and presented his arguments in mathematical form in his great work *Die Galvanische Kette* 1827.

Oistrakh David Fyodorovich (1908–1974). Soviet violinist. He was celebrated for performances of both standard and contemporary Russian repertoire. Shostakovich wrote both his violin concertos for him. His son *Igor* (1931–   ) is equally renowned as a violinist.

O'Keeffe Georgia (1887–1986). US painter. She is known chiefly for her large, semi-abstract studies of flowers and bones, such as *Black Iris* 1926 (Metropolitan Museum of Art, New York) and the *Pelvis Series* of the 1940s. Her mature style stressed contours and subtle tonal transitions, which often transformed the subject into a powerful and erotic abstract image. In 1946 she settled in New Mexico, where the desert landscape inspired many of her paintings. She was married 1924–46 to photographer and art exhibitor Alfred Stieglitz, in whose gallery her work was first shown.

Suggested reading
Castro, Jan Garden *The Art and Life of Georgia O'Keeffe* (1985)
Eisler, Benita *O'Keeffe and Stieglitz: An American Romance* (1991)
O'Keeffe, Georgia *Art and Letters* (selected by Sarah Greenough) (1987)
Peters, Sarah Whitaker *Becoming O'Keeffe: The Early Years* (1991)
Robinson, Roxana *Georgia O'Keeffe: A Life* (1990)

Okeghem Johannes (Jean d') (*c.* 1421–*c.* 1497). Flemish composer of church music. His works include the antiphon *Alma Redemptoris Mater* and the richly contrapuntal *Missa Prolationum/Prolation Mass* employing complex canonic imitation in multiple parts at different levels. He was court composer to Charles VII, Louis XI, and Charles VIII of France.

Okri Ben (1959–   ). Nigerian novelist, broadcaster, and journalist. His novel *The Famished Road* won the UK Booker Prize 1991. He published his first book *Flowers and Shadows* 1980, and wrote his second, *The Landscapes Within* 1982, while still a student at university

Okri *Nigerian writer Ben Okri, winner of the 1991 Booker Prize with the novel* The Famished Road. *His lyrical, visionary style belies his often gruesome perceptions of Africa and his understanding of everyday life as being full of 'ordinary miracles'.*

in Essex, England. He worked for the BBC World Service as a broadcaster 1984–85 and was poetry editor of *West Africa* magazine 1980–87. Short story collections include *Incidents at the Shrine* 1987 and *Stars of the New Curfew* 1988. His first book of poems, *An African Elegy* 1992, is based on contemporary Africa. More recent work includes *Astonishing the Gods* 1995.

Ōkubo Toshimichi (1831–1878). Japanese samurai leader from Satsuma province in S Japan, whose opposition to the Tokugawa shogunate made him a leader in the Meiji restoration 1866–88. He served as finance and home minister in the Meiji government, but was assassinated by a former samurai from Satsuma in May 1878.

Okuma Shigenobu (1838–1922). Japanese politician and prime minister 1898 and 1914–16. He presided over Japanese pressure for territorial concessions in China, before retiring 1916.

Olaf five kings of Norway, including:

Olaf (I) Tryggvesson (*c.* 969–1000). King of Norway from 995. He began the conversion of Norway to Christianity and was killed in a sea battle against the Danes and Swedes.

Olaf (II) Haraldsson (*c.* 995–1030). King of Norway from 1015. He offended his subjects by his centralizing policy and zeal for Christianity, and was killed in battle by Norwegian rebel chiefs backed by Canute of Denmark. He was declared the patron saint of Norway 1164.

Olaf V (1903–1991). King of Norway from 1957, when he succeeded his father, Haakon VII. After the German invasion of Norway 1940 Olav, as crown prince, became a rallying point for his compatriots by holding out against German air raids for two months and later, in exile in England, playing an important part in liaison with resistance movements in Norway as well as building up the Free Norwegian forces in Britain.

Olazabal Jose Maria (1966–   ). Spanish golfer, one of the leading players on the European circuit. After a distinguished amateur career he turned professional 1986. He was a member of the European Ryder Cup teams 1987, 1989, and 1991.

He won the English amateur championship 1984 and the Youths title the following year. He finished second in the European money list in his second year as a professional.

Olbers Heinrich Wilhelm Matthäus (1758–1840). German astronomer, a founder member of the Celestial Police, a group of astronomers who attempted to locate a supposed missing planet between Mars and Jupiter. During his search he discovered two asteroids, Pallas 1802 and Vesta 1807. Also credited to Olbers are a number of comet discoveries, a new method of calculating cometary orbits, and the stating of Olbers' paradox. Olbers' paradox is the question, put forward in 1826: If the universe is infinite in extent and filled with stars, why is the sky dark at night? Olbers explained the darkness of the night sky by assuming that space is not absolutely transparent and that some interstellar matter absorbs a very minute percentage of starlight. This effect is sufficient to dim the light of the stars, so that they are seen as points against a dark sky. In fact, darkness is now generally accepted as a by-product of the red shift caused by stellar recession. He practised as a physician in Bremen 1781–1823, but was a keen amateur astronomer, with an observatory at the top of his house.

Olbrich Joseph Maria (1867–1908). Viennese architect. He worked under Otto Wagner and was opposed to the over-ornamentation of Art Nouveau. His major buildings, however, remain Art Nouveau in spirit: the Vienna Sezession 1897–98, the Hochzeitsturm 1907, and the Tietz department store in Düsseldorf, Germany, 1906–09.

Oldenbarneveldt Johan van (1547–1619). Dutch politician, a leading figure in the Netherlands' struggle for independence from Spain. He helped William the Silent negotiate the Union of Utrecht 1579. As leader of the Republican party he opposed the war policy of stadholder (magistrate) Maurice of Orange and negotiated a 12-

year truce with Spain 1609. His support of the Remonstrants (Arminians) in the religious strife against Maurice and the Gomarists (Calvinists) effected his downfall and he was arrested and executed.

Oldenburg Claes Thure (1929–). US Pop artist. He organized happenings and made assemblages, but is best known for 'soft sculptures', gigantic replicas of everyday objects and foods, made of stuffed canvas or vinyl. One characteristic work is *Lipstick* 1969 (Yale University).
Suggested reading
Fuchs, Rudolf H *Claes Oldenburg: Large Scale Projects* (1980)
Rose, Barbara *Claes Oldenburg* (1970)

Oldenburg Henry (1615–1677). German official, residing in London from 1652, who founded and edited in 1665 the first-ever scientific periodical, *Philosophical Transactions*. He was secretary to the Royal Society 1663–77 and through his extensive correspondence acted as a clearing house for the science of the day.

Oldfield Barney (Berna Eli) (1878–1946). US racing-car driver. Henry Ford employed him as a driver for his experimental racing car 1902 and in the following year Oldfield set the world land speed record of 60 mph/96.6 kph. In 1910 he reached a speed in excess of 130 mph/209 kph.

Born in Wauseon, Ohio, USA, Oldfield established a reputation as a successful bicycle racer as a youth. A familiar figure at races across the country, he retired from competitive driving 1918 and spent the rest of his career as a consultant to various automobile and tyre makers.

Oldfield Bruce (1950–). English fashion designer. He set up his own business 1975. His evening wear is worn by the British royal family, film stars, and socialites.

Old Pretender nickname of ◊James Edward Stuart, the son of James II of England.

Olds Ransom Eli (1864–1950). US car manufacturer. He experimented with steam-powered prototype automobiles from 1886. In 1895 he produced a gas-powered car and in the following year founded the Olds Motor Vehicle Company. Reorganizing the operation as the Olds Motor Works, he produced his popular Oldsmobiles from 1899 in Detroit. He pioneered the assembly-line method of car production that would later be refined by Henry Ford.

After selling the Olds Motor Works 1904, Olds established the Reo Motor Car Company, serving as its president 1904–24 and chair of the board 1924–36.

Olga, St (*c.* 890–*c.* 969). the wife of Igor, the Scandinavian prince of Kiev. Her baptism around 955 was a decisive step in the Christianization of Russia.

Oliphant Margaret (born Wilson) (1828–1897). Scottish writer. The author of 98 novels, 25 non-fictional works, 50 short stories, and 300 articles, she was one of the first women writers to live entirely on writing, which she did while bringing up her children unaided, following her husband's death. She wrote her first novel at 17, while nursing her sick mother, and had a novel published at 21. Her major work is the series *The Chronicles of Carlingford* 1863–66, including *The Perpetual Curate*, and *Hester*.

Olivares Count-Duke of (born Gaspar de Guzmán) (1587–1645). Spanish prime minister 1621–43. He overstretched Spain in foreign affairs and unsuccessfully attempted domestic reform. He committed Spain to recapturing the Netherlands and to involvement in the Thirty Years' War 1618–48, and his efforts to centralize power led to revolts in Catalonia and Portugal, which brought about his downfall.

Oliver Isaac (*c.* 1560–1617). English painter of miniatures. Originally a Huguenot refugee, he studied under Nicholas Hilliard. He became a court artist in the reign of James I. His sitters included the poet John Donne.

Oldfield English fashion designer Bruce Oldfield. Having studied fine art, he turned to fashion design in the late 1960s and worked for Yves Saint-Laurent before showing his first collection 1975. He has received international acclaim for both his custom-made clothes and his ready-to-wear designs. His haute-couture creations are worn by the rich and famous.

Oliver King (Joseph) (1885–1938). US jazz cornet player, bandleader, and composer. His work with Louis Armstrong 1922–24, on numbers like 'Canal Street Blues', took jazz beyond the confines of early Dixieland. His other compositions include 'Snake Rag' 1923 and 'Dr Jazz' 1927.

Born in Louisiana, Oliver began his career with New Orleans brass bands but was based mainly in Chicago from 1919 and in New York from the mid-1920s. He led his own band (called first the Creole Jazz Band and later the Dixie Syncopators) 1918–27 and 1931–37. The two-part cornet improvisations he created with Armstrong are seen as the high point of 1920s jazz. Oliver later moved towards a swing style.

Olivier Laurence Kerr, Baron Olivier (1907–1989). English actor and director. For many years associated with the Old Vic theatre, he was director of the National Theatre company 1962–73. His stage roles include Henry V, Hamlet, Richard III, and Archie Rice in John Osborne's *The Entertainer* 1957 (filmed 1960). His acting and direction of filmed versions of Shakespeare's plays received critical acclaim for example, *Henry V* 1944 and *Hamlet* 1948 (Academy Award). Knighted 1947, baron 1970.

Olivier appeared on screen in many films, including *Wuthering*

Olivier English actor Laurence Olivier in Terence Rattigan's film Sleuth. Olivier played most of the great Shakespearean roles and his contribution to British theatre generally is widely recognized. He was knighted 1947 and made a life peer 1970, as well as receiving many honours from the theatre world. (Image Select)

Heights 1939, *Rebecca* 1940, *Sleuth* 1972, *Marathon Man* 1976, and *The Boys from Brazil* 1978. The Olivier Theatre (part of the National Theatre on the South Bank, London) is named after him. He was married to Vivien Leigh 1940–60, and to Joan Plowright from 1961 until his death.

Suggested reading
Daniels, R L *Laurence Olivier* (1980)
Holden, A *Laurence Olivier* (1988)
Olivier, Laurence *Confessions of an Actor* (1982)
Olivier, Tarquin *My Father Laurence Olivier* (1992)
Spoto, Donald *Laurence Olivier: A biography* (1992)

Olmsted Frederick Law (1822–1903). US landscape designer. He became interested in scientific farming and founded a successful nursery business 1844. Appointed superintendent of New York's Central Park 1857, Olmsted and his partner Calvert Vaux directed its design and construction. After the American Civil War 1861–65, he became a sought-after planner of public parks, designing the grounds of the World's Columbian Exposition 1893. A keen observer of social and economic conditions, he published his travel journals of the South as *Journeys and Explorations in the Cotton Kingdom* 1861.

Olson Charles John (1910–1970). US poet and theoretician. He was a leader of the Black Mountain school of experimental poets and originator of the theory of 'composition by field'. His *Maximus Poems* published in full 1983, an open-ended, erudite, and encyclopedic fusion of autobiography and history set in Gloucester, Massachusetts, were a striking attempt to extend the American epic poem beyond Ezra Pound's *Cantos* or William Carlos Williams' *Patterson*.

Set out in his influential essay on 'Projective Verse' 1950, Olson's theory, which is the poetic equivalent of Abstract Expressionist and abstract painting, demanded that the measure be based on breath rather than metre. It also demanded that reality be re-enacted rather than described, so that the poet draws associations from the moment of composition, and the reader relives the process of its creation. As well as works of linguistic scholarship and archaeology, Olson published an acclaimed study of Melville, *Call Me Ishmael* 1947.

Olympias (*c.* 375–316 BC). Macedonian queen. The daughter of the king of Epirus, she married Philip II of Macedon 357 BC, and was the mother of Alexander the Great. When Philip left her for Cleopatra, niece of Attalus, she is said to have instigated his assassination 337 BC. She gained much influence during Alexander's reign, and after his death plotted to secure power for her grandson by killing Alexander's half-brother and successor. The Macedonian general Cassander besieged her at Pydna, and executed her on its surrender.

O'Malley King (*c.* 1858–1953). Australian politician, probably born in Canada and educated in the USA. He migrated in the 1880s and was elected to the House of Representatives as an independent but supporting Labor. He was minister for home affairs 1910–13 and 1915–16 and was instrumental in the foundation of the Commonwealth Bank and in securing land for the federal capital.

Omar alternative spelling of ◊Umar, 2nd caliph of Islam.

Omar Sheik Abdel-Rahman (1938–   ). Egyptian cleric who campaigns for the establishment of a theocratic Muslim state. He is associated with the Gama'a Islamic group. He actively supported the mujaheddin in the Afghan War. During the 1980s Sheik Omar was imprisoned several times for his connection with militant Islamic groups opposed to the Egyptian government. Members of Gama'a have been charged in connection with the 1993 World Trade Center bomb in New York.

Omar Khayyám (*c.* 1050–*c.* 1123). Persian astronomer, mathematician, and poet. In the West, he is chiefly known as a poet through Edward Fitzgerald's version of *The Rubaiyat of Omar Khayyám* 1859. Khayyám was born in Nishapur. He founded a school of astronomical research and assisted in reforming the calendar. The result of his observations was the *Jalālī* era, begun 1079. He wrote a study of algebra, which was known in Europe as well as in the East.

Omayyad alternative spelling of ◊Umayyad dynasty.

Onassis Aristotle Socrates (1906–1975). Turkish-born Greek shipowner. In 1932 he started what became the largest independent shipping line and during the 1950s he was one of the first to construct supertankers. In 1968 he married Jacqueline Kennedy, widow of US president John F Kennedy.

Onassis Jacqueline Lee (born Bouvier) (1929–1994). US publisher and former first lady. She shone as first lady when husband John F Kennedy became US president 1961, and is remembered for the melancholy dignity with which she conducted herself after Kennedy's assassination 1963. She married the elderly Greek shipping billionaire Aristotle Onassis 1968. After his death 1975, Jackie worked as an editor at the New York publishers Viking and Doubleday.

Born into an affluent French Catholic family, Jackie suffered a series of misfortunes which she rose above with grace and fortitude. As a photographer for the *Times Herald* she met and captivated senator John Kennedy; they married 1953. She had a miscarriage and a stillborn child before her children, Caroline and John, were born; a third child died in infancy. Her marriage was put under strain by Kennedy's compulsive womanizing. However, Jackie shone as first lady when Kennedy became US president 1961. She transformed the White House, hosting glittering parties attended by prominent intellectuals and artists, and charmed world leaders, notably France's president Charles de Gaulle. Her televised tour of the presidential home broke new ground, giving the public a unique insight into the 'American Camelot' she and her husband had created.

Jackie's second marriage, in 1968, to the elderly Greek shipping billionaire Aristotle Onassis dismayed and angered some Americans; the marriage was not a happy one. After his death, she worked as an editor, and clearly enjoyed this phase of her life, saying 'One of the things I like about publishing is that you don't promote the editor, you promote the book and the author'. Her greatest success was the commissioning of Michael Jackson's bestselling autobiography *Moonwalk*.

Ondaatje (Philip) Michael (1943–). Ceylon-born Canadian writer. He won the 1992 Booker Prize for his novel *The English Patient* about four people in a villa in Italy at the end of World War II.

Born in Colombo in what is now Sri Lanka, and educated in the UK, he emigrated to Canada 1962. His first published poetry was *The Dainty Monsters* 1967. *The Collected Works of Billy the Kid* 1970 and *There's a Trick with a Knife I'm Learning to Do* 1979 both won the Governor-General's Award for poetry. His other novels are *Coming Through Slaughter* 1976 and *In the Skin of a Lion* 1987. His memoirs *Running in the Family* were published 1992.

Our lives are merely strange dark interludes in the electric display of God the Father.

EUGENE O'NEILL
Strange Interlude 1928

O'Neill Eugene Gladstone (1888–1953). US playwright. He is widely regarded as the greatest US dramatist. O'Neill was born in New York City, the son of stage actors James O'Neill and Ella Quinlan. His tumultuous family relationships would later provide much material for his plays. He had varied experience as gold prospector, sailor, and actor. His plays, although tragic, are characterized by a down-to-earth quality and are often experimental in form, influenced by German Expressionism, Strindberg, and Freud. They were a radical departure from the romantic and melodramatic American theatre entertainments. They include the Pulitzer prize-winning plays *Beyond the Horizon* 1920 and *Anna Christie* 1921, as well as *The Emperor Jones* 1920, *The Hairy Ape* 1922, *Desire Under the Elms* 1924, *The Iceman Cometh* 1946, and the posthumously produced autobiographical drama *A Long Day's Journey into Night* 1956 (written 1941), also a Pulitzer prize winner. He was awarded the Nobel Prize for Literature 1936.

Other plays include *The Great God Brown* 1925, *Strange Interlude* 1928 (which lasts five hours), *Mourning Becomes Electra* 1931 (a trilogy on the theme of Orestes from Greek mythology), and *A Moon for the Misbegotten* 1947 (written 1943).

Suggested reading
Berlin, N *Eugene O'Neill* (1982)
Bogard, T *Contour in Time* (1988)
Floyd, V *The Plays of Eugene O'Neill: A New Assessment* (1984)
Gelb, A and B *O'Neill* (1962)
Prasad, H M *The Dramatic Art of Eugene O'Neill* (1987)

O'Neill Terence, Baron O'Neill of the Maine (1914–1990). Northern Irish Unionist politician. In the Ulster government he was minister of finance 1956–63, then prime minister 1963–69. He resigned when opposed by his party on measures to extend rights to Roman Catholics, including a universal franchise. Baron 1970.

O'Neill Tip (Thomas Philip) (1912–1994). US Democratic Party politician, speaker of the House of Representatives 1977–86. An Irish-American 'New Deal' liberal, he was the last Democrat leader from the old school of machine politics. He entered the Massachusetts state legislature 1936, and the US House of Representatives 1952. Plain-speaking, big-hearted, and possessed with a natural authority, O'Neill was immensely popular.

O'Neill was born in a working-class district in Cambridge, Massachusetts; his political thinking was conditioned by the Great Depression. He entered the Massachusetts state legislature 1936 and the US House of Representatives 1952, taking over a seat vacated by John F Kennedy. Through a mixture of stalwart partisanship, legislative shrewdness, and skilful alliance building, O'Neill ascended the Democratic Capitol Hill hierarchy. As speaker from 1977, he took charge of a House that was becoming more atomistic and difficult to control. From 1981 he worked with Republican president, Ronald Reagan. O'Neill abhorred Reagan's 'New Right' policies and described him as 'the least knowledgeable president' he had ever met. On retirement from Congress 1986, O'Neill became something of a media celebrity, writing a best-selling autobiography and being paid handsomely for advertising endorsements.

Onetti Juan Carlos (1909–1994). Uruguayan novelist whose bleak, realist work features protagonists at odds with their shabby, urban surroundings. His novels include *El pozo/The Pit* 1939 and *La vida breve/A Brief Life* 1950. He was awarded the Spanish Cervantes Award 1980, and the Jose Enrique Rodo Prize (Uruguay) 1991.

Onsager Lars (1903–1976). Norwegian-born US physical chemist. He worked on the application of the laws of thermodynamics to systems not in equilibrium, and received the 1968 Nobel Prize for Chemistry.

After working in Zürich, Switzerland, as research assistant to Dutch chemist Peter Debye, Onsager emigrated to the USA in 1928. As a lecturer first at Brown University and from 1933 at Yale, he was a failure: the students named his courses 'Sadistical Mechanics' and 'Advanced Norwegian I and II'.

At Brown University Onsager submitted a PhD thesis on what is now a classic work on reversible processes, but the authorities turned it down. It was published in 1931 but ignored until the late 1940s; in 1968 it earned Onsager the Nobel prize. At Yale his paper called 'Solutions to the Mathieu equation of period 4π and certain related functions' was passed in incomprehension among the chemistry, physics, and mathematics departments before Onsager got his PhD. In Zürich Onsager put forward a modification to the Debye–Hückel ionization theory. Now known as the Onsager limiting law, this gave better agreement between calculated and actual conductivities.

Investigating the connection between microscopic reversibility and transport processes, Onsager found that the key to the problem is the distribution of molecules and energy caused by random thermal motion. Ludwig Boltzmann had shown that the nature of thermal equilibrium is statistical and that the statistics of the spontaneous deviation is determined by the entropy. Using this principle Onsager derived a set of equations known as Onsager's law of reciprocal relations, sometimes called the fourth law of thermodynamics.

In 1949, he established a firm statistical basis for the theory of liquid crystals.

Oort Jan Hendrik (1900–1992). Dutch astronomer. In 1927, he calculated the mass and size of our Galaxy, the Milky Way, and the Sun's distance from its centre, from the observed movements of stars around the Galaxy's centre. In 1950 Oort proposed that comets exist in a vast swarm, now called the *Oort cloud*, at the edge of the solar system. He spent most of his career at Leiden, becoming professor 1935 and director of the observatory 1945.

Oort confirmed the calculations of astronomers Bertil Lindblad and Harlow Shapley and went on to show that the stars in the Milky Way were arranged like planets revolving round a sun, in that the stars nearer the centre of the Galaxy revolved faster round the centre than those farther out. He established radio observatories at Dwingeloo and Westerbork, which put the Netherlands in the forefront of radio astronomy.

Oparin Alexandr Ivanovich (1894–1980). Russian biochemist who in the 1920s developed one of the first of the modern theories about the origin of life on Earth, postulating a primeval soup of biomolecules.

In 1929 he became professor of plant biochemistry at Moscow State University. He was a cofounder of the Bakh Institute of Biochemistry in Moscow 1935, and its director from 1946.

Oparin's ideas about the origin of life contained three basic premises: that the first organisms arose in the ancient seas, which contained many already formed organic compounds that the organisms used as nutriment; that there was a constant, virtually limitless supply of external energy in the form of sunlight; and that true life was characterized by a high degree of structural and functional organization, contrary to the prevailing view that life was basically molecular. Oparin's theory, first published 1924, stimulated much research into the origin of life, notably US chemist Stanley Miller's attempt in 1953 to reproduce primordial conditions in the laboratory. Oparin also researched into enzymology and did much to provide a technical basis for industrial biochemistry in the USSR. His works include *The Origin of Life on Earth* 1936.

Oppenheimer *US physicist J Robert Oppenheimer led the Manhattan Project, which produced the atomic bomb. When later he opposed the construction of the hydrogen bomb and advocated the international control of atomic energy, he was accused of communist sympathies. A man of wide learning, he wrote several non-technical books, including* Science and the Common Understanding *1954.*

Ophuls Max. Adopted name of Max Oppenheimer (1902–1957). German film director. His style is characterized by an ironic, bittersweet tone and intricate camera movement. He worked in Europe and the USA, attracting much critical praise for such films as *Letter from an Unknown Woman* 1948, *La Ronde* 1950, and *Lola Montes* 1955.

Opie John (1761–1807). English artist. Born in St Agnes, Cornwall, he was a portrait painter in London from 1780, later painting historical pictures and genre scenes. He became a professor at the Royal Academy 1805 and his lectures were published posthumously 1809. Among his best known paintings are the portraits of his wife, Amelia Opie, and Mary Wollstonecraft (National Portrait Gallery). He contributed to Boydell's Shakespeare Gallery and painted the historical *Murder of James I of Scotland* (Guildhall Art Gallery).

Opie Peter Mason (1918–1982) and Iona Margaret Balfour (1923–   ). Husband-and-wife team of folklorists who specialized in the myths and literature of childhood. Their books include the *Oxford Dictionary of Nursery Rhymes* 1951 and *The Lore and Language of Schoolchildren* 1959. In 1987 their collection of children's books was sold to the Bodleian Library, Oxford, for £500,000.

Öpik Ernst Julius (1893–1985). Estonian astronomer whose work on the nature of meteors and comets was instrumental in the development of heat-deflective surfaces for spacecraft on their re-entry into the Earth's atmosphere.

Öpik was born near Rakvere and studied at Tartu, where he spent most of his academic career 1921–44. He then moved to Germany, becoming professor at the Baltic University in 1945. Three years later, Öpik moved to Northern Ireland, where he eventually became director of the Armagh Observatory. From 1956 onward he held a concurrent post at the University of Maryland, USA.

Öpik was the originator of a method for counting meteors that requires two astronomers to scan simultaneously. His theories on surface events in meteors upon entering the Earth's atmosphere at high speed (the ablation, or progressive erosion, of the outer layers) proved to be extremely important in the development of heat shields and other protective devices to enable a spacecraft to withstand the friction and the resulting intense heat upon re-entry.

Much of Öpik's other work was directed at the analysis of comets that orbit our Sun. He postulated that the orbit of some of these comets may take them as far away as 1 light year.

Oppenheim Meret (1913–1985). German-Swiss painter and designer. She was renowned as the creator of the celebrated Surrealist-Dada object *Breakfast in Fur* 1936 (Museum of Modern Art, New York): a teacup, saucer, and spoon covered in animal fur.

Oppenheim studied art in Paris in the 1920s and in the early 1930s became the model and muse of the Surrealist painter and photographer Man Ray. Her own paintings are replete with mythological and fairytale figures. Among the many surreal objects she created is a wooden table with bird's legs and feet in gold-plated bronze (private collection, Paris). She also designed jewellery for the couturier Elsa Schiaparelli.

In some sort of crude sense ... the physicists have known sin; and this is a knowledge which they cannot lose.

J ROBERT OPPENHEIMER
on the hydrogen bomb in a lecture at Massachusetts Institute of Technology 25 Nov 1947 *Physics in the Contemporary World*

Oppenheimer J(ulius) Robert (1904–1967). US physicist. As director of the Los Alamos Science Laboratory 1943–45, he was in charge of the development of the atom bomb (the Manhattan Project). When later he realized the dangers of radioactivity, he objected to the development of the hydrogen bomb, and was alleged to be a security risk 1953 by the US Atomic Energy Commission (AEC).

Investigating the equations describing the energy states of the atom, Oppenheimer showed in 1930 that a positively charged particle with the mass of an electron could exist. This particle was detected in 1932 and called the positron.

Between 1929 and 1942 he was on the staff of both the University of California, Berkeley, and the California Institute of Technology. After World War II he returned briefly to California and then in 1947 was made director of the Institute of Advanced Study at Princeton University. Oppenheimer also served as chair of the General Advisory Committee to the AEC 1946–52.

During World War II he reported to the Federal Bureau of Investigation friends and acquaintances who he thought might be communist agents; physicist David Bohm was one such.

Suggested reading
Goodchild, P *J Robert Oppenheimer: Shatterer of Worlds* (1985)
Rabi, I and others *Oppenheimer* (1969)
Smith, A K and Weiner, C (eds) *Robert Oppenheimer: Letters and Recollections* (1981)

Oppolzer Theodor Egon Ritter von (1841–1886). Austrian astronomer and mathematician whose interest in asteroids, comets, and eclipses led to his compiling meticulous lists of such bodies and events for the use of other astronomers.

Oppolzer was born in Prague (now in the Czech Republic) and studied medicine, but had a private observatory. In 1866 he became lecturer in astronomy at the University of Vienna, and professor 1875. He was made director of the Austrian Geodetic Survey in 1873.

Oppolzer sought, by observation and calculation, to establish the orbits of asteroids. He was the originator of a novel technique for correcting orbits he found to be inaccurate.

In 1868, Oppolzer participated in an expedition to study a total eclipse of the Sun. Afterwards, he decided to calculate the time and path of every eclipse of the Sun and every eclipse of the Moon for as long a period as possible. The resulting *Canon der Finsternisse* 1887 covered the period 1207 BC–AD 2163.

Orange, House of Royal family of the Netherlands. The title is derived from the small principality of Orange in S France, held by the family from the 8th century to 1713. They held considerable possessions in the Netherlands, to which, after 1530, was added the German county of Nassau.

From the time of William, Prince of Orange, the family dominated Dutch history, bearing the title of stadholder (magistrate) for the greater part of the 17th and 18th centuries. The son of Stadholder William V became King William I 1815.

Orbison Roy (1936–1988). US pop singer and songwriter. He specialized in slow, dramatic ballads, such as 'Only the Lonely' 1960 and 'Running Scared' 1961. His biggest hit was the jaunty 'Oh, Pretty Woman' 1964.

Born in Texas, Orbison began in the mid-1950s as a rockabilly singer on Sun Records. In the 1970s he turned to country material but made a pop comeback 1988 as a member of the Traveling Wilburys with Bob Dylan, George Harrison (ex-Beatle), Tom Petty (1952–   ), and Jeff Lynne (1947–   ).

We seek him here, we seek him there, / Those Frenchies seek him everywhere. / Is he in heaven? Is he in hell? / That demmed, elusive Pimpernel?

BARONESS ORCZY
Scarlet Pimpernel 1905

Orczy Emma Magdalena Rosalia Marie Josepha Barbara, Baroness Orczy (1865–1947). Hungarian-born English novelist. She wrote the historical adventure *The Scarlet Pimpernel* 1905. The foppish Sir Percy Blakeney, bold rescuer of victims of the French Revolution, appeared in many sequels.

Ore Oystein (1899–1968). Norwegian mathematician whose work concentrated on the fields of abstract algebra, number theory, and the theory of graphs.

In 1926 he became professor at Oslo, but moved a year later to Yale in the USA. In 1945 he returned to Norway.

Ore investigated linear equations in noncommutative fields, summarizing his work in a book on abstract algebra 1936. He then turned to an examination of number theory, and in particular of algebraic numbers.

Ore also wrote a book (1967) on the four-colour problem, the theory that maps require no more than four colours for each region of the map to be coloured but with no zone sharing a common border with another zone of the same colour. German mathematician August Möbius had raised this problem 1840.

Orellana Francisco de (c. 1500–c. 1549). Spanish explorer who travelled with Francesco Pizarro from Guayaquil, on the Pacific coast of South America, to Quito in the Andes. He was the first person known to have navigated the full length of the Amazon from the Napo River to the Atlantic Ocean 1541–43.

In all my work, my final concern is not with musical but with spiritual exposition.

CARL ORFF
quoted in Andreas Liess *Carl Orff* 1966

Orff Carl (1895–1982). German composer. An individual stylist, his work is characterized by sharp dissonances and percussion. Among his compositions are the cantata *Carmina Burana* 1937 and the opera *Antigone* 1949.

Orford, 1st Earl of title of the British politician Robert ◊Walpole.

Organ (Harold) Bryan (1935–   ). English portraitist. His subjects have included Harold Macmillan, Michael Tippett, Elton John, and the Prince and Princess of Wales.

Origen (c. 185–c. 254). Christian theologian, born in Alexandria, who produced a fancifully allegorical interpretation of the Bible. He also compiled a vast synopsis of versions of the Old Testament, called the *Hexpla*.

Origen taught in Alexandria and Caesarea. The Palestinian historian Eusebius says that Origen castrated himself to ensure his celibacy, but since Origen disapproves of such actions in his biblical commentaries, this may be just malicious gossip. He was imprisoned and tortured during the persecution of Christians ordered by the Roman emperor Decius in 250.

He took Jesus' saying 'There are eunuchs who made themselves eunuchs for the kingdom of heaven's sake' in an absurdly literal way. He lost no time in carrying out the saviour's words, endeavouring to do it unnoticed by his pupils.

Eusebius on ORIGEN
in *Church History* bk 2 ch 3

By drawing on Greek philosophy and on Scripture, Origen produced interpretations of the Bible that disturbed the more orthodox. For example, he held that the Fall occurred when spiritual beings became bored with the adoration of God and turned their attention to inferior things.

Oratory is just like prostitution: you must have little tricks.

VITTORIO ORLANDO
Time 8 Dec 1952

Orlando Vittorio Emanuele (1860–1952). Italian politician, prime minister 1917–19. He attended the Paris Peace Conference after World War I, but dissatisfaction with his handling of the Adriatic settlement led to his resignation. He initially supported Mussolini but was in retirement 1925–46, when he returned to the assembly and then the senate.

Ormandy Eugene. Assumed name of Jenö Ormandy Blau (1899–1985). Hungarian-born US conductor. He was music director of the Philadelphia Orchestra 1936–80. Originally a violin virtuoso, he championed the composers Rachmaninov and Shostakovich.

Ormonde James Butler, 1st Duke of Ormonde (1610–1688). Irish general. He commanded the Royalist troops in Ireland 1641–50 during the Irish rebellion and the English Civil War, and was lord lieutenant 1644–47, 1661–69, and 1677–84. He was created a marquess 1642 and a duke 1661.

Orozco José Clemente (1883–1949). Mexican muralist painter. His work was inspired by the Mexican revolution of 1910, such as the series in the Palace of Government, Guadalajara, 1949. *Mankind's Struggle* 1930 (New School for Social Research, New York) is typical.

Initially a student of architecture, he turned to painting 1909 and subsequently worked both in Mexico and the US. His art, sombre and dramatic, contains many images of death and suffering, and shows the passionate concern with Mexico's history that inspired its artists after the revolution that began 1910. In later works, this feeling for humanity took a more generalized form. His frescoes include those for the Palace of Fine Arts, Mexico City, 1934, and for the Mexican Supreme Court, 1941. He also produced many easel pictures and lithographs.

Suggested reading
Helm, MacKinley *Man of Fire: J C Orozco: An Interpretive Memoir* (1953)
Orozco, José *José Clemente Orozco: An Autobiography* (trs 1962)

Orpen William Newenham Montague (1878–1931). Irish portraitist and genre artist, active mainly in London. He was elected a member of the Royal Academy 1919. KBE 1918.

A fellow student with Augustus John at the Slade School. In portraiture he achieved a distinct style of a somewhat mannered and mechanical brilliance. He painted modern 'conversation pieces' of note, these including his *Homage to Manet* (group of George

Moore and others) and his *Café Royal* (with portraits of its *habitués*). His many war paintings and drawings of 1914–18 culminated in his portrayal (edged with satire) of the Peace Treaty delegates at Versailles.

Orr Bobby (Robert Gordon) (1948–). Canadian ice-hockey player who played for the Boston Bruins 1967–76 and the Chicago Blackhawks 1976–79 of the National Hockey League. He was voted the best defence every year 1967–75, and was Most Valuable Player 1970–72. He was the first defence to score 100 points in a season, and was leading scorer 1970 and 1975.

Orsini Felice (1819–1858). Italian political activist, a member of the Carbonari secret revolutionary group, who attempted unsuccessfully to assassinate Napoleon III in Paris Jan 1858. He was subsequently executed, but the Orsini affair awakened Napoleon's interest in Italy and led to a secret alliance with Piedmont at Plombières 1858, directed against Austria.

Ortega Saavedra Daniel (1945–). Nicaraguan socialist politician, head of state 1981–90. He was a member of the Sandinista Liberation Front (FSLN) which overthrew the regime of Anastasio Somoza 1979, later becoming its secretary general. US-sponsored Contra guerrillas opposed his government from 1982.

A participant in underground activities against the Somoza regime from an early age, Ortega was imprisoned and tortured several times. He became a member of the national directorate of the FSLN and fought in the two-year campaign for the Nicaraguan Revolution. Ortega became a member of the junta of national reconstruction, and its co-ordinator two years later. The FSLN won the free 1984 elections, but in Feb 1990, Ortega lost the presidency to US-backed Violeta Chamorro.

The poet begins where the man ends. The man's lot is to live his human life, the poet's to invent what is nonexistent.

JOSÉ ORTEGA Y GASSET
Velasquez, Goya, and the Dehumanization of Art 1927

Ortega y Gasset José (1883–1955). Spanish philosopher and critic. He considered communism and fascism the cause of the downfall of Western civilization. His *Toward a Philosophy of History* 1941 contains philosophical reflections on the state and an interpretation of the meaning of human history.

Orton Joe (John Kingsley) (1933–1967). English dramatist. In his black comedies, surreal and violent action takes place in genteel and unlikely settings. Plays include *Entertaining Mr Sloane* 1964, *Loot* 1966, and *What the Butler Saw* 1968. His diaries deal frankly with his personal life. He was murdered by his lover Kenneth Halliwell.

Orwell George. Pen name of Eric Arthur Blair (1903–1950). British author. His books include the satirical fable *Animal Farm* 1945, which included such slogans as 'All animals are equal, but some are more equal than others', and the prophetic *Nineteen Eighty-Four* 1949, portraying the catastrophic excesses of state control over the individual. A deep sense of social conscience and antipathy towards political dictatorship characterize his work.

Orwell was born in India and educated in England. He served for five years in the Burmese police force, an experience reflected in the novel *Burmese Days* 1935. Life as a dishwasher and tramp were related in *Down and Out in Paris and London* 1933, and service for the Republican cause in the Spanish Civil War in *Homage to Catalonia* 1938. He also wrote numerous essays.

Suggested reading
Crick, B *George Orwell: A Life* (1980)
Hammond, J R *A George Orwell Companion* (1982)
Stansky, P and Abrahams, W *The Unknown Orwell* (1972)
Stansky, P and Abrahams, W *Orwell: Transformations* (1980)
Williams, R *Orwell* (1970)
Woodcock, G *The Crystal Spirit* (1966)

Osborn Henry Fairfield (1857–1935). US palaeontologist who did much to promote the acceptance of evolutionary theory in the USA. He emphasized that evolution was the result of pressures from four main directions: external environment, internal environment, heredity, and selection.

In 1891 he became professor of biology at Columbia. He was staff palaeontologist with the US Geological Survey 1900–24 and president of the American Museum of Natural History 1908–33.

Osborn's evolutionary studies focused on the problem of the adaptive diversification of life. He was particularly concerned with the parallel but independent evolution of related lines of descent, and with the explanation of the gradual appearance of new structural units of adaptive value.

Osborn wrote an influential textbook, *The Age of Mammals* 1910.

All letters ... should be free and easy as one's discourse.

DOROTHY OSBORNE
Letters of Dorothy Osborne to William Temple Sept 1653

Osborne Dorothy, Lady Temple (1627–1695). English letter-writer. In 1655 she married Sir William Temple (1628–99), to whom she addressed her letters, written 1652–54 and first published 1888.

Osborne John James (1929–1994). English dramatist. He became one of the first Angry Young Men (anti-establishment writers of the 1950s) of British theatre with his debut play, *Look Back in Anger* 1956. Other plays include *The Entertainer* 1957, *Luther* 1960, *Inadmissible Evidence* 1964, *A Patriot for Me* 1965, *West of Suez* 1971, and *Watch It Come Down* 1976. With *Déjà-Vu* 1992 he returned unsuccessfully to Jimmy Porter, the hero of the epoch-making *Look Back in Anger*.

Osborne was born into a lower middle class family in London. In the first volume of his autobiography, *A Better Class of Person* 1981, he describes with great candour his love for his father, a quiet, modest man who died when Osborne was young, and his frank detestation of his mother, a woman whose coldness, ignorance, and calculation he never forgave. In the second volume, *Almost a Gentleman* 1991, his anger had not lessened, his opinions about his mother and others to whom he took exception remaining vitriolic, uninhibited, and unapologetic. The same passion, scintillating intelligence and righteous indignation characterizes *Damn you, England* 1994, a collection of occasional writings.

Don't clap too hard – it's a very old building.

JOHN OSBORNE
The Entertainer 1957

Look Back in Anger, which appeared when he was in his late 20s, quickly made him a celebrity, and brought a new energy and urgency into British drama. Its central character's self-pitying rages against the 'system' caught exactly the mood of a generation disillusioned by the gulf between their expectations and the drab reality of a postwar Britain in decline. The play paved the way for the extraordinary generation of playwrights that included Harold Pinter, John Arden, Robert Bolt, Edward Bond, and Arnold Wesker.

Osborne's plays are first and foremost character studies, although they also reflect broader social issues. Other works include *Hotel in Amsterdam* 1968, *West of Suez* 1971, *Too Young to Fight, Too Old to Forget* 1985, and *Dejavu* 1992.

Osborne also had a successful career in films. Forming a film company with the director Tony Richardson, he made highly acclaimed versions of *Look Back in Anger*, starring Richard Burton, and *The Entertainer*, starring Laurence Olivier. His adaptations for cinema include *Tom Jones* 1963, which brought him an Oscar for best screenplay, *Hedda Gabler* 1972, and *The Picture of Dorian Gray* 1973.

Suggested reading
Anderson, M *Anger and Detachment: A Study of Arden, Osborne and Pinter* (1976)

Ferrar, H *John Osborne* (1973)
Goldstone, H *Coping with Vulnerability: The Achievement of John Osborne* (1988)
Hinchcliffe, A *John Osborne* (1984)
Osborne, John *A Better Class of Person* (autobiography 1981)
Osborne, John *Almost a Gentleman* (autobiography 1981)

Oscar two kings of Sweden and Norway:

Oscar I (1799–1859). King of Sweden and Norway from 1844, when he succeeded his father, Charles XIV. He established freedom of the press, and supported Denmark against Germany 1848.

Don't let them shut the theatres for me.

OSCAR II
Last words 1907

Oscar II (1829–1907). King of Sweden and Norway 1872–1905, king of Sweden until 1907. He was the younger son of Oscar I, and succeeded his brother Charles XV. He tried hard to prevent the separation of his two kingdoms but relinquished the throne of Norway to Haakon VII 1905. He was an international arbitrator in Samoa, Venezuela, and the Anglo-American dispute.

I cast actors from rock because they're sensitive to what people want. They're performers. Their antennae are screwed on right. They don't mind getting right in there and having a go at the truth.

NAGISA OSHIMA
on rock 'n' roll and cinema in *Photoplay* Sept 1983

Oshima Nagisa (1932–). Japanese film director. His violent and sexually explicit *Ai no corrida/In the Realm of the Senses* 1977 caused controversy when first released. His other work includes *Koshikei/Death by Hanging* 1968 and *Merry Christmas Mr Lawrence* 1983, which starred the singer David Bowie.

Osman I or Uthman I (1259–1326). Turkish ruler from 1299. He began his career in the service of the Seljuk Turks, but in 1299 he set up a kingdom of his own in Bithynia, NW Asia, and assumed the title of sultan. He conquered a great part of Anatolia, so founding a Turkish empire. His successors were known as 'sons of Osman', from which the term Ottoman Empire is derived.

Ossian (Celtic *Oisin*) legendary Irish hero, invented by the Scottish writer James Macpherson. He is sometimes represented as the son of Finn Mac Cumhaill, about 250, and as having lived to tell the tales of Finn and the Ulster heroes to St Patrick, about 400. The publication 1760 of Macpherson's poems, attributed to Ossian, made Ossian's name familiar throughout Europe.

Ostade Adriaen van (1610–1685). Dutch painter, trained at Haarlem in the studio of Frans Hals, though following the example of his fellow pupil, Brouwer, in devoting himself to peasant, village and alehouse scenes. His *Boors making Merry* (Dulwich Gallery) is a good instance. He made etchings and painted some delicate watercolours in the same genre as his oils.

Östberg Ragnar (1866–1945). Swedish architect who designed the City Hall, Stockholm, Sweden 1911–23.

Ostrovsky Alexander Nikolaevich (1823–1886). Russian dramatist. He was a founder of the modern Russian theatre. He dealt satirically with the manners of the merchant class in numerous plays, for example *The Bankrupt* (or *It's All in the Family*) 1849. His best-known play is a family tragedy, *The Storm* 1860. His fairy-tale play *The Snow Maiden* 1873 inspired the composers Tchaikovsky and Rimsky-Korsakov.

Other peoples still live under the regime of individualism, whereas we [Germans] live under the regime of organization.

WILHELM OSTWALD
in J Labadie (ed) *L'Allemagne, a-t-elle le Secret de L'organisation?* 1916

Ostwald (Friedrich) Wilhelm (1853–1932). Latvian-born German chemist who devised the Ostwald process (the oxidation of ammonia over a platinum catalyst to give nitric acid). His work on catalysts laid the foundations of the petrochemical industry. Nobel Prize for Chemistry 1909.

He was professor at Riga 1881–87 and at Leipzig 1887–1906, and was from 1898 the first director of Leipzig's Physicochemical Institute.

From 1909 Ostwald became interested in the methodology and organizational aspects of science, in a world language, internationalism, and pacifism. He also built a laboratory for colour research.

Many carried away earth from where he fell in battle, until so much had been taken away as to make a hole as deep as a man's height.

Bede on ST OSWALD
in *Church History* bk 3, ch 9

Oswald, St (*c.* 605–642). King of Northumbria from 634, after killing the Welsh king Cadwallon. He became a Christian convert during exile on the Scottish island of Iona. With the help of St Aidan he furthered the spread of Christianity in N England.

Oswald was defeated and killed by King Penda of Mercia. His feast day is 9 Aug.

Othman alternative spelling of ◊Uthman, third caliph of Islam.

Othman I another name for the Turkish sultan ◊Osman I.

Otho I (1815–1867). King of Greece 1832–62. As the 17-year-old son of King Ludwig I of Bavaria, he was selected by the European powers as the first king of independent Greece. He was overthrown by a popular revolt.

Otis Elisha Graves (1811–1861). US engineer who developed a lift that incorporated a safety device, making it acceptable for passenger use in the first skyscrapers. The device, invented 1852, consisted of vertical ratchets on the sides of the lift shaft into which spring-loaded catches would engage and lock the lift in position in the event of cable failure.

Otis was born in Halifax, Vermont, and became a builder and mechanic. During the construction of a factory in Yonkers, New York, he had to make a hoist and invented his safety device to prevent accidents to the workforce.

Otis patented and began manufacturing his invention. At the Crystal Palace Exposition in New York 1854, he demonstrated it by letting himself be hoisted into the air, and then a mechanic cut the hoisting rope. This was a grand advertisement and the orders started to come in. In 1857, the first public passenger lift was installed in New York. Generally the lifts were powered by steam engines and in 1860 Otis patented and improved the double oscillatory machine specially designed for his lifts. Also from the workshops of his company, Otis invented and patented railway trucks and brakes, a steam plough, and a baking oven.

I'm not a philosopher. Guilty bystander, that's my role.

PETER O'TOOLE
Sunday Times 20 May 1990

O'Toole Peter Seamus (1932–). Irish-born English actor. He made his name as *Lawrence of Arabia* 1962, and then starred in such films as *Becket* 1964 and *The Lion in Winter* 1968. Subsequent appearances include *The Ruling Class* 1972, *The Stuntman* 1978, and *High Spirits* 1988.

Otto Nikolaus August (1832–1891). German engineer who in 1876 patented an effective internal-combustion engine. Otto was born in Holzhausen, Nassau. In 1861 he built a small experimental gas engine, and three years later, with two others, formed a company to market such engines. At the Paris Exhibition of 1867 the firm's product won a gold medal in competition with 14 other gas engines. A new factory, the Gasmotorenfabrik, was built at Deutz near Cologne in 1869. Otto concentrated on the administrative side of the business, and in 1872 Gottlieb Daimler and Wilhelm Maybach joined on the engineering side.

Otto first designed a successful vertical atmospheric gas engine in 1867. In 1876, he described the four-stroke engine. His patent was invalidated 1886 when his competitors discovered that Alphonse Beau de Rochas (1815–1893) had described the principle of the four-stroke cycle in an obscure pamphlet, but Otto is believed to have reached his results independently of Rochas.

Otto Rudolf (1869–1937). German Lutheran theologian. In his chief work, *The Idea of the Holy* 1917, he explores the sense of the numinous, which is common to all strong religious experiences and beyond reason, knowledge, or any other term. He was professor of systematic theology at the University of Marburg 1919–37.

Otto four Holy Roman emperors, including:

Otto I (912–973). Holy Roman emperor from 962. He restored the power of the empire, asserted his authority over the pope and the nobles, ended the Magyar menace by his victory at the Lechfeld 955, and refounded the East Mark, or Austria, as a barrier against them.

Otto IV (*c.* 1182–1218). Holy Roman emperor, elected 1198. He engaged in controversy with Pope Innocent III, and was defeated by the pope's ally, Philip of France, at Bouvines 1214.

Otway Thomas (1652–1685). English dramatist. His plays include the tragedies *Alcibiades* 1675, *Don Carlos* 1676, *The Orphan* 1680, and *Venice Preserv'd* 1682.

Oughtred William (1575–1660). English mathematician, credited as the inventor of the slide rule 1622. His major work *Clavis mathematicae/The Key to Mathematics* 1631 was a survey of the entire body of mathematical knowledge of his day. It introduced the '×' symbol for multiplication, as well as the abbreviations 'sin' for sine and 'cos' for cosine.

Ouida pen name of Marie Louise de la Ramée (1839–1908). English romantic novelist. Her work includes *Under Two Flags* 1867 and *Moths* 1880.

Ouspensky Peter Demianovich (1878–1947). Russian mystic. He became a disciple of the occultist George Gurdjieff 1914 but broke with him 1924. He expanded Gurdjieff's ideas in terms of other dimensions of space and time. His works include *In Search of the Miraculous.*

Ouspensky was born in Moscow and became a journalist. Other works include *Tertium Organum* 1912 and *A New Model of the Universe.*

The Bayard of India, sans peur et sans reproche.

Sir Charles Napier's description of JAMES OUTRAM
at a public dinner for him at Sakhar 5 Nov 1842

Outram James (1803–1863). British general, born in Derbyshire. He entered the Indian Army 1819, served in the Afghan and Sikh wars, and commanded in the Persian campaign of 1857. On the outbreak of the Indian Mutiny, he co-operated with General Henry Havelock (1795–1857) to raise the siege of Lucknow, and held the city until relieved by Sir Colin Campbell (later Baron Clyde). KCB 1856, baronet 1858.

Ovid (Publius Ovidius Naso) (43 BC–AD 17). Latin poet. His poetry deals mainly with the themes of love (*Amores* 20 BC, *Ars amatoria/The*

Art of Love 1 BC), mythology (*Metamorphoses* AD 2), and exile (*Tristia* AD 9–12). Born at Sulmo, Ovid studied rhetoric in Rome in preparation for a legal career, but soon turned to literature. In 8 BC he was banished by Augustus to Tomi, on the Black Sea, where he died. Sophisticated, ironical, and self-pitying, his work was highly influential during the Middle Ages and Renaissance.

Suggested reading
Fränkel, H *Ovid: A Poet Between Two Worlds* (1945)
Mack, Sara *Ovid* (1988)
Solodow, J B *The World of Ovid's Metamorphoses* (1988)

Ovitz Michael (1947–). US media entrepreneur, president of the Disney entertainment conglomerate from 1995. As founder of the Creative Artists Agency 1975 and its chair until 1995, he was one of the most powerful people in Hollywood.

Ovitz was born in Chicago and studied at the University of California in Los Angeles. He acted as intermediary between the Japanese and the American corporations in the purchase of Columbia Pictures by Sony 1989 and of MCA/Universal by Matsushita 1990, as well as helping to extricate Matsushita from the deal in 1994.

Owen David Anthony Llewellyn (1938–). British politician, Labour foreign secretary 1977–79. In 1981 he was one of the founders of the Social Democratic Party (SDP), and became its leader 1983. Opposed to the decision of the majority of the party to merge with the Liberals 1987, Owen stood down, but emerged 1988 as leader of a rump SDP, which was eventually disbanded 1990. In 1992 he replaced Lord Carrington as European Community (now European Union) mediator in the peace talks on Bosnia-Herzegovina. He resigned from the post 1995, and retired from active politics.

Suggested reading
Harris, Kenneth *David Owen* (1987)

Owen Richard (1804–1892). British anatomist and palaeontologist. He attacked the theory of natural selection and in 1860 published an anonymous and damaging review of Charles Darwin's work. As director of the Natural History Museum, London, he was responsible for the first public exhibition of dinosaurs. KCB 1884.

He became professor at the Royal College of Surgeons and 1858–62 at the Royal Institution. In 1856, he was made the first superintendent of the Natural History Departments of the British Museum, and was promoted to director when the collections were moved to South Kensington.

Owen published more than 360 monographs on recent and fossil invertebrates and vertebrates, notably the pearly nautilus, the moa and other birds of New Zealand, the dodo from Mauritius, and the *Archaeopteryx* – his reconstruction of that extinct bird on comparative anatomical principles is regarded as a classic. Other works include *History of British Fossil Reptiles* 1849–84 and a popular textbook, *Palaeontology* 1860.

Owen Robert (1771–1858). British socialist, born in Wales. In 1800 he became manager of a mill at New Lanark, Scotland, where by improving working and housing conditions and providing schools he created a model community. His ideas stimulated the co-operative movement (the pooling of resources for joint economic benefit).

From 1817 Owen proposed that 'villages of co-operation', self-supporting communities run on socialist lines, should be founded; these, he believed, would ultimately replace private ownership. His later attempt to run such a community in the USA (called New Harmony) failed.

He organized the Grand National Consolidated Trades Union 1833, in order that the unions might take over industry and run it co-operatively, but this scheme collapsed 1834. In *A New View of*

All things I thought I knew; but now confess / The more I know I know, I know the less.

ROBERT OWEN
Works bk VI ch 39

Society 1813, he claimed that personal character is wholly determined by environment. He had earlier abolished child employment, established sickness and old-age insurance, and opened educational and recreational facilities at his cotton mills in the north of England.

Suggested reading
Harrison, J *Robert Owen and the Owenites in Britain and America* (1969)
Morton, A L *The Life and Ideas of Robert Owen* (1962)
Owen, Robert *The Life of Robert Owen Written by Himself* (1857, reprinted 1970)
Podmore, Frank *Robert Owen* (1971)

It is pock-marked like the body of foulest disease, and its odour is the breath of cancer...No Man's Land under snow is like the face of the moon, chaotic, crater-ridden, uninhabitable, awful, the abode of madness.

WILFRED OWEN
Letter 19 Jan 1917

Owen Wilfred Edward Salter (1893–1918). English poet. His verse, owing much to the encouragement of Siegfried Sassoon, expresses his hatred of war, for example 'Anthem for Doomed Youth', published 1921. He was killed in action a week before the Armistice.

Suggested reading
Hibbard, D *Owen the Poet* (1986)
Owen, Harold *Journey from Obscurity: Wilfred Owen 1893–1918* (3 vols, 1963–65)
Simcox, K *Wilfred Owen: Anthem for a Doomed Youth* (1988)
Stallworthy, J *Wilfred Owen: A Biography* (1974)

Owens Jesse (James Cleveland) (1913–1980). US track and field athlete who excelled in the sprints, hurdles, and long jump. At the 1936 Berlin Olympics he won four gold medals. The Nazi leader Hitler is said to have stormed out of the stadium at the 1936 Berlin Olympic Games, in disgust at the black man's triumph. Owens held the world long-jump record for 25 years 1935–60. At Ann Arbor, Michigan, on 25 May 1935, he broke six world records in less than an hour.

Suggested reading
Baker, William J *Jesse Owens: An American Life* (1986)

At fifty you begin to be tired of the world, and at sixty the world is tired of you.

COUNT OXENSTJERNA
Reflections and Maxims

Oxenstjerna Axel Gustafsson, Count (1583–1654). Swedish politician, chancellor from 1612. He pursued Gustavus Adolphus's foreign policy, acted as regent for Queen Christina, and maintained Swedish interests during and after the Thirty Years' War. Count 1645.

Oxford Edward de Vere, 17th Earl of Oxford (1550–1604). English lyric poet, sometimes suggested as the real author of Shakespeare's works. Earl 1562.

Oxford and Asquith, Earl of title of British Liberal politician Herbert Henry ◊Asquith.

Oxley John Joseph William Molesworth (*c.* 1783–1828). English-born pioneer, surveyor, and explorer in Australia who, in 1817, followed the Lachlan River until blocked by marshes. This led him to the incorrect assumption that country in S New South Wales and W Victoria would be of little use to pastoralists.

Oyono Ferdinand Léopold (1929–). Cameroon novelist. Written in French, his work describes Cameroon during the colonial era, for example *Une Vie de boy/Houseboy* 1956 and *Le Vieux Nègre et la médaille/The Old Man and the Medal* 1956.

Oz Amos. Adopted name of Amos Klausner (1939–). Israeli writer. His poetic novels and short stories document events in Israeli and kibbutz life; for example, the novel *My Michael* 1972, set in Jerusalem in the 1950s. He is a spokesperson for more liberal Israelis who oppose Jewish extremism towards the Palestinians.

Oz was born in Jerusalem, the son of Russian immigrants from Poland who arrived 1933, and educated at the Hebrew University, Jerusalem, and in the UK at Oxford. He moved to a kibbutz 1954 and became editor of the *Seventh Day* periodical. His first novel, *Elsewhere, Perhaps* 1966, depicts life on a kibbutz near the Syrian border. *Touch the Water, Touch the Wind* 1973 is set against the background of the history of Israel between World War II and the Six-Day War. *Where the Jackals Howl and Other Stories* was published 1981. His nonfiction works include *In the Land of Israel* 1983, *Israel, Palestine, and Peace* 1994, and *Under this Blazing Light: Essays* 1995.

Özal Turgut (1927–1993). Turkish Islamic right-wing politician, prime minister 1983–89, president 1989–93. He was responsible for improving his country's relations with Greece, but his prime objective was to strengthen Turkey's alliance with the USA.

Özal worked for the World Bank 1971–79. In 1980 he was deputy to prime minister Bülent Ulusu under the military regime of Kenan Evren, and, when political pluralism returned 1983, he founded the Islamic, right-of-centre Motherland Party (ANAP) and led it to victory in the elections of that year. In the 1987 general election he retained his majority and Nov 1989 replaced Evren as Turkey's first civilian president for 30 years. He died in office and was succeeded by Süleiman Demirel.

Ozbek (Ibrahim Mehmet) Rifat (1953–). Turkish fashion designer. His opulent clothing is often inspired by different ethnic groups. He showed his first collection in London 1984, changed direction 1990 with a collection that was entirely white, and began showing designs in Milan 1991, with a collection inspired by native American dress.

Ozu Yasujiro (1903–1963). Japanese film director. He became known in the West only in his last years. *Tokyo Monogatari/Tokyo Story* 1953 has low camera angles and a theme of middle-class family life, which typify his work. His other major films include *Late Spring* 1949 and *Autumn Afternoon* 1962.

P

Pabst G(eorg) W(ilhelm) (1885–1967). German film director. His films include *Die Büchse der Pandora/Pandora's Box* and *Das Tagebuch einer Verlorenen/The Diary of a Lost Girl* 1929, both starring Louise Brooks, the antiwar story *Westfront 1918* 1930, and *Die Dreigroschenoper/The Threepenny Opera* 1931.

Pachelbel Johann (1653–1706). German organist and composer. Although his only well-known work today is the *Canon and Gigue* in D major for three violins and continuo, he was a leading progressive composer of keyboard and religious works, influencing J S Bach.

Pachomius, St (*c*. 292–346). Egyptian Christian, the founder of the first Christian monastery, near Dendera on the river Nile. Originally for Copts (Egyptian Christians), the monastic movement soon spread to include Greeks.

I'm nuts, I'm weird but I'm great.

AL PACINO
in *Cinema and TV* South America 4 Oct 1974

Pacino Al(fredo James) (1940–   ). US film actor. He has played powerful, introverted but violent roles in films such as *The Godfather* 1972, *Serpico* 1973, and *Scarface* 1983. *Dick Tracy* 1990 added comedy to his range of acting styles. More recent roles include *Glengarry Glen Ross* 1992 and *Scent of a Woman* 1992, for which he won an Academy Award.

Paganini *The violinist Niccolò Paganini was one of the foremost virtuosos of the 19th century. He exploited the use of novel effects, such as pizzicatos and harmonics, which were adopted more commonly by his successors. His influence on later artists, including Chopin, Liszt and Schumann, was considerable.*

Packer Kerry Francis Bullmore (1937–   ). Australian media proprietor. He is chair of Consolidated Press Holdings (CPH), which he privatized in 1983, a conglomerate founded by his father which produces such magazines as the *Australian Women's Weekly* and the *Bulletin*. CPH also has interests in radio and television stations. In 1977 he created World Series Cricket, which introduced one-day matches and coloured kit to the game.

Kerry Packer's father was the media magnate Frank Packer (1906–1974) who began as a cadet reporter on one of *his* father's papers and grew to be the most powerful media owner in Australia. He had interests in horse racing and yachting and in 1962 and 1970 unsuccessfully contested the America's Cup.

If I don't practise for one day, I know it; if I don't practise for two days, the critics know it; it I don't practise for three days, the audience knows it.

JAN PADEREWSKI
quoted in Shapiro *An Encyclopaedia of Quotations about Music* 1978

Paderewski (Ignacy) Jan (1860–1941). Polish pianist, composer, and politician. After his debut in Vienna 1887, he became celebrated in Europe and the USA as an interpreter of the piano music of Chopin and as composer of the nationalist *Polish Fantasy* 1893 for piano and orchestra and the *Polonia* symphony 1903–09.

During World War I he helped organize the Polish army in France; in 1919 he became prime minister of the newly independent Poland, which he represented at the Peace Conference, but continuing opposition forced him to resign the same year. He resumed a musical career 1922, was made president of the Polish National Council in Paris 1940, and died in New York.

Páez José Antonio (1790–1873). Venezuelan soldier and political leader, the first president of Venezuela 1830, president and dictator 1831–46 and 1861–63. An illiterate ranch hand, Páez came to lead the *llaneros* (cowboys) of the Orinoco plains, converting them to the nationalist cause. While Simón Bolívar pursued the cause of Gran Colombia (Colombia, Ecuador, and Venezuela), Páez led the call for a separate Venezuela, which was achieved 1830. He ruled the new state, sometimes through nominees, from then until 1848, and became one of the country's largest landowners.

Páez faced a series of revolts, the most serious being in 1835–36, and opposition increased during an economic crisis that began in the 1840s. In 1848 he led an uprising against the government he himself had chosen but was defeated and expelled 1850. He returned after the 1858 revolution, but continuing instability forced him to leave again the next year.

Paganini Niccolò (1782–1840). Italian violinist and composer. He was a concert soloist from the age of nine. A prodigious technician, he drew on folk and gypsy idioms to create the modern repertoire of virtuoso techniques.

His dissolute appearance, wild love life, and amazing powers of expression, even on a single string, fostered rumours of his being in league with the devil. His compositions include six concertos and various sonatas and variations for violin and orchestra, sonatas for violin and guitar, and guitar quartets.

Page Earle Christmas Grafton (1880–1961). Australian politician, leader of the Country Party 1920–39 and briefly prime minister in April 1939. He represented Australia in the British war cabinet 1941–42 and was minister of health 1949–55. GCMG 1938.

Page Frederick Handley (1885–1962). British aircraft engineer, founder 1909 of one of the earliest aircraft-manufacturing companies and designer of long-range civil aeroplanes and multi-engined bombers in both world wars; for example, the Halifax, flown in World War II. Knighted 1942.

Paget James (1814–1899). English surgeon, one of the founders of pathology. He described two conditions now named after him: Paget's disease of the nipple and Paget's disease of the bone. Baronet 1871.

He was one of the original 300 fellows of the Royal College of Surgeons of England in 1843, and was professor there 1847–52. Having tended the Princess of Wales 1878, he was appointed surgeon extraordinary to Queen Victoria.

Paget's disease of the nipple was described 1874 and is an eczematous skin eruption that indicates an underlying carcinoma of the breast, although the eruption is not simply an extension of the cancer cells inside the breast.

When Paget described the disease of the bone in 1877, he referred to it as osteitis deformans. This implies an inflammation of the bone, which is not accurate, and it is now called osteodystrophia deformans. This condition can affect the elderly. The bones soften, giving rise to deformity of the limbs, which may also fracture easily. If the skull is affected, bony changes cause enlargement of the head, and pressure on the VIIIth cranial nerve can cause deafness.

Paglia Camille (1947–). US writer and academic. An opponent of women's studies, she believes that the great accomplishments of Western civilization have been achieved by men as a result of the male determination to conquer nature. This is set out in *Sexual Personae: Art and Decadence from Nefertiti to Emily Dickinson* 1990. She became professor of humanities in the University of Arts, Philadelphia, 1984.

She was born in Endicott, New York. Self-assertive, combatively verbose, and combining paeans to rock stars with an erudite surface dazzle, Paglia quickly became popular with the media. She celebrates the glamour of women and their difference from men in such books as *Sex, Art, and American Culture* 1992 and *Vamps and Tramps* 1995.

Pagnol Marcel Paul (1895–1974). French film director, producer, author, and playwright. His work includes *Fanny* 1932 and *Manon des sources* 1952 (novels, filmed 1986). His autobiographical *La Gloire de mon père/My Father's Glory* 1957 was filmed 1991. He regarded the cinema as recorded theatre; thus his films, although strong on character and background, fail to exploit the medium fully as an independent art form.

Pahlavi dynasty Iranian dynasty founded by Reza Khan (1877–1944), an army officer who seized control of the government 1921 and was proclaimed shah 1925. During World War II, Britain and the USSR were nervous about his German sympathies and occupied Iran 1941–46. They compelled him to abdicate 1941 in favour of his son Muhammad Reza Shah Pahlavi, who took office in 1956, with US support, and was deposed in the Islamic revolution of 1979.

Paige Satchel Leroy Robert (1906–1982). US baseball player. As a pitcher, he established a near-legendary record, leading the Kansas City Monarchs of the Negro National League to the championship 1942. In 1948, with the end of racial segregation in the major leagues, Paige joined the Cleveland Indians. He later played with the St Louis Browns 1951–53.

My country is the world, and my religion is to do good.
THOMAS PAINE
The Rights of Man 1791

Paine Thomas (1737–1809). English left-wing political writer. He was active in the American and French revolutions. His pamphlet *Common Sense* 1776 ignited passions in the American Revolution; others include *The Rights of Man* 1791 and *The Age of Reason* 1793.

He advocated republicanism, deism, the abolition of slavery, and the emancipation of women.

Paine, born in Thetford, Norfolk, was a friend of US scientist and politician Benjamin Franklin and went to America 1774, where he published several republican pamphlets and fought for the colonists in the revolution. In 1787 he returned to Britain. *The Rights of Man* is an answer to the conservative theorist Burke's *Reflections on the Revolution in France*. In 1792, Paine was indicted for treason and escaped to France, to represent Calais in the National Convention. Narrowly escaping the guillotine, he regained his seat after the fall of Robespierre. Paine returned to the USA 1802 and died in New York.
Suggested reading
Ayer, A J *Paine* (1989)
Williamson, Audrey *Thomas Paine: His Life, Work and Times* (1973)

Paisley Ian Richard Kyle (1926–). Northern Ireland politician and cleric, leader of the Democratic Unionist Party from 1972. A member of the Northern Ireland parliament from 1969, he has represented North Antrim in the House of Commons since 1974. An almost fanatical loyalist, he resigned his Commons seat 1985 in protest against the Anglo-Irish Agreement, but returned 1986 to continue his opposition to closer co-operation with the South. His blunt and forthright manner, stentorian voice, and pugnaciousness are hallmarks of his political career.

He has been a member of the European Parliament since 1979. He was ordained 1946.

Pakenham William Christopher (1861–1933). British admiral. Pakenham joined the Royal Navy 1874. Prior to World War I he served with the Japanese fleet during the Russo-Japanese war 1904. In World War I, he commanded the 3rd cruiser squadron before taking charge of the 2nd battle cruiser squadron at the Battle of Jutland 1916. He succeeded Admiral Beatty as commander of the battle cruiser force Dec 1916. After the war, he became president of the Royal Naval College 1919–20 and then commander in chief North Atlantic and West Indies. KCB 1916.

Pakula Alan J(ay) (1928–). US film director. Formerly a producer, his compelling films include *Klute* 1971, *The Parallax View* 1974, and *All the President's Men* 1976. His later work includes *Sophie's Choice* 1982 and *Presumed Innocent* 1990.

Pala dynasty NE Indian hereditary rulers, influential between the 8th and 13th centuries. Based in the agriculturally rich region of Bihar and Bengal, the dynasty was founded by Gopala, who had been elected king, and reached its peak under his son Dharmapala (reigned *c.* 770–810).

The Palas, who patronized Buddhism at a time when it was in decline in the rest of India, maintained close trading relations with the countries of SE Asia to which many Buddhist monks later fled after the dynasty's fall, 1196.

Palamas Kostes (1859–1943). Greek poet. He enriched the Greek vernacular by his use of it as a literary language, particularly in his poetry, such as in *Songs of My Fatherland* 1886 and *The Flute of the King* 1910, which expresses his vivid awareness of Greek history.

Palance Jack. Stage name of Walter Jack Palahnuik (1921–). US film actor. Often cast as a brooding villain, his films include *Shane* 1953, *Contempt* 1963, and *Batman* 1989. He received an Academy Award as best supporting actor in *City Slickers* 1991.

Palestrina Giovanni Pierluigi da (*c.* 1525–1594). Italian composer. He wrote secular and sacred choral music, and is regarded as

---

This severe ascetic music, calm, and horizontal as the line of the ocean, monotonous by virtue of its serenity, anti-sensuous, and yet so intense in its contemplativeness that it verges sometimes on ecstasy.
Charles Gounod on PALESTRINA
quoted in James Harding *Gounod* 1973

the most perfect exponent of Renaissance counterpoint. Apart from motets and madrigals, he also wrote 105 masses, including *Missa Papae Marcelli*.

Suggested reading
Anderson, Nicholas *Baroque Music: From Monteverdi to Handel* (1994)
Arnold, Denis and others *Italian Baroque Masters* (1980)
Roche, Jerome *Palestrina* (1971)

Paley Grace (1922–). US short-story writer, critic, and political activist. Her stories express Jewish and feminist domestic experience with highly ironic humour, as in *The Little Disturbances of Man* 1960 and *Later the Same Day* 1985. Her *Collected Stories* appeared 1994.

Paley William (1743–1805). English Christian theologian and philosopher. He taught at Cambridge University for many years, and became archdeacon of Carlisle 1782. He put forward the argument from design theory, which reasons that the complexity of the universe necessitates a superhuman creator and that the existence of this being (God) can be deduced from a 'design' seen in all living creatures. His views were widely held until challenged by Charles Darwin. His major treatises include *The Principles of Moral and Political Philosophy* 1785, *A View of the Evidences of Christianity* 1794, and *Natural Theology* 1802.

Palissy Bernard (1510–1589). French potter. He made richly coloured rustic pieces, such as dishes with realistic modelled fish and reptiles. He was favoured by the queen, Catherine de' Medici, but was imprisoned in the Bastille as a Huguenot 1588 and died there.

Palladio Andrea (1508–1580). Italian Renaissance architect who created harmonious and balanced classical structures. He designed numerous palaces and country houses in and around Vicenza, Italy, making use of Roman classical forms, symmetry, and proportion. The Villa Malcontenta and the Villa Rotonda are examples of houses designed from 1540 for patrician families of the Venetian Republic. He also designed churches in Venice and published his studies of classical form in several illustrated books.

His ideas were revived in Britain in the early 17th century by Inigo Jones and in the 18th century by Lord Burlington and Colen Campbell, and later by architects in Italy, the Netherlands, Germany, Russia, and the USA. Examples of 'Palladian' buildings include George Washington's home at Mount Vernon, USA, the palace of Tsarskoe Selo in Russia, and Prior Park, England.

Suggested reading
Ackerman, James S *Palladio* (1966)
Farber, J and Reed, H *Palladio's Architecture and Its Influence* (1980)
Puppi, Lionello *Andrea Palladio* (1975)

Pallava dynasty hereditary Hindu rulers who dominated SE India between the 4th and 9th centuries. The dynasty's greatest kings were Simhavisnu (ruled *c.* 575–600) and Narasimhavarman I (ruled 630–668). Their capital was Kanchi, SW of Madras.

Under the Pallavas, maritime trade with Sri Lanka and SE Asia flourished, as did music, painting, literature, and architecture. Structural stone temples replaced rock buildings, the most impressive example being the sculptured Shore Temple at the seaport of Mahabalipuram, dedicated to the god Shiva.

Palma Ricardo (1833–1919). Peruvian writer. Curator of the Peruvian National Library and founder of the Peruvian Academy 1887, he wrote poems and romantic plays but is best known for his *Tradiciones peruanas/Peruvian Traditions* 1872–1910, a series of impudently fanciful sketches of the pageantry and intrigue of colonial Peru drawing on folk tale, legend, and gossip as well as historical material.

Palme (Sven) Olof Joachim (1927–1986). Swedish social-democratic politician, prime minister 1969–76 and 1982–86. Palme, educated in Sweden and the USA, joined the Social Democratic Labour Party (SAP) 1949 and became secretary to the prime minister 1954. He led the SAP youth movement 1955–61. In 1963 he entered government and held several posts before becoming leader of the SAP 1969. As prime minister he carried out constitutional reforms, turning the Riksdag into a single-chamber parliament and stripping the monarch of power, and was widely respected for his support of Third World countries. Palme was shot by an unknown assassin in the centre of Stockholm while walking home with his wife after an evening visit to a cinema.

Palmer A(lexander) Mitchell (1872–1936). US public official. He held office in the US House of Representatives 1909–15. A Quaker, he declined an appointment as secretary of war under President Wilson, and served instead as custodian of alien property during World War I. As US attorney general 1919–21, he led the controversial 'Palmer raids' against alleged political radicals during the Red Scare.

Palmer Arnold Daniel (1929–). US golfer who helped to popularize the professional sport in the USA in the 1950s and 1960s. He won the Masters 1958, 1960, 1962, and 1964; the US Open 1960; and the British Open 1961 and 1962.

Born in Pennsylvania, he won the US amateur title 1954, and went on to win all the world major professional trophies except the US PGA Championship. In the 1980s he enjoyed a successful career on the US Seniors Tour.

Palmer Geoffrey Winston Russell (1942–). New Zealand Labour politician, deputy prime minister and attorney-general 1984–89, prime minister 1989–90. A graduate of Victoria University, Wellington, Palmer was a law lecturer in the USA and New Zealand before entering politics, becoming Labour member for Christchurch in the House of Representatives 1979. He succeeded David Lange on Lange's resignation as prime minister but resigned himself the following year.

Palmer Samuel (1805–1881). English landscape painter and etcher. Palmer's expressive landscapes have a visionary quality. He was largely self-taught, though given some instruction by John Linnell, whose daughter he married. Greatly inspired in his early work by a meeting with William Blake, and the latter's engravings for Thornton's *Virgil*, he lived for a while at Shoreham, Kent, with other young enthusiasts, known as 'the Ancients', producing small pastoral scenes of remarkable beauty and intensity of feeling in oil, watercolour and sepia. These early works, now highly regarded, have had a distinct influence on the imaginative treatment of landscape in modern English art, and fine examples are in the Tate Gallery, Victoria and Albert Museum, London, and Ashmolean Museum, Oxford. Neither a visit to Italy, 1837–39, nor a later life spent at Redhill under the aegis of his father-in-law benefited his art, which declined into garishness and mediocrity.

Palmerston Henry John Temple, 3rd Viscount Palmerston (1784–1865). British politician. Initially a Tory, in Parliament from 1807, he was secretary-at-war 1809–28. He broke with the Tories 1830 and sat in the Whig cabinets of 1830–34, 1835–41, and 1846–51 as foreign secretary. His foreign policy was marked by distrust of France and Russia, against whose designs he backed the independence of Belgium and Turkey. He became home secretary in the coalition government of 1852. He was prime minister 1855–58 (when he rectified Aberdeen's mismanagement of the Crimean War, suppressed the Indian Mutiny, and carried through the Second Opium War) and 1859–65 (when he almost involved Britain in the American Civil War on the side of the South). He was responsible for the warship *Alabama* going to the Confederate side in the American Civil War. He was popular with the people and made good use of the press, but his high-handed attitude annoyed Queen Victoria and other ministers. Palmerston succeeded to an Irish peerage 1802.

Suggested reading
Chamberlain, M *Lord Palmerston* (1988)
Pemberton, B *Lord Palmerston* (1954)
Ridley, J *Lord Palmerston* (1981)

Palumbo Peter Garth (1935–). English property developer. As chair of the Arts Council 1989–94, he advocated a close partnership between public and private funding of the arts, and a greater role for the regions. His planned skyscraper by the German architect

Ludwig Mies van der Rohe beside the Mansion House, London, was condemned by Prince Charles as 'a giant glass stump'.

Panchen Lama 10th incarnation (1935–1989). Tibetan spiritual leader, second in importance to the Dalai Lama. A protégé of the Chinese since childhood, the 10th Panchen Lama was not universally recognized. When the Dalai Lama left Tibet 1959, the Panchen Lama was deputed by the Chinese to take over, but was stripped of power 1964 for refusing to denounce the Dalai Lama. He did not appear again in public until 1978. The Tibetan Gedhun Choekyi Nyima (1989–) was identified by the Dalai Lama as the new incarnation of the Panchen Lama 1995.

Pandit Vijaya Lakshmi (born Swarup Kumari Nehru) (1900–1990). Indian politician, member of parliament 1964–68. She was involved, with her brother Jawaharlal Nehru, in the struggle for India's independence and was imprisoned three times by the British. She was the first woman to serve as president of the United Nations General Assembly, 1953–54, and held a number of political and diplomatic posts until her retirement 1968.

Pandya dynasty (3rd century BC–16th century AD). S Indian hereditary rulers based in the region around Madurai (its capital). The dynasty extended its power into Kerala (SW India) and Sri Lanka during the reigns of kings Kadungon (ruled 590–620), Arikesar Maravarman (670–700), Varagunamaharaja I (765–815), and Srimara Srivallabha (815–862). Pandya influence peaked in Jatavarman Sundara's reign 1251–68. After Madurai was invaded by forces from the Delhi sultanate 1311, the Pandyas declined into merely local rulers.

Paneth Friedrich Adolf (1887–1958). Austrian chemist who contributed to the development of radioactive tracer techniques. He worked on unstable metal hydrides and developed sensitive methods for determining trace amounts of helium. From 1929 to the end of his life, meteorites dominated his interests.

Paneth was born in Vienna. He studied and worked at a number of European institutions, including the university of Glasgow, the Vienna Institute for Radium Research, and the Prague Institute of Technology. In 1929 he became professor at Königsberg, but left Germany for the UK in 1933 because of the rise of the Nazis. He was professor at Durham 1939–53, and during World War II he was head of the chemical division of the Joint British and Canadian Atomic Energy Team in Montreal. In 1953 Paneth returned to Germany to become director of the Max Planck Institute for Chemistry in Mainz.

Paneth worked out that radium D and thorium B are isotopes of lead and that radium E and thorium C are isotopes of bismuth. He prepared a new tin hydride, SnH_4, and investigated its properties.

In the late 1930s Paneth succeeded in obtaining measurable amounts of helium by the neutron bombardment of boron: he had induced an artificial transmutation. He then began to investigate the trace elements in the stratosphere, and determined the helium, ozone, and nitrogen dioxide content of the atmosphere.

Panetta Leon E(dward) (1938–). US Democrat politician, White House Chief of Staff from June 1995. An advocate of spending cuts and tax increases in order to deal with the budget deficit, he was director of the Office of Management and Budget 1993–94.

Panetta was born in Monterey, California. He was civil-rights officer of the Department of Health, Education, and Welfare under President Richard Nixon, concerned with the desegregation of schools, but resigned 1970. He was a member of the House of Representatives 1977–93. As chair of the Budget Committee 1989–93, he was a leading architect of President George Bush's 1990 tax-raising budget.

Pankhurst Emmeline (born Goulden) (1858–1928). English suffragette. Founder of the Women's Social and Political Union 1903, she launched the militant suffragette campaign 1905. In 1926 she joined the Conservative Party and was a prospective Parliamentary candidate.

She was supported by her daughters Christabel Pankhurst (1880–1958), political leader of the movement, and Sylvia Pankhurst (1882–1960). The latter was imprisoned nine times under the 'Cat and Mouse Act', and was a pacifist in World War I.

Suggested reading

Castle, Barbara *Sylvia and Christabel Pankhurst* (1987)
Hoy, Linda *Emmeline Pankhurst* (1985)
Mitchell, David *The Fighting Pankhursts* (1967)
Pankhurst, Emmeline *My Own Story* (1914, rep 1970)
Pankhurst, Richard *Sylvia Pankhurst: Artist and Crusader* (1979)
Romero, Patricia E *Sylvia Pankhurst: Portrait of a Radical* (1987)

Is not a woman's life, is not her health, are not her limbs more valuable than panes of glass? There is no doubt of that, but most important of all, does not the breaking of glass produce more effect upon the Government?

EMMELINE PANKHURST
Speech 16 Feb 1912

Panofsky Erwin (1892–1968). German art historian who lived and worked in the USA from 1931. He pioneered iconography, the study of the meaning of works of art, in such works as *Studies in Iconology* 1939 and *Meaning in the Visual Arts* 1955, and in so doing profoundly influenced the development of art history as a discipline.

Panufnik Andrzej (1914–1991). Polish-born composer and conductor. He was a pupil of the Austrian composer and conductor Felix Weingartner (1863–1942). He came to Britain 1954 and became a British citizen 1961. His music is based on the dramatic interplay of symbolic motifs.

Paolozzi Eduardo Luigi (1924–). English sculptor and graphic artist. He was a major force in the Pop art movement in London in the mid-1950s. In the 1940s he produced collages using images taken from popular magazines. From the 1950s he worked primarily as a sculptor, typically using bronze casts of pieces of machinery to create robot-like structures. *Cyclops* 1957 (Tate Gallery, London) is an example. He also designed the mural decorations for Tottenham Court Road tube station, London, installed 1983–85. Knighted 1989.

Papa Doc nickname of François ◊Duvalier, president of Haiti 1957–71.

Papandreou Andreas (1919–1996). Greek socialist politician, founder of the Pan-Hellenic Socialist Movement (PASOK); prime minister 1981–89 and again 1993–96. He lost the 1989 election after being implicated in an alleged embezzlement scandal, involving the diversion of funds to the Greek government from the Bank of Crete, headed by George Koskotas. In Jan 1992 a trial cleared Papandreou of all corruption charges.

Son of a former prime minister, he studied law in Athens and at Harvard. He was director of the Centre for Economic Research in Athens 1961–64, and economic adviser to the Bank of Greece. He was imprisoned April–Dec 1967 for his political activities, after which he founded PASOK. After another spell in overseas universities, he returned to Greece 1974. He was leader of the opposition 1977–81, and became Greece's first socialist prime minister. He was re-elected 1985, but defeated 1989 after damage to his party and himself from the Koskotas affair. After being acquitted Jan 1992, Papandreou's request for a general election was rejected by the government. However, PASOK won the Oct 1993 general election, and he again became head of government. Following his hospitalization with pneumonia Nov 1995, Papandreou resigned the premiership Jan 1996.

Papen Franz von (1879–1969). German right-wing politician. As chancellor 1932, he negotiated the Nazi–Conservative alliance that made Hitler chancellor 1933. He was envoy to Austria 1934–38 and ambassador to Turkey 1939–44. Although acquitted at the Nuremberg trials, he was imprisoned by a German denazification court for three years.

Papin Denis (1647–*c.* 1712). French physicist and technologist who in 1679 invented a vessel that was the forerunner of the pressure cooker and the autoclave, together with a safety valve.

His first job was as assistant to Dutch physicist Christiaan Huygens in Paris, and in 1675 he went to London as secretary to scientist and inventor Robert Hooke. Papin spent 1681–84 in Venice, returned to London and a job at the Royal Society, then became professor of mathematics at Marburg 1687–96. He returned to London in 1707.

Papin worked with Huygens and Irish physicist Robert Boyle on an air pump and invented the condensing pump. It was in London with Boyle that he invented the 'steam digester' – a vessel with a tightly fitting lid that prevented steam from escaping. The high pressure generated caused the boiling point of the water to rise considerably.

In 1690, Papin suggested a cylinder-and-piston steam engine, but his scheme was unworkable, because he proposed to use one vessel as both boiler and cylinder. He proposed the first steam-driven boat in 1690 and in 1707 he built a paddle boat, but the paddles were turned by human power and not by steam.

Papineau Louis Joseph (1786–1871). Canadian politician. He led a mission to England to protest against the planned union of Lower Canada (Quebec) and Upper Canada (Ontario), and demanded economic reform and an elected provincial legislature. In 1835 he gained the co-operation of William Lyon Mackenzie in Upper Canada, and in 1837 organized an unsuccessful rebellion of the French against British rule in Lower Canada. He fled the country, but returned 1847 to sit in the United Canadian legislature until 1854.

Papp Joseph (born Papirofsky) (1921–1991). US theatre director. He was the founder of the New York Shakespeare Festival 1954 held in an open-air theatre in the city's Central Park. He also founded the New York Public Theater 1967, an off-Broadway forum for new talent, which staged the first productions of the musicals *Hair* 1967 and *A Chorus Line* 1975. Productions directed by Papp include *The Merchant of Venice* and a musical version of *The Two Gentlemen of Verona* (Tony award 1972). Many of Papp's productions achieved great success when transferred to Broadway.

Pappus of Alexandria (*c.* 300–*c.* 350). Greek mathematician, astronomer, and geographer whose book *Synagogue/Collection* deals with nearly the whole body of Greek geometry, mostly in the form of commentaries on texts the reader is assumed to have to hand.

Nothing is known of his life and many of his writings survive only in translations from the original Greek. Without the *Collection*, much of the geometrical achievement of his predecessors would have been lost for ever. It reproduces known solutions to problems in geometry, and also frequently gives Pappus' own solutions, or improvements and extensions to existing solutions. For example, he handles the problem of inscribing five regular solids in a sphere in a way quite different from Euclid.

Among Pappus' other works are a commentary on Ptolemy's *Almagest* and a commentary on Euclid's *Elements*. Pappus is also believed to be the author of the *Description of the World*, a geographical treatise that has come down to us only in Armenian and bearing the name of Moses of Khoren as its author.

Paracelsus adopted name of Theophrastus Bombastus von Hohenheim (1493–1541). Swiss physician, alchemist, and scientist who developed the idea that minerals and chemicals might have medical uses (iatrochemistry). He introduced the use of laudanum (which he named) for pain-killing purposes. His rejection of traditional lore

and insistence on the value of observation and experimentation make him a leading figure in early science.

Overturning the contemporary view of illness as an imbalance of the four humours, Paracelsus sought an external agency as the source of disease. This encouraged new modes of treatment, supplanting, for example, bloodletting, and opened the way for new ideas on the source of infection.

Paracelsus was extremely successful as a doctor. His descriptions of miners' diseases first identified silicosis and tuberculosis as occupational hazards. He recognized goitre as endemic and related to minerals in drinking water, and originated a medical account of chorea, rather than believing this nervous disease to be caused by possession by spirits. Paracelsus was the first to distinguish the congenital from the infectious form of syphilis, and showed that it could be treated with carefully controlled doses of a mercury compound.

Paracelsus was born in Einsiedeln, Schwyz canton. Like many of his contemporaries, he became a wandering scholar, studying at Vienna, Basel, and several universities in Italy. He was a military surgeon in Venice and the Netherlands and is said to have visited England, Scotland, Russia, Egypt, and Constantinople. Having practised as a physician in Austria, he became professor of medicine at Basel 1527, but scandalized other academics by lecturing in German rather than Latin and by his savage attacks on the classical medical texts – he burned the works of Galen and Avicenna in public – and was forced to leave Basel 1528. In 1541 he was appointed physician to Duke Ernst of Bavaria.

Paracelsus was the disseminator in Europe of the medieval Islamic alchemists' theory that matter is composed of only three elements: salt, sulphur, and mercury. His study of alchemy helped to develop it into chemistry and produced new, nontoxic compounds for medicinal use; he discovered new substances arising from the reaction of metals and described various organic compounds, including ether. He was the first to devise such advanced laboratory techniques as the concentration of alcohol by freezing. Paracelsus also devised a specific nomenclature for substances already known but not precisely defined, and his attempt to construct a system of grouping chemicals according to their susceptibility to similar processes was the first of its kind.

Pardo Bazán Emilia (1852–1921). Spanish writer. She was the author of more than 20 novels, 600 short stories, and many articles. *Los Pazos de Ulloa/The House of Ulloa* 1886 and its sequel *La madre naturaleza/Mother Nature* 1887, set in her native Galicia, describe the decline of the provincial aristocracy.

Paré Ambroise (*c.* 1509–1590). French surgeon who introduced modern principles to the treatment of wounds. Paré was born in Mayenne *département* and trained in Paris. His book *La Méthode de traicter les playes faites par les arquebuses et aultres bastons à feu/Method of Treating Wounds Inflicted by Arquebuses and Other Guns* 1545 became a standard work in European armies, and was followed by a number of works on anatomy. As a military surgeon, Paré developed new ways of treating wounds and amputations, which greatly reduced the death rate among the wounded. He abandoned the practice of cauterization (sealing with heat), using balms and soothing lotions instead, and used ligatures to tie off blood vessels.

Paré eventually became chief surgeon to Charles IX. He also made important contributions to dentistry and childbirth, and invented an artificial hand.

Parer Damien (1912–1944). Australian photographer, noted particularly for his World War II work when, as official cameraman with the Second AIF, he photographed troops in action in Tobruk, Syria, and Greece. He was killed while covering the landing of American forces at Peleliu in the Pacific. He won an Academy Award with his film *Kokoda Front* 1942.

Pareto Vilfredo (1848–1923). Italian economist and political philosopher. A vigorous opponent of socialism and liberalism, he justified inequality of income on the grounds of his empirical observation (*Pareto's law*) that income distribution remained constant whatever efforts were made to change it.

Pareto was born in Paris. He produced the first account of society as a self-regulating and interdependent system that operates independently of human attempts at voluntary control. A founder of welfare economics, he put forward a concept of 'optimality', which contends that optimum conditions exist in an economic system if no one can be made better off without at least one other person becoming worse off.

Give me fruitful error any time, full of seeds, bursting with its own corrections. You can keep your sterile truth for yourself.

VILFREDO PARETO
Mind and Society 1916

Paretsky Sara (1947–). US crime writer. Her series of mystery novels featuring a tough-minded feminist private detective, V I Warshawski, includes *Deadlock* 1984 and *Bloodshot* 1988.

Paretsky was born in Ames, Iowa. She was marketing manager of a Chicago insurance company before turning to writing. Her books are generally set in Chicago. Her first novel was *Indemnity Only* 1982; others include *Killing Orders* 1985, *Guardian Angel* 1991, and *Tunnel Vision* 1994.

Paris Henri d'Orléans, Comte de (1908–). Head of the royal house of France. He served in the Foreign Legion under an assumed name 1939–40, and in 1950, on the repeal of the *loi d'exil* of 1886 banning pretenders to the French throne, returned to live in France.

It is dangerous to write against a man who can easily do you wrong.

MATTHEW PARIS
after the death of King John on 18 Oct 1216 *Chronica Maiora*

Paris Matthew (*c.* 1200–1259). English chronicler. He entered St Albans Abbey 1217, and wrote a valuable history of England up to 1259.

Park Merle Florence (1937–). Rhodesian-born English ballerina. She joined the Sadler's Wells Ballet 1954, and by 1959 was a principal soloist with the Royal Ballet. She combined elegance with sympathetic appeal in such roles as Cinderella. DBE 1986.

Park Mungo (1771–1806). Scottish explorer who traced the course of the Niger River 1795–97. He disappeared and probably drowned during a second African expedition 1805–06. He published *Travels in the Interior of Africa* 1799.

Park spent 18 months in the Niger Basin while tracing the river. Even though he did not achieve his goal of reaching Timbuktu, he proved that it was feasible to travel through the interior of Africa.

Suggested reading
Brent, P *Black Nile: Mungo Park and the Search for the Niger* (1977)
Schiffers, H *The Quest for Africa* (1957)
Tames, R *Mungo Park* (1973)

Park Chung Hee (1917–1979). President of South Korea 1963–79. Under his rule South Korea had one of the world's fastest-growing economies, but recession and his increasing authoritarianism led to his assassination 1979.

Parker Bonnie (1911–1934). US criminal; see ◊Bonnie and Clyde.

Parker Charlie (Charles Christopher 'Bird', 'Yardbird') (1920–1955). US alto saxophonist and jazz composer. He was associated with the trumpeter Dizzy Gillespie in developing the bebop style. His skilful improvisations inspired performers on all jazz instruments.

Parker was born in Kansas City, a hub of jazz music. The young Parker studied the work of saxophonist Lester Young and played in several conventional jazz and dance bands. Joining the Earl Hines Orchestra 1942–43 brought him into collaboration with Gillespie, and in their early recordings together ('Salt Peanuts', 'Groovin' High' 1945) bebop began to take shape. 'Ko-Ko' and 'Billie's Bounce' 1945 were recorded with a group that included Miles Davis on trumpet. Among other Parker compositions are 'Yardbird Suite' and 'Ornithology' (late 1940s). Parker was also very influential as a live performer; primitive bootleg tapes were made by fans, and live albums include *Quintet of the Year* 1953, again with Gillespie.

Suggested reading
Giddens, Gary *Celebrating Bird: The Triumph of Charlie Parker* (1986)
Priestly, Brian *Charlie Parker* (1984)
Reisner, R G *Bird* (1977)

Parker Dorothy (born Rothschild) (1893–1967). US writer and wit. She was a leading member of the literary circle known as the Algonquin Round Table. She reviewed for the magazines *Vanity Fair* and the *New Yorker*, and wrote wittily ironic verses, collected in several volumes including *Not So Deep as a Well* 1936, and short stories. She also wrote screenplays in Hollywood, having moved there from New York City along with other members of her circle.

Suggested reading
Frewin, Leslie *The Late Mrs Dorothy Parker* (1987)
Keats, John *You Might As Well Live: The Life and Times of Dorothy Parker* (1970)
Meade, Marion *Dorothy Parker* (1988)

Execution of laws and orders must be the first and the last part of good governance, although I yet admit moderations for times, places, multitudes.

MATTHEW PARKER
on the enforcement of his *Advertisements* 1566
in C R N Routh *Who's Who in Tudor England* 1990

Parker Matthew (1504–1575). English cleric. He was converted to Protestantism at Cambridge University. He received high preferment under Henry VIII and Edward VI, and as archbishop of Canterbury from 1559 was largely responsible for the Elizabethan religious settlement (the formal establishment of the Church of England).

It we don't convert our colony (New South Wales) into a great and prosperous nation, it will be a miracle of error ... a gigantic sin.

HENRY PARKES
Speech at Melbourne 16 Mar 1867

Parkes Henry (1815–1896). Australian politician, born in the UK. He promoted education and the cause of federation, and suggested the official name 'Commonwealth of Australia'. He was five times premier of New South Wales 1872–91. Parkes, New South Wales, is named after him. KCMG 1877.

Parkinson Cecil Edward (1931–). British Conservative politician. He was chair of the party 1981–83, and became minister for trade and industry, but resigned Oct 1984 following disclosure of an affair with his secretary. In 1987 he rejoined the cabinet as secretary of state for energy, and in 1989 became transport secretary. He left the cabinet when John Major became prime minister 1990 and later announced his intention to retire from active politics.

Parkinson Cyril Northcote (1909–1993). English writer and historian, celebrated for his study of public and business administration, *Parkinson's Law* 1958, which included the dictum: 'Work expands to fill the time available for its completion.'

It is now known ... that men enter local politics solely as a result of being unhappily married.

CYRIL NORTHCOTE PARKINSON
Parkinson's Law ch 10 1958

Parkinson James (1755–1824). British neurologist who first described Parkinson's disease.

Parkinson Norman. Adopted name of Ronald William Smith (1913–1990). English fashion and portrait photographer. He caught the essential glamour of each decade from the 1930s to the 1980s. Long associated with the magazines *Vogue* and *Queen*, he was best known for his colour work, and from the late 1960s took many official portraits of the royal family.

Parkinson Sydney (c. 1745–1771). Scottish artist, employed on James Cook's 1770 voyage to the Pacific as a natural illustrator draughtsman. He made 955 drawings and his journal, edited by his brother Stanfield, was published 1773.

The great strength (of his prose) comes from his acute sense of specific place and ... fact, and ... brilliant control of the pace of his narrative.

David Leven on FRANCIS PARKMAN
in *History as Romantic Art*

Parkman Francis (1823–1893). US historian and traveller who chronicled the European exploration and conquest of North America in such books as *The California and Oregon Trail* 1849 and *La Salle and the Discovery of the Great West* 1878. Parkman viewed the defeat by England of the French at Quebec 1759 (described in his *Montcalm and Wolfe* 1884) as the turning point of North American history, in so far as it swung the balance of power in North America towards the British colonies, which would form the United States of America.

Parmenides (c. 510–450 BC). Greek pre-Socratic philosopher, head of the Eleatic school (so called after Elea in S Italy). Against

Heraclitus's doctrine of Becoming, Parmenides advanced the view that non-existence was impossible, that everything was permanently in a state of being. Despite evidence of the senses to the contrary, motion and change are illusory – in fact, logically impossible – because their existence would imply a contradiction. Parmenides saw speculation and reason as more important than the evidence of the senses.

Never will this prevail, that what is not is. Restrain your thought from this road of enquiry.

PARMENIDES
quoted in Plato *Sophist* Fragment B 7.1–2

Parmigianino (Girolamo) Francesco (Maria Mazzola) (1503–1540). Italian Mannerist painter and etcher. He was active in Parma and elsewhere. He painted religious subjects and portraits in a graceful, sensual style, with elongated figures, for example *Madonna of the Long Neck* about 1535 (Uffizi, Florence).

A member of an artist family and taught by his uncles, he became one of the most distinguished of the Mannerist followers of Correggio, exaggerating the height and slenderness of his figures with graceful effect. His early work was done in Parma, where he decorated the south transept of the cathedral 1522. In 1523 he went to Rome, being employed by Clement VII, and is said to have been painting his *Vision of St Jerome* (National Gallery) when imperialist troops burst into his studio during the sack of the city 1527. He was able to escape without harm to Bologna and returned to Parma 1531. From then on he was ostensibly occupied with frescoes in the church of Santa Maria della Staccata, but delayed so long in their execution that he was finally thrown into prison for breach of contract. On his release he fled to Casal Maggiore, where he died soon afterwards. His drawings were numerous and much prized by English collectors in the 17th and 18th centuries, and he also produced original etchings and designs from which chiaroscuro woodcuts were made.

Parmigianino was the first Italian artist to make original etchings (rather than copies of existing paintings).

Parnell Charles Stewart (1846–1891). Irish nationalist politician. He supported a policy of obstruction and violence to attain Home Rule, and became the president of the Nationalist Party 1877. In 1879 he approved the Land League, and his attitude led to his imprisonment 1881. His career was ruined 1890 when he was cited as co-respondent in a divorce case.

Parnell, born in County Wicklow, was elected member of Parliament for Meath 1875. He welcomed Gladstone's Home Rule Bill, and continued his agitation after its defeat 1886. In 1887 his reputation suffered from an unfounded accusation by *The Times* of complicity in the murder of Lord Frederick Cavendish, chief secretary to the lord-lieutenant of Ireland. Three years later came the adultery scandal, and for fear of losing the support of Gladstone, Parnell's party deposed him. He died suddenly of rheumatic fever at the age of 45.

Suggested reading
Bew, Peter *Parnell* (1980)
Lyons, Francis *Charles Stewart Parnell* (1977)
Schlesinger, Arthur, Jr (ed) *Charles Stewart Parnell* (1989)

Parr Catherine (1512–1548). Sixth wife of Henry VIII of England. She had already lost two husbands when in 1543 she married Henry VIII. She survived him, and in 1547 married Lord Seymour of Sudeley (1508–1549).

She had character, spirit, and much shrewdness, besides great kindness of heart. She managed Henry VIII more successfully than any other of his wives.

C R N Routh on CATHERINE PARR
in *Who's Who in Tudor England* 1990

Parnell Irish politician, member of Parliament, and president of the Land League, Charles Parnell made Home Rule for Ireland a live issue. In spite of his great ability, his relationship with Katharine O'Shea (whom he later married) led to his political downfall.

Parra, de las Teresa (1889–1936). Venezuelan novelist. *Ifigenia* 1922 contrasts a world of dull provincial respectability with the Paris where de las Parra was educated; the heroine sacrifices herself and renounces her true love for a rich but dull husband. *Las memorias de Mamá Blanca* 1929 recalls her idyllic childhood.

I cannot stand Parry's orchestration: it's dead and is never more than an organ part arranged.

Edward Elgar on HUBERT PARRY
quoted in *Elgar Newsletter* 1978

Parry (Charles) Hubert (Hastings) (1848–1918). English composer. His works include songs, motets, and the setting of Milton's 'Blest Pair of Sirens' and Blake's 'Jerusalem'. Knighted 1898, baronet 1902.

Parry William Edward (1790–1855). English admiral and Arctic explorer. He made detailed charts during explorations of the Northwest Passage (the sea route between the Atlantic and Pacific oceans) 1819–20, 1821–23, and 1824–25. He made an attempt to reach the North Pole 1827. The Parry Islands, Northwest Territories, Canada, are named after him. Knighted 1829.

Parsons Charles Algernon (1854–1931). English engineer who invented the Parsons steam turbine 1884, a landmark in marine engineering and later universally used in electricity generation to drive an alternator.

Parsons developed more efficient screw propellers for ships and suitable gearing to widen the turbine's usefulness, both on land and sea. He also designed searchlights and optical instruments, and developed methods for the production of optical glass.

Parsons was born in London and studied at Trinity College, Dublin, and at Cambridge. He worked for various engineering firms in NE England until 1889, when he set up his first company near Newcastle-upon-Tyne. He developed turbo-generators of various kinds and increasing capacities, which formed the basic machinery for national (and much of international) electricity production.

With new propulsion machinery devised by Parsons, his steamship *Turbinia* reached a record-breaking speed of 34.5 knots in 1897. Parsons' turbines fitted to the liners *Lusitania* and *Mauritania* gave them high speed with less vibration, and developed some 70,000 hp/52,000 kW. KCB 1911.

Parsons Louella (1893–1972). US newspaper columnist. Working for the Hearst syndicate, she moved to Hollywood 1925 and began a gossip column and a popular radio programme *Hollywood Hotel* 1934. For over 40 years she exerted great influence (some damaging) over the lives of stars and studios. She published her memoirs as *The Gay Illiterate* 1944 and *Tell It to Louella* 1961.

Parsons Talcott (1902–1979). US sociologist who attempted to integrate all the social sciences into a science of human action. He was converted to functionalism under the influence of the anthropologist Bronislaw Malinowski. In *The Social System* 1951, Parsons argued that the crucial feature of societies, as of biological organisms, is homeostasis (maintaining a stable state), and that their parts can be understood only in terms of the whole.

Parsons began his career as a biologist and later became interested in economics and sociology. He studied in Heidelberg, Germany. He taught sociology at Harvard from 1931 until his death, and set up the Department of Social Relations there. He published more than 150 books and articles.

Like the German sociologist Max Weber, whose work he translated, Parsons wanted to describe convincingly logical types of social relation applicable to all groups, however small or large. His great achievement was to construct a system or general theory of social action to include all its aspects, drawing on several disciplines and reinterpreting previous theories. His first attempt at this systematization appeared in *The Structure of Social Action* 1937, followed by *Essays in Sociological Theory, Pure and Applied* 1942.

Parsons William, 3rd Earl of Rosse (1800–1867). Irish astronomer, engineer, and politician who built the largest telescope then in use. He found 15 spiral nebulae and named the Crab nebula. He was among the first to take photographs of the Moon. Earl 1841.

Parsons was born in York and studied at Oxford. As the eldest son of a titled landowner, he was elected to Parliament while still an undergraduate to represent King's County, a seat he then held for 13 years. In 1831 he became Lord Lieutenant of County Offaly, and in 1841, on the death of his father, he entered the House of Lords. During and after the potato famine of 1846, Parsons worked to alleviate the living conditions of his tenants.

Determined to construct a large telescope, Parsons learned to cast and grind mirrors. Fourteen years after his experiments began, he was able to make a 92-cm/36-in solid mirror, and in 1842 he cast the 'Leviathan of Parsonstown', a disc 1.8 m/72 in in diameter which weighed nearly 4 tonnes and was incorporated into a telescope with a focal length of 16.2 m/54 ft. It took three years to put together. He also invented a clockwork drive for the large equatorial mounting of an observatory.

Oh I wish you joy / And I wish you happiness / But above all this I wish you love.

DOLLY PARTON
Lyrics to 'I will always love you' which Parton wrote and
sang in the 1982 film *The Best Little Whorehouse in Texas*

Parton Dolly Rebecca (1946–). US country singer and songwriter. Her combination of cartoonlike sex-symbol looks and intelligent, assertive lyrics made her popular beyond the genre, with hits like 'Jolene' 1974, but deliberate crossover attempts were less successful. She has also appeared in films, beginning with *9 to 5* 1980.

Partridge Eric Honeywood (1894–1979). New Zealand lexicographer. He studied at Oxford University and settled in England to write a number of dictionaries, including *A Dictionary of Slang and Unconventional English* 1934 and 1970, and *Dictionary of the Underworld, British and American* 1950.

Pascal Blaise (1623–1662). French philosopher and mathematician. He contributed to the development of hydraulics, the calculus, and the mathematical theory of probability. In mathematics, Pascal is known for his work on conic sections and, with Pierre de Fermat, on the probability theory. In physics, Pascal's chief work concerned fluid pressure and hydraulics. Pascal's principle states that the pressure everywhere in a fluid is the same, so that pressure applied at one point is transmitted equally to all parts of the container. This is the principle of the hydraulic press and jack.

Pascal's triangle is a triangular array of numbers in which each number is the sum of the pair of numbers above it. In general the nth ($n = 0, 1, 2,...$) row of the triangle gives the binomial coefficients ^nC_r, with $r = 0, 1,..., n$.

His *Pensées* 1670 was part of an unfinished defence of the Christian religion.

Pascal was born in Clermont-Ferrand. In Paris in his teens he met mathematicians Descartes and Fermat. From 1654 Pascal was closely involved with the Jansenist monastery of Port Royal. He defended a prominent Jansenist, Antoine Arnauld (1612–1694), against the Jesuits in his *Lettres provinciales/Provincial Letters* 1656. His last project was to design a public transport system for Paris, which was inaugurated 1662.

Between 1642 and 1645, Pascal constructed a machine to carry out the processes of addition and subtraction, and then organized the manufacture and sale of these first calculating machines. (At

---

I have made this letter longer than usual because I lack the time to make it shorter.

BLAISE PASCAL
Lettres Provinciales 1656

least seven of these 'computers' still exist. One was presented to Queen Christina of Sweden in 1652.)

Pascal's work in hydrostatics involved repeating the experiment by Italian physicist Evangelista Torricelli to prove that air pressure supports a column of mercury. This led rapidly to investigations of the use of the mercury barometer in weather forecasting.

Suggested reading
Coleman, Francis X J *Neither Angel nor Beast: The Life and Work of Blaise Pascal* (1986)
Davidson, Hugh *Blaise Pascal* (1983)
Menhard, J *Pascal: His Life and Works* (1952)
Mortimer, Ernest *Blaise Pascal: The Life and Work of a Realist* (1959)
Nelson, Robert *Pascal* (1982)

Pasmore (Edwin John) Victor (1908–). English painter. He was a founder-member of the Euston Road School (which favoured a subdued, measured style) in the 1930s. He painted landscapes and, from 1947, abstract paintings and constructions, reviving the early ideas of the Constructivists.

Pasolini Pier Paolo (1922–1975). Italian film director, poet, and novelist. His early work is coloured by his experience of life in the poor districts of Rome, where he lived from 1950. From his Marxist viewpoint, he illustrates the decadence and inequality of society, set in a world ravaged by violence and sexuality. Among his films are *Il vangelo secondo Mateo/The Gospel According to St Matthew* 1964, *The Decameron* 1970, *I racconti de Canterbury/The Canterbury Tales* 1972, and *Salò/Salo – The 120 Days of Sodom* 1975, which included explicit scenes of sexual perversion.

Pasolini's writings include the novels *Ragazzi di vita/The Ragazzi* 1955 and *Una vita violenta/A Violent Life* 1959, filmed with success as *Accattone* 1961.

Suggested reading
Friedrich, Pia *Pier Paolo Pasolini* (1982)
Leprohon, Pierre *The Italian Cinema* (1972)
Siciliano, Enzo *Pasolini: A Biography* (1982)
Willemen, Paul (ed) *Pier Paolo Pasolini* (1977)

Passfield Baron Passfield. Title of the Fabian socialist Sidney ◊Webb.

Passy Frédéric (1822–1912). French economist who shared the first Nobel Peace Prize 1901 with Jean-Henri Dunant. Passy founded the International League for Permanent Peace 1867 and, with the English politician William Cremer (1828–1908), the Inter-Parliamentary Conferences on Peace and on Arbitration 1889.

To live life to the end is not a childish task.

BORIS PASTERNAK
Doctor Zhivago 1957

Pasternak Boris Leonidovich (1890–1960). Russian poet and novelist. His novel *Dr Zhivago* 1957 was banned in the USSR as a 'hostile act', and was awarded a Nobel prize (which Pasternak declined). The ban on *Dr Zhivago* has since been lifted and Pasternak has been posthumously rehabilitated.

Born in Moscow, he remained in Russia when his father, the artist Leonid Pasternak (1862–1945), emigrated. His volumes of lyric poems include *A Twin Cloud* 1914 and *On Early Trains* 1943, and he translated Shakespeare's tragedies into Russian.

Suggested reading
Fleishman, L (ed) *Boris Pasternak and His Times* (1988)
Gifford, H *Pasternak* (1977)
Hingley, Ronald *Boris Pasternak* (1983)
Pasternak, Boris *I Remember: Sketch for an Autobiography* (trs 1959)

Pasteur Louis (1822–1895). French chemist and microbiologist who discovered that fermentation is caused by microorganisms and developed the germ theory of disease. He also created a vaccine for rabies, which led to the foundation of the Pasteur Institute in Paris 1888.

Pasteur saved the French silkworm industry by identifying two microbial diseases that were decimating the worms. He discovered the pathogens responsible for anthrax and chicken cholera, and developed vaccines for these diseases. He inspired his pupil Joseph Lister's work in antiseptic surgery. Pasteurization to make dairy products free from the tuberculosis bacteria is based on his discoveries.

He was professor at Strasbourg 1849–63, moving to the Ecole Normale Supérieure to institute a teaching programme that related chemistry, physics, and geology to the fine arts. Also in 1863 he became dean of the new science faculty at Lille University, where he initiated the novel concept of evening classes for workers. In 1867 a laboratory was established for him with public funds, and from 1888 to his death he headed the Pasteur Institute.

A query from an industrialist about wine- and beer-making prompted Pasteur's research into fermentation. Using a microscope he found that properly aged wine contains small spherical globules of yeast cells whereas sour wine contains elongated yeast cells. He proved that fermentation does not require oxygen, yet it involves living microorganisms, and that to produce the correct type of fermentation (alcohol-producing rather than lactic acid-producing) it is necessary to use the correct type of yeast. Pasteur also realized that after wine has formed, it must be gently heated to about 50°C/122°F – pasteurized – to kill the yeast and thereby prevent souring during the ageing process.

Suggested reading
Dubos, René *Louis Pasteur: Free Lance of Science* (1986)
Nicolle, J *Louis Pasteur: The Story of His Major Discoveries* (1961)

Paston family family of Norfolk, England, whose correspondence and documents (known as the Paston letters) for 1422–1509 throw valuable light on the period.

Patch Alexander McCarrell (1889–1945). US general. He became commander of US XIV Corps on Guadalcanal 1942. In 1944 he commanded the US 7th Army which landed in S France and fought northward through Alsace to join the Allied troops which had landed in Normandy. His army crossed the Rhine 26 March 1945.

Patel Sardar Vallabhbhai Javerabhai (1875–1950). Indian political leader. A fervent follower of Mahatma Gandhi and a leader of the Indian National Congress, he was deputy prime minister 1947–50, after independence.

Patel participated in the satyagraha (the struggle for Indian independence by nonviolent, non-cooperative means) in Kaira in 1918. He was a member of the right wing of the Indian National Congress and supported the conservative opposition to the reform of Hindu law as it applied to the lack of rights of Hindu women.

Pater Walter Horatio (1839–1894). English scholar, essayist and art critic. He published *Studies in the History of the Renaissance* 1873, which expressed the idea of 'art for art's sake' that influenced the Aesthetic Movement. His other works include the novel *Marius the Epicurean* 1885, in which the solitary hero, living under the Roman imperium of Marcus Aurelius, meditates on beauty, Paganism, and Christianity; *Imaginary Portraits* 1887; and *Appreciations with an Essay on Style* 1889.

Suggested reading
Buckler, W E *Walter Pater* (1987)
Fletcher, Iain *Walter Pater* (1971)
Levey, Michael *The Case of Walter Pater* (1978)
Williams, C *Transfigured World* (1990)

Paterson Banjo (Andrew Barton) (1864–1941). Australian journalist and folk poet. Early acquaintance with drovers, squatters, and even bushrangers in New South Wales gave him material for his collection *The Man from Snowy River and Other Verses* 1895. He elaborated a horsily Arcadian myth of Australian life and published novels and travel sketches, but is best known for the song 'Waltzing Matilda' which he wrote about 1895 and performed to the Scots melody 'Craigielee'.

Paterson William (1745–1806). Irish-born US Supreme Court justice and political leader. Born in Ireland, Paterson emigrated to

America with his family 1747 and graduated from Princeton University 1763. Admitted to the bar 1769, he served as a member of the provincial congress 1775–76 and as New Jersey attorney general 1776–83. A member of the Constitutional Convention 1787, he was elected one of New Jersey's first US senators 1789. After serving as New Jersey governor 1790–93, Paterson was appointed to the US Supreme Court by President Washington, serving as associate justice 1793–1806. He was noted for his vigorous prosecution of cases under the Sedition Act of 1798.

Pathé Charles (1863–1957). French film pioneer. He began his career selling projectors 1896 and with the profits formed Pathé Frères with his brothers. In 1901 he embarked on film production and by 1908 had become the world's biggest producer, with branches worldwide. He also developed an early colour process and established a weekly newsreel, *Pathé Journal*. During World War I he faced stiff competition from the USA, and his success in Europe suffered as a consequence of the war. In 1929 he handed over control of his company, which continued to produce a large number of films after his retirement.

Patinir Joachim, (also Patenier or Patinier) (*c.* 1485–1524). Flemish painter of religious works. He was active in Antwerp. His visionary landscape backgrounds dwarf his figures. He is known to have worked with Quentin Matsys and to have painted landscape backgrounds for other artists' works.

We love, Fool, for the good we do, / Not that which unto us is done.
                                                                    COVENTRY PATMORE
The Angel in the House bk 1, canto 6, 'A Riddle Solved' 1854–64

Patmore Coventry Kersey Dighton (1823–1896). English poet and critic. He was a librarian at the British Museum 1846–66, and as one of the Pre-Raphaelite Brotherhood published the sequence of poems *The Angel in the House* 1854–63 and the collection of odes *The Unknown Eros* 1877.

Paton Alan Stewart (1903–1988). South African writer. Paton was born in Pietermaritzburg. He became a schoolmaster and in 1935 the principal of a reformatory near Johannesburg, which he ran along enlightened lines. His novel *Cry, the Beloved Country* 1948 focused on racial inequality in South Africa. Later books include the study *Land and People of South Africa* 1956 and *The Long View* 1968; *Debbie Go Home* 1961 (short stories); political and social studies; and his autobiography *Towards the Mountain* 1980.

For it is the dawn that has come, as it has come for a thousand centuries, never failing. But when that dawn will come, of our emancipation from the fear of bondage and the bondage of fear, why, that is a secret.
                                                                    ALAN PATON
Last words of Cry the Beloved Country 1948

Patou Jean (1880–1936). French clothes designer. He opened a fashion house 1919 and was an overnight success. His swimsuits and innovative designs were popular in the 1920s and he dominated both the couture and the ready-to-wear sectors of the fashion world until his death. He had a great influence on the designers he employed, many of whom went on to make names for themselves. He created the perfume Joy 1926.

Patrick, St (*c.* 389–*c.* 461). Patron saint of Ireland. Born in Britain, probably in S Wales, he was carried off by pirates to six years' slavery in Antrim, Ireland, before escaping either to Britain or Gaul – his poor Latin suggests the former – to train as a missionary. He is variously said to have landed again in Ireland 432 or 456, and his work was a vital factor in the spread of Christian influence there. His symbols are snakes and shamrocks; feast day 17 March.

Patrick is credited with founding the diocese of Armagh, of which he was bishop, though this was probably the work of a 'lost apostle' (Palladius or Secundinus). Of his writings only his *Confessio* and an *Epistola* survive.

Suggested reading
Hanson, R P *The Life and Writings of the Historical Saint Patrick* (1968)
Thompson, E A *Who Was Saint Patrick ?* (1986)

Patten Chris(topher Francis) (1944–). British Conservative politician, governor of Hong Kong from 1992. A director of the Conservative Party research department, he held junior ministerial posts under Prime Minister Margaret Thatcher, despite his reputation of being to the left of the party, and eventually joined the cabinet. As environment secretary 1989–90, he was responsible for administering the poll tax. He was Conservative Party chair 1990–92, orchestrating the party's campaign for the 1992 general election, in which he lost his parliamentary seat. He accepted the governorship of Hong Kong for the crucial five years prior to its transfer to China. His prodemocracy, anti-Chinese stance won the backing of many Hong Kong residents, but was criticized by members of its business community.

Patterson Harry (1929–). English novelist. He has written many thrillers under his own name, including *Dillinger* 1983, as well as under the pseudonym Jack Higgins, including *The Eagle Has Landed* 1975.

Patterson P(ercival) J(ames) (1935–). Jamaican politician and lawyer, prime minister from 1992. After training and practising as a lawyer, he became a leading member of the People's National Party (PNP), serving as minister for development, planning, and production 1989–92 and deputy prime minister and minister for finance and planning 1991. He had taken over the prime ministerial portfolio for several periods during 1990 when his leader, Michael Manley, had been unwell and was widely seen as Manley's natural successor. However, in 1991 there were allegations that taxes amounting to some US\$30 million, owed to the Jamaican government by the international oil company, Shell, had been waived and Patterson, as finance minister, and the mining and energy minister, Horace Clarke, resigned. Despite this, when, in March 1992, Manley's health deteriorated to the extent that he felt obliged to retire, the PNP elected Patterson to succeed him by almost a three-to-one majority, automatically making him prime minister. In March 1993 he secured his own popular mandate by calling a snap general election and securing a landslide victory.

Patti Adelina (Adela Juana Maria) (1843–1919). Anglo-Italian soprano. She was renowned for her performances of Lucia in *Lucia di Lammermoor* and Amina in *La sonnambula*. At the age of 62 she was persuaded out of retirement to make a number of gramophone recordings, thus becoming one of the first opera singers to be recorded.

Patton George Smith (1885–1945). US general in World War II, known as 'Blood and Guts'. During World War I, he formed the first US tank force and led it in action 1918. He was appointed to command the 2nd Armored Division 1940 and became commanding general of the First Armored Corps 1941. In 1942 he led the Western Task Force that landed at Casablanca, Morocco. After commanding the 7th Army, he led the 3rd Army across France and into Germany, and in 1945 took over the 15th Army.

Suggested reading
Blumenson, Martin *Patton* (1985)
D'Este, Carlo *A Genius for War: A Life of General George S Patton* (1995)
Farago, Ladislas *Patton* (1964)
Farago, Ladislas *The Last Days of Patton* (1981)
Hogg, I V *Patton: The Biography of General George S Patton* (1982)

Paul Elliot Harold (1891–1958). US author. His works include the novel *Indelible* 1922, about two young musicians, and the travel book *The Narrow Street/The Last Time I Saw Paris* 1940.

Paul Les. Adopted name of Lester Polfuss (1915–). US inventor of the solid-body electric guitar in the early 1940s. He was also a pioneer of recording techniques including overdubbing and electronic echo. The Gibson Les Paul guitar was first marketed 1952 (the first commercial solid-body guitar was made by Leo Fender). As a guitarist in the late 1940s and 1950s he recorded with the singer Mary Ford (1928–1977).

Paul, St (*c*. AD 3–*c*. 68). Christian missionary and martyr; in the New Testament, one of the apostles and author of 13 epistles. The Jewish form of his name is Saul. He was born in Tarsus (now in Turkey), son of well-to-do Pharisees, and had Roman citizenship. Originally opposed to Christianity, he took part in the stoning of St Stephen. He is said to have been converted by a vision on the road to Damascus. After his conversion he made great missionary journeys, for example to Philippi and Ephesus, becoming known as the Apostle of the Gentiles (non-Jews). On his return to Jerusalem after his missionary journeys, he was arrested, appealed to Caesar, and (as a citizen) was sent to Rome for trial about 57 or 59. After two years in prison, he may have been released before his final arrest and execution under the emperor Nero.

St Paul's theology was rigorous on such questions as sin and atonement, and his views on the role of women were adopted by the Christian church generally. His emblems are a sword and a book; feast day 29 June.

Suggested reading
Beker, J C *Paul the Apostle* (1980)
Coggan, Donald *Paul: Portrait of a Revolutionary* (1984)
Maccoby, Hyam *The Myth Maker: Paul and the Invention of Christianity* (1986)
Meeks, W A *The First Urban Christians: The Social World of the Apostle Paul* (1982)
Sanders, E P *Paul* (1991)

Paul Wolfgang (1913–1993). German nuclear physicist. He made fundamental contributions to molecular beam spectroscopy, mass spectrometry, and electron acceleration technology. In 1989 he shared the Nobel Prize for Physics with US scientists Norman Ramsey and Hans Dehmelt, for his development of the ion trap, or Paul trap, used to store single atoms long enough to make useful measurements.

In 1957 he helped found the famous DESY accelerator laboratory in Hamburg. From 1964–67, Paul was director of the nuclear physics laboratory of CERN, the joint European laboratory for particle physics in Geneva.

Paul became professor and director of the Physics Institute at the University of Bonn 1952, a post that he held until he retired 1981. At Bonn, he developed the sextupole focusing of molecular beams, the radio frequency quadrupole mass spectrometer, and the ion trap. With colleagues he built two electron accelerators.

Paul (1901–1964). King of the Hellenes (Greece) from 1947, when he succeeded his brother George II. He was the son of Constantine I. In 1938 he married Princess Frederika (1917–   ), daughter of the Duke of Brunswick.

Paul six popes, including:

[His] prevalently philosophic attitude was often construed by his critics as timidity, indecision, and uncertainty.

Encyclopaedia Britannica on PAUL VI
1990

Paul VI (Giovanni Battista Montini) (1897–1978). He was born near Brescia, Italy. He spent more than 25 years in the Secretariat of State under Pius XI and Pius XII before becoming archbishop of Milan in 1954. In 1958 he was created a cardinal by Pope John, and in 1963 he succeeded him as pope, taking the name of Paul as a symbol of ecumenical unity. His encyclical *Humanae Vitae/Of Human Life* 1968 reaffirmed the church's traditional teaching on birth control, thus following the minority report of the commission originally appointed by Pope John rather than the majority view.

Suggested reading
Barrett, W E *Shepherd of Mankind: A Biography of Pope Paul VI* (1964)
Smith, J E *Humanae Vitae: A Generation Later* (1991)

Paul I (1754–1801). Tsar of Russia from 1796, in succession to his mother Catherine II. Mentally unstable, he pursued an erratic foreign policy and was assassinated.

The Pauli principle must be characterized as a fundamental law of physics.

WOLFGANG PAULI
Nobel prize citation 1945

Pauli Wolfgang (1900–1958). Austrian-born Swiss physicist who originated the exclusion principle: in a given system no two fermions (electrons, protons, neutrons, or other elementary particles of half-integral spin) can be characterized by the same set of quantum numbers. He also predicted the existence of neutrinos. The neutrino was proposed in 1930 to explain the production of beta radiation in a continuous spectrum; it was eventually detected 1956. Nobel prize 1945.

The exclusion principle, announced 1925, involved adding a fourth quantum number to the three already used (n, l, and m). This number, s, would represent the spin of the electron and would have two possible values. The principle also gave a means of determining the arrangement of electrons into shells around the nucleus, which explained the classification of elements into related groups by their atomic number.

Pauli was born in Vienna and studied in Germany at Munich. He then went to Göttingen as an assistant to German physicist Max Born, moving on to Copenhagen to study with Danish physicist Niels Bohr. From 1928 Pauli was professor of experimental physics at the Eidgenössische Technische Hochschule, Zürich, though he spent World War II in the USA at the Institute for Advanced Study, Princeton.

Pauling Linus Carl (1901–1994). US theoretical chemist and biologist whose ideas on chemical bonding are fundamental to modern theories of molecular structure. He also investigated the properties and uses of vitamin C as related to human health. He won the Nobel Prize for Chemistry 1954 and the Nobel Peace Prize 1962, having campaigned for a nuclear test-ban treaty.

In Europe 1925–27, he met the chief atomic scientists of the day. He became professor at Caltech 1931, and was director of the Gates and Crellin Laboratories 1936–58 and of the Linus Pauling Institute of Science and Medicine in Menlo Park, California 1973–75.

He was a pioneer in the application of quantum mechanical principles to the structures of molecules, relating them to interatomic distances and bond angles by X-ray and electron diffraction, magnetic effects, and thermochemical techniques. In 1928, Pauling introduced the concept of hybridization of bonds. This provided a clear basic insight into the framework structure of all carbon compounds, that is, of the whole of organic chemistry. He also studied electronegativity of atoms and polarization (movement of electrons) in chemical bonds. Electronegativity values can be used to show why certain substances, such as hydrochloric acid, are acid, whereas others, such as sodium hydroxide, are alkaline. Much of this work was consolidated in his book *The Nature of the Chemical Bond* 1939.

In his researches on blood in the 1940s, Pauling investigated immunology and sickle-cell anaemia. Later work confirmed his conviction that the disease is genetic and that normal haemoglobin and the haemoglobin in sickle cells differ in electrical charge. Pauling's work provided a powerful impetus to Crick and Watson in their search for the structure of DNA.

Pauling was co-author of *Introduction to Quantum Mechanics* 1935; he published two textbooks, *General Chemistry* 1948 and *College Chemistry* 1950.

During the 1950s he became politically active, his especial concern being the long-term genetic damage resulting from atmospheric nuclear bomb tests. In this, he conflicted with the US establishment and with several of his science colleagues. He was denounced as a pacifist, and a communist, his passport was withdrawn 1952–54, and he was obliged to appear before the US Senate Internal Security Committee. One item in his sustained wide-ranging campaign was his book *No More War!* 1958. He presented to the UN a petition signed by 11,021 scientists from 49 countries urging an end to nuclear weapons testing, and during the 1960s spent several years on a study of the problems of war and peace at the Center for the Study of Democratic Institutions in Santa Barbara, California.

Suggested reading
Moore, Ruth *The Coil of Life* (1961)
Serafini, Anthony *Linus Pauling: A Man and His Science* (1989)

He had a look which both terrified you and filled you with reverence.

Bede on PAULINUS
in *Church History* bk 2, ch 16

Paulinus (died *c.* 644). Roman missionary to Britain who joined St Augustine in Kent 601, converted the Northumbrians 625, and became the first archbishop of York. Excavations 1978 revealed a church he built in Lincoln.

Pavarotti With the luxurious warmth and versatility of his voice, Italian lyric tenor Luciano Pavarotti has done much to popularize opera. His own popularity has grown steadily since his 1963–64 concert tour, and he has appeared in several films and made many recordings.

Pauling Double Nobel prize-winning American chemist Linus Pauling. Pauling won the prize for chemistry in 1954 following his work investigating the nature of the chemical bond. In 1962 he also won the peace prize following his campaign for a nuclear test ban treaty. (Image Select)

Paulus Friedrich von (1890–1957). German field marshal in World War II, responsible for much of the detailed planning of Operation Barbarossa, the German invasion of the Soviet Union 1941, and commander of the forces that besieged Stalingrad (now Volgograd) 1942–43. He was captured and gave evidence for the prosecution at the Nuremberg trials before settling in East Germany.

The man should have shot himself ... Beyond the life of the individual is the Nation ... He could have ... ascended into eternity and national immortality, but he prefers to go to Moscow.

Adolf Hitler on FRIEDRICH VON PAULUS' surrender at Stalingrad 1943

Pausanias (lived 2nd century AD). Greek geographer, author of a valuably accurate description of Greece compiled from his own travels, *Description of Greece*, also translated as *Itinerary of Greece*.

Pavarotti Luciano (1935–). Italian tenor. He has an impressive dynamic range. His operatic roles have included Rodolfo in *La Bohème*, Cavaradossi in *Tosca*, the Duke of Mantua in *Rigoletto*, and Nemorino in *L'Elisir d'amore*. He gave his first performance in the title role of *Otello* in Chicago, USA, 1991. He has done much to popularize opera, performing to wide audiences outside the opera houses including open-air concerts in New York and London city parks.

He collaborated with José Carreras and Placido Domingo in a recording of operatic hits coinciding with the World Cup soccer series in Rome 1990; his rendition of 'Nessun Dorma' from Puccini's *Turandot* was adopted as the theme music for the series.

Pavese Cesare (1908–1950). Italian poet, translator, and novelist. Imprisoned for anti-Fascist journalism, he published his poems *Lavorare stanca/Hard Labour* 1936 on his release. His translations and critical writings introduced Italian readers to modern English and American writers, notably Joyce and Melville, who influenced his fascination with myth, symbol, and archetype. His novel *La luna e i falò/The Moon and the Bonfires* appeared 1950.

Pavlov Ivan Petrovich (1849–1936). Russian physiologist who studied conditioned reflexes in animals. His work had a great impact on behavioural theory and learning theory. Nobel Prize for Physiology or Medicine 1904.

Pavlov was born in Ryazan and studied in St Petersburg at the university and the Imperial Medical Academy, where he became professor 1890.

Studying the physiology of the circulatory system and the regulation of blood pressure, Pavlov devised animal experiments such as the dissection of the cardiac nerves of a living dog to show how the nerves that leave the cardiac plexus control heartbeat strength.

Pavlov's work relating to human behaviour and the nervous system also emphasized the importance of conditioning. He deduced that the inhibitive behaviour of a psychotic person is a means of self-protection. The person shuts out the world and, with it, all damaging stimuli. Following this theory, the treatment of psychiatric patients in Russia involved placing a sick person in completely calm and quiet surroundings.

Pavlov summarized his Nobel prize-winning work in *Die Arbeit der Verdauungsdrüsen/Lectures on the Work of the Principal Digestive Gland* 1897.

Suggested reading
Babkin, B P *Pavlov: A Biography* (1949)
Gray, Jeffrey *Pavlov* (1979)

Pavlov Valentin (1937–   ). Soviet communist politician, prime minister Jan–Aug 1991. He served in the Finance Ministry, the State Planning Committee (Gosplan), and the State Pricing Committee before becoming minister of finance 1989. In Jan 1991 he replaced Nikolai Ryzhkov as prime minister, with the brief of halting the gathering collapse of the Soviet economy. In Aug 1991 he was a member of the eight-person junta which led the abortive anti-Gorbachev

Pavlov, Ivan *Russian physiologist Ivan Pavlov, who developed the idea of the 'conditional reflex', after showing that if a bell was sounded whenever a dog was presented with food, the dog would eventually begin to salivate whenever the bell was rung, regardless of whether food was presented.* (Ann Ronan/Image Select)

attempted coup. In the midst of the coup, he relinquished his position as premier, citing health reasons. He was arrested when the coup was finally thwarted but released under an amnesty 1994.

Pavlova Anna (1881–1931). Russian dancer. Prima ballerina of the Imperial Ballet from 1906, she left Russia 1913, and went on to become one of the world's most celebrated exponents of classical ballet. With London as her home, she toured extensively with her own company, influencing dancers worldwide with roles such as Mikhail Fokine's *The Dying Swan* solo 1907. She was opposed to the modern reforms of Diaghilev's Ballets Russes, adhering strictly to conservative aesthetics.

Suggested reading
Fonteyn, Margot *Portrait of a Dancer* (1984)
Franks, A H (ed) *Pavlova* (1956)
Kerensky, O *Anna Pavlova* (1973)
Lazzarini, R *Pavlova: Repertoire of a Legend* (1980)
Money, K *Anna Pavlova* (1982)

An artist should know all about love and learn to live without it.

ANNA PAVLOVA
Attributed remark

Paxton Joseph (1801–1865). English architect. He was also garden superintendent to the Duke of Devonshire from 1826. He designed the Great Exhibition building 1851 (the Crystal Palace), which was revolutionary in its structural use of glass and iron. Knighted 1851.

Payne-Gaposchkin Cecilia Helena (born Payne) (1900–1979). English-born US astronomer who studied stellar evolution and galactic structure. Her investigation of stellar atmospheres during the 1920s gave some of the first indications of the overwhelming abundance of the lightest elements (hydrogen and helium) in the Galaxy.

Payne was born in Wendover, Buckinghamshire, and studied at Cambridge and at Harvard College Observatory in Cambridge, Massachusetts, under US astronomer Harlow Shapley. In 1927 she was appointed an astronomer at the observatory, and in 1956 she became the first woman professor at Harvard.

Payne-Gaposchkin employed a variety of spectroscopic techniques in the investigation of stellar properties and composition, especially variable stars. Her studies of the Large and Small Magellanic Clouds were carried out in collaboration with her husband Sergei I Gaposchkin. Other areas of her interest included the devising of methods to determine stellar magnitudes, the position of variable stars on the Hertzsprung–Russell diagram, and novae.

Paz (Estenssoro) Victor (1907–   ). President of Bolivia 1952–56, 1960–64, and 1985–89. He founded and led the Movimiento Nacionalista Revolucionario (MNR) which seized power 1952. His regime extended the vote to Indians, nationalized the country's largest tin mines, embarked on a programme of agrarian reform, and brought inflation under control.

After holding a number of financial posts, Paz entered politics in the 1930s and in 1942 founded the MNR. In exile in Argentina during one of Bolivia's many periods of military rule, he returned in 1951 and became president in 1952. He immediately embarked on a programme of political reform, retaining the presidency until 1956 and being re-elected 1960–64 and again in 1985, returning from near-retirement at the age of 77. During his long career he was Bolivian ambassador to London 1956–59 and a professor at London University 1966. Following an indecisive presidential contest 1989, Paz was replaced by Jaime Paz Zamora of the Movement of the Revolutionary Left (MIR).

We are condemned to kill time: Thus we die little by little.

OCTAVIO PAZ
Cuento de los Jardines

Paz Octavio (1914–   ). Mexican poet and essayist. His works reflect many influences, including Marxism, Surrealism, and Aztec mythology. His long poem *Piedra del sol/Sun Stone* 1957 uses contrasting images, centring upon the Aztec Calendar Stone (representing the Aztec universe), to symbolize the loneliness of individuals and their search for union with others. Nobel Prize for Literature 1990.

Peabody George (1795–1869). US philanthropist. Peabody started working at 11 and made a fortune from a dry-goods business in Baltimore, followed by an investment banking business in Boston and London, where he lived from 1837. Among his gifts were museums at Yale and Harvard Universities, more than $2 million to develop education in the southern states, including a teaching college in Tennessee, an Arctic expedition, and many innovative housing schemes in London for rehousing tenement dwellers.

Peacock Thomas Love (1785–1866). English satirical novelist and poet. Peacock worked for the East India Company from 1819 and was instrumental in the development of the earliest gunboats during the 1830s. His works include *Headlong Hall* 1816, *Melincourt* 1817, and *Nightmare Abbey* 1818, which has very little plot, consisting almost entirely of conversation. With a prevailing comic tone, the author satirizes contemporary ideas, outlooks, and attitudes. His other works include *Crotchet Castle* 1831 and *Gryll Grange* 1860.

Marriage may often be a stormy lake, but celibacy is almost always a muddy horsepond.

THOMAS LOVE PEACOCK
Melincourt 1817

Peake Mervyn Laurence (1911–1968). English writer and illustrator. His novels include the grotesque fantasy trilogy *Titus Groan* 1946, *Gormenghast* 1950, and *Titus Alone* 1959. He illustrated most of his own work and produced drawings for an edition of *Treasure Island* 1949, and other works. Among his collections of verse are *The Glassblowers* 1950 and the posthumous *A Book of Nonsense* 1972.

Peale name of an American artist family, most notable of whom was Charles Willson (1741–1826). He studied under Benjamin West in London, 1767–70, and worked successfully as a portrait painter in Philadelphia. He painted several portraits of George Washington and of other famous men of his time (Independence Hall, Philadelphia). His brother James (1749–1831), whom he taught, was a miniaturist, and his sons (whom he named after old masters) were also painters; Rembrandt (1778–1860) was a portraitist and lithographer, Raphaelle (1774–1825) a still-life painter, and Titian Ramsey (1800–1885) an animal draughtsperson.

Peale Norman Vincent (1898–). US Methodist leader. Through his radio programme and book *The Art of Living* 1948, he became one of the best-known religious figures in the USA. His *The Power of Positive Thinking* 1952 became a national bestseller. Peale was elected president of the Reformed Church in America in 1969.

Peano Giuseppe (1858–1932). Italian mathematician who was a pioneer in symbolic logic. His concise logical definitions of natural numbers were devised in order to derive a complete system of notation for logic. He also discovered a curve that fills topological space.

Peano was born near Cuneo, Piedmont, and studied at Turin. On graduating, he joined the staff of the university and remained there for the rest of his life, first becoming a professor there in 1890. He was also professor at Turin Military Academy 1886–1901.

Peano's first work in logic, published in 1888, contained his rigorously axiomatically derived postulates for natural numbers. He acknowledged his debt for some of the work to German mathematician Richard Dedekind. Some of Peano's work was used by English philosopher Bertrand Russell.

Peano also applied the axiomatic method to other fields, such as geometry, first in 1889 and again in 1894. A treatise on this work contained the beginnings of geometrical calculus. Peano provided new definitions of the length of an arc of a curve and of the area of a surface. *Formulario mathematico* 1895–1908, comprising his work and that of collaborators, contains 4,200 theorems.

Pears Peter Neville Luard (1910–1986). English tenor. He was the life companion of Benjamin Britten and with him co-founded the Aldeburgh Festival. He inspired and collaborated with Britten in a rich catalogue of song cycles and operatic roles, exploiting a distinctively airy and luminous tone, from the title role in *Peter Grimes* 1947 to Aschenbach in *Death in Venice* 1973. Knighted 1978.

Ireland's historic claim is for separation. Ireland has authorised no man to abate that claim.

PATRICK HENRY PEARSE
Collected Works 'Ghosts' 1917

Pearse Patrick Henry (1879–1916). Irish poet. He was prominent in the Gaelic revival, a leader of the Easter Rising 1916. Proclaimed president of the provisional government, he was court-martialled and shot after its suppression.

When something had to be done he did it, and entirely disregarded logic or economics or force.

James Stephens on PATRICK HENRY PEARSE
in *Dictionary of National Biography Missing Persons* 1993

Pearson Drew (Andrew Russell) (1897–1969). US newspaper correspondent who from 1932 wrote the syndicated column 'Washington Merry-Go-Round'. After his death the column was taken over by newspaper columnist and writer Jack Anderson (1922–).

Pearson Karl (1857–1936). British statistician who followed Francis Galton in introducing statistics and probability into genetics and who developed the concept of eugenics (improving the human race by selective breeding). He introduced the term standard deviation into statistics.

Pearson was born in London and studied at Cambridge, where he persuaded the authorities to abolish the mandatory classes in Christianity for undergraduates. In 1884 he became professor of mathematics at University College, London; from 1911 he was professor of eugenics at London University. In order to publish work on statistics as applied to biological subjects, he founded 1901 the journal *Biometrika*, which he edited until his death.

Pearson's discoveries included the Pearson coefficient of correlation (1892), the theory of multiple and partial correlation (1896), the coefficient of variation (1898), work on errors of judgement (1902), and the theory of random walk (1905).

Pearson's *Biometrika* for 1901 is a book of tables of the ordinates, integrals, and other properties of Pearson's curves.

Pearson Lester Bowles (1897–1972). Canadian politician, leader of the Liberal Party from 1958, prime minister 1963–68. As foreign minister 1948–57, he represented Canada at the United Nations, playing a key role in settling the Suez Crisis 1956. Nobel Peace Prize 1957.

Pearson served as president of the General Assembly 1952–53 and helped to create the UN Emergency Force (UNEF) that policed Sinai following the Egypt–Israel war of 1956. As prime minister, he led the way to formulating a national medicare (health insurance) law.

Suggested reading
Bothwell, R *Pearson: His Life and World* (1978)
Pearson, Lester *Memoirs* (1973–75)
Thordarson, Bruce *Lester Pearson: Diplomat and Politician* (1974)

The grim fact is that we prepare for war like precocious giants and for peace like retarded pygmies.

LESTER PEARSON
News summaries 15 March 1955

Peary Robert Edwin (1856–1920). US polar explorer who, after several unsuccessful attempts, became the first person to reach the North Pole on 6 April 1909. He sailed to Cape Sheridan in the *Roosevelt* with his aide Matthew Henson, and they then made a sledge journey to the Pole. In 1988 an astronomer claimed Peary's measurements were incorrect.

Suggested reading
Herbert, W *The Noose of Laurels* (1989)
Hunt, William *To Stand at the Pole: The Dr Cook-Admiral Peary North Pole Controversy* (1982)
Weems, J E *Peary* (1988)

Peck (Eldred) Gregory (1916–). US film actor. He specialized in strong, upright characters, but also had a gift for light comedy. His films include *Spellbound* 1945, *Duel in the Sun* 1946, *Gentleman's Agreement* 1947, *Roman Holiday* 1953, *To Kill a Mockingbird* 1962, for which he won an Academy Award, and (cast against type as a Nazi doctor) *The Boys from Brazil* 1974.

Peckinpah Sam (David Samuel) (1926–1984). US film director. Mainly Westerns, his films were usually associated with slow-motion, blood-spurting violence. His best work, such as *The Wild Bunch* 1969, exhibits a magisterial grasp of staging and construction.

Pedro two emperors of Brazil:

Pedro I (1798–1834). Emperor of Brazil 1822–31. The son of John VI of Portugal, he escaped to Brazil on Napoleon's invasion, and was appointed regent 1821. He proclaimed Brazil independent 1822 and was crowned emperor, but abdicated 1831 and returned to Portugal.

Pedro II (1825–1891). Emperor of Brazil 1831–89. He proved an enlightened ruler, but his antislavery measures alienated the landowners, who compelled him to abdicate.

It is a great misfortune to him to write in a style that would disgrace a washerwoman.
George IV on ROBERT PEEL
in *Letters* 1812

Peel Robert (1788–1850). British Conservative politician. As home secretary 1822–27 and 1828–30, he founded the modern police force and in 1829 introduced Roman Catholic emancipation. He was prime minister 1834–35 and 1841–46.

Peel, born in Lancashire, entered Parliament as a Tory 1809. After the passing of the Reform Bill of 1832, which he had resisted, he reformed the Tories under the name of the Conservative Party, on a basis of accepting necessary changes and seeking middle-class support. He fell from prime ministerial office because his repeal of the Corn Laws 1846 was opposed by the majority of his party. He and his followers then formed a third party standing between the Liberals and Conservatives; the majority of the Peelites, including Gladstone, subsequently joined the Liberals. 2nd baronet 1830.

Suggested reading
Gash, N *Sir Robert Peel* (1961–72)
Lever, Tresham *The Life and Times of Sir Robert Peel* (1942)
Read, Donald *Sir Robert Peel* (1987)

His golden locks time hath to silver turn'd; / O time too swift, O swiftness never ceasing!
GEORGE PEELE
'A Farewell to Arms'

Peele George (c. 1558–c. 1597). English dramatist. He wrote a pastoral, *The Arraignment of Paris* 1584; a fantastic comedy, *The Old Wives' Tale* 1595; and a tragedy, *David and Bethsabe* 1599.

Péguy Charles Pierre (1873–1914). French Catholic socialist. He established a socialist publishing house in Paris. From 1900 he published on political topics *Les Cahiers de la quinzaine*/*Fortnightly Notebooks* and on poetry, including *Le Mystère de la charité de Jeanne d'Arc*/*The Mystery of the Charity of Joan of Arc* 1897.

He who does not bellow the truth when he knows the truth makes himself the accomplice of liars and forgers.
CHARLES PÉGUY
Lettre du Provincial 21 Dec 1899

Pei Ieoh Ming (1917–). Chinese-born US Modernist architect. Pei became a US citizen 1948. He is noted for his innovative High-Tech structures, particularly the use of glass walls. His projects include the 70-storey Bank of China, Hong Kong, 1987 – Asia's tallest building at 368 m/1,209 ft – and the glass pyramid in front of the Louvre, Paris, 1989. Other works by him are Dallas City Hall, Texas; East Building, National Gallery of Art, Washington DC 1978; John F Kennedy Library Complex and the John Hancock Tower, Boston 1979; and the National Airlines terminal at Kennedy Airport, New York.

Peierls Rudolf Ernst (1907–1995). German-born British physicist who contributed to the early theory of the neutron–proton system. He helped to develop the atomic bomb 1940–46. Knighted 1968.

Peierls was born in Berlin and studied at universities in Germany and Switzerland under leading atomic physicists. From 1933 he worked in the UK, and was professor at Birmingham 1937–63 and at Oxford 1963–74.

In 1940, at Birmingham, Austrian physicist Otto Frisch and Peierls made an estimate of the energy released in a nuclear chain reaction, which indicated that a fission bomb would make a weapon of terrifying power. They drew the attention of the British government to this in 1940, and Peierls was placed in charge of a small group concerned with evaluating the chain reaction and its efficiency. In 1943, when Britain decided not to continue its work on nuclear energy, Peierls moved to the USA to help in the work of the Manhattan Project, first in New York and then at Los Alamos.

Peirce Charles Sanders (1839–1914). US philosopher and logician, founder of pragmatism (which he later called pragmaticism), who argued that genuine conceptual distinctions must be correlated with some differences of practical effect. He wrote extensively on the logic of scientific enquiry, suggesting that truth could be conceived of as the object of an ultimate consensus. His works include *How to Make Our Ideas Clear* 1878; his *Collected Papers* were published posthumously 1931–58.

Pelagius (c. 360–c. 420). British theologian. He taught that each person possesses free will (and hence the possibility of salvation), denying Augustine's doctrines of predestination and original sin. Cleared of heresy by a synod in Jerusalem 415, he was later condemned by the pope and the emperor.

Pelé adopted name of Edson Arantes do Nascimento (1940–). Brazilian soccer player. A prolific goal scorer, he appeared in four World Cup competitions 1958–70 and led Brazil to three championships (1958, 1962, 1970). He spent most of his playing career with the Brazilian team Santos, before ending it with the New York Cosmos in the USA.

Suggested reading
Pelé and Fish, Robert *My Life and the Beautiful Game* (1977)

His understanding was more solid than brilliant.
Archdeacon Coxe on HENRY PELHAM
in *Memoirs of the Pelham Administration* 1829

Pelham Henry (1696–1754). British Whig politician. He held a succession of offices in Robert Walpole's cabinet 1721–42, and was prime minister 1743–54. His brother Thomas Pelham-Holles, 1st Duke of Newcastle, succeeded him as prime minister.

Pelletier Pierre-Joseph (1788–1842). French chemist whose extractions of a range of biologically active compounds from plants founded the chemistry of the alkaloids. The most important of his discoveries was quinine, used against malaria.

Pelletier was born in Paris and qualified as a pharmacist. He was professor at the Ecole de Pharmacie 1825–40.

Pelletier began with the analysis of gum resins and the colouring matter in plants. In 1817, together with chemist Joseph Caventou (1795–1877), he isolated the green pigment in leaves, which they named chlorophyll. In 1818 they turned to plant alkaloids: strychnine 1818, brucine and veratrine 1819, and quinine 1820 whose powerful effects made it possible to specify chemical compounds in pharmacology instead of the imprecise plant extracts and mixtures used previously.

Working with chemist Jean Baptiste Dumas, Pelletier obtained firm evidence for the presence of nitrogen in alkaloids 1823. He later carried out researches on strychnine and developed procedures for its extraction.

In 1832 Pelletier discovered a new opium alkaloid, narceine; he also claimed to have been the first to isolate thebaine (which he called paramorphine). In a study (1837–38) of an oily by-product of pine resin he discovered toluene (now methylbenzene).

Pelsaert François (1590–1630). Belgian-born Dutch East India Company official and commander of the *Batavia* which was wrecked off the W Australian coast near Houtman Abrolhos in 1629. Pelsaert probably slept one night on the mainland before setting off on an open-boat voyage to Batavia (now Jakarta) to seek assistance for the 300 survivors. He was the first European to record the existence of wallabies.

Pelton Lester Allen (1829–1918). US engineer who developed a highly efficient water turbine used to drive both mechanical devices and hydroelectric power turbines using large heads of water. The Pelton wheel remains the only hydraulic turbine of the impulse type in common use today.

From Ohio, Pelton joined the California gold rush at the age of 20. He observed the water wheels used at the mines to power machinery, and came up with improvements. By 1879 he had tested a prototype at the University of California. A patent was granted 1889, and he later sold the rights to the Pelton Water Wheel Company of San Francisco.

The energy to drive these wheels was supplied by powerful jets of water which struck the base of the wheel on hemispherical cups. Pelton's discovery was that the wheel rotated more rapidly, and hence developed more power, with the jet striking at the inside edge of the cups, rather than the centre; he built a wheel with split cups. By the time of his death, Pelton wheels developing thousands of horsepower in hydroelectric schemes at efficiencies of more than 90% were in operation.

Penda (c. 577–654). King of Mercia, an Anglo-Saxon kingdom in England, from about 632. He raised Mercia to a powerful kingdom, and defeated and killed two Northumbrian kings, Edwin 632 and Oswald 642. He was killed in battle by Oswy, king of Northumbria.

Penderecki Krzysztof (1933–). Polish composer. His expressionist works, such as the *Threnody for the Victims of Hiroshima* 1961 for strings, employ cluster and percussion effects. He later turned to religious subjects and a more orthodox style, as in the *Magnificat* 1974 and the *Polish Requiem* 1980–83. His opera *The Black Mask* 1986 uncovered a new vein of surreal humour.

Pendlebury John Devitt Stringfellow (1904–1941). British archaeologist. Working with his wife, he became the world's leading expert on Crete. In World War II he was deputed to prepare guerrilla resistance on the island, was wounded during the German invasion, and shot by his captors.

Penn Irving (1917–). US fashion, advertising, portrait, editorial, and fine art photographer. In 1948 he made the first of many journeys to Africa and the Far East, resulting in a series of portrait photographs of local people, avoiding sophisticated technique. He was associated for many years with *Vogue* magazine in the USA.

Penn William (1644–1718). English member of the Society of Friends (Quakers), born in London. He joined the Society 1667, and in 1681 obtained a grant of land in America (in settlement of a debt owed by the king to his father) on which he established the colony of Pennsylvania as a refuge for persecuted Quakers.

Penn made religious tolerance a cornerstone of his administration of the colony. He maintained good relations with neighbouring colonies and with the Indians in the area, but his utopian ideals were not successful for the most part. In 1697 he presented a plan, never acted upon, for a union among the colonies. In 1701 he established, with his Charter of Privileges, a bicameral legislature as the government for Pennsylvania.

Suggested reading
Dunn, Mary M *William Penn: Politics and Conscience* (1967)
Dunn, R S and M M *The World of William Penn* (1986)
Endy, M B, Jr *William Penn and Early Quakerism* (1973)
Wildes, H *William Penn* (1974)

Penney William George (1909–1991). English scientist who worked at Los Alamos, New Mexico, 1944–45, developing the US atomic bomb. He also headed the team that constructed Britain's first atomic bomb and directed its testing programme at the Monte Bello Islands off Western Australia 1952. He subsequently directed the UK hydrogen bomb project, tested on Christmas Island 1957, and developed the advanced gas-cooled nuclear reactor used in some UK power stations. KBE 1952, baron 1967.

Penney was born in Sheerness, Kent, and studied at London and Cambridge, and in the USA at Wisconsin. A mathematician by training, he became an explosives expert. He was director of the Atomic Weapons Research Establishment 1953–59 and chair of the UK Atomic Energy Authority 1964–67. He was rector of Imperial College, London, 1967–73.

Pennington Mary Engle (1872–1952). US chemist who set standards for food refrigeration. She also designed both industrial and household refrigerators.

Pennington was born in Nashville, Tennesse, and studied at the University of Pennsylvania but was initially denied a degree on account of her sex. In 1898 she opened her own Philadelphia Clinical Laboratory. She was head of the Food Research Laboratory of the Department of Agriculture 1908–19. From 1922 she worked as an independent consultant on the storage, handling, and transportation of perishable goods.

In Philadelphia, from research into the preservation of dairy products, Pennington developed standards of milk inspection that were later used by health boards across the USA. During World War I she conducted experiments into railway refrigeration cars and recommended the standards that remained in use into the 1940s. As a consultant, she turned her interest to frozen food.

Pennycuick Colin James (1933–). English zoologist who has studied the various processes involved in flight. He discovered that many migratory birds have minimal energy reserves and must stop to feed at regular intervals. The destruction of the intermediate feeding places of these birds could lead to their extinction, even if their summer and winter quarters are conserved. In 1964 he became a lecturer at Bristol University, with a break 1971–73 spent researching at Nairobi University in Kenya.

Pennycuick's research is unusual in that it interrelates an extremely large number of factors and therefore gives a very detailed account of flight. In flying vertebrates, for example, he has investigated the mechanics of flapping; the aerodynamic effects of the feet and tail; the physiology of gaseous exchange; heat disposal; the relationship between the size and anatomy of a flying creature and the power it develops; and the frequency of wing beats. Pennycuick has also hypothesized that migratory birds navigate using the Sun's altitude and its changing position.

Penrose Lionel Sharples (1898–1972). English physician and geneticist who carried out pioneering work on mental retardation and Down's syndrome. He was the first to demonstrate the significance of the mother's age.

He was director of psychiatric research for Ontario, Canada, 1939–45. In 1945 he became professor of eugenics at London University.

While working as research medical officer at the Royal Eastern Counties Institution, Colchester, 1930–39, Penrose produced an influential survey of patients and their families (*A Clinical and Genetic Study of 1,280 Cases of Mental Defect* 1938), showing that there were many different types and causes of mental defect and that normality and subnormality were on a continuum.

Early in his career, Penrose advanced the study of schizophrenia and developed a test for its diagnosis. His subsequent work concentrated on the causes of Down's syndrome.

Penrose Roger (1931–). English mathematician who formulated some of the fundamental theorems that describe black holes, including the singularity theorems, developed jointly with English physicist Stephen Hawking, which state that once the gravitational collapse of a star has proceeded to a certain degree, singularities (which form the centre of black holes) are inevitable. Penrose has also proposed a new model of the universe.

While he worked for his doctorate at Cambridge in 1957, Penrose and his father were devising geometrical figures, the construction of which is three-dimensionally impossible. (They became well known when incorporated by Dutch artist M C Escher into a couple of his disturbing lithographs.) Penrose was professor at Birkbeck College, London, 1966–73, and then moved to Oxford University.

The existence of a trapped surface within an 'event horizon' (the interface between a black hole and space-time), from which little or no radiation or information can escape, implies that some events remain hidden to observers outside the black hole. Penrose has put forward the hypothesis of 'cosmic censorship' – that all singularities are so hidden – which is now widely accepted.

Calculations in the world of ordinary objects (including Einstein's general theory of relativity) use real numbers, whereas the world of quantum theory often requires a system using complex numbers, containing imaginary components that are multiples of the square root of –1. Penrose holds that all calculations about both the macroscopic and microscopic worlds should use complex numbers, requiring reformulation of the major laws of physics and of space-time. He has proposed a model of the universe whose basic building blocks are what he calls 'twistors'.

His works include *The Emperor's New Mind: Concerning Computers, Minds, and the Laws of Physics* 1989 and *Shadows of the Mind: A Search for the Missing Science of Consciousness* 1994.

Penston Michael (1943–1990). British astronomer at the Royal Greenwich Observatory 1965–90. From observations made with the Ultraviolet Explorer Satellite of hot gas circulating around the core of the galaxy NGC 4151, he and his colleagues concluded that a black hole of immense mass lay at the galaxy's centre.

NGC 4151 is the brightest of a class of objects known as Seyfert galaxies, which are like scaled-down versions of quasars. Supermassive black holes had long been suspected to lie at the centres of such objects, because of their strange behaviour, but Penston's result was the first direct observational evidence in favour of this theory.

Penzias Arno Allan (1933–). German-born US radio engineer who in 1964, with radioastronomer Robert Wilson, was the first to detect cosmic background radiation. This radiation had been predicted on the basis of the 'hot Big Bang' model of the origin of the universe. Penzias and Wilson shared the 1978 Nobel Prize for Physics.

In 1961 he joined the staff of the Radio Research Laboratory of the Bell Telephone Company, becoming its director 1976 and vice president of research 1981. Concurrently he has held a series of academic positions at Princeton, Harvard, and from 1975 as professor at the State University of New York at Stony Brook.

In 1963, Penzias and Wilson were assigned by Bell to the tracing of radio noise that was interfering with the development of a communications programme involving satellites. By May 1964 they had detected a surprisingly high level of microwave radiation which had

no apparent source (that is, it was uniform in all directions). The temperature of this background radiation was 3.5K (–269.7°C/ –453.4°F), later revised to 3.1K (–270°C/–454.1°F).

They took this enigmatic result to physicist Robert Dicke at Princeton, who had predicted that this sort of radiation should be present in the universe as a residual relic of the intense heat associated with the birth of the universe following the Big Bang. His department was in the process of constructing a radio telescope designed to detect precisely this radiation when Penzias and Wilson presented their data.

Penzias's later work has been concerned with developments in radioastronomy, instrumentation, satellite communications, atmospheric physics, and related matters.

Pepin the Short (*c.* 714–*c.* 768). King of the Franks from 751. The son of Charles Martel, he acted as Mayor of the Palace to the last Merovingian king, Childeric III, deposed him and assumed the royal title himself, founding the Carolingian dynasty. He was Charlemagne's father.

Peppard George (1928–1994). US actor with a gift for laconic understatement. He played leading roles in several early-1960s productions, including *Breakfast at Tiffany's* 1961 and *The Carpetbaggers* 1964. From 1983 to 1986 he played the grizzled, cigar-chomping leader of *The A-Team*, in an NBC TV series. In his later years he appeared in occasional stage productions, and toured in the USA in *The Lion in Winter* 1992.

Pepusch Johann Christoph (1667–1752). German composer. He settled in England about 1700 and contributed to John Gay's ballad operas *The Beggar's Opera* and *Polly*.

Pepys Samuel (1633–1703). English diarist. Born in London, he entered the navy office 1660, and was secretary to the Admiralty 1672–79, publishing *Memoires of the Navy* 1690. His diary 1659–69 was a unique record of both the daily life of the period and his own intimate feelings. Written in shorthand, it was not deciphered until 1825. Pepys was imprisoned 1679 in the Tower of London on suspicion of being connected with the Popish Plot. He was reinstated 1684 but finally deprived of his post after the 1688 Revolution, for suspected disaffection.

Suggested reading
Bryant, A *Samuel Pepys* (1933-38)
Ollard, R *Samuel Pepys* (1974)
Trease, G *Samuel Pepys and his World* (1978)

Perahia Murray (1947–). US pianist and conductor. He is noted for urbane interpretations of Chopin, Schumann, and Mendelssohn. He has recorded all of the Mozart piano concertos with the English Chamber Orchestra, conducting from the keyboard.

Perceval Spencer (1762–1812). British Tory politician. He became chancellor of the Exchequer 1807 and prime minister 1809. He was shot in the lobby of the House of Commons 1812 by a merchant who blamed government measures for his bankruptcy.

Percival Arthur (1887–1966). British general. He took command of British forces in Malaya June 1941 and barely had time to consider his position before the Japanese invaded Dec 1941. He was keenly aware of the deficiencies in his defences but could extract no further support from Britain and was forced to surrender 15 Feb 1942. He was imprisoned in Manchuria but was present aboard the USS *Missouri* to see the Japanese formally surrender 2 Sept 1945.

Percy family name of dukes of Northumberland; seated at Alnwick Castle, Northumberland, England.

Percy Henry ('Hotspur') (1364–1403). English soldier, son of the 1st Earl of Northumberland. In repelling a border raid, he defeated the Scots at Homildon Hill in Durham 1402. He was killed at the battle of Shrewsbury while in revolt against Henry IV.

Percy Thomas (1729–1811). English scholar and bishop of Dromore from 1782. He discovered a manuscript collection of songs, ballads, and romances, from which he published a selection as *Reliques of Ancient English Poetry* 1765, which was influential in the Romantic revival.

Peregrinus Petrus. Adopted name of Peregrinus de Maricourt (*c.* 1220–*c.* 1270/90). French scientist and scholar who published *Epistola de magnete* 1269. In it he described a simple compass (a piece of magnetized iron on a wooden disc floating in water) and outlined the laws of magnetic attraction and repulsion.

Peregrinus was an engineer in the French army under Louis IX, and was active in Paris in the middle of the 13th century. There he advised English scientist Roger Bacon. Peregrinus took part in the siege of Lucera in Italy in 1269.

His ideas on magnetism, based largely on experiment, were taken up 250 years later by English physicist William Gilbert.

Love is not the dying moan of a distant violin – it is the triumphant twang of a bedspring.

S J PERELMAN
Attributed remark

Perelman S(idney) J(oseph) (1904–1979). US humorist. His work was often published in the *New Yorker* magazine, and he wrote film scripts for the Marx Brothers. He shared an Academy Award for the script of *Around the World in 80 Days* 1956.

Peres Shimon (born Perski) (1923–   ). Israeli socialist politician, prime minister 1984–86 and 1995–96. Peres emigrated from Poland to Palestine 1934, but was educated in the USA. In 1959 he was elected to the Knesset (Israeli parliament). He was leader of the Labour Party 1977–92, when he was replaced by Rabin. Peres was prime minister, then foreign minister, under a power-sharing agreement with the leader of the Consolidation Party (Likud), Yitzhak Shamir. From 1989 to 1990 he was finance minister in a Labour–Likud coalition. As foreign minister in Yitzhak Rabin's Labour government from 1992, he negotiated the 1993 peace agreement with the Palestine Liberation Organization (PLO). He was awarded the 1994 Nobel Prize for Peace jointly with Rabin and PLO leader, Yassir Arafat. Following the assassination of Rabin Nov 1995, Peres succeeded him as prime minister, and pledged to continue with the peace process in which they had both been so closely involved. His party lost the 1996 elections.

Perey Marguérite Catherine (1909–1975). French nuclear chemist who discovered the radioactive element francium in 1939. Her career, which began as an assistant to Marie Curie 1929, culminated with her appointment as professor of nuclear chemistry at the University of Strasbourg 1949 and director of its Centre for Nuclear Research 1958.

Pérez de Cuéllar Javier (1920–   ). Peruvian diplomat, secretary general of the United Nations 1982–91. A delegate to the first UN General Assembly 1946–47, he subsequently held several ambassadorial posts. He raised the standing of the UN by his successful diplomacy in ending the Iran–Iraq War 1988 and securing the independence of Namibia 1989. He was unable to resolve the Gulf conflict resulting from Iraq's invasion of Kuwait 1990 before combat against Iran by the UN coalition began Jan 1991, but later in 1991 he negotiated the release of Western hostages held in Beirut. In 1994 it was thought that he might seek the Peruvian presidency.

Pérez Galdós Benito (1843–1920). Spanish novelist. His works include the 46 historical novels in the cycle *Episodios nacionales* and the 21-novel cycle *Novelas españolas contemporáneas*, which includes *Doña Perfecta* 1876 and the epic *Fortunata y Jacinta* 1886–87, his masterpiece. In scale he has been compared to the French writer Honoré de Balzac and the English novelist Charles Dickens.

Pérez Jiménez Marcos (1914–   ). Venezuelan president 1952–58. He led the military junta that overthrew the Acción Democrática government of Rómulo Gallegos 1948, was made provisional president 1952, and approved as constitutional president by

Congress 1953. His regime had a reputation as the most repressive in Venezuelan history. It also encouraged European immigration and undertook massive public works in the capital, Caracas.

Peri Jacopo (1561–1633). Italian composer. He served the Medici family, the rulers of Florence. His experimental melodic opera *Euridice* 1600 established the opera form and influenced Monteverdi. His first opera, *Dafne* 1597, is now lost.

Periander Greek tyrant of Corinth about 625–585 BC. Under his reign, and that of his father Cypselus, Corinthian wealth and influence greatly expanded. He conquered Epidaurus and annexed Corcyra (Corfu). He was a patron of men of letters and was one of the Seven Sages of Greece.

Pericles (*c.* 495–429 BC). Athenian politician who was effective leader of the city from 443 BC and under whom Athenian power reached its height. His policies helped to transform the Delian League into an Athenian empire, but the disasters of the Peloponnesian War led to his removal from office 430 BC. Although quickly reinstated, he died soon after.

Suggested reading
Bowra, C M *Periclean Athens* (1966)
Burns, A *Pericles and Athens* (1970)
Ehrenberg, Victor *Sophocles and Pericles* (1954)
Kagan, Donald *Pericles of Athens and the Birth of Democracy* (1990)

During the whole period of peacetime when Pericles was at the head of affairs the state was wisely led and firmly guided, and it was under him that Athens was at her greatest.

Thucydides on PERICLES
in *History* 2.65

Perkin William Henry (1838–1907). British chemist. In 1856 he discovered mauve, the dye that originated the aniline-dye industry and the British synthetic-dyestuffs industry generally. Knighted 1906.

Perkin was born in London and studied at the Royal College of Chemistry. He was only 18 when he discovered and patented the process for mauve. With the help of his father he set up a factory to manufacture the dye. Perkin's factory introduced new dyes based on the alkylation of magenta, and in 1868 he established a new route for the synthesis of alizarin. By 1871 Perkin's company was producing one tonne of alizarin every day. He sold the factory and retired from industry in 1874 to continue his academic research.

In the late 1860s, Perkin prepared unsaturated acids by the action of acetic anhydride on aromatic aldehydes, a method known as the Perkin synthesis. In 1868 he synthesized coumarin, the first preparation of a synthetic perfume.

I have learned more about love, selflessness, and human understanding in this great adventure in the world of AIDS than I ever did in the cut-throat, competitive world in which I spent my life.

ANTHONY PERKINS
Statement published posthumously, *Independent on Sunday* 20 Sept 1992

Perkins Anthony (1932–1992). US film actor. He is remembered as the mother-fixated psychopath Norman Bates in Alfred Hitchcock's *Psycho* 1960 and *Psycho II* 1982. He played shy but subtle roles in *Friendly Persuasion* 1956, *The Trial* 1962, and *The Champagne Murders* 1967. He also appeared on the stage in London and New York.

Perkins Frances (1882–1965). US public official. She became the first female cabinet officer when she served as secretary of labour under F D Roosevelt 1933–45. Under Truman she was a member of the federal civil service commission 1946–53.

Perlman Itzhak (1945–   ). Israeli violinist. He is one of the great virtuosos in modern times, combining a brilliant technique and distinctive tone with concern for every detail. His repertory spans the works of the 19th and 20th centuries. Perhaps his most notable interpretation is that of Tchaikovsky's Violin Concerto in D 1878.

Perls Laura (born Lore Posner) (1906–1990). German-born US psychotherapist who, together with her husband, Fritz, helped develop the gestalt method of psychotherapy. The gestalt treatment relies on a wide range of techniques to treat emotional illness, including some derived from theatre and dance movement. Perls and her husband founded the New York Institute for Gestalt Therapy 1952.

Perón (María Estela) Isabel (born Martínez) (1931–   ). President of Argentina 1974–76, and third wife of Juan Perón. She succeeded him after he died in office, but labour unrest, inflation, and political violence pushed the country to the brink of chaos. Accused of corruption, she was held under house arrest for five years. She went into exile in Spain.

Perón Evita (María Eva, born Duarte) (1919–1952). Argentine populist leader. A successful radio actress, she married Juan Perón in 1945. When he became president the following year, she became his chief adviser and virtually ran the health and labour ministries, devoting herself to helping the poor, improving education, and achieving women's suffrage. She was politically astute and sought the vice-presidency 1951, but was opposed by the army and withdrew.

Suggested reading
Fraser, Nicholas and Navarro, Marysa *Eva Perón* (1980)
Perón, Eva *My Mission in Life* (trs 1953)
Taylor, Julie M *Evita Perón: The Myths of a Woman* (1979)

Perón Juan Domingo (1895–1974). Argentine politician, dictator 1946–55 and from 1973 until his death. A professional army officer, Perón took part in the right-wing military coup that toppled Argentina's government 1943 and his popularity with the *descamisados* ('shirtless ones') led to his election as president 1946. His populist appeal to the poor was enhanced by the charisma and political work of his second wife Eva (Evita) Perón. After her death in 1952 his popularity waned and he was deposed in a military coup 1955. He returned from exile to the presidency 1973, but died in office 1974, and was succeeded by his third wife Isabel Perón. He instituted social reforms, but encountered economic difficulties.

Suggested reading
Crossweller, Robert *Perón* (1987)
DeChancie, J *Juan Perón* (1987)
Page, J A *Perón* (1983)

Perot (Henry) Ross (1930–   ). US industrialist and independent politician, unsuccessful presidential candidate 1992. Critical of the economic policies of the main political parties, he entered the 1992 presidential contest as a self-financed, independent candidate. Despite securing no electoral college votes, Perot had the highest popular vote of any third presidential candidate since Theodore Roosevelt. In Sept 1995 he established the Independent Party to support a third-party challenger for the 1996 presidential elections.

He was born in a Texas border town and, after service in the US Navy and then with IBM, he established his own company, Electronic Data Systems, quickly becoming a billionaire.

Perrault Charles (1628–1703). French writer who published a collection of fairy tales, *Contes de ma mère l'oye/Mother Goose's Fairy Tales* 1697. These are based on traditional stories and include 'The Sleeping Beauty', 'Little Red Riding Hood', 'Blue Beard', 'Puss in Boots', and 'Cinderella'.

Perrault was a member of the French Academy and a champion of what was then modern in literature against the classical style. He set out these views in *Le Parallèle des anciens et des modernes* 1688–97. He retold French folk tales in verse (*Grisélidis, avec le conte de Peau d'âne et celui des souhaits ridicules* 1694) before writing the prose versions for which he is now known.

Perret Auguste (1874–1954). French architect. He was a pioneer in the use of reinforced concrete. Noted for the exposed concrete frames of his buildings, his most developed work is the church of Notre Dame de Raincy 1922–23. Perret's thinking on standardized building components was later to influence Le Corbusier.

Perrin Jean Baptiste (1870–1942). French physicist who produced the crucial evidence that finally established the atomic nature of matter. Assuming the atomic hypothesis, Perrin demonstrated how the phenomenon of Brownian motion could be used to derive precise values for Avogadro's number. Nobel prize 1926.

Perrin also contributed to the discovery that cathode rays are electrons. His experiments included imposing a negative electric charge on a fluorescent screen onto which various rays were focused. As the negative charge was increased, the intensity of fluorescence fell.

He worked at the Sorbonne from 1897, becoming professor 1910, but in 1940, during World War II, his outspoken antifascism caused him to flee the German occupation. He went to New York. His book *Les Atomes/Atoms* 1913 describes his Nobel prize-winning study of Brownian motion.

Perry Fred(erick John) (1909–1995). English lawn-tennis player, the last Briton to win the men's singles at Wimbledon, 1936. He also won the world table-tennis title 1929. Perry later became a television commentator and a sports-goods manufacturer.

Perry Matthew Calbraith (1794–1858). US naval officer, commander of the expedition of 1853 that reopened communication between Japan and the outside world after 250 years' isolation. Evident military superiority enabled him to negotiate the Treaty of Kanagawa 1854, giving the USA trading rights with Japan.

Perry was born in Newport, Rhode Island. He fought in the War of 1812 and the Mexican War 1847. In the early 1800s he helped to found the African state of Liberia for free US blacks. Perry arrived in the Bay of Edo (Tokyo) in July 1853 to demand the opening of Japanese ports to US ships, and returned in Feb 1854 with a larger force. The steamships were thought by some to be floating volcanoes, and a telegraph line was also brought to demonstrate technical as well as military superiority.

Suggested reading
Morison, Samuel *Old Bruin: Commodore Matthew C Perry* (1967)
Perry, Matthew C *The Japan Expedition, 1852–1854: The Personal Journal of Commodore Matthew C Perry* (ed Roger Pineau 1968)
Walworth, Arthur *Black Ships off Japan* (1946)

Perry Oliver Hazard (1785–1819). US naval officer. Born in South Kingston, Rhode Island, he began his naval career 1799 as a midshipman and saw action in the Tripolitan War. During the Anglo-American War 1812–14 he played a decisive role in securing American control of Lake Erie. Ordered there in 1813, he was responsible for the decisive victory over the British at the Battle of Put-in-Bay and participated in the Battle of the Thames. He died of fever while on a cruise to South America.

Perry William James (1927–   ). US Democrat politician, defence secretary from 1994. As a mathematician and head of research at the Defense Department 1977–81, he was involved in the early development of stealth technology.

Before moving to the Defense Department 1967 as a technical consultant, Perry was director of electronic military laboratories in Mountain View, California, 1954–64. He was professor and co-director of the Center for International Security and Arms Control at Stanford University, California, 1989–93.

It is enough for the poet to be the bad conscience of his time. I am sure there must be others.

SAINT-JEAN PERSE
Letter Dec 1941

Perse Saint-John. Pen name of (Marie René Auguste) Alexis Saint-Léger (1887–1975). French poet and diplomat. Entering the foreign service 1914, he was secretary general 1933–40. He then emigrated permanently to the USA, and was deprived of French citizenship by the Vichy government. His first book of verse, *Eloges* 1911, reflects the ambience of the West Indies, where he was born and raised. His later works include *Anabase* 1924, an epic poem translated by T S Eliot 1930. He was awarded a Nobel prize 1960.

Pershing John Joseph (1860–1948). US general. He served in the Spanish War 1898, the Philippines 1899–1903, and Mexico 1916–17. He commanded the US Expeditionary Force sent to France 1917–18. In World War I, he stuck to the principle of using US forces as a coherent formation, and refused to attach regiments or brigades to British or French divisions.

Suggested reading
Goldhurst, Richard *Pipe Clay and Drill: John J Pershing, the Classic American Soldier* (1976)
Pershing, John J *My Experiences in the World War* (1931)
Smyth, D *Pershing* (1986)

Perugino Pietro. Original name of Pietro di Cristoforo Vannucci (*c.* 1446–1523). Italian painter. He was active chiefly in Perugia and taught Raphael, who absorbed his graceful figure style.

He is said to have been a pupil of Fiorenzo di Lorenzo and probably an assistant to Verrocchio, his style being formed at Florence. Frescoes in the Palazzo Communale at Perugia, 1475, were an early undertaking. In 1480 he was one of the artists chosen by Sixtus IV to embellish his newly finished Sistine Chapel, his fresco of *The Delivery of the Keys to St Peter* showing that sense of space he was to transmit to his pupil Raphael, who worked under him at Florence 1500–04. Among principal works were his frescoes for the Collegio del Cambio, Perugia, the *Crucifixion with Saints*, 1496 (Florence, Santa Maria Maddalena de' Pazzi), accounted his masterpiece, and the altarpiece *Virgin and Child with St Michael and St Raphael* (National Gallery, London), in which, it has been speculatively suggested, there is a trace of the young Raphael's handiwork. Its gentle and youthful human types and also its serene sky and background, receding space being emphasized by tall, thin trees, indicate clearly enough the source of Raphael's early style, though Perugino was left behind by the great onward movement of the Renaissance in which Raphael attained his full stature. He painted a ceiling for one of Raphael's Stanze in the Vatican 1508, but otherwise his later years were spent in Florence, Perugia, Siena, and other cities and in producing repetitive works with a simple charm. There are delightful portraits by him in the Uffizi.

Perutz Max Ferdinand (1914–). Austrian-born British biochemist who shared the 1962 Nobel Prize for Chemistry with his co-worker John Kendrew for work on the structure of the haemoglobin molecule.

Perutz, born and educated in Vienna, moved to Britain in 1936 to work on X-ray crystallography at the Cavendish Laboratory, Cambridge. After internment in Canada as an enemy alien during World War II, he returned to Cambridge and in 1947 was appointed head of the new Molecular Biology Unit of the Medical Research Council (MRC). From 1962 he was chair of the MRC's new Laboratory of Molecular Biology.

Perutz first applied the methods of X-ray diffraction to haemoglobin in 1937, but it was not until 1953 that he discovered that if he added a single atom of a heavy metal such as gold or mercury to each molecule of protein, the diffraction pattern was altered slightly. By 1960 he had worked out the precise structure of haemoglobin. Later, Perutz tried to interpret the mechanism by which the haemoglobin molecule transports oxygen in the blood, realizing that an inherited disorder such as sickle-cell anaemia could be caused by a mutation of this molecule.

Peruzzi Baldassare Tommaso (1481–1536). Sienese High Renaissance architect. His most important buildings are found in Rome. His first significant work is the Villa Farnesina 1509–11, inspired by Raphael and yet more delicately decorative. He succeeded Raphael as architect to St Peter's 1520, but returned to Siena 1527, after the Sack of Rome, where he worked with Antonio da Sangallo the Younger on the Villa Caprarola 1530. His final work, the Palazzo Massimo alle Colonne, Rome, 1532–36, reflects in its unorthodoxy a move away from Renaissance Classicism towards Mannerism.

Pessoa Fernando Antonio Nogueira (1888–1935). Portuguese poet. Born in Lisbon, he was brought up in South Africa and was bilingual in English and Portuguese. His verse is considered to be the finest written in Portuguese in the 20th century. He wrote under three assumed names, which he called 'heteronyms' – Alvaro de Campos, Ricardo Reis, and Alberto Caeiro – for each of which he invented a biography.

Pestalozzi Johann Heinrich (1746–1827). Swiss educationalist who advocated the French philosopher Jean-Jacques Rousseau's 'natural' principles (of natural development and the power of example), and described his own theories in *Wie Gertrude ihre Kinder lehrt/How Gertrude Teaches her Children* 1801. He stressed the importance of mother and home in a child's education. International Children's Villages named after Pestalozzi have been established; for example, at Sedlescombe, East Sussex, UK.

Suggested reading
Gutek, Gerald *Pestalozzi and Education* (1968)
Heafford, M *Pestalozzi: His Thought and its Relevance Today* (1967)
Silber, K *Pestalozzi: The Man and His Work* (1974)

Pétain (Henri) Philippe (1856–1951). French general and right-wing politician. His defence of Verdun 1916 during World War I made him a national hero.

In 1917 Pétain was created French commander in chief, although he became subordinate to Marshal Foch 1918. He suppressed a rebellion in Morocco 1925–26. As a member of the Higher Council of National Defence he advocated a purely defensive military policy, and was strongly conservative in politics. He became head of state 16 June 1940 and signed an armistice with Germany 22 June, convinced that Britain was close to defeat and that France should get the best terms possible. Removing the seat of government to Vichy, a health resort in central France, he established an authoritarian regime. Although his

Pétain *Henri Philippe Pétain, French general and politician. Pétain was a national hero in World War I, but collaborated with the Germans in World War II. After the war he was sentenced to death for treason, but this was later commuted to life imprisonment. He died in prison in 1951.* (Image Select)

Vichy government collaborated with the Germans he dismissed his deputy Pierre Laval who wanted to side with the Axis powers Dec 1940. The Germans had Laval reinstated April 1942 and in Nov occupied the Vichy area of France, reducing Pétain's 'government' to a puppet regime. On the Allied invasion he was taken to Germany, but returned 1945 and was sentenced to death for treason, the sentence later being commuted to life imprisonment.

Suggested reading
Griffiths, Richard *Pétain: A Biography of Marshal Philippe Pétain of Vichy* (1970)
Lottmann, Herbert *Pétain: Hero or Traitor: The Untold Story* (1984)

To make a union with Great Britain would be a fusion with a corpse.

PHILIPPE PÉTAIN
in response to Churchill's proposal of an Anglo-French union 1940

Peter Laurence J (1910–1990). Canadian writer and teacher, author (with Raymond Hull) of *The Peter Principle* 1969, in which he outlined the theory that people tend to be promoted into positions for which they are incompetent.

Peter, St (lived 1st century). Christian martyr, the author of two epistles in the New Testament and leader of the apostles. He is regarded as the first bishop of Rome, whose mantle the pope inherits. Originally a fisherman of Capernaum, on the Sea of Galilee, Peter may have been a follower of John the Baptist, and was the first to acknowledge Jesus as the Messiah. Tradition has it that he later settled in Rome; he was martyred during the reign of the emperor Nero, perhaps by crucifixion. Bones excavated from under the Basilica of St Peter's in the Vatican 1968 were accepted as those of St Peter by Pope Paul VI. His real name was Simon, but he was nicknamed Kephas ('Peter', from the Greek for 'rock') by Jesus, as being the rock upon which he would build his church. His emblem is two keys; feast day 29 June.

Suggested reading
Grant, Michael *Saint Peter* (1994)
Murphy, W F *Upon this Rock* (1987)
O'Connor, D W *Peter in Rome* (1960)
Taylor, W M *Peter, The Apostle* (1990)
Thiede, Carsten P *Simon Peter: From Galilee to Rome* (1986)
Thomas, W *The Apostle Peter: His Life and Writings* (1984)

You are Peter, and on this rock I will build my church and to you I will give the keys of the kingdom of heaven.

Words of Jesus to ST PETER, quoted in the Bible, Matthew 16:18

Peter three tsars of Russia:

Peter (I) the Great (1672–1725). Tsar of Russia from 1682 on the death of his brother Tsar Feodor; he assumed control of the government 1689. He attempted to reorganize the country on Western lines; the army was modernized, a fleet was built, the administrative and legal systems were remodelled, education was encouraged, and the church was brought under state control. On the Baltic coast, where he had conquered territory from Sweden, Peter built his new capital, St Petersburg.

After a successful campaign against the Ottoman Empire 1696, he visited Holland and Britain to study Western techniques, and worked in Dutch and English shipyards. In order to secure an outlet to the Baltic, Peter undertook a war with Sweden 1700–21, which resulted in the acquisition of Estonia and parts of Latvia and Finland. A war with Persia 1722–23 added Baku to Russia.

Two things are necessary in government – order and defence.

PETER (I) THE GREAT
Letter to his son Alexis 11 Oct 1715

Suggested reading
Cracraft, J *For God and Peter the Great* (1982)
De Jong, A *Fire and Water: A Life of Peter the Great* (1979)
Massie, R *Peter the Great* (1981)
Troyat, H *Peter the Great* (1988)

Peter II (1715–1730). Tsar of Russia from 1727. Son of Peter the Great, he had been passed over in favour of Catherine I 1725 but succeeded her 1727. He died of smallpox.

Peter III (1728–1762). Tsar of Russia 1762. Weak-minded son of Peter I's eldest daughter, Anne, he was adopted 1741 by his aunt Elizabeth, Empress of Russia, and at her command married the future Catherine II 1745. He was deposed in favour of his wife and probably murdered by her lover, Alexius Orlov.

It was not enough to tear from my head the crown of Russia: they must have my life besides!

PETER III
Last words before being strangled on the orders of his wife, Catherine the Great, 1762

Peter I (1844–1921). King of Serbia from 1903. He was the son of Prince Alexander Karageorgevich and was elected king when the last Obrenovich king was murdered 1903. He took part in the retreat of the Serbian army 1915, and in 1918 was proclaimed first king of the Serbs, Croats, and Slovenes (renamed Yugoslavia in 1921).

Peter II (1923–1970). King of Yugoslavia 1934–45. He succeeded his father, Alexander I, and assumed the royal power after the overthrow of the regency 1941. He escaped to the UK after the German invasion, and married Princess Alexandra of Greece 1944. He was dethroned 1945 when Marshal Tito came to power and the Soviet-backed federal republic was formed.

Peter Damian, St real name Pietro Damianai (1007–1072). Italian monk who was associated with the initiation of clerical reform by Pope Gregory VII.

Peter Lombard (1100–1160). Italian Christian theologian whose *Sententiarum libri quatuor* considerably influenced Catholic doctrine.

Peter the Hermit (c. 1050–c. 1115). French priest whose eloquent preaching of the First Crusade sent thousands of peasants marching against the Turks, who massacred them in Asia Minor. Peter escaped and accompanied the main body of crusaders to Jerusalem.

Petipa Marius (1822–1910). French choreographer. He emigrated to St Petersburg 1847, becoming ballet master of the Imperial Ballet 1862. He created some of the most important ballets in the classical repertory. For the Imperial Ballet in Russia he created masterpieces such as *Don Quixote* 1869, *La Bayadère* 1877, *The Sleeping Beauty* 1890, *Swan Lake* 1895 (with Ivanov), and *Raymonda* 1898. His ballets were grand, evening-length works complete with exotic costumes and richly decorated sets. A feature of Petipa's ballets were the divertissements that brought the often thin storyline to a halt to allow the soloists a chance to display their virtuosity. These were contrasted with the shifting patterns and formations of the corps de ballet.

Petit Alexis Thérèse (1791–1820). French physicist, co-discoverer with Pierre Dulong of Dulong and Petit's law, which states that, for a solid element, the product of relative atomic mass and specific heat capacity is approximately constant.

Petit was born in Vesoul, Haute-Saône, and studied in Paris at the Ecole Polytechnique, becoming professor there 1815.

Petit's early research was conducted in collaboration with French scientist Dominique Arago. They examined the effect of temperature on the refractive index of gases. Their results led Petit to become an early supporter of the wave theory of light.

Petit and Dulong began their collaboration 1815, and in 1819 announced their law of atomic heats. Chemists who at that time were having difficulty determining atomic weights (and distinguishing them from equivalent weights) now had a method of estimating the approximate weight merely by measuring the specific heat of a sample of the element concerned.

Petöfi Sándor (1823–1849). Hungarian nationalist poet. He published his first volume of poems 1844. He expressed his revolutionary ideas in the semi-autobiographical poem 'The Apostle', and died fighting the Austrians in the battle of Segesvár.

To be able to say how much you love is to love but little.
                                                            PETRARCH
                                                    To Laura in Death poem 16

Petrarch Francesco, (Italian Petrarca) (1304–1374). Italian poet. He was a devotee of the Classical tradition. His *Il Canzoniere* is composed of sonnets in praise of his idealized love, 'Laura', whom he first saw 1327 (she was a married woman and refused to become his mistress). The dialogue *Secretum meum/My Secret* is a spiritual biography.

From 1337 he often stayed in secluded study at his home at Vaucluse, near Avignon, then the residence of the popes. Eager to restore the glories of Rome, he wanted to return the papacy there. He was a friend of the poet Boccaccio, and supported the political reformer Cola di Rienzi's attempt to establish a republic 1347.
Suggested reading
Foster, K *Petrarch* (1987)
Mann, Nicholas *Petrarch* (1984)
Wilkins, E H *Life of Petrarch* (1961)

Petrie (William Matthew) Flinders (1853–1942). English archaeologist who excavated sites in Egypt (the pyramids at Gîza, the temple at Tanis, the Greek city of Naucratis in the Nile delta, Tell el Amarna, Naqada, Abydos, and Memphis) and Palestine from 1880. Petrie's work was exacting and systematic, and he developed dating sequences of pottery styles that correlated with dynastic and predynastic events. Knighted 1923.

Others achieve fame by energy, Petronius by laziness.
                                                    Tacitus on PETRONIUS
                                                    in *Annals* 16.18

Petronius Gaius, known as Petronius Arbiter, (died 1st century). Roman author of the licentious romance *Satyricon*. He was a companion of the emperor Nero and supervisor of his pleasures.

Pevsner Antoine (1886–1962). Russian-born sculptor and painter, a French citizen from 1930. Pevsner studied in Kiev and Paris and for a period painted in a Cubist style, for example *Carnaval* 1915 (Tretyakov Gallery, Moscow). He spent World War I in Oslo with his brother and the two experimented with constructions that substituted thin, overlapping planes for solid mass. Antoine went on to teach in Moscow and then Berlin, where he helped organize the 'First Russian Art Exhibition' 1922, consisting of avant-garde works. By 1921–22 Russian official tolerance of experimental art was on the wane, and Pevsner settled in Paris 1923. A pioneer of Russian Constructivism, his work was entirely abstract but distinguished by the mathematical precision of its spiralling curves and planes, as in *Developable Column* 1942 (Museum of Modern Art, New York). Like his brother Naum Gabo, he worked with celluloid and wire, but also copper, brass sheet, and bronze.

Pevsner Nikolaus Bernhard Leon (1902–1983). Anglo-German art historian. Born in Leipzig, he fled from the Nazis to England. He became an authority on architecture, especially English. His *Outline of European Architecture* was published 1942 (followed by numerous other editions). In his series *The Buildings of England* (46 volumes) 1951–74, he built up a first-hand report on every notable building in the country.

Pfeffer Wilhelm Friedrich Philipp (1845–1920). German physiological botanist who was the first to measure osmotic pressure, in

1877. He also showed that osmotic pressure varies according to the temperature and concentration of the solute.

Pfeffer was born in Grebenstein, near Kassel, and studied at Göttingen. His first professorship was at Bonn 1873, and from 1887 he was at Leipzig.

Pfeffer made the first ever quantitative determinations of osmotic pressure, using a semipermeable container of sugar solution immersed in a vessel of water. He connected a mercury-filled manometer to the top of the semi-permeable container. Pfeffer's work on osmosis was of fundamental importance in the study of cells, because semi-permeable membranes surround all cells and play a large part in controlling their internal environment.

Pfeffer also studied respiration, photosynthesis, protein metabolism, and transport in plants. His *Handbuch der Pflanzenphysiologie/ Physiology of Plants* 1881 was an important text for many years.

Pfeiffer Michelle (1959–). US actress, one of the major Hollywood female stars of the late 1980s and 1990s. A fine-boned, fragile beauty, she has successfully avoided being typecast. Her films include *Dangerous Liaisons* 1988; *The Fabulous Baker Boys* 1989, in which she sang; *Frankie and Johnny* 1991, in which she played a frumpy, lonely waitress; *Batman Returns* 1992 as Catwoman; *The Age of Innocence* 1993; and *Wolf* 1994. Her other films include *Grease 2* 1982, *Married to the Mob*, *Tequila Sunrise* both 1988, *The Russia House* 1990, and *Love Field* 1992.

Whatever amusing invention appears in my retelling of old stories should be assessed on its merits, not by the weight of the author's reputation.
                                                            PHAEDRUS
                                                    Fables bk 2 preface

Phaedrus (*c.* 15 BC–*c.* AD 50). Roman fable writer. He was born a slave in Macedonia and later freed by Emperor Augustus. The allusions in his fables (modelled on those of Aesop) caused him to be brought to trial by a minister of Emperor Tiberius. His work was popular in the Middle Ages.

Phalaris (*c.* 570–*c.* 554 BC). Tyrant of the Greek colony of Acragas (Agrigento) in Sicily. He is said to have built a hollow bronze bull in which his victims were roasted alive. He was killed in a revolt.

The *Letters of Phalaris* attributed to him were proved by the British scholar Richard Bentley to be a forgery of the 2nd century AD.

Phidias produced the great golden statue of Athena, and is inscribed on the base as the craftsman who made it.
                                                    Plutarch on PHIDIAS
                                                    in *Life of Pericles* ch 13.9

Phidias or Pheidias (lived mid-5th century BC). Greek sculptor, active in Athens. He was a friend of the political leader Pericles, who made him superintendent of public works in Athens. He supervised the sculptural programme for the Parthenon (most of it is preserved in the British Museum, London, and known as the Elgin marbles). He also executed the colossal statue of Zeus at Olympia, one of the Seven Wonders of the World.

Philby H(arry) St John (Bridger) (1885–1960). British explorer. As chief of the British political mission to central Arabia 1917–18, he was the first European to visit the southern provinces of Najd. In 1932, he crossed the Rub 'al Khali desert. He wrote *The Empty Quarter* 1933 and *Forty Years in the Wilderness* 1957.

Philby Kim (Harold Adrian Russell) (1912–1988). British intelligence officer from 1940 and Soviet agent from 1933. He was liaison

To betray, you must first belong. I never belonged.
                                                            KIM PHILBY
                                                    Sunday Times 17 Dec 1967

officer in Washington 1949–51, when he was confirmed to be a double agent and asked to resign. Named in 1963 as having warned Guy Burgess and Donald Maclean (similarly double agents) that their activities were known, he fled to the USSR and became a Soviet citizen and general in the KGB. A fourth member of the ring was Anthony Blunt.

'He betrayed his country' – yes, perhaps he did, but who among us has not committed treason to something or someone more important than a country?

Graham Greene on KIM PHILBY
in Philby's *My Silent War* 1968

Philip 'King'. Name given to Metacomet by the English (c. 1639–1676). American chief of the Wampanoag people. Born in Rhode Island, Metacomet was the son of Wampanoag chieftain Massasoit. In 1662, after the death of his father and elder brother, he assumed power and was called 'King Philip' by the English colonists. During the growing tension over Indian versus settlers' land rights, Philip was arrested and his people were disarmed 1671. Full-scale hostilities culminated in 'King Philip's War' 1675, and Philip was defeated and murdered 1676. Although costly to the English, King Philip's War ended Indian resistance in New England.

When a man opens the car door for his wife, it's either a new car or a new wife.

PHILIP, DUKE OF EDINBURGH
quoted in *Observer* 6 March 1988

Philip Duke of Edinburgh (1921–). Prince of the UK, husband of Elizabeth II, a grandson of George I of Greece and a great-great-grandson of Queen Victoria. He was born in Corfu, Greece, but brought up in England. He was educated at Gordonstoun and Dartmouth Naval College. During World War II he served in the Mediterranean, taking part in the battle of Matapan, and in the Pacific. A naturalized British subject, taking the surname Mountbatten March 1947, he married Princess Elizabeth in Westminster Abbey 20 Nov 1947, having the previous day received the title Duke of Edinburgh. In 1956 he founded the Duke of Edinburgh's Award Scheme to encourage creative achievement among young people. He was created a prince of the UK 1957, and awarded the Order of Merit 1968.
Suggested reading
Hall, Unity *Philip* (1988)
Judd, Denis *Prince Philip: A Biography* (1980)
Parker, John *Prince Philip: A Critical Biography* (1990)

Philip six kings of France, including:

Philip II (Philip Augustus) (1165–1223). King of France from 1180. As part of his efforts to establish a strong monarchy and evict the English from their French possessions, he waged war in turn against the English kings Henry II, Richard I (with whom he also went on the Third Crusade), and John (whom he defeated, along with Emperor Otto IV, at the decisive battle of Bouvines in Flanders 1214).

Philip IV the Fair (1268–1314). King of France from 1285. He engaged in a feud with Pope Boniface VIII and made him a prisoner 1303.
Clement V (1264–1314), elected pope through Philip's influence 1305, moved the papal seat to Avignon 1309 and collaborated with Philip to suppress the Templars, a powerful order of knights. Philip allied with the Scots against England and invaded Flanders.

Philip VI (1293–1350). King of France from 1328, first of the house of Valois, elected by the barons on the death of his cousin, Charles IV. His claim was challenged by Edward III of England, who defeated him at Crécy 1346.

Philip II of Macedon (382–336 BC). King of Macedonia from 359 BC. He seized the throne from his nephew, for whom he was

regent, defeated the Greek city states at the battle of Chaeronea (in central Greece) 338 and formed them into a league whose forces could be united against Persia. He was assassinated while he was planning this expedition, and was succeeded by his son Alexander the Great.
Philip's tomb was discovered at Vergina, N Greece, in 1978.
Suggested reading
Adams, W *Philip II* (1982)
Hogarth, D G *Philip and Alexander of Macedon* (1897, rep 1984)
Perlman, Samuel *Philip and Athens* (1973)

What a life is ours if we must live to suit the convenience of the asses.

PHILIP II OF MACEDON's
comment on the priorities of a military
campaign. Quoted in Plutarch *Sayings of Philip* 13

Philip five kings of Spain, including:

Philip (I) the Handsome (1478–1506). King of Castile from 1504, through his marriage 1496 to Joanna the Mad (1479–1555). He was the son of the Holy Roman emperor Maximilian I.

Philip II (1527–1598). King of Spain from 1556. He was born at Valladolid, the son of the Habsburg emperor Charles V, and in 1554 married Queen Mary of England. On his father's abdication 1556 he inherited Spain, the Netherlands, and the Spanish possessions in Italy and the Americas, and in 1580 he annexed Portugal. His intolerance and lack of understanding of the Netherlanders drove them into revolt. Political and religious differences combined to involve him in war with England and, after 1589, with France. The defeat of the Spanish Armada (the fleet sent to invade England in 1588) marked the beginning of the decline of Spanish power.
Suggested reading
Lynch, John *Spain under the Hapsburgs* (1969)
Grierson, Edward *King of Two Worlds* (1974)
Parker, Geoffrey *Philip II* (1978)
Pierson, P *Philip II of Spain* (1975)

He declined into a depressed hypochondriac, totally enslaved to his iron-willed wife ... and generally inclining to lassitude, religiosity, gloom, eccentricity and insanity.

E N Williams on PHILIP V
in *Penguin Dictionary of English and European History 1485–1789* 1980

Philip V (1683–1746). King of Spain from 1700. A grandson of Louis XIV of France, he was the first Bourbon king of Spain. He was not recognized by the major European powers until 1713.

Philip Neri, St (1515–1595). Italian Roman Catholic priest who organized the Congregation of the Oratory. He built the oratory over the church of St Jerome, Rome, where prayer meetings were held and scenes from the Bible performed with music, originating the musical form oratorio. Feast day 26 May.

Philip, St (lived 1st century AD). In the New Testament, one of the 12 apostles. He was an inhabitant of Bethsaida (N Israel), and is said to have worked as a missionary in Anatolia. Feast day 3 May.

Philip the Good (1396–1467). Duke of Burgundy from 1419. He engaged in the Hundred Years' War as an ally of England until he made peace with the French at the Council of Arras 1435. He made the Netherlands a centre of art and learning.

Philippa of Hainault (c. 1314–1369). Daughter of William III, Count of Holland; wife of King Edward III of England, whom she married in York Minster 1328, and by whom she had 12 children (including Edward the Black Prince, Lionel Duke of Clarence, John Duke of Lancaster, Edmund Duke of York, and Thomas Duke of Gloucester). She was admired for her clemency and successfully pleaded for the lives of the six burghers of Calais who surrendered to save the town from destruction 1347.

Philips Anton (1874–1951). Dutch industrialist and founder of an electronics firm. The Philips Bulb and Radio Works 1891 was founded with his brother Gerard, at Eindhoven. Anton served as chair of the company 1921–51, during which time the firm became the largest producer of electrical goods outside the USA.

He permanently inspired the colony ... with habitual respect for law and deference to constituted authority.

C A Harris on ARTHUR PHILLIP's rule in
New South Wales, in *Dictionary of National Biography*

Phillip Arthur (1738–1814). British vice admiral, founder and governor of the convict settlement at Sydney, Australia, 1788–1792, and hence founder of New South Wales.

Phillips Jayne Anne (1952–). US writer. Her first novel *Machine Dreams* 1984 dealt vividly with the impact of the Vietnam War on small-town America. Other works include the short-story collection *Fast Lanes* 1987 and *Shelter* 1994.

One, on God's side, is a majority.

WENDELL PHILLIPS
Lecture at Brooklyn 1859

Phillips Wendell (1811–1884). US reformer. Born in Boston and educated at Harvard University, Phillips was admitted to the bar 1834. After attending the World Anti-Slavery Convention in London 1840, he became an outspoken proponent of the abolition of slavery. In addition he espoused a variety of other social causes, including feminism, prohibition of alcohol, unionization, and improved treatment of American Indians. Critical of the Mexican War 1846–48 and the conduct of the American Civil War 1861–65 by President Lincoln, Phillips was a reform candidate for governor of Massachusetts 1870.

Philo Judaeus (lived 1st century AD). Jewish philosopher of Alexandria who in AD 40 undertook a mission to Caligula to protest against the emperor's claim to divine honours. In his writings Philo Judaeus attempts to reconcile Judaism with Platonic and stoic ideas.

Philopoemen (c. 253–182 BC). Greek general of the Achaean League. He crushed the Spartans at Mantinea 208 BC and defeated Nabis, tyrant of Sparta, 192 BC. He was captured by the Messenians and executed.

Phiz pseudonym of Hablot Knight Browne (1815–1882). English artist who illustrated the greater part of the *Pickwick Papers* and other works by Charles Dickens.

Phoenix River (1970–1993). US film actor, one of the 'Brat Pack', a group of young American actors who gained popularity with young cinema-goers in the mid-1980s. He came to prominence in the teenage 'rites of passage' film *Stand By Me* 1986, and went on to create several telling screen portraits of disaffected youth, most notably in the role of a narcoleptic rent boy in *My Own Private Idaho* 1991.

Phryne (lived 4th century BC). Greek courtesan, famed for her beauty. She is said to have been the model for the *Aphrodite of Cnidos* by the Athenian sculptor Praxiteles.

Phyfe Duncan (c. 1768–1854). Scottish-born US furniture-maker. Born in Scotland, Phyfe emigrated to America with his family 1784. He settled in Albany, New York, and learned the cabinet-maker's trade. Establishing his own workshop in New York City 1792, he gained a national reputation. Although derived from earlier English and Greco-Roman designs, the Phyfe style was distinctive in its simplicity of line with elaborate ornamentation and carving. In 1837 he reorganized his firm as Duncan Phyfe and Sons. He remained active until his retirement in 1847.

Piacentini Marcello (1881–1960). Italian architect. He worked closely with the Fascist regime, and was its most successful urban architect, carrying out numerous official commissions in a grandiose Neo-Classical style. Among them were the Palace of Justice in Milan, 1933–40, the Hotel Ambasciatori, Rome, 1926, the Piazza della Vittoria, Brescia, and the Via della Consiliazione, Rome, 1932, which opened up an axial vista to St Peter's. Between 1937 and 1942 he assisted in the planning of Mussolini's satellite town EUR (Esposizione Universale di Roma) near Rome. He was also an architectural writer and teacher.

Piaf Edith. Stage name of Edith Giovanna Gassion (1915–1963). French singer and songwriter, a cabaret singer in Paris from the late 1930s. She is remembered for the defiant song 'Je ne regrette rien/I Regret Nothing' and 'La Vie en rose' 1946.
Suggested reading
Crosland, Margaret *Piaf* (1985)
Lange, Monique *Piaf* (trs 1981)
Piaf, Edith *The Wheel of Fortune* (autobiography) (trs 1965)

Piaget Jean (1896–1980). Swiss psychologist whose studies of the development of thought processes in children have been influential in early-childhood research and on school curricula and teaching methods.

The subjects of Piaget's studies of intellectual development were his own children. He postulated four main stages in the development of mental processes: sensorimeter (birth to the age of two), pre-operational (two to seven), concrete operational (seven to twelve), and formal operational, characterized by the development of logical thought.

He was a child prodigy in zoology, and by the age of 15 had gained an international reputation for his work on molluscs. Subsequently he studied at Neuchâtel, Zürich, and Paris, where he researched into the reasons why children fail intelligence tests. This gained him the directorship of the Institut J J Rousseau in Geneva 1921. During his subsequent career Piaget held many academic positions, some of them concurrent. In 1955 he founded the International Centre of Genetic Epistemology at Geneva University. He also held several positions with UNESCO at various times.

Piaget's works include *La Naissance de l'intelligence chez l'enfant/The Origins of Intelligence in the Child* 1936 and *The Child's Construction of Reality* 1936.
Suggested reading
Atkinson, C *Making Sense of Piaget* (1984)
Boden, M A *Piaget* (1979)
Flavell, J H *The Developmental Psychology of Jean Piaget* (1963)
Modgil, S and C *Jean Piaget* (1982)
Singer, D G and Revenson, T A *A Piaget Primer* (1978)

Piano Renzo (1937–). Italian High Tech architect. With Richard Rogers, he designed the Pompidou Centre, Paris, 1970–77. Among his other buildings are Kansai Airport, Osaka, Japan and a sports stadium in Bari, Italy, 1989, both employing new materials and making imaginative use of civil-engineering techniques.

Piazzi Giuseppe (1746–1826). Italian astronomer who in 1801 identified the first asteroid, which he named Ceres.

He studied in various Italian cities and in 1764 entered the Theatine Order as a monk. In 1779 he became professor of mathematics at the Palermo Academy in Sicily. When it was decided to establish observatories in Palermo and Naples, Piazzi travelled to observatories in England and France to obtain advice and equipment. He was director of Palermo Observatory from 1790 and from 1817 also of Naples Observatory. Additional responsibilities included the reformation of the Sicilian system of weights and measures 1812.

In 1803, Piazzi published his first catalogue of fixed stars, which located 6,748 stars with unprecedented accuracy.

Picabia Francis (1879–1953). French painter. He was a Cubist from 1909. On his second visit to New York, 1915–16, he joined with Marcel Duchamp in the Dadaist revolt and later took the movement to Barcelona. He was also associated with the Surrealists for a time. His work, which appears in many styles, is generally provocative, anarchic, and experimental.

Picard (Charles) Emile (1856–1941). French mathematician whose work was mainly in the fields of mathematical analysis and algebraic geometry. He formulated two theorems on integral functions. He applied mathematical principles as much as possible to other branches of science, particularly physics and engineering.

At the age of 23 he was appointed professor in Toulouse, but returned to Paris two years later and became professor at the Sorbonne 1885. Picard's work on the integrals attached to algebraic surfaces, together with the associated topological questions, developed into an area of algebraic geometry that had applications in topology and function theory. Much of Picard's work was recorded in the three-volume *Traité d'analyse*.

Picasso Pablo Ruiz y (1881–1973). Spanish artist. Active chiefly in France, he was one of the most inventive and prolific talents in 20th-century art. Picasso was the son of a painter and drawing master, José Ruiz Blasco, using as surname the birth name of his mother, Maria Picasso y Lopez. He began to paint and draw at an early age under his father's tuition, and fraternized with the artists and writers of Barcelona. He first went to Paris 1900 and settled there permanently 1904. To begin with his work was concerned with the social scene, after the fashion of Degas, Forain, and Toulouse-Lautrec, but between 1901 and 1904 he turned to austere figure studies, blue being the dominant colour. Circus pictures followed, delicate and more varied in colour ('rose period', 1905–06). An epoch-making change in his art followed when between 1907 and 1909, together with Georges Braque, he developed Cubism, from the study of Cézanne combined with that of Negro sculpture and primitive art. *Les Demoiselles d'Avignon* 1907 (Museum of Modern Art, New York), marks the birth of the Cubist movement, to which Picasso adhered until 1914. Like Braque, he practised successively its 'analytic' form (construction in depth) and its 'synthetic' form (more decorative and two-dimensional in effect). A feature of his Cubist still life, 1912–14, was the use of collage. He reverted to a Neo-Classical style 1920–24, in painting and in outline etchings of classical themes. He met Diaghilev and designed the *décor* of a number of ballets 1917–1927. A new and imaginative phase of his art began *c*. 1925, and coincided with the development of Surrealism. The bull, a traditional Spanish emblem of conflict and tragedy, began to appear in paintings and etchings, and the *Guernica*, painted 1937 during the Spanish Civil War (New York, Museum of Modern Art), was a fierce pictorial comment on a deplorable bombing incident, making use of this symbolism. Further images of violence and horror produced during and after World War II provoked much criticism. A Surrealistic practice in works after 1938 of combining two different views of a head in the same 'double image' often produced a monstrous distortion which also caused protest. In other works, however, a certain humour appears, and Picasso moved freely from one style and one medium to another, using all with astonishing freedom and virtuosity.

He practised sculpture, devised metal constructions, designed pottery (from 1946 at Villauris near Antibes) and produced a great number of prints, etchings, aquatints and lithographs. His graphic art is one of his most distinctive achievements, including his illustrations to Ovid and Balzac, his Minotaur etchings, and his aquatints for Buffon's *Natural History* (published 1942). His prodigious facility was shown in the 180 drawings of artist and model produced 1953–54. His restless energy has been impressively conveyed by a film showing him at work. Picasso has affected the whole course of modern art and no later artist of the School of Paris has rivalled him as an international influence, though the non-figurative art of today has found other sources of inspiration. His paintings are widely distributed in the world's principal public galleries and in many private collections.

Suggested reading

Berger, J *The Success and Failure of Picasso* (1965)
Cirlot, J E *Picasso: Birth of a Genius* (1972)
Fabre, J *Picasso* (1985)
Gedo, M *Picasso* (1980)
Mailer, Norman *Portrait of Picasso as a Young Man: An Interpretive Biography* (1995)
O'Brien, P *Pablo Ruiz Picasso* (1976)
Penrose, R *Picasso: His Life and Work* (1958)

Piccard Auguste Antoine (1884–1962). Swiss scientist. Auguste Piccard was born and educated in Basel, and joined the balloon section of the Swiss army 1915. From 1922 he was professor of physics at Brussels, Belgium. In 1931–32, he and his twin brother, Jean Félix (1884–1963), made ascents to 17,000 m/55,000 ft in a balloon of his own design, resulting in useful discoveries concerning stratospheric phenomena such as cosmic radiation. He also built and used, with his son Jacques Ernest (1922–   ), bathyscaphs for research under the sea. Jacques Piccard twice, in 1953 and 1960, set a world record with the depth he reached in a bathyscaph. The second time he descended to 10,917 m/35,820 ft in the Mariana Trench near Guam in the Pacific Ocean.

Pickering Edward Charles (1846–1919). US astronomer who was a pioneer in three practical areas of astronomical research: visual photometry, stellar spectroscopy, and stellar photography. He established an international astronomical colour index: a measure of the apparent colour of a star and thus of its temperature.

He was director of the Harvard College Observatory from 1876. Unusually for his generation, he encouraged women to take up astronomy as a career.

As a basis for the more than 1.5 million photometric readings he carried out, Pickering made two critical decisions. First, he adopted a scale on which a change of one magnitude represented a change of a factor of 2.512 in brightness. Second, choosing the Pole Star (Polaris), then thought to be of constant brightness, as the standard magnitude and arbitrarily assigning a value of 2.1 to it, he redesigned the photometer to reflect a number of stars round the meridian at the same time so that comparisons were immediately visible. In 1908 Harvard published a catalogue with the magnitudes of more than 45,000 stars.

The *Henry Draper Catalogue* 1918 contained the spectra of no fewer than 225,000 stars, work begun by Pickering and classified according to the new system devised by Annie Jump Cannon.

The first *Photographic Map of the Entire Sky*, published 1903, contained photographs taken at Harvard and at its sister station in the southern hemisphere, at Arequipa in Peru, where Pickering's brother William Pickering (1858–1938) was director. In addition, Pickering built up a 300,000-plate Harvard photographic library.

Pickett George Edward (1825–1875). US military leader. Born in Richmond, Virginia, Pickett graduated from West Point military academy 1846 and was commended for bravery during the Mexican War 1846–48. After service in Texas 1849–55, he was transferred to the Pacific Northwest. At the outbreak of the American Civil War 1861, he joined the Confederate army, rising to the rank of brigadier general 1862. Although he saw action in many battles, he is best remembered for leading the bloody, doomed 'Pickett's Charge' at Gettysburg 1863. After the end of the Civil War 1865 Pickett declined further military appointments and retired to private life.

Pickett Wilson (1941–   ). US soul singer with a punchy, confident delivery. His first big hit was 'In the Midnight Hour' 1965. Other pop and rhythm-and-blues hits were 'Land of 1,000 Dances' 1966, 'Mustang Sally' 1967, and 'Don't Let the Green Grass Fool You' 1971. After he left the Atlantic label 1973, his star waned.

Pickford Mary. Stage name of Gladys Mary Smith (1893–1979). Canadian-born US actress. The first star of the silent screen, she was known as 'America's Sweetheart', and played innocent ingenue roles into her thirties. In 1919 she formed United Artists with Charlie Chaplin, D W Griffith, and her second husband (1920–35) Douglas Fairbanks. Her films include *Rebecca of Sunnybrook Farm* 1917, *Pollyanna* 1920, *Little Lord Fauntleroy* 1921, and *Coquette* 1929, her

---

She was the girl every young man wanted to have ... as his sister.

Alistair Cooke on MARY PICKFORD
quoted in Leslie Halliwell *Filmgoer's Companion* 1965

first talkie (Academy Award). She was presented a special Academy Award 1976.

Suggested reading
Pickford, Mary *Sunshine and Shadow* (autobiography) (1955)
Windeler, Robert *Sweetheart* (1974)

Pico della Mirandola Giovanni, Count (1463–1494). Italian mystic philosopher. Born at Mirandola, of which his father was prince, he studied Hebrew, Chaldean, and Arabic, showing particular interest in the Jewish and theosophical system, the kabbala. His attempt to reconcile the religious base of Christianity, Islam, and the ancient world earned Pope Alexander VI's disapproval.

Pidgeon Walter (1897–1984). Canadian film actor. Usually appearing as a softly spoken, handsome lead actor, Pidgeon's Hollywood career spanned nearly 50 years, including such films as *How Green Was My Valley* 1941 (John Ford), *Mrs Miniver* 1942, and *Man Hunt* 1941 (Fritz Lang).

Pieck Wilhelm (1876–1960). German communist politician. He was a leader of the 1919 Spartacist revolt and a founder of the Socialist Unity Party 1946. He opposed both the Weimar Republic and Nazism. From 1949 he was president of East Germany; the office was abolished on his death.

Pierce Franklin (1804–1869). 14th president of the USA, 1852–56. Born in Hillsboro, New Hampshire, Pierce was admitted to the bar 1827. He served in the New Hampshire state legislature 1829–33. A Democrat, he held office in the US House of Representatives 1833–37, and the US Senate 1837–42. Returning to New Hampshire from the Senate 1942, he served briefly as US attorney and saw action in the Mexican War 1846–48. Chosen as a compromise candidate of the Democratic party, he was elected president 1852. Despite his expansionist foreign policy, North–South tensions grew more intense, and Pierce was denied renomination 1856.

Suggested reading
Bisson, W *Franklin Pierce* (1990)
Lorant, S *Glorious Burden* (1976)
Nichols, Roy F *Franklin Pierce: Young Hickory of the Granite Hills* (1958)

Pierce Webb (1926–1991). US country singer and songwriter. He developed the honky-tonk style and enjoyed two decades of hit records in the US country-music charts. He was one of the first artists to have a pedal-steel guitar on his recordings (inconspicuous on his debut 'Wondering' 1952, strongly featured on 'Slowly' 1954), an instrument that later became almost ubiquitous in country music. His hits include 'Back Street Affair' 1952, 'There Stands the Glass' 1953 (both written by Pierce), and 'In the Jailhouse Now' 1955. By the 1970s his sound had dated and he was largely neglected until a duet album with Willie Nelson 1982 revived his fortunes.

Piercy Marge (1937–). US poet and novelist. Her fiction takes a passionate look at the fringes of American social life and the world of the liberated woman. Her novels include *Small Changes* 1972, the utopian *Woman on the Edge of Time* 1979, *Fly Away Home* 1984, a war novel *Gone to Soldiers* 1987, and *Summer People* 1989.

Pierné (Henri Constant) Gabriel (1863–1937). French composer and conductor. He succeeded César Franck as organist to the church of Ste Clothilde, Paris, and conducted the Colonne Orchestra from 1903. His numerous ballets include *Cydalise et le chèvre-pied*/*Cydalise and the Satyr* 1923, containing the 'Entry of the Little Fauns'.

Piero della Francesca (c. 1420–1492). Italian painter. Active in Arezzo and Urbino, he was one of the major artists of the 15th century. His work has a solemn stillness and unusually solid figures, luminous colour, and carefully calculated compositional harmonies. It includes a fresco series, *The Legend of the True Cross* (San Francesco, Arezzo), begun about 1452, and the *Flagellation of Christ* (Galleria della Marche, Palazzo Ducale, Urbino), a small-scale work painted in the 1450s, which is notable for its use of perspective.

He was the pupil of Domenico Veneziano, and is first mentioned 1439 when he was an assistant of Domenico, then painting frescoes in Sant' Egidio in Florence. He returned to his native town, Borgo, no doubt with a valuable store of Florentine science, including that of perspective, and was much employed there on pictures and frescoes. He also worked at Urbino, where he had the patronage of the Duke Federigo Montefeltro and his wife, of whom he painted famous portraits (Uffizi). He visited Rome, though nothing remains of his work there, and Ferrara, Rimini, and Arezzo, where he painted his masterpieces of fresco 1452–60. He returned regularly to Borgo, to which he seems to have been very attached. He gave up painting when about 60, as his sight was failing, and devoted himself to mathematical and philosophical studies. Two written treatises remain on the laws of perspective and mathematics. His great works include the profoundly impressive fresco at Borgo, *The Resurrection*, and the *Madonna with the Duke of Urbino as Donor* (Milan, Brera). The two famous paintings in the National Gallery, London, the *Baptism of Christ* and the *Nativity*, though closely related in style, are considered to be an early and late work respectively. The oil method of his Urbino portraits suggests some acquaintance with Netherlandish painting, but in general the art of Piero is strongly individual in its poetry and contemplative spirit, and the feeling of intellectual force conveyed by its abstract treatment of space and form.

Suggested reading
Angelini, A *Piero della Francesca* (1985)
Clark, Kenneth *Piero della Francesca* (1951)
Ginzburg, C *The Enigma of Piero* (1988)
Hendy, P *Piero della Francesca and the Early Renaissance* (1968)
Lightbown, R *Piero della Francesca* (1992)

Piero di Cosimo (c. 1462–c. 1521). Italian painter. He was known for his inventive pictures of mythological subjects, often featuring fauns and centaurs. *Mythological Scene* about 1510 (National Gallery, London) is typical. He also painted religious subjects and portraits.

The son of Lorenzo di Piero, he was the pupil of Cosimo Rosselli, whose Christian name he adopted. Though influenced by Signorelli and Leonardo, he had a personal and whimsical imagination, which gives a vivid life to his representations of the satyrs and centaurs of classical fable, and also shows itself in the various animals he introduced into his pictures. His *Perseus and Andromeda* (Uffizi) presents a typically fantastic dragon, and his mythological picture, formerly known as *The Death of Procris* (National Gallery), faintly like the work of his contemporary Botticelli in its delicate pathos, introduces, as well as its famous dog, the strangest of fauns. Another distinctive masterpiece is the *Venus, Mars and Cupid* (Berlin). He assisted Cosimo Rosselli in his frescoes in the Sistine Chapel 1481–82. He was also the author of some strongly characterized portraits that have an element of Leonardesque caricature. He was the master of Andrea del Sarto.

Pietilä Reima Frans Ilmari (1923–1993). Finnish architect. Influenced by Alvar Aalto, his buildings reflect the natural Finnish landscape of forests, lakes, and rocks in their free-flowing forms. The Embassy of Finland, New Delhi, 1983–85, has a faceted roof shape, recalling the snow sculptures found in the winter ice around the Gulf of Finland.

He was a member of CIAM and one of a group of Scandinavian architects who sought to explore the possibilities for regional variation within the context of the Modern Movement. His other works include the Finnish Pavilion at the Brussels World Fair 1956–58 and the Kaleva Church, Tampere 1959–66.

Pietro da Cortona (Pietro Berrettini) (1596–1669). Italian painter and architect. He was a major influence in the development of the High Baroque. He studied at Cortona under a Florentine painter, Andrea Commodi, and then in Rome, where he attracted the notice of Urban VIII and enjoyed the patronage of a succession of pontiffs. In 1620–40 he produced paintings for the Marchese Sacchetti (Rome, Capitoline Gallery), frescoes for Cardinal Francesco Barberini in Santa Bibiana and other Roman churches, and his masterpiece, the allegorical ceiling painting for the Barberini Palace, 1633–39 (Rome, Galleria Nazionale), in which the illusionist effect of figures foreshortened and floating in space as seen from below was contrived with immense skill and daring.

Outside Rome he worked only in Florence (decorations for the Pitti Palace, 1640–47), refusing invitations to go to France and Spain. He later resumed work in Rome in the Pamfili and Barberini palaces. He collaborated with the theologian Ottonelli in a treatise on painting and sculpture, 1653, and as architect was responsible for the façade of Santa Maria in Via Lata and the church of San Martino in which he was buried.

Pigalle Jean Baptiste (1714–1785). French sculptor. Pigalle studied in Rome 1736–39. In Paris he gained the patronage of Madame de Pompadour, the mistress of Louis XV. In 1744 he carved the marble *Mercury* (Louvre, Paris), a lively, naturalistic work. His subjects range from the intimate to the formal, and include portraits. His works include *Venus, Love and Friendship* 1758 (Louvre, Paris), a nude statue of *Voltaire* 1776 (Institut de France, Paris), and the grandiose *Tomb of Maréchal de Saxe* 1753 (Strasbourg).

Piggott Lester Keith (1935–). English jockey. He adopted a unique high riding style and is renowned as a brilliant tactician. A champion jockey 11 times between 1960 and 1982, he has ridden a record nine Derby winners. Piggott retired from riding 1985 and took up training. In 1987 he was imprisoned for tax evasion. He returned to racing in 1990 and has ridden 4,460 winners, including a record 30 Classics to the start of the 1994 season.

He was associated with such great horses as Nijinsky, Sir Ivor, Roberto, Empery, and The Minstrel. Piggott won all the major races, including the English classics.

Pigou Arthur Cecil (1877–1959). British economist whose notion of the 'real balance effect' (the 'Pigou effect') contended that employment was stimulated by a fall in prices, because the latter increased liquid wealth and thus demand for goods and services.

Pike Magnus Alfred (1908–1992). British food scientist and broadcaster. He enjoyed an extraordinary period of celebrity following his retirement 1973, co-presenting *Don't Ask Me*, which became the most popular science series on British television. Pike had a mission to explain, which he achieved brilliantly. Much in demand as a lecturer, his arms flailed as he sought the clearest answers to the questions his audience asked.

Pike was author of the standard work *The Manual of Nutrition* 1945. He ran Genochil Research Station, Scotland 1955–73, after which he became secretary of the British Association for the Advancement of Science.

Pike Zebulon Montgomery (1779–1813). US explorer and military leader. Pike, born in Lamberton, New Jersey, joined the army at age 15 and served in the Department of the West. In 1805 he was sent by the governor of the Louisiana Territory to explore the source of the Mississippi River. In 1806 he was sent to explore the Arkansas River and to contest Spanish presence in the area. After crossing Colorado and failing to reach the summit of the peak later named after him, he was captured by the Spanish, who released him 1807. Promoted to brigadier general, he was killed in action in the Anglo-American War 1812–14.

Pilate Pontius (died *c.* AD 36). Roman procurator of Judea AD 26–36. The New Testament Gospels describe his reluctant ordering of Jesus' crucifixion, but there has been considerable debate about his actual role in it. Pilate was unsympathetic to the Jews; his actions several times provoked riots, and in AD 36 he was recalled to Rome to account for the brutal suppression of a Samaritan revolt. The Greek historian Eusebius says he committed suicide after Jesus' crucifixion, but another tradition says he became a Christian, and he is regarded as a saint and martyr in the Ethiopian Coptic and Greek Orthodox churches.

Pilcher Percy Sinclair (1867–1899). English aviator who was the first Briton to make a successful flight in a heavier-than-air craft, called the *Bat*, 1895. Like Otto Lilienthal, Pilcher made flights only downhill from gliders, using craft resembling the modern hang glider. Pilcher's next successful aircraft was the *Hawk*, launched 1896 at Eynsford, Kent, by a tow line. He was killed 1899 flying the *Hawk* near Rugby in the Midlands.

Pilsudski Józef Klemens (1867–1935). Polish nationalist politician, dictator from 1926. Born in Russian Poland, he founded the Polish Socialist Party 1892 and was twice imprisoned for anti-Russian activities. During World War I he commanded a Polish force to fight for Germany and evicted the Russians from E Poland but fell under suspicion of intriguing with the Allies and was imprisoned by the Germans 1917–18. When Poland became independent 1919, he was elected chief of state, and led a Polish attack on the USSR 1920, driving the Soviets out of Poland. He retired 1923, but in 1926 led a military coup that established his dictatorship until his death.
Suggested reading
Jedrzejewicz, W *Pilsudski: A Life for Poland* (1990)
Pilsudski, Joseph *Memoirs* (trs 1931, rep 1972)
Reddaway, W F *Marshal Pilsudski* (1939)

Pincus Gregory Goodwin (1903–1967). US biologist who, together with Min Chueh Chang (1908–) and John Rock (1890–1984), developed the contraceptive pill in the 1950s. As a result of studying the physiology of reproduction, Pincus conceived the idea of using synthetic hormones to mimic the condition of pregnancy in women. This effectively prevents impregnation.

He joined the staff of Harvard 1930, and in 1944 cofounded the Worcester Foundation for Experimental Biology in Shrewsbury, Massachusetts. It was there he began his research on steroid hormones, which was encouraged by birth-control pioneer Margaret Sanger. The pill was first marketed 1960.

A shadow in a dream is Man.

PINDAR
Pythian VIII

Pindar (*c.* 518–*c.* 438 BC). Greek lyric poet. He is noted for his surviving choral songs, or odes, written in honour of victors in the Greek athletic games at Delphi, Olympia, Nemea, and the Isthmus of Corinth.
Suggested reading
Bowra, C M *Pindar* (1964)
Norwood, Gilbert *Pindar* (1945)
Race, William *Pindar* (1986)

Pindling Lynden Oscar (1930–). Bahamian politician, prime minister 1967–92. After studying law in London, he returned to the island to join the newly formed Progressive Liberal Party and then became the first black prime minister of the Bahamas.

Pinero Arthur Wing (1855–1934). English dramatist. A leading exponent of the 'well-made' play, he enjoyed great contemporary success with his farces, beginning with *The Magistrate* 1885. More substantial social drama followed with *The Second Mrs Tanqueray* 1893, and comedies including *Trelawny of the 'Wells'* 1898. Knighted 1909.

Pinkerton Allan (1819–1884). US detective, born in Glasgow, Scotland. He founded Pinkerton's National Detective Agency 1852 and built up the federal secret service from the espionage system he developed during the American Civil War. He thwarted an early assassination plot against Abraham Lincoln and compiled the nation's most complete files on criminal activity. His agency became increasingly involved in the suppression of labour unrest. His men fought brutal battles against striking steelworkers 1892 and the Molly Maguires, a secret Irish coalminers' organization.

Pink Floyd British psychedelic rock group, formed 1965. The original members were Syd Barrett (1946–), Roger Waters (1944–), Richard Wright (1945–), and Nick Mason (1945–). Their albums include *The Dark Side of the Moon* 1973 and *The Wall* 1979, with its spin-off film starring Bob Geldof. They were the most successful group to emerge from London's hippie scene in the late 1960s.

Pinkham Lydia E(stes) (1819–1893). US entrepreneur and patent-medicine proprietor who claimed she could cure any 'female complaint'. Pinkham began her manufacturing business in a cellar kitchen where she developed and mixed her own formulae. Although her claims of cures were never substantiated, her mixtures became increasingly popular, as was the Department of Advice she set up with an all-female staff to deal with the huge volume of enquiries the Lydia E Pinkham Medicine Co attracted.

Pinochet (Ugarte) Augusto (1915–   ). Military ruler of Chile from 1973, when a coup backed by the US Central Intelligence Agency ousted and killed President Salvador Allende. Pinochet took over the presidency and governed ruthlessly, crushing all opposition. He was voted out of power when general elections were held Dec 1989 but remained head of the armed forces. In 1990 Pinochet's attempt to reassert political influence was firmly censured by President Patricio Aylwin.

Pinter Harold (1930–   ). English dramatist, originally an actor. He specializes in the tragicomedy of the breakdown of communication, broadly in the tradition of the Theatre of the Absurd – for example, *The Birthday Party* 1958 and *The Caretaker* 1960. Later plays include *The Homecoming* 1965, *Old Times* 1971, *Betrayal* 1978, and *Moonlight* 1993.

Suggested reading
Anderson, M *Anger and Detachment: A Study of Arden, Osborne and Pinter* (1976)
Almansi, G and Henderson, S *Harold Pinter* (1983)
Bold, A (ed) *Harold Pinter: You Never Heard Such Silence* (1984)
Gussow, Mel *Conversations with Pinter* (1994)
Hayman, R *Harold Pinter* (1975)
Thompson, D T *Harold Pinter: The Player's Playwright* (1985)

Pinturicchio (or Pintoricchio) pseudonym of Bernardino di Betto (c. 1454–1513). Italian painter. He was active in Rome, Perugia, and Siena. His chief works are the frescoes in the Borgia Apartments in the Vatican, painted in the 1490s, and in the Piccolomini Library of Siena Cathedral, 1503–08. He is thought to have assisted Perugino in decorating the Sistine Chapel, Rome.

Piozzi Hester Lynch (born Salusbury) (1741–1821). Welsh writer. She published *Anecdotes of the Late Samuel Johnson* 1786 and their correspondence 1788. Johnson had been a constant visitor to her house in Streatham, London, when she was married to her first husband, Henry Thrale, but after Thrale's death Johnson was alienated by her marriage to the musician Gabriele Mario Piozzi (1740–1809). *Thraliana*, her diaries and notebooks of the years 1766–1809, was published 1942.

Piper John Egerton Christmas (1903–1992). English painter, printmaker, and designer. His subjects include traditional Romantic views of landscape and architecture. As an official war artist in World War II he depicted bomb-damaged buildings. He also designed theatre sets and stained-glass windows for Coventry Cathedral and the Catholic Cathedral, Liverpool.

Pippard (Alfred) Brian (1920–   ). English physicist who applied microwaves to the study of superconductivity. The research he initiated has transformed understanding of the dynamical laws governing the motion of electrons in metals. Knighted 1975.

Pippard was born in London and studied at Cambridge, returning there after World War II. In 1960 he became professor.

Pippard worked on the way in which electric currents flow without resistance in a thin layer at the surface of the metal. He measured the thickness (about $1000 \text{ Å}/10^{-7} \text{ m}$) of this penetration layer and examined variations with temperature and purity. When he tried to change the properties at one point by applying a disturbance, he influenced the metal over a distance greater than the penetration layer thickness. Because of this, he said that the electrons of superconductors possess a property which he called 'coherence', and that impurities in the metal could shorten the coherence length. From this starting point, he worked out an equation relating current to magnetic field.

Piran, St (lived c. 5 AD). Christian missionary sent to Cornwall by St Patrick. There are remains of his oratory at Perranzabuloe, and he is the patron saint of Cornwall and its nationalist movement. Feast day 5 March.

Pirandello Luigi (1867–1936). Italian playwright, novelist, and short-story writer. His plays, which often deal with the themes of illusion and reality, and the tragicomic absurdity of life, include *Sei personaggi in cerca d'autore*/*Six Characters in Search of an Author* 1921, and *Enrico IV*/*Henry IV* 1922. The themes and innovative techniques of his plays anticipated the work of Brecht, O'Neill, Anouilh, and Genet. His novel *Il fu Mattia Pascal*/*The Late Mattia Pascal* 1904 was highly acclaimed, along with many short stories. Nobel prize 1934.

Suggested reading
Bentley, Eric *The Pirandello Commentaries* (1986)
Giudice, Gaspare *Pirandello: A Biography* (trs 1975)
Starkie, Enid *Luigi Pirandello* (1965)

Piranesi Giambattista (Giovanni Battista) (1720–1778). Italian architect and graphic artist. He is most significant for his powerful etchings of Roman antiquities and as an influential theorist of architecture, advocating imaginative use of Roman models. His series of etchings *Prisons of Invention* about 1745–61 depict imaginary prisons, vast and gloomy. Only one of his architectural designs was built, Sta Maria del Priorato, Rome.

Pirenne Henri (1862–1935). Belgian historian, author of a seven-volume *Histoire de Belgique*/*History of Belgium* 1900–32. He also wrote numerous books and articles on the Middle Ages, including *Belgian Democracy: Its Early History* 1910. In *Mohammed and Charlemagne* 1939, he argued that the Middle Ages properly began with the rise of Islam, which disrupted Western European trade in the Mediterranean and thus led to a decline in European towns.

Pirquet Clemens von (1874–1929). Austrian paediatrician and pioneer in the study of allergy.

Pisanello nickname of Antonio Pisano (c. 1395–c. 1455). Italian artist. He was active in Verona, Venice, Naples, Rome, and elsewhere. His panel paintings reveal a rich International Gothic style. He was also an outstanding portrait medallist. His frescoes in the Palazzo Ducale in Mantua were rediscovered after World War II.

His early life was spent at Verona, where he was trained in the 'International Gothic' style which flourished there. He was associated with one of the main Italian practitioners of the style, Gentile da Fabriano, completing frescoes (now destroyed) by Gentile, in Venice and Rome. As a painter and producer of portrait medallions he made a triumphal progress from one Italian court to another, working for the Gonzagas in Mantua, the Visconti in Pavia, Sigismondo Malatesta in Rimini, Lionello d'Este in Ferrara, and from 1448, for Alfonso of Aragon in Naples. Of the few examples of his frescoes that remain, the *Annunciation* in the church of San Fermo, Verona, 1423–24, and the *St George* at Santa Anastasia, Verona, 1437–38, show his ornate manner, and on a small scale *The Legend of St Eustace* and *Virgin with St Anthony and St George* (National Gallery) are exquisite examples of his art. He excelled in relief portraiture, and his drawings from nature, especially his animal studies, show an observation surpassing the conventions of the belated Gothic style. The most important collection of his drawings is that of the *Codex Vallardi* of the Louvre, Paris, and the Victoria and Albert Museum, London, has a notable collection of the medals.

Pisano Andrea (c. 1290–c. 1348). Italian sculptor. He made the earliest bronze doors for the Baptistery of Florence Cathedral, completed 1336. He completed the campanile for the cathedral, designed by Giotto.

Piscator Erwin (1893–1966). German theatre director. He introduced the idea of epic theatre, using slide-projection, music, dance, and film to create a revolutionary social drama in the *Red Revue* 1921 and in *Hoppla, That's Life!* 1927. While in the USA 1939–51 he produced an adaptation of Tolstoy's *War and Peace* 1942, but returned to directing in Germany 1951, where he produced plays by Rolf Hochhuth.

Pisistratus (c. 605–527 BC). Athenian politician. Although of noble family, he assumed the leadership of the peasant party, and seized power 561 BC. He was twice expelled, but recovered power from 546 BC until his death. Ruling as a tyrant under constitutional forms, he was the first to have the Homeric poems written down, and founded Greek drama by introducing the Dionysiac peasant festivals into Athens.

Pisistratus administered the city's affairs moderately, more like a citizen than a tyrant.

Aristotle on PISISTRATUS
in *Constitution of Athens* ch 16.2

Pissarro Camille (1830–1903). French Impressionist painter. He experimented with various styles, including Pointillism, in the 1880s.

After showing a desire to paint in the Danish West Indies where he was born, he made a definite start in Paris at the age of 25, working at the Académie Suisse, where he met Claude Monet, and being influenced, like most young painters of the time, by Corot and Courbet. His early work, subdued in tone and simple in composition, already showed the feeling of open air which he developed in country retreats at Pontoise and Louveciennes before 1870. His house was occupied and most of his pictures destroyed in the German invasion, and he was in England with Monet 1870–71, living in south London and painting pictures of the Crystal Palace, Sydenham, and Upper Norwood. On his return he pursued a course parallel with that of Monet in the rendering of light by colour, with blues, purples, and greens prevailing. He produced works of great beauty and exhibited at all the Impressionist exhibitions. He settled at Eragny 1884 but made frequent visits to Le Havre, Rouen, and Paris, with excellent views of the boulevards of the capital and of the waterfronts being the results, though his most typical paintings represent the quiet countryside and its peasantry. He was consistent in style, though under the influence of Seurat he practised a systematic

Pitt , William the Younger *William Pitt the Younger entered Parliament at the age of 22 and two years later became England's youngest prime minister.*

division of colour 1886–88. His own influence on others was beneficent, and by introducing both Cézanne and Gauguin to Impressionism he set them on their respective paths to maturity. He lived in the UK from 1890.
Suggested reading
Lloyd, Christopher *Pissarro* (1981)
Pissarro, Camille (ed John Rewald) *Letters to His Son Lucien* (trs 1943)
Reid, Martin *Pissarro* (1993)
Rewald, John *Camille Pissarro* (1963)

Piston Walter Hamor (1894–1976). US composer and teacher. He wrote a number of textbooks, including *Harmony* 1941 and *Orchestration* 1955. His Neo-Classical works include eight symphonies, a number of concertos, chamber music, the orchestral suite *Three New England Sketches* 1959, and the ballet *The Incredible Flutist* 1938.

Pitman Isaac (1813–1897). English teacher and inventor of Pitman's shorthand. He studied Samuel Taylor's scheme for shorthand writing, and in 1837 published his own system, Stenographic Soundhand, fast, accurate, and adapted for use in many languages. Knighted 1894.

A simplified Pitman Script, combining letters and signs, was devised 1971 by Emily D Smith. His grandson (Isaac) James Pitman (1901–1985) devised the 44-letter Initial Teaching Alphabet in the 1960s to help children to read.

Pitt William, 'the Elder', 1st Earl of Chatham (1708–1778). British Whig politician, 'the Great Commoner'.

Entering Parliament 1735, Pitt led the Patriot faction opposed to the Whig prime minister Robert Walpole and attacked Walpole's successor, Carteret, for his conduct of the War of the Austrian Succession. As paymaster of the forces 1746–55, he broke with tradition by refusing to enrich himself; he was dismissed for attacking the Duke of Newcastle, the prime minister. Recalled by popular demand to form a government on the outbreak of the Seven Years' War 1756, he was forced to form a coalition with Newcastle 1757. A 'year of victories' ensued 1759, and the French were expelled from India and Canada. In 1761 Pitt wished to escalate the war by a declaration of war on Spain. George III disagreed and Pitt resigned, but was again recalled to form an all-party government 1766. He championed the Americans against the king, though rejecting independence, and collapsed during his last speech in the House of Lords – opposing the withdrawal of British troops – and died a month later. Earl 1766.
Suggested reading
Ayling, Stanley *The Elder Pitt* (1976)
Middleton, R *The Bells of Victory* (1985)
Plumb, J H *Chatham* (1953)

Pitt William, 'the Younger' (1759–1806). British Tory prime minister 1783–1801 and 1804–06. Son of William Pitt the Elder, he entered Cambridge University at 14 and Parliament at 22. He was the Whig Shelburne's chancellor of the Exchequer 1782–83, and with the support of the Tories and king's friends became Britain's youngest prime minister 1783. He reorganized the country's finances and negotiated reciprocal tariff reduction with France. In 1793, however, the new French republic declared war and England fared badly. Pitt's policy in Ireland led to the 1798 revolt, and he tried to solve the Irish question by the Act of Union 1800, but George III rejected the Catholic emancipation Pitt had promised as a condition, and Pitt resigned 1801.

On his return to office 1804, he organized an alliance with Austria, Russia, and Sweden against Napoleon, which was shattered at Austerlitz. In declining health, he died on hearing the news, saying:

Necessity is the plea for every infringement of human freedom. It is the argument of tyrants; it is the creed of slaves.

WILLIAM PITT THE YOUNGER
Speech in House of Commons 18 Nov 1783

'Oh, my country! How I leave my country!' He was buried in Westminster Abbey.

Suggested reading
Ehrman, John *The Younger Pitt: The Years of Acclaim* (1969)
Ehrman, John *The Younger Pitt: The Reluctant Transition* (1983)
Mackesy, Piers *War Without Victory: The Downfall of Pitt, 1799–1802* (1984)
Reilly, Robin *Pitt the Younger, 1759–1806* (1978)

Pitt-Rivers Augustus Henry Lane-Fox (1827–1900). English archaeologist. He made a series of model archaeological excavations on his estate in Dorset, England, and developed the concept of stratigraphy (identifying layers of soil within a site with successive archaeological stages). The Pitt-Rivers Museum, Oxford, contains some of his collection.

Pius twelve popes, including:

Pius IV (Giovanni Angelo Medici) (1499–1565). Pope from 1559. He reassembled the Council of Trent and completed its work 1563.

Pius V (Michele Ghislieri) (1504–1572). Pope from 1566. He excommunicated Elizabeth I of England, and organized the expedition against the Turks that won the victory of Lepanto.

Pius VI (Giovanni Angelo Braschi) (1717–1799). Pope from 1775. He strongly opposed the French Revolution, and died a prisoner in French hands.

Pius VII (Gregorio Barnaba Chiaramonte) (1742–1823). Pope from 1800. He concluded a concordat (papal agreement) with France 1801 and took part in Napoleon's coronation, but relations became strained. Napoleon annexed the papal states, and Pius was imprisoned 1809–14. After his return to Rome 1814, he revived the Jesuit order.

Pius IX (Giovanni Maria Mastai-Ferretti) (1792–1878). Pope from 1846. He never accepted the incorporation of the papal states and of Rome in the kingdom of Italy. He proclaimed the dogmas of the Immaculate Conception of the Virgin 1854 and papal infallibility 1870; his pontificate was the longest in history.

Originally a liberal, he became highly reactionary as papal territories were progressively lost. He refused to set foot outside the Vatican after the Italian occupation of Rome, regarding himself as a prisoner, and forbade Catholics to take any part in politics in Italy. He centred power in the Vatican, refusing compromise with modern spiritual ideas. His devotion inspired a cult following that continues to this day.

The first stage in his canonization was begun 1985.

Pius X (Giuseppe Melchiore Sarto) (1835–1914). Pope from 1903, canonized 1954. He condemned Modernism in a manifesto 1907.

Pius XI (Achille Ratti) (1857–1939). Pope from 1922. He signed the concordat (papal agreement) with Mussolini 1929.

Pius XII (Eugenio Pacelli) (1876–1958). Pope from 1939. He was conservative in doctrine and politics, and condemned Modernism. He proclaimed the dogma of the bodily assumption of the Virgin Mary 1950 and in 1951 restated the doctrine (strongly criticized by many) that the life of an infant must not be sacrificed to save a mother in labour. He was criticized for failing to speak out against atrocities committed by the Germans during World War II and has been accused of collusion with the Nazis.

Suggested reading
Falconi, Carlo *The Silence of Pius XII* (trs 1970)
Friedlander, Saul *Pius XII and the Third Reich* (1966)

Pixii Hippolyte (1808–1835). French inventor who in 1832 made the first practical electricity generator. It could produce both direct current and alternating current.

Pixii was an instrument-maker, trained by his father. Learning of Michael Faraday's electromagnetic induction and his suggestions for making a simple dynamo, Pixii constructed a device that consisted of a permanent horseshoe magnet, rotated by means of a treadle, and a coil of copper wire above each of the magnet's poles. The two coils were linked and the free ends of the wires connected to terminals, from which a small alternating current was obtained when the magnet rotated. This device was first exhibited at the French Academy of Sciences in Paris 1832. Later, at the suggestion of physicist André Marie Ampère, a commutator (a simple switching device for reversing the connections to the terminals as the magnet is rotated) was fitted so that Pixii's generator could produce direct-current electricity. This revised generator was taken to Britain in 1833 and exhibited in London.

Pizarro Francisco (*c.* 1475–1541). Spanish conquistador who took part in the expeditions of Vasco Núñez de Balboa and others. He began exploring the NW coast of South America 1524, and conquered Peru 1531 with 180 followers. The Inca king Atahualpa was seized and murdered. In 1535 Pizarro founded the Peruvian city of Lima. Internal feuding led to Pizarro's assassination.

His half-brother Gonzalo Pizarro (*c.* 1505–1548) explored the region east of Quito 1541–42. He made himself governor of Peru 1544, but was defeated and executed.

Suggested reading
Hemmings, John *The Conquest of the Incas* (1970)
Innes, H *The Conquistadors* (1969)

Plaatje Solomon Tshekiso (1875–1932). Pioneer South African black community leader who was the first secretary general and founder of the African National Congress 1912.

Place Francis (1771–1854). English Radical. He showed great powers as a political organizer, and made Westminster a centre of pro-labour union Radicalism. He secured the repeal of the anti-union Combination Acts 1824.

A cocksure radical individualist ... he worked, not for revolution but for social betterment.

E L Woodward on FRANCIS PLACE
in *The Age of Reform 1815–1870* 1962

Plage Götz Dieter (1936–1993). German wildlife photographer known especially for his films for Anglia Television's *Survival* series. A man of action who often took considerable risks, his films brought a narrative drama and excitement to natural history photography. Films include *Gorilla* 1974, *Orphans of the Forest* 1975, about orangutans threatened with extinction, and *Tiger! Tiger!* 1977.

Plaidy Jean. Pen name of Eleanor Hibbert (*c.* 1910–1993). English historical novelist. A prolific writer, she produced many novels on historical themes under three different pseudonyms: Jean Plaidy, Victoria Holt, and Philippa Carr.

The name Plaidy was taken from Plaidy Beach in Cornwall. She and her husband, George Hibbert, lived near Looe in Cornwall during World War II and she subsequently made frequent use of Cornish place-names in her fiction. The novels under this name were fictionalized English history and were often particularly concerned with episodes involving queens and princesses.

Under the name Victoria Holt she published *Mistress of Mellyn* 1961, a Victorian gothic-style romance set in Cornwall. The author's identity was kept a closely guarded secret. Thirty more Victoria Holt novels were published, all of them set in the second half of the last century. A final novel, *The Black Opal*, was published posthumously. She also wrote, under the name Philippa Carr, a series of novels set in various historical periods from Tudor times to World War II, aiming to show how historical events affected the lives of individuals. The central character in each is an English gentlewoman, and the series became known as the 'Daughters of England'. An immensely popular writer, Hibbert received quantities of fan mail and apparently answered each letter personally.

Planchon Roger (1931–). French theatre director, actor, and dramatist. After early productions of the plays of Adamov and Brecht, he established a theatre company in Villeurbanne, outside Lyon, France, 1957; it inherited the name Théâtre National

Populaire 1973. Major productions of Shakespeare (*Henry V* 1957) and Molière (*Tartuffe* 1962 and 1973) were followed by Pinter's *No Man's Land* 1979 and Racine's *Athalie* 1980.

Planck Max Karl Ernst (1858–1947). German physicist who framed the quantum theory 1900. His research into the manner in which heated bodies radiate energy led him to report that energy is emitted only in indivisible amounts, called 'quanta', the magnitudes of which are proportional to the frequency of the radiation. His discovery ran counter to classical physics and is held to have marked the commencement of the modern science. Nobel Prize for Physics 1918.

He became professor at Kiel 1885, but moved 1888 to Berlin as director of the newly founded Institute for Theoretical Physics. He was also professor of physics at Berlin 1892–1926. Appointed president of the Kaiser Wilhelm Institute 1930, he resigned 1937 in protest at the Nazis' treatment of Jewish scientists. In 1945, after World War II, the institute was renamed the Max Planck Institute and moved to Göttingen. Planck was reappointed its president.

Planck's idea that energy must consist of indivisible particles, not waves, was revolutionary. But an explanation for photoelectricity was provided by Albert Einstein in 1905 using Planck's quantum theory, and in 1913 Danish physicist Niels Bohr successfully applied the quantum theory to the atom.

Planck's constant, a fundamental constant (symbol h), is the energy of one quantum of electromagnetic radiation divided by the frequency of its radiation.

Suggested reading

Jammer, Max *The Conceptual Development of Quantum Mechanics* (1966)

Planck, Max *Scientific Autobiography and Other Papers* (trs 1949)

An important scientific innovation rarely makes its way by gradually winning over and converting its opponents: it rarely happens that Saul becomes Paul. What does happen is that its opponents gradually die out, and that the growing generation is familiarized with the ideas from the beginning.

MAX PLANCK
quoted in G Holton *Thematic Origins of Scientific Thought* 1973

Plantagenet English royal house, reigning 1154–1399, whose name comes from the nickname of Geoffrey, Count of Anjou (1113–1151), father of Henry II, who often wore in his hat a sprig of broom, *planta genista*. In the 1450s, Richard, Duke of York, took 'Plantagenet' as a surname to emphasize his superior claim to the throne over Henry VI's.

Plaskett John Stanley (1865–1941). Canadian astronomer and engineer who discovered many new binary stars, including Plaskett's Twins, previously thought to be a single, massive star. He also carried out research into stellar radial velocities.

From 1903 he was in charge of astrophysical work at the new Dominion Observatory in Ottawa. He designed a 1.8-m/72-in reflector telescope for the Dominion Astrophysical Observatory in Victoria, and was its director 1917–35. He then supervised the construction of a 205-cm/82-in mirror for the MacDonald Observatory at the University of Texas.

Plaskett's work on the radial velocities of galactic stars enabled him to confirm the contemporary discovery of the rotation of the Galaxy and to indicate the most probable location of its gravitational centre. This led to a study of the motion and distribution of galactic interstellar matter, particularly calcium.

Plater Alan Frederick (1935–). English dramatist. He is best known as a writer for television (18 episodes of *Z Cars* and 30 episodes of *Softly Softly*). His TV and radio scripts and plays reflect his northern working-class origins, left-wing political beliefs, and love of jazz.

A series of collaborative local musical commentaries began with a coal-mining community in *Close the Cookhouse Door* 1968, followed by the fiercely anti-establishment *Simon Says!* 1970. Plater is a great supporter of regional theatre, especially in Hull, for which he wrote *Sweet Sorrow* 1990, a celebration of the poet Philip Larkin. He has adapted for TV works by Anthony Trollope and Olivia Manning and his own *Beiderbecke* trilogy (written 1985–92).

Dying, / Is an art, like everything else. / I do it exceptionally well.

SYLVIA PLATH
'Lady Lazarus'

Plath Sylvia (1932–1963). US poet and novelist. Her powerful, highly personal poems, often expressing a sense of desolation, are distinguished by their intensity and sharp imagery. Her *Collected Poems* 1981 was awarded a Pulitzer prize. Her autobiographical novel *The Bell Jar* 1961 deals with the events surrounding a young woman's emotional breakdown.

Plath was born in Boston, Massachusetts, attended Smith College, and was awarded a Fulbright scholarship to study at Cambridge University, England. Here she met the poet Ted Hughes, whom she married 1956; they separated 1962. She committed suicide while living in London. Collections of her poems include *The Colossus* 1960 and *Ariel* 1965, published after her death.

Suggested reading

Annas, P *A Disturbance of Mirrors* (1988)

Roenblatt, J *Sylvia Plath* (1979)

Stevenson, A *Bitter Fame* (1989)

Wagner-Martin, L *Sylvia Plath: A Biography* (1987)

Platini Michel (1955–). French footballer who was the inspiration of the French team that won the 1984 European Championship. He was the first to be elected European Footballer of the Year on three successive years 1983–85. After starting his career in France with Nancy and St Etienne, he moved to Italy in 1982 where he played for Juventus. He represented his country on 72 occasions, scoring a record 41 goals and playing in three World Cups. He became manager of the French national team in 1988.

Plato (*c.* 427–347 BC). Greek philosopher. He was a pupil of Socrates, teacher of Aristotle, and founder of the Academy school of philosophy. He was the author of philosophical dialogues on such topics as metaphysics, ethics, and politics. Central to his teachings is the notion of Forms, which are located outside the everyday world – timeless, motionless, and absolutely real.

Plato's philosophy has influenced Christianity and European culture, directly and through Augustine, the Florentine Platonists during the Renaissance, and countless others.

Of his work, some 30 dialogues survive, intended for performance either to his pupils or to the public. The principal figure in these ethical and philosophical debates is Socrates and the early ones employ the Socratic method, in which he asks questions and traps the students into contradicting themselves; for example, *Iron*, on poetry. Other dialogues include the *Symposium*, on love, *Phaedo*, on immortality, and *Apology* and *Crito*, on Socrates' trial and death. It is impossible to say whether Plato's Socrates is a faithful representative of the real man or an articulation of Plato's own thought.

Plato's philosophy rejects scientific rationalism (establishing facts through experiment) in favour of arguments, because mind, not matter, is fundamental, and material objects are merely imperfect copies of abstract and eternal 'ideas'. His political philosophy is expounded in two treatises, *The Republic* and *The Laws*, both of

---

Blessed is such a wise man, and blessed too are those who hear the words of wisdom from his lips..

PLATO
Laws 711e

which describe ideal states. Platonic love is inspired by a person's best qualities and seeks their development.

Plautus (*c*. 250–*c*. 184 BC). Roman comic dramatist. Born in Umbria, he settled in Rome and was active before and after 200 BC, writing at least the 21 comedies that survive in his name, many of them based on Greek originals by playwrights such as Menander. Shakespeare drew on his *Menaechmi* for *The Comedy of Errors*.

Player Gary Jim (1935–). South African golfer who won major championships in three decades and the first British Open 1959. A match-play specialist, he won the world title five times. His total of nine 'majors' is the fourth (equal) best of all time. He is renowned for wearing all-black outfits. In the 1980s he was a successful Seniors player.

Playfair William Henry (1789–1857). Scottish Neo-Classical architect. He was responsible for much of the design of Edinburgh New Town in the early 19th century. His Royal Scottish Academy 1822 and National Gallery of Scotland 1850 in Greek style helped to make Edinburgh the 'Athens of the North'.

Playford Thomas (1896–1981). Australian Liberal Country League politician. He was premier of South Australia 1938–65, a record term in Australia and the Commonwealth of Nations, during which time his programmes attracted immigration and secondary industry to the state.

> *There are two types: Toupée actors and non-toupée actors.*
> DONALD PLEASENCE
> in *Daily Mail* 1965

Pleasence Donald (1919–1995). English character actor, who specialized in sinister or mysterious roles; for example, as the devious, aggressive tramp in Pinter's *The Caretaker* 1960 which he also played in the film version of 1963. His other films include *Dr Crippen* 1962, *Will Penny* 1968 and *The Eagle Has Landed* 1976 (as the Nazi Himmler). He was one of the most prolific of British film and television actors.

Pleasence made his first film appearance in 1954 and, after graduating to featured roles, only occasionally returned to the stage, though he had success as a Nazi war criminal in *The Man in the Glass Booth* 1968, and in 1990 reprised the tramp's role in a revival of *The Caretaker*. In more sympathetic guise, he played the investigating psychiatrist in the influential horror film *Halloween* 1978. Other films include Roman Polanski's *Cul de Sac* 1966, *Soldier Blue* 1970, and *The Last Tycoon* 1976. He played James Bond's adversary Blofeld in *You Only Live Twice* 1967.

Plečnik Jože (1872–1957). Austro-Hungarian architect whose work combines classical tradition with modernist elements. Born in Ljubljana, Slovenia, he went to school in Austria, trained with Otto Wagner, and himself taught at Prague from 1911. In 1930 he won a competition to rebuild Prague Castle as the architectural palace of Czechoslovakia, his most important work (completed 1935). His other work includes the National University Library in his native Ljubljana (1936–41).

Plekhanov Georgi Valentinovich (1857–1918). Russian Marxist revolutionary and theorist, founder of the Menshevik party. He led the first populist demonstration in St Petersburg, became a Marxist and, with Lenin, edited the newspaper *Iskra* (spark). In 1903 his opposition to Lenin led to the Bolshevik–Menshevik split. He returned to Russia 1917 but died in Finland.

> *He took up Marxism with such enthusiasm because he discerned in it a scientific explanation of history, and hence the uncertainty that the revolutionaries ... would no longer sacrifice their hopes ... in vain.*
> Geoffrey Hosking on GEORGI PLEKHANOV
> *History of the Soviet Union* 1985

Plethon George Gemisthos (*c*. 1353–*c*. 1452). Byzantine philosopher who taught for many years at Mistra in Asia Minor. A Platonist, he maintained a resolutely anti-Christian stance and was the inspiration for many of the ideas of the 15th-century Florentine Platonic Academy.

Plimsoll Samuel (1824–1898). English social reformer, born in Bristol. He sat in Parliament as a Radical 1868–80, and through his efforts the Merchant Shipping Act was passed in 1876, providing for Board of Trade inspection of ships, and the compulsory painting of a Plimsoll line to indicate safe loading limits.

> *The only certainty is that nothing is certain.*
> PLINY THE ELDER
> *Historia Naturalis* bk 2, ch 7

Pliny the Elder (Gaius Plinius Secundus) (*c*. AD 23–79). Roman scientific encyclopedist and historian. Pliny was born in Como, completed his studies in Rome and took up a military career in Germany, where he became a cavalry commander and friend of Vespasian. He kept out of harm's way while Nero was on the throne, but when in AD 69 Vespasian was made emperor, Pliny returned to Rome and took up various public offices. In AD 79 he was in command of a fleet in the bay of Naples when the volcano Vesuvius erupted. Going to take a closer look, he was killed by poisonous fumes. Many of his works have been lost, but in *Historia naturalis*/*Natural History*, probably completed AD 77, Pliny surveys all the known sciences of his day, notably astronomy, meteorology, geography, mineralogy, zoology, and botany.

Pliny states that he has covered 20,000 subjects of importance drawn from 100 selected writers, to whose observations he has added many of his own. Botany, agriculture, and horticulture appear to interest him most. To Pliny the world consisted of four elements: earth, air, fire, and water. The light substances were prevented from rising by the weight of the heavy ones, and vice versa. This is the earliest theory of gravity.

According to Pliny, the Earth was surrounded by seven stars: the Sun, the Moon, Mercury, Venus, Mars, Jupiter, and Saturn. Pliny took the Moon to be larger than the Earth, since it obscured the Sun during an eclipse.

Pliny the Younger (Gaius Plinius Caecilius Secundus) (*c*. AD 61–113). Roman administrator. He was the nephew of Pliny the Elder. His correspondence is of great interest; among his surviving letters are those describing the eruption of Vesuvius, his uncle's death, and his correspondence with the emperor Trajan.

> *I know that no higher tribute can be paid to my reputation than some favour from so exalted a ruler as yourself.*
> PLINY THE YOUNGER
> Remark to the emperor Trajan. *Letters* 10.13.

Plisetskaya Maya Mikhailovna (1925–). Soviet ballerina and actress. She attended the Moscow Bolshoi Ballet School and became prima ballerina of the Bolshoi Ballet 1945. An extremely strong yet supple dancer of flamboyant exuberance, she is noted for her fast spins, scissorlike jumps, and head-to-heel backward kicks, which she displayed to best advantage in the role of Kitri in *Don Quixote*. Her other noted classical role is Odette/Odile in *Swan Lake*. She is also associated with *Carmen Suite* 1967. She has acted dramatic roles in such films as *Anna Karenina* 1968.

Plomer William Charles Franklyn (1903–1973). South African novelist. He was the author of *Turbot Wolfe* 1925, an early criticism of South African attitudes to race. He settled in London 1929 and wrote two autobiographical volumes.

Plotinus (AD 205–270). Egyptian-born Roman philosopher who originated neo-Platonism. Plotinus studied from the age of 28 under

Ammonius Saccas (died AD 243) in Alexandria. He taught first in Alexandria and in 244 went to Rome, where he founded a philosophy school. His treatises in Greek, the *Enneads*, were edited by his pupil Porphyry (AD 232–c. 305). They deal with most topics of ancient philosophy except politics. He held that the ultimate goal of mystical union with the One or Good (the source of all being) can be achieved by intense moral and intellectual discipline. From the One or Good, the various levels of reality emanate timelessly.

The first level is the Divine Intellect, in which the Ideas (Plato called them Forms) are living intelligences and archetypes of the things of the world of sense. The next level is the Soul, the active principle forming and ordering the visible universe. People can choose to live on the level of the lower Soul (Nature) or the higher Soul (Intellect).

Plücker Julius (1801–1868). German mathematician and physicist. He made fundamental contributions to the field of analytical geometry and was a pioneer in the investigations of cathode rays that led eventually to the discovery of the electron.

He was professor of mathematics at Bonn 1828–33 and again 1836–47, when he became professor of physics there.

Plücker introduced six equations of higher plane curves which have been named Plücker's coordinates. His work led to the foundation of line geometry. He was one of the first to recognize the potential of gas spectroscopy in analysis, and found the first three hydrogen lines.

Experimenting with electrical discharge in gases at high pressures, Plücker found in 1858 that the discharge caused a fluorescent glow to form on the glass walls of the vacuum tube, and that the glow could be made to shift by applying an electromagnet to the tube, thus creating a magnetic field. It was left to one of his students to show that the glow was produced by cathode rays.

Gentlemen, we may not make history tomorrow, but we shall certainly change the geography.

HUBERT PLUMER
Remark to his staff before the Battle of Messines 1917
in which mines were extensively employed

Plumer Hubert Charles Onslow, 1st Viscount Plumer (1857–1932). British major-general in World War I. Plumer spent much of the war on the Western Front around the Ypres area, scene of much heavy fighting. He was responsible for the planning and execution of the attack on Messines 1917, generally considered to be one of the best-organized British operations of the war. He was highly popular with his troops (who referred to him as 'Daddy') as he planned carefully, organized meticulously, and generally executed his plans at far less cost in lives than any of his contemporaries could have managed. After the Armistice he marched his army to the Rhine as part of the forces of occupation. He was made a field-marshal 1919, and was appointed governor of Malta. KCB 1906, baron 1919, viscount 1929.

I must be permitted to devote myself to the signs of the soul in men.

PLUTARCH
Life of Alexander 1

Plutarch (c. AD 46–c. 120). Greek biographer and essayist. His *Parallel Lives* comprise paired biographies of famous Greek and Roman soldiers and politicians, followed by comparisons between the two. Thomas North's 1579 translation inspired Shakespeare's Roman plays. Plutarch lectured on philosophy in Rome and was appointed procurator of Greece by Emperor Hadrian.

Pocahontas Matoaka (c. 1595–1617). American Indian alleged to have saved the life of English colonist John Smith when he was captured by her father, Powhatan. She was kidnapped 1613 by an Englishman, Samuel Argall, and later married colonist John Rolfe (1585–1622) and was entertained as a princess at the English court

of James I. Pocahontas' marriage and conversion to Christianity brought about a period of peaceful relations between Indians and settlers. She fell ill on her journey back to Virginia; her ship docked at Gravesend, Kent, where she died.
Suggested reading
Barbour, Philip L *Pocahontas and Her World* (1969)
Mossiker, Frances *Pocahontas: The Life and the Legend* (1976)
Woodward, G S *Pocahontas* (1969)

Po Chü-i alternative transliteration of ◊Bo Zhu Yi, Chinese poet.

Poe was the first great nonstop literary drinker of the American nineteenth century. He made the indulgences of Coleridge and De Quincey seem like a bit of mischief in the kitchen with the cooking sherry.

James Thurber on EDGAR ALLAN POE
in *Alarms and Diversions* pt 1 'The Moribundant Life' 1957

Poe Edgar Allan (1809–1849). US writer and poet. Poe, born in Boston, was orphaned 1811 and joined the army 1827 but was court-martialled 1830 for deliberate neglect of duty. He failed to earn a living by writing, became an alcoholic, and in 1847 lost his wife (commemorated in his poem 'Annabel Lee'). His verse, of haunting lyric beauty, influenced the French Symbolists (for example, 'Ulalume' and 'The Bells'). His short stories are renowned for their horrific atmosphere, as in 'The Fall of the House of Usher' 1839 and 'The Masque of the Red Death' 1842, and for their acute reasoning (ratiocination), as in 'The Gold Bug' 1843 and 'The Murders in the Rue Morgue' 1841 (in which the investigators Legrand and Dupin anticipate Conan Doyle's Sherlock Holmes). His poems include 'The Raven' 1845. His novel *The Narrative of Arthur Gordon Pym of Nantucket* 1838 has attracted critical attention.
Suggested reading
Dayan, J *Fables of the Mind* (1987)
Kennedy, J G *Poe, Death and Life of Writing* (1987)
Quinn, Arthur *Edgar Allan Poe: A Critical Biography* (1969)

Thought is only a flash between two long nights, but the flash is everything.

JULES HENRI POINCARÉ
Attributed remark

Poincaré Jules Henri (1854–1912). French mathematician who developed the theory of differential equations and was a pioneer in relativity theory. He suggested that Isaac Newton's laws for the behaviour of the universe could be the exception rather than the rule. However, the calculation was so complex and time-consuming that he never managed to realize its full implication.

Poincaré wrote on the philosophy of science. He believed that some mathematical ideas precede logic, and stressed the role played by convention in scientific method. He also published the first paper devoted entirely to topology (the branch of geometry that deals with the unchanged properties of figures). He was professor at the Sorbonne from 1881.

Poincaré Raymond Nicolas Landry (1860–1934). French politician, prime minister 1912–13, president 1913–20, and again prime minister 1922–24 (when he ordered the occupation of the Ruhr, Germany) and 1926–29.

An accumulation of facts is no more science than a pile of bricks is a house.

RAYMOND POINCARÉ
La Science et 1'Hypothèse 1902

Poindexter John Marlane (1936–). US rear admiral and Republican government official. A doctor in nuclear physics, Poindexter served in the US Navy, rising to become deputy head of naval educational training 1978–81. From 1983 he worked closely with the National Security Council head, Robert McFarlane, and took over when McFarlane left Dec 1985. As a result of the Irangate scandal, Poindexter was forced to resign 1986, along with his assistant, Oliver North. Poindexter retired from the navy Dec 1987, and was found guilty on all counts April 1990, but his convictions were overturned on appeal Nov 1991.

Poiret Paul (1879–1944). French fashion designer. He was influential in the early part of the 20th century. He founded his own fashion house 1904 and two years later began loosening the shape of his designs, producing soft, amorphous gowns which were simple and elegant, followed by Eastern-inspired outfits 1909. He introduced the hobble skirt 1911 which, although it freed the hips, confined the ankles and attracted much criticism.

Poiseuille Jean Léonard Marie (1799–1869). French physiologist who made a key contribution to our knowledge of the circulation of blood in the arteries. He also studied the flow of liquids in artificial capillaries. In 1842 he was elected to the Académie de Médicine in Paris.

Poiseuille improved on earlier measurements of blood pressure by using a mercury manometer and filling the connection to the artery with potassium carbonate to prevent coagulation. He used this instrument, known as a hemodynamometer, to show that blood pressure rises during expiration (breathing out) and falls during inspiration (breathing in). He also discovered that the dilation of an artery fell to less than $\frac{1}{20}$ of its normal value during a heartbeat.

Poisson Siméon Denis (1781–1840). French applied mathematician and physicist. In probability theory he formulated the Poisson distribution. Poisson's ratio in elasticity is the ratio of the lateral contraction of a body to its longitudinal extension. The ratio is constant for a given material.

Much of Poisson's work involved applying mathematical principles in theoretical terms to contemporary and prior experiments in physics, particularly with reference to electricity, magnetism, heat, and sound. Poisson was also responsible for a formulation of the 'law of large numbers', which he introduced in his work on probability theory, *Recherches sur la probabilité des jugements/Researches on the Probability of Opinions* 1837.

Poisson was born in Pithiviers, Loirel, and studied in Paris at the Ecole Polytechnique, where he became professor 1806. In 1808 he was appointed astronomer at the Bureau des Longitudes, and the following year he was appointed professor of mechanics at the Faculty of Sciences. From 1820 he was an administrator at the highest level in France's educational system.

Poisson's works include *Treatise on Mechanics* 1833, *Mathematical Theory of Heat* 1835, and *Researches on the Movement of Projectiles in Air* 1835, the first account of the effects of the Earth's rotation on motion.

I hate to think that my avenues of critical expression were circumscribed by my colour.

SIDNEY POITIER
Showtime 1967

Poitier Sidney (1924–). US actor and film director. He was Hollywood's first black star. His films as an actor include *Something of Value* 1957, *Lilies of the Field* 1963, *In the Heat of the Night* 1967, and *Sneakers* 1992, and as director *Stir Crazy* 1980.

Polanski Roman (1933–). Polish film director. His films include *Repulsion* 1965, *Cul de Sac* 1966, *Rosemary's Baby* 1968,

---

TV has changed the world by changing people's attitudes. When they are born with a TV set in their room – well, you can't fool them any more.

ROMAN POLANSKI
Time Dec 1967

Tess 1979, *Frantic* 1988, *Bitter Moon* 1992, and *Death and the Maiden* 1995.

He suffered a traumatic childhood in Nazi-occupied Poland, and later his wife, actress Sharon Tate, was the victim of murder by the Charles Manson 'family'. He left the USA for Europe and his tragic personal life is perhaps reflected in a fascination with horror and violence in his work.

Polanyi Michael ·(1891–1976). Hungarian-born British chemist, social scientist, and philosopher. As a scientist, he worked on thermodynamics, X-ray crystallography, and physical adsorption. As a philosopher and social scientist, he was concerned about the conflicts between personal freedom and central planning, and the impact of the conflict upon scientists.

Polanyi, born in Budapest, studied medicine there and later turned to chemistry. In 1933 he resigned from the Kaiser Wilhelm Institute in Berlin over the dismissal of Jewish scientists, and moved to Manchester University, England, as professor of physical chemistry. He was professor of social studies at Manchester 1948–58, and then moved to Oxford.

Polanyi introduced the idea of the existence of an attractive force between a solid surface and the atoms or molecules of a gas; he also suggested that the adsorbed surface is a multilayer and not subject to simple valency interactions.

He advocated that scientific research need not necessarily have a pre-stated function and expressed the belief that a commitment to the discovery of truth is the prime reason for being a scientist. He also analysed the nature of knowledge, skills, and discovery. Polanyi's works include *Personal Knowledge* 1958, *Knowing and Being* 1969, and *Scientific Thought and Social Reality* 1974.

Pole Reginald (1500–1558). English cardinal from 1536 who returned from Rome as papal legate on the accession of Mary I in order to readmit England to the Catholic church. He succeeded Cranmer as archbishop of Canterbury 1556.

Politian (Angelo Poliziano). Pen name of Angelo Ambrogini (1454–1494). Italian poet, playwright, and exponent of humanist ideals. He was tutor to Lorenzo de Medici's children, and professor at the University of Florence; he wrote commentaries and essays on Classical authors.

Polk James Knox (1795–1849). 11th president of the USA 1845–49, a Democrat, born in North Carolina. He allowed Texas

Polk As 11th president of the USA, James Polk settled the Oregon Boundary dispute with Britain and successfully conducted the Mexican War, which resulted in the annexation of California. Devoted to the Democratic principles of his predecessors, Thomas Jefferson and Andrew Jackson, Polk set up a revenue tariff and an independent treasury.

admission to the Union, and forced the war on Mexico that resulted in the annexation of California and New Mexico.

Suggested reading
Bergieron, Paul *James K Polk* (1989)
McCoy, Charles *Polk and the Presidency* (1960)
Polk, James K *The Diaries of James K Polk* (1911, ed by Allan Nevins 1952)
Sellers, C G *James K Polk* (1957–66)

Pollaiuolo Antonio del (*c*. 1432–1498) and Piero (*c*. 1441–1496) Italian artists. They were active in Florence. Both brothers were painters, sculptors, goldsmiths, engravers, and designers. Antonio is said to have been the first Renaissance artist to make a serious study of anatomy. The *Martyrdom of St Sebastian* about 1475 (National Gallery, London) is considered a joint work. The brothers also executed two papal monuments in St Peter's basilica, Rome. The major individual works are Piero's set of *Virtues* in Florence and Antonio's engraving *The Battle of the Nude Men* about 1465. Antonio's work places a strong emphasis on the musculature of the human figure in various activities.

Pollen Arabella (1961–). English fashion designer. She achieved instant success 1981 when she sold one of her first coat designs to the Princess of Wales. She has become familiar for her classic styles – tailored, sophisticated shapes in bright-coloured wool and cotton. In 1991 she launched Pollen B, a line of clothing directed at a younger market, which is simpler in design and cheaper than her main collection.

Pollock (Paul) Jackson (1912–1956). US painter. He was a pioneer of Abstract Expressionism and one of the foremost exponents of action painting. His style is characterized by complex networks of swirling, interwoven lines of great delicacy and rhythmic subtlety. In the early 1940s Pollock moved from a vivid Expressionist style, influenced by Mexican muralists such as Siqueiros and by Surrealism, towards a semi-abstract style. The paintings of this period are colourful and vigorous, using enigmatic signs and mysterious forms. From 1947 he developed his more violently expressive abstracts, placing large canvases on the studio floor and dripping or hurling paint across them. He was soon recognized as the leading Abstract Expressionist and continued to develop his style, producing even larger canvases in the 1950s.

Suggested reading
Frascina, F (ed) *Pollock and After* (1985)
Friedman, B *Jackson Pollock: Energy Made Visible* (1972)
Naifeh, S and Smith, G *Jackson Pollock: An American Genius* (1988)
O'Connor, F *Jackson Pollock* (1967)
Potter, J (ed) *To A Violent Grave: An Oral Biography of Jackson Pollock* (1985)

I have not told half of what I saw.
MARCO POLO
Last words

Polo Marco (1254–1324). Venetian traveller and writer. He joined his father (Niccolo) and uncle (Maffeo), who had travelled to China as merchants (1260–69), when they began a journey overland back to China (1271). Once there, he learned Mongolian and served the emperor Kubla Khan until he returned to Europe by sea 1292–95. He was captured while fighting for Venice against Genoa, and, while in prison 1296–98, dictated an account of his travels. These accounts have remained the primary source of information about the Far East until the 19th century.

Suggested reading
Hart, H H *Marco Polo, Venetian Adventurer* (1967)
Humble, R *Marco Polo* (1975)
Severin, T *Tracking Marco Polo* (1986)
Wood, Frances *Did Marco Polo go to China ?* (1995)

Pol Pot (also known as Saloth Sar, Tol Saut, and Pol Porth) (*c*. 1925–). Cambodian politician and leader of the Khmer Rouge communist movement that overthrew the government 1975. Pol Pot was a member of the anti-French resistance under Ho Chi Minh in the 1940s. In 1975 he proclaimed Democratic Kampuchea with himself as premier. His policies were to evacuate cities and put people to work in the countryside. The Khmer Rouge also carried out a systematic extermination of the Western-influenced educated and middle classes (1–4 million). After widespread atrocities against the civilian population, his regime was deposed by a Vietnamese invasion 1979. Pol Pot continued to help lead the Khmer Rouge despite officially resigning from all positions in 1989. Rumours of his death reached the West 1996.

Pólya George (1887–1985). Hungarian mathematician who worked on function theory, probability, and applied mathematics. Pólya's theorem 1920 is a solution of a problem in combinatorial analysis theory and method.

From 1914 he lectured at the Swiss Federal Institute of Technology in Zürich, becoming professor 1928. In 1940 he emigrated to the USA, ending his career at Stanford University, Palo Alto, California, 1946–53.

Pólya published studies on analytical functions in 1924 and on algebraic functions in 1927. He also worked on linear homogeneous differential equations (1924) and transcendental equations (1930). One of his studies in mathematical physics was an investigation into heat propagation 1931.

Other subjects he examined included the study of complex variables, polynomials, and number theory.

The fairest of names, but the worst of realities – mob rule.
POLYBIUS
History bk vi 57

Polybius (*c*. 200–*c*. 118 BC). Greek politician and historian. He was involved with the Achaean League against the Romans and, following the defeat of the Macedonians at Pydna 168 BC, he was taken as a political hostage to Rome. He returned to Greece 151 and was present at the capture of Carthage by his friend Scipio 146. The first part of his history of Rome in 40 books, covering the years 220–146, survives intact.

Who is so worthless or so indolent as not to wish to know by what means and under what government the Romans have come to dominate the world?
POLYBIUS
History bk i ch 1

Polycarp, St (*c*. 69–*c*. 155). Christian martyr allegedly converted by St John the Evangelist. As bishop of Smyrna (modern Izmir, Turkey), he carried on a vigorous struggle against various heresies for over 40 years. He was burned alive at a public festival. Feast day 26 Jan.

Polycrates (lived 6th century BC). Tyrant of Samos, *c*. 540–522 BC. He established an effective navy of over 100 ships and was master of the Aegean basin. He was also a promoter of ambitious building projects, and patron of poets such as Anacreon. He was crucified by the Persians in about 522 BC.

The story is told that in order to ward off disaster, he must throw away his most precious possession. He threw his favourite ring into the sea but it was returned to him in the belly of a fish.

Polygnotus (*c*. 500–*c*. 440 BC). Greek painter, who developed the art of large-scale narrative painting in Athens. Polygnotus settled in Athens in the time of Cimon. Although none of his work survives, Pausanias describes in detail his *Sack of Troy* on the walls of the painted Stoa of Attalus in the agora (marketplace) in Athens. He also executed a mural painting of the *Rape of the Leucippidae* in the shrine of the Dioscuri. He was admired for his composition of figures and depictions of facial characteristics. His most famous works were the *Sack of Troy* and *Ulysses in the Underworld* at Delphi. He excelled in the delineation of character in the human face, and this quality of his work receives unqualified praise from Aristotle and other ancient critics. He had numerous pupils and followers.

Polykleitos or Polyclitus (lived 5th century BC). Greek sculptor. His *Spear Carrier* 450–440 BC (only Roman copies survive) exemplifies the naturalism and harmonious proportions of his work. He created the legendary colossal statue of Hera in Argos, in ivory and gold.

After us the deluge.

MADAME DE POMPADOUR
quoted in Du Haussay *Mémoires* 1821

Pompadour Jeanne Antoinette Poisson, Marquise de, (known as Madame de Pompadour) (1721–1764). Mistress of Louis XV of France from 1744, born in Paris. She largely dictated the government's ill-fated policy of reversing France's anti-Austrian policy for an anti-Prussian one. She acted as the patron of the Enlightenment philosophers Voltaire and Diderot.
Suggested reading
Behrens, C *The Ancien Régime* (1967)
Mitford, Nancy *Madame de Pompadour* (1964)
Smythe, David *Madame de Pompadour: Mistress of France* (1953)

Wherever in Italy I stamp my foot there will spring up infantry and cavalry.

POMPEY THE GREAT
quoted in Plutarch *Life of Pompey* ch 57.5

Pompey the Great (Gnaeus Pompeius Magnus) (106–48 BC). Roman soldier and politician. From 60 BC to 53 BC, he was a member of the First Triumvirate with Julius Caesar and Marcus Livius Crassus.

Originally a supporter of Sulla, Pompey became consul with Crassus in 70 BC. He defeated Mithridates VI Eupator of Pontus, and annexed Syria and Palestine. He married Caesar's daughter Julia (died 54 BC) in 59 BC. When the Triumvirate broke down after 53 BC, Pompey was drawn into leadership of the senatorial faction. On the outbreak of civil war 49 BC he withdrew to Greece, was defeated by Caesar at Pharsalus 48 BC, and was murdered in Egypt.
Suggested reading
Greenhalgh, Peter *Pompey: The Roman Alexander* (1980)
Greenhalgh, Peter *Pompey: The Republican Prince* (1981)
Leach, John *Pompey the Great* (1978)
Seager, Robin *Pompey: A Political Biography* (1979)

Pompidou Georges Jean Raymond (1911–1974). French conservative politician, president 1969–74. An adviser on General de Gaulle's staff 1944–46, Pompidou held administrative posts until he became director-general of the French House of Rothschild 1954, and even then continued in close association with de Gaulle, helping to draft the constitution of the Fifth Republic 1958–59. He was elected to the presidency on de Gaulle's resignation. He negotiated a settlement with the Algerians 1961 and, as prime minister 1962–68, with the students in the revolt of May 1968.

A statesman is a politician who places himself at the service of the nation. A politician is a statesman who places the nation at his service.

GEORGES POMPIDOU
Observer Dec 1973

Pomus and Shuman Doc (Jerome Solon Felder) Pomus (1925–1991) and Mort Shuman (1936–   ). US pop-music songwriting partnership 1956–65. The team wrote hits for the Drifters ('Save the Last Dance for Me' 1960) and Elvis Presley ('Little Sister' and 'His Latest Flame' 1961). Fluent in a number of styles, they were innovators in none.

Much of their material was written for prefabricated pop stars like Fabian ('I'm a Man' 1959) or, like 'Teenager in Love' for Dion and the Belmonts 1959, in imitation of a recent hit. Between 1960 and 1963 Pomus and Shuman were one of the songwriting teams working in the Brill Building, the New York hit factory.

Ponce de León Juan (*c.* 1460–1521). Spanish soldier and explorer. He is believed to have sailed with Columbus 1493, and served 1502–04 in Hispaniola. He conquered Puerto Rico 1508, and was made governor 1509. In 1513 he was the first European to reach Florida. He returned to Spain 1514 to report his 'discovery' of Florida (which he thought was an island), and was given permission by King Ferdinand to colonize it. He died in Cuba from an arrow wound.

Poncelet Jean-Victor (1788–1867). French mathematician and military engineer who advanced projective geometry. His book *Traité des propriétés projectives des figures* 1822 deals with the properties of plane figures that remain unchanged when projected.

He took part in Napoleon's campaign against Russia, and was captured. During his two years as a prisoner of war, he began his work on geometry. On his release 1814, he returned to Metz and was engaged on projects in military engineering there until 1824, when he became professor of mechanics at a local military school. In 1830 he was elected a member of Metz Municipal Council and secretary of the Conseil-Général of the Moselle. He moved to the University of Paris 1838 and ended his career as commandant of the Ecole Polytechnique with the rank of general.

Poncelet had been a pupil of Gaspard Monge, the originator of modern synthetic geometry, but Poncelet also used analytical geometry and contributed greatly to the development of the relatively new synthetic (projective) geometry. He became the centre of controversy over the principle of continuity, and developed the circular points at infinity.

Poncelet developed a new model of a variable counterweight drawbridge, which he described and publicized in 1822. His most important technical contributions were concerned with hydraulic engines, such as Poncelet's water wheel, with regulations and with dynamometers, as well as in devising various improvements to his own fortification techniques.

Pond John (1767–1836). English astronomer who as Astronomer Royal 1811–35 reorganized and modernized Greenwich Observatory. Instituting new methods of observation, he went on to produce a catalogue of more than 1,000 stars in 1833.

He travelled in several Mediterranean and Middle Eastern countries, making astronomical observations wherever possible. When he returned to England in 1798, he established a small private observatory near Bristol. The observations he published led to his appointment as Astronomer Royal.

At the age of 15, Pond noticed errors in the observations being made at the Greenwich Observatory and began a thorough investigation of the declination of a number of fixed stars. By 1806 he had publicly demonstrated that the quadrant at Greenwich had become deformed with age and needed replacing. It was this in particular that prompted his programme to modernize the whole observatory.

Pons Jean-Louis (1761–1831). French astronomer who discovered 37 comets. He was the first to recognize the return of Encke's comet.

At the age of 28 he became a porter and doorkeeper at the Marseille Observatory. Noting his interest in astronomy, the directors of the observatory gave him instruction, and he turned out to be good at practical observation. Pons was made assistant astronomer 1813 and assistant director 1818. In 1819 he became director of a new observatory at Lucca, N Italy, moving to the Florence Observatory 1822.

In 1818 Pons discovered three small, tailless comets, among which was one that he claimed had first been seen in 1805 by Johann Encke of the Berlin Observatory. Alerted to this possibility, Encke carried out further observations and calculations, and finally ascribed to it a period of 1,208 days – which meant that it would return in 1822. Its return was duly observed, in Australia, only the second instance ever of the known return of an identified comet. Encke wanted the comet to be named after Pons, but it continued to be called after its discoverer.

Ponti Gio(vanni) (1891–1979). Italian designer and architect. He was a pioneer of the Modern Movement in Italy. His masterpiece is the Pirelli skyscraper in Milan, designed with Pier Luigi Nervi, 1957–60, which is 126 m/415 ft high and remarkable for its slender hexagonal plan, with tapering ends. He was the founder, and editor for many years, of the influential architectural periodical *Domus*.

Pontiac (*c.* 1720–1769). North American Indian, chief of the Ottawa from 1755. Allied with the French forces during the French and Indian War, Pontiac was hunted by the British after the French withdrawal. He led the 'Conspiracy of Pontiac' 1763–64 in an attempt to resist British persecution. He achieved remarkable success against overwhelming odds, but eventually signed a peace treaty 1766. Pontiac was born near Detroit. He was murdered by a Peoria Indian in Illinois at the instigation of a British trader.

Pontormo Jacopo da, (Jacopo Carucci) (1494–1557). Italian Mannerist painter. Pontormo worked in Andrea del Sarto's workshop from 1512. An early work, *Joseph in Egypt* about 1515 (National Gallery, London), is already Mannerist. Active in Florence, he developed a dramatic style, with lurid colours, demonstrated in *The Deposition* about 1525 (Sta Felicità, Florence). This is an extraordinary composition of interlocked figures, with rosy pinks, lime yellows, and pale apple greens illuminating the scene. The same distinctive colours occur in the series of frescoes he painted 1522–25 for the Certosa monastery outside Florence.

Overfed white kids with nice complexions. Do you fools have any brains?

IGGY POP
quoted in Irwin Stambler *The Encyclopedia of Pop, Rock and Soul* 1989. One of many insults Pop is alleged to have shouted at his fans during concerts.

Pop Iggy. Stage name of James Newell Osterberg (1947–   ). US rock singer and songwriter. Initially known as Iggy Stooge, he was lead singer with a seminal garage band called the Stooges (1967–74), whose self-destructive proto-punk performances became legendary. His solo career began with *The Idiot* 1977 and *Lust for Life* 1977, composed and produced by David Bowie, who also contributed to *Blah, Blah, Blah* 1986.

Know then thyself, presume not God to scan, / The proper study of mankind is man.

ALEXANDER POPE
Essay on Man 2 1733–34

Pope Alexander (1688–1744). English poet and satirist. He established his reputation with the precocious *Pastorals* 1709 and 'Essay on Criticism' 1711, which were followed by a parody of the heroic epic *The Rape of the Lock* 1712–14 and 'Eloisa to Abelard' 1717. Other works include a highly Neo-Classical translation of Homer's *Iliad* and *Odyssey* 1715–26.

Pope had a biting wit, which he expressed in the form of heroic couplets. As a Catholic, he was subject to discrimination, and he was embittered by a deformity of the spine. His edition of Shakespeare attracted scholarly ridicule, for which he revenged himself by a satire on scholarly dullness, the *Dunciad* 1728. His philosophy, including *Essay on Man* 1733–34 and *Moral Essays* 1731–35, was influenced by the politician and philosopher Henry Bolingbroke. His finest mature productions are his *Imitations of the Satires of Horace* 1733–38 and his personal letters. Among his friends were the writers Swift, Arbuthnot, and Gay. His line 'A little learning is a dang'rous thing' is often misquoted.

Suggested reading
Gordon, I *Preface to Pope* (1993)
Gurr, E *Pope* (1971)
Mack, M *Alexander Pope: A Life* (1986)
Quennell, P *Alexander Pope: The Education of a Genius, 1688–1728* (1968)

Rogers, P *An Introduction to Pope* (1975)

Pope-Hennessy John Wyndham (1913–1994). English art historian and museum curator. He first joined the staff of the Victoria and Albert Museum in 1938 as a member of the department of painting, although his work there was interrupted by World War II, which he spent largely in the Air Ministry. He pioneered the study in Britain of Italian Renaissance sculpture, of which he was a great connoisseur, and was director and secretary of the Victoria and Albert Museum 1967–73, and director of the British Museum 1974–76. Knighted 1971.

Pope-Hennessy realized that the study of sculpture remained relatively underdeveloped in comparison with painting, and dedicated himself to a new catalogue of the Victoria and Albert Museum's collection; his work was published in three volumes 1964, and immediately became standard reference works. In 1976, he became consultative chairman of the Department of European Painting at the Metropolitan Museum of Art in 1976, and spent 10 years in New York, combining his museum work with teaching at the Institute of Fine Arts. In 1992 he made his final home in Florence, and in 1993 he published a book on Donatello, and was made an honorary citizen of Siena.

Popov Alexander Stepanovich (1859–1905). Russian physicist who devised the first aerial, in advance of Marconi (although he did not use it for radio communication). He also invented a detector for radio waves.

Popova Liubov Sergeevna (born Eding) (1889–1924). Russian artist and designer. In 1912 she studied painting in Paris, returning to France and Italy 1914. Like Rodchenko and Stepanova, she taught art and design after the 1917 revolution; by 1921 she had abandoned easel painting in favour of productivist art. Influenced by Futurism and Constructivism, in 1916 she began designing textiles and rugs, and in 1917 collaborated with Vladimir Tatlin on the decoration of the Café Pittoresque in Moscow. Like Varvara Stepanova, in the 1920s she designed textiles for Moscow's First State Textile Printing Factory. In 1922 she designed a stark, functional set and costumes for Vfezolod Meierkhold's production of *The Magnanimous Cuckold*.

Popper Karl Raimund (1902–1994). Austrian philosopher of science. His theory of falsificationism says that although scientific generalizations cannot be conclusively verified, they can be conclusively falsified by a counter-instance; therefore, science is not certain knowledge but a series of 'conjectures and refutations', approaching, though never reaching, a definitive truth. For Popper, psychoanalysis and Marxism are falsifiable and therefore unscientific. Knighted 1965.

One of the most widely read philosophers of the century, Popper's book *The Open Society and its Enemies* 1945 became a modern classic. In it he investigated the long history of attempts to formulate a theory of the state. Animated by a dislike of the views of Freud and Marx, Popper believed he could show that their hypotheses about hidden social and psychological processes were falsifiable.

His major work on the philosophy of science is *The Logic of Scientific Discovery* 1935. Other works include *The Poverty of Historicism* 1957 (about the philosophy of social science), *Conjectures and Refutations* 1963, and *Objective Knowledge* 1972.

Born and educated in Vienna, Popper served for a while as an assistant to the psychologist Alfred Adler before emigrating to New Zealand in 1937. Returning to Europe, he became a naturalized British subject 1945 and was professor of logic and scientific method at the London School of Economics 1949–69. He opposed Wittgenstein's view that philosophical problems are merely pseudo-problems. Popper's view of scientific practice has been criticized by T S Kuhn and other writers.

Every solution of a problem raises new unsolved problems.

KARL POPPER
Conjectures and Refutations 1963

Suggested reading
Magee, Bryan *Popper* (1973)
Miller, David (ed) *A Pocket Popper* (selections from Popper's works) (1983)
O'Hear, A *Karl Popper* (1982)
Popper, Karl *Unended Quest: An Intellectual Autobiography* (1976)

Porritt Jonathon (1950–). British environmental campaigner, director of Friends of the Earth 1984–90. He has stood in both British and European elections as a Green (formerly Ecology) Party candidate.

Green consumerism is a target for exploitation. There's a lot of green froth on top, but murkiness lurks underneath.

JONATHON PORRITT
Speech at a Friends of the Earth Conference 1989

Porsche Ferdinand (1875–1951). German car designer and engineer who designed the Volkswagen Beetle, first mass produced 1945. By 1972 more than 15 million had been sold, making it the world's most popular model. Porsche sports cars were developed by his son Ferry Porsche from 1948.

Ferdinand Porsche designed his first racing car in the mid-1930s, which was successfully developed by Auto-Union for their racing team. Ferry's Porsche Company produced Grand Prix čars, sports cars, and prototypes. Their Formula One racing car was not successful and it was at sports-car and Can-Am racing that they proved to be more dominant.

He was technical director with Daimler-Benz 1923–29 and formed his own company 1931. In 1932 he devised the first torsion-bar suspension system, which was incorporated in the Volkswagen prototype he began working on 1934. In 1936, he received a contract from the German government to develop the Volkswagen and plan the factory where it would be built. World War II halted this development, so Porsche designed the Leopard and Tiger tanks used by German Panzer regiments and helped to develop the V1 flying bomb.

In the 1930s Porsche also designed light tractors, and worked on aviation engines and plans and designs for wind-driven power plants – large windmills with automatic sail adjustment.

Porson Richard (1759–1808). British Classical scholar, professor of Greek at Cambridge from 1792 and editor of the Greek dramatists Aeschylus and Euripides.

Portal Charles Frederick Algernon, 1st Viscount Portal of Hungerford (1893–1971). British air chief marshal in World War II. Chief of the Air Staff 1940–45, he was an advocate of strategic bombing and at the Casablanca Conference Jan 1943 reached agreement with the US on a combined bomber offensive to destroy German military industrial capability. Portal was unable to control Harris, commanding RAF Bomber Command, who considered such a policy a 'panacea' and instead preferred simple area bombing. KCB 1940, baron 1945, viscount 1946.

Porter Cole (Albert) (1892–1964). US composer and lyricist. He wrote mainly musical comedies. His witty, sophisticated songs like 'Let's Do It' 1928, 'I Get a Kick Out of You' 1934, and 'Don't Fence Me In' 1944 have been widely recorded and admired. His shows, many of which were made into films, include *The Gay Divorce* 1932 (filmed 1934 as *The Gay Divorcee*) and *Kiss Me Kate* 1948.

Suggested reading
Eells, George *The Life That Late He Led: A Biography of Cole Porter* (1967)
Schwartz, Charles *Cole Porter* (1977)

In olden days a glimpse of stocking / Was looked on as something shocking / Now, heaven knows, / Anything goes.

COLE PORTER
'Anything Goes'

Porter Edwin Stratton (1869–1941). US director, a pioneer of silent films. His 1903 film *The Great Train Robbery* lasted an unprecedented 12 minutes and contained an early use of the close-up. More concerned with the technical than the artistic side of his films, which include *The Teddy Bears* 1907 and *The Final Pardon* 1912, Porter abandoned film-making 1916.

Porter Eric (1928–1995). English actor. His numerous classical roles include title roles in *Uncle Vanya*, *Volpone*, and *King Lear*; on television he played Soames Forsyte in *The Forsyte Saga*.

Porter George (1920–). English chemist. From 1947 he and Ronald Norrish developed a technique by which flashes of high energy are used to bring about extremely fast chemical reactions. They shared a Nobel prize 1967. Knighted 1972.

After World War II he carried out research at Cambridge under Norrish. Porter was professor at Sheffield 1955–66, director of the Royal Institution 1966–85, and president of the Royal Society 1985–90. In the 1960s he made many appearances on British television.

Porter began using quick flashes of light to study transient species in chemical reactions, particularly free radicals and excited states of molecules. In 1950 he could detect entities that exist for less than a microsecond; by 1975, using laser beams, he had reduced the time limit to a picosecond (10^{-12} sec). His early work dealt with reactions involving gases (mainly chain reactions and combustion reactions), but he later extended the technique to solutions and also studied the processes that occur in the first nanosecond of photosynthesis in plants. He developed a method of stabilizing free radicals by trapping them in the structure of a supercooled liquid (a glass), a technique called matrix isolation.

Porter Hal (1911–1984). Australian novelist, short-story writer, playwright, and poet. He is best known for his short stories, collected in seven volumes, and for his three autobiographical works *The Watcher on the Cast-Iron Balcony* 1963, *The Paper Chase* 1966, and *The Extra* 1975.

Love is purely a creation of the human imagination ... the most important example of how the imagination continually outruns the creature it inhabits.

KATHERINE ANNE PORTER
quoted in *Contemporary Novelists* 1976

Porter Katherine Anne Maria Veronica Callista Russell (1890–1980). US writer. She published three volumes of short stories *Flowing Judas* 1930, *Pale Horse, Pale Rider* 1939, and *The Leaning Tower* 1944; a collection of essays, *The Days Before* 1952; and the allegorical novel *Ship of Fools* 1962 (filmed 1965). Her *Collected Short Stories* 1965 won a Pulitzer prize.

Suggested reading
Givner, Joan *Katherine Anne Porter* (1984)
Hill, Kathryn *Katherine Anne Porter* (1989)
Lopez, Enrique Hank *Conversations with Katherine Anne Porter* (1981)
Stout, Janis P *Katherine Anne Porter: A Sense of the Times* (1995)

Porter Michael (1947–). US management theorist and expert on competitive strategy. His first book, *Competitive Strategy* 1980, set out his theory on strategies for competitive advantage and is regarded by many as the definitive work in the field. He applied the same theory to countries in his *Competitive Advantage of Nations* 1990 to explain why some countries are richer than others.

His 'competitive strategy' theory is based on an analysis of a company's competitive position within its environment, using the 'five forces' that drive competition. These forces are: the relative strength of buyers or customers; the relative strength of suppliers; the relative ease with which potential new competitors can enter the market; the potential availability of substitutes; and rivalry between competing firms. Porter is professor of management at Harvard Business School.

Porter Rodney Robert (1917–1985). English biochemist. In 1962 he proposed a structure for human immunoglobulin (antibody) in which the molecule was seen as consisting of four chains. He was awarded the 1972 Nobel Prize for Physiology or Medicine.

He became professor of immunology at St Mary's Hospital Medical School, London, 1960; from 1967 he was professor of biochemistry at Oxford.

Basing his research on the work of US immunologist Karl Landsteiner, Porter studied the structural basis of the biological activities of antibodies, proposing in 1962 a structure for gammaglobulin. He also worked on the structure, assembly, and activation mechanisms of the components of a substance known as complement. This is a protein that is normally present in the blood, but disappears from the serum during most antigen–antibody reactions. In addition, Porter investigated the way in which immunoglobulins interact with complement components and with cell surfaces.

Portillo Michael Denzil Xavier (1953–   ). British Conservative politician, employment secretary 1994–95, and defence secretary from 1995. Representative of the right wing of the party in John Major's government, his progress up the ministerial ladder was swift, leading some admirers to regard him as Major's eventual successor. He is an avowed 'Thatcherite', convinced of the supremacy of the market and suspicious of the encroaching powers of the European Union (EU).

After a short spell in industry, Portillo joined the research department at Conservative Central Office where his role as adviser to several government ministers give him an appetite for active politics. He entered the Commons 1984 in the London Southgate by-election. His appointment as employment secretary 1994 made him directly responsible for UK policy on the controversial EU Social Chapter, the *bête noire* of right-wing Tories.

A blunt man who had a gift for making enemies and who, though quite incorruptible, liked wealth.

C P Hill on WILLIAM BENTINCK, 1ST EARL OF PORTLAND
in *Who's Who in History* vol II 1965

Portland William Bentinck, 1st Earl of Portland (1649–1709). Dutch politician who accompanied William of Orange to England 1688, and was created an earl 1689. He served in William's campaigns. KG 1697.

Portland William Henry Cavendish Bentinck, 3rd Duke of Portland (1738–1809). British politician, originally a Whig, who in 1783 became nominal prime minister in the Fox–North coalition government. During the French Revolution he joined the Tories, and was prime minister 1807–09. Duke 1762.

Portsmouth Louise Renée de Kéroualle, Duchess of Portsmouth (1649–1734). Mistress of Charles II of Britain, she was a Frenchwoman who came to England as Louis XIV's agent 1670, and was hated by the public. Duchess 1673.

Potemkin Grigory Aleksandrovich, Prince (1739–1791). Russian politician. He entered the army and attracted the notice of Catherine II, whose friendship he kept throughout his life. He was an active administrator who reformed the army, built the Black Sea Fleet, conquered the Crimea 1783, developed S Russia, and founded the Kherson arsenal 1788 (the first Russian naval base on the Black Sea).

Potter Dennis Christopher George (1935–1994). English playwright and journalist. He distinguished himself as the most important dramatist for television in its history, greatly extending the boundaries of the art-form. Plays include *Pennies from Heaven* 1978 (feature film 1981), *Brimstone and Treacle* 1976 (transmitted 1987, feature film 1982), and *The Singing Detective* 1986. His posthumous plays were *Cold Lazarus* and *Karaoke*, both 1995.

Potter's television dramas exhibit a serious concern for social issues, and are characterized by a marked avoidance of euphemism or delicacy. Highly inventive in form, they explore the medium's technical possibilities, employing devices such as overlap, fantasy sequences, and flashback.

He was a journalist and TV critic before becoming known as a playwright. He was recruited by the BBC 1959 and worked on current-affairs programmes and documentaries. He left 1961 and became a political features writer for the *Daily Herald*. Then, when only 29, he was afflicted by the hereditary disease, psoriatic arthropathy, which kept him at home for most of the rest of his life. He turned to television criticism, writing for the *New Statesman* and then for the *Sunday Times*.

He started to write television plays in the mid-1960s. Four were screened 1965–66, two of which, *Stand Up Nigel Barton* and *Vote Vote Vote for Nigel Barton*, were autobiographical. Many of his plays went beyond the bounds of public taste – *Son of Man* 1969 depicted a working-class Christ, and *Brimstone and Treacle*, banned 1976, was about the Devil curing a brain-damaged girl by raping her. Potter often incorporated popular music into his works, for example in the six-part series *Pennies from Heaven*, in which the action is interrupted by songs lip-mimed by the characters. Something similar happened in *The Singing Detective*.

New drugs enabled him to produce, direct, and narrate his four-part *Blackeyes* 1989, about the sexual exploitation of a model by the advertising-industry. In addition to over 30 plays and series, Potter wrote screenplays for Hollywood and four novels.

It is said that the effect of eating too much lettuce is 'soporific'.

BEATRIX POTTER
Tale of the Flopsy Bunnies 1909

Potter (Helen) Beatrix (1866–1943). English writer and illustrator of children's books. Her first little book was *The Tale of Peter Rabbit* 1900, followed by *The Tailor of Gloucester* 1902, based on her observation of family pets and wildlife around her home in the English Lake District. Her tales are told with a childlike wonder, devoid of sentimentality, and accompanied by delicate illustrations. Other books in the series include *The Tale of Mrs Tiggy Winkle* 1904, *The Tale of Jeremy Fisher* 1906, and a sequel to Peter Rabbit, *The Tale of the Flopsy Bunnies* 1909. She grew up in London but was a self-taught naturalist. Her diaries, written in a secret code, were translated and published 1966. Her Lake District home is now a museum.

Potter was also an accomplished mycologist. She was the first person to report the symbiotic relationship between lichen and fungi, and to catalogue the fungi of the British Isles. She was excluded from professional scientific societies because of her sex.

Suggested reading
Hobbs, A S *Beatrix Potter's Art* (1990)
Lane, Margaret *The Tale of Beatrix Potter* (1968)
MacDonald, R K *Beatrix Potter* (1986)
Potter, Beatrix (ed L Linder) *The Journals of Beatrix Potter* (1990)

Potter Paulus (1625–1654). Dutch painter and etcher. He was active in Delft, The Hague, and Amsterdam. He specialized in rural scenes; his paintings of animals include *The Young Bull* 1647 (Mauritshuis, The Hague).

A good general rule is to state that the bouquet is better than the taste, and vice versa.

STEPHEN POTTER
One-Upmanship ch 14 1952

Potter Stephen Meredith (1900–1969). English author. He wrote humorous studies in how to outwit and outshine others, including *Gamesmanship* 1947, *Lifemanship* 1950, and *One Upmanship* 1952.

Poulenc Francis Jean Marcel (1899–1963). French composer and pianist. A self-taught composer of witty and irreverent music, he was a member of the group of French composers known as *Les Six*. Among his many works are the operas *Les Mamelles de Tirésias/The Breasts of Tiresias* 1947 and *Dialogues des Carmélites/Dialogues of the Carmelites* 1957, and the ballet *Les Biches/The Little Darlings* 1923.

My music is my portrait.

FRANCIS POULENC
quoted in Pierre Bernac *Francis Poulenc* 1977

Poulsen Valdemar (1869–1942). Danish engineer who in 1900 was the first to demonstrate that sound could be recorded magnetically – originally on a moving steel wire or tape; his device was the forerunner of the tape recorder.

Pound (Alfred) Dudley (Pickman Rogers) (1877–1943). British admiral of the fleet. As First Sea Lord and chief of the British naval staff 1939–43, he was responsible for the effective measures taken against the German submarine U-boats in World War II. KCB 1933.

His verve as a driver of motor-cars led occasionally to remonstrances addressed to the First Sea Lord from the chief commissioner of police.

R V Brockman on DUDLEY POUND
in *Dictionary of National Biography*

Pound Ezra Loomis (1885–1972). US poet and cultural critic. He is regarded as one of the most important figures of 20th-century literature, and his work revolutionized modern poetry. His *Personae* and *Exultations* 1909 established and promoted the principles of Imagism, and influenced numerous poets, including T S Eliot. His largest work was his series of *Cantos* 1925–69 (intended to number 100), a highly complex, eclectic collage, which sought to create a unifying, modern cultural tradition.

He lived in London 1909–21 and then moved to Paris 1921–25, where he became a friend of the writers Gertrude Stein and Ernest Hemingway. He then settled in Rapallo, Italy. His anti-Semitism and sympathy with the fascist dictator Mussolini led him to broadcast from Italy in World War II, and he was arrested by US troops 1945. Found unfit to stand trial, he was confined in a mental hospital until 1958. His first completely modern poem was 'Hugh Selwyn Mauberley' 1920. He also wrote versions of Old English, Provençal, Chinese, ancient Egyptian, and other verse.
Suggested reading
Brocker, P *A Student's Guide to the Selected Poems of Ezra Pound* (1979)
Conrad, Peter *Ezra Pound and his World* (1980)
Flory, W S *The American Ezra Pound* (1989)
Kenner, Hugh *The Pound Era* (1971)
Kenner, Hugh *The Poetry of Ezra Pound* (1985)
Stock, Noel *The Life of Ezra Pound* (1970)
Tytell, J *Ezra Pound* (1987)

Pound Roscoe (1870–1964). US jurist. He was the leading exponent of what became known as sociological jurisprudence: the idea that the law must be sufficiently flexible to take into account social realities in order to provide the maximum of people's wants with the minimum of friction and waste. He regarded this as a form of social engineering that required the balancing of competing interests, classified as individual, public, and social interests. His main published work is the five-volume *Jurisprudence*.

Poussin Nicolas (1594–1665). French painter. Active chiefly in Rome, he was also court painter to Louis XIII 1640–43. He was the foremost exponent of 17th-century Baroque Classicism. He painted mythological and literary scenes in a strongly Classical style; for example, *Et in Arcadia Ego* 1638–39 (Louvre, Paris).

Among his great works are *The Inspiration of the Poet*, 1636 (Louvre), *Bacchanalian Festival*, painted for Richelieu before 1641 (National Gallery, London), *The Arcadian Shepherds*, 1638–39 (Louvre), *Diogenes throwing away the Cup*, 1648 (Louvre), and *The Entombment* (National Gallery of Ireland). A superb self-portrait at the age of 56 is in the Louvre.
Suggested reading
Blunt, Anthony *Poussin* (1967–68)
Friedlaender, W *Nicolas Poussin: A New Approach* (1966)
Wright, C *French Painters of the 17th Century* (1986)

The excellence of the painting depended less on rules of art than on great genius.

Philippe de Champaigne on NICOLAS POUSSIN
in a lecture at the Royal Academy of Painting and Sculpture
7 Jan 1668 (referring to *Rebecca and Eleazer* by Poussin)

Powell Adam Clayton, Jr (1908–1972). US political leader. A leader of New York's black community, he was elected to the city council 1941. He was appointed to the US Congress 1944, and later became chair of the House Education and Labor Committee. Following charges of corruption, he was denied his seat in Congress 1967. Re-elected 1968, he won back his seniority by a 1969 decision of the US Supreme Court.

Powell Anthony Dymoke (1905–   ). English novelist. He wrote the series of 12 volumes *A Dance to the Music of Time* 1951–75 that begins shortly after World War I and chronicles a period of 50 years in the lives of Nicholas Jenkins and his circle of upper-class friends.

He fell in love with himself at first sight and it is a passion to which he has always remained faithful.

ANTHONY POWELL
Acceptance World 1955

Powell Cecil Frank (1903–1969). English physicist who investigated the charged subatomic particles in cosmic radiation by using photographic emulsions carried in weather balloons. This led to his discovery of the pion (π meson) 1947, a particle whose existence had been predicted by Japanese physicist Hideki Yukawa 1935. He collaborated with Italian physicist Giuseppe Occhialini (1907–   ), and together they published *Nuclear Physics in Photographs* 1947, which became a standard text on the subject. Powell was awarded a Nobel prize 1950.

Powell was born in Tonbridge, Kent, and studied at Cambridge, where he carried out research at the Cavendish Laboratory under Ernest Rutherford and C T R Wilson, taking photographs of particle tracks in a cloud chamber. From 1928 Powell worked at the Wills Physics Laboratory at Bristol University, becoming professor 1948.

Powell Colin Luther (1937–   ). US general, chair of the Joint Chiefs of Staff from 1989–93 and, as such, responsible for the overall administration of the Allied forces in Saudi Arabia during the Gulf War 1991. A Vietnam War veteran, he first worked in government 1972 and was national security adviser 1987–89. Following intense media speculation, in Nov 1995 Powell announced that he would not seek the Republican party's presidential nomination in 1996, citing family reasons.

Powell was born in New York, the son of Jamaican immigrants; he joined the army in the 1950s, was sent to Vietnam 1962 and volunteered to return 1968. He worked for Caspar Weinberger and Frank Carlucci at the Office of Management and Budget 1972, before being posted to Korea 1973.

He returned to Washington as assistant to Carlucci at the Defense Department 1981–83 and as adviser to Weinberger 1983–86 and was promoted to general. After a year in West Germany he was recalled to Washington following the Irangate scandal, first as assistant to Carlucci and then replacing him as national security adviser. In 1989 he was made a four-star general and chair of the Joint Chiefs of Staff, a position from which he retired 1993.

As I look ahead, I am filled with foreboding. Like the Roman, I seem to see 'the River Tiber foaming with much blood'.

ENOCH POWELL
Speech at Conservative Political Centre, Birmingham 20 Apr 1968

Powell (John) Enoch (1912–). British Conservative politician. He was professor of Greek at the University of Sydney, Australia 1937–39 when he resigned to enter the British army, becoming its youngest brigadier 1944 at the age of 32. At the end of World War II he joined the Conservative Party Research department. He was an MP for Wolverhampton from 1950. He was minister of health 1960–63, and contested the party leadership 1965. In 1968 he made a speech against immigration that led to his dismissal from the shadow cabinet. He resigned from the party 1974, and was Official Unionist Party member for South Down, Northern Ireland 1974–87.

Powell John Wesley (1834–1902). US geologist whose enormous and original studies produced lasting insights into erosion by rivers, volcanism, and mountain formation. His greatness as a geologist and geomorphologist stemmed from his capacity to grasp the interconnections of geological and climatic causes.

Powell was born in New York State and self-educated. In the 1850s he became secretary of the Illinois Society of Natural History. Fighting in the Civil War, he had his right arm shot off, but continued in the service, rising to the rank of colonel. After the end of the war, Powell became professor of geology in Illinois, while continuing with intrepid fieldwork (he was one of the first to steer a way down the Grand Canyon).

In 1870, Congress appointed Powell to lead an official survey of the natural resources of the Utah, Colorado, and Arizona area. Powell was appointed director of the US Geological Survey 1881. He drew attention to the aridity of the American southwest, and campaigned for irrigation projects and dams, for the geological surveys necessary to implement adequate water strategies, and for changes in land policy and farming techniques. Failing to win political support on such matters, he resigned in 1894 from the Geological Survey.

Powell Lewis Stanley (1907–). US jurist. He practised in Virginia, becoming president of the American Bar Association 1964–65 and president of the American College of Trial Lawyers 1968–69. He was associate justice of the US Supreme Court 1971–87 under President Nixon. A conservative, Powell voted to restrict Fifth Amendment guarantees against self-incrimination and for capital punishment. In *United States* v *Nixon* 1974, he sided with the majority in limiting executive privilege. He retired from the Court 1987 for health reasons.

Powell Michael Latham (1905–1990). English film director and producer. Some of his most memorable films were made in collaboration with Hungarian screenwriter Emeric Pressburger. The two men formed a company, the Archers, 1942, which engaged provocatively with British cultural and ethical values. They produced a succession of ambitious and richly imaginative films, including *A Matter of Life and Death* 1946, *Black Narcissus* 1947, and *The Red Shoes* 1948. Powell's films range from *The Life and Death of Colonel Blimp* 1943 to the opera movie *The Tales of Hoffman* 1951, but after the partnership with Pressburger was amicably dissolved, he went on to make generally less rewarding films. The most distinctive was the voyeuristic horror story *Peeping Tom* 1960. He was the author of several books, including his autobiography *A Life in Movies* 1986.

Powell Mike (1963–). US long jumper who in 1991 broke US athlete Bob Beamon's world long-jump record of 8.90 m (which had stood since 1968) with a leap of 8.95 m. At the same time, he dealt Carl Lewis his first long-jump defeat since 1981. Powell also topped the world long-jump rankings in 1990.

Powell William (1892–1984). US film actor. He co-starred with Myrna Loy in the *Thin Man* series 1934–47. He also played suave leading roles in *My Man Godfrey* 1936, *Life with Father* 1947, and *Mister Roberts* 1955. He retired 1955.

Powys John Cowper (1872–1963). English novelist. His mystic and erotic books include *Wolf Solent* 1929 and *A Glastonbury Romance* 1933. He was one of three brothers:

Theodore Francis Powys (1875–1953) is best known for the novel *Mr Weston's Good Wine* 1927, and the autobiography of Llewelyn Powys (1884–1939), *Skin for Skin*, was published 1925.

Poynter Edward John (1836–1919). English artist. He was the first head of the Slade School of Fine Art, London, 1871–75, and president of the Royal Academy in succession to John Everett Millais. He produced decorous nudes, mosaic panels for Westminster Palace 1870, and scenes from ancient Greece and Rome. Knighted 1896, baronet 1902.

Poynting John Henry (1852–1914). English physicist, mathematician, and inventor. He devised an equation by which the rate of flow of electromagnetic energy (now called the Poynting vector) can be determined. In 1891 he made an accurate measurement of Isaac Newton's gravitational constant.

From 1880 he was professor of physics at Mason College, Birmingham (which became Birmingham University in 1900).

In *On the Transfer of Energy in the Electromagnetic Field* 1884, Poynting published the equation by which the magnitude and direction of the flow of electromagnetic energy can be determined.

In 1903, he suggested the existence of an effect of the Sun's radiation that causes small particles orbiting the Sun to gradually approach it and eventually plunge in. This idea was later developed by US physicist Howard Percy Robertson (1903–1961) and is now known as the Poynting–Robertson effect. Poynting also devised a method for measuring the radiation pressure from a body; his method can be used to determine the absolute temperature of celestial objects.

Poynting's other work included a statistical analysis of changes in commodity prices on the stock exchange 1884.

Pozsgay Imre (1933–). Hungarian socialist politician, presidential candidate for the Hungarian Socialist Party from 1989. Pozsgay joined the ruling Hungarian Socialist Workers' Party (HSWP) 1950 and was a lecturer in Marxism-Leninism and an ideology chief in Bacs county 1957–70. He was minister of education and culture from 1976 before becoming head of the Patriotic People's Front umbrella organization 1982. Noted for his reformist social-democratic instincts, he was brought into the HSWP politburo in 1988 as a move towards political pluralism began. Having publicly declared that 'communism does not work', he helped remould the HSWP into the new Hungarian Socialist Party 1989 and was selected as its candidate for the presidency. Influential in the democratization of Hungary 1988–89, he was rejected by the electorate in the parliamentary elections of March 1990, coming a poor third in his constituency.

Prandtl Ludwig (1875–1953). German physicist who put fluid mechanics on a sound theoretical basis and originated the boundary-layer theory. His work in aerodynamics resulted in major changes in wing design and streamlining of aircraft.

In 1901 he became professor at the Technische Hochschule in Hanover; and from 1904 he was professor of applied mechanics at Göttingen. There he constructed the first German wind tunnel in 1909 and built up a centre for aerodynamics.

In a paper of 1904, Prandtl proposed that no matter how small the viscosity of a fluid, it is always stationary at the walls of the pipe. This thin static region or boundary layer has a profound influence on the flow of the fluid, and an understanding of the effects of boundary layers was developed to explain the action of lift and drag on aerofoils during the following half century. In 1907, Prandtl investigated supersonic flow.

In 1926, Prandtl developed the concept of mixing length – the average distance that a swirling fluid element travels before it dissipates its motion – and produced a theory of turbulence.

Prasad Rajendra (1884–1963). Indian politician. Prasad was trained as a lawyer, and was a loyal follower of Mahatma Gandhi. He was national president of the Indian National Congress several times between 1934 and 1948 and India's first president after independence 1950–62.

Praxiteles (lived mid-4th century BC). Greek sculptor. He was active in Athens. His *Aphrodite of Cnidus c.* 350 BC (known through Roman copies) is thought to have initiated the tradition of life-size free-standing female nudes in Greek sculpture. The works credited to him include the statue of Hermes carrying Dionysus.

The Merry Courtesan is believed to represent Phryne, and connoisseurs detect in the figure Praxiteles' love for her and the reward promised him by the expression on the courtesan's face.

Pliny the Elder on PRAXITELES
in *Natural History* bk 34, ch 70

Prelog Vladimir (1906–). Bosnian-born Swiss organic chemist who studied alkaloids and antibiotics. The comprehensive molecular topology that evolved from his work on stereochemistry is gradually replacing classical stereochemistry. He shared a Nobel prize 1975.

In 1935 he went back to Yugoslavia to lecture at Zagreb, but in 1941, after the German occupation at the beginning of World War II, Prelog moved to the Federal Institute of Technology, Zürich, where he became professor 1957.

Alkaloids were the subject of Prelog's early research, and he derived the structures of quinine, strychnine, and steroid alkaloids from plants of the genera *Solanum* and *Veratrum*. His studies of lipid extracts from animal organs also resulted in the discovery of various steroids and the elucidation of their structures. He investigated metabolic products of microorganisms and with a number of other researchers isolated various new complex natural products that have interesting biological properties. These include antibiotics and bacterial growth factors.

Premadasa Ranasinghe (1924–1993). Sri Lankan right-wing politician, prime minister 1978–88, president from 1988, having gained popularity through overseeing a major house-building and poverty-alleviation programme. He launched an initiative to provide universal housing and alleviate poverty. He also adopted a Sinhala nationalist stance 1987 and refused to support the Indo-Sri Lankan Accord signed by Jayawardene and Indian prime minister Rajiv Gandhi.

As president, Premadasa negotiated the Indian peacekeeping force's withdrawal from the northern Jaffna peninsula, and secured a 15-month ceasefire with the Tamil Tiger separatist forces. He sanctioned harsh action against the southern-based Marxist JVP movement, which cost at least 5,000 lives Aug–Sept 1989. These forthright actions brought back political stability and revived Sri Lanka's economy. Alienated by Premadasa's autocratic style, UNP rivals, including former national security minister Lalith Athulathmudali (also assassinated 1993) and Gamani Dissanayake, left to form the new Democratic United National Front. He was assassinated in office by a suicide bomber in the centre of Colombo; the Tamil Tigers denied responsibility.

Preminger Otto Ludwig (1906–1986). Austrian-born US film producer, director, and actor. His films include *Margin for Error* 1942, *Laura* 1944, *The Moon Is Blue* 1953, *The Man with the Golden Arm* 1955, *Anatomy of a Murder* 1959, *Advise and Consent* 1962, *Rosebud* 1974, and *The Human Factor* 1980. His films are characterized by an intricate technique of storytelling and a masterly use of the wide screen and the travelling camera.

Prendergast Maurice Brazil (1859–1924). US painter. His early youth was spent in Boston but he went to Paris 1886, studying at the Académie Julian. He was influenced by *les Nabis*, notably Pierre Bonnard and Edouard Vuillard. He also worked in Italy for some time before settling in New York. In his use of colour he advanced towards the Post-Impressionist standpoint, and he is of note among the pioneer observers of city life. He created a decorative style in watercolours and in oils, using small translucent pools of colour. His work was inspired by Impressionism and Post-Impressionism. *Umbrellas in the Rain, Venice* 1899 (Museum of Fine Arts, Boston) is typical.

Prescott John Leslie (1938–). British Labour Party politician, deputy leader from 1994. A former merchant sailor and trade-union official, he was member of parliament for Kingston-on-Hull (East) 1970–83 and MP for Hull East from 1983. In 1975, he became a member of the European Parliament, despite being opposed to Britain's membership of the European Community. A strong parliamentary debater and television performer, he was sometimes critical of his colleagues. He unsuccessfully challenged for the leadership 1988 and 1992, but was finally elected deputy leader 1994, after losing to Anthony Blair in the contest.

Prescott William Hickling (1796–1859). US historian, author of *History of the Reign of Ferdinand and Isabella, the Catholic* 1838, *History of the Conquest of Mexico* 1843, and *History of the Conquest of Peru* 1847.

He narrates events with considerable skill, but the causes of the events ... he does not appreciate. He tells the fact for the fact's sake.

Theodore Parker on WILLIAM HICKLING PRESCOTT
in *The American Scholar*

Presley Elvis Aron (1935–1977). US singer and guitarist, the most influential performer of the rock-and-roll era. With his recordings for Sun Records in Memphis, Tennessee, 1954–55 and early hits such as 'Heartbreak Hotel', 'Hound Dog', and 'Love Me Tender', all 1956, he created an individual vocal style, influenced by Southern blues, gospel music, country music, and rhythm and blues. His records continued to sell in their millions into the 1990s.

Presley was born in Tupelo, Mississippi. His first records were regional hits in the South, and he became a nationwide star 1956, Sun having sold his recording contract to RCA at the instigation of his new manager, the self-styled Colonel Tom Parker (1909–), a former carnival huckster. Of the four films Presley made in the 1950s, *Loving You* 1957 and *Jailhouse Rock* 1957 offer glimpses of the electrifying stage performer he then was. After his army service 1958–60, the album *Elvis Is Back* 1960 and some gospel-music recordings made that year were outstanding, but from then on his work deteriorated quickly. Parker pushed him into a demeaning career divided between Hollywood and Las Vegas. By the time of his death, Presley had long been a caricature. His early contribution to rock music was, however, inestimable, and his Memphis home, Graceland, draws millions of visitors each year.

Suggested reading
Cotton, L *All Shook Up* (1985)
Gibson, R and Shaw, S *Elvis* (1987)
Goldman, Albert *Elvis* (1981)
Guralnick, Peter *Last Train to Memphis: The Rise of Elvis Presley* (1994)
Hopkins, Jerry *Elvis: The Final Years* (1981)
Sauer, W *Elvis Presley* (1984)

Pressburger Emeric (1902–1988). Hungarian film producer, screenwriter, and director. He was known for his partnership with Michael Powell. Forming the production company the Archers 1942, Powell and Pressburger collaborated on 14 films between 1942 and 1956, such as *The Red Shoes* 1948.

Prester John Legendary Christian prince. During the 12th and 13th centuries, Prester John was believed to be the ruler of a powerful empire in Asia. From the 14th to the 16th century, he was generally believed to be the king of Abyssinia (now Ethiopia) in NE Africa.

Suggested reading
Rachewiltz, Igor de *Prester John and Europe's Discovery of East Asia* (1972)
Silverberg, Robert *The Realm of Prester John* (1972)

Preston Margaret Rose (1875–1963). Australian painter, wood engraver, and linocut artist whose style was influenced by Aboriginal bark paintings. Her still lifes, characterized by strong, simple shapes, feature Australian flora and she is also known for a series of woodcuts of Sydney Harbour scenes.

Preston Peter John (1938–). British newspaper editor and executive. In 1975 he became editor of the moderate left-wing daily *Guardian* and from 1988 he was also its company chair.

Previn André George (1929–). German-born US conductor and composer. After early success as a composer and arranger for film, he studied conducting with Pierre Monteux 1951. He was principal conductor of the London Symphony Orchestra 1968–79 and was appointed music director of Britain's Royal Philharmonic Orchestra 1985 (a post he relinquished the following year, staying on as principal conductor until 1991). He was also principal conductor of the Los Angeles Philharmonic 1986–89 and is now a guest conductor of many orchestras in Europe and the USA. His compositions include concertos for piano 1971 and guitar 1984; he has conducted Gershwin and Mozart concertos from the keyboard and recorded many US and British composers. Knighted 1996.

Prévost Pierre (1751–1839). Swiss physicist who first showed, in 1791, that all bodies radiate heat, no matter how hot or cold they are. In challenging the notion then prevalent that cold was produced by the entry of cold into an object rather than by an outflow of heat, Prévost made a basic advance in our knowledge of energy.

Prévost was born in Geneva and studied and travelled widely. For a year he was professor of literature at Geneva, then worked in Paris on the translation of a Greek drama. Returning to Geneva 1786, he became active in politics as well as carrying out research into magnetism and heat. He was professor of philosophy and general physics at Geneva 1793–1823. In his later years, Prévost chose to study the human ageing process. He used himself for his observations, noting down in detail every sign of advancement that his mind, body, and mirror showed.

Previn *The conductor and pianist André Previn. He has had a long-lasting relationship with the London Symphony Orchestra, currently holding the position of Conductor Laureate. His many recordings include persuasive accounts of English music.*

Prévost found by experiment that dark, rough-textured objects give out and absorb more radiation than smooth, light-coloured bodies, given that both are at the same temperature. He conceived of heat as being a fluid composed of particles and this led to Prévost's theory of heat exchanges. If several objects at different temperatures are placed together, they exchange heat by radiation until all achieve the same temperature. They then remain at this temperature if they are receiving as much heat from their surroundings as they radiate away.

Prévost d'Exiles Antoine François (1697–1763). French novelist. Known as Abbé Prévost, he combined a military career with his life as a monk. His *Manon Lescaut* 1731 inspired operas by Massenet and Puccini.

Price Leontyne (1927–). US opera singer. She played a leading singing role in Ira Gershwin's revival of his musical *Porgy and Bess* 1952–54. Gaining a national reputation, she made her operatic debut in San Francisco 1957. She appeared at La Scala in Milan 1959 and became a regular member of the Metropolitan Opera in New York 1961.

Price Vincent (1911–1993). US actor. He made his film debut 1938 after a stage career. His gift for both Gothic grandiosity and judicious self-parody made him a popular star of horror films. He made his mark on the genre in *House of Wax* 1953, and later starred in a succession of free adaptations from Edgar Allan Poe made by Roger Corman 1960–64, including *The House of Usher* 1960 and *The Pit and the Pendulum* 1961. Price also played several non-horror roles, such as that of a gigolo in *Laura* 1944, and *Leave Her To Heaven* 1945. More recently he appeared in *The Whales of August* 1987 and *Edward Scissorhands* 1991.

Prichard Katharine Susannah (1884–1969). Australian novelist, short-story writer, and poet, born in Fiji. She is best known for her novels which include *Working Bullocks* 1926, about timber workers in Western Australia, *Coonardoo* 1929, dealing with the relationship between a white man and an Aboriginal woman, and the goldfields trilogy *The Roaring Nineties* 1946, *Golden Miles* 1948, and *Winged Seeds* 1950. She was a founding and lifelong member of the Communist Party of Australia.

Priestley J(ohn) B(oynton) (1894–1984). English novelist and playwright. His first success was a novel about travelling theatre, *The Good Companions* 1929. He followed it with a realist novel about London life, *Angel Pavement* 1930. As a playwright he was often preoccupied with theories of time, as in *An Inspector Calls* 1945.

Priestley had a gift for family comedy, for example, the play *When We Are Married* 1938. He was also known for his wartime broadcasts and literary criticism, such as *Literature and Western Man* 1960. Later novels include *Lost Empires* 1965 and *The Image Men* 1968.

Most of us could do with a smaller, plainer, more companionable world.

J B PRIESTLEY
Delight ch 105 1949

Priestley Joseph (1733–1804). English chemist and Unitarian minister. He identified oxygen 1774 and several other gases. Dissolving carbon dioxide under pressure in water, he began a European craze for soda water. Swedish chemist Karl Scheele independently prepared oxygen in 1772, but his tardiness in publication resulted in Priestley being credited with the discovery.

Priestley discovered nitric oxide (nitrogen monoxide, NO) 1772 and reduced it to nitrous oxide (dinitrogen monoxide, N_2O). In the same year he became the first person to isolate gaseous ammonia by collecting it over mercury (previously ammonia was known only in aqueous solution). In 1774 he found a method for producing sulphur dioxide (SO_2).

Priestley was born near Leeds and became a cleric; as a Dissenter, he was barred from English universities. A meeting with US polymath Benjamin Franklin 1766 aroused his interest in science. As librarian and literary companion to Lord Shelburne 1773–80, Priestley accompanied him to France in 1774 and there met chemist Antoine Lavoisier. Priestley moved to Birmingham 1780 and joined the Lunar Society, an association of inventors and scientists that included James Watt, Matthew Boulton, Josiah Wedgwood, and Erasmus Darwin. In 1791 Priestley's chapel and house were sacked by a mob because of his support for the French Revolution. He fled to London, then emigrated to the USA 1794, settling in Pennsylvania.

Priestley's early work was in physics, particularly electricity and optics. He established that electrostatic charge is concentrated on the outer surface of a charged body and that there is no internal force. From this observation he proposed an inverse square law for charges, by analogy with gravitation.

Suggested reading
Gibbs, F W *Joseph Priestley: Adventurer in Science and Champion of Truth* (1965)

Gillam, John *The Crucible: The Story of Joseph Priestley* (1954)

Kieft, Lester and Willeford, Bennett R, Jr (eds) *Joseph Priestley: Scientist, Theologian, and Metaphysician* (1979)

Priestley, Joseph *Autobiography of Joseph Priestley* (1806, ed Jack Lindsay 1976)

Prigogine Ilya, Viscount Prigogine (1917–). Russian-born Belgian chemist who, as a highly original theoretician, has made major contributions to the field of thermodynamics. Earlier theories had considered systems at or about equilibrium; Prigogine began to study 'dissipative' or nonequilibrium structures frequently found in biological and chemical reactions. Nobel Prize for Physics 1977. Viscount 1989.

Prigogine was born in Moscow. He studied at Brussels and became professor there 1951, and in 1959 director of the Instituts Internationaux de Physique et de Chemie. He was professor at the Enrico Fermi Institute at the University of Chicago 1961–66, and from 1967 director of the Center for Statistical Mechanics and Thermodynamics at the University of Texas in Austin, concurrently with his professorship in Brussels.

When Prigogine began studying dissipative systems in the 1940s, it was not understood how a more orderly system, such as a living creature, could arise spontaneously and maintain itself despite the universal tendency towards disorder. It is now known that order can be created and preserved by processes that flow 'uphill' in the thermodynamic sense, compensated by 'downhill' events. Dissipative systems can exist only in harmony with their surroundings. Close to equilibrium, their order tends to be destroyed.

These ideas have been applied to examine how life originated on Earth, to ecosystems, to the preservation of world resources, and even to the prevention of traffic jams.

Primaticcio Francesco (1504–1570). Italian Mannerist painter, sculptor, architect, and decorator. He was influential in the development of the Fontainebleau School in France. He learnt his skills under Giulio Romano in the Palazzo del Tè at Mantua. Summoned to France by François I 1532, he worked with Rosso at Fontainebleau, developing an innovatory combination of painting and stucco work.

A genial eccentric with a Falstaffian approach to political life, he governed by a form of personal improvisation which ensured that he bore the blame for his regime's failures.

Paula Preston on PRIMO DE RIVERA
in *Spanish Civil War* 1986

Primo de Rivera Miguel, Marqués de Estella (1870–1930). Spanish soldier and politician, dictator from 1923 as well as premier from 1925. He was captain-general of Catalonia when he led a coup against the ineffective monarchy and became virtual dictator of Spain with the support of Alfonso XIII. He resigned 1930.

Primus Pearl (1919–1994). US dancer, choreographer, and dance teacher who pioneered an awareness and understanding of the

African American tradition in dance. Primus was born in Trinidad and raised in the USA. As a medical student unable to find a laboratory job, she applied to the national Youth Administration and was directed into dance. She studied contemporary technique at the New Dance Group School as well as with Martha Graham and Charles Weidman. When she made her professional debut as a dancer and choreographer 1943, including then unusual African themes in her programme, she immediately received critical acclaim. Primus also looked at contemporary black American experience; early dances include her solo *Strange Fruit*, in which a woman reacts to a lynching, as well as *The Negro speaks of Rivers*, based on a poem by Langston Hughes.

Prince former stage name of Prince Rogers Nelson (1959–). US pop musician. He composes, arranges, and produces his own records and often plays all the instruments. His albums, including *1999* 1982 and *Purple Rain* 1984, contain elements of rock, funk, and jazz. His stage shows are energetic and extravagant. Prince has now changed his name to a symbol.

His band the Revolution broke up after four years 1986. His hits include 'Little Red Corvette' from *1999*, 'Kiss' from *Parade* 1986, and 'Sign O' the Times' from the album of the same name 1987. He has also starred in several films, including *Graffiti Bridge* 1990. His home town of Minneapolis, Minnesota, has become a centre for recording as a result of his success.

Prince Hal (Harold Smith) (1928–). US director of musicals. He directed, among others, *Cabaret* 1968 and *Follies* 1971 on Broadway in New York, and *Evita* 1978 and *Sweeney Todd* 1980 in London's West End.

Prince Imperial title of ◊Eugène, son of Emperor Napoleon III of France.

Pringsheim Ernst (1859–1917). German physicist whose experimental work on the nature of thermal radiation led directly to the quantum theory. In 1881 he developed a spectrometer that made the first accurate measurements of wavelengths in the infrared region. He was professor at Berlin 1896–1905 and at Breslau from 1905.

Pringsheim began in 1896 to collaborate with Otto Lummer on a study of black-body radiation. This led to a verification of the Stefan–Boltzmann law that relates the energy radiated by a body to its absolute temperature, but in 1899 they found anomalies in laws that had been devised to express the energy of the radiation in terms of its frequency and temperature. The results encouraged Max Planck to find a new radiation law that would account for the experimental results and in 1900, Planck arrived at such a law by assuming that the energy of the radiation consists of indivisible units that he called quanta. This marked the founding of the quantum theory.

Prior James Michael Leathes, Baron Prior (1927–). British Conservative politician. He held ministerial posts from 1970. As employment secretary he curbed trade-union activity with the Employment Act 1980, and was Northern Ireland secretary 1981–84. After his resignation 1984 he became chair of the General Electric Company. Baron 1987.

Prior Matthew (1664–1721). British poet and diplomat. He was associated under the Whigs with the negotiation of the treaty of Ryswick 1697 ending the war with France and under the Tories with that of Utrecht 1714 ('Matt's Peace') ending the War of the Spanish Succession, but on the Whigs' return to power he was imprisoned by the government leader Walpole 1715–17. His gift as a poet was for light occasional verses.

Cur'd yesterday of my disease, / I died last night of my physician.

MATTHEW PRIOR
'The Remedy Worse than the Disease'

Pritchett V(ictor) S(awdon) (1900–). English short-story writer, novelist, and critic. His style is often witty and satirical. His short stories were gathered in *Collected Stories* 1982 and *More Collected Stories* 1983. His critical works include *The Living Novel* 1946 and biographies of the Russian writers Turgenev 1977 and Chekhov 1988. His *Complete Short Stories* was published 1990. Knighted 1975.

Procopius (*c.* 495–565). Greek historian. As secretary to Justinian's general, Belisarius, he wrote a history of the campaigns of the Eastern Roman Empire against the Goths and the Vandals. He also wrote extensively on architecture, and was the author of *The Secret History*, a relatively scandalous account of the leading figures of the age.

Profumo John Dennis (1915–). British Conservative politician, secretary of state for war from 1960 to June 1963, when he resigned on the disclosure of his involvement with Christine Keeler, mistress also of a Soviet naval attaché. In 1982 Profumo became administrator of the social and educational settlement Toynbee Hall in London.

Prokhorov Aleksandr Mikhailovich (1916–). Russian physicist whose fundamental work on microwaves with Nikolai Basov led to the construction of the first practical maser (the microwave equivalent of the laser). They shared the 1964 Nobel Prize for Physics with Charles Townes.

I have to hear the Russian language echoing in my ear, I have to speak to people so that they give me back what I lack here; their songs, my songs.

SERGEY PROKOFIEV
quoted in Wolfgang Stahr *Notes on Piano Concertos* 1993

Prokofiev Sergey Sergeyevich (1891–1953). Soviet composer. Born near Ekaterinoslav, he studied at St Petersburg under Rimsky-Korsakov and achieved fame as a pianist. He left Russia 1918 and lived for some time in the USA and in Paris, but returned 1927 and again 1935. His music includes operas such as *The Love for Three Oranges* 1921; ballets for Sergei Diaghilev, including *Romeo and Juliet* 1935; seven symphonies including the *Classical Symphony* 1916–17; music for film, including Eisenstein's *Alexander Nevsky* 1938; piano and violin concertos; songs and cantatas (for example, that composed for the 30th anniversary of the October Revolution); and *Peter and the Wolf* 1936 for children, to his own libretto after a Russian folk tale. Prokofiev was essentially a classicist in his use of form, but his extensive and varied output demonstrates great lyricism, humour, and skill.

Suggested reading
Gutman, D *Prokofiev* (1988)
Hanson, Lawrence and Elisabeth *Prokofiev: The Prodigal Son* (1964)
Prokofiev, S *Sergei Prokofiev: Materials, Article, Interviews* (1978)
Prokofiev, S *Prokofiev by Prokofiev: A Composer's Memoirs* (1979)
Robinson, H *Sergei Prokofiev* (1984)

Propertius Sextus (*c.* 47–15 BC). Roman elegiac poet. A member of Maecenas' circle, he is best known for his highly personal love poems addressed to his mistress 'Cynthia'.

Prost Alain Marie Pascal (1955–). French motor-racing driver who was world champion 1985, 1986, 1989, and 1993, and the first French world drivers' champion. To the end of the 1993 season he had won 51 Grand Prix from 199 starts. He retired 1993.

He raced in Formula One events from 1980 and had his first Grand Prix win in France 1981, driving a Renault. In 1984 he began driving for the McLaren team. He moved to Ferrari in 1990 for two years but was without a drive at the start of the 1992 season. He drove for Williams 1993, winning his fourth world championship before finally retiring at the end of the season. He is known as 'the Professor'.

Proudhon Pierre Joseph (1809–1865). French anarchist, born in Besançon. He sat in the Constituent Assembly of 1848, was imprisoned for three years, and had to go into exile in Brussels. He published *Qu'est-ce que la propriété/What is Property?* 1840 and *Philosophie de la misère/Philosophy of Poverty* 1846.

Suggested reading
Hoffman, R L *Revolutionary Justice: The Social and Political Theory of Pierre-Joseph Proudhon* (1971)
Hyams, Edward *Pierre-Joseph Proudhon: His Revolutionary Life, Mind and Works* (1979)
Woodcock, George *Pierre-Joseph Proudhon: His Life and Work* (1972)

Property is theft.

PIERRE JOSEPH PROUDHON
What is Property? 1840

Proust Joseph Louis (1754–1826). French chemist. He was the first to state the principle of constant composition of compounds – that compounds consist of the same proportions of elements wherever found.

Proust was born in Angers and trained as an apothecary. In the 1780s he went to Spain and spent the next 20 years in Madrid. He taught at various academies and carried out his research in a laboratory provided by his patron, King Charles IV of Spain. In 1808, Napoleon invaded Spain and French soldiers wrecked Proust's laboratory. He returned to France a poor man.

French chemist Claude Berthollet had stated that the composition of compounds could vary, depending on the proportions of reactants used to produce them. In 1799 Proust prepared and analysed copper carbonate produced in various ways and compared the results with those obtained by analysing mineral deposits of the same substance; he found that they all had the same composition. Similar results with other compounds led Proust to propose the law of constant composition. After a long controversy Berthollet conceded that Proust was right.

A work of art that contains theories is like an object on which the price tag has been left.

MARCEL PROUST
Remembrance of Things Past: 'Time Regained' 1913–27

Proust Marcel (1871–1922). French novelist and critic. Born at Auteuil, Proust was a delicate, asthmatic child; until he was 35 he moved in the fashionable circles of Parisian society, but after the death of his parents 1904–05 he went into seclusion in a cork-lined room in his apartment, and devoted the rest of his life to writing his masterpiece. His immense autobiographical work *A la Recherche du temps perdu/Remembrance of Things Past* 1913–27, consisting of a series of novels, is the expression of his childhood memories coaxed from his subconscious; it is also a precise reflection of life in France at the end of the 19th century.

Suggested reading
Hayman, Ronald *Proust* (1990)
Hindus, M *A Reader's Guide to Marcel Proust* (1962)
Hughes, E *Marcel Proust* (1984)
Maurois, André *Proust* (trs 1984)
May, Derwent *Proust* (1983)
Painter, George *Marcel Proust: A Biography* (1959–65)
Shattuck, Roger *Marcel Proust* (1974)

Prout William (1785–1850). British physician and chemist. In 1815 Prout published his hypothesis that the relative atomic mass of every atom is an exact and integral multiple of the mass of the hydrogen atom. The discovery of isotopes (atoms of the same element that have different masses) in the 20th century bore out his idea.

In 1827, Prout became the first scientist to classify the components of food into the three major divisions of carbohydrates, fats, and proteins.

He set up a medical practice in London and established a private chemical laboratory. From 1813 he wrote about and gave lectures in 'animal chemistry'.

Studying various natural secretions and products, Prout became convinced that they derive from the chemical breakdown of body tissues. In 1818, he isolated urea and uric acid for the first time, and six years later he found hydrochloric acid in digestive juices from the stomach.

In his anonymous paper of 1815, Prout concluded, from the determinations of atomic weights that had been made, that hydrogen was the basic building block of matter. In 1920 Ernest Rutherford named the proton – the hydrogen nucleus, which is a constituent of every atomic nucleus – after Prout.

Prout also studied the gases of the atmosphere and in 1832 made accurate measurements of the density of air. The Royal Society adopted his design for a barometer as the national standard.

Prud'hon Pierre Paul (1758–1823). French Romantic painter. He became drawing instructor and court painter to the wives of the emperor Napoleon.

After winning the Prix de Rome 1784, Prud'hon visited Italy but, unlike his contemporary Jacques-Louis David, he was unaffected by the Neo-Classical vogue; his style is indebted to the Italian painter Correggio.

In classical subjects he was voluptuous rather than sculptural, this causing David to describe him as the 'Boucher of our time'. He was patronized by the imperial family (and designed the cradle of the king of Rome), but his life was a sad one, an early and unfortunate marriage causing him years of misery, while his attachment to his pupil, Constance Mayer, ended, to his inconsolable grief, in her suicide. Notable works are his portrait of the Empress Josephine at Malmaison, 1805 (Louvre), *Psyche transported by the Zephyrs*, 1808 (Louvre), and *Justice and Divine Vengeance pursuing Crime*, 1808, commissioned for the hall of the criminal court in the Palais de Justice, and now in the Louvre. An artist of the transition from the 18th to the 19th century, he seems a Romantic in his emotionalism.

Plenty is the child of peace.

WILLIAM PRYNNE
Histriomastix act 1 sc 1 1632

Prynne William (1600–1669). English Puritan. He published in 1632 *Histriomastix*, a work attacking stage plays; it contained aspersions on the Queen, Henrietta Maria, for which he was pilloried and lost his ears. In 1637 he was again pilloried and branded for an attack on the bishops. He opposed the execution of Charles I, and actively supported the Restoration.

Pryor Richard (1940–). US comedian, film actor, and screenwriter. His acutely observed character monologues, peppered with profanities, and searing indictments of racial and social hypocrisies made Pryor one of the foremost comedians of his generation. He co-scripted *Blazing Saddles* 1974 with Mel Brooks, and formed an acting partnership with Gene Wilder (1935–) in a series of comedy 'buddy movies' including *Silver Streak* 1976 and *Stir Crazy* 1980. His film career, however, has never matched the potent impact of his stand-up routines, captured in such filmed live performances as *Richard Pryor – Live in Concert* 1979 and *Richard Pryor – Live on Sunset Strip* 1982.

As a comedian, Pryor used his highly volatile personal life as prime subject matter for his act, including his heart attacks, his drug abuse, and brushes with the police. As an actor, his first memorable role was in *Lady Sings the Blues* 1972, followed by roles in *Uptown Saturday Night* 1974, and *Car Wash* 1976. He also appeared in *Superman III* 1983. He directed *Richard Pryor Here and Now* 1983, one of his four filmed live performances; and the semi-autobiographical *Jo Jo Dancer, Your Life is Calling* 1986. Pryor has also won several Grammy awards for his comedy albums.

Przhevalsky Nikolai Mikhailovitch (1839–1888). Russian explorer and soldier. In 1870 he crossed the Gobi Desert to Beijing and then went on to the upper reaches of the Chang Jiang River. His attempts to penetrate Tibet as far as Lhasa failed on three occasions, but he continued to explore the mountain regions between Tibet and Mongolia, where he made collections of plants and animals, including

a wild camel and a wild horse (the species is now known as *Przhevalsky's horse*).

The Kirghiz town of Karakol on the eastern shores of Lake Issyk Kul where he died was renamed Przhevalsky in 1889.

Psellus Michael Constantine (*c.* 1018–*c.* 1079). Byzantine academician, philosopher, administrator, historian, and poet. A voluminous writer on almost all academic subjects from physics to jurisprudence, Psellus was strongly influenced by neo-Platonism and the earlier Christian writers. His many letters offer a remarkable insight into the society of his time.

A dead man does not bite.

PTOLEMY
on the need to kill Pompey. Quoted in Plutarch *Life of Pompey* ch 77.4

Ptolemy (Claudius Ptolemaeus) (*c.* AD 100–*c.* 170). Egyptian astronomer and geographer. His *Almagest* developed the theory that Earth is the centre of the universe, with the Sun, Moon, and stars revolving around it. In 1543 the Polish astronomer Copernicus proposed an alternative to the Ptolemaic system. Ptolemy's *Geography* was a standard source of information until the 16th century. Ptolemy produced vivid maps of Asia and large areas of Africa.

He may have been born in the town of Ptolemais Hermii, on the banks of the Nile. He worked in Alexandria and had an observatory on the top floor of a temple.

The *Almagest* (he called it *Syntaxis*) contains all his works on astronomical themes. Probably inspired by Plato, Ptolemy began with the premise that the Earth was a perfect sphere. All planetry orbits were circular, but those of Mercury and Venus, and possibly Mars (Ptolemy was not sure), were epicyclic (the planets orbited a point that itself was orbiting the Earth). The sphere of the stars formed a dome with points of light attached or pricked through.

In his thesis on astrology, *Tetrabiblios*, Ptolemy suggests that some force from the stars may influence the lives and events in the human experience.

Ptolemy dynasty of kings of Macedonian origin who ruled Egypt over a period of 300 years; they included:

Ptolemy I (*c.* 367–283 BC). Ruler of Egypt from 323 BC, king from 304. He was one of Alexander the Great's generals, and established the dynasty and Macedonian organization of the state in Alexandria.

Because Ptolemy was a king, lying would have been more dishonourable for him than for anyone else.

Arrian on PTOLEMY I
in preface to *History of Alexander*

Ptolemy II (308–246 BC). Ruler of Egypt 283–246 BC. He consolidated Greek control and administration, constructing a canal from the Red Sea to the Nile as well as the museum, library, and the Pharos (lighthouse) at Alexandria, one of the Seven Wonders of the World. He was the son of Ptolemy I.

Ptolemy XIII (63–47 BC). Joint ruler of Egypt with his sister-wife Cleopatra in the period preceding the Roman annexation of Egypt. He was killed fighting against Julius Caesar.

Pucci Emilio, Marchese di Barsento (1914–1992). Italian couturier, champion skier, and politician. In 1934 he was a member of the Italian Olympic ski team, and shortly afterwards went to the USA to read social science at university. After returning to Florence and completing his studies 1941, he enrolled in the Italian Air Force during World War II, where he rose to the rank of lieutenant colonel.

Pucci became known after photographs of him, wearing his own designs on the Italian ski slopes, appeared in *Harpers Bazaar* 1948. In 1950 he established his own couture house at the family home, Palazzo Pucci. His designs were popular in the mid-1950s to mid-1960s. Produced in bright colours (turquoise, acid yellow, and

Puccini The composer Giacomo Puccini (1858–1924). One of the last great Romantic composers, Puccini also introduced 20th-century elements of realism (verismo) into his operas. Although his music was successful with the public, many critics have not been able to recognize his genius. (Image Select)

almond green), his designs became the symbol of a new casual chic, and contributed to the growth of the Italian fashion industry after World War II.

In 1964 he stood for parliament and served as a deputy in Rome for nine years. He was also active in Florentine city politics.

Puccini Giacomo (Antonio Domenico Michele Secondo Maria) (1858–1924). Italian opera composer. His music shows a strong gift for melody and dramatic effect and his operas combine exotic plots with elements of *verismo* (realism). They include *Manon Lescaut* 1893, *La Bohème* 1896, *Tosca* 1900, *Madame Butterfly* 1904, and the unfinished *Turandot* 1926.
Suggested reading
Ashbrook, W *The Operas of Puccini* (1985)
Jackson, S *Monsieur Butterfly: The Story of Giacomo Puccini* (1974)
Marek, G R *Puccini* (1951)
Weaver, W and Hume, P *Puccini* (1977)

God touched me with His little finger and said, 'Write for the theatre, only for the theatre'.

GIACOMO PUCCINI
quoted in Joseph Wechsberg *The Opera* 1972

Pudovkin Vsevolod Illarionovich (1893–1953). Russian film director. His films include the silent *Mother* 1926, *The End of St Petersburg* 1927, and *Storm over Asia* 1928; and the sound films *Deserter* 1933 and *Suvorov* 1941.

Puget Pierre (1620–1694). French Baroque sculptor, painter, and architect. He developed a powerful and expressive style. He created a muscular statue of the tyrant *Milo of Crotona* 1671–82 (Louvre, Paris) for the garden of the palace of Versailles. Puget worked in Italy 1640–43 and was influenced by Michelangelo and Pietro da Cortona. After 1682 he failed to gain further court patronage because of his stubborn temperament and his severe style.

Pugh Clifton Ernest (1924–   ). Australian artist. His bush landscapes often depict the savage world of the hunter and hunted, as in *Memory of a Feral Cat* 1960 (Mertz Collection, USA). A noted portraitist, he won the Archibald Prize in 1965, 1971, and 1972.

Pugin Augustus Welby Northmore (1812–1852). English architect. He collaborated with Charles Barry in the detailed design of the Houses of Parliament. He did much to instigate the Gothic Revival in England, largely through his book *Contrasts* 1836.
Suggested reading
Clark, Kenneth *The Gothic Revival* (1950)
Harries, J *Pugin* (1973)
Stanton, Phoebe *Pugin* (1972)

P'u-i Henry, (or *Pu-Yi*) (1906–1967). Last emperor of China (as Hsuan Tung) from 1908 until his deposition 1912; he was restored for a week 1917. After his deposition he chose to be called Henry. He was president 1932–34 and emperor 1934–45 of the Japanese puppet state of Manchukuo. Captured by Soviet troops, he was returned to China 1949 and put on trial in the new People's Republic of China 1950. Pardoned by Mao Zedong 1959, he became a worker in a botanical garden in Beijing.

Puig Manuel (1932–1990). Argentine novelist whose works owe much to the Hollywood cinema of the 1940s and 1950s. His book *El beso de la mujer araña/Kiss of the Spider Woman* 1976 was filmed 1985 and adapted as a musical 1992. Later novels such as *La traición de Rita Hayworth/Betrayed by Rita Hayworth* (1968) and *Cae la Noche Tropical/Tropical Night Falling* 1988 ironically demonstrate the extent to which modern life is shaped by the 'trashier' aspects of popular culture.

Pulaski Casimir (1747–1779). Polish patriot and military leader. He was forced into exile after participating in the unsuccessful Polish defence against the Russian invasion 1770–72. Hired by Silas Deane and Benjamin Franklin in their campaign to recruit for the American Revolution 1775–83, he was placed in command of the Continental cavalry 1777. He saw action at Valley Forge 1777–78 and after a dispute with General Anthony Wayne, was given an independent cavalry command. He died in action in the siege of Savannah.

Pulitzer Joseph (1847–1911). Hungarian-born US newspaper publisher. Pulitzer came to the US 1864 and became a citizen 1867. A Democrat, he merged two St Louis newspapers and published 1878 the successful St Louis *Post-Dispatch*. He acquired *The World* 1883 in New York City and, as a publisher, his format set the style for the modern newspaper. He made *The World* into a voice of the Democratic Party. During a circulation battle with rival publisher William Randolph Hearst's papers, he and Hearst were accused of resorting to 'yellow journalism,' or sensationalism. After his death, funds provided in his will established 1912 the school of journalism at Columbia University and the annual Pulitzer prizes in journalism, literature, and music (from 1917).

Pullman George Mortimer (1831–1897). US engineer and entrepreneur who developed the Pullman railway car. In an attempt to improve the standard of comfort of rail travel, he built his first Pioneer sleeping car 1864. It was not the first sleeping carriage but it was the most luxurious. Pullman cars were initially staffed entirely by black porters whose only income was from tips.

He formed the Pullman Palace Car Company 1867 and in 1881 the town of Pullman, Illinois, was built for his workers. One of the most famous strikes in US labour history took place at Pullman in 1894. In 1937 the Brotherhood of Sleeping Car Porters became the first black union recognized by a US corporation.

Purcell Henry (c. 1659–1695). English Baroque composer. Born at Westminster, he became a chorister at the Chapel Royal, and subsequently was a pupil of Dr John Blow. In 1677 he was appointed composer to the Chapel Royal, and in 1679 organist at Westminster Abbey. As composer to the king, Purcell set to music odes or anthems. His music balances high formality with melodic expression of controlled intensity, for example, the opera *Dido and Aeneas* 1689 and music for Dryden's *King Arthur* 1691 and for *The Fairy Queen* 1692. He wrote more than 500 works, ranging from secular operas and incidental music for plays to cantatas and church music.

Suggested reading
Burden, M (ed) *The Purcell Companion* (1995)
Duffy, Maureen *Henry Purcell* (1994)
Westrup, J A *Purcell* (1973)
Zimmerman, F *Henry Purcell* (1983)

Here lies Henry Purcell Esquire, who left life and is gone to that blessed place where only his harmony can be exceeded.

Epitaph for HENRY PURCELL in Westminster Abbey

Purchas Samuel (*c.* 1577–1626). English compiler of travel books. His collection *Purchas, his Pilgrimage* 1613, was followed by another in 1619, and in 1625 by *Hakluytus Posthumus or Purchas his Pilgrimes*, based on papers left by the geographer Richard Hakluyt. He was rector of St Martin's, Ludgate 1614–26.

Purdy James Amos (1923–). US novelist. His first novel, *Malcolm* 1959, concerns the quest of a teenage boy for his lost father and is set in a world of bizarre depravity. It was followed by *The Nephew* 1960 and *Cabot Wright Begins* 1964. His novels, like his poetry and plays, deal with extreme emotional states and dramatic transformations. They typically treat homosexual subjects with stylistic elegance and a flair for strange or grotesque images. One of the latest is *Out with the Stars* 1991.

Purkinje Jan Evangelista (1787–1869). Czech physiologist who made pioneering studies of vision, the functioning of the brain and heart, pharmacology, embryology, and cells and tissue. Purkinje described 1819 the visual phenomenon in which different-coloured objects of equal brightness in certain circumstances appear to the eye to be unequally bright; this is now called the Purkinje effect.

In 1823 he was appointed professor at Breslau (now Wroclaw in Poland) – perhaps through the influence of German poet Wolfgang von Goethe, who had befriended him. In addition to his scientific work, Purkinje also translated the poetry of Goethe and Friedrich von Schiller. At Breslau, Purkinje founded the world's first official physiological institute. In 1850, he returned to Prague University.

In 1832, he was the first to describe what are now known as Purkinje's images: a threefold image of a single object seen by one person reflected in the eye of another person. This effect is caused by the object being reflected by the surface of the cornea and by the anterior and posterior surfaces of the eye lens.

Purkinje cells are large nerve cells with numerous dendrites found in the cortex of the cerebellum; he discovered these 1837, and the Purkinje fibres in the ventricles of the heart 1839. Also in 1839, in describing the contents of animal embryos, Purkinje was the first to use the term 'protoplasm' in the scientific sense.

In 1823 he recognized that fingerprints can be used as a means of identification. He discovered the sweat glands in skin, described ciliary motion, and observed that pancreatic extracts can digest protein. In 1837 he outlined the principal features of the cell theory.

Pusey Edward Bouverie (1800–1882). English Church of England priest from 1828. In 1835 he joined J H Newman in issuing the *Tracts for the Times*. After Newman's conversion to Catholicism, Pusey became leader of the High Church Party, or Puseyites, striving until his death to keep them from conversion. He was professor of Hebrew at Oxford University. His work is continued through Pusey House at Oxford, founded in his memory, which contains his library.

Purcell *The composer Henry Purcell as painted by John Closterman in 1695. One of the greatest of all English composers since Byrd and before Elgar, Purcell contributed to all genres, sacred and secular. He was influenced by both the French and Italian styles.* (Image Select)

Pushkin Aleksandr Sergeyevich (1799–1837). Russian poet and writer. His works include the novel in verse *Eugene Onegin* 1823–31 and the tragic drama *Boris Godunov* 1825. Pushkin's range was wide, and his willingness to experiment freed later Russian writers from many of the archaic conventions of the literature of his time.

Pushkin was born in Moscow. He was exiled 1820 for his political verse and in 1824 was in trouble for his atheistic opinions. He wrote ballads such as *The Gypsies* 1827, and the prose pieces *The Captain's Daughter* 1836 and *The Queen of Spades* 1834. He was mortally wounded in a duel with his brother-in-law.

Suggested reading
Bayley, John *Pushkin: A Comparative Commentary* (1971)
Magarshak, David *Pushkin: A Biography* (1967)
Troyat, Henri *Pushkin* (trs 1970)

Putnik Radomir (1847–1917). Serbian field marshal. He fought in the Serbo-Bulgar war 1885 and was commander in chief of the Serbian Army in the Balkan Wars 1912–13. Effectively in command of Serbian forces in World War I, in the first months his tactics outfought the Austrians at almost every turn. However, eventually the greater numerical strength of the Austro-German combination told and he was forced to retreat across the mountains of Montenegro and Albania to the Adriatic Oct–Nov 1915.

Puttnam David Terence (1941–). English film producer. He played a major role in reviving the British film industry internationally in the 1980s. Films include *Chariots of Fire* 1981 (Academy Award for best film), *The Killing Fields* 1984, and *Memphis Belle* 1990. He was briefly head of Columbia Pictures in the mid-1980s.

Puvis de Chavannes Pierre Cécile (1824–1898). French Symbolist painter. His major works are vast decorative schemes in pale colours, mainly on mythological and allegorical subjects, for public buildings such as the Panthéon and Hôtel de Ville in Paris. His work influenced Paul Gauguin. The Boston Public Library, Massachusetts, also owns several of his murals. His *Poor Fisherman* 1881 (Louvre, Paris) is a much admired smaller work.

Pu-Yi alternative transliteration of the name of the last Chinese emperor, Henry ◊P'u-i.

Pye John David (1932–). English zoologist who has studied the way bats use echolocation, and also the use of ultrasound in other animals. In 1973 he became professor at Queen Mary College, London.

A surprisingly large number of animals use ultrasound (which has a frequency above about 20 kHz and is inaudible to humans) – bats, whales, porpoises, dolphins, and many insects, for example. Because of the lack of detection devices, the phenomenon was not discovered until 1935.

In 1971 Pye calculated the resonant frequencies of the drops of water in fog and found that these frequencies coincided with the spectrum of frequencies used by bats for echolocation. In other words, bats cannot navigate in fog. Pye also found that ultrasound seems to be important in the social behaviour of rodents and insects.

Pyke Margaret (1893–1966). British birth-control campaigner. In the early 1930s she became secretary of the National Birth Control Association (later the Family Planning Association, FPA), and campaigned vigorously to get local councils to set up family-planning clinics. She became chair of the FPA in 1954.

It is better taste somehow that a man should be unfaithful to his wife away from home.

BARBARA PYM
Jane and Prudence ch 7 1953

Pym Barbara Mary Crampton (1913–1980). English novelist. Her closely observed novels of village life include *Some Tame Gazelle* 1950, *The Sweet Dove Died* 1978, and *A Few Green Leaves* 1980.

Pym Francis Leslie, Baron Pym (1922–). British Conservative politician. He was defence secretary 1979–81, and succeeded Lord Carrington as foreign minister 1982, but was dismissed in the post-election reshuffle 1983. Baron 1987.

Pym John (1584–1643). English Parliamentarian, largely responsible for the petition of right 1628. As leader of the Puritan opposition in the Long Parliament from 1640, he moved the impeachment of Charles I's advisers the Earl of Strafford and William Laud, drew up the Grand Remonstrance, and was the chief of five members of Parliament Charles I wanted arrested 1642. The five hid themselves and then emerged triumphant when the king left London.

A parliament is that to the Commonwealth which the soul is to the body.

JOHN PYM
Speech in House of Commons 17 Apr 1640

Pyman Frank Lee (1882–1944). English organic chemist who worked on pharmaceuticals, particularly studying the properties of glyoxalines (glyoxal is ethanedial).

Pyman took a job in the Experimental Department of the Wellcome Chemical Works in Dartford, Kent. He was professor at Manchester and head of the Department of Applied Chemistry at the College of Technology 1919–27 and then became director of research at the Boots Pure Drug Company's laboratories at Nottingham.

The glyoxalines are cyclic amidines with therapeutic properties, and Pyman studied especially the relationship between their chemical constitution and their physiological action. Study of the constitution of the anhydro-bases made from glycoside revealed the existence of a substance whose molecules contained a ten-membered heterocyclic

ring. He also examined alkaloids, and became the first person to isolate a natural substance containing an asymmetric nitrogen atom.

Pynaker Adam (1622–1673). Dutch landscape painter. His style reflects Italianate influence in the way it combines cloudless skies with the effect of clear, golden light on a foreground of trees and foliage. *Landscape with Sportsmen and Game* about 1665 (Dulwich College Art Gallery, London) is a typical work.

Pynchon Thomas (1937–). US novelist. With great stylistic verve, he created a bizarre, labyrinthine world in his books, the first of which was *V* 1963, a parodic detective story in pursuit of the endlessly elusive Lady V. It was followed by the shorter comic quest novel, *The Crying of Lot 49* 1966, before his gargantuan tour-de-force *Gravity's Rainbow* 1973, which represents a major achievement in 20th-century literature, with its fantastic imagery and esoteric language, drawn from mathematics and science. After a collection of earlier written short stories *Slow Learner* 1984, he published his fourth novel, *Vineland* 1990, a reworking of earlier preoccupations.

Pyrrho (*c.* 360–*c.* 270 BC). Greek philosopher, founder of Scepticism, who maintained that since certainty was impossible, peace of mind lay in renouncing all claims to knowledge.

Pyrrhus (319–272 BC). King of Epirus, Greece, from 307, who invaded Italy 280, as an ally of the Tarentines against Rome. He twice defeated the Romans but with such heavy losses that a Pyrrhic victory has come to mean a victory not worth winning. He returned to Greece 275 after his defeat at Beneventum, and was killed in a riot in Argos.

Pythagoras (*c.* 580–500 BC). Greek mathematician and philosopher who formulated Pythagoras' theorem. Pythagoras' theorem states that in a right-angled triangle, the area of the square of the hypotenuse (the longest side) is equal to the sum of the areas of the squares drawn on the other sides. Much of Pythagoras' work concerned numbers, to which he assigned mystical properties. For example, he classified numbers into triangular ones (1, 3, 6, 10...), which can be represented as a triangular array, and square ones (1, 4, 9, 16...), which form squares. He also observed that any two adjacent triangular numbers add to a square number (for example, $1 + 3 = 4$; $3 + 6 = 9$; $6 + 10 = 16...$).

Pythagoras was born on the island of Samos and may have been obliged to flee the despotism of its ruler. He went on to found a school and religious brotherhood in Croton, S Italy. Its tenets included the immortality and transmigration of the soul. As a mathematical and philosophical community the Pythagorean brotherhood extended science; politically its influence reached the western Greek colonies. This caused conflict which saw Pythagoras exiled to Metapontum, on the Gulf of Taranto, until he died. The school continued for 50 or 60 years before being totally suppressed.

Using geometrical principles, the Pythagoreans were able to prove that the sum of the angles of any regular-sided triangle is equal to that of two right angles (using the theory of parallels), and to solve any algebraic quadratic equations having real roots. They formulated the theory of proportion (ratio), which enhanced their knowledge of fractions, and used it in their study of harmonics upon their stringed instruments: the harmonic of the octave was made by touching the string at $\frac{1}{2}$ its length, of a fifth at $\frac{2}{3}$ its length, and so on. Pythagoras himself is said to have made this the basis of a complete system of musical scales and chords.

Suggested reading
Gorman, Peter *Pythagoras: A Life* (1978)
O'Meara, Dominic *Pythagoras Revived: Mathematics and Philosophy in Late Antiquity* (1989)
Stanley, Thomas *Pythagoras* (1989)

There is geometry in the humming of the strings. There is music in the spacings of the spheres.

PYTHAGORAS
quoted in Aristotle *Metaphysics*

Pythagorus of Rhegium (lived 5th century BC). Greek sculptor. He was born on the island of Samos and settled in Rhegium (Reggio di Calabria), Italy. He made statues of athletes and is said to have surpassed his contemporary Myron in this field.

Pythagoras of Rhegium was the first sculptor to show the sinews and veins, and to represent the hair more carefully.

Pliny the Elder on PYTHAGORAS OF RHEGIUM
in *Natural History* bk 34 ch 59

Pytheas has led many people into error by saying that he traversed the whole of Britain on foot, giving the island a circumference of 5,000 miles.

Strabo on PYTHEAS
in *Geographica* bk 2 ch 4

Pytheas (lived 4th century BC). Greek navigator from Marseille who explored the coast of W Europe at least as far north as Denmark, sailed around Britain, and reached what he called Thule, the most northern place known (possibly the Shetlands).

Qaboos bin Said (1940–   ). Sultan of Oman, the 14th descendant of the Albusaid family. Opposed to the conservative views of his father, he overthrew him 1970 in a bloodless coup and assumed the sultanship. Since then he has followed more liberal and expansionist policies, while maintaining his country's position of international nonalignment.

Qaddafi alternative form of ◊Khaddhafi, Libyan leader.

Qin dynasty (221–206 BC). China's first imperial dynasty. It was established by Shi Huangdi, ruler of the Qin, the most powerful of the Zhou era warring states. The power of the feudal nobility was curbed and greater central authority exerted over N central China, which was unified through a bureaucratic administrative system.

Writing and measurement systems were standardized, state roads and canals built, and border defence consolidated into what became known as the Great Wall. On the debit side, the dynasty is identified with injustice, oppression, and a literary inquisition which came to be known as 'the burning of the books'.

Qing last ruling dynasty in China from 1644; see ◊Manchu.

Quant Mary (1934–   ). English fashion designer. She popularized the miniskirt in the UK and was one of the first designers to make clothes specifically for the teenage and early twenties market, producing bold, simple outfits which were in tune with the 'swinging London' of the 1960s. Her designs were sharp, angular, and streetwise, and she combined spots, stripes, and checks in an original way. Her Chelsea boutique was named Bazaar. In the 1970s she extended into cosmetics and textile design.

Quantrill William Clarke (1837–1865). US pro-slavery outlaw who became leader of an irregular unit on the Confederate side in the American Civil War. Frank and Jesse James were members of his gang (called Quantrill's Raiders).

Quantz Johann Joachim (1697–1773). German flautist and composer. He composed 300 flute concertos, but is best remembered for writing the treatise 'On Playing the Transverse Flute' 1752. He improved the flute's adaptability by adding the second key and devising a sliding tuning mechanism.

Poetry is the revelation of a feeling that the poet believes to be interior and personal [but] which the reader recognizes as his own.

SALVATORE QUASIMODO
Speech 1960

Quasimodo Salvatore (1901–1968). Italian poet. His early collections, such as *Acque e terre/Waters and Land* 1930, established his reputation as an exponent of 'hermetic' poetry, spare, complex, and private. Later collections, including *Nuove poesie/New Poetry* 1942 and *Il falso e vero verde/The False and True Green* 1956, reflect a growing preoccupation with the political and social problems of his time. Nobel prize 1959.

Quayle (John) Anthony (1913–1989). English actor and director. From 1948–56 he directed at the Shakespeare Memorial Theatre, and appeared as Falstaff in *Henry IV*, Petruchio in *The Taming of the Shrew*, and played the title role in *Othello*. He played nonclassical parts in *Galileo*, *Sleuth*, and *Old World*. He founded the Compass Company 1984. His numerous film appearances include *Lawrence of Arabia* 1962. Knighted 1985.

Quayle (James) Dan(forth) (1947–   ). US Republican politician, vice president 1989–93. Born into a rich and powerful Indianapolis newspaper-owning family, Quayle was admitted to the Indiana bar 1974, and was elected to the House of Representatives 1976 and to the Senate 1980. When George Bush ran for president 1988, he selected Quayle as his running mate, admiring his conservative views and believing that Quayle could deliver the youth vote. This choice encountered heavy criticism because of Quayle's limited political experience. As Bush's vice president, Dan Quayle attracted criticism for, among other things, his enlistment in the 1960s in the Indiana National Guard, which meant that he was not sent overseas during the Vietnam War.

Queensberry John Sholto Douglas, 8th Marquess of Queensberry (1844–1900). British patron of boxing. In 1867 he formulated the Queensberry Rules, which form the basis of today's boxing rules.

He was the father of Lord Alfred Douglas and it was his misspelled insult to Oscar Wilde that set in motion the events leading to the playwright's imprisonment. Marquess 1858.

Queneau Raymond (1903–1976). French Surrealist poet and humorous novelist. His works include *Zazie dans le métro/Zazie in the Metro* 1959, a portrayal of a precocious young Parisian woman.

Quennell Peter Courtney (1905–1992). English biographer and critic. He edited the journal *History Today* 1951–79, and wrote biographies of famous literary and social figures of England: the poet Lord Byron 1935, art critic John Ruskin 1949, poet Alexander Pope 1968, and Samuel Johnson, the lexicographer and conversationalist known as Dr Johnson, 1972.

Quercia Jacopo della (c. 1374–1438). Sienese sculptor. He was a contemporary of Donatello and Ghiberti. His major works were a fountain for his hometown of Siena, the Fonte Gaia 1414–19 (Palazzo Pubblico, Siena), and the main portal at San Petronio, Bologna, 1425–38. His turbulent style and powerful figures influenced Michelangelo, whose painting *The Creation of Adam* 1511 (Sistine Chapel, Vatican) was inspired by Jacopo's relief panel of the same subject at San Petronio.

Quesnay François (1694–1774). French economic philosopher. He was the head of the Physiocratic School – the first systematic school of political economy. He held that land was the main source of wealth, and advocated non-interference by government in economic matters. Quesnay was consulting physician to Louis XV at Versailles, where he became interested in economics. His political economy is summed up in his *Tableau économique/Economic Scene* 1758.

Quetelet Lambert Adolphe Jacques (1796–1874). Belgian statistician. He developed tests for the validity of statistical information, and gathered and analysed statistical data of many kinds. From his work on sociological data came the concept of the 'average person'.

Quevedo y Villegas Francisco Gómez de (1580–1645). Spanish novelist and satirist. His picaresque novel *La vida del buscón/The Life of a Scoundrel* 1626 follows the tradition of the roguish hero who has a series of adventures. *Sueños/Visions* 1627 is a brilliant series of satirical portraits of contemporary society.

Quiller-Couch Arthur Thomas (1863–1944). British scholar and writer who usually wrote under the pseudonym 'Q'. He edited several anthologies, including *The Oxford Book of English Verse* 1900, and wrote a number of critical studies, such as *On the Art of Writing*

1920. Among his novels are *The Splendid Spur* 1889 and *The Ship of Stars* 1899. He was professor of English literature at Cambridge University from 1912 until his death. Knighted 1910.

Quilter Roger Cuthbert (1877–1953). English composer. He wrote song settings of Shakespeare and Alfred Lord Tennyson, including 'Now Sleeps the Crimson Petal' 1904, and others, as well as incidental music, such as *A Children's Overture* 1920, and chamber music.

Quimby Fred(erick) (1886–1965). US film producer. He was head of MGM's short films department 1926–56. Among the cartoons produced by this department were the *Tom and Jerry* series and those directed by Tex Avery.

Quincy Josiah (1772–1864). US public official. A staunch Federalist, he served in the US House of Representatives 1805–13, opposing the trade policies of the Jefferson administration and the Louisiana Purchase of 1803. As an opponent of US involvement in the Anglo-American War 1812–14, he resigned from Congress and returned to Boston, where he was mayor 1823–28.

Quine Willard Van Orman (1908–   ). US philosopher and logician with a highly scientific view of the world. He is often described as a nominalist because he believes that universals do not have any real existence outside of thought and language, and a pragmatist because he holds that our minds group together properties in the ways that are most useful for us.

According to Quine, 'to be is to be the value of a variable' in a system of formal logic. By this, he means that we commit ourselves to the existence of something only when we can say that it has a quality or feature, and that existence itself is not a quality or feature.

Quine's theory of the indeterminacy of translation states that assured translation between two languages (or even within one language) is impossible in principle, because the designation of any two words or phrases as synonymous is impossible to justify completely. This is set out in *Word and Object* 1960.

He was professor of philosophy at Harvard from 1936 until his retirement. He also wrote *Two Dogmas of Empiricism* 1951 and *Philosophy of Logic* 1970.

Suggested reading
Gibson, Roger F, Jr (ed) *The Philosophy of W V Quine* (1982)
Orenstein, Alex *Willard Van Orman Quine* (1977)

I never saw a lavatory until I was ten. I spent the first twenty years of my life almost continually hungry.

ANTHONY QUINN
Publicity release for the film *A Star for Two* 1990

Quinn Anthony Rudolph Oaxaca (1916–   ). Mexican-born US actor. In films from 1935, his roles frequently displayed volatile machismo and he often played larger-than-life characters. He is famous for the title role in *Zorba the Greek* 1964; other films include *Viva Zapata!* 1952 (Academy Award for best supporting actor) and Fellini's *La strada* 1954.

Quintero Serafin Alvárez and Joaquin Alvárez. Spanish dramatists. See ◊Alvárez Quintero.

Quintilian (Marcus Fabius Quintilianus) (*c.* AD 35–*c.* 100). Roman rhetorician. He was born at Calagurris, Spain, taught rhetoric in Rome from AD 68, and composed the *Institutio Oratoria/ The Education of an Orator*, in which he advocated a simple and sincere style of public speaking.

Quisling Vidkun Abraham Lauritz Jonsson (1887–1945). Norwegian politician. Leader from 1933 of the Norwegian Fascist Party, he aided the Nazi invasion of Norway 1940 by delaying mobilization and urging non-resistance. He was made premier by Hitler 1942, and was arrested and shot as a traitor by the Norwegians 1945. His name became a generic term for a traitor who aids an occupying force.

R

Rabelais François (*c.* 1495–1553). French satirist, monk, and physician. His name has become synonymous with bawdy humour. He was educated in the Renaissance humanist tradition and was the author of satirical allegories, including *La Vie inestimable de Gargantua/The Inestimable Life of Gargantua* 1535 and *Faits et dits héroïques du grand Pantagruel/Heroic Deeds and Sayings of the Great Pantagruel* 1533, about two giants (father and son).
Suggested reading
Bakhtin, M *Rabelais and His World* (trs 1971)
Frame, D M *François Rabelais* (1977)
Putnam, Samuel *The Portable Rabelais* (1977)
Screech, M *Rabelais* (1979)

I go to seek a great perhaps.

FRANÇOIS RABELAIS
Attributed remark on his deathbed

Rabi Isidor Isaac (1898–1988). Russian-born US physicist who developed techniques to measure accurately the strength of the weak magnetic fields generated when charged elementary particles, such as the electron, spin about their axes. The work won him the 1944 Nobel Prize for Physics.

The government of Israel has decided to recognize the PLO as the representative of the Palestinian people.

YITZHAK RABIN
On signing a peace agreement with the
Palestine Liberation Organization, Sept 1993

Rabin Yitzhak (1922–1995). Israeli Labour politician, prime minister 1974–77 and 1992–95. He was minister for defence under the conservative Likud coalition government 1984–90. His policy of favouring Palestinian self-government in the occupied territories contributed to the success of the centre-left party in the 1992 elections. In Sept 1993 he signed a historic peace agreement with the Palestinian Liberation Organization (PLO), providing for a phased withdrawal of Israeli forces. He was awarded the 1994 Nobel Prize for Peace jointly with Israeli foreign minister, Shimon Peres, and PLO leader, Yassir Arafat. He was shot and killed by a young Israeli extremist while attending a peace rally in Tel Aviv Nov 1995. He was succeeded by Shimon Peres.
Suggested reading
Rabin, Yitzhak *Rabin Memoirs* (trs 1979)
Slater, Robert *Rabin of Israel* (1993)

Rabuka Sitiveni Ligamamada (1948–). Fijian soldier and politician, prime minister from 1992. Rabuka joined the Fijian army at an early age and was trained at Sandhurst military academy, England. He commanded a unit of the United Nations peacekeeping force in Lebanon, for which he was awarded the OBE. In May 1987 Rabuka removed the new Indian-dominated Fijian government at gunpoint, but the governor-general regained control within weeks; in Sept he staged a second coup and proclaimed Fiji a republic, withdrawing from the Commonwealth. He gave way to a civilian government Dec 1987 and served as home-affairs minister, but resigned the post 1990. He was nominated premier May 1992, and re-elected to the post 1994.

Rachel stage name of Elisa Félix (1821–1858). French tragic actress. She excelled in fierce, passionate roles, notably Phaedra in Racine's tragedy *Phèdre*, which she took on tour to Europe, the USA, and Russia.

Rachmaninov Sergei Vasilevich (1873–1943). Russian composer, conductor, and pianist. After the 1917 Revolution he emigrated to the USA. His music is melodious and emotional and includes operas, such as *Francesca da Rimini* 1906, three symphonies, four piano concertos, piano pieces, and songs. Among his other works are the *Prelude in C-Sharp Minor* 1882 and *Rhapsody on a Theme of Paganini* 1934 for piano and orchestra.
Suggested reading
Norris, Geoffrey *Rakhmaninov* (1976)
Piggott, P *Rachmaninov* (1978)
Threlfal, R *Sergei Rachmaninov* (1973)
Walker, Robert *Rachmaninoff: His Life and Times* (1979)

Racine Jean Baptiste (1639–1699). French dramatist. He was an exponent of the classical tragedy in French drama, taking his subjects from Greek mythology and observing the rules of classical Greek drama. Most of his tragedies have women in the title role, for example *Andromaque* 1667, *Iphigénie* 1674, and *Phèdre* 1677.

An orphan, Racine was educated by Jansenists at Port Royal, but later moved away from an ecclesiastical career to success and patronage at court. His ingratiating flattery won him the success he craved 1677 when he was appointed royal historiographer. After the failure of *Phèdre* in the theatre he no longer wrote for the secular stage but, influenced by Madame de Maintenon, wrote two religious dramas, *Esther* 1689 and *Athalie* 1691, which achieved posthumous success.
Suggested reading
Brereton, Geoffrey *Jean Racine: A Critical Biography* (1973)
Butler, Philip *Racine* (1974)
France, P *Racine's Rhetoric* (1965)
Pocock, G *Corneille and Racine: Problems of Tragic Form* (1973)
Turnell, Martin *Jean Racine: Dramatist* (1972)
Weinberg, B *The Art of Jean Racine* (1963)

I loved you when you were inconstant. What should I have done if you had been faithful?

JEAN RACINE
Andromaque IV. v 1667

Radcliffe Ann (born Ward) (1764–1823). English novelist. An exponent of the Gothic novel or 'romance of terror', she wrote, for example, *The Mysteries of Udolpho* 1794. She was one of the first novelists to include vivid descriptions of landscape and weather.

Radcliffe-Brown Alfred Reginald (1881–1955). English anthropologist. Influenced by Emile Durkheim, he developed the theory of structural functionalism in which aspects of society were analysed in terms of their contribution to the overall social structure or system.

Radić Stjepan (1871–1928). Yugoslav nationalist politician, founder of the Croatian Peasant Party 1904. He led the Croat national movement within the Austro-Hungarian Empire and advocated a federal state with Croatian autonomy. His opposition to Serbian supremacy within Yugoslavia led to his assassination in parliament.

Raeburn Henry (1756–1823). Scottish portrait painter. Active mainly in Edinburgh, he developed a technique of painting with broad brushstrokes directly on the canvas without preparatory drawing. He was appointed painter to George IV 1823. *The Reverend Robert Walker Skating* about 1784 (National Gallery of Scotland, Edinburgh) is typical of his work.

Rafsanjani *The president of Iran, Ali Akbar Rafsanjani. He is viewed as the most pragmatic and influential member of Iran's post-Khomeini collective leadership.*

Largely self-taught, he began by painting miniatures, married a widow of some fortune, and went to London *c.* 1778. On the advice of Reynolds, he went to Italy 1785, returning to Edinburgh 1787 to become its foremost portrait painter. His subjects were the notable figures of literature and law in the great period of Edinburgh's intellectual eminence, and the chieftains of the Highland clans. He excelled in male rather than female portraits, his broad brush-stroke being well adapted to convey rugged dignity of feature. He made the most of a limited range in composition and colour, and his full-lengths have dramatic force, as in the *Macdonell of Glengarry* of the National Gallery of Scotland (a main repository of his art). He exhibited regularly at the Royal Academy in London 1792–1823, and, as well as being president of the Royal Scottish Academy (1812), was RA 1815. He was also appointed His Majesty's Limner for Scotland. Knighted 1822.

Raeder Erich (1876–1960). German admiral. Chief of Staff in World War I, he became head of the navy 1928. He successfully evaded the restrictions of the Versailles treaty while expanding the navy in 1930s. He was behind the successful U-boat campaign against Britain and launched attacks against the Arctic convoys supplying the USSR. Following the humiliation of the Battle of Barents Sea Dec 1942, Hitler threatened to remove big guns from battleships and install them as coastal defence weapons. This was too much for Raeder and he resigned 1943. Sentenced to life imprisonment at the Nuremberg trials of war criminals, he was released 1955 on grounds of ill health.

Rafaelson Bob (Robert) (1933–). US film director. He gained critical acclaim for his second film, *Five Easy Pieces* 1971. Other films include *The King of Marvin Gardens* 1972, *Stay Hungry* 1976, and *The Postman Always Rings Twice* 1981.

Rafferty Chips. Stage name of John William Goffage (1909–1971). Australian film actor and producer who through his many film roles portrayed the typical outback Australian. His films include *Forty Thousand Horsemen* 1940, *Smiley* 1956, *The Sundowners* 1960, *They're a Weird Mob* 1966 and *Wake in Fright* 1971. In 1953 he formed Southern International Films, and produced a steady stream of films through the 1950s.

Raffles (Thomas) Stamford (1781–1826). British colonial administrator, born in Jamaica. He served in the British East India Company, took part in the capture of Java from the Dutch 1811, and while governor of Sumatra 1818–23 was responsible for the acquisition and founding of Singapore 1819. Knighted 1817.
Suggested reading
Collis, Maurice *Raffles* (1966)
Wurtzburg, C E *Raffles of the Eastern Isles* (1954)

Rafsanjani Hojatoleslam Ali Akbar Hashemi (1934–). Iranian politician and cleric, president from 1989. Rafsanjani was born near Kerman, SE Iran, to a family of pistachio farmers. At 14 he went to study Islamic jurisprudence with Khomeini in the Shi'ites holy city of Qom and qualified as an *alim* (Islamic teacher). During the period 1964–78, he acquired considerable wealth through his construction business but kept in touch with his exiled mentor Ayatollah Khomeini, and was repeatedly imprisoned for fundamentalist political activity. When Khomeini returned after the revolution of 1979–80, Rafsanjani became the speaker of the Iranian parliament and, after Khomeini's death, state president and effective political leader. His attitude became more moderate in the 1980s, and as president he normalized relations with the UK 1990. He was re-elected with a reduced majority 1993.

Raft George (1895–1980). US film actor. He was often cast as a sharp-eyed gangster (as in *Scarface* 1932). His later work included a self-satirizing cameo in *Some Like It Hot* 1959.

Raglan FitzRoy James Henry Somerset, 1st Baron Raglan (1788–1855). English general. He took part in the Peninsular War under Wellington, and lost his right arm at Waterloo. He commanded the

Raglan *English general FitzRoy Somerset, 1st Baron Raglan, took over the command of the British forces in the Crimea 1854. He won the battles of Alma and Inkerman, but was responsible for the ambiguous order that led to the loss of the Light Brigade at Balaclava.*

British forces in the Crimean War from 1854. The raglan sleeve, cut right up to the neckline with no shoulder seam, is named after him.
Suggested reading
Hibbert, Christopher *The Destruction of Lord Raglan* (1966)
Palmer, Alan *The Banner of War: The Story of the Crimean War* (1987)

Rahere (died 1144). Minstrel and favourite of Henry I of England. In 1123, having recovered from malaria while on a pilgrimage to Rome, he founded St Bartholomew's priory and St Bartholomew's hospital in London.

Rahman Sheik Mujibur (1920–1975). Bangladeshi nationalist politician, president 1975. He was arrested several times for campaigning for the autonomy of East Pakistan. He won the elections 1970 as leader of the Awami League but was again arrested when negotiations with the Pakistan government broke down. After the civil war 1971, he became prime minister of the newly independent Bangladesh. He was presidential dictator Jan–Aug 1975, when he was assassinated.

Rahman Tunku (Prince) Abdul (1903–1990). Malaysian politician, first prime minister of independent Malaya 1957–63 and of Malaysia 1963–70.

Born at Kuala Keda, the son of the sultan and his sixth wife, a Thai princess, the Tunku studied law in England. After returning to Malaya he founded the Alliance Party 1952. The party was successful in the 1955 elections, and the Tunku became prime minister of Malaya on gaining independence 1957, continuing when Malaya became part of Malaysia 1963. His achievement was to bring together the Malay, Chinese, and Indian peoples within the Alliance Party, but in the 1960s he was accused of showing bias towards Malays. Ethnic riots followed in Kuala Lumpur 1969 and, after many attempts to restore better relations, the Tunku retired 1970. In his later years he voiced criticism of the authoritarian leadership of Mahathir bin Mohamed.

Rahner Karl (1904–1984). German Catholic theologian. In his 16-volume *Schriften zur Theologie/Theological Investigations* 1954–84, he attempted a systematic exploration linking the historical and the transcendent, especially by relating salvation history to the history of evolution and the world.

Rahner joined the Jesuits 1922, studying first philosophy and then theology. He was professor at Munich 1964–67 and Münster 1967–71. He was considered too radical by many in the Catholic church but was one of the more influential advisers to the Second Vatican Council.

Raikes Robert (1735–1811). English printer who started the first Sunday school (for religious purposes) in Gloucester 1780 and who stimulated the growth of weekday voluntary 'ragged schools' for poor children.

Raine Kathleen Jessie (1908–   ). English poet. She wrote a three-volume autobiography, *Farewell Happy Fields* 1973, *The Land Unknown* 1975, and *The Lion's Mouth* 1977, which reflect both the Northumberland landscape of her upbringing and the religious convictions that led to her brief conversion to Roman Catholicism 1944. Her volumes of poetry include *Stone and Flower* 1943, *Collected Poems* 1981, and *Living with Mystery* 1992. She is a well-known authority on William Blake.

Rainier III (1923–   ). Prince of Monaco from 1949. He married US film actress Grace Kelly 1956.

Rains Claude (1889–1967). British-born US character actor. On the London stage from the age of 11, he graduated to Broadway and then Hollywood. He achieved success with his first film role as the unseen hero of *The Invisible Man* 1933, followed by a string of roles opposite Bette Davis (*Now, Voyager* 1942, *Mr Skeffington* 1945, and *Deception* 1946). He became noted for playing suave and sardonic figures such as the police chief in *Casablanca* 1942, Prince John in *Adventures of Robin Hood* 1938, and the mother-dominated Nazi in Alfred Hitchcock's *Notorious* 1946.

Rainwater (Leo) James (1917–   ). US physicist who with the Danes Aage Bohr and Ben Mottelson shared the 1975 Nobel Prize for Physics for their work on the structure of the atomic nucleus.

Rainwater was born in Council, Idaho, and studied at the California Institute of Technology and at Columbia University, where he became professor of physics 1952. During 1942–46, he worked on the Manhattan Project to construct the atom bomb.

In 1950, Rainwater wrote a paper in which he observed that most of the particles in the nucleus of an atom form an inner nucleus, while the other particles form an outer nucleus. Each set of particles is in constant motion at very high velocity and the shape of each set affects the other set. He postulated that if some of the outer particles moved in similar orbits, this would create unequal centrifugal forces of enormous power, which could be strong enough permanently to deform an ideally symmetrical nucleus. This was confirmed experimentally by Bohr and Mottelson, and paved the way for nuclear fusion.

Rais Gilles de (1404–1440). French marshal who fought alongside Joan of Arc. In 1440 he was hanged for the torture and murder of 140 children, but the court proceedings were irregular. He is the historical basis of the Bluebeard character.

So the heart be right, it is no matter which way the head lies.

WALTER RALEIGH
When asked which way he preferred to lay his head on the block, quoted in W Stebbing *Sir Walter Raleigh* 1899

Raleigh Walter, or Ralegh (c. 1552–1618). English adventurer, writer, and courtier to Queen Elizabeth I. Born in Devon, England, Raleigh became a confidant of Queen Elizabeth I and was knighted 1584. After initiating several unsuccessful attempts 1584–87 to establish a colony in North America, he led a gold-seeking expedition to the Orinoco River in South America 1595 (described in his *Discoverie of Guiana* 1596). He distinguished himself in expeditions against Spain in Cádiz 1596 and the Azores 1597.

After James I's accession to the English throne 1603, Raleigh was condemned to death on a charge of conspiracy, but was reprieved and imprisoned in the Tower of London, where he wrote his unfinished *History of the World*. Released 1616 to lead a second expedition to the Orinoco, which failed disastrously, he was beheaded on his return under the charges of his former sentence. He is traditionally credited with introducing the potato to Europe and popularizing the use of tobacco.
Suggested reading
Coote, Stephen *The Play of Passion: The Life of Sir Walter Raleigh* (1993)
Irwin, R *That Great Lucifer* (1960)
Greenblatt, S *Sir Walter Raleigh: The Renaissance Man* (1973)
Lacey, R *Sir Walter Raleigh* (1974)
Sinclair, A *Sir Walter Raleigh and the Age of Discovery* (1984)
Winton, J *Sir Walter Raleigh* (1975)

Ramakrishna adopted name of Gadadhar Chatterjee (1836–1886). Hindu sage, teacher, and mystic (dedicated to achieving oneness with or a direct experience of God or some force beyond the normal world). Ramakrishna claimed that mystical experience was the ultimate aim of religions, and that all religions which led to this goal were equally valid.

Ramakrishna's most important follower, Swami Vivekananda (1863–1902), set up the Ramakrishna Society 1897, which now has centres for education, welfare, and religious teaching throughout India and beyond.

Raman Chandrasekhara Venkata (1888–1970). Indian physicist who in 1928 discovered what became known as the Raman effect: the scattering of monochromatic (single-wavelength) light when passed through a transparent substance. The Raman spectra produced are used to obtain information on the structure of molecules. Knighted 1929. Nobel prize 1930.

He joined the civil service as an accountant in Calcutta but pursued his studies privately. His work on vibration in sound and the theory of musical instruments and on diffraction led to his becoming professor of physics at the University of Calcutta 1917–33. From 1948 he was director of the Raman Research Institute, built for him by the government in Bangalore.

Raman showed 1921 that the blue colour of the sea is produced by the scattering of light by water molecules. Continuing to work on the scattering of light, he arrived at the Raman effect. It is caused by the internal motion of the molecules encountered, which may impart energy to the light photons or absorb energy in the resulting collisions. Raman scattering therefore gives precise information on the motion and shape of molecules.

Raman's other research included the effects of sound waves on the scattering of light in 1935 and 1936, the vibration of atoms in crystals in the 1940s, the optics of gemstones, particularly diamonds, and of minerals in the 1950s, and the physiology of human colour vision in the 1960s.

Ramanuja (c. 1017–1137). Indian teacher and philosopher of Vaishnavism, the worship of the Hindu god Vishnu. He taught the path of self-surrender to a personal God and laid the foundation for the bhakti movement in Hinduism. He looked upon individual souls as distinct from God and advocated devotion as superior to knowledge. He countered Sankara's *advaita* (non-dual) philosophy of pure monism with *vishishtadvaita*, 'non-duality in difference'.

Ramanujan Srinivasa Ayengar (1887–1920). Indian mathematician who did original work especially in function theory and number theory.

Ramanujan was born near Kumbakonam, Madras (now Tamil Nadu), and taught himself mathematics from just one textbook, *A Synopsis of Elementary Results in Pure and Applied Mathematics* by G S Carr, published 1880. In 1914 he won a scholarship to Cambridge, England, but tuberculosis forced him to return to India 1919.

Carr's textbook, and particularly the section on pure mathematics, was the basis of all Ramanujan's work. From the knowledge he gained he was able to proceed beyond the material published and develop his own results in many fields, but also kept 'discovering' already well-known theorems.

With his mentor, Cambridge mathematician G H Hardy, Ramanujan published a theory on the methods for partitioning an integer into a sum of smaller integers, called summands. In function theory he found accurate approximations to π, and worked on modular, elliptic, and other functions.

His collected papers were published by Hardy 1927.

Ramaphosa (Matamela) Cyril (1953–   ). South African politician, secretary general of the African National Congress from 1991. He was a chief negotiator in the constitutional talks with the South African government that led to the first universal suffrage elections May 1994, and was subsequently elected by parliament to chair the assembly that would write the country's new permanent constitution. He is seen by some as Mandela's natural successor.

Trained as a lawyer, Ramaphosa was a successful organizer of the National Union of Mineworkers from 1981.

Rambert Marie. Adopted name of Cyvia Myriam Rambam (1888–1982). Polish-born British ballet dancer and teacher. One of the major innovative and influential figures in modern ballet, she worked with the Diaghilev ballet 1912–13, opened the Rambert School 1920, and in 1926 founded the Ballet Rambert which she directed. It became a modern-dance company from 1966 with Norman Morrice as director, and was renamed the Rambert Dance Company 1987. Rambert became a British citizen 1918. DBE 1962.
Suggested reading
Bradley, L *Sixteen Years of Ballet Rambert, 1930–1946* (1946)
Clarke, M *Dancers of Mercury* (1962)

Rambouillet Catherine de Vivonne, Marquise de Rambouillet (1588–1665). French society hostess, whose salon at the Hôtel de Rambouillet in Paris included the philosopher Descartes and the writers La Rochefoucauld and Madame de Sévigné. The salon was ridiculed by the dramatist Molière in his *Les Précieuses ridicules* 1659.

Ram Das (1534–1581). Indian religious leader, fourth guru (teacher) of Sikhism 1574–81, who founded the Sikh holy city of Amritsar.

Harmony alone can stir the emotions. It is the one source from which melody directly emanates, and draws its power.

JEAN-PHILIPPE RAMEAU
Observations sur notre instinct pour la musique 1734

Rameau Jean-Philippe (1683–1764). French organist and composer. His *Traité de l'harmonie/Treatise on Harmony* 1722 established academic rules for harmonic progression, and his varied works include keyboard and vocal music and many operas, such as *Castor and Pollux* 1737.

Ramée Louise de la. English novelist who wrote under the name ◊Ouida.

Rameses alternative spelling of ◊Ramses, name of kings of ancient Egypt.

Ram Mohun Roy (1770–1833). Indian religious reformer, founder 1830 of Brahma Samaj, a mystic cult.

Ramón y Cajal Santiago (1852–1934). Spanish cell biologist and anatomist whose research revealed that the nervous system is based on units of nerve cells (neurons). He shared the 1906 Nobel Prize for Physiology or Medicine.

Ramón y Cajal was born in Petilla de Aragon, studied at Zaragoza, and then joined the army medical service. He was professor at Valencia 1884–87, at Barcelona 1887–92, and at Madrid 1892–1921. In 1900 he became director of the new Instituto Nacional de Higiene, and in 1921 of the Cajal Institute in Madrid, founded in his honour.

Ramón y Cajal demonstrated that the axons of neurons end in the grey matter of the central nervous system and never join the endings of other axons or the cell bodies of other nerve cells – findings indicating that the nervous system is not a network. In 1897 he investigated the human cerebral cortex, described several types of neurons, and demonstrated that structure might be related to the localization of a particular function to a specific area. Within the cell body he found neurofibrils 1903, and recognized that the cell body itself was concerned with conduction.

His books include *Structure of the Nervous System of Man and other Vertebrates* 1904 and *The Degeneration and Regeneration of the Nervous System* 1913–14.

Ramos Fidel ('Eddie') (1928–   ). Philippine politician, president from 1992. He was Corazon Aquino's staunchest ally as defence secretary, and was later nominated her successor. As president, he launched a commission to consult with militant rebel groups, and, as part of a government move to end corruption and human-rights abuses, purged the police force. These and other initiatives won him popular support and in the 1995 elections his supporters won a sweeping victory.

Ramphal Shridath Surendranath ('Sonny') (1928–   ). Guyanese politician. He was minister of foreign affairs and justice 1972–75 and secretary general of the British Commonwealth 1975–90. Knighted 1970.

Difficult acting with a chimp? No, no. The emotions were the same. In a way it was like playing opposite Paul Newman. The chimpanzee reacted differently, that's all.

CHARLOTTE RAMPLING
Publicity release for *Mas, Mon Amour* 1986

Rampling Charlotte (1946–). English film actress. She has appeared in, among other films, *Georgy Girl* 1966, *The Damned* 1969, *The Night Porter/Il Portiere di Notti* 1974, *Farewell My Lovely* 1975, and *D.O.A.* 1988.

Rams Dieter (1932–). German industrial designer. He is best known for his electrical appliance designs for the Braun company with which he has worked as chief designer since 1955. Rams is the leading German designer of the postwar years and epitomizes the country's contribution to international design.

He was trained at the Hochschüle für Gestaltung in Ulm, Germany, which was committed to the stark, geometric aesthetic which has characterized Rams's many designs, among them his 'T3' transistor radio 1958 and his 'ET44' electronic calculator 1977. He is active in Frankfurt.

Ramsay Allan (1686–1758). Scottish poet. He published *The Tea-Table Miscellany* 1724–37 and *The Evergreen* 1724, collections of ancient and modern Scottish song, including revivals of the work of such poets as William Dunbar and Robert Henryson. He was the father of painter Allan Ramsay.

Ramsay Allan (1713–1784). Scottish portrait painter. After studying in Edinburgh, Scotland and later in Italy, he established himself as a portraitist in London, England, becoming artist to King George III 1760.

Unlike his younger contemporary and rival, Reynolds, he sought for grace rather than grandeur in European models, acquiring in his earlier work a Baroque elegance from his studies in Naples and Rome, and profiting by the example of Solimena and Batoni. He later delighted in the Rococo delicacy of the French in Nattier, Perronneau, and Quentin de la Tour. This European cultivation made him highly esteemed when he returned from Italy 1736. He is noted for the charm of his female portraiture, especially 1754–66, as in his masterpiece of 1755, *The Artist's Wife*, the portrait of Margaret Lindsay, his second wife (National Gallery of Scotland). He was devoted to drawing, and the value of this study can be seen in his admirable full-length portraits, for example of Lady Mary Coke (Collection, Marquess of Bute). After the 1760s he delegated much to assistants and 'drapery men', such as Joseph van Hacken, taking up literary pursuits and being one of the circle of the lexicographer Dr Johnson.

Ramsay Bertram Home (1883–1945). British admiral in World War II. He was responsible for organizing Operation Dynamo, the evacuation of about 350,000 British and Allied troops from Dunkirk in the face of the German army 1940. He then served with the Allied force which invaded N Africa 1942 and planned the Allied landings in Sicily 1943. In 1943 he became naval commander in chief for the D-Day landings and supervised the amphibious aspects of the operation. He commanded the naval side of the clearing of the Scheldt Estuary late 1944. He was killed in an aircraft accident Jan 1945. KCB 1942.

Ramsay William (1852–1916). Scottish chemist who, with Lord Rayleigh, discovered argon 1894. In 1895 Ramsay produced helium and in 1898, in co-operation with Morris Travers, identified neon, krypton, and xenon. In 1903, with Frederick Soddy, he noted the transmutation of radium into helium, which led to the discovery of the density and relative atomic mass of radium. KCB 1902. Nobel prize 1904.

In his book *The Gases of the Atmosphere* 1896, Ramsay repeated a suspicion he had stated 1892 that there was an eighth group of new elements at the end of the periodic table. During the next decade Ramsay and Travers sought the remaining rare gases by the fractional distillation of liquid air.

In 1880 he was appointed professor at the newly created University College of Bristol (later Bristol University) and a year later became principal of the College. From 1887 he was professor at University College, London.

Helium was known from spectrographic evidence to be present on the Sun but yet to be found on Earth. Certain uranium minerals were known to produce an unidentified inert gas on heating, and Ramsay obtained sufficient of the gas to send a sample to English scientist William Crookes for spectrographic analysis. Crookes confirmed that it was helium.

Ramses or Rameses. 11 kings (pharaohs) of ancient Egypt, including:

Ramses II or Rameses II. King (pharaoh) of ancient Egypt about 1290–1224 BC, the son of Seti I. He campaigned successfully against the Hittites, and built two rock temples at Abu Simbel in S Egypt.
Suggested reading
Freed, Rita *Rameses the Great* (1987)
MacQuitty, William *Ramasses the Great* (1978)
Montet, Pierre *Lives of the Pharaohs* (1968)

Ramses III or Rameses III. King (pharaoh) of ancient Egypt about 1194–1163 BC. He won victories over the Libyans and the Sea Peoples and asserted his control over Palestine.

Ramsey Ian Thomas (1915–1972). English theologian. He argued that the essential character of religious language is in its 'disclosures', which allow a deeper level of perception of religious truth. He offered a new slant on the problem of analogy – how the language of this world can be the vehicle of a religious dimension beyond this world.

Ramus Petrus. Latinized name of Pierre de la Ramée (1515–1572). French philosopher and logician. He sought to improve the syllogistic logic of Greek philosopher Aristotle with the rhetoric of Roman orator Cicero. In the 17th century, Ramism was a serious rival to Aristotelian logic in Britain, New England, and Germany.

Aristotelian logic had also been criticized by Italian scholar Lorenzo Valla. Francis I suppressed Ramus's works 1544, but Henry II lifted the ban 1547. From 1551, Ramus was professor of philosophy and eloquence at the Collège de France. Around 1561 he became a Protestant. He was murdered by hired assassins. His works include *Dialectique/Dialectic* 1555.

Rand Ayn. Adopted name of Alice Rosenbaum (1905–1982). Russian-born US novelist. Born and educated in St Petersburg, Rand came to the USA 1926 and settled in Chicago. She became a US citizen 1931. She worked as a scriptwriter in Hollywood and edited *The Objectivist*, a magazine that promoted Objectivism, her theory of self-interest and laissez-faire capitalism that is presented in her novels. Her novel *The Fountainhead* 1943, describing an idealistic architect who destroys his project rather than see it altered, displays her persuasive blend of vehement anticommunism and fervent philosophy of individual enterprise. Her allegorical novel *Atlas Shrugged* 1957 was also a bestseller. Her beliefs won her a cult following. Her other works include *We, the Living* 1936, *The Virtue of Selfishness* 1965, *Capitalism* 1966, *The New Left* 1971, and *Philosophy: Who Needs It?* 1982.

Rand Sally (born Helen Gould Beck) (1904–1979). US exotic dancer. Born in Hickory County, Missouri, USA, Rand joined the circus as an acrobat as a teenager. During the 1930s she worked as a dancer in Chicago and developed her trademark nude dance routine to Chopin and Debussy, which featured the coy use of huge ostrich fans. Playing a role in the 1965 burlesque revival on Broadway, she continued to dance until 1978. She moved to Hollywood where she played supporting roles in a number of silent films.

Randell William Richard (1824–1911). Australian boat builder, born in England. He was the first steam navigator on the Murray River.

Randolph Asa Philip (1889–1979). US labour and civil rights leader. He founded the periodical *Messenger* 1917 and after successfully organizing railroad workers, he served as the president of the Brotherhood of Sleeping Car Porters 1925–68. Devoting himself to the cause of unionization, especially among black Americans, he was named a vice president of the American Federation of Labor and Congress of Industrial Organizations (AFL-CIO) 1957. He was one of the organizers of the 1963 civil-rights march on Washington.

Ranjit Singh (1780–1839). Indian maharajah. He succeeded his father as a minor Sikh leader 1792, and created a Sikh army that conquered Kashmir and the Punjab. In alliance with the British, he established himself as 'Lion of the Punjab', ruler of the strongest of the independent Indian states.

Ranjitsinhji K S, Maharajah Jamsaheb of Nawanagar (1872–1933). Indian prince and cricketer who played for Sussex and England. A top batsman, he scored 3,065 runs in 1900, and five double centuries in one season. KCSI 1917.

Rank J(oseph) Arthur, 1st Baron Rank (1888–1972). English film magnate. Having entered films 1933 to promote the Methodist cause, by the mid-1940s he controlled, through the Rank Organization, half the British studios and more than 1,000 cinemas. The Rank Organization still owns the Odeon chain of cinemas, although film is now a minor part of its activities. Baron 1957.

He did not mean that he would achieve a God-like impartiality, but that he would write history as he found it rather than to prove any dogma.

Agatha Ramm on LEOPOLD VON RANKE
in Blackwell's Dictionary of Historians 1988

Ranke Leopold von (1795–1886). German historian whose quest for objectivity in history had great impact on the discipline. His attempts to explain 'how it really was' dominated both German and outside historical thought until 1914 and beyond. His *Weltgeschichte/World History* (nine volumes 1881–88) exemplified his ideas.

Ranke pioneered empirical research and the analysis of sources. His ideas were often regarded as the beginning of 'modern' history. He published extensively on a wide range of topics, including the development of the German peoples and *Die romischen Papste, ihre Kirche und ihr Staat im 16. und 17. Jahrhundert/History of the Popes in the 16th and 17th Centuries* 1834–36. He was professor of history at Berlin University from 1825 until his death.

Rankine William John Macquorn (1820–1872). Scottish engineer and physicist who was one of the founders of the science of thermodynamics, especially in reference to the theory of steam engines. From 1855 he was professor at Glasgow. In 1849 he delivered two papers on the subject of heat, and in 1849 he showed the further modifications required to French physicist Sadi Carnot's theory of thermodynamics.

In *A Manual of the Steam Engine and other Prime Movers* 1859, Rankine described a thermodynamic cycle of events (the Rankine cycle), which came to be used as a standard for the performance of steam-power installations where a considerable vapour provides the working fluid. Rankine here explained how a liquid in the boiler vaporized by the addition of heat converts part of this energy into mechanical energy when the vapour expands in an engine. As the exhaust vapour is condensed by a cooling medium such as water, heat is lost from the cycle. The condensed liquid is pumped back into the boiler.

Ransom John Crowe (1888–1974). US poet and critic. He published his romantic but anti-rhetorical verse in, for example, *Poems About God* 1919, *Chills and Fever* 1924, and *Selected Verse* 1947.

Born in Tennessee, Ransom was a leader of the Southern literary movement that followed World War I. As a critic and teacher he was a powerful figure in the New Criticism movement, which shaped much literary theory from the 1940s to the 1960s. He founded the respected literary magazine *The Kenyon Review*.

Grab a chance and you won't be sorry for a might-have-been.

ARTHUR RANSOME
We Didn't Mean to Go to Sea ch 2 1937

Ransome Arthur Michell (1884–1967). English journalist (correspondent in Russia for the *Daily News* during World War I and the

Revolution) and writer of adventure stories for children, such as *Swallows and Amazons* 1930 and *Peter Duck* 1932. The original dinghy, the inspiration of the *Amazon* in *Swallows and Amazons*, was restored in 1991 and put on show in the Windermere Steamboat Museum.

Ransome Robert (1753–1830). English ironfounder and agricultural engineer, whose business earned a worldwide reputation in the 19th and 20th centuries. He introduced factory methods for the production of an improved range of ploughs from 1789. The firm remained at the forefront of advances in agricultural mechanization in connection with steam engines, threshing machines, and lawnmowers.

Rao P(amulaparti) V(enkata) Narasimha (1921–). Indian politician, prime minister of India 1991–96 and Congress (I) leader. He governed the state of Andhra Pradesh as chief minister 1971–73, and served in the Congress (I) cabinets of Indira and Rajiv Gandhi as minister of external affairs 1980–85 and 1988–90 and of human resources 1985–88. He took over the party leadership after the assassination of Rajiv Gandhi. Elected prime minister the following month, he instituted a reform of the economy. He survived a vote of confidence 1993 but was defeated and left office 1996.

Rao Raja (1909–). Indian writer. Rao was born at Hassan, Karnataka. He studied at Montpellier and the Sorbonne in France. He wrote about Indian independence from the perspective of a village in S India in *Kanthapura* 1938 and later, in *The Serpent and the Rope* 1960, about a young cosmopolitan intellectual seeking enlightenment. Collections of stories include *The Cow of the Barricades* 1947 and *The Policeman and the Rose* 1978.

Raoult François Marie (1830–1901). French chemist. In 1882, while working at the University of Grenoble, Raoult formulated one of the basic laws of chemistry. Raoult's law enables the relative molecular mass of a substance to be determined by noting how much of it is required to depress the freezing point of a solvent by a certain amount.

Raphael Sanzio (Raffaello Sanzio) (1483–1520). Italian painter. He was one of the greatest artists of the High Renaissance, active in Perugia, Florence, and Rome (from 1508), where he painted frescoes in the Vatican and for secular patrons. His religious and mythological scenes are harmoniously composed; his dignified portraits enhance the character of his sitters. Many of his designs were engraved, and much of his later work was the product of his studio.

Raphael was born in Urbino, the son of Giovanni Santi (died 1494), a court painter. In 1499 he went to Perugia, where he worked with Perugino, whose graceful style is reflected in Raphael's *Marriage of the Virgin* 1504. This work also shows his early concern for harmonious disposition of figures in the pictorial space. In Florence 1504–08 he studied the works of Leonardo da Vinci, Michelangelo, Masaccio, and Fra Bartolommeo. His paintings of this period include the *Ansidei Madonna*. Pope Julius II commissioned him to decorate the papal apartments (the Stanze della Segnatura) in the Vatican. Raphael's first fresco series there, *The School of Athens* 1509, is a complex but classically composed grouping of Greek philosophers and mathematicians, centred on the figures of Plato and Aristotle. A second series of frescoes, 1511–14, includes the dramatic and richly coloured *Mass of Bolsena*. Raphael received many commissions and within the next few years he produced mythological frescoes in the Villa Farnesina in Rome (1511–12), cartoons for tapestries for the Sistine Chapel, Vatican, the *Sistine Madonna* about 1512, and portraits, for example of Baldassare Castiglione *c.* 1515. His last great work, *The Transfiguration* 1519–20, anticipates Mannerism.

Suggested reading
Beck, James *Raphael* (1976)
Fischel, Oskar *Raphael* (1964)
Freeberg, S J *Painting in Italy 1500–1600* (1975)
Jones, R and Penny, N *Raphael* (1983)
Pope-Hennessy, J *Raphael* (1970)

Rattle *The conductor Simon Rattle. He has worked closely with the City of Birmingham Symphony Orchestra since 1980 and is renowned for his eclectic programmes, which favour music of the 20th century. In recent years his repertory has widened and he has performed 19th-century classics in his distinctive energetic style.*

Rasmussen Poul Nyrup (1943–). Danish economist and politician, prime minister from 1993. Leader of the Social Democrats from 1992, he succeeded Poul Schluter as prime minister, heading the first majority coalition government since 1982. He was returned to power in the 1994 general election.

Following his country's initial rejection of the Maastricht Treaty, he negotiated exemptions from the Treaty's key provisions, including those on defence, and won the nation's backing in a second referendum May 1993.

Rasputin (Russian 'dissolute'; born Grigory Efimovich Novykh) (1871–1916). Siberian Eastern Orthodox mystic who acquired influence over the tsarina Alexandra, wife of Nicholas II, and was able to make political and ecclesiastical appointments. His abuse of power and notorious debauchery (reputedly including the tsarina) led to his murder by a group of nobles.

Rasputin, the illiterate son of a peasant, began as a wandering 'holy man'. Through the tsarina's faith in his power to ease her son's suffering from haemophilia, he became a favourite at the court, where he instigated wild parties under the slogan 'Sin that you may obtain forgiveness'. A larger-than-life character, he even proved hard to kill: when poison had no effect, his assassins shot him and dumped him in the river Neva.
Suggested reading
Minney, R J *Rasputin* (1972)
Wilson, C *Rasputin and the Fall of the Romanovs* (1964)

Rathbone (Philip St John) Basil (1892–1967). South African-born British character actor. He specialised in playing villains, and also played Sherlock Holmes (the fictional detective created by Arthur Conan Doyle) in a series of films. He worked mainly in Hollywood, in such films as *The Adventures of Robin Hood* 1938 and *The Hound of the Baskervilles* 1939.

Two profiles pasted together.

Dorothy Parker on BASIL RATHBONE
quoted in Leslie Halliwell *Filmgoer's Companion* 1965

Rathenau Walther (1867–1922). German politician. He was a leading industrialist and was appointed economic director during World War I, developing a system of economic planning in combination with capitalism. After the war he founded the Democratic Party, and became foreign minister 1922. The same year he signed the Rapallo Treaty of Friendship with the USSR, cancelling German and Soviet counterclaims for indemnities for World War I, and soon after was assassinated by right-wing fanatics.

Do you know what 'le vice Anglais' – the English vice – really is? Not flagellation, not pederasty – whatever the French believe it to be. It's our refusal to admit our emotions. We think they demean us, I suppose.

TERENCE RATTIGAN
In Praise of Love II 1973

Rattigan Terence Mervyn (1911–1977). English dramatist. His play *Ross* 1960 was based on the character of T E Lawrence (Lawrence of Arabia). Rattigan's work ranges from the comedy *French Without Tears* 1936 to the psychological intensity of *The Winslow Boy* 1946. Other plays include *The Browning Version* 1948 and *Separate Tables* 1954. Knighted 1971.

Rattle Simon (1955–). English conductor, principal conductor of the City of Birmingham Symphony Orchestra (CBSO) from 1979. He was assistant conductor with the Bournemouth Symphony Orchestra 1974–76 and with the BBC Scottish Symphony Orchestra 1977–79. He was the driving force behind the funding and building of a new concert hall for the CBSO, Symphony Hall, completed 1991. He has built the CBSO into a world class orchestra, with a core repertoire of early 20th century music; he has also commissioned new works. A popular and dynamic conductor, he achieves a characteristically clear and precise sound. Knighted 1994.

Ratushinskaya Irina (1954–). Soviet dissident poet. Sentenced 1983 to seven years in a labour camp plus five years in internal exile for criticism of the Soviet regime, she was released 1986. Her strongly Christian work includes *Grey is the Colour of Hope* 1988.

Rau Johannes (1931–). German socialist politician. The son of a Protestant pastor, Rau became state premier of North Rhine–Westphalia 1978. In Jan 1987 he stood for chancellor of West Germany but was defeated by the incumbent conservative coalition.

Raul Julia (1940–1994). US film actor. He became known with his appearances on the children's television series *Sesame Street*, and from 1971 onwards had numerous minor film roles. The first film in which he achieved a significant impact, however, was as a jailed political activist in a totalitarian South American state in *Kiss of the Spider Woman* 1985. Julia went on to appear in a number of other films, including *The Morning After* 1986, *Moon Over Parador* 1988, and as Harrison Ford's defence lawyer in *Presumed Innocent* 1990. He achieved widespread popular recognition shortly before his early death for his mockingly stylish embodiment of Gomez in the two films derived from the Charles Addams cartoons, *The Addams Family* 1991 and *Addams Family Values* 1993.

Rauschenberg Robert (born Milton Rauschenberg) (1925–). US Pop artist. He has created happenings and incongruous multimedia works, such as *Monogram* 1959 (Moderna Museet, Stockholm), a stuffed goat daubed with paint and wearing a car tyre around its body. In the 1960s he returned to painting and used the silk-screen printing process to transfer images to canvas. He also made collages.

Suggested reading

Alloway, L *Robert Rauschenberg* (1976)

Tomkins, Calvin *Ahead of the Game: Four Versions of the Avant-Garde* (1962)

Tomkins, Calvin *Off the Wall: Robert Rauschenberg and the Art World of Our Time* (1981)

I still have so much music in my head. I have said nothing. I have so much more to say.

MAURICE RAVEL
quoted in Helene Jourdan-Morhange *Ravel et nous* 1945

Ravel (Joseph) Maurice (1875–1937). French composer and pianist. His work is characterized by its sensuousness, exotic harmonics, and dazzling orchestral effects. Examples are the piano pieces *Pavane pour une infante défunte*/*Pavane for a Dead Infanta* 1899 and *Jeux d'eau*/*Waterfall* 1901, and the ballets *Daphnis et Chloë* 1912 and *Boléro* 1928.

Suggested reading

Demuth, Norman *Ravel* (1947)

Myers, R *Ravel: Life and Works* (1960)

Orenstein, A *Ravel* (1975)

Stuckenschmidt, H H *Maurice Ravel* (1968)

Rawlings Jerry John (1947–). Ghanaian politician, president from 1981. Rawlings first took power in a military coup 1979, pledging to root out widespread corruption and promote 'moral reform'. Within four months he had restored civilian government, but threatened a further coup if politicians were to put their own interests before those of the nation. Alleging renewed corruption in government circles, he seized power again 1981 and, despite promising a speedy return to civilian rule, remained as military leader for more than a decade. Following a referendum supporting multiparty politics 1992, Rawlings left the air force (in which he had been a flight lieutenant) and successfully contested the presidency as a civilian under the new constitution.

Criticized by many traditional politicians and senior military figures as an opportunist adventurer, he retained his popular appeal and successfully made the transition from military leader to constitutionally elected head of state.

Rawlinson Henry Creswicke (1810–1895). English orientalist and political agent in Baghdad in the Ottoman Empire from 1844. He deciphered the Babylonian cuneiform and Old Persian scripts of Darius I's trilingual inscription at Behistun, Persia, continued the excavation work of A H Layard, and published a *History of Assyria* 1852. KCB 1856, baronet 1891.

Rawlinson Henry Seymour, 1st Baron Rawlinson (1864–1925). British soldier in World War I. He joined the Rifle Brigade 1884 and then transferred to the Coldstream Guards 1892 after service in India and Burma. He became a divisional commander 1910 and in 1914 was made director of recruiting but within a month went to France at the head of 7th Division which he led through Belgium to Ypres and Neuve Chapelle. He was given command of the 4th (New) Army 1915. He was responsible for the main attack on the Somme 1916 and played a decisive part in stemming the German Spring Offensive and then the Allied offensive which ended the war. In early 1918 he became British representative at the Council of Versailles but was hastily recalled to the front in March. In 1920 he was appointed commander in chief of the army in India. 2nd baronet 1895, baron 1819.

Rawls John (1921–). US philosopher. In *A Theory of Justice* 1971, he revived the concept of the social contract and its enforcement by civil disobedience. He argued that if we did not know which

Ravel *The composer Maurice Ravel. Along with Debussy he was the leading impressionist composer. His works are often intricately crafted; Stravinsky compared him to a Swiss watchmaker. He was an innovator of pianistic and orchestral techniques, especially when evoking exotic musical ideas.* (Image Select)

position we were to occupy in society, we would choose to live in a society in which there was equal liberty and the minimum of social and economic inequalities. His ideas have influenced left-of-centre parties throughout the world. He taught at Princeton, Cornell, the Massachusetts Institute of Technology, and Harvard.

Rawsthorne Alan (1905–1971). British composer. His *Theme and Variations* for two violins 1938 was followed by other tersely energetic works including *Symphonic Studies* 1939, the overture *Street Corner* 1944, *Concerto for Strings* 1950, and a vigorously inventive sonata for violin and piano, 1959.

Ray John (1627–1705). English naturalist who devised a classification system accounting for some 18,000 plant species. It was the first system to divide flowering plants into monocotyledons and dicotyledons, with additional divisions made on the basis of leaf and flower characters and fruit types. In *Methodus plantarum nova* 1682, Ray first set out his system. He also established the species as the fundamental unit of classification. Ray believed that fossils are the petrified remains of dead animals and plants. This concept, which appeared in his theological writings, did not gain general acceptance until the late 18th century.

In 1670 Ray, with Francis Willughby's help, published *Catalogus plantarum Angliae*/*Catalogue of English Plants*. Ray and Willughby then began working on a definitive catalogue and classification of all known plants and animals. *Historia generalis plantarum* 1686–1704 covered about 18,600 species (most of which were European) and contained much information on the morphology, distribution, habitats, and pharmacological uses of individual species as well as

---

He that uses many words for the explaining of any subject, doth, like the cuttle fish, hide himself for the most part in his own ink.

JOHN RAY
On the Creation

general aspects of plant life, such as diseases and seed germination.

Ray also wrote several books on zoology, giving details of individual species in addition to classification: *Synopsis methodica animalium quadrupedum et serpentini generis/Synopsis of Quadrupeds* 1693, *Historia insectorum/History of Insects* 1710, and *Synopsis methodica avium et piscium/Synopsis of Birds and Fish* 1713.

It is marvelous that we are / the only species that creates / gratuitous forms. / To create is divine, to reproduce / is human.

MAN RAY
Objets de Mon Affection, 'Original Graphic Multiples'

Ray Man. Adopted name of Emmanuel Rabinovich Rudnitsky (1890–1976). US photographer, painter, and sculptor. He was active mainly in France and was associated with the Dada movement. His pictures often showed Surrealist images, for example the photograph *Le Violon d'Ingres* 1924.

Man Ray was born in Philadelphia, but lived mostly in Paris from 1921. He began as a painter and took up photography in 1915, the year he met the Dada artist Duchamp in New York. In 1922 he invented the rayograph, a black-and-white image obtained without a camera by placing objects on sensitized photographic paper and exposing them to light; he also used the technique of solarization (partly reversing the tones on a photograph). His photographs include portraits of many artists and writers.

Suggested reading
Baldwin, Neil *Man Ray* (1988)
Penrose, Roland *Man Ray* (1975)
Ray, Man *Self Portrait* (autobiography) (1963)
Schwarz, Arturo *Man Ray* (1977)

Ray Nicholas. Adopted name of Raymond Nicholas Kienzle (1911–1979). US film director. He was critically acclaimed for his socially aware dramas that concentrated on the individual as an outsider, such as *They Live by Night* 1948 and *Rebel Without a Cause* 1955. Other films include *In a Lonely Place* 1950 and *55 Days at Peking* 1963.

Ray Satyajit (1921–1992). Indian film director. He was internationally known for his trilogy of life in his native Bengal: *Pather Panchali, Unvanquished,* and *The World of Apu* 1955–59. Later films include *The Music Room* 1963, *Charulata* 1964, *The Chess Players* 1977, and *The Home and the World* 1984.

Suggested reading
Seton, Marie *Portrait of a Director: Satyajit Ray* (1971)

Rayburn Samuel Taliaferro (1882–1961). US political leader. A Democrat, he was elected to the US Congress 1912. He supported President Roosevelt's New Deal programme 1933, and was elected majority leader 1937 and Speaker of the House 1940. With the exception of two terms, he served as Speaker until his death. His tenure in the House 1912–61 was the longest on record.

Born in Roane County, Tennessee, USA, and raised in Texas, Rayburn received a law degree from the University of Texas 1908. He served in the state legislature 1907–12. A leader of the Democratic party, Rayburn chaired the national conventions in 1948, 1952, and 1956.

Rayet George Antoine Pons (1839–1906). French astronomer who, in collaboration with Charles Wolf (1827–1918), detected a new class of peculiar white or yellowish stars whose spectra contain broad hydrogen and helium emission lines. These stars are now called *Wolf–Rayet stars.*

He worked in the new weather forecasting service created by astronomer Urbain Leverrier at the Paris Observatory until dismissed over a disagreement about the practical forecasting of storms. From 1876 Rayet was professor of astronomy at Bordeaux, and from 1879 also director of the new observatory at nearby Floirac.

At the Paris Observatory, Rayet collaborated with Charles Wolf and in 1865 they photographed the penumbra of the Moon during an eclipse. In 1866 a nova appeared, and after its brilliance had significantly diminished, Rayet and Wolf discovered bright bands in its spectrum – a phenomenon that had never been noticed in stellar spectra before. The bands were the result of a phase that can occur in the later stages of evolution of a nova. The two astronomers went on to investigate whether permanently bright stars exhibit this phenomenon and in 1867 they discovered three such stars in the constellation of Cygnus. Wolf–Rayet stars are now known to be relatively rare.

Some proofs command assent. Others woo and charm the intellect. They evoke delight and an overpowering desire to say 'Amen, Amen'.

H E Hunter on JOHN WILLIAM STRUTT, 3RD BARON RAYLEIGH
in *The Divine Proportion* 1970

Rayleigh John William Strutt, 3rd Baron Rayleigh (1842–1919). English physicist who wrote the standard treatise *The Theory of Sound* (1877–78), experimented in optics and microscopy, and, with William Ramsay, discovered argon. Baron 1873. Nobel prize 1904.

He set up a laboratory at his home and was professor of experimental physics at Cambridge 1879–84, making the Cavendish Laboratory an important research centre.

In 1871, Rayleigh explained that the blue colour of the sky arises from the scattering of light by dust particles in the air, and was able to relate the degree of scattering to the wavelength of the light. He also made the first accurate definition of the resolving power of diffraction gratings, which led to improvements in the spectroscope. He completed in 1884 the standardization of the three basic electrical units: the ohm, ampere, and volt. His insistence on accuracy prompted the designing of more precise electrical instruments.

After leaving Cambridge, Rayleigh continued to do research in a broad range of subjects including light and sound radiation, thermodynamics, electromagnetism, and mechanics.

An inconsistency in the Rayleigh–Jeans equation, published by Rayleigh 1900 (amended 1905 by James Jeans), which described the distribution of wavelengths in black-body radiation, led to the formulation shortly after of the quantum theory by German physicist Max Planck.

Read Herbert Edward (1893–1968). English art critic, poet, and academic. His writings during the 1930s made modern art accessible to the public. His books include *The Meaning of Art* 1931 and the influential *Education through Art* 1943. He was one of the founders of the Institute of Contemporary Arts in London.

Take courage, my friend, the devil is dead!

CHARLES READE
The Cloister and the Hearth ch 24 1861

Reade Charles (1814–1884). English novelist and playwright. He wrote the historical epic, set in the 15th century, *The Cloister and the Hearth* 1861.

Reagan Ronald Wilson (1911–). 40th president of the USA 1981–89, a Republican. He was governor of California 1966–74, and a former Hollywood actor. Reagan was a hawkish and popular president. He adopted an aggressive policy in Central America, attempting to overthrow the government of Nicaragua, and invading Grenada 1983. In 1987, Irangate was investigated by the Tower

Politics is supposed to be the second oldest profession. I have come to realize that it bears a very close resemblance to the first.

RONALD REAGAN
at a conference in Los Angeles 2 Mar 1977

Commission; Reagan admitted that US–Iran negotiations had become an 'arms for hostages deal', but denied knowledge of resultant funds being illegally sent to the Contras in Nicaragua. He increased military spending (sending the national budget deficit to record levels), cut social programmes, introduced deregulation of domestic markets, and cut taxes. His Strategic Defense Initiative, announced 1983, proved controversial owing to the cost and unfeasibility. He was succeeded by vice president George Bush.

Reagan was born in Tampico, Illinois, the son of a shoe salesman who was bankrupted during the Depression. He became a Hollywood actor 1937 and appeared in 50 films, including *Bedtime for Bonzo* 1951 and *The Killers* 1964. As president of the Screen Actors' Guild 1947–52, he became a conservative, critical of the bureaucratic stifling of free enterprise, and named names before the House Un-American Activities Committee. He joined the Republican Party 1962, and his term as governor of California was marked by battles against students.

Having lost the Republican presidential nomination 1968 and 1976 to Nixon and Ford respectively, Reagan won it 1980 and defeated President Carter. He was wounded in an assassination attempt 1981. The invasion of Grenada, following a coup there, generated a revival of national patriotism, and Reagan was re-elected by a landslide 1984. His insistence on militarizing space through the Strategic Defense Initiative, popularly called Star Wars, prevented a disarmament agreement when he met the Soviet leader Gorbachev 1985 and 1986, but a 4% reduction in nuclear weapons was agreed 1987. In 1986, he ordered the bombing of Tripoli, Libya, in alleged retaliation for the killing of a US soldier in Berlin by a guerrilla group.

Suggested reading
Blumenthal, S and Edsall, T B *The Reagan Legacy* (1988)
Boyarsky, B *Ronald Reagan: His Life and Rise to Presidency* (1981)
Palmer, John L (ed) *Perspectives on the Reagan Years* (1986)
Wills, Garry *Reagan's America: Innocents at Home* (1987)

Reardon Ray (1932–   ). Welsh snooker player. One of the leading players of the 1970s, he was six times world champion 1970–78.

Réaumur Réné Antoine Ferchault de (1683–1757). French scientist. His work on metallurgy *L'Arte de convertir le fer forge en acier* 1722 described how to convert iron into steel and stimulated the development of the French steel industry. He produced a six-volume work 1734–42 on entomology, *L'Histoire des insectes/History of Insects*, which threw much new light on the social insects. He also contributed to other areas of science.

Reber Grote (1911–   ). US radio engineer who pioneered radio astronomy. He attempted to map all the extraterrestrial sources of radio emission that could be traced. He built his own apparatus for studying cosmic radio waves, and held posts at several US institutions. From 1954 he worked mainly in Australia at the Commonwealth Scientific and Industrial Research Organization in Tasmania, though he spent 1957–61 at the National Radio Astronomy Observatory at Green Back, West Virginia.

Reber's first instrument was a bowl-shaped reflector 9 m/30 ft in diameter, with an antenna at its focus, built in the back garden of his Illinois home in 1957. For a number of years, Reber's was probably the only radio telescope in existence. With it, he could identify only a general direction from which radio waves were coming. The most intense radiation he recorded emanated from the direction of Sagittarius, near the centre of the Galaxy.

In Hawaii a new radio telescope was constructed, sensitive to lower frequencies, and he worked there 1951–54. His last project, in Tasmania, was to complete a map of radio sources emitting waves around 144 m/473 ft in length.

Récamier Jeanne Françoise Juliet Adélaide (born Bernard) (1777–1849). French society hostess, born in Lyon. At the age of 15 she married Jacques Récamier (died 1830), an elderly banker, and held a salon of literary and political celebrities.

Red Cloud (Sioux name *Mahpiua Luta*) (1822–1909). American Sioux Indian leader. Paramount chief of the Oglala Sioux from

Reagan *Ronald Reagan, US president 1981–89. Despite, or perhaps because of, his fundamentalist rhetoric and his emphasis on high defence spending and military intervention, Reagan was a popular president and was easily re-elected 1984 for a second term.*

1860, he led the armed resistance to the advance of white settlers along the Bozeman Trail. He signed the Fort Laramie Treaty 1869 which gave the Indians a large area in the Black Hills of Dakota. He resisted any involvement in the war which culminated in the Battle of Little Bighorn 1876.

Born in the area of modern Nebraska, Red Cloud led his followers to the Red Cloud Agency in Nebraska after Custer's last stand at Little Bighorn. From there they were moved to the Pine Ridge Agency in South Dakota 1878; Red Cloud continued to seek compromise with the government.

Suggested reading
Andrist, Ralph *The Long Death: The Last Days of the Plains Indians* (1969)
Josephy, A M *The Patriot Chiefs* (1961)
Olsen, James *Red Cloud and the Sioux Problem* (1965)

Redding Otis (1941–1967). US soul singer and songwriter. He had a number of hits in the mid-1960s such as 'My Girl' 1965, 'Respect' 1967, and '(Sittin' on the) Dock of the Bay' 1968, released after his death in a plane crash.

Robert Redford is the centre of America – blonde, blue-eyed, tall and thin.

Barry Levinson on ROBERT REDFORD
quoted in *Film Yearbook* 1986

Redford (Charles) Robert (1937–   ). US actor and film director. His blond good looks and versatility earned him his first starring role in *Barefoot in the Park* 1967, followed by *Butch Cassidy and the Sundance Kid* 1969 and *The Sting* 1973 (both with Paul Newman). His other films as an actor include *All the President's Men* 1976, *Out of Africa* 1985, and *Indecent Proposal* 1993. He directed *Ordinary People* 1980, *The Milagro Beanfield War* 1988, *A River Runs Through It* 1992, and *Quiz Show* 1994. He established the Sundance Institute in Utah for the development of film-making 1981.

I have a very low regard for cynics. I think it's the beginning of dying.

ROBERT REDFORD
Time 29 March 1976

Redgrave Michael Scudamore (1908–1985). English actor. His stage roles included Hamlet and Lear (Shakespeare), Uncle Vanya (Chekhov), and the schoolmaster in Rattigan's *The Browning Version* (filmed 1951). On screen he appeared in *The Lady Vanishes* 1938, *The Importance of Being Earnest* 1952, and *Goodbye Mr Chips* 1959. He was the father of actresses Vanessa and Lynn Redgrave. Knighted 1959.

Redgrave Steven Geoffrey (1962–). English oarsman. Gold medallist at three successive Olympics, winning the coxed fours 1984 and the coxed pairs 1988 and 1992. He also won four gold medals at the World Championships 1986–93, gold at the World Indoor Championships 1991, and was a member of the winning four-man bobsleigh team at the national bobsleigh championships 1989.

Redgrave Vanessa (1937–). English actress. She has played Shakespeare's Lady Macbeth and Cleopatra on the stage, Ellida in Ibsen's *Lady From the Sea* 1976 and 1979, and Olga in Chekhov's *Three Sisters* 1990. She won an Academy Award for best supporting actress for her title role in the film *Julia* 1976; other films include *Wetherby* 1985 and *Howards End* 1992. She is active in left-wing politics.

Redhead Brian (1929–1994). English journalist and broadcaster, best known as co-host of Radio 4's *Today* programme 1975–94, where he won over listeners with his jaunty, confident manner and often idiosyncratic interviewing style. Redhead worked for the *Manchester Guardian* from 1954, becoming northern editor 1964, and he was appointed editor of the *Manchester Evening News* 1969. He left newspaper journalism to join the *Today* team 1975. His highly idiosyncratic and unpredictable broadcasts gained a large and devoted following.

Redman Roderick Oliver (1905–1975). English astronomer who was chiefly interested in stellar spectroscopy and the development of spectroscopic techniques, and in solar physics.

Redman worked mainly at the Cambridge observatories and organized their re-equipping after World War II. He became professor 1947 and in 1972 was made director of the amalgamated observatories and Institute of Theoretical Physics. He also established a solar observatory in Malta.

Redman applied the method of photographic photometry to the study of elliptical galaxies and in the 1940s, in Pretoria, South Africa, also to the study of bright stars, for which he developed the narrow-band technique, which was of great value in stellar photometry.

He went all over the world in order to observe total eclipses of the Sun, during which he was able to identify thousands of the emission lines in the chromospheric spectrum and to investigate the chromospheric temperature.

Redman's final contribution to astronomy was his initiation of a large stellar photometry programme.

What you have done for Frenchmen in Quebec ... for Dutchmen in the Transvaal, you should now do for Irishmen in Ireland.

JOHN REDMOND
Speech in favour of Irish Home Rule in
the House of Commons 30 Mar 1908

Redmond John Edward (1856–1918). Irish politician, Charles Parnell's successor as leader of the Nationalist Party 1890–1916. The 1910 elections saw him holding the balance of power in the House of Commons, and he secured the introduction of a Home Rule bill, which was opposed by Protestant Ulster. Redmond supported the British cause on the outbreak of World War I, and the bill was passed though its operation was suspended until the war's end. The growth of the nationalist party Sinn Féin (the political wing of the Irish Republican Army) and the 1916 Easter Rising ended his hopes and his power.

Redon Odilon (1840–1916). French Symbolist painter and graphic artist. He used fantastic symbols and images, sometimes mythological. From the 1890s he painted still lifes, flowers, and landscapes. His work was much admired by the Surrealists.

Redon initially worked mostly in black and white, producing charcoal drawings and lithographs, but from 1890 his works, in both oils and pastels, were often brilliantly coloured. The head of Orpheus is a recurring motif in his work.

Suggested reading
Druick, Douglas *Odilon Redon* (1994)
Hobbs, Richard *Odilon Redon* (1977)

Redouté Pierre Joseph (1759–1840). French flower painter. He was patronized by Empress Josephine and the Bourbon court. He taught botanical drawing at the Museum of Natural History in Paris and produced volumes of sumptuous, highly detailed flowers, notably *Les Roses* 1817–24.

Redwood John (1951–). British Conservative politician. He was Welsh Secretary 1993–95, when he resigned to contest the Conservative leadership following John Major's decision to challenge his critics within the party by forcing a leadership election.

Although he was defeated, Redwood fought a creditable campaign, increasing his public profile and establishing himself as a serious potential leader from the right of the party. His seemingly unemotional character, which earned him the nickname 'Vulcan', was to some extent dispelled by his performance during the campaign, and even his fiercest critics have had to acknowledge his intellectual ability.

Reed Carol (1906–1976). English film producer and director. The illegitimate son of actor Herbert Beerbohm Tree, who died when Reed was 11, he followed his father onto the stage as an actor before finding work at Ealing studios as a dialogue coach. He was an influential figure in the British film industry of the 1940s. His films include *Odd Man Out* 1947, *The Third Man* 1949, *The Fallen Idol* 1950, *Our Man in Havana* 1959, and the Academy Award-winning musical *Oliver!* 1968. *The Fallen Idol* and *The Third Man* were both written for him by Graham Greene. Knighted 1952.

Reed Ishmael Scott (1938–). US novelist. His novels parody and satirize notions of historical fact, exploiting traditions taken from jazz and voodoo. They include *The Free-Lance Pallbearers* 1967, *Mumbo Jumbo* 1972, *Reckless Eyeballing* 1986, and *Japanese by Spring* 1993. His poetry includes the collection *Chattanooga* 1973.

Reed John (1887–1920). US journalist and author. As a supporter of the Bolsheviks, Reed published his account of the Russian Revolution in *Ten Days that Shook the World* 1919. Later indicted in the US for sedition, Reed fled to the Soviet Union, where he died in exile.

Suggested reading
O'Connor, Richard and Walker, Dale *The Lost Revolutionary* (1967)
Rosenstone, Robert *Romantic Revolutionary* (1975)

I can't listen to it any more. It makes me too taut and nervous. And it brings back too many bad trips.

LOU REED
on his sombre album *Berlin*, talking to
Steven Gains *Sunday News* 6 Jan 1974

Reed Lou (Louis Firbank) (1942–). US rock singer, songwriter, and guitarist. He was a member 1965–70 and 1993 of the New York avant-garde group the Velvet Underground, perhaps the most influential band of the period. His solo work deals largely with urban alienation and angst, and includes the albums *Berlin* 1973, *Street Hassle* 1978, and *New York* 1989. His best-known recording is 'Walk on the Wild Side' from the album *Transformer* 1972.

Reed (Robert) Oliver (1938–). English actor. He appeared in such films as *Women in Love* 1969, *The Devils* 1971, and *Castaway* 1987. He is the nephew of the director Carol Reed.

Reed Walter (1851–1902). US physician and medical researcher who isolated the aedes mosquito *Aedes aegypti* as the sole carrier of yellow fever. This led to the local eradication of the deadly virus disease by destruction of mosquito breeding grounds. His breakthrough work was carried out during a yellow-fever epidemic 1900–01 in Cuba.

He joined the Army Medical Corps 1875, served as an army surgeon in Arizona 1876–89 and Baltimore 1890–93, and was professor at the Army Medical College 1893–1902.

His 1898 research into the causes and transmission of typhoid fever brought about significant control of the disease in army camps. He also worked on malaria and diphtheria.

Rees Lloyd Frederic (1895–1988). Australian landscape artist. His paintings of Sydney Harbour and the southern New South Wales coast span more than half a century. They range in style from the sombre tones of his early work and the thickly layered oils of his middle years to the large-scale, pale-coloured, abstract but still recognizable landscapes of his later years.

Rees-Mogg William, Baron Rees-Mogg (1928–). British journalist, editor of *The Times* 1967–81, chair of the Arts Council 1982–89, and from 1988 chair of the Broadcasting Standards Council. In 1993 he challenged the government over ratification of the Maastricht Treaty, notably the government's right to transfer foreign policy decisions to European Community (now European Union) institutions. His challenge was rejected by the High Court. Knighted 1981, baron 1988.

Reeve Christopher (1952–). US actor best known for playing the title role in the film *Superman* 1978 and its three sequels. Reeve appeared as both the muscle-bound hero and his mild-mannered, bespectacled alter ego, and the films owe much of their success to his charm, humour, and sense of irony. Reeve also tried to play as many different parts as possible; subsequent films include *Deathtrap* 1981 and *The Bostonians* 1984, and he appeared in more than 110 stage productions in the USA and England. He became paralysed from the neck down in a 1995 horse-riding accident.

Reeves William Pember (1857–1932). New Zealand politician and writer. He was New Zealand minister of education 1891–96, and director of the London School of Economics 1908–19. He wrote poetry and the classic history of New Zealand, *Long White Cloud* 1898.

Regan Donald Thomas (1918–). US Republican political adviser to Ronald Reagan. He was secretary of the Treasury 1981–85, and chief of White House staff 1985–87, when he was forced to resign because of widespread belief in his complicity in the Irangate scandal.

Creation must be completely free: Every fetter one imposes on oneself by taking into account playability or public taste leads to disaster.

MAX REGER
in a letter to Kerndl 1900

Reger (Johann Baptist Joseph) Max(imilian) (1873–1916). German composer and pianist. He was professor at the Leipzig Conservatoire from 1907. His works embody a particular blend of contrapuntal ingenuity and Romantic sentimentality, and include *Four Symphonic Poems* 1913, sonatas, Romantic character pieces, and orchestral variations and fugues on themes by Beethoven, Mozart, and other less well known composers.

Regiomontanus (Johannes Müller) (1436–1476). German astronomer who compiled astronomical tables, translated Ptolemy's *Almagest* from Greek into Latin, and assisted in the reform of the Julian calendar.

Johannes Müller adopted the name Regiomontanus as a Latinized form of his birthplace Königsberg while studying at Vienna. At the age of 15, he was appointed to the Faculty of Astronomy at Vienna. In 1471 he moved to Nuremberg, where he installed a printing press in his house and so became one of the first publishers of astronomical and scientific literature. He went to Rome in 1475, invited by the

pope to assist in amending the notoriously incorrect ecclesiastical calendar.

In 1467, Regiomontanus started compiling trigonometric and astronomical tables, but these too were not published until more after his death. Regiomontanus's *Ephemerides* 1474 was the first publication of its kind to be printed (by himself); it gave the positions of the heavenly bodies for every day from the year 1475 to 1506.

After Regiomontanus's death, the statement 'the motion of the stars must vary a tiny bit on account of the motion of the Earth' was found in his handwriting. This has led some people to believe that Regiomontanus gave Copernicus the idea that the Earth moves round the Sun.

Regnault Henri Victor (1810–1878). German-born French physical chemist who showed that Boyle's law applies only to ideal gases. He also invented an air thermometer and a hygrometer, and discovered carbon tetrachloride (tetrachloromethane).

Regnault was born in Aachen and studied in Paris at the Ecole Polytechnique and the Ecole des Mines as well as in various parts of Europe. He returned to the Ecole Polytechnique in 1836 as an assistant to Joseph Gay-Lussac and in 1840 succeeded him as professor of chemistry. He became professor of physics at the Collège de France in 1841. From 1854 Regnault lived and worked in Sèvres as director of the porcelain factory and was still engaged in research there when, in 1870, all his instruments and books were destroyed by Prussian soldiers.

In chemistry, Regnault studied the action of chlorine on ethers, leading to the discovery of vinyl chloride (monochloroethene), dichloroethylene (dichloroethene), trichloroethylene (trichloroethene), and carbon tetrachloride (tetrachloromethane).

In 1842 Regnault was commissioned to redetermine all the physical constants involved in the design and operation of steam engines. This led him to study the thermal properties of gases. He measured the coefficients of expansion of various gases and by 1852 had shown how real gases depart from the behaviour required by Boyle's law.

Regnault also calculated that absolute zero is at −273°C/−459°F. He redetermined the composition of air, and performed experiments on respiration in animals.

Rehnquist William Hubbs (1924–). Chief justice of the US Supreme Court from 1986. Under his leadership, the Court has established a reputation for conservative rulings on such issues as abortion and capital punishment.

Active within the Republican Party, Rehnquist was appointed head of the office of legal counsel by President Nixon in 1969 and controversially defended such measures as pre-trial detention and wiretapping. He became an associate justice of the Supreme Court in 1972. As chief justice, he wrote the majority opinion for such cases as *Morrison v Olson* 1988, in which the Court ruled that a special court can appoint special prosecutors to investigate crimes by high-ranking officials, and *Hustler v Falwell* 1988, in which the Court ruled that public figures cannot be compensated for stress caused by parody that cannot possibly be taken seriously. Rehnquist dissented in *Texas v Johnson* 1989, in which the Court ruled that the burning of the US flag in protest is protected by individual rights set forth in the First Amendment. In 1990 he dissented on the Court's ruling that it is unconstitutional for states to have the right to require a teenager to notify her parents before having an abortion.

As an associate justice, Rehnquist argued in dissent for the death penalty in *Furman v Georgia* 1972, and again in dissent against the right to abortion in *Roe v Wade* 1973. Writing for the majority, Rehnquist held in *Rostken v Goldberg* 1981 that it is constitutional to exclude women for registering for the draft.

He was appointed chief justice by President Reagan.

Rehoboam King of Judah about 932–915 BC, son of Solomon. Under his rule the Jewish nation split into the two kingdoms of Israel and Judah. Ten of the tribes revolted against him and took Jeroboam as their ruler, leaving Rehoboam only the tribes of Judah and Benjamin.

Reich Robert B(ernard) (1946–). US Democrat politician and political economist, secretary of labour from 1993. In *Minding America's Business: The Decline and Rise of the American Economy* 1982, he proposed the diversion of government financial incentives away from declining manufacturing industries to those employing new technology.

Reich entered the Justice Department 1974, became director of policy planning at the Federal Trade Commission 1976, and a lecturer in political economy at the John F Kennedy School of Government, Harvard University, 1981. His other books include *New Deals: The Chrysler Revival and the American System*, an analysis of government intervention to bail out the car manufacturer Chrysler 1979; *Tales of a New America* 1987; *The Resurgent Liberal (and Other Unfashionable Prophecies)* 1989; and *The Work of Nations: Preparing Ourselves for 21st Century Capitalism* 1991, where he called for the education of a skilled and flexible workforce, able to adapt to new techniques.

Reich Steve (1936–). US composer. His Minimalist music employs simple patterns carefully superimposed and modified to highlight constantly changing melodies and rhythms; examples are *Phase Patterns* for four electronic organs 1970, *Music for Mallet Instruments, Voices, and Organ* 1973, and *Music for Percussion and Keyboards* 1984.

Reich Wilhelm (1897–1957). Austrian physician who emigrated to the USA 1939. He combined Marxism and psychoanalysis to advocate the positive effects of directed sexual energies and sexual freedom. His works include *Die Sexuelle Revolution/The Sexual Revolution* 1936–45 and *Die Funktion des Orgasmus/The Function of the Orgasm* 1948.

He held the view that neuroses were the result of repressed sexual energy that could be released only through orgasm. He extended Freud's hypothesis that sexuality determines personality, and concluded that orgastically potent individuals will spontaneously seek to do what is good and right.

Suggested reading
Reich, Ilse Ollendorf *Wilhelm Reich: A Personal Biography* (1969)
Rycroft, Charles *Reich* (1971)
Sharaf, Myron *Fury on Earth* (1983)
Wilson, Colin *The Quest for Wilhelm Reich* (1981)

Reichenau Walther von (1884–1942). German field marshal in World War II. He commanded 10th Army in the invasion of Poland 1939 and 6th Army in the invasion of Belgium and France 1940. He remained in command of 6th Army and led it in Operation Barbarossa 1941, playing a major role in the victory at Kiev. He was rewarded with the command of Army Group South but suffered a heart attack shortly after and died.

Reichstadt, Duke of title of Napoleon II, son of Napoleon I.

Reichstein Tadeus (1897–1996). Swiss biochemist who investigated the chemical activity of the adrenal glands. By 1946 Reichstein had identified a large number of steroids secreted by the adrenal cortex, some of which would later be used in the treatment of Addison's disease. Reichstein shared the 1950 Nobel Prize for Physiology or Medicine with Edward Kendall and Philip Hench.

Reid George Houstoun (1845–1918). Australian politician, born in Scotland; premier of New South Wales 1894–99, prime minister 1904–05. While premier he brought in reforms in the areas of taxation, public administration, land law, and social legislation. He was an equivocal supporter of federation but entered the first federal parliament as leader of the conservative Free Trade Party. In 1904 he was able to form a coalition government but his majority was not secure enough for his government to forward initiatives and he was defeated after ten months. He retired from parliament in 1908. KCMG 1909.

Reid arrived in Australia in 1852 and worked at the Colonial Treasury and Crown Law Office in Sydney before entering parliament. After his retirement he became the first Australian high commissioner to London 1910–16 and was then a member of the House of Commons.

Reid Thomas (1710–1796). Scottish mathematician and philosopher. His *Enquiry into the Human Mind on the Principles of Common Sense* 1764 attempted to counter the sceptical conclusions of Scottish philosopher David Hume. He believed that the existence of the material world and the human soul is self-evident 'by the consent of ages and nations, of the learned and unlearned'. In 1794 he succeeded Adam Smith as professor of moral philosophy at Glasgow. He was also a Presbyterian minister.

Reinhardt Django (Jean Baptiste) (1910–1953). Belgian jazz guitarist and composer. He was co-leader, with Stephane Grappelli, of the Quintet du Hot Club de France 1934–39. He had a lyrical acoustic style and individual technique, and influenced many US musicians.

Reinhardt Max. Adopted name of Max Goldmann (1873–1943). Austrian producer and director. His Expressionist style was predominant in German theatre and film during the 1920s and 1930s. Directors such as Murnau and Lubitsch and stars such as Dietrich worked with him. He co-directed the film *A Midsummer Night's Dream* 1935, a play he directed in numerous stage productions.

In 1920 Reinhardt founded the Salzburg Festival. When the Nazis came to power, he lost his theatres and, after touring Europe as a guest director, went to the USA, where he produced and directed. He founded an acting school and theatre workshop in Hollywood.

Reisz Karel (1926–). Czech film director. He was originally a film critic. He lived in Britain from 1938, and later in the USA. His first feature film, *Saturday Night and Sunday Morning* 1960, was a critical and commercial success. His other films include *Morgan* 1966, *The French Lieutenant's Woman* 1981, and *Sweet Dreams* 1986. He has subsequently directed plays in London.

Remarque Erich Maria (1898–1970). German novelist. He was a soldier in World War I. His *All Quiet on the Western Front* 1929, one of the first anti-war novels, led to his being deprived of German nationality. He lived in Switzerland 1929–39, and then in the USA.

Rembrandt Harmensz van Rijn (1606–1669). Dutch painter and etcher. He was one of the most prolific and significant artists in Europe of the 17th century.

The fourth son of a prosperous miller, he first studied painting in the studio of Jan van Swanenburgh at Leyden, in which he spent three years, then for some six months under Pieter Lastman at Amsterdam. Through these two painters, especially Lastman, and other contemporaries who had visited Italy, such as Honthorst, he acquired the dramatic use of light and shade they had learned from Caravaggio. It appears already in his early works, *The Philosopher* (National Gallery, London) being a remarkable example. In 1631 he settled at Amsterdam, and ten brilliant and happy years followed. In 1632 he became celebrated for his group portrait of the Amsterdam Guild of Surgeons around an opened corpse, *The Anatomy Lesson of Dr Tulp* (The Hague, Mauritshuis). In 1634 he married the daughter of wealthy parents, Saskia van Uilenburgh, who became the centre of his life and art. *Self-Portrait with Saskia* (Gemäldegalerie, Dresden) is a joyous work, and he painted Saskia in various other roles (for example as *Flora* in the National Gallery portrait of 1635). Rembrandt prospered in portrait painting. He spent lavishly on an art collection and personal finery. In 1641 his son Titus was born.

The year 1642, however, saw a change of fortune. Saskia died, and the famous group known as *The Night Watch* (*The Militia Company of Captain Frans Banning Cocq and Lieutenant Willem van Ruytenburch*, Rijksmuseum) marked the beginning of a decline in popularity, being unconventional in arrangement and not giving the equal importance to each person portrayed that his clients wished for. The years which followed seem sombre. Rembrandt became bankrupt. His housekeeper Hendrickje Stoffels, however, took care of him and Titus, and acted as model, and his industry remained intense. In spiritual quality his work increased in power, including such superb late masterpieces as *The Syndics of the Cloth Guild* and *The Jewish Bride* (Rijksmuseum). Between 600 and 700 paintings, 300 etchings, and nearly 2,000 drawings show the development of his genius. His self-portraits, from youth to old age, are an analytic study of his appearance and state of mind, most moving being those of his last years; in general Rembrandt is greatly inspired in the representation of the aged. In landscape (taking some hints from Hercules Seghers and van Goyen) he could produce such a magnificent work as *The Stone Bridge* (Rijksmuseum). In biblical subjects he progressed from the theatrical magnificence of *The Woman taken in Adultery* (National Gallery, London), with its small figures and immense background, to an intensely human interpretation of Christian stories. Rembrandt's technical resources match his thought. In oils his rich impasto creates living substance and solids. In many etchings, and in his drawings, another faculty comes into play; he is swift, free and fresh, though in etching he also achieves such elaborate triumphs as the *Hundred Guilder* print (*Christ healing the Sick*) and the *Three Trees*. Rembrandt was buried in the Wester Kerk at Amsterdam, and his house in the city is now a Rembrandt museum.

Suggested reading
Clark, K *An Introduction to Rembrandt* (1978)
Haak, B *Rembrandt: His Life, his Work, his Time* (1969)
Rosenberg, J *Rembrandt: Life and Work* (1981)
White, C *Rembrandt and his World* (1964)
White, C *Rembrandt: Self-Portraits* (1982)

Remick Lee (1935–1991). US film and television actress. Although often typecast as a flirt early in her career, she later delivered intelligent and affecting portrayals of an extensive range of characters. Among her best-known films were *The Long Hot Summer* 1958, *Anatomy of a Murder* 1959, *Sanctuary* 1961, and *No Way to Treat a Lady* 1968. Her last film role was in *The Europeans* 1979, in which she gave a warm and amusing performance.

Remington Eliphalet (1793–1861). US inventor, gunsmith, and arms manufacturer and founder (with his father) of the Remington firm. He supplied the US army with rifles in the Mexican War 1846–48, then in 1856 the firm expanded into the manufacture of agricultural implements. His son Philo continued the expansion.

Remington Frederic (1861–1909). US artist and illustrator. He was known for his paintings, sculptures, and sketches of scenes of the American West, which he recorded during several trips to the region. His lively images of cowboys and horses include the sculpture *The Outlaw* 1906 (Los Angeles County Museum of Art).

Remington Philo (1816–1889). US inventor of the breech-loading rifle that bears his name. He began manufacturing typewriters 1873, using the patent of Christopher Sholes, and made improvements that resulted five years later in the first machine with a shift key, thus providing lower-case letters as well as capital letters. US humorist Mark Twain bought one of the earliest Remington typewriters, becoming the first author to provide his publisher with a typescript.

The Remington rifle and carbine, which had a falling block breech and a tubular magazine, were developed in collaboration with his father Eliphalet Remington. Philo and Eliphalet Remington made many improvements to guns and their manufacture; for example, a special lathe for the cutting of gunstocks, a method of producing extremely straight gun barrels, and the first US drilled rifle barrel from cast steel.

Renan (Joseph) Ernest (1823–1892). French theologian and historian. His *La Vie de Jésus/The Life of Jesus*, published 1863, controversially denied the supernatural element of Christ's life and mission. It was the first work in a series on the history of the origins of Christianity. Renan was professor of Hebrew at the Collège de France.

A man is happy who in the flower of youth wins fortune and glory, and whose thread runs out before bitter old age.

MARY RENAULT
The King Must Die 1958

Renault Mary. Pen name of (Eileen) Mary Challans (1905–1983). English historical novelist. She specialized in stories about ancient Greece, with a trilogy on Theseus and two novels on Alexander the Great: *Fire from Heaven* 1970 and *The Persian Boy* 1972.

Rendell Ruth Barbara (1930–). English novelist and short-story writer. She is the author of a detective series featuring Chief Inspector Wexford. Her psychological crime novels explore the minds of people who commit murder, often through obsession or social inadequacy, as in *A Demon in my View* 1976 and *Heartstones* 1987. *Lake of Darkness* 1980 won the Arts Council National Book Award (Genre Fiction) for that year. She also writes under the pseudonym Barbara Vine.

René (France) Albert (1935–). Seychelles left-wing politician, the country's first prime minister after independence and president from 1977 after a coup. In 1964 René founded the left-wing Seychelles People's United Party, pressing for complete independence. When this was achieved, in 1976, he became prime minister and James Mancham, leader of the Seychelles Democratic Party, became president. René seized the presidency in 1977 and set up a one-party state. He has followed a non-nuclear policy of nonalignment. In 1993 René and his party, the People's Progressive Front, won the country's first free elections in 16 years.

Renger-Patzsch Albert (1897–1966). German photographer. He was a leading figure of the New Photography movement which emphasized objectivity of vision. His influential book *Die Welt ist schön/The World is Beautiful* 1928 was a disparate collection of objects, from plants to industrial machinery, all photographed in the same way.

Rendell English novelist Ruth Rendell first achieved success with her series of detective novels written around the main character, Detective Chief Inspector Wexford. Obsessive love and personal inadequacy are frequent themes in her novels. She also writes under the pen name Barbara Vine.

Reni Guido (1575–1642). Italian painter. Active in Bologna and Rome about 1600–14, his idealized works include the fresco *Aurora* 1613–14 (Casino Rospigliosi, Rome). His workshop in Bologna produced numerous religious images, including Madonnas.

He first studied at Bologna under the Flemish painter Denis Calvaert, but afterwards entered the academy of the Carracci and became one of the principal adherents of Annibale Carracci. He went to Rome about 1600, where, though belonging to an opposite camp, he seems to have been influenced to some extent by Caravaggio. He was, however, more greatly impressed by Raphael and antique sculpture. It is a Raphaelesque grace that characterizes his most celebrated work, the ceiling painting of *Aurora*. Apart from a visit to Naples 1621 he worked mainly in Bologna. He was esteemed among the great masters for his skill in composition and the silvery colour of his later manner until the 19th century. Guido was then, and has since been, criticized for sweetness of sentiment and empty theatricality. He had many pupils and his historical importance in the development of the Baroque style is unquestionable.

Rennenkampf Paul Karlovich (1854–1918). Russian general. He served in China and the Russo-Japanese war before taking charge of the invasion of E Prussia in World War I. After some initial success he was forced to retreat following the Russian defeat at the Battle of Tannenberg Aug 1914. He attacked again with reinforcements, drove the Germans back from the river Niemen line, and once more invaded E Prussia. He was then transferred to the Warsaw Front where he argued with General Russky and was retired late 1914. He lived in retirement for the rest of the war until he was murdered by the Bolsheviks 1918.

Rennie John (1761–1821). Scottish engineer. He started his own engineering business about 1791, and built the London and East India docks, as well as construction work on harbours in the UK, Malta, and Bermuda. He built three bridges over the River Thames in London, later demolished: Waterloo Bridge 1811–17, Southwark Bridge 1814–19, and London Bridge 1824–34; he also built other bridges, canals, and dams (Rudyard dam, Staffordshire, 1800). Waterloo Bridge was demolished 1934–36 and replaced 1944; London Bridge was demolished 1968, bought by a US oil company and reassembled at Lake Havana, Arizona.

Reno Janet (1939–). US lawyer, US attorney general under President Clinton. Having been appointed to the post in 1993, she took full responsibility in the same year for the attack by the Federal Bureau of Investigation on the compound of the Branch Davidian cult at Waco, Texas, in which 86 died.

Reno was born in Miami, Florida. As chief prosecutor for Dade County, Florida, 1978–93, she concentrated on helping disadvantaged children to grow into responsible citizens. She is a Democrat and is the first woman to be appointed Attorney General.

The exchange of two fantasies and the coming together of two epidermises.

JEAN RENOIR
Definition of love in the film *La Règle du Jeu* 1939

Renoir Jean (1894–1979). French film director. His films, characterized by their humanism and naturalistic technique, include *Boudu sauvé des eaux*/*Boudu Saved from Drowning* 1932, *La Grande Illusion* 1937, and *La Règle du jeu*/*The Rules of the Game* 1939. In 1975 he received an honorary Academy Award for his life's work. He was the son of the painter Pierre-Auguste Renoir.

Suggested reading
Durgnat, Raymond *Jean Renoir* (1974)
Faulkner, Christopher *The Social Cinema of Jean Renoir* (1986)
Gilliatt, Penelope *Jean Renoir: Essays, Conversations and Reviews* (1975)
Renoir, Jean *My Life and My Films* (1974)

Renoir Pierre-Auguste (1841–1919). French Impressionist painter. He met Monet and Sisley in the early 1860s, and together they formed the nucleus of the Impressionist movement. He developed a lively, colourful painting style with feathery brushwork (known as his 'rainbow style') and painted many voluptuous female nudes, such as *The Bathers* about 1884–87 (Philadelphia Museum of Art, USA). In his later years he turned to sculpture.

One of the five sons of a poor tailor (and himself pursued by poverty for 40 years), he began his career in a porcelain factory painting designs on china, then earned a little money by copying 18th-century pictures on fans and similar work. In 1862 he entered the atelier of Gleyre, where he made friends with Monet, Sisley and Bazille. With them he worked at Fontainebleau, and with Monet on the Seine near Paris, a favourite subject with both being the bathing place, 'La Grenouillère'. His early pictures show the influence of Courbet, for example the portrait of Sisley and his wife, 1868 (Cologne), but after the Franco-Prussian War (in which he served as cuirassier), with Monet at Argenteuil, he produced riverscapes completely Impressionist in their atmospheric colour, such as the *Regatta, Argenteuil*, 1874. While associated with Impressionism, and exhibiting at the Impressionist exhibitions in the 1870s, Renoir was never a theorist, or addicted primarily to landscape, and many beautiful works show his main delight to be in human life and the female model. *The Loge*, 1874 (Courtauld Gallery, London), a work painted in the studio, *Dancing at the Moulin de la Galette*, 1876 (main version, Louvre), and *Madame Charpentier and her Daughters*, 1879 (New York, Metropolitan Museum), are good examples. A reaction against Impressionism began in the 1880s after he had visited Italy, where he was influenced by the Graeco-Roman paintings from Pompeii at Naples, and by a stay at L'Estaque with Cézanne (who was also concerned with solid and permanent qualities in painting). A harder, linear manner resulted, as in *The Umbrellas*, c. 1884 (National Gallery, London), and *The Bathers*. This gave way to his later style, in which figures were treated loosely but plastically, with a colour of Mediterranean warmth.

Severely affected by arthritis from 1902, he continued to paint, and in 1913, though entirely crippled, he guided assistants in the production of sculpture, for example *Venus Victrix* (Tate Gallery, London). Many of his sculptures are monumental female nudes not unlike those of Maillol. His vast output is widely distributed, with many important works in the United States, where his genius was early and enthusiastically recognized.

Suggested reading
Gaunt, W *Renoir* (1983)
Renoir, J *Renoir, My Father* (1962)
Rouart, D *Renoir* (1985)
White, B *Renoir: His Life, Art and Letters* (1984)

Repin Ilya Efimovich (1844–1930). Russian painter of portraits, and historical and genre subjects. He studied at the Academy of Fine Arts, St Petersburg, then travelled in France and Italy. In 1894 he was appointed professor of historical painting at the St Petersburg Academy. He was noted for his portraits of Tolstoy and Mussorgsky, and such scenes of Russian life as his *Volga Boatmen*, *The Return from Siberia*, and *The Cossacks' Jeering Reply to the Sultan Mahomet IV*.

Repington Charles à Court (1858–1925). British soldier and journalist. He joined the Rifle Brigade 1878 and served in Afghanistan, Burma, and the Sudan before being on the staff during the South African War 1899–1902. He started work for the *Times* 1902 after being forced to resign from the army following an affair with another officer's wife. He retained his contacts in the army and it was thanks to them that he exposed the shell scandal 1915.

Repton Humphry (1752–1818). English garden designer. He worked for some years in partnership with English architect John Nash. Repton preferred more formal landscaping than Capability Brown, and was responsible for the landscaping of some 200 gardens and parks. He coined the term 'landscape gardening'.

Resnais Alain (1922–). French film director. His work is characterized by the themes of memory and unconventional concepts of time. His films include *Hiroshima, mon amour* 1959, *L'Année dernière à Marienbad/Last Year at Marienbad* 1961, and *Providence* 1977.

Respighi Ottorino (1879–1936). Italian composer. His works include the symphonic poems *Fontane di Roma/The Fountains of Rome* 1917 and *Pini di Roma/The Pines of Rome* 1924 (incorporating the recorded song of a nightingale), operas, and chamber music. He was a student of Rimsky-Korsakov.

Retz Jean François Paul de Gondi, Cardinal de Retz (1614–1679). French politician. A priest with political ambitions, he stirred up and largely led the insurrection known as the Fronde. After a period of imprisonment and exile he was restored to favour 1662 and created abbot of St Denis.

Reuter (Paul) Julius de, Baron. Adopted name of Israel Beer (1816–1899). German founder of the international news agency Reuters. He began a continental pigeon post 1849 at Aachen, Germany, and in 1851 set up a news agency in London. In 1858 he persuaded the press to use his news telegrams, and the service became worldwide.

Revans Reginald William (1907–   ). British management expert, originator of the 'action learning' method of management improvement in which, for example, each department of a firm probes the problem-avoiding system of some other department until the circle is completed, with resultant improved productivity.

Revere Paul (1735–1818). American revolutionary, a Boston silversmith, who carried the news of the approach of British troops to Lexington and Concord. Revere, who took part in the Boston Tea Party, was a courier for the Continental Congress, often riding from Boston to Philadelphia. On 18 April 1775 he alerted rebels in New Hampshire that the British, under General Thomas Gage were transporting supplies from Fort William and Mary. The New Hampshire militia captured quantities of munitions that proved decisive at the Battle of Bunker Hill. On 19 April the first shots of the Revolution were fired at Lexington. Longfellow's poem 'The Midnight Ride of Paul Revere' commemorates the event.

Revere was active throughout the Revolution and printed the first continental money. Revere's silver *Sons of Liberty* punchbowl 1768 (Museum of Fine Arts, Boston, USA) is a notable piece. He also produced propaganda prints exposing British atrocities in the war.
Suggested reading
Buhler, Kathryn *Paul Revere* (1956)
Forbes, Esther *Paul Revere and the World He Lived In* (1942, rep 1962)
Green, M *Paul Revere: The Man Behind the Legend* (1964)

Rey Fernando. Stage name of Fernando Casado Arambillet Veiga (1912–1994). Spanish actor who appeared in several films by Luis Buñuel, including *Viridiana* 1961 and *Le Charme discret de la Bourgeoisie/The Discreet Charm of the Bourgeoisie* 1972. He played villains in many European-made action and adventure films, most notably in the role of the sardonic drug-running mastermind of *The French Connection* 1971.

Reynaud Paul (1878–1966). French prime minister in World War II, who succeeded Edouard Daladier in March 1940 but resigned in June after the German breakthrough. He was imprisoned by the Germans until 1945, and again held government offices after the war.

Reynolds Albert (1933–   ). Irish politician, prime minister 1992–94. He joined Fianna Fáil 1977, and held various government posts including minister for industry and commerce 1987–88 and minister of finance 1989–92. He became prime minister when Charles Haughey was forced to resign Jan 1992, but his government was defeated on a vote of confidence Nov 1992. He succeeded in forming a Fianna Fáil–Labour coalition but resigned as premier and party leader Nov 1994 after Labour disputed a judicial appointment he had made and withdrew from the coalition.

He fostered closer relations with Britain and in Dec 1993 he and UK prime minister John Major issued a joint peace initiative for Northern Ireland, the 'Downing Street Declaration', which led to a general cease-fire the following year.

When an actor marries an actress they both fight for the mirror.

BURT REYNOLDS
Guardian 12 Mar 1988

Reynolds Burt (1936–   ). US film actor. He appeared in adventure films and comedies including *Deliverance* 1972, *Hustle* 1975, and *City Heat* 1984. He directed a few films, including *Sharkey's Machine* 1981.

A mere copier of nature can never produce anything great.

JOSHUA REYNOLDS
Discourse to Students of the Royal Academy 14 Dec 1770

Reynolds Joshua (1723–1792). English portrait painter. He was active in London from 1752 and became the first president of the Royal Academy 1768. His portraits display a facility for striking and characterful compositions in a consciously grand manner. He often borrowed classical poses, for example *Mrs Siddons as the Tragic Muse* 1784 (San Marino, California).

Reynolds was apprenticed to the portrait painter Thomas Hudson (1701–1779). From 1743 he practised in Plymouth and London and 1749–52 completed his studies in Rome and Venice, concentrating on the antique and High Renaissance masters. After his return to London he became the leading portraitist of his day with pictures such as *Admiral Keppel* 1753–54 (National Maritime Museum, London). In his influential *Discourses on Art* 1769–91, he argued in favour of the 'Grand Manner', a style based on the Classical past rather than the mundane present.
Suggested reading
Hudson, D *Sir Joshua Reynolds* (1959)
Reynolds, Joshua (ed) *Discourses on Art* (1959)
Waterhouse, E *Reynolds* (1973)

Reynolds Osborne (1842–1912). Irish physicist and engineer who studied fluid flow and devised the Reynolds number, which gives a

Reynolds, Albert *Irish politician and prime minister Albert Reynolds (right) with Irish Labour Party leader Dick Spring. Albert Reynolds was prime minister 1992–94. With UK prime minister John Major he issued the Downing Street Declaration 1993.* (Image Select)

numerical criterion for determining whether fluid flow under specified conditions will be smooth or turbulent. From 1868 he was professor at Owens College (now Manchester University).

Reynolds showed, using dye, that the flow of a liquid will be turbulent unless it has a high viscosity, low density, and an open surface. He applied much of what he had learned about turbulent flow to the behaviour of the water in river channels and estuaries. For one study he made an accurate model of the mouth of the river Mersey, and pioneered the use of such models in marine and civil engineering projects. He also worked on multistage steam turbines, and, using the experimental steam engine which he designed for his engineering department, he determined the mechanical equivalent of heat so accurately that it has remained one of the classical determinations of a physical constant.

Rhee Syngman (1875–1965). Korean right-wing politician. A rebel under Chinese and Japanese rule, he became president of South Korea from 1948 until riots forced him to resign and leave the country 1960. He established a repressive dictatorship and was an embarrassing ally for the USA.

Rhine Joseph Banks (1895–1980). US parapsychologist who carried out many groundbreaking laboratory experiments in parapsychology. Some are described in his book *Extra-Sensory Perception* 1934, which made ESP a common term.

Rhine conducted this work from 1927 onwards at Duke University, North Carolina. He was the first to make use of Zener cards in card-guessing experiments to investigate telepathy and precognition. They were named after K E Zener, a psychologist colleague, and each shows one of five simple graphic symbols. Rhine also investigated psychokinesis in experiments where subjects tried to influence the fall of dice. This work is described in *The Reach of the Mind* 1947.

Rhodes Cecil John (1853–1902). South African politician, born in the UK, prime minister of Cape Colony 1890–96. Aiming at the formation of a South African federation and the creation of a block of British territory from the Cape to Cairo, he was responsible for the annexation of Bechuanaland (now Botswana) in 1885. He formed the British South Africa Company in 1889, which occupied Mashonaland and Matabeleland, thus forming Rhodesia (now Zambia and Zimbabwe).

Rhodes went to Natal in 1870. As head of De Beers Consolidated Mines and Goldfields of South Africa Ltd, he amassed a large fortune. He entered the Cape legislature 1881, and became prime minister 1890, but the discovery of his complicity in the Jameson Raid forced him to resign 1896. Advocating Anglo-Afrikaner co-operation, he was less alive to the rights of black Africans, despite the final 1898 wording of his dictum: 'Equal rights for every civilized man south of the Zambezi.'

The Rhodes scholarships were founded at Oxford University, UK, under his will, for students from the Commonwealth, the USA, and Germany.

Suggested reading
Flint, John *Cecil Rhodes* (1974)
Marlowe, John *Cecil Rhodes* (1972)
Roberts, Brian *Cecil Rhodes: Flawed Colossus* (1987)
Rotberg, Robert *Cecil Rhodes* (1988)

Rhodes Wilfred (1877–1973). English cricketer. He took more wickets than anyone else in the game – 4,187 wickets 1898–1930 – and also scored 39,802 first-class runs. Playing for Yorkshire, Rhodes made a record 763 appearances in the county championship. He took 100 wickets in a season 23 times and completed the 'double' of 1,000 runs and 100 wickets in a season 16 times (both records). He played his 58th and final game for England, against the West Indies 1930, when he was 52 years old, the oldest ever Test cricketer.

Rhodes Zandra Lindsey (1940–). English fashion designer. She is known for the extravagant fantasy and luxury of her dress creations. She founded her own fashion house 1968. She began by designing and printing highly individual textiles. Her fabrics –

chiffon, silk, and tulle – are frequently handprinted with squiggles, zigzags, and other patterns. Her evening dresses are often characterized by their uneven handkerchief hems. She designs wedding and evening dresses embroidered in India, and saris for the top end of the Indian fashion market.

> *The perpetual hunger to be beautiful and that thirst to be loved which is the real curse of Eve.*
>
> JEAN RHYS
> *The Left Bank* 1927

Rhys Jean. Adopted name of Ella Gwendolen Rees Williams (1890?–1979). English novelist. Her works include *Wide Sargasso Sea* 1966, a recreation, set in a Caribbean island, of the life of the mad wife of Rochester from Charlotte Brontë's *Jane Eyre*.

Ribalta Francisco (1565–1628). Spanish painter. He was active in Valencia from 1599. Around 1615 he developed a dramatic Baroque style using extreme effects of light and shade (recalling Caravaggio), as in *Christ Embracing St Bernard* about 1620–28 (Prado, Madrid).

He worked in his youth in Madrid, where he seems to have been influenced by the paintings of such Italian Mannerists as Sebastiano del Piombo. After 1599 he lived and worked in Valencia, developing those 'tenebrist' effects of dark shadow, in which he was the first artist in Spain to express a sombre fervour (distinct from the spiritual exaltation of El Greco) appropriate to scenes of torture and martyrdom. He has sometimes been supposed to have derived his style from the study of Caravaggio, but he had begun to cultivate it before Caravaggio started to paint. *The Crucifixion* (Hermitage), *Christ embracing St Bernard* (Prado), *The Last Supper* (Valencia), and *The Vision of Father Simón* (National Gallery, St Petersburg) are among his principal works. Ribera is said to have studied with him. Ribalta's son, Juan (1596–1628), was his pupil and collaborated with him.

> *My last wish is that Germany rediscovers her unity and that an alliance is made between East and West.*
>
> JOACHIM VON RIBBENTROP
> Last words before being hanged 1946

Ribbentrop Joachim von (1893–1946). German Nazi politician and diplomat. Born in the Rhineland, Ribbentrop was awarded the Iron Cross in World War I, and from 1919 became wealthy as a wine merchant. He joined the Nazi party 1932 and acted as Hitler's adviser on foreign affairs; he was German ambassador to Britain 1936–38. A political lightweight and social climber, his loyalty was useful to Hitler since he posed no threat, although he was regarded with contempt by his colleagues. As foreign minister 1938–45, he negotiated the non-aggression pact between Germany and the USSR (the Ribbentrop–Molotov pact 1939). He was tried at Nuremberg as a war criminal 1946 and hanged.

Ribera José (Jusepe) de (1591–1652). Spanish painter. He was active in Italy from 1616 under the patronage of the viceroys of Naples. His early work shows the impact of Caravaggio, but his colours gradually lightened. He painted many full-length versions of saints as well as mythological figures and genre scenes, which he produced without preliminary drawing.

He may possibly have studied under Ribalta in his early days, but by 1616 had settled in Naples, where his life was mainly spent. Naples was then under Spanish rule, and Ribera, known as 'Lo Spagnoletto', often emphasized his Spanish origin by adding 'Jativa' or 'Valencia' to his signature, but his style was derived from Caravaggio and his Neapolitan followers. Like Ribalta and in the spirit of his time and country, he painted gloomy religious subjects of martyrdom and torture, though these were varied by realistic studies of common types in which the 'naturalism' derived from Caravaggio was opposed to the 'idealism' of the School of Bologna. He enjoyed great favour with the Spanish viceroys of Naples, though he is said to have terrorized such rivals as Guido Reni and Domenichino with threats and acts of violence. Many of his works went back to Spain, and he may be directly credited with having introduced into his native country the Caravaggesque light and shade and attitude to art. Though he never abandoned his brown shadows, he made some progress towards richness and luminosity of colour in his mature work, of which the *Martyrdom of St Bartholomew*, ?1639 (Prado), is an example. One of his last paintings, the *Boy with a Club Foot*, 1652 (Louvre), is a masterpiece of realism, while such studies of types (represented as celebrities of antiquity) as his *Aesop* and *Archimedes* (Prado) are in a vein which Velazquez pursued.

Ricardo David (1772–1823). English economist, author of *Principles of Political Economy* 1817. Among his discoveries were the principle of comparative advantage (that countries can benefit by specializing in goods they produce efficiently and trading internationally to buy others), and the law of diminishing returns (that continued increments of capital and labour applied to a given quantity of land will eventually show a declining rate of increase in output).

Suggested reading
Gootzeit, M J *David Ricardo* (1975)
Hollander, S *The Economics of David Ricardo* (1979)

Ricardo Harry Ralph (1885–1974). English engineer who played a leading role in the development of the internal-combustion engine. During World War I and World War II, his work enabled British forces to fight with the advantage of technically superior engines. His work on combustion and detonation led to the octane-rating system for classifying fuels for petrol engines. Knighted 1948.

Ricardo was born in London. At the age of 12 he built a steam engine, and as a student at Cambridge he designed and built a motorcycle, with its power unit. In 1905 he designed and built a two-cylinder, two-stroke engine and a four-cylinder version to power his uncle's large car. During World War I, Ricardo worked on aircraft engines and designed the engine for the Mark V tank. In 1917 he set up a research and consultancy company, which worked on engine development and categorization of fuels according to their ease of detonation.

Ricardo designed an effective combustion chamber, which was also used in his aircraft engines during World War II.

Ricci Nina (1883–1970). French fashion designer. By 1905 she was designing clothes, and in 1932 set up a boutique specializing in dresses for mature, elegant women. Her L'Air du Temps perfume was sold in Lalique bottles. Her son Robert Ricci (1905–1988) managed the business from 1945.

Ricci Sebastiano (1659–1734). Venetian painter. He worked throughout Italy as well as in Vienna. Between 1712 and 1716 he was in London where he painted *The Resurrection* for the chapel of the Royal Hospital, Chelsea. Ricci's revival of the Venetian tradition of history painting was so successful that many of his paintings were indistinguishable from those of the Veronese. Ricci's lighter palette paved the way for Tiepolo.

The English Royal Collection has many works by Ricci.

Ricci-Curbastro Gregorio (1853–1925). Italian mathematician whose systematization of absolute differential calculus (the Ricci calculus) enabled Albert Einstein to derive the theory of relativity. From 1880 he was professor of mathematical physics at Padua. He was also a magistrate and local councillor.

By introducing an invariant element – an element that can also be used in other systems – Ricci-Curbastro was able to modify differential calculus so that the formulas and results retained the same form regardless of the system of variables used. In 1896, he applied the absolute calculus to the congruencies of lines on an arbitrary Riemann variety; later, he used the Riemann symbols to find the contract tensor, now known as the Ricci tensor (which plays a fundamental role in the theory of relativity). He also discovered the invariants that occur in the theory of the curvature of varieties.

With a former pupil, Tullio Levi-Civita, he published *Méthodes de calcul différentiel absolu et leurs applications*, describing the use of intrinsic geometry as an instrument of computation dealing with normal congruencies, geodetic laws, and isothermal families of surfaces. The work also shows the possibilities of the analytical, geometric, mechanical, and physical applications of the new calculus.

Rice Elmer. Adopted name of Elmer Reizenstein (1892–1967). US dramatist. His works include *The Adding Machine* 1923 and *Street Scene* 1929, which won a Pulitzer prize and was made into an opera by Kurt Weill. Many of his plays deal with such economic and political issues as the Depression (*We, the People* 1933) and racism (*American Landscape* 1939).

For when the One Great Scorer comes to mark against your name, / He writes – not that you won or lost – but how you played the Game.

GRANTLAND RICE
'Alumnus Football'

Rice Grantland (1880–1954). US sports journalist. Gaining a reputation for vivid sports writing, he worked for the *New York Herald Tribune* 1914–30. After 1930 he wrote the column 'The Spotlight', setting the standard for modern sports journalism. He succeeded Walter Camp in selecting the annual All-America football team.

Born in Murfreesboro, Tennessee, USA, and educated at Vanderbilt University, Rice joined the staff of the *Nashville News* 1901 and was hired by the *New York Mail* 1911. His autobiography, *The Tumult and the Shouting*, was published 1954.

Rice Peter (1935–1992). British structural engineer. He was responsible for some of the most exciting buildings of the 1970s and 1980s: the Sydney Opera House, the Pompidou Centre in Paris, and the Lloyd's building in London.

His first employment was with Ove Arup; at the age of 23 he was assigned to raise the sail-like roofs of the Sydney Opera House, designed by Finnish architect Joern Utzon. There followed the Centre Pompidou, the Menil Art Collection Museum in Houston, the San Nicola World Cup Stadium in Bari, the Kansai International Airport in Japan, and the Pavilion of the Future at the Seville Expo. In Britain, he is known for the terminal at Stansted Airport as well as the Lloyd's building. The architects with whom he collaborated – notably Richard Rogers, Renzo Piano and Norman Foster – held him in high regard. Piano, the Italian architect with whom he built the Centre Pompidou and the Menil museum, said he designed structures 'like a pianist who can play with his eyes shut; he understands the basic nature of structures so well that he can afford to think in the darkness about what might be possible beyond the obvious'.

In July 1992 Rice received the UK's Royal Gold Medal for Architecture, an honour rarely awarded to engineers. In his acceptance speech, he remarked that structural engineers were often seen as reducing every soaring idea an architect might have by insisting on rationality in design. The structural engineer's true role, Rice said, was not to reduce and restrict, but to explore materials and structures as had the great Victorian engineers and medieval cathedral builders; rigour and imagination could go hand in hand.

I am notorious ... I will go down in history as another Lady Hamilton.

MANDY RICE-DAVIES
à propos of the Profumo scandal 1963

Rice-Davies Mandy (Marilyn) (1944–). English model. She achieved notoriety in 1963 following the revelations of the affair between her friend Christine Keeler and war minister John Profumo, and his subsequent resignation.

Rich Adrienne (1929–). US radical feminist poet, writer, and critic. Her poetry is both subjective and political, concerned with female consciousness, peace, and gay rights. Her works include *On Lies, Secrets and Silence* 1979, *The Fact of a Doorframe: Poems, 1950–84* 1984, and *What is Found There: Notebooks on Poetry and Politics* 1994.

In the 1960s her poetry was closely involved with the student and antiwar movements in the USA but since then she has concentrated on women's issues. In 1974, when given the National Book Award, she declined to accept it as an individual, but with Alice Walker and Audrey Rich accepted it on behalf of all women.

The connections between and among women are the most feared, the most problematic, and the most potentially transforming force on the planet.

ADRIENNE RICH
Chrysalis no. 7 1979

Richard Cliff. Stage name of Harry Roger Webb (1940–). English pop singer. Initially influenced by Elvis Presley, he soon became a Christian family entertainer. One of his best-selling early records was 'Livin' Doll' 1959 and he had hits in the UK through the 1980s. His original backing group was the Shadows (1958–68 and later re-formed). During the 1960s, he starred in a number of musical films including *Summer Holiday* 1962. Knighted 1996.

The Shadows had solo instrumental hits in the early 1960s and their lead guitarist, Hank Marvin (1941–), inspired many British rock guitarists.

Even those to whom his performance was unfamiliar could not fail to give credit to Cliff Richard's talent and mastery.

Comment in *Sovestskaya Kulturn* on CLIFF RICHARD
during his tour of Russia.

Richard three kings of England:

Richard (I) the Lion-Heart (French *Coeur-de-Lion*) (1157–1199). King of England from 1189, who spent all but six months of his reign abroad. He was the third son of Henry II, against whom he twice rebelled. In the third Crusade 1191–92 he won victories at Cyprus, Acre, and Arsuf (against Saladin), but failed to recover Jerusalem. While returning overland he was captured by the Duke of Austria, who handed him over to the emperor Henry VI, and he was held prisoner until a large ransom was raised. He then returned briefly to England, where his brother John I had been ruling in his stead. His later years were spent in warfare in France, where he was killed.

Himself a poet, he became a hero of legends after his death. He was succeeded by John I.
Suggested reading
Brundage, J *Richard Lion Heart* (1974)
Gibb, Christopher *Richard the Lionheart and the Crusades* (1985)
Gillingham, John *Richard the Lionheart* (1979)
Harvey, J H *The Plantagenets* (1970)

A man of the greatest honour and bravery, but he is imprudent ... and shows too great recklessness of his own life.

Saladin on RICHARD (I) THE LION-HEART
to the bishop of Salisbury in Jerusalem after the truce of 2 Sept 1192

Richard II or Richard of Bordeaux (1367–1400). King of England from 1377, effectively from 1389, son of Edward the Black Prince. Richard was born in Bordeaux. He succeeded his grandfather Edward III when only ten, the government being in the hands of a council of regency. His fondness for favourites resulted in conflicts with Parliament, and in 1388 the baronial party, headed by the Duke of Gloucester, had many of his friends executed. Richard recovered control 1389, and ruled moderately until 1397, when he had Gloucester murdered and his other leading opponents executed or banished, and assumed absolute power. In 1399 his cousin Henry Bolingbroke, Duke of Hereford (later Henry IV), returned from exile to lead a revolt; Richard II was deposed by Parliament and imprisoned in Pontefract Castle, where he died mysteriously.
Suggested reading
Cheetham, A *The Life and Times of Richard II*
Tuck, A *Richard II and the English Nobility* (1973)

His reign is the first attempt of an English king to rule as an autocrat on principle.

V H Galbraith on RICHARD II
in *A New Life of Richard II*

Richard III (1452–1485). King of England from 1483. The son of Richard, Duke of York, he was created Duke of Gloucester by his brother Edward IV, and distinguished himself in the Wars of the Roses. On Edward's death 1483 he became protector to his nephew Edward V, and soon secured the crown for himself on the plea that Edward IV's sons were illegitimate. He proved a capable ruler, but the suspicion that he had murdered Edward V and his brother undermined his popularity. In 1485 Henry, Earl of Richmond (later Henry VII), raised a rebellion, and Richard III was defeated and killed at Bosworth. Scholars now tend to minimize the evidence for his crimes as Tudor propaganda.
Suggested reading
Gillingham, John *Richard III: A Medieval Kingship* (1993)
Hammond, P W and Sutton, A F *Richard III: The Road to Bosworth Field* (1985)
Hicks, Michael *Richard III: The Man Behind the Myth* (1991)
Horrox, Rosemary *Richard III: A Study in Service* (1989)
Ross, Charles *Richard III* (1981)
Seward, Desmond *Richard III, England's Black Legend* (1983)
Weir, Alison *The Princes in the Tower* (1992)
Williamson, Audrey *The Mystery of the Princes in the Tower* (1978)

He appears to have been unusually clear-sighted in what he wanted to achieve, particularly singleminded and determined in its pursuit, and utterly ruthless in its implementation.

Michael Hicks on RICHARD III
in *Who's Who in Later Medieval England* 1991

Richard of Wallingford (*c.* 1292–1335). English mathematician, abbot of St Albans from 1326. He was a pioneer of trigonometry, and designed measuring instruments.

Richards Frank. Pen name of Charles Harold St John Hamilton (1876–1961). English writer. He wrote for the children's papers *Magnet* and *Gem* and invented Greyfriars public school and the fat boy Billy Bunter.

The fat greedy owl of the Remove.

FRANK RICHARDS
on Billy Bunter in *Magnet* vol 3, no 72

Richards Gordon (1904–1986). English jockey and trainer who was champion on the flat a record 26 times between 1925 and 1953. He started riding 1920 and rode 4,870 winners from 21,834 mounts before retiring 1954 and taking up training. He rode the winners of all the classic races but only once won the Epsom Derby (on Pinza 1953). In 1947 he rode a record 269 winners in a season and in 1933 at Nottingham/Chepstow he rode 11 consecutive winners. Knighted 1953.

Richards I(vor) A(rmstrong) (1893–1979). English literary critic. He collaborated with C K Ogden and wrote *Principles of Literary Criticism* 1924. In 1939 he went to Harvard University, USA, where he taught detailed attention to the text and had a strong influence on contemporary US literary criticism.

If [poetry] is capable of saving us; it is a perfectly possible means of overcoming chaos.

I A RICHARDS
Science and Poetry 1925

Richards Theodore William (1868–1928). US chemist who determined as accurately as possible the relative atomic masses of a large number of elements. He also investigated the physical properties of the elements, such as atomic volumes and the compressibilities of nonmetallic solid elements. Nobel prize 1914.

Richards was born in Germantown, Pennsylvania, and studied at Harvard, where he was professor from 1901.

Introducing various new analytical techniques, Richards made accurate atomic weight measurements for 25 elements; and his co-workers determined 40 more. In 1913, he detected differences in the atomic weights of ordinary lead and samples extracted from uranium minerals (which had arisen by radioactive decay) – one of the first convincing demonstrations of the uranium decay series and confirming English chemist Frederick Soddy's prediction of the existence of isotopes.

Richards Viv (Isaac Vivian Alexander) (1952–). West Indian cricketer, captain of the West Indies team 1986–91. He has played for the Leeward Islands and, in the UK, for Somerset and Glamorgan. A prolific run-scorer, he holds the record for the greatest number of runs made in Test cricket in one calendar year (1,710 runs in 1976). He retired from international cricket after the West Indies tour of England in 1991 and from first class cricket at the end of the 1993 season.

Richardson Dorothy Miller (1873–1957). English novelist. Her works were collected under the title *Pilgrimage* 1938. She was the first English novelist to use the 'stream of consciousness' method in *Pointed Roofs* 1915. Her contemporary, English novelist and critic Virginia Woolf recognized and shared this technique as part of the current effort to express women's perceptions in spite of the resistance of man-made language, and she credited Richardson with having invented 'the psychological sentence of the feminine gender'.

Richardson Henry Handel. Pen name of Ethel Florence Lindesay Richardson (1870–1946). Australian novelist. Richardson was born in Melbourne. In 1888 she went to study piano in Leipzig, Germany, and her first novel, *Maurice Guest* 1908, is based on these years. The trilogy *The Fortunes of Richard Mahony*, published as *Australia Felix* 1917, *The Way Home* 1925, and *Ultima Thule* 1929, traces the career of a gold-rush migrant from the early 1850s to the mid-1870s and draws heavily on the life of her father. She was the first Australian writer to win a reputation abroad. Her works include *The Getting of Wisdom* 1910, based on her schooldays and filmed 1977. She left Australia when only 18.

Suggested reading
Elliott, William D *Henry Handel Richardson: A Critical Study* (1975)
Green, Dorothy *Ulysses Bound: Henry Handel Richardson and Her Fiction* (1973)
Palmer, N *Henry Handel Richardson: A Study* (1950)
Richardson, Henry Handel *Myself When Young* (autobiography) (1948)

Richardson Henry Hobson (1838–1886). US architect. He was distinguished for his revival of the Romanesque style. He designed churches, university buildings, homes, railway stations, and town libraries. He had a strong influence on Louis Sullivan. His buildings include Sever Hall 1878 and Austin Hall 1881 at Harvard University, and the monumental Marshall Field Wholesale Warehouse, Chicago, 1885–87. His best-known work is Trinity Church in Copley Square, Boston, 1873–77.

Richardson Miranda (1958–). English stage, film, and television actress. Her credits span both comic and serious productions, from her role as Elizabeth I in the black comedy television series *Blackadder* 1986–87 to the murderess Ruth Ellis in her first film *Dance with a Stranger* 1985 and the unbalanced Vivien Haigh-Wood, wife of T S Eliot, in *Tom and Viv* 1994.

Richardson made her West End debut 1980. Plays include *A Lie of the Mind* 1987, *Etta Jenks* 1990, and *The Changeling* and *Mountain Language* 1988. Films include *Empire of the Sun* 1987, *Enchanted April* 1991, *The Crying Game* 1992, and *Damage* (BAFTA award for best supporting actress) and *Century* both 1993.

Richardson Owen Willans (1879–1959). British physicist. He studied the emission of electricity from hot bodies, giving the name thermionics to the subject. At Cambridge University, he worked under J J Thomson in the Cavendish Laboratory. Nobel prize 1928. Knighted 1939.

The art of acting lies in keeping people from coughing.

RALPH RICHARDSON
quoted in Leslie Halliwell *Filmgoer's Companion* 1965

Richardson Ralph David (1902–1983). English actor. He played many stage parts, including Falstaff (Shakespeare), Peer Gynt (Ibsen), and Cyrano de Bergerac (Rostand). He shared the management of the Old Vic theatre with Laurence Olivier 1944–50. In later years he revealed himself as an accomplished deadpan comic.

Later stage successes include David Storey's *Home* 1970 and Pinter's *No Man's Land* 1976. His films include *Things to Come* 1936, *Richard III* 1956, *Our Man in Havana* 1959, *The Wrong Box* 1966, *The Bed Sitting Room* 1969, and *O Lucky Man!* 1973. Knighted 1947.

Richardson Samuel (1689–1761). English novelist. Born in Derbyshire, Richardson was brought up in London and apprenticed to a printer. He set up his own business in London 1719, becoming printer to the House of Commons. All his six young children died, followed by his wife 1731, which permanently affected his health. He was one of the founders of the modern novel. *Pamela* 1740–41, written in the form of a series of letters and containing much dramatic conversation, was sensationally popular all across Europe, and was followed by *Clarissa* 1747–48 and *Sir Charles Grandison* 1753–54.

An examination of Richardson's skeleton 1994 showed that he suffered from the painful bone disorder diffuse idiopathic skeletal hyperostosis, in which bony outgrowths form around the joints.

The heart that is able to partake of the distress of another, cannot wilfully give it.

SAMUEL RICHARDSON
History of Sir Charles Grandison vol 3, letter 32 1753

Richardson Tony (Cecil Antonio) (1928–1991). English director and producer. With George Devine he established the English Stage Company 1955 at the Royal Court Theatre, with productions such as John Osborne's *Look Back in Anger* 1956. His films include *Saturday Night and Sunday Morning* 1960, *A Taste of Honey* 1961, *The Loneliness of the Long Distance Runner* 1962, *Tom Jones* 1963, *Joseph Andrews* 1977, and *Blue Sky* 1991.

Richelieu Armand Jean du Plessis de (1585–1642). French cardinal and politician. Born in Paris of a noble family, he entered the church and was created bishop of Luçon 1606 and a cardinal 1622. Through the influence of Marie de' Medici he became Louis XIII's chief minister 1624, a position he retained until his death. His secretary Père Joseph was the original Grey Eminence. Richelieu was chief minister from 1624. He aimed to make the monarchy absolute; he ruthlessly crushed opposition by the nobility and destroyed the political power of the Huguenots, while leaving them religious freedom. Abroad, he sought to establish French supremacy by breaking the power of the Habsburgs; he therefore supported the Swedish king Gustavus Adolphus and the German Protestant princes against Austria and in 1635 brought France into the Thirty Years' War.

Richelieu French statesmen and chief minister to Louis XIII, Cardinal Armand de Richelieu. Whilst tolerant of the religion of the Huguenots, Richelieu nevertheless sabotaged their military and political power, aiming to establish the absolute authority of the crown. (Image Select)

Suggested reading
Gowan, C D'O *The Background of the French Classics* (1960)
O'Connell, D P *Richelieu* (1968)
Wedgwood, C V *Richelieu and the French Monarchy* (1962)

Richier Germaine (1904–1959). French sculptor. Richier trained in Paris 1925–29 under Émile-Antoine Bourdelle (1861–1929) but developed her spiky, threatening, anthropomorphized figures in Switzerland during World War II. She gained a major reputation after World War II with her febrile, Expressionist sculptures based on animal life, for example *The Ant* 1953 (Bayerische Staatsgemäldesammlungen, Munich). Her highly original style was much imitated during the 1950s.

Richler Mordecai (1931–). Canadian novelist. His novels, written in a witty, acerbic style, include *The Apprenticeship of Duddy Kravitz* 1959 and *St Urbain's Horseman* 1971. Later works include *Joshua Then and Now* 1980, *Home Sweet Home* 1984, and *Solomon Gursky Was Here* 1990.
Suggested reading
Sheps, G D (ed) *Mordecai Richler* (1971)
Ramraj, Victor *Mordecai Richler* (1983)
Woodcock, George *Mordecai Richler* (1970)

Richmond John (1960–). English fashion designer. He produces unconventional street and clubland designs. He worked in the Richmond–Cornejo partnership 1984–87, creating upmarket leather jackets and separates, before setting up his own fashion label 1987. He continued to experiment with leather, producing jackets with tattoo-printed sleeves 1989 and jackets covered with graffiti 1990. In 1989 he expanded his range with the 'Destroy' line which combines the basic elements of his signature with lower prices. He staged his first solo show 1991.

Richter Burton (1931–). US particle physicist. In the 1960s he designed the Stanford Positron–Electron Accelerating Ring (SPEAR), a machine designed to collide positrons and electrons at high energies. In 1974 Richter and his team used SPEAR to produce a new subatomic particle, the ψ meson. This was the first example of a particle formed from a charmed quark, the quark whose existence had been postulated by Sheldon Glashow ten years earlier. Richter shared the 1976 Nobel Prize for Physics with Samuel Ting, who had discovered the particle independently.

Richter Charles Francis (1900–1985). US seismologist, deviser of the Richter scale used to measure the strength of the waves from earthquakes.

Richter Jean Paul (Johann Paul Friedrich) (1763–1825). German author. He created a series of comic eccentrics in works such as the romance *Titan* 1800–03 and *Die Flegeljahre/The Awkward Age* 1804–05.

Richter Sviatoslav Teofilovich (1915–). Russian pianist. He was an outstanding interpreter of Schubert, Schumann, Rachmaninov, and Prokofiev.

Richthofen Ferdinand Paul Wilhelm, Baron von (1833–1905). German geographer and traveller who carried out extensive studies in China 1867–70 and subsequently explored Java, Thailand, Myanmar (Burma), Japan, and California.

Richthofen Manfred, Freiherr von (the 'Red Baron') (1892–1918). German aviator. In World War I he commanded the 11th Chasing Squadron, known as 'Richthofen's Flying Circus', and shot down 80 aircraft before being killed in action.

Originally a cavalryman (Lancer) he transferred to the air corps and eventually became the most famous 'ace' of the German service. A phenomenal shot, he relied more upon that than upon any tactical skill, and by Feb 1917 had over 20 Allied aircraft to his credit. He scored his 80th victory April 1918, when he received the Order of the Red Eagle with Crowns and Swords. He was shot down behind British lines on the Somme 21 April 1918 and buried with full military honours.
Suggested reading
Burrows, William *Richthofen: A True History of the Red Baron* (1969)

Rickenbacker Edward Vernon (1890–1973). US racing-car driver, aviator, and airline executive. A racing-car driver in his youth, by 1917 he had established a land speed record of 134 mph/216 kph. He was a leading US fighter pilot during World War I and was later awarded the Congressional Medal of Honor for his wartime service. He purchased Eastern Airlines 1938 leaving briefly to serve as an adviser to the War Department during World War II. Taking on special missions, he ditched his plane in the Pacific Ocean, drifting for 23 days before being rescued.

Ricketts Howard Taylor (1871–1910). US pathologist who discovered the *Rickettsia* (named after him), a group of unusual microorganisms that have both viral and bacterial characteristics. The ten known species in the *Rickettsia* genus are all pathogenic in human beings, causing such diseases as Rocky Mountain spotted fever and typhus.

From 1902 he worked at Chicago University. In 1909 he went to Mexico City to investigate typhus, and while there he became fatally infected with the disease.

Ricketts began studying Rocky Mountain spotted fever in 1906 and discovered that the disease is transmitted to human beings by the bite of a particular type of tick that inhabits the skins of animals. In 1908, he found the causative microorganisms in the blood of infected animals and in the bodies and eggs of ticks. In his studies of typhus in Mexico, Ricketts demonstrated that the microorganisms are transmitted to humans by the body louse. Before he died from the disease, he also showed that typhus can be transmitted to monkeys, and that, after recovery, they are immune to further attacks.

Rickey Branch Wesley (1881–1965). US baseball executive. Born in Stockdale, Ohio, USA, Rickey received a law degree from the

University of Michigan 1911. Always active in athletics, he signed as a catcher with the St Louis Browns 1905–06. With the New York Yankees 1907, he then retired as a player. In 1913 he accepted a managerial job with the Browns. As president of the Brooklyn Dodgers 1942–50, he made baseball history by signing Jackie Robinson, the first black American to play in the major leagues. As president of the St Louis Cardinals 1917 and manager 1919–25, he pioneered the minor-league system of developing talent.

Rickover Hyman George (1900–1986). Russian-born US naval officer. Rickover emigrated to the USA with his family 1906 and graduated from the US Naval Academy 1922. After further studies in engineering, he became a specialist in the electrical division of the Bureau of Ships. During World War II, he worked on the atomic-bomb project, headed the navy's nuclear reactor division, and served on the Atomic Energy Commission. He was responsible for the development of the first nuclear submarine, the *Nautilus*, 1954. He was promoted to the rank of admiral 1973. After retiring 1982, he became an outspoken critic of the dangers of nuclear research and development.

Ricoeur Paul (1913–). French philosopher. Under the influence of existentialism and Sigmund Freud, he reflected at length on the nature of language and interpretation, subjectivity and the will. His works include *Le Volontaire et l'involontaire/Freedom and Nature: the Voluntary and the Involuntary* 1950, *L'Homme faillible/Fallible Man* 1960, and *La Symbolique du mal/The Symbolism of Evil* 1960. He taught at the Sorbonne and elsewhere.

Riding Laura (born Reichenthal) (1901–1991). US poet. She was a member of the Fugitive Group of poets that flourished in the southern USA 1915–28. She went to England 1926 and worked with the writer Robert Graves. Having published her *Collected Poems* 1938, she wrote no more verse, but turned to linguistics in order to analyse the expression of 'truth'.

Gentle by nature, devoid of rancour ... firm in his opinions, bold in opposition ... a man of independent judgment ... invincible faith and undaunted courage.

C R N Routh on NICHOLAS RIDLEY
Who's Who in Tudor England 1990

Ridley Nicholas (*c.* 1500–1555). English Protestant bishop. He became chaplain to Henry VIII 1541, and bishop of London 1550. He took an active part in the Reformation and supported Lady Jane Grey's claim to the throne. After Mary's accession he was arrested and burned as a heretic.

Ridley Nicholas (1929–1993). British Conservative politician, cabinet minister 1983–90. After a period in industry he became active as a 'dry' right-winger in the Conservative Party. He served under Harold Macmillan, Edward Heath, and Alec Douglas-Home, but did not become a member of the cabinet until 1983. His apparent disdain for public opinion caused his transfer, in 1989, from the politically sensitive Department of the Environment to that of Trade and Industry.

Ridley was born in Newcastle upon Tyne, and after a privileged education at Eton and Balliol College, Oxford, he spent his early career in industry around Tyneside before entering politics. He entered Parliament as member for Tewkesbury 1959 and represented it until 1992. He held junior government posts before being made minister of state in the Department of Trade and Industry 1970–72 under Edward Heath. In his mistrust of Brussels bureaucracy, he was ideologically in tune with Margaret Thatcher, who gave him progressively senior portfolios, including transport 1983–86, environment 1986–89, and trade and industry 1989–90. His article denigrating Germany in the *Spectator* 1990, eventually cost him his ministerial post and his political career.

Rie Lucie (born Gomperz) (1902–). Austrian-born potter. She worked in England from the 1930s. Her pottery, exhibited all over the world, is simple and pure in form, showing a debt to English potter Bernard Leach.

Riebeeck Johan Anthoniszoon van (1619–1677). Dutch colonizer and ship's surgeon, chosen by the Dutch East India Company to found a settlement at Table Bay, South Africa. He landed in April 1652 and proceeded to establish and extend Cape Colony in the face of many hardships. He returned to Holland in 1662.

Riefenstahl Leni (Berta Helene Amalie) (1902–). German filmmaker. She trained as a dancer, appearing in films in the 1920s, but in the early 1930s formed her own production company, and directed and starred in *Das blaue Licht/The Blue Light* 1932. Her film of the Nazi rallies at Nuremberg, *Triumph des Willens/Triumph of the Will* 1934, vividly illustrated Hitler's charismatic appeal but tainted her career. She followed this with a filmed two-part documentary on the 1936 Berlin Olympic Games – *Olympiad: Fest der Volker/Festival of the Nations* and *Olympiad: Fest der Schönheit/Festival of Beauty*. After World War II she was imprisoned by the French for four years for her Nazi propagandist work. Unable to pursue her film career after being blacklisted, she turned to photography and is known for the volumes of photographs that have resulted from her visits to Africa, including *The Last of the Nuba* 1973 and *Mein Afrika/My Africa* 1982.

Riel Louis (1844–1885). French-Canadian rebel, a champion of the Métis (an Indian-French people); he established a provisional government in Winnipeg in an unsuccessful revolt 1869–70 and was hanged for treason after leading a second revolt in Saskatchewan 1885.
Suggested reading
Davidson, W M *Louis Riel* (1955)
Stanley, G F G *Louis Riel* (1963)
Walsh, F G *The Trial of Louis Riel* (1965)

Riemann Georg Friedrich Bernhard (1826–1866). German mathematician whose system of non-Euclidean geometry, thought at the time to be a mere mathematical curiosity, was used by Albert Einstein to develop his general theory of relativity. Riemann made a breakthrough in conceptual understanding within several other areas of mathematics: the theory of functions, vector analysis, projective and differential geometry, and topology.

Riemann took into account the possible interaction between space and the bodies placed in it; until then, space had been treated as an entity in itself, and this new point of view was to become a central concept of 20th-century physics. He spent his academic career at Göttingen, becoming professor 1859.

Riemann's paper on the fundamental postulates of Euclidean geometry, written in the early 1850s but not published until 1867, was to open up the whole field of non-Euclidean geometry and become a classic in the history of mathematics. He also published a paper on hypergeometric series, invented 'spherical' geometry as an extension of hyperbolic geometry, and in 1855–56 lectured on his theory of Abelian functions, one of his fundamental developments in mathematics.

He developed the Riemann surfaces to study complex function behaviour. These multiconnected, many-sheeted surfaces can be dissected by cross-cuts into a singly connected surface. By means of these surfaces he introduced topological considerations into the theory of functions of a complex variable, and into general analysis. He showed, for example, that all curves of the same class have the same Riemann surface.

Riemenschneider Tilman (*c.* 1460–1531). German sculptor. He was the head of a large and successful workshop in Würzburg from 1483 and an active participant in the political and religious struggles of his time. He is best known for his limewood sculptures, such as *St Matthew* 1495–1505 (Berlin-Dahlem, Staatliche Museum). The deep serenity of his figures stands in marked contrast to his dramatic life.

Rienzi Cola di (*c.* 1313–1354). Italian political reformer. In 1347, he tried to re-establish the forms of an ancient Roman republic. His second attempt seven years later ended with his assassination.

Riesman David (1909–). US sociologist, author of *The Lonely Crowd: A Study of the Changing American Character* 1950. He made a distinction among 'inner-directed', 'tradition-directed', and 'other-directed' societies; the first using individual internal values, the second using established tradition, and the third, other people's expectations, to develop cohesiveness and conformity within a society.

Rietvelt Gerrit Thomas (1888–1964). Dutch architect. He was associated with the De Stijl group. He designed the Schroeder House in Utrecht 1924 and is known for his rectilinear Red-Blue Chair 1918.

Rifkind Malcolm Leslie (1946–). British lawyer and Conservative politician, foreign secretary from 1995. Rifkind initially embarked on an academic career but was called to the Scottish Bar 1975 and in the same year entered politics, winning the Edinburgh Pentland seat. A junior minister in the Scottish Office from 1979, he progressed through the Foreign and Commonwealth Office to become Scottish secretary 1986 and transport secretary 1990. As defence secretary 1992–95, his incisive intellect enabled him to manage the 'peace dividend', with its inevitable rundown of parts of the armed forces, more successfully than some of his predecessors.

Rigaud Hyacinthe (1659–1743). French portraitist. He was court painter to Louis XIV from 1688. His portrait of *Louis XIV* 1701 (Louvre, Paris) is characteristically majestic, with the elegant figure of the king enveloped in ermine and drapery.

He first studied at Montpellier and Lyons, and went to Paris 1681. Though he won the Prix de Rome 1685, he was advised by Le Brun to stay in Paris instead of going to Italy, becoming a successful court painter to Louis XIV; after Louis's death to the regent, Philippe d'Orléans; and later to Louis XV. The style of his earlier portraits, formal and grandiose, culminates in the pomp of his *Louis XIV*. He later developed a more intimate and natural approach, some works showing the influence of Rembrandt, seven paintings by whom were in his possession 1703. Many replicas were required of him and he had a busy studio, few works being entirely the product of his own hand.

Rigg Diana (1938–). English actress. Her stage roles include Bianca in *The Taming of the Shrew* 1961, Cordelia in *King Lear* 1964, and Héloïse in *Abelard and Héloïse* 1970; television roles include Emma Peel in *The Avengers* 1965–67, Clytemnestra in *The Serpent Son* 1979, and Lady Deadlock in *Bleak House* 1985. She became the hostess for *Mystery Theater* on US public television 1989. DBE 1994.

Riis Jacob August (1849–1914). Danish-born US journalist, photographer, and reformer. Riis emigrated to the USA 1870. After working at a succession of jobs, he was hired as a reporter for the *New York Tribune* 1877. As police reporter for the *New York Evening Sun* 1888–99, he was exposed to the grim realities of urban life, and his photographic exposé of conditions in the New York slums, *How the Other Half Lives* 1890, made the American public aware of the poverty in its own midst.

Riley Bridget Louise (1931–). English painter. She was a pioneer of Op art. In the early 1960s she invented her characteristic style, arranging hard-edged black and white dots or lines in regular patterns to create disturbing effects of scintillating light and movement. *Fission* 1963 (Museum of Modern Art, New York) is an example. She introduced colour in the late 1960s and experimented with silkscreen prints on Perspex.

Riley James Whitcomb (1849–1916). US poet. Born in Greenfield, Indiana, Riley had little formal education and worked at a series of odd jobs before becoming the editor of a local newspaper. In 1877 he began to contribute light verse to the *Indianapolis Journal*. His first collection of poems, *The Old Swimmin' Hole*, was published 1883. His later collections include *Rhymes of Childhood* 1890 and *Home Folks* 1900. His use of the Midwestern vernacular and familiar themes earned him the unofficial title 'The Hoosier Poet'.

Rilke Rainer Maria (1875–1926). Austrian writer. Rilke was born in Prague. He travelled widely and worked for a time as secretary to

the sculptor Rodin. His prose works include the semi-autobiographical *Die Aufzeichnungen des Malte Laurids Brigge/The Notebook of Malte Laurids Brigge* 1910. His verse is characterized by a form of mystic pantheism that seeks to achieve a state of ecstasy in which existence can be apprehended as a whole. His poetical works include *Die Sonnette an Orpheus/Sonnets to Orpheus* 1923 and *Duisener Elegien/Duino Elegies* 1923. He died in Switzerland.

> *I hold this to be the highest task for a bond between two people: that each protects the solitude of the other.*
> RAINER MARIA RILKE
> Letter to Paula Modersohn-Becker 12 Feb 1902

Suggested reading
Baron, Frank and others (eds) *Rilke: The Alchemy of Alienation* (1980)
Butler, Elizabeth *Rainer Maria Rilke* (1941, rep 1973)
Hendry, J F *Sacred Threshold* (1983)
Peters, H F *Rainer Maria Rilke: Masks and Man* (1960)
Prater, D *A Ringing Glass* (1986)

Rimbaud (Jean Nicolas) Arthur (1854–1891). French Symbolist poet. His verse was chiefly written before the age of 20, notably *Les Illuminations* published 1886. From 1871 he lived with the poet Paul Verlaine. Although the association ended after Verlaine attempted to shoot him, it was Verlaine's analysis of Rimbaud's work 1884 that first brought him recognition. Rimbaud then travelled widely, working as a trader in North Africa 1880–91.

Suggested reading
Fowlie, Wallace *Rimbaud* (1965)
Hackett, C A *Rimbaud: A Critical Introduction* (1981)
Lawler, James *Rimbaud's Theatre of the Self* (1992)
Starkie, Enid *Arthur Rimbaud* (1961)

Rimington Stella (1935–). British public servant and director-general of the counter-intelligence security service (MI5) 1992–96. Rimington joined MI5 1969 as a desk officer and progressed to become director of counter-terrorism. She was promoted to senior deputy director-general 1990 and in 1992 became the first woman to hold the top post. She was the first head of MI5 to be named publicly, and in July 1993 published a booklet containing hitherto undisclosed details on the service, including its history, organization, and constitutional role.

> *Rimsky was ... deeply and unshowingly generous, and unkind only to admirers of Tchaikovsky.*
> Igor Stravinsky on NIKOLAY RIMSKY-KORSAKOV
> in *Memories and Commentaries* 1960

Rimsky-Korsakov Nikolay Andreyevich (1844–1908). Russian nationalist composer. His operas include *The Maid of Pskov* 1873, *The Snow Maiden* 1882, *Mozart and Salieri* 1898, and *The Golden Cockerel* 1907, a satirical attack on despotism that was banned until 1909. He also wrote an influential text on orchestration. Other works include the symphonic poem *Sadko* 1867, the programme symphony *Antar* 1869, and the symphonic suite *Scheherazade* 1888. He also completed works by other composers, for example, Mussorgsky's *Boris Godunov*.

Suggested reading
Abraham, Gerald *Rimsky-Korsakov: A Short Biography* (1948)
Rimsky-Korsakov, Nikolay *Chronicle of My Musical Life* (trs 1942)

Ringling Charles (1863–1926). US circus promoter. Born in McGregor, Iowa, Ringling started a vaudeville act 1882 with his brothers, John, Albert, Otto, and Alfred. The touring act eventually became a small circus and grew more popular after the purchase of an elephant 1888. With Charles as business manager, the Ringling Brothers Circus toured widely. With its three rings and large cast, the Ringlings' circus was touted as the 'Greatest Show on Earth,' the byword still most associated with the modern Ringling Brothers and Barnum and Bailey Circus (which the Ringling brothers acquired 1907).

Riopelle Jean-Paul (1923–). Canadian artist. He was active in Paris from 1946. He moved from automatism in the 1950s to an Abstract Expressionist style, producing colourful thickly painted canvases. He also produced sculptures. His *Encounter* 1956 is a typically rough-textured canvas.

Ripley Robert LeRoy (1893–1949). US cartoonist, creator of the syndicated column 'Believe It or Not!', a highly popular compendium of bizarre facts. Born in Santa Rosa, California, Ripley began drawing cartoons as a teenager and was hired by the sports department of the *San Francisco Bulletin* 1910. In 1913 he became a sports cartoonist for the *New York Globe* and later began to present sports records in the series called 'Believe It or Not!' Moving from sports to all kinds of oddities and obscure facts, Ripley took his column to the *New York Evening Post* in 1923 and later to national syndication. Through radio and film appearances and continued syndication, Ripley became a national celebrity and master of the bizarre.

Ritter Johann Wilhelm (1776–1810). German physicist who carried out early work on electrolytic cells and discovered ultraviolet radiation. Ritter was born in Samnitz, Silesia (now in Poland), and studied medicine at Jena. Until 1804 he also taught at Jena and at Gotha, before moving to Munich as a member of the Bavarian Academy of Science.

In 1800, Ritter electrolysed water to produce hydrogen and oxygen and two years later developed a dry battery, both of which phenomena convinced him that electrical forces were involved in chemical bonding. He also compiled an electrochemical series. At about the same time he was studying the effect of light on chemical reactions, and from the darkening of silver chloride in light he discovered ultraviolet radiation.

I dreamed of a hillbilly heaven.

TEX RITTER
Title of his 1961 hit, which he co-wrote

Ritter Tex (Woodward Maurice) (1905–1974). US singer and actor. He was popular as a singing cowboy in B-films in the 1930s and 1940s (*Arizona Trail* 1943). He sang the title song to *High Noon* 1952.

Rivadavia Bernardino (1780–1845). Argentine politician, first president of Argentina 1826–27. Rivadavia was secretary to the revolutionary junta 1811–12 and a minister in the Rodríguez administration 1820–23. War with Brazil over Uruguay 1825–28 forced him to call the congress which wrote the central constitution 1826, and elected him to the presidency. An enigmatic and controversial figure, he is variously regarded as a democrat, republican, monarchist, and traitor. During his rule he made a number of social reforms including extending the franchise to all males over 20 and encouraging freedom of the press. Unable to control the provincial caudillos, he was forced to resign and spent most of his remaining years in exile in Europe.

Rivera Diego (1886–1957). Mexican painter. He was active in Europe until 1921. An exponent of Social Realism, he received many public commissions for murals exalting the Mexican revolution. A vast cycle on historical themes (National Palace, Mexico City) was begun 1929. In the 1930s he visited the USA and with Ben Shahn produced murals for the Rockefeller Center, New York (later overpainted because he included a portrait of Lenin).
Suggested reading
Arquin, Florence *Diego Rivera* (1971)
Detroit Institute of Arts *Diego Rivera: A Retrospective* (1986)
Rivera, Diego and March, Gladys *My Art, My Life* (1960)
Wolfe, Bertram *The Fabulous Life of Diego Rivera* (1963)

Rivera José Fructuoso (*c.* 1788–1854). Uruguayan general and politician, president 1830–34, 1839–43. Rivera fought under José Artigas and submitted to Brazilian occupation before rejoining the revolution 1825. When he became president his financial mismanagement and favouritism provoked open dissent. He led a revolt

1836 against his successor Manuel Oribe (1792–1857), during which he became the focus of the Colorado Party. During his second term in office he declared war on Argentina.

Rivera Primo de. Spanish politician; see ◊Primo de Rivera.

Rivers William Halse Rivers (1864–1922). English anthropologist and psychologist. His systematic study of kinship relations and his emphasis on fieldwork helped to establish anthropology as a more scientific discipline.

As a psychologist he argued that perception was culturally conditioned, and he applied the theories of Sigmund Freud in his treatment of World War I shell-shock victims.

My Farce from my Elbow

BRIAN RIX
Title of autobiography 1977

Rix Brian Norman Roger, Baron Rix (1924–). English actor and manager. He first became known for his series of farces at London's Whitehall Theatre, notably *Dry Rot* 1954–58. He made several films for cinema and television, including *A Roof Over My Head* 1977, and promotes charities for the mentally disabled. Knighted 1986, baron 1992.

Rizzio David (*c.* 1533–1566). Italian adventurer at the court of Mary Queen of Scots. After her marriage to Darnley, Rizzio's influence over her incited her husband's jealousy, and he was murdered by Darnley and his friends.

Roach Hal (Harald Eugene) (1892–1992). US film producer. He was active from the 1910s to the 1940s, producing many comedies. Born in Elmira, New York state, he had an adventurous youth, including a spell as a gold prospector in Alaska, before entering films as a stunt man and bit player 1912. He turned producer on the strength of a modest legacy 1915. Directing many of his earlier efforts himself, he concentrated on two-reel shorts; these included vehicles for Charlie Chase and Zasu Pitts as well as the classic shorts of Laurel and Hardy, with whom he retained links after switching to feature-length production during the 1930s. His work includes *The Music Box* 1932, *Way Out West* 1936, and *Of Mice and Men* 1939. After World War II, during which he produced training and propaganda films, he turned to television, with mixed fortunes. Although his production company folded in the late 1950s, he remained sporadically active on the fringes of the film industry.

Now all is over. Let the piper play 'Return No More'.

ROBERT MACGREGOR (ROB ROY)
Last words 1734

Rob Roy nickname of Robert MacGregor (1671–1734). Scottish Highland Jacobite outlaw. After losing his estates, he lived by cattle theft and extortion. Captured, he was sentenced to transportation but pardoned 1727. He is a central character in Walter Scott's historical novel *Rob Roy* 1817.
Suggested reading
Frewin, L R *Legends of Rob Roy* (1954)

Robbe-Grillet Alain (1922–). French writer. Robbe-Grillet qualified as an agronomist and worked in Africa and the West Indies as a research biologist before turning to writing. He was the leading theorist of *le nouveau roman* ('the new novel'), for example his own *Les Gommes/The Erasers* 1953, *La Jalousie/Jealousy* 1957, and *Dans le Labyrinthe/In the Labyrinth* 1959, which concentrates on the detailed description of physical objects. He also wrote the script for the film *L'Année dernière à Marienbad/Last Year at Marienbad* 1961.

Robbia, della Italian family of sculptors and architects. They were active in Florence. Luca della Robbia (1400–1482) created a number of major works in Florence, notably the marble *cantoria* (singing gallery) in the cathedral 1431–38 (Museo del Duomo), with lively groups of choristers. Luca also developed a characteristic style of glazed terracotta work. Andrea della Robbia (1435–1525), Luca's nephew and pupil, and Andrea's sons continued the family business, inheriting the formula for the vitreous terracotta glaze. The blue-and-white medallions of foundling children 1463–66 on the Ospedale degli Innocenti, Florence, are typical. Many later works are more elaborate and highly coloured, such as the frieze 1522 on the façade of the Ospedale del Ceppo, Pistoia.

Robbins Jerome (1918–   ). US dancer and choreographer. First a chorus boy on Broadway, then a soloist with the newly formed American Ballet Theater 1941–46, Robbins was associate director of the New York City Ballet 1949–59. His first ballet, *Fancy Free* 1944, was a great success (and was adapted with Leonard Bernstein into the musical *On the Town* 1944). He was co-director of the New York City Ballet 1969–83 (with George Balanchine). His ballets are internationally renowned and he is considered the greatest US-born ballet choreographer. Other Robbins ballets include *Dancers at a Gathering* 1969, *The Goldberg Variations* 1971, and *Glass Pieces* 1983 (based on W H Auden's poem). He also choreographed the musicals *The King and I* 1951, *West Side Story* 1957, and *Fiddler on the Roof* 1964.

Robbins Lionel Charles, Baron Robbins (1898–   ). English economist who stressed the role of scarcity and constraints in economic decisionmaking. He defined economics as 'the science which studies human behaviour as a relationship between ends and scarce means which have alternative uses'.

Robbins made a distinction between positive and normative economics. Positive economics is concerned with hypotheses about economic relationships that can be tested by empirical evidence. Normative economics involves value judgements, such as 'unemployment should be reduced to 5%'. Robbins's view was that economists should not make value judgements and should concern themselves with positive economics. Baron 1959.

He chaired a committee of inquiry to review the pattern of higher education, which recommended the extension of degree courses to polytechnics (now mostly universities) in its report, now known as the Robbins Report, 1963.

Robbins Tim (1958–   ). US actor. Tall and rangy, with a mercurial talent for comic characterization, he won fame in the leading role of the Hollywood satire *The Player* 1992. He has scripted and directed one film, *Bob Roberts* 1993, a humorous view of political campaigning in which he also played the title role. Other films in which he has appeared include *Top Gun* 1985, *Bull Durham* 1988, *Cadillac Man* 1990, and *Short Cuts* 1993.

Robert two dukes of Normandy:

Robert (I) the Devil Duke of Normandy from 1027. Also known as 'the Magnificent', he was the father of William the Conqueror, and was legendary for his cruelty. He became duke after the death of his brother Richard III, in which he may have been implicated.

The 'Robert the Devil' who is the hero of three Old French romances is a mythical figure, the product of an unholy copulation between a demon and the duchess of Normandy who, after a life of terrible brutality, became a famously holy hermit.

Robert II (*c.* 1054–1134). Eldest son of William the Conqueror, succeeding him as Duke of Normandy (but not on the English throne) 1087. His brother William II ascended the English throne, and they warred until 1096, after which Robert took part in the First Crusade. When his other brother Henry I claimed the English throne 1100, Robert contested the claim and invaded England unsuccessfully 1101. Henry invaded Normandy 1106, and captured Robert, who remained a prisoner in England until his death.

Robert three kings of Scotland:

Robert (I) the Bruce (1274–1329). King of Scotland from 1306, and grandson of Robert de Bruce. He shared in the national uprising led by William Wallace and, after Wallace's execution 1305, rose once more against Edward I of England, and was crowned at Scone 1306. He defeated Edward II at Bannockburn

1314. In 1328 the treaty of Northampton recognized Scotland's independence and Robert as king.

Suggested reading
Barrow, G W S *Robert Bruce* (1965)

Robert II (1316–1390). King of Scotland from 1371. He was the son of Walter (1293–1326), steward of Scotland, who married Marjory, daughter of Robert the Bruce. He was the first king of the house of Stuart.

Robert III (*c.* 1340–1406). King of Scotland from 1390, son of Robert II. He was unable to control the nobles, and the government fell largely into the hands of his brother, Robert, Duke of Albany (*c.* 1340–1420).

Robert Guiscard (*c.* 1015–1085). Norman adventurer and duke of Apulia. Robert, also known as 'the Wizard', carved out a fiefdom centred on Apulia in southern Italy, of which he became duke 1059.

Robert was the son of an obscure Norman, Tancred de Hauteville, and from *c.* 1047 he helped his family in its struggles with the Byzantines, ejecting them from Calabria and defeating the Byzantine-Lombard-Papal army at Civitate 1053, where he briefly took Pope Leo IX prisoner. He benefited from the schism between the Orthodox and Catholic churches 1054, because his success against the Byzantines and his plan to rid Sicily of Arabs brought him back into papal favour. One result was his investiture with the duchy of Apulia and lordship of Calabria and Sicily 1059. Incursions into papal territory earned him excommunication 1075, and the following year he defeated the Pope's Lombard allies and captured Salerno, which he made his capital. Amicable relations with Pope Gregory VII were restored 1080, allowing him to wage war against the Byzantines along the Adriatic coast 1081–82. After a pause to prevent Gregory VII falling to Holy Roman Emperor Henry IV 1083, he returned to his Illyrian campaigns, dying at the siege of Cephalonia, in Greece.

In a society devoted to drunkenness, he seems to have been comparatively temperate, and, though living by plunder ... comparatively humane.

J K Laughton on BARTHOLOMEW ROBERTS
in *Dictionary of National Biography*

Roberts Bartholomew (*c.* 1682–1722). British merchant-navy captain who joined his captors when taken by pirates in 1718. He became the most financially successful of all the sea rovers until surprised and killed in battle by the British navy.

Roberts Charles George Douglas (1860–1943). Canadian poet, short-story writer, and novelist. He is known as 'the father of Canadian literature'. His early *Orion, and Other Poems* 1880 influentially demonstrated that Canadian poets could creatively assimilate Tennysonian Romanticism, but later volumes such as *The Vagrant of Time* 1927 developed a more modern idiom. His 24 volumes of short fiction, starting with *Earth's Enigmas* 1896, included some of the first and most realistic animal stories as well as tales of outdoor adventure. He also wrote historical romances such as *Barbara Ladd* 1902, set during the American Revolution. Knighted 1935.

Roberts David (1796–1864). Scottish painter whose oriental paintings were the result of several trips to the Middle East. Roberts progressed from interior decorator to scene painter at Drury Lane Theatre, London. From 1831 he travelled around the Mediterranean producing topographical views. Many of these were published in books, including the six-volume *The Holy Land, Syria, Idumea, Arabia, Egypt & Nubia* 1842–49.

Roberts Frederick Sleigh, 1st Earl Roberts (1832–1914). British field marshal. Born in India, Roberts joined the Bengal Artillery 1851, and served through the Indian Mutiny, receiving the VC, and the Abyssinian campaign of 1867–68. During the Afghan War of 1878–80 he occupied Kabul.

After serving in Afghanistan and making a victorious march to Kandahar, he became commander in chief in India 1885–93 and in Ireland 1895–99. He then received the command in South Africa, where he occupied Bloemfontein and Pretoria. During the Second South African War 1899–1902 he made possible the annexation of the Transvaal and Orange Free State. KCB 1878, baron 1892, earl 1900.

Roberts Richard (1789–1864). Welsh engineer and inventor of such machinery as a screw-cutting lathe and a metal-planing machine. Roberts was born in Montgomeryshire and became a toolmaker. Moving to London, he worked as an apprentice to English engineer Henry Maudslay. In 1814 Roberts set up in business in Manchester. From 1828 to 1842 he was a partner in the firm of Sharpe, Thomas and Company, which manufactured machines to his design. When the Liverpool and Manchester Railway opened 1830, the firm began building locomotives. Their products were bought by railway companies throughout Europe. When the firm split up, Roberts retained the part of the company known as the Globe Works.

In 1824, at the request of some manufacturers, Roberts built a self-acting spinning mule which was a vast improvement on that devised by Samuel Crompton in 1779. In 1845 he invented an electromagnet. He also designed a steam brake and a system of standard gauges to which all his work was constructed. In 1848 he invented a machine for punching holes in steel plates. Incorporating the Jacquard method, he devised a machine for punching holes of any pitch or pattern in bridge plates and boiler plates.

Roberts Tom (Thomas William) (1856–1931). Australian painter. He was the founder of the Heidelberg School, which introduced Impressionism to Australia. Born in England, he arrived in Australia 1869, returning to Europe to study 1881–85. He received official commissions, including one to paint the opening of the first Australian federal parliament, but is better known for his scenes of pioneering life.

Robertson Pat (Marion Gordon) (1930–). US Republican politician and religious broadcaster. A born-again evangelical Christian, he founded the Christian Broadcasting Network (CBN) 1961. He is the host of its daily talk show, *The 700 Club*, and was a candidate for the Republican presidential nomination 1988.

A 'Bible conservative', he believes in 'traditional values'. In 1981 he started the Freedom Council to recruit evangelical Christians for political action.

Robertson was born in Lexington, Virginia, studied at the New York Theological Seminary, and was ordained into the Southern Baptist Church 1961. He launched CBN after buying a run-down television station in Portsmouth, Virginia, and it grew into a large network. He founded CBN University 1977, and built the CBN Center in Virginia Beach. His books include his autobiography *Shout It from the Housetops* 1972, and *The New World Order* 1991.

Robertson Robert (1869–1949). Scottish chemist who worked on explosives for military use, such as TNT (trinitrotoluene, 2,4,6-trinitromethylbenzene), and made improvements to cordite. KBE 1918.

Working at the Royal Gunpowder Factory in Essex, he was put in charge of the main laboratory in 1900 and transferred to the Research Department at Woolwich Arsenal, London, 1907. In 1921 Robertson became the government chemist. He left government service in 1936 for the Royal Institution, but returned to Woolwich for the duration of World War II.

Robertson's appointment to Woolwich in 1907 coincided with the analysis of defects in British ammunition that had been revealed during the South African War. The new explosives tetryl (trinitrophenylmethylnitramine) and amatol were developed.

His investigations as government chemist included the carriage of dangerous goods by sea, the determination of sulphur dioxide and nitrous gases in the atmosphere, the elimination of sulphur dioxide from the emissions at power stations, the possible effects on health of tetraethyl lead additives to petrol, and the preservation of photographic reproductions of valuable documents.

[He was] the founder of 'cup-and-saucer drama'.

Commonly used description of THOMAS WILLIAM ROBERTSON

Robertson Thomas William (1829–1871). English dramatist. Initially an actor, he had his first success as a dramatist with *David Garrick* 1864, which set a new, realistic trend in English drama; later plays included *Society* 1865 and *Caste* 1867.

Robertson William (1721–1793). Scottish historian who wrote a history of Scotland in the reigns of Mary and James VI (1759), and one of the reign of the emperor Charles V (1769).

...'Orace, you're for 'ome!

WILLIAM ROBERTSON
to General Smith-Dorrien, when relieving him of his command

Robertson William Robert (1860–1933). British general in World War I, the only man ever to rise from private to field marshal in the British army. Robertson enlisted as a trooper in the cavalry 1877, was commissioned 1888, and made KCVO 1913.

He served in France in World War I until he was appointed Chief of the Imperial General Staff Dec 1915. He resigned 1918 after a difference of opinion with Lloyd George over the direction of the war. He was awarded £10,000 and a baronetcy for his war services 1919. Promoted to full general 1916, he finally became a field marshal 1920.

Robeson Paul (1898–1976). US bass singer and actor. He graduated from Columbia University as a lawyer, but limited opportunities led him instead to the stage. He appeared in Eugene O'Neill's play *The Emperor Jones* 1924 and the Jerome Kern musical *Show Boat* 1927, in which he sang 'Ol' Man River'. He played *Othello* 1930, and his films include *Sanders of the River* 1935 and *King Solomon's Mines* 1937. An ardent advocate of black rights, he had his passport withdrawn 1950–58 after a highly public visit to Russia. His last years were spent in England.
Suggested reading
Duberman, Martin *Paul Robeson* (1989)
Hamilton, Virginia *Paul Robeson* (1974)
Robeson, Paul *Here I Stand* (autobiography) (1958)
Robeson, Susan *The Whole World in His Hands* (1981)

Any institution which does not suppose the people good, and the magistrate corruptible, is evil.

MAXIMILIEN DE ROBESPIERRE
Declaration of the Rights of Man 24 Apr 1793

Robespierre Maximilien François Marie Isidore de (1758–1794). French politician in the French Revolution. Robespierre, a lawyer, was elected to the National Assembly of 1789–91. His defence of democratic principles made him popular in Paris, while his disinterestedness won him the nickname of 'the Incorruptible'. As leader of the Jacobins in the National Convention, he supported the execution of Louis XVI and the overthrow of the right-wing republican Girondins, and in July 1793 was elected to the Committee of Public Safety. His zeal for social reform and his attacks on the excesses of the extremists made him enemies on both right and left; a conspiracy was formed against him, and in July 1794 he was overthrown and executed by those who actually perpetrated the Reign of Terror. Many believe that he was a scapegoat for the Reign of Terror since he ordered only 72 executions personally.
Suggested reading
Jordan, David *The Revolutionary Career of Maximilien Robespierre* (1985)
Rudé, G E *Robespierre* (1975)
Schama, Simon *Citizens: A Chronicle of the French Revolution* (1988)

Robin Hood in English legend, an outlaw and champion of the poor against the rich, said to have lived in Sherwood Forest, Nottinghamshire, during the reign of Richard I (1189–99). He feuded with the sheriff of Nottingham, accompanied by Maid Marian and a band of followers known as his 'merry men'. He appears in many popular ballads from the 13th century, but his first datable appearance is in William Langland's *Piers Plowman* in the late 14th century. He became popular in the 15th century.

Traditionally he is a nobleman who remained loyal to Richard during his exile and opposed the oppression of King John. His companions included Little John, so-called because of his huge stature, Friar Tuck, a jovial cleric, and Alan a Dale. There may be some historical basis for the legend, but many of the customs and practices associated with his name suggest that he is a character of Mayday celebrations. He is claimed to have been buried at Kirklees Hall, Yorkshire.

Robinson Edward G. Stage name of Emmanuel Goldenberg (1893–1973). US film actor. Born in Romania, he emigrated with his family to the USA 1903. He was noted for his gangster roles, such as *Little Caesar* 1930, but also gave strong performances in psychological dramas such as *Scarlet Street* 1945.

He also performed in dramatic and comedy roles in film and on the stage, and was a great art collector. He wrote two autobiographical volumes, *My Father, My Son* 1958 and *All My Yesterdays* 1973. His other films include *Dr Ehrlich's Magic Bullet* 1940, *Double Indemnity* 1944, *The Ten Commandments* 1956, *A Hole in the Head* 1959, and *Soylent Green* 1973.

Robinson Edwin Arlington (1869–1935). US poet. His verse, dealing mainly with psychological themes in a narrative style, is collected in volumes such as *The Children of the Night* 1897, which established his reputation. He was awarded three Pulitzer Prizes for poetry: *Collected Poems* 1922, *The Man Who Died Twice* 1925, and *Tristram* 1928.

Robinson, Mary The independent candidate Mary Robinson's victory in the 1990 presidential election was seen as a turning point in Irish politics. A Catholic married to a Protestant, she became the first president since 1945 not to have been backed by the dominant Fianna Fáil party.

Robinson, Edward G US film actor Edward G Robinson (passenger) in Little Caesar 1930. He became famous playing gangsters in such films as Little Caesar and Key Largo 1948 (with Humphrey Bogart), though in his long career he played a wide variety of roles. Other films include Double Indemnity 1944, Scarlet Street 1945, and The Cincinnati Kid 1965.

Robinson George Augustus (1788–1866). English Methodist lay preacher in Australia, who was appointed in 1829 to 'effect an intercourse with the natives' in Tasmania. His mission led to the capture of almost all the Tasmanian Aborigines still alive. His aim was to save the Aborigines from further slaughter by the white settlers and to Christianize and Europeanize them. His Aboriginal settlements were ultimately not successful and by the end of the century the Tasmanian Aborigines had died out. Robinson was also appointed chief protector of Aborigines in Port Phillip in 1838 but was unable to protect them from the settlers' desire to take over the land.

Robinson Henry Crabb (1775–1867). English writer. His diaries, journals, and letters are a valuable source of information on his literary friends Charles Lamb, Samuel Taylor Coleridge, William Wordsworth, and Robert Southey.

Robinson was a lawyer with literary interests. He travelled much in Germany and helped to popularize the work of German writers, particularly J W Goethe, in the UK. He was a cofounder of University College and the Athenaeum club, both in London.

Robinson Henry Peach (1830–1901). English photographer. He studied as a painter before taking up photography 1851. By careful composition and the combination of several negatives in one print, he produced images that closely imitated the effects and subject matter of Victorian painting.

Robinson Jackie (Jack Roosevelt) (1919–1972). US baseball player. In 1947 he became the first black American in the major leagues, playing second base for the Brooklyn Dodgers and winning rookie of the year honours. In 1949 he was the National League's batting champion and was voted the league's most valuable player. He had a career batting average of .311.

Robinson Joan Violet (born Maurice) (1903–1983). British economist who introduced Marxism to Keynesian economic theory. She expanded her analysis in *Economics of Perfect Competition* 1933.

Robinson John Arthur Thomas (1919–1983). British Anglican cleric, bishop of Woolwich 1959–69. A left-wing Modernist, he wrote *Honest to God* 1963, which was interpreted as denying a personal God.

Robinson Mary (1944–). Irish Labour politician, president from 1990. Robinson was born in County Mayo and educated at Trinity College, Dublin, and Harvard University, USA. She became a professor of law at 25. A strong supporter of women's rights, she has campaigned for the liberalization of Ireland's laws prohibiting divorce and abortion. As a member of the Labour Party, she tried unsuccessfully to enter the Dáil (parliament) in 1990, and then surprisingly won the presidency of her country, defeating the Fianna Fáil frontrunner Brian Lenihan.

Robinson Robert (1886–1975). English chemist, Nobel prizewinner 1947 for his research in organic chemistry on the structure of many natural products, including flower pigments and alkaloids. He formulated the electronic theory now used in organic chemistry. Knighted 1939.

Robinson's studies of the sex hormones, bile acids, and sterols were fundamental to the methods now used to investigate steroid compounds. His discovery that certain synthetic steroids could produce the same biological effects as the natural oestrogenic sex hormones paved the way for the contraceptive pill.

He first became professor at Sydney, Australia, 1912, returning to the UK 1915 and ending his career at Oxford 1929–55.

Robinson studied the composition and synthesis of anthocyanins (red and blue plant pigments) and anthoxanthins (yellow and brown pigments), and related their structure to their colour.

In his research on alkaloids he worked out the structure of morphine in 1925 and by 1946 he had devised methods of synthesizing strychnine and brucine, which influenced all structural studies of natural compounds that contain nitrogen.

During World War II, Robinson investigated the properties of the antibiotic penicillin and elucidated its structure. His methods were later applied to structural investigations of other antibiotics.

Robinson Smokey (William) (1940–). US singer, songwriter, and record producer. He was associated with Motown records from its conception. He was lead singer of the Miracles 1957–72 (hits include 'Shop Around' 1961 and 'The Tears of a Clown' 1970) and his solo hits include 'Cruisin' ' 1979 and 'Being With You' 1981. His light tenor voice and wordplay characterize his work.

He explained how to develop a basic plot and stick to it. He explained how every song should be a complete story.

SMOKEY ROBINSON
on Berry Gordy who taught him his song-writing technique,
quoted in Irwin Stambler, *The Encyclopedia
of Pop, Rock and Soul* 1989

Robinson Sugar Ray. Adopted name of Walker Smith (1920–1989). US boxer, world welterweight champion 1945–51; he defended his title five times. Defeating Jake LaMotta 1951, he took the middleweight title. He lost the title six times and won it seven times. He was involved in the 'Fight of the Century' with Randolph Turpin of the UK 1951, and was narrowly beaten for the light-heavyweight title by Joey Maxim of the USA 1952. He retired at the age of 45.

Robinson W(illiam) Heath (1872–1944). English cartoonist and illustrator. He made humorous drawings of bizarre machinery for performing simple tasks, such as raising one's hat. A clumsily designed apparatus is often described as a 'Heath Robinson' contraption.

Robinson William Leefe (1895–1919). British fighter pilot. During an air-raid Sept 1916, he shot down the first German airship to be brought down over the UK, for which he was awarded the Victoria Cross.

Robsart Amy (c. 1532–1560). Wife of Robert Dudley, the Earl of Leicester.

Robson Flora McKenzie (1902–1984). English actress. A stalwart of both stage and screen, she was notable as Queen Elizabeth I in the film *Fire Over England* 1937 and Mrs Alving in *Ghosts* 1958, an adaptation of the 19th-century play by Norwegian dramatist Henrik Ibsen. DBE 1960.

Rocard Michel Louis Léon (1930–). French socialist politician, prime minister 1988–91; leader of the Socialist Party (PS) 1993–94. Rocard trained at the prestigious Ecole Nationale d'Administration, where he was a classmate of Jacques Chirac. He became leader of the radical Unified Socialist Party (PSU) 1967, standing as its presidential candidate 1969. A former radical, he joined the PS 1973, emerging as leader of its moderate social-democratic wing.

Having gone over to the PS, Rocard unsuccessfully challenged Mitterrand for the party's presidential nomination 1981. After serving as minister of planning and regional development 1981–83 and of agriculture 1983–85, he resigned April 1985 in opposition to the government's introduction of proportional representation. In May 1988, however, as part of a strategy termed 'opening to the centre', the popular Rocard was appointed prime minister by Mitterrand. Following his resignation 1991, after his government only just survived a vote of no confidence, he was viewed as a presidential candidate. He replaced Laurent Fabius as PS leader April 1993 but resigned June 1994 after his party polled poorly in the European elections. He was replaced by Henri Emmanuelli.

Roche Stephen (1959–). Irish cyclist. One of the outstanding riders in Europe in the 1980s, he was the first British winner of the Tour de France in 1987 and the first English-speaking winner of the Tour of Italy the same year, as well as the 1987 world professional road-race champion.

Rochester John Wilmot, 2nd Earl of Rochester (1647–1680). English poet and courtier. He fought gallantly at sea against the Dutch, but chiefly led a debauched life at the court of Charles II. He wrote graceful (but often obscene) lyrics, and his *A Satire against Mankind* 1675 rivals Swift. He was a patron of the English poet John Dryden. Earl 1658.

Rockefeller John D(avison) (1839–1937). US millionaire, founder of Standard Oil 1870 (which achieved control of 90% of US refineries by 1882). The activities of the Standard Oil Trust led to an outcry against monopolies and the passing of the Sherman Anti-Trust Act of 1890. A lawsuit of 1892 prompted the dissolution of the trust, only for it to be refounded in 1899 as a holding company. In 1911, this was also declared illegal by the Supreme Court. He founded the philanthropic Rockefeller Foundation 1913, to which his son John D(avison) Rockefeller Jr (1874–1960) devoted his life.

Rockingham Charles Watson Wentworth, 2nd Marquess of Rockingham (1730–1782). British Whig politician, prime minister 1765–66 and 1782 (when he died in office); he supported the American claim to independence. Marquess 1750.

Rockne Knute Kenneth (1888–1931). Norwegian-born US American football coach. His greatest contribution to football was the extensive use of sophisticated formations and the forward pass. He established an unparalleled lifetime record of 105 wins, 12 losses, and 5 ties – with 5 undefeated, untied seasons.

Rockne emigrated to the USA with his family 1893. As a student at Notre Dame University 1910–14, he was a star football player and became the school's head football coach 1918. Serving in that position until his death, his book *Coaching, the Way of the Winner* was published 1925. His memoirs, *Autobiography*, appeared 1931.

Rockwell Norman (1894–1978). US painter and illustrator. He designed magazine covers, mainly for *The Saturday Evening Post*, and cartoons portraying American life. His whimsical view of the ordinary activities of the nation at work and at play earned him huge popularity. There is a museum of his work at Stockbridge, Massachusetts.
Suggested reading
Buechner, Thomas *Norman Rockwell* (1970)
Finch, Christopher *Rockwell's America* (1975)
Walton, Donald *A Rockwell Portrait* (1978)

Rodchenko Alexander Mikhailovich (1891–1956). Russian avant-garde painter, designer, and photographer. The aim of his work, in all media, was to create a visual language that would reflect the new revolutionary times. His paintings were abstract works based on severe geometrical shapes; under the influence of Tatlin he made three-dimensional constructions of wood, cardboard, and metal. His photographs of everyday objects were presented in close-up, from strange angles or from high viewpoints, an approach similar to that of the Hungarian Laszlo Moholy-Nagy; they document the early years of the Soviet era.

Roddick Anita Lucia (1943–). British entrepreneur, founder of the Body Shop, which now has branches worldwide. Roddick started with one shop in Brighton, England, 1976, selling only natural toiletries in refillable plastic containers.

Rodgers Jimmie (James Charles) (1897–). US country singer, songwriter, and guitarist. He was the genre's first important recording star. His blues-influenced vocals established an enduring style for country singers and he popularized yodelling. Not only his vocal style but also the content of his songs influenced country music for decades to come: the hard-done-by, hard-drinking, broken-hearted drifter is a persona of Rodgers' creation. The use of steel-guitar backing, now commonplace in country music, was also pioneered by Rodgers. Rodgers, born in Mississippi, was known as 'the Singing Brakeman' after his employment on the railway. His recordings, including 13 that were titled 'Blue Yodel' (in a numbered series), were made between 1927 and his death from tuberculosis; one of the last was called 'TB Blues'.

Many of his Blue Yodels are better known by alternative titles: 'Blue Yodel 1' is 'T for Texas', 'Blue Yodel 8' is 'Mule Skinner Blues'. Other songs include 'Waiting for a Train' and 'In the Jailhouse Now'.

Rodgers Richard Charles (1902–1979). US composer. He collaborated with librettist Lorenz Hart (1895–1943) on songs like 'Blue Moon' 1934 and musicals like *On Your Toes* 1936. With Oscar Hammerstein II, he wrote many musicals, including *Oklahoma!* 1943, *South Pacific* 1949, *The King and I* 1951, and *The Sound of Music* 1959.

Rodin (René François) Auguste (1840–1917). French sculptor. He is considered the greatest of his day. He freed sculpture from the idealizing conventions of the time by realistic treatment of the human figure, introducing a new boldness of style and expression. Examples are *Le Penseur/The Thinker* 1880 (Musée Rodin, Paris), *Le Baiser/The Kiss* 1886 (marble version in the Louvre, Paris), and *The Burghers of Calais* 1884–86 (copy in Embankment Gardens, Westminster, London).

Rodin failed the entrance examination for the Ecole des Beaux Arts, and never attended. He started as a mason, began to study in museums, and in 1875 visited Italy, where he was inspired by the work of Michelangelo. His early statue *The Age of Bronze* 1877 (Musée Rodin, Paris) was criticized for its total naturalism and accuracy. In 1880 he began the monumental bronze *Gates of Hell* for the Ecole des Arts Décoratifs in Paris (inspired by Ghiberti's bronze doors in Florence), a project that occupied him for many years and was unfinished at his death. Many of the figures designed for the gate became independent sculptures. During the 1890s he received two notable commissions, for statues of the writers Balzac 1893–97 (Musée Rodin, Paris) and Victor Hugo 1886–90 (Musée Rodin, Paris). He also produced many drawings.

Suggested reading
Champigneulle, Bernard *Rodin* (1967)
Elsen, A E *Auguste Rodin: Readings on his Life and Work* (1965)
Jianou, I *Rodin* (1970)

Rodney George Brydges, 1st Baron Rodney (1718–1792). British admiral. In 1762 he captured Martinique, St Lucia, and Grenada from the French. In 1780 he relieved Gibraltar by defeating a Spanish squadron off Cape St Vincent. In 1782 he crushed the French fleet under Count de Grasse off Dominica, for which he was raised to the peerage. He had become a baronet in 1764.

Rodnina Irina Konstantinovna (1949–). Soviet ice skater. Between 1969 and 1980 she won 23 world, Olympic, and European gold medals in pairs competitions. Her partners were Alexei Ulanov and then Alexsandr Zaitsev.

Rodrigo Joaquín (1902–). Spanish composer. His works are filled with Spanish folklore or ambience, as in the well-known *Concierto de Aranjuez* 1939 or the *Concerto heroico* 1943. He has always composed in a conservative, lucid Neo-Classical style that is less adventurous than Manuel de Falla but nevertheless as effective and colourful.

Roe (Edwin) Alliott Verdon (1877–1958). English aircraft designer, the first Briton to construct and fly an aeroplane, in 1908. He designed the Avro series of aircraft from 1912. Roe was born in Patricroft, near Manchester, was apprenticed to a railway company, then entered the motor industry. He became interested in aircraft design, and his biplane flew a distance of 23 m/75 ft nearly a year before the first officially recognized flight in England by John Moore-Brabazon (1884–1964). In 1910 Roe founded the firm of A V Roe and Company, manufacturing aircraft, but in 1928 he left the firm and turned his attention to the design of flying boats. He founded the Saunders–Roe Company based on the Isle of Wight.

The first aircraft from the Manchester works was the Avro 500, one of the first machines to be ordered for use by the British army. Two of these formed the strength of the Central Flying School of the Royal Flying Corps.

In 1913 the company produced its first seaplane, a large biplane known as the Avro 503. The Avro 504, also 1913, was considerably in advance of its contemporaries, and would be used for decades of safe flying instruction. Although not basically a military aircraft, it was used extensively in World War I. Many modifications followed; the 504H was the first aircraft to be successfully launched by catapult. Knighted 1929.

Time and speed are desperate shackles and terribly difficult to fight. But it's worth having a go.

NICOLAS ROEG
in *Films Illustrated* July 1980

Roeg Nicolas Jack (1928–). English film director and writer. He was formerly a cinematographer. His striking visual style is often combined with fractured, disturbing plots, as in *Performance* 1970, *Don't Look Now* 1973, *The Man Who Fell to Earth* 1976, and *The Witches* 1989. His other films include *Walkabout* 1971, *Bad Timing* 1980, *Castaway* 1986, and *Track 29* 1988.

All lovers live by longing, and endure: / Summon a vision and declare it pure.

THEODORE ROETHKE
Four for Sir John Davies IV 'The Vigil'

Roethke Theodore Huebner (1908–1963). US poet. His lyrical, visionary, and exclusively personal poetry drew on theological and mystical sources. It derived much of its detail and imagery from the greenhouses and plants in his father's large nursery business in Michigan. Collections include *Open House* 1941, *The Lost Son* 1948, *The Waking* 1953 (Pulitzer prize), and the posthumous *Collected Poems* 1968.

Suggested reading
Chaney, N *Theodore Roethke: The Poetics of Wonder* (1982)
Malkoff, Karl *Theodore Roethke: An Introduction to the Poetry* (1966)
Parini, Jay *Theodore Roethke: An American Romantic* (1979)
Seager, Allan *The Glass House: The Life of Theodore Roethke* (1968)

Roger II (1095–1154). King of Sicily from 1130, the second son of Count Roger I of Sicily (1031–1101).

Roger succeeded his brother Simon as count 1105. By 1122 he had seized Calabria from his cousins and put down revolts by its barons. He secured the duchy of Apulia 1127 following the death of his cousin Duke William, grandson of Robert Guiscard. Pope Honorius II (died 1130) invested him as duke of Apulia, Calabria, and Sicily 1128, and two years later, on the authority of the antipope Anacletus II, he was crowned King of Sicily. In 1139 Roger captured

Pope Innocent II, forcing him to confirm this title, with lordship over Norman Italy. Having put down a series of rebellions he proclaimed the Assizes of Ariano 1140, a comprehensive set of laws by which his realms were to be pacified. Aiming to establish a Mediterranean empire at the expense of the Byzantines, Roger used his powerful navy to capture Malta and to establish control in North Africa from Tripoli to Tunis.

Roger modelled his government on Byzantine autocracy, but encouraged toleration among the cultures and religions of his people. His Palermo court was a cultural centre where Latin, Greek, and Arab scholars mixed freely. His daughter Constance married the future Holy Roman emperor Henry VI, and on the death of Roger's grandson William II 1189, Henry inherited the kingdom of Sicily.

Rogers Carl Ransom (1902–1987). US psychologist who developed the client-centred approach to counselling and psychotherapy. This stressed the importance of clients making their own decisions and developing their own potential (self-actualization). He emphasized the value of genuine interest on the part of a therapist who is also accepting and empathetic. Rogers's views became widely employed.
Suggested reading
Evans, Richard *Carl Rogers: The Man and His Ideas* (1975)
Rogers, Carl *Client-Centered Therapy* (1951)
Rogers Carl *On Becoming a Person* (1961)
Rogers, Carl *On Becoming Carl Rogers* (1980)

Rogers Ginger. Stage name of Virginia Katherine McMath (1911–1995). US actress, dancer, and singer. Born in Independence, Missouri, Rogers became a dancer in vaudeville, partly on the strength of winning a charleston competition. From New York nightclub appearances she graduated to Broadway shows, including *Crazy for You* 1930. Prompted by her indefatigable mother Lela, she moved to Hollywood and had small parts in various films, typically (as in *42nd Street* 1933) as a wisecracking member of the chorus line. She worked from the 1930s to the 1950s, often starring with Fred Astaire in such films as *Top Hat* 1935 and *Swing Time* 1936. Rogers first appeared with Astaire when both had secondary roles in *Flying Down to Rio* 1933. Their dance numbers together made them the most celebrated dance duo in screen history.

Although Rogers's aspirations to dramatic roles were vindicated by her winning an Academy Award for playing the title role in *Kitty Foyle* 1940, comedy remained her forte, and she seemed more at home in such films as *Roxie Hart* 1942 and *The Major and the Minor* 1942.

In the years after World War II her screen career started to decline. Despite a popularly received reunion with Astaire in *The Barkleys of Broadway* 1949, few of her subsequent films achieved much impact. Her last screen role was as Jean Harlow's mother in the low-budget *Harlow* 1965, but she subsequently enjoyed considerable success in the theatre. Having already starred in US touring productions of such shows as *Annie Get Your Gun*, she took over from Carol Channing in 1966 in the Broadway musical *Hello, Dolly!*, and in London in 1969 played the lead in *Mame*.

'Form follows profit' is the aesthetic principle of our times.
RICHARD ROGERS
Times 13 Feb 1991

Rogers Richard George (1933–). English High Tech architect. His works include the Pompidou Centre in Paris 1977 (jointly with Renzo Piano), the Lloyd's of London building in London 1986, and the Reuters building at Blackwall Yard, London, 1992 (which won him a RIBA award). Knighted 1991.

When my times comes, just skin me and put me right up there on Trigger.

ROY ROGERS's own suggested epitaph

Rogers Roy. Stage name of Leonard Slye (1912–). US actor. He moved over to cinema from radio and was one of the original singing cowboys of the 1930s and 1940s. Although he was confined to B-films for most of his career, he appeared opposite Bob Hope and Jane Russell in *Son of Paleface* 1952.

I don't make jokes – I just watch the government and report the facts.
WILL ROGERS
in *Saturday Review* 25 Aug 1962

Rogers Will(iam Penn Adair) (1879–1935). US humorist and columnist for *The New York Times* from 1922, whose wry comments on current affairs won him national popularity. He specialized in aphorisms and homespun philosophy ('Everybody is ignorant, only on different subjects').

Born in Oologah Indian Territory (now Oklahoma), Rogers ended his formal education 1898 to work as a cowboy in Texas. He later travelled widely, performing in Wild West shows from 1902 and starting his own vaudeville act of rope twirling and humorous banter 1905. After beginning a Broadway career in 1915, which included Ziegfeld's Follies (1916–18, 1922, 1924–25), he moved to California to appear in motion pictures.

Among his numerous books are *The Cowboy Philosopher on Prohibition* 1919 and *Ether and Me* 1929. *A Connecticut Yankee* 1931 and *State Fair* 1933 were two of his most popular films. Rogers was killed in a plane crash in Alaska with famed pilot Wiley Post.

Roget Peter Mark (1779–1869). English physician, one of the founders of the University of London, and author of a *Thesaurus of English Words and Phrases* 1852, a text constantly revised and still in print, offering synonyms.

Röhm Ernst (1887–1934). German leader of the Nazi Brownshirts, the SA (Sturmabteilung). On the pretext of an intended SA putsch (uprising) by the Brownshirts, the Nazis had some hundred of them, including Röhm, killed 29–30 June 1934. The event is known as the Night of the Long Knives.

Rohmer Eric. Adopted name of Maurice Henri Joseph Schérer (1920–). French film director and writer. He was formerly a critic and television-documentary director. Part of the French New Wave, his films are often concerned with the psychology of self-deception. They include *Ma Nuit chez Maud/My Night at Maud's* 1969, *Le Genou de Claire/Claire's Knee* 1970, *Die Marquise von O/The Marquise of O* 1976, and *Un Conte d'Hiver/A Winter's Tale* 1992.

Rohmer Sax. Pen name of Arthur Sarsfield Ward (1883–1959). English crime writer. He created the sinister Chinese character Fu Manchu.

Roh Tae-woo (1932–). South Korean right-wing politician and general, president 1988–93. A Korean Military Academy classmate of Chun Doo-hwan, Roh fought in the Korean War and later, during the 1970s, became commander of the 9th Special Forces Brigade and Capital Security Command. Roh retired as a four-star general July 1981 and served as minister for national security, foreign affairs, and, later, home affairs under President Chun, and became chair of the ruling Democratic Justice Party 1985. He was elected president 1988, amid allegations of fraud and despite being connected with the massacre of about 2,000 anti-government demonstrators 1980. In Oct 1995 Roh admitted publicly to secretly amassing £400 million during his term in office, of which he retained £140 million for personal use; he was arrested Nov on corruption charges.

Rohwedder Detler (1932–1991). German Social Democrat politician and business executive. In Aug 1990 he became chief executive of Treuhand, the body concerned with the privatization or liquidation of some 8,000 East German businesses. His attempt to force market-oriented solutions on Treuhand was controversial, many preferring a more interventionist stance. He was assassinated the following April.

Rokossovsky Konstantin Konstantinovich (1896–1968). Soviet soldier. He came to prominence as commander of the 16th Army defending Moscow 1941 and played an important role in pushing the Germans back from Soviet territory. He commanded the 1st Byelorussian Front 1944 and advanced as far as Warsaw where he paused while the Polish Home Army rose against the Germans. When both Poles and Germans had been virtually destroyed, he captured Warsaw Jan 1945. He then advanced across Poland, took Danzig, and isolated the German armies in Kurland, finally making contact with the British at Wismar 5 May 1945. Following the war, he was appointed commander in chief of Soviet forces in Poland, despite the role he had played during the war in crushing Polish independence.

Roland (died *c.* 778). French hero whose real and legendary deeds of valour and chivalry inspired many medieval and later romances, including the 11th-century *Chanson de Roland* and Ariosto's *Orlando furioso*. A knight of Charlemagne, Roland was killed 778 with his friend Oliver and the 12 peers of France at Roncesvalles (in the Pyrenees) by Basques. He headed the rearguard during Charlemagne's retreat from his invasion of Spain.

Roland de la Platière Jeanne Marie Manon (born Philipon) (1754–1793). French intellectual politician whose salon from 1789 was a focus of democratic discussion. Her ideas were influential after her husband Jean Marie Roland de la Platière (1734–1793) became minister of the interior 1792. As a supporter of the Girondin party, opposed to Robespierre and Danton, she was condemned to the guillotine 1793 without being allowed to speak in her own defence. While in prison she wrote *Mémoires*.

Pray for the repose of His soul. He was so tired.

FREDERICK ROLFE ('Baron Corvo')
Hadrian VII ch 24 1904

Rolfe Frederick William (1860–1913). English writer. He called himself Baron Corvo. A Roman Catholic convert, frustrated in his desire to enter the priesthood, he wrote the novel *Hadrian VII* 1904, in which the character of the title rose from being a poor writer to become pope. In *Desire and Pursuit of the Whole* 1934 he wrote about his homosexual fantasies and friends, earning the US poet W H Auden's description of him as 'a master of vituperation'.

Rolland Romain (1866–1944). French author and musicologist. He was a leading supporter of pacificism and internationalism. He was associated with Charles Péguy on the influential journal *Les Cahiers de la quinzaine/Fortnightly Notebooks* where he published his best-known novel cycle *Jean-Christophe* 1904–12, about a German composer. He also wrote several biographies and critical works, including *Michelangelo* 1906, *Beethoven* 1910, and *Tolstoy* 1911. The Nobel Prize for Literature was awarded to him 1915.

He collected his plays as *Le Théâtre de la revolution/Theatre of Revolution* 1904 and *Les Tragédies de la foi/Tragedies of Faith* 1913.

Rolle de Hampole Richard (*c.* 1300–1349). English hermit and author of English and Latin works. These include the mystic *Meditation of the Passion*.

Rolling Stones, the British band formed 1962, once notorious as the 'bad boys' of rock. Original members were Mick Jagger (1943–), Keith Richards (1943–), Brian Jones (1942–1969), Bill Wyman (1936–), Charlie Watts (1941–), and the pianist Ian Stewart (1938–1985). A rock-and-roll institution, the Rolling Stones were still performing and recording in the 1990s.

Oh can't you see I am fadin' fast / And this shoot will be my last.

THE ROLLING STONES
Drug-influenced lyrics to 'Sister Morphine' 1971, on the album *Sticky Fingers*

The Stones' earthy sound was based on rhythm and blues, and their rebel image was contrasted with the supposed wholesomeness of the early Beatles. Classic early hits include 'Satisfaction' 1965 and 'Jumpin' Jack Flash' 1968. The albums from *Beggars Banquet* 1968 to *Exile on Main Street* 1972 have been rated among their best work; others include *Some Girls* 1978 and *Steel Wheels* 1989.

Suggested reading
Hoffman, D *The Rolling Stones: The Early Years* (1985)
Norman, Philip *The Life and Good Times of the Rolling Stones* (1989)
Palmer, Robert *Rolling Stones* (1983)
Shofield, Carey *Jagger* (1985)

Rollins Sonny (Theodore Walter) (1930–). US tenor saxophonist and jazz composer. A leader of the hard-bop school, he is known for the intensity and bravado of his music and for his skilful improvisation.

Rollo 1st duke of Normandy (*c.* 860–*c.* 932). Viking leader. He left Norway about 875 and marauded, sailing up the Seine to Rouen. He besieged Paris 886, and in 912 was baptized and granted the province of Normandy by Charles III of France. He was its duke until his retirement to a monastery 927. He was an ancestor of William the Conqueror.

Rolls Charles Stewart (1877–1910). British engineer who joined with Henry Royce in 1905 to design and produce cars. Rolls trained as a mechanical engineer at Cambridge, where he developed a passion for engines of all kinds. After working at the railway works in Crewe, he set up a business in 1902 as a motor dealer. In 1906 a light model 20, driven by Rolls, won the Tourist Trophy and also broke the Monte Carlo-to-London record. Rolls was the first to fly nonstop across the English Channel and back 1910. Before the business could flourish, he died in a flying accident.

Every man who feels well is a sick man neglecting himself.

JULES ROMAINS
Knock, or the Triumph of Medicine 1923

Romains Jules. Pen name of Louis Henri Jean Farigoule (1885–1972). French novelist, playwright, and poet. His plays include the farce *Knock, ou le triomphe de la médecine/Dr Knock* 1923 and *Donogoo* 1930, and his novels include *Mort de quelqu'un/Death of a Nobody* 1911, *Les Copains/The Boys in the Back Room* 1913, and *Les Hommes de bonne volonté/Men of Good Will* (27 volumes) 1932–47.

Romains developed the theory of Unanimism, which states that every group has a communal existence greater than that of the individual, which intensifies the individual's perceptions and emotions.

Romano Giulio. See ◊Giulio Romano, Italian painter and architect.

Romanov dynasty rulers of Russia from 1613 to the Russian Revolution 1917. Under the Romanovs, Russia developed into an absolutist empire. The pattern of succession was irregular until 1797. The last tsar, Nicholas II, abdicated March 1917 and was murdered July 1918, together with his family.

Suggested reading
Bergamini, John *The Tragic Dynasty: The History of the Romanovs* (1969)
Cowles, Virginia *The Romanovs* (1971)
Kluchevsky, V *The Rise of the Romanovs* (1970)

Romer Alfred Sherwood (1894–1973). US palaeontologist and comparative anatomist who made influential studies of vertebrate evolution. Romer was born in White Plains, New York, and studied at Amherst College and Columbia University. From 1934 he was professor of biology at Harvard; he also became director of the Museum of Comparative Zoology 1946.

Romer spent almost all his career investigating vertebrate evolution. Using evidence from palaeontology, comparative anatomy, and embryology, he traced the basic structural and functional changes that took place during the evolution of fishes to primitive terrestrial vertebrates and from these to modern vertebrates. In these studies he emphasized the evolutionary significance of the relationship between the form and function of animals and the environment. His *The Vertebrate Body* 1949 is still a standard textbook today.

Römer Ole (or Olaus) Christensen (1644–1710). Danish astronomer who first calculated the speed of light, in 1679. This was all the more remarkable in that most scientists of his time considered light to be instantaneous in propagation.

In 1671 Jean Picard (1620–1682), who had been sent by the French Academy to verify the exact position of Tycho Brahe's observatory, was impressed by Römer's work and invited him back to Paris with him. In Paris, Römer was made a member of the Academy and tutor to the crown prince. He conducted observations, designed and improved scientific instruments, and submitted various papers to the Academy. He returned to Denmark in 1681 to take up the dual post of Astronomer Royal to Christian V and director of the Royal Observatory in Copenhagen. He also accepted a number of civic duties.

It was through the precision of both his observations and his calculations that Römer not only demonstrated that light travels at a finite speed but also put a rate to it. Noticing that the length of time between eclipses of the satellite Io by Jupiter was not constant, he realized that it depended on the varying distance between the Earth and Jupiter. He was able to announce in Sept 1679 that the eclipse of Io by Jupiter predicted for 9 Nov would occur ten minutes later than expected. Römer's prediction was borne out; his interpretation of the delay provoked a sensation. He said that the delay was caused by the time it took for the light to traverse the extra distance across the Earth's orbit.

Rommel Erwin Johannes Eugen (1891–1944). German field marshal. He served in World War I, and in World War II he played an important part in the invasions of central Europe and France. He was commander of the N African offensive from 1941 (when he was nicknamed 'Desert Fox') until defeated in the Battles of El Alamein and he was expelled from Africa March 1943. Rommel was commander in chief for a short time against the Allies in Europe 1944 but (as a sympathizer with the Stauffenberg plot against Hitler) was forced to commit suicide.

Suggested reading
Douglas-Home, C *Rommel* (1973)
Irving, D *The Trail of the Fox: The Life of Field Marshal Erwin Rommel* (1977)
Mitcham, S *Rommel's Desert War* (1984)
Rutherford, W *Rommel* (1981)

Romney George (1734–1802). English portrait painter. He was active in London from 1762. He became, with Gainsborough and Reynolds, one of the most successful portrait painters of the late 18th century. After provincial training, and practice in portraiture at Kendal and York, he came to London 1762, leaving behind a wife from whom he remained separated until towards the end of his life. A visit to Italy, 1773–75, filled him with the ambition to paint classical and imaginative compositions, and 1782–85 he drew and painted Emma Hart (Lady Hamilton), whom he admired obsessively, in many preliminary studies for the classic themes he was ill-fitted to carry out. He went back to Lancashire broken in health and spirit 1789. His best work is to be found in the straightforward realism of *The Beaumont Family* (National Gallery, London) or the unassuming charm of *The Parson's Daughter* (Tate Gallery, London).

Romulus Augustulus (born *c.* AD 461). Last Roman emperor in the West. He was made emperor by his father the patrician Orestes about 475 but was compelled to abdicate 476 by Odoacer, leader of the barbarian mercenaries, who nicknamed him Augustulus (meaning 'Little Augustus'), because of his youth. Orestes was executed and Romulus Augustulus was sent to live on a pension in Campania. The date of his death is unknown.

Ronsard Pierre de (1524–1585). French poet. He was the leader of the *Pléiade* group of poets. Under the patronage of Charles IX, he published original verse in a lightly sensitive style, including odes and

love sonnets, such as *Odes* 1550, *Les Amours/Lovers* 1552–53, and the 'Marie' cycle, *Continuation des amours/Lovers Continued* 1555–56.

Röntgen Wilhelm Konrad, (or Roentgen) (1845–1923). German physicist who discovered X-rays 1895. While investigating the passage of electricity through gases, he noticed the fluorescence of a barium platinocyanide screen. This radiation passed through some substances opaque to light, and affected photographic plates. Developments from this discovery revolutionized medical diagnosis. Nobel prize 1901.

He was professor at Giessen 1879–88, then director of the Physical Institute at Würzburg, and ended his career in the equivalent position at Munich 1900–20.

It was at Würzburg Röntgen conducted the experiments that resulted in the discovery of the rays formerly named after him; they are now called X-rays. Today, the unit of radiation exposure is called the roentgen, or röntgen (symbol R). He refused to make any financial gain out of his findings, believing that the products of scientific research should be made freely available to all.

Röntgen worked on such diverse topics as elasticity, heat conduction in crystals, specific heat capacities of gases, and the rotation of plane-polarized light. In 1888 he made an important contribution to electricity when he confirmed that magnetic effects are produced by the motion of electrostatic charges.

Roon Albrecht Theodor Emil, Graf von (1803–1879). Prussian field marshal. As war minister from 1859, he reorganized the army and made possible the victories over Austria 1866 and those in the Franco-Prussian War 1870–71.

Röntgen German physicist Wilhelm Röntgen. Röntgen won the Nobel Prize for Physics in 1901 following his discovery of X-rays. The roentgen, named after him, is a unit of radiation exposure. (Image Select)

Roosevelt , Franklin D *The US president Franklin D Roosevelt 1936. A Democrat he became the 32nd president of the USA 1933. His presidency saw the Great Depression, the launch of the New Deal, and World War II.* (Image Select)

I was a fourteen year old boy for thirty years.

MICKEY ROONEY
in Leslie Halliwell *Filmgoer's Companion* 1965

Rooney Mickey. Stage name of Joe Yule (1922–). US actor. He began his career aged two in his parents' stage act. He played Andy Hardy in the Hardy family series of B-films (1937–47) and starred opposite Judy Garland in several musicals, including *Babes in Arms* 1939. He also gave memorable performances in *Boys' Town* 1935, as Puck in *A Midsummer Night's Dream* 1935, and the title role in *Baby Face Nelson* 1957.

No one can make you feel inferior without your consent.

ELEANOR ROOSEVELT
in *Catholic Digest*

Roosevelt (Anna) Eleanor (1884–1962). US social worker, lecturer, and First Lady; her newspaper column 'My Day' was widely syndicated. She influenced New Deal policies, especially supporting desegregation. She was a delegate to the UN general assembly and chair of the UN commission on human rights 1946–51, and helped to draw up the Declaration of Human Rights at the UN 1945. She was married to President Franklin D Roosevelt.

The niece of Theodore Roosevelt, she was educated in Europe. After her husband's death 1945, she continued to work on civil rights for US blacks and for human rights worldwide. Within the Democratic Party she formed the left-wing Americans for Democratic Action group 1947.

Suggested reading
Hershan, Stella *A Woman of Quality* (1970)
Lash, Joseph *Eleanor and Franklin* (1971)
Lash, Joseph *Eleanor: The Years Alone* (1972)
Roosevelt, Eleanor *Autobiography* (1961)
Wiesen Cook, Blanche *Eleanor Roosevelt* (1992)

Roosevelt Franklin D(elano) (1882–1945). 32nd president of the USA 1933–45, a Democrat. He served as governor of New York

I pledge you – I pledge myself – to a new deal for the American people.

FRANKLIN D ROOSEVELT
Speech 1932

1929–33. Born in Hyde Park, New York, of a wealthy family, Roosevelt was educated in Europe and at Harvard and Columbia universities, and became a lawyer. In 1910 he was elected to the New York state senate. He held the assistant secretaryship of the navy in Wilson's administrations 1913–21, and did much to increase the efficiency of the navy during World War I. He suffered from polio from 1921 but returned to politics, winning the governorship of New York State in 1929. When he first became president 1933, Roosevelt inculcated a new spirit of hope by his skilful 'fireside chats' on the radio and his inaugural-address statement: 'The only thing we have to fear is fear itself.' Surrounding himself by a 'Brain Trust' of experts, he immediately launched his reform programme. Banks were reopened, federal credit was restored, the gold standard was abandoned, and the dollar devalued. During the first hundred days of his administration, major legislation to facilitate industrial and agricultural recovery was enacted. In 1935 he introduced the Utilities Act, directed against abuses in the large holding companies, and the Social Security Act, providing for disability and retirement insurance. The presidential election 1936 was won entirely on the record of the New Deal. During 1935–36 Roosevelt was involved in a conflict over the composition of the Supreme Court, following its nullification of major New Deal measures as unconstitutional. In 1938 he introduced measures for farm relief and the improvement of working conditions. In his foreign policy, Roosevelt endeavoured to use his influence to restrain Axis aggression, and to establish 'good neighbour' relations with other countries in the Americas. Soon after the outbreak of war, he launched a vast rearmament programme, introduced conscription, and provided for the supply of armaments to the Allies on a 'cash-and-carry' basis. In spite of strong isolationist opposition, he broke a long-standing precedent in running for a third term; he was re-elected 1940. He announced that the USA would become the 'arsenal of democracy'. Roosevelt was eager for US entry into the war on behalf of the Allies. In addition to his revulsion for Hitler, he wanted to establish the USA as a world power, filling the vacuum he expected to be left by the break-up of the British Empire. He was restrained by isolationist forces in Congress, and some argued that he welcomed the Japanese attack on Pearl Harbor.

Public opinion, however, was in favour of staying out of the war. The Japanese then attacked the naval base at Pearl Harbor in Hawaii. The deaths at Pearl Harbor 7 Dec 1941 incited public opinion, and the USA entered the war. From this point on, Roosevelt concerned himself solely with the conduct of the war. He participated in the Washington 1942 and Casablanca 1943 conferences to plan the Mediterranean assault, and the conferences in Quebec, Cairo, and Tehran 1943, and Yalta 1945, at which the final preparations were made for the Allied victory. He was re-elected for a fourth term 1944, but died 1945.

Suggested reading
Alsop, Joseph *The Life and Times of Franklin D Roosevelt* (1982)
Burns, James *Roosevelt: The Lion and the Fox* (1956)
Freidel, Frank *Franklin D Roosevelt* (1952–73)
Heinrich, W *The Threshold of War: Franklin D Roosevelt and the American Entry into World War II* (1988)
Lash, Joseph *Eleanor and Franklin* (1971)
Leuchtenburg, William *Franklin D Roosevelt and the New Deal* (1963)
Schlesinger, Arthur, Jr *The Age of Roosevelt* (1957–60)

Roosevelt Theodore (1858–1919). 26th president of the USA 1901–09, a Republican. Roosevelt, born in New York, was elected to the state legislature 1881. He was assistant secretary of the Navy 1897–98, and during the Spanish–American War 1898 commanded a volunteer force of 'rough riders'. After serving as governor of New York 1898–1900 he became vice president to McKinley, whom he succeeded as president on McKinley's assassination 1901. At age 42, Roosevelt was the youngest person to become president of the USA. In office he became more liberal. He tackled business monopolies, initiated measures for the conservation of national resources, and introduced the Pure Food and Drug Act. He campaigned against the great trusts (associations of enterprises that reduce competition), while carrying on a jingoist foreign policy designed to enforce US supremacy over Latin America. He won the Nobel Peace Prize 1906 for his part in ending the Russo-Japanese war. Alienated after his retirement by the conservatism of his successor Taft, Roosevelt formed the Progressive or 'Bull Moose' Party. As their candidate he unsuccessfully ran for the presidency 1912. During World War I he strongly advocated US intervention.

Suggested reading
Burton, David *Theodore Roosevelt* (1973)
Collins, Michael *That Damned Cowboy* (1989)
Harbaugh, William *The Life and Times of Theodore Roosevelt* (1975)
McCullough, David *Mornings on Horseback: The Story of an Extraordinary Family, A Vanished Way of Life, and the Unique Child Who Became Theodore Roosevelt* (1981)
Norton, A A *Theodore Roosevelt* (1980)
Roosevelt, Theodore *Autobiography* (1913)

I wish to preach, not the doctrine of ignoble ease, but the doctrine of the strenuous life.

THEODORE ROOSEVELT
Speech 1899

Rorty Richard McKay (1931–   ). US philosopher. His main concern has been to trace the personal and social implications of our changing perception of human identity, and his work draws inspiration from US philosopher John Dewey and German social theorist Jürgen Habermas.

In his *Contingency, Irony and Solidarity* 1989, Rorty argues that language, self, and community are determined by history and are not expressions of an essential human nature. When we accept that human identity is not fixed, he argues, we then need to reconcile two seemingly conflicting consequences: at the personal level, the possibility of autonomy and self-creation; and at the public level, the need to create a freer and less cruel society.

Be silent, unless what you have to say is better than silence.

SALVATOR ROSA
Motto on self-portrait *c.* 1645

Rosa Salvator (1615–1673). Italian Baroque painter, etcher, poet, and musician. He was active in Florence 1640–49 and subsequently in Rome. Born near Naples, he studied art under an uncle, Paolo Greco, and his father-in-law, Francesco Fracanzo (a follower of Ribera). The painter Lanfranco bought his *Hagar*, and started him on a prosperous career to which his paintings lend more of an atmosphere of romantic violence than it actually contained.

Whether or no he consorted with bandits, he invented a type of romantic art in his rocky landscapes with ruins and brigandlike figures, inspired by southern Italy, and with Claude Lorraine is one of the founders of the picturesque tradition so influential in 18th-century Britain. Following the example of Aniello Falcone he also painted some battle scenes. Good examples of his art are *Saul and the Witch of Endor* and *Battlepiece* (Louvre), both from the collection of Louis XIV, and the *Bridge* (Pitti).

Rosas Juan Manuel de (1793–1877). Argentine soldier, gaucho (cowboy), and dictator 1835–52. Rosas used his private gaucho army to overthrow the Liberal regime of Bernardino Rivadavia 1827. A Buenos Aires Federalist, he was governor of that city 1829–32 and, when he was also dictator of Argentina, presided over a reign of terror. While appealing to the urban masses, he allowed

Roosevelt, Theodore *Theodore Roosevelt US Statesman and president (1901–9). He wrote several historical works, including* The Naval War of 1812 *(1882) and* The Winning of the West *1889–96.*

huge land sales at absurdly low prices that benefited the landed aristocracy, including Rosas's wealthy Creole family.

A manipulative and ruthless operator against centralists, once he became dictator, he began a cult of personality which included his image being displayed on church altars. Rosas supported the Uruguayan Blancos led by Manuel Oribe (1792–1857) by besieging Montevideo for nine years from 1843. This led to his downfall when a key aide, Justo José de Urquiza, changed sides and relieved the city 1852. Rosas spent the rest of his life in Britain.

Roscellinus Johannes (*c.* 1050–*c.* 1122). French philosopher regarded as the founder of scholasticism because of his defence of nominalism (the idea that classes of things are simply names and have no objective reality) against Anselm.

Roscellinus was born in Compiègne and was the teacher of Peter Abelard in Brittany. Accused of heresy in 1092, he moved to England; after his conflict with Anselm, he moved to Rome. His views are known mainly from the writings of Anselm and Abelard.

Roscius Gallus Quintus (*c.* 126–62 BC). Roman actor who was so gifted that his name became a byword for a great actor.

Rose Frederick George Godfrey (1915–1991). English anthropologist and socialist, who studied the Australian Aborigines. He held academic posts in East Germany from 1956. He published books in German and English, among them *The Traditional Mode of Production of the Australian Aborigine* 1987.

It is beginning to be hinted that we are a nation of amateurs.

ARCHIBALD ROSEBERY
Address 1900

Rosebery Archibald Philip Primrose, 5th Earl of Rosebery (1847–1929). British Liberal politician. He was foreign secretary 1886 and 1892–94, when he succeeded Gladstone as prime minister, but his government survived less than a year. After 1896 his imperialist views gradually placed him further from the mainstream of the Liberal Party. Earl 1868.

Rosenberg Alfred (1893–1946). German politician, born in Tallinn, Estonia. He became the chief Nazi ideologist and was minister for eastern occupied territories 1941–44. He was tried at Nuremberg 1946 as a war criminal and hanged.

Death could drop from the dark / As easily as song.

ISAAC ROSENBERG
'Returning, We Hear the Larks'

Rosenberg Isaac (1890–1918). English poet of the World War I period. Trained as an artist at the Slade School in London, Rosenberg enlisted in the British army 1915. He wrote about the horror of life on the front line, as in 'Break of Day in the Trenches'. Like that of his contemporary Wilfred Owen, Rosenberg's work is now ranked with the finest World War I poems, although he was largely unpublished during his lifetime. After serving for 20 months in the front line, he was killed on the Somme.

Rosenberg Julius (1918–1953) and Ethel Greenglass (1915–1953). US married couple, convicted of being leaders of a nuclear-espionage ring passing information from Ethel's brother via courier to the USSR. The Rosenbergs were executed after much public controversy and demonstration. They were the only Americans executed for espionage during peacetime.

Both were born in New York City; Julius owned a radio repair shop and was a member of the Communist Party. Despite an offer of clemency from the government, they both maintained their innocence right up to their executions. Other implicated Party members received long prison terms. The Cold War atmosphere was one of widespread fear of the Soviet Union, and several major spy scandals had occurred at this time. The death penalty was ruled as justified because of the danger to the US from their actions. Recently published journals kept by Khrushchev further implicate the Rosenbergs.

Suggested reading
Meeropol, Michael and Robert *We Are Your Sons: The legacy of Ethel and Julius Rosenberg* (memoir by their children) (1975)
Radosh, Ronald and Milton, Joyce *The Rosenberg File* (1983)
Wexley, John *The Judgment of Julius and Ethel Rosenberg* (1977)

Rosenquist James Albert (1933–   ). US painter and printmaker. He was a seminal figure in American Pop art. In his paintings, fragmented images drawn from advertising and the mass media are enlarged to huge proportions and juxtaposed against each other in a deadpan manner, as in *I Love You with My Ford* 1961 (Moderna Museet, Stockholm).

Rosenquist worked as an industrial sign and billboard painter in the early 1950s. While studying and working in New York 1955–57, he met Robert Rauschenberg and Jasper Johns and began painting his first colossal-scale works 1960–61. His renowned *F-111*, fully 26 m/85 ft in length and first shown 1965, includes an American military aeroplane and child under a hairdryer among its images, reading as a comment on war and helplessness.

Rosmer Ernst. Pseudonym of Elsa Bernstein (1866–1925). German dramatist who wrote several naturalistic plays influenced by Ibsen, including *Dämmerung/Twilight* 1893; tragedies such as *Nausikaa* 1906; and a fairytale melodrama *Königskinder* 1894, which subsequently became the libretto for an opera by Engelbert Humperdinck. She survived being sent to Theresienstadt concentration camp during World War II. Her pseudonym was taken from Ibsen's play *Rosmersholm* 1886.

Ross Betsy (born Griscom) (1752–1836). American seamstress remembered as the maker of the first US flag. According to popular legend, she was approached 1776 by family acquaintance George Washington to create an official flag for the new nation. Despite little historical substantiation, it is believed by many that the familiar red and white stripes with white stars on a field of blue was Ross's original concept.

Born in Philadelphia to a devout Quaker family, Ross married upholsterer John Ross 1773. When he died 1776, she took over his business. Becoming famous after the war, she continued in the upholstery business until her retirement 1827.

Ross James Clark (1800–1862). English explorer who discovered the north magnetic pole 1831. He also went to the Antarctic 1839. Ross Island, Ross Sea, and Ross Dependency are named after him. Knighted 1843.

He is associated with his uncle John Ross and William Parry in Arctic exploration.

Ross John (1777–1856). Scottish rear admiral and explorer. He served in wars with France and made voyages of Arctic exploration in 1818, 1829–33, and 1850. KCB 1834.

Ross Martin. Pen name of Violet Florence ◊Martin, Irish novelist.

Ross Ronald (1857–1932). British physician and bacteriologist, born in India. From 1881 to 1899 he served in the Indian Medical Service, and during 1895–98 identified mosquitoes of the genus *Anopheles* as being responsible for the spread of malaria. Nobel prize 1902. KCB 1911.

On retiring from the Indian Medical Service in 1899, he returned to Britain, eventually becoming professor of tropical medicine at Liverpool. During World War I he was consultant on malaria to the War Office, and when the Ross Institute of Tropical Diseases was opened 1926, he became its first director.

While on leave in England in 1894, Ross became acquainted with Scottish physician Patrick Manson, who suggested that malaria was spread by a mosquito. Returning to India, Ross collected mosquitoes, identifying the various species and dissecting their internal organs. In 1897 he discovered in an *Anopheles* mosquito a cyst containing the parasites that had been found in the blood of malarial patients.

Later, using caged birds with bird malaria, Ross was able to study the entire life history of the parasite inside a mosquito, and the mode of transmission to the victim.

Rossellini Roberto (1906–1977). Italian film director. His World War II trilogy, *Roma città aperta/Rome, Open City* 1945, *Paisà/Paisan* 1946, and *Germania anno zero/Germany Year Zero* 1947, reflects his humanism, and is considered a landmark of European cinema.

He and actress Ingrid Bergman formed a creative partnership which produced *Stromboli* 1949 and seven other films over a six-year period, which were neither critical nor box-office successes. After their divorce, Rossellini returned to form with *General della Rovere* 1959, and then went on to make films for television, such as *La Prise de pouvoir par Louis XIV/The Rise of Louis XIV* 1966, a feature-length film for French television.

Rossetti Christina Georgina (1830–1894). English poet. She was the sister of Dante Gabriel Rossetti and a devout High Anglican. Her verse includes *Goblin Market and Other Poems* 1862 and expresses unfulfilled spiritual yearning and frustrated love. She was a skilful technician and made much use of irregular rhyme and line length.

Suggested reading
Battiscombe, Georgina *Christina Rossetti* (1981)
Bellas, Ralph *Christina Rossetti* (1977)
Thomas, Frances *Christina Rossetti* (1992)

My name is Might-have-been; / I am also called No-more, Too-late, Farewell.

DANTE GABRIEL ROSSETTI
'A Superscription'

Rossetti Dante Gabriel (1828–1882). English painter and poet. He was a founding member of the Pre-Raphaelite Brotherhood (PRB) 1848. As well as romantic medieval scenes, he produced many idealized portraits of women, including the spiritual *Beata Beatrix* 1864. His verse includes 'The Blessed Damozel' 1850. His sister was the poet Christina Rossetti.

Rossetti, the son of an exiled Italian, formed the PRB with the painters Millais and Hunt but developed a broader style and a personal subject matter, related to his poetry. He was a friend of the critic Ruskin, and of William Morris and his wife Jane, who became Rossetti's lover and the subject of much of his work. His *Poems* 1870 were recovered from the grave of his wife Elizabeth Siddal (1834–1862), also a painter, whom he had married 1860, and were attacked as of 'the fleshly school of poetry'.

Suggested reading

Doughty, Oswald *Dante Gabriel Rossetti: A Victorian Romantic* (1960)

Dobbs, Brian and Judy *Dante Gabriel Rossetti: An Alien Victorian* (1977)

Gaunt, William *The Pre-Raphaelite Dream* (1966)

Rossi Aldo (1931–). Italian architect and theorist. He has been strongly influenced by Rationalist thought and by Neo-Classicism. A pioneer of Neo-Rationalism, his main works include the Gallaratese II apartment complex, Milan, 1969–73; the Modena cemetery, 1973; and the floating, demountable theatre Teatro del Mondo, Venice, 1979. Of his 1980s commissions both the Friedrichstadt apartments, Berlin, 1981–87, and the funerary chapel in Guissano, Italy, 1987, are notable.

Delight must be the basis and aim of this art. Simple melody – clear rhythm!

GIOACCHINO ROSSINI
Letter 1868

Rossini Gioacchino Antonio (1792–1868). Italian composer. His first success was the opera *Tancredi* 1813. In 1816 his opera buffa *Il barbiere di Siviglia/The Barber of Seville* was produced in Rome. During 1815–23 he produced 20 operas, and created (with Donizetti and Bellini) the 19th-century Italian operatic style.

After *Guillaume Tell/William Tell* 1829, Rossini gave up writing opera and his later years were spent in Bologna and Paris. Among the works of this period are the *Stabat Mater* 1842 and the piano music arranged for ballet by Respighi as *La Boutique fantasque/The Fantastic Toyshop* 1919.

Suggested reading

Coe, Richard N *Life of Rossini* (1970)

Harding, James *Rossini* (1971)

Kendall, Alan *Gioacchino Rossini: The Reluctant Hero* (1992)

Till, Nicholas *Rossini: His Life and Times* (1983)

Rossler Rudolf (1897–1958). German spy who spied for the Allies in World War II. An ex-soldier, he had many friends in high places who were as opposed to the Nazi party as he was, and he received valuable information from them.

He moved to Switzerland 1933 and set up in business as a publisher. He had advance notice of many German operations, and with the aid of Swiss military intelligence passed the information to the Allies. He was recruited by the Soviet director of intelligence in Switzerland under the code-name 'Lucy', after which his information was relayed directly to Moscow, including details of the German plans at Stalingrad and Kursk. Eventually the operations of the 'Lucy Ring' became too blatant for the Swiss to tolerate and they moved against it 1944, ending Rossler's activities. He never revealed the names of his contacts in the German High Command.

Rosso Giovanni Battista di Jacopo (called Rosso Fiorentino) (1494–1540). Italian painter. He studied under Andrea del Sarto and worked in Florence 1513–23. His dramatic style, like that of his friend Pontormo, exemplifies early Italian Mannerism. In 1530 he was invited to France by François I and worked at Fontainebleau with Primaticcio. Together they founded the Fontainebleau School style, a Mannerist fusion of French and Italian taste.

Rostand Edmond (1868–1918). French poetic dramatist. He wrote *Cyrano de Bergerac* 1898 and *L'Aiglon* 1900 (based on the life of Napoleon III), in which Sarah Bernhardt played the leading role.

Rostropovich Mstislav Leopoldovich (1927–). Russian cellist and conductor. He became an exile 1978 because of his sympathies with political dissidents. Prokofiev, Shostakovich, Khachaturian,

and Britten wrote pieces for him. Since 1977 he has directed the National Symphony Orchestra, Washington, DC.

Roth Joseph (1894–1939). Austrian novelist and critic. He depicted the decay of the Austrian Empire before 1914 in such novels as *Savoy Hotel* 1924, *Radetsky Marsch/The Radetsky March* 1932, and (after he moved to Paris 1933) *Die hundert Tage/The Hundred Days* 1936. He worked as a journalist during the 1920s in several European capitals. His novels defy easy classification; he stayed aloof from literary groups of his time.

Because to be bad, Mother, that's the real struggle: to be bad – and enjoy it! That's what makes men of us boys, Mother ... LET'S PUT THE ID BACK IN YID!

PHILIP ROTH
Portnoy's Complaint 1969

Roth Philip Milton (1933–). US novelist. His witty, sharply satirical, and increasingly fantastic novels depict the moral and sexual anxieties of 20th-century Jewish-American life, most notably in *Goodbye Columbus* 1959 and *Portnoy's Complaint* 1969.

Roth's series of semi-autobiographical novels about a writer, Nathan Zuckerman, consist of *The Ghost Writer* 1979, *Zuckerman Unbound* 1981, *The Anatomy Lesson* 1984, and *The Counterlife* 1987. The novel *Operation Shylock: A Confession* 1993, is a fantasy about his fictional double; and his memoir *Patrimony* 1991 concerns his father's death.

Rossini The composer Gioacchino Rossini in a cartoon by André Gill (1867). Most famous for the filigree of his comic operas, Rossini retired as a composer for the stage at the age of 37, Guillaume Tell being his last and one of his most successful operas. (Image Select)

Rothenstein William (1872–1945). English painter, writer, and teacher. His work includes decorations for St Stephen's Hall, Westminster, London, and portrait drawings. He was principal of the Royal College of Art 1920–35, where he encouraged the sculptors Jacob Epstein and Henry Moore, and the painter Paul Nash. Knighted 1931. His elder son John Knewstub Maurice Rothenstein (1901–) was director of the Tate Gallery, London, 1938–64.

Rothermere Harold Sidney Harmsworth, 1st Viscount Rothermere (1868–1940). British newspaper proprietor, brother of Lord Northcliffe. Baron 1914, viscount 1919.

Rothermere Vere Harold Esmond Harmsworth, 3rd Viscount Rothermere (1925–). British newspaper proprietor. As chair of Associated Newspapers (1971–) he controls the right-wing *Daily Mail* (founded by his great-uncle Lord Northcliffe) and *Mail on Sunday* (launched 1982), the London *Evening Standard*, and a string of regional newspapers. Viscount 1978.

In 1971 Rothermere took control of the family newspapers. He closed the *Daily Sketch* and successfully transformed the *Mail* into a tabloid. In 1977 he closed the London *Evening News* with heavy loss of jobs, but obtained a half-share of the more successful *Evening Standard*, and gained control of the remainder 1985.

Rothko Mark. Adopted name of Marcus Rothkovich (1903–1970). Russian-born US painter. He was an Abstract Expressionist and a pioneer, towards the end of his life, of Colour Field painting (an abstract style dominated by areas of unmodulated, strong colour). Rothko produced several series of large-scale paintings in the 1950s and 1960s, examples of which are owned by Harvard University, the Tate Gallery, London, and a chapel in Houston, Texas.
Suggested reading
Ashton, D *About Rothko* (1983)
Waldman, D *Mark Rothko* (1978)

Rothschild European family active in the financial world for two centuries. Mayer Amschel (1744–1812) set up as a moneylender in Frankfurt-am-Main, Germany, and business houses were established throughout Europe by his ten children.

Nathan Meyer (1777–1836) settled in England, and his grandson Nathan Meyer (1840–1915) was created a baron in 1885. Lionel Walter (1868–1937) succeeded his father as 2nd Baron Rothschild and was an eminent naturalist. His daughter Miriam (1908–) is an entomologist, renowned for her studies of fleas. Of the French branch, Baron Eric de Rothschild (1940–) owns Château Lafite and Baron Philippe de Rothschild (1902–) owns Château Mouton-Rothschild, both leading red Bordeaux-producing properties in Pauillac, SW France.

Rothschild (Nathaniel Mayer) Victor, 3rd Baron (1910–1990). English scientist and public servant. After working in military intelligence during World War II he joined the zoology department at Cambridge University 1950–70, at the same time serving as chair of the Agricultural Research Council 1948–58 and Shell Research 1963–70. In 1971 he was asked by prime minister Edward Heath to head his new think tank, the Central Policy Review Staff, a post he held until 1974.

Rouault Georges Henri (1871–1958). French painter, etcher, illustrator, and designer. He was one of the major religious artists of the 20th century. Early in his career he was associated with the Fauves but created his own style using rich, dark colours and heavy outlines. His subjects include sad clowns, prostitutes, and evil lawyers. From about 1940 he painted mainly religious works.

Rouault was born in Paris, the son of a cabinet-maker. He served an apprenticeship as a boy with a painter of stained glass, and later studied at the École des Beaux-Arts under Gustave Moreau. After the death of Moreau 1898 he was made curator of the Musée Gustave Moreau. He had met Matisse at the Beaux-Arts and exhibited with him and the Fauves of 1905, though the trend of his ideas had more affinity with those of the German Expressionists than of his French contemporaries. He seemed to be directed, either by suffering as a personal emotion, or by a sense of the existence of

suffering in the world, to paintings of sad clowns and even to harsh social comment as in *Les Noces* (Tate Gallery, London), and later to religious paintings tragic in spirit. This sense of tragedy was impressively conveyed by sombre tones and distortions of form, though as time went on he gave his religious themes something of the dusky richness of stained glass (no doubt with some reminiscence of his early training). He illustrated books for Ambroise Vollard, the dealer to whom all his productions were reserved for many years, the etched plates for *Miserere*, 1948 (executed 1922–27), being a notable achievement. In both etchings and lithographs he showed all the quality of his painting.

Roubiliac Louis François, (or Roubillac) (c. 1705–1762). French sculptor. A Huguenot, he fled religious persecution to settle in England 1732. He became a leading sculptor of the day, creating a statue of German composer Georg Handel for Vauxhall Gardens 1737. He also produced lively statues of historic figures, such as Newton, and an outstanding funerary monument, the *Tomb of Lady Elizabeth Nightingale* 1761.

Rouget de Lisle Claude-Joseph (1760–1836). French army officer. While in Strasbourg 1792, he composed 'La Marseillaise', the French national anthem.

Rousseau Henri Julien Félix, 'Le Douanier' (1844–1910). French painter. A self-taught naive artist, his subjects include scenes of the Parisian suburbs and exotic junglescapes, painted with painstaking detail; for example, *Tropical Storm with a Tiger* 1891 (National Gallery, London).

Rousseau served in the army for some years, then became a toll collector (hence *Le Douanier*, 'the customs official'), and finally took up full-time painting 1885. He exhibited at the Salon des Indépendants 1886–1910 and was associated with the group led by Picasso and the poet Apollinaire.
Suggested reading
Alley, R *Portrait of a Primitive: The Art of Henri Rousseau* (1978)
Le Pichon, Y *The World of Henri Rousseau* (1982)
Vallier, D *Henri Rousseau* (1964)

Rousseau Jean-Jacques (1712–1778). French social philosopher and writer. His book *Du Contrat social/Social Contract* 1762, emphasizing the rights of the people over those of the government, was a significant influence on the French Revolution. In the novel *Emile* 1762, he outlined a new theory of education.

Rousseau was born in Geneva, Switzerland. *Discourses on the Origins of Inequality* 1754 made his name: he denounced civilized society and postulated the paradox of the superiority of the 'noble savage'. In *Social Contract* he argued that government is justified only if sovereignty stays with the people. He thereby rejected representative democracy in favour of direct democracy, modelled on the Greek polis and the Swiss canton, and stated that a government could be legitimately overthrown if it failed to express the general will of the people. *Emile* was written as an example of how to elicit the unspoiled nature and abilities of children, based on natural development and the power of example.

Rousseau's ideas were condemned by philosophers, the clergy, and the public, and he lived in exile in England for a year, being helped by Scottish philosopher David Hume until they fell out. He was a contributor to the *Encyclopédie* and also wrote operas. *Confessions*, published posthumously 1782, was a frank account of his occasionally immoral life and was a founding work of autobiography.
Suggested reading
Cranston, Maurice *The Noble Savage: Jean-Jacques Rousseau* (1983)
Blanchard, William *Rousseau and the Spirit of Revolt* (1967)
De Beer, Gavin *Jean-Jacques Rousseau and His World* (1972)
Grimsley, Ronald *The Philosophy of Rousseau* (1973)
Rousseau, Jean-Jacques *Confessions* (1782, several translations)

Rousseau (Pierre Etienne) Théodore (1812–1867). French landscape painter of the Barbizon School. Born in Paris, he came under the influence of the English landscape painters Constable and Bonington, sketched from nature in many parts of France, and settled in Barbizon 1848.

He was a pupil of his cousin, Pau de St Martin, and two other minor landscapists. His lack of success in the Salons, which earned him the title of 'le grand refusé' caused him to withdraw to the forest of Fontainebleau, which to his romantic spirit was the essence of the wild. Joined at the village of Barbizon by Dupré, Diaz, and Millet, he may be called the founder of the Barbizon School. The melancholy which Baudelaire remarked on in his darkly toned pictures of forest glades was due to his own temperament and the mood caused by the mental derangement of his wife, but he is notable also for an objective devotion to nature. Success came to him late, signalled by the *salon* assigned to him at the Exposition Universelle of 1855.

Roux Wilhelm (1850–1924). German anatomist and zoologist who carried out research into developmental mechanics in embryology. He also investigated the mechanisms of functional adaptations, examining the physical stresses that cause bones, cartilage, and tendons to adapt to malformations and diseases.

At Breslau (now Wroclaw in Poland) from 1879, he eventually became director of his own Institute of Embryology. He was professor at Innsbruck, Austria, 1889–95, when he became director of the Anatomical Institute at Halle.

Roux's embryological investigations were performed mainly on frogs' eggs. Puncturing the eggs at the two-cell stage of development (a technique Roux pioneered), he found that they grew into half-embryos: the fate of the parts had already been determined. He also researched into the earliest structures in amphibian development.

Rowbotham Sheila (1943–). British socialist, feminist, historian, lecturer, and writer. Her pamphlet *Women's Liberation and the New Politics* 1970 laid down fundamental approaches and demands of the emerging women's movement. Rowbotham taught in schools and then became involved with the Workers' Educational Association. An active socialist since the early 1960s, she has contributed to several left-wing journals. Her books include *Hidden from History*, *Women's Consciousness, Man's World* both 1973, *Beyond the Fragments* 1979, and *The Past is Before Us* 1989.

Rowe Nicholas (1674–1718). English dramatist and poet. His dramas include *The Fair Penitent* 1703 and *The Tragedy of Jane Shore* 1714, in which English actress Mrs Siddons played. He edited Shakespeare, and was poet laureate from 1715.

Rowland Henry Augustus (1848–1901). US physicist who developed the concave diffraction grating 1882, which made the analysis of spectra much faster and more accurate. He also carried out the precise determination of certain physical constants.

Rowland was born in Honesdale, Pennsylvania, and studied at the Rensselaer Polytechnic Institute at Troy, New York, later joining its staff. From 1876 he was professor at Johns Hopkins in Baltimore, and made the physics laboratories at the newly established university among the best equipped in the world.

Rowland provided in 1875 the first demonstration that an electric current could be regarded as a sequence of electric charges in motion, by showing that a rapidly rotating charged body was able to deflect a magnet.

Rowland was able to produce greatly improved diffraction gratings and went on to introduce a concave metal or glass grating. This was self-focusing and thus eliminated the need for lenses, which absorbed some wavelengths of the spectrum. He put his invention to use 1886–95 by remapping the solar spectrum, publishing the wavelengths for 14,000 lines with an accuracy ten times better than his predecessors had managed.

Rowland Tiny (Roland W). Adopted name of Roland Fuhrhop (1917–). British entrepreneur, co-chief executive and managing director of Lonrho 1961–1994, and owner from 1981 of the *Observer* Sunday newspaper.

Born in India, he emigrated to Rhodesia 1947. In 1961 he merged his business interests with the London and Rhodesian Mining and Land Company, now known as Lonrho. After acquiring the *Observer*, he made an unsuccessful bid for the Harrods department store in London. Roland announced his resignation as managing director of Lonrho Nov 1994, following a long-running power struggle with his joint-chief executive.

Rowlandson Thomas (1757–1827). English painter and illustrator, a caricaturist of Georgian social life. His series of drawings *Tour of Dr Syntax in Search of the Picturesque* was published 1809 and its two sequels followed 1812–21.

Rowlandson studied at the Royal Academy schools and in Paris. Impoverished by gambling, he turned from portrait painting to caricature around 1780. Other works include *The Dance of Death* 1815–16 and illustrations for works by the novelists Tobias Smollett, Oliver Goldsmith, and Laurence Sterne.

Rowley William (c. 1585–c. 1642). English actor and dramatist. He collaborated with Thomas Middleton on *The Changeling* 1622 and with Thomas Dekker and John Ford on *The Witch of Edmonton* 1621.

Rowling Bill (Wallace Edward) (1927–1995). New Zealand Labour politician, party leader 1969–75, prime minister 1974–75. KCMG 1983.

Rowntree B(enjamin) Seebohm (1871–1954). English entrepreneur and philanthropist. Much of the money he acquired as chair (1925–41) of the family firm of confectioners, H I Rowntree, he used to fund investigations into social conditions. The three Rowntree Trusts, which were founded by his father Joseph Rowntree (1836–1925) in 1904, fund research into housing, social care, and social policy, support projects relating to social justice, and give grants to pressure groups working in these areas.

Rowntree joined the York-based family business in 1889 after studying at Owens College (later the University of Manchester). The introduction of company pensions (1906), a five-day working week (1919), and an employee profit-sharing scheme (1923) gave him a reputation as an enlightened and paternalistic employer. An associate of David Lloyd George, he was director of the welfare department of the Ministry of Munitions during World War I.

His pioneering study of working-class households in York 1897–98, published as *Poverty, A Study of Town Life* 1900, was a landmark in empirical sociology; it showed that 28% of the population fell below an arbitrary level of minimum income, and 16% experienced 'primary poverty'. Rowntree also wrote on gambling, unemployment, and business organization.

Rowse A(lfred) L(eslie) (1903–). English popular historian. He published a biography of Shakespeare 1963, and in *Shakespeare's Sonnets: The Problems Solved* 1973 controversially identified the 'Dark Lady' of Shakespeare's sonnets as Emilia Lanier, half-Italian daughter of a court musician, with whom the Bard is alleged to have had an affair 1593–95. His other works include the scholarly *Tudor Cornwall: Portrait of a Society* 1941, 1969 and *Shakespeare the Man* 1973.

Roy Manabendra Nath. Adopted name of Narendranath Bhattacharya (1887–1954). Founder of the Indian Communist Party in exile in Tashkent 1920. Expelled from the Comintern 1929, he returned to India and was imprisoned for five years. A steadfast communist, he finally became disillusioned after World War II and developed his ideas on practical humanism.

Roy Rajah Ram Rohan. Bengali religious and social reformer known as ◊Ram Mohun Roy.

Royce (Frederick) Henry (1863–1933). British engineer, who so impressed Charles Rolls by the car he built 1904 that Rolls-Royce Ltd was formed 1906 to produce automobiles and aero-engines. Baronet 1930.

Royce was born in Huntingdonshire and became an apprentice engineer with the Great Northern Railway. He worked on the pioneer scheme 1882–83 to light London's streets with electricity, and as chief electrical engineer on the project to light the streets of Liverpool. In 1884 he founded the firm of F H Royce and Company, manufacturing electric cranes and dynamos. He built three cars of his first design 1904 and soon afterwards teamed up with Rolls.

Royce Josiah (1855–1916). US idealist philosopher who in *The Conception of God* 1895 and *The Conception of Immortality* 1900 interpreted Christianity in philosophical terms.

Rubbia Carlo (1934–). Italian physicist and 1989–93 director-general of CERN, the European nuclear research organization. In 1983 he led the team that discovered the weakons (W and Z particles), the agents responsible for transferring the weak nuclear force. Rubbia shared the Nobel Prize for Physics 1984 with his colleague Simon van der Meer (1925–).

Rubbia was born in Gorizia and studied at Pisa, Rome, and in the USA at Columbia. He worked at CERN from 1960 and concurrently served as professor of physics at Harvard 1972–88.

Rubbra Edmund (1901–1986). English composer. He studied under German composer Gustav Holst and specialized in contrapuntal writing, as exemplified in his study *Counterpoint* 1960. His compositions include 11 symphonies, chamber music, and songs.

Rubens Peter Paul (1577–1640). Flemish painter. He was born of an Antwerp family in Westphalia, where his father, Jan Rubens, a lawyer, had gone into exile. On the latter's death 1587, his widow returned to Antwerp, where Peter Paul was educated at the Jesuit school, and at 16 he was prepared for courtly life as a page of the Countess Lalaing. He studied art under 'Romanist' masters, Tobias Verhaecht, Adam van Noort, and Otto van Veen, and 1598 was a member of the Painters' Guild at Antwerp. He went to Italy, and worked 1600–08 as court painter to Vincenzo Gonzaga, Duke of Mantua, painting many portraits of the nobility, and 1603 went to Spain on the duke's behalf. His study of the Italian masters, especially of Titian and Veronese at Venice, was a major factor in the development of his powers. He returned to Antwerp equipped for splendid undertakings, in 1609 being appointed painter to the Brussels court of the Archduke Albert and the Infanta Isabella, and gathering a brilliant cohort of assistants around him. A triumphant release of force appears in the great religious compositions of 1609–21 for the cathedral and the Church of the Jesuits at Antwerp, in which Rubens seems to express the essence of the Counter-Reformation, using all the compositional and theatrical devices of the Baroque style. This decorative magnificence on a vast scale was applied, 1622–25, to secular use in the cycle of the *Life of Marie de' Medici*, at whose invitation he visited Paris. His happy marriage with Isabella Brant was ended by her death 1626, and Rubens was now often away from the stately home he had built at Antwerp (since 1946 renovated as a Rubens museum). Diplomatic missions took him to Spain, 1628, where he painted Philip IV and met Velazquez; and to London, 1629–30, where he was made an honorary MA of Cambridge University and commissioned to paint the ceiling (extant and now restored) for the Banqueting Hall, Whitehall. On his return to Antwerp 1630 he married Helena Fourment, a girl of 16, who inspired a number of portraits and appears also in various religious and mythological works. In 1635 he bought a country residence, the Castle of Steen, and during the last five years of his life was occupied with paintings for the Torre de la Parada, Philip IV's hunting lodge near Madrid, and, for his personal satisfaction, with landscapes.

The Olympian energy of Rubens was stupendous. In less than 40 years he produced more than 3,000 paintings, more than 400 drawings. He created masterpieces in every genre: religious, for example *The Descent from the Cross*, c. 1611–14 (Antwerp); portraiture, the so-called *Chapeaude Pailles*, c. 1620 (National Gallery, London); peasant life, the *Kermesse*, c. 1622 (Louvre); allegory, *War and Peace*, c. 1629–30 (National Gallery, London); landscape, the *Château de Steen*, c. 1635–37 (National Gallery, London). As a colourist and technician he is remarkable, and he devised a classic oil method of thinly painted shadow and loaded highlight. His studio-factory was a model of efficient administration, his assistants so able, and his own supervision so well directed, that the standard of works not due to his hand alone is consistently high. He summoned into being a whole school of engravers, occupied in reproducing his works. In addition he was a great collector, of ancient marbles and gems, pictures, manuscripts, and books, a classical scholar who knew and corresponded with people of learning throughout Europe, and a diplomat who spoke five languages. His influence on painters – Velazquez, Watteau, Delacroix, Constable among them – was enormous.

Suggested reading
Fletcher, J *Peter Paul Rubens* (1968)
Gerson, N *Peter Paul Rubens: A Biography of a Giant* (1973)
Jaff, M *Rubens and Italy* (1977)
White, C *Rubens and his World* (1968)

Rubik Ernö (1944–). Hungarian architect who invented the Rubik cube, a multicoloured puzzle that can be manipulated and rearranged in only one correct way, but about 43 trillion wrong ones. Intended to help his students understand three-dimensional design, it became a fad that swept around the world.

Rubin Jerry (1938–1994). US activist, financier, and businessman. A radical political activist in the sixties, he co-founded the US Youth International Party, whose members were known as 'Yippies'. He gained international fame for his disruptive actvities for the anti-Vietnam war protest movement.

Following a visit to Cuba in 1964, Rubin became active in the Free Speech Movement in Berkeley, California. In 1967 he campaigned to have a pig elected president. In 1968, along with Abbie Hoffman and Tom Hayden, he became the media focus in the 'Battle of Chicago', the conflict between the police and protesters around the National Democratic Convention. At the subsequent 1969 trial, he was a member of the 'Chicago Seven', tried for conspiracy and inciting riots, although all seven were later aquitted. He wrote about his activism in a best-selling autobiography *Do It! Scenarios of the Revolution* 1970.

In the 1980s he renounced his earlier anti-capitalist activities and became a successful Wall Street securities analyst and later an independent entrepreneur, claiming that power 'really comes out of the cheque book'.

Rubin Robert Edward (1938–). US Democrat politician, treasury secretary from 1995. He was economic policy adviser to President Bill Clinton 1993–95, and is head of the National Economic Council. Rubin was born in New York. He worked for Goldman Sachs & Co 1966–92 and was its co-chair 1990–92.

Rubinstein Anton Grigorievich (1829–1894). Russian pianist and composer. One of the great virtuosos of his day, he did not join the Russian nationalist movement of his contemporaries, The Five. His music follows a more Western European style, but although solidly constructed it lacks the imaginative touch of genius.

Rubinstein Artur (1887–1982). Polish-born US pianist. His early encounters with Joseph Joachim and the Belgian violinist, conductor, and composer Eugène Ysaye (1858–1931) link his interpretations of Beethoven, Mozart, and Chopin with the virtuoso Romantic tradition. He was also a noted interpreter of de Falla.

He studied in Warsaw and Berlin and for 85 of his 95 years appeared with the world's major symphony orchestras.

Rubinstein Helena (1870–1965). Polish-born cosmetics tycoon, who emigrated to Australia 1902, where she started a cosmetics business. She moved to Europe 1904 and later to the USA, opening salons in London, Paris, and New York.

Rublev Andrei, or Rublyov (c. 1360–c. 1430). Russian icon painter. He is considered the greatest exponent of the genre in Russia. Only one documented work of his survives, the *Old Testament Trinity* about 1411 (Tretyakov Gallery, Moscow). This shows a basically Byzantine style, but with a gentler expression.

He was probably the pupil at Moscow of Theophanes the Greek and Daniel Chyorny, with whom he collaborated. The two works which represent his genius are the fragments of a *Last Judgment*, 1408, in the Cathedral of Vladimir, and the Icon of the Holy Trinity (now in the Moscow Museum of History), a work of majestic simplicity and feeling far transcending the conventional icon.

He is known to have worked with Theophanes the Greek in the Cathedral of the Annunciation in Moscow. In later life Rublev became a monk. The Russian film director Andrei Tarkovsky made a film of his life 1966.

Rude François (1784–1855). French Romantic sculptor. Rude was a supporter of Napoleon, together with the painter David, and in 1814 both artists went into exile in Brussels for some years. He produced the *Marseillaise* 1833, also known as *The Volunteers of 1792*, a low-relief scene on the Arc de Triomphe, Paris, showing the capped figure of Liberty leading the revolutionaries. Rude's other works include a bust of *David* 1831 and the monument *Napoleon Awakening to Immortality* 1854 (both in the Louvre, Paris).

You are freed henceforward from the torment of my presence ... death alone can save my good name.

Last letter from RUDOLPH to his wife after
his suicide pact with Mary Vetseva 1889

Rudolph (1858–1889). Crown prince of Austria, the only son of Emperor Franz Joseph. He married Princess Stephanie of Belgium in 1881, and they had one daughter, Elizabeth. In 1889 he and his mistress, Baroness Marie Vetsera, were found shot in his hunting lodge at Mayerling, near Vienna. The official verdict was suicide, although there were rumours that the deed was done by Jesuits, Hungarian nobles, or the baroness's husband.

From an early age he showed progressive views that brought him into conflict with his father. He conceived and helped to write a history of the Austro-Hungarian empire.

Rudolph two Holy Roman emperors:

Rudolph I (1218–1291). Holy Roman emperor from 1273. Originally count of Habsburg, he was the first Habsburg emperor and expanded his dynasty by investing his sons with the duchies of Austria and Styria.

Rudolph II (1552–1612). Holy Roman emperor from 1576, when he succeeded his father Maximilian II. His policies led to unrest in Hungary and Bohemia, which led to the surrender of Hungary to his brother Matthias 1608 and religious freedom for Bohemia.

Ruffin David (1941–1991). US pop singer, member of the vocal group the Temptations 1962–68 and lead baritone on many of their hits, including 'My Girl' 1965. The Temptations were Motown Records' most popular male group.

Born in Mississippi, Ruffin 'heard gospel before I could think'; in Detroit he recorded on local labels before joining the Temptations. Their first hit, 'The Way You Do the Things You Do' 1964, was written by Smokey Robinson, with Eddie Kendricks on lead vocal. Ruffin became lead singer starting with 'My Girl' 1965, which sold a million copies, followed by 'Since I Lost My Baby' and 'It's Growing' the same year, and many others. 'I Wish It Would Rain' 1968 also has Ruffin on lead, but he left after 'Cloud Nine' that year.

He had a few solo hits, notably 'My Whole World Ended' 1969 and 'Walk Away From Love' 1975. When the Temptations reformed for various projects, including the LP *Reunion* 1982, Ruffin took part.

Ruffini Paolo (1765–1822). Italian mathematician, philosopher, and physician. He published a theorem stating that it was impossible to give a general solution to equations of greater than the fourth degree using only radicals (such as square roots, cube roots, and so on). This became known as the Abel–Ruffini theorem when endorsed by Norwegian mathematician Niels Abel.

Ruffini was born in Valentano, Viterbo, and studied at Modena. From 1788 he was a professor there, though when Napoleon entered Modena in 1796, Ruffini found himself appointed an official of the French republic. Two years later he refused to swear the oath of allegiance to the republic and was for a time barred from teaching.

Ruffini made a substantial contribution to the theory of equations, developing the so-called theory of substitutions, which was the forerunner of modern group theory. His work became incorporated into the general theory of the solubility of algebraic equations developed by the ill-starred French mathematician Evariste Galois.

In addition, Ruffini considered the possibility that living organisms had come into existence as the result of chance, thus anticipating more modern work on probability.

Ruggles Carl (1876–1971). US composer. He was an associate, during the 1920s and 1930s, of the experimentalist composers Charles Ives, Edgard Varèse, and Henry Cowell, trying to forge a new direction in music. His instrumental forms were, however, more conservative than those of other composers, as in his best-known work *Sun-Treader* 1932 for orchestra, which, typically, uses elements of serialism but in a polyphonic texture.

Ruhmkorff Heinrich Daniel (1803–1877). German-born French instrument-maker who invented the Ruhmkorff induction coil 1851, a type of transformer for direct current that outputs a high voltage from a low-voltage input.

Ruhmkorff was born in Hanover and went to Paris in 1819. Working as a porter in the laboratory of physicist Charles Chevalier (1804–1850), he became interested in electrical equipment and soon began to manufacture scientific instruments. He opened his own workshop in 1840, and eventually became famous throughout Europe for his scientific apparatus.

Ruhmkorff's first notable invention was a thermoelectric battery 1844. The principles of the induction coil had been worked out by English scientist Michael Faraday in 1831. Ruhmkorff's induction coil consisted of a central cylinder of soft iron on which were wound two insulated coils: an inner primary coil comprising only a few turns of relatively thick copper wire, and an outer secondary coil with a large number of turns of thinner copper wire. An interrupter automatically made and broke the current in the primary coil, thereby inducing an intermittent high voltage in the secondary coil.

Ruisdael Jacob Isaakszoon van, or Ruysdael (c. 1628–1682). Dutch landscape painter. He painted rural scenes near his native town of Haarlem and in Germany, and excelled in depicting gnarled and weatherbeaten trees. A notable example of his work is *The Jewish Cemetery* about 1660 (Gemäldegalerie, Dresden). The few figures in his pictures were painted by other artists.

He was possibly a pupil of his uncle, Salomon van Ruisdael, and of Cornelisz Vroom. He painted many views in the region of Haarlem, and of Amsterdam, where he lived 1659–81, afterwards returning to his native city. His only known journey abroad is to Caen, where he took a degree in medicine 1676, presumably at that late stage of his career with a view to practice. However, his work gives some evidence of journeys along the Rhine and on the German border, and either like Everdingen he went to Norway and Sweden, or else in one phase he borrowed crags, waterfalls, and pinewoods from Everdingen. He is, however, primarily an interpreter of typical Dutch landscape, of dunes, coastal gleams, low horizons over which great clouds sweep, and quiet patches of woodland, his dark greens and greys infusing a personal and romantic melancholy. He had a worthy pupil in Hobbema, but was posthumously the master of both English and French landscape painters, greatly influencing Gainsborough, Constable, and the Barbizon School. The large collection of his works in the National Gallery, London, illustrates every type of subject he painted.

Suggested reading

Kahr, Madlyn Millner *Dutch Painting in the Seventeenth Century* (1978)

Levey, Michael *Ruisdael: Jacob van Ruisdael and Other Painters of His Family* (1977)

Stechow, Wolfgang *Dutch Landscape Painting in the Seventeenth Century* (1966)

Rumford Benjamin Thompson, Count von (1753–1814). American-born British physicist and inventor. In 1798, impressed by the seemingly inexhaustible amounts of heat generated in the boring of a cannon, he published his theory that heat is a mode of vibratory motion, not a substance. Rumford devised the domestic range – the 'fire in a box' – and fireplaces incorporating all the features now considered essential in open fires and chimneys, such as the smoke shelf and damper.

Rumford spied for the British in the American Revolution, and was forced to flee from America to England 1776. He travelled in Europe, and was knighted and created a count of the Holy Roman Empire for services to the elector of Bavaria 1784. In Bavaria he became war and police minister as well as grand chamberlain to the elector. In Bavaria, Rumford employed beggars from the streets to manufacture military uniforms, and took responsibility for feeding them. A study of nutrition led him to devise many recipes, emphasizing vegetable soup and potatoes. Meanwhile soldiers were being employed in gardening to produce the vegetables. His search for an alternative to alcoholic drinks led to the promotion of coffee and the design of the first percolator. He cofounded the Royal Institution in London 1799, and two years later moved to France.

He invented the Rumford shadow photometer and established the standard candle, which was the international unit of luminous intensity until 1940. He also devised a calorimeter to compare the heats of combustion of various fuels.

Rumford even planned the large park in Munich called the Englischer Garten.

It frequently happens that in the ordinary affairs ... of life opportunities present themselves of contemplating the most curious operations of nature.

BENJAMIN THOMPSON, COUNT VON RUMFORD
addressing the Royal Society 1798

Runcie Robert Alexander Kennedy, Baron Runcie (1921–   ). English cleric, archbishop of Canterbury 1980–91, the first to be appointed on the suggestion of the Church Crown Appointments Commission (formed 1977) rather than by political consultation. He favoured ecclesiastical remarriage for the divorced and the eventual introduction of the ordination of women. Baron 1991.

Runciman Walter, 1st Viscount Runciman (1870–1949). British Liberal politician. He entered Parliament in 1899 and held various ministerial offices between 1908 and 1939. In Aug 1938 he undertook an abortive mission to Czechoslovakia to persuade the Czech government to make concessions to Nazi Germany. Viscount 1937.

Liberal confusions and discords were ... to deny him the highest political positions ... Not given his full chance, he was not given his full due.

Archibald Hurd on WALTER, 1ST VISCOUNT RUNCIMAN
in *Dictionary of National Biography*

Rundstedt (Karl Rudolf) Gerd von (1875–1953). German field marshal in World War II. Largely responsible for the German breakthrough in France 1940, he was defeated on the Ukrainian front 1941.

After his defeat in the Ukraine he resigned Nov 1941 because of Hitler's order that there should be no withdrawals. He was rehabilitated 1942 and was responsible for the construction of the Atlantic Wall and the defence of 'Fortress Europe'. As commander in chief in France from 1942, he resisted the Allied invasion 1944 and in Dec launched the temporarily successful Ardennes offensive. He had his hands tied in resisting the Allied invasion of Europe by having to have every decision approved by Hitler. Recognizing the position as hopeless, he advocated peace and was dismissed but again recalled Sept 1944. He was captured 1945, but war-crime charges were dropped 1949 owing to his ill-health.

Runge Philipp Otto (1777–1810). German Romantic painter. His portraits, often of children, have a remarkable clarity and openness. He also illustrated fairy tales by German folklorists the brothers Grimm.

Runyon (Alfred) Damon (1880–1946). US journalist, primarily a sports reporter, whose short stories in *Guys and Dolls* 1932 deal

wryly with the seamier side of New York City life in his own invented jargon.

'My boy,' he says, 'always try to rub up against money, for if you rub up against money long enough, some of it may rub off on you.'

DAMON RUNYON
'A Very Honorable Guy'

Rupert Prince, or Rupert of the Rhine (1619–1682). English Royalist general and admiral, born in Prague, son of the Elector Palatine Frederick V and James I's daughter Elizabeth. Defeated by Cromwell at Marston Moor and Naseby in the Civil War, he commanded a privateering fleet 1649–52, until routed by Admiral Robert Blake, and, returning after the Restoration, was a distinguished admiral in the Dutch Wars. He founded the Hudson's Bay Company. Duke of Cumberland and Earl of Holderness 1644.

Suggested reading
Ashley, Maurice *Rupert of the Rhine* (1976)
Morah, Patrick *Prince Rupert of the Rhine* (1976)
Thompson, George Malcolm *Warrior Prince* (1976)

He was the last knight-errant – the first liberal politician.

George Edinger on PRINCE RUPERT
in *Rupert of the Rhine* 1936

Rupprecht (1869–1955). Crown prince of Bavaria and general in the German army with a distinguished record in World War I. European princes were often given high commands, but Prince Rupprecht was unusual in also having sound military ability. He joined the German army 1886 and worked his way up, becoming general 1904 and inspector-general of the Bavarian Corps 1913. He commanded the 6th Army, largely composed of Bavarian units, in Lorraine 1914 then fought on the Lys and in the first Battle of Ypres Oct–Nov 1914. In 1917 he commanded the German front from the North Sea to the river Oise and led his army group in the German Spring Offensive 1918. He went into exile upon Bavaria declaring itself a republic 1918.

He was a descendant of Charles I of England and, according to some authorities, the rightful heir to the throne of England.

Rush Benjamin (1745–1813). American physician and public official. Born in Bayberry, Pennsylvania, Rush was educated at the College of New Jersey, and graduated as a Doctor of Medicine at the University of Edinburgh 1768. Committed to the cause of the American Revolution 1775–83, he was a signatory of the Declaration of Independence 1776 and was named surgeon general of the Continental army 1777. His involvement in agitation against Washington's leadership led to his resignation. After the war, Rush served on the medical faculty of the University of Pennsylvania 1780–97 and was active in public-health programmes. From 1797 he was treasurer of the US Mint.

One of the extraordinary things about human events is that the unthinkable becomes thinkable.

SALMAN RUSHDIE
Guardian 8 Nov 1990

Rushdie (Ahmed) Salman (1947–   ). British writer. He was born in India of a Muslim family. His novel *The Satanic Verses* 1988 (the title refers to verses deleted from the Koran) offended many Muslims with alleged blasphemy. In 1989 the Ayatollah Khomeini of Iran called for Rushdie and his publishers to be killed.

Rushdie was born in Bombay and later lived in Pakistan before moving to the UK. His earlier novels in the magic-realist style include *Midnight's Children* 1981, which deals with India from the date of independence and won the Booker Prize, and *Shame* 1983, set in an imaginary parallel of Pakistan. The furore caused by the publication of *The Satanic Verses* led to the withdrawal of British diplomats from Iran. In India and elsewhere, people were killed in demonstrations against the book and Rushdie was forced to go into hiding. *Haroun and the Sea of Stories*, a children's book, was published 1990, and the novel *The Moor's Last Sigh* 1995.

Rusk (David) Dean (1909–1994). US Democrat politician. He was secretary of state to presidents J F Kennedy and L B Johnson 1961–69, and became unpopular through his involvement with the Vietnam War.

Rusk was born in Georgia, the son of a Presbyterian minister, and studied politics at Oxford University as a Rhodes scholar. He taught political science on his return to the USA, before military service during the World War II, where he was involved in intelligence and guerrilla operations in Burma (now Myanmar). He joined the US State Department after the war and progressed to becoming assistant secretary for Far Eastern affairs 1950–51. He was prominent in Korean War negotiations; convinced of the need not to appease communist expansionism, he played a key part in the US decision to defend South Korea against invasion by North Korea.

In 1952, when the Republican general Dwight Eisenhower was elected US president, Rusk left the State Department to become president of the internationalist Rockefeller Foundation. John F Kennedy appointed Rusk as his secretary of state on assuming the presidency 1961. Rusk advised against the unsuccessful April 1961 Bay of Pigs invasion of Cuba. During the Cuban missile crisis the following year, when the Soviet leader Nikita Khrushchev backed down, he commented famously: 'We're standing eyeball to eyeball, and the other fellow just blinked.'

Despite criticism from peace campaigners, Rusk never wavered in his advocacy of a firm interventionist line in Vietnam in an effort to halt the perceived spread of communism. He continued as secretary of state under President Lyndon Johnson, before retiring 1969 to teach international law at the University of Georgia. Liberal on social issues but hawkish and internationalist on external matters, Rusk was an archetypal 'defence Democrat'.

When we build, let us think that we build for ever.

JOHN RUSKIN
Seven Lamps of Architecture 1849

Ruskin John (1819–1900). English art critic and social critic. He published five volumes of *Modern Painters* 1843–60 and *The Seven Lamps of Architecture* 1849, in which he stated his philosophy of art. His writings hastened the appreciation of painters considered unorthodox at the time, such as J M W Turner and the Pre-Raphaelite Brotherhood. His later writings were concerned with social and economic problems.

In *The Stones of Venice* 1851–53, Ruskin drew moral lessons from architectural history. From 1860 he devoted himself to social and economic problems, in which he adopted an individual and radical outlook exalting the 'craftsman'. He became increasingly isolated in his views. To this period belongs a series of lectures and pamphlets (*Unto this Last* 1860, *Sesame and Lilies* 1865 on the duties of men and women, *The Crown of Wild Olive* 1866).

Ruskin was born in London, and was educated at Oxford. In 1848 he married Euphemia 'Effie' Chalmers Gray, but six years later the marriage was annulled. Ruskin was Slade professor of art at Oxford 1869–79, and he made a number of social experiments, such as St George's Guild, for the establishment of an industry on socialist lines. His last years were spent at Brantwood, Cumbria.

Ruskin College was founded in Oxford 1899 by an American, Walter Vrooman, to provide education in the social sciences for working people. It is supported by trade unions and other organizations.

Suggested reading
Bell, Q *Ruskin* (1963)
Clark, L *Ruskin Today* (1964)
Hunt, J D *The Wider Sea: A Life of John Ruskin* (1982)
Kemp, W *The Desire of My Eyes: The Life and Work of John Ruskin* (1991)
Rosenberg, J D *The Darkening Glass: A Portrait of Ruskin* (1961)

Life without industry is guilt, and industry without art is brutality.

JOHN RUSKIN
Lectures on Art 3 1870

Russ Joanna (1937–   ). US writer of feminist science fiction. Her work includes the novel *The Female Man* 1975 and her short stories have been collected in *The Zanzibar Cat* 1983.

Russell Bertrand Arthur William, 3rd Earl Russell (1872–1970). British philosopher and mathematician who contributed to the development of modern mathematical logic and wrote about social issues. His works include *Principia Mathematica* 1910–13 (with A N Whitehead), in which he attempted to show that mathematics could be reduced to a branch of logic; *The Problems of Philosophy* 1912; and *A History of Western Philosophy* 1946. He was an outspoken liberal pacifist. Earl 1931. Nobel Prize for Literature 1950.

Russell was born in Monmouthshire, the grandson of Prime Minister John Russell. He studied mathematics and philosophy at Trinity College, Cambridge, where he became a lecturer 1910. His

Rushdie *Indian-born English writer Salman Rushdie. He was put under sentence of death when his novel* The Satanic Verses, *an imaginative exploration of verses omitted from the Koran, was condemned as blasphemous by the Muslim religious leader Ayatollah Khomeini. The violent response to the book – public demonstrations, the murder of several people associated with its publication – caused Rushdie, in hiding and under close guard, to undertake a profound reappraisal of his beliefs and in 1990 he converted to Islam.*

Russell, Bertrand *English philosopher and mathematician Bertrand Russell (right) meeting United Nations secretary general U Thant in London 1962. During a long, wide-ranging intellectual career Russell wrote numerous books on philosophy, education, morals, and religion. A life-long campaigner on a range of social issues, he was imprisoned 1961 at the age of 89 for taking part in a nuclear disarmament demonstration in London.*

pacifist attitude in World War I lost him the lectureship, and he was imprisoned for six months for an article he wrote in a pacifist journal. His *Introduction to Mathematical Philosophy* 1919 was written in prison. He and his wife ran a progressive school 1927–32. After visits to the USSR and China, he went to the USA 1938 and taught at many universities. In 1940, a US court disqualified him from teaching at City College of New York because of his liberal moral views. He later returned to England and resumed his fellowship at Trinity College.

Three passions, simple but overwhelmingly strong, have governed my life: the longing for love, the search for knowledge, and unbearable pity for the suffering of mankind.

BERTRAND RUSSELL
Autobiography Prologue 1967

Russell was a life-long pacifist except during World War II. From 1949 he advocated nuclear disarmament and until 1963 was on the Committee of 100, an offshoot of the Campaign for Nuclear Disarmament.

Among his other works are *Principles of Mathematics* 1903, *Principles of Social Reconstruction* 1917, *Marriage and Morals* 1929, *An Enquiry into Meaning and Truth* 1940, *New Hopes for a Changing World* 1951, and *Autobiography* 1967–69.

Suggested reading
Ayer, A J *Russell* (1972)
Clark, Ronald W *The Life of Bertrand Russell* (1975)
Jager, Ronald *The Development of Bertrand Russell's Philosophy* (1972)
Moorhead, Caroline *Bertrand Russell: A Life* (1992)
Pears, D F *Bertrand Russell and the British Tradition in Philosophy* (1967)
Russell, Bertrand *The Autobiography of Bertrand Russell* (1967–69)
Watling, John *Bertrand Russell* (1970)

Mathematics may be defined as the subject in which we never know what we are talking about, nor whether what we are saying is true.

BERTRAND RUSSELL
Mysticism and Logic 1918

Russell Charles Taze (1852–1916). US religious figure, founder of the Jehovah's Witness sect 1872.

Russell Dora Winifred (born Black) (1894–1986). English feminist who married Bertrand Russell 1921. The 'openness' of their marriage (she subsequently had children by another man) was a matter of controversy.

She was educated at Girton College, Cambridge, of which she became a fellow. In 1927 the Russells founded the progressive Beacon Hill School in Hampshire. She was a founding member of the National Council for Civil Liberties in 1934. After World War II she actively supported the Campaign for Nuclear Disarmament.

Russell Frederick Stratten (1897–1984). English marine biologist who studied the life histories and distribution of plankton. He also discovered a means of distinguishing between different species of fish shortly after they have hatched, when they are almost identical in appearance. Knighted 1965.

From 1924 he worked for the Marine Biological Association in Plymouth, becoming its director 1945.

Having investigated the different types of behaviour of individual species of fish at various times of the year, and the distribution of two kinds of plankton, Russell was able to establish certain types of plankton as indicators of different types of water in the English Channel and the North Sea. He also offered a partial explanation for the difference in abundance of herring in different areas. Russell's studies of plankton and of water movements provided valuable information on which to base fishing quotas, the accuracy of which is essential to prevent overfishing and the depletion of fish stocks.

Russell also elucidated the life histories of several species of medusa by rearing the hydroids from parent medusae, and he published *The Medusae of the British Isles* 1953–70.

In the lost boyhood of Judas, / Christ was betrayed.

GEORGE WILLIAM RUSSELL (AE)
'Germinal'

Russell George William (1867–1935). Irish poet and essayist. An ardent nationalist, he helped found the Irish national theatre, and his poetry, published under the pseudonym 'AE', includes *Gods of War* 1915 and reflects his interest in mysticism and theosophy.

Russell Henry Norris (1877–1957). US astronomer who was the first to put in graphic form what became known as the Hertzsprung–Russell diagram 1913.

Russell was born in Oyster Bay, New York, and studied at Princeton, where in 1905 he was made professor and director of the observatory. In 1921 he moved to the Mount Wilson Observatory, California.

Like Ejnar Hertzsprung, Russell concluded that stars could be grouped in two main classes, one much brighter than the other. He used Annie Cannon's system of spectral classification, which also indicated surface temperature. Most of the stars were grouped together in what became known as the 'main sequence', but there was a group of very bright stars outside the main sequence. Russell put forward the theory that all stars progress at one time or another either up or down the main sequence, depending on whether they are contracting (and therefore becoming hotter) or expanding (thus cooling), but the progression he proposed was discredited within a decade.

Russell's lifelong study of binary stars resulted in a method for calculating the mass of each star from a study of its orbital behaviour.

He pioneered a system using both orbits and masses in order to compute distance from Earth.

His stentorian 'view–halloo' could be sworn to by every rustic between Dartmoor and Exmoor.

Thomas Seccombe on JACK RUSSELL
in *Dictionary of National Biography*

Russell Jack (John) (1795–1883). British 'sporting parson', who bred the short-legged, smooth-coated Jack Russell terrier.

They held up The Outlaw for five years. And Howard Hughes had me doing publicity for it every day, five days a week for five years.

JANE RUSSELL
on the controversial film *The Outlaw*
in *Cinéma, Cinéma*, Antenne 2 (French TV) 1985

Russell Jane (1921–). US actress. She was discovered by producer Howard Hughes, and promoted as a 'pin-up girl'. Her first film, *The Outlaw* 1943, was not properly released for several years because of censorship problems. Other films include *The Paleface* 1948, *Gentlemen Prefer Blondes* 1953, and *The Revolt of Mamie Stover* 1957.

If peace cannot be maintained with honour, it is no longer peace.

JOHN RUSSELL
Speech 1853

Russell John, 1st Earl Russell, known until 1861 as Lord John Russell (1792–1878). British Liberal politician, son of the 6th Duke of Bedford. He entered the House of Commons 1813 and supported Catholic emancipation and the Reform Bill. He held cabinet posts 1830–41, became prime minister 1846–52, and was again a cabinet

Russell, John *John Russell, British Liberal politician, was created 1st Earl Russell in 1861. As a young MP of aristocratic background, he helped frame the 1832 Reform Bill and championed its passage through parliament.*

minister until becoming prime minister again 1865–66. He retired after the defeat of his Reform Bill 1866.

As foreign secretary in Aberdeen's coalition 1852 and in Palmerston's second government 1859–65, Russell assisted Italy's struggle for unity, although his indecisive policies on Poland, Denmark, and the American Civil War provoked much criticism. He had a strained relationship with Palmerston. Earl 1861.

Russell John Peter (1858–1931). Australian artist. Having met Tom Roberts while sailing to England, he became a member of the French Post-Impressionist group.

I've not read one review of Mahler. I know it's a good film. The critics who recognize it as such are good critics. Those who do not are bad critics.

KEN RUSSELL
Film Illustrated 1980

Russell Ken (Henry Kenneth Alfred) (1927–). English film director. His work, typified by stylistic extravagance, includes *Women in Love* 1969, *The Music Lovers* 1971, *Mahler* 1974, *Tommy, Lisztomania* both 1975, *Altered States* 1979, and *Gothic* 1986. Highly controversial, his work is often criticized for self-indulgence, containing gratuitous sex and violence, but is also regarded for its vitality and imagination. He has made television biographies of the lives of the composers Elgar, Delius, and Richard Strauss.

If I do not take his life, he will soon have mine.

Charles II on WILLIAM, LORD RUSSELL, showing no mercy in 1683

Russell William, Lord (1639–1683). British Whig politician. Son of the 1st Duke of Bedford, he was among the founders of the Whig Party, and actively supported attempts in Parliament to exclude the Roman Catholic James II from succeeding to the throne. In 1683 he was accused, on dubious evidence, of complicity in the Rye House Plot to murder Charles II, and was executed. He used the courtesy title Lord Russell from 1678.

Russell William Howard (1820–1907). British journalist, born in Ireland. He was the correspondent for *The Times* during the Crimean War, and created a sensation by exposing the mismanagement of the campaign.

Russell, William *English journalist William H Russell, special correspondent for The Times during the Crimean War, photographed by Roger Fenton. Russell's dispatches, which exposed the sufferings of the British soldiers, inspired the work of Florence Nightingale.*

Russell of Liverpool Edward Frederick Langley Russell, 2nd Baron Russell of Liverpool (1895–1981). British barrister. As deputy judge advocate-general, British Army of the Rhine, 1946–47 and 1948–51, he was responsible for all war-crime trials in the British Zone of Germany 1946–50. He published *The Scourge of the Swastika* 1954 and *The Trial of Adolf Eichmann* 1962. Baron 1920.

Russky Nicholas Vladimirovich (1855–1919). Russian general. He served as a Chief of Staff in the Russo-Japanese war 1905 and then as minister of war. In World War I he won considerable acclaim for his victories over the Austrians on the Galician front. Following the Russian Revolution March 1917, he helped secure the abdication of the tsar, but he fell foul of the Council of Workers' and Soldiers' Deputies and was dismissed, to be murdered Jan 1919.

Rust Mathias (1968–   ). German aviator who, in May 1987, piloted a light plane from Finland to Moscow, landing in Red Square. Found guilty of 'malicious hooliganism', he was imprisoned until 1988. His exploit, carefully timed to take place on the USSR's 'national border-guards' day', highlighted serious deficiencies in the Soviet air-defence system and led to the dismissal of the defence minister.

Rust, despite pleading that his actions had been designed to promote world peace, was sentenced to four years' imprisonment by the Soviet authorities. After serving 14 months in a KGB prison in Lefortovo, he was released and sent home as a humanitarian gesture by the Gorbachev administration. In April 1991, he was sentenced to two and a half years' imprisonment for attempted manslaughter in 1989, when he stabbed a student nurse who spurned his advances.

Rutherford, Ernest New Zealand-born physicist Ernest Rutherford. Rutherford described atomic structure. The vast majority of an atom's mass is made up of neutrons and protons which exist in an infinitesimally small nucleus. The nucleus is surrounded by space in which electrons orbit. (Image Select)

Rustaveli Shota (*c.* 1172–*c.* 1216). Georgian poet. He was the author of the Georgian national epic *Vekhis-tqaosani/The Man [or Knight] in the Panther's Skin*, which draws on ancient Greek and Eastern philosophy in the celebration of heroism, courtly love, and comradeship.

Ruth Babe (George Herman) (1895–1948). US baseball player, regarded by many as the greatest of all time. He played in ten World Series and hit 714 home runs, a record that stood from 1935 to 1974 and led to the nickname 'Sultan of Swat'.

Ruth started playing 1914 as a pitcher-outfielder for the Boston Braves before moving to the Boston Red Sox later that year. He joined the New York Yankees 1920 and became one of the best hitters in the game. He hit 60 home runs in the 1927 season (a record beaten 1961 by Roger Maris). He is still the holder of the record for most bases in a season: 457 in 1921. Yankee Stadium is known as 'the house that Ruth built' because of the money he brought into the club.

Suggested reading
Creamer, Robert *Babe* (1974)
Ruth, George Herman and Considine, Bob *The Babe Ruth Story* (autobiography) (1948)
Smelser, Marshall *The Life That Ruth Built: A Biography* (1975)

Rutherford Ernest, 1st Baron Rutherford of Nelson (1871–1937). New Zealand-born British physicist, a pioneer of modern atomic science. He was in 1911 the first to recognize the nuclear nature of the atom. Nobel prize 1908. Knighted 1914, baron 1931.

Rutherford produced the first artificial transformation, changing one element to another, in 1919, bombarding nitrogen with alpha particles and getting hydrogen and oxygen. After further research he announced that the nucleus of any atom must be composed of hydrogen nuclei; at Rutherford's suggestion, the name 'proton' was given to the hydrogen nucleus in 1920. He speculated that uncharged particles (neutrons) must also exist in the nucleus.

In 1934, using heavy water, Rutherford and his co-workers bombarded deuterium with deuterons and produced tritium. This may be considered the first nuclear fusion reaction.

Rutherford was born near Nelson on South Island and studied at Christchurch. In 1895 he went to Britain and became the first research student to work under English physicist J J Thomson at the Cavendish Laboratory, Cambridge. Rutherford obtained 1898 his first academic position with a professorship at McGill University, Montréal, Canada, which then boasted the best-equipped laboratory in the world. He returned to the UK 1907, to Manchester University. From 1919 he was director of the Cavendish Laboratory, where he directed the construction of a particle accelerator, and was also professor of natural philosophy at the Royal Institution from 1921.

Rutherford began investigating radioactivity 1897 and had by 1900 found three kinds of radioactivity with different penetrating power: alpha, beta, and gamma rays. When he moved to Montréal, he began to use thorium as a source of radioactivity instead of uranium. English chemist Frederick Soddy helped Rutherford identify its decay products, and in 1903 they were able to to explain that radioactivity is caused by the breakdown of the atoms to produce a new element. In 1904 Rutherford worked out the series of transformations that radioactive elements undergo and showed that they end as lead.

In 1914, Rutherford found that positive rays consist of hydrogen nuclei and that gamma rays are waves that lie beyond X-rays in the electromagnetic spectrum.

Suggested reading
Bunge, Mario and Shea, William (eds) *Rutherford and Physics at the Turn of the Century* (1979)

Anyone who expects a source of power from the transformation of these atoms is talking moonshine.

ERNEST RUTHERFORD
in *Physics Today* Oct 1970

Chadwick, J (ed) *The Collected Papers of Lord Rutherford of Nelson* (1962–65)
Feather, N *Lord Rutherford* (1973)
Wilson, David *Rutherford: Simple Genius* (1983)

Rutherford Margaret (1892–1972). English film and theatre actress. She specialized in formidable yet jovially eccentric roles. She played Agatha Christie's Miss Marple in four films in the early 1960s and won an Academy Award for her role in *The VIPs* 1963.

One of the great character actresses, she became mildly successful in the mid-1930s but went on to her greatest success when she played Miss Marple. Other films include *Blithe Spirit* 1945, *Passport to Pimlico* 1949, *Mouse on the Moon* 1943, and Orson Welles' *Chimes at Midnight* 1966. DBE 1967.

[She] usually seemed to be playing somebody's slightly dotty spinster aunt.

Leslie Halliwell on MARGARET RUTHERFORD
in his *Filmgoer's Companion* 1965

Rutherfurd Lewis Morris (1816–1892). US spectroscopist and astronomical photographer. He produced a classification scheme of stars based on their spectra that turned out to be similar to that of Italian astronomer Angelo Secchi.

In 1856 he had his own observatory built and spent the rest of his life working there.

From 1858 Rutherfurd produced many photographs that were widely admired of the Moon, Jupiter, Saturn, the Sun, and stars down to the fifth magnitude. He went on to map the heavens by photographing star clusters, and devised a new micrometer that could measure the distances between stars more accurately.

In 1862 he began to make spectroscopic studies of the Sun, Moon, Jupiter, Mars, and 16 fixed stars. To help this work, Rutherfurd devised highly sophisticated diffraction gratings.

Rutledge Wiley Blount, Jr (1894–1949). US jurist and associate justice of the US Supreme Court 1943–49. He was known as a liberal, often dissenting from conservative Court decisions, such as in *Wolf* v *Colorado* 1949, which allowed illegally obtained evidence to be used against a defendant in state courts.

Rutskoi Aleksander (1947–). Russian politician, founder of the reformist Communists for Democracy group, and vice president of the Russian Federation 1991–93. During the abortive Aug 1991 coup he led the Russian delegation to rescue Soviet leader Mikhail Gorbachev from his forced confinement in the Crimea. In Sept 1993, with Rusian Khasbulatov, he led the insurrection against Russian president Boris Yeltsin. Both men were arrested and imprisoned but then released 1994 on the instructions of the federal assembly. Shortly after his release, Rutskoi, as leader of the Russian Social Democratic People's Party, professed his support for a reconstituted Soviet Union. In 1995 he became leader of the Derzhava (Great Power) nationalist party.

A former air officer and highly decorated Afghan war veteran, Rutskoi became increasingly critical of the Yeltsin administration, especially its price liberalization reforms. In 1992 Yeltsin placed Rutskoi in charge of agricultural reform.

Ruysdael Jacob van. See ◊Ruisdael, Dutch painter.

Ruyter Michiel Adriaanszoon de (1607–1676). Dutch admiral who led his country's fleet in the wars against England. On 1–4 June 1666 he forced the British fleet under Rupert and Albemarle to retire into the Thames, but on 25 July was heavily defeated off the North Foreland, Kent. In 1667 he sailed up the Medway, burning three men-of-war at Chatham, and capturing others. Ruyter was mortally wounded in an action against the French fleet off Messina and died at Syracuse, Sicily.

Ružička Leopold Stephen (1887–1976). Swiss chemist who began research on natural compounds such as musk and civet secretions. In the 1930s he investigated sex hormones, and in 1934 succeeded in extracting the male hormone androsterone from 31,815 litres/7,000 gallons of urine and synthesizing it. Born in Croatia, Ružička settled in Switzerland in 1929. Ružička shared the 1939 Nobel Prize for Chemistry with Adolf Butenandt.

[A] strong featured American leading actor who never seemed to get the roles he deserved.

Leslie Halliwell on ROBERT RYAN
in his *Filmgoer's Companion* 1965

Ryan Robert (1913–1973). US film and theatre actor. He was equally impressive in leading and character roles. He was memorable playing the anti-Semitic murderer in *Crossfire* 1947 and an equally villainous role in *Bad Day at Black Rock* 1954. His films include *The Set-Up* 1949, *God's Little Acre* 1958, and *The Wild Bunch* 1969.

Rydberg Johannes Robert (1854–1919). Swedish physicist who discovered a mathematical expression that gives the frequencies of spectral lines for elements. It includes a constant named the Rydberg constant after him.

Rydberg was born in Halmstad and studied at Lund, where he spent his whole career, becoming professor 1897.

Rydberg began by classifying spectral lines into three types: principal (strong, persistent lines), sharp (weaker but well-defined lines), and diffuse (broader lines). Each spectrum of an element consists of several series of these lines superimposed on each other. He then sought to find a mathematical relationship that would relate the frequencies of the lines in a particular series. In 1890, he achieved this by using a quantity called the wave number, which is the reciprocal of the wavelength. The formula expresses the wave number in terms of a constant common to all series (the Rydberg constant), two constants that are characteristic of the particular series, and an integer. The lines are then given by changing the value of the integer.

Rydberg then went on to produce another formula, which would express the frequency of every line in every series of an element.

Ryder Albert Pinkham (1847–1917). US painter. He developed one of the most original styles of his time. He painted with broad strokes that tended to simplify form and used yellowish colours that gave his works an eerie, haunted quality. His works are poetic, romantic, and filled with unreality; *Death on a Pale Horse* about 1910 (Cleveland Museum of Art) is typical.

Rylance Mark (1960–). English actor and director, from 1995 the artistic director of Shakespeare's Globe Theatre, London. He received the 1994 Olivier Award for best actor for his role as Benedick in *Much Ado About Nothing*. Films include *Prospero's Books* 1991, *Angels and Insects* 1994, *Institute Bejamenta* 1994, and *Loving* 1995. In 1991 he formed his own theatre company, Phoebus Cart. Rylance has also appeared in several television films, earning high praise for his performance as the kicked-about tramp in BBC2's award-winning *The Grass Arena* 1993.

The dogma of the Ghost in the Machine.

GILBERT RYLE
The Concept of Mind ch 1 1949

Ryle Gilbert (1900–1976). British philosopher. His *The Concept of Mind* 1949 set out to show that the distinction between an inner and an outer world in philosophy and psychology cannot be sustained. He ridiculed the mind–body dualism of the French philosopher René Descartes as the doctrine of 'the Ghost in the Machine'.

Ryle Martin (1918–1984). English radioastronomer. At the Mullard Radio Astronomy Observatory, Cambridge, he developed the technique of sky-mapping using 'aperture synthesis', combining smaller dish aerials to give the characteristics of one large one. His work on the distribution of radio sources in the universe brought confirmation of the Big Bang theory. He was knighted 1966, and won, with his co-worker Antony Hewish, the Nobel Prize for Physics 1974.

During World War II he was involved in the development of radar. After the war he joined the Cavendish Laboratory in Cambridge, and in 1959 he became the first Cambridge professor of radioastronomy, responsible for most of the radiotelescope developments. He was Astronomer Royal 1972–82.

Larger and larger radio telescopes were built at the Cambridge sites, resulting in the Cambridge Catalogue Surveys, numbered 1C–5C, giving better and better maps of radio sources in the northern sky. The 3C survey, published 1959, is used as reference by all radioastronomers. The 4C survey catalogued 5,000 sources.

The first 'supersynthesis' telescope, in which a fixed aerial maps a band of the sky using solely the rotation of the Earth, and another aerial maps successive rings out from it concentrically, was built in 1963, and a 5-km/3-mi instrument was completed in 1971. The programmes for which it is in use includes the mapping of extragalactic sources and the study of supernovae and newly born stars. It can provide as sharp a picture as the best ground-based optical telescopes.

Rysbrack Jan Michiel (1694–1770). Dutch-born sculptor, whose style was one of restrained Baroque. He settled in England 1720 and produced portrait busts and tombs in Westminster Abbey, London.

He also created the equestrian statue of William III in Queen Square, Bristol, 1735.

Ryzhkov Nikolai Ivanovich (1929–). Soviet Communist politician. He held governmental and party posts from 1975 before being brought into the Politburo and serving as prime minister 1985–90 under Gorbachev. A low-profile technocrat, Ryzhkov was the author of unpopular economic reforms.

An engineering graduate from the Urals Polytechnic in Ekaterinburg (formerly Sverdlovsk), Ryzhkov rose to become head of the giant Uralmash engineering conglomerate. A member of the Communist Party from 1959, he became deputy minister for heavy engineering 1975. He then served as first deputy chair of Gosplan (the central planning agency) 1979–82 and Central Committee secretary for economics 1982–85 before becoming prime minister. He was viewed as a more cautious and centralist reformer than Gorbachev. In 1990 he was nearly forced to resign, as a result of the admitted failure of his implementation of the perestroika economic reform programme, and he survived only with the support of Gorbachev. He stepped down as Soviet premier following a serious heart attack late Dec 1990. In June 1991, he unsuccessfully challenged Boris Yeltsin for the presidency of the Russian Federation.

S

Saarinen Eero (1910–1961). Finnish-born US architect. He was renowned for his wide range of innovative Modernist designs, experimenting with different structures and shapes. His works include the US embassy, London, 1955–61, the TWA Kennedy terminal, New York, 1956–62, and Dulles Airport, Washington, DC, 1958–63. He collaborated on a number of projects with his father, Eliel Saarinen.

Saarinen (Gottlieb) Eliel (1873–1950). Finnish-born US architect and town planner. He founded the Finnish Romantic school. His best-known European project is the Helsinki railway station 1905–14. In 1923 he emigrated to the USA, where he is remembered for his designs for the Cranbrook Academy of Art in Bloomfield Hills, Michigan, 1926–43, and Christ Church, Minneapolis, 1949.

Sabah Sheik Jabir al-Ahmad al-Jabir al-(1928–). Emir of Kuwait from 1977. He suspended the national assembly 1986, after mounting parliamentary criticism, ruling in a feudal, paternalistic manner. On the invasion of Kuwait by Iraq 1990 he fled to Saudi Arabia, returning to Kuwait March 1991. In 1992 a reconstituted national assembly was elected.

Sabatier Paul (1854–1941). French chemist. He found in 1897 that if a mixture of ethylene and hydrogen was passed over a column of heated nickel, the ethylene changed into ethane. Further work revealed that nickel could be used to catalyse numerous chemical reactions. Nobel prize 1912.

From 1884 he was professor at Toulouse. With his assistant Abbé Jean-Baptiste Senderens (1856–1936), Sabatier extended the nickel-catalyst method to the hydrogenation of other unsaturated and aromatic compounds, and synthesized methane by the hydrogenation of carbon monoxide. He later showed that at higher temperatures the same catalysts can be used for dehydrogenation, enabling him to prepare aldehydes from primary alcohols and ketones from secondary alcohols.

Sabatier later explored the use of oxide catalysts, such as manganese oxide, silica, and alumina. Different catalysts often gave different products from the same starting material. Alumina, for example, produced olefins (alkenes) with primary alcohols, which yielded aldehydes with a copper catalyst.

Sabatini Gabriela (1970–). Argentine tennis player who in 1986 became the youngest Wimbledon semifinalist for 99 years. She was ranked number three in the world behind Monica Seles and Steffi Graf in 1991.

Sábato Ernesto (1911–). Argentine novelist and social critic. Trained as a physicist, he was removed from his university post 1945 for opposition to the Perón government. He depicted an existential antihero in his successful novel *El túnel*/*The Outsider* 1948. Both in essays such as 'Hombres y engranajes/Men and Gears' 1951 and novels such as *Abaddón el exterminador*/*Abaddón the Exterminator* 1974 he has explored the excesses of scientific rationalism in an overmechanized modern society.

Sabin Albert Bruce (1906–1993). Russian-born US microbiologist who developed a highly effective, live vaccine against polio. The earlier vaccine, developed by physicist Jonas Salk, was based on heat-killed viruses. Sabin was convinced that a live form would be longer-lasting and more effective, and in 1957 he succeeded in weakening the virus so that it lost its virulence. The vaccine can be given by mouth.

After a period at the Rockefeller Institute of Medical Research, he was appointed professor at the University of Cincinnati College of Medicine 1946–60. He became interested in polio research while working at the Rockefeller Institute. In 1936, he and a co-worker were able to make polio viruses from monkeys grow in tissue cultures from the brain cells of a human embryo. He concentrated on developing a live-virus vaccine because it would not, like the Salk vaccine, have to be injected. Sabin succeeded in finding virus strains of all three types of polio, each producing its own variety of antibody. The single-dose vaccine worked by inducing a harmless infection of the intestinal tract, causing rapid antibody formation and thereby providing lasting immunity.

Sabin was unable to test his new vaccine in America because, at an earlier stage of the Salk vaccine's development in 1954, a faulty batch caused paralytic polio in some children. However, Sabin managed to interest the Russians in his vaccine, and subsequently was able to report 1959 that 4.5 million vaccinations had been successfully carried out. The vaccine was commercially available by 1961.

Sabin Florence Rena (1871–1953). US medical researcher who studied the development of the lymphatic system and tuberculosis. She also campaigned to modernize US public health laws. Sabin was the first woman to be elected to the National Academy of Sciences.

Sabine Edward (1788–1883). Irish geophysicist who made intensive studies of terrestrial magnetism. He was able to link the incidence of magnetic storms with the sunspot cycle. KCB 1869.

Sabine was born in Dublin and educated at the Royal Military Academy, Woolwich, London. He served in the Royal Artillery, rising to the rank of major general in 1859.

In 1818, Sabine was official astronomer on an expedition to explore the Northwest Passage. The following year he went to the Arctic, and 1821–22 to the southern hemisphere. Sabine collaborated with English mathematician Charles Babbage from 1826 on a survey of magnetism in Britain, a project that was repeated by Sabine himself in the late 1850s.

At Sabine's urging, an expedition to establish observatories in the southern hemisphere was sent out in 1839 and with the data thus accumulated, Sabine in 1851 discovered a 10–11-year periodic fluctuation in the number of magnetic storms. He then correlated this magnetic cycle with data German astronomer Samuel Schwabe had collected on a similar variation in solar activity.

I'm Abu the thief, son of Abu the thief, grandson of Abu the thief.

SABU's lines from the film *The Thief of Baghdad* 1940

Sabu stage name of Sabu Dastagir (1924–1963). Indian child actor. He was the hero of *The Thief of Bagdad* 1940. He performed in Britain and the USA until the 1950s. Other films include *Elephant Boy* 1937 and *Black Narcissus* 1947.

Sacher Paul (1906–). Swiss conductor. In 1926 he founded the Basel Chamber Orchestra, for which he has commissioned a succession of works from contemporary composers including Bartók's *Divertimento* 1939, Stravinsky's Concerto in D for strings 1946, and Boulez's *Messagesquisse* 1977.

Sacher-Masoch Leopold von (1836–1895). Austrian novelist. His books dealt with the sexual pleasure of having pain inflicted on oneself, hence masochism.

Sachs Hans (1494–1576). German poet and composer. Working as a master shoemaker in Nuremberg, he composed 4,275

Meisterlieder/Mastersongs, and figures prominently in Wagner's opera *Die Meistersinger von Nürnberg*.

Sackville Thomas, 1st Earl of Dorset (1536–1608). English poet. He collaborated with Thomas Norton on *Gorboduc* 1561, written in blank verse, one of the earliest English tragedies. Baron Buckhurst 1567, earl 1604.

Sackville-West Vita (Victoria Mary) (1892–1962). English writer. She was the wife of Harold Nicolson from 1913; *Portrait of a Marriage* 1973 by their son Nigel Nicolson described their married life. Her novels include *The Edwardians* 1930 and *All Passion Spent* 1931; she also wrote the long pastoral poem *The Land* 1926. The fine gardens around her home at Sissinghurst, Kent, were created by her and her husband. Virginia Woolf based the novel *Orlando* 1928 on Sackville-West.

Sadat (Muhammad) Anwar (1918–1981). Egyptian politician. Succeeding Nasser as president 1970, he restored morale by his handling of the Egyptian campaign in the 1973 war against Israel. In 1974 his plan for economic, social, and political reform to transform Egypt was unanimously adopted in a referendum. In 1977 he visited Israel to reconcile the two countries, and shared the Nobel Peace Prize with Israeli prime minister Menachem Begin 1978. He was assassinated by Islamic fundamentalists.

Sade Donatien Alphonse François, Comte de, known as the Marquis de Sade (1740–1814). French writer. He was imprisoned for sexual offences and finally committed to an asylum. He wrote plays and novels dealing explicitly with a variety of sexual practices, including sadism, deriving pleasure or sexual excitement from inflicting pain on others.

S'adi (or Saadi) pen name of Sheik Moslih Addin (c. 1184– c. 1291). Persian poet. He was the author of *Bustan/Tree-garden* and *Gulistan/Flower-garden*.

To jealousy, nothing is more frightful than laughter.

FRANÇOISE SAGAN
The Masquerade ch 9 1966

Sagan Carl Edward (1934–1996). US physicist and astronomer who popularized astronomy through writings and broadcasts. His main research was on planetary atmospheres. His books include *Broca's Brain: Reflections on the Romance of Science* 1979 and *Cosmos* 1980, based on his television series of that name. Sagan also did research into the origin of life on Earth, the probable climatic effects of nuclear war, and the possibility of life on other planets.

He became professor of astronomy and space science at Cornell University 1970, and provided data for several NASA space-probe missions, especially *Mariner 9* to Mars.

In the early 1960s Sagan determined the surface temperature of Venus. He then turned his attention to the early planetary atmosphere of the Earth, and, like US chemist Stanley Miller before him, was able to produce amino acids by irradiating a mixture of methane, ammonia, water, and hydrogen sulphide. In addition, his experiment produced glucose, fructose, nucleic acids, and traces of adenosine triphosphate (ATP, used by living cells to store energy).

Other works by Sagan are *Cosmic Connection: An Extraterrestrial Perspective* 1973 and the science-fiction novel *Contact* 1985.

Our loyalties are to the species and the planet. We speak for Earth. Our obligation to survive is owed not just to ourselves but also to that Cosmos, ancient and vast, from which we spring.

CARL SAGAN
Cosmos 1980

Sagan Françoise. Pen name of Françoise Quoirez (1935–). French novelist. Her studies of love relationships include *Bonjour Tristesse/Hello Sadness* 1954, *Un Certain Sourire/A Certain Smile* 1956, and *Aimez-vous Brahms?/Do You Like Brahms?* 1959. In lucidly dispassionate prose she describes how amoral characters seek to escape solitude in brief liaisons.

Sage Kings legendary rulers of China c. 2800–c. 2200 BC. Of the three sovereigns and five emperors based in the Huang He (Yellow River) region, Huang-tu (reigned c. 2697 BC) is credited with defeating the barbarians. The era has been associated with the domestication of animals, agricultural development, the gradual replacement of stone implements with bronze, and the formation of larger tribal confederacies.

Saigō Takamori (1827–1877). Japanese general and conservative politician who helped in the Meiji restoration and then rebelled against it. Saigō was a minor official from Satsuma in Kyushu, a province traditionally at odds with the shogunate. With Ōkubo Toshimichi, he led the successful samurai rebellion 1867–68 against the Tokugawa shogunate. Saigō became a government minister 1871. He became commander in chief 1872 and one of the leading figures in the Meiji government. Disapproving of the Meiji government and in particular the introduction of conscription, which threatened the samurai way of life, he resigned 1873 after his plan for a war of redemption against Korea had been rejected. He led the Satsuma rebellion 1877. He committed suicide after the failure of the rebellion, realising that defeat meant the end of the samurai class.

Saint-Claire Deville Henri Etienne (1818–1881). French inorganic chemist who worked on high-temperature reactions and was the first to extract metallic aluminium in any quantity.

He studied science and medicine in France and in 1845 became professor at Besançon. In 1851 he moved to the Ecole Normale in Paris and from 1859 he was at the Sorbonne.

In 1827, German chemist Friedrich Wöhler had isolated small quantities of impure aluminium from its compounds by heating them with metallic potassium. Saint-Claire Deville substituted the safer sodium. He first had to prepare sufficient sodium metal, but by 1855 he had obtained enough aluminium to cast a block weighing 7 kg/15 lb. The process was put into commercial production and within four years the price of aluminium had fallen to onehundredth of its former level.

Saint-Denis Michel (1897–1971). French theatre director and actor. He founded both the Compagnie des Quinze 1930 and the London Theatre Studio 1936–39. From 1946 to 1952 he was director of the Old Vic Theatre School, and became an artistic adviser for the Lincoln Center in New York 1957, and later for the Royal Shakespeare Company in Britain 1962.

Sainte-Beuve Charles Augustin (1804–1869). French critic and historian. A champion of Romanticism, he wrote widely on French literature and culture, his articles appearing in the *Revue des deux mondes/Review of the Two Worlds* from 1831 as 'Causeries du lundi/Monday Chats' 1851–62. His outstanding work as a historian was *Port Royal* 1840–59, a study of Jansenism which also includes descriptions of the 17th-century literary figures Corneille, Molière, and Racine.

One can be a brother only in something. Where there is no tie that binds men, men are not united but merely lined up.

ANTOINE DE SAINT-EXUPÉRY
Flight to Arras ch 23 1987 ed

Saint-Exupéry Antoine Marie Roger de (1900–1944). French author and pilot. He wrote the autobiographical *Vol de nuit/Night Flight* 1931 and *Terre des hommes/Wind, Sand, and Stars* 1939. His children's book *Le Petit Prince/The Little Prince* 1943 is also an adult allegory. He disappeared in World War II on a mission over occupied France.

Saint-Gaudens Augustus (1848–1907). Irish-born US sculptor. He was one of the leading Neo-Classical sculptors of his time. His monuments include the *Admiral Farragut* 1878–81 in Madison Square Park, New York City, and the Adams Memorial 1891 in Rock Creek Cemetery, Washington, DC.

St Joseph (John) Kenneth (Sinclair) (1912–1994). British pioneer of aerial photography in archaeology. He was responsible for the discovery of thousands of previously unknown archaeological sites, and can be said to have redrawn the archaeological map of Britain singlehandedly.

During World War II he was employed by the RAF on the interpretation of aerial photographs, and it was this experience that showed him their potential. He became a lecturer in geology at Cambridge University 1945, and began persuading the university to create a new department devoted to the new discipline of aerial photography. By 1949 he had become the university's first curator of aerial photography, and was appointed director of the department 1962, and professor of air photographic studies 1973. For the first few years the department depended on borrowed access to RAF training flights, until the university purchased its own survey aircraft and employed a professional pilot.

St Joseph pinpointed more than 200 previously unknown forts and marching camps, proving that the Roman general Agricola's raid into Scotland *c.* AD 80 penetrated much further than had been thought. St Joseph also worked over Ireland, Denmark, Holland, N France, SW Germany, and Hungary, and was influential in encouraging archaeologists all over Europe to take to the air. Cambridge University's collection of over 300,000 photographs was made open and accessible, and became an invaluable teaching facility. St Joseph published several books and numerous papers on the subject, including *The Uses of Air Photography* 1966 and *Roman Britain from the Air* 1983, with S S Frere.

Power belongs to the self-possessed.

LOUIS ANTOINE DE SAINT-JUST
to Robespierre when the latter gave way to passion
at a meeting of the Committee of Public Safety

Saint-Just Louis Antoine Léon Florelle de (1767–1794). French revolutionary. A close associate of Robespierre, he became a member of the Committee of Public Safety 1793, and was guillotined with Robespierre.

Elected to the National Convention in 1792, he was its youngest member at 25 and immediately made his mark by a radical speech condemning King Louis XVI ('one cannot reign without guilt'). His later actions confirm the tone of his book *The Spirit of the Revolution* 1791 in which he showed his distrust of the masses and his advocacy of repression. On his appointment to the Committee of Public Safety he was able to carry out his theories by condemning 'not merely traitors, but the indifferent', including Danton and Lavoisier, although his own death was to follow within weeks.

Saint-Laurent Yves Henri Donat Mathieu (1936–). French fashion designer. He has had an exceptional influence on fashion in the second half of the 20th century. He began working for Christian Dior 1955 and succeeded him as designer on Dior's death 1957. He established his own label 1962 and went on to create the first 'power-dressing' looks for men and women: classic, stylish city clothes.

In 1966 Saint-Laurent established a chain of boutiques called Rive Gauche selling his ready-to-wear line. By the 1970s he had popularized a style of women's day wear that was inspired by conventionally 'masculine' garments such as blazers, trousers, and shirts. He launched a menswear collection 1974. He continues to produce tailored, stylish designs, but his main influence was in the 1960s–70s.

Saint-Pierre Jacques Henri Bernadin de (1737–1814). French author. He wrote the sentimental romance *Paul et Virginie* 1789.

Saint-Saëns (Charles) Camille (1835–1921). French composer, pianist and organist. Born in Paris, he studied at the Conservatoire. In 1857 he became organist at the Church of the Madeleine in Paris.

Among his many lyrical Romantic pieces are concertos, the symphonic poem *Danse macabre* 1875, the opera *Samson et Dalila* 1877, and the orchestral *Carnaval des animaux/Carnival of the Animals* 1886.

There are two kinds [of conductors]: one takes the music too fast, and the other too slow. There is no third.

CAMILLE SAINT-SAËNS
quoted in Thomas Beecham *A Mingled Chime* 1944

Saint-Simon (Claude) Henri de Rouvroy, Comte de (1760–1825). French socialist who fought in the American Revolution and was imprisoned during the French Revolution. He advocated an atheist society ruled by technicians and industrialists in *Du système industriel/The Industrial System* 1821.
Suggested reading
Carlisle, Robert *The Proffered Crown* (1988)
Dondo, Mathurin *The French Faust: Henri de Saint-Simon* (1955)
Manuel, Frank *The New World of Henri de Saint-Simon* (1955)

Saint-Simon Louis de Rouvroy, Duc de (1675–1755). French soldier, courtier, and politician. His *Mémoires* 1691–1723 are unrivalled as a description of the French court.

Every day I saw the huge material, intellectual and nervous resources of thousands of people being poured into the creation of a means of total destruction, something capable of annihilating all human civilisation. I noticed that the control levers were in the hands of people who, though talented in their own ways, were cynical.

ANDREI SAKHAROV
Sakharov Speaks 1974

Sakharov Andrei Dmitrievich (1921–1989). Soviet physicist, an outspoken human-rights campaigner who with Igor Tamm (1895–1971) developed the hydrogen bomb. He later protested against Soviet nuclear tests and was a founder of the Soviet Human Rights Committee 1970, winning the Nobel Peace Prize 1975. For criticizing Soviet action in Afghanistan, he was in internal exile 1980–86.

Sakharov was elected to the Congress of the USSR People's Deputies 1989, where he emerged as leader of its radical reform grouping before his death later the same year.

In the early 1960s, Sakharov was instrumental in breaking biologist Trofim Lysenko's hold over Soviet science and in giving science some political immunity. Sakharov's scientific papers in the 1960s concerned the structure of the universe. He also began publicly to argue for a reduction of nuclear arms by all nuclear powers, an increase in international co-operation, and the establishment of civil liberties in Russia. Such books as *Sakharov Speaks* 1974, *My Country and the World* 1975, and *Alarm and Hope* 1979 made him an international figure but also brought harassment from the Soviet authorities.
Suggested reading
Bailey, George *The Making of Andrei Sakharov* (1989)
Bonner, Elena *Alone Together* (a memoir by his wife) (trs 1986)
Lozansky, Edward and Sakharov, Andrei (eds) *Andrei Sakharov and Peace* (1985)
Sakharov, Andrei *Alarm and Hope* (trs 1978)

Saki pen name of H(ector) H(ugh) Munro (1870–1916). Burmese-born British writer. He served with the Military Police in

---

A little inaccuracy sometimes saves tons of explanation.

SAKI
'Comments of Moung Ka'

Burma, and was foreign correspondent of the *Morning Post* 1902–08. He produced ingeniously witty and bizarre short stories, often with surprise endings. He also wrote two novels, *The Unbearable Bassington* 1912 and *When William Came* 1913. He was killed in action on the western front in World War I.

Sakyamuni the historical Buddha, called Shaka in Japan (because Gautama was of the Sakya clan).

Saladin or Sala-ud-din (1138–1193). Born a Kurd, sultan of Egypt from 1175, in succession to the Atabeg of Mosul, on whose behalf he conquered Egypt 1164–74. He subsequently conquered Syria 1174–87 and precipitated the Third Crusade by his recovery of Jerusalem from the Christians 1187. Renowned for knightly courtesy, Saladin made peace with Richard I of England 1192.
Suggested reading
Ehrenkreutz, A *Saladin* (1972)
Lane-Poole, S *Saladin and the Fall of the Kingdom of Jerusalem* (1964)
Newby, P H *Saladin in his Time* (1983)

Ali Asuli writing ... 900 years ago divided his pharmacopeia into ... 'Diseases of the Rich' and 'Diseases of the Poor'.

ABDUS SALAM
Scientific World No 3 1967

Salam Abdus (1926–1996). Pakistani physicist who proposed a theory linking the electromagnetic and weak nuclear forces. In 1979 he became the first person from his country to receive a Nobel prize.
Salam shared the Nobel prize with US physicists Sheldon

Salinger J D Salinger's first and only novel The Catcher in the Rye *1951, which describes an adolescent's rejection of the 'phony' world of adults, soon became a cult classic. In the mid-1960s, by which time he had published three sets of closely related short stories, Salinger became a recluse and published nothing else.*

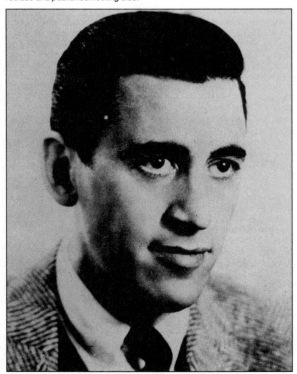

Glashow and Steven Weinberg for unifying the theories of electromagnetism and the weak force, the force responsible for a neutron transforming into a proton, an electron, and a neutrino during radioactive decay. Building on Glashow's work, Salam and Weinberg independently arrived at the same theory 1967.

He attended Government College in Lahore before going to Cambridge University in England. From 1957 he was professor at Imperial College, London, and he was chief scientific adviser to the president of Pakistan 1961–74. Salam was also instrumental in setting up the International Centre for Theoretical Physics in Trieste, Italy, to stimulate science and technology in developing countries.

Personally ascetic, quiet and unambitious, he ruled Portugal firmly, through a corporative system which used the ideas of fascism without its style and insignia.

Alan Palmer on SALAZAR
in *Penguin Dictionary of Twentieth Century History* 1979

Salazar António de Oliveira (1889–1970). Portuguese prime minister 1932–68 who exercised a virtual dictatorship. During World War II he maintained Portuguese neutrality but fought long colonial wars in Africa (Angola and Mozambique) that impeded his country's economic development as well as that of the colonies.
A corporative constitution on the Italian model was introduced 1933, and until 1945 Salazar's National Union, founded 1930, remained the only legal party. Salazar was also foreign minister 1936–47.

Saleh Ali Abdullah (1942–). Yemeni politician and soldier, president from 1990. He became president of North Yemen on the assassination of its president (allegedly by South Yemen extremists) 1978, and was re-elected to the post 1983 and 1988. In 1990 he was elected president of a reunified Yemen, but within three years differences between north and south had resurfaced and civil war re-erupted 1994. Saleh's army inflicted a crushing defeat on the southern forces of Vice President al-Baidh, who fled into exile, and a new ruling coalition was formed.

Salieri Antonio (1750–1825). Italian composer. He taught Beethoven, Schubert, and Liszt, and was the musical rival of Mozart, whom it has been suggested, without proof, that he poisoned, at the emperor's court in Vienna, where he held the position of court composer.

Salinas de Gortari Carlos (1948–). Mexican politician, president 1988–94, a member of the dominant Institutional Revolutionary Party. Educated in Mexico and the USA, he taught at Harvard and in Mexico before joining the government in 1971. He thereafter held a number of posts, mostly in the economic sphere, including finance minister. He narrowly won the 1988 presidential election, despite allegations of fraud. During his presidency he was confronted with problems of drug trafficking and violent crime, including the murder of his nominated successor, Luis Donaldo Colosio, 1994. He went into exile 1995 after his brother Raul was implicated in the assassination of another high-ranking PRI official and held in jail. It was later revealed that his brother had more than $84 million in a Swiss bank account.

Salinger J(erome) D(avid) (1919–). US writer. He wrote the classic novel of mid-20th-century adolescence *The Catcher in the Rye* 1951. He developed his lyrical Zen themes in 'Franny and Zooey' 1961 and 'Raise High the Roof Beam, Carpenters' and 'Seymour: An Introduction' 1963, short stories about a Jewish family named Glass, after which he stopped publishing.
Suggested reading
Hamilton, Ian *In Search of J D Salinger* (1988)
Lundquist, J *J D Salinger* (1978)

Salisbury Harrison E(vans) (1908–1993). US journalist. Moscow correspondent for the *New York Times* 1949–54, he won the Pulitzer Prize for international reporting 1955 for his series Russia Reviewed about the terror under Stalin. He was the first journalist to visit Hanoi during the Vietnam War with a North Vietnam visa and US permission.

Remaining with the *New York Times*, he reported on racial tension in Birmingham, Alabama, 1960. During his 1966 visit to Hanoi he sent eyewitness reports on the US bombing of civilian targets, contributing to the growing movement against the Vietnam War in the USA. His books include *Moscow Journal: The End of Stalin* 1961 and *The 900 Days: The Siege of Leningrad* 1969; *Behind the Lines* 1967, in which he argued that US bombing of North Vietnam would prolong the war; and *Orbit of China* 1967 and *The Long March: The Untold Story* 1986.

Salisbury Robert Cecil, 1st Earl of Salisbury. Title conferred on Robert ◊Cecil, secretary of state to Elizabeth I of England.

Salisbury Robert Arthur Talbot Gascoyne-Cecil, 3rd Marquess of Salisbury (1830–1903). British Conservative politician. He entered the Commons 1853 and succeeded to his title 1868. As foreign secretary 1878–80, he took part in the Congress of Berlin, and as prime minister 1885–86, 1886–92, and 1895–1902 gave his main attention to foreign policy, remaining also as foreign secretary for most of this time. Marquess 1868.

Suggested reading
Kennedy, Aubrey Leo *Salisbury, 1830–1903: Portrait of a Statesman* (1953)
Taylor, Robert *Lord Salisbury* (1975)

Salisbury Robert Arthur James Gascoyne-Cecil, 5th Marquess of Salisbury (1893–1972). British Conservative politician. He was Dominions secretary 1940–42 and 1943–45, colonial secretary 1942, Lord Privy Seal 1942–43 and 1951–52, and Lord President of the Council 1952–57. Baron 1941, marquess 1947.

Salk Jonas Edward (1914–1995). US physician and microbiologist. In 1954 he developed the original vaccine that led to virtual eradication of paralytic polio in industrialized countries.

He began working on virus epidemics in the 1940s. He was director of the Salk Institute for Biological Studies, University of California, San Diego, 1963–75.

Salk set about finding a way of treating the polio virus so that it was unable to cause the disease but was still able to produce an antibody reaction in the human body. He collected samples of spinal cord from many polio victims and grew the virus in a live-cell culture medium, and used formaldehyde (methanol) to render the virus inactive. By 1952 he had produced a vaccine effective against the three strains of polio virus common in the USA; he tested it on monkeys, and later on his own children. In 1955, in a big publicity campaign, some vaccine was prepared without adequate precautions and about 200 cases of polio, with 11 deaths, resulted from the clinical trials. More stringent control prevented further disasters.

Sallinen Tyko Konstantin (1879–1955). Finnish Expressionist painter. Inspired by Fauvism on visits to France 1909 and 1914, he created visionary works relating partly to his childhood experiences of religion. He also painted Finnish landscape and peasant life, such as *Washerwoman* 1911 (Ateneum, Helsinki).

Everyone who wishes to rise above the lower animals should strive his hardest to avoid living all his days in obscurity.

GAIUS SALLUST
Catilinarian Conspiracy preface

Sallust Gaius Sallustius Crispus (86–*c.* 34 BC). Roman historian, a supporter of Julius Caesar. He wrote vivid accounts of Catiline's conspiracy and the Jugurthine War.

Salmond Alex(ander Elliott Anderson) (1954–). Scottish politician, leader of the Scottish National Party (SNP) from 1990. He joined the SNP and in 1987 was elected to the House of Commons, representing Banff and Buchan. He became SNP leader 1990 and,

through his ability to project a moderate image, did much to improve his party's credibility, even though its proposals to make Scotland an independent member of the European Union (EU) went far beyond the limits of what the majority of Sottish electors would support.

Harmony makes small things grow; lack of it makes great things decay.

GAIUS SALLUST
Jugurthine Wars ch 10.6

Salmond John Maitland (1881–1968). British air marshal in World War I. After service in the South African War 1901–02, he learned to fly at his own expense and joined the Royal Flying Corps 1912 as an instructor. Promoted to major-general 1918 he transferred to the Royal Air Force, became air vice-marshal, and was knighted 1919. In 1918 he succeeded Air Marshal Trenchard as commander of the Independent Air Force in France and was responsible for much of the strategic bombing campaign that followed.

Salome (lived 1st century AD). In the New Testament, granddaughter of the king of Judea, Herod the Great. Rewarded for her skill in dancing, she requested the head of John the Baptist from her stepfather Herod Antipas.

Salomon Haym (*c.* 1740–1785). Polish-born American financier. Salomon travelled extensively throughout Europe before settling permanently in New York 1772 where he became a successful merchant. A supporter of American independence, he supplied provisions to the Continental troops during the American Revolution 1861–65. Accused of being a spy by the British 1776, he was briefly arrested and was captured and sentenced to death 1778. After escaping, he raised large public subscriptions for the continuance of the war.

Salk US microbiologist and immunologist Jonas Edward Salk, developer of the first successful polio vaccine, shown at a World Health Organization conference 1962. Salk's vaccine was first administered during a trial 1954 and was found to be 80–90% effective. By the end of 1955, over 7 million people had been innoculated. (WHO/Jean Mohr/Image Select)

Salonen Esa-Pekka (1958–   ). Finnish conductor and composer. He studied French horn, and made his UK conducting debut 1983 with the London Philharmonia Orchestra. Appointed chief conductor of the Swedish Radio Symphony Orchestra 1985, he became music director of the Los Angeles Philharmonic Orchestra 1992.

Salonen made the first recording of Lutoslawski's Symphony No 3 1986. His hard-edged, relentless style has been compared to that of conductor Pierre Boulez. His compositions include *Horn Music I* 1976 and Concerto for Saxophone and Orchestra 1980.

Salzedo Carlos (1885–1961). French-born harpist and composer. He studied in Paris and moved to New York, where he cofounded the International Composers' Guild. He did much to promote the harp as a concert instrument, and invented many unusual sounds.

Samaranch Juan Antonio, Marquis of (1920–   ). Spanish president of the International Olympic Committee (IOC) from 1980. He was responsible for transforming the amateur Olympic Games by allowing professional athletes to take part.

Samaranch was a roller-hockey player in the 1940s, became a banker and property developer, and financed the world roller-hockey championships in Barcelona 1951. A member of the Spanish Olympic Committee from 1954, he became a member of the IOC 1966. He was sports minister 1966–70 and ambassador to the USSR 1977–80. The Los Angeles Olympic Games 1984 were the first to be financed through corporate sponsorship rather than with government money and from then on there were many bids from cities wanting to host the Games.

Re-elected 1989 and 1993, Samaranch opened the Olympic Museum in Lausanne, Switzerland, 1993, near the headquarters of the IOC. He was created Marquis of Samaranch 1992.

Sampras Pete (1971–   ). US tennis player, winner of Wimbledon for three consecutive years. At the age of 19 years and 28 days, he became the youngest winner of the US Open 1990. A fine server and volleyer, Sampras also won the inaugural Grand Slam Cup in Munich 1990.

Samson (lived 11th century BC). In the Old Testament, a hero of Israel. He was renowned for exploits of strength against the Philistines, which ended when his lover Delilah had his hair, the source of his strength, cut off, as told in the Book of Judges.

Samsonov Aleksandr Vassilievich (1859–1914). Russian general. He joined the cavalry 1875, served in the Russo-Turkish war, became a general 1902 and commanded a Siberian Cossack brigade in the Russo-Japanese war 1905. In 1914 he was given command of the Army of the Narev and invaded E Prussia. After some initial victories and advancing as far as Allenstein (now Olzstyn, Poland), he was completely defeated at Tannenberg and committed suicide 31 Aug 1914.

Samuel (lived 11th century BC). In the Old Testament, the last of the judges who ruled the ancient Hebrews before their adoption of a monarchy, and the first of the prophets; the two books bearing his name cover the story of Samuel and the reigns of kings Saul and David.

Man does not live by GNP alone.
PAUL SAMUELSON
Economics 1948

Samuelson Paul Anthony (1915–   ). US economist, awarded a Nobel prize 1970 for his application of scientific analysis to economic theory. His books include *Economics* 1948, a classic textbook, and *Linear Programming and Economic Analysis* 1958. He became professor at the Massachusetts Institute of Technology 1940.

Sanctorius Sanctorius (1561–1636). Italian physiologist who pioneered the study of metabolism and invented the clinical thermometer and a device for measuring pulse rate.

Sanctorius introduced quantitative methods into medicine. For 30 years he weighed both himself and his food, drink, and waste products. He determined that over half of normal weight loss is due to 'insensible perspiration'.

What constitutes adultery is not the hour which a woman gives her lover, but the night which she afterwards spends with her husband.
GEORGE SAND
Attributed remark

Sand George. Pen name of Amandine Aurore Lucie Dupin (1804–1876). French author. Her prolific literary output was often autobiographical. In 1831 she left her husband after nine years of marriage and, while living in Paris as a writer, had love affairs with Alfred de Musset, Chopin, and others. Her first novel *Indiana* 1832 was a plea for women's right to independence. Her other novels include *la Mare au diable/The Devil's Pool* 1846 and *la Petite Fadette/The Little Fairy* 1848. In 1848 she retired to the château of Nohant, in central France.

Poetry is the opening and closing of a door, leaving those who look through to guess about what is seen during a moment.
CARL SANDBURG
'Poetry Considered'

Sandburg Carl August (1878–1967). US poet. He worked as a farm labourer and a bricklayer, and his poetry celebrates ordinary life in the USA, as in *Chicago Poems* 1916, *The People, Yes* 1936, and *Complete Poems* 1950 (Pulitzer prize). In free verse, it is reminiscent of Walt Whitman's poetry. Sandburg also wrote a monumental biography of Abraham Lincoln, *Abraham Lincoln: The Prairie Years* 1926 (two volumes) and *Abraham Lincoln: The War Years* 1939 (four volumes; Pulitzer prize). *Always the Young Strangers* 1953 is his autobiography.

Sandby Paul (1725–1809). English painter. He is often called 'the father of English watercolour'. He specialized in Classical landscapes, using both watercolour and gouache, and introduced the technique of aquatint to England.

Sandby was born in Nottingham. He and his brother, Thomas Sandby (1721–98), came to London 1742, being employed in the Military Drawing Office in the Tower of London. Paul was a draughtsperson in the survey of the Highlands that followed the 45 rebellion, and stayed in Scotland some years, making drawings and etchings of Scottish scenery and character. Subsequently he often stayed at Windsor with his brother, who was appointed Deputy Ranger of Windsor Forest, and some of his best work (Royal Collection) is of Windsor Castle and its environs. He also travelled widely in Britain, being one of the first to depict the beauties of Welsh scenery. His landscapes in gouache and watercolour have a great 18th-century charm. He was a founder member of the Royal Academy 1768. The romantic features in his paintings, such as ruined castles and stormy skies, paved the way for the full-bodied romanticism of Girtin and Turner. His brother was an architectural draughtsperson of some merit.

Sander August (1876–1964). German portrait photographer. His long-term project was to create a vast composite portrait, *Man of the Twentieth Century*. Concentrating on German society, he turned his dispassionate gaze on every walk of life – from butchers to bankers – in a way that combined the individual with the archetypal. Much of his work was destroyed when his Cologne studio was bombed 1944.

Sanders George (1906–1972). Russian-born British actor. He was often cast as a smooth-talking cad. Most of his film career was spent in the USA where he starred in such films as *Rebecca* 1940, *The Moon and Sixpence* 1942, *The Picture of Dorian Gray* 1944, and *All About Eve* 1950 (Academy Award for best supporting actor).

During World War II he played the maverick detectives 'The Saint' and 'The Falcon' in a series of films.

I was beastly but never coarse. A high-class sort of heel.
GEORGE SANDERS
quoted in Leslie Halliwell *Filmgoer's Companion* 1965

Sándor György (1912–). Hungarian-born US pianist. He is renowned for his performances and recordings of works by Prokofiev and Bartók (who was his teacher). He has transcribed for piano *L'Apprenti sorcier/The Sorcerer's Apprentice* by Dukas.

I'll be at your Board, when at leisure from cricket.
JOHN MONTAGU, 4TH EARL OF SANDWICH
Message to the First Lord of the Admiralty on his appointment
as a Lord Commissioner of the Admiralty June 1745

Sandwich John Montagu, 4th Earl of Sandwich (1718–1792). British politician. He was an inept First Lord of the Admiralty 1771–82 during the American Revolution, and his corrupt practices were blamed for the British navy's inadequacies. Earl 1729.

The Sandwich Islands (Hawaii) were named after him, as are sandwiches, which he invented so that he could eat without leaving the gaming table.

Sandys (Edwin) Duncan, Baron Duncan-Sandys (1908–1987). British Conservative politician. As minister for Commonwealth relations 1960–64, he negotiated the independence of Malaysia 1963. Baron 1974.

Sangallo Antonio Giamberti da, (the Younger) (c. 1483–1546). Florentine High Renaissance architect. He worked under Bramante and Peruzzi in Rome. His masterpiece is the monumental Palazzo Farnese, Rome (begun 1513, completed by Michelangelo). Sangallo took over as chief architect of St Peter's 1539 and expanded on Bramante's original plan, but it was left to Michelangelo, his successor, to make the building a convincing whole.

Sanger Frederick (1918–). English biochemist, the first person to win a Nobel Prize for Chemistry twice: the first in 1958 for determining the structure of insulin, and the second in 1980 for work on the chemical structure of genes.

Sanger's second Nobel prize was shared with two US scientists, Paul Berg and Walter Gilbert, for establishing methods of determining the sequence of nucleotides strung together along strands of RNA and DNA. He also worked out the structures of various enzymes and other proteins.

Sanger was born in Gloucestershire and studied at Cambridge, where he spent his whole career. In 1961 he became head of the Protein Chemistry Division of the Medical Research Council's Molecular Biology Laboratory.

Between 1943 and 1953, Sanger and his co-workers determined the sequence of 51 amino acids in the insulin molecule. By 1945 he had discovered a compound, Sanger's reagent (2,4-dinitrofluorobenzene), which attaches itself to amino acids, and this enabled him to break the protein chain into smaller pieces and analyse them using paper chromatography.

From the late 1950s, Sanger worked on genetic material, and in 1977 he and his co-workers announced that they had established the sequence of the more than 5,000 nucleotides along a strand of RNA from a bacterial virus called R17. They later worked out the order for mitochondrial DNA, which has approximately 17,000 nucleotides.

Sanger Margaret Louise (born Higgins) (1883–1966). US health reformer and crusader for birth control. As a nurse, she saw the deaths and deformity caused by self-induced abortions and became committed to providing health and birth-control education to the poor. In 1914 she founded the National Birth Control League. In 1917 she was briefly sent to prison for opening a public birth-control clinic in Brooklyn 1916. She founded and presided over the American Birth Control League 1921–28, the organization that later became the Planned Parenthood Federation of America, and the International Planned Parenthood Federation 1952. Her *Autobiography* appeared 1938.

San Martín José de (1778–1850). South American revolutionary leader. He served in the Spanish army during the Peninsular War, but after 1812 he devoted himself to the South American struggle for independence, playing a large part in the liberation of Argentina, Chile, and Peru from Spanish rule.

Sansovino Jacopo (born Tatti) (1486–1570). Florentine Renaissance architect and sculptor. He studied and began his career in Rome but fled after the sack of the city 1527 to Venice, where most of his major works are found. Notable are the Loggetta in St Mark's Square 1537–40 and the richly decorated Library and Mint opposite the Doge's Palace 1537–45. Palladio was greatly influenced by his work.

Santa Anna Antonio López de (c. 1795–1876). Mexican revolutionary who became general and dictator of Mexico for most of the years between 1824 and 1855. He led the attack on the Alamo fort in Texas 1836.

A leader in achieving independence from Spain in 1821, he pursued a chequered career of victory and defeat and was in and out of office as president or dictator for the rest of his life.

Santa Cruz Andrés (1792–1865). President of Bolivia 1829–34, 1839, 1841–44, and 1853–55. Strong-willed and conservative, he dabbled in political intrigue before and after his intermittent rule as dictator. He established order in the new state and increased expenditure on education and road building.

Santa Cruz was made a grand marshal after his part in the Battles of Junín and Ayacucho which brought about the independence of Peru 1824. Two years later Simón Bolívar named him president of Peru's council of ministers, but the Peruvian congress rejected him. As president, he formed the Peru-Bolivian Confederation 1836 but its economic and strategic power threatened Chile and Argentina who forced its break-up 1839.

Santayana George (born Jorge Augustín Nicolás Ruiz de Santayana) (1863–1952). Spanish-born US philosopher and critic. He developed his philosophy based on naturalism and taught that everything has a natural basis.

Born in Madrid, Santayana grew up in Spain and the USA and graduated from Harvard University. He taught at Harvard 1889–1912. His books include *The Life of Reason* 1905–06, *Skepticism and Animal Faith* 1923, *The Realm of Truth* 1937, *Background of My Life* 1945; volumes of poetry; and the best-selling novel *The Last Puritan* 1935.

Sant'Elia Antonio (1888–1916). Italian architect. His drawings convey a Futurist vision of a metropolis with skyscrapers, traffic lanes, and streamlined factories.

Santer Jacques (1937–). Luxembourg politician, prime minister 1984–94. In Jan 1995 he succeeded Jacques Delors as president of the European Commission.

The manner of his selection as European Commission president, as a compromise alternative to the rejected Belgian prime minister, Jean-Luc Dehaene, weakened his standing as a worthy successor to Delors. However, Santer made a personal appeal to the newly-elected European Parliament, of which he had been a member 1975–79, claiming that his aspirations for closer European union were at least as strong as those of Dehaene.

Sānusī Sidi Muhammad ibn 'Ali as- (c. 1787–1859). Algerian-born Muslim religious reformer. He preached a return to the puritanism of early Islam and met with much success in Libya, where he founded the sect named after him. He made Jaghbub his centre.

San Yu (1919–). Myanmar (Burmese) politician, president 1981–88. A member of the Revolutionary Council that came to power 1962, he became president 1981 and was re-elected 1985. He was forced to resign July 1988, along with Ne Win, after riots in Yangon (formerly Rangoon).

Sapir Edward (1884–1939). German-born US language scholar and anthropologist who initially studied the Germanic languages but later, under the influence of Franz Boas, investigated indigenous

American languages. He is noted for the view now known as linguistic relativity: that people's ways of thinking are significantly shaped (and even limited) by the language(s) they use. His main work is *Language: An Introduction to the Study of Speech* 1921.

Sapper pen name of (Herman) Cyril McNeile (1888–1937). British author of the adventure story *Bulldog Drummond* 1920 and its sequels; he was a lieutenant-colonel in the Royal Engineers until 1919.

Some say a formation of horseman, infantry, / or ships is the loveliest thing on the black / earth, but I maintain it is whatever / a person loves.

SAPPHO OF MYTILENE
fragment 16: 1–4

Sappho (*c*. 610–*c*. 580 BC). Greek lyric poet. A native of Lesbos and contemporary of the poet Alcaeus, she was famed for her female eroticism (hence lesbianism). The surviving fragments of her poems express a keen sense of loss, and delight in the worship of the goddess Aphrodite.

Sarazen Gene (Eugene) (1902–). US golfer. He won the first of his two US open titles in 1922 at the age of 20 and a couple of months later added the US PGA title, which he retained the following year. He won the British Open in 1932 and the Masters in 1935, when he became the first person to complete a 'set' of major titles.

Sardou Victorien (1831–1908). French dramatist. He was a leading exponent of the 'well-made' play. He wrote plays with roles for Sarah Bernhardt – for example, *Fédora* 1882 and *La Tosca* 1887 (the basis for the opera by Puccini). George Bernard Shaw coined the expression 'Sardoodledom' to express his disgust with Sardou's contrived dramatic technique.

Sargent (Harold) Malcolm (Watts) (1895–1967). English conductor. He was professor at the Royal College of Music from 1923, chief conductor of the BBC Symphony Orchestra 1950–57, and continued as conductor in chief of the annual Henry Wood promenade concerts at the Royal Albert Hall.

He championed Vaughan Williams and Holst and conducted the first performances of Walton's oratorio *Belshazzar's Feast* 1931 and opera *Troilus and Cressida* 1954. Knighted 1947.
Suggested reading
Reid, Charles *Malcolm Sargent* (1968)

Every time I paint a portrait I lose a friend.

JOHN SINGER SARGENT
quoted in N Bentley and E Esar *Treasury of Humorous Quotations* 1951

Sargent John Singer (1856–1925). US portrait painter. Born in Florence of American parents, he studied there and in Paris, then settled in London around 1885.

He quickly became a successful society portrait painter, though not in the sense that he flattered: he brilliantly depicted a type of society, and Anglo-American society in general. His paintings of the Wertheimer family (Tate Gallery) constitute a remarkable family record, and for 25 years he portrayed a long series of celebrities, including Roosevelt, Rockefeller, Chamberlain, Ellen Terry, and many others. In various ways he reacted against the demands of portraiture: in the much criticized murals for the Boston Library, 1890; in his war pictures, for example *Gassed*, 1920 (Imperial War Museum); and in the watercolours in which after 1910 he found his main pleasure, his views of Venice in this medium being notable works. He may most readily be compared in portraiture with British artists, especially Sir Thomas Lawrence. The superficiality of which he is often accused may also be said to be that of the society he depicted, and he remains one of the outstanding recorders of an age.
Suggested reading
Hills, Patricia *John Singer Sargent* (1986)
Mount, Charles Merrill *John Singer Sargent* (1969)

Lubin, David *Act of Portrayal: Eakins, Sargent, James* (1985)
Olson, Stanley *John Singer Sargent: His Portrait* (1986)
Ormond, Richard *John Singer Sargent* (1970)

Sargeson Frank. Pen name of Norris Frank Davey (1903–1982). New Zealand writer. His work includes short stories and novels, such as *The Hangover* 1967 and *Man of England Now* 1972.
Suggested reading
Rhodes, H Winston *Frank Sargeson* (1969)
Sargeson, Frank *Once is Enough* (autobiography) (1973)
Sargeson, Frank *More Than Enough* (autobiography) (1975)
Sargeson, Frank *Never Enough!* (autobiography) (1977)

Sargon two Mesopotamian kings:

Sargon I king of Akkad *c*. 2334–*c*. 2279 BC, and founder of the first Mesopotamian empire. Like Moses, he was said to have been found floating in a cradle on the local river, in his case the Euphrates.

Sargon II (died 705). King of Assyria from 722 BC, who assumed the name of his predecessor. To keep conquered peoples from rising against him, he had whole populations moved from their homelands, including the Israelites from Samaria.

Sarmiento Domingo Faustino (1811–1888). Argentina's first civilian president 1868–74, regarded as one of the most brilliant Argentines of the 19th century. An outspoken critic of the dictator Juan Manuel de Rosas, Sarmiento spent many years in exile. As president, he doubled the number of schools, creating the best education system in Latin America, and encouraged the establishment of libraries and museums. He also expanded trade, extended railroad building, and encouraged immigration.

Sarney (Costa) José (1930–). Brazilian politician, member of the centre-left Democratic Movement, president 1985–90. Sarney was elected vice president 1985 and within months, on the death of President Neves, became head of state. Despite earlier involvement with the repressive military regime, he and his party won a convincing victory in the 1986 general election. In Dec 1989, Ferdinando Collor de Mello of the Party for National Reconstruction was elected to succeed Sarney in March 1990.

Sarnoff David (1891–1971). Russian-born US broadcasting pioneer, head of the Radio Corporation of America (RCA) from 1930. A telegraph operator for Marconi Wireless from 1906, he became commercial manager of the company when it was taken over by RCA 1919. Named RCA president 1930 and board chair 1947, Sarnoff was an early promoter of TV broadcasting during the 1940s and the first to manufacture colour sets and transmit colour programmes in the 1950s.

Saro-Wiwa Ken (1931–1995). Nigerian writer, environmentalist, and political leader of the Ogoni people. He was imprisoned 1994 for his political activity and, despite widespread international opposition and condemnation, was executed by the military leadership Nov 1995. Saro-Wiwa's works include the book *On a Darkling Plain*, about the Biafran civil war, and the script for a popular television comedy series. In 1994 he won the international Right Livelihood Award for his work for the Ogoni.

Saroyan William (1908–1981). US author. He wrote short stories, such as 'The Daring Young Man on the Flying Trapeze' 1934, idealizing the hopes and sentiments of the 'little man'. His plays, preaching a gospel of euphoric enjoyment, include *The Time of Your Life* (Pulitzer prize; refused) 1939, about eccentricity; *My Heart's in the Highlands* 1939, about an uplifting bugle-player; *Love's Old Sweet Song* 1941, and *Talking to You* 1962. He published three volumes of autobiography, including *Obituaries* 1979.

Sarrail Maurice Paul Emmanuel (1856–1929). French general. He was appointed commander of the Army of the Orient, the French element in the Salonika expedition, Aug 1915 and became commander in chief of the Allied forces in Salonika Jan 1916. He made little impression in this role and was replaced 1917, then placed on the reserve early 1918.

Sarraute Nathalie Ilyanova (born Tchernik) (1900–). Russian-born French novelist. Her books include *Portrait d'un inconnu/Portrait of a Man Unknown* 1948, *Les Fruits d'or/The Golden Fruits* 1964, and *Vous les entendez?/Do You Hear Them?* 1972. An exponent of the *nouveau roman*, Sarraute bypasses plot, character, and style for the half-conscious interaction of minds.

Sartre Jean-Paul (1905–1980). French author and philosopher, a leading proponent of existentialism. He published his first novel, *La Nausée/Nausea*, 1937, followed by the trilogy *Les Chemins de la Liberté/Roads to Freedom* 1944–45 and many plays, including *Huis Clos/In Camera* 1944. In the later work *Critique de la raison dialectique/Critique of Dialectical Reason* 1960 he tried to produce a fusion of existentialism and Marxism.

Sartre was born in Paris, and was the long-time companion of the feminist writer Simone de Beauvoir. During World War II he was a prisoner for nine months, and on his return from Germany joined the Resistance. As a founder of existentialism, he edited its journal *Les Temps modernes/Modern Times*, and expressed its tenets in his novels and plays. According to Sartre, people's awareness of their own freedom takes the form of anxiety, and they therefore attempt to flee from this awareness into what he terms *mauvaise foi* ('bad faith'); this is the theory he put forward in *L'Etre et le néant/Being and Nothingness*. In *Crime passionel/Crime of Passion* 1948 he attacked aspects of communism while remaining generally sympathetic. In his later work Sartre became more sensitive to the social constraints on people's actions. He refused the Nobel Prize for Literature 1964 for 'personal reasons', but allegedly changed his mind later, saying he wanted it for the money.

Suggested reading
Cohen-Solal, Annie *Sartre: A Life* (trs 1987)
Danto, Arthur C *Sartre* (1975)
Grene, Marjorie *Sartre* (1983)
Hayman, Ronald *Writing Against: A Biography of Sartre* (1986)
Murdoch, Iris *Sartre: Romantic Rationalist* (1987)
Sartre, Jean Paul *Words* (autobiography) (trs 1964)

Sassou-Nguesso Denis (1943–). Congolese socialist politician, president 1979–92. He progressively consolidated his position within the ruling left-wing Congolese Labour Party (PCT), at the same time as improving relations with France and the USA. In 1990, in response to public pressure, he agreed that the PCT should abandon Marxism–Leninism and that a multiparty system should be introduced.

Sassetta Stefano di Giovanni (*c.* 1392–1450). Sienese painter. His work remained true to the International Gothic style of the 14th-century Sienese school, while reflecting contemporary discoveries in spatial representation by Florentine artists. His major work, a masterpiece of devotional art, was the altarpiece for San Francesco in Sansepolcro 1437–44 (Villa i Tatti, Florence/National Gallery, London/Louvre, Paris).

Sassoon Siegfried Loraine (1886–1967). English writer. He wrote the autobiography *Memoirs of a Foxhunting Man* 1928. Educated at Cambridge, Sassoon enlisted in the army 1915, serving in France and Palestine. His *War Poems* 1919 express the disillusionment of his generation. He published many volumes of poetry and three volumes of childhood autobiography, *The Old Century and Seven More Years* 1938, *The Weald of Youth* 1942, and *Siegfried's Journey* 1945. He wrote a biography of the novelist George Meredith 1948 and published *Collected Poems* 1961.

Sassoon Vidal (1928–). English hairdresser. He was patronized by pop stars and models from the early 1950s. He created many new hairstyles, including the shape 1959, a layered cut tailored to the bone structure – a radical change from the beehive hairstyles of the 1950s. He stopped cutting 1974.

Satie Erik Alfred Leslie (1866–1925). French composer. His piano pieces, such as the three *Gymnopédies* 1888, are precise and tinged with melancholy, and parody romantic expression with surreal commentary. His aesthetic of ironic simplicity, as in the *Messe des pauvres/Poor People's Mass* 1895, acted as a nationalist antidote to the perceived excesses of German Romanticism.

Mentor of the group of composers *Les Six*, he promoted the concept of *musique d'ameublement* ('furniture music'), anticipating the impact of radio. His *Parade* for orchestra 1917 includes a typewriter, and he invented a new style of film music for René Clair's *Entr'acte* 1924.

Suggested reading
Gillmor, A M *Erik Satie* (1988)
Harding, James *Erik Satie* (1971)
Harding, James *The Ox on the Roof: Scenes from Musical Life in Paris in the Twenties* (1972)
Volta, O (ed) *Satie: His World Through His Letters* (1989)

Satō Eisaku (1901–1975). Japanese conservative politician, prime minister 1964–72. He ran against Hayato Ikeda (1899–1965) for the Liberal Democratic Party leadership and succeeded him as prime minister, pledged to a more independent foreign policy. He shared a Nobel Prize for Peace in 1974 for his rejection of nuclear weapons. His brother Nobosuke Kishi (1896–1987) was prime minister of Japan 1957–60.

Saul (lived 11th century BC). in the Old Testament, the first king of Israel. He was anointed by Samuel and warred successfully against the neighbouring Ammonites and Philistines, but fell from God's favour in his battle against the Amalekites. He became jealous and suspicious of David and turned against him and Samuel. After being wounded in battle with the Philistines, in which his three sons died, he committed suicide.

Saunders Cicely Mary Strode (1918–). English philanthropist, founder of the hospice movement, which aims to provide a caring and comfortable environment in which people with terminal illnesses can die. She was the medical director of St Christopher's Hospice in Sydenham, S London, 1967–85, and later became its chair. She wrote *Care of the Dying* 1960. DBE 1980.

Saunders Clarence (1881–1953). US retailer who opened the first self-service supermarket, Piggly-Wiggly, in Memphis, Tennessee, 1919.

Saussure Ferdinand de (1857–1913). Swiss language scholar, a pioneer of modern linguistics and the originator of the concept of structuralism as used in linguistics, anthropology, and literary theory.

He taught at the universities of Paris and Geneva. His early work, on the Indo-European language family, led to a major treatise on its vowel system. *Cours de linguistique générale/Course in General Linguistics* 1916 was posthumously derived mainly from his lecture notes by his students Charles Bally and Albert Séchehaye.

Saussurean concepts include: (1) language seen as both a unified and shared social system (*langue*) and as individual and idiosyncratic speech (*parole*); (2) language described in synchronic terms (as a system at a particular time) and in diachronic terms (as changing through time).

Saussure Horace Bénédict de (1740–1799). Swiss geologist who made the earliest detailed and first-hand study of the Alps. He was a physicist at the University of Geneva. The results of his Alpine survey appeared in his classic work *Voyages des Alpes/Travels in the Alps* 1779–86.

Savage Michael Joseph (1872–1940). New Zealand Labour politician. As prime minister 1935–40, he introduced much social-security legislation.

Savalas Telly (Aristotle) (1926–1994). US actor who played the title role in the TV police series *Kojak* 1973–78. He made the hard-bitten but socially conscious Lieutenant Kojak one of television's most distinctive cop heroes. He had previously played many film roles as villains, including *Birdman of Alcatraz* 1962 and *The Dirty Dozen* 1967. His trademark was a shaven head.

Savery Thomas (*c.* 1650–1715). British engineer who invented the steam-driven water pump 1696. It was the world's first working steam engine, though the boiler was heated by an open fire.

The pump used a boiler to raise steam, which was condensed (in a separate condenser) by an external spray of cold water. The partial vacuum created sucked water up a pipe; steam pressure was then used to force the water away, after which the cycle was repeated. Savery patented his invention 1698, but it appears that poor-quality work and materials made his engines impractical.

Savery was born in Devon. His first patent was in 1696 for a machine for cutting, grinding, and polishing mirror glass. He also invented a mechanism for measuring the distance sailed by a ship. From 1705 to 1714 he was treasurer for Sick and Wounded Seamen. In 1714 he was appointed surveyor of the waterworks at Hampton Court and he designed a pumping system, driven by a water wheel, for supplying the fountains.

His pump was called the Miner's Friend and was intended to raise water from mines, but there are no records of any engines being installed in mines. An engine built at York Buildings waterworks had continuous problems with blowing steam joints.

Savimbi Jonas Malheiro (1934–). Angolan soldier and right-wing revolutionary.

The struggle for independence from Portugal escalated 1961 into a civil war. In 1966 Savimbi founded the right-wing National Union for the Total Independence of Angola (UNITA), which he led against the left-wing People's Movement for the Liberation of Angola (MPLA), led by Agostinho Neto. Neto, with Soviet and Cuban support, became president when independence was achieved 1975, while UNITA, assisted by South Africa, continued its fight. A cease-fire was agreed June 1989, but fighting continued, and the truce was abandoned after two months. A further truce was signed May 1991. Civil war re-erupted Sept 1992 following an election victory for the ruling party, a result which Savimbi disputed. Representatives of UNITA and the government signed a peace agreement 1994. Savimbi subsequently agreed to accept the post of vice president.

Savonarola Girolamo (1452–1498). Italian reformer, a Dominican friar and an eloquent preacher. His crusade against political and religious corruption won him popular support, and in 1494 he led a revolt in Florence that expelled the ruling Medici family and established a democratic republic. His denunciations of Pope Alexander VI led to his excommunication in 1497, and in 1498 he was arrested, tortured, hanged, and burned for heresy.
Suggested reading
Cronin, Vincent *The Florentine Renaissance* (1967)
Ridolfi, Roberto *Life of Girolamo Savonarola* (trs 1959)
Weinstein, Donald *Savonarola and Florence* (1970)

Sawchuk Terry (Terrance Gordon) (1929–1970). Canadian ice-hockey player, often considered the greatest goaltender of all time. He played for Detroit, Boston, Toronto, Los Angeles, and New York Rangers 1950–67, and holds the National Hockey League (NHL) record of 103 shut-outs (games in which he did not concede a goal).

Saw Maung (1929–). Myanmar (Burmese) soldier and politician. Appointed head of the armed forces in 1985 by Ne Win, he led a coup to remove Ne Win's successor, Maung Maung, in 1988 and became leader of a totalitarian 'emergency government', which remained in office despite being defeated in the May 1990 election. In April 1992 he was replaced as chair of the ruling military junta, prime minister, and commander of the armed forces by Than Shwe.

Saxe (Hermann) Maurice, Comte de (1696–1750). Soldier, illegitimate son of the Elector of Saxony, who served under Prince Eugène of Savoy and was created marshal of France in 1743 for his exploits in the War of the Austrian Succession.

Saxe-Coburg-Gotha Saxon duchy. Albert, the Prince Consort of Britain's Queen Victoria, was a son of the 1st Duke, Ernest I (1784–1844), who was succeeded by Albert's elder brother, Ernest II (1818–1893). It remained the name of the British royal house until 1917, when it was changed to Windsor.

Saxe-Weimar-Eisenach Duchess of. Title of Anna ◊Amalia, patron of German literature.

As I grow older and older, / And totter towards the tomb, / I find that I care less and less / Who goes to bed with whom.
DOROTHY SAYERS
'That's Why I Never Read Modern Novels'

Sayers Dorothy L(eigh) (1893–1957). English writer of crime novels. Her stories feature the detective Lord Peter Wimsey and the heroine Harriet Vane, and include *Strong Poison* 1930, *The Nine Tailors* 1934, and *Gaudy Night* 1935. She also wrote religious plays for radio, and translations of Dante.

Scalia Antonin (1936–). US jurist and associate justice of the US Supreme Court 1986– . From 1971 he worked as a lawyer in the executive branch of the federal government, ultimately becoming assistant attorney general 1974, where he advised the Gerald Ford White House in the Watergate scandal. He concurred with the majority in *Texas* v *Johnson* 1989, that ruled constitutional the burning of the US flag in protest. He dissented in *Edwards* v *Aguillard* 1987 when the Court ruled that states may not mandate the teaching of the theory of creationism to counteract the teaching of the theory of evolution.

Only a fool wants a confrontation and only a fool wants a strike.
ARTHUR SCARGILL
quoted in *Observer* 6 Nov 1977

Scargill Arthur (1938–). British trade-union leader. Scargill became a miner on leaving school and was soon a union and political activist, in the Young Communist League 1955–62, and then a member of the Labour Party from 1966 and president of the Yorkshire miners' union 1973–81. He became a fiery and effective orator. Elected president of the National Union of Miners (NUM) 1981, he embarked on a collision course with the Conservative government of Margaret Thatcher. The damaging strike of 1984–85 split the miners' movement. During the 1984–85 miners' strike he was criticized for not seeking an early NUM ballot to support the strike decision. In 1990 an independent inquiry, commissioned by the NUM, found him guilty of breach of duty and maintaining double accounts during the strike. In 1995, criticizing what he saw as the Labour party's lurch to the right, he announced that he would establish a rival, independent party.

This son of mine is an eagle whose wings are grown; he ought not to stay idle in the nest and I ought not to hinder his flight.
ALESSANDRO SCARLATTI
on Domenico Scarlatti, to Ferdinand de' Medici, 1705

Scarlatti (Giuseppe) Domenico (1685–1757). Italian composer. The eldest son of Alessandro Scarlatti, he lived most of his life in Portugal and Spain in the service of the Queen of Spain. He wrote over 500 sonatas for harpsichord, short pieces in binary form demonstrating the new freedoms of keyboard composition and inspired by Spanish musical idioms.
Suggested reading
Kirkpatrick, Ralph *Domenico Scarlatti* (1955)
Sitwell, S *A Background for Domenico Scarlatti* (1935)

Scarlatti (Pietro) Alessandro (Gaspare) (1660–1725). Italian Baroque composer. He was maestro di capella at the court of Naples and developed the opera form. He composed more than 100 operas, including *Tigrane* 1715, as well as church music and oratorios.
Suggested reading
Anderson, Nicholas *Baroque Music: From Monteverdi to Handel* (1994)

Dent, Edward *Alessandro Scarlatti: His Life and Works* (1959)
Grout, Donald *Alessandro Scarlatti* (1979)

Scarman Leslie George, Baron Scarman (1911–). English judge and legal reformer. A successful barrister, he was a High Court judge 1961–73 and an appeal-court judge 1973–77, prior to becoming a law lord. He gradually shifted from a traditional position to a more reformist one, calling for liberalization of divorce laws 1965 and campaigning for a bill of rights 1974. As chair of the inquiry into the Brixton riots 1981, he proposed positive discrimination in favour of black people. He campaigned for the release of the Birmingham Six and the Guildford Four. Knighted 1961, baron 1977.

Scarpa Carlo (1906–1978). Italian architect. His emphasis on craftsmanship and fine detail shows the influence of the Art Nouveau tradition. His works include the restoration of the Castelvecchio Museum, Verona, 1964, which displays both reverence for, and an inventive dialogue with, the past and the artworks displayed. His other projects include the Brion Cemetery at San Vito d'Altivole, near Treviso, 1970–72, and the Banco Popolare, Verona, 1973–75, his last major work.

Scharoun Hans Bernhard (1893–1972). German architect. He was one of the greatest 20th-century exponents of the organic tradition in architecture. The concert hall for the Berlin Philharmonic Orchestra, completed 1963, is the most dramatic expression of his ideas on organic design, integrating audience and orchestra on various levels.

Scharoun studied architecture at Berlin Technical College 1912–14, later becoming associated with the influential Deutscher Werkbund movement, which called for high standards in industrial design. His first major project was the Schminke House, Lobau, Saxony 1932–33, notable for the lightness of its exposed steel-frame structure. The rise to power of the Nazis brought his career to a temporary halt but he was involved in plans for the rebuilding of Berlin 1946, and subsequently produced many influential competition designs. Other postwar works of note are the Maritime Museum, Berlin, 1970, and the National Library, Berlin, 1978.

Scheele Karl Wilhelm (1742–1786). Swedish chemist and pharmacist who isolated many elements and compounds for the first time, including oxygen, about 1772, and chlorine 1774, although he did not recognize it as an element. He showed that oxygen is involved in the respiration of plants and fish.

In the book *Abhandlung von der Luft und dem Feuer/Experiments on Air and Fire* 1777, Scheele argued that the atmosphere was composed of two gases. One, which supported combustion (oxygen), he called 'fire air', and the other, which inhibited combustion (nitrogen), he called 'vitiated air'. He thus anticipated Joseph Priestley's discovery of oxygen by two years.

Although offered academic positions in Germany and England, from 1775 he ran a pharmacy in the small town of Köping on Lake Malären in Västmanland.

Scheele's discoveries include arsenic acid, benzoic acid, calcium tungstate (scheelite), citric acid, copper arsenite (Scheele's green), glycerol, hydrogen cyanide and hydrocyanic acid, hydrogen fluoride, hydrogen sulphide, lactic acid, malic acid, manganese, nitrogen, oxalic acid, permanganates, and uric acid. He also discovered that the action of light modifies certain silver salts (50 years before they were first used in photographic emulsions).

Scheer Reinhard (1863–1928). German admiral in World War I, commander of the High Sea Fleet from 1915 and commander of the German forces at the Battle of Jutland.

Scheiner Christoph (1573–1650). German astronomer who carried out one of the earliest studies of sunspots and made significant improvements to the helioscope and the telescope. In about 1605 he invented the pantograph, an instrument used for copying plans and drawings to any scale.

Scheiner was born near Mindelheim, Bavaria, and studied at Ingolstadt, where he became professor of mathematics and Hebrew 1610. There he began to make astronomical observations and organized public debates on current issues in astronomy. In 1616

Scheiner was invited to the court in Innsbruck, Austria, and the following year he was ordained to the priesthood. From 1633 he lived in Vienna and from 1639 in Neisse (now Nysa in Poland).

Scheiner built his first telescope in 1611, one of the first properly mounted telescopes. He projected the image of the Sun onto a white screen so that it would not damage his eyes. When he detected spots on the Sun, he believed they were small planets circling the Sun. His Jesuit superiors did not wish him to publish his observations in case he might discredit their order, so he communicated his discovery to a friend who under a pseudonym passed it on to astronomers Galileo and Kepler. Galileo nonetheless identified Scheiner and claimed priority for the discovery of sunspots, hinting that Scheiner was guilty of plagiarism. Scheiner also concluded that Venus and Mercury revolve around the Sun, but because of his religious beliefs, he did not extend this observation to the Earth.

In his *Sol ellipticus* 1615 and *Refractiones caelestes* 1617, Scheiner drew attention to the elliptical form of the Sun near the horizon, which he explained as being due to the effects of refraction. In his major work, *Rosa ursina sive sol* 1626–30, he accurately described the inclination of the axis of rotation of the sunspots to the plane of the ecliptic.

Schellenberg Walter (1911–1952). German SS general. He joined the SD 1934 and formed the first Einsatzgruppen 1938. He also organized the kidnapping of three British Secret Service agents in Holland 1939. After the fall of Admiral Canaris 1944 he became head of the Combined Intelligence Service and was involved with Himmler's abortive attempt to arrange peace talks with the Allies. He escaped to Sweden but later surrendered to the Allies, and was sentenced to six years' imprisonment 1949.

Schelling Friedrich Wilhelm Joseph von (1775–1854). German philosopher who developed a 'philosophy of identity' (*Identitäts-philosophie*), in which subject and object are seen as united in the absolute. Schelling began as a follower of J.G Fichte, but moved away from subjective idealism, which treats the external world as essentially immaterial. His early philosophy influenced G W F Hegel, but his later work criticizes Hegel, arguing that being necessarily precedes thought.

Schepisi Frederic Alan (1939–). Australian film director, based in the USA. He established his reputation with two important films made at the height of the revival of the Australian film industry *Devil's Playground* 1976 and *The Chant of Jimmie Blacksmith* 1978 both of which he also wrote and produced. Other films include *Iceman* 1984, *Plenty* 1985, and *The Russia House* 1990. In 1988 he returned to Australia to direct *Evil Angels*, based on the trial of Lindy Chamberlain.

Scherchen Hermann (1891–1966). German conductor. He collaborated with Schoenberg 1911–12, and in 1919 founded the journal *Melos* to promote contemporary music. He moved to Switzerland 1933, and was active as a conductor and teacher. He wrote two texts, *Handbook of Conducting* and *The Nature of Music*. During the 1950s he founded a music publishing house, Ars Viva Verlag, and an electronic studio at Gravesano.

Schiaparelli Elsa (*c.* 1890–1973). Italian couturier and knitwear designer. Her innovative fashion ideas included padded shoulders, sophisticated colours ('shocking pink'), and the pioneering use of zips and synthetic fabrics. She was widely influential in the 1930s; her outlook had much in common with the Surrealists, some of whom she commissioned to design fabric prints and jewellery. She had a productive partnership with Salvador Dali, creating lobster-printed skirts, a coat with drawers for pockets, based on Dali's painting *City of Drawers*, and a range of hats based on objects such as a shoe, an ice-cream cone, and a lamb chop.

In her 1938 'Circus' collection she introduced buttons in the shape of acrobats. She held her last show 1954.

Schiaparelli Giovanni Virginio (1835–1910). Italian astronomer who drew attention to linear markings on Mars, which gave rise to popular belief that they were canals. Fanciful stories of advanced life on Mars proliferated on the basis of the 'canals'. These markings were soon shown by French astronomer Eugène Antoniadi to be optical effects and not real lines. Schiaparelli also gave observational evidence for the theory that all meteor showers are fragments of disintegrating comets.

From 1860 he was astronomer at the Brera Observatory in Milan. He discovered asteroid 69 (Hesperia) 1861, but mainly studied comets until more sophisticated instruments became available at Milan, and then turned his attention to the planets. He also studied ancient and medieval astronomy. Schiaparelli concluded that Mercury and Venus revolved in such a way as always to present the same side to the Sun. Other observations included a study of binary stars in order to deduce their orbital systems.

Schiele Egon (1890–1918). Austrian Expressionist artist. Originally a landscape painter, he was strongly influenced by Art Nouveau, in particular Gustav Klimt, and developed a contorted linear style, employing strong colours. His subject matter includes portraits and openly erotic nudes. In 1911 he was arrested for alleged obscenity.

Suggested reading
Comini, Alessandra *Schiele in Prison* (1973)
Comini, Alessandra *Schiele's Portraits* (1974)
Comini, Alessandra *Schiele* (1976)
Mitsch, Erwin *The Art of Egon Schiele* (trs 1988)
Whitford, Frank *Schiele* (1981)

Schillebeeckx Edward Cornelis Florentius Alfons (1914–). Belgian Catholic theologian who explored the meaning of modern biblical scholarship and engaged with secular philosophy. His book *Jesus: An Experiment in Christology* was the first major Catholic book to consider Jesus in the light of these studies, rather than from a doctrinal perspective.

Against stupidity the gods themselves struggle in vain.
FRIEDRICH VON SCHILLER
Maid of Orleans 1801

Schiller (Johann Christoph) Friedrich von (1759–1805). German dramatist, poet, and historian. He wrote *Sturm und Drang* ('storm and stress') verse and plays, including the dramatic trilogy *Wallenstein* 1798–99. Much of his work concerns aspirations for political freedom and the avoidance of mediocrity.

He was a qualified surgeon, but after the success of the play *Die Räuber/The Robbers* 1781, he devoted himself to literature and completed his tragedies *Die Verschwörung des Fiesko zu Genua/Fiesco, or, the Genoese Conspiracy* and *Kabale und Liebe/Love and Intrigue* 1783. Moving to Weimar 1787, he wrote his more mature blank-verse drama *Don Carlos* and the hymn 'An die Freude/Ode to Joy', later used by Beethoven in his ninth symphony. As professor of history at Jena from 1789 he completed a history of the Thirty Years' War and developed a close friendship with Goethe after early antagonism. His essays on aesthetics include the piece of literary criticism 'über naive und sentimentalische Dichtung/Naive and Sentimental Poetry'. Schiller became the foremost German dramatist with his classic dramas *Wallenstein, Maria Stuart* 1800, *Die Jungfrau von Orleans/ The Maid of Orleans* 1801, and *Wilhelm Tell/William Tell* 1804.

Schindler Oskar (1908–1974). Czechoslovak industrialist and Jewish benefactor. A flamboyantly successful businessman, he set up a factory in Cracow, Poland, soon after the German invasion of 1939. He established good relations with the occupying forces and, through gifts and lavish entertainment, persuaded them to let him employ Jewish workers. He saved many hundreds of Jews from death in concentration camps by bribing the Nazis to release them into his 'custody'.

His activities, which earned him the gratitude and respect of the Zionist movement, were recorded in the form of a novel *Schindler's Ark* 1982, by Australian author Thomas Keneally, and later translated into an Oscar-winning film *Schindler's List* by Steven Spielberg.

Schindler Rudolph (1887–1953). Austrian architect who settled in the USA 1913. Initially influenced by Otto Wagner, he worked for Frank Lloyd Wright 1916–21 and later Richard Neutra. His design for Lovell Beach House, Newport Beach, 1925–26, reflects the work of the Dutch De Stijl group while anticipating the horizontal planes of Wright's Falling Water project.

Schinkel Karl Friedrich (1781–1841). Prussian Neo-Classical architect. His major works include the Old Museum, Berlin, 1823–30, the Nikolaikirche in Potsdam 1830–37, and the Roman Bath 1833 in the park of Potsdam.

Schlegel August Wilhelm von (1767–1845). German Romantic author and translator of Shakespeare. His *Über dramatische Kunst und Literatur/Lectures on Dramatic Art and Literature* 1809–11 broke down the formalism of the old classical criteria of literary composition. Friedrich von Schlegel was his brother.

Schlegel (Karl Wilhelm) Friedrich von (1772–1829). German literary critic. With his brother August, he was a founder of the Romantic movement, and a pioneer in the comparative study of languages.

Schleiden Matthias Jakob (1804–1881). German botanist who identified the fundamental units of living organisms when, in 1838, he announced that the various parts of plants consist of cells or derivatives of cells. This was extended to animals by Theodor Schwann the following year.

He was professor at Jena 1831–62 and at Dorpat, Estonia, 1862–64, after which he returned to Germany.

The existence of cells had been discovered by British physicist Robert Hooke 1665, but Schleiden was the first to recognize their importance. He also noted the role of the nucleus in cell division, and the active movement of intracellular material in plant tissues.

Schlemmer Oskar (1888–1943). German choreographer, sculptor, painter, teacher, and designer. He was a member of the Bauhaus school of artists during the 1920s. His paintings and sculptures are characterized by stylized, mannequinlike figures. His explorations of form, colour, light, and motion resulted in a series of dances which were radically different from the prevailing Ausdruckstanz style of the time. His dances are extremely simple and lack explicit emotional statements; they include *Triadic Ballet* 1922 (music by Paul Hindemith) and *Bauhaus Dances* 1926.

Schlesinger Arthur Meier, Jr (1917–). US historian. His first book, *The Age of Jackson*, won a Pulitzer prize 1945. Becoming active in Democratic politics, he served as a speechwriter in the presidential campaigns of Adlai Stevenson 1956 and John Kennedy 1960.

Born in Columbus, Ohio, USA, the son of a prominent historian, Schlesinger was educated at Harvard University and served as an intelligence officer during World War II. He was presidential assistant for Latin American Affairs 1961–64 and in 1967 became a professor at the City College of New York.

Schlesinger John Richard (1926–). English film and television director. He was responsible for such British films as *Billy Liar* 1963 and *Darling* 1965. His first US film, *Midnight Cowboy* 1969 (Academy Award), was a big commercial success and was followed by *Sunday, Bloody Sunday* 1971, *Marathon Man* 1976, *Yanks* 1979, and *Pacific Heights* 1990.

Schlick (Friedrich Albert) Moritz (1882–1936). German philosopher, physicist, and founder of the Vienna Circle. Schlick, born in Berlin, became professor of the philosophy of the inductive sciences in Vienna, Austria, 1922. Under the influence of the early Ludwig Wittgenstein and the logical positivism of the German-born US philosopher and logician Rudolf Carnap (1891–1970), Schlick concluded that all philosophical problems arise from the inadequacy of language. The task of philosophy is to clarify the question in dispute. If the question cannot be ascertained in principle by scientific methods, then the question is meaningless. He based meaning on the possibility of immediate sense-experience. The inaccessibility of this private experience of meaning led Wittgenstein to his 'use' theory of meaning.

He was assassinated 1936 by a demented student, an event that hastened the break-up of the Vienna Circle. His publications include *Allgemeine Erkenntnislehre/General Theory of Knowledge* 1918.

I have gazed upon the face of Agamemnon

HEINRICH SCHLIEMANN
Telegram allegedly sent to the king of Greece.
Quoted in Michael Wood *In Search of the Trojan War* p 72 1985

Schliemann Heinrich (1822–1890). German archaeologist. He earned a fortune in business, retiring in 1863 to pursue his lifelong ambition to discover a historical basis for Homer's *Iliad*. In 1870 he began excavating at Hissarlik, Turkey, a site which yielded the ruins of nine consecutive cities and was indeed the site of Troy. His later excavations were at Mycenae 1874–76, where he discovered the ruins of the Mycenaean civilization.
Suggested reading
Brackman, Arnold *The Dream of Troy* (1974)
Moorhead, Caroline *The Lost Treasure of Troy* (1995)
Schliemann, Heinrich *Memoirs of Heinrich Schliemann* (trs 1978)
Traill, David *Schliemann of Troy: Treasure and Deceit* (1995)

Schlüter Poul Holmskov (1929–   ). Danish right-wing politician, leader of the Conservative People's Party (KF) from 1974 and prime minister 1982–93. His centre-right coalition survived the 1990 election and was reconstituted, with Liberal support. In Jan 1993 Schlüter resigned, accused of dishonesty over his role in an incident involving Tamil refugees. He was succeeded by Poul Nyrup Rasmussen.
Having joined the KF in his youth, he trained as a lawyer and then entered the Danish parliament (Folketing) in 1964.

Schmidt Bernhard Voldemar (1879–1935). Estonian lens- and mirror-maker who devised a special lens to work in conjunction with a spherical mirror in a reflecting telescope. The effect of this was to nullify 'coma', the optical distortion of focus away from the centre of the image, and thus to bring the entire image into a single focus.
Schmidt was born on the island of Naissaar. He lost most of his right arm in a childhood experiment with gunpowder. He studied engineering in Göteborg, Sweden, and at Mittweida in Germany. He stayed in Mittweida making lenses and mirrors for astronomers; in 1905 he made a 40-cm/27-in mirror for the Potsdam Astrophysical Observatory. From 1926 he was attached to the Hamburg Observatory. He worked on the mountings and drives of the telescopes, as well as on their optics. It was in Hamburg that he perfected his lens and built it into the observatory telescope, specifically for use in photography.
By replacing the parabolic mirror of a telescope with a spherical one plus his correcting lens, Schmidt could produce an image that was sharply focused at every point (generally on a curved photographic plate, although on later models he used a second lens to compensate for the use of a flat photographic plate).

[His] combination of power and self-denial made him ... like a caged lion. But as he had himself erected the bars he sniffed around them with ... reasonable content.

ROY JENKINS on HELMUT SCHMIDT
in *Gallery of 20th Century Portraits* 1988

Schmidt Helmut Heinrich Waldemar (1918–   ). German socialist politician, member of the Social Democratic Party (SPD), chancellor of West Germany 1974–83.
Schmidt was elected to the Bundestag (federal parliament) in 1953. He was interior minister for Hamburg 1961–65, defence minister 1969–72, and finance minister 1972–74. He became federal chancellor (prime minister) on Willy Brandt's resignation in 1974. Re-elected 1980, he was defeated in the Bundestag in 1982 following the switch of allegiance by the SPD's coalition allies, the Free Democratic Party. As chancellor, Schmidt introduced social reforms

and continued Brandt's policy of Ostpolitik. With the French president Giscard d'Estaing, he instigated annual world and European economic summits. He was a firm supporter of NATO and of the deployment of US nuclear missiles in West Germany during the early 1980s. Schmidt retired from federal politics at the general election of 1983, having encountered growing opposition from the SPD's left wing, who opposed his stance on military and economic issues.
Suggested reading
Carr, Jonathan *Helmut Schmidt* (1985)
Childs, David and Johnson, Jeffrey *West Germany: Politics and Society* (1981)

Schmidt-Rottluff Karl (1884–1976). German Expressionist painter and printmaker. He was a founding member of *die Brücke* in Dresden 1905, active in Berlin from 1911. Inspired by Vincent van Gogh and Fauvism, he developed a vigorous style of brushwork and a bold palette. He painted portraits and landscapes and produced numerous woodcuts and lithographs.

The notes I handle no better than many pianists. But the pauses between the notes – ah, that is where the art resides!

ARTUR SCHNABEL
in *Chicago Daily News* 11 June 1958

Schnabel Artur (1882–1951). Austrian pianist, teacher, and composer. He taught music at the Berlin State Academy 1925–30, but settled in the USA 1939 where, in addition to lecturing, he composed symphonies and piano works. He excelled at playing Beethoven and trained many pianists.

Schneerson Menachem Mendel (1902–1994). Russian-born US rabbi, leader from 1950 of the Lubavitch right-wing orthodox Judaic movement. A charismatic figure, he was regarded by some of his followers as a Messiah. His advice was prized as practical and wise, and respected by many people unconnected with the movement. Under his guidance, the Lubavitch movement expanded worldwide, and the community's publishing division is now the world's largest distributor of Jewish books.

Schneider Romy. Stage name of Rosemarie Albach-Retty (1938–1982). Austrian film actress. She starred in *Boccaccio '70* 1962, *Der Prozess/The Trial* 1963, and *Ludwig* 1972.

Women always want to be our last love, and we their first.

ARTHUR SCHNITZLER
quoted in F Ungar (ed) *Practical Wisdom*

Schnitzler Arthur (1862–1931). Viennese dramatist. A doctor with an interest in psychiatry, he was known for his psychological dramas exploring egotism, eroticism, and self-deception in Viennese bourgeois life. *Reigen/Merry-Go-Round* 1897, a cycle of dramatic dialogues depicting lust, caused a scandal when performed 1920 but made a successful French film as *La Ronde* 1950, directed by Max Ophuls. His novel *Leutnant Gustl* 1901 pioneered interior monologue in fiction.

The introduction of my method of composing with twelve notes does not facilitate composing; on the contrary, it makes it more difficult.

ARNOLD SCHOENBERG
Style and Idea, translated by Dika Newlin 1950

Schoenberg Arnold Franz Walter (1874–1951). Austro-Hungarian composer, a US citizen from 1941. After Romantic early works such as *Verklärte Nacht/Transfigured Night* 1899 and the *Gurrelieder/Songs of Gurra* 1900–11, he experimented with atonality

Schoenberg *The composer Arnold Schoenberg. After escaping the Nazis in 1933 he settled in the USA as a lecturer, eloquently preaching the laws of harmony despite his serialist compositional philosophy.*

The son of the goldsmith, Kaspar Schongauer, he became a freeman of Colmar 1455. From about 1473 he worked in Colmar, where the monastery church has his one entirely authenticated painting, *The Madonna of the Rosearbour*. In 1488 he became a citizen of Breisach. His line engravings are classics of that art, which set a standard widely followed. The young Dürer admired and copied his work, sought him out at Colmar and, though Schongauer died before they could meet, worked in his studio.

> *Buying books would be a good thing if one could also buy the time to read them in.*
>
> ARTHUR SCHOPENHAUER
> *Essays and Aphorisms* 1970

Schopenhauer Arthur (1788–1860). German philosopher whose *The World as Will and Idea* 1818, inspired by Immanuel Kant and ancient Hindu philosophy, expounded an atheistic and pessimistic world view: an irrational will is considered as the inner principle of the world, producing an ever-frustrated cycle of desire, of which the only escape is aesthetic contemplation or absorption into nothingness.

Having postulated a world of suffering and disappointment, he based his ethics on compassion. His notion of an irrational force at work in human beings strongly influenced both the philosopher Friedrich Nietzsche and the founder of psychiatry, Sigmund Freud. The theory also struck a responsive chord in the composer Richard Wagner, the German novelist Thomas Mann, and the English writer Thomas Hardy.

Suggested reading
Copleston, Frederick *Arthur Schopenhauer: Philosopher of Pessimism* (1975)
Gardiner, Patrick *Schopenhauer* (1963)
Hamlyn, David *Schopenhauer* (1985)
Magee, Bryan *The Philosophy of Schopenhauer* (1988)

Schreiner Olive Emilie Albertina (1855–1920). South African novelist and supporter of women's rights. Her autobiographical *The Story of an African Farm* 1883 describes life on the South African veld. Other works include *Trooper Peter Halket of Mashonaland* 1897, a fictional attack on the expansionist policies of Cecil Rhodes, and the feminist classic *Women and Labour* 1911.

> *A living organism ... feeds upon negative entropy ... Thus the device by which an organism maintains itself stationary at a fairly high level of orderliness (fairly low level of entropy) really consists in continually sucking orderliness from its environment.*
>
> ERWIN SCHRÖDINGER
> *What is Life?* 1944

(absence of key), producing works such as *Pierrot lunaire/ Moonstruck Pierrot* 1912 for chamber ensemble and voice, before developing the twelve-tone system of musical composition.

After 1918, Schoenberg wrote several Neo-Classical works for chamber ensembles. He taught at the Berlin State Academy 1925–33. The twelve-tone system was further developed by his pupils Alban Berg and Anton Webern. Driven from Germany by the Nazis, Schoenberg settled in the USA 1933, where he influenced music scoring for films. Later works include the opera *Moses und Aron* 1932–51.

Suggested reading
MacDonald, Malcolm *Schoenberg* (1976)
Reich, Willi *Schoenberg: A Critical Biography* (trs 1971)
Rosen, Charles *Schoenberg* (1975)
Stuckenschmidt, H H *Schoenberg* (trs 1959)

Schoenheimer Rudolf (1898–1941). German-born US biochemist who introduced the use of isotopes as tracers to study biochemical processes in 1935.

Schoenheimer was born and educated in Berlin. In 1933 he emigrated to the USA, working at the University of Columbia. He committed suicide.

Schoenheimer used deuterium to replace some of the hydrogen atoms in molecules of fat, which he fed to laboratory animals. On analysing the body fat of rats four days later, he found that about half of the labelled fat was being stored. This meant that, contrary to previous belief, there was a constant changeover in the body between stored fat and fat that was used. Schoenheimer used the isotope nitrogen-15 (prepared by US chemist Harold Urey, also at Columbia) to label amino acids, the basic building blocks of proteins, and again found that component molecules of the body are continually being broken down and built up. He summarized his findings in his book *The Dynamical State of Bodily Constituents* 1942.

Schongauer Martin (*c*. 1450–1491). German painter and engraver. His many fine engravings of religious subjects elevated the status of engraving from that of a craft to an art. Deeply influenced by Rogier van Weyden, he in turn influenced many of his contemporaries.

Schrödinger Erwin (1887–1961). Austrian physicist who advanced the study of wave mechanics to describe the behaviour of electrons in atoms. He produced in 1926 a solid mathematical explanation of the quantum theory and the structure of the atom. Nobel prize 1933.

Schrödinger's mathematical description of electron waves superseded matrix mechanics, developed 1925 by Max Born and Werner Heisenberg, which also described the structure of the atom mathematically but, unlike wave mechanics, gave no picture of the atom. It was later shown that wave mechanics is equivalent to matrix mechanics.

Schrödinger was born and educated in Vienna. He was professor at Zürich, Switzerland, 1921–33. With the rise of the Nazis in Germany, Schrödinger went to Oxford, England, 1933. Homesick, he returned to Austria in 1936 to take up a post at Graz, but the Nazi takeover of Austria in 1938 forced him into exile, and he worked at the Institute for Advanced Studies in Dublin, Ireland, 1939–56. He spent his last years at the University of Vienna.

French physicist Louis de Broglie had in 1924, using ideas from Albert Einstein's special theory of relativity, shown that an electron or any other particle has a wave associated with it. In 1926 both Schrödinger and de Broglie published the same wave equation, which Schrödinger later formulated in terms of the energies of the electron and the field in which it was situated. He solved the equation for the hydrogen atom and found that it fitted with energy levels proposed by Danish physicist Niels Bohr.

In the hydrogen atom, the wave function describes where we can expect to find the electron. Although it is most likely to be where Bohr predicted it to be, it does not follow a circular orbit but is described by the more complicated notion of an orbital, a region in space where the electron can be found with varying degrees of probability. Atoms other than hydrogen and also molecules and ions can be described by Schrödinger's wave equation but such cases are very difficult to solve.

The task is ... to think what nobody has yet thought, about that which everybody sees.

ERWIN SCHRÖDINGER
quoted in L Bertalanffy *Problems of Life* 1952

Schrödinger *Nobel laureate Austrian physicist Erwin Schrödinger. Schrödinger's equation describes the wave function associated with an electron. He shared the Nobel Prize for Physics with Paul Dirac and Werner Heisenberg in 1933. (Image Select)*

Schubert *The composer Franz Schuber, after the portrait by Rieder. Schubert is best-known for his melodic gift, which was put to good use in more than 600 Lieder. His harmonic language and often-cyclic conception of works foreshadow later developments of the 19th century. (Image Select)*

Schubert Franz Peter (1797–1828). Austrian composer. His ten symphonies include the incomplete eighth in B minor (the 'Unfinished') and the 'Great' in C major. He wrote chamber and piano music, including the 'Trout Quintet', and over 600 *lieder* (songs) combining the Romantic expression of emotion with pure melody. They include the cycles *Die schöne Müllerin/The Beautiful Maid of the Mill* 1823 and *Die Winterreise/The Winter Journey* 1827.

Suggested reading

Brown, M J *Schubert: A Critical Biography* (1958)
Brown, M J *The New Grove Schubert* (1983)
Deutsch, O *The Schubert Reader* (1947)
Einstein, A *Schubert: A Musical Portrait* (1951)
Osborne, Charles *Schubert and His Vienna* (1985)
Reed, John *Schubert* (1987)
Woodford, P *Schubert: His Life and Times* (1978)

Though I have worked very hard at the Winterreise the last five years, every time I come back I am amazed not only by the extraordinary mastery of it ... but by the renewal of the magic; the mystery remains.

Benjamin Britten on FRANZ SCHUBERT'S
Winterreise, on receiving the first Aspen Award, 1964

Schultz Theodore William (1902–). US economist, a specialist in agricultural economics. He shared the 1979 Nobel prize with Arthur Lewis for his work on the problems of developing countries.

Schulz Charles M(onroe) (1922–). US cartoonist who created the *Peanuts* strip, syndicated by United Features Syndicate from 1950. His characters Snoopy, Charlie Brown, Lucy, and Linus have been merchandised worldwide and featured in a 1967 musical, *You're a Good Man, Charlie Brown*.

Schumacher Fritz (Ernst Friedrich) (1911–1977). German economist who believed that the increasing size of institutions,

Schumann, Robert *The composer Robert Schumann . After permanently damaging a finger as a result of over-practising, he gave up his career as a pianist to devote himself full-time to composition. His wife Clara was a fine pianist in her own right.* (Image Select)

coupled with unchecked economic growth, creates a range of social and environmental problems. He argued his case in books like *Small is Beautiful* 1973, and established the Intermediate Technology Development Group.

Schumacher studied at Oxford and held academic posts there and in the USA at Columbia in the 1930s and 1940s. After World War II he was economic adviser to the British Control Commission in Germany 1946–50 and to the UK National Coal Board 1950–70. He also served as president of the Soil Association and as director of the Scott-Bader Company, which manufactures polymers and is based on common ownership. He advised many governments on problems of rural development. His book *A Guide for the Perplexed* 1977 deals with philosophy.

Schumacher Michael (1969–). German motor-racing driver. He began his career in the Mercedes-Benz junior team; he joined the Jordan Formula One team 1991, but was poached by Benetton almost immediately. He won his first Grand Prix in Belgium 1992. Hailed by many as a gifted 'natural' driver, he won his world drivers' championship title for the first time 1994, and again 1995.

Schuman Robert (1886–1963). French politician. He was prime minister 1947–48, and as foreign minister 1948–53 he proposed in May 1950 a common market for coal and steel (the Schuman Plan), which was established as the European Coal and Steel Community 1952, the basis of the European Community (now the European Union).

Schuman William Howard (1910–). US composer and teacher. His music is melodic, if sometimes tempered by polytonality, and often emphasizes motoric rhythm or other intense rhythms, as in *American Festival Overture* 1939. His large-scale conception suits the orchestral medium, for which he has written nine symphonies. He has also written chamber and vocal works.

Schumann Clara Josephine (born Wieck) (1819–1896). German pianist and composer. She wrote a Concerto in A Minor for piano and orchestra 1835–36, a Piano Trio about 1846, and romances for piano. She married Robert Schumann 1840 (her father had been his piano

teacher). During his life and after his death she was devoted to popularizing his work, appearing frequently in European concert halls.

Suggested reading
Chissell, J *Clara Schumann: A Dedicated Spirit* (1983)
Reich, Nancy *Clara Schumann: The Artist and the Woman* (1985)

Schumann Robert Alexander (1810–1856). German composer and writer. His songs and short piano pieces portray states of emotion with great economy. Among his compositions are four symphonies, a violin concerto, a piano concerto, sonatas, and song cycles, such as *Dichterliebe/Poet's Love* 1840. Mendelssohn championed many of his works.

He also wrote much chamber music. His music criticism was published in his *Neue Zeitschrift für Musik/New Musical Journal* 1835–44. Born at Zwickau, Saxony, he taught at Leipzig Conservatoire and was musical director at Düsseldorf 1850–53. After a suicide attempt in 1854, he was sent to an asylum near Bonn, where he died.

Suggested reading
Brion, M *Schumann and the Romantic Age* (1956)
Chissell, J *Schumann* (1967)
Moore, Gerald *Poet's Love: The Songs and Cycles of Schumann* (1981)
Ostwald, P F *Schumann: Music and Madness* (1985)
Taylor, Ronald *Robert Schumann: His Life and Work* (1982)
Walker, Alan (ed) *Robert Schumann: The Man and his Music* (1974)

Schumpeter Joseph A(lois) (1883–1950). Austrian-born US economist and sociologist. Schumpeter was born in Moravia, now the Czech Republic, and migrated to the USA 1932. He was deeply interested in mathematics, and he took part in the founding of the Econometric Society 1930. In *Capitalism, Socialism and Democracy* 1942 he contended that Western capitalism, impelled by its very success, was evolving into a form of socialism because firms would become increasingly large and their managements increasingly divorced from ownership, while social trends were undermining the traditional motives for entrepreneurial accumulation of wealth.

His writings established him as an authority on economic theory as well as the history of economic thought. Among other standard reference works, he wrote the *History of Economic Analysis*, published posthumously 1954.

Schurz Carl (1829–1906). German-born US editor and political leader. Born in Germany, Schurz emigrated to the USA 1852, studied law, and was admitted to the Wisconsin bar 1859. Named US minister to Spain 1861–62, he returned to see action as a staff officer in the American Civil War (1861–65). After working briefly as editor of the *Detroit Post* 1866, he moved to St Louis. He held office in the US Senate 1869–75 and served as secretary of the interior under President Hayes 1877–81. He was editor of the *New York Evening Post* 1881–83. A harsh critic of government corruption, he was president of the National Civil Service Reform League 1892–1901.

Schuschnigg Kurt von (1897–1977). Austrian chancellor 1934–38, in succession to Dollfuss. He tried in vain to prevent Nazi annexation (*Anschluss*) but in Feb 1938 he was forced to accept a Nazi minister of the interior, and a month later Austria was occupied and annexed by Germany. He was imprisoned in Germany until 1945, when he went to the USA; he returned to Austria 1967.

Schütz Heinrich (1585–1672). German early Baroque composer. He was musical director to the Elector of Saxony from 1614. His works include *The Seven Last Words* about 1645, *Musicalische Exequien* 1636, and the *Deutsche Magnificat/German Magnificat* 1671. He increased the range and scope of instrumental and choral polyphony and was an important precursor of J S Bach.

Schuyler Philip John (1733–1804). American public official. A member of the Continental Congress 1775–77, he was named general in command of the Department of New York at the outbreak of the American Revolution 1775. Replaced in 1777, he returned to the Continental Congress 1778–81. A supporter of the US Constitution, Schuyler became one of New York's first US senators 1789–91 and later served 1797–98.

Schwabe Samuel Heinrich (1789–1875). German astronomer who was the first to measure the periodicity of the sunspot cycle. This may be considered as marking the beginning of solar physics.

Schwabe was born in Dessau, studied at Berlin, and worked as a pharmacist. In 1829 he sold his pharmacy and became an astronomer. He published 109 scientific papers and left 31 volumes of astronomical data to the Royal Astronomical Society.

Schwabe began to watch the Sun in 1825 with a 5-cm/2-in telescope and noticed sunspots, making daily counts of them for most of the rest of his life. In 1843 he was able to announce a periodicity: he declared that the sunspots waxed and waned in number according to a ten-year cycle.

In 1827 Schwabe rediscovered the eccentricity of Saturn's rings, and in 1831 he drew a picture of the planet Jupiter on which the Great Red Spot was shown for the first time.

Schwann Theodor (1810–1882). German physiologist who, with Matthias Schleiden, is credited with formulating the cell theory, one of the most fundamental concepts in biology. Schwann also did important work on digestion, fermentation, and the study of tissues.

He spent 1834–38 working as an assistant to German physiologist Johannes Peter Müller at the Museum of Anatomy in Berlin. In 1839, however, Schwann's work on fermentation attracted so much adverse criticism that he left Germany for Belgium, where he was professor at Louvain 1839–48 and then at Liège.

In 1836, Schwann isolated from the lining of the stomach a chemical responsible for protein digestion, which he called pepsin. This was the first enzyme to be isolated from animal tissue.

Schwann showed 1836–37 that the fermentation of sugar is a result of the life processes of living yeast cells (he later coined the term 'metabolism' to denote the chemical changes that occur in living tissue).

In *Mikroskopische Untersuchungen über die übereinstimmung in der Struktur und dem Wachstum der Tiere und Pflanzen/Microscopical Researches on the Similarity in the Structure and Growth of Animals and Plants* 1839, he concluded that all organisms consist entirely of cells or of products of cells and that the life of each individual cell is subordinated to that of the whole organism. In addition, he noted that an egg is a single cell that eventually develops into a complex organism.

Schwartz Delmore (1913–1966). US poet, short-story writer, and critic. He is noted for lyric poetry of intelligent phrasing and subtle tone. His books include *In Dreams Begin Responsibilities* (stories) 1938, *The World is a Wedding* 1948, *New and Selected Poems (1938–1958) 1959: Summer Knowledge* 1959, and *Selected Essays* 1970. He co-edited the influential magazine *Partisan Review* 1943–55.

Schwarzenegger Arnold (1947–). Austrian-born US film actor. He was one of the biggest box-office attractions of the late 1980s and early 1990s. He starred in sword-and-sorcery films such as *Conan the Barbarian* 1982 and later graduated to large-scale budget action movies such as *Terminator* 1984, *Predator* 1987, *Terminator II* 1991, and *True Lies* 1994.

Schwarzenegger began his career as a body-builder and won numerous medals including the 1969 Mr Universe competition. He came to the attention of Hollywood in *Pumping Iron* 1976, a documentary about body-building. He was cast in a series of roles which made much of his physique and little of his character, thus overcoming fears over the apparent obstacle of his Austrian accent. The power of his onscreen personality soon enabled him to play a variety of roles, including comic roles in *Twins* 1988 and *Kindergarten Cop* 1991.

Schwarzkopf Norman, (nicknamed 'Stormin' Norman') (1934–). US general. A graduate of the military academy at West Point, Schwarzkopf obtained a master's degree in guided-missile engineering. He became an infantryman and later a paratrooper, and did two tours of service in Vietnam. He was a battalion commander in the Vietnam War and deputy commander of the 1983 US invasion of Grenada.

He was supreme commander of the Allied forces in the Gulf War 1991. He planned and executed a blitzkrieg campaign, 'Desert Storm', sustaining remarkably few Allied casualties in the liberation of Kuwait. Maintaining the 28-member Arab-Western military coalition against Iraq 1991 extended his diplomatic skills, and his success in the Gulf War made him a popular hero in the USA. He retired from the army Aug 1991.

Schwarzkopf (Olga Maria) Elisabeth (Friederike) (1915–). German operatic soprano. Her fame rests on her interpretations of Mozart and Richard Strauss roles and of German *lieder* (songs). Her art brings a classical poise and precision to the expression of romantic emotion.

Schwarzschild Karl (1873–1916). German astronomer and theoretical physicist who was the first to substitute a photographic plate at the telescope in place of the eye and then measure densities with a photometer. He designed and constructed some of his own instruments.

In 1902 he was appointed professor at Göttingen and director of the observatory. From 1909 he was director of the Astrophysical Observatory at Potsdam. He was the father of Martin Schwarzschild.

In 1900, he suggested that the geometry of space was possibly not in conformity with Euclidean principles. (This was 16 years before the publication of Albert Einstein's general theory of relativity.) He later gave the first exact solution of Einstein's field equations.

Schwarzschild introduced the concept of radiative equilibrium in astrophysics and was probably the first to see how radiative processes were important in conveying heat in stellar atmospheres. In 1906, he published work on the transfer of energy at and near the surface of the Sun.

He devised a multi-slit interferometer and used it to measure the separation of close double stars. During a total solar eclipse 1905, he obtained spectrograms that gave information on the chemical composition of regions at various heights on the Sun. He later designed a spectrographic objective that provided a quick, reliable way to determine the radial velocities of stars.

Schwarzschild Martin (1912–). German-born US astronomer whose most important work was in the field of stellar structure and evolution. He greatly narrowed the estimated range of mass that stars can have.

Schwarzschild was born in Potsdam, the son of astronomer Karl Schwarzschild. After studying at Göttingen, he emigrated to the USA 1935. He was professor at Columbia 1947–51 and at Princeton from 1951.

Schwarzschild worked out a quantity (Z_{He}) for the total mass density of the elements heavier than helium, using the density of hydrogen as one unit. The values of Z_{He} are smallest for old stars (0.003) and largest for young stars (0.04), implying that the most recently formed stellar objects were formed out of a medium of interstellar gas and dust that was already enriched with heavy elements. These elements were probably produced in stellar interiors and expelled by the oldest stars.

In 1938, Schwarzschild suggested that the star's deepest interior pulsates, but that in the outermost regions the elements of gas do not all vibrate in unison, causing a lag in the light curve by the observed amount.

Schweitzer Albert (1875–1965). French Protestant theologian, organist, and missionary surgeon. He founded the hospital at Lambaréné in Gabon in 1913, giving organ recitals to support his work there. He wrote a life of German composer J S Bach and *Von reimarus zu Wrede/The Quest for the Historical Jesus* 1906. He was awarded the Nobel Peace Prize in 1952 for his teaching of 'reverence for life'.

Suggested reading
Brabazon, James *Albert Schweitzer: A Comprehensive Biography* (1975)
Cousins, Norman *Albert Schweitzer's Mission* (1985)

Reverence for Life.

ALBERT SCHWEITZER
My Life and Thought ch 13 1933

McKnight, Gerald *Verdict on Schweitzer* (1964)
Schweitzer, Albert *My Life and Thought* (trs 1933)

Schwinger Julian Seymour (1918–1994). US quantum physicist. His research concerned the behaviour of charged particles in electrical fields. This work, expressed entirely through mathematics, combines elements from quantum theory and relativity theory into a new theory called quantum electrodynamics, the most accurate physical theory of all time. Schwinger shared the Nobel Prize for Physics 1963 with Richard Feynman and Sin-Itiro Tomonaga (1906–1979).

Described as the 'physicist in knee pants', he entered college in New York at the age of 15, transferred to Columbia University and graduated at 17. At the age of 29 he became Harvard University's youngest full professor.

He went to work on nuclear physics problems at Berkeley (in association with J Robert Oppenheimer) and at Purdue University. From 1943 to 1945 he worked on problems relating to radar at the Massachusetts Institute of Technology and, after the war, moved to Harvard, where he developed his version of quantum electrodynamics. He calculated the anomalous magnetic moment of the electron soon after its discovery. In 1957, Schwinger anticipated the existence of two different neutrinos associated with the electron and the muon (heavy electron), which was confirmed experimentally in 1963. He also speculated that weak nuclear forces are carried by massive, charged particles. This was confirmed in 1983 at CERN (the European Laboratory for Particle Physics) in Geneva. In 1972 Schwinger became Professor of Physics at the University of California, Los Angeles.

Schwitters Kurt (1887–1948). German artist. He was a member of the Dada movement. He moved to Norway 1937 and to England 1940. From 1918 he developed a variation on collage, using discarded items such as buttons and bus tickets to create pictures and structures. He called these art works *Merz*, and produced a magazine of the same name from 1923. Later he created *Merzbauen* (Merz houses), extensive constructions of wood and scrap, most of which were destroyed.

Sciascia Leonardo (1921–1989). Sicilian novelist. He used the detective novel to explore the hidden workings of Sicilian life, as in *Il giorno della civetta/Mafia Vendetta* 1961.

Scipio Publius Cornelius (lived 3rd century BC). Roman general, father of Scipio Africanus Major. Elected consul 218, during the Second Punic War, he was defeated by Hannibal at Trebia and killed by the Carthaginians in Spain.

I do not disregard the power of fortune, and know well tht everything we do is subject to a thousand chances.

SCIPIO AFRICANUS MAJOR
quoted in Livy *From the Foundation of the City* bk 30, ch 31

Scipio Africanus Major Publius Cornelius (236–*c.* 183 BC). Roman general. He defeated the Carthaginians in Spain 210–206 BC, invaded Africa 204 BC, and defeated Hannibal at Zama 202 BC.

Scipio Africanus Minor Publius Cornelius (*c.* 185–129 BC). Roman general, the adopted grandson of Scipio Africanus Major, also known as Scipio Aemilianus. He destroyed Carthage 146, and subdued Spain 133. He was opposed to his brothers-in-law, the Gracchi.

A glorious moment, Polybius; but I have a dread foreboding that some day the same doom will be pronounced on my country.

The reaction of SCIPIO AFRICANUS MINOR to the destruction of Carthage in 146 BC. Quoted in Polybius *History* bk 38, ch 1

Scofield (David) Paul (1922–). English actor. His wide-ranging roles include the drunken priest in Graham Greene's *The Power and*

the Glory 1956, Lear in *King Lear* 1962, and Salieri in Peter Shaffer's *Amadeus*. He appeared as Sir Thomas More in both stage and film versions of Robert Bolt's *A Man for All Seasons* (stage 1960–61, film 1966).

Scoones Geoffry Alan Percival (1893–1975). British general in World War II. He was commander of the British IV Corps on the India–Burma border 1944 and was responsible for the defence of Kohima and Imphal and the defeat of the Japanese Ha-Go offensive against India. After this he led IV Corps in an offensive which drove the Japanese across the Chindwin river and into central Burma. In Dec 1944 he was given command of central India and in 1945 was made KBE.

Scopas (lived 4th century BC). Greek sculptor, whose intense and brooding style was influential in the development of the early Classicists. He carved the decorations for the Mausoleum at Halicarnassus and for the temples of Artemis at Ephesus and Athena Alea at Tegea.

I hate shooting – getting up at 5.30 am. I prefer noon to midnight. I'm not awake until 3pm.

MARTIN SCORSESE
Antenne 2 (French TV) 10 Jan 1991

Scorsese Martin (1942–). US director, screenwriter, and producer. His films concentrate on complex characterization and the themes of alienation and guilt. Drawing from his Italian-American Catholic background, his work often deals with sin and redemption, as in his first major film *Boxcar Bertha* 1972. His influential, passionate, and forceful movies include *Mean Streets* 1973, *Taxi Driver* 1976, *Raging Bull* 1980, *The Last Temptation of Christ* 1988, *GoodFellas* 1990, *Cape Fear* 1991, and *The Age of Innocence* 1993.

Scorsese's other major films include *Alice Doesn't Live Here Anymore* 1974 (featuring his only lead female protagonist), the musical *New York New York* 1977, and *The King of Comedy* 1982.

Scott Douglas (1913–1990). English industrial designer who produced a remarkable variety of classic designs, including the London Transport Routemaster bus (a red double-decker which went into service 1968) and the Raeburn cooker. He set up Britain's first professional product-design course and Mexico's first design school.

Scott was born in London, and trained from the age of 13 to be a silversmith. Working for lighting manufacturers, he produced Art Deco and Neo-Greek light fittings for town halls and cinemas, and streetlamp designs still in use in the 1990s in Australia and Cyprus. He then moved to the office of US designer Raymond Loewy. After World War II, Scott set up his own practice, designing rugged yet streamlined household items, including hand whisks, television cameras, and power boats.

Scott Francis Reginald (1899–1985). Canadian poet. A distinguished academic, constitutional lawyer, and leftist social critic, he was intellectually as well as poetically committed to social justice and regeneration through love and renewed contact with nature. His collections include *Overtures* 1945 and *The Dance is One* 1973. His volume of satirical verse *The Eye of the Needle* appeared 1957.

Scott George C(ampbell) (1927–). US actor. He often played tough, authoritarian film roles. His work includes *Dr Strangelove* 1964, *Patton* 1970, *The Hospital* 1971, and *Firestarter* 1984.

Scott (George) Gilbert (1811–1878). English architect. As the leading practical architect of the mid-19th-century Gothic Revival in England, Scott was responsible for the building or restoration of many public buildings and monuments, including the Albert Memorial 1863–72, the Foreign Office in Whitehall 1862–73, and the St Pancras Station Hotel 1868–74, all in London.

Scott Giles Gilbert (1880–1960). English architect. He was the grandson of (George) Gilbert Scott. He designed Liverpool Anglican Cathedral (begun 1903; completed 1978), Cambridge University Library 1931–34, Battersea Power Station 1932–34, and

Waterloo Bridge, London, 1939–45. He supervised the rebuilding of the House of Commons after World War II.

Scott Paul Mark (1920–1978). English novelist. Born in Southgate, North London, he served for three years in the Indian Army in India 1943–46 but otherwise lived all his life in Southgate. He was the author of *The Raj Quartet* consisting of *The Jewel in the Crown* 1966, *The Day of the Scorpion* 1968, *The Towers of Silence* 1972, and *A Division of the Spoils* 1975, dealing with the British Raj in India. Other novels include *Staying On* 1977, which is set in post-independence India.

Scott Percy Moreton (1853–1924). British admiral. He joined the Royal Navy 1866 and was a fierce advocate of gunnery training and improvements and a strong believer in the future of the submarine. He commanded a cruiser squadron 1907–09, was made KCVO 1910, created a baronet 1913, and retired with admiral's rank 1913. Recalled to duty 1914, he was given command of London's air defences in the early stages of World War I and placed them on a sound footing before retiring for a second time.

Scott Peter Markham (1909–1989). British naturalist, artist, and explorer, founder of the Wildfowl Trust at Slimbridge, Gloucestershire, England, 1946, and a founder of the World Wildlife Fund (now World Wide Fund for Nature). He was knighted in 1973.

He was the son of Antarctic explorer R F Scott; he studied at Cambridge, in Germany, and at the Royal Academy School, London. In 1936 he represented Britain in the Olympic Games, gaining a bronze medal for the single-handed sailing event. During World War II he served with the Royal Navy. In 1949 he led his first expedition, which was to explore the uncharted Perry River area in the Canadian Arctic. Scott also led ornithological expeditions to

Scott, George C *Craggy, rasp-voiced US actor George C Scott achieved fame as the first actor to refuse an Academy Award (for his role in Patton 1970). He has played many roles, though he has seldom received the acclaim his authority and characterization merit.*

Iceland, Australasia, the Galápagos Islands, the Seychelles, and the Antarctic. He was the first president of the World Wildlife Fund 1961–67.

Scott's paintings were usually either portraits or bird studies. He published many books on birds, including *Key to the Wild Fowl of the World* 1949 and *Wild Geese and Eskimos* 1951, and an autobiography 1961, *The Eye of the Wind*.

Scott Randolph. Stage name of Randolph Crane (1903–1987). US actor. He began his career in romantic films before becoming one of Hollywood's leading Western stars in the 1940s. His films include *Roberta* 1934, *Jesse James* 1939, *The Tall T* 1956, and *Ride the High Country* 1962.

Scott Ridley (1939–). English film director and producer. Having started as a set designer, Scott graduated to directing episodes of the television series *Z Cars* before leaving the BBC 1967. He completed his first film *The Duellists* 1977. His work includes some of the most visually spectacular and influential films of the 1980s and 1990s, such as *Alien* 1979 and *Blade Runner* 1982. Criticized for sacrificing storyline and character development in favour of ornate sets, Scott replied with *Thelma and Louise* 1991, a carefully wrought story of female bonding and adventure. Among his other films are *Legend* 1985, *Someone to Watch Over Me* 1987, *Black Rain* 1989, and *1492 – The Conquest of Paradise* 1992.

> *Great God! this is an awful place.*
>
> ROBERT FALCON SCOTT
> on the South Pole, in his diary 17 Jan 1912

Scott Robert Falcon, (known as Scott of the Antarctic) (1868–1912). English explorer who commanded two Antarctic expeditions, 1901–04 and 1910–12. On 18 Jan 1912 he reached the South Pole, shortly after Norwegian Roald Amundsen, but on the return journey he and his companions died in a blizzard only a few miles from their base camp. His journal was recovered and published in 1913.

Born at Devonport, he entered the navy in 1882. With Scott on the final expedition were Wilson, Laurence Oates, Bowers, and Evans.
Suggested reading
Brent, P *Captain Scott and the Antarctic Tragedy* (1974)
Huntford, R *Scott and Amundsen* (1979)
Huxley, E *Scott of the Antarctic* (1978)

Scott Rose (1847–1925). Australian social reformer and suffragette. She was a founding member of the Women's Literary Society in 1889 from whose members the Womanhood Suffrage League of New South Wales was formed in 1891. Her report on conditions at Sydney's Darlinghurst Gaol led to the establishment, in 1906, of a separate prison for women. She was first president of the Women's Political Educational League, and in 1910 was instrumental in raising the age of consent to 16.

Scott Terry. Stage name of Owen John Scott (1927–1994). English comic actor. He achieved popularity on television partnering June Whitfield in *Happy Ever After* and *Terry and June* 1974–88, in which he epitomized suburban man, by turns timorous and truculent. His wide-ranging career also encompassed theatre, films, and radio. Scott played supporting roles in films, including seven of the *Carry On* series (he played Cardinal Wolsey in *Carry On Henry* 1970). He was a pantomime dame at the London Palladium for three seasons, and performed in West End stage farces such as *The Mating Game* 1972. In private life he was a lay preacher.

Scott Walter (1771–1832). Scottish novelist and poet. Born in Edinburgh, Scott was lamed for life following an early attack of poliomyelitis. His first literary works were translations of German ballads, and in 1797 he married Charlotte Charpentier or Carpenter, of French origin. His *Minstrelsy of the Scottish Border* appeared 1802, and from then he combined the practice of literature with his legal profession. *The Lay of the Last Minstrel* 1805 was an immediate success, and so too were *Marmion* 1808, *The Lady of* the Lake 1810, *Rokeby* 1813, and *Lord of the Isles* 1815. Out of the proceeds he purchased and rebuilt the house of Abbotsford on the Tweed, but Byron had to some extent now captured the lead with a newer style of verse romance, and Scott turned to prose fiction. *Waverley* was issued 1814, and gave its name to a long series of historical novels, including *Guy Mannering* 1815, *The Antiquary* 1816, *Old Mortality* 1816, *Rob Roy* 1817, *The Heart of Midlothian* 1818, and *The Bride of Lammermoor* 1819. *Ivanhoe* transferred the scene to England; *Kenilworth* 1821, *Peveril of the Peak* 1823, *The Talisman* 1825, and *The Fair Maid of Perth* 1828 followed.

O what a tangled web we weave, / When first we practise to deceive!

WALTER SCOTT
Marmion VI. 17 1808

In 1820 Scott was created a baronet, but in 1826 he was involved in financial ruin through the bankruptcy of Constable, his chief publisher, with whom fell Ballantyne & Co, the firm of printers and publishers in which Scott had been for many years a sleeping partner. Refusing to accept bankruptcy, he set himself to pay off the combined debts of £114,000. *Woodstock* 1826, a life of Napoleon, and *Tales of a Grandfather* 1827–30 are among the chief products of these last painful years. The last outstanding liabilities were cleared after his death on the security of copyrights. Continuous overwork ended in a nervous breakdown.

He died at Abbotsford on 21 Sept 1832. His *Journal* was issued 1890, and his life by J G Lockhart, his son-in-law, 1837.

Suggested reading

Brown, D *Walter Scott and the Historical Imagination* (1979)
Calder, A and J *Scott* (1971)
Mayhead, R *Walter Scott* (1968)
Wilson, A N *The Laird of Abbotsford: A View of Sir Walter Scott* (1980)

Scott Winfield (1786–1866). US military leader. Born in Petersburg, Virginia, Scott attended the College of William and Mary and began his military career 1807. As a colonel in the Anglo-American War 1812–14, he won distinction at the battles of Chippewa and Lundy's Lane. Promoted to brigadier general, he saw action in the Black Hawk War 1832 and Seminole Wars 1835–37. In 1841 he became general in chief of the army. During the Mexican War 1846–48 he led the capture of Veracruz and Mexico City. An unsuccessful Whig candidate for president 1852, Scott was still head of the army at the outbreak of the American Civil War 1861 but retired from active service in the same year.

Scribe Augustin Eugène (1791–1861). French dramatist. He achieved recognition with *Une Nuit de la garde nationale/Night of the National Guard* 1815, and with numerous assistants produced many plays of technical merit but little profundity, including *Bertrand et Raton/The School for Politicians* 1833.

Scripps James Edmund (1835–1906). US newspaper publisher who established the *Detroit Evening News* 1873, and with his younger brother Edward Wyllis Scripps (1854–1926) created the first US national newspaper chain 1880 with the *St Louis Evening Chronicle* and the *Cincinnati Post*.

Born in London, England, Scripps began his newspaper career in Chicago 1857. He later moved to Michigan and became part owner of the *Detroit Daily Advertiser* in the early 1860s. Together with his brother he founded the *Cleveland Press* 1878. He was also active in Republican politics.

Scruton Roger Vernon (1944–). British philosopher and right-wing social critic, professor of aesthetics at Birkbeck College, London, from 1985. Advocating the political theories of Edmund

---

Hospitality is the only form of gift that imposes itself as an obligation.

ROGER SCRUTON
Meaning of Conservatism 1980

Burke in such books as *The Meaning of Conservatism* 1980, he influenced the free-market movements in E Europe.

Scudamore Peter Michael (1958–). British National Hunt jockey who was champion jockey 1982 (shared with John Francome) and from 1986 to 1992. In 1988–89 he rode a record 221 winners. In April 1993 he announced his retirement from the sport, with a world record 1,677 winners. He has won over 30% of his races.

Scullin James Henry (1876–1953). Australian Labor politician. He was leader of the Federal Parliamentary Labor Party 1928–35, and prime minister and minister of industry 1929–31.

Seaborg Glenn Theodore (1912–). US nuclear chemist. For his discovery of plutonium and research on the transuranic elements, he shared a Nobel prize 1951 with his co-worker Edwin McMillan.

During part of World War II he was at the metallurgical laboratory at Chicago University, where much of the early work on the atomic bomb was carried out. He was professor at the University of California at Berkeley 1945–61, and chair of the Atomic Energy Commission 1961–71, encouraging the rapid growth of the US nuclear-power industry. He returned to Berkeley 1971.

Transuranic elements are all radioactive and none occurs to any appreciable extent in nature; they are synthesized by transmutation reactions. Seaborg was involved in the identification of plutonium (atomic number 94) 1940, americium (95) 1944–45, curium (96) 1944, berkelium (97) 1949, californium (98) 1950, einsteinium (99) 1952, fermium (100) 1953, mendelevium (101) 1955, and nobelium (102) 1957.

Searle Ronald William Fordham (1920–). English cartoonist and illustrator. He created the schoolgirls of St Trinian's characters 1941 and has made numerous cartoons of cats. His drawings, as a Japanese prisoner of war during World War II, established him as a serious artist. His sketches of places and people include *Paris Sketch Book* 1950 and *Rake's Progress* 1955.

Sebastian, St (died c. 258). Roman soldier, traditionally a member of Emperor Diocletian's bodyguard until his Christian faith was discovered. He was condemned to be killed by arrows. Feast day 20 Jan.

Sebastian is said to have survived being shot full of arrows (the manner in which he is usually depicted) and was finally beaten to death with clubs. He has been regarded since the 4th century as a protector against plague. A large number of images of him were created during the Renaissance, which may be explained as an opportunity to depict the male nude.

Sebastiano del Piombo (Sebastiano Luciani) (c. 1485–1547). Italian painter of the High Renaissance. Born in Venice, he was a pupil of Giorgione and developed a similar style of painting. In 1511 he moved to Rome, where his friendship with Michelangelo (and rivalry with Raphael) inspired him to his greatest works, such as *The Raising of Lazarus* 1517–19 (National Gallery, London). He also painted powerful portraits.

Secchi Pietro Angelo (1818–1878). Italian astronomer and astrophysicist who classified stellar spectra into four classes based on their colour and spectral characteristics. He was the first to classify solar prominences, huge jets of gas projecting from the Sun's surface.

Secchi was born in Reggio nell'Emilia and became a Jesuit priest, lecturing in physics and mathematics at the Collegio Romano from 1839. In 1848 he was driven into exile for being a Jesuit and went first to Stonyhurst College, England, then to Georgetown University in Washington DC. He returned to Italy 1849 as director of the observatory at the Collegio Romano and professor of astronomy.

With English astronomer William Huggins, Secchi was the first person to adapt spectroscopy to astronomy in a systematic manner and he made the first spectroscopic survey of the heavens. He proposed that the differences in stellar spectra reflected differences in chemical composition. His classification system of 1867 is the basis of the modern system.

Secchi was among the first to use the new technique of photography for astronomical purposes. By 1859 he had a complete set of photographs of the Moon.

Frank and genial in manner and abounding in self-confidence ... he divined what the people of New Zealand wanted, and sought to satisfy their needs.

A B White on RICHARD SEDDON
in *Dictionary of National Biography*

Seddon Richard John (1845–1906). New Zealand Liberal politician, prime minister 1893–1906.

Sedgwick Adam (1785–1873). English geologist who contributed greatly to understanding the stratigraphy of the British Isles, using fossils as an index of relative time. Together with Scottish geologist Roderick Murchison, he identified the Devonian system in SW England.

Sedgwick was born in Dent, Yorkshire, and studied mathematics at Cambridge, where he became professor of geology 1818.

An energetic champion of field work, Sedgwick explored such diverse districts as the Isle of Wight, Devon and Cornwall, the Lake District, and NE England. In the 1830s, he unravelled the stratigraphic sequence of fossil-bearing rocks in North Wales, naming the oldest of them the Cambrian period (now dated at 500–570 million years ago). In South Wales, his companion Murchison had concurrently developed the Silurian system. The question of where the boundary lay between the older Cambrian and the younger Silurian sparked a dispute that was not resolved until 1879, when Charles Lapworth (1842–1920) coined the term Ordovician for the middle ground.

Seebohm Frederick, Baron Seebohm (1909–1990). English banker and philanthropist. Seebohm joined Barclays Bank at 20, progressing to become chair 1965–72. He was highly influential in the banking world, and chaired numerous governmental and quasi-governmental committees. He was knighted 1970 and made a life peer 1972.

Seeckt Hans von (1866–1936). German general. In World War I, he planned the German offensive against Soissons, the Austro-German campaign in Galicia, and the conquest of Serbia 1915. Following the war, he became commander in chief of the new German Army 1921 and throughout the 1920s concentrated upon building up the 100,000 strong army into a highly-trained cadre which, from 1933 onward, was able to expand into the Reichswehr.

Seeger Pete(r) (1919–   ). US folk singer and songwriter. He wrote antiwar protest songs, such as 'Where Have All the Flowers Gone?' 1956 and 'If I Had a Hammer' 1949. Seeger was active in left-wing politics from the late 1930s and was a victim of the witch-hunt of Senator Joe McCarthy in the 1950s. As a member of the vocal group the Weavers 1948–58, he popularized songs of diverse ethnic origin and had several hits.

Seferis George. Assumed name of Georgios Stylianou Seferiades (1900–1971). Greek poet and diplomat. Although his poems are modernist in technique, drawing on Symbolism and Surrealism, they are steeped in a classical past and have a spare and elegant clarity. He published his first volume, *Turning Point*, 1931 and his *Collected Poems* 1950. Nobel prize 1963.

He was ambassador to Lebanon 1953–57 and to the UK 1957–62.

Segal Walter (1907–1985). Swiss-born British architect. He pioneered community architecture in the UK. From the 1960s he developed proposals for end-users to design and build their own housing, using simple construction methods and standardized low-tech building components, such as timber framing and pre-cut cladding boards. Houses built by the Lewisham Self-Build Housing Association, London, 1977–80, are examples of his system in practice.

Segar Elzie Crisler (1894–1938). US cartoonist, creator of Popeye the sailor 1929. His characters appeared in comic strips and animated films. He also created the hamburger-loving Wimpy and the adventurous baby Swee'pea.

Segovia Andrés (1893–1987). Spanish virtuoso guitarist. He transcribed J S Bach for guitar and Ponce, Castelnuovo-Tedesco, de Falla, and Villa-Lobos composed some of their best-known music for him. Segovia's artistry did much to rehabilitate the guitar as a concert instrument and to promote the music of Spain. He taught lutenist Julian Bream and guitarist John Williams.

Electric guitars are an abomination, whoever heard of an electric violin? An electric cello? Or for that matter an electric singer?

ANDRÉS SEGOVIA
on the Beatles in *Words Without Music*, 1968

Segrè Emilio Gino (1905–1989). Italian-born US physicist who in 1955 discovered the antiproton, a new form of antimatter. He shared the 1959 Nobel Prize for Physics with his co-worker Owen Chamberlain. Segrè discovered the first synthetic element, technetium (atomic number 43), in 1937.

Segrè was born near Rome and studied there, working with Enrico Fermi. Segrè became professor at Palermo 1936 but was forced into exile by the Fascist government and, apart from wartime research at Los Alamos, New Mexico, worked from 1938 at the University of California at Berkeley, where he became professor 1947.

In 1940 Segrè discovered another new element, now called astatine (atomic number 85). He again met up with Fermi, now at Columbia University, to discuss using plutonium-239 instead of uranium-235 in atomic bombs. Segrè began working on the production of plutonium at Berkeley and then moved to Los Alamos to study the spontaneous fission of uranium and plutonium isotopes.

In 1947, Segrè started work on proton–proton and proton–neutron interaction, using a cyclotron accelerator at Berkeley. This was how he detected the antiproton, which confirmed the relativistic quantum theory of English physicist Paul Dirac.

Seguin Marc (1786–1875). French engineer who, in 1825, built the first successful suspension bridge in Europe using cables of iron wire. He also invented the multitubular boiler. Seguin's first suspension bridge was built in Geneva in association with Swiss engineer Henri Dufour (1786–1875). Over the next 20 years, Seguin and his brothers erected cable suspension bridges in France, beginning with one over the river Rhône at Tournon in 1827. Seguin established France's first modern railway between Lyon and St Etienne, completed 1832.

In physics, Seguin argued that matter consisted of small, dense molecules constantly on the move in miniature solar systems and that magnetic, electrical, and thermal phenomena were the result of their particular velocities and orbits. He identified heat as molecular velocity and explained that its conversion to a mechanical effect occurs when the molecules transmit their velocities to external objects. In *De l'Influence des chemins de fer* 1839 he tried unsuccessfully to determine the numerical relationship between heat and mechanical power.

Seidler Harry (1923–   ). Austrian-born architect in Australia who studied under W Gropius, and whose work shows strong German Bauhaus influence. He is known for both functional-style domestic architecture and large public structures, including Australia Square Tower, Sydney 1967, the Australian Embassy, Paris 1977, and high-rise buildings in Mexico and Hong Kong.

Seifert Jaroslav (1901–1986). Czech poet. He won state prizes under the communists, but became an original member of the Charter 77 human-rights movement. His works include *Mozart in Prague* 1970, *Umbrella from Piccadilly* 1978, and *The Prague Column* 1979. Nobel prize 1984.

Seki Kowa (also called Takakazu) (c. 1642–1708). Japanese mathematician who created a new mathematical notation system and used it to discover many of the theorems and theories that were being – or were shortly to be – discovered in the West.

Much of his reputation stems from the social reform he introduced in order to develop the study of mathematics in Japan and make it widely accessible.

He introduced Chinese ideograms to represent unknowns and variables in equations, and although he was obliged to confine his work to equations up to the fifth degree – his algebraic alphabet (*endan-jutsu*) was not suitable for general equations of the *n*th degree – he was able to create equations with literal coefficients of any degree and with several variables, and to solve simultaneous equations. In this way he was able to derive the equivalent of $f(x)$, and thereby to arrive at the notion of a discriminant – a special function of the root of an equation expressible in terms of the coefficients.

Another of Seki's contributions was the rectification of the circle; he obtained a value for π that was correct to the 18th decimal place. Seki is also credited with major discoveries in calculus.

Selby Hubert (1928–   ). US novelist. His acclaimed first novel, *Last Exit to Brooklyn* 1964, vividly depicted urban vice and violence. It was the subject of obscenity trials in Britain 1966 and 1967. Similar portrayals followed in his later novels *The Room* 1971, *The Demon* 1976, *Requiem for a Dream* 1978, and in the stories of *Song of the Silent Snow* 1986.

Old friends are best. King James used to call for his old shoes; they were easiest for his feet.

JOHN SELDEN
Table Talk, 'Friends' 1689

Selden John (1584–1654). English antiquarian and opponent of Charles I's claim to the divine right of kings (the doctrine that the monarch is answerable to God alone), for which he was twice imprisoned. His *Table Talk* 1689 consists of short essays on political and religious questions.

Seles Monica (1973–   ). Yugoslavian lawn-tennis player who won her first Grand Slam title, the French Open, at the age of 16. She dominated the major events in 1991 but withdrew from Wimbledon and consequently missed the chance to achieve the Grand Slam. In 1991 she became the youngest woman player ever to achieve number-one ranking.

In 1993 she was stabbed by a fan of her rival, Steffi Graf, on court during the Hamburg Open. The enforced break from the game meant her missing most major tournaments 1993–95. She beat Martina Navratilova July 1995 in her first public match since the stabbing.

Seleucus I Nicator (*c.* 358–280 BC). Macedonian general under Alexander the Great and founder of the Seleucid Empire. After Alexander's death 323 BC, Seleucus became governor and (312 BC) ruler of Babylonia, founding the city of Seleucia on the river Tigris. He conquered Syria and had himself crowned king 306 BC, but his expansionist policies brought him into conflict with the Ptolemies of Egypt, and he was assassinated. He was succeeded by his son Antiochus I.

Selfridge Harry Gordon (1858–1947). US entrepreneur who in 1909 founded Selfridges in London, the first large department store in Britain.

Selkirk Alexander (1676–1721). Scottish sailor marooned 1704–09 in the Juan Fernández Islands in the S Pacific. His story inspired Daniel Defoe to write *Robinson Crusoe*.

Sellers Peter (originally Richard Henry Sellers) (1925–1980). English comedian and film actor. He was noted for his skill at mimicry. He made his name in the madcap British radio programme *The Goon Show* 1949–60. His films include *The Ladykillers* 1955, *I'm All Right Jack* 1960, *Dr Strangelove* 1964, five *Pink Panther* films 1964–78 (as the bumbling Inspector Clouseau), and *Being There* 1979.

Selous Frederick Courteney (1851–1917). British explorer and writer. His pioneer journey in the present-day Zambia and Zimbabwe area opened up the country to Europeans. He fought in the first Matabele War (1893) and was killed in the E African campaign in World War I.

The Selous Scouts were a multi-ethnic counter-insurgency force in Rhodesia 1973–80.

I have never believed in the infallibility of governments – If a Minister is right oftener than he is wrong it is a considerable achievement.

SELWYN LLOYD
in *New York Times* 'Ideas and Men' 23 May 1965

Selwyn Lloyd (John) Selwyn Brooke Lloyd, Baron Selwyn Lloyd (1904–1978). British Conservative politician. He was foreign secretary 1955–60 and chancellor of the Exchequer 1960–62. He was responsible for the creation of the National Economic Development Council, but the unpopularity of his policy of wage restraint in an attempt to defeat inflation forced his resignation. He was Speaker of the House of Commons 1971–76. Baron 1976.

Selznick David O(liver) (1902–1965). US film producer. His early work includes *King Kong, Dinner at Eight*, and *Little Women*, all 1933. His independent company, Selznick International (1935–40), made such lavish films as *Gone with the Wind* 1939, *Rebecca* 1940, and *Duel in the Sun* 1946. His last film was *A Farewell to Arms* 1957.

Sembène Ousmane (1923–   ). Senegalese writer and film director. His novels, written in French, include *Le Docker noir* 1956, about his experiences as a union leader in Marseille; *Les Bouts de bois/God's Bits of Wood* 1960; *Le Mandat/The Money Order* 1966; and *Xala* 1974, the last two of which he made into films (1968 and 1975). He later directed the film *Camp de Thiaroye* 1988.

Semenov Nikolai Nikolaevich (1896–1986). Russian physical chemist who studied chemical chain reactions, particularly branched-chain reactions, which can accelerate with explosive velocity. For his work in this area, in 1956 he became the first Russian to gain the Nobel Prize for Chemistry.

Semenov was born in Saratov and studied at Petrograd (now St Petersburg). He became professor at the Physical-Technical Institute there 1928. He was director of the Institute for Chemical Physics at the Soviet Academy of Sciences 1931–44, and then moved to Moscow State University.

Semenov did his Nobel prizewinning work in the 1920s and summarized his results in his book *Chemical Kinetics and Chain Reactions* 1934. Semenov also played an important part in resisting narrow interpretations of Marxism–Leninism in its application to chemistry.

Semiramis (lived 9th century BC). Greek name for Sammuramat, an Assyrian queen, later identified with the chief Assyrian goddess Ishtar.

Semmelweis Ignaz Philipp (1818–1865). Hungarian obstetrician who unsuccessfully pioneered asepsis (better medical hygiene), later popularized by the British surgeon Joseph Lister.

Semmelweis was an obstetric assistant at the General Hospital in Vienna at a time when 10% of women were dying of puerperal (childbed) fever. He realized that the cause was infectious matter carried on the hands of doctors treating the women after handling corpses in the postmortem room. He introduced aseptic methods (hand-washing in chlorinated lime), and mortality fell to almost zero. Semmelweis was dismissed for his efforts, which were not widely adopted at the time.

Semmes Raphael (1809–1877). American naval officer. At the outbreak of the American Civil War 1861, he joined the Confederate navy and attacked Union shipping in the Atlantic. He was placed in command of the Confederate cruiser *Alabama* 1862, losing the ship in a battle with the USS *Kearsarge* in the English Channel 1864.

Semonides (lived 7th century BC). Greek poet. What little of his work survives includes a satirical poem extending the misogyny of Hesiod's myth of Pandora, and a reflection on the unhappy life of men.

Senanayake Don Stephen (1884–1952). First prime minister of independent Sri Lanka (formerly Ceylon) 1947–52. Active in politics from 1915, he became leader of the United National Party and negotiated independence from Britain 1947. A devout Buddhist, he promoted Sinhalese-Tamil racial harmony and rural development.

Senanayake Dudley Shelton (1911–1973). Prime minister of Sri Lanka 1952–53, 1960, and 1965–70; son of Don Senanayake, he sought to continue his father's policy of communal reconciliation.

Sendak Maurice Bernard (1928–). US writer and book illustrator. Born in Brooklyn, New York, he attended the Art Students League and illustrated books for other authors. *Kenny's Window* 1956 was the first book that he both wrote and illustrated. *Very Far Away* 1957 and *The Sign on Rosie's Door* 1960 soon followed. His children's books with their deliberately arch illustrations include *Where the Wild Things Are* 1963, *In the Night Kitchen* 1970, and *Outside Over There* 1981. He also designed several works for the stage, including an operatic version of *Where the Wild Things Are* and a production of Mozart's *The Magic Flute*.

No-one can lead a happy life, or even a bearable one, without the pursuit of wisdom.

SENECA
Letters 16

Seneca Lucius Annaeus (*c.* 4 BC–*c.* AD 65). Roman stoic playwright, author of essays and nine tragedies. He was tutor to the future emperor Nero but lost favour after Nero's accession to the throne and was ordered to commit suicide. His tragedies were accepted as classical models by 16th-century dramatists.

Suggested reading
Griffin, Miriam *Seneca: A Philosopher in Politics* (1975)
Hardeman, T P *The Philosophy of Lucius Annaeus Seneca* (1956)
Sorenson, V *Seneca: The Humanist at the Court of Nero* (trs 1984)

Senefelder (Johann Nepomuk Franz) Alois (1771–1834). German engraver, born in Prague. He is thought to have invented lithography.

Senghor Léopold Sédar (1906–). Senegalese politician and writer. Senghor studied at the Sorbonne in Paris 1935–39 (the first West African to complete the *agrégation* there), where he was a strong advocate of pride in his native Africa, developing the literary movement known as *négritude*, celebrating black identity and lamenting the baneful impact of European culture on traditional black culture.

He served in the French army during World War II, and was in a German concentration camp 1940–42; his wartime experience aided him in leading his country, French West Africa, to independence 1956 as Senegal. He was the first president of independent Senegal 1960–80. Previously he was Senegalese deputy to the French National Assembly 1946–58, and founder of the Senegalese Progressive Union.

His works, written in French, include *Songs of the Shade* 1945, *Ethiopiques* 1956, and *On African Socialism* 1961. He was a founder of the journal *Présence Africaine*.

Suggested reading
Blair, D *African Literature in French* (1976)
Hymans, Jacques *Léopold Sédar Senghor* (1971)
Peters, J A *A Dance of Masks* (1978)

Senna Ayrton (1960–1994). Brazilian motor-racing driver who was killed at the 1994 San Marino Grand Prix at Imola. He won his first Grand Prix in Portugal 1985 and won 41 Grand Prix in 161 starts, including a record six wins at Monaco. Senna was world champion in 1988, 1990, and 1991.

He started his Formula One career with Toleman 1984, and went to Lotus 1985–87, before joining McLaren 1988 and winning his first World Championship. He moved to the Williams team 1993, convinced they could regain him the world title. He was on pole position for a record 65th time when he died at 260 kph/160 mph at the Tamburello corner at Imola.

Your king misleads you when he says that the Lord your God will save you from the grip of the Assyrian king.

SENNACHERIB
Boast to the Jewish defenders of Jerusalem,
the Bible, 2 Chronicles 32: 10–11

Sennacherib (died 681 BC). King of Assyria from 705 BC. Son of Sargon II, he rebuilt the city of Nineveh on a grand scale, sacked Babylon 689, and defeated Hezekiah, king of Judah, but failed to take Jerusalem. He was assassinated by his sons, and one of them, Esarhaddon, succeeded him.

A mother never gets hit with a custard-pie. Mothers-in-law, yes. But mothers, never.

MACK SENNETT
quoted in Leslie Halliwell *Filmgoer's Companion* 1965

Sennett Mack. Stage name of Michael Sinnott (1880–1960). Canadian-born US film producer. He was originally an actor. In 1911 he founded the Keystone production company, responsible for slapstick silent films featuring the Keystone Kops, Fatty Arbuckle, and Charlie Chaplin. He did not make the transition to sound with much enthusiasm and retired 1935. His films include *Tillie's Punctured Romance* 1914, *The Shriek of Araby* 1923, and *The Barber Shop* (sound) 1933.

Sequoya George Guess (*c.* 1770–1843). American Indian scholar and leader. After serving with the US army in the Creek War 1813–14, he made a study of his own Cherokee language and created a syllabary which was approved by the Cherokee council 1821. This helped thousands of Indians towards literacy and resulted in the publication of books and newspapers in their own language.

Sequoya went on to write down ancient tribal history. In later life he became political representative of the Western tribes in Washington, negotiating for the Indians when the US government forced resettlement in Indian territory in the 1830s.

A type of giant redwood tree, the sequoia, is named after him, as is a national park in California.

Sergel Johan Tobias (1740–1814). German-born Swedish Neo-Classical sculptor. He was active mainly in Stockholm. His portraits include *Gustaf III* 1790–1808 (Royal Palace, Stockholm); he also made terracotta figures such as *Mars and Venus* (National Museum, Stockholm).

Sergius, St of Radonezh (born Barfolomey Kirillovich) (1314–1392). Patron saint of Russia, who founded the Eastern Orthodox monastery of the Blessed Trinity near Moscow 1334. Mediator among Russian feudal princes, he inspired the victory of Dmitri, Grand Duke of Moscow, over the Tatar khan Mamai at Kulikovo, on the upper Don, 1380.

Serkin Rudolf (1903–1991). Austrian-born US pianist and teacher. Serkin first appeared at the age of 12 with the Vienna Symphony. He played with the New York Philharmonic orchestra in Switzerland 1936. Emigrating to the USA 1939, he joined the piano faculty of the Curtis Institute in Philadelphia, where he taught until 1975, serving as director from 1968 to 1975. He is remembered for the quality and sonority of his energetic interpretations of works by J S Bach and Mozart, Beethoven, Schubert, and Brahms. He founded, with German violinist Adolf Busch, the Marlboro Festival for chamber music in Vermont, and served as its director from 1952 until his death.

Serlio Sebastiano (1475–1554). Italian architect and painter. He was the author of *L'Architettura* 1537–51, which set down practical rules for the use of the Classical orders and was used by architects of the Neo-Classical style throughout Europe.

Serota Nicholas Andrew (1946–). British art-gallery director. He was director of the Whitechapel Art Gallery from 1976 to 1987, when he became director of the Tate Gallery, London.

Serra Junipero Blessed (1713–1784). Spanish missionary and explorer in America. A Franciscan friar, he pursued a missionary career and served in Querétaro 1750–58. He was transferred to Baja California with the expulsion of the Jesuits from Mexico 1767 and in 1769 led a missionary expedition to Alta California. He subsequently established several missions throughout the region.

Serra Richard (1939–). US sculptor. A leading exponent of the Minimalist school, he is noted for the element of risk present in his precariously balanced sculptures. His signature works of the 1970s–80s are powerful, site-specific sculptures (both outdoor and indoor), built from huge, curving steel plates with rusting surfaces, as in *Sight-Point* 1971–75 (Stedelijk Museum, Amsterdam).

Serra made innovative, splashed pieces of molten and rolled lead in the 1960s before graduating in the 1970s to his ingenious constructions of steel plates and rods.

Servan-Schreiber Jean Jacques (1924–). French Radical politician, and founder of the magazine *L'Express* 1953. His *Le Défi américain* 1967 maintained that US economic and technological dominance would be challenged only by a united left-wing Europe. He was president of the Radical Party 1971–75 and 1977–79.

I will burn, but this is a mere incident. We will continue our discussion in eternity.

MICHAEL SERVETUS
to his judges

Servetus Michael (Miguel Serveto) (1511–1553). Spanish Christian Anabaptist theologian and physician. He was a pioneer in the study of the circulation of the blood and found that it circulates to the lungs from the right chamber of the heart. He was burned alive by the church reformer Calvin in Geneva, Switzerland, for publishing attacks on the doctrine of the Trinity.

Service Robert William (1874–1958). Canadian author. He wrote ballads of the Yukon in the days of the Gold Rush, for example *The Shooting of Dan McGrew* 1907.
Suggested reading
Klinck, Carl *Robert Service: A Biography* (1976)
Service, Robert *Ploughman of the Moon* (autobiography) (1945)

Sesshū Tōyō (1420–1506). Japanese artist. He is generally considered to be one of Japan's greatest painters. He visited China 1467–68 and, though scornful of contemporary Chinese painting, was influenced by several Chinese styles. His highly individualistic work, combining subtle tones and sharp, energetic lines, helped to establish a tradition of realism in landscape painting.

Sessions Roger Huntington (1896–1985). US composer. His international Modernist style secured an American platform for serious German influences, including Hindemith and Schoenberg, and offered an alternative to the lightweight, fashionable Modernism of Milhaud and Paris. An able symphonist, his works include *The Black Maskers* (incidental music) 1923, eight symphonies, and Concerto for Orchestra 1971.

Born in Brooklyn, New York, he attended Harvard and Yale, then studied under Ernest Bloch. He became a leading teacher of composition, serving on the faculties of Boston University, Princeton University, the University of California at Berkeley, and the Juilliard School of Music.

Seton Ernest Thompson (born Ernest Seton Thompson) (1860–1946). Canadian author and naturalist. He illustrated his own books with drawings of animals. He was the founder of the Woodcraft Folk youth movement, a non-religious alternative to the scouting movement.

Seton St Elizabeth Ann (born Bayley) (1774–1821). US religious leader and social benefactor. A convert to Roman Catholicism, she founded schools for the poor. Known as 'Mother Seton,' she was proclaimed the first American saint 1975.

Born in New York, USA, Seton was devoted to the service of the poor and established the Society for the Relief of Poor Widows with Small Children 1797. After a trip to Italy and the death of her first husband, she joined the Roman Catholic Church 1805.

Seurat Georges Pierre (1859–1891). French artist. He originated, with Paul Signac, the Neo-Impressionist technique of Pointillism (painting with small dabs rather than long brushstrokes).

At 16 he went to the École des Beaux-Arts, where he remained for four years, showing a remarkable early proficiency in figure drawing. Masters whose work he studied were Delacroix (frescoes at St Sulpice) and Piero della Francesca, with whom he shows an affinity in his sense of formal and geometrical beauty. An early masterpiece was *La Baignade* of 1884 (Tate Gallery, London), in which the atmospheric effect of Impressionist painting was combined with a new solidity of form and composition.

At this time Seurat, together with his friend Signac, was interested in the colour theories of various scientists, especially the 'simultaneous contrast' and interplay of complementary colours expounded by Eugène Chevreul, with the purpose of giving a new range of vibration in the rendering of light and its effect on any surface. The method, known as 'Divisionism', of using three sets of complementaries (red and green, blue and orange, and violet and yellow) in small separate touches, was first systematically applied in Seurat's famous *A Sunday Afternoon on the Island of La Grande Jatte*, 1886 (Art Institute of Chicago), the final product of many oil sketches and drawings. Seurat practised Divisionism in a number of other works, including such beautiful landscapes as the *Bridge at Courbevoie* (Courtauld Gallery, London), the broken colour being in a sense 'Neo-Impressionist', in the term devised by his friend Felix Fénéon, though the ordered geometric scheme of composition was carefully worked out. Urban and industrial landscapes and views of the Seine and the Normandy coast were followed by compositions suggested by a metropolitan gaiety, in which the simple opposition of verticals and horizontals characterizing his landscapes is replaced by a more lively geometry, interpreting movement as in *Le Chahut* (Kröller-Müller Museum, the Netherlands) and *Le Cirque* (Louvre, Paris). As a draughtsperson Seurat was also exceptional, his drawings, executed with a greasy conté crayon on rough paper, conveying a remarkable richness of light and shade.
Suggested reading
Broude, Norma (ed) *Seurat in Perspective* (1978)
Carr-Gomm, S *Seurat* (1993)
Russell, John *Seurat* (1965)
Thomson, R *Seurat* (1985)

Severin Tim (Giles Timothy) (1940–). Writer, historian, and traveller who has re-enacted several 'classic' voyages. In 1961 he led a motorcycle team along the Marco Polo route in Asia and four years later canoed the length of the Mississippi. His Brendan Voyage 1977 followed the supposed transatlantic route taken by St Brendan in the 7th century; the Sinbad Voyage took him from Oman to China 1980–81; the Jason Voyage followed the ancient route of the Argonauts in search of the Golden Fleece 1984; the Ulysses Voyage took him from Troy to Ithaca 1985; and a journey on horseback retraced the route to the Middle East taken by the Crusaders 1987–88.

Severini Gino (1883–1966). Italian painter. As a member of the Futurist group, he was influenced by both Cubism and the Neo-Impressionism of Seurat and developed a semi-abstract style, using patterns to suggest movement. His *Suburban Train Arriving in Paris* 1915 (Tate Gallery, London) is typical of this period. From the 1920s he worked in a Neo-Classical mode. He expounded his ideas in a book *Du Cubisme au Classicism* 1921.

Be united, reward the soldiers, despise all else.

LUCIUS SEPTIMIUS SEVERUS
Dying words to his sons, quoted in Dio Cassius *History* bk 77, ch 15

Severus Lucius Septimius (146–211). Roman emperor. He held a command on the Danube when in 193 the emperor Pertinax was murdered. Proclaimed emperor by his troops, Severus had to fight campaigns against his rivals, Pescennius Niger in Syria (died AD 194) and Clodius Albinus, who was defeated at Lyons AD 197. Severus was an able administrator. He was born in N Africa at Leptis Magna, and was the only African to become emperor. He died at York while campaigning in Britain against the Caledonians.

Severus of Antioch (*c.* 467–538). Christian bishop, one of the originators of the Monophysite heresy. As patriarch of Antioch from 512, Severus was the leader of opposition to the doctrine agreed at the Council of Chalcedon 451 in an attempt to unite factions of the early church. Severus insisted that Christ existed in one nature only. He was condemned by Emperor Justin I in 518, and left Antioch for Alexandria, never to return.

Sévigné Marie de Rabutin-Chantal, Marquise de Sévigné (1626–1696). French writer. In her letters to her daughter, the Comtesse de Grignan, she paints a vivid picture of contemporary customs and events.

Seward William Henry (1801–1872). US public official. A leader of the Republican party, he was appointed secretary of state by President Lincoln 1860. Although seriously wounded in the 1865 assassination of Lincoln, Seward continued to serve as secretary of state under President Andrew Johnson to 1868, purchasing Alaska for the USA from Russia for $7.2 million 1867.

Seward was born in Florida, New York, educated at Union College, and became a lawyer 1822. He was elected to the New York state senate 1830 and served as governor 1838–42 and US senator 1849–61.

Sewell Anna (1820–1878). English author. Her only published work, *Black Beauty* 1877, tells the life story of a horse. Her aim in writing the book was "to induce kindness, sympathy, and understanding treatment of horses".

Disabled by a childhood accident, her regular outings in a horse-drawn carriage provided material for the book. She wrote *Black Beauty* during the last years of her life when she was confined indoors.

Sewell Henry (1807–1879). New Zealand politician, born in England; first prime minister of New Zealand after self-government was achieved 1856. Lack of ministerial support led to his replacement after two weeks.

Sexton Anne (born Harvey) (1928–1974). US poet. She studied with Robert Lowell and wrote similarly confessional poetry, as in *To Bedlam and Part Way Back* 1960 and *All My Pretty Ones* 1962. She committed suicide, and her *Complete Poems* appeared posthumously 1981.
Suggested reading
McClatchy, J D (ed) *Anne Sexton* (1978)
Sexton, Anne *No Evil Star: Selected Essays, Interviews and Prose* (1985)
Wood Middlebrook, Diane *Anne Sexton: A Biography* (1991)

Sextus Empiricus (*c.* AD 160–*c.* 210). Greek physician and philosopher. He was an exponent of scepticism of an agnostic, not a dogmatic, kind – that is, he rejected the view that knowledge was demonstrably impossible, and he insisted on keeping an open mind on this as on other questions. His most important work is the *Outlines of Pyrrhonism* – a summary of the scepticism of Greek philosopher Pyrrho and his successors.

His other surviving works are *Against the Learned* and *Against the Dogmatists*. Sextus' work is a valuable source for the history of philosophy, because of his impartiality in presenting the arguments of his opponents. Little is known of his life.

Seyfert Carl Keenan (1911–1960). US astronomer and astrophysicist who studied the spectra of stars and galaxies, and identified and classified the type of galaxy that now bears his name. A Seyfert galaxy has a small, bright centre caused by hot gas moving at high speed around a massive central object, possibly a black hole. Almost all Seyferts are spiral galaxies. They seem to be closely related to quasars, but are about 100 times fainter.

Seyfert was born in Cleveland, Ohio, and studied at Harvard. He was director of Barnard Observatory 1946–51, and from 1951 professor at Vanderbilt University and director of the observatory there. He was a member of the National Defence Research Committee.

In 1943, Seyfert was studying 12 active spiral galaxies with bright nuclei. His investigations showed that these galaxies contain hydrogen as well as ionized oxygen, nitrogen, and neon. On the basis of their spectra, Seyfert divided the galaxies into two types, I and II. Seyfert galaxies emit radio waves, infrared energy, X-rays, and nonthermal radiation. The gases at their centres are subject to explosions which cause them to move violently, with speeds of many thousands of kilometres per second relative to the centre of the galaxy in the case of type I, and of several hundreds of kilometres per second in the case of type II.

In 1951, Seyfert began a study of the objects now known as Seyfert's Sextet: a group of diverse extragalactic objects, of which five are spiral nebulae and one an irregular cloud. One member of the group is moving away from the others at a velocity nearly five times that at which the others are receding from each other.

Seymour family names of the dukes of Somerset (seated at Maiden Bradley, Wiltshire, England), and marquesses of Hertford (seated at Ragley Hall, Warwickshire, England); they first came to prominence through the marriage of Jane Seymour to Henry VIII.

Seymour Jane (*c.* 1509–1537). Third wife of Henry VIII, whom she married in 1536. She died soon after the birth of her son Edward VI.

Seymour Lynn (born Lynn Springbett) (1939–). Canadian ballerina. She is known for her rare dramatic talent. She was principal dancer of the Royal Ballet from 1959 and artistic director of the Munich State Opera Ballet 1978–80. She formed a partnership with Christopher Gable in such ballets as *The Invitation* 1960, *The Two Pigeons* 1961, and *Romeo and Juliet* 1966 (a role which she had to teach to Margot Fonteyn and four other ballerinas before she could dance it onstage).

Although officially retired from dancing 1987, she has continued to dance in such roles as Titiana in *Onegin*. She has also choreographed ballets including *Rashomon* 1976 and *Wolfi* 1987, on the death of Mozart.

Sforza Italian family that ruled the duchy of Milan 1450–99, 1512–15, and 1522–35. Its court was a centre of Renaissance culture and its rulers prominent patrons of the arts.

The family's original name was Attendoli but it took the name Sforza (Italian 'force') in the early 13th century. Francesco Sforza (1401–1466) obtained Milan by marriage 1441 to the Visconti heiress; then his son Galeazzo (1444–1476) ruled and became a patron of the arts. After his assassination, his brother Ludovico il Moro (1451–1508) seized power, made Milan one of the most powerful Italian states, and became a great patron of artists, especially Leonardo da Vinci. He was ousted by Louis XII of France 1499, restored 1512–15, then ousted again. His son Francesco (1495–1535) was re-established 1522 by Emperor Charles V. Francesco had no male heirs, and Milan passed to Charles 1535.

Shackleton Ernest Henry (1874–1922). Irish Antarctic explorer. In 1907–09, he commanded an expedition that reached 88° 23' S latitude, located the magnetic South Pole, and climbed Mount Erebus.

He was a member of Scott's Antarctic expedition 1901–04, and also commanded the expedition 1914–16 to cross the Antarctic, when he had to abandon his ship, the *Endurance*, crushed in the ice of the Weddell Sea. He died on board the *Quest* on his fourth expedition 1921–22 to the Antarctic. Knighted 1909.
Suggested reading
Fisher, M and J *Shackleton* (1957)
Huntford, Roland *Shackleton* (1986)
Worsley, Frank *Shackleton's Boat Journey* (1977)

Shadwell Thomas (*c.* 1642–1692). English dramatist and poet. His plays include *Epsom-Wells* 1672 and *Bury-Fair* 1689. He was involved in a violent feud with the poet Dryden, whom he attacked in *The Medal of John Bayes* 1682 and succeeded as poet laureate 1689.

The haste of a fool is the slowest thing in the world.

THOMAS SHADWELL
A True Widow III. i 1679

Shaffer Peter Levin (1926–   ). English dramatist. His psychological dramas include *Five Finger Exercise* 1958, the historical epic *The Royal Hunt of the Sun* 1964, *Equus* 1973, *Amadeus* 1979, about the envy provoked by the composer Mozart, and *Gift of the Gorgon* 1993.

Shafi'i Muhammad ibn Idris al-Shafi'i (767– AD 820). Muslim jurist, founder of one of the four main schools of Sunni Islamic law. He based the law on four points: the Koran, the sayings of Muhammad, *ijma* (the consensus of the whole Muslim community, and analogical reasoning.

Shafi'i was born in Palestine, a descendant of Muhammad's grandfather Abd al-Muttalib, and was educated in Gaza and Mecca. He wrote his first book, *Al-Usul/The Foundations*, in Baghdad. He then returned to Mecca and travelled to Egypt where he met Imam Malik. He died in Cairo, where his tomb is still a place of pilgrimage.

Shaftesbury Anthony Ashley Cooper, 1st Earl of Shaftesbury (1621–1683). English politician, a supporter of the Restoration of the monarchy. He became lord chancellor in 1672, but went into opposition in 1673 and began to organize the Whig Party. He headed the Whigs' demand for the exclusion of the future James II from the succession, secured the passing of the Habeas Corpus Act 1679, then, when accused of treason 1681, fled to Holland. Baronet 1631, baron 1661, earl 1672.

Shaftesbury Anthony Ashley Cooper, 3rd Earl of Shaftesbury (1671–1713). English philosopher, author of *Characteristics of Men, Manners, Opinions, and Times* 1711 and other ethical speculations. Earl 1699.

Shakespeare *The English dramatist and poet William Shakespeare. This portrait appeared on the title page of the edition of his works published 1623.*

Of all the artificial relations formed between mankind, the most capricious and variable is that of author and reader.

ANTHONY ASHLEY COOPER, 3RD EARL OF SHAFTESBURY
Characteristics vol iii 227 1711

Shaftesbury Anthony Ashley Cooper, 7th Earl of Shaftesbury (1801–1885). British Tory politician. He strongly supported the Ten Hours Act of 1847 and other factory legislation, including the 1842 act forbidding the employment of women and children underground in mines. He was also associated with the movement to provide free education for the poor. Earl 1851.

I cannot bear to leave the world with all the misery in it.

ANTHONY ASHLEY COOPER, 7TH EARL OF SHAFTESBURY
aged eighty-four, quoted in G W E Russell
Collections and Recollections 1904 ed

Shah Jahan (1592–1666). Mogul emperor of India from 1628, under whom the dynasty reached its zenith. Succeeding his father Jahangir, he extended Mogul authority into the Deccan plateau (E India), subjugating Ahmadnagar, Bijapur, and Golconda 1636, but lost Kandahar in the NW to the Persians 1653. His reign marked the high point of Indo-Muslim architecture, with Delhi being rebuilt as Shahjahanabad, while the Taj Mahal and Pearl Mosque were constructed at Agra. On falling seriously ill 1658 he was dethroned and imprisoned by his son Aurangzeb.

Suggested reading
Gascoigne, Bamber and Christina *The Great Moghuls* (1971)
Lal, Muni *Shahjahan* (1986)

Shahn Ben(jamin) (1898–1969). Lithuanian-born US artist. A Social Realist, his work includes drawings and paintings on the Dreyfus case and the Sacco-Vanzetti case in which two Italian anarchists were accused of murders. He painted murals for the Rockefeller Center, New York (with the Mexican artist Diego Rivera), and the Federal Security Building, Washington, 1940–42.

Suggested reading
Morse, J D (ed) *Ben Shahn* (1972)
Rodman, S *Portrait of an Artist as an American: Ben Shahn* (1951)
Shahn, Ben *The Shape of Content* (1957)
Shahn, Bernarda *Ben Shahn* (1972)

Shaka or **Chaka** (*c.* 1787–1828). Zulu chief who formed a Zulu empire in SE Africa. He seized power from his half-brother 1816 and then embarked on a bloody military campaign to unite the Zulu clans. He was assassinated by his two half-brothers.

His efforts to unite the Zulu peoples of Nguni (the area that today forms the South African province of Natal) initiated the period of warfare known as the Mfecane.

Shakespeare William (1564–1616). English dramatist and poet. Established in London by 1589 as an actor and a dramatist, he is considered the greatest English dramatist. His plays, written in blank verse with some prose, can be broadly divided into lyric plays, including *Romeo and Juliet* and *A Midsummer Night's Dream*; comedies, including *The Comedy of Errors*, *As You Like It*, *Much Ado About Nothing*, and *Measure For Measure*; historical plays, such as *Henry VI* (in three parts), *Richard III*, and *Henry IV* (in two parts), which often showed cynical political wisdom; and tragedies, such as *Hamlet*, *Macbeth*, and *King Lear*. He also wrote numerous sonnets.

Born in Stratford-on-Avon, the son of a wool dealer, he was educated at the grammar school, and in 1582 married Anne Hathaway. They had a daughter, Susanna, 1583, and twins Hamnet (died 1596) and Judith 1595. Early plays, written around 1589–93, were the tragedy *Titus Andronicus*; the comedies *The Comedy of Errors*, *The Taming of the Shrew*, and *The Two Gentlemen of Verona*; the three parts of *Henry VI*; and *Richard III*. About 1593 he came under the patronage of the Earl of Southampton, to whom he dedicated his

Shakespeare: the plays

title	performed/written (approximate)
Early plays	
Henry VI Part I	1589–92
Henry VI Part II	1589–92
Henry VI Part III	1589–92
The Comedy of Errors	1592–93
The Taming of the Shrew	1593–94
Titus Andronicus	1593–94
The Two Gentlemen of Verona	1594–95
Love's Labours Lost	1594–95
Romeo and Juliet	1594–95
Histories	
Richard III	1592–93
Richard II	1595–97
King John	1596–97
Henry IV Part I	1597–98
Henry IV Part II	1597–98
Henry V	1599
Roman plays	
Julius Caesar	1599–1600
Antony and Cleopatra	1607–08
Coriolanus	1607–08
The 'great' or 'middle' comedies	
A Midsummer Night's Dream	1595–96
The Merchant of Venice	1596–97
Much Ado About Nothing	1598–99
As You Like It	1599–1600
The Merry Wives of Windsor	1600–01
Twelfth Night	1601–02
The great tragedies	
Hamlet	1601–02
Othello	1604–05
King Lear	1605–06
Macbeth	1605–06
Timon of Athens	1607–08
The 'dark' comedies	
Troilus and Cressida	1601–02
All's Well That Ends Well	1602–03
Measure for Measure	1604–05
Late plays	
Pericles	1608–09
Cymbeline	1609–10
The Winter's Tale	1610–11
The Tempest	1611–12
Henry VIII	1612–13

long poems *Venus and Adonis* 1593 and *The Rape of Lucrece* 1594; he also wrote for him the comedy *Love's Labour's Lost*, satirizing the explorer Walter Raleigh's circle, and seems to have dedicated to him his sonnets written around 1593–96, in which the mysterious 'Dark Lady' appears. From 1594 Shakespeare was a member of the Chamberlain's (later the King's) company of players, and had no rival as a dramatist, writing, for example, the lyric plays *Romeo and Juliet*, *A Midsummer Night's Dream*, and *Richard II* 1595–97, followed by *King John* and *The Merchant of Venice* 1596–97. The Falstaff plays of 1597–99 – *Henry IV* (parts I and II), *Henry V*, and *The Merry Wives of Windsor* (said to have been written at the request of Elizabeth I) – brought his fame to its height. He wrote *Julius Caesar* 1599. The period ended with the lyrically witty *Much Ado*

About Nothing, *As You Like It*, and *Twelfth Night*, about 1598–1601. With *Hamlet* begins the period of the great tragedies, 1601–08: *Othello*, *Macbeth*, *King Lear*, *Timon of Athens*, *Antony and Cleopatra*, and *Coriolanus*. This 'darker' period is also reflected in the comedies *Troilus and Cressida*, *All's Well That Ends Well*, and *Measure for Measure* around 1601–04. It is thought that Shakespeare was only part author of *Pericles*, which is grouped with the other plays of around 1608–11 – *Cymbeline*, *The Winter's Tale*, and *The Tempest* – as the mature romance or 'reconciliation' plays of the end of his career. During 1613 it is thought that Shakespeare collaborated with John Fletcher on *Henry VIII* and *Two Noble Kinsmen*. He had already retired to Stratford about 1610, where he died on 23 April 1616. He was buried in the chancel of Holy Trinity, Stratford, and within a few years a monument was erected over his grave.

For the first 200 years after his death, Shakespeare's plays were frequently performed in cut or revised form (Nahum Tate's *King Lear* was given a happy ending), and it was not until the 19th century, with the critical assessment of Samuel Coleridge and William Hazlitt, that the original texts were restored. Appreciation of Shakespeare's plays in the present century has become analytical, examining in detail such aspects as language, structure, contemporary theatrical conditions, and the social and intellectual context of his work. His plays were collected and edited by John Hemige and Henry Condell, two of Shakespeare's former colleagues from the King's company, into the *First Folio* 1623. Later editions were published 1632, 1664, and 1685 as the Second, Third and Fourth Folios, respectively.

Shalmaneser five Assyrian kings, including:

Shalmaneser III king of Assyria 859–824 BC who pursued an aggressive policy and brought Babylon and Israel under the domination of Assyria.

Shamil Imam (*c.* 1798–1871). Caucasian warlord from the Lezgi people who led resistance to the Russian encroachment; he was also a Muslim religious leader. He united the people of the N Caucasus against the Russians and was captured 1859 only after 30 years of struggle.

Our image has undergone a change from David fighting Goliath to being Goliath.

YITZHAK SHAMIR
on Israel, *Observer* Jan 1989

Shamir Yitzhak Yernitsky (1915–). Polish-born Israeli right-wing politician; prime minister 1983–84 and 1986–92; leader of the Likud (Consolidation Party) until 1993. He was foreign minister under Menachem Begin 1980–83, and again foreign minister in Shimon Peres' unity government 1984–86.

In Oct 1986, he and Peres exchanged positions, Shamir becoming prime minister and Peres taking over as foreign minister. Shamir was re-elected 1989 and formed a new coalition government with Peres; this broke up 1990 and Shamir then formed a government without Labour membership and with religious support. He was a leader of the Stern Gang of guerrillas (1940–48) during the British mandate rule of Palestine.

Shang dynasty or Yin dynasty (*c.* 1500–*c.* 1066 BC). China's first fully authenticated dynasty, which saw the start of the Bronze Age. Shang rulers dominated the Huang He (Yellow River) plain of N China, developing a complex agricultural civilization which used a written language. The dynasty's existence was verified in the 1920s by the discovery of inscribed oracle bones ('dragon bones') at its capital situated at Anyang, N Henan.

Shankar Ravi (1920–). Indian composer and musician. A virtuoso of the sitar, he has been influential in popularizing Indian music in the West. He has composed two concertos for sitar and orchestra 1971 and 1981, and film music, including scores for Satyajit Ray's *Pather Panchali* 1955 and Richard Attenborough's *Gandhi* 1982, and founded music schools in Bombay and Los Angeles.

Shankara (*c.* 700–*c.* 750). Hindu philosopher who wrote commentaries on some of the major Hindu scriptures, as well as hymns and essays on religious ideas. Shankara was responsible for the final form of the Advaita Vedanta school of Hindu philosophy, which teaches that Brahman, the supreme being, is all that exists in the universe, everything else is illusion. Shankara was fiercely opposed to Buddhism and may have influenced its decline in India.

Shannon Claude Elwood (1916–). US mathematician who founded the science of information theory. He argued that entropy is equivalent to a shortage of information content (a degree of uncertainty), and obtained a quantitative measure of the amount of information in a given message.

Shannon reduced the notion of information to a series of yes/no choices, which could be presented by a binary code. Each choice, or piece of information, he called a 'bit'. In this way, complex information could be organized according to strict mathematical principles. He also wrote the first effective program for a chess-playing computer.

His book *The Mathematical Theory of Communication* 1949 was written with W Weaver (1894–1978).

From 1941 he worked at the Bell Telephone Laboratories, but he also held academic positions at MIT from 1956, and in 1958 he left Bell to become professor of science.

As early as 1938 Shannon began examining the question of a mathematical approach to language. His methods, although devised in the context of engineering and technology, were soon seen to have applications not only to computer design but to virtually every subject in which language was important, such as linguistics, psychology, cryptography, and phonetics; further applications were possible in any area where the transmission of information in any form was important.

Shapiro Karl Jay (1913–). US poet and critic. He is noted for the sparkling wit of his poetry and for his denunciation of Modernists (Ezra Pound, T S Eliot, and W B Yeats), and the New Criticism. His conception of the Jew as a prototype of the modern human informed his striking *V Letter and Other Poems* 1945 (Pulitzer prize) and *Poems of a Jew* 1958. Later volumes include *Adult Bookstore* 1976 and *The Younger Son* 1988.

Shapley Harlow (1885–1972). US astronomer who established that the Galaxy was much larger than previously thought. The Sun was not at the centre of the Galaxy as then assumed, but two-thirds of the way out to the rim; globular clusters were arranged in a halo around the Galaxy.

He worked at Mount Wilson Observatory, California, 1914–21, and was then appointed director of the Harvard College Observatory. Alleged by Senator Joseph McCarthy in 1950 to be a communist, he was interrogated by the House of Representatives Committee on Un-American Activities.

Shapley obtained nearly 10,000 measurements of the sizes of stars in order to analyse some 90 eclipsing binaries. He also showed that Cepheid variable stars were pulsating single stars, not double stars. He discovered many previously unknown Cepheid variables and devised a statistical procedure to establish the distance and luminosity of a Cepheid variable. Shapley's surveys recorded tens of thousands of galaxies in both hemispheres.

Sharaff Irene (1910–1993). US stage and film designer. The designer of costumes and sometimes also sets for some of the best-known musicals in both theatre and cinema, she provided a key element in a range of important productions, varying from the Oriental silks and Victorian crinolines of *The King and I* (stage 1950, film 1956) to the jeans and T-shirts of *West Side Story* (stage 1958, film 1961). She also designed costumes for several Samuel Goldwyn productions, including *Guys and Dolls* 1956. Her film work encompassed various non-musicals, among them *Who's Afraid of Virginia Woolf?* 1966 and her last film, *Mommie Dearest* 1981.

Sharif Omar. Stage name of Michael Chalhoub (1932–). Egyptian-born actor (of Lebanese parents). He was Egypt's top male star before breaking into international films after his successful appearance in *Lawrence of Arabia* 1962. His films include *Dr Zhivago* 1965 and *Funny Girl* 1968.

> *Space is out of this world.*
>
> HELEN SHARMAN
> Speech May 1991

Sharman Helen (1963–). The first Briton to fly in space, chosen from 13,000 applicants for a 1991 joint UK–Soviet space flight. Sharman, a research chemist, was launched on 18 May 1991 in *Soyuz TM-12* and spent six days with Soviet cosmonauts aboard the *Mir* space station.

> *Folk music is the ungarbled and ingenuous expression of the human mind and on that account it must reflect the essential and basic qualities of the human mind.*
>
> CECIL SHARP
> *English Folk Song* 1907

Sharp Cecil James (1859–1924). English collector and compiler of folk dance and song. His work ensured that the English folk-music revival became established in school music throughout the English-speaking world. He led a movement to record a threatened folk-song tradition for posterity, publishing *English Folk Song* 1907 (two volumes). In the USA he tracked down survivals of English song in the Appalachian Mountains and elsewhere.

> *[He had] the most inflexible of human wills united to the gentlest of human hearts.*
>
> James Stephen on GRANVILLE SHARP
> in *Dictionary of National Biography*

Sharp Granville (1735–1813). English philanthropist. He was prominent in the anti-slavery movement and in 1772 secured a legal decision 'that as soon as any slave sets foot on English territory he becomes free'.

Sharpey-Schafer Edward Albert (born Schäfer) (1850–1935). English physiologist, one of the founders of endocrinology. He made important discoveries relating to the hormone adrenaline, and to the pituitary and other endocrine, or ductless, glands. He also introduced the supine position for artificial respiration, which improved on existing techniques. Knighted 1913.

Schäfer was born in London and studied at University College; he later took the name Sharpey-Schafer to honour one of his professors, and himself became professor there 1883. From 1899 he was professor at Edinburgh.

In 1894 Sharpey-Schafer and his co-worker George Oliver (1841–1915) discovered that an extract from the central part of an adrenal gland injected into the bloodstream of an animal caused a rise in blood pressure by vasoconstriction. They also noted that the smooth muscles of the animal's bronchi relaxed. These effects were caused by the action of the hormone adrenaline.

Sharpey-Schafer also suspected that another hormone was produced by the islets of Langerhans in the pancreas. He adopted for it the name 'insulin' (from the Latin for 'island').

Shastri Lal Bahadur (1904–1966). Indian politician, prime minister 1964–66. He campaigned for national integration, and secured a declaration of peace with Pakistan at the Tashkent peace conference 1966.

Before independence, he was imprisoned several times for civil disobedience. Because of his small stature, he was known as 'the Sparrow'.

Shaw Artie. Stage name of Arthur Arshawsky (1910–). US jazz clarinettist, bandleader, and composer. He became famous in the swing era when his version of Cole Porter's 'Begin the Beguine' was a number-one hit in the USA 1938. Other hits (all with different line-ups) were 'Back Bay Shuffle' 1939 (his own composition), 'Frenesi' 1941, and 'Stardust' 1942. He retired 1952.

> *He is a daring pilgrim who has set out from the grave to find the cradle. He started from points of view that no one else was clever enough to discover, and he is at last discovering points of view which no one else was ever stupid enough to ignore.*
>
> G K Chesterton on GEORGE BERNARD SHAW
> in *Essays* 'Shaw the Puritan' 1936

Shaw George Bernard (1856–1950). Irish dramatist. He was also a critic and novelist, and an early member of the socialist Fabian Society. His plays combine comedy with political, philosophical, and polemic aspects, aiming to make an impact on his audience's social conscience as well as their emotions.

Born in Dublin, the son of a civil servant, Shaw went to London 1876, where he became a brilliant debater and supporter of the Fabians, and worked as a music and drama critic. He wrote five unsuccessful novels before his first play, *Widowers' Houses*, was privately produced 1892. Attacking slum landlords, it allied him with the realistic, political, and polemical movement in the theatre, pointing to people's responsibility to improve themselves and their social environment. His first public production was *Arms and the Man*, a cynical view of war.

The volume *Plays: Pleasant and Unpleasant* 1898 also included *The Philanderer; Mrs Warren's Profession*, dealing with prostitution and banned until 1902; and *Arms and the Man* 1894. *Three Plays for Puritans* 1901 contained *The Devil's Disciple* 1897, *Caesar and Cleopatra* 1899 (a companion piece to Shakespeare's *Antony and Cleopatra*), and *Captain Brassbound's Conversion* 1899, written for the actress Ellen Terry. *Man and Superman* 1903 expounds his ideas of evolution by following the character of Don Juan into hell for a debate with the devil.

The 'anti-romantic' comedy *Pygmalion*, first performed 1913, was written for the actress Mrs Patrick Campbell (and after Shaw's death converted to a musical as *My Fair Lady*). Later plays included *Heartbreak House* 1920, *Back to Methuselah* 1922, and the historical *St Joan* 1923.

Altogether Shaw wrote more than 50 plays and became a byword for wit. His theories were further explained in the voluminous prefaces to the plays, and in books such as *The Intelligent Woman's Guide to Socialism and Capitalism* 1928. He was also an unsuccessful advocate of spelling reform and a prolific letter-writer.

Suggested reading
Ganz, A *George Bernard Shaw* (1983)
Gibbs, A M *The Art and Mind of Shaw* (1983)
Henderson, A *George Bernard Shaw: Man of the Century* (1957)
Holroyd, M *George Bernard Shaw* (1988)
Pearson, H *Bernard Shaw: His Life and Personality* (1942)
Purdon, C B *A Guide to the Plays of Bernard Shaw* (1963)

Shaw (Richard) Norman (1831–1912). English architect, born in Edinburgh. He was the leader of the trend away from Gothic and Tudor styles back to Georgian designs. In partnership with W E Nesfield (1835–1888), he began working in the Arts and Crafts tradition, designing simple country houses using local materials, in a style known as Old English. The two then went on to develop the Queen Anne style, inspired by 17th-century Dutch domestic architecture, of which Shaw's design for Swan House, Chelsea, London 1876, is a fine example. Shaw's later style was Imperial Baroque, as in the Piccadilly Hotel 1905.

Shaw (William) Napier (1854–1945). English meteorologist who introduced the millibar as the meteorological unit of atmospheric pressure (in 1909, but not used internationally until 1929). He also invented the tephigram, a thermodynamic diagram widely used in meteorology, in about 1915. Knighted 1915.

Shaw was born in Birmingham and studied at Cambridge, where he worked at the Cavendish Laboratory for experimental physics 1877–1900. He was director of the Meteorological Office 1905–20, and professor of meteorology at the Royal College of Science (part of London University) 1920–24.

Shaw pioneered the study of the upper atmosphere by using instruments carried by kites and high-altitude balloons. His work on pressure fronts formed the basis of a great deal of later work in the field.

His books include *Life History of Surface Air Currents* 1906 and *The Air and its Ways* 1923 (both with his colleague R Lempfert) and (with J. S. Owens) *The Smoke Problem of Great Cities* 1925, an early work on atmospheric pollution. Shaw's *Manual of Meteorology* 1926–31 is still a standard reference work.

Shawn William. Adopted name of William Chon (1907–1992). US journalist, editor 1952–87 of the *New Yorker* cultural magazine, where he nurtured many outstanding writers.

Shawn grew up in Chicago, where he was briefly the Midwest editor of the *International Illustrated News*. He started at the *New Yorker* 1933 as a reporter, went on to become associate editor and then managing editor. As managing editor 1939–52, responsible for the factual output, he helped establish the magazine's famous commitment to absolute accuracy. He then succeeded the magazine's founding editor, Harold Ross, who died in 1951.

Shawn is generally credited with having transformed the *New Yorker* from being an entertaining magazine to one of the USA's most influential cultural institutions. During his tenure as editor, some of the country's finest writers were contributors, including film critic Pauline Kael, fiction writers J D Salinger, John Cheever, and John Updike, and poets W H Auden and James Merrill.

Renowned for his shyness and courtesy, Shawn was held in great affection and respect by those who worked for him. When, in 1987, the Newhouse family of media magnates removed Shawn and appointed a new editor, Robert Gottlieb, 154 writers and contributors signed a letter asking Gottlieb to withdraw. After he left the *New Yorker*, Shawn worked as a special editor for the publisher Farrar, Straus and Giroux.

Shays Daniel (c. 1747–1825). American political agitator. In 1786 he led Shays Rebellion, an armed uprising of impoverished farmers, against the refusal of the state government to offer economic relief. The riot was suppressed 1787 by a Massachusetts militia force, but it drew public attention to the plight of the western farmers and the need for a stronger central government. Shays was pardoned 1788.

Shchedrin N. Pen name of Mikhail Evgrafovich Saltykov (1826–1889). Russian writer. His works include *Fables* 1884–85, in which he depicts misplaced 'good intentions', and the novel *The Golovlevs* 1880. He was a satirist of pessimistic outlook. He was exiled for seven years for an early story that proved too liberal for the authorities, but later held official posts.

Shearer (Edith) Norma (1900–1983). Canadian-born US actress. She starred in silent films and in talkies such as *Private Lives* 1931, *Romeo and Juliet* 1936, *Marie Antoinette* 1938, and *The Women* 1939. She was married to MGM executive Irving Thalberg and retired after *Her Cardboard Lover* 1942.

Sheeler Charles (1883–1965). US painter. He was known for his paintings of factories, urban landscapes, and machinery, as in *Upper Deck* 1929 (Fogg Art Museum, Cambridge, Massachusetts). He was associated with Precisionism, a movement that used sharply defined shapes to represent objects. His method was to photograph his subjects before painting them.

> *The Jesuit of Berkeley Square.*
>
> George III on WILLIAM PETTY, 2ND EARL OF SHELBURNE
> quoted in *The Correspondence of George III with Lord North* 1927–28

Shelburne William Petty, 2nd Earl of Shelburne (1737–1805). British Whig politician. He was an opponent of George III's

American policy, and as prime minister in 1783, he concluded peace with the United States of America.

He was created Marquess of Lansdowne in 1784.

Shelley Mary Wollstonecraft (born Godwin) (1797–1851). English writer. She was the daughter of Mary Wollstonecraft and William Godwin. In 1814 she eloped with the poet Percy Bysshe Shelley, whom she married 1816. Her novels include *Frankenstein* 1818, *The Last Man* 1826, and *Valperga* 1823.
Suggested reading
Dunn, J *Moon in Eclipse: A Life of Mary Shelley* (1978)
Nitchie, E *Mary Shelley, Author of Frankenstein* (1953)
Spark, M *Child of Light* (1951)

Shelley Percy Bysshe (1792–1822). English lyric poet. He was a leading figure in the Romantic movement. He fought all his life against religion and for political freedom. Born near Horsham, Sussex, he was educated at Eton public school and University College, Oxford, where his collaboration in a pamphlet *The Necessity of Atheism* 1811 caused his expulsion. While living in London he fell in love with 16-year-old Harriet Westbrook, whom he married 1811. He visited Ireland and Wales, writing pamphlets defending vegetarianism and political freedom, and in 1813 published privately *Queen Mab*, a poem with political freedom as its theme. Meanwhile he had become estranged from his wife and in 1814 left England with Mary Wollstonecraft Godwin, whom he married after Harriet drowned herself 1816. *Alastor*, written 1815, was followed by the epic *The Revolt of Islam*, and by 1818 Shelley was living in Italy. Here he produced the tragedy *The Cenci* 1818; the satire on Wordsworth, *Peter Bell the Third* 1819; and the lyric drama *Prometheus Unbound* 1820. Other works of the period are 'Ode to the West Wind' 1819; 'The Cloud' and 'The Skylark', both 1820; 'The Sensitive Plant' and 'The Witch of Atlas'; 'Epipsychidion' and, on the death of the poet Keats, 'Adonais' 1821; the lyric drama *Hellas* 1822; and the prose *Defence of Poetry* 1821. In July 1822 Shelley was drowned while sailing near Viareggio, and his ashes were buried in Rome.
Suggested reading
Blunden, Edmund *Shelley: A Life Story* (1965)
Cameron, K N *The Young Shelley: Genesis of a Radical* (1951)
Cameron, K N *Shelley: The Golden Years* (1974)
Holmes, R *Shelley, The Pursuit* (1974)
Tomalin, C *Shelley and his World* (1980)
White, N I *Shelley* (1972)

Shen Chou (1427–1509). Chinese painter. He depicted sensitive landscapes. His style drew on the work of the old masters of Chinese painting and, possibly, also on that of Japanese artist Sesshū.

Laws are generally found to be nets of such a texture, as the little creep through, the great break through, and the middle-sized are alone entangled in.

WILLIAM SHENSTONE
Essays, 'On Politics' 1764–69

Shenstone William (1714–1763). English poet and essayist. His poems include *Poems upon Various Occasions* 1737, the Spenserian *Schoolmistress* 1742, elegies, odes, songs, and ballads.

Shepard Alan Bartlett (1923–). US astronaut, the fifth person to walk on the Moon. Shepard was born in New Hampshire and studied at the US Naval Academy in Annapolis. After working as a naval pilot and test pilot, he was selected to be a NASA astronaut 1959. He was the first American in space, as pilot of *Mercury-Redstone 3* the suborbital mission on board the *Freedom 7* capsule May 1961, and commanded the *Apollo 14* lunar landing mission 1971. He resigned 1974.

Shepard E(rnest) H(oward) (1879–1976). English illustrator. He illustrated books by A A Milne (*Winnie-the-Pooh* 1926) and Kenneth Grahame (*The Wind in the Willows* 1908).

Shepard Sam (born Samuel Shepard Rogers) (1943–). US dramatist and actor. His work combines colloquial American dialogue

with striking visual imagery, and includes *The Tooth of Crime* 1972 and *Buried Child* 1978, for which he won a Pulitzer prize. *Seduced* 1979 is based on the life of the recluse Howard Hughes. He has acted in a number of films, including *The Right Stuff* 1983, *Fool for Love* 1986, based on his play of the same name, and *Steel Magnolias* 1989, and directed the film *Silent Tongue* 1994.

Shephard Gillian Patricia (1940–). British Conservative politician, education and employment secretary from 1995. After a career in education as an extra-mural lecturer and an education officer and schools' inspector, Shephard entered politics in her mid-forties, winning the South-West Norfolk seat 1987. She made steady progress through ministerial ranks, entering the cabinet as secretary of state for employment 1992, and then moved rapidly through agriculture to education. She became education secretary 1994 at a time when relations between government and the profession were particularly fraught. Her open conciliatory approach did much initially to alleviate the situation, although teachers' patience rapidly dissipated in the face of on-going cuts in education budgets. In the cabinet reshuffle that followed Prime Minister John Major's successful re-election bid for the party leadership July 1995, she was also given responsiblity for employment.

Of two virtues have I ever cherished an honest pride. Never have I stooped to friendship with Jonathan Wild ... and though an undutiful son, I never damned my mother's eyes.

JACK SHEPPARD
Last words 1724

Sheppard Jack (John) (1702–1724). English criminal. Born in Stepney, E London, he was an apprentice carpenter, but turned to theft and became a popular hero by escaping four times from prison. He was finally caught and hanged.

Sher Antony (1949–). South African-born actor. A versatile performer in contemporary and classic drama, his roles include *Richard III* 1984, Shylock in *The Merchant of Venice* 1987, the title role in Peter Flannery's *Singer* 1989, and Tamburlaine in Marlowe's tragedy 1992. For television, he played Howard Kirk in Malcolm Bradbury's *The History Man* 1981.

Sheraton Thomas (1751–1806). English designer of elegant inlaid furniture. He was influenced by his predecessors Hepplewhite and Chippendale. He published the *Cabinet-maker's and Upholsterer's Drawing Book* 1791.

The only good Indian is a dead Indian.

PHILIP SHERIDAN
Attributed remark, at Fort Cobb Jan 1869

Sheridan Philip Henry (1831–1888). Union general in the American Civil War. Recognizing Sheridan's aggressive spirit, General Ulysses S Grant gave him command of his cavalry in 1864, and soon after of the Army of the Shenandoah Valley, Virginia. Sheridan laid waste to the valley, cutting off grain supplies to the Confederate armies. In the final stage of the war, Sheridan forced General Robert E Lee to retreat to Appomattox and surrender.

Following the war, Sheridan led troops at the Mexican border and hastened the collapse of the regime of Emperor Maximilian. Sheridan served as military governor of Texas and Louisiana during Reconstruction; his policies were so harsh that he was removed by President Andrew Johnson. He was general in chief of the US army 1883–88.

Sheridan Richard Brinsley (1751–1816). Irish dramatist and politician. His social comedies include *The Rivals* 1775, celebrated for the character of Mrs Malaprop, and *The School for Scandal* 1777. He also wrote a burlesque, *The Critic* 1779. In 1776 he became lessee of the Drury Lane Theatre. He became a member of Parliament 1780.

He entered Parliament as an adherent of Charles Fox. A noted orator, he directed the impeachment of the former governor general of India, Warren Hastings, and was treasurer to the Navy 1806–07. His last years were clouded by the burning down of his theatre 1809, the loss of his parliamentary seat 1812, and by financial ruin and mental breakdown.

Suggested reading
Auburn, Mark *Sheridan's Comedies* (1977)
Ayling, Stanley *A Portrait of Sheridan* (1985)
Sherwin, Oscar *Uncorking Old Sherry* (1960)

Sherman Roger (1721–1793). American public official. He was one of the signatories of the Declaration of Independence 1776, the Articles of Confederation 1781, and the US Constitution 1788. A supporter of American independence, he was a member of the Continental Congress 1774–81 and 1783–84. At the Constitutional Convention 1787 he introduced the 'Connecticut Compromise', providing for a bicameral federal legislature. Sherman served in the US House of Representatives 1789–91 and the US Senate 1791–93.

There is many a boy here to-day who looks on war as all glory, but, boys, it is all hell.

WILLIAM SHERMAN
Speech 1880

Sherman William Tecumseh (1820–1891). Union general in the American Civil War. He served in the Mexican War and then became a banker. Early in the Civil War he served at the First Battle of Bull Run 1861 and Shiloh 1862. He replaced General U S Grant as commander of the West 1864 and launched his Georgia campaign. In 1864 he captured and burned Atlanta; continued his march eastward, to the sea, laying Georgia waste; and then drove the Confederates northward.

Despite the ruthlessness of his campaign to capture Atlanta and the widespread destruction he inflicted as he marched to the sea, he was conciliatory in victory, offering terms that had to be repudiated by President A Johnson. After the war, there was a move to nominate Sherman for president, but he announced that he would not run if nominated and would not serve if elected. He succeeded Grant as commander of the army 1869–83.

Suggested reading
Lucas, M B *Sherman and the Burning of Columbia* (1988)
Merrill James M *William Tecumseh Sherman* (1971)
Sherman, William Tecumseh *Memoirs* (1875, rep 1957)
Williams, T H *McClelan, Sherman and Grant* (1962)

A useful corrective to the romantic conception of war.

G B Shaw's verdict on R C SHERRIFF's *Journey's End*
quoted in *The Bloomsbury Theatre Guide* 1988

Sherriff R(obert) C(edric) (1896–1975). English dramatist. He is remembered for the antiheroic war play *Journey's End* 1928. Later plays include *Badger's Green* 1930 and *Home at Seven* 1950.

Sherrington Charles Scott (1857–1952). English neurophysiologist who studied the structure and function of the nervous system. *The Integrative Action of the Nervous System* 1906 formulated the principles of reflex action. Nobel Prize for Physiology or Medicine 1932. GBE 1922.

He showed that when one set of antagonistic muscles is activated, the opposing set is inhibited. This theory of reciprocal innervation is known as Sherrington's law. Sherrington also identified the regions of the brain that govern movement and sensation in particular parts of the body.

Sherrington was born in London and studied there at St Thomas's Hospital and at Cambridge. He became professor at London University's veterinary institute 1891, at Liverpool 1895, and was professor of physiology at Oxford 1913–35. During World War I,

for three months he worked incognito as a labourer in a munitions factory, and the observations he made there did much to improve safety for factory workers.

One of Sherrington's findings, published 1894, was that the nerve supply to muscles contains 25–50% sensory fibres, as well as motor fibres concerned with stimulating muscle contraction. The sensory fibres carry sensation to the brain so that it can determine, for example, the degree of tension in the muscles. Sherrington divided the sense organs into three groups: interoceptive, characterized by taste receptors; exteroceptive, such as receptors that detect sound, smell, light, and touch; and proprioceptive, which involve the function of the synapse (Sherrington's word) and respond to events inside the body.

In 1906 Sherrington investigated the scratch reflex of a dog, using an electric 'flea', and found that the reflex stimulated 19 muscles to beat rhythmically five times a second, and brought into action a further 17 muscles which kept the dog upright. The exteroceptive sensors initiated the order to scratch, and the proprioceptors initiated the muscles to keep the animal upright.

Sherrington also carried out significant work in the development of antitoxins, particularly those for cholera and diphtheria.

Sherwood Robert Emmet (1896–1955). US dramatist. His plays include *The Petrified Forest* 1935, the melodrama *Idiot's Delight* 1936, *Abe Lincoln in Illinois* 1938, and *There Shall Be No Night* 1940. For each of the last three he received a Pulitzer prize.

Sherman, William US general William Tecumseh Sherman who as a leader of the Union forces in the American Civil War was second only to Ulysses Grant. Attempting to destroy Confederate supplies and morale, he waged an economic campaign against the civilian population of Georgia and the Carolinas, laying waste to the countryside.

Shevardnadze *Although reputedly unpopular and authoritarian as secretary of the Georgian Communist Party in the 1970s, Edvard Shevardnadze won worldwide renown for his work on disarmament. After the collapse of the Soviet Union, he became president of Georgia, but had to fight a bloody civil war with supporters of the former president Zviad Gamsakhurdia.*

A member of the Algonquin Round Table, Sherwood worked as a magazine editor during the 1920s. Later he became Franklin Roosevelt's speechwriter and adviser and held various political offices. After World War II he produced little important theatrical material except for the Academy Award-winning film *The Best Years of Our Lives* 1946.

His ironic pessimism grew darker.

Phyllis Hartnoll on ROBERT SHERWOOD in
Oxford Companion to the Theatre 1983

Shevardnadze Edvard Amvrosievich (1928–). Georgian politician, Soviet foreign minister 1985–91, head of the state of Georgia from 1992. A supporter of Gorbachev, he was first secretary of the Georgian Communist Party from 1972 and an advocate of economic reform. In 1985 he became a member of the Politburo, working for détente and disarmament. In July 1991, he resigned from the Communist Party (CPSU) and, along with other reformers and leading democrats, established the Democratic Reform Movement. In March 1992 he was chosen as chair of Georgia's ruling military council, and in Oct was elected speaker of parliament (equivalent to president). He survived an assassination attempt 1995.

On 20 Dec 1990, he dramatically resigned as foreign minister in protest against what he viewed as the onset of a dictatorship in the USSR, as reactionary forces, particularly within the military, regained the ascendancy. Following the abortive anti-Gorbachev attempted coup Aug 1991 (in which he stood alongside Boris

Yeltsin) and the dissolution of the CPSU, his Democratic Reform Party stood out as a key force in the 'new politics' of Russia and the USSR. Shevardnadze turned down an offer from President Gorbachev to join the post-coup Soviet security council, but subsequently agreed to join Gorbachev's advisory council. In March 1992, following the ousting of President Gamsakhurdia, he was chosen as chair of Georgia's ruling State Council, and in the first parliamentary elections in Oct was elected speaker of parliament, with 90% of the vote.

Shevardnadze inherited a nation riven by a continuing civil war and secessionist movement in Abkhazia. Reluctantly, he turned to Russia for military aid to crush the insurgencies and attempted to disband private militias. He was directly elected executive president Nov 1995.

Shevchenko Taras Hryhorovych (1814–1861). Ukrainian national poet. Born a serf, he was freed (for 2,500 roubles) in St Petersburg, where he then studied art. His sensationally successful first collection *Kobzar/Folk Minstrel* 1840 romantically glorified the Ukraine's Cossack past. It was followed by the long poem *Haidamaky/The Haidamaks* 1841. His protest against injustice and tsarist oppression in the Ukraine led to a ban on publication of his poems and eventual exile and penal servitude for subversive activity.

Shidehara Kijuro (1872–1951). Japanese politician and diplomat, prime minister 1945–46. As foreign minister 1924–27 and 1929–31, he promoted conciliation with China, and economic rather than military expansion. After a brief period as prime minister 1945–46, he became speaker of the Japanese Diet (parliament) 1946–51.

Shi Huangdi or Shih Huang Ti (*c.* 259–*c.* 210 BC). Emperor of China who succeeded to the throne of the state of Qin in 246 BC and had reunited China as an empire by 228 BC. He burned almost all existing books in 213 BC to destroy ties with the past; rebuilt the Great Wall of China; and was buried in Xian, Shaanxi province, in a tomb complex guarded by 10,000 life-size terracotta warriors (excavated in the 1980s). He had so overextended his power that the dynasty and the empire collapsed with the death of his weak successor in 207 BC.

Shilton Peter (1949–). English international footballer, an outstanding goalkeeper, who has set records for the highest number of Football League appearances (995 to start of 1994/95 season) and England caps (125). First capped by England 1970 he retired from international football 1990, after the England–West Germany World Cup semifinal. He was manager of Plymouth Argyle 1992–95.

Shilts Randy Martin (1951–1994). US journalist and writer. As a reporter on the *San Francisco Chronicle* from 1981, he pioneered awareness of the AIDS epidemic in the USA. *The Mayor of Castro Street: The Life and Times of Harvey Milk* 1982 is his biography of a local politician murdered 1978 as well as an analysis of prejudice against homosexuals in US politics.

Shilts was one of the first openly gay reporters in the USA, writing for the *Advocate* in the 1970s. In *And the Band Played On: Politics, People, and the AIDS Epidemic* 1987 he exposed the Reagan administration's inadequate handling of the AIDS crisis. His last book was *Conduct Unbecoming: Lesbians and Gays in the US Military* 1993.

Shimazaki Tōson (1872–1943). Japanese poet and novelist. His work explores the clash of old and new values in rapidly modernizing Japan. He published romantic poetry in the 1890s and *Hakai/Broken Commandment* 1906, the first Japanese naturalist novel, as well as the confessional novel *Ie/The House* 1910–11. *Yoake mae/Before the Dawn* 1935 is an account of the struggle for the restoration of the Empire 1862 from the perspective of a rural community.

Shirer William L(awrence) (1904–1993). US journalist, author, and historian. A columnist and commentator for the Columbia Broadcasting System (CBS), from 1937 to 1941 he covered the events leading up to World War II. He remained with CBS until 1947 and worked for the Mutual Broadcasting System 1947–49.

In 1937 Shirer was appointed CBS man in Vienna, reporting on Hitler's seizure of Austria March 1938. Moving to Geneva and later Berlin, he covered, in characteristically calm, clearly worded reports, Hitler's rapid advance into E Europe, including the invasion of Czechoslovakia and the Blitzkrieg against Poland. His greatest scoop came with the signing of the Armistice in Compiègne June 1940 when, due to an engineer's error, Shirer's report went on the air before the Führer had himself announced the event. Six months later, frustrated by Nazi censorship, he returned to the USA. From 1942 to 1948 he wrote for the *Herald Tribune*, returning to Germany to cover the Nuremberg trials. Later blacklisted by McCarthy, he left broadcasting to dedicate himself to lecturing and writing. His minutely observed diary records were published 1941 as *Berlin Diary: The Journal of a Foreign Correspondent 1934–41*. Later, he set them in a historical context in his monumental study of Hitlerism *The Rise and Fall of the Third Reich* 1960. His other works include *The Sinking of the Bismarck* 1962, *The Collapse of the Third Republic: An Enquiry into the Fall of France in 1940* 1969, *Gandhi: A Memoir* 1980, and *The Nightmare Years: 1930–1940* 1984.

Shnitke Alfred Garriyevich, or Schnittke (1934–). Russian composer. He has experimented with integral serialism and unusual instrumental textures, which are characteristically rich with a prominent use of strings, often using quotations and parodies. Among his many works are ... *pianissimo...* 1969 for orchestra, *Sinfonia* 1972, the oratorio *Nagasaki* 1958, and *Minnesang/Lovesong* 1981 for 48 voices.

Shockley William Bradford (1910–1989). US physicist and amateur geneticist who worked with John Bardeen and Walter Brattain on the invention of the transistor. They were jointly awarded a Nobel prize 1956. During the 1970s Shockley was criticized for his claim that blacks were genetically inferior to whites in terms of intelligence. He donated his sperm to the bank in S California established by the plastic-lens millionaire Robert Graham for the passing-on of the genetic code of geniuses.

Shoemaker Willie (William Lee) (1931–). US jockey 1949–90. He rode 8,833 winners from 40,351 mounts and his earnings exceeded $123 million. He retired Feb 1990 after finishing fourth on Patchy Groundfog at Santa Anita, California. He was the leading US jockey ten times. Standing 1.5 m/4 ft 11 in tall, he weighed about 43 kg/95 lb.

Sholes Christopher Latham (1819–1890). American printer and newspaper editor who, in 1867, invented the first practicable typewriter in association with Carlos Glidden and Samuel Soulé. In 1873, they sold their patents to Remington & Sons, a firm of gunsmiths in New York, who developed and sold the machine commercially. In 1878 Sholes developed a shift-key mechanism that made it possible to touch-type.

Sholokhov Mikhail Aleksandrovich (1905–1984). Russian novelist. His *And Quiet Flows the Don* 1926–40, hailed in the Soviet Union as a masterpiece of Socialist Realism, depicts the Don Cossacks through World War I and the Russian Revolution. His authorship of the novel was challenged by Alexander Solzhenitsyn. Nobel prize 1965.

Shore Dinah (Frances Rose) (1917–1994). US pop singer, actress, and television talk-show hostess who was one of the best-selling female vocalists of the 1940s, with hits including 'The Gypsy' 1946, 'Doin' What Comes Natur'lly' 1946, and 'Buttons and Bows' 1948. She also appeared in a number of musical films, but became best known as a television personality over a 40 year period from 1951.

A Soviet composer's reply to just criticism.
DMITRY SHOSTAKOVICH
Epigraph to his fifth symphony

Shostakovich Dmitry Dmitriyevich (1906–1975). Soviet composer. His music is tonal, expressive, and sometimes highly dramatic; it was not always to official Soviet taste. He wrote 15 symphonies, chamber and film music, ballets, and operas, the latter including *Lady Macbeth of Mtsensk* 1934, which was suppressed as 'too divorced from the proletariat', but revived as *Katerina Izmaylova* 1963.

His son Maxim (1938–), a conductor, defected to the West after his father's death.

Suggested reading
Kay, Norman F *Shostakovich* (1971)
MacDonald, Ian *The New Shostakovich* (1990)
Roseberry, Eric *Shostakovich: His Life and Times* (1982)
Shostakovich, Dimitri *Testimony: The Memoirs of Dmitri Shostakovich* (1979)

Shovell Cloudesley (1650–1707). English admiral who took part, with George Rooke (1650–1709), in the capture of Gibraltar 1704. In 1707 his flagship *Association* was wrecked off the Isles of Scilly and he was strangled for his rings by an islander when he came ashore. Knighted 1689.

Shrapnel Henry (1761–1842). British army officer who invented shells containing bullets, to increase the spread of casualties, first used 1804; hence the word shrapnel to describe shell fragments.

He received a commission in the Royal Artillery in 1779, and in the following year he went to Newfoundland, returning to England 1783. He served in the Duke of York's unsuccessful campaign against France 1793, being wounded in the siege of Dunkirk. In 1804, he was appointed inspector of artillery at the Royal Arsenal in Woolwich, London. He retired with the rank of lieutenant general. Shrapnel had spent several thousand pounds of his own money in perfecting his inventions. The Treasury eventually granted him a pension of £1,200 a year for life.

Shrapnel's shell was fused and filled with musket balls, plus a small charge of black powder to explode the container after a predetermined period of time. The first shells were round; later they were of an elongated form with added velocity. Shrapnel's shells continued to be used until World War I.

Shultz George Pratt (1920–). US Republican politician, economics adviser to President Reagan 1980–82, and secretary of state 1982–89. Shultz taught as a labour economist at the University of Chicago before serving in the 1968–74 Nixon administration. His posts included secretary of labor 1969–70 and secretary of the treasury 1972–74.

Shuman Mort (1936–). See ◊Pomus and Shuman, US pop-music writing partnership.

Shushkevich Stanislav (1934–). Belarus politician, president 1991–94. Shushkevich, the son of a poet who died in the gulag, was deputy rector for science at the Lenin State University in Minsk. He entered politics as a result of his concern at the Soviet cover-up of the Chernobyl disaster 1986. He was elected to parliament as a nationalist 'reform communist' 1990 and played a key role in the creation of the Commonwealth of Independent States as the successor to the Soviet Union. A supporter of free-market reforms, he opposed alignment of Belarus' economic and foreign policy with that of neighbouring Russia.

Shuster Joe (Joseph) (1914–1992). Canadian-born US cartoonist who, with writer Jerry Siegel (1914–), created the world's first comic-strip superhero, Superman, 1938. It spawned 44 different comic-book series, radio shows, film serials, animated cartoons, television shows, and four of the highest-grossing films in cinema history.

Shute Nevil. Pen name of Nevil Shute Norway (1899–1960). English novelist. Among his books are *A Town Like Alice* 1949 and *On the Beach* 1957. He settled in Australia 1950, having previously flown his own plane to Australia 1948–49 to research material for his books. *On the Beach* was filmed 1959.

Siad Barre Mohamed (1921–1995). Somalian soldier and politician, president of Somalia 1969–91. Born in the Ogaden region, a member of the Marehan clan, Siad Barre, despite only a rudimentary education, rose from the rank of ordinary police officer in Italian-controlled Somalia to become brigadier general of police when his country achieved independence 1960, and commander in chief of the armed forces five years later. When the Somalian president died in 1969, Siad Barre, with 20 fellow army officers and five police officers, seized power, suspended the constitution, and began to rule by decree. His repressive regime became increasingly discredited and in Jan 1991 his opponents forced him out of office.

He left the capital, Mogadishu, to return to his own clan area, from where he hoped to rally support and return to power. In April 1992 he went into exile in Kenya, where he became a source of embarrassment to the government of President Arap Moi, who eventually persuaded him to accept the protection of Nigeria, where he died.

Pay no attention to what the critics say; there has never been a statue set up in honour of a critic.

JEAN SIBELIUS
Attributed remark

Sibelius Jean Julius Christian (1865–1957). Finnish composer. His works include nationalistic symphonic poems such as *En saga* 1893 and *Finlandia* 1900, a violin concerto 1904, and seven symphonies.

He studied the violin and composition at Helsinki and went on to Berlin and Vienna. In 1940 he abruptly ceased composing and spent the rest of his life as a recluse. Restoration of many works to their original state has helped to dispel his conservative image and reveal unexpectedly radical features.

Suggested reading
James, B D *The Music of Jean Sibelius* (1983)
Layton, R *Sibelius* (1987)
Layton, R *Sibelius and his World* (1970)
Tyrell, J and others *New Grove Turn of the Century Masters* (1985)

Sibelius *The composer Jean Sibelius. Most of his works date from after 1897, when the Finnish government voted to give him an annual grant to enable him to compose full-time. He was an ardent nationalist, transferring his passion for Finland into his music. (Image Select)*

Sibley Antoinette (1939–). English dancer. Joining the Royal Ballet 1956, she became principal soloist 1960. Her roles included Odette/Odile in *Swan Lake*, Giselle, and the title role in Kenneth MacMillan's *Manon* 1974. A dancer of exceptional musicality and grace, she excelled in Frederick Ashton's *The Dream* 1964. She formed an ideal partnership with Anthony Dowell. A knee injury 1976 brought her career to a five-year standstill, but in 1981 she returned to dance in Helpmann's *Hamlet* and since then has been a regular guest artist with the Royal Ballet.

Sickert Walter Richard (1860–1942). English artist. His Impressionist cityscapes of London and Venice, portraits, and domestic and music-hall interiors capture subtleties of tone and light, often with a melancholic atmosphere. He studied at the Slade School of Art.

Sickert was born in Munich, the eldest son of the Danish painter Oswald Adalbert Sickert. The family moved to London 1868, and as a young man Sickert worked with Whistler in Chelsea, taking, like his master, to etching. He met Degas in Paris 1883, and founded his style and attitude to art on him rather than on Whistler. Often called an Impressionist, he was only so to the same limited extent as Degas, constructing a picture with deliberation from swift notes made on the spot, and never painting in the open air. He worked at Dieppe, 1885–1905, with occasional visits to Venice, and music-hall paintings and views of Venice and Dieppe executed in dark, rich tones belong to this period. In his 'Camden Town' period, 1905–14, he explored the little back rooms, shabby lodging-houses and dingy streets, his zest for urban life and his personality gathering a group of younger artists about him. Although the modern art that may be dated from Cézanne was a closed book to him, he thus brought together 1911 the English Post-Impressionists of the Camden Town Group. His later work became broader in treatment and lighter in tone, a late innovation being the 'Echoes', in which he freely adapted the work of Victorian illustrators.

His verve and quality as an artist claim general modern respect, though the prejudices expressed in his writings (collected 1947 under the title *A Free House*) date both in substance and style of wit. His third wife, Thérèse Lessore, whom he married 1926, was also a painter.

Suggested reading
Connett, Maureen *Walter Sickert and the Camden Town Group* (1992)
Sickert, Walter *A Free House* (1947)
Sutton, Denys *Walter Sickert* (1976)

Siddons Sarah (born Kemble) (1755–1831). English actress. She toured the provinces with her father Roger Kemble (1721–1802), until she appeared in London to immediate acclaim in Otway's *Venice Preserv'd* 1774. This led to her appearing with David Garrick at Drury Lane. Her majestic presence made her suited to tragic and heroic roles such as Lady Macbeth, Zara in Congreve's *The Mourning Bride*, and Constance in *King John*. She retired 1812.

Sidgwick Nevil Vincent (1873–1952). English theoretical chemist who made contributions to the theory of valency and chemical bonding.

Sidgwick was born in Oxford and studied there and in Germany. He spent his entire career at Oxford, becoming professor 1935.

Sidgwick became absorbed by the study of atomic structure and its importance in chemical bonding. He explained the bonding in coordination compounds (complexes), with a convincing account of the significance of the dative bond. Together with his students he demonstrated the existence and wide-ranging importance of the hydrogen bond.

His works include *The Organic Chemistry of Nitrogen* 1910, *The Electronic Theory of Valency* 1927, *Some Physical Properties of the Covalent Link in Chemistry* 1933, and the definitive *The Chemical Elements and their Compounds* 1950.

Sidmouth Viscount. Title of Henry ◊Addington, British Tory prime minister 1801–04.

Sidney Algernon (1622–1683). English Republican politician. He was a cavalry officer in the Civil War on the Parliamentary side, and was wounded at the Battle of Marston Moor 1644. He was elected to the Long Parliament 1646, but retired from politics when Cromwell dissolved the Rump 1653. After the Restoration he lived in exile on the Continent, but on returning to England 1677 continued to oppose the monarchy. He was arrested after the Rye House Plot 1683, convicted of high treason, and executed.

Who shoots at the mid-day sun, though he be sure he shall never hit the mark; yet as sure he is he shall shoot higher than who aims but at a bush.

PHILIP SIDNEY
Arcadia II 1590

Sidney Philip (1554–1586). English poet and soldier. He wrote the sonnet sequence *Astrophel and Stella* 1591, *Arcadia* 1590, a prose romance, and *Apologie for Poetrie* 1595, the earliest work of English literary criticism.

Sidney was born in Penshurst, Kent. He entered Parliament 1581, and was knighted 1583. In 1585 he was made governor of Vlissingen in the Netherlands, and died at Zutphen, fighting the Spanish.

Suggested reading

Buxton, J *Sir Philip Sidney and the English Renaissance* (1954)
Hamilton, A C *Sir Philip Sidney* (1977)
Muir, Kenneth *Sir Philip Sidney* (1960)

I'd let my wife, children and animals starve before I'd subject myself to something like that again.

DON SIEGEL
on working on *Jinxed* with Bette Midler, *Premiere* Nov 1989

Siegel Don(ald) (1912–1991). US film director. He specialized in thrillers, Westerns, and police dramas. Two of his low-budget features, the prison film *Riot in Cell Block 11* 1954 and the science-fiction story *Invasion of the Body Snatchers* 1956, are widely recognized for transcending their lack of resources. Siegel moved on to bigger budgets, but retained his taut, acerbic view of life in such films as the Clint Eastwood vehicles *Coogan's Bluff* 1969, *The Beguiled*, and *Dirty Harry* both 1971.

Siemens Ernst Werner von (1816–1892). German electrical engineer and inventor who discovered the dynamo principle 1867. He organized in 1870 the construction of the Indo-European telegraph system between London and Calcutta via Berlin, Odessa, and Tehran.

In 1847 he founded, with scientific instrument-maker Johan Halske (1814–1890), the firm of Siemens-Halske to manufacture and construct telegraph systems. In addition, he co-operated with his brothers who founded Siemens Brothers in the UK. As scientific consultant to the British government, Siemens helped to design the first cable-laying ship. He also helped to establish scientific standards of measurement.

Siemens's inventions include a process for gold- and silver-plating and a method for providing the wire in a telegraph system with seamless insulation, using gutta-percha.

Siemens introduced the double-T armature and succeeded in connecting the armature, the electromagnetic field, and the external load of an electric generator in a single current. His companies became pioneers in the development of electric traction – making trams, for example – and also electricity-generating stations.

Sienkiewicz Henryk Adam Alexander (1846–1916). Polish author. His books include *Quo Vadis?* 1895, set in Rome at the time of Nero, and the 17th-century historical trilogy *With Fire and Sword*, *The Deluge*, and *Pan Michael* 1890–93. *Quo Vadis?* was the basis of several spectacular films.

Sieyès Emmanuel-Joseph (1748–1836). French cleric and constitutional theorist who led the bourgeois attack on royal and aristocratic privilege in the States General (parliament) 1788–89.

Active in the early years of the French Revolution, he later retired from politics, but re-emerged as an organizer of the coup that brought Napoleon I to power in 1799.

I survived.

EMMANUEL-JOSEPH SIÈYES'S
answer on being asked what he had done during the French Revolution

---

Siger of Brabant (*c.* 1240–*c.* 1282). Netherlandish philosopher, a follower of Averroës, who taught at the University of Paris, and whose distinguishing between reason and Christian faith led to his works being condemned as heretical 1270. He refused to recant and was imprisoned. He was murdered in prison.

Sigismund (1368–1437). Holy Roman emperor from 1411. He convened and presided over the Council of Constance 1414–18, where he promised protection to the religious reformer Huss, but imprisoned him after his condemnation for heresy and acquiesced in his burning. King of Bohemia from 1419, he led the military campaign against the Hussites.

Signac Paul (1863–1935). French artist. In 1884 he joined with Georges Seurat in founding the Salon des Artistes Indépendants and developing the technique of Pointillism.

When 21 he exhibited in the first Salon des Indépendants, with which he was associated until 1934, and in 1886 he joined with Seurat in the scientific use of spectrum colour. He painted with separate mosaic-like blocks of pure colour, as distinct from the dots or 'Pointillism' of Seurat, and remained the practitioner and propagandist of this method throughout his life. Without the individual genius which makes Seurat unique, he produced many striking landscapes and seascapes of the Normandy and Brittany coasts and the Mediterranean, his love of ships and the sea finding expression in many admirable watercolours as well as oils. In his well-known book *D'Eugène Delacroix au Néo-Impressionisme*, published 1899, he acclaimed Delacroix as the precursor of the new art of colour he and Seurat pursued.

Signorelli Luca (*c.* 1450–1523). Italian painter. He was active in central Italy. He was the pupil of Piero della Francesca, but was also much influenced by the Florentine, Pollaiuolo, and his study of anatomy and physical movement. He was one of the group of painters chosen to decorate the Sistine Chapel 1481–83. His most famous work is the series of frescoes in the Brizio chapel of the cathedral of Orvieto, 1499, an undertaking begun by Fra Angelico 1447. The 'Overthrow of Antichrist', the 'Destruction of the World by Fire', the 'Resurrection of the Dead and Punishment of the Damned', and the 'Blessed ascending to Heaven' were the themes painted with tremendous force and unusual effects of colour, the frescoes being noted above all for figures in an expressive violence of action, which gave inspiration to Michelangelo for his *Last Judgment*. A masterpiece on canvas was his *Pan* (Berlin), destroyed during World War II. His later years were spent at Cortona in less ambitious effort, running a workshop producing altarpieces.

Sihanouk Norodom (1922–). Cambodian politician, king 1941–55 and from 1993. He abdicated 1955 in favour of his father, founded the Popular Socialist Community, and governed as prime minister 1955–70. His government was overthrown in a military coup led by Lon Nol. With Pol Pot's resistance front, he overthrew Lon Nol 1975 and again became prime minister 1975–76, when he was forced to resign by the Khmer Rouge. Based in North Korea, he became the recognized head of the Democratic Kampuchea government in exile 1982, leading a coalition of three groups opposing the Vietnamese-installed government. International peace conferences aimed at negotiating a settlement repeatedly broke down, fighting intensified, and the Khmer Rouge succeeded in taking some important provincial capitals. A peace agreement was eventually signed in Paris 23 Oct 1991. He returned from exile Nov 1991 under the auspices of a United Nations-brokered peace settlement to head a coalition intended to comprise all Cambodia's warring factions (the Khmer Rouge, however, continued fighting).

He was re-elected king after the 1993 elections, in which the royalist party won a majority.

Sikorski Wladyslaw Eugeniusz (1881–1943). Polish general and politician; prime minister 1922–23, and 1939–43 of the Polish government in exile in London during World War II.

He was in Paris when the Germans took Poland and became commander in chief of the 100,000-strong Free Polish Forces, who he took to the UK 1940. Following the German invasion of the USSR 1941, he concluded an agreement with the Soviet Union to re-establish Poland's pre-war boundaries, but the treatment of Polish prisoners in Soviet hands soured relations. The revelation of the Katyn Wood massacre 1943 nearly caused a serious rift, only averted by strong intervention from Churchill. He was killed in an aeroplane crash near Gibraltar in controversial circumstances. Following his death, the government-in-exile's influence seriously declined.

Sikorsky Igor Ivan (1889–1972). Ukrainian-born US engineer who built the first successful helicopter 1939 (commercially produced from 1943). His first biplane flew 1910, and in 1929 he began to construct multi-engined flying boats.

The first helicopter was followed by a whole series of production designs using one, then two, piston engines. During the late 1950s piston engines were replaced by the newly developed gas-turbine engines.

Sikorsky was born in Kiev and was inspired to make a helicopter by the notebooks of Italian Renaissance inventor Leonardo da Vinci. In 1908 he met US aviation pioneer Wilbur Wright in France, and in 1909 Sikorsky began to construct his first helicopter, but had to abandon his attempts until better materials and engines became available.

Instead, he built fixed-wing aeroplanes and began a lifelong practice of taking the controls on the first flight. In 1911 his S-5 aeroplane flew for over an hour and achieved altitudes of 450 m/ 1,480 ft. His aeroplanes *Le Grand* and the even larger *Ilia Mourometz* had four engines, an enclosed cabin for crew and passengers, and even a toilet. They became the basis for the four-engined bomber that Russia used during World War I.

Following the revolution, he emigrated to the USA 1918. He founded the Sikorsky Aero Engineering Corporation, which was taken over by the United Aircraft Corporation. Sikorsky continued to work as a designer and engineering manager until 1957. His S-40 American Clipper flying boat 1931 allowed Pan American Airways to develop routes in the Caribbean and South America.

Silayev Ivan Stepanovich (1930–   ). Soviet politician, prime minister of the USSR Aug–Dec 1991.

A member of the Communist Party 1959–91 and of its Central Committee 1981–91, Silayev emerged as a reformer in 1990, founding the Democratic Reform Movement (with former foreign minister Shevardnadze).

An engineer, Silayev worked 1954–74 in the military-industrial complex in Gorky (now Nizhni-Novgorod) and then in the central aviation and machine-tools industries, becoming Soviet deputy prime minister 1985. Chosen to become prime minister of the Russian republic by its new radical president Boris Yeltsin, Silayev formulated an ambitious plan of market-centred reform. After the failure of the Aug 1991 anti-Gorbachev attempted coup, he was appointed Soviet prime minister and given charge of the economy.

Sillitoe Alan (1928–   ). English novelist. He wrote *Saturday Night and Sunday Morning* 1958, about a working-class man in Nottingham, Sillitoe's home town. He also wrote *The Loneliness of the Long Distance Runner* 1959, *Life Goes On* 1985, many other novels, and poems, plays, and children's books. His autobiography *Life Without Armour* appeared 1995.

Sills Beverly. Stage name of Belle Miriam Silverman (1929–   ). US operatic soprano. Her high-ranging coloratura is allied to a subtle emotional control in French and Italian roles, notably as principal in Donizetti's *Lucia di Lammermoor* and Puccini's *Manon Lescaut*.

She sang with touring companies and joined the New York City Opera 1955. In 1979 she became director of New York City Opera and retired from the stage 1980.

Silone Ignazio. Pen name of Secondo Tranquilli (1900–1978). Italian novelist. His novel *Fontamara* 1933 deals with the hopes and disillusionment of a peasant village from a socialist viewpoint. His other works include *Una manciata di more/A Handful of Blackberries* 1952.

Sim Alastair George Bell (1900–1976). Scottish comedy actor. Possessed of a marvellously expressive face, he was ideally cast in eccentric roles, as in the title role in *Scrooge* 1951. His other films include *Inspector Hornleigh* 1939, *Green for Danger* 1945, and *The Belles of St Trinians* 1954.

Simenon Georges Joseph Christian (1903–1989). Belgian crime writer. Initially a pulp fiction writer, in 1931 he created Inspector Maigret of the Paris Sûreté who appeared in a series of detective novels.

Suggested reading
Bresler, Fenton *The Mystery of Georges Simenon* (1983)
Eskin, Stanley *Simenon: A Critical Biography* (1987)
Marnham, Patrick *The Man Who Was Not Maigret: A Portrait of Georges Simenon* (1992)
Simenon, Georges *Intimate Memoirs* (trs 1984)

Simeon Stylites, St (c. 390–459). Syrian Christian ascetic who practised his ideal of self-denial by living for 37 years on a platform on top of a high pillar (Greek *stulos*). Feast day 5 Jan.

Simmel Georg (1858–1918). German sociologist who attempted to construct a formal system of sociology, abstracted from history and the detail of human experience, in *Soziologie, Untersuchungen über die Formen der Vergesellschaftung/Sociology, Investigations into the Forms of Socialization* 1908. In *Die Philosophie des Geldes/The Philosophy of Money* 1900, he explored the effects of the money economy on human behaviour. He also wrote essays on aspects of culture and society. Simmel was professor at Strasbourg University 1914–18.

Simmons Jean (1929–   ). English actress. Of dark, elegant looks, she played Ophelia in Laurence Olivier's film of *Hamlet* 1948, and later in Hollywood starred in such films as *Black Narcissus* 1947, *Guys and Dolls* 1955, and *Spartacus* 1960.

Simnel Lambert (c. 1475–c. 1535). English impostor, a joiner's son who under the influence of an Oxford priest claimed to be Prince Edward, one of the Princes in the Tower. Henry VII discovered the plot and released the real Edward for one day to show him to the public. Simnel had a keen following and was crowned as Edward VI in Dublin 1487. He came with forces to England to fight the royal army, and attacked it near Stoke-on-Trent 16 June 1487. He was defeated and captured, but was contemptuously pardoned. He is then said to have worked in the king's kitchen.

Simon Claude Eugène Henri (1913–   ). French novelist. Originally an artist, he abandoned 'time structure' and story line in such innovative novels as *La Route de Flandres/The Flanders Road* 1960, *Le Palace* 1962, and *Histoire* 1967 in order to depict the constant flux of experience. His later novels include *Les Géorgiques* 1981 and *L'Acacia* 1989. Nobel prize 1985.

Simon Franz Eugen (1893–1956). German-born British physicist who developed methods of achieving extremely low temperatures (nearly as low as one millionth of a degree above absolute zero). He experimentally established the validity of the third law of thermodynamics. Knighted 1954.

He became professor at the Technical University in Breslau 1931, but, with the rise to power of the Nazis, emigrated to the UK 1933 and spent the rest of his career at Oxford, as professor from 1945. During World War II, Simon worked on the atomic bomb.

Simon solidified gases by the use of high pressure, and showed that helium could be solidified at a temperature ten times as high as its liquid/gas critical point. He worked on the properties of fluids at high pressure and low temperature, and in 1932 he worked out a cheap and simple method for generating liquid helium.

In the 1930s, Simon developed magnetic cooling to investigate properties of substances below 1K. He then went on to investigate nuclear cooling, showing that the cooling effect is limited by interaction energies.

Simon Herbert Alexander (1916–). US social scientist. He researched decisionmaking in business corporations, and argued that maximum profit was seldom the chief motive. He was awarded the Nobel Prize for Economics 1978.

He has sat on the fence so long the iron has entered his soul.

David Lloyd George on 1ST VISCOUNT SIMON
attributed.

Simon John Allsebrook Simon, 1st Viscount Simon (1873–1954). British Liberal politician. He was home secretary 1915–16, but resigned over the issue of conscription. He was foreign secretary 1931–35, home secretary again 1935–37, chancellor of the Exchequer 1937–40, and lord chancellor 1940–45. Knighted 1910, viscount 1940.

Simon (Marvin) Neil (1927–). US dramatist and screenwriter. His stage plays (which were made into films) include the wryly comic *Barefoot in the Park* 1963 (filmed 1967), *The Odd Couple* 1965 (filmed 1968), and *The Sunshine Boys* 1972 (filmed 1975), and the more serious, autobiographical trilogy *Brighton Beach Memoirs* 1983 (filmed 1986), *Biloxi Blues* 1985 (filmed 1988), and *Broadway Bound* 1986 (filmed 1991). He has also written screenplays and co-written musicals. The musicals include *Sweet Charity* 1966, *Promises, Promises* 1968, and *They're Playing Our Song* 1978.

Simon Paul (1942–). US pop singer and songwriter. In a folk-rock duo with Art Garfunkel (1942–), he had such hits as 'Mrs Robinson' 1968 and 'Bridge Over Troubled Water' 1970. Simon's solo work includes the critically acclaimed album *Graceland* 1986, for which he drew on Cajun and African music.

The success of *Graceland* and subsequent tours involving African musicians helped to bring world music to international attention, but Simon had always had an eclectic ear and had, for example, as early as 1971 used reggae rhythm on the song 'Mother and Child Reunion' and a Latin beat on 'Me and Julio Down by the Schoolyard'. A Brazilian drumming group, Olodum, featured on his *The Rhythm of the Saints* 1990.

Simone Martini (*c.* 1284–1344). Italian painter. He was a master of the Sienese school. A pupil of Duccio, he continued the bright colours and graceful linear patterns of Sienese painting while introducing a fresh element of naturalism. His patrons included the city of Siena, the king of Naples, and the pope. Two of his frescoes are in the Town Hall in Siena: the *Maestà* about 1315 and a portrait (on horseback) of the local hero Guidoriccio da Fogliano (the attribution of the latter is disputed). Sometime in the 1320s or 1330s Simone worked at Assisi where he decorated the chapel of St Martin with scenes depicting the life of the saint, regarded by many as his masterpiece.

French Gothic art and the Gothic element in the sculpture of the Pisani contributed to give his art a new direction, dominant in Siena for the following two centuries. A link with France and court life was first established by his visit to Naples 1317, where he painted for Robert of Anjou his altarpiece in the church of San Lorenzo, showing St Louis crowning Robert, King of Naples. In 1339 he went on public business to Avignon and remained in that centre of an exiled Papacy and a chivalric culture for the rest of his life. There he was the friend of Petrarch and painted a portrait (now lost) of Petrarch's Laura. In Avignon he exerted a great influence on French art and the development of an international Gothic style. An interesting signed and dated work of the Avignon period is the *Christ returning to His Parents after disputing with the Doctors*, 1342 (Liverpool, Walker Art Gallery), and an important product of his studio is the polyptych (three panels of Sts Ambrose, Michael and Augustine) in the Fitzwilliam Museum, Cambridge.

Go, tell the Spartans, thou who passest by, / That here obedient to their laws we lie.

SIMONIDES
Epigrams

Simonides (*c.* 556–*c.* 448 BC). Greek choral poet and epigrammatist. His longer poems include hymns composed to celebrate victories in the athletic games of Greece, and other competition pieces for choral performance. He was extremely successful, internationally famous, and reputedly avaricious. He wrote the epigram above on the Spartans who died fighting the Persians at Thermopylae in 480 BC. His work exists in fragments only.

Simpson (Cedric) Keith (1907–1985). British forensic scientist, head of department at Guy's Hospital, London, 1962–72. His evidence sent John Haig (an acid-bath murderer) and Neville Heath to the gallows. In 1965 he identified the first 'battered baby' murder in England.

Simpson George Clark (1878–1965). English meteorologist who studied atmospheric electricity, ionization and radioactivity in the atmosphere, and the effect of radiation on the polar ice. KCB 1935.

In 1905 he became the first lecturer in meteorology at a British university (Manchester), and began working at the Meteorological Office; he was its director 1920–38. With the outbreak of World War II, he returned from retirement to take charge of Kew Observatory, continuing research into the electrical structure of thunderstorms until 1947.

Simpson travelled widely. In 1902 he visited Lapland to investigate atmospheric electricity. He spent a period inspecting meteorological stations throughout India and Burma; travelled to the Antarctic in 1910 on Captain Scott's last expedition; and visited Mesopotamia during World War I as a meteorological adviser to the British Expeditionary Force. Later he was a member of the Egyptian government's Nile Project Commission.

Simpson's revised form of the Beaufort scale of wind speed was in international use 1926–39.

Simpson concluded that excessive solar radiation would increase the amount of cloud and that the resultant increase in precipitation would lead to enlargement of the polar ice caps, which might explain the ice ages.

Simpson George Gaylord (1902–1984). US palaeontologist who studied the evolution of mammals. He applied population genetics to the subject and to analyse the migrations of animals between continents.

From 1927 he worked at the American Museum of Natural History, becoming curator 1942. He was professor at Columbia 1945–59, at Harvard 1959–70, and at Arizona from 1967.

Simpson's work in the 1930s concerned early mammals of the Mesozoic era and the Palaeocene and Eocene epochs, which entailed many extensive field trips throughout the Americas and to Asia to study fossil remains. In the 1940s he began applying genetics to mammalian evolution and classification.

He wrote several textbooks, including *The Meaning of Evolution* 1949, *The Major Features of Evolution* 1953, and *The Principles of Animal Taxonomy* 1961, which were influential in establishing the neo-Darwinian theory of evolution.

Simpson James Young (1811–1870). Scottish physician, the first to use ether as an anaesthetic in childbirth 1847, and the discoverer, later the same year, of the anaesthetic properties of chloroform, which he tested by experiments on himself. Baronet 1866.

Simpson was born near Linlithgow and studied at Edinburgh, where he became professor of midwifery 1840. From 1847 he was requested to attend Queen Victoria during her stays in Scotland. By this time he had a thriving private practice and was making pioneering advances in gynaecology; he was eventually appointed physician to Queen Victoria.

Simpson's *Account of a New Anaesthetic Agent* 1847 aroused opposition from Calvinists, who regarded labour pains as God-given. It was

Simpson, Wallis *Mrs Wallis Simpson, the Duchess of Windsor, in a photograph taken 1936. Mrs Simpson, who had been divorced twice, married Edward VIII 1937. He abdicated in order to marry her, because of constitutional objections to his marrying a divorced woman.* (Image Select)

Queen Victoria's endorsement of Simpson's use of chloroform during the birth of her seventh child 1853 that made his techniques universally adopted.

Dotty highjinks that satirise the vacuity of the dreary, conventional world.

T J Shank on N F SIMPSON 1963

Simpson N(orman) F(rederick) (1919–). English dramatist. His plays *A Resounding Tinkle* 1957, *The Hole* 1958, and *One Way Pendulum* 1959 show the logical development of an abnormal situation, and belong to the Theatre of the Absurd. He also wrote a novel, *Harry Bleachbaker* 1976.

Simpson O(renthal) J(ames) (1947–). former professional American football player, film and TV actor, and sports commentator. In 1995 he was charged with two counts of first-degree murder relating to the June 1994 fatal stabbings of his wife Nicole and her friend Ronald Goldman; he was found not guilty Oct 1995. The issue of race featured prominently in the case, and allegations of racial bias have been made against both the Los Angeles Police Department and the largely African-American jury.

Simpson was one of the greatest running backs in American football history. He led the University of Southern California's Trojans to a Rose Bowl championship and the number one ranking in the country 1967, and in 1968 he set records for the most ball carrying and the most yards gained in a single season. He played as halfback for the Buffalo Bills 1969–78 and the San Francisco 49'ers 1978–79. He was named National Football Player of the Decade 1979, and was inducted into the Pro Football Hall of Fame 1985.

On his retirement from professional sport, he started a new career as a TV commentator 1979–86 and also appeared in several TV and cinema films.

Simpson Thomas (1710–1761). English mathematician and writer who devised Simpson's rule, which simplifies the calculation of areas under graphic curves. He also worked out a formula that can be used to find the volume of any solid bounded by a ruled surface and two parallel planes.

In 1735 or 1736 he moved to London and worked as a weaver at Spitalfields, teaching mathematics in his spare time. It was there that he published his first mathematical works, which won some acclaim. Soon after 1740 he was elected to the Royal Academy of Stockholm, and in 1743 he was appointed professor of mathematics at the Royal Academy in Woolwich, London.

Simpson's first mathematical work, in 1737, was a treatise on 'fluxions' (calculus). This was followed by *The Nature and Laws of Chance* 1740, *The Doctrine of Annuities and Reversions* 1742, *Mathematical Dissertation on a Variety of Physical and Analytical Subjects* 1743, *A Treatise of Algebra* 1745, *Elements of Geometry* 1747, *Trigonometry, Plane and Spherical* 1748, *Select Exercises in Mathematics* 1752, and *Miscellaneous Tracts on Some Curious Subjects in Mechanics, Physical Astronomy and Special Mathematics* 1757.

Simpson Wallis Warfield, Duchess of Windsor (1896–1986). US socialite, twice divorced. She married Edward VIII 1937, who abdicated in order to marry her. He was given the title Duke of Windsor by his brother, George VI, who succeeded him.

Sims William Sowden (1858–1936). US admiral. He joined the US navy 1878, was naval attaché to France 1898, and later became fleet intelligence officer to the Asiatic Fleet. On the entry of the USA into World War I, he was placed in command of all US naval operations in European waters and was made a vice-admiral 1918. He won a Pulitzer prize for his book *Victory at Sea* 1920.

Sinan (1489–1588). Ottoman architect. He was chief architect to Suleiman the Magnificent from 1538. Among the hundreds of buildings he designed are the Suleimaniye mosque complex in Istanbul 1551–58 and the Selimiye mosque in Adrianople (now Edirne) 1569–74.

The charm which once made him irresistible was lost in the predictable whims of a spoiled child.

Leslie Halliwell on FRANK SINATRA
in *Filmgoer's Companion* 1965

Sinatra Frank (Francis Albert) (1915–). US singer and film actor. Celebrated for his phrasing and emotion, especially on love ballads, he is particularly associated with the song 'My Way'. In the 1940s he sang such songs as 'Night and Day' and 'You'd Be So Nice to Come Home To' with Harry James's and Tommy Dorsey's bands; many of his later recordings were made with arranger Nelson Riddle (1921–1985). After a slump in his career, he established himself as an actor. His films from 1941 include *From Here to Eternity* 1953 (Academy Award), *Guys and Dolls* 1955, and *Some Came Running* 1959. His later career includes film, television, and club appearances, and setting up a record company, Reprise, 1960.

Ol' blue eyes is back.

FRANK SINATRA
Name of his TV special in 1973, and later the name of an album

Suggested reading
Howlett, John *Frank Sinatra* (1980)
Kelley, Kitty *His Way* (1986)
Petkov, Steven and Mustazza, Leonard *The Frank Sinatra Reader* (1995)
Rockwell, John *Sinatra: An American Classic* (1984)

Sinclair Clive Marles (1940–). British electronics engineer who produced the first widely available pocket calculator, pocket and wristwatch televisions, a series of home computers, and the innovative but commercially disastrous C5 personal transport (a low cyclelike three-wheeled vehicle powered by a washing-machine motor). Knighted 1983.

Sinclair Upton Beall (1878–1968). US novelist. His polemical concern for social reform was reflected in his prolific output of documentary novels. His most famous novel, *The Jungle* 1906, is an important example of naturalistic writing, which exposed the horrors of the Chicago meat-packing industry and led to a change in food-processing laws. His later novels include *King Coal* 1917, *Oil!* 1927, and his 11-volume Lanny Budd series 1940–53, including *Dragon's Teeth* 1942, which won a Pulitzer prize.
Suggested reading
Bloodworth, William A, Jr *Upton Sinclair* (1977)
Sinclair, Upton *The Autobiography of Upton Sinclair* (1962)

Sinden Donald Alfred (1923–). English actor. A performer of great versatility and resonant voice, his roles ranged from Shakespearean tragedies to light comedies, such as *There's a Girl in My Soup* 1966, *Present Laughter* 1981, and the television series *Two's Company*.

Sinding Christian August (1856–1941). Norwegian composer. His works include four symphonies, piano pieces (including *Rustle of Spring*), and songs. His brothers Otto (1842–1909) and Stephan (1846–1922) were a painter and sculptor respectively.

Sometimes love is stronger than man's convictions.
ISAAC BASHEVIS SINGER
quoted in *New York Times Magazine* 26 Nov 1978

Singer Isaac Bashevis (1904–1991). Polish-born US novelist and short-story writer. He lived in the USA from 1935. His works, written in Yiddish, often portray traditional Jewish life in Poland and the USA, and the loneliness of old age. They include *The Family Moskat* 1950 and *Gimpel the Fool and Other Stories* 1957. Nobel prize 1978.

Written in an often magical storytelling style, his works combine a deep psychological insight with dramatic and visual impact. Many of his novels were written for serialization in New York Yiddish newspapers. Among his works are *The Slave* 1960, *Shosha* 1978, *Old Love* 1979, *Lost in America* 1981, *The Image and Other Stories* 1985, and *The Death of Methuselah* 1988. He also wrote plays and books for children.
Suggested reading
Friedman, L S *Understanding Isaac Bashevis Singer* (1988)
Sinclair, C *The Brothers Singer* (1983)
Singer, Isaac Bashevis *In My Father's Court* (autobiography) (1966)

Singer Isaac Merrit (1811–1875). US inventor of domestic and industrial sewing machines. Within a few years of opening his first factory 1851, he became the world's largest sewing-machine manufacturer (despite infringing the patent of Elias Howe), and by the late 1860s more than 100,000 Singer sewing machines were in use in the USA alone.

Singer was born in Pittstown, New York, and became a machinist. During his early working life he patented a rock-drilling machine and later a metal- and wood-carving one. One day he was asked to carry out some repairs to a Lerow and Blodgett sewing machine. Singer decided he could add many improvements to the design. Eleven days later he produced a new model, which he patented.

Singer used the best of Howe's design and altered some of the other features. The basic mechanism was the same: as the handle

turned, the needle paused at a certain point in its stroke so that the shuttle could pass through the loop formed in the cotton. When the needle continued, the threads were tightened, forming a secure stitch. To make his machines available to the widest market, Singer became the first manufacturer to offer hire-purchase terms. Singer's machines were very reliable and long-lived. So, in order to reduce the supply of second-hand machines, he would break up any old machines taken in part exchange.

Singh Vishwanath Pratap (1931–). Indian politician, prime minister 1989–90. As a member of the Congress (I) Party, he held ministerial posts under Indira Gandhi and Rajiv Gandhi, and from 1984 led an anti-corruption drive. He was minister of commerce 1976–77 and 1983, Uttar Pradesh chief minister 1980–82, minister of finance 1984–86, and of defence 1986–87, when he revealed the embarrassing Bofors scandal. Respected for his probity and sense of principle, Singh emerged as one of the most popular politicians in India. When he unearthed an arms-sales scandal 1988, he was ousted from the government and party and formed a broad-based opposition alliance, the Janata Dal, which won the Nov 1989 election. Mounting caste and communal conflict split the Janata Dal and forced him out of office Nov 1990.

Singh, Gobind see ◊Gobind Singh, Sikh guru.

Siodmak Robert (1900–1973). US film director of brooding melodramas and thrillers of the mid-1940s, including *The Spiral Staircase* and *The Killers* both 1946. Away from the genre of film noir of which Siodmak was master, his work was less striking.

Brought up in Germany, he was heralded as an important new talent in German cinema with *Farewell* 1930, but fled to Hollywood in 1941 to escape the Nazis. He ended his career back in Europe.

Siqueiros David Alfaro (1896–1974). Mexican painter. He was a prominent Social Realist and outstanding member of the Mexican muralist movement of the 1930s. A lifelong political activist, his work championed his revolutionary ideals.

He was the master of a vigorous style, typified by massed, churning figures and the use of foreshortening and multiple viewpoints, as in the mural *Portrait of the Bourgeoisie* 1939 (Electrical Workers' Union, Mexico City).

In the 1920s Siqueiros worked with Diego Rivera and Jose Orozco on allegorical frescoes for the National Preparatory School, Mexico City – the first of many such mural commissions. Unlike the others, he incorporated elements of fantasy, such as human-and-machine hybrids. His easel paintings and woodcuts, like his murals, express deeply felt themes of protest, for example *Echo of a Scream* 1937 (Museum of Modern Art, New York). He also worked and taught in the USA, where he influenced the Abstract Expressionist Jackson Pollock.

Siraj-ud-Daula (1728–1757). Nawab of Bengal, India, from April 1756. He captured Calcutta from the British in June 1756 and imprisoned some of the British in the Black Hole of Calcutta (a small room in which a number of them died), but was defeated in 1757 by Robert Clive, and lost Bengal to the British at the Battle of Plassey. He was killed in his capital, Murshidabad.

Sirk Douglas. Adopted name of Claus Detlef Sierck (1900–1987). German film director. He was known for such extravagantly lurid Hollywood melodramas as *Magnificent Obsession* 1954, *All that Heaven Allows* 1956 and *Written on the Wind* 1957, praised for their implicit critiques of American bourgeois society.

Siskind Aaron (1903–1991). US art photographer. He began as a documentary photographer and in 1940 made a radical change towards a poetic exploration of forms and planes, inspired by the Abstract Expressionist painters.

Sisley Alfred (1839–1899). French Impressionist painter. Lyrical and harmonious, his work is distinctive for its lightness of touch and subtlety of tone. Unlike most other Impressionists, Sisley developed his style slowly and surely, without obvious changes.

His father was a wealthy businessman in Paris and the boy was sent to England at 18, destined for a commercial career, but he was afterwards allowed to study art, and worked under Gleyre with Monet and Renoir. He devoted himself exclusively to landscape, exhibited at the first Impressionist exhibition of 1874, and is a close partner of Monet in atmospheric colour. He began virtually as an amateur, but the loss of the family fortune compelled him to paint in earnest for a living. Despite a lifelong struggle with financial difficulty, his art shows an admirable consistency and quality. Apart from two short stays in England, when he painted on the Thames, he lived and worked in the valley of the Seine and near Paris, settling finally in a small dwelling at Moret. *The Floods at Port-Marly* (Louvre 1876) and *Bridge at Sèvres* (Tate Gallery) are beautiful examples of his art, which figures in many galleries.

Sisulu Walter Max Ulyate (1912–). South African civil-rights activist, one of the first full-time secretary generals of the African National Congress (ANC), in 1964, with Nelson Mandela. He was imprisoned following the 1964 Rivonia Trial for opposition to the apartheid system and released, at the age of 77, as a gesture of reform by President F W de Klerk 1989. In 1991, when Mandela became ANC president, Sisulu became his deputy.

Sitter Willem de (1872–1934). Dutch astronomer, mathematician, and physicist, who contributed to the birth of modern cosmology. He was influential in English-speaking countries in bringing the relevance of the general theory of relativity to the attention of astronomers. He was professor of theoretical astronomy at the University of Leiden from 1908 as well as director of its observatory from 1919.

In 1911 de Sitter outlined how the motion of the constituent bodies of our Solar System might be expected to deviate from predictions based on Newtonian dynamics if Albert Einstein's special relativity theory were valid. After the publication of Einstein's general theory of relativity 1915, de Sitter expanded his ideas and introduced the 'de Sitter universe' (as distinct from the 'Einstein universe'). His model later formed an element in the theoretical basis for the steady-state hypothesis regarding the creation of the universe. He presented further models of a nonstatic universe: he described both an expanding universe and an oscillating one.

Sitting Bull (Indian name Tatanka Iyotake) (*c.* 1834–1890). North American Indian chief who agreed to Sioux resettlement 1868. When the treaty was broken by the USA, he led the Sioux against Lieutenant Colonel Custer at the Battle of the Little Bighorn 1876. He was pursued by the US Army and forced to flee to Canada. He was allowed to return 1881, and he toured in the Wild West show of 'Buffalo Bill' Cody. He settled on a Dakota reservation and was killed during his arrest on suspicion of involvement in Indian agitations.
Suggested reading
Adams, Alexander *Sitting Bull* (1973)
Carroll, J M (ed) *The Arrest and Killing of Sitting Bull: A Documentary* (1986)
Miller, David *Custer's Fall: The Indian Side of the Story* (1985)
Utley, Robert *The Last Days of the Sioux Nation* (1963)

Sitwell Edith Louisa (1887–1964). English poet. Her series of poems *Façade* was performed as recitations to the specially written music of William Walton from 1923. Her verse has an imaginative and rhythmic intensity. DBE 1954.
Suggested reading
Glendinning, Victoria *Edith Sitwell: A Unicorn Among Lions* (1981)
Lehmann, John *A Nest of Tigers: Edith, Osbert and Sacheverell Sitwell in Their Times* (1968)
Pearson, John *Façades: Edith, Osbert and Sacheverell Sitwell* (1978)
Sitwell, Edith *Taken Care Of* (autobiography) (1965)

Jane, Jane / Tall as a crane, / The morning light creaks down again.

EDITH SITWELL
Façade, 'Aubade' 1922

The British Bourgeoisie / Is not born, / And does not die, / But, if it is ill, / It has a frightened look in its eyes.

OSBERT SITWELL
At the House of Mrs Kinfoot 1921

Sitwell (Francis) Osbert (Sacheverell) (1892–1969). English poet and author. He was the elder brother of Edith and Sacheverell Sitwell. He wrote art criticism; novels, including *A Place of One's Own* 1941; and a series of five autobiographical volumes 1945–62. 5th baronet 1943.

Sitwell Sacheverell (1897–1988). English poet and art critic. His work includes *Southern Baroque Art* 1924 and *British Architects and Craftsmen* 1945; poetry; and prose miscellanies such as *Of Sacred and Profane Love* 1940 and *Splendour and Miseries* 1943. 6th baronet 1969.

Sivaji or Shivaji (1627–1680). Founder of the Maratha state in W India, which lasted until 1818. He came from a Maratha noble family, and gained a reputation as a skilled warrior and defender of Hindu interests in successful confrontations with the Muslim rulers of Bijapur and the emperor Aurangzeb. He was crowned rajah (king) 1674 and remains a Hindu hero. Sivaji was a superb organizer, setting up an equitable land system which helped to finance his military exploits. He was an innovative fighter, using guerrilla tactics of speed and surprise.

Sixtus five popes, including:

Sixtus IV (born Francesco della Rovere) (1414–1484). Pope from 1471. He built the Sistine Chapel in the Vatican, which is named after him.

Sixtus V (born Felice Peretti) (1521–1590). Pope from 1585. He supported the Spanish Armada against Britain and the Catholic League against Henry IV of France.

Skelton John (*c.* 1460–1529). English poet. He was tutor to the future Henry VIII. His satirical poetry includes the rumbustious *The Tunnyng of Elynor Rummynge* 1516, and political attacks on Wolsey, such as *Colyn Cloute* 1522.

Education is what survives when what has been learnt has been forgotten.

B F SKINNER
in *New Scientist* 21 May 1964

Skinner B(urrhus) F(rederic) (1904–1990). US psychologist, a radical behaviourist who rejected mental concepts, seeing the organism as a 'black box' where internal processes are not significant in predicting behaviour. He studied operant conditioning (influencing behaviour patterns by reward or punishment) and held that behaviour is shaped and maintained by its consequences.

He invented the 'Skinner box', an enclosed environment in which the process of learned behaviour can be observed. In it, a rat presses a lever, and learns to repeat the behaviour because it is rewarded by food. Skinner also designed a 'baby box', a controlled, soundproof environment for infants. His own daughter was partially reared in such a box until the age of two.

His radical approach rejected almost all previous psychology; his text *Science and Human Behavior* 1953 contains no references and no bibliography. His other works include *Walden Two* 1948 and *Beyond Freedom and Dignity* 1971. Both these books argue that an ideal society can be attained and maintained only if human behaviour is modified – by means of such techniques as conditioning – to fit society instead of society adapting to the needs of individuals. He was professor at Indiana 1945–48 and at Harvard 1948–74.

Skinner attempted to explain even complex human behavior as a series of conditioned responses to outside stimuli. He opposed the use of punishment, arguing that it did not effectively control behaviour and had unfavourable side effects.

Suggested reading
Carpenter, Finley *A Skinner Primer: Behind Freedom and Dignity* (1984)
Skinner, B F *Walden Two* (1948)
Skinner, B F *Beyond Freedom and Dignity* (1971)

Skolem Thoralf Albert (1887–1963). Norwegian mathematician who did important work on Diophantine equations and who helped to provide the axiomatic foundations for set theory in logic.

Skolem was born at Sandsvaer and educated at Oslo, where he became professor 1938. He wrote 182 scientific papers, but they remained largely unread, partly because they were written in Norwegian.

Skolem's main work was in the field of formal mathematical logic. From papers published in the 1920s emerged what is now known as the Löwenheim–Skolem theorem, one consequence of which is Skolem's paradox: if an axiomatic system (such as axiomatic set theory) is consistent (that is, satisfiable), then it must be satisfiable within a countable domain; but Georg Cantor had shown the existence of a neverending sequence of transfinite powers in mathematics (that is, uncountability). Skolem's answer was that there *is* no complete axiomatization of mathematics.

Before such subjects as model theory, recursive function theory, and axiomatic set theory had become separate branches of mathematics, he introduced a number of the fundamental notions that gave rise to them.

Skolimowski Jerzy (1938–). Polish film director. Formerly a writer, he is active in both his own country and other parts of Europe. His films include *Deep End* 1970, *The Shout* 1978, *Moonlighting* 1982, and *Torrents of Spring* 1989.

Skorzeny Otto (1908–1975). German colonel. He commanded various special forces units in World War II and was a specialist in irregular warfare.

He commanded the special unit which rescued Mussolini from imprisonment Sept 1943 and kidnapped the son of Admiral Horthy Oct 1944, forcing Horthy to abdicate and thus foiling his plan to sue for a separate peace. In Dec 1944 he caused chaos in the Battle of the Bulge with the deployment of squads of English-speaking soldiers, dressed in US uniforms and driving US vehicles, inserted behind the US lines to mystify and confuse. He was tried for war crimes at Nuremberg and acquitted.

I was once a Chopinist, then a Wagnerist, now I am only a Scriabinist.

ALEXANDER SKRYABIN
in 1903, quoted in Faubion Bowers *Scriabin* 1969

Skryabin Alexander Nikolayevich, or Scriabin (1872–1915). Russian composer and pianist. His visionary tone poems such as *Prometheus* 1911, and symphonies such as *Divine Poem* 1903, employed unusual scales and harmonies.

Slade Felix (1790–1868). English art collector who bequeathed most of his art collection to the British Museum and endowed Slade professorships in fine art at Oxford, Cambridge, and University College, London. The Slade School of Fine Arts, opened 1871, is a branch of the latter.

Slater Samuel (1768–1835). British-born US industrialist whose knowledge of industrial technology and business acumen as a mill owner and banker made him a central figure in the New England textile industry.

Slater was born in England. He trained in machinery manufacture and worked as a mechanical supervisor in a textile mill. Emigrating to the USA 1789, he was quickly hired by several American machine manufacturing firms. In 1791 he supervised the construction of a mill, based on the design of the English model, in Providence, Rhode Island. He established his own manufacturing company 1798.

Slayton Deke (Donald Kent) (1924–1993). US astronaut, one of the original seven chosen by NASA in 1959 for the Mercury series

of flights. Grounded for health reasons, he became director of NASA's flight-crew operations for ten years. In 1972 he was returned to flight status, and in 1975 he finally flew in space, then the oldest person to have done so at the age of 51.

He subsequently left NASA to join a private company, Space Services Incorporated, which unsuccessfully attempted to develop rockets for a commercial launch service.

Sleep Wayne (1948–). English dancer. He was a principal dancer with the Royal Ballet 1973–83. He formed his own company, Dash, 1980, and in 1983 adapted his TV *Hot Shoe Show* for the stage, fusing classical, modern, jazz, tap, and disco. He also acted in the musical *Cats* 1981.

Slessor Kenneth Adolf (1901–1971). Australian poet. A journalist and war correspondent, he is remembered for his superbly pictorial verse, particularly 'Five Visions of Captain Cook' 1931 and his best-known work, the title poem of his collection *Five Bells* 1939, an elegy for his friend Joe Lynch. 'Beach Burial' 1944 illustrates the futility of war in the bewildered pity of battle-hardened soldiers in the presence of casualties.

Suggested reading
Jaffa, Herbert C *Kenneth Slessor* (1971)
Stewart, Douglas *A Man of Sydney* (1977)

Slidell John (1793–1871). American public official and diplomat. Born in New York and educated at Columbia University, Slidell moved to New Orleans 1819 and was admitted to the bar. He served as district attorney 1829–33 and US congressman 1843–45. He was named minister to Mexico by President Polk 1845–48 and later served in the US Senate from 1853 to the outbreak of the American Civil War 1861, when he resigned and joined the Confederacy. He was captured and imprisoned by the US navy, living in exile in France after his release 1862.

In a battle nothing is ever as good or as bad as the first reports of excited men would have it.

WILLIAM SLIM
Unofficial History 1959

Slim William Joseph, 1st Viscount Slim (1891–1970). British field marshal in World War II. He served in the North Africa campaign 1941 then commanded the 1st Burma Corps 1942–45, stemming the Japanese invasion of India, and then forcing them out of Burma (now Myanmar) 1945. He was governor-general of Australia 1953–60. KCB 1944, viscount 1960.

Slipher Vesto Melvin (1875–1969). US astronomer who established that spiral nebulae lie beyond our Galaxy. He also discovered the existence of particles of matter in interstellar space. His work in spectroscopy increased our knowledge of planetary and nebular rotation, planetary and stellar atmospheres, and diffuse and spiral nebulae.

Slipher was born in Mulberry, Indiana, attended Indiana University, and in 1902 joined the Lowell Observatory in Arizona. He was director of the observatory 1926–52.

Slipher measured the period of rotation for Venus, Mars, Jupiter, Saturn, and Uranus. His work on Jupiter first showed the existence of bands in the planet's spectrum, and he and his colleagues were able to identify the bands as belonging to metallic elements, including iron and copper. He also showed that the diffuse nebula of the Pleiades had a spectrum similar to that of the stars surrounding it and concluded that the nebula's brightness was the result of light reflected from the stars.

Slipher's measurements of the radial velocities of spiral nebulae 1912–25 suggested that they must be external to our Galaxy. This paved the way for an understanding of the motion of galaxies and for cosmological theories that explained the expansion of the universe.

Sloan John French (1871–1951). US painter. Born in Lock Haven, Pennsylvania, USA, he started as a newspaper illustrator for several Philadelphia newspapers. Encouraged to paint by Robert Henri, he helped organize 'the Eight', a group of realists who were against academic standards, and was a founder member of the Ashcan School. He moved to New York 1904 and helped to organize the avant-garde Armory Show 1913. His paintings of working-class urban life pioneered the field of American realism. He was president of the Society of Independent Artists 1918–44 and taught at the Art Students League 1916–37.

Suggested reading
Brookes, V W *John Sloan: A Painter's Life* (1955)
Goodrick, L *John Sloan* (1952)
Scott, D *John Sloan* (1975)
St John, B *John Sloan* (1971)
Sloan, John *Gist of Art* (1939)

Sloane Hans (1660–1753). British physician, born in County Down, Ireland. He settled in London, and in 1721 founded the Chelsea Physic Garden. He was president of the Royal College of Physicians 1719–35, and in 1727 succeeded the physicist Isaac Newton as president of the Royal Society. His library, which he bequeathed to the nation, formed the nucleus of the British Museum. 1st baronet 1716.

Slovo Joe (1926–1995). South African lawyer and politician, general secretary of the South African Communist Party 1986–91, Chief of Staff of Umkhonto we Sizwe (Spear of the Nation), the armed wing of the African National Congress (ANC) 1985–87, and minister of housing in President Mandela's government 1994–95. He was one of the most influential figures in the ANC, and spent 27 years in exile.

Born in Lithuania, Slovo emigrated to South Africa as a child with his parents, who had originally intended to settle in Argentina. Forced by poverty to leave school to take manual work before finishing his formal education, he soon became an industrial shop steward, where he secured benefits for white workers but, to his dismay, not for blacks. Despite his restricted education, he won a place to read law at Witwatersrand University, where he graduated with high honours. His early involvement with the South African Communist Party was consolidated when, in 1949, he married Ruth First, the daughter of the party's treasurer. As a partnership, they became a legend and their home a meeting place for radicals. In 1982 Ruth First was killed by a terrorist bomb in Mozambique.

After Mandela and F W de Klerk, Slovo was perhaps the most significant figure in South Africa's recent history in that he was white and yet respected and trusted by the ANC and able to persuade Mandela that the ANC could embrace all shades of opinion and all races and colours. During his exile from South Africa, Slovo travelled widely from his base in Mozambique, preparing for a guerrilla war which, he was convinced, was the only way of removing the hated system of apartheid and the regime that had installed it. A believer in the fundamental tenets of communism from an early age, he admitted in the 1980s that his uncritical support of the undemocratic Soviet regimes had been misguided. Slovo died after a progressively severe terminal illness, having lived long enough to see his vision of a multiracial, nondiscriminatory South Africa fulfilled.

Sluter Claus (c. 1380–1406). N European Gothic sculptor. Probably of Dutch origin, he was active in Dijon, France. His work includes the *Well of Moses* about 1395–1403 (now in the grounds of a hospital in Dijon) and the kneeling mourners, or *pleurants*, for the tomb of his patron Philip the Bold, Duke of Burgundy (Dijon Museum and Cleveland Museum, Ohio). In its striking realism, his work marks a break with the International Gothic style prevalent at the time.

Smalley Richard E (1943–). US chemist who, with colleagues Robert Curl and Harold Kroto, discovered buckminsterfullerene (carbon 60) 1985. Smalley also pioneered the technique used to discover buckminsterfullerene, supersonic jet laser-beam spectroscopy.

Smart Christopher (1722–1771). English poet. In 1756 he was confined to an asylum, where he wrote *A Song to David* and *Jubilate Agno/Rejoice in the Lamb*, the latter appreciated today for its surrealism.

For I will consider my cat Jeoffrey. / For he is the servant of the Living God duly and daily serving him.

CHRISTOPHER SMART
Jubilate Agno Fragment B, 1. 154

Smeaton John (1724–1792). England's first civil engineer. He rebuilt the Eddystone lighthouse in the English Channel 1756–59, having rediscovered high-quality cement, unknown since Roman times.

Smeaton was born near Leeds and qualified as a lawyer, but then became a maker of scientific instruments. Smeaton adopted the term 'civil engineer' in contradistinction to the fast-growing number of engineers graduating from military colleges. He was also a consultant in the field of structural engineering, and from 1757 onwards he was responsible for projects including bridges, power stations operated by water or wind, steam engines, and river and harbour facilities.

Smeaton's research led to the abandonment of the established undershot water wheel (which operates through the action of the flow of water against blades in the wheel) in favour of the overshot wheel (which is operated by water moving the wheel by the force of its weight). Experimenting with models, Smeaton showed that overshot wheels were twice as efficient as undershot ones.

Smeaton performed extensive tests on the experimental steam engine of Thomas Newcomen, which led to improvements in its design and efficiency.

By the grace of God and with his help I shall one day be a Liszt in technique and a Mozart in composition.

BEDŘICH SMETANA
Diary 1845

Smetana Bedřich (1824–1884). Bohemian composer. He established a Czech nationalist style in, for example, the operas *Prodaná Nevěsta/The Bartered Bride* 1866 and *Dalibor* 1868, and the symphonic suite *Má Vlast/My Country* 1875–80. He conducted the National Theatre of Prague 1866–74.

Smiles Samuel (1812–1904). Scottish writer. He was the author of the popular Victorian didactic work *Self Help* 1859. Here, as in *Character* 1871, *Thrift* 1875, and *Duty* 1880, he energetically advocated self-improvement, largely through emulation of the successful. His works propagated the values of the time, such as diligence, frugality, honesty, sobriety, and independence.

The shortest way to do many things is to do only one thing at once.

SAMUEL SMILES
Self Help 1859

Smirke Robert (1781–1867). English architect. Although his domestic architecture was Gothic Revival, he is best known for his Neo-Classical public buildings, such as the British Museum, London, 1823–47. Although often compared unfavourably to those of his contemporary in Germany, Karl Friedrich Schinkel, his designs have a powerful architectural presence and are invariably academically correct in detail. Knighted 1832.

Smith Adam (1723–1790). Scottish economist, often regarded as the founder of political economy. He was born in Kirkcaldy, and was professor of moral philosophy at Glasgow 1752–63. His *The Wealth of Nations* 1776 defined national wealth in terms of consumable goods and the labour that produces them, rather than in terms of bullion, as prevailing economic theories assumed. The ultimate cause of economic growth is explained by the division of labour – dividing a production process into several repetitive operations, each carried out by different workers, is more efficient. Smith advocated the free working of individual enterprise, and the necessity of 'free trade'.

In *Theory of Moral Sentiments* 1759, Smith argued that the correct way to discern the morally right is to ask what a hypothetical impartial spectator would regard as fitting or proper.

Suggested reading
Campbell, R H and Skinner, A S *Adam Smith* (1982)
Fay, C R *The World of Adam Smith* (1960)
Raphael, D *Adam Smith* (1985)
Ross, Ian Simpson *The Life of Adam Smith* (1996)

Smith Al(fred Emanuel) (1873–1944). US political leader who served four terms as governor of New York but was unsuccessful as a candidate for the presidency. Smith, born in New York, left school in his teens and became involved in local Democratic politics. After serving in the New York state assembly 1905–15 he became New York County sheriff 1915–17. In 1918 he was elected governor of New York. He was defeated for re-election 1920 but was victorious in 1922, 1924, and 1926. In 1928 he became the first Roman Catholic to receive a presidential nomination. In his lively, yet unsuccessful, campaign against Herbert Hoover he was called the 'Happy Warrior'.

Smith Bessie (Elizabeth) (1894–1937). US jazz and blues singer. Known as the 'Empress of the Blues', she established herself in the 1920s after she was discovered by Columbia Records. She made over 150 recordings accompanied by such greats as Louis Armstrong and Benny Goodman. Her popularity waned in the Depression, and she died after a car crash when she was refused admission to a whites-only hospital.

Suggested reading
Albertson, Chris *Bessie* (1973)

Smith David Roland (1906–1965). US sculptor and painter. His work made a lasting impact on sculpture after World War II.

Smetana The composer Bedřich Smetana. Although Bohemian by birth, Smetana was educated in Germany and did not speak Czech like a native. He nevertheless wrote music in a Czech nationalist style, for example Má vlast/My homeland *and* Dalibor. (Image Select)

Trained as a steel welder in a car factory, his pieces are large open-work metal abstracts.

Smith turned first to painting and then, about 1930, to sculpture. Using welded steel, he created abstract structures influenced by the metal sculptures of Picasso and Julio González. In the 1940s and 1950s he developed a more linear style. The *Cubi* series of totemlike abstracts, some of them painted, was designed to be placed in the open air.

Smith Francis Graham (1923–). English radioastronomer who with his colleague Martin Ryle mapped the radio sources in the sky in the 1950s. Smith discovered the strongly polarized nature of radiation from pulsars 1968, and estimated the strength of the magnetic field in interstellar space. He was Astronomer Royal 1982–90. Knighted 1986.

Smith was born in Roehampton, Surrey, and studied at Cambridge. During World War II he was assigned to the Telecommunications Research Establishment, and when he returned to Cambridge, he joined the radio research department at the Cavendish Laboratory. He was appointed professor of astronomy at Manchester 1964 and worked at Jodrell Bank until 1974. He was director of the Royal Greenwich Observatory 1976–81. In 1981, he moved back to Jodrell Bank to become director there.

In 1948, Smith and Ryle, investigating a source of radio waves in the constellation of Cygnus, detected a second source in the constellation Cassiopeia. Smith spent the following years trying to determine the precise location of both sources. Finally, astronomers at Mount Palomar, California, were able to pinpoint optical counterparts. Cassiopeia A was shown to derive from a supernova explosion within our Galaxy; Cygnus A is a double radio galaxy.

Smith and Ryle were the first to publish (in 1957) a paper on the possibility of devising an accurate navigational system that depended on the use of radio signals from an orbiting satellite.

In 1962 Smith installed a radio receiver in *Ariel II*, one of a series of joint US–UK satellites, enabling it to make the first investigation of radio noise above the ionosphere.

Smith F(rederick) E(dwin). British Conservative politician. See ◊Birkenhead.

Smith Hamilton Othanel (1931–). US microbiologist who shared the 1978 Nobel Prize for Physiology or Medicine with his colleague Daniel Nathans for their work on restriction enzymes, special enzymes that can cleave genes into fragments.

Smith was born in New York and studied at the University of California, Berkeley, and at Johns Hopkins University. In 1964 he returned to Johns Hopkins, becoming professor 1973.

Werner Arber (1929–), a Swiss microbiologist, discovered restriction enzymes in the 1960s. Smith, working independently of Arber, verified Arber's findings and was also able to identify the gene fragments. Smith collaborated with Nathans on some of this work.

As a result of the work of Nathans, Smith, and Arber (who also shared the Nobel prize), it is now possible to determine the chemical formulas of the genes in animal viruses, to map these genes, and to study the organization and expression of genes in higher animals.

He was popular with his colleagues and subordinates, who were fascinated by his daring energy and originality, and admired his rough and ready wit.

R H Vetch on HARRY SMITH
in *Dictionary of National Biography*

Smith Harry George Wakelyn (1787–1860). British general. He served in the Peninsular War (1808–14) and later fought in South Africa and India. He was governor of Cape Colony 1847–52. The towns of Ladysmith and Harrismith, South Africa, are named after his wife and him respectively. 1st baronet 1846.

Smith Ian Douglas (1919–). Rhodesian politician. He was a founder of the Rhodesian Front 1962 and prime minister 1964–79. In 1965 he made a unilateral declaration of Rhodesia's independence

Smith, John *English explorer John Smith. He was captured during an expedition through Indian territory but saved by Pocahontas, daughter of Chief Powhatan, who secured his release.*

and, despite United Nations sanctions, maintained his regime with tenacity.

In 1979 he was succeeded as prime minister by Bishop Abel Muzorewa, when the country was renamed Zimbabwe. He was suspended from the Zimbabwe parliament April 1987 and resigned in May as head of the white opposition party. In 1992 he helped found a new opposition party, the United Front.

The gaining provinces addeth to the King's Crown; but the reducing heathen people to civility and true religion bringeth honour to the King of Heaven.

JOHN SMITH
to his followers in Virginia, quoted in E Arber (ed)
Travels and Works of Captain John Smith vol I 1910

Smith John (1580–1631). English colonist. After an adventurous early life he took part in the colonization of Virginia, acting as president of the North American colony 1608–09. He explored New England in 1614, which he named, and published pamphlets on America and an autobiography. His trade with the Indians may have kept the colonists alive in the early years.

During an expedition among the American Indians he was captured, and his life is said to have been saved by the intervention of the chief's daughter Pocahontas.
Suggested reading
Barbour, Philip *The Three Worlds of Captain Smith* (1964)
Emerson, E H *Captain John Smith* (1971)
Fox, Joseph *Captain John Smith* (1985)

Smith John (1938–1994). British Labour politician, party leader 1992–94. He was trade and industry secretary 1978–79 and from 1979 held various shadow cabinet posts, culminating in that of shadow chancellor 1987–92. As leader of the opposition, he won a

reputation as a man of transparent honesty and a formidable parliamentarian. His sudden death from a heart attack shocked British politicians of all parties.

Smith John Maynard. British biologist, see ◊Maynard Smith.

Smith Joseph (1805–1844). US founder of the Mormon religious sect. Born in Vermont, he received his first religious call in 1820, and in 1827 claimed to have been granted the revelation of the *Book of Mormon* (an ancient American prophet), inscribed on gold plates and concealed a thousand years before in a hill near Palmyra, New York State. He founded the Church of Jesus Christ of Latter-day Saints in Fayette, New York, 1830. The Mormons were persecuted for their beliefs and Smith was killed by an angry mob in Illinois.
Suggested reading
Brodie, F M *No Man Knows My History: The Life of Joseph Smith* (1971)
Bushman, Richard *Joseph Smith and the Beginnings of Mormonism* (1985)
Hill, Donna *Joseph Smith* (1977)

Smith Keith Macpherson (1890–1955) and Ross Macpherson (1892–1922). Australian aviators and brothers who made the first England–Australia flight 1919. Both KBE 1919.

Smith Maggie (Margaret Natalie Cross) (1934–). English actress. She is notable for her commanding presence, fluting voice, and throwaway lines. Her films include *The Prime of Miss Jean Brodie* 1969 (Academy Award), *California Suite* 1978, *A Private Function* 1984, *A Room with a View* and *The Lonely Passion of Judith Hearne* both 1987, and *Sister Act* 1992. DBE 1990.

Smith Matthew Arnold Bracy (1879–1959). English artist. Influenced by the Fauves, he was known for his exuberant treatment of nudes, luscious fruits and flowers, and landscapes.

He studied at the Slade School and in Paris, working for a short time in Matisse's school 1911. His mature style developed in the 1920s. In a series of nudes, landscapes (Cornwall and South of France), and flower and still-life paintings he displayed a sumptuousness of colour in which he had no modern British rival. Knighted 1954.

Smith Patti (1946–). US rock singer and songwriter. Her album *Horses* 1975 contributed to the genesis of the New Wave. Her risk-taking performances and punk sensibility made her a significant influence. In 1978 she had a hit with Bruce Springsteen's 'Because the Night'.

Horses was followed by *Radio Ethiopia* 1976, *Easter* 1978, and *Waves* 1979. She made a comeback 1988 with *Dream of Life*.

Smith Paul (1946–). English clothes designer. His clothes are stylistically simple and practical. He opened his first shop 1970, selling designer menswear alongside his own designs, and showed his first collection in Paris 1976. He launched a toiletry range 1986, a children's wear collection 1991, and women's wear 1994. His designs were sold in 27 countries by 1993 and there were 78 Paul Smith shops in Japan alone.

I was much too far out all my life/And not waving but drowning.

STEVIE SMITH
'Not Waving but Drowning'

Smith Stevie (Florence Margaret) (1902–1971). English poet and novelist. She published her first book, *Novel on Yellow Paper*, 1936, and her first collection of poems, *A Good Time Was Had by All*, 1937. She wrote a further eight volumes of eccentrically direct verse illustrated with her equally eccentric line drawings, including *Not Waving but Drowning* 1957, and two more novels. *Collected Poems* was published 1975.

Smith Sydney (1771–1845). English writer. He was one of the founders of the *Edinburgh Review* 1802, and contributed to it for 25

1815 that he published *A Delineation of the Strata of England and Wales*, a geological map using a scale of five miles to the inch. Between 1816 and 1824 he published *Strata Identified by Organized Fossils* and *Stratigraphical System of Organized Fossils*, a descriptive catalogue. He also issued various charts and sections, and geological maps of 21 counties.

Smith-Dorrien Horace Lockwood (1858–1930). British general. Potentially one of Britain's best generals of World War I, he was denied the opportunity to realize this potential by petty spite.

He was sent to France to take command of 2nd Corps in the retreat from Mons and held the Germans at Le Cateau Aug 1914, which incurred the displeasure of Sir John French, since it was against his orders. Later, French refused to allow him to shorten his line at Ypres in order to avoid unnecessary casualties. After the first gas attacks at Ypres he was instructed to direct fresh attacks, which he considered wasteful of lives; he protested to French, who took the opportunity to relieve him. He then went to take charge of operations in East Africa but suffered from pneumonia and was invalided home. He became Governor of Gibraltar 1918. KCB 1907.

Smithson Alison Margaret (born Gill) (1928–1993) and Peter Denham (1923–) English architects, teachers, and theorists. They are known for their development in the 1950s and 1960s of the style known as Brutalism, for example, Hunstanton School, Norfolk, 1954. Notable among their other designs are the Economist Building, London, 1964, and Robin Hood Gardens, London, 1968–72. Their style reflected the influence of Le Corbusier and Mies van der Rohe in its symmetry and clarity of form.

Alison Smithson made significant contributions to post-war architectural theory as a leading member of Team X, a group formed to prepare for the 10th congress of the urban-planning body CIAM (Congrès Internationaux d'Architecture Moderne) in Dubrovnik 1956. The team called for personal responsibility and attention to detail, in contrast to the grandiose schemes that had dominated the work of the organization since its foundation in the 1920s.

The Smithsons were also active members of the Independent Group at the Institute of Contemporary Art, London, in the early 1950s, and made an original contribution to the London Whitechapel Gallery's *This Is Tomorrow* exhibition 1956. The same year saw their *House of the Future* at the Ideal Home Exhibition in London, which drew on futuristic car design and innovative mechanical services.

Smithson James Louis Macie (1765–1829). British chemist and mineralogist whose bequest of $100,000 led to the establishment of the Smithsonian Institution.

Smithson Robert (1938–1973). US sculptor and experimental artist. He is celebrated for his huge outdoor earthwork *Spiral Jetty* 1970 – a spiralling stone causeway that extended into Great Salt Lake, Utah, but of which only photographs remain. He began by exhibiting mirrored constructions and open boxes filled with quarry stones or coal, but turned to outdoor earthworks in the late 1960s, which he elaborated with maps, drawings, and instant photographs. He saw his outdoor pieces, which he frequently called 'non-sites', as akin to the 'ancient mysteries' of archaeological finds and a turning away from the conventions of museum gallery art. Since his death in a plane crash, he has become something of a cult figure.

Smollett Tobias George (1721–1771). Scottish novelist. He wrote the picaresque novels *Roderick Random* 1748, *Peregrine Pickle* 1751, *Ferdinand Count Fathom* 1753, *Sir Launcelot Greaves* 1760–62, and *Humphrey Clinker* 1771. His novels are full of gusto and vivid characterization.

I am pent up in frowzy lodgings, where there is not room to swing a cat.

TOBIAS SMOLLETT
Humphry Clinker vol 1 (letter from Matthew Bramble 8 June) 1771

Smith, John *John Smith who succeeded Neil Kinnock as leader of the British Labour Party 1992. He continued Kinnock's reform of the party, determined in particular to redefine the vital but often difficult relationship between the Labour Party and the labour unions. His sudden death from a heart attack 12 May 1994 shocked the nation.*

years. A popular and witty preacher, he became a canon of St Paul's Cathedral 1831.

Smith was ordained 1794. Although he preached to packed audiences, he had many enemies, because he attacked evangelists, Methodists, and followers of Edward Pusey, but supported Catholic emancipation. Smith moved in influential Whig circles and was a member of the Holland House group. In a speech on the rejection of the Reform Bill 1831, he compared the House of Lords to Mrs Partington (a popular fictitious character) resisting the Atlantic Ocean with a mop.

Smith Willi (1948–1987). US fashion designer. He set up WilliWear Ltd 1976, making casual ready-to-wear lines. Previously he designed knitwear.

Smith William (1769–1839). English geologist who produced the first geological maps of England and Wales, setting the pattern for geological cartography. Often called the founder of stratigraphical geology, he determined the succession of English strata across the whole country, from the Carboniferous up to the Cretaceous. He also established their fossil specimens. Working as a canal engineer, he observed while supervising excavations that different beds of rock could be identified by their fossils, and so established the basis of stratigraphy.

Smith was born in Churchill, Oxfordshire, and became a drainage expert, a canal surveyor, and a mining prospector.

Smith was not the first geologist to recognize the principles of stratigraphy nor the usefulness of type fossils. His primary accomplishment lay in mapping. He began in 1799 but it was not until

Suggested reading
Bruce, D *Radical Doctor Smollett* (1964)
Grant, D *Tobias Smollett* (1977)
Spector, R D *Tobias Smollett* (1968)

Smuts Jan Christian (1870–1950). South African politician and soldier; prime minister 1919–24 and 1939–48. He supported the Allies in both world wars and was a member of the British imperial war cabinet 1917–18.

During the Second South African War (1899–1902) Smuts commanded the Boer forces in his native Cape Colony. He subsequently worked for reconciliation between the Boers and the British. On the establishment of the Union of South Africa, he became minister of the interior 1910–12 and defence minister 1910–20. During World War I he commanded the South African forces in E Africa 1916–17. He was prime minister 1919–24 and minister of justice 1933–39; on the outbreak of World War II he succeeded General Hertzog as premier. He was made a field marshal in 1941.

Smuts received the Order of Merit in 1947. Although more of an internationalist than his contemporaries, Smuts was a segregationalist, voting in favour of legislation that took away black rights and land ownership.

Suggested reading
Hancock, William Keith *Smuts* (1962–68)
Smuts, J C *Jan Christian Smuts* (a biography by his son) (1952)
Williams, Basil *Botha, Smuts and South Africa* (1946)

Smyth Ethel Mary (1858–1944). English composer. She studied in Leipzig. Her works include *Mass in D* 1893 and operas *The Wreckers* 1906 and *The Boatswain's Mate* 1916. In 1911 she was imprisoned as an advocate of women's suffrage. DBE 1922.

Smythson Robert (*c.* 1535–1614). English architect. He built Elizabethan country houses, including Longleat 1568–75, Wollaton Hall 1580–88, and Hardwick Hall 1590–97. Their castlelike silhouettes, symmetry, and large gridded windows are a uniquely romantic English version of Classicism.

Snell Willebrord van Roijen (1581–1626). Dutch mathematician and physicist who devised the basic law of refraction, known as Snell's law, in 1621. This states that the ratio between the sine of the angle of incidence and the sine of the angle of refraction is constant. He also founded the method of determining distances by triangulation.

Snell was born in Leiden, where he studied and eventually became professor. Snell developed the method of triangulation in 1615, starting with his house and the spires of nearby churches as reference points. He used a large quadrant over 2 m/7 ft long to determine angles, and by building up a network of triangles, was able to obtain a value for the distance between two towns on the same meridian. From this, Snell made an accurate determination of the radius of the Earth.

The laws describing the reflection of light were well known in antiquity, but the principles governing the refraction of light were little understood. Snell's law was published by French mathematician Descartes in 1637. He expressed the law differently from Snell, but could easily have derived it from Snell's original formulation. Whether Descartes knew of Snell's work or discovered the law independently is not known.

The official world. The corridors of power.
C P SNOW
Homecomings ch 22 1956

Snow C(harles) P(ercy). Baron Snow (1905–1980). English novelist and physicist. He held government scientific posts in World War II and 1964–66. His sequence of novels *Strangers and Brothers* 1940–64 portrayed English life from 1920 onwards. His *The Two Cultures and the Scientific Revolution* (Cambridge Rede lecture 1959) discussed the absence of communication between literary and scientific intellectuals in the West, and added the phrase 'the two cultures'

to the language. Knighted 1957, baron 1964.
Suggested reading
Karl, F *C P Snow: The Politics of Conscience* (1963)
Schusterman, David *C P Snow* (1975)
Snow, Philip *Stranger and Brother: A Portrait of C P Snow* (1983)

It would be desirable if every government, when it comes to power, should have its old speeches burned.
PHILIP, 1ST VISCOUNT SNOWDEN
quoted in C E Bechofer Roberts *Philip Snowden* ch 12

Snowden Philip, 1st Viscount Snowden (1864–1937). British right-wing Labour politician, chancellor of the Exchequer 1924 and 1929–31. He entered the coalition National Government in 1931 as Lord Privy Seal, but resigned in 1932. Viscount 1931.

Snowdon Anthony Charles Robert Armstrong-Jones, 1st Earl of Snowdon (1930–). English photographer. He is especially known for his portraits. He was consultant to the Council of Industrial Design and editorial adviser to *Design Magazine* 1961–87; artistic adviser to Sunday Times Publications 1962–90; and photographer for the *Telegraph Magazine* from 1990. He has also made several films for television. In 1960 he married Princess Margaret; they were divorced 1978. Earl 1961.

Snyder Gary Sherman (1930–). US poet. He was a key figure in the poetry renaissance in San Francisco during the 1950s. He combined an early interest in ecological issues with studies of Japanese, Chinese and North American Indian cultures and myths. Associated with the Beat Generation of writers, he was the protagonist of Jack Kerouac's novel *The Dharma Bums* 1958. Snyder's works include *Earth House Hold* 1969, the Pulitzer prize-winning poetry collection *Turtle Island* 1974, and *No Nature* 1992.

Snyder Solomon Halbert (1938–). US pharmacologist and neuroscientist who has studied the chemistry of the brain, and co-discovered the receptor mechanism for the body's own opiates, the encephalins. From 1965 he worked at the Johns Hopkins Medical School, becoming professor 1970.

In the early 1970s, in collaboration with his research student Candace Pert (1946–), Snyder realized that the very specific effects of synthetic opiates given in small doses suggested that they must bind to highly selective target receptor sites. Using radioactively labelled compounds, they located such receptors in specialized areas of the mammalian brain and from this finding deduced that there might be natural opiatelike substances in the brain that used these sites. These chemicals, the encephalins, were discovered by others shortly afterwards.

Continuing to examine the relationships of chemicals to neural functioning, Snyder has made a particular study of the receptor sites for the benzodiazepine drugs, which are widely used in psychiatry.

Snyders Frans (1579–1657). Flemish painter. His subjects were hunting scenes and still lifes. Based in Antwerp, he was a pupil of Brueghel the Younger and later assisted Rubens and worked with Jordaens. In 1608–09 he travelled in Italy. He excelled at painting fur, feathers, and animals fighting.

Soames (Arthur) Christopher (John), Baron Soames (1920–1987). British Conservative politician. He held ministerial posts 1958–64, was vice president of the Commission of the European Communities 1973–77 and governor of (Southern) Rhodesia in the period of its transition to independence as Zimbabwe, Dec 1979–April 1980. He became GCMG 1972 and was created a life peer 1978.

There was a touch of bombast about him, but ... underneath there was a large reservoir of imaginative statesmanship.
Roy Jenkins on CHRISTOPHER SOAMES
Gallery of 20th Century Portraits 1988

Soane John (1753–1837). English architect. His refined Neo-Classical designs anticipated contemporary taste. He designed his own house in Lincoln's Inn Fields, London, 1812–13, now the Soane Museum. Little remains of his extensive work at the Bank of England, London. Knighted 1831.

Soares Mario Alberto Nobre Lopes (1924–). Portuguese socialist politician, president from 1986. Exiled 1970, he returned to Portugal 1974, and, as leader of the Portuguese Socialist Party, was prime minister 1976–78. He resigned as party leader 1980, but in 1986 he was elected Portugal's first socialist president.

Sobchak Anatoly (1937–). Soviet centrist politician, mayor of St Petersburg from 1990, cofounder of the Democratic Reform Movement (with former foreign minister Shevardnadze), and member of the Soviet parliament 1989–91.

Sobchak was born in Siberia, studied law at the University of Leningrad and became professor of economic law there 1983. He was elected to parliament in the semi-free poll of March 1989, chaired the congressional commission into the massacre of Georgian nationalists, and became a leading figure in the radical Interregional Group of deputies.

He left the Communist Party 1990 after only two years' membership and in May 1991 was elected mayor of Leningrad (renamed St Petersburg later the same year). When tanks advanced on the city during the coup attempt in Aug, Sobchak negotiated an agreement to ensure that they remained outside, and upheld the democratic cause. He prominently resisted the abortive anti-Gorbachev attempted coup of Aug 1991.

Sobers Garry (Garfield St Auburn) (1936–). West Indian test cricketer and arguably the world's finest ever all rounder. Sobers started playing first-class cricket in 1952. He held the world individual record for the highest test innings with 365 not out, until beaten by Brian Lara 1994. He played county cricket for Nottinghamshire and, in a match against Glamorgan at Swansea 1968, he became the first to score six sixes in an over in first-class cricket. He played for the West Indies on 93 occasions, and was captain 39 times. He was knighted for services to cricket 1975.

Sobieski John. Alternative name for ◊John III, king of Poland.

Nothing can harm a good man, either in life or after death.

SOCRATES
quoted in Plato *Apology* 42

Socrates (c. 469–399 BC). Athenian philosopher. He wrote nothing but was immortalized in the dialogues of his pupil Plato. In his desire to combat the scepticism of the sophists, Socrates asserted the possibility of genuine knowledge. In ethics, he put forward the view that the good person never knowingly does wrong. True knowledge emerges through dialogue and systematic questioning and an abandoning of uncritical claims to knowledge.

The effect of Socrates' teaching was disruptive since he opposed tyranny. Accused in 399 on charges of impiety and corruption of youth, he was condemned by the Athenian authorities to die by drinking hemlock.

Suggested reading
Gulley, Norman *The Philosophy of Socrates* (1968)
Navia, L E *Socrates: The Man and His Philosophy* (1989)
Vlastos, Gregory (ed) *The Philosophy of Socrates* (1971)
Vlastos, Gregory *Socrates: Ironist and Moral Philosopher* (1991)

Soddy Frederick (1877–1956). English physical chemist who pioneered research into atomic disintegration and coined the term isotope. He was awarded a Nobel prize 1921 for investigating the origin and nature of isotopes. Soddy was professor at Aberdeen 1914–19 and at Oxford 1919–36. He opposed military use of atomic power.

The displacement law, introduced by Soddy in 1913, explains the changes in atomic mass and atomic number for all the radioactive intermediates in the decay processes.

After his chemical discoveries, Soddy spent some 40 years developing a theory of 'energy economics', which he called 'Cartesian economics'. He argued for the abolition of debt and compound interest, the nationalization of credit, and a new theory of value based on the quantity of energy contained in a thing.

Soddy and Rutherford postulated that radioactive decay is an atomic or subatomic process, and formulated a disintegration law. They also predicted that helium should be a decay product of radium, a fact that Soddy proved spectrographically in 1903.

His works include *Chemistry of the Radio-Elements* 1912–14, *The Interpretation of the Atom* 1932, and *The Story of Atomic Energy* 1949.

Söderberg Hjalmar Eric Fredrik (1869–1941). Swedish writer. His work includes the short, melancholy novels *Förvillelser/Aberrations* 1895, *Martin Bircks ungdom/The Youth of Martin Birck* 1901, *Doktor Glas/Dr Glass* 1906, and the play *Gertrud* 1906.

Sokolovsky Vasily (1897–1968). Soviet general in World War II. Chief of Staff to the West Front Army from 1941, he took command of it 1943, led it in the counter-offensive after the Battle of Kursk and liberated Smolensk. His progress then slowed and he was removed from command and became Chief of Staff to the 1st Ukrainian Front. In 1945 he became deputy commander of 1st Byelorussian Front for the attack on Berlin, captured the *Führerbunker*, and verified Hitler's corpse from dental records. After the war he became commander in chief of Soviet Forces in Germany.

Solander Daniel Carl (1736–1782). Swedish botanist. In 1768, as assistant to Joseph Banks, he accompanied the explorer James Cook on his first voyage to the S Pacific, during which he made extensive collections of plants.

Solander was born in Norrland and studied under Swedish botanist Linnaeus. In 1771 he became secretary and librarian to Banks and in 1773 became keeper of the natural-history department of the British Museum. Named after him are a genus of Australian plants and a cape at the entrance to Botany Bay.

Solomon (c. 974–c. 937 BC). In the Old Testament, third king of Israel, son of David by Bathsheba. During a peaceful reign, he was famed for his wisdom and his alliances with Egypt and Phoenicia. The much later biblical Proverbs, Ecclesiastes, and Song of Songs are attributed to him. He built the temple in Jerusalem with the aid of heavy taxation and forced labour, resulting in the revolt of N Israel.

The so-called King Solomon's Mines at Aqaba, Jordan (copper and iron), are of later date.

Mark this: until he is dead, keep the word happy in reserve. Till then, a man is not happy, only lucky.

SOLON's response when Croesus tried to demonstrate that he was the happiest of men. Quoted in Herodotus *History* 1. 32

Solon (c. 638–c. 558 BC). Athenian statesman. As one of the chief magistrates about 594 BC, he carried out the cancellation of all debts from which land or liberty was the security and the revision of the constitution that laid the foundations of Athenian democracy. He was one of the Seven Sages of Greece.

Soloviev Vladimir Sergeyevich (1853–1900). Russian philosopher and poet. His blending of neo-Platonism and Christian mysticism attempted to link all aspects of human experience in a doctrine of divine wisdom. His theories, expressed in poems and essays, influenced Symbolist writers such as Alexander Blok.

Solti Georg (1912–). Hungarian-born British conductor. He was music director at the Royal Opera House, Covent Garden, London, 1961–71, and became director of the Chicago Symphony Orchestra 1969. He was also principal conductor of the London Philharmonic Orchestra 1979–83. KBE 1971. *See illustration on page 800.*

Solti *The conductor and pianist Georg Solti. During his long and distinguished career as conductor, Solti has galvanized performances in all genres, especially 19th-century music. He gave the first complete studio recording of the* Ring *cycle and his sets of symphonies convey all the excitement of the concert hall.*

A young conductor has to compromise. He will put more energy in and get less back.

GEORG SOLTI
interviewed in *Classic CD* 1995

Solvay Ernest (1838–1922). Belgian industrial chemist who in the 1860s invented the ammonia-soda process, also known as the Solvay process, for making the alkali sodium carbonate. It is a multistage process in which carbon dioxide is generated from limestone and passed through brine saturated with ammonia. Sodium hydrogen carbonate is isolated and heated to yield sodium carbonate. All intermediate by-products are recycled so that the only ultimate by-product is calcium chloride.

In 1860 he went to work at a gasworks, and there learned about the industrial handling of ammonia both as a gas and as an aqueous solution. Within a year he had discovered and patented the reactions that are the basis of the Solvay process. Trial production failed; for two years Solvay knew he had the chemistry right, but could not solve the considerable problems of chemical engineering. He built his first factories 1863 and 1873.

Solvay soon realized that there was more money to be made from granting licences to other manufacturers than there was in making soda. Throughout the world, the Solvay process replaced the old Leblanc process, which was more expensive and polluting. Solvay became a very rich man and entered politics, becoming a member of the Belgian senate and a minister of state.

Solyman I alternative spelling of ◊Suleiman, Ottoman sultan.

Solzhenitsyn Alexander Isayevich (1918–   ). Soviet novelist. He became a US citizen 1974. He was in prison and exile 1945–57 for anti-Stalinist comments. Much of his writing is semi-autobiographical and highly critical of the system, including *One Day in the Life of Ivan Denisovich* 1962, which deals with the labour camps under

Stalin, and *The Gulag Archipelago* 1973, an exposé of the whole Soviet labour-camp network. This led to his expulsion from the USSR 1974. He was awarded a Nobel prize 1970.

Other works include *The First Circle* and *Cancer Ward*, both 1968, and his historical novel *August 1914* 1971. His autobiography, *The Oak and the Calf*, appeared 1980. He has adopted a Christian position, and his criticism of Western materialism is also stringent. In 1991, cleared of the original charges of treason, he returned to Russia.

Suggested reading
Ericson, E *Solzhenitsyn: The Moral Vision* (1980)
Feuer, Katheryn (ed) *Solzhenitsyn: A Collection of Critical Essays* (1976)
Kodjak, A *Alexander Solzhenitsyn* (1978)
Rothberg, A *Aleksandr Solzhenitsyn: The Major Novels* (1971)
Scammell, M *Solzhenitsyn: A Biography* (1984)

He failed to carry out his objects because he lacked patience, hated compromise, and consistently underrated the strength of the forces opposed to him.

A F Pollard on EDWARD SEYMOUR, 1ST DUKE OF SOMERSET
in *Dictionary of National Biography*

Somerset Edward Seymour, 1st Duke of Somerset (*c.* 1506–1552). English politician. Created Earl of Hertford after Henry VIII's marriage to his sister Jane, he became Duke of Somerset and protector (regent) for Edward VI in 1547. His attempt to check enclosure (the transfer of land from common to private ownership) offended landowners and his moderation in religion upset the Protestants, and he was beheaded on a fake treason charge in 1552. Knighted 1523, viscount 1536, earl 1537.

Somerville Edith Anna Oenone (1861–1949). Irish novelist. She wrote stories of Irish life jointly with her cousin, Violet Martin ('Martin Ross'). Their works include *Some Experiences of an Irish RM* 1899.

Somerville Mary (born Fairfax) (1780–1872). Scottish scientific writer who produced several widely used textbooks, despite having just one year of formal education. Somerville College, Oxford, is named after her.

Her main works were *Mechanism of the Heavens* 1831 (a translation of French astronomer Pierre Laplace's treatise on celestial mechanics), *On the Connexion of Physical Sciences* 1834, *Physical Geography* 1848, and *On Molecular and Microscopic Science* 1869.

Somes Michael George (1917–1994). British ballet dancer, teacher, *répétiteur*, and guardian of the Royal Ballet's Frederick Ashton repertoire. Somes was praised by critics for his elegant deportment, superb elevation, and exceptional musicality. He was also an important long-time partner of Margot Fonteyn.

The first leading male dancer to be developed from what was then called the Vic-Wells Ballet School, Somes was awarded a scholarship in 1934, and soon established himself as one of the most gifted dancers of his generation. His early appearances with the Sadler's Wells ballet began to reveal his lyricism and musicality, which inspired Frederick Ashton to create roles for him in such works as *A Wedding Bouquet* 1937, *Les Patineurs* 1937, and *Horoscope* 1938, in which Somes first danced with Margot Fonteyn. Although war service and injury interrupted his career and prevented him from developing real virtuosity, when he returned to the company his partnership with Fonteyn continued, and they created further important roles in Ashton's ballets *Symphonic Variations* 1946, *Scenes de Ballets* 1948, and *Ondine* 1958.

During the 1950s, Somes increasingly became a model for male dancers. In later years he continued to perform in character parts, and also served as assistant company director under Ashton. From 1970 his association with the Royal Ballet took the shape of chief *répétiteur* and teacher. When he left the company in 1984 (under slightly acrimonious circumstances – he was known for his fierce temper), he staged several Ashton ballets in many different countries. This work continued up until his death, and is considered to be Somes's greatest legacy to ballet.

Sommeiller Germain (1815–1871). French engineer who built the Mont Cenis Tunnel, 12 km/7 mi long, between Switzerland and France. The tunnel was drilled with his invention the pneumatic drill.

Sommerfeld Arnold Johannes Wilhelm (1868–1951). German physicist who demonstrated that difficulties with Niels Bohr's model of the atom, in which electrons move around a central nucleus in circular orbits, could be overcome by supposing that electrons adopt elliptical orbits. This led him in 1916 to predict a series of spectral lines based on the relativistic effects that would occur with elliptical orbits. Friedrich Paschen (1865–1945) undertook the spectroscopic work required and confirmed Sommerfeld's predictions.

He was professor at the Mining Academy in Clausthal 1897–1900, at the Technical Institute in Aachen 1900–06, and then moved to Munich University as director of the Institute of Theoretical Physics, specially established for him. Sommerfeld built his institute into a leading centre of physics.

Sommerfeld was active as a theoretician both in physics and engineering, and he produced a four-volume work on the theory of gyroscopes 1897–1910 with mathematician Felix Klein. Sommerfeld's other works include *Atombau und Spektrallinien/ Atomic Structure and Spectral Lines* 1919 and *Wellenmechanischer Ergänzungsband/Wave Mechanics* 1929.

Sommerville Duncan MacLaren Young (1879–1934). British mathematician who made significant contributions to the study of non-Euclidean geometry.

In 1915 he emigrated to New Zealand as professor at Victoria University College, Wellington.

Sommerville explained how non-Euclidean geometries arise from the use of alternatives to Euclid's postulate of parallels, and showed

Somerville, Mary Scottish mathematician and astronomer Mary Somerville, who helped popularize science in the early 19th century. She strongly supported the emancipation and education of women, and Somerville College at Oxford is named after her. (Ann Ronan/Image Select)

that both Euclidean and non-Euclidean geometries – such as hyperbolic and elliptic geometries – can be considered as sub-geometries of projective geometry. He stated that projective geometry is the invariant theory associated with the group of linear fractional transformations.

Somoza Debayle Anastasio (1925–1980). Nicaraguan soldier and politician, president 1967–72 and 1974–79. The second son of Anastasio Somoza García, he succeeded his brother Luis Somoza Debayle (1922–1967; president 1956–63) as president of Nicaragua in 1967, to head an even more oppressive regime. He was removed by Sandinista guerrillas in 1979, and assassinated in Paraguay 1980.

Somoza García Anastasio (1896–1956). Nicaraguan soldier and politician, president 1937–47 and 1950–56. A protégé of the USA, who wanted a reliable ally to protect their interests in Central America, he was virtual dictator of Nicaragua from 1937 until his assassination in 1956. He exiled most of his political opponents and amassed a considerable fortune in land and businesses. Members of his family retained control of the country until 1979, when they were overthrown by popular forces.

Sondheim Stephen Joshua (1930–). US composer and lyricist. He wrote the lyrics for Leonard Bernstein's *West Side Story* 1957 and composed witty and sophisticated musicals, including *A Little Night Music* 1973, *Pacific Overtures* 1976, *Sweeney Todd* 1979, *Into the Woods* 1987, and *Sunday in the Park with George* 1989.

Song dynasty or Sung dynasty (10th–13th centuries). Chinese imperial family 960–1279, founded by northern general Taizu (Zhao Kuangyin 928–76). A distinction is conventionally made between the Northern Song period 960–1126, when the capital was at Kaifeng, and Southern Song 1127–1279, when it was at Hangzhou (Hangchow). A stable government was supported by a thoroughly centralized administration. The dynasty was eventually ended by Mongol invasion.

During the Song era, such technologies as shipbuilding, firearms, clock-making, and the use of the compass far outstripped those of Europe. Painting, poetry, and ceramics flourished, as did economic development, particularly in the rice-growing SE. NE China remained independent of the Song, being ruled by the Liao and Jin dynasties.

Existence is no more than the precarious attainment of relevance in an intensely mobile flux of past, present, and future.

SUSAN SONTAG
Styles of Radical Will, 'Thinking Against Oneself: Reflections on Cioran' 1969

Sontag Susan (1933–). US critic, novelist, and screenwriter. Her novel *The Benefactor* appeared 1963, and she established herself as a critic with the influential cultural essays of 'Against Interpretation' 1966 and 'Styles of Radical Will' 1969. More recent studies, showing the influence of French structuralism, are *On Photography* 1976 and the powerful *Illness as Metaphor* 1978 and *Aids and its Metaphors* 1989.

Soong Ching-ling (1890–1981). Chinese politician, wife of the Guomindang nationalist leader Sun Yat-sen; she remained a prominent figure in Chinese politics after his death, being a vice chair of the People's Republic of China from 1959.

Soper Donald Oliver, Baron Soper (1903–). British Methodist minister, superintendent of the West London Mission, Kingsway Hall, 1936–78. He is well known for his readiness of wit in debate and through television appearances. His books include *All His Grace* 1957 and *Aflame with Faith*, and as a speaker at Hyde Park Corner he has influenced many. In 1965 he became a life peer.

Sophia Electress of Hanover (1630–1714). Twelfth child of Frederick V, elector palatine of the Rhine and king of Bohemia, and Elizabeth, daughter of James I of England. She married the elector of

Hanover in 1658. Widowed in 1698, she was recognized in the succession to the English throne in 1701, and when Queen Anne died without issue in 1714, her son George I founded the Hanoverian dynasty.

A clever, witty and lively old woman, broad in her interests, international in outlook ... abler and less parochial than her son [George I].

C P Hill on SOPHIA, ELECTRESS OF HANOVER
in *Who's Who in History* vol III 1965

Sophocles (*c.* 496–406 BC). Athenian dramatist. He is attributed with having developed tragedy by introducing a third actor and scene-painting, and ranked with Aeschylus and Euripides as one of the three great tragedians. He wrote some 120 plays, of which seven tragedies survive. These are *Antigone* 443 BC, *Oedipus the King* 429, *Electra* 410, *Ajax, Trachiniae, Philoctetes* 409 BC, and *Oedipus at Colonus* 401 (produced after his death).

Sophocles lived in Athens when the city was ruled by Pericles, a period of great prosperity; he was a devout man, and assumed public office. A regular winner of dramatic competitions, he first defeated Aeschylus at the age of 27. In his tragedies heroic determination leads directly to violence unless, as in *Philoctetes* and *Oedipus at Colonus*, it contains an element of resignation. Among his other works are a lost treatise on the chorus, and a large surviving fragment of one of his satyr-dramas, *Ichneutai*.

Suggested reading
Kitto, H D F *Sophocles: Dramatist and Philosopher* (1958)
Segal, Charles *Tragedy and Civilization: An Interpretation of Sophocles* (1981)
Winnington-Ingram, R P *Sophocles* (1980)

Sophocles, well, he always took life as it came – he's probably taking death as it comes too.

Aristophanes on SOPHOCLES
The Frogs line 82

Sopwith Thomas Octave Murdoch (1888–1989). English designer of the Sopwith Camel biplane, used in World War I, and joint developer of the Hawker Hurricane fighter plane used in World War II. Knighted 1953.

From a Northumbrian engineering family, Sopwith gained a pilot's licence 1910 and soon after set a British aerial duration record for a flight of 3 hours 12 minutes. In 1912 he founded the Sopwith Aviation Company, which in 1920 he wound up and reopened as the Hawker Company, after the chief test pilot Harry Hawker. The Hawker Company was responsible for the Hawker Hart bomber, the Hurricane, and eventually the vertical take-off Harrier jump jet.

Sorby Henry Clifton (1826–1908). English geologist whose discovery 1863 of the crystalline nature of steel led to the study of metallography. Thin-slicing of hard minerals enabled him to study the constituent minerals microscopically in transmitted light. He later employed the same techniques in the study of iron and steel under stress.

In addition to microscopic study, Sorby used a Nicol prism to distinguish the different component minerals by the effect they produced on polarized light.

Sorby also extrapolated from laboratory models and small-scale natural processes in the expectation of explaining vast events in geological history.

He published *On the Microscopical Structure of Crystals* 1858.

Sorel Georges Eugène (1847–1922). French philosopher who believed that socialism could only come about through a general strike; his theory of the need for a 'myth' to sway the body of the people was used by fascists.

Sørensen Søren Peter Lauritz (1868–1939). Danish chemist who in 1909 introduced the concept of using the pH scale as a measure of the acidity of a solution. On Sørensen's scale, still used today, a pH of 7 is neutral; higher numbers represent alkalinity, and lower numbers acidity.

Sorokhin Pitirim Alexandrovich (1889–1968). Russian-born sociologist who worked in the USA. His detailed knowledge of history, including first-hand experience of the Russian Revolutions of 1917, led him to make an analysis of macro social change.

In *Social and Cultural Dynamics* 1937–41, he perceived recurring patterns of change within the history of civilization. He saw the current age as being in a crisis of hedonism and violence which could only be cured by altruism.

Soros George (1930–). Hungarian-born US financier and philanthropist. He made over $1 billion (£650 million) from the collapse of sterling Sept 1992, which he helped bring about, from speculating against the currency on the international markets.

Soros began as a securities analyst and made his fortune from investment and currency speculation, becoming one of the most powerful private investors in the world. He donated $250 million of his money in various forms of nonmilitary aid to development programmes in former Eastern Bloc countries, including the establishment of a series of Society Foundations offering scholarships, technical assistance, and modernization programmes for business education. In some countries his enormous financial power was resented and he was accused of using his disbursements to try to influence the politics of the formative post-Soviet era democracies of Eastern Europe.

Sōseki Natsume. Pen name of Natsume Kinnosuke (1867–1916). Japanese novelist. Sōseki was born in Tokyo and studied English literature there and (1900–03) in the UK. He became well known with his debut novel, *Wagahai wa neko de aru/I Am a Cat* 1905, followed by the humorous *Botchan* 1906, but found a more serious, sensitive style in his many later novels, such as *Sore kara/And Then* 1909. He also studied classical Chinese literature and Zen Buddhism and wrote on literary theory. His works are deep psychological studies of urban intellectual lives. Strongly influenced by English literature, his later works are somewhat reminiscent of Henry James; for example, the unfinished *Meian/Light and Darkness* 1916. Sōseki is regarded as one of Japan's greatest writers.

Sottsass Ettore, Jr (1917–). Austrian-born product and furniture designer. He was active in Milan, Italy, from 1945. Sottsass is the best known of the Italian 'radical' designers of the 1960s who challenged the values of establishment design.

His work in the areas of typewriters and office furniture, including his red plastic portable 'Valentine' typewriter 1969 and 'Synthesis 45' 1969, for the Olivetti company has, since 1958, ensured him a living as a freelance designer while his more experimental, personal projects in the areas of furniture and ceramics, among them his 'Yantra' series of one-off ceramic vases 1970, have marked him out as one of the most innovative designers of his generation. Sottsass was the prime mover behind the Memphis group which made an international impact with its zany designs 1981–87.

Noted for his courage in battle and his opportunism in politics ... [he] built a reputation for vigour, boldness, and method.

Encyclopaedia Britannica on NICOLAS JEAN DE DIEU SOULT
1990

Soult Nicolas Jean de Dieu (1769–1851). Marshal of France. He held commands in Spain in the Peninsular War, where he sacked the port of Santander 1808, and was Chief of Staff at the Battle of Waterloo. He was war minister 1830–40.

Souphanouvong Prince (1902–1995). Laotian politician, president 1975–86.

Souphanouvong was born in Luang Prabang, the youngest of the 22 sons of Prince Boun Khong, the *uparat* (or regent) in the royal house. He became attracted to radical politics when studying civil engineering in Paris, France, and on his return to Laos 1938, working as a civil engineer for the French colonial authorities, he opposed the re-establishment of French control after the close of World War II. After an abortive revolt against French rule in 1945, he led the guerrilla organization Pathet Lao (Land of the Lao).

He joined the Lao Issara (Free Laos) nationalist movement in 1946 and spent the period to 1949 in exile in Thailand. When moderate elements within the Lao Issara, including his half-brother Prince Souvanna Phouma, made a semiautonomy agreement with France 1949, Souphanouvong, who had also been educated in Hanoi and whose wife was Vietnamese, joined the Vietminh, or Communist Party of Indochina, which was dominated by Vietnamese communists. The Pathet Lao was formed by Souphanouvong in 1950 as a Laotian breakaway group.

Assisted by North Vietnam, the Pathet Lao spent much of the next 15 years waging a guerrilla war, first against the French (to 1954) and then, after independence, against the rightist pro-Western regime, which was headed from 1958 by Souvanna Phouma. By contrast with his half-brother, Souphanouvong was dubbed the 'Red Prince'.

In 1975 Souphanouvong, who had briefly held positions in coalition governments formed in 1957–58, 1962, and 1973, became the first president of the communist Lao People's Democratic Republic. This was largely a ceremonial position and the real controlling force in the new state was Kaysone Phomvihane, leader of the Lao People's Revolutionary Party (LPRP). Following a stroke in 1986, Souphanouvong stepped down as head of state, but remained a member of the LPRP'S ruling politburo until 1991.

Sousa John Philip (1854–1932). US bandmaster and composer of marches. He wrote 'The Stars and Stripes Forever!' 1897. He became known as a brilliant bandmaster during his tenure as leader of the Marine Band 1880–92. He went on to form the Sousa Band 1892 and toured internationally with this group until his death. In addition to about 140 stirring marches, he composed operettas, symphonic poems, suites, waltzes, and songs.

Souter David Hackett (1939–). US jurist, appointed as associate justice of the US Supreme Court by President Bush 1990. After private practice in New Hampshire, Souter served as state assistant and deputy attorney general before being appointed state attorney general 1976. He became a judge on the state trial court 1978 and was named to the state supreme court 1983. He was appointed by President Bush to the US Court of Appeals for the First Circuit 1990 and to the Supreme Court later in the same year.

South James (1785–1867). English astronomer who published two catalogues of double stars 1824 and 1826, the former with John Herschel. For this catalogue, they were awarded the gold medal of the Astronomical Society 1826. Knighted 1830.

He became a member of the Royal College of Surgeons before renouncing medicine at the age of 31 in order to devote himself to astronomy. His marriage in 1816 made him wealthy enough to establish observatories in London and in Paris and equip them with the best telescopes available.

South had an argumentative temperament, and his public criticism of the Royal Society for participating in the decline of the sciences in Britain offended other Fellows.

Southampton Henry Wriothesley, 3rd Earl of Southampton (1573–1624). English courtier, patron of Shakespeare. Shakespeare dedicated *Venus and Adonis* and *The Rape of Lucrece* to him and may have addressed him in the sonnets. Earl 1581.

Southerne Thomas (1660–1746). English playwright and poet. He was the author of the tragi-comedies *Oroonoko* 1695–96 and *The Fatal Marriage* 1694.

For love is but discovery: / When that is made, the pleasure's done.

THOMAS SOUTHERNE
Sir Anthony Love act 2, song 1691

Southey Robert (1774–1843). English poet and author. He abandoned his early revolutionary views, and from 1808 contributed regularly to the Tory *Quarterly Review*. He was a friend of Coleridge and Wordsworth. In 1813 he became poet laureate but he is better known for his *Life of Nelson* 1813, and for his letters.

Live as long as you may, the first twenty years are the longest half of your life.

ROBERT SOUTHEY
The Doctor ch 130 1837

Soutine Chaïm (1893–1943). Lithuanian-born French Expressionist artist. Using brilliant colours and thick, energetically applied paint, he created intense, emotionally charged works, mostly landscapes and portraits. *Page Boy* 1927 (Albright-Knox Art Gallery, Buffalo, New York) is typical.

He worked for a while in the art school at Vilna, and then found his way to Paris, where he lived a poverty-stricken life among painters and poets. He was driven by poverty to attempt suicide 1912. He was the close friend of Modigliani, on whose death he retired for a while to Céret, painting tormented canvases that reflected despair. After 1923, however, when Zborowski, the dealer to whom Modigliani introduced him, arranged an exhibition, he had a measure of success in Paris. The Expressionist distortion of his work recalls van Gogh, and he shows a remarkable intensity of colour in his still life, a plucked fowl being a characteristic subject.

Soyer Alexis Benoît (1809–1858). French chef who worked in England. Soyer was chef at the Reform Club, London, and visited the Crimea to advise on nutrition for the British army. He was a prolific author of books of everyday recipes, such as *Shilling Cookery for the People* 1855.

Soyinka (Akinwande Olu)Wole (1934–). Nigerian author and dramatist. His plays explore Yoruba myth, ritual, and culture, with the early *Swamp Dwellers* 1958 and *the Lion and the Jewel* 1959, culminating with *A Dance of the Forests* 1960, written as a tragic vision of Nigerian independence. Tragic inevitability is the theme of *Madmen and Specialists* 1970 and of *Death and the King's Horseman* 1976, but he has also written sharp satires, from *The Jero Plays* 1960 and 1973 to the indictment of African dictatorship in *A Play of Giants* 1984. He was the first African to receive the Nobel Prize for Literature, 1986. A recent volume of poetry, *From Zia with Love*, appeared 1992.

Suggested reading
Maduakor, Obi *Wole Soyinka* (1988)
Moore, Gerald *Wole Soyinka* (1972)
Soyinka, Wole *Aké: The Years of Childhood* (autobiography) (1982)
Soyinka, Wole *Ibadan: The Penkelemes Years: A Memoir 1946–1965* (1994)

All of you are exhausted. I find it comforting that, beginning with our very first day, we find ourselves in such complete unanimity.

PAUL-HENRI SPAAK
Speech concluding the first General
Assembly meeting of the United Nations 1945

Spaak Paul-Henri (1899–1972). Belgian socialist politician. From 1936 to 1966 he held office almost continuously as foreign minister or prime minister. He was an ardent advocate of international peace.

Spacek Sissy (Mary Elizabeth) (1949–). US film actress. Of waiflike looks, she starred in *Badlands* 1973 and *Carrie* 1976, in which she played a repressed telekinetic teenager. Other films include *Coal Miner's Daughter* 1979 (Academy Award) and *Missing* 1982.

Spark *Scottish novelist Muriel Spark. Her novels, which are witty, finely structured satires, blend fantasy and sharply observed realism to express essentially spiritual themes. She has also written biographies and poetry.*

My cousin, Rip Torn, persuaded me not to change my name: You shouldn't change what you are, in search of success.

SISSY SPACEK
in *Photoplay* 1977

Spallanzani Lazzaro (1729–1799). Italian biologist. He disproved the theory that microbes spontaneously generate out of rotten food by showing that they would not grow in flasks of broth that had been boiled for 30 minutes and then sealed. Spallanzani also concluded that the fundamental factor in digestion is the solvent property of gastric juice – a term first used by him. He studied respiration, proving that tissues use oxygen and give off carbon dioxide.

He was professor at Reggio College 1754–60, at Modena University 1760–69, and from 1769 at Pavia. He was also a priest.

In 1771, while examining a chick embryo, Spallanzani discovered vascular connections between arteries and veins – the first time this had been observed in a warm-blooded animal. He studied the effects of growth on the circulation in chick embryos and tadpoles, and showed that the arterial pulse is caused by sideways pressure on the expansile artery walls from heartbeats transmitted by the bloodstream.

Spallanzani also studied the migration of swallows and eels, the flight of bats, and the electric discharge of torpedo fish. In addition to his biological work, Spallanzani pioneered the science of vulcanology.

Spark Muriel Sarah (born Camberg) (1918–). Scottish novelist. She is a Catholic convert, and her enigmatic satires include *The*

Ballad of Peckham Rye 1960, *The Prime of Miss Jean Brodie* 1961, *The Only Problem* 1984, and *Symposium* 1990.
Suggested reading
Bold, A *Muriel Spark* (1986)
Page, N *Muriel Spark* (1990)
Whittaker, R *The Faith and Fiction of Muriel Spark* (1982)

'I am putting old heads on your young shoulders ... and all my pupils are the crème de la crème.'

MURIEL SPARK
The Prime of Miss Jean Brodie 1961

Spartacus (died 71 BC). Thracian gladiator who in 73 BC led a revolt of gladiators and slaves in Capua, near Naples, and swept through southern Italy and Cisalpine Gaul. He was eventually caught by Roman general Crassus 71 BC. The fate of Spartacus is not known, although his followers were executed in mass crucifixions.

Spear (Augustus John) Ruskin (1911–1990). English artist. His portraits include Laurence Olivier (as Macbeth), Francis Bacon, and satirical representations of Margaret Thatcher.

Spector Phil (1940–). US record producer. He is known for the 'wall of sound', created using a large orchestra, which distinguished his work in the early 1960s with vocal groups such as the Crystals and the Ronettes. He withdrew into semi-retirement 1966 but his influence can still be heard.

Spee Maximilian Johannes Maria Hubert, Count von (1861–1914). German admiral, born in Copenhagen. He defeated a British squadron in a naval battle at Coronel Nov but 1914 went down with his flagship in the 1914 battle of the Falkland Islands. The *Graf Spee* battleship was named after him.

Speer Albert (1905–1981). German architect and minister in the Nazi government during World War II. He was appointed Hitler's architect and, like his counterparts in Fascist Italy, chose an overblown Classicism to glorify the state, for example, his plan for the Berlin and Nuremberg Party Congress Grounds 1934. He built the New Reich Chancellery, Berlin, 1938–39 (now demolished) but his designs for an increasingly megalomaniac series of buildings in a stark Classical style were never realized, notably the Great Assembly Hall for Berlin.

As armaments minister he raised the index of arms production from 100 Jan 1942 to 322 by July 1944. In the latter months of the war he concentrated on frustrating Hitler's orders for the destruction of German industry in the face of the advancing Allies. After the war, he was sentenced to 20 years imprisonment for his employment of slave labour.
Suggested reading
Schmidt, Matthias *Albert Speer: The End of a Myth* (trs 1984)
Sereny, Gitta *Albert Speer: His Battle with Truth* (1995)
Speer, Albert *Inside the Third Reich* (memoirs) (trs 1970)

Speke John Hanning (1827–1864). British explorer. He joined British traveller Richard Burton on an African expedition in which they reached Lake Tanganyika 1858; Speke became the first European to see Lake Victoria.

His claim that it was the source of the Nile was disputed by Burton, even after Speke and James Grant made a second confirming expedition 1860–63. Speke shot himself, in England, the day before he was due to debate the matter publicly with Burton. This may have been an accident, though the timing was strange.

Spemann Hans (1869–1941). German embryologist who discovered the phenomenon of embryonic induction – the influence exerted by various regions of an embryo that controls the development of cells into specific organs and tissues. Nobel Prize for Physiology or Medicine 1935. In 1908 he was appointed professor at Rostock. He was director of the Kaiser Wilhelm Institute of Biology in Berlin 1914–19, and professor at Freiburg-im-Breisgau 1919–35.

Spemann carried out his research on newt embryos. He found that embryos split in half at an early stage of development either died or developed into a whole embryo, but if they were divided at a later stage, half-embryos formed. Next he transplanted various embryonic parts to other areas of the embryo and to different embryos, and demonstrated that one area of embryonic tissue influences the development of neighbouring tissues.

In another series of experiments, Spemann found that embryonic tissue from newts always gives rise to newt organs, even when transplanted into a frog embryo, and that frog tissue always develops into frog organs in a newt embryo.

In the course of this work, Spemann pioneered techniques of microsurgery.

Spence Basil Urwin (1907–1976). Scottish architect. His works include Coventry Cathedral 1951 and the British embassy in Rome. He was professor of architecture at the Royal Academy, London, 1961–68. Knighted 1960.

Spence William Guthrie (1846–1926). Australian labour leader and politician, born in Scotland. He founded the Australian Workers' Union in 1894, amalgamating the shearers' and rural workers' unions. From 1901 to 1917 he was a Labor member of the House of Representatives and a member of the Fisher ministry during World War I. After the split over conscription, he represented the Nationalist Party 1917–19. His book *Australia's Awakening* 1909 expounded the principle of industrial unionism.

Spencer Herbert (1820–1903). British philosopher. Spencer was born in Derby and was largely self-taught; he worked as a railway engineer before entering journalism, and was a subeditor on *The Economist*. He wrote *Social Statics* 1851, expounding his laissez-faire views on social and political problems. In 1862 he began his ten-volume *System of Synthetic Philosophy*, in which he extended Charles Darwin's theory of evolution to the entire field of human knowledge. The chief of the ten volumes are *First Principles* 1862 and *Principles of Biology* 1864–67, *Principles of Sociology* 1876–96, and *Principles of Ethics* 1879–93. Other works are *Principles of Psychology* 1855, *Essays on Education* 1861, *The Study of Sociology* 1873, *Man versus the State* 1884, and *Autobiography* 1904.

The Republican form of Government is the highest form of government; but because of this it requires the highest type of human nature – a type nowhere, at present existing.

HERBERT SPENCER
Essays, 'The Americans' 1857

Spencer Stanley (1891–1959). English painter. He was born and lived in Cookham-on-Thames, Berkshire, and recreated the Christian story in a Cookham setting. His detailed, dreamlike compositions had little regard for perspective and used generalized human figures in a highly original manner. Knighted 1959.

Examples are *Christ Carrying the Cross* 1920 and *Resurrection: Cookham* 1923–27 (both Tate Gallery, London) and murals of army life for the oratory of All Souls' at Burghclere, Berkshire.

Suggested reading
Collis, Louise *A Private View of Stanley Spenser* (1972)
Pople, Kenneth *Stanley Spencer: A Biography* (1991)
Robinson, Duncan *Stanley Spencer* (1990)
Rothenstein, John *Stanley Spenser the Man: Correspondence and Reminiscences* (1979)
Spenser, Gilbert *Stanley Spenser* (memoir by his brother) (1961)

Spencer-Churchill family name of the dukes of Marlborough, whose seat is Blenheim Palace, Oxfordshire, England.

Spencer Jones Harold (1890–1960). English astronomer who made a determination of solar parallax, using observations of the asteroid Eros. He also studied the speed of rotation of the Earth, and the motions of the Sun, Moon, and planets. Knighted 1943.

He worked at the Royal Observatory, Greenwich, 1913–23; was His Majesty's Astronomer on the Cape of Good Hope, South Africa, 1923–33; and ended his career as the tenth Astronomer Royal 1933–55.

While at the Cape of Good Hope, Spencer Jones published a catalogue containing the radial velocities of the southern stars, calculated the orbits of a number of spectroscopic binary stars, and made a spectroscopic determination of the constant of aberration. In 1925, he obtained and described a long series of spectra of a nova which had appeared in the constellation of Pictor.

Spencer Jones proved that fluctuations in the observed longitudes of the Sun, Moon, and planets are due not to any peculiarities in their motion, but to fluctuations in the angular velocity of rotation of the Earth. He also investigated the Earth's magnetism and oblateness, and he estimated the mass of the Moon.

Spender Stephen Harold (1909–1995). English poet and critic. Educated at University College, Oxford, he founded with Cyril Connolly the magazine *Horizon* (of which he was co-editor 1939–41) and was co-editor of *Encounter* 1953–67. He became professor of English at University College, London, 1970. His earlier poetry has a left-wing political content, as in *Twenty Poems* 1930, *Vienna* 1934, *The Still Centre* 1939, and *Poems of Dedication* 1946. Other works include the verse drama *Trial of a Judge* 1938, the autobiography *World within World* 1951, and translations. His *Journals 1939–83* were published 1985. Knighted 1983.

Who live under the shadow of a war, / What can I do that matters?

STEPHEN SPENDER
'Who Live Under the Shadow'

Speke *On a Royal Geographical Society expedition to equatorial Africa, English explorer John Speke discovered Lakes Tanganyika (with Richard Burton) and Victoria. He later confirmed his theory that Lake Victoria was the source of the Nile 1860.*

Spielberg *US film director Steven Spielberg on the set of* The Color Purple. *His films are characterized by a combination of nail-biting action and tenderness.* (Image Select)

Spengler Oswald (1880–1936). German philosopher whose *Decline of the West* 1918 argued that civilizations go through natural cycles of growth and decay. He was admired by the Nazis.

Spenser Edmund (c. 1552–1599). English poet. He has been called the 'poet's poet' because of his rich imagery and command of versification. Born in London and educated at Cambridge University, in 1580 he became secretary to the Lord Deputy in Ireland and at Kilcolman Castle completed the first three books of *The Faerie Queene*. In 1598 Kilcolman Castle was burned down by rebels, and Spenser with his family narrowly escaped. His major work is the moral allegory *The Faerie Queene*, of which six books survive (three published 1590 and three 1596). Other books include *The Shepheard's Calendar* 1579, *Astrophel* 1586, the love sonnets *Amoretti* and the *Epithalamion* 1595. He died in London, and was buried in Westminster Abbey.

Suggested reading

Hamilton, A C (ed) *Essential Articles for the Study of Edmund Spenser* (1972)
Hough, Graham *A Preface to the Faerie Queene* (1961)
Judson, A C *Edmund Spenser: A Biography* (1945)
Kermode, Frank *Shakespeare, Spenser, Donne* (1971)

Sperry Elmer Ambrose (1860–1930). US engineer who developed various devices using gyroscopes, such as gyrostabilizers (for ships and torpedoes) and gyro-controlled autopilots. The first gyrostabilizers dated from 1912, and during World War I Sperry designed a pilotless aircraft that could carry up to 450 kg/990 lb of explosives a distance of 160 km/100 mi under gyroscopic control – the first flying bomb. By the mid-1930s Sperry autopilots were standard equipment on most large ships.

Sperry was born in Cortland County, New York. He set up his own research and development enterprise 1888, then formed a mining-machinery company and, moving to Cleveland, Ohio, in 1893, developed and manufactured trams. He was president of the Sperry Gyroscope Company until 1926.

Sperry's first invention was a generator with characteristics suited to arc lighting. He produced a superior storage battery (accumulator), teaching himself chemistry in the process. He was also active in internal-combustion engine research and developed ways of detecting substandard railway track.

Sperry's gyrostabilizer, patented 1908, mounted the gyro with its axis vertical in the hold of the ship. The axis was free to move in a fore and aft direction, but not from side to side. He used an electric motor to precess the gyro (tilt its rotor) artificially just as the ship began to roll. The gyro responded by exerting a force to one side or the other. Since it was fixed rigidly to the ship in the plane, the ship's roll was largely counteracted.

Sperry introduced many of the concepts now common in control theory, cybernetics, and automation.

Spiegelman Art (1948–). US cartoonist. He won a Pulitzer prize in 1992 for *Maus: A Survivor's Tale I: My Father Bleeds History* 1986 and *Maus: A Survivor's Tale II: And Here My Troubles Began* 1991, graphic novels dealing with his father's experiences in Poland before and during World War II, when he was in Auschwitz concentration camp, and with his relationship with his father. In the comic-strip drawings, Jews are portrayed as mice.

Spiegelman was born in Stockholm, Sweden, but emigrated to the USA with his family 1951. In San Francisco during the 1970s he published cartoons in underground magazines. He founded *Raw* magazine 1980. In 1992 he began working as an artist for the prestigious *New Yorker* magazine. There was an exhibition of his work at the Museum of Modern Art, New York, 1991.

Spielberg Steven (1947–). US film director, writer, and producer. His credits include such phenomenal box-office successes as *Jaws* 1975, *Close Encounters of the Third Kind* 1977, *Raiders of the Lost Ark* 1981, *ET* 1982, and *Jurassic Park* (winner of three Academy Awards) and *Schindler's List*, based on Thomas Keneally's novel, which won seven Academy Awards, including those for Best Picture and Best Director, 1993. Immensely popular, his films often combine heartfelt sentimentality and a childlike sensibility. He also directed *Indiana Jones and the Temple of Doom* 1984, *The Color Purple* 1985, *Empire of the Sun* 1987, *Indiana Jones and the Last Crusade* 1989, and *Hook* 1991.

Spillane Mickey (Frank Morrison) (1918–). US crime novelist. He began by writing for pulp magazines and became an internationally best-selling author with books featuring private investigator Mike Hammer, a violent vigilante who wages an amoral war on crime. His most popular novels include *I, the Jury* 1947 and *Kiss Me Deadly* 1953 (both made into films in the *noir* style in the 1950s).

By the time of his 12th Mike Hammer novel, *The Killing Man* 1989, Spillane's books had achieved sales in excess of 180 million. His other works include *Day of the Guns* 1964, *The Long Wait* 1951, and *The Delta Factor* 1968. He also wrote *Vengeance is Mine* 1950, *The Death Dealers* 1965, *Survival... Zero* 1970, *The Last Cop Out* 1973, and *The Day the Sea Rolled Back* 1979.

All things excellent are as difficult as they are rare.
BENEDICT SPINOZA
Ethics V. xiii 1677

Spinoza Benedict, or Baruch (1632–1677). Dutch philosopher who believed in a rationalistic pantheism that owed much to Descartes's mathematical appreciation of the universe. Mind and matter are two modes of an infinite substance that he called God or Nature, good and evil being relative. He was a determinist, believing that human action was motivated by self-preservation.

Ethics 1677 is his main work. *A Treatise on Religious and Political Philosophy* 1670 was the only one of his works published during his life, and was attacked by Christians. He was excommunicated by the Jewish community in Amsterdam on charges of heretical thought and practice 1656. He was a lens-grinder by trade.

Suggested reading

Allison, Henry *Benedict de Spinoza: An Introduction* (1975)
Hampshire, Stuart *Spinoza* (1975)
Kennington, Richard (ed) *The Philosophy of Baruch Spinoza* (1980)
Scruton, Roger *Spinoza* (1986)

Spitz Mark Andrew (1950–). US swimmer. He won a record seven gold medals at the 1972 Olympic Games, all in world record times. He won 11 Olympic medals in total (four in 1968) and set 26 world records between 1967 and 1972. After retiring in 1972 he became a movie actor, and two of his films were elected candidates for 'The Worst of Hollywood'.

Spitzer Lyman (1914–). US astrophysicist who developed influential theories about the formation of stars and planetary systems. Spitzer was born in Toledo, Ohio, and studied at Yale, with a year in the UK at Cambridge. He stayed at Yale until 1947, when he moved to Princeton as head of the Astronomy Department.

Spitzer proposed that only a magnetic field could contain gases at temperatures as high as 100 million degrees, by which point hydrogen gas fuses to form helium, and he devised a figure-of-eight design to describe this field. His model was important to later attempts to bring about the controlled fusion of hydrogen.

Spitzer criticized the theory that our planetary system is the result of a gas cloud or gaseous filaments breaking off from the Sun to become planetary fragments. He showed that a gas would be dispersed into interstellar space long before it had cooled sufficiently to condense into planets.

The more different people have studied different methods of bringing up children the more they have come to the conclusion that what good mothers and fathers instinctively feel like doing for their babies is best after all.
BENJAMIN SPOCK
The Common Sense Book of Baby and Child Care 1946

Spock Benjamin McLane (1903–). US paediatrician and writer on child care. His *Common Sense Book of Baby and Child Care* 1946 urged less rigidity in bringing up children than had been advised by previous generations of writers on the subject, but this was misunderstood as advocating permissiveness. He was also active in the peace movement, especially during the Vietnam War.

In his later work he stressed that his common-sense approach had not implied rejecting all discipline, but that his main aim was to give parents the confidence to trust their own judgement rather than rely on books by experts who did not know a particular child.

Spode Josiah (1754–1827). English potter. Around 1800, he developed bone porcelain (made from bone ash, china stone, and china clay), which was produced at all English factories in the 19th century. Spode became potter to King George III 1806.

Spohr Ludwig (Louis) (1784–1859). German violinist, composer, and conductor. He travelled throughout Europe as a soloist and leader of orchestras, playing with the London Philharmonic Society 1820. His music reflects his career as a violinist, including 15 violin concertos, chamber music, and 9 symphonies. He was one of the first conductors to use a baton.

Spooner William Archibald (1844–1930). English academic after whom the spoonerism is named. He was an Anglican cleric and warden of New College, Oxford, 1903–24, with a tendency to transpose the initial sounds of words, as in 'Let us drink to the queer old Dean'. Most spoonerisms are apocryphal.

Spooner was elected a fellow of New College 1867, and lectured on ancient history, philosophy, and divinity. 'You have tasted two whole worms, hissed all my mystery lectures, and been caught fighting a liar in the quad. You must leave Oxford by the next town drain.' is often cited as an example of a spoonerism, though he probably never said it.

Spranger Bartholomeus (1544–1611). Flemish Mannerist painter. He trained in Antwerp and worked in Paris, Rome, and Vienna before becoming court painter to Rudolph II in Prague. His paintings, which are mostly of mythological or allegorical subjects, are often highly erotic.

Sprengel Christian Konrad (1750–1816). German botanist. Writing in 1793, he described the phenomenon of dichogamy, the process whereby stigma and anthers on the same flower ripen at different times and so guarantee cross-fertilization.

Spring Richard ('Dick') (1950–). Irish Labour Party leader from 1982. He entered into coalition with Garret FitzGerald's Fine Gael 1982 as deputy prime minister (with the posts of minister for the environment 1982–83 and minister for energy 1983–87). In 1993 he became deputy prime minister to Albert Reynolds in a Fianna Fáil–Labour Party coalition, with the post of minister for foreign affairs. He withdrew from the coalition Nov 1994 in protest over a judicial appointment made by Reynolds, and the following month formed a new coalition with Fine Gael.

Springsteen Bruce (1949–). US rock singer, songwriter, and guitarist. His music combines melodies in traditional rock idiom and reflective lyrics about working-class life and the pursuit of the American dream on such albums as *Born to Run* 1975, *Born in the USA* 1984, and *Human Touch* 1992. *Darkness at the Edge of Town* 1978, *The River* 1980, and the solo acoustic *Nebraska* 1982 reinforced his reputation as a songwriter. His vast stadium concerts with the E Street Band were marked by his ability to overcome the distance between audience and artist, making him one of rock's finest live performers.

Spruance Raymond Amos (1886–1969). US admiral in World War II. During the Battle of Midway June 1942, Spruance took over command when Admiral Fletcher's flagship was crippled and sank all four Japanese carriers. He then became Chief of Staff to Admiral Nimitz and was given command of the 5th Central Pacific Fleet Aug 1943, leading it at Tarawa, Kwajaliewn, Truk, the Battle of the Philippine Sea, Okinawa, and Iwo Jima. He was involved in the planning for the invasion of Japan, and after the war succeeded Nimitz as commander in chief of the Pacific Fleet.

Squanto also known as Tisquantum (c. 1580–1622). American Pawtuxet Indian ally of the Plymouth colonists. Kidnapped by the English and taken to England 1605, he returned to New England 1619 as a guide for Captain John Slaine. His own tribe having been wiped out by an epidemic, Squanto settled among the Wampanoag people, serving as interpreter for Chief Massasoit in his dealings with the Pilgrims.

Sraffa Piero (1898–). Italian-born economist, in the UK from 1927, a critic of neoclassical economics. In 1926 he suggested that, contrary to orthodox theory, firms could influence the price of a product even if there were a large number of firms competing against each other. He also pointed out the difficulties of applying supply-and-demand analysis to capital in his book *Production of Commodities by Means of Commodities* 1960. He suggested that these difficulties, related to the problem of defining capital precisely, meant that the idea that prices are wholly determined by the interaction of supply and demand was flawed.

Staël Anne Louise Germaine Necker, Madame de (1766–1817). French author. She wrote semi-autobiographical novels such as *Delphine* 1802 and *Corinne* 1807, and the critical work *De l'Allemagne* 1810, on German literature. She was banished from Paris by Napoleon 1803 because of her advocacy of political freedom.

Stahl Franklin William (1929–). US molecular biologist who, with Matthew Meselson, confirmed that replication of the genetic material DNA is semiconservative (that is, the daughter cells each receive one strand of DNA from the original parent cell and one newly replicated strand). In 1970 he became professor at the University of Oregon and a research associate of the Institute of Molecular Biology.

Working at the California Institute of Technology, Meselson and Stahl began experimenting with viruses in 1957, and then carried out their successful experiment with bacteria to prove the semiconservative nature of DNA replication. The concept was first suggested by Francis Crick and James Watson, who pioneered the study of DNA.

In 1961, working with scientists Sidney Brenner and François Jacob, Meselson and Stahl demonstrated that ribosomes require instructions in order to be able to manufacture proteins, and can make different proteins from those normally produced by a particular cell. They also showed that messenger RNA supplies the instructions to the ribosomes.

Stahl has also researched into the genetics of bacteriophages.

Stahl Georg Ernst (1660–1734). German chemist who developed the theory that objects burn because they contain a combustible substance, phlogiston. Substances rich in phlogiston, such as wood, burn almost completely away. Metals, which are low in phlogiston, burn less well. Chemists spent much of the 18th century evaluating Stahl's theories before these were finally proved false by Antoine Lavoisier.

He became a physician to the duke of Saxe-Weimar in 1687. As professor of medicine at Halle 1694–1716, he also lectured in chemistry. From 1716 he was physician to King Frederick I of Prussia.

The phlogiston theory was the first attempt at a rational explanation for combustion and what we would term oxidation. Doubt crept in only when chemists began weighing the products of such reactions, which should always have been lighter, having lost phlogiston. Stahl accounted for observations to the contrary by suggesting that phlogiston was weightless or could even have negative weight.

Stainer John (1840–1901). English organist and composer. He became organist of St Paul's 1872. His religious choral works are *The Crucifixion* 1887, an oratorio, and *The Daughter of Jairus* 1878, a cantata. Knighted 1888.

Stakhanov Aleksei Grigorievich (1906–1977). Soviet miner who exceeded production norms; he gave his name to the Stakhanovite movement of the 1930s, when workers were offered incentives to simplify and reorganize work processes in order to increase production.

It is hard to conceive such a grand figure as Stalin ... We have not known ... one great initiative, slogan, directive in our policy, the author of which was not Stalin.

Sergei Kirov on JOSEPH STALIN
at the Leningrad Party Conference 1934,
showing the depths of the current Stalin-worship in the Party.

Stalin Joseph. Adopted name (Russian 'steel') of Joseph Vissarionovich Djugashvili (1879–1953). Soviet politician. Stalin was born in Georgia, the son of a shoemaker. Educated for the priesthood, he was expelled from his seminary for Marxist propaganda. He became a member of the Social Democratic Party 1898, and joined Lenin and the Bolsheviks 1903. He was repeatedly exiled to Siberia 1903–13. He then became a member of the Communist Party's Politburo, and sat on the October Revolution committee 1917. Stalin rapidly consolidated a powerful following (including Molotov); in 1921 he became commissar for nationalities in the Soviet government, responsible for the decree granting equal rights to all peoples of the Russian Empire, and was appointed general secretary of the Communist Party 1922. After Lenin's death 1924, Stalin sought to create 'socialism in one country' and clashed with Trotsky, who denied the possibility of socialism inside Russia until revolution had occurred in W Europe. Stalin won this ideological struggle by 1927, and a series of five-year plans was launched to collectivize industry and agriculture from 1928. All opposition was eliminated in the Great Purge 1936–38. During World War II, Stalin intervened in the military direction of the campaigns against Nazi Germany. He managed to not only bring the USSR through the war but helped it emerge as a superpower, although only at an immense cost in human suffering to his own people. He met Churchill and Roosevelt at Tehran 1943 and at Yalta 1945, and took part in the Potsdam conference. After the war, Stalin quickly turned E Europe into a series of Soviet satellites and maintained an autocratic rule domestically. He disposed of all real and imagined enemies. His anti-Semitism caused, for example, the execution of 19 Jewish activists in 1952 for a 'Zionist conspiracy'. His role was denounced after his death by Khrushchev and other members of the Soviet regime.

Suggested reading
Jonge, Alex de *Stalin and the Shaping of the Soviet Union* (1986)
McNeal, R H *Stalin* (1988)
Richards, Michael *Stalin* (1979)
Smith, E E *The Young Stalin* (1967)
Tucker, R C *Stalin in Power* (1990)
Ulam, Adam *Stalin* (1973)
Urban, George *Stalinism* (1982)

I really am a manifestation of my own fantasy.

SYLVESTER STALLONE
quoted in Leslie Halliwell *Filmgoer's Companion* 1965

Stallone Sylvester Enzio (1946–). US film actor, director, and screenwriter. At first a bit player, he rocketed to fame as the boxer in *Rocky* 1976, which won the Oscar for Best Picture, and its sequels. Other films include *First Blood* 1982 and the subsequent *Rambo* series from 1985 and the comedy *Stop! Or My Mom Will Shoot* 1992. He wrote the screenplays for all five of the *Rocky* series, and directed three of them.

Stallworthy Jon Howie (1935–). English poet and biographer. The collection *Root and Branch* 1969 showed him to be a meticulous chronicler of mainly familial and emotional themes. He has written biographies of the poets Wilfred Owen 1985 and Louis MacNeice 1995.

In 1992 Stallworthy became professor of English literature at Oxford. His poetry includes *A Familiar Tree* 1978, reflecting his own family history – he was the son of two third-generation New Zealanders.

Standish Myles (1584–1656). American colonial military leader. Born in Lancashire, England, Standish began his military career as a mercenary in the Dutch rebellion against the Spanish. As military adviser to the Pilgrims, he arrived in New England 1621 and obtained a charter for Plymouth colony from England 1925. He negotiated with the Wampanoag people and supervised the Plymouth colonists' military training, and became one of the colony's chief investors 1627. Although one of the most influential figures in colonial New England, he is best remembered through US poet Henry Longfellow's *The Courtship of Miles Standish* 1863.

Stanford (Amasa) Leland (1824–1893). US public official and railroad developer. Born in Watervliet, New York, Stanford was educated at Cazenovia Seminary and was admitted to the bar 1848. Settling in California 1856, he became a successful merchant in Sacramento. Elected governor of California 1861, he became president of the Central Pacific Railroad in the same year, and was one of the founders of the Southern Pacific Railroad 1870. He served in the US Senate 1885–93.

In the orchestra, percussion instruments are effective in inverse proportion to their number.

CHARLES STANFORD

Stanford Charles Villiers (1852–1924). Irish composer and teacher. He was a leading figure in the 19th-century renaissance of British music. His many works include operas such as *Shamus O'Brien* 1896, seven symphonies, chamber music, and church music. Among his pupils were Vaughan Williams, Gustav Holst, and Frank Bridge. Knighted 1902.

Stanhope Hester Lucy (1776–1839). English traveller who left England in 1810 to tour the east Mediterranean with Bedouins and eventually settled there. She adopted local dress and became involved in Middle Eastern politics.

Stanislavsky Konstantin Sergeivich Alekseyev (1863–1938). Russian actor, director, and teacher of acting. Stanislavsky co-founded the Moscow Art Theatre 1898 and directed productions of Chekhov and Gorky. His ideas, which were described in the autobiography *My Life in Art* 1924 and the manuals *An Actor Prepares* 1936, *Building a Character* 1950, and *Creating a Role* 1961, had considerable influence on acting techniques in Europe and the USA. He rejected the declamatory style of acting in favour of a more realistic approach, concentrating on the psychological basis for the development of character. The Actors Studio is based on his methods. As a director, he is acclaimed for his productions of the great plays of Chekhov.

Suggested reading
Benedetti, Jean *Stanislavsky: An Introduction* (1982)
Edwards, Christine *The Stanislavsky Heritage* (1965)
Magarshack, David *Stanislavsky: A Life* (1950)

Stanley family name of earls of Derby.

Dr Livingstone, I presume?

HENRY MORTON STANLEY
on meeting David Livingstone at Lake Tanganyika
Nov 1871, in *How I Found Livingstone* 1872

Stanley Henry Morton. Adopted name of John Rowlands (1841–1904). Welsh-born US explorer and journalist who made four expeditions to Africa. Stanley worked his passage over to America when he was 18. He fought on both sides in the US Civil War. He worked for the *New York Herald* from 1867, and in 1871 he was sent by the editor James Gordon Bennett (1795–1872) to find the ailing Livingstone, which he did on 10 Nov. He and David Livingstone met at Ujiji 1871 and explored Lake Tanganyika. He traced the course of the river Zaïre (Congo) to the sea 1874–77, established the Congo Free State (Zaire) 1879–84, and charted much of the interior 1887–89. From Africa he returned to the UK and was elected to Parliament 1895. GCB 1899.

Suggested reading
Hall, Richard *Stanley: An Adventurer Explored* (1974)
McLynn *Stanley* (1989–91)
Stanley, Henry Morton *The Autobiography of Henry M Stanley* (1909, rep 1969)

Stanley John (1713–1786). English composer and organist. His works, which include organ voluntaries (solos) and concertos for strings, influenced Handel. He succeeded William Boyce as Master of the King's Musick 1779.

Stanley Wendell Meredith (1904–1971). US biochemist who crystallized the tobacco mosaic virus (TMV) in 1935. He demonstrated that, despite its crystalline state, TMV remained infectious. Together with John Northrop and James Sumner, Stanley received the 1946 Nobel Prize for Chemistry.

Stansfield Lisa (1965–). English pop singer. Her soulful vocals with slick productions have won her several of the UK record industry's Brit Awards. She had a UK number-one hit with 'All Around the World' 1989. Her albums *Affection* 1989 and *Real Love* 1992 also enjoyed chart success in the UK and the USA.

Stansfield Smith Colin (1932–). English architect. Under his leadership from 1973 the work of Hampshire County Architects Department has come to represent the best of public English architecture in recent times. The schools built are generally organic modern buildings that relate to their rural context. Bishopstoke Infants' School is housed under a sweeping teepeelike tiled roof.

Stanton Edwin McMasters (1814–1869). US public official, secretary of war 1862–68. A lawyer and a Democrat, he was appointed US attorney general by President Buchanan 1860 and then secretary of war by Republican president Lincoln 1862.

Stanton Elizabeth (born Cady) (1815–1902). US feminist who, with Susan B Anthony, founded the National Woman Suffrage Association 1869, the first women's movement in the USA, and was its first president. She and Anthony wrote and compiled the *History of Women's Suffrage* 1881–86. Stanton also worked for the abolition of slavery.

She organized the International Council of Women in Washington DC. Her publications include *Degradation of Disenfranchisement* and *Solitude of Self* 1892, and in 1885 and 1898 she published a two-part feminist critique of the Bible: *The Woman's Bible*.

Eyes are the greatest tool in film. Mr Capra taught me that, sure, it's nice to say very good dialogue, if you can get it. But great movie acting – watch the eyes.

BARBARA STANWYCK
in *LA Times* 5 April 1987

Stanwyck Barbara. Stage name of Ruby Stevens (1907–1990). US film actress. Of commanding presence, she was equally at home in comedy or melodrama. Stanwyck made her first film appearance 1927 after early experience in vaudeville and on Broadway, rapidly assumed star status and continued to be active in the cinema until 1965. She was well suited to the roles of independently minded women, however perverse. She excelled as the confidence trickster of *The Lady Eve* 1941 and as the temptress of *Double Indemnity* 1944. Her films include *Stella Dallas* 1937 and *Executive Suite* 1954. In later years she appeared frequently on television, notably as the matriarchal star of *The Big Valley*. She never achieved the top rung of stardom, but in 1944 was said to be the highest paid woman in the USA.

Starck Philippe Patrick (1949–). French product, furniture, and interior designer. He brought French design to international attention in the 1980s with his innovative and elegant designs, notably those for a room in the Elysée Palace 1982 and for the Café Costes in Paris 1984. The wooden and metal chair he designed for the Café

Stanton, Edwin Edwin McMasters Stanton, secretary of state during the American Civil War. A keen abolitionist, he opposed those who after the war wanted to make concessions to the South on the issue of slavery. His dismissal by President Johnson on this issue led to Johnson's impeachment.

became a huge international success. Reproductions numbered over 400,000 in 1990. Starck also designed the interior of New York's Royalton Hotel 1988. His high international profile characterized the 'designer' decade.

Stark Freya Madeline (1893–1993). English traveller, mountaineer, and writer who for a long time worked in South America. Often travelling alone in dangerous territories, she described her explorations in the Middle East in many books, including *The Valley of the Assassins* 1934, *The Southern Gates of Arabia* 1936, and *A Winter in Arabia* 1940. The first volume of her autobiography, *The Traveller's Prelude*, which she began soon after World War II, was published 1950, followed by *Beyond Euphrates* 1951, *The Coast of Incense* 1953, and *Dust in the Lion's Paw* 1961. Becoming interested in the history and archaeology of Asia Minor, she learned the language and explored distant regions of Turkey, which she wrote about in *Ionia: a Quest* 1954 and *The Lycian Shore* 1956. In her 70s and 80s she travelled to Afghanistan, Nepal, and again to Iraq for a journey on a raft down the Euphrates. She continued writing; her last book, *Rivers in Time*, appeared 1982. DBE 1972.

Stark Johannes (1874–1957). German physicist. In 1902 he predicted, correctly, that high-velocity rays of positive ions (canal rays) would demonstrate the Doppler effect, and in 1913 showed that a strong electric field can alter the wavelength of light emitted by atoms (the Stark effect). Nobel Prize for Physics 1919.

Stark modified in 1913 the photo-equivalence law proposed by Albert Einstein in 1906. Now called the Stark–Einstein law, it states that each molecule involved in a photochemical reaction absorbs only one quantum of the radiation that causes the reaction.

He became professor 1906 at the Technische Hochschule in Hanover and subsequently held other academic posts until 1922, when he attempted to set up a porcelain factory. This scheme failed, largely because of the depressed state of the German economy. Stark joined the Nazi party 1930 and three years later became president of the Reich Physical-Technical Institute and also president of the German Research Association. But his attempts to become an important influence in German physics brought him into conflict with the authorities and he was forced to resign in 1939. After World War II, he was sentenced to four years' imprisonment by a denazification court 1947.

Starling Ernest Henry (1866–1927). English physiologist who, with William Bayliss, discovered secretin and in 1905 coined the word 'hormone'. He formulated Starling's law, which states that the force of the heart's contraction is a function of the length of muscle fibres. He is considered one of the founders of endocrinology.

Starling and Bayliss researched the nervous mechanisms that control the activities of the organs of the chest and abdomen, and together they discovered the peristaltic wave in the intestine. In 1902 they found the hormone secretin. Secretin is produced by the small intestine of vertebrates and stimulates the pancreas to secrete its digestive juices when acid chyme passes from the stomach into the duodenum. It was the first time that a specific chemical substance had been seen to act as a stimulus for an organ at a distance from its site of origin.

Starling was born and educated in London, and was professor of physiology at University College, London, 1899–1923.

Starling also studied the conditions that cause fluids to leave blood vessels and enter the tissues. In 1896 he demonstrated the Starling equilibrium: the balance between hydrostatic pressure, causing fluids to flow out of the capillary membrane, and osmotic pressure, causing the fluids to be absorbed from the tissues into the capillary.

Stas Jean Servais (1813–1891). Belgian analytical chemist who made the first accurate determinations of atomic weights (relative atomic masses).

Stas was born in Louvain and studied medicine there. He went to Paris 1837 as assistant to French chemist Jean Baptiste Dumas. From 1840 to 1869 Stas was professor at the Ecole Royale Militaire in Brussels, and advised the Belgian government on military topics. He was also commissioner of the Mint, but disagreed with the monetary policy of the government and retired 1872. He was openly critical of the part played by the Christian church in education.

While he was working with Dumas in Paris, Stas helped to redetermine the atomic weights of oxygen and carbon. In the 1850s and 1860s, Stas measured the atomic weights of many elements, using oxygen = 16 as a standard. His results discredited English physicist William Prout's hypothesis that all atomic weights are whole numbers, provided the foundation for the work of Dmitri Mendeleyev and others on the periodic system, and remained the standard of accuracy for 50 years.

Statius (c. 45–96). Roman poet. He was the author of the *Silvae*, occasional poems of some interest; the epic *Thebaïd*, which tells the story of the sons of Oedipus; and an unfinished epic *Achilleïs*. He was admired by Dante and Chaucer.

Staudinger Hermann (1881–1965). German organic chemist, founder of macromolecular chemistry, who carried out pioneering research into the structure of albumen and cellulose. Nobel prize 1953.

To measure the high molecular weights of polymers he devised a relationship, now known as Staudinger's law, between the viscosity of polymer solutions and their molecular weight.

He became professor 1908 at the Technische Hochschule in Karlsruhe, moved to Zürich, Switzerland, 1912, and from 1926 was at the University of Freiburg-im-Breisgau, where in 1940 he was made director of the Chemical Laboratory and Research Institute for Macromolecular Chemistry.

He devised a new and simple synthesis of isoprene (the monomer for the production of the synthetic rubber polyisoprene) in 1910.

Most chemists thought that polymers were disorderly conglomerates of small molecules, but from 1926 Staudinger put forward the view that polymers are giant molecules held together with ordinary chemical bonds. To give credence to the theory, he made chemical changes to polymers that left their molecular weights almost unchanged; for example, he hydrogenated rubber to produce a saturated hydrocarbon polymer.

In his book *Macromolekulare Chemie und Biologie* 1947, Staudinger anticipated the molecular biology of the future.

God save our sacred Germany.

Stauffenberg Claus von (1907–1944). German colonel in World War II who, in a conspiracy to assassinate Hitler (the July Plot), planted a bomb in the dictator's headquarters conference room in the Wolf's Lair at Rastenburg, East Prussia, 20 July 1944. Hitler was merely injured, and Stauffenberg and 200 others were later executed by the Nazi regime.

Stead Christina Ellen (1902–1983). Australian writer. She lived in Europe and the USA 1928–68. An exploratory, psychological writer, imaginatively innovative in form and style, she disclosed elements of the irrational, even the grotesque, in the subconscious of her characters. Her novels include *The Man Who Loved Children* 1940, *Dark Places of the Heart* 1966 (published as *Cotter's England* in the UK), and *I'm Dying Laughing* 1986.

Suggested reading

Brydon, Diana *Christina Stead* (1987)
Lidoff, Joan *Christina Stead* (1982)
Rowley, Hazel *Christina Stead* (1995)
Sheridan, Susan *Christina Stead* (1988)
Williams, Chris *Christina Stead: A Life in Letters* (1989)

Stebbins Joel (1878–1966). US astronomer, the first to develop the technique of electric photometry in the study of stars. He was professor at the University of Illinois 1913–22 and at Wisconsin 1922–48, as well as director of the Washburn Observatory. He continued research at the Lick Observatory until 1958.

In 1906 Stebbins began attempting to use electronic methods in photometry. At first only the brightest objects in the sky (such as the Moon) could be studied in this manner. From 1909 to 1925 he devoted much of his time to improving the photoelectric cell and using it to study the light curves of eclipsing binary stars. As the sensitivity of the device was increased, he could observe variations in the light of cooler stars.

During the 1930s Stebbins applied photoelectric research to the nature and distribution of interstellar dust and its effects on the transmission of stellar light. He analysed the degree of reddening of the light of hot stars and of globular clusters. His discoveries contributed to an understanding of the structure and size of our Galaxy.

Steed Henry Wickham (1871–1956). British journalist. Foreign correspondent for *The Times* in Vienna 1902–13, he was then foreign editor 1914–19 and editor 1919–22.

Steel David Martin Scott (1938–   ). British politician, leader of the Liberal Party 1976–88. Steel was president of the students' union while at Edinburgh University, and less than three years later became a member of Parliament. He entered into a compact with the Labour government 1977–78, and into an alliance with the Social Democratic Party (SDP) 1983. Having supported the Liberal–SDP merger (forming the Social and Liberal Democrats), he resigned the leadership 1988, becoming the Party's foreign affairs spokesman. At the 1994 party conference, he announced that he would not seek re-election to the next parliament. He is the president of Liberal International. KBE 1990.
Suggested reading
Bartram, Peter *David Steel: His Life and Politics* (1981)

Steele Edward John (1948–   ). Australian immunologist whose research into the inheritance of immunity has lent a certain amount of support to the Lamarckian theory of the inheritance of acquired characteristics, thus challenging modern theories of heredity and evolution. Steele found that mice that have been made immune to certain antigens can pass on this acquired immunity to first and second generations of their offspring.

Steele was born in Darwin, Northern Territory, and educated at the University of Adelaide. He carried out research at the Ontario Cancer Institute, Canada, 1977–80, and then moved to the UK to work at the Medical Research Council in Harrow, Middlesex.

Steele Richard (1672–1729). Irish essayist who founded the journal *The Tatler* 1709–11, in which Joseph Addison collaborated. They continued their joint work in *The Spectator*, also founded by Steele, 1711–12, and *The Guardian* 1713. He also wrote plays, such as *The Conscious Lovers* 1722.

Steen Jan Havickszoon (c. 1626–1679). Dutch painter. He studied under Adriaen van Ostade and Jan van Goyen, whose daughter he married. He worked at The Hague, Delft (where he had a brewery) and Leiden, where in his later years he kept an inn. His great sensitivity as an artist saved his humorous genre scenes from triviality. A well-known picture is *The Prince's Birthday* (Rijksmuseum). He painted humorous genre scenes, mainly set in taverns or bourgeois households, as well as portraits and landscapes.

Steer Philip Wilson (1860–1942). English artist. The son of Philip Steer, a portrait painter, he studied art in Paris under Bouguereau and Cabanel, but was more influenced by the French Neo-Impressionism of the 1880s, and in beauty of colour and effective simplicity of design his paintings of Walberswick (Tate Gallery, London) and Cowes, executed between 1886 and 1892, were a signal contribution to the early exhibitions of the New English Art Club. Later he returned to English tradition, leaning towards Constable and Turner, his *Chepstow Castle* (Tate Gallery, London) being a Turnerian view as Constable might have handled it. He revived the art of direct watercolour painting, and also painted some able portraits and figure studies suggested by Gainsborough's 'fancy pictures', but is of note mainly as an English Impressionist in landscape.

Stefan Josef (1835–1893). Austrian physicist who established one of the basic laws of heat radiation in 1879, since known as the Stefan–Boltzmann law. This states that the heat radiated by a hot body is proportional to the fourth power of its absolute temperature.

Stefan was born in Klagenfurt and studied at Vienna, becoming professor there 1863 and director of the Institute for Experimental Physics 1866.

Stefan deduced his radiation law from experiments done by Irish physicist John Tyndall with a platinum wire. From his law, Stefan was able to make the first accurate determination of the surface temperature of the Sun, obtaining a value of approximately 6,000°C/11,000°F.

In 1884 Ludwig Boltzmann, a former student of Stefan's, gave a theoretical explanation of Stefan's law based on thermodynamic principles and kinetic theory. Boltzmann pointed out that it held only for perfect black bodies, and Stefan had been able to derive the law because platinum approximates to a black body.

Stefanik Milan Ratislav (1884–1919). Slovakian general. He joined the French Army as a private soldier 1914 and rapidly rose to the rank of general. He went to the Italian front 1916 and flew several missions to drop propaganda pamphlets on Czech troops of the Austro-Hungarian army. Active in rallying Czech and Slovak troops from all areas, he worked with the Czech legion in Siberia 1918 and on the formation of the Czechoslovakian republic 1918 he became commander in chief and war minister. He was killed 1919 in a flying accident while on his way to Prague.

I have seen the future; and it works.
LINCOLN STEFFENS
of the newly formed Soviet Union, in a letter to Marie Howe 3 April 1919

Steffens (Joseph) Lincoln (1866–1936). US investigative journalist. Intent on exposing corruption and fraud in high places, he initiated the style known as 'muckraking' while working for *McClure's* magazine. He later covered the Mexican Revolution and befriended the Soviet leader Lenin.

An expert in financial affairs, Steffens was editor of the *New York Commercial Advertiser* 1897–1901 before moving on to *McClure's* (managing editor 1901–06) where he joined forces with writers Ida Tarbell (1857–1944) and Ray Stannard Baker (1870–1946). His *Autobiography* appeared 1931.

Steichen Edward Jean (1879–1973). Luxembourg-born US photographer, who with Alfred Stieglitz helped to establish photography as an art form. His style evolved during his career from painterly impressionism to realism. He recorded both world wars, and was also an innovative fashion and portrait photographer. During World War I he helped to develop aerial photography, and in World War II he directed US naval-combat photography. He turned to fashion and advertising 1923–38, working mainly for *Vogue* and *Vanity Fair* magazines. He was in charge of the Museum of Modern Art's photography collection 1947–62, where in 1955 he organized the renowned 'Family of Man' exhibition.

It sounds pompous, but it's the nearest thing I can do to being God. I'm trying to create human beings and so does he.
ROD STEIGER
Remark, London 10 Oct 1970

Steiger Rod(ney Stephen) (1925–   ). US character actor. Of the Method school, his films includes *On the Waterfront* 1954, *The Pawnbroker* 1965, *In the Heat of the Night* 1967 (Academy Award), and *W C Fields and Me* 1976.

Stein (Mark) Aurel (1862–1943). Hungarian archaeologist and explorer who carried out projects for the Indian government in Chinese Turkestan and Tibet 1900–15. Knighted 1912.

Stein Gertrude (1874–1946). US writer. Born in Allegheny, Pennsylvania, Stein went to Paris 1903 after medical school at Johns

Hopkins University and lived there, writing and collecting art, for the rest of her life. She settled in with her brother, also a patron of the arts, and a companion/secretary, Alice B Toklas (1877–1967), and in her home she held court to a 'lost generation' of expatriate US writers and modern artists (Picasso, Matisse, Braque, Gris). Her work includes the self-portrait *The Autobiography of Alice B Toklas* 1933. She also wrote *Three Lives* 1910, *The Making of Americans* 1925, *Composition as Explanation* 1926, *Tender Buttons* 1914, *Mrs Reynolds* 1952, and the operas (with composer Virgil Thomson) *Four Saints in Three Acts* 1929 and *The Mother of Us All* 1947. A tour of the USA 1934 resulted in *Everybody's Autobiography* 1937. She influenced authors Ernest Hemingway, Sherwood Anderson, and F Scott Fitzgerald with her radical prose style. Drawing on the stream-of-consciousness psychology of William James and on the geometry of Cezanne and the Cubist painters in Paris, she evolved a 'continuous present' style made up of constant repetition and variation of simple phrases.

Suggested reading
Bridgman, Richard *Gertrude Stein in Pieces* (1970)
Hobhouse, Janet *Everybody Who Was Anybody* (1975)
Hoffman, Michael *Gertrude Stein* (1976)
Mellow, James *Charmed Circle: Gertrude Stein and Company* (1974)

A rose is a rose is a rose, is a rose.

GERTRUDE STEIN
'Sacred Emily'

Stein Peter (1937–). German theatre director. He was artistic director of the politically radical Berlin Schaubühne 1970–85. Stein's early productions included Edward Bond's *Saved* 1967 and Goethe's *Torquato Tasso* 1969. These foreshadowed the spectacular staging of Ibsen's *Peer Gynt* 1971, and his exploratory show *Shakespeare's Memory* 1976. His final productions for the Schaubühne included Genet's *The Blacks* 1983 and Chekhov's *Three Sisters* 1984.

Stein has directed the plays of the German dramatist Botho Strauss, including *The Park* 1984, and operas for the Welsh Opera: Verdi's *Otello* 1986, and Debussy's *Pelléas et Mélisande* 1992.

Steinbeck John Ernst (1902–1968). US novelist. His realist novels, such as *In Dubious Battle* 1936, *Of Mice and Men* 1937, and *The Grapes of Wrath* 1939 (Pulitzer prize) (filmed 1940), portray agricultural life in his native California, where migrant farm labourers from the Oklahoma dust bowl struggled to survive. Nobel prize 1962.

Born in Salinas, California, Steinbeck worked as a labourer to support his writing career, and his experiences supplied him with authentic material for his books. He first achieved success with *Tortilla Flat* 1935, a humorous study of the lives of Monterey *paisanos* (farmers). His early naturalist works are his most critically acclaimed. Later books include *Cannery Row* 1944, *The Wayward Bus* 1947, *East of Eden* 1952, *Once There Was a War* 1958, *The Winter of Our Discontent* 1961, and *Travels with Charley* 1962. He also wrote screenplays for films, notably *Viva Zapata!* 1952. His best-known short story is the fable 'The Pearl'.

Suggested reading
Benson, J J *The True Adventures of John Steinbeck, Writer* (1984)
Kiernan, Thomas *The Intricate Music: A Biography of John Steinbeck* (1979)
Levant, H *The Novels of John Steinbeck: A Critical Study* (1975)
Timmerman, J H *John Steinbeck's Fiction* (1986)

Steinberg Saul (born Jacobson) (1914–). Romanian-born US artist. Embarking on a career as a painter and cartoonist, he emigrated to the USA 1942. During World War II he served as an American intelligence officer in Italy. He was inducted into the US National Institute of Arts and Letters 1968. He is known for the cartoons he contributed to the *New Yorker* and other magazines. His work portrays a childlike personal world with allusions to the irrational and absurd.

Steinem Gloria (1934–). US journalist and liberal feminist who emerged as a leading figure in the US women's movement in the late 1960s. She was also involved in radical protest campaigns against racism and the Vietnam War. She cofounded the Women's Action Alliance 1970 and *Ms* magazine. In 1983 a collection of her articles was published as *Outrageous Acts and Everyday Rebellions*.

A woman without a man is like a fish without a bicycle.

GLORIA STEINEM
Attributed remark

Steiner (Francis) George (1929–). French-born US critic and writer. His books, which focus on the relationships between the arts, culture, and society, include *The Death of Tragedy* 1960, *In Bluebeard's Castle* 1971, a novella about Hitler, *The Portage to San Cristobal of A.H.* 1981, and *Proofs and Three Parables* 1993.

Steiner Jakob (1796–1863). Swiss mathematician, the founder of modern synthetic, or projective, geometry. He discovered the Steiner surface (also called the Roman surface), which has a double infinity of conic sections on it, and the Steiner theorem.

After training as a teacher in Germany, he was admitted to the University of Berlin 1822. By 1825 he was teaching at the university and in 1834 a professorship of geometry was created for him, which he held for the rest of his life.

His first published paper, which appeared in 1826, contained his discovery of the geometrical transformation known as inversion geometry.

The Steiner theorem states that two pencils (collections of geometric objects) by which a conic is projected from two of its points are projectively related.

In the Steiner–Poncelet theorem, an extension of work done by French mathematician Jean Poncelet in 1822, Steiner proved that any Euclidean figure could be generated using only a straight rule if the plane of construction had a circle with its centre marked drawn on it already.

His most important work is *Systematische Entwicklung der Abhängigkeit geometrischer Gestalten von Einander* 1832.

Steiner Max(imilian Raoul Walter) (1888–1971). Austrian-born US film composer. With Erich Korngold, he brought the style of Mahler and Richard Strauss to Hollywood movie scores. He pioneered the use of the click-track for feature films to guarantee absolute co-ordination of music and film action. His richly sentimental scores include *King Kong* 1934, *Gone with the Wind* 1939, and *Casablanca* 1942.

Steiner Rudolf (1861–1925). Austrian philosopher, occultist, and educationalist who formulated his own mystic and spiritual teaching, which he called anthroposophy. This rejected materialism and aimed to develop the whole human being, intellectually, socially, and, above all, spiritually. A number of Steiner schools follow a curriculum laid down by him with a strong emphasis on the arts.

Steiner first made a detailed study of the thought of the German writer Goethe, and then turned to theosophy before developing anthroposophy. He believed that people are reincarnated several times before attaining complete self-consciousness.

The many subjects on which he lectured include the arts, medicine – where he reintroduced the concept of the humours – and agriculture, where his theory of biodynamics suggested that plants germinate better at different points in the lunar cycle. He also designed and built a cultural centre, the Goethanum, in Dornach, Switzerland, in a geometrical expressionist style. It became the world centre of anthroposophy.

Suggested reading
Harward, A C *The Faithful Thinker* (1961)
Steiner, Rudolf *The Course of My Life* (trs 1951)
Wilson, Colin *Rudolf Steiner: The Man and His Vision* (1985)

Steinmetz Charles Proteus (1865–1923). US engineer who formulated the Steinmetz hysteresis law in 1891, which describes the dissipation of energy that occurs when a system is subject to an alternating magnetic force. He worked on the design of alternating current transmission and from 1894 to his death served as consulting engineer to General Electric.

Stella Frank Philip (1936–). US painter. He was a pioneer of the hard-edged geometric trend in abstract art that followed Abstract Expressionism. From around 1960 he also experimented with shaped canvases.

Stella Joseph (1877–1946). Italian-born US painter. Born in Naples, Italy, Stella emigrated to the USA 1902 and studied art at the Art Students' League, New York, USA, and the New York School of Art. He exhibited at the Armory Show 1913 and with the Société Anonyme, of which he was a member. He was one of America's leading Futurists. His works are mostly mechanical and urban scenes, although his later paintings include tropical landscapes. His Futurist-inspired views of New York City include *Brooklyn Bridge* 1917–18 (Yale University Art Gallery, Connecticut).

Beauty is only the promise of happiness.
STENDHAL
De l'amour ch 17, footnote 1965

Stendhal pen name of Marie Henri Beyle (1783–1842). French novelist. Stendhal was born in Grenoble. He served in Napoleon's armies and took part in the ill-fated Russian campaign. Failing in his hopes of becoming a prefect, he lived in Italy from 1814 until suspicion of espionage drove him back to Paris 1821, where he lived by literary hackwork. From 1830 he was a member of the consular service, spending his leaves in Paris. His novels *Le Rouge et le noir/The Red and the Black* 1830 and *La Chartreuse de Parme/The Charterhouse of Parma* 1839 were pioneering works in their treatment of disguise and hypocrisy; a review of the latter by fellow novelist Balzac in 1840 furthered Stendhal's reputation.

Suggested reading
Adams, R N *Stendhal: Notes on a Novelist* (1959)
Alter, Robert and Cosman, Carol *A Lion for Love: A Critical Biography of Stendhal* (1979)
Hemmings, F W J *Stendhal* (1964)
Keates, Jonathan *Stendhal* (1994)
Stendhal *The Life of Henri Brulard* (autobiography) (trs 1958)

Stenmark Ingemar (1956–). Swedish skier who won a record 85 World Cup races 1974–87, including a record 13 in 1979. He won a total of 18 titles, including the overall title three times.

Steno Nicolaus. Latinized form of Niels Steensen (1638–1686). Danish anatomist and naturalist, one of the founders of stratigraphy. To illustrate his ideas, Steno sketched what are probably the earliest geological sections.

In 1666 he was appointed personal physician to the grand duke of Tuscany, and became royal anatomist in Copenhagen 1672. Returning to Italy, he was ordained a Catholic priest 1675, and gave up science on being appointed vicar-apostolic to N Germany and Scandinavia.

As a physician he discovered Steno's duct of the parotid (salivary) gland, and investigated the workings of the ovaries. Showing that a pineal gland resembling the human one is found in other creatures, he used this finding to challenge French philosopher René Descartes's claim that the gland was the seat of the human soul.

Steno's examination of quartz crystals disclosed that, despite differences in the shapes, the angle formed by corresponding faces is invariable for a particular mineral. This constancy is known as Steno's law.

Having found fossil teeth far inland closely resembling those of a shark he had dissected, in his *Sample of the Elements of Myology* 1667 Steno championed the organic origin of fossils. On the basis of his palaeontological findings, he set out a view of geological history, contending that sedimentary strata had been deposited in former seas.

Stephan Peter (1943–). English therapeutic immunologist. In 1981, he developed Omnigen, a total cellular extract and serum for treating premature cellular degeneration. Stephan was born in Middlesbrough, Yorkshire.

He learned about cell therapy from his father, who died in 1964, leaving his son to run his Harley Street clinic at the age of only 21. He studied homeopathic medicine and graduated in 1970.

The concept of cell therapy is that by injecting healthy cells into the body, the general state of health of the body can be improved. Stephan's treatment involves injecting an organ-specific RNA (nucleic acid copied from the genetic material DNA) to boost the cellular RNA and then injecting tissue-specific antisera. These antisera travel to the defective cells and kill them while at the same time they stimulate the body's immune system, and the healthy cells become active and reproduce.

Stephan's recent work has been concerned with the substance that is formed before the production of the antibody from which he prepares his sera. This substance seems to have beneficial effects which may be used therapeutically.

Stephen (c. 1097–1154). King of England from 1135. A grandson of William the Conqueror, he was elected king 1135, although he had previously recognized Henry I's daughter Matilda as heiress to the throne. Matilda landed in England 1139, and civil war disrupted the country until 1153, when Stephen acknowledged Matilda's son, Henry II, as his own heir.

Stephen Leslie (1832–1904). English critic. He was the first editor of the *Dictionary of National Biography* and father of the novelist Virginia Woolf. KCB 1902.

Stephen I (St Stephen of Hungary) (c. 975–c. 1038). King of Hungary from 997, when he succeeded his father. He completed the conversion of Hungary to Christianity and was canonized in 1803.

Stephen, St (lived c. AD 35). The first Christian martyr; he was stoned to death. Feast day 26 Dec.

Stephens Alexander Hamilton (1812–1883). American public official. Stephens was born in Taliaferro County, Georgia, educated at the University of Georgia, and qualified as a lawyer in 1834. A leader of the Whig party, he served in the US House of Representatives 1843–59 and was an opponent of the Mexican War 1846–48 and a strong defender of slavery. In 1861 he was chosen as vice president of the Confederacy. Arrested and briefly imprisoned at the end of the American Civil War 1865, he served again as US Congressman 1872–82. He served in the Georgia state legislature 1836–41 and as governor of Georgia 1882–83.

Stephens John Lloyd (1805–1852). US explorer in Central America, with British architect and illustrator Frederick Catherwood. He recorded his findings of ruined Mayan cities in his two-volume *Incidents of Travel in Central America, Chiapas and Yucatan* 1841–43. The journey was undertaken without maps and on mules.

Stephenson George (1781–1848). English engineer who built the first successful steam locomotive. He also invented a safety lamp independently of Humphrey Davy in 1815. He was appointed engineer of the Stockton and Darlington Railway, the world's first public railway, in 1821, and of the Liverpool and Manchester Railway in 1826. In 1829 he won a prize with his locomotive *Rocket*.

Experimenting with various gradients, Stephenson found that a slope of 1 in 200, common enough on roads, reduced the haulage power of a locomotive by 50% (on a completely even surface, a tractive force of less than 5 kg/11 lb would move a tonne). Friction was virtually independent of speed. It followed that railway gradients should always be as low as possible, and cuttings, tunnels, and embankments were therefore necessary. He also advocated the use of malleable iron rails instead of cast iron. The gauge for the Stockton and Darlington railway was set by Stephenson at 1.4 m/4 ft 8 in, which became the standard gauge for railways in most of the world.

Stephenson was born near Newcastle-upon-Tyne and received no formal education. He worked at a coal mine, servicing the steam pumping engine, and it was there he built his first locomotive in

1814. After the Liverpool and Manchester railway opened 1830, he worked as a consultant engineer to several newly emerging railway companies, all in the north of England or the Midlands.

In his first locomotive, Stephenson introduced a system by which exhaust steam was redirected into the chimney through a blast pipe, bringing in air with it and increasing the draught through the fire. This development made the locomotive truly practical.

With his son Robert, he established locomotive works at Newcastle. The Stockton and Darlington Railway was opened 1825 by Stephenson's engine *Locomotion*, travelling at a top speed of 24 kph/15 mph.

Stephenson was engaged to design the railway from Manchester to Liverpool, but there was an open competition for the most efficient locomotive. Three other engines were entered, but on the day of the trials the *Rocket* was the only locomotive ready on time. It weighed 4.2 tonnes, half the weight of *Locomotion*.

Suggested reading
Davies, Hunter *A Biographical Study of the Father of the Railways: George Stephenson* (1977)
Robbins, R M *George and Robert Stephenson* (1966)
Rolt, L T *George Stephenson* (1960)
Rolt, L T *The Railway Revolution: George and Robert Stephenson* (1962)

Stephenson Robert (1803–1859). English civil engineer who constructed railway bridges such as the high-level bridge at Newcastle-upon-Tyne, England, and the Menai and Conway tubular bridges in Wales. He was the son of George Stephenson. The successful *Rocket* steam locomotive was built under his direction 1829, as were subsequent improvements to it.

Stephenson was born near Newcastle-upon-Tyne, and began his working life assisting his father in the survey of the Stockton and Darlington Railway in 1821. He managed the locomotive factory his father had established in Newcastle, with a three-year break in South America, superintending some gold and silver mines in Colombia. In 1833 he became engineer for a projected railway from Birmingham to London. The line was completed 1838, and from then on he was engaged on railway work for the rest of his life.

In 1844 construction began, under Stephenson's supervision, of a railway line from Chester to Holyhead. His bridge for the Menai Straits, in which the railway tracks were completely enclosed in parallel iron tubes, was so successful that he adopted the same design for other bridges. One such, the Victoria Bridge over the St Lawrence at Montréal, Canada, built 1854–59, was for many years the longest bridge in the world.

Suggested reading
Robbins, R M *George and Robert Stephenson* (1966)
Rolt, L T *The Railway Revolution: George and Robert Stephenson* (1962)

Steptoe Patrick Christopher (1913–1988). English obstetrician who pioneered in vitro fertilization. Steptoe, together with biologist Robert Edwards, was the first to succeed in implanting in the womb an egg fertilized outside the body. The first 'test-tube baby' was born in 1978. Steptoe developed laparoscopy for exploring the interior of the abdomen without a major operation. He worked at Oldham General Hospital 1951–78, and from 1969 was director of the Centre for Human Reproduction.

In 1968 Edwards and Steptoe began to collaborate on the fertilization of human eggs. Steptoe treated volunteer patients with a fertility drug to stimulate maturation of the eggs in the ovary. In 1971, Edwards and Steptoe were ready to introduce an eight-celled embryo into the uterus of a volunteer patient who hoped to become pregnant, but their attempts were unsuccessful. In 1977 it was decided to abandon the use of the fertility drug and remove the egg at precisely the right natural stage of maturity; once fertilized, the egg was reimplanted in the mother two days later. This pregnancy came to term and the baby was delivered by Caesarean section.

Stern Isaac (1920–). Russian-born US violinist. He is both a fine concert soloist and chamber music player; his tone is warm and his style impeccable. He has premiered works by the US composers William Schuman and Leonard Bernstein.

Stern Otto (1888–1969). German physicist who demonstrated by means of the Stern–Gerlach apparatus that elementary particles have wavelike properties as well as the properties of matter that had been demonstrated. Nobel Prize for Physics 1943.

He worked with Albert Einstein in Prague and Zürich. In 1923 Stern became professor at Hamburg and director of the Institute of Physical Chemistry. With the rise of the Nazis, he emigrated to the USA in 1933 and set up a department for the study of molecular beams at the Carnegie Technical Institute in Pittsburgh.

In 1920 Stern and Walther Gerlach (1899–1979) carried out their experiment, which consisted of passing a narrow beam of silver atoms through a strong magnetic field. Classical theory predicted that this field would cause the beam to broaden, but quantum theory predicted that the beam would split into two separate beams. The result, showing a split beam, was the first clear evidence for space quantization – the phenomenon that, in a magnetic field, certain atoms behave like tiny magnets which can only take up particular orientations with respect to the direction of the field. Stern went on to improve this molecular-beam technique and in 1931 was able to detect the wave nature of particles in the beams.

In 1933, Stern measured the magnetic moment of the proton and the deuteron, and demonstrated that the proton's magnetic moment was 2.5 times greater than expected.

Sternberg Josef von (1894–1969). Austrian film director. He lived in the USA from childhood. He is best remembered for his seven films with Marlene Dietrich, including *Der blaue Engel/The Blue Angel* 1930, *Blonde Venus* 1932, and *The Devil Is a Woman* 1935, all of which are marked by his expressive use of light and shadow.

Sterne Laurence (1713–1768). Irish writer. Sterne, born in Clonmel, Ireland, took orders 1737 and became vicar of Sutton-in-the-Forest, Yorkshire, in the next year. In 1741 he married Elizabeth Lumley, producing an unhappy union largely because of his infidelity. He had a sentimental love affair with Eliza Draper, of which the *Letters of Yorick to Eliza* 1775 is a record. He created the comic anti-hero Tristram Shandy in *The Life and Opinions of Tristram Shandy, Gent* 1759–67, an eccentrically whimsical and bawdy novel which foreshadowed many of the techniques and devices of 20th-century novelists, including James Joyce. His other works include *A Sentimental Journey through France and Italy* 1768.

Suggested reading
Cash, Arthur H *Laurence Sterne: The Early and Middle Years* (1975)
Cash, Arthur H *Laurence Sterne: The Later Years* (1986)
Dilworth, E N *The Unsentimental Journey of Laurence Sterne* (1948)
Thomson, David *Wild Excursions: The Life and Fiction of Laurence Sterne* (1972)
Traugott, J *Tristram Shandy's World* (1954)

Stesichorus (*c.* 630–*c.* 550 BC). Greek choral poet. He lived and wrote mostly in Sicily. His lyrical narratives, incorporating direct speech, had a profound influence on later Greek tragedy, but his work survives only in fragments.

Steuben Friedrich Wilhelm Ludolf Gerhard Augustin, Baron von (1730–1794). Prussian military leader in the American Revolution 1775–83. Born in Prussia, Steuben began his military career in the Seven Years' War 1756–63. After leaving active duty 1763, he was a functionary in the court of Hohenzollern-Hechingen 1764–75 and was made a baron. He left Europe to seek employment as an officer in the American Revolution. After joining George Washington at Valley Forge 1778, he was named inspector general of the Continental army. He later saw action in the South and was present at the victory of Yorktown 1781.

Stevens Alfred (1818–1875). English sculptor, painter, and designer. He created the Wellington monument, St Paul's Cathedral, London, begun 1858. He was devoted to High Renaissance art, especially to Raphael, and studied in Italy 1833–1842.

Other works of design were the lions for the British Museum railings, the mosaics of prophets for the spandrels under the dome of St

Paul's, and a scheme of decoration for the old Dorchester House, Park Lane. His principal legacy as a pictorial artist is an immense number of beautiful chalk and pencil drawings, studies for his larger undertakings, fully represented at the Tate Gallery. His distinction as a portrait painter is shown by his *Mrs Leonard Collmann* (National Gallery, London).

Stevens David Robert, Baron Stevens of Ludgate (1936–). British financier and newspaper publisher, chair of United Newspapers (a provincial newspaper and magazine group based in the north of England) from 1981 and of Express Newspapers from 1985 (the right-wing *Daily* and *Sunday Express*, the tabloid *Daily Star*, and a few provincial papers). Weekly averages for the period Jan–June 1991 showed that the *Daily Express* sold 1,564,596 copies, the *Sunday Express* 1,622,846 copies, and the *Daily Star* 878,891 copies.

Stevens George (1904–1975). US film director. He began as a director of photography and went on to make such films as *Swing Time* 1936 and *Gunga Din* 1939. His reputation grew steadily, as did the length and ambition of his films. His later work included *A Place in the Sun* 1951, *Shane* 1953, and *Giant* 1956.

Stevens John Paul (1920–). US jurist and associate justice of the US Supreme Court from 1975, appointed by President Ford. A moderate whose opinions and dissents were wide-ranging, he opined that the death penalty is not by definition cruel and unusual punishment in *Jurek v Texas* 1976, and that the burning of the US flag in protest is unconstitutional in *Texas v Johnson*.

Stevens Nettie Maria (1861–1912). US biologist whose experiments with a species of beetle showed that sex was determined by a specific chromosome. This was the first direct evidence that the units of heredity postulated by Austrian biologist Gregor Mendel were associated with chromosomes.

She spent research periods at marine and zoological laboratories in Europe, and was an associate professor at Bryn Mawr from 1905. Stevens studied regenerative processes in lower invertebrates. From there she moved on to working on the development of the roundworm, examining its regenerative properties after exposure to ultraviolet radiation, and showed that even in very early embryonic life, cells were restricted in their regenerative capabilities.

Stevens Siaka Probin (1905–1988). Sierra Leone politician, president 1971–85. He was the leader of the moderate left-wing All People's Congress (APC), from 1978 the country's only legal political party.

Stevens became prime minister in 1968 and in 1971, under a revised constitution, became Sierra Leone's first president. He created a one-party state based on the APC, and remained in power until his retirement at the age of 80.

If sex were all, then every trembling hand / Could make us squeak, like dolls, the wished-for words.

WALLACE STEVENS
'Le Monocle de Mon Oncle'

Stevens Wallace (1879–1955). US poet. An insurance company executive, he was not recognized as a major poet until late in his life. His volumes of poems include *Harmonium* 1923, *The Man with the Blue Guitar* 1937, and *Transport to Summer* 1947. *The Necessary Angel* 1951 is a collection of essays. An elegant and philosophical poet, he won a Pulitzer prize 1954 for his *Collected Poems*.
Suggested reading
Bloom, Harold *Wallace Stevens* (1977)
Brazeau, Peter *Parts of the World: Wallace Stevens Remembered* (1983)
Brown, Ashley and Haller, Robert *The Achievement of Wallace Stevens* (1962)
Kermode, Frank *Wallace Stevens* (1960)

Stevenson Adlai Ewing (1900–1965). US Democrat politician. As governor of Illinois 1949–53 he campaigned vigorously against corruption in public life, and as Democratic candidate for the presidency 1952 and 1956 was twice defeated by Eisenhower. In 1945 he was chief US delegate at the founding conference of the United Nations.
Suggested reading
Cochran, Bert *Adlai Stevenson* (1969)
Darling, Grace and David *Stevenson* (1977)
Sievers, R M *The Last Puritan? Adlai E Stevenson* (1983)

Stevenson Juliet Anne Virginia (1956–). English stage and film actress. A Royal Shakespeare Company actress 1978–86, her work includes *Yerma* 1987, *Hedda Gabler* 1988, and *Death and the Maiden* 1991–92. Film roles include *Truly, Madly, Deeply* 1991, *The Trial* 1993, and *The Secret Rapture* 1994.

For my part, I travel not to go anywhere, but to go. I travel for travel's sake. The great affair is to move.

ROBERT LOUIS STEVENSON
Travels with a Donkey 1879

Stevenson Robert (1772–1850). Scottish engineer who built many lighthouses, including the Bell Rock lighthouse 1807–11.

Stevenson Robert Louis Balfour (1850–1894). Scottish novelist and poet. Stevenson was born in Edinburgh. He studied at the university there and qualified as a lawyer, but never practised. Early works include *An Island Voyage* 1878 and *Travels with a Donkey* 1879. In 1879 he met the American Fanny Osbourne in France and followed her to the USA, where they married 1880. In the same year they returned to Britain, and he subsequently published a volume of stories, *The New Arabian Nights* 1882, and essays; for example, 'Virginibus Puerisque' 1881 and 'Familiar Studies of Men and Books' 1882. He wrote the adventure novel *Treasure Island* 1883. Later works included the novels *Kidnapped* 1886, *The Master of Ballantrae* 1889, *The Strange Case of Dr Jekyll and Mr Hyde* 1886, and the anthology *A Child's Garden of Verses* 1885. The humorous *The Wrong Box* 1889 and the novels *The Wrecker* 1892 and *The Ebb-tide* 1894 were written in collaboration with his stepson, Lloyd Osbourne (1868–1920). In 1890 he settled at Vailima, in Samoa, where he sought a cure for his tuberculosis.
Suggested reading
Bell, I *Robert Louis Stevenson: Dreams of Exile* (1992)
Daiches, D *Robert Louis Stevenson and his World* (1973)
McLynn, F *Robert Louis Stevenson: A Biography* (1993)
Pope-Hennessy, J *Robert Louis Stevenson* (1974)

Stevinus Simon (*c.* 1548–1620). Flemish scientist who, in physics, developed statics and hydrodynamics; he also introduced decimal notation into Western mathematics. He began work in Antwerp as a clerk and then entered Dutch government service, using his engineering skills to become quartermaster-general to the army. He designed sluices that could be used to flood parts of Holland to defend it from attack.

In statics Stevinus made use of the parallelogram of forces and in dynamics he made a scientific study of pulley systems. In hydrostatics he noted that the pressure exerted by a liquid depends only on its height and is independent of the shape of the vessel containing it. He is supposed to have carried out an experiment (later attributed to Italian physicist Galileo) in which he dropped two unequal weights from a tall building to demonstrate that they fell at the same rate.

Stevinus wrote in the vernacular (a principle he advocated for all scientists). His book on mechanics is *De Beghinselen der Weeghcoust* 1586.

Stewart Douglas Alexander (1913–1985). Australian poet, playwright and critic born in New Zealand. He is best known for the verse-drama *Fire on the Snow* 1939 about the tragic expedition of Captain Robert Scott to the South Pole in 1912.
Suggested reading
Semmler, Clement *Douglas Stewart* (1974)
Stewart, Douglas *Springtime in Taranaki: An Autobiography in Youth* (1984)

Stewart Jackie (John Young) (1939–). Scottish motor-racing driver. His first win was in 1965, and he started in 99 races. With manufacturer Ken Tyrrell, Stewart built up one of the sport's great partnerships. His last race was the 1973 Canadian Grand Prix. He pulled out of the next race (which would have been his 100th) because of the death of his team-mate Francois Cevert. Until surpassed by Alain Prost (France) 1987, Stewart held the record for the most Formula One Grand Prix wins (27). He is now a motor-racing commentator.

I kept my own western costume for most of my films. The hat in particular. I wore it in every western until one day it completely disintegrated.

JAMES STEWART
speaking in London June 1966

Stewart James Maitland (1908–). US actor. He made his Broadway debut 1932 and soon after worked in Hollywood. Speaking with a soft, slow drawl, he specialized in the role of the stubbornly honest, ordinary American in such films as *Mr Smith Goes to Washington* 1939, *The Philadelphia Story* 1940 (Academy Award), *It's a Wonderful Life* 1946, *Harvey* 1950, *The Man from Laramie* 1955, and *Anatomy of a Murder* 1959. His films with director Alfred Hitchcock include *Rope* 1948, *Rear Window* 1954, *The Man Who Knew Too Much* 1956, and *Vertigo* 1958.

Stewart Potter (1915–1985). US jurist, appointed associate justice of the US Supreme Court 1958–81 by President Eisenhower. Seen as a moderate, he is known for upholding civil rights for minorities and for opinions on criminal procedure. He dissented in both *Escabedo* v *Illinois* 1964 and in *In re Gault* 1967, which gave juveniles due process rights.

Stewart (Robert) Michael (Maitland), Baron Stewart of Fulham (1906–1990). English Labour politician, member of Parliament 1945–79. He held ministerial office in the governments of Clement Attlee and Harold Wilson, rising to foreign secretary 1968. Baron 1969.

Stieglitz Alfred (1864–1946). US photographer. After forming the Photo Secession group in 1903, he started up the magazine *Camera Work*. Through exhibitions at his gallery '291' in New York he helped to establish photography as an art form. His works include *Winter, Fifth Avenue* 1893 and *Steerage* 1907. In 1924 he married the painter Georgia O'Keeffe, who was the model in many of his photographs.

Stieltjes Thomas Jan (1856–1894). Dutch-born French mathematician who contributed greatly to the theory of series and is often called the founder of analytical theory. His analysis of continued fractions, in particular, has had immense influence in the development of mathematics.

He worked at the Leiden Observatory 1877–83. In 1884 he became professor of mathematics at Groningen. From 1886 he taught at the University of Toulouse, France.

Stieltjes studied almost all the problems in analysis then known – the theory of ordinary and partial differential equations, Euler's gamma functions, elliptic functions, interpolation theory, and asymptotic series. His researches also raised the mathematical status of discontinuous functions and divergent series.

His memoir 'Recherches sur les fractions continues', completed just before he died and published in two parts (1894 and 1895), was a milestone in mathematical history. Stieltjes was the first mathematician to give a general treatment of continued fractions as part of complex analytical function theory.

Stilicho, our new Scipio, conqueror of a second Hannibal more savage than the first.

Claudian on FLAVIUS STILICHO
in *On Stilicho's Consulship* preface 21

Stilicho Flavius (AD 365–408). Roman general of Vandal origin, who campaigned successfully against the Visigoths and Ostrogoths. He virtually ruled the western empire as guardian of Honorius (son of Theodosius I) from 395, but was later executed on Honorius' orders.

Still Clyfford (1904–1980). US painter. Self-taught, Still painted flickering, semi-abstract landscapes of western America during the 1930s and 1940s prior to arriving at his own forceful style about 1947. The broadening of his technique coincided with his moral stance against extraneous detail and his exploration of simplified fields of dark and light colour. He was a pioneer and central figure of Abstract Expressionism. His vast, thickly painted canvases are characterized by jagged areas of raw colours. *1954* 1954 (Albright-Knox Art Gallery, Buffalo, New York) is typical.

Stilwell Joseph Warren ('Vinegar Joe') (1883–1946). US general in World War II. Born in Palatka, Florida, Stilwell graduated from West Point 1904. In 1942 he became US military representative in China, when he commanded the Chinese forces co-operating with the British (with whom he quarrelled) in Burma (now Myanmar); he later commanded all US forces in China, Burma, and India until recalled to the USA 1944 after differences over nationalist policy with the Guomindang (nationalist) leader Chiang Kai-shek. Subsequently he commanded the US 10th Army on the Japanese island of Okinawa.

Stimson Henry Lewis (1867–1950). US politician. He was war secretary in Taft's cabinet 1911–13, Hoover's secretary of state 1929–33, and war secretary 1940–45.

I decided to become a teenager at 25.

STING
quoted in B Cohen *Sting: Every Breath He takes* 1984

Sting stage name of Gordon Sumner (1951–). English pop singer, songwriter, bass player, and actor. As a member of the trio the Police 1977–83, he had UK number-one hits with 'Message in a Bottle' 1979, 'Walking on the Moon' 1979, and 'Every Breath You Take' 1983. 'Don't Stand So Close to Me' was the best-selling single in the UK 1980. In his solo career he has often drawn on jazz, as on the albums *The Dream of Blue Turtles* 1985, *Nothing Like the Sun* 1987, and *Soul Cages* 1991.

Emerging during the punk era, the Police were one of the first white pop groups to use a reggae-based sound. In his solo work, Sting has continued to blend music styles from all over the world into a Western rock format. His films include *Quadrophenia* 1979, *Brimstone and Treacle* 1982, and *Dune* 1984.

Stirling (Archibald) David (1915–1990). English army colonel and creator of the Special Air Service, which became the elite regiment of the British Army from 1942. In 1967 he cofounded the Watchguard organization, based in Guernsey, employing ex-SAS soldiers to provide bodyguards for Middle East rulers and others. He resigned from this organization in 1972. Knighted 1990.

Stirling James (1791–1865). Scottish naval officer and colonial administrator, the first governor of Western Australia 1828–39. Having explored the west coast of Australia in 1827, he persuaded the government to proclaim Western Australia a British colony (originally under the name of the Swan River Colony), and returned there with the first settlers in 1829.

Stirling James Frazer (1926–1992). Scottish architect. He was possibly the most influential of his generation. While in partnership with James Gowan (1924–), he designed the Leicester University Engineering Building 1959–63 in a Constructivist vein. He later adopted a more eclectic approach, exemplified in his considered masterpiece, the Staatsgalerie at Stuttgart, Germany 1977–83, which blended Constructivism, Modernism, and several strands of Classicism. He also designed the Clore Gallery 1982–86 to house the Tate Collection of the Tate Gallery, London. The last of his designs completed in his lifetime was the B Braun Factory in Melsungen, Germany, 1992. Knighted 1983.

Stirling Robert (1790–1878). Scottish inventor of the first practicable hot-air engine 1816. The Stirling engine has a high thermal efficiency and a large number of inherent advantages, such as flexibility in the choice of fuel, that could make it as important as the internal-combustion engine.

He was ordained a Presbyterian minister in 1816, responsible for the parish of Galston, Ayrshire, 1824–76. He also designed and made scientific instruments.

The patent on the first air engine (and related patents until 1840) was taken out jointly with his younger brother James, a mechanical engineer. Their first engine appeared 1818. It had a vertical cylinder about 60 cm/2 ft in diameter, produced about 1.5 kW/2 hp pumping water from a quarry, and ran for two years before the hot sections of the cylinder burned out.

In 1824, the brothers started work on improved engines and in 1843 converted a steam engine at a Dundee factory to operate as a Stirling engine. It is said to have produced 28 kW/37 hp and to have used less coal per unit of power than the steam design it replaced. However, the hot parts burned out continually.

The Stirling-cycle engine differs from the internal-combustion engine in that the working fluid (in Stirling's case, air) remains in the working chambers. The heat is applied from an external source, so anything from wood to nuclear fuel can be used. It also means that combustion can be made to take place under the best conditions, making the control of emissions (pollution) considerably easier. The burning of the fuel is continuous, not intermittent as in an internal-combustion engine, so there is less noise and vibration.

Stirner Max. Pseudonym of Johannes Kaspar Schmidt (1806–1856). German anarchist thinker. He argued that the state, class, and humanity were meaningless abstractions, and that only individuals mattered. In his extreme form of egoism, the aim of human life is the fulfilment of one's own will. His main work is *Der Einzige und sein Eigentum/The Ego and his Own* 1845.

Stock Alfred (1876–1946). German inorganic chemist who prepared many of the hydrides of boron (called boranes). He introduced sensitive tests for mercury and devised improved laboratory techniques for dealing with the metal to minimize the risk of poisoning.

He was director of the Chemistry Department at the Technische Hochschule in Karlsruhe 1926–36. By 1923 he was suffering from chronic mercury poisoning.

Stock began studying the boron hydrides – general formula B_xH_y – in 1909 at Breslau. In 1912 he devised a high-vacuum method for separating mixtures of them. In the 1960s boron hydrides found their first practical use as additives to rocket fuel.

In 1921, Stock prepared beryllium (scarcely known before in the metallic state) by electrolysing a fused mixture of sodium and beryllium fluorides. This method made beryllium available for industrial use, as in special alloys and glasses and for making windows in X-ray tubes.

Musical form is life-form, thought-form, made audible.
KARLHEINZ STOCKHAUSEN
quoted in Karl H Wörner *Stockhausen: Life and Work* 1973

Stockhausen Karlheinz (1928–   ). German composer of avant-garde music. He has continued to explore new musical sounds and compositional techniques since the 1950s. His major works include *Gesang der Jünglinge* 1956, *Kontakte* 1960 (electronic music), and *Sirius* 1977.

Since 1977 all his works have been part of *LICHT*, a cycle of seven musical ceremonies intended for performance on the evenings of a week. He has completed *Donnerstag* 1980, *Samstag* 1984, *Montag* 1988, and *Dienstag* 1992. Earlier works include *Klavierstücke I–XIV* 1952–85, *Momente* 1961–64, and *Mikrophonie I* 1964.
Suggested reading
Cott, Jonathan *Stockhausen: Conversations with the Composer* (1974)
Harvey, Jonathan *The Music of Stockhausen: An Introduction* (1975)

Maconie, Robin *The Works of Karlheinz Stockhausen* (1976)
Würner, Karl *Stockhausen: Life and Work* (trs 1973)

Stockwood (Arthur) Mervyn (1913–1995). British Anglican cleric. As bishop of Southwark 1959–80, he expressed unorthodox views on homosexuality and in favour of the ordination of women.

There was one great tomb more lordly than all the rest ... On it was but one word DRACULA.
BRAM STOKER
Dracula ch 27 'Dr Van Helsing's Memo 5 Nov' 1897

Stoker Bram (Abraham) (1847–1912). Irish novelist, actor, theatre manager, and author. His novel *Dracula* 1897 crystallized most aspects of the traditional vampire legend and became the source for all subsequent fiction and films on the subject. Stoker wrote a number of other stories and novels of fantasy and horror, such as *The Lady of the Shroud* 1909. A civil servant 1866–78, he subsequently became business manager to the theatre producer Henry Irving.
Suggested reading
Farson, Daniel *The Man Who Wrote Dracula* (1975)
Ludlam, H *A Biography of Dracula: The Life Story of Bram Stoker* (1962)
McNally, R T and Florescu, Radu *In Search of Dracula* (1972)

Stokes George Gabriel (1819–1903). Irish physicist who studied the viscosity (resistance to relative motion) of fluids. This culminated in Stokes' law, $F = 6\pi\eta rv$, which applies to a force acting on a sphere falling through a liquid, where η is the liquid's viscosity and r and v are the radius and velocity of the sphere. 1st baronet 1889.

In 1852 Stokes gave the first explanation of the phenomenon of fluorescence, a term he coined. He noticed that ultraviolet light was being absorbed and then re-emitted as visible light. This led him to use fluorescence as a method to study ultraviolet spectra.

Stokes was born in Sligo, Ireland; he studied at Cambridge, where he became professor of mathematics 1849.

Stokes's investigation into fluid dynamics in the late 1840s led him to consider the problem of the ether, the hypothetical medium for the propagation of light waves. He showed that the laws of optics held if the Earth pulled the ether with it in its motion through space, and from this he assumed the ether to be an elastic substance that flowed with the Earth.

Stokes realized in 1854 that the Sun's spectrum is made up of spectra of the elements it contains. He concluded that the dark Fraunhofer lines are the spectral lines of elements absorbing light in the Sun's outer layers.

Stokes William (1804–1878). Irish physician who, with John Cheyne, gave his name to Cheyne–Stokes breathing, or periodic respiration.

Stokes studied clinical medicine at the Meath Hospital, Dublin, and at Edinburgh. He returned to Dublin and held a post at the Meath Hospital. When Stokes referred to Cheyne's paper on periodic respiration in his book *The Diseases of the Heart and Aorta*, the phenomenon became known by both their names. Stokes's name was also applied to Stokes–Adams attacks after his paper 'Observations on Some Cases of Permanently Slow Pulse' 1846.

He is a very fine man I am sure and interested in many things – but not, I think, in music.
Jean Sibelius on STOKOWSKI
quoted in Charles N Gattey *Peacocks on the Podium* 1982

Stokowski Leopold Antoni Stanislaw (1882–1977). US conductor. An outstanding innovator, he promoted contemporary music with enthusiasm, was an ardent popularist, and introduced changes in orchestral seating. He co-operated with Bell Telephone Laboratories in early stereophonic recording experiments in the mid-1930s. He was also a major collaborator with Walt Disney in the programming and development of 'Fantasound' optical surround-sound recording technology for the animated film *Fantasia* 1940.

Stone Harlan Fiske (1872–1946). US jurist. He was associate justice to the US Supreme Court 1925–41 and chief justice 1941–46 under President Roosevelt. During World War II he authored opinions favouring federal war powers and regulation of aliens.

As an associate justice, Stone favoured judicial restraint, the making of decisions on constitutional rather than personal grounds. He dissented from numerous conservative decisions opposing President F D Roosevelt's New Deal legislation. He supported voting rights and use of the Constitution's commerce clause to justify federal legislation regulating interstate commerce.

Stone (John) Richard (Nicholas) (1913–   ). British economist, a statistics expert whose system of 'national income accounting' has been adopted in many countries. Nobel Prize for Economics 1984. Knighted 1978.

> *In education, in marriage, in religion, in everything, disappointment is the lot of women. It shall be the business of my life to deepen this disappointment in every woman's heart until she bows down to it no longer.*
>
> LUCY STONE
> Speech Oct 1855

Stone Lucy (1818–1893). US feminist orator and editor. Married to the radical Henry Blackwell in 1855, she gained wide publicity when, after a mutual declaration rejecting the legal superiority of the man in marriage, she chose to retain her own surname. The term 'Lucy Stoner' was coined to mean a woman who advocated doing the same.

Stone was born in Massachusetts, attended Oberlin College, and gave public lectures from 1847 against black slavery and for women's rights. In the 1860s she helped to establish the American Woman Suffrage Association and founded and edited the Boston *Woman's Journal*, a suffragist paper that was later edited by her daughter Alice Stone Blackwell (1857–1950).
Suggested reading
Blackwell, Alice *Lucy Stone: Pioneer of Women's Rights* (1930, rep 1971)
Hays, Elinor R *Morning Star: A Biography of Lucy Stone* (1961)

Stone Oliver (1946–   ). US film director, screenwriter, and producer. Although working in Hollywood's mainstream, he has tackled traditionally 'difficult' social and political themes with great success. A former infantryman in Vietnam, Stone is perhaps best known for his trilogy of films on the Vietnam war *Platoon* 1986, *Born on the Fourth of July* 1989, which dealt with America's treatment of its war veterans, and *Heaven and Earth* 1993, the biography of a Vietnamese woman. His other notable films include *Wall Street* 1987, the epic-scaled *JFK* 1991, and *Natural Born Killers* 1994, an ultra-violent satire on media irresponsibility.

He won his first Academy Award for his screenplay for *Midnight Express* 1978. His other film credits include *Scarface* 1983 (screenplay), *Salvador* 1986 (director, screenplay, producer), *Reversal of Fortune* 1990 (producer), and *The Doors* 1991 (director, screenplay).

Stone Robert Anthony (1937–   ). US novelist and journalist. His *Dog Soldiers* 1974 is a classic novel about the moral destructiveness of the Vietnam War. *A Flag for Sunrise* 1982 similarly explores the political and moral consequences of US intervention in a corrupt South American republic. Among his other works is *Children of Light* 1986.

Stonehouse John Thomson (1925–1988). British Labour Party politician. An active member of the Co-operative Movement, he entered Parliament in 1957 and held junior posts under Harold Wilson before joining his cabinet in 1967. In 1974 he disappeared in Florida in mysterious circumstances, surfacing in Australia amid suspicions of fraudulent dealings. Extradited to Britain, he was tried

and imprisoned for embezzlement. He was released in 1979, but was unable to resume a political career.

Stopes Marie Charlotte Carmichael (1880–1958). Scottish birth-control campaigner. Stopes was born in Edinburgh and studied botany at University College, London, and in Germany at Munich. She taught at the University of Manchester 1905–11, as the first woman to be appointed to the science staff there. Her field was palaeobotanical research into fossil plants and primitive cycads. With her husband H V Roe (1878–1949), an aircraft manufacturer, she founded Britain's first birth-control clinic in London 1921. She wrote plays and verse as well as the best-selling manual *Married Love* 1918, in which she urged women to enjoy sexual intercourse within their marriage, a revolutionary view for the time. Her other works include *Wise Parenthood* 1918 and *Radiant Motherhood* 1921. The Well Woman Centre in Marie Stopes House, London, commemorates her work.
Suggested reading
Briant, Keith *Passionate Paradox* (1962)
Hall, Ruth *Marie Stopes: Passionate Crusader* (1977)
Rose, June *Marie Stopes and the Sexual Revolution* (1992)

Stopford Montagu George North (1892–1971). British general in World War II. He commanded an infantry brigade in France and Belgium 1940 and was given command of 33 Corps in India 1943. With this corps he relieved Kohima and Imphal 1944 and then advanced into central Burma to capture Mandalay 25 March 1945 and continued to Rangoon. He was appointed Commander of 12th Army just before the war ended. KBE 1944.

> *Eternity's a terrible thought. I mean, where's it all going to end?*
>
> TOM STOPPARD
> *Rosencrantz and Guildenstern Are Dead* II 1967

Stoppard Tom (born Thomas Straussler) (1937–   ). Czechoslovak-born British dramatist. His works use wit and wordplay to explore logical and philosophical ideas. His play *Rosencrantz and Guildenstern are Dead* 1967 was followed by comedies including *The Real Inspector Hound* 1968, *Jumpers* 1972, *Travesties* 1974, *Dirty Linen* 1976, *The Real Thing* 1982, *Hapgood* 1988, *Arcadia* 1993, and *Indian Ink* 1995. He has also written for radio, television, and the cinema.
Suggested reading
Jenkins, Anthony *The Theatre of Tom Stoppard* (1987)
Sammells, Neil *Tom Stoppard: The Artist as Critic* (1988)

> *Halfway through the writing I discovered it was taking place in a lunatic asylum.*
>
> DAVID STOREY's explanation of his 1970 play
> *Home*, quoted in *The Bloomsbury Theatre Guide* 1988

Storey David Malcolm (1933–   ). English dramatist and novelist. His plays include *In Celebration* 1969, *Home* 1970, *Early Days* 1980, *The March on Russia* 1989, and *Stages* 1992. Novels include *This Sporting Life* 1960.

Storey Helen (1959–   ). English fashion designer. She launched her own label 1984, opened Boyd and Storey with fellow fashion designer Karen Boyd 1987, and in 1989 designed a range of shoes for Dr Martens UK. Her first solo catwalk show was staged 1990 and she launched a menswear collection 1991.

Story Joseph (1779–1845). US jurist and associate justice of the US Supreme Court 1811–45 under President Madison. Born in Marblehead, Massachusetts, Story was a graduate of Harvard College and practised law in Massachusetts. He served in the Massachusetts legislature 1805–08 and the US House of Representatives 1808–09, before returning to the Massachusetts legislature, of which he became speaker 1811. He wrote several decisions defining the role of federal courts in admiralty law. The most notable was *United States v Schooner Amistad* 1841, in which the Court ordered black slaves who had seized a slaving ship repatriated to Africa.

Stoss Veit. Also known as Wit Stwosz (*c.* 1450–1533). German sculptor and painter. He was active in Nuremberg and Poland. He carved a wooden altarpiece with high relief panels in St Mary's, Kraków, a complicated design with numerous figures that centres on the *Death of the Virgin* 1477–89.

Stoss was born in Nuremberg and returned there from Poland. The figure of *St Roch* about 1510 in Sta Annunziata, Florence, shows his characteristic Flemish realism and bold drapery. Most of his sculptures were brightly painted.

Stout Robert (1844–1930). New Zealand politician, born in Scotland; prime minister 1884–87. He arrived in New Zealand in 1863 and was a school teacher and lawyer before entering parliament 1875 as a member of the Radical Party. During his prime ministership he legislated that all land purchases should be made through government commissioners and supported the temperance movement. KCMG 1886.

Stow (Julian) Randolph (1935–). Australian novelist and poet. Many of his novels are set in the northwest of Australia, and include *To the Islands* 1958, revised 1982, which won the Miles Franklin Award, the semi-autobiographical *Merry-Go-Round in the Sea* 1965, set in Geraldton where Stow was born and spent his childhood, and the popular children's novel *Midnite* 1967.

Stowe Harriet Elizabeth Beecher (1811–1896). US suffragist, abolitionist, and author. Stowe was a daughter of Congregationalist minister Lyman Beecher and in 1836 married C E Stowe, a professor of theology. Her antislavery novel *Uncle Tom's Cabin* was first published serially 1851–52. The inspiration came to her in a vision 1848, and the book brought immediate success. Her book was radical in its time and did much to spread antislavery sentiment, but in the 20th century was criticized for sentimentality and racism.
Suggested reading
Adams, John *Harriet Beecher Stowe* (1963)
Hendrick, Joan D *Harriet Beecher Stowe: A Life* (1994)
Wagenknecht, Edward C *Harriet Beecher Stowe: The Known and the Unknown* (1965)
Wilson, Edmund *Patriotic Gore* (1962)

With famous places you have to put up with the boring bits of geography like mine.
        STRABO
        Geography bk 14, ch 1.9

Strabo (*c.* 63 BC–*c.* AD 24). Greek geographer and historian who travelled widely to collect first-hand material for his *Geography*.

Strachey (Giles) Lytton (1880–1932). English critic and biographer. He was a member of the Bloomsbury Group of writers and artists. His *Landmarks in French Literature* was written 1912. The mocking and witty treatment of Cardinal Manning, Florence Nightingale, Thomas Arnold, and General Gordon in *Eminent Victorians* 1918 won him recognition. His biography of *Queen Victoria* 1921 was more affectionate.
Suggested reading
Holroyd, Michael *Lytton Strachey: The New Biography* (1994)
Sanders, C R *Lytton Strachey: His Mind and Art* (1957)

Stradivari Antonio (Latin form Stradivarius) (*c.* 1644–1737). Italian stringed instrument-maker, generally considered the greatest of all violin-makers. He was born in Cremona and studied there with Niccolò Amati. He produced more than 1,100 instruments from his family workshops, over 600 of which survive. The secret of his skill is said to be in the varnish but is probably a combination of fine proportioning and ageing.

Strafford Thomas Wentworth, 1st Earl of Strafford (1593–1641). English politician, originally an opponent of Charles I, but from 1628 on the Royalist side. He ruled despotically as Lord Deputy of Ireland 1632–39, when he returned to England as Charles's chief adviser and received an earldom. He was impeached in 1640 by Parliament, abandoned by Charles as a scapegoat, and beheaded. Knighted 1611, baron 1628, earl 1640.

Put not your trust in princes, nor in the sons of men: for in them there is no salvation.
        THOMAS WENTWORTH, 1ST EARL OF STRAFFORD
    quoted in Bulstrode Whitelocke *Memorials of English Affairs* 1682. On discovering Charles I had signed the Bill of Attainder, sentencing him to death.

Strand Paul (1890–1976). US photographer and film-maker. He studied with Lewis Hine and was encouraged by Alfred Stieglitz. After his early, near-abstract studies of New York, he turned to predominantly rural subjects which celebrate human dignity in a clear and straightforward manner. His portfolios, which include *Photographs of Mexico* 1940 and *Time in New England*, were always meticulously printed.

Strange Curtis Northrup (1955–). US golfer, professional from 1976. Strange was born in Virginia. He won his first tournament in 1979 (Pensacola Open). He became the first person to win $1 million in a season in 1988. He has won over 20 tournaments, including two 'majors', the 1988 and 1989 US Opens. In 1989 he became the fourth person to win $5 million in a golfing career.

Strasberg Lee (born Israel Strassberg) (1901–1982). US actor and artistic director of the Actors Studio from 1948. He developed

Stowe Harriet Beecher Stowe, author of *Uncle Tom's Cabin* 1851–52. With its vivid depiction of the suffering of families torn apart by slavery, the novel greatly influenced the abolitionist cause.

Strauss, Richard *The composer and conductor Richard Strauss. His life may be divided compositionally into two phases: the early orchestral works (including the tone poems) and the operas, which were written from the turn of the century and later. He was no relation to Johann Strauss.* (Image Select)

Method acting from Stanislavsky's system; pupils have included Marlon Brando, Paul Newman, Julie Harris, Kim Hunter, Geraldine Page, Al Pacino, and Robert De Niro.

I never felt Lee Strasberg could act, and I fail to see how someone who can't act can teach acting.

Paul Henreid
on LEE STRASBERG's technique, quoted in
Leslie Halliwell *Filmgoer's Companion* 1965

Strassburg Gottfried von (lived *c.* 1210). German poet. He was the author of the unfinished epic *Tristan und Isolde*, which inspired the German composer Wagner.

Straus Oskar (1870–1954). Austrian composer. A pupil of Max Bruch, he was chief conductor and composer at the Überbrettl cabaret, becoming a master of light satirical stage pieces. He is remembered for the operetta *The Chocolate Soldier* 1908.

Strauss Botho (1944–   ). German dramatist and critic. His stark plays focus on problems of identity and the disintegration of personality. They include *Big and Little* 1978 and *The Park* 1984, his adaptation of *A Midsummer Night's Dream*.

Strauss Franz-Josef (1915–1988). German conservative politician, leader of the West German Bavarian Christian Social Union (CSU) party 1961–88, premier of Bavaria 1978–88.

Born and educated in Munich, Strauss, after military service 1939–45, joined the CSU and was elected to the *Bundestag* (parliament) in 1949. He held ministerial posts during the 1950s and 1960s and became leader of the CSU 1961. In 1962 he lost his post as minister of defence when he illegally shut down the offices of *Der Spiegel* for a month, after the magazine revealed details of a failed NATO exercise. In the 1970s, Strauss opposed Ostpolitik (the policy of reconciliation with the East). He left the *Bundestag* to become premier of Bavaria in 1978, and was heavily defeated in 1980 as chancellor candidate. From 1982 Strauss sought to force changes in economic and foreign policy of the coalition under Chancellor Kohl.

Strauss Johann Baptist (1825–1899). Austrian conductor and composer. He was the son of composer Johann Strauss (1804–1849). In 1872 he gave up conducting and wrote operettas, such as *Die Fledermaus/The Flittermouse* 1874, and numerous waltzes, such as *The Blue Danube* and *Tales from the Vienna Woods*, which gained him the title 'the Waltz King'.
Suggested reading
Fantel, Hans *Johann Strauss* (1974)
Gartenberg, Egon *Johann Strauss: The End of an Era* (1974)
Wechsberg, Joseph *The Waltz Emperors* (1973)

Haven't I the right, after all, to write what music I please? I cannot bear the tragedy of the present time. I want to create joy. I need it.

RICHARD STRAUSS
remark, 1924

Strauss Richard Georg (1864–1949). German composer and conductor. He followed the German Romantic tradition but had a strongly personal style, characterized by his bold, colourful orchestration. He first wrote tone poems such as *Don Juan* 1889, *Till Eulenspiegel's Merry Pranks* 1895, and *Also sprach Zarathustra/Thus Spake Zarathustra* 1896. He then moved on to opera with *Salome* 1905 and *Elektra* 1909, both of which have elements of polytonality. He reverted to a more traditional style with *Der Rosenkavalier/The Knight of the Rose* 1909–10.
Suggested reading
Del Mar, Norman *Richard Strauss* (1962–72)
Jefferson, Alan *The Life of Richard Strauss* (1973)
Strauss, Richard *Recollections and Reflections* (trs 1953)
Wilhelm, Kurt *Richard Strauss: An Intimate Portrait* (trs 1989)

I did not like Le Sacre then. I have conducted it fifty times since. I do not like it now.

Pierre Monteux on IGOR STRAVINSKY
quoted in Charles Reid *Thomas Beecham* 1961

Stravinsky Igor Fyodorovich (1882–1971). Russian composer, later of French (1934) and US (1945) nationality. He studied under Rimsky-Korsakov and wrote the music for the Diaghilev ballets *The Firebird* 1910, *Petrushka* 1911, and *The Rite of Spring* 1913 (controversial at the time for their unorthodox rhythms and harmonies). His versatile work ranges from his Neo-Classical ballet *Pulcinella* 1920 to the choral-orchestral *Symphony of Psalms* 1930. He later made use of serial techniques in such works as the *Canticum Sacrum* 1955 and the ballet *Agon* 1953–57.

Stravinsky was born near St Petersburg. Having lived in Paris from 1920, he went to the USA in 1939. His works also include symphonies, concertos (for violin and piano), chamber music, and operas; for example, *The Rake's Progress* 1951 and *The Flood* 1962.
Suggested reading
Craft, Robert *Stravinsky* (1986)
Kobler, John *Firebird: A Biography of Igor Stravinsky* (1988)
Stravinsky, Igor *Chronicles of My Life* (1936)
Tierney, Neil *The Unknown Country: A Life of Igor Stravinsky* (1977)
Vlad, Roman *Stravinsky* (1967)
White, Eric *Stravinsky: The Composer and his Work* (1966)
Young, P M *Stravinsky* (1966)

Strawson Peter Frederick (1919–   ). English philosopher who studied the distortions that logical systems impose on ordinary language. He also analysed the ways in which we distinguish individual things, concluding that the location of things in space and time is fundamental to all the various ways in which we distinguish individuals of any kind. He called his approach 'descriptive metaphysics' and he identified Immanuel Kant as a fellow practitioner.

Strawson was born in London. He taught at Oxford from 1948, becoming professor of metaphysics 1968. His publications include *Introduction to Logical Theory* 1952, *Individuals: An Essay in Descriptive Metaphysics* 1959, and *The Bounds of Sense* 1966. Knighted 1977.

You can't get spoiled if you do your own ironing.
MERYL STREEP
in *Film Yearbook* 1985

Streep Meryl (Mary Louise) (1949–). US actress. A leading star of the 1980s and 1990s, she is known for her strong character roles, portrayed with emotionally dramatic intensity, and her accomplished facility with a wide variety of accents. Her films include *The Deer Hunter* 1978, *Kramer vs Kramer* 1979 (Academy Award for best supporting actress), *The French Lieutenant's Woman* 1981, *Sophie's Choice* 1982 (Academy Award), *Out of Africa* 1985, *Ironweed* 1988, *A Cry in the Dark* 1989, and the comedy *Death Becomes Her* 1992.

Stravinsky *The composer Igor Stravinsky, painted by J E Blanche. Along with Schoenberg he was the most important figure of the early 20th century. He did not embrace serial technique until late in his career, his earlier works favouring first a rhythmically vital dissonant style and then Neo-Classicism. (Image Select)*

Street George Edmund (1824–1881). English Victorian architect. He was a pupil of Gilbert Scott. He practised in Oxford from 1852, where Webb and Morris were among his assistants, before moving to London 1855. He designed and restored hundreds of churches in a vigorous, continental Gothic Revival style, notably St James the Less, Vauxhall Bridge Road, London, 1860–61, and St Philip and St James, Oxford, 1860–62.

His principal secular work is the Law Courts, the Strand (won in competition 1866; opened 1882), the foremost Gothic Revival building in England after the Houses of Parliament. It has a vaulted Great Hall 70 m/230 ft long, 15 m/48 ft wide, and 25 m/82 ft high.

Street J(abez) C(urry) (1906–1989). US physicist who, with Edward C Stevenson, discovered the muon (an elementary particle) in 1937. He was head of the Massachusetts Institute of Technology Radiation Laboratory during World War II.

Street Jessie Mary (born Grey) (1889–1970). Australian feminist, humanist, peace worker, reformer, and writer. She was involved in the suffragette movement in England and later helped to found the Family Planning Association of Australia, and was active in the campaign for equal pay for women. She initiated the movement that resulted in the 1967 referendum which granted citizenship to Australian Aborigines.

Streeton Arthur Ernest (1867–1943). Australian artist. He was a founder of the Heidelberg School and pioneered Impressionistic renderings of Australia's landscape. Knighted 1937.

Strehler Giorgio (1921–). Italian stage director. He founded the Piccolo Teatro in Milan 1947, and has specialized in productions of Goldoni with *The Servant of Two Masters* 1947 influenced by the popular *commedia dell'arte*; of Brecht with *Galileo* 1963; and of Shakespeare with *King Lear* 1972 and *The Tempest* 1978. His distinctive combination of lyricism with naturalism has also been expressed in productions of Mozart's operas.

The moral immune system of this country has been weakened and attacked, and the AIDS virus is the perfect metaphor for it.
BARBRA STREISAND
in *Guardian* 26 Nov 1992

Streisand Barbra Joan (1942–). US singer and actress who became a film star in *Funny Girl* 1968 (Academy Award). Her subsequent films include *What's Up Doc?* 1972, *The Way We Were* 1973, and *A Star Is Born* 1979. She directed, produced, and starred in *Yentl* 1983 and directed and starred in *Prince of Tides* 1991.

I hated singing. I wanted to be an actress. But I don't think I'd have made it any other way.
BARBRA STREISAND
Playboy Oct 1972

Stresemann Gustav (1878–1929). German politician, chancellor in 1923 and foreign minister from 1923 to 1929 of the Weimar Republic. During World War I he was a strong nationalist but his views became more moderate under the Weimar Republic. His achievements included reducing the amount of war reparations paid by Germany after the Treaty of Versailles 1919; negotiating the Locarno Treaties 1925; and negotiating Germany's admission to the League of Nations. He shared the 1926 Nobel Peace Prize with Aristide Briand.

Strindberg (Johan) August (1849–1912). Swedish dramatist and novelist. Born in Stockholm, he lived mainly abroad after 1883, having been unsuccessfully prosecuted for blasphemy 1884 following publication of his short stories *Giftas/Marrying*. His life was stormy and his work has been criticized for its hostile attitude to women, but he is regarded as one of Sweden's greatest writers. His plays are in a variety of styles including historical dramas, symbolic dramas (the two-part *Dödsdansen/The Dance of Death* 1901) and 'chamber plays' such as *Spöksonaten/The Ghost [Spook] Sonata* 1907. *Fadren/The Father* 1887 and *Fröken Julie/Miss Julie* 1888 are among his best-known works. His prose works include the satirical novel *Röda rummet/The Red Room* 1879, about bohemian life in Stockholm, and the autobiography *Tjänstekvinnans son/The Son of a Servant* 1886.

Suggested reading
Lagercrantz, Olof *August Strindberg* (trs 1984)
Lamm, M *August Strindberg* (trs 1971)
Meyer, M *Strindberg: A Biography* (1985)
Morgan, M *August Strindberg* (1986)
Ollen, Gunnar *August Strindberg* (1984)

Stroessner Alfredo (1912–). Military leader and president of Paraguay 1954–89. As head of the armed forces from 1951, he seized power in a coup in 1954 sponsored by the right-wing ruling Colorado Party. Accused by his opponents of harsh repression, his regime spent heavily on the military to preserve his authority. Despite criticisms of his government's civil-rights record, he was re-elected seven times and remained in office until ousted in an army-led coup 1989, after which he gained asylum in Brazil.

Stroheim Erich von. Assumed name of Erich Oswald Stroheim (1885–1957). Austrian actor and director. In Hollywood from 1914, he was successful as an actor in villainous roles. His career as a director, which produced films such as *Foolish Wives* 1922, was wrecked by his extravagance (*Greed* 1923) and he returned to acting in such films as *La Grande Illusion* 1937 and *Sunset Boulevard* 1950.

Strömgren Bengt Georg Daniel (1908–1987). Swedish-born Danish astronomer whose 1940 hypothesis about the so-called Strömgren spheres – zones of ionized hydrogen gas surrounding hot stars embedded in gas clouds – proved fundamental to our understanding of the structure of interstellar material.

He studied in Denmark at Copenhagen, where he became professor 1938; in 1940 he succeeded his father Elis Strömgren as director of the observatory there. From 1946 he held mainly US academic posts; he was professor at the University of Chicago 1951–57 and director of both the Yerkes and McDonald observatories, and was a member of the Institute for Advanced Study at Princeton 1957–67.

Some gaseous nebulae that can be observed within our Galaxy are luminous. Strömgren proposed that this light was caused by hot stars within obscuring layers of gas in the nebulae. He suggested that these stars ionize hydrogen gas and that the dimensions of the ionized zone (the Strömgren sphere) depend on both the density of the surrounding gas and the temperature of the star. His calculations of the sizes of these zones have been confirmed by observations.

Strömgren's other work included an analysis of the spectral classification of stars by means of photoelectric photometry, and research into the internal composition of stars.

Struve F(riedrich) G(eorg) W(ilhelm) von (1793–1864). German-born Russian astronomer, a pioneer in the observation of double stars and one of the first to measure stellar parallax, in 1830. He was the founder of a dynasty of astronomers that spanned four generations.

Struve was born in Altona, Schleswig-Holstein. To avoid conscription into the German army, he fled to Estonia and studied at Dorpat (now Tartu). He became professor there 1813, and director of the Dorpat Observatory 1817. In 1839 he became the first director of Pulkovo Observatory near St Petersburg, and was succeeded 1862 by his son Otto Wilhelm Struve.

Struve published a catalogue of about 800 double stars 1822, and instigated an extensive observational programme. The number of such stars known had increased to more than 3,000 by 1827. In addition, Struve described more than 500 multiple stars in a paper 1843.

In 1846 Struve published his observations of the absorption of stellar light in the galactic plane, which he correctly deduced to be caused by the presence of interstellar material.

Struve made significant contributions to geodesy with his survey of Livonia 1816–19 and his measurements of the arc of meridian 1822–27.

Struve (Gustav Wilhelm) Ludwig (Ottovich) von (1858–1920). Russian astronomer, an expert on the occultation of stars during a total lunar eclipse, and on stellar motion.

Struve was born in Pulkovo, near St Petersburg. The son of Otto Wilhelm von Struve, he followed the family tradition by studying astronomy at Dorpat (now Tartu, Estonia). He began his research at Pulkovo Observatory, and visited observatories in many European countries. In 1894 he moved to the University of Kharkov, where he became professor 1897 and director of the observatory. From 1919 he was professor at Tauris University in Simferopol.

Struve was interested in precession and he investigated the whole question of motion within the Solar System. This led him to work on the positions and motions of stars, and to an estimation of the rate of rotation of the Galaxy.

Struve (Karl) Hermann von (1854–1920). Russian astronomer, an expert on Saturn. His other work was largely concerned with features of the Solar System, although he shared the family interest in stellar astronomy.

Struve was born in Pulkovo, near St Petersburg, and studied at Dorpat (now Tartu, Estonia), travelled in Europe and visited major centres of astronomical research. He began his career at Pulkovo Observatory (founded by his grandfather Wilhelm von Struve), becoming its director 1890. In 1895 he moved to Germany, first as professor at Königsberg, and from 1904 as director of the Observatory of Berlin-Babalsberg (the Neubabalsberg Observatory from 1913).

Among the many features of the Solar System studied by Struve were the transit of Venus, the orbits of Mars and Saturn, the satellites (especially Iapetus and Titan) of Saturn, and Jupiter and Neptune. Struve's 1898 paper on the ring system of Saturn formed the basis of much of his later research.

Struve Otto von (1897–1963). Russian-born US astronomer who developed a nebular spectrograph to study interstellar gas clouds. In 1938 he showed that ionized hydrogen is present in interstellar matter. He also determined that the interstellar hydrogen is concentrated in the galactic plane.

Struve was born in Kharkov, where his father Ludwig von Struve was director of the observatory. He served in the Imperial Russian Army on the Turkish front during World War I, then graduated from Kharkov. Conscripted into the counter-revolutionary White Army during the Civil War in 1919, he fled to Turkey in 1920 and emigrated to the USA 1921. He worked at the Yerkes Observatory, becoming its director 1932. He was professor of astrophysics at Chicago 1932–50 and at the University of California at Berkeley 1950–59. He was also the founder of the McDonald Observatory in Texas, and the first director of the National Radioastronomy Observatory at Green Bank, West Virginia. In 1962 he was appointed joint professor of the Institute for Advanced Study at Princeton and the California Institute of Technology.

Struve did early work on stellar rotation and demonstrated the rotation of blue giant stars and the relationship between stellar temperature (and hence spectral type) and speed of rotation. In 1931 he found, as he had anticipated, that stars that spun at a high rate deposited gaseous material around their equators.

Struve believed that the establishment of a planetary system should be thought of as the normal course of events in stellar evolution and not a freak occurrence.

Struve Otto Wilhelm von (1819–1905). Russian astronomer who made an accurate determination of the constant of precession. He discovered about 500 double stars.

Struve was born in Dorpat (now Tartu), Estonia, studied there, and worked at the Pulkovo Observatory, near St Petersburg, from 1839. From 1847 to 1862 he was also a military adviser in St Petersburg. In 1862 he succeeded his father F G W von Struve as director of the observatory.

Struve studied Saturn's rings, discovered a satellite of Uranus, and calculated the mass of Neptune. He also concerned himself with the measurement of stellar parallax, the movement of the Sun through space, and the structure of the universe, although he was among those astronomers who erroneously believed our Galaxy to be the extent of the whole universe.

Strzelecki Paul Edmund de (1797–1873). Polish-born explorer and scientist in Australia 1839–42 who, during his journeys in SE Australia, named the highest peak in the Snowy Mountains after the Polish patriot Tadeusz Kosciuszko. In 1839 Strzelecki found traces of gold near Hartley, on the W slopes of the Blue Mountains, New South Wales, but the news was suppressed by Governor Gipps who feared its effect upon the convict colony. KCMG 1869.

Stuart or Stewart. Royal family who inherited the Scottish throne in 1371 and the English throne in 1603, holding it until 1714, when Queen Anne died without heirs and the house of Stuart was replaced by the house of Hanover.

Stuart Lady Arabella (1575–1615). Claimant to the English throne. She was the cousin of James I and next in succession to him to both Scottish and English thrones after Elizabeth I. She was the focus of the main plot to eliminate James, and was imprisoned 1609 when James became suspicious. On her release 1610 she secretly married William Seymour, another claimant to the throne, and they were both imprisoned. She died insane in the Tower of London.

Stuart Gilbert Charles (1755–1828). American portrait painter, who first studied at Newport, Rhode Island, but went to England 1755, becoming a pupil of the American painter Benjamin West. He assimilated the methods of English portraiture and was successful in London, though he got into debt and his financial embarrassments caused him to retreat to Ireland. He worked, 1778–93 (again with success), in Dublin. He returned to America to paint George Washington, three versions resulting in the *Atheneaum* portrait of which he made many replicas. His freshness of colour and the calm dignity of his heads make him outstanding. He painted many distinguished Americans besides Washington, and among his artist sitters were Copley, West, and Reynolds.

Stuart James 'Athenian' (1713–1788). English architect. He is notable for his role in the Greek Revival movement. His small but distinctive output includes the Doric Temple at Hagley Park, Worcestershire, 1758, and decorative schemes for a number of rooms in Spencer House, London (begun 1760).

Stuart John McDouall (1815–1866). Scottish-born Australian explorer. He went with Charles Sturt on his 1844 expedition, and in 1860, after two unsuccessful attempts, crossed the centre of Australia from Adelaide in the southeast to the coast of Arnhem Land. He almost lost his life on the return journey.

Stubbs George (1724–1806). English artist. He is renowned for his paintings of horses. After the publication of his book of engravings *The Anatomy of the Horse* 1766, he was widely commissioned as an animal painter. The dramatic *Lion Attacking a Horse* 1770 (Yale University Art Gallery, New Haven, Connecticut) and the peaceful *Reapers* 1786 (Tate Gallery, London) show the variety of mood in his painting.

Stubbs was largely self-taught, and as a young man he practised portrait painting at York and elsewhere in the north of England while studying human and animal anatomy. In 1754 he went to Rome, continuing to study nature and anatomy. Before settling in London 1759 he rented a farm and carried out a series of dissections of horses, which resulted in his book *The Anatomy of the Horse*, 1766. He found much employment among the sporting aristocracy for paintings of racehorses. Not only an expert animal painter, he has come to be regarded as one of the major English artists of the 18th century in power of design and composition and all-round ability. Examples are the spacious *Gimcrack with a Groom, Jockey and Stable-lad on Newmarket Heath*, painted for Viscount Bolingbroke, and his beautiful pictures of haymakers and reapers. He also painted some works in enamel colours on Wedgwood plaques.

Suggested reading
Egerton, J *George Stubbs: Anatomist and Animal Painter* (1976)
Taylor, Basil *Animal Painting in England* (1955)
Taylor, Basil *Stubbs* (1971)

Stukeley William (1687–1765). English antiquarian and pioneer archaeologist, who made some of the earliest accurate observations about Stonehenge 1740 and Avebury 1743. He originated the popular (but erroneous) idea that both were built by Druids.

Sturdee Frederick Charles Doveton (1859–1925). British admiral. He became chief of the war staff 1914 and was sent by Lord Fisher to find the German admiral von Spee after the British defeat at Coronel, which he did at the Battle of the Falkland Islands 8 Dec 1914. He commanded the fourth battle squadron at the Battle of Jutland 1916 and was promoted to full admiral 1917, then Admiral of the Fleet 1921. He was commander in chief of the important naval base at the Nore on the Thames Estuary 1918–21. He received a grant of £10,000 for his war services. KCB 1913, 1st baronet 1916.

Sturgeon William (1783–1850). English physicist and inventor who made the first electromagnets. He also invented a galvanometer in 1836.

He was in the army 1802–20, and in 1824 became a lecturer in science and philosophy at the East India Royal Military College of Addiscombe. In 1832 he was appointed to the lecturing staff of the Adelaide Gallery of Practical Science, and in 1840 he moved to Manchester to become superintendent of the Royal Victoria Gallery of Practical Science. When this failed, he became an itinerant lecturer. In 1836 he established *Annals of Electricity*, the first English-language journal devoted wholly to electricity. It ran until 1843, after which he founded other publications.

In 1828 Sturgeon put into practice the idea of a solenoid, first proposed by French physicist André Ampère, by wrapping wire round an iron core and passing a current through the wire. He found that a magnetic field was formed, which seemed to be concentrated in the iron core and disappeared as soon as the current was switched off. His device was capable of lifting 20 times its own weight.

Sturges Preston. Adopted name of Edmund Preston Biden (1898–1959). US film director and writer. He enjoyed great success with a series of comedies in the early 1940s, including *Sullivan's Travels* 1941, *The Palm Beach Story* 1942, and *The Miracle of Morgan's Creek* 1943.

Sturluson Snorri (1179–1241). Icelandic author. He wrote the Old Norse poems called Edda and the *Heimskringla*, a saga chronicle of Norwegian kings until 1177.

Sturt Charles (1795–1869). British explorer and soldier. Born in India, he served in the army, and in 1827 discovered with the Australian explorer Hamilton Hume the river Darling. In 1828 he sailed down the Murrumbidgee River in SE Australia to the estuary of the Murray in circumstances of great hardship, charting the entire river system of the region. Drawn by his concept of a great inland sea, he set out for the interior in 1844, crossing what is now known as the Sturt Desert, but failing to penetrate the Simpson Desert.

Stuyvesant Peter (*c.* 1592–1672). Dutch colonial leader in America. Born in Holland, Stuyvesant first worked as an official of the Dutch West India Company. Appointed director general of New Netherland 1646, he arrived there in 1647. He reorganized the administration of the colony and established a permanent boundary with Connecticut by the Treaty of Hartford 1650. Forced to surrender the colony to the British 1664, Stuyvesant remained there for the rest of his life.

Styne Jule (Julius Kerwin) (1905–1994). English-born US composer of songs, mainly for musicals and films. His first hit song was 'Sunday' 1926. Amongst those he taught as a voice coach was the singer Ethel Merman, who later became a big star on Broadway, and the child star Shirley Temple. His work includes the score for the musicals *Gentlemen Prefer Blondes* 1949, *Gypsy* 1959, and *Funny Girl* 1964, and he won an Academy Award for the theme song to the film *Three Coins in the Fountain* 1954.

The lyricist Sammy Cahn was his most frequent collaborator, beginning with 'I've Heard That Song Before' for the film *Youth on Parade* 1942. Other films for which they wrote songs include *Follow the Boys* 1944, *Anchors Aweigh* 1945, and *The Kid from Brooklyn*

1946. In 1947 they turned to the Broadway stage with the musical *High Button Shoes*, which was to run for two years.

At one time, Styne played the piano in a strip club, and *Gypsy*, one of his biggest successes, was based on the autobiography of a stripper called Gypsy Rose Lee, with lyrics by Stephen Sondheim. *Funny Girl* was based on the life of the vaudeville star Fanny Brice. Another notable musical for which Styne wrote the score was *Bells Are Ringing* 1956 by Betty Comden and Adolph Green.

Styron William Clark (1925–). US novelist. Born in Virginia, many of his novels had a Southern setting. His novels *Lie Down in Darkness* 1951, *The Confessions of Nat Turner* 1967 (Pulitzer prize), and *Sophie's Choice* 1979 (filmed 1982) all won critical and popular acclaim. *Confessions* caused controversy and protest from black critics for its fictionalization of the leader of a slave revolt in 19th-century Virginia. *A Tidewater Morning* appeared 1993. He also wrote the short memoir of a descent into depression and madness, *Darkness Visible* 1991.

Suárez González Adolfo (1932–). Spanish politician, prime minister 1976–81. A friend of King Juan Carlos, he was appointed by the king to guide Spain into democracy after the death of the fascist dictator Franco. Following a career in the National Movement that spanned 18 years, Suárez was made prime minister by the king 1976. He called and won the first free elections in Spain for more than 40 years as leader of the Union of the Democratic Centre (UCD) 1977. He resigned the premiership 1981, and in the following year founded the Democratic and Social Centre party (CDS).

Suchocka Hanna (1946–). Polish politician, prime minister 1992–93. Formerly a lecturer in law, Suchocka served on the legislation committee of the Polish parliament (*Sejm*), where her abilities brought her to the attention of influential politicians. She was chosen as prime minister by President Walesa because her unaligned background won her the support of seven of the eight parties that agreed to join a coalition government.

In 1992 she replaced prime minister Waldemar Pawlak, who was unable to form a viable government, but was later, in turn, replaced by Pawlak. In 1993 she lost a vote of confidence prior to her centrist coalition being ousted in a general election.

Suckling John (1609–1641). English Cavalier poet and dramatist. An ardent Royalist, he played an active part in the Civil War, fleeing to France where he may have committed suicide. He tried to effect Lord Strafford's escape from the Tower of London. His chief lyrics appeared in *Fragmenta Aurea* and include his best-known one, 'Why so pale and wan, fond lover?' Knighted 1630.

Sucre Antonio José de (1795–1830). South American revolutionary leader. As chief lieutenant of Simón Bolívar, he won several battles in freeing the colonies of Ecuador and Bolivia from Spanish rule, and in 1826 became president of Bolivia. After a mutiny by the army and invasion by Peru, he resigned in 1828 and was assassinated in 1830 on his way to join Bolívar.

Suess Eduard (1831–1914). Austrian geologist who helped pave the way for the theories of continental drift. He suggested that there had once been a great supercontinent, made up of the present southern continents; this he named Gondwanaland, after a region of India.

He was professor at Vienna from 1861, and served as a member of the Reichstag for 25 years.

As a palaeontologist, Suess investigated the fossil mammals of the Danube Basin. He carried out research into the structure of the Alps, the tectonic geology of Italy, and seismology. The possibility of a former landbridge between N Africa and Europe caught his attention.

In his book *The Face of the Earth* 1885–1909, Suess analysed the physical agencies contributing to the Earth's geographical evolution. He offered an encyclopedic view of crustal movement, the structure and grouping of mountain chains, sunken continents, and the history of the oceans. He also made significant contributions to rewriting the structural geology of each continent.

Suetonius Tranquillus is a most upright, honest and learned man.

Pliny the Younger
recommending SUETONIUS to the Emperor Trajan. *Letters* bk 10 ch 94

Suetonius (Gaius Suetonius Tranquillus) (*c.* AD 69–*c.* 140). Roman historian. He was the author of *Lives of the Caesars* (Julius Caesar to Domitian).

So many men, so many opinions.

SUETONIUS
Phormio

Sufi, al- (903–986). Persian astronomer whose importance lies in his compilation of a valuable catalogue of 1,018 stars with their approximate positions, magnitudes, and colours.

Sugar Alan Michael (1947–). British entrepreneur, founder in 1968 of the Amstrad electronics company, which holds a strong position in the European consumer electronics and personal-computer market. In 1985 he introduced a complete word-processing system at the price of £399. Subsequent models consolidated his success internationally.

It is neither right nor natural for Frenchmen to be subject to Englishmen, but rather for Englishmen to be subject to Frenchmen.

SUGER
referring to William II's campaign against
France 1097–1098 in *Life of Louis VI*

Suger (*c.* 1081–1151). French historian and politician. He was regent of France during the Second Crusade. In 1122 he was elected abbot of St Denis, Paris, and was counsellor to, and biographer of, Louis VI and Louis VII. He began the reconstruction of St Denis as the first large-scale Gothic building.

Suharto Thojib I (1921–). Indonesian politician and general, president from 1967. Formerly Chief of Staff under Sukarno, he dealt harshly with a left-wing attempt to unseat his predecessor and then assumed power himself. He ended confrontation with Malaysia, invaded East Timor 1975, and reached a co-operation agreement with Papua New Guinea 1979. His authoritarian rule has met with domestic opposition from the left, but the Indonesian economy has enjoyed significant growth. He was re-elected 1973, 1978, 1983, 1988, and 1993.

Sui dynasty (581–618). Chinese ruling family which reunited China after the strife of the Three Kingdoms era. There were two Sui emperors: Yang Qien (Yang Chien, 541–604), and Yangdi (Yang-ti, ruled 605–17). Though short-lived, the Sui re-established strong centralized government, rebuilding the Great Wall and digging canals which later formed part of the Grand Canal system. The Sui capital was Chang'an.

Sukarno Achmed (1901–1970). Indonesian nationalist, president 1945–67. During World War II he co-operated in the local administration set up by the Japanese, replacing Dutch rule. After the war he became the first president of the new Indonesian republic, becoming president-for-life in 1966; he was ousted by Suharto.

Sukenick Ronald (1932–). US postmodern novelist and theoretician. His innovative and laconic style marks the collection *The Death of the Novel and Other Stories* 1969 and such novels as *Up* 1968 and *Out* 1973. Later works include *Blown Away* 1986 and a volume of essays *In Form: Digressions on the Act of Fiction* 1985.

Sukhomlinov Vladimir Aleksandrovich (1848–1926). Russian soldier. He first came to prominence during the Russo-Japanese war 1904–05, after which he reorganized the Russian Army and became minister for war 1909–15. He was responsible for the mobilization plans of 1914 which put the Russian Army into the field much faster than the Germans expected, but early Russian defeats were blamed upon his failure to stockpile sufficient munitions and equipment, and he was sentenced to life imprisonment for accepting bribes from army contractors. He was released 1918 and went into exile in Finland.

Suleiman or Solyman (c. 1494–1566). Ottoman sultan from 1520, known as the Magnificent and the Lawgiver. Under his rule, the Ottoman Empire flourished and reached its largest extent. He made conquests in the Balkans, the Mediterranean, Persia, and N Africa. He was a patron of the arts, a poet, and an administrator.

Suleiman captured Belgrade in 1521, the Mediterranean island of Rhodes in 1522, defeated the Hungarians at Mohács in 1526, and was halted in his advance into Europe only by his failure to take Vienna, capital of the Austro-Hungarian Empire, after a siege Sept–Oct 1529. In 1534 he turned more successfully against Persia, and then in campaigns against the Arab world took almost all of N Africa and the Red Sea port of Aden. Only the Knights of Malta inflicted severe defeat on both his army and fleet when he tried to take Valletta in 1565.

Suggested reading
Inalcik, Halil *The Ottoman Empire: The Classical Age* (1973)
Merriman, Robert *Suleiman the Magnificent, 1520–1566* (1944)

How can you be an honest man when your father left you nothing and yet you are so rich?

Contemporary comment on LUCIUS CORNELIUS SULLA
quoted in Plutarch's *Life of Sulla* ch 1.2

Sulla Lucius Cornelius (138–78 BC). Roman general and politician, a leader of the senatorial party. He was nicknamed Felix ('Lucky'). Forcibly suppressing the democrats by marching on Rome in 88 BC, he departed for a successful campaign against Mithridates VI of Pontus. The democrats seized power in his absence, but on his return in 82 Sulla captured Rome and massacred all opponents. The reforms he introduced as dictator, which strengthened the Senate, were conservative and short-lived. He retired 79 BC.

I've always been a contrapuntalist.

ARTHUR SULLIVAN
on falling from a punt, quoted in Caryl Brahms *Gilbert and Sullivan* 1975

Sullivan Arthur Seymour (1842–1900). English composer. He wrote operettas in collaboration with William Gilbert, including *HMS Pinafore* 1878, *The Pirates of Penzance* 1879, *Patience* (which ridiculed the Aesthetic Movement) 1881, *The Mikado* 1885, *The Yeomen of the Guard* 1888, and *The Gondoliers* 1889. Their partnership broke down 1896. Sullivan also composed serious instrumental, choral, and operatic works – for example, the opera *Ivanhoe* 1890 – which he valued more highly than the operettas. Knighted 1883.

Suggested reading
Ayre, Leslie *The Gilbert and Sullivan Companion* (1972)
Brahms, Caryl *Gilbert and Sullivan* (1975)
Eden, D *Gilbert and Sullivan* (1986)
Hibbert, Christopher *Gilbert and Sullivan and Their Victorian World* (1976)
Hughes, Gervase *The Music of Arthur Sullivan* (1960)

Sullivan Harry Stack (1892–1949). US psychoanalyst. He was the chief exponent of the dynamic–cultural school of psychoanalysis, which emphasized the role of ongoing interpersonal relationships rather than infantile sexuality in the formation of abnormal behaviour. Although this view incurred considerable criticism from orthodox Freudian psychoanalysts, Sullivan argued that many psychological afflictions were amenable to this approach, including schizophrenia, with which he claimed to achieve considerable therapeutic success.

Sullivan Jim (1903–1977). Welsh-born rugby player. He played rugby union for Cardiff before joining Wigan Rugby League Club in 1921. He kicked 193 goals in 1933–34 (a record at the time) and against Flimby and Fothergill in 1925 he kicked 22 goals, still a record. A great goal-kicker, he kicked a record 2,867 points in a 25-year Rugby League career covering 928 matches.

Sullivan John L(awrence) (1858–1918). US boxer. Born in Boston, Sullivan briefly attended Boston College before beginning a professional boxing career. He won the heavyweight championship from Paddy Ryan 1882 and in the following years toured widely throughout the USA and British Isles. In 1892 he lost his title to James 'Gentleman Jim' Corbett in the first championship bout held according to the Marquess of Queensberry rules. After his retirement from the ring, Sullivan became a popular vaudevillian and was a saloon-keeper in New York.

Sullivan Louis Henry (1856–1924). US architect. He was a leader of the Chicago School and an early developer of the skyscraper. His skyscrapers include the Wainwright Building, St Louis, 1890, the Guaranty Building, Buffalo, 1894, and the Carson, Pirie and Scott Store, Chicago, 1899. He was the teacher of Frank Lloyd Wright. Sullivan was influential in the anti-ornament movement.

Suggested reading
Connely, W *Louis Sullivan As He Lived: The Shaping of American Architecture* (1960)
Morrison, Hugh *Louis Sullivan: Prophet of Modern Architecture* (1971)
Paul, S *Louis Sullivan: An Architect in American Thought* (1962)
Sullivan, Louis *The Autobiography of an Idea* (1924)
Twombly, Robert *Louis Sullivan: His Life and Work* (1986)

Sullivan Pat(rick) (1887–1933). Australian-born US animator and cartoonist. He wrote and drew a newspaper comic strip called 'Sammie Johnson', turned it into a silent animated film 1916, and created the first cartoon-film hero to achieve world fame, *Felix the Cat* 1920.

Sully Maximilien de Béthune, Duc de Sully (1560–1641). French politician, who served with the Protestant Huguenots in the Wars of

Sullivan, Arthur Arthur Sullivan, English composer whose prolific partnership with W S Gilbert produced 14 comic operas. It was a collaboration that lasted from 1871 to 1896, broken by a three-year interruption caused by a quarrel over invoices at the Savoy Theatre. He also wrote a Te Deum *1872*, cantatas, and hymn-tunes such as 'Onward Christian Soldiers'.

Religion, and, as Henry IV's superintendent of finances 1598–1611, aided French recovery. He became Duke 1606.

The English take their pleasures sadly after the fashion of their country.

DUC DE SULLY
Possibly originally referring to his visit to
England in June 1603, Memoirs c. 1630

Sully-Prudhomme (René François) Armand (1839–1907). French poet. He wrote philosophical verse including *Les Solitudes/Solitude* 1869, *La Justice/Justice* 1878, and *Le Bonheur/Happiness* 1888. He was awarded the Nobel Prize for Literature 1901.

Summerson John Newenham (1904–1992). English architectural scholar and critic, whose books include *Georgian London* 1945, *Heavenly Mansions* 1949, and *The Classical Language of Architecture* 1964. He was curator of Sir John Soane's museum 1945–84. Knighted 1958.

Sumner Charles (1811–1874). US political leader. Born in Boston and educated at Harvard University, Sumner was admitted to the bar 1833. He travelled in Europe before teaching at Harvard, lecturing on abolitionism and pacifism. Elected to the US Senate as a Free Soil Democrat 1852, he was defeated by South Carolina congressman Preston Brooks 1856 for his uncompromising abolitionist views on the issue of slavery. During the American Civil War 1861–65, he was a Republican leader in Congress. A supporter of Radical Reconstruction, he opposed President Grant's re-nomination 1872.

Sumner James Batcheller (1887–1955). US biochemist. In 1926 he succeeded in crystallizing the enzyme urease and demonstrating its protein nature. For this work Sumner shared the 1946 Nobel Prize for Chemistry with John Northrop and Wendell Stanley.

A Proteus ever acting in disguise; / A finished statesman, intricately wise, / A second Machiavel, who soar'd above / The little tyes of gratitude and love.

Lampoon on ROBERT SPENCER, 2ND EARL OF SUNDERLAND
(imitating Dryden) entitled 'Faction Displayed' in State Poems 1716 vol iv

Sunderland Robert Spencer, 2nd Earl of Sunderland (1640–1702). English politician, a sceptical intriguer who converted to Roman Catholicism to secure his place under James II, and then reverted with the political tide. In 1688 he fled to Holland (disguised as a woman), where he made himself invaluable to the future William III. Now a Whig, he advised the new king to adopt the system, which still prevails, of choosing the government from the dominant party in the Commons. Earl 1643.

Sung dynasty (960–1279). Chinese imperial family; see ◊Song dynasty.

Sun Ra adopted name of Herman P Blount (1914–1993). US jazz keyboard player, bandleader, and composer, whose eccentricity matched his avant-garde experimental music. His big band, the Arkestra, formed in the 1950s, combined free-form and traditional jazz, African percussion, and synthesizer effects.

Sun Ra's broad outlook and pioneering explorations of the Moog synthesizer led to a collaboration with US rock group the MC5 on their 1969 debut; other musicians who cite him as an influence range from funk master George Clinton to art rockers Sonic Youth and British techno producers. Sun Ra's more than 300 compositions were often released on his own Saturn label. They include 'Brainville' 1956, 'Cosmic Explorer' 1970, and the albums *Sound of Joy* 1957 and *Heliocentric Worlds of Sun Ra* 1965.

Sun Yat-sen or Sun Zhong Shan (1867–1925). Chinese revolutionary leader, founder of the Guomindang (nationalist party) 1894, and provisional president of the Republic of China 1912 after playing a vital part in deposing the emperor.

Sun Yat-sen was the son of a Christian farmer. After many years in exile he returned to China during the 1911 revolution that overthrew the Manchu dynasty. In an effort to bring unity to China, he resigned as provisional president 1912 in favour of the military leader Yuan Shikai. As a result of Yuan's increasingly dictatorial methods, Sun established an independent republic, of which he was president, in S China based in Canton 1921. He was criticized for lack of organizational ability, but his 'three people's principles' of nationalism, democracy, and social reform are accepted by both the nationalists and the Chinese communists.

Sun Zhong Shan Pinyin transliteration of Sun Yat-sen.

Contented with thine own estate; / Neither wish death nor fear his might.

HENRY HOWARD, EARL OF SURREY
The Happy Life (translation of Martial Epigrams)

Surrey Henry Howard, Earl of Surrey (*c.* 1517–1547). English courtier and poet. With Thomas Wyatt, he introduced the sonnet to England and was a pioneer of blank verse. He was executed on a poorly based charge of high treason.

Surtees John (1934–). British racing driver and motorcyclist, the only person to win world titles on two and four wheels. After winning seven world motorcycling titles 1956–60, he turned to motor racing and won the world title in 1964. He later produced his own racing cars.

Surtees R(obert) S(mith) (1805–1864). English novelist. He created Jorrocks, a sporting grocer, and in 1838 published *Jorrocks's Jaunts and Jollities*. He excels in his observation of characters from country life.

Three things I never lends – my 'oss, my wife, and my name.

R S SURTEES
Hillingdon Hall ch 33 1888

Sutcliff Rosemary (1920–1992). English historical novelist. She wrote for both adults and children, and her books include *The Eagle of the Ninth* 1954, *Tristan and Iseult* 1971, and *The Road to Camlann* 1981. Her settings range from the Bronze Age to the 18th century, but her favourite period was the Roman occupation of Britain.

For a Legion to serve ... generation after generation, among tribes who believe it to be accursed is not good for that Legion.

ROSEMARY SUTCLIFFE
The Eagle of the Ninth ch 13 1954

Sutcliffe Frank Meadow (1853–1941). English photographer. He lived in the seaside town of Whitby, North Yorkshire, and photographed its inhabitants and environs in a consistently naturalistic style for most of his life.

Sutherland Donald McNichol (1934–). Canadian-born US film actor. He often appears in offbeat roles. He starred in *M.A.S.H.* 1970, and his subsequent films include *Klute* 1971, *Don't Look Now* 1973, *Ordinary People* 1980, and *Revolution* 1985. He is the father of actor Kiefer Sutherland.

Sutherland Earl Wilbur (1915–1974). US physiologist, discoverer of cyclic AMP, a chemical 'messenger' made by a special enzyme in the wall of living cells. Many hormones operate by means of this messenger. Nobel Prize for Physiology or Medicine 1971.

He was director of the Department of Medicine at Western Reserve (now Case Western Reserve) University in Cleveland 1953–63, then moved to Vanderbilt University, Nashville, and in

1973 to the University of Miami Medical School.

Sutherland began studying hormones at Washington under biochemists Carl and Gerty Cori and then spent the 1950s doing research on his own. At that time it was thought that hormones, carried in the bloodstream, activated their target organs directly. Sutherland showed that the key to the process – the activating agent of the organ concerned – is cyclic adenosine 3,5 monophosphate (cyclic AMP). The arrival of a hormone increases the organ's cellular level of cyclic AMP, which in turn triggers or inhibits the cellular activity.

Sutherland Gordon Brims Black McIvor (1907–1980). Scottish physicist who used infrared spectroscopy to study molecular structure. He elucidated the structure of a wide range of substances, from proteins to diamonds. Knighted 1960.

He was at Cambridge 1934–49, then went to the USA as professor at the University of Michigan. In 1956 he returned to Britain to become director of the National Physical Laboratory. He was master of Emmanuel College, Cambridge, 1964–77.

Working with English physicist William Penney, Sutherland showed that the four atoms of hydrogen peroxide (H_2O_2) do not lie in the same plane but that the molecule's structure resembles a partly opened book, with the oxygen atoms aligned along the spine and the O–H bonds lying across each cover. Later, during World War II, Sutherland and his research group at Cambridge analysed fuel from crashed German aircraft in order to discover their sources of oil. At Michigan he was one of the first to use spectroscopy to study biophysical problems; he also continued his investigations into simpler molecules and crystals.

Sutherland Graham Vivian (1903–1980). English painter, graphic artist, and designer. He was active mainly in France from the late 1940s. He painted portraits, landscapes, and religious subjects, often using a semi-abstract style. He first studied engraving and etching, his early prints showing some affinity with the work of Samuel Palmer, but began to paint from 1930, and during that decade acquired a Surrealist appreciation of the strangeness and metaphorical suggestion of natural form. This developed into the characteristic thorns, sinister tree shapes, and distillations of landscape of the 1940s. As official war artist from 1941, his sense of strangeness found vivid expression in paintings of bomb devastation. The *Crucifixion*, 1946, for the church of St Matthew, Northampton, the *Origins of the Land* (for the Festival of Britain, 1951, Tate Gallery, London), the excursions into portraiture, among which the *Somerset Maugham* is especially striking, and his designs for the *Christ in Glory* tapestry of Coventry Cathedral, 1962, show varied aspects of his art. Its essence, however, is the imaginative symbolism that has gained him international repute. Other work includes ceramics and designs for posters, stage costumes, and sets.

Suggested reading
Berthoud, Roger *Graham Sutherland* (1982)
Cooper, Douglas *The Work of Graham Sutherland* (1961)
Hayes, John *The Art of Graham Sutherland* (1980)

Sutherland Ivan Edward (1938–). US electronics engineer who pioneered the development of computer graphics, the method by which computers display pictorial (as opposed to alphanumeric) information on screen.

In Salt Lake City, Utah, he founded the Evans and Sutherland Computer Corporation and was professor at Utah 1972–76. In 1976 he moved to the California Institute of Technology.

The Sketchpad project was the first system of computer graphics that could be altered by the operator in the course of its use. Sketchpad used complex arrangements of the data fed into the computer to produce representations of the objects in space as well as geometrical detail. Programs could be altered using light pens, which touch the surface of the screen. Sutherland worked on this at MIT 1960–63.

At Utah, Sutherland worked on the design of a colour graphics system able to represent fine distinctions of colour as well as accurate perspective. The image could be moved, rotated, made larger or smaller to give a realistic image of the object, rendering the computer suitable for use in engineering and architectural design.

Sutherland Joan (1926–). Australian soprano. She is noted for her commanding range and impeccable technique. She made her debut England 1952, in *The Magic Flute*; later roles included *Lucia di Lammermoor*, Donna Anna in *Don Giovanni*, and Desdemona in *Otello*. She retired from the stage 1990. DBE 1979.

Suggested reading
Adams, Brian *La Stupenda* (1983)
Braddon, R R *Joan Sutherland* (1962)
Greenfield, Edward *Joan Sutherland* (1973)

Sutton-Pringle John William (1912–1982). British zoologist who established much of our knowledge of the anatomical mechanisms involved in insect flight. Sutton-Pringle studied at Cambridge, where he spent his whole academic career.

Most insects have two hindwings and two forewings, and in many species each pair of wings acts in unison. Not all species use both pairs of wings for flight; in the housefly, for example, the hindwings are reduced in size and serve as balancing organs during flight.

Insect flight is achieved by simple up-and-down movements of the wings. In aphids, for example, these wing movements are brought about by the contractions of two separate sets of muscles. When moving through the air, the front edge of the wings remains rigid while the back edge bends. This causes the development of a localized region of high-pressure air behind the insect, which propels the insect forwards. The faster the wing beats, the greater the displacement of the posterior wing edges, the greater the pressure exerted on the insect from behind, and therefore the faster the insect flies.

Suu Kyi Aung San (1945–). Myanmar (Burmese) politician and human rights campaigner, leader of the National League for Democracy (NLD), the main opposition to the military junta. Educated in India and Oxford University from 1960, she later worked at the United Nations and settled in the UK. In protest against human-rights abuses and the brutal suppression of dissent in Burma she formed, on her return there from the UK 1988, the NLD opposition movement to campaign for democratic reform. When the NLD won the 1990 elections, the junta refused to surrender power, and placed Suu Kyi under house arrest; she was released 1995. She was awarded the Nobel Prize for Peace 1991 in recognition of her 'nonviolent

Sutherland, Joan *The soprano Joan Sutherland. Her highly flexible voice is well-suited to a variety of roles, but her greatest success was in Italian bel canto opera of the 18th and 19th centuries. She has a huge range and was one of the foremost coloratura sopranos of the century.*

struggle for democracy and human rights' in Myanmar. She is the daughter of former Burmese premier Aung San.

Suvorov Aleksandr Vasilyevich (1729–1800). Russian field marshal, victorious against the Turks 1787–91, the Poles 1794, and the French army in Italy 1798–99 in the Revolutionary Wars.

Suzman Helen Gavronsky (1917–). South African politician and human-rights activist. A university lecturer concerned about the inhumanity of the apartheid system, she joined the white opposition to the ruling National Party and became a strong advocate of racial equality, respected by black communities inside and outside South Africa. In 1978 she received the United Nations Human Rights Award. She retired from active politics in 1989.

Suzuki D(aisetz) T(eitaro) (1870–1966). Japanese scholar and follower of Zen Buddhism. His books in English first introduced Zen thought to the general public in the West. While studying in Tokyo, Suzuki underwent Zen training and rose to become professor of Buddhist philosophy at Otani University 1921. He spent much time in the USA 1897–1908 and from 1949 onwards, lecturing at many universities and explaining the Japanese Buddhist philosophy and practice of Zen Buddhism in Western terms. His works include *Essays in Zen Buddhism* 1927 (second series 1933) and *An Introduction to Zen Buddhism* 1934.

Suzuki Harunobu (1725–1770). Japanese artist. He was a leading exponent of ukiyo-e and one of the first printmakers to use colour effectively. His work displays a sure sense of composition and line and features domestic scenes, courtesans, and actors among its subjects.

Suzuki Zenkō (1911–). Japanese politician. Originally a socialist member of the Diet in 1947, he became a conservative (Liberal Democrat) in 1949, and was prime minister 1980–82.

Švankmajer Jan (1934–). Czech film-maker whose surrealist films combine puppets, stop-motion animation, and live actors. Švankmajer was born and educated in Prague, studying puppetry and design and then working in marionette theatre. His first film was *The Last Trick* 1964; others include *Punch and Judy* 1966, *Jabberwocky* 1971, and *Food* 1992. His full-length films are *Alice* 1988, and *Faust* 1994.

Svedberg Theodor (1884–1971). Swedish chemist. In 1924 he constructed the first ultracentrifuge, a machine that allowed the rapid separation of particles by mass. This can reveal the presence of contaminants in a sample of a new protein, or distinguish between various long-chain polymers. Nobel Prize for Chemistry 1926.

Svedberg was born near Gävle, studied at Uppsala and spent his career there, as professor 1912–49 and head of the Institute of Nuclear Chemistry 1949–67.

Svedberg prepared a number of new organosols from more than 30 metals. Through an ultramicroscope, he studied the particles in these sols and confirmed Albert Einstein's theories about Brownian movement.

Svedberg discovered that thorium-X crystallizes with lead and barium salts (but not with others), anticipating English chemist Frederick Soddy's demonstration of the existence of isotopes.

Svedberg also investigated, about 1923, the chemistry involved in the formation of latent images in photographic emulsions.

Working on synthetic polymers, Svedberg introduced electron microscopy to study natural and regenerated cellulose, X-ray diffraction techniques to investigate cellulose fibres, and electron diffraction to analyse colloidal micelles and crystallites.

Svendsen Johan Severin (1840–1911). Norwegian composer, violinist, and conductor. After a career as a virtuoso violinist, he took up composing. He was a friend of Grieg, who admired his orchestrational technique. His style, though Romantic, shows elements of Norwegian folk music. He wrote two symphonies and other orchestral works, as well as chamber and vocal works. He was the greatest Scandinavian conductor of his period.

Svevo Italo. Pen name of Ettore Schmitz (1861–1928). Italian novelist, encouraged by James Joyce. His work includes *As a Man Grows Older* 1898 and his comic masterpiece *Confessions of Zeno* 1923, one of the first novels to be based on Freudian analysis.

Swammerdam Jan (1637–1680). Dutch naturalist who is considered a founder of both comparative anatomy and entomology. Based on their metamorphic development, he classified insects into four main groups, three of which are still used in a modified form in insect classification. He was also probably the first to discover red blood cells when he observed oval particles in frog's blood in 1658.

Swammerdam was born in Amsterdam and studied medicine at Leiden but never practised as a physician. From 1673 he was under the influence of a religious zealot.

He accurately described and illustrated the life cycles and anatomies of many insect species, including bees, mayflies, and dragonflies.

Swammerdam also provided a substantial body of new knowledge about vertebrates. He anticipated the discovery of the role of oxygen in respiration by postulating that air contained a volatile element that could pass from the lungs to the heart and then to the muscles, providing the energy for muscle contraction.

In his work on human and mammalian anatomy, he discovered valves in the lymphatic system (now called Swammerdam valves). He also investigated the human reproductive system and was one of the first to show that female mammals produce eggs, analogous to birds' eggs.

His manuscripts were not published in full until 1737, when Hermann Boerhaave published *Biblia naturae/Bible of Nature*, a two-volume Latin translation of Swammerdam's Dutch text, with illustrations engraved from Swammerdam's drawings.

Swan Joseph Wilson (1828–1914). English inventor of the incandescent-filament electric lamp and of bromide paper for use in developing photographs. Knighted 1904.

Swan took out more than 70 patents. He made a miner's electric safety lamp which was the ancestor of the modern miner's lamp. In the course of this invention he devised a new lead cell (battery) which would not spill acid. He also attempted to make an early type of fuel cell.

Swan was born in Sunderland and went to work in a chemical firm. Interested in electric lighting from about 1845, he began making filaments by cutting strips of paper and baking them at high temperatures to produce a carbon fibre. In making the first lamps, he connected the ends of a filament to wire (itself a difficult task), placed the filament in a glass bottle, and attempted to evacuate the air and seal the bottle with a cork. Usually the filament burned away very quickly in the remaining air, blackening the glass at the same time. Only after the invention of the vacuum pump 1865 was Swan able to produce a fairly durable incandescent lamp. For this he made a new type of filament from cotton thread partly dissolved by sulphuric acid. He patented the process in 1880 and began manufacturing lamps. In 1882 US inventor Thomas Edison initiated litigation for patent infringement against Swan, but this was dismissed and the joint company Edison and Swan United Electric Light Company came into being in 1883.

A wet process for producing photographic prints, using a gelatine film impregnated with carbon or other pigment granules and photosensitized using potassium dichromate, was patented by Swan in 1864. This was known as the carbon or autotype process.

Swann Donald Ibrahim (1923–1994). British composer, pianist, and entertainer. With his partner, Michael Flanders, he is best remembered for the inimitable wit and humour of their various 'Drop of a Hat' reviews. The songs they wrote, including the immensely popular 'Hippopotamus' and other funny animal numbers, were sung at various revues by such stars as Joyce Grenfell and Ian Wallace. Flanders and Swann would perform together only at private gatherings but in 1956 were eventually persuaded to offer their 'after-dinner ferrago', 'At the Drop of a Hat' at a small theatre in Notting Hill Gate. They soon transferred to the Fortune Theatre in the West End where the review ran for over two years. They went to New York, then toured North America. A second review, 'At the Drop of Another Hat', just as popular, was presented first at the

Haymarket Theatre in the West End, then on tour in Australia, New Zealand, Hong Kong, and the USA. There were 'Hats' for over ten years. When the partnership ended 1967, Swann tried his hand at more serious works – opera, a *Te Deum*, more songs – though none became quite so popular.

Swanson Gloria. Stage name of Gloria Josephine Mae Svenson (*c.* 1897–1983). US actress. A star of silent films, she became the epitome of glamour during the 1920s. She was second only to Mary Pickford in fame and in 1926 she formed her own production company with Joseph Kennedy as her financial backer. She retired 1932 but made several major comebacks. Her work includes *Sadie Thompson* 1928, *Queen Kelly* 1928 (unfinished), and *Sunset Boulevard* 1950.

Swedenborg Emanuel (born Svedberg) (1688–1772). Swedish mystic and scientist. In *Divine Love and Wisdom* 1763, he concluded that the Last Judgement had taken place in 1757, and that the New Church, of which he was the prophet, had now been inaugurated. His writings are the scriptures of the sect popularly known as Swedenborgians, and his works are kept in circulation by the Swedenborg Society, London.

As assessor to the Swedish Royal College of Mines, Swedenborg carried out research that anticipated many later discoveries in the fields of engineering, navigation, and astronomy. In *Opera Philosophica et Mineralia/Philosophical and Logical Works* 1734, he attempted to explain the natural world as having a spiritual foundation. From 1744 he devoted himself exclusively to religious speculation, claiming access to God via the angels, and formulating a 'doctrine of correspondence' whereby all things in the material world have spiritual counterparts. This doctrine resembled neo-Platonism and influenced the Romantics, notably William Blake, and the French theorists of Symbolism.

Suggested reading
Jonsson, Inge *Emanuel Swedenborg* (trs 1971)
Toksvig, Signe *Emanuel Swedenborg: Scientist and Mystic* (1948)
Wunch, William *An Outline of Swedenborg's Teaching* (1975)

Sweelinck Jan Pieterszoon (1562–1621). Dutch composer, organist, harpsichordist, and teacher. He was the first composer to write an independent part for the pedal keyboard (pedalboard) in organ works, a technique which reached its peak in J S Bach's organ compositions. He taught many of the next generation's organists of the German school.

Sweet Henry (1845–1912). British philologist, author of works on Old and Middle English, who took to England German scientific techniques of language study. He was said to be the original of Professor Higgins in George Bernard Shaw's play *Pygmalion*.

He employed his Wit to the noblest Purposes, in ridiculing as well Superstition in Religion as infidelity, and several Errors and immoralities which sprung from time to time in his Age; and lastly, in the Defence of his Country, against several pernicious schemes of wicked Politicians.

Henry Fielding on JONATHAN SWIFT
in *True Patriot* 5 Nov 1745

Swift Jonathan (1667–1745). Irish satirist and Anglican cleric. He wrote *Gulliver's Travels* 1726, an allegory describing travel to lands inhabited by giants, miniature people, and intelligent horses. Other works include *The Tale of a Tub* 1704, attacking corruption in religion and learning; contributions to the Tory paper *The Examiner*, of which he was editor 1710–11; the satirical pamphlet *A Modest Proposal* 1729, which suggested that children of the poor should be eaten; and many essays and pamphlets.

Swift, born in Dublin, became secretary to the diplomat William Temple (1628–1699) at Moor Park, Surrey, where his friendship with the child 'Stella' (Hester Johnson 1681–1728) began 1689. Returning to Ireland, he was ordained in the Church of England

1694, and in 1699 was made a prebendary of St Patrick's, Dublin. In 1710 he became a Tory pamphleteer, and obtained the deanery of St Patrick 1713.

His *Journal to Stella* is a series of letters, 1710–13, in which he described his life in London. 'Stella' remained the love of his life, but 'Vanessa' (Esther Vanhomrigh 1690–1723), a Dublin woman who had fallen in love with him, jealously wrote to her rival 1723 and so shattered his relationship with both women. From about 1738 his mind began to fail.

Murry, J M *Jonathan Swift: A Critical Biography* (1955)
Nokes, D *Jonathan Swift, A Hypocrite Reversed: A Critical Biography* (1985)

Bright with names that men remember, loud with names that men forget.

ALGERNON CHARLES SWINBURNE
'Eton: An Ode'

Swinburne Algernon Charles (1837–1909). English poet. He attracted attention with the choruses of his Greek-style tragedy *Atalanta in Calydon* 1865, but he and Rossetti were attacked 1871 as leaders of 'the fleshly school of poetry', and the revolutionary politics of *Songs before Sunrise* 1871 alienated others.

We were as nearly bored as enthusiasm would permit.

Anonymous critic on a SWINBURNE play
quoted in Christopher Hassall *Edward Marsh* ch 6 1959

Swinburne James (1858–1958). Scottish engineer, a pioneer in electrical engineering and plastics. Baronet 1934.

During 1881–85 he worked for English inventor Joseph Swan, setting up electric-lamp factories in France and the USA. Swinburne was then employed as assistant to English engineer Rookes Crompton, particularly involved in the development of dynamos.

In 1894 Swinburne set up his own laboratory. Some of his research focused on the reaction between phenol and formaldehyde, but when he came to patent the product in 1907, he was by just one day beaten to the idea by Belgian chemist Leo Baekeland (with his invention of Bakelite). Swinburne was able to obtain a patent on the production of a lacquer, however, and set up his own Damard Lacquer Company in Birmingham. Baekeland bought him out in the early 1920s and formed Bakelite Limited, Great Britain, of which Swinburne became the first chair.

Swinburne's inventions included the watt-hour meter and the 'hedgehog' transformer for stepping up medium-voltage alternating current to high voltages for long-distance power transmission. The words 'motor' and 'stator' are thought to have been coined by him.

Swineshead Richard (lived *c.* 1340). British scientist and leading member of a group of natural scientists associated with Merton College, Oxford, who attempted to analyse and quantify the various forms of motion.

Swineshead was known as 'the Calculator'.

Swings Pol(idore F F) (1906–1983). Belgian astrophysicist who used spectroscopy to identify the elements in astronomical bodies, especially comets. Swings was born in Ransart, near Charleroi, and studied at Liège, where he was professor 1932–75, with several years as visiting professor at a number of US universities.

From his study of cometary atmospheres, he is credited with the discovery of the Swings bands and the Swings effect. Swings bands are emission lines resulting from the presence of certain atoms of carbon; the Swings effect was discovered with the aid of a slit spectrograph and is attributed to fluorescence resulting partly from solar radiation.

Swings also made spectroscopic studies of interstellar space and investigated stellar rotation, as well as nebulae, novae, and variable stars.

Swinton Ernest Dunlop (1868–1951). British soldier and historian. He served in South Africa and in World War I, and was the inventor of the tank in 1916.

Returning to London on leave Christmas 1914 he was pondering the problem of overcoming trenches and barbed wire when he saw a Holt tractor towing a gun. This inspired him to draw up a paper proposing a 'power-driven, bullet-proof, armed engine capable of destroying machine guns, breaking through entanglements and climbing earthworks'. This paper eventually reached Churchill, who set up the Admiralty Landships Committee, and from it emerged the tank. Swinton later commanded tanks in action, and drew up the tactical and operational manuals which governed their employment. He was Chichele professor of military history at Oxford, 1925–39. KBE 1923.

Swithun, St or Swithin (c. 800–c. 862). English priest, chancellor of King Ethelwolf and bishop of Winchester from 852. According to legend, the weather on his feast day (15 July) is said to continue as either wet or fine for 40 days.

Sydenham Thomas (1624–1689). English physician, the first person to describe measles and to recommend the use of quinine for relieving symptoms of malaria. His original reputation as the 'English Hippocrates' rested upon his belief that careful observation is more useful than speculation. His *Observationes medicae* was published in 1676.

Sydow Max (Carl Adolf) von (1929–). Swedish actor. He was associated with the director Ingmar Bergman. He made his US debut as Jesus in *The Greatest Story Ever Told* 1965. His other films include *The Seventh Seal* 1957, *The Exorcist* 1973, *Hannah and Her Sisters* 1986, and *The Ox* 1991.

Sykes Percy Molesworth (1867–1945). English explorer, soldier, and administrator who surveyed much of the territory in SW Asia between Baghdad, the Caspian Sea, and the Hindu Kush during World War I (1914–18). KCIE 1915.

In 1894 he was the first British consul to Kerman (now in Iran) and Persian Baluchistan. Later he raised and commanded the South Persian Rifles. His histories of Persia and Afghanistan were published in 1915 and 1940.

Sylow Ludwig Mejdell (1832–1918). Norwegian mathematician who in 1872 published his fundamental theorem on groups and the type of subgroups now named after him. For 40 years he taught mathematics in a school in Halden. From 1898 he was professor at Christiania.

Sylow collaborated with Sophus Lie, then professor of mathematics at Christiania, on producing an edition of the works of Norwegian mathematician Niels Abel, published 1881; it was followed by Sylow's edition of Abel's letters in 1901.

Sylvester James Joseph (1814–1897). English mathematician who was one of the discoverers of the theory of algebraic invariants. He coined the term 'matrix' in 1850 to describe a rectangular array of numbers out of which determinants can be formed.

He became professor of natural philosophy at University College, London, 1837. In 1841 he went to the USA to become professor at the University of Virginia, but resigned 1845 and returned to England. For the next ten years he abandoned academic life, although he took in private pupils, including nursing pioneer Florence Nightingale. In 1844 he joined an insurance company, and in 1850 he became a barrister. In 1855 he returned to academic life, becoming professor of mathematics at the Royal Military Academy in Woolwich, London.

In 1877 he again went to the USA, becoming professor at the newly founded Johns Hopkins University in Baltimore. Returning to the UK, he was from 1883 professor at Oxford.

Sylvester laid the foundations, with English mathematician Arthur Cayley (with whom he did not collaborate), of modern invariant algebra. He also wrote on the nature of roots in quintic equations and on the theory of numbers, especially in partitions and Diophantine analysis.

Symington William (1763–1831). Scottish engineer who built the first successful steamboat. He invented the steam road locomotive in

1787 and a steamboat engine in 1788. His steamboat *Charlotte Dundas* was completed in 1802.

Symonds John Addington (1840–1893). British critic who spent much of his life in Italy and Switzerland, and campaigned for homosexual rights. He wrote *The Renaissance in Italy* 1875–86. His frank memoirs were finally published 1984.

And I would have, now love is over, / An end to all, an end: / I cannot, having been your lover, / Stoop to become your friend!

ARTHUR SYMONS
'After Love'

Symons Arthur William (1865–1945). Welsh critic. He was a follower of Walter Pater, and friend of the artists Toulouse-Lautrec and Aubrey Beardsley, the poets Stéphane Mallarmé and W B Yeats, and the novelist Joseph Conrad. He introduced T S Eliot to the poetry of Jules Laforgue and wrote *The Symbolist Movement in Literature* 1900.

Symons Julian Gustave (1912–1995). British author. Although best known for his crime novels, he also worked as a critic, editor, poet, essayist, biographer, and historian. Symons became deeply involved in anarchist and literary circles in London, writing poetry and editing the influential poetry magazine *The Twentieth Century*. His first detective novel, *The Immaterial Murder Case* 1945, was a spoof in which he introduced many of the literary figures of the period. By the time he wrote his second, *The Thirty First of February* 1950, he had begun to use his writing to investigate the psychology of relationships and to comment upon the structure of society. His novels, in which he develops his theme with wit and intellectual flair, include *The End of Solomon Grundy* 1964, *The Man Who Lost His Wife* 1970, and *The Blackheath Poisonings* 1978, one of several works with a Victorian setting.

Some of his best writings on the crime novel are contained in *Bloody Murder* 1972; among his many other works are biographies of Edgar Allen Poe, Charles Dickens, Thomas Carlyle, and Dashiell Hammett (a favourite author); social histories, such as *The General Strike* 1957 and *The Thirties* 1960; and a brief autobiography, *Notes from Another Country* 1972. As a critic and editor, he encouraged several generations of young writers.

The Playboy of the Western World

J M SYNGE
Title of play 1907

Synge J(ohn) M(illington) (1871–1909). Irish dramatist. He was a leading figure in the Irish dramatic revival of the early 20th century. His six plays reflect the speech patterns of the Aran Islands and W Ireland. They include *In the Shadow of the Glen* 1903, *Riders to the Sea* 1904, and *The Playboy of the Western World* 1907, which caused riots at the Abbey Theatre, Dublin, when first performed.

Synge Richard Laurence Millington (1914–1994). British biochemist who improved paper chromatography (a means of separating mixtures) to the point where individual amino acids could be identified. He developed the technique, known as partition chromatography, with his colleague Archer Martin 1944. They shared the 1952 Nobel Prize for Chemistry.

From 1967 until his retirement in 1974 he worked as a biochemist at the Food Research Institute of the Agricultural Research Council in Norwich.

Martin and Synge worked together at Cambridge and at the Wool Industries Research Association in Leeds. Their chromatographic method became an immediate success, widely adopted. It was soon demonstrated that not only the type but the concentration of each amino acid can be determined.

In the early 1940s there were only crude chromatographic techniques available for separating proteins in reasonably large samples;

no method existed for the separation of the amino acids that make up proteins. Martin and Synge developed the technique of paper chromatography, using porous filter paper to separate out amino acids using a solvent. A minute quantity of the amino acid solution is placed at the tip of the filter paper; once dry it is dipped (or suspended) in a solvent. As the solvent passes the mixture the amino acids move with it, but they do so at different rates and so become separated. Once dry the paper is sprayed with a developer and the amino acids show up as dark dots. Synge and Martin announced their technique 1944; it was soon being applied to a wide variety of experimental problems.

Paper chromatography is so precise that it can be used to identify amino acid concentration, as well as type, enabling Synge to work out the exact structure of the antibiotic peptide Gramicidin-S, a piece of research important to Frederick Sanger's determination of the structure of insulin 1953.

In 1948 Synge moved to the Rowett Research Institute, Aberdeen, where he remained in charge of protein chemistry until 1967. He then moved to Norwich where he became honorary professor of biology at the University of East Anglia. Synge was very active in the peace movement, and after his retirement in 1976, he became treasurer of the Norwich Peace Council. He died in Norwich.

Szasz Thomas (1920–　　). Hungarian-born US psychiatrist. In his book *The Myth of Mental Illness* 1961, he argued that the concept of mental illness was false. Believing that individuals should take responsibility for their own actions, he supported the policy of moving mental patients out of hospital and into the community.

Szasz was born in Budapest but emigrated to the USA 1938. He was professor of psychiatry at SUNY Health Science Center, Syracuse, New York, 1956–90, and it was there he developed his anti-psychiatry philosophy. He saw psychiatrists as concerned less with treating mental illness than with defining normal behaviour, acting as social police. His many books include *Law, Liberty and Psychiatry* 1963, *Ideology and Insanity* 1970, *Schizophrenia: The Sacred Symbol of Psychiatry* 1976, *The Myth of Psychotherapy* 1978, *Insanity: The Idea and Its Consequences* 1987, and *Cruel Compassion: Psychiatric Control of Society's Unwanted* 1994.

Szent-Györgyi Albert von Nagyrapolt (1893–1986). Hungarian-born US biochemist who isolated vitamin C and studied the chemistry of muscular activity. He was awarded the Nobel Prize for Physiology or Medicine 1937.

In 1928 Szent-Györgyi isolated a substance from the adrenal glands that he named hexuronic acid; he also found it in oranges and paprika, and in 1932 proved it to be vitamin C.

He was active in the anti-Nazi underground movement during World War II; after the war he became professor at Budapest. In 1947 he emigrated to the USA, where he became director of the National Institute of Muscle Research at Woods Hole, Massachusetts. From 1975 he was scientific director of the National Foundation for Cancer Research.

Szent-Györgyi also studied the uptake of oxygen by muscle tissue. In 1940 he isolated two kinds of muscle protein and named the combined compound actomyosin. When adenosine triphosphate (ATP) is added to it, a change takes place in the relationship of the two components which results in the contraction of the muscle.

In the 1960s Szent-Györgyi began studying the thymus gland, and isolated several compounds from the thymus that seem to be involved in the control of growth.

His last work was *Electronic Biology and Cancer* 1976.

Don't lie if you don't have to.

LEO SZILARD
in *Science* vol 176 p 966 1972

Szilard Leo (1898–1964). Hungarian-born US physicist who, in 1934, was one of the first scientists to realize that nuclear fission, or atom splitting, could lead to a chain reaction releasing enormous amounts of instantaneous energy. He emigrated to the USA in 1938 and there influenced Albert Einstein to advise President Roosevelt to begin the nuclear-arms programme. After World War II he turned his attention to the newly emerging field of molecular biology.

Szymanowski Karol Maliej (1882–1937). Polish composer. He wrote piano music, violin concertos, four symphonies, a *Stabat Mater* 1926, and the opera *Król Roger/King Roger* 1918–24, in richly glamorous idiom drawing on national folklore and French impressionist style. He was director of the Conservatoire in Warsaw from 1926.

T

respectively. He also wrote a *Life of Agricola* 97 (he married Agricola's daughter 77) and a description of the Germanic tribes, *Germania* 98.

I shall write without anger or bias.

TACITUS
Annals bk 1 ch 1

Tafawa Balewa Alhaji Abubakar (1912–1966). Nigerian politician, prime minister from 1957 to 1966, when he was assassinated in a coup d'état. Tafawa Balewa entered the House of Representatives 1952, was minister of works 1952–54, and minister of transport 1954–57. KBE 1960.

Taft Robert Alphonso (1889–1953). US right-wing Republican senator from 1939, and a candidate for the presidential nomination 1940, 1944, 1948, and 1952. He sponsored the Taft–Hartley Labor Act 1947, restricting union power. He was the son of President William Taft.

Taft William Howard (1857–1930). 27th president of the USA 1909–13, a Republican. Born in Cincinnati, Ohio, Taft graduated from Yale University and Cincinnati Law School. His first interest was always the judiciary, although he accepted a post as governor of the Philippines and took responsibility for the construction of the Panama Canal. He was secretary of war 1904–08 in Theodore Roosevelt's administration, but as president his conservatism provoked Roosevelt to stand against him in the 1912 election. Taft served as chief justice of the Supreme Court 1921–30.

His single term as president was characterized by struggles against progressives, although he prosecuted more trusts than had his predecessor. As chief justice of the Supreme Court, he supported a minimum wage.

Suggested reading
Anderson, Judith *William Howard Taft: An Intimate History* (1981)
Coletta, P *The Presidency of William Howard Taft* (1973)
Steven, B *William Howard Taft: The President Who Became Chief Justice* (1970)

Tagliacozzi Gaspare (1546–1599). Italian surgeon who pioneered plastic surgery. He was the first to repair noses lost in duels or through syphilis. He also repaired ears. His method involved taking flaps of skin from the arm and grafting them into place.

Her popularity was such that hairstyles were copied from her and 'Taglioniser' became a verb.

Christy Adair on MARIE TAGLIONI in
Woman and Dance; Sylphs and Sirens 1992

Taglioni Marie (1804–1884). Italian dancer. A ballerina of ethereal style and exceptional lightness, she was the first to use pointe work, or dancing on the toes, as an expressive part of ballet rather than as sheer technique. She created many roles, including the title role in *La Sylphide* 1832, first performed at the Paris Opéra, and choreographed by her father Filippo (1771–1871).

Marie's brother Paolo (1808–1884) was a choreographer and ballet master at Berlin Court Opera 1856–83, and his daughter Marie (1833–1891) danced in Berlin and London, creating many roles in her father's ballets.

Taft, William *William Taft, 27th US president and later chief justice, the only person to have headed both the executive and the judicial branches of the US government. As chief justice of the US Supreme Court, Taft improved the efficiency of the judicial machinery by securing the passage of the Judiciary Act 1925.*

Tabor David (1913–). English physicist who worked mainly in tribology, the study of friction and wear between solid surfaces. From 1946 he worked at Cambridge in the Cavendish Laboratory, becoming professor 1973.

Tabor showed that the low friction of Teflon is due not to poor adhesion but to molecular structure, and worked on the self-lubrication of polymers by incorporating surface materials into the polymer itself. A study of the friction of rubber led to the introduction of high-hysteresis rubber into vehicle tyres as a means of increasing their skid-resistance.

Tabor researched into the shear properties of molecular films of long-chain organic molecules as an extension of earlier work on the mechanism of boundary lubrication, and showed that the shear strength of these materials rises sharply when they are subjected to high pressure. This sheds light on the mechanism of thin film lubrication.

When they make a desolation they call it peace.

TACITUS
Agricola

Tacitus Publius Cornelius (*c.* AD 56–*c.* 120). Roman historian. A public orator in Rome, he was consul under Nerva 97–98 and proconsul of Asia 112–113. He wrote histories of the Roman Empire, *Annales* and *Historiae*, covering the years AD 14–68 and 69–97

Tagore Rabindranath (1861–1941). Bengali Indian writer. He translated into English his own verse *Gitanjali* ('song offerings') 1912 and his verse play *Chitra* 1896. Nobel Prize for Literature 1913.

An ardent nationalist and advocate of social reform, he resigned his knighthood in 1919, given in 1918, as a gesture of protest against British repression in India.

Suggested reading
Bose, A *Rabindranath Tagore* (1958)
Chakravarty, Amiya (ed) *A Tagore Reader* (1961)
Dutta, Krishna and Robinson, Andrew *Rabindranath Tagore: The Myriad-Minded Man* (1995)
Kripalani, H R *Rabindranath Tagore: A Biography* (1962)
Lago, Mary *Rabindranath Tagore* (1976)

There are four types of men in the world: lovers, opportunists, lookers-on and imbeciles. The happiest are the imbeciles.

HIPPOLYTE TAINE
Vie et opinions de Thomas Graingorge 1867

Taine Hippolyte Adolphe (1828–1893). French critic and historian. He analysed literary works as products of period and environment, as in *Histoire de la littérature anglaise/History of English Literature* 1863 and *Philosophie de l'art/Philosophy of Art* 1865–69.

Taira or Heike. In Japanese history, a military clan prominent in the 10th–12th centuries and dominant at court 1159–85. Their destruction by their rivals, the Minamoto, 1185 is the subject of the 13th-century literary classic *Heike Monogatari/The Tale of the Heike*.

Takemitsu Toru (1930–1996). Japanese composer. He was mainly self-taught and was initially influenced by Schoenberg, Messiaen, and *musique concrète*. Like other composers of his generation (such as Ligeti), he was interested in the treatment of texture. His use of the electronic medium is well exemplified in *Relief statique* 1955.

Takeshita Noboru (1924–). Japanese right-wing politician. Elected to parliament as a Liberal Democratic Party (LDP) deputy 1958, he became president of the LDP and prime minister Oct 1987. He and members of his administration were shown in the Recruit scandal to have been involved in insider-trading and he resigned April 1989.

Talbot William Henry Fox (1800–1877). English pioneer of photography. He invented the paper-based calotype process 1841, the first negative/positive method. Talbot made photograms several years before Louis Daguerre's invention was announced.

In 1851 he made instantaneous photographs by electric light and in 1852 photo engravings. *The Pencil of Nature* 1844–46 by Talbot was the first book illustrated with photographs to be published.

He was elected Liberal member of Parliament for Chippenham 1833. During a trip to Italy he tried to capture the images obtained in a camera obscura and by 1835 had succeeded in fixing outlines of objects laid on sensitized paper. Images of his home, Lacock Abbey, Wiltshire, followed. Talbot was also a mathematician and classical scholar, and was one of the first to decipher the cuneiform inscriptions of Nineveh, Assyria.

In Talbot's calotype process, writing paper was coated successively with solutions of silver nitrate and potassium iodide, forming silver iodide. The iodized paper was made more sensitive by brushing with solutions of gallic acid and silver nitrate, and then it was exposed (either moist or dry). The latent image was developed with an application of gallo-silver nitrate solution, and when the image became visible, the paper was warmed for one to two minutes. It was fixed with a solution of potassium bromide (later replaced by sodium hyposulphite). Calotypes did not have the sharp definition of daguerreotypes and were generally considered inferior.

Talbot patented an enlarger in 1843. In the decade to 1851, he took out some patents that contained previously published claims, but in 1852 he cleared the way for amateurs to use processes developed in other countries.

Suggested reading
Arnold, A J P *Talbot: Pioneer of Photography and Man of Science* (1977)
Hannavy, J *Fox Talbot* (1984)
Newhall, Beaumont *The History of Photography: 1839 to the Present Day* (1982)

Taliesin (lived *c.* 550). Legendary Welsh poet, a bard at the court of the king of Rheged in Scotland. Taliesin allegedly died at Taliesin (named after him) in Dyfed, Wales.

Talleyrand-Périgord Charles Maurice de (1754–1838). French politician and diplomat. As bishop of Autun 1789–91 he supported moderate reform during the French Revolution, was excommunicated by the pope, and fled to the USA during the Reign of Terror (persecution of anti-revolutionaries). He returned and became foreign minister under the Directory 1797–99 and under Napoleon 1799–1807. He represented France at the Congress of Vienna 1814–15.

As he did live, so also did he die,/ In mild and quiet sort,/ (O! happy man).

epitaph for THOMAS TALLIS in St Alphege, Greenwich

Tallis Thomas (*c.* 1505–1585). English composer. He was a master of counterpoint. His works include *Tallis's Canon* ('Glory to thee my God this night') 1567, the antiphonal *Spem in alium non habui* (about 1573) for 40 voices in various groupings, and a collection of 34 motets, *Cantiones sacrae*, 1575 (of which 16 are by Tallis and 18 by Byrd). In 1575 Elizabeth I granted Tallis and Byrd the monopoly for printing music and music paper in England.

Suggested reading
Doe, Paul *Thomas Tallis* (1968)
Wulstan, David *Tudor Music* (1985)

Talman William (1650–1719). English architect. He was a contemporary of Christopher Wren, to whom he is often compared, although Wren's output was significantly more accomplished and prolific. Influenced by French and Italian Baroque, Talman worked on Chatsworth House, Derbyshire, 1687–96, designing the east front and the monumental south front, which is characterized by severe rusticated masonry and heavy keystones.

Tamayo Rufino (1899–1991). Mexican painter and printmaker. His work, nurtured by both European Modernism and pre-Columbian indigenous art, demonstrates a clear break with the rhetoric and pictoralism of the preceding generation of Mexican muralists. His mainly easel-sized paintings, with their vibrant colours and cryptic, semi-abstract figures, display strong Cubist, Expressionist, and Surrealist elements, as in *Women Reaching for the Moon* 1946 (Cleveland Museum of Art, Cleveland, Ohio).

Tamayo painted many important murals 1933–77 as well as smaller-scale works. His choice of subject matter – Mexican folklore, people, fauna, and flora – reveals his passion for his native country, for example *Watermelons* 1968 (Rufino Tamayo Museum, Mexico City). Among important commissions was his mural, *Prometheus Bringing Fire to Man* 1958, for the UNESCO Building, Paris.

Tambo Oliver (1917–1993). South African nationalist politician, in exile 1960–90, president of the African National Congress (ANC) 1977–91. Because of poor health, he was given the honorary post of national chair July 1991, and Nelson Mandela resumed the ANC presidency.

Tambo first met Mandela at Fort Hare University, but was expelled for organizing a student protest, and joined the African National Congress (ANC) 1944. With Mandela, he helped found the ANC Youth League, becoming its vice-president; together they also established a law practice in Johannesburg 1952.

A devout Christian, Tambo applied to join the priesthood, but before he could be accepted as a candidate, received a year's imprisonment for subversive activities 1956. When the ANC was banned 1960, as ANC deputy president, he was advised to go into exile and left South Africa to set up an external wing. Before long the organization's main leaders had been imprisoned or killed, and Tambo worked tirelessly from his London base as acting ANC president, becoming president 1977. His return to South Africa Dec 1990 was rapturously received.

Tamerlane or Tamburlaine or Timur i Leng ('Timur the Lame') (1336–1405). Mongol ruler of Samarkand, in Uzbekistan, from 1369 who conquered Persia, Azerbaijan, Armenia, and Georgia. He defeated the Golden Horde 1395, sacked Delhi 1398, invaded Syria and Anatolia, and captured the Ottoman sultan in Ankara 1402; he died invading China. He was a descendant of the Mongol leader Genghis Khan and the great-grandfather of Babur, founder of the Mogul Empire.

Tan Amy (An-mei Ruth) (1952–   ). US writer. Her first novel, *The Joy Luck Club* 1989, tells the story of four Chinese immigrant mothers and their American daughters. She was screenwriter and producer of the film of *The Joy Luck Club* 1993.

Tan was born in Oakland, California, to Chinese immigrant parents. She worked as a freelance business writer in the 1980s. Her other novels are *The Kitchen God's Wife* 1991, inspired by her mother's life in China before the communist revolution; *The Moon Lady* 1992; and *The Chinese Siamese Cat* 1994.

Tanaka Kakuei (1918–1993). Japanese right-wing politician, leader of the dominant Liberal Democratic Party (LDP) and prime minister 1972–74. Tanaka was minister of finance 1962–65 and of international trade and industry 1971–72, before becoming LDP leader. In 1974 he had to resign the premiership because of allegations of corruption and in 1976 he was arrested for accepting bribes from the Lockheed Corporation while premier. He was found guilty 1983, but remained in the Diet as an independent deputy pending appeal. He was also implicated in the 1988–89 Recruit scandal of insider trading.

The son of a small cattle trader in rural western Japan, Tanaka trained at night school as a quantity surveyor and made his fortune as a building contractor. In 1947 he was elected to Japan's House of Representatives and used his personal wealth and connections to build up a powerful faction within the LDP. Tanaka's meteoric political rise culminated in his becoming post-war Japan's youngest prime minister 1972. As premier he was initially popular, having a raffish common touch and a charisma generally lacking in Japanese politicians. The Tanaka political dynasty survived Kakuei's death – his daughter, Makiko, representing his former parliamentary seat from 1993.

Tandy Jessica (1909–1994). English film and theatre actress. One of the greatest classical theatre actresses of her day, she played all the major Shakespearean heroines, including Ophelia alongside John Gielgud's Hamlet 1934. In the US she created the role of Blanche DuBois in the premiere of Tennessee Williams's *A Streetcar Named Desire* 1947. She often played supporting film roles, including parts in *Dragonwyck* 1946 and *The World according to Garp* 1963. Her most successful film was *Driving Miss Daisy* 1989, for which she won an Academy Award.

Born in London, she made her first stage appearance in Birmingham in 1927 and her West End debut two years later. In 1940, following her divorce from the actor Jack Hawkins, she moved to the US and in 1942 married the actor Hume Cronyn. She and Cronyn frequently acted together, both in such modern plays as *The Fourposter* (Broadway 1951) and in a variety of classic revivals.

Her film appearances also included Alfred Hitchcock's *The Birds* 1963, but remained occasional until the 1980s, when she suddenly became in demand for character roles. She appeared with Cronyn in *Honky Tonk Freeway* 1981 and *Cocoon* 1985 and alone in several other films, including *Used People* 1992.

Taney Roger Brooke (1777–1864). US lawyer. Born in Calvert County, Maryland, Taney was educated at Dickinson College and became a barrister 1799. He served as a Maryland state senator

1816–21 and state attorney general 1827–31. He was President Jackson's attorney general 1831, and US secretary of the treasury 1833–35. In 1835 he was appointed chief justice of the US Supreme Court. In the Dred Scott case 1857 he ruled that Congress had no right to ban slavery in the territories, a decision that seriously aggravated sectional tensions.

Tang dynasty (7th–10th centuries). The greatest of China's imperial dynasties, which ruled 618–907. Founded by the Sui official Li Yuan (566–635), it extended Chinese authority into central Asia, Tibet, Korea, and Annam, establishing what was then the world's largest empire. The dynasty's peak was reached during the reign (712–56) of Emperor Minghuang (Hsuan-tsung).

The Tang dynasty set up a centralized administrative system based on the Han examination model. Buddhism continued to spread and the arts and science flourished. Printing was invented, gunpowder first used, and seaborne and overland trade and cultural contacts were widened.

Tange Kenzo (1913–   ). Japanese Modernist architect. His works include the National Gymnasium, Tokyo, for the 1964 Olympics with its vast catenary steel roof, and the crescent-shaped city of Abuja, which replaced Lagos as the capital of Nigeria 1992. In 1991 he completed the 70-storey City Hall, Tokyo – Japan's tallest building.

Tanguy Yves (1900–1955). French Surrealist painter. He lived in the USA from 1939. His inventive canvases feature semi-abstract creatures in a barren landscape. Tanguy was first inspired to paint by the works of de Chirico and in 1925 he joined the Surrealist movement. He soon developed his characteristic style with bizarre, slender forms in a typically Surrealist wasteland.

Tanizaki Jun-ichirō (1886–1965). Japanese novelist. His works include a version of Murasaki's *The Tale of Genji* 1939–41, *The Makioka Sisters* in three volumes 1943–48, and *The Key* 1956.

Tanner Beatrice Stella. Unmarried name of actress Mrs Patrick ◊Campbell.

Tansley Arthur George (1871–1955). English botanist, a pioneer in the science of plant ecology. He co-ordinated a large project to map the vegetation of the British Isles; the results were published in *Types of British Vegetation* 1911. He was also instrumental in the formation of organizations devoted to the study of ecology and the protection of wildlife. Knighted 1950.

He founded the journal *New Phytologist* 1902, remaining its editor for 30 years. As co-founder of the British Ecological Society 1913, he also edited its *Journal of Ecology* 1916–38. From 1923 to 1924 he abandoned botany to study under Sigmund Freud, the founder of psychoanalysis, in Austria. Tansley was professor of botany at Oxford 1927–39, and chair of Nature Conservancy 1949–53.

In *The British Islands and their Vegetation* 1939, Tansley showed how vegetation is affected by soil, climate, the presence of wild and domesticated animals, previous land management, and contemporary human activities. He also reviewed all known accounts of British flora and then linked the two themes, thereby demonstrating which factors are important in influencing the various types of vegetation.

Tàpies Antoni (1923–   ). Spanish abstract painter. He is noted for his highly textured paintings created from mixed media. In works such as *Large Brown Triangle* 1963 (Musée National d'Art Moderne, Centre Pompidou, Paris), he uses monochromatic, earthy tones and broken surfaces – either painted with graffiti or incised with a few lines – to express the passage of time and traces left by human beings.

Self-taught, Tàpies began to paint in a Surrealist vein 1945–46, and in 1957 was a founder member of the El Paso group. His paintings of the late 1950s and early 1960s employ thick coatings of tar, bitumen, sand, and clay and such waste materials as wire, paper, rope, straw, and rags. In later works, real objects are affixed to the picture plane, such as mirrors and clothing, and assemblages created from furniture, for example *Wardrobe* 1973 (Fundacío Antoni Tàpies, Barcelona).

Tarantino Quentin (1963–   ). US film director and screenwriter whose films are characterized by a fragmented structure and often explicit violence. His first feature, *Reservoir Dogs* 1992, deals with the aftermath of an unsuccessful jewel heist. His second, *Pulp Fiction* 1994, is more humorous and intertwines several storylines; it won the Palme d'Or at Cannes. Tarantino also wrote the screenplay of *True Romance* 1993, and the screen story of *Natural Born Killers* 1994, though he disowned Oliver Stone's completed film.

Tarbell Ida Minerva (1857–1944). US journalist whose exposés of corruption in high places made her one of the most prominent 'muckrakers' in the USA. Born in Erie County, Pennsylvania, USA, Tarbell was educated at Allegheny College and the Sorbonne, Paris, France, and became an editor of the *Chautauquan* 1883. She was an editor and contributor to *McClure's Magazine* 1894–1906. Her book *The History of the Standard Oil Company* 1904 sparked antitrust reform. Her autobiography, *All in a Day's Work*, appeared 1939. From 1906 to 1915 she worked on the staff of the *American Magazine*.

Arguments only confirm people in their own opinions.
BOOTH TARKINGTON
in *Looking Forward to the Great Adventure* 1926

Tarkington (Newton) Booth (1869–1946). US novelist. His novels for young people, which include *Penrod* 1914, are classics. He was among the best-selling authors of the early 20th century with works such as *Monsieur Beaucaire* 1900 and novels of the Midwest, including *The Magnificent Ambersons* 1918 (filmed 1942 by Orson Welles).

Tarkovsky Andrei Arsenyevich (1932–1986). Soviet film director. His work is characterized by an epic style combined with intense personal spirituality. His films include *Solaris* 1972, *Mirror* 1975, *Stalker* 1979, and *The Sacrifice* 1986.
Suggested reading
Tarkovsky, Andrey *Time Within Time: The Diaries, 1970–86* (trs 1991)
Turovskaya, Maya *Tarkovsky: Cinema as Poetry* (1989)

Tarleton Richard (died 1588). Elizabethan theatrical clown. He was the most celebrated clown of his time. A member of the Queen's Men theatre company from 1583, he was renowned for the jig, a doggerel song-and-dance routine, and for his extempore humour, which influenced some of the characters in Shakespeare's plays.

Tarquinius Superbus (Tarquin the Proud) (lived 6th century BC). Last king of Rome 534–510 BC. He abolished certain rights of Romans, and made the city powerful. According to legend, he was deposed when his son Sextus raped Lucretia.

Tartaglia adopted name of Niccolò Fontana (*c.* 1499–1557). Italian Renaissance mathematician and physicist who specialized in military problems, topography, and mechanical physics.

Tartaglia was born in Brescia, Lombardy. He was called Tartaglia ('stammerer') because of a speech defect resulting from a wound caused by French soldiers sacking the town when he was 12. Although self-educated, he taught in Verona 1516–33. He then moved to Venice, where he eventually became professor of mathematics.

Tartaglia solved the problems of calculating the volume of a tetrahedron from the length of its sides, and of inscribing within a triangle three circles tangent to one another.

He delighted in planning the disposition of artillery, surveying the topography in relation to the best means of defence, and in designing fortifications. He also attempted a study of the motion of projectiles, and formulated Tartaglia's theorem: the trajectory of a projectile is a curved line everywhere, and the maximum range at any speed of its projection is obtained with a firing elevation of 45°.

When Tartaglia translated Euclid's *Elements* into Italian 1543, it was the first translation of Euclid into a contemporary European language.

Tartini Giuseppe (1692–1770). Italian composer and violinist. In 1728 he founded a school of violin playing in Padua. A leading exponent of violin technique, he composed numerous sonatas and concertos for strings, including the *Devil's Trill* sonata, about 1714.

Tasman Abel Janszoon (*c.* 1603–1659). Dutch navigator. In 1642, he was the first European to see Tasmania. He also made the first European sightings of New Zealand, Tonga, and Fiji. He called Tasmania Van Diemen's Land in honour of the governor-general of the Netherlands Indies; it was subsequently renamed in his honour 1856.

Tasso Torquato (1544–1595). Italian poet. He was the author of the romantic epic poem of the First Crusade *Gerusalemme liberata/Jerusalem Delivered* 1574, followed by the *Gerusalemme conquistata/Jerusalem Conquered*, written during the period from 1576 when he was mentally unstable.

At first a law student at Padua, he overcame his father's opposition to a literary career by the success of his romantic poem *Rinaldo* 1562, dedicated to Cardinal Luigi d'Este, who took him to Paris. There he met the members of the *Pléiade* group of poets. Under the patronage of Duke Alfonso d'Este of Ferrara, he wrote his pastoral play *Aminta* 1573.

Tate Jeffrey Philip (1943–). English conductor. He was appointed chief conductor and artistic director of the Rotterdam Philharmonic Orchestra 1991. He assisted at Covent Garden, London 1970–77 and under Boulez at Bayreuth, S Germany 1976 before making a remarkable operatic debut at the New York Metropolitan Opera 1980 with Berg's expressionist masterpiece *Lulu*.

Principal conductor of the English Chamber Orchestra 1985, principal conductor of the Royal Opera House, Covent Garden, London, 1986–91, and principal guest conductor since 1991, he has specialized in Mozart symphonies and piano concertos, the latter with his wife Mitsuko Uchida as soloist.

Tate Nahum (1652–1715). Irish poet. He wrote an adaptation of Shakespeare's *King Lear* with a happy ending. He also produced a version of the psalms and hymns; among his poems is 'While shepherds watched'. He became British poet laureate 1692.

Tate Phyllis Margaret Duncan (1911–1987). British composer. Her works include concerto for saxophone and strings 1944, the opera *The Lodger* 1960, based on the story of Jack the Ripper, and *Serenade to Christmas* for soprano, chorus, and orchestra 1972.

Tati Jacques. Stage name of Jacques Tatischeff (1908–1982). French comic actor, director, and writer. He portrayed Monsieur Hulot, the embodiment of polite opposition to modern mechanization, in a series of films beginning with *Les Vacances de M Hulot/Monsieur Hulot's Holiday* 1953, and including *Mon Oncle/My Uncle* 1959 and *Playtime* 1968.
Suggested reading
Gilliatt, Penelope *Jacques Tati* (1976)
Maddock, Brent *The Films of Jacques Tati* (1977)

Tatlin Vladimir Yevgrafovich (1885–1953). Russian artist. He was a cofounder of Constructivism. After encountering Cubism in Paris 1913 he evolved his first Constructivist works, using raw materials such as tin, glass, plaster, and wood to create abstract sculptures that he suspended in the air. He worked as a stage designer 1933–52.

Although unbuilt, his design for a monument to the Third International 1919 came to symbolize the Constructivist style: a large, openwork, spiralling tower of glass and painted steel, with geometric shapes revolving within its central core.

Tatum Art(hur) (1910–1956). US jazz pianist. He is considered among the most technically brilliant of jazz pianists and his technique and chromatic harmonies influenced many musicians, such as Oscar Peterson (1925–). He worked mainly as a soloist in the 1930s and improvised with the guitarist Tiny Grimes (1916–) in a trio from 1943.

Tatum Edward Lawrie (1909–1975). US microbiologist. For his work on biochemical genetics, he shared the 1958 Nobel Prize for Physiology or Medicine with his co-workers George Beadle and Joshua Lederberg.

He worked with Beadle at Stanford 1937–41 and with Lederberg at Yale, where he became professor 1946. He ended his career at the Rockefeller Institute for Medical Research from 1957.

Beadle and Tatum used X-rays to cause mutations in bread mould, studying particularly the changes in the enzymes of the various mutant strains. This led them to conclude that for each enzyme there is a corresponding gene. From 1945, with Lederberg, Tatum applied the same technique to bacteria and showed that genetic information can be passed from one bacterium to another. The discovery that a form of sexual reproduction can occur in bacteria led to extensive use of these organisms in genetic research.

Taube Henry (1915–). US chemist who established the basis of inorganic chemistry through his study of the loss or gain of electrons by atoms during chemical reactions. He was awarded a Nobel prize 1983 for his work on electron transference between molecules in chemical reactions.

Taussig Helen Brooke (1898–1986). US cardiologist who developed surgery for 'blue' babies. Such babies never fully develop the shunting mechanism in the circulatory system that allows blood to be oxygenated in the lungs before passing to the rest of the body. The babies are born chronically short of oxygen and usually do not survive without surgery.

Tavener John Kenneth (1944–). English composer. He has written austere vocal works including the dramatic cantata *The Whale* 1968 and the opera *Thérèse* 1979. *The Protecting Veil*, composed 1987 for cello and strings alone, became a best-selling classical recording.

Tavener draws on Eastern European idioms and Orthodox Christian traditions; he described his chamber opera *Mary of Egypt* 1991, premiered at Aldeburgh Music Festival 1992, as 'a moving icon'.

Taverner John (*c.* 1495–1545). English organist and composer. He wrote masses and motets in polyphonic style, showing great contrapuntal skill, but as a Protestant renounced his art. He was imprisoned 1528 for heresy, and, as an agent of Thomas Cromwell, assisted in the dissolution of the monasteries.
Suggested reading
Josephson, David *John Taverner* (1979)
Wulstan, David *Tudor Music* (1985)

Taylor, Elizabeth Elizabeth Taylor in the title role of the 1963 film *Cleopatra*.

Tawney Richard Henry (1880–1962). English economic historian and social critic and reformer. He had a great influence on the Labour Party, especially during the 1930s, although he never became an MP. His *Labour and the Nation* was the party's manifesto for the 1931 general election.

After leaving Oxford University, he taught for the Workers' Educational Association while working on *The Agrarian Problem in the 16th Century* 1912. He helped found the Economic History Society 1926 and became the joint editor of its journal, the *Economic History Review*.

As a committed Christian, Tawney based his socialism on moral values. His classic *Religion and the Rise of Capitalism* 1926 examined morals and economic practice in England 1588–1640, his special period. One of his most widely read books is *The Acquisitive Society* 1921 (later abridged as *Labour and the Nation*), in which he criticized capitalism because it encourages acquisitiveness and so corrupts everyone. In *Equality* 1931, he argued for urgent improvements in social services to deal with some of the glaring inequities of the class system.

Taylor A(lan) J(ohn) P(ercivale) (1906–1990). English historian and television lecturer. His books include *The Struggle for Mastery in Europe 1848–1918* 1954, *The Origins of the Second World War* 1961, and *English History 1914–1945* 1965.

Taylor lectured at Manchester University 1930–38 and was a fellow of Magdalen College, Oxford, 1938–76. International history lecturer at Oxford University 1953–63, he established himself as an authority on modern British and European history and did much to popularize the subject, giving the first televised history lectures.
Suggested reading
Sisman, Adam *A J P Taylor: A Biography* (1994)
Taylor, A J P *Letters to Eva, 1969–83* (1991)
Taylor, A J P *A Personal History* (1983)

Taylor C(ecil) P(hilip) (1929–1981). Scottish dramatist. His stage plays include *Bread and Butter* 1966, *And a Nightingale Sang...* 1979, and *Good* 1981, a study of intellectual complicity in Nazi Germany. His work was first produced by the Traverse Theatre in Edinburgh; he also wrote extensively for television and radio.

Taylor Elizabeth (born Coles) (1912–1975). English novelist. Her books include *At Mrs Lippincote's* 1946 and *Angel* 1957. She is a shrewd observer of nuances of character and emotion.

Some of my best leading men have been dogs and horses.

ELIZABETH TAYLOR
in *The Times* 18 Feb 1981

Taylor Elizabeth Rosemond (1932–). English-born US actress. She graduated from juvenile leads to dramatic roles, becoming one of the most glamorous stars of the 1950s and 1960s. Her films include *National Velvet* 1944, *Cat on a Hot Tin Roof* 1958, *Butterfield 8* 1960 (Academy Award), *Cleopatra* 1963, and *Who's Afraid of Virginia Woolf?* 1966 (Academy Award). Her husbands have included the actors Michael Wilding (1912–1979) and Richard Burton (twice).
Suggested reading
Kelley, Kitty *Elizabeth Taylor: The Last Star* (1982)
Maddox, Brenda *Who's Afraid of Elizabeth Taylor* (1977)
Sheppard, Dick *Elizabeth* (1974)

Marriage is a great institution.

ELIZABETH TAYLOR
in *Film Yearbook* 1987

Taylor Frederick Winslow (1856–1915). US engineer and management consultant, the founder of scientific management. His ideas, published in *Principles of Scientific Management* 1911, were based on the breakdown of work to the simplest tasks, the separation of planning from execution of tasks, and the introduction of time-and-motion studies. His methods were clearly expressed in assembly-line factories, but have been criticized for degrading and alienating workers and producing managerial dictatorship.

Taylor Paul Belville (1930–). US choreographer and dancer. Among his works, which often display immense charm, musicality, and humour, are *Aureole* 1962 and *Esplanade* 1975. He danced with Merce Cunningham 1953–54 and Martha Graham 1958–62 before founding his own modern dance company 1954.

Taylor Robert (1714–1788). English Neo-Palladian architect and sculptor. He was immensely successful during his lifetime, although little of his work has survived. Stone Building in Lincoln's Inn Fields, London 1775, is the finest extant example. Knighted 1682.

Taylor Zachary (1784–1850). 12th president of the USA 1849–50. A veteran of the War of 1812 and a hero of the Mexican War (1846–48), he was nominated for the presidency by the Whigs in 1848 and was elected, but died less than one and a half years into his term. He was succeeded by Vice President Millard Fillmore.
Suggested reading
Bauer, K J *Zachary Taylor* (1985)
McKinley, S B and Bent, S *Old Rough and Ready* (1946)
Nichols, E J *Zach Taylor's Little Army* (1963)

Tchaikovsky Pyotr Il'yich (1840–1893). Russian composer. His strong sense of melody, personal expression, and brilliant orchestration are clear throughout his many Romantic works, which include six symphonies, three piano concertos, a violin concerto, operas (for example, *Eugene Onegin* 1879), ballets (for example, *The Nutcracker* 1891–92), orchestral fantasies (for example, *Romeo and Juliet* 1870), and chamber and vocal music.

Professor of harmony at Moscow 1865, he later met Balakirev, becoming involved with the nationalist movement in music. He was the first Russian composer to establish a reputation with Western audiences.
Suggested reading
Brown, David *Tchaikovsky Remembered* (reminiscences and
    contemporary documents) (1993)
Evans, E *Tchaikovsky* (1966)
Strutte, Wilson *Tchaikovsky: His Life and Times* (1978)
Volkoff, Vladimir *Tchaikovsky* (1975)

Teague Walter Dorwin (1883–1960). US industrial designer. Active in New York, he was a pioneer of industrial design in the 1930s. His first client was Eastman Kodak and he is best known for his redesign of Kodak's 'Box Brownie' camera 1934 and his remodelling of Texaco's gas stations at the end of the decade, both in the popular 'streamline' style of the day.

He is often called the 'Dean of industrial design', implying his leadership in the field. He chaired the Board of Design for the New York World's Fair 1939.

Tebaldi Renata (1922–). Italian dramatic soprano. She was renowned for the nobility and warmth of her voice in Puccini operas.

Tebbit Norman Beresford, Baron Tebbit (1931–). British Conservative politician. His first career was as an airline pilot, when he held various trade-union posts. He was minister for employment 1981–83, minister for trade and industry 1983–85, chancellor of the Duchy of Lancaster 1985–87, and chair of the party 1985–87. As his relations with Margaret Thatcher cooled, he returned to the back benches 1987. He was injured in a bomb blast during the 1984 Conservative Party conference in Brighton, East Sussex. Created a life peer 1992.

Tebbutt John (1834–1916). Australian astronomer who made detailed observations of the orbits of comets and minor planets over a 50-year period, beginning in 1854, from an observatory he built at his home in Windsor, near Sydney. He published more than 300 scientific papers and was the first person to see the 'Great Comet' of 1861 (later named Tebbutt's comet).

Tecumseh (1768–1813). North American Indian chief of the Shawnee. He attempted to unite the Indian peoples from Canada to Florida against the encroachment of white settlers, but the defeat of

Tchaikovsky *The composer Pyotr Tchaikovsky in a drawing by W I Bruckman. Although he distanced himself from Balakirev's circle of nationalist composers, Tchaikovsky's love of his country and its folk song ensured that a Russian flavour remained.* (Image Select)

his brother Tenskwatawa, 'the Prophet', at the battle of Tippecanoe in Nov 1811 by W H Harrison, governor of the Indiana Territory, largely destroyed the confederacy built up by Tecumseh. He was commissioned a brigadier general in the British army during the War of 1812, and died in battle.
Suggested reading
Drake, B *Life and Times of Tecumseh and His Brother* (1841, rep
    1969)
Edmunds, R D *Tecumseh and the Quest for Indian Leadership* (1984)
Klinck, C F *Tecumseh: Fact and Fiction in Early Records* (1961)
Sugden, J *Tecumseh's Last Stand* (1985)

Tedder Arthur William, 1st Baron Tedder (1890–1967). UK marshal of the Royal Air Force in World War II. He was air officer commanding RAF Middle East 1941–43, where his method of pattern bombing became known as 'Tedder's carpet'. As deputy supreme commander under US general Eisenhower 1943–45, he was largely responsible for the initial success of the 1944 Normandy landings. KCB 1942, baron 1946.

Teilhard de Chardin Pierre (1881–1955). French Jesuit theologian, palaeontologist, and philosopher. He developed a creative synthesis of nature and religion, based on his fieldwork and fossil studies. Publication of his *Le Phénomène humain/The Phenomenon of Man*, written 1938–40, was delayed (owing to his unorthodox views) until after his death by the embargo of his superiors. He saw humanity as being in a constant process of evolution, moving towards a perfect spiritual state.

He was born in the Puy-de-Dôme; he entered the Society of Jesus 1899, was ordained 1911, and during World War I was a stretcher bearer, taking his final vows 1918. From 1951 until his death he lived in the USA.

Suggested reading
De Lubac, Henri *Teilhard de Chardin: The Man and His Meaning* (1965)
King, T M *Teilhard de Chardin* (1988)
Speaight, Robert *Teilhard de Chardin: A Biography* (1967)

Tej Bahadur (1621–1675). Indian religious leader, ninth guru (teacher) of Sikhism 1664–75, executed for refusing to renounce his faith.

Te Kanawa Kiri Janette (1944–   ). New Zealand soprano. Te Kanawa's first major role was the Countess in Mozart's *The Marriage of Figaro* at Covent Garden, London, 1971. Her voice combines the purity and intensity of the upper range with an extended lower range of great richness and resonance. Apart from classical roles, she has also featured popular music in her repertoire, such as the 1984 recording of Leonard Bernstein's *West Side Story*. DBE 1982.

I have always aimed at facility. Music ought not to be an effort.

TELEMANN
quoted in C Headington The Bodley Head History of Western Music 1974

Telemann Georg Philipp (1681–1767). German Baroque composer, organist, and conductor. He conducted at the Johanneum, Hamburg, from 1721. His prolific output of concertos for both new and old instruments, including violin, viola da gamba, recorder, flute, oboe, trumpet, horn, and bassoon, represent a methodical and fastid-

Te Kanawa *Her glowing mezzo-soprano, graduating to soprano, gives an impression of sustained physical and emotional power. Drawing on the rich vocal traditions of her native New Zealand, Kiri Te Kanawa brings dignity and intelligence to both lyric and passionate operatic roles.*

ious investigation into the tonal resonances and structure of the new Baroque orchestra, research noted by J S Bach. Other works include 25 operas, numerous sacred cantatas, and instrumental fantasias.

Suggested reading
Anderson, Nicholas *Baroque Music: From Monteverdi to Handel* (1994)
Petzholdt, R *Georg Philipp Telemann* (trs 1974)

Telford Thomas (1757–1834). Scottish civil engineer who opened up N Scotland by building roads and waterways. He constructed many aqueducts and canals, including the Caledonian canal 1802–23, and erected the Menai road suspension bridge 1819–26, a type of structure scarcely tried previously in England. In Scotland he constructed over 1,600 km/1,000 mi of road and 1,200 bridges, churches, and harbours.

Telford was born in Westerkirk, Dumfries, and began as a stonemason. Moving to London, he found employment building additions to Somerset House in the Strand under the supervision of architect William Chambers. Recognizing his talents, the rich and famous were soon consulting him about their own buildings.

In 1786, Telford was appointed official surveyor to the county of Shropshire. There he built three bridges over the river Severn, among other structures. He also rebuilt many Roman roads to meet the need for faster travel.

As engineer to the Ellesmere Canal Company from 1793, Telford was responsible for the building of aqueducts over the Ceirog and Dee valleys in Wales, using a new method of construction consisting of troughs made from cast-iron plates and fixed in masonry. In 1963 the new town of Telford, Shropshire, 32 km/20 mi NW of Birmingham, was named after him.

Suggested reading
Pearce, R M *Thomas Telford* (1973)
Penfold, A (ed) *Thomas Telford: Engineer* (1980)
Rolt, L T C *Thomas Telford* (1958)

Teller Edward (1908–   ). Hungarian-born US physicist known as the father of the hydrogen bomb. He worked on the fission bomb – the first atomic bomb – 1942–46 (the Manhattan Project) and on the fusion bomb, or H-bomb, 1946–52. In the 1980s he was one of the leading supporters of the Star Wars programme (Strategic Defense Initiative).

Teller was born in Budapest and studied there and at various German universities. He left Germany 1933 when the Nazis came to power, and emigrated to the USA 1935, becoming professor at George Washington University, Washington DC. He joined the University of Chicago 1942 to work on atomic fission, and then moved to Los Alamos. By the end of World War II, Teller had designed an H-bomb, and in 1951 he was given responsibility for constructing one. It was successfully tested on Eniwetok Atoll in the Pacific Ocean in 1952. By then, a second nuclear-weapons research facility had opened, the Lawrence-Livermore Laboratory near Berkeley, California. Teller was Livermore's associate director 1954–75, as well as professor at the University of California from 1953.

The original idea of using a fission explosion to ignite a thermonuclear (fusion) explosion in deuterium (heavy hydrogen) came from Italian-born physicist Enrico Fermi. Polish-born mathematician Stanislaw Ulam (1909–1985) then suggested a configuration in which shock waves from the fission explosion would compress and heat the deuterium, causing it to explode. Teller modified this idea to use X-rays from the first explosion, rather than shock waves.

Temin Howard Martin (1934–1994). US virologist concerned with cancer research. For his work on the genetic inheritance of viral elements he shared the 1975 Nobel Prize for Physiology or Medicine with David Baltimore (1938–   ) and Renato Dulbecco (1914–   ). From 1960 he worked at the University of Wisconsin, becoming professor 1969.

Temin's prizewinning research was on a virus that has a mechanism which incorporates its material into mammalian genes. He discovered that beneficial mutations outside the germ line are naturally selected and that the mechanism adds genetic information from outside into the germ line.

I stopped believing in Santa Claus at an early age.
Mother took me to see him in a department store, and he
asked me for my autograph.

SHIRLEY TEMPLE
Comment by the child-star in adult life, quoted
in Leslie Halliwall *Filmgoer's Companion* 1965

Temple Shirley (1928–   ). US actress. She became the most successful child star of the 1930s. Her films include *Bright Eyes* 1934 (Academy Award), in which she sang 'On the Good Ship Lollipop', *Curly Top* 1935, and *Rebecca of Sunnybrook Farm* 1938. Her film career virtually ended by the time she reached adolescence. As Shirley Temple Black, she became active in the Republican Party and was US chief of protocol 1976–77. She was appointed US ambassador to Czechoslovakia 1989.

Temple William (1881–1944). English church leader, archbishop of Canterbury 1942–44. He was a major ecumenical figure who strove to achieve church unity. His theological writings constantly sought to apply Christian teachings to contemporary social conditions, as in his *Christianity and the Social Order* 1942.

Templer Gerald Walter Robert (1898–1979). British field marshal. He served in both world wars, but is especially remembered for his work as high commissioner in Malaysia 1952–54, during the period of fighting against communist insurgents. KBE 1949.

Tench Watkin (c. 1759–1833). English-born military officer and author in Australia. He arrived in New South Wales with the First Fleet in command of a detachment of marines. While in the colony he discovered the Nepean River and recorded the life of the settlement in a daily journal. This was published in two volumes *Narrative of the Expedition to Botany Bay, with an Account of New South Wales* and *Complete Account of the Settlement at Port Jackson* 1793.

Teng Hsiao-ping alternative spelling of ◊Deng Xiaoping, Chinese politician.

Teniers family of Flemish painters, active in Antwerp. David Teniers the Younger (David II, 1610–1690) became court painter to Archduke Leopold Wilhelm, governor of the Netherlands, in Brussels. He painted humorous scenes of peasant life, full of vitality, inspired by Brouwer. As curator of the archduke's art collection, he made many copies of the pictures and a collection of engravings, *Theatrum Pictorium* 1660. His father, David Teniers the Elder (David I, 1582–1649), painted religious pictures.

Tennant Kylie (1912–1988). Australian novelist and biographer. Her novels include *Tiburon* 1935, set in rural New South Wales and showing the narrow-mindedness of small-town life, *The Battlers* 1941, about the struggles of a band of unemployed itinerants, and *All the Proud Tribesmen* 1959, winner of the 1960 Children's Book Award. She was made an AO in 1980.

Tenniel John (1820–1914). English illustrator and cartoonist. He joined the satirical magazine *Punch* 1850, and for over 50 years was one of its leading cartoonists. He is known for his illustrations for Lewis Carroll's *Alice's Adventures in Wonderland* 1865 and *Through the Looking-Glass* 1872. Knighted 1893.

Tennstedt Klaus (1926–   ). German conductor. A noted interpreter of Mozart, Beethoven, Bruckner, and Mahler, he was musical director of the London Philharmonic Orchestra 1983–87.

Alfred is always carrying a bit of chaos around with him
and turning it into cosmos.

Thomas Carlyle on ALFRED TENNYSON
quoted in J L Lowes *Convention and Revolt in Poetry* 1930

Tennyson Alfred, 1st Baron Tennyson (1809–1892). English poet. Tennyson was born at Somersby, Lincolnshire. He was poet laureate 1850–92. His verse has a majestic, musical quality. His works include 'The Lady of Shalott', 'The Lotus Eaters', 'Ulysses', 'Break, Break, Break', 'The Charge of the Light Brigade'; the longer narratives *Locksley Hall* 1832 and *Maud* 1855; the elegy *In Memoriam* 1850; and a long series of poems on the Arthurian legends *The Idylls of the King* 1857–85.

The death of A H Hallam (a close friend during his years at Cambridge) 1833 prompted the elegiac *In Memoriam*, unpublished until 1850, the year in which he succeeded Wordsworth as poet laureate and married Emily Sellwood. Baron 1884.

Suggested reading
Albright, D *Tennyson: The Muses Tug-of-War* (1987)
Martin, R B *Tennyson: The Unquiet Heart* (1980)
Ricks, C *Tennyson* (1972)

Tenzing Norgay known as Sherpa Tenzing (1914–1986). Nepalese mountaineer. In 1953 he was the first, with Edmund Hillary, to reach the summit of Mount Everest. He had previously made 19 Himalayan expeditions as a porter. He subsequently became a director of the Himalayan Mountaineering Institute, Darjeeling.

Terauchi Count Hisaichi (1879–1945). Japanese field marshal in World War II; commander of the Southern Army from Sept 1941 to the end of the war, with headquarters in Saigon. He was not a strategist and frequently persisted in reinforcing operations which had no chance of success. Totally indifferent to human life, he sacrificed his troops and wasted no sympathy on prisoners. He was responsible for building the Burma railway, in which 17,000 prisoners of war died. He died from a stroke Sept 1945.

Terborch Gerard (1617–1681). Dutch painter. His works are small-scale portraits and genre scenes, mainly of soldiers at rest or wealthy families in their homes. He travelled widely in Europe. *The Peace of Münster* 1648 (National Gallery, London) is an official group portrait.

Terbrugghen Hendrick (1588–1629). Dutch painter. He was a leader of the Utrecht School with Honthorst. He visited Rome around 1604 and was one of the first northern artists to be inspired by the works of Caravaggio. He painted religious subjects and genre scenes.

Fortune favours the brave.

TERENCE
Phormio 203

Terence (Publius Terentius Afer) (c. 190–c. 159 BC). Roman dramatist. Born in Carthage, he was taken as a slave to Rome where he was freed and came under the patronage of the Roman general Scipio Africanus Minor. His surviving six comedies (including *The Eunuch* 161 BC) are subtly characterized and based on Greek models. They were widely read and performed during the Middle Ages and the Renaissance.

Teresa Mother (born Agnes Gonxha Bojaxhiu) (1910–   ). Roman Catholic nun. She was born in Skopje, Macedonia, and at 18 entered a Calcutta convent and became a teacher. In 1948 she became an Indian citizen and founded the Missionaries of Charity, an order for men and women based in Calcutta that helps abandoned children and the dying. She was awarded the Nobel Peace Prize 1979.

Teresa, St (1515–1582). Spanish mystic who founded an order of nuns 1562. She was subject to fainting fits, during which she saw visions. She wrote *The Way to Perfection* 1583 and an autobiography, *Life of the Mother Teresa of Jesus*, 1611. In 1622 she was canonized, and in 1970 was made the first female Doctor of the Church. She was born in Avila.

Tereshkova Valentina Vladimirovna (1937–   ). Soviet cosmonaut, the first woman to fly in space. In June 1963 she made a three-day flight in *Vostok 6*, orbiting the Earth 48 times. *See illustration on page 840.*

Terragni Giuseppe (1904–1942). Italian architect. He was largely responsible for introducing the Modern Movement to Italy. As a

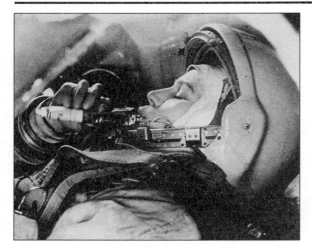

Tereshkova *Russian cosmonaut and first woman in space Valentina Tereshkova, shown in the command module of* Vostok 6. *During her historic flight she made 48 orbits of the Earth with a total duration of nearly 71 hours.* (Ann Ronan/Image Select)

leading member of Gruppo 7, he advocated a return to the principles of Rationalism, inciting widespread opposition from the orthodox architectural establishment. Notable among his designs are the Novecomum block of flats, Como, 1927, and his masterpiece, the Casa del Fascio, Como, 1932–36, a crystalline white cube, devoid of ornament but clearly exhibiting its structure.

Terry Alfred Howe (1827–1890). US military leader. Terry was born in Hartford, Connecticut, educated at Yale University, and became a barrister 1849. He served with distinction in the American Civil War 1861–65. During the Civil War he was colonel of the 2nd Connecticut militia and was promoted to brigadier general 1865. After the war he commanded the Department of Dakota and also served in the Department of the South 1869–72. He was George Custer's commander in the 1876 Sioux War and later negotiated with Sitting Bull, supervising the opening of the Northern Plains.

Terry (Alice) Ellen (1847–1928). English actress. She was leading lady to Henry Irving from 1878. She excelled in Shakespearean roles, such as Ophelia in *Hamlet*. She was a correspondent of long-standing with the dramatist G B Shaw. GBE 1925.

Terry (John) Quinlan (1937–). English Post-Modernist architect. He works in a Neo-Classical idiom. His projects include country houses, for example Merks Hall, Great Dunmow, Essex, 1982, and the larger-scale riverside project at Richmond, London, commissioned 1984.

Terry-Thomas stage name of Thomas Terry Hoar Stevens (1911–1990). English film comedy actor. He portrayed upper-class English fools and cads in such films as *I'm All Right Jack* 1959, *It's a Mad, Mad, Mad, Mad World* 1963, and *How to Murder Your Wife* 1965.

Tertullian Quintus Septimius Florens (*c.* AD 155–*c.* 222). Carthaginian theologian, one of the so-called Fathers of the Church and the first major Christian writer in Latin. He became a leading exponent of Montanism.

Tesla Nikola (1856–1943). Croatian-born US physicist and electrical engineer who invented fluorescent lighting, the Tesla induction motor 1882–87, and the Tesla coil, and developed the alternating current (AC) electrical supply system.

The Tesla coil is an air core transformer with the primary and secondary windings tuned in resonance to produce high-frequency, high-voltage electricity. Using this device, Tesla produced an electric spark 40 m/135 ft long in 1899. He also lit more than 200 lamps over a distance of 40 km/25 mi without the use of intervening wires. Gas-filled tubes are readily energized by high-frequency currents and so lights of this type were easily operated within the field of a large Tesla coil. Tesla soon developed all manner of coils which have since found numerous applications in electrical and electronic devices.

He emigrated to the USA 1884, and from 1888 was associated with industrialist George Westinghouse, who bought and successfully exploited Tesla's patents, leading to the introduction of alternating current for power transmission. Tesla neglected to patent many of his discoveries and made little profit from them.

Tesla was very interested in the possibility of radio communication and as early as 1897 he demonstrated remote control of two model boats on a pond. He extended this to guided weapons, in particular a remote-control torpedo. In 1900 he began to construct a broadcasting station on Long Island, New York, in the hope of developing 'World Wireless', but lost his funding. He also outlined a scheme for detecting ships at sea, which was later developed as radar. One of his most ambitious ideas was to transmit electricity to anywhere in the world without wires by using the Earth itself as an enormous oscillator.

Tetley Glen (1926–). US choreographer and dancer. He was the first choreographer to attempt the blending of ballet with modern dance idioms without strict adherence to the conventions of either, as in his first major work, *Pierrot lunaire* 1962, set to Schoenberg. Closely associated with the Netherlands Dance Theatre throughout the 1960s, he became director of the Stuttgart Ballet 1974–76, and often worked with the Ballet Rambert, as with his *The Tempest* 1979.

Terry, Ellen *British actress Dame Ellen Terry, who played Mamilius in* The Winter's Tale *at the age of eight. She went on to become the leading Shakespearean actress of her time and had roles written for her by both George Bernard Shaw and James Barrie.*

In 1986, he staged *Alice*, based on Lewis Carroll's Wonderland stories, for the National Ballet of Canada, subsequently becoming the company's associate artistic adviser 1987.

As a dancer, Tetley performed with Martha Graham 1957–59; the American Ballet Theater 1960; and Robbins' company Ballets: USA 1961. His ballets include *The Anatomy Lesson* 1964, *Mutations* 1970 (with Hans van Manen), and *Summer's End* 1980.

I've never had a gramophone; I never had a picture of myself in my life.

MAGGIE TEYTE
BBC broadcast 1959

Teyte Maggie (Margaret) (1888–1976). English lyric soprano. She brought a French intimacy of style to her Mozartian roles, such as Cherubino in *The Marriage of Figaro*, and was coached as Mélisande in *Pelléas et Mélisande* by the opera's composer, Debussy. DBE 1958.

Yes, I am a fatal man, Madame Fribsbi. To inspire hopeless passion is my destiny.

WILLIAM MAKEPEACE THACKERAY
Pendennis ch 23 1848

Thackeray William Makepeace (1811–1863). English novelist and essayist. The son of an East India Company official, he was educated at Cambridge. He studied law, and then art in Paris, before ultimately becoming a journalist in London. He was a regular contributor to *Fraser's Magazine* and *Punch*. His first novel was *Vanity Fair* 1847–48, followed by *Pendennis* 1848, *Henry Esmond* 1852 (and its sequel *The Virginians* 1857–59), and *The Newcomes* 1853–55, in which Thackeray's tendency to sentimentality is most marked. Other works include *The Book of Snobs* 1848 and the fairy tale *The Rose and the Ring* 1855.

Suggested reading
Carey, John *Thackeray* (1977)
Ennis, Lambert *Thackeray: The Sentimental Cynic* (1950)
Ray, Gordon N *Thackeray: The Uses of Adversity, 1811–1846* (1955)
Ray, Gordon N *Thackeray: The Age of Wisdom, 1847–1863* (1958)
Sutherland, John *Thackeray at Work* (1974)

The women of Alexander inflicted a greater punishment on the Persians on behalf of Greece than all her famous commanders.

THAÏS
Comment after recommending the burning of the Persian
palace. Quoted in Plutarch *Life of Alexander* ch 38.4

Thaïs (lived 4th century BC). Greek courtesan, mistress of Alexander the Great and later wife of Ptolemy I, king of Egypt. She allegedly instigated the burning of Persepolis.

Thalberg Irving Grant (1899–1936). US film-production executive. Born in Brooklyn, New York, Thalberg was hired 1918 as assistant to Carl Laemmle, president of Universal Pictures Corporation in New York. Having moved to Hollywood 1919, Thalberg, 'the boy genius,' was named head of the studio 1923, and in 1924 he became production supervisor of the newly formed Metro-Goldwyn-Mayer (MGM). He was responsible for such prestige films as *Ben Hur* 1926 and *Mutiny on the Bounty* 1935. With Louis B Mayer, he built up MGM into one of the biggest Hollywood studios of the 1930s.

Thales (*c.* 624–*c.* 547 BC). Greek philosopher and scientist. He made advances in geometry, predicted an eclipse of the Sun 585 BC, and, as a philosophical materialist, theorized that water was the first principle of all things. He speculated that the Earth floated on water, and so proposed an explanation for earthquakes. He lived in Miletus in Asia Minor.

Thales explained such events as earthquakes in terms of natural phenomena, rather than in the usual terms of activity by the gods. Aristotle records that, when he was reproached for being impractical, Thales, having predicted that weather conditions the next year would be conducive to a large olive harvest, bought up all the olive presses in Miletus and exploited his monopoly to make a large profit.

In five fundamental propositions Thales laid down the foundations on which classical geometry was raised. (1) A circle is bisected by its diameter. (2) In an isosceles triangle the two angles opposite the equal sides are themselves equal to each other. (3) When two straight lines intersect, four angles are produced, the opposite ones being equal. (4) The angle in a semicircle is a right angle. (5) Two triangles are congruent if they have two angles and one side that are respectively equal to each other. He is also said to have introduced the notion of proof by the deductive method.

Asked why he had no children he replied 'Because I love children'.

THALES
Remark attributed to Thales in Diogenes
Laertius *Lives of the Philosophers* bk 1, ch 26

Thant, U (1909–1974). Burmese diplomat, secretary general of the United Nations 1962–71. He helped to resolve the US-Soviet crisis over the Soviet installation of missiles in Cuba, and he made the controversial decision to withdraw the UN peacekeeping force from the Egypt–Israel border 1967.

Tharp Twyla (1941–). US modern-dance choreographer and dancer. A phenomenal success in the 1970s, Tharp's work both entertains and challenges audiences with her ability to create serious and beautifully constructed ballets with an often amusing or flippant veneer. Reflecting her eclectic training, she has fused many dance styles including ballet, jazz, modern, tap, and avant-garde dance. Her works, frequently set to popular music, include *Eight Jelly Rolls* 1971, *Deuce Coupe* 1973 (music by the Beach Boys), and *Push Comes to Shove* 1976 with Mikhail Baryshnikov, which was one of the most popular works of the decade.

In the 1980s Tharp focused on integrating emotional content into dance, as in *The Catherine Wheel* 1983, set to music by David Byrne (of Talking Heads), in which members of an archetypal American family are pitted against one another in an emotional battleground. She has been instrumental in preserving the classical technique within the framework of modern dance.

If Margaret Thatcher wins on Thursday, I warn you not to be ordinary, I warn you not to be young, I warn you not to fall ill, and I warn you not to grow old.

Neil Kinnock on MARGARET THATCHER
Speech at Bridgend 7 June 1983

Thatcher Margaret Hilda (born Roberts), Baroness Thatcher (1925–). British Conservative politician, prime minister 1979–90. Margaret Thatcher was born in Grantham, the daughter of a grocer, and studied chemistry at Oxford before becoming a barrister. As minister for education 1970–74 she faced criticism for abolishing free milk for schoolchildren over eight. She was nevertheless an unexpected victor in the 1975 leadership election when she defeated Edward Heath. As prime minister she sharply reduced public spending to bring down inflation, but at the cost of generating a recession: manufacturing output fell by a fifth, and unemployment rose to over three million. Her popularity revived after her sending a naval force to recapture the Falkland Islands 1982. Her second term of office was marked by the miners' strike 1984–85, which ended in defeat for the miners and indicated a shifted balance of power away from the unions. In Oct 1984 she narrowly avoided an IRA bomb that exploded during the Conservative Party conference. Her election victory 1987 made her the first prime minister in 160 years to be elected for a third term, but she became increasingly isolated by her autocratic, aloof stance, which allowed little time for cabinet debate. An astute Parliamentary tactician, she tolerated little disagreement, either from the opposition or from within her own party. In 1986 defence minister Michael Heseltine resigned after supporting a European-led plan for the rescue of the Westland helicopter company. In 1989 Nigel Lawson resigned as chancellor when she publicly supported her financial adviser Alan Walters against him. The introduction of the poll tax from 1989 was widely unpopular. Finally, Geoffrey Howe resigned as home secretary in Nov 1990 over her public denial of an earlier cabinet consensus over the single European currency and she was forced to resign.

I am extraordinarily patient, provided I get my own way in the end.

MARGARET THATCHER
in *Observer* 4 Apr 1989

Thatcher was the most influential peacetime Conservative prime minister of the 20th century. She claimed to have 'rolled back the frontiers of the state' by reducing income-tax rates, selling off council houses, and allowing for greater individual choice in areas such as education. However, such initiatives often resulted paradoxically in greater central government control. She left the opposition Labour Party in disarray, and forced it to a fundamental review of its policies. Her vindictiveness against the left was revealed in her crusade against local councils, which she pursued at the cost of a concern for social equity. In 1991, after three months of relative quiescence on the back benches, she made it evident that she intended to remain an active voice in domestic and international politics. She was created a life peer 1992. Her first speech in the House of Lords was an attack on the government's policies.

Since leaving public office, she has devoted herself to the development of her individual philosophy through the 'Thatcher Foundation'.

Suggested reading
Harris, Kenneth *Thatcher* (1988)
Jenkins, Peter *Mrs Thatcher's Revolution* (1987)
Minogue, Kenneth and Biddiss, Michael *Thatcherism: Personality and Politics* (1987)
Thatcher, Margaret *The Downing Street Years* (memoirs) (1993)
Thatcher, Margaret *The Path to Power* (memoirs) (1995)
Young, Hugo *The Iron Lady* (1989)

Theiler Max (1899–1972). South African–born US microbiologist who developed an effective vaccine against yellow fever, which gained him the 1951 Nobel Prize for Physiology or Medicine. He also researched into various other diseases, including Weil's disease and poliomyelitis.

In 1922 he emigrated to the USA. From 1930 to 1964 he worked at the Rockefeller Institute for Medical Research (now Rockefeller University), New York City, becoming director of the Virus Laboratory there in 1950. He ended his career as professor at Yale.

Theiler used albino mice in his work on yellow fever, and eventually combined the mouse-adapted viral strain with serum from the blood of people who had recovered from yellow fever and injected the mixture into humans. This produced immunity without affecting the kidneys, and was the first safe vaccine against yellow fever.

However, human serum containing antibodies against yellow fever is difficult to obtain. Theiler therefore began culturing the virus in chick embryos, and in 1937 he developed vaccine 17-D, still the main form of protection against yellow fever.

When voting for the prize of bravery, everyone put his own name first but the majority agreed in putting Themistocles second ...

HERODOTUS on THEMISTOCLES
Adjudication of the prize for valour at Salamis, *History* bk 8, ch 123

Themistocles (c. 528–c. 462 BC). Athenian soldier and politician. Largely through his success in persuading the Athenians to build a navy, Greece was saved from Persian conquest. He fought with distinction in the Battle of Salamis 480 BC during the Persian War. About 470 he was accused of embezzlement and conspiracy against Athens, banished and fled to Asia, where Artaxerxes, the Persian king, received him with favour.

For I too am a clear voice of the Muses, and all call me the best of singers; but I am slow to credit them, truly I am.

THEOCRITUS
Remark of Simichidas, usually identified with Theocritus himself, *Idyll* 7: 37–9

Theocritus (c. 310–c. 250 BC). Greek poet. His *Idylls* became models for later pastoral poetry. Probably born in Syracuse, he spent much of his life in Alexandria under the Greek dynasty of the Ptolemies.

Theodora (c. 508–548). Byzantine empress from 527. The daughter of a bear-keeper, Theodora became an actress and she was originally the mistress of Emperor Justinian before marrying him in 525. She earned a reputation for charity, courage, and championing the rights of women. She was the most influential woman in Europe, since Justinian consulted her on all affairs of state.

Theodorakis Mikis (1925–). Greek composer. He was imprisoned 1967–70 for attempting to overthrow the military regime of Greece. His work includes oratorios, ballets, song cycles, and film scores, of which the best known is *Zorba the Greek*.

Theodoric of Freiburg (c. 1250–1310). German scientist and monk. He studied in Paris 1275–77. In his work *De iride/On the Rainbow* he describes how he used a water-filled sphere to simulate a raindrop, and determined that colours are formed in the raindrops and that light is reflected within the drop and can be reflected again, which explains secondary rainbows.

A poor Roman plays the Goth, a rich Goth the Roman.

Anonymous on THEODORIC THE GREAT
in *Valesianus* ch 12, 61

Theodoric the Great (c. 455–526). King of the Ostrogoths from 474 in succession to his father. He invaded Italy 488, overthrew King Odoacer (whom he murdered) and established his own Ostrogothic kingdom there, with its capital in Ravenna. He had no strong successor, and his kingdom eventually became part of the Byzantine Empire of Justinian.

Just as a ceaseless motion makes the sky go round, just as the seas are stirred up by the waves, and the sun does not know how to keep still, you are in ceaseless motion.

Pacatus on THEODOSIUS (I) THE GREAT
Panegyric of Theodosius 10.1

Theodosius (I) the Great (c. AD 346–395). Roman emperor. Appointed emperor of the East 379, he fought against the Goths successfully, and established Christianity throughout the region. He invaded Italy 393, restoring unity to the empire, and died in Milan. He was buried in Constantinople.

A pious Christian and adherent of the Nicene creed, he dealt severely with heretics, ordering the death penalty for some extreme sects. In 390 he ordered the massacre of 7,000 citizens of Thessalonica to avenge the killing of one of his generals, an act for which he did penance.

Theodosius II (401–450). Byzantine emperor from 408 who defeated the Persians 421 and 441, and from 441 bought off Attila's Huns with tribute.

It is not proper to compare a man, meaning Attila, with a god, meaning Theodosius.

Priscus on THEODOSIUS II
fragment 11.2; Blockley

Theon of Smyrna (lived *c.* AD 130). Greek astronomer and mathematician. In his celestial mechanics, the planets, Sun, Moon, and the sphere of fixed stars were all set at intervals congruent with an octave. His only surviving work, *Expositio rerum mathematicarum ad legendum Platoneum utilium*, is in two manuscripts, one on mathematics and one on astronomy and astrology.

Theon collated and organized discoveries made by his predecessors, and articulated the interrelationships between arithmetic, geometry, music, and astronomy. The section on mathematics deals with prime, geometrical, and other numbers in the Pythagorean pantheon; the section on music considers instrumental music, mathematical relations between musical intervals, and the harmony of the universe.

The astronomical section is by far the most important. Theon puts forward what was then known about conjunctions, eclipses, occultations, and transits. Other subjects covered include descriptions of eccentric and epicyclic orbits, and estimates of the greatest arcs of Mercury and Venus from the Sun.

At Novgorod Theophanes painted the well known monochrome figures over which the highlights scurry in eccentric, flickering brush strokes.

Kurt Weitzmann on THEOPHANES THE GREEK
in *The Icon* 1978

Theophanes the Greek (*c.* 1330–1405). Byzantine painter. Active in Russia, he influenced painting in Novgorod, where his frescoes in the church of Our Saviour of the Transfiguration are dated to 1378. He also worked in Moscow with Andrei Rublev. Another Theophanes of later date (16th century) was a leading artist of the Byzantine school of Crete which had flourished in its monasteries from the beginning of the 14th century.

Theophrastus (*c.* 372–*c.* 287 BC). Greek philosopher, regarded as the founder of botany. A pupil of Aristotle, Theophrastus took over the leadership of his school 323 BC, consolidating its reputation. Of his extensive writings, surviving work is mainly on scientific topics, but includes the *Characters*, a series of caricatures which may have influenced the comic dramatist Menander.

Theophrastus covered most aspects of botany: descriptions of plants, classification, plant distribution, propagation, germination, and cultivation. He distinguished between two main groups of flowering plants – dicotyledons and monocotyledons in modern terms – and between flowering plants and cone-bearing trees (angiosperms and gymnosperms).

Theophrastus was born on Lesvos but studied in Athens at the Academy, which he then headed until his death.

Theophrastus classified plants into trees, shrubs, undershrubs, and herbs. He described and discussed more than 500 species and varieties of plants from lands bordering the Atlantic and Mediterranean. He noted that some flowers bear petals whereas others do not, and observed the different relative positions of the petals and ovary. In his work on propagation and germination, Theophrastus described the various ways in which specific plants and trees can grow: from seeds, from roots, from pieces torn off, from a branch or twig, or from a small piece of cleft wood.

Theremin Leon (1896–1993). Russian inventor of the theremin 1922, a monophonic synthesizer, and of other valve-amplified instruments in the 1930s. Following commercial and public success in the USA and Hollywood, he returned to Russia 1938 to imprisonment and obscurity. After 1945 he continued acoustic research in Moscow and reappeared at a Stockholm electronic music symposium 1990.

The theremin was played without being touched by converting the operator's arm movements into musical tones. The instrument could produce a wide range of sounds and was used to make eerie sound effects for films. He also invented an electronic dance platform, called the terpsitone, in which a dancer's movements were converted into musical tones. Other inventions included a stringless electronic cello, the first syncopated rhythm machine, a colour television system, and a security system which was installed at Sing Sing and Alcatraz Prisons.

Theremin was educated as a physicist and musician. In 1922 he demonstrated his theremin to Lenin and was sent on a tour which included sell-out concerts in Berlin, Paris, London, and New York. He established a studio in New York, where he lived 1927–38. He was then ordered to return to the USSR and sent to a Siberian labour camp during the great Stalin purge. During World War II he worked in a military laboratory, producing a radio-controlled aircraft, tracking systems for ships and submarines, and television systems which are still in use. He also invented a miniature listening device, or 'bug', for the KGB. For this he received the Stalin Prize, first class, and was allowed to live in Moscow, where he became professor of acoustics at the Moscow Conservatory of Music. He was sacked and his laboratory closed when a chance encounter with a reporter from the *New York Times* resulted in a newspaper article which revealed his earlier imprisonment. He continued his acoustics research, and work aimed at reversing the ageing process, until he died.

Thérèse of Lisieux, St (born Thérèse Martin) (1873–1897). French saint. She was born in Alençon, and entered a Carmelite convent in Lisieux at 15, where her holy life induced her superior to ask her to write her spiritual autobiography. She advocated the 'Little Way of Goodness' in small things in everyday life, and became known as the 'Little Flower of Jesus'. She died of tuberculosis and was canonized 1925.

Writing is made with the fingers, and all writing, even the clumsy kind, exposes in its loops and slants a yearning deeper than an intention, the soul of the writer flapping on the clothes peg of his exclamation mark.

PAUL THEROUX
Saint Jack ch 1 1973

Theroux Paul Edward (1941–   ). US novelist and travel writer. His works include the novels *Saint Jack* 1973, *The Mosquito Coast* 1981, *Doctor Slaughter* 1984, and *Chicago Loop* 1990. His accounts of his travels by train, notable for their sharp depiction of the socio-economic divides, include *The Great Railway Bazaar* 1975, *The Old Patagonian Express* 1979, *The Kingdom by the Sea* 1983, and *Riding the Iron Rooster* 1988.

Therry John Joseph (1791–1864). Australian pioneer Roman Catholic priest, born in Ireland. In 1820 he was sent to the colony at his own request to minister to Irish convicts. In 1821 he laid the foundation stone for St Mary's Church, Sydney (where St Mary's Cathedral, consecrated 1870 now stands).

Thesiger Wilfred Patrick (1910–   ). English explorer and writer. His travels and military adventures in Abyssinia (now Ethiopia and Eritrea), North Africa, and Arabia are recounted in a number of books, including *Arabian Sands* 1959, *The Marsh Arabs* 1964, *Desert, Marsh and Mountain* 1979, and the autobiographical *The Life of My Choice* 1987 and *Kenya Days* 1994.

The inventor of tragedy.

THESPIS
commonly ascribed epithet

Thespis (lived 6th century BC). Greek poet. He is said to have introduced the first actor into dramatic performances (previously presented by choruses only), hence the word thespian for an actor.

He is also said to have invented tragedy and to have introduced the wearing of linen masks.

Thibault Jacques Anatole François. French writer who wrote as Anatole ◊France.

Everything must be taken seriously, nothing tragically.

LOUIS ADOLPHE THIERS
Speech at French National Assembly 24 May 1973

Thiers Louis Adolphe (1797–1877). French politician and historian, first president of the Third Republic 1871–73. He held cabinet posts under Louis Philippe, led the parliamentary opposition to Napoleon III from 1863, and as head of the provisional government 1871 negotiated peace with Prussia and suppressed the briefly autonomous Paris Commune. His economic policies facilitated the nation's recovery after the Franco-Prussian War.

His books include *Histoire de la Révolution française/History of the French Revolution* 1823–27.

Albion is still in the chains of slavery. I quit it without regret.

ARTHUR THISTLEWOOD
Statement at the end of his trial 1820

Thistlewood Arthur (1770–1820). English Radical. A follower of the pamphleteer Thomas Spence (1750–1814), he was active in the Radical movement and was executed as the chief leader of the Cato Street Conspiracy to murder government ministers.

Thom René Frédéric (1923–). French mathematician who developed catastrophe theory in 1966. He is a specialist in the fields of differentiable manifolds and topology.

He was professor at Strasbourg 1954–63 and then at the Institute of Advanced Scientific Studies at Bures-sur-Yvette.

Thom formulated a precise series associated with 'space spherical bundles' and demonstrated that the fundamental class of open spherical bundles showed topological invariance and formed a differential geometry. In his work on the theory of forms Thom showed that there are complete homological classes that cannot be the representation of any differential form, and formulated auxiliary spaces, now known as Thom spaces.

In 1956, Thom developed the theory of transversality, and contributed to the examination of singularities of smooth maps. This work laid the ground for his statement of the catastrophe theory, which is, in fact, a model, not yet an explanation. He proposed seven 'elementary catastrophes', which he hoped would be sufficient to describe processes within human experience of space-time dimensions. The seven elementary catastrophes are the fold, cusp, swallow-tail, butterfly, hyperbolic, elliptic, and parabolic. Of these, the cusp is both the simplest and the most useful.

In his book *Stabilité structurelle et morphogenèse/Structural Stability and Morphogenesis* 1972, Thom discusses how the concept of structural stability may be applied to the life sciences. He also introduces the notion of the 'universal unfolding' of a singularity.

Thomas Clarence (1948–). US Supreme Court justice (1991–). Born in Savannah, Georgia, he received a law degree from Yale University Law School (1974). President Reagan appointed him head of the civil rights division of the Department of Education 1981 and the head of the Equal Employment Opportunities Commission 1982. Thomas served there until 1990, when President Bush appointed him a justice on the US Court of Appeals. It was widely believed that his Republican views and opposition to abortion, rather than his legal experience, caused him to be nominated to the Supreme Court the following year, and the nomination was not supported by the National Association for the Advancement of Colored People, which would normally back a black nominee. After extremely bitter and sensational confirmation hearings, in which he was accused of sexual harassment by former colleague Anita Hill, Thomas was confirmed by the Senate by 52 votes to 48, the narrowest margin for any nominee to the Supreme Court in the 20th century, and took his seat on the Court.

Do not go gentle into that good night, / Rage, rage against the dying of the light.

DYLAN THOMAS
'Do Not Go Gentle into That Good Night'

Thomas Dylan Marlais (1914–1953). Welsh poet. Born in Swansea, son of the English teacher at the local grammar school where he was educated, he worked as a reporter on the *South Wales Evening Post*, then settled as a journalist in London and published his first volume *Eighteen Poems* 1934. His poems, characterized by complex imagery and a strong musicality, include the celebration of his 30th birthday 'Poem in October' and the evocation of his youth 'Fern Hill' 1946. His 'play for voices' *Under Milk Wood* 1954 describes with humour and compassion a day in the life of the residents of a small Welsh fishing village, Llareggub. The short stories of *Portrait of the Artist as a Young Dog* 1940 are autobiographical. He died in New York where he had made a number of reading and lecture tours. He lived in Laugharne, South Wales.

Suggested reading
Ferris, P *Dylan Thomas: A Biography* (1977)
FitzGibbon, C *The Life of Dylan Thomas* (1965)
Thomas, C *Leftover Life to Kill* (1957)
Thomas, C and Tremlett, G *Caitlin* (1986)
Tindall, W Y *A Reader's Guide to Dylan Thomas* (1962)

Thomas Lewis (1913–1993). US physician and academic, best known as a writer of essays on science, especially medicine and biology, for the nonscientist. Essays include 'The Lives of a Cell' 1974 and 'Medusa and the Snail' 1979.

During World War II he served in the navy, carrying out medical experiments in the Pacific. After the war, he continued his medical career; he was dean of the New York University School of Medicine 1966–72 and of the Yale School of Medicine 1972–73, and was president and chief executive of the Memorial Sloan Kettering Cancer Center 1973–80.

Thomas Lowell Jackson (1892–1981). US journalist, a radio commentator for the Columbia Broadcasting System (CBS) 1930–76. Born in Woodington, Ohio, Thomas was educated at Northern Indiana University and the University of Denver and joined the staff of the *Chicago Journal* 1912. After receiving an MA from Princeton 1915, he served as a special observer for President Wilson during World War I. His first-person account of the Arab Revolt was published as *With Lawrence in Arabia* 1924. Travelling to all World War II theatres of combat and to remote areas of the world, he became one of America's best-known journalists.

Thomas Michael Tilson (1944–). US conductor and pianist. His career was launched 1969 when he took over from an unwell William Steinberg in the middle of a Boston Symphony Orchestra concert, subsequently becoming principal guest conductor for the orchestra 1969–74. He was appointed principal conductor of the London Symphony Orchestra 1988. An enthusiastic proponent of 'authentic' restorations of modern repertoire, he has championed US composers. He has made first recordings of Steve Reich's *The Desert Music* 1983, the complete symphonies of Charles Ives, and a reconstruction of George Gershwin's original *Rhapsody in Blue*.

Thomas Norman Mattoon (1884–1968). US political leader, six times Socialist candidate for president 1928–48. Born in Marion, Ohio, USA, Thomas graduated from Princeton University 1905 and after study at the Union Theological Seminary was ordained a Presbyterian minister 1911. As pastor of the East Harlem Church he first confronted the problem of urban poverty and joined the Socialist Party 1918, leaving the ministry for political activism two years later. One of the founders of the American Civil Liberties Union 1920, he also served as a director of the League for Industrial

Democracy 1922–37. He was a brilliant speaker and published *A Socialist's Faith* 1951.

Thomas (Philip) Edward (1878–1917). English poet and prose writer. He met the US poet Robert Frost and began writing poetry under his influence. His poems, like his essays, were quiet, stern, melancholy evocations of rural life. *Poems* was published Oct 1917 after his death in World War I, followed by *Last Poems* 1918. His wife Helen Thomas (1877–1967) published the biographical volumes *As it Was* 1926, and *World without End* 1931.

Suggested reading
Cooke, William *Edward Thomas: A Critical Biography* (1970)
Marsh, Jan *Edward Thomas* (1978)
Thomas, Helen *As It Was* (memoir by his wife) (1926)
Thomas, Helen *World Without End* (memoir by his wife) (1931)

Thomas R(onald) S(tuart) (1913–). Welsh poet. His verse contrasts traditional Welsh values with encroaching 'English' sterility. His poems, including *The Stones of the Field* 1946, *Song at the Year's Turning* 1955, and *Laboratories of the Spirit* 1975, excel at the portrayal of the wild beauty of the Welsh landscape and the religious spirit that the harshness of life there engenders. His *Collected Poems* appeared 1993.

Thomas Seth (1785–1859). US clock manufacturer. Born in Wolcott, Connecticut, Thomas trained as a carpenter and cabinetmaker. In 1807 he joined a partnership in Plymouth, Connecticut, for the production of clocks. Establishing his own firm 1812, he became enormously successful in the manufacture of affordable shelf clocks. In 1853 the firm was reorganized as the Seth Thomas Clock Company and continued to prosper into the 20th century. Its headquarters were based in Plymouth Hollow, Connecticut, now renamed Thomaston.

Thomas Sidney Gilchrist (1850–1885). English metallurgist and inventor who, with his cousin Percy Gilchrist, developed a process for removing phosphorus impurities from the iron melted during steel manufacture.

Thomas was born in London and for most of his life worked as a police-court clerk. His deep interest was in industrial chemistry; he experimented systematically at home and attended the laboratories of various chemistry teachers.

The steel produced from phosphoric ores (such as most British, French, German, and Belgian iron ore) was brittle and of little use. Towards the end of 1875 Thomas arrived at a theoretical solution to the problem of how to dephosphorize pig iron when it was loaded into a Bessemer converter. He thought of adding lime, or the chemically similar magnesia or magnesian limestone, to the lining of the converter or furnace. Gilchrist, a chemist at a large ironworks, helped him try out this idea, and Thomas's patent was filed in 1878. The slag that formed as a by-product of this process found use in the developing artificial fertilizer industry.

Thomas à Kempis adopted name of Thomas Hämmerken (c. 1380–1471). German Augustinian monk. His *De Imitatio Christi*/*Imitation of Christ* is probably the most widely known Christian devotional work ever written. It was an expression of the strain of pious devotion known as *devotio moderna*.

Thomas à Kempis lived at the monastery of Zwolle in the Netherlands. He took his name from his birthplace Kempen, near Cologne. He also wrote hymns, sermons, and biographies.

Thomas Aquinas Medieval philosopher; see ◊Aquinas, St Thomas.

Unless I see the mark of the nails on Jesus' hands, when I put my fingers into the place where the nails were, I will not believe that he lives.

ST THOMAS
in the Bible, John 20:25

Thomas, St (died AD 53). In the New Testament, one of the 12 Apostles, said to have preached in S India, hence the ancient churches there were referred to as the 'Christians of St Thomas'. He is not the author of the Gospel of St Thomas, the Gnostic collection of Jesus' sayings.

Thompson Benjamin. Original name of Count ◊Rumford, American-born physicist.

Thompson D'Arcy Wentworth (1860–1948). Scottish biologist and classical scholar who interpreted the structure and growth of organisms in terms of the physical forces to which every individual is subjected throughout its life. He also hypothesized, in his book *On Growth and Form* 1917, that the evolution of one species into another results mainly from transformations involving the entire organism. Knighted 1937.

He was professor at Dundee 1884–1917, and then at St Andrews. In 1896 and 1897 he went on expeditions to the Pribilof Islands as a member of a British–American commission on fur-seal hunting in the Bering Sea. He was also one of the British representatives on the International Council for the Exploration of the Sea.

In the 1942 revised edition of *On Growth and Form*, Thompson admitted that his evolutionary theory did not adequately account for the cumulative effect of successive small modifications.

Thompson wrote many papers on fisheries and oceanography. He also published works on classical natural history, including *A Glossary of Greek Birds* 1895 and an edition of Aristotle's *Historia animalium* 1910.

Thompson Daley Francis Morgan (1958–). English decathlete who broke the world record four times since winning the Commonwealth Games decathlon title 1978. He won two more Commonwealth titles (1982, 1986), two Olympic gold medals (1980, 1984), three European medals (silver 1978; gold 1982, 1986), and a world title (1983). He retired in 1992.

Thompson David (1770–1857). Canadian explorer and surveyor who mapped extensive areas of W Canada, including the Columbia River, for the Hudson's Bay Company 1789–1811.

Thompson Emma (1959–). English actress. She has worked in cinema, theatre, and television, ranging from song-and-dance to

Thomas, Michael Tilson US conductor Michael Tilson Thomas is also a pianist and composer. His concerts for the Berkshire Music Centre, Ojai Music Festival, and New York Philharmonic Young People's Concerts established him firmly in the Bernstein and Boulez tradition of innovative programming and positive support of contemporary music.

Shakespeare, often playing variations on the independent woman. In 1989 she married actor-director Kenneth Branagh, and has appeared in all his films to date, including the role of Katharine in *Henry V* 1989, a dual role in *Dead Again* 1991, and as Beatrice in *Much Ado About Nothing* 1993; the couple separated 1995. Away from Branagh, she won an Academy Award for her performance in *Howards End* 1992, and appeared in *The Remains of the Day* 1993. She both acted in, and wrote the screenplay for the film *Sense and Sensibility* 1995, for which she won a second Academy Award (best adapted screenplay).

Thompson Flora Jane (1876–1947). English novelist. Her trilogy *Lark Rise to Candleford* 1945 describes Victorian rural life.

The angels keep their ancient places; / Turn but a stone, and start a wing! / 'Tis ye, 'tis your estrangèd faces, / That miss the many-splendoured thing.

FRANCIS THOMPSON
'Kingdom of God'

Thompson Francis (1859–1907). English poet. Born in Preston, he settled in London, where he fell into poverty and ill health. Wilfrid and Alice Meynell arranged the publication of his poems in 1893, including 'The Hound of Heaven'. In this and in *Sister Songs* 1895 and *New Poems* 1897 Thompson, who was a Roman Catholic, expressed a mystic view of life.

Thompson Hunter Stockton (1939–). US writer and journalist. A proponent of the New Journalism school of reporting, which made the writer an essential component of the story, Thompson mythologized himself as the outrageous Doctor Gonzo in his political journalism of the 1960s. These articles were mainly published in *Rolling Stone* magazine. An acute observer of the decadence and depravity in American life, he wrote such books as *Hell's Angels* 1966, *Fear and Loathing on the Campaign Trail '72* 1973, and the reportage novel *Fear and Loathing in Las Vegas* 1971. He also wrote the collections *Generation of Swine* 1988 and *Songs of the Doomed* 1990.

Thompson Jack (1940–). Stage name of John Payne Thompson, Australian television and film actor who began acting at university and came to prominence in the television series *Spyforce* 1971–72. His films include *Sunday Too Far Away* 1975, *Breaker Morant* 1980, *The Man from Snowy River* 1982 and *Merry Christmas, Mr Lawrence* 1983.

Thompson Jim (James Myers) (1906–1977). US writer. A prolific author, he was critically neglected until after his death, when he acquired a cult status for his books' powerful and original use of pulp, 'hard-boiled' genres, which he imbued with a horrific, pathological violence. His novels include *The Killer Inside Me* 1952 and *The Grifters* 1963 (filmed 1990).

Thompson John Taliaferro (1860–1940). US general and weapons designer. He invented the Thompson sub-machine gun 1920, which became famous as the 'Tommy gun'.

Thompson joined the artillery 1882, transferred to the Ordnance Department 1890, and spent the rest of his military career in developing small arms, particularly the Springfield M1903 rifle and Colt M1911 pistol. He retired from the army Nov 1914 and joined the Remington Arms Company as chief engineer.

When the USA entered the war 1917 he was recalled to duty and converted the British Enfield rifle to the US .303 in calibre design. He was promoted to brigadier general and given responsibility for supplying small arms and ammunition to the American Expeditionary Force in France, and was awarded the Distinguished Service Medal for his services. He retired from the army again Dec 1918 and returned to designing small arms.

Thompson Richard (1949–). English virtuoso guitarist, songwriter, and singer. His work spans rock, folk, and avant-garde. He was a member of pioneering folk-rock group Fairport Convention 1966–71, contributing to albums like *What We Did on Our Holidays* 1968. With his wife Linda Thompson he made several albums,

among them *Shoot Out the Lights* 1982. Later solo work includes *Rumor and Sigh* 1991.

Thomsen Christian Jürgensen (1788–1865). Danish archaeologist. He devised the classification of prehistoric cultures into Stone Age, Bronze Age, and Iron Age.

Thomson Elihu (1853–1937). US inventor. He founded, with E J Houston (1847–1914), the Thomson–Houston Electric Company 1882, later merging with the Edison Company to form the General Electric Company. He made advances into the nature of the electric arc and invented the first high-frequency dynamo and transformer.

Thomson George Paget (1892–1975). English physicist whose work on interference phenomena in the scattering of electrons by crystals helped to confirm the wavelike nature of particles. He shared a Nobel prize 1937. Knighted 1943.

In the USA, C J Davisson made the same discovery independently, earlier the same year, using a different method.

Thomson was born and educated at Cambridge, the son of physicist J J Thomson. His first professorship was 1922–30 at Aberdeen, and he moved to Imperial College, London, 1930–52. During World War II, Thomson headed many government committees, including one concerned with atomic weapons.

During the mid-1920s, Thomson carried out a series of experiments hoping to verify French physicist Louis de Broglie's hypothesis that electrons possess duality, acting both as particles and as waves. The experiment involved bombarding very thin metal (aluminium, gold, and platinum) and celluloid foils with a narrow beam of electrons. The beam was scattered into a series of rings. Applying mathematical formulas to measurements of the rings, together with a knowledge of the crystal lattice, Thomson showed in 1927 that all the readings were in complete agreement with de Broglie's theory.

Thomson J(oseph) J(ohn) (1856–1940). English physicist who discovered the electron 1897. His work inaugurated the electrical theory of the atom, and his elucidation of positive rays and their application to an analysis of neon led to the discovery of isotopes. Nobel prize 1906. Knighted 1908.

Using magnetic and electric fields to deflect positive rays, Thomson found in 1912 that ions of neon gas are deflected by different amounts, indicating that they consist of a mixture of ions with different charge-to-mass ratios. English chemist Frederick Soddy had earlier proposed the existence of isotopes and Thomson proved this idea correct when he identified, also in 1912, the isotope neon-22. This work was continued by his student Frederick Aston.

Thomson was born near Manchester and studied there and at Cambridge, where he spent his entire career. As professor of experimental physics 1884–1918, he developed the Cavendish Laboratory into the world's leading centre for subatomic physics. His son was George Paget Thomson.

Investigating cathode rays, Thomson proved that they were particulate and found their charge-to-mass ratio to be constant and with a value nearly 1,000 times smaller than that obtained for hydrogen ions in liquid electrolysis. He also measured the charge of the cathode-ray particles and found it to be the same in the gaseous discharge as in electrolysis. Thus he demonstrated that cathode rays are fundamental, negatively charged particles; the term 'electron' was introduced later.

Suggested reading
Rayleigh R J *The Life of Sir J J Thomson* (1942)
Thomson, George *J J Thomson and the Cavendish Laboratory of His Day* (1965)

Thomson James (1700–1748). Scottish poet. His descriptive blank verse poem *The Seasons* 1726–30 was a forerunner of the Romantic movement. He also wrote the words of 'Rule, Britannia'.

Thomson James (1834–1882). Scottish poet. Born in Renfrewshire, he became an army schoolmaster and a journalist. He is remembered for his despairing poem 'The City of Dreadful Night' 1874. He also wrote as 'BV' (Bysshe Vanolis).

An Image sits, stupendous, superhuman, / The Bronze colossus of a wingèd Woman.

JAMES THOMSON
City of Dreadful Night XVI 1874

Thomson James (1822–1892). Northern Irish physicist and engineer who discovered 1849 that the melting point of ice decreases with pressure. He was also an authority on hydrodynamics and invented the vortex waterwheel 1850.

Thomson was born in Belfast, the brother of the future Lord Kelvin. At the age of only ten he began to attend Glasgow University, obtaining an MA in 1839. He held a succession of engineering posts before settling in Belfast in 1851 as a civil engineer. He was professor of civil engineering at Belfast 1857–73 and at Glasgow 1873–89.

The vortex water wheel was a smaller and more efficient turbine than those in use at the time, and it came into wide use. Thomson continued his investigations into whirling fluids, making improvements to pumps, fans, and turbines.

Thomson's discovery about the melting point of ice led him to an understanding of the way in which glaciers flow. He also carried out painstaking studies of the phase relationships of solids, liquids, and gases, and was involved in both geology and meteorology, producing scientific papers on currents and winds.

Rhapsodies ... are not a very difficult formula, if one can think up enough tunes.

VIRGIL THOMSON
Modern Music 1935

Thomson Virgil (1896–1989). US composer and critic. He studied in France with Nadia Boulanger 1921–22 and returned to Paris 1925–40, mixing with Gertrude Stein and her circle. He is best known for his opera *Four Saints in Three Acts* 1927–33 to a libretto by Stein, and the film scores *The Plow That Broke the Plains* 1936 and *Louisiana Story* 1948. His music is notable for a refined absence of expression, his criticism for trenchant matter-of-factness, both at odds with the prevailing US musical culture.

Suggested reading
Hoover, Kathleen and Cage, John *Virgil Thomson* (1959)
Nicholls, D *American Experimental Music, 1890–1940* (1989)
Thomson, Virgil *Virgil Thomson on Virgil Thomson* (1966)
Tommasini, A (ed) *Virgil Thomson's Musical Portraits* (1986)

Thomson William. Irish physicist, see Lord ◊Kelvin.

Thoreau Henry David (1817–1862). US author. One of the most influential figures of 19th-century US literature, he is best known for his vigorous defence of individualism and the simple life. Thoreau was born in Concord, Massachusetts, and graduated from Harvard. His friend the transcendentalist Ralph Waldo Emerson encouraged him to write and offered him land near Walden Pond on which to set up his experiment 1845–47 in living a life close to nature, requiring little manual labour and allowing him time to write. His work *Walden, or Life in the Woods* 1854 stimulated the back-to-nature movement, and he completed some 20 volumes based on his daily nature walks. His essay 'Civil Disobedience' 1849, prompted by his refusal to pay taxes, advocated peaceful resistance to unjust laws and had a wide impact, even in the 20th century.

Thoreau's other works include *A Week on the Concord and Merrimack Rivers* 1849 and, published posthumously, *Excursions* 1863, *The Maine Woods* 1864, *Cape Cod* 1865, and *A Yankee in Canada* 1866.

Suggested reading
Harding, Walter *A Thoreau Handbook* (1959)
Harding, Walter *The Days of Henry Thoreau* (1965)
Paul, S *The Shores of America: Thoreau's Inward Exploration* (1958)
Richardson, Robert, Jr *Henry Thoreau: The Life of the Mind* (1986)
Schneider, Richard *Henry David Thoreau* (1987)
Wagenknecht, E H *Henry David Thoreau* (1981)

Thomson, J J *English physicist and discoverer of the electron J J Thomson. In 1876, he won a scholarship to Trinity College, Cambridge, where he eventually succeeded Lord Rayleigh as Cavendish Professor of Experimental Physics. Thomson revolutionized the Cavendish Laboratory, turning it into the greatest research institution in the world – seven of his research assistants went on to win Nobel prizes. Thomson died 1940 and was buried near Newton in the nave of Westminster Abbey.* (Image Select)

Thorndike (Agnes) Sybil (1882–1976). English actress. George Bernard Shaw wrote *St Joan* for her. The Thorndike Theatre (1969), Leatherhead, Surrey, England, is named after her. She was married to the actor Sir Lewis Casson (1885–1972), with whom she often appeared. DBE 1931.

Thorndike Edward Lee (1874–1949). US educational psychologist whose experiments in behaviour of cats and dogs in a 'puzzle box' brought him to the conclusion that learning was improved when it achieved a satisfactory result. He extended this theory to human learning and found that students were encouraged by good results, but that being wrong did not teach them to correct their errors.

Thorpe (John) Jeremy (1929–). British Liberal politician, leader of the Liberal Party 1967–76. From a family of MPs, Thorpe first trained as a barrister, then became a Liberal MP 1959 and party leader 1967. A flamboyant campaigner, party fortunes advanced under his leadership, but he was forced to step down 1976 following allegations that he had had a homosexual affair with Norman Scott, and that he had conspired in an attempted murder of his lover. He was acquitted of all charges 1979, but lost his parliamentary seat at the general election.

Thorpe Jim (James Francis) (1888–1953). US athlete. Born in Prague, Oklahoma, Thorpe attended the Carlisle Indian School in Pennsylvania. A member of the 1912 US Olympic Team in Stockholm, he won gold medals for the decathlon and pentathlon but was forced to return them when he admitted that he had played semiprofessional baseball. He played major-league baseball 1913–19 and was an outstanding player of professional football

1917–29. His Olympic medals were restored to him by the Amateur Athletic Union 1973.

Thorvaldsen Bertel, or Thorwaldsen (*c.* 1770–1844). Danish Neo-Classical sculptor. He went to Italy on a scholarship 1796 and stayed in Rome for most of his life, producing portraits, monuments, and religious and mythological works. Much of his work is housed in the Thorvaldsen Museum, Copenhagen.

Thothmes. four kings (pharaohs) of ancient Egypt of the 18th dynasty, including:

Thothmes I king (pharaoh) of ancient Egypt, reigned *c.* 1504–*c.* 1492 BC. He campaigned in Syria.

Thothmes III king (pharaoh) of ancient Egypt, reigned *c.* 1479–*c.* 1425 BC. He extended the empire to the river Euphrates, and conquered Nubia. He was a grandson of Thothmes I.

Thubron Colin Gerald Dryden (1939–). English travel writer and novelist. He is noted for his lyrical prose. Among his books are *Mirror to Damascus* 1967, *The Hills of Adonis: A Journey through Lebanon* 1968, and *Behind the Wall: A Journey through China* 1987. He also wrote the novels *A Cruel Madness* 1985 and *Turning Back the Sun* 1991.

My work is not a piece of writing designed to meet the taste of an immediate public, but was done to last for ever.

THUCYDIDES
Histories 1.22

Thucydides (*c.* 455–*c.* 400 BC). Athenian historian. He exercised military command in the Peloponnesian War with Sparta, but was banished from Athens in 424. In his *History of the Peloponnesian War*, he gave a detailed account of the conflict down to 411.
Suggested reading
Adcock, Frank *Thucydides and his History* (1963)
Connor, W Robert *Thucydides and the Science of History* (1984)
Hornblower, Simon *Thucydides* (1987)
Romilly, J de *Thucydides and Athenian Imperialism* (1963)

Thunderbolt Captain. Alias of Australian bushranger Frederick ◊Ward.

Thunders Johnny. Stage name of John Anthony Genzale (1952–1991). US rock guitarist, singer, and songwriter. Lead guitarist with the glam-rock garage band the New York Dolls 1971–75, he fronted his own group, the Heartbreakers, 1975–77. Moving to London 1976, they became part of the punk movement. Thunders' subsequent solo work includes the album *So Alone* 1978.

Thünen Johann Heinrich von (1785–1850). German economist and geographer who believed that the success of a state depends on the wellbeing of its farmers. His book *The Isolated State* 1820, a pioneering study of land use, includes the earliest example of marginal productivity theory, a theory that he developed to calculate the natural wage for a farmworker. He has been described as the first modern economist.

Thurber James Grover (1894–1961). US humorist. His short stories, written mainly for the *New Yorker* magazine, include 'The Secret Life of Walter Mitty' 1932. His stories and sketches are collected in *Is Sex Necessary?* (with E B White) 1929, *The Middle-Aged Man on the Flying Trapeze* 1935, *The Last Flower* 1939, and *My World and Welcome to It* 1942. He also wrote adult fairy tales – *Many Moons* 1943, *The Great Quillow* 1944, *The White Deer* 1945, *The 13 Clocks* 1950, and *The Wonderful O* 1957 – and a play, *The Male Animal* 1940. His doodle drawings include fanciful impressions of dogs. Partially blind from childhood, he became totally blind in the last ten years of his life but continued to work.

Suggested reading
Arner, Robert *James Thurber: An Introduction* (1979)
Bernstein, Burton *Thurber* (1975)
Kenney, Catherine *Thurber's Anatomy of Confusion* (1984)

Thynne family name of marquesses of Bath; seated at Longleat, Wiltshire, England.

Thyssen Fritz (1873–1951). German industrialist who based his business on the Ruhr iron and steel industry. Fearful of the communist threat, Thyssen became an early supporter of Hitler and contributed large amounts of money to his early political campaigns. By 1939 he had broken with the Nazis and fled first to Switzerland and later to Italy, where in 1941 he was sent to a concentration camp. Released 1945, he was ordered to surrender 15% of his property.

Tiberius (Tiberius Claudius Nero) (42 BC–AD 37). Roman emperor, the stepson, adopted son, and successor of Augustus from AD 14. He was a cautious ruler whose reign was marred by the heavy incident of trials for treason or conspiracy. Tiberius fell under the influence of Sejanus who encouraged the emperor's fear of assassination and was instrumental in Tiberius's departure from Rome to Caprae (Capri). He never returned to Rome.

Tibullus Albius (*c.* 48–*c.* 19 BC). Roman elegiac poet, a friend of the poets Horace and Ovid. Two books of poems, addressed to his patron Valerius Messalla Corvinus, are extant. His pastoral poems were known throughout the Middle Ages.

Tieck (Johann) Ludwig (1773–1853). German Romantic poet and collector of folk tales. He dramatized some of the tales, such as 'Puss in Boots'.

Tiepolo Giovanni Battista (Giambattista) (1696–1770). Italian painter. He was one of the first exponents of Italian Rococo and created monumental Rococo decorative schemes in palaces and churches in NE Italy, SW Germany, and Madrid 1762–70. His style is light-hearted, his colours light and warm, and he made great play with illusion. Tiepolo painted religious and, above all, historical or allegorical pictures, for example, scenes from the life of Cleopatra, 1745 (Palazzo Labia, Venice) and from the life of Frederick Barbarossa, 1757 (Kaisersaal, Würzburg Palace). His sons were among his many assistants.

He studied under the minor painter, Gregorio Lazzarini, but the source of his light and fanciful Rococo style may be found in Sebastiano Ricci. Influenced also by Crespi and Piazzetta in such early works as the *Sacrifice of Isaac*, *c.* 1715–16 (Venice, Ospedaletto), and his paintings in the church of the Scalzi, he shed their dark effects of chiaroscuro to attain a luminous and aerial atmosphere in which he rivals Veronese, who also led him to cover vast wall spaces with sumptuous effects of architecture and splendidly attired groups of figures. Until 1750, with immense virtuosity and a quality of brush-stroke and colour entirely his own, he covered the walls and ceilings of many villas and palaces in Venice and elsewhere in northern Italy, the series of *Antony and Cleopatra* (Palazzo Labia) being a culminating achievement. The decoration of the Villa San Sebastiano at Malmarana, near Vicenza, 1737, with scenes from the *Iliad*, *Orlando Furioso* and *Gerusalemme Liberata* was another of many notable works in Italy. He went to Würzburg 1751–53 to decorate the Prince Bishop's Palace, being assisted by his sons, Giovanni Domenico and Lorenzo. In 1755 he was elected president of the Venetian Academy and in 1762 was invited to Spain by Charles III, there carrying out a scheme of decoration for the Palacio Real, and painting altarpieces for San Pasquale at Aranjuez. These were later replaced by pictures by Mengs, his competitor and opponent in style.

Tiepolo's drawings (well exemplified in the Victoria and Albert Museum, London) are also of exceptional brilliance. He married the sister of Francesco Guardi 1719. Of his two sons the more notable as an artist was Giovanni Domenico (1727–1802). As a painter the latter assisted and imitated his father, and in his later years produced some original and satiric scenes of Italian comedy and Venetian life. Like his father he was a facile and able draughtsperson.

Suggested reading
Alpers, Svetlana and Baxandall, Michael *Tiepolo and the Pictorial Intelligence* (1994)
Barcham, William L *Tiepolo* (1992)
Levey, Michael *Giambattista Tiepolo: His Life and Art* (1986)

Tiffany Louis Comfort (1848–1933). US artist and glassmaker. He was the son of Charles Louis Tiffany, who founded Tiffany and Company, the New York City jewellers. In 1881 he founded his own decorating firm. By 1893, he began producing his glass art objects, which remained popular through the 1920s and enjoyed a resurgence of popularity from the 1950s on. He produced stained-glass windows, iridescent Favrile (from Latin *faber* 'craftsman') glass, and lampshades in the Art Nouveau style. He used glass that contained oxides of iron and other elements to produce rich colours.

Tikhonov Nikolai Aleksandrovich (1905–). Soviet politician. He was a close associate of President Brezhnev, joining the Politburo 1979, and was prime minister (chair of the Council of Ministers) 1980–85. In April 1989 he was removed from the Central Committee.

Tilden Samuel Jones (1814–1886). US politician. Born in New Lebanon, New York, Tilden was educated at Yale and New York universities, and became a barrister 1841. A Democrat, he was governor of New York 1874–76, elected on a reform ticket. He received the Democratic presidential nomination 1876, and although he received a plurality of popular votes, the 1877 electoral college awarded the majority of electoral votes to Rutherford B Hayes.

Tillich Paul Johannes (1886–1965). Prussian-born US theologian, best remembered for his *Systematic Theology* 1951–63. Tillich received his PhD from the University of Breslau 1911. Ordained a pastor in the Evangelical Lutheran Church 1912, he served as a chaplain during World War I. Appointed to a professorship at Frankfurt 1929, he was removed by the Nazis and fled to the USA 1933. He was professor of theology at the Union Theological Seminary 1933–55, Harvard University 1955–62, and the University of Chicago 1962–65.

Suggested reading
Armbruster, Carl *The Vision of Paul Tillich* (1967)
McLeod, Alastair *Tillich* (1973)
Pauck, Wilhelm and Marion *Paul Tillich: His Life and Thought* (1976)
Thomas, J Heywood *Tillich: An Appraisal* (1963)
Tillich, Hanna *From Time to Time* (memoir by his wife) (1976)

Tilly Jan Tserklaes, Count von (1559–1632). Flemish commander of the army of the Catholic League and imperial forces in the Thirty Years' War. Notorious for his storming of Magdeburg, E Germany, 1631, he was defeated by the Swedish king Gustavus Adolphus at Breitenfeld and at the river Lech in SW Germany, where he was mortally wounded.

Timoshenko Semyon Konstantinovich (1895–1970). Soviet general in World War II; he was an old companion of Stalin and one of the few people he was prepared to trust. After commanding a sector in the Winter War against Finland 1939–40 he became Commissar of Defence. When the German invasion took place 1941 he took command of the West Front but was too late to do more than delay the German advance. Transferred to the Southwest Front he mounted a powerful but mistimed offensive to recapture Kharkov which was soundly defeated by the Germans who then swept him aside and advanced to Stalingrad and the Caucasus. Timoshenko was then moved to a less active area for a short time before being assigned to Moscow to work on strategic planning for the rest of the war.

Timothy (died *c*. AD 97). In the New Testament, companion to St Paul, both on his missionary journeys and in prison. Two of Paul's epistles are addressed to him.

Timur i Leng alternative spelling of ◊Tamerlane, Mongol ruler.

Tinbergen Jan (1903–). Dutch economist. He shared a Nobel prize 1969 with Ragnar Frisch for his work on econometrics (the mathematical-statistical expression of economic theory).

Tinbergen Niko(laas) (1907–1988). Dutch-born British zoologist who specialized in the study of instinctive behaviour. One of the founders of ethology, the scientific study of animal behaviour in natural surroundings, he shared a Nobel prize 1973 with Konrad Lorenz (with whom he worked on several projects) and Karl von Frisch.

Tinbergen investigated other aspects of animal behaviour, such as learning, and also studied human behaviour, particularly aggression, which he believed to be an inherited instinct that developed when humans changed from being predominantly herbivorous to being hunting carnivores.

Tinbergen was born in The Hague and educated at Leiden, where he became professor 1947. From 1949 he was in the UK at Oxford, and established a school of animal-behaviour studies there.

In *The Study of Instinct* 1951, Tinbergen showed that the aggressive behaviour of the male three-spined stickleback is stimulated by the red coloration on the underside of other males (which develops during the mating season). He also demonstrated that the courtship dance of the male is stimulated by the sight of the swollen belly of a female that is ready to lay eggs.

In *The Herring Gull's World* 1953, Tinbergen described the social behaviour of gulls, emphasizing the importance of stimulus–response processes in territorial behaviour.

Ting Samuel Chao Chung (1936–). US physicist. In 1974 he and his team at the Brookhaven National Laboratory, New York, detected a new subatomic particle, which he named the J particle. It was found to be identical to the ψ particle discovered in the same year by Burton Richter and his team at the Stanford Linear Accelerator Center, California. Ting and Richter shared the Nobel Prize for Physics 1976.

Tintoretto adopted name of Jacopo Robusti (1518–1594). Italian painter, so named because his father was a dyer (Italian *tintore*). He was active in Venice. His dramatic religious paintings are spectacularly lit and full of movement, such as his huge canvases of the lives of Christ and the Virgin in the Scuola di San Rocco, Venice, 1564–88. He was a student of Titian and an admirer of Michelangelo. His *Miracle of St Mark Rescuing a Slave* 1548 (Accademia, Venice) marked the start of his successful career. In the Scuola di San Rocco he created a sequence of heroic scenes with bold gesture and foreshortening, a flickering, unearthly light, and dramatic distortions of space. He also painted canvases for the Doge's Palace.

Except for a visit to Mantua he never seems to have left Venice, where his unremitting labour produced a vast output of religious paintings, portraits, and a number of allegorical and mythological subjects. They include his great *Miracle of St Mark*, his decorations for the Scuola di San Rocco (including the vast *Christ before Pilate* and *Last Supper*), 1560, and the overwhelming *Paradise* for the Doge's Palace, 1590. These great works show a never-failing imagination; a wonderfully dramatic sense of movement, space, and lighting in composition; and superb use of colour. The effects he observed (and utilized in his painted compositions) from focusing light on small wax models grouped inside a box had a considerable influence on later painters. His originality in portraiture can be appreciated in the *Doge Mocenigo* (Venice, Accademia), *Self-Portrait* (Louvre, Paris) and *Vincenzo Morosini* (National Gallery, London). Masterpieces, apart from his religious works on a decorative scale, are his *Susanna and the Elders* (Vienna), *St George and the Dragon*, with its sense of rushing movement (National Gallery, London), and the *Origin of the Milky Way*, one of the most beautiful of painted allegories. The Scuola di San Rocco works inspired a famous panegyric by Ruskin, who, in *The Stones of Venice* and other writings, did much to rescue his fame from neglect. His art may be looked on as a foundation of that of El Greco.

His son Domenico was his assistant in his later works and carried on his workshop, in which another son, Marco, and his daughter, Marietta, were also trained.

Suggested reading
Freeberg, S J *Painting in Italy 1500–1600* (1975)
Hartt, Frederick *Italian Renaissance Art* (1987)
Newton, Eric *Tintoretto* (1952)
Pignatti, T and Valcanover, F *Tintoretto* (1985)

Tiomkin Dimitri (1899–1979). Russian composer. He lived in the USA from 1925 and from 1930 wrote Hollywood film scores, including music for *Duel in the Sun* 1946, *The Thing* 1951, and *Rio Bravo* 1959. His score for *High Noon* 1952 won him an Academy Award.

Tippett Michael Kemp (1905–   ). English composer. He first made his name in World War II with his oratorio *A Child of Our Time* 1944, and was briefly imprisoned as a conscientious objector 1943. His works include the operas *The Midsummer Marriage* 1952, *The Knot Garden* 1970, and *New Year* 1989; four symphonies; *Songs for Ariel* 1962; and choral music including *The Mask of Time* 1982. Knighted 1966.

Suggested reading
Kemp, Ian *Tippett: The Composer and His Music* (1984)
Matthews, David *Michael Tippett* (1980)
Tippett, Michael *Those Twentieth Century Blues* (autobiography) (1991)
White, E W *Tippett and His Operas* (1979)

Tipu Sultan (c. 1750–1799). Sultan of Mysore (now Karnataka) in SW India from the death of his father, Hyder Ali, 1782. He died of wounds when his capital, Seringapatam, was captured by the British. His rocket brigade led Sir William Congreve (1772–1828) to develop the weapon for use in the Napoleonic Wars.

Tirpitz Alfred Friedrich von (1849–1930). German admiral. As secretary for the navy 1897–1916, he created the German navy and planned the World War I U-boat campaign.

Tirso de Molina pen name of Gabriel Téllez (c. 1571–1648). Spanish dramatist and monk. He claimed to have written more than 300 plays, of which 80 are extant, including comedies, historical and biblical dramas, and a series based on the legend of Don Juan.

Tiselius Arne Wilhelm Kaurin (1902–1971). Swedish chemist who developed a powerful method of chemical analysis known as electrophoresis. Electrophoresis is the diffusion of charged particles through a fluid under the influence of an electric field. It can be used to separate molecules of different sizes, which diffuse at different rates. He applied his new techniques to the analysis of animal proteins. Nobel prize 1948.

Tiselius was born in Stockholm and studied at Uppsala, where he spent his career. From 1938 he was director of the Institute of Biochemistry.

Working at Princeton in the USA 1934–35, Tiselius investigated zeolite minerals, which have a unique capacity to exchange their water of crystallization for other substances, the crystal structure remaining intact even after the water has been removed under vacuum. He studied the optical changes that occur when the dried crystals are rehydrated.

Tiselius first used electrophoresis in the 1920s. In the 1930s he separated the proteins in horse serum and revealed for the first time the existence of three components which he named α-, β-, and γ-globulin. Later he developed new techniques in chromatography.

Tiselius founded the Nobel Symposia, which take place every year in each of the five prize fields to discuss the social, ethical, and other implications of the award-winning work.

Tissot James (Joseph Jacques) (1836–1902). French painter. He produced detailed portraits of Victorian high society during a ten-year stay in England, as in *Ball on Shipboard* 1874 (Tate Gallery, London). In the 1880s Tissot visited Palestine. His religious works were much admired.

Titian anglicized form of Tiziano Vecellio (c. 1487–1576). Italian painter. Active in Venice, he was one of the greatest artists of the

High Renaissance. In 1533 he became court painter to Charles V, Holy Roman emperor, whose son Philip II of Spain later became his patron. Titian's work is richly coloured, with inventive composition. He produced a vast number of portraits, religious paintings, and mythological scenes, including *Bacchus and Ariadne* 1520–23 (National Gallery, London), *Venus and Adonis* 1554 (Prado, Madrid), and the *Pietà* about 1575 (Accademia, Venice).

He was born in a mountainous district of the Venetian Alps (from which his landscape backgrounds seem often to derive) and was apprenticed as a boy of nine to mosaicists (Zuccati) in Venice, afterwards being the pupil of Giovanni Bellini, like Giorgione, with whom he worked. It is assumed that they collaborated, 1507–08, on the decoration of the Fondaco de' Tedeschi (now destroyed). Titian seems to have finished pictures left incomplete at Giorgione's death 1510 (for example the *Concert*, Pitti Gallery). From the sensuous and poetic suggestion of Giorgione he quickly developed a personal style. The most famous of his early works are the so-called *Sacred and Profane Love* (Rome, Borghese), *L'Homme au Gant* (Louvre), *Christ and the Tribute Money* (Dresden), and *Flora* (Uffizi). After about 1518, the expansion of his powers and his rise to European eminence were steady and continuous. The masterpiece *Bacchus and Ariadne* was painted 1522, and the great religious works, the *Assumption* (Church of the Frari, Venice) and *Entombment* (Louvre), belong to this period. In 1533 he was introduced to the Emperor Charles V, who sat for his portrait. The admiration of Charles V and his successor, Philip II, for Titian accounts for the presence of so many of his masterpieces in the imperial collections and the Prado, Madrid. Titian was now internationally famous, rulers competing for his 'poetical compositions' or 'poesie' (as he termed his mythological scenes with their sumptuous nude figures), and for his portraits. He worked in a number of centres: in Venice, where in 1537 he painted his *Battle of Cadore* (destroyed by fire 1577); in Milan, where in 1541 he was with the emperor; in Rome, 1545, at the invitation of the Pope; in Augsburg, 1548, where he painted Philip of Spain. From this time onwards he painted mainly at Venice, the splendid Indian summer of his art producing works profound in feeling and characterized by remarkable developments in technique.

His method was complex and deliberate. On a solid foundation in a red earth colour the cooler tones were laid, and films or glazes of transparent colour applied at intervals, the artist sometimes softening the effect with finger rather than brush and adding crisp touches of definition. In this way he achieved his inimitable depth of colour and feeling of rich material texture. In the style of his old age, a broken richness of colour and a preoccupation with effects of light might be called 'impressionist'.

Suggested reading
Hope, C *Titian* (1980)
Morassi, Antonio *Titian* (1964)
Rosand, David *Titian* (1978)
Steer, John *Venetian Painting: A Concise History* (1970)
Wethey, Harold E *The Paintings of Titian* (1970)
Wilde, J *Venetian Art from Bellini to Titian* (1974)
Williams, J *The World of Titian* (1968)

Tito adopted name of Josip Broz (1892–1980). Yugoslav communist politician, in effective control of Yugoslavia from 1943. Born in Croatia, Tito served in the Austrian army during World War I, was captured by the Russians, and fought in the Red Army during the civil wars. Returning to Yugoslavia 1923, he became prominent as a communist and during World War II as partisan leader against the Nazis. He organized the National Liberation Army to carry on guerrilla warfare against the German invasion 1941, and was created marshal 1943. In 1943 he established a provisional government and gained Allied recognition (previously given to the Chetniks) 1944, and with Soviet help proclaimed the federal republic 1945. As prime minister, he settled the Yugoslav minorities question on a federal basis, and in 1953 took the newly created post of president (for life from 1974). In 1948 he was criticized by the USSR and other communist countries for his successful system of decentralized profit-sharing workers' councils, and became a leader of the nonaligned movement. He followed a foreign policy of 'positive neutralism'.

Suggested reading
Auty, Phyllis *Tito: A Biography* (1970)
Deakin, F W *The Embattled Mountain* (1971)
Djilas, Milovan *Tito* (1980)
Ormcanin, Ivo *Tito* (1984)
Ridley, Jasper *Tito: A Biography* (1994)

Friends, without a good deed I have lost a day.
TITUS
quoted in Suetonius *Titus* ch 8

Titus (Titus Flavius Vespasianus) (AD 39–81). Roman emperor from AD 79. Eldest son of Vespasian, he captured Jerusalem 70 to end the Jewish revolt in Roman Palestine. He completed the Colosseum, and helped to mitigate the suffering from the eruption of Vesuvius in 79, which destroyed Pompeii and Herculaneum.

Tobin James (1918–). US Keynesian economist. He was awarded a Nobel prize 1981 for his 'general equilibrium' theory, which states that other criteria than monetary considerations are applied by households and firms when making decisions on consumption and investment.

Tocqueville Alexis Charles Henri Clérel de (1805–1859). French politician, sociologist, and historian, author of the first analytical study of the strengths and weaknesses of US society, *De la Démocratie en Amérique/Democracy in America* 1835. He also wrote a penetrating description of France before the Revolution, *L'Ancien Régime et la Révolution/The Old Regime and the Revolution* 1856.

Elected to the Chamber of Deputies 1839, Tocqueville became vice president of the Constituent Assembly and minister of foreign affairs 1849. He retired after Napoleon III's coup 1851. No other 19th-century liberal thinker saw the problems of contemporary democratic society quite as clearly as Tocqueville.

Suggested reading
Boesche, R *The Strange Liberalism of Alexis de Tocqueville* (1987)
Brogan, Hugh *Tocqueville* (1973)
Jardin, André *Tocqueville: A Biography* (trs 1988)
Lerner, Max *Tocqueville and American Civilization* (1966)
Siedentop, Larry *Tocqueville* (1994)

Todd Alexander Robertus, Baron Todd (1907–1997). Scottish organic chemist who won a Nobel prize 1957 for his work on the role of nucleic acids in genetics. He also synthesized vitamins B_1, B_{12}, and E. Knighted 1954, baron 1962.

Todd was born in Glasgow and studied there and in Germany at Frankfurt. He was professor at Manchester 1938–44 and Cambridge 1944–71.

Todd began his work on the synthesis of organic molecules 1934 with vitamin B_1. In the late 1940s and early 1950s he worked on nucleotides; he synthesized adenosine triphosphate (ATP) and adenosine diphosphate (ADP), the key substances in generating energy in the body. He developed new methods for the synthesis of all the major nucleotides and their related coenzymes, and established in detail the chemical structures of the nucleic acids, such as DNA (deoxyribonucleic acid), the hereditary material of cell nuclei. During the course of this work, which provided the essential basis for further developments in the fields of genetics and of protein synthesis in living cells, Todd also devised an approach to the synthesis of the nucleic acids themselves.

Todd Ann (1909–1993). British film actress. Born in Hartford, Cheshire, Todd trained for the stage and rapidly achieved a West End reputation in a string of light comedies. Her film debut came in 1931, and of her pre-war films, the best remembered is probably *Things To Come* 1936. She achieved lasting fame for her role as the put-upon concert pianist heroine of the romantic melodrama *The Seventh Veil* 1945. She went to Hollywood for one film, Hitchcock's *The Paradine Case* 1948, then played in three major British films directed by David Lean (to whom she was married 1947–57); *The*

Passionate Friends 1949, *Madeleine* 1950, and *The Sound Barrier* 1959, but they failed to establish her fully as a box-office name.

During the 1950s, her screen appearances became sporadic, though she was active on the stage, playing Lady Macbeth during the Old Vic season 1954–55. A robbery during which she sustained an injury dealt something of a blow to her career, but she went on to direct several travel films, and much later made a comeback to screen acting in *The Human Factor* 1979, based on the Graham Greene novel.

Todd Ron(ald) (1927–). British trade-union leader. He rose from shop steward to general secretary of Britain's largest trade union, the Transport and General Workers' Union, a post he held 1985–92. Although a Labour Party supporter, he criticized its attitude toward nuclear disarmament.

Todt Fritz (1891–1942). German engineer who was responsible for building the first autobahns (German motorways) and, in World War II, the Siegfried Line of defence along Germany's western frontier, and the Atlantic Wall.

Todt's success as minister for road construction led Nazi dictator Hitler to put him in charge of completing the Siegfried Line 1938. His Organization Todt, formed for this task, continued constructing defences on the Atlantic Coast using forced labour until 1944. He was made minister for arms and munitions 1940. In 1942, alarmed at the attrition of equipment on the Eastern Front, he advised Hitler to end the war with the USSR. He was killed in an air crash on the way back from this meeting.

Togare stage name of Georg Kulovits (1900–1988). Austrian wild-animal tamer and circus performer. Togare invented the character of the exotic and fearless Oriental lion tamer after watching Douglas Fairbanks in the 1924 film *The Thief of Bagdad.*

Togliatti Palmiro (1893–1964). Italian politician who was a founding member of the Italian Communist Party 1921 and effectively its leader for almost 40 years from 1926 until his death.

Togliatti trained as a lawyer, served in the army, and was wounded during World War I. He was associated with the revolutionary wing of the Italian Socialist Party that left to form the Communist Party 1921. He edited the newspaper *Il Comunista* 1922–24 and became a member of the party's central committee. He was in Moscow when Mussolini outlawed the party, and stayed there to become a leading member of the Comintern, joining the Secretariat 1935. Returning to Italy after Mussolini's downfall, he advocated coalition politics with other leftist and democratic parties, a policy which came to fruition in the elections of 1948 where the communists won 135 seats.

Tōgō Heihachirō (c. 1846–1934). Japanese admiral who commanded the fleet at the battle of Tsushima 1905, when Japan defeated the Russians and effectively ended the Russo-Japanese War of 1904–05.

Tōjō Hideki (1884–1948). Japanese general and premier 1941–44 during World War II. Promoted to Chief of Staff of Japan's Guangdong army in Manchuria 1937, he served as minister for war 1940–41 where he was responsible for negotiating the tripartite Axis alliance with Germany and Italy 1940. He was held responsible for defeats in the Pacific 1944 and forced to resign. After Japan's defeat, he was hanged as a war criminal.

His main concern was winning the war in China, but both he and the Japanese Army felt this was being hampered by the Western powers denying Japan vital resources. He brought Japan into the war to take Allied colonial possessions in the Pacific and SE Asia, which put Japan in a position of strength in subsequent negotiations. As part of this strategy, he ordered the occupation of Indo-China 1941 and maintained peace negotiations with the USA right until the attack on Pearl Harbor 1941.

Suggested reading
Browne, C *Tojo: The Last Banzai* (1967)
Butow, R *Tojo and the Coming of War* (1961)

Tolstoy, Leo *Russian novelist Count Leo Tolstoy wrote his greatest novels,* War and Peace *and* Anna Karenina, *while living on his estate at Yasnaya Polyana. Between 1857 and 1861 he fostered an interest in educational reforms on two trips to western Europe, establishing a school for peasants on his return to the estate.*

Tokugawa military family that controlled Japan as shoguns 1603–1868. Tokugawa Ieyasu (1542–1616) was the Japanese general and politician who established the Tokugawa shogunate. The Tokugawa were feudal lords who ruled about one-quarter of Japan. Undermined by increasing foreign incursions, they were overthrown by an attack of provincial forces from Chōshū, Satsuma, and Tosa, who restored the Meiji emperor to power.

Toland Gregg (1904–1948). US director of film photography. He used deep focus to good effect in such films as *Wuthering Heights* 1939, *Citizen Kane* 1941, *The Grapes of Wrath* 1940, and *The Best Years of our Lives* 1946.

Tolansky Samuel (1907–1973). English physicist who analysed spectra to investigate nuclear spin and magnetic and quadrupole moments. He used multiple-beam interferometry to explore the fine details of surface structure. From 1947 he was professor at London University.

Tolansky made a particular study of the spectrum of mercury. He also studied the hyperfine structure of the spectra of halogen gases such as chlorine and bromine, and of arsenic, iron, copper, and platinum.

During World War II, Tolansky was asked to ascertain the spin of uranium-235, which is the isotope capable of fission in a nuclear chain reaction. Although he had to use samples in which the proportion was only 0.7%, he was fairly successful.

Tolkien J(ohn) R(onald) R(euel) (1892–1973). English writer. He created the fictional world of Middle Earth in *The Hobbit* 1937 and

One Ring to rule them all, One Ring to find them, / One Ring to bring them all and in the darkness bind them.

J R R TOLKIEN
Lord of the Rings pt 1 ch 2 1954

the trilogy *The Lord of the Rings* 1954–55, fantasy novels peopled with hobbits, dwarves, and strange magical creatures. His work developed a cult following in the 1960s and had many imitators. At Oxford University he was professor of Anglo-Saxon 1925–45 and Merton professor of English 1945–59.

Tolstoy Alexei Nikolaievich (1882–1945). Russian novelist and dramatist, a soldier of the counter-revolutionary White Army who later came under the patronage of Stalin. His works include the trilogy of novels *The Road to Calvary* 1921–41 and the historical *Peter the Great* 1929–34.

All happy families resemble each other, but each unhappy family is unhappy in its own way.

LEO TOLSTOY
Anna Karenina 1877

Tolstoy Leo Nikolaievich (1828–1910). Russian novelist. Tolstoy was born of noble family at Yasnaya Polyana, near Tula, and fought in the Crimean War. His first published work was *Childhood* 1852, the first part of the trilogy that was completed with *Boyhood* 1854 and *Youth* 1857. *Tales from Sebastopol* was published 1856. He wrote *War and Peace* 1863–69 and *Anna Karenina* 1873–77. From 1880 Tolstoy underwent a profound spiritual crisis and took up various moral positions, including passive resistance to evil, rejection of authority (religious or civil) and private ownership, and a return to basic mystical Christianity. He was excommunicated by the Orthodox Church, and his later works were banned.

Later books include *What I Believe* 1883 and *The Kreutzer Sonata* 1889, and the novel *Resurrection* 1900. His desire to give up his property and live as a peasant disrupted his family life, and he finally fled his home and died of pneumonia at the railway station in Astapovo.
Suggested reading
Berlin, Isaiah *The Hedgehog and the Fox: An Essay on Tolstoy's View of History* (1953)
Christian, R F *Tolstoy: A Critical Introduction* (1970)
Gifford, Henry *Tolstoy* (1982)
Hechy, Leo *Tolstoy the Rebel* (1975)
Rowe, W W *Leo Tolstoy* (1986)
Troyat, Henri *Tolstoy* (1965)
Wilson, A N *Tolstoy: A Biography* (1988)

Tomasi Giuseppe. Prince of Lampedusa. Italian writer; see ◊Lampedusa.

Tomba Alberto (1964–). Italian skier who became the Olympic and World Cup slalom and giant-slalom champion in 1988. He won the World Cup giant-slalom championships again in 1991. Tomba's gold medal in the giant slalom at the 1992 Albertville Winter Olympics enabled him to become the first skier to retain his Olympic gold medal.

Tombaugh Clyde William (1906–). US astronomer who discovered the planet Pluto 1930. Tombaugh, born in Streator, Illinois, became an assistant at the Lowell Observatory in Flagstaff, Arizona, in 1929, and photographed the sky in search of an undiscovered but predicted remote planet.

The new planet would be dim, so each photograph could be expected to show anything between 50,000 and 500,000 stars. And, because of its distance from the Earth, any visible motion would be very slight. Tombaugh solved the problem by comparing two photographs of the same part of the sky taken on different days. The photographic plates were focused at a single point and alternately flashed rapidly on to a screen. A planet moving against the background of stars would appear to move back and forth on the screen. Tombaugh found Pluto on 18 Feb 1930, from plates taken three weeks earlier. He continued his search for new planets across the entire sky; his failure to find any placed strict limits on the possible existence of planets beyond Pluto.

Tone (Theobald) Wolfe (1763–1798). Irish nationalist, prominent in the revolutionary society of the United Irishmen. In 1798 he accompanied the French invasion of Ireland, was captured and condemned to death, but slit his own throat in prison.

At bottom ... a sober, modest, brave man ... whom circumstances rather than predilection turned into a rebel.
Robert Dunlop on WOLFE TONE
in *Dictionary of National Biography*

Tönnies Ferdinand Julius (1855–1936). German social theorist and philosopher, one of the founders of the sociological tradition of community studies and urban sociology through his key work, *Gemeinschaft – Gesellschaft* 1887. Tönnies contrasted the nature of social relationships in traditional societies and small organizations (*Gemeinschaft*, 'community') with those in industrial societies and large organizations (*Gesellschaft*, 'association'). He was pessimistic about the effect of industrialization and urbanization on the social and moral order, seeing them as a threat to traditional society's sense of community.

With all my heart. Whose wife shall it be?
JOHN HORNE TOOKE
in reply to a suggestion that he take a wife

Tooke John Horne (1736–1812). British politician who established a Constitutional Society for parliamentary reform 1771. He was elected a member of Parliament 1801.

Toplady Augustus Montague (1740–1778). British Anglican priest, the author of the hymn 'Rock of Ages' 1775.

Torquemada Tomás de (1420–1498). Spanish Dominican monk, confessor to Queen Isabella I. In 1483 he revived the Inquisition on her behalf, and at least 2,000 'heretics' were burned; Torquemada also expelled the Jews from Spain 1492, with a resultant decline of the economy.

Torres Luis Vaez de (lived 17th century). Spanish navigator who, in 1605, sailed with an expedition under the command of Pedro Fernandez de Quiros in search of the supposed southland (*Terra Australis Incognito*). His navigation through the strait between New Guinea and Australia earned him the honour of the strait being named after him.

Torres-García Joaquin (1874–1949). Uruguayan artist. In Paris from 1926, he was influenced by Mondrian and others and, after visiting Madrid 1932, by Inca and Nazca pottery. His mature style is based on a grid pattern derived from the aesthetic proportions of the golden section.

Torricelli Evangelista (1608–1647). Italian physicist who established the existence of atmospheric pressure and devised the mercury barometer 1644. In 1643 Torricelli filled a long glass tube, closed at one end, with mercury and inverted it in a dish of mercury. Atmospheric pressure supported a column of mercury about 76 cm/30 in long; the space above the mercury was a vacuum. Noticing that the height of the mercury column varied slightly from day to day, he came to the conclusion that this was a reflection of variations in atmospheric pressure.

When physicist Galileo read Torricelli's *De motu gravium naturaliter descendentium et proiectorum* 1641, which dealt with movement, he invited him to Florence, where he served as Galileo's secretary for the three months till his death. From 1642 Torricelli was professor of mathematics at Florence.

Tortelier Paul (1914–1990). French cellist. His powerfully intuitive style brought him widespread fame as a soloist. Romantic in temperament, he specialized in the standard 19th-century repertoire, from Bach's solo suites to Elgar, Walton, and Kodály. Tortelier came to prominence 1947 as soloist in Richard Strauss' *Don Quixote* in London under English conductor Thomas Beecham. From 1956 he taught at the Paris Conservatoire, where his pupils included English cellist Jacqueline du Pré.

Torvill and Dean Jayne Torvill (1957–) and Christopher Dean (1959–) British ice-dance champions. They won the world title four times 1981–84 and were the 1984 Olympic champions. They turned professional shortly thereafter, but returned to international competition 1994 and immediately won the European Championship. They retired again from competitive ice dance after a bronze medal in the same year at the Olympic Games in Lillehammer, Norway.

Can't you read? The score demands con amore, and what are you doing? You are playing it like married men!
ARTURO TOSCANINI
Attributed remark, during rehearsal with an Austrian orchestra

Toscanini Arturo (1867–1957). Italian conductor. He made his mark in opera as three-times musical director of La Scala, Milan, 1898–1903, 1906–08, and 1921–29, and subsequently as conductor 1937–54 of the NBC Symphony Orchestra which was established for him by NBC (National Broadcasting Company) Radio. His wide-ranging repertoire included Debussy and Respighi, and he imparted an Italianate simplicity to Mozart and Beethoven when exaggerated solemnity was the trend in Germany.
Suggested reading
Horowitz, J *Understanding Toscanini* (1987)
Sachs, H *Toscanini* (1978)
Taubman, Howard *The Maestro: The Life of Arturo Toscanini* (1951)

A man gifted with remarkable discretion, energetic in the extreme, and held in high repute among the Goths.
Procopius on TOTILA
in *Wars* 7.2.7

Totila (died 522). King of the Ostrogoths, who warred with the Byzantine emperor Justinian for Italy, and was killed by General Narses at the battle of Taginae 552 in the Apennines.

Totò (1898–1967). Stage name of Antonio de Curtis Gagliardi Ducas Comneno di Bisanzio. Italian comedian who moved to films from the music hall. His films, such as *Totò le Moko* 1949 and *L'Oro di Napoli/Gold of Naples*, made him something of a national institution.

Toulouse-Lautrec Henri Marie Raymond de (1864–1901). French artist. Associated with the Impressionists, he was active in Paris, where he painted entertainers and prostitutes in a style characterized by strong colours, bold design, and brilliant technical skill. From 1891 his lithographic posters were a great success, skilfully executed and yet retaining the spontaneous character of sketches. His later work was to prove vital to the development of poster art.

At 18 he entered the studio of Bonnat and later of Cormon, but abandoned academic tuition 1884 and took his own studio in the rue Tourlaque, where he remained for 13 years. His main activity as an artist belongs to the decade 1885–95, when his life revolved round Montmartre. At home in society of every grade and in the haunts of gaiety or vice, he drew and observed in the cafés, cabarets and *maisons closes*, giving a wonderful picture of what has been called 'midnight civilization'. Among his cast of characters are Yvette Guilbert, La Goulue, Valentin, Chocolate the Negro dancer, and Jane Avril. Although detached in outlook, he shared in the excesses of the 1890s, which brought him broken in health to a sanatorium 1899. There he drew and painted from memory the series *Au Cirque*. In 1901, nearing final collapse, he joined his mother at the family château, where he died aged 37. He was impressed by Degas, owes something also to Forain, and brilliantly adapted the design and technique of the Japanese print to his own purpose in colour lithography, his posters for the Moulin Rouge and other resorts being classics of their kind. The usual oil method of painting does not seem to have been congenial to him, and he was interested neither in light nor form as such, but in the intensity of mood and expression that he conveyed with the utmost mastery.

Peinture à l'essence, oil diluted with petrol and used on board, giving a matt effect, was a favoured medium, enabling him to sketch swiftly and vividly in paint, but it is in drawings and lithographs that he is unique.

Suggested reading
Bouret, Jean *The Life and Work of Toulouse-Lautrec* (1966)
Hanson, Elizabeth *The Tragic Life of Toulouse-Lautrec* (1956)
Lucie-Smith, Edward *Toulouse-Lautrec* (1977)

Toungoo dynasty (1539–1752). Burmese family of rulers that reunified the country (now Myanmar) after the collapse of Pagan. The dynasty was founded by Tabinshweti and its most famous king was Bayinnaung. Its capital was at Pegu until 1634, then at Ava, which was captured 1752 by the Mon people as they overthrew the dynasty.

Tourneur Cyril (1575–1626). English dramatist. Little is known about his life, but *The Atheist's Tragedy* 1611 and *The Revenger's Tragedy* 1607 (thought by some scholars to be by Thomas Middleton) are among the most powerful of Jacobean dramas.

Toussaint L'Ouverture Pierre Dominique (*c.* 1743–1803). Haitian revolutionary leader, born a slave. He joined the insurrection of 1791 against the French colonizers and was made governor by the revolutionary French government. He expelled the Spanish and British, but when the French emperor Napoleon reimposed slavery he revolted, was captured, and died in prison in France. In 1983 his remains were returned to Haiti.

Suggested reading
James, C L R *Black Jacobins: Toussaint L'Ouverture and the San Domingo Revolution* (1963)
Moran, Charles *Black Triumvirate: A Study of L'Ouverture, Dessalines, Christophe* (1957)
Parkinson, W *This Gilded African* (1978)
Schlesinger, A M, Jr (ed) *Toussaint L'Ouverture: Haitian Liberator* (1989)

Tower John Goodwin (1925–1991). US Republican politician, a senator for Texas 1961–83. Tower, in 1961 the first Republican to be elected senator for Texas, emerged as a military expert in the Senate, becoming chair of the Armed Services Committee in 1981. After his retirement from the Senate in 1983, he acted as a consultant to arms manufacturers and chaired the 1986–87 Tower Commission, which investigated aspects of the Irangate arms-for-hostages scandal. Despite having been a paid arms-industry consultant, he was selected 1989 by President Bush to serve as defence secretary, but the Senate refused to approve the appointment because of Tower's previous heavy drinking.

Townes Charles Hard (1915–). US physicist who in 1953 designed and constructed the first maser. A maser (acronym for *m*icrowave *a*mplification by *s*timulated *e*mission of *r*adiation) is a high-frequency microwave amplifier or oscillator in which the signal to be amplified is used to stimulate unstable atoms into emitting energy at the same frequency. Atoms or molecules are raised to a higher energy level and then allowed to lose this energy by radiation emitted at a precise frequency. For this work, he shared the 1964 Nobel prize. He was professor at Columbia 1950–61, at the Massachusetts Institute of Technology 1961–67, and from 1967 at the University of California, Berkeley.

Ammonia molecules can occupy only two energy levels and, Townes argued, if a molecule in the high energy level can be made to absorb a photon of a specific frequency, then the molecule should fall to the lower energy level, emitting two photons of the same frequency and producing a coherent beam of single-frequency microwave radiation. Townes had to develop a method (now called population inversion) for separating the relatively scarce high-energy molecules from the more common lower energy ones. He succeeded by using an electric field that focused the high-energy ammonia molecules into a resonator.

In 1958 Townes published a paper that demonstrated the theoretical possibility of producing an optical maser to produce a coherent beam of single-frequency visible light.

Townsend John Sealy Edward (1868–1957). Irish mathematical physicist who studied the kinetics of electrons and ions in gases. He was the first to obtain a value for the charge on the electron, in 1898, and to explain how electric discharges pass through gases. From 1900 Townsend was professor at Oxford. Knighted 1941.

Townsend studied the conductivity of gases ionized by the newly discovered X-rays and in 1897 developed a method for producing ionized gases using electrolysis. In 1898, he began the first study of diffusion in gases that had been ionized (or electrified) by means of the so-called Townsend discharge of a weak current through low-pressure gases. In Townsend's collision theory of ionization, collisions by negative ions (electrons) could induce the formation of secondary ions, thus carrying an electric charge through a gas.

Townsend also studied the electrical conditions that led to the production of a spark in a gas, and the confusing role played in this by the positive ions that are produced simultaneously with the electrons.

During the 1920s, Townsend was involved with the measurement of the average fraction of energy lost by an electron in a single collision.

Townsend Sue (Susan) (1946–). English humorous novelist. She is the author of *The Secret Diary of Adrian Mole, aged 13$\frac{3}{4}$* 1982 and later sequels. Other novels include *Rebuilding Coventry* 1985 and *The Queen and I* 1992.

Never minister had cleaner hands than he had.

Lord Chesterfield on CHARLES TOWNSHEND
Letters (Mahon ed) vol ii

Townshend Charles (1725–1767). British politician, chancellor of the Exchequer 1766–67. The Townshend Acts, designed to assert Britain's traditional authority over its colonies, resulted in widespread resistance. Among other things they levied taxes on imports (such as tea, glass, and paper) into the North American colonies. Opposition in the colonies to taxation without representation precipitated the American Revolution.

Townshend Charles, 2nd Viscount Townshend (known as 'Turnip' Townshend) (1674–1738). English politician and agriculturalist. He was secretary of state under George I 1714–17, when dismissed for opposing the king's foreign policy, and 1721–30, after which he retired to his farm and did valuable work in developing crop rotation and cultivating winter feeds for cattle (hence his nickname). Viscount 1687.

Townshend did not, in fact, originate the new techniques with which his name has become associated. Turnips, for example, were already being grown in East Anglia, England, as a fodder crop from at least the 1660s, and it is unlikely that he ever adopted the four-course turnips–barley–clover–wheat rotation. This was not taken up until many years after his death. Through the successful development of his agricultural estate at Rainham in W Norfolk, however, Townshend brought a range of improved cultivation practices to wider public notice.

Townshend Charles Vere Ferrers (1861–1924). British soldier. He served with the Royal Marines in India, where he came to prominence by his defence of Chitral 1893, before returning to Africa. His loss of Kut-al-Imara during World War I and subsequent indifference to the brutal treatment of his men was further compounded by his offer to act as an intermediary between the British and Turkish governments. He was ignored by the British and never received another military appointment. KCB 1917.

Townshend Pete(r Dennis Blandford) (1945–). UK rock musician. He was a founder member of the Who. His solo albums include *Empty Glass* 1980.

Toynbee Arnold (1852–1883). English economic historian who coined the term 'industrial revolution' in his *Lectures on the Industrial Revolution*, published 1884. Toynbee Hall, an education settlement in the east end of London, was named after him.

Civilization is a movement and not a condition, a voyage and not a harbour.

ARNOLD TOYNBEE
in *Reader's Digest* Oct 1958

Toynbee Arnold Joseph (1889–1975). English historian whose *A Study of History* 1934–61 was an attempt to discover the laws governing the rise and fall of civilizations. He was the nephew of the economic historian Arnold Toynbee.
Suggested reading
McNeill, W H *Arnold J Toynbee: A Life* (1989)
Stromberg, Ronald *Arnold J Toynbee: Historian for an Age of Crisis* (1972)
Winetrout, Kenneth *Arnold J Toynbee* (1975)

America is a large, friendly dog in a very small room. Every time it wags its tail it knocks over a chair.

ARNOLD TOYNBEE
Broadcast news summary 14 July 1954

Toyotomi Hideyoshi. Adopted name of Kinoshita Tōkichirō (1537–1598). Japanese warlord, one of the three military leaders who unified Japan in the 16th century (Momoyama period). Successful military campaigns and alliances gave him control of central and SW Japan by 1587 and E Japan by 1590. His invasion of Korea 1592–98 was, however, defeated.

Skilled in siege strategy, Hideyoshi rose in the service of Oda Nobunaga (1534–1582), the first of the three great Momoyama warlords, and on the death of Nobunaga took over the leadership of his troops, subduing Kyushu island in the SW. He reached an agreement with his main rival, Tokugawa Ieyasu, in E central Honshu, and had himself appointed regent (*kanpaku*) by the emperor 1585, chancellor (*dajōdaijin*) 1586, and retired regent (*taiko*) 1592, the last being the title by which he is still known in Japan; he did not take the title of shogun. He was an able administrator, introducing new land and tax systems and ordering the disarmament of all but the samurai class. He instigated land surveys and in 1590 a population census.

In Hollywood sometimes you're dead before you're dead.

SPENCER TRACY
in *Sunday Express* 1960

Tracy Spencer (1900–1967). US actor. He was distinguished for his understated, seemingly effortless, natural performances. His films include *Captains Courageous* 1937 and *Boys' Town* 1938 (for both of which he won Academy Awards), and he starred with Katharine Hepburn in nine films, including *Adam's Rib* 1949 and *Guess Who's Coming to Dinner* 1967, his final appearance. His other films include *Bad Day at Black Rock* 1955, *The Last Hurrah* 1958, *The Old Man and the Sea* 1958, and *Inherit the Wind* 1960.
Suggested reading
Davidson, Bill *Spencer Tracy: Tragic Idol* (1988)
Deschner, D *The Complete Films of Spencer Tracy* (1987)
Kanin, Garson *Tracy and Hepburn* (1971)

Tradescant John (1570–c. 1638). English gardener and botanist who travelled widely in Europe and is thought to have introduced the cos lettuce to England from the Greek island of that name. He was appointed gardener to Charles I and was succeeded by his son, John Tradescant the Younger (1608–1662). The younger Tradescant undertook three plant-collecting trips to Virginia in North America. The Tradescants introduced many new plants to Britain, including the acacia, lilac, and occidental plane. Tradescant senior is generally considered the earliest collector of plants and other natural-history objects.

In 1604 the elder Tradescant became gardener to the earl of Salisbury, who in 1610 for the first time sent him abroad to collect plants. In 1620 he accompanied an official expedition against the North African Barbary pirates and brought back to England gutta-percha and various fruits and seeds. Later, when he became gardener to Charles I, Tradescant set up his own garden and museum in London. In 1624 he published a catalogue of 750 plants grown in his garden.

The Tradescants' collection of specimens formed the nucleus of the Ashmolean Museum in Oxford. Swedish botanist Carolus Linnaeus named the genus *Tradescantia* (the spiderworts) after the younger Tradescant.

I within did flow / With seas of life, like wine. / I nothing of this world did know, / But 'twas divine!

THOMAS TRAHERNE
'Wonder'

Traherne Thomas (*c.* 1637–1674). English Christian mystic. His moving lyric poetry and his prose *Centuries of Meditations* were unpublished until 1903.

Trajan (Marcus Ulpius Trajanus) (AD 52–117). Roman emperor and soldier, born in Seville. He was adopted as heir by Nerva, whom he succeeded AD 98. He was a just and conscientious ruler, corresponded with Pliny about the Christians, and conquered Dacia (Romania) 101–07 and much of Parthia (113–17), bringing the empire to its greatest extent. Trajan's Column, erected in the Forum he had constructed, commemorates his Dacian victories.

The public interest must be our sole concern.

TRAJAN
quoted in Pliny *Letters* bk 10.22

Traven B(en). Pen name of Albert Otto Max Feige (*c.* 1882–1969). German-born US novelist. His true identity was not revealed until 1979. His books include the bestseller *The Death Ship* 1926 and *The Treasure of the Sierra Madre* 1934, which was made into a film starring Humphrey Bogart 1948.

Born in a part of Germany now in Poland, he was in turn known as the anarchist Ret Marut, Traven Torsvan, and Hollywood scriptwriter Hal Croves. Between the two world wars he lived in obscurity in Mexico and avoided recognition.

Travers Ben(jamin) (1886–1980). English dramatist. He wrote (for actors Tom Walls, Ralph Lynn, and Robertson Hare) the 'Aldwych farces' of the 1920s, so named from the London theatre in which they were played. They include *A Cuckoo in the Nest* 1925 and *Rookery Nook* 1926.

Travers Morris William (1872–1961). English chemist who, with Scottish chemist William Ramsay, between 1894 and 1908 first identified what were called the inert or noble gases: krypton, xenon, and radon.

Travers was born in London and studied there at University College, where he became professor 1903. He went to Bangalore 1906 as director of the new Indian Institute of Scientists, but returned to Britain at the outbreak of World War I and directed the manufacture of glass at Duroglass Limited. In 1920 he became involved with high-temperature furnaces and fuel technology, including the gasification of coal.

Travers helped Ramsay to determine the properties of the newly discovered gases argon and helium. They also heated minerals and meteorites in the search for further gases, but found none. Then in 1898 they obtained a large quantity of liquid air and subjected it to fractional distillation. Spectral analysis of the least volatile fraction revealed the presence of krypton. They examined the argon fraction for a constituent of lower boiling point, and discovered neon. Finally xenon, occurring as an even less volatile companion to krypton, was identified spectroscopically.

Travers continued his researches in cryogenics and made the first accurate temperature measurements of liquid gases. He also helped to build several experimental liquid air plants in Europe.

Travolta John (1954–). US film actor. Tall, dark, and athletic, he achieved teenage heart-throb status in *Saturday Night Fever* 1977 and *Grease* 1978. His career subsequently faltered but he regained some popularity in the comedy *Look Who's Talking* 1989 and its sequels. He won plaudits as a serious actor in the role of an underworld killer in *Pulp Fiction* 1994.

He fell in love with magnificence.

J L Palmer on HERBERT BEERBOHM TREE
in *Dictionary of National Biography*

Tree Herbert Draper Beerbohm (1853–1917). English actor and theatre manager. Noted for his lavish Shakespeare productions, he was founder of the Royal Academy of Dramatic Art (RADA). He was the half-brother of Max Beerbohm. Knighted 1909.

Trefusis Violet (1894–1972). British society hostess and writer. Daughter of Mrs Keppel, who was later the mistress of Edward VII, she had a disastrous marriage to cavalry officer Denys Trefusis and a passionate elopement with the writer Vita Sackville-West.

Treitschke Heinrich von (1834–1896). German historian. At first a Liberal, he later adopted a Pan-German standpoint. He is known for the *Deutsche Geschichte im 19 Jahrhundert/History of Germany in the 19th Century* 1879–94.

Trenchard Hugh Montague, 1st Viscount Trenchard (1873–1956). British aviator and police commissioner. He commanded the Royal Flying Corps in World War I 1915–17, and 1918–29 organized the Royal Air Force, becoming its first marshal 1927. As commissioner of the Metropolitan Police 1931–35, he established the Police College at Hendon and carried out the Trenchard Reforms, which introduced more scientific methods of detection. KCB 1918, baronet 1919, baron 1930, viscount 1936.

Trésaguet Pierre-Marie-Jérôme (1716–1796). French civil engineer who introduced improved methods of road building.

Trésaguet was born in Nevers and worked for the Corps des Ponts et Chaussées on civil engineering projects. He eventually rose to inspector general.

Trésaguet realized that lasting improvement to roads could be made only by providing a solid foundation, one that could withstand winter rains and frost, and the effects of traffic. He chose to dig out the roadbed to a depth of about 25 cm/10 in and lay first a course of uniform flat stones, laid on edge to permit drainage. Well hammered in, they provided a solid base on top of which he spread a layer of much smaller stones for a smoother surface. His roads were built 5.4 m/18 ft wide, with a crown that rose 15 cm/6 in above the outside edge.

His method was first used for a main road that ran from Paris to the Spanish border, via Toulouse. It proved so successful that many other countries copied the idea.

Scottish civil engineer Thomas Telford put the principle into practice when he was surveyor to the county of Shropshire.

Tressell Robert. Pseudonym of Robert Noonan (1868–1911). English author. *The Ragged Trousered Philanthropists*, published in an abridged form 1914, gave a detailed account of the poverty of working people's lives.

Treurnicht Andries Petrus (1921–1993). South African Conservative Party politician. A former minister of the Dutch Reformed Church, he was elected to the South African parliament as a National Party member 1971 but left it 1982 to form a new right-wing Conservative Party, opposed to any dilution of the apartheid system.

Born at Piketberg, Treurnicht was a student at Stellenbosch and Cape Town universities, acquiring a doctorate in political philosophy. He was a minister of the Dutch Reformed Church 1946–60,

later becoming the editor of its influential journal *Die Kerkbode*. In this capacity he came to the attention of prime minister Hendrik Verwoerd, who was seeking some philosophical justification for the policy of apartheid. Treurnicht provided this and, having sampled the fringe of politics, decided to commit himself wholeheartedly, and was elected MP for Waterbury 1971.

He occupied a number of governmental posts, including education and training 1976–78, plural relations and development 1978–79, public works, statistics, and tourism 1979–80, and state administration and statistics 1980–82. He broke away from the National Party when it accepted a proposal to create a tricameral parliament in which whites, coloureds, and Indians would be represented in separate chambers. His party, which sought the establishment of an independent Boer republic, gained ground in the 1987 and 1989 elections but dropped back in 1992. Towards the end of his life Treurnicht softened the party's approach and participated in multiparty constitutional talks.

Trevelyan George Macaulay (1876–1962). British historian. Regius professor of history at Cambridge 1927–40, he pioneered the study of social history, as in his *English Social History* 1942.

Trevelyan George Otto (1838–1928). British politician and historian, a nephew of the historian Lord Macaulay, whose biography he wrote 1876. Succeeded to baronetcy 1886.

Trevino Lee Buck (1939–). US golfer who won his first major title, the 1968 US Open, as a virtual unknown, and won it again in 1971. He has also won the British Open and US PGA titles twice, and is one of only five players to have won the US Open and British Open in the same year. He played in six Ryder Cup matches and was nonplaying captain in 1985.

Trevithick Richard (1771–1833). English engineer, constructor of a steam road locomotive 1801, the first to carry passengers, and probably the first steam engine to run on rails 1804. Trevithick also built steamboats, river dredgers, and threshing machines.

Trevithick was born in Illogan, Cornwall. As a boy he was fascinated by mining machinery and the large stationary steam engines that worked the pumps. He made a working model of a steam road locomotive 1797 and went on to build various full-sized engines.

Trevithick's road locomotive *Puffing Devil* made its debut on Christmas Eve 1801, but burned out while he and his friends were celebrating their success at a nearby inn. He then made a larger version which he drove from Cornwall to London the following year, at a top speed of 19 kph/12 mph.

By 1804 he had produced his first railway locomotive, able to haul 10 tonnes and 70 people for 15 km/9.5 mi on rails used by horse-drawn trains at a mine in Wales. He set up in London 1808 giving novelty rides on the engine *Catch-me-who-can*. Then in 1816 he left England for Peru. When he returned, after making and losing a fortune, he found that steam transport had become a thriving concern. Trevithick had been overtaken, and he died a poor man.

We are all [neurotically] ill: but even a universal sickness implies an idea of health.

LIONEL TRILLING
The Liberal Imagination 'Art and Neurosis' 1950

Trilling Lionel (1905–1975). US author and literary critic. Born in New York, USA, and educated at Columbia University, Trilling joined the Columbia English Department faculty 1932. He received his PhD 1938 and was appointed professor 1948. His novel *The Middle of the Journey* 1947 is based on the character of Whittaker Chambers, who was to be a protagonist of the Alger Hiss case. His books of criticism include *The Liberal Imagination* 1950, *Beyond Culture* 1965, and *The Experience of Literature* 1967. He also produced annotated editions of the works of English poets Matthew Arnold and John Keats.

Tristan Flora (1803–1844). French socialist writer and activist. She was the author of *Promenades dans Londres/The London Journal*

1840, a vivid record of social conditions, and *L'Union ouvrière/Workers' Union* 1843, an outline of a workers' utopia.

Tristano Lennie (Lennard Joseph) (1919–1978). US jazz pianist and composer. An austere musician, he gave an academic foundation to the school of cool jazz in the 1940s and 1950s, which was at odds with the bebop tradition. He was also active as a teacher.

Trollope Anthony (1815–1882). English novelist. He went to Ireland at the age of 26 as a junior Post Office official and his first two novels had Irish themes. He became a post office clerk 1834, introduced the pillar box 1853, and achieved the position of surveyor before retiring 1867. He tried unsuccessfully to enter Parliament as a Liberal. He delineated provincial English middle-class society in a series of novels set in or around the imaginary cathedral city of Barchester. *The Warden* 1855 began the series, which includes *Barchester Towers* 1857, *Doctor Thorne* 1858, and *The Last Chronicle of Barset* 1867. His political novels include *Can You Forgive Her?* 1864, *Phineas Finn* 1867–69, and *The Prime Minister* 1875–76.

Suggested reading
Mullen, R *Anthony Trollope: A Victorian and his World* (1990)
Snow, C P *Trollope: His Life and Art* (1975)
Trollope, Anthony *Autobiography* (1883, several recent editions)
Wright, A *Anthony Trollope* (1983)

Tromp Maarten Harpertszoon (1597–1653). Dutch admiral. He twice defeated the occupying Spaniards 1639. He was defeated by English admiral Blake May 1652, but in Nov triumphed over Blake in the Strait of Dover. In Feb–June 1653 he was defeated by Blake and Monk, and was killed off the Dutch coast. His son, Cornelius Tromp (1629–1691), also an admiral, fought a battle against the English and French fleets in 1673.

Any contemporary of ours who wants peace and comfort before anything has chosen a bad time to be born.
LEON TROTSKY
quoted in *Observer* 26 March 1933

Trotsky Leon. Adopted name of Lev Davidovitch Bronstein (1879–1940). Russian revolutionary. Trotsky became a Marxist in the 1890s and was imprisoned and exiled for opposition to the tsarist regime. He lived in W Europe from 1902 until the 1905 revolution, when he was again imprisoned but escaped to live in exile until 1917, when he returned to Russia. He joined the Bolshevik party and took a leading part in the seizure of power 1917 and raising the Red Army that fought the Civil War 1918–20. Although as a young man Trotsky admired Lenin, when he worked with him organizing the revolution of 1917, he objected to Lenin's dictatorial ways. He was second in command until Lenin's death, and was minister for foreign affairs 1917–18 and minister for war 1918–Jan 1925. In the struggle for power that followed Lenin's death 1924, Stalin defeated Trotsky, and this and other differences with the Communist Party led to his exile 1929. He settled in Mexico, where he was assassinated at Stalin's instigation. Trotsky believed in world revolution and in permanent revolution, and was an uncompromising, if liberal, idealist.

Official Soviet recognition of responsibility for his assassination through the secret service came in 1989. Trotsky's later works are critical of the Soviet regime; for example, *The Revolution Betrayed* 1937. His greatest work is his magisterial *History of the Russian Revolution* 1932–33.

Suggested reading
Deutscher, Isaac *The Prophet Armed* (1954)
Deutscher, Isaac *The Prophet Unarmed* (1959)
Deutscher, Isaac *The Prophet Outcast* (1963)
Mandel, Ernest *Trotsky: A Study in the Dynamic of His Thought* (1979)
Segal, Ronald *Leon Trotsky: A Biography* (1979)
Trotsky, Leon *My Life* (trs 1930)

Troyanos Tatiana (1938–1993). US opera singer. Her repertoire was wide but she was especially noted for her singing of trouser roles, particularly as the composer in Richard Strauss's *Ariadne auf Naxos* and Octavian in his *Der Rosenkavalier*.

Troyanos was born in New York. Her father was Greek, her mother of German origin. She studied *Lieder* and oratorio, though not opera, at the Juilliard School with Hans Heinz. She made her operatic debut 1963 with the New York City Opera, singing Hippolyta in Benjamin Britten's *A Midsummer Night's Dream* and stayed with them for two years. She then went to Germany and sang for the Hamburg State Opera for ten years, during which time she sang Dorabella in Mozart's *Così fan Tutti*, several Verdi roles, and Baba the Turk in Stravinsky's *The Rake's Progress*, which the company brought to the Metropolitan Opera, New York 1967. Troyanos also sang in Munich, Vienna, and Salzburg. From 1971 she appeared frequently in the United States, where her performances included the title role in Handel's *Ariodante* in Washington and Charlotte in Massenet's *Werther* in Chicago. In Boston 1971 she sang Romeo in Bellini's *I Capuleti ed i Montecci* (based on *Romeo and Juliet*); some years later she sang this role at Covent Garden. Her debut with the Metropolitan Opera was in 1976, when she sang Octavian, and stayed for 16 years. Her roles there included Hansel in Humperdinck's *Hansel und Gretel*, Orlovsky in Johann Strauss's *Die Fledermaus*, Adalgisa in Bellini's *Norma* (which she also sang at La Scala), and Queen Isabella in Philip Glass's 1992 commemorative opera about Christopher Columbus, *The Voyage*.

Troyat Henri. Pen name of Lev Tarassoff (1911–). Russian-born French writer. His 77 books include novels and political and literary biographies. His novel *L'Araignée/The Web* 1938 won the Prix Goncourt.

Tarassoff was born in Moscow, but his family moved to Paris 1920 after the Russian Revolution, and many of his books draw on his Russian background. He published his first novel 1934. *Tant que la Terre durera/My Father's House* 1947–50, a trilogy, is a historical saga of a White Russian family from 1905 until its exile in France after the Revolution, and the five-part *Les Semailles et les moissons/The Seed and the Fruit* 1953–58 tells the story of a family in the Corrèze *département* from the end of World War I to the liberation from the Nazis 1944. Troyat has written biographies of the writers Mikhail Lermontov, Fyodor Dostoevsky, Nicolai Gogol, and Leo Tolstoy, and of the Russian rulers Catherine the Great, Peter the Great, and Ivan the Terrible. He was elected to the French Academy 1959.

Trudeau Pierre Elliott (1919–). Canadian Liberal politician. He was prime minister 1968–79 and 1980–84. In 1980, having won again by a landslide on a platform opposing Quebec separatism, he helped to defeat the Quebec independence movement in a referendum. He repatriated the constitution from Britain 1982, but by 1984 had so lost support that he resigned.

Suggested reading
Butson, T *Pierre Trudeau* (1986)
Radwanski, George *Trudeau* (1978)

In James Dean today's youth discovers itself.
FRANÇOIS TRUFFAUT
on *Antenne* (French TV) 26 Sept 1956

Truffaut François (1932–1984). French New Wave film director and actor. He was formerly a critic. A romantic and intensely humane film-maker, he wrote and directed a series of semi-autobiographical films starring Jean-Pierre Léaud, beginning with *Les Quatre Cent Coups/The 400 Blows* 1959. His other films include *Jules et Jim*, *Fahrenheit 451* 1966, *L'Enfant sauvage/The Wild Child* 1970, and *La Nuit américaine/Day for Night* 1973 (Academy Award).

His passion in cinema led to a job as film critic for *Cahiers du cinéma* during the 1950s before embarking on his career as director. His later work includes *The Story of Adèle H* 1975 and *Le Dernier Métro/The Last Metro* 1980. He played one of the leading roles in Steven Spielberg's *Close Encounters of the Third Kind* 1977.

Suggested reading
Allen, D *Finally Truffaut* (1986)
Insdorf, A *François Truffaut* (1978)
Monaco, James *The New Wave* (1976)

Truganini (*c.* 1812–1876). Australian Aborigine, thought to be the last full-blooded Tasmanian Aborigine. Her tribe was violently disrupted by European sealers, whalers, and timber merchants. In the 1830s, with her husband, Wooraddy, she assisted George Robinson in rounding up the remnants of her people to protect them from murder. She accompanied Robinson to the unsuccessful Aboriginal settlement on Flinders Island and later to Port Phillip. In 1856 the few remaining Tasmanian Aborigines from the groups who had been taken to Flinders Island were moved to Oyster Bay on the E coast of Tasmania where they tried to resume their traditional lifestyle. By 1873 all but Truganini had died and she moved to Hobart. After her death, against her stated wishes, her body was exhumed for scientific research. From 1904–47 her skeleton was on display at the Tasmanian Museum. Her bones were eventually cremated and the ashes scattered on the D'Entrecasteaux Channel by Aboriginal rights workers.

Trujillo Molina Rafael Leónidas (1891–1961). Dictator of the Dominican Republic 1930–61. As commander of the Dominican Guard, he seized power and established a ruthless autocracy aided by a powerful police force. He owned all the mass media and the transport and communications systems in the Dominican Republic as well as 80% of the land and the country' banks, services, and utilities. He also owned around 45% of all sources of production. He was assassinated.

The buck stops here.

HARRY S TRUMAN
Sign on his presidential desk

Truman Harry S (1884–1972). 33rd president of the USA 1945–53, a Democrat. Born in Lamar, Missouri, he ran a clothing store that was bankrupted by the Great Depression. He became a senator 1934. In Jan 1945 he became vice president to F D Roosevelt, and president when Roosevelt died in April that year. He used the atom bomb against Japan, launched the Marshall Plan to restore W Europe's economy, and nurtured the European Community (now the European Union) and NATO (including the rearmament of West Germany).

In 1948 he was elected for a second term in a surprise victory over Thomas Dewey (1902–1971), governor of New York. At home, he had difficulty converting the economy back to peacetime conditions, and failed to prevent witch-hunts on suspected communists such as Alger Hiss. In Korea, he intervened when the South was invaded, but sacked General MacArthur when the general's policy threatened to start World War III. Truman's decision not to enter Chinese territory, betrayed by the double agent Kim Philby, led to China's entry into the war.

Suggested reading
Alonzo, L (ed) *Harry S Truman and the Fair Deal* (1974)
Ferrell, Robert *Harry S Truman and the Modern American Presidency* (1983)
Jenkins, Roy *Truman* (1986)
Kirkendall, R (ed) *The Harry S Truman Encyclopedia* (1989)
McCoy, D R *The Presidency of Harry S Truman* (1984)
Miller, R *Truman: The Rise to Power* (1986)

Trumbull John (1756–1843). American artist. He was known for his series of historical paintings of war scenes from the American revolution (1775–83), the most famous of which was his depiction of the signing of the Declaration of Independence 1776.

His first works were inspired by Copley. He had a year under West in London, 1785, and afterwards turned from individual portraiture to painting scenes from the American Revolution, including the likenesses of those still living who had taken part. In his spirited battle pictures he was no unworthy successor of Copley. In 1817 he was commissioned by Congress to paint four revolutionary themes for the Rotunda of the Capitol at Washington.

Trump Donald John (1946–). US millionaire property financier who for his headquarters in 1983 built the skyscraper Trump Tower in New York. He owns three casinos in Atlantic City, New Jersey.

The son of a builder, Trump studied finance and in 1974 negotiated his first big property deal, rebuilding the Commodore Hotel, Manhattan, with financial help from the Hyatt Corporation. In addition to Trump Tower on Fifth Avenue, he built nearby Trump Parc and bought the Plaza Hotel in 1983. One of his casinos is named Trump's Castle.

Trumpler Robert Julius (1886–1956). Swiss-born US astronomer who studied and classified star clusters found in our Galaxy. He also took part in observational tests of the general theory of relativity 1922.

In 1915 he moved to the USA; he was professor of astronomy at the University of California from 1930.

At the Allegheny Observatory in Pennsylvania, Trumpler noted that galactic star clusters contain an irregular distribution of different classes of stars, and these observations paved the way for later theories about stellar evolution. In 1930 he showed that interstellar material was responsible for obscuring some light from galaxies, which had led to overestimations of their distances from Earth.

Working at the Lick Observatory, near Chicago, he studied the planet Mars, concluding that some of the supposed 'canals' observed by Italian astronomer Giovanni Schiaparelli could be volcanic faults. Trumpler's hypothesis, made in 1924, did not gain real support until the return of the photographs taken by the *Mariner 9* space probe to Mars, more than 50 years later.

Truth Sojourner. Adopted name of Isabella Baumfree, later Isabella Van Wagener (*c.* 1797–1883). US antislavery and women's-suffrage campaigner. Born a slave, she ran away and became involved with religious groups. In 1843 she was 'commanded in a vision' to adopt the name Sojourner Truth. She published an autobiography, *The Narrative of Sojourner Truth*, in 1850. She worked as a fund-raiser for the North during the American Civil War.

Ts'ao Chan alternative transcription of Chinese novelist ◊Cao Chan.

Ts'ao Ts'ao Chinese general AD 155–220; see ◊Cao Cao.

Tschiffley Aimé Felix (1895–1954). Swiss writer and traveller whose 16,000-km/10,000-mi journey on horseback from Buenos Aires to New York was known as 'Tschiffley's Ride', recounted in *Southern Cross to Pole Star* 1933.

Tschumi Bernard (1944–). Swiss-born architect. An exponent of Deconstructionism, he has drawn far more than he has built. In his competition-winning proposals for Parc de la Villette in Paris (begun 1982), a series of striking red pavilions, lining the main route to the park, are the scheme's most obvious architectural manifestations. These are, in effect, follies, accentuating the anti-functional Deconstructionist ethic.

Tsiolkovsky Konstantin Eduardovich (1857–1935). Russian scientist who developed the theory of space flight. He published the first practical paper on astronautics 1903, dealing with space travel by rockets using liquid propellants, such as liquid oxygen.

Tsiolkovsky was born in the Spassk district and had little formal education; he was deaf from the age of ten. He never actually constructed a rocket, but his theories and designs were fundamental in helping to establish the reality of space flight.

In 1883 Tsiolkovsky proved that it is feasible for a rocket-propelled craft to travel through the vacuum of space. He calculated that in order to achieve flight into space, speeds of 11.26 km/7 mi per second or 40,232 kph/25,000 mph would be needed – the escape velocity for Earth. Known solid fuels were too heavy, so Tsiolkovsky worked out how to use liquid fuels. He also suggested the 'piggyback' or step principle, with one rocket on top of another. When the lower one was expended, it could be jettisoned (reducing the weight) while the next one fired and took over.

Tsvetayeva Marina Ivanovna (1892–1941). Russian poet. Most of her work was written after she left the USSR 1923. She wrote mythic, romantic, frenetic verse, including *The Demesne of the Swans*, written in the 1920s but not published until 1957. Her *Selected Poems* was translated 1971.

Suggested reading
Karlinsky, Simon *Marina Tsvetaeva* (1985)
Proffer, Ellendea (ed) *Tsvetaeva: A Pictorial Biography* (1985)
Schweitzer, Viktoria *Tsvetaeva* (1992)

Tswett Mikhail Semyonovich (1872–1919). Italian-born Russian scientist who made an extensive study of plant pigments and developed the technique of chromatography to separate them.

Tswett was born in Asti and studied at Geneva, Switzerland. He worked in Warsaw from 1901, and during World War I organized the evacuation of the Botany Department of the Warsaw Polytechnic Institute to Moscow and Gorky. In 1917 he was appointed professor of botany at Yuriev University (Estonia), but under threat of German invasion had to move once again, to Voronezh.

Tswett showed that green leaves contain more than one type of chlorophyll, and by 1906 he had devised an adsorption method of separating the pigments. He ground up leaves in petroleum ether and let the liquid trickle down a glass tube filled with powdered chalk or alumina. As the mixture seeped downwards, each pigment showed a different degree of readiness to attach itself to the adsorbent, and in this way the pigments became separated as different-coloured layers in the tube. Tswett called the new technique chromatography because the result of the analysis was 'written in colour' along the length of the adsorbent column. Eventually he found six different pigments.

Tubman Harriet Ross (1821–1913). US abolitionist. Born a slave in Maryland, she escaped to Philadelphia (where slavery was outlawed) 1849. She set up the Underground Railroad, a secret network of sympathizers, to help slaves escape to the North and Canada. During the American Civil War she spied for the Union army. She spoke against slavery and for women's rights, and founded schools for emancipated slaves after the Civil War.

Tubman William Vacanarat Shadrach (1895–1971). Liberian politician. The descendant of US slaves, he was a lawyer in the USA. After his election to the presidency of Liberia 1944 he concentrated on uniting the various ethnic groups. Re-elected several times, he died in office of natural causes, despite frequent assassination attempts.

Tucker Albert (1914–). Australian Surrealist and Symbolist painter. Self-taught, his early work has much in common with the strong colours and forms of German Expressionism. His Surrealist paintings include *The Futile City* 1940, which shows the influence of de Chirico and T S Eliot's 'Hollow Men' poems, and *The Intruders* 1964, which features his 'Antipodean Heads': blank-eyed creatures in which man and the harsh Australian outback environment are fused.

Tuckwell Barry Emmanuel (1931–). Australian-born British horn player. Heralded as the greatest virtuoso of his generation, he seems to play technically formidable passages effortlessly. He has appeared both as a soloist and as a member of the Tuckwell Wind Quintet.

Tudjman Franjo (1922–). Croatian nationalist leader and historian, president from 1990. During World War II Tudjman joined Tito's partisan force and rose to the rank of major general before leaving the army 1960. He was expelled from the League of Communists of Yugoslavia 1967 for Croatian nationalist writings and imprisoned for separatist activities 1972–74 and 1981–84. In 1990 he was elected president, having campaigned under a nationalist, anti-Serbia banner. As leader of the centre-right Croatian Democratic Union (CDU), he led the fight for Croatian independence. During the 1991–92 civil war, his troops were hampered by lack of arms and the military superiority of the Serb-dominated federal army, but Croatia's independence was recognized following a successful United Nations-negotiated cease-fire Jan 1992. Tudjman was re-elected Aug 1992 and again Oct 1995.

He was criticized for his hesitant conduct during the 1991–92 civil war but, despite many soldiers having opted to fight under the banner of the better-equipped right-wing extremist faction by Dec 1991, Tudjman retained the vocal support of the majority of Croatians.

In 1993, in violation of the 1992 UN peace accord, Tudjman launched an offensive to recapture Serb-held territory in the disputed Krajina enclave, and further offensives into W Slavonia and Krajina 1995, which created more than 150,000 Serb refugees and were allegedly accompanied by widespread human-rights violations. In Aug 1995 Krajina was recaptured from the Serbs, and Serbia subsequently agreed to gradually hand back control over Eastern Slavonia. Tudjman called an early election Oct 1995, seeking a popular mandate to continue with his militaristic policies, but, although re-elected, his party failed to win the two-thirds majority for which he had hoped.

Tudor Antony (born William Cook) (1908–1987). English choreographer, dancer, and teacher. He introduced psychological drama into ballet. His first works were for the Rambert company (for example, *Lilac Garden* 1936). He was one of the founding choreographers for the American Ballet Theater 1940 and created several works for it, including *Pillar of Fire* 1942, *Romeo and Juliet* 1943, and *The Tiller in the Fields* 1978.

Tudor dynasty (1485–1603). English dynasty, descended from the Welsh Owen Tudor (c. 1400–1461), second husband of Catherine of Valois (widow of Henry V of England). Their son Edmund married Margaret Beaufort (1443–1509), the great-granddaughter of John of Gaunt, and was the father of Henry VII, who became king by overthrowing Richard III 1485. The dynasty ended with the death of Elizabeth I 1603.

The Tudors were portrayed in a favourable light in Shakespeare's history plays.

Tu Fu or Du Fu (712–770). Chinese poet of the Tang dynasty. With Li Po, he was one of the two greatest Chinese poets. He wrote about the social injustices of his time, peasant suffering, and war, as in *The Army Carts* on conscription, and *The Beauties*, comparing the emperor's wealth with the lot of the poor.

Tull Jethro (1674–1741). English agriculturist who about 1701 developed a drill that enabled seeds to be sown mechanically and spaced so that cultivation between rows was possible in the growth period. Tull was born in Berkshire, studied at Oxford and qualified as a barrister, but took up farming about 1700.

The seed drill was a revolutionary piece of equipment, designed to incorporate three previously separate actions into one: drilling, sowing, and covering the seeds. The drill consisted of a box capable of delivering the seed in a regulated amount, a hopper mounted above it for holding the seed, and a plough and harrow for cutting the drill (groove in the soil) and turning over the soil to cover the sown seeds. His chief work, *Horse-Hoeing Husbandry*, was published 1733.

Tull also developed a plough with blades set in such a way that grass and roots were pulled up and left on the surface to dry. Basically the design of a plough is much the same today.

Suggested reading
Fussell, G E *Jethro Tull* (1973)

Tunney Gene James Joseph (1898–1978). US boxer. Born in New York, Tunney attended LaSalle Academy and worked as a steamship clerk 1912–17. As an amateur boxer, he won the US armed-forces championship in Paris, France, 1919. As a professional he won the US light-heavyweight title 1922. He began to fight as a heavyweight in 1924 and was the upset winner over heavyweight champion Jack Dempsey 1926. Tunney retained the title against Dempsey in the famous 'Long Count' bout 1927 and retired undefeated 1928. After his retirement from boxing, he became successful in business and published *A Man Must Fight* 1932 and *Arms for Living* 1941.

Tunnicliffe C(harles) F(rederick) (1901–1979). English painter of birds. He worked in Anglesey. His many books include *Bird Portraiture* 1945 and *Shorelands Summer Diary* 1952.

Túpac Amarú adopted name of José Gabriel Condorcanqui (*c.* 1742–1781). Peruvian Indian revolutionary leader, executed for his revolt against Spanish rule 1780; he claimed to be descended from the last chieftain of the Incas.

Turenne Henri de la Tour d'Auvergne, Vicomte de Turenne (1611–1675). French marshal under Louis XIV, known for his siege technique. He fought for the Protestant alliance during the Thirty Years' War, and on both sides during the wars of the Fronde.

Turgenev Ivan Sergeievich (1818–1883). Russian writer. He is notable for poetic realism, pessimism, and skill in characterization. His works include the play *A Month in the Country* 1849, and the novels *A Nest of Gentlefolk* 1858, *Fathers and Sons* 1862, and *Virgin Soil* 1877. His series *A Sportsman's Sketches* 1852 criticized serfdom.

Suggested reading
Freeborn, Richard *Turgenev: The Novelists's Novelist* (1960)
Magarshack, David *Turgenev* (1954)
Pritchett, V S *The Gentle Barbarian: The Life and Work of Turgenev* (1977)
Schapiro, L *Turgenev: His Life and Times* (1978)

[The American] people is the hope of the human race. It may become the model.

ANNE ROBERT JACQUES TURGOT
Letter to Dr Richard Price 1778

Turgot Anne Robert Jacques (1727–1781). French finance minister 1774–76, whose reforming economies led to his dismissal by a hostile aristocracy.

Turing Alan Mathison (1912–1954). English mathematician and logician. In 1936 he described a 'universal computing machine' that could theoretically be programmed to solve any problem capable of solution by a specially designed machine. This concept, now called the Turing machine, foreshadowed the digital computer.

Turing is believed to have been the first to suggest (in 1950) the possibility of machine learning and artificial intelligence. His test for distinguishing between real (human) and simulated (computer) thought is known as the Turing test: with a person in one room and the machine in another, an interrogator in a third room asks questions of both to try to identify them. When the interrogator cannot distinguish between them by questioning, the machine will have reached a state of humanlike intelligence.

Turing was born in London and studied at Cambridge. During World War II he worked on the Ultra project in the team that cracked the German Enigma cipher code. After the war he worked briefly on the project to design the general computer known as the Automatic Computing Engine, or ACE, and was involved in the pioneering computer developed at Manchester University from 1948.

Turing was concerned with mechanistic interpretations of the natural world and attempted to erect a mathematical theory of the chemical basis of organic growth. He was able to formulate and solve complicated differential equations to express certain examples of symmetry in biology and also certain phenomena such as the shapes of brown and black patches on cows.

He committed suicide following a prosecution for a minor homosexual offence.

Suggested reading
Herken, R *The Universal Turing Machine* (1988)
Hodges, Andrew *Alan Turing: The Enigma* (1983)

Turnbull William (1922–). Scottish painter and sculptor. He became internationally known in his early career for his primitive, totemlike figures. From 1962, he explored Minimalist form, employing identical, pre-fabricated units to produce austere, vertical, and repetitive structures grouped on a mathematically devised ground plan, as in *5 x 1* 1966 (Tate Gallery, London).

Turnbull was a founder-member of the Independent Group at the Institute of Contemporary Arts (ICA), London, 1952.

Turner Big Joe (Joseph Vernon) (1911–1985). US blues singer. He was considered the greatest of the blues 'shouters'. His raucously joyful work with boogie-woogie pianist Pete Johnson (1904–1967) influenced early rock and roll. Turner was born in Kansas City, Missouri, and became part of the jazz scene there. His hits include 'Honey Hush' 1953 and 'Shake, Rattle, and Roll' 1954.

Turner Charles Henry (1867–1923). US biologist who carried out research into insect behaviour patterns. He was the first to prove that insects can hear and distinguish pitch and that cockroaches learn by trial and error.

Turner was born in Cincinnati, studied there, and went on to teach at schools and colleges. He also wrote nature stories for children and was active in the civil-rights movement in St Louis.

From 1892 until his death, Turner conducted experiments on ants, bees, moths, spiders, and cockroaches. In French literature the turning movement of the ant towards its nest was given the name 'Turner's circling'.

Turner published over 50 papers on neurology, animal behaviour, and invertebrate ecology, including his dissertation 'The homing of ants: an experimental study of ant behaviour' 1907.

Turner Ethel Sybil (1872–1958). Australian novelist and children's writer. She is best known for *Seven Little Australians* 1894, about the lives and adventures of the large Woolcott family who live in a rambling house on the Parramatta River nick-named 'Misrule' and its sequel *The Family at Misrule* 1895. She published 27 full-length novels and numerous collections of short stories and anthologies of verse and fiction.

Turner Eva (1892–1990). English operatic soprano. She was prima donna of the Carl Rosa Opera Company 1916–24. Her incomparable top range and generous tone survive in a magnificent *Turandot* recorded 1928 under Thomas Beecham. DBE 1962.

He touches the historian, the social scientist, the intellectual, the antiquarian, the mass subconscious mind, and the average citizen – an intuitive genius.

H R Lamar on FREDERICK JACKSON TURNER
quoted in Marcus Cunliffe and R W Winks (eds) *Postmasters*

Turner Frederick Jackson (1861–1932). US historian, professor at Harvard University 1910–24. He emphasized the significance of the frontier in US historical development, attributing the distinctive character of US society to the influence of changing frontiers over three centuries of westward expansion.

Turner John Napier (1929–). Canadian Liberal politician, prime minister 1984. He was elected to the House of Commons 1962 and served in the cabinet of Pierre Trudeau until resigning 1975. He succeeded Trudeau as party leader and prime minister 1984, but lost the 1984 and 1988 elections. Turner resigned as leader 1989, and returned to his law practice. He was replaced as Liberal Party chief by Herbert Gray in Feb 1990.

Turner Joseph Mallord William (1775–1851). English landscape painter. He was one of the most original artists of his day. He travelled widely in Europe, and his landscapes became increasingly Romantic, with the subject often transformed in scale and flooded with brilliant, hazy light. Many later works anticipate Impressionism; for example, *Rain, Steam and Speed* 1844 (National Gallery, London).

A precocious talent, Turner went to the Royal Academy schools 1789. In 1792 he made the first of several European tours, from which numerous watercolour sketches survive. His early oil paintings show Dutch influence, but by the 1800s he had begun to paint landscapes in the 'Grand Manner', reflecting the styles of Claude Lorrain and Richard Wilson.

Many of his most dramatic works are set in Europe or at sea; for example, *Shipwreck* 1805, *Snowstorm: Hannibal Crossing the Alps*

1812 (both Tate Gallery, London), and *The Slave Ship* 1839 (Museum of Fine Arts, Boston, Massachusetts).

His use of colour was enhanced by trips to Italy (1819, 1828, 1835, 1840), and his brushwork became increasingly free. Early in his career he was encouraged by the portraitist Thomas Lawrence and others, but he failed to achieve recognition and became a reclusive figure. Later he was championed by the critic John Ruskin in his book *Modern Painters* 1843.

Turner was also devoted to literary themes and mythologies; for example, *Ulysses Deriding Polyphemus* 1829 (Tate Gallery). In his old age he lived as a recluse in Chelsea under an assumed name. He died there, leaving to the nation more than 300 paintings, nearly 20,000 watercolours, and 19,000 drawings. In 1987 the Clore Gallery extension to the Tate Gallery, London, was opened (following the terms of his will) to display the collection of the works he had left to the nation.

Suggested reading

Gaunt, W *Turner* (1983)
Gowing, L *Turner: Imagination and Reality* (1966)
Lindsay, J *JMW Turner: His Life and Work* (1966)
Wilton, A *JMW Turner* (1982)

A successful man is one who makes more money than his wife can spend. A successful woman is one who can find such a man.

LANA TURNER
Attributed remark 1980

Turner Lana (Julia Jean Mildred Frances) (1920–1995). US actress. She was known as the 'Sweater Girl' during World War II and appeared in melodramatic films of the 1940s and 1950s such as *Peyton Place* 1957. Her other films include *The Postman Always Rings Twice* 1946, *The Three Musketeers* 1948, and *Imitation of Life* 1959.

Turner Nat (1800–1831). US slave and Baptist preacher. Believing himself divinely appointed, he led 60 slaves in a revolt – the Southampton Insurrection of 1831 – in Southampton County, Virginia. Before he and 16 of the others were hanged, at least 55 slave-owners had been killed. He eluded capture for 6 weeks following the uprising, which so alarmed slave owners that repressive measures forbidding the educating of any blacks were swiftly enacted. Widespread torture and execution followed as owners exacted retribution, and the abolition movement in the south was abandoned.

Turner Robert Edward III ('Ted') (1938–). US businessman and sportsman who developed a conglomerate that includes WTBS, a sports and entertainment cable television channel; CNN, a cable television news network; MGM/UA Entertainment Company; the Atlanta Braves baseball team; and the Atlanta Hawks basketball team. He won the America's Cup 1977.

Born in Cincinnati, Ohio, USA, Turner attended Brown University but left 1960 to work for the family-owned billboard advertising company, which he headed after his father's suicide 1963. He was the prime promoter of the Goodwill Games, first held in Moscow 1986. He is married to actress Jane Fonda.

I don't like to know when anyone [special] is in the house because when I do it gets to me ... I forget a line or something.

TINA TURNER
in an interview with Dave Thomson in *The Face* Jan 1984

Turner Tina. Adopted name of Annie Mae Bullock (1940–). US rhythm-and-blues singer. She recorded 1960–76 with her husband Ike Turner (1931–), including *River Deep, Mountain High* 1966, produced by Phil Spector. In the 1980s she achieved success as a solo artist, recording such albums as *Private Dancer* 1984, and as a live performer.

Turner, Lana *Lana Turner, US film actress who was known as the 'Sweater Girl' after her appearance in* They Won't Forget, *1937. Her later work in such films as* The Postman Always Rings Twice *shows her considerable acting talent in more demanding roles.*

Turner Victor Witter (1920–1983). Scottish-born US social anthropologist who studied the Ndembu people of Zambia. His book *Schism and Continuity in an African Society* 1957 describes how social structure and conflict in certain social relationships gives rise to 'social dramas'.

In *The Forest of Symbols: Aspects of Ndembu Ritual* 1967, *The Ritual Process* 1969, and other works, he explored the complexities of symbolism in ritual. This led on to his developing the concept of 'communitas', a bonding social relationship that occurs in 'liminality'. Liminality occurs during changes in an individual's, or group's, social status and cultural or psychological state; for example, during rites of passage and on pilgrimages. These concepts are further elaborated in articles collected in *Dramas, Fields, and Metaphors: Symbolic Action in Human Society* 1974.

Turpin Ben (1874–1940). US comedian. A star of silent films, his hallmarks were his cross-eyed grimace and a taste for parodying his fellow actors. His work includes *The Shriek of Araby* 1923, *A Harem Knight* 1926, and *Broke in China* 1927.

Turpin Dick (Richard) (1705–1739). English highwayman. The son of an innkeeper, he turned to highway robbery, cattle-thieving, and smuggling, and was hanged at York, England. His legendary ride from London to York on his mare Black Bess is probably based on one of about 305 km/190 mi from Gad's Hill to York completed in 15 hours in 1676 by highwayman John Nevison (1639–84).

The cult of the criminal, so strong then in England ... made a hero out of unpromising material.

Geoffrey Treasure on DICK TURPIN
in *Who's Who in Early Hanoverian England* 1991

Tussaud Madame (born Anne Marie Grosholtz) (1761–1850). French wax-modeller. In 1802 she established an exhibition of wax models of celebrities in London. It was destroyed by fire 1925, but reopened 1928. Originally housed in the Strand, the exhibition was transferred to Baker Street in 1883 and to its present site in Marylebone Road in 1884. Born in Strasbourg, she went to Paris as a young girl 1766 to live with her wax-modeller uncle, Philippe Curtius, whom she soon surpassed in working with wax. During the French Revolution they were forced to take death masks of many victims and leaders (some still exist in the Chamber of Horrors).

Tutankhamen (14th century BC). King (pharaoh) of ancient Egypt of the 18th dynasty, about 1333–1323 BC. A son of Akhenaton (also called Amenhotep IV), he was about 11 at his accession. In 1922 his tomb was discovered by the British archaeologists Lord Carnarvon and Howard Carter in the Valley of the Kings at Luxor, almost untouched by tomb robbers. The contents included many works of art and his solid-gold coffin, which are now displayed in a Cairo museum.
Suggested reading
Desroches-Noblecourt, Christine *Tutankhamen* (1954)
Edwards, I E S *Tutankhamun: The Tomb and its Treasures* (1977)
Hobson, Christine *The World of the Pharaohs* (1987)
Magnusson, Magnus *Tutankhamun* (1972)

Tutin Dorothy (1931–). English actress. Her roles include most of Shakespeare's leading heroines (among them Portia, Viola, and Juliet) for the Royal Shakespeare Company, and Lady Macbeth for the National Theatre Company. She has also acted in the first productions of plays by John Osborne and Harold Pinter.

Tutu Desmond Mpilo (1931–). South African priest, Anglican archbishop of Cape Town and general secretary of the South African Council of Churches 1979–84. One of the leading figures in the struggle against apartheid in the Republic of South Africa, he was awarded the 1984 Nobel Peace Prize.

Tvardovsky Alexander (1910–1971). Russian poet and editor. Early work such as *Path to Socialism* 1931 and *The Land of Muravia* 1936 (Stalin Prize 1941) repudiates individualism and commends collectivized farming. His humorous wartime poem 'Vasili Tyorkin' 1941–45 was extremely popular. As editor of the journal *Novy Mir* 1950–54 and 1958–70, he encouraged innovative and outspoken writers such as Solzhenitsyn. *By Right of Memory* 1967–69, an attempt to tell the whole truth about his times, was banned by the censor.

There was never yet an uninteresting life. Such a thing is an impossibility. Inside of the dullest exterior there is a drama, a comedy, and a tragedy.

MARK TWAIN
The Refuge of the Derelicts ch 4

Twain Mark. Pen name of Samuel Langhorne Clemens (1835–1910). US writer. He established his reputation with the comic masterpiece *The Innocents Abroad* 1869 and two classic American novels, in dialect, *The Adventures of Tom Sawyer* 1876 and *The Adventures of Huckleberry Finn* 1885. He also wrote satire, as in *A Connecticut Yankee at King Arthur's Court* 1889.

Born in Florida, Missouri, Twain grew up along the Mississippi River in Hannibal, Missouri, the setting for many of his major works, and was employed as a riverboat pilot before he moved west; taking a job as a journalist, he began to write. The tale 'The Celebrated Jumping Frog of Calaveras County' was his first success. After a trip by boat to Palestine, he wrote *The Innocents Abroad*. As his writing career blossomed, he also became successful as a lecturer. In 1870 he married, and a few years later he and his wife settled in Hartford, Connecticut. *Huckleberry Finn* is Twain's masterpiece, for its use of the vernacular, vivid characterization and descriptions, and its theme, underlying the humour, of man's inhumanity to man.

He also wrote *Roughing It* 1872, *The Gilded Age* 1873, *Old Times on the Mississippi* 1875, *The Prince and the Pauper* 1882, *Life on the Mississippi* 1883, *Pudd'nhead Wilson* 1894, and *Personal Recollections of Joan of Arc* 1896. His later works, such as *The Mysterious Stranger*, unpublished until 1916, are less humorous and more pessimistic. He is recognized as one of America's finest and most characteristic writers.
Suggested reading
Blair, W *Mark Twain and Huck Finn* (1960)
Budd, L J *Our Mark Twain: The Making of His Public Personality* (1983)
Gibson, W H *The Art of Mark Twain* (1976)
Hill, H *Mark Twain, God's Fool* (1973)
Kaplan, J *Mark Twain and his World* (1974)

Tweed William Marcy ('Boss') (1823–1878). US politician. Born in New York City, USA, Tweed worked briefly as a clerk in his father's factory. Becoming involved in municipal politics, he served as an alderman 1852–56 and emerged as the leader of Tammany Hall (a New York City Democratic club, founded 1789). He held office in the US House of Representatives 1853–55. In various municipal offices, and from 1867 in New York state senate, he controlled government spending and accumulated a fortune estimated at somewhere between $45 million and $200 million. He was convicted of forgery and larceny and sent to jail 1873–75, when he escaped to Spain. His anonymity was subverted by a Thomas Nast cartoon, from which Tweed was recognized and sent back to New York. He died in prison.

Twort Frederick William (1877–1950). English bacteriologist, the original discoverer in 1915 of bacteriophages (often called phages), the relatively large viruses that attack and destroy bacteria. He also researched into Johne's disease, a chronic intestinal infection of cattle.

From 1909 he was superintendent of the Brown Institute, a pathology research centre, and he was also professor of bacteriology at the University of London from 1919.

While working with cultures of *Staphylococcus aureus* (the bacterium that causes the common boil), Twort noticed that colonies of these bacteria were being destroyed. He isolated the substance that produced this effect and found that it was transmitted indefinitely to subsequent generations of the bacterium. He then suggested that the substance was a virus. Twort was unable to continue this work, and the importance of bacteriophages was not recognized until the 1950s.

Twort also discovered that vitamin K is needed by growing leprosy bacteria, which opened a new field of research into the nutritional requirements of microorganisms.

Tyler Wat (died 1381). English leader of the Peasants' Revolt of 1381. He was probably born in Kent or Essex, and may have served in the French wars. After taking Canterbury, he led the peasant army to Blackheath, outside London, and went on to invade the city. At Mile End King Richard II met the rebels and promised to redress their grievances, which included the imposition of a poll tax. At a further conference at Smithfield, London, Tyler was murdered.

Tyler John (1790–1862). 10th president of the USA 1841–45, succeeding William H Harrison, who died after only a month in office. Tyler's government annexed Texas 1845.

Tyler was the first US vice president to succeed to the presidency. A 'president without a party', he was repudiated by the Whig Party, and the Democrats refused to recognize him. He remained constantly at odds with the cabinet and Congress until elections forced the Whigs from power and enabled Tyler to reorganize his cabinet.

Tylor Edward Burnett (1832–1917). English anthropologist. Often called 'the father of anthropology', he was the leading evolutionary anthropologist of the 19th century. His definition of culture in his book *Primitive Culture* 1871 was the first anthropological definition of the term; most modern definitions have derived from it.

He developed a theory of animism (the notion that spirits inhabit inanimate objects) as the most primitive religion, and believed that many customs, such as wearing earrings, were 'survivals' from a primitive stage of culture. His *Anthropology* 1881 was the first text-book on the subject, and in 1884 he became the first person to hold an academic position in anthropology when he became a lecturer at Oxford.

A good drama critic is one who perceives what is happening in the theatre of his time. A great drama critic also perceives what is not happening.

KENNETH TYNAN
Tynan Right and Left 1967

Tynan Kenneth Peacock (1927–1980). English theatre critic and author, a leading cultural figure of the radical 1960s. A strong opponent of censorship, he devised the nude revue *Oh Calcutta!* 1969, first staged in New York, USA. His publications include *A View of the English Stage 1944–63* 1975.

Tyndale William (c. 1492–1536). English translator of the Bible. The printing of his New Testament (the basis of the Authorized Version) was begun in Cologne 1525 and, after he had been forced to flee, completed in Worms. Tyndale introduced some of the most familiar phrases to the English language, such as 'filthy lucre', and 'God forbid'. He was strangled and burned as a heretic at Vilvorde in Belgium.

Suggested reading
Dickens, A G *The English Reformation* (1964)
Elton, G R *Reform and Reformation: England, 1509–1558* (1978)
Mozley, J F *Tyndale* (1937)
Williams, Charles *William Tyndale* (1969)

Tyndall John (1820–1893). Irish physicist who 1869 studied the scattering of light by invisibly small suspended particles in colloids.

Known as the Tyndall effect, it was first observed with colloidal solutions, in which a beam of light is made visible when it is scattered by minute colloidal particles (whereas a pure solvent does not scatter light). Similar scattering of blue wavelengths of sunlight by particles in the atmosphere makes the sky look blue (beyond the atmosphere, the sky is black).

He became professor at the Royal Institution 1853 and was also professor at the Royal School of Mines 1859–68. As superintendent of the Royal Institution from 1867, he did much to popularize science in Britain and also in the USA, where he toured from 1872 to 1873.

Having established that there are dust particles suspended in the air, Tyndall was able to show that the air contains living microorganisms. This confirmed the work of French chemist Louis Pasteur that rejected the spontaneous generation of life, and it also inspired Tyndall to develop methods of sterilizing by heat treatment.

Tyndall also carried out experimental work on the absorption and transmission of heat by gases, especially water vapour and atmospheric gases, which was important in the development of meteorology.

Tyrtaeus (lived 7th century BC). Spartan war poet, reputedly also a general. His poems are a resolute expression of early Spartan militarism.

Tyson Mike (Michael Gerald) (1966–). US heavyweight boxer, undisputed world champion from Aug 1987 to Feb 1990. He won the World Boxing Council heavyweight title 1986 when he beat Trevor Berbick to become the youngest world heavyweight champion. He beat James 'Bonecrusher' Smith for the World Boxing Association title 1987 and later that year became the first undisputed champion since 1978 when he beat Tony Tucker for the International Boxing Federation title.

He turned professional 1985. Of Tyson's first 25 opponents, 15 were knocked out in the first round. He was undefeated until 1990, when he lost the championship in an upset to James 'Buster' Douglas. Tyson was scheduled to fight again for the championship, but was convicted of rape and imprisoned 1992. He was released from prison March 1995.

Tzu-Hsi alternative transliteration of ◊Zi Xi, dowager empress of China.

U

U2 Irish rock group formed 1977 by singer Bono Vox (born Paul Hewson, 1960–), guitarist Dave 'The Edge' Evans (1961–), bassist Adam Clayton (1960–), and drummer Larry Mullen (1961–). The band's albums include *The Unforgettable Fire* 1984, *The Joshua Tree* 1987, and *Achtung Baby* 1992.

Uccello Paolo. Adopted name of Paolo di Dono (1397–1475). Italian painter. Active in Florence, he was one of the first to experiment with perspective. His surviving paintings date from the 1430s onwards. Decorative colour and detail dominate his later pictures.

He was trained as a goldsmith, and *c.* 1407–12 was apprentice to Ghiberti when the latter was working on the doors of the Florentine baptistery. In 1415 he entered the Physicians' Guild at Florence as a painter. He worked mainly in Florence, with an interlude from 1425 at Venice, where he is said to have produced a mosaic for the façade of St Mark's. He bought a house in Florence 1442 and evidently prospered for a time, though his old age was reputedly spent in poverty and isolation. He is famous for his study of perspective, though he used it imaginatively rather than with scientific accuracy or consistency. His works in fresco include his painting (in imitation of an equestrian statue) of the English *condottiere*, Sir John Hawkwood (known as Giovanni Acuto), 1436, in the cathedral at Florence, and a series in the Chiostro Verde of Santa Maria Novella, Florence, the principal composition being the *Deluge* of *c.* 1445. He is, however, most celebrated for his panel pictures, notably the three pictures, *Rout of San Romano*, of the battle between the Florentines and the Sienese, 1432, painted for the Medici (Uffizi, FLorence; Louvre, Paris; and National Gallery, London). They were intended to be framed together, but each gives an effect of completeness and is wonderfully rich in design. Other remarkable works, showing his originality and vividness of imagination, are the *Hunt* (Ashmolean, Oxford) and *St George and the Dragon* (*c.* 1460 National Gallery, London). A series of portraits by him (Louvre) suggests that he admired particularly Giotto, Donatello, Brunelleschi, and the mathematician Antonio Manetti.

Udall Nicholas (*c.* 1505–1556). English schoolmaster and dramatist. He was the author of *Ralph Roister Doister* dated by various scholars around 1540/53, printed 1566–67. It is the first known English comedy and is based on the plays of the Roman comic dramatists Plautus and Terence.

Uelsmann Jerry (1934–). US photographer who produced dreamlike images, created by synthesizing many elements into one with great technical skill.

Uhland Johann Ludwig (1787–1862). German poet. He was the author of ballads and lyrics in the Romantic tradition.

Ulam Stanislaw Marcin (1909–1985). Polish-born US mathematician. Ulam was born and educated in Lvov (now in Ukraine). On the invitation of mathematician John Von Neumann, he emigrated to the USA 1936 and joined the Institute for Advanced Study at Princeton. He was a member of the Manhattan Project, which produced the first atom bomb, 1943–45, and from 1946 collaborated with Edward Teller on the design of the hydrogen bomb, solving the problem of how to ignite the bomb. All previous designs had collapsed.

Ulanova Galina Sergeyevna (1910–). Soviet dancer. She was prima ballerina of the Bolshoi Ballet 1944–62. A dancer of eloquent simplicity and lightness, she excelled as Juliet and Giselle and created the role of Katerina in Prokofiev's *The Stone Flower*.

Ulbricht Walter (1893–1973). East German communist politician, in power 1960–71. He lived in exile in the USSR during Hitler's rule 1933–45. A Stalinist, he became first secretary of the Socialist Unity Party in East Germany 1950 and (as chair of the Council of State from 1960) was instrumental in the building of the Berlin Wall 1961. He established East Germany's economy and recognition outside the Eastern European bloc.

Ullmann Liv Johanne (1938–). Norwegian actress. She is notable for her work with the Swedish director Ingmar Bergman. Her films include *Persona* 1966, *Pope Joan* and *Lost Horizon* both 1972, and *Autumn Sonata* 1978. She directed her first film, *Sophie* 1992.

Ulugh Beg (Turkish 'great lord') title of Muhammad Taragay (1394–1449). Mongol mathematician and astronomer, ruler of Samarkand from 1409 and of the Mongol Empire from 1447. He built an observatory from which he made very accurate observations of the Sun and planets. He published a set of astronomical tables, called the *Zij* of Ulugh Beg.

Ulugh Beg was born at Sulaniyya in central Asia and brought up at the court of his grandfather Tamerlane. At the age of 15 Ulugh Beg became ruler of the city of Samarkand and the province of Maverannakhr. In 1447 he succeeded his father, Shahrukh, to the throne, but was assassinated two years later in a coup by his son.

In 1420 Ulugh Beg founded an institution of higher learning, or 'madrasa', in Samarkand. It specialized in astronomy and higher mathematics. Four years later he built a three-storey observatory and a sextant. By observing the altitude of the Sun at noon every day, he was able to deduce the Sun's meridianal height, its distance from the zenith, and the inclination of the ecliptic.

The *Zij* of Ulugh Beg and his school is written in Tajik. It consists of a theoretical section and tables of calendar calculations, of trigonometry, and of the positions of planets, as well as a star catalogue of 1,018 stars. This includes 992 stars whose positions Ulugh Beg redetermined with unusual precision.

Umar (*c.* 581–644). Adviser of the prophet Muhammad. In 634 he succeeded Abu Bakr as caliph (civic and religious leader of Islam), and conquered Syria, Palestine, Egypt, and Persia. He was assassinated by a slave. The Mosque of Omar in Jerusalem is attributed to him.

Umayyad dynasty Arabian dynasty of the Islamic empire who reigned as caliphs (civic and religious leaders of Islam) 661–750, when they were overthrown by Abbasids. A member of the family, Abd al-Rahmam, escaped to Spain and in 756 assumed the title of Emir of Córdoba. His dynasty, which took the title of caliph in 929, ruled in Córdoba until the early 11th century.

Umberto two kings of Italy:

Umberto I (1844–1900). King of Italy from 1878, who joined the Triple Alliance 1882 with Germany and Austria-Hungary; his colonial ventures included the defeat at Aduwa, Abyssinia, 1896. He was assassinated by an anarchist.

Umberto II (1904–1983). Last king of Italy 1946. On the abdication of his father, Victor Emmanuel III, he ruled 9 May–13 June 1946, when he had to abdicate since a referendum established a republic. He retired to Portugal.

The chiefest sanctity of a temple is that it is a place to which men go to weep in common.
MIGUEL DE UNAMUNO
Tragic Sense of Life, 'The Man of Flesh and Bone' 1913

Unamuno Miguel de (1864–1936). Spanish writer of Basque origin. He was exiled 1924–30 for criticism of the military directorate of Primo de Rivera. His works include mystic poems and the study *Del sentimiento trágico de la vida/The Tragic Sense of Life* 1913, about the conflict of reason and belief in religion.

Underwood (George Claude) Leon (1890–1975). English painter, graphic artist, and sculptor. He travelled to Iceland, the USA, Mexico, and West Africa, devoting several books to masks, wood carvings, and bronzes. His rhythmic figures are powerful symbols of human myth.

Underwood Rory (1963–). English rugby union player who made his international debut 1984, and became the first English player to reach 50 international appearances. His 35 tries are also an English record. He helped England to win successive Grand Slams 1991 and 1992.

Undset Sigrid (1882–1949). Norwegian novelist. She was the author of *Kristin Lavransdatter* 1920–22, a strongly Catholic novel set in the 14th century. She was awarded the Nobel Prize for Literature 1928.

Ungaretti Giuseppe (1888–1970). Italian poet. His spare, lyrical poems, employing experimental verse forms and complex imagery, made him the principal figure of the 'hermetic' school of Italian poetry (from *ermetico* 'obscure'). His works include *Allegria di naufragi/The Joy of Shipwrecks* 1919, *Sentimento del tempo/The Sense of Time* 1933, and *Il dolore/Grief* 1947.

Unitas John Constantine (1933–). US football player. Born in Pittsburgh, USA, Unitas was a football star for the University of Louisville. He was drafted by the Pittsburgh Steelers of the National Football League (NFL) 1955 where he played for one season. He was signed by the Baltimore Colts 1956 and as Colt quarterback for 17 seasons, Unitas led the team to five NFL championship titles in the years 1958–71. Following his release from the Colts, Unitas played for the San Diego Chargers 1973. He was one of the greatest passers in the history of the game.

Uno Sōsuke (1922–). Japanese conservative politician, member of the Liberal Democratic Party (LDP). He held various cabinet posts from 1976, and was designated prime minister in June 1989 in an attempt to restore the image of the LDP after several scandals. He resigned after only a month in office when his affair with a prostitute became public knowledge.

Unwin Raymond (1863–1940). English town planner. He put the garden city ideals of Ebenezer Howard into practice, overseeing Letchworth, Hertfordshire (begun 1903), Hampstead Garden Suburb, outside London (begun 1907), and Wythenshawe, outside Manchester (begun 1927). Knighted 1932.

Updike John Hoyer (1932–). US writer. Updike was born in Shillington, Pennsylvania, and graduated from Harvard University. Associated with the *New Yorker* magazine from 1955, he soon established a reputation for polished prose, poetry, and criticism. His novels include *The Poorhouse Fair* 1959, *The Centaur* 1963, *Couples* 1968, *The Witches of Eastwick* 1984, *Roger's Version* 1986, and

S. 1988, and deal with the tensions and frustrations of contemporary US middle-class life and their effects on love and marriage.

The yearning for an afterlife is the opposite of selfish; it is love and praise for the world that we are privileged, in this complex interval of light, to witness and experience.
JOHN UPDIKE
Self-Consciousness: Memoirs ch 6 1989

Two characters recur in his novels: the former basketball player 'Rabbit' Angstrom, who matures in the series *Rabbit, Run* 1960, *Rabbit Redux* 1971, *Rabbit is Rich* 1981 (Pulitzer prize), and *Rabbit at Rest* 1990 (Pulitzer prize); and the novelist Henry Bech, who appears in *Bech: A Book* 1970 and *Bech is Back* 1982. Other novels by Updike include *Of the Farm* 1965, *A Month of Sundays* 1972, *Marry Me* 1976, *The Coup* 1978, and *Memories of the Ford Administration* 1992. His short-story collections include *The Same Door* 1959, *Pigeon Feathers* 1962, *Museums and Women* 1972, and *Problems* 1979. His body of work includes essay collections, such as *Hugging the Shore* 1983, and the play *Buchanan Dying* 1974.

Suggested reading
Greiner, D T *John Updike's Novels* (1985)
Hendin, Josephine *Vulnerable People: A View of American Fiction since 1945* (1978)
Newman, Judie *John Updike* (1988)
Updike, John *Self-Consciousness: Memoirs* (1989)
Uphaus, Suzanne *John Updike* (1980)

America is a vast conspiracy to make you happy.
JOHN UPDIKE
Problems 'How to love America and Leave it at the Same Time' 1980

Urban six popes, including:

Urban II (c. 1042–1099). Pope 1088–99. He launched the First Crusade at the Council of Clermont in France 1095.

Urban VIII (Maffeo Barberini) (1568–1644). Pope 1623–44. His policies during the Thirty Years' War were designed more to maintain the balance of forces in Europe and prevent one side from dominating the papacy than to further the Counter-Reformation. He extended the papal dominions and improved their defences. During his papacy, Galileo was summoned 1633 to recant the theories that the Vatican condemned as heretical.

Urey Harold Clayton (1893–1981). US chemist. In 1932 he isolated heavy water and discovered deuterium, for which he was awarded the 1934 Nobel Prize for Chemistry.

During World War II he was a member of the Manhattan Project, which produced the atomic bomb, and after the war he worked on tritium (another isotope of hydrogen, of mass 3) for use in the hydrogen bomb, but later he advocated nuclear disarmament and world government. He became professor of chemistry at Columbia 1934, and was at Chicago 1945–58.

After deuterium, Urey went on to isolate heavy isotopes of carbon, nitrogen, oxygen, and sulphur. His group provided the basic information for the separation of the fissionable isotope uranium-235 from the much more common uranium-238.

Urey also developed theories about the formation of the Earth. He thought that the Earth had not been molten at the time when its materials accumulated. In 1952, he suggested that molecules found in its primitive atmosphere could have united spontaneously to give rise to life. The Moon, he believed, had a separate origin from the Earth.

Urquhart Robert Elliot (1901–1988). British general of World War II. Served with the 51st Highland Division in N Africa 1942 and then in Sicily and Italy. He returned to the UK and in 1944 was given command of 1st Airborne Division which he led at Arnhem.

Urquiza Justo José de (1801–1870). Argentine president 1854–60, regarded as the organizer of the Argentine nation. Governor of Entre

Ustinov *English actor, dramatist, and director Peter Ustinov is easily recognized by his mellifluous, drawling voice and shambling manner. He has appeared in many films, almost always in light or comic roles, and has written many plays, as well as novels and an autobiography that gives full range to his skill as a raconteur.*

Ríos from 1841, he set up a progressive administration. Supported by Brazil and Uruguay, he defeated the unpopular dictator Juan Manuel de Rosas in the Battle of Caseros 1852. As president he fostered internal economic development and created the Argentine Confederation 1853 which united the country's provinces, but he failed to bring Buenos Aires into it.

Ursula, St (lived 4th century AD). English legendary saint, supposed to have been martyred with 11 virgins (misread as 11,000 in the Middle Ages) by the Huns in the Rhineland.

Usher James (1581–1656). Irish priest, archbishop of Armagh from 1625. He was responsible for dating the creation to the year 4004 BC, a figure that was inserted in the margin of the Authorized Version of the Bible until the 19th century.

Ussher alternative spelling of James Usher.

Ustinov Peter Alexander (1921–). English stage and film actor, writer, and director. He won an Academy Award for *Spartacus* 1960. He wrote, produced, directed, and acted in several films, including *Romanoff and Juliet* 1961, *Billy Budd* 1962, and *Lady L* 1965. Other film appearances include *Topkapi* 1964, *Death on the Nile* 1978, and *Evil under the Sun* 1981. He published his autobiography *Dear Me* 1983. Knighted 1990.

> *Comedy is the only way I know of being serious.*
>
> PETER USTINOV
> in *Time* 8 Aug 1983

Utagawa Kuniyoshi. Japanese printmaker; see ◊Kuniyoshi Utagawa.

Utamaro Kitagawa (1753–1806). Japanese colour-print artist of the ukiyo-e school, known for his muted colour prints of beautiful women engaged in everyday activities, including informal studies of prostitutes. His style was distinctive: his subject is often seen close up, sometimes from unusual angles or viewpoints, and he made use of sensuous lines and highly decorative textiles. He was one of the first Japanese artists to become known in the West.
Suggested reading
Kondo, Ichitaro *Kitagawa Utamaro* (1956)
Smith, Lawrence *Ukiyo-E: Images of Unknown Japan* (1989)
Stern, Harold P *Master Prints of Japan* (1969)

Uthman (c. 574–656). Third caliph (leader of the Islamic empire) from 644, a son-in-law of the prophet Muhammad. Under his rule the Arabs became a naval power and extended their rule to N Africa and Cyprus, but Uthman's personal weaknesses led to his assassination. He was responsible for the compilation of the authoritative version of the Koran, the sacred book of Islam.

Uthman I another name for the Turkish sultan ◊Osman I.

Utrillo Maurice (1883–1955). French artist. He painted townscapes of his native Paris, many depicting Montmartre, often from postcard photographs. His almost naive style (he was self-taught) is characterized by his subtle use of pale tones and muted colours.

Utrillo was the son of Suzanne Valadon. He showed early signs of a neurosis that drove him to alcoholism, and he was encouraged by his mother to paint as a therapeutic measure when 18. He instantly took to art, and from 1903 produced views of Montmagny, where he and his mother lived for a while, and cathedrals and villages taken from picture postcards. After an Impressionist phase he arrived at his characteristic 'white period', c. 1909–14, painting in pictures of great beauty the streets and the peeling plaster of white walls in Montmartre, his native quarter, for which he had a deep affection. His style changed from about 1917, for a time deteriorating. Brighter colour and a more rudimentary kind of drawing characterized his later work, though in its final phases it showed some return to the style for which he is most esteemed. He produced gouaches as well as oil-paintings.
Suggested reading
De Polnay, Peter *Enfant Terrible: The Life and World of Maurice Utrillo* (1969)
Werner, Alfred *Maurice Utrillo* (1981)

Utzon Joern (1918–). Danish architect whose design for the Sydney Opera House won an international competition in 1957. He was born in Copenhagen and is also known as a designer of furniture, lamps, and glassware.

Vail Alfred Lewis (1807–1859). US communications pioneer. Vail was born in Morristown, New Jersey, educated at New York University, and worked as a mechanic at his father's iron foundry. A close associate of Samuel Morse 1837, he developed an improved design for the telegraph mechanism, beginning production of the new model 1838. With US Congressional funding for a telegraph line between Washington and Baltimore, Vail renewed his working relationship with Morse 1844.

His book *The American Electro Magnetic Telegraph* was published 1845, and he retired from business 1849.

Valdemar alternative spelling of ◊Waldemar, four kings of Denmark.

Valdivia Pedro de (c. 1497–1554). Spanish explorer who travelled to Venezuela about 1530 and accompanied Francisco Pizarro on his second expedition to Peru. He then went south into Chile, where he founded the cities of Santiago 1541 and Valdivia 1544. In 1552 he crossed the Andes to explore the Negro River. He was killed by Araucanian Indians.

Valentine, St according to tradition, a bishop of Terni martyred in Rome, now omitted from the calendar of saints' days as probably non-existent. His festival was 14 Feb, but the custom of sending 'valentines' to a loved one on that day seems to have arisen because the day accidentally coincided with the Roman mid-February festival of Lupercalia.

Valentino trade name of Valentino Garavani (1932–). Italian fashion designer. He opened his fashion house in Rome 1959. He opened his first ready-to-wear boutique ten years later, before showing the line in Paris from 1975. He launched his menswear collection 1972. His designs are characterized by simplicity – elegantly tailored suits and coats, usually marked with a V in the seams.

Valentino Mario (1927–1991). Italian shoe designer. He built an international empire of boutiques and shoe, leather-goods, cosmetics, and ready-to-wear ranges. Valentino was born in Naples and began his career designing specialist shoes, a sector in which he reached fame in the 1950s. His commercial flair steered him towards many areas. By 1956 he had a shoe-manufacturing company in Naples and a number of shops around the world. He attracted custom from international socialites such as Sophia Loren, Ava Gardner, and Jacqueline Onassis. He was instrumental in furthering the careers of the designers Giorgio Armani and Gianni Versace, employing both of them on his leather ranges; Karl Lagerfeld still designs Valentino shoes.

> *Here was one who was catnip to women ... he had youth and fame ... and yet he was very unhappy.*
>
> H L Mencken on RUDOLPH VALENTINO
> quoted in Leslie Halliwell *Filmgoer's Companion* 1965

Valentino Rudolph. Adopted name of Rodolfo Alfonso Guglielmi di Valentina d'Antonguolla (1895–1926). Italian-born US film actor and dancer. He was the archetypal romantic lover of the Hollywood silent era. His screen debut was 1919, but his first starring role was in *The Four Horsemen of the Apocalypse* 1921. His subsequent films include *The Sheik* 1921 and *Blood and Sand* 1922.

Valentino came to the USA 1913 and worked as a gardener and a dancer in New York City before appearing as a dancer in a 1918 Hollywood film. He became the screen idol of his day, in such films as *Monsieur Beaucaire* 1924, *The Eagle* 1925, and *Son of the Sheik* 1926.

Suggested reading
Oberfist, Robert *Rudolph Valentino: The Man Behind the Myth* (1962)
Walker, Alexander *Rudolph Valentino* (1976)

Valera Éamon de. Irish politician; see ◊de Valera.

Valéry Paul Amboise (1871–1945). French poet and mathematician. His poetry, which combines delicate lyricism with intellectual rigour, includes *La Jeune Parque/The Young Fate* 1917 and *Charmes/Enchantments* 1922, which contains 'Le Cimetière marin/The Graveyard by the Sea', one of the major poems of 20th-century French literature. He also wrote critical essays and many volumes of journals, which he regarded as among his most important work.

After publishing Symbolist-inspired verse in the 1890s, he abandoned poetry for nearly 20 years, devoting himself to the study of philosophy and mathematics before publishing *La Jeune Parque*.

Valentino, Rudolph *Italian-born US film actor Rudolph Valentino in* The Sheik *1921. Combining real acting ability and good looks, Valentino became an international star in the 1920s through silent films such as* The Sheik *and* The Four Horsemen of the Apocalypse *1921, and* Blood and Sand *1922. As the archetypal romantic hero, he had a huge following.*

Valla Lorenzo (1407–1457). Italian philosopher, translator, and historian. He attacked scholasticism and promoted classical literature, advocating an alliance between faith and eloquence. He influenced the Dutch humanist Erasmus and the German Protestant Martin Luther.

Valla, born in Rome, was historian and secretary to King Alfonso of Naples 1435–1448, when he returned to Rome as secretary to Pope Nicholas V. He proved some of the most hallowed documents in the papal curia to be forgeries, notably the Donation of Constantine, which purported to give the pope temporal sovereignty over the Roman emperor. Valla criticized Aristotelian logic, and believed that medieval philosophy and logic had had a bad effect on theology.

His works include *Elegantiarum libri/On the Elegancies of the Latin Tongue* 1471, the first Latin grammar to be written since the Middle Ages, and *Annotationes in Novum Testamentum/Annotations on the New Testament* 1444.

Vallandigham Clement Laird (1820–1871). US political leader. Born in New Lisbon, Ohio, USA, and educated at Washington and Jefferson College, Vallandigham was admitted to the bar 1842 before entering the state legislature 1845–47. He served in the US House of Representatives 1858–63. A staunch Democrat, he supported Stephen Douglas for president 1860 and opposed many of President Lincoln's war policies. He was arrested for sedition 1862

Van Allen US physicist James Van Allen, who discovered the magnetosphere. Using V2 rockets left over from World War II, Van Allen measured cosmic-ray intensities in the upper atmosphere and recorded anomalously high values. When the US government launched the Explorer satellites in 1958, their onboard geiger counters showed that the Earth's magnetic field trapped high-speed charged particles in two doughnut-shaped zones, which were named Van Allen belts or, more commonly, the magnetosphere. (NASA/Image Select)

and deported to the Confederacy. Returning to Ohio 1864, he remained a strong foe of the radical Republicans until his death.

Valle José Cecilio del (1776–1834). Central American Conservative politician. Valle was elected mayor of Guatemala city 1820 towards the end of Spanish colonial rule. To avert social revolution, he joined the provisional junta which took control of Central America 1821, and led its annexation into Agustin de Iturbide's Mexican empire. When this fell 1824, he was elected first president of the Federation of Central America, but was denied the post on a technicality. He died as the votes that would have made him president were being counted.

Vallee Rudy (Hubert Prior) (1901–1986). US singer, actor, and bandleader. Establishing a clean-cut, college-boy image, he became one of the most popular crooners (indicating a smooth, intimate style) of the 1920s. He formed his band the Connecticut Yankees 1928 and hosted a radio programme with the theme song 'My Time Is Your Time' (recorded 1929). From 1929 he appeared in films and stage musicals.

Vallee was born in Island Pond, Vermont, and raised in Maine. After studying at the University of Maine and Yale, he travelled widely, making appearances in England and throughout the USA. In the 1920s he sang through a megaphone, which became a trademark. He served in World War I and in the Coast Guard in World War II. Vallee started as a saxophone player and toured with local bands throughout his teenage years. On leaving college he became a singer, making records like 'The Vagabond Lover' 1929 and 'Brother, Can You Spare a Dime?' 1932. In Hollywood and on Broadway he began as a romantic lead but turned to comedy in the 1940s; his films include *George White's Scandals* 1934, *Palm Beach Story* 1942, and *How to Succeed in Business Without Really Trying* 1966. His performing career lasted into the 1980s.

Valle-Inclán Ramón María de (1866–1936). Spanish author and poet. His works, made notorious by their frank eroticism, were influenced by French Symbolism. They include the four novels *Sonatas* 1902–05 and, set in South America, the novel *Tirano Banderas/The Tyrant* 1926.

Vallejo Mariano Guadalupe (1808–1890). American military leader in colonial California. Born in Monterey, California, Vallejo chose a military career early in life. Stationed in Alta California he helped put down an Indian uprising at San Jose 1829. During the 1830s, he opposed the rule of autocratic governors sent from Mexico City and in 1838 became the military commander of the province. He was briefly imprisoned during the Bear Flag revolt 1849 before becoming a citizen of the state of California, serving as a member of the state senate.

Valois branch of the Capetian dynasty, originally counts of Valois in France, members of which occupied the French throne from Philip VI 1328 to Henry III 1589.

Vámbéry Arminius (1832–1913). Hungarian traveller and writer who crossed the deserts of Central Asia to Khiva and Samarkand dressed as a dervish, a classic journey described in his *Travels and Adventures in Central Asia* 1864.

As professor of oriental languages in Budapest he continued to write about the language and ethnography of the Turks and the Tatars, supporting the notion that British rule in the East was beneficial.

Van Allen James Alfred (1914–). US physicist whose instruments aboard the first US satellite *Explorer 1* 1958 led to the discovery of the Van Allen belts, two zones of intense radiation around the Earth. He pioneered high-altitude research with rockets after World War II.

He organized and led scientific expeditions to Peru 1949, the Gulf of Alaska 1950, Greenland 1952 and 1957, and Antarctica 1957 to study cosmic radiation. From 1951 he was professor at Iowa. He participated 1953–54 in Project Matterhorn, which was concerned with the study of controlled thermonuclear reactions, and he was responsible for the instrumentation of the first US satellites.

After the end of World War II, Van Allen began utilizing unused German V2 rockets to measure levels of cosmic radiation in the outer atmosphere, the data being radioed back to Earth. He then conceived of rocket-balloons (rockoons), which began to be used in 1952. They consisted of a small rocket which was lifted by means of a balloon into the stratosphere and then fired off.

Van Basten Marco (1964–). Dutch footballer. He started his career with top Dutch side Ajax and won many domestic honours. In 1987 he transferred to AC Milan for 3.3 million. A celebrated striker, he helped the Netherlands to win the European Championship in 1988 and scored two goals for AC Milan in the European Cup final in 1989.

Love, like fortune, turns upon a wheel, and is very much given to rising and falling.

JOHN VANBRUGH
False Friend I. i 1702

Vanbrugh John (1664–1726). English Baroque architect and dramatist. He designed Blenheim Palace, Oxfordshire, and Castle Howard, Yorkshire, and wrote the comic dramas *The Relapse* 1696 and *The Provok'd Wife* 1697. Knighted 1714. He was imprisoned in France 1688–93 as a political hostage during the war between France and the Grand Alliance (including Britain).
Suggested reading
Beard, Geoffrey *The Work of Sir John Vanbrugh* (1986)
Downes, Kerry *Vanbrugh: Biography* (1987)
Holland, N N *The First Modern Comedies* (1959)

Van Buren Martin (1782–1862). Eighth president of the US 1837–41, a Democrat, who had helped establish the Democratic Party. He was secretary of state 1829–31, minister to Britain 1831–33, vice president 1833–37, and president during the Panic of 1837, the worst US economic crisis until that time, caused by land speculation in the West. Refusing to intervene, he advocated the establishment of an independent treasury, one not linked to the federal government, worsening the depression and losing the 1840 election.
Suggested reading
Curtis, James *The Fox at Bay: Martin Van Buren and the Presidency* (1970)
Niven, John *Martin Van Buren and the Romantic Age of American Politics* (1983)
Van Buren, Martin *Autobiography* (1920, rep 1973)
Wilson, Major L *The Presidency of Martin Van Buren* (1984)

Vance Cyrus Roberts (1917–). US Democratic politician, secretary of state 1977–80. He was United Nations negotiator in the peace talks on Bosnia-Herzegovina 1992–93, resigning from the post due to ill health. Together with European Community negotiator Lord Owen, he devised the Vance–Owen peace plan for dividing the republic into ten semi-autonomous provinces. The plan was rejected by the Bosnian Serbs.

Van Cortlandt Stephanus (1643–1700). Dutch-American colonial official. Born in New Amsterdam (New York from 1664), Van Cortlandt was the son of a prominent family of Dutch settlers. He was a prosperous merchant and expanded his landholdings after the English conquest of the colony in 1664. A colonel in New York provincial militia, he served on the governor's council and in 1677 became the first native-born mayor of New York. He was a local judge 1677–91 and justice of the provincial supreme court 1691–1700.

Vancouver George (1757–1798). British navigator who made extensive exploration of the W coast of North America. He accompanied James Cook on two voyages, and served in the West Indies. He also surveyed parts of Australia, New Zealand, Tahiti, and Hawaii.

van de Graaff Robert Jemison (1901–1967). US physicist who from 1929 developed a high-voltage generator, which in its modern form can produce more than a million volts.

He worked at the Massachusetts Institute of Technology 1931–60. In 1946 he set up the High Voltage Engineering Corporation with his collaborator John Trump.

Trump and van de Graaff had modified the generator so that it would produce hard X-rays for use in radiotherapy in treating internal tumours (the first machine was installed in a Boston hospital 1937). In the 1940s they began commercial production, and developed the van de Graaff generator for a wide variety of scientific, medical, and industrial research purposes. The tandem principle of particle acceleration and a new insulating core transformer invented by van de Graaff contributed to these advances.

Vandenberg Arthur Hendrick (1884–1951). US public official. Born in Grand Rapids, Michigan, USA, Vandenberg briefly attended the University of Michigan Law School. He left to join the staff of the *Grand Rapids Herald*, of which he became editor 1906 and later became active in state politics. A Republican, he was appointed to a US Senate seat 1928 and remained in that office for the next 23 years. Although initially an isolationist, he supported F D Roosevelt's war policies and was a supporter of the United Nations 1945. He was chair of the Senate Foreign Relations Committee 1946–48.

Vanderbilt Cornelius (1794–1877). US industrialist who made a fortune of more than $100 million in steamships and (from the age of 70) by financing railways.

Vanderbilt William Henry (1821–1885). US financier and railway promoter. Born in New Brunswick, New Jersey, USA, son of financier Cornelius Vanderbilt, he became the head of a railway trust and was strongly opposed to government regulation of the railway industry. Given control of the Staten Island Railroad 1857, he was named vice president of the New York and Harlem Railroad 1864, acquired other railways, and became president of the New York Central Railroad 1877. Vanderbilt was famous for his contemptuous phrase 'The public be damned'. He retired in 1883.

van der Laan Hans (1904–1991). Dutch architect of monasteries. He studied architecture in the 1920s in Delft before entering the Benedictine order, where he was ordained as a priest 1934. His earliest work was a guest wing added to the abbey in Oosterhaut 1938; his most significant work is the monastery in Vaals 1956–1982. Here the strength and clarity of mass and void evoke an elementary Classicism.

Vandermonde Alexandre-Théophile (1735–1796). French musician and musical theorist who wrote original and influential papers on algebraic equations and determinants.

Vandermonde was born in Paris. He played a part in the founding of the Conservatoire des Arts et des Métiers and served as its director after 1782. Vandermonde wrote four mathematical papers, all between 1771 and 1773. The first considered the solvability of algebraic equations. He found formulas for solving general quadratic equations, cubic equations, and quartic equations. The second and third papers are less important; the fourth paper is controversial, and includes the Vandermonde determinant.

van der Post Laurens Jan (1906–1996). South African writer. His books, many of them autobiographical, reflect his openness to diverse cultures and his belief in the importance of intuition, individualism, and myth in human experience. His best-known works, which record the disappearing culture of the Bushmen of the Kalahari, are *The Lost World of the Kalahari* 1958, *The Heart of the Hunter* 1961, and *Testament to the Bushmen* 1984.

His first novel, *In a Province* 1934, was an indictment of racism in South Africa; later works include *Flamingo Feather* 1955, *The Hunter and the Whale* 1967, *A Story like the Wind* 1972, and *A Far-off Place* 1974. He wrote about Japanese prisoner-of-war camps in *The Seed and the Sower* 1963 (filmed as *Merry Christmas Mr Lawrence*). He was knighted 1981. *See illustration on page 870.*

Van Devanter Willis (1859–1941). US jurist. Born in Marion, Indiana, USA, Van Devanter was educated at Asbury University and received a law degree from the University of Cincinnati 1881.

van der Post *South African writer Laurens van der Post. Throughout his work – novels, essays, travel books, and autobiographies – he expressed his concern that modern man needs to regain a harmony between the unconscious, feminine element of the psyche and the conscious, masculine element. He applied this search for psychic harmony to race (he was forced to leave South Africa for running an anti-apartheid periodical) and also to ecology, and was a close adviser to Prince Charles.*

Settling in Cheyenne, Wyoming, he served as city attorney 1887–88 and chief justice of the territorial supreme court 1888–90. He was appointed US Supreme Court justice 1910–37 by President Taft. Active in Republican politics, he served as assistant US attorney general 1897–1903 and federal circuit judge 1903–10. A staunch conservative, Van Devanter was a bitter opponent of the New Deal until his retirement.

van Diemen Anthony (1593–1645). Dutch admiral; see ◊Diemen, Anthony van.

Van Doren Harold (1895–1957). US pioneer industrial designer. He was active in Philadelphia from 1930. His first client was the Toledo Scale Company for which he designed a corporate identity. Key products include a green plastic radio in the image of a sky-scraper 1930–31 and a streamlined child's scooter 1936. In 1940 he published a seminal text entitled *Industrial Design*.

Van Doren Mark Albert (1894–1972). US poet and writer. Born in Hope, Illinois, USA, Van Doren was educated at the University of Illinois and received his PhD 1920 from Columbia University, where he taught English 1920–59. He published his first collection, *Spring Thunder*, 1924. His anthology *Collected Poems* 1939 won a

Pulitzer prize. He was an editor of *The Nation* 1924–28 and published the novels *The Transients* 1935 and *Windless Cabins* 1940. His autobiography appeared 1958 and his last collection of poems, *Good Morning*, 1973.

van Dyck Anthony. Flemish painter; see ◊Dyck, Anthony van.

Death is but a little word, but 'tis a great work to die.
HENRY VANE
spoken on the scaffold 1662

Vane Henry (1613–1662). English politician. In 1640 he was elected a member of the Long Parliament, and was knighted in the same year. He was prominent in the impeachment of Archbishop Laud and in 1643–53 was in effect the civilian head of the Parliamentary government. At the Restoration of the monarchy he was executed.

Vane John Robert (1927–). British pharmacologist who discovered the wide role of prostaglandins in the human body, produced in response to illness and stress. He shared the 1982 Nobel Prize for Physiology or Medicine with Sune Bergström (1916–) and Bengt Samuelson (1934–) of Sweden.

van Eyck Aldo. Dutch architect; see ◊Eyck, Aldo van.

van Eyck Jan. Flemish painter; see ◊Eyck, Jan van.

van Gogh Vincent. Dutch painter; see ◊Gogh, Vincent van.

van Leyden Lucas. Dutch painter; see ◊Lucas van Leyden.

van Meegeren Hans. Dutch forger; see ◊Meegeren, Hans van.

Van Rensselaer Stephen (1764–1839). American public official and soldier. Born in New York, Van Rensselaer was educated at Harvard University and inherited extensive real estate holdings. He served in the New York state assembly 1789–91, in the state senate 1791–96, and as a major general in the militia. A commander during the Anglo-American War of 1812–14 he suffered a serious defeat at Queenstown, Canada. He was a US congressman 1822–29. As president of the New York Canal Commission 1825–39 he oversaw the construction of the Erie Canal.

Perhaps his most original feat was to have a play in French run for four months in Paris when ... at the embassy.
Neville Bland on ROBERT VANSITTART
in *Dictionary of National Biography*

Vansittart Robert Gilbert, 1st Baron Vansittart (1881–1957). British diplomat, noted for his anti-German polemic. He was permanent undersecretary of state for foreign affairs 1930–38 and chief diplomatic adviser to the foreign secretary 1938–41. KCB 1929, baron 1941.

van't Hoff Jacobus Henricus (1852–1911). Dutch physical chemist. He explained the 'asymmetric' carbon atom occurring in optically active compounds. His greatest work – the concept of chemical affinity as the maximum work obtainable from a reaction – was shown with measurements of osmotic and gas pressures, and reversible electrical cells. He was the first recipient of the Nobel Prize for Chemistry, in 1901. He was professor at Amsterdam 1878–96 and at the Prussian Academy of Sciences in Berlin from 1896.

In 1874 van't Hoff postulated that the four valencies of a carbon atom are directed towards the corners of a regular tetrahedron. This allows it to be asymmetric (connected to four different atoms or groups) in certain compounds, and it is these compounds that exhibit optical activity. Van't Hoff ascribed the ability to rotate the plane of polarized light to the asymmetric carbon atom in the molecule, and showed that optical isomers are left- and right-handed forms (mirror images) of the same molecule.

Van't Hoff's first ideas about chemical thermodynamics and

affinity were published in 1877, and consolidated in his *Etudes de dynamique chimique* 1884. He applied thermodynamics to chemical equilibria, developing the principles of chemical kinetics and describing a new method of determining the order of a reaction. He deduced the connection between the equilibrium constant and temperature in the form of an equation known as the van't Hoff isochore.

Van Vleck John Hasbrouck (1899–1980). US physicist, considered one of the founders of modern magnetic theory. He shared the 1977 Nobel Prize for Physics with his student Philip Anderson. He became professor at Minnesota 1927 and was professor at Harvard 1934–69.

Using wave mechanics, Van Vleck devised a theory that gives an accurate explanation of the magnetic properties of individual atoms in a series of chemical elements. He also introduced the idea of temperature-independent susceptibility in paramagnetic materials – now called Van Vleck paramagnetism. His formulation of the ligand field theory is one of the most useful tools for interpreting the patterns of chemical bonds in complex compounds. This theory explains the magnetic, electrical, and optical properties of many elements and compounds by considering the influences exerted on the electrons in particular atoms by other atoms nearby.

Varah (Edward) Chad (1911–   ). British priest who founded the Samaritans.

Varda Agnès (1928–   ). French film director. Favouring a documentary form throughout her career, she explored feminist themes in such films as *Cléo de Cinq à Sept/Cleo from Five to Seven* 1961, and *L'Une Chante, L'Autre Pas/One Sings the Other Doesn't* 1977. She has also made short films on political topics, and the film *Jacquot de Nantes* 1991, on the youth of her late husband, the director Jacques Demy (1931–1990).

Vardon Harry (Henry William) (1870–1937). British golfer, born in Jersey. He won the British Open a record six times 1896–1914. Vardon was the first UK golfer to win the US Open 1900. He formed a partnership with James Braid and John Henry Taylor, which became known as 'the Great Triumvirate', and dominated British golf in the years up to World War I.

There is no avant-garde: only some people a bit behind.
EDGAR VARÈSE
Attributed remark

Varèse Edgar Victor Achille Charles (1883–1965). French composer. He left Paris for New York 1916 where he cofounded the New Symphony Orchestra 1919 with the French-born US harpist Carlos Salzédo (1885–1961) to promote modern and pre-classical music. Renouncing the values of tonality, he discovered new resources of musical expression in the percussion sonorities of *Ionisation* 1929–31, the swooping sound of two theremins in *Hyperprism* 1933–34, and the combination of taped and live instrumental sounds in *Déserts* 1950–54.
Suggested reading
Bernard, Jonathan *The Music of Edgar Varèse* (1987)
Varèse, Louise *Varèse: A Looking-Glass Diary* (by his wife) (1972)

Vargas Getúlio Dorneles (1883–1954). President of Brazil 1930–45 and 1951–54. He overthrew the republic 1930 and in 1937 set up a totalitarian, pro-fascist state known as the Estado Novo. Ousted by a military coup 1945, he returned as president 1951 but, amid mounting opposition and political scandal, committed suicide 1954.

Vargas Llosa (Jorge) Mario (Pedro) (1936–   ). Peruvian novelist. He wrote *La ciudad y los perros/The Time of the Hero* 1963 and *La guerra del fin del mundo/The War at the End of the World* 1982. As a writer he belongs to the magic realist school. *La tía Julia y el escribidor/Aunt Julia and the Scriptwriter* 1977 is a humorously autobiographical novel.

His other works are *Historia de Mayta/The Real Life of Alejandro Mayta* 1985, an account of an attempted revolution in Peru in 1958, and *The Storyteller* 1990.

In his political career, Vargas Llosa began as a communist and turned to the right; he ran unsuccessfully for the presidency 1990.
Suggested reading
Vargas Llosa, Mario *A Fish in Water: A Memoir* (trs 1994)
Vargas Llosa, Mario *A Writer's Reality* (1991)

Varley John (1778–1842). English painter. His watercolour landscapes were painted in a sublime manner, and he was one of the most influential early watercolourists. He was a friend of English poet and artist William Blake.

He was in youth a protégé of Dr Monro and became well known as a teacher of art, David Cox and Samuel Palmer being among the many he trained or encouraged. Views of North Wales are of note in his own work, but his large output tended towards a mechanical facility. It was for him that Blake drew his famous 'visionary heads'. His brother Cornelius (1781–1873) painted architectural subjects in watercolour. His younger brother, William Fleetwood (1785–1856), his son, Albert Fleetwood, and two grandsons were also watercolourists.

Vasa dynasty Swedish royal house founded by Gustavus Vasa. He liberated his country from Danish rule 1520–23 and put down local uprisings of nobles and peasants. By 1544 he was secure enough to make his title hereditary. His grandson, Gustavus Adolphus, became king 1611 and led the armies of the Protestant princes in the Thirty Years' War until his death. The dynasty ended 1809 when Gustavus IV was deposed by a revolution and replaced by his uncle Charles XIII. With no heir to the throne, the crown was offered 1810 to one of Napoleon's generals, Bernadotte, who became King Charles John until his death in 1844.

Vasarély Victor (1908–   ). Hungarian-born French Op artist. In the 1940s he developed precise geometric compositions, full of visual puzzles and effects of movement, which he created with complex arrangements of hard-edged geometric shapes and subtle variations in colours.

He was active in Paris from 1930, then in the south of France from 1960. He initially worked as a graphic artist, concentrating on black and white artwork.

Vasari Giorgio (1511–1574). Italian art historian, architect, and painter. In his *Lives of the Most Excellent Architects, Painters and Sculptors* 1550 (enlarged and revised 1568), he proposed the theory of a Renaissance of the arts beginning with Giotto and culminating with Michelangelo. He designed the Uffizi Palace, Florence, as well as palaces and churches in Pisa and Arezzo.

He studied art in Florence for a short while with Michelangelo, for whom he had an unbounded admiration, and also with Andrea del Sarto and Baccio Bandinelli. He studied the work of Raphael in Rome. He was successful as an architect and decorative painter, and in 1547 built himself a house at Arezzo, now a museum, which he decorated lavishly. As a painter he has never been highly rated, though of interest as an instance of the Mannerist exaggeration which the devotion to Michelangelo produced. His *Lives*, however, is a classic, and, though corrected in a number of particulars by modern research, remains of the greatest value as a largely unbiased account of the progress of Italian art from the Middle Ages to the Renaissance.
Suggested reading
Blunt, Anthony *Artistic Theory in Italy, 1450–1600* (1962)
Boase, T S R *Giorgio Vasari: The Man and the Book* (1975)
Rubin, Patricia L *Giorgio Vasari: Art and History* (1995)

Vasco da Gama Portuguese navigator; see ◊Gama.

Vasilevsky Alexandr M (1895–1977). Soviet general, Marshal of the Soviet Union. Appointed Chief of Staff 1942 he was responsible for planning most major Soviet operations of World War II, including the Stalingrad counter-offensive and the defence of the Kursk salient. In March 1945 he took command of the 3rd Byelorussian Front when its commander was killed and completed the conquest of E Prussia and the Baltic states. He was appointed commander in chief Far East May 1945, and planned and executed the invasion of Manchuria, Korea, and the Kurile and Sakhalin islands of Japan.

Vaughan, Sarah *US jazz vocalist Sarah Vaughan, noted for her mastering of such vocal techniques as vibrato, vocal leaps, 'skat' singing, and improvization. Her vocal control and the beauty of her tone were the hallmarks of her singing, and she made a major vocal contribution to the development of bebop.*

Vassar Matthew (1792–1868). British-born US entrepreneur and educational philanthropist. Born in England, Vassar arrived in the USA with his family 1796. He worked in his father's brewery in Poughkeepsie before establishing his own firm 1811, and successfully expanded his business interests and real-estate investments. A proponent of higher education for women, he endowed Vassar Female College in Poughkeepsie, New York, 1861. The school opened 1865 with a full college curriculum and became one of the finest women's educational institutions in the USA.

Vassiliou Georgios Vassos (1931–   ). Greek-Cypriot politician and entrepreneur, president of Cyprus 1988–93. A self-made millionaire, he entered politics as an independent and in 1988 won the presidency, with Communist Party support. He subsequently, with United Nations help, tried to heal the rift between the Greek and Turkish communities, but was unsuccessful. In the Feb 1993 presidential elections he was narrowly defeated by Glafkos Clerides.

Vatutin Nikolai A (1901–1944). Soviet general. Appointed commander of the Southwest Front 1942 he took part in the action at Stalingrad; he attempted an offensive but was soundly defeated by von Manstein. After this he conducted a successful defence of the southern sector of the Kursk salient and then counter-attacked to Kharkov and liberated much of the Ukraine. A further advance liberated Kiev, but he was ambushed by anti-Soviet partisans near Rovno Feb 1945 and fatally wounded.

Vauban Sébastien le Prestre de (1633–1707). French marshal and military engineer. In Louis XIV's wars he conducted many sieges and rebuilt many of the fortresses on France's east frontier.

Vaucouleurs Gerard Henri De (1918–   ). French-born US astronomer; see ◊De Vaucouleurs.

Vaughan Henry (1622–1695). Welsh poet. He published several volumes of metaphysical religious verse and prose devotions. His mystical outlook on nature influenced later poets, including Wordsworth.

Vaughan Sarah Lois (1924–1990). US jazz singer. She began by singing bebop with such musicians as Dizzy Gillespie and later moved effortlessly between jazz and romantic ballads, her voice having a range of nearly three octaves. She toured very widely and had several hit singles, including 'Make Yourself Comfortable' 1954, 'Mr Wonderful' 1956, and 'Broken-Hearted Melody' 1959.

Vaughan Williams Ralph (1872–1958). English composer. His style was tonal and often evocative of the English countryside through the use of folk themes. Among his works are the orchestral *Fantasia on a Theme by Thomas Tallis* 1910; the opera *Sir John in Love* 1929, featuring the Elizabethan song 'Greensleeves'; and nine symphonies 1909–57.

He studied at Cambridge, the Royal College of Music, with Max Bruch in Berlin, and Maurice Ravel in Paris. His choral poems include *Toward the Unknown Region* (Whitman) 1907 and *On Wenlock Edge* (Housman) 1909, *A Sea Symphony* 1910, and *A London Symphony* 1914. Later works include *Sinfonia Antartica* 1953, developed from his film score for *Scott of the Antarctic* 1948, and symphony no. 9 1957. He also wrote *A Pastoral Symphony* 1922, sacred music for unaccompanied choir, the ballad opera *Hugh the Drover* 1924, and the operatic morality play *The Pilgrim's Progress* 1951.

Suggested reading
Day, James *Vaughan Williams* (1975)
Kennedy, M *The Works of Vaughan Williams* (1964)
Mellers, W *Vaughan Williams and the Vision of Albion* (1989)
Vaughan Williams, Ralph *The Making of Music* (1955)
Vaughan Williams, Ursula *R V W: A Biography of Ralph Vaughan Williams* (1964)

Vauquelin Louis Nicolas (1763–1829). French chemist who worked mainly in the inorganic field, analysing minerals. He discovered the elements chromium (1797) and beryllium.

Vauquelin was born in Saint-André d'Héberôt, Calvados, and was apprenticed to an apothecary. Moving to Paris, he became a laboratory assistant at the Jardin du Roi and was befriended by a professor of chemistry. In 1791 he was made a member of the Academy of Sciences and from that time he helped to edit the journal *Annales de Chimie*, although he left the country for a while during the height of the French Revolution. On his return in 1794 he became professor of chemistry at the Ecole des Mines in Paris, and in 1802 was appointed assayer to the Mint. From 1809 he was professor at the University of Paris. He was elected to the Chamber of Deputies in 1828.

In organic chemistry, Vauquelin also made some significant discoveries. In 1806, working with asparagus, he isolated the amino acid aspargine, the first one to be discovered. He also discovered pectin and malic acid in apples, and isolated camphoric acid and quinic acid.

Vaux James Hardy (born 1782). English-born convict, three times transported to Australia for robbery. During his second period in New South Wales 1810–29, he wrote an autobiography *Memoirs of James Hardy Vaux* which was published in England 1819 with an appendix *Vocabulary of the Flash Language*, which Vaux claimed to have compiled. This was re-edited and re-published 1964 and serves as a source of convict language usage.

Veblen Thorstein Bunde (1857–1929). US social critic. Veblen was born in Cato, Wisconsin, raised in Minnesota, educated at Carleton College and received his PhD from Yale University 1884. He taught at Chicago, Stanford, and Missouri universities and edited the *Journal of Political Economy* 1892–1905. His insights on culture and economics were expressed in his books *The Theory of the Leisure Class* 1899 and *The Theory of Business Enterprise* 1904. He was a founder of the New School for Social Research in New York 1919.

Conspicuous consumption of valuable goods is a means of reputability to the gentleman of leisure.

THORSTEIN VEBLEN
The Theory of the Leisure Class 1899

Veeck William Louis, (1914–1986). US baseball executive and pioneer of new marketing techniques. Born in Chicago, USA, Veeck was the son of the owner of major league baseball's Chicago Cubs, and attended Kenyon College. He became part owner of the Cleveland Indians, and helped guide them to a World Series victory 1948.

As owner of St Louis Browns 1951–53 and Chicago White Sox 1959–61, he introduced innovations in the sale of television rights and the drafting of amateurs that later became standard in professional sports.

Vega Lope Felix de Carpio (1562–1635). Spanish poet and dramatist. He was born in Madrid, served with the Armada 1588, and in 1613 took holy orders. He was one of the founders of modern Spanish drama. He wrote epics, pastorals, odes, sonnets, novels, and, reputedly, over 1,500 plays (of which 426 are still in existence), mostly tragicomedies. He set out his views on drama in *Arte nuevo de hacer comedias/The New Art of Writing Plays* 1609, in which he defended his innovations while reaffirming the classical forms. *Fuenteovejuna* about 1614 has been acclaimed as the first proletarian drama.

Veidt Conrad (1893–1943). German film actor. He was memorable as the sleepwalker in *Das Kabinett des Dr Caligari/The Cabinet of Dr Caligari* 1919 and as the evil caliph in *The Thief of Bagdad* 1940. An international film star from the 1920s, he moved to Hollywood in the 1940s, where he played the Gestapo officer in *Casablanca* 1942.

Veil Simone (1927–). French politician. A survivor of Hitler's concentration camps, she was minister of health 1974–79 and framed the French abortion bill. She was president of the European Parliament 1979–82. She held a cabinet post as minister for health, urban, and social affairs 1993–95.

Velázquez Diego Rodríguez de Silva y (1599–1660). Spanish painter. He was the outstanding Spanish artist of the 17th century. In 1623 he became court painter to Philip IV in Madrid, where he produced many portraits of the royal family as well as occasional religious paintings, genre scenes, and other subjects. Notable among his portraits is *Las Meninas/The Maids of Honour* 1656 (Prado, Madrid), while *Women Frying Eggs* 1618 (National Gallery of Scotland, Edinburgh) is a typical genre scene.

His pictures (which he signed *Diego Velasquez* or *Diego de Silva Velasquez*) do not, it is estimated, number more than 170. Copies and versions were produced by his assistants, among whom were Juan Paréja and Juan del Mazo. His immediate influence in Spain was small, though Goya was to declare as the source of his inspiration 'Rembrandt, Velazquez and Nature', and many great artists since, such as Manet, have been inspired by this most 'painterly' of great painters.

His first master was Francisco de Herrera, from whom he went to the more cultivated guidance of Francisco Pacheco, whose daughter, Juana, he married 1618. His early works produced at Seville were *bodegones*, 'kitchen pictures', of the type then popular, with peasant figures and carefully detailed still-life detail, showing strongly the influence of Caravaggio's 'naturalism'. Examples are the *Christ in the House of Martha and Mary* (National Gallery, London), the *Cook* (National Gallery of Scotland) and the *Water Carrier* (Apsley House). He went to Madrid on a short visit 1622. He was recalled in the following year by Philip IV's minister, Olivares, and gained immediate success and prompt appointment as painter to the king. A painting that established his reputation was *Los Borracho/The Topers* of 1629. At this time he met Rubens in Madrid and was also stimulated by his first visit to Italy 1629–31. He studied and copied the great Venetians in Venice, and went on to Rome and Naples, where he met Ribera. His *Forge of Vulcan* (Prado) attempts a reconciliation of the mythological theme as treated by Italians, and his native sense of realism. From 1631 he settled to an assiduous court routine which entailed various official duties as well as painting, broken only by a second visit to Italy (Genoa, Venice, Naples and Rome), 1649–51. Paintings of the royal family, for example the full-length *Philip IV* (National Gallery, London) and *Prince Baltasar*

Carlos dressed as a Hunter (Prado) mainly occupied him, though to this period belongs the great *Surrender of Breda (Las Lanzas)* (Prado), painted before 1635 to commemorate the successful siege of Breda by Spinola. The second visit to Italy (to buy pictures and to gain information useful for the organization of a proposed Spanish Royal Academy) produced Velazquez's portrait of Innocent X, his remarkable landscape sketch of the Gardens of the Villa Medici (Prado), and the *Rokeby Venus* (National Gallery, London), in which he sought to emulate Titian. His later years are marked not by prolific output but by a remarkable series of masterpieces. His portraits of Philip IV's second wife, Mariana of Austria, and of the Infanta Margarita, combine exquisite colour with breadth of design. In the famous group pictures – the *Las Meninas/Maids of Honour* and the view inside the royal tapestry works *Las Hilanderas*, both in the Prado – intricate themes are perfectly resolved.

Suggested reading

Brown, D *The World of Velázquez* (1969)
Kahr, M M *Velázquez: The Art of Painting* (1976)
Lopez-Rey, J *Velázquez' Work and World* (1968)

Velde, van de name of a Dutch painter family. Essaias (*c.* 1591–1630) was a painter of landscape, battle-pieces and genre, who worked at Haarlem and as a court painter at The Hague, mainly noted for his small landscapes with figures. His brother, Willem the Elder (1610/11–1693), was a marine painter who took part in the naval warfare between Holland and England, but in 1672 was summoned to England together with his son to paint for Charles II. His son, Willem the Younger (1633–1707), who had studied at Amsterdam under his father and Simon de Vlieger, collaborated with him and is the more eminent of the two. The brother of Willem the Younger, Adriaen (1636–1672), was an animal and landscape painter.

Velázquez *A self-portrait by the Spanish painter Velázquez. Velázquez was the most prominent artist in 17th-century Spain, and was court painter to Philip IV. He produced religious scenes and depictions of everyday life as well as portraits of the royal family.* (Image Select)

Vendôme Louis Joseph, Duc de Vendôme (1654–1712). Marshal of France under Louis XIV, he lost his command after defeat by the British commander Marlborough at Oudenaarde, Belgium, 1708, but achieved successes in the 1710 Spanish campaign during the War of the Spanish Succession.

Veneziano Domenico. Italian painter; see ◊Domenico Veneziano.

Vening Meinesz Felix Andries (1887–1966). Dutch geophysicist who originated the method of making very precise gravity measurements in the stable environment of a submarine. The results he obtained were important in the fields of geophysics and geodesy. He was able to discount the model of the Earth's shape that proposed a flattening at the equator.

Employed by the government to take part in a gravimetric survey of the Netherlands, he took measurements at over 50 sites. He was professor at Utrecht 1927–57 and also at Delft 1938–57. Between 1923 and 1939 he undertook 11 scientific expeditions in submarines.

Vening Meinesz realized that measurements of the Earth's gravitational field could yield indications of the internal features of the Earth. He developed a device requiring the measurement of the mean periods of two pendulums that swing from the same apparatus. The mean of the two periods is not affected by disturbances in the horizontal plane, and so can be used to determine the local gravitational force accurately.

Underwater studies led to the discovery of low-gravity belts in the Indonesian archipelago. Vening Meinesz proposed that these were the result of a downward buckling of the crust causing light sediments to fill the resulting depressions. This is the origin of the concept of the syncline.

Venizelos Eleuthérios Kyriakos (1864–1936). Greek politician born in Crete, leader of the Cretan movement against Turkish rule until the union of the island with Greece in 1905. He later became prime minister of the Greek state on five occasions, 1910–15, 1917–20, 1924, 1928–32, and 1933, before being exiled to France in 1935.

Having led the fight against Turkish rule in Crete, Venizelos became president of the Cretan assembly and declared the union of the island with Greece in 1905. As prime minister of Greece from 1910, he instituted financial, military, and constitutional reforms and took Greece into the Balkan Wars 1912–13. As a result, Greece annexed Macedonia, but attempts by Venizelos to join World War I on the Allied side led to his dismissal by King Constantine. Leading a rebel government in Crete and later in Salonika, he declared war on Bulgaria and Germany and secured the abdication of King Constantine.

As prime minister again from 1917 he attended the Paris Peace Conference in 1919. By provoking a war with Turkey over Anatolia in 1920 he suffered an electoral defeat. On his last return to office in 1933, he was implicated in an uprising by his supporters and fled to France, where he died.

Venn John (1834–1923). English logician whose diagram, known as the Venn diagram, is much used in the teaching of elementary mathematics. The Venn Diagram represents sets and the logical relationships between them. Sets are drawn as circles. An area of overlap between two circles contains elements that are common to both sets, and thus represents a third set. Circles that do not overlap represent sets with no elements in common (disjoint sets). Venn was born in Hull, Yorkshire, and studied at Cambridge. He became a priest, but abjured his clerical orders 1883. From 1862 he was a Cambridge college lecturer in moral sciences.

The use of geometrical representations to illustrate syllogistic logic was not new. Venn adopted the method of illustrating propositions by means of exclusive and inclusive circles, and added the new device of shading the segments of the circles to represent the possibilities that were excluded by the propositions at issue. Later, he extended his method by proposing a series of circles dividing the plane into compartments, so that each successive circle should intersect all the compartments already existing. This idea, taken up and refined by Charles Dodgson (the writer Lewis Carroll), led to the use of the closed compartment enclosing the whole diagram to define what is now known as the universal set.

Venn published three standard texts: *The Logic of Chance* 1866, *Symbolic Logic* 1881, and *The Principles of Empirical Logic* 1889.

Ventris Michael George Francis (1922–1956). English architect. Deciphering Minoan Linear B, the language of the tablets found at Knossos and Pylos, he showed that it was a very early form of Greek, thus revising existing views on early Greek history. *Documents in Mycenaean Greek*, written with John Chadwick (1920–), was published shortly after he died.

Venturi Robert Charles (1925–). US architect. He pioneered Post-Modernism through his books *Complexity and Contradiction in Architecture* 1967 (Pulitzer prize 1991) and *Learning from Las Vegas* 1972. In 1986 he was commissioned to design the Sainsbury Wing extension to the National Gallery, London, opened 1991. He is famous for his slogan 'Less is a bore', countering German architect Ludwig Mies van der Rohe's 'Less is more'.
Suggested reading
Jencks, Charles A *The Language of Post-Modern Architecture* (1977)
Maxwell, Robert and Stern, Robert *Venturi and Rauch* (1977)
Venturi, Robert *Complexity and Contradiction in Architecture* (1967)

Vercingetorix (died 46 BC). Gallic chieftain. Leader of a revolt of all the tribes of Gaul against the Romans 52 BC; he lost, was captured, displayed in Julius Caesar's triumph 46 BC, and later executed. This ended the Gallic resistance to Roman rule.

Verdi Giuseppe Fortunino Francesco (1813–1901). Italian opera composer of the Romantic period. He took his native operatic style to new heights of dramatic expression. In 1842 he wrote the opera *Nabucco*, followed by *Ernani* 1844 and *Rigoletto* 1851. Other works include *Il trovatore* and *La traviata* both 1853, *Aïda* 1871, and the masterpieces of his old age, *Otello* 1887 and *Falstaff* 1893. His *Requiem* 1874 commemorates Alessandro Manzoni.

During the mid-1800s, Verdi became a symbol of Italy's fight for independence from Austria, frequently finding himself in conflict with the Austrian authorities, who felt that his operas encouraged Italian nationalism.
Suggested reading
Gatti, Carlo *Verdi: The Man and his Music* (1955)
Hussey, D *Verdi* (1963)
Martin, George *Verdi* (1963)
Phillips-Matz, Mary Jane *Verdi: A Biography* (1993)
Walker, F *The Man Verdi* (1962)
Weaver, W *Verdi: A Documentary Study* (1977)

Verge John (1782–1861). English-born architect in Australia whose buildings, most in the Colonial Regency style of architecture, include the country house Camden Park, near Sydney 1835, and Elizabeth Bay House, Sydney 1837.

Vergil alternative spelling of ◊Virgil, Roman poet.

Verlaine Paul Marie (1844–1896). French lyric poet. He was acknowledged as the leader of the Symbolist poets. His volumes of verse, strongly influenced by the poets Charles Baudelaire and Arthur Rimbaud, include *Poèmes saturniens/Saturnine Poems* 1866, *Fêtes galantes/Amorous Entertainments* 1869, and *Romances sans paroles/Songs without Words* 1874. In 1873 he was imprisoned for shooting and wounding Rimbaud. His later works reflect his attempts to lead a reformed life.
Suggested reading
Chadwick, Charles *Verlaine* (1973)
Coulon, Marcel *Poet Under Saturn: The Tragedy of Verlaine* (1970)
Raitt, A W *Life and Letters in France in the 19th Century* (1965)

Vermeer Jan (1632–1675). Dutch painter. He was active in Delft. Most of his pictures are genre scenes, characterized by a limpid clarity, a distinct air of stillness, and colour harmonies often based on yellow and blue. He frequently depicted solitary women in domestic settings, as in *The Lacemaker* about 1655 (Louvre, Paris).

He was probably the pupil of Carel Fabritius, and was admitted to the Delft Guild of Painters 1653, being Master of the Guild 1662 and again 1670. He died in poverty, the obligations of a large family no doubt being a contributory cause, and he was evidently not a prolific painter – less than 40 authentic works remain. After his death he was forgotten until the French critic 'W Bürger' (Théophile Thoré) rediscovered him 1866. In balance and simplicity of design, and in his exquisite sense of colour and of colour in light, he attains a serene perfection. Italian influence may be discerned in his early work, for example *Diana and her Nymphs* (The Hague) and *The Courtesan* (Dresden), but independent genius appears in his masterpieces: the two great exterior views the *View of Delft* (The Hague) and *The Little Street* (Rijksmuseum); the interiors in which he transcended the brilliance of de Hooch, Terborch and Metsu, such as the *Lady standing at the Virginals* (National Gallery, London) and *The Painter's Studio* (Vienna) – unsold at the time of his death; and such remarkable studies as the *Maidservant pouring Milk* (Rijksmuseum), the *Girl with a Turban* (The Hague), and the *Girl with a Flute* (National Gallery, Washington).

Suggested reading
Blankert, A *Vermeer of Delft* (1978)
Gowing, L *Vermeer* (1970)
Koningsberger, H *The World of Vermeer* (1967)
Slatkes, L *Vermeer and his Contemporaries* (1981)
Wheelock, A K *Vermeer* (1978)

Verne Jules (1828–1905). French author. He wrote tales of adventure that anticipated future scientific developments: *Five Weeks in a Balloon* 1862, *Journey to the Centre of the Earth* 1864, *Twenty Thousand Leagues under the Sea* 1870, and *Around the World in Eighty Days* 1873.

Suggested reading
Butcher, William *Verne's Journey to the Centre of the Self* (1990)
Costello, Peter *Jules Verne: Inventor of Science Fiction* (1978)

Verdi *Italian composer Giuseppe Verdi in a print published in 1886, the year before his* Otello *appeared. He was one of the greatest opera composers of all time, but his music was once devalued by scholars for following predictable formulae until, ironically, German critics of the 1920s recognized his genius.* (Image Select)

Evans, A B *Jules Verne Rediscovered* (1988)
Evans, I O *Jules Verne and His Work* (1965)
Jules-Verne, Jean *Jules Verne* (trs 1976)

As for the Yankees, they have no other ambition than to take possession of this new continent of the sky [the Moon], and to plant upon the summit of its highest elevation the star-spangled banner of the United States.

JULES VERNE
1865

Verney Edmund (1590–1642). English courtier, knight-marshal to Charles I from 1626. He sat as a member of both the Short and the Long Parliaments and, though sympathizing with the Parliamentary position, remained true to his allegiance: he died at his post as royal standard bearer at the Battle of Edgehill. Knighted 1611.

The Verney papers, a collection of his memoirs and other personal papers, are a valuable record of this and later periods. His son Ralph (1613–96) supported the Parliamentarians.

Vernier Pierre (*c.* 1580–1637). French engineer and instrument-maker who invented a means of making very precise measurements with what is now called the vernier scale.

He was working as a military engineer for the Spanish Habsburgs, then the rulers of Franche-Comté, when he realized the need for a more accurate way of reading angles on the surveying instruments he used in map-making. In 1630 he was appointed to the service of the count of Burgundy, for whom he built fortifications.

In 1631 Vernier published *La construction, l'usage, et les propriétez du quadrant nouveau mathématique/The construction, uses and properties of a new mathematical quadrant*, in which he explained his method.

Old Grog

Nickname given to EDWARD VERNON (after his grogram coat) by Thomas and J C Robertson Byerley in *The Percy Anecdotes 1820–1822*. The name was afterwards given to the mixed liquor (brandy/rum with water) that he compelled British sailors to take.

Vernon Edward (1684–1757). English admiral who captured Portobello from the Spanish in the Caribbean 1739, with a loss of only seven men.

Veronese Paolo (Paolo Caliari) (*c.* 1528–1588). Italian painter. He was active mainly in Venice (from about 1553). He specialized in grand decorative schemes, such as his ceilings in the Doge's Palace in Venice, with their *trompe l'oeil* effects and inventive detail. Whether religious, mythological, historical, or allegorical, his paintings celebrate the power and splendour of Venice.

He was the pupil of a minor painter, Antonio Badile, but learned much from the study of Titian and Tintoretto. Some part of his youth was also spent in the shop of his brother Antonio, who dealt in the embroidery and rich stuffs that were to play an important decorative part in his painting. From 1555 he lived in Venice, producing those huge decorative compositions with their representation of splendid architecture and crowds of luxuriously dressed figures for which he is famous. Many of his best paintings and frescoes are at Venice in the Doge's Palace, the church of San Sebastiano, the Accademia, and the Villa Masiera, but masterpieces elsewhere are the great *Marriage at Cana*, 1562–63 (Louvre), the *Family of Darius before Alexander*, ? *c.* 1570 (National Gallery), and the *Finding of Moses* (Washington, Mellon Collection). The *Marriage at Cana* is typical in its pomp and luxury, containing more than 130 figures, including portraits of many celebrities of the time – Charles V, Francis I, Sultan Soliman II, Titian, Bassano, Tintoretto, Aretino – together with an assortment of fools, dwarfs, Negro pages and dogs, in a grandiose architectural setting.

This, and a work similarly conceived, the *Supper in the House of Levi* (Venice, Accademia), were considered irreverent in their treatment of a religious theme and caused Veronese to be questioned by the Inquisition 1573. In composition, in painting the figure, and in tapestry-like schemes of colour, Veronese ranks with the greatest Venetians, and his work inspired the last brilliant efflorescence of mural painting in the 18th century as represented by Tiepolo. Veronese was assisted in his huge undertakings by his brother Benedetto and his sons Carlo and Gabriel, who carried on his studio after his death.

Veronica, St (lived 1st century AD). Woman of Jerusalem who, according to tradition, lent her veil to Jesus to wipe the sweat from his brow on the road to Calvary, whereupon the image of his face was printed upon it. A relic alleged to be the actual veil is preserved in St Peter's Basilica, Rome.

Verrocchio Andrea del (Andrea di Cione) (c. 1435–1488). Italian painter, sculptor, and goldsmith. He ran a large workshop in Florence and received commissions from the Medici family. The vigorous equestrian statue of *Bartolomeo Colleoni* begun about 1480 (Campo SS Giovanni e Paolo, Venice) was his last work.

He studied as a goldsmith under Giuliano Verrocchi and was probably also a pupil of Donatello. He is famous principally as a sculptor, his bronze equestrian statue of Bartolommeo Colleoni being one of the great masterpieces of that art. As a painter he is less eminent; indeed only one picture, the *Baptism of Christ* (Uffizi), is attributed to him with certainty; but his studio-workshop, in which painting was one of many activities, was an important Florentine training ground, and Verrocchio has a secondary fame as the master (and for some years employer) of Leonardo da Vinci, while Lorenzo di Credi was his principal assistant in painting. A wellgrounded tradition has it that Leonardo painted the angel (at left) in the *Baptism* (Uffizi). His hand has also been traced in the background of the *Virgin and Child* (Sheffield).

Versace Gianni (1946–   ). Italian fashion designer. He opened his own business and presented a menswear collection 1978. He has diversified into women's wear, accessories, perfumes, furs, and costumes for opera, theatre, and ballet. He uses simple shapes and strong colours to create provocative clothing.

Verwoerd Hendrik Frensch (1901–1966). South African rightwing Nationalist Party politician, prime minister 1958–66. As minister of native affairs 1950–58, he was the chief promoter of apartheid legislation (segregation by race). He made the country a republic 1961. He was assassinated 1966.

Vesalius Andreas (1514–1564). Belgian physician who revolutionized anatomy. His great innovations were to perform postmortem dissections and to make use of illustrations in teaching anatomy. The dissections (then illegal) enabled him to discover that Galen's system of medicine was based on fundamental anatomical errors. Vesalius's book *De humani corporis fabrica/On the Structure of the Human Body* 1543, together with the main work of astronomer Copernicus, published in the same year, marked the dawn of modern science.

Vesalius was born in Brussels and studied at Louvain, Paris, and Padua in Italy, where he was professor 1537–42. He became court physician to Charles V, and later to his son Philip II of Spain. On his way back from a pilgrimage to Jerusalem, Vesalius died in a shipwreck off Greece.

Dissatisfied with the instruction he had received, Vesalius resolved to make his own observations, which disagreed with Galen's. For instance, he disproved that men had a rib less than women – a belief that had been widely held until then. He also believed, contrary to Aristotle's theory of the heart being the centre of the mind and emotion, that the brain and the nervous system are the centre.

Between 1539 and 1542 Vesalius prepared his masterpiece, a book that employed talented artists to provide the anatomical illustrations.

Vesey Denmark (c. 1767–1822). American resistance leader. Probably born on the Caribbean island of St Thomas, Vesey was purchased 1781 and taken to Charleston, South Carolina, 1783. He established himself as a carpenter 1800. Buying his freedom for $600 in 1800, he became an outspoken and eloquent critic of the institution of slavery. Arrested 1822 on suspicion of fomenting a rebellion among local slaves, he and five other black leaders were hanged despite a lack of evidence against them.

Vespasian (Titus Flavius Vespasianus) (AD 9–79). Roman emperor from AD 69. Proclaimed emperor by his soldiers while he was campaigning in Palestine, he reorganized the eastern provinces, and was a capable administrator. He was responsible for the construction of the Colosseum in Rome, which was completed by his son Titus.

He was commander of the Second Legion during the invasion of Britain AD 42–43.

An emperor ought to die standing.

VESPASIAN
Dying words during an attack of diarrhoea,
quoted in Suetonius *Vespasian* ch 24

Vespucci Amerigo (1454–1512). Florentine merchant. The Americas were named after him as a result of the widespread circulation of his accounts of his explorations. His accounts of the voyage 1499–1501 include descriptions of places he could not possibly have reached (the Pacific Ocean, British Columbia, Antarctica).

Veuster Joseph de (1840–1889). Belgian missionary, known as Father Damien. He entered the order of the Fathers of the Sacred Heart at Louvain, went to Hawaii, and from 1873 was resident priest in the leper settlement at Molokai. He eventually became infected and died there.

Vian Philip Louis (1894–1968). British admiral of the fleet in World War II. In 1940 he was the hero of the *Altmark incident*, and in 1941 commanded the destroyers that chased the *Bismarck*.

He later evacuated British troops from Norway and then moved to the Mediterranean to escort convoys to Malta. In 1943 he commanded a naval force covering the invasion of Sicily and then a carrier support force during the invasion of Italy. In 1944 he commanded the Eastern Task Force in the D-Day landings and then went to the Far East to command the Pacific carrier squadron, taking part in the landings at Okinawa. KBE 1942.

Vickers Jon(athan Stewart) (1926–   ). Canadian tenor. He has sung in all the major opera houses. With a ringing tone, clear enunciation, and deep involvement in his characterizations, he has proved outstanding in lead roles in Wagner's *Tristan und Isolde*, Britten's *Peter Grimes*, and Verdi's *Otello*.

Vico Giambattista (Giovanni Battista) (1668–1744). Italian philosopher, considered the founder of the modern philosophy of history. Vico was born in Naples and was professor of rhetoric there 1698. He became historiographer to the king of Naples 1735. He argued that we can understand history more adequately than nature, since it is we who have made it. He believed that the study of language, ritual, and myth was a way of understanding earlier societies. His cyclical theory of history (the birth, development, and decline of human societies) was put forward in *New Science* 1725.

Vico postulated that society passes through a cycle of four phases: the divine, or theocratic, when people are governed by their awe of the supernatural; the aristocratic, or 'heroic' (Homer, *Beowulf*); the democratic and individualistic; and chaos, a fall into confusion that startles people back into supernatural reverence. This is expressed in his dictum *verum et factum convertuntur* ('the true and the made are convertible'). His belief that the study of language and rituals was a better way of understanding early societies was a departure from the traditional ways of writing history either as biographies or as preordained God's will.

Suggested reading
Berlin, Isaiah *Vico and Herder* (1976)
Burke, Peter *Vico* (1985)
Tagliacozzo, Giorgio (ed) *Vico and Contemporary Thought* (1978)

Victor Emmanuel three kings of Italy, including:

Victor Emmanuel II (1820–1878). First king of united Italy from 1861. He became king of Sardinia on the abdication of his father Charles Albert 1849. In 1855 he allied Sardinia with France and the UK in the Crimean War. In 1859 in alliance with the French he defeated the Austrians and annexed Lombardy. By 1860 most of Italy had come under his rule, and in 1861 he was proclaimed king of Italy. In 1870 he made Rome his capital.

Victor Emmanuel III (1869–1947). King of Italy from the assassination of his father, Umberto I, 1900. He acquiesced in the Fascist regime of Mussolini from 1922 and, after the dictator's fall 1943, relinquished power to his son Umberto II, who co-operated with the Allies. Victor Emmanuel formally abdicated 1946.

Victoria (1819–1901). Queen of the UK from 1837, when she succeeded her uncle William IV, and empress of India from 1876. In 1840 she married Prince Albert of Saxe-Coburg and Gotha. Her relations with her prime ministers ranged from the affectionate (Melbourne and Disraeli) to the stormy (Peel, Palmerston, and Gladstone). Her golden jubilee 1887 and diamond jubilee 1897 marked a waning of republican sentiment, which had developed with her withdrawal from public life on Albert's death 1861.

Only child of Edward, Duke of Kent, fourth son of George III, she was born 24 May 1819 at Kensington Palace, London. She and Albert had four sons and five daughters. After Albert's death 1861 she lived mainly in retirement. Nevertheless, she kept control of affairs, refusing the Prince of Wales (Edward VII) any active role. From 1848 she regularly visited the Scottish Highlands, where she had a house at Balmoral built to Prince Albert's designs. She died at Osborne House, her home in the Isle of Wight, 22 Jan 1901, and was buried at Windsor.

Suggested reading
Charlot, Monica *The Young Queen* (1991)
Hibbert, Christopher *Queen Victoria in Her Letters and Journals* (1985)
Longford, Elizabeth *Queen Victoria* (1965)
Richardson, Joanna *Victoria and Albert* (1977)
Weintraub, Stanley *Victoria: Biography of a Queen* (1987)
Woodham-Smith, Cecil *Queen Victoria* (1972)

There is something about a bureaucrat that does not like a poem.

GORE VIDAL
Sex, Death and Money preface

Vidal Gore (born Eugene Luther Vidal) (1925–). US writer and critic. Much of his fiction deals satirically with history and politics and includes the novels *Myra Breckinridge* 1968, *Burr* 1973, and *Empire* 1987, plays and screenplays, including *Suddenly Last Summer* 1958, and essays, such as 'Armageddon?' 1987. His autobiography *Palimpsest* appeared 1995.

Vidocq François Eugène (1775–1857). French criminal who became a spy for the Paris police 1809, and rose to become chief of the detective department.

Vidor King Wallis (1896–1982). US film director. He made such epics as *The Big Parade* 1925 and *Duel in the Sun* 1946. He has been praised for his stylistic experimentation and socially concerned themes. He received an honorary Academy Award 1979. His other films include *The Crowd* 1928 and *Guerra e Pace/War and Peace* 1956.

He was instrumental in setting up the Screen Directors' Guild 1936 and was a crucial figure in 1930s Hollywood.

Viète François (1540–1603). French mathematician who developed algebra and its notation. He was the first mathematician to use letters of the alphabet to denote both known and unknown quantities, and is credited with introducing the term 'coefficient' into algebra.

Viète was born in Fontenay-le-Comte in the Poitou region and studied law at Poitiers. In 1570 he moved to Paris and was employed by Charles IX until 1584, when persecution of the Huguenots forced him to flee to Beauvoir-sur-Mer. It was in these years that his most fruitful algebraic research was carried out. On the accession of Henry IV in 1589, Viète returned to the royal service, and deciphered coded messages captured during war with Spain. He was dismissed from the court in 1602.

Viète's mathematical achievements were the result of his interest in cosmology; for example, a table giving the values of six trigonometrical lines based on a method originally used by Egyptian astronomer Ptolemy. Viète was the first person to use the cosine law for plane triangles and he also published the law of tangents.

His works include *Canon mathematicus seu ad triangula* 1579, *In artem analytica isogoge* 1591, and *De aequationum recognitione et emandatione* 1615.

Vigée-Lebrun (Marie) Elisabeth (Louise) (1755–1842). French portrait painter. She was trained by her father (a painter in pastels) and Greuze. She became painter to Queen Marie Antoinette in the 1780s; many royal portraits survive, executed in a flattering Rococo style.

At the outbreak of the Revolution 1789 she left France and travelled in Europe, staying in St Petersburg, Russia, 1795–1802. She resettled in Paris 1809. She published an account of her travels, *Souvenirs* 1835–37, written in the form of letters.

Vigeland (Adolf) Gustav (1869–1943). Norwegian sculptor. He studied in Oslo and Copenhagen and with Rodin in Paris 1892. His programme of sculpture in Frogner Park, Oslo, conceived 1900, was never finished: heavy and monumental in style, it consists of allegorical groups of figures and animals surrounding a fountain.

Vignola Giacomo Barozzi da (1507–1573). Italian Mannerist architect. He is largely remembered for his architectural textbook *Regole delle cinque ordini/On the Five Orders* 1562. He appears to have designed much of the complex plan for the Villa Giulia, Rome 1551–55, a building whose idiosyncratic Classicism influenced the development of contemporary Post-Modernism. From 1559 Vignola worked on the completion of Peruzzi's design for the Villa Caprarola, and later succeeded Michelangelo as architect to St Peter's, Rome.

The Gesù church in Rome, another of Vignola's highly influential designs, was built 1568–75 for the Jesuits.

Vigny Alfred Victor, Comte de (1797–1863). French Romantic writer. His works, pervaded by an air of melancholy stoicism, include the historical novel *Cinq-Mars* 1826, the play *Chatterton* 1835, and poetry, for example, *Les Destinées/Destinies* 1864.

Vigo Jean. Adopted name of Jean Almereyda (1905–1934). French film director. His work was intensely lyrical, Surrealist-tinged, and experimental. He made only two shorts, *A Propos de Nice* 1930 and *Taris Champion de natation* 1934; and two feature films, *Zéro de conduite* 1933 and *L'Atalante* 1934.

A truly creative musician is capable of producing, from his own imagination, melodies that are more authentic than folk-lore itself.

HEITOR VILLA-LOBOS
quoted in Joseph Machlis *Introduction to Contemporary Music* 1963

Villa-Lobos Heitor (1887–1959). Brazilian composer and conductor. He absorbed Russian and French influences in the 1920s to create Neo-Baroque works in Brazilian style, using native colours and rhythms. His gift for melody is displayed in the *Chôros* (serenades) series 1920–29 for various ensembles, and the series of nine *Bachianas Brasileiras* 1930–45, treated in the manner of Bach. His other works include guitar and piano solos, chamber music, choral works, film scores, operas, and 12 symphonies.

Villard Henry (born Ferdinand Heinrich Gustav Hilgard) (1835–1900). German-born US journalist and financier. He covered the American Civil War 1861–65 for the New York *Herald* and *Tribune*.

An astute investor, he was president of the Edison General Electric Co 1890–92 and the *New York Evening Post* 1881–1900.

Born in Germany, Villard emigrated to the USA 1853 and settled in Illinois. He was president of the Oregon and California Railroad 1876, served as president of the Northern Pacific Railroad 1881–84, and was Northern Pacific's chair of the board 1889–93.

Villard Oswald Garrison (1872–1949). US editor and civil rights leader. A founder of the National Association for the Advancement of Colored People (NAACP), he was active in antiwar movements. He was president of the *New York Evening Post* 1900–18 and editor of the magazine *The Nation* 1918–32. His autobiography, *Fighting Years*, appeared 1939.

Born in Germany during the European travels of his father Henry Villard, he was educated at Harvard University and joined the staff of the *Philadelphia Press* 1893. After selling the *Post* 1918 he concentrated on its subsidiary, *The Nation*.

A capable soldier who delighted to describe, as if in a real-life epic, the wonderful events he had seen.

Colin Morris on GEOFFROY DE VILLEHARDOUIN
in *Blackwell's Dictionary of Historians* 1988

Villehardouin Geoffroy de (*c.* 1160–*c.* 1213). French historian. He was the first to write in the French language. He was a leader of the Fourth Crusade, of which his *Conquest of Constantinople* (about 1209) is an account.

Villiers de l'Isle Adam (Jean Marie Philippe) Auguste, Comte de (1838–1889). French poet. He was the inaugurator of the Symbolist movement. His work includes the drama *Axel* 1890; *Isis* 1862, a romance of the supernatural; verse; and short stories.

Villon François (1431–*c.* 1465). French poet. He used satiric humour, pathos, and lyric power in works written in the slang of the time. Among the little of his work that survives, *Petit Testament* 1456 and *Grand Testament* 1461 are prominent (the latter includes the 'Ballade des dames du temps jadis/Ballad of the Ladies of Former Times').

He was born in Paris and dropped his surname (Montcorbier or de Logos) to assume that of one of his relatives, a canon, who sent him to study at the Sorbonne, where he graduated 1449 and took his MA 1452. In 1455 he stabbed a priest in a street fight and had to flee the city. Pardoned the next year, he returned to Paris but was soon in flight again after robbing the College of Navarre. He stayed briefly at the court of the duke of Orléans until sentenced to death for an unknown offence, from which he was saved by the amnesty of a public holiday. Theft and public brawling continued to occupy his time, in addition to the production of the *Grand Testament* 1461. A sentence of death in Paris, commuted to ten-year banishment 1463, is the last that is known of his life.

Vincent de Paul, St (*c.* 1580–1660). French Roman Catholic priest and founder of the two charitable orders of Dazarists 1625 and Sisters of Charity 1634. After being ordained 1600, he was captured by Barbary pirates and held as a slave in Tunis until he escaped 1607. He was canonized 1737; feast day 19 July.

Vincent of Beauvais (*c.* 1190–1264). French scholar, encyclopedist, and Dominican priest. A chaplain to the court of Louis IX, he is remembered for his *Speculum majus/Great Mirror* 1220–44, a reference work summarizing contemporary knowledge on virtually every subject, including science, natural history, literature, and law. It also contained a history of the world from the creation. It is noteworthy for its positive attitude to classical literature, which had undergone a period of eclipse in the preceding centuries.

Vinson Frederick Moore (1890–1953). US jurist. He held office in the US House of Representatives 1924–28 and 1930–38 and was appointed chief justice of the US Supreme Court 1946–53 by President Truman. He defended federal intervention in social and economic matters, and dissented in *Youngstown Sheet and Tube Co* v

Sawyer 1952, revoking presidential nationalization of the steel industry during the Korean War.

Born in Louisa, Kentucky, USA, Vinson received his undergraduate and law degrees from Centre College and became a lawyer active in Democratic politics. He was appointed judge of the US Court of Appeals for the District of Columbia 1939.

Viollet-le-Duc Eugène Emmanuel (1814–1879). French architect. A leader of the Gothic Revival in France, he is known mostly for his writings, notably *Entretiens* in two volumes 1863 and 1872. He argued for a Rationalist interpretation of the Gothic style and the structural use of new materials such as iron. His most famous restorations were carried out on the Sainte Chapelle and Notre Dame in Paris; he also restored the old city of Carcassone from 1844.

Vionnet Madeleine (1876–1975). French fashion designer. She started a dressmaking apprenticeship when she was 12 years old and worked in Paris until moving to London around 1897 to work for the dressmaker Kate O'Reilly. She returned to Paris 1901 and joined the fashion house Callot Soeurs, before working for the fashion house of Doucet in 1907. In 1912 she opened her own house (although it was closed 1914–22 because of World War I). During the 1920s and 1930s she achieved critical acclaim when she developed the bias cut (cutting the fabric at an angle of 45 degrees from the selvage across the thread that runs lengthways through the fabric). This enabled her to create simple fluid shapes in crêpe de chine, satin, and gaberdine. She also became known for her draped and handkerchief-pointed dresses. By 1934 she had changed her look to clinging skirts, bare backs, and light crêpe de chine evening dresses. She retired 1939.

Virchow Rudolf Ludwig Carl (1821–1902). German pathologist, the founder of cellular pathology. Virchow was the first to describe leukaemia (cancer of the blood). In his book *Die cellulare Pathologie/Cellular Pathology* 1858, he proposed that disease is not due to sudden invasions or changes, but to slow processes in which normal cells give rise to abnormal ones.

Viren Lasse (1949–). Finnish long-distance runner who won the 5,000 metres and 10,000 metres at the 1972 Munich and 1976 Montréal Olympics, becoming the first Olympic athlete successfully to defend both titles at these distances.

Virgil (Publius Vergilius Maro) (70–19 BC). Roman poet. He wrote the *Eclogues* 37 BC, a series of pastoral poems; the *Georgics* 30 BC, four books on the art of farming; and his epic masterpiece, the *Aeneid* 30–19 BC. He was patronized by Maecenas on behalf of Octavian (later the emperor Augustus).

Born near Mantua, Virgil was educated in Cremona and Mediolanum (Milan), and later studied philosophy and rhetoric at Rome. He wrote his second work, the *Georgics*, in honour of his new patron, Maecenas, to whom he introduced Horace. He passed much of his later life at Naples and devoted the last decade of it to the composition of the *Aeneid*, often considered the most important poem in Latin literature, of which he is said to have read parts to the emperor Augustus. Later Christian adaptations of his work, in particular of the prophetic *Fourth Eclogue*, greatly enhanced his mystical status in the Middle Ages, resulting in his adoption by Dante as his guide to the underworld in the *Divine Comedy*.

Suggested reading
Camps, W A *An Introduction to the Aeneid* (1969)
Gramdsen, K W *Virgil* (1990)
Griffin, Jasper *Virgil* (1986)
Johnson, W R *Darkness Visible: A Study of Vergil's 'Aeneid'* (1976)
Otis, B *Virgil: A Study in Civilized Poetry* (1963)
Williams, R D and Pattie, T S *Virgil: His Poetry Through the Ages* (1982)

Virtanen Artturi Ilmari (1895–1973). Finnish chemist who from 1920 made discoveries in agricultural chemistry. Because green fodder tends to ferment and produce a variety of harmful acids, it cannot be preserved for long. Virtanen prevented the process from starting by acidifying the fodder. In this form it lasted longer and remained nutritious. Nobel Prize for Chemistry 1945.

Visconti dukes and rulers of Milan 1277–1447. They originated as north Italian feudal lords who attained dominance over the city as a result of alliance with the Holy Roman emperors. Despite papal opposition, by the mid-14th century they ruled 15 other major towns in northern Italy. The duchy was inherited by the Sforzas 1447.

They had no formal title until Gian Galeazzo (1351–1402) bought the title of duke from Emperor Wenceslas IV (1361–1419). On the death of the last male Visconti, Filippo Maria, 1447, the duchy was passed to the Sforzas 1450 after a short-lived republic.

Visconti Luchino (1906–1976). Italian film, opera, and theatre director. The film *Ossessione* 1942 pioneered Neo-Realist cinema despite being subject to censorship problems from the fascist government. His later works include *Rocco and His Brothers* 1960, *The Leopard* 1963, *The Damned* 1969, and *Death in Venice* 1971. His powerful social commentary led to clashes with the Italian government and Roman Catholic Church.
Suggested reading
Marcini, E *Luchino Visconti* (1986)
Nowell-Smith, Geoffrey *Visconti* (1973)
Stirling, Monica *A Screen of Time* (1979)
Tonetti, C *Luchino Visconti* (1983)

I have composed detailed prescriptions so that, Augustus, by attending to them you can personally understand the nature of past and future constructions.

POLLIO VITRUVIUS
On Architecture bk 1 preface

Vitruvius (Marcus Vitruvius Pollio) (lived 1st century BC). Roman architect. His ten-volume interpretation of Roman architecture, *De architectura*, provided an impetus for the Renaissance; it was first printed in Rome 1486. Although often obscure, his writings have had a lasting influence on Western perceptions of Classical architecture, mainly through the work of Leon Battista Alberti, and later Raphael and Palladio.

Vitry Philippe de (1291–1361). French composer, poet, and theorist. One of the masters of ars nova, his works are characterized by contrapuntal intricacy. He wrote four treatises on ars nova and some of his motets survive today.

Vitus, St (lived early 4th century). Christian saint, perhaps Sicilian, who was martyred in Rome early in the 4th century. Feast day 15 June.

Vivaldi Antonio Lucio (1678–1741). Italian Baroque composer, violinist, and conductor. He wrote 23 symphonies; 75 sonatas; over 400 concertos, including *The Four Seasons* 1725 for violin and orchestra; over 40 operas; and much sacred music. His work was largely neglected until the 1930s. Known as the 'Red Priest', because of his flaming hair colour, Vivaldi spent much of his church career teaching music at a girl's orphanage. He wrote for them and for himself.
Suggested reading
Booth, John *Vivaldi* (1989)
Kendall, Alan *Vivaldi* (1989)
Kolneder, Walter *Antonio Vivaldi: His Life and Work* (trs 1970)
Robbins Landon, H C *Vivaldi: Voice of the Baroque* (1994)
Talbot, Michael *Vivaldi* (1978)

Vladimir I (St Vladimir of Kiev) (956–1015). Russian saint, prince of Novgorod, and grand duke of Kiev. Converted to Christianity 988, he married Anna, Christian sister of the Byzantine emperor Basil II, and established the Byzantine rite of Orthodox Christianity as the Russian national faith.
Feast day 15 July.

Vlaminck Maurice de (1876–1958). French painter and graphic artist who was largely self-taught. An early adherent of Fauvism, he is best known for his vibrant, brilliantly coloured landscapes. He later abandoned Fauve colour, his works becoming more sombre and Expressionist. Initially he was inspired by van Gogh but by 1908 Cézanne had become the chief influence. He was also a writer of poetry, novels, and essays, a violinist, racing cyclist, farmer, and collector of African art.

He began to study painting when 19 and worked in company with André Derain. He was greatly impressed by the van Gogh exhibition of 1901, and made the typically Fauve announcement that 'one should paint with pure vermilion, Veronese green and cobalt', and he was associated with Matisse, Derain and others in the Fauvist Salon of 1905. His mature work, however, did not pursue the implications of using pure colour. Following van Gogh only in emphasis, it was marked by heavy impasto and sudden transitions from dark to light, which gave dramatic effect to the stormy skies and snowbound villages of his characteristic landscapes. These, and still lifes in the same key, were his main products.

Vlasov Andrey Andreyevich (1900–1946). Soviet general in World War II. He was captured by the Germans May 1942 and, feeling he had been badly treated by Stalin, began making anti-Soviet broadcasts for the Germans. In Nov 1944 he began forming a 'Russian Liberation Army' from disaffected prisoners-of-war. He was captured by the Soviets May 1945 and executed for treason.

Vogel Hans-Jochen (1926–). German socialist politician, chair of the Social Democratic Party (SPD) 1987–91. A former leader of the SPD in Bavaria and mayor of Munich, he served in the Brandt and Schmidt West German governments in the 1970s as housing and then justice minister and then, briefly, as mayor of West Berlin.

A centrist, compromise figure, Vogel unsuccessfully contested the 1983 federal election as chancellor candidate for the SPD and in 1987 replaced Brandt as party chair; he left that post 1991 and later in the year stood down as SPD parliamentary leader.

Vogel Hermann Carl (1842–1907). German astronomer who discovered spectroscopic binary stars. By measuring the Doppler effect in the spectral lines of stars to ascertain their velocity, he ended the controversy over the value of Christian Doppler's theory for investigating motion in the universe.

Vogel was born and educated in Leipzig and in 1863 began working at the observatory there. From 1882 he was director of the Potsdam Observatory near Berlin.

Vogel worked intensively on the spectroscopic properties of planets, nebulae, the northern lights, comet III 1871, and the Sun, and examined the spectra of some 4,000 stars. He used spectrophotometry to study Nova Cygni in 1876 and his results provided the first evidence that changes occur in the spectrum of a nova during its fading phase.

Vogel's discovery of spectroscopic binary stars arose from a study of the periodic displacements of the spectral lines of the stars Algol and Spica, eclipsing binary stars whose components could not, at the time, be detected as separate entities by optical means. From his spectrographs, Vogel derived the dimensions of this double star system, the diameter of both components, the orbital velocity of Algol, the total mass of the system and in 1889, he derived the distance between the two component stars from each other.

Voight Jon (1938–). US film actor. He starred as the naive hustler in *Midnight Cowboy* 1969. Subsequent films include *Deliverance* 1972, *Coming Home* 1977 (Academy Award), and *Runaway Train* 1985.

Volcker Paul Adolph (1927–). US economist. As chair of the board of governors of the Federal Reserve System 1979–87, he controlled the amount of money in circulation in the USA. He was succeeded by Alan Greenspan.

Volhard Jacob (1834–1910). German chemist who devised various significant methods of organic synthesis, and a method of quantitatively analysing for an element via silver chloride. Bromides can also be determined using this technique.

Volhard was born in Darmstadt and studied at Giessen. He held professorial appointments at three German universities: Munich 1864–79, Erlangen 1879–82, and Halle 1882–1910.

During the 1860s Volhard developed methods for the syntheses of the amino acids sarcosine (*N*-methylaminoethanoic acid) and creatine, and the heterocyclic compound thiophen; he also did research on guanidine and cyanimide.

Volhard's method of preparing halogenated organic acids has become known as the Hell–Volhard–Zelinsky reaction, in which the acid is treated with chlorine or bromine in the presence of phosphorus. The reaction is also useful for syntheses because the substituted halogen atom(s) can easily be replaced by a cyanide group (by treatment with potassium cyanide), which in the presence of an aqueous acid and ethyl alcohol (ethanol) yields the corresponding malonic ester (diethylpropandioate), from which barbiturate drugs can be synthesized.

Volonté Gian Maria (1933–1994). Italian film and stage actor. His international popularity was based on 'spaghetti Westerns' of the 1960s. In Italy he was active in left-wing politics and gave commanding performances in a succession of films with political themes.

Volonté was born in Milan and studied at Rome's National School of Dramatic Art. He made his stage debut in 1957, going on to play a wide range of roles and to make his first film 1960. In 1964 his stage production of the Swiss dramatist Rolf Hochhuth's *The Vicar*, which indicted the wartime stance of Pope Pius XII, was banned after one performance.

In the cinema, Volonté appeared under the pseudonym John Wells as the sadistic chief villain in *Per un pugno di dollari/A Fistful of Dollars* 1964, and as a crazed killer in its sequel *Per qualche dollari in piu/For a Few Dollars More* 1965. In the succeeding years he took leading roles in a number of more serious Italian films. As well as his playing of a corrupt police chief in *Indagine su un cittadino al di spora di ogni sospetto/Investigation of a Citizen Above Suspicion* 1969, these included two works by Francesco Rosi, *Il caso Mattei/The Mattei Affair* 1972 and *Lucky Luciano* 1973, in which Volonté gave a memorable impersonation of the Italian–American gangster. In one of his last films, *Porte aperte/Open Doors* 1990, his performance as a judge investigating a murder case contained in full measure the intelligence and authority of his best-known portrayals.

Volta Alessandro Giuseppe Antonio Anastasio, Count (1745–1827). Italian physicist who invented the first electric cell (the voltaic pile, 1800), the electrophorus (an early electrostatic generator, 1775), and an electroscope.

In 1776 Volta discovered methane by examining marsh gas found in Lago Maggiore. He then made the first accurate estimate of the proportion of oxygen in the air by exploding air with hydrogen to remove the oxygen. In about 1795, Volta recognized that the vapour pressure of a liquid is independent of the pressure of the atmosphere and depends only on temperature.

Volta was born in Como; he became professor there 1775 and was professor at Pavia 1778–1819. The volt is named after him.

Volta's electrophorus consisted of a disc made of turpentine, resin, and wax, which was rubbed to give it a negative charge. A plate covered in tin foil was lowered by an insulated handle on to the disc, which induced a positive charge on the lower side of the foil. The negative charge that was likewise induced on the upper surface was removed by touching it to ground the charge, leaving a positive charge on the foil. This process could then be repeated to build up a greater and greater charge. Volta went on to realize from his electrostatic experiments that the quantity of charge produced is proportional to the product of its tension and the capacity of the conductor.

Volta repeated and built on Italian physiologist Luigi Galvani's experiments with metals and the muscles of dead animals, and in 1792, Volta concluded that the source of the electricity was in the junction of two different metals and not, as Galvani thought, in the animals. Volta even succeeded in producing a list of metals in order of their electricity production based on the strength of the sensation they made on his tongue, thereby deriving the electromotive series.

In 1800 Volta described two arrangements of conductors that produced an electric current. One was a pile of silver and zinc discs separated by cardboard moistened with brine, and the other a series of glasses of salty or alkaline water in which bimetallic curved electrodes were dipped. Volta's electric cell was a sensation, for it enabled high electric currents to be produced for the first time.

If God did not exist, it would be necessary to invent him.
VOLTAIRE
Épîtres

Voltaire pen name of François-Marie Arouet (1694–1778). French writer, the embodiment of the 18th-century Enlightenment. He wrote histories, books of political analysis and philosophy, essays on science and literature, plays, poetry, and the satirical fable *Candide* 1759, his best-known work. A trenchant satirist of social and political evils, he was often forced to flee from his enemies and was twice imprisoned. His works include *Lettres philosophiques sur les Anglais/Philosophical Letters on the English* 1733 (essays in favour of English ways, thought, and political practice), *Le Siècle de Louis XIV/The Age of Louis XIV* 1751, and *Dictionnaire philosophique* 1764.

Voltaire was born in Paris, the son of a notary, and used his pen name from 1718. He was twice imprisoned in the Bastille and exiled from Paris 1716–26 for libellous political verse. *Oedipe/Oedipus*, his first essay in tragedy, was staged 1718. While in England 1726–29 he dedicated an epic poem on Henry IV, *La Henriade/The Henriade*, to Queen Caroline, and on returning to France published the successful *Histoire de Charles XII/History of Charles XII* 1731, and produced the play *Zaïre* 1732.

He took refuge with his lover, the Marquise de Châtelet, at Cirey in Champagne, where he wrote the play *Mérope* 1743 and much of *Le Siècle de Louis XIV*. Among his other works are histories of Peter the Great, Louis XV, and India; the satirical tale *Zadig* 1748; *La Pucelle/The Maid* 1755, on Joan of Arc; and the tragedy *Irène* 1778. From 1751 to 1753 he stayed at the court of Frederick II (the Great) of Prussia, who had long been an admirer, but the association ended in deep enmity. From 1754 he established himself near Geneva, and after 1758 at Ferney, just across the French border.

His remains were transferred 1791 to the Panthéon in Paris.

Suggested reading
Besterman, T *Voltaire* (1969)
Crocker, L G (ed) *The Age of Enlightenment* (1969)
Gay, Peter *Voltaire's Politics: The Poet as Realist* (1988)
Hearsey, John *Voltaire* (1976)
Mitford, Nancy *Voltaire in Love* (1957)
Wade, Ira *The Intellectual Development of Voltaire* (1969)

Volterra Vito (1860–1940). Italian mathematician whose chief work was in the fields of function theory and differential equations. His chief method, hit upon as a young boy, was based on dividing a problem into a small interval of time and assuming one of the variables to be constant during each time period.

He was professor at Pisa 1883–92, Turin 1892–1900, and Rome 1900–31. During World War I he established the Italian Office of War Inventions, where he designed armaments and proposed that helium be used in place of hydrogen in airships. After the war he became increasingly involved in politics, speaking in the Senate and voicing his opposition to the Fascist regime. For his views he was eventually dismissed from his academic post and banned from taking part in any Italian scientific meeting.

At the age of 13, after reading Jules Verne's novel *From the Earth to the Moon*, Volterra became interested in projectile problems and came up with a plausible determination for the trajectory of a spacecraft which had been fired from a gun. His solution was based on the device of breaking time down into small intervals during which it could be assumed that the force was constant. The trajectory could thus be viewed as a series of small parabolic arcs. This was the essence of the argument he developed in detail 40 years later in a series of lectures at the Sorbonne, France.

Volterra contributed especially to the foundation of the theory of functionals, the solution of integral equations with variable limits, and the integration of hyperbolic partial differential equations. His papers on partial differential equations of the early 1890s included the solution of equations for cylindrical waves.

He also brought his knowledge of mathematics to bear on biological matters, constructing a model for population change in which the prey and the predator interact in a continuous manner.

Volterra's main works are *The Theory of Permutable Functions* 1915 and *The Theory of Functionals and of Integral and Integro-differential Equations* 1930.

von Braun Wernher Magnus Maximilian (1912–1977). German rocket engineer who developed military rockets (V1 and V2) during World War II and later worked for the space agency NASA in the USA.

During the 1940s his research team at Peenemünde on the Baltic coast produced the V1 (flying bomb) and supersonic V2 rockets.

In the 1950s von Braun was part of the team that produced rockets for US satellites (the first, *Explorer 1*, was launched early 1958) and early space flights by astronauts.

Von Braun was born in Wirsitz (now in Poland) and studied at Berlin and in Switzerland at Zürich. In 1930 he joined a group of scientists who were experimenting with rockets, and in 1938 he became technical director of the Peenemünde military rocket establishment; he joined the Nazi Party 1940. In the last days of the war in 1945 von Braun and his staff, not wishing to be captured in the Soviet-occupied part of Germany, travelled to the West to surrender to US forces. Soon afterwards von Braun began work at the US Army Ordnance Corps testing grounds at White Sands, New Mexico. In 1952 he became technical director of the army's ballistic-missile programme. He held an administrative post at NASA 1970–72.

von Gesner Konrad. Swiss naturalist. See ◊Gesner, Konrad von.

von Karajan Herbert. Austrian conductor. See ◊Karajan, Herbert von.

Vonnegut Kurt, (1922–). US writer. His early works, *Player Piano* 1952 and *The Sirens of Titan* 1959, used the science-fiction genre to explore issues of technological and historical control. He turned to more experimental methods with his highly acclaimed, popular success *Slaughterhouse-Five* 1969, a novel that mixed a world of fantasy with the author's experience of the fire-bombing of Dresden during World War II. His later novels, marked by a bittersweet spirit of absurdist anarchy and folksy fatalism, include *Breakfast of Champions* 1973, *Slapstick* 1976, *Jailbird* 1979, *Deadeye Dick* 1982, *Galapagos* 1985, *Hocus Pocus* 1990, and *The Face* 1992.

His short stories are collected in *Welcome to the Monkey House* 1968, and he has written two volumes of autobiography, *Palm Sunday* 1981 and *Fates Worse Than Death: An Autobiograpahical Collage of the 1980s* 1992.

Suggested reading
Giannone, Richard *Vonnegut: A Preface to His Novels* (1977)
Klinkowitz, Jerome *Kurt Vonnegut* (1982)
Lundquist, James *Kurt Vonnegut* (1977)
Schatt, Stanley *Kurt Vonnegut* (1976)

In mathematics you don't understand things. You just get used to them.

JOHN VON NEUMANN
Attributed remark

Von Neumann John (born Johann) (1903–1957). Hungarian-born US scientist and mathematician, a pioneer of computer design. He invented his 'rings of operators' (called Von Neumann algebras) in the late 1930s, and also contributed to set theory, game theory, quantum mechanics, cybernetics (with his theory of self-reproducing automata, called Von Neumann machines), and the development of the atomic and hydrogen bombs.

He designed and supervised the construction of the first computer able to use a flexible stored program (named MANIAC-1) at the Institute for Advanced Study at Princeton 1940–1952. This work laid the foundations for the design of all subsequent programmable computers.

In 1930 he emigrated to the USA, where he became professor at Princeton 1931, and from 1933 he was a member of the Institute for Advanced Study there. He also held a number of advisory posts with the US government 1940–54.

Von Neumann's book *The Mathematical Foundations of Quantum Mechanics* 1932 defended mathematically the uncertainty principle of German physicist Werner Heisenberg. In 1944, Von Neumann showed that matrix mechanics and wave mechanics were equivalent.

The monumental *Theory of Games and Economic Behavior* 1944, written with Oskar Morgenstern (1902–1977), laid the foundations for modern game theory.

Von Neumann originated the basic ideas of game theory in 1928 by proving that a quantitative mathematical model could be constructed for determining the best strategy – the one that, in the long term, would produce maximal gains and minimal losses in any game, even one of chance or one with more than two players. Games for which this theory found immediate use were business, warfare, and the social sciences.

Vorontsov-Vel'iaminov Boris Aleksandrovich (1904–). Russian astronomer and astrophysicist. In 1930, independently of Swiss astronomer Robert Trumpler, Vorontsov-Vel'iaminov demonstrated the occurrence of the absorption of stellar light by interstellar dust. As a result, it became possible to determine astronomical distances and, in turn, the size of the universe more accurately.

Vorontsov-Vel'iaminov was professor at Moscow from 1934. Analysing the Hertzsprung–Russell diagram, with reference to the evolution of stars, he made particularly important contributions to the study of the blue-white star sequence, which was the subject of a book he published in 1947.

In 1959 Vorontsov-Vel'iaminov recorded and listed the positions of 350 interacting galaxies clustered so closely that they seem to perturb each other slightly in structure. Besides this catalogue, he compiled a more extensive catalogue of galaxies in 1962, in which he listed and described more than 30,000 examples.

Voroshilov Klement Efremovich (1881–1969). Marshal of the USSR. He joined the Bolsheviks 1903 and was arrested many times and exiled, but escaped. He became a Red Army commander in the civil war 1918–20, a member of the central committee 1921, commissar for war 1925, member of the Politburo 1926, and marshal 1935. He was removed as war commissar 1940 after defeats on the Finland front and failing to raise the German siege of Leningrad. He was a member of the committee for defence 1941–44 and president of the Presidium of the USSR 1953–60.

Vorster John (born Balthazar Johannes) (1915–1983). South African Nationalist politician, prime minister 1966–78, and president 1978–79. During his term as prime minister some elements of apartheid were allowed to lapse, and attempts were made to improve relations with the outside world. He resigned the presidency because of a financial scandal.

Voysey Charles Francis Annesley (1857–1941). English architect and designer. He designed country houses which are characteristically asymmetrical with massive buttresses, long sloping roofs, and roughcast walls, for example, The Cottage, Bishop's Itchington, Warwickshire, 1888–89. He also designed textiles and wallpaper in the Arts and Crafts tradition.

Vranitzky Franz (1937–). Austrian socialist politician, federal chancellor from 1986. A banker, he entered the political arena through the moderate, left-of-centre Socialist Party of Austria (SPÖ), and became minister of finance 1984. He succeeded Fred Sinowatz as federal chancellor 1986, heading an SPÖ-ÖVP (Austrian People's Party) coalition, which was returned in the Oct 1994 general election.

Vuillard (Jean) Edouard (1868–1940). French painter and printmaker. He was a founding member of *les Nabis*. His work is mainly decorative, with an emphasis on surface pattern that reflects the influence of Japanese prints. With Pierre Bonnard he produced numerous lithographs and paintings of simple domestic interiors, works that are generally categorized as Intimiste.

He was closely linked with Bonnard, his friend from youth, and took a parallel direction in art. He was a member of the Nabi group, though, as he said, there was 'nothing of the revolutionary' about him. The term Intimiste, applied both to him and to Bonnard, refers particularly aptly to the gentle and seclusive spirit in which Vuillard painted lamplit domestic interiors. He was less venturesome and more academic in tendency than Bonnard, though in colour lithography he developed, with the inspiration of Japanese prints, some brilliant and unconventional designs. He produced a number of decorations, for the Comédie des Champs Élysées, 1913, Palais de Chaillot, 1937, and the Palais des Nations, Geneva, 1938. His notebooks and diaries were left to the Bibliothèque Nationale on the condition that they were not opened until 1980.

Vygotsky Lev Semionovich (1896–1934). Soviet psychologist whose work on language and linguistic development is based on his supposition that higher cognitive processes are a product of social development. From early research into the rules and development of tool-use and sign-use behaviour, Vygotsky turned to symbolic processes in language, focusing on the semantic structure of words and the way in which meanings of words change from emotive to concrete and then become more abstract.

Vygotsky, born in Orsha, Byelorussia (now Belarus), was active in a number of other fields during his brief academic career, notably the psychological analysis of art and fables; child psychology, including the problems of deaf and retarded children; and the psychological analysis of brain-injured adults. His major works include *Thought and Language* 1937, *Selected Psychological Studies* 1956, and *Development of the Higher Mental Processes* 1960.

Confession is the queen of evidence.

D Burg and G Teifer on ANDREI VYSHINSKY in *Solzhenitsyn* 1972

Vyshinsky Andrei Yanuaryevich (1883–1954). Soviet politician. As commissar for justice, he acted as prosecutor at Stalin's treason trials 1936–38. He was foreign minister 1949–53 and often represented the USSR at the United Nations.

Vysotsky Vladimir Semenovich (1938–1980). Russian ballad singer and actor famous during the 1970s for his popular songs, circulated privately since he was forbidden to publish the words. The satirical ballads he wrote and performed told of Russian hypocrisy, Stalin's prison camps, food lines, and other Soviet ills.

W

Wace Robert (*c.* 1100–*c.* 1175). Anglo-Norman poet and chronicler of early chivalry. His major works, both written in Norman French, were *Roman de Brut* (also known as *Geste des Bretons*) 1155, containing material relating to the Arthurian legend, and *Roman de Rou* (or *Geste des Normanz*) 1160–62, covering the history of Normandy.

He was born in Jersey to a noble family, educated at Paris and Caen in Normandy, and made prebend of Bayeux by the gift of Henry II. *Roman de Brut*, dedicated to Eleanor of Aquitaine, was adapted from Geoffrey of Monmouth's *Historia Regum Britanniae*. *Roman de Rou*, dedicated to Henry II, was a chronicle of the dukes of Normandy.

Waddington David Charles, Baron Waddington (1929–   ). British Conservative politician, home secretary 1989–90. He trained as a barrister, and became a member of Parliament 1978. A Conservative whip from 1979, Waddington was a junior minister in the Department of Employment and in the Home Office before becoming chief whip 1987. In 1990 he was made a life peer and became leader of the House of Lords in John Major's government.

Wade (Sarah) Virginia (1945–   ). English tennis player who won the Wimbledon singles title in the Silver Jubilee year of 1977 after fifteen years of striving. She also won the US Open in 1968 and the 1972 Australian Open. She holds a record number of appearances for the Wightman and Federation Cup teams and her total of eight Grand Slam titles is a post-war British record equalled only by Ann Jones.

Wagenfeld Wilhelm (1900–1990). German architect and industrial designer. A graduate of the Bauhaus design school in Weimar, Germany, Wagenfeld went on to become one of the country's leading proponents of the machine style (a geometric, undecorated style deemed appropriate for industrial products) in the areas of metal and glass goods.

Major clients were the Jenaer Glassworks 1930–34, for which he designed a tea diffuser 1932; the Lausitzer Glassworks 1935–38, where he designed his 'Cube' dishes 1938; and from 1954 the Württembergische Metallwarenfabrik (WMF).

Wagner Honus (John Peter) (1874–1955). US baseball player. Born in Mansfield, Pennsylvania, USA, Wagner began his professional baseball career 1895 and was signed as a shortstop by the Louisville club of the National League 1897. He was acquired by the Pittsburgh Pirates 1899 and remained there until his retirement 1917. He had an impressive lifetime batting average of .329. In addition to his fielding skills, he was a great runner; his career record of 722 stolen bases won him the nickname 'the Flying Dutchman'.

Wagner Otto (1841–1918). Viennese architect. Initially working in the Art Nouveau style, for example the Vienna Stadtbahn 1894–97, he later rejected ornament for Rationalism, as in the Post Office Savings Bank, Vienna, 1904–06. He influenced such Viennese architects as Josef Hoffmann, Adolf Loos, and Joseph Olbrich.

Wagner Robert (1910–1991). US politician, mayor of New York City 1954–65. He demolished slum areas, built public housing, and was instrumental in introducing members of ethnic minorities into City Hall.

Wagner Robert F(erdinand) (1877–1953). US Democratic senator 1927–49, a leading figure in the development of welfare provision in the USA, especially in the New Deal era. He served as a Democrat in the state assembly 1905-09 and senate 1909-18 and as a justice of the state supreme court 1919-26. He helped draft much

new legislation, including the National Industrial Recovery Act 1933, the Social Security Act 1936, and the National Labor Relations Act 1935, known as the Wagner Act.

Where the speech of men stops short, then the art of music begins.

RICHARD WAGNER
A Happy Evening

Wagner (Wilhelm) Richard (1813–1883). German opera composer. He revolutionized the 19th-century conception of opera, envisaging it as a wholly new art form in which musical, poetic, and scenic elements should be unified through such devices as the leitmotif. His operas include *Tannhäuser* 1845, *Lohengrin* 1848, and *Tristan und Isolde* 1865. In 1872 he founded the Festival Theatre in Bayreuth; his masterpiece *Der Ring des Nibelungen*/*The Ring of the Nibelung*, a sequence of four operas, was first performed there 1876. His last work, *Parsifal*, was produced 1882.

Wagner's early career was as director of the Magdeburg Theatre, where he unsuccessfully produced his first opera *Das Liebesverbot*/*Forbidden Love* 1836. He lived in Paris 1839–42 and conducted the Dresden Opera House 1842–48. He fled Germany to escape arrest for his part in the 1848 revolution, but in 1861 he was

Wagner, Richard *The composer Richard Wagner. Probably the most influential composer of the Romantic movement, he conceived of opera as a continuous flow of music, unbounded by conventional form and traditional cadences. His plots were of epic proportion. (Image Select)*

allowed to return. He won the favour of Ludwig II of Bavaria 1864 and was thus able to set up the Festival Theatre in Bayreuth. The Bayreuth tradition was continued by his wife Cosima (Liszt's daughter, whom he married after her divorce from Hans von Bülow); by his son Siegfried Wagner (1869–1930), a composer of operas such as *Der Bärenhäuter*; and by later descendants.

Suggested reading
Deathridge, John and Dahlhaus, Carl *The New Grove Wagner* (1984)
Gregor-Dellin, Martin *Richard Wagner: His Life, His Work, His Century* (1983)
Gutman, Robert *Richard Wagner: The Man, His Mind and His Music* (1968)
Newman, Ernest *The Life of Richard Wagner* (1933–47)
Osborne, Charles *Wagner and his World* (1977)
Wagner, Richard *My Life* (1911, later editions available)
Westernhagen, Curt von *Wagner: A Biography* (1978)

Wagner-Jauregg Julius (1857–1940). Austrian neurologist. He received a Nobel prize in 1927 for his work on the use of induced fevers in treating mental illness.

Wain John Barrington (1925–1994). English poet and novelist. His first novel, *Hurry on Down* 1953, expresses the radical political views of the 'Angry Young Men' of the 1950s. He published several volumes of verse, collected in *Poems 1949–79*, and was professor of poetry at Oxford 1973–80.
Suggested reading
Salwak, D *John Wain* (1981)
Wain, John *Sprightly Running* (autobiography) (1962)
Wain, John *Dear Shadows: Portraits from Memory* (1986)

Wainwright Alfred (1907–1991). English walker and author of guidebooks. His first articles appeared 1955 in a local paper, and he eventually produced over 40 meticulously detailed books, including volumes on the Lake District, Pennine Way, and other areas of N England.

Waite Edgar Ravenswood (1866–1928). Australian ornithologist and zoologist. He was a member of several expeditions into the subantarctic islands, New Guinea, and central Australia which contributed significantly to scientific knowledge of vertebrates. His published work includes more than 200 scientific papers, *Popular Account of Australian Snakes* 1898 and *The Fishes of South Australia* 1923.

Waite Morrison Remick (1816–1888). US lawyer and chief justice of the USA from 1874, appointed by President Grant. He presided over constitutional challenges to Reconstruction 1865–77, but is best remembered for his decisions upholding the right of states to regulate public utilities.

Born in Lyme, Connecticut, USA, and educated at Yale University, Waite settled in Ohio, where he was admitted to the bar 1839. After serving in the state legislature 1849–50, he returned to private practice. A staunch Republican, he was named US counsel in the 1871 *Alabama* claims case.

Politics come from man. Mercy, compassion and justice come from God.

TERRY WAITE
quoted in *Observer* 13 Jan 1985

Waite Terry (Terence Hardy) (1939–). British religious adviser to the archbishop of Canterbury (then Dr Robert Runcie) 1980–87. As the archbishop's special envoy, Waite disappeared 20 Jan 1987 while engaged in secret negotiations to free European hostages in Beirut, Lebanon. He was taken hostage by an Islamic group and released 18 Nov 1991. His kidnapping followed six conversations he held with the US agent Col Oliver North, who appeared to be hoping to ransom US hostages through Waite.

Waits Tom (1949–). US singer, songwriter, musician, and actor, with a characteristic gravelly voice. His songs typically deal with urban street life and have jazz-tinged arrangements, as on *Rain Dogs* 1985. He has written music for and acted in several films, including Jim Jarmusch's *Down by Law* 1986.

Waits developed a beatnik hobo persona on his early albums (*Closing Time* 1973, *Nighthawks at the Diner* 1976, *Small Change* 1977) with songs like 'The Piano Has Been Drinking' and 'Tom Traubert's Blues'. His later work has a spare, twisted jazz feel and suggests the influence of German songwriter Kurt Weill; for example, *Swordfishtrombones* 1983 and *Bone Machine* 1992. As an actor, his films include Francis Ford Coppola's *One from the Heart* 1982 and *Ironweed* 1987.

He collaborated with writer William Burroughs and composer Robert Wilson on the opera *Black Ride* 1992.

Anything I write isn't valid for me unless I can perform it on stage or use it in an album.

TOM WAITS
quoted in Irwin Stambler *The Encyclopedia of Pop, Rock and Soul* 1989

Wajda Andrzej (1926–). Polish film and theatre director. He was one of the major figures in postwar European cinema. His films have great intensity and are frequently concerned with the predicament and disillusion of individuals caught up in political events. His works include *Ashes and Diamonds* 1958, *Man of Marble* 1977, *Man of Iron* 1981, *Danton* 1982, and *Korczak* 1990.
Suggested reading
Michatek, Boleslaw *The Cinema of Andrzej Wajda* (trs 1973)
Sulik, Boleslaw *A Change of Tack: Making the Shadow Line* (1976)
Wajda, Andrzej *Double Vision: My Life in Films* (trs 1989)

His main contribution to the development of the colonies was ... his view that, under proper control, Australia could take an almost unlimited number of suitable settlers.

E L Woodward on EDWARD GIBBON WAKEFIELD
in *The Age of Reform 1815–1870* 1963

Wakefield Edward Gibbon (1796–1862). British colonial administrator. He was imprisoned 1826–29 for abducting an heiress, and became manager of the South Australian Association, which founded a colony 1836. He was an agent for the New Zealand Land Company 1839–46, and emigrated there in 1853. His son Edward Jerningham Wakefield (1820–1879) wrote *Adventure in New Zealand* 1845.

Waksman Selman Abraham (1888–1973). US biochemist, born in Ukraine. He coined the word 'antibiotic' for bacteria-killing chemicals derived from microorganisms. Waksman was awarded a Nobel prize in 1952 for the discovery of streptomycin, an antibiotic used against tuberculosis. Waksman, in the USA from 1910, was professor of soil microbiology at Rutgers University in New Jersey.

Walcott Derek Walton (1930–). St Lucian poet and playwright. His work fuses Caribbean and European, classical and contemporary elements, and deals with the divisions within colonial society and his own search for cultural identity. His works include the long poem *Omeros* 1990, and his adaptation for the stage of Homer's *Odyssey* 1992; his *Collected Poems* were published 1986. He won the Nobel Prize for Literature 1992.

Walcott was educated at the University of the West Indies. He has taught writing at the universities of Columbia, Yale, and Harvard. He contributed greatly to the development of an indigenous West Indian theatre, and for 25 years ran a theatre in Trinidad. Other plays include *Dream on Monkey Mountain* 1970, *O Babylon!* 1978, and *Remembrance* 1980.
Suggested reading
Baugh, Edward *Derek Walcott: Memory as Vision* (1978)
Hammer, Robert *Derek Walcott* (1981)

Walcott Jersey Joe. Adopted name of Arnold Raymond Cream (1914–1994). US boxer who won the world heavyweight championship 1951, at the age of 37. He won the championship at his fifth attempt, successfully defeating Ezzard Charles, and subsequently lost his title in an epic 13-round fight against a young Rocky Marciano, a defeat which effectively ended his boxing career.

Cream was born in Merchantville, New Jersey, and had by 1930 begun his professional career – illegally, since he was too young. His adopted name was in honour of Joe Walcott, a Barbadian who held the world welterweight title at the turn of the century. He met little success and retired 1944. Then, in 1945, he had the opportunity to take part in an exhibition fight against reigning champion Joe Louis, who was on a tour. As both boxers were short of money, as were their trainers and managers, it became a title fight. Walcott knocked Louis down twice and was robbed of the decision.

After his retirement, he kept in touch with boxing as a referee and as New Jersey's state commissioner for boxing until 1988. He refereed several world title fights, including a return fight between Muhammad Ali and Sonny Liston which lasted just a few seconds.

Wald George (1906–). US biochemist who explored the chemistry of vision. He discovered the role played in night vision by the retinal pigment rhodopsin, and later identified the three primary-colour pigments. Nobel Prize for Physiology or Medicine 1967.

He spent his academic career at Harvard from 1935, becoming professor of biology 1948. In the 1970s he spoke out against the US role in the Vietnam War.

Studying rhodopsin, which occurs in the rods (dim-light receptors) of the retina, Wald discovered in 1933 that this substance consists of the colourless protein opsin in combination with retinal, a yellow carotenoid compound that is the aldehyde of vitamin A. Rhodopsin molecules are split into these two compounds when they are struck by light, and the enzyme alcohol dehydrogenase then further reduces the retinal to form vitamin A. In the dark the process is reversed, but over a period of time some of the retinal is lost. This deficiency has to be made up from vitamin A, and if the body's stores are inadequate, night blindness results.

In the 1950s Wald found the retinal pigments that detect red and yellow-green light, and a few years later the pigment for blue light. All these are related to vitamin A, and in the 1960s he demonstrated that the absence of one or more of them results in colour blindness.

Wald Lillian D (1867–1940). US public health administrator and founder of New York City's Henry Street Settlement House 1895. In 1912 she founded the National Organization for Public Health Nursing and was also active in union and antiwar activities.

Born in Cincinnati, Ohio, USA, Wald graduated from the New York Hospital Training School for Nurses 1891. She later worked as a nurse in some of New York's poorest neighbourhoods, providing medical, nutritional, educational, and social-welfare programmes for children and adults. Her memoirs, *House on Henry Street*, appeared 1915.

Waldemar or Valdemar. Four kings of Denmark, including:

Waldemar (I) the Great (1131–1182). King of Denmark from 1157, who defeated rival claimants to the throne and overcame the Wends on the Baltic island of Rügen 1169.

Waldemar (II) the Conqueror (1170–1241). King of Denmark from 1202. He was the second son of Waldemar the Great and succeeded his brother Canute VI. He gained control of land north of the river Elbe (which he later lost), as well as much of Estonia, and he completed the codification of Danish law.

Waldemar IV (1320–1375). King of Denmark from 1340, responsible for reuniting his country by capturing Skåne (S Sweden) and the island of Gotland 1361. However, the resulting conflict with the Hanseatic League led to defeat by them, and in 1370 he was forced to submit to the Peace of Stralsund.

Walden (Alastair) Brian (1932–). British journalist and, from 1977, television presenter. He was a Labour member of Parliament 1964–77. Walden was a university lecturer before entering Parliament. Disillusioned with party politics, he cut short his parliamentary career in 1977 and became presenter of the current-affairs TV programme *Weekend World*, with a direct and uninhibited style of interviewing public figures. He also contributes to the *Sunday Times* and *Evening Standard* newspapers.

Waldheim Kurt (1918–). Austrian politician and diplomat, president 1986–92. He was secretary general of the United Nations 1972–81, having been Austria's representative there 1964–68 and 1970–71.

He was elected president of Austria despite revelations that during World War II he had been an intelligence officer in an army unit responsible for transporting Jews to death camps. His election therefore led to some diplomatic isolation of Austria, and in 1991 he announced that he would not run for re-election.

Suggested reading
Bassett, Richard *Waldheim and Austria* (1988)
Herzstein, R E *Waldheim: The Missing Years* (1988)
Waldheim, Kurt *In the Eye of the Storm* (autobiography) (trs 1986)

Walesa Lech (1943–). Polish trade-union leader, president of Poland 1990–95. He founded Solidarity (Solidarność) in 1980, an organization, independent of the Communist Party, which forced substantial political and economic concessions from the Polish government 1980–81 until being outlawed. He was awarded the Nobel Prize for Peace 1983. By 1994 Walesa's public approval rating had slumped dramatically.

As an electrician at the Lenin shipyard in Gdańsk, Walesa became a trade-union organizer and led a series of strikes that drew wide public support. In Dec 1981 Solidarity was outlawed and Walesa arrested, after the imposition of martial law by the Polish leader Gen Jaruzelski. Walesa, a devout Catholic, was released 1982.

After leading a further series of strikes during 1988, he negotiated an agreement with the Jaruzelski government in April 1989 under the terms of which Solidarity once more became legal and a new, semi-pluralist 'socialist democracy' was established.

Waldheim Former Austrian chancellor Kurt Waldheim, elected in 1986 despite his wartime service with the Nazi German army in Yugoslavia. He was secretary general of the United Nations 1972–81, responsible for several peacekeeping missions in the Middle East, Asia, and other areas, none of which ended hostilities.

The coalition government elected Sept 1989 was dominated by Solidarity. Rifts appeared, but Walesa went on to be elected president Dec 1990. In 1991 Walesa left Solidarity and in 1993 publicly disassociated himself from the party. Criticized for being arrogant and out of touch, in Oct 1994 he was censured by parliament for violating the constitution. He was narrowly defeated in the 1995 presidential elections by his communist challenger, Alexander Kwasniewski.

Wales, Prince of title conferred on the eldest son of the UK's sovereign. Prince Charles was invested as 21st prince of Wales at Caernarvon 1969 by his mother, Elizabeth II.

High about me, triangular and sharp, / Like a cluster of sword-points many summits rose.

ARTHUS WALEY
The Temple (from the Chinese poem of Po Ch-i) 1923

Waley Arthur David (born Schloss) (1889–1966). English orientalist who translated from both Japanese and Chinese, including such classics as the Japanese *The Tale of Genji* 1925–33 and *The Pillow-book of Sei Shōnagon* 1928, and the 16th-century Chinese novel *Monkey* 1942. He never visited the Far East.

Walker Alice Malsenior (1944–). US poet, novelist, critic, and essay writer. She has been active in the US civil-rights movement since the 1960s and, as a black woman, wrote about the double burden of racist and sexist oppression, about colonialism, and the quest for political and spiritual recovery. Her novel *The Color Purple* 1982 (filmed 1985), told in the form of letters, won a Pulitzer prize. Her other works include *Possessing the Secret of Joy* 1992, which deals passionately with female circumcision.

She was born in Eatonton, Georgia, and wrote the novels *The Third Life of Grange Copeland* 1970, *Meridian* 1976, and *The Temple of My Familiar* 1989. Walker's collections of poems include *Once* 1968 and *Revolutionary Petunias* 1973; her short stories and essays are collected in *Love and Trouble: Stories of Black Women* 1973 and *In Search of Our Mothers' Gardens: Womanist Prose* 1983.

Walker Jimmy (James John) (1881–1946). US public official. Born in New York, USA, Walker attended St Francis Xavier College and was admitted to the bar 1912. Becoming active in Democratic party politics, he served in the state assembly 1909–15 and the state senate 1915–25, where he became a protégé of Al Smith. In 1925 Walker was elected mayor of New York City and in that position became a popular personality, familiarly known to his constituents as 'Jimmy'. Although Walker made great improvements to the city's infrastructure, he was charged with graft and forced to resign 1932.

Walker Peter Edward, Baron Walker of Worcester (1932–). British Conservative politician, energy secretary 1983–87, secretary of state for Wales 1987–90. As energy secretary, he managed the government's response to the national miners' strike 1984–85 that resulted in the capitulation of the National Union of Miners. He retired from active politics 1990. Baron 1992.

Walker Sebastian (1942–1991). English publisher. Formerly a sales representative, Walker worked his way up to director of the Chatto and Windus publishing house 1977–79, and founded Walker Books Ltd 1978. Walker Books produce some 300 children's books a year, with an emphasis on high quality, following a broadly anti-sexist and antiracist line. In 1989, Walker Books won four of the five main children's-book awards.

Walker T-Bone (Aaron Thibeaux) (1910–1975). US blues guitarist, singer, and songwriter. His sophisticated guitar technique incorporated jazz idioms and he was one of the first to use an electrically amplified guitar, from the mid-1930s. He was born in Texas but active mainly in California, and often worked with jazz musicians. His recordings include 'Call It Stormy Monday' 1946 and the album *T-Bone Blues* 1960.

Walker William (1824–1860). US adventurer who for a short time established himself as president of a republic in NW Mexico, and

was briefly president of Nicaragua 1856–57. He was eventually executed and is now regarded as a symbol of US imperialism in Central America.

Wall Max. Stage name of Maxwell George Lorimer (1908–1990). English music-hall comedian. Wall was born in London, the son of a Scots comedian, and became a well-known dancer before radio enabled his verbal comedy to reach a wider audience. In the 1950s his career declined dramatically after he left his wife and children. Towards the end of his career he appeared in starring roles as a serious actor, in John Osborne's *The Entertainer* 1974, in Pinter's *The Caretaker* 1977, and in Samuel Beckett's *Waiting for Godot* 1980. In his solo comedy performances his trademark was an eccentric walk.

Wallace Alfred Russel (1823–1913). Welsh naturalist who collected animal and plant specimens in South America and SE Asia, and independently arrived at a theory of evolution by natural selection similar to that proposed by Charles Darwin.

In 1858, Wallace wrote an essay outlining his ideas on evolution and sent it to Darwin, who had not yet published his. Together they presented a paper to the Linnean Society that year. Wallace's section, entitled 'On the Tendency of Varieties to Depart Indefinitely from the Original Type', described the survival of the fittest. Although both thought that the human race had evolved to its present physical form by natural selection, Wallace was of the opinion that humans' higher mental capabilities had arisen from some 'metabiological' agency.

Wallace was born in Usk. While working as a schoolteacher, he met English naturalist Henry Bates; together they planned a collecting trip to the Amazon, and arrived in South America 1848. When Wallace was returning to the UK 1852, his ship sank and although he survived, all his specimens were lost except those that had been shipped earlier. From 1854 to 1862 he explored the Malay Peninsula and archipelago, from which he collected more than 125,000 specimens, and in 1869–70 he made an expedition to Borneo and Maluku.

Wallace's works include *A Narrative of Travels on the Amazon and Rio Negro* 1853, *On the Law Which Has Regulated the Introduction of New Species* 1855, *The Malay Archipelago* 1869, *Contributions to the Theory of Natural Selection* 1870; and a pioneering work on zoogeography, *Geographical Distribution of Animals* 1876.
Suggested reading
Fichman, M *Alfred Russel Wallace* (1981)
George, W B *Biologist Philosopher: A Study of the Life and Writings of Alfred Russel Wallace* (1964)
McKinney, H Lewis *Wallace and Natural Selection* (1972)

Segregation now, segregation tomorrow and segregation forever!

GEORGE WALLACE
Inaugural speech as governor of Alabama Jan 1963

Wallace George Corley (1919–). US politician who was opposed to integration; he was governor of Alabama 1963–67, 1971–79, and 1983–87. He contested the presidency in 1968 as an independent (the American Independent Party) and in 1972 campaigned for the Democratic nomination but was shot at a rally and became partly paralysed.

Wallace Henry Agard (1888–1965). US editor and public official. Born in Adair County, Iowa, USA, Wallace was educated at Iowa State College and in 1910 joined the staff of the family-owned periodical *Wallace's Farmer*. Although his father was a prominent Republican, the younger Wallace joined the Democratic party 1928. Appointed secretary of the treasury by Franklin Roosevelt 1933 he served as vice president during Roosevelt's third term 1941–45. He later broke with Truman and, after serving as editor of the *New Republic* 1946–47, was the unsuccessful Progressive Party candidate for president 1948.

Wallace Irving (1916–1990). US novelist. He was one of the most popular writers of the 20th century. He wrote 17 works of nonfiction and 16 novels; they include *The Chapman Report* 1960, a novel inspired by the Kinsey Report on sexual behaviour, and *The Prize* 1962.

Wallace Lew(is) (1827–1905). US general and novelist. He served in the Mexican War and the American Civil War and subsequently became governor of New Mexico and minister to Turkey. He was credited with saving Washington, DC, from capture by Confederate forces and served on the tribunal that tried those accused of conspiring to assassinate Abraham Lincoln. He wrote several historical novels, including *The Fair God* 1873 and *Ben Hur* 1880 which was filmed twice, in 1926 and 1959.

Wallace Richard (1818–1890). English art collector. He inherited a valuable art collection from his father, the Marquess of Hertford, which was given 1897 by his widow to the UK as the Wallace Collection, containing many 18th-century French paintings. Baronet 1871.

What is a highbrow? He is a man who has found something more interesting than women.

EDGAR WALLACE
New York Times 24 Jan 1932

Wallace (Richard Horatio) Edgar (1875–1932). English writer of thrillers. His prolific output includes *The Four Just Men* 1905; a series set in Africa and including *Sanders of the River* 1911; crime novels such as *A King by Night* 1926; and melodramas such as *The Ringer* 1926.

Wallace William (*c.* 1272–1305). Scottish nationalist who led a revolt against English rule 1297, won a victory at Stirling, and assumed the title 'governor of Scotland'. Edward I defeated him at Falkirk 1298, and Wallace was captured and executed. He was styled Knight in a charter of 1298.

Liberty is the best of all things; never live beneath the noose of a servile halter.

WILLIAM WALLACE
from a medieval proverb

Wallas Graham (1858–1932). English political scientist, the first professor of political science at the London School of Economics. Wallas was an early member of the Fabian Society and contributed to *Fabian Essays in Socialism* 1888. He left the society 1904 because it had become antiliberal.

In *Human Nature in Politics* 1908 he argued that certain nonrational factors, such as prejudice, custom, and accident, were more likely to affect politics than rational calculation. *The Great Society* 1914 expressed concern for the individual in modern industrial society which was becoming increasingly centralized.

Wallenberg Raoul (1912–*c.* 1947). Swedish business executive who attempted to rescue several thousand Jews from German-occupied Budapest 1944, during World War II. He was taken prisoner by the Soviet army 1945 and was never heard from again.

In Hungary he tried to rescue and support Jews in safe houses, and provided them with false papers to save them from deportation to extermination camps. After the arrival of Soviet troops in Budapest, he reported to the Russian commander Jan 1945 and then disappeared. The Soviet government later claimed that he died of a heart attack July 1947. However, rumours persisted into the 1980s that he was alive and held in a Soviet prison camp. In the 1990s the Russians said that he had died as claimed.
Suggested reading
Bierman, John *Righteous Gentile* (1981)

Wallenstein Albrecht Eusebius Wenzel von (1583–1634). German general who, until his defeat at Lützen 1632, led the Habsburg armies in the Thirty Years' War. He was assassinated.

Haughty and ambitious, he was indifferent to religion, but somewhat neurotically under the spell of astrology.

E N Williams on WALLENSTEIN
in *Penguin Dictionary of English and European History 1485–1789* 1980

Go, lovely Rose! / Tell her, that wastes her time and me, / That now she knows, / When I resemble her to thee, / How sweet and fair she seems to be.

EDMUND WALLER
'Go, Lovely Rose!'

Waller Edmund (1606–1687). English poet. He managed to eulogize both Cromwell and Charles II. He is now mainly remembered for lyrics such as 'Go, lovely rose'.

Waller Fats (Thomas Wright) (1904–1943). US jazz pianist and composer. He had a forceful stride piano style. His songs, many of which have become jazz standards, include 'Ain't Misbehavin'' 1929, 'Honeysuckle Rose' 1929, and 'Viper's Drag' 1934.

An exuberant, humorous performer, Waller toured extensively and appeared in several musical films, including *Stormy Weather* 1943. His first recordings were on piano rolls and in the 1920s he recorded pipe-organ solos. In the 1930s he worked with a small group (as Fats Waller and his Rhythm Boys), before leading a big band 1939–42.
Suggested reading
Machlin, Paul *Stride: The Music of Fats Waller* (1985)
Vance, Joel *Fats Waller: His Life and Times* (1977)

Wallis Barnes Neville (1887–1979). British aeronautical engineer who designed the airship R-100, and during World War II perfected the 'bouncing bombs' used by the Royal Air Force Dambusters Squadron to destroy the German Möhne and Eder dams in 1943. He also assisted in the development of the Concorde supersonic airliner and developed the swing wing aircraft. Knighted 1968.

Wallis was born in Derbyshire and trained as a marine engineer. From shipbuilding he turned to the design of airships and then to aeroplanes. He joined the Vickers Company 1911 and worked there as a designer until the end of World War II, moving to the British Aircraft Corporation 1945.

In the G4–31 biplane 1932, Wallis introduced a lattice-work system derived from the wire-netting used to contain the gas bags on the airship R-100. A full geodesic structure was first employed in the monoplane that became the Wellesley bomber. In the Wallis lattice pattern, if one series of members was in tension, the opposite members were in compression, so that the system was stress-balanced in all directions. The Wellesley was responsible for a great technical advance in design in the mid-1930s, which eventually produced the Wellington bomber of World War II.

Wallis Hal (Harold Brent) (1899–1986). US film producer. Born in Chicago, USA, Wallis left school early. After moving to Los Angeles 1922, he joined the staff of the Warner Brothers studios. He was named publicity director 1924 and was promoted to studio manager 1928, distinguishing himself as a shrewd business operator. He had a keen eye for choosing potential box-office successes. He was chief executive in charge of production at Warner Brothers 1933–44, when he left to establish his own company, Hal Wallis Productions, which releases through Paramount.

Wallis John (1616–1703). English mathematician and cleric who made important contributions to the development of algebra and analytical geometry. He was one of the founders of the Royal Society.

Wallis was born in Ashford, Kent, and studied at Cambridge. In 1640 he was ordained in the Church of England. He moved to London 1645 and assisted the Parliamentary side by deciphering captured coded letters during the Civil War. From 1649 he was professor of geometry at Oxford, and in 1658 he was appointed keeper of the university archives. In 1660 Charles II chose him as his royal chaplain. After the revolution of 1688–89, which drove James II from the throne, Wallis was employed by William III as a decipherer.

Wallis also conducted experiments in speech and attempted to teach, with some success, congenitally deaf people to speak. His method was described in his *Grammatica linguae anglicanae* 1652.

Wallis's *Arithmetica infinitorum* 1655 was the most substantial single work on mathematics yet to appear in England. It introduced the symbol ∞ to represent infinity, the germ of the differential calculus, and, by an impressive use of interpolation (the word was Wallis's invention), the value for π. His *Mechanica* 1669–71 was the fullest treatment of the subject then existing, and his *Algebra* 1685 introduced the principles of analogy and continuity into mathematics.

Walpole Horace, 4th Earl of Orford (1717–1797). English novelist, letter writer and politician, the son of Robert Walpole. He was a Whig member of Parliament 1741–67. He converted his house at Strawberry Hill, Twickenham (then a separate town SW of London), into a Gothic castle; his *The Castle of Otranto* 1764 established the genre of the Gothic, or 'romance of terror', novel. More than 4,000 of his letters have been published. Earl 1791.
Suggested reading
Fothergill, Brian *The Strawberry Hill Set: Horace Walpole and His Circle* (1983)
Lewis, W S *Horace Walpole* (1961)
Lewis, W S *Rescuing Robert Walpole* (1978)
Smith, W H (ed) *Horace Walpole: Writer, Politician, Connoisseur* (1968)

Walpole Hugh Seymour (1884–1941). English novelist, born in New Zealand. His books include *The Cathedral* 1922 and *The Old Ladies* 1924. He also wrote the historical 'Lakeland Saga' of the *Herries Chronicle* 1930–33. Knighted 1937.

They now ring the bells, but they will soon wring their hands.

ROBERT WALPOLE
Remark when war against Spain was declared 1739

Walpole Robert, 1st Earl of Orford (1676–1745). British Whig politician, the first 'prime minister' as First Lord of the Treasury and chancellor of the Exchequer 1715–17 and 1721–42. He encouraged trade and tried to avoid foreign disputes (until forced into the War of Jenkins' Ear with Spain 1739).

Opponents thought his foreign policies worked to the advantage of France. He held favour with George I and George II, struggling against Jacobite intrigues, and received an earldom when he eventually retired 1742. KB 1725.
Suggested reading
Dickinson, H T *Walpole and the Whig Supremacy* (1973)
Plumb, J H *Sir Robert Walpole* (1956–1961)

Walpurga, St (*c.* 710–*c.* 779). English abbess who preached Christianity in Germany. Walpurgis Night, the eve of 1 May (one of her feast days), became associated with witches' sabbaths and other superstitions. Her feast day is 25 Feb.

Walras (Marie Esprit) Léon (1834–1910). French economist. In his *Éléments d'économie politique pure* 1874–77 he attempted to develop a unified model for general equilibrium theory (a hypothetical situation in which demand equals supply in all markets). He also originated the theory of diminishing marginal utility of a good (the increased value to a person of consuming more of a product).

Walsh Raoul (1887–1980). US film director. He was originally an actor. A specialist in tough action stories, he made a number of outstanding films, including *The Thief of Bagdad* 1924, *The Roaring Twenties* 1939, *Objective Burma* 1945, *White Heat* 1949, and *The Tall Men* 1955.

Walsingham Francis (*c.* 1530–1590). English politician who, as secretary of state from 1573, both advocated a strong anti-Spanish

policy and ran the efficient government spy system that made it work. Knighted 1577.

Walter Hubert (died 1205). Archbishop of Canterbury 1193–1205. As justiciar (chief political and legal officer) 1193–98, he ruled England during Richard I's absence and introduced the offices of coroner and justice of the peace.

Walter John (1739–1812). British newspaper editor, founder of *The Times* (originally the *Daily Universal Register* 1785, but renamed 1788).

Walter Lucy (*c.* 1630–1658). Mistress of Charles II, whom she met while a Royalist refugee in The Hague, Netherlands, 1648; the Duke of Monmouth was their son.

Walters Alan Arthur (1926–). British economist and government adviser 1981–89. He became economics adviser to Prime Minister Thatcher, but his publicly stated differences with the policies of her chancellor Nigel Lawson precipitated, in 1989, Lawson's resignation from the government as well as Walters' own departure.

Walters held the post of economics professor at the London School of Economics 1968–75 and has been professor of political economy at the Johns Hopkins University, Baltimore, from 1976. He was also economics adviser to the World Bank 1976–80. Knighted 1983.

Walther von der Vogelweide (*c.* 1170–1230). German poet. The greatest of the Minnesingers, his songs dealt mainly with courtly love. Of noble birth, he lived in his youth at the Austrian ducal court in Vienna, adopting a wandering life after the death of his patron in 1198. His lyrics deal mostly with love, but also with religion and politics.

Walton Ernest Thomas Sinton (1903–1995). Irish physicist who collaborated with John Cockcroft on investigating the structure of the atom. In 1932 they succeeded in splitting the atom; for this experiment they shared the 1951 Nobel Prize for Physics. Walton and Cockcroft built the first successful particle accelerator. This used an arrangement of condensers to produce a beam of protons and was completed in 1932.

Walton was born in County Waterford and studied at Trinity College, Dublin, and 1927–34 at the Cavendish Laboratory in Cambridge, England. He returned to Trinity and was professor there 1947–74.

Using the proton beam to bombard lithium, Walton and Cockcroft observed the production of large quantities of alpha particles, showing that the lithium nuclei had captured the protons and formed unstable beryllium nuclei which instantaneously decayed into two alpha particles travelling in opposite directions. They detected these alpha particles with a fluorescent screen. Later they investigated the transmutation of other light elements using proton beams, and also deuterons (nuclei of deuterium) derived from heavy water.

I am, Sir, a Brother of the Angle

IZAAK WALTON
Compleat Angler ch 1 1653

Walton Izaak (1593–1683). English author. He was born in Stafford and settled in London as an ironmonger. He is known for his classic fishing text *Compleat Angler* 1653. He also wrote short biographies of the poets George Herbert and John Donne and the theologian Richard Hooker.

Walton William Turner (1902–1983). English composer. Among his works are *Façade* 1923, a series of instrumental pieces designed to be played in conjunction with the recitation of surrealist poems by Edith Sitwell; the oratorio *Belshazzar's Feast* 1931; and *Variations on a Theme by Hindemith* 1963. He also composed a viola concerto 1929, two symphonies 1935, a violin concerto 1939, and a sonata for violin and pianoforte 1950. Knighted 1951.
Suggested reading
Howes, Frank *The Music of William Walton* (1974)
Kennedy, Michael *Portrait of Walton* (1989)

Sadie, Stanley *20th Century English Masters* (1986)
Tierney, N *William Walton* (1985)
Walton, Susana *William Walton: Behind the Façade* (1988)

Wanamaker John (1838–1922). US retailer who developed the modern department store. Born in Philadelphia, USA, Wanamaker worked as a delivery boy and store clerk, founding the dry-goods firm of Brown and Wanamaker with his brother-in-law 1861. He established his own firm, John Wanamaker and Company, 1869. Renting an abandoned railroad depot 1876, he merchandised goods in distinct departments; he publicized his stores through extensive advertising.

Wanamaker Sam (1919–1993). US actor and director, the founder of, and driving force in, the project to build an authentic replica of Shakespeare's Globe Theatre in its original location on the south bank of the Thames opposite St Paul's Cathedral, London.

As an actor he appeared in many films, including *Those Magnificent Men in Their Flying Machines* 1965 and *The Spy Who Came in from the Cold* 1966, and directed several films including *Catlow* 1971. His opera productions include Michael Tippett's *King Priam* at Covent Garden, London 1962 and Sergei Prokofiev's *War and Peace* at the Sydney Opera House, Australia 1973.

He was born Samuel Watenmaker in Chicago, the son of Russian-Jewish immigrants, and was educated at Drake University, Iowa. He acted in the city's Civic Repertory Theater and soon appeared on Broadway. He served in the US Marine Corps during World War II, returning to Broadway afterwards. He went to London 1952, during the McCarthy era, to make the film *Give Us This Day*, and stayed. He was a dynamic actor, especially in US plays, and a brilliant director. In 1956 he played the leading role in N Richard Nash's comedy, *The Rainmaker*, and directed Bertolt Brecht's *The Threepenny Opera* at the Royal Court Theatre, London.

Although not a notable Shakespearean actor, his devotion to Shakespeare and his determination, despite considerable opposition and against all the odds, to see the world's most famous theatre rebuilt have ensured his own fame.

Wang An (1920–1990). Chinese-born US engineer, founder of Wang Laboratories 1951, one of the world's largest computer companies in the 1970s. In 1948 he invented the computer memory core, the most common device used for storing computer data before the invention of the integrated circuit (chip).

Wang emigrated to the USA 1945. He developed his own company with the $500,000 he received from IBM from the sale of his patent. One of his early contracts was the first electronic scoreboard, installed at New York's Shea Stadium. His company took off in 1964 with the introduction of a desktop calculator. Later, Wang switched with great success to the newly emerging market for word-processing systems based on cheap silicon chips, turning Wang Laboratories into a multibillion-dollar company. But with the advent of the personal computer, the company fell behind. Wang Laboratories made a loss of $400 million 1989.

Wang Zhen (1908–1993). Chinese communist political leader. He was veteran of the Long March. Born in the south-central province of Hunan, Wang began his career in the labour movement, working initially on the railways. He joined the Chinese Communist Party 1927, and until the 1950s was an important army commander and political officer. He took part in the Long March 1934–35 when the communists retreated northwards under the attack of the Nationalist forces. Following the communist victory 1949 Wang directed the forced 'liberation' and Han Chinese colonization of the largely Muslim far-western province of Xinjiang. He became a full member of the CCP's influential central committee 1956.

An unswerving Marxist, Wang escaped the purge during the ultra-leftist Cultural Revolution 1966–69. He was the only member of the subsequent reformist administration of Deng Xiaoping to do so. He became vice-premier 1975 and joined the CCP's Politburo 1978. Advancing age forced Wang to retire as vice-premier 1980, but he served as vice-chairman of the Central Advisory Committee 1985–87, a body set up by Deng to accommodate senior party figures. In his position as a party elder, he worked, via his protégés, to defend 'Mao's revolution'. In 1986 he was influential in securing the ousting of the liberal-minded CCP leader Hu Yaobang. A hard-line Marxist, he strongly supported the Tiananmen Square crackdown against the student-led pro-democracy movement June 1989.

Wankel Felix (1902–1988). German engineer who developed by 1956 the rotary engine that bears his name. Wankel was born in Luhran. In 1927 he became a partner in an engineering works before opening his own research establishment. Later he carried out work for the German Air Ministry. At the end of World War II he began to work for a number of German motor manufacturers at the Technische Entwicklungstelle in Lindow; he was made its director 1960.

During the 1930s Wankel carried out a systematic investigation of internal-combustion engines, particularly rotary engines. The German motor firm NSU sponsored the development of his engine with a view to its possible use in motorcycles. Eventually he rearranged his early designs and produced a successful prototype of a practical engine in 1956.

Wankel engines are easily connected together in pairs. They have few moving parts compared with an ordinary motorcar engine; there are no piston rods or camshafts. The saving in engine weight means that slightly less power is required from engines of this type when they are used in cars. Companies throughout the world have bought the rights to manufacture and use the Wankel engine.

Warbeck Perkin (c. 1474–1499). Flemish pretender to the English throne. Claiming to be Richard, brother of Edward V, he led a rising against Henry VII in 1497, and was hanged after attempting to escape from the Tower of London.

Warburg Otto Heinrich (1883–1970). German biochemist who in 1923 devised a manometer (pressure gauge) sensitive enough to measure oxygen uptake of respiring tissue. By measuring the rate at which cells absorb oxygen under differing conditions, he was able to show that enzymes called cytochromes enable cells to process oxygen. Nobel Prize for Physiology or Medicine 1931.

Later he discovered the mechanism of the conversion of light energy to chemical energy that occurs in photosynthesis. He also demonstrated that cancerous cells absorb less oxygen than normal cells.

In 1913 he went to the Kaiser Wilhelm (later Max Planck) Institute for Cell Physiology in Berlin, becoming a professor there in 1918 and its director in 1931. In 1941 Warburg, being part-Jewish, was removed from his post but such was his international prestige that he was soon reinstated. In 1944 he was nominated for a second Nobel prize but Nazi rules prevented him from accepting the award.

Warburg discovered that in both charcoal systems and living cells, the uptake of oxygen is inhibited by the presence of cyanide or hydrogen sulphide, which combine with heavy metals.

He also showed that, in the dark, carbon monoxide inhibits the respiration of yeast but does not do so in the light. He was aware that heavy metals form complexes with carbon monoxide and that the iron complex is dissociated by light, which provided further evidence for the existence of an iron-containing respiratory enzyme. He then investigated the efficiency of light in overcoming the carbon monoxide inhibition of respiration, and determined the photochemical absorption spectrum of the respiratory enzyme, which proved to be a haemoprotein (a protein with an iron-containing group) similar to haemoglobin; he called it iron oxygenase.

Ward (Aaron) Montgomery (1843–1913). US retailer who pioneered the mass marketing of clothing and personal items through the mails. Serving the needs of farm families in remote rural areas, he constantly expanded his catalogue from its inception in 1872. He moved the firm's headquarters to the Ward Tower in Chicago 1900.

Born in Chatham, New Jersey, USA, Ward left school in his teens to become a travelling representative for several Midwestern dry-goods firms. He retired from the day-to-day operations of the firm in 1886.

Ward Artemus. Pen name of Charles Farrar Browne (1834–1867). US humorist. He achieved great popularity with comic writings such as *Artemus Ward: His Book* 1862 and *Artemus Ward: His Travels* 1865, and with his deadpan lectures. He influenced Mark Twain.

My pollertics, like my religion, bein of a exceedin accommodatin character.

ARTEMUS WARD
Artemus Ward: His Book, 'The Crisis' 1862

Ward Barbara, Baroness Jackson of Lodsworth (1914–1981). British economist. She became president of the Institute for Environment and Development 1973. DBE 1974. In 1976 she received a life peerage as Baroness Jackson of Lodsworth. Her books include *Policy for the West* 1951, *The Widening Gap* 1971 and her best-known work, *Only One Earth* (with René Dubois) 1972.

Ward Frederick (1836–1870). Australian bushranger, known as 'Captain Thunderbolt'. He operated in the 1860s first in the Hunter Valley area of New South Wales, later in the New England area and Queensland, gaining a reputation as a chivalrous bushranger. He was shot by troopers in May 1870.

Ward Mrs Humphry (born Mary Augusta Arnold) (1851–1920). English novelist. She wrote didactic books such as *Robert Elsmere* 1888, a study of religious doubt. She was an opponent of women's suffrage on the grounds that public life would dissipate women's potent influence on family and home. She was the niece of Matthew Arnold.
Suggested reading
Jones, E Huws *Mrs Ward* (1973)
Sutherland, John *Mrs Humphry Ward: Eminent Victorian, Pre-Eminent Edwardian* (1990)
Ward, Mrs Humphry *Recollections* (1918)

Ward Leslie (1851–1922). English caricaturist, known under the pseudonym 'Spy' for his caricatures in *Vanity Fair*. Knighted 1918.

Wardell Robert (1793–1834). Australian barrister and newspaper editor born in England. In 1824, with William Wentworth, he founded the *Australian* and through its pages campaigned vigorously for self-government for the colony.

Warhol Andy. Adopted name of Andrew Warhola (1928–1987). US Pop artist and film-maker. He made his name in 1962 with paintings of Campbell's soup cans, Coca-Cola bottles, and film stars. In his New York studio, the Factory, he and his assistants produced series of garish silk-screen prints. His films include *Chelsea Girls* 1966 and *Trash* 1970.

Warhol was born in Pittsburgh, Pennsylvania, where he studied art. In the 1950s he became a leading commercial artist in New York. With the breakthrough of Pop art, his bizarre personality and flair for self-publicity made him a household name. He was a pioneer of multimedia events with the 'Exploding Plastic Inevitable' touring show 1966 featuring the Velvet Underground rock group. In 1968 he was shot and nearly killed by a radical feminist, Valerie Solanas.

In the 1970s and 1980s Warhol was primarily a society portraitist, although his activities included a magazine (*Interview*) and a cable TV show. In May 1994 a museum of his works was opened in Pittsburgh, the largest museum in the country to be dedicated solely to the works of one artist.

His early silk-screen series dealt with car crashes and suicides, Marilyn Monroe, Elvis Presley, and flowers. His films, beginning with *Sleep* 1963 and ending with *Bad* 1977, have a strong improvisational element. His books include *The Philosophy of Andy Warhol (From A to B and Back Again)* 1975 and *Popism* 1980.
Suggested reading
Bockris, V *Warhol* (1989)
Bourdon, D *Warhol* (1989)
Koch, S *Stargazer: Andy Warhol's World and his Films* (1983)
Ratcliff, C *Andy Warhol* (1983)
Shanes, E *Warhol* (1993)
Warhol, Andy *Diaries* (1988)

Warlock Peter. Pen name of Philip Arnold Heseltine (1894–1930). English composer. His style was influenced by the music of the Elizabethan age and by that of Delius. His works include the orchestral suite *Capriol* 1926 based on 16th-century dances, and the song cycle *The Curlew* 1920–22. His works of musical theory and criticism were published under his real name.

He who has heard the cry of a curlew on a lone and desolate moor has heard the music of this richly gifted personality.

Eric Fenby on PETER WARLOCK
in *Delius as I Knew Him* 1936

Warming Johannes Eugenius Bülow (1841–1924). Danish botanist whose pioneering studies of the relationships between plants and their natural environments established plant ecology as a new discipline within botany.

He studied at Copenhagen and at German universities. While still a student, he spent 1863–66 at Lagoa Santa, Brazil, where he undertook a study of tropical vegetation. In 1882 he became professor at the Royal Institute of Technology in Stockholm, Sweden. He went on an expedition to Greenland in 1884 and to Norway in 1885, after which he returned to Copenhagen to become professor and director of the Botanical Gardens, positions he held until 1911. His last major expedition, 1890–92, was to the West Indies and Venezuela.

Warming investigated the relationships between plants and various environmental conditions, such as light, temperature, and rainfall, and attempted to classify types of plant communities (he defined a plant community as a group of several species that is subject to the same environmental conditions, which he called ecological factors). In *Plantesamfund/Oecology of Plants* 1895 he also formulated a programme for future research into the subject.

Warner Deborah (1959–). English theatre director. She founded the Kick Theatre company 1980. Discarding period costume and furnished sets, she adopted an uncluttered approach to the classics, including productions of many Shakespeare plays and Sophocles' *Electra*.

Warner Rex Ernest (1905–1986). English novelist. His later novels, such as *The Young Caesar* and *Imperial Caesar* 1958–60, are based on classical themes, but he is better remembered today for his earlier works, such as *The Aerodrome* 1941, which are disturbing parables based on the political situation of the 1930s.

Warren Earl (1891–1974). US jurist and chief justice of the US Supreme Court 1953–69. He served as governor of California 1943–53. As chief justice, he presided over a moderately liberal court, taking a stand against racial discrimination and ruling that segregation in schools was unconstitutional. He headed the commission that investigated 1963–64 President Kennedy's assassination.

Warren Frank (1952–). British boxing promoter who helped bring world-title fights to commercial television. He set up the London Arena in the Docklands. In 1989 he was seriously wounded in a shotgun attack.

Warren Joseph (1741–1775). American colonial physician and revolutionary leader. Born in Roxbury, Massachusetts, and educated at Harvard University, Warren established a private medical practice in Boston. Opposing British colonial rule in Massachusetts, he sent Paul Revere and William Dawes to warn the countryside of the approach of the British 1775. Appointed major general of the Massachusetts militia, he was killed at the Battle of Bunker Hill 1775.

Warren Robert Penn (1905–1989). US poet and novelist. He is the only author to have received a Pulitzer prize for both prose and poetry. His work explored the moral problems of the South. His most important novel, *All the King's Men* 1946 (Pulitzer prize 1947), depicts the rise and fall of a back-country demagogue modelled on the career of Huey Long. He also won Pulitzer prizes for *Promises*

1968 and *Now and Then: Poems* 1976–78. He was a senior figure of the New Criticism, and the first official US poet laureate 1986–88.
Suggested reading
Casper, L *Robert Penn Warren: The Dark and Bloody Ground* (1960)
Guttenberg, Barnett *Web of Being: The Novels of Robert Penn Warren* (1975)
Watkins, F C and Hiers, J T (eds) *Robert Penn Warren Talking: Interviews 1950–1978* (1980)

Wit and satire are transitory and perishable, but nature and passion are eternal.

JOSEPH WARTON
in 'Essay on the Writings and Genius of Pope' 1756 and 1782

Warton Joseph (1722–1800). English poet. His verse and 'Essay on the Writings and Genius of Pope' 1756–82 marked an 'anti-Classical' reaction. He was headmaster of Winchester 1766–93.

Warton Thomas Wain (1728–1790). English critic. He was professor of poetry at Oxford 1757–67 and published the first *History of English Poetry* 1774–81. He was poet laureate from 1785.

Warwick Richard Neville, 1st or 16th Earl of Warwick (1428–1471). English politician, called 'the Kingmaker'. During the Wars of the Roses he fought at first on the Yorkist side against the Lancastrians, and was largely responsible for placing Edward IV on the throne. Having quarrelled with him, he restored Henry VI in 1470, but was defeated and killed by Edward at Barnet, Hertfordshire. Earl 1449.

An able soldier and statesman, who with singular perseverance and consistency devoted his life to ... the house of York.

C W Oman on RICHARD NEVILLE, 1ST OR 16TH EARL OF WARWICK
in *Warwick the Kingmaker* 1891

Washington Booker T(aliaferro) (1856–1915). US educationist, pioneer in higher education for black people in the South. He was the founder and first principal of Tuskegee Institute, Alabama, in 1881, originally a training college for blacks, and now an academic institution. He maintained that economic independence was the way to achieve social equality. He was the son of a slave, and his books include the autobiography *Up from Slavery* 1901.
Suggested reading
Harlan, Louis R *Booker T Washington: The Making of a Black Leader, 1856–1901* (1972)
Hawkins, Hugh (ed) *Booker T Washington and His Critics* (1962)
Washington, Booker T *Up From Slavery* (autobiography) (1901, rep 1963)

Washington George (1732–1799). Commander of the American forces during the American Revolutionary War and 1st president of the United States 1789–97; known as 'the father of his country'. George Washington was born at Pope's Creek, Westmoreland County, Virginia. He was of British descent, his great-grandfather, John Washington, having migrated from Sulgrave Manor, Northamptonshire, in 1657. Largely self-taught, he began his career as a land surveyor, but inheriting the Mount Vernon estate from his brother Lawrence, Washington settled down as a country gentleman. Governor Dinwiddie soon made him lieutenant-colonel of the Virginia military. In April 1754 Washington was ordered to drive the French out of Fort Duquesne. He succeeded, but was in turn besieged in Fort Necessity, and was forced to accept surrender terms.
In 1758 Washington resigned command of the Virginia troops and married a rich widow, Martha Custis. The union of their plantations made Washington one of the wealthiest men in his state. He entertained lavishly, and thus came into contact with notable men from all over the British colonies in America. He was elected in 1759 to the Virginia House of Burgesses, and re-elected. He soon displayed a growing interest in disputes between the colonies and the British Crown, and Virginia elected him one of its delegates to the first

Continental Congress. In Philadelphia he bought arms and ammunition, which he sent to Virginia, and when the congress adjourned he returned to Virginia to take up active training of the raw soldiers. When the second Continental Congress met in Philadelphia the general feeling among New Englanders was that they must have a Southern man to lead them, since only thus could they be sure of uniting all the colonies in one common cause. War had already started, and John Adams proposed Washington as commander-in-chief of the colonial armies and on 15 June 1775 Washington took over the command.
The American troops often lacked arms, munitions, food, and clothes; and Washington had to combat faction and treachery among his generals, including the episode of Benedict Arnold's treachery. When he took charge of the American forces at Boston he won a notable success. His occupation of Dorchester Heights compelled Howe to evacuate Boston in March 1776. He then had a succession of reverses, notably at the battle of Brooklyn Heights, but in New Jersey he turned and beat his enemy at Trenton and Princeton. Following defeats in the battles of the Brandywine and Germantown in the autumn of 1777, Washington led his 11,000 men into winter camp at Valley Forge, 32 km/ 20 mi from Philadelphia. The spring brought better news for the Americans. The French were coming into the war. Clinton, who succeeded Howe, had been ordered to give up Philadelphia and return to New York. Washington harassed his troops, notably at the battle of Monmouth. When Clinton reached New York, Washington took up a position at White Plains and for three years, while fighting was going on elsewhere, the two armies watched each other.
At last, Washington's chance came when Cornwallis met with difficulties in North Carolina, withdrew his army to Virginia, and finally shut himself up in Yorktown. Here Washington, who had hurried south, forced him to surrender (1781). When the British finally moved out of New York for home the American army under Washington entered the town. A few days afterwards, on 4 Dec 1783, Washington went via Philadelphia to Annapolis, Maryland, where Congress was sitting. Here on 23 Dec he resigned his commission as commander of the armies.
For four years he strove to recoup his shattered fortunes. At length it was decided to call a convention to frame a constitution, and Washington was chosen as one of the Virginia delegation. The convention opened on 13 May 1787 in Philadelphia, and Washington was unanimously chosen to preside. Others wrote the constitution, but it was Washington who did much to remove difficulties. He was unanimously chosen first president of the republic. He was inaugurated on 30 April 1789.
As president, Washington alienated his secretary of state, Thomas Jefferson, who resigned in 1793, by accepting the fiscal policy championed by Alexander Hamilton and overseeing the payment of the foreign and domestic debt incurred by the new nation. He also shaped the powers of the presidency, assuming some implied powers not specified in the Constitution – among them, the power to create a national bank, and the introduction of an excise tax.
Washington wished to retire at the end of his first term, but at the instance of the rival leaders, Thomas Jefferson and Alexander Hamilton, he was elected to a second term by a unanimous vote. His neutral policy towards the French Revolution angered the pro-French Jefferson party. He was also widely criticized for signing Jay's Treaty 1794 that resolved outstanding differences with Britain, enabling trading links to be re-established. Under the terms of Pinckney's Treaty 1795 the US made territorial gains from Spain.
He declined a third term, and on giving up office, he made a famous farewell address, warning the country against entangling alliances and advising it to keep aloof from European quarrels.

I can't tell a lie, Pa; you know I can't tell a lie. I did cut it [a prized cherry tree] with my hatchet.

Purported remark of the young GEORGE WASHINGTON
in M L Weems *Life of George Washington* 10th ed ch 2 1962

Suggested reading

Alden, John *George Washington: A Biography* (1984)
Cunliffe, Marcus *George Washington: Man and Monument* (1958)
Emery, N *Washington* (1976)
Nettels, C P *George Washington and American Independence* (1951)

Wassermann August Paul von (1866–1925). German professor of medicine. In 1907 he discovered a diagnostic blood test for syphilis, known as the Wassermann reaction.

Waterhouse Alfred (1830–1905). English architect. He was a leading exponent of Victorian Neo-Gothic, typically using multi-coloured tiles and bricks. His works include the Natural History Museum, London, 1868.

Waterhouse Keith Spencer (1929–   ). English journalist, novelist, and dramatist. His second novel, *Billy Liar* 1959, a whimsical day in the life of a fantasy-prone undertaker's clerk, became a successful play and film. His play *Jeffrey Bernard Is Unwell* 1989 was based on the dissolute life of a *Spectator* columnist.

Waterhouse's Yorkshire working-class background and early job experience helped produce *Billy Liar*, which he adapted for the stage in collaboration with Willis Hall (1929–   ). They went on to write a long line of plays, musical revues, and films together; for example, the screenplays *Whistle Down the Wind* 1961 and *A Kind of Loving* 1962 (adapted from a novel by Stan Barstow). Waterhouse was a journalist on the *Daily Mirror* for many years. Further novels include *Jubb* 1963, on life in a new town; *Maggie Muggins* 1981, a study of urban female alcoholism; and *Unsweet Charity* 1992.

Waterston John James (1811–1883). Scottish physicist who first formulated the essential features of the kinetic theory of gases 1843–45. He also estimated the temperature of the Sun 1857.

Watson, James *American biologist James Watson who shared the Nobel Prize for Physiology or Medicine with Francis Crick and Maurice Wilkins in 1962. Watson and Crick determined the structure of the genetic material DNA at the Cavendish Laboratory in Cambridge, England. The characters and work underlying the discovery are described in Watson's book* The Double Helix. *(Image Select)*

Waterston was born and educated in Edinburgh. He moved to London 1833 to do surveying for the railways, and then took a job in the Hydrographers' Department of the Admiralty. In 1839 he went to India as teacher of the East India Company's cadets in Bombay, returning to Edinburgh 1857 to devote all his efforts to research. His work was repeatedly rejected or ignored, causing him to withdraw from the scientific community.

Waterston's first scientific paper, published when he was only 19, concerned a model which he proposed might explain gravitational force without the necessity for postulating an effect that operated at great distances.

In 1843, Waterston wrote a book on the nervous system in which he attempted to apply molecular theory to physiology. It included several fundamental features of the kinetic theory of gases, among them the idea that temperature and pressure are related to the motion of molecules. He formulated kinetic theory more fully in a paper submitted to the Royal Society in 1845, but this was turned down, delaying progress by about 15 years.

Waterston wrote other papers on sound, capillarity, latent heat, and various aspects of astronomy.

Waterton Charles (1782–1865). British naturalist who travelled extensively in South and North America 1804–24. In the UK, he was the first person to protest against pollution from industry, and created a nature reserve around his home in Yorkshire. Publications include *Wanderings in South America* 1825.

Watkins Gino (Henry George) (1907–1932). English polar explorer whose expeditions in Labrador and Greenland helped to open up an Arctic air route during the 1930s. He was drowned in a kayak accident while leading an expedition in Greenland.

Watling Thomas (born 1762). Convict and artist in Australia, born in Scotland. Transported for forgery, he arrived in Sydney in 1791 where he produced detailed paintings and drawings of the Aborigines, of the settlement, and of natural history. His *A Direct North General View of Sydney Cove* 1794 (Dixson Galleries, Sydney) is the first oil painting executed in Australia.

Watson James Dewey (1928–   ). US biologist whose research on the molecular structure of DNA and the genetic code, in collaboration with Francis Crick, earned him a shared Nobel prize in 1962. Based on earlier works, they were able to show that DNA formed a double helix of two spiral strands held together by base pairs. Crick and Watson published their work on the proposed structure of DNA in 1953, and explained how genetic information could be coded.

He initially specialized in viruses but shifted to molecular biology and in 1951 he went to the Cavendish Laboratory at Cambridge University, where he performed the work on DNA with Crick. In 1953 Watson returned to the USA. He became professor at Harvard 1961 and director of the Cold Spring Harbor Laboratory of Quantitative Biology 1968, and was head of the US government's Human Genome Project 1989–92.

Crick and Watson envisaged DNA replication occurring by a parting of the two strands of the double helix, each organic base thus exposed linking with a nucleotide (from the free nucleotides within a cell) bearing the complementary base. Thus two complete DNA molecules would eventually be formed by this step-by-step linking of nucleotides, with each of the new DNA molecules comprising one strand from the original DNA and one new strand.

Watson John Broadus (1878–1958). US psychologist, founder of behaviourism. He rejected introspection (observation by an individual of his or her own mental processes) and regarded psychology as the study of observable behaviour, within the scientific tradition.

Suggested reading

Cohen, David *J B Watson: The Founder of Behaviorism* (1979)
Watson, John B *Psychology from the Standpoint of a Behaviorist* (1919)

Watson Tom (Thomas Sturges) (1949–   ). US golfer who won the British Open five times (1975, 1977, 1980, 1982, 1983) and by 1990 was ranked third in career earnings in professional golf.

Watson, born in Kansas City, turned professional 1971 and has won more than 30 tournaments on the US Tour, including the Masters and US Open. In 1988 he succeeded Jack Nicklaus as the game's biggest money winner, but was overtaken by Tom Kite 1989.

Watson-Watt Robert Alexander (1892–1973). Scottish physicist who developed a forerunner of radar. He proposed in 1935 a method of radiolocation of aircraft – a key factor in the Allied victory over German aircraft in World War II. Knighted 1942.

Watson-Watt was born in Brechin, Angus, and educated at the University of St Andrews. He spent a long career in government service (1915–52).

Watson-Watt patented in 1919 a device concerned with radiolocation by means of short-wave radio waves. By 1935 he had made it possible to follow an aeroplane by the radio-wave reflections it sent back. By 1938, radar stations were in operation, and during the Battle of Britain in 1940 radar made it possible for the British to detect incoming German aircraft as easily by night as by day, and in all weathers including fog. Early in 1943 microwave aircraft-interceptor radars were operational, ending night-bombing raids on Britain.

The first radar sets specifically designed for airborne surface-vessel detection were flown in 1943. Before the USA joined the war, Watson-Watt went there to advise on the setting-up of radar systems.

Watt James (1736–1819). Scottish engineer who developed the steam engine in the 1760s. He made Thomas Newcomen's steam engine vastly more efficient by cooling the used steam in a condenser separate from the main cylinder. Steam engines incorporating governors, sun-and-planet gears, and other devices of his invention were successfully built by him in partnership with Matthew Boulton and were vital to the Industrial Revolution. Watt also devised the horsepower as a description of an engine's rate of working.

Between 1767 and 1774, he made his living as a canal surveyor. In 1775 Boulton and Watt went into partnership and manufactured Watt's engines at the Soho Foundry, near Birmingham. In 1782

Watt *Scottish engineer and inventor James Watt shown repairing a small working model of Newcomen's steam engine in his workship at Glasgow University. Watt noticed several defects in Newcomen's engine and built his own, which incorporated a separate condenser. Watt's improvements to the design increased the efficiency of the engine by a factor of three and provided a practical way of producing power for British industry during the Industrial Revolution. (Ann Ronan/Image Select)*

Watt improved his machine by making it drive on both the forward and backward strokes of the piston, and a sun-and-planet gear produced rotary motion. This highly adaptable engine was quickly adopted by cotton and woollen mills.

Watt also invented artistic instruments and a chemical copying process for documents.

Suggested reading
Dickinson, H W and Vowles, H P *James Watt and the Industrial Revolution* (1943)
Robinson, E H and Musson, James (eds) *James Watt and the Steam Revolution: A Documentary History* (1969)

Watteau (Jean) Antoine (1684–1721). French Rococo painter. Watteau was born in Valenciennes. At first inspired by Flemish genre painters, he produced tavern and military scenes. His early years in Paris, from 1702, introduced him to fashionable French paintings and in particular to decorative styles and theatrical design. He was also influenced by Giorgione and Rubens. He developed a new category of genre painting known as the *fête galante*: fanciful scenes depicting elegantly dressed young people engaged in outdoor entertainment. One of these pictures, *The Embarkation for Cythera* 1717 (Louvre, Paris), won him membership in the French Academy.

Suggested reading
Brookner, Anita *Watteau* (1967)
Posner, Donald *Antoine Watteau* (1984)
Vidal, Mary *Watteau's Painted Conversations* (1992)

Watts Alan Witson (1915–1973). British-born US philosopher. Educated in England, Watts was a longtime student of Eastern religions and published *The Spirit of Zen* 1936. He emigrated to the USA 1939, graduated from the Seabury-Weston Theological Seminary, and was ordained in the Episcopal Church 1944. Briefly serving as chaplain at Northwestern University, he moved to California and taught philosophy at the College of the Pacific 1951–57. As a popular lecturer and author, he became a spiritual leader of the 'beat generation' of the 1950s. His books include *The Way of Zen* 1957.

Watts George Frederick (1817–1904). English painter and sculptor. He painted allegorical, biblical, and classical subjects, investing his work with a solemn morality, as in *Hope* 1886 (Tate Gallery, London). Many of his portraits are in the National Portrait Gallery, London. As a sculptor he executed *Physical Energy* 1904 for Cecil Rhodes' memorial in Cape Town, South Africa; a replica is in Kensington Gardens, London. He was a forerunner of Symbolism.

He frequented the studio of the sculptor Behnes as a boy and studied in the Royal Academy Schools 1835. In 1842 he won the prize of £300 in the competition for wall-painting designs for Westminster, and went to Italy and met Lord and Lady Holland, with whom he stayed in Florence, and who became his patrons. The Renaissance pattern of patron and household genius was later repeated in his 30 years' stay at Little Holland House in Kensington with Mr and Mrs Thoby Prinsep. Insulated from the world, he worked on allegories, symbolic frescoes, and portraits of those he admired. In his portraits of eminent Victorians such as the *Morris* and *Tennyson* (National Portrait Gallery), idealism and reality were combined with distinguished result, while his portrayal of the young Ellen Terry, his first wife, has much beauty. He is better known for such cloudily philosophic works of the 1880s as *Hope* and *Love and Death* (Tate Gallery), while his *Mammon* shows the desire of his age to teach and uplift. The influence of the Venetians and of the Elgin Marbles is traceable in his style, but failings in colour and form too often give painful prominence to his didacticism and ill-defined thought. His equestrian statue *Physical Energy*, however, matches subject to style in a work of great originality.

His second wife had the gallery built at Compton, Surrey (near his house, 'Limnerslease'), where there is a permanent collection of his work.

Watts Isaac (1674–1748). English Nonconformist writer of hymns, including 'O God, our help in ages past'.

How doth the little busy bee / Improve each shining hour.
ISAAC WATTS
Divine Songs for Children, 'Against Idleness and Mischief' 1715

Watts-Dunton Walter Theodore (1832–1914). English writer. He was the author of *Aylwin* 1898, a novel of gypsy life, poems, and critical work. He was a close friend of the painter Rossetti, the writer Borrow, and the poet Swinburne, who shared his house at Putney for many years.

Waugh Evelyn Arthur St John (1903–1966). English novelist. His social satires include *Decline and Fall* 1928, *Vile Bodies* 1930, and *The Loved One* 1948. A Roman Catholic convert from 1930, he developed a serious concern with religious issues in *Brideshead Revisited* 1945. *The Ordeal of Gilbert Pinfold* 1957 is largely autobiographical.

Suggested reading
Bradbury, Malcolm *Evelyn Waugh* (1964)
Hastings, Selina *Evelyn Waugh: A Biography* (1994)
Lane, C W *Evelyn Waugh* (1981)
Pryce-Jones, D (ed) *Evelyn Waugh and His World* (1973)

Wavell Archibald Percival, 1st Earl Wavell (1883–1950). British field marshal in World War II. As commander in chief in the Middle East, he successfully defended Egypt against Italy July 1939 and successfully conducted the North African war against Italy 1940–41. He was transferred as commander in chief in India in July 1941, and became Allied Supreme Commander after Japan entered the war. He was unable to prevent Japanese advances in Malaya and Burma and Churchill became disillusioned with him. He was made viceroy of India 1943–47. KCB 1939, viscount 1943, earl 1947.

In the general judgement of Whitehall, the greatest administrator of his time, perhaps of any time in the country's history.
Lord Salter on JOHN ANDERSON, 1ST VISCOUNT WAVERLEY
in *Dictionary of National Biography*

Waverley John Anderson, 1st Viscount Waverley (1882–1958). British administrator. He organized civil defence for World War II, becoming home secretary and minister for home security in 1939. Anderson shelters, home outdoor air-raid shelters, were named after him. He was chancellor of the Exchequer 1943–45. KCB 1919, viscount 1952.

Wayne Anthony ('Mad Anthony') (1745–1796). American Revolutionary War officer and Indian fighter. He secured a treaty 1795 that made possible the settlement of Ohio and Indiana. He built Fort Wayne, Indiana, USA.

A surveyor and farmer, he was briefly active in politics before the Revolution. He assisted Benedict Arnold in his retreat from Quebec, held a variety of increasingly important commands, was with George Washington at Valley Forge 1777–78, took Stony Point, New York, and was then trapped by Cornwallis' superior force at Green Spring, Virginia, but escaped and served under General Greene in Georgia before retiring to farming and business interests. President Washington recalled him 1792 as a major general to command the Army of the West against the Indians.

Wayne John ('Duke'). Stage name of Marion Michael Morrison (1907–1979). US actor. He played the archetypal Western hero: plain-speaking, brave, and solitary. His films include *Stagecoach* 1939, *Red River* 1948, *She Wore a Yellow Ribbon* 1949, *The Searchers*

Any one who has been to an English public school will always feel comparatively at home in prison.
EVELYN WAUGH
Decline and Fall pt 3, ch 4 1928

Wayne, John *US film actor John Wayne in* The Man Who Shot Liberty Valance *1961. Wayne started his film career 1927, using the name Duke Morrison. He went on to make over 175 films.*

1956, *Rio Bravo* 1959, *The Man Who Shot Liberty Valance* 1962, and *True Grit* 1969 (Academy Award). He was active in conservative politics.

Wayne also appeared in many war films, such as *The Sands of Iwo Jima* 1945, *In Harm's Way* 1965, and *The Green Berets* 1968. His other films include *The Quiet Man* 1952, *The High and the Mighty* 1954, and *The Shootist* 1976, his last.

Suggested reading
Bishop, George *John Wayne* (1979)
Carpozi, George, Jr *John Wayne* (1979)
Zmijewsky, Boris and others *The Complete Films of John Wayne* (1983)
Zolotow, Maurice *Shooting Star* (1974)

Wazyk Adam (1905–). Polish writer who made his name with *Poem for Adults* 1955, a protest against the regime that preceded the fall of the Stalinists in 1956. In 1957 he resigned with others from the Communist Party, disappointed by First Secretary Gomulka's illiberalism. He also wrote novels and plays.

Weaver Sigourney (1949–). US actress. Tall, stately, and fine-boned, Weaver attained star status for her role as the resourceful heroine in Ridley Scott's *Alien* series of films 1979–91. She showed a talent for understated comedy in *Ghostbusters* 1984 and *Ghostbusters II* 1989. She played the anthropologist Dian Fossey in *Gorillas in the Mist* 1988. Her other notable films include *Working Girl* 1988 and *The Year of Living Dangerously* 1982.

Webb Aston (1849–1930). English architect. He was responsible for numerous public buildings at the turn of the century. His work in London includes the main section of the Victoria and Albert Museum 1891–1909, Admiralty Arch 1908–09, and the façade of Buckingham Palace 1912–13. Knighted 1904.

If I ever felt inclined to be timid as I was going into a room full of people, I would say to myself, 'You're the cleverest member of one of the cleverest families in the cleverest class of the cleverest nation in the world, why should you be frightened?'.

BEATRICE WEBB
quoted in Bertrand Russell *Autobiography*

Webb (Martha) Beatrice (born Potter) (1858–1943) and Sidney James, 1st Baron Passfield (1859–1947). English social reformers, writers, and founders of the London School of Economics (LSE) 1895. They were early members of the socialist Fabian Society, and were married in 1892. They argued for social insurance in their minority report (1909) of the Poor Law Commission, and wrote many influential books, including *The History of Trade Unionism* 1894, *English Local Government* 1906–29, and *Soviet Communism* 1935.

Sidney Webb was professor of public administration at the LSE 1912–27. He was a member of the Labour Party executive 1915–25, entered Parliament 1922, and was president of the Board of Trade 1924, dominions secretary 1929–30, and colonial secretary 1929–31. He became a baron 1929. Beatrice wrote *The Co-operative Movement in Great Britain* 1891, *My Apprenticeship* 1926, and *Our Partnership* 1948.

Suggested reading
MacKenzie, Jeanne *A Victorian Courtship: The Story of Beatrice Potter and Sidney Webb* (1979)
Muggeridge, Kitty and Adam, Ruth *Beatrice Webb: A Life, 1858–1943* (1967)
Seymour-Jones, Carole *Beatrice Webb: Woman of Conflicts* (1992)
Webb, Beatrice *Our Partnership* (memoirs) (1926, rep 1975)

Webb Mary Gladys (born Meredith) (1881–1927). English novelist. She wrote of country life and characters, for example in *Precious Bane* 1924, which became known through a recommendation by Stanley Baldwin.

Webb Philip Speakman (1831–1915). English architect. He was a leading figure (along with Richard Norman Shaw and Charles Voysey) of the Arts and Crafts movement, which was instrumental in the revival of English domestic architecture in the late 19th century. He mostly designed private houses, notably the Red House, Bexley Heath, Sussex, 1859, for William Morris. Other houses include Joldwyns, Surrey, 1873, Clouds, East Knoyle, Wiltshire, 1876–91, and Standen, East Grinstead, 1891–94.

Webber Andrew Lloyd. English composer of musicals: see ◊Lloyd Webber.

What love is to man, music is to the arts and mankind, for it is actually love itself, the purest, most ethereal language of the emotions.

CARL MARIA VON WEBER
Review of Hoffmann's *Undine* 1817

Weber Carl Maria Friedrich Ernst von (1786–1826). German composer. He established the Romantic school of opera with *Der Freischütz/The Marksman* 1821 and *Euryanthe* 1823. He was kapellmeister (chief conductor) at Breslau 1804–06, Prague 1813–16, and Dresden 1816. He died during a visit to London where he produced his opera *Oberon* 1826, written for the Covent Garden Theatre.

Weber Ernst Heinrich (1795–1878). German anatomist and physiologist. He applied hydrodynamics to study blood circulation, and formulated Weber's law, relating response to stimulus. Weber's law (also known as the Weber–Fechner law) states that sensation is proportional to the logarithm of the stimulus. It is the basis of the scales used to measure the loudness of sounds.

In 1825, with his brother Wilhelm Weber, he made the first experimental study of interference in sound.

Weber Heinrich (1842–1913). German mathematician whose chief work was in the fields of algebra and number theory. He demonstrated Norwegian mathematician Niels Abel's theorem in its most general form.

Weber was born and educated in Heidelberg, where he became professor 1869. He then taught at a number of institutions in Germany and Switzerland.

Weber proved German mathematician Leopold Kronecker's theorem that the absolute Abelian fields are cyclotomic; that is, that they are derived from the rational numbers by the adjunction of roots of unity.

Weber's work in such subjects as heat, electricity, and electrolytic dissociation was contained in his *Die partiellen Differentialgleichungen der mathematischen Physik* 1900–01, which was essentially a reworking of, and a commentary upon, a book of the same title based on lectures given by Bernhard Riemann and written by Karl Hattendorff. Weber's *Lehrbuch der Algebra* 1896 became a standard text.

Weber Max (1864–1920). German sociologist, one of the founders of modern sociology. He emphasized cultural and political factors as key influences on economic development and individual behaviour.

Weber argued for a scientific and value-free approach to research, yet highlighted the importance of meaning and consciousness in understanding social action. His ideas continue to stimulate thought on social stratification, power, organizations, law, and religion.

Key works include *The Protestant Ethic and the Spirit of Capitalism* 1902, *Economy and Society* 1922, *The Methodology of the Social Sciences* 1949, and *The Sociology of Religion* 1920.

Suggested reading
Bendix, R *Max Weber: An Intellectual Portrait* (1960)
Mitzman, A *The Iron Cage: An Historical Interpretation of Max Weber* (1969)
Weber, M S *Max Weber: A Biography* (1975)

Weber Max (1881–1961). Russian-born US painter and sculptor. Born in Russia, he emigrated to New York 1891, where he studied painting. He travelled through Europe 1905–09. Influenced by Parisian avant-garde painters of the Cubist and Futurist schools, he was a prominent figure in importing these styles to the USA and also created Futuristic sculpture.

Weber Wilhelm Eduard (1804–1891). German physicist who studied magnetism and electricity. Working with mathematician Karl Gauss, he made sensitive magnetometers to measure magnetic fields, and instruments to measure direct and alternating currents. He also built an electric telegraph. The SI unit of magnetic flux, the weber, is named after him.

Weber defined an electromagnetic unit for electric current which was applied to measurements of current made by the deflection of the magnetic needle of a galvanometer. In 1846, he developed the electrodynamometer, in which a current causes a coil suspended within another coil to turn when a current is passed through both. In 1852, Weber defined the absolute unit of electrical resistance.

Weber was born in Wittenberg, the brother of Ernst Weber, and studied at Halle. In 1831 he became professor at Göttingen; he lost this post after making a political protest 1837, but was reinstated 1849.

At Göttingen, he built a 3-km/2-mi telegraph to connect the physics laboratory with the astronomical observatory where Gauss worked, and this was the first practical telegraph to operate anywhere in the world. Gauss and Weber organized a network of observation stations 1836–41 to correlate measurements of terrestrial magnetism made around the world.

Weber put forward in 1871 the view that atoms contain positive charges that are surrounded by rotating negative particles and that the application of an electric potential to a conductor causes the negative particles to migrate from one atom to another. He also provided similar explanations of thermal conduction and thermoelectricity.

Doomed to a total failure in a deaf world of ignorance and indifference, he inexorably kept on cutting out his diamonds, his dazzling diamonds, the mines of which he knew to perfection.

Igor Stravinsky on WEBERN
quoted in Kilnoder *Anton Webern* 1968

Webern Anton Friedrich Wilhelm von (1883–1945). Austrian composer. He wrote spare, enigmatic miniatures combining a pastoral poetic with severe structural rigour. A Renaissance musical scholar, he became a pupil of Arnold Schoenberg, whose twelve-tone system he reinterpreted as abstract design in works such as the *Concerto for Nine Instruments* 1931–34 and the *Second Cantata* 1941–43. His constructivist aesthetic influenced the postwar generation of advanced composers. He was mistakenly shot during the Allied occupation of Austria.

Webster Daniel (1782–1852). US politician and orator. He sat in the US House of Representatives 1813–27 and the Senate 1827–41, 1845–50, at first as a Federalist and later as a Whig. He was secretary of state 1841–43 and 1850–52, and negotiated the Webster-Ashburton Treaty 1842, which fixed the Maine–Canada boundary. His 'seventh of March' speech in the Senate 1850 helped secure a compromise on the slavery issue. He argued that the Congress was powerless under the Constitution to interfere with slavery, and he maintained that the break-up of the Union would produce an even greater evil. He was born in Salisbury, New Hampshire.

Webern *The composer Anton Webern. One of the three composers of the Second Viennese School, Webern was artistically the most strict and concise of the group. Although he received very little recognition during his lifetime, he is acknowledged as having had an enormous impact on future composers.* (Image Select)

Is not old wine wholesomest, old pippins toothsomest, old wood burn brightest, old linen wash whitest? Old soldiers, sweethearts are surest, and old lovers are soundest.

JOHN WEBSTER
Westward Hoe II ii 1607

Webster John (c. 1580–c. 1625). English dramatist. He ranks after Shakespeare as the greatest tragedian of his time, and is the Jacobean whose plays are most frequently performed today. His two great plays *The White Devil* 1612 and *The Duchess of Malfi* 1614 are dark, violent tragedies obsessed with death and decay.

Webster Noah (1758–1843). US lexicographer whose books on grammar and spelling and *American Dictionary of the English Language* 1828 standardized US English. Webster learned 26 languages and began the scientific study of etymology. Following the American Revolution, he was prompted by patriotic sentiment to create schoolbooks that would impart that sentiment to young students. His *Blue-Backed Speller* sold nearly 100 million copies in a century. In 1833 he published a revision of the *Authorized Version of English Bible*.

Weddell James (1787–1834). British Antarctic explorer. In 1823, he reached 75°S latitude and 35°W longitude, in the Weddell Sea, which is named after him.

Wedderburn Joseph Henry Maclagan (1882–1948). Scottish mathematician who opened new lines of thought in the subject of mathematical fields and who had a deep influence on the development of modern algebra.

He taught in the USA at Princeton 1909–45, though during World War I he saw active duty in France as a soldier in the British army.

The first paper that Wedderburn published, 'Theorem on Finite Algebra' 1905, was a milestone in algebraic history. By introducing new methods, he showed that it was possible to arrive at a complete understanding of the structure of semi-simple algebras over any field.

From that foundation he went on to derive the two theorems to which his name has become attached. The first was contained in his paper 'On Hyper-Complex Numbers' 1907, in which he demonstrated that a simple algebra consists of matrices of a given degree with elements taken from a division of algebra.

The first Wedderburn theorem states that 'if the algebra is a finite division algebra (that is, that it has only a finite number of elements and always permits division by a non-zero element), then the multiplication law must be commutative, so that the algebra is actually a finite field'.

Wedderburn's second theorem states that a central-simple algebra is isomorphic to the algebra of all $n \times n$ algebras. He arrived at it by an investigation of skew fields with a finite number of elements.

His discovery that every field with a finite number of elements is commutative under multiplication led to a complete classification of all semi-simple algebras with a finite number of elements.

Wedekind Frank (1864–1918). German dramatist. He was a forerunner of Expressionism with *Frühlings Erwachen/The Awakening of Spring* 1891, and *Der Erdgeist/The Earth Spirit* 1895 and its sequel *Der Marquis von Keith. Die Büchse der Pandora/Pandora's Box* 1904 was the source for Berg's opera *Lulu.*

Wedgwood C(icely) V(eronica) (1910–   ). British historian. An authority on the 17th century, she has published studies of *Cromwell* 1939 and *The Trial of Charles I* 1964. DBE 1968, OM 1969.

[Her work is] elegant and undogmatic, history as a 'velvet study', as pleasing as edifying.

Ivan Roots on C V WEDGWOOD
in *Blackwell's Dictionary of Historians* 1988

Wedgwood Josiah (1730–1795). English pottery manufacturer. He set up business in Staffordshire in the early 1760s to produce his agateware as well as unglazed blue or green stoneware (jasper) decorated with white Neo-Classical designs, using pigments of his own invention.

Wedgwood was born in Burslem, Staffordshire, and worked in the family pottery. Eventually he set up in business on his own at the Ivy House Factory in Burslem, and there he perfected cream-colonial earthenware, which became known as queen's ware because of the interest and patronage of Queen Charlotte in 1765. In 1768 he expanded the company into the Brick House Bell Works Factory. He then built the Etruria Factory, using his engineering skills in the design of machinery and the high-temperature beehive-shaped kilns, which were more than 4 m/12 ft wide.

Suggested reading
Burton, Anthony *Josiah Wedgwood* (1976)
Kelly, Alison *The Story of Wedgwood* (1962)
Meteyard, Eliza *The Life of Josiah Wedgwood* (1865, rep 1970)
Reilly, Robin *Josiah Wedgwood, 1730–1795* (1992)
Wedgwood, Barbara Boyd and Wedgwood, Hensleigh *The Wedgwood Circle, 1730–1897* (1980)

Weems Mason Locke (1759–1825). American writer and cleric. His biography *The Life and Memorable Actions of George Washington*, published around 1800, contained the first published version of the 'cherry-tree' legend which was responsible for much of the Washington myth. He also wrote lives of Francis Marion 1809 and Benjamin Franklin 1815.

Born in Anne Arundel County, Maryland, USA, Weems studied for the ministry in England and was ordained in the Anglican church 1784. Returning to America, he served as a parish cleric until 1792. Thereafter he still insisted on being addressed as 'Parson Weems'. After becoming the sales agent of a Philadelphia publisher, Weems settled in Virginia 1795 and became an author.

Wegener Alfred Lothar (1880–1930). German meteorologist and geophysicist whose theory of continental drift, expounded in *Origin of Continents and Oceans* 1915, was originally known as 'Wegener's hypothesis'. His ideas can now be explained in terms of plate tectonics, the idea that the Earth's crust consists of a number of plates, all moving with respect to one another.

Wegener was born in Berlin and studied at Heidelberg, Innsbruck, and Berlin. From 1924 he was professor of meteorology and geophysics at Graz, Austria. He completed three expeditions to Greenland and died on a fourth.

Wegener supposed that a united supercontinent, Pangaea, had existed in the Mesozoic. This had developed numerous fractures and had drifted apart some 200 million years ago. During the Cretaceous, South America and Africa had largely been split, but not until the end of the Quaternary had North America and Europe finally separated; the same was true of the break between South America and Antarctica. Australia had been severed from Antarctica during the Eocene.

Wei Jingsheng (1951–). Chinese prodemocracy activist and essayist, imprisoned 1979–93 for attacking the Chinese communist system. He is regarded as one of China's most important political dissidents.

The son of a Communist Party official in Anhui province, Wei joined the Red Guards in the Cultural Revolution 1966. In 1978 he joined the Democracy Movement of reformist dissidents in Beijing and published essays critical of the government in the journal *Explorations*, which he cofounded. In 1979, he was arrested and sentenced to 15 years' imprisonment 'for handing military secrets to foreigners'. Within the six months following his early release Sept 1993, he was re-arrested twice and placed under interrogation by the Chinese authorities. He was re-arrested again Nov 1995 on the capital charge of trying to overthrow the government.

Weick Fred (1899–1993). US aeronautical engineer. His designs include the Erco Ercoupe 1936, remarkable for its safety and simplicity of design, and the Piper Cherokee in the 1950s, the first cheap

Wedgwood *English potter Josiah Wedgwood in a portrait by Joshua Reynolds (1782). Responsible for the development of several new wares, Wedgwood's most famous contribution was the production of unglazed blue jasper ware, which he decorated with Neo-Classical figures.*

all-metal aircraft, of which over 30,000 have since been built.

He developed the fully enclosed engine cowling that streamlined and reduced the drag of cumbersome radial aero engines, and a novel form of undercarriage that he called 'tricycle landing gear', which has since become the standard configuration. Impressed by the safety of the Erco Ercoupe, the US Civil Aeronautics Authority reduced the time for a trainee pilot to fly solo from eight to five hours when flying an Ercoupe.

Weick became interested in aviation as a child. On graduating from the University of Illinois as a mechanical engineer, he took a job converting surplus bombers into mail planes. He made his first solo flight 1923 – a 100-mile journey in bad weather – but it was not until 1939 that he bothered to obtain a pilot's licence. In 1923 he joined the Bureau of Aeronautics in Washington DC, working on propeller technology. He was invited to run the propeller research wind tunnel of the National Advisory Committee for Aeronautics (NACA), the forerunner of NASA. Whilst working for NACA, he developed the streamlined cowl and continued his pioneering work on propeller design. His interest in aircraft stability and control led him to develop a safe, simple aeroplane for private owners – the Weick W-1, which first flew 1934. In 1936 he was invited by the Engineering and Research Corporation (Erco) of Washington DC to develop a commercial version of the W-1, and the Ercoupe was born.

Weierstrass Karl Theodor Wilhelm (1815–1897). German mathematician who deepened and broadened the understanding of functions. He demonstrated in 1871 that there exist continuous functions in an interval which have derivatives nowhere in the interval.

Weierstrass was born in Ostenfelde, Westphalia, and trained as a teacher. From 1856 he was professor at the Royal Polytechnic School in Berlin as well as the university.

Weierstrass's breakthrough came with a paper 1854 that solved the inversion of hyperelliptic integrals. He did much to clarify basic concepts such as 'function', 'derivative', and 'maximum'. His development of the modern theory of functions was described in his *Abhandlungen aus der Funktionlehre* 1886, a text derived chiefly from his students' lecture notes. In the 1890s Weierstrass planned the publication of his life's work, again to be compiled from lecture notes. Two volumes were published before his death and five more appeared during the next three decades.

Weigel Helene (1900–1971). Austrian actress and director. She co-founded the Berliner Ensemble with her husband Berthold Brecht 1949 and took leading roles in productions of his plays, visiting London 1956 and 1965. She took over direction of the Ensemble after Brecht's death 1956.

Weil André (1906–). French mathematician who worked on number theory and group theory, and contributed to the generalization of algebraic geometry. He was a founder member of a secretive group that published mathematical papers under the pseudonym Nicolas Bourbaki.

Weil was born and educated in Paris, the brother of political writer Simone Weil. In 1930 he went to India for two years as professor at Aligarh Muslim University. Returning to France, he took up a similar post at Strasbourg University. In 1940 he emigrated, and was professor at the University of São Paolo, Brazil, 1945–47. He moved to the USA and the University of Chicago 1947–58, and then transferred to the Institute for Advanced Study at Princeton.

In 1929, Weil extended some work by Henri Poincaré; this resulted in the postulation of what is now called the Mordell–Weil theorem, which is closely connected to the theory of Diophantine equations.

Weil worked on quadratic forms with algebraic coefficients and extended Austrian mathematician Emil Artin's work on the theory of quadratic number fields. Weil's chief work was *Foundations of Algebraic Geometry* 1946.

Weil Simone (1909–1943). French writer who became a practising Catholic after a mystical experience in 1938. Apart from essays, her works (advocating political passivity) were posthumously published, including *Waiting for God* 1951, *The Need for Roots* 1952, and *Notebooks* 1956.

She worked for the Republicans in the Spanish Civil War, and during World War II worked briefly for the Free French leader General de Gaulle in London. She died in an English sanatorium.

Suggested reading
Cabaud, Jacques *Simone Weil* (trs 1965)
Coles, Robert *Simone Weil: A Modern Pilgrimage* (1987)
Pétrement, Simone *Simone Weil: A Life* (trs 1976)
Rees, Richard *Simone Weil: Sketch for a Portrait* (1966)

I write for today. I don't care about posterity.
KURT WEILL
quoted in David Ewen *American Composers* 1982

Weill Kurt Julian (1900–1950). German composer. He was a US citizen from 1943. He wrote chamber and orchestral music and collaborated with Bertolt Brecht on operas such as *Die Dreigroschenoper/The Threepenny Opera* 1928 and *Aufsteig und Fall der Stadt Mahagonny/The Rise and Fall of the City of Mahagonny* 1930, all attacking social corruption (*Mahagonny* caused a riot at its premiere in Leipzig). He tried to evolve a new form of music theatre, using subjects with a contemporary relevance and the simplest musical means. In 1935 he left Germany for the USA where he wrote a number of successful scores for Broadway, among them the antiwar musical *Johnny Johnson* 1936 (including the often covered 'September Song') and *Street Scene* 1947 based on an Elmer Rice play set in the Depression.

Suggested reading
Sanders, Ronald *The Days Grow Short* (1980)
Schebera, Jurgen *Kurt Weill: An Illustrated Life* (1995)

Weinberg Steven (1933–). US physicist who in 1967 demonstrated, together with Abdus Salam, that the weak nuclear force and the electromagnetic force (two of the fundamental forces of nature) are variations of a single underlying force, now called the electroweak force. Weinberg and Salam shared a Nobel prize in 1979.

Weinberg and Salam's theory involved the prediction of a new interaction, the neutral current (discovered in 1973), which required the presence of charm.

Weinberger Caspar Willard (1917–). US Republican politician. He served under presidents Nixon and Ford, and was Reagan's defence secretary 1981–87.

Weizmann Chaim Weizmann, Russian-born chemist and Zionist leader. He did scientific work for the UK in both world wars, and was head of the Hebrew University in Jerusalem.

Weir Peter Lindsay (1944–). Australian film director who has latterly worked in the USA. His films ranged from melodramas to comedies, but frequently are marked by an an atmospheric quality and often contain a strong spiritual element. His Australian films include *Picnic at Hanging Rock* 1975 and *Gallipoli* 1981. Among his American films are *Witness* 1985, *Dead Poets Society* 1989, the comedy *Green Card* 1990, and *Fearless* 1993.

Weiser (Johann) Conrad (1696–1760). American colonial public official in Berks County, Pennsylvania from 1729. Born in Germany, Weiser emigrated to America 1710, settling in New York's Hudson Valley. Weiser served as judge of Berks County 1752–60 and as colonel of the militia. Familiar with the language and customs of the local Iroquois Indians, he was frequently used as an official interpreter in government dealings with them. Owing to his efforts, peace conferences were held in Philadelphia in 1731 and 1736.

Weismann August Friedrich Leopold (1834–1914). German biologist, one of the founders of genetics. He postulated that every living organism contains a special hereditary substance, the 'germ plasm', and in 1892 he proposed that changes to the body do not in turn cause an alteration of the genetic material.

This 'central dogma' of biology remains of vital importance to biologists supporting the Darwinian theory of evolution. If the genetic material can be altered only by chance mutation and recombination, then the Lamarckian view that acquired bodily changes can subsequently be inherited becomes obsolete.

From 1863 he taught at Freiburg; persuading the university to build a zoological institute and museum, he became its director. Failing eyesight forced him to turn from microscopy to theoretical work in the 1860s.

Weismann realized that the germ plasm controls the development of every part of the organism and is transmitted from one generation to the next in an unbroken line of descent. Since repeated mixing of the germ plasm at fertilization would lead to a progressive increase in the amount of hereditary material, he predicted that there must be a type of nuclear division.

Weissmuller Johnny (Peter John) (1904–1984). US film actor. Formerly an Olympic swimmer, he played Tarzan in a long-running series of films for MGM and RKO including *Tarzan the Ape Man*

1932, *Tarzan and His Mate* 1934, and *Tarzan and the Mermaids* 1948. He later starred in the *Jungle Jim* series of B-movies.

Me Tarzan, you Jane.

JOHNNY WEISSMULLER
in *Photoplay Magazine* June 1932 (the words did not occur in the film script of *Tarzan, the Ape Man*)

Weizmann Chaim Azriel (1874–1952). Zionist leader, the first president of Israel (1948–52), and a chemist. He conducted the negotiations leading up to the Balfour Declaration 1924, by which Britain declared its support for an independent Jewish state.

Born in Russia, he became a naturalized British subject, and as director of the Admiralty laboratories 1916–19 discovered a process for manufacturing acetone, a solvent. He became head of the Hebrew University in Jerusalem, then in 1948 became the first president of the new republic of Israel.

Suggested reading
Goodman, Paul (ed) *Chaim Weizmann: A Tribute* (1959)
Litvinoff, Barnet *Weizmann: Last of the Patriarchs* (1976)
Weizmann, Chaim *Trial and Error* (autobiography) (1949)

Weizsäcker Carl Friedrich von (1912–). German theoretical physicist who investigated the way in which energy is generated in the cores of stars. He also developed a theory that planetary systems were formed as a natural by-product of stellar evolution, condensing from vortices of gas.

He was professor at Strasbourg 1942–44. During World War II, he was a member of the research team investigating the feasibility of constructing nuclear weapons and harnessing nuclear energy, although he did not want his team to develop a weapon for the Nazi government. In 1946 he became director of a department in the Max Planck Institute of Physics in Göttingen. He was professor of philosophy at Hamburg 1957–69, and in 1970 he became a director of the Max Planck Institute.

In 1938, Weizsäcker and German-born physicist Hans Bethe independently proposed the same theory of stellar evolution, which accounted both for the very high temperatures in stellar cores and for the production of ionizing and particulate radiation by stars. They proposed that hydrogen atoms fused to form helium via a proton–proton chain reaction.

Weizsäcker Richard, Baron von (1920–). German Christian Democrat politician, president 1984–94. He began his career as a lawyer and was also active in the German Protestant church and in Christian Democratic Union party politics. He was elected to the West German Bundestag (parliament) 1969 and served as mayor of West Berlin from 1981, before being elected federal president 1984.

Welch (Maurice) Denton (1915–1948). English writer and artist. His works include the novel *In Youth is Pleasure* 1944 and the autobiographical *A Voice Through a Cloud* 1950.

Being a sex symbol was rather like being a convict.

RAQUEL WELCH
quoted in *Observer* 25 Feb 1979

Welch Raquel. Stage name of Raquel Tejada (1940–). US actress. She was a sex symbol of the 1960s in such films as *One Million Years BC* 1966, *Myra Breckinridge* 1970, and *The Three Musketeers* 1973.

Welch Robert Henry Winborne, Jr (1899–1985). US anticommunist crusader and business executive. Born in Chowan County, North Carolina, USA, Welch was educated at the University of North Carolina and joined the family candy business in Boston 1922. Over the years, he supported conservative political causes and by the 1950s had become an outspoken anticommunist. He founded the extreme right-wing John Birch Society 1958 in memory of the American Baptist missionary. A supporter of the losing Republican presidential candidate Barry Goldwater 1964, Welch

later became increasingly venomous in his accusations against supposed communist agents and sympathizers.

Weldon Fay (1931–). English novelist and dramatist. Her work deals with feminist themes, often in an ironic or comic manner. Novels include *The Fat Woman's Joke* 1967, *Female Friends* 1975, *Remember Me* 1976, *Puffball* 1980, *The Life and Loves of a She-Devil* 1984 (made into a film with Meryl Streep 1990), *The Hearts and Lives of Men* 1987, and *Splitting* 1995. She has also written plays for the stage, radio, and television.

I don't believe in happiness: why should we expect to be happy? In such a world as this, depression is rational, rage reasonable.

FAY WELDON
Interview in *Observer* 16 April 1995

Welensky Roy (originally Roland) (1907–1991). Rhodesian politician. He was instrumental in the creation 1953 of the Central African Federation, comprising Northern Rhodesia (now Zambia), Southern Rhodesia (now Zimbabwe), and Nyasaland (now Malawi), and was prime minister 1956–63, when the federation was disbanded. His Southern Rhodesian Federal Party was defeated by Ian Smith's Rhodesian Front in 1964. In 1965, following Smith's Rhodesian unilateral declaration of Southern Rhodesian independence from Britain, Welensky left politics. Knighted 1953.

Welhaven Johan Sebastian Cammermeyer (1807–1873). Norwegian poet. He was professor of philosophy at Christiania (now Oslo) 1839–68. A supporter of the Dano-Norwegian culture, he is considered one of the greatest Norwegian masters of poetic form. His works include the satiric *Norges Damring/The Dawn of Norway* 1834.

Welles (George) Orson (1915–1985). US actor and film and theatre director. His first film was *Citizen Kane* 1941, which he produced, directed, and starred in. Using innovative lighting, camera angles and movements, it is a landmark in the history of cinema, yet

Welles, Orson *Orson Welles as Harry Lime in* The Third Man *1949. By his mid-twenties Welles had established himself as an outstanding director, writer, and actor with his first film* Citizen Kane, *an influential film widely accepted as a classic. As an actor he appeared most memorably – though briefly – in Carol Reed's* The Third Man.

Wellington *Portrait of Arthur Wellesley, British soldier and statesman. He was created Duke of Wellington as part of the honours for his victory over Napoleon in the Peninsular Wars. He was nicknamed the 'Iron Duke' by his troops for his notoriously harsh discipline. (Image Select)*

he subsequently directed very few films in Hollywood, and worked mainly in Europe. His performances as an actor include the character of Harry Lime in *The Third Man* 1949.

In 1937 he founded the Mercury Theater, New York, with John Houseman, where their repertory productions included a modern-dress version of *Julius Caesar*. Welles' realistic radio broadcast of H G Wells' *The War of the Worlds* 1938 caused panic and fear of Martian invasion in the USA. His films include *The Magnificent Ambersons* 1942, *The Lady from Shanghai* 1948 with his wife Rita Hayworth, *Touch of Evil* 1958, and *Chimes at Midnight* 1966, a Shakespeare adaptation.

Suggested reading
Bessy, Maurice *Orson Welles* (1971)
Cowie, Peter *The Cinema of Orson Welles* (1978)
Leaming, Barbara *Orson Welles: A Biography* (1985)

[It is not true that] there was a cabal preventing Orson [Welles] making more films. He simply never fulfilled himself after that magnificent start. His own fault – lack of self-discipline.

Robert Wise on ORSON WELLES
Paris Passion Dec 1989

Welles Gideon (1802–1878). US politician, one of the founders of the Republican Party 1854. Born in Glastonbury, Connecticut, USA, and educated at Norwich University, Welles served as editor of the *Hartford Times* 1826–36. Originally a Democrat he served in the state legislature 1827–35 and held other state and federal offices before co-founding the Republican Party. Welles was appointed secretary of the navy by President Lincoln 1861 and in that position supervised the expansion of the Union naval forces and advocated the development of ironclads (wooden, iron-plated warships). An opponent of President Grant, he joined the Liberal Republicans 1872.

Wellesley family name of dukes of ◊Wellington; seated at Stratfield Saye, Berkshire, England.

Wellesley Richard Colley, Marquess Wellesley (1760–1842). British administrator; brother of the 1st Duke of Wellington. He was governor-general of India 1798–1805, and by his victories over the Marathas of W India greatly extended the territory under British rule. He was foreign secretary 1809–12, and lord lieutenant of Ireland 1821–28 and 1833–34. Baron 1797, marquess 1799.

Wellesz Egon Joseph (1885–1974). Austrian-born British composer and musicologist. He taught at Vienna University 1913–38, specializing in the history of Byzantine, Renaissance, and modern music. He moved to England 1938 and lectured at Oxford from 1943. His compositions include operas such as *Alkestis* 1924; symphonies, notably the Fifth 1957; ballet music; and a series of string quartets.

You must build your House of Parliament upon the river: so ... that the populace cannot exact their demands by sitting down around you.

ARTHUR WELLESLEY, 1ST DUKE OF WELLINGTON
quoted in Sir William Fraser *Words on Wellington*,
on the rebuilding of Parliament after the fire of 1834

Wellington Arthur Wellesley, 1st Duke of Wellington (1769–1852). British soldier and Tory politician. As commander in the Peninsular War, he expelled the French from Spain 1814. He defeated Napoleon Bonaparte at Quatre-Bras and Waterloo 1815, and was a member of the Congress of Vienna. As prime minister 1828–30, he was forced to concede Roman Catholic emancipation. KB 1804, viscount 1809, earl 1812, marquess 1812, duke 1814.

Wellington was born in Ireland, the son of an Irish peer, and sat for a time in the Irish parliament. He was knighted for his army service in India and became a national hero with his victories of 1808–14 in the Peninsular War and as general of the allies against Napoleon. At the Congress of Vienna he opposed the dismemberment of France and supported restoration of the Bourbons. As prime minister he modified the Corn Laws but became unpopular for his opposition to parliamentary reform and his lack of opposition to Catholic emancipation. He was foreign secretary 1834–35 and a member of the cabinet 1841–46. He held the office of commander in chief of the forces at various times from 1827 and for life from 1842. His home was Apsley House in London.

Suggested reading
Longford, E *Wellington: The Years of the Sword* (1969)
Longford, E *Wellington: The Pillar of State* (1972)
Weller, J *Wellington at Waterloo* (1967)

Human history becomes more and more a race between education and catastrophe.

H G WELLS
Outline of History 1920

Wells H(erbert) G(eorge) (1866–1946). English writer. He is best remembered for his 'scientific romances' such as *The Time Machine* 1895 and *The War of the Worlds* 1898. His later novels had an anti-establishment, anti-conventional humour remarkable in its day, for example *Kipps* 1905 and *Tono-Bungay* 1909. His many other books include *Outline of History* 1920 and *The Shape of Things to Come* 1933, a number of his prophecies from which have since been fulfilled. He also wrote many short stories.

Suggested reading
Coren, M *The Invisible Man: The Life and Liberties of H G Wells* (1993)
Dickson, L *H G Wells: His Turbulent Life and Times* (1969)
Mackenzie, N and J *The Time Traveller* (1973)
West, A *Aspects of a Life* (1984)
Wells, H G *Experiment in Autobiography* (1934)

Wells Horace (1815–1848). US dentist who discovered nitrous oxide anaesthesia and, in 1844, was the first to use the gas in dentistry.

Wells was born in Hartford, Vermont. He set up a dental practice in Hartford, Connecticut, in partnership with William Morton, who later pioneered the use of ether as an anaesthetic. In 1844, while watching an exhibition of the effects of laughing gas (nitrous oxide) staged by a travelling show, Wells observed that the gas induced anaesthesia. He tried it first on himself and then used it to perform tooth extractions on his patients. In 1845 Wells went to Boston where, with the help of Morton (then no longer his partner) and others, he arranged to give a demonstration at the Massachusetts General Hospital. However, the patient cried out and, although the patient later claimed to have felt no pain, the audience believed that the demonstration had failed.

After this, Wells gave up his dental practice and became a travelling sales representative, selling canaries and then showerbaths in Connecticut. Once Morton had given a successful demonstration of ether anaesthesia, Wells went to Paris 1847 to try to establish his priority in using anaesthesia. At about this time he also began experimenting on himself with nitrous oxide, ether, and various other intoxicating chemicals; as a result he became addicted to chloroform. He committed suicide in prison.

Wells Ida Bell (1862–1931). US journalist and political activist. Born in Holly Springs, Mississippi, USA, Wells was educated in a segregated school and became a teacher in Memphis, Tennessee. Losing her job in 1891 as the result of a suit she had filed against state segregation laws, she began a career of political activism after moving to New York City. She later married and settled in Chicago 1895. She joined the staff of *New York Age* 1891 and embarked on extensive lecture tours. She served as secretary of the National Afro-American Council 1898–1902 and as a Chicago probation officer 1913–16.

Wells Mary Esther (1943–1992). US pop and rhythm-and-blues singer, one of Motown Records' first stars. She had a number-one hit with 'My Guy' 1964, written and produced, like most of her material, by Smokey Robinson.

Wells began singing in school and in church in her native Detroit, Michigan, and auditioned for Berry Gordy, Motown's founder, in 1961 with her own song 'Bye Bye Baby', which became an R&B hit. She made a significant contribution to the early success of the company, backed by the production and songwriting skills of Robinson on clever midtempo numbers like 'The One Who Really Loves You', 'You Beat Me to the Punch', 'Two Lovers' (all hits 1962), and 'Laughing Boy' 1963. But after 'My Guy', as she turned 21, she left Motown, and a legal battle ensued over her contract. Her unrealistic hopes of becoming a film star were crushed, she never again found the same chart success or even a label where she could settle, and she died in poverty.

Welsbach Carl Auer, Baron von (1858–1929). Austrian chemist and engineer who discovered two rare-earth elements and invented the incandescent gas mantle and a lighter flint.

He showed that didymium, previously thought to be an element, actually consisted of two very similar but different elements: praseodymium and neodymium. He also found that another rare earth element, cerium, added as its nitrate salt to a cylindrical fabric impregnated with thorium nitrate, produced a fragile mantle that glowed with white incandescence when heated in a gas flame. The 'Welsbach mantle' was patented 1885.

Most lighter flints consist of Welsbach's invention *Mitschmetall*, a pyrophoric mixture containing about 50% cerium, 25% lanthanum, 15% neodymium, and 10% other rare metals and iron. When it is struck or scraped, it produces hot metal sparks. *Mitschmetall* is also used as a deoxidizer in vacuum tubes and as an alloying agent for magnesium.

Welty Eudora Alice (1909–   ). US novelist and short-story writer. Her works reflect life in the American South and are notable for their creation of character and accurate rendition of local dialect. Her novels include *Delta Wedding* 1946, *Losing Battles* 1970, and *The Optimist's Daughter* 1972. *The Collected Stories of Eudora Welty* appeared in 1982. The autobiographical work *One Writer's Beginnings* 1984 is a warm recounting of the people, places, and incidents that influenced Welty's work.

Suggested reading
Evans, Elizabeth *Eudora Welty* (1981)
Kreyling, Michael *Eudora Welty's Achievement of Order* (1980)
Welty, Eudora *One Writer's Beginnings* (1984)

Wenceslas, St (c. 907–929). Duke of Bohemia who attempted to Christianize his people and was murdered by his brother. He is patron saint of the Czech Republic and the 'good King Wenceslas' of a popular carol. Feast day 28 Sept.

Wenner-Gren Axel Leonard (1881–1961). Swedish industrialist who founded the Electrolux Company 1921, manufacturing electrical appliances, and developed a monorail system.

Wenner-Gren was born in Uddevalla, educated in Germany, and began his career working for the Swedish Electric Lamp Company, where he eventually became a majority shareholder. In 1921 he founded the Electrolux Company to manufacture vacuum cleaners and, later, refrigerators. He then acquired one of country's largest wood-pulp mills and the Bofors munition works. From the profits, he donated a large sum for the foundation of an institute for the development of scientific research in Sweden, the Wenner-Gren Foundation for Nordic Co-operation and Research.

Wenner-Gren's monorail, the Alweg line, consisted of a concrete beam carried on concrete supports. The cars straddled the beam on rubber-tyred wheels, and there were also horizontal wheels in two rows on each side of the beam. The system was used, for example, for the 13.3-km/8.3-mi line in Japan from Tokyo to Haneda Airport.

Democracy he disclaimed and detested as based on an utterly false theory ... that of human equality.

A P Martin on WILLIAM CHARLES WENTWORTH
in *Dictionary of National Biography*

Wentworth William Charles (1793–1872). Australian politician, newspaper publisher, and explorer, who was a member of the expedition which made the first successful crossing of the Blue Mountains, New South Wales, in 1813.

In 1824 he began to publish, without government permission, the outspoken newspaper the *Australian* which became a political mouthpiece in his campaign for self-government and for trial by jury in New South Wales. The Legislative Council which came into being in 1842 was largely as he had proposed, and he took his place on it as an elected member.

In 1855 he was in Britain to steer the New South Wales constitution through Parliament, and campaigned for Australian federalism and self-government. He was the son of D'Arcy Wentworth (c. 1762–1827), surgeon of the penal settlement on Norfolk Island. He settled in Britain in 1862. A town and shire in SW New South Wales and a waterfall in the Blue Mountains are named after him.

Werfel Franz (1890–1945). Austrian poet, dramatist, and novelist. He was a leading Expressionist. His works include the poem 'Der Weltfreund der Gerichtstag'/'The Day of Judgment' 1919; the plays *Juarez und Maximilian* 1924 and *Das Reich Gottes in Böhmen*/*The Kingdom of God in Bohemia* 1930; and the novels *Verdi* 1924 and *Das Lied von Bernadette*/*The Song of Bernadette* 1941.

Born in Prague, he lived in Germany, Austria, and France, and in 1940 escaped from a French concentration camp to the USA, where he died. In 1929 he married Alma Mahler, daughter of the composer Gustav Mahler.

Wergeland Henrik Arnold (1808–1845). Norwegian lyric poet. He was a leader of the Norwegian revival and is known for his epic *Skabelsen, Mennesket, og Messias*/*Creation, Humanity, and Messiah* 1830.

Werner Abraham Gottlob (1749–1817). German geologist, one of the first to classify minerals systematically. He also developed the later discarded theory of neptunism – that the Earth was initially covered by water, with every mineral in suspension; as the water receded, layers of rocks 'crystallized'.

Although both forms of aphasia result from brain damage, Wernicke found that the locus of the damage differed, sensory aphasia being induced by lesions to the left temporal lobe, motor aphasia by lesions to the left posterior frontal lobe. He used the differential clinical features of the two aphasias to formulate a general theory of the neural bases of language.

Wernicke also described a form of encephalopathy induced by thiamine deficiency which bears his name.

Wertheimer Max (1880–1943). Czech-born psychologist and founder, with Koffka and Kohler, of gestalt psychology. While travelling on a train 1910 he saw that a light flashing rapidly from two different positions seemed to be one light in motion. This type of perception became the basis for his gestalt concept.

Wesker, unusually for a British playwright, had a very overt, idealist-socialist 'message'.

Arthur Marwick on ARNOLD WESKER in *British Society since 1945* 1982

Wesker Arnold (1932–). English dramatist. His socialist beliefs were reflected in the successful trilogy *Chicken Soup with Barley, Roots*, and *I'm Talking About Jerusalem* 1958–60. He established a catchphrase with *Chips with Everything* 1962. His autobiography, *As Much as I Dare* was published 1994.

In 1961, Wesker tried unsuccessfully to establish a working-class theatre with trade-union backing at the Round House in London. Later plays include *The Merchant* 1978 and *Lady Othello* 1987.

Wesley Charles (1707–1788). English Methodist, brother of John Wesley and one of the original Methodists at Oxford. He became a principal preacher and theologian of the Wesleyan Methodists, and wrote some 6,500 hymns.

Beware you be not swallowed up in books! An ounce of love is worth a pound of knowledge.

JOHN WESLEY
quoted in R Southey *Life of Wesley* ch 16 1820

Wesley John (1703–1791). English founder of Methodism. When the pulpits of the Church of England were closed to him and his followers, he took the gospel to the people. For 50 years he rode about the country on horseback, preaching daily, largely in the open air. His sermons became the doctrinal standard of the Wesleyan Methodist Church.

He was born at Epworth, Lincolnshire, where his father was the rector, and went to Oxford University together with his brother Charles, where their circle was nicknamed Methodists because of their religious observances. He was ordained in the Church of England 1728 and returned to his Oxford college 1729 as a tutor. In 1735 he went to Georgia, USA, as a missionary. On his return he experienced 'conversion' 1738, and from being rigidly High Church developed into an ardent Evangelical. His *Journal* gives an intimate picture of the man and his work.

Suggested reading
Ayling, Stanley *John Wesley* (1979)
Pudney, John *John Wesley and his World* (1978)
Tuttle, Robert *John Wesley: His Life and Work* (1978)

Wesley Samuel (1776–1837). English organist and composer. Son of the well known composer of hymns, Charles Wesley, he was regarded as the best organist of his day. In 1787 a fall left him with a recurrent illness, ending his career. He wrote many masses, motets, anthems (including *In exitu Israel*), and also secular music.

West Benjamin (1738–1820). American Neo-Classical painter. He was active in London from 1763. He enjoyed the patronage of George III for many years and was a noted history painter. His *The Death of General Wolfe* 1770 (National Gallery, Ottawa) began a vogue for

Wesker *The English playwright Arnold Wesker. His early plays, based largely on his own experiences of growing up in London's East End, helped to bring social realism ('kitchen sink' drama) to British theatre in the late 1950s and 1960s.*

Werner was born in Silesia and studied at the Mining School at Freiberg, Saxony, and the University of Leipzig. From 1775 he taught at the Freiberg Akademie.

Werner's geology was particularly important for establishing a physically based stratigraphy, grounded on precise mineralogical knowledge. He linked the order of the strata to the history of the Earth, and related studies of mineralogy and strata.

Werner Alfred (1866–1919). French-born Swiss chemist. He was awarded a Nobel prize in 1913 for his work on valency theory, which gave rise to the concept of coordinate bonds and coordination compounds.

Werner demonstrated that different three-dimensional arrangements of atoms in inorganic compounds gives rise to optical isomerism (the rotation of polarized light in opposite directions by molecules that contain the same atoms but are mirror images of each other).

Werner was born in Mulhouse, Alsace, and studied in Switzerland at the Zürich Polytechnic, becoming professor there 1895.

In addition to ionic and covalent bonds, Werner proposed the existence of a set of coordination bonds resulting from an attractive force from the centre of an atom acting uniformly in all directions. The number of groups, or ligands, that can thus be bonded to the central atom depends on its coordination number and determines the structure (geometry) of the resulting molecules. Neutral ligands (such as ammonia and water) leave the central atom's ionic charge unchanged; ionic ligands (such as chloride or cyanide ion) alter the central charge accordingly.

Wernicke Carl (1848–1905). German neurologist and psychiatrist. He is known for his study of aphasia. In *The Aphasic Syndrome* 1874, he described what later became known as sensory aphasia (that is, defects in, or loss of, speech and expression) as distinct from motor aphasia, first described by French surgeon Paul Pierre Broca (1824–1880).

painting recent historical events in contemporary costume. He became president of the Royal Academy, London, 1792.

Suggested reading
Alberts, Robert *Benjamin West* (1978)
Dillenberger, John *Benjamin West* (1977)

Give a man a free hand and he'll try to put it all over you.

MAE WEST
as Frisco Doll in the film *Klondike Annie* 1936

West Mae (1892–1980). US vaudeville, stage, and film actress. She wrote her own dialogue, setting herself up as a provocative sex symbol and the mistress of verbal innuendo. She appeared on Broadway in *Sex* 1926, *Drag* 1927, and *Diamond Lil* 1928, which was the basis of the film (with Cary Grant) *She Done Him Wrong* 1933. Her other films include *I'm No Angel* 1933, *My Little Chickadee* 1940 (with W C Fields), *Myra Breckinridge* 1969, and *Sextette* 1977. Both her plays and her films led to legal battles over censorship.

Two of her often quoted lines are 'It's better to be looked over than to be overlooked', and 'Beulah, peel me a grape'. Her autobiography, *Goodness Had Nothing to Do with It*, was published 1959. The 'Mae West', a naval inflatable life-jacket, was affectionately named after her.

West Morris Langlo (1916–   ). Australian novelist. An abandoned vocation with the Christian Brothers and experience as secretary to a former Australian prime minister and as Vatican correspondent for the *Daily Mail* contributed to the recurring themes of Catholicism in crisis, political power, and moral dilemma in his novels. He first attracted international attention with the award-winning *Devil's Advocate* 1959, filmed 1977.

Later novels include *The Shoes of the Fisherman* 1963, about a fictional pope, *The Clowns of God* 1981, and *The World is Made of Glass* 1983, an imaginative reconstruction of the psychological and moral ordeal of one of Jung's female patients. *Moon in my Pocket* 1945 is West's semi-autobiographical account of his disillusionment with the Catholic church. He has also written plays.

West Nathanael. Pen name of Nathan Wallenstein Weinstein (1903–1940). US writer. He is noted as an idiosyncratic black-humour parodist. His surrealist-influenced novels capture the absurdity and extremity of American life and the dark side of the American Dream. His most powerful novel, *The Day of the Locust* 1939, is a vivid exploration of the apocalyptic violence given release by the fantasies created by Hollywood, where West had been a screenwriter.

His other work consisted of *The Dream Life of Balso Snell* 1931, a surreal comedy written in Paris; *Miss Lonelyhearts* 1933, a black farce about a newspaper agony columnist who feels the misfortunes of his correspondents; and a *A Cool Million* 1934, which satirizes the rags-to-riches dream of success. West and his wife died in a car accident.

There is no such thing as conversation. It is an illusion. There are intersecting monologues, that is all.

REBECCA WEST
There Is No Conversation, 'The Harsh Voice' 1 1921

West Rebecca. Pen name of Cicily Isabel Fairfield (1892–1983). Irish journalist and novelist, an active feminist from 1911. *The Meaning of Treason* 1959 deals with the spies Burgess and Maclean. Her novels have political themes and include *The Fountain Overflows* 1956 and *The Birds Fall Down* 1966. DBE 1959.

Wester-Wemyss Rosslyn Erskine Wemyss, 1st Baron (1864–1933). (more commonly known as Sir Rosslyn Wemyss) British admiral. He commanded the naval squadron at Gallipoli 1916 and provided naval support for the subsequent evacuation. He became First Sea Lord 1917, a post he held until 1919 when he was

West, Mae *US film and vaudeville actress Mae West who wrote and delivered some of the most often quoted lines in film history. She specialized in glamorous roles, made memorable by her languid and suggestive delivery of the dialogue.*

raised to the peerage. He became admiral of the fleet 1920. KCB 1916, baron 1919.

Westgarth William (1815–1889). Scottish-born merchant, politician, and historian in Australia, prominent in the development of Victoria where he lived 1840–57. He published several essays, pamphlets, and books including *The Colony of Victoria* 1864 and *Half a Century of Australasian Progress* 1889.

Westinghouse George (1846–1914). US inventor and founder of the Westinghouse Corporation 1886. He patented a powerful air brake for trains 1869, which allowed trains to run more safely with greater loads at higher speeds. In the 1880s he turned his attention to the generation of electricity. Unlike Thomas Edison, Westinghouse introduced alternating current (AC) into his power stations.

Westinghouse was born in Central Bridge, New York, and ran away from school at 15 to fight in the Civil War. In 1865 he took out the first of more than 400 patents. He formed various companies to manufacture his inventions, several based in Pittsburgh and nearby in Turtle Creek Valley, where in 1889 Westinghouse built a model town for his workers. During 1907–08 a series of financial crises and takeovers caused him to lose control of the Westinghouse Industries.

Westinghouse helped to standardize railway components, including the development of a completely new signalling system. He also developed a system of gas mains. In the 1880s Westinghouse got his engineers to design equipment suitable for a new high-tension (voltage) AC system. He also secured the services of Croatian physicist Nikola Tesla. In 1895 the Westinghouse Electric Company harnessed Niagara Falls to generate electricity for the lights and trams of the nearby town of Buffalo.

Resentful that AC current was chosen as the standard for domestic electricity supply, Edison, who supported DC current transmission, coined the term 'Westinghoused' to describe the fate of someone who had been executed by electric chair.

Westmacott Richard (1775–1856). English Neo-Classical sculptor. He studied under Antonio Canova in Rome and was elected to the Royal Academy, London 1811, becoming a professor there 1827–54. His works include monuments in Westminster Abbey and in St Paul's Cathedral, and the *Achilles* statue in Hyde Park, all in London. Knighted 1837.

Westmoreland William Childs (1914–). US military leader who served as commander of US forces in Vietnam 1964–68. He was an aggressive advocate of expanded US military involvement there.

Born in Spartanburg County, South Carolina, USA, Westmoreland was a 1936 graduate of West Point military academy. He served in various administrative capacities at the Pentagon 1953–58. In Vietnam 1963–68, he ended his active military career as army Chief of Staff 1968–72.

Weston Brett (1911–1993). US photographer, whose main subjects were the American landscape and epic natural phenomena. During the Depression of the 1930s he made a living as a portrait photographer and then worked as a government photographer, a movie cameraman and a truck driver before joining the US Signal Corps in World War II. He returned to photography after the war, firstly in New York and then touring the USA, which the award of a Guggenheim fellowship enabled him to do. Unlike many post-war photographers, he had no interest in politics or social ills, his images being mostly of landscapes and abstracts of nature. His work is to be found in many US museums and other collections. His published portfolios include *San Francisco* 1938, *Japan* 1970, *Europe* 1973, and *Portraits of My Father* 1976. He was the son of Edward Weston.

Weston Edward (1886–1958). US photographer. A founding member of the 'f/64' group (after the smallest lens opening), a school of photography advocating sharp definition. He is noted for the technical mastery, composition, and clarity in his California landscapes, clouds, gourds, cacti, and nude studies. In his photography, Weston aimed for realism. He never used artificial light and seldom enlarged, cropped, or retouched his negatives. His aesthetic principle dominated American photography for many years.

Westwood Vivienne (1941–). English fashion designer. She first attracted attention in the mid-1970s as co-owner of a shop with the rock-music entrepreneur Malcolm McLaren (1946–), which became a focus for the punk movement in London. Early in the 1980s her 'Pirate' and 'New Romantics' looks gained her international recognition.

Westwood's dramatic clothes continue to have a wide influence on the public and other designers. Recently she has designed clothes and accessories for mail-order companies and young people's high-street fashion stores.

Suggested reading
Vermorel, Fred *Fashion & Perversity: A Life of Vivienne Westwood and the Sixties Laid Bare* (1976)

Weyden Rogier van der (*c.* 1399–1464). Netherlandish artist. He was official painter to the city of Brussels from 1436. He painted portraits and religious subjects, such as *The Last Judgment* about 1450 (Hôtel-Dieu, Beaune). His refined style had considerable impact on Netherlandish painting.

He became official painter to the city of Brussels 1436, visited Italy (where he was regarded with admiration) 1450 and had a busy workshop at Brussels until his death 1464. Though he signed no paintings, his work is as distinct as that of Jan van Eyck, and the products of his studio, now in many of the world's galleries, exerted a dominant influence in northern Europe during the late 15th century. A lucid and graceful mode of composition, a feeling for relief (suggesting that he made use of effects observed in Gothic sculpture), and a warm humanity, observable in the play of human expression in which he had no contemporary rival, characterize his work and account for his eminent position. These qualities are displayed in his *Descent from the Cross* (Escurial and other versions). The *Pietà* (The Hague), the great polyptych of the *Last Judgment*, the *Seven Sacraments* (Antwerp), and the *Adoration of the Magi*

(Berlin) are among his main religious works, while his portraits, such as the *Portrait of a Lady* (Washington), have a comparable quality.

Suggested reading
Cuttler, Charles *Northern Painting: From Pucelle to Bruegel* (1968)
Davies, Martin *Rogier van der Weyden* (1972)
Whinney, Margaret *Early Flemish Painting* (1968)

In three weeks England will have her neck wrung like a chicken.

Said by MAXIME WEYGAND at the fall of France 1940 and quoted in Winston Churchill *Their Finest Hour* ch 10 1949 (Churchill answered: 'some chicken, some neck')

Weygand Maxime (1867–1965). French general. In World War I he was Chief of Staff to Marshal Foch and chief of the Allied general staff 1918. In 1940, as French commander in chief, he advised surrender to Germany, and was subsequently high commissioner of N Africa 1940–41. He was a prisoner in Germany 1942–45, and was arrested after his return to France; he was released 1946, and in 1949 the sentence of national infamy was quashed.

Weyl Hermann (1885–1955). German mathematician and mathematical physicist who studied mainly topological space and the geometry of Bernhard Riemann, but also quantum mechanics and number theory.

He was professor at the Technische Hochschule in Zürich, Switzerland, 1913–30, and then at Göttingen, but the unfavourable political climate of Nazi Germany prompted him to move to the Institute for Advanced Study at Princeton, USA.

As a colleague of Albert Einstein during 1913, Weyl became interested in the developing general theory of relativity and came to believe (erroneously) that he had found a way to a grand unification of gravitation and electromagnetism. Weyl was able to anticipate the nonconservation of parity, which has since been found to be characteristic of weak interactions between leptons (a class of subatomic particles).

Weyl's most important work on Riemann surfaces was the definition of the complex manifold of the first dimension, which has been important in all later work on the theory of both complex and differential manifolds. Weyl's works include *Raum-Zeit-Materie/ Space-Time-Matter* 1918. He also published works on philosophy, logic, and the history of mathematics.

Whale James (1886–1957). English film director. He went to Hollywood to film his stage success *Journey's End* 1930, and then directed four horror films: *Frankenstein* 1931, *The Old Dark House* 1932, *The Invisible Man* 1933, and *Bride of Frankenstein* 1935. He also directed the musical *Show Boat* 1936.

Wharton Edith Newbold (born Jones) (1862–1937). US novelist. Her work, known for its subtlety and form and influenced by her friend Henry James, was mostly set in New York society. It includes *The House of Mirth* 1905, which made her reputation; the grim, uncharacteristic novel of New England *Ethan Frome* 1911; *The Custom of the Country* 1913; and *The Age of Innocence* 1920 (Pulitzer prize).

Suggested reading
Auchincloss, L *Edith Wharton* (1971)
Benstock, S *Edith Wharton: No Gifts from Chance* (1994)
Lewis, R W B *Edith Wharton* (1985)
Wolff, C G *A Feast of Words: The Triumph of Edith Wharton* (1977)

Wheatley Dennis Yates (1897–1977). English thriller and adventure novelist. His works include a series dealing with black magic and occultism, but he also wrote crime novels in which the reader was invited to play the detective, as in *Murder off Miami* 1936, with real clues such as ticket stubs.

Wheatstone Charles (1802–1875). English physicist and inventor. With William Cooke, he patented a railway telegraph 1837, and, developing an idea of Samuel Christie (1784–1865), devised the

Wheatstone bridge, an electrical network for measuring resistance. He also invented the concertina. Knighted 1868.

In 1834 Wheatstone made the first determination of the velocity of electricity along a wire. He also improved on early versions of the dynamo so that current was generated continuously.

Wheatstone was born in Gloucester and joined the family business making musical instruments. His work in acoustics led to his appointment as professor of experimental physics at King's College, London, 1834, a position he retained for the rest of his life.

In 1827 Wheatstone invented a device called the kaleidophone, which visually demonstrated the vibration of sounding surfaces by causing an illuminated spot to vibrate and produce curves by the persistence of vision. He went on to investigate the transmission of sound in instruments and discovered modes of vibration in air columns 1832 and vibrating plates 1833. Wheatstone showed in 1835 that spectra produced by spark discharges from metal electrodes have different lines and colours formed by different electrodes. He predicted correctly that with development, spectroscopy would become a technique for the analysis of elements. In 1860, he demonstrated how the visual combination of two similar pictures in a stereoscope gives an illusion of three dimensions.

Wheeler (Robert Eric) Mortimer (1890–1976). English archaeologist. As director-general of archaeology in India in the 1940s he excavated sites of the Indus valley civilization. While Wheeler was keeper of the London Museum 1926–44, his digs included Caerleon in Wales 1926–27 and Maiden Castle in Dorset 1934–37. He helped to popularize archaeology by his television appearances. Knighted 1952.

Wheeler adhered to the rules for stratigraphic excavation set down by General Pitt-Rivers, despite the sometimes less-than-scientific methodology pursued by his contemporaries. After a number of spectacular excavations in Britain, Wheeler was appointed director-general of archaeology in India 1944–48.

He investigated the cities of a forgotten civilization known as the Indus valley civilization. It flourished in the later 3rd millennium. Two major cities were excavated, Mohenjo Daro and Harappa. Wheeler revealed a society that was advanced enough to produce ceremonial and state architecture and a complex water, drainage, and waste-disposal system.

Suggested reading

Clark, Ronald *Sir Mortimer Wheeler* (1960)

Hawkes, Jacquetta *Mortimer Wheeler: Adventurer in Archaeology* (1982)

Wheeler, Mortimer *Still Digging* (autobiography) (1955)

Wherrett Richard (1940–). Australian actor and theatrical director working mainly in Sydney. He was associate director at the Old Tote Theatre Company and from 1974 was co-artistic director of the Nimrod Theatre where he directed new plays by local authors such as Alex Buzo and Steve J Spears. Wherrett's best-known production, *The Elocution of Benjamin Franklin* opened in Sydney in 1976, in London, in 1978 and in New York in 1979. He was foundation director of the Sydney Theatre Company 1979–90.

Whewell William (1794–1866). British physicist and philosopher who coined the term 'scientist' along with such words as 'Eocene' and 'Miocene', 'electrode', 'cathode', and 'anode'. He produced two works of great scholarship, *The History of the Inductive Sciences* 1837 and *The Philosophy of the Inductive Sciences* 1840. Most of his career was connected with Cambridge University, where he became the Master of Trinity College.

Whipple Fred Lawrence (1906–). US astronomer whose hypothesis in 1949 that the nucleus of a comet is like a dirty snowball was confirmed 1986 by space-probe studies of Halley's comet. He was professor at Harvard 1950–77 and director of the Smithsonian Astrophysics Observatory 1955–73.

In addition to discovering six new comets, Whipple proposed that the nucleus of a comet consisted of a frozen mass of water, ammonia, methane, and other hydrogen compounds together with silicates, dust, and other materials. As the comet's orbit brought it

Wheatstone *English physicist Charles Wheatstone who, as well as performing important experimental work in the fields of acoustics and electricity, was also an eminent inventor. Wheatstone introduced the term microphone and invented the concertina, kaleidoscope and the first electric telegraph. Ironically, he did not actually invent the Wheatstone bridge (an instrument for determining resistances in a circuit), but instead played a major role in applying the device to new physical problems. (Ann Ronan/Image Select)*

nearer to the Sun, solar radiation would cause the frozen material to evaporate, thus producing a large amount of silicate dust which would form the comet's tail.

Whipple also worked on ascertaining cometary orbits and defining the relationship between comets and meteors. In the 1950s he became active in the programme to devise effective means of tracking artificial satellites.

Whipple George Hoyt (1878–1976). US physiologist whose research interest concerned the formation of haemoglobin in the blood. He showed that anaemic dogs, kept under restricted diets, responded well to a liver regime, and that their haemoglobin quickly regenerated. This work led to a cure for pernicious anaemia. He shared the 1934 Nobel Prize for Physiology or Medicine with George Minot (1885–1950) and William Murphy (1892–1987).

Whistler James Abbott McNeill (1834–1903). US painter and etcher. He was active in London from 1859. Influenced by Japanese prints, he painted riverscapes and portraits that show subtle composition and colour harmonies: for example, *Arrangement in Grey and Black: Portrait of the Painter's Mother* 1871 (Louvre, Paris).

He settled in Chelsea, London, and painted views of the Thames including *Old Battersea Bridge* about 1872–75 (Tate Gallery, London). In 1877 the art critic John Ruskin published an article on his *Nocturne in Black and Gold: The Falling Rocket* (now in Detroit) that led to a libel trial in which Whistler was awarded symbolic damages of a farthing (a quarter of an old penny). Whistler described the trial in his book *The Gentle Art of Making Enemies* 1890.

Suggested reading

Anderson, Ronald and Koval, Anne *Whistler: Beyond the Myth* (1994)

Fleming, Gordon *James Abbott McNeill Whistler: A Life* (1993)

Sutton, Denys *Nocturne: The Art of James McNeill Whistler* (1963)

Taylor, Hilary *James McNeill Whistler* (1978)

Whistler Rex (Reginald John) (1905–1944). English artist. He painted fanciful murals, for example *In Pursuit of Rare Meats*

1926–27 in the Tate Gallery restaurant, London. He also illustrated many books and designed stage sets. He was killed in World War II. His brother Laurence Whistler (1912–) is a glass engraver and poet.

White Byron Raymond (1917–). US jurist. He worked to elect John F Kennedy to the presidency 1960 and was appointed by him as associate justice of the Supreme Court, serving 1962–93. Born in Fort Collins, Colorado, USA, White graduated from the University of Colorado 1938. He studied at Oxford University, UK, as a Rhodes scholar 1939 and entered Yale Law School 1940. He graduated from Yale 1946 after service with the US navy in World War II. He served as law clerk 1946–47 to Supreme Court associate justice Fred M Vinson. He served as deputy attorney general 1961–62, before being appointed to the Supreme Court. He was a moderate conservative, usually dissenting on the rights of criminals, but upholding the right of accused citizens to trial by jury.

White Edward Douglass, Jr (1845–1921). US jurist. Elected to the US Senate 1891, President Cleveland nominated him as associative justice to the US Supreme Court 1893 and under President Taft he was nominated as chief justice 1910. During his office the Court made important decisions on US economic policy as in *United States v E C Knight and Co* 1895 when he joined the majority in weakening the Sherman Antitrust Act by removing manufacture of goods from its purview.

Born in Lafourche Parish, Louisiana, USA, White attended Mount St Mary's College (Maryland), the Jesuit College (New Orleans), and Georgetown University, but left his college studies to serve in the Confederate Army. After the American Civil War 1865 he studied law at the University of Louisiana Law School in New Orleans; he was admitted to the bar 1868. Becoming active in Democratic politics, he was elected to the state senate 1874 and was a justice of the Louisiana supreme court 1878–80.

Democracy is the recurrent suspicion that more than half of the people are right more than half of the time.

E B WHITE
in *New Yorker* 3 July 1944

White E(lwyn) B(rooks) (1899–1985). US writer. He was long associated with the *New Yorker* magazine and renowned for his satire, such as *Is Sex Necessary?* 1929 (with the humorist James Thurber). With William Strunk, Jr, he published *The Elements of Style* 1935, considered a definitive style manual for the English language. White also wrote children's classics: *Stuart Little* 1945, *Charlotte's Web* 1952, and *The Trumpet of the Swan* 1970.

'I say it's spinach, and I say the hell with it.'

E B WHITE
Caption in *New Yorker* 28 Dec 1928

White Gilbert (1720–1793). English naturalist and cleric. He was the author of *The Natural History and Antiquities of Selborne* 1789, which records the flora and fauna of an area of Hampshire.

White studied at Oxford. Although assigned to parishes elsewhere, he chose to live in his native Selborne. White's book is based on a diary of his observations and on letters to two naturalist friends over a period of about 20 years. Elegantly written, *The Natural History* contains descriptions of rural life and acute observations of a wide variety of natural-history subjects, such as the migration of swallows, the recognition of three distinct species of British leaf warblers, and the identification of the harvest mouse and the noctule bat as British species.

White also wrote *Calendar of Flora and the Garden* 1765, an account of observations he made in his garden in 1751, and *Naturalist's Journal* (begun in 1768).

White Patrick Victor Martindale (1912–1990). Australian writer. White, a member of an established Australian pastoralist family, was born in London and educated in Australia and England. After graduating from Cambridge he lived and wrote in London and in 1940 joined the RAF as an intelligence officer. In the 1940s he returned to settle in Australia. He did more than any other to put Australian literature on the international map. His partly allegorical novels explore the lives of early settlers in Australia and often deal with misfits or inarticulate people. They include *The Aunt's Story* 1948, *The Tree of Man* 1955, and *Voss* 1957 (based on the ill-fated 19th-century explorer Leichhardt). As well as a novelist, he was a playwright, short-story writer, and poet. Nobel Prize for Literature 1973. His autobiography, *Flaws in the Glass*, appeared 1981.

Suggested reading
Kiernan, B *Patrick White* (1980)
Walsh, W *Patrick White* (1977)
Weigel, J *Patrick White* (1983)
White, Patrick *Flaws in the Glass* (autobiography) (1981)

White Stanford (1853–1906). US architect. He was a co-founder of the architectural firm of McKim, Mead and White. One of the most prominent US architects of the 19th century, he specialized in the Renaissance style and designed, among many famous projects, the original Madison Square Garden and the Washington Square Arch, both in New York City. A flamboyant and arrogant personality, he was murdered in the rooftop restaurant of Madison Square Garden by the husband of a former lover.

There were magicians in the forest ... There were even a few dragons, though they were rather small ones.

T H WHITE
The Sword in the Stone ch 2 1939

White T(erence) H(anbury) (1906–1964). English writer. He retold the Arthurian legend in four volumes of *The Once and Future King* 1938–58.

Whitefield George (1714–1770). British Methodist evangelist. He was a student at Oxford University and took orders 1738, but was suspended for his unorthodox doctrines and methods. For many years he travelled through Britain and America, and by his preaching contributed greatly to the Great Awakening. Whitefield's Tabernacle was built for him in Tottenham Court Road, London (1756; bombed 1945 but rebuilt).

Intelligence is quickness to apprehend as distinct from ability, which is capacity to act wisely on the thing apprehended.

ALFRED WHITEHEAD
Dialogues 15 Dec 1939

Whitehead Alfred North (1861–1947). English philosopher and mathematician. In his 'theory of organism', he attempted a synthesis of metaphysics and science. His works include *Principia Mathematica* 1910–13 (with Bertrand Russell), *The Concept of Nature* 1920, and *Adventures of Ideas* 1933.

Whitehead's research in mathematics involved a highly original attempt – incorporating the principles of logic – to create an extension of ordinary algebra to universal algebra (*A Treatise of Universal Algebra* 1898), and a meticulous re-examination of the relativity theory of Albert Einstein.

He was professor of applied mathematics at London University 1914–24 and professor of philosophy at Harvard University, USA, 1924–37.

At the International Congress of Philosophy in 1900, Whitehead and Russell heard Italian mathematician Giuseppe Peano describe

---

A science which hesitates to forget its founders is lost.

ALFRED WHITEHEAD
Attributed remark

---

the method by which he had arrived at his axioms concerning the natural numbers, and they spent the next ten years on their project to deduce mathematics from logic in a general and fundamental way. Other works include *Principles of Natural Knowledge* 1919, *Science and the Modern World* 1925, and *Process and Reality* 1929.

Whitehead John Henry Constantine (1904–1960). British mathematician who studied the more abstract areas of differential geometry, and of algebraic and geometrical topology.

Whitehead was born in Madras, India, and studied at Oxford, where he became professor 1947. Some of his most significant work was in the study of knots. In geometry a knot is a two-dimensional representation of a three-dimensional curve that because of its dimensional reduction (by topological distortion) appears to have nodes (to loop onto itself). Whitehead wrote a textbook together with Oswald Veblen (1880–1960), *Foundations of Differential Geometry* 1932.

Whitehead Robert (1823–1905). English engineer who invented the self-propelled torpedo 1866. He devised methods of accurately firing torpedoes either above or below water from the fastest ships, no matter what the speed or bearing of the target.

Whitehead developed the torpedo for the Austrian Empire. Typically it was 4 m/13 ft long, could carry a 9-kg/20-lb dynamite warhead, and by 1889 had a speed of 29 knots. It was powered by compressed air and had a balancing mechanism and, later, gyroscopic controls. In 1876 he developed a servomotor, which controlled the steering gear and gave the torpedo a truer path through the water.

Whitehead was born in Bolton, Lancashire, and apprenticed to an engineering company. In 1847 he set up his own business in Milan (then part of Austria), moving to Trieste 1848 and Fiume 1856.

Whitehead designed pumps for draining part of the Lombardy marshes and made improvements to silk-weaving looms. From 1856, in Fiume, he built naval marine engines; he designed and built the engines of the ironclad warship *Ferdinand Max*.

Whitehouse Mary (1910–). British media activist. A founder of the National Viewers' and Listeners' Association, she has campaigned to censor radio and television for their treatment of sex and violence.

Whitelaw William Stephen Ian, 1st Viscount Whitelaw (1918–). British Conservative politician. As secretary of state for Northern Ireland he introduced the concept of power sharing. He was chief Conservative whip 1964–70, and leader of the House of Commons 1970–72. He became secretary of state for employment 1973–74, but failed to conciliate the trade unions. He was chair of the Conservative Party 1974 and home secretary 1979–83, when he was made a viscount. He resigned 1988.

Whiteley Brett (1939–1992). Australian painter. He achieved international recognition in 1961 with exhibitions in London, the purchase of his *Untitled Red* by the Tate Gallery, London (the youngest ever painter to be so honoured), and the award of the Paris Biennale Prix International. During his London period he produced a set of paintings and drawings based on the murderer, John Christie. He is also known for landscapes, such as the Lavender Bay series which includes *The Balcony* 1975 (Art Gallery of New South Wales, Sydney) and *The Jacaranda Tree* which won the 1977 Wynne Prize. In 1977–78 he became the first artist to win the Archibald, Wynne, and Sulman prizes.

Whiteman Paul (1890–1967). US dance-band and swing-orchestra leader. He specialized in 'symphonic jazz'. He commissioned George Gershwin's *Rhapsody in Blue*, conducting its premiere 1924.

I do not mind the Liberals, still less ... the Country party, calling me a bastard. In some circumstances, I am only doing my job if they do.

GOUGH WHITLAM
Speech 9 June 1974

Whitlam (Edward) Gough (1916–). Australian politician, leader of the Labor Party 1967–78 and prime minister 1972–75. He cultivated closer relations with Asia, attempted redistribution of wealth, and raised loans to increase national ownership of industry and resources. When the opposition blocked finance bills in the Senate, following a crisis of confidence, Whitlam refused to call a general election, and was dismissed by the governor-general (Sir John Kerr). He was defeated in the subsequent general-election by Malcolm Fraser.

Suggested reading
Kelly, Paul *The Unmaking of Gough* (1976)
Oakes, Laurie and Solomon, David *The Making of an Australian Prime Minister* (1973)
Reid, Alan *The Whitlam Adventure* (1976)

Whitman Christine (born Todd) (1946–). US Republican politician, governor of New Jersey from 1994. She is on the left of her party on social issues, but fiscally conservative.

She was born in New Jersey, the daughter of a millionaire, and began her career working for President Richard Nixon. As governor, she cut state income tax and appointed the first African-American to the state's supreme court. Although she supports feminism and minority rights, she has been tipped as a future presidential candidate.

Whitman Walt(er) (1819–1892). US poet. He published *Leaves of Grass* 1855, which contains the symbolic 'Song of Myself'. It used unconventional free verse (with no rhyme or regular rhythm) and scandalized the public by its frank celebration of sexuality.

Born at West Hill (Huntington, Long Island), New York, as a young man Whitman worked as a printer, teacher, and journalist. In 1865 he published *Drum-Taps*, a volume inspired by his work as an army nurse during the Civil War. *Democratic Vistas* 1871 is a collection of his prose pieces. He also wrote an elegy for Abraham Lincoln, 'When Lilacs Last in the Dooryard Bloom'd'. He preached a

Whitman, Walt US poet Walt Whitman, whose breaking away from conventional form made him one of the most influential writers of his generation. The main themes in his poetry include the sacredness of the self, the beauty of death, the equality of all people, brotherly love, and the immortality of the soul.

particularly American vision of individual freedom and human brotherhood. Such poets as Ezra Pound, Wallace Stevens, and Allen Ginsberg show his influence in their work.

Suggested reading

Allen, G W *A Reader's Guide to Walt Whitman* (1970)

Chase, R *Walt Whitman Reconsidered* (1955)

Zweig, P *Walt Whitman: The Making of a Poet* (1984)

Whitney Eli (1765–1825). US inventor who in 1794 patented the cotton gin, a device for separating cotton fibre from its seeds. Whitney's machine had a wooden cylinder bearing rows of spikes set 1.3 cm/0.5 in apart, which extended between the bars of a grid set so closely together that only the cotton lint (and not the seeds) could pass through. A revolving brush cleaned the cotton off the spikes and the seeds fell into another compartment. The machine was hand-cranked, and one gin could produce about 23 kg/50 lb of cleaned cotton per day – a 50-fold increase in a worker's output. Also a manufacturer of firearms, he created a standardization system that was the precursor of the assembly line.

His cotton gin was so easy to copy and manufacture that he eventually gave up defending his patent and in 1798 turned to the manufacture of firearms in New Haven, Connecticut. He used machine tools to make arms with fully interchangeable parts, and introduced division of labour and mass production.

In 1818 he made a small milling machine, with a power-driven table that moved horizontally beneath and at right angles to a rotating cutter.

Whittam Smith Andreas (1937–). British newspaper editor, founder and editor from 1986 of the centrist daily the *Independent* and cofounder 1990 of the *Independent on Sunday*.

Whitten-Brown Arthur (1886–1948). British aviator. After serving in World War I, he took part in the first nonstop flight across the Atlantic as navigator to Captain John Alcock 1919. KBE 1919.

Whittier John Greenleaf (1807–1892). US poet. He was a powerful opponent of slavery, as shown in the verse *Voices of Freedom* 1846. Among his other works are *Legends of New England in Prose and Verse*, *Songs of Labor* 1850, and the New England nature poem 'Snow-Bound' 1866. He was also a journalist and humanitarian. Many of his poems have been set to music, and are sung as church hymns.

He would hardly have been permanently remembered had not his benefactions ... mostly posthumous ... associated him with ... prominent London buildings.

James Tait on DICK WHITTINGTON
in *Dictionary of British Biography*

Whittington Dick (Richard) (*c.* 1358–1423). English cloth merchant who was mayor of London 1397–98, 1406–07, and 1419–20. According to legend, he came to London as a poor boy with his cat when he heard that the streets were paved with gold and silver. His cat first appears in a play 1605.

Whittle Frank (1907–1996). British engineer who patented the basic design for the turbojet engine 1930. In the Royal Air Force he worked on jet propulsion 1937–46. In May 1941 the Gloster E 28/39 aircraft first flew with the Whittle jet engine. Both the German (first operational jet planes) and the US jet aircraft were built using his principles. Knighted 1948.

Whittle was born in Coventry and joined the RAF as an apprentice, later training as a fighter pilot. He had the idea for a jet engine 1928 but could not persuade the Air Ministry of its potential until 1935, when he formed the Power Jets Company. He retired from the RAF with the rank of air commodore 1948 and took up a university appointment in the USA.

Whitworth Joseph (1803–1887). English engineer who established new standards of accuracy in the production of machine tools and precision measuring instruments. He devised standard gauges and screw threads, and introduced new methods of making gun barrels. Baronet 1869.

Whitworth was born in Stockport, Cheshire, and left school at 14. He worked for English engineer Henry Maudslay in his London workshops 1825–33, then moved to Manchester and set up in business as a toolmaker. From this, a large factory developed. He was concerned with the training, lives, and leisure time of his workers, and donated large sums to educational organizations.

Whitworth brought standardization to his company and the engineering industry as a whole by developing means of measuring to tolerances never before possible, so that shafts, bearings, gears, and screws could be interchanged. The Whitworth company produced many machines for cutting, shaping, and planing. Whitworth also designed a knitting machine and a horse-drawn mechanical roadsweeper.

At the Whitworth works, guns of all sizes were produced, and Whitworth supervised many experiments to investigate the forces acting on the breech and barrel of a gun. He also made advances in the design of rifling for the barrels of small-calibre weapons.

Anyway, anyhow, anywhere.

THE WHO
Song title, written by Townsend/Daltry 1965

Who, the English rock group, formed 1964, with a hard, aggressive sound, high harmonies, and a propensity for destroying their instruments on stage. Their albums include *Tommy* 1969, *Who's Next* 1971, and *Quadrophenia* 1973.

Originally a mod band, the Who comprised Pete Townshend (1945–), guitar and songwriter; Roger Daltrey (1944–), vocals; John Entwistle (1944–), bass; and Keith Moon (1947–1978), drums.

Whymper Edward (1840–1911). English mountaineer. He made the first ascent of many Alpine peaks, including the Matterhorn 1865, and in the Andes scaled Chimborazo and other mountains. He wrote *Scrambles amongst the Alps* 1871 and *Zermatt and the Matterhorn* 1897.

Wickham Henry (1846–1928). British planter who founded the rubber plantations of Sri Lanka and Malaysia, and broke the monopoly in rubber production then held by Brazil. He collected rubber seeds from Brazil, where they grew naturally, cultivated them at Kew Gardens, Surrey, and re-exported them to the Far East.

Widmark Richard (1914–). US actor. He made his film debut in *Kiss of Death* 1947 as a psychopath. He subsequently appeared in a variety of roles including *The Alamo* 1960, *Madigan* 1968, and *Coma* 1978.

Widor Charles Marie Jean Albert (1844–1937). French composer and organist. He created the solo organ symphony, which in effect treats the instrument itself as an orchestra of variously coloured pipes and stops. He wrote ten such symphonies; the famous *Toccata* *c.* 1880 is the finale of his Fifth Symphony.

Influenced to an extent by César Franck, Widor succeeded him as professor at the Paris Conservatoire. Among his other works are operas, ballets, and a treatise on orchestration.

Wieland Christoph Martin (1733–1813). German poet and novelist. After attempts at religious poetry, he came under the influence of Voltaire and Rousseau, and wrote novels such as *Die Geschichte des Agathon/The History of Agathon* 1766–67 and the satirical *Die Abderiten* 1774 (translated as *The Republic of Fools* 1861); and tales in verse such as *Musarion oder Die Philosophie der Grazien* 1768, *Oberon* 1780, and others. He translated Shakespeare into German 1762–66.

Wieland Heinrich Otto (1877–1957). German organic chemist who determined the structures of steroids and related compounds. He also studied other natural compounds, such as alkaloids and pterins, and contributed to the investigation of biological oxidation. Nobel prize 1927. He spent most of his career at the University and

Technische Hochschule of Munich. During World War I he researched into chemical warfare.

In 1912 Wieland showed that bile acids have similar structures to that of cholesterol. Later he worked out what he thought was the basic skeleton of a steroid molecule (for which he was awarded the Nobel prize), but it was found to be incorrect. In 1932 he and his co-workers produced a somewhat modified structure, which is still accepted today.

Wieland did other work with the bile acids, demonstrating their role in converting fats into water-soluble cholic acids (a key process in digestion). He determined the structures of, and synthesized many, toadstool poisons, such as phalloidine from the deadly *Amanita* fungus. He also began research into the composition and synthesis of pterins, the pigments that give the colour to butterflies' wings.

Wieland proved experimentally that biological oxidation (the process within living tissues by which food substances such as glucose are converted to carbon dioxide and energy) was in fact a catalytic dehydrogenation. This was in direct opposition to the findings of Otto Warburg, who had shown that biological oxidation was an addition of oxygen, and the controversy sparked debate and research. In the end both dehydrogenation and oxidation were shown to occur.

Wien Wilhelm Carl Werner Otto Fritz Franz (1864–1928). German physicist who studied radiation and established the principle, since known as Wien's law, that the wavelength at which the radiation from an idealized radiating body is most intense is inversely proportional to the body's absolute temperature. (That is, the hotter the body, the shorter the wavelength.) For this and other work on radiation, he was awarded the 1911 Nobel Prize for Physics.

Wiene Robert (1880–1938). German film director. He is known for the bizarre Expressionist film *Das Kabinett des Dr Caligari/The Cabinet of Dr Caligari* 1919. He also directed *Orlacs Hände/The Hands of Orlac* 1924, *Der Rosenkavalier* 1926, and *Ultimatum* 1938.

Wiener Norbert (1894–1964). US mathematician, credited with the establishment of the science of cybernetics in his book *Cybernetics* 1948. In mathematics, he laid the foundation of the study of stochastic processes (those dependent on random events), particularly Brownian motion.

Wiener was born in Columbia, Missouri, and received his PhD from Harvard at the age of 19. He then went to Europe to study under leading mathematicians (Bertrand Russell at Cambridge, England, and David Hilbert at Göttingen, Germany). From 1919 he taught at the Massachusetts Institute of Technology, becoming professor 1932.

Wiener devoted much of his efforts to methodology, developing mathematical approaches that could usefully be applied to continuously changing processes.

During World War II, Wiener worked on the control of anti-aircraft guns (which required him to consider factors such as the machinery itself, the gunner, and the unpredictable evasive action on the part of the target's pilot), on filtering 'noise' from useful information for radar, and on coding and decoding. His investigations stimulated his interest in information transfer and processes such as information feedback.

Wiesel Elie (Eliezer) (1928–). US academic and human-rights campaigner, born in Romania. He was held in Buchenwald concentration camp during World War II, and has assiduously documented wartime atrocities against the Jews in an effort to alert the world to the dangers of racism and violence. Nobel Peace Prize 1986.

Wiggin Kate Douglas (born Smith) (1856–1923). US writer. She was a pioneer in the establishment of kindergartens in the USA, and wrote the children's classic *Rebecca of Sunnybrook Farm* 1903 and its sequels.

Wigglesworth Vincent Brian (1899–1994). English entomologist whose research covered many areas of insect physiology, especially the role of hormones in growth and metamorphosis. Knighted 1964.

During World War I he served in France, and then qualified in medicine at St Thomas's Hospital, London. He was director of the Agricultural Research Council Unit of Insect Physiology at Cambridge 1943–67, as well as professor of biology at Cambridge 1952–66.

Wigglesworth's work on insect metamorphosis was carried out mainly on the bloodsucking insect *Rhodnius prolixus*. He demonstrated that the hormones responsible for growth and moulting, and for preventing the development of adult characteristics until the insect larva is fully grown, are produced in specific areas of the brain.

Wigglesworth investigated many other aspects of insect anatomy and physiology, including the mechanisms involved in hatching; the mode of action of adhesive organs in walking; the role of the outer waxy layer on insects' bodies in preventing water loss; the respiration of insect eggs; insect sense organs and their use in orientation; and the functions of insect blood cells.

His book *The Principles of Insect Physiology* 1939 became the standard text on insect physiology.

Wigley Dafydd (1943–). Welsh politician, president of Plaid Cymru, the Welsh nationalist party, 1981–84 and from 1991. He aims to see Wales as a self-governing nation within the European Community. Wigley worked as an industrial economist 1964–74, and published *An Economic Plan for Wales* 1970. He has been Plaid Cymru member of Parliament for Caernarfon since Feb 1974, and sponsored the Disabled Persons Act 1981.

Wigman Mary (born Marie Wiegman) (1886–1973). German dancer and choreographer. She was a pioneer of the Ausdruckstanz school of modern dance. She was noted for her solos exploring the darker, melancholic sides of human nature. Much of her movements were angular and distorted, tending towards the ground rather than balletic elevation.

Wigman studied eurythmics with Emile Jaques-Dalcroze and later became Rudolf von Laban's assistant during World War I. Some of her early compositions were performed in silence to assert dance's independence from music.

Wigner Eugene Paul (1902–1995). Hungarian-born US physicist who introduced the notion of parity, or symmetry theory, into nuclear physics, showing that all nuclear processes should be indistinguishable from their mirror images. For this and other work on nuclear structure, he shared the 1963 Nobel Prize for Physics.

The Wigner effect is a rapid rise in temperature in a nuclear reactor pile when, under particle bombardment, such materials as graphite deform, swell, then suddenly release large amounts of energy. This was the cause of the fire at the British Windscale plant 1957.

Educated at the Lutheran Gymnasium in Budapest, Wigner took up postgraduate studies in Berlin where he was present at Albert Einstein's seminars in the 1920s. He emigrated to the USA in 1930, and became a US citizen 1937.

He was one of the scientists who persuaded President Roosevelt to commit the USA to developing the atom bomb. In 1960, he was awarded the Atoms for Peace Award, in recognition of his vigorous support for the peaceful use of atomic energy. He taught as a professor of mathematics at Princeton University for 40 years until his retirement 1971.

Wilander Mats (1964–). Swedish lawn-tennis player. He won his first Grand Slam event 1982 when he beat Guillermo Vilas to win the French Open, and had won eight Grand Slam titles by 1990. He played a prominent role in Sweden's rise to the forefront of men's tennis in the 1980s, including Davis Cup successes.

Wilberforce Samuel (1805–1873). British Anglican bishop of Oxford 1845–69, and from 1869 of Winchester. He defended Anglican orthodoxy against Tractarianism, the Oxford Movement for the revival of English Roman Catholicism.

Wilberforce William (1759–1833). English reformer who was instrumental in abolishing slavery in the British Empire. He entered Parliament 1780; in 1807 his bill for the abolition of the slave trade was passed, and in 1833, largely through his efforts, slavery was abolished throughout the empire.

Suggested reading
Furneaux, Robin *William Wilberforce* (1974)
Pollock, John *Wilberforce* (1977)
Warner, O M *William Wilberforce and His Times* (1962)

God Almighty has set before me two great objects, the suppession of the Slave Trade and the reformation of manners.

WILLIAM WILBERFORCE
Diary 1787

Wilbur Richard Purdy (1921–). US poet. He is noted for his cultural conservatism, urbane wit, and the elegance of his verse in such volumes as *The Beautiful Changes* 1947 and *Things of This World* 1956. He also published children's verse, as in *Loudmouse* 1963 and *Opposites* 1973.

Wilcox Stephen (1830–1893). US inventor who, with Herman Babcock, designed a steam-tube boiler which was developed into one of the most efficient sources of high-pressure steam.

After leaving school he went to work on improving old machines and inventing new ones, such as a hot-air engine for operating fog signals. In about 1856 Wilcox patented a steam-tube boiler which was not entirely successful. Ten years later, with his boyhood friend Babcock, he designed an improved safety water-tube boiler, and they formed a company to manufacture this. Throughout his inventing career Wilcox acquired nearly 50 patents.

The Babcock–Wilcox boiler, patented 1867, had straight tubes inclined to the horizontal and connected together at their ends, through which the hot water gradually rose by convection. The firebox surrounded the tubes to give rapid heating, and there was a reservoir of hot water above the firebox and tubes, with steam above the water. These steam engines were used in the first American electricity generating stations and played an important part in the subsequent development of electric lighting.

He realized that, in a big and crowded city, crime may be organized as a business ... the first of the racketeers.

Geoffrey Treasure on JONATHAN WILD
in *Who's Who in Early Hanoverian England* 1991

Wild Jonathan (*c.* 1682–1725). English criminal who organized the thieves of London and ran an office that, for a payment, returned stolen goods to their owners. He was hanged at Tyburn.

Wild was the subject of Henry Fielding's satire *Jonathan Wild the Great* 1743 and the model for Macheath in John Gay's *The Beggar's Opera* 1728.

Wilde Cornel(ius Louis) (1915–1989). Austrian-born US actor and film director. He worked in the USA from 1932. He starred as the composer and pianist Chopin in *A Song to Remember* 1945, and directed *The Naked Prey* 1966, *Beach Red* 1967, and *No Blade of Grass* 1970, among other films.

Wilde also starred in *Leave Her to Heaven* 1945 and *Forever Amber* 1947. He produced, directed, and starred (with his wife Jean Wallace) in several films from 1955, including *Storm Fear* 1955, *Maracaibo* 1958, and *Beach Red* 1967.

Yet each man kills the thing he loves, ... / The coward does it with a kiss, / The brave man with a sword!

OSCAR WILDE
Ballad of Reading Gaol 1898

Wilde Oscar Fingal O'Flahertie Wills (1854–1900). Irish writer. With his flamboyant style and quotable conversation, he dazzled London society and, on his lecture tour 1882, the USA. He published his only novel, *The Picture of Dorian Gray*, 1891, followed by

a series of sharp comedies, including *A Woman of No Importance* 1893 and *The Importance of Being Earnest* 1895. In 1895 he was imprisoned for two years for homosexual offences; he died in exile.

Wilde was born in Dublin and studied at Dublin and Oxford, where he became known as a supporter of the Aesthetic movement ('art for art's sake'). He published *Poems* 1881, and also wrote fairy tales and other stories, criticism, and a long, anarchic political essay, 'The Soul of Man Under Socialism' 1891. His elegant social comedies include *Lady Windermere's Fan* 1892 and *An Ideal Husband* 1895. The drama *Salome* 1893, based on the biblical character, was written in French; considered scandalous by the British censor, it was first performed in Paris 1896 with the actress Sarah Bernhardt in the title role.

Among his lovers was Lord Alfred Douglas, whose father provoked Wilde into a lawsuit that led to his social and financial ruin and imprisonment. The long poem *Ballad of Reading Gaol* 1898 and a letter published as *De Profundis* 1905 were written in jail to explain his side of the relationship. After his release from prison 1897, he lived in France and is buried in Paris.

Suggested reading
Ellmann, R *Oscar Wilde* (1987)
Holland, V *Oscar Wilde* (1966)
Hyde, M *Oscar Wilde: A Biography* (1976)
Kohl, N *Oscar Wilde* (1989)
Worth, K *Oscar Wilde* (1983)

I've met a lot of hardboiled eggs in my time, but you're twenty minutes.

BILLY WILDER
in the film *Ace in the Hole* 1951

Wilder Billy (Samuel) (1906–). Austrian-born US screenwriter and film director. He worked in the USA from 1934. He directed and co-scripted the cynical *Double Indemnity* 1944, *The Lost Weekend* (Academy Award for best director) 1945, *Sunset Boulevard* 1950, *Some Like It Hot* 1959, and *The Apartment* (Academy Award) 1960.

I've never met anyone as utterly mean as Marilyn Monroe. Nor as utterly fabulous on the screen. And that includes Garbo.

BILLY WILDER
in *Photoplay* September 1982

Wilder Thornton Niven (1897–1975). US dramatist and novelist. He won Pulitzer prizes for the novel *The Bridge of San Luis Rey* 1927, and for the plays *Our Town* 1938 and *The Skin of Our Teeth* 1942. His farce *The Matchmaker* 1954 was filmed 1958. In 1964 it was adapted into the hit stage musical *Hello, Dolly!*, also made into a film. His plays are innovative in that they are overtly philosophical, they generally employ no props or scenery, and the characters often directly address the audience.

The comic spirit is given to us in order that we may analyze, weigh, and clarify things in us which nettle us, or which we are outgrowing, or trying to reshape.

THORNTON WILDER
Interview in Malcolm Cowley (ed) *Writers at Work*, first series 1959

Wilfrid, St (634–709). Northumbrian-born bishop of York from 665. He defended the cause of the Roman Church at the Synod of Whitby 664 against that of Celtic Christianity. Feast day 12 Oct.

Wilkes John (1727–1797). British Radical politician, imprisoned for his political views; member of Parliament 1757–64 and from 1774. Wilkes, born in Clerkenwell, London, entered Parliament as a Whig 1757. His attacks on the Tory prime minister Bute in his paper

The North Briton led to his being outlawed 1764; he fled to France, and on his return 1768 was imprisoned. He was four times elected MP for Middlesex, but the Commons refused to admit him and finally declared his opponent elected. This secured him strong working-and middle-class support, and in 1774 he was allowed to take his seat in Parliament. He championed parliamentary reform, religious toleration, and US independence.

Suggested reading
Christie, I R *Wilkes, Wyvill and Reform* (1962)
Kronenberger, L *John Wilkes* (1974)
Rudé, G F E *Wilkes and Liberty* (1962)

Nothing has been so obnoxious to me through life as a dead calm.

Horace Blackley on JOHN WILKES in *Life of John Wilkes*

Wilkes Maurice Vincent (1913–   ). English mathematician who led the team at Cambridge University that built the EDSAC (electronic delay storage automatic calculator) 1949, one of the earliest of the British electronic computers. During World War II he became involved with the development of radar. He was director of the Cambridge Mathematical Laboratory 1946–80.

In the late 1940s Wilkes and his team began to build the EDSAC. At the time, electronic computers were in their infancy. Wilkes chose the serial mode, in which the information in the computer is processed in sequence (and not several parts at once, as in the parallel type). This design incorporated mercury delay lines (developed at the Massachusetts Institute of Technology, USA) as the elements of the memory.

In May 1949 the EDSAC ran its first program and became the first delay-line computer in the world. From early 1950 it offered a regular computing facility to the members of Cambridge University, the first general-purpose computer service. Much time was spent by the research group on programming and on the compilation of a library of programs. The EDSAC was in operation until 1958.

EDSAC II came into service 1957. This was a parallel-processing machine and the delay line was abandoned in favour of magnetic storage methods.

Wilkie David (1785–1841). Scottish genre and portrait painter. He was active in London from 1805. His paintings are in the 17th-century Dutch tradition and include *The Letter of Introduction* 1813 (National Gallery of Scotland, Edinburgh).

The son of a parish minister, he studied at the Trustees' Academy, Edinburgh, and the Royal Academy Schools, but engravings after Teniers and Ostade suggested the pictures of popular life in which he was to excel. *The Village Politicians*, 1805, won instant success and was followed by such other works as *The Blind Fiddler* (Tate Gallery) and *The Penny Wedding* (Royal Collection). After 1825, when he visited Italy and Spain, his style changed under the influence of Velazquez and Murillo. He died on the way home from a visit to Constantinople and Palestine.

Wilkins George Hubert (1888–1958). Australian polar explorer, a pioneer in the use of surveys by both aircraft and submarines. He studied engineering, learned to fly 1910, and visited both polar regions. In 1928 he flew from Barrow (Alaska) to Green Harbour (Spitsbergen), and in 1928–29 made an Antarctic flight that proved that Graham Land is an island. He also planned to reach the North Pole by submarine. Knighted 1928.

Suggested reading
Thomas, Lowell *Sir Hubert Wilkins* (1961)
Wilkins, George Hubert *Under the North Pole* (1931)

Wilkins Maurice Hugh Frederick (1916–   ). New Zealand-born British molecular biologist. In 1962 he shared the Nobel Prize for Physiology or Medicine with Francis Crick and James Watson for his work on the molecular structure of nucleic acids, particularly DNA, using X-ray diffraction.

Wilkins began his career as a physicist working on luminescence and phosphorescence, radar, and the separation of uranium iso-

Wilkes, John British Radical politician John Wilkes. Wilkes championed the rights of the individual , but was also a notorious xenophobe who constantly ridiculed the Scots as an alien and tyrannical nation. Samuel Johnson's definition of patriotism as 'the last refuge of the scoundrel' was written with Wilkes in mind.

topes, and worked in the USA during World War II on the development of the atomic bomb. After the war he turned his attention from nuclear physics to molecular biology, and studied the genetic effects of ultrasonic waves, nucleic acids, and viruses by using ultraviolet light. He became professor of biophysics at London 1970.

Studying the X-ray diffraction pattern of DNA, he discovered that the molecule has a double helical structure and passed on his findings to Crick and Watson.

Wilkins William (1778–1839). English architect. He pioneered the Greek Revival in England with his design for Downing College, Cambridge, 1807–20. Other works include the main block of University College London 1827–28, and the National Gallery, London, 1834–38.

Wilkinson Geoffrey (1921–1996). English inorganic chemist who shared a Nobel prize 1973 for his pioneering work on the organometallic compounds of the transition metals. Knighted 1976.

Wilkinson was born near Manchester and studied at Imperial College, University of London. He held numerous posts in North America, and was assistant professor at Harvard 1951–56. He then moved back to Imperial College, where he was professor of inorganic chemistry, retiring 1988.

Wilkinson's Nobel-prizewinning work was done with US chemist R B Woodward. An organometallic molecule consists of a metal atom sandwiched between carbon rings. The synthetic compound they were investigating, ferrocene, turned out to have a single iron atom sandwiched between two five-sided carbon rings; materials were later created with other metals and four-, six-, seven-, and eight-membered carbon rings.

Wilks Samuel Stanley (1906–1964). US statistician whose work in data analysis enabled him to formulate methods of deriving valid information from small samples. He also concentrated on the developments and applications of techniques for the analysis of variance. He studied architecture at Texas and statistics at Iowa. He spent his career at Princeton, becoming professor 1944.

Wilks's investigations of the analysis of variance were devoted especially to multivariate analysis. Two of his most original contributions were the Wilks criterion and his multiple correlation coefficient.

The US College Entrance Examination Board, which carries out extensive educational tests, found his assistance invaluable in analysing their results. Seeking also to apply these methods to industrial problems, Wilks did fundamental work in the establishment of the theory of statistical tolerance.

Willard Frances Elizabeth Caroline (1839–1898). US educationalist and campaigner. Committed to the cause of the prohibition of alcohol, culminating in the Prohibition 1920–33, she served as president of the Women's Christian Temperance Union 1879–98. She was also elected president of the National Council of Women 1888.

Born in Churchville, New York, USA, and raised in Wisconsin, Willard was educated at the Northwestern Female College in Evanston, Illinois. After a career as a teacher, she was appointed dean of women at Northwestern University 1873.

Willem Dutch form of William.

William (full name William Arthur Philip Louis) (1982–). Prince of the UK, first child of the Prince and Princess of Wales.

William four kings of England:

William (I) the Conqueror (c. 1027–1087). King of England from 1066. He was the illegitimate son of Duke Robert the Devil and succeeded his father as duke of Normandy 1035. Claiming that his relative King Edward the Confessor had bequeathed him the English throne, William invaded the country 1066, defeating Harold II at Hastings, Sussex, and was crowned king of England.

He was crowned in Westminster Abbey on Christmas Day 1066. He completed the establishment of feudalism in England, compiling detailed records of land and property in the Domesday Book, and kept the barons firmly under control. He died in Rouen after a fall from his horse and is buried in Caen, France. He was succeeded by his son William II.

Suggested reading
Ashley, Maurice *The Life and Times of William I* (1973)
Barlow, F *William I and the Norman Conquest* (1965)
Douglas, D C *William the Conqueror: The Norman Impact on England* (1964)

By the splendour of God I have taken possession of my realm; the earth of England is in my two hands.

WILLIAM I
on falling over when coming ashore at Pevensey with
his invasion army 28 Sept 1066, quoted in E A Freeman
The History of the Norman Conquest vol iii ch 15 1974

William (II) Rufus ('the Red') (c. 1056–1100). King of England from 1087, the third son of William the Conqueror. He spent most of his reign attempting to capture Normandy from his brother Robert II, duke of Normandy. His extortion of money led his barons to revolt and caused confrontation with Bishop Anselm. He was killed while hunting in the New Forest, Hampshire, and was succeeded by his brother Henry I.

Shoot, Walter, in heaven's name; as if it were a devil.

WILLIAM II
Last words to Walter Tirel, while hunting in the New
Forest, 1100. Tirel shot and the arrow killed the king.

Suggested reading
Grinnell-Milne, D W *The Killing of William Rufus* (1968)
Slocombe, G *The Sons of the Conqueror* (1960)

William (III) of Orange (1650–1702). King of Great Britain and Ireland from 1688, the son of William II of Orange and Mary, daughter of Charles I. He was offered the English crown by the parliamentary opposition to James II. He invaded England 1688 and in 1689 became joint sovereign with his wife, Mary II. He spent much of his reign campaigning, first in Ireland, where he defeated James II at the battle of the Boyne 1690, and later against the French in Flanders. He was succeeded by Mary's sister, Anne.

Far better qualified to save a nation than to adorn a court.

T B Macaulay on WILLIAM (III) OF ORANGE
in *History of England* 1848

Born in the Netherlands, William was made *stadtholder* (chief magistrate) 1672 to resist the French invasion. He forced Louis XIV to make peace 1678 and then concentrated on building up a European alliance against France. In 1677 he married his cousin Mary, daughter of the future James II. When invited by both Whig and Tory leaders to take the crown from James, he landed with a large force at Torbay, Devon. James fled to France, and his Scottish and Irish supporters were defeated at the battles of Dunkeld 1689 and the Boyne 1690.

Suggested reading
Baxter, S B *William III* (1966)
MacCubbin, R P and Hamilton-Phillips, M (eds) *The Age of William and Mary* (1988)
Ogg, David *William III* (1956)
Robb, N A *William of Orange* (1962-66)

Every bullet has its billet.

WILLIAM (III) OF ORANGE
quoted in John Wesley *Journal* 6 June 1765

William IV (1765–1837). King of Great Britain and Ireland from 1830, when he succeeded his brother George IV; third son of George III. He was created duke of Clarence 1789, and married Adelaide of Saxe-Meiningen (1792–1849) 1818. During the Reform Bill crisis he secured its passage by agreeing to create new peers to overcome the hostile majority in the House of Lords. He was succeeded by Victoria.

Suggested reading
Allen, W G *King William IV* (1960)
Zeigler, P *King William IV* (1971)

His ignorance, weakness and levity put him in a miserable light, and prove him to be one of the silliest old gentlemen in his dominions.

Charles Grenville on WILLIAM IV
in his Diary 17 May 1832

William two emperors of Germany:

William I (1797–1888). King of Prussia from 1861 and emperor of Germany from 1871; the son of Friedrich Wilhelm III. He served in the Napoleonic Wars 1814–15 and helped to crush the 1848 revolution. After he succeeded his brother Friedrich Wilhelm IV to the throne of Prussia, his policy was largely dictated by his chancellor Bismarck, who secured his proclamation as emperor.

William II (1859–1941). Emperor of Germany from 1888, the son of Frederick III and Victoria, daughter of Queen Victoria of Britain. In 1890 he forced Chancellor Bismarck to resign and began to direct foreign policy himself, which proved disastrous. He encouraged warlike policies and built up the German navy. In 1914 he first approved Austria's ultimatum to Serbia and then, when he realized war was inevitable, tried in vain to prevent it. In 1918 he fled to Holland, after Germany's defeat and his abdication.

Suggested reading
Aronson, Theo *The Kaisers* (1971)
Balfour, Michael *The Kaiser and His Times* (1972)
Kurtz, Harold *The Second Reich: Kaiser Wilhelm II and His Germany* (1970)
Palmer, Alan *The Kaiser* (1978)

Though he would have hated to be told so, he was a bourgeois monarch.

Michael Balfour on WILLIAM II
in *The Kaiser and his Times* 1964

William three kings of the Netherlands:

William I (1772–1844). King of the Netherlands 1815–40. He lived in exile during the French occupation 1795–1813 and fought against the emperor Napoleon at Jena and Wagram. The Austrian Netherlands were added to his kingdom by the Allies 1815, but secured independence (recognized by the major European states 1839) by the revolution of 1830. William's unpopularity led to his abdication 1840.

William II (1792–1849). King of the Netherlands 1840–49, son of William I. He served with the British army in the Peninsular War and at Waterloo. In 1848 he averted revolution by conceding a liberal constitution.

William III (1817–1890). King of the Netherlands 1849–90, the son of William II. In 1862 he abolished slavery in the Dutch East Indies.

Almost all the chief towns of modern Scotland trace their erection or the grant of privileges to his reign.

A J G Mackay on WILLIAM THE LION
in *Dictionary of National Biography*

William the Lion (1143–1214). King of Scotland from 1165. He was captured by Henry II while invading England 1174, and forced to do homage, but Richard I abandoned the English claim to suzerainty for a money payment 1189. In 1209 William was forced by King John to renounce his claim to Northumberland.

In his youth ... the most perfect type of chivalry; in his old age and in history ... one of the noblest of medieval soldier-statesmen.

C L Kingsford on WILLIAM THE MARSHALL
in *Dictionary of National Biography*

William the Marshall 1st Earl of Pembroke (c. 1146–1219). English knight, regent of England from 1216. After supporting the dying Henry II against Richard (later Richard I), he went on a crusade to Palestine, was pardoned by Richard, and was granted an earldom 1189. On King John's death he was appointed guardian of the future Henry III, and defeated the French under Louis VIII to enable Henry to gain the throne.

He grew up as a squire in Normandy and became tutor in 1170 to Henry, son of Henry II of England. William's life was a model of chivalric loyalty, serving four successive kings of England.

William the Silent (1533–1584). Prince of Orange from 1544. William, brought up at the court of Charles V, was appointed governor of Holland by Philip II of Spain 1559, but joined the revolt of 1572 against Spain's oppressive rule and, as a Protestant from 1573, became the national leader and first stadholder. He was known as 'the Silent' because of his absolute discretion. He briefly succeeded in uniting the Catholic south and Protestant northern provinces, but

the former provinces submitted to Spain while the latter formed a federation 1579 (Union of Utrecht) which repudiated Spanish suzerainty 1581. He was assassinated by a Spanish agent.

Suggested reading
Parker, Geoffrey *The Dutch Revolt* (1989)
Wedgwood, C V *William the Silent* (1944)

As long as he lived he was the guiding-star of a whole nation, and when he died the little children cried in the streets.

J L Motley on WILLIAM THE SILENT
in *The Rise and Fall of the Dutch Republic* pt vi 1876

William of Malmesbury (c. 1080–c. 1143). English historian and monk. He compiled the *Gesta regum/Deeds of the Kings* c. 1120–40 and *Historia novella*, which together formed a history of England to 1142.

To select sources intelligently, to employ them truthfully and imaginatively, and to render them in elegant Latin.

Rodney M Thomson on WILLIAM OF MALMESBURY's conception
of the historian's task in *Blackwells's Dictionary of Historians* 1988

William of Wykeham (c. 1323–1404). English politician, bishop of Winchester from 1367, Lord Chancellor 1367–72 and 1389–91, and founder of Winchester College (public school) 1378 and New College, Oxford 1379.

Williams Frederic Calland (1911–1977). English electrical and electronics engineer who developed cathode-ray-tube storage devices used in many early computers. He was professor at Manchester from 1946. He took part in building the first stored-program computer 1948. Knighted 1976.

During World War II, Williams played a major part in the development of radar and allied devices, and in the design of the feedback systems known as servomechanisms. Visiting the Massachusetts Institute of Technology, USA, he learned of attempts to use cathode-ray tubes to store information as dots on the screen, and in 1946 began to develop this system in the UK. The phosphor in the tubes allowed an image to persist for only a fraction of a second, and at first he transferred information to and from two tubes; later he designed the appropriate circuitry to repeat the dots in one tube so that they would persist indefinitely.

Together with M H A Newman, Williams built a computer which began operation in June 1948. After modification, the machine went into production with Ferranti Limited.

In the 1950s Williams began work on electrical machines, principally induction motors and induction-excited alternators. During his later years he worked on an automatic transmission for motor vehicles.

Williams Frederick Ronald (1927–1982). Australian landscape painter. His bush paintings make a feature and a source of beauty of the monotony and repetitions that occur in the Australian countryside. In *Upwey Landscape* 1966 (Australian National Gallery, Canberra) he moves between a figurative and abstract interpretation – the tree-dotted plain stretching to the horizon conveys an impression of the Australian bush in general rather than a comment on any one part of it. His non-figurative approach brought him into conflict with the Antipodean Group of artists early in his career.

Williams George (1821–1905). Founder of the Young Men's Christian Association (YMCA). Knighted 1894.

Williams (George) Emlyn (1905–1987). Welsh actor and dramatist. His plays, in which he appeared, include *Night Must Fall* 1935 and *The Corn Is Green* 1938. He was also acclaimed for his solo performance as the author Charles Dickens. Williams gave early encouragement to the actor Richard Burton.

Williams (Hiram) Hank (1923–1953). US country singer, songwriter, and guitarist. Williams was born in Alabama, learned guitar

Williams, John *Classical guitar virtuoso John Williams. He studied with the Spanish guitarist Segovia and at the Royal College of Music, London. As a well-known and accomplished musician, he has recorded and toured widely – performing alone, with chamber groups, and as soloist with many international orchestras.*

from a black street singer, and formed his band the Drifting Cowboys 1937. Their sparse honky-tonk (dance-hall) sound featured fiddle and steel guitar. 'Lovesick Blues' 1949, which Williams did not write, was his first number-one country hit and he quickly became the genre's biggest star. He was the author of dozens of country standards and one of the originators of modern country music. His songs are characteristically mournful and blues-influenced, like 'Your Cheatin' Heart' 1953, but also include the uptempo 'Jambalaya' 1952 and the proto-rockabilly 'Hey, Good-Lookin'' 1951.

He is credited with more than 100 songs, including 'Move It On Over' 1947, 'I'm So Lonesome I Could Cry' 1949, 'Why Don't You Love Me' 1950, 'You Win Again' 1952, 'Kaw-Liga' 1952, and 'I'll Never Get Out of This World Alive' (posthumous hit 1953).

Williams John Christopher (1942–). Australian guitarist. He has been resident in London since 1952. After studying with Segovia, he made his formal debut 1958. His extensive repertoire includes contemporary music and jazz; he recorded the Rodrigo *Concerto de Aranjuez* (1939) three times. He was a founder member of the pop group Sky 1979–84.

Williams J(ohn) P(eter) R(hys) (1949–). Welsh rugby union player. With 55 appearances for his country, he is Wales's most capped player. He played in three Grand Slam winning teams and twice toured with winning British Lions teams. He played for Bridgend and London Welsh.

Williams Robin (1952–). US actor and comedian. His rapid-fire, stream-of-consciousness delivery and hyperactive stage presence first came to attention in the comedy television series *Mork and Mindy* 1978–82. Many attempts have been made to create a suitable film milieu for Williams's unique comic persona, most successfully as the subversive disc jockey in *Good Morning, Vietnam* 1987, but he has also excelled in straight dramatic performances, such as *Dead Poets Society* 1989 and *Seize the Day* 1986.

He began his career as a stand-up comic in the late 1970s and still continues to deliver his free-association comic rants in live performances and television specials. His film debut in a leading role was in Robert Altman's *Popeye* 1980, the screen version of the popular

cartoon series. His other films include *The World According to Garp* 1982, *Moscow on the Hudson* 1984, *Cadillac Man*, and *Awakenings* both 1990, *The Fisher King* 1991, the voice of the Genie in Disney's *Aladdin* 1993, and *Mrs Doubtfire* 1993.

Williams Roger (*c.* 1603–1683). American colonist, founder of the Rhode Island colony 1636, based on democracy and complete religious freedom. He tried to maintain good relations with the Indians of the region, although he fought against them in the Pequot War and King Philip's War. He was the colony's president 1654–57; there he founded the first Baptist Church in America.

Williams Shirley Vivien Teresa Brittain, Baroness Williams of Crosby (1930–). British Social Democrat Party politician. She was Labour minister for prices and consumer protection 1974–76, and education and science 1976–79. She became a founder member of the SDP (Social Democrat Party) 1981, its president 1982, but lost her parliamentary seat 1983. In 1988 she joined the newly-merged Social and Liberal Democratic Party (SLDP). She is the daughter of the socialist writer Vera Brittain. Baroness 1993.

Williams Ted (Theodore Samuel) (1918–). US baseball player. Born in San Diego, California, USA, Williams was signed by the Boston Red Sox and made his major league debut 1939. Named rookie of the year, he went on to a 19-season career with the Red Sox (interrupted by service in World War II and the Korean War). Establishing a lifetime batting average of .344, he was six times the American League batting champion and twice won the most valuable player award. In 1947 he became the second player ever to twice win the Triple Crown (leading the league in batting, home runs, and runs batted in for a season).

We're all of us guinea pigs in the laboratory of God. Humanity is just a work in progress.

TENNESSEE WILLIAMS
Camino Real 1953

Williams Tennessee (Thomas Lanier) (1911–1983). US dramatist. His work is characterized by fluent dialogue and searching analysis of the psychological deficiencies of his characters. His plays, usually set in the Deep South against a background of decadence and degradation, include *The Glass Menagerie* 1945, *A Streetcar Named Desire* 1947, and *Cat on a Hot Tin Roof* 1955, the last two of which earned Pulitzer prizes. His other plays include *Suddenly Last Summer* 1958 and *Sweet Bird of Youth* 1959. After writing *The Night of the Iguana* 1961, also awarded a Pulitzer prize, he entered a period of ill health, and none of his subsequent plays succeeded. However, his earlier work earned him a reputation as one of America's pre-eminent dramatists.

Suggested reading
Hirsch, F *A Portrait of the Artist: The Plays of Tennessee Williams* (1979)
Leverich, Lyle *Tom: The Unknown Tennessee Williams* (1995)
Londre, F H *Tennessee Williams* (1980)
Williams, Tennessee *Memoirs* (1975)

Liquor and love / rescue the cloudy sense / banish its despair / give it a home.

WILLIAM CARLOS WILLIAMS
'World Narrowed to a Point'

Williams William Carlos (1883–1963). US poet, essayist, and theoretician. He was associated with Imagism and Objectivism. One of the most original and influential of modern poets, he is noted for advancing poetics of visual images and colloquial American rhythms, conceiving the poem as a 'field of action'. His epic, five-book poem *Patterson* 1946–58 is written in a form of free verse that combines historical documents, newspaper material, and letters, to celebrate his home town in New Jersey. *Pictures from Brueghel* 1963 won him, posthumously, a Pulitzer prize. His vast body of prose work includes novels, short stories, essays, and the play *A Dream of Love* 1948.

Suggested reading
Guimond, J *The Art of William Carlos Williams* (1968)
Mariani, P *William Carlos Williams: A New World Naked* (1981)
Wagner, L *A Reference Guide to William Carlos Williams* (1978)
Whitaker, T *William Carlos Williams* (1968)
Williams, William Carlos *Autobiography* (1951)

Williams-Ellis (Bertram) Clough (1883–1978). English architect. He designed the fantasy resort of Portmeirion, N Wales. Knighted 1972.

Williamson Alexander William (1824–1904). British organic chemist who made significant discoveries concerning alcohols and ethers, catalysis, and reversible reactions. He was the first to explain the action of a catalyst in terms of the formation of an intermediate compound. He was professor at University College, London, 1849–87.

Williamson was the first to make 'mixed' ethers, with two different alkyl groups, and his method is still known as the Williamson synthesis. It involves treating an alkoxide with an alkyl halide (haloalkane).

Some of the reactions of alcohols and ethers are reversible (that is, the products of a reaction may recombine to form the reactants), a phenomenon first noted and described by Williamson in the early 1850s. If the rate of the forward reaction is the same as that of the reverse reaction, all compounds in the process coexist and the system is said to be in 'dynamic equilibrium' (a term also introduced by Williamson).

Williamson David Keith (1942–). Australian dramatist and scriptwriter. He is noted for his witty fast-moving dialogue and realistic plots and settings. His plays include *The Removalists* 1971, which won awards in both Australia and in the UK, *Don's Party* 1971, *The Department* 1975, *The Club* 1977, *Travelling North* 1979, and *The Perfectionist* 1981. His play *Siren* 1990 opened simultaneously in Sydney and Melbourne. Williamson's screenplays include *Stork* 1971, *Eliza Fraser* 1976, *Gallipoli* 1981, and *The Year of Living Dangerously* 1982 (co-writer).

Williamson Henry (1895–1977). English author. His stories of animal life include *Tarka the Otter* 1927. He described his experiences in restoring an old farm in *The Story of a Norfolk Farm* 1941 and wrote the fictional, 15-volume sequence *Chronicles of Ancient Sunlight*.

Williamson J(ames) C(assius) (1845–1913). US-born actor who became Australia's most successful theatrical entrepreneur. In 1882 in partnership with two rival theatre managers he formed an organization, known popularly as the 'Firm', which became Australia's leading theatrical management company. It controlled theatres in Sydney, Melbourne, Adelaide, and Brisbane and brought to Australia famous performers from overseas. In 1911 the name of the company changed to J C Williamson Ltd. It continued operations until 1982.

Williamson Malcolm Benjamin Graham Christopher (1931–). Australian composer, pianist, and organist. He settled in Britain 1953. His works include operas such as *Our Man in Havana* 1963, symphonies, and chamber music.

He became Master of the Queen's Musick 1975.

Willis Bruce (1955–). US actor. He first attracted attention in the television series *Moonlighting*, which displayed his gift for laconic comedy. He has cultivated a 'tough guy' image in films, notably as a resourceful detective in *Die Hard* 1988 and its two sequels 1990 and 1995, and as a prizefighter in *Pulp Fiction* 1994. Other films include *The Last Boy Scout* 1991 and *The Player* 1992.

Willis supplied the narrating voice of the baby in the successful comedy *Look Who's Talking* 1989 and its sequel 1990. He co-authored the story of the comedy-thriller *Hudson Hawk* 1991, in which he starred, but the film proved to be a box-office flop. He won an Emmy award in 1987 for *Moonlighting*. Willis is married to actress Demi Moore (1963–).

Willis Norman David (1933–). British trade-union leader. A trade-union official since leaving school, he was the general secretary of the Trades Union Congress (TUC) 1984–93. He presided over the TUC at a time of falling union membership, hostile legislation from the Conservative government, and a major review of the role and policies of the Labour Party.

Willis Ted (1914–1992). English writer and politician. He became a theatre critic for the communist newspaper *The Daily Worker*, and producer and writer for the left-wing Unity Theatre. He created one of British television's most popular characters, Constable Dixon (later Sergeant), the main character in the television series *Dixon of Dock Green* that ran for 22 years. He was also author of numerous novels, plays, and scripts for films, radio, and television.

Willis was also a scriptwriter for the long-running radio series *Mrs Dale's Diary*, and wrote several other scripts and plays for television, though none achieved the outstanding success of *Dixon of Dock Green*. His first book was his autobiography, *Whatever Happened to Tom Mix* 1970. After this he began a new career as a writer of thrillers, the first of which was *Death May Surprise Us* 1974, about the kidnapping of a prime minister. His last book was another volume of autobiography, *Evening All* 1991. He was made a Labour life peer 1970, one of the first life peers.

Willkie Wendell Lewis (1892–1944). US politician who was the Republican presidential candidate 1940. Born in Elwood, Indiana, USA, Willkie was educated at Indiana University, and became a barrister 1916. After service in World War I, he became corporate counsel for a private utility and an outspoken opponent of the economic policies of the New Deal, for which reason he was nominated as the 1940 Republican presidential candidate. After losing to F D Roosevelt, he continued as a leader of the liberal wing of the Republican Party. Becoming committed to the cause of international co-operation, he published *One World* 1942.

Wills Bob (James Robert) (1905–1975). US country fiddle player and composer. Wills began playing 1920 and went on to do local radio shows. As leader of the band known from 1934 as Bob Wills and his Texas Playboys, Wills became a pioneer of Western swing and a big influence on US popular music. His songs include 'San Antonio Rose' 1938. The band was named and renamed after the commercial sponsor's product (for a time they were the Light Crust Doughboys, for example). Their repertory drew on blues, popular ballads, and jazz, as well as country, with much original material.

Wills Helen Newington (1905–). US tennis player. She won her first US women's title 1923 and her first Wimbledon championship 1927. In the course of an unparalleled amateur tennis career, he went on to win the US title six more times and Wimbledon seven more times. She won two gold medals in the 1924 Paris Olympics. From 1929 to 1937 she played under her married name, Helen Wills Moody.

Wills William John (1834–1861). English-born Australian explorer who in 1860, with Burke, undertook an expedition to cross the continent south-north. Both men died of starvation after they had pushed on ahead to the waters of the Gulf of Carpentaria and on their return to Cooper Creek missed, by hours only, the relief party which had been waiting for them.

Willstätter Richard (1872–1942). German organic chemist who investigated plant pigments – such as chlorophyll – and alkaloids, determining the structure of cocaine, tropine, and atropine. Nobel prize 1915.

In 1905 he became professor at the Technische Hochschule in Zürich, Switzerland; he worked at the Kaiser Wilhelm Institute in Berlin 1912–16. In 1916 he became professor at Munich, but resigned in 1925 because of mounting anti-Semitism. At the start of World War II in 1939 he left Germany for Switzerland.

Willstätter showed that chlorophyll is made up of four components: two green ones, chlorophyll *a* and *b*, and two yellow ones, carotene and xanthophyll, and established the ratio in which they occur. In order to separate the complex substances, he redeveloped the technique of chromatography.

Willstätter also worked on quinones and, by following English chemist William Perkin's method of oxidizing aniline (phenylamine) with chromic acid, determined the structure of the dyestuff aniline black. Later he studied enzymes and catalytic hydrogenation, particularly in the presence of oxygen. He worked on the degradation of cellulose, investigated fermentation, and pioneered the use of hydrogels for absorption.

Wilson A(ndrew) N(orman) (1950–   ). English novelist and biographer. His first novel was *The Sweets of Pimlico* 1977. Among the subjects of his biographies have been the novelists Leo Tolstoy 1988 and C S Lewis 1990, and Jesus 1992.

The fiction trilogy that began with *Incline Our Hearts* 1988 revealed a combination of absurdist comedy and High Tory wit; a more recent novel is *The Vicar of Sorrows* 1993. 'Lilibet' 1984, a verse account of Queen Elizabeth II's early years, was ill received. Wilson was literary editor of the *Spectator* 1981–83, and in 1990 was appointed to the same post in the London *Evening Standard*.

I have no concern for the common man except that he should not be so common.

ANGUS WILSON
No Laughing Matter 1967

Wilson Angus Frank Johnstone (1913–1991). English novelist, short-story writer, and biographer. His acidly humorous books include *Anglo-Saxon Attitudes* 1956 and *The Old Men at the Zoo* 1961. In his detailed portrayal of English society he extracted high comedy from its social and moral grotesqueries.

Wilson was first known for his short-story collections *The Wrong Set* 1949 and *Such Darling Dodos* 1950. His other major novels include *Late Call* 1964, *No Laughing Matter* 1967, and *Setting the World on Fire* 1980. He also published critical works on Zola,

Wilson, Harold *Labour politician Harold Wilson was prime minister during a period of rapid social change in Britain. His premiership saw the introduction of comprehensive education, new laws on divorce and abortion, and the reduction of the voting age to 18. It was also a period beset by economic problems and the rapid decline of Britain as a world power.*

Dickens, and Kipling. Knighted 1980.
Suggested reading
Drabble, Mary *Angus Wilson: A Biography* (1995)
Gardner, A *Angus Wilson* (1985)

Wilson Brian. US pop musician and producer, founder member of the ◊Beach Boys.

Wilson Charles Thomson Rees (1869–1959). Scottish physicist who in 1911 invented the Wilson cloud chamber, an apparatus for studying subatomic particles. A cloud chamber consists of a vessel fitted with a piston and filled with air or other gas, supersaturated with water vapour. When the volume of the vessel is suddenly expanded by moving the piston outwards, the vapour cools and a cloud of tiny droplets forms on any nuclei, dust, or ions present. As fast-moving ionizing particles collide with the air or gas molecules, they show as visible tracks. Wilson shared a Nobel prize 1927 and was professor at Cambridge 1925–34.

Wilson originally devised the cloud chamber to simulate clouds in his laboratory. From 1895 to 1899, he carried out many experiments and established that the nucleation of droplets can take place in the absence of dust particles. He also demonstrated that once the gas is supersaturated with water vapour, nucleation can occur and is greatly improved by exposure to X-rays. This showed that ions are the nucleation sites on which water droplets form in the absence of dust.

Wilson realized 1910 that the cloud chamber could possibly show the track of a charged particle moving through it, and applying a magnetic field to the chamber would cause the track to curve, giving a measure of the charge and mass of the particle. The adapted Wilson cloud chamber immediately became vital to the study of radioactivity.

During 1900–10, Wilson studied electrical conduction in dust-free air by means of a gold-leaf electroscope he devised.

Wilson Colin Henry (1931–   ). English author. He wrote *The Outsider* 1956 and thrillers, including *Necessary Doubt* 1964. Later works, such as *Mysteries* 1978, are about the occult.

Wilson Edmund (1895–1972). US critic and writer. *Axel's Castle* 1931 is a survey of symbolism, and *The Wound and the Bow* 1941 a study of art and neurosis. He also produced the satirical sketches in *Memoirs of Hecate County* 1946.

Wilson Edward Osborne (1929–   ). US zoologist whose books have stimulated interest in biogeography, the study of the distribution of species, and sociobiology, the evolution of behaviour. He is a world authority on ants. Wilson was born in Birmingham, Alabama. His works include *Sociobiology: The New Synthesis* 1975, *On Human Nature* 1978, and *The Diversity of Life* 1992.

Wilson Henry Hughes (1864–1922). British soldier. He had a mixed career in World War I; following an uninspiring performance during the retreat from Mons 1914 he was given a liaison post with the French HQ. He was dismissed from this position 1916 after rowing with General Pétain, but was appointed by Lloyd George to serve on the Versailles Council 1917. Following the war, he became involved in Irish politics and was murdered by two Sinn Fein gunmen in London June 1922. Baronet 1919.

Wilson Henry Maitland ('Jumbo'), 1st Baron Wilson (1881–1964). British field marshal in World War II. He was commander in chief in Egypt 1939, led the unsuccessful Greek campaign of 1941, was commander in chief in the Middle East 1943, and in 1944 was supreme Allied commander in the Mediterranean. KCB 1940, baron 1946.

Wilson (James) Harold, Baron Wilson of Rievaulx (1916–1995). British Labour politician, party leader from 1963, prime minister 1964–70 and 1974–76. His premiership was dominated by the issue of UK admission to membership of the European Community (now the European Union), the social contract (unofficial agreement with the trade unions), and economic difficulties.

Wilson, born in Huddersfield, West Yorkshire, studied at Jesus College, Oxford, where he gained a first-class degree in philosophy, politics, and economics. During World War II he worked as a civil servant, and in 1945 stood for Parliament and won the marginal seat of Ormskirk. Assigned by prime minister Clement Attlee to a junior post in the Ministry of Works, he progressed to become president of the Board of Trade 1947–51 (when he resigned because of social-service cuts). In 1963 he succeeded Hugh Gaitskell as Labour leader and became prime minister the following year, increasing his majority 1966. He formed a minority government Feb 1974 and achieved a majority of three Oct 1974. He resigned 1976 and was succeeded by James Callaghan. He was knighted 1976 and made a peer 1983.

If I had the choice between smoked salmon and tinned salmon, I'd have it tinned, with vinegar.
HAROLD WILSON
in Observer 11 Nov 1962

In terms of electoral success Wilson was an outstanding party leader, winning four of the five general elections he fought and causing Labour to be described as the 'natural party of government'. In preventing division between the left and the right of his party, he was frequently obliged to trim his policies to secure the support of the opposing wings. His attempts to rejuvenate British industry and enterprise were not always successful; perhaps his greatest achievement was setting up the Open University.

Following the Labour victory in the 1964 general election, Wilson announced his intention to revitalize British industry and created the Department of Economic Affairs (DEA) in order to thwart what he saw as the negative influence of the Treasury. The attempt predictably failed and the DEA was subsequently abandoned.

In 1966, despite opposition from within his own party as well as outside, he decided to reapply for British membership of the European Community (EC). With his deputy George Brown, he toured the European capitals, canvassing support. Their efforts were to no avail; the application was vetoed by the French president Charles de Gaulle.

Wilson turned his attention to industrial relations and awaited the report of the Donovan Royal Commission on Trade Unions and Employers' Associations, which he had set up in 1965. When it reported in 1968, an attempt to implement its recommendations, through the White Paper *In Place of Strife*, was blocked by opposition from trade unions and from within the cabinet.

The two years before Wilson's unexpected resignation were primarily occupied with the problems of reconciling EC membership (achieved by Edward Heath's government 1970–74), with calls within the Labour Party for withdrawal, and the revival of the economy without uncontrollable inflation. He solved the first through a referendum, which endorsed EC membership, and tackled the second by means of an incomes policy.

He retired in 1976, leaving his successor, James Callaghan, to finish what he had started. Despite rumours of undercover plots to remove him, Wilson steadfastly claimed that it had long been his intention to retire from public life after his 60th birthday. There was speculation that he had detected early signs of a diminution in his powers of memory which persuaded him to leave before they deteriorated further.

Suggested reading
Haines, Joe *The Politics of Power* (1977)
Smith, Dudley *Harold Wilson: A Critical Biography* (1964)
Wilson, Harold *Memoirs: The Making of a Prime Minister, 1916–64* (1986)
Ziegler, Philip *Wilson: The Authorised Life* (1993)

Wilson John Tuzo (1908–1993). Canadian geologist and geophysicist who established and brought about a general understanding of the concept of plate tectonics.

Born in Ottawa, Wilson studied geology and physics – an original combination that led directly to the development of the science of geophysics – at the University of Toronto, and obtained his doctoral degree at Princeton University, New Jersey, USA. His particular interest was the movement of the continents across the Earth's surface – then a poorly understood and not widely accepted concept known as 'continental drift'. He spent 28 years as professor of geophysics at the University of Toronto, retiring 1974 just as interest in

plate tectonics was developing worldwide. From then on he was the director-general of the Ontario Science Centre and later the chancellor of York University, Toronto, finally retiring 1987. In 1957 he was the president of the International Union of Geodesy and Geophysics – the most senior administrative post in the field.

Wilson's great strength was in education. He pioneered hands-on interactive museum exhibits, and could explain complex subjects like the movement of continents, the spreading of ocean floors, and the creation of island chains by using astonishingly simple models. He was an active outdoor man, leading expeditions into the remote north of Canada, and he made the first ascent of Mount Hague in Montana, USA, 1935. The Wilson Range in Antarctica is named after him.

Wilson Pete (1933–). US Republican politician, governor of California from 1991. He was senator from California 1983–91, and mayor of San Diego, California, 1971–83.

Wilson was born in Lake Forest, Illinois. He pioneered controlled urban growth in San Diego, encouraging public transport, discouraging the use of private cars, and concentrating development in rural areas. As governor of California (he had defeated Dianne Feinstein in the election), he increased taxes in order to reduce the large budget deficit. He was re-elected 1994.

Wilson Richard (1714–1782). Welsh painter. His landscapes are infused with an Italianate atmosphere and recomposed in a Classical manner. His work influenced the development of English landscape painting, and Turner in particular.

His father gave him a classical education and he studied art in London, 1729, under an obscure portrait painter, Thomas Wright. Until 1750 he practised portraiture with some success, painting the Prince of Wales (George III) and his brother, the Duke of York (National Portrait Gallery), as well as Flora Macdonald (National Gallery of Scotland). He also painted some landscapes before going to Italy 1750, and during his stay there (until 1756) was encouraged to devote himself to landscape. He painted at Rome and Naples, having several pupils, and producing a type of 'classical landscape' deriving partly from Claude and Gaspard Poussin but also from Cuyp, whose golden light Wilson greatly admired, while his convention for painting foliage seems to have been based on Ruisdael. His originality lay, however, in a structural simplicity of design, breadth of treatment, and luminous atmosphere directly studied in nature. It is possible that this departure from the artificialities then in vogue accounts for his lack of success when he returned to England. He was often unsuccessful, in introducing mythology (as in his *Niobe*), in remembered Italian scenes (which were uneven in quality and sometimes evidently 'potboilers'), and in his views of England and Wales. Yet he created masterpieces, among them *The River Dee* (Barber Institute, Birmingham), *Cader Idris* (National Gallery), and *Snowdon* (Nottingham). He retired shortly before his death to live near Llanberis, and left an achievement fully appreciated by the following generation.

Wilson Robert (1941–). US avant-garde theatre director. He specializes in non-narrative, elaborately visual theatre productions such as *Deafman Glance* 1971, *Ka Mountain* at the Shiraz Festival, Iran, 1972, and *The Life and Times of Joseph Stalin* 1973. Later productions include *Einstein on the Beach* 1976 and 1992, operatic productions of Euripides' tragedies *Medea* 1984 and *Alcestis* 1986, *The Black Rider* 1990, and *Alice* 1992. Wilson has worked consistently outside the USA, and has collaborated closely with the German dramatist Heiner Müller.

Wilson Robert Woodrow (1936–). US radioastronomer who, with Arno Penzias, in 1964–65 detected the cosmic background radiation, which is thought to represent a residue of the primordial Big Bang. He and Penzias shared the 1978 Nobel Prize for Physics for their work on microwave radiation.

In 1963 he joined the Bell Telephone Laboratories in New Jersey; he was made head of the Radiophysics Department in 1976.

In 1964, Wilson and Penzias tested a radiotelescope and receiver system for the Bell Telephone Laboratories with the intention of tracking down all possible sources of static that were causing interference in satellite communications. They found a high level of isotropic background radiation at a wavelength of 7.3 cm/2.9 in, with a temperature of 3.1K (−276°C/−529°F). This radiation was a hundred times more powerful than any that could be accounted for on the basis of any known sources.

Unable to explain this signal, Wilson and Penzias contacted Princeton University, where it was immediately realized that their findings confirmed predictions of residual microwave radiation from the beginning of the universe.

Wilson Teddy (Theodore Shaw) (1912–1986). US bandleader and jazz pianist. He toured with Benny Goodman 1935–39 and during that period recorded in small groups with many of the best musicians of the time; some of his 1930s recordings feature the singer Billie Holiday. Wilson led a big band 1939–40 and a sextet 1940–46.

The world must be made safe for democracy.

WOODROW WILSON
Address to Congress 2 Apr 1917

Wilson (Thomas) Woodrow (1856–1924). 28th president of the USA 1913–21, a Democrat. He kept the USA out of World War I until 1917, and in Jan 1918 issued his 'Fourteen Points' as a basis for a just peace settlement.

At the peace conference in Paris he secured the inclusion of the League of Nations in individual peace treaties, but these were not ratified by Congress, so the USA did not join the League. Nobel Peace Prize 1919.

Wilson, born in Virginia, became president of Princeton University 1902. In 1910 he became governor of New Jersey.

Wilson, Woodrow *The 28th president of the USA, Democrat Woodrow Wilson. He won the presidential election on his neutrality in the face of World War I, but public sentiment kindled by U-boat attacks on the Allies forced him to enter the hostilities.* (Image Select)

Elected president 1912 against Theodore Roosevelt and William Taft, he initiated anti-trust legislation and secured valuable social reforms in his progressive 'New Freedom' programme. He strove to keep the USA neutral during World War I but the German U-boat campaign forced him to declare war 1917. In 1919 he suffered a stroke from which he never fully recovered.

Suggested reading
Bailey, T A *Woodrow Wilson and the Great Betrayal* (1945)
Cooper, John *The Warrior and the Priest: Woodrow Wilson and Theodore Roosevelt* (1983)
Levin, N G *Woodrow Wilson and World Politics* (1968)
Link, Arthur (ed) *Woodrow Wilson: A Profile* (1968)

Winchell Walter (1897–1972). US journalist, born in New York. He was a columnist for the *New York Mirror* 1929–69, and his bitingly satiric writings were syndicated throughout the USA.

Winckelmann Johann Joachim (1717–1768). German art historian. The son of a cobbler, Winckelmann spent his early career as a schoolmaster in Prussia. By converting to Catholicism, he was able to move to Rome, where he became Commissioner of Antiquities to the Holy See. He worked in Rome from 1755. His studies of ancient Greece and Rome were an inspiration for the Neo-Classicism movement, provided the basis for modern art history, and influenced the direction of education in Germany. They include *Geschichte der Kunst des Altertums/History of the Art of Antiquity* 1764, in which he defines art as the expression of the spirit of an age.

Windsor Duchess of. Title of Wallis Warfield ◊Simpson.

Windsor Duke of. Title of ◊Edward VIII.

Wingate Orde Charles (1903–1944). British soldier. In 1936 he established a reputation for unorthodox tactics in Palestine. In World War II he served in the Middle East and organized guerrilla forces in Ethiopia, and later led the Chindits, the 3rd Indian Division, in guerrilla operations against the Japanese army in Burma (now Myanmar). He was killed in an aeroplane accident in Burma.

Winnicott Donald Woods (1896–1971). British psychoanalyst and child psychiatrist. In his early work, Winnicott studied the relationship between mother and child, developing the view that, for the infant, the mother mediates development of the self. His theories were developed in three volumes summarizing his clinical experience, entitled *Collected Papers: Through Paediatrics to Psychoanalysis* 1958, *The Maturational Process and the Facilitating Environment* 1965, and *Playing and Reality* 1971.

Although often regarded as an exponent of object-relations theory, he was a critic of Kleinian approaches to therapy, arguing that only a technique which could allow regression to early childhood might help individuals for whom premature parental demands had impaired the course of ego development.

Winsor Frederick Albert (1763–1830). German inventor, one of the pioneers of gas lighting in the UK and France. Winsor was born in Brunswick. He went to Britain before 1799 and became interested in the technology and economics of fuels. In 1802 he went to Paris to investigate the 'thermo-lamp' which French engineer Philippe Lebon had patented in 1799. Returning to Britain, he started a gasworks and in 1807 lit one side of Pall Mall, London, with gas lamps. In 1804–09 he was granted various patents for gas furnaces and purifiers.

His application to Parliament for a charter for the Light and Heat Company having failed, Winsor once more moved to France, but in Paris his company made little progress and was liquidated 1819.

The distilling retort Winsor used consisted of an iron pot with a fitted lid. The lid had a pipe in the centre leading to the conical condensing vessel, which was compartmented inside with perforated divisions to spread the gas to purify it of hydrogen sulphide and ammonia. The device was not very successful, and the gas being burned was impure and emitted a pungent smell.

Winsor published *Description of the Thermo-lamp Invented by Lebon of Paris* 1802, *Analogy between Animal and Vegetable Life, Demonstrating the Beneficial Application of the Patent Light Stoves to all Green and Hot Houses* 1807, and others.

Winterhalter Franz Xavier (1805–1873). German portraitist. He became court painter to Grand Duke Leopold at Karlsruhe, then, in 1834, moved to Paris and enjoyed the patronage of European royalty.

Winter King, the name given to Frederick V because he was king of Bohemia for one winter (1619–20).

I asked why he was a priest, and he said if you have to work for anybody an absentee boss is best.

JEANETTE WINTERSON
The Passion ch 1 1987

Winterson Jeanette (1959–   ). English novelist. Her autobiographical first novel *Oranges Are Not the Only Fruit* 1985, humorously describes her upbringing as an Evangelical Pentecostalist in Lancashire, and her subsequent realization of her homosexuality. Later novels include *The Passion* 1987, *Sexing the Cherry* 1989, *Written On the Body* 1992, and *Art and Lies* 1994.

Winthrop John (1588–1649). American colonist and first governor of the Massachusetts Bay Colony. A devout Puritan and one of the founders of the Massachusetts Bay Company 1628, he served as Massachusetts governor or deputy governor until his death. He first arrived in New England with a large group of settlers 1630. He was a founder of the city of Boston the same year.

Born in England and educated at Cambridge University, Winthrop studied law at Gray's Inn and became a barrister 1628. Deeply conservative, he favoured the prosecution and banishment of Anne Hutchinson 1638. His *History of New England from 1630 to 1649* was published 1825.

Wise Robert Earl (1914–   ). US film director. He began as a film editor, making his directing debut with a horror film, *Curse of the Cat People* 1944; he progressed to such large-scale projects as *The Sound of Music* 1965 and *Star* 1968. His other films include *The Body Snatcher* 1945 and *Star Trek: The Motion Picture* 1979.

Wise Stephen Samuel (1874–1949). Hungarian-born US religious leader. Ordained as a reform rabbi 1893, he served congregations in New York City 1893–1900 and Portland, Oregon, 1900–07, after which he became rabbi of the Free Synagogue in New York. He was president of the American Jewish Congress 1924–49.

Born in Budapest, Wise emigrated to the USA with his family 1875. Educated at the City College of New York, he received a PhD from Columbia University 1901. An ardent Zionist, he attended the Versailles Peace Conference 1919.

Wise Thomas James (1859–1937). British bibliographer. He collected the Ashley Library of first editions, chiefly English poets and dramatists 1890–1930, acquired by the British Museum at his death, and made many forgeries of supposed privately printed first editions of Browning, Tennyson, and Swinburne. His activities were revealed 1934, and in 1956 it was found that he had perfected his own copies of 17th-century plays by abstracting leaves from copies belonging to the British Museum.

Wiseman Nicholas Patrick Stephen (1802–1865). British Catholic priest who became the first archbishop of Westminster 1850.

Wishart George (*c.* 1513–1546). Scottish Protestant reformer burned for heresy, who probably converted John Knox.

Wister Owen (1860–1938). US novelist. He created the Western genre. He was born in Philadelphia, a grandson of the English actress Fanny Kemble, and became known for stories of cowboys, including *The Virginian* 1902. He also wrote *Roosevelt: The Story of a*

When you call me that, smile!

OWEN WISTER
The Virginian ch 2 1902

Friendship 1880–1919 1930, about his relationship with US president Theodore Roosevelt.

Withering William (1741–1799). English physician, botanist, and mineralogist who investigated the drug digitalis (from the foxglove plant), which he initially used as a diuretic to treat oedema.

From 1775 he had a practice in Birmingham, where he met prominent contemporary scientists; he later became physician at Birmingham General Hospital. Because he publicly expressed his sympathies with the French Revolution, in 1791 his house was attacked by a mob.

Withering began studying *Digitalis purpurea* in 1775, after noting its use in traditional herbal remedies. He worked out precise dosages of dried foxglove leaves for oedema, and also suggested the possible use of the drug in the treatment of heart disease. It is now widely used for treating heart failure.

Withering published *Account of the Foxglove* 1785.

His *Botanical Arrangement* 1776, based on the system of Swedish botanist Linnaeus, became a standard work, and his activities in geology are remembered through the mineral ore witherite (barium carbonate), which was named after him.

Witkiewicz Stanislaw Ignacy (1885–1939). Polish dramatist and novelist. His surrealist plays only became widely known after World War II: these include *The Water Hen* 1921, *The Crazy Locomotive* 1923, *The Madman and the Nun* 1925, and the tragedy *The Pragmatists* (written 1918). Many of his plays were produced by the director Tadeusz Kantor.

Cultured, arrogant, ruthless and realistic ... showing short-term political skill of a high order, though not long-term statesmanship.

E N Williams on JOHANN DE WITT
in *Penguin Dictionary of English and European History 1485–1789* 1980

Witt Johann de (1625–1672). Dutch politician, grand pensionary of Holland and virtual prime minister from 1653. His skilful diplomacy ended the Dutch Wars of 1652–54 and 1665–67, and in 1668 he formed a triple alliance with England and Sweden against Louis XIV of France. He was murdered by a rioting mob.

Witt Katarina (1965–   ). German ice-skater. She was 1984 Olympic champion (representing East Germany) and by 1990 had won four world titles (1984–85, 1987–88) and six consecutive European titles (1983–88). After four years as a professional she returned to competitive skating in 1993.

Wittgenstein Ludwig Josef Johann (1889–1951). Austrian philosopher. *Tractatus Logico-Philosophicus* 1922 postulated the 'picture theory' of language: that words represent things according to social agreement. He subsequently rejected this idea, and developed the idea that usage was more important than convention.

The picture theory said that it must be possible to break down a sentence into 'atomic propositions' whose elements stand for elements of the real world. After he rejected this idea, his later philosophy developed a quite different, anthropological view of language: words are used according to different rules in a variety of human activities – different 'language games' are played with them. The traditional philosophical problems arise through the assumption that words (like 'exist' in the sentence 'Physical objects do not really exist') carry a fixed meaning with them, independent of context.

Wittgenstein was born in Vienna and studied in the UK at Cambridge, where he taught in the 1930s and 1940s, becoming professor 1939. His *Philosophical Investigations* 1953 and *On Certainty* 1969 were published posthumously.

Suggested reading
Bloor, D *Wittgenstein* (1983)
Finch, Henry Le Roy *Wittgenstein* (1995)
Grayling, A C *Wittgenstein* (1989)
Kenny, Anthony *Wittgenstein* (1973)
Malcolm, Norman *Wittgenstein: A Memoir* (1958)
Monk, Ray *Wittgenstein: The Duty of Genius* (1990)

Wittgenstein Paul (1887–1961). Austrian pianist. He was a brother of the philosopher Ludwig Wittgenstein. Despite losing his right arm in World War I he continued a career as a pianist, cultivating a virtuoso left-arm technique. He commissioned Ravel's *Concerto for the Left Hand* 1929–30, Prokofiev's concerto no 4 in B flat 1931, and concert works from Richard Strauss, Benjamin Britten, and others.

Wittig Georg (1897–1987). German chemist whose method of synthesizing olefins (alkenes) from carbonyl compounds is a reaction often termed the Wittig synthesis. For this achievement he shared the 1979 Nobel Prize for Chemistry. He was professor at Freiburg 1937–44, Tübingen 1944–56, and Heidelberg 1956–67.

Witz Konrad (*c.* 1400–*c.* 1445). German-born Swiss painter. His sharply observed realism suggests that he was familiar with the work of contemporary Flemish artists such as Jan van Eyck. Lake Geneva is the setting for a biblical story in his best-known work, *The Miraculous Draught of Fishes* 1444 (Musée d'Art et d'Histoire, Geneva), representing one of the earliest recognizable landscapes in European art.

Witz was the son of a painter who worked for the Duke of Burgundy. He went with his father to Burgundy and the Netherlands, and derived some inspiration from these sources. He worked mainly at Basel, developing a strength and sureness of design in which he departed from the 'soft' manner of German art at the time. His great powers can be seen in the *Annunciation, c.* 1445 (Nuremberg), but unquestionably his masterpiece is *The Miraculous Draught of Fishes*, with its beautifully rendered landscape background.

Witzleben Erwin von (1881–1944). German field marshal in World War II. He commanded the 1st German Army in France 1940 and became commander in chief in the West May 1941 but retired for health reasons 1942. He had long been involved with a circle of officers opposed to Hitler and was drawn into the July Plot 1944, being nominated as the future commander in chief after Hitler had been killed. When the plot failed he was arrested and hanged Aug 1944.

Jeeves, of course, is a gentleman's gentleman, not a butler, but if the call comes, he can buttle with the best of them.

P G WODEHOUSE
Stiff Upper Lip, Jeeves ch 1 1963

Wodehouse P(elham) G(renville) (1881–1975). English novelist. He became a US citizen 1955. His humorous novels portray the accident-prone world of such characters as the socialite Bertie Wooster and his invaluable and impeccable manservant Jeeves, and Lord Emsworth of Blandings Castle with his prize pig, the Empress of Blandings.

From 1906, Wodehouse also collaborated on the lyrics of Broadway musicals by Jerome Kern, Gershwin, and others. He spent most of his life in the USA. Staying in France 1941, during World War II, he was interned by the Germans; he made some humorous broadcasts from Berlin, which were taken amiss in Britain at the time, but he was later exonerated, and became KBE 1975. His work is admired for its style and geniality, and includes *Indiscretions of Archie* 1921, *Uncle Fred in the Springtime* 1939, and *Aunts Aren't Gentlemen* 1974.

Suggested reading
Connolly, Joseph *P G Wodehouse* (1980)
Donaldson, Frances *P G Wodehouse* (1982)
Edwards, Owen Dudley *P G Wodehouse* (1977)
Wodehouse, P G *Wodehouse on Wodehouse* (autobiography) (1957)

Woffington Peg (Margaret) (*c.* 1714–1760). Irish actress. She played in Dublin as a child and made her debut at Covent Garden, London, 1740. She acted in many Restoration comedies, often taking male roles, such as Lothario in Rowe's *The Fair Penitent*.

Organic chemistry just now is enough to drive one mad. It gives one the impression of a primeval, tropical forest full of the most remarkable things, a monstrous and boundless thicket, with no way of escape, into which one may well dread to enter.

FRIEDRICH WÖHLER
Letter to Berzelius 28 Jan 1835

Wöhler Friedrich (1800–1882). German chemist who in 1828 became the first person to synthesize an organic compound (urea) from an inorganic compound (ammonium cyanate). He also devised a method 1827 that isolated the metals aluminium, beryllium, yttrium, and titanium from their ores. He was professor at Göttingen from 1836.

Until Wöhler's landmark synthesis of urea there had been a basic misconception in scientific thinking that the chemical changes undergone by substances in living organisms were not governed by the same laws as inanimate substances.

Wöhler worked with German chemist Justus von Liebig on a number of important investigations. In 1830, they proved the polymerism of cyanates and fulminates; in 1837, they investigated uric acid and its derivatives.

Wöhler discovered quinone (cyclohexadiene-1,4-dione), hydroquinone or quinol (benzene-1,4-diol), and calcium carbide. He isolated boron and silicon.

I sent him a song five years ago, and asked him to mark a cross in the score wherever he thought it was faulty ... Brahms sent it back unread, saying, 'I don't want to make a cemetery of your composition.'

HUGO WOLF
quoted in L P Lochner *Fritz Kreisler* 1951

Wolf Hugo Filipp Jakob (1860–1903). Austrian composer. His more than 250 *lieder* (songs) included the *Mörike-Lieder/Mörike Songs* 1888 and the two-volume *Italienisches Liederbuch/Italian Songbook* 1891, 1896. He brought a new concentration and tragic eloquence to the art of lieder. Among his other works are the opera *Der Corregidor/The Magistrate* 1895 and orchestral works, such as *Italian Serenade* 1892.

Wolf Maximilian Franz Joseph Cornelius (1863–1932). German astronomer who developed new photographic methods for observational astronomy. He discovered several new nebulae, both within the Milky Way and outside our Galaxy; more than 200 asteroids; and in 1883 a comet, which now bears his name.

Wolf was born and educated in Heidelberg, where he spent most of his career, becoming professor 1893. He used a small private observatory 1885–96, and then became the director of a new observatory at Königstuhl, near Heidelberg, built at his instigation.

Wolf was the first to use time-lapse photography in astronomy, a technique he used for detecting asteroids. In 1903 he discovered the first of the so-called Trojan satellites (number 588, later named Achilles), whose orbits are in precise synchrony with that of Jupiter's; they form a gravitationally stable configuration between Jupiter and the Sun. This kind of triangular three-bodied system had been analysed and predicted theoretically by Joseph Lagrange in the 1770s.

Independently of US astronomer Edward Barnard, Wolf discovered that the dark 'voids' in the Milky Way are in fact nebulae which are obscured by vast quantities of dust, and he studied their spectral characteristics and distribution.

Wolf was the first to observe Halley's comet when it approached the Earth in 1909.

Wolf Naomi (1962–). US feminist writer. In *The Beauty Myth: How Images of Beauty are Used Against Women* 1990, she attributes the prevalence of eating disorders to the exaggerated importance given to a woman's appearance.

She argues that the cosmetics and diet industries force women to be preoccupied with attaining an ideal of beauty, thereby lowering their self-esteem. In *Fire with Fire: The New Female Power and How it will Change the Twenty-First Century* 1993, she proposes that women are powerful enough to move on from traditional feminism.

Wolfe Gene (1931–). US writer. He is known for the science-fiction series *The Book of the New Sun* 1980–83, with a Surrealist treatment of stock themes, and for the urban fantasy *Free, Live Free* 1985.

Oh! he is mad, is he? Then I wish he would bite some other of my generals.

George II
replying to a complaint that General JAMES WOLFE was a madman

---

Wolfe James (1727–1759). British soldier who served in Canada and commanded a victorious expedition against the French general Montcalm in Quebec on the Plains of Abraham, during which both commanders were killed. The British victory established their supremacy over Canada.

Wolfe fought at the battles of Dettingen, Falkirk, and Culloden. With the outbreak of the Seven Years' War (the French and Indian War in North America), he was posted to Canada and played a conspicuous part in the siege of the French stronghold of Louisburg 1758. He was promoted to major-general 1759.

Suggested reading
Garrett, R *General Wolfe* (1975)
Schama, S *Dead Certainties* (1991)

Most of the time we think we're sick, it's all in the mind.

THOMAS WOLFE
Look Homeward, Angel pt 1, ch 1 1929

Wolfe Thomas Clayton (1900–1938). US novelist. He is noted for the unrestrained rhetoric and emotion of his prose style. He wrote four long and hauntingly powerful autobiographical novels, mostly of the South: *Look Homeward, Angel* 1929, *Of Time and the River* 1935, *The Web and the Rock* 1939, and *You Can't Go Home Again* 1940 (the last two published posthumously).

Born in Asheville, North Carolina, Wolfe studied playwriting at the University of North Carolina and Harvard University. He settled in New York City, with hopes of becoming a dramatist. His first novel, *Look Homeward, Angel*, was a realistic, brutal view of the South and Southern family life, the result of six years of work with Scribner's editor Maxwell Perkins. He also wrote *The Story of a Novel* 1936 and the short-story collections *From Death to Morning* 1935 and *The Hills Beyond* 1941.

Suggested reading
Donald, David Herbert *Look Homeward: A Biography of Thomas Wolfe* (1987)
Evans, E *Thomas Wolfe* (1984)
Turnbull, A *Thomas Wolfe* (1968)
Wolfe, Thomas *The Autobiography of an American Novelist* (1983)

Wolfe Tom (Thomas Kennerly Wolfe, Jr) (1931–). US journalist and novelist. In the 1960s he was a founder of the 'New Journalism', which brought fiction's methods to reportage. Wolfe recorded US mores and fashions in pop-style essays in, for example, *The Kandy-Kolored Tangerine-Flake Streamline Baby* 1965. His sharp social eye is applied to the New York of the 1980s in his novel *The Bonfire of the Vanities* 1988 (filmed 1990).

Born in Richmond, Virginia, Wolfe graduated from Yale University and worked as a journalist for both newspapers and magazines. He also wrote *The Electric Kool-Aid Acid Test* 1968; *Radical Chic and Mau-Mauing the Flak Catchers* 1970; *The Painted Word* 1975, about art; *The Right Stuff* 1979, about the first US astronauts

(filmed 1983); and *From Bauhaus to Our House* 1981, about modern architecture.

Wolff Christian (1679–1754). German philosopher, mathematician, and scientist who invented the terms 'cosmology' and 'teleology'. He was science adviser to Peter the Great of Russia 1716–25. He was professor of mathematics at Halle 1707–23 and professor of mathematics and philosophy at Marburg 1723–40.

Wolff worked in many fields, including theology, psychology, botany, and physics. His philosophy was influenced by Gottfried Leibniz and scholasticism. His numerous works include *Vernunftige Gedanken von Gott, der Welt und der Seele der Menschen/Rational Ideas on God, the World and the Soul of Man* 1720.

Wolff Heinz Siegfried (1928–). German-born British biomedical engineer who works on high-technology instruments and the application of technology to medicine.

Born in Berlin, Wolff left Germany for the UK as a boy. He studied physiology at London and then worked at the Medical Research Council (MRC)'s National Institute for Medical Research, where he specialized in the development of instrumentation. Formerly director of the Biomedical Division of the MRC's Clinical Research Centre, he is currently director of the Institute for Bioengineering at Brunel University in the UK.

Wolff's interests range from the invention of new high technology instruments to the widespread and sensible application of technology to the problems of the elderly and the disabled. He believes that

Wolfe, Tom US journalist and novelist Tom Wolfe, a foremost exponent of the 'New Journalism'. Since the 1960s he has cast a perceptive and satirical eye over popular US culture, capturing periods or movements in such phrases as 'radical chic' and 'the me decade'. His deflation of contemporary political ideas have led some critics to see him as essentially racist and anti-liberal.

small, specialized pieces of equipment that can be worked by doctors and nurses may be preferable to large centralized units to which patients have to go for tests or treatment. Machines should be simple to use, should show when they are not working properly, and should be designed so that they can be repaired on the spot by the operator.

Wolff Kaspar Friedrich (1733–1794). German surgeon and physiologist who is regarded as the founder of embryology. He introduced the idea that initially unspecialized cells later differentiate to produce the separate organs and systems of the plant or animal body.

Wolff was born in Berlin and studied at Halle and the Berlin Medical School. In 1766 he accepted an invitation from Catherine II of Russia to take the post of Academician for anatomy and physiology in St Petersburg. He remained there until his death.

Wolff produced his revolutionary work *Theoria generationis* in 1759. Until that time it was generally believed that each living organism develops from an exact miniature of the adult within the seed or sperm – the so-called preformation or homunculus theory. In fact, Wolff's view that plants and animals are composed of cells was still a subject of controversy, and his findings were largely ignored for more than 50 years.

His name is also associated with, among other parts of the anatomy, the Wolffian body, a structure in an animal embryo that eventually develops into the kidney.

Wolf-Ferrari Ermanno (1876–1948). Italian composer. His operas include *Il segreto di Susanna/Susanna's Secret* 1909 and the realistic tragedy *I gioielli di Madonna/The Jewels of the Madonna* 1911.

Wölfflin Heinrich (1864–1945). Swiss art historian and writer on aesthetics. His analyses of style in painting, such as *Kunstgeschichtliche Grundbegriffe/Principles of Art History* 1915, have been very influential, advocating a formalist approach and the study of concrete properties such as line, colour, and form. His significance is now seen chiefly in his establishing art history as a rigorous intellectual discipline.

Wolfit's Lear is a ruined piece of nature.

James Agate on DONALD WOLFIT
in *Autobiography* 1946

Wolfit Donald (1902–1968). English actor and manager. He formed his own theatre company 1937, and excelled in the Shakespearean roles of Shylock and Lear, and Volpone (in Ben Jonson's play). Knighted 1957.

Wolfson Isaac (1897–1991). British store magnate and philanthropist, chair of Great Universal Stores from 1946. He established the Wolfson Foundation 1955 to promote health, education, and youth activities, founded Wolfson College, Cambridge, 1965, and (with the Ford Foundation) endowed Wolfson College, Oxford, 1966. Baronet 1962.

Wollaston William Hyde (1766–1828). English chemist and physicist who discovered in 1804 how to make malleable platinum. He went on to discover the new elements palladium 1804 and rhodium 1805. He also contributed to optics through the invention of a number of ingenious and still useful measuring instruments.

Wollaston was born in East Dereham, Norfolk, and studied medicine at Cambridge.

Wollaston initiated the technique of powder metallurgy when working with platinum. Using aqua regia (a mixture of concentrated nitric and hydrochloric acids), he dissolved the platinum from crude platina, a mixed platinum–iridium ore. He then prepared ammonium platinichloride, which he decomposed by heating to yield fine grains of platinum metal. The grains were worked using heat, pressure, and hammering to form sheets, which he sold to industrial chemists. He donated much of the profits to various scientific societies to help finance their researches.

In 1807 he developed the *camera lucida*, which was to inspire William Fox Talbot to his discoveries in photography. A supporter

of John Dalton's atomic theory, Wollaston suggested 1808 that a knowledge of the arrangements of atoms in three dimensions would be a great leap forward. As a member of a Royal Commission in 1819, Wollaston was instrumental in the rejection of the decimal system of weights and measures.

I do not wish them [women] to have power over men; but over themselves.

MARY WOLLSTONECRAFT
Vindication of the Rights of Woman ch 4 1792

Wollstonecraft Mary (1759–1797). British feminist, member of a group of radical intellectuals called the English Jacobins, whose book *A Vindication of the Rights of Women* 1792 demanded equal educational opportunities for women. She married William Godwin and died giving birth to a daughter, Mary (later Mary Shelley).
Suggested reading
Flexner, Eleanor *Mary Wollstonecraft* (1972)
Godwin, William *Memoirs of Mary Wollstonecraft Godwin* (1798)
Tims, Margaret *Mary Wollstonecraft: A Social Pioneer* (1976)
Tomalin, Claire *The Life and Death of Mary Wollstonecraft* (1975)
Wollstonecraft, Mary *A Vindication of the Rights of Women* (1792, modern editions available)

Surely John Bull will not endanger his birthright, his liberty, his property, simply in order that men and women may cross between England and France without running the risk of sea-sickness.

GARNET WOLSELEY
On the Channel Tunnel proposals of 1882

Wolseley Garnet Joseph, 1st Viscount Wolseley (1833–1913). British army officer. He fought in the Crimean War 1853–56 and then commanded in both the Ashanti War 1873–74 and last part of the Zulu War 1879–80. He campaigned in Egypt, but was too late to relieve General Gordon at Khartoum. As commander in chief 1895–1900, he began modernizing the army. KCMG 1870, baron 1882, viscount 1885.

Wolsey Thomas (c. 1475–1530). English cleric and politician. In Henry VIII's service from 1509, he became archbishop of York 1514, cardinal and lord chancellor 1515, and began the dissolution of the monasteries.

His reluctance to further Henry's divorce from Catherine of Aragon led to his downfall 1529. He was charged with high treason 1530 but died before being tried.
Suggested reading
Guy, J A *The Cardinal's Court* (1977)
Gwyn, Peter *The King's Cardinal: The Rise and Fall of Thomas Wolsey* (1990)
Harvey, Nancy L *Thomas Cardinal Wolsey* (1980)
Ridley, Jasper *The Statesman and the Fanatic: Thomas Wolsey and Thomas More* (1982)
Williams, Neville *The Cardinal and the Secretary: Thomas Wolsey and Thomas Cromwell* (1976)

We say God is colourless, but everything we do tends to draw a distinction. Religion is a very racial thing.

STEVIE WONDER
in an interview with Robert Hilburn *Los Angeles Times* 1980

Wonder Stevie. Stage name of Steveland Judkins Morris (1950–). US pop musician, singer, and songwriter. He is associated with Motown Records, and had his first hit, 'Fingertips', at the age of 12. Later hits, most of which he composed and sang, and on which he also played several instruments, include 'My Cherie Amour' 1973, 'Master Blaster (Jammin')' 1980, and the album *Innervisions* 1973.

Wood Grant (1892–1942). US painter. He was based mainly in his native Iowa. Though his work is highly stylized, he struck a note of hard realism in his studies of farmers, notably in *American Gothic* 1930 (Art Institute, Chicago). He also painted landscapes and somewhat humorous scenes: for example, *Daughters of Revolution* 1932 (Cincinnati Art Museum), which satirized membership in patriotic societies.

Wood Haydn (1882–1959). British composer. A violinist, he wrote a violin concerto among other works, and is known for his songs, which include 'Roses of Picardy', associated with World War I.

Dead! ... and never called me mother.

MRS HENRY WOOD
East Lynne (dramatized by T A Palmer) 1861

Wood Mrs Henry (born Ellen Price) (1814–1887). English novelist. She was a pioneer of crime fiction and her works include the melodramatic *East Lynne* 1861.

Wood Henry Joseph (1869–1944). English conductor. He studied at the Royal Academy of Music and became an organist and operatic conductor. From 1895 until his death, he conducted the London Promenade Concerts, now named after him. He promoted a national interest in music and encouraged many young composers. As a composer he is remembered for the *Fantasia on British Sea Songs* 1905, which ends each Promenade season. Knighted 1911.

Wood John, the Elder (*c.* 1705–1754). English architect. He was known as 'Wood of Bath' because of his many works in that city. His plan to restore the Roman character of Bath in strict Palladian style was only partially realized. His designs include Queen Square 1729–36 and the Circus 1754, a circular space with streets radiating out from it, which was not yet built by the time he died. His son, John Wood, the Younger (1728–1782) carried on his work, and himself designed the impressive Royal Crescent 1767–75 and Assembly Rooms 1769–71.

Wood Natalie. Stage name of Natasha Gurdin (1938–1981). US film actress. She started out as a child star. Her films include *Miracle on 34th Street* 1947, *Rebel Without a Cause* 1955, *The Searchers* 1956, and *Bob and Carol and Ted and Alice* 1969. Other films include *Splendor in the Grass* 1961 and *Gypsy* 1962. She was married to actor Robert Wagner and died by drowning.

Woodforde James (1740–1803). British cleric who held livings in Somerset and Norfolk, and whose diaries 1758–1802 form a record of rural England.

Woodger Joseph Henry (1894–1981). English biologist who attempted to provide biology with a systematic and logical foundation on which observations, theories, and methods could be based. He taught at the Middlesex Hospital Medical School from 1924 and became professor there 1947.

Woodger developed the idea that one of the characteristics of a living system is the organization of its substance, and that this order is of a hierarchical nature. Thus the components of an organism can be classified on a scale of increasing size and complexity: molecular, macromolecular, cell components, cells, tissues, organs, and organisms. Each class exhibits specifically new modes of behaviour, which cannot be interpreted as being merely additive phenomena from the previous class. Living matter shows not only spatial hierarchical order but also divisional hierarchies (each cell or group of cells has a parent cell), and he showed that many difficulties in biological theory arose originally through viewing an organism as a series of components ordered in space but not in time.

Woodger's works include the textbook *Elementary Morphology and Physiology* 1924, *Biological Principles: a critical study* 1929, and *The Technique of Theory Construction* 1939.

Woodward Joanne Gignilliat (1930–   ). US actress. She is active in film, television, and theatre. She was directed by her husband Paul Newman in the film *Rachel Rachel* 1968, and also starred in *The*

Three Faces of Eve 1957, *They Might Be Giants* 1971, and *Harry and Son* 1984. She has appeared with Newman in several films, including *Mr and Mrs Bridge* 1990.

Woodward Robert Burns (1917–1979). US chemist who worked on synthesizing a large number of complex molecules. These included quinine 1944, cholesterol 1951, chlorophyll 1960, and vitamin B_{12} 1971. Nobel prize 1965. He worked throughout his career at Harvard, becoming professor 1950.

In 1947 Woodward worked out the structure of penicillin and two years later that of strychnine. In the early 1950s, he began to synthesize steroids, and in 1954 he synthesized the poisonous alkaloid strychnine and lysergic acid, the basis of the hallucinogenic drug LSD. In 1956 he made reserpine, the first of the tranquillizing drugs, Turning his attention again to antibiotics, he and his co-workers produced a tetracycline 1962 and cephalosporin C in 1965. The synthesis of vitamin B_{12} was made in collaboration with Swiss chemists and took ten years.

Woodworth Robert Sessions (1869–1962). US psychologist. He collaborated with Edward Thorndike in examining individual learning differences and later attempted to derive objective tests of emotional stability. Although his contributions to research were limited, he published a number of general texts on psychology including *Experimental Psychology* 1938, *Contemporary Schools of Psychology* 1931, and *Dynamics of Behavior* 1958.

He became professor of psychology at Cornell University 1909 and in 1914 was elected president of the American Psychological Association. In 1956 he received the first Gold Medal award of the American Psychological Foundation for his exceptional contribution as an integrator and organizer of psychological science.

Woolcott Marion Post (1910–1990). US documentary photographer. She is best known for her work for the Farm Security Administration (with Walker Evans and Dorothea Lange), showing the conditions of poor farmers in the late 1930s in Kentucky and the deep South.

The poet gives us his essence, but prose takes the mould of the body and mind entire.

VIRGINIA WOOLF
The Captain's Death Bed 'Reading' 1950

Woolf (Adeline) Virginia (born Stephen) (1882–1941). English novelist and critic. In novels such as *Mrs Dalloway*, *To the Lighthouse* 1927, and *The Waves* 1931, she used a 'stream of consciousness' technique to render inner experience. In *A Room of One's Own* 1929, *Orlando* 1928, and *The Years* 1937, she examines the importance of economic independence for women and other feminist principles.

Her first novel, *The Voyage Out* 1915, explored the tensions experienced by women who want marriage and a career. After the death of her father, Leslie Stephen, she and her siblings moved to Bloomsbury, forming the nucleus of the Bloomsbury Group. She produced a succession of novels, short stories, and critical essays, which include *The Common Reader* 1925, 1932. With her husband, Leonard Woolf, she founded the Hogarth Press 1917. She was plagued by bouts of depression and committed suicide 1941.

Suggested reading
Bell, Q *Virginia Woolf* (1972)
Daiches, D *Virginia Woolf* (1945)
Gordon, L *Virginia Woolf: A Writer's Life* (1985)
King, J *Virginia Woolf* (1994)
Woolf, Virginia *Diaries* (1978, ed A O Bell)

Woollcott Alexander Humphreys (1887–1943). US theatre critic and literary figure. He was *The New York Times*' theatre critic 1914–22, a regular contributor to *The New Yorker* from its inception 1925, and hosted the radio interview programme *Town Crier* 1929–42. He appeared on stage in *The Man Who Came to Dinner* 1939 as a character based on himself. Woollcott was a member of the Algonquin Hotel Round Table of wits in New York City, together with Robert Benchley and Dorothy Parker.

A broker is a man who takes your fortune and runs it into a shoestring.

ALEXANDER WOOLLCOTT
quoted in S H Adams *Alexander Woollcott* 1946

Woollett William (1735–1785). British engraver. In 1775 he was appointed engraver to George III.

Woolley (Charles) Leonard (1880–1960). British archaeologist. He excavated at Carchemish in Syria, Tel el Amarna in Egypt, Atchana (the ancient Alalakh) on the Turkish-Syrian border, and Ur in Iraq. He is best remembered for the work on Ur, which he carried out for the British Museum and Pennsylvania University Museum 1922–29.

Besides his scholarly excavation reports he published popular accounts of his work – *Ur of the Chaldees* 1929 and *Digging Up the Past* 1930 – which helped to promote archaeology to a non-specialist audience. Knighted 1935.

Woolley Richard van der Riet (1906–1986). English astronomer whose work included observational and theoretical astrophysics, stellar dynamics and the dynamics of the Galaxy. Knighted 1963.

He was director of the Commonwealth Observatory at Mount Stromlo, Canberra, Australia, 1939–55, and Astronomer Royal at Herstmonceux, Sussex, England, 1956–70. The observatory at Mount Stromlo was devoted mainly to solar physics, and Woolley devoted much of his time there to the study of photospheric convection, emission spectra of the chromosphere, and the solar corona. He pioneered the observation of monochromatic magnitudes and constructed colour magnitude arrays for globular clusters.

During the 15 years that he spent as Astronomer Royal, his personal interests were globular clusters, the evolution of galactic orbits, improvements of radial velocities, and a re-evaluation of RR Lyrae luminosities.

Woolman John (1720–1772). American Quaker, born in Ancocas (now Rancocas), New Jersey. He was one of the first antislavery agitators and left an important *Journal*. He supported those who refused to pay a tax levied by Pennsylvania, to conduct the French and Indian War, on the grounds that it was inconsistent with pacifist principles.

Woolrich Cornell (1903–1968). US writer of suspense fiction. He also wrote under the names William Irish and George Hopley (his middle names). His stories are marked by a bleak, alienated despair and create a sinister, nightmare world. Despite their sometimes clichéd plots, many of these stories were made into films, such as *Black Angel* 1943 (filmed 1946), greatly contributing to the *film noir* genre. He spent most of his adult life as a recluse living in hotels with his mother, writing prolifically until the 1950s.

Woolsey Theodore Dwight (1801–1889). US educationalist. Born in New York, USA, and educated at Yale University, Woolsey studied classics in Europe and was appointed to the Yale faculty as a professor of Greek 1831. President of Yale University 1846–71, he oversaw its expansion into a modern university with specialized departments and graduate degrees. He was the author of *Political Science* 1878 and *Communism and Socialism* 1880. After his retirement as president, Woolsey remained a member of the Yale Corporation 1871–85.

Woolworth Frank Winfield (1852–1919). US entrepreneur. He opened his first successful 'five and ten cent' store in Lancaster, Pennsylvania, in 1879, and, together with his brother C S Woolworth (1856–1947), built up a chain of similar stores throughout the USA, Canada, the UK, and Europe.

Woosnam Ian (1958–). Welsh golfer who, in 1987, became the first UK player to win the World Match-Play Championship. He has since won many tournaments, including the World Cup 1987, World Match-Play 1990, and US Masters 1991. Woosnam was Europe's leading moneywinner in 1987 (as a result of winning the $1 million Sun City Open in South Africa) and again in 1990. He was ranked Number One in the world for 50 weeks in 1991–92.

Wootten George Frederick (1893–1970). Australian military officer and solicitor. Promoted major-general during World War II, he commanded the 9th Australian Division in the New Guinea and Borneo campaigns and accepted the surrender of the Japanese in Borneo in 1945. KBE 1958.

Wootton Barbara Frances, Baroness Wootton of Abinger (1897–1988). British educationist and economist. She taught at London University, and worked in the fields of politics, media, social welfare, and penal reform. Her books include *Freedom under Planning* 1945 and *Social Science and Social Pathology* 1959. She was given a life peerage 1958.

We saw a raven very high above us. It called out, and the dome of the sky seemed to echo the sound.

DOROTHY WORDSWORTH
Journals 27 July 1800

Wordsworth Dorothy (1771–1855). English writer. She lived with her brother William Wordsworth as a companion and support from 1795 until his death, and her many journals describing their life at Grasmere in the Lake District and their travels provided inspiration and material for his poetry.
Suggested reading
Ellis, A M *Rebels and Conservatives: Dorothy and William Wordsworth and Their Circle* (1967)
Gittings, R and Manton, J *Dorothy Wordsworth* (1985)
Gunn, E *A Passion for the Particular: Dorothy Wordsworth: A Portrait* (1981)

Wordsworth William (1770–1850). English Romantic poet. Wordsworth was born in Cockermouth, Cumbria, and educated at Cambridge University. In 1791 he returned from a visit to France, having fallen in love with Marie-Anne Vallon, who bore him an illegitimate daughter. In 1802 he married Mary Hutchinson. In 1797 he moved with his sister Dorothy to Somerset to be near Coleridge, collaborating with him on *Lyrical Ballads* 1798 (which included 'Tintern Abbey'). From 1799 he lived in the Lake District, and later works include *Poems* 1807 (including 'Intimations of Immortality') and *The Prelude* (written by 1805, published 1850). *The Prelude* was written to form part of the autobiographical work *The Recluse*, never completed. He was appointed poet laureate 1843.
Suggested reading
Byatt, A S *Unruly Times: Wordsworth and Coleridge in Their Time* (1970)
Danby, J *The Simple Wordsworth* (1960)
Davies, Hunter *William Wordsworth: A Biography* (1980)
Hamilton, Paul *Wordsworth: A Critical Introduction* (1986)
Nesbitt, G L *Wordsworth: The Biographical Background of His Poetry* (1970)

Poetry is the breath and finer spirit of all knowledge.

WILLIAM WORDSWORTH
Preface to *Lyrical Ballads* 1798

Worner Manfred (1934–1994). German politician, NATO secretary-general 1988–94. He was elected for the Conservative Christian Democratic Union (CDU) to the West German Bundestag (parliament) 1965 and, as a specialist in strategic affairs, served as defence minister under Chancellor Kohl 1982–88. A proponent of closer European military collaboration, he succeeded the British politician Peter Carrington as secretary-general of NATO July 1988.

Worrall Denis John (1935–). South African politician, member of the white opposition to apartheid. Worrall, a former academic and journalist, joined the National Party (NP) and was made ambassador to London 1984–87. On his return to South Africa he resigned from the NP and in 1988 established the Independent Party (IP), which later merged with other white opposition parties to form the reformist DP, advocating dismantling of the apartheid system and universal adult suffrage. A co-leader of the Democratic Party (DP), he was elected to parliament 1989.

Worth Charles Frederick (1825–1895). English couturier. He began work in a draper's shop in London, and served a seven-year apprenticeship, at Swan and Edgar, before working for a silk mercer for a short period and then moving to Paris 1845. After working at Maison Gagelin for five years he opened a dressmaking department in the store before opening his own house 1858 in Paris. He became known for creating ornate and opulent evening gowns and for influencing the shapes of women's clothing. An experimental designer, he introduced a variety of outfits such as the tunic dress, a knee-length tunic worn over a long skirt, during the 1860s, followed by the bustle towards the end of the decade. He was patronized by European royalty.

How happy is he born and taught / That serveth not another's will; / Whose armour is his honest thought / And simple truth his utmost skill!

HENRY WOTTON
'Character of a Happy Life'

Wotton Henry (1568–1639). English poet and diplomat under James I, provost of Eton public school from 1624. He defined an ambassador as 'an honest man sent to lie abroad for the good of his country', a comment which caused much amusement in later centuries due to the misunderstanding of the Tudor use of lie – i.e. stay. He was knighted 1603. *Reliquiae Wottonianae* 1651 includes the lyric 'You meaner beauties of the night'.

Woyrsch Remus von (1847–1925). German general. He joined the army 1866 and fought in the Franco-Prussian War 1870–71. In World War I, he was one of Hindenburg's staff during the first attacks on Russia 1914, and in 1915 commanded various formations in SW Poland, as far as the Vistula. Operating with Kovess, he captured Ivangorod 4 Aug 1915. In 1916 he commanded the German 9th Army on the Eastern Front before being retired on reaching the age of 70.

Wrangel Ferdinand Petrovich, Baron von (1797–1870). Russian vice admiral and Arctic explorer, after whom Wrangel Island (Ostrov Vrangelya) in the Soviet Arctic is named.

Wrangel Peter Nicolaievich, Baron von (1878–1928). Russian general, born in St Petersburg. He commanded a division of Cossacks in World War I, and in 1920, after succeeding Anton Denikin as commander in chief of the White Army, was defeated by the Bolsheviks in the Crimea.

Wray Fay (1907–   ). US film actress. She starred in *King Kong* 1933 after playing the lead in Erich von Stroheim's *The Wedding March* 1928, and appearing in *Doctor X* and *The Most Dangerous Game* both 1932. She continued in intermittent screen roles until 1958.

Si monumentum requiris circumspice [If you would see his monument look around].

CHRISTOPHER WREN
Inscription in St Paul's Cathedral, London, attributed to Wren's son

---

Wren Christopher (1632–1723). English architect. His ingenious use of a refined and sober Baroque style can be seen in his best-known work, St Paul's Cathedral, London, 1675–1710, and in the many churches he built in London including St Mary-le-Bow, Cheapside, 1670–77 and St Bride's, Fleet Street, 1671–78. Other works include the Sheldonian Theatre, Oxford, 1664–69; Greenwich Hospital, London, begun 1694; and Marlborough House, London, 1709–10 (now much altered). Knighted 1672.

Wren studied mathematics, and in 1660 became a professor of astronomy at Oxford University. His opportunity as an architect came after the Great Fire of London 1666. He prepared a plan for rebuilding the city on Classical lines, incorporating piazzas and broad avenues, but it was not adopted. Instead, Wren was commissioned to rebuild St Paul's Cathedral and 51 City churches, showing great skill both in varying the designs and in fitting his buildings into the irregular sites of the destroyed churches. The west towers of Westminster Abbey, often attributed to him, were the design of his pupil Nicholas Hawksmoor.

Suggested reading
Downes, Kerry *Christopher Wren* (1971)
Dutton, Ralph *The Age of Wren* (1951)
Sekler, Eduard *Wren and His Place in European Architecture* (1956)
Whinney, Margaret *Wren* (1971)

Doubtless you wonder how a man may be an Etonian one year and a trooper in a French Hussar Regiment the next.

P C WREN
Beau Sabreur ch 2 1926

Wren P(ercival) C(hristopher) (1875–1941). English novelist. He wrote adventure novels including *Beau Geste* 1924, dealing with the Foreign Legion.

Wren, Christopher *English architect Christopher Wren, in an early 20th-century chromolithograph after a portrait by Godfrey Kneller. Wren designed St Paul's Cathedral, London, and 51 London churches. He also worked as a mathematician and astronomer. He died in London and is buried in St Paul's Cathedral. (Image Select)*

Wright Almroth Edward (1861–1947). English bacteriologist who developed a vaccine against typhoid fever. He established a new discipline within medicine, that of therapeutic immunization by vaccination, which was aimed at treating microbial diseases rather than preventing them. Knighted 1906.

Wright was born near Richmond, Yorkshire, and studied at Trinity College, Dublin, Ireland, and at German universities. He was professor of pathology at the Army Medical School 1892–1902, and at St Mary's Hospital in London 1902–46. In 1911, Wright went to South Africa, where he introduced prophylactic inoculation against pneumonia for workers in the Rand gold mines. On returning to England, he was appointed director of the Department of Bacteriology of the newly founded Medical Research Committee (later Council).

By 1896 Wright had succeeded in developing an effective antityphoid vaccine, which he prepared from killed typhoid bacilli. Preliminary trials of the vaccine on troops of the Indian Army proved its effectiveness and the vaccine was subsequently used successfully among the British soldiers in the Boer War. He also originated vaccines against enteric tuberculosis and pneumonia.

Wright proved that the human bloodstream contains bacteriotropins (opsonins) in the serum and that these substances can destroy bacteria by phagocytosis.

Wright Frank Lloyd (1869–1959). US architect. He is known for 'organic architecture', in which buildings reflect their natural surroundings. From the 1890s, he developed his celebrated prairie house style, a series of low, spreading houses with projecting roofs. He later diversified, employing reinforced concrete to explore a variety of geometric forms. Among his buildings are his Wisconsin home, Taliesin East, 1925, in prairie-house style; Falling Water, near Pittsburgh, Pennsylvania, 1936, a house of cantilevered terraces straddling a waterfall; and the Guggenheim Museum, New York, 1959, a spiral ramp rising from a circular plan.

Wright also designed buildings in Japan 1915–22, most notably the Imperial Hotel in Tokyo 1916. In 1938 he built his winter home in the Arizona Desert, Taliesin West, and established an architectural community there. He always designed the interiors and furnishings for his projects, to create a total environment for his patrons.

Suggested reading
Gill, Brendan *Many Masks: A Life of Frank Lloyd Wright* (1987)
Secrest, M *Frank Lloyd Wright* (1992)
Storer, W *The Architecture of Frank Lloyd Wright* (1974)
Twombly, Robert C *Frank Lloyd Wright: His Life and Architecture* (1979)
Wright, Frank Lloyd *On Architecture* (1941)
Wright, Frank Lloyd *An Autobiography* (1943)

Wright Joseph (1734–1797). English painter. He was known as Wright of Derby, from his birthplace. He painted portraits, landscapes, and groups performing scientific experiments. His work is often dramatically lit – by fire, candlelight, or even volcanic explosion. Several of his subjects are highly original: for example *The Experiment on a Bird in the Air Pump* 1768 (National Gallery, London). His portraits include the reclining figure of *Sir Brooke Boothby* 1781 (Tate Gallery, London).

Wright Joseph (1855–1930). English philologist. He was professor of comparative philology at Oxford University 1901–25, and recorded English local speech in his six-volume *English Dialect Dictionary* 1896–1905.

Wright Judith Arundell (1915–). Australian poet. Her chief volumes of poetry are *The Moving Image* 1946, containing 'South of My Days' and 'Bullocky', *Woman to Man* 1949, *The Other Half* 1966, and *Alive: Poems 1971–1972* 1973. She is well known as a literary critic and anthologist, and as a conservationist.

Suggested reading
Hope, A D *Judith Wright* (1975)
Thomson, A K *Critical Essays on Judith Wright* (1968)
Walker, Shirley *The Poetry of Judith Wright* (1981)

Wright Louis Tompkins (1891–1952). US physician, surgeon, and civil-rights leader who specialized in head injuries and fractures, but also venereal disease and cancer.

From 1919 he worked at the Harlem Hospital, New York, rising to director of surgery 1942 and director of the medical board of Harlem Hospitals 1948. He was the first black doctor to be appointed to a municipal hospital position in New York City. In 1929 he also became the first black police surgeon in the history of the city. Wright was chair of the board of directors of the National Association for the Advancement of Colored People for 17 years.

Wright originated the intradermal method of vaccination against smallpox 1918. He devised a brace for neck fractures, a blade for the treatment of fractures of the knee joint, and a plate made of tantalum for the repair of recurrent hernias. He also became an authority on the venereal disease lymphogranuloma venereum, and was the first physician to experiment with the antibiotics Aureomycin and Terramycin. In 1948, Wright moved into the field of cancer research and studied the effectiveness of chemotherapeutic drugs.

Wright Peter (1916–1995). British intelligence agent. Wright joined MI5 in 1955 and was a consultant to the director-general 1973–76, when he retired. His book *Spycatcher* 1987, written after his retirement, caused an international stir when the British government tried unsuccessfully to block its publication anywhere in the world because of its damaging revelations about the secret service. In *Spycatcher* he claimed, among other things, that Roger Hollis, head of MI5 (1955–65), had been a Soviet double agent; this was later denied by the KGB.

Wright Richard (1908–1960). US novelist. He was one of the first to depict the condition of black people in 20th-century US society with his powerful tragic novel *Native Son* 1940 and the autobiography *Black Boy* 1945.

Between 1932 and 1944 he was active in the Communist Party. Shortly thereafter he became a permanent expatriate in Paris. His other works include *White Man, Listen!* 1957, originally a series of lectures.

Suggested reading
Fabre, Michel *The Unfinished Quest of Richard Wright* (trs 1973)
Webb, Constance *Richard Wright: A Biography* (1968)

Wright Sewall (1889–1988). US geneticist and statistician. During the 1920s he helped modernize Charles Darwin's theory of evolution, using statistics to model the behaviour of populations of genes. Wright's work on genetic drift centred on a phenomenon occurring in small isolated colonies where the chance disappearance of some types of gene leads to evolution without the influence of natural selection.

Wright Thomas (1711–1786). English astronomer and teacher. He was the first to propose that the Milky Way is a layer of stars, including the Sun, in his *An Original Theory or New Hypothesis of the Universe* 1750.

Wright was born near Durham and apprenticed to a clockmaker. He taught mathematics and lectured on popular scientific subjects. In his book, Wright described the Milky Way as a flattened disc, in which the Sun does not occupy a central position. Furthermore, he stated that nebulae lie outside the Milky Way. These views were more than 150 years ahead of their time. However, he believed that the centre of the system was occupied by a divine presence.

Wright's other work included thoughts on the particulate nature of the rings of Saturn, and reflections on such diverse fields as architecture and reincarnation.

Wright brothers Orville (1871–1948) and Wilbur (1867–1912). US inventors; brothers who pioneered piloted, powered flight. In 1899 the Wrights flew a large kite with controls for warping the wings to achieve control of direction and stability. These were the forerunners of ailerons. They then built a small wind tunnel and tested various wing designs and cambers, compiling the first accurate tables of lift and drag. Inspired by Otto Lilienthal's gliding, they perfected their piloted glider 1902. In 1903 they built a powered machine, a 12-hp 341-kg/750-lb plane, and became the first to make a successful powered flight, near Kitty Hawk, North Carolina. Orville flew 36.6 m/120 ft in 12 sec; Wilbur, 260 m/852 ft in 59 sec.

They built their piloted glider while running a bicycle business in Dayton. In 1905 the Wrights offered their aeroplane design to the US War Department, though they did not exhibit the planes publicly until 1908–09, when they took them to Europe. From 1909 they manufactured aeroplanes, but Orville sold his interest in the Wright Company 1915, after Wilbur's death.

Suggested reading
Crouch, T D *The Bishop's Boys: A Life of Wilbur and Orville Wright* (1989)
Degan, Paula and Wescott, Lyranne *Wind and Sand: The Story of the Wright Brothers* (1983)
Howard, Fred *Wilbur and Orville* (1987)

Wundt Wilhelm Max (1832–1920). German physiologist who regarded psychology as the study of internal experience or consciousness. His main psychological method was introspection; he also studied sensation, perception of space and time, and reaction times.

Wurtz Charles Adolphe (1817–1884). French organic chemist who discovered ethylamine, the first organic derivative of ammonia, 1849 and ethylene glycol (1,2-ethanediol) 1856.

In 1844 he moved to Paris and worked at the Sorbonne, where he became professor 1874. He also held public office as mayor of the Seventh Arrondissement of Paris and as a senator.

Wurtz initially worked on the oxides and oxyacids of phosphorus; in 1846 he discovered phosphorus oxychloride ($POCl_3$). He later turned to organic chemistry. In 1855, Wurtz discovered a method of producing paraffin hydrocarbons (alkanes) using alkyl halides (haloalkanes) and sodium in ether. The method was named the Wurtz reaction.

Wurtz discovered aldol (3-hydroxybutanal) while investigating the polymerization of acetaldehyde (ethanal), devised a method of making esters from alkyl halides, and in 1867, with German chemist Friedrich Kekulé, synthesized phenol from benzene.

Wu Tao-tzu (*c.* 680–*c.* 740). Chinese painter, a native of Yang-ti, Honan. He is known for his murals in Buddhist and Taoist temples. He is considered the greatest master of the T'ang Dynasty and one of the greatest of all Chinese artists, though his work can only be estimated by copies, as none of his work survives.

Wyatt James (1746–1813). English architect. A contemporary of the Adam brothers, he designed in the Neo-Gothic style. His over-enthusiastic 'restorations' of medieval cathedrals earned him the nickname 'Wyatt the Destroyer'.

They flee from me, that sometime did me seek.

THOMAS WYATT
'Remembrance'

Wyatt Thomas (*c.* 1503–1542). English poet. He was employed on diplomatic missions by Henry VIII, and in 1536 was imprisoned for a time in the Tower of London, suspected of having been the lover of Henry's second wife, Anne Boleyn. In 1541 Wyatt was again imprisoned on charges of treason. With the Earl of Surrey, he introduced the sonnet to England. Knighted 1537.

Woman's love is but a blast, / And turneth like the wind.

THOMAS WYATT
'The Careful Lover Complaineth'

Wyatville Jeffrey. Adopted name of Jeffrey Wyatt (1766–1840). English architect. He remodelled Windsor Castle, Berkshire. He was a nephew of the architect James Wyatt. Knighted 1828.

The woman that marries to love better will be as much mistaken as the wencher that marries to live better. Marrying to increase love is like gaming to become rich; you only lose what little stock you had before.

WILLIAM WYCHERLEY
Country Wife IV 1675

Wycherley William (1640–*c.* 1716). English Restoration dramatist. His first comedy, *Love in a Wood*, won him court favour 1671, and later bawdy works include *The Country Wife* 1675 and *The Plain Dealer* 1676.

Wycliffe John (*c.* 1320–1384). English religious reformer. Having studied at Oxford University, he became Master of Balliol College there, and sent out bands of travelling preachers. Allying himself with the party of John of Gaunt, which was opposed to ecclesiastical influence at court, he attacked abuses in the church, maintaining that the Bible rather than the church was the supreme authority. He criticized such fundamental doctrines as priestly absolution, confession, and indulgences, and set disciples to work on translating the Bible into English. He was denounced as a heretic, but died peacefully at Lutterworth.

Suggested reading
Carrick, J C *Wycliffe and the Lollards* (1977)
McFarlane, K B *John Wycliffe and the Beginnings of English Nonconformity* (1952)
Stacey, John *John Wycliffe and Reform* (1964)

Wyeth Andrew Newell (1917–). US painter. His portraits and landscapes, usually in watercolour or tempera, are naturalistic, minutely detailed, and often convey a strong sense of the isolation of the countryside; for example, *Christina's World* 1948 (Museum of Modern Art, New York).

Suggested reading
Corn, Wanda (ed) *The Art of Andrew Wyeth* (1973)
Hoving, Thomas *Two Worlds of Andrew Wyeth* (1978)
Wilmerding, John *Andrew Wyeth: The Helga Pictures* (1987)
Wyeth, Andrew *Autobiography* (1995)

Wyeth N(ewel) C(onvers) (1882–1944). US artist. He was the foremost US illustrator of his time as well as an accomplished muralist. He illustrated over 20 children's classics, including *Treasure Island, The Adventures of Tom Sawyer, Robin Hood*, and *The Yearling*. Wyeth's students included his daughter Henriette and his son Andrew.

Wyler William (1902–1981). German-born film director. He lived in the USA from 1922. Noted for his adroit, painstaking style, he directed *Wuthering Heights* 1939, *Mrs Miniver* 1942, *Ben Hur* 1959, and *Funny Girl* 1968, among others.

Wylie (lived 19th century). An Aborigine of the King George Sound tribe who accompanied the explorer Eyre on his 1840–41 expedition. He was Eyre's sole companion for much of the journey, saving him from probable death.

I tell you, a triffid's in a damn sight better position to survive than a blind man.

JOHN WYNDHAM
The Day of the Triffids ch 4 1951

Wyndham John. Pen name of John Wyndham Parkes Lucas Beynon Harris (1903–1969). English science-fiction writer. He wrote *The Day of the Triffids* 1951, *The Chrysalids* 1955, and *The Midwich Cuckoos* 1957. A recurrent theme in his work is people's response to disaster, whether caused by nature, aliens, or human error.

Wynne-Edwards Vero Copner (1906–1997). English zoologist who argued that animal behaviour is often altruistic and that animals will behave for the good of the group, even if this entails individual sacrifice. His study *Animal Dispersal in Relation to Social Behaviour* was published 1962.

The theory that animals are genetically programmed to behave for the good of the species has since fallen into disrepute. From this dispute grew a new interpretation of animal behaviour, seen in the work of biologist E O Wilson.

Wyss Johann David (1743–1818). Swiss author. He is remembered for the children's classic *Swiss Family Robinson* 1812–13.

X

Xavier, St Francis (1506–1552). Spanish Jesuit missionary. He went to the Portuguese colonies in the East Indies, arriving at Goa 1542. He was in Japan 1549–51, establishing a Christian mission that lasted for 100 years. He returned to Goa in 1552, and sailed for China, but died of fever there. He was canonized 1622.

Xenakis Iannis (1922–). Romanian-born Greek composer. He studied music in Paris 1947–51 while practising as an engineering draughtsman for French architect Le Corbusier. Compositions such as *Metastaseis/After Change* 1953–54 for 61 players apply stochastic principles (for example, describing particle motion in fluids) to the composition of densely-textured effects in which change is perceived globally. Later works, including a setting of the *Oresteia* 1965–66 for choir and ensemble, draw on Greek mythology.

Prosperity creates presumption in most men, but adversity brings sobriety to all.

XENOPHON

Xenophon (*c*. 430–354 BC). Greek historian, philosopher, and soldier. He was a disciple of Socrates (described in Xenophon's *Symposium*). In 401 he joined a Greek mercenary army aiding the Persian prince Cyrus, and on the latter's death took command. His *Anabasis* describes how he led 10,000 Greeks on a 1,600-km/1,000-mile march home across enemy territory. His other works include *Memorabilia*, *Apology*, and *Hellenica/A History of My Times*.
Suggested reading
Anderson, J K *Xenophon* (1974)

Dillery, John *Xenophon and the History of His Times* (1996)
Schmeling, Gareth *Xenophon of Ephesus* (1980)
Xenophon *Anabasis* (trs H D Rouse 1947)

I will bridge the Hellespont and march an army through Europe into Greece and punish the Athenians for their outrage gainst my father.

XERXES
quoted in Herodotus *History* bk 7 ch 8

Xerxes (*c*. 519–465 BC). King of Persia from 486 BC when he succeeded his father Darius. In 480, at the head of a great army which was supported by the Phoenician navy, he crossed the Dardanelles over a bridge of boats. He captured and burned Athens, but the Persian fleet was defeated at Salamis and Xerxes was forced to retreat. His general Mardonius remained behind in Greece, but was defeated by the Greeks at Plataea 479. Xerxes was eventually murdered in a court intrigue.
Suggested reading
Green, Peter *Xerxes at Salamis* (1970)
Smith, J S *Greece and the Persians* (1989)

Xia dynasty or Hsia dynasty. China's first legendary ruling family, *c*. 2200–*c*. 1500 BC, reputedly founded by the model emperor Yu the Great. He is believed to have controlled floods by constructing dykes. Archaeological evidence suggests that the Xia dynasty really did exist, as a Bronze Age civilization where writing was being developed, with its capital at Erlidou (Erh-li-t'ou) in Henan (Honan).

Y

Yahya Khan Agha Muhammad (1917–1980). Pakistani president 1969–71. His mishandling of the Bangladesh separatist issue led to civil war, and he was forced to resign.

Yahya Khan fought with the British army in the Middle East during World War II, escaping German capture in Italy. Later, as Pakistan's chief of army general staff, he supported General Ayub Khan's 1958 coup and in 1969 became military ruler. Following defeat by India 1971, he resigned and was under house arrest 1972–75.

Yalow Rosalyn Sussman (1921–). US physicist who developed radioimmunoassay (RIA), a technique for detecting minute quantities of hormones present in the blood. It can be used to discover a range of hormones produced in the hypothalamic region of the brain. She shared the Nobel Prize for Physiology or Medicine 1977.

In the 1940s she started working in the Radioisotope Unit of the Veterans Administration Hospital in the Bronx, New York, with a medical doctor, Sol Berson. When he died 1972, Yalow was appointed director of the laboratory.

To measure the concentration of a natural hormone, a solution containing a known amount of the radioisotope-labelled form of the hormone and its antibody is prepared. When a solution containing the natural hormone is added to the first solution, some of the labelled hormone is displaced from the hormone–antibody complex. The fraction of labelled hormone displaced is proportional to the amount of the natural hormone (which is unknown).

Yamagata Aritomo (1838–1922). Japanese soldier, politician, and prime minister 1889–91 and 1898–1900. As war minister 1873 and chief of the imperial general staff 1878, he was largely responsible for the modernization of the military system. He returned as chief of staff during the Russo-Japanese War 1904–05 and remained an influential political figure until he was disgraced in 1921 for having meddled in the marriage arrangements of the crown prince.

Yamamoto Gombei (1852–1933). Japanese admiral and politician. As prime minister 1913–14, he began Japanese expansion into China and initiated political reforms. He became premier again 1923 but resigned the following year.

Yamamoto Isoroku (1884–1943). Japanese admiral in World War II. He was appointed chief of naval aviation 1938 and given command of the combined fleet 1939. Long convinced that Japan would eventually fight the USA, he began planning the attack on Pearl Harbor early 1940. After the raid he was quick to appreciate the significance of the US carrier force escaping the damage, and prepared plans to entrap and destroy them, but this backfired and instead he lost most of his own carriers in the Battle of Midway.

He planned a series of naval offensives 1943 and set out on a tour of bases in the Solomon Islands to explain his strategy and raise morale. US forces intercepted signals giving his itinerary and shot down his aircraft 18 April 1943.

Yamamoto Kansai (1944–). Japanese fashion designer. He opened his own house 1971. The presentation of his catwalk shows made him famous, with dramatic clothes in an exciting atmosphere. He blends the powerful and exotic designs of traditional Japanese dress with Western sportswear to create a unique, abstract style.

Yamamoto Yohji (1943–). Japanese fashion designer. He formed his own company 1972 and showed his first collection 1976. He is an uncompromising, nontraditionalist designer who swathes and wraps the body in unstructured, loose, voluminous garments.

Yamashita Tomoyuki (1885–1946). Japanese general in World War II. He commanded the 25th Army in the invasion of Malaya and Singapore 1941, conducting a quick and effective campaign which earned him the title 'Tiger of Malaya' in Japan.

His success in Malaya angered the premier Tōjō who thought Yamashita was seeking his place, and he was sent to Manchuria to command an army group. After Tōjō fell from grace 1944, Yamashita was brought out of obscurity and sent to defend the Philippines. He conducted a skilful defensive campaign but was eventually forced to surrender after the Japanese capitulation Sept 1945. He was arrested for war crimes and executed 1946.

Yanayev Gennady (1937–). Soviet communist politician, leader of the Aug 1991 anti-Gorbachev attempted coup, after which he was arrested and charged with treason. He was released 1994 under an amnesty. He was vice president of the USSR 1990–91.

Yanayev rose in the ranks as a traditional, conservative-minded communist bureaucrat to become a member of the Politburo and Secretariat, and head of the official Soviet trade-union movement from 1990. In Dec 1990 he was President Gorbachev's surprise choice for vice president. In Aug 1991, however, Yanayev became titular head of the eight-member 'emergency committee' that launched the reactionary coup against Gorbachev.

Yang Shangkun (1907–). Chinese communist politician. He held a senior position in the party 1956–66 but was demoted during the Cultural Revolution. He was rehabilitated 1978, elected to the Politburo 1982, and served as state president 1988–93.

The son of a wealthy Sichuan landlord and a veteran of the Long March 1934–35 and the war against Japan 1937–45, Yang rose in the ranks of the Chinese Communist Party before being purged for alleged revisionism in the Cultural Revolution. He is viewed as a trusted supporter of Deng Xiaoping.

All changed, changed utterly: / A terrible beauty is born.

W B YEATS
'Easter 1916'

Yeats Jack Butler (1871–1957). Irish painter and illustrator. His vivid scenes of Irish life, for example *Back from the Races* 1925 (Tate Gallery, London), and Celtic mythology reflected a new consciousness of Irish nationalism. He was the brother of the poet W B Yeats.

His youth was spent in Sligo and his early work consisted mainly of pen and watercolour drawings, lively impressions of country and sporting life and character in Ireland. From 1930 he devoted himself to oil paintings with an emotional violence of colour that might be called Expressionist, and in his later years was considered the most eminent representative of Ireland in art.

Suggested reading
Booth, John *Jack B Yeats: A Vision of Ireland* (1992)
Pyle, Hilary *Jack B Yeats: A Biography* (1989)
Rosenthal, T G *The Art of Jack B Yeats* (1993)

Yeats W(illiam) B(utler) (1865–1939). Irish poet. He was a leader of the Celtic revival and a founder of the Abbey Theatre in Dublin. His early work was romantic and lyrical, as in the poem 'The Lake Isle of Innisfree' and the plays *The Countess Cathleen* 1892 and *The Land of Heart's Desire* 1894. His later books of poetry include *The Wild Swans at Coole* 1917 and *The Winding Stair* 1929. He was a senator of the Irish Free State 1922–28. Nobel Prize for Literature 1923.

Yeats was born in Dublin. His early poetry includes *The Wind Among the Reeds* 1899, and he drew on Irish legend for his poetic plays, including *Deirdre* 1907, but broke through to a new sharply resilient style with *Responsibilities* 1914. In his personal life there was also a break: the beautiful Maude Gonne, to whom many of his poems had been addressed, refused to marry him, and in 1917 he married Georgie Hyde-Lees, whose work as a medium reinforced his leanings towards mystic symbolism, as in the prose work *A Vision* 1925 and 1937. Among his later volumes of verse are *The Tower* 1928 and *Last Poems and Two Plays* 1939. His other prose works include *Autobiographies* 1926, and *Dramatis Personae* 1936.

Suggested reading
Bloom, Harold *Yeats* (1970)
Donoghue, D *William Butler Yeats* (1971)
Ellmann, R *Eminent Domain* (1967)
Jeffares, A N *W B Yeats: A New Biography* (1989)
O'Donnell, W *The Poetry of William Butler Yeats: An Introduction* (1986)
Unterecker, J *A Reader's Guide to William Butler Yeats* (1959)

Yeltsin Boris Nikolayevich (1931–). Russian politician, president of the Russian Soviet Federative Socialist Republic (RSFSR) 1990–91, and president of the newly independent Russian Federation from 1991. He directed the Federation's secession from the USSR and the formation of a new, decentralized confederation, the Commonwealth of Independent States (CIS), with himself as the most powerful leader. A referendum 1993 supported his policies of price deregulation and accelerated privatization, despite severe economic problems and civil unrest.

Born in Sverdlovsk (now Ekaterinburg), Yeltsin began his career in the construction industry. He joined the Communist Party of the Soviet Union (CPSU) in 1961 and became district party leader. Brought to Moscow by Mikhail Gorbachev and Nikolai Ryzhkov in 1985, he was appointed secretary for construction and then, in Dec 1985, Moscow party chief. His demotion to the post of first deputy chair of the State Construction Committee Nov 1987 was seen as a blow to Gorbachev's perestroika initiative and a victory for the conservatives grouped around Yegor Ligachev. He was re-elected March 1989 with an 89% share of the vote, defeating an official Communist Party candidate, and was elected to the Supreme Soviet in May 1989. A supporter of the Baltic states in their calls for greater independence, Yeltsin demanded increasingly more radical economic reform. In 1990 he renounced his CPSU membership and was elected president of the RSFSR, the largest republic of the USSR.

Advocating greater autonomy for the constituent republics within a federal USSR, Yeltsin prompted the Russian parliament June 1990 to pass a decree giving the republic's laws precedence over those passed by the Soviet parliament. In April 1991, he was voted emergency powers by congress, enabling him to rule by decree, and two months later was popularly elected president. In the abortive Aug 1991 coup, Yeltsin, as head of a democratic 'opposition state' based at the Russian parliament building, played a decisive role, publicly condemning the usurpers and calling for the reinstatement of President Gorbachev.

As the economic situation deteriorated within Russia, Yeltsin's leadership came under increasing challenge. An attempted coup by parliamentary leaders was successfully thwarted Sept–Oct 1993, but unexpected far-right gains in assembly elections in Dec forced him to compromise his economic policies and rely increasingly on the support of the military. From early 1995 he came under criticism for his apparent sanctioning of a full-scale military offensive in the breakaway republic of Chechnya. His hospitalization with a heart condition July, and again in Oct, 1995 raised speculation as to his possible successors. However, he won the 1996 presidential elections with a substantial majority.

Suggested reading
Morrison, John *Boris Yeltsin: From Bolshevik to Democrat* (1991)
Steele, Jonathan *Eternal Russia: Yeltsin, Gorbachev and the Mirage of Democracy* (1994)
Solovyov, Vladimir and Klepikova, Elena *Boris Yeltsin: A Political Biography* (1992)

Yersin Alexandre Emile Jean (1863–1943). Swiss bacteriologist who discovered the bubonic plague bacillus in Hong Kong 1894 and prepared a serum against it. The bacillus was discovered independently, in the same epidemic, by Japanese bacteriologist Shibasaburō Kitasato, who published his results before Yersin did.

Yesenin Sergei Aleksandrovich. Alternative form of ◊Esenin, Russian poet.

Yevele Henry de (died 1400). English architect. He was the mason of the naves of Westminster Abbey, begun 1375, Canterbury Cathedral 1379–1405, and Westminster Hall 1394, with its majestic hammerbeam roof.

Yevtushenko Yevgeny Aleksandrovich (1933–). Soviet poet. He aroused controversy with his anti-Stalinist 'Stalin's Heirs' 1956, published with Khrushchev's support, and 'Babi Yar' 1961, which attacked Russian as well as Nazi anti-Semitism. His other works include the long poem *Zima Junction* 1956, the novel *Berries* 1981, and *Precocious Autobiography* 1963.

'Wherefore shrink from me? What have I done that you should fear me? You have been listening to evil tales, my child'

CHARLOTTE M YONGE
The Little Duke 1895

Yonge Charlotte M(ary) (1823–1901). English novelist. Her books deal mainly with family life, and are influenced by the High Church philosophy of the Oxford Movement. She published *The Heir of Redclyffe* 1853.

York English dynasty founded by Richard, Duke of York (1411–60). He claimed the throne through his descent from Lionel, Duke of Clarence (1338–1368), third son of Edward III, whereas the reigning monarch, Henry VI of the rival house of Lancaster, was descended from the fourth son. The argument was fought out in the Wars of the Roses. York was killed at the Battle of Wakefield 1460, but next year his son became King Edward IV, in turn succeeded by his son Edward V and then by his brother Richard III, with whose death at Bosworth the line ended. The Lancastrian victor in that battle was crowned Henry VII and consolidated his claim by marrying Edward IV's eldest daughter, Elizabeth.

York Alvin Cullum ('Sergeant') (1887–1964). US war hero. Although a conscientious objector, York was drafted as a private in the 82nd Infantry Division in World War I and promoted to the rank of sergeant. At the Battle of the Argonne Forest 8 Oct 1918, York led a charge against a German position in which he and his comrades captured 132 prisoners and 35 machine guns. He was awarded the Congressional Medal of Honour and the French *Croix de Guerre*. A film biography, *Sergeant York*, appeared 1940.

York Duke of. Title often borne by younger sons of British sovereigns, for example George V, George VI, and Prince Andrew from 1986.

A well meaning and an honest man, but ... scarcely on a level with the ordinary scale of human intellect.

James Fenimore Cooper on FREDERICK AUGUSTUS, DUKE OF YORK
Gleanings in Europe: England 1928

York Frederick Augustus, Duke of York (1763–1827). Second son of George III. He was an unsuccessful commander in the Netherlands 1793–99 and British commander in chief 1798–1809. Duke 1784.

The nursery rhyme about the 'grand old duke of York' who marched his troops up the hill and down again commemorates him, as does the Duke of York's column in Waterloo Place, London.

Yoshida Shigeru (1878–1967). Japanese conservative (Liberal Party) politician who served as prime minister of US-occupied Japan for most of the post–World War II period 1946–54. He was foreign minister 1945–46.

Young Arthur (1741–1820). English writer and publicizer of the new farm practices associated with the agricultural revolution. When the Board of Agriculture was established 1792, Young was appointed secretary, and was the guiding force behind the production of a county-by-county survey of British agriculture.

His early works, such as *Farmer's Tour through the East of England* and *A Six Months' Tour through the North of England*, contained extensive comment and observations gathered during the course of a series of journeys around the country. He published the *Farmers' Calendar* 1771, and in 1784 began the *Annals of Agriculture*, which ran for 45 volumes, and contained contributions from many eminent farmers of the day.

Young Brigham (1801–1877). US Mormon religious leader, born in Vermont. He joined the Mormon Church, or Church of Jesus Christ of Latter-day Saints, 1832, and three years later was appointed an apostle. After a successful recruiting mission in Liverpool, England, he returned to the USA and, as successor of Joseph Smith (who had been murdered), led the Mormon migration to the Great Salt Lake in Utah 1846, founded Salt Lake City, and headed the colony until his death.

Suggested reading
Arrington, Leonard *Brigham Young: American Moses* (1985)
Bringhurst, Newell *Brigham Young* (1986)
Stott, Clifford *Search for Sanctuary* (1984)

Young Charles Augustus (1834–1908). US astronomer who made some of the first spectroscopic investigations of the Sun. He was the first person to observe the spectrum of the solar corona.

He was professor at the Western Reserve College, Hudson, Ohio, 1856–66; at Dartmouth College 1866–77; and at Princeton 1877–1905.

Young discovered a layer in the solar atmosphere in which the dark hues of the Sun's spectrum are momentarily reversed at the moment of a total solar eclipse. He published a series of papers relating his spectroscopic observations of the solar chromosphere, solar prominences, and sunspots. He also compiled a catalogue of bright spectral lines in the Sun and used these to measure its rotational velocity. Young wrote several best-selling textbooks: *General Astronomy* 1888, *Lessons in Astronomy* 1891, and *Manual of Astronomy* 1902.

Young Cy (Denton True) (1867–1955). US baseball player. As a pitcher of unequalled skill and stamina, he established a lifetime record of 511 victories. In 16 seasons, he finished with 20 or more wins, 5 times exceeding 30. He was nicknamed 'Cy' for his 'cyclone' pitch.

Born in Gilmore, Ohio, USA, Young played for the Cleveland Nationals 1890–98, the St Louis Cardinals 1899–1900, the Boston Red Sox 1901–08, the Cleveland Indians 1909–11, and the Boston Braves 1911.

Young David Ivor, Baron Young of Graffham (1932–). British Conservative politician, chair of the Manpower Services Commission (MSC) 1982–84, secretary for employment from 1985, trade and industry secretary 1987–89, when he retired from politics. He was subsequently criticized by a House of Commons select committee over aspects of the privatization of the Rover car company. Baron 1984.

Procrastination is the thief of time.

EDWARD YOUNG
Night Thoughts on Life, Death and Immortality i, 393 1742

Young Edward (1683–1765). English poet and dramatist. A country clergyman for much of his life, he wrote his principal work *Night Thoughts on Life, Death and Immortality* 1742–45 in defence of Christian orthodox thinking. His other works include dramatic tragedies, satires, and a long poem, *Resignation*, published 1726.

Young John Watts (1930–). US astronaut. His first flight was on *Gemini 3* 1965. He landed on the Moon with *Apollo 16* 1972, and was commander of the first flight of the space shuttle *Columbia* 1981.

Young was born in San Francisco. He became a NASA astronaut

in 1962, and chief of the Astronaut Office in 1975. He flew on *Apollo 10* in 1969 and commanded the ninth space-shuttle flight in 1983.

Young John Zachary (1907–). English zoologist who discovered and studied the giant nerve fibres in squids, contributing greatly to knowledge of nerve structure and function. He also did research on the central nervous system of octopuses, demonstrating that memory stores are located in the brain. He set up a unit at Oxford to study nerve regeneration in mammals. In 1945 he became the first non-medical scientist in Britain to hold a professorship in anatomy, at London.

Young discovered that certain nerve fibres of squids are about 100 times the diameter of mammalian neurons and are covered with a relatively thin myelin sheath (unlike mammalian nerve fibres, which have thick sheaths). These properties make them easy to experiment on and to obtain intracellular nerve material.

Turning his attention to the central nervous system, Young showed that octopuses can learn to discriminate between different orientations of the same object. When presented with horizontal and vertical rectangles, for example, the octopuses attacked one but avoided the other. He also demonstrated that octopuses can learn to recognize objects by touch. In addition, Young proposed a model to explain the processes involved in memory. Young published the textbooks *The Life of Vertebrates* 1950 and *The Life of Mammals* 1957.

Young Lester Willis (1909–1959). US tenor saxophonist and jazz composer. He was a major figure in the development of his instrument for jazz music from the 1930s and was an accompanist for the singer Billie Holiday, who gave him the nickname 'President', later shortened to 'Pres'.

Young Michael. Baron Young of Dartington (1915–). British social entrepreneur, creator of the Open University, the Consumers' Association 1957, and some 30 other organizations.

Young's first project was the Institute for Community Studies set up in the East End of London 1952. He established a number of bodies concerned with education, such as the National Extension Colleges, the University of the Third Age, the College of Health (for National Health Service patients), and the Advisory Centre for Education. He has also been active in neighbourhood development schemes and Social Democrat politics, setting up the Tawney Society and the journal *Samizdat* in the 1980s. Baron 1978.

Young Neil (1945–). Canadian rock guitarist, singer, and songwriter. He lived in the USA from 1966. Young was a member of Buffalo Springfield, a hippie folk-rock group, 1966–68, and from 1969 a part-time member of Crosby, Stills, Nash, and Young, primarily a vocal-harmony group. His high, plaintive voice and loud, abrasive guitar make his work instantly recognizable, despite abrupt changes of style throughout his career. *Rust Never Sleeps* 1979 and *Arc Weld* 1991 (both with the group Crazy Horse) are among his best work.

Young Terence (1915–1994). British film director who worked in Hollywood and Europe. He carved a niche in popular cinema by masterminding three of the early James Bond action films. The first of these, *Dr No* 1962, was quite modestly budgeted but evinced a cynical, luxurious flair that made it a box-office hit and launched a continuing tradition. His later projects include the suspense thriller *Wait Until Dark* 1967 and the period tear-jerker *Mayerling* 1968. His last film was the little-regarded mystery *The Jigsaw Man* 1984.

Young Thomas (1773–1829). British physicist, physician, and Egyptologist who revived the wave theory of light and identified the phenomenon of interference in 1801. He also established many important concepts in mechanics.

In 1793, Young recognized that focusing of the eye (accommodation) is achieved by a change of shape in the lens of the eye, the lens being composed of muscle fibres. He also showed that astigmatism is due to irregular curvature of the cornea. In 1801, he became the first to recognize that colour sensation is due to the presence in the retina of structures that respond to the three colours red, green, and violet.

He was professor of natural philosophy at the Royal Institution 1801–03 and worked as a physician at St George's Hospital, London, from 1811.

Young assumed that light waves are propagated in a similar way to sound waves, and proposed that different colours consist of different frequencies. He obtained experimental proof for the principle of interference by passing light through extremely narrow openings and observing the interference patterns produced.

In mechanics, Young was the first to use the terms 'energy' for the product of the mass of a body with the square of its velocity and 'labour expended' for the product of the force exerted on a body 'with the distance through which it moved'. He also stated that these two products are proportional to each other. He introduced an absolute measurement in elasticity, now known as Young's modulus.

From 1815 onwards, Young published papers on Egyptology; his account of the Rosetta stone played a crucial role in the stone's eventual decipherment.

Younghusband Francis Edward (1863–1942). British soldier and explorer, born in India. He entered the army 1882 and 20 years later accompanied the mission that opened up Tibet. He wrote travel books on India and Central Asia and works on comparative religion. KCIE 1904.

Young Pretender nickname of ◊Charles Edward Stuart, claimant to the Scottish and English thrones.

Yourcenar Marguerite. Pen name of Marguerite de Crayencour (1903–1987). French writer. She first gained recognition as a novelist in France in the 1930s with books such as *La Nouvelle Euridyce/The New Euridyce* 1931. Her evocation of past eras and characters, exemplified in *Les Mémoires d'Hadrien/The Memoirs of Hadrian* 1951, brought her acclaim as a historical novelist. In 1939 she settled in the USA. In 1980 she became the first woman to be elected to the French Academy.

Ypres, 1st Earl of title of Sir John ◊French, British field marshal.

Ysaye Eugène-Auguste (1858–1931). Belgian violinist, conductor, and composer. One of the greatest and most individual virtuosos of his day, he toured as a soloist and conductor throughout Europe and America. Although he never studied composition formally, he mastered writing in a Romantic style.

Yuan dynasty (1279–1368). Mongol rulers of China, after Kublai Khan defeated the Song dynasty. Much of Song China's administrative infrastructure survived and internal and foreign trade expanded. The Silk Road to the west was re-established and the Grand Canal extended north to Beijing to supply the court with grain.

The Mongol conquest was particularly brutal, and relations with the Chinese were never easy, resulting in the recruitment of foreigners such as central Asian Muslims to act as officials. The Venetian traveller Marco Polo also served at the court. After the death of Temur (ruled 1294–1307), there was increasing internal disorder and economic discontent. This was the first dynasty to control territories S of the Chang Jiang.

Yuan Shikai (1859–1916). Chinese soldier and politician, leader of Republican China 1911–16. He assumed dictatorial powers 1912, dissolving parliament and suppressing Sun Yat-sen's Guomindang. He died soon after proclaiming himself emperor.

Although committed to military reform, Yuan betrayed the modernizing emperor Guangxu and sided with the Empress Dowager Zi Xi during the Hundred Days' Reform 1898. With a power base in N China, he was appointed prime minister and commander in chief after the 1911 revolution against the Manchu Qings and was made president 1912. He lost credibility after submitting to Japan's Twenty-one demands 1915, ceding territory to Japan.

Yudenich Nikolai Nikolaevich (1862–1933). Russian general. He saw service in the Russo-Japanese war 1904–05 and in World War I. He defeated the Turkish offensive in the Caucasus led by Enver Pasha 1915 and carried out offensives against the Turks 1916. He turned up again in Finland 1919, commanding White Russian forces in an offensive against the Bolsheviks near Petrograd (now St Petersburg) but was defeated and went into retirement.

Yukawa Hideki (1907–1981). Japanese physicist. In 1935 he discovered the strong nuclear force that binds protons and neutrons together in the atomic nucleus, and predicted the existence of the subatomic particle called the meson. Nobel prize 1949.

Yukawa was born and educated in Kyoto and spent his career at Kyoto University, becoming professor 1939 and director of the university's newly created Research Institute for Fundamental Physics from 1953.

Yukawa's theory of nuclear forces postulated the existence of a nuclear 'exchange force' that counteracted the mutual repulsion of the protons and therefore held the nucleus together. He predicted that this exchange force would involve the transfer of a particle (the existence of which was then unknown), and calculated the range of the force and the mass of the hypothetical particle, which would be radioactive, with an extremely short half-life. The muon, or μ meson, discovered 1936, fitted part of the description, and the pion, or π meson, discovered 1947, fitted all of it.

In 1936 Yukawa predicted that a nucleus could absorb one of the innermost orbiting electrons and that this would be equivalent to emitting a positron. These innermost electrons belong to the K electron shell, and this process of electron absorption by the nucleus is known as K capture.

✦ Z ✦

Zadkine Ossip (1890–1967). French Cubist sculptor. Born in Russia, he was active in Paris from 1909. His art represented the human form in dramatic, semi-abstract terms, as in the monument *To a Destroyed City* 1953 (Schiedamse, Rotterdam).

Zahir Shah Muhammad (1914–). King of Afghanistan 1933–73. Zahir, educated in Kabul and Paris, served in the government 1932–33 before being crowned king. He was overthrown 1973 by a republican coup and went into exile. He became a symbol of national unity for the Mujaheddin Islamic fundamentalist resistance groups. In 1991 the Afghan government restored Zahir's citizenship.

Zahir ud-Din Muhammad first Mogul emperor of India; see ◊Babur.

Zamenhof Lazarus Ludovik (1859–1917). Polish inventor of the international language Esperanto in 1887.

Zampieri Domenico. Italian Baroque painter, known as ◊Domenichino.

For God's sake don't say yes until I've finished talking.
DARRYL F ZANUCK
quoted in Philip French *The Movie Moguls* 1969

Zanuck Darryl F(rancis) (1902–1979). US film producer. He founded 20th Century Pictures in 1933, which merged the following year with Fox to form 20th Century-Fox. His ability to gauge public tastes and endless dynamism made him one of the most forceful executives in Hollywood. In addition to supervising his studio's output, he personally produced such prestige films as *The Grapes of Wrath* 1940 and *All About Eve* 1950.

He began his career writing scenarios for canine star, Rin Tin Tin, and then became head of production at Warner Bros, where he championed contemporary 'torn from the headlines' material in the early sound era. He became an independent producer 1956, but in 1962 was persuaded back to Fox and elected company president, remaining at the studio until 1971.

Zanzotto Andrea (1921–). Italian poet. A teacher from the Veneto, he has published much verse, including the collection *La beltà*/*Beauty* 1968, with a strong metaphysical element.

Zapata Emiliano (1879–1919). Mexican Indian revolutionary leader. He led a revolt against dictator Porfirio Díaz (1830–1915) from 1911 under the slogan 'Land and Liberty', to repossess for the indigenous Mexicans the land taken by the Spanish. By 1915 he was driven into retreat, and was assassinated.
Suggested reading
Knight, A *The Mexican Revolution* (1986)
Parkinson, Roger *Zapata: A Biography* (1975)
Womack, John, Jr *Zapata and the Mexican Revolution* (1968)

Rock journalism is people who can't write interviewing people who can't talk for people who can't read.
FRANK ZAPPA
quoted in L Botts *Loose Talk*

Zappa Frank (Francis Vincent) (1940–1993). US rock musician, bandleader, and composer. His crudely satirical songs (*Joe's Garage* 1980), deliberately bad taste, and complex orchestral and electronic compositions (*Hot Rats* 1969, *Jazz from Hell* 1986) make his work

hard to categorize. His group the Mothers of Invention 1965–73 was part of the 1960s avant-garde, and the Mothers' hippie parody *We're Only in It for the Money* 1967 was popular with its target.

Zarathustra another name for the Persian religious leader ◊Zoroaster.

Zassenhaus Hans Julius (1912–). German mathematician who mainly studied group theory and number theory. Zassenhaus groups form part of the basis for the contemporary development of finite group theory.

Zassenhaus was born in Koblenz and studied at Hamburg. He was professor at Montréal, Canada, 1949–59. Transferring to the USA, he finally became professor at Ohio State 1964.

Group theory is the study of systems in which the product of any two members of a system results in another member of the same system (for example, even numbers). Zassenhaus's most significant results were obtained in his investigations into finite groups. In group extensions he postulated with Issai Schur (1875–1941) what has become known as the Schur–Zassenhaus theory.

Zassenhaus also made contributions to the study of Lie algebras, the geometry of numbers, and applied mathematics.

Zatopek Emil (1922–). Czech runner. At the Olympic Games in Helsinki 1952 he won gold medals for the 5,000 metres, the 10,000 metres, and the marathon. He retired as a runner 1958, having set 18 world records during his career, including those for 10 miles, 15 miles, and 30,000 metres.

He broke 13 world long-distance records between 1948 and 1954, winning the gold medal for the 10,000-metre world record of 28 minutes 54.2 seconds 1949.

Zatopek was born in Koprövnice, Czechoslovakia. He began running in the early 1940s, and in 1946 cycled from Prague to Berlin to run in a 5,000-metre race. He was deprived of his rank of colonel after voicing his opposition to the Soviet invasion of Czechoslovakia 1968, and later involved himself with the work of the Czech national sports institute.

Zeami Motokiyo (1363–1443). Japanese dramatist and drama theorist. He developed the dramatic dance form practised by his father Kan'ami into Nō drama, for which he wrote over 100 plays, many of which are still in the contemporary repertoire. He also wrote a series of manuals (*Kadensho*) 1440–42, which dealt with discipline required in performance and the philosophical theory of Nō drama.

Zedekiah (lived early 6th century). Last king of Judah 597–586 BC. Placed on the throne by Nebuchadnezzar, he rebelled, was forced to witness his sons' execution, then was blinded and sent to Babylon. The witness to these events was the prophet Jeremiah, who describes them in the Old Testament.

Zeeman Erik Christopher (1925–). British mathematician concerned with catastrophe theory and its applications to the physical, biological, and behavioural sciences, and with dynamical systems. For example, he has constructed catastrophe models of heartbeat and the propagation of nerve impulses.

In 1964 he became professor at Warwick, where he founded and became director of the Mathematics Research Centre.

Zeeman's interest in catastrophe theory arose from his study of topology and brain modelling. If two elementary catastrophes (two conflicting behavioural drives, for example) are plotted as axes on the horizontal plane – called the control surface – and the complementary result (the resulting behaviour) is plotted on a third axis perpendicular to the first two, resultant points can be plotted for the entire control surface, and when connected they form a surface of their own. Catastrophe theory reveals that in the middle of the surface is a pleat, which becomes narrower towards the back. For Zeeman, all the points on the surface represent the most probable behaviour, with the exception of those on the pleated middle part, which represent the least likely behaviour. At the edge of the pleat, the sheet on which the behaviour points have been travelling folds under and is wiped out. The behaviour state falls to the bottom sheet of the graph and there is a sudden change in behaviour.

Zeeman Pieter (1865–1943). Dutch physicist who discovered 1896 that when light from certain elements, such as sodium or lithium (when heated), is passed through a spectroscope in the presence of a strong magnetic field, the spectrum splits into a number of distinct lines. His discovery, known as the Zeeman effect, won him a share of the 1902 Nobel Prize for Physics with Hendrik Lorentz.

He was professor at Amsterdam 1900–35, and from 1923 director of a new laboratory named the Zeeman Laboratory.

Lorentz proposed that light is caused by the vibration of electrons and suggested that imposing a magnetic field on light would result in a splitting of spectral lines by varying the wavelengths of the lines. Using a sodium flare between the poles of a powerful electromagnet and producing spectra with a large concave diffraction grating, Zeeman was able to detect a broadening of the spectral lines when the current was activated. In 1897 he refined the experiment and was successful in resolving the broadening of the narrow blue-green spectral line of cadmium produced in a vacuum discharge into a triplet of three component lines.

Zeeman's attention turned to the velocity of light in moving media and he was able to show that the results were in agreement with the theory of relativity.

In my productions the principals are of the least importance.

FRANCO ZEFFIRELLI
quoted in Robert Jacobson *Reverberations* 1975

Zeffirelli Franco Corsi (1923–   ). Italian theatre, opera and film director, and stage designer. He is acclaimed for his stylish designs and lavish productions. His films include *Romeo and Juliet* 1968, *La Traviata* 1983, *Otello* 1986, and *Hamlet* 1990.

Zeiss Carl (1816–1888). German optician. He opened his first workshop in Jena 1846, and in 1866 joined forces with Ernst Abbe (1840–1905) producing cameras, microscopes, and binoculars.

Zeitzler Kurt (1895–1963). German general in World War II. A favourite of Hitler, in 1942 as Chief of the General Staff he supported von Paulus's request to withdraw from Stalingrad. Hitler refused, von Paulus was destroyed, and thereafter Hitler paid more attention to his Chief of Staff. After several defeats at Soviet hands, Hitler lost patience and July 1944 replaced him with Guderian.

Zel'dovich Yakov Borisovich (1914–1987). Soviet astrophysicist, originally a specialist in nuclear physics. His cosmological theories led to more accurate determinations of the abundance of helium in older stars.

Zel'dovich was born in Minsk, studied at Leningrad (now St Petersburg), and in 1931 began work at the Soviet Academy of Sciences. During World War II he contributed research towards the war effort. He later worked at the Institute of Cosmic Research at the Space Research Institute of the Soviet Academy of Sciences in Moscow.

During the 1930s, Zel'dovich was involved in a research programme aimed at discovering the mechanism of oxidation of nitrogen during an explosion. He also wrote about the chemical reactions of explosions, the subsequent generation of shockwaves, and the related subjects of gas dynamics and flame propagation.

Zel'dovich participated in early work on the mechanism of fission during the radioactive decay of uranium. In the 1950s he developed an interest in cosmology and in such subjects as quark annihilation

and neutrino detection. In 1967 he proposed that in its initial stages the universe was uniform in all directions, but that as it has expanded, this isotropy has diminished.

Zelenka Jan Dismas (1679–1745). Bohemian composer. He wrote lightweight orchestral works, trio sonatas, and solemn religious works including Magnificats in D 1725 and C 1727. He worked at the court of Dresden and became director of church music 1729. His compositions were rediscovered in the 1970s.

Zemeckis Robert (1952–   ). US film director and screenwriter responsible for some of the most commercially successful films of the 1980s such as the hit romantic adventure *Romancing the Stone* 1984. He has combined technical ingenuity and humorous invention, notably in the sci-fi comedy *Back to the Future* 1986 and its two sequels, *Who Framed Roger Rabbit?* 1988, which combined animation and live action, and the black farce *Death Becomes Her* 1992.

Zenger John Peter (1697–1746). American colonial printer and newspaper editor. Born in Germany, Zenger emigrated to New York 1710 and was apprenticed to a printer. Establishing his own press 1726, Zenger became active in local political affairs. In 1733 he founded the *New York Weekly Journal* through which he publicized his opposition to New York governor William Cosby. In 1734 he was arrested for seditious libel. Acquitted by a jury in 1735, he published *A Brief Narrative of the Case and Trial of John Peter Zenger* 1736 and remained a spokesman for the principle of freedom of the press.

Zeng Guofan or Tseng Kuo-fan (1811–1872). Chinese imperial official who played a crucial role in crushing the Taiping Rebellion. He raised the Hunan army 1852 to organize resistance to this revolt, eventually capturing Nanjing 1864. The regional influence he acquired made him in some ways a forerunner of the 20th-century Chinese warlords.

Fearful that Zeng's provincial army might grow too powerful, the government refused him money, forcing him to extract local financial support. He became a supporter of the Self-strengthening movement for military modernization, and was governor general of Liangjiang in E central China 1860–65, setting up the Jiangnan Arsenal in Shanghai for the manufacture of modern weapons and the study of Western science and technology.

Whatever must be accomplished in matters of war must be done by valour alone.

ZENOBIA
Response to the Roman demand to
surrender, quoted in *Life of Aurelian* ch 27

Zenobia (lived 3rd century). Queen of Palmyra AD 266–272. She assumed the crown as regent for her sons, after the death of her husband Odaenathus, and in 272 was defeated at Emesa (now Homs) by Aurelian and taken captive to Rome.

Zeno of Citium (c. 335–262 BC). Greek founder of the stoic school of philosophy in Athens, about 300 BC.

What is moving is moving neither in the place in which it is nor in the place in which it is not.

ZENO OF ELEA
quoted in Diogenes Laertius *Lives of the Philosophers* bk 9, ch 72

Zeno of Elea (c. 490–c. 430 BC). Greek philosopher who pointed out several paradoxes that raised 'modern' problems of space and time. For example, motion is an illusion, since an arrow in flight must occupy a determinate space at each instant, and therefore must be at rest.

Zeppelin Ferdinand Adolf August Heinrich, Count von (1838–1917). German airship pioneer. His first airship was built and tested 1900. During World War I a number of zeppelins bombed England. They were also used for luxury passenger transport but the construction of hydrogen-filled airships with rigid keels was abandoned after several disasters in the 1920s and 1930s. Zeppelin also helped to pioneer large multi-engine bomber planes.

In the 1860s he joined an expedition to North America to explore the sources of the Mississippi River, and in 1870 at Fort Snelling, Minnesota, he made his first ascent in a (military) balloon. Zeppelin rose to the rank of brigadier general before retiring from the army 1891. He devoted himself to the study of aeronautics, and by 1906 he had developed a practical airship. The German government then subsidized him with a National Zeppelin Fund.

In World War I zeppelins were used extensively for air raids on Britain and France 1915–16 but the large size and slow speed of the zeppelin made it a relatively easy target, and it remained in use only as a supply transport.

Zermelo Ernst Friedrich Ferdinand (1871–1953). German mathematician who made important contributions to the development of set theory, particularly in developing the axiomatic set theory that now bears his name.

In 1905 he became professor at Göttingen, eventually moving to Freiburg, where he resigned his post 1935 in protest at the Nazi regime, but was reinstated 1946.

In 1900 Zermelo provided an ingenious proof to the well-ordering theorem, which states that every set can be well ordered (that is, can be arranged in a series in which each subclass – not being null – has a first term). He said that a relation $a < b$ (a comes before b) can be introduced such that for any two statements a and b, either $a = b$, or $a < b$ or $b < a$. If there are three elements a, b, and c, then if $a b$ and $b < c$, then $a < c$. This gave rise to the Zermelo axiom that every class can be well ordered.

In 1904 Zermelo defined the axiom of choice, the use of which had previously been unrecognized in mathematical reasoning. The first formulations of axioms for set theory – an axiom system for German mathematician Georg Cantor's theory of sets – were made by Zermelo in 1908.

Zernike Frits (1888–1966). Dutch physicist who developed the phase-contrast microscope 1935. Earlier microscopes allowed many specimens to be examined only after they had been transformed by heavy staining and other treatment. The phase-contrast microscope allowed living cells to be directly observed by making use of the difference in refractive indices between specimens and medium. Nobel Prize for Physics 1953.

Zeroual Lamine (1941–). Algerian politican and soldier, president from 1994. He was brought into government 1993 as defence minister, and the following year became commander-in-chief of the armed forces. Appointed president at a time of increasing civil strife, he initially attempted dialogue and reconciliation with imprisoned Islamic fundamentalist leaders. After this failed, Zeroual increasingly resorted to military tactics to counter the unrest. Following his victory in a direct presidential election Nov 1995, he attempted to reopen dialogue with the outlawed Islamic Salvation Front (FIS).

Zetterling Mai Elisabeth (1925–1994). Swedish actress and director. After gaining early success with her sexually provocative role in the film *Frenzy* 1945, she played in several West End theatre productions in London, including *The Seagull* 1948 and *A Doll's House* 1953. She subsequently returned to Sweden to launch a career as a director, often exploring feminist issues in films such as *Loving Couples* 1964.

Zeuxis (lived 5th century BC). Greek painter belonging to the Ionic School, apparently influenced by Apollodoros, and the contemporary and rival of Parrhasios. He excelled in the subtle use of colour and shading, and painted imaginative portraits of such mythical figures as Penelope and Helen. His reputed masterpiece was the picture of Helen which he painted for Crotona. According to legend his picture of grapes was so realistic as to deceive the birds, who tried to eat them. None of his works are still in existence.

Zhang Yimou (1950–). Chinese film director and screenwriter. The foremost member of the 'Fifth Generation' of film-makers that

graduated from the Beijing Film Academy in the early 1980s, Zhang has spearheaded renewed international interest in Chinese filmmaking. His films are notable for the use of sumptuous colours as imagery to underpin the storyline. Many of his films deal with the social and sexual pressures on women in Chinese history. His films include *Hong Gaoliang/Red Sorghum* 1988, *Du Hong Denglong Gao Gao Gua/Raise the Red Lantern* 1991, and *Qiuju da Guansi/The Story of Qiu Ju* 1992.

Zhang worked as the cinematographer on Chen Kaige's *Yellow Earth* and *The Big Parade* before making *Red Sorghum*. His other films include *Daihao 'Meizhoubao'/Codename 'Cougar'* 1989 and *Judou/Ju Dou* 1990.

Zhao Ziyang (1919–). Chinese politician, prime minister 1980–87 and secretary of the Chinese Communist Party 1987–89.

Zhao, son of a wealthy landlord from Henan province, joined the Communist Youth League 1932 and worked underground as a CCP official during the liberation war 1937–49. He rose to prominence in the party in Guangdong from 1951. As a supporter of the reforms of Liu Shaoqi, he was dismissed during the 1966–69 Cultural Revolution, paraded through Canton in a dunce's cap, and sent to Inner Mongolia.

He was rehabilitated by Zhou Enlai 1973 and sent to China's largest province, Sichuan, as first party secretary 1975. Here he introduced radical and successful market-oriented rural reforms. Deng Xiaoping had him inducted into the Politburo 1977. After six months as vice premier, Zhao was appointed prime minister 1980 and assumed, in addition, the post of CCP general secretary Jan 1987. His reforms included self-management and incentives for workers and factories. His economic reforms were criticized for causing inflation, and his liberal views of the prodemocracy demonstrations that culminated in the student occupation of Tiananmen Square June 1989 led to his downfall.

Zhelev Zhelyu (1935–). Bulgarian politician, president from 1990. The son of peasants, he became professor of philosophy at Sofia University. He was a member of the Bulgarian Communist Party 1961–65, when he was expelled for his criticisms of Lenin. In 1989 he became head of the opposition Democratic Forces coalition. He is a proponent of market-centred economic reform and social peace. He was made president of Bulgaria 1990 after the demise of the 'reform communist' regime, and was directly elected to the post 1992.

Zheng He (1371–1433). Chinese admiral and emperor during the Ming dynasty. A Muslim court eunuch, he undertook maritime expeditions 1405–33 to India, the Persian Gulf, and E Africa, demonstrating China's early command of the compass and shipbuilding techniques.

Zhirinovsky Vladimir (1946–). Russian politician, leader of the far-right Liberal Democratic Party of Russia (LDPR) from 1991. His strong, sometimes bizarre views, advocating the use of nuclear weapons and the restoration of the Russian empire, initially cast him as a lightweight politician. However, his ability to win third place out of six candidates in Russia's first free presidential elections 1991, and the success of his party in winning nearly 23% of the vote and 15% of the seats in the Dec 1993 federal assembly elections, forced a reassessment.

His complex, unpredictable personality is tellingly revealed in his autobiography *Last Thrust to the South* which has been likened to Hitler's *Mein Kampf*. He has been seen as a threat to democratic progress in Russia.

Zhivkov Todor (1911–). Bulgarian Communist Party (BCP) leader 1954–89, prime minister 1962–71, president 1971–89. Zhivkov, a printing worker, joined the BCP 1932 and was active in the resistance 1941–44. After the war, he was elected to the National Assembly and soon promoted into the BCP secretariat and Politburo. As BCP first secretary, Zhivkov became the dominant political figure in Bulgaria after the death of Vulko Chervenkov 1956. Zhivkov was elected to the new post of state president 1971 and lasted until the Eastern bloc upheavals of 1989. His period in office was one of caution and conservatism. In 1990 he was charged with embezzlement during his time in office. His trial began Feb 1991 but was subsequently postponed indefinitely on health grounds.

Zhou dynasty or Chou dynasty (c. 1066–256 BC). Chinese succession of rulers, under whose rule cities emerged and philosophy flourished. The dynasty was established by the Zhou, a seminomadic people from the Wei Valley region, W of the great bend in the Huang He (Yellow River). Zhou influence waned from 403 BC, as the Warring States era began.

The founder was Wu Wang, 'the Martial', who claimed that Shang dynasty misrule justified the transfer of the 'mandate of heaven'. Under the Zhou, agriculture and commerce developed further, iron implements and metal coins came into use, cities grew up, and the philosophies of Confucius, Lao Zi, Mencius, and Taoism flowered. The Western Zhou controlled feudal vassal states in the Wei Valley, basing their capital at Hao, near Xian, until 771 BC. A new capital was later set up at Luoyang, to serve the Eastern Zhou. Zhou society had a very similar structure to later feudal European and Japanese periods, with strict divisions and hereditary classes.

Zhou Enlai or Chou En-lai (1898–1976). Chinese politician. Zhou, a member of the Chinese Communist Party (CCP) from the 1920s, was prime minister 1949–76 and foreign minister 1949–58. He was a moderate Maoist and weathered the Cultural Revolution. He played a key role in foreign affairs.

Born into a declining mandarin gentry family near Shanghai, Zhou studied in Japan and Paris, where he became a founder member of the overseas branch of the CCP. He adhered to the Moscow line of urban-based revolution in China, organizing communist cells in Shanghai and an abortive uprising in Nanchang 1927. In 1935 Zhou supported the election of Mao Zedong as CCP leader and remained a loyal ally during the next 40 years. He served as liaison officer 1937–46 between the CCP and Chiang Kai-shek's nationalist Guomindang government. In 1949 he became prime minister, an office he held until his death Jan 1976.

Zhou, a moderator between the opposing camps of Liu Shaoqi and Mao Zedong, restored orderly progress after the Great Leap Forward (1958–60) and the Cultural Revolution (1966–69), and was the architect of the Four Modernizations programme 1975. Abroad, Zhou sought to foster Third World unity at the Bandung Conference 1955, averted an outright border confrontation with the USSR by negotiation with Prime Minister Kosygin 1969, and was the principal advocate of détente with the USA during the early 1970s.

Zhu De or Chu Teh (1886–1976). Chinese Red Army leader from 1931. He devised the tactic of mobile guerrilla warfare and organized the Long March to Shaanxi 1934–36. He was made a marshal 1955.

The son of a wealthy Sichuan landlord, Zhu served in the Chinese Imperial Army before supporting Sun Yat-sen in the 1911 revolution. He studied communism in Germany and Paris 1922–25 and joined the Chinese Communist Party (CCP) on his return, becoming commander in chief of the Red Army. Working closely with Mao Zedong, Zhu organized the Red Army's Jiangxi break-out 1931 and led the 18th Route Army during the liberation war 1937–49. He served as head of state (chair of the Standing Committee of the National People's Congress) 1975–76.

Zhukov Georgi Konstantinovich (1896–1974). Marshal of the USSR in World War II and minister of defence 1955–57. Zhukov joined the Bolsheviks and the Red Army 1918 and led a cavalry regiment in the Civil War 1918–20. His army defeated the Japanese forces in Mongolia 1939. As Chief of Staff from 1941, he defended Moscow 1941, counter-attacked at Stalingrad (now Volgograd) 1942, organized the relief of Leningrad (now St Petersburg) 1943, and led the offensive from the Ukraine March 1944 which ended in the fall of Berlin. At the end of World War II, he headed the Allied delegation that received the German surrender, and subsequently commanded the Soviet occupation forces in Germany. Under the Khrushchev regime he was denounced 1957 for obstructing party work and encouraging a Zhukov cult, but was restored 1965.

Zia Begum Khaleda (1945–). Bangladeshi conservative politician, prime minister from 1991. As leader of the Bangladesh Nationalist Party (BNP) from 1984, she successfully oversaw the transition from presidential to democratic parliamentary government.

In 1958 she married Captain Zia ur Rahman who assumed power in a military coup 1976. He became president 1977, and was assassinated 1981. Begum Khaleda Zia then entered opposition politics, becoming leader of the BNP 1984. In 1990 she helped form a seven-party alliance, whose pressure for a more democratic regime resulted in the toppling of General Ershad, a long-standing military ruler, during whose regime she had been detained seven times. From Dec 1994 she faced a mounting campaign against her government, with opposition MPs boycotting parliament and the longest general strike in the country's history being called.

If the Court sentences the blighter to hang, then the blighter will hang.

MOHAMMED ZIA UL-HAQ
of the death sentence imposed on former president Zulfikar Ali Bhutto 1979

Zia ul-Haq Muhammad (1924–1988). Pakistani general, in power from 1977 until his death, probably an assassination, in an aircraft explosion. He became army Chief of Staff 1976, led the military coup against Zulfikar Ali Bhutto 1977, and became president 1978. Zia introduced a fundamentalist Islamic regime and restricted political activity.

Zia was a career soldier from a middle-class Punjabi Muslim family. As army Chief of Staff, his opposition to the Soviet invasion of Afghanistan 1979 drew support from the USA, but his refusal to commute the death sentence imposed on Zulfikar Ali Bhutto was widely condemned. He lifted martial law 1985.

Ziegler Karl (1898–1973). German organic chemist. In 1963 he shared the Nobel Prize for Chemistry with Giulio Natta of Italy for his work on the chemistry and technology of large polymers. He combined simple molecules of the gas ethylene (ethene) into the long-chain plastic polyethylene (polyethene).

Ziegler and Natta discovered 1953 a family of stereo-specific catalysts capable of introducing an exact and regular structure to various polymers. This discovery formed the basis of nearly all later developments in synthetic plastics, fibres, rubbers, and films derived from such olefins as ethylene (ethene) and butadiene (but-1,2:3,4-diene).

From 1943 he was director of the Kaiser Wilhelm (later Max Planck) Institute for Coal Research in Mülheim.

In 1933, Ziegler discovered a method of making compounds that contain large rings of carbon atoms. Later he carried out research on the organic compounds of aluminium. Using electrochemical techniques, he prepared various other metal alkyls from the aluminium ones, including tetraethyl lead, which was used as an additive to petrol.

Zinnemann Fred(erick) (1907–). Austrian film director. He lived in the USA from 1921, and latterly in the UK. His films include *High Noon* 1952, *From Here to Eternity* 1953 (Academy Award), *A Man For All Seasons* 1966 (Academy Award), *The Day of the Jackal* 1973, and *Five Days One Summer* 1982.

Zinoviev Grigory Yevseyevich (1883–1936). Russian communist politician whose name was attached to a forgery, the Zinoviev letter, inciting Britain's communists to rise, which helped to topple the Labour government 1924.

Armed warfare must be preceded by a struggle against the inclinations to compromise which are embedded among the majority of British workmen.

ZINOVIEV
Letter to the British Communist Party 15 Sept 1924 quoted
in *The Times* 25 Oct 1924. Alleged by some to be a forgery.

A prominent Bolshevik, Zinoviev returned to Russia 1917 with Lenin and played a leading part in the Revolution. He became head of the Communist International 1919. As one of the 'Old Bolsheviks', he was seen by Stalin as a threat. He was accused of complicity in the murder of the Bolshevik leader Sergei Kirov 1934, and was tried and shot.

Suggested reading
Carr, E M *The Russian Revolution* (1951–53)
Rabinowitch, Alexander *The Bolsheviks Come to Power* (1976)
Zinoviev, Grigory *History of the Bolshevik Party* (1923, trs 1973)

Zinovyev Aleksander Aleksandrovich (1922–). Russian satirical writer and mathematician. He now lives in Munich, Germany. His first book *Ziyayushchie vysoty*/*Yawning Heights* 1976, a surreal, chaotic narrative, represents a formal negation of the socialist realist novel and the promised 'great Future' of Soviet ideology. He complicates the quasi-scientific stance of his writing by deliberate disorganization, even in his treatise *Kommunizm kak realnost*/*The Reality of Communism* 1981.

Zi Xi or Tz'u-hsi (*c.* 1834–1908). Empress dowager of China. She was presented as a concubine to the emperor Xianfeng. On his death 1861 she became regent for her young son Tongzhi (1856–1875) until 1873 and, after his death, for her nephew Guangxu (1871–1908) until 1889. A ruthless conservative, she blocked the Hundred Days' Reform launched in 1898 and assumed power again, having Guangxu imprisoned. Her policies helped deny China a peaceful transition to political and economic reform.

Zoë (*c.* 978–1050). Byzantine empress who ruled from 1028 until 1050. She gained the title by marriage to the heir apparent Romanus III Argyrus, but was reputed to have poisoned him (1034) in order to marry her lover Michael. He died 1041 and Zoë and her sister Theodora were proclaimed joint empresses. Rivalry led to Zoë marrying Constantine IX Monomachus with whom she reigned until her death.

Zoffany Johann (or John) (1733–1810). British portrait painter, of German origin. He was based in London from about 1761. Under the patronage of George III he painted many portraits of the royal family and the English aristocracy. He spent several years in Florence (1770s) and India (1780s).

Zog Ahmed Bey Zogu (1895–1961). King of Albania 1928–39. He became prime minister of Albania 1922, president of the republic 1925, and proclaimed himself king 1928. He was driven out by the Italians 1939 and settled in England.

Zola Émile Edouard Charles Antoine (1840–1902). French novelist and social reformer. Born in Paris, Zola was a journalist and clerk until his *Contes à Ninon*/*Stories for Ninon* 1864 enabled him to devote himself to literature. With *La Fortune des Rougon*/*The Fortune of the Rougons* 1867 he began a series of some 20 naturalistic novels, portraying the fortunes of a French family under the Second Empire. They include *Le Ventre de Paris*/*The Underbelly of Paris* 1873, *Nana* 1880, *Germinal* 1885 and *La Débâcle*/*The Debacle* 1892. In 1898 he published *J'accuse*/*I Accuse*, a pamphlet indicting the persecutors of Dreyfus, for which he was prosecuted for libel but later pardoned. Among later novels are the trilogy *Trois Villes*/*Three Cities* 1894–98, and *Fécondité*/*Fecundity* 1899.

Suggested reading
Hemmings, F W H *The Life and Times of Émile Zola* (1977)
Josephson, Matthew *Zola and His Time* (1985)
Richardson, Joanna *Zola* (1978)
Walker, Philip *Zola* (1985)
Wilson, Angus *Émile Zola: An Introductory Study of His Novels* (1952)

Zoroaster or Zarathustra (*c.* 638–*c.* 553 BC). Persian prophet and religious teacher, founder of Zoroastrianism. Zoroaster believed that he had seen God, Ahura Mazda, in a vision. His first vision came at the age of 30 and, after initial rejection and violent attack, he converted King Vishtaspa. Subsequently, his teachings spread rapidly, becoming the official religion of the kingdom.

Zorrilla y Moral José (1817–1893). Spanish poet and playwright. He based his plays chiefly on national legends, such as the *Don Juan Tenorio* 1844.

Zsigmondy Richard Adolf (1865–1929). Austrian-born German chemist who devised and built an ultramicroscope in 1903. The microscope's illumination was placed at right angles to the axis. (In a conventional microscope the light source is placed parallel to the instrument's axis.) Zsigmondy's arrangement made it possible to observe particles with a diameter of 10-millionth of a millimetre. Nobel Prize for Chemistry 1925.

Zsigmondy was born in Vienna and studied at Munich. He stayed in Germany, becoming professor at Göttingen 1908.

Working at the Glass Manufacturing Company in Jena 1897–1900, Zsigmondy became concerned with coloured and turbid glasses and he invented a type of milk glass. This aroused his interest in colloids, because it is colloidal inclusions that give glass its colour or opacity. His belief that the suspended particles in gold sols are kept apart by electric charges was generally accepted, and the sols became model systems for much of his later work on colloids.

Using the ultramicroscope Zsigmondy was able to count the number of particles in a given volume and indirectly estimate their sizes. He showed that colour changes in sols reflect changes in particle size caused by coagulation when salts are added, and that the addition of agents such as gelatin stabilizes the colloid by inhibiting coagulation.

Zuckerman Solly, Baron Zuckerman (1904–1993). South African-born British zoologist, educationalist, and establishment figure. He did extensive research on primates, publishing a number of books that became classics in their field, including *The Social Life of Monkeys and Apes* 1932 and *Functional Affinities of Man, Monkeys and Apes* 1933. He was chief scientific adviser to the British government 1964–71.

Born in Cape Town, where he was demonstrator in anatomy at the university, Zuckerman came to London in the 1920s and soon established himself as a leading anatomist with the Zoological Society. He joined the faculty of Oxford University 1934 and during World War II, as a government scientific adviser, investigated the biological effects of bomb blasts. He was professor of anatomy at Birmingham University 1946–68, and was created a peer 1971. As chief scientific adviser to the government during Harold Wilson's premiership, he had his own office within the Cabinet Office, with direct access to the prime minister himself. He published his autobiography *From Apes to Warlords* 1978.

Zukofsky Louis (1904–1978). US poet. He combined poetry, prose, criticism, musical notation, and drama in his complex epic *A* (complete publication 1979). He was a major theorist and practitioner of Objectivism. Zukofsky also published fiction, translations, and works of criticism and aesthetics including *Bottom: On Shakespeare* 1963 and *Prepositions* 1967. His short lyric poems were collected in two volumes 1965 and 1966.

Zurbarán Francisco de (1598–*c.* 1664). Spanish painter. Based in Seville, he painted religious subjects in a powerful, austere style, often focusing on a single figure in prayer.

He came from a peasant family, and was apprenticed as a boy to a painter in Seville, Juan de las Roelas. He settled in Seville 1628, painting many religious works for churches and monasteries. He was the friend of the young Velazquez, and was influenced in style by him and by the dark manner of painting then cultivated in southern Spain and derived from Ribera and the Neapolitan School. He lived in Madrid in later life, and was appointed one of the painters to Philip IV 1650. But his austere and simple art suffered in competition with the sensational productions of Murillo. Characteristic of his work are paintings of monks at prayer or in solitary meditation. He also painted a number of portraits of women, in 17th-century dress but described, according to a poetic custom of the time, as female saints. The charming *St Margaret* of the National Gallery, London is an example. A third remarkable aspect of his art is to be found in his still life, in which there is the same concentrated simplicity as in his figures. A masterpiece of this kind is the *Oranges, Lemons and a Rose* (Uffizi).

Zweig Arnold (1887–1968). German novelist, playwright, and poet. He is remembered for his realistic novel about a Russian peasant in the German army *Der Streit um den Sergeanten Grischa/The Case of Sergeant Grischa* 1927.

Zweig Stefan (1881–1942). Austrian writer. He was the author of plays, poems, and many biographies of writers (including Balzac and Dickens) and historical figures (including Marie Antoinette and Mary Stuart). He and his wife, exiles from the Nazis from 1934, despaired at what they saw as the end of civilization and culture and committed suicide in Brazil.

Zwicky Fritz (1898–1974). Swiss astronomer who predicted the existence of neutron stars 1934. He discovered 18 supernovae and determined that cosmic rays originate in them. Zwicky observed that most galaxies occur in clusters, each of which contains several thousand galaxies. He made spectroscopic studies of the Virgo and Coma Berenices clusters and calculated that the distribution of galaxies in the Coma Berenices cluster was statistically similar to the distribution of molecules in a gas when its temperature is at equilibrium. Beginning 1936, he compiled a catalogue of galaxies and galaxy clusters in which he listed 10,000 clusters.

Zwicky was born in Varna, Bulgaria, but his parents were Swiss and he retained his Swiss nationality throughout his life. He studied at the Federal Institute of Technology in Zürich, then moved to the USA 1925 to join the California Institute of Technology, where he spent his whole career.

Zwicky was among the first to suggest that there is a relationship between supernovae and neutron stars. He suggested in the early 1930s that the outer layers of a star that explodes as a supernova leave a core that collapses upon itself as a result of gravitational forces.

Zwingli Ulrich (1484–1531). Swiss Protestant, born in St Gallen.

He was ordained a Roman Catholic priest 1506, but by 1519 was a Reformer and led the Reformation in Switzerland with his insistence on the sole authority of the Scriptures. He was killed in a skirmish at Kappel during a war against the cantons that had not accepted the Reformation.

Suggested reading

Chadwick, Owen *The Reformation* (1964)
Potter, G R *Zwingli* (1976)
Spitz, Lewis *The Protestant Reformation* (1984)
Stephens, W P *The Theology of Huldrych Zwingli* (1985)

Zworykin Vladimir Kosma (1889–1982). Russian-born US electronics engineer who invented a television camera tube and developed the electron microscope.

During World War I he worked as a radio officer in Russia. In 1919 he emigrated to the USA. He joined the Westinghouse corporation in Pittsburgh, Pennsylvania, and in 1923 took out a patent for the iconoscope (his TV camera tube), followed a year later by the kinescope (a TV receiver tube). In 1929 he demonstrated an improved electronic television system and became director of electronic research for the Radio Corporation of America (RCA), where he rose to vice president 1947.

The iconoscope tube uses an electron beam to scan the charge pattern on a signal plate, which corresponds to the pattern of light and dark of an image focused on it by a lens. Zworykin's inventions also included an early form of electric eye and an electronic image tube sensitive to infrared light, which was the basis for World War II inventions for seeing in the dark. In 1957 he patented a device that uses ultraviolet light and television to throw a colour picture of living cells on a screen, which opened up new prospects for biological investigation.

He worked with James Hillier (1915–) on the development of the electron microscope, a device Hillier constructed while a member of Zworykin's research group at RCA.

Appendices

Academy Award winners

best picture	best director	best actor	best actress
1928 Wings	Frank Borzage *Seventh Heaven* and Lewis Milestone *Two Arabian Nights*	Emil Jannings *The Way of All Flesh, The Last Command*	Janet Gaynor *Seventh Heaven, Street Angel, Sunrise*
1929 The Broadway Melody	Frank Lloyd *The Divine Lady*	Warner Baxter *In Old Arizona*	Mary Pickford *Coquette*
1930 All Quiet on the Western Front	Lewis Milestone *All Quiet on the Western Front*	George Arliss *Disraeli*	Norma Shearer *The Divorcee*
1931 Cimarron	Norman Taurog *Skippy*	Lionel Barrymore *A Free Soul*	Marie Dressler *Min and Bill*
1932 Grand Hotel	Frank Borzage *Bad Girl*	Fredric March *Dr Jekyll and Mr Hyde* and Wallace Beery *The Champ*	Helen Hayes *The Sin of Madelon Claudet*
1933 Cavalcade	Frank Lloyd *Cavalcade*	Charles Laughton *The Private Life of Henry VIII*	Katharine Hepburn *Morning Glory*
1934 It Happened One Night	Frank Capra *It Happened One Night*	Clark Gable *It Happened One Night*	Claudette Colbert *It Happened One Night*
1935 Mutiny on the Bounty	John Ford *The Informer*	Victor McLaglen *The Informer*	Bette Davis *Dangerous*
1936 The Great Ziegfeld	Frank Capra *Mr Deeds Goes to Town*	Paul Muni *The Story of Louis Pasteur*	Luise Rainer *The Great Ziegfeld*
1937 The Life of Emile Zola	Leo McCarey *The Awful Truth*	Spencer Tracy *Captains Courageous*	Luise Rainer *The Good Earth*
1938 You Can't Take It With You	Frank Capra *You Can't Take It With You*	Spencer Tracy *Boys Town*	Bette Davis *Jezebel*
1939 Gone With the Wind	Victor Fleming *Gone With the Wind*	Robert Donat *Goodbye Mr Chips*	Vivien Leigh *Gone With the Wind*
1940 Rebecca	John Ford *The Grapes of Wrath*	James Stewart *The Philadelphia Story*	Ginger Rogers *Kitty Foyle*
1941 How Green Was My Valley	John Ford *How Green Was My Valley*	Gary Cooper *Sergeant York*	Joan Fontaine *Suspicion*
1942 Mrs Miniver	William Wyler *Mrs Miniver*	James Cagney *Yankee Doodle Dandy*	Greer Garson *Mrs Miniver*
1943 Casablanca	Michael Curtiz *Casablanca*	Paul Lukas *Watch on the Rhine*	Jennifer Jones *The Song of Bernadette*
1944 Going My Way	Leo McCarey *Going My Way*	Bing Crosby *Going My Way*	Ingrid Bergman *Gaslight*
1945 The Lost Weekend	Billy Wilder *The Lost Weekend*	Ray Milland *The Lost Weekend*	Joan Crawford *Mildred Pierce*
1946 The Best Years of Our Lives	William Wyler *The Best Years of Our Lives*	Fredric March *The Best Years of Our Lives*	Olivia de Havilland *To Each His Own*
1947 Gentleman's Agreement	Elia Kazan *Gentleman's Agreement*	Ronald Coleman *A Double Life*	Loretta Young *The Farmer's Daughter*
1948 Hamlet	John Huston *Treasure of Sierra Madre*	Laurence Olivier *Hamlet*	Jane Wyman *Johnny Belinda*
1949 All the King's Men	Joseph L Mankiewicz *A Letter to Three Wives*	Broderick Crawford *All the King's Men*	Olivia de Havilland *The Heiress*
1950 All About Eve	Joseph L Mankiewicz *All About Eve*	José Ferrer *Cyrano de Bergerac*	Judy Holliday *Born Yesterday*
1951 An American in Paris	George Stevens *A Place in the Sun*	Humphrey Bogart *The African Queen*	Vivien Leigh *A Streetcar Named Desire*
1952 The Greatest Show on Earth	John Ford *The Quiet Man*	Gary Cooper *High Noon*	Shirley Booth *Come Back Little Sheba*
1953 From Here to Eternity	Fred Zinnemann *From Here to Eternity*	William Holden *Stalag 17*	Audrey Hepburn *Roman Holiday*
1954 On the Waterfront	Elia Kazan *On the Waterfront*	Marlon Brando *On the Waterfront*	Grace Kelly *The Country Girl*
1955 Marty	Delbert Mann *Marty*	Ernest Borgnine *Marty*	Anna Magnani *The Rose Tattoo*
1956 Around the World in 80 Days	George Stevens *Giant*	Yul Brynner *The King and I*	Ingrid Bergman *Anastasia*
1957 The Bridge on the River Kwai	David Lean *The Bridge on the River Kwai*	Alec Guinness *The Bridge on the River Kwai*	Joanne Woodward *The Three Faces of Eve*
1958 Gigi	Vincente Minnelli *Gigi*	David Niven *Separate Tables*	Susan Hayward *I Want to Live!*
1959 Ben Hur	William Wyler *Ben Hur*	Charlton Heston *Ben Hur*	Simone Signoret *Room at the Top*
1960 The Apartment	Billy Wilder *The Apartment*	Burt Lancaster *Elmer Gantry*	Elizabeth Taylor *Butterfield 8*
1961 West Side Story	Robert Wise and Jerome Robbins *West Side Story*	Maximillian Schell *Judgment at Nuremberg*	Sophia Loren *Two Women*
1962 Lawrence of Arabia	David Lean *Lawrence of Arabia*	Gregory Peck *To Kill a Mockingbird*	Anne Bancroft *The Miracle Worker*
1963 Tom Jones	Tony Richardson *Tom Jones*	Sidney Poitier *Lilies of the Field*	Patricia Neal *Hud*
1964 My Fair Lady	George Cukor *My Fair Lady*	Rex Harrison *My Fair Lady*	Julie Andrews *Mary Poppins*
1965 The Sound of Music	Robert Wise *The Sound of Music*	Lee Marvin *Cat Ballou*	Julie Christie *Darling*
1966 A Man for All Seasons	Fred Zinnemann *A Man for All Seasons*	Paul Scofield *A Man for All Seasons*	Elizabeth Taylor *Who's Afraid of Virginia Woolf?*
1967 In the Heat of the Night	Mike Nichols *The Graduate*	Rod Steiger *In the Heat of the Night*	Katharine Hepburn *Guess Who's Coming to Dinner*
1968 Oliver!	Sir Carol Reed *Oliver!*	Cliff Robertson *Charly*	Katharine Hepburn *The Lion in Winter* and Barbra Streisand *Funny Girl*
1969 Midnight Cowboy	John Schlesinger *Midnight Cowboy*	John Wayne *True Grit*	Maggie Smith *The Prime of Miss Jean Brodie*
1970 Patton	Franklin J Schaffner *Patton*	George C Scott *Patton*	Glenda Jackson *Women in Love*
1971 The French Connection	William Friedkin *The French Connection*	Gene Hackman *The French Connection*	Jane Fonda *Klute*
1972 The Godfather	Bob Fosse *Cabaret*	Marlon Brando *The Godfather*	Liza Minnelli *Cabaret*
1973 The Sting	George Roy Hill *The Sting*	Jack Lemmon *Save the Tiger*	Glenda Jackson *A Touch of Class*

Academy Award winners (continued)

1974 *The Godfather Part II*	Francis Ford Coppola *The Godfather Part II*	Art Carney *Harry and Tonto*	Ellen Burstyn *Alice Doesn't Live Here Anymore*
1975 *One Flew Over the Cuckoo's Nest*	Milos Forman *One Flew Over the Cuckoo's Nest*	Jack Nicholson *One Flew Over the Cuckoo's Nest*	Louise Fletcher *One Flew Over the Cuckoo's Nest*
1976 *Rocky*	John G Avildsen *Rocky*	Peter Finch *Network*	Faye Dunaway *Network*
1977 *Annie Hall*	Woody Allen *Annie Hall*	Richard Dreyfuss *The Goodbye Girl*	Diane Keaton *Annie Hall*
1978 *The Deer Hunter*	Michael Cimino *The Deer Hunter*	Jon Voight *Coming Home*	Jane Fonda *Coming Home*
1979 *Kramer vs Kramer*	Robert Benton *Kramer vs Kramer*	Dustin Hoffman *Kramer vs Kramer*	Sally Field *Norma Rae*
1980 *Ordinary People*	Robert Redford *Ordinary People*	Robert De Niro *Raging Bull*	Sissy Spacek *Coal Miner's Daughter*
1981 *Chariots of Fire*	Warren Beatty *Reds*	Henry Fonda *On Golden Pond*	Katharine Hepburn *On Golden Pond*
1982 *Gandhi*	Richard Attenborough *Gandhi*	Ben Kingsley *Gandhi*	Meryl Streep *Sophie's Choice*
1983 *Terms of Endearment*	James L Brooks *Terms of Endearment*	Robert Duvall *Tender Mercies*	Shirley Maclaine *Terms of Endearment*
1984 *Amadeus*	Milos Forman *Amadeus*	F Murray Abraham *Amadeus*	Sally Field *Places in the Heart*
1985 *Out of Africa*	Sydney Pollack *Out of Africa*	William Hurt *Kiss of the Spider Woman*	Geraldine Page *The Trip to Bountiful*
1986 *Platoon*	Oliver Stone *Platoon*	Paul Newman *The Color of Money*	Marlee Matlin *Children of a Lesser God*
1987 *The Last Emperor*	Bernardo Bertolucci *The Last Emperor*	Michael Douglas *Wall Street*	Cher *Moonstruck*
1988 *Rain Man*	Barry Levinson *Rain Man*	Dustin Hoffman *Rain Man*	Jodie Foster *The Accused*
1989 *Driving Miss Daisy*	Oliver Stone *Born on the Fourth of July*	Daniel Day-Lewis *My Left Foot*	Jessica Tandy *Driving Miss Daisy*
1990 *Dances With Wolves*	Kevin Costner *Dances With Wolves*	Jeremy Irons *Reversal of Fortune*	Kathy Bates *Misery*
1991 *The Silence of the Lambs*	Jonathan Demme *The Silence of the Lambs*	Anthony Hopkins *The Silence of the Lambs*	Jodie Foster *The Silence of the Lambs*
1992 *Unforgiven*	Clint Eastwood *Unforgiven*	Al Pacino *Scent of a Woman*	Emma Thompson *Howard's End*
1993 *Schindler's List*	Steven Spielberg *Schindler's List*	Tom Hanks *Philadelphia*	Holly Hunter *The Piano*
1994 *Forrest Gump*	Robert Zemeckis *Forrest Gump*	Tom Hanks *Forrest Gump*	Jessica Lange *Blue Sky*
***1995** Braveheart*	Mel Gibson *Braveheart*	Nicolas Cage *Leaving Las Vegas*	Susan Sarandon *Dead Man Walking*

Assassinations

	victim	details of assassination
681 BC	Sennacherib of Assyria	murdered by his two sons
514	Hipparchus, tyrant of Athens	killed by Harmodius and Aristogeiton, two Athenians
336	Philip II of Macedon	killed by Pausanias, a Spartan regent and general
44	Julius Caesar, Roman dictator	stabbed by Brutus, Cassius, and others in Senate
AD 41	Caligula, Roman emperor	murdered by Cassius Chaerea, an officer of his guard
96	Domitian, Roman dictator	stabbed in his bedroom by Stephanus, a freed slave
1170	Thomas à Becket	killed by four knights (Fitzorse, Tracy, Morville, and Brito) in Canterbury Cathedral, England
1437	James I of Scotland	murdered in court residence, a Dominican monastery, by assassins led by Sir Robert Graham
1488	James III of Scotland	murdered by an unknown person following defeat of royal army at Sauchieburn
1567	Lord Darnley, husband of Mary Queen of Scots	blown up near Edinburgh while suffering from smallpox; suspected assassin: the Earl of Bothwell
1584	William the Silent, Prince of Orange	shot at Delft by Balthasar Gérard
1589	Henry III of France	stabbed by Jacques Clément, a fanatical Dominican
1610	Henry IV of France	murdered by Ravaillac, a Catholic fanatic
1628	Duke of Buckingham	stabbed at Portsmouth, England en route for La Rochelle, by John Felton, a discontented subaltern
1634	Prince Wallenstein, German general	killed in private train by Devereux
1793	Jean Paul Marat, French revolutionary	stabbed in bath by Charlotte Corday
1801	Paul I of Russia	strangled by army officers who had conspired to force his abdication
1812	Spencer Perceval, British prime minister	shot while entering lobby of the House of Commons by John Bellingham, a bankrupt Liverpool broker
1865	Abraham Lincoln, US president	shot by actor J Wilkes Booth in theatre
1881	James A Garfield, US president	shot at station by Charles Guiteau, a disappointed office-seeker
1881	Alexander II of Russia	died from injuries after bomb was thrown near his palace by Nihilists
1882	Lord Frederick Cavendish, chief secretary for Ireland	murdered by 'Irish Invincibles' in Phoenix Park, Dublin
1894	Marie François Carnot, French president	murdered by Italian anarchist in Lyon
1897	Antonio Cánovas del Castillo, Spanish premier	shot by Italian anarchist Angiolillo at the bath of Santa Agueda, Vitoria
1900	Umberto I of Italy	murdered by anarchist G Bresci in Monza
1901	William McKinley, US president	shot by anarchist Leon Czolgosz in Buffalo, New York
1903	Alexander Obrenovich, King of Serbia, and his wife Draga	murdered by military conspirators

Assassinations (continued)

	victim	details of assassination
1913	George I of Greece	murdered by a Greek, Schinas, in Salonika
1914	Archduke Francis Ferdinand	shot in car by Gavrilo Princip in Sarajevo (sparked World War I); an alleged Serbian plot
1914	Jean Jaurès, French socialist	shot by nationalist in café
1916	Rasputin, Russian monk	shot and dumped in river Neva by a group of nobles led by Prince Feliks Yusupov
1922	Michael Collins, Irish Sinn Féin leader, head of state for ten days	killed in an ambush between Bandon and Macroom in Irish Republic
1934	Dr Engelbert Dollfuss, Austrian chancellor	shot by Nazis in the Chancellery
1934	Alexander I of Yugoslavia	murdered; Italian fascists or Croatian separatists suspected
1935	Huey Long, corrupt American politician	murdered by Dr Carl Austin Weiss
1940	Leon Trotsky, exiled Russian communist leader	killed with an ice axe in Mexico by Ramon de Rio
1942	Reinhard Heydrich, second in command of the Nazi secret police	murdered by Czech resistance fighters
1948	Mahatma Gandhi, Indian nationalist leader	shot by a Hindu fanatic, Nathuran Godse
1948	Count Folke Bernadotte, Swedish diplomat	murdered by Jewish extremists in ambush in Jerusalem
1951	Abdullah I of Jordan	murdered by member of Jehad faction
1951	Liaquat Ali Khan, prime minister of Pakistan	murdered in Rawalpindi by fanatics advocating war with India
1958	Faisal II of Iraq	murdered with his entire household during a military coup
1959	Solomon Bandaranaike, Ceylonese premier	murdered by Buddhist monk Talduwe Somarama
1959	Rafael Trujillo Molina, Dominican Republic dictator	machine-gunned in car by assassins including General J T Díaz
1963	John F Kennedy, US president	shot in car by rifle fire in Dallas, Texas; alleged assassin, Lee Oswald, himself shot two days later while under heavy police escort
1963	Malcolm X (Little), US leading representative of the Black Muslims	shot at political rally
1966	Hendrik Verwoerd, South African premier	stabbed by parliamentary messenger (later ruled mentally disordered)
1968	Rev Martin Luther King, US black civil rights leader	shot on hotel balcony by James Earl Ray in Memphis, Tennessee
1968	Robert F Kennedy, US senator	shot by Arab immigrant Sirhan Sirhan in the Hotel Ambassador, Los Angeles
1975	King Faisal of Saudi Arabia	murdered by his nephew
1976	Christopher Ewart Biggs, British ambassador to Republic of Ireland	car blown up by IRA landmine
1978	Aldo Moro, president of Italy's Christian Democrats and five times prime minister	kidnapped by Red Brigade guerrillas and later found dead
1979	Airey Neave, British Conservative MP and Northern Ireland spokesperson	killed by IRA bomb while driving out of House of Commons car park
1979	Lord Mountbatten, uncle of Duke of Edinburgh	killed by IRA bomb in sailing boat off coast of Ireland
1979	Park Chung Hee, president of South Korea	shot in restaurant by chief of Korean Central Intelligence Agency
1980	John Lennon, singer and songwriter	shot outside his apartment block in New York
1981	Anwar al-Sadat, president of Egypt	shot by rebel soldiers while reviewing military parade
1984	Indira Gandhi, Indian prime minister	murdered by members of her Sikh bodyguard
1986	Olof Palme, Swedish prime minister	shot in Stockholm as he walked home with his wife
1988	General Zia ul-Haq, military leader of Pakistan	killed in air crash owing to sabotage
1991	Rajiv Gandhi, former Indian prime minister	killed by a bomb during an election campaign
1992	Muhammad Boudiaf, president of Algeria's ruling High State Council	murdered during a speech
1992	Paolo Borsellino, chief prosecutor in anti-Mafia investigations	killed by a car bomb
1992	Giovanni Lizzio, senior police official involved in anti-Mafia investigations	shot dead by gunmen on motorcycles
1992	Sadegh Sharafkandi, Iranian Kurdish opposition leader	shot dead by masked gunmen
1992	Pedro Huillca, leader of the General Federation of Peruvian Workers	shot by eight people with submachine guns
1993	Chris Hani, secretary general of the South African Communist Party	shot outside his home in a Johannesburg suburb
1993	Ranasinghe Premadasa, Sri Lankan president	killed by a suicide bomber in Colombo during the May Day parade
1993	Lalith Athulathmudali, leader of Sri Lanka's opposition party	shot dead at a campaign rally
1993	Melchior Ndadaye, president of Burundi	killed in a military coup
1993	Mouin Shabaytah, Lebanese PLO military leader	shot by gunmen in Sidon, Lebanon
1994	Luis Donaldo Colosio Murrieta, Mexican presidential candidate for the PRI	shot dead following a campaign speech in Tijuana
1994	Cyprien Ntaryamira, president of Burundi	killed in a plane crash caused by gunfire
1994	Juvenal Habyarimana, president of Rwanda	killed in a plane crash caused by gunfire
1995	Yitzhak Rabin, Israeli prime minister	shot following speech at a propeace rally in Tel Aviv
1995	Maurizio Gucci, former fashion designer	shot dead in Milan
1996	Yahya Ayyash, operative of the Islamic fundamentalist organization Hamas	killed by a booby-trapped cellular phone

Australia: prime ministers from 1901

term	name	party
1901–03	Edmund Barton	Protectionist
1903–04	Alfred Deakin	Protectionist
1904	John Watson	Labor
1904–05	G Reid	Free Trade–Protectionist coalition
1905–08	Alfred Deakin	Protectionist
1908–09	Andrew Fisher	Labor
1909–10	Alfred Deakin	Fusion
1910–13	Andrew Fisher	Labor
1913–14	J Cook	Liberal
1914–15	Andrew Fisher	Labor
1915–23	William Morris Hughes	Labor (National Labor from 1917)
1923–29	Stanley Bruce	National–Country Coalition
1929–32	J H Scullin	Labor
1932–39	Joseph Aloysius Lyons	United Australia–Country coalition
1939	Earle Page	United Australia–Country Coalition
1939–41	R G Menzies	United Australia
1941–41	A W Fadden	Country–United Australia coalition
1941–45	John Curtin	Labor
1945	F M Forde	Labor
1945–49	J B Chifley	Labor
1949–66	R G Menzies	Liberal–Country coalition
1966–67	Harold Holt	Liberal–Country coalition
1967–68	John McEwen	Liberal–Country coalition
1968–71	J G Gorton	Liberal–Country coalition
1971–72	William McMahon	Liberal–Country coalition
1972–75	Gough Whitlam	Labor
1975–83	Malcolm Fraser	Liberal–National coalition
1983–91	Robert Hawke	Labor
1991–96	Paul Keating	Labor
1996–	John Howard	Liberal–National coalition

Canada: prime ministers from 1867

term	name	party
1867–73	John A Macdonald	Conservative
1873–78	Alexander Mackenzie	Liberal
1878–91	John A Macdonald	Conservative
1891–92	John J Abbott	Conservative
1892–94	John S D Thompson	Conservative
1894–96	Mackenzie Bowell	Conservative
1896	Charles Tupper	Conservative
1896–1911	Wilfred Laurier	Liberal
1911–20	Robert L Borden	Conservative
1920–21	Arthur Meighen	Conservative
1921–26	William L M King	Liberal
1926–26	Arthur Meighen	Conservative
1926–30	William L M King	Liberal
1930–35	Richard B Bennett	Conservative
1935–48	William L M King	Liberal
1948–57	Louis S St Laurent	Liberal
1957–63	John G Diefenbaker	Conservative
1963–68	Lester B Pearson	Liberal
1968–79	Pierre E Trudeau	Liberal
1979–80	Joseph Clark	Progressive Conservative
1980–84	Pierre E Trudeau	Liberal
1984	John Turner	Liberal
1984–93	Brian Mulroney	Progressive Conservative
1993	Kim Campbell	Progressive Conservative
1993–	Jean Chretien	Liberal

Booker Prize for Fiction

1969	P H Newby *Something to Answer For*
1970	Bernice Rubens *The Elected Member*
1971	V S Naipaul *In a Free State*
1972	John Berger *G*
1973	J G Farrell *The Siege of Krishnapur*
1974	Nadine Gordimer *The Conservationist*; Stanley Middleton *Holiday* (joint winners)
1975	Ruth Prawer Jhabvala *Heat and Dust*
1976	David Storey *Saville*
1977	Paul Scott *Staying On*
1978	Iris Murdoch *The Sea, The Sea*
1979	Penelope Fitzgerald *Offshore*
1980	William Golding *Rites of Passage*
1981	Salman Rushdie *Midnight's Children*
1982	Thomas Keneally *Schindler's Ark*
1983	J M Coetzee *The Life and Times of Michael K*
1984	Anita Brookner *Hotel du Lac*
1985	Keri Hulme *The Bone People*
1986	Kingsley Amis *The Old Devils*
1987	Penelope Lively *Moon Tiger*
1988	Peter Carey *Oscar and Lucinda*
1989	Kazuo Ishiguro *The Remains of the Day*
1990	A S Byatt *Possession*
1991	Ben Okri *The Famished Road*
1992	Barry Unsworth *Sacred Hunger*; Michael Ondaatje *The English Patient* (joint winners)
1993	Roddy Doyle *Paddy Clarke Ha Ha Ha*
1994	James Kelman *How Late It Was, How Late*
1995	Pat Barker *The Ghost Road*
1996	Graham Swift *Last Orders*

Canterbury, archbishops of

1414	Henry Chichele (1362–1414)
1443	John Stafford (?–1452)
1452	John Kemp (c. 1380–1454)
1454	Thomas Bouchier (1410–1486)
1486	John Morton (c. 1429–1500)
1501	Henry Deane (?–1503)
1503	William Warham (1450–1532)
1533	Thomas Cranmer (1489–1556)
1556	Reginald Pole (1500–1558)
1559	Matthew Parker (1504–1575)
1576	Edmund Grindal (1519–1583)
1583	John Whitgift (1530–1604)
1604	Richard Bancroft (1544–1610)
1611	George Abbot (1562–1633)
1633	William Laud (1573–1645)
1660	William Juxon (1582–1663)
1663	Gilbert Sheldon (1598–1677)
1678	William Sancroft (1617–1693)
1691	John Tillotson (1630–1694)
1695	Thomas Tenison (1636–1715)
1716	William Wake (1657–1737)
1737	John Potter (c. 1674–1747)
1747	Thomas Herring (1693–1757)
1758	Matthew Hutton (1693–1758)
1758	Thomas Secker (1693–1768)
1768	Hon. Frederick Cornwallis (1713–1783)
1783	John Moore (1730–1805)
1805	Charles Manners-Sutton (1755–1828)
1828	William Howley (1766–1848)
1848	John Bird Sumner (1780–1862)
1862	Charles Longley (1794–1868)
1868	Archibald Campbell Tait (1811–1882)
1883	Edward White Benson (1829–1896)
1896	Frederick Temple (1821–1902)
1903	Randall Thomas Davidson (1848–1930)
1928	Cosmo Gordon Lang (1864–1945)
1942	William Temple (1881–1944)
1945	Geoffrey Fisher (1887–1972)
1961	Michael Ramsey (1904–1988)
1974	Donald Coggan (1909–)
1980	Robert Runcie (1921–)
1991	George Carey (1935–)

Elizabeth II: line of succession

Charles, Prince of Wales, eldest son of Elizabeth II (1948–)
Prince William, eldest son of Charles (1982–)
Prince Henry (Harry), second son of Charles (1984–)
Andrew, Duke of York, second son of Elizabeth II (1960–)
Princess Beatrice, eldest daughter of Andrew (1988–)
Princess Eugenie, second daughter of Andrew (1990–)
Prince Edward, youngest son of Elizabeth II (1964–)
Anne, Princess Royal, daughter of Elizabeth II (1950–)
Peter Phillips, son of Anne (1977–)
Zara Phillips, daughter of Anne (1981–)
Princess Margaret, sister of Elizabeth II (1930–)
Viscount Linley, son of Margaret (1961–)
Lady Sarah Armstrong-Jones, daughter of Margaret (1964–)
Richard, Duke of Gloucester, son of brother of George VI (father of
    Elizabeth II) (1944–)
Alexander, Earl of Ulster, son of Gloucester (1974–)
Lady Davina Windsor, eldest daughter of Gloucester (1977–)
Lady Rose Windsor, youngest daughter of Gloucester (1980–)
Edward, Duke of Kent, son of brother of George VI (1935–)
Edward, Baron Downpatrick, grandson of Kent (1988–)
Lord Nicholas Windsor, son of Kent (1970–)
Lady Helen Windsor, daughter of Kent (1964–)
Lord Frederick Windsor, son of Michael (1979–)
Lady Gabriella Windsor, daughter of Michael (1981–)
Alexandra, sister of Kent (1936–)
James, son of Alexandra (1964–)
Marina, daughter of Alexandra (1966–)
George Lascelles, 7th Earl of Harewood, son of sister of George IV
    (1923–)
David, Viscount Lascelles, eldest son of Harewood (1950–)
Hon Alexander Lascelles, son of Viscount Lascelles (1980–)
Hon Edward Lascelles, youngest son of Viscount Lascelles (1982–)
Hon James Lascelles, second son of Harewood (1953–)
Rowan Lascelles, son of Hon James Lascelles (1977–)
Tewa Lascelles, youngest son of Hon James Lascelles (1985–)
Sophie Lascelles, daughter of Hon James Lascelles (1973–)
Hon Jeremy Lascelles, youngest son of Harewood (1955–)
Thomas Lascelles, son of Hon Jeremy Lascelles (1982–)
Ellen Lascelles, daughter of Hon Jeremy Lascelles (1984–)
Amy Lascelles, youngest daughter of Hon Jeremy Lascelles (1986–)
Hon Gerald Lascelles, younger brother of Harewood (1924–)
Henry Lascelles, son of Hon Gerald Lascelles (1953–)

England: sovereigns

reign	name	relationship	reign	name	relationship
West Saxon kings			*House of York*		
901–25	Edward the Elder	son of Alfred the Great	1461–70,		
925–40	Athelstan	son of Edward I	1471–83	Edward IV	son of Richard, Duke of York
940–46	Edmund	half-brother of Athelstan	1483	Edward V	son of Edward IV
946–55	Edred	brother of Edmund	1483–85	Richard III	brother of Edward IV
955–59	Edwy	son of Edmund	*House of Tudor*		
959–75	Edgar	brother of Edwy	1485–1509	Henry VII	son of Edmund Tudor, Earl of Richmond
975–78	Edward the Martyr	son of Edgar			
978–1016	Ethelred II	son of Edgar	1509–47	Henry VIII	son of Henry VII
1016	Edmund Ironside	son of Ethelred	1547–53	Edward VI	son of Henry VIII
Danish kings			1553–58	Mary I	daughter of Henry VIII
1016–35	Canute	son of Sweyn I of Denmark, who conquered England 1013	1558–1603	Elizabeth I	daughter of Henry VIII
			House of Stuart		
1035–40	Harold I	son of Canute	1603–25	James I	great-grandson of Margaret (daughter of Henry VII)
1040–42	Hardicanute	son of Canute			
West Saxon kings (restored)			1625–49	Charles I	son of James I
1042–66	Edward the Confessor	son of Ethelred II	1649–60	*the Commonwealth*	
1066	Harold II	son of Godwin	*House of Stuart (restored)*		
Norman kings			1660–85	Charles II	son of Charles I
1066–87	William I	illegitimate son of Duke Robert the Devil	1685–88	James II	son of Charles I
			1689–1702	William III and Mary	son of Mary (daughter of Charles I); daughter of James II
1087–1100	William II	son of William I			
1100–35	Henry I	son of William I	1702–14	Anne	daughter of James II
1135–54	Stephen	grandson of William II	*House of Hanover*		
House of Plantagenet			1714–27	George I	son of Sophia (granddaughter of James I)
1154–89	Henry II	son of Matilda (daughter of Henry I)			
1189–99	Richard I	son of Henry II	1727–60	George II	son of George I
1199–1216	John	son of Henry II	1760–1820	George III	son of Frederick (son of George II)
1216–72	Henry III	son of John			
1272–1307	Edward I	son of Henry III	1820–30	George IV (regent 1811–20)	son of George III
1307–27	Edward II	son of Edward I			
1327–77	Edward III	son of Edward II	1830–37	William IV	son of George III
1377–99	Richard II	son of the Black Prince	1837–1901	Victoria	daughter of Edward (son of George III)
House of Lancaster			*House of Saxe-Coburg*		
1399–1413	Henry IV	son of John of Gaunt	1901–10	Edward VII	son of Victoria
1413–22	Henry V	son of Henry IV	*House of Windsor*		
1422–61,			1910–36	George V	son of Edward VII
1470–71	Henry VI	son of Henry V	1936	Edward VIII	son of George V
			1936–52	George VI	son of George V
			1952–	Elizabeth II	daughter of George VI

France: rulers

title of ruler	name	date of accession	title of ruler	name	date of accession
kings	Pepin III/Childerich III	751	**kings**	Henri IV	1574
	Pepin III	752		Louis XIII	1610
	Charlemagne/Carloman	768		Louis XIV	1643
	Louis I	814		Louis XVI	1774
	Lothair I	840		National Convention	1792
	Charles II (the Bald)	843		Directory (five members)	1795
	Louis II	877	**first consul**	Napoléon Bonaparte	1799
	Louis III	879	**emperor**	Napoléon I	1804
	Charles III (the Fat)	882	**king**	Louis XVIII	1814
	Odo	888	**emperor**	Napoléon I	1815
	Charles III (the Simple)	893	**kings**	Louis XVIII	1815
	Robert I	922		Charles X	1824
	Rudolf	923		Louis XIX	1830
	Louis IV	936		Henri V	1830
	Lothair II	954		Louis-Philippe	1830
	Louis V	986	**heads of state**	Philippe Buchez	1848
	Hugues Capet	987		Louis Cavaignac	1848
	Robert II	996	**president**	Louis Napoléon Bonaparte	1848
	Henri I	1031	**emperor**	Napoléon III	1852
	Philippe I	1060	**presidents**	Adolphe Thiers	1871
	Louis VI	1108		Patrice MacMahon	1873
	Louis VII	1137		Jules Grevy	1879
	Philippe II	1180		François Sadui-Carnot	1887
	Louis VIII	1223		Jean Casimir-Périer	1894
	Louis IX	1226		François Faure	1895
	Philippe III	1270		Emile Loubet	1899
	Philippe IV	1285		Armand Fallières	1913
	Louis X	1314		Raymond Poincaré	1913
	Jean I	1316		Paul Deschanel	1920
	Philippe V	1328		Alexandre Millerand	1920
	Charles IV	1322		Gaston Doumergue	1924
	Philippe VI	1328		Paul Doumer	1931
	Jean II	1350		Albert Le Brun	1932
	Charles V	1356		Philippe Pétain (Vichy government)	
	Charles VI	1380			1940
	Charles VII	1422		provisional government	1944
	Louis XI	1461		Vincent Auriol	1947
	Charles VIII	1483		René Coty	1954
	Louis XII	1498		Charles de Gaulle	1959
	François I	1515		Alain Poher	1969
	Henri II	1547		Georges Pompidou	1969
	François II	1559		Alain Poher	1974
	Charles IX	1560		Valéry Giscard d'Estaing	1974
	Henri III	1574		François Mitterrand	1981
				Jacques Chirac	1995

Holy Roman Emperors

reign	name
Carolingian kings and emperors	
800–14	Charlemagne (Charles the Great)
814–40	Louis the Pious
840–55	Lothair I
855–75	Louis II
875–77	Charles II the Bald
881–87	Charles III the Fat
891–94	Guido of Spoleto
892–98	Lambert of Spoleto (co-emperor)
896–901	Arnulf (rival)
901–05	Louis III of Provence
905–24	Berengar
911–18	Conrad I of Franconia (rival)
Saxon kings and emperors	
918–36	Henry I the Fowler
936–73	Otto I the Great
973–83	Otto II
983–1002	Otto III
1002–24	Henry II the Saint
Franconian (Salian) emperors	
1024–39	Conrad II
1039–56	Henry III the Black
1056–1106	Henry IV
1077–80	Rudolf of Swabia (rival)
1081–93	Hermann of Luxembourg (rival)
1093–1101	Conrad of Franconia (rival)
1106–25	Henry V
1126–37	Lothair II
Hohenstaufen kings and emperors	
1138–52	Conrad III
1152–90	Frederick Barbarossa
1190–97	Henry VI
1198–1215	Otto IV
1198–1208	Philip of Swabia (rival)
1215–50	Frederick II
1246–47	Henry Raspe of Thuringia (rival)
1247–56	William of Holland
1250–54	Conrad IV
1254–73	no ruler (the Great Interregnum)

reign	name
rulers from various noble families	
1257–72	Richard of Cornwall (rival)
1257–73	Alfonso X of Castile (rival)
1273–91	Rudolf I, Habsburg
1292–98	Adolf I of Nassau
1298–1308	Albert I, Habsburg
1308–13	Henry VII, Luxembourg
1314–47	Louis IV of Bavaria
1314–25	Frederick of Habsburg (co-regent)
1347–78	Charles IV, Luxembourg
1378–1400	Wenceslas of Bohemia
1400	Frederick III of Brunswick
1400–10	Rupert of the Palatinate
1411–37	Sigismund, Luxembourg
Habsburg emperors	
1438–39	Albert II
1440–93	Frederick III
1493–1519	Maximilian I
1519–56	Charles V
1556–64	Ferdinand I
1564–76	Maximilian II
1576–1612	Rudolf II
1612–19	Matthias
1619–37	Ferdinand II
1637–57	Ferdinand III
1658–1705	Leopold I
1705–11	Joseph I
1711–40	Charles VI
1742–45	Charles VII of Bavaria
Habsburg-Lorraine emperors	
745–65	Francis I of Lorraine
1765–90	Joseph II
1790–92	Leopold II
1792–1806	Francis II

Ireland: kings and queens

445–452	Niall of the Nine Hostages (king of Tara; traditional ancestor of claimants to the high kingship)
452–463	Lóegaire (son)
463–482	Ailill Molt (grandnephew of Niall)
482–507	Lugaid (son of Lóegaire)
507–534	Muirchertach I (great-grandson of Niall)
534–544	Tuathal Máelgarb (great-grandson of Niall)
544–565	Diarmait I (great-grandson of Niall)
565–566	Domnall Ilchelgach (brother; co-regent)
566–569	Ainmire (fourth in descent from Niall)
569–572	Bétán I (son of Muirchertach I)
569–572	Eochaid (son of Domnall Ilchelgach; co-regent)
572–586	Báetán II (fourth in descent from Niall)
586–598	Áed (son of Ainmire)
598–604	Áed Sláine (son of Diarmait I)
598–604	Colmán Rímid (son of Báetán I; co-regent)
604–612	Áed Uaridnach (son of Domnall Ilchelgach)
612–615	Máel Cobo (son of Áed)
615–628	Suibne Menn (grandnephew of Muirchertach I)
628–642	Domnall (son of Áed)
642–654	Conall Cáel (son of Máel Cobo)
642–658	Cellach (brother; co-regent)
658–665	Diarmait II (son of Áed Sláine)
658–665	Blathmac (brother; co-regent)
665–671	Sechnussach (son)
671–675	Cennfáelad (brother)
675–695	Fínsnechta Fledach (grandson of Áed Sláine)
695–704	Loingsech (grandson of Domnall)
704–710	Congal Cennmagair (grandson of Domnall)
710–722	Fergal (great-grandson of Áed Uaridnach)
722–724	Fogartach (great-grandson of Diarmait II)
724–728	Cináed (fourth in descent from Áed Sláine)
728–734	Flaithbertach (son of Loingsech; deposed, died 765)
734–743	Áed Allán (son of Fergal)
743–763	Domnall Midi (seventh in descent from Diarmait I)
763–770	Niall Frossach (son of Fergal; abdicated, died 778)
770–797	Donnchad Midi (son of Domnall Midi)
797–819	Áed Oirdnide (son of Niall Frossach)
819–833	Conchobar (son of Donnchad Midi)
833–846	Niall Caille (son of Áed ed Oirdnide)
846–862	Máel Sechnaill I (nephew of Conchobar)
862–879	Áed Findliath (son of Niall Caille)
879–916	Flann Sinna (son of Máel SechnailII)
916–919	Niall Glúndub (son of Áed Findliath)
919–944	Donnchad Donn (son of Flann Sinna)
944–956	Congalach Cnogba (tenth in descent from Áed Sláine)
956–980	Domnall ua Néill (grandson of Niall Glúundub)
980–1002	Máel Sechnaill II (grandson of Donnchad Donn; deposed)
1002–1014	Brian Bóruma (Dál Cais; king of Munster)
1014–1022	Máel Sechnaill II (restored; interregnum 1022–72)
1072–1086	Tairrdelbach I (grandson of Brian Bóruma; king of Munster)
1086–1119	Muirchertach II (son)
1119–1121	Domnall ua Lochlainn (fourth in descent from Domnall ua Néill; king of Ailech)
1121–1156	Tairrdelbach II (Ua Conchobair; king of Connacht)
1156–1166	Muirchertach III (grandson of Domnall ua Lochlainn)
1166–1186	Ruaidrí (son of Tairrdelbach II; deposed, died 1198; regional kingships under English domination)

Japan: prime ministers from 1945

term	name	party
1945–46	Kijuro Shidehara	coalition
1946–47	Shigeru Yoshida	Liberal
1947–48	Tetsu Katayama	coalition
1948–48	Hitoshi Ashida	Democratic
1948–54	Shigeru Yoshida	Liberal
1954–56	Ichiro Hatoyama	Liberal*
1956–57	Tanzan Ishibashi	LDP
1957–60	Nobusuke Kishi	LDP
1960–64	Hayato Ikeda	LDP
1964–72	Eisaku Sato LDP	
1972–74	Kakuei Tanaka	LDP
1974–76	Takeo Miki LDP	
1976–78	Takeo Fukuda	LDP
1978–80	Masayoshi Ohira	LDP
1980–82	Zenko Suzuki	LDP
1982–87	Yasuhiro Nakasone	LDP
1987–89	Noboru Takeshita	LDP
1989–89	Sosuke Uno LDP	
1989–91	Toshiki KaifuLDP	
1991–93	Kiichi Miyazawa	LDP
1993–94	Morohiro Hosokawa	JNP-led coalition
1994–94	Tsutoma Hata	Shinseito-led coalition
1994–96	Tomiichi Murayama	SDPJ-led coalition
1996–	Ryutaro Hashimoto	LDP

* The conservative parties merged 1955 to form the Liberal Democratic Party (LDP, Jiyu-Minshuto).

New Zealand: prime ministers

J Ballance	(Liberal)	1891
R J Seddon	(Liberal)	1893
W Hall-Jones	(Liberal)	1906
Joseph Ward	(Liberal)	1906
T MacKenzie	(Liberal)	1912
W F Massey	(Reform)	1912
J G Coates	(Reform)	1925
Joseph Ward	(United)	1928
G W Forbes	(United)	1930
M J Savage	(Labour)	1935
P Fraser	(Labour)	1940
S G Holland	(National)	1949
K J Holyoake	(National)	1957
Walter Nash	(Labour)	1957
K J Holyoake	(National)	1960
J Marshall	(National)	1972
N Kirk	(Labour)	1972
W Rowling	(Labour)	1974
R Muldoon	(National)	1975
D Lange	(Labour)	1984
G Palmer	(Labour)	1989
J Bolger	(National)	1990

Nobel Prize for Chemistry

1901 Jacobus van't Hoff (Netherlands): laws of chemical dynamics and osmotic pressure

1902 Emil Fischer (Germany): sugar and purine syntheses

1903 Svante Arrhenius (Sweden): electrolytic theory of dissociation

1904 William Ramsay (UK): inert gases in air and their locations in the periodic table

1905 Adolf von Baeyer (Germany): organic dyes and hydroaromatic compounds

1906 Henri Moissan (France): isolation of fluorine and adoption of electric furnace

1907 Eduard Buchner (Germany): biochemical researches and discovery of cell-free fermentation

1908 Ernest Rutherford (New Zealand): atomic disintegration, and the chemistry of radioactive substances

1909 Wilhelm Ostwald (Germany): catalysis, and principles of equilibria and rates of reaction

1910 Otto Wallach (Germany): alicyclic compounds

1911 Marie Curie (Poland): discovery of radium and polonium, and the isolation and study of radium

1912 Victor Grignard (France): discovery of Grignard reagent; Paul Sabatier (France): catalytic hydrogenation of organic compounds

1913 Alfred Werner (Switzerland): bonding of atoms within molecules

1914 Theodore Richards (USA): accurate determination of the atomic masses of many elements

1915 Richard Willstäter (Germany): research into plant pigments, especially chlorophyll

1916–17 no award

1918 Fritz Haber (Germany): synthesis of ammonia from its elements

1919 no award

1920 Walther Nernst (Germany): work on thermochemistry

1921 Frederick Soddy (UK): work on radioactive substances, especially isotopes

1922 Francis Aston (UK): mass spectrometry of isotopes of radioactive elements, and enunciation of the whole-number rule

1923 Fritz Pregl (Austria): microanalysis of organic substances

1924 no award

1925 Richard Zsigmondy (Austria): heterogeneity of colloids

1926 Theodor Svedberg (Sweden): investigation of dispersed systems

1927 Heinrich Wieland (Germany): constitution of bile acids and related substances

1928 Adolf Windaus (Germany): constitution of sterols and related vitamins

1929 Arthur Harden (UK) and Hans von Euler-Chelpin (Germany): fermentation of sugar, and fermentative enzymes

1930 Hans Fischer (Germany): analysis of haem (the iron-bearing group in haemoglobin) and chlorophyll, and the synthesis of haemin (a compound of haem)

1931 Carl Bosch (Germany) and Friedrich Bergius (Germany): invention and development of chemical high-pressure methods

1932 Irving Langmuir (USA): surface chemistry

1933 no award

1934 Harold Urey (USA): discovery of deuterium (heavy hydrogen)

1935 Irène and Frédéric Joliot-Curie (France): synthesis of new radioactive elements

1936 Peter Debye (Netherlands): work on molecular structures by investigation of dipole moments and the diffraction of X-rays and electrons in gases

1937 Norman Haworth (UK): work on carbohydrates and ascorbic acid (vitamin C); Paul Karrer (Switzerland): work on carotenoids, flavins, retinol (vitamin A) and riboflavin (vitamin B_2)

1938 Richard Kuhn (Austria): carotenoids and vitamins

1939 Adolf Butenandt (Germany): work on sex hormones; Leopold Ruzicka (Switzerland) polymethylenes and higher terpenes

1940–42 no prizes awarded

1943 Georg von Hevesy (Sweden): use of isotopes as tracers in chemical processes

1944 Otto Hahn (Germany): discovery of nuclear fission

1945 Artturi Virtanen (Finland): agriculture and nutrition, especially fodder preservation

1946 James Sumner (USA): crystallization of enzymes; John Northrop (USA) and Wendell Stanley (USA): preparation of pure enzymes and virus proteins

1947 Robert Robinson (UK): biologically important plant products, especially alkaloids

1948 Arne Tiselius (Sweden): electrophoresis and adsorption analysis, and discoveries concerning serum proteins

1949 William Giauque (USA): chemical thermodynamics, especially at very low temperatures

1950 Otto Diels (Germany) and Kurt Alder (Germany): discovery and development of diene synthesis

1951 Edwin McMillan (USA) and Glenn Seaborg (USA): chemistry of transuranic elements

1952 Archer Martin (UK) and Richard Synge (UK): invention of partition chromatography

1953 Hermann Staudinger (West Germany): discoveries in macromolecular chemistry

1954 Linus Pauling (USA): nature of chemical bonds, especially in complex substances

1955 Vincent Du Vigneaud (USA): investigations into biochemically important sulphur compounds, and the first synthesis of a polypeptide hormone

1956 Cyril Hinshelwood (UK) and Nikoly Semenov (USSR): mechanism of chemical reactions

1957 Alexander Todd (UK): nucleotides and nucleotide coenzymes

1958 Frederick Sanger (UK): structure of proteins, especially insulin

1959 Jaroslav Heyrovsky (Czechoslovakia): polarographic methods of chemical analysis

1960 Willard Libby (USA): radiocarbon dating in archaeology, geology, and geography

1961 Melvin Calvin (USA): assimilation of carbon dioxide by plants

1962 Max Perutz (UK) and John Kendrew (UK): structures of globular proteins

1963 Karl Ziegler (West Germany) and Giulio Natta (Italy): chemistry and technology of high polymers

1964 Dorothy Crowfoot Hodgkin (UK): crystallographic determination of the structures of biochemical compounds, notably penicillin and cyanocobalamin (vitamin B_{12})

1965 Robert Woodward (USA): organic synthesis

1966 Robert Mulliken (USA): molecular orbital theory of chemical bonds and structures

1967 Manfred Eigen (West Germany), Ronald Norrish (UK), and George Porter (UK): investigation of rapid chemical reactions by means of very short pulses of energy

1968 Lars Onsager (USA): discovery of reciprocal relations, fundamental for the thermodynamics of irreversible processes

1969 Derek Barton (UK) and Odd Hassel (Norway): concept and applications of conformation

1970 Luis Federico Leloir (Argentina): discovery of sugar nucleotides and their role in carbohydrate biosynthesis

1971 Gerhard Herzberg (Canada): electronic structure and geometry of molecules, particularly free radicals

1972 Christian Anfinsen (USA), Stanford Moore (USA), and William Stein (USA): amino-acid structure and biological activity of the enzyme ribonuclease

1973 Ernst Fischer (West Germany) and Geoffrey Wilkinson (UK): chemistry of organometallic sandwich compounds

1974 Paul Flory (USA): physical chemistry of macromolecules

Nobel Prize for Chemistry (continued)

1975 John Cornforth (Australia): stereochemistry of enzyme-catalysed reactions; Vladimir Prelog (Yugoslavia): stereochemistry of organic molecules and their reactions

1976 William N Lipscomb (USA): structure and chemical bonding of boranes (compounds of boron and hydrogen)

1977 Ilya Prigogine (USSR): thermodynamics of irreversible and dissipative processes

1978 Peter Mitchell (UK): biological energy transfer and chemiosmotic theory

1979 Herbert Brown (USA) and Georg Wittig (West Germany): use of boron and phosphorus compounds, respectively, in organic syntheses

1980 Paul Berg (USA): biochemistry of nucleic acids, especially recombinant-DNA; Walter Gilbert (USA) and Frederick Sanger (UK): base sequences in nucleic acids

1981 Kenichi Fukui (Japan) and Roald Hoffmann (USA): theories concerning chemical reactions

1982 Aaron Klug (UK): crystallographic electron microscopy: structure of biologically important nucleic-acid–protein complexes

1983 Henry Taube (USA): electron-transfer reactions in inorganic chemical reactions

1984 Bruce Merrifield (USA): chemical syntheses on a solid matrix

1985 Herbert A Hauptman (USA) and Jerome Karle (USA): methods of determining crystal structures

1986 Dudley Herschbach (USA), Yuan Lee (USA), and John Polanyi (Canada): dynamics of chemical elementary processes

1987 Donald Cram (USA), Jean-Marie Lehn (France), and Charles Pedersen (USA): molecules with highly selective structure-specific interactions

1988 Johann Deisenhofer (West Germany), Robert Huber (West Germany), and Hartmut Michel (West Germany): three-dimensional structure of the reaction centre of photosynthesis

1989 Sydney Altman (USA) and Thomas Cech (USA): discovery of catalytic function of RNA

1990 Elias James Corey (USA): new methods of synthesizing chemical compounds

1991 Richard R Ernst (Switzerland): improvements in the technology of nuclear magnetic resonance (NMR) imaging

1992 Rudolph A Marcus (USA): theoretical discoveries relating to reduction and oxidation reactions

1993 Kary Mullis (USA): invention of the polymerase chain reaction technique for amplifying DNA; Michael Smith (Canada): development of techniques for splicing foreign genetic segments into an organism's DNA in order to modify the proteins produced

1994 George A Olah (USA): development of technique for examining hydrocarbon molecules

1995 Sherwood Roland (USA), Mario Molina (Mexico), and Paul Crutzen (Netherlands): explaining the mechanisms of the ozone layer

1996 Robert F Curl (USA), Harold W Kroto (UK), and Richard E Smalley (USA): discovery of fullerenes

Nobel Prize for Economics

1969 Ragnar Frisch (Norway) and Jan Tinbergen (Netherlands): work in econometrics

1970 Paul A Samuelson (USA): scientific analysis of economic theory

1971 Simon Kuznets (USA): research on the economic growth of nations

1972 Sir John Hicks (UK) and Kenneth J Arrow (USA): contributions to general economic equilibrium theory

1973 Wassily Leontief (USA): work on input analysis

1974 Gunnar Myrdal (Sweden) and Friedrich von Hayek (UK): analysis of the interdependence of economic, social, and institutional phenomena

1975 Leonid V Kantorovich (Russia) and Tjalling C Koopmans (USA): contributions to the theory of optimum allocation of resources

1976 Milton Friedman (USA): consumption analysis, monetary theory, and economic stabilization

1977 Bertil Ohlin (Sweden) and James Meade (UK): contributions to theory of international trade

1978 Herbert A Simon (USA): decision-making processes in economic organization

1979 W Arthur Lewis (UK) and Theodore W Schultz (USA): analysis of economic processes in developing nations

1980 Lawrence R Klein (USA): development and analysis of empirical models of business fluctuations

1981 James Tobin (USA): empirical macroeconomic theories

1982 George Stigler (USA): work on the economic effects of governmental regulation

1983 Gerard Debrau (USA): mathematical proof of supply and demand theory

1984 Sir Richard Stone (UK): development of a national income accounting system

1985 Franco Modigliani (USA): analysis of household savings and financial markets

1986 James McGill Buchanan (USA): political theories advocating limited government role in the economy

1987 Robert M Solow (USA): contributions to the theory of economic growth

1988 Maurice Allais (France): contributions to the theory of markets and efficient use of resources

1989 Trygve Haavelmo (Norway): testing fundamental econometric theories

1990 Harry Markowitz, Merton Miller, and William Sharpe (USA): pioneering theories on managing investment portfolios and corporate finances

1991 Ronald H Coase (USA): work on value and social problems of companies

1992 Gary S Becker (USA): work linking economic theory to aspects of human behaviour, drawing on other social sciences

1993 Robert Fogel and Douglass North (USA): creating a new method of studying economic history (cliometrics)

1994 John F Nash and John C Harsanyi (USA), and Reinhard Selten (Germany): work on 'game theory', which investigates decision-making in a competitive environment

1995 Robert E Lucas Jr (USA): developing the 'rational expectations' school, which questions a government's ability to steer the economy

1996 James A Mirrlees (UK) and William Vickrey (USA): contributions to the economic theory of incentives under asymmetric information

Nobel Prize for Literature

1901	René F A Sully-Prodhomme (French)
1902	Theodor Mommsen (German)
1903	Bjornsterne Bjornsen (Norwegian)
1904	Frédéric Mistral (French)
1905	Henryk Sienkiwicz (Polish)
1906	Giosue Carducci (Italian)
1907	Rudyard Kipling (British)
1908	Rudolk Eucken (German)
1909	Selma Lagerlöf (Swedish)
1910	Paul von Heyse (German)
1911	Maurice Maeterlinck (Belgian)
1912	Gerhart Hauptmann (German)
1913	Rabindranath Tagore (Indian)
1914	no award
1915	Romain Rolland (French)
1916	Verver von Heidenstan (Swedish)
1917	Karl Gjellerup (Danish)
1918	no award
1919	Carl Spitteler (Swiss)
1920	Knut Hamsun (Norwegian)
1921	Anatole France (French)
1922	Jacinto Benavente y Martinez (Spanish)
1923	William Butler Yeats (Irish)
1924	Wladyslaw Stanislaw Reymont (Polish)
1925	George Bernard Shaw (Irish)
1926	Grazia Deledda (Italian)
1927	Henri Bergson (French)
1928	Sigrid Undsey (Norwegian)
1929	Thomas Mann (German)
1930	Sinclair Lewis (American)
1931	Erik Axel Karlfeldt (Swedish)
1932	John Galsworthy (British)
1933	Ivan Bunin (Russian)
1934	Luigi Pirandello (Italian)
1935	no award
1936	Eugene O'Neill (American)
1937	Roger Martin du Gard (French)
1938	Pearl Buck (American)
1939	Frans Enil Sillanpää (Finnish)
1940–43	no award
1944	Johannes V Jensen (Danish)
1945	Gabriela Mistral (Chilean)
1946	Hermann Hesse (German-born Swiss)
1947	André Gide (French)
1948	T S Eliot (American-born English)
1949	William Faulkner (American)
1950	Bertrand Russell (British)
1951	Pär Lagerkvist (Swedish)

1952	François Mauriac (French)
1953	Sir Winston Churchill (British)
1954	Ernest Hemingway (American)
1955	Halldór Laxness (Icelandic)
1956	Juan Ramón Jiménez (Spanish)
1957	Albert Camus (French)
1958	Boris Pasternak, declined award (Russian)
1959	Salvatore Quasimodo (Italian)
1960	Saint-John Perse (French)
1961	Ivo Andric (Yugoslav)
1962	John Steinbeck (American)
1963	George Seferis (Greek)
1964	Jean-Paul Sartre, declined award (French)
1965	Mikhail Sholokhov (Russian)
1966	Shmuel Yosef Agnon (Israeli); Nelly Sachs (German-born Swedish)
1967	Miguel Angel Asturias (Guatemalan)
1968	Kawabata Yasunari (Japanese)
1969	Samuel Beckett (Irish)
1970	Aleksandr Solzhenitsyn (Russian)
1971	Pablo Neruda (Chilean)
1972	Heinrich Böll (German)
1973	Patrick White (Australian)
1974	Eyvind Johnson (Swedish); Harry Martinson (Swedish)
1975	Eugenio Montale (Italian)
1976	Saul Bellow (American)
1977	Vicente Aleixandre (Spanish)
1978	Isaac Bashevis Singer (American)
1979	Odysseus Lytis (Greek)
1980	Czeslaw Milosz (Polish-American)
1981	Elias Canetti (Bulgarian-born German)
1982	Gabriel García Márquez (Colombian)
1983	William Golding (British)
1984	Jaroslav Seifert (Czech)
1985	Claude Simon (French)
1986	Wole Soyinka (Nigerian)
1987	Joseph Brodsky (Russian-American)
1988	Naguib Mahfouz (Egyptian)
1989	Camilo José Cela (Spanish)
1990	Octavio Paz (Mexican)
1991	Nadine Gordimer (South African)
1992	Derek Walcott (Santa Lucian)
1993	Toni Morrison (American)
1994	Kenzaburo Oe (Japanese)
1995	Seamus Heaney (Irish)
1996	Wislawa Szymborska (Polish)

Nobel Prize for Medicine or Physiology

1901 Emil von Behring (Germany): discovery that the body produces antitoxins, and development of serum therapy for diseases such as diphtheria

1902 Ronald Ross (UK): role of the *Anopheles* mosquito in transmitting malaria

1903 Niels Finsen (Denmark): use of ultraviolet light to treat skin diseases

1904 Ivan Pavlov (Russia): physiology of digestion

1905 Robert Koch (Germany): investigations and discoveries in relation to tuberculosis

1906 Camillo Golgi (Italy) and Santiago Ramón y Cajal (Spain): fine structure of nervous system

1907 Charles Laveran (France): discovery that certain protozoa can cause disease

1908 Ilya Mechnikov (Russia) and Paul Ehrlich (Germany): work on immunity

1909 Emil Kocher (Switzerland): physiology, pathology, and surgery of the thyroid gland

1910 Albrecht Kossel (Germany): study of cell proteins and nucleic acids

1911 Allvar Gullstrand (Sweden): refraction of light through the different components of the eye

1912 Alexis Carrel (USA): techniques for connecting severed blood vessels and transplanting organs

1913 Charles Richet (France): allergic responses

1914 Robert Bárány (Austria): physiology and pathology of the equilibrium organs of the inner ear

1915–18 no award

1919 Jules Bordet (Belgium): work on immunity

1920 August Krogh (Denmark): discovery of mechanism regulating the dilation and constriction of blood capillaries

1921 no award

1922 Archibald Hill (UK): production of heat in contracting muscle; Otto Meyerhof (Germany): relationship between oxygen consumption and metabolism of lactic acid in muscle

1923 Frederick Banting (Canada) and John Macleod (UK): discovery and isolation of the hormone insulin

1924 Willem Einthoven (Netherlands): invention of the electrocardiograph

1925 no award

1926 Johannes Fibiger (Denmark): discovery of a parasite *Spiroptera carcinoma* that causes cancer

1927 Julius Wagner-Jauregg (Austria): use of induced malarial fever to treat paralysis caused by mental deterioration

1928 Charles Nicolle (France): role of the body louse in transmitting typhus

1929 Christiaan Eijkman (Netherlands): discovery of a cure for beriberi, a vitamin-deficiency disease; Frederick Hopkins (UK): discovery of trace substances, now known as vitamins, that stimulate growth

1930 Karl Landsteiner (USA): discovery of human blood groups

1931 Otto Warburg (Germany): discovery of respiratory enzymes that enable cells to process oxygen

1932 Charles Sherrington (UK) and Edgar Adrian (UK): function of neurons (nerve cells)

1933 Thomas Morgan (USA): role of chromosomes in heredity

1934 George Whipple (USA), George Minot (USA), and William Murphy (USA): treatment of pernicious anaemia by increasing the amount of liver in the diet

1935 Hans Spemann (Germany): organizer effect in embryonic development

1936 Henry Dale (UK) and Otto Loewi (Germany): chemical transmission of nerve impulses

1937 Albert Szent-Györgyi (Hungary): investigation of biological oxidation processes and of the action of ascorbic acid (vitamin C)

1938 Corneille Heymans (Belgium): mechanisms regulating respiration

1939 Gerhard Domagk (Germany): discovery of the first antibacterial sulphonamide drug

1940–42 no award

1943 Carl Dam (Denmark): discovery of vitamin K; Edward Doisy (USA): chemical nature of vitamin K

1944 Joseph Erlanger (USA) and Herbert Gasser (USA): transmission of impulses by nerve fibres

1945 Alexander Fleming (UK): discovery of the bactericidal effect of penicillin; Ernst Chain (UK) and Howard Florey (Australia): isolation of penicillin and its development as an antibiotic drug

1946 Hermann Muller (USA): discovery that X-ray irradiation can cause mutation

1947 Carl Cori (USA) and Gerty Cori (USA): production and breakdown of glycogen (animal starch); Bernardo Houssay (Argentina): function of the pituitary gland in sugar metabolism

1948 Paul Müller (Switzerland): discovery of the first synthetic contact insecticide DDT

1949 Walter Hess (Switzerland): mapping areas of the midbrain that control the activities of certain body organs; Antonio Egas Moniz (Portugal): therapeutic value of prefrontal leucotomy in certain psychoses

1950 Edward Kendall (USA), Tadeus Reichstein (Poland), and Philip Hench (USA): structure and biological effects of hormones of the adrenal cortex

1951 Max Theiler (South Africa): discovery of a vaccine against yellow fever

1952 Selman Waksman (USA): discovery of streptomycin, the first antibiotic effective against tuberculosis

1953 Hans Krebs (UK): discovery of the Krebs cycle; Fritz Lipmann (USA): discovery of coenzyme A, a nonprotein compound that acts in conjunction with enzymes to catalyse metabolic reactions leading up to the Krebs cycle

1954 John Enders (USA), Thomas Weller (USA), and Frederick Robbins (USA): cultivation of the polio virus in the laboratory

1955 Hugo Theorell (Sweden): nature and action of oxidation enzymes

1956 André Cournand (USA), Werner Forssmann (Germany), and Dickinson Richards Jr (USA): technique for passing a catheter into the heart for diagnostic purposes

1957 Daniel Bovet (Switzerland): discovery of synthetic drugs used as muscle relaxants in anaesthesia

1958 George Beadle (USA) and Edward Tatum (USA): discovery that genes regulate precise chemical effects; Joshua Lederberg (USA): genetic recombination and the organization of bacterial genetic material

1959 Severo Ochoa (USA) and Arthur Kornberg (USA): discovery of enzymes that catalyse the formation of RNA (ribonucleic acid) and DNA (deoxyribonucleic acid)

1960 Macfarlane Burnet (Australia) and Peter Medawar (UK): acquired immunological tolerance of transplanted tissues

1961 Georg von Békésy (USA): investigations into the mechanism of hearing within the cochlea of the inner ear

1962 Francis Crick (UK), James Watson (USA), and Maurice Wilkins (UK): discovery of the double-helical structure of DNA and of the significance of this structure in the replication and transfer of genetic information

1963 John Eccles (Australia), Alan Hodgkin (UK), and Andrew Huxley (UK): ionic mechanisms involved in the communication or inhibition of impulses across neuron (nerve cell) membranes

1964 Konrad Bloch (USA) and Feodor Lynen (West Germany): cholesterol and fatty-acid metabolism

Nobel Prize for Medicine or Physiology (continued)

1965 François Jacob (France), André Lwoff (France), and Jacques Monod (France): genetic control of enzyme and virus synthesis

1966 Peyton Rous (USA): discovery of tumour-inducing viruses; Charles Huggins (USA): hormonal treatment of prostatic cancer

1967 Ragnar Granit (Sweden), Haldan Hartline (USA), and George Wald (USA): physiology and chemistry of vision

1968 Robert Holley (USA), Har Gobind Khorana (USA), and Marshall Nirenberg (USA): interpretation of genetic code and its function in protein synthesis

1969 Max Delbruck (USA), Alfred Hershey (USA), and Salvador Luria (USA): replication mechanism and genetic structure of viruses

1970 Bernard Katz (UK), Ulf von Euler (Austria), and Julius Axelrod (USA): storage, release, and inactivation of neurotransmitters

1971 Earl Sutherland (USA): discovery of cyclic AMP, a chemical messenger that plays a role in the action of many hormones

1972 Gerald Edelman (USA) and Rodney Porter (UK): chemical structure of antibodies

1973 Karl von Frisch (Austria), Konrad Lorenz (Austria), and Nikolaas Tinbergen (Netherlands): animal behaviour patterns

1974 Albert Claude (USA), Christian de Duve (Belgium), and George Palade (USA): structural and functional organization of the cell

1975 David Baltimore (USA), Renato Dulbecco (USA), and Howard Temin (USA): interactions between tumour-inducing viruses and the genetic material of the cell

1976 Baruch Blumberg (USA) and Carleton Gajdusek (USA): new mechanisms for the origin and transmission of infectious diseases

1977 Roger Guillemin (USA) and Andrew Schally (USA): discovery of hormones produced by the hypothalamus region of the brain; Rosalyn Yalow (USA): radioimmunoassay techniques by which minute quantities of hormone may be detected

1978 Werner Arber (Switzerland), Daniel Nathans (USA), and Hamilton Smith (USA): discovery of restriction enzymes and their application to molecular genetics

1979 Allan Cormack (USA) and Godfrey Hounsfield (UK): development of the CAT scan

1980 Baruj Benacerraf (USA), Jean Dausset (France), and George Snell (USA): genetically determined structures on the cell surface that regulate immunological reactions

1981 Roger Sperry (USA): functional specialization of the brain's cerebral hemispheres; David Hubel (USA) and Torsten Wiesel (Sweden): visual perception

1982 Sune Bergström (Sweden), Bengt Samuelson (Sweden), and John Vane (UK): discovery of prostaglandins and related biologically reactive substances

1983 Barbara McClintock (USA): discovery of mobile genetic elements

1984 Niels Jerne (Denmark), Georges Köhler (West Germany), and César Milstein (UK): work on immunity and discovery of a technique for producing highly specific, monoclonal antibodies

1985 Michael Brown (USA) and Joseph L Goldstein (USA): regulation of cholesterol metabolism

1986 Stanley Cohen (USA) and Rita Levi-Montalcini (Italy): discovery of factors that promote the growth of nerve and epidermal cells

1987 Susumu Tonegawa (Japan): process by which genes alter to produce a range of different antibodies

1988 James Black (UK), Gertrude Elion (USA), and George Hitchings (USA): principles governing the design of new drug treatment

1989 Michael Bishop (USA) and Harold Varmus (USA): discovery of oncogenes, genes carried by viruses that can trigger cancerous growth in normal cells

1990 Joseph Murray (USA) and Donnall Thomas (USA): pioneering work in organ and cell transplants

1991 Erwin Neher (Germany) and Bert Sakmann (Germany): discovery of how gatelike structures (ion channels) regulate the flow of ions into and out of cells

1992 Edmund Fisher (USA) and Erwin Krebs (USA): isolating and describing the action of the enzyme responsible for reversible protein phosphorylation, a major biological control mechanism

1993 Phillip Sharp (USA) and Richard Roberts (UK): discovery of split genes (genes interrupted by nonsense segments of DNA)

1994 Alfred Gilman (USA) and Martin Rodbell (USA): discovery of a family of proteins (G proteins) that translate messages – in the form of hormones or other chemical signals – into action inside cells

1995 Edward B Lewis and Eric F Wieschaus (USA), and Christiane Nüsslein-Volhard (Germany): discovery of genes which control the early stages of the body's development

1996 Peter C Doherty (Australia) and Rolf M Zinkernagel (Switzerland): discovery of how the immune system recognizes virus-infected cells

Nobel Prize for Peace

1901 Jean Henri Dunant (Switzerland): founder of the Red Cross; Frédéric Passy (France): advocate of international arbitration and peace

1902 Elie Ducommun (Switzerland) and Charles Albert Gobat (Switzerland): work for peace within the International Peace Bureau

1903 Sir William Cremer (UK): advocate of international arbitration

1904 Institute of International Law

1905 Bertha von Suttner (Austria): influential peace novels

1906 Theodore Roosevelt (USA): mediation at end of Russo-Japanese war 1904

1907 Ernesto Teodoro Moneta (Italy): founder of International League for peace and president of International Peace Conference 1906; Louis Renault (France): international arbitration

1908 Klas Pontus Arnoldson (Sweden): mediating dissolution of Norwegian–Swedish Union; Fredrik Bajer (Denmark): work for female emancipation and the peace movement

1909 Baron d'Estournelles de Constant (France): diplomat; Auguste Beernaert (Belgium): work at the Hague Peace Conferences

1910 International Peace Bureau

1911 Tobias Asser (Netherlands): forming the Permanent Court of Justice (1899 Hague Peace Conference); Alfred Fried (Austria): cofounder of German peace movement

1912 Elihu Root (USA): international arbitration

1913 Henri Lafontaine (Belgium): president of International Peace Bureau

1914–16 no award

1917 International Red Cross Committee

1918 no award

1919 Woodrow Wilson (USA)

1920 Léon Bourgeois (France): advocate of the League of Nations and international cooperation

1921 Karl Branting (Sweden): conciliatory international diplomacy; Christian Lous Lange (Norway): work as secretary-general of Inter-Parliamentary Union

1922 Fridtjof Nansen (Norway): relief work after World War I

1923–24 no award

1925 Austen Chamberlain (UK): work on the Locarno Pact 1925; Charles G Dawes (USA): reorganization of German reparation payments

1926 Aristide Briand (France) and Gustav Stresemann (Germany): work for European reconciliation

1927 Ferdinand Buisson (France): cofounder of League of Human Rights 1898; Ludwig Quidde (Germany): work for peace in Germany

1928 no award

1929 Frank B Kellogg (USA): Kellogg–Briand Pact 1928

1930 Nathan Söderblom (Sweden): efforts for peace through church unity

1931 Jane Addams (USA): support of women's suffrage; Nicholas Murray Butler (USA): work in forming Carnegie Endowment for International Peace

1932 no award

1933 Sir Norman Angell (UK): work on the economic futility of war

1934 Arthur Henderson (UK): work for disarmament

1935 Carl von Ossietzky (Germany): opposition to Nazi rearmament

1936 Carlos Saavedra Lamas (Argentina): efforts to end the Chaco War 1932–35

1937 Viscount Cecil of Chetwood (UK): drafting the League of Nations Covenant 1919

1938 Nansen International Office for Refugees

1939–43 no award

1944 International Red Cross Committee

1945 Cordell Hull (USA): for his part in organizing the United Nations

1946 Emily Greene Balch (USA): leader of the women's movement for peace; John R Mott (USA): for work in international missionary movements

1947 American Friends Service Committee (USA) and Friends Service Council (UK): promotion of peace through social service

1948 no award

1949 Lord Boyd-Orr (UK): work on nutritional requirements

1950 Ralph Bunche (USA): negotiating the Arab–Israeli truce 1949

1951 Léon Juhaut (France): cofounder of International Confederation of Free Trade Unions

1952 Albert Schweitzer (Germany): medical and other work in Africa

1953 George C Marshall (USA): Marshall (European recovery) plan

1954 Office of the United Nations High Commissioner for Refugees

1955–56 no award

1957 Lester B Pearson (Canada): efforts to solve the Suez Crisis 1956

1958 Dominique Georges Pire (Belgium): aid to displaced Europeans after World War II

1959 Philip Noel-Baker (UK): advocate of world disarmament

1960 Albert Lutuli (South Africa): nonviolent struggle against apartheid

1961 Dag Hammarskjöld (Sweden): Secretary-General of the United Nations (posthumously awarded)

1962 Linus Pauling (USA): campaigns for the control of nuclear weapons and nuclear testing

1963 International Red Cross Committee: for relief work after natural disasters

1964 Martin Luther King Jr (USA): black civil rights leader

1965 United Nations Children's Fund

1966–67 no award

1968 René Cassin (France): principal author of the UN Declaration of Human Rights

1969 International Labour Organization

1970 Norman E Borlaug (USA): agricultural technology

1971 Willy Brandt (Germany): reconciliation between West and East Germany

1972 no award

1973 Henry Kissinger (USA) and Le Duc Tho (North Vietnam) (declined): peace settlement of the Vietnam War

1974 Eisaku Sato (Japan): antinuclear policies; Sean MacBride (Ireland): campaign for human rights

1975 Andrei D Sakharov (Russia): advocacy of human rights and disarmament

1976 Mairead Corrigan and Betty Williams (Northern Ireland): campaigning to end sectarian strife in Northern Ireland

1977 Amnesty International: work to secure the release of political prisoners

1978 Menachem Begin (Israel) and Anwar el-Sadat (Egypt): Israel–Egypt peace treaty 1979

1979 Mother Teresa of Calcutta (Macedonia): help with the destitute in India

1980 Adolfo Pérez Esquivel (Argentina): work for human rights in Latin America

1981 United Nations High Commissioner for Refugees

1982 Alva Myrdal (Sweden) and Alfonso García Robles (Mexico): advocacy of nuclear disarmament

1983 Lech Walesa (Poland): the Solidarity movement

1984 Desmond Tutu (South Africa): peaceful anti-apartheid work

1985 International Physicians for the Prevention of Nuclear War

1986 Elie Wiesel (France): writer and human-rights activist

1987 Oscar Arias Sánchez (Costa Rica): promoting peace in Central America

1988 United Nations peacekeeping forces

1989 The Dalai Lama (Tibet): spiritual and exiled temporal leader

1990 Mikhail Gorbachev (Russia): promoting greater openness in the USSR and helping to end the Cold War

1991 Aung San Suu Kyi (Burma): nonviolent campaign for democracy

1992 Rigoberta Menchu (Guatemala): campaign for indigenous people

1993 Nelson Mandela and Frederik Willem de Klerk (South Africa): work towards dismantling apartheid and negotiating transition to nonracial democracy

1994 Yassir Arafat (Palestine) and Yitzhak Rabin and Shimon Peres (Israel): agreement of an accord on Palestinian self-rule

1995 Joseph Rotblat (UK) and the Pugwash Conferences on Science and World Affairs: campaign against nuclear weapons

1996 Carlos Filipe Ximenes Belo and José Ramos-Horta (East Timor): solution to conflict in East Timor

Nobel Prize for Physics

1901 Wilhelm Röntgen (Germany): discovery of X-rays

1902 Hendrik Lorentz (Netherlands) and Pieter Zeeman (Netherlands): influence of magnetism on radiation phenomena

1903 Antoine Becquerel (France): discovery of spontaneous radioactivity; Pierre Curie (France) and Marie Curie (Poland): researches on radiation phenomena

1904 John Strutt (Lord Rayleigh, UK): densities of gases and discovery of argon

1905 Philipp von Lenard (Germany): work on cathode rays

1906 Joseph J Thomson (UK): theoretical and experimental work on the conduction of electricity by gases

1907 Albert Michelson (USA): measurement of the speed of light through the design and application of precise optical instruments such as the interferometer

1908 Gabriel Lippmann (France): photographic reproduction of colours by interference

1909 Guglielmo Marconi (Italy) and Karl Braun (Germany): development of wireless telegraphy

1910 Johannes van der Waals (Netherlands): equation describing the physical behaviour of gases and liquids

1911 Wilhelm Wien (Germany): laws governing radiation of heat

1912 Nils Dalen (Sweden): invention of light-controlled valves, which allow lighthouses and buoys to operate automatically

1913 Heike Kamerlingh Onnes (Netherlands): studies of properties of matter at low temperatures

1914 Max von Laue (Germany): discovery of diffraction of X-rays by crystals

1915 William Bragg (UK) and Lawrence Bragg (UK): X-ray analysis of crystal structures

1916 no award

1917 Charles Barkla (UK): discovery of characteristic X-ray emission of the elements

1918 Max Planck (Germany): formulation of quantum theory

1919 Johannes Stark (Germany): discovery of Doppler effect in rays of positive ions, and splitting of spectral lines in electric fields

1920 Charles Guillaume (Switzerland): precision measurements through anomalies in nickel–steel alloys

1921 Albert Einstein (Switzerland): theoretical physics, especially law of photoelectric effect

1922 Niels Bohr (Denmark): structure of atoms and radiation emanating from them

1923 Robert Millikan (USA): discovery of the electric charge of an electron, and study of the photoelectric effect

1924 Karl Siegbahn (Sweden): X-ray spectroscopy

1925 James Franck (USA) and Gustav Hertz (Germany): laws governing the impact of an electron upon an atom

1926 Jean Perrin (France): confirmation of the discontinuous structure of matter

1927 Arthur Compton (USA): transfer of energy from electromagnetic radiation to a particle; Charles Wilson (UK): invention of the Wilson cloud chamber, by which the movement of electrically charged particles may be tracked

1928 Owen Richardson (UK): thermionic phenomena and associated law

1929 Louis Victor de Broglie (France): discovery of wavelike nature of electrons

1930 Venkata Raman (India): discovery of the scattering of single-wavelength light when it is passed through a transparent substance

1931 no award

1932 Werner Heisenberg (Germany): creation of quantum mechanics

1933 Erwin Schrödinger (Austria) and Paul Dirac (UK): development of quantum mechanics

1934 no award

1935 James Chadwick (UK): discovery of the neutron

1936 Victor Hess (Austria): discovery of cosmic radiation; Carl Anderson (USA): discovery of the positron

1937 Clinton Davisson (USA) and George Thomson (UK): diffraction of electrons by crystals

1938 Enrico Fermi (USA): use of neutron irradiation to produce new elements, and discovery of nuclear reactions induced by slow neutrons

1939 Ernest O Lawrence (USA): invention and development of cyclotron, and production of artificial radioactive elements

1940–42 no award

1943 Otto Stern (Germany): molecular-ray method of investigating elementary particles, and discovery of magnetic moment of proton

1944 Isidor Isaac Rabi (USA): resonance method of recording the magnetic properties of atomic nuclei

1945 Wolfgang Pauli (Austria): discovery of the exclusion principle

1946 Percy Bridgman (USA): development of high-pressure physics

1947 Edward Appleton (UK): physics of the upper atmosphere

1948 Patrick Blackett (UK): application of the Wilson cloud chamber to nuclear physics and cosmic radiation

1949 Hideki Yukawa (Japan): theoretical work predicting existence of mesons

1950 Cecil Powell (UK): use of photographic emulsion to study nuclear processes, and discovery of pions (pi mesons)

1951 John Cockcroft (UK) and Ernest Walton (Ireland): transmutation of atomic nuclei by means of accelerated subatomic particles

1952 Felix Bloch (USA) and Edward Purcell (USA): precise nuclear-magnetic measurements

1953 Frits Zernike (Netherlands): invention of phase-contrast microscope

1954 Max Born (Germany): statistical interpretation of wave function in quantum mechanics; Walther Bothe (Germany): coincidence method of detecting the emission of electrons

1955 Willis Lamb (USA): structure of hydrogen spectrum; Polykarp Kusch (USA): determination of magnetic moment of the electron

1956 William Shockley (USA), John Bardeen (USA), and Walter Houser Brattain (USA): study of semiconductors, and discovery of transistor effect

1957 Yang Chen Ning (USA) and Lee Tsung-Dao (China): investigations of weak interactions between elementary particles

1958 Pavel Cherenkov (USSR), Ilya Frank (USSR), and Igor Tamm (USA): discovery and interpretation of Cherenkov radiation

1959 Emilio Segrè (Italy) and Owen Chamberlain (USA): discovery of the antiproton

1960 Donald Glaser (USA): invention of the bubble chamber

1961 Robert Hofstadter (USA): scattering of electrons in atomic nuclei, and structure of protons and neutrons; Rudolf Mössbauer (Germany): resonance absorption of gamma radiation

1962 Lev Landau (USSR): theories of condensed matter, especially liquid helium

1963 Eugene Wigner (USA): discovery and application of symmetry principles in atomic physics; Maria Goeppert-Mayer (USA) and Hans Jensen (Germany): discovery of the shell-like structure of atomic nuclei

1964 Charles Townes (USA), Nikolai Basov (USSR), and Aleksandr Prokhorov (USSR): quantum electronics leading to construction of oscillators and amplifiers based on maser–laser principle

1965 Sin-Itiro Tomonaga (Japan), Julian Schwinger (USA), and Richard Feynman (USA): quantum electrodynamics

1966 Alfred Kastler (France): development of optical pumping, whereby atoms are raised to higher energy levels by illumination

1967 Hans Bethe (USA): theory of nuclear reactions, and discoveries concerning production of energy in stars

1968 Luis Alvarez (USA): elementary-particle physics, and discovery of resonance states, using hydrogen bubble chamber and data analysis

1969 Murray Gell-Mann (USA): classification of elementary particles, and study of their interactions

1970 Hannes Alfvén (Sweden): magnetohydrodynamics and its applications in plasma physics; Louis Néel (France): antiferromagnetism and ferromagnetism in solid-state physics

1971 Dennis Gabor (UK): invention and development of holography

1972 John Bardeen (USA), Leon Cooper (USA), and John Robert Schrieffer (USA): theory of superconductivity

Nobel Prize for Physics (continued)

1973   Leo Esaki (Japan) and Ivar Giaver (USA): tunnelling phenomena in semiconductors and superconductors; Brian Josephson (UK): theoretical predictions of the properties of a supercurrent through a tunnel barrier

1974   Martin Ryle (UK) and Antony Hewish (UK): development of radioastronomy, particularly aperture-synthesis technique, and the discovery of pulsars

1975   Aage Bohr (Denmark), Ben Mottelson (Denmark), and James Rainwater (USA): discovery of connection between collective motion and particle motion in atomic nuclei, and development of theory of nuclear structure

1976   Burton Richter (USA) and Samuel Ting (USA): discovery of the psi meson

1977   Philip Anderson (USA), Nevill Mott (UK), and John Van Vleck (USA): electronic structure of magnetic and disordered systems

1978   Pyotr Kapitza (USSR): low-temperature physics; Arno Penzias (Germany) and Robert Wilson (USA): discovery of cosmic background radiation

1979   Sheldon Glashow (USA), Abdus Salam (Pakistan), and Steven Weinberg (USA): unified theory of weak and electromagnetic fundamental forces, and prediction of the existence of the weak neutral current

1980   James W Cronin (USA) and Val Fitch (USA): violations of fundamental symmetry principles in the decay of neutral kaon mesons

1981   Nicolaas Bloemergen (USA) and Arthur Schawlow (USA): development of laser spectroscopy; Kai Siegbahn (Sweden): high-resolution electron spectroscopy

1982   Kenneth Wilson (USA): theory for critical phenomena in connection with phase transitions

1983   Subrahmanyan Chandrasekhar (USA): theoretical studies of physical processes in connection with structure and evolution of stars; William Fowler (USA): nuclear reactions involved in the formation of chemical elements in the universe

1984   Carlo Rubbia (Italy) and Simon van der Meer (Netherlands): contributions to the discovery of the W and Z particles (weakons)

1985   Klaus von Klitzing (Germany): discovery of the quantized Hall effect

1986   Erns Ruska (Germany): electron optics, and design of the first electron microscope; Gerd Binnig (Germany) and Heinrich Rohrer (Switzerland): design of scanning tunnelling microscope

1987   Georg Bednorz (Germany) and Alex Müller (Switzerland): superconductivity in ceramic materials

1988   Leon M Lederman (USA), Melvin Schwartz (USA), and Jack Steinberger (Germany): neutrino-beam method, and demonstration of the doublet structure of leptons through discovery of muon neutrino

1989   Norman Ramsey (USA): measurement techniques leading to discovery of caesium atomic clock; Hans Dehmelt (USA) and Wolfgang Paul (Germany): ion-trap method for isolating single atoms

1990   Jerome Friedman (USA), Henry Kendall (USA), and Richard Taylor (Canada): experiments demonstrating that protons and neutrons are made up of quarks

1991   Pierre-Gilles de Gennes (France): work on disordered systems including polymers and liquid crystals; development of mathematical methods for studying the behaviour of molecules in a liquid on the verge of solidifying

1992   Georges Charpak (Poland): invention and development of detectors used in high-energy physics

1993   Joseph Taylor (USA) and Russell Hulse (USA): discovery of first binary pulsar (confirming the existence of gravitational waves)

1994   Clifford G Shull (USA) and Bertram N Brockhouse (Canada): development of technique known as 'neutron scattering' which led to advances in semiconductor technology

1995   Frederick Reines (USA): discovery of the neutrino; Martin L Perl (USA): discovery of the tau lepton

1996   David M Lee (Usa), Douglas D Osheroff (USA) and Robert C Richardson (USA): discovery of superfluidity in helium–3

Poets laureate

1668   John Dryden (1631–1700)
1689   Thomas Shadwell (1642?–1692)
1692   Nahum Tate (1652–1715)
1715   Nicholas Rowe (1674–1718)
1718   Laurence Eusden (1688–1730)
1730   Colley Cibber (1671–1757)
1757   William Whitehead (1715–1785)
1785   Thomas Warton (1728–1790)
1790   Henry James Pye (1745–1813)

1813   Robert Southey (1774–1843)
1843   William Wordsworth (1770–1850)
1850   Alfred, Lord Tennyson (1809–1892)
1896   Alfred Austin (1835–1913)
1913   Robert Bridges (1844–1930)
1930   John Masefield (1878–1967)
1968   Cecil Day Lewis (1904–1972)
1972   Sir John Betjeman (1906–1984)
1984   Ted Hughes (1930–   )

Popes

name	date reign began	name	date reign began	name	date reign began	name	date reign began	name	date reign began
St Peter	42	St Felix IV	526	Benedict III	855	Urban II	1088	Sixtus IV	1471
St Linus	67	Boniface II	530	St Nicholas I	858	Paschal II	1099	Innocent VIII	1484
St Anacletus (Cletus)	76	John II	533	Adrian II	867	Gelasius II	1118	Alexander VI	1492
St Clement I	88	St Agapetus I	535	John VIII	872	Callistus II	1119	Pius III	1503
St Evaristus	97	St Silverius	536	Marinus I	882	Hororius II	1124	Julius II	1503
St Alexander I	105	Vigilius	537	St Adrian III	884	Innocent II	1130	Leo X	1513
St Sixtus I	115	Pelagius I	556	Stephen V (VI)	885	Celestine II	1143	Adrian VI	1522
St Telesphorus	125	John III	561	Formosus	891	Lucius II	1144	Clement VII	1523
St Hyginus	136	Benedict I	575	Boniface VI	896	Eugene III	1145	Paul III	1534
St Pius I	140	Pelagius II	579	Stephen VI (VII)	896	Anastasius IV	1153	Julius III	1550
St Anicetus	155	St Gregory I		Romanus	897	Adrian IV	1154	Marcellus II	1555
St Soterus	166	(the Great)	590	Theodore II	897	Alexander III	1159	Paul IV	1555
St Eleutherius	175	Sabinianus	604	John IX	898	Lucius III	1181	Pius IV	1559
St Victor I	189	Boniface III	607	Benedict IV	900	Urban III	1185	St Pius V	1566
St Zephyrinus	199	St Boniface IV	608	Leo V	903	Gregory VIII	1187	Gregory XIII	1572
St Callistus I	217	St Deusdedit		Sergius III	904	Clement III	1187	Sixtus V	1585
St Urban I	222	(Adeodatus I)	615	Anastasius III	911	Celestine III	1191	Urban VII	1590
St Pontian	230	Bondiface V	619	Landus	913	Innocent III	1198	Gregory XIV	1590
St Anterus	235	Honorius I	625	John X	914	Honorius III	1216	Innocent IX	1591
St Fabius	236	Severinus	640	Leo VI	928	Gregory IX	1227	Clement VIII	1592
St Cornelius	251	Severinus	640	Stephen VII (VIII)	928	Celestine IV	1241	Leo XI	1605
St Lucius I	253	John IV	640	John XI	931	Innocent IV	1243	Paul V	1605
St Stephen I	254	Theodore I	642	Leo VII	936	Alexander IV	1254	Gregory XV	1621
St Sixtus II	257	St Martin I	649	Stephen VII (IX)	939	Urban IV	1261	Urban VIII	1623
St Dionysius	259	St Eugene I	654	Marinus II	942	Clement IV	1265	Innocent X	1644
St Felix I	269	St Vitalian	657	Agapetus II	946	Gregory X	1271	Alexander VII	1655
St Eutychian	275	Adeodatus II	672	John XII	955	Innocent V	1276	Clement IX	1667
St Caius	283	Donus	676	Leo VIII	963	Adrian V	1276	Clement X	1670
St Marcellinus	296	St Agatho	678	Benedict V	964	John XXI	1276	Innocent XI	1676
St Marcellus I	308	St Leo II	682	John XIII	965	Nicholas III	1277	Alexander VIII	1689
St Eusebius	309	St Benedict II	684	Benedict VI	973	Martin IV	1281	Innocent XII	1691
St Melchiades	311	John V	685	Benedict VII	974	Honorius IV	1285	Clement XI	1700
St Sylvester I	314	Conon	686	John XIV	983	Nicholas IV	1288	Innocent XIII	1721
St Marcus	336	St Sergius I	687	John XV	985	St Celestine V	1294	Benedict XIII	1724
St Julius I	337	John VI	701	Gregory V	996	Boniface VIII	1294	Clement XII	1730
Liberius	352	John VII	705	Sylvester II	999	Benedict XI	1303	Benedict XIV	1740
St Damasus I	366	Sisinnius	708	John XVII	1003	Clement V	1305	Clement XIII	1758
St Siricius	384	Constantine	708	John XVIII	1004	John XXII	1316	Clement XIV	1769
St Anastasius I	399	St Gregory II	715	Sergius IV	1009	Benedict XII	1334	Pius VI	1775
St Innocent I	401	St Gregory III	731	Benedict VIII	1012	Clement VI	1342	Pius VII	1800
St Zosimus	417	St Zachary	741	John XIX	1024	Innocent IV	1352	Leo XII	1823
St Boniface I	418	Stephen II (III)*	752	Benedict IX	1032	Urban V	1362	Pius VIII	1829
St Celestine I	422	St Paul I	757	Gregory VI	1045	Gregory XI	1370	Gregory XVI	1831
St Sixtus III	432	Stephen III (IV)	768	Clement II	1046	Urban VI	1378	Pius IX	1846
St Leo I (the Great)	440	Adrian I	772	Benedict IX**	1047	Boniface IX	1389	Leo XIII	1878
St Hilary	461	St Leo III	795	Damasus II	1048	Innocent VII	1404	St Pius X	1903
St Simplicius	468	Stephen IV (V)	816	St Leo IX	1049	Gregory XII	1406	Benedict XV	1914
St Felix III	483	St Paschal I	817	Victor II	1055	Martin V	1417	Pius XI	1922
St Gelasius I	492	Eugene II	824	Stephen IX (X)	1057	Eugene IV	1431	Pius XII	1939
Anastasius II	496	Valentine	827	Nicholas II	1059	Nicholas V	1447	John XXIII	1958
St Symmachus	498	Gregory IV	827	Alexander II	1061	Callistus III	1455	Paul VI	1963
St Hormisdas	514	Sergius II	844	St Gregory VII	1073	Pius II	1458	John Paul I***	1978
St John I	523	St Leo IV	847	Victor III	1086	Paul II	1464	John Paul II	1978

* The original Stephen II died before consecration, and was dropped from the list of popes in 1961; Stephen III became Stephen II and the numbers of the other popes named Stephen were also moved up.

** Benedict IX was driven from office for scandalous conduct; but returned briefly 1047.

*** John Paul I died after only 33 days as Pontiff.

Pulitzer Prize for Fiction (American)

1917	no award		**1958**	James Agee *A Death in the Family*
1918	Ernest Poole *His Family*		**1959**	Robert Lewis Taylor *The Travels of Jamie McPheeters*
1919	Booth Tarkington *The Magnificent Ambersons*		**1960**	Allen Drury *Advise and Consent*
1920	no award		**1961**	Harper Lee *To Kill a Mockingbird*
1921	Edith Wharton *The Age of Innocence*		**1962**	Edwin O'Connor *The Edge of Sadness*
1922	Booth Tarkington *Alice Adams*		**1963**	William Faulkner *The Reivers*
1923	Willa Cather *One of Ours*		**1964**	no award
1924	Margaret Wilson *The Able McLaughlins*		**1965**	Shirley Ann Grau *The Keepers of the House*
1925	Edna Ferber *So Big*		**1966**	Katherine Anne Porter *The Collected Stories of Katherine Anne Porter*
1926	Sinclair Lewis *Arrowsmith*		**1967**	Bernard Malamud *The Fixer*
1927	Louis Bromfield *Early Autumn*		**1968**	William Styron *The Confessions of Nat Turner*
1928	Thornton Wilder *The Bridge at San Luis Rey*		**1969**	N Scott Momaday *House Made of Dawn*
1929	Julia Peterkin *Scarlet Sister Mary*		**1970**	Jean Stafford *Collected Stories*
1930	Oliver LaFarge *Laughing Boy*		**1971**	no award
1931	Margaret Ayer Barnes *Years of Grace*		**1972**	Wallace Stegner *Angle of Repose*
1932	Pearl S Buck *The Good Earth*		**1973**	Eudora Welty *The Optimist's Daughter*
1933	T S Stribling *The Store*		**1974**	no award
1934	Caroline Miller *Lamb in His Bosom*		**1975**	Michael Shaara *The Killer Angels*
1935	Josephine Winslow Johnson *Now in November*		**1976**	Saul Bellow *Humboldt's Gift*
1936	Harold L Davis *Honey in the Horn*		**1977**	no award
1937	Margaret Mitchell *Gone With the Wind*		**1978**	James Alan McPherson *Elbow Room*
1938	John Phillips Marquand *The Late George Apley*		**1979**	John Cheever *The Stories of John Cheever*
1939	Marjorie Kinnan Rawlings *The Yearling*		**1980**	Norman Mailer *The Executioner's Song*
1940	John Steinbeck *The Grapes of Wrath*		**1981**	John Kennedy Toole *A Confederacy of Dunces*
1941	no award		**1982**	John Updike *Rabbit is Rich*
1942	Ellen Glasgow *In This Our Life*		**1983**	Alice Walker *The Color Purple*
1943	Upton Sinclair *Dragon's Teeth*		**1984**	William Kennedy *Ironweed*
1944	Martin Flavin *Journey in the Dark*		**1985**	Alison Lurie *Foreign Affairs*
1945	John Hersey *A Bell for Adano*		**1986**	Larry McMurtry *Lonesome Dove*
1946	no award		**1987**	Peter Taylor *A Summons to Memphis*
1947	Robert Penn Warren *All the King's Men*		**1988**	Toni Morrison *Beloved*
1948	James A Michener *Tales of the South Pacific*		**1989**	Anne Tyler *Breathing Lessons*
1949	James Gould Cozzens *Guard of Honor*		**1990**	Oscar Hijuelos *The Mambo Kings Play Songs of Love*
1950	A B Guthrie Jr *The Way West*		**1991**	John Updike *Rabbit at Rest*
1951	Conrad Richter *The Town*		**1992**	Jane Smiley *A Thousand Acres*
1952	Herman Wouk *The Caine Mutiny*		**1993**	Robert Olen Butler *A Good Scent from a Strange Mountain*
1953	Ernest Hemingway *The Old Man and the Sea*		**1994**	E Annie Proulx *The Shipping News*
1954	no award		**1995**	Carol Shields *The Stone Diaries*
1955	William Faulkner *A Fable*		**1996**	Richard A Ford *Independence Day*
1956	Mackinley Kantor *Andersonville*			
1957	no award			

Russian rulers 1547–1917

House of Rurik			Theodore III	1676–82
Ivan 'the Terrible'	1547–84		Peter I 'Peter the Great' and Ivan V (brothers)	1682–96
Theodore I	1584–98		Peter I, as tsar	1689–1721
Irina	1598		Peter I, as emperor	1721–25
			Catherine I	1725–27
House of Godunov			Peter II	1727–30
Boris Godunov	1598–1605		Anna Ivanovna	1730–40
Theodore II	1605		Ivan VI	1740–41
			Elizabeth	1741–62
usurpers			Peter III	1762
Dimitri III	1605–06		Catherine II 'Catherine the Great'	1762–96
Basil IV	1606–10		Paul I	1796–1801
			Alexander I	1801–25
interregnum 1610–13			Nicholas I	1825–55
			Alexander II	1855–81
House of Romanov			Alexander III	1881–94
Michael Romanov	1613–45		Nicholas II	1894–1917
Alexis	1645–76			

Scotland: kings and queens 1005–1603

from the unification of Scotland to the union of the crowns of Scotland and England

reign	name	reign	name
Celtic kings		*English domination*	
1005	Malcolm II	1292–96	John Baliol
1034	Duncan I	1296–1306	annexed to England
1040	Macbeth	*House of Bruce*	
1057	Malcolm III Canmore		
1093	Donald III Donalbane	1306	Robert I the Bruce
1094	Duncan II	1329	David II
1094	Donald III (restored)	*House of Stuart*	
1097	Edgar		
1107	Alexander I	1371	Robert II
1124	David I	1390	Robert III
1153	Malcolm IV	1406	James I
1165	William the Lion	1437	James II
1214	Alexander II	1460	James III
1249	Alexander III	1488	James IV
1286–90	Margaret of Norway	1513	James V
		1542	Mary
		1567	James VI
		1603	union of crowns

United Kingdom: prime ministers from 1721

term	name	party	term	name	party
1721–42	Sir Robert Walpole	Whig	1866–68	Earl of Derby	Conservative
1742–43	Earl of Wilmington	Whig	1868	Benjamin Disraeli	Conservative
1743–54	Henry Pelham	Whig	1868–74	W E Gladstone	Liberal
1754–56	Duke of Newcastle	Whig	1874–80	Benjamin Disraeli	Conservative
1756–57	Duke of Devonshire	Whig	1880–85	W E Gladstone	Liberal
1757–62	Duke of Newcastle	Whig	1885–86	Marquess of Salisbury	Conservative
1762–63	Earl of Bute	Tory	1886	W E Gladstone	Liberal
1763–65	George Grenville	Whig	1886–92	Marquess of Salisbury	Conservative
1765–66	Marquess of Rockingham	Whig	1892–94	W E Gladstone	Liberal
1767–70	Duke of Grafton	Whig	1894–95	Earl of Rosebery	Liberal
1770–82	Lord North	Tory	1895–1902	Marquess of Salisbury	Conservative
1782	Marquess of Rockingham	Whig	1902–05	Arthur James Balfour	Conservative
1782–83	Earl of Shelburne	Whig	1905–08	Sir H Campbell-Bannerman	Liberal
1783	Duke of Portland	coalition	1908–15	H H Asquith	Liberal
1783–1801	William Pitt the Younger	Tory	1915–16	H H Asquith	coalition
1801–04	Henry Addington	Tory	1916–22	David Lloyd George	coalition
1804–06	William Pitt the Younger	Tory	1922–23	Andrew Bonar Law	Conservative
1806–07	Lord Grenville	coalition	1923–24	Stanley Baldwin	Conservative
1807–09	Duke of Portland	Tory	1924	Ramsay MacDonald	Labour
1809–12	Spencer Perceval	Tory	1924–29	Stanley Baldwin	Conservative
1812–27	Earl of Liverpool	Tory	1929–31	Ramsay MacDonald	Labour
1827	George Canning	coalition	1931–35	Ramsay MacDonald	national coalition
1827–28	Viscount Goderich	Tory	1935–37	Stanley Baldwin	national coalition
1828–30	Duke of Wellington	Tory	1937–40	Neville Chamberlain	national coalition
1830–34	Earl Grey	Tory	1940–45	Sir Winston Churchill	coalition
1834	Viscount Melbourne	Whig	1945–51	Clement Attlee	Labour
1834–35	Sir Robert Peel	Whig	1951–55	Sir Winston Churchill	Conservative
1835–41	Viscount Melbourne	Whig	1955–57	Sir Anthony Eden	Conservative
1841–46	Sir Robert Peel	Conservative	1957–63	Harold Macmillan	Conservative
1846–52	Lord Russell	Liberal	1963–64	Sir Alec Douglas-Home	Conservative
1852	Earl of Derby	Conservative	1964–70	Harold Wilson	Labour
1852–55	Lord Aberdeen	Peelite	1970–74	Edward Heath	Conservative
1855–58	Viscount Palmerston	Liberal	1974–76	Harold Wilson	Labour
1858–59	Earl of Derby	Conservative	1976–79	James Callaghan	Labour
1859–65	Viscount Palmerston	Liberal	1979–90	Margaret Thatcher	Conservative
1865–66	Lord Russell	Liberal	1990–	John Major	Conservative

United States: presidents and elections

year elected/took office	president	party	losing candidate(s)	party
1789	1. George Washington	Federalist	no opponent	
1792	re-elected		no opponent	
1796	2. John Adams	Federalist	Thomas Jefferson	Democrat–Republican
1800	3. Thomas Jefferson	Democrat–Republican	Aaron Burr	Democrat–Republican
1804	re-elected		Charles Pinckney	Federalist
1808	4. James Madison	Democrat–Republican	Charles Pinckney	Federalist
1812	re-elected		DeWitt Clinton	Federalist
1816	5. James Monroe	Democrat–Republican	Rufus King	Federalist
1820	re-elected		John Quincy Adams	Democrat–Republican
1824	6. John Quincy Adams	Democrat–Republican	Andrew Jackson	Democrat–Republican
		Henry Clay	Democrat–Republican	
		William H Crawford	Democrat–Republican	
1828	7. Andrew Jackson	Democrat	John Quincy Adams	National Republican
1832	re-elected		Henry Clay	National Republican
1836	8. Martin Van Buren	Democrat	William Henry Harrison	Whig
1840	9. William Henry Harrison	Whig	Martin Van Buren	Democrat
1841	10. John Tyler[1]	Whig		
1844	11. James K Polk	Democrat	Henry Clay	Whig
1848	12. Zachary Taylor	Whig	Lewis Cass	Democrat
1850	13. Millard Fillmore[2]	Whig		
1852	14. Franklin Pierce	Democrat	Winfield Scott	Whig
1856	15. James Buchanan	Democrat	John C Fremont	Republican
1860	16. Abraham Lincoln	Republican	Stephen Douglas	Democrat
			John Breckinridge	Democrat
			John Bell	Constitutional Union
1864	re-elected		George McClellan	Democrat
1865	17. Andrew Johnson[3]	Democrat		
1868	18. Ulysses S Grant	Republican	Horatio Seymour	Democrat
1872	re-elected		Horace Greeley	Democrat–Liberal Republican
1876	19. Rutherford B Hayes	Republican	Samuel Tilden	Democrat
1880	20. James A Garfield	Republican	Winfield Hancock	Democrat
1881	21. Chester A Arthur[4]	Republican		
1884	22. Grover Cleveland	Democrat	James Blaine	Republican
1888	23. Benjamin Harrison	Republican	Grover Cleveland	Democrat
1892	24. Grover Cleveland	Democrat	Benjamin Harrison	Republican
			James Weaver	People's
1896	25. William McKinley	Republican	William J Bryan	Democrat–People's
1900	re-elected		William J Bryan	Democrat
1901	26. Theodore Roosevelt[5]	Republican		
1904	re-elected		Alton B Parker	Democrat
1908	27. William H Taft	Republican	William J Bryan	Democrat
1912	28. Woodrow Wilson	Democrat	Theodore Roosevelt	Progressive
			William H Taft	Republican
1916	re-elected		Charles E Hughes	Republican
1920	29. Warren G Harding	Republican	James M Cox	Democrat
1923	30. Calvin Coolidge[6]	Republican		
1924	re-elected		John W Davis	Democrat
			Robert M LaFollette	Progressive
1928	31. Herbert Hoover	Republican	Alfred E Smith	Democrat
1932	32. Franklin D Roosevelt	Democrat	Herbert Hoover	Republican
			Norman Thomas	Socialist
1936	re-elected		Alfred Landon	Republican
1940	re-elected		Wendell Willkie	Republican
1944	re-elected		Thomas E Dewey	Republican
1945	33. Harry S Truman[7]	Democrat		
1948	re-elected		Thomas E Dewey	Republican
			J Strom Thurmond	States' Rights
			Henry A Wallace	Progressive
1952	34. Dwight D Eisenhower	Republican	Adlai E Stevenson	Democrat
1956	re-elected		Adlai E Stevenson	Democrat
1960	35. John F Kennedy	Democrat	Richard M Nixon	Republican
1963	36. Lyndon B Johnson[8]	Democrat		

United States: presidents and elections (continued)

year elected/took office	president	party	losing candidate(s)	party
1964	re-elected		Barry M Goldwater	Republican
1968	37. Richard M Nixon	Republican	Hubert H Humphrey	Democrat
			George C Wallace	American Independent
1972	re-elected		George S McGovern	Democrat
1974	38. Gerald R Ford[9]	Republican		
1976	39. Jimmy Carter	Democrat	Gerald R Ford	Republican
1980	40. Ronald Reagan	Republican	Jimmy Carter	Democrat
			John B Anderson	Independent
1984	re-elected		Walter Mondale	Democrat
1988	41. George Bush	Republican	Michael Dukakis	Democrat
1992	42. Bill Clinton	Democrat	George Bush	Republican

[1] became president on death of Harrison
[2] became president on death of Taylor
[3] became president on assassination of Lincoln
[4] became president on assassination of Garfield
[5] became president on assassination of McKinley
[6] became president on death of Harding
[7] became president on death of F D Roosevelt
[8] became president on assassination of Kennedy
[9] became president on resignation of Nixon

Wales: sovereigns and princes 844–1282

844–78	Rhodri the Great
878–916	Anarawd
915–50	Hywel Dda (Hywel the Good)
950–79	Iago ab Idwal
979–85	Hywel ab Ieuaf (Hywel the Bad)
985–86	Cadwallon
986–99	Maredudd ab Owain ap Hywel Dda
999–1008	Cynan ap Hywel ab Ieuaf
1018–23	Llywelyn ap Seisyll
1023–39	Iago ab Idwal ap Meurig
1039–63	Gruffydd ap Llywelyn ap Seisyll
1063–75	Bleddyn ap Cynfyn
1075–81	Trahaern ap Caradog
1081–1137	Gruffydd ap Cynan ab Iago
1137–70	Owain Gwynedd
1170–94	Dafydd ab Owain Gwynedd
1194–1240	Llywelyn Fawr (Llywelyn the Great)
1240–46	Dafydd ap Llywellyn
1246–82	Llywellyn ap Gruffydd ap Llywellyn

Wales, Princes of

1301	Edward (II)
1343	Edward (the Black Prince)
1376	Richard (II)
1399	Henry of Monmouth (V)
1454	Edward of Westminster
1471	Edward of Westminster (V)
1483	Edward
1489	Arthur Tudor
1504	Henry Tudor (VIII)
1610	Henry Stuart
1616	Charles Stuart (I)
c. 1638	Charles (II)
1688	James Francis Edward (Old Pretender)
1714	George Augustus (II)
1729	Frederick Lewis
1751	George William Frederick (III)
1762	George Augustus Frederick (IV)
1841	Albert Edward (Edward VII)
1901	George (V)
1910	Edward (VII)
1958	Charles Philip Arthur George

Chronological Index

The entries in this index are arranged first by date of birth, and then, if dates of birth are the same, by dates of death. When two entries have the same dates of birth and death, they appear in alphabetical order. Where date of birth is unknown, the entries appear under date of death. When only the era during which a person lived is known, the entry is at the beginning of the appropriate century.

30th–11th centuries BC

Menes *c.* 3050 BC. King of Egypt
Imhotep *c.* 2630 BC– . Egyptian physician and architect
Khufu *c.* 2550 BC. Egyptian king of Memphis
Sargon I 24th–23rd centuries BC. King of Akkad
Abraham *c.* 2300 BC. Founder of the Jewish nation
Isaac *c.* 22nd century BC. Old Testament Hebrew patriarch
Ishmael *c.* 22nd century BC. Traditional ancestor of the Arab people
Hammurabi died *c.* 1750 BC. King of Babylon
Abijah *c.* 16th century BC. King of Judah
Thothmes I died *c.* 1492 BC. King of Egypt
Hatshepsut *c.* 1473–*c.* 1458 BC. Queen of Egypt
Thothmes III died *c.* 1425 BC. King of Egypt
Akhenaton 14th century BC. King of Egypt
Nefertiti 14th century BC. Queen of Egypt
Tutankhamen 14th century BC. King of Egypt
Amenhotep III 1391–1353 BC. King of Egypt
Aaron *c.* 13th century BC. Old Testament figure, elder brother of Moses
Joshua 13th century BC. Old Testament Hebrew leader
Moses *c.* 13th century BC. Old Testament Hebrew lawgiver and judge
Ramses II died *c.* 1224 BC. King of Egypt
Deborah 12th century BC. Old Testament prophet and judge
Ramses III died *c.* 1166 BC. King of Egypt
Abner *c.* 11th century BC. Old Testament figure, cousin of Saul
Delilah 11th century BC. Old Testament figure, Philistine mistress of Samson
Eli 11th century BC. Old Testament priest
Gideon 11th century BC. Old Testament judge
Samson 11th century BC. Old Testament Hebrew judge
Samuel 11th century BC. Old Testament Hebrew judge
Saul 11th century BC. King of Israel
David *c.* 1060–*c.* 970 BC. King of Israel

10th–6th centuries BC

Absalom *c.* 10th century BC. Old Testament figure, son of King David
Jeroboam 10th century BC. King of Israel
Solomon *c.* 974–*c.* 937 BC. King of Israel
Rehoboam died *c.* 913 BC. King of Judah
Semiramis 9th century BC. Queen of Assyria
Shalmaneser III 9th century BC. King of Assyria
Ahab *c.* 875–854 BC. King of Israel
Jehosophat *c.* 873–849 BC. King of Judah
Elijah mid-9th century BC. Old Testament prophet
Elisha mid-9th century BC. Old Testament prophet
Jehu *c.* 842–815 BC. King of Israel
Hesiod 8th century BC. Greek poet
Hezekiah 8th century BC. King of Judah
Homer 8th century BC. Greek epic poet
Hosea 8th century BC. Old Testament prophet
Isaiah 8th century BC. Old Testament prophet
Micah 8th century BC. Old Testament Hebrew prophet

Sargon II died 705 BC. King of Assyria
Alcman 7th century BC. Greek lyric poet
Arion 7th century BC. Greek writer
Draco 7th century BC. Athenian politician
Jeremiah 7th–6th centuries BC. Old Testament prophet
Jonah 7th century BC. Old Testament prophet
Mimnermus 7th century BC. Greek poet
Nāhum 7th century BC. Old Testament Hebrew prophet
Semonides 7th century BC. Greek poet
Tyrtaeus 7th century BC. Spartan war poet
Sennacherib died 681 BC. King of Assyria
Esarhaddon died 669 BC. King of Assyria
Josiah *c.* 647–609 BC. King of Judah
Solon *c.* 638–*c.* 558 BC. Athenian statesman
Zoroaster *c.* 638–*c.* 553 BC. Persian prophet and religious teacher
Nebuchadnezzar *c.* 630–*c.* 562 BC. King of Babylonia
Stesichorus *c.* 630–*c.* 550 BC. Greek poet
Periander 625 BC–585 BC. Greek tyrant of Corinth
Thales *c.* 624–*c.* 547 BC. Greek philosopher and scientist
Alcaeus *c.* 611–*c.* 580 BC. Greek lyric poet
Sappho *c.* 610–*c.* 580 BC. Greek poet
Anaximander *c.* 610–*c.* 546 BC. Greek astronomer and philosopher
Pisistratus *c.* 605–527 BC. Athenian politician
Lao Zi *c.* 604–531 BC. Chinese philosopher
Zedekiah early 6th century BC. King of Judah
Amasis II 6th century BC. King of Egypt
Belshazzar 6th century BC. Last king of Babylon
Cambyses 6th century BC. King of Persia
Corinna 6th century BC. Greek poet
Daniel 6th century BC. Old Testament prophet
Hecataeus 6th–5th centuries BC. Greek historian and geographer
Polycrates 6th century BC. Tyrant of Samos
Tarquinius Superbus 6th century BC. King of Rome
Thespis 6th century BC. Greek poet
Ezekiel *c.* 600 BC. Old Testament prophet
Mahavira *c.* 599–527 BC. Indian sage
Pythagoras *c.* 580–500 BC. Greek mathematician and philosopher
Phalaris *c.* 570–*c.* 554 BC. Greek tyrant of Acragas
Cleisthenes *c.* 570–*c.* 508 BC. Athenian statesman
Buddha *c.* 563–483 BC. Religious leader, founder of Buddhism
Darius (I) the Great *c.* 558–486 BC. King of Persia
Simonides *c.* 556–*c.* 448 BC. Greek poet
Hipparchus *c.* 555–514 BC. Tyrant of Athens
Confucius 551–479 BC. Chinese sage
Aesop mid-6th century BC. Greek fable writer
Exekias *c.* 550–525 BC. Athenian potter
Miltiades the Younger *c.* 550–489 BC. Athenian general
Croesus died 546 BC. Last king of Lydia
Heraclitus *c.* 544–*c.* 483 BC. Greek philosopher
Gelon *c.* 540–478 BC. Tyrant of Syracuse
Aristides *c.* 530–468 BC. Athenian politician
Epicharmus *c.* 530–*c.* 440 BC. Greek comic writer
Cyrus the Great died 529 BC. Founder of the Persian Empire
Themistocles *c.* 528–*c.* 462 BC. Athenian soldier and politician
Aeschylus *c.* 525–*c.* 456 BC. Athenian dramatist
Euphronius *c.* 520–470 BC. Greek vase painter
Xerxes *c.* 519–465 BC. King of Persia

Pindar *c.* 518–*c.* 438 BC. Greek poet
Cimon *c.* 512–449 BC. Athenian general
Parmenides *c.* 510–450 BC. Greek philosopher
Myron *c.* 500–440 BC. Greek sculptor
Polygnotus *c.* 500–*c.* 440 BC. Greek painter

5th–1st centuries BC

Alcamenes 5th century BC. Athenian classical sculptor
Ananda 5th century BC. Favourite disciple of the Buddha
Callicrates 5th century BC. Athenian architect
Cincinnatus, Lucius Quinctius 5th century BC. Roman general
Ezra 500 BC. Old Testament scribe
Hippodamus 5th century BC. Greek architect and town planner
Job 5th century BC. Old Testament Hebrew leader
Nehemiah 5th century BC. Hebrew governor of Judaea
Polykleitos 5th century BC. Greek sculptor
Pythagorus of Rhegium 5th century BC. Greek sculptor
Zeuxis 5th century BC. Greek painter
Aristagoras died 497 BC. Tyrant of Miletus
Sophocles *c.* 496–406 BC. Athenian dramatist
Pericles *c.* 495–429 BC. Athenian politician
Empedocles *c.* 493–433 BC. Greek philosopher
Zeno of Elea *c.* 490–*c.* 430 BC. Greek philosopher
Euripides *c.* 485–*c.* 406 BC. Athenian tragic dramatist
Herodotus *c.* 484–*c.* 424 BC. Greek historian
Leonidas died *c.* 480 BC. Greek epigrammatist
Nicias *c.* 470–413 BC. Athenian politician and general
Mo Tzu *c.* 470–*c.* 391 BC. Chinese philosopher
Socrates *c.* 469–399 BC. Athenian philosopher
Critias *c.* 460–403 BC. Athenian politician and orator
Hippocrates *c.* 460–*c.* 377 BC. Greek physician
Democritus *c.* 460–*c.* 370 BC. Greek philosopher
Lysias *c.* 459–*c.* 380 BC. Greek orator
Thucydides *c.* 455–*c.* 400 BC. Athenian historian
Phidias mid-5th century BC. Greek sculptor
Alcibiades 450–404 BC. Athenian politician and general
Alexander I died *c.* 450 BC. King of Macedonia
Eupolis *c.* 445–*c.* 411 BC. Greek comic dramatist
Aristophanes *c.* 445–*c.* 380 BC. Greek comedy dramatist
Aspasia *c.* 440 BC. Greek courtesan
Isocrates 436–338 BC. Athenian orator
Aristippus *c.* 435–356 BC. Greek philosopher
Dionysius the Elder *c.* 430 BC–367 BC. Greek tyrant of Syracuse
Xenophon *c.* 430–354 BC. Greek historian, philosopher, and soldier
Plato *c.* 427–347 BC. Greek philosopher
Cleon died 422 BC. Athenian politician and general
Epaminondas *c.* 420–362 BC. Theban general and politician
Diogenes *c.* 412–*c.* 323 BC. Greek philosopher
Eudoxus, of Cnidus *c.* 400–*c.* 347 BC. Greek mathematician and astronomer
Apelles 4th century BC. Greek painter
Camillus, Marcus Furius 4th century BC. Roman general and statesman
Dionysius the Younger 4th century BC. Greek tyrant of Syracuse
Lysippus 4th century BC. Greek sculptor
Phryne 4th century BC. Greek courtesan
Pytheas 4th century BC. Greek navigator
Scopas 4th century BC. Greek sculptor
Thaïs 4th century BC. Greek mistress of Alexander the Great
Caecus, Appius Claudius 4th–3rd centuries BC. Roman politician
Lysander died 395 BC. Spartan military leader
Aeschines 389–314 BC. Athenian orator
Heraklides of Pontus 388–315 BC. Greek philosopher and astronomer
Aristotle 384–322 BC. Greek philosopher
Demosthenes *c.* 384–322 BC. Athenian orator
Philip II 382–336 BC. King of Macedonia

Antigonus 382–301 BC. General of Alexander the Great
Olympias *c.* 375–316 BC. Macedonian queen
Mencius, Latinized name of Mengzi *c.* 372–*c.* 289 BC. Chinese philosopher and moralist
Theophrastus *c.* 372–*c.* 287 BC. Greek philosopher
Chuang Tzu *c.* 370–300 BC. Chinese philosopher
Ptolemy I *c.* 367–283 BC. Ruler of Egypt
Pyrrho *c.* 360–*c.* 270 BC. Greek philosopher
Seleucus I, Nicator *c.* 358–280 BC. Macedonian general
Alexander the Great 356–323 BC. King of Macedon
Praxiteles mid-4th century BC. Greek sculptor
Chandragupta Maurya 346–297 BC. Ruler of N India
Menander *c.* 342–291 BC. Greek dramatist
Epicurus 341–270 BC. Greek philosopher
Zeno of Citium *c.* 335–262 BC. Greek philosopher
Alexander I died 330 BC. King of Epirus, Greece
Euclid *c.* 330–*c.* 260 BC. Greek mathematician
Herophilus of Chalcedon *c.* 330–*c.* 260 BC. Greek physician
Antiochus I *c.* 324–*c.* 261 BC. King of Syria
Alexander IV 323–310 BC. King of Macedonia
Aristarchus of Samos *c.* 320–*c.* 250 BC. Greek astronomer
Pyrrhus 319–272 BC. King of Epirus
Theocritus *c.* 310–*c.* 250 BC. Greek poet
Callimachus *c.* 310–*c.* 240 BC. Greek poet and critic
Ptolemy II 308–246 BC. Ruler of Egypt
Erasistratus *c.* 304–*c.* 250 BC. Greek physician and anatomist
Hsun Tzu 300–230 BC. Chinese philosopher
Apollonius of Rhodes 3rd century BC. Greek poet
Scipio, Publius Cornelius 3rd century BC. Roman general
Archimedes *c.* 287–212 BC. Greek mathematician
Antiochus II *c.* 286–*c.* 246 BC. King of Syria
Eratosthenes *c.* 276–*c.* 194 BC. Greek geographer and mathematician
Asoka *c.* 273–*c.* 228 BC. Mauryan emperor of India
Aratus of Sicyon 271–213 BC. Greek soldier and politician
Hamilcar Barca *c.* 270–228 BC. Carthaginian general
Apollonius of Perga *c.* 262–*c.* 190 BC. Greek mathematician
Fabius Maximus *c.* 260–203 BC. Roman general
Shi Huangdi *c.* 259–*c.* 210 BC. Emperor of China
Philopoemen *c.* 253–182 BC. Greek general
Plautus *c.* 250–*c.* 184 BC. Roman dramatist
Hannibal 247–*c.* 182 BC. Carthaginian general
Antiochus (III) the Great *c.* 241–187 BC. King of Syria
Ennius, Quintus *c.* 239–169 BC. Roman poet
Scipio Africanus Major, Publius Cornelius 236–*c.* 183 BC. Roman general
Cato, Marcus Porcius 234–149 BC. Roman politician
Flaminius, Gaius died 217 BC. Roman consul and general
Antiochus IV *c.* 215–164 BC. King of Syria
Polybius *c.* 200–*c.* 118 BC. Greek politician and historian
Chang Ch'ien 2nd century BC. Chinese explorer
Terence *c.* 190–*c.* 159 BC. Roman dramatist
Hipparchus *c.* 190–*c.* 120 BC. Greek astronomer and mathematician
Scipio Africanus Minor, Publius Cornelius *c.* 185–129 BC. Roman general
Lucilius, Gaius *c.* 180–*c.* 102 BC. Roman poet
Accius, Lucius 170–*c.* 85 BC. Roman tragic poet
Gracchus, Tiberius Sempronius *c.* 163–133 BC. Roman reformer
Antiochus VII *c.* 159–129 BC. King of Syria
Marius, Gaius *c.* 157–86 BC. Roman general and politician
Gracchus, Gaius Sempronius *c.* 153–121 BC. Roman reformer
Meleager *c.* 140–170 BC. Greek philosopher and epigrammatist
Sulla, Lucius Cornelius 138–78 BC. Roman general and politician
Roscius Gallus, Quintus *c.* 126–62 BC. Roman actor
Mithridates VI Eupator *c.* 120–63 BC. King of Pontus
Crassus, Marcus Licinius *c.* 115–53 BC. Roman general
Lucullus, Lucius Licinius *c.* 110–*c.* 56 BC. Roman general and consul
Catiline *c.* 108–62 BC. Roman politician
Pompey the Great 106–48 BC. Roman soldier and politician

1st–5th centuries AD

Cecilia, St 2nd or 3rd century. Christian patron saint of music
Christopher, St 3rd century. Patron saint of travellers
Diogenes Laertius 3rd century. Greek writer
Zenobia 3rd century. Queen of Palmyra
Decius, Gaius Messius Quintus Traianus c. 201–251. Roman emperor
Plotinus 205–270. Roman philosopher
Alexander Severus 208–235. Roman emperor
Cyprian, St c. 210–258. Christian martyr
Longinus, Cassius 213–273. Greek philosopher
Aurelian c. 215–275. Roman emperor
Diocletian, (Gaius Aurelius Valerius Diocletianus) 245–313. Roman emperor
Helena, St c. 248–c. 328. Roman empress
Diophantus c. 250. Greek mathematician
Arius c. 250–336. Egyptian priest
Anthony, St c. 251–356. Egyptian founder of Christian monasticism
Denis, St died c. 258. Bishop of Paris
Sebastian, St died c. 258. Roman soldier
Eusebius c. 260–340. Bishop of Caesarea
Constantine the Great c. 285–337. First Christian emperor of Rome
Pachomius, St c. 292–346. Egyptian monk
Athanasius, St 298–373. Bishop of Alexandria
Pappus of Alexandria c. 300–c. 350. Greek mathematician, astronomer, and geographer
Ammianus Marcellinus 4th century. Roman soldier and historian
Catherine of Alexandria, St early 4th century. Christian martyr
Nicholas, St 4th century. Bishop of Myra
Ursula, St 4th century. English saint
George, St died c. 303. Christian martyr
Alban, St died c. 305. First Christian martyr in England
Apollinarius of Laodicea c. 310–c. 390. Bishop of Laodicea in Phrygia
Martin, St c. 316–c. 400. French monk, bishop of Tours
Basil, St c. 330–379. Cappadocian monk
Jovian (Flavius Claudius Jovianus) c. 331–364. Roman emperor
Julian the Apostate 332–363. Roman emperor
Ambrose, St c. 340–397. Christian leader and theologian
Jerome, St c. 340–420. Christian leader and scholar
John Chrysostom, St c. 345–407. Bishop of Constantinople
Theodosius (I) the Great c. AD 346–395. Roman emperor
Augustine of Hippo, St, (Aurelius Augustinus) 354–430. Christian leader and writer
Pelagius c. 360–c. 420. British theologian
Stilicho, Flavius 365–408. Roman general
Claudian c. 370–404. Roman poet
Alaric c. 370–410. King of the Visigoths
Hypatia c. 370–c. 415. Greek philosopher
Cyril of Alexandria, St 376–444. Bishop of Alexandria
Eutyches c. 384–c. 456. Greek theologian
Patrick, St c. 389–c. 461. Patron saint of Ireland
Simeon Stylites, St c. 390–459. Syrian Christian ascetic
Leo (I) the Great, (St Leo) c. 390–461. Pope
Marcian 396–457. Eastern Roman emperor
Avianus c. 400. Roman fable writer
Kālidāsa 5th century. Indian poet and dramatist
Theodosius II 401–450. Byzantine emperor
Attila c. 406–453. King of the Huns
Odoacer c. 433–493. King of Italy
Bridget, St 453–523. Irish saint
Horsa died c. 455. Anglo-Saxon leader
Theodoric the Great c. 455–526. King of the Ostrogoths
Romulus Augustulus born c. 461. Roman emperor
Clovis 465–511. Merovingian king of the Franks
Severus of Antioch c. 467–538. Christian bishop
Narses c. 478–c. 573. Byzantine general
Boethius, Anicius Manlius Severinus 480–524. Roman philosopher
Benedict, St c. 480–c. 547. Founder of Christian monasticism in the West

Justinian I c. 483–565. Byzantine emperor
Hengist died c. 488. Anglo-Saxon leader
Procopius c. 495–565. Greek historian
Piran, St c. 500 AD. Patron saint of Cornwall

6th – 10th centuries

Alboin 6th century. King of the Lombards
Arthur 6th century. Legendary British king
Bodhidharma 6th century. Indian Buddhist and teacher
Cadwallon 6th century. King of Gwynedd, N Wales
David, St 5th–6th centuries. Patron saint of Wales
Belisarius c. 505–565. Roman general
Theodora c. 508–548. Byzantine empress
Kentigern, St c. 518–603. Scottish monk, bishop of Glasgow
Columba, St 521–597. Irish abbot and missionary
Totila died 522. King of the Ostrogoths
Gregory of Tours, St c. 538–594. French bishop of Tours
Gregory (I) the Great c. 540–604. Pope
Columban, St 543–615. Irish abbot
Taliesin c. 550. Welsh poet
Ethelbert c. 552–616. King of Kent
Isidore of Seville c. 560–636. Spanish writer and missionary
Abbās 566–652. Uncle of the prophet Muhammad
Muhammad c. 570–632. Founder of Islam
Abu Bakr 573–634. First caliph of Islam
Uthman c. 574–656. Caliph of Islam
Heraclius c. 575–641. Byzantine emperor
Penda c. 577–654. King of Mercia
Umar c. 581–644. Adviser of the prophet Muhammad
Edwin c. 585–633. King of Northumbria
Harsha-Vardhana c. 590–c. 647. Supreme ruler of N India
Ali c. 598–661. Fourth caliph of Islam
Aidan, St c. 600–651. Irish monk
Cadwalader 7th century. Welsh hero
Caedmon 7th century. Earliest known English poet
Augustine, St died 605. English saint, first archbishop of Canterbury
Oswald, St c. 605–642. King of Northumbria
Ayesha 611–678. Wife of the prophet Muhammad
Hasan 625–670. Grandson of the prophet Muhammad
Adamnan, St c. 625–704. Irish monk
Husayn 627–680. Grandson of the prophet Muhammad
Wilfrid, St 634–709. Northumbrian bishop
Aldhelm, St c. 640–709. English prelate and scholar
Paulinus died c. 644. Roman missionary
Abd al-Malik ibn Marwan 647–705. Caliph of the Umayyad dynasty
Birinus, St died c. 650. English saint and bishop
Bede c. 673–735. English theologian and historian
John of Damascus, St c. 676–c. 754. Eastern Orthodox theologian
Wu Tao-tzu c. 680–c. 740. Chinese painter
Leo (III) the Isaurian c. 680–741. Byzantine emperor
Boniface, St 680–754. English Benedictine monk
Cuthbert, St died 687. Christian saint
Charles Martel c. 688–741. Frankish ruler
Shankara c. 700–c. 750. Hindu philosopher
Abū Hanīfah, al-Nu'man c. 700–780. Sunni religious leader and jurist
Cynewulf early 8th century. Anglo-Saxon poet
Li Po c. 705–762. Chinese poet
Walpurga, St c. 710–c. 779. English abbess
Tu Fu 712–770. Chinese poet
Pepin the Short c. 714–c. 768. King of the Franks
Malik, Abu Abdallah Malik ibn Anas 716–795. Muslim jurist
Geber, Latinized form of Jabir ibn Hayyan c. 721–c. 776. Arab alchemist
Abd-ar-Rahmān I 731–788. Emir of Córdoba
Abd-ar-Rahmān died 732. Moorish chief

11th century

12th century

13th century

15th century

Essex, Robert Devereux, 2nd Earl of Essex 1566–1601. English soldier and politician
James I 1566–1625. King of England and Scotland
Alleyn, Edward 1566–1626. English actor
Nashe, Thomas 1567–1601. English poet and satirist
Burbage, Richard c. 1567–1619. English actor
Campion, Thomas 1567–1620. English poet and musician
Francis of Sales, St 1567–1622. French bishop and theologian
Champlain, Samuel de 1567–1635. French pioneer, soldier, and explorer
Alexander, William 1567–1640. Scottish poet
Monteverdi, Claudio Giovanni Antonio 1567–1643. Italian composer
Aloysius, St 1568–1591. Italian Jesuit
Brueghel, Jan 1568–1625. Flemish painter; see ◊Brueghel family
Wotton, Henry 1568–1639. English poet and diplomat
Urban VIII (Maffeo Barberini) 1568–1644. Pope
Jahangir 1569–1627. Mogul emperor of India
Fawkes, Guy 1570–1606. English conspirator
Lippershey, Hans c. 1570–c. 1619. Dutch lensmaker
Coperario, John c.1570–1626. English composer
Middleton, Thomas c. 1570–1627. English dramatist
Aytoun, Robert 1570–1638. Scottish poet
Tradescant, John 1570–c. 1638. English gardener and botanist
Heywood, Thomas c. 1570–c. 1650. English actor and dramatist
Abbās I, the Great c. 1571–1629. Shah of Persia
Kepler, Johannes 1571–1630. German mathematician and astronomer
Cotton, Robert Bruce 1571–1631. English antiquary
Tirso de Molina c. 1571–1648. Spanish dramatist and monk
Donne, John 1572–1631. English poet
Dekker, Thomas c. 1572–c. 1632. English dramatist and pamphleteer
Jonson, Ben(jamin) 1572–1637. English dramatist, poet, and critic
Catesby, Robert 1573–1605. English conspirator
Caravaggio, Michelangelo Merisi da 1573–1610. Italian painter
Southampton, Henry Wriothesley, 3rd Earl of Southampton 1573–1624. English courtier
Marie de' Medici 1573–1642. Queen consort and regent of France
Laud, William 1573–1645. English cleric, archbishop of Canterbury
Scheiner, Christoph 1573–1650. German astronomer
Jones, Inigo 1573–1652. English architect
Anne of Denmark 1574–1619. Queen consort of James VI of Scotland
Fludd, Robert 1574–1637. British physician and alchemist
Stuart, Lady Arabella 1575–1615. Claimant to the English throne
Boehme, Jakob 1575–1624. German mystic
Tourneur, Cyril 1575–1626. English dramatist
Reni, Guido 1575–1642. Italian painter
Oughtred, William 1575–1660. English mathematician
Marston, John 1576–1634. English satirist and dramatist
Herrera, de, Francisco (the Elder) 1576–1656. Spanish painter
de la Warr, Thomas West 1577–1618. US colonial administrator
Purchas, Samuel c. 1577–1626. English compiler of travel books
Joseph, Père 1577–1638. French monk and politician
Burton, Robert 1577–1640. English philosopher
Rubens, Peter Paul 1577–1640. Flemish painter
Christian IV 1577–1648. King of Denmark and Norway
Elsheimer, Adam 1578–1610. German painter and etcher
Ferdinand II 1578–1637. Holy Roman emperor
Harvey, William 1578–1657. English physician
Fletcher, John 1579–1625. English dramatist
Calvert, George, 1st Baron Baltimore 1579–1632. English politician
Helmont, Jean Baptiste van 1579–1644. Belgian scientist
Snyders, Frans 1579–1657. Flemish painter
Squanto c. 1580–1622. North American Pawtuxet Indian
Webster, John c. 1580–c. 1625. English dramatist
Smith, John 1580–1631. English colonist
Vernier, Pierre c. 1580–1637. French engineer and inventor

Minuit, Peter c. 1580–1638. Dutch colonial administrator
Quevedo y Villegas, Francisco Gómez de 1580–1645. Spanish novelist and satirist
Vincent de Paul, St c. 1580–1660. French priest
Leven, Alexander Leslie c. 1580–1661. Scottish general
Gunter, Edmund 1581–1626. English mathematician
Snell, Willebrord van Roijen 1581–1626. Dutch mathematician and physicist
Domenichino 1581–1641. Italian painter and architect
Usher, James 1581–1656. Irish priest, archbishop of Armagh
Hals, Frans c. 1581–1666. Flemish painter
India, Sigismondo d' c. 1582–1629. Italian composer
Teniers, David 'the Elder' 1582–1649. Flemish religious painter; see ◊Teniers family
Allegri, Gregorio 1582–1652. Italian composer
Gibbons, Orlando 1583–1625. English composer
Wallenstein, Albrecht Eusebius Wenzel von 1583–1634. German general
Massinger, Philip 1583–1640. English dramatist
Frescobaldi, Girolamo 1583–1643. Italian composer
Grotius, Hugo 1583–1645. Dutch jurist and politician
Herbert, Edward 1583–1648. English philosopher
Oxenstjerna, Axel Gustafsson, Count 1583–1654. Swedish chancellor
Holborne, Anthony 1584–1602. English composer
Beaumont, Francis 1584–1616. English dramatist and poet
Baffin, William 1584–1622. English explorer and navigator
Pym, John 1584–1643. English Parliamentarian
Miyamoto, Musashi c. 1584–1645. Japanese samurai
Selden, John 1584–1654. English antiquarian
Standish, Myles 1584–1656. American colonial military leader
Avercamp, Hendrick 1585–1634. Dutch landscape painter
Jansen, Cornelius Otto 1585–1638. Dutch theologian
Richelieu, Armand Jean du Plessis de 1585–1642. French cardinal and politician
Rowley, William c. 1585–c. 1642. English actor and dramatist
Drummond, William 1585–1649. Scottish poet
Cotton, John 1585–1652. American Puritan leader
Schütz, Heinrich 1585–1672. German composer
Ford, John c. 1586–c. 1640. English poet and dramatist
Arundel, Thomas Howard 1586–1646. English politician and patron of the arts
Hooker, Thomas 1586–1647. British colonial religious leader
Olivares, Count-Duke of 1587–1645. Spanish prime minister
Tarleton, Richard died 1588. English theatrical clown
Terbrugghen, Hendrick 1588–1629. Dutch painter
Le Nain, Antoine c. 1588–1648. French painter
Mersenne, Marin 1588–1648. French mathematician and philosopher
Winthrop, John 1588–1649. American colonist and administrator
Rambouillet, Catherine de Vivonne, Marquise de Rambouillet 1588–1665. French society hostess
Hobbes, Thomas 1588–1679. English political philosopher
Abul Hasan 1589–1616. Mogul painter
Verney, Edmund 1590–1642. English courtier
Honthorst, Gerrit van 1590–1656. Dutch painter
Bradford, William 1590–1657. British colonial administrator
Massasoit c. 1590–1661. North American Wampanoag Indian leader
Velde, van de, Essaias c. 1591–1630. Dutch painter; see ◊Velde, van de family
Hutchinson, Anne Marbury 1591–1643. American colonial religious leader
Essex, Robert Devereux, 3rd Earl of Essex 1591–1646. English soldier
Ribera, José (Jusepe) de 1591–1652. Spanish painter
Lenthall, William 1591–1662. English lawyer
Guercino, Il 1591–1666. Italian painter
Herrick, Robert 1591–1674. English poet and cleric
Callot, Jacques 1592/93–1635. French engraver and painter

1601–50

Seki, Kowa c. 1642–1708. Japanese mathematician
Newton, Isaac 1642–1727. English physicist and mathematician
Duval, Claude 1643–1670. English criminal
la Salle, René Robert Cavelier, Sieur de la Salle 1643–1687. French explorer
Van Cortlandt, Stephanus 1643–1700. Dutch-American colonial official
Burnet, Gilbert 1643–1715. English historian and bishop
Jeffreys of Wem, George, 1st Baron Jeffreys of Wem 1644–1689. Welsh judge
Bashō 1644–1694. Japanese poet
Biber, Heinrich Ignaz Franz von 1644–1704. Bohemian composer and violinist
Abraham a Sancta Clara 1644–1709. German preacher
La Vallière, Louise Françoise de la Baume le Blanc 1644–1710. Mistress of Louis XIV of France
Römer, Ole (or Olaus) Christensen 1644–1710. Danish astronomer
Kino, Eusebio Francisco c. 1644–1711. Jesuit missionary
Penn, William 1644–1718. American Quaker colonist
Stradivari, Antonio c. 1644–1737. Italian stringed instrumentmaker
La Bruyère, Jean de 1645–1696. French essayist
Joliet (or Jolliet), Louis 1645–1700. Canadian explorer
Kidd, 'Captain' William c. 1645–1701. Scottish pirate
Charpentier, Marc-Antoine c. 1645–1704. French composer
Hardouin-Mansart, Jules 1646–1708. French architect
Leibniz, Gottfried Wilhelm 1646–1716. German mathematician, philosopher, and diplomat
Flamsteed, John 1646–1719. English astronomer
Kneller, Godfrey 1646–1723. English painter
Bacon, Nathaniel 1647–1676. American colonial leader
Rochester, John Wilmot, 2nd Earl of Rochester 1647–1680. English poet and courtier
Bayle, Pierre 1647–1706. French critic and philosopher
Papin, Denis 1647–c. 1712. French physicist
Oates, Titus 1648–1705. English conspirator
Blow, John 1648–1708. English composer
Aldrich, Henry 1648–1710. English ecclesiastic
Gibbons, Grinling 1648–1720. Dutch woodcarver
Monmouth, James Scott, 1st Duke of Monmouth 1649–1685. Claimant to the British throne
Claverhouse, John Graham c. 1649–1689. Scottish soldier
Portland, William Bentinck, 1st Earl of Portland 1649–1709. Dutch politician
Portsmouth, Louise Renée de Kéroualle, Duchess of Portsmouth 1649–1734. Mistress of Charles II of England
Gwyn, Nell (Eleanor) 1650–1687. English actress
Cassegrain c. 1650–1700. French inventor
William (III) of Orange 1650–1702. King of Great Britain and Ireland
Shovell, Cloudesley 1650–1707. English admiral
Savery, Thomas c. 1650–1715. British engineer
Talman, William 1650–1719. English architect
Marlborough, John Churchill, 1st Duke of Marlborough 1650–1722. English soldier
Collier, Jeremy 1650–1726. British cleric

1651–1700

Cruz, Juana Inés de la, Sor 1651–1695. Mexican poet and dramatist
Dampier, William 1651–1715. English explorer and hydrographic surveyor
Fénelon, François de Salignac de la Mothe 1651–1715. French writer and ecclesiastic
Otway, Thomas 1652–1685. English dramatist
Tate, Nahum 1652–1715. Irish poet
Lee, Nathaniel c. 1653–1692. English dramatist
Benbow, John 1653–1702. English admiral
Pachelbel, Johann 1653–1706. German organist and composer
Corelli, Arcangelo 1653–1713. Italian composer and violinist

Chikamatsu, Monzaemon 1653–1725. Japanese dramatist
Bernoulli, Jakob 1654–1705. Swiss mathematician
Vendôme, Louis Joseph, Duc de Vendôme 1654–1712. Marshal of France
Abbadie, Jacques 1654–1727. French ecclesiastic and writer
Charles XI 1655–1697. King of Sweden
Fletcher, Andrew of Saltoun 1655–1716. Scottish patriot
Har Krishen 1656–1664. Eighth guru of Sikhism
Halley, Edmond 1656–1742. English astronomer
Frederick I 1657–1713. King of Prussia
Delalande, Michel-Richard 1657–1726. French organist and composer
Ogata, Kōrin 1658–1716. Japanese painter and designer
Mary of Modena 1658–1718. Queen consort of James II of England
Purcell, Henry c. 1659–1695. English composer
Ricci, Sebastiano 1659–1734. Venetian painter
Rigaud, Hyacinthe 1659–1743. French artist
Scarlatti, (Pietro) Alessandro (Gaspare) 1660–1725. Italian composer
George I 1660–1727. King of Great Britain and Ireland
Defoe, Daniel 1660–1731. English writer
Stahl, Georg Ernst 1660–1734. German chemist
Fux, Johann Joseph 1660–1741. Austrian composer
Southerne, Thomas 1660–1746. English playwright and poet
Sloane, Hans 1660–1753. British physician
Charles II 1661–1700. King of Spain
Iberville, Pierre Le Moyne, Sieur d' 1661–1706. French colonial administrator and explorer
Halifax, Charles Montagu, 1st Earl of Halifax 1661–1715. British financier
Harley, Robert 1661–1724. British politician
Hawksmoor, Nicholas 1661–1736. English architect
Mary II 1662–1694. Queen of England, Scotland, and Ireland
Atterbury, Francis 1662–1732. English bishop and politician
Bentley, Richard 1662–1742. English classical scholar
Mather, Cotton 1663–1728. American theologian and writer
Newcomen, Thomas 1663–1729. English steam pioneer
Byng, George 1663–1733. British admiral
Eugène 1663–1736. Prince of Savoy
Bracegirdle, Anne c. 1663–1748. English actress
Prior, Matthew 1664–1721. British poet and diplomat
Vanbrugh, John 1664–1726. English architect and dramatist
Alberoni, Giulio 1664–1752. Spanish-Italian priest and politician
Anne 1665–1714. Queen of Great Britain and Ireland
Cristofori, Bartolommeo di Francesco 1665–1731. Italian harpsichordmaker
Gobind Singh 1666–1708. Tenth guru of Sikhism
Centlivre, Susannah c. 1667–c. 1723. English dramatist and actress
Arbuthnot, John 1667–1735. Scottish writer and physician
Swift, Jonathan 1667–1745. Irish satirist
Lovat, Simon Fraser c. 1667–1747. Scottish Jacobite
Bernoulli, Johann 1667–1748. Swiss mathematician
Pepusch, Johann Christoph 1667–1752. German composer
Moivre, Abraham De 1667–1754. French mathematician
Couperin, François le Grand 1668–1733. French composer
Boerhaave, Hermann 1668–1738. Dutch physician and chemist
Archer, Thomas 1668–1743. English architect
Vico, Giambattista (Giovanni Battista) 1668–1744. Italian philosopher
Hildebrandt, Johann Lucas von 1668–1745. Austrian architect
Le Sage, Alain-René 1668–1747. French novelist and dramatist
Coram, Thomas 1668–1751. English philanthropist
Clarke, Jeremiah c. 1669–1707. English composer
Congreve, William 1670–1729. English dramatist and poet
Berwick, James Fitzjames, 1st Duke of Berwick 1670–1734. French marshal
Shaftesbury, Anthony Ashley Cooper, 3rd Earl of Shaftesbury 1671–1713. English philosopher
Rob Roy 1671–1734. Scottish outlaw
Grandi, Guido 1671–1742. Italian mathematician

Albinoni, Tomaso 1671–1751. Italian composer
Addison, Joseph 1672–1719. English writer
Peter (I) the Great 1672–1725. Tsar of Russia
Steele, Richard 1672–1729. Irish essayist
Rowe, Nicholas 1674–1718. English dramatist and poet
Townshend, Charles 1674–1738. English politician and
    agriculturalist
Tull, Jethro 1674–1741. English agriculturist
Watts, Isaac 1674–1748. English hymn writer
Nash, 'Beau' (Richard) 1674–1762. British dandy
Hotteterre, Jacques-Martin 1674–1763. French musician
Saint-Simon, Louis de Rouvroy, Duc de 1675–1755. French
    soldier, courtier, and politician
Selkirk, Alexander 1676–1721. Scottish sailor
Campbell, Colen 1676–1729. Scottish architect
Boyle, Charles 1676–1731. Irish soldier and diplomat
Nithsdale, William Maxwell, 5th Earl of Nithsdale 1676–1744.
    English Jacobite leader
Walpole, Robert 1676–1745. British prime minister
Farquhar, George c. 1677–1707. Irish dramatist
Darby, Abraham 1677–1717. English iron manufacturer
Hales, Stephen 1677–1761. English scientist
Joseph I 1678–1711. Holy Roman emperor
Vivaldi, Antonio Lucio 1678–1741. Italian composer
Bolingbroke, Henry St John, 1st Viscount Bolingbroke 1678–1751.
    British politician and political philosopher
Zelenka, Jan Dismas 1679–1745. Bohemian composer
Wolff, Christian 1679–1754. German philosopher, mathematician,
    and scientist
Bienville, Jean Baptiste Le Moyne, Sieur de 1680–1768. French
    colonial administrator
Bering, Vitus Jonassen 1681–1741. Danish explorer
Telemann, Georg Philipp 1681–1767. German composer
Charles XII 1682–1718. King of Sweden
Roberts, Bartholomew c. 1682–1722. British merchant-navy
    captain
Wild, Jonathan c. 1682–1725. English criminal
Gibbs, James 1682–1754. Scottish architect
Morgagni, Giovanni Battista 1682–1771. Italian anatomist
Caroline of Anspach 1683–1737. Queen consort of George II of
    Great Britain
Philip V 1683–1746. King of Spain
Réaumur, Réné Antoine Ferchault de 1683–1757. French scientist
George II 1683–1760. King of Great Britain and Ireland
Rameau, Jean-Philippe 1683–1764. French organist and composer
Young, Edward 1683–1765. English poet and dramatist
Watteau, (Jean-)Antoine 1684–1721. French painter
Catherine I 1684–1727. Empress of Russia
Kent, William 1684–1748. English architect
Vernon, Edward 1684–1757. English admiral
Gay, John 1685–1732. English poet and dramatist
Charles VI 1685–1740. Holy Roman emperor
Bach, Johann Sebastian 1685–1750. German composer
Berkeley, George 1685–1753. Irish philosopher and cleric
Scarlatti, (Giuseppe) Domenico 1685–1757. Italian composer
Handel, Georg Friedrich 1685–1759. German composer
Ketch, Jack died 1686. English executioner
Fahrenheit, Gabriel Daniel 1686–1736. Dutch physicist
Ramsay, Allan 1686–1758. Scottish poet
Law, William 1686–1761. English cleric
Neumann, (Johann) Balthasar 1687–1753. German architect
Geminiani, Francesco 1687–1762. Italian violinist and composer
Stukeley, William 1687–1765. English antiquarian and
    archaeologist
Frederick William I 1688–1740. King of Prussia
Pope, Alexander 1688–1744. English poet and satirist
Marivaux, Pierre Carlet de Chamblain de 1688–1763. French
    novelist and dramatist
James Francis Edward Stuart 1688–1766. Claimant to the British
    throne

Swedenborg, Emanuel 1688–1772. Swedish mystic and scientist
Adam, William 1689–1748. Scottish architect; see ◊Adam family
Montesquieu, Charles Louis de Secondat, Baron de la Brède
    1689–1755. French historian
Richardson, Samuel 1689–1761. English novelist
Montagu, Lady Mary Wortley 1689–1762. English society hostess
Carey, Henry c. 1690–1743. English poet and musician
Lancret, Nicolas 1690–1743. French painter
Cave, Edward 1691–1754. British printer
Lecouvreur, Adrienne 1692–1730. French actress
Butler, Joseph 1692–1752. English priest and theologian
Tartini, Giuseppe 1692–1770. Italian composer and violinist
Bradley, James 1693–1762. English astronomer
Newcastle, Thomas Pelham-Holles, 1st Duke of Newcastle
    1693–1768. British prime minister
Harrison, John 1693–1776. English clock- and instrumentmaker
Rysbrack, Jan Michiel 1694–1770. British sculptor
Chesterfield, Philip Dormer Stanhope, 4th Earl of Chesterfield
    1694–1773. English politician and writer
Quesnay, François 1694–1774. French economic philosopher
Voltaire 1694–1778. French writer and philosopher
Burlington, Richard Boyle, 3rd Earl of Burlington 1695–1753.
    Anglo-Irish architectural patron
Saxe, (Hermann) Maurice, Comte de 1696–1750. French marshal
Mahmud I 1696–1754. Ottoman sultan
Pelham, Henry 1696–1754. British prime minister
Weiser, (Johann) Conrad 1696–1760. American colonial public
    official
Tiepolo, Giovanni Battista (Giambattista) 1696–1770. Italian
    painter
Oglethorpe, James Edward 1696–1785. English colonizer of
    Georgia
Charles VII 1697–1745. Holy Roman emperor
Zenger, John Peter 1697–1746. American printer and newspaper
    editor
Anson, George 1697–1762. English admiral
Dupleix, Joseph-François 1697–1763. French colonial
    administrator
Prévost d'Exiles, Antoine François 1697–1763. French novelist
Hogarth, William 1697–1764. English painter and engraver
Leclair, Jean-Marie 1697–1764. French violinist and composer
Canaletto, Antonio 1697–1768. Italian painter
Quantz, Johann Joachim 1697–1773. German flautist and
    composer
Maclaurin, Colin 1698–1746. Scottish mathematician
Calas, Jean 1698–1762. French Protestant
Metastasio 1698–1782. Italian poet and librettist
Chardin, Jean-Baptiste-Siméon 1699–1779. French painter
Thomson, James 1700–1748. Scottish poet
Bernoulli, Daniel 1700–1782. Swiss mathematical physicist

1701–25

Celsius, Anders 1701–1744. Swedish astronomer, physicist, and
    mathematician
Cruden, Alexander 1701–1770. Scottish biblical scholar
La Condamine, Charles Marie de 1701–1774. French soldier and
    geographer
Sheppard, Jack (John) 1702–1724. English criminal
Bayes, Thomas 1702–1761. English mathematician
Edwards, Jonathan 1703–1758. US theologian
Boucher, François 1703–1770. French painter
Wesley, John 1703–1791. English founder of Methodism
Cramer, Gabriel 1704–1752. Swiss mathematician
Byng, John 1704–1757. British admiral
Aram, Eugene 1704–1759. English murderer
Kay, John 1704–c. 1780. English inventor
Turpin, Dick (Richard) 1705–1739. English highwayman
Wood, John, the Elder c. 1705–1754. English architect

Appert, Nicolas François *c.* 1750–1841. French pioneer of food preservation

Herschel, Caroline Lucretia 1750–1848. English astronomer

1751–75

André, John 1751–1780. British army major
Ledyard, John 1751–1789. American explorer
Gordon, Lord George 1751–1793. British agitator
Sheraton, Thomas 1751–1806. English designer
Sheridan, Richard Brinsley 1751–1816. Irish dramatist and politician
Madison, James 1751–1836. Fourth president of the USA
Eldon, John Scott, 1st Earl of Eldon 1751–1838. English politician
Prévost, Pierre 1751–1839. Swiss physicist
Chatterton, Thomas 1752–1770. English poet
Cozens, John Robert 1752–1797. English painter
Clark, George Rogers 1752–1818. American military leader and explorer
Repton, Humphry 1752–1818. English garden designer
Clementi, Muzio 1752–1832. Italian pianist and composer
Freneau, Philip Morin 1752–1832. US poet
Legendre, Adrien-Marie 1752–1833. French mathematician
Jacquard, Joseph Marie 1752–1834. French textile manufacturer
Nash, John 1752–1835. English architect
Ross, Betsy 1752–1836. American seamstress
Engleheart, George 1752–1839. English painter
Burney, Fanny (Frances) 1752–1840. English novelist and diarist
Utamaro, Kitagawa 1753–1806. Japanese artist
Blanchard, Jean Pierre François 1753–1809. French balloonist
Hidalgo y Costilla, Miguel 1753–1811. Mexican priest and revolutionary leader
Rumford, Benjamin Thompson, Count von Rumford 1753–1814. British physicist
Achard, Franz Karl 1753–1821. German chemist
Inchbald, Elizabeth 1753–1821. English author and actress
Carnot, Lazare Nicolas Marguerite 1753–1823. French general and politician
Crompton, Samuel 1753–1827. British inventor
Bewick, Thomas 1753–1828. English wood engraver
Ransome, Robert 1753–1830. English ironfounder and agricultural engineer
Soane, John 1753–1837. English architect
Brissot, Jacques Pierre 1754–1793. French revolutionary leader
Louis XVI 1754–1793. King of France
Roland de la Platière, Jeanne Marie Manon 1754–1793. French politician
Paul I 1754–1801. Tsar of Russia
Barlow, Joel 1754–1812. US poet and diplomat
Bligh, William 1754–1817. English sailor
Bowdler, Thomas 1754–1825. English editor
L'Enfant, Pierre Charles 1754–1825. US architect
Proust, Joseph Louis 1754–1826. French chemist
Spode, Josiah 1754–1827. English potter
Crabbe, George 1754–1832. English poet
McCauley, Mary Ludwig Hays 1754–1832. American war heroine
Martin, Richard 1754–1834. Irish landowner and lawyer
Talleyrand-Périgord, Charles Maurice de 1754–1838. French politician and diplomat
Murdock, William 1754–1839. Scottish inventor and technician
Coke, Thomas William, 1st Earl of Leicester 1754–1842. English agricultural pioneer
Hale, Nathan 1755–1776. American revolutionary soldier
Marie Antoinette 1755–1793. Queen consort of Louis XVI of France
Evans, Oliver 1755–1819. US engineer
Louis XVIII 1755–1824. King of France
Parkinson, James 1755–1824. British neurologist
Brillat-Savarin, Jean Anthelme 1755–1826. French gastronome

Flaxman, John 1755–1826. English sculptor and illustrator
Stuart, Gilbert Charles 1755–1828. American painter
Barras, Paul François Jean Nicolas, Count 1755–1829. French revolutionary
Siddons, Sarah 1755–1831. English actress
Marshall, John 1755–1835. US politician and jurist
Vigée-Lebrun, (Marie) Elisabeth (Louise) 1755–1842. French painter
Mozart, (Johann Chrysostom) Wolfgang Amadeus 1756–1791. Austrian composer and performer
Collins, David 1756–1810. British administrator in Australia
Lee, Henry 1756–1818. American military and political leader
Raeburn, Henry 1756–1823. Scottish painter
Chladni, Ernst Florens Friedrich 1756–1827. German physicist
Burr, Aaron 1756–1836. US vice president
Godwin, William 1756–1836. English philosopher and novelist
McAdam, John Loudon 1756–1836. Scottish engineer
Fitzherbert, Maria Anne 1756–1837. Wife of the Prince of Wales (later George IV)
Trumbull, John 1756–1843. American artist
Vancouver, George 1757–1798. British navigator
Hamilton, Alexander 1757–1804. US politician
Gillray, James 1757–1815. English caricaturist
Canova, Antonio, Marquese d'Ischia 1757–1822. Italian sculptor
Kemble, (John) Philip 1757–1823. English actor-manager
Blake, William 1757–1827. English poet and artist
Rowlandson, Thomas 1757–1827. English artist
Charles Augustus 1757–1828. Grand Duke of Saxe-Weimar
Lafayette, Marie Joseph Paul Yves Roch Gilbert de Motier 1757–1834. French soldier and politician
Telford, Thomas 1757–1834. Scottish civil engineer
Charles X 1757–1836. King of France
Addington, Henry, 1st Viscount Sidmouth 1757–1844. British prime minister
Robespierre, Maximilien François Marie Isidore de 1758–1794. French politician
Nelson, Horatio 1758–1805. English admiral
Dessalines, Jean Jacques *c.* 1758–1806. Emperor of Haiti
King, Philip Gidley 1758–1808. English governor of New South Wales
Hoppner, John 1758–1810. English painter
Grose, Francis 1758–1814. English colonial administrator
Masséna, André 1758–1817. Marshal of France
Prud'hon, Pierre Paul 1758–1823. French painter
Gall, Franz Joseph 1758–1828. Austrian anatomist
Monroe, James 1758–1831. Fifth president of the USA
Nasmyth, Alexander 1758–1840. Scottish painter
Olbers, Heinrich Wilhelm Matthäus 1758–1840. German astronomer
Webster, Noah 1758–1843. US lexicographer
Danton, Georges Jacques 1759–1794. French revolutionary
Burns, Robert 1759–1796. Scottish poet
Wollstonecraft, Mary 1759–1797. British feminist
Schiller, Johann Christoph Friedrich von 1759–1805. German dramatist, poet, and historian
Lunardi, Vincenzo 1759–1806. Italian balloonist
Pitt, William, the Younger 1759–1806. British prime minister
Porson, Richard 1759–1808. British scholar
Fouché, Joseph, Duke of Otranto 1759–1820. French politician
Weems, Mason Locke 1759–1825. American writer and cleric
Cockerill, William 1759–1832. English engineer
Tench, Watkin *c.* 1759–1833. Australian military officer
Wilberforce, William 1759–1833. English reformer
Grenville, William Wyndham 1759–1834. British politician
Redouté, Pierre Joseph 1759–1840. French painter
Beauharnais, Alexandre, Vicomte de 1760–1794. French liberal aristocrat and general
Desmoulins, (Lucie Simplice) Camille (Benoist) 1760–1794. French revolutionary
Babeuf, François-Noël 1760–1797. French revolutionary journalist

Clinton, De Witt 1769–1828. US politician
Lawrence, Thomas 1769–1830. English painter
Cuvier, Georges Léopold Chrétien Frédéric Dagobert 1769–1832.
  French comparative anatomist
Accum, Friedrich Christian 1769–1838. German chemist
Hardy, Thomas Masterman 1769–1839. British sailor
Smith, William 1769–1839. English geologist
Abinger, James Scarlett 1769–1844. British politician and judge
Campbell, Robert 1769–1846. Australian pioneer settler
Brunel, Marc Isambard 1769–1849. British engineer
Mehmet Ali 1769–1849. Governor of Egypt
Soult, Nicolas Jean de Dieu 1769–1851. Marshal of France
Wellington, Arthur Wellesley, 1st Duke of Wellington 1769–1852.
  British soldier and prime minister
Humboldt, (Friedrich Wilhelm Heinrich) Alexander 1769–1859.
  German scientist and explorer
Belgrano, Manuel 1770–1820. Argentine revolutionary
Thistlewood, Arthur 1770–1820. English Radical
Beethoven, Ludwig van 1770–1827. German composer and pianist
Canning, George 1770–1827. British prime minister
Liverpool, Robert Banks Jenkinson, 2nd Earl Liverpool 1770–1828.
  British prime minister
Caley, George 1770–1829. English botanist and explorer
Huskisson, William 1770–1830. British politician
Hegel, Georg Wilhelm Friedrich 1770–1831. German philosopher
Ram Mohun Roy 1770–1833. Indian religious reformer
Hogg, James 1770–1835. Scottish novelist and poet
Clark, William 1770–1838. US explorer; see ◊Lewis and Clark
Frederick William III 1770–1840. King of Prussia
Hölderlin, (Johann Christian) Friedrich 1770–1843. German poet
Sequoya, George Guess c. 1770–1843. American Indian scholar
  and leader
Thorvaldsen, Bertel c. 1770–1844. Danish sculptor
Wordsworth, William 1770–1850. English poet
Thompson, David 1770–1857. Canadian explorer and surveyor
Czartoryski, Adam Jerzy 1770–1861. Polish president and general
Bichat, Marie François Xavier 1771–1802. French physician
Fra Diavolo c. 1771–1806. Italian brigand
Park, Mungo 1771–1806. Scottish explorer
Brown, Charles Brockden 1771–1810. US novelist and magazine
  editor
Maudslay, Henry 1771–1831. English engineer and toolmaker
Scott, Walter 1771–1832. Scottish novelist and poet
Trevithick, Richard 1771–1833. English engineer
Senefelder, (Johann Nepomuk Franz) Alois 1771–1834. German
  engraver
Smith, Sydney 1771–1845. English writer
Cumberland, Ernest Augustus 1771–1851. King of Hanover
Place, Francis 1771–1854. English Radical
Wordsworth, Dorothy 1771–1855. English writer
Cramer, Johann Baptist 1771–1858. German composer and pianist
Owen, Robert 1771–1858. British social reformer
Novalis 1772–1801. German poet
Ricardo, David 1772–1823. English economist
Schlegel, (Karl Wilhelm) Friedrich von 1772–1829. German
  literary critic
Coleridge, Samuel Taylor 1772–1834. English poet
Fourier, (François Marie) Charles 1772–1837. French socialist
Maelzel, Johann Nepomuk 1772–1838. German inventor
William I 1772–1844. King of the Netherlands
Stevenson, Robert 1772–1850. Scottish engineer
Quincy, Josiah 1772–1864. US public official
Young, Thomas 1773–1829. British physicist, physician, and
  Egyptologist
Mill, James 1773–1836. Scottish philosopher
Bowditch, Nathaniel 1773–1838. US astronomer
Mohs, Friedrich 1773–1839. German mineralogist
Holland, Henry Richard Vassall Fox, 3rd Baron Holland
  1773–1840. British politician
Harrison, William Henry 1773–1841. Ninth president of the USA

Colles, Abraham 1773–1843. Irish surgeon
Jeffrey, Francis, Lord 1773–1850. Scottish lawyer and literary critic
Louis Philippe 1773–1850. King of France
Tieck, (Johann) Ludwig 1773–1853. German poet and folklorist
Cayley, George 1773–1857. English aviation pioneer
Brown, Robert 1773–1858. Scottish botanist
Metternich, Klemens Wenzel Nepomuk Lothar, Prince von
  Metternich 1773–1859. Austrian politician
Brisbane, Thomas Makdougall 1773–1860. Scottish colonial
  administrator
Lewis, Meriwether 1774–1809. US explorer; see ◊Lewis and Clark
Flinders, Matthew 1774–1814. English navigator
Seton, St Elizabeth Ann 1774–1821. US religious leader
Lycett, Joseph c. 1774–1825. Australian painter
Bickford, William 1774–1834. English inventor
Henry, William 1774–1836. English chemist and physician
Bentinck, Lord William Henry Cavendish 1774–1839. British
  colonial administrator
Friedrich, Caspar David 1774–1840. German painter
Bell, Charles 1774–1842. Scottish anatomist and surgeon
Southey, Robert 1774–1843. English poet and author
Baily, Francis 1774–1844. British astronomer
Chapman, John ('Johnny Appleseed') 1774–1845. US pioneer and
  folk hero
Lawson, William 1774–1850. English pastoralist and explorer
Beaufort, Francis 1774–1857. British admiral and hydrographer
Biot, Jean Baptiste 1774–1862. French physicist
Girtin, Thomas 1775–1802. English painter
Malus, Etienne Louis 1775–1812. French physicist
Austen, Jane 1775–1817. English novelist
Lowell, Francis Cabot 1775–1817. US industrialist
Lewis, Matthew Gregory 1775–1818. English writer
Lamb, Charles 1775–1834. English essayist and critic
Ampère, André Marie 1775–1836. French physicist and
  mathematician
Bonaparte, Lucien 1775–1840. Prince of Canino; see ◊Bonaparte
  family
Crockford, William 1775–1844. British gambler
O'Connell, Daniel 1775–1847. Irish politician
Turner, Joseph Mallord William 1775–1851. English painter
Grotefend, Georg Friedrich 1775–1853. German scholar
Kemble, Charles 1775–1854. English actor-manager
Schelling, Friedrich Wilhelm Joseph von 1775–1854. German
  philosopher
Bolyai, (Farkas) Wolfgang 1775–1856. Hungarian mathematician
Westmacott, Richard 1775–1856. English sculptor
Vidocq, François Eugène 1775–1857. French criminal and spy
Bahadur Shah II 1775–1862. Last of the Mogul emperors of India
Beecher, Lyman 1775–1863. US preacher
Landor, Walter Savage 1775–1864. English poet and essayist
Robinson, Henry Crabb 1775–1867. English writer

1776–1800

Ritter, Johann Wilhelm 1776–1810. German physicist
Hoffmann, Amadeus (Ernst Theodor Wilhelm) 1776–1822.
  German composer and writer
Germain, Sophie 1776–1831. French mathematician
Niebuhr, Barthold Georg 1776–1831. German historian
Valle, José Cecilio del 1776–1834. Central American politician
Constable, John 1776–1837. English artist
Wesley, Samuel 1776–1837. English organist and composer
Stanhope, Hester Lucy 1776–1839. English traveller
Avogadro, Amedeo, Conte di Quaregna 1776–1856. Italian
  physicist
Fraser, Simon 1776–1862. Canadian explorer
Runge, Philipp Otto 1777–1810. German painter
Kleist, (Bernd) Heinrich (Wilhelm) von 1777–1811. German
  dramatist

Michelet, Jules 1798–1874. French historian

Mosquera, Tomás Cipriano de 1798–1878. Colombian general and political thinker

Pushkin, Aleksandr Sergeyevich 1799–1837. Russian poet and writer

Hood, Thomas 1799–1845. English poet and humorist

Balzac, Honoré de 1799–1850. French writer

Almeida-Garrett, João Baptista da Silva Leitão 1799–1854. Portuguese poet and politician

Catherwood, Frederick 1799–1854. English topographical and archaeological artist

Garrett, Almeida 1799–1854. Portuguese poet, novelist, and dramatist

Acton, Eliza 1799–1859. English cookery writer and poet

Oscar I 1799–1859. King of Sweden and Norway

Fellows, Charles 1799–1860. English archaeologist

Lonsdale, William 1799–1864. English colonial administrator

Bell, Patrick 1799–1869. Scottish inventor

Derby, Edward George Geoffrey Smith Stanley, 14th Earl of Derby 1799–1869. British prime minister

Poiseuille, Jean Léonard Marie 1799–1869. French physiologist

Argelander, Friedrich Wilhelm August 1799–1875. Prussian astronomer

Cameron, Simon 1799–1889. US political leader

Turner, Nat 1800–1831. US slave and Baptist preacher

Aarestrup, Carl Ludvig Emil 1800–1856. Danish poet

Brown, John 1800–1859. US slavery abolitionist

Macaulay, Thomas Babington 1800–1859. English historian

Goodyear, Charles 1800–1860. US inventor

Ross, James Clark 1800–1862. English explorer

Parsons, William 1800–1867. Irish astronomer, engineer, and politician

Clarendon, George William Frederick Villiers 1800–1870. British diplomat and politician

McGuffey, William Holmes 1800–1873. US educator

Fillmore, Millard 1800–1874. 13th president of the USA

Migne, Jacques Paul 1800–1875. French curate and religious publisher

Talbot, William Henry Fox 1800–1877. English photographic pioneer

Pusey, Edward Bouverie 1800–1882. English priest

Wöhler, Friedrich 1800–1882. German chemist

Holloway, Thomas 1800–1883. English manufacturer and philanthropist

Dumas, Jean Baptiste André 1800–1884. French chemist

Barnes, William 1800–1886. English poet and cleric

Chadwick, Edwin 1800–1890. English social reformer

Bancroft, George 1800–1891. US diplomat and historian

Moltke, Helmuth Carl Bernhard, Count von Moltke 1800–1891. Prussian general

1801–10

Bonington, Richard Parkes 1801–1828. English painter

Bellini, Vincenzo 1801–1835. Italian composer of operas

Cole, Thomas 1801–1848. US painter

Bradshaw, George 1801–1853. British publisher

d'Orsay, Alfred Guillaume Gabriel 1801–1857. French dandy

Müller, Johannes Peter 1801–1858. German comparative anatomist

Baedeker, Karl 1801–1859. German editor and publisher

Flores, Juan José 1801–1864. Ecuadorian president

Elkington, George Richards 1801–1865. English inventor

Paxton, Joseph 1801–1865. English architect

Plücker, Julius 1801–1868. German mathematician and physicist

Farragut, David Glasgow 1801–1870. US admiral

Urquiza, Justo José de 1801–1870. Argentine president

Seward, William Henry 1801–1872. US public official

Labrouste, (Pierre François) Henri 1801–1875. French architect

La Trobe, Charles Joseph 1801–1875. Australian administrator

Lane, Edward William 1801–1876. English traveller and translator

Young, Brigham 1801–1877. US Mormon leader

Martens, Conrad 1801–1878. Australian painter

Miller, William 1801–1880. Welsh crystallographer

Shaftesbury, Anthony Ashley Cooper, 7th Earl of Shaftesbury 1801–1885. British politician

Fechner, Gustav Theodor 1801–1887. German psychologist

Woolsey, Theodore Dwight 1801–1889. US educationalist

Newman, John Henry 1801–1890. English cardinal and theologian

Airy, George Biddell 1801–1892. English astronomer

Abel, Niels Henrik 1802–1829. Norwegian mathematician

Bentinck, Lord (William) George (Frederic Cavendish) 1802–1848. English politician

Hess, Germain Henri 1802–1850. Russian chemist

Coleridge, Sara 1802–1852. English editor and writer

Bolyai, János 1802–1860. Hungarian mathematician

Wiseman, Nicholas Patrick Stephen 1802–1865. British priest, archbishop of Westminster

Fourneyron, Benoit 1802–1867. French engineer

Dumas, Alexandre (Dumas *père*) 1802–1870. French author

Hill, David Octavius 1802–1870. Scottish photographer; see ◊Hill and Adamson

Landseer, Edwin Henry 1802–1873. English painter, sculptor, and engraver

Wheatstone, Charles 1802–1875. English physicist and inventor

Martineau, Harriet 1802–1876. English journalist, economist, and novelist

Welles, Gideon 1802–1878. US politician

Child, Lydia Maria Francis 1802–1880. US writer and social critic

Hugo, Victor Marie 1802–1885. French poet, novelist, and dramatist

Dix, Dorothea Lynde 1802–1887. US educator and medical reformer

Hopkins, Mark 1802–1887. US educator and religious leader

Allen, Horatio 1802–1890. US civil engineer

Grey, Henry George 1802–1894. British politician

Kossuth, Lajos 1802–1894. Hungarian revolutionary leader

Lacenaire, Pierre-François 1803–1836. French criminal

Tristan, Flora 1803–1844. French socialist writer and activist

Beddoes, Thomas Lovell 1803–1849. English poet and dramatist

Doppler, Christian Johann 1803–1853. Austrian physicist

Blackburn, James 1803–1854. Australian engineer

Adam, Adolphe Charles 1803–1856. French composer

Stephenson, Robert 1803–1859. English civil engineer

Outram, James 1803–1863. British general

Brooke, James 1803–1868. British colonial administrator

Berlioz, (Louis) Hector 1803–1869. French composer

Mérimée, Prosper 1803–1870. French author

Beaufoy Merlin, Henry 1803–1873. Australian documentary photographer

Liebig, Justus, Baron von 1803–1873. German chemist

Lytton, Edward George Earle Lytton Bulwer 1803–1873. English writer

Ruhmkorff, Heinrich Daniel 1803–1877. French instrumentmaker

Abbott, Jacob 1803–1879. US author

Roon, Albrecht Theodor Emil, Graf von 1803–1879. Prussian field marshal

Borrow, George Henry 1803–1881. English author and traveller

Challis, James 1803–1882. English astronomer

Emerson, Ralph Waldo 1803–1882. US philosopher, essayist, and poet

Hansom, Joseph Aloysius 1803–1882. English architect and inventor

Whitworth, Joseph 1803–1887. English engineer

Ericsson, John 1803–1889. US engineer

Adler, Nathan Marcus 1803–1890. Chief rabbi of the British Empire

Jacobi, Carl Gustav Jacob 1804–1851. German mathematician

Glinka, Mikhail Ivanovich 1804–1857. Russian composer

Hawthorne, Nathaniel 1804–1864. US writer
Cobden, Richard 1804–1865. British politician and economist
Lenz, Heinrich Friedrich Emil 1804–1865. Russian physicist
Aldridge, Ira Frederick 1804–1867. US actor
Baxter, George 1804–1867. English engraver and printmaker
Odoyevsky, Vladimir 1804–1869. Russian writer
Pierce, Franklin 1804–1869. 14th president of the USA
Sainte-Beuve, Charles Augustin 1804–1869. French critic and historian
Feuerbach, Ludwig Andreas 1804–1872. German philosopher
Sand, George 1804–1876. French author
Stokes, William 1804–1878. Irish physician
Disraeli, Benjamin 1804–1881. British prime minister and novelist
Gould, John 1804–1881. English zoologist
Schleiden, Matthias Jakob 1804–1881. German botanist
Taglioni, Marie 1804–1884. Italian dancer
Weber, Wilhelm Eduard 1804–1891. German physicist
Owen, Richard 1804–1892. British anatomist and palaeontologist
Burnes, Alexander 1805–1841. Scottish soldier, linguist, and diplomat
Smith, Joseph 1805–1844. US founder of the Mormon sect
Stephens, John Lloyd 1805–1852. US explorer
Dirichlet, (Peter Gustav) Lejeune 1805–1859. German mathematician
Tocqueville, Alexis Charles Henri Clérel de 1805–1859. French politician, sociologist, and historian
Locke, Joseph 1805–1860. English railway engineer
O'Brien, James Bronterre 1805–1864. Irish Chartist
Surtees, R(obert) S(mith) 1805–1864. English novelist
Fitzroy, Robert 1805–1865. British vice admiral and meteorologist
Hamilton, William Rowan 1805–1865. Irish mathematician
Graham, Thomas 1805–1869. Scottish chemist
Maurice, (John) F(rederick) D(enison) 1805–1872. English cleric and social reformer
Mazzini, Giuseppe 1805–1872. Italian nationalist
Wilberforce, Samuel 1805–1873. English cleric, bishop of Oxford
Winterhalter, Franz Xavier 1805–1873. German artist
Andersen, Hans Christian 1805–1875. Danish writer of fairy tales
Bournonville, August 1805–1879. Danish dancer and choreographer
Garrison, William Lloyd 1805–1879. US editor and reformer
Blanqui, (Louis) Auguste 1805–1881. French revolutionary politician
Palmer, Samuel 1805–1881. English artist
Ainsworth, William Harrison 1805–1882. English historical novelist
Guys, Constantin 1805–1892. French illustrator
Lesseps, Ferdinand Marie, Vicomte de Lesseps 1805–1894. French engineer
Martineau, James 1805–1900. British preacher
Hotham, Charles 1806–1855. English governor of Australia
Stirner, Max 1806–1856. German anarchist
Brunel, Isambard Kingdom 1806–1859. British engineer and inventor
Barrett Browning, Elizabeth 1806–1861. English poet
Chisholm, Jesse c. 1806–c. 1868. US pioneer
Maclise, Daniel 1806–1870. Irish painter
De Morgan, Augustus 1806–1871. British mathematician
Juárez, Benito Pablo 1806–1872. Mexican president
Lever, Charles James 1806–1872. Irish novelist
Maury, Matthew Fontaine 1806–1873. US oceanographer
Mill, John Stuart 1806–1873. English philosopher and economist
Le Play, Frédéric (Pierre Guillaume) 1806–1882. French social scientist
Amari, Michele 1806–1889. Italian historian, orientalist, and politician
Vail, Alfred Lewis 1807–1859. US communications pioneer
Lee, Robert E(dward) 1807–1870. US Confederate general
Agassiz, Jean Louis Rodolphe 1807–1873. US palaeontologist
McClure, Robert John le Mesurier 1807–1873. British admiral

Welhaven, Johan Sebastian Cammermeyer 1807–1873. Norwegian poet
Ledru-Rollin, Alexandre Auguste 1807–1874. French politician
Sewell, Henry 1807–1879. New Zealand prime minister
Alter, David 1807–1881. US inventor and physicist
Garibaldi, Giuseppe 1807–1882. Italian soldier
Longfellow, Henry Wadsworth 1807–1882. US poet
Abd al-Kader c. 1807–1883. Algerian nationalist
Adams, Charles Francis 1807–1886. US political leader and journalist
Johnston, Joseph Eggleston 1807–1891. US Confederate general
Whittier, John Greenleaf 1807–1892. US poet
Pixii, Hippolyte 1808–1835. French inventor
Espronceda, José de 1808–1842. Spanish poet
Wergeland, Henrik Arnold 1808–1845. Norwegian poet
Nerval, Gérard de 1808–1855. French writer and poet
Balfe, Michael William 1808–1870. Irish composer and singer
Chase, Salmon Portland 1808–1873. US public official and chief justice
Napoleon III 1808–1873. Emperor of the French
Johnson, Andrew 1808–1875. 17th president of the USA
Chisholm, Caroline 1808–1877. English welfare worker and philanthropist
Norton, Caroline Elizabeth Sarah 1808–1877. British writer
Daumier, Honoré Victorin 1808–1879. French artist
Bourdon, Eugène 1808–1884. French engineer and instrumentmaker
Davis, Jefferson 1808–1889. US politician
Nasmyth, James 1808–1890. Scottish machine-tool manufacturer
Vallejo, Mariano Guadelupe 1808–1890. American military leader
Devonshire, William Cavendish, 7th Duke of Devonshire 1808–1891. British aristocrat
Cook, Thomas 1808–1892. British travel agent
Manning, Henry Edward 1808–1892. English cardinal
Fish, Hamilton 1808–1893. US public figure and diplomat
MacMahon, Marie Edmé Patrice Maurice, Comte de MacMahon 1808–1893. Marshal of France
Mendelssohn (-Bartholdy), (Jakob Ludwig) Felix 1809–1847. German composer
Poe, Edgar Allan 1809–1849. US writer and poet
Gogol, Nicolai Vasilyevich 1809–1852. Russian writer
Soyer, Alexis Benoît 1809–1858. French chef
Lincoln, Abraham 1809–1865. 16th president of the USA
Proudhon, Pierre Joseph 1809–1865. French anarchist
Carson, Kit (Christopher) 1809–1868. US frontier settler and guide
Grassmann, Hermann Günther 1809–1877. German mathematician and linguist
Semmes, Raphael 1809–1877. US naval officer
Alvarado, Juan Bautista 1809–1882. Californian insurgent
Darwin, Charles Robert 1809–1882. English naturalist
Liouville, Joseph 1809–1882. French mathematician
Fitzgerald, Edward 1809–1883. English poet and translator
McCormick, Cyrus Hall 1809–1884. US inventor
Hamlin, Hannibal 1809–1891. US vice president
Haussmann, Georges Eugène 1809–1891. French administrator
Kinglake, Alexander William 1809–1891. British historian
Morphett, John 1809–1892. Australian pioneer and politician
Tennyson, Alfred 1809–1892. English poet
Kemble, Fanny (Frances Anne) 1809–1893. English actress
Holmes, Oliver Wendell 1809–1894. US writer and physician
Gladstone, William Ewart 1809–1898. British prime minister
Montt, Manuel 1809–1900. Chilean president
Mácha, Karel Hynek 1810–1836. Czech poet
Chopin, Frédéric François 1810–1849. Polish composer and pianist
Fuller, (Sarah) Margaret 1810–1850. US author and reformer
Schumann, Robert Alexander 1810–1856. German composer and writer
Musset, (Louis Charles) Alfred de 1810–1857. French poet and playwright
Cavour, Camillo Benso di, Count 1810–1861. Italian prime minister of Piedmont

Hohenlohe-Schillingsfürst, Prince Chlodwig Karl Victor von 1819–1901. German chancellor

Victoria 1819–1901. Queen of Great Britain and Ireland

Stokes, George Gabriel 1819–1903. Irish physicist

Gregory, Augustus Charles 1819–1905. Australian explorer

Struve, Otto Wilhelm von 1819–1905. Russian astronomer

McClintock, Francis Leopold 1819–1907. Irish polar explorer

Frith, William Powell 1819–1909. English painter

Howe, Julia Ward 1819–1910. US feminist and antislavery campaigner

Brontë, Anne 1820–1849. English novelist; see ◊Brontë sisters

Falcón, Juan Crisóstomo 1820–1870. Venezuelan president

Melgarejo, Mariano c. 1820–1871. Bolivian dictator

Vallandigham, Clement Laird 1820–1871. US political leader

Rankine, William John Macquorn 1820–1872. Scottish engineer and physicist

Carboni, Raffaello 1820–1875. Italian writer, poet, and goldminer

Sewell, Anna 1820–1878. English author

Victor Emmanuel II 1820–1878. King of Italy

Nègre, Charles 1820–1880. French photographer

Le Gray, Gustave 1820–1882. French photographer

Lind, Jenny (Johanna Maria) 1820–1887. Swedish soprano

Augier, (Guillaume Victor) émile 1820–1889. French dramatist

Sherman, William Tecumseh 1820–1891. US Civil War general

Tyndall, John 1820–1893. Irish physicist

Engels, Friedrich 1820–1895. German philosopher

Doulton, Henry 1820–1897. English ceramicist

Grove, George 1820–1900. English scholar

Alishan, Leon 1820–1901. Armenian poet and historian

Spencer, Herbert 1820–1903. British philosopher

Anthony, Susan B(rownell) 1820–1906. US pioneering campaigner for women

Russell, William Howard 1820–1907. British journalist

Nadar 1820–1910. French photographer and caricaturist

Nightingale, Florence 1820–1910. English nurse

Tenniel, John 1820–1914. English illustrator and cartoonist

1821–30

Adamson, Robert 1821–1848. Scottish photographer

Nicholson, John 1821–1857. British general and colonial administrator

Rachel 1821–1858. French actress

Burke, Robert O'Hara 1821–1861. Australian explorer

Barth, Heinrich 1821–1865. German geographer and explorer

Baudelaire, Charles Pierre 1821–1867. French poet

Forrest, Nathan Bedford 1821–1877. US Confederate military leader

Nekrasov, Nikolai Alekseevich 1821–1878. Russian poet and publisher

Flaubert, Gustave 1821–1880. French writer

Amiel, Henri Frédéric 1821–1881. Swiss philosopher and writer

Dostoevsky, Fyodor Mihailovich 1821–1881. Russian novelist

Mariette, Auguste Ferdinand François 1821–1881. French Egyptologist

Vanderbilt, William Henry 1821–1885. US financier and railway promoter

Alecsandri, Vasile 1821–1890. Romanian poet and dramatist

Burton, Richard Francis 1821–1890. British explorer and translator

Baker, Samuel White 1821–1893. English explorer

Brown, Ford Madox 1821–1893. English painter

Helmholtz, Hermann Ludwig Ferdinand von 1821–1894. German physiologist, physicist, and inventor

Cayley, Arthur 1821–1895. English mathematician

Virchow, Rudolf Ludwig Carl 1821–1902. German pathologist

Mitre, Bartólomé 1821–1906. Argentine president

Blackwell, Elizabeth 1821–1910. US physician

Eddy, Mary Baker 1821–1910. US founder of the Christian Science movement

Barton, Clara 1821–1912. US health worker

Tubman, Harriet Ross 1821–1913. US abolitionist

Dalziel, John 1822–1860. English wood engraver; see ◊Dalziel family

Murger, (Louis) Henri 1822–1861. French writer

Cadell, Francis 1822–1879. Australian navigator, shipowner and merchant

Lissajous, Jules Antoine 1822–1880. French physicist

Mendel, Gregor Johann 1822–1884. Austrian biologist and monk

Grant, Ulysses S(impson) 1822–1885. US Civil War general

Angas, George French 1822–1886. Australian naturalist and artist; see ◊Angas family

Arnold, Matthew 1822–1888. English poet and critic

Clausius, Rudolf Julius Emanuel 1822–1888. German physicist

Boucicault, Dion(ysus) Larner 1822–1890. Irish dramatist and actor

Franck, César Auguste 1822–1890. Belgian composer

Schliemann, Heinrich 1822–1890. German archaeologist

Thomson, James 1822–1892. Northern Irish physicist and engineer

Hayes, Rutherford Birchard 1822–1893. 19th president of the USA

Pasteur, Louis 1822–1895. French chemist and microbiologist

Goncourt, Edmond de 1822–1896. French writer

Hughes, Thomas 1822–1896. English writer

Bonheur, Rosa (Marie Rosalie) 1822–1899. French painter

Lenoir, (Jean Joseph) Etienne 1822–1900. French engineer

Hermite, Charles 1822–1901. French mathematician

Olmsted, Frederick Law 1822–1903. US landscape designer

Red Cloud 1822–1909. North American Sioux Indian leader

Petipa, Marius 1822–1910. French choreographer

Galton, Francis 1822–1911. English scientist, inventor, and explorer

Passy, Frédéric 1822–1912. French economist

Petöfi, Sándor 1823–1849. Hungarian poet

Abd al-Mejid I 1823–1861. Sultan of Turkey

Tweed, William Marcy ('Boss') 1823–1878. US politician

Colfax, Schuyler 1823–1885. US political leader

Judson, Edward Zane Carroll 1823–1886. US author

Ostrovsky, Alexander Nikolaevich 1823–1886. Russian dramatist

Andrássy, Gyula 1823–1890. Hungarian prime minister

Kronecker, Leopold 1823–1891. German mathematician

Betti, Enrico 1823–1892. Italian mathematician

Lalo, (Victor Antoine) Edouard 1823–1892. French composer

Renan, (Joseph) Ernest 1823–1892. French theologian and historian

Parkman, Francis 1823–1893. US historian and traveller

Brady, Mathew B c. 1823–1896. US photographer

Patmore, Coventry Kersey Dighton 1823–1896. English poet and critic

Li Hongzhang 1823–1901. Chinese politician

Yonge, Charlotte M(ary) 1823–1901. English novelist

Angas, John Howard 1823–1903. Australian politician; see ◊Angas family

Whitehead, Robert 1823–1905. English engineer

Dalziel, Thomas Bolton 1823–1906. English wood engraver; see ◊Dalziel family

Amsler-Laffon, Jakob 1823–1912. Swiss mathematical physicist

Wallace, Alfred Russel 1823–1913. Welsh naturalist

Fabre, Jean Henri Casimir 1823–1915. French entomologist

Walker, William 1824–1860. US adventurer

Jackson, 'Stonewall' (Thomas Jonathan) 1824–1863. US Confederate general

Hofmeister, Wilhelm Friedrich Benedikt 1824–1877. German botanist

Burnside, Ambrose Everett 1824–1881. US military leader and politician

Street, George Edmund 1824–1881. English architect

Dayananda Sarasvati, originally Mula Sankara 1824–1883. Hindu religious reformer

Doyle, Richard 1824–1883. English caricaturist and illustrator

Smetana, Bedřich 1824–1884. Bohemian composer

Venn, John 1834–1923. English logician
Baring-Gould, Sabine 1834–1924. English author
Eliot, Charles William 1834–1926. US educator
Jevons, William Stanley 1835–1882. British economist
Stefan, Josef 1835–1893. Austrian physicist
Giles, (William) Ernest (Powell) 1835–1897. Australian explorer
Beltrami, Eugenio 1835–1899. Italian mathematician
Villard, Henry 1835–1900. US journalist
Butler, Samuel 1835–1902. English author
Chaillu, Paul Belloni du 1835–1903. US explorer
Scripps, James Edmund 1835–1906. US newspaper publisher
Carducci, Giosuè 1835–1907. Italian poet
Leopold II 1835–1909. King of the Belgians
Lombroso, Cesare 1835–1909. Italian criminologist
Newcomb, Simon 1835–1909. US mathematician
Lafarge, John 1835–1910. US painter and ecclesiastical designer
Schiaparelli, Giovanni Virginio 1835–1910. Italian astronomer
Twain, Mark 1835–1910. US writer
Cronje, Piet Arnoldus 1835–1911. Boer commander
Jackson, John Hughlings 1835–1911. English neurophysiologist
Austin, Alfred 1835–1913. English poet
Pius X 1835–1914. Pope
Gorst, J(ohn) E(ldon) 1835–1916. English politician
Baeyer, Johann Friedrich Wilhelm Adolf von 1835–1917. German organic chemist
Cui, César Antonovich 1835–1918. Russian composer and writer
Carnegie, Andrew 1835–1919. US industrialist and philanthropist
Saint-Saëns, (Charles) Camille 1835–1921. French composer
Matsukata, Masayoshi, Prince 1835–1924. Japanese prime minister
Beeton, Mrs 1836–1865. British cookery writer
Ward, Frederick 1836–1870. Australian bushranger
Cavendish, Lord Frederick Charles 1836–1882. British administrator
Green, Thomas Hill 1836–1882. English philosopher
Ramakrishna 1836–1886. Hindu sage, teacher, and mystic
Delibes, (Clément Philibert) Léo 1836–1891. French composer
Gould, Jay (Jason) 1836–1892. US financier
Lobengula 1836–1894. King of Matabeleland
Sacher-Masoch, Leopold von 1836–1895. Austrian novelist
Besant, Walter 1836–1901. English writer
Harte, (Francis) Bret 1836–1902. US writer
Tissot, James (Joseph Jacques) 1836–1902. French painter
Fantin-Latour, (Ignace) Henri (Jean Théodore) 1836–1904. French painter
Aldrich, Thomas Bailey 1836–1907. US poet and editor
Campbell-Bannerman, Henry 1836–1908. British prime minister
Homer, Winslow 1836–1910. US painter and lithographer
Gilbert, W(illiam) S(chwenk) 1836–1911. English humorist and dramatist
Alma-Tadema, Lawrence 1836–1912. Dutch painter
Chamberlain, Joseph 1836–1914. British politician
Anderson, Elizabeth Garrett 1836–1917. English physician
Poynter, Edward John 1836–1919. English artist
Lockyer, (Joseph) Norman 1836–1920. English scientist
Allbutt, Thomas Clifford 1836–1925. British physician
Chéret, Jules 1836–1932. French lithographer and poster artist
Adam, Juliette 1836–1936. French writer
Quantrill, William Clarke 1837–1865. US proslavery outlaw
Hickok, 'Wild Bill' 1837–1876. US pioneer and law enforcer
Draper, Henry 1837–1882. US astronomer
Boulanger, Georges Ernest Jean Marie 1837–1891. French general
Carnot, (Marie François) Sadi 1837–1894. French president
Isaacs, Jorge 1837–1895. Colombian writer
Newlands, John Alexander Reina 1837–1898. English chemist
Moody, Dwight Lyman 1837–1899. US evangelist
Hanna, Mark 1837–1904. US politician
Cleveland, (Stephen) Grover 1837–1908. 22nd and 24th president of the USA
Swinburne, Algernon Charles 1837–1909. English poet
Balakirev, Mily Alexeyevich 1837–1910. Russian composer

Morgan, J(ohn) P(ierpont) 1837–1913. US financier
Murray, James Augustus Henry 1837–1915. Scottish philologist
Dewey, George 1837–1917. US naval officer
Itagaki, Taisuke 1837–1919. Japanese military and political leader
Howells, William Dean 1837–1920. US novelist and editor
Hyatt, John Wesley 1837–1920. US inventor
Booth, John Wilkes 1838–1865. US actor and assassin
Bizet, Georges (Alexandre César Léopold) 1838–1875. French composer of operas
Gambetta, Léon Michel 1838–1882. French prime minister
Richardson, Henry Hobson 1838–1886. US architect
Clay, Frederic 1838–1889. English composer
Villiers de l'Isle Adam, (Jean Marie Philippe) Auguste, Comte de 1838–1889. French poet
Chatterji, Bankim Chandra 1838–1894. Indian novelist
Daly, (John) Augustin 1838–1899. US theatre manager
Hunt, John Horbury 1838–1904. Australian architect
Irving, Henry 1838–1905. English actor
Perkin, William Henry 1838–1907. British chemist
Hill, Octavia 1838–1912. English social reformer
Muir, John 1838–1914. US conservationist
Brentano, Franz 1838–1916. German-Austrian philosopher and psychologist
Mach, Ernst 1838–1916. Austrian philosopher and physicist
Zeppelin, Ferdinand Adolf August Heinrich, Count von Zeppelin 1838–1917. German airship pioneer
Adams, Henry Brooks 1838–1918. US historian and novelist
Bruch, Max 1838–1920. German composer
Bryce, James 1838–1922. British politician
Jordan, (Marie Ennemond) Camille 1838–1922. French mathematician
Okuma, Shigenobu 1838–1922. Japanese prime minister
Solvay, Ernest 1838–1922. Belgian industrial chemist
Wanamaker, John 1838–1922. US retailer
Yamagata, Aritomo 1838–1922. Japanese soldier and prime minister
Morley, Edward Williams 1838–1923. US physicist
Morley, John 1838–1923. British politician and writer
Trevelyan, George Otto 1838–1928. British politician and historian
Hankel, Hermann 1839–1873. German mathematician
Custer, George Armstrong 1839–1876. US general
Mussorgsky, Modest Petrovich 1839–1881. Russian composer
Leclanché, Georges 1839–1882. French engineer
Przhevalsky, Nikolai Mikhailovitch 1839–1888. Russian explorer and soldier
Ballance, John 1839–1893. New Zealand prime minister
Kundt, August Adolph Eduard Eberhard 1839–1894. German physicist
Pater, Walter Horatio 1839–1894. English scholar and art critic
George, Henry 1839–1897. US economist
Willard, Frances Elizabeth Caroline 1839–1898. US educationalist and campaigner
Sisley, Alfred 1839–1899. French painter
Bentley, John Francis 1839–1902. English architect
Gibbs, Josiah Willard 1839–1903. US physicist and chemist
Cézanne, Paul 1839–1906. French painter
Rayet, George Antoine Pons 1839–1906. French astronomer
Sully-Prudhomme, (René François) Armand 1839–1907. French poet
Buller, Redvers Henry 1839–1908. British military commander
Machado de Assis, Joaquim Maria 1839–1908. Brazilian writer and poet
Ouida 1839–1908. English novelist
Holstein, Friedrich August von 1839–1909. German diplomat
Mond, Ludwig 1839–1909. British chemist
MacWhirter, John 1839–1911. Scottish painter
Furness, Frank Heyling 1839–1912. US architect
Carol I 1839–1914. First king of Romania
Peirce, Charles Sanders 1839–1914. US philosopher and logician

de Morgan, William Frend 1839–1917. English pottery designer
Chardonnet, (Louis-Marie) Hilaire Bernigaud, Comte de 1839–1924. French chemist
Rockefeller, John D(avison) 1839–1937. US millionaire
Kilvert, (Robert) Francis 1840–1879. English cleric
Veuster, Joseph de 1840–1889. Belgian missionary
Balmaceda, José Manuel 1840–1891. Chilean president
Emin Pasha, Mehmed 1840–1892. German explorer, physician, and linguist
Symonds, John Addington 1840–1893. British critic
Tchaikovsky, Pyotr Il'yich 1840–1893. Russian composer
Gall c. 1840–1894. American Sioux Indian leader
Daudet, Alphonse 1840–1897. French novelist
Stainer, John 1840–1901. English organist and composer
Krafft-Ebing, Richard, Baron von 1840–1902. German psychiatrist and neurologist
Nast, Thomas 1840–1902. US illustrator
Zola, Émile Edouard Charles Antoine 1840–1902. French novelist and social reformer
Joseph, Chief c. 1840–1904. North American Indian leader
Abbe, Ernst 1840–1905. German physicist
Cleve, Per Teodor 1840–1905. Swedish chemist and geologist
Baker, Benjamin 1840–1907. English engineer
Svendsen, Johan Severin 1840–1911. Norwegian composer, violinist, and conductor
Whymper, Edward 1840–1911. English mountaineer
Bebel, (Ferdinand) August 1840–1913. German socialist
Holland, John Philip 1840–1914. Irish engineer
Mahan, Alfred Thayer 1840–1914. US military strategist and historian
Rothschild, Nathan Meyer, 1st Baron 1840–1915. English financier; see ◊Rothschild family
Booth, Charles 1840–1916. English sociologist
Maxim, Hiram Stevens 1840–1916. British inventor
Redon, Odilon 1840–1916. French artist
Rodin, (René François) Auguste 1840–1917. French sculptor
Dunlop, John Boyd 1840–1921. Scottish inventor
Blunt, Wilfrid Scawen 1840–1922. English poet
Cobden-Sanderson, Thomas James 1840–1922. English bookbinder and painter
Gardner, Isabella Stewart 1840–1924. US art collector
Monet, Claude 1840–1926. French painter
Hardy, Thomas 1840–1928. English novelist and poet

1841–50

Oppolzer, Theodor Egon Ritter von 1841–1886. Austrian astronomer and mathematician
Chabrier, (Alexis) Emmanuel 1841–1894. French composer
Morisot, Berthe Marie Pauline 1841–1895. French painter
Dvořák, Antonín Leopold 1841–1904. Czech composer
Stanley, Henry Morton 1841–1904. US explorer
Itō, Hirobumi 1841–1909. Japanese prime minister
Edward VII 1841–1910. King of Great Britain and Ireland
Wagner, Otto 1841–1918. Viennese architect
Laurier, Wilfrid 1841–1919. Canadian prime minister
Renoir, Pierre-Auguste 1841–1919. French painter
Fisher, John Arbuthnot 1841–1920. British admiral
Darrell, George (Frederick Price) 1841–1921. Australian actor-manager and dramatist
Croker, Richard 1841–1922. US politician
Hudson, W(illiam) H(enry) 1841–1922. British author
Warming, Johannes Eugenius Bülow 1841–1924. Danish botanist
Fayol, Henri 1841–1925. French management expert
Ader, Clément 1841–1926. French aviation pioneer and inventor
Clemenceau, Georges 1841–1929. French prime minister and journalist
Holmes, Oliver Wendell 1841–1935. US jurist

Lanier, Sidney 1842–1881. US flautist and poet
Burnaby, Frederick Gustavus 1842–1885. English soldier and traveller
Mallarmé, Stéphane 1842–1898. French poet
Lie, (Marius) Sophus 1842–1899. Norwegian mathematician
Sullivan, Arthur Seymour 1842–1900. English composer
Vogel, Hermann Carl 1842–1907. German astronomer
McKillop, Mary Helen (Mother Mary of the Cross) 1842–1909. Australian nun and teacher
James, William 1842–1910. US psychologist and philosopher
Alfaro, Eloy 1842–1912. Ecuadorian president
Massenet, Jules Emile Frédéric 1842–1912. French composer
Reynolds, Osborne 1842–1912. Irish physicist and engineer
Weber, Heinrich 1842–1913. German mathematician
Bierce, Ambrose Gwinett 1842–c. 1914. US author
Alverstone, Richard Everard Webster 1842–1915. British politician and lawyer
Darboux, (Jean) Gaston 1842–1917. French mathematician
Abd al-Hamid II 1842–1918. Last sultan of Turkey
Adams, Charles Follen 1842–1918. US humourous dialect poet
Rayleigh, John William Strutt, 3rd Baron Rayleigh 1842–1919. English physicist
Kropotkin, Peter Alexeivich, Prince Kropotkin 1842–1921. Russian anarchist
Dewar, James 1842–1923. Scottish chemist and physicist
Marshall, Alfred 1842–1924. English economist
Breuer, Josef 1842–1925. Viennese pioneer of psychoanalysis
Giolitti, Giovanni 1842–1928. Italian prime minister
McKinley, William 1843–1901. 25th president of the USA
Myers, F(rederic) W(illiam) H(enry) 1843–1901. English psychic researcher
Grieg, Edvard Hagerup 1843–1907. Norwegian composer
Koch, (Heinrich Hermann) Robert 1843–1910. German bacteriologist
Dilke, Charles Wentworth 1843–1911. British politician
Furphy, Joseph 1843–1912. Australian writer
Ward, (Aaron) Montgomery 1843–1913. US retailer
Gill, David 1843–1914. Scottish astronomer
Goltz, Wilhelm Leopold Colmar, Freiherr von der 1843–1916. German soldier
James, Henry 1843–1916. US novelist
Liberty, Arthur Lasenby 1843–1917. English retailer
Hertling, Count Georg Friedrich von 1843–1919. German chancellor
Patti, Adelina (Adela Juana Maria) 1843–1919. Anglo-Italian soprano
Pérez Galdós, Benito 1843–1920. Spanish novelist
Cambon, Pierre Paul 1843–1924. French diplomat
Doughty, Charles Montagu 1843–1926. English travel writer
Golgi, Camillo 1843–1926. Italian cell biologist
Chamberlin, Thomas Chrowder 1843–1928. US geophysicist
Jekyll, Gertrude 1843–1932. English gardener and writer
Bernadette, St, of Lourdes (originally Maries Bernard Soubirous) 1844–1879. French saint
Riel, Louis 1844–1885. French-Canadian rebel
Hopkins, Gerard Manley 1844–1889. English poet and priest
Verlaine, Paul Marie 1844–1896. French poet
Nietzsche, Friedrich Wilhelm 1844–1900. German philosopher
Queensberry, John Sholto Douglas, 8th Marquess of Queensberry 1844–1900. British patron of boxing
Umberto I 1844–1900. King of Italy
D'Oyly Carte, Richard 1844–1901. English theatrical producer
Boltzmann, Ludwig Eduard 1844–1906. Austrian physicist
Rimsky-Korsakov, Nikolay Andreyevich 1844–1908. Russian composer
Rousseau, Henri Julien Félix 'Le Douanier' 1844–1910. French painter
Lang, Andrew 1844–1912. Scottish historian and folklorist
Hagenbeck, Carl 1844–1913. German zoo proprietor
Menelik II 1844–1913. Emperor of Abyssinia

Plekhanov, Georgi Valentinovich 1857–1918. Russian Marxist revolutionary
Barnard, Edward Emerson 1857–1923. US astronomer
Conrad, Joseph 1857–1924. English novelist
Coué, Emile 1857–1926. French psychological healer
Atget, Eugène 1857–1927. French photographer
Veblen, Thorstein Bunde 1857–1929. US social critic
Taft, William Howard 1857–1930. 27th president of the USA
Lethaby, William Richard 1857–1931. English architect
Doumer, Paul 1857–1932. French president
Plumer, Hubert Charles Onslow, 1st Viscount Plumer 1857–1932. British major general
Reeves, William Pember 1857–1932. New Zealand politician and writer
Ross, Ronald 1857–1932. British physician and bacteriologist
Elgar, Edward (William) 1857–1934. English composer
Hutier, Oskar von 1857–1934. German general
Ligget, Hunter 1857–1935. US general
Osborn, Henry Fairfield 1857–1935. US palaeontologist
Tsiolkovsky, Konstantin Eduardovich 1857–1935. Russian scientist
Garrod, Archibald Edward 1857–1936. English physician
Pearson, Karl 1857–1936. British statistician
Abel, John Jacob 1857–1938. US biochemist
Darrow, Clarence Seward 1857–1938. US lawyer
Lévy-Bruhl, Lucien 1857–1939. French anthropologist and philosopher
Pius XI 1857–1939. Pope
Wagner-Jauregg, Julius 1857–1940. Austrian neurologist
Baden-Powell, Robert Stephenson Smyth 1857–1941. British general, founder of the Scout Association
Voysey, Charles Francis Annesley 1857–1941. English architect and designer
Henry, Alice 1857–1943. Australian journalist and suffragette
Koller, Carl 1857–1944. Austrian ophthalmologist
Lonsdale, Hugh Cecil Lowther 1857–1944. British sporting enthusiast
Tarbell, Ida Minerva 1857–1944. US journalist
Sherrington, Charles Scott 1857–1952. English neurophysiologist
Rudolph 1858–1889. Crown prince of Austria
Diesel, Rudolf Christian Karl 1858–1913. German engineer
Gourmont, Rémy de 1858–1915. French critic and novelist
Durkheim, Emile 1858–1917. French sociologist
Alexander, George 1858–1918. English actor-manager
Simmel, Georg 1858–1918. German sociologist
Sullivan, John L(awrence) 1858–1918. US boxer
Leoncavallo, Ruggero 1858–1919. Italian composer
Roosevelt, Theodore 1858–1919. 26th president of the USA
Struve, (Gustav Wilhelm) Ludwig (Ottovich) von 1858–1920. Russian astronomer
Law, Andrew Bonar 1858–1923. British prime minister
Castro, Cipriano 1858–1924. Venezuelan dictator
Duse, Eleonora 1858–1924. Italian actress
Nesbit, E(dith) 1858–1924. English children's author
Puccini, Giacomo (Antonio Domenico Michele Secondo Maria) 1858–1924. Italian opera composer
Repington, Charles à Court 1858–1925. British soldier and journalist
Achad Haam 1858–1927. Jewish writer and Zionist leader
Carroll, James 1858–1927. New Zealand Maori politician
Pankhurst, Emmeline 1858–1928. English suffragette
Welsbach, Carl Auer, Baron von 1858–1929. Austrian chemist and engineer
Eijkman, Christiaan 1858–1930. Dutch bacteriologist
Smith-Dorrien, Horace Lockwood 1858–1930. British general
Russell, John Peter 1858–1931. Australian artist
Ysaye, Eugène-Auguste 1858–1931. Belgian violinist, conductor, and composer
Brieux, Eugène 1858–1932. French dramatist
Peano, Giuseppe 1858–1932. Italian mathematician

Wallas, Graham 1858–1932. English political scientist
Fowler, Henry Watson 1858–1933. English scholar; see ◊Fowler brothers
Ochs, Adolph Simon 1858–1935. US newspaper publisher
Sims, William Sowden 1858–1936. US admiral
Bose, Jagadis Chunder 1858–1937. Indian physicist and plant physiologist
House, Edward Mandell 1858–1938. US politician and diplomat
Carter, Herbert James 1858–1940. Australian entomologist
Dolmetsch, (Eugène) Arnold 1858–1940. English musician
Dubois, Marie Eugène François Thomas 1858–1940. Dutch palaeontologist
Hadfield, Robert Abbott 1858–1940. British chemist and metallurgist
Hobson, John Atkinson 1858–1940. British economist
Lagerlöf, Selma Ottiliana Lovisa 1858–1940. Swedish novelist
Gaetano, Mosca 1858–1941. Italian political scientist
Boas, Franz 1858–1942. US anthropologist
Forsyth, Andrew Russell 1858–1942. Scottish mathematician
Antoine, André 1858–1943. French theatre director
Burns, John Elliot 1858–1943. British labour leader
Webb, (Martha) Beatrice 1858–1943. English social reformer
Smyth, Ethel Mary 1858–1944. English composer
Lugard, Frederick John Dealtry 1858–1945. British colonial administrator
Planck, Max Karl Ernst 1858–1947. German physicist
Selfridge, Harry Gordon 1858–1947. US entrepreneur
Gustavus V 1858–1950. King of Sweden
O'Malley, King c. 1858–1953. Australian politician
Swinburne, James 1858–1958. Scottish engineer
Billy the Kid 1859–1881. US outlaw
Seurat, Georges Pierre 1859–1891. French artist
Popov, Alexander Stepanovich 1859–1905. Russian physicist
Cesaro, Ernesto 1859–1906. Italian mathematician
Curie, Pierre 1859–1906. French scientist
Thompson, Francis 1859–1907. English poet
Jaurès, (Auguste Marie Joseph) Jean (Léon) 1859–1914. French politician
Samsonov, Aleksandr Vassilievich 1859–1914. Russian general
Yuan Shikai 1859–1916. Chinese soldier and politician
Pringsheim, Ernst 1859–1917. German physicist
Zamenhof, Lazarus Ludovik 1859–1917. Polish inventor of Esperanto
Herbert, Victor 1859–1924. US conductor
Prendergast, Maurice Brazil 1859–1924. US painter
Sharp, Cecil James 1859–1924. English folklorist
Camp, Walter Chauncey 1859–1925. US football coach
Curzon, George Nathaniel 1859–1925. British politician and viceroy of India
Sturdee, Frederick Charles Doveton 1859–1925. British admiral
Arrhenius, Svante August 1859–1927. Swedish physical chemist
Jerome, Jerome K(lapka) 1859–1927. English journalist and writer
Duguit, Léon 1859–1928. French jurist
Cajori, Florian 1859–1930. US historian
Doyle, Arthur Conan 1859–1930. Scottish writer
Belasco, David 1859–1931. US dramatist and producer
Grahame, Kenneth 1859–1932. Scottish author
Hume, Fergus 1859–1932. British writer
Ehrenfels, (Maria) Christian (Julius Leopold Karl) von 1859–1933. Austrian philosopher and psychologist
Gilbert, Cass 1859–1934. US architect
Dreyfus, Alfred 1859–1935. French army officer
Hassam, (Frederick) Childe 1859–1935. US painter
Jellicoe, John Rushworth 1859–1935. British admiral
Junkers, Hugo 1859–1935. German aeroplane designer
Demachy, Robert 1859–1936. French photographer
Housman, A(lfred) E(dward) 1859–1936. English poet and classical scholar
Wise, Thomas James 1859–1937. British bibliographer
Alexander, Samuel 1859–1938. Australian philosopher

Husserl, Edmund Gustav Albrecht 1859–1938. German philosopher
Ellis, (Henry) Havelock 1859–1939. English psychologist
Lansbury, George 1859–1940. British politician
Bergson, Henri Louis 1859–1941. French philosopher
Van Devanter, Willis 1859–1941. US jurist
William II 1859–1941. Emperor of Germany
Palamas, Kostes 1859–1943. Greek poet
Janet, Pierre Marie Félix 1859–1947. French psychiatrist
Webb, Sidney James, 1st Baron Passfield 1859–1947. English social reformer
Dewey, John 1859–1952. US philosopher
Hamsun, Knut Pedersen 1859–1952. Norwegian novelist
Eastwood, Alice 1859–1953. US botanist
Bashkirtseff, Marie 1860–1884. Russian diarist and painter
Laforgue, Jules 1860–1887. French poet
Wolf, Hugo Filipp Jakob 1860–1903. Austrian composer
Chekhov, Anton Pavlovich 1860–1904. Russian dramatist
Finsen, Niels Ryberg 1860–1904. Danish physician
Herzl, Theodor 1860–1904. Austrian Zionist
Leno, Dan 1860–1904. English comedian
Albone, Dan 1860–1906. English inventor
Hope, John Adrian Louis 1860–1908. Scottish governor general of Australia
Linlithgow, John Adrian Louis Hope, 1st Marquess Linlithgow 1860–1908. British governor general of Australia
MacDowell, Edward Alexander 1860–1908. US composer
Albéniz, Isaac 1860–1909. Spanish nationalist composer and pianist
Fröding, Gustaf 1860–1911. Swedish poet
Mahler, Gustav 1860–1911. Austrian composer and conductor
Rolfe, Frederick William 1860–1913. English writer
Buchner, Eduard 1860–1917. German chemist
Bayliss, William Maddock 1860–1924. English physiologist
Bryan, William Jennings 1860–1925. US politician
Lummer, Otto Richard 1860–1925. German physicist
Katō, Taka-akira 1860–1926. Japanese prime minister
Oakley, Annie 1860–1926. US sharpshooter
Einthoven, Willem 1860–1927. Dutch physiologist
Low, Juliette Gordon 1860–1927. Founder of the Girl Scouts in the USA
Frampton, George James 1860–1928. English sculptor
Hollerith, Herman 1860–1929. US inventor
Sperry, Elmer Ambrose 1860–1930. US engineer
Robertson, William Robert 1860–1933. British general
Poincaré, Raymond Nicolas Landry 1860–1934. French president
Addams, Jane 1860–1935. US social reformer and feminist
Gilman, Charlotte Anna 1860–1935. US poet
Isaacs, Rufus Daniel 1860–1935. British lawyer and politician
Haldane, John Scott 1860–1936. Scottish physiologist
Barrie, J(ames) M(atthew) 1860–1937. Scottish dramatist and novelist
Filene, Edward Albert 1860–1937. US store owner
Horniman, Annie Elizabeth Fredericka 1860–1937. English repertory theatre pioneer
Wister, Owen 1860–1938. US novelist
Mucha, Alphonse Maria 1860–1939. Czech painter and designer
Thompson, John Taliaferro 1860–1940. US general and weapons designer
Volterra, Vito 1860–1940. Italian mathematician
Paderewski, (Ignacy) Jan 1860–1941. Polish pianist, composer, and politician
Sickert, Walter Richard 1860–1942. English artist
Steer, Philip Wilson 1860–1942. English artist
Carver, George Washington 1860–1943. US agricultural chemist
Jespersen, (Jens) Otto (Harry) 1860–1943. Danish linguist
Roberts, Charles George Douglas 1860–1943. Canadian writer
Boberg, Ferdinand 1860–1945. Swedish architect
Lalique, René 1860–1945. French designer
Murray, Archibald James 1860–1945. British general

Seton, Ernest Thompson 1860–1946. Canadian author and naturalist
Pershing, John Joseph 1860–1948. US general
Thompson, D'Arcy Wentworth 1860–1948. Scottish biologist and classical scholar
Ensor, James Sidney, Baron Ensor 1860–1949. Belgian painter and printmaker
Hyde, Douglas 1860–1949. Irish president
Orlando, Vittorio Emanuele 1860–1952. Italian prime minister
Inge, William Ralph 1860–1954. English philosopher and cleric
Charpentier, Gustave 1860–1956. French composer
Moses, 'Grandma' 1860–1961. US painter

1861–70

Remington, Frederic 1861–1909. US artist
Crippen, Hawley Harvey 1861–1910. US murderer
Stevens, Nettie Maria 1861–1912. US biologist
Spee, Maximilian Johannes Maria Hubert 1861–1914. German admiral
Lane, William 1861–1917. Australian political journalist
Kaledin, Alexander Maximovich 1861–1918. Russian soldier
Falkenhayn, Erich Georg Anton Sebastian von 1861–1922. German soldier
Townshend, Charles Vere Ferrers 1861–1924. British soldier
Steiner, Rudolf 1861–1925. Austrian philosopher, occultist, and educationalist
Bateson, William 1861–1926. English geneticist
Diaz, Armando 1861–1928. Italian general
Haig, Douglas 1861–1928. British military commander
Svevo, Italo 1861–1928. Italian novelist
Horne, Henry Sinclair 1861–1929. British general
Nansen, Fridtjof 1861–1930. Norwegian explorer and scientist
Burali Forti, Cesare 1861–1931. Italian mathematician
Melba, Nellie 1861–1931. Australian soprano
Cowan, Edith Dircksey 1861–1932. Australian social worker and politician
Turner, Frederick Jackson 1861–1932. US historian
Pakenham, William Christopher 1861–1933. British admiral
Allenby, (Edmund) Henry Hynman 1861–1936. British field marshal
Guillaume, Charles Edouard 1861–1938. Swiss physicist
Méliès, Georges 1861–1938. French film pioneer
Kennelly, Arthur Edwin 1861–1939. US engineer
Mayo, William James 1861–1939. US surgeon
Naismith, James 1861–1939. US inventor of basketball
Heath, Thomas Little 1861–1940. English mathematical historian
Murray, (John) Hubert (Plunkett) 1861–1940. Australian administrator
Tagore, Rabindranath 1861–1941. Bengali writer
Maillol, Aristide (Joseph Bonaventure) 1861–1944. French sculptor and graphic artist
Hopkins, Frederick Gowland 1861–1947. English biochemist
Horta, Victor, Baron Horta 1861–1947. Belgian architect
Whitehead, Alfred North 1861–1947. English philosopher and mathematician
Wright, Almroth Edward 1861–1947. English bacteriologist
Ferdinand 1861–1948. King of Bulgaria
Somerville, Edith Anna Oenone 1861–1949. Irish novelist
Kingsley, Mary Henrietta 1862–1900. English ethnologist
Henry, O 1862–1910. US short-story writer
Cody, Samuel Franklin 1862–1913. US aviation pioneer
Boveri, Theodor Heinrich 1862–1915. German biologist
Kulpe, Oswald 1862–1915. German psychologist and philosopher
Martin, Violet Florence 1862–1915. Irish novelist
Debussy, (Achille-) Claude 1862–1918. French composer
Klimt, Gustav 1862–1918. Austrian painter
Botha, Louis 1862–1919. South African soldier and politician
Adam, Paul-Auguste-Marie 1862–1920. French novelist

1871–80

Perkins, Frances 1882–1965. US public official
Coburn, Alvin Langdon 1882–1966. British photographer
Morgan, Ann Haven 1882–1966. US zoologist
Hopper, Edward 1882–1967. US painter and etcher
Kaiser, Henry John 1882–1967. US industrialist
Kodály, Zoltán 1882–1967. Hungarian composer and educationist
Babcock, Harold Delos 1882–1968. US astronomer and physicist
Kimmel, Husband E 1882–1968. US admiral
Nash, Walter 1882–1968. New Zealand prime minister
Chukovsky, Kornei Ivanovich 1882–1969. Russian critic and poet
Traven, B(en) c. 1882–1969. US novelist
Born, Max 1882–1970. British physicist
Dowding, Hugh Caswall Tremenheere, 1st Baron Dowding 1882–1970. British air chief marshal
Stravinsky, Igor 1882–1971. Russian composer
Gustavus VI 1882–1973. King of Sweden
Joy, Alfred Harrison 1882–1973. US astronomer
Malipiero, Gian Francesco 1882–1973. Italian composer
Maritain, Jacques 1882–1973. French philosopher
Goldwyn, Samuel 1882–1974. US film producer
Jackson, Alexander Young 1882–1974. Canadian painter
de Valera, Eamon 1882–1975. Irish president
Thorndike, (Agnes) Sybil 1882–1976. English actress
Stokowski, Leopold Antoni Stanislaw 1882–1977. US conductor
Abetti, Giorgio 1882–1982. Italian astrophysicist
Hulme, T(homas) E(rnest) 1883–1917. British philosopher, critic, and poet
Hašek, Jaroslav 1883–1923. Czech writer
Kafka, Franz 1883–1924. Czech novelist
Chaney, Lon (Alonso) 1883–1930. US star of silent films
Gibran, Kahlil 1883–1931. Lebanese-American writer and artist
Bull, Olaf Jacob Martin Luther 1883–1933. Norwegian poet
Kamenev, Lev Borisovich 1883–1936. Russian Bolshevik leader
Zinoviev, Grigory Yevseyevich 1883–1936. Russian politician
Fairbanks, Douglas, Sr 1883–1939. US actor
Laval, Pierre 1883–1945. French prime minister
Mussolini, Benito Amilcare Andrea 1883–1945. Italian dictator
Ramsay, Bertram Home 1883–1945. British admiral
Webern, Anton (Friedrich Wilhelm von) 1883–1945. Austrian composer
Keynes, John Maynard 1883–1946. English economist
Stilwell, Joseph Warren 1883–1946. US general
Blaskowitz, Johann Albrecht 1883–1948. German general
Orozco, José Clemente 1883–1949. Mexican painter
Chareau, Pierre 1883–1950. French designer
Haworth, (Walter) Norman 1883–1950. English organic chemist
Schumpeter, Joseph A(lois) 1883–1950. US economist
Wavell, Archibald Percival, 1st Earl Wavell 1883–1950. British field marshal
Horton, Max Kennedy 1883–1951. British admiral
Bax, Arnold Edward Trevor 1883–1953. English composer
Ghormley, Robert Lee 1883–1953. US admiral
Mises, Richard von 1883–1953. Austrian mathematician and aerodynamicist
Vargas, Getúlio Dorneles 1883–1954. Brazilian president
Vyshinsky, Andrei Yanuaryevich 1883–1954. Soviet politician
Ortega y Gasset, José 1883–1955. Spanish philosopher and critic
Utrillo, Maurice 1883–1955. French artist
Donovan, William Joseph 1883–1959. US public official
Hinton, William Augustus 1883–1959. US bacteriologist and pathologist
Rohmer, Sax 1883–1959. English crime writer
Teague, Walter Dorwin 1883–1960. US industrial designer
Meštrović, Ivan 1883–1962. Yugoslav sculptor
Alanbrooke, Alan Francis Brooke 1883–1963. British army officer
Cunningham, Andrew Browne 1883–1963. British admiral
Williams, William Carlos 1883–1963. US poet, essayist, and theoretician
Eskola, Pentti Eelis 1883–1964. Finnish geologist
Hess, Victor Francis 1883–1964. Austrian physicist

Sheeler, Charles 1883–1965. US painter
Varèse, Edgar Victor Achille Charles 1883–1965. French composer
Sanger, Margaret Louise 1883–1966. US health reformer and crusader
Severini, Gino 1883–1966. Italian painter
Attlee, Clement Richard 1883–1967. British politician
Bruce, Stanley Melbourne 1883–1967. Australian prime minister
Ansermet, Ernest Alexandre 1883–1969. Swiss conductor
Gropius, Walter Adolf 1883–1969. German architect
Jaspers, Karl Theodor 1883–1969. German philosopher
Goldberg, Rube (Reuben Lucius) 1883–1970. US cartoonist
Heckel, Erich 1883–1970. German painter, lithographer, and illustrator
Ricci, Nina 1883–1970. French fashion designer
Warburg, Otto Heinrich 1883–1970. German biochemist
Burt, Cyril Lodowic 1883–1971. British psychologist
Chanel, Coco (Gabrielle) 1883–1971. French fashion designer
Mackenzie, (Edward Montague) Compton 1883–1972. Scottish author
Budenny, Semyon Mikhailovich 1883–1973. Soviet general
Neill, A(lexander) S(utherland) 1883–1973. Scottish educationist
Knopf, Eleanora Frances 1883–1974. US geologist
Maufe, Edward Brantwood 1883–1974. English architect
Nice, Margaret 1883–1974. US ornithologist
Cunningham, Imogen 1883–1976. US photographer
Williams-Ellis, (Bertram) Clough 1883–1978. English architect
Flecker, (Herman) James Elroy 1884–1915. English poet
Stefanik, Milan Ratislav 1884–1919. Slovakian general
Modigliani, Amedeo 1884–1920. Italian artist
Black, Davidson 1884–1934. Canadian anatomist
Sapir, Edward 1884–1939. US language scholar
Walpole, Hugh Seymour 1884–1941. English novelist
Malinowski, Bronislaw Kasper 1884–1942. British anthropologist
Reichenau, Walther von 1884–1942. German field marshal
Yamamoto, Isoroku 1884–1943. Japanese admiral
Birkhoff, George David 1884–1944. US mathematician
Langdon, Harry Philmore 1884–1944. US film comedian
Donoghue, Steve (Stephen) 1884–1945. British jockey
Beneš, Eduard 1884–1948. Czechoslovak president
Tōjō, Hideki 1884–1948. Japanese general and prime minister
Bergius, Friedrich Karl Rudolph 1884–1949. German chemist
Beckmann, Max 1884–1950. German artist
Fraser, Peter 1884–1950. New Zealand prime minister
Huston, Walter 1884–1950. US actor
Blamey, Thomas Albert 1884–1951. Australian field marshal
Flaherty, Robert Joseph 1884–1951. US film director
Meyerhof, Otto 1884–1951. US biochemist
Vandenberg, Arthur Hendrick 1884–1951. US public official
Senanayake, Don Stephen 1884–1952. Ski Lankan prime minister
Lugosi, Bela 1884–1956. US film actor
Ferguson, Harry George 1884–1960. Northern Irish engineer
Bachelard, Gaston 1884–1962. French philosopher and scientist
Piccard, Auguste Antoine 1884–1962. Swiss scientist
Roosevelt, (Anna) Eleanor 1884–1962. US social worker, writer, and first lady
Ben Zvi, Izhak 1884–1963. Israeli president
Prasad, Rajendra 1884–1963. Indian president
O'Casey, Sean 1884–1964. Irish dramatist
Arden, Elizabeth 1884–1966. US beauty expert
Auriol, Vincent 1884–1966. French politician
Debye, Peter 1884–1966. US physicist
Funk, Casimir 1884–1967. US biochemist
Ransome, Arthur Michell 1884–1967. English journalist and children's author
Thomas, Norman Mattoon 1884–1968. US political leader
Compton-Burnett, Ivy 1884–1969. English novelist
Dornier, Claude 1884–1969. German pioneer aircraft designer
Gallegos, Rómulo 1884–1969. Venezuelan president and writer
Prichard, Katharine Susannah 1884–1969. Australian novelist
Daladier, Edouard 1884–1970. French prime minister

Laurel, Stan 1890–1965. US film comedian; see ◊Laurel and Hardy
Hopper, Hedda 1890–1966. US actress and celebrity reporter
Heyrovský, Jaroslav 1890–1967. Czech chemist
Muller, Hermann Joseph 1890–1967. US geneticist
Tedder, Arthur William 1890–1967. UK air marshal
Whiteman, Paul 1890–1967. US bandleader
Zadkine, Ossip 1890–1967. French sculptor
Crompton, Richmal 1890–1969. English writer
Eisenhower, Dwight David ('Ike') 1890–1969. 34th president of the USA
Ho Chi Minh 1890–1969. North Vietnamese president
de Gaulle, Charles André Joseph Marie 1890–1970. French general and president
Bragg, (William) Lawrence 1890–1971. British physicist
Gale, Humphrey Middleton 1890–1971. British general
Herbert, A(lan) P(atrick) 1890–1971. English politician and writer
Rickenbacker, Edward Vernon 1890–1973. US racing-car driver
Schiaparelli, Elsa c. 1890–1973. Italian couturier and knitwear designer
Bush, Vannevar 1890–1974. US electrical engineer
Martin, Frank 1890–1974. Swiss composer, pianist, and harpsichordist
Melnikov, Konstantin Stepanovich 1890–1974. Soviet architect
Underwood, (George Claude) Leon 1890–1975. English artist
Casey, Richard Gardiner 1890–1976. Australian diplomat, politician, and governor-general
Christie, Agatha Mary Clarissa 1890–1976. English detective novelist
Lang, Fritz 1890–1976. Austrian film director
Ray, Man 1890–1976. US photographer, painter, and sculptor
Strand, Paul 1890–1976. US photographer and filmmaker
Wheeler, (Robert Eric) Mortimer 1890–1976. English archaeologist
Gabo, Naum 1890–1977. US sculptor
Marx, Julius 'Groucho' 1890–1977. US film comedian; see ◊Marx Brothers
Rhys, Jean c. 1890–1979. English novelist
Martinez, Maria Montoya 1890–1980. Pueblo Indian potter
Porter, Katherine Anne Maria Veronica Callista Russell 1890–1980. US writer
Soong Ching-ling 1890–1981. Chinese politician
Forde, Francis Michael 1890–1983. Australian prime minister
Molotov, Vyacheslav Mikhailovich 1890–1986. Soviet politician

1891–1900

Gaudier-Brzeska, Henri 1891–1915. French sculptor
Gramsci, Antonio 1891–1937. Italian Marxist
Mandelstam, Osip Emilevich 1891–1938. Russian poet
Gertler, Mark 1891–1939. English painter
Bulgakov, Mikhail Afanasyevich 1891–1940. Russian novelist and playwright
Banting, Frederick Grant 1891–1941. Canadian physician
Todt, Fritz 1891–1942. German engineer
Rommel, Erwin Johannes Eugen 1891–1944. German field marshal
Model, Walter 1891–1945. German field marshal
Konoe, Fumimaro, Prince 1891–1946. Japanese prime minister
Wright, Louis Tompkins 1891–1952. US physician, surgeon, and civil-rights leader
Prokofiev, Sergey Sergeyevich 1891–1953. Soviet composer
Rodchenko, Alexander Mikhailovich 1891–1956. Russian painter
Bothe, Walther Wilhelm Georg 1891–1957. German physicist
Colman, Ronald Charles 1891–1958. English film actor
Paul, Elliot Harold 1891–1958. US author
Spencer, Stanley 1891–1959. English painter
Marx, Leonard 'Chico' 1891–1961. US film comedian; see ◊Marx Brothers
Trujillo Molina, Rafael Leónidas 1891–1961. Dictator of the Dominican Republic

Low, David Alexander Cecil 1891–1963. British cartoonist
Fraenkel, Abraham Adolf 1891–1965. Israeli mathematician
Scherchen, Hermann 1891–1966. German conductor
Ehrenburg, Ilya Grigorievich 1891–1967. Soviet writer
Heartfield, John (Helmut Hertzfelde) 1891–1968. German painter and graphic artist
Alexander, Harold Rupert Leofric George 1891–1969. British field marshal
Dix, Otto 1891–1969. German painter
Carnap, Rudolf 1891–1970. German philosopher
Slim, William Joseph, 1st Viscount Slim 1891–1970. British field marshal
Sarnoff, David 1891–1971. US broadcasting pioneer
Humason, Milton Lasell 1891–1972. US astronomer
Nijinksa, Bronislava 1891–1972. Russian choreographer and dancer
Lipchitz, Jacques 1891–1973. Lithuanian sculptor
Chadwick, James 1891–1974. English physicist
Fairweather, Ian 1891–1974. Australian artist
Lagerkvist, Pär Fabian 1891–1974. Swedish writer
Warren, Earl 1891–1974. US jurist and chief justice
Bliss, Arthur Edward Drummond 1891–1975. English composer and conductor
Ernst, Max 1891–1976. German artist
Polanyi, Michael 1891–1976. Hungarian chemist
Nervi, Pier Luigi 1891–1979. Italian engineer
Ponti, Gio(vanni) 1891–1979. Italian designer and architect
Dönitz, Karl 1891–1980. German admiral
Miller, Henry Valentine 1891–1980. US writer
McKell, William John 1891–1985. Australian governor general
Harriman, (William) Averell 1891–1986. US diplomat
Northrop, John Howard 1891–1987. US chemist
Michelucci, Giovanni 1891–1990. Italian architect
Richthofen, Manfred, Freiherr von 1892–1918. German aviator
Alcock, John William 1892–1919. British aviator
Smith, Ross Macpherson 1892–1922. Australian aviator
Akutagawa, Ryūnosuke 1892–1927. Japanese writer
Hinkler, Herbert John Louis 1892–1933. Australian pilot
Dollfuss, Engelbert 1892–1934. Austrian chancellor
Benjamin, Walter 1892–1940. German critic
Dodds, Johnny (John M) 1892–1940. US jazz clarinetist
Tsvetayeva, Marina Ivanovna 1892–1941. Russian poet
Wood, Grant 1892–1942. US painter
Brand, Max 1892–1944. US novelist and poet
Leigh-Mallory, Trafford Leigh 1892–1944. British air chief marshal
Willkie, Wendell Lewis 1892–1944. US politician
Alekhine, Alexander 1892–1946. French chess master
Lubitsch, Ernst 1892–1947. German film director
Forrestal, James Vincent 1892–1949. US politician
Handley, Tommy (Thomas Reginald) 1892–1949. English radio comedian
Sullivan, Harry Stack 1892–1949. US psychoanalyst
Millay, Edna St Vincent 1892–1950. US poet
Betti, Ugo 1892–1953. Italian dramatist
Cruwell, Ludwig 1892–1953. German general
Honegger, Arthur 1892–1955. Swiss composer
Childe, V(ere) Gordon 1892–1957. Australian archaeologist
Hardy, Oliver 1892–1957. US film comedian; see ◊Laurel and Hardy
Amanullah Khan 1892–1960. Emir of Afghanistan
Aldington, Richard 1892–1962. English poet, novelist, and critic
Compton, Arthur Holly 1892–1962. US physicist
Sackville-West, Vita (Victoria Mary) 1892–1962. English writer
Haldane, J(ohn) B(urdon) S(anderson) 1892–1964. British physiologist, geneticist, and author
Porter, Cole (Albert) 1892–1964. US composer and lyricist
Appleton, Edward Victor 1892–1965. British physicist
Daglish, Eric Fitch 1892–1966. English artist and author
Gregg, Norman McAlister 1892–1966. Australian ophthalmic surgeon

Smith, Bessie (Elizabeth) 1894–1937. US jazz and blues singer
Segar, Elzie Crisler 1894–1938. US cartoonist
Roth, Joseph 1894–1939. Austrian novelist and critic
Babel, Isaak Emmanuilovich 1894–1941. Russian writer
Boris III 1894–1943. Tsar of Bulgaria
Rutledge, Wiley Blount, Jr 1894–1949. US jurist
Bishop, William Avery 1894–1956. Canadian fighter pilot
Kinsey, Alfred Charles 1894–1956. US sexologist
Céline, Louis Ferdinand 1894–1961. French novelist
Hammett, (Samuel) Dashiell 1894–1961. US crime novelist
Thurber, James Grover 1894–1961. US humorist
cummings, e(dward) e(stlin) 1894–1962. US poet
Huxley, Aldous (Leonard) 1894–1963. English writer
Davis, Stuart 1894–1964. US painter
Kuznetsov, Vasilly 1894–1964. Soviet general
Wiener, Norbert 1894–1964. US mathematician
Aaltonen, Wäinö (Valdemar) 1894–1966. Finnish sculptor
Lemaître, Georges Edouard 1894–1966. Belgian cosmologist
Morgan, Frederick Edgworth 1894–1967. British general
Vian, Philip Louis 1894–1968. British admiral
Sternberg, Josef von 1894–1969. Austrian film director
Copland, Douglas Berry 1894–1971. Australian economist and diplomat
Khrushchev, Nikita Sergeyevich 1894–1971. Soviet president
Edward VIII 1894–1972. King of Great Britain and Northern Ireland
Trefusis, Violet 1894–1972. British society hostess and writer
Van Doren, Mark Albert 1894–1972. US poet and writer
Romer, Alfred Sherwood 1894–1973. US palaeontologist and comparative anatomist
Benny, Jack 1894–1974. US comedian
Bose, Satyendra Nath 1894–1974. Indian physicist
Brennan, Walter 1894–1974. US actor
Piston, Walter Hamor 1894–1976. US composer and teacher
Kenyatta, Jomo c. 1894–1978. Kenyan president
Leese, Oliver William Hargreaves 1894–1978. British general
Menzies, Robert Gordon 1894–1978. Australian prime minister
Rockwell, Norman 1894–1978. US painter and illustrator
Dessau, Paul 1894–1979. German composer
Fiedler, Arthur 1894–1979. US conductor
Partridge, Eric Honeywood 1894–1979. New Zealand lexicographer
Renoir, Jean 1894–1979. French film director
Oparin, Alexandr Ivanovich 1894–1980. Russian biochemist
Böhm, Karl 1894–1981. Austrian conductor
Woodger, Joseph Henry 1894–1981. English biologist
Nicholson, Ben(jamin Lauder) 1894–1982. English artist
Kapitza, Peter (Pyotr Leonidovich) 1894–1984. Soviet physicist
Priestley, J(ohn) B(oynton) 1894–1984. English novelist and playwright
Kertész, André 1894–1986. US photographer
Lartigue, Jacques-Henri Charles Auguste 1894–1986. French photographer
Macmillan, (Maurice) Harold 1894–1986. British prime minister
Russell, Dora Winifred 1894–1986. English feminist
Hess, (Walter Richard) Rudolf 1894–1987. German Nazi leader
Graham, Martha 1894–1991. US dancer and choreographer
McCudden, James Thomas Byford 1895–1918. British fighter pilot
Robinson, William Leefe 1895–1919. British fighter pilot
Esenin, or Yesenin, Sergey Aleksandrovich 1895–1925. Soviet poet
Valentino, Rudolph 1895–1926. US film actor
Bagritsky, Eduard 1895–1934. Russian poet
Cierva, Juan de la 1895–1936. Spanish engineer
Mitchell, R(eginald) J(oseph) 1895–1937. English aircraft designer
Friedeburg, Hans von 1895–1945. German admiral
Moholy-Nagy, Laszlo 1895–1946. US photographer
Bernadotte, Folke, Count 1895–1948. Swedish diplomat
Coningham, Arthur 1895–1948. British air marshal
Ruth, Babe (George Herman) 1895–1948. US baseball player
Liaquat Ali Khan, Nawabzada 1895–1951. Prime minister of Pakistan

Eluard, Paul 1895–1952. French poet
George VI 1895–1952. King of Great Britain
Tschiffley, Aimé Felix 1895–1954. Swiss writer and traveller
Alvaro, Corrado 1895–1956. Italian novelist
Arlen, Michael 1895–1956. Bulgarian writer
Bor-Komorowski, Tadeusz 1895–1956. Polish general and resistance leader
Van Doren, Harold 1895–1957. US pioneer industrial designer
Humphrey, Doris 1895–1958. US choreographer, dancer, and teacher
Nagy, Imre 1895–1958. Hungarian prime minister
Hammerstein, Oscar, II 1895–1960. US lyricist and librettist
Bedell Smith, Walter 1895–1961. US general
Zog, Ahmed Bey Zogu 1895–1961. King of Albania
Flagstad, Kirsten Malfrid 1895–1962. Norwegian soprano
Hindemith, Paul 1895–1963. German composer and teacher
Zeitzler, Kurt 1895–1963. German general
Domagk, Gerhard Johannes Paul 1895–1964. German pathologist
Lange, Dorothea 1895–1965. US photographer
Lindblad, Bertil 1895–1965. Swedish astronomer
Sargent, (Harold) Malcolm (Watts) 1895–1967. English conductor
Cárdenas, Lázaro 1895–1970. Mexican president and general
Giono, Jean 1895–1970. French novelist
Liddell Hart, Basil Henry 1895–1970. British military strategist
Timoshenko, Semyon Konstantinovich 1895–1970. Soviet general
Clark, Wilfrid Edward Le Gros 1895–1971. English anatomist and surgeon
Hoth, Hermann 1895–1971. German general
Tubman, William Vacanarat Shadrach 1895–1971. Liberian president
Balenciaga, Cristóbal 1895–1972. Spanish couturier
Hartley, L(eslie) P(oles) 1895–1972. English novelist
Hoover, J(ohn) Edgar 1895–1972. US director of the FBI
Wilson, Edmund 1895–1972. US critic and writer
Fadden, Artie (Arthur William) 1895–1973. Australian prime minister
Ford, John 1895–1973. US film director
Frisch, Ragnar Anton Kittil 1895–1973. Norwegian economist
Horkheimer, Max 1895–1973. German social theorist
Virtanen, Artturi Ilmari 1895–1973. Finnish chemist
Abbott, William 1895–1974. Member of US comedy duo ◊Abbott and Costello
Pagnol, Marcel Paul 1895–1974. French film director
Perón, Juan Domingo 1895–1974. Argentine president
Bulganin, Nikolai Aleksandrovich 1895–1975. Soviet politician and military leader
Hogben, Lancelot Thomas 1895–1975. English zoologist and geneticist
Berkeley, Busby 1895–1976. US choreographer and film director
Dam, Carl Peter Henrik 1895–1976. Danish biochemist
Minkowski, Rudolph Leo 1895–1976. US astrophysicist
Gerhardie, William Alexander 1895–1977. English novelist
Vasilevsky, Alexandr M 1895–1977. Soviet general
Williamson, Henry 1895–1977. English author
Leavis, F(rank) R(aymond) 1895–1978. English literary critic
Diefenbaker, John George 1895–1979. Canadian prime minister
Massine, Léonide 1895–1979. Russian choreographer and dancer
Raft, George 1895–1980. US film actor
Rhine, Joseph Banks 1895–1980. US parapsychologist
Russell of Liverpool 1895–1981. British barrister
Freud, Anna 1895–1982. British child psychoanalyst
Orff, Carl 1895–1982. German composer
Baillie, Isobel 1895–1983. British soprano
Dempsey, Jack (William Harrison) 1895–1983. US boxer
Fuller, (Richard) Buckminster 1895–1983. US architect
Halas, George Stanley 1895–1983. US athlete and sports promoter
Graves, Robert Ranke 1895–1985. English poet and author
Horrocks, Brian Gwynne 1895–1985. British general
Chase, William C 1895–1986. US general
Arup, Ove 1895–1988. Danish engineer

1901–5

Hergé 1907–1983. Belgian artist
Hellman, Lillian Florence 1907–1984. US dramatist
Hooker, Stanley George 1907–1984. English engineer
Segal, Walter 1907–1985. British architect
Simpson, (Cedric) Keith 1907–1985. British forensic scientist
Eliade, Mircea 1907–1986. Romanian philosopher and
    anthropologist
Tinbergen, Niko(laas) 1907–1988. British zoologist
Du Maurier, Daphne 1907–1989. English novelist
Olivier, Laurence Kerr 1907–1989. English actor and director
Bowlby, (Edward) John (Mostyn) 1907–1990. English psychologist
Foot, Hugh Mackintosh, Baron Caradon 1907–1990. British
    politician
MacLennan, (John) Hugh 1907–1990. Canadian novelist and
    essayist
Stanwyck, Barbara 1907–1990. US film actress
Ashcroft, Peggy 1907–1991. English actress
Inoue, Yasushi 1907–1991. Japanese writer
McMillan, Edwin Mattison 1907–1991. US physicist
McPartland, Jimmy (James Duigald) 1907–1991. US cornet player
Miles, Bernard James, Baron Miles 1907–1991. English actor and
    producer
Moravia, Alberto 1907–1991. Italian novelist
Wainwright, Alfred 1907–1991. English walker and author of
    guidebooks
Welensky, Roy 1907–1991. Rhodesian prime minister
Bovet, Daniel 1907–1992. Swiss physiologist
Shawn, William 1907–1992. US journalist
Charteris, Leslie Charles Bowyer Yin 1907–1993. US novelist
Hart, H(erbert) L(ionel) A(dolphus) 1907–1993. English jurist and
    philosopher
Calloway, Cab(ell) 1907–1994. US band leader and singer
Burger, Warren 1907–1995. US jurist and chief justice
Nu, U (Thakin) 1907–1995. Myanmar prime minister
Peierls, Rudolf Ernst 1907–1995. British physicist
Whittle, Frank 1907–1996. British engineer
Todd, Alexander Robertus 1907–1997. Scottish organic chemist
Barzun, Jacques Martin 1907– . US historian
Duwez, Pol 1907– . US scientist
Fry, Christopher Harris 1907– . English dramatist
Hailsham, Quintin McGarel Hogg, Baron Hailsham 1907– .
    British lawyer and politician
Heinlein, Robert A(nson) 1907– . US science-fiction writer
Hope, A(lec) D(erwent) 1907– . Australian poet and critic
Karamanlis, Konstantinos 1907– . Greek prime minister
Meade, James Edward 1907– . British economist
Niemeyer, (Soares Filho) Oscar 1907– . Brazilian architect
Paz, (Estenssoro) Victor 1907– . President of Bolivia
Powell, Lewis Stanley 1907– . US jurist
Revans, Reginald William 1907– . British management expert
Wray, Fay 1907– . US film actress
Yang Shangkun 1907– . Chinese president
Young, J(ohn) Z(achary) 1907– . English zoologist
Zinnemann, Fred(erick) 1907– . Austrian film director
Herbrand, Jacques 1908–1931. French mathematician
Lombard, Carole 1908–1942. US film actress
Pavese, Cesare 1908–1950. Italian poet, translator, and novelist
McCarthy, Joe (Joseph Raymond) 1908–1957. US politician
Wright, Richard 1908–1960. US novelist
Merleau-Ponty, Maurice 1908–1961. French philosopher
Roethke, Theodore Huebner 1908–1963. US poet
Fleming, Ian Lancaster 1908–1964. English author
Murrow, Edward R(oscoe) 1908–1965. US broadcast journalist
Holt, Harold Edward 1908–1967. Australian prime minister
Landau, Lev Davidovich 1908–1968. Russian physicist
Adamov, Arthur 1908–1970. French poet
Balchin, Nigel Marlin 1908–1970. English author
Lin Biao 1908–1971. Chinese politician
Powell, Adam Clayton, Jr 1908–1972. US political leader
Allende (Gossens), Salvador 1908–1973. Chilean politician

Johnson, Lyndon Baines 1908–1973. 36th president of the USA
Bronowski, Jacob 1908–1974. British scientist
Oistrakh, David Fyodorovich 1908–1974. Soviet violinist
Schindler, Oskar 1908–1974. Czechoslovak industrialist and Jewish
    benefactor
Skorzeny, Otto 1908–1975. German colonel
Crawford, Joan 1908–1977. US film actress
Libby, Willard Frank 1908–1980. US chemist
Manning, Olivia Mary 1908–1980. English novelist
Betancourt, Rómulo 1908–1981. Venezuelan president
Saroyan, William 1908–1981. US author
Johnson, Celia 1908–1982. English actress
Tati, Jacques 1908–1982. French comic actor
Buckler, Ernest Redmond 1908–1984. Canadian novelist
Gibberd, Frederick Ernest 1908–1984. English architect and town
    planner
Hoxha, Enver 1908–1985. Albanian head of state
Redgrave, Michael Scudamore 1908–1985. English actor
Beauvoir, Simone de 1908–1986. French socialist, feminist, and
    writer
Gardner, Helen Louise 1908–1986. English scholar and critic
Kaldor, Nicholas, Baron Kaldor 1908–1986. British economist
Lancaster, Osbert 1908–1986. English cartoonist and writer
Larsson, Lars-Erik 1908–1986. Swedish composer, conductor, and
    critic
Sandys, (Edwin) Duncan, Baron Duncan-Sandys 1908–1987.
    British politician
Strömgren, Bengt Georg Daniel 1908–1987. Danish astronomer
Tudor, Antony 1908–1987. English choreographer, dancer, and
    teacher
McMahon, William 1908–1988. Australian prime minister
Davis, Bette 1908–1989. US film actress
Karajan, Herbert von 1908–1989. Austrian conductor
Frank, Ilya Mikhailoivich 1908–1990. Russian physicist
Harrison, Rex (Reginald Carey) 1908–1990. English actor
Wall, Max 1908–1990. English music-hall comedian
Bardeen, John 1908–1991. US physicist
Lean, David 1908–1991. English film director
Manzù, Giacomo 1908–1991. Italian sculptor
Maskell, Dan 1908–1992. British tennis commentator
Messiaen, Olivier Eugène Prosper Charles 1908–1992. French
    composer, organist, and teacher
Morley, Robert 1908–1992. English actor and playwright
Pike, Magnus Alfred 1908–1992. British food scientist and
    broadcaster
Ameche, Don 1908–1993. US actor
Marshall, Thurgood 1908–1993. US jurist and civil-rights leader
Salisbury, Harrison E(vans) 1908–1993. US journalist
Wang, Zhen 1908–1993. Chinese political leader
Wilson, John Tuzo 1908–1993. Canadian geologist
Alfvén, Hannes Olof Gösta 1908–1995. Swedish astrophysicist
Ambartsumian, Viktor Amazaspovich 1908– . Soviet-Armenian
    astronomer
Balthus 1908– . French painter
Barr, Murray Llewellyn 1908– . Canadian anatomist and
    geneticist
Bradman, Don(ald George) 1908– . Australian cricketer
Carter, Elliott Cook 1908– . US composer
Cartier-Bresson, Henri 1908– . French photographer
Cooke, (Alfred) Alistair 1908– . US journalist
Edwards, George Robert 1908– . British aircraft designer
Eldem, Sedad Hakki 1908– . Turkish architect
Fuchs, Vivian Ernest 1908– . British explorer and geologist
Galbraith, John Kenneth 1908– . US economist
Grappelli, Stephane 1908– . French jazz violinist
Karsh, Yousuf 1908– . Canadian photographer
Lévi-Strauss, Claude 1908– . French anthropologist
Martin, (John) Leslie 1908– . English architect
Mellanby, Kenneth 1908– . British ecologist and entomologist
Mills, John Lewis Ernest Watts 1908– . English actor

Chandrasekhar, Subrahmanyan 1910–1995. US astrophysicist
Bowles, Paul Frederick 1910– . US writer and composer
Candela, (Outeriño) Félix 1910– . Spanish architect and engineer
Casson, Hugh Maxwell 1910– . English architect
Cockerell, Christopher Sydney 1910– . English engineer
Cousteau, Jacques Yves 1910– . French oceanographer and
   conservationist
Fraenkel-Conrat, Heinz Ludwig 1910– . US biochemist
Giap, Vo Nguyen 1910– . Vietnamese military leader and
   politician
Hunt, (Henry Cecil) John, Baron Hunt 1910– . British
   mountaineer
Kurosawa, Akira 1910– . Japanese director
Latsis, John 1910– . Greek shipping tycoon
Markova, Alicia 1910– . English ballet dancer
Martin, Archer John Porter 1910– . British biochemist
Merton, Robert King 1910– . US sociologist
Mitford, Diana 1910– . English socialite; see ◊Mitford sisters
Schuman, William Howard 1910– . US composer and teacher
Shaw, Artie 1910– . US jazz clarinettist and bandleader
Teresa, Mother 1910– . Roman Catholic nun
Thesiger, Wilfred Patrick 1910– . English explorer and writer
Ulanova, Galina Sergeyevna 1910– . Soviet dancer
Wedgwood, C(icely) V(eronica) 1910– . British historian
Whitehouse, Mary 1910– . British media activist

1911–15

Parker, Bonnie 1911–1934. US criminal; see ◊Bonnie and Clyde
Harlow, Jean 1911–1937. US film actress
Schellenberg, Walter 1911–1952. German SS general
Austin, J(ohn) L(angshaw) 1911–1960. British philosopher
Seyfert, Carl Keenan 1911–1960. US astronomer
Burgess, Guy Francis de Moncy 1911–1963. British spy
O'Brien, Flann 1911–1966. Irish humorist, novelist, and essayist
Peake, Mervyn Laurence 1911–1968. English writer and illustrator
Goodman, Paul 1911–1972. US writer and social critic
Jackson, Mahalia 1911–1972. US gospel singer
Senanayake, Dudley Shelton 1911–1973. Sri Lankan prime
   minister
Dean, Dizzy (Jay Hanna) 1911–1974. US baseball player
Pompidou, Georges Jean Raymond 1911–1974. French president
Herrmann, Bernard 1911–1975. US film composer
Harrisson, Tom (Thomas Harnett) 1911–1976. British
   anthropologist
Rattigan, Terence Mervyn 1911–1977. English dramatist
Schumacher, Fritz (Ernst Friedrich) 1911–1977. German
   economist
Williams, Frederic Calland 1911–1977. English electrical and
   electronics engineer
Humphrey, Hubert Horatio 1911–1978. US political leader
Lynen, Feodor Felix Konrad 1911–1979. German biochemist
Oberon, Merle 1911–1979. British actress
Ray, Nicholas 1911–1979. US film director
McLuhan, (Herbert) Marshall 1911–1980. Canadian
   communication theorist
Charnley, John 1911–1982. English orthopaedic surgeon
Frei, Eduardo 1911–1982. Chilean president
Williams, Tennessee (Thomas Lanier) 1911–1983. US dramatist
Porter, Hal 1911–1984. Australian writer
Chernenko, Konstantin Ustinovich 1911–1985. Soviet president
Turner, Big Joe (Joseph Vernon) 1911–1985. US blues singer
Hubbard, L(afayette) Ron(ald) 1911–1986. US founder of
   Scientology
Tate, Phyllis Margaret Duncan 1911–1987. British composer
Alvarez, Luis Walter 1911–1988. US physicist
Fuchs, (Emil Julius) Klaus 1911–1988. German spy
Ball, Lucille Desirée 1911–1989. US comedy actress
Goddard, Paulette 1911–1990. US film actress

Le Duc Tho 1911–1990. North Vietnamese diplomat
Spear, Ruskin 1911–1990. English artist
Terry-Thomas 1911–1990. English film actor
Frisch, Max Rudolf 1911–1991. Swiss dramatist
Burkitt, Denis Parsons 1911–1993. British surgeon
Cantinflas 1911–1993. Mexican comedian
Golding, William Gerald 1911–1993. English novelist
Price, Vincent 1911–1993. US actor
Weston, Brett 1911–1993. US photographer
Jerne, Niels Kaj 1911–1994. Danish microbiologist
Djilas, Milovan 1911–1995. Yugoslav dissident
Fangio, Juan Manuel 1911–1995. Argentine racing-car driver
Fowler, William Alfred 1911–1995. US astrophysicist
Hordern, Michael Murray 1911–1995. English actor
Lyttleton, Raymond Arthur 1911–1995. English astronomer and
   physicist
Rogers, Ginger 1911–1995. US actress, dancer, and singer
Maclean, Fitzroy Hew 1911–1996. Scottish writer and diplomat
Bernhard Leopold 1911– . Prince of the Netherlands
Bjelke-Petersen, Joh(annes) 1911– . Australian premier of
   Queensland
Calvin, Melvin 1911– . US chemist
Castle, Barbara Anne 1911– . British politician
Curnow, Allen 1911– . New Zealand poet and dramatist
Dassin, Jules 1911– . US film director
Elytis, Odysseus 1911– . Greek poet
Gorton, John Grey 1911– . Australian prime minister
Katz, Bernard 1911– . British biophysicist
Mahfouz, Naguib 1911– . Egyptian novelist and playwright
Matta, (Roberto Sebastien Antonio Matta Eschaurren) 1911– .
   French painter
Menotti, Gian Carlo 1911– . US composer
Miłosz, Czesław 1911– . Polish-American writer
Ne Win 1911– . Myanmar president
Reagan, Ronald Wilson 1911– . 40th president of the USA
Reber, Grote 1911– . US radio engineer
Sábato, Ernesto 1911– . Argentine novelist and social critic
Scarman, Leslie George, Baron Scarman 1911– . English judge
   and legal reformer
Suzuki, Zenkō 1911– . Japanese prime minister
Troyat, Henri 1911– . French writer
Varah, (Edward) Chad 1911– . British founder of the Samaritans
Zhivkov, Todor 1911– . Bulgarian president
Johnson, Robert c. 1912–1938. US blues guitarist
Parer, Damien 1912–1944. Australian photographer
Braun, Eva 1912–1945. German mistress of Adolf Hitler
Wallenberg, Raoul 1912–c. 1947. Swedish business executive
Ferrier, Kathleen Mary 1912–1953. English contralto
Turing, Alan Mathison 1912–1954. English mathematician and
   logician
Pollock, (Paul) Jackson 1912–1956. US painter
Louis, Morris 1912–1962. US painter
Tafawa Balewa, Alhaji Abubakar 1912–1966. Nigerian prime
   minister
Guthrie, Woody (Woodrow Wilson) 1912–1967. US folk singer
   and songwriter
Henie, Sonja 1912–1969. Norwegian skater
Taylor, Elizabeth 1912–1975. English novelist
Braun, Wernher von 1912–1977. German scientist
von Braun, Wernher Magnus Maximilian 1912–1977. German
   rocket engineer
John Paul I 1912–1978. Pope
Deller, Alfred 1912–1979. English singer
Hutton, Barbara 1912–1979. US heiress
Kenton, Stan (Stanley Newcomb) 1912–1979. US jazz musician
Glover, Denis 1912–1980. New Zealand poet
Drysdale, (George) Russell 1912–1981. Australian artist
Johnson, Pamela Hansford, Lady Snow 1912–1981. British novelist
Cheever, John 1912–1982. US writer
Jurgens, Curt (Curd Jürgens) 1912–1982. German actor

Paul, Les 1915– . US inventor
Pinochet (Ugarte), Augusto 1915– . Chilean president
Profumo, John Dennis 1915– . British politician
Richter, Sviatoslav Teofilovich 1915– . Russian pianist
Samuelson, Paul Anthony 1915– . US economist
Schwarzkopf, (Olga Maria) Elisabeth (Friederike) 1915– . German soprano
Shamir, Yitzhak Yernitsky 1915– . Israeli prime minister
Sinatra, Frank (Francis Albert) 1915– . US singer and film actor
Taube, Henry 1915– . US chemist
Townes, Charles Hard 1915– . US physicist
Wright, Judith Arundell 1915– . Australian poet
Young, Michael 1915– . British social entrepreneur

1916–20

Aung San 1916–1947. Burmese politician
Burns, John Horne 1916–1953. US novelist
Mills, C(harles) Wright 1916–1962. US sociologist
Blomdahl, Karl-Birger 1916–1968. Swedish composer
Grable, Betty (Elizabeth Ruth) 1916–1973. US film actress
Finch, Peter William Mitchell 1916–1977. English film actor
Moro, Aldo 1916–1978. Italian prime minister
Neave, Airey Middleton Sheffield 1916–1979. British intelligence officer and politician
Ginastera, Alberto Evaristo 1916–1983. Argentine composer
Hayden, Sterling 1916–1986. US film actor
Eames, Ray (Kaiser) 1916–1988. US designer
Dahl, Roald 1916–1990. British writer
Hutton, Len (Leonard) 1916–1990. English cricketer
Lockwood, Margaret Mary 1916–1990. English actress
Wallace, Irving 1916–1990. US novelist
Brickhill, Paul Chester Jerome 1916–1991. Australian writer
Gaillard, Slim (Bulee) 1916–1991. US jazz musician
Giles, Carl Ronald 1916–1995. British cartoonist
Herriot, James 1916–1995. English writer
Wilson, (James) Harold 1916–1995. British prime minister
Wright, Peter 1916–1995. British intelligence agent
Mitterrand, François 1916–1996. French president
Babbitt, Milton 1916– . US composer and theorist
Bandaranaike, Sirimavo 1916– . Sri Lankan prime minister
Ben Bella, Mohammed Ahmed 1916– . Algerian president
Botha, P(ieter) W(illem) 1916– . South African president
Cela, Camilo José 1916– . Spanish novelist
Crick, Francis Harry Compton 1916– . English molecular biologist
Cronkite, Walter Leland 1916– . US broadcast journalist
De Havilland, Olivia Mary 1916– . US actress
Dicke, Robert Henry 1916– . US physicist
Douglas, Kirk 1916– . US film actor
Dutilleux, Henri 1916– . French composer
Eysenck, Hans Jürgen 1916– . British psychologist
Ford, Glenn (Gwyllym Samuel Newton) 1916– . US actor
Ginzburg, Vitalii Lazarevich 1916– . Russian astrophysicist
Hanbury-Brown, Robert 1916– . British radio astronomer
Heath, Edward Richard George 1916– . British prime minister
McCarthy, Eugene Joseph 1916– . US politician
Menuhin, Yehudi, Baron Menuhin 1916– . British violinist and conductor
Mintoff, Dom(inic) 1916– . Maltese prime minister
Peck, (Eldred) Gregory 1916– . US film actor
Prokhorov, Aleksandr Mikhailovich 1916– . Russian physicist
Quinn, Anthony Rudolph Oaxaca 1916– . US actor
Shannon, Claude Elwood 1916– . US mathematician
Simon, Herbert Alexander 1916– . US social scientist
West, Morris Langlo 1916– . Australian novelist
Whitlam, (Edward) Gough 1916– . Australian prime minister
Wilkins, Maurice Hugh Frederick 1916– . British molecular biologist

Lipatti, Dinu 1917–1950. Romanian pianist
Kennedy, John F(itzgerald) ('Jack') 1917–1963. 35th president of the USA
McCullers, (Lula) Carson 1917–1967. US novelist
Niland, D'Arcy Francis 1917–1967. Australian writer
Nyholm, Ronald Sydney 1917–1971. Australian chemist
Lowell, Robert Traill Spence, Jr 1917–1977. US poet
Maudling, Reginald 1917–1979. British politician
Park Chung Hee 1917–1979. President of South Korea
Woodward, Robert Burns 1917–1979. US chemist
Yahya Khan, Agha Muhammad 1917–1980. Pakistani president
Monk, Thelonious Sphere 1917–1982. US jazz pianist and composer
Gandhi, Indira Priyadarshani 1917–1984. Indian prime minister
Böll, Heinrich Theodor 1917–1985. German novelist
Porter, Rodney Robert 1917–1985. English biochemist
Marcos, Ferdinand Edralin 1917–1989. Filipino president
Bohm, David Joseph 1917–1992. British physicist
Cheshire, (Geoffrey) Leonard 1917–1992. British pilot
Nolan, Sidney Robert 1917–1992. Australian artist
Burgess, Anthony 1917–1993. English novelist, critic, and composer
Burr, Raymond 1917–1993. Canadian actor
Gillespie, Dizzy (John Birks) 1917–1993. US jazz trumpeter
Tambo, Oliver 1917–1993. South African politician
Shore, Dinah (Frances Rose) 1917–1994. US pop singer and actress
Somes, Michael George 1917–1994. British ballet dancer
Mitford, Jessica 1917–1996. US writer; see ◊Mitford sisters
Allyson, June 1917– . US film actress
Bastos, Augusto Roa 1917– . Paraguayan writer
Bedford, John Robert Russell, 13th Duke of Bedford 1917– . English peer
Causley, Charles Stanley 1917– . English poet
Clarke, Arthur C(harles) 1917– . English science-fiction writer
Cornforth, John Warcup 1917– . Australian chemist
Cunningham, John 1917– . British fighter pilot
Duve, Christian René de 1917– . Belgian biochemist
Fontaine, Joan 1917– . US film actress
Hardy, Frank (Francis) 1917– . Australian political writer
Healey, Denis Winston, Baron Healey 1917– . British politician
Hooker, John Lee 1917– . US blues guitarist
Huxley, Andrew Fielding 1917– . English physiologist
Kendrew, John Cowdery 1917– . English biochemist
Lynch, Jack (John Mary) 1917– . Irish prime minister
Lynn, Vera Margaret Lewis 1917– . English singer
Mitchum, Robert Charles Duran 1917– . US film actor
Nakasone, Yasuhiro 1917– . Japanese prime minister
Nkomo, Joshua 1917– . Zimbabwean vice president
Pei, Ieoh Ming 1917– . US architect
Penn, Irving 1917– . US photographer
Prigogine, Ilya, Viscount Prigogine 1917– . Belgian chemist
Rainwater, (Leo) James 1917– . US physicist
Rowland, Tiny (Roland W) 1917– . British entrepreneur
Schlesinger, Arthur Meier, Jr 1917– . US historian
Sottsass, Ettore, Jr 1917– . Italian designer
Suzman, Helen Gavronsky 1917– . South African politician
Vance, Cyrus Roberts 1917– . US politician
Weinberger, Caspar Willard 1917– . US politician
White, Byron Raymond 1917– . US jurist
Wyeth, Andrew Newell 1917– . US painter
Bolo, Paul (Pasha) died 1918. French traitor and confidence trickster
Gibson, Guy Penrose 1918–1944. British bomber pilot
Birch, John M 1918–1945. US missionary
Rosenberg, Julius 1918–1953. US spy
James, Elmore 1918–1963. US blues guitarist
Nasser, Gamal Abdel 1918–1970. Egyptian president
Holden, William 1918–1981. US film actor
Sadat, (Muhammad) Anwar 1918–1981. Egyptian president

1921–25

Nono, Luigi 1924–1990. Italian composer
Vaughan, Sarah Lois 1924–1990. US jazz singer
Bevan, Brian 1924–1991. Australian rugby league player
Hart, Judith Constance Mary, Baroness Hart 1924–1991. British
    politician
Abe Kōbō 1924–1993. Japanese novelist and playwright
Premadasa, Ranasinghe 1924–1993. Sri Lankan president
Slayton, Deke (Donald Kent) 1924–1993. US astronaut
Clavell, James du Maresq 1924–1994. British writer, film director,
    and producer
Feyerabend, Paul K 1924–1994. US philosopher
Mancini, Henry 1924–1994. US composer
Bolt, Robert Oxton 1924–1995. English dramatist and screenwriter
Mastroianni, Marcello 1924–1997. Italian film actor
Bacall, Lauren 1924– . US actress
Barre, Raymond 1924– . French politician
Berger, Thomas Louis 1924– . US writer
Bernstein, Basil Bernard 1924– . British sociologist
Berrigan, Philip 1924– . US Roman Catholic priest, opponent of
    the Vietnam War
Black, James Whyte 1924– . British physiologist
Brando, Marlon 1924– . US actor
Bush, George Herbert Walker 1924– . 41st president of the USA
Bykau, Vasil 1924– . Belorussian writer
Caro, Anthony (Alfred) 1924– . English sculptor
Carter, Jimmy 1924– . 39th president of the USA
Chisholm, Shirley Anita St Hill 1924– . US politician
Day, Doris 1924– . US film actress
Demirel, Süleyman 1924– . Turkish president
Denktaş, Rauf R 1924– . President of the Turkish Republic of
    North Cyprus
Dollfus, Audouin Charles 1924– . French physicist and astronomer
Donen, Stanley 1924– . US film director
Frame, Janet Paterson 1924– . New Zealand novelist
Frank, Robert 1924– . US photographer
Freud, Clement Raphael 1924– . British journalist and politician
Gass, William Howard 1924– . US experimental writer
Guillemin, Roger Charles Louis 1924– . US endocrinologist
Haig, Alexander Meigs 1924– . US general and politician
Herbert, Zbigniew 1924– . Polish poet and essayist
Heston, Charlton 1924– . US film actor
Hewish, Antony 1924– . English radio astronomer
Huxley, Hugh Esmor 1924– . English physiologist
Kaunda, Kenneth David 1924– . Zambian president
Kim Dae Jung 1924– . South Korean politician
Kimura, Motō 1924– . Japanese biologist
Koch, Ed(ward Irving) 1924– . US politician
Lighthill, (Michael) James 1924– . British mathematician
Lumet, Sidney 1924– . US film director
Lyotard, Jean François 1924– . French philosopher
Mandelbrot, Benoit B 1924– . French mathematician
Manley, Michael (Norman) 1924– . Jamaican prime minister
Marriner, Neville 1924– . English conductor and violinist
Moi, Daniel arap 1924– . Kenyan president
Murayama, Tomiichi 1924– . Japanese trade unionist and prime
    minister
Nykvist, Sven 1924– . Swedish director of photography
Obote, (Apollo) Milton 1924– . Ugandan president
Paolozzi, Eduardo Luigi 1924– . Scottish sculptor and graphic
    artist
Poitier, Sidney 1924– . US actor and film director
Pugh, Clifton Ernest 1924– . Australian artist
Rehnquist, William 1924– . US chief justice
Rix, Brian Norman Roger 1924– . English actor and director
Servan-Schreiber, Jean Jacques 1924– . French politician
Soares, Mario Alberto Nobre Lopes 1924– . Portuguese president
Takeshita, Noboru 1924– . Japanese prime minister
Pol Pot c. 1925– . Cambodian prime minister
Fanon, Frantz Omar 1925–1961. French political writer
Lumumba, Patrice Emergy 1925–1961. Congolese prime minister

O'Connor, (Mary) Flannery 1925–1964. US novelist and short-
    story writer
Bruce, Lenny 1925–1966. US comedian
Kennedy, Robert Francis 1925–1968. US politician and lawyer
Mishima, Yukio 1925–1970. Japanese novelist
Lispector, Clarice 1925–1977. Brazilian writer
Boumédienne, Houari 1925–1978. Algerian politician
Sellers, Peter 1925–1980. English comedian and film actor
Somoza Debayle, Anastasio 1925–1980. Nicaraguan president
Burton, Richard 1925–1984. Welsh stage and screen actor
Ashley, Laura 1925–1985. Welsh designer
Hudson, Rock 1925–1985. US film actor
Stonehouse, John Thomson 1925–1988. British politician
Davis, Sammy, Jr 1925–1990. US entertainer
Duarte, José Napoleon 1925–1990. El Salvadorean president
Pomus, Doc (Jerome Solon Felder) 1925–1991. US songwriter; see
    ◊Pomus and Shuman
Tower, John Goodwin 1925–1991. US politician
Hill, Benny 1925–1992. English comedian
Bérégovoy, Pierre Eugène 1925–1993. French prime minister
Moore, Charles 1925–1993. US architect
Baker, Howard Henry 1925–1994. US politician
Mercouri, Melina 1925–1994. Greek actress and politician
Wain, John Barrington 1925–1994. English poet and novelist
Zetterling, Mai Elisabeth 1925–1994. Swedish actress and director
Durrell, Gerald Malcolm 1925–1995. English conservationist and
    writer
Aldiss, Brian Wilson 1925– . English science-fiction writer
Alia, Ramiz 1925– . Albanian president
Altman, Robert 1925– . US film director and producer
Amin (Dada), Idi 1925– . Ugandan president
Astley, Thea 1925– . Australian novelist and short-story writer
Benn, Tony (Anthony Neil Wedgwood) 1925– . British politician
Berio, Luciano 1925– . Italian composer
Boulez, Pierre 1925– . French composer and conductor
Brook, Peter Stephen Paul 1925– . English theatre director
Buckley, William F(rank) 1925– . US political writer
Cameron, Alastair Graham Walter 1925– . US astrophysicist
Christopher, Warren 1925– . US politician
Cohan, Robert Paul 1925– . US choreographer
Curtis, Tony 1925– . US film actor
Delors, Jacques Lucien Jean 1925– . French politician and head of
    the European Commission
Edwards, Robert Geoffrey 1925– . British physiologist
Esaki, Leo 1925– . Japanese physicist
Fischer-Dieskau, Dietrich 1925– . German baritone
Haughey, Charles James 1925– . Irish prime minister
Hawkes, John Clendennin Burne Jr 1925– . US novelist
Izetbegović, Alija 1925– . Bosnia-Herzegovinan president
King, B B (Riley) 1925– . US blues guitarist and singer
Larsen, Henning 1925– . Danish architect
Lederberg, Joshua 1925– . US geneticist
Lemmon, Jack (John Uhler III) 1925– . US actor
Leonard, Elmore John, Jr 1925– . US novelist
McCowen, Alec (Alexander Duncan) 1925– . English actor
MacCready, Paul Beattie 1925– . US ship designer
Mackerras, (Alan) Charles (MacLaurin) 1925– . Australian
    conductor
McWhirter, Norris Dewar 1925– . British editor
Mahathir bin Mohamed 1925– . Malaysian prime minister
Masire, Quett Ketumile Joni 1925– . Botswanan president
Medvedev, Vadim Andreyevich 1925– . Soviet politician
Mugabe, Robert (Gabriel) 1925– . Zimbabwean president
Muzorewa, Abel (Tendekayi) 1925– . Zimbabwean prime
    minister and bishop
Mwinyi, Ali Hassan 1925– . Tanzanian president
Neizvestny, Ernst Iosifovich 1925– . Russian artist and sculptor
Newman, Paul 1925– . US actor and director
Plisetskaya, Maya Mikhailovna 1925– . Soviet ballerina and
    actress

1926–30

Eisner, Thomas 1929–   . US entomologist
Field, George Brooks 1929–   . US astrophysicist
Foley, Thomas S(tephen) 1929–   . US politician
French, Marilyn 1929–   . US feminist writer
Friel, Brian 1929–   . Northern Irish dramatist
Gehry, Frank Owen 1929–   . US architect
Gell-Mann, Murray 1929–   . US physicist
Grange, Kenneth Henry 1929–   . English industrial designer
Habermas, Jürgen 1929–   . German social theorist
Haitink, Bernard 1929–   . Dutch conductor
Harnoncourt, Nikolaus 1929–   . German conductor, cellist, and
   musicologist
Hassan II 1929–   . King of Morocco
Hawke, Bob (Robert James Lee) 1929–   . Australian prime
   minister
Herzog, Bertram 1929–   . German computer scientist
Iskander, Fazil Abdulovich 1929–   . Georgian writer
Kent, Bruce 1929–   . British peace campaigner
Kundera, Milan 1929–   . Czech writer
Le Guin, Ursula K(roeber) 1929–   . US science-fiction writer
Le Roy Ladurie, Emmanuel Bernard 1929–   . French historian
Mayhew, Patrick (Barnabas Burke) 1929–   . British politician
Moss, Stirling 1929–   . English racing-car driver
Mössbauer, Rudolf (Ludwig) 1929–   . German physicist
Müller, Heiner 1929–   . German dramatist
Nujoma, Sam 1929–   . Namibian president
Oldenburg, Claes Thure 1929–   . US artist
Oyono, Ferdinand Léopold 1929–   . Cameroon novelist
Palmer, Arnold Daniel 1929–   . US golfer
Patterson, Harry 1929–   . English novelist
Previn, André George 1929–   . US conductor
Rich, Adrienne 1929–   . US poet and feminist
Ryzhkov, Nikolai Ivanovich 1929–   . Soviet prime minister
Saw Maung 1929–   . Myanmar soldier and prime minister
Schlüter, Poul Holmskov 1929–   . Danish prime minister
Sills, Beverly 1929–   . US soprano
Simmons, Jean 1929–   . English actress
Stahl, Franklin William 1929–   . US molecular biologist
Steiner, (Francis) George 1929–   . US critic
Sydow, Max (Carl Adolf) von 1929–   . Swedish actor
Thorpe, (John) Jeremy 1929–   . British politician
Turner, John Napier 1929–   . Canadian prime minister
Waddington, David Charles 1929–   . British politician
Waterhouse, Keith Spencer 1929–   . English journalist, novelist,
   and dramatist
Wilson, E(dward) O(sborne) 1929–   . US zoologist
Mboya, Tom (Thomas Joseph) 1930–1969. Kenyan politician
Colombo, Joe Cesare 1930–1971. Italian industrial designer
MacArthur, Robert Helmer 1930–1972. US ecologist
McQueen, Steve (Terrence Steven) 1930–1980. US film actor
Bulatović, Miodrag 1930–1991. Serbian writer
Baudouin 1930–1993. King of the Belgians
Frink, Elisabeth 1930–1993. English sculptor
Herron, Ron(ald James) 1930–1994. English architect
Grosz, Károly 1930–1996. Hungarian prime minister
Takemitsu, Toru 1930–1996. Japanese composer
Achebe, Chinua (Albert Chinualumogo) 1930–   . Nigerian
   novelist
Aldrin, Edwin Eugene ('Buzz') 1930–   . US astronaut
Arden, John 1930–   . English dramatist
Armstrong, Neil Alden 1930–   . US astronaut
Assad, Hafez al 1930–   . Syrian Ba'athist politician
Baker, James Addison III 1930–   . US politician
Ballard, J(ames) G(raham) 1930–   . English novelist
Bart, Lionel 1930–   . English composer
Barth, John Simmons 1930–   . US novelist and short-story writer
Biffen, (William) John 1930–   . British politician
Brathwaite, Edward Kamau 1930–   . West Indian historian and
   poet
Calne, Roy Yorke 1930–   . British surgeon

Carlucci, Frank Charles 1930–   . US politician
Chabrol, Claude 1930–   . French film director
Charles, Ray 1930–   . US singer, songwriter, and pianist
Choong, Eddy (Ewe Beng) 1930–   . Malaysian badminton player
Coleman, Ornette 1930–   . US jazz saxophonist and composer
Connery, Sean Thomas 1930–   . Scottish film actor
Cooper, Leon Niels 1930–   . US physicist
Dawe, (Donald) Bruce 1930–   . Australian poet
Derrida, Jacques 1930–   . French philosopher
Eagleburger, Lawrence S(idney) 1930–   . US government official
Eastwood, Clint(on) 1930–   . US film actor and director
Ershad, Hussain Muhammad 1930–   . Bangladeshi president
Fraser, (John) Malcolm 1930–   . Australian prime minister
Garbus, Martin 1930–   . US lawyer
Godard, Jean-Luc 1930–   . French film director
Goldsmith, Jerry (Jerrald) 1930–   . US composer
Hall, Peter Reginald Frederick 1930–   . English theatre and opera
   director
Hughes, Ted (Edward James) 1930–   . English poet
Hurd, Douglas (Richard) 1930–   . English politician
Iliescu, Ion 1930–   . Romanian president
Johns, Jasper 1930–   . US painter, sculptor, and printmaker
Kohl, Helmut 1930–   . German chancellor
Kovac, Michal 1930–   . Slovak president
Landy, John Michael 1930–   . Australian athlete
Maazel, Lorin Varencove 1930–   . US conductor and violinist
Marcos, Imelda Romualdez 1930–   . Filipino politician
Margaret 1930–   . Princess of the UK
Meselson, Matthew Stanley 1930–   . US molecular biologist
Miller, Stanley Lloyd 1930–   . US chemist
Mobutu, Sese Seko Kuku Ngbeandu Wa Za Banga 1930–   .
   Zairean president
O'Brien, (Josephine) Edna 1930–   . Irish writer
O'Connor, Sandra Day 1930–   . US jurist
Perot, Ross 1930–   . US industrialist and politician
Pindling, Lynden (Oscar) 1930–   . Bahamian prime minister
Pinter, Harold 1930–   . English dramatist
Rendell, Ruth Barbara 1930–   . English novelist and short-story
   writer
Robertson, Pat (Marion Gordon) 1930–   . US politician and
   religious broadcaster
Rocard, Michel 1930–   . French prime minister
Rollins, Sonny (Theodore Walter) 1930–   . US jazz saxophonist
Sarney (Costa), José 1930–   . Brazilian president
Silayev, Ivan Stepanovich 1930–   . Soviet prime minister
Snowdon, Anthony Charles Robert Armstrong-Jones, 1st Earl of
   Snowdon 1930–   . English photographer
Snyder, Gary Sherman 1930–   . US poet
Sondheim, Stephen Joshua 1930–   . US composer and lyricist
Soros, George 1930–   . US financier
Taylor, Paul Belville 1930–   . US choreographer and dancer
Walcott, Derek Walton 1930–   . St Lucian poet and playwright
Williams, Shirley Vivien Teresa Brittain, Baroness Williams of
   Crosby 1930–   . British politician
Woodward, Joanne Gignilliat 1930–   . US actress
Young, John Watts 1930–   . US astronaut

1931–35

Dean, James Byron 1931–1955. US actor
Cooke, Sam 1931–1964. US soul singer and songwriter
Acheampong, Ignatius Kutu 1931–1979. Ghanaian army officer
   and politician
Ailey, Alvin 1931–1989. US dancer, choreographer, and director
Barthelme, Donald 1931–1989. US writer
Mantle, Mickey Charles 1931–1995. US baseball player
Saro-Wiwa, Ken 1931–1995. Nigerian writer and political leader
Abish, Walter 1931–   . US writer
Auerbach, Frank Helmuth 1931–   . British painter

1936–40

Lubbers, Rudolph Franz Marie (Ruud) 1939– . Dutch prime minister
McCabe, John 1939– . English pianist and composer
McKellen, Ian Murray 1939– . English actor
Masekela, Hugh 1939– . South African trumpet player
Matura, Mustapha 1939– . British dramatist
Mauger, Ivan Gerald 1939– . New Zealand speedway racer
Mnouchkine, Ariane 1939– . French theatre director
Moorcock, Michael John 1939– . English writer
Mulroney, Brian 1939– . Canadian prime minister
Oz, Amos 1939– . Israeli writer
Reno, Janet 1939– . US attorney general
Schepisi, Frederic Alan 1939– . Australian film director
Scott, Ridley 1939– . English film director and producer
Serra, Richard 1939– . US sculptor
Seymour, Lynn 1939– . Canadian ballerina
Sibley, Antoinette 1939– . English dancer
Souter, David Hackett 1939– . US jurist
Stewart, Jackie (John Young) 1939– . Scottish motor-racing driver
Thompson, Hunter Stockton 1939– . US writer and journalist
Thubron, Colin Gerald Dryden 1939– . English travel writer and novelist
Trevino, Lee Buck 1939– . US golfer
Waite, Terry (Terence Hardy) 1939– . English envoy
Lennon, John Winston 1940–1980. English singer and songwriter
Hailwood, Mike (Stanley Michael Bailey) 1940–1981. English motorcyclist
Chatwin, (Charles) Bruce 1940–1989. English writer
Carter, Angela 1940–1992. English novelist and short-story writer
Zappa, Frank (Francis Vincent) 1940–1993. US rock musician
Raul, Julia 1940–1994. US film actor
Aidoo, Ama Ata 1940– . Ghanaian dramatist and writer
Alaïa, Azzedine 1940– . Tunisian fashion designer
Archer, Jeffrey Howard, Baron Archer of Weston-super-Mare 1940– . English writer and politician
Arias Sanchez, Oscar 1940– . Costa Rican president
Bausch, Pina 1940– . German choreographer
Bell, John Anthony 1940– . Australian actor and theatrical director
Bertolucci, Bernardo 1940– . Italian film director
Black, Conrad Moffat 1940– . Canadian newspaper publisher
Blyth, Chay (Charles) 1940– . British sailing adventurer
Boycott, Geoffrey 1940– . English cricketer
Brodsky, Joseph Alexandrovich 1940– . Russian poet
Broome, David 1940– . British show jumper
Christie, Julie Frances 1940– . English film actress
Clarke, Kenneth Harry 1940– . British politician
Coetzee, J(ohn) M(ichael) 1940– . South African author
Constantine II 1940– . King of the Hellenes
Dehaene, Jean-Luc 1940– . Belgian prime minister
de Maizière, Lothar 1940– . German politician
De Palma, Brian Russell 1940– . US film director
Disch, Thomas M(ichael) 1940– . US novelist and poet
Edgar, David 1940– . English dramatist
Fassett, Kaffe 1940– . US knitwear and textile designer
Herr, Michael 1940– . US writer
Hibberd, Jack (John Charles) 1940– . Australian dramatist
Hogan, Paul 1940– . Australian actor
Josephson, Brian David 1940– . Welsh physicist
Kenzo, trade name of Kenzo Takada 1940– . Japanese fashion designer
Kingston, Maxine Hong 1940– . US writer
McBride, Willie John (William James) 1940– . Irish rugby union player
Makarova, Natalia Romanovna 1940– . Russian ballerina
Margrethe II 1940– . Queen of Denmark
Mason, Bobbie Ann 1940– . US writer
Mitchell, Juliet 1940– . British psychoanalyst and writer
Nadir, Asil 1940– . Turkish Cypriot entrepreneur
Nazarbayev, Nursultan 1940– . President of Kazakhstan

Nicklaus, Jack William 1940– . US golfer
Noriega, Manuel (Antonio Morena) 1940– . Panamanian soldier and political leader
Nunn, Trevor Robert 1940– . English stage director
Pacino, Al(redo) James 1940– . US film actor
Pelé 1940– . Brazilian footballer
Pryor, Richard 1940– . US comedian and film actor
Qaboos bin Said 1940– . Sultan of Oman
Rhodes, Zandra Lindsey 1940– . English fashion designer
Richard, Cliff 1940– . English pop singer
Robinson, Smokey (William) 1940– . US singer, songwriter, and record producer
Rothschild, Eric de 1940– . French winemaker; see ◊Rothschild family
Severin, Tim (Giles Timothy) 1940– . British writer, historian, and traveller
Shephard, Gillian Patricia 1940– . British politician
Sinclair, Clive Marles 1940– . British electronics engineer
Spector, Phil 1940– . US record producer
Starr, Ringo 1940– . Member of English pop group the ◊Beatles
Thompson, Jack 1940– . Australian actor
Turner, Tina 1940– . US rhythm-and-blues singer
Welch, Raquel 1940– . US actress
Wherrett, Richard 1940– . Australian actor and director

1941–45

Redding, Otis 1941–1967. US soul singer and songwriter
Lee, Bruce 1941–1973. US film actor
Clark, (Harold) Gene 1941–1991. US rock and folk singer
Ruffin, David 1941–1991. US pop singer
Moore, Bobby (Robert Frederick) 1941–1993. English footballer
Nilsson, Harry 1941–1994. US singer and songwriter
Ando, Tadao 1941– . Japanese architect
Ashdown, Paddy (Jeremy John Durham) 1941– . English politician
Babangida, Ibrahim 1941– . Nigerian soldier and president
Baez, Joan 1941– . US folk singer
Carmichael, Stokely 1941– . US civil-rights activist
Dawkins, (Clinton) Richard 1941– . British zoologist
Debray, Régis 1941– . French Marxist theorist
Domingo, Placido 1941– . Spanish lyric tenor
Dunaway, (Dorothy) Faye 1941– . US film actress
Dylan, Bob 1941– . US singer and songwriter
Ephron, Nora 1941– . US writer
Frears, Stephen Arthur 1941– . English film director
Geingob, Hage Gottfried 1941– . Namibian prime minister
Goh Chok Tong 1941– . Singapore prime minister
Gould, Stephen Jay 1941– . US palaeontologist and writer
Holbrooke, Richard 1941– . US diplomat
Howard, Michael 1941– . British politician
Jackson, Jesse Louis 1941– . US politician and cleric
Klaus, Václav 1941– . Czech prime minister
Kristeva, Julia 1941– . French psychoanalyst
McKay, Heather Pamela 1941– . Australian squash player
Milošević, Slobodan 1941– . Serbian president
Muti, Riccardo 1941– . Italian conductor
Neville, Aaron 1941– . US singer; see the ◊Neville Brothers
Pickett, Wilson 1941– . US soul singer
Puttnam, David Terence 1941– . English film producer
Tharp, Twyla 1941– . US choreographer
Theroux, Paul Edward 1941– . US novelist and travel writer
Watts, Charlie 1941– . British rock musician, member of the ◊Rolling Stones
Westwood, Vivienne 1941– . English fashion designer
Wilson, Robert 1941– . US theatre director
Zeroual, Lamine 1941– . Algerian president
Jones, Brian 1942–1969. British rock musician, member of the ◊Rolling Stones

Hendrix, Jimi (James Marshall) 1942–1970. US rock guitarist
Walker, Sebastian 1942–1991. English publisher
Hani, Chris (Martin Thembisile) 1942–1993. South African antiapartheid activist
Jarman, Derek 1942–1994. English film director
Alexeev, Vasiliy 1942– . Soviet weightlifter
Ali, Muhammad 1942– . US boxer
Allende, Isabel 1942– . Chilean novelist
Barenboim, Daniel 1942– . Israeli pianist and conductor
Brenton, Howard 1942– . English dramatist
Carson, Willie (William Fisher Hunter) 1942– . Scottish jockey
Caslavska, Vera 1942– . Czechoslovak gymnast
Comme des Garçons 1942– . Japanese fashion designer
Conti, Tom 1942– . Scottish actor
Court, Margaret 1942– . Australian tennis player
Crawford, Michael 1942– . English actor and singer
Crichton, Michael 1942– . US novelist, screenwriter, and director
Crowley, John 1942– . US science-fiction writer
Dos Santos, José Eduardo 1942– . Angolan president
Eusebio 1942– . Portuguese footballer
Ford, Harrison 1942– . US film actor
Franklin, Aretha 1942– . US soul singer
Garner, Helen 1942– . Australian writer
Gemayel, Amin 1942– . Lebanese president
Gibson, Mike (Cameron Michael Henderson) 1942– . Irish rugby player
González Márquez, Felipe 1942– . Spanish prime minister
Greenaway, Peter 1942– . English film director
Handke, Peter 1942– . Austrian novelist and playwright
Hawking, Stephen William 1942– . English physicist
Herzog, Werner 1942– . German film director
Hoskins, Bob (Robert William) 1942– . English actor
Irving, John Winslow 1942– . US novelist
Jong, Erica Mann 1942– . US novelist and poet
Keeler, Christine 1942– . British prostitute
Keillor, Garrison Edward 1942– . US writer and humorist
Khaddafi, Moamer al 1942– . Libyan revolutionary leader
Kim Jong Il 1942– . North Korean president
Kinnock, Neil Gordon 1942– . British politician
Klein, Calvin (Richard) 1942– . US fashion designer
Lamont, Norman Stewart Hughson 1942– . British politician
Lange, David Russell 1942– . New Zealand prime minister
McCartney, (James) Paul 1942– . English singer and songwriter
Mbeki, Thebo 1942– . South African politician
Meciar, Vladimir 1942– . Slovak prime minister
Palmer, Geoffrey Winston Russell 1942– . New Zealand prime minister
Passmore, George 1942– . English painter and performance artist; see ◊Gilbert and George
Reed, Lou (Louis Firbank) 1942– . US rock singer and songwriter
Saleh, Ali Abdullah 1942– . Yemeni president
Scorsese, Martin 1942– . US director, screenwriter, and producer
Simon, Paul 1942– . US pop singer and songwriter
Streisand, Barbra Joan 1942– . US singer, actress, and film producer
Williams, John Christopher 1942– . Australian guitarist
Williamson, David Keith 1942– . Australian dramatist and scriptwriter
Wilson, Brian 1942– . Member of US pop group the ◊Beach Boys
Wilson, Brian 1942– . US pop musician and producer
Joplin, Janis 1943–1970. US blues and rock singer
Baader, Andreas 1943–1977. German political activist
Penston, Michael 1943–1990. British astronomer
Nutter, Tommy 1943–1992. English tailor
Wells, Mary Esther 1943–1992. US singer
Ashe, Arthur Robert, 1943–1993. US tennis player and coach
Goria, Giovanni 1943–1994. Italian prime minister
Agostini, Giacomo 1943– . Italian motorcyclist
Banks, Jeff 1943– . English fashion designer
Bell Burnell, (Susan) Jocelyn 1943– . British astronomer

Botta, Mario 1943– . Swiss architect
Carey, Peter Philip 1943– . Australian novelist
Cecil, Henry Richard Amherst 1943– . Scottish racehorse trainer
Chappell, Ian Michael 1943– . Australian cricketer
Chiluba, Frederick 1943– . Zambian president
Cimino, Michael 1943– . US film director
Cronenberg, David 1943– . Canadian filmmaker
Deneuve, Catherine 1943– . French actress
De Niro, Robert 1943– . US film actor
Dowell, Anthony James 1943– . English ballet dancer
Eyre, Richard (Charles Hastings) 1943– . English stage and film director
Ferneyhough, Brian John Peter 1943– . English composer
Fischer, Bobby (Robert James) 1943– . US chess player
Gardiner, John Eliot 1943– . English conductor
Gingrich, Newt (Newton Leroy) 1943– . US politician
Harrison, George 1943– . Member of English pop group the ◊Beatles
Isaacs, Susan 1943– . US novelist and screenwriter
Jagger, Mick 1943– . British rock musician, member of the ◊Rolling Stones
Kawakubo, Rei 1943– . Japanese fashion designer
Khasbulatov, Rusian 1943– . Russian vice president
Killy, Jean-Claude 1943– . French skier
King, Billie Jean 1943– . US tennis player
Kingsley, Ben (Krishna Banji) 1943– . British actor
Lafontaine, Oskar 1943– . German politician
Leigh, Mike 1943– . English dramatist and filmmaker
Lubovitch, Lar 1943– . US choreographer
McDowell, Malcolm Taylor 1943– . English actor
Major, John 1943– . British prime minister
Mitchell, Joni 1943– . Canadian singer, songwriter, and guitarist
Mladic, Ratko 1943– . Bosnian general
Muluzi, Bakili 1943– . Malawi president
Namath, Joe (Joseph William) 1943– . US football player
North, Oliver 1943– . US Marine lieutenant colonel
Ondaatje, (Philip) Michael 1943– . Canadian writer
Proesch, Gilbert 1943– . English painter and performance artist; see ◊Gilbert and George
Rasmussen, Poul Nyrup 1943– . Danish prime minister
Richards, Keith 1943– . British rock musician, member of the ◊Rolling Stones
Roddick, Anita Lucia 1943– . British entrepreneur
Rowbotham, Sheila 1943– . British feminist and historian
Sassau-Nguesso, Denis 1943– . Congolese president
Shepard, Sam 1943– . US dramatist and actor
Smalley, Richard E 1943– . US chemist
Stephan, Peter 1943– . English immunologist
Tate, Jeffrey Philip 1943– . English conductor
Walesa, Lech 1943– . Polish trade-union leader and president
Wigley, Dafydd 1943– . Welsh politician
Yamamoto, Yohji 1943– . Japanese fashion designer
Mendes, Chico (Filho Francisco) 1944–1988. Brazilian environmentalist and labour leader
Gandhi, Rajiv 1944–1991. Indian prime minister
Everett, Kenny 1944–1995. British broadcaster
Blakemore, Colin Brian 1944– . English physiologist
Burns, Terence 1944– . British economist
Crossley, Paul Christopher Richard 1944– . English pianist
Daltrey, Roger 1944– . English rock musician; see ◊Who, the
Davis, Angela Yvonne 1944– . US black activist
Demme, Jonathan 1944– . US film director and screenwriter
De Savary, Peter John 1944– . British entrepreneur
Douglas, Michael Kirk 1944– . US film actor and producer
Entwistle, John 1944– . English rock musician; see ◊Who, the
Farrelly, Bernard 1944– . Australian surfer
Ferré, Gianfranco 1944– . Italian couturier
Fiennes, Ranulph Twisleton-Wykeham 1944– . British explorer
Keating, Paul John 1944– . Australian prime minister
Leakey, Richard Erskine Frere 1944– . Kenyan anthropologist

1951–55

Roche, Stephen 1959– . Irish cyclist
Storey, Helen 1959– . English fashion designer
Thompson, Emma 1959– . English actress
Warner, Deborah 1959– . English theatre director
Winterson, Jeanette 1959– . English novelist
Senna, Ayrton 1960–1994. Brazilian motor-racing driver
Andrew, (full name Andrew Albert Christian Edward) 1960– . Prince of the UK, Duke of York
Aouita, Said 1960– . Moroccan runner
Benjamin, George William John 1960– . English composer, conductor, and pianist
Branagh, Kenneth Charles 1960– . Northern Irish actor and director
Burton, Tim 1960– . US film director
Cauthen, Steve 1960– . US jockey
Christie, Linford 1960– . English sprinter
Egoyan, Atom 1960– . Canadian filmmaker
Galliano, John 1960– . English fashion designer
Lendl, Ivan 1960– . US tennis player
Lineker, Gary 1960– . English footballer
Maradona, Diego Armando 1960– . Argentine footballer
Marsalis, Branford 1960– . US saxophonist
Richmond, John 1960– . English fashion designer
Rylance, Mark 1960– . English actor and director

1961–65

Bruno, Frank 1961– . English boxer
Comaneci, Nadia 1961– . Romanian gymnast
Diana 1961– . Princess of Wales
Gretzky, Wayne 1961– . Canadian ice-hockey player
lang, k d 1961– . Canadian singer
LeMond, Greg 1961– . US racing cyclist
Lewis, Carl (Frederick Carlton) 1961– . US athlete
McAuley, Dave 1961– . Irish boxer
Marsalis, Wynton 1961– . US trumpet player
Pollen, Arabella 1961– . English fashion designer
Campese, David 1962– . Australian rugby union player
Clark, Michael 1962– . Scottish dancer
Cruise, Tom 1962– . US film actor
Davies, Jonathan 1962– . Welsh rugby league player
Farr-Jones, Nick (Nicholas) 1962– . Australian rugby union player
Foster, Jodie 1962– . US film actress and director
Grant, Hugh 1962– . English actor
Gullit, Ruud 1962– . Dutch footballer
Hastings, Andrew Gavin 1962– . Scottish rugby union player
Nasrin, Tashima 1962– . Bangladeshi writer and feminist
Redgrave, Steven Geoffrey 1962– . English oarsman
Wolf, Naomi 1962– . US feminist writer
Flett, John 1963–1991. English fashion designer
Borodina, Olga 1963– . Russian mezzo-soprano
Bubka, Sergey Nazarovich 1963– . Russian pole vaulter
Davies, Laura 1963– . English golfer
Hammer 1963– . US rap vocalist

Houston, Whitney 1963– . US soul singer
Jordan, Michael Jeffrey 1963– . US basketball player
Kasparov, Gary Kimovich 1963– . Russian chess player
Khan, Jahangir 1963– . Pakistani squash player
Lynagh, Michael 1963– . Australian rugby union player
Powell, Mike 1963– . US athlete
Sharman, Helen 1963– . British astronaut
Tarantino, Quentin 1963– . US film director and screenwriter
Underwood, Rory 1963– . English rugby union player
Edward, (full name Edward Antony Richard Louis) 1964– . Prince of the UK
Ellis, Bret Easton 1964– . US novelist
Fenech, Jeff (Jeffrey) 1964– . Australian boxer
Gross, Michael 1964– . German swimmer
McColgan, Elizabeth 1964– . Scottish athlete
Moorhouse, Adrian 1964– . English swimmer
Tomba, Alberto 1964– . Italian skier
Van Basten, Marco 1964– . Dutch footballer
Wilander, Mats 1964– . Swedish tennis player
Carling, Will(iam) David Charles 1965– . English rugby union player
Cash, Pat 1965– . Australian tennis player
Hanley, Ellery 1965– . English rugby league player
Hirst, Damien 1965– . English artist
Stansfield, Lisa 1965– . English pop singer
Witt, Katarina 1965– . German ice skater

1966–

Björk 1966– . Icelandic pop singer
Cantona, Eric 1966– . French footballer
Edberg, Stefan 1966– . Swedish tennis player
Gunnell, Sally 1966– . British hurdler
Hick, Graeme Ashley 1966– . English cricketer
Lewis, Lennox 1966– . British boxer
Olazabal, Jose Maria 1966– . Spanish golfer
Tyson, Mike (Michael Gerald) 1966– . US boxer
Cobain, Kurt 1967–1994. US rock singer
Becker, Boris 1967– . German tennis player
Gascoigne, Paul 1967– . English footballer
Atherton, Michael Andrew 1968– . English cricketer
Rust, Mathias 1968– . German aviator
Graf, Steffi 1969– . German tennis player
Lara, Brian 1969– . Trinidadian cricket player
Schumacher, Michael 1969– . German motor-racing driver
Phoenix, River 1970–1993. US film actor
Hendry, Stephen 1970– . Scottish snooker player
Sabatini, Gabriela 1970– . Argentine tennis player
Sampras, Pete 1971– . US tennis player
Martinez, Conchita 1972– . Spanish tennis player
Seles, Monica 1973– . Yugoslavian tennis player
Hamed, Nassem ('Prince')1974– . English boxer
William 1982– . Prince of the UK
Henry, (Charles Albert David) 1984– . Prince of the UK